A

TOPOGRAPHICAL DICTIONARY

OF

ENGLAND,

IN FOUR VOLUMES.

A TOPOGRAPHICAL DICTIONARY OF ENGLAND

By Samuel Lewis

VOLUME I

CLEARFIELD

Originally published, London, 1831
Reprinted, four volumes in two, 1996, by
Genealogical Publishing Co., Inc.
Baltimore, Maryland

Reprinted in the original four-volume format, 2018, by
Genealogical Publishing Company for
Clearfield Company
Baltimore, Maryland

ISBN Volume I: 9780806358673
Set ISBN: 9780806315089

A

TOPOGRAPHICAL DICTIONARY

OF

ENGLAND,

COMPRISING THE

SEVERAL COUNTIES, CITIES, BOROUGHS, CORPORATE AND MARKET TOWNS,
PARISHES, CHAPELRIES, AND TOWNSHIPS,
AND THE ISLANDS OF GUERNSEY, JERSEY, AND MAN,

WITH

HISTORICAL AND STATISTICAL DESCRIPTIONS;

ILLUSTRATED BY

MAPS OF THE DIFFERENT COUNTIES AND ISLANDS

AND EMBELLISHED WITH

ENGRAVINGS OF THE ARMS OF THE CITIES, BISHOPRICKS, UNIVERSITIES, COLLEGES, CORPORATE TOWNS, AND BOROUGHS; AND OF THE SEALS OF THE SEVERAL MUNICIPAL CORPORATIONS.

BY SAMUEL LEWIS.

IN FOUR VOLUMES.

VOL. I.

LONDON:
PUBLISHED BY S. LEWIS AND CO., 87, ALDERSGATE-STREET.
M.DCCC.XXXI.

PREFACE.

In introducing to the Public the "Topographical Dictionary of England," it may be necessary to state that, although some few works, bearing a similar title, have been published within the last thirty years, yet no work of sufficient authority, as a book of general reference, has appeared since the time of Camden; the publication, therefore, of a Dictionary, affording a more comprehensive and faithful delineation of the kingdom, had become a desideratum. Of the many local histories and other works, which at the time of their publication might have afforded an accurate account of the places they describe, the greater number having been published long since, and there being several counties and considerable towns of which no authentic history had been given, it was found impossible to compile from existing authorities a Topographical Dictionary in any degree deserving the public patronage. It was determined therefore to make a general Survey of the whole Kingdom, and several gentlemen were engaged to procure, by personal examination and enquiry, the fullest information upon the various subjects contemplated in the plan of the work; and, in order to facilitate their enquiries, and to preserve uniformity in the arrangement of the information, they were furnished with printed questions, embracing every object to which their attention was to be directed.

The islands of Guernsey and Jersey, with the smaller dependent islands, and the Isle of Man, though not forming integral portions of England, are so closely connected with it, that it was considered that a detail of their history, and a minute and faithful description of their peculiar systems of government, laws, customs, &c., would form an interesting feature in the work: with this view gentlemen were sent to visit those islands, and were for many months employed in collecting the requisite information, and in revising and correcting the proof sheets on the spot.

Previously to the commencement of the present undertaking, a clergyman residing in the neighbourhood of Ashby de la Zouch had projected a work somewhat similar, the materials for which he proposed to collect by transmitting, through several peers of the realm and members of parliament, printed queries to the officiating clergymen throughout the kingdom; but, finding that his letters were only partially answered, and that the present publication upon a more extensive plan was in progress, he relinquished his design, and transferred to the Proprietors more than three thousand letters, which he had received, containing much original and useful information.

It was at first intended to confine the plan of the work to a topographical and statistical account of the several places; but, considering that a summary of the history of such as either are, or have been, of importance, would increase its value, and render it more complete, it was determined to introduce a concise narrative of the principal events which have marked their progress from their origin to the present time. To effect this, several other gentlemen were employed at the British Museum, the London Institution, and other libraries, to select from authentic records and manuscripts the most important occurrences in the history of each place.

To render the account of every town and place of importance as correct as possible, prior to its being finally put to press, proof sheets were forwarded to those resident gentlemen who had previously furnished local information, in order that, in their revisal of them, they might introduce any changes which had subsequently taken place, or improvements that might be at that time in progress: these were in general promptly examined and returned, but in some instances inevitable delay was occasioned by the absence of the parties to whom they were addressed.

Though this essential precaution may have retarded the publication, it has conduced materially to the accuracy, of the work. For a similar reason, the time employed in the Survey has been longer than was at first anticipated; it having been thought advisable that the persons engaged in that arduous and important service should protract the period originally prescribed for their researches, rather than compromise the interests of the work by omitting to avail themselves of every possible source of intelligence. And here the Proprietors beg to return their unfeigned thanks for the kind attention uniformly manifested, and the valuable information liberally communicated, to their agents, during the three years they were employed in their pursuits; and gratefully to acknowledge the prompt and powerful assistance received from the resident nobility, gentry, and clergy, and persons holding official situations, many of whom have transmitted original manuscripts, containing much valuable information never before published.

It may be necessary to state that, in the arrangement, all places having the same general name are classed together according to the alphabetical order of their distinguishing epithets,—as Norton (King's), Norton (South); and always precede those of which the name is a compound term,—as Norton-Conyers, Norton-Lindsey, &c., which follow in the same order; but when, as in some instances, it is difficult to ascertain which is the primary and which the adjunct term, if the first occurring in the alphabetical order be not the proper name of the place, a reference is given to the other name, under which the description will be found.

For the greater facility of reference, the following arrangements have been adopted. First, with respect to COUNTIES:—the name, and whether an inland or maritime county,—its relative situation, superficial extent in square miles and statute acres, and population, according to the census of 1821;—historical summary;—province, diocese, archdeaconries, and deaneries;—number of parishes, stating how many are rectories, vicarages, and perpetual curacies;—lathes, rapes, hundreds, or other civil divisions of a like kind, but differing in name;—cities, boroughs, sea-ports, corporate and market towns;—courts of assize and general quarter session, and where held;—number of acting magistrates;—amount of parochial rates, and the portion assigned for the relief of the poor;—climate, agriculture, soil, and the quantity of land devoted to tillage and pasture;—predominant breeds of cattle;—extent of forests, woods, commons, marshes, lakes, &c.;—geology;—manufactures and commerce;—navigable rivers, canals, and railways;—principal turnpike roads;—Roman stations and roads;—encampments and other relics of antiquity;—remains of religious houses;—ancient churches and fonts;—ancient castles;—principal modern seats;—mineral springs, and natural curiosities.

Secondly, in Cities, Boroughs, and Corporate and Market Towns:—name and situation;—distance and bearing from the county town and from London;—population, according to the census of 1821;—origin, and etymology of name;—historical summary;—local description;—scientific and literary institutions;—places and sources of amusement;—commerce, trade, and manufactures;—markets and fairs;—municipal government, of what officers composed, and when and how chosen;—privileges and immunities, courts of justice, prisons, &c.;—parliamentary representation, elective franchise, and when granted, number of electors, and how they obtain their freedom, returning officer, and the prevailing influence;—ecclesiastical and religious establishments;—nature of the livings;—in what archdeaconry and diocese, or, if of exempt jurisdiction, to whom the peculiar belongs;—amount at which the living is rated in the king's books;—endowment, whether by private benefaction, royal bounty, or parliamentary grant,—patron,—tutelar saint and architectural description of the churches;—dissenting places of worship, and of what denominations;—scholastic and charitable foundations and endowments;—benevolent institutions;—ancient monastic establishments, with the amount of revenue at the dissolution;—antiquities;—mineral springs;—natural phenomena;—eminent natives and residents;—title, if any, which the place confers, and on what family.

Thirdly, in Parishes:—name and situation;—distance and bearing from the nearest market or post town;—chapelries, townships, &c., which they comprise;—population, according to the census of 1821;—nature of the living;—the archdeaconry and diocese in which it is included, and, if of exempt jurisdiction, the peculiar court to which it belongs;—amount at which each living is rated in the king's books;—endowment by private benefaction, royal bounty, or parliamentary grant;—patron;—tutelar saint and architectural description of the church;—dissenting places of worship, and of what denominations;—schools, hospitals, and other charitable institutions;—monastic establishments, encampments, relics of antiquity, and miscellaneous information.

In Townships, Chapelries, Hamlets, and Tythings, forming civil divisions of parishes, the same arrangement of subjects has been observed as in the parishes themselves: these, though enumerated under the head of the parishes to which they belong, and with which their population is collectively returned, are also separately inserted in the work, and their respective population given under their several heads. But, with regard to the great number of villages and hamlets which are not recognized divisions, it has, from their general want of importance, been thought unnecessary to notice them, with the exception of such as may possess some historical interest, or geological features, in which case they are described under the heads of their respective parishes.

It has been found difficult to determine precisely by what title to designate those places which, though formerly only chapelries, have, by virtue of their endowment by the Governors of Queen Anne's bounty, for the augmentation of the maintenance of the clergy, become perpetual curacies, and in a great measure independent of the incumbents of the parishes to which they belonged. Though, from some partial dependence on the mother church, arising either from the right of appointing the curate, or from a reservation either of the whole, or a portion, of the tithes, and in some instances of the surplice fees, they may be still considered chapelries; yet for all civil purposes they possess full parochial rights, and are consequently, in many instances, described as parishes.

It has also, in many instances, been difficult to obtain correct information respecting the patronage of the livings, many of the incumbents having been appointed by the purchaser of a next presentation only; and, in some cases, where the living has been held for a long term, the advowson has passed into other hands: the information obtained on the spot has, therefore, frequently differed from that communicated by the registrars of the several dioceses, who have kindly afforded considerable assistance on all ecclesiastical affairs.

The augmentations have been taken from a work recently published by Mr. Hodgson, Secretary to the Governors of the bounty of Queen Anne, but they do not afford any just criterion of the present value of the living, the money having been, in many instances, vested in land and other property, and in some, either the whole, or a considerable portion, having been expended on the repair of the glebe house. The amount of the revenues of the several monastic establishments, at the time of their dissolution, has been adopted from the valuation published by Mr. Speed, from a catalogue of religious houses drawn up by Mr. Burton.

Respecting scholastic foundations and endowments, and other charitable institutions, great facility has been afforded by the reports of the Commissioners appointed by act of parliament to enquire concerning charities; yet, with regard to such as were not included in those already published, much difficulty was experienced, as it became necessary to depend almost exclusively upon the information obtained from the parties by whom they were immediately superintended.

The distances of the several places have been measured by a chartometer on the most recent maps;—the market towns from the county town and from London, and the parishes and townships from the nearest market or post town; so that by adding, or deducting, the distance of any parish or township from the market town, according to its bearing, which may be seen by a reference to the county map, its distance from London may be easily ascertained. The admeasurement has generally been made from the respective churches; but, in townships or other places having no church, it has been taken from the centre of the village.

In describing the various specimens of ecclesiastical architecture, it has been thought advisable to lay aside the terms of designation which, till within a recent period, have been almost universally adopted. The term "Saxon" has been hitherto improperly applied to a numerous class of buildings, of which scarcely any specimens existed in this country till long after the Saxon period; and the term "Gothic," whatever may have been its origin, has neither reference to date, nor to distinction of character. Of truly Saxon architecture there are few, if any, well-authenticated examples; and, consequently, with reference to buildings supposed to be of this class, a decided opinion has not been expressed. For the sake of distinctness and classification, these interesting structures have been referred respectively to the Norman, the early English, the decorated English, and the later English, styles of architecture. The first of these styles is appropriately designated Norman, as having been generally adopted by that people; and the three last mark distinctly the successive periods of that style which is called English, not only as having been brought to its highest state of perfection in this country, but as displaying characteristics which distinguish it from that of any other. The Norman style, though some few specimens previously existed, was more extensively brought into practice subsequently to the Conquest, and continued till the end of the reign of Henry II.; the most ancient part of Winchester cathedral is a fine specimen. The early English style, which originated in the former, and in its earliest period is scarcely to be distinguished from it, was introduced in the beginning of the reign of Richard I., and prevailed till the end of that of Edward I.; in its progress it assumed a character peculiarly its own, by which it is easily distinguished from the later Norman: the purest specimen is Salisbury cathedral. The decorated English style was introduced at the beginning of the reign of Edward II., and continued till the end of that of Edward III.; the chapter-house at York is, perhaps, the richest and the purest specimen. The later English style was introduced in the reign of Richard II., attained its highest degree of perfection in that of Henry VII., and continued in considerable purity till the end of the reign of Henry VIII., since which period there is scarcely any building entirely of that character; the finest specimen is Henry the Seventh's chapel at Westminster.

The Maps accompanying the work are engraved on steel plates, from drawings made from the best authorities, and corrected up to the present time. The Seals of the several cities, boroughs, corporate towns, bishopricks, universities, colleges, &c., are engraved from drawings made from impressions in wax, furnished by the respective corporate bodies; and, notwithstanding they have generally been either enlarged or reduced to one scale, for the sake of uniformity, great care has been taken to preserve, in every instance, an exact *fac-simile* of the original. The mutilated state of many of the seals rendered it almost impossible to decypher the legends; but this difficulty has been kindly removed by Sir George Nayler, and other gentlemen at the Heralds' College, who have also furnished the Arms of several of the towns.

The Proprietors cannot indulge the hope that, in a work of such magnitude, compiled from such a variety of sources, and containing notices so numerous and diversified, some errors have not occurred: indeed, the information collected upon the spot, even from the most intelligent persons, has frequently been so contradictory, as to require much labour and perseverance to reconcile and verify it. They have, however, regardless of expense, used the most indefatigable exertions to attain correctness, and to render the work as complete as possible; and they, therefore, trust that occasional inaccuracies will receive the indulgence of the Subscribers, who both in number and respectability are greater than have hitherto appeared in support of any similar undertaking.

In conclusion, they beg respectfully to inform those gentlemen who have also subscribed for the Dictionaries of the remaining portions of the United Kingdom, that the Survey of Wales is nearly completed, and that surveys of Scotland and Ireland are also in progress; and that they will thankfully acknowledge the receipt of any original information respecting any town or district in those countries.

SUBSCRIBERS.

*THE KING'S MOST EXCELLENT MAJESTY

*HER MOST GRACIOUS MAJESTY THE QUEEN

*HIS LATE MOST GRACIOUS MAJESTY GEORGE THE FOURTH

*HIS ROYAL HIGHNESS THE LATE DUKE OF YORK
*HIS ROYAL HIGHNESS THE DUKE OF CUMBERLAND
*HIS ROYAL HIGHNESS THE DUKE OF SUSSEX
*HIS ROYAL HIGHNESS THE DUKE OF CAMBRIDGE
*HER ROYAL HIGHNESS THE PRINCESS AUGUSTA
*HIS ROYAL HIGHNESS THE DUKE OF GLOUCESTER
*HER ROYAL HIGHNESS THE DUCHESS OF KENT
*HER ROYAL HIGHNESS THE DUCHESS OF CUMBERLAND

*HIS ROYAL HIGHNESS PRINCE LEOPOLD OF SAXE COBURG

Aaron, Mr. J., Bradford-street, Birmingham
Abbot, George, Esq., Mark-lane, London
*Abbot, W., Esq., Canterbury
*Abbot, W., Esq., Doctors Commons, London
*Abbotson, E. G., Esq., Burton, Westmorland
Abbott, Wm., Esq., A.B., Queens coll., Oxford
*Abbott, Mr. John, Conduit-street, London
*Abbott, John Edward, Esq., Frederick-place, do.
Abbotts, Mr. Thomas, Skinner-street, do.
*Abbs, Major, Pinner, Middlesex
*A'Beckett, Wm., Esq., Golden-square, London
Abell, Mr. John, Bishop's Froome, Herefordshire
Abell, J., Esq., Mitchel-Dean, Gloucestershire
Abell and Clutterbuck, Messrs., Gloucester
ABERCORN, The Most Noble the Marquis of
*ABERDEEN, The Right Hon. the Earl of
*ABERGAVENNY, The Rt. Hon. the Earl of
Abernethy, J., Esq., Brasenose college, Oxford
*ABINGDON, The Right Honorable the Earl of
Abington, W., Esq., East India House, London
Ablett, Joseph, Esq., Ruthin, Denbigh
*Abraham, R., Esq., Russell-square, London
Abraham, Thos., Esq., Dunster, Somersetshire
*Absolom, C. S., Esq., Trinity coll., Cambridge
Ackers, Messrs. James and Joseph, Liverpool
Ackers, James, Esq., Trinity coll., Cambridge
Ackers, William, Esq., Prescot, Lancashire
*Ackland, R. J., Esq., Boulston, Haverford-West
*Acland, Sir J. P., Bart., Fairfield, Sussex
Acland, Sir T. D., Bart., M.P., Killerton, Devon
Acland, P. P. P., Esq., Fairfield, Somersetshire
Acton, Mrs. C., Lower Brook-st., Ipswich
*Acton, John, Esq., Burslem, Staffordshire
*Acton, Samuel, Esq., Finsbury-square, London
Acton, Wm., Esq., Wolverton, near Worcester
Acton, Rev. W., L. L. B., Ayott St. Lawrence,
*Actor, E.F., Esq. Trinity-hall, Cambrid. [Herts.
Acworth, George, Esq., Rochester
*Adair, A., Esq., Heatherton-park, Somersetshire
*Adair, Henry, Esq., Exeter college, Oxford
*Adams, C. H., Esq., Walsall, Staffordshire
Adams, Mr. C., Chequer-yard, London
Adams, Edward George, Esq., Norwich
*Adams, Edward R., Esq., Beckenham, Kent
*Adams, Mr. Edward, Bucklershard, Hants.
*Adams, E., R., Jun., Esq., Caius coll., Camb.
Adams, G., Esq., Lindridge, Worcestershire
*Adams, J., Esq., Reading, Berks.
*Adams, James, Esq., Walsall, Staffordshire
*Adams, John, Esq., Manchester [London
*Adams, Rev. R. L., A. M., Grosvenor-place,
*Adams, Samuel, Esq., Ware, Herts.
Adams, Mr. Thomas, Windsor
*Adams, W., Esq., Cobridge, Staffordshire
*Adams, Wm., Esq., Fenton-hall, Stoke, do.
Adams and Hooper, Messrs., Norwich
*Adamson, Jas., Esq., Ely-place, Holborn, Lond.
*Adamson, Mr. John, Lime-street, do.
*Adamthwaite, J. A., Esq., St. Michael's-alley, Cornhill, London
Adcock, Mr. Benjamin, Windsor [London
*Addams, R., Esq., L.L.D., Doctors Commons,
Addenbrooke, Henry, Esq., Hagley, Worcestersh.
Addenbrooke, John, Esq., Stourbridge
Adderley, R., Esq., Barlaston-hall, Staffordshire
Addey, Mr. John, Blind Institution, Norwich
Addington, H. J., Esq., Burrington, Somerset
Addis, Rev. B. J., Portico, Lancashire
*Addis, Mr. C., Yatton Chapel, Herefordshire
Addis, Mr. John, Hope-Mansell, do.
*Addis, Richard, Esq., Alton-court, Ross, do.
*Addison, R., Esq., Fleet-st., London
Addison, Richard, Esq., Liverpool
*Addison, Samuel, Esq., Wednesbury, Staffordsh.
*Addison, T., Esq., Aigburth, Liverpool
Addison, Thomas, Esq., Leyland, Lancashire
*Adey, D.G., Esq., Markgate-priory, Hertfordsh.
Adkins, Rev. Thomas, Southampton
*Adlington, T. E., Esq., Clement's-inn, London
Adlington, Thos., Esq., Upper Tooting, Surrey
ADMIRALTY, The Right Honorable the Lords Commissioners of the
Adnam, Mr. William, Harwell, Berks.
*Adolphus, John, Esq., Temple, London
*Adshead, A., Esq., Stalybridge, Lancashire
Agar, Benjamin, Esq., Brockfield, near York
Agar, Mr. Francis, Windsor
*Agar, Thomas, Esq., Maidstone
Agard, Henry, Esq., Liverpool
Agg, W. J., Esq., Howletts, Cheltenham
Ainsley, George, Esq., Preston, Lancashire
*Ainsley, Joseph, Esq., Hart-street, London
*Ainslie, M. F., Esq., Hall-Garth, Lancashire
*Ainsworth, James, Esq., Manchester
Ainsworth, Mr. J. M., Bristol-st., Birmingham
*Ainsworth, Nicholas, Esq., Newton, Cheshire

Those marked with an Asterisk (*) are Subscribers for large paper Copies.

*Ainsworth, T., Esq., Ulverstone, Lancashire
*Ainsworth, Thomas, Esq., Preston, do.
Aird, W. F., Esq., King's-Arms-yard, London
Aitchison, Capt., R. N., Eling, near Southampton
*Aitkins, John M., Esq., Chapel-st., Grosvenor-
*Aiton, John T., Esq., Windsor [place, London
*Alban, W. Y., Esq., Lincoln's-inn, London
Albott, Messrs. G. and C., Birmingham
*Aldersey, J. S., Esq., Bedford-square, London
Aldersey, J., Esq., Wrexham, Denbighshire
*Aldersey, Robert, Esq., Chester
*Aldersey, Samuel, Esq., Aldersey-hall, Cheshire
Alderson, Christopher, Esq., Harthill, York
Alderson, Robert, Esq., Norwich
*Alderson, Ralph, Esq., Preston, Lancashire
Alderson, T. J., Esq., Chancery-lane, London
Alderton, Christ., Esq., Magdalene hall, Oxford
Aldham, H., Esq., Worcester college, do.
Aldhouse, Rev. S., St. Peter's col., Cambridge
*Aldridge, John, Esq., Lincoln's-inn, London
*Aldridge, R., Esq., St. Leonard's Forest, Sussex
*Aldridge, W. Esq., Stroud, Gloucestershire
Alexander, Dykes, Esq., Ipswich, Suffolk
Alexander, G., Esq., M. D., Rochdale
Alexander, H., Esq., Cork-st., Bond-st., London
*Alexander, Henry, Esq., Carey-street, do.
*Alexander, H., Esq., Wickham-Park, Surrey
Alexander, James, Esq., Doncaster, Yorkshire
Alexander, Richard, Esq., Corsham, Wilts.
Alexander, R. C., Esq., Wadham college, Oxford
Alexander, Samuel, Esq., Ipswich, Suffolk
Alexander, William, Esq., Preston, Lancashire
*Alexander, Mr. W., Yarmouth, Norfolk
*Algar, Mr. Joseph, King-st., Holborn, London
Algar, Mr. Robert, Back-Inn, Norwich
*Allaway, Mr. George, Reading, Berks.
Allaway, Mr. Wm., Lydbrook, Gloucestershire
*Alkin, J. J., Esq., Hunters-place, nr. Maidstone
*Allan, Mr. John, Hackney-road, Middlesex
*Allan, Robert Henry, Esq., Durham
Allan, Mr. W., Primrose-street, London
Allatt, Dr., Bolton-street, Piccadilly, do.
*Allchin, T., Esq., East Malling, near Maidstone
Allchin, W. H., Esq., do. do.
Allcott, Jas., Esq., Bosbury, Hereford
Allee, Mr. L. T., Rookley, Hants.
Allen, B. F., Esq., Preston, Lancashire
Allen, Captain, R. N., Devonport
*Allen, Francis, Esq., Hereford
Allen, George, Esq., Broxbourne, Herts.
Allen, Mr. George, jun., Manchester
Allen, H., Esq., Crane-hall, Ipswich, Suffolk
Allen, J. W., Esq., Frith-st., Soho-sq., London
*Allen, Rev. James T., Shobdon, Herefordshire
*Allen, J., Esq., jun., West-borough, Maidstone
Allen, Mr. James, Leominster
Allen, Mr. John, Judd-street, London
Allen, Mundeford, Esq., Furnival's-inn, do.
Allen, Oswald, Esq., York
*Allen, Rev. W., A. M., Bolton, Lancashire
*Allen, Wm., Esq., Aldermanbury, London
*Allen, Wm., Esq., Marsden-sq., Manchester
Allen, Mr. Wm., St. Peter's, Mancroft, Norwich
*Allerton, R., Esq., Norfolk-street, London
Allies, Rev. T., A.M., Clifton-downs, near Bristol
*Allin, Mr. W., High-street, Birmingham
Alloway, Mr. Jno., Bray, nr. Maidenhead, Berks.
Allport, H. C., Esq., Aldridge, Staffordshire
*Allport, Josiah, Esq., Atherstone, Warwickshire
*Allport, Samuel, Esq., Bull-street, Birmingham
Allpress, Jno., Esq., Broughton, Huntingdonsh.
Allpress, R. W., Esq., St. Ives, do.
Allsop, Mr. Jas., Wellow, near Romsey, Hants.
*Allsop, Thomas, Esq., Oadby, Leicestershire
Allsop and Son, Messrs., Burton on Trent
Allvey, Samuel, Esq., M. D., Huntingdon
*Allwood, John, Esq., Bloomsbury-sq., London
*Allwood, Rev. Robert, Clifton, near Bristol
Alsop, John, Esq., Lea-bridge, Derbyshire
Alsop, Luke, Esq., Lea-hall, do.
*Alston, R. G., Esq., Christ-church col., Oxford
*Alston, William, Esq., Blackburn, Lancashire
Althorpe, J. C., Esq., Dunnington-hall, near Worksop
*Alto, Mr. Thomas, Great Warner-st., London
Alty, Thomas, Esq., Bickerstaffe, Lancashire
ALVANLEY, The Right Honorable Lord
Alven, F., Esq., Walbrook, London
Alves, Duncan D., Esq., Lime-st.-square, do.
*Amery, Richard, Esq., Bartington, Cheshire
*Ames, G. H., Esq., Rodney-house, near Bristol
*Ames, Levi, Esq., Hereford-street, London
AMHERST, The Right Honorable Earl
Amor, T., Esq., Abberley, Worcestershire
Amor, T., Esq., Nursling, near Southampton
Amphlett, Mr. Edmund, Worcester
Amphlett, Mr. John, do.
Amphlett, John, Esq., Clent, Worcestershire
Anders, John, Esq., Wyndham-street, Bryan-stone-square, London [Lincoln
*Anderson, Rev. Sir C. J., Bart., Lea-hall,
*Anderson, Charles, Esq., Lea, Lincolnshire
*Anderson, Christopher, Esq., Ealing, Middlesex
Anderson, G., Esq., Great St. Thomas Apostle,
*Anderson, Mr. George, Durham [London
*Anderson, John, Esq., West Wickham, Kent
Anderson, Joseph, Esq., M. D., Liverpool
Anderson, Joshua, Esq., Carlisle, Cumberland
*Anderson, Thos., Esq., Trinity col., Cambridge
*Anderson, Mr. T., Southampton-build., London
*Anderson, William, Esq., Cambridge
Anderton, James, Esq., Liverpool
Anderton, Peter, Esq., Datchett, near Windsor
*Anderton, Samuel G., Esq., Manchester
Anderton, Thos., Esq., Liverpool
Anderton, Mr. Wm., jun., Birmingham
Andras, Mr. J., High-street, Eton, Bucks.
*Andrew, C., Esq., Laysters, Herefordshire
Andrew, Mr. J., Shirleywich, Staffordshire
Andrew, Jas., Esq., Gee-cross, nr. Manchester
*Andrew, John, Esq., Manchester
Andrew, John, Esq., Wirksworth, Derbyshire
Andrews, Mr. George, Hertford
Andrews, G. P., Esq., Birchin-lane, London
Andrews, Mr. George, Durham
Andrews, Mr. J. L. B., Newport, Isle of Wight
*Andrews, R., Esq., Stanmore, Middlesex
Andrews, Mr. R. P., Lisson-grove, London
Andrews, Miss, Alton, Hants.
Andrews, Richard, Esq., Farnham, Surrey
Andrews, Richard B., Esq., Epping, Essex
Andrews, Thomas, Esq., East Malling, Kent
Andrews, Thomas, Esq., Canterbury
Andrews, T. W., Esq., Nursling, Hants.
Andrews, William, Esq., Salisbury
*Andrews, W., Esq., Royton-hall, Lancashire
*Angell, S., Esq., Langbourne-chambers, London
Angell and Rastall, Messrs., Lincolns-inn-fields
*ANGLESEY, The Most Noble the Marquis of
Angus, Mr. J., Camden Town, Middlesex
*Anning, Mr. William, Hungerford
*Ansdell, R., Esq., Northwich, Cheshire
Ansley, S. H., Esq., Houghton-Hill, Hunts.
*ANSON, The Right Honorable Lord Viscount
Anson, Lieut.-General Sir William
*Anson, Edw. J., Esq., Lawrence-Pountney-lane,
*Anstice, J. P., Esq., Broad-st., do. [London
Anstice, R., Esq., Bridg-water, Somersetshire
Anstie, G. W., Esq., Devizes, Wilts.
Anthony, Capt. C., R. N., Preston, Lancashire
Anthony, Mr. Charles, Hereford
*Antrobus, G. Crawford, Esq., Eaton-hall, Chesh.
*Antwis, Samuel, Esq., Aston, Frodsham, do.
*Antwis, William, Esq., do. do. do.
Apperley, R., Esq., Fownhope, Herefordshire
Apperley, W. H., Esq., Withington, do.
*Appleby, George, Esq., Durham
*Appleby, S., Esq., Raymond-buildings, London
Appleby, Thomas, Esq., Salford, Lancashire
Appleby & Charnock, Mess., Gray's-inn, Lond.
Appleby, Walker, & Co., Messrs., Renishaw,
Appleford, Mr. John, Windsor [Derbyshire
*Applegath, Augustus, Esq., Crayford, Kent
*Appleton, John Grigg, Esq., Evesham
*Appleton, R. W., Esq., Everton, Liverpool
*Appleton, R. W., Esq., St. Michael's-alley, Cornhill, London
*Appleyard, R. S., Esq., Bloomsbury-sq., London
*Arabin, R. St. Julian, Esq., Trinity college, Cambridge
*Arbuthnot, The Rt. Hon. Sir C., Bart., M.P.
Arbuthnot, Edmd., Esq., Newtown-house, Hants.
Arbuthnot, George, Esq., Wimpole-st., London
*Archdeacon, Mr. Wm., Marsh-place, Reading
Archer, C. R., Esq., Christ-church col., Oxford
Archer, Penton, Esq., Puckle-Church-hall, Glou-
*Archer, Thomas, Esq., Chelmsford [cestershire
Archibald, Mr. A., Thayer-street, London
Archibald, J., Esq., Holmer, Herefordshire
*Archdall, Gen. M., M.P., Conduit-st., London
*Archdall, E. M., Esq., Lincoln's-inn-fields, do.
ARDEN, The Right Honorable Lord
Arden, Mr. T., Weobley, Herefordshire
*Arderne, R., Esq., Utkinton, Cheshire
*Argles, E., Esq., Great James-street, London
*ARGYLL, His Grace the Duke of
*Arkwright, C., Esq., Dunstall, Staffordshire
*Arkwright, P., Esq., Rock-house, Derbyshire
Arkwright, R., Esq., Willersley, do., 2 Copies
Arkwright, Robert, Esq., Stoke, near Bakewell
*Arlick, George, Esq., Park-row, Leeds
*Armfield, R., Esq., Cateaton-street, London
*Armitstead, Arthur, Esq., Lancaster
*Armitstead, John, Esq., do.
*Armitstead, L., Esq., Cranage-Hall, Cheshire
*Armitstead, Rev. W., M.A., West Kirby, do.
Armstrong, Mr. C., Lisson-grove, Middlesex
Armstrong, John, Esq., Preston, Lancashire
*Armstrong, J. J. W., Esq., Audlem, Cheshire
Armstrong, Mr. Robert, Lambeth, Surrey
*Armstrong, Mr. S., Tor Mills, Cheshire
*Armytage, Lieut.-Col., Abbots-Langley, Herts.
Arnold, E., Esq., M.D., Whisendine, Rutlandsh.
*Arnold, Rev. J. W., M.A., Burrington, Somerset
Arnold, S. P., Esq., Aldersgate-street, London
Arnold, T. J., Esq., Staple-inn, do.
Arnold, Rev. T., D. D., Rugby, Warwickshire
*Arnold, W. H., Esq., Tokenhouse-yard, Lond.
*ARRAN, The Right Honorable the Earl of
*Arrundell, W., Esq., Newton in Mackerfield, Lancashire
*Arthur, Mr. C., Bensington, Oxfordshire
Arundale, George, Esq., Park-st., Camden Town
*Arundell, The Honorable Henry
Asbridge, Rev. J., Eversley, Hants.
Asbury, Jacob Vale, Esq., Enfield, Middlesex
*Ash, C., Esq., Ashleigh, near Taunton
*Ash, Rev. J. G., Catsfield, Sussex
Ash, Mrs., Hastings, do.
Ashbourn, G., Esq., Croxton-Keyrial, Leicestersh.
Ashby, W. A., Esq., Ashford, Derbyshire
*Ashley, Thomas, Esq., Coppice-hall, Cheshire
*Ashpitel, W. H., Esq., Clapton-sq., Hackney
*Ashton, Benjamin, Esq., Hyde, Cheshire
Ashton, Edward, Esq., Prescot, Lancashire
*Ashton, H., Esq., Sandiway-lodge, Cheshire
Ashton, Henry, Esq., Toxteth-park, Liverpool
Ashton, John, Esq., do.
Ashton, James, Esq., Newton, Cheshire
Ashton, Robert, Esq., Hyde, do.
*Ashton, R., Esq., Ramsbottom, near Bury, Lan-
*Ashton, R., Esq., New Inn, London [cashire
*Ashton, T., Esq., Hyde, near Stockport, Cheshire
*Ashton, W. G., Esq., Cambridge
*ASHTOWN, The Right Honorable Lord
Ashurst, W. H., Esq., Waterstock, Oxford
*Ashwin, James, Esq., Bretforton, Worcestersh.
Ashwood, Mr., E., Allensmore, Hereford
*Ashworth, Giles, Esq., Friday-st., Manchester
*Ashworth, Henry, Esq., Bolton, Lancashire
Ashworth, Percy, Esq., Wadham col., Oxford
*Ashworth, Rev. Thomas, M. A., Grasmere, Westmorland
*Askew, H., Esq., Emanuel college, Cambridge
*Askew, W., Esq., Upper Thames-street, London
Askwith, William, Esq., Proctor, York

*Aslatt, Mr. John, Southampton
*Aspinall, J., Esq., Standon-hall, Lancashire
Aspinall, James, Esq., Liverpool
Aspinall, R., Esq., do.
*Aspinall, W., Esq., Manchester
*Aspinall and Templeman, Messrs., London
Astbury, J., Esq., Stone, Staffordshire
*Astbury, J. M., Esq., Manchester
*Astell, Tooke, and Thornton, Messrs., London
Astley, Sir J., Bart., M.P., Everleigh-house, Wilts
*Astley, J.W., Esq., Fellow of King's col., Cam-
Aston, Mr. Edw., Tipton, Staffordshire [bridge
*Aston, George, Esq., Clapham-road, Surrey
*Aston, Mr. James, Tipton, Staffordshire
Aston, John, Esq., Barlaston, do.
Aston, John, Esq., Hereford
*Aston, John P., Esq., Manchester
Atcheson, Rev. Anthony Singleton, S. C. L., Great Budworth, Cheshire
*Atherley, E. C., Esq., York-place, London
Atherton, Nathan, Esq., Calne, Wilts.
*Atherton, John, Esq., Hollingworth, Cheshire
Atherton, Mr. William, Poplar, Middlesex
Athorpe, J. C., Esq., Dunnington, York
Atkins, Mr. G., Commercial-road, London
Atkins, Mr. Henry James, Windsor
Atkins, Miss, Stamford, Lincolnshire
Atkins, L. D., Esq., Bath
*Atkins and Son, Messrs., Portsmouth
Atkins, Thomas, Esq., New-street, Birmingham
*Atkins, Mr.W., Kimbridge, near Romsey, Hants.
Atkinson, D. F., Esq., Liverpool
*Atkinson, Edward P., Esq., Runcorn, Cheshire
*Atkinson, Joseph, Esq., Preston, Lancashire
*Atkinson, Miss, Dalton, Yorkshire
*Atkinson, J. R., Esq., Clay-pit-house, Leeds
Atkinson, Mr. M., Bakewell, Derbyshire
Atkinson, T. W., Upper Stamford-st., Blackfriars
*Atkinson, W., Esq., Paternoster-row, London
*Atkinson, W. W., Esq., Burton, Lancashire
*Atkinson, W., Esq., University college, Oxford
*Atkinson, Mess. W. and A., New Broad-street-court, London
*Atlas Fire and Life Insurance Company, do.
Attenborough, Mr. Henry, Nottingham
*Attfield, Mr., Kingston upon Thames [Bucks.
Attkins, Rev. H. T., M. A., Langley-house,
Attkins, Rev. Thomas, Egham, Surrey
*Attree, William, Esq., Brighton
*Attree and Clarke, Messrs., do.
*Attwood, Francis, Esq., Salisbury
Attwood, Rev. H. A. S., M. A., Kenilworth
Atwood, Mr. W., Claston, Herefordshire
*Auber, Peter, Esq., East India-house, London
*Aubertin, Rev. Peter, Chipstead, Surrey
*Aubrey, Lewis, Esq., Snatchupend, Hertfordsh.
Audit Office, Somerset-place, London, 2 Copies
AUDLEY, The Right Honorable Lord
*Aughtie, H.W., Esq., Cheapside, London
*Austen, Colonel, Seven-Oaks, Kent
*Austen, George L., Esq., do.
Austen, R. A., Esq., Oriel college, Oxford
*Austen and Hobson, Mess., Gray's-inn, London
*Auster, C. H., Esq., Birmingham
*Austin, Charles, Esq., Luton, Bedfordshire
Austin, Capt. Francis W., R. N., C. B., Gosport
*Austin, J. P., Esq., Grosmont, Monmouth
Austin, Mr. James, Slough, Bucks.
Austin, W. Piercy, Esq., Exeter college, Oxford
*Aveling, Mr. T., Whittlesea, Huntingdonshire
*Avern, Mr. William, Paradise-st., Birmingham
Avery, J. R., Esq., Boscastle, Cornwall
Avery, Mr. Thomas, Monmouth
*Avison, Thomas, Esq., Liverpool
Axford, F., Esq., Bridg-water, Somersetshire
Ayer, John, Esq., Heslington, near York
*Ayerst, R. G., Esq., Batts-house, Somersetshire
Ayling, Rev. H., Guildford, Surrey
Ayling, Mr. John, Chertsey, do.
*Aylmer, G. W., Esq., Tonbridge Wells
Ayscough, T., Esq., Raymond-buildgs., London
Ayton, W. C., Esq., Millman-street, do.

*Babington, C.C., Esq., St. John's col., Cambr.
Babington, Mr., Horncastle, Lincolnshire
*Babson, Robert, Esq., Ramsbury
Backhouse, Mr. H., Hunt's-bank, Manchester
*Backhouse, Rev. J. B., Deal, Kent
Bacon, Charles, Esq., Donnington, Berks.
Bacon, George, Esq., Nottingham
Bacon, John, Esq., Stratford upon Avon
*Bacon, N., Esq., St. Albans
*Bacon, R. W., Esq., King's college, Cambridge
Bacon, W. V., Esq., Norwich
*Badcock, H., Esq., Taunton, Somersetshire
*Badcock, Rev. J., do., do.
*Baddeley, Henry, Esq., Lemon-street, London
*Badger, Messrs. Thomas and Isaac, Dudley
Badley, D. B., Esq., Hanley, Staffordshire
*Baggallay, R., jun., Esq., Camberwell, Surrey
Bagge, W., Esq., Lynn, Norfolk
Bagnall, J., Esq., West Bromwich, Staffordsh.
*BAGOT, The Right Honorable Lord
Bagot, Rev. R., M.A., Wolstanton, Staffordsh.
Bagott, Robert, Esq., Liverpool
*Bagshaw, John, Esq., Manchester
*Bagshaw, Thomas, Esq., Altrincham, Cheshire
Bagshaw, Rev. W., Banner-cross, Yorkshire
*Bagshaw, W. J., Esq., The Oakes, Derbyshire
*Bailey, C., Esq., Chippenham, Wiltshire
*Bailey, Mr. George, Old Broad-street, London
*Bailey, J., Esq., Blackburn, Lancashire
Bailey, J., jun., Esq., Brasenose col., Oxford
*Bailey, Philip, Esq., Nottingham
Bailey, Wm., jun., Esq., Lane-End, Staffordshire
Baillie, R., Esq., Tadcaster, Yoskshire
*Bailward, J., Esq., Bradford, Wilts.
*Bain, Alexander, Esq., Burton-crescent, London
Bainbridge, Joseph, Esq., Newcastle upon Tyne
Bainbrigge, T. P., Esq., Derby
*Bainbrigge, W., Esq., Cannon-row, Westminster
*Baines, James, Esq., Ludlow, Shropshire
*Baines, John, Esq., Six-clerks'-office, London
*Baird, D., Esq., M. D., Duke-street, Liverpool
*Baird, Mr. John, Newcastle upon Tyne
*Bairstow, John, Esq., Preston, Lancashire
*Baker, Miss, Baddow-lane, Chelmsford
*Baker, B., Esq., Maldon-hall, Essex
Baker, Charles, Esq., Southampton
Baker, Captain, R. N., Swaffham, Norfolk
Baker, Edward, Esq., Avon-Side, Stoke-Bishop
Baker, Rev. F., Wily, Wiltshire
*Baker, G. T., Esq., Fort-William, Cork
*Baker, Mr. G., Clapton, Middlesex
*Baker, J., Esq., East Malling, near Maidstone
Baker, Jno., Esq., Wood-st., Cheapside, Lond.
Baker, J. E., Esq., Accomb-lodge, York
*Baker, J. R., Esq., Chalk, near Gravesend
Baker, Richard, Esq., Wadham coll., Oxford
Baker, Samuel, Esq., jun., Rochester
Baker, Slade, Esq., Bewdley, Worcestershire
Baker, Rev. T., Yarmouth, Norfolk
Baker, Rev. Thomas, Whitburn, Durham
*Baker, Capt. Thomas, Rochester, Kent
*Baker, William, Esq., Hertford
*Baker, William, Esq., Fenton, Staffordshire
*Baker, Mess. J. & B., Gibraltar-house, Chatham
Baker, Messrs. J. and W., Monmouth
Baldock, W. H., Esq., Pelham, near Canterbury
Baldwin, Lieut.-col., Frodsham, Cheshire
*Baldwin, C., Esq., Camberwell, Surrey
*Baldwin, Charles, Esq., Bridge-st., Blackfriars
Baldwin, Rev. G., M. A., Leyland, Lancashire
*Baldwin, H., Esq., Lancaster
*Baldwin, J., Esq., Colne, Lancashire
*Baldwin, Richard, Esq., Preston, do.
*Baldwin, Major T. J., Leyland, do.
*Baldwin, Mrs., Liverpool
Baldwin, W., Esq., Upton-Bishop, Herefordsh.
Baldwin, Mr. William, Bilston, Staffordshire
*Balfour, Rev. J., M. A., Lower Peover, Cheshire
Balguy, B. T., Esq., Derby
*Balguy, Charles G., Esq., Nottingham
*Balguy, John, Esq., Godling, Nottinghamshire
*Balguy, T., Esq., Duffield, Derbyshire

*Ball, E., Esq., Wardleworth, Rochdale
*Ball, William E., Esq., Hereford
Ballard, M., Esq., Wood-st., Cheapside, Lond.
*Ballard, Philip, Esq., Westhide, Herefordshire
Ballinger, C., Esq., Great Brampton, do.
*Balme, Mr. John, Leeds, Yorkshire
Balmer, John, Esq., Acton-Grange, Cheshire
Balston, C., Esq., Corpus-Christi college, Oxford
*Baly, Joseph, Esq., Warwick
Bambridge, Mr. G., Bridewell, Norwich
*Bamford, James, Esq., Milk-street, Cheapside
Bamford, Mr. Jas. E., Egham, Surrey
*Bamford, William, Esq., Rugeley, Staffordshir
Bampfylde, Rev. C. F., Dunkerton, Somersetsh.
Banaster, George, Esq., Tewkesbury
Banbury, Thomas, Esq., Coventry
*Bancks, William, Esq., Brierly, Staffordshire
*BANDON, The Right Honorable the Earl of
*Banister, T. M., Esq., Brunswick-sq., London
*Bankes, M. Esq., Winstanley-hall, near Wigan
*Bankes, Roger, Esq., Newton, Cheshire
*Bankes, Wm., Esq., Weston, near Runcorn, do.
Banks, Sir Edw., Knt., Adelphi-terrace, London
Banks, George, Esq., Hunslet-lane, Leeds
*Banks, Mr. G., Ettingshall, Staffordshire
Banks, Joseph, Esq., Lothbury, London
*Banks, S., Esq., St. John's college, Cambridge
*Banks, Mr. William, Bilston, Staffordshire
*Bannehi, William, Esq., New-st., Southwark
*Banner, Mr. Henry, Holloway, Middlesex
*Banner, John M., Esq., Liverpool
Banner, Thomas, Esq., Daresbury, Cheshire
Banning, William, Esq., Liverpool
Bannister, J., Esq., Wall-heath, Staffordshire
Banting, Mr. Joseph, St. Giles', Oxford
*Banting, Mr. Thomas, Pall-Mall, London
*Bantook, William J., Esq., Kennington, Surrey
BANTRY, The Right Honorable the Earl of
*Barber, C. C., Esq., Chancery-lane, London
*Barber, C. H., Esq., Lincoln's-inn, do.
*Barber, Joseph, Esq., Billiter-street, do.
*Barber, J., Esq., Water-street, Manchester
Barber, John, Esq., Derby
Barber, John, Esq., Sheffield
Barber, J. H., Esq., Nottingham
Barber, J. M., Esq., New-inn, London
Barber, Rev. L., President of Downside college, Stratton on the Fosse, Somersetshire
*Barber, T. F. P. H., Esq., Moorgreen, Notts.
Barber, Mr. Richard, Walsall, Staffordshire
Barber, Rev. W., M. A., Duffield
Barber, Mr. B. J., Norwich
Barber, Carter, and Allen, Sandbach, Cheshire
*Barbor, R., Esq., Charter-house, London
*Barclay, Alex., Esq., Teddington, Middlesex
*Barclay, Mr. A., York . . . . 3 Copies
Barclay, J. P., Esq., Wickham-Market, Suffolk
*Bardsley, Mr. J., Hooley-hill, Lancashire
Bardswell, Charles, Esq., jun., Liverpool
Barfield, John, Esq., Thatcham, Berks.
*Barge, Thomas, jun., Esq., Manchester
Barham, J. F., Esq., Queen-Anne-st., London
*Barham, Rev. W. F., Trinity col., Cambridge
Baring, Sir Thos. M. P., Stratton-park, Hants.
*Baring, A., Esq., M. P., Grange-park, do.
*Baring, C., Esq., Christ-church col., Oxford
Baring, Henry, Esq., Somerly-house, Hants.
Barker, Rev. A., Baslow, Derbyshire
Barker, Carter, and Allen, Messrs., Sandbach,
*Barker, F. D., Esq., Cambridge [Cheshire
*Barker, G., Esq., Gray's-inn-square, London
*Barker, George, Esq., Birmingham
Barker, H., Esq., Christ-church college, Oxford
*Barker, Henry J., Esq., Middlewich, Cheshire
*Barker, John, Esq., Wolverhampton
Barker, Mr. John, Ulverstone, Lancashire
Barker, Rev. J., A. M., East-Church, Kent
Barker, J. F., Esq., Great Malvern, Worcestersh.
*Barker, J. F., Esq., Brasenose college, Oxford
*Barker, J. W., Esq., Bakewell, Derbyshire
*Barker, Peter, Esq., Northwich, Cheshire
*Barker, Richard, Esq., Chester

Barker, Samuel, Esq., Barnby-Moor, Notts.
* Barker, Thomas, Esq., Oldham, Lancashire
Barker, Mr. William, King-st., Holborn, London
* Barker, W., Esq., Pendleton, near Manchester
* Barker, Walter, Esq., South-bank, Regent's-park, London
Barker, Mr. W., Coleharbour-st., Hackney-road
Barkworth, John, Esq., Anlaby, Yorkshire
* Barley, E., Esq. March, Cambridgeshire
Barlow, Rev. G., Burgh, near Ipswich
* Barlow, G., Esq., Sidney-Sussex col., Cambr.
Barlow, G. F., Esq., Wetherby, Yorkshire
* Barlow, Henry, Esq., Highfield, Cheshire
* Barlow, H. M., Esq., Wadham coll., Oxford
* Barlow, J. H., Esq., Stoke-Newington, Middlesex
Barlow, J., Esq., Blackburn, Lancashire
* Barlow, J. P., Esq., Doctors Commons, London
* Barlow, John, Esq., Maidstone, Kent
Barlow, Rev. John, Uckfield, Sussex
* Barlow, Mr. R., Worsley, near Manchester
* Barnard, Alfred, Esq., Norwich
Barnard, Benjamin, Esq., Ham common, Surrey
* Barnard, Mr. Francis, Watford, Herts.
Barnard, Rev. H. W., Pilton, Somersetshire
* Barnard, Mr. P., Watling-street, London
* Barnard, W. H., Esq., Upper Tooting, Surrey
* Barnard, W. V., Esq., Lowestoft, Suffolk
Barneby, Rev. Thomas, Bromyard, Herefordshire
Barneby, Mrs., Buckenhill, do.
* Barnes, Rev. E. W., M. A., Richmond, Yorkshire
* Barnes, G., Esq., Christ-church coll., Oxford
Barnes, Rev. Henry, Monmouth
Barnes, Mr. Philip, All Saints'-green, Norwich
* Barnes, Robert, Esq., Manchester
* Barnes, R., Esq., Great Budworth, Cheshire
Barnes, Thomas, Esq., New-Mills, Derbyshire
Barnes, Thomas, Esq., Canonbury, Islington
* Barnes, William, Esq., Manchester
* Barnett, John, Esq., Bristol
Barnett, Joseph, Esq., Colwall, Hereford
Barnewall, Robert, Esq., Liverpool
Barns, Rev. J., Warton, Lancashire
* Barnston, Roger, Esq., Chester
* Barnston, Roger Harry, Esq., Crew-hall, Chesh.
Barnwell, Rev. J., Stogursey, Somersetshire
* Baronneau, Mrs., New Lodge, near Barnet
* Barr, Wallis, Esq., Blackman-street, London
* Barras, George, Esq., Newcastle upon Tyne
* Barras, John, Esq., Gateshead, Durham
* Barratt, John, Esq., Altrincham, Cheshire
Barrett, Mr. George, Reading, Berks.
Barrett, Mr. I. S., Stockport, Cheshire
Barrie, Commodore, C. B.,
* Barrington, Lady, Swainstone-house, Isle of Wight
* Barron, Capt. T., Berners-street, London
* Barrow, Mrs., Burton in Kendal, Westmorland
Barrow, G. H., Esq., Southwell, Nottinghamsh.
Barrow, Rev. J. N., Stanmore, Middlesex
Barrow, John, Esq., Wedmore, Somersetshire
Barrow, R., Esq., Raymond-buildings, London
* Barrow, Richard, jun., Esq., Manchester
* Barrow, Simon, Esq., Lansdown-grove, Bath
* Barrow, T. W., Esq., Manchester
* Barry, C., Esq., Ely-place, London
* Barry, David, Esq., Swinton-street, do.
* Barry, Thomas, Esq., Sawbridgeworth, Herts.
* Barter, John, Esq., Wolverhampton
Barth, W., Esq., Yarmouth, Norfolk
* Bartholmew, George D., Esq., Reading, Berks.
* Barthrop, R., Esq., Clapham-road-place, Surrey
Bartlemere, Wm., Esq., Rochdale, Lancashire
* Bartlett and Beddome, Messrs., Nicholas-lane, London
Bartley, N., Esq., Martin's-lane, Cannon-st., do.
Barton, Ashton W., Esq., Coventry
* Barton, E., Esq., Great Tower-street, London
* Barton, Jeffrey L., Esq., Bishopsgate-st., do.
* Barton, Rev. John, A. M., East Church, Kent
* Barton, M., Esq., St. John's college, Cambridge
Barton, Richard G., Esq., Windsor
* Barton, Samuel, Esq., Old Broad-st., London
* Barton, Samuel, Esq., Manchester
* Barton, Thomas, Esq., Altrincham, Cheshire
* Barton, William L., Bishopsgate-street, London
Barton, W., Esq., King's-Arms-buildings, do.
* Barton and Co., Messrs., Ardwick, Manchester
Bartrop, Robert F., Esq., Chertsey, Surrey
* Barttelot, H., Esq., Bishops-Hull, Somersetshire
Barwell, Osborn, Esq., Dawney-house, do.
Barwick, Rev. John, Charing, Kent
Baseley, Henry, Esq., Leamington, Warwicksh.
Baskerville, Henry, Esq., Bristol
* Baskerville, T. B. M., Esq., Hay, Brecon
* Baskerville, T. B. M., Esq., Rockley-house, near Marlborough
Basnett, Rev. T. B., Cloughs, Staffordshire
* Bassett, G., Esq., Norfolk-street, London
Bassford, Mr. Stephen, Bilston, Staffordshire
* Bassil, Robert S., Esq., Tag's-end, Hertfordsh.
Bastard, E. P., Esq., Ketley, near Yealhampton
Batchellor, Rev. W., Charlton, near Bath
Batchelor, Mr. John, Eling, near Southampton
* Batchelor, Mr. J. G., do.
Bate, Robert, Esq., Bridg-water, Somersetshire
Bateman, Mrs. Anne, Stratford upon Avon
* Bateman, I., Esq., Knypersley-hall, Staffordsh.
* Bateman, J., Esq., Southampton-buildings, Lond.
Bateman, Mr. John, Norwich
* Bateman, Joseph, Esq., Chester
* Bateman, Thomas, Esq., Manchester
Bateman, W., Esq., Middleton, Derbyshire
Bates, Rev. C. C., A. M., Castleton, do.
* Bates, J. E., Esq., Christ-church coll., Oxford
* Bates, John, Esq., Long-lane, Bermondsey
* Bates, Mr. John, Smithfield, London
Bateson, J. T., Esq., Lancaster
* BATH, The Most Noble the Marquis of
* Bath, Mr. Thomas, Forbury, Reading, Berks.
* Bath, Mr. William, Bilston, Staffordshire
Bathe, William, Esq., Aldersgate-street, London
Bather, The Venerable and Reverend Archdeacon, M. A., Shrewsbury
Batho, W. M., Esq., America-square, London
* Bathurst, The Right Honorable C. B.
Batt, Thomas, Esq., Abergavenny
* Batten, Edmund, Esq., Yeovil, Somersetshire
Batten, Edwd., Esq., Wandsworth-road, Surrey
Batten, Mr. Henry N., Clapham, do.
Batten, Rev. S. E., M. A., Harrow, Middlesex
* Batten, Thomas, Esq., Coleford, Gloucestersh.
Batterbee, Mr. J., Gray's-inn-lane, London
Battersby, A. G. H., Esq., Clifton, near Bristol
Battersby, C., Esq., Hindley, Lancashire
Battersby, J., Esq., Wigan, do.
Battersby, Rev. R., Lathom, do.
* Battiscomb, Rev. H., King's coll., Cambridge
* Battison, Richard, Esq., Lymm, Cheshire
* Battye, J., Esq., Rochdale, Lancashire
* Battye, R. C., Esq., Park-row, Leeds, Yorkshire
Baugh, Rev. J. W., Ripple, Worcester
* Bawden, J., Esq., Chard, Somersetshire
Baxendale, Messrs., & Co., King's-Arms-yard, Coleman-street, London
Baxter, Mr. I., Lewes, Sussex
Baxter, Rev. R. W., Kingsthorpe, near Northampton
Baxter, Robert, Esq., Doncaster
* Baxter, Robert, Esq., Dee-hills, Chester
* Baxter Stafford S., Esq., Atherstone, Warwicksh.
* Baxter, Mr. William, Oxford
Bayford, John, Esq. Doctors Commons, London
Bayle, P., Esq., M. D., Clarendon-square, do.
* Bayley, A., Esq., Stalybridge, Lancashire
* Bayley, E. B., Esq., Broughton, nr. Manchester
Bayley, Rev. E. G., A. M., Ampthill, Bedfordsh.
Bayley, Rev. H. V., D. D., Sub-Dean of Lincoln
* Bayley, James, Esq., Stapeley-cottage, Cheshire
Bayley, Jno., Esq., Essex-court, Temple, London
* Bayley, John, Esq., F. R. S. and S. A., Upper Harley-street, do.
* Bayley, W., Esq., Broughton, near Manchester
* Bayley, Rev. W. F., M. A., F. R. S., & F. A. S., Precincts, Canterbury
* Bayliff, Mr. R., sen., Queen-square, Hoxton
* Bayliff, Mr. R., jun., do., do.
* Bayliff, T. L., Esq., St. John's coll., Oxford
* Baylis, John, Esq., Ponder's End, Middlesex
* Baylis, Joseph, Esq., Kidderminster
Bayly, John B., Esq., Devizes, Wilts.
Bayly, Wentworth, Esq., Foxleaze-park, Hants.
Bayne, Rev. T. V., Jesus college, Oxford
Bayne, W. J., Esq., M. D., Trinity coll., Camb.
* Baynes, Mr. Cornelius, Weston, Cheshire
* BAYNING, The Right Honorable Lord
* Baynton, Rev. H., Bromham, near Devizes
* Bays, William P., Esq., Wisbeach, Cambridge
* Bazett, Farquhar, Crawford, and Co., Messrs., Old Broad-street, London
Bazing, W. H., Esq., Southampton-st., Reading
* Bazley, J. H., Esq., Bolton, Lancashire
Bazley, T., jun., Esq., Manchester
* Beach, M. H. H., Esq., Christ-church col., Oxford
* Beach, Mr. W., Loveday-st., Birmingham
Beacham, Mr. J. P., Theatre Royal, Norwich
Beachcroft, Samuel, Esq., Canterbury
Beadle, Charles, Esq., Erith, Kent
Beadon, R., Esq., Taunton, Somersetshire
* Beadon, Rev. J. W., Christian-Malford, Wilts.
* Beadon, W., Esq., Gotten-house, Somersetshire
* Beal, Richard, Esq., Malling, near Maidstone
* Beale, Richard, Esq., Biddenden, Kent
* Bean, J. C., Esq., Clement's-inn, London
Beard, John, Esq., Bold-street, Liverpool
* Beard, Joseph, Esq., Wrenbury, Cheshire
Beard, Mr. William, Heaton-Norris, Lancashire
* Beard, Thomas, Esq., Lewes, Sussex
* Beardsworth, Mr. John, Birmingham
Beare, Mr. Samuel S., Norwich
Beart, J., Esq., Yarmouth, Norfolk
Beasley, Thomas, Esq., L. L. D., Uxbridge
Beattie, Mr. G., North Audley-st., London
* Beauchamp, R. F., Esq., Walford-house, Somersetshire
BEAUFORT, His Grace the Duke of
* Beaumont, Mr. F., Buckland, near Reigate
* Beaumont, J., Esq., Wetherby, Yorkshire
* Beaumont, J., Esq., Barrow on Trent, Derbysh.
Beaumont, J. B., Esq., County Fire-office, Lond.
* Beaumont, R. H., Esq., Gravesend, Kent
Beaumont, Rev. T., M. A., Budgford-hill, Notts.
* Beaver, H., Esq., New Cannon-st., Manchester
* Beavor, J. P., Esq., Clifford-street, London
* Beazley, Edward, Esq., Mincing-lane, do.
* Bebb, Joseph, Esq., Bloomsbury-square, do.
* Beck, John, Esq., Clement's-lane, do.
Beck, Peter, Esq., Shrewsbury
* Beck, T. A., Esq., Hawkshead, Lancashire
* Becke, Cecil, Esq., Devonshire-st., London
* Becker, H., Esq., Foxdenton-hall, near Manchester
Beckett, The Honorable W. K.
* Beckett, A., Esq., Sutton-hall, Cheshire
* Beckett, Ashton, Esq., Audlem, do.
Beckett, Thos., Esq., Mile-End-road, London
* Beckwick, A. A. H., Esq., Norwich
Beckwith, Rev. H. A., Collingham, York
Beckwith, Rev. J. F., East Retford, Notts.
* BECTIVE, The Right Honorable the Earl of
Beddall, Mrs., Congleton, Cheshire
* BEDFORD, His Grace the Duke of
* Bedford, George, Esq., Brighton
* Bedford, John, Esq., Abbey-house, Pershore
* Bedford, Rev. R. G., A. M., Clifton, Bristol
Bedford, William, Esq., Oriel college, Oxford
* Bedingfield, F. P., Esq., Catsfield, Sussex
Bedman, William, Esq., Maidstone, Kent
Bedwell, C., Esq., Ely, Cambridgeshire
* Bedwell, B. B., Esq., East Bergholt, Suffolk
* Bedwell, P., Esq., St. John-street, Clerkenwell
Beechey, W. N., Esq., Harley-street, London
* Beechey, Mr. W. F., Cold-Arbour, Oxford
Beedham, John, Esq., Kimbolton, Hunts.
* Beek, C. T., Esq., Lincoln's-inn, London
* Beeman, Mr. Isaac, Nelson-square, do.
BEERHAVEN, The Right Hon. Lord Viscount
* Beeston, R., Esq., Wood-street, Cheapside
Beete, Joseph, Esq., Clifton, Gloucestershire
* Beetholme, J. L., Esq., Ambleside, Cumberland

Becthólme, J. L., Esq., St. John-street, London
Beethorn, Rev. J., M. A., Lancaster
Beilby, W. Turton, Esq., Kingston upon Hull
Belcombe, H. S., Esq., M. D., York
*BELFAST, The Right Honorable the Earl of
Bell, Mr., Broughton, near Stockbridge, Hants.
Bell, Charles, Esq., Ware, Herts.
Bell, E., Esq., Fleet-street, London
Bell, James, Esq., Frowse-mills, Norwich
Bell, Joseph, Esq., Austin-Friars, London
Bell, Mr. John, Romsey, Hants.
*Bell, Rev. T., M. A., Garstang, Lancashire
*Bell, Thomas, Esq., Norwich
Bell, William, Esq., Bow Church-yard, London
Bell, W. B., Esq., Shaftesbury, Dorset
Bell, Mr. W. B., Doctors Commons, London
Bell, J. & H., Mess., Itchen-Ferry, Southampton
*Bell, J. & S., Messrs., Gough-square, London
*Bellamy, Mrs. A., Goodrich, Herefordshire
*Bellamy, Rev. T., Chetnole, Dorset
Bellamy, W. H., Esq., Hereford
*Bellchambers, Mr., Birmingham
*Bellhouse, David, Esq., Manchester
*Bellhouse, James, Esq., do.
*Bellhouse, W., Esq., Park-place, Leeds [bridge
Bellingham, J. G., Esq., St. John's col., Cam-
Bellott, S., Esq., Brook-house, Coombs, Derby-
*Belson, F., Esq., University col., Oxford [shire
*Benbow, Mr. C., Taplow-mills, Bucks.
*Benbow, Mr. Hurley, near Maidenhead, Berks.
*Benett, John, Esq., Trinity col., Cambridge
*Benfield, R., Esq., Whitmore-house, Hoxton
*Benham, Thomas, Esq., Southampton
*Benham, W. P., Esq., Hawkhurst, Kent
*Beningfield, Mr. S., Mark-lane, London
Benn, Rev. Jno., Farringdon, near Alton, Hants.
Benner, Mr. W., Ross, Herefordshire
Bennet, Mr. J. D., Newark, Nottinghamshire
Bennet, P., Esq., Rougham-hall, Suffolk
Bennett, Mr. C., Clehonger, Herefordshire
*Bennett, Edward, Esq., Wolverhampton
Bennett, George, Esq., Banwell, Somersetshire
Bennett, Geo., A. M., F. L. S., Staines, Middlesex
Bennett, Rev. H., Marchington, Staffordshire
*Bennett, Jas., Esq., Wallingford, Berks.
*Bennett, J., Esq., Simondsley, Derbyshire
*Bennett, J., Esq., Horseferry-road, Westminster
*Bennett, J. B. H., Esq., Tutbury, Staffordshire
*Bennett, Mr. J., Brampton-Abbots, Herefordsh.
*Bennett, Mr. J., Ingestone-Foy, do.
*Bennett, James, Esq., Cadbury-house, Somerset
Bennett, Mr. J., Tretire, Herefordshire
Bennett, Mr. R., Kennington-house, Surrey
Bennett, Mr. Richard, Wantage, Berks.
Bennett, Mr. R., jun., Hope-Ash, Hereford
*Bennett, Mr. S. T., Worthing, Sussex
Bennett, S. W., Esq., Brighton
Bennett, Capt. T., R. N., Hereford
*Bennett, Mr. Thomas, Fawley, Herefordshire
Bennett, W., Esq., Chapel le Frith, Derbysh.
*Bennett, William, Esq., St. John's coll., Cam-
Bennett, William, Esq., Dudley [bridge
*Bennett, William, Esq., Ringmere, Sussex
Bennett, Mr. William, Stretford, Herefordshire
Bennett, Rev. W. C., Westbury, Wilts.
*Bennison, Mr. R., South-row, St. Pancras
*Bennison, Mr. T., High Holborn, London
*Bensley, Thomas, Esq., Clapham Rise, Surrey
*Bensley, Mr. Benjamin, Andover, Hants.
*Bensley, Mr. Thomas, do., do.
Bensley, Mr. John, All Saints'-green, Norwich
*Benson, E. O., Esq., Wadham coll., Oxford
Benson, Rev. H. B., Heckington, near Sleaford
Benson, James, Esq., Manchester
Benson, Mr. John, Birmingham [ersetshire
*Benson, Rev. J., Norton under Hambdon, Som-
*Benson, Rev. J., D. D., Hounslow, Middlesex
*Benson, Rev. Martin, Merstham, Surrey
*Benson, R. Moore, Esq., Birmingham
*Benson, Rev. W., Wolverhampton
Benson, Mr. W., Bull-street, Birmingham
*Bent, James. Esq., Mitholm, Lancashire

Bent, Thomas, Esq., M. D., Derby
Bent, W., Esq., M. D., Newcastle under Line
Bentley, Henry, Esq., Liverpool
*Bentley, John, Esq., Cheapside, London
Bentley, R. T., Esq., Bedford-street, do.
Bentley and Wear, Messrs., Shelton, Staffordsh.
*Benwell, Henry, Esq., Greenwich, Kent
*Benwell and Co., Messrs., Henley, Oxfordshire
*Benyon, Rev. E. R., Downham, Essex
*BERESFORD, The Right Hon. Lord Viscount
BERESFORD, The Right Hon. Lord George
Beresford, James, Esq., Macclesfield
Berkeley, John, Esq., Longdon, Worcestershire
*Berkely, R., jun., Esq., Spetchley, nr. Worcester
*Berkshire Chronicle, Proprietors of the
*Bernard, The Honorable Francis
Bernard, H. I., Esq., Wells, Somersetshire
Bernard, John, Esq., Sutton, near Shrewsbury
Bernard, T., Esq., M. P., Castle-Bernard, Ireland
*Berners, The Venerable and Rev. Archdeacon
Berridge, Rev. B., Algarkirk, Lincolnshire
Berridge, Mr. William, Windsor
Berriman, Mr. Thomas, Brook-house, Herefordsh.
*Berry, Henry, Esq., Furnivals-inn, London
Berry, J. W. M., Esq., Brasenose coll., Oxford
*Berry, Joseph, Esq., Hatton-Hall, Cheshire
*BERWICK, The Right Honorable Lord
*Best, Norris, Esq., Bilston, Staffordshire
Bestow, Mr. W., Wood-street, Cheapside, Lond.
Beswick, John, Esq., Rochdale, Lancashire
*Beswick, Mr. Samuel, Kennington, Surrey
*Bethell, Rev. G., M. A., Fellow of Eton college
Bethell, Richard, Esq., M. P., Rise, Yorkshire
*Bethell, R., Esq., Chancery-lane, London
Bethune, G., Esq., Trinity college, Oxford
Beton, B., Esq., Watling-street, London
*Bettington, J. H., Esq., Guildford-street, do.
Betts, Mr. I. P., Smithfield Bars, do.
*Bevan, J., Esq., Edvin-Loach, Worcestershire
Bevan, Robert, Esq., M. D., Monmouth
Bevan, Thomas, Esq., Balliol college, Oxford
Beverley, C. J., Esq., Bethnal-green, London
*Beverley, John, Esq., Leeds
*Bewley, Mr. Thomas, Strand, London
*Bewsher, Rev. James, Richmond, Surrey
BEXLEY, The Right Honorable Lord
*Beynon, Rev. E. T., Carshalton, Surrey
Bibbs, B., Esq., Hall-house, Ledbury
*Bibly, John, Esq., Bucklow-Hill, Cheshire
Bickersteth, R., Esq., Liverpool
Bickerstoff, R., Esq., Preston, Lancashire
*Bickham, Charles C., Esq., Reading, Berks.
*Bickmore, Rev. B., B. A., Caldicott-lodge, Hertfordshire
Bicknell, C., Esq., Spring-gardens, London
Bicknell, J., Esq., Staple's-inn, do.
*Biddulph, Benj., Esq., Burghill, Herefordshire
Biden, Miss A., Houghton, Hunts.
Bidwell, Charles, Esq., Ely
*Bidwell, L. S., Esq., Thetford, Norfolk
Bielby, Mr. Robson, Birmingham
*Biffin, Mr. John, Plumtree-street, Bloomsbury
*Bigbie, Thomas, Esq., Mark-lane, London
*Bigg, E. S., Esq., Southampton-buildings, do.
Biggs, Mr. R., Devizes, Wiltshire [land
Bigland, Capt., R. N., Milnthorpe, Westmor-
*Bigland, G., Esq., Cartmel, Lancashire
*Bignold, Pulley, & Co., Messrs., Norwich, and Bridge-street, London . . . . . 2 Copies
Bill, John, jun., Esq., Farley-hall, Staffordshire
Billing, Robert, Esq., Worcester coll., Oxford
*Billinge, J., Esq., Warnford-court, London
Billinge, Thomas, Esq., Cateaton-street, do.
*Billinge, William, Esq., Bull-street, Birmingham
*Billington, Rev. J., Kennington, Kent
*Bilton, Mr. T. H., Newman-st., Oxford-st., Lond.
*Binckes, Mr. J. M., New Church-st., Alpha-road
Bindloss, E., Esq., Magdalene col., Cambridge
*Bindloss, Son, and Bowman, Messrs., Manchester
*Bingham, Major-Gen. Sir George R., K. C. B.
*Bingham, Colonel, Rochester, Kent [and F. S.

*Bingham, Rev. T., M. A., Norbury, Derbyshire
*Bingham, W., Esq., St. Mary-hall, Oxford
*Bingley, Robert, Esq., Royal Mint, London
*Binley, Mr. James C., Chancery-lane, do.
*Binns, Mr. Abraham, Oldham, Lancashire
*Binns, Charles, Esq., New-Mills, Derby
Binns, Joseph, Esq., Lancaster
Binns, Mr. N., King-street, Norwich
*Binns, Thomas, Esq., Essex-street, London
*Binyon, A., Esq., Mayfield, near Manchester
Birch, Mr. Charles, Hales-Owen
Birch, James, Esq., Rainford, Lancashire
Birch, Joseph, Esq., St. James'-place, London
Birch, T., Esq., Diana-place, New-road, do.
Birchall, John, Esq., Prescot, Lancashire
*Birchall, Mr. J. S., James-st., Covent-garden
Bird, Rev. C. S., Culverlands, Burghfield, Berks.
Bird, Rev. Charles John, A. M., F. A. S., Mordiford, Herefordshire
Bird, Mr. George M., Sydenham, Kent
Bird, Rev. J., Preston, Lancashire
Bird, John, Esq., Staunton-Lacy, do.
Bird, John, Esq., Kensington, Liverpool
*Bird, John G., Esq., West Derby, near do.
Bird, Mr. J. S., Ledbury, Herefordshire
*Bird, Thomas, Esq., Hereford
Bird, T., jun., Esq., Upton upon Severn
*Bird, Mr. William, Cambridge
*Birds, Rev. D., Ellesmere, Shropshire
*Birkett, Mr. H. T., Wallingford, Berkshire
*Birmingham Canal Company
Birmingham Library
*Birmingham News Room
*Birnie, Sir Richard, Knt.
*Birnie, J. R., Esq., Basingstoke, Hants. 2 Copies
*Birt, Rev. J., D. D., Canterbury
*Bischoff, Charles, Esq., Torrington-sq., London
Bish, Thomas, Esq., Cornhill, do.
*Bishop, Mrs., Sunbury-house, Middlesex
*Bishop, G., Esq., West-Borough, Maidstone
Bishop, Rev. Henry, Ardleigh, Essex
Bishop, J., Esq., Castle-Froome, Hereford
Bishop, J. W., Esq., Lombard-street, London
*Bishop, Thomas, Esq., Tenterden, Kent
Bishop, T. H., Esq., Newbury, Berkshire
*Bishop, W., Esq., Shelton-hall, Staffordshire
*Bishops and Harrington, Messrs., Finsbury-place, London
*Bishton, G., Esq., Neachley, Shropshire
*Bishton, T., Esq., Kilsal, do.
*Bisp, D., Esq., Lea, near Ross, Herefordshire
Bispham, T., Esq., Prescot, Lancashire
Bissland, Rev. T., Winchmore-hill, Middlesex
Bissell, Benjamin, Esq., Tipton, Staffordshire
Bissel, Mr. I., jun. do. do.
Bissell, Mr. Simeon, do. do.
*Black, James, Esq., Regent-street, London
*Blackburn, James, Esq., Lothbury, do.
Blackburn, James, Esq., Birmingham
*Blackburn, W., Esq., Low Harrogate, Yorksh.
*Blackburn Mail Newspaper, the Proprietors of the
Blackburn, Thomas, Esq., Liverpool
*Blackburne, Isaac, Esq., Didsbury, Lancashire
Blackley, Mr. William, Canterbury
Blacklow, S. J., Esq., Frith-st., Soho, London
*Blackman, James, Esq., M. D., and F. R. S., Shurdington, Gloucestershire
*Blackmore, Robert, Esq., Chapel-street, Lond.
*Blackstone, W. S., Esq., Christ-ch. col., Oxford
*Blackwell, S., Esq., Sarratt-hall, Hertfordshire
Blackwood, Vice-Admiral Sir H., Bart.
Blackwood, R., Esq., Oriel college, Oxford
*Blacow, Rev. R., A. M., Liverpool
Blades, John, Esq., Ludgate-hill, London
*Blagborne, J., Esq., M. D., Manchester
Blagg, J. M., Esq., Cheadle, Staffordshire
*Blagg, Thomas Ward, Esq., St. Albans
*Blagrave, John, Esq., Calcot-park, Reading
Blair, James, Esq., Uttoxeter, Staffordshire
*Blair, S., Esq., Bolton, Lancashire
Blair, Thomas, Esq., Walton-grove, Surrey

*Blake, Sir Francis, M. P., Tilmouth-park, Durham
Blake, D., Esq., Receiver-General's-office, Nor-
*Blake, F. J., Esq., Norwich [wich
Blake, George, Esq., Halton, Cheshire
*Blake, George, Esq., Liverpool
Blake, M., Esq., M. D., Taunton, Somerset
Blake, William, Esq., Swanton-Abbott, Norfolk
*Blake, William, Esq., Welwyn, Herts.
*Blaker, Harry, Esq., Brighton, Sussex
Blakeway, Mr. Charles, Shelderton, Salop
Blakeway, Mr. Richard, Middleton, Herefordsh.
*Bland, H., Esq., Garrow-hill, near York
Blandy, Rev. F. J., Downton, Wiltshire
Blandy, Mr. William, Reading, Berks.
*Blandy and Andrews, Messrs., do., do.
Blane, R., Esq., Winkfield-park, near Windsor
*Blanshard, W., Esq., Temple, London
Blayds, Rev. H., Norton St. Philips, Somerset
Blayney, Thomas, Esq., Evesham, Worcestersh.
*Bleadon, John, Esq., Lothbury, London
Blease, Peter, Esq., Liverpool
*Bleeck, Alfred, Esq., Redcliffe-parade, Bristol
Bleeck, Rev. W., Oare, near Pewsey, Berks.
*Blencowe, E., Esq., Wadham college, Oxford
Blewitt, R. J., Esq., Gloucester
Blick, Rev. E., M. A., Walton on Trent, Der-
*Bligh, Capt., R.N., Millbrook, Hants. [byshire
Bligh, Rev. J., L. L. B., Derby
*Bliss, C., Esq., Witton on Wye, Herefordshire
*Bliss, James, Esq., Oriel college, Oxford
*Blisset, J., Esq., Letton, Herefordshire
Blofield, R. Clealand, Esq., Vauxhall, Surrey
*Blofield, Rev. T. C., Hoveton-house, Norfolk
Blogg, Mr. William, Norwich
*Blomfield, Rev. G. B., M.A., Tattenhall, Chesh.
Bloodworth, Thomas, Esq., Kimbolton, Hunts.
*Bloome and Gatliff, Messrs., Leeds
Blott, William, Esq., Wytton, near Huntingdon
Blount, George, Esq., Liverpool
*Blount, Rev. W., Sedgeley-park, Staffordshire
*Blount, Mr. William, Gt. Cumberland-st., Lond.
*Bloxham, Rev. Charles, Badsey, Worcestershire
Bloxham, Rev. R., D.D., Rugby, Warwicksh.
Bloxham, Henry, Esq., Ellesmere, Shropshire
Bloxham, J. M., Esq., Hales-Owen, do.
Bloxham, Thomas, Esq., Liverpool
*Bloxsome, O., Esq., Doughty-st., London
*Bloxsome, E., Esq., Wadham college, Oxford
*Bloxsome, W. H., Esq., Dursley, Gloucestersh.
Blundell, Byron, Esq., Liverpool
Blundell, Mr. B., Speen, near Newbury, Berks.
Blundell, C., Esq., Ince, Lancashire
Blunden, G., Esq., East Malling, Kent
Blunt, Lieut.-Gen. R., Shirley-lodge, Hants.
Blunt, Mr. Robert, Windsor
Blurton, Webb, & Co., Messrs., Burton on Trent
Blyth, John, Esq., Goswell-street, London
*Boardman, R., Esq., Bolton, Lancashire
Boddington, E., Esq., Stockton, Worcestershire
Boddy, W., Esq., Beaconsfield, Buckinghamsh.
*Bodenham, Chas., Esq., Rotherwas, Herefordsh.
*Bodicoate, H. V., Esq., Lindfield, Sussex
Bodingfield, T. T., Esq., Ditchingham-hall,
Bodmar, William, Esq., Maidstone [Norfolk
Bogue, George, Esq., Pinner-house, Middlesex
*Bogue & Lambert, Messrs., Raymond-buildings, London
Boissier, Rev. P. E., Sunninghill, Berks.
Bold, Rev. Thomas, Liverpool
Boldero, Rev. G., Ixworth, Suffolk
*Bolders, Rev. George, A.M., do., do.
Boldran, Mr. W., Aldbrough, Yorkshire
Bolger, Thomas, Esq., Fiskerton, Notts.
*Bolingbroke, H., Esq., Claremont.-sq., London
Bolland, Mr. George, York . . . . . . 2 Copies
*Bolling, E., Esq., Bolton, Lancashire
*Bolling, W., Esq., do. do.
*BOLTON, The Right Honorable Lord
Bolton, Mr. George, Norwich
*Bolton, H., Esq., Colne, Lancashire
Bolton, Rev. Henry, Radcliffe-lodge, Notts.
*Bolton, John, Esq., Liverpool
*Bolton, John, Esq., Preston, Lancashire
Bolton, R., Esq., Wigan, do.
Bolton, T., Esq., Brickworth, near Salisbury
Bolton, Mr. Thomas, Birmingham
*Bolton, W. G., Esq., Austin-friars, London
Bolus, Mr. T., High-street, Birmingham
*Bomford, Mr. T., Hay, Brecon [near Bristol
*Bompass, George G., Esq., M. D., Fish-ponds,
*Bond, B., Esq., Canterbury's-Margaretting
Bond, Rev. Essex H., B. A., Merton, Surrey
*Bond, J. M., Esq., Basinghall-street, London
*Bond, Stephen, Esq., Westmorland-st., do.
*Bond, Winfrid, Esq., Clapham, Surrey
*Bond, W., Esq., Caius college, Cambridge
*Boner, N., Esq., Hurst, Sussex
Bonner, B., Esq., Gloucester
Bonnett, Rev. Charles S., Avington, Hants.
Bonney, Rev. T., A. M., Rugeley, Staffordshire
Bonnor, William, Esq., Ross-Foreign
Bonomi, Ignatius, Esq., Durham
*Bonsor, Joseph, Esq., Polesden, Surrey
Bontflower, Charles, Esq., Colchester
Booker, Mr. E., Edmonton, Middlesex
*Booker, Josias, Esq., Liverpool
Booker, Rev. L., L. L. D., F. R. S. L., Dudley
*Boolteby, B., Esq., Christ-church col., Oxford
Boor, J., Esq., Warminster, Wiltshire
*Boote, James, Esq., Hankelow, Cheshire
*Booth, Benjamin, Esq., Manchester
*Booth, Mr. George, Liverpool
*Booth, Mr. George, jun., do. [Cheshire
*Booth, Joseph, Esq., Oak-cottage, nr. Nantwich,
*Booth, John G., Esq., Hornsey, Middlesex
Booth, J., Esq., Manchester
Booth, Mr. J., Easy-row, Birmingham
*Booth, Mr. James, Littlefield, Derbyshire
Booth, Peter, Esq., Chapel en le Frith, do.
Booth, Richard, Esq., Old Basing-house, Hants.
*Booth, Mr. Robert, Chisworth, Derbyshire
*Booth, Mr. S., Charlesworth, do.
*Booth, T., Esq., Edenfield, Lancashire
*Booth, William, Esq., Stanstead, Ware, Herts.
*Booth, W. J., Esq., Red Lion-square, London
*Boothby, Sir W., Bart., Ashbourn-hall, Derbyshire
Boothroyd, John, Esq., Stockport, Cheshire
Borland, J., Esq., M. D., Teddington, Middsx.
*Borough, C. B., Esq., Chetwynd-park, Shropsh.
*Borrodaile, William, Esq., Clapham, Surrey
*Bosanquet, Richard, Esq., Maidstone, Kent
BOSCAWEN, The Right Honorable Lord
Boscawen, The Honorable and Reverend J. E.
Bosley, Mr. John, Hereford
*Bosley, Robert, Esq., Glossop, Derbyshire
Bosley, Mr. Thomas, Ledbury, Herefordshire
Bostock, George, Esq., Macclesfield
*Bostock, J. B., Esq., George-street, Mansion-house, London
*Bostock, T., Esq., Malpas, Cheshire
*Boston Permanent Library, Lincolnshire
*Bosworth, W., Esq., Queen's col., Cambridge
Botfield, B., Esq., Christ-church col., Oxford
*Botfield, W., Esq., Decker-hill-hall, Shropshire
*Bott, Michael, Esq., Nantwich, Cheshire
*Bottomley, G., Esq., Croydon, Surrey
Bouch, John, Esq., Monument-yard, London
Boules, Rev. R., Yarmouth, Norfolk
Boulger, William, Esq., Queen's college, Oxford
Boult, Mr. Zachariah, Bray, Berks.
*Boultbee, T. P., Esq., Ruddington, Notts.
*Boulter, Mr. Daniel, Reading, Berks.
*Boulton, Frederick, Esq., Dalston, Middlesex
Boulton, John, Esq., Hanley, Staffordshire
Boulton, William, Esq., Queen's college, Oxford
*Bourne, James, Esq., Dudley
Bourne, J. C., Esq., Cheadle, Staffordshire
Bourne, Mr. J. W., Church-Gresley, Derbysh.
*Bourne, Ralph, Esq., Hilderstone-hall, Staffordsh.
*Bourne, Mr. Stephen, Bridge-st., Blackfriars
Bourne, John, Esq., Fenton, Staffordshire
Bourne, Timothy, Esq., Liverpool
*Bousfield, Mr. G., Gracechurch-street, London
Boutcher, G., Esq., Long-lane, Bermondsey
*Bover, George, Esq., Stockton-lodge, Cheshire
Bouverie, E., Esq., Delapree-abbey, Northamptonshire
*Bouverie, Major-Gen. Sir H., Knt., K. C. B., Rotherham, Kent
*Bovill, William, Esq., Upper Tooting, Surrey
*Bowden, J. S., Esq., Aldermanbury, London
*Bowden, N., Esq., Little St. Thomas-Apostle, do.
Bowden, Thomas, Esq., Coleshill, Bucks.
Bowdler, Chs., Esq., Doctors Commons, London
*Bowdon, Mr. J., Kingston upon Hull, Yorkshire
Bowen, B., Esq., Harrow, Middlesex
*Bowen, Mr. Thomas, Woofferton, Herefordshire
Bowen, W. W. W., Esq., St. Peter's college, Cambridge
Bower, C. Esq., Clifford's-inn, London
Bower, Henry, Esq., F. S. A., Doncaster
*Bower, J. H., Esq., Chancery-lane, London
Bower, John, Esq., M. D., Broxholme, near Doncaster
*Bower, Ralph, jun., Esq., New-Mills, Derbysh.
*Bowes, The Honorable J. B.
Bowker, W., Esq., Gray's-inn-square, London
Bowle, Rev. I., Salisbury
*Bowler, J., Esq., Denton, Lancashire
*Bowler, W., Esq., Dean-street, London
Bowles, Mr. B., Hertford
Bowles, Chas., Esq., Shaftesbury, Dorsetshire
Bowles, Rev. W. L., Salisbury
*Bowley, Mr. Thomas, Duke-street, London
Bowling, William, Esq., Jesus college, Oxford
*Bowman, Joseph, Esq., Wood-street, London
*Bowman, Rev. W., Queenborough, Kent
*Bownas, G., Esq., Newcastle upon Tyne
Bowring, William, Esq., Queen's col., Oxford
*Bowser, R., Esq., Bishop-Auckland, Durham
Bowstead, Rev. T. S., Liverpool
Bowyer, Mr. Edw., Ragland, Monmouthshire
Bowyer, Rev. H., Sunningwell, Berks.
*Bowyer, John, Esq., Petworth, Sussex
Bowyer, Robert, Esq., Pall-Mall, London
Bowyer, Mr. Thos., Buckden, Huntingdonshire
*Bowyer, W. W., Esq., Brasenose coll., Oxford
Box, Mr. John, Broughton, Hants.
*Boxall, Mr. Jonathan, Brighton, Sussex
Boyall, Mr. Richard, Belton, Lincolnshire
Boyce, F. L., Esq., Norwich
Boycott, William, jun., Esq., Kidderminster
Boyd, G., Esq., Acomb, Yorkshire
Boyd, William, Esq., Pinner-Green, Middlesex
*Boydell, John, Esq., Trevallyn-hall, Denbighsh.
Boydell, Samuel, Esq., Ilchester
Boyer, Edward, Esq., Scarisbrick, Lancashire
*Boyer, H., Esq., Barton upon Irwell, near Manchester
Boyles, Rev. C. J., Buriton, Hants
Boynell, E., Esq., Smithwick-hall, Shireland
*Boys, Edward, Esq., St. Albans
*Boys, James, Esq., Rochester, Kent
Boys, Jacob, Esq., Brighton, Sussex
Boys, W., Esq., Bridg-water, Somersetshire
*Boys, Mr. W., East Bourne, Sussex
*Bozon, F., Esq., Pinner's-hall, London
*Brabant, Edward, Esq., Middlewich, Cheshire
*Brabant, John Thomas, Esq., do., do.
*Brace, Major, Canterbury
Brackenbury, Ralph, Esq., Liverpool
*Brackenbury, Rev. R. C. N., M. A., St. Margaret's, Canterbury
Braddon, H., Esq., Surrey-street, London
Bradburne, H. H., Esq., Fossway-house, near Lichfield
*Bradburne, Jas., Esq., Great Neston, Cheshire
Bradby, Captain Thomas, Southampton
Bradby, Mr. John, Mottisfont, Hants.
*Braddick, J., Esq., Boughton-mount, Maidstone
Brade, W., Esq., Mount-pleasant, Liverpool
*BRADFORD, The Right Honorable the Earl of
Bradford, Mr. J. P., Leominster
*Bradford, John W., Esq., Langford, near Bristol

Bradford, Mr. Richard, Windsor
*Bradford, Rev. W. M., Beaconsfield, Bucks.
*Bradley, Edward, Esq., Reading, Berks.
Bradley, John, Esq., Liverpool
Bradley, Richard, Esq., Tipton, Staffordshire
Bradley, Rev. W., Atherstone, Warwickshire
*Bradock, J., jun., Esq., Fenchurch-st., London
*Bradshaw, A. H., Esq., Charles-street, do.
Bradshaw, F., Esq., Blunt-hall, Derbyshire
Bradshaw, H., Esq., St. Helen's-place, London
*Bradshaw, R. J., Esq., Halton-hall, Lancaster
*Bradshaw, Rev. W., Over Kellet, do.
Brady, Mr. T., Cannon-street, London
Bragge, William, Esq., Oxford [Kent
*Braham, Rev. W. S. H., M. A., Willesborough,
Braikenridge, G. W., Esq., Brislington, Somerset
Braikenridge, John, Esq., do., do.
*Brailsford, Richard, Esq., Enfield, Middlesex
Brain, Mr. George, Tipton, Staffordshire
Braine, Mr. Robert, Oxford [square, London
*Braithwaite, John, Esq., Bath-place, Fitzroy-
*Braithwaite, J., Esq., Home-Lacy, Herefordsh.
*Bramley, Rev. T. J., A. M., Enfield, Middlesex
Bramwell, Mr. W., North Shields, Northumb.
Branbury, Mr. P., Walcot-place, Lambeth
*Brancker, J., Esq., Croft-lodge, Westmorland
*Brancker, P. W., Esq., Liverpool
Brancker, Thomas, Esq., do.
*Brand, John, Esq., Lime-street-sq., London
*Brand, T., Esq., Christ-church college, Oxford
Brandling, C. J., Esq., Newcastle upon Tyne
*Brandling, John, Esq., Stand-house, do.
Brandling, R. W., Esq., do.
*Brandon & Catlow, Mess., Cheadle, Staffordshire
*Brandt, Rev. Francis, Gawsworth, Cheshire
Bransby, Rev. J. H., Dudley
Branson, Thomas, Esq., Sheffield, Yorkshire
Branthwaite, Mr. Richard, Cwm-Dows, near Newport, Monmouthshire
*Branton, Mrs., Micklefield-green, Herts.
Brasenose College, Library of, Oxford
Brasse, Rev. John, D. D., Cheshunt, Herts.
*Brassey, Rev. W., Weymouth, Dorset [bridge
*Braune, G. M., Esq., Sidney-Sussex col., Cam-
*Bray, J., Esq., St. Martin's-lane, London
*Bray, Joseph, Esq., Preston, Lancashire
*Bray, Joseph, Esq., Back-square, Manchester
Bray, P., Esq., Bromyard, Herefordshire
Bray, R., Esq., Great Russel-street, London
*Bray, Mr. W. F., Liverpool-street, do.
*Breakspear, Rev. Robert, M. A., P. G. S., Aud-
Breakspear, Mr., Birmingham [lem, Cheshire
Brearey, Mrs., Middlethorpe, Yorkshire
*Brearley, Mr. William, Birmingham
Bree, Stapylton, Esq., Queen's coll., Cambridge
*Breedon, J. S., Esq., Pangbourn, Berks.
*Breeds, James, Esq., Hastings, Sussex
Bremridge, J., Esq., Walbrook-buildings, Lond.
Bremridge, R., Esq., Chancery-lane, do.
Brenan, R., Esq., Great Eastcheap, do.
Brent, Mr. John, Canterbury
Brent, W. B., Esq., Old-sq., Lincoln's-inn, Lond.
*Brereton, Francis Wm., Esq., Tooting, Surrey
Brereton, Rev. John, L. L. D., Bedford
Breton, Captain P., Polygon, Southampton
*Brettle, G., Esq., Wood-st., Cheapside, London
*Brewer, Rev. H., Preston, Lancashire
Brewer, Jehoiada, Esq., Caira, Monmouthshire
*Brewer, John, jun., Esq., Newport, do.
*Brewer, Marmaduke, Esq., do. do.
*Brewer, S. K., Esq., Brighton, Sussex
Brickman, Mr. W. H., Worle, Somersetshire
Briddon, John, Esq., Manchester
Bridge, John, Esq., Ludgate-hill, London
*Bridge, Mr. John, New-Mills, Derbyshire
*Bridge, S., Esq., South Petherton, Somersetshire
*Bridge, S. F., Esq., Wellington, do.
*Bridge, T. F. H., Esq., Christ-church coll., Oxford
*Bridgeman, The Honorable and Reverend G.
*Bridgeman, George, Esq., Wigan
*Bridgen and Cousins, Messrs., Southampton
Bridger, E. D., Esq., Chilcombe, Hants.

Bridges, Sir B. W. B., Goodnestone-lodge, Kent
*Bridges, A. H., Esq., Oriel college, Oxford
Bridges, Mr. James, Chalfont-St. Giles, Bucks.
*Bridges, Thos., Esq., Tooting, Surrey [Oxford
*Bridges, Rev. T. E., D. D., Corpus-Christi col.,
*Bridges, T. C., Esq., Sufton-Court, Herefordsh.
Bridget, J., Esq., Derby
Bridle, Mr. William, Bath [countess
BRIDPORT, The Right Hon. Lady Vis-
*Bridson, T. R., Esq., Bolton, Lancashire
*Brierley, J., Esq., Ardwick, Manchester
*Brierley, S., Esq., Salford, Lancashire
*Brierly, Mrs. S., Brighton, Sussex
*Briggs, Abraham, Esq., Heckington, Lincolnsh.
*Briggs, C., Esq., Bolton, Lancashire
*Briggs, Edward, Esq., Preston, do.
*Brigham, William, Esq., Manchester
*Bright, John, Esq., Wadham college, Oxford
*Brindle, J., Esq., Manchester
Brindley, J. N., Esq., Temple, London
Brindley, Mr. Joseph, Longport, Staffordshire
Brinton, Mr. William, Kidderminster [hampton
*Briscoe, G., Esq., Oldfallings-hall, near Wolver-
Briscoe, S. S., Esq., King's Swinford, Staffordsh.
*Bristol, The Corporation of the Poor of
*Bristow, William, Esq., Liverpool
*Bristowe, Simon, Esq., do.
*Britain, Mr. John, Wetherby, Yorkshire
*British Traveller Newspaper, Proprietors of the
Brittain, Mr. G., Ripley, Derbyshire
*Brittain, Robert, Esq., Hoole-Bank, Chester
*Brittain, Samuel, Esq., Upton, Cheshire
Brittain, Verdon, Esq., Sheffield, Yorkshire
*Brittlebank, T., Esq., Ashbourn, Derbyshire
Britton, D., Esq., Barnstaple, Devonshire
Broadbent, John, Esq., Liverpool
*Broadbent, Richard, Esq., Altrincham, Cheshire
*Broadbent, William, Esq., do. do.
Broadhurst, J., Esq., West-heath-cottage, do.
*Broadhurst, J., Esq., Nantwich, do.
*Broadley, H., Esq., Melton-hill, Yorkshire
*Broadley, John, Esq., F. S. A., F. R. S. L., F. L. S., F. Z. S., South Ella, Yorkshire
Broadmead, P., Esq., Milverton, Somersetshire
*Brockbanck, J. B., Esq., Manchester
*Brockholes, Joseph, Esq.
*Brockholes, T. F., Esq., Garstang, Lancashire
*Brocklebank, Rev. J., M. A., Delamere, Cheshire
*Brocklebank, Rev. R. B., M. A., Kidnal, do.
*Brockman, Rev. J. D., Cheriton, Kent
*Brockman, Rev. Tatton, Frant, Sussex
Brodbelt, T., Esq., Bolton, Lancashire
*Broderip, E., Esq., Trinity college, Oxford
*Broderip, Edmund, jun., Esq., Wells, Somerset.
*Brodhurst, J. E., Esq., Mansfield, Notts.
*Brodhurst, William, Esq., do., do.
*Brodicate, H. V., Esq., Lindfield, Sussex
*Brodie, Alfred, Esq., Trinity coll., Cambridge
*Brodie, A. C., Esq., Lucknam-park, Wiltshire
Brodie, P. B., Esq., Lincoln's-inn-fields, Lond.
Brodie, Mr. W. B., Salisbury
*Brodribb, E., Esq., Upper Thames-st., London
Brokenbrow, W., Esq., Bath
*Bromage, Snead, and Co., Messrs., Monmouth
*Bromehead, Rev. A. C., Eckington, Derbyshire
Bromehead, Wm., Esq., Lincoln college, Oxford
Bromfield, B., Esq., Wavertree, Liverpool
*Bromfield, W., Esq., High-Ash-house, Cheshire
Bromilow, W., Esq., Merton-bank, Lancashire
Bromilow, W. jun., Esq., St. Helens, do.
*Bromley, Mr. James, Ashton under Line
*Bromley, Mr. John, do.
*Bromley, Robert, Esq., Clapham-Rise, Surrey
*Bromley, William, Esq., Gray's-inn-sq., London
*Bromley, William, Esq., Euston-square, do.
Brook, B. W., Esq., Egham, Surrey
*Brook, T., Esq., King's-Arms-yard, London
*Brooke, Sir Richard, Bart., Norton, Cheshire
Brooke, Rev. C., Ufford, Suffolk
*Brooke, Mr. Charles, Trafalgar-street, Leeds
*Brooke, A. J., Esq., Horningsheath, Suffolk
Brooke, C. W., Esq., Capel, do.

Brooke, F. C., Esq., Christ-church col., Oxford
*Brooke, George, Esq., Chester
Brooke, Rev. J., Everton, near Liverpool
*Brooke, James B., Esq., Ashton under Line
*Brooke, Rev. John, M. A., Shiffnall, Shropshire
*Brooke, John, Esq., Stockport, Cheshire
*Brooke, John, Esq., Dewsbury, Yorkshire
Brooke, Rev. Joseph, Gamston, Notts.
Brooke, Peter, Esq., Bridgford-hill, do.
Brooke, Richard, Esq., Liverpool
*Brooke, S. B., Esq., Old Jewry, London
Brooke, Rev. Thos., M. A., Wistaston, Cheshire
*Brooke, W., Esq., King's college, Cambridge
Brookes, Charles, Esq., Walsall, Staffordshire
*Brookes, Francis, Esq., Stafford
Brookes, Rev. G. J., Christ's Hospital, London
*Brookes, H., Esq., Tarporley, Cheshire
Brooking, A., Esq., Trinity college, Cambridge
*Brooks, Mr. Charles, Southampton
*Brooks, D., Esq., do.
Brooks, G. Eyre, Esq., New Bond-st., London
Brooks, Rev. J. W., East Retford, Notts.
*Brooks, Mr. George, Ashton under Line
Brooks, James, Esq., Henley upon Thames
Brooks, Jno., Esq., Lincoln's-inn-fields, Lond.
*Brooks, James, Esq., jun., Norwich
Brooks, John, Esq., Wantage, Berks.
Brooks, S. P., Esq., Ross, Herefordshire
Brooks, William, Esq., Furnival's-inn, London
*Brooksbank & Farn, Mess., Gray's-inn-sq., do.
*Brooksby, Rev. T., West Hanningfield, Essex
Broom, John, Esq., Kidderminster
*Broome, William, Esq., Manchester
Broomhead, B., Esq., Darley-dale, Derbyshire
Broomhead, H., Esq., Sheffield, Yorkshire
*Bros, T., Esq., Upper Clapton, Middlesex
Brothers, Lieut., R. N., Addlestone, Surrey
*Brotherton, J., Esq., Salford, Lancashire
*Broughton, Lieut.-Gen. Sir J. D., Bart., Doddington-hall, Cheshire
Broughton, A., Esq., Reigate, Surrey
*Broughton, B., Esq., Tokenhouse-yard, London
*Broughton, H. A., Esq., Gt. Marlborough-st., do.
Broughton, J., Esq., Peterborough
Broughton, T., Esq., Boston, Lincolnshire
Browmfield, James, Esq., Norwich
Brown, Mr., Alderman, do.
*Brown, Mrs. Anne, Belvidere-hall, Cheshire
*Brown, A. J., Esq., Hatton-garden, London
Brown, Mr. B., Aldermanbury, do.
*Brown, Capt., R. N., Mint-house, Edinburgh
*Brown, Edward, Esq., Oldham, Lancashire
*Brown, Rev. G., Lancaster
*Brown, G., Esq., Water-street, Manchester
Brown, G. C., Esq., M. D., Sheffield
Brown, George, jun., Esq., Liverpool
Brown, Mr. George, Monmouth
Brown, Mr. G., Neville, Ware, Herts.
Brown, H., Esq., Hanley, Staffordshire
Brown, Humphrey, jun., Esq., Tewkesbury
*Brown, Mr. H., Gravesend, Kent
*Brown, James, Esq., Wolverhampton
*Brown, James, Esq., Harehills-grove, Leeds
*Brown, J., Esq., Cook's-court, London
Brown, J., Esq., Lewston, Herefordshire
Brown, Mr. J., Camden-Town, Middlesex
Brown, Mr. James, Hertford
Brown, Mr. James, Windsor
Brown, Mr. J., Swadlincote, Derbyshire
Brown, John, Esq., Lea-castle, Kidderminster
*Brown, John, Esq., jun., Bishopsgate-st., Leeds
*Brown, Mr. John, Windsor
*Brown, Mr. John, Waltham-Abbey, Essex
Brown, Mr. John, Earith, Huntingdonshire
Brown, Mr. John, Tring, Hertfordshire
*Brown, Mr. Joseph, Ledbury, Herefordshire
Brown, J., Esq., Holdfast, nr. Upton on Severn
Brown, Jos., Esq., Princes-st., Cornhill, London
*Brown, Mr. Nicholas, Leeds, Yorkshire
Brown, R., Esq., Preston, Lancashire
Brown, Rev. Thos., Fen-Stanton, Huntingdonsh.
*Brown, Rev. T., Tonbridge, Kent

* Brown, T., Esq., Dove-crt., Lombard-st., Lond.
Brown, T., Esq., Trinity-house, do.
Brown, T., Esq., Great Berkhampstead, Herts.
Brown, Mr. Thomas, Lichfield-st., Birmingham
Brown, T. D., Esq., Worcester college, Oxford
* Brown, Rev. W., M. A., Stonesfield, Oxfordsh.
* Brown, William, Esq., St. Albans
* Brown, William, Esq., Chalk, Kent
Brown, William, Esq., Cheapside, London
* Brown, W., Esq., Russell-square, do.
Brown, William, Esq., Gloucester
Brown, W., Esq., Everton, near Liverpool
* Brown, W. J., Esq., Gt. Winchester-st., Lond.
* Brown, W. R., Esq., Brasenose college, Oxford
* Brown, Wm. Williams, Esq., Leeds, Yorkshire
* Brown and Son, Messrs., Reading, Berks.
* Brown and Danson, Messrs., Kings'-Arms-yard, Coleman-street, London, ...2 Copies
* Brownbill, N., Esq., Chorley, Lancashire
* Browne, A., Esq., Wood-st., Cheapside, London
Browne, A. P., Esq., Dulverton, Somersetshire
Browne, B., Esq., Wokingham, Berks.
* Browne, C., Esq., Norwich
* Browne, David, Esq., Macclesfield, Cheshire
* Browne, John, Esq., jun., Norwich
* Browne, J., Esq., Bishop's Froome, Herefordsh.
* Browne, Mackley, Esq., Parliament-st., London
Browne, O. E., Esq., Nailsworth, Gloucestersh.
Browne, Robert, Esq., Margaret-street, London
Browne, T., Esq., Brislington, near Bristol
* Browne, Thomas, Esq., Kingston upon Hull
* Browne, Thomas, Esq., Fenchurch-st., London
Browne, Champion, and Co., Messrs., Bridgwater, Somersetshire
Brownell, Charles, Esq., Richview, Yorkshire
* Browning, C. C., Esq., Lincoln's-inn, London
Browning, Mr. H., South-street, Finsbury
Brownlow, C., Esq., M.P., Park-place, Lond.
* Brownrigg, Sir R., Bart., Helstone-house, Herefordsh.
* Bruce, Rev. Thomas, Westbere, Kent
* Bruce, W. A., Esq., Bath
Brunel, M.J., Esq., Bridge-st., Blackfriars, London
Brunel, T., Esq., do., do., do.
Bruton, Mr. James, Hereford
* Brutton, Robert, Esq., Old Broad-st., London
* Bryans, Rev. Francis, M.A., Farndon, Cheshire
Bryant, Mr. Charles, Huntingdon
* Bryant, Edward, Esq., Southampton
Bryant, Mr. Isaac, George-st., Hampstead-road
Bryant, Mr. Jeremiah, Buckden, Huntingdonsh.
Brydges, Mr. James, Castle-Froome, Herefordsh.
Brymer, Rev. W.T.P., M.A., West Charlton, Somersetshire
* BUCCLEUCH, His Grace the Duke of
* Buchan, Mr. H., Southampton
* Buck, A., Esq., Burnley, Lancashire
Buck, Charles, Esq., Preston, do.
Buck, G., Esq., Glass-Hayes, Lyndhurst, Hants.
* Buck, R., Esq., Bolton, Lancashire
Buck, Mr. Thomas, Sunderland
* Buckbanck, J. B., Esq. Manchester
Buckham, Rev. P. W., Oundle, Northampton
* BUCKINGHAM, Her Grace the Duchess of
Buckingham, J. H., Esq., Gaddesden, Herts.
Buckland, C. E., Esq., Shaftesbury, Dorsetshire
* Buckland, R., Esq., Bouverie-street, London
* Buckland and Smith, Messrs., Furnival's-inn, do.
Buckle, Capt., R.N., St. James's-square, Bath
* Buckle, Miss J. B., Chacely-lodge, Worcester
* Buckle, Joseph, Esq., York
Buckler, T., Esq., Broomy-hill, Herefordshire
* Buckley, J., Esq., Todmorden, Lancashire
* Buckley, N., Esq., Carrhill, do.
* Buckmaster, J. J., Esq., Falmouth
Bucknell, W., Esq., Crowcombe, Somerset.
Buckner, Colonel, Wick, Sussex
* Buckston, Rev. G., M.A., Bradborne, Derbysh.
* Buckton, F., Esq., 11, Furnival's-inn, London
* Buckton, G., Esq., Doctors Commons, do.
* Buckton, James, Esq., do., do.
* Buckton, John, Esq., Canterbury
* Budd, T. H., Esq., Bedford-row, London
Buddle, John, Esq., Walls-End, Northumberland
* Budge, Sealy, Esq., South Petherton, Somerset.
Budgen, John, Esq., Trinity college, Oxford
* Bulcock, W., Esq., Blackburn
* Bull, Rev. J., M.A., Clipston, Northamptonsh.
Bull, Rev. S. Neville, Harwich, Essex
Bull, Mr. Samuel, Weobley, Herefordshire
Bull, Thomas, Esq., Digbeth, Birmingham
* Bullen, C., Esq., Southampton
* Bullen, Mr. G., Cherry-Hinton, nr. Cambridge
Bullen, J., Esq., New-inn, London
Bullen, Robert U., Esq., Taunton, Somersetsh.
Buller, A., Esq., Oriel college, Oxford
Buller, E. Esq., Dilhorne-hall, Staffordshire
Buller, H. J., Esq., Trinity college, Oxford
Bulley, Frederick, Esq., Magdalene college, do.
* Bulley, W. W., Esq., Liverpool
Bullock, J. Esq., Congleton, Cheshire
* Bullock, E., Esq., West Bromwich, Staffordshire
* Bullock, George, Esq., North Coker, Somerset.
Bullock, J. B., Esq., Gray's-inn, London
Bullock, Mr. John, Newport, Monmouthshire
* Bulman, J., Esq., Preston, Lancashire
Bulmer, John, Esq., York
* Bulmer, John, Esq., Osborne-st., Whitechapel
* Bulmer, William, Esq., Watling-street, London
Bunbury, Sir H., Bart., M.P., Bury St. Edmunds
* Bunbury, H., Esq., Oriel college, Oxford
* Bunney, William, jun., Esq., Hull
Bunyard and Sons, Messrs., Maidstone
* Burbury, D. W., Esq., Warwick
Burchell, William, Esq., Godalming, Surrey
Burdekin, G., Esq., Blackburn, Lancashire
Burden, Miss Martha, East Ilsley, Berks.
* Burder, John, Esq., Parliament-street, London
Burdett, Sir F., Bart., M. P., Ramsbury, Wilts.
* Burdsall, Rev. J., Manchester
Burford, John, Esq., Royal Exchange Assurance Office, London
* Burge, Mr. W., Hungerford, Berks.
Burge, Mr. William, Kintbury, do.
Burgess, Henry, Esq., Lombard-st., London
* Burgess, Henry, Esq., Styall, Cheshire
* Burgess, J., Esq., Churbrook, Nantwich, do.
* Burgess, J. R., Esq., Oriel college, Oxford
* Burgess, Messrs. J. and A., Worsley, near Manchester
Burgess, Mr. S. W., Manchester
* Burgess, Thomas, Esq., Curzon-street, May-fair
* Burgess, Thomas, Esq., Kingsley, Cheshire
* Burgess, W. R., Esq., Hartford-bridge, Hants.
Burgman, F., Esq., Trinity college, Oxford
Burk and Kennebrook, Messrs., Norwich
Burke, Rev. John, Usk, Monmouthshire
Burlin, Francis, Esq., Marlowes, Hertfordshire
* Burlingham, Miss Ann, Evesham, Worcestersh.
* Burlinson, Mr. John, Sunderland
Burlton, F. J., Esq., Leominster, Herefordshire
Burlton, Richard, Esq., The Hill, do., do.
* Burman, T. T. P., Esq., Henley in Arden
* Burman, W. S., Esq., Smithfield, Birmingham
Burmester, C., Esq., Weston under Penyard
* Burn, Mr. Edmund, Lower Shadwell, London
* Burn, John J., Esq., Gray's-inn-sq., do.
Burn, W. B., Westmorland-place, do.
* Burne, Thomas, Esq., Watling-street, do.
* Burne, Thomas, Esq., Manchester
* Burne, Rev. W. W., Grittleton, Wiltshire
Burnell, P. P., Esq., Winkbourn-hall, Notts.
* Burnell, T., Esq., Coleman-street, London
* Burnett, John F., Esq., May-place, Kent
Burnie, Joseph, Esq., Liverpool
* Burningham, Mr. J., Billericay, Essex
Burningham, Thomas, Esq., Froyle, Hants.
Burningham, T., jun., Esq., Trinity col., Oxford
Burns, Charles, Esq., Liverpool
Burnside, F., Esq., Lincoln's-inn-fields, London
* Burnside, Rev. J., Plumtree, Nottinghamshire
Burr, George, Esq., Tovil, near Maidstone, Kent
Burra and Neild, Messrs., King-st., Cheapside
Burrell, John, Esq., Durham
* Burridge, Mr. G. F., Mincing-lane, London
Burridge, Rev. W., Bradford, Wiltshire
* Burrough, Sir James, Knt., Bedford-sq., Lond.
Burrough, M., Esq., Corsham, Wiltshire
* Burrough, Mr. T. W., Wycombe, Bucks.
Burroughes, Mrs., Hoveton-hall, Norfolk
* Burroughs, Rev. E., M.A., Long Stratton, Suffolk
Burroughs, G. J., Esq., Shepton-Mallet
* Burroughs, Rev. Lynch, A. M., Offley, Herts.
Burroughs, Rev. T., Hemingford-Grey, Hunts.
* Burrow, George W., Esq., Holly-house, Hoxton
* Burrow, G., Esq., Lancaster
Burrow, Mr. J. C., Bishopsgate-st., London
Burrow, Samuel, Esq., Norton, Herefordshire
* Burrows, F., Esq., Great Queen-street, London
Burrows, S., Esq., M. D., Yatton, Somerset
Burrup, John, Esq., Gloucester
Burt, C. J. T., Esq., Mitre-court, London
Burt, T., Esq., Ironmonger-lane, do.
* Burt, T., Esq., Reigate, Surrey
* Burt, T. R., Esq., East Grinstead, Sussex
* Burton, Sir Francis, Knt., Coyningham-hall, Yorkshire
* Burton, Decimus, Esq., Regent-street, London
* Burton, Rev. E., D.D., Christ-ch. coll., Oxford
* Burton, Rev. Henry, M. A., Atcham, Shropsh.
* Burton, Henry, Esq., M. P., Hotham, York
Burton, H. S., Esq., Balliol college, Oxford
Burton, John S., Esq., Norwich
* Burton, Mr. John, Renville, Kent
* Burton, Mr., Brook-st., Grosvenor-sq., London
Burton, Mr. L., Newcastle-street, do.
Burton, R., Esq., Wood-street, Cheapside do.
Burton, Rev. R. L., M. A., Shrewsbury
Burton, Richard, Esq., Hotham, York
* Burton, Robert, Esq., Longnor, Shropshire
* Burton, Septimus, Esq., Lincoln's-inn, London
* Burton, Capt. Thos., New-bridge-st., do.
Burton, Thomas, Esq., Egham, Surrey
Burtt, Mr. James, Clifton, Bristol
* Bury, A., Esq., Salford, Lancashire
* Bury, Rev. Charles, B. A., Shrewsbury
* Bury, C. R., Esq., Manchester
* Bury, J., Esq., White-Ash, near Blackburn
* Bury, James, Esq., Ardwick, near Manchester
* Bury, T. Esq., Clayton-mills, do.
* Bury, S. H., Esq., Weymouth-street, London
* Bury, Thomas, Esq., Liverpool
* Bury, T., jun., Esq., Salford, Lancashire
Bury, William, Esq., New Bridge-street, London
* Busby, J., Esq., Winchester-st., Pentonville, do.
* Bush, A., Esq., Swallow-place, Regent-st., do.
Bush, Elijah, Esq., Trowbridge, Wilts.
Bush, H., Esq., Clifton, Bristol
Bush, John, Esq., Kings-Down-parade, do.
* Bush, John, Esq., Bradford, Wilts.
Bush, Robert, Esq., sen., Clifton, Bristol
Bush, Samuel, Esq., Frome, Somersetshire
Bushell, Henry, Esq., Rochester, Kent
* Bushell, John, Esq., Preston, Lancashire
* Bushell, Joseph, Esq., do., do.
* Bushnell, James, Esq., Reading, Berks.
Busigny, William, Esq., Stockbridge, Hants.
Busk, Jacob H., Esq., Ponsborne, Herts.
Buswell, Charles, Esq., Northampton
Butcher, Robert, Esq., Bungay, Suffolk
Butcher, Mr. William, Cheshunt, Herts.
* Butcher, William, Esq., Norwich
* BUTE, The Most Noble the Marquis of, 2 Copies
* Butler, Charles, Esq., Cheapside, London
* Butler, E. T., Esq., Erith, Kent
* Butler, G., Esq., Woolston, near Farringdon, Berkshire
Butler, John, Esq., Woolwich, Kent
* Butler, John, Esq., Bouverie-street, London
Butler, Mr. J., Henley upon Thames
Butler, Mr. J., Smithfield, London
* Butler, R. F., Esq., Barton-hall, Staffordshire
* Butler, Mr. Richard, Farringdon-street, London
Butler, W. H., Esq., Kenilworth, Warwickshire
* Butt, Captain, R. N., Romsey, Hants.
* Butt, William, Esq., Bognor, Sussex
* Butt, Mr. W., Bar-gate, Southampton
Butt, Mr. William, Bosbury, Herefordshire
* Buttenshaw, Mr. E., Holborn-bridge, London

*Butterfield, Richard, Esq., Keighley, Yorkshire
Butterfield, Rev. W., M.A., Shirland, Derbysh.
Butterton, Rev. G. A., Fellow of St. John's college, Cambridge
Butterworth, J., Esq., Grange, Bermondsey
*Butterworth, T., Esq., Rochdale, Lancashire
*Butterworth, Mr. C., Manchester
*Butterworth, Mr., Wood-st., Cheapside, Lond.
Buttery, John, Esq., Nottingham
*Button, Mr. Edward, Wallingford, Berks.
Buxton, Sir Robert John, Bart., Shadwell-lodge, Norfolk
Buxton, Thomas, Esq., Preston, Lancashire
*Buxton, T. F., Esq., M.P., ... 3 Copies
*Byam, Rev. R. B., A.M., Feltham, Middlesex
*Byde, C. P., Esq., Lincoln's-inn-fields, London
Byde, Rev. John, Bengeo, Herts.
*Byfield, Mr. John, Brooksby-street, Islington
*Bygrave, J., Esq., Gray's-inn, London
Bygrave, Thomas, Esq., Clement's-inn, do.
*Byng, T., Esq., Merton college, Oxford
Byng, W. B., Esq., Staines, Middlesex
*Byrd, Rev. W., Badsey, Worcestershire
*Byrom, W., Esq., Liverpool
Byron, Rev. John, Leatherhead, Surrey
*Byron, Mr. R., Ashton under Line, Lancashire
*Byron, Thomas, Esq., M. P., Nottingham-pl.
Bythesea, Rev. G., Freshford, Somersetshire
Bythesea, Rev. H. F., Nettleton, Wiltshire

*Cadogan, H., Esq., Oriel coll., Oxford
*Cafe, Mr. H. S., Great Marlborough-st., London
Cahill, R. S., Esq., Westbrook-park, Surrey
Cahusac, William, Esq., Bexley, Kent
*Caiger and Wells, Messrs., Southampton
*Caius college, Library of, Cambridge
*Calcroft, Robert, Esq., Grantham, Lincolnshire
*Caldecott, Charles, Esq., Tilston, Cheshire
*Calder, Sir Henry B., Bart., Feltham, Middsx.
Caldwell, T., Esq., Prescot, Lancashire
CALEDON, The Right Honorable the Earl of
Caley, Mr. John, Windsor
Callaghan, Colonel, Stanhope, Durham
Callaghan, N., Esq., Durham
Callander, John, Esq., M. D., Eye, Suffolk
*Callender, R. B., Esq., Bristol
Calrow, Joseph, Esq., Liverpool
Calrow, R., Esq., Walton-lodge, Lancashire
*Calrow, Thomas, Esq., Bury, do.
*Calrow, William, Esq., Woodhill, do., do.
*Calverley, Thomas, Esq., Ewell, Surrey
*Calvert, C., Esq., M.P., Twickenham, Middlesex
*Calvert, F., Esq., Lincoln's-inn-fields, London
Calvert, N., Esq., M. P., Ware, Herts.
Calvert, Rev. T. J., D.D., Manchester
Cam, Samuel, Esq., Hereford
*Cam, William, Esq., Basinghall-st., London
Cam and Booth, Messrs., Maiden-lane, do.
Camberbeach, Mr. T., Audenshaw, Lancashire
Cambridge, John, Esq., Bury St. Edmund's
*CAMDEN, The Most Noble the Marquis of
Cameron, A. A., Esq., London-road, Reading
Cameron, Charles, Esq., Queen's coll., Oxford
*Cameron, I., Esq., Easebourne, Sussex
Camp, G., Esq., New-inn, London
Camp, Messrs. I. and D., Cheshunt, Herts.
Campbell, Major-General Sir C., K. C. B., M. T. S., G. M. I., and T.S.
*Campbell, A. G., Esq., Upper Eaton-st., Pimlico
*Campbell, C. M., Esq., Bennington-park, Herts.
Campbell, D., Esq., M. D., Lancaster
*Campbell, Rev. D., Crowcombe, Somersetshire
Campbell, F. W., Esq., Birkfield-lodge, Suffolk
*Campbell, J., Esq., M.D., Ashton under Line
*Campbell Rev. J. T., B.A., Cholmondeley-castle, Cheshire
*Campbell, Mumford, Esq., Sutton at Hone, Kent
Campbell, Robert John, Esq., Norwich
*Campin, Mr. T., St. Paul's Churchyard, Lond.
Campion, A., Esq., Henrietta-street, do.
*Campion, H., Esq., Malling Deanery, Sussex
*Campion, James, Esq., Waltham-Cross, Essex
Campion, T. F., Esq., Gray's-inn-square, Lond.
*Campion, W. J., Esq., Denny, Sussex
*Cancellor, J. H., Esq., Gray's-inn, London
*Candler, T., Esq., Copthall-court, do.
Candy, Mr. Charles, Friday-street, do.
Cane, Rev. T. C., Southwell, Notts.
Cannan, D., Esq., Lothbury, London
Cannock, Mr. J., Weston under Penyard
*Cannon, John, Esq., Queen's college, Oxford
*Cansdell, Mr. Wm., Bishopsgate-street, London
*CANTERBURY, His Grace the Lord Archbishop of . . . . 2 Copies
Canterbury, The Very Reverend the Dean and Chapter of
*Capel, P. S., Esq., Bridewell-precinct, London
Capel, Cuertons, and Cundy, Messrs., do.
*Capper, George, Esq., Crosby-square, do.
*Capron, A., Esq., Midhurst, Sussex
*CARBERY, The Right Honorable Lord
Cardale, John B., Esq., Bedford-row, London
Carew, Gerald, Esq., Wadham college, Oxford
Carew, H., Esq., Queen's college, Cambridge
*Carew, Miss, Crowcombe-court, Somersetshire
Carew, L. G. W., Esq., do., do.
*Carew, W. H. P., Esq., Oriel college, Oxford
Carige, I. H., Esq., Great Alne, Warwickshire
Carleill, W., Esq., Longstone-hall, Derbyshire
CARLISLE, The Right Honorable the Earl of
*CARLISLE, The Hon. & Rt. Rev. Lord Bishop of
*Carlisle, The Worshipful the Corporation of
*Carlisle Journal, The Proprietor of the
*Carlisle, Richard, Esq., Manchester
Carlisle, Rev. W., A. M., Belmont, Staffordshire
*Carmalt, Rev. William, Putney, Surrey
*Carmichael, A. G., Esq., Trinity coll., Cambridge
Carmichael, Lieut.-Col. J., Staines, Middlesex
*Carne, Joseph, Esq., Trinity coll., Cambridge
Carnell, John, Esq., Tonbridge, Kent
Carpendale, Rev. W., Horsington, Somersetshire
*Carpenter, Lieut. Colonel, Northaw, Herts.
*Carpenter, Captain D. T., Sunbury, Middlesex
*Carpenter, H., Esq., Tooley-street, Borough
Carpenter, Mr. Robert H., Hereford
Carpenter & Son, Messrs., Old Bond-st., Lond.
Carr, Rev. Charles, Winchester, Hants.
*Carr, George, Esq., Christ-ch. col., Cambridge
Carr, John F., Esq., Horbury, Yorkshire
*Carr, Mr. John, Norwich
*Carr, Ralph, Esq., Chepstow, Monmouthshire
Carr, Ralph, Esq., Park-crescent, London
Carr, Robert, Esq., Wakefield, Yorkshire
Carr, Samuel, Esq., Eversden, Cambridge
Carr, Rev. Samuel, Colchester
*Carr, T., Esq., John-st., Bedford-row, London
*Carr, Thomas, Esq., Clitham-castle
*Carr, William, Esq., Enfield, Middlesex
Carr, Mr. Wm. Hardy, Cottingham, Yorkshire
*Carr & Hargreaves, Mess., Preston, Lancashire
*CARRICK, The Right Honorable the Earl of
*Carruthers, J., Esq., Tonbridge Wells, Sussex
Carson, John, Esq., Everton, Liverpool
*Carter, Chas., Esq., St. Katharine's-dock, Lon.
Carter, Mr. Edward, Camden Town, Middlesex
*Carter, Henry, Esq., Tombland, Norwich
*Carter, J., Esq., St. John's college, Oxford
*Carter, J., Esq., Bread-st., Cheapside, London
*Carter, J. S., Esq., Trinity college, Cambridge
Carter, Mr. Joseph, Gloucester
Carter, Rev. M., D. D., Eton college
*Carter, Peter, Esq., Northwich, Cheshire
Carter, R. H., Esq., Gloucester
*Carter, Major T., Little Wittenham, Berks.
*Carter, T. T., Esq., Christ-church college, Oxford, and Eton college, near Windsor
*Carter, J. M., Esq., Hertford
*Carter, W., Esq., Millbrook, near Southampton
*Carter, W. F., Esq., Christ's college, Cambridge
*Carter, H. W., Esq., M. D., F. R. S. E., Canterbury
*Carter and Dewes, Messrs., Coventry
Carther, Christopher, Esq., Knaresborough
*Carthew, Rev. Thomas, Woodbridge, Suffolk
*Cartmel, Thomas, Esq., Farleton, Lancashire
*Cartwright, C., Esq., Dudley, Worcestershire
*Cartwright, Rev. E., F. A. S., Arundel
*Cartwright, H., Esq., Great Fenton, Staffordsh.
Cartwright, Thomas, Esq., Wolverhampton, do
*Cartwright, Thomas, Esq., West Dean, Sussex
*Cartwright, Rev. W. H., M.A., Dudley
*Cartwright, W. B., Esq., Cateaton-st., London
*Carwithen, G. H. J., Esq., Oriel college, Oxford
*Cary, H., Esq., Martock Mill-cottage, Somerset
*CARYSFORT, The Right Hon. the Earl of
*Case, J. A., Esq., Liverpool
Case, J. D., Esq., do.
Case, G. A., Esq., Belmont, Shrewsbury
*Case, Thos., Esq., Summer-hill, near Liverpool
*Casey, James D., Esq., Gray's-inn, London
Cash, Newman, Esq., Leeds, Yorkshire
*Casley, J., Esq., Furnival's-inn, London
*Cass, Frederick, Esq., East Barnet, Herts.
*Cass, George, Esq., Ware, do.
Cass, J. T., Esq., Caldecott, Huntingdonshire
Cass, Mr. John, Ware, Hertfordshire
*CASSILLIS, The Right Honorable the Earl of
Castell, Rev. W., Brooke, near Norwich
Castell, Mr. W. S., Chertsey, Surrey, 2 Copies
*Castle, A., jun., Esq., Kentish-Town, Middsx.
Castle, Augustus, Esq., Staples-inn, London
*Caslon, H., Esq., Chiswell-street, Finsbury, do.
*Cater, William, Esq., Ware, Herts.
*Catharine-hall, Library of, Cambridge
*Catherwood, Mr. F., Lancaster-place, London
Catt, Mr. J. M., Hackney-road, Middlesex
Catterall, Paul, Esq., Preston, Lancashire
*Cattly, William, Esq., Barnet, Herts.
*Caulfeild, Rev. E., Chippenham, Wiltshire
*Caunt, John, Esq., Nottingham
Caunter, Rev. R. M'Donald, L. L. B., Harrow, Middlesex
*Causer, Mr. Edward, Stourbridge
*Cauty, Henry J., Esq., Birmingham
Cave, Sir W. B., Bart., Stretton-hall, Derbyshire
*Cave, D., Esq., Cleve-hill-house, Gloucestershire
*Cave, F. R. B., Esq., Wootton-park, Staffordsh.
Cave, George, Esq., Cleve-Dale, near Bristol
*Cave, John, Esq., Brentry, do.
*Cave, R. O., Esq., Suffolk-street, London
Cavell, Mr. James, Southampton
*Cavendish, W., Esq., M.P., Devonshire-pl., Lon.
*Cawley, Rev. James, Runcorn-heath, Cheshire
Cayley, W., Esq., Christ-church coll., Oxford
Cazenove, James, Esq., Old Broad-st., London
Ceeley, Robert, Esq., Aylesbury, Bucks.
Chabot, P. J., Esq., Lincoln's-inn, London
Chadborn, John, Esq., Gloucester
Chaddock, Thomas, Esq., Congleton, Cheshire
*Chadwick, C., Esq., Mavesyn-Ridware, Staffordshire
*Chadwick, Mr. Edward, Ashton under Line
Chadwick, Henry, Esq., Preston, Lancashire
Chadwick, H. M., Esq., Leventhorp-house, Yorkshire
Chadwick, James, Esq., Bolton, Lancashire
*Chadwick, J., Esq., Rochdale, do.
*Chadwick, John, Esq., Ashton under Line
*Chadwick, Samuel, Esq., Heywood, Lancashire
Chadwick, S., Esq., Pool-stock-house, do.
*Chadwick, Thomas, Esq., Heap, near Bury, do.
*Chaffey, R., Esq., M. D., Martock, Somerset.
*Chaffey, R., Esq., East Stoke, Sub-Hamdon, do.
*Chafy, Rev. William, D. D., Vice-Chancellor of the University, Cambridge
*Chalk, Mr. William, Milton
*Chalk & Hall, Messrs., Worcester
*Challenor, Miss, Belle-Vue, Tarporley, Cheshire
Challinor, Charles, Esq., Liverpool
Chamberlain, J., Esq., Hanley-castle, Worcestershire
*Chamberlain, Mr. J., Norwich
Chamberlain, Rev. J., Leicester
*Chamberlain, Mr. Robert, Norwich
Chamberlayne, Rev. J., M. A., Etwall, Derbyshire
*Chamberlayne, T., Esq., Magdalene col., Oxford
Chambers, B., Esq., Tibshelf, Derbyshire

Chambers, I., Esq., Nutt-place, Hertford
*Chambers, Mr. James, Clifford, Herefordshire
*Chambers, R. J., Esq., Bishopsgate-st., London
Champion, Mr. James, Nettlebed, Oxfordshire
Champion, Mr. William, Reading, Berks.
*Champney, George, Esq., York
*CHANCELLOR, The Rt. Hon. the Lord High
*Chandler, G. H., Esq., Wadham coll., Oxford
Chandler, Rev. G., Treeton, Rotheram, York
*Chandler, Mr. J., St. Paul's Churchyard, Lond.
Chantler, Wm., Esq., Grappenhall, Cheshire
*Chantrell, R. D., Esq., Leeds, Yorkshire [Lon.
*Chapeaurouge, Messieurs de, Fenchurch-street,
Chaplin, Francis, Esq., Riseholme, near Lincoln
Chaplin, Rev. Henry B., Blankney, Lincolnsh.
Chaplin, V., Esq., Bucklersbury, London
Chapman, Sir John, Knt., Windsor, Berks.
Chapman, Mr. Edmund, do., do.
Chapman, Mr. Edmund, Cheshunt, Herts.
*Chapman, James, Esq., Manchester
*Chapman, James, Esq., Reigate, Surrey
*Chapman, Rev. J., Haslemere, do.
Chapman, R. E., Esq., Took's-court, London
*Chapman, Thos., jun., Esq., Middle-Temple, do.
Chapman, Mr. Sam., Leeds, Yorkshire [London
Chapman, W. H., Esq., Charter-house-square,
*Chapman, William, Esq., Richmond, Surrey
*Chappe, Paul, Esq., Manchester
*Chappell, T. B., Esq., Park-street, London
Chard, C. H., Esq., Thame, Oxfordshire
*Charge, John, Esq., Spital, near Chesterfield
Charles, A., Esq., St. Margaret's-st., Canterbury
Charles, John R., Esq., Thanet-place, London
*Charles, P., Esq., M. D., Putney, Surrey
Charles, Mr. William, Yatton, Herefordshire
*Charlesworth, Edward P., Esq., M.D., Lincoln
*Charlesworth, J., Esq., Lofthouse, Wakefield
*Charlesworth, Thomas, Esq., Leeds, Yorkshire
*CHARLEVILLE, The Right Hon. the Earl of
*Charlton, Mr. James, Gateshead, Durham
*Charlton, P., Esq., Wytheford-hall, Shropshire
*Charlton, William, Esq., Chiswell-hall
*Charnock, Mr. John, Leeds, Yorkshire
Charnock, Rev. J., A.M., Bishopton-close, do.
*Charrington, E., Esq., Brasenose coll., Oxford
Charrington, Jno., Esq., Mile-End-road, London
Charsley, Robert, Esq., Mark-lane, do.
*Chater, Thomas, Esq., Newcastle upon Tyne
*Chatfield, Mr. W., Charlotte-street, London
*Chatham Royal Marine Library
Chatteris, Thos., Esq., Waltham-Abbey, Essex
*Chauvel, Rev. A. R., L. L. B., Great Stanmore, Middlesex
*Chayter, W. C., Esq., Durham
*Chaytor, William, Esq., Wilton-castle, do.
Cheek, J. M. G., Esq., Evesham
Cheek, Thomas, Esq., Hertford
Cheese, E. W., Esq., Ridgeborne, Herefordshire
*Cheetham, D., Esq., Stalybridge, Lancashire
*Cheetham, Josiah, Esq., Vale-house, Cheshire
*Cheffins, George, Esq., Hoddesden, Herts.
Cheffins, Mr. Joshua, Bishop-Stortford, Essex
*Cheffins, Mr. Lewin, Cheshunt, Herts.
Cheffins, Peter James, Esq., Amwell, do.
Chellingworth, H., Esq., Upton-Bishop, Here-
*Cheshire, Thos., Esq., Peterborough [fordshire
CHESTER, The Right Rev. Lord Bishop of
*Chester, Public Library of the City of
Chester, Rev. Charles, L. L. B., Ayott St. Peter, Hertfordshire
Chester, Rev. W., Auckland St. Helen, Durham
*Chester, W. H. C., Esq., Emanuel col., Cambridge
*CHESTERFIELD, The Right Hon. the Earl of
*Cheston, Rev. J. B., Longford-house, near
Chettleburgh, Mr. Robt., Norwich [Gloucester
Chetwode, Sir John, Bart., Chetwode, Bucks.
*Chetwode, Rev. H., Lower Whitley, Cheshire
Chew, T. C., Esq., Manchester
Cheyney, Mr. C., Wherwell, Hants.
*CHICHESTER, The Right Hon. the Earl of
*CHICHESTER, The Rt. Rev. Lord Bishop of
*Chichester, Lieut.-Col. A., Horsham, Sussex
*Chilcote, G. H., Esq., Bond-court, Walbrook
Child, Mr. John, Clapham, Surrey
Child, Samuel H., Esq., Wolverhampton
Child, Smith, Esq., Newfield, Staffordshire
Child J., Esq., Upper Thames-street, London
*Childe, C. F., Esq., St. John's coll., Cambridge
*Childe, W. L., Esq., Christ-church coll., Oxford
*Childers, Rev. Eardley, Maidenhead, Berks.
Chilton & Son, Messrs., Chancery-lane, London
*Chinn, Henry, Esq., The Close, Lichfield
*Chinn, Thomas B., Esq., do., do.
*Chippendale, John, Esq., Hillingdon, Middsx.
*Chisholm, A. W., Esq., Trinity coll., Cambridge
*Chisholm, Rev. Charles, Eastwell, Kent
Chisholme, R., Esq., M. D., Canterbury, do.
*Chisholme, W., Esq., Lincoln's-inn-fields, Lond.
*Chitty, George, Esq., Shaftesbury, Dorsetshire
Chitty, P. M., Esq., do., do.
Cholmeley, H. D., Esq., St. John's coll., Oxford [London
*Cholmeley, H. J., Esq., M. D., Bridge-street,
*Cholmeley, J. M., Esq., Magdalene col., Oxford
*CHOLMONDELEY, The Most Noble the Marquis of
*Cholmondeley, Chs., Esq., Knutsford, Cheshire
*Choppin, Francis Hume, Esq., Enfield, Middlsx.
Chorlton, Samuel, Esq., Hyde, Cheshire
*Chrees, W., Esq., Wolverhampton
Christ Church College Library, Oxford
*Christian, J., Esq., Isle of Man
Christie, James, Esq., Carshalton, Surrey
Christie, Rev. John, Shaftesbury, Dorsetshire
*Christie, P., Esq., Hoddesdon, Herts.
Christie, Messrs. J. and R., Mark-lane, London
*Christmas, Mr. Charles J., Knutsford, Cheshire
Christmas, Mr. T., jun., Godmanchester, Hunts.
Christophers, J., Esq., New Broad-street, Lond.
Christopherson, Mr. H., Brighton
*Christy, John, Esq., Gracechurch-st., London
Chubb, M., Esq., Bridg-water, Somersetshire
*Chubb, Thomas N., Esq., Salisbury, Wilts.
Church, J., Esq., Woodside, Hatfield, Herts.
*Church, James, Esq., Green-street, Kent
*Church, J. T., Esq., Great James-street, London
Churchill, John S., Esq., Wells, Somersetshire
Churchill, Miss, Sunning-hill, Berks.
*Churchman, C. B., Esq., Kensington-square
*Chute, Mrs., The Vine, near Basingstoke, Hants.
*Chuter, H., Esq., Carey-street, London [land
Clanney, W. R., Esq., M. D., F. R. S., Sunder-
*CLANWILLIAM, The Rt. Hon. the Earl of
*Clapham, Henry, Esq., Leeds, Yorkshire
*Clapham, John, Esq., jun., do., do.
*Clapham, John Peel, Esq., do., do.
*Clapham, Samuel, Esq., do., do.
*Clapham, Samuel, Esq., Cheshunt, Herts.
*Clapham, Thomas, Esq., Chelmsford, Essex
*Clapham, W., Esq., Burton, Westmorland
Clapp, Rev. J. C., Coulston, Wilts.
*CLARE, The Right Honorable the Earl of
*Clare, John, Esq., Sankey, Lancashire
Clare, Rev. T., Great Staughton, Hunts.
CLARENDON, The Right Hon. the Earl of
*Claridge, Mr. R., Curzon-st., May-fair, London
*Clark, Mr. Andrew, Bear-garden, Bankside, do.
*Clark, D., Esq., Dronfield, Derbyshire
Clark, Mr. Edward, Reading, Berks.
Clark, Mr. Francis, Cotherston, York
Clark, G., Esq., Newgate-street, London
Clark, Henry, Esq., Lyndhurst, Hants. [London
Clark, John, Esq., Sessions-house, Old Bailey,
*Clark, John, Esq., K. B., Temple, London
*Clark, J. H., Esq., Holles-street, do.
Clark, Joseph, Esq., Maidenhead, Berks.
Clark, Mr. Joseph, King's-head, Chelsea
Clark, Lieut. W., R. N., Langhaugh, Galushiels
Clark, L., Esq., Ludlow, Shropshire
*Clark, R., Esq., Bridewell-hospital, London
*Clark, Richard, Esq., Lancaster
Clark, Mr. Richard, Stoke-Lacy, Herefordshire
Clark, Robert, Esq., Farnham, Surrey
Clark, Mr. Robert, Albany-road, Mile-end
*Clark, R., Esq., Guildhall
*Clark, Sam., Esq., East India-house, London
Clark, Thomas, Esq., Farnham, Surrey
*Clark, Thomas, Esq., Russell-place, London
*Clark, W., Esq., Stonefield-street, Islington
Clark, Mr. William, Wolverhampton
*Clarke, Sir S. H., Bart., Southgate, Middlesex
Clarke, The Venerable and Reverend Archdeacon, Downton, Wilts
*Clarke, Rev. A., L.L.D., Haydon-hall, Middsx.
Clarke, Mr. Alexander, Newport, Isle of Wight
*Clarke, A., Esq., Bishopsgate Churchyard, Lond.
Clarke, Bramhall, Esq., Liverpool
*Clarke, Charles, Esq., Derby
Clarke, H., Esq., Basinghall-street, London
Clarke, H., Esq., Trinity coll., Cambridge
*Clarke, J. A. G., Esq., Kinnersley-castle, Herefordshire
Clarke, J. G., Esq., Newcastle upon Tyne
*Clarke, John, Esq., Dairy-house, Ashley, Chesh.
*Clarke, John, Esq., Bowdon-downs, do.
*Clarke, Mr. Jno., Green-Heys, near Manchester
Clarke, Mr. J., Maiden-lane, Wood-st., London
Clarke, Mr. Joseph, Maidstone, Kent
Clarke, N., Esq., Trowbridge, Wilts.
*Clarke, Ralph, Esq., Fishbourne, Sussex
*Clarke, Robert, Esq., Wallingford, Berks.
*Clarke, R. G., Esq., Craven-street, London
*Clarke, T., Esq., Altrincham, Cheshire
Clarke, Thomas, Esq., Tenbury, Worcestershire
*Clarke, T. E., Esq., Chard, Somersetshire
Clarke, Thomas T., Esq., Swakeleys, Middlesex
*Clarke, William, Esq., Penn, Bucks.
Clarke, Rev. W. B., A.M., Bergholt, Suffolk
Clarke, W. L., Esq., Belle-Vue, Bristol
Clarke, W. W., Esq., Wadham college, Oxford
Clarke, Mr. William, Compton, Berks.
Clarke, Rev. Unwin, Eastham, Cheshire
*Clarkson, C., Esq., Rockhill-lodge, nr. Sydenham
Clarkson, George, Esq., Essex-st., Strand, Lond.
Clarkson, Mr. G., Barnard-castle, Durham
Clarkson, Rev. Isaac, Wednesbury, Staffordshire
*Clarkson, T. L., Esq., Christ's coll., Cambridge
*Clarkson, W. G., Esq., Doctors Commons
*Claughton, T., Esq., Bloomsbury-sq., London
Claxson, Rev. B. S., D. D., Gloucester
Clay, E., Esq., Grinstead-park, near Colchester
*Clay, Rev. J., B. D., Walton le Dale, Lancash.
*Clay, T., Esq., Little Abington, Cambridgesh.
Clay, William, Esq., Liverpool
*Clay, William, Esq., Twickenham, Middlesex
*Clay, W. W. P., Esq., Southwell, Notts.
*Claydon, Charles, Esq., Cambridge
Claye, Rev. W., A. M., Westhorpe, Southwell,
Clayette, J., Esq., Strangeways, Manchester
*Clayton, David S., Esq., Worth, Cheshire [Notts.
Clayton, Lieut.-Gen., R. B. & D.C.L., Clifton
*Clayton, E., Esq., Preston, Lancashire
Clayton, I., Esq., Upton-Bishop, Herefordshire
*Clayton, John, Esq., Newcastle upon Tyne
Clayton, J., Esq., John-st., Bedford-row, Lond.
*Clayton, Thomas, Esq., Colne, Lancashire
*Clayton, Thomas D., Esq., Preston, do.
*Clayton, William, Esq., Adlington, Cheshire
Cleave, John, Esq., Hereford
*Clegg, Charles, Esq., David-street, Manchester
Clegg, Henry, Esq., Houghton-house
*Clegg, J., Esq., High Crompton, Lancashire
*Clegg, James, Esq., Heywood, do.
*Clegg, Robert B., Esq., Pendleton, Manchester
*Cleghorn, Henry, Esq., Gateshead, Durham
Cleland, Mr. James, Cheapside, London
*Clement, H., Esq., Exeter coll., Oxford
Clement, Thomas, Esq., Alton, Hants.
Clement, W., Esq., Morning Chronicle-office, Strand, London
*Clements, Mr. J., St. Stephen's, Norwich
Clements, Mr. J., jun., Pillgwenlly, Monmouth-
-Clementson, John H., Esq., Liverpool [shire
*Clementson, R., Esq., Coleman-street, London
*Cleminson, James, Esq., Ulverstone, Lancash.

Cleminson, Rev. W., Grantham, Lincolnshire
*Clemonston, Geo., Esq., Newcastle upon Tyne
*Clennell, T., Esq., do.
*Cleobury, T. M., Esq., Chancery-lane, Lond.
Clerk, Walter, Esq., East Bergholt, Suffolk
Clever, Mr. William, Maidstone, Kent
*Cleworth, James, Esq., Atherton, Lancashire
*Cliff, R., Esq., Bank-chambers, London
Clifford, C.T., Esq., Kenilworth, Warkwickshire
*Clifford, Mr. E., John-street, Adelphi, London
Clinnick, Miss, West Hide, Herefordshire
CLINTON, The Right Honorable Lord
*Clinton, Rev. C. I. F., A.M., Cromwell, Notts.
*Clinton, Rev. H., B.A., Caius coll., Cambridge
*Clisby, T. W., Esq., Brighton
Clive, J. H., Esq., Newcastle under Line
*Cloake, Mr. Henry, Uckfield, Sussex
*Close, Thomas, Esq., Nottingham
*Clough, H. G., Esq., M.D., Norton-st., Portland-road, London
*Clough, James, Esq., Dock-street, Leeds
*Clough, J. H., Esq., Plas Llanfair, Anglesey
Clowes, W., Esq., Parliament-st., Westminster
*Clowes, W. L., Esq., Yeldersley-hall, Derbysh.
*Clowes, Orme, and Wedlake, Messrs., King's-bench-walk, Temple, London
Clubb, Mr. Isaac, Bullocksmithy, Cheshire
Clubbe, J., Esq., Earl-Soham-lodge, Suffolk
*Cludde, Edward, Esq., Arleton, Salop
*Clues, Josiah, Esq., Winnington, Cheshire
*Cluley, Mr. William, Altrincham, do.
Clulow, W. W., Esq., Enfield, Middlesex
*Clutterbuck, H., Esq., St. Peter's coll., Cambdg.
*Clutterbuck, Peter, Esq., Red-hall, Herts.
*Clutterbuck, T., Esq., Chippenham, Wiltshire
*Clutterbuck, T., Esq., Stroud
*Clutterbuck, T., Esq., Micklefield-hall, Herts.
Clutton, Rev. John, D.D., Hereford
Clutton, Thomas, Esq., New college, Oxford
*Clutton, Carter, & Co., Messrs., Southwark
*Coales, John, Esq., St. Albans
*Coape, H. C., Esq., Christ-church coll. Oxford
*Coates, B. D., Esq., Ashton under Line
Coates, Henry, Esq., Salisbury
*Coates, John, Esq., Wadham college, Oxford
Coates, John, jun., Esq., Ripon, Yorkshire
Coates, Joseph, Esq., Eyton, Herefordshire
Coates, Mr. Joseph, Monmouth
Coates, P. E., Esq., Stanton-court, Somersetsh.
Coates, Mr. Richard, Leominster, Herefordsh.
Coates, Mr. Richard, Norwich,
*Coates, Miss S., Springfield, near Chelmsford
Coates, Mr. Samuel, Leominster, Herefordshire
*Coates, Thomas, Esq., Secretary to the Society for the Diffusion of Useful Knowledge, Gray's-inn, London
Coates, John, Esq., Temple, London
*Coates, Mr. Thomas, Gas-works, Sunderland
*Cobb, George, Esq., Clement's-inn, London
Cobb, G., Esq., The Trump, near Monmouth
*Cobb, James, Esq., Yarmouth, Norfolk
Cobbett, Mr. Thomas, Farnham, Surrey
*Cobbin, Mr. R., Slough, Bucks.
*Cobbold, Thomas, Esq., Cotton, Norfolk
*Cobden, Mr. Richard, Windsor
Cobham, C., Esq., Little Amwell, near Hertford
*Cobham, Nathaniel, Esq., Ware, Hertfordshire
*Cobham, Wm., jun., Esq., do., do.
Cobley, Mr. T., jun., Essex-st., Whitechapel
*Cobley, Mr. Thomas, Ashton under Line
*Cock, C., Esq., Southampton-row, London
Cock, Simon, Esq., New Bank-buildings, do.
*Cockburn, The Right Hon. Sir C., M.P., K.C.B.
Cockcroft, John, Esq., M.D., Liverpool
*Cocke, William, Esq., Dover
*Cocker, A. R., Esq., Nassau-street, London
Cocker, Henry, Esq., Hathersage, Derbyshire
*Cocker, James, Esq., Bolton, Lancashire
Cocker, Saxon, Esq., Sloane-street, Chelsea
*Cockeran, Rev. H., Kingsdon, Somersetshire
Cocks, W. C., Esq., Ross, Herefordshire
Cocks & Son, Messrs. James, Reading, Berks.
Cocksedge, R., Esq., Norwich
*Cocksey, Thomas, Esq., Bolton, Lancashire
*Cockshott, James, Esq., Rodney-st., Liverpool
Cocum, John, Esq., Windsor
Codd, B., Esq., Gainsborough, Lincolnshire
Coddington, Rev. H., Trinity coll., Cambridge
*Codington, Mr. W., Gainsborough, Lincolnshire
Codrington, R., Esq., Bridg-water, Somerset
*Coe, James, Esq., Hatton-garden, London
Coe, J. H., Esq., Clifford's-inn, do.
Coghlan, Rev. W., Ormskirk, Lancashire
*Cohen, Isaac, Esq., Hampton, Middlesex
Coke, D. Ewes, Esq., Brookhill, Derbyshire
*Coke, E., Esq., Langford-hall, do.
Coke, Rev. Francis, Lower-Moor, Herefordshire
*Coke, John, Esq., Debdale, near Mansfield
Colbatch, John, Esq., Brighton
Colbeck, Thomas, Esq., Hertford
*Colborne, W., Esq., Chippenham, Wiltshire
COLCHESTER, The Right Honorable Lord
*Colchester, M., Esq., Mitchell-Dean, Gloucestershire
*Colclough, J., Esq., Lincoln's-inn-fields, Lond.
Coldwell, Rev. W. E., M.A., Stafford
COLE, The Right Honorable Lord Viscount
Cole, Mr. Alderman, St. Giles', Norwich
*Cole, Edward, Esq., Great Charlotte-st., London
Cole, G., Esq., Wolverhampton
*Cole, George C., Esq., Seven-Oaks, Kent
Cole, Mr. George, Kimbolton, Huntingdonshire
*Cole, Jesse, Esq., Thayer-st., Manchester-sq.
*Cole, John, Esq., Serjeant's-inn, London
*Cole, O. B., Esq., Christ-church coll., Oxford
*Cole, S. T., Esq., Twickenham, Middlesex
*Cole, T. B., Esq., Garstang, Lancashire
*Cole, T. R., Esq., Basinghall-st., London
*Cole, William, jun., Esq., Chester
Cole, W. N., Esq., Highbury-terrace, Islington
*Cole and Child, Messrs., Lothbury, London
Coleby, Mr. George, Norwich
*Coleman, Charles, Esq., Maidstone, Kent
*Coleman, J., Esq., Pontefract, Yorkshire
Coleman, John, Esq., Norwich
*Coleman, W., Esq., Langley, near Chippenham
Coleman, William, Esq., Queen's coll., Oxford
*Coleman, William, Esq., Solton, near Dovor
*Coleridge, Rev. E., Eton college
*Coles, Edward, Esq., Taunton, Somersetshire
*Coles, Rev. George, Croydon, Surrey
Coles, Rev. I. J., Clifton-wood, near Bristol
*Coles, James, Esq., Old Change, London
Coles, W., Esq., Elm-street-road, Mary-le-bone
*Coley, Wm. P., Esq., Old Broad-st., London
*Colguitt, Thomas, Esq., Liverpool
Collet, E. J., Esq., M. P.
Collet, J., Esq., Stratford on Avon, Warwicksh.
*Collier, Miss, Bowdon-downs, Cheshire
Collier, John, Esq., Plymouth
*Collier, Robert, Esq., Crawley, Oxfordshire
Collier, Robert, Esq., Gloucester
Collier, Mr. Thomas, Hereford
*Collier, Marchant, Birch, and Steel, Messrs., Carey-street, London
Collin, George, Esq., Pidnambury, Essex
*Colling, Joseph, Esq., Parsons-street, London
Collings, D. Harrison, Esq., Sandbridge, Wilts.
Collings, Mr. James, Waltham-Abbey, Essex
*Collings, Richard J., Esq., Ashford, Kent
Collins, Anthony, Esq., Lime-street, London
Collins, Francis, Esq., Leominster, Herefordsh.
Collins, Rev. J., D. D., Southall-Park, Middlesex
*Collins, Rev. John, M.A., Frodsham, Cheshire
*Collins, Mr. John, Godalming, Surrey
Collins, John S., Esq., Ross, Herefordshire
*Collins, Richard, Esq., Manchester
Collins, W., Esq., Kirkman-bank, Knaresbro'.
Collinson, John, Esq., Doncaster, Yorkshire
*Collinson, Richard, Esq., Queen's coll., Oxford
Collis, Major Charles, Milverton, Somerset
Collis, Mr. Thomas, Stourbridge
Collishaw, Joseph, Esq., Swinton, Notts.
Collison, Thomas, Esq., Liverpool [London
*Collison and Co., Messrs., Skinner's-place,
Collrett, Mr. W., Bucklersbury, London
Collyer, William, Esq., Chilland, Hants.
*Colmore, Mr. T., New-street, Birmingham
*Colnaghi, M., Esq., Cockspur-st., London
*Colquhoun, James, Esq., Woolwich
Colson, J., Esq., Southampton
Colt, E. H. V., Esq., Queen's coll., Oxford
*Colt, James, Esq., Leominster, Herefordshire
*Colt, O., Esq., Nursling, Hants.
Colthurst, Sir Nicholas Conway, Ardrum, Cork
Colton, William B., Esq., Liverpool
Colvile, J. W., Esq., Trinity coll., Cambridge
*Colville, Sir John, Knt., Duffield-hall, Derbysh.
*Colwell, Mr. D., Ashted, Warwickshire
Colyer, William, Esq., Greenhythe, Kent
*Combe, J., Esq., Staples-inn, London
*Comberbeach, Mr. T., Audenshaw, Lancashire
COMBERMERE, The Rt. Hon. Lord Viscount
Comely, Mr. James, Compton, near Winchester
COMMANDER IN CHIEF'S OFFICE, His Majesty's
*Commeline, Samuel, Esq., Gloucester
*Compson, Rev. J. E., A. M., Shrewsbury
*Compson, John, Esq., Bromsgrove
*Compton, G., Esq., Chilworth, Hants.
Compton, J. T., Esq., Urchfont, near Devizes
Compton, S. W., Esq., Walford, Herefordshire
Condlyffe, William, Esq., Leek, Staffordshire
Condyington, Edward, Esq., Liverpool
*Congreve, Miss, Iscoyd Park, Cheshire
*Congreve, Richard, Esq., Burton, do.
Congreve, W., Esq., Aldermaston-house, Berks.
*Conington, Rev. R., Fishtoft, Lincolnshire
Connop, Henry, sen., Esq., Yarpole, Herefordsh.
Connop, Mr. J., Fownhope, do.
*Conroy, Sir John, K.C.H., Kensington Palace
*Conroy, E., Esq., Christ-church coll., Oxford
Constable, Sir Clifford, Bart.
*Constable, Rev. R., Cowfold, Sussex
*Constable & Kirk, Mess., Symond's-inn, London
CONYNGHAM, The Most Noble the Marquis [of
Cooch, Samuel Edward, Esq., Huntingdon
*Coode, H., Esq., Guildford-street, London
Coode, Thomas, Esq., St. Austell, Cornwall
*Cook, Lieut.-Gen. Sir G., Hanfield, Middlesex
Cook, John, Esq., Ledbury, Herefordshire
*Cook, John Earley, Esq., Nunsbury, Herts.
*Cook, S., Esq., Booth-st., Spitalfields, London
Cook, Rev. Thomas, Kidderminster
Cook, William, Esq., Furnival's-inn, London
Cook, William, Esq., Hertford
Cook, William, Esq., Worcester college, Oxford
Cook and Co., Messrs. G., Southampton
Cooke, Rev. Charles, Samer, Suffolk
*Cooke, Edward, Esq., Queen's college, Oxford
*Cooke, J., Esq., Pendlebury, near Manchester
*Cooke, John, Esq., Ross, Herefordshire
Cooke, Joseph, Esq., Lawford, Essex
Cooke, Rev. Joseph, Newark, Nottinghamshire
*Cooke, H., Esq., Kingsland-road, Middlesex
Cooke, H. P., Esq., Mortimer's-cross, Hereford.
*Cooke, Isaac, Esq., Liverpool
Cooke, J. Esq., Balliol college, Oxford
Cooke, J. D., Esq., Brampton-Bryan, Hereford.
Cooke, Launcelot, Esq., Abchurch-lane, Lond.
Cooke, P. B., Esq., Gloucester
*Cooke, Richard Harry, Esq., York
*Cooke, Mr. Richard, Ludlow, Salop
Cooke, Samuel, Esq., Salford, Lancashire
*Cooke, Samuel N., Esq., New-inn, London
Cooke, Mr. Thomas, Hereford
*Cooke, W., Esq., Kensington, Liverpool
Cooke, Rev. William, College, Hereford
*Cooke, W. H., Esq., Sheerness, Kent
Cookesley, H. P., Esq., Trinity coll., Cambridge
*Cookesley, Rev. W. G., A. M., King's coll., do.
*Cookney, J. T., Esq., Bedford-row, London
Cooksey and Mallin, Messrs., Great-bridge, [Staffordsh.
*Cookson, A., Esq., M.D., Lincoln
Cookson, E., Esq., University college, Oxford

*Cookson, John, Esq., Lancaster
Cookson, Joseph, Esq., Clifton, Gloucestershire
*Cookson, Rev. J. W., B. A., Coddington, Chesh.
*Coombe, J. N., Esq., St. John's coll., Oxford
*Coombe, George A., Esq., Arundel, Sussex
*Coombs, Henry, Esq., Salisbury, Wiltshire
*Coombs, Rev. J. A., Salford, Lancashire
Coombs, Mr. J., Doctors Commons, London
*Coope, W. T., Esq., St. Mary-hall, Oxford
Cooper, Sir Astley P., Bart., F. R. S., Gadesbridge, Herts.
*Cooper, A. P., Esq., Whitehill, Berkhampstead
*Cooper, Rev. C. B., A. M., Hemel-Hempstead
*Cooper, C. P., Esq., Lincoln's-inn, London
*Cooper, Mr. Edward, jun., Henley in Arden
*Cooper, F. Y., Esq., Taunton, Somersetshire
*Cooper, Mr. H., Islington, Middlesex
Cooper, Henry, Esq., Canterbury
Cooper, Mr. Henry, Ludgate-hill, Birmingham
Cooper, Mr. John, Reading, Berks.
Cooper, Mr. John James, do., do.
*Cooper, Mr. Joseph, Chisworth, Derbyshire
*Cooper, Robert, Esq., York
Cooper, Mr. R., Camden Town, Middlesex
Cooper, R. H., Esq., Worcester college, Oxford
Cooper, Rev. Samuel, Wistow, Huntingdonshire
Cooper, Thomas, Esq., Daw-end, Staffordshire
*Cooper, Thomas, Esq., Hankelow-hall, Cheshire
*Cooper, Mr. Thomas, Manchester
*Cooper, Rev. W., A. B., Bradford, Yorkshire
Cooper, William, Esq., Shrewsbury
*Cooper, Wm., Esq., Maidenhead, Berks.
*Cooper, Mr. W., Stoke, near Colnbrook, Bucks.
*Cooper, W. S., Esq., Furnival's-inn, London
Cooper, Mr. W., Cheshunt, Herts.
*Coote, R. H., Esq., Lincoln's-inn, London
Coote, Mr. William, St. Ives, Huntingdonshire
Cope, Rev. J., Middleton, Lancashire
Cope, Thomas, Esq., Buckden, Huntingdonshire
Cope, Thomas, Esq., Coventry
*Copeland, T., Esq., Lincoln's-inn-fields, Lond.
*Copeland, William, Esq., Gray's-inn-sq., do.
*Coppard, T., Esq., Horsham, Sussex
Coppin, J. M., Esq., Stratford on Avon
Coppock, William, Esq., Stockport, Cheshire
*Cor, Rev. Thomas Coleridge, Crediton, Devon
*Corbet, Sir Andrew, Bart., Acton-Reynold, Salop
*Corbet, A. V., Esq., do., do.
*Corbet, A. W., Esq., Sandorne-castle, do.
*Corbet, David, Esq., M. D., Worcester
*Corbet, Richard, Esq., Adderley, Shropshire
*Corbett, Edwin, Esq., Winsford, Cheshire
*Corbett, J., Esq., Ledbury, Hereford
Corbett, R., Esq., Bilston, Staffordshire
Corbould, Mr., Newbury, Berks.
Corby, Rob., Esq., Withingham, near Norwich
*Corderoy, W., Esq., High-street, Mary-le-bone
Cordery, Mr. H., Longstock, Hants.
Cordery, Mr. Thomas, Winchester, do.
Coren, A. E., Esq., South Moreton, Berks.
Corfield, Rev. R., A. M., Pitchford, Shropshire
*Corfield, Mr. William, St. Andrew's, Norwich
*Cork, J. D., Esq., Exeter college, Oxford
*Cork, Robert, Esq., King's-road, London
*CORK AND ORRERY, The Rt. Hon. the Earl of
Corker, Henry, Esq., Hathersage, Derby
*Corker, Messrs. G. & T., Edmonton, Middlesex
Corkhill, J. A., Esq., Wadebridge, Cornwall
Cornelius, Mr. Bernard, Epsom, Surrey
Corner, G. R., Esq., Canterbury-sq., Southwark
*Cornewall, Sir George, Bart., Moccas-court, Herefordshire
*Corney, John, Esq., Arundel-park, Sussex
*Corpus-Christi college Library, Oxford
*Corrie, J., Esq., Finchley, Middlesex
Corry, George, Esq., Preston, Lancashire
Cort, John, Esq., Liverpool
*Cort, John, Esq., Blackburn, Lancashire
Cossham, J. T., Esq., Lodge-st., Bristol
Cossum, Messrs. W. and C., Maidenhead, Berks.
*Costar and Waddell, Messrs., Oxford
*Coster, J. W., Esq., Prince's-st., Spitalfields

Cotgreave, Sir J., Knt., Nethwelgh-house, Chester
*Cother, W., Esq., Christ-church col., Oxford
*Cottam, Adam, Esq., Whalley, near Blackburn
*Cotterell, Mr. G., Whitecross-street, London
*Cottingham, G., Esq., Bolton, Lancashire
Cottingham, N. N., Esq., Waterloo-road, Lond.
*Cottingham, T., Esq., Little Neston, Cheshire
Cottingham, Parish Officers of
*Cottle, Rev. H. W., Cholsey, Berks.
*Cotton, Rev. C., Christ's-hospital, Hertford
Cotton, Rev. C., Evelyn, Dalbury, Derbyshire
*Cottrell, Mr. C., Waterloo-bridge-road, London
Coulman, R. J., Esq., Wadworth-hall, York
Coulter, M., Esq., Friday-street, London
*Coupland, Mr., Southampton
*Courier Newspaper, The Proprietors of the
*Court, William, Esq., Middlewich, Cheshire
Court, Mr. William, Monmouth
*Courtenay, H. Hugh, Esq. Merton coll., Oxford
*Courtenay, W., Esq., Duke-st., Westminster
*COURTOWN, The Right Hon. the Earl of
*Cove, Richard, Esq., Milford, near Salisbury
*COVENTRY, The Right Hon. the Earl of
Coventry, The Honorable William
Covey, Charles, Esq., Basingstoke, Hants.
*Covey, W. H., Esq., Uckfield, Sussex
Cowan, Mr. T. C., Charlotte-st. Park-st. Bristol
*Cowderoy, T., Esq., Froxfield, Berks.
*Cowe, Rev. J., M. A., Sunbury, Middlesex
Cowell, W. A., Esq., Pangbourn, Berks.
*Cowen, George, Esq., Dalston, Cumberland
Cowley, Mr. T., Queenhill, Worcestershire
*Cowne, S., Esq., Connaught-terrace, London
*COWPER, The Right Honorable Earl
Cowtan, Mr. M., Canterbury
*Cox, Charles, Esq., Wilford, near Nottingham
Cox, E. S., Esq., Brailsford, Derbyshire
*Cox, E. T. J., Esq., Lancaster
*Cox, James, Esq., Croydon, Surrey
*Cox, Mr. John, Wrington, Somersetshire
Cox, Rev. Joseph, Gainsborough, Lincolnshire
Cox, Mr. Joseph, Dudley, Worcestershire
Cox, Rev. R. C., Dover
Cox, R., Esq., Corpus-Christi coll., Cambridge
*Cox, Samuel, Esq., Beaminster, Dorsetshire
*Cox, S. C., Esq., Chancery-chambers, London
*Cox, Rev. T., Coleridge, Crediton, Devon.
Cox, Rev. J. S., Pembroke college, Oxford
*Cox, Rev. W. H., Queen's college, do.
Cox, Mr. W. C., Taunton, Somersetshire
*Cox, W. J., Esq., Misterton, do.
Cox, William, Esq., Hereford
*Coxwell, Rev. Charles S., Evershot, Dorset.
Coxwell, Rev. C., Dowdeswell, Gloucestershire
*Crabtree, Jno, Esq., Hebden-bridge, Yorkshire
*Crabtree, Richard, Esq., Wokingham, Berks.
*Craddock, John, Esq., Nuneaton, Warwickshire
*Cradock, Mr. J., Carey-street, London
Cragg, John, Esq., Threckingham, Lincolnshire
*Crakanthorpe, Harvey, Esq., Eastham, Cheshire
*Crallan, T., Esq., Ardwick, near Manchester
*Cram, David, Esq., Newcastle upon Tyne
Cram, G. W., Esq., do.
*Cramlington, H., Esq., do.
*Crampton, J. N., Lincoln's-inn-fields, London
Crane, Benj., Esq., College-yard, Worcester
*Crane, Mr. E., Newington Causeway, Southwark
*Crane, Henry, Esq., Wolverhampton
*Crane, Mr. Joseph, Kidderminster
Crane, S. G., Esq., Preston, Lancashire
Crane, Thomas, jun., Esq., do., do.
*Cranke, J., Esq., Ulverstone, do.
*Cranke, William, Esq., Urswick, do.
CRANSTOUN, The Right Honorable Lord
*Craps, Rev. John, Portland-place, Lincoln
*CRAVEN, The Right Honorable the Earl of
*Craven, T., Esq., Nelson-street, Whitechapel
Crawcorn, B., Esq., Norwich
Crawford, C. J., Esq., Wadham coll., Oxford
Crawshall, G., Esq., Stanhope, Durham
Crawshaw, Mr. James, Sheffield
Crawter, Mr. Henry, Cheshunt, Herts.

*Crawter and Sons, Messrs., Southampton-buildings, London
Cree, Mr. John, Addlestone, Surrey
*Crees and Son, Messrs., Arundel, Sussex
Creese, Mr. John, Teddington, Worcestershire
Creghe, Rev. Stephen, York
*Cremer, Thomas, Esq., Norwich
*Cresford, Mr. S., Cambridge
*Cressy, E., Esq., F.A.S., Suffolk-st., London
*Creswell, Charles, Esq., Birchin-lane, do.
*Creswell, Richard, Esq., Ravenstone, Derbysh.
Creswick, Thomas, Esq., Hatfield, Herts.
*CREWE, The Right Honorable Lord
*Crewe, Sir George, Bart., Calk-abbey, Derbysh.
Crewe, Rev. Charles, Longdon, Worcestershire
Crewe, Rev. H. R., Stanton by Bridge, Derbysh.
Crewe, Robert, Esq., Marchwood, Hants.
Cribb, Mr. W., King-st., Covent-garden, London
*Crighton, Mr. J., Manchester
*Crighton, Mr. W., do.
*Crisford, Mr. S., Bourn-bridge, Cambridgesh.
*Crisp, Mr. T. W., Castle-ditch, Norwich
*Critchley, Henry, Esq., Macclesfield, Cheshire
*Crocker, H. G., Esq., Northover, Somersetshire
Crockett, Mr. Thomas, New-street, Birmingham
Croft, John, Esq., Hitchin, Herts.
*Croft, Mr. John, Hampstead heath, Middlesex
Croft, Mr. Philip, King's Caple, Herefordshire
*Crofts, Rev. P. G., Malling-house, Sussex
*Crofts, Robert, Esq., Dumpton, Kent
*Crofts, Mr., Chancery-lane, London
Croggon, Mr. R. W., Cornhill, do.
Croker, John W., Esq., M. P., Admiralty, do.
*Crompton, A., Esq., Lincoln's-inn, do.
Crompton, Mr. George, Hereford
*Crompton, George, Esq., Chorley, Lancashire
*Crompton, James, Esq., Bolton, do.
*Crompton, J., Esq., Kersley, near do., do.
*Crompton, T. B., Esq., Farnworth, do.
*Crook, John, Esq., Rochdale, do.
*Crook, Mr. J. C., Watling-street, London
Crook, Richard S., Esq., Liverpool
Crook, Thomas, Esq., do.
*Crooke, Rev. James, Manchester
*Crooke, G. W., Esq., Liverpool
Crooks, Mr. W., St. Andrew's-hill, London
*Croome, D., Esq., Berkeley, Gloucestershire
Croose, Mr. George, Hereford
Cropper, J., jun., Esq., Toxteth-Park, Liverpool
*Crosfield, J., Esq., Warrington, Lancashire
*Croskell, Rev., William, Durham
*Croskey, J. D., Esq., Mansion-house-st., Lond.
*Crosland, John, Esq., Torrington-square, do.
*Crosley, James, Esq., Leeds, Yorkshire, 2 Copies
Cross, Henry, Esq., Liverpool
*Cross, James, Esq., Blackburn, Lancashire
*Cross, John, Esq., Bolton, do.
*Cross, Thomas, Esq., do., do.
*Cross, William, Esq., Blackburn, do.
*Crossdaile, T. P., Esq., Royal Mint, London
*Crosse, Rev. J., Powlett, near Bridg-water
Crosse, T., Esq., Lewinthorpe-House, Leeds
Crossley, John, Esq., Chalfont St. Giles, Bucks.
*Crossley, John, Esq., F.A.S., Rochdale
Crossley, Robert, Esq., do.
*Crossley, Mess. J. and Sons, Fallen-Royd, Lancashire
Crouch, Jno., Esq., St. Cross, Winchester, Hants.
Croudson, John, Esq., Wigan, Lancashire
Crowder, John, Esq., London
Crowdy, Rev. Anthony, Swindon, Wilts.
*Crowdy, R. W., Esq., Farringdon, Berkshire
*Crowdy, William, Esq., Highworth, Wilts.
Crowdy, William Morse, Esq., Swindon, do.
Crowe, S., Esq., George-st., Euston-sq., Lond.
Crowley, Mr. Henry, Alton, Hants.
*Crowley, John, Esq., Wolverhampton
Crowther, Mr. G. H., Chester
Crowther, Samuel, Esq., Hayfield, Derbyshire
*Crowther, S. F., Esq., Wednesbury, Staffordsh.
Croxon and Co., Messrs., Ellesmere, Shropsh.
*Crozier, William, Esq., Gateshead, Durham
Crump & Sons, Messrs., Temple-st., Birmingham

Cruse, Mr. Thomas, Calne, Wiltshire
Cruso, J., jun., Esq., Leek, Staffordshire
Cruttwell, C. H., Esq., Hertford
Cruttwell, T. M., Esq., Bath
Cubitt, Mr. George, Norwich
Cuddon, James, Esq., do.
Culledge, C., Esq., March, Cambridgeshire
Culley, Samuel, Esq., Norwich
Cullum, Sir Thos. Grey, Bart., Hardwick-house
Cullum, Mr. George, Judd-street, London
Culshaw, W., Esq., Aughton, Lancashire
Cuming, Mr. C., Trumpington, near Cambridge
*Cuming, John, Esq., Greyswood, Surrey
Cumming, John, Esq., Trent-Park, Middlesex
*Cumming, George, Esq., M. D., Chester
Cummins, John, Esq., Linton, Herefordshire
*Cummins, Mr. T., Redman's-row, Mile-end
Cummins, W., Esq., Dymock, Gloucestershire
Cundall, Benjamin, Esq., Norwich
Cunliffe, Sir Foster, Bart., F.S.A., Acton-park, Denbighshire
*Cunliffe, John, Esq., Garstang, Lancashire
Cunliffes, Brookes, and Co., Mess., Blackburn
*Cunningham, B., Esq., Chippenfield-house, Herts.
*Cunningham, C., Esq., Christ-church college, [Oxford
*Cunningham, J., Esq., Clifton, Gloucestershire
*Cunningham, R., Esq., Castletown, I. of Man
Cunyngham, W. A., Esq., Temple, London
*Curling, William, Esq., Hitchin, Herts.
Currer, Rev. D. R., Clifton-house, near York
*Currie, James, Esq., London
Currie, Rev. J., A.M., Much Hadham, Herts.
*Currie, Mark, Esq., Hayes, Middlesex
*Curry, P. F., Esq., Liverpool
Curry, Colonel W. S., Lismore Castle, Ireland
*Curteis, H. B., Esq., Peasmarsh, Sussex
Cursham, William, Esq., Nottingham
Curteis, George, Esq., Canterbury
Curteis and Kingsford, Messrs., do.
*Curties, Jeremiah, Esq., Tenterden, Kent
*Curtis, Sir William, Bart., Southgate, Middlesex
Curtis, J. A., Esq., do., do.
Curtis, A., Esq., Bridge-street, Blackfriars
Curtis, Charles B., Esq., Lombard-st., London
*Curtis, Charles A., Esq., Abingdon, Berks.
Curtis, Rev. G. W., Padworth, do.
Curtis, H. P., Esq., Romsey, Hants.
*Curtis, J., Esq., Southampton-buildings, Lond.
*Curtis, T. A., Esq., Staple's-inn, do.
*Curtis, Thomas, Esq., Lombard-street, do.
Curtis & Harvey, Messrs., do., do.
Curtler, F. G., Esq., Droitwich, Worcestershire
Curtler, John, Esq., Bromsgrove, do.
Curtler, Thomas G., Esq., Droitwich, do.
*Curtois, Rev. Peregrine, Longhills, near Lincoln
Curtoys, Chs., Esq., Northampton-sq., London
*Curwen, H. C., Esq., Windermere, Westmorl.
*Curwen, Rev. John, Harrington, Cumberland
*Curwen, R. E., Esq., York-pl., Portman-sq.
Curzon, The Honorable Vice-Admiral
*Curzon, Honorable N., Farnagh, near Derby
*Cusins, Teeling, Esq., Brook-st., Hanover-sq.
*Cussons, Thomas, Esq., Oldham, Lancashire
*Cust, Richard, Esq., Carlisle, Cumberland
CUSTOMS, The Honorable the Commissioners of His Majesty's
*Cutbush, Mr. Henry, Maidstone
*Cutbush, Mr. Richard J., do.
Cuthbert, Rev. W., Doncaster, Yorkshire
*Cutten, C., Esq., Quality-court, London
*Cutto, A., Esq., Canterbury-square, Southwark

DACRE, The Right Honorable Lord
*Daglish, R., Esq., Wigan, Lancashire
Daintree, R., Esq., Hemingford-Abbots, Hunts.
Dainty, Thomas R., Esq., North-rode, Cheshire
Daker, Job, Esq., Skerton, Lancashire
Dakeyne, Edward, Esq., Darley-dale, Derbysh.
Dale, Adam, Esq., York
*Dale, H., Esq., North Shields, Northumberland
Dale, Mr. John, Manchester
*Dale, Mr. R., Wood-street, Cheapside, London
Dale, Mr. Thomas A., Liverpool
*Dale, Rev. Thos., University-chambers, London
*Dalgleish, Mr. Simeon, Maiden-lane, do.
*Dallas, Lieut.-Gen. Sir Thomas, K. C. B.
Dallin, Rev. James, York
Dallinger, Mr. Jos., St. Peter's, Norwich
Dallinger, J., Esq., Hertford
*DALMENY, The Right Honorable Lord
*Dalton, Christopher, Esq., Watford, Herts.
*Dalton, George, Esq, Dudley, Worcestershire
Dalton, Thomas, Esq., Hollingworth, Cheshire
*Daly, D., Esq., Christ-church college, Oxford
Daly, J., Esq., Darlington-place, Maida-hill
Daly, James, Esq., Dunsandle, Ireland
*Dampier, C. E., Esq., Gray's-inn, London
Dampier, Rev. J., Codford St. Peter, Wilts.
Dance, Lieut.-Colonel Sir C. Webb, Herstborne-Manor-place
Danger, William, Esq., Congresbury, Bath
*Dangerfield, John, Esq., Ely-place, London
*Daniel, A., Esq., Exeter college, Oxford
*Daniel, G., Esq., Thanet-pl., Strand, London
*Daniel, James W., Esq., Beaminster, Dorset.
*Daniel, John, Esq., St. John's coll., Cambridge
Daniel, Mr. Jno., Abergavenny, Monmouthshire
Daniel, R., Esq., Stoke upon Trent, Staffordsh.
*Daniel, T., Esq., jun., Sneed-park, near Bristol
*Daniell, Rev. G. W., Frome, Somersetshire
*Daniell, T., Esq., Little Berkhampstead, Herts.
*Daniell, Wm., Esq., Abercarne, Monmouthshire
*Danks, Isaiah, Esq., Wolverhampton, Staffordsh.
*Danks, Samuel, Esq., Wednesbury, do.
*Dann, Henry, Esq., St. John's coll., Oxford
*Darby, George, Esq., Hastings, Sussex
Darby, Mr. G., Hertford
Darby, Mr. S., Cookham, Berks.
Darbyshire, C. J., Esq., Bolton, Lancashire
Darbyshire, Edw., Esq., Great Lever, do.
*Dare, Mr. George, Bermondsey, Southwark
*Darley, A. H., Esq., Christ's coll., Cambridge
Darley, R., Esq., Trinity-pl., Charing-cross, Lon.
*Darlington, John, Esq., Comberbach, Cheshire
DARNLEY, The Right Honorable the Earl of
Dart, Joseph, Esq., East Budleigh, Devonshire
*DARTMOUTH, The Right Hon. the Earl of
Darwall, C. H., Esq., Walsall, Staffordshire
*Darwell, T., Esq., Standish-Hall, Lancashire
*Darwen, John, Esq., Edgbaston, Birmingham
*Dasent, William, Esq., Saxmundham, Suffolk
*Dash, Mr. Thos., Windsor
*Dashwood, Sir G., Bart., Kirtlington-park, Oxon
Dashwood, Rev. Augustus, Deerham, Norfolk
*Daubeney, Lieut.-Colonel, Crescent, Bath
Daubeney, G. M., Esq., Cote, near Bristol
Davencey, C. B., Esq., Norwich
Davenport, Mr. G., Kimbolton, Herefordshire
Davenport, Henry, Esq.
*Davenport, John, Esq., Westwood, Staffordshire
*Davenport, Mr. John, Dunham-Massey, Chesh.
*Davenport, W., Esq., Church-row, Hampstead
Davey, William, Esq., Redruth, Cornwall
Davidson, Thos., Esq., Newcastle upon Tyne
Davidson, W. F., Esq., Doctors Commons
*Davies, B., Esq., Devonshire-square, London
*Davies, C. R., Esq., South Petherton, Somerset.
Davies, Rev. D., D.D., Emsworth, Hants.
Davies, Rev. W., D.D., F.A.S., F.R.S.L., Rockhampton, Gloucestershire
Davies, Rev. D. W., M. A., Cranbrook, Kent
Davies, D., Esq., Palsgrave-place, London
*Davies, Mr. Daniel, Hereford
*Davies, E., Esq., Shepton-Mallet, Somersetsh.
*Davies, E., Esq., Ebley-house, Gloucestershire
Davies, Edward, Esq., Salisbury
Davies, G. A. A., Esq., Crickhowell, Breconsh.
*Davies, Mr. George, Hereford
*Davies, Rev. H., Stoke-Edith, Herefordshire
Davies, Henry, Esq., Monmouth
Davies, H. G., Esq., Astmore-bridge, Cheshire
*Davies, Rev. J. B., A. M., Usk, Monmouthsh.
*Davies, Rev. J. J., Tottenham, Middlesex
*Davies, James, Esq., Threadneedle-st., London
Davies, John, Esq., Great Mollington, Cheshire
Davies, John, Esq., Hertford
*Davies, Jno., Esq., Devonshire-square, London
*Davies, Mr. J., Tarrington, Herefordshire
Davies, Mr. John, Newbury, Berks.
Davies, Mr. John, Hay, Brecon
Davies, R. W. P., Esq., Worcester coll., Oxford
*Davies, Mr. Rice, Bayswater, London
*Davies, Robert, Esq., Wells, Somersetshire
*Davies, Rev. S., B. C. L., Cherry-Hinton, near [Cambridge
Davies, S., Esq., Southwark
*Davies, Samuel, Esq., Winsford, Cheshire
Davies, Rev. T. M., Trevilan, Cardiganshire
*Davies, Thomas, Esq., Tarporley, Cheshire
Davies, Mr. T., Dudley, Worcestershire
Davies, Mr. Thomas, Ross, Herefordshire
Davies, William, Esq., Wantage, Berks.
Davies, W. H., Esq., Lea, nr. Ross, Herefordsh.
Davies, Mrs., Croft-castle, do.
*Davis, A., Esq., M.D., Westbrook, do.
Davis, A., Esq., Nicholas-lane, London
Davis, Charles, Esq., Bircher, Herefordshire
Davis, F. Henry, Esq., Clapham Rise, Surrey
Davis, Mr. F. W., Windsor
Davis, Rev. Jas., Chepstow, Monmouthshire
Davis, J., Esq., Upper Berkeley-st., London
*Davis, Rev. John, Ashwick, Somersetshire
*Davis, J., Esq., Bernard-st., Russell-square
*Davis, Mr. John Smyth, Hereford
Davis, J. W., Esq., Hertford
Davis, R., Esq., Walbrook, London
Davis, Mr. S., Tipton, Staffordshire
*Davis, Thomas, Esq., Warminster, Wiltshire
*Davis, T. B., Esq., Cerne, Dorsetshire
*Davis, W. R., Esq., Loudwater, Bucks.
Davis, William, Esq., Blechingley, Surrey
*Davise, John, Esq., Liverpool
*Davison, D. W., Esq., Clement's-inn, London
*Davison, H., Esq., Penkridge, Staffordshire
*Davison, J. M., Esq., Beamish-park, Durham
Davison, Wm., Esq., Bread-street, London
Davy, Christopher, Esq., Furnival's-inn, do.
Davy, D. E., Esq., Ufford, Suffolk
Davy, Mr. John K., Tewkesbury
*Davy, Mr. William, Norwich
Dawe, Mr. Edward, Monmouth
*Dawes, Matthew, Esq., Bolton, Lancashire
*Dawes, Samuel, Esq., Handsworth, Staffordshire
*Dawes, Wm. Bower, Esq., Bolton, Lancashire
*Dawes and Chatfield, Messrs., Angel-court, London
Dawes and Son, Messrs., West Bromwich, near [Birmingham
Dawkins, Mr. Geo., Wherwell, Hants.
*Dawkins, G. H., Esq., Portland-place, London
*Dawnay, W. H., Esq., Christ-ch. coll., Oxford
*Daws, John, Esq., Ripley, Surrey
Dawson, Mr., Great Marlborough-st., London
Dawson, Abraham, Esq., Newcastle upon Tyne
*Dawson, Geo., Esq., Size-lane, Bucklersbury
*Dawson, H. P., Esq., Brasenose coll., Oxford
*Dawson, G. R., Esq., M.P., Grosvenor-square, 2 Copies
Dawson, James, Esq., Newington, Liverpool
*Dawson, Mr. J., Castle-street, London
*Dawson, J. V., Esq., Symond's-inn, do.
Dawson, Richard, Esq., Liverpool
*Dawson, Richard Crosbie, Esq., do.
*Dawson, Thos., Esq., Grasmere, Westmorland
*Dawson, William, Esq., Dunkinfield, Cheshire
Day, A., Esq., Milverton, Somersetshire
*Day, Rev. C., L. L. B., Rushmere, Ipswich
*Day, D., Esq., Rochester
Day, Mr. Edward, Birmingham
Day, George G., Esq., St. Ives, Hunts.
Day, H. J., Esq., St. Neots, do.
Day, H. T., Esq., Wickham-Market, Suffolk
*Day, John, Esq. Sheerness, Kent
*Day, Jno., Esq., Water-lane, Tower-hill, Lond.
Day, Peter, Esq., Norwich
*Day, Ralph, Esq., Sarratt-house, Herts.

Day, Mr. Starling, Norwich
*Day, Thomas, Esq., Maidstone
Day, William, Esq., Market-place, Norwich
Day, Mr. William, St. Neots, Hunts
Day and Co., Messrs., Gracechurch-st., London
Dayers, Thomas, Esq., Dilwyn, Herefordshire
Deacon, Mr. C., Skinner-street, London
*Deacon, Henry, Esq., Portsmouth
Deacon, John, Esq., Doctors Commons, Lond.
Deacon, Mr. John, Oundle, Northamptonshire
Deacon, Mr. Thomas, Skinner-street, London
*Deacon, William, Esq., Hertford
Deacon, Harrison and Co., Messrs., Wakefield
*Deadman, John, Esq., Arnos-vale, near Bristol
*Deakin, Mr. William, Birmingham
Dean, Mr. G., Clapton-square, Middlesex
Dean, Rev. E. N., Weston under Penyard
Dean, Rev. J., D.D., St. Mary-hall, Oxford
Dean, J., Esq., Winnington, Cheshire
*Dean, Richard T., Esq., Knutsford, do.
*Dean, Samuel, Esq., Witton, do.
*Dean, Rev. Thomas, Colwall, Herefordshire
*Dean, William, Esq., Bilston, Staffordshire
*Dean, William, Esq., Guildford-street, London
*Dean, William, Esq., Bolton, Lancashire
*Dean, Mr. William, Friday-street, London
*Deane, Henry, Esq., Exeter college, Oxford
*Deane, John, Esq., Reading, Berks.
*Deane, Robert M., Esq., do., do.
Deane, T.P., Esq., St. John's coll., Oxford
Deane, Rev., W. H., Hintlesham, Suffolk
Dear, Charles, Esq., Enfield, Middlesex
*Dear, Charles, Esq., Hertford
*Dearden, James, Esq., Rochdale, Lancashire
*Dearden, Thomas F., Esq., do., do.
*D'Arville, Rev. F., Thornbury, Gloucestershire
Death, Mr. James, Waltham-Abbey, Essex
Debenham, Mr., King-st., Covent-garden, Lon.
De Beauvoir, R. P. W. B., Esq., Englefield-house, Berks.
De Carle, Mr. Robert, jun., Norwich
Dee, Thomas, Esq., Broughton, Hants.
*Deedes, E., Esq., Jesus college, Cambridge
De Jersey, H., Esq., Old Jewry, London
*Delafosse, Rev. D. C., A.M., Richmond, Surrey
De Lasaux, Mr. Thomas J., Canterbury, Kent
De Levante, W., Esq., Princes-street, London
Deighton, Mr. Thomas, Kidderminster
DELAMERE, The Right Honorable Lord
*Delaunay, G., Esq., Crumpsall, near Manchester
*Delisser, Alexander, Esq., Judd-st., London
*Dell, W. W., Esq., Southampton-buildings, do.
*Dell, George, Esq., Dover
Delmar, Mr. James, Canterbury
Delmar, William, Esq., Kenfield, Kent
Delph, N., Esq., Edmonton, Middlesex
*Demaine, Rev. H., Ashford, Kent
*Dempster, Mr. Rich., Brighton, Sussex
Dendy, Arthur, Esq., Dorking, Surrey
*Denew, Mr. J., Charles-st., Berkeley-sq., Lond.
*Denham, Joseph, Esq., Bolton, Lancashire
*Denham, Richard, Esq., Bury, do.
Denison, George, Esq., Oriel college, Oxford
Denison, Henry, Esq., Liverpool
*Denison, T., Esq., Tottenham-court-road, Lond.
*Denne, Henry, Esq., Canterbury
Denne, T., Esq., Christ-church college, Oxford
Denning, Miss S. H., Castle School, Monmouth
Dennis, Capt. I., Leominster, Herefordshire
*Denshire, H., Esq., Clare-hall, Cambridge
Dent, George, Esq., M. D., Stafford
Denton, N., Esq., Denton, Lancashire [Lond.
Denton and Barker, Messrs., Gray's-inn-square,
*Depear, Mr. M., Manchester
Derby, C. G., Esq., Inner Temple, London
*Derbyshire, W., jun., Esq., Salford, Lancash.
Dermer, Wm., Esq., M. D., Farnham, Surrey
Derry, F. B., Esq., New Burchen-Castle, Frome
*Derry, Richard, Esq., Pencombe, Herefordshire
Desborough, Mrs., Hemingford-Grey, Hunts.
Devas, William, Esq., Watling-street, London

De Vear, F. T., Esq., Norwich
*Devereux, R., Esq., Christ-church coll., Oxford
Devereux, Thos., Esq., Bromyard, Herefordshire
*Devereux, William, Esq., do., do.
Devisme, Rev. J. E., Stanton-Drew, Somerset.
DEVONSHIRE, His Grace the Duke of
Dew, Mr. Daniel, Ross, Herefordshire
*Dew, Geo., Esq., Coat, near Martock, Somerset.
Dew, T., Esq., Bampton-Abbas, Herefordshire
Dew, Thomas, Esq., Boroughbridge, Yorkshire
Dew, Mr. W., Pencreig, Marston, Hereford
*Dewe, Mr. John L., Reading, Berks.
*Dewe, Rev. S., Chatham, Kent
*Dewes, Capt. Edward, Hadley, Middlesex
*Dewgard, Major, Tewkesbury, Gloucestershire
*Dewhurst, Henry, Esq., Preston, Lancashire
*Dewhurst, Samuel D., Esq., Salford, do.
*Dewhurst, Thomas, Esq., Preston, do.
Dewhurst, Messrs. D. and J., do., do.
*Dewis, J., Esq., Wood-st., Cheapside, London
Dewsbury, P. R., Esq., Tring, Hertfordshire
Dewse, Thomas, Esq., York
Deykes, T., Esq., Little Sansfield, Hereford
Deykin, Mr. Jas., Birmingham
De Lannoy, Wm., Esq., Friday-st., Cheapside
*De Pavia, — Esq., Broad-street, do.
*De Starck, Rev. H. G., Fisherton, Wiltshire
Dibley, George, Esq., Newbury, Berks.
*Dicas, John, Esq., Austin-Friars, London
Diceonson, C., Esq., Wrightington, Lancashire
Dick, P. T., Esq., M. D., Castle-Cary, Somersetshire
*Dickens, Commissary-Gen., Hadley, Middlsx.
Dickens, Thomas, Esq., Leatherhead, Surrey
*Dickenson, J. D., Esq., Tavistock-place, Lond.
*Dickenson, J., Esq., King's-Langley, Herts
*Dickins, F., Esq., Queen-st., Cheapside, Lond.
Dickins, Mr. Thomas, Hereford
*Dickinson, Mrs. Ann, Ware, Herts.
Dickinson, Mr. George, Buckland, Kent
*Dickinson, Isaac, Esq., Ulverstone, Lancashire
*Dickinson, Jno., Esq., New Broad-st., London
*Dickinson, P., Esq., West Retford, Notts.
*Dickman, J., Esq., Newgate-st., London
Dickson, Rev. M., Pitminster, Somersetshire
Dickson, Peter, Esq., M. C., Southampton
Dickson, Mr. W., Triangle, Hackney, Middsx.
*Diggles, Peter, Esq., Bolton, Lancashire
*Dighton, Gen. T., Newland, Gloucestershire
Dighton, Rev. Edward, Cranmore, Somerset
*Dighton, Rev. Jas., Stone-Easton, do.
*Dignam, Thos., Esq., Little Distaff-lane, Lond.
Dikes, W.H., Esq., F. G. S., Kingston upon Hull
Dillon, Mr. J., Hereford
*Dillwyn, John, Esq., Oriel college, Oxford
*Dilly, Mr. Thomas, Governor of Oxford Castle
*Dilworth, James, Esq., Preston, Lancashire
*DIMSDALE, The Honorable Baron
*Dimsdale, C. T., Esq., Tolmers, near Hertford
Dinham, W. B., Esq., Magdalene hall, Oxford
*Disney, Edgar, Esq., St. Peter's coll., Cambdg.
*Ditchburn, Mr. Henry, Gravesend, Kent
Ditchburn, Thos., Esq., Corbet-court, London
*Ditchfield, Peter, Esq., Bolton, Lancashire
*Divett, Miss, Westerham, Kent
*Divett, John, Esq., Trinity coll., Cambridge
Dix, Charles, Esq., Basinghall-street, London
*Dix, Richard, Esq., Symond's-inn, do.
*Dix, Robert, Esq., Ely, Cambridgeshire
Dix, Samuel, Esq., Norwich
*Dixie, Capt. R. N., Chertsey, Surrey
Dixon, Dixon, Esq., Newcastle upon Tyne
Dixon, E., Esq., Ashwood-house, near Dudley
*Dixon, Henry, Esq., Oxford
Dixon, Mr. James, Henley upon Thames
*Dixon, John, Esq., Knells, Cumberland
*Dixon, John, Esq., Peel-street, Manchester
Dixon, John, Esq., Sheffield, Yorkshire
Dixon, John, Esq., St. Swithin's-lane, London
*Dixon, Mr. John, Wolverhampton
Dixon, Mr. J. M., Ipswich
Dixon, Mr. Matthew, Upton upon Severn

*Dixon, Peter, Esq., Warwick-bridge, Carlisle
Dixon, R., Esq., Chancery-lane, London
*Dixon, Thomas, Esq., Preston, Lancashire
*Dixon, T., Esq., New Boswell-court, London
Dixon, Mr. Thomas, Norwich
Dixon, William, Esq., Custom-house, London
Dixon, Rev. W. H., Bishopthorpe, Yorkshire
Dixon, Messrs. C. & W., Walsall, Staffordshire
*Dixson, T. G., Esq., Deal, Kent
*Dobb, John, Esq., Timperley, Cheshire
*Dobie, A., Esq., Palsgrave-place, London
*Dobinson, William, Esq., Carlisle
*Dobson, Benjamin, Esq., Bolton, Lancashire
Dobson, J., Esq., Newcastle upon Tyne
*Dobson, John, Esq., Gateshead, Durham
*Dobson, John, Esq., Queen's college, Oxford
*Dobson, Lepton, Esq., Park-square, Leeds
Dobson, T., Esq., jun., Chancery-lane, London
Docker, Edmund, Esq., Sambrook-court, do.
Dockray, John, Esq., Rossendale, Lancashire
*Dodd, G. R., Esq., Tokenhouse-yard, London
*Dodd, Rev. H. A., Newcastle upon Tyne
*Dodds, Joseph, Esq., Lambeth, Surrey
Dodds, W., Esq., Gosberton, Lincolnshire
*Dodgson, Rev. C., A.M., Daresbury, Cheshire
*Dodgson, Rev. W. J. T., B.A., Nantwich, do.
Dodgson, John, Esq., Blackburn
Dodsley, John, Esq., Skegby-hall, Notts.
Dodson, John, Esq., Lancaster
*Dodson, William, Esq., Holford, Cheshire
*Dodsworth, Sir E., Bart., Newland-park, York
*Dodwell, H., Esq., Bray, Maidenhead, Berks.
*Dolphin, J. W., Esq., Worcester coll., Oxford
*Donald, Rev. A., M.A., King's Langley, Herts.
*Donald, Joseph, Esq., Runcorn, Cheshire
*Donavan, Alexander, Esq., Uckfield, Sussex
*Done, James, Esq., Bickley-hall, Cheshire
*Donkin, Henry, Esq., Durham [Tyne
*Donkin and Stable, Messrs., Newcastle upon
Donn, Robert, Esq., St. John's college, Camb.
*Donne, E., Esq., York-place, Portman-square
Donne, J., Esq., Michael-Church, Herefordshire
*Donnison, Wm., Esq., University coll., Oxford
*Donton, Rev. J., M.A., Weathampstead, Herts.
Doran, Capt. J. G., Southampton
Dore, Mr. W. H., Bath
*Dorell, Edward, Esq., Charing, Kent
DORMER, The Right Honorable Lord
*Dornell, R. W., Esq., Grange, Sunderland
*Dorning, William, Esq., Manchester
*Dorrien, T., Esq., Berkhampstead, Herts.
*Dossetor, Mr. Thomas, Poultry, London
Dottin, A. R., Esq., M. P., Southampton
Douce, A. E., Esq., Maidstone, Kent
*DOUGLAS, The Most Noble the Marquis of
Douglas, Rev. J., Newland, Gloucestershire
Dover, H. J., Esq., Gt. Winchester-st., London
*Doveton, Rev. J. F., Mells, Somerset.
*Dowdeswell, Rev. E. C., D. D., Stanford-Rivers, Essex
*Dowdeswell, Mrs., Cheltenham
*Dowdeswell, G., Esq., Redmarley, Worcestersh.
*Dowdeswell, J. E., Esq., M. P., Pull-court, do.
*Dowding, Frederick, Esq., Bath
Dowding, W., Esq., China-court, Herefordshire
*Dowell, Mr. John, Clifford-court, do.
Dowell, Mr. Joseph, Bradford-st., Birmingham
*Dowell, Mr. Thos., Bage, Dorston, Herefordsh.
Dowle, James, Esq., Forhampton, Worcestersh.
Dowle, Mr. James, Chepstow, Monmouthshire
Dowle, Mr. John, Langannock, Herefordshire
*Dowle, Mr. W., Sheepcot Clifford, do.
*Dowling, Rev. J. G., Crypt, Gloucestershire
*DOWNES, the Right Honorable Lord
*Downes, John, Esq., Christ's coll., Cambridge
Downes, J., Esq., Longland, Herefordshire
*Downes, John, Esq., Nantwich, Cheshire
*Downes, J. F., Esq., Ashford-Carbonell, Salop.
*Downes, Dawson, and Turner, Messrs., London-wall, London
Downing, Francis, Esq., Dudley
*DOWNSHIRE, the Most Noble Marquis of
Dows, Mr. John, Newbury, Berks.

Dowson, John William, Esq., Norwich
Dowson, Mr. Wm., Great Surrey-street, London
* Dowton, William, Esq., Vauxhall, Surrey
Doyden, William, Esq., Kingston upon Hull
* Drake, F., Esq., Cook's-court, London
* Drake, F. H. N., Esq., Colyton-house, Devonsh.
Drake, Rev. G. T., B. C. L., Malpas, Cheshire
Drake, Hinton E. S., Esq., Bath
Drake, J. D., Esq., Brasenose college, Oxford
* Drake, J. R., Esq., Christ-church coll., do.
* Drake, R., Esq., Clare hall, Cambridge
Drake, W. W., Esq., Poultry, London
Drake, W. W., Esq., Walthamstow, Essex
* Drake, Mr., Walden, Herts.
Drake, Mr. W., Kingsclere, Berks.
Dransfield, James, Esq., Birmingham
Draper, Robt., Esq., Kenilworth, Warwickshire
Draper, Thomas, Esq., Wiln-Mills, Derbyshire
* Drawbridge, F. K., Esq., Arundel-st., London
* Drax, J. S. W., Esq., Lower Grosvenor-st., do.
Drayson, W., Esq., Waltham Abbey, Essex
* Drew, D., Esq., Inrolment-Office, London
Drew, Mr. James, Sellack, Herefordshire
Drew, Mr. William, Preston, do.
* Driver, Messrs. E. and G. N., Whitehall
* Driver, Rev. J., A. M., Ellel, near Lancaster
* Druce, Mr. Samuel, Ensham, near Oxford
* Drummond, A. B., Esq., Cadland, Hants.
* Drummond, A. M., Esq., Charing-Cross, Lond.
Drummond, D. J. K., Esq., Worcester college, Oxford
* Drummond, Geo., Esq., Wilton-crescent, Bath
Drummond, Henry, Esq., Belgrave-sq., London
Drummond, Rev. James, A. M., Down, Kent
* Drury, Rev. A., A.M., Upper Sunbury, Middsx.
Drury, Rev. G., Claydon, Suffolk
* Drury, Rev. Henry, A. M., Harrow, Middsx.
Dryden, William, Esq., Hull, Yorkshire
* Drysdale, W. F., Esq., Lyon's-inn, London
* Dubbins, Mr. Edward, Brighton, Sussex
* Duberley, Sir James, Knt., Gainshall
* Duberley, W., Esq., Dursley, Gloucestershire
Duboulay, A., Esq., St. Alban's hall, Oxford
* Duboulay, J., Esq., Exeter college, do.
* Duck, Mr. James, Speenhamland, Berks.
Duckworth, Sir J., Bart., Wearhouse, Devon
* Duckworth, T., Esq., Ardwick, nr. Manchester
* Ducord, P. J., Esq., Newland, Gloucestershire
* Dudding, John, Esq., New-road, Lincoln
DUDLEY, The Right Honorable the Earl of
Dudley, Crews, Esq., Oxford
Dudley, Rev. J., Himley, Staffordshire
* Dudley, J., Esq., Winsford-lodge, Cheshire
* Dudley, John, Esq., Wharton-lodge, do.
* Dudley, William, Esq., Cheapside, London
* Dufaur, F., Esq., Millman-street, do.
Duffield, Rev. M. D., Widford Rectory, Herts.
* Duffield, T., Esq., Marcham-park, Berks.
Duffin, William, Esq., York
* Dufty, Rich., Esq., Nottingham
* Dugdale, Adam, Esq., Liverpool
Dugdale, R., Esq., Compton-Bassett, Wilts.
Dugdale, Thomas, Esq., Blackburn, Lancash.
Duggan, Mr. John, Kington, Herefordshire
Dugood, Mrs., Owen's-row, Islington
* Duke, A., Esq., Guildford, Surrey
Duke, Rev. E., M. A., F. A. S., and L. S., Lake-house, Somerset
Duke, W., Esq., Magdalene hall, Oxford
* Dukes, Thomas Farmer, Esq., Shrewsbury
Dumvile, P. W., Esq., Manchester
* Dumville, T. Bond, Esq., Knutsford, Cheshire
* Duncan, The Honorable Captain Henry, R.N.
Duncan, A., Esq., Church-court, Old Jewry, [London
* Duncan, A., Esq., Gray's-inn, do.
* Duncan, William, Esq., Manchester
* DUNCANNON, The Right Honorable Lord
* Duncombe, Adolphus, Esq., Christ-church college, Oxford
* Duncombe, T. S., Esq., M. P., Queen-street, [May-fair
* Duncumb, Rev. Thomas, Sheen, Surrey
Dundas, R. A., Esq., M.P., Eaton-square, Lon.

Dundas, C., Esq., M. P., Barton-court, Berks.
* DUNGANNON, The Rt. Hon. Lord Viscount
* DUNGLAS, The Right Honorable Lord
Dunlap, A., Esq., St. John's college, Oxford
Dunlop, Walter, Esq., Bury, Lancashire
Dunlop, Walter, Esq., Rochdale, do.
Dunn, Mr. George, Ledbury, Herefordshire
Dunn, Mr. John, Tower-street, London
Dunn, Mr. Jonathan, Nottingham
* Dunn, Mrs., Upton upon Severn, Worcestersh.
* Dunn, Rev. Salisbury, B.A., Amwell, Herts.
* Dunn, Mr. Samuel, Delamere Forest, Cheshire
Dunne, Thomas, Esq., Bircher, Herefordshire
Dunning, Joseph, Esq., Leeds
* Dunnington, J., Esq., St. John's col., Cambridge
* Dunstan, Mr. John, Chester
* Dunstan, Mr. Richard, Manchester
* Duppa, Rev. J. W., Pudleston-ct., Herefordshire
* Dupré, Rev. M. T., M. A., Berkhampstead
* Dupuis, Rev. G. J., Eton college
Durell, Capt. T. P., R.N., Taunton Somerset.
* DURHAM, The Right Rev. Lord Bishop of
* DURHAM, The Right Honorable Lord
* Durham, Subscription Library
* Durlacher, L., Esq., Old Burlington-st., London
Durnford, James, Esq., Upper George-st., do.
Durnford, Rev. Richard, Chilbolton, Hants.
* Durrant, George, Esq. Norwich
* Durrant, Mr. William, do.
* Dutton, C., Esq., Bridenbury, Herefordshire
* Dutton, L. C., Esq., Warrington, Lancashire
* Dutton, R., Esq., Middlewich, Cheshire
* Duxbury, Giles, Esq., Manchester
Du Boulay, F., Esq., Clare hall, Cambridge
* Du Gard, Thomas, Esq., M. D., Shrewsbury
* Du Pré, James, Esq., Wilton-park, Bucks.
Dwyer, Mr. Jas., South Main-street, Cork
Dyer, H. S., Esq., Worcester college, Oxford,
* Dyer, John, Esq., Chief Clerk of the Admiralty
Dyer, J., Esq., Wotton under Edge, Gloucester
Dyke, Henry, Esq., Brighton, Sussex
* Dyke, Thos., Esq., Doctors Commons, London
Dyke, Mr. Thomas, Monmouth
Dymock, Major Edw., Penley-hall, Shropshire
Dymock, T. F., Esq., Hatch-Beauchamp, So- [merset.
* Dymock, Rev. W. G., do., do.
Dyne, Edmund, Esq., Bruton, do.
* Dyne, Wm., Esq., Lincoln's-inn-fields, London
* Dyneley, Chas., Esq., Doctors Commons, do.
* Dyneley and Gatty, Messrs., Gray's-inn, do.
DYNEVOR, The Right Honorable Lord
* Dyott, Lieut.-General William
Dyson, G., Esq., New-sq., Lincoln's-inn
Dyson, James, Esq., Newark, Nottinghamshire
* Dyson, John, Esq., Watford, Herts.
* Dyster, John, Esq., Leadenhall-st., London

Eade, G., Esq., Upper Thames-street, London
Eades, Mr. J., Delph-Clay-works, Staffordshire
Eager, Richard, Esq., Guildford, Surrey
Eager, Richard, Esq., Ripley, do.
Eagle, F. K., Esq., Milden-hall, Suffolk
* Eagle, William, Esq., Gravesend, Kent
Eagles, E., Esq., jun., Bedford
* Eagleton, Mr. Joseph, Bilston, Staffordshire
Earle, Charles, Esq., Everton, Liverpool
* Earle, Nicholas, Esq., Ashton under Line
Earle, R., Esq., Spekelands, near Liverpool
* Earle, William, Esq., Fenchurch-st., London
* Earnshaw, S., Esq., St. John's coll., Cambridge
Eashnent, J. W., Wincanton, Somerset
* Eason, Mrs. Elizabeth, South Petherton, do.
Easterby, Rich., Esq., Preston, Lancashire
* EAST INDIA COMPANY, The Honorable the Court of Directors of the . . 3 Copies
* Easton, John, Esq., Hereford
Eaststaff, Mr. Thomas, Reading, Berks.
Eastwick, Rev. J., Hemingford-Grey, Hunts.
* Eastwood, E. L., Esq., Crescent-place, Black-friars, London
* Eaton, H., Esq., New-Inn, London

Eaton, Mr. William, Ashford-Carbonell, Salop
Ebden, John, Esq., Hawleigh, Suffolk
* Ebdon, Rev. T., Durham
Ebsworth, H., Esq., Sambrook-court, London
* Eccles, Aaron, Esq., Marple, Cheshire
Eccles, John, Esq., M.D., Birmingham
* Eccles, John, Esq., Blackburn, Lancashire
* Eccles, Joseph, Esq., do., do.
* Eccles, William, Esq., do., do.
Eccles, Mr. W., Hatton-Garden, London
* Eccleston, Miss, Lytham, Lancashire
Eckersley, William, Esq., Wigan, do.
* Eckley, Rev. E., Tillington-court, Herefordsh.
Eckley, J. E., Esq., Trinity college, Oxford
* Eckley, Rev. John, Creden-hill, Herefordshire
Ede, Jas., Esq., Ridgway-castle, Southampton
Ede, Limbery, Esq., Friday-street, London
* Eden, The Honorable R. H.
Eden, The Honorable and Rev. R. T.
* Eden, The Honorable and Rev. William
* Eden, James, Esq., Bolton, Lancashire
Eden, John, Esq., Liverpool
Eden, Rev. R., Corpus-Christi college, Oxford
Edenborough, W., Esq., Coleman-street, Lond.
Edgall, Rev. Edward, Alvington, Devon
* Edge, A., Esq., Essex-street, London
* Edge, Mr. Charles, Bennett's-hill, Birmingham
* Edge, T. W., Esq., Strelley-hall, Notts.
* Edge, William, Esq., Manchester
Edgecomb, Mr. H., Tewkesbury [mersetshire
Edgell, Capt., R. N., Standerwick-court, So-
* Edgell, F., Esq., Basinghall-street, London
* Edleston, Richard, Esq., Blackburn, Lancash.
* Edleston, Richard, Esq., Nantwich, Cheshire
* Edmonds, Charles, Esq., Change-alley, London
* Edmonds, C., Esq., Bridge-st., Southwark
Edmonds, Ezekiel, Esq., Bradford, Wilts.
* Edmonds, R. T., Esq., South Petherton, Somerset
* Edmondson, J., Esq., Grass-Yard-hall, Lancash.
* Edmonstone, Rev. G., Potterne, near Devizes
Edmund, St., Hall Library, Oxford
* Edmunds, F. O., Esq., Warndworth, York
* Edmunds, G., Esq., Lincoln's-inn, London
Edmunds, John, Esq., Middleton, Herefordshire
* Edmunds, William, Esq., Margate, Kent
Edney, Mr. William, Chilworth, Hants.
* Edridge, A. L., Esq., Pockeredge
* Edridge, Thomas, Esq., Chippenham, Wilts.
Edwards, Mr. Charles, Monmouth
Edwards, Rev. E., A. B., Ellesmere, Shropshire
Edwards, Rev. E., M. A., Offord-Cluny, Hunts.
* Edwards, Rev. Edward, Ware, Herts.
Edwards, Mr. E., Blackley, near Manchester
Edwards, Mr. E., Islington, Middlesex
Edwards, George, Esq., Farningham, Kent
* Edwards, Henry, Esq., Hatton-Garden, London
Edwards, Mr. Henry, Bunshill, Herefordshire
Edwards, Rev. John, Warboys, Huntingdonshire
Edwards, Rev. John, Head Master of the Grammar School, Bury St. Edmund's, Suffolk
Edwards, Mr. John, Gough-sq., Birmingham
Edwards, J. S., Esq., Home-Lacy, Herefordsh.
* Edwards, R. G., Esq., Lothbury, London
* Edwards, R. P., Esq., Wedmore, Somersetshire
* Edwards, Samuel, Esq., Hentland, Herefordsh.
* Edwards, Samuel V., Esq., Trinity coll., Oxford
Edwards, S., Esq., Kenilworth, Warwickshire
* Edwards, T., Esq., Brislington, near Bristol
Edwards, T., Esq., Broadward, Herefordshire
* Edwards, Mr. Thomas, Daresbury, Cheshire
* Edwards, W., Esq., Great Elm, Somersetshire
Edwards, W., Esq., Framlingham, Suffolk
Edwards, W., Esq., Leominster, Herefordshire
* Edwards, Rev. W., Winford, Somersetshire
Edwards, Mr. Wm., Peterborough
Edy, John, Esq., Ledbury, Herefordshire
Egan, Charles, Esq., Wilton-street, London
Egan, F., Esq., Liverpool
* Egan, Mr. John, Essex-street, Strand, London
Egar, Richard, Esq., Guildford, Surrey
* Egerton, The Reverend Sir Philip Grey, Bart., M.P., Oulton-park, Cheshire

*Egerton, F. T., Esq., Roche-court, Salisbury
*Egerton, Rev. John, A.M., Bunbury, Cheshire
*Egerton, Mrs. Susanna, Stretton-hall, do.
Egerton, S., Esq., Christ-church coll., Oxford
*Eggar, Mr. Thomas, Harrow, Middlesex
Egginton, J. S., Esq., Kirk-Ella, Yorkshire
Egginton, Samuel H., Esq., Ferriby, do.
*Eicke, Charles, Esq., Old Broad-st., London
Ekin, William, Esq., Huntingdon
*Ekin, Mr. William, Cambridge
*Eldridge, T., Esq., Stock-house, Chelmsford
Elkington, F. R., Esq., Birmingham
*Elkington, Messrs., W. and Son, do.
*Elkins, John, Esq., Newman-street, London
Ellames, P., Esq., Allerton-hall, near Liverpool
*Elleray, Rev. J., Over Knutsford, Cheshire
Ellerton, Rev. Joseph, Baswich, Staffordshire
Elles, Mr. T., Oxford-st., Whitechapel, London
*Ellice, Edward, Esq., Trinity coll., Cambridge
Ellice and Co., Messrs., Leadenhall-st., London
Ellidge, J. P., Esq., Hereford
*Elliot, Andrew, Esq., Carlisle
Elliot, Mr. James, Clehonger, Herefordshire
*Elliott, Henry, Esq., Gutter-lane, London
*Elliott, John, Esq., Rochdale, Lancashire
Elliott, Mr. J., Early, near Reading, Berks.
*Elliott, J. F., Esq., Cateaton-street, London
*Elliott, Rev. Richard, Devizes, Wilts.
*Ellis, The Right Honorable and Honorable G. James W. Agar, M.P.
Ellis, Major, York
*Ellis, C., Esq., Verulam-buildings, London
Ellis, Charles, Esq., Maidstone, Kent
*Ellis, James J., Esq., jun., Barming, do.
Ellis, John, Esq., Ware, Herts.
*Ellis, John, Esq., Trinity college, Cambridge
Ellis, Mr. John, Dewsbury, Yorkshire
*Ellis, John L., Esq., Petworth, Sussex
Ellis, Mr. N. G., York
Ellis, R., Esq., St. Mildred's-court, London
*Ellis, Richard, Esq., Fenchurch-street, do.
*Ellis, W., Esq., Cadogan-place, Sloane-street
*Ellisen, P. D., Esq., Manchester
*Ellison, Luke, Esq., Standish-hall, Lancashire
*Ellison, Michael, Esq., Sheffield, Yorkshire
Ellison, Rev. Noel T., Huntispill, Somerset.
Ellison, R., Esq., Christ-church coll., Oxford
*Ellison, Thos., Esq., Glossop-hall, Derbyshire
Ellison, Mr. Thomas, Nantwich, Cheshire
Ellis, Mr. Joseph, Richmond, Surrey
*Elliston's Library, Leamington, Warwickshire
*Ellithorn, Abraham, Esq., Lancaster
Elmes, J., Esq., St. Bride's-passage, London
*ELPHIN, The Right Reverend Lord Bishop of
*Elsted, P., Esq., Dover, Kent
*Elton, Henry, Esq., Winford, near Bristol
*Elvy, F. B., Esq., Maidstone, Kent
*Elwell, Edw., Esq., Wednesbury, Staffordshire
*Elwes, R. C., Esq., Great Billinghouse, near Northampton
*Elwin, H., Esq., Corpus-Christi coll., Cambridge
Elwood, A., Esq., Bungay, Suffolk
*Elwood, R., Esq., Nantwich, Cheshire
*ELY, The Most Noble the Marquis of
*ELY, The Right Reverend Lord Bishop of
Ely, The Very Rev. the Dean and Chapter of
*Ely, Mr. Anthony, Chanston, Herefordshire
*Emary, Mr. Charles, Battle, Sussex
*Emary, Mr. F., Hastings, do.
*Emary, Mr. T. R., do., do.
*Emery, George, Esq., Banwell, Somersetshire
*Emery, T. B., Esq., Glastonbury, do.
*Emly, Henry, Esq., Temple, London
*Enfield, H., Esq., Holborn-court, do.
Enfield, H., Esq., Nottingham
*Engall, Mr. John, Home-park, Windsor
*England, T. H., Esq., Bower-Henton, Somerset.
England & Shackles, Messrs., Kingston upon Hull
*Engleheart, N. B., Esq., Doctors Commons
English, Sir J. H., Knt., Gt. Warley-house, Essex
*English, John, Esq., Feckenham, Worcestersh.
*English, John, Esq., Lynn, Norfolk
English, T. W., Esq., M.D., Chepstow, Monmouthshire
*ENNISKILLEN, The Right Hon. the Earl of
*Entwisle, T., Esq., Pendlebury, Manchester
*Entwistle, R., Esq., Brasenose college, Oxford
Errington, George H., Esq., Casina, Colchester
ERROL, The Right Honorable the Earl of
Escott, Robert K., Esq., Ongar-hill, Surrey
*Escott, Rev. T. S., M.A., Hartrow, Somerset
*Esdaile, E. J., Esq., Cothelstone-house, do.
*Espinasse, J., Esq., Temple, London
*Essell, George, Esq., Precincts, Rochester
Essen, G. T. Pitter, Esq., Pembroke coll., Oxford
ESSEX, The Right Honorable the Earl of
*Estcourt, W. J. B., Esq., Balliol coll., Oxford
*Etherington, Mr. C., Heckmondwike, near Leeds
Etough, Rev. Dr., Croxton-Keyrial, Leicestersh.
*Etwall, William, Esq., Trinity college, Oxford
Euing, Mr. W. R., Liverpool
*Eustace, Thos. M., Esq., Ilminster, Somerset.
*Evans, Mr. J., Great Guildford-st., Southwark
Evans, Mrs., Linton-Grove, Notts.
Evans, Charles, Esq., Ludlow, Shropshire
*Evans, Charles, Esq., Manchester
Evans, Edw., Esq., Leominster, Herefordshire
*Evans, Edward, Esq., Royton, Lancashire
Evans, Evan, Esq., Carnarvon
Evans, Rev. G. S., West Ilsley, Berks.
*Evans, Rev. G. W. D., Herne-Bay, Kent
*Evans, Henry, Esq., Bull-street, Birmingham
Evans, Hugh, Esq., Oxford
*Evans, James, Esq., Stoke-Lacy, Herefordshire
*Evans, John, Esq., Took's-court, London
Evans, John, Esq., Wood-st., Cheapside, do.
Evans, John, Esq., Chepstow, Monmouthshire
Evans, Mr. John, Oxford
*Evans, Mr. John, Broad-street, Worcester
*Evans, Owen, Esq., Little Hampton, Sussex
*Evans, Richard, Esq., sen., Wolverhampton
*Evans, Richard, Esq., jun., do.
Evans, R., Esq., Queen-st., Cheapside, London
*Evans, Samuel, Esq., Derby
Evans, Thomas, Esq., Selsey, Sussex
Evans, Thos., Esq., M. D., Ross, Herefordsh.
*Evans, Thomas D., Esq., do., do.
*Evans, T. J., Esq., Hemel-Hempstead, Herts
*Evans, Mr. T., jun., Great Guildford-st., Lond.
Evans, T. B., Esq., St. Giles', Norwich
Evans, Walter M., Esq., Holborn-court, Lond.
Evans, Rev. W., Pusey, Berks.
Evans, Rev. William, Kingsland, Herefordshire
Evans, William, Esq., Allestrey, near Derby
Evans, William, Esq., Bath
Evans, Mr. W. M., Gloucester
*Evans, Mr. W., Llangattock, Brecon.
*Evatt, Major-General, Fordwich, Kent
Eveleigh, W. G., Esq., Oriel coll., Oxford
*Evelyn, Lynden, Esq., Regent's-park, London
*Everard, Reverend Edward, D.D., Brighton
Everard, Scarlet, Esq., Lynn, Norfolk
Evered, John, Esq., Bridg-water, Somersetshire
Everett, Mr. Frederick P., Reading, Berks.
Everett, Rev. G. F., Landford, Wiltshire
Everett, Henry, Esq., Salisbury do.
*Everett, Joseph, Esq., Heytesbury, do.
*Everingham, James, Esq., Cobham, Surrey
Everingham, James, Esq., Kirby-st., London
Evers, Mr. Samuel, Stourbridge, Worcestershire
Everset, Mr. William, Ware, Herts.
*Every, Sir H., Bart., Egginton-hall, Derbyshire
*Ewan, Thomas, Esq., Wray, Lancashire
*Ewart, J., Esq., M.P., Mossley-hill, nr. Liverpool
Ewart, Simon, Esq., Carlisle
*Ewbank, W. Withers, Esq., Christ's coll., Camb.
*Ewer, James, Esq., Holywell
*Ewington, W., Esq., Finsbury-square, London
Exall, William, Esq., Alton, Hants.
*EXCISE, The Honorable the Commissioners of His Majesty's
EXETER, The Right Reverend Lord Bishop of
Exeter college Library, Oxford
*Exley, John, Esq., Egham, Surrey
Exnam, Rev Wm., M. A., Harrow, Middlesex
*Exton, R., Esq., Brasenose college, Oxford
Exton, S., Esq., M.D., Peter-Church, Hereford
Eyes, Charles, Esq., Liverpool
Eyes, Edward, Esq., do.
*Eyles, Major, Coleshill-house, near Amersham
Eyre, The Venerable & Rev. Archdeacon, M.A.
Eyre, Rev. Charles W., Carlton, Notts.
*Eyre, Francis, Esq., Trinity college, Cambridge
Eyre, Henry, Esq., Botleigh-Grange, Hants.
*Eyre and Coverdale, Messrs., Gray's-inn, Lond.
*Eyres, Charles, Esq., Caius college, Cambridge
*Eyton, Thomas, Esq., Eyton, Shropshire

*Faber, T. H., Esq., Bishop-Auckland, Durham
*Fagg, Sir John, Bart., Mystole-house, Kent
*Fagg, John F., Esq., Westbere, do.
*Failden, Rev. R. H., A. M., Walton le Dale
*Fairbairn, James, Esq., Botcharby, Carlisle
*Fairclough, Charles, Esq., Liverpool
Fairclough, William, Esq., do.
Fairs, John, Esq., Brighton
Fairthorne and Lofty, Messrs., King-st., Cheapside, London
Faithful, Henry, Esq., Brighton
Faithfull, Edward, Esq., Tring, Herts.
Falcon, John, Esq., Garston-house, do.
Falconer, J., Esq., Doncaster
Falkner, Joseph, Esq., Swaffham, Norfolk
*Falland, W. E., Esq., Hull
*Falle, J., Esq., Sidney-Sussex coll., Cambridge
*Fallowfield, J., Esq., Preston, Lancashire
*Fallows, Mr. John, New-street, Birmingham
*FALMOUTH, The Right Honorable the Earl of
*Fane, Lieutenant-Colonel, M.P., Sutton, Surrey
*Fane, J., Esq., M. P., Wormsley, Oxfordshire
*Fanning, Wm., Esq., Manor-house, Finchley
*Farden, Richard, Esq., New-inn, London
*Farmer, Samuel, Esq., Nonsuch-park
*Farmer, Jasper, Esq., Treage, Herefordshire
*Farnell, John, Esq., Isleworth, Middlesex
FARNHAM, The Right Honorable Lord
Farnworth, Rev. W. T., Prescot, Lancashire
Farquhar, R., Esq., Pont-y-pool, Monmouthshire
Farquhar, W. M., Esq., Christ-ch. coll., Oxford
*Farquharson, R., Esq., do., do.
Farquharson, Lieut.-Col., Newcastle upon Tyne
Farr, Mr. Edward, Hatfield, Hertfordshire
Farr, George, Esq., do., do.
*Farrar, F., Esq., Doctors Commons, London
*Farrar, George, Esq., Park-street, Islington
Farrar, H., Esq., Lincoln's-inn, London
*Farrer, H., Esq., Kirklinton-hall, Cumberland
Farrer, Akinson, and Parkinson, Messrs., Lincoln's-inn-fields, London
Farrington, John, Esq., Walsall, Staffordshire
Farrington, Wm., Esq., Leyland, Lancashire
Farris, Mr. Thomas, Canterbury, Kent
Farrow, Mr. Edward L., Newbury, Berks.
*Faulconer, Thos. C., Esq., Newhaven, Sussex
*Faulkner, H., Esq., Kensington . . . 2 Copies
*Faulkner, Mr. Isaac, Manchester
*Faulkner, Mr. Joseph, Lymm, Cheshire
Faux, William, Esq., Earith, Huntingdonshire
Favell, Beddome, and Co., Messrs., Fenchurch-street, London
Fawcett, Major, Cliffe-hall, near Devizes
*Fawcett, J., Esq., Holborn-court, Grays-inn
*Fawcett, John, Esq., Carlisle, Cumberland
Fawcett, W., Esq., Trump-st., Cheapside, Lon.
Fawssett, John, Esq., Jesus college, Cambridge
*Fayerman, Arnoll T., Esq., M. D., Norwich
Fearby, John, Esq., Poppleton-lodge, York
*Fearnley, J. E., Esq., Ratcliff-cross, London
Fearon, Henry, B., Esq., Holborn-hill, do.
Featherby, Mr. Robert, High-street, Lincoln
Featherstone, Sir G. R., Bart., Ardagh, Longford, Ireland
*Featherstonhaugh, J. R., Esq., Islington
Feilder, Rev. H. T., Walton le Dale, Lancash.
*Fell, C., jun., Esq., Sharples, near Bolton, do.

Fell, J., jun., Esq., St. Peter's coll., Cambridge
*Fell, William, Esq., Pennington, Lancashire
*Fell, William, Esq., Ambleside, Westmorland
Fellowes, Rev. R., L. L. D., Reigate, Surrey
Fellowes, W. H., Esq., jun., Ch.-ch. col., Oxford
Fellows, C., Esq., Lansdown-place, London
*Fellows, E., Esq., Weymouth-street, do.
*Fellows, Thos., Esq., Money-hill-house, Herts.
Fellows and Son, Messrs., Dudley
Fendall, J., Esq., Elm-court, Temple, London
*Fendall, Rev. John, Miserden, Gloucester
*Fenna, John, Esq., Tattenhall-hall, Cheshire
*Fenner, G., Esq., Exchequer-office, Temple
*Fennes, John, Esq., Dovor
*Fenton, C. E., Esq., Doctors Commons, London
*Fenton, James, Esq., Crimble, near Rochdale
*Fenton, Jno. T., Esq., Trinity coll., Cambridge
Fenton, Perrot, Esq., Doctors Commons, Lond.
*Fenwick, John, Esq., Durham
*Fenwick, S. F., Esq., Leyton, Essex
Fenwick, Thomas, Esq., Newcastle upon Tyne
Fenwick, Thomas, Esq., Tynemouth
*Fereday, J. T., Esq., The Ellows, Staffordshire
*Fereday, W. T., Esq., Ford-house, do.
Ferguson, A., Esq., Wood-st., Cheapside, Lond.
Ferguson, John, Esq., Carlisle
*Ferguson, Joseph, Esq., do.
Ferguson, Richard, Esq., do.
Ferguson, Thomas, Esq., Windle, Lancashire
*Ferguson, Hood, and Jacox, Messrs., Wood-street, Cheapside, London
*Fernie, Ebenezer, Esq., Cornhill, London
*Ferns, T. M., Esq., Stockport, Cheshire
*Ferrer, George, Esq., Calver-hill, Herefordshire
*Ferrer, William, Esq., Garmage, do.
FERRERS, The Right Honorable Earl
*Fetherstonhaugh, C. S., Esq., Kirk-Oswald, Cumberland
*FEVERSHAM, The Right Honorable Lord
*Few, C., Esq., Covent-garden, London
Fewtrell, W., Esq., Kington, Herefordshire
*Ficklin, T. T., Esq., Cambridge
*Fickling, Robert, Esq., Norwich
*Fidler, Rev. D., B. D., Westmorland, Jamaica
*Fidler, Thomas, Esq., Richmond, Surrey
Field, Mr. Abraham, Canterbury
*Field, Mr. Benjamin, Botolph-lane, London
Field, Mr. Daniel, Garford, Berks.
Field, James, Esq., Lothbury, London
Field, Joseph, Esq., Hatfield, Hertfordshire
*Field, Robert, Esq., Cartmel, Lancashire
*Field, Mr. William, Botolph-lane, London
*Fielden, John, Esq., Mollington-hall, Chester
Fielden, Rev. R. M., Kirk-Langley, Derbyshire
*Fielden and Brothers, Messrs., Todmorden, Lancashire
*Fieldes, J., Esq., Strangeways, Manchester
*Fielding, Rev. Allen, Sturry, Kent
*Fielding, Rev. H., M. A., Manchester
*Fielding, Rev. Henry, Blean, near Canterbury
*Fielding, H. B., Esq., Stodday-lodge, Lancaster
*Fielding, J., Esq., Garstang, do.
FIFE, The Right Honorable the Earl of
Figes, Mr. Thomas, Romsey, Hants.
*Figgins, Mr. V., West-street, West Smithfield
*Fildes, James, Esq., Strangeways, Manchester
Filer, Mr. Martin, Winchester
Fillingham, G., Esq., Syerston-hall, Notts.
*Filmer, E., Esq., Oriel college, Oxford
*Finch, Charles, Esq., Fisherton, Wilts.
*Finch, Mr. Charles, jun., Cambridge
Finch, John, Esq., Red-heath-hall, Herts.
Finch, Joseph, Esq., Harrow-road, Middlesex
*Finch, Joseph, Esq., Newcastle upon Tyne
*Finch, W., Esq., M. D., Salisbury
Finley, Jno., Esq., Trinity college, Cambridge
*Finley, Robert, Esq., Canterbury
*Finney, Samuel, Esq., Cheshunt, Herts.
Finney, Mr. Thomas, Ashton under Line
Finney, Mr. T., Tottenham, Middlesex
Finsham, John, Esq., Portsmouth
Firmstone, G., Esq., King's Swinford, Stafford
Firmstone, J. P., Esq., Wolverhampton
Firmstone, Wm., Esq., Wordsley, Staffordshire
*First Fruits Office, Temple . . . . . . 2 Copies
*Firth, Mr. James F., Newington-place
*Firth, T., Esq., Dane-bridge, Northwich, Chesh.
*Fish, Rev. John, A. B., Thurstaston, do.
Fish, Rev. Joseph, Ellesmere, Shropshire
Fish, William, Esq., Maidstone, Kent
Fisher, F., Esq., Doncaster, Yorkshire
Fisher, George, Esq., Liverpool
Fisher, J. G., Esq., Yarmouth, Norfolk
*Fisher, J., Esq., Dalton, Lancashire
*Fisher, Rev. James, Duckinfield, Cheshire
Fisher, James H., Esq., Davies-street, Grosvenor-square, London
*Fisher, Rev. John H., M. A., Fellow of Trinity college, Cambridge
Fisher, J., Esq., West Bromwich, Staffordshire
*Fisher, J., Esq., Langford-court, Somersetshire
*Fisher, John, Esq., Measham, Derbyshire
Fisher, J. E., Esq., Llanwarne-court, Hereford
*Fisher, Joseph, Esq., Cleeve, Somersetshire
Fisher, Mr. J., Chancery-lane, London
Fisher, Richard, Esq., Queen's college, Oxford
*Fisher, Richard, Esq., Newark, Notts.
*Fisher, Mr. Robert, Nettlebed, Oxfordshire
*Fisher, S., Esq., Queen-st., Cheapside, London
*Fisher, Thomas, Esq., East India-house, do.
Fisher, T. M., Esq., Gray's-inn, do.
Fisher, Mr. Thomas M., Manchester
*Fisher, William, Esq., Wallbrook, London
*Fishlake, Rev. J. R., Little Cheverell, Wilts.
*Fitch, John, Esq., Union-street, Borough
*Fitch, Joseph, Esq., Edmonton, Middlesex
*Fitch, Wm., Esq., Little Tower-street, London
Fitchett and Wagstaff, Messrs., Warrington
Fitzgerald, The Right Honorable W. Vesey, M. P.
Fitzgerald, Jas., Esq., Wherstead-lodge, Ipswich
Fitzgibbon, The Honorable R. Hobart, M. P.
*Fitzherbert, Sir Henry, Bart., Tessington-hall, Derbyshire [Staffordshire
*Fitzherbert, Thomas, Esq., Swinnerton-hall,
Fitzhugh, Wm., Esq., Southampton
*Fitzjames, J., Esq., St. John's coll., Cambridge
Fitzpatrick, Mr. R. J., Barkston, Lincolnshire
*FITZWILLIAM, The Right Honorable Earl
Fitzwilliams, John, Esq., Oldbury, Salop
*Flack, John, Esq., Ware, Hertfordshire
Flanagan, Mr. W., Wolverhampton
Flanders, Wm., Esq., Colebrook-row, Islington
Fleet, Mr. W., Brighton, Sussex
*Fleetwood, J. W., Esq., Penkridge, Staffordshire
*Fleming, Reverend Sir Richard, Bart., Grassmere, Westmorland
Fleming, Rev. F., Rydal, do.
Fleming, J., Esq., M. P., Stoneham-park, Hants
*Fleming, John, Esq., Blackburn, Lancashire
*Fleming, Joseph, Esq., Old Jewry, London
*Fleming, T., Esq., Pendleton, near Manchester
Fleming, T. B., Esq., Chancery-lane, London
Flersheim, S., Esq., Manchester
Fletcher, Lieut.-Gen., Preston, Lancashire
*Fletcher, Mr. Alderman, Chester
Fletcher, Rev. Charles, Southwell, Notts.
Fletcher, Rev. Lloyd, B. A., Overton, Flintshire
Fletcher, Mr. Charles, Salford, Lancashire
Fletcher, Mr. G. M., Walsall, Staffordshire
*Fletcher, H. S., Esq., Queen's college, Oxford
*Fletcher, Jno., Esq., Tokenhouse-yard, London
*Fletcher, John, Esq., Liverpool
Fletcher, John, Esq., Preston, Lancashire
*Fletcher, J. B., Esq., St. John's col., Cambridge
Fletcher, John, Esq., Stanton upon Arrow, He-
*Fletcher, Rev. Joseph, Bewdley [refordshire
*Fletcher, Joseph, Esq., Rochdale, Lancashire
*Fletcher, Matthew, Esq., Bury, do.,
Fletcher, Rev. N., Lee-house, Romsey, Hants.
*Fletcher, Ralph, Esq., Bolton, Lancashire
Fletcher, Rev. R., Blackburn, do.
*Fletcher, Mr. Samuel, Ridgefield, Manchester
Fletcher, W., Esq., Tean, Staffordshire
Fletcher, Rev. William, Woodbridge, Suffolk
Fletcher and Sons, Messrs., Walsall, Staffordsh.
*Fletcher and Young, Messrs., Millbrook, near Southampton
*Flint, Sir Charles W., Knt., Brodsworth-house, Doncaster
*Flint, Mr. Thomas, Burlington Arcade, London . . 2 Copies
*Flood, Mr. John, Arundel, Sussex
*Floud, H., Esq., Upper Tooting, Surrey
*Flower, Farnham, Esq., Chilcompton, Somerset.
*Fogg, Ralph, Esq., Salford, Lancashire
*Foley, Edward, Esq., Stoke-Edith-park
*Foley, Rev. T. P., Old Swinford, Worcestershire
*Foljambe, T., Esq., Wakefield, Yorkshire
Follett, Rev. R. F., Taunton, Somersetshire
*Fooks, Thomas, Esq., Sherborne, Dorsetshire
*Fooks, Thomas B., Esq., Dartford, Kent
*Foord, James, Esq., Ospringe, do.
Foot, Samuel, Esq., Salisbury
Forbes, Dr., Argyle-street, London
*Forbes, Edward, Esq., Douglas, Isle of Man
Forbes, Hugh, Esq., St. Mary hall, Oxford
Forbes, William, Esq., Sleaford, Lincoln
Ford, Colonel, Sandbach, Cheshire
Ford, Charles, Esq., Great Queen-st., London
Ford, A., Esq., Stamp-office, Somerset-house
Ford, Rev. F., Tilford, Farnham, Surrey
Ford, Mr. Henry, Baynes-row, Clerkenwell
*Ford, J., Esq., Hemel-Hempstead, Herts.
*Ford, R. M., Esq., Lansdown-place, East Bath
*Fordham, J. W., Esq., Broxbourne, Herts.
*Fordham, John Edward, Esq., Royston, do.
FORESTER, The Right Honorable Lord
Forester, G. T., Esq., Brasenose coll., Oxford
Forester, R. F., Esq., M. D., F. L. S., Derby
*Forman, Colonel, Greenwich
*Forrest, Roger, Esq., Blackburn, Lancashire
*Forrest, Thomas, Esq., Greenhythe, Kent
Forrister, G., Esq., Lane-End, Staffordshire
Forster, Messrs. C. and J., Walsall, do.
*Forster, F., Esq., Margate, Kent
*Forster, E., Esq., Tower-street, London
*Forster, George, Esq., Newcastle upon Tyne
*Forster, H., Esq., Corpus-Christi coll., Cambrid.
*Forster, John, Esq., Carlisle, Cumberland
*Forster, Jno., Esq., Southend, Lewisham, Kent
*Forster, John, Esq., Upper Thames-st., London
*Forster, J. W., Esq., Old Broad-street, do.
*Forster, Rev. L., Blackburn, Lancashire
*Forster, Mathew, Esq., Newcastle upon Tyne
Forster, Percival, Esq., Durham
Forster, Wm., Esq., Knaresborough, Yorkshire
*Fort, John, Esq., Blackburn, Lancashire
Fortescue, Rev. F., Knottesford, Warwickshire
Fosbery, Wm., Esq., Everton, Liverpool
*Fosbrooke, L., Esq., Shardlow-hall, Derbyshire
Fosbrooke, Rev. Y., St. Briavell's, Gloucestersh.
*Foster, Rev. A., Kingston, Somersetshire
*Foster, Andrew, Esq., Wadham college, Oxford
Foster, Mr. Charles Burton, Windsor
*Foster, Ebenezer, jun., Esq., Cambridge
*Foster, Rev. F. W., D. D., Ockbrook, Derbysh.
Foster, Henry, Esq., Heptonstall Slack, Yorksh.
*Foster, J., Esq., F. S. A., F. R. S. E., Liverpool
*Foster, Rev. John, M. A., Sarratt, Herts.
*Foster, John, Esq., East India-house, London
*Foster, Jno., Esq., Springside-house, Blackburn
*Foster, John, Esq., Yarmouth, Norfolk
*Foster, Mr. J. M., Cambridge
Foster, M., Esq., Liverpool
*Foster, Oswald, Esq., Hitchin, Herts.
*Foster, Richard, jun., Esq., Cambridge
Foster, Thomas, Esq., Liverpool
*Foster, Wm., Esq., Lawton-street, do.
Fothergill, R., Esq., Caerleon, Monmouthshire
Fothergill, Thomas, Esq., Whitwell, Herts.
*Foudrinier, J. C., Esq., Angel-court, Throgmorton-street, London
*Foulds, James, Esq., Colne, Lancashire
Foulks, A., Esq., Redland-house, near Bristol
*Fowden, William, Esq., Oxford-st., Manchester
Fowke, Mrs., Walton on Thames, Surrey

Fowke, W., Esq., Stafford
Fowler, Mr. Samuel, Stourbridge, Worcestershire
* Fowler, William, Esq., Birmingham
Fowler, William, Esq., St. Neots, Hunts.
* Fowler, Rev. William, B. A., Baldock, Herts.
* Fowls, John, Esq., Northwich, Cheshire
Fowls, Samuel, Esq., do., do.
* Fox, The Honorable Mrs., Chertsey, Surrey
Fox, Miss, Huntingdon
Fox, Mr. Charles, Enfield, Middlesex
* Fox, Mr. Charles, St. Mary's, Southampton
* Fox, Charles Jas., Esq., M. D., Margate, Kent
* Fox, Edward Long, Esq., M. D., Brislington-house, Somersetshire
* Fox, G., Esq., Bramham-park, Leeds
Fox, Rev. J., D. D., Queen's college, Oxford
Fox, John, Esq., Newcastle upon Tyne
Fox, John, Esq., Nottingham
* Fox, J. E., Esq., Finsbury-circus, London
* Fox, Rev. Thomas, H. L., Hinton, Dorsetshire
Fox, Rev. Thomas, South Newton, Wiltshire
* Fox, William, Esq., Northwich, Cheshire
Fox, W., Esq., Doctors Commons, London.
* Foxcroft, Henry, Esq., Lancaster
* Foxlowe, Rev. F., M. A., Elmton, Derbyshire
* Frampton, F. A., Esq., Tavistock-sq., London
* Frampton, W. H., Esq., Gray's-inn-sq., do.
* France, James F., Esq., Bostock-hall, Cheshire
* Francis, Mr. Alderman, Norwich
* Francis, Rev. Edward, Milton, near Gravesend
* Francis, Mr. Edward Parke, Hertford
Francis, W. W., Esq., Colchester
Francis, Smith, & Hawkes, Mess., Birmingham.
* Francis and Urquhart, Messrs., Monument-yard,
* Frank, Mr. E. B., Doncaster, Yorkshire [Lond.
* Frankland, Mr. T., Reading, Berks.
Franklin, E., Esq., Belle-Vue, Westbury, Wilts.
Franklyn, Henry, Esq., Ludlow, Shropshire
Franklyn, James N., Esq., Clifton, near Bristol
* Franklyn, R., Esq., Totteridge-house, Herts.
* Franklyn, Richard, Esq., Royal Mint, London
Frankum, Thomas, Esq., Abingdon, Berks.
* Fraser, Rev. Henry W., Bowdon, Cheshire
* Fraser, John, Esq., Six Clerks'-office, London
Fraser, John William, Esq., Bath
* Fraser, Mr. W., Cleveland-court, St. James's
Fraser, Mr. W., Farnham, Surrey
Frazer, Augustus S., Esq., Woolwich, Kent
Free, R., Esq., Claremont-place, Rotherhithe
Free, W. H., Esq., St. Mary-Axe, London
Freeborn, J. J. S., Esq., Bensington, Oxon
* Freeland, J. B., Esq., Chichester, Sussex
* Freeman, C., Esq., Hidcote, Worcestershire
* Freeman, E. B., Esq., Suckley, do.
* Freeman, Mrs. E. L., Tottenham, Middlesex
Freeman, Jno., Esq., Withington, Herefordshire
Freeman, John, Esq., Whitbourne, do.
* Freeman, John, Esq., Kent-road, London
Freeman, Mr. John, Smallburgh, Norwich
Freeman, Major J. D., Castle Cor, Ireland
* Freeman, Luke, Esq., Guildford-st., London
Freeman, Rev. Matthew, Mellor, Derbyshire
Freeman, Thos., Esq., Laysters, Herefordshire
Freeman, Thomas, Esq., Brighton
Freeman, W. P. W., Esq., Fawley-court, Bucks.
* Freemantle, Sir W., Knt., Stanhope-st., Lond.
Freer, Rev. Geo., St. Neots, Huntingdonshire
* Freer, Rev. T. Lane, Handsworth, Staffordshire
Fremantle, W. R., Esq., Christ-ch. coll., Oxford
Freme, J. R., Esq., Toxteth-park, Liverpool
* Freme, Messrs. W. and J., do.
* French, Rev. P. A., Sydenham, Kent
French, W. J., Esq., Wilton
* French, William, Esq., Caius coll., Cambridge
Frend, Mr. George, Canterbury, Kent
* Frere, B., Esq., Callow, Walford, Herefordsh.
* Freshfield and Son, Messrs., New Bank-buildings, London
Freston, Rev. T., Whitcomb, Gloucestershire
* Fretwell, Mr. Jno., Gainsborough, Lincolnshire
Friend, Robert, Esq., Preston, Lancashire
* Fripp, Daniel, Esq., Bristol
Fripp, William, Esq., jun., Bristol
* Frisby, William H., Esq., Mark-lane, London
Frith, John, Esq., Bank-hall, Derbyshire
Frith, Peter, Esq., Sheffield
* Frodsham, Robert, Esq., Liverpool
* Fromow, Mr. P. J., Wooburn, Bucks.
* Frost, Chas., Esq., F. S. A., Hull, Yorkshire
* Frost, James F., Esq., Water-st., Manchester
* Frost, John, Esq., Howland-street, London
Frost, Matthew, jun., Esq., Calver, Derbyshire
* Frost, Thomas, Esq., Manchester
Frost, Rev. W. B., Dedham, Essex
Froude, Rev. R. H., Oriel college, Oxford
* Froude, Wm., Esq., do., do.
Fry, Joseph, Esq., Plashot-house, Essex
Fry, Joseph, Esq., Liverpool
* Fryer, James, Esq., Bewdley, Worcester
Fryer, J. R., Esq., Proctor, York
Fryer, Thomas, Esq., Chatteris, Cambridge
* Fryer, William, Esq., Newcastle upon Tyne
* Fryzer, Samuel, Esq., Tewkesbury
* Fulcher, Thomas, Esq., East Grinstead, Sussex
* Fuller, John, Esq., Neston-park, Wilts.
* Fuller, John, Esq., Croydon, Surrey
Fuller, Mr. John, Caversham, Oxfordshire
Fuller, Mr. John H., Maidenhead, Berks
* Fuller, Rev. R. F., East Grinstead, Sussex
* Fuller, Rev. Thomas, Wartling, do.
Fuller, Mr. Thomas, Cliffe, Lewes, do.
* Fuller, W., Esq., Fleet-street, London
* Fuller, Mr. William H., Reading, Berks.
Fullerton, John, Esq., Thyburgh-castle, near Rotherham
* Fullerton, J., jun., Esq., Forest-hill, Notts.
* Fulwell, T. K., Esq., Tyldesley-hall, Bolton
Furlong, Mr. Robert, Cheshunt, Herts.
* Furnival, G., jun., Esq., Warrington, Lancash.
* Furnival, John, Esq., do., do.
Furnivall, John, Esq., Egham, Surrey
Furnivall, Mr. J., Dowgate-hill, London
Fussell, H. D., Esq., Sidney-Sussex coll., Cam-
* Fussell, Jas., Esq., Frome, Somerset. [bridge
* Fussell, Rev. J., Doulting, do.
Fussell, Mr. Jonathan, Old-street, London
* Fussell, T., Esq., Mells, Somerset
* Fyfe, James, Esq., Harbledown, Kent
* Fyler, T. B., Esq., M. P., Dover-st., Piccadilly
Fynmore, Thomas, Esq., Camberwell, Surrey

Gabb, Rev. Geo. W., Llanwenarth, Monmouth
Gabb, R., Esq., Abergavenny, do.
Gadsden, James, Esq., Kingston upon Hull
Gadsden, R., Esq., Furnival's-inn, London
GAGE, The Right Honorable Lord Viscount
Gage, Mr. E., Pownall-terrace, Lambeth, Surrey
Gale, A. A. W., Esq., Shepton-Mallet
* Gale, A. R., Esq., Wadham college, Oxford
* Gale, Rev. J., Angersleigh, Somerset
Gale, Mr. R. C., Winchester
* Gale, Mr. Robert, Chapel-walks, Manchester
* Gale, William, Esq., Ulverstone, Lancashire
* Galindo, Percy, Esq., Monmouth
* Galliard, Charles J., Esq., Nantwich, Cheshire
Galliers, John, Esq., Coxhall, Herefordshire
* Gallon, Richard, Esq., Hawkeshead, Lancashire
* Galloway, Rev. James, M. A., Aldbury, Herts.
Galton, J. H., Esq., Hadzor-house, Droitwich
GALWAY, The Right Honorable Lord Viscount
* Gambier, S. J., Esq., Magdalene col., Cambdg.
* Gambier, William, Esq., Sacomb-park, Herts.
Gamlen, R., Esq., Verulam-buildings, London
* Gandolfe, Mrs., Blackmore-park, Worcestersh.
* Gape, Thomas Foreman, Esq., St. Albans
* Gapper, T. A., Esq., Wincanton, Somerset
* Garbett, Edward W., Esq., Jermyn-st., London
Garbett, Rev. J., A. M., Birmingham
* Gardener, Mr. J., Newcastle upon Tyne [Notts.
* Gardiner, J. G. C., Esq., Thurgarton-priory,
Gardiner, J., Esq., Instone-Bishops, Herefordsh.
Gardiner, Mr. John, Hereford
* Gardiner, J., Esq., Manchester
Gardiner, R. W., Esq., Hopton, Stoke-Lacy
* Gardiner, R., Esq., East Hoathly, Sussex
* Gardiner, S., Esq., Deptford
* Gardner, Mr. Andrew, Kennington
Gardner, B., Esq., Hyde, near Bromyard
* Gardner, E., Esq., Stamford Hill, Middlesex
* Gardner, Rev. F., B. D., Warburton, Cheshire
* Gardner, John, Esq., Garstang, Lancashire
* Gardner, John, Esq., Marlborough, Wiltshire
* Gardner, R., Esq., Malpas, Cheshire
Gardner, P. T., Esq., Fen-Stanton, Hunts.
* Gardner, Thomas, Esq., Gloucester
Gardner, Thomas, jun., Esq., Liverpool
Garforth, W., Esq., York
* Garforth, Mr. W., Duckinfield, Cheshire
* Garlick, J. P., Esq., Park-row, Leeds
Garlike, T. C., Esq., Clare hall, Cambridge
* Garling, H., Esq., Little James-street, London
Garner, Mr. William, General Post-office, do.
* Garnett, R., Esq., Oak-hill, near Manchester
* Garnett, Rev. W., M. A., Haughton-hall, Chesh.
Garnham, J., Esq., Gorleston, Suffolk
Garnham, Mr. W., Yarmouth, Norfolk
Garnier, Rev. Thomas, Bishop's Stoke, Hants.
Garnier, T., Esq., Worcester college, Oxford
* Garnier, Rev. William, Winchester, Hants.
* Garrard, Thomas, Esq., F. A. S., Bristol
* Garratt, John, Esq., Kingston, Surrey
Garratt, Mr. Moses, Hereford
* Garrett, J., Esq., Queen's college, Oxford
Garrett, Mr. J., Stafford
* Garrett, R., Esq., jun., New Broad-st.-ct., Lond.
* Garrick, C. P., Esq., Richmond, Surrey
* Garrold, T., Esq., Boulstone, Herefordshire
Garry, W. H., Esq., Furnival's-inn, London
* Garside, Mr. James, Ashton under Line
* Garside, John, Esq., Portwood, Cheshire
Garton, John, Esq., Matlock, Derbyshire
Garton, W., Esq., St. Helens, Lancashire
* Gartside, Mr. J., Ashton under Line
* Garven, E., Esq., Warrington, Lancashire
Garwood, W., Esq., York
Gascoyne, R. O., Esq., Parlington-hall, York
* Gaskarth, Mess. J. and J., Altrincham, Chesh.
Gaskell, Benjamin, Esq., Wakefield, York
* Gaskell, H., Esq., Warrington, Cheshire
Gaskell, Rev. J., A. M., Duckinfield, do.
* Gaskell, Rev. T., Newton, near Manchester
* Gaskill and Son, Mess., Bullocksmithy, Chesh.
* Gate, Rev. Joseph, Bidstone, do.
Gater, W. H., Esq., West-End, Southampton
* Gates, John, Esq., Peterborough
Gates, W., Esq., Northampton
Gath, Samuel, Esq., Liverpool
* Gathorne, Rev. John, M. A., Kirkby-Lonsdale
* Gatty, Haddan, & Gatty, Messrs., Angel-court, Throgmorton-street, London
* Gaunt, Matthew, Esq., Leeds, Yorkshire
Gaunt, Matthew, Esq., Leek, Staffordshire
* Gaunt, Richard, Esq., do., do.
Gauntlet, Rev. F., Badgworth, Somersetshire
* Gayter, Joseph, Esq., Moor, Cheshire
* Gayton, C., Esq., Trinity college, Cambridge
Gaze, Marker, Esq., Norwich
* Geary, Sir W. R. P., Bart., Oxenheath, Kent
* Geary, Henry, Esq., St. Albans
* Gee, Mr. Joel, jun., Duckinfield, Cheshire
* Gee, Mr. John, Market-square, Nottingham
* Gee, Robert, Esq., Cambridge
* Geldard, John, Esq., Enfield, Middlesex
Gell, E. S., Esq., Watling-street, London
* Gell, P., Esq., Hopton-hall, Derbyshire
Gell, Rev. Philip, M. A., Matlock, do.
Gell, Rev. R., A. M., Wirksworth, do.
* Gem, W. H., Esq., Birmingham
Gentry, Mr. R., Waltham-Abbey, Essex
* George, A., Esq., Enfield, Middlesex
George, Mr. Edmund, Abercarne, Monmouthsh.
George, Mr. George, Yarpole, Herefordshire
George, Rev. J., Grosmont, Monmouth
George, Rev. James, Hereford
George, Mr. John, do.

*George, Rev. P., Durham
George, Robert, Esq., Chatham
George, Mr. Thomas, Patteshall, Herefordshire
George, Rev. W., North Petherton, Somersetsh.
*George, Mr. William, Bircher, Herefordshire
George, Mr. William, Warham
*Gerard, Sir John, Bart., New-hall, Lancashire
Gerard's Reading Society, Gee-cross, do.
German, W., Esq., Peckham, Surrey
Gerock, Mr. C., Cornhill, London
Gervis, Henry, Esq., Thorverton, near Exeter
*Gibb, Duncan, Esq., Liverpool
*Gibb, William, Esq., Manchester
*Gibbon, W. F., Esq., Nantwich, Cheshire
*Gibbons, E. H., Esq., Little Hampton, Sussex
Gibbons, Joseph, Esq., Toxteth-park, Liverpool
*Gibbons, M., Esq., Fleet-street, London
*Gibbs, Mr. Alex., Worship-square, do.
*Gibbs, F., Esq., Harewood, near Leeds
Gibbs, H. G., Esq., Broad-street, London
*Gibbs, James, Esq., Jermyn-street, do.
Gibbs, John, Esq., Gray's-inn-square, do.
Gibbs, John, Esq., Westbury, Wiltshire
*Gibbs, Joseph, Esq., Crayford, Kent
*Gibbs, Miss M., Wootton, Warwickshire
*Gibbs, Mr., Southampton
*Gibbs, Samuel, Esq., Cheshunt, Herts.
*Gibbs and Yorke, Messrs., do., do.
*Gibson, Alexander, Esq., Philpot-lane, London
*Gibson, C., Esq., Quornmore-park, Lancashire
*Gibson, Edward, Esq., Kingston upon Hull
*Gibson, Mr. James, Northwich, Cheshire
*Gibson, John, Esq., Jermyn-street, London
*Gibson, R., Esq., Heathly-heath, Lymm, Chesh.
*Gibson, R., Esq., Beckenham, Kent
*Gibson, Rev. Rob., A. M., Beaumont Grange, Lancashire
Gibson, T., Esq., Milk-st., Cheapside, London
Gibson, Thomas, Esq., Ulverstone, Lancashire
Gibson, Mr. William, Manchester [fordshire
*Gifford, Thos. W., Esq., Chillington-hall, Staf-
*Gifford, Reverend J. G., Fulham, Middlesex
*Gilbert, Edward, Esq., Waterloo-place, London
Gilbert, John, Esq., Rollstone, Monmouth
*Gilbert, Rev. Gilbert, M.A., Richmond, Surrey
*Gilbert, Henry, Esq., Dover, Kent
*Gilbert, Mrs. Mary, Waterloo-place, London
*Gilbert, T., Esq., King-st., Bloomsbury-sq., do.
Gilbertson, Mr. James, Hertford
Gilbertson, Mr. J. M., do.
Gilbertson, W.W., Esq., Speldhurst-place, Lond.
*Gildhart, Rev. Fred., L. C. B., West Wickham
*Giles, F., Esq., Salisbury-st., Strand, London
Giles, George Duke, Esq., Clement's-inn, do.
Giles, J. A., Esq., Corpus-Christi coll., Oxford
Giles, Robert H., Esq., Gravesend, Kent
*Giles, Mr. R. F., Fareham, Hants
Gill, Mr. E. W., Hereford
Gill, George, Esq., Millman-street, London
*Gill, George, Esq., Bank Chambers, do.
*Gill, Hamilton, Esq., Shenley-lodge, Herts.
Gill, James, Esq., Ocle-Pitchard, Herefordsh.
*Gill, Thos., Esq., Lincoln's-inn-fields, London
*Gillam, Robert, Esq., Worcester
Gillet, Richard, Esq., Spital, near Chesterfield
*Gilliat, A. G., Esq., Portswood-lodge, Hants.
*Gilliat, W. H., Esq., Liverpool
Gillies, Jas., Esq., Court-Eskley, Herefordshire
Gillow, Francis, Esq., Minster, Kent
*Gillow, Richard, Esq., Leighton-hall, Lancash.
*Gillow, R., Esq., Clifton-hall, near Lancaster
Gilpin, Bernard, Esq., Ulverstone, Lancashire
Gilpin, Rev. Martin, Stockport, Cheshire
*Gilpin, Perry, Esq., East Sheen, Surrey
*Gilpin, William, Esq., do., do.
*Gilson, Mr. Thomas, Bucklersbury, London
*Ginders, Jer., Esq., Ingestrie, Staffordshire
Giradot, Rev. John, A. M., Averham, Notts.
*Girardot, J. C., Esq., Little Bookham, Surrey
*Girdleston, Wing, & Jackson, Mess., Wisbeach
*Girot and Co., Mess., Walbrook-build., Lond.
Gisborne, T., Esq., Horwich-house, Derbyshire
*Gist, J., Esq., Wormington-Grange, Gloucester
*Gist, Samuel Gist, Esq., Dixton
*Gladdish, Wm., Esq., Cliff-cottage, Gravesend
Gladstone, Rev. J., Bootle, near Liverpool
Gladstone, John, Esq., Seaforth, near do.
Gladstone, W. E., Esq., Christ-ch. col., Oxford
Gladwin, Rev. C. T., L. L. B., Liverpool
*Glanville, John, Esq., Wedmore, Somersetshire
Glascodine, Mr. Henry, Bristol
*Glasgow, R. R., Esq., Trinity coll., Cambridge
Gleadow, Rev. R., M.A., Frodesley, Shropshire
Gleadow, T. Ward, Esq., Kingston upon Hull
*Gleave, William, Esq., Mill-crooks, near York
*Glegg, Baskerville, Esq., Backford-hall, Chester
Glegg, Mr. John, Bracondale, Norwich
Glenister, Mr. J. R., Tring, Herts.
*Globe Insurance Company, London
*Glossop, Rev. H., A. M., Isleworth, Middlesex
*GLOUCESTER, The Rt. Rev. Lord Bishop of
*Glover, Charles, Esq., Altrincham, Cheshire
Glover, J., Esq., Stoke-house, Wakefield
Glover, Mr. J. F., Newark, Notts.
Glover, Mr. Stephen, Derby
Glover, William C., Esq., Shiffnall, Stafford
*Glynes, C. W., Esq., Vine-street, America-square, London
*Glynn, Sir S., Bart., Hawarden-castle, Flintsh.
Glynn, John, Esq., St. John's coll., Cambridge
*Glynne, ——Esq., Christ-church coll., Oxford
*Goddard, Edward, Esq., Cookham, Berks.
*Goddard, G., Esq., Thavies-inn, London
Goddard, H. R., Esq., Brasenose coll., Oxford
Goddard, John, Esq., Coventry
*Goddard, Mr. William, Eton, Bucks.
Godfrey, Edward Smith, Esq., Newark
Godfrey, James, Esq., Warwick
Godfrey, T. S., Esq., Beaconsfield-house, Newark
*Godfrey, Wm., Esq., Bishop's Cleeve, Gloucestershire [park, London
Goding, T., Esq., St. George's-place, Hyde-
Godsall, J., Esq., Winforton-court, Herefordsh.
*Godson, Stephen, Esq., Worcester
Godwin, Mr. Thomas, Winchester, Hants.
Goertz, Mr. H. L., Windsor
Goffe, Mr. John, Enfield, Middlesex
*Golden, Jno., Esq., Gainsborough, Lincolnshire
Golding, A. G., Esq., Custom-house, London
*Golding, Edward, Esq., Maiden-Erlegh, Berks.
*Goldney, Rev. C., A. M., Stratford, Suffolk
Goldney, Gabriel, Esq., Clifton, Bristol
Goldney, Mr. T., Norman-st., St. Luke's, Lond.
Goldring, G., Esq., Jamaica-place, Limehouse
Goldsmith, George, Esq., Watford
Goldsmith, Mr. J. W., Great Knight-Rider-st., London
Goldthorpe, R., Esq., Cleckheaton, near Leeds
Goldwyer, Henry, Esq., Bristol
Golightly, C., Esq., Oriel college, Oxford
Golightly, Richard, Esq., Liverpool
Gondy, Thomas, Esq., Preston, Lancashire
*Gonne, T. G., Esq., Trinity coll., Cambridge
Gooch, Sir T. S., Bart., Binacre-hall, Suffolk
Gooch, B., Esq., Yarmouth, Norfolk
Gooch, C., Esq., do., do.
Gooch, Rev. R., Frostendge-lodge, Suffolk
*Gooch, T., Esq., London-wall, London
Good, Edw., Esq., Leominster, Herefordshire
Good, Rev. John Everett, Salisbury
Good, John, Esq., Bockleton, Herefordshire
*Good, Mrs., Guildford-st., Russell-sq., London
Goodall, Mr. Edw., Camden Town, Middlesex
Goodall, Rev. Joseph, D.D., Eton college
Goodbarne, Mr. Thomas, Bunhill-row, London
*Goodchild, J., Esq., Bishop-Wearmouth, Dur-
Goodchild, Mr. J. D., Hambledon, Bucks. [ham
*Goode, Samuel, Esq., Lynn, Norfolk
Goode, Thomas, Esq., Dudley
Gooden, W., Esq., Compton-house, Dorset
*Goodhall, E. and R., Messrs., Coventry
*Goodhall, Henry H., Esq., Crutched-friars,
Goodhall, J., Esq., Warwick [London
*Goodhart, Emanuel, Esq., Langley-park, Kent
*Gooding, J., Esq., Southwold, Suffolk
*Goodlad, Joseph, Esq., Bury, Lancashire
*Goodlad, William, Esq., do., do.
Goodliff, Richard, Esq., Wood-Walton, Hunts.
*Goodman, B., Esq., Norwich
*Goodman, Rev. Godfrey, Bredon, Worcestersh.
*Goodman, J. R., Esq., Trinity coll., Cambridge
*Goodrich, James, Esq., Bath
*Goodrich, W. T. P., Esq., Oriel coll., Oxford
*Goodridge, Mr. James, Bath
*Goodwin, Charles, Esq., Lynn, Norfolk
Goodwin, F., Esq., Mappleton, Derbyshire
Goodwin, F. G., Esq., Wigwell-Grange, do.
Goodwin, George, Esq., Buxton, do.
*Goodwin, G., Esq., Harlow, Essex
Goodwin, James, Esq., Norwich
*Goodwin, P., Esq., Harlow, Essex
Goodyer, Mr. T., Aldersgate-street, London
Goolden, John, Esq., Bristol
Goolden, Richard, Esq., Maidenhead, Berks.
Goose, Robert, Esq., Hellesdon, Norfolk
GORDON, His Grace the Duke of
*Gordon, Mrs., Marlow, Bucks.
Gordon, Alexander, Esq., Dudley
*Gordon, A., Esq., East Bourne, Sussex
*Gordon, The Very Reverend George, D. D., Dean of Lincoln
*Gordon, Colonel Robert, Walmer, Kent
Gordon, Rev. W., Spaxton, Somersetshire
*Gordon, William, Esq., Haffield, Ledbury
*Gore, Vice-Admiral Sir J., K. C. B., Datchet. near Windsor
Gore, F. R., Esq., Walbrook, London
Gore, Mr. Jas., Much-Walton, near Liverpool
Gore and Son, Messrs., Liverpool
Gorham, George J., Esq., St. Neots, Hunts.
Goring, H., Esq., Holywell, Oxford
*Goring, Harry D., Esq., Yapton, Sussex
Gorst, Edward, Esq., Preston, Lancashire
*GORT, The Right Honorable Lord Viscount
*Gorton, T., Esq., jun., Chancery-lane, London
GOSFORD, The Right Honorable the Earl of
Gosling, Charles, Esq., Strand, London
*Gosling, H., Esq., Jermyn-st., St. James's, do.
Gosling, T. M., Esq., Brasenose coll., Oxford
Gosset, Rev. T. S., Old Windsor [London
*Gossett, M., Esq., George-st., Mansion-house,
*Goucé, L. E., Esq., Ombersley, Worcestershire
Gough, J. E., Esq., Hereford
Gough, F. W., Esq., do.
Gough, Mr. William, Windsor
*Goulburn, Edw., Esq., Regent's-park, London
*Gould, I. H., Esq., Smithfield, do.
*Gould, Mr. J., Wood-street, do.
Gould, J. B., Esq., Magdalene hall, Oxford
*Gould, J. M., Esq., Broad-street, London
*Gould, J. N., Esq., Little Hempston, Devon.
*Gould, Rowland, Esq., Macclesfield, Cheshire
Gould, Mr. Thomas, Alcester, Warwickshire
*Gould, Mr. W. E., Gracechurch-street, London
*Gouldsmith, Latreille, & Co., Old Jewry, do.
Gover, Mr. W., Winchester, Hants.
Govett, Edward, Esq., Taunton, Somersetshire
Govett, Rev. Robert, Staines, Middlesex
*Gowland, E., Esq., Great Dover-st., London
*Gowland, J. S., Esq., Cagebrook, Herefordshire
Gowland, R., Esq., Lincoln's-inn-fields, Lond.
*Gowne, G., Esq., Chichester, Sussex
Graburn, Mr. James, Winchester, Hants.
*Grace, Richard, Esq., Arley-park, Cheshire
Grady, Mr. John, Pratt-st., Lambeth, Surrey
Grafham, Mr. E., Chertsey, do.
*GRAFTON, His Grace the Duke of
*Graham, Sir B. B., Bart., Norton-Conyers, York
Graham, Sir Robt., Bart., Esk, Cumberland
Graham, George, Esq., Harwich
Graham, H., Esq., York
*Graham, I. Eysam, Esq., The Sheet, Salop
*Graham, Rev. J., D.D., Christ's coll., Cambdg.
*Graham, W., Esq., Christ-church coll., Oxford
Graham and Galsworthy, Messrs., London
Graham, Kinderly, and Domville, Messrs., do.

Granger, Mr. Charles, Wolverhampton
*Granger, T. H., Esq., Leeds
*Grant, Lieutenant General, Sir William Keir, K.C.B., and G.H.M.T., Crescent, Bath
*Grant, D., Esq., Manchester
Grant, George, Esq., Liverpool
*Grant, John, Esq., Bolton, Lancashire
*Grant, R. J., Esq., Sanderstead-court, Surrey
*Grant, Rev. Robert, Bradford-Abbas, Dorset.
*Grant, Thomas, Esq., Deal, Kent
*Grant, William, Esq., Bolton, Lancashire
*Grantham, Stephen, Esq., Stoneham, Sussex
*GRANVILLE, The Rt. Hon. Lord Viscount
*Granville, C., Esq., Colwich-house, Staffordshire
Granville, Dr., Grafton-st., Berkeley-sq., London
*Grape, Mr. James, Clifton-st., Finsbury-sq., do.
*Grassett, W., Esq., Sundridge, Kent [London
*Gratorex, T. C., Esq., Bush-lane, Cannon-st.,
*Gratrix, T., Esq., Southgate, Manchester
*Gratwick, W. G. K., Esq., Angmering, Sussex
Graves, C. G., Esq., Army-pay-office, London
*Graves, H. A., Esq., London-street, do.
Graves, John, Esq., Bath
Gravesend Book Society, Gravesend, Kent
Gray, Mr. Edward, Manchester
*Gray, John, Esq., Carlisle, Cumberland
Gray, Rev. Joseph, Chelmsford, Essex
*Gray, Nathan, Esq., March, Cambridgeshire
Gray, R., Esq., Brompton-crescent, Middlesex
Gray, William, Esq., Magdalene college, Oxford
Gray, William, Esq., York
*Grayson, Mr. Robert, Leeds
*Grazebrook, George, Esq., Stourbridge
*Grazebrook, J. W., Esq., City-road, London
*Greatwood, Robert, Esq., Birmingham
Greaves, G., Esq., Ashbourn, Derbyshire
*Greaves, James, Esq., Partington, Cheshire
*Greaves, J., Esq., Pendleton, near Manchester
Greaves, John R., Esq., Liverpool
Greaves, Mr. John, Barford, near Warwick
Greaves, W., Esq., Mayfield-hall, Staffordshire
Green, Rev. C., M.A., Jesus coll., Cambridge
*Green, Charles, Esq., Teddington, Middlesex
*Green, D. F., Esq., Warminster, Wilts.
Green, Rev. G. W., Court Henry, Carmarthensh.
*Green, George J., Esq., Birmingham
*Green, Mr. George, Abergavenny
Green, Henry, Esq., Liverpool
*Green, H. G., Esq., Staple-inn, London
Green, Isaac, Esq., Essendon, Hertfordshire
Green, Rev. James, Upton upon Severn
Green, James, Esq., Holcombe, Somersetshire
*Green, J., Esq., Blackfriars, London
*Green, J., Esq., Upper Thames-street, do.
*Green, J., Esq., Poulton, Lancelyn-hall, Chesh.
*Green, J. F., Esq., Ware, Herts.
*Green, J., Esq., Worcester
*Green, John, Esq., Sandford-st., Manchester
*Green, Mr. P., Fish-street-hill, London
*Green, R., Esq., Headington-hill, near Oxford
*Green, Rev. R., A.M., Newcastle upon Tyne
*Green, Mr. Richard, Brighton, Sussex
Green, Samuel, Esq., Bluntisham, Hunts.
*Green, Thomas, Esq., Athelington, Suffolk
Green, Thomas, Esq., Worcester coll., Oxford
*Green, Thomas, Esq., Walbrook, London
Green, Thomas, Esq., Yarmouth, Norfolk
Green, Thomas, Esq., Orleton, Herefordshire
*Green, W., Esq., Upper Charlotte-street, Fitzroy-square, London
Green, William, Esq., Liverpool
Green, W., Esq., Stanway-hall, Colchester
*Green, W. A. H., Esq., Lenham, Kent
Green and Hartley, Messrs., Broad-st., London
Green and Jordon, Messrs., Ware, Herts.
*Green and Son, Messrs., Maidstone, Kent
*Green, Pemberton, & Crawley, Messrs., Salisbury-square, Fleet-street, London
*Greenall, Edw., Esq., Wilderspool, Warrington
Greenall, Peter, Esq., St. Helens, Lancashire
Greene, Rev. E. H., Lawford-hall, Suffolk
*Greene, Thos., Esq., M.P., Kirkby-Lonsdale

Greene, William, Esq., Liverpool
*Greener, William, Esq., Newcastle upon Tyne
*Greenfield, B. W., Esq., Corpus-Christi coll., Cambridge
*Greenfield, J. Esq., Brasenose coll., Oxford
*Greenfield, J. S., Esq., Thelwall, Cheshire
Greenfield, Wm., Esq., Gray's-inn-sq., London
*Greenhalgh, G. I. H., Esq., L.L.B., Bury
*Greenhalgh, John, Esq., Manchester
*Greenham, J., Esq., Ludgate-street, London
Greenhill, B. C., Esq., Worcester coll., Oxford
Greenhill, Russell Robt., Esq., Wendover
Greenhow, E., Esq., North Shields, Northum-
Greenlaw, Rev. W., Blackheath, Kent [berland
Greenly, Rev. John, A.M., Salisbury
Greenly, W., Esq., Titley-court, Herefordshire
Greenough, W. A., Esq., Wigan, Lancashire
Greenslade, W., Esq., Trinity coll., Cambridge
*Greenway, Gleattell, Esq., Warwick
*Greenwood, Charles, Esq., Wallingford, Berks.
Greenwood, C., Esq., Audley-square, London
Greenwood, Rev. John, Royston, Herts.
Greenwood, John, Esq., Prestwich, Lancashire
Greenwood, John, Esq., Preston, do.
*Greenwood, Robert, Esq., Chelmsford
Greenwood, Mr. Robert, Bell-alley, London
*Greenwood, Thomas, Esq., Wallingford, Berks.
*Greenwood, Mr. T., St. John's-sq., Clerkenwell
*Greenwood & Co., Mess., Charing-cross, Lond.
*Greet, T. G., Esq., Queenborough, Kent
Greetham, C. S., Esq., Portsmouth
*Gregg, George, Esq., Skinners'-hall, London
Gregg, James, jun., Esq., Ledbury, Herefordsh.
*Gregory, Rev. Edward, Lower Hardres, Kent
*Gregory, Reverend John, Elmstone, do.
*Gregory, J., Esq., Clement's-inn, London
Gregory, M. H., Esq., Maiden-lane, do.
Gregory, Thomas, Esq., York
*Gregory, Mr. W., Serle's-place, London
*Gregson, B. Padgett, Esq., Lancaster
*Gregson, Henry, Esq., do.
*Gregson, Mr. J. T., Bishop-Wearmouth
*Gregson, John, Esq., do.
Gregson, T., Esq., Hare-court, Temple, London
Greive, General, York
Grellier, James, Esq., Douglas, Isle of Man
*Grenfell, P. S. L., Esq., Lombard-st., London
*GRENVILLE, The Right Honorable Lord
*Grenville, Mr., Cleveland-square
Gresley, Mr. John, Iver, Bucks.
Gresley, N., Esq., Christ-church coll., Oxford
Gresley, R., Esq., Stowe-house, Staffordshire
*Gretton, G. H. L., Esq., Elmstone-Hardwicke, near Cheltenham
Gretton, Philip, Esq., Colchester
Greville, A., Esq., Sun-court, Cornhill, London
Greville, Henry, Esq., Blandford-street, Finsbury-square, London
Greville, Rev. J., Duston, near Northampton
*GREY, The Right Honorable Earl
Grey, C. S., Esq., Trinity college, Cambridge
Grey, H., jun., Esq., Water-lane, Tower-st., London
Grice, John Le, Esq., Bury St. Edmunds
*Grice, Joseph, Esq., Handsworth, Staffordshire
Griffin, Mr. Charles, Snowhill, London
Griffin, Henry, Esq., Queen's college, Oxford
*Griffin, Rev. John, Solihull, Warwickshire
Griffin, John, Esq., Hemel-Hempstead, Herts.
Griffin, Thomas, Esq., Shelton, Staffordshire
Griffith, G. D., Esq., Jesus college, Oxford
*Griffith, T., Esq., Gray's-inn-place, London
*Griffith, Rev. Thomas, M.A. Llangollen, N.W.
Griffith, Rev. W., Hentland, Herefordshire
Griffith, William, Esq., Hereford
Griffith, Mr. W., Frome, Somersetshire
Griffiths, Chs., Esq., Chepstow, Monmouthshire
*Griffiths, Charles, Esq., Gloucester
Griffiths, Mr. E., Norton, Herefordshire
Griffiths, George, Esq., Pentonville, Middlesex
*Griffiths, J., Esq., Wadham college, Oxford
*Griffiths, J., Esq., Hereford

Griffiths, J., Esq., The Weir, Hereford
Griffiths, J., Esq., Witley, Worcestershire
*Griffiths, Jas., Esq., Deddington, Oxfordshire
Griffiths, John, Esq., Crispin-st., Spitalfields,
*Griffiths, Price, Esq., Hereford [London
*Griffiths, L. D., Esq., do.
*Griffiths, W., Esq., Monmouth
Griffiths, Mr. W., Church-street, Shoreditch
*Griffiths, Mr. W. H., Shrewsbury
*Grime, W. B., Esq., Water-st., Manchester
Grimes, Captain J., Hoddesdon, Hertfordshire
Grimes, Mr. T., Colchester
Grimmer, William, Esq., Norwich [shire
Grimshaw, J., Esq., Audenshaw-lodge, Lanca-
*Grimshaw, S., Esq., Brasenose coll., Oxford
*Grimshaw, Samuel, Esq., Partington, Cheshire
Grindrod, J., Esq., M.D., Liverpool
Grinnell, Mr. John, Pershore, Worcestershire
Gripper, Mr. Thomas, Hertford
*Grissell, T., Esq., York-road, Westminster
Grist, Mr. P., Davies-street, London
Gritton, J. F., Esq., Queen-hithe, Kent
Grobety, Mr. Benjamin, Newbury, Berks.
Groocock, Mr. W. A., St. Ives, Huntingdonshire
Groom, Captain J., Bromfield, near Ludlow
*Groom, John, Esq., Audlem, Cheshire
*Groome, John A., Esq., King's Langley, Herts.
Groser, Mr. William, Maidstone, Kent
Grossmith, Mr., Castle-street, Reading, Berks.
GROSVENOR, The Right Honorable Earl
*Grosvenor, The Right Honorable Robert, M.P.
Grosvenor, J., Esq., Lower Egdon, Herefordsh.
Grosvenor, T. F., Esq., Leek, Staffordshire
*Grote, Charles, Esq., Leadenhall-st., London
*Grout, George, Esq., Norwich
*Grout, Joseph, Esq., Gutter-lane, London
*Grove, Rev. Charles, Oldstock, Wiltshire
Grove, John, Esq., M.D., Salisbury, do.
*Grover, C. E., Esq., Hemel-Hempstead, Herts.
Groves, W. J., Esq., Trinity college, Oxford
*Groves, Mr. W. W., Brighton, Sussex
*Grubb, Mr. A., Bow-street, London
*Grundy, Dennis, Esq., Bury, Lancashire
*Grundy, George, Esq., do., do.
*Grundy, John, Esq., do., do.
*Grundy, Robert, Esq., do., do.
*Grundy, Samuel, Esq., do., do.
*Grundy, Thomas, Esq., do., do.
*Grylls, Glynn, Esq., Helston, Cornwall
*Guardian Assurance Company, London
*Gudgeon, James, Esq., Stow-Market, Suffolk
*Guerin, Rev. T., West Bagborough, Somersetsh.
Guest and Sons, Messrs. E., Dudley
Guiball, James, Esq., Liverpool
*GUILDFORD, The Right Hon. the Earl of
*Guildhall Library of the Corporation of London
*Guille, Edw., Esq., St. John's coll., Cambridge
Guillemard, J., Esq., St. John's college, Oxford
*Guise, Sir B. W., Bart., M.P., Highnam-coast, Gloucestershire
Gulson, Edward, Esq., Coventry, Warwickshire
*Gumpel and Co., Messrs., Manchester
Gunning, Mr. John, Bristol
Gunning, Matt., Esq., Much-Hadham, Herts.
*Gunning, P., Esq., Merton college, Oxford
*Gurney, J., Esq., Lakenham-Grove, Norwich
*Gurney, J. J., Esq., Lombard-street, London
*Gurney, S., Esq., do., do.
Gurney, Mr. Richard, Norwich
Gutch, I. M., Esq., Bristol
Gutteridge, James, Esq., Munden, Herts.
Gutteridge, Mr. Samuel, Hertford
*Gutterson, Thomas, Esq., Enfield, Middlesex
Guy, Mr. Robert, Southampton
Gwatkin, Rev. R., St. John's coll., Cambridge
Gwillim, John, Esq , Hereford
*Gwillim, John, Esq., How-castle, Herefordsh.
*Gwillim, John, Esq., London-wall, London
Gwinnell, T. C., Esq., Gray's-inn-sq., do.
*Gwinnett, Samuel, Esq., Stratford upon Avon
Gwyn, H., Esq., Trinity college, Oxford
*Gwynne, S., Esq., Surrey-square, London

Hacking, Wm., Esq., Blackburn, Lancashire
* Hackney, The Trustees of the Parish of
* Haddersich, W., Esq., Stafford
Haddon, Mr. John, Castle-street, City-road
* Hadfield, Captain G., Hollingworth, Cheshire
* Hadfield, Joseph, Esq., Lees-hall, Derbyshire
Hadler, Mr. Thomas, Rochester, Kent
Hadsley, Miss M., Priory, Ware, Herts.
Hadwen, R. S., Esq., Pancras-lane, London
Haggitt, Rev. D'Arcy, Pershore, Worcestersh.
* Hague, Jonathan G., Esq., Ashton under Line
* Haile, Francis, Esq., Park-hall, Notts.
Hailstone, E., Esq., Southampton-buildings, London
Hailstone, Rev. J., M. A., F. R. S., F. L. S., Trumpington, near Cambridge
* Hailstone, John, Esq., Trinity coll., Cambridge
Haines, G., Esq., M. D., Godalming, Surrey
Haines, Richard, Esq., Southampton
Haines, Mr. Richard, Tipton, Staffordshire
* Haines, William, Esq., Birmingham
* Haines, Mr. William, Newgate-street, London
* Haldon, Mr. C., Oxford
Hale, Mr. G. L., Broadstairs, Kent
* Hale, John, Esq., Busford
* Hale, John R. B., Esq., Oriel college, Oxford
Hale, Mr. Samuel, Poultry, London
Hale, William, Esq., Acomb, Yorkshire
Hale, William, Esq., King's Walden, Herts.
Hale, William, Esq., Bath
Hales, J., Esq., Cobridge, Staffordshire
Hales, Thomas, Esq., Coddington, Herefordsh.
Haliburton, A., Esq., Douglas-Bank, Lancash.
Haliburton, John, Esq., Preston, do.
* Halkyard, Henry, Esq., Oldham, do.
Hall, Alexander, Esq., Austin-friars, London
Hall, B., Esq., Llanover-court, Monmouthshire
Hall, Rev. F. B., Fulbourn St. Vigors, Cambridgeshire
* Hall, Edward, Esq., Dalton, Lancashire
* Hall, Francis, Esq., Park-hall, Notts.
* Hall, Francis, Esq., Saffron-Walden, Essex
Hall, Rev. George, Tenbury, Worcestershire
* Hall, G., Esq., M. D., Brighton
Hall, Mr. Giles, Blagdon, Somersetshire
Hall, G. C., Esq., Alfreton, Derbyshire
Hall, H., Esq., Newcastle under Line
Hall, Mr. Henry, Romsey, Hants
* Hall, James, Esq., Redbrook, Gloucestershire
Hall, James W. R., Esq., Ross, Herefordshire
* Hall, John, Esq., Lancaster
* Hall, John, Esq., Bury, Lancashire
* Hall, John, Esq., Manchester
* Hall, John, Esq., St. Mary-Axe, London
Hall, John, Esq., West Derby, near Liverpool
Hall, Joseph, Esq., Castleton, Derbyshire
Hall, J., Esq., Bury of Weston, Pembridge, Herefordshire
Hall, J. H., Esq., Risley-hall, Derbyshire
Hall, J. R., Esq., Christ-church college, Oxford
Hall, Mr. J. V., Maidstone, Kent
* Hall, R., Esq., Great James-street, London
* Hall, Richard, Esq., Totteridge, Herts.
Hall, Mr. R., Park-place, Leeds
Hall, T., Esq., St. John's college, Cambridge
Hall, Mr. Thomas, Eardisley, Herefordshire
Hall, William, Esq. Hatfield, do.
* Hall, William, Esq., Warrington, Lancashire
* Hall, Messrs. James and J., Salford, do.
Hall and Brownley, Messrs., New Boswell-court, London
* Hall and Sons, Messrs., Dartford, Kent
* Hall, Thompson, and Co., Messrs., Salter's-hall, London
Hallen, Thomas, Esq., Kidderminster
Halley, R., Esq., St. Neots, Huntingdonshire
Halliday, John E., Esq., Taunton
* Hallifax, Rev. R. F., Richard's Castle, Salop
* Halliley, Mr. Ed., Albion-st., Leeds, Yorkshire
* Halliley, John, Esq., Dewsbury, do.
* Hallowes, Thos., Esq., Glapwell-hall, Derbysh.
Hallows, Joseph, Esq., Enfield, Middlesex
* Hallworth, Mr. Samuel, Ashton under Line
Halsall, R. J., Esq., Middleton, Lancashire
* Halsted, L., Esq., Hood-house, do.
* Halsted, Thomas, Esq., Woodcote, Sussex
Halton, Capt., R. N., Carlisle [byshire
Halton, Rev. J., M. A., South Winfield, Der-
Halton, Mrs. L., Thruxton, Hants.
* Halton, Peter, Esq., Aston, Frodsham, Cheshire
Hamber, Mr. T., Southampton-buildings, Lond.
Hamer, Mr. H., Springfield, Bootle, nr. Liverpool
* Hamersley, E., Esq., Trinity college, Cambridge
* Hamilton, Rev. A., Newport, Isle of Wight
* Hamilton, Charles, Esq., Kensworth, Herts.
* Hamilton, Rev. I. V., Sandwich, Kent
* Hamilton, J. Esq., Dean-street, Soho, London
* Hamilton, J., Esq., Hemel-Hempstead, Herts.
Hamilton, Rev. James, Hackington, Kent
Hamilton, J., Esq., Brasenose college, Oxford
* Hamilton, Joseph, Esq., Manchester
* Hamilton, Rev. R., D. D., F. R. S., and S. A., Kensington, Middlesex
Hamman, James, Esq., Bow-lane, London
* Hamman, John, Esq., do., do.
Hammerton, H., Esq., Burnley, Lancashire
* Hammerton, T. E., Esq., Todmorden, do.
Hammond, Rev. A. A., Southampton
* Hammond, Mr. Chas., Petham, nr. Canterbury
Hammond, Mr. Chas. W., Enfield, Middlesex
* Hammond, H., Esq., Furnival's-inn, London
* Hammond, H., Esq., Church-st., Manchester
Hammond, Henry, Esq., Windsor
* Hammond, I. W., Esq., Nantwich, Cheshire
Hammond, J., Esq., Leominster, Herefordshire
Hammond, J., Esq., Queen's coll., Cambridge
* Hammond, Wm., Esq., Southgate, Middlesex
* Hammond, W., jun., Esq., Whetstone, Herts.
* Hampson, William, Esq., Duckinfield, Cheshire
Hanbury, Alfred, Esq., St. Mary hall, Oxford
* Hanbury, Rev. John, Thatcham, Berks.
Hanbury, Sampson, Esq., Ware, Herts.
* Hanbury, W., Esq., Moreton-Colwich, Stafford.
* Hancock, W., Esq., Aston-bank, Flintshire
* Hancock, Wm., jun., Esq., do., do.
Hancock, Mr. W., Disley, near Stockport, Chesh.
* Hancock and Griesback, Messrs., Fenchurch-street, London
Hancock, Messrs. P. and W., Wiveliscombe,
Hancoks, Mr. William, Wolverley [Somerset.
* Hand, Rev. Charles, Northwich, Cheshire
* Handforth, Rev. John, Ashton under Line
* Handley, W., Esq., St. John's coll., Cambridge
* Handly, William F., Esq., Newark, Notts.
* Hands, Benjamin, Esq., Hornsey, Middlesex
Hands, Mr. D., Birmingham
Hands, John, Esq., St. Paul's square, do.
Handy, Miss, Wacton, Herefordshire [shire
Hanford, C. E., Esq., Wooler's-hill-hall, Che-
Hanisson, R. S., Esq., Bourn-Abbey, Lincolnsh.
* Hankes, Mr. Alderman, Norwich
Hankins, Richard, Esq., Bartestree, Hereford
Hankins, Wm., Esq., Pigeon-house, do.
* Hankinson, Chas., Esq., Hale, Cheshire
* Hanley, W. L., Esq., Furnival's-inn, London
* Hanmer, Sir John, Bart., Hanmer-hall, Flintsh.
* Hanmer, J. W., Esq., Lincoln's-inn, London
* Hannah, Rev. John, Grosvenor-st., Manchester
* Hannam, H. P., Esq., Northbourne-court, Kent
* Hannington, Smith, Esq., Brighton
* Hanrott, P. A., Esq., Gt. Ormond-st., London
Hanrott & Metcalfe, Messrs., Lincoln's-inn, do.
Hansby, M. W., Esq., Ragland, Monmouthshire
Hansom, Mr. Joseph, York
Hanson, R. D., Esq., Philpot-lane, London
Hanson, Thomas, Esq., Birmingham
* Hanson, Rev. W. H., B. A., Fellow and Tutor, Caius college, Cambridge
Harbard, William Oliver, Esq., Liverpool
* Harbin, George, Esq., Newton-house, Yeovil
Harbroe, Edward, Esq., Ripley, Surrey
* Hardcastle, James, Esq., Bolton, Lancashire
* Hardcastle, W., Esq., Covent-garden, London
Harden, Nathaniel, Hadley, Middlesex
Harden, Mr. William, Clapham, Surrey
* Hardey, Henry, Esq., Lymm, Cheshire
* Hardey, Peter, Esq., do., do.
* Hardey, Samuel, Esq., Altrincham, do.
* Hardey, Thomas, Esq., Lymm, do.
* Hardey, Thomas B., Esq., Preston, Lancashire
Harding, W., Esq., Lombard-street, London
* Harding, John, Esq., Heald, Cheshire
* Harding, Thomas, Esq., Ware, Herts.
Harding, W., Esq., Latimers, Bucks
* Harding, W. S., Esq., Birmingham
Harding, Messrs. W. & J. P., Burslem, Staffordsh.
Hardman, Mr. J. Symonds, Hereford
* Hardman, Thos., Esq., Quay-st., Manchester
* Hardman, Thomas, Esq., do.
* Hardman, W., Esq., Bury, Lancashire
* Hardman, W., jun., Esq., do., do.
Hardwick, Benj., Esq., Lawrence-lane, London
Hardwick, John, Esq., Credenhill, Herefordsh.
Hardwick, Joseph, Esq., Lulham, do.
* HARDWICKE, The Right Hon. the Earl of
Hardwicke, Rev. Charles, Gloucester
Hardy, Mr. Charles, Norwich
Hardy, E. W., Esq., Bath
Hardy, J., Esq., Old Broad-street, London
Hardy, J., Esq., Heath, near Wakefield, Yorksh.
* Hardy, Mr. Samuel, Islington Spa, London
Hardy, Mr. Thomas, Sunderland
Hardy, Mr. W. E., Ilchester, Somersetshire
* Hardy, Turner, and Walkington, Messrs. Grantham, Lincolnshire
Hardyman, Captain L. F., R. N., and C. B., Upton-house, near Romsey, Hants.
* Hare, H., Esq., Wadham college, Oxford
Hare, Rev. J. C., M. A., Fellow and Tutor of Trinity college, Cambridge
Hare, Joseph, Esq., Cannon-street, London
* Hare, W., Esq., Rochdale, Lancashire
* Hare and Co., Messrs. John, Bristol
* Harence, H., Esq., Christ-church coll., Oxford
* HAREWOOD, The Right Honorable the Earl of
* Harford, H., Esq., Bray, Berkshire
Harford, J. S., Esq., Blaize-Castle, near Bristol
* Harford, S., Esq., Sirhoroy, Monmouthshire
* Harford, W. H., Esq., Barley-wood, Somerset.
Hargreave, O., Esq., Southampton-buildings, London
* Hargreaves, B., Esq., Accrington, Lancashire
* Hargreaves, George, Esq., Newchurch, do.
* Hargreaves, H., Esq., Spring-field, Lancaster
* Hargreaves, James, Esq., Burnley, Lancashire
* Hargreaves, John, Esq., Blackburn, do.
* Hargreaves, W., Esq., Burnley, do.
* Hargreaves, William, Esq., Leeds
Harington, H., Esq., Magdalene hall, Oxford
* Harker, Thomas, Esq., Broxbourn, Herts.
Harland, Sir Robert, Bart., Orwell-park, Suffolk
* Harle, John, Esq., Newcastle upon Tyne
* Harman, E., Esq., Theobalds, Hertfordshire
* Harman, J., Esq., Caius college, Cambridge
Harman, J., Esq., Howard-street, London
* Harman, John, Esq., Croydon, Surrey
* Harman, Rev. Thomas, Nockholt, Kent
* Harman, Thomas, Esq., Wombwell-hall, do.
* Harman and Co., Messrs., Adam's-court, Old Broad-street, London
* Harmer, Daniel, Esq., Elton, Lancashire
* Harmer, James, Esq., Hatton-garden, London
* Harmood, H., Esq., Wilmington-house, Kent
Harnett, J., Esq., Northumberland-st., London
* Harper, Edward, Esq., Great Queen-street, do.
* Harper, George, Esq., Whitchurch, Shropshire
* Harper, J. H., Esq., Davenham-hall, Cheshire
* Harper, R. J., Esq., Needwood-forest, Stafford
* Harper, Pearce, and Co., Messrs., Gracechurch-street, London
Harrington, E. C., Esq., Worcester coll., Oxford
* Harrington, James, Esq., Woodbank, Carlisle
* Harrington, Mr. T., Pershore, Worcestershire
Harriot, George, Esq., Ormskirk, Lancashire
* Harris, The Honorable G. F. R.
Harris, B., Esq., Leominster, Herefordshire

*Harris, Chas., Esq., Gracechurch-street, London
*Harris, Charles, Esq., Trinity college, Oxford
*Harris, Edmund R., Esq., Preston, Lancashire
*Harris, Francis, Esq., Benthall-hall, Shropshire
Harris, Mr. James, Egham, Surrey
Harris, Mr. James, Holme, Herefordshire
*Harris, John, Esq., Bank of England, London
Harris, Jno., Esq., Kington, Herefordshire
*Harris, Joseph, Esq., Shrubbery, Worcester
Harris, Mr. Joseph, Tipton, Staffordshire
Harris, Mr. Richard, Newton, Herefordshire
*Harris, Thomas, Esq., Seven-Oaks, Kent
Harris, Mr. T., Reading, Berks.
Harris, Rev. William, Wallingford, do.
Harris, Mr. W., Holborn, London
*Harrison, A., Esq., Stalybridge, Lancashire
*Harrison, Mrs. Alice, Woodbourn, Isle of Man
*Harrison, Mr. B., Charlesworth, Derbyshire
*Harrison, B., Esq., Ambleside, Westmorland
Harrison, C., Esq., Trinity coll., Cambridge
*Harrison, C. L., Esq., Furnival's-inn, London
*Harrison, Mr. George, Buckland, Kent
Harrison, H., Esq., Manchester [byshire
*Harrison, Rev. J., M. A., Duffield-bank, Der-
Harrison, J. S., Esq., King's-Arms-yard, Lond.
*Harrison, James, Esq., Bury, Lancashire
Harrison, James, Esq., Chorley, do.
*Harrison, James, Esq., Manchester
Harrison, James, Esq., Birmingham
Harrison, Mr. James, Liverpool
Harrison, John, Esq., Snelston-hall, Derbyshire
Harrison, John, Esq., Belper, do.
*Harrison, Jno., Esq., Newly-bridge, Lancashire
Harrison, John, Esq., Liverpool
Harrison, Mr. John, Derby
Harrison, L. W., Esq., Hoddesdon, Hertfordsh.
*Harrison, R., Esq.
*Harrison, Rich., Esq., Warrington, Lancashire
Harrison, Mr. Richard, Birmingham
*Harrison, Robert, Esq., Nantwich, Cheshire
*Harrison, Roger, Esq., Frodsham, do
Harrison, R. S., Esq., Bourne Abbey, Lincoln
*Harrison, Stephen W., Esq., North Shields
*Harrison, T., Esq., Walbrook-buildings, London
*Harrison, W., Esq., Cheshunt, Hertfordshire
*Harrison, Wm., Esq., Primrose-lodge, Cheshire
*Harrison, Wm., Esq., Water-st., Manchester
Harrison, Mr. William, Portsmouth
Harrison, Mr. W. L., Chelmsford
*Harrison, Watson, & Locke, Messrs., Kingston upon Hull
*Harrop, Isaac, Esq., Altrincham, Cheshire
*Harrop, John, Esq., do., do.
*Harrop, Miss, Hale-Lodge, do.
*Harrop, John, Esq., Ashton under Line
*Harrop, J., Esq., Bardsley, Lancashire
*Harrop & Vaudrey, Messrs., Stockport, Cheshire
*HARROWBY, The Right Honorable the Earl of
Hart, Gen. G. V., M.P., Duke-st., St. James's
*Hart, Thomas, Esq., Uttoxeter, Stafford
*Harter, George G., Esq., Trinity coll., Oxford
Hartland, John A., Esq., Tewkesbury
Hartland, Mr. Robert, Bosbury, Herefordshire
Hartley, E., Esq., Boston, Lincolnshire
*Hartley, J., Esq., New Bridge-street, London
*Hartley, Rev. W. H. H., Bucklebury-house, Berkshire
Hartley, W., Esq., Clitheroe, Lancashire
Hartley, William Powell, Esq., Bristol
Hartnell, Mr. Aaron, do.
Harvey, Colonel John, Thorpe-lodge, Norwich
*Harvey, Audley, Esq., Bath
*Harvey, Capt., R. N., Ramsgate, Kent
*Harvey, Edward, Esq., Newington, Surrey
Harvey, George, Esq., Thorpe, near Norwich
*Harvey, H. D., Esq., Wiveliscombe, Somerset.
Harvey, H. W., Esq., Ripple, Kent
*Harvey, J., Esq., Hankelow Mills, Cheshire
Harvey, John, Esq., Ludgate-street, London
*Harvey, Mr. Robert, Oxford-street, do.
Harvey, Mr. Robert, Dunster Mills, Somerset.
*Harvey, Thomas, Esq., Wandsworth, Surrey

Harvey, Mr. Thomas, Westgate, Bath
*Harvey, W., Esq., Parrock-house, Gravesend
*Harvey, W. W., Esq., King's coll., Cambridge
Harvey, Messrs. W. and E., Liverpool [London
Harvey and Darton, Messrs., Gracechurch-st.,
*Harwar, Mr. Charles, Oldham, Lancashire
Harward, Rev. Jno., Hartlebury, Worcestershire
Harward, Rev. Thomas, Winterfold, Chaddesley
*Harwood, Capt., R. N., Maismore-lodge, near Gloucester
Haselgrove, Mr. J., Shirley, near Southampton
Hasell, E. W., Esq., Penrith, Cumberland
*Hasker, John, Esq., Newbury, Berks.
*Hasker, Thomas, Esq., Chinham, Hants.
*Haslam, Samuel H., Esq., Kirkby-Lonsdale
Haslam, Brothers, Messrs., Swanwick, Derby
Hassal, John S., Esq., Liverpool
*Hassall, Stephen, Esq., Wem, Salop.
Hassell, William, Esq., Bristol
*Hassell, Rev. Wm., Allensmore, Herefordshire
*Hassells, Rev. C. S., M. A., Caverswall, Staffordshire [London
*Hast, Wm., Esq., Vine-street, America-square,
Hasted, Rev. H., Bury St. Edmund's, Suffolk
*Haster, John, Esq., Chichester, Sussex
*Hastings, Sir C. A., Bart., M.P., Willesley-hall, Derbyshire
Hastings, Charles, Esq., M. D., Worcester
Haswell, Capt. J., Stepney, Brimfield, Hereford
Hatch, Rev. Mr., Yarmouth, Norfolk
Hatchard and Son, Messrs., Piccadilly, London 2 Copies
Hatfield, Weston, Esq., Huntingdon and Cambridge Gazette-office . . . . 4 Copies
*Hathorn and Co., Messrs. George, London
*Hathway, Nicholas, Esq., Hereford
*Hatley, Captain, R. N., Lauriston, Dover
Hattatt, Henry, Esq., Broughton, Hants.
Hatton, Mr. Charles, Speenhamland, Berks.
*Hautenville, W., Esq., Clifton, near Bristol
Havard, Mr. Thomas, Bromyard, Herefordshire
*Havers, Thomas, Esq., Helton-hall, Norfolk
*Hawar, Charles, Esq., Oldham
*Haweis, J. O. W., Esq., Queen's coll., Oxford
Hawes, Messrs. Benjamin, T., and W., London
*Hawes, Rev. Herbert, D. D., Prebend of Sarum
Hawke, Charles M., Esq., Thavies-inn, London
Hawker, J., Esq., F. S. A., Richmond Herald
*Hawkes, A., Esq., King's Swinford, Staffordsh.
*Hawkes, Mr. Francis, Reading, Berks.
*Hawkes, Rev. James, Nantwich, Cheshire
Hawkes, R., Esq., Wells, Somersetshire
*Hawkes, T., Esq., Himley, Staffordshire
*Hawkes, Thomas, Esq., Frome, Somersetshire
*Hawkes & Co., Messrs., Bishop-Stortford, Essex
Hawkings, J., Esq., Albion-place, Blackfriars
*Hawkins, Sir John C., Bart., Kelston-house, Somersetshire
Hawkins, Rev. C., Kelston, near Bath
*Hawkins, Mr. Daniel, Bishopsgate-st., London
*Hawkins, Frederick, Esq., Birmingham
Hawkins, Jas., Esq., Newport, Monmouthshire
*Hawkins, John, Esq., Bye-lands, Herts.
*Hawkins, Mr. Joseph, Hatfield-street, London
*Hawkins, Thos., Esq., Staunton, Worcestersh.
*Hawks, Thomas, Esq., Gray's-inn, London
*Hawkyard, Joel, Esq., Ashton under Line
*Haworth, A. L., Esq., Bolton, Lancashire
*Haworth, Henry, Esq., Blackburn, do.
Haworth, T., Esq., Barham-wood, Middlesex
*Hay, Rev. W. R., M. A., Rochdale, Lancashire
Haycock, Mr. Edward, Shrewsbury
Haydon, Joseph, Esq., Guildford, Surrey
Haydon, Thomas, Esq., Queen-street, London
Haydon, Mr. W., Mill-Mead, Guildford, Surrey
Hayes, Sir H. B., Knt.
Hayes, Rev. James, Wybunbury, Cheshire
*Hayes, Thomas, Esq., Downing-street, London
*Hayes, William, Esq., Temple, do.
*Hayes, William, Esq., Frodsham, Cheshire
Hayes and Russell, Messrs., Liverpool
Hayles, Mr. Charles, Portsmouth

*Haynes, Miss, Hereford
*Haynes, R., Esq., Pembroke college, Oxford
*Haynes, Robert, Esq., Westbury, Wilts.
Haynes, Mr. W., Bristol
Hays, H. J. W. C. R., Esq., Tewkesbury
*Haythorne, John, Esq., Hill-house, near Bristol
*Haythorne, John, Esq., Oriel college, Oxford
Haythorne, Rev. Jos., Congresbury, Somerset.
Hayton, Amos, Esq., Queen's college, Oxford
*Hayton, T. W., Esq., Gwersyllt, near Wrexham
Hayton, W. C., Esq., Moreton-court, Hereford-
*Hayward, C., Esq., New-Road, Lincoln [shire
Hayward, Mr. H., Maidstone, Kent
Hayward, James, Esq., Wokingham, Berks.
*Hayward, J., Esq., West Chinnock, Somerset.
Hayward, J. B., Esq., South Petherton, do.
*Hayward, Oliver, Esq., Yeovil, do.
*Hayward, John, Esq., Dartford, Kent
*Hayward, W., Esq., Watlington, near Oxford
*Hayward, W., Esq., Hackney-road, Middlesex
Hayward, W. R., Esq., Essex-ct., Temple, Lond.
Haywood, Edwin, Esq., Salford, Worcestershire
Haywood, Francis, Esq., Liverpool [wickshire
Haywood, Mr. P. H., Henley in Arden, War-
*Hazard, Mrs., Gravesend, Kent
Hazell, Mr. James, Newbury, Berks.
*Hazledine, James, Esq., Lymm, Cheshire
Heach, Mr. Thomas, Queenhill, Worcestershire
Heacock, Philip, Esq., Buxton, Derbyshire
Head, George, Esq., Carlisle, Cumberland
*Headington, R. C., Esq., Broad-street-buildings, London
*Headington, W., Esq., Walbrook, do.
Headlam, Rev. John, M. A., Wycliffe, Yorkshire
*Headlam, Thomas, Esq., Aigburth, Liverpool
Headland, E., Esq., Featherstone-build., London
*Headland, Henry, Esq., King's-road, do.
Heal, Mr. A., Old Compton-street, Soho, do.
Heale, Mr. John, Yatton, Somersetshire
Healing, William, Esq., Liverpool
*Heap, John, Esq., Manchester
Hearn, William, Esq., Isle of Wight
Hearon, W. H., Esq., Fulford, Yorkshire
*Heath, B. R., Esq., Trinity coll., Cambridge
Heath, John, Esq., Calne, Wiltshire
Heath, J. B., Esq., Bloomsbury-place, London
*Heath, Matthew, Esq., Furnival's-inn, do.
Heath, T., Esq., Hoxton Town, Middlesex
*Heath, Thomas, Esq., Warwick
*Heathcote, Sir W., Bart., M.P., Hursley, Hants
Heathcote, A. W., Esq., Darley-dale, Derbysh.
*Heathcote, Capt. Gilbert, R. N., Southampton
*Heathcote, G., Esq., New college, Oxford
*Heathcote, J. E., Esq., Trinity coll., Cambridge
Heathcote, John, Esq., Leek, Stafford
*Heathcote, Rev. Thomas, Seend, Wiltshire
*Heathcote, Unwin, Esq., Shephalbury, Herts.
*Heathcote, Unwin, Esq., Upper Harley-street,
Heather, Charles, Esq., Hereford [London
*Heather, Henry, Esq., Haslemere, Surrey
*Heaven, W. H., Esq., Pilton, near Shepton-
*Heaver, John, Esq., Ware, Herts. [Mallet
*Heaver, Michael, Esq., Broxburn, do.
*Heaword, Jos., Esq., Heaton-Mersey, Lancash.
Hebbert, J, Esq., Islington, near Birmingham
Heckford, Rev. J., Somersham, Hunts.
Heddell, Mr. Thomas, Hereford
Hedgeman, Richard, Esq., King-street, Norwich
Hedger, H., Esq., Stone-lodge, Ipswich, Suffolk
Hedges, Henry, Esq., Hayes, Middlesex
*Hedges, John A., Esq., Wallingford, Berks.
Heeles, Mr. Josiah, Ramsey, Isle of Man
*Heginbottom, W., Esq., Hurst-Brook, Lancash.
Helder, William, Esq., Clement's-inn, London
Hellier, Rev. T. Shaw, Lincoln coll., Cambridge
*Hellier, J. S., Esq., Woodhouse, near Wolverhampton
*Hellyer, Mr. W. S., Redbridge, Southampton
*Helps, Thomas, Esq., Treasurer of St. Bartholomew's Hospital, London
*Helyar, William, Esq., East Coker, Somerset
Heming, Rev. J., Kimbolton, Huntingdonshire

Heming, J. P., Esq., Acton-Beauchamp, Worcestershire
*Heming, Richard, Esq., Hillingdon, Middlesex
*Hemington, J., Esq., Trumpington, nr. Cambr.
*Hemingway, Edw., Esq., Bank-street, Leeds
Hemming, R., Esq., Kingsland, Herefordshire
Hemmings, W., Esq., Ledbury, do.
Hemsley, H., Esq., Token-house-yard, London
Henan, J., Esq., Verulam-buildings, do.
*Henderson, Lieut.-Col. George, Southampton
Hendy, Charles M., Esq., Liverpool
*Heneage, G. H. W., Esq., Compton-Bassett, [Wilts.
Henlon and Johnston, Messrs., Dublin
*HENNIKER, The Right Honorable Lord
*Henniker, The Honorable Major
*Henry, A., Esq., Haydon-square, Whitechapel
Hensley, Rev. Charles, Gainsborough
*Henslow, J., Esq., St. Peter's, St. Alban's
*Hensman, Boswell, Esq., Walbrook, London
Hensman, John, Esq., Northampton
*Henson, John, Esq., Bouverie-street, London
*Henty, Robert, Esq., Chichester, Sussex
*Henty, William, Esq., East Lavant, do.
Hepple, R., Esq., Staindrop, Durham
*Heraud, Mr. J. A., Carey-street, London
Herbert, The Honorable Sidney
*Herbert, A., Esq., Stoke-house, near Coventry
Herbert, Mr. D., Hereford
*Herbert, J. M., Esq., St. John's coll., Cambridge
Herbert, John L., Esq., Oriel college, Oxford
Herbert, Mr. J., Hatton-garden, London
*Herbert, Rev. W. A., Eldersfield, Worcestersh.
Herbert, Mr. William, Huntingdon
Herbert, Mr., Reading, Berks.
HEREFORD, The Rt. Rev. Lord Bishop of
*Hereford, R., Esq., Lugwardine, Herefordshire
*Herley, C., Esq., Great Winchester-st., Lond.
*Herley, Mess. C., and Co., do., do.
*Heron, Lieut. General, Moor-hall, Cheshire
*Hertslet, Charles, Esq., Norfolk-st., Strand
*Heselden, Mr. R., Northam, near Southampton
*Hesketh, Mrs., Preston, Lancashire
*Hesketh, P., Esq., Rossall-hall, near Preston
*Hesketh, Rev. William, Liverpool
*Heslop, Thomas D., Esq., Ripley, Yorkshire
*Heslop, W. F., Esq., Manchester
*Hetherington, John, Esq., Barge-yard, London
Hetley, H., Esq., Bulbridge-house, Salisbury
*Hetley, Richard, Esq., Britford, Wiltshire
Hetling, William Ernest, Esq., Bristol
*Heward, Henry, Esq., Waltham-Cross, Essex
*Hewdey, Mr. William, Hanover-place, Leeds
*Hewes, Thomas Cheek, Esq., Manchester
*Hewetson, H., Esq., Cateaton-street, London
*Hewetson, Mr. J., Tottenham-court-road, do.
Hewett, William, Esq., East Ilsley, Berks.
*Hewgill, Rev. Francis, Saundby, Notts.
*Hewitt, Charles, Esq., Norwich
Hewitt, Mr. I., Waltham-Cross, Essex
Hewitt, T. S., Esq., Tokenhouse-yard, London
*Hewitt, W., Esq., Trinity college, Cambridge
*Hewlett, Mr. Alfred, St. Aldate's, Oxford
Hewlett, Rev. J., Abingdon, Berks.
*Hewlett, Mr. Thomas, Harrow, Middlesex
*Hex, Thomas, Esq., Stocklinch, Somersetshire
*Hey, Wm., Esq., M. D., Albion-street, Leeds
*Heydon, Thomas, Esq., jun., Warwick
Heyes, John, Esq., Prescot, Lancashire
*Heyes, Joseph, Esq., Great Lever, near Bolton
Heygate, J., Esq., jun., Hampstead, Middlesex
Heywood, Eliezer, Esq., Brampton, Hunts.
Heyworth, James, Esq., Everton, near Liverpool
*Heyworth, John, Esq., Bacup, Lancashire
*Hiatt, Mr. Richard, Dymock, Gloucestershire
Hibberson, Jas., Esq., Bowden-hall, Derbysh.
*Hibbert, Robert, Esq., Chalfont-lodge, Bucks.
Hibel, Mr. Thomas, Newbury, Berks
*Hick, Benjamin, Esq., Bolton, Lancashire
*Hick, Charles, Esq., York
*Hick, Robert, Esq., Leeds, Yorkshire
*Hick, Samuel, Esq., do., do.
Hickie, Mr. D., Bracondale, Norfolk
Hickie, D. B., Esq., L.L.D., Hawkeshead, Lancashire
*Hicklin, Benjamin, Esq., Wolverhampton
Hickman, Mr. Benjamin, Ludlow, Shropshire
*Hickman, Mr. Charles R., Oxford
*Hickman, Mr. E., King's Caple, Herefordshire
Hickman, Mr. G. R., Tipton, Staffordshire
Hickman, Rev. H., Old Swinford, Worcestersh.
*Hickman, Henry Bacon, Esq., Gainsborough
*Hickman, R., Esq., Shackerley-house, Salop
Hickman, Jos., Esq., Hertingfordbury, Hertford
*Hicks, B. W., Esq., Dursley, Gloucestershire
Hicks, Sir W., Bart., Whitcomb-park, do.
*Hicks, F., Esq., Bartlett's-buildings, London
*Hicks, G. H., Esq., M. D., Baldock, Herts.
Hicks, J., Esq., Liverpool
Hicks, John, jun., Esq., do.
*Hicks, J. K., Esq., Jesus coll., Cambridge
Hicks, P. W. H., Esq., Northampton
Hicks, Mr. William, Sonning, Berks.
*Higford, John, Esq.
*Higgin, John, Esq. Ulverstone, Lancashire
Higgin, John, Esq., Lancaster Castle
*Higgin, John, jun., Esq., Lancaster
*Higgin, R., Esq., Cannon-street, Manchester
*Higginbotham, S., Esq., Macclesfield, Cheshire
Higgins, Mr. C. D., Falcon-st., Fleet-st., Lond.
Higgins, Mr. C., Eastnor, Herefordshire
Higgins, Rev. E., Brasenose college, Oxford
Higgins, J. A., Esq., Ledbury, Herefordshire
Higgins, Samuel, Esq., do., do.
*Higgins, William, Esq., Hay, Brecon
*Higginson, J., Esq., Queen's college, Oxford
Higginson, Mr. W. C., Stockport, Cheshire
Higgott, Thomas, Esq., Uttoxeter, Staffordshire
Higgs, Mr. George, Reading, Berks. [tershire
Higgs, Mr. John, Tardebigg Grange, Worces-
*Higman, Rev. J. P., M. A., F. R. S, Fellow and Tutor of Trinity coll., Cambridge
*Higson, Thomas, Esq., Manchester [cestershire
Hildebrand, Rev. J. B., Melton-Mowbray, Lei-
Hilder, Charles, Esq., Salehurst, Sussex
*Hilder, James, Esq., do., do.
*Hilditch, Tho., Esq., Blackden-hall, Cheshire
*Hildyard, Rev. H. S., B. A., Tutor of St. Peter's college, Cambridge
*Hildyard, T. B., Esq., Flintham-house, Notts.
*Hildyard, Rev. W., M. A., Trinity hall, Camb.
Hilhouse, G., Esq., Coombe-house, near Bristol
HILL, The Right Honorable Lord Arthur
*Hill, Sir Dudley, Knt., K.C.B., Molesey, Surrey
*Hill, The Right Honorable and Hon. W. Noel
*Hill, The Honorable and Reverend R. Noel
*Hill, Sir Robert, K.C.B., Prees, Salop
*Hill, Sir Rowland, Bart., M. P., Hawkeston-hall, Shropshire
*Hill, Charles, Esq., Brasenose college, Oxford
*Hill, C. S., Esq., Sunderland
Hill, Rev. Edward, B. A., Wigan
*Hill, Edward, Esq., Emanuel coll., Cambridge
*Hill, Mr. E., Inner Temple, London
*Hill, Francis, Esq., Wood-st., Cheapside, do.
*Hill, G. W., Esq., Worcester
Hill, J. D., Esq., Trinity college, Oxford
*Hill, Henry, Esq., Wolverhampton
Hill, Rev. John, Oakley, Monmouth
*Hill, Rev. John, Banbury, Oxfordshire
Hill, John, Esq., Milton, Herefordshire
*Hill, John, Esq., Paulton, Somersetshire
*Hill, John, Esq., Ashley-hall, Cheshire
*Hill, Mr. John, Enfield, Middlesex
Hill, Mr. John, Worcester
*Hill, John Moody, Esq., Rood-lane, London
*Hill, Nathaniel, Esq., Drogheda, Ireland
Hill, Philip L., Esq., Wiveliscombe, Somerset.
Hill, Mr. R., Weston super Mare, Somersetshire
Hill, Robert, Esq., Newcastle, Staffordshire
Hill, R. C., Esq., Stallington-hall, do.
Hill, Rev. Thomas, Badgeworth
Hill, Rev. T., Shurdington, Gloucestershire
*Hill, Rev. Thomas, Staunton, Worcestershire
*Hill, Rev. Thomas, Sutton, Herefordshire
Hill, Thomas, Esq., Dymock, Gloucestershire
Hill, Thomas, Esq., Blaenavon, Abergavenny
Hill, Mr. Thomas, Ledbury, Herefordshire
Hill, William, Esq., Hagley, near Hereford
*Hill, Rev. W. H., Newland, Gloucestershire
*Hill, Wm., Esq., Crescent, Salford, Lancashire
Hill & Son, Messrs., Tipton-green, Staffordshire
*Hillary, Sir Wm., Bart., Douglas, Isle of Man
*Hills, Mr. Robert, Maidstone, Kent
*Hills, Walter, Esq., do., do. [shire
Hillworth, W. R., Esq., Langdon, Worcester-
*HILSBOROUGH, The Rt. Hon. the Earl of
*Hilton, Giles, Esq., Faversham, Kent
*Hilton, Henry, Esq., Darwen-lodge, Blackburn
Hilton, Rev. J., Sarre, Isle of Thanet
*Hilton, James, Esq., per Messrs. Longman
Hinckes, J., Esq., F. A. S., Tettenhall, Stafford
Hinckley, Arthur, Esq., Hints-hall, Lichfield
Hind, Rev. John, M. A., Sidney-Sussex coll., Cambridge [Gloucestershire
*Hind, Thomas, Esq., Vollenham Hempstead,
*Hinde, E., Esq., Sunderland
*Hinde, Rev. John, Winwick, near Warrington
*Hinde, Mr. J., Winchester-street, London
*Hinde, W., Esq., Undercroft-hall, Lancashire
*Hindes, and Co., Messrs., Dolphinholme, near Lancaster
*Hindle, Captain W. F., Torkington-lodge, near Stockport, Cheshire
Hindle, John F., Esq., Chorley, Lancashire
*Hindle, John F., jun., Esq., Garstang, do.
Hindley, C., Esq., Berner's-street, London
*Hindley, Charles, Esq., Duckinfield, Cheshire
Hindley, Isaac, Esq., Baldock, Herts.
Hindley, Robert, Esq., Salford, Lancashire
*Hinds, B., Esq., Downshire-hall, Hampstead
*Hinds, T. M., Esq., do., do.
Hinds, Rev. J. T., B. A., Stone, Staffordshire
*Hine, Mr. George, Shrewsbury
*Hines, John, Esq., Durham
*Hinton, Rev. Jas., A. M., St. Aldate's, Oxford
*Hinves, Mr. George, jun., Southampton
*HIPPESLEY, Lady, Stone-Easton-park, Somersetshire
Hippius, C. J., Esq., Finsbury-circus, London
*Hirst, J., Esq., Great Ropus, near Brentwood
Hiscock, Leonard, Esq., Portsmouth
*Hiscock and Sons, Messrs., Newbury, Berks.
Hitch, Mr. Caleb, Ware, Herts.
Hitch, Mr. William Coles, Hertford
*Hitchings, George, Esq., St. Aldate's, Oxford
*Hitchock, S. P., Esq., Manchester
Hoar, Charles, Esq., Maidstone, Kent
Hoare, Sir R. C., Bart., F. R. A. and S. A., Stourhead, Wilts
*Hoare, P. R., Esq., Whatley, Somersetshire
*Hoare, W. H., Esq., St. John's coll., Cambridge
*Hobart, The Honorable and Very Reverend H. L., D. D., Dean of Windsor
Hobart, Henry, Esq., Norwich
*Hobart, Mr. H. C., Greek-st., Soho-sq., London
*Hobbs, Mr. John W., Windsor
Hobbs, Rev. T., Cotlington, near Bridg-water
Hobbs, W. H., Esq., New-inn, London
*Hobden, H. W., Esq., Warrington, Lancashire
Hobhouse, Thos. B., Esq., Balliol coll., Oxford
Hobler, Francis, Esq., Walbrook, London
Hoblyn, Rev. R., Pultney-street, Bath
Hoblyn, Thomas, Esq., Sloane-street, London
Hoblyn, Rev. W., Whatley, Somersetshire
*Hobson, C., Esq., Raymond's-buildings, Lond.
*Hobson, Mr. John, Macclesfield, Cheshire
Hobson, John, Esq., Manchester
*Hobson, Richard, Esq., M. D., Leeds, Yorkshire
Hobson, Rev. W., Ellesmere, Shropshire
Hockley, Joseph, Esq., Guildford, Surrey
Hodd, Mr. Stephen T., Brighton
*Hodding, J. M., Esq., Salisbury, Wiltshire
Hodges, Rev. C. B., M. A., Congleton, Cheshire
*Hodges, Edward, Esq., Reading, Berks.
Hodges, James, Esq., Haywood-lodge
Hodges, Mr. James, Woodside, Herefordshire

*Hodges, R., Esq., Colton, Staffordshire
*Hodges, T. L., Esq., M.P., Hemsted-place, Kent
*Hodgetts, Samuel Wilmot, Esq., Paddington
Hodgkins, Mr. J., Great-Bridge, Tipton, Staf-
Hodgkinson, G., Esq., Newark, Notts. [fordsh.
*Hodgkinson, J., Esq., Stamford-street, London
*Hodgkinson, R., Esq., Atherton, Lancashire
Hodgkinson, R., Esq., Morton Grange, Notts.
*Hodgson, Adam, Esq., Liverpool
*Hodgson, Mr. Brian, Canterbury
Hodgson, Christopher, Esq., Secretary to His Grace the Archbishop of Canterbury, Bounty-office, Westminster
Hodgson, Fred., Esq., Roehampton, Surrey
Hodgson, J., Esq., jun., Queen's coll., Oxford
Hodgson, Jno., Esq., Upper Islington, Liverpool
*Hodgson, Mr. John, Budge-row, Cannon-st.,
Hodgson, J. R., Esq., Manchester [London
Hodgson, Rev. R., Burnley-wood, Lancashire
Hodgson, Rev. T. D., East Woodhay, Hants.
Hodgson, Rev. W., M. A., St. Peter's college, Cambridge
Hodgson, W., Esq., Castle-street, London
*Hodgson, W., Esq., Bishop-Auckland, Durham
Hodgson, W. A., Esq., Queen's college, Oxford
*Hodgson, W. N., Esq., Carlisle
*Hodson, C.T., Esq., Burton on Trent, Stafford-
*Hodson, J., Esq., King's-road, London [shire
*Hodson, Richard, Esq., Ludlow, Shropshire
*Hodson, Samuel, Esq., Peel-street, Manchester
*Hoffman, George H., Esq., Margate, Kent
*Hogarth, D., Esq., Yarmouth, Norfolk
*Hogg, Colonel Adam, Wimbledon, Surrey
*Hoggart, C. L., Esq., Old Broad-st., London
*Hoggart, Robert, Esq., Fenchurch-st., do.
Hoghton, Mr. Benj., Waltham-Abbey, Essex
*Hoghton, H. B., Esq., Bold-hall, Lancashire
Holbert, J., Esq., King's-Arms-yard, London
Holbrook, James, Esq., Monmouth
Holbrook, Thomas, Esq., Ledbury, Herefordsh.
*Holcomb, Rev. G., D. D., West Lake, Notts.
Holden, E. A., Esq., Corpus-Christi coll., Oxford
*Holden, Rev. J. R., Upminster, Essex
Holden, R., Esq., Baker-st., Portman-square,
*Holden, R. G., Esq., Watling-st., do. [London
Holden, W. D., Esq., Aston-lodge, Derbyshire
*Holden, Wm., Esq., Bedford-place, London
*Holder, Rev. C., Thornbury, Gloucestershire
Holder, Mr. John, Egham, Surrey
Holder, Mr. Thomas, Chertsey, do.
Holding, W., Esq., Kingsclere, Hants.
Holditch, Rev. H., M. A., Fellow of Caius coll., Cambridge
Holdsworth, T. H., Esq., Lincoln's-inn, London
*Holdsworth, W., Esq., Bilbrough, Yorkshire
*Holdsworth, Wm., Esq., West-gate, Wakefield
Hole, Mr. Charles, Greenham, Newbury, Berks.
*Holland, Charles, Esq., Liverpool
*Holland, Mr. C. W., Cheltenham
Holland, Mr. Henry, Gray's-inn-lane, London
*Holland, James, Esq., Altrincham, Cheshire
*Holland, John, Esq., Heybrook, Rochdale
Holland, Rev. K., St. Ives, Huntingdonshire
*Holland, Peter, Esq., Knutsford, Cheshire
*Holland, R., Esq., Bolton, Lancashire [shire
Holland, Rev. T. E. M., Stoke-Bliss, Hereford-
*Holland, T.D., Esq., Heighington, Lincolnshire
*Holleday, and Brown, Messrs., Watford, Herts.
Hollest, John, Esq., Farnham, Surrey
Holliday, John E., Esq., Taunton, Somerset.
Hollings, J., Esq., Hill-End, Herefordshire
Hollingshead, B. R., Esq., Liverpool
*Hollingsworth, John, Esq., Ware, Herts.
*Hollingsworth, Thos., Esq., Hayle-place, Kent
*Hollingworth, E., Esq., Port-st., Manchester
*Hollingworth, Capt. R., Hollingworth, Cheshire
Hollins, Henry, Esq., Pleasley, Derbyshire
*Hollis, C., Esq., Upper Stamford-street, London
Hollis, Wm., Esq., Mountain, Monmouthshire
Holloway, Charles, Esq., Hereford
Holloway, Mr. R., Burghfield, Reading, Berks.
*Holman, Henry, Esq., Hurst, Sussex
*Holme, J., Esq., Hudcar, Bury, Lancashire
Holme, Rev. William, Loughborough [ham
*Holmes, Edward, Esq., Mosely, near Birming-
*Holmes, George, Esq., Bury, Lancashire
Holmes, Mr. George, Birmingham
*Holmes, J., Esq., F.A.S., East Retford, Notts.
*Holmes, James, Esq., Montague-st., London
Holmes, James, Esq., Godmanchester, Hunts.
*Holmes, John, Esq., High Bailiff for the Borough of Southwark
Holmes, John P., Esq., Alconbury-hill, Hunts.
Holmes, W., Esq., Lyon's-inn, London
Holmes, Wm., Esq., M.P., Grafton-st., do.
*Holmes, Wm., Esq., Arundel, Sussex
Holmes and Son, Mess. H., Liverpool [Lewes
*Holroyd, J. B., Esq., Barcombe-house, near
*Holroyd, Thomas, Esq., Regent's-park, London
*Holroyde, E., Esq., Manchester
*Holt, George, Esq., Rochdale, Lancashire
*Holt, J., Esq., Bispham-hall, near Wigan, do.
*Holt, John, Esq., Bacup, do.
*Holt, John, jun., Esq., Tottenham, Middlesex
*Holt, Thomas, Esq., Bath
Holt, Thomas, Esq., Liverpool
*Holt, Thomas, Esq., Manchester
Holt, Messrs. T. & J., Aldermanbury, London
Holt, Mr. T. W., Wigton
*Holt, Wm, Esq., Threadneedle-street, London
Holt, Mr. William, Lymm, Cheshire [chester
Holt, Messrs. M. and R., Hulme, near Man-
Holtaway, J. H., Esq., Took's-court, London
*Holworthy, Jas., Esq., Brookfield, Derbyshire
*Holyoake, John, Esq., Bromsgrove
*Homball, James, Esq., Trump-street, King-st., Cheapside
*Homersham, E., Esq., North-place, Kingsland
Homersham, Mr. E., Canterbury, Kent
Homersham, Mr. George, do., do.
Homfray, Rev. John, B. A., F.A.S., Yarmouth
*Homfray, S., Esq., Newport, Monmouthshire
Homewood, Edw., Esq., Sandling, Kent
Hone, J. Terry, Esq., Middle Temple, London
*Hone, Rev. J. F., Tirley, Gloucestershire
Hone, Mr. N. T., Reading, Berks.
*Hone, Mr. William, do., do.
*Honey, Rev. W. E., Baverstock, Wiltshire
*Honywood, P. J., Esq., B.A., Trinity col., Oxford
*Hood, Sir A., Knt., Bart., Glastonbury, Somersetshire
*Hood, T., Esq., West Bromwich, Staffordshire
Hood, Thos., Esq., Winchmore-hill, Middlsx.
Hood, Mr. T., Doctors Commons, London
*Hooker, H. J., Esq., Staples-inn, do.
*Hooks, John W., Esq., Dartford, Kent
Hoole, Mr. J., Addle-street, Aldermanbury,
*Hooman, Geo., Esq., Kidderminster [London
Hooman, James, Esq., do.
Hooper, B., Esq., Essendonbury, Hertfordshire
Hooper, C. J., Esq., Bermondsey, Surrey
Hooper, Edw. J., Esq., Ludgate-hill, London
*Hooper, George, Esq., Putson, Herefordshire
*Hooper, George, Esq., Cottington, Kent
Hooper, Rev. John, Westbury, Wilts.
Hooper, Jno., Esq., M.D., Buntingford, Herts.
*Hooper, Joseph, Esq., North-crescent, Hertford
Hooper, Mrs. M. D. H., Ware, Herts.
*Hooper, Thomas, Esq., Staunton, Worcester
Hooper, Mr. Thomas, Hay, Brecon [London
Hooper, William T., Esq., East India-house,
Hope, Rev. C. S., All Saints, Derby
Hope, Henry P., Esq., per Mr. Lindsell
*Hope, Mr. John, Hay, Brecon
*Hope, Thomas, Esq., Haymarket, London
Hopkins, Rev. A., Clent, Staffordshire
*Hopkins, Carey Bonham, Esq., Crayford, Kent
Hopkins, James, Esq., Arundel, Sussex
Hopkins, Mr. James, Dover-road, London
Hopkins, Thomas, Esq., Boston, Lincolnshire
Hopkins, W., Esq., Dymock, Gloucestershire
*Hopkins, Rev. W. T., Nuffield, Oxfordshire
Hopkins and Arlett, Messrs., Essex-st., London
Hopkinson, George, jun., Esq, Nottingham
*Hopkinson, Mr. L. W., Millbrook, Southampton
*Hopton, John, Esq., Brasenose coll., Oxford
*Hopton, Rev. W., Kemerton-ct., Gloucestersh.
Hopwood, Mr. J. J., Chancery-lane, London
*Hordern, Alexander, Esq., Temple, do.
*Hordern, Rev. James, Oldham, Lancashire
*Hordern, Henry, Esq., Wolverhampton
Hordern, J., Esq., Sardon, Staffordsh. [chester
*Hordern, Rev. P., Cheetham Library, Man-
*Hore, Christopher, Esq., Cambridge
*Hore, Rev. T., B. D., Ham Common, Surrey
Horlock, H., Esq., Magdalene hall, Oxford.
*Horlocke, I. J., Esq., Rock-abbey, Glouces-
*Horn, Mr. H., Maidstone, Kent [tershire
Horn, Rob., Esq., Turnstall-lodge, Sunderland
*Hornby, E., Esq., Burton in Kendal, Westmorland
Hornby, E. G., Esq., Ellel-hall, Lancashire
*Hornby, E. I. O., Esq., Portsmouth
*Hornby, E. O., Esq., Brasenose coll., Oxford
Hornby, Hugh, Esq., Sandown, Lancashire
*Hornby, Rev. Hugh, M. A., Preston, do.
*Hornby, Rev. J. J., Winwick do.
*Hornby, John, Esq., Blackpool, do.
*Hornby, Joseph, Esq., Kirkham, do.
Hornby, T., Esq., St. Swithin's-lane, London
Hornby, Rev. T., M.A., Kirkham, Lancashire
Horncastle, Thomas, Esq., Southwark
Horne, Mr. J., Old Change, Cheapside, Lond.
Horne, John De, Esq., Lexdon, near Colchester
*Horne, S., Esq., King's Caple, Herefordshire
*Horner, J., Esq., Bucklersbury, London
Horner, Mr. Richard, Newbury, Berks.
Horner, Rev. Wm., Kirkdale, near Liverpool
Horner, T. S., Esq., Mell's-park, Somersetshire
*Hornidge, S. G., Clement's-inn Chambers, London [cester
*Hornyold, T. C., Esq., Blackmore-park, Wor-
*Horrocks, G., Esq., Preston, Lancashire
Horrocks, John, Esq., do., do.
*Horrocks, P., Esq., Albany-terrace, Regent's-park, London
*Horrocks, S., jun., Esq., Preston, Lancashire
Horsfall, Charles, Esq., Everton, near Liverpool
Horsfall, J., Esq., Leeds, Yorkshire
*Horton, D., Esq., Ley Iron-works, near Dudley
*Horton, Edward, Esq., Montague-st., London
Horton, Mr. Edward, Paddington-green, do.
*Horton, Mr. Henry, Edmund-st., Birmingham
Horton, Mr. Isaac, West Bromwich, Staffordsh.
Horton, T., Esq., Toll-End, Tipton, do.
Horton, John, Esq., Dover, Kent
Horton, Mr. Joshua, Great Bridge, Staffordshire
*Horton, Messrs. J. T. and John, Birmingham
Horwood, Thomas, Esq., Temple, London
Hosburgh, Capt. Jas., Herne-hill, Camberwell
Hoskins, A., Esq., Lincoln's-inn-fields, London
Hoskins, George, Esq., Liverpool
Hoskins, Mr. G., Slough, Bucks.
*Hoskins, K., Esq., Strickstenny, Herefordshire
*Hoskyns, Sir Hungerford, Bart., Harewood, Herefordshire
Hoskyns, Rev. B., Newton-cottage, Hereford
Hotchkis, John, Esq., Crickhowell
*Hotham, Edwin, Esq., New college, Oxford
Houblon, C. A., Esq., Christ-church coll., Oxford
*Hough, William, Esq., Tranmore, Cheshire
*Hougham, William, Esq., Canterbury, Kent
Houghton, Mr. Dugdale, Birmingham
Houghton, J. R., Esq., Earl-street, London
*Houghton, Richard, Esq., Liverpool
Houghton, T., Esq., Ormskirk, Lancashire
*Houldsworth, Thos., Esq., M. P., Manchester
*Houldsworth, W., Esq., Farnsfield, Notts.
Hoult, John, Esq., Wadsley-bridge, Yorkshire
Houlton, Col. J., Fareby Castle, Durham
Hounsfield, B., Esq., Clough-house, nr. Sheffield
*Houseman, J., Esq. Essex-st., Strand, London
*Housman, W., Esq., Woodchester-house, Glou-
*Hovell, Thomas, Esq., Cambridge [cestershire
*Hovenden, Rev. V., Trinity coll., do.
How, Mr. John, Everton, near Liverpool

* How, William W., Esq., Shrewsbury
Howard, The Honorable W. G.
* Howard, Edward J., Esq., Duke-street, London
* Howard, Geo., Esq., Hemel-Hempstead, Herts.
* Howard, Henry, Esq., Disley, Cheshire
* Howard, John, Esq., Stockport, do.
Howard, John, Esq., Ripon, Yorkshire
Howard, L., Esq., Cannon-street, London
* Howard, P.H., Esq., M.P., Corby-castle, Carlisle
* Howard, Robert, Esq., Sloane-square, London
Howard, T. B., Esq., Norfolk-st., Strand, do.
* Howard, William, Esq., Southampton
* HOWE, The Right Honorable Earl
* Howe, G., Esq., Somerset-house, London
* Howe, Joseph, Esq., Coventry
Howell, Rev. Charles, Alton, Hants.
* Howell, John, Esq., Wickham-place, Kent
Howell, John, Esq., Hatton-garden, London
Howell, S., Esq., Brampton-Abbots, Hereford
Howell, William, Esq., Hereford
Howells, Rev. Edward, College, do.
Howes, Mr. Jasper, Wymondham
Howson, Rev. H., Southwell, Notts.
Howson, Messrs. Edmund, & Sons, Huntingdon
Hoy, W., Esq., Higham-lodge, Suffolk
Hoyle, Mr. G. W., Watling-street, London
Hoyle, Henry, Esq., Hey Haslingden, Lancash.
* Hoyle, James, Esq., Rochdale, do.
* Hoyle, John, Esq., Haslingden, do.
* Hoyle, T., Esq., Mayfield, Manchester
* Hubball, T. M., Esq., Stafford
* Hubbard, George, Esq., Cheadle, Staffordshire
Hubbard, Mr. J., Reading, Berks.
* Hubbard, T., Esq., Trinity college, Cambridge
Hubbersty, J. L., Esq., Lincoln's-inn, London
Hubbersty, P., Esq., Wirksworth, Derbyshire
Hubbertsey, Z., Esq., Burton-street, London
* Huddleston, G., Esq., Gray's-inn-road, do.
Huddlestone, George, Esq., Ulverstone
* Hudson, George, Esq., York
Hudson, J., Esq., St. Swithin's-lane, London
* Hudson, James, Esq., Ware, Herts.
* Hudson, Rev. J., A.M., Kendal, Westmorland
* Hudson, Mr. John, Chichester, Sussex
Hudson, Thomas B., Esq., Old Jewry, London
* Hughes, Edward, Esq., Altrincham, Cheshire
* Hughes, Edw. Ball, Esq., Oatlands, Surrey
* Hughes, Mrs. Ball, do., do.
Hughes, F., Esq., Stafford
Hughes, Rev. H. H., B. D., Fellow and Tutor of St. John's college, Cambridge
* Hughes, Henry, Esq., Basinghall-st., London
* Hughes, Mr. Henry, Monmouth
* Hughes, H. R., Esq., Bache-hall, Chester
Hughes, Rev. John, A.M., Cranford, Middlsx.
* Hughes, J. H., Esq., King-street, Portman-sq.
Hughes, J. H., Esq., Magdalene college, Oxford
Hughes, Rev. Jenkin, B. A., Abergavenny
Hughes, R., Esq., Hadland Dilwyn, Herefordsh.
Hughes, R., Esq., Much-Marcle, do.
Hughes, T., Esq., Newport, Monmouthshire
Hughes, Thomas, Esq., Grosmont, do.
Hughes, Mr. Thomas, Bolton, Lancashire
* Hughes, William, Esq., Bury, do.
Hughes, William, Esq., Southampton [Lond.
Hughes, W. L., Esq., M. P., South Audley-st.,
Hughes, Mr. W., King's Swinford, Staffordshire
Hukes, Rev. H. W., Mitchell-Dean, Glouces-
* Hulke and Son, Messrs., Deal, Kent [tershire
* Hulkes, Thomas W., Esq., Stroud, do.
Hull, Rev. John, M. A., Lancaster
Hull, Samuel, Esq., Uxbridge, Middlesex
* Hulley, Jasper, Esq., One-house, Cheshire
Hulley, Mr. Thomas, Reading, Berks.
Hulls, John, Esq., Gloucester
* Hulls, Thomas, Esq., Corse, Gloucestershire
Hulme, Ardern, Esq., Hampton-Wick, Middlsx.
* Hulme, Rev. George, Shinfield, Berks.
Hulme, Rev. George, Arely, Worcestershire
* Hulme, J., Esq., Ashton upon Mersey, Chesh.
* Hulme, J. H., Esq., Manchester
* Hulme, James, Esq., Bolton, Lancashire

* Hulme, John, Esq., Cannon-street, Manchester
Hulme and Sons, Messrs. Lane-End, Staffordshire
* Hulse, Field Marshal, Sir S., Knt.
Hulse, Edw., Esq., Christ-church coll., Oxford
Hulton, Edward H., Esq., Southampton
* Hulton, J. D., Esq., Trinity coll., Cambridge
* Hulton, John, Esq., Blackley, near Manchester
* Hulton, Wm., Esq., Hulton-park, Lancashire
Hulton, William Adam, Esq., Preston, do.
* Hume, Adolphus Wm., Esq., Reading, Berks.
* Hume, Rev. G., Melksham, Wiltshire
Hume, Rev. J. R., Calne, do.
Hume, Rev. Thomas H., Salisbury
Hume and Co., Messrs., Gt. Titchfield-st., Lond.
* Humfrey, Rev. John, Wroxham, Norfolk
* Humfrey, L. C., Esq., Temple, London
Humfrey, Richard, Esq., Berkeley-sq., Bristol
* Humphreys, Mr. J. B., Southampton
Humphreys, Mr. Richard, Winchester, Hants.
* Humphreys, Rob., Esq., Chippenham, Wilts.
* Humphreys, S. M., Esq., Brasenose coll., Oxford
Humphreys, Mr. W. E., Carmarthen, South Wales
Humphries, John, Esq., Ripon, Yorkshire
Humphries, W., Esq., Broadway, Ludgate-hill,
* Humphrys, George, Esq., Manchester [Lond.
Hundleby, G., Esq., Herne-hill, Camberwell
Hunley, J., Esq., Knightwick, Worcestershire
* Hunloke, James, Esq., Birdholme, Derbyshire
* Hunt, Edward, Esq., Southampton
* Hunt, Mr. George, do.
* Hunt, H., Esq., Lothbury, London
* Hunt, Jackson K., Esq., Lincoln's-inn, do.
Hunt, Mr. James, Oxford
Hunt, James, Esq., Preston, Lancashire
* Hunt, Rowland, Esq., Exeter
Hunt, Mr. R. G., Liverpool
Hunt, T. F., Esq., St. James's-palace, London
* Hunt, Mr. W., New Mills, Derbyshire
* Hunt, W. A., Esq., East India-house, London
Hunt and Son, Messrs., Stourbridge
* Hunter, Sir R., Knt., Brighton, Sussex
* Hunter, Abraham, Esq., Newcastle upon Tyne
* Hunter, C. V., Esq., Kilburne-hall, Derbyshire
Hunter, J., Esq., Dorset-place, London
* Hunter, Jno., Esq., Grosvenor-street, do.
* Hunter, John, Esq., Liverpool [Cheshire
Hunter, Rev. J., B. D., Ashton upon Mersey,
* Hunter, P., Esq., Leatherhead, Surrey
* Hunter, William, Esq., Manchester
Hunter, Mr. W., Brancepeth, Durham
* HUNTINGFIELD, The Right Hon. Lord
* Huntley, G. H., Esq., Howden Villa, Northumberland
Huntley, Rev. J. F., M. A., Kimbolton, Hunts.
Huntley, Rev. R. W., All Souls' college, Oxford
Hurcourt, George, Esq., Chertsey, Surrey
Hurle, John, Esq., Clifton, Bristol
* Hurley, Charles, Esq., Gray's-inn-sq., London
* Hurley and Co., Messrs., Lewes, Sussex
Hurlock, Rev. J. T., D.D., Langham, Essex
* Hurlstone, A. P., Esq., Clement's-inn, London
Hurry, William, jun., Esq., Liverpool
Hurst, William, Esq., Doncaster, Yorkshire
* Hurt, C., jun., Wirksworth, Derbyshire
* Hurt, Francis, Esq., Alderwasley, do.
Husband, Mr. T. W., Long Ashton, Somerset.
* Husenbeth, Rev. F.C., Cossey-hall, near Norwich
* Huskisson, Capt. T., R. N., Fitzroy-sq., Lond.
* Huskisson, T., Esq., Navy Pay Office, do.
* Hussey, E., Esq., Christ-church coll., Oxford
Hussey, James, Esq., Balliol college, do.
Hussey, P., Esq., Wyrley-grove, Staffordshire
* Hutchings, Thomas, Esq.
* Hutchins, E., Esq., Thornbury, Gloucestershire
* Hutchins, Wm., Esq., Keynsham, near Bristol
Hutchinson, The Honorable J. H.
Hutchinson, C., Esq., Bishop-Wearmouth
* Hutchinson, F., Esq., Newcastle upon Tyne
Hutchinson, H.C., Esq., Welham, Notts.
Hutchinson, Henry, Esq., Liverpool
* Hutchinson, Rev. J., M.A., Ashton under Line

Hutchinson, J., Esq., jun., Durham
Hutchinson, James, Esq., Bury, Lancashire
* Hutchinson, John, Esq., do., do.
Hutchinson, S., Esq., Durham
Hutchinson, Stoakly, Esq., Colne, Hunts.
Hutchinson, T., Esq., Bishop's-crt., Herefordsh.
Hutchinson, Mr. T., St. Ives, Huntingdonshire
* Hutchinson, W. H., Esq., Liverpool
Hutchinson, W. K., Esq., Bury, Lancashire
Hutchinson, W. R., Esq., Furnival's-inn, Lond.
Hutchinson, William Thomas, Esq., Sunderland
Hutchinson, Mr. William, Liverpool
* Hutton, Edward, Esq., Burton, Westmorland
Hutton, G. H., Esq., Carlton on Trent, Notts.
* Hutton, H., Esq., Trinity college, Oxford
Hutton, Rev. Jno., Granby, Nottinghamshire
Hutton, Rev. J. Harriman, Stockbridge, Hants.
Hutton, W., Esq., Great Burton, Lincolnshire
* Huyshe, Rev. R., East Coker, Somersetshire
Hyatt, J. F., Esq., Newcastle under Line
* Hyde, George, Esq., Tintwistle-hall, Cheshire
* Hyde, J. B., Esq., Worcester
* Hyde, James, Esq., Dukinfield, Cheshire
* Hyde, John, Esq., Ospringe, Kent
* Hyde, Rev. John, Witney, Oxfordshire
Hyde, Saville J., Esq., Quorndon, Leicestershire
* Hyde, Thomas, Esq., Mayfield, Manchester
* Hyde, William, Esq., Heswall, Cheshire
Hyett, Mr. B., Grafton-street, London

Ibbetson, H., Esq., Doctors Commons, London
Ibbotson, J., Esq., Chapel en le Frith, Derby-
Ibbotsons, Brothers, Messrs., Sheffield [shire
* Ikin, T., Esq., Swinthorpe-house, York
* Ilbert, P. A., Esq., Trinity college, Oxford
* Iliff, Rev. Fred., M. A., Shrewsbury
* Illidge, J., Esq., St. Paul's Churchyard, London
* Illingworth, W., Esq., F.A.S., Gray's-inn-sq., do.
Ilott, Mr. Jno., Benham, near Newbury, Berks.
* Ilott, Thomas, Esq., Bromley, Kent
Impey, W. J., Esq., Inner Temple, London
* Ince, Townsend, Esq., Christleton, Cheshire
* Inderwick, Mr. John, Prince's-street, London
Inett, Mr. Thos., Brockhampton, Herefordshire
Inett, Mr. W., Norton, do.
Ingalton, Mr. William, Eton
Inge, Rev. C., M. A., Rugeley, Staffordshire
* Inge, Wm. T., Esq., Thorpe-hall, near Lichfield
Ingham, Joseph, Esq., York
* Ingilby, Sir W. A., Bart., Ripley-park, Yorksh.
Ingilby, W. A., Esq., M. P., Harrogate, do.
* Ingilby, Miss, Minster-yard, Lincoln
Ingleby, Joseph, Esq., Cheadle, Staffordshire
* Ingledew, Henry, Esq., Newcastle upon Tyne
* Inglis, A. D., Esq., Beckenham-place, Kent
* Inglis, W., Esq., Crown-ct., Philpot-lane, Lond.
Ingram, R. H. W., Esq., Temple, do.
Ingram, Rev. J., D. D., Trinity coll., Oxford
* Ingram, T. W., Esq., Birmingham
Ings, Edward, Esq., Devizes, Wilts.
Inkersole, John, Esq., sen., St. Neots, Hunts.
Inkersole, Mr. Thomas, do., do.
Inman, Richard, Esq., Preston, Lancashire
* Inman, Thomas, Esq., Silverdale, do.
* Innes, Rev. George, Warwick
* Innes, John, Esq., Little Tower-street, London
* Ion, Joseph, Esq., Basinghall-street, do.
Ions, Mr. J. W., Canterbury, Kent
* Ireland, W., Esq., Aldermanbury, London
Ireland, E. L., Esq., Kirk-hall, Derbyshire
* Ireland, Rev. Jno., Nunney, Somerset
Irish Society, The
* Irwin, J. L., Esq., Christ-church coll., Oxford
* Isaacs, E., Esq., St. Mary-Axe, London
* Isaacson, Hawes, Esq., Monmouth
Isherwood, John, Esq., Marple-hall, Cheshire
* Isherwood, R., Esq., Doctors Commons, Lond.
Ivaotts, Mr. James, Guildhall, do.
Ives, William, Esq., Monmouth
* Iveson, James, Esq., Hedon, Yorkshire
* Iveson, J., Esq., Tottenham-park, Marlborough

*Ivimey, J., Esq., Harper-street, London
Izod, Mr. Jas., Turnagain-lane, Cannon-st., do.
Izon, Mr. J. Y., West Bromwich, Staffordshire

*Jackson, C., Esq., Somerset-house, London
Jackson, G., Esq., Bolton, Lancashire
*Jackson, G. V., Esq., Christ's coll., Cambridge
*Jackson, George, Esq., Hertford
*Jackson, George, Esq., Preston, Lancashire
*Jackson, J., Esq., Bury St. Edmund's, Suffolk
*Jackson, Rev. John, M. A., Over, Cheshire
*Jackson, John, Esq., Settle, Yorkshire
Jackson, John, Esq., Ulverstone
*Jackson, John, Esq., Warrington
*Jackson, John J., Esq., Lincroft, Yorkshire
*Jackson, Mr. John, Moor, Cheshire
*Jackson, Jonathan, Esq., Manchester
*Jackson, Joseph, Esq., East Retford, Notts.
*Jackson, Joseph, Esq., Norwich
*Jackson, Peter, Esq., Cogshall-hall, Cheshire
*Jackson, Richard, Esq., Lancaster
*Jackson, R., Esq., Hurst-bank-lodge, Lancash.
Jackson, Captain Samuel, Millbrook, Hants.
*Jackson, S. B., Esq., New-inn, London
*Jackson, T., Esq., Ambleside, Westmorland
Jackson, Thomas, Esq., Ferriby, Yorkshire
*Jackson, T. H., Esq., East Farleigh, Kent
Jackson, T. M., Esq., Lincoln college, Oxford
Jackson, W., Esq., Brighton [Lancashire
*Jackson, William, Esq., Ashton in Mackerfield,
Jackson, W., Esq., Temple, London
Jacombs, J., Esq., Wood-street, Cheapside, do.
*Jacques, W. S., Esq., Clifton, Bristol
*Jadis, H., Esq., Bryanstone-square, London
*Jaffray, Richard, Esq., New Broad-street, do.
Jalland, W. E., Esq., Kingston upon Hull
Jago, R. H., Esq., King-st., Holborn, London
James, Edward, Esq., Uxbridge
James, Mr. F. W., Worcester
*James, H., Esq., Worcester college, Oxford
James, Henry, Esq., Balliol college, do.
James, H. G., Esq., Huntingdon
*James, Hosken, Esq., Truro, Cornwall
James, James, Esq., Aylesbury, Bucks.
*James, James, Esq., Swansea, South Wales
*James, Mr. James, Ross, Herefordshire
James, J., Esq., Bradford-street, Birmingham
*James, J., Esq., St. John's college, Cambridge
James, John, Esq., Houghton-lodge, Hants.
*James, John, Esq., Lombard-st., London
*James, J., Esq., Queen's coll., Oxford
James, John, Esq., Stretton, Herefordshire
*James, John, Esq., Wrington, Somersetshire
*James, John, Esq., Walsall, Staffordshire
James, Mr. John, Camden Town, Middlesex
James, Richard, Esq., Walsall, Staffordshire
*James, Rob., Esq., Glastonbury, Somersetshire
*James, Rev. Thomas, Sallack, Herefordshire
James, Rev. Thomas, Sherborne, Dorsetshire
*James, Thomas, Esq., Wrington, Somersetshire
James, Thomas, Esq., Oriel college, Oxford
James, Mr. Thos., Monnington, Herefordshire
James, Mr. T., Ludlow, Shropshire [fordshire
James, W., jun., Esq., Tupsley-court, Here-
*James, Wm., Esq., Barrack-lodge, near Carlisle
*James, W. C., Esq., Timsbury, Somersetshire
*James, Sir W. J., Bart., Freshford-house, do.
*James, W. R., Esq., Ely-place, London
James, Mr. William, Hereford
*Janaway, W., Esq., Hythe, Kent
Jane, Mr. Wm. H., Newport, Monmouthshire
*Janion, J. S., Esq., Castle-hill-house, Cheshire
*Janion, Richard, Esq., Rock Savage, do.
*Janson, Alfred, Esq., Tottenham, Middlesex
*Jaques, Mr. Edward, Commercial-street, Leeds
Jaques, Mr. John O., Fell-street, London
Jardine, Thomas, Esq., Bolton, Lancashire
*Jarratt, Rev. John, M. A., Stoke, Somersetshire
Jarratt, Rev. Robert, Wellington, do.
*Jarratt, William, Esq., Queen's college, Oxford
*Jarrett, Mrs., Camerton-house, Somersetshire
Jarrett, John, Esq., Marelands, Hants.
*Jarvis, Daniel, Esq., Margate, Kent
Jarvis, Messrs., Lynn, Norfolk
*Jay, Cyrus, Esq., Gray's-inn-place, London
Jay, Thomas, Esq., Hereford
*Jay, Thomas, Esq., Dunsdale, Herefordshire
*Jeakes, Commodore, Lower Halliford, Middlesex
Jeans, Rev. George, Pembroke college, Oxford
Jearrad, Mr. Charles, Adam-st. (East), London
Jeavons, Mr. Jonah, Tipton, Staffordshire
Jefferson, Mr., Douglas, Isle of Man
Jeffrey, Mr. Russell, Basingstoke, Hants.
*Jeffreys, H., Esq., Christ-church coll., Oxford
*Jeffreys, M., Esq., do., do.
*Jeffreys, Samuel, Esq., Sutton, Salop.
Jeffreys, Thomas, Esq., M. D., Liverpool
Jeffreys, Thomas, Esq., do.
Jeffreys, W. E., Esq., Shrewsbury
Jeffries, E. C., Esq., Pembridge, Herefordshire
Jeffries, Thos., Esq., Lyonshall, do.
*Jekyll, Rev. Geo., West Coker, Somersetshire
Jellicoe, Samuel, Esq., Shirley, Southampton
*Jellicoe, W., Esq., Binerthorne-hall, Shropshire
Jemmett, Charles E., Esq., Kingston, Surrey
Jemmett, George Elwick, Esq., Ashford, Kent
*Jemmett, Mr. William, Egham, Surrey
Jenkins, A. H., Esq., Gloucester
Jenkins, Mr. H. C., Brighton
Jenkins, Rev. James, Llanfoist, Monmouthshire
Jenkins, James, Esq., Chepstow, do.
Jenkins, John, Esq., Staines's-mill, Middlesex
Jenkins, John, Esq., Caerleon, Monmouthshire
Jenkins, Mr. J. D., Pillgwenlly, do.
Jenkins, Thomas M., Esq., Ross, Herefordshire
*Jenkins, William, Esq., Barnard's-inn, London
*Jenkins, Mr. Wm., Bradford-st., Birmingham
*Jenkins and Abbott, Messrs., New-inn, London
*Jenks, Miss A. Eliza, Bilston, Staffordshire
Jenks, J., Esq., Bishop's Grendon, Herefordsh.
*Jenks, Thomas, Esq.
Jenks, William, Esq., Horsnett, Herefordshire
*Jenkyn, Rev. James, M. A., St. Alban's
*Jenner, Sir H., Knt., L.L.D., Chiselhurst, Kent
Jenner, Thomas, Esq., Windsor
*Jennett, Mr. William, Gerrard-street, London
*Jennings, Henry, Esq., Leeds
Jennings, Mrs., Elgin-house, Egham, Surrey
*Jennings, John, Esq., Evershot, Dorsetshire
Jennings, J., Esq., Dormington, Herefordshire
*Jennings, John Finch, Esq., Dover
*Jennings, Mr. John, Sittingbourne, Kent
*Jennings, R. W., Esq., Doctors Commons
Jennings, Mr. S., Chalfont St. Peter's, Bucks.
Jennings, Thomas, Esq., Rolstone, Monmouth
*Jervoise, Rev. Sir S. C., Bart., Idsworth-park, Hants
*Jervoise, G. P., Esq., Herriard-house, do.
Jerwood, J., Esq., St. John's coll., Cambridge
*Jesse, John, Esq., Ardwick, near Manchester
Jesson, H., Esq., Trysall, near Wolverhampton
*Jessop, W., Esq., Butterby-hall, Derbyshire
Jeston, Thos. W., Esq., Henley upon Thames
Jesus College Library, Oxford
*Jillard, W. P., Esq., Oakhill-cottage, Somerset
Jinkings, Edward, Esq., Maidstone, Kent
*Jobling and Chambers, Messrs., Bedford-street, Covent-garden, London
*Jodrell F., Esq., Henbury-hall, Cheshire
*Jodrell, F. B., Esq., Christ-church coll., Oxford
*Johnson, Rev. Arthur, Little Baddow, Essex
Johnson, Rev. B. E., M. A., Lymm, Cheshire
*Johnson, Rev. C. T., Enborne, Berks. [shire
Johnson, F. G. G., Esq., Cloud-house, Stafford-
*Johnson, Mr. George, Newcastle upon Tyne
Johnson, Henry, Esq., Shannon-court, Bristol
Johnson, Rev. J., St. Owen-street, Hereford
*Johnson, J., Esq., Cateaton-street, London
Johnson, John, Esq., Doncaster
Johnson, John, Esq., Tarvin, Cheshire
Johnson, Mr. J., Artillery-road, Westminster
Johnson, Mr. John, Norwich
Johnson, Mr. John, Quality-court, London
*Johnson, Mr. J. H., Chesterton, near Cambridge
*Johnson, Mr. Joshua, Lant-street, Borough
Johnson, M. B., Esq., Cheshunt, Herts.
*Johnson, Mrs. Mary, Northwich, Cheshire
*Johnson, P. N., Esq., Hatton-garden, London
*Johnson, Rev. R. P., Ashton upon Mersey,
Johnson, R. W., Esq., Gloucester [Cheshire
*Johnson, Richard, Esq., Bread-street, London
Johnson, Thomas, Esq., Lichfield
Johnson, W., Esq., Hemel-Hempstead, Herts.
*Johnson, William, Esq., Budge-row, London
Johnson, Mr. W., Tibbington Colliery, Stafford
Johnson, Wm., Esq., Stamford-hill, Middlesex
*Johnson, W. F., Esq., Deansgate, Manchester
Johnson, W. C., Esq., Merton college, Oxford
Johnson and Sons, Messrs., Liverpool
*Johnson, Barry, & Harris, Mess., Birmingham
Johnston, Geo., Esq., Barnstaple, Devonshire
*Johnston, Hugh, Esq., Danson-Park, Kent
Johnston, Rev. Thomas, Broughton, Hunts.
Johnston, Rev. T. Bryan, Clutton, Somersetshire
*Johnstone, B. B., Esq., Sallack, Herefordshire
*Johnstone, Sir G. F., Bart., Woodeaton, Oxon
*Johnstone, Mr. J., Southampton-buildgs, Lond.
*Johnstone, W. B., Esq., Provader, Kent
*Joliffe, Sir W. G. H., Bt., M. P., Merstham, Surrey
*Jolliffe, G. E., Esq., M. P., Crawley, Sussex
*Jolliffe, G. H., Esq., Crewkerne, Somersetshire
Jolliffe, J. T., Esq., Ammerdown, do.
*Jones, Mrs. Black Lees, Kingsley, Cheshire
Jones, Alexander, Esq., Usk, Monmouthshire
Jones, Amos, Esq. Ross, Herefordshire
Jones, Rev. B., Gloucester
Jones, Rev. C., Canon-Pion, Herefordshire
Jones, Mr. Charles, Hope-Mansell, do.
*Jones, Colonel, Woolwich, Kent
*Jones, Edmund, Esq., Liverpool
*Jones, E. J., Esq., Rowlstone, Herefordshire
Jones, Mr. E., Longdon, Worcestershire
Jones, Mr. Edward, Fencott, Herefordshire
Jones, Mr. F., Maidstone, Kent
*Jones, F. J. W., Esq., St. John's coll., Camb
*Jones, G., Esq., Birchin-lane, London
*Jones, George, Esq., Birmingham
Jones, George, Esq., Alcester, Warwickshire
Jones, Mr. G., King-street, Old Kent-road
Jones, Rev. H., A. B., Burton on Trent, Staf-
*Jones, H. G., Esq., Gray's-inn, Lond. [fordsh.
*Jones, Rev. J., Hereford
*Jones, Rev. Henry, Northop, Flintshire
Jones, Mr. Henry, Newport, Monmouthshire
*Jones, Mr. Hugh, Basingstoke, Hants.
Jones, Mr. James, Bradford-street, Birmingham
Jones, J., Esq., L. L. D., Islington, Middlesex
Jones, J., Esq., M. P., Carmarthen, S. Wales
*Jones, John, Esq., Manchester
*Jones, J. O., Esq., John-st., Bedford-row, Lond.
*Jones, J., Esq., Tarporley, Cheshire
*Jones, John, Esq., Lincoln's-inn, London
Jones, John, Esq., L. L. D., Islington
Jones, Mr. John, Ware, Herts.
*Jones, Joseph, Esq., Chester
Jones, Joseph, Esq., Measham, Derbyshire
*Jones, Joseph, jun., Esq., Oldham, Lancashire
Jones, Captain, L. P., Weston super Mare, So-
*Jones, Rev. M. W., Ospringe, Kent [mersetshire
*Jones, Major, Wefre-hall, Flintshire
Jones, P., Esq., Keynsham, near Bristol
*Jones, P., Esq., Sugwas, Herefordshire
Jones, R., Esq., Ludlow, Salop
Jones, R., Esq., Clement's-inn, London
*Jones, R., Esq., Morden-lodge, Surrey
Jones, Rich., Esq., Leamington, Warwickshire
Jones, Richard, Esq., Liverpool
*Jones, Richard, Esq., Middlewich, Cheshire
Jones, Mr. Richard, Clement's-inn, London
Jones, Mr. Richard Thomas, Hereford
Jones, Robert, Esq., Liverpool
Jones, Samuel, Esq., London-wall, London
*Jones, Rev. T., Hempstead, Gloucestershire
*Jones, Thomas, Esq., High-street, Southwark
Jones, Thomas, Esq., Ailstone-hill, Herefordsh.

Jones, Thomas, Esq., Plas-grove, Wrexham
Jones, Thos,, Esq., sen., Jesus college, Oxford
Jones, Thos., Esq., do., do.
*Jones, Thomas, Esq., Newcastle upon Tyne
Jones, Thomas, Esq., Warwick
*Jones, Thomas, Esq., Stapleton, near Bristol
Jones, Thomas Herbert, Esq., Abergavenny
*Jones, Thomas W., Esq., Hough, Cheshire
Jones, Rev. William, Monmouth
*Jones, William, Esq., Cholmondeley, Cheshire
*Jones, William, Esq., Crosby-square, London
*Jones, Wm., jun., Esq., Oldham, Lancashire
Jones, W., Esq., Llanarth, Monmouthshire
*Jones, W., Esq., Wadham college, Oxford
*Jones, W. H., Esq., Lincoln's-inn, London
Jones, Mr. W., Canon-bridge, Herefordshire
Jones, Mr. William, Hentland, do.
Jones, Mr. William, Strand, London
Jones, Mr. W. D., Chalfont St. Peter's, Bucks.
Jones, Misses, Wandsworth-road, Surrey
*Jones and Horton, Messrs., Gray's-inn, London
*Jones and Howard, Messrs., Mincing-lane, do.
Jones and Bodman, Mess., Fish-street-hill, do.
Jones, Son, & Foster, Mess., Bilston, Staffordsh.
*Jordan, H., Esq., Lincoln's-inn-fields, London
*Jordan, Rich., Esq., M.D., Hoddesdon, Herts.
*Jordan, Wm., Esq., Somerset-square, Bristol
Josse, Rev. Abbé, Gloucester
*Joule, John, Esq., Stone, Staffordshire
*Jourdain, W. C., Esq., Artillery-place, London
Jowett, S., Esq., Woodhall-Reddish, Lancash.
*Joy, H. H., Esq., Hartham-park, Wiltshire
*Joy, John, Esq., Cheam, Surrey
Joyce, Mr. John, Beckington, Somersetshire
Joyning, Mr. Robert, Enfield, Middlesex
*Juby, John, Esq., Norwich
Judd, J. P., Esq., Trinity college, Cambridge
*Judge, J. B., Esq., Ramsgate, Kent
Judson, John Henry, Esq., Ware, Herts.
Jukes, Mr. G., Hanley-castle, Worcestershire
*Jump, W., Esq., Wisbeach, Cambridgeshire
Jupp, Wm., Esq., Old Broad-street, London

*Kadslake, W. H., Esq., Oriel college, Oxford
Kadwell, Mr. C., Greenwich, Kent
*Katenbeck, Mr. A., Edmonton, Middlesex
Kay, Alexander, Esq., Manchester
Kay, J. R., Esq., Longholme, Lancashire
*Kay, James, Esq., Pendleton, do.
*Kay, James O., Esq., Bury, do.
*Kay, John, Esq., Aldersgate-street, London
*Kay, John, Esq., Bury, Lancashire
*Kay, Robert, Esq., Bolton, do.
*Kay, Robert, Esq., Heywood, do.
*Kay, Samuel, Esq., Ashton under Line
*Kaye, Chas., Esq., Throgmorton-street, London
Keane, E., Esq., Inner Temple-lane, do.
Keane, Captain James, Hereford
*Kearsey, Thomas, Esq., Lothbury, London
*Kearsley, E., Esq., Hindley, Lancashire
*Kearsley, James, Esq., Over Halton, do.
*Kearsley, J. H., Esq., Higher-hall, do.
*Kearsley, Thomas, Esq., Bolton, do.
*Keating, T., Esq., St. Paul's Churchyard, Lon.
Keats, Rev. R., Wiveliscombe, Somersetshire
*Keddell, T., Esq., Sheerness, Kent
Kedgrave, Mark, Esq., Catton, Norfolk
Kedward, John, Westhide, Herefordshire
*Keel, Mr. John, Rickford, Somersetshire
*Keeling, Edward, Esq., Tower-street, London
*Keeling, Rev. W., Pendleton, near Manchester
*Keen, Thomas, Esq., Garlick-hill, London
*Keen, Mr. W., Canterbury, Kent
Keene, Rev. C. E., A. M., Buckland, Surrey
*Keene, Saml. B., Esq., Furnival's-inn, London
*Keene, Wm. Charles, Esq., Lincoln's-inn, do.
*Keenlyside, John, Esq., Newcastle upon Tyne
Keenlyside, T. W., Esq., do.
*Keens, Michael, Esq., Isleworth, Middlesex
*Keep, William A., Esq., Lambeth, Surrey
*Keith, William, Esq., Manchester

Kelham, Robt. K., Esq., Bleasby-hall, Notts.
Kell, William, Esq., Gateshead, Durham
Kelly, P., Esq., L. L. D., Finsbury-sq., London
*Kelsall, H., Esq., Chester
Kelsall, Henry, Esq., Rochdale, Lancashire
*Kelsall, Joseph, Esq., Liverpool
Kelsall, Robert, Esq., Rochdale, Lancashire
Kelsey, F. J., Esq., Salisbury, Wilts.
*Kemp, R. P., Esq., Yarmouth, Norfolk
*Kemp, Thomas Read, Esq., M.P., Brighton
*Kemplay, Rich., Esq., St. John's-place, Leeds
*Kempson, E., Esq., Graiseley-hall, Staffordsh.
*Kempson, Rev. H., Brewood, do.
Kempson, H. C., Esq., Birmingham
*Kempson, Mr. John, do.
Kempson, Mr. P., Islington, near do.
*Kendall, Nicholas, Esq., Pelynt, Cornwall
Kendall, T. G., Esq., Liverpool
*Kendrick, James, Esq., M. D., Warrington
Kenedy, A. G., Esq., M. D., Uttoxeter, Staffordshire
Kennedy, Rev. B. Hall, Head Master of Harrow School, Middlesex [chester
*Kennedy, J., Esq., Ardwick-house, near Manchester
Kennedy, C. S., Esq., Ulverstone, Lancashire
Kennell, J. P., Esq., London University
*Kennett, Matthew, Esq., Dover
*Kennett, J. J., Esq., Eythorn, Kent
Kenrick, A., Esq., jun., West Bromwich
*Kenrick, George C., Esq., Uxbridge
*Kenrick, Rev. Jarvis, Bletchingley, Surrey
*Kensit, J. G., Esq., Skinners'-hall, London
Kent, B. G., Esq., Earl's Croom, Worcester
*Kent, Joseph Henry, Esq., Nantwich, Cheshire
Kent, Samuel, Esq., Upton upon Severn, do.
*Kent, William, Esq., Nantwich, do.
*Kent, W. O., Esq., Stratford on Avon
*Kent, Messrs. T. & G., Falcon-square, London
*Kenward, Thomas, Esq., Battle, Sussex
*Kenworthy, John, Esq., Manchester
KENYON, The Right Honorable Lord
*Kenyon, The Honorable E.
Kenyon, Mrs. Elizabeth, Swinley, Lancashire
Kenyon, Mr. Thomas C., Leeds, Yorkshire
*Ker, Mr. Charles, Canal-street, Manchester
Ker, William, Esq., Liverpool
Kerfoot, T. H., Esq., Bread-street, London
Kerly, Rev. R. W., Grosvenor-place, Bath
Kerr, Henry J. C., Sutton, Herefordshire
*Kerr, W. F., Esq., St. John's coll., Cambridge
Kerrison, Sir E., Bart., M.P., Brome-hall, Suffolk
*Kerrison, Robert Masters, M.D., Esq., New Burlington-street, London
Kerrison, Roger, Esq., Tombland, Norwich
*Kershaw, James, Esq., Whitfield, Derbyshire
*Kershaw, John, Esq., Hurst, do.
Kershaw, John, Esq., Bury, Lancashire
Kershaw, Philip, Esq., Accrington, do.
*Kershaw, Thomas, Esq., Ormskirk, do.
*Kersitman, Major H. G., Taunton, Somerset
*Kesteven, Messrs. J. and J., York-street, Covent-garden, London
Kett, G. S., Esq., Brooke-hall, Norwich
Kewley, Rev. T., St. Anne, Isle of Man
*Kewney, J., Esq., Nottingham
*Key, Mr. Joseph, Lower Brook-street, London
Kibblewhite, J., Esq., Gray's-inn-place, do.
*Kidgell, Thomas, Esq., Pangbourn, Berks.
*Kidman, Mr. J., Linton, Cambridgeshire
*Kidman, Mr. Thomas, do., do.
Kidson, John, Esq., Sunderland
Kilby, Rev. Thomas, Wakefield, Yorkshire
KILCOURSIE, The Right Hon. Lord Visct.
KILMOREY, The Right Hon. the Earl of
Kimber, J., Esq., Red-cross-street, London
Kimberly, Geo., Esq., Emscote, Warwickshire
Kimberly, Mr. Samuel, Tipton, Staffordshire
Kimpton, J. H., Esq., Hertford
*Kinder, Thomas, Esq., St. Alban's
Kinder, Mr. W., John-st., Bedford-row, Lond.
*King, The Honorable Captain J. W., R. N.
*King, The Ven. and Rev. Archdeacon, A.M.

*King, Major, Ashby de la Launde, Lincolnshire
King, A., Esq., Lyon's-inn, London
King, Charles, Esq., Abingdon, Berks.
King, Charles, Esq., Bolton-street, London
*King, Mr. George, Redbridge, Hants.
King, Mr. George, Norwich
*King, H., Esq., Bedford-place, London
*King, J., Esq., Walford-place, Herts.
*King, Rev. J., A. M., Lattimers, Bucks.
King, Rev. James, Henley on Thames
*King, James, Esq., Rochdale, Lancashire
King, Mr. James, Southampton
King, Mr. John, do.
King, Mr. John, Ipswich
*King, Rev. Josh., M. A., Woodchurch, Cheshire
King, Joseph, Esq., Liverpool
King, Mr. J., Birmingham
King, J. B., Esq., Stock Exchange, London
King, Mr. Samuel, Bethel-street, Norwich
King, Thomas, Esq., Redcliffe Parade, Bristol
King, William R., Esq., Serjeant's-inn, London
King, Mr. William, Newton-Stacey, Hants.
King & Lukin, Messrs., Gray's-inn-sq., London
Kinglake, Wm., Esq., Taunton, Somersetshire
*KINGSBOROUGH, The Rt. Hon. Lord Visc.
*King's College Library, Cambridge
Kingsbury, M. B., Esq., Bungay, Suffolk
Kingsbury, Thos., Esq., Bathwick-priory, Bath
Kingsford, Rev. Edward, Newport, near Lincoln
*Kingsford, Edward, Esq., Canterbury
*Kingsford, Henry, Esq., do.
Kingsford, Mr. Sampson, do.
*KINGSLAND, The Rt. Hon. Lord Viscount
*Kingsmill, Rev. Henry, Southampton
*Kingsmill, Henry, Esq., Trinity coll., Oxford
Kingsmill, John, Esq., Lymington, Hants.
*Kingsmill, Wm., Esq., Trinity college, Oxford
*KINGSTON, The Right Honorable the Earl of
*Kingston, Mr. T., St. Alban's
Kingston upon Hull, The Worshipful the Mayor and Corporation of
*Kington, Thomas, Esq., Clifton, Bristol
*Kinleside, Rev. William, Angmering, Sussex
*Kinnear, Mr. Charles, Frith-street, London
*Kinnersley, T., Esq., Clough-hall, Staffordsh.
*KINSALE, The Right Honorable Lord
*Kinsman, J. K., Esq., Essex-street, London
*Kipling, Robert, Esq., Cateaton-street, do.
*Kipling, Mr. William, Poultry, do.
Kippax, G., Esq., Hare-hill, East Retford, Notts.
Kirby, Charles, Esq., Knaresborough
Kirby, Rev. John, A. M., Mayfield, Sussex
*Kirby, J. B., Esq., Inner Temple-lane, London
Kirby, Wm., Esq., Wood-st., Cheapside, do.
*Kirk, W., Esq., Bishop-Wearmouth, Durham
Kirk, Mr. William, Sunderland
*Kirkbank, Rev. J. T., M. A., Dalton, Lancash.
Kirkby, Henry, Esq., Sheffield
Kirke, William, Esq., East Retford, Notts.
Kirkes, Morecroft, Esq., Cartmel, Lancashire
*Kirkland, John, Esq., Roehampton, Surrey
*Kirkman & Rutherford, Mess., Cannon-st., Lon.
Kirkpatrick, Edward, Esq., Southampton
*KIRKWALL, The Right Hon. Lord Viscount
Kitchen, George, Esq., Sheffield, Yorkshire
Kitchen, Mr. Richard, do., do.
*Kitchingham, Mr. J., Crooked-lane, London
Kitson, Rev. Edward, Balliol college, Oxford
Kittmer, Benjamin, Esq., Norwich
*Knapp, H., Esq., Haberdashers'-hall, London
Knatchbull, N. J., Esq., Christ-ch. col., Oxford
Knatchbull, W. F., Esq., Babington, Somerset.
Knight, Charles, Esq., Tavistock-st., London
*Knight, Edward, Esq., Chawton-house, Hants.
*Knight, Edw., Esq., Godmersham-park, Kent
Knight, Edward, Esq., M. D., Stafford
*Knight, H., Esq., Shepton-Mallet, Somerset.
*Knight, James, Esq., Mold, Flintshire
*Knight, James, Esq., Manchester [Surrey
*Knight, Admiral Sir J., K.C.B., Camberwell,
*Knight, John, Esq., Southampton
Knight, John, Esq., Farnham, Surrey

*Knight, Mr. John, Rupert-street, London
*Knight, Joseph, Esq., Verulam-buildings, do.
Knight, Thomas, Esq., Alton, Hants.
*Knight, W., Esq., Goswell-street, London
Knight, Messrs., Winchester
Knight and Co., Messrs. Jno., Farnham, Surrey
Knighton, Sir Wm., Bart., M.D., Charlston, Dorsetshire
*Knighton, W., Esq., Christ-church coll., Oxford
*Knobel, J. F., Esq., Chapel-street, London
*Knobel, W., Esq., Upper Montague-street, do.
Knocker, Edward, Esq., Dover
Knott, Mr. Edward, Easton, Herefordshire
Knott, N., Esq., Lambrook, Somersetshire
*Knott, Saml., Esq., Fairfield, near Manchester
Knowles, Mr. Francis, Lawrence-lane, London
Knowles, George, Esq., Preston, Lancashire
Knowles, Mr. G. B., Snowhill, Birmingham
*Knowles, J., Esq., Bolton, Lancashire
*Knowles, John, Esq., Manchester
*Knowles, J., Esq., Mincing-lane, London
*Knowles, Joshua, Esq., Bury, Lancashire
*Knowles, N., Esq., Bedford-square, London
Knowlton, T., Esq., Darley-dale, Derbyshire
Knox, The Honorable Thomas, M.P.
*Knox, Hen., Esq., Trinity college, Cambridge
Knox, Rev. Thomas, D.D., Tonbridge, Kent
*Knyfton, T. T., Esq., Uphill, Somersetshire
Kough, Thomas Harley, Esq., Shrewsbury
Kruger, Baron De
*Kruger, J., Esq., Nicholas-lane, London
*Kuhff, Henry, Esq., Catherine-hall, Cambridge
*Kynaston, Sir E., Bart., Hardwick-hall, Salop
Kynaston, H., Esq., Christ-church coll., Oxford

*Labouchere, H., Esq., M.P., Hamilton-pl., Lon.
Lace, Miller, and Lace, Messrs., Liverpool
*Lacon, John, E., Esq., Ormsby, Norfolk
La Coste, Messrs. T. and G., Chertsey, Surrey
Lacy, John, Esq., jun., The Close, Salisbury
*Lacy, R., Esq., Clayton-hall, near Ripon
Ladbrooke, Mr. Henry, Norwich
*Ladbrooke, James W., Esq., Reigate, Surrey
Ladbury, S., Esq., Newton, Lancashire
*Lade, J. H., Esq., Boughton-Blean, Kent
*Laidlaw, James, Esq., Trinity college, Oxford
*Laing, David, Esq., F.S.A., Chapel-place, Poultry, London
*Laing, J., Esq., North Shields, Northumberland
*Lainson, Henry, Esq., Bread-street, London
*Lainson, John, Esq., do., do.
*Laird, William, Esq., Birkenhead, Cheshire
Lakin, B., Esq., Whitchurch, Salop.
Lamb, The Honorable George, M.P.
Lamb, H., Esq., Ryton, Newcastle upon Tyne
*Lamb, Rev. J., D.D., Chipping-Warden, Northamptonshire
*Lamb, John F., Esq., Deddington, Oxfordshire
Lamb, Mr. J., Bishop's Hampton, Herefordsh.
*Lamb, Thomas, Esq., Horsham, Sussex
*Lamb, Thomas, Esq., Lancaster
*Lamb, W., Esq., Hay Car, near do.
*Lamb, Wm. Ellis, Esq., Witney, Oxfordshire
*Lambard, W., Esq., Seven-Oaks, Kent
*Lambert, Frank, Esq., Chertsey, Surrey
Lambert, J. F., Esq., Lincoln's-inn, London
Lambert, W. G., Esq., Corpus-Christi col., Oxford
Lambert, Rev. W., Camberwell, Surrey
*Lambert, W., Esq., Woodmanstone, do.
*Lambirth, H., Esq., Writtle, Essex
Lampet, E. B., Esq., Corpus-Christi coll., Camb.
Lamprey, Stephen, Esq., Maidstone
Landon, Saml., Esq., Sunbury-park, Middlesex
Landon, The Very Rev. W., D.D., Worcester college, Oxford
Landor, Rev. R., Birlingham, Worcestershire
Landor, Walter, Esq., Rugeley, Staffordshire
*Lane, Charles, Esq., Montague-street, London
Lane, Mr. George, Hereford
*Lane, J., Esq., Wombourne, Staffordshire
Lane, James, Esq., Grosmont, Monmouthshire
*Lane, James R., Esq., Hereford
Lane, John, Esq., Ledbury, Herefordshire
*Lane, John, Esq., Goldsmiths'-hall, London
*Lane, Joseph, Esq., Stockport, Cheshire
*Lane, Rev. J., Withington, Gloucestershire
*Lane, Richard, Esq., Manchester
*Lane, Robert, Esq., Ryelands, Herefordshire
*Lane, Mr. T., Canon-Pion, do.
*Lane, Theophilus, Esq., Hereford
Langford, Robert, Esq., Gower-street, London
Langham, Sir J., Bart., Cottesbrook, Northamptonshire [London
*Langham, Messrs. J. & S., Bartlett's-buildings,
Langley, C. H., Esq., Wellington, Somerset.
*Langley, H., Esq., Dover, Kent
*Langslow, R., Esq., Essex-court, Temple, Lon.
*Langston, Thomas, Esq., Manchester
Langston, Mr. W., Uxbridge
Langton, Col. Gore, Grosvenor-square, London
*Langton, S. Z., Esq., Bedford-row, do.
*Langworthy, V., Esq., Ilminster, Somersetshire
*Lansdown, J., Esq., Regent's-park, London
LANSDOWNE, The Most Noble the Marquis of
*Lant, George, Esq., Coventry
Lanwarne, Mr. H., Hereford
Lanwarne, Mr. T., Willmaston
*Laporte, Mr. Charles, Petty Cury, Cambridge
*Laprimaudaze, C. J., Esq., St. John's col., Oxford
*Lardner, John H., Esq., Rye, Sussex [ford
*Larkin, Charles, Esq., Rochester, Kent
*Larkin, Rev. W., A. B., Hadham-ford-house,
Larkum, Mr. Jas., Stockport, Cheshire [Herts.
Larratt, Daniel, Esq., Thurlby, Lincolnshire
Lascelles, Mr. G., Brough, Westmorland
*Laslett, William, Esq., Worcester
Latcham, Charles, Esq., Bristol [Surrey
*Laterrierre, Pierre de Sales, Esq., M.D., Tooting,
*Latham, G., Esq., Ashton in Mackerfield, Lancashire
*Latham, Rev. R., M. A., Sandbach, Cheshire
*Latham, R., Esq., King's college, Cambridge
*Latimer, G., Esq., Pembroke college, Oxford
La Touche, P., Esq., Corpus-Christi col., do.
Latouche, Robert, Esq., Bury-street, London
*Latter, Robert Booth, Esq., Bromley, Kent
*Laugharne, Rev. H., Rowington, Warwickshire
Launt, Mr. Anthony, Thames-street, London
*Laurence, Charles, jun., Esq., Battle, Sussex
*Laurence, James, Esq., do., do.
Laurence, Mr. J. T., Digbeth, near Birmingham
Laurence, R. F., Esq., Christ-church col., Oxford
*Laurie, Robert, Esq., Broxbourne, Herts.
*Lautour, J. A., Esq., Hexton-house, do.
Lavender, Mr. S., Manchester
*Laver, T. C., Esq., M.D., Hunter-street, Lond.
*Lavington, Mr. Francis, Twyford, Hants.
Law, Mr. C., Upper Thames-street, London
*Law, Evan, Esq., Horsted-place, Sussex
Law, Rev. Henry, Standon, Herts.
Law, James, Esq., Accrington, Lancashire
*Law, Richard, Esq., Carlisle
*Lawes, J. B., Esq., Rothamsted-house, Herts.
Lawford, Mr. Edward, Leighton, Bedfordshire
Lawford, Edward, Esq., Drapers'-hall, London
Lawley, F., Esq., M.P., Grosvenor-sq., do.
Lawrence, Rev. B., M.A., Darley, Derbyshire
Lawrence, Henry, Esq., Rodney-st., Liverpool
*Lawrence, Isaac, Esq., Watling-street, London
*Lawrence, John, Esq., do., do.
*Lawrence, Thomas, Esq., Salisbury, Wilts.
Lawrence, W., Esq., Whitehall-place, London
*Lawrence, W. R., Esq., Queen's coll., Oxford
*Lawrence, William, Esq., Maldon, Essex
*Lawrence, W. J., Esq., Holborn-court, London
Lawrence, Mr. W., Carey-street, do.
*Lawrie, John, Esq., Adelphi, do.
*Lawrinson, Mr. James, Manchester
Laws, Ralph, Esq., Sunderland
Lawson, Mrs. C., Guildford, Surrey
Lawter, Robert, jun., Esq., Norwich
Lawton, George, Esq., York
*Lawton, William, Esq., Birkenhead, Cheshire
Lax, Rev. Professor, Trinity coll., Cambridge, and St. Ibbs, Hertfordshire
*Laxon, William, Esq., Coventry
Laxton, W., Esq., Watford, Herts.
*Lay, Mr. J., Great Titchfield-street, London
Laycock, Thomas, Esq., Appleton, Yorkshire
*Layton, Mr. Charles, Windsor
Layton, J., Esq., Camden Town, Middlesex
Layton, Rev. W., A.M., Ipswich, Suffolk
Lea, Mr. Joseph, Vow-Church, Hereford
*Leach, Thomas, Esq., Preston, Lancashire
Leach, Walter, Esq., Chilcompton, Somerset.
*Leach, Tweedale & Co., Messrs., London
*Leacroft, Thomas, Esq., Chester
Leacroft, W. S., Esq., Southwell, Notts.
Leadbitter, Robert, Esq., Newcastle upon Tyne
*Leadbitter, W., Esq., do.
Leader, G. P., Esq., Wormwood-street, London
*Leader, J. T., Esq., Christ-church col., Oxford
*Leaf, Henry, Esq., Manchester
*Leaf, W., Esq., jun., Old Change, London
Leake, George, Esq., Mecklenburgh-sq., do.
Lean, James, Esq., Clifton-hill, near Bristol
Lean, Joel, Esq., Fishpond-house, do.
*Leary, D., Esq., Parliament-street, London
*Leather, James, Esq., Beeston-park, Leeds
Leather, J. T., Esq., Sheffield
Leather, Peter, Esq., Liverpool
*Leather, Peter, Esq., Stretton, Cheshire
*Le Blanc, J., Esq., Temple, London
*Leche, John H., Esq., West Kirby, Cheshire
Le Corneu, Rev. J., M.A., Hathersage, Derbysh.
Le Cren, Henry, Esq., Mincing-lane, London
Ledger, George William, Esq., Dover
Ledger, W., Esq., do.
Ledsam, J. F., Esq., Edgbaston, Birmingham
Lee, Mrs. Anne, Wallingford, Berks.
*Lee, Daniel, Esq., Manchester
*Lee, George, Esq., Petworth, Sussex
Lee, J., Esq., Hereford
Lee, J. Martineau, Esq., Norwich
*Lee, James, Esq., East Retford, Notts.
Lee, John, Esq., Wakefield, Yorkshire
Lee, Lee, Esq., Chorley, Lancashire
*Lee, Robert, Esq., Hull
Lee, Mr. S., Bowling-green-lane, Clerkenwell
Lee, W. T., Esq., Heath, Yorkshire
*Lee, Messrs. J. and Co., Hammersmith
*Lee and Hunt, Messrs., Birmingham
*Leech, J., Esq., Chatham-place, London
*Leech, John, Esq., Stalybridge, Lancashire
Leech, Thomas, Esq., Liverpool
Leek, Mr. Richard, Abberley, Worcestershire
*Leeke, F. G. Y., Esq., Yaxley-hall, Suffolk
*Leeming, John, Esq., Manchester
Lees, Edward, Esq., Ashton under Line
*Lees, Miss, Runcorn-hill, Cheshire [Lancashire
*Lees, E., Esq., Wernith-lodge, near Oldham,
*Lees, James, Esq., Manchester
*Lees, James, Esq., Dukinfield, Cheshire
*Lees, James, Esq., Newton, do.
*Lees, James, Runcorn, Esq., Cheshire
*Lees, John, Esq., Padfield-brook, Derbyshire
Lees, John, Esq., Newton-Solney, do.
*Lees, John, Esq., Manchester
Lees, John, Esq., Ashton under Line
*Lees, John F., Esq., Brasenose coll., Oxford
*Lees, Messrs. J. and J., Manchester
*Lees, Robert, Esq., Dukinfield, Cheshire
Lees, William, Esq., Whiston, Lancashire
*Lees, William H., Esq., Gorton, do.
*Lees, William, Esq., Tower of London
*Leeves, William, Esq., Chichester, Sussex
Le Fevre, C. S., Esq., M.P., Heckfield, Hants.
*Le Fevre, Samuel, Esq., Southampton
Le Fevre, Thos. B., Esq., Birmingham
Le Frome, C. S., Esq., Hetchfield, Hants.
*Leger, A. B. St., Esq., Brasenose coll., Oxford
*Leggatt, H., Esq., Adelphi-terrace, London
Legge, The Honorable and Reverend
*Legh, George John, Esq., High Leigh, Cheshire
*Legh, H. C., Esq., Brasenose college, Oxford

*Legh, John, Esq., King's college, Cambridge
Legh, Rev. Peter, Golborn-park, Lancashire
Legh, T., Esq., M. P., Lyme-park, Cheshire
*Legh, William, Esq., Windsor, Berks.
Le Gros, J. S., Esq., Downing col., Cambridge
*Leicester, Peter, Esq., Altrincham, Cheshire
*Leifchild, William, Esq., Finch-lane, London
*Leigh, C., Esq., Stoneleigh-abbey, Warwicksh.
*Leigh, Egerton P., Esq., Langley-place, Bucks.
Leigh, George, Esq., Brasenose college, Oxford
Leigh, Henry Jas., Esq., Taunton, Somerset
*Leigh, James, Esq., Northenden, Cheshire
*Leigh, John, jun., Esq., Liverpool
*Leigh, Joseph, Esq., Belmont, Cheshire
Leigh, J. S., Esq., Liverpool
*Leigh, Peter, Esq., Ashton under Line
*Leigh, Robert, Esq., Taunton, Somersetshire
*Leigh, Richard, Esq., Dartford, Kent
*Leigh, Rev. W., A. M., Bilston, Staffordshire
Leigh, W., Esq., Charlotte-street, Bristol
Leighton, T. K., Esq., Magdalene coll., Oxford
*Leighton, W., Esq., Preston, Lancashire
Leishman and Welsh, Messrs., Liverpool
*Leith, James, Esq., Deal, Kent
Le Marchant, Robert, Esq., Birmingham
*Lemon, J., Esq., Enfield, Middlesex
Lendon, Rev. W. S., B. A., Totteridge, Herts.
*Lennard, Geo. B., Esq., Lincoln's-inn, London
*Lepine, Mr. Charles, Newgate-street, do.
*LESLIE, The Right Honorable Lady Mary
*Lethbridge, Sir T. B., Bart., Sandhill-park, So-
*Lett, Thomas, Esq., Lambeth, Surrey [merset
*Lettsom, William N., Esq., Gray's-inn, London
*Levason and Jones, Messrs., Chester
Levett, N., Esq., Milford, Pembrokeshire
*Levett, T., Esq., Packington-hall, Staffordshire
*Levett, T., Esq., Lichfield
*Levyssolm, E. H., Esq., Manchester
*Lewer, E. N., Esq., Eaton-street, Pimlico
*Lewer, Mr. William H., Duke-st., Westminster
Lewes, Rev. D., Langharne Bodenham, Hereford
Lewin, E. B. H., Esq., St. Peter's col., Cambdg.
*Lewin, R. H., Esq., March, Cambridgeshire
Lewin, Thomas, Esq., Bexley, Kent
Lewington, John, Esq., Maidenhead, Berks.
*Lewis, Miss, Llanddyfnan, Anglesey [London
*Lewis, C., Esq., Stamp Office, Somerset-house,
Lewis, Mr. Charles, Newbury, Berks.
*Lewis, Rev. D., D.D., F.A.S., Twickenham
Lewis, D. B., Esq., Rochester, Kent
*Lewis, Rev. E., Chepstow, Monmouthshire
*Lewis, Edward, Esq., Bryn-Edwin, Cheshire
*Lewis, E. S., Esq., Christ-church coll., Oxford
*Lewis, Rev. F., Home-Lacy, Herefordshire
Lewis, Mr. George, High-street, Shadwell
*Lewis, Rev. J., Ingatestone, Essex
Lewis, J., Esq., Prestbury, Gloucestershire
Lewis, Rev. I., A. M., Long Ashton, Somerset
*Lewis, James, Esq., Clifton, Gloucestershire
Lewis, J., Esq., Hanley-castle, Worcestershire
Lewis, John, Esq., Jesus college, Oxford
Lewis, Mr. J., Ross, Herefordshire
Lewis, Mr. John, High Holborn, London
Lewis, Mr. John, Newport, Monmouthshire
Lewis, Richard, Esq., Llantillio-Grossenny, do.
*Lewis, Mr. S., Regent's-park, London
Lewis, T., Esq., Brinsop, Herefordshire
Lewis, Col. Thomas, St. Pierre, Monmouthshire
Lewis, Thomas Plomer, Esq., Canterbury, Kent
*Lewis, Rev. W., M. A., Abbots Langley, Herts.
Lewis, W. Anthony, Esq., Basingstoke, Hants.
Lewis, Wm. H., Esq., Trinity college, Oxford
*Lewis, W. T., Esq., Ludlow, Shropshire
*Lewtas, Richard, Esq., Manchester
*Ley, James P., Esq., Queen's coll., Cambridge
Ley, J. H., Esq., Cotton-garden, Westminster
LICHFIELD and COVENTRY, The Honor-
able and Right Reverend Lord Bishop of
Lidbetter, George, Esq., Uckfield, Sussex
Liddell, The Honorable Henry T.
Liddell, Charles, Esq., York
*Liddell, George, Esq., Kingston upon Hull

Liddow, J. W., Esq., Hemel-Hempstead, Herts.
*Lidster, John, Esq., Stalybridge, Lancashire
Light, Capt. J. H., Brimfield-cross, Herefordsh.
Light, Mr. Richard, Fletchwood, Eling, Hants.
*Lightfoot, John, Esq., Keswick, Cumberland
*Lightfoot, T., Esq., Old Burlington-st., London
*Lightfoot, Mr. Thomas, Liverpool
Lightoller, T., Esq., Chorley, Lancashire
*Lignum, Edward, Esq., Manchester
Lillington, W., Esq., Elmden-hall, Warwicksh.
*Lilly, John, Esq., Manchester
Lilly, Mr. Joseph, Royston, Herts.
*Lillyman, J., Esq., Dalby-terrace, Islington
Lilwall, Mr. W., Kington, Herefordshire
Lima, Joaquin Je de St., Esq., St. Helen's-
place, London
*LIMERICK, The Right Honorable the Earl of
LINCOLN, The Rt. Reverend Lord Bishop of
Lincoln College Library, Oxford
*Lincoln Library
Lincoln New Library
Lincoln's-inn Library, London
*Lindesay, George, Esq., Durham
*Lindon, W., Esq., Cheetham-hill, Manchester
Lindsay, P., Esq., Liverpool
*Lindsay, William, Esq., do.
Lindsell, T., Esq., St. Ives, Huntingdonshire
Lindsell, William, Esq., Brampton-mills, do.
*Lingard, R. R., Esq., Heaton-Norris, Cheshire
*Lingard, Thomas, Esq., Water-st., Manchester
Lingen, Henry, Esq., The Lodge, Hereford
*Lingham, G. A., Esq., Little St. Thos. Apostle,
Linnecar, E. H., Esq., Aldermanbury [London
Lintall, Daniel, Esq., Caldicot-house, Berks.
Lintall, Thomas, Esq., do., do.
Lippitt, Mr. Henry, Lindridge, Worcestershire
Lipscomb, Mr. Charles, Alton, Hants.
Lipscomb, G., Esq., M.D., Whitchurch, Bucks.
Liptrap, S. D., Esq., Laura-place, Southampton
LISLE, The Right Honorable Lord
Lister, T. H., Esq., Armitage-park, Staffordsh.
*Lister, John, Esq., Blackburn, Lancashire
*Litchfield, Thos., Esq., Twickenham, Middlesex
Litherland, Nathan, Esq., Liverpool
*Little, Archibald, Esq., Shabden-park, Surrey
*Little, William, Esq., Coventry
Littledale, Thomas, Esq., Liverpool [London
*Littleton, E. J., Esq., M.P., Grosvenor-place,
Littlewood, J. W., Esq., Doncaster
Littlewood, Rev. Samuel, Devizes, Wilts.
*Livermore, Mr. M., Bank Chambers, London
LIVERPOOL, The Rt. Honorable the Earl of
Liverpool, The Worshipful the Mayor and Cor-
Liverpool Library [poration of
*Liverpool Select Vestry
*Livesey, John, Esq., Bolton, Lancashire
*Livingston, James, Esq., Manchester
LLANDAFF, The Right Rev. Lord Bishop of
Llewellin, John, Esq., Jesus college, Oxford
*Llord, George, Esq., Acomb, Yorkshire
Lloyd, C., Esq., Christ-church coll., Oxford
*Lloyd, C. W., Esq., Magdalene col., Cambrdg.
*Lloyd, Edmd., Esq., Thornbury, Gloucestersh.
*Lloyd, E. A., Esq., Frederick's-place, London
*Lloyd, Edward J., Esq., Oldfield-hall, Cheshire
*Lloyd, Edward J., Esq., Lincoln's-inn, London
Lloyd, Mr. Enoch, Hanley-castle, Worcestersh.
Lloyd, H.W., Esq., Magdalene coll., Cambdg.
Lloyd, George, Esq., Wellcombe, Warwickshire
Lloyd, John, Esq., Ludlow, Shropshire
Lloyd, John D., Esq., Queen's college, Oxford
*Lloyd, J. P., Esq., Christ-church college, do.
Lloyd, John Pusser, Esq., Southampton
Lloyd, Mr. John W., Hay, Brecon
*Lloyd, Lionel, Esq., Manchester
Lloyd, Llewellin, Esq., Liverpool
*Lloyd, L., Esq., Upper Stamford-street, London
*Lloyd, Rev. Rees, Newchurch, Monmouth
*Lloyd, Rev. Thomas, Hertford
Lloyd, T., Esq., Hanley-castle, Worcestershire
Lloyd, William, Esq., Ludlow, Shropshire
*Lloyd, Mr. William, Hereford

Lloyd, W. Walker, Esq., Birmingham
*Lloyds', The Committee of, London
Loaden, W., jun., Esq., Great James-st., do.
Loch, John, Esq., M. P., Wimbledon, Surrey
*Lock, Henry, Esq., Norwich
Lock, Mr. R. H., Maiden-la., Cheapside, Lond.
*Locke, C., Esq., Millbrook, near Southampton
Locke, F. A. S., Esq., Devizes
*Locke, P. W., Esq., St. John's col., Cambridge
*Locke, Wadham, Esq., Devizes, Wilts.
Locke, W. O., Esq., M. D., F. L. S., Swaffham
Locke, Mr. W. F., Coleford, Gloucestershire
*Locket, William Jeffrey, Esq., Derby
Lockett, Mr. Richard, Hereford
*Lockett, Joseph, Esq., Manchester
*Lockett, Thomas, Esq., do.
*Lockett, Rev. W., B. D., Davenham, Cheshire
*Lockhart, Rev. A., Stone, Bucks.
Lockwood, Rev. J. C., Croydon, Surrey
Lockwood, Rev. F. V., Mersham, Kent
*Lockwood, H. J., Esq., Magdalene coll., Cam-
*Lockwood, William, Esq., York [bridge
*Loder, E., Esq., Great Winchester-st., London
Loder, Mr. John, Woodbridge, Suffolk
Loder, Mr. Rob., Brighton, Sussex [bridge
Lodge, Rev. J., M.A., Magdalene college, Cam-
Lodge, Rev. John, Bosbury, Herefordshire
*Lodge, John, Esq., Lancaster
Lodge, Thomas, Esq., Preston, Lancashire
Logger, S., Esq., Handburres, Herefordshire
*Lomas, G., Esq., Farnworth, Lancashire
*Lomas, Rev. John, Manchester
*Lomas, Thomas, Esq., Strangeways, near do.
Lomax, Charles, Esq., Weobley, Herefordshire
Lomax, James, Esq., jun., Bristol
*Lomax, James, Esq., Wirrall, Cheshire
*Lomax, Mr. James, Stockport, do.
*Lomax, John, Esq., Master of the Grammar
School, Hales-Owen, Shropshire
Lomax, R. G., Esq., Clayton-hall, nr. Blackburn
Lomax, Richard, Esq., Bury, Lancashire
*Lomax, Robert, Esq., Bolton, do.
Lomax, Samuel, Esq., Rochdale, do.
*LONDON, The Right Honorable and Right
Reverend Lord Bishop of
London Assurance Company, Birchin-l., Lond.
*London Institution, Finsbury-circus, do.
*London Institution, City of, Aldersgate-street
*Loney, Joseph, Esq., Macclesfield, Cheshire
*Long, H.G.S., Esq., Upton upon Severn
*Long, Jno., jun., Esq., Coulston-house, Wilts.
*Long, Peter, Esq., Chester
Long, Peter B., Esq., Ipswich, Suffolk
*Long, Walter, Esq., Chalcote-house, Wilts.
Long and Austen, Messrs., Gray's-inn, London
Longden, John R., Esq., Doctors Commons, do.
Longfield, Colonel John, Longueville, Ireland
Longmore, George, Esq., Judd-street, London
*Longmore, Philip, Esq., Hertford
*Longsdon, P., Esq., Ardwick, near Manchester
Longworth, W., Esq., Malvern, Worcestershire
*LONSDALE, The Right Honorable the Earl of
*Lonsdale, Mr. Ralph, Regent-street, London
*Looker, John, Esq., Oxford
*Loraine, R. G., Esq., Lincoln's-inn, London
*Loraine, W., Esq., Lumley-park, Durham
*Lord, Rev. Henry, D.D., Barfreston, Kent
*Lord, Mr. James, Ashton under Line
Lord, Jno., Esq., Bushley-park, Worcestershire
*Lord, John, Esq., Wigan, Lancashire
Lord, Joseph, Esq., Kersley, do.
Losh, Miss, Woodside, Carlisle
Losh, James, Esq., Warrington, Lancashire
Losh, Wilson, and Bell, Messrs., Newcastle
*Loud, G. H., Esq., Buckland, Kent [upon Tyne
*LOUGHBOROUGH, The Right Hon. Lord
*Lousley, Mr. Job, Hampstead Norris, Berks.
*Lovegrove, Joseph, Esq., Horsham, Sussex
Lovegrove, Mr. Robert, Reading, Berks.
*Lovegrove, Thomas, Esq., do., do.
Lovell, E., Esq., Coventry-street, London
*Lovell, Edmund, Esq., Wells, Somersetshire

* Lovell, Edward, Esq., Wells, Somersetshire
Lovell, G., Esq., jun., Rookley-house, Hants.
Loveridge, Mr. J., Ledbury, Herefordshire
Loveridge, Mr. Thomas, Ross, do.
Low, Archibald, Esq., Portsea, Hants.
Low, Mr. William, jun., Speen, Berks.
Lowden, John, Esq., Heigham, Norfolk
Lowe, Francis, Esq., Somersham, Hunts.
* Lowe, George, Esq., Over Whitley, Cheshire
* Lowe, James, Esq., Warrington, Lancashire
* Lowe, John, Esq., Bent-house, Cheshire
* Lowe, John, Esq., Dukinfield, do.
Lowe, J., Esq., Buttas, King's-Pion, Herefordsh.
* Lowe, J., Esq., Liverpool
* Lowe, Mr. J. B., Jermyn-street, London
Lowe, Messrs. J. and W., Temple, do.
Lowe, T. B., Esq., Wolverhampton
* Lowe, William, Esq., Nantwich, Cheshire
Lowe, William, Esq., Nottingham
Lowndes, W., Esq., Congleton, Cheshire
Lowndes, W., Esq., Lawton-house, do.
Lowndes and Gatty, Messrs., London
Lowndes and Robinson, Messrs., Liverpool
Lowne, Mr. Charles, Norwich
Lowrey, John, Esq., North Shields
* Lowry, Richard, Esq., Carlisle
* Lowry, Rev. T., D. D., Crosby-house, do.
Lowten, Thos., Esq., Lansdown-place, London
* Lowther, The Honorable Colonel, M. P.
* Lowther, Launcelot, Esq., Bradford, Wilts.
* Loyd, Edward, Esq., Green-hill, Manchester
Lubbock, W. J., Esq., Leamington, Warwicksh.
Lucas, Bernard, Esq., Hasland, Derbyshire
* Lucas, Joseph, Esq., Hitchin, Herts.
* Lucas, J., Esq., Wymondley, do.
* Lucas, J. R., Esq., Backwell, Somersetshire
Lucas, Mr. J. P., High-street, Birmingham
Lucas, Rev. T., Yarmouth, Norfolk,
* Lucas, William, Esq., Hitchin, Herts.
Lucas and Cook, Messrs., Liverpool [minster
* Lucas, Messrs. W. C. & E., Millbank-st., West-
* Lucombe, Mr. Thomas, Brighton, Sussex
* Lucy, Mr. William, Birmingham
* Ludlow, H. G. G., Esq., Christ's coll., Cambrdg.
Ludlow, W. H., Esq., Seend, Wilts.
Luke, Rev. T., Taunton, Somersetshire
* Lumley, The Honorable Lieut.-Gen. Sir Wm.
Lumley, John, Esq., Hermitage-house, Berks.
* Lumley, J. O., Esq., New-inn, London
Lunn, Rev. Francis, Butleigh, Somersetshire
* Lunnon, William, Esq., Beaconsfield, Bucks.
Lupton, Harry, Esq., Thame, Oxfordshire
Lupton, Rev. Thomas, Garswood, Lancashire
* Lupton and Adamthwaite, Messrs., Salford, do.
Lury, Mrs. W., Bristol
Lushington, C., Esq., Christ-ch. coll., Oxford
Lutener, W., Esq., Newton, Montgomeryshire
* Luttly, B. C., Esq., Dyers'-hall, London
Luttrell, F. F., Esq., Kilve-court, Somersetshire
Luttrell, Rev. A. P., East Quantoxhead, do.
Luttrell, J. F., Esq., M.P., Dunster-castle, do.
* Lutwidge, Charles, Esq., Kingston upon Hull
Luxmore, C., Esq., Red Lion-square, London
* Lyall, George, Esq., New Broad-street, do.
Lyddon, R., Esq., Wellington, Somersetshire
Lyddon, R., Esq., South Petherton, do.
* Lyde, L., Esq., Stone-buildings, Lincoln's-inn,
* Lye, B. L., Esq., Bath [London
* Lye, John B., Esq., M. D., Hereford
* Lyle, Joseph, Esq., St. Columb, Cornwall
* Lyle, Samuel, Esq., St. Austell, do.
* Lynch, X. Y., Esq., Aldermanbury, London
* Lyne, Davie and Co., Messrs., do.
Lynes, Rev. John, Elmley-Lovett, Worcester
* Lynn, G. G., Esq., Keswick, Cumberland
* Lyon, Charles, Esq., Binchester, Durham
* Lyon, G., Esq., Bruch-hall, near Manchester
* Lyon, Joseph, Esq., do.
Lyon, Joseph, Esq., Liverpool
* Lyon, Thomas, Esq., Appleton-hall, Cheshire
* Lysaght, Capt. A., R.N., Campden-place, Bath
* Lyster, Henry, Esq., Ronton-castle, Salop

* Lytham, Miss E., Preston, Lancashire
* Lythgoe, J., Esq., Essex-street, Strand, London
LYTTLETON, The Right Honorable Lord
Lywood, L., Esq., Newton-Stacev, Hants.

Maason, Richard, Esq., Cholstrey, Herefordsh.
* Mabbot, W. C., Esq., Uckfield, Sussex
* Maberly, Joseph, Esq., Bedford-row, London
* Mabson, J., Esq., St. Mary's-sq., Birmingham
* MACCLESFIELD, The Rt. Hon. the Earl of
Macclesfield Library, Cheshire
Macdonald, The Ven. Archdeacon, Salisbury
Macdonogh, Rev. T. M., St. Arrans, Monmouth
Machell, Mr. John, Liverpool
* Machell, J., Esq., Newly-bridge, Lancashire
* Machell, J. P., Esq., Ulverstone, do.
* Machin, H., Esq., Gateford-Hill, Notts.
Machin, William, Esq., Burslem, Staffordshire
Macilwain, George, Esq., Ely-place, London
Mackensey, J., Esq., Maidstone, Kent
Mackenzie, T., Esq., M.D., Newcastle under Line
* Mackeson, J., Esq., Leigh-house, Bradford,
* Mackey, Bryan, Esq., Poultry, London [Wilts.
* Mackey, William H., Esq., Bath
* Mackie, Mrs., Westerham, Kent
Mackie, Mrs. Sarah, Norwich
Mackinnon, W. A., Esq., Hyde-park-pl., Lond.
* Mackmurdo, G., Esq., Broad-street, do.
* Mackmurdo, E., Esq., New Broad-street, do.
Mackreth, Rev. T., B. D., Halton, Lancashire
Mackworth, W. H., Esq., Balliol coll., Oxford
Macpherson, W., Esq., Kent-road, London
Macqueen, Mr. James, Bakewell, Derbyshire
* Madan, G., Esq., Christ-church coll., Oxford
Maddison, Geo., Esq., Jesus coll., Cambridge
Maddison, J., Esq., Green-park-buildgs., Bath
* Maddison, Rev. I. F., West Monkton, Somer-
* Maddock, Finchett, Esq., Chester [setshire
* Maddy, Rev. Benjamin, B. A., Shrewsbury
* Maddy, Edwin, Esq., Gloucester
* Mader, James, Esq., Bacup, Lancashire
Madox, James F., Esq., Austin-friars, London
Maffey, Mr. J., East-street, Southampton
Magdalene College Library, Oxford
Magenis, R., Esq., Grosvenor-place, London
Mahony, J. M., Esq., Quality-court, do.
* Mahony, Mr. J. M., Red Lion-square, do.
Mailes, P., Esq., Woolhope, Herefordshire
* Main, R., Esq., Picket-st., Temple-bar, Lond.
* Mainwaring, Sir H.M., Bart., Over Peover-hall, Cheshire
Mainwaring, Rev. A., Barrow, Suffolk
Mainwaring, C., Esq., Whitmore-hall, Staffords.
* Mainwaring, Chas. K., Esq., Otley-park, Salop
Mainwaring, Rev. J., Bromborough-park, Ches-
Mainwaring, Mr. William, Dudley [ter
Maister, Major General
* Maitland, E. F., Esq., Bryanstone-sq., London
Maitland, E. P. R., Esq., do., do.
Maitland, Rev. S. R., Gloucester Spa
Majendie, Rev. G., Magdalene college, Oxford
Majendie, Rev. Henry, Speen, Berks.
* Major, David B., Esq., Canterbury
* Major, Thomas, Esq., Hungerford
Makalien, Mr. Alfred, Strangeways, Manchester
Malbon, Jas., Esq., East India-house, London
* Malborn, John, Esq., Walton, Cheshire
* Malcolm, Neill, Esq., Bexley, Kent
* Malden, Mr. I., Bear-st., Leicester-sq., London
Malden, J., Esq., M. D., Worcester
* Maley, Richard, Esq., Bicester, Oxfordshire
* Malkin, Robert, Esq., Chesterfield, Derbyshire
Mallaby, Joseph, Esq., Liverpool
* Mallalieu, Mr. John, Manchester
* Mallett, George, Esq., Bolton, Lancashire
* Malley, Edward, Esq., Warrington, do.
Mallison, Rev. R., Arkholme, do.
* MALMESBURY, The Right Hon. the Earl of
Malpas, Charles, Esq., Bilton, Warwickshire
* Maltby, Rev. E., D.D., Lincoln's-inn, London
* Maltby, Thomas, Esq., Golding, Notts.

Maltby, Rev. W., B. A., Pleasley, Derbyshire
Man, C., Esq., Thames-street, London
Man, James, Esq., Brick-hill, do.
* Man, Mr. John, Lancaster
Manbry, William, Esq., Queen's coll., Oxford
Manby, Capt. R. N., Yarmouth, Norfolk
* Manby, Rev. J., A. M., Lancaster
Manchester Fire and Life Assurance Company
* Manchester, Overseer's Office
Manchester Subscription Library
* Manclarke, R. B., Esq., Ashbourn, Derbyshire
* Mangles, Mrs. James, Woodbridge, Surrey
Mangles, John, Esq., Circus, Bath
* Mangles, Mr. P., Guildford, Surrey
* Manifold, Joseph, Esq., Kingsley, Cheshire
Manley, I. S., Esq., Thickbroom, near Lichfield
* Manley, W. E., Esq., Tyldesley, Lancashire
* Mann, Charles, Esq., Aldgate High-st., Lond.
* Mann, James, Esq., Mile-End, do.
* Mann, Thomas, Esq., Andover, Hants.
* Mann, Rev. W. H. G., M. A., Bowden, Chesh.
Mann, William, Esq., Larkfield, Lancashire
* Mann, William, Esq., Liverpool
Manners, Mr. C. W., Bath, Somersetshire
* Manning, A., Esq., Dedham, Essex
* Manning, A, Esq., Hertford-street, London
* Manning, John, Esq., Dyer's-buildings, do.
* Mansfield, I., Esq., John-st., Bedford-row, do.
Mant and Son, Messrs., Winchester
* Mantell, Sir Thomas, Knt., Dover
Manton, Rev. H., Great Ponton, Lincolnshire
Manton, Mr. John, Spittlegate, do.
Marchant, Mr. John, Ware, Hertfordshire
Marcon, George R., Esq., Swaffham, Norfolk
* Mare, M., Esq., Hatherton, Cheshire
Mares, John, Esq., Maidstone, Kent
Marfell, Mr. T., Weston under Penyard
* Margerison, E., Esq., Burnley, Lancashire
* Margerison, T., Esq., do., do.
Margetts, Messrs., Huntingdon
* Markham, Wm., Esq., Becca-hall, near Leeds
Markham, Mr. William, Enfield, Middlesex
* Markland, W., Esq., Devonshire-sq., London
MARLBOROUGH, His Grace the Duke of
Marmaduke, The Honorable E.
* Marriage, Joseph, Esq., Chelmsford
* Marriage, Joseph, jun., Esq., do.
* Marriage, Thomas, jun., Esq., do.
* Marriner, Mr. John, Cheapside, London
Marriott, H., Esq., Marple, Cheshire
* Marriott, Major-Gen., Avonbank, Worcestersh.
Marriott, Charl s, Esq., Sellersbrook
* Marriott, Rev. G., A. B., Farnworth, Lancash.
Marriott, Rev. W. M. Smith, Horsmonden, Kent
* Marris, Francis, Esq., Manchester
* Marsden, —, Esq., Guildford-st., London
* Marsden, W., Esq., Thavies-inn, do.
Marsh, Rev. G. P., Boughton-Blean, Kent
Marsh, H. C., Esq., St. John's coll., Cambrid.
Marsh, J. R., Esq., Golden-hill, Staffordshire
Marsh, Mr. J., Chesterfield, Derbyshire
Marsh, Mr. Jos., Wood-st., Cheapside, London
* Marsh, Mrs. S., Lloyd-house, Staffordshire
* Marsh, Samuel C., Esq., Norwich
Marsh, T., Esq., Coleford, Gloucestershire
* Marsh and Swann, Messrs., Cambridge
* Marshall, B. A., Esq., St. Peter's college, do.
Marshall, Mr. F., Leamington, Warwickshire
Marshall, H., Esq., Godalming, Surrey
* Marshall, Mr. Isaac, Bradford-st., Birmingham
Marshall, J., Esq., Harrogate, Yorkshire
* Marshall, John, Esq., Hallstead, Cumberland
Marshall, John, Esq., Liverpool
* Marshall, John, Esq., Northwich, Cheshire
* Marshall, John, Esq., jun., Headingley, Leeds
* Marshall, John, Esq., Wallingford, Berks.
Marshall, Mr. John, Watling-street, London
Marshall, M., Esq., Chew-Magna, Somerset.
Marshall, P. B., Esq., Shepton-Mallet, do.
* Marshall, Richard, Esq., Wray, Lancashire
Marshall, Mr. Sam., Newport, Monmouthshire
Marshall, T. H., Esq., Leeds

*Marshall, William, Esq., Preston, Lancashire
Marsham, The Right Hon. and Rev. D. D.
*Marshe, Rev. J. B., Preston, Lancashire
*Marsland, G., Esq., Brasenose coll., Oxford
*Marsland, Thomas, Esq., Stockport, Cheshire
Marsland, Mr. William, Baguley-hall, do.
Marston, Robert, Esq., Norwich
*Marten, Lieut. Col., Stratford-place, London
*Martin, Rev. C. H., Maismore, near Gloucester
Martin, Charles, Esq., Vintners'-hall, London
Martin, Downs, Esq., Godmanchester, Hunts.
Martin, Edward, Esq., Brampton-lodge, do.
*Martin, G., Esq., Birchwood-house, Surrey
*Martin, G. A., Esq., Waltham-Cross, Hertford
*Martin, Sir Henry W., Bart., Lockinge, Berks.
*Martin, I. A., Esq., Sidbrook, Somersetshire
Martin, J. J., Esq., Upton upon Severn
*Martin, Rev. J., Bunbury, Cheshire
Martin, Mr. John, Wistow, Hunts.
Martin, John W., Esq., Twining, Gloucestersh.
Martin, M., Esq., Holborn court, London
*Martin, Nathaniel, Esq., Leman-street, do.
Martin, R., Esq., Weston under Penyard
*Martin, T., Esq., Horsham, Sussex
*Martin, Thos., Esq., Bradford-st., Birmingham
Martin, T., Esq., Knapton's-green, Herefordsh.
Martin, William, Esq., Lord Chamberlain's-Office, St. James's, London
Martin, W. B., Esq., Hickling, Notts.
*Martindale, J., Esq., Chester le Street, Durham
Martindale, R., Esq., Temple, London [shire
*Martland, R., Esq., M. D., Blackburn, Lanca-
Martyn, Mr. Edward, Taunton, Somersetshire
Martyn, Rev. Francis, Walsall, Staffordshire
*Martyn, Richd. W., Esq., Somerton, Somerset.
Marwood, Edward, Esq., Liverpool
Mash, J. B., Esq., Lord Chamberlain's-office, St. James's, London
*Maskill, Mr. R. S., Basinghall-street, do.
Maslen, Rev. C., Hertford
*Mason, Mr. Edward, Maidstone, Kent
*Mason, F., Esq., Penkridge, Staffordshire
*Mason, George, Esq., Broughton, Lancashire
*Mason, Rev. George, Cuckney, Notts.
Mason, Horatio, Esq., Calver, Derbyshire
*Mason, H. W., Esq., Amersham, Bucks.
*Mason, J., Esq., Bilston, Staffordshire
Mason, J., Esq., Spring-grove, near Birmingham
Mason, Mr. John, Bosbury, Herefordshire
*Mason, Mr. John, Cippenham, Bucks.
Mason, Mr. R. K., Reading, Berks.
*Mason, Thomas, Esq., Lancaster
Mason, Thomas, Esq., Stratford on Avon
Mason, Thomas, Esq., Walsall, Staffordshire
*Mason, Mr. T., Farringdon-street, London
*Mason, William, Esq., Cuckney, Notts.
Massey, Lieut. Colonel, Hatfield Manor, York
*Massey, John, Esq., Burnley, Lancashire
*Massey, Jos., jun., Esq., Greenhill-house, do.
*Massey, Richard, Esq., Moston-hall, Cheshire
Massey, Thomas George, Esq., Liverpool
Massey, Thomas H., Esq., Newark, Notts.
*Massingberd, Mrs. C., Minster-yard, Lincoln
Massingham, Mr. J., Guildford, Surrey
Masterman, H., Esq., Millbrook, Southampton
*Masterman, Wm., Esq., Nicholas-lane, Lond.
*Masterman and Stonehouse, Messrs., Newport, Monmouthshire
*Masters, John, Esq., Berkeley-square, Bristol
Masters, John S., Esq., Greenwich, Kent
Masters, Mr. John H., Canterbury
Mather, John, Esq., Liverpool
*Mather, Mr. Thomas, jun., Manchester
*Mathew, Nathaniel, Esq., Tottenham, Middlsx.
Mathews, Mr. W. Franks, Westminster
Mathews, W. H., Esq., King's Charlton, Gloucestershire
Mathews, Mr. W., Ploville, Herefordshire
*Mathias, J., Esq., Brasenose college, Oxford
*Mathison, G. F., Esq., Royal Mint, London
*Matley, R., Esq., Mottram, Cheshire
*Matson, Mr. J., St. Margaret at Cliffe, Kent
*Matson, John, Esq., Martin's-lane, London
*Matthews, David, Esq., Brampton, Cumberland
Matthews, J., Esq., Much-Marcle, Herefodsh.
Matthews, Mr. James, Biddlestone, do.
*Matthews, John, Esq., Gravesend, Kent
*Matthews, John, Esq., Hungerford, Berks.
Matthews, P., Esq., Burton Linton, Herefordsh.
Matthews, Richard, Esq., Bircher, do.
*Matthews, S., Esq., Enfield, Middlesex
Matthie, Rev. Hugh, Chaseley, Worcester
*Maude, F., Esq., Highfield-hall, Yorkshire
*Maude, Jacob, Esq., Selaby-hall, Durham
Maude, Joseph, Esq., Queen's college, Oxford
*Maude, W., Esq., Langham-hall, nr. Colchester
*Maudsley, Henry, Esq., Lambeth, Surrey
*Maugham, Mr. G., Ramsbottom, Lancashire
Maule, George Frederick, Esq., Huntingdon
Maule, John, Esq., do.
*Maulkin, Robert, Esq., Bury St. Edmunds
Maullin and Co., Messrs., Birmingham
Maund, Mr. G., Pencombe, Herefordshire
Maunsell, P., Esq., Thorpe-Malsor, Northamp-
*Maury, William, Esq., Liverpool [ton
Mawdesley, Rev. T., M. A., Chelford, Cheshire
Mawson, George, Esq., East Ilsley, Berks.
*Maxfield, Capt. W., Sunbury, Middlesex
Maxwell, Archibald, Esq., Liverpool
Maxwell, J. G., Esq., Hartford, Hunts.
May, Mr. B. W., Duke-st., Grosvenor-sq., Lon.
May, Charles, Esq., Limehouse, Middlesex
May, George, Esq., Reading, Berks.
May, James, Esq., do., do.
May, Mr. John, Birmingham
May, T., Esq., L. L. D., Enfield, Middlesex
*May, Thomas, Esq., Basingstoke, Hants.
*May, W. B., Esq., Hadlow-court-castle, Kent
May, Mr. W. H., George-st., Mansion-house,
May, W. J., Esq., Easthorpe, Notts. [London
May, Mr. William, Burghfield, Berks.
Maybrey, J., Esq., Willersley-court, Herefordsh.
Mayer, Thomas, Esq., Newcastle, Staffordshire
*Mayhew, Thomas, Esq., Saxmundham
*Maynard, Edward G., Esq., Chesterfield
*Maynard, F. H., Esq., Durham
Mayne, Colonel W., Caversham, Berks.
Mayne, F. T., Esq., Telfont-house, Wilts.
Mayne, H. G., Esq., Camberwell, Surrey
*Mayo, Mr. T., Twickenham, Middlesex
*Mayor, Geo., Esq., Little Distaff-lane, London
Mayos, Walter, Esq., Llangarran, Herefordsh.
Maze, Peter, Esq., Rownham-lodge, Bristol
Mc Doughall, A., Esq., Parliament-st., London
*Mead, E., Esq., Hemel-Hempstead, Herts.
*Meade, Lieut.-Gen. R., Eastham-hall, Norfolk
*Meadows, D. R., Esq., Witnesham, Suffolk
*Meadows, Rev. Philip, Great Bealings, do.
*Meares, Robert, Esq., Frome, Somersetshire
*Mears, Mr. Thomas, Whitechapel, London
*Measure, John, Esq., Lincoln's-inn, do.
Mecey, Mr. J., Southampton
*Meddowcroft, W., Esq., Gray's-inn, London
*Mee, J., Esq., East Retford, Notts.
*Meek, James, Esq., Ilfracombe, Devonshire
Meek, Mr. Joseph, Ross, Herefordshire
*Meeke, Wm. B., Esq., Broom, Staffordshire
*Meetherke, Adolphus, Esq., Julians, Herts.
*Meigh, Charles, Esq., Hanley, Staffordshire
*Meigh, Job, Esq., Bank-house, do.
Meiklam, J., Esq., Corpus-Christi coll., Oxford
*Mellard, Rev. W., M. A., Caddington, Beds.
Meller, T. W., Esq., Trinity coll., Cambridge
Mellersh, Wm., Esq., St. John's coll., do.
*Mellor, Edwin, Esq., Ashton under Line
Mellors and Russell, Messrs., Liverpool
*Melly, A., Esq., do.
*Melmoth, J., Esq., Sherborne, Dorsetshire
MELVILLE, The Right Hon. Lord Viscount
*Melville, D., Esq., Wood-st., Cheapside, Lond.
*Mercer, Mrs. Elizabeth, East Farleigh, Kent
*Mercer, Messrs. John and Thomas, Maidstone
*Mercer, J., Esq., Chorlton-lodge, Cheshire
*Mercer, Nicholas, Esq., Henley upon Thames
Mercer, Mr. S., Hyde, near Stockport, Cheshire
Mercer, Samuel, Esq., East Farleigh, Kent
*Mercer, Capt. W., R. N., Ross, Herefordshire
*Mere, A. De la, Esq., Caius coll., Cambridge
*Meredith, J., Esq., Tattenhall, Cheshire
*Meredith, Jas. B., Esq., Gray's-inn, London
*Meredith, John, Esq., Old-square, Birmingham
Meredith, Mr. John, Kington, Herefordshire
*Meredith, Michael, Esq., Liverpool-st., London
Merivale, H., Esq., Trinity college, Oxford
Merrick, George, Esq., Clifton, near Bristol
*Merrick, T., Esq., Denham-lodge, Middlesex
*Merrifield, G., Esq., Ely-place, London
Merriman, Rob., Esq., Avenbury, Herefordshire
*Merriman, S., Esq., M. D., Brook-st., London
Merriman, Thomas, Esq., Marlborough, Wilts.
*Merritt, Miss, Portsmouth
*Merry, Anthy., Esq., Dedham, Essex
*Merry, Mr. Robert, Norwich
*Merry, Thomas, Esq., Bolton, Lancashire
*Merry, W., Esq., Wood-st., Cheapside, Lond.
Messiter, G., Esq., Frome, Somersetshire
*Messiter, G., Esq., Wincanton, do.
Mesure, Mr. Lemon, High Holborn, London
Metcalfe, C. J., Esq., Roxton-house, Bedford
Metcalfe, G., Esq., Gainsborough, Lincolnsh.
Methuen, Rev. T. A., Allcannings, nr. Devizes
Metropolitan Police, The Commissioners of the
*Meux, Henry, Esq., Theobald's-park, Herts.
*Meyler, Rev. T., Marlborough, Wilts.
*Meynell, G., Esq., Meynell-Langley, Derby
*Meynell, George, Esq., York [shire
Meynell, H. C., Esq., Hoarcross-hall, Stafford-
Meyrick, T., Esq., High-wood, Herefordshire
*Meyrick, William, Esq., Red Lion-sq., London
*Michael, Mr. Joseph, M. C., Stamford
*Michaud, L., Esq., Brighton, Sussex
Michell, Edward, Esq., Chippenham, Wilts.
Michell, J. C., Esq., Queen's-square, London
*Micklam, Mr. James, Wells-st., Oxford-st., do.
*Middlemore, Messrs. R. and Son, Birmingham
*MIDDLETON, The Right Honorable Lord
Middleton, Sir W. F., Bart., Crowfield-hall, Suff.
Middleton, C. S., Esq., Everton, Lancashire
*Middleton, M. M., Esq., Leam, Derbyshire
*Midgley, Messrs. W. & Son, Rochdale, Lancash.
*MIDLETON, The Right Hon. Lord Viscount
Milbank, Sir J. P., Bart., Millbrook, Southampton
*Milburn, Alexander, Esq., Millman-st., London
Miles, John, Esq., North-end, Hampstead
*Miles, John, Esq., Watford, Herts.
Miles, L., Esq., Queen's college, Oxford
*Miles, P. J., Esq., Leigh-court, near Bristol
*Miles, William, Esq., Clifton, do.
*Military, Royal, College, Sandhurst
*Miller, Miss A., Pennoxston-house, Herefordsh.
Miller, George, Esq., Farnham, Surrey
*Miller, Henry, Esq., Frome, Somersetshire
Miller, Henry, Esq., Norwich
Miller, Mr. Henry, King's Caple, Herefordsh.
Miller, Mr. J., Canterbury
*Miller, Miss, Froyle, near Alton, Hants.
*Miller, James, Esq., New-inn, London
*Miller, John, Esq., Enfield, Middlesex
*Miller, John, Esq., Clifton, Gloucestershire
Miller, Mr. John, Pall-Mall, London
Miller, Mr. John, Chatham, Kent
*Miller, J. T., Esq., New Bridge-street, London
Miller, Rev. J., Durham
Miller, Rev. M. H., Maidstone, Kent
Miller, Rev. Robert, D. D., Dedham, Essex
*Miller, R., Esq., York-st., Portman-sq., Lond.
Miller, William, Esq., Preston, Lancashire
Miller, W. E., Esq., Castle-Cary, Somerset
Miller, Mr. Wm., Speen, near Newbury, Berks.
Miller, Messrs. J. & Co., Wood-st., Cheapside
Millers, Rev. G., Ely, Cambridgeshire
Millican, Mr. Joseph, Lymm, Cheshire
*Millikin & Son, Messrs. R., Dublin . . 2 Copies
*Millington, John, Esq., Doughty-street, London
*Millington, W. M., Esq., Manchester
Millner, Rev. William, Bristol

Mills, Lieut.-Col., Wilmington, Durham
*Mills, Francis B., Esq., Bicester, Oxfordshire
*Mills, John, Esq., Stratford on Avon
*Mills, John, Esq., Bistern, Ringwood, Hants.
Mills, J. F., Esq., Lexdon-park, nr. Colchester
Mills, Miss, Stowe-hill, near Lichfield
Mills, Richard, Esq., Eltham, Kent
Mills, Rev. Thomas, Stutton, Suffolk
*Mills, Thos. M., Esq., Taunton, Somersetshire
*Mills, Mr. Thomas, sen., Windsor
Mills, Mr. William, Egham, Surrey
*Mills and Co., Mess., Paradise-st., Birmingham
*Millward, Rev. James, Solihull, Warwickshire
*Milne, Jas., Esq., High Crompton, Lancashire
*Milne, Mr. John, Greenfield Shaw, do.
*Milne, Joshua, Esq., High Crompton, do.
*Milner, C., Esq., Preston-hall, Aylesford, Kent
Milner, Mr. Henry, Kington, Herefordshire
*Milner and Sons, Messrs. J., Manchester
*Milner, Thos., Esq., Strangeways, do.
Milnes, H., Esq., Leominster, Herefordshire
Milnes, James, Esq., Ashover, Derbyshire
Milnes, William, Esq., Stubbinedge-hall, do.
Milsum, Mr. James, Wantage, Berks.
*Milton, William, Esq., Hereford
*Milward, B., Esq., Keynsham, near Bristol
*Milward, Richard, Esq., Hexgrave-park, Notts.
Minchin, W., Esq., solicitor for the affairs of His Majesty's Duchy of Lancaster
*MINT OFFICE, His Majesty's
Minter, Mr. John, Canterbury
Minton, Mr. G., Cheapside, London
Minton, Mr. Robert, jun., Hereford
Mitchell, J., Esq., Christ-church coll., Oxford
Mitchell, John, Esq., Charles-street, London
Mitchell, Dr. John, Kington, Herefordshire
*Mitchell, John, Esq., Royd-house, Lancashire
Mitchell, Mr. John, Enfield, Middlesex
Mitchell, W. T., Esq., New Kent-road, London
Mitford, J. R., Esq., Christ-church coll., Oxford
*Moccas, T. P., Esq.
*Mogg, C. W. C., Esq., Caius coll., Cambridge
Mogg, Rev. H. H., Chewton-Mendip, Somerset.
*Mogg, Rev. Rees, Clutton, do.
Mogridge, J., Esq., Reading, Berks. [mingham
*Moilliet, J. L., Esq., Hampstead-hall, near Bir-
Moises, Rev. W. B., Felton, Northumberland
Mold, Henry, Esq., Belper, Derbyshire
Mold, John, Esq., Alderwasley, do.
Mole, Mr. Thomas, Cheshunt, Herts.
*Mole, Mr. Wm., Paradise-street, Birmingham
*Molineux, C. H., Esq., Wolverhampton
Mollenhaver, J. H., Esq., Liverpool
*Molling, Frederick, Esq., Eltham, Kent
Molyneux, J. M., Esq., Guildford, Surrey
*Molyneux, T. C., Esq., Stapelands, nr. Liverpool
Monck, J. B., Esq., Coley-park, Berks.
Monckton, G., Esq., Stretton, Staffordshire
*Monckton, John, Esq., Maidstone, Kent
Money, Mr. John, Donnington, Berks.
*Money, Rev. J. K., Much Marcle, Herefordsh.
*Money, Rev. W., Wetham-house, Devizes
*Moneyment, Mr. G., Castle-meadow, Norwich
*Monger, Mr. William R., Ewell, Surrey
*Monins, Rev. J., Ringswould, Kent
Monk, John, Esq., Manchester
Monk, John, Esq., Waltham-Cross, Herts.
*Monk, William, Esq., Preston, Lancashire
*Monkhouse, C. J., Esq., Craven-st., Strand, Lond.
*Monkhouse, Rev. J., Whitney, Herefordshire
Monkhouse, Wm., Esq., Queen's coll., Oxford
*Monkton, The Honorable Edward
Monnington, Rev. G., Brampton-Bryan, Hereford
*Monro, Robert, Esq., Busbridge-hall, Surrey
*MONSON, The Right Honorable Lord
Monteith, R., Esq., Trinity college, Cambridge
MONTFORT, The Right Honorable Lord
*Montresor, Lieut.-Gen., Ospringe-house, Kent
Moody, A., Esq., Kingsden, Somersetshire
Moody, Mr. Robert, Romsey, Hants.
*Moogin, J. G., Esq., Mark-lane, London
*Moon, Mr. James, Gutter-lane, do.
*Moon, Mr. James, Dover
*Moon, Mr. William, Tottenham, Middlesex
*Moor, George, Esq., Durham
Moore, The Right Hon. and Rev. Edward
*Moore, C. R., Esq., Christ-church coll., Oxford
*Moore, C. A., Esq., Dursley, Gloucestershire
Moore, D., Esq., Bordesley-pk., nr. Birmingham
Moore, Edw., Esq., Stone, Staffordshire
Moore, G. P., Esq., Trinity college, Oxford
Moore, Rev. Henry, Willingdon, Sussex
*Moore, H., Esq., Corpus-Christi coll., Cambdg.
Moore, John L., Esq., Lower Chadnor, Dilwyn,
Moore, Mr. John, Tewkesbury [Herefordshire
*Moore, Rev. R., M. A., Preston, Lancashire
Moore, Mr. R., Dudley
*Moore, Saml. M., Esq., Ardwick, Manchester
*Moore, Thomas, Esq., Ruddington, Notts.
*Moore, Thomas, Esq., Worcester
*Moore, T., Esq., North Ouram, near Halifax
Moore, Mr. T., Weston-Beggard, Herefordshire
Moore, Mr. Thomas, Tipton, Staffordshire
*Moore, Mr. Thomas, Holland-place, Kensington
Moore, Rev. W., Brimpsfield, Gloucestershire
Moore, William, Esq., Liverpool
Moore, W., Esq., Wychdon-lodge, Staffordshire
Moore, Mr. W., Buxton, Derbyshire
*Moore, W. B., Esq., Church-st., Westminster
*Moore and Son, Messrs., Doctors Coms., Lond.
*Moore, Messrs. J. & Son, Douglas, Isle of Man
Moorhouse, C., Esq., Congleton, Cheshire
Moorsom, Admiral Sir Rt., K. C. B., Rochester
Morant, G., Esq., per Mr. Hailes
Mordaunt, Sir J., Bart., Walton, Warwickshire
*Morell, Rev. T., L. L. D., Wymondley, Herts.
*Mores, W. G., Esq., Cockspur-street, London
*Moresby, Christop., Esq., Frome, Somersetshire
Morgan, C., Esq., Rupperra, Glamorganshire
Morgan, Caleb, Esq., Haywards, Herefordshire
*Morgan, Charles, Esq., Kentchurch, do.
Morgan, Rev. H. C., Byford, do.
Morgan, Francis, Esq., Mortimers, Berks.
*Morgan, F. D., Esq., Waterloo-bridge, Lond.
*Morgan, George, Esq., Macknade, Kent
Morgan, Rev. Hugh, Hereford
Morgan, John, Esq., Holborn-court, London
Morgan, J., Esq., Great James-street, do.
*Morgan, J. B., Esq., Doctors Commons, do.
*Morgan, J. R., Esq., Bethnal-green do.
*Morgan, Thomas, Esq., Savage-gardens, do.
Morgan, Rev. Thomas, D. D., Portsmouth
Morgan, Mrs. Walter, Bacton, Monmouth
Morgan, William, Esq., Wadham coll., Oxford
Morgan, William, Esq., Abergavenny
Morgan, Brown and Co., Messrs., Bristol
*Morland, Benjamin, Esq., Marcham, Berks.
Morland, Rev. George, Lancaster
Morland, Wm., Esq., jun., West Ilsley, Berks.
*Morley, H., Esq., Hatton-garden, London
Morley, R., Esq., Ripon, Yorkshire
*Morning Journal, The Proprietors of the
*Morning Post, do.
Morpeth, John, Esq., Carlisle
Morphett, N., Esq., Bream's-buildings, London
Morrall, Edward, Esq., Plas-Warren, Salop.
*Morrell, R. P, Esq., Magdalene college, Oxford
*Morre, Col. J. K., Much Marcle, Herefordshire
Morrice, Walter, Esq., Eling, Southampton
*Morrieé, Rev. Henry, M. A., Ashwell, Herts.
*Morris, Christopher, Esq., Wigan, Lancashire
*Morris, Mr. D., Tipton, Staffordshire
Morris, Mr. Ebbenezer, Lewes, Sussex
*Morris, E., Esq., Sidney-Sussex coll., Cambrid.
Morris, George, Esq., Gloucester
Morris, J., Esq., Abergavenny, Monmouthshire
*Morris, Rev. J., M. A., Feltham, Middlesex
Morris, James, Esq., Perry-ditch, Herefordshire
Morris, Mr. James, Colnbrook, Bucks.
Morris, Rev. John, Rolstone, Monmouth
Morris, John, Esq., sen., Derby
Morris, John, Esq., Bury-Stockton, Herefordsh.
*Morris, John, Esq., Wingfield-house, Wiltshire
Morris, Mr. John, Marden, Herefordshire
Morris, J., Esq., Northumberland-st., London
*Morris, Rev. J., A. M., Feltham, Middlesex
*Morris, L. S., Esq., Christ's coll., Cambridge
Morris, Mr. N. D., Hereford
Morris, P., Esq., Newbury Bishop, do.
*Morris, R., Esq., Christ-church coll., Oxford
Morris, Robert, Esq., Wigan, Lancashire
*Morris, T. S., Esq., Coventry
*Morris, Thomas, Esq., Custom-house, London
Morris, Mr. T. C., Wilson-st., Finsbury, do.
Morris, Mr. Thomas, Tipton, Staffordshire
*Morris, Mr. Walter, Shucknall, Herefordshire
*Morris, W. H., Esq., Lincoln's-inn, London
*Morris and Smith, Messrs., Regent-st., do.
*Morrison and Co., Messrs. James, Fore-st., do.
*Mort, Mr. John, jun., Altrincham, Cheshire
*Mortfield, T. C., Esq., Haltiwell
Mortimer, Miss A., Bishopthorpe, York
*Mortimer, Thomas, Esq., Manchester
*Mortimer, T. H., Esq., Albany, London
Mortimore, R., Esq., Chippenham, Wilts.
Mortlock, William, Esq., Cambridge
MORTON, The Right Honorable the Earl of
Morton, Mr. Charles, Croydon, Surrey
Morton, George, Esq., Dymock, Gloucester
*Morton, Mr. George, Liverpool
*Morton, James, Esq., Holborn-hill, London
*Morton, Mr. T., Sharston, Cheshire
Morver, G., Esq., Wilham, East Retford, Notts.
*Moseley, Sir Oswald, Bart., D. C. L., Rolleston-hall, Staffordshire
*Moseley, W., Esq., Lincoln's-inn-fields, Lond.
*Mosely, David, Esq., Bullocksmithy, Cheshire
*Mosely, Walter, Esq., Winterdyne, Bewdley
*Moses, Moses, Esq., Abercarne, Monmouthshire
*Mosley, A. N. E., Esq., Congreve-house, Derbys.
Mosley, J. E., Esq., Burton on Trent, Stafford.
Mosman, Mr. Adam, Liverpool
*Mosman, Mrs. Raithby, Lincolnshire
*Moss, Mr. Frederick, Wellington-st., London
Moss, Mr. George, Canterbury
*Moss, J., Esq., Otter's-pool, near Liverpool
*Moss, James, Esq., Moor-hall, Cheshire
Moss, Mr. James, Liverpool
Moss, John, Esq., Derby
Moss, William, Esq., Ironmonger-lane, London
Mott, George, Esq., Fenchurch-street, do.
Mott, Julius, Esq., Loughborough, Leicestersh.
*Mott, R. D., Esq., Gloucester-street, London
Mott, John, Esq., The Close, Lichfield
*Mott, T. T., Esq., Christ-church college, Oxford
Mott, T. S., Esq., Much Hadham, Herts.
Mould, Mr. Lestock Joseph, Enfield, Middlesex
Mould, Rev. W., Willersley, Gloucestershire
Moultrie, Rev. J., Windsor, and Rugby, War-
*Mounsey, G. G., Esq., Carlisle [wickshire
*Mounsey, James, Esq., Preston, Lancashire
*Mount, Charles, Esq., Watling-street, London
Mount, G., Esq., King's-Arms-yard, Coleman-
Mount, Mr. H., Nackington, Kent [street, do.
Mount, R. M., Esq., Canterbury
*Mount, Mr. W., do.
Mount, William, Esq., Wasing-place, Berks.
*MOUNTCASHEL, The Rt. Hon. the Earl of
*Mountcastle, Mr. W., Manchester
*MOUNTCHARLES, The Rt. Hon. the Earl of
*Mountford, R., Esq., Shiffnall, Shropshire
Mourilyan, J., Esq., Sandwich, Kent
Mousley, Thomas, Esq., Hanley, Staffordshire
Mousley, W. Eaton, Esq., Derby
*Moxhay, E., Esq., Threadneedle-street, London
Moxon, J., Esq., Twickenham-lodge, Middlesex
*Moxon, Mr. James, Southampton
*Muggeridge, Richard M., Esq., Proprietor of the Herts. Mercury
Muirhead, Mr. James, Buxton, Derbyshire
*Mulcaster, Major-Gen., Nackington, Kent
*Mules, Charles H., Esq., Ilminster, Somerset.
Mules, Rev. James, Wellington, do.
*Mules, William, Esq., Dedham, Essex
Mullett, Mr. William, London-wall, London
Mullins, John, Esq., Fenchurch-street, do.

Mullock, Mr. R., Newport, Monmouthshire
Mundy, F., Esq., M.P., Markeaton, Derbyshire
*Mundy, Mr. B., Broad-street, London
Mundy, E. M., Esq., Shipley-hall, Derbyshire
*Munn, J., Esq., Tenterden, Kent
Munn, Mr. John, Maidstone, do.
*Munn, John R., Esq., Worcester coll., Oxford
*Munn, Lewis, Esq., Sarratt, Herts.
*Munro, George, Esq., City-road, London
*Munro, T. Esq., Lowestoft, Suffolk
*Munt, Matthew, Esq., Cheshunt, Herts.
*Muriel, Mr. Charles, High-street, Borough
*Murly, Edward, Esq., Crewkerne, Somerset.
*Murphy, Messrs. James and Edward, Union-court, Broad-street, London
Murphy, John, Esq., Welbeck-street, do.
Murphy, Joseph, Esq., Park-square, Leeds
*Murphy, R., Esq., B. A., Caius col., Cambdg.
Murray, The Honorable Charles J.
*Murray, Lieut. Gen. Sir Geo., K.C.B. & G.H.
Murray, Admiral Robert, Liverpool
Murray, Alexand., Esq., Symond's-inn, London
Murray, C. Knight, Esq., Green-street, do.
*Murray, Capt. J., R.N., New Broad-st., do.
*Murray, J., Esq., Sidney-Sussex col., Cambridge
*Murray, John, Esq., Liverpool
*Murray, T. L., Esq., Great Ormond-st., London
Murray, William, Esq., London-street, do.
Murray, William, Esq., Blacon-hall, Cheshire
*Murray and Son, Messrs. C., Chancery-lane,
*Murrell, B., Esq., Northfleet, Kent [London
Murrell, Rev. Thos., Bentworth, Alton, Hants.
*Musgrave, Rev. R. A., Compton-Bassett, Wilts.
Musgrove, John, Esq., Austin-friars, London
Muspratt, James, Esq., Liverpool
Mustard, David, Esq., Colchester
*Musters, John, Esq., Colwick-hall
*Musters, W., Esq., Corpus-Christi col., Oxford
Mutlon, Mr. E., Leominster, Herefordshire
*Myers, Rev. John, Somerby, Lincolnshire
*Myers, J. P., Esq., Broughton, Lancashire
Mylins, H., Esq., Gt. Winchester-st., London
*Mylrea, The Rev. and Venerable Archdeacon, Isle of Man
Mynors, H. E., Esq., Keynsham, near Bristol
*M'All, Rev. R. S., M. A., Manchester
*M'Alpin, D., Esq., Bread-street, London
*M'Andrew, Robert, Esq., Liverpool
M'Bayne, L., Esq., Clifton, near Bristol
M'Bean, Mrs. Anne, Windsor
*M'Candlish, Capt. J., R.N., Salford, Lancash.
*M'Cartney, John, Esq., M. D., Liverpool
*M'Clintock, Captain I., Londonderry
*M'Connochie, John, Esq., Burnley, Lancashire
*M'Cullock, Rev. T., S. C. L., Wormley, Herts.
M'Donald, Colin, Esq., Liverpool
M'Donald, Mr. G., Jermyn-street, London
*M'Dowall, Rev. W., M. A., Luton, Bedfordsh.
M'Dowall, Mr. William, Lisson-grove, London
*M'Gibbon, B. W., Esq., Hay, Brecon.
M'Gillivray, Simon, Esq., Canada-house, do.
M'Iver, Evan, Esq., Liverpool
M'Kenzie, Mrs., St. Neots, Huntingdonshire
M'Michael, G., Esq., Skinner-street, London
*M'Michael, Mr. John B., Birmingham
*M'Mullan, Mrs., St. George's-place, London
*M'Mullen, Mr. Edward, Hertford
M'Mullen, Mr. William, do.
M'Nab, William, Esq., Ware, Herts.
*M'Pherson, R. R. J., Esq., Queen's coll., Oxford
*M'Quod, W., Esq., Derby-street, London
M'William, R., Esq., Torrington-sq., do.

*Nabb, Robert, Esq., Manchester
*Naftel, Andrew, Esq., Bittern, Hants.
*Nailer, Mr. George, Gainsborough, Lincolnshire
*Nairn, Fasham, Esq., Barnett's-place, Sussex
*Nalder, Francis, Esq., Cheapside, London
*Nash, A., Esq., Trinity college, Cambridge
Nash, Mr. E., Guildford, Surrey
Nash, F. J., Esq., Bishop-Stortford, Essex
*Nash, F. J., Esq., Trinity college, Cambridge
Nash, John, Esq., Regent-street, London
Nash, Mr. John, Windsor
Nash, Lieut. William, R. N., Chertsey, Surrey
*Nash, Wm., Esq., Budge-row, London
*Nash, W. W., Esq., Royston, Herts.
Naters, R., Esq., Sandyford, Northumberland
NAVY, The Right Honorable the Lords Commissioners of His Majesty's
Naylor, John, Esq., Wakefield, Yorkshire
Naylor, G. P., Esq., Sheffield [Liverpool
Naylor, J. T., Esq., Kensington-house, near
Naylor, Rev. T., South Brent, Somersetshire
*Neald, Jos., jun., Esq., M.P., Alderton, Wilts.
Nealds, John, Esq., Guildford, Surrey
Neale, C., Esq., Mansfield-Woodhouse, Notts.
*Neale, E. V., Esq., Oriel college, Oxford
*Neale, Rev. J., Boddington, Gloucestershire
Neale, Mr. John, Speenhamland, Berks.
Neale, Mr. Philip, Norwich
*Neale, Mrs. Susanna, Shepperton, Middlesex
Neale, W., Esq., Melton-Mowbray, Leicestersh.
*Neame, Mr. George, Canterbury
Neame, Mr. John, Selling, Kent
Neat, John, Esq., Upton-Scudamore, Wilts.
Neden, J., Esq., Lydiate, Lancashire
Need, Jno., Esq., Mansfield-Woodhouse, Notts.
Need, N., Esq., Uttoxeter, Staffordshire
*Needham, John, Esq., Wigan, Lancashire
*Needs, James, Esq., Hastings, Sussex
Neeves, Mr. Benjamin, Wokingham, Berks.
Negus, E., Esq., Friday-st., Cheapside, London
*Neild, Wm., Esq., Mayfield, near Manchester
*Nelson, Rev. John, Vicar-Gen., Isle of Man
Nelson, Mr. John, Milk-st., Cheapside, London
*Nelson, P., Esq., Essex-street, do.
*Nelson, Mr. Philip, Wallingford, Berks.
Nesham, J. D., Esq., Lincoln's-inn-fields, Lon.
Ness, J., Esq., Dyer's-buildings, do.
*Netherton, Rev. John, Bromsgrove
Neve, Rev. C., A. B., Brierley-hill, Staffordshire
*Nevile, Rev. E., M. A., Prees, Shropshire
*Nevill, W., Esq., Maiden-la., Cheapside, London
*NEVILLE, The Right Hon. Lord Viscount
*Neville, James, Esq., Blackburn, Lancashire
New, Mr. Henry, St. Mary's-sq., Birmingham
*Newall, Mrs., Rochdale, Lancashire
*Newall, William, Esq., Littleborough, do.
*Newall, William, Esq., Manchester
*Newark, H., Esq., Wood-st., Cheapside, Lond.
Newark Library, Newark, Nottinghamshire
*Newbald, C., Esq., Tooley-street, London
*Newbald, John, Esq., Southwark, do.
*Newbery, Jacob, Esq., Reading, Berks. [Lond.
*Newbon and Son, Messrs., Doctors Commons,
Newbould, W., Esq., Broomhill, near Sheffield
*NEWBURGH, The Right Hon. the Earl of
*NEWBURGH, The Right Hon. the Countess of
Newbury, Henry, Esq., Manchester
*Newby, Geo., Esq., Witton le Wear, Durham
Newby, James, Esq., Cartmel, Lancashire
*NEWCASTLE, His Grace the Duke of
*Newcastle upon Tyne, The Worshipful the Mayor and Corporation of [ciety of
*Newcastle upon Tyne, The Philosophical So-
Newcome, Rev. T., F. A. S., Shenley, Herts.
Newdegate, C. N., Esq., Harefield-place, Mid-
*Newdick, S., Esq., Reigate, Surrey [dlesex
*Newell, G. W., Esq., Holyport, Bray, Berks.
*Newland, B., Esq., Midhurst, Sussex
*Newland, Charles, Esq., Chichester, do.
*Newman, Edwin, Esq., Yeovil, Somersetshire
*Newman, Mr. George, Hertford
*Newman, John, Esq., Town-hall, Southwark
*Newman, Mr. John, Tooley-street, London
Newman, Mr. J. R. G., Newmarket
Newman, R. T., Esq., Guildhall, London
*Newman, Mrs. S., Brighton, Sussex
*Newman, T., Esq., Hertingfordbury, Hertford
*Newman, Mr. T., Cherry-Hinton, Cambridge
Newman, Mr. Wm., Cockspur-street, London
Newman, W. B., Esq., Corsham, Wilts.
*Newman, W. L., Esq., Guildhall, London
Newman, Mr. T., Barnet, Herts.
*Newnham, Rev. W. M., Chilcompton, Somerset.
Newnham, William, Esq., Farnham, Surrey
Newport, The Right Hon. Sir J., Bart., M.P.
NEWRY, The Right Honorable Lord Viscount
Newsam, Rev. Jas., Sharrow, Yorkshire
*Newsham, John, Esq., Blackburn, Lancashire
Newsham, Richard, jun., Esq., Preston, do.
Newsham, Thomas, Esq., Wigan, do.
Newton, Edmund, Esq., Norwich
*Newton, George, Esq., Atherton, Lancashire
Newton, George W., Esq., Cornhill, London
*Newton, G. W., Esq., High Peak, Derby
Newton, Henry, Esq., York
*Newton Jas., Esq., Doctors Commons, London
*Newton, James, Esq., Cheadle-heath, Cheshire
*Newton, Jno., Esq., Walton on Thames, Surrey
*Newton, Robert, Esq., Bowbridge, Derbyshire
*Newton, R. A., Esq., Bensington, Oxfordshire
*Newton, Samuel, Esq., Atherton, Lancashire
*Newton, Mr. Samuel, Ashton under Line
Newton, T., Esq., Lugwardine, Herefordshire
*Newton, Mr. T., Wallingford, Berks
*Newton, Wm., Esq., Holborn-court, London
*Newton, Wm., Esq., Ambleside, Westmorland
Newton, Wm., Esq., Chancery-lane, London
Newton, William, Esq., Altrincham, Cheshire
*Newton & Son, Mess. M., Ancoats, Manchester
Newton and Son, Messrs. Isaac, Knaresborough
Nichol, R., Esq., Queen-st., Cheapside, London
Nicholas, A., Esq., Newport, Monmouthshire
Nicholas, Mr. Edw., do., do.
*Nicholas, Rev. G. F., M. A., King's college,
Nicholas, John, Esq., Liverpool [Cambridge
Nicholas, Mr. Thomas, Hereford
*Nicholetts, J., Esq., South Petherton, Somerset.
Nicholl, John, Esq., Furnival's-inn, London
*Nicholl, J. R., Esq., Exeter college, Oxford
*Nicholl, R., Esq., Greenhill-grove, Herts.
*Nicholls, Devereux J., Esq., Altrincham, Chesh.
Nicholls, George J., Esq., Bourn, Lincolnshire
Nicholls, H., Esq., Buckworth, Huntingdonshire
*Nicholls, John, Esq., Bewdley, Worcestershire
Nicholls, Thos., Esq., Axbridge, Somersetshire
*Nicholls, T., Esq., Manchester
*Nicholls, T., Esq., Hemel-Hempstead, Herts.
Nicholls, W. P., Esq., Norwich
Nichols, John, Esq., Bewdley, Worcestershire
Nichols, Mr. John, Farnham, Surrey
Nichols, Mr. Richard, Wakefield
Nicholson, C., Esq., Barford, Wilts.
Nicholson, G., Esq., Landsdown-place, London
*Nicholson, George, Esq., Hertford
*Nicholson, Mr. James, Manchester
Nicholson, John, Esq., Queen's college, Oxford
*Nicholson, J., Esq., Lancaster-place, London
*Nicholson, P., Esq., Well-st., Gray's-inn-la., do.
Nicholson, Rich., Esq., Ripon, Yorkshire
Nicholson, Mr. Samuel, Rochester, Kent
*Nicholson, T., Esq., Hertford
Nicholson, William, Esq., Preston, Lancashire
*Nicholson, Messrs. J. and W., St. John-street,
*Nicholson and Barr, Messrs., Leeds [London
Nicholson and Hoole, Messrs., Sheffield
Nicklin, Mr. Richard, Tipton, Staffordshire
Nicklin, Mr. Thomas, do., do.
Nicoll, Rev. A., L. L. D., Christ-church coll.,
*Nicoll, S. W., Esq., York [Oxford
*Nicolls, General, Chichester
*Nicols, Rev. B., Buntingford, Hertfordshire
*Nield, J. W., Esq., Altrincham, Cheshire
Nightingale, J., Esq., Rochester, Kent
Nightingale, R. T., Esq., Blackheath, do.
*Nightingale, W. G., Esq., Embley, near Romsey, Hants., and Lea-Hurst, Derbyshire
Nisbet, James, Esq., Thatcham, Berks.
*Nixon, Rev. F. Russel, M. A., Plaistow, Essex
*Nixson, Paul, Esq., Carlisle and Stonehouse-Dent, Yorkshire
*Noakes, John, jun., Esq., Great Mongeham, Kent
*Noakes, Joseph, Esq., Deal, do.

*Noakes, William, Esq., Woolwich, Kent
*Noble, C. J., Esq., Henley in Arden, Warwick-
*Noble, George, Esq., Preston, Lancashire [shire
*Noble, John, Esq., do., do.
*Noble, John, Esq., Fleet-street, London
*Noel, Sir G. N, Bart., M.P., Exton-park, Rutland.
*Noel, Mrs. P., Belbroughton, Worcestershire
Noke, Mr. Thomas, Windsor
*Nokes, William, Esq., Woolwich, Kent
*Norbrook, Mr. W., Fish-street-hill, London
*Norbury, John, Esq., jun., Northwich, Cheshire
*Norgate, Benjamin H., Esq., Norwich
*Norie, Mr. J. W., Leadenhall-street, London
*Norman, Rev. C. M., M. A., St. Albans
*Norman, Edward, Esq., Mistley, Essex
Norman, Rev. G., Stafford
Norman, George, Esq., Circus, Bath
Norman, Rev. H., High Offley, Staffordshire
*Norman, Wm., Esq., Langport, Somersetshire
*NORMANTON, The Right Hon. the Earl of
Norris, Charles, Esq., Norwich
Norris, Rev. H. H., South Hackney, Middlesex
*Norris, H., Esq., South Petherton, Somerset.
*Norris, John, Esq., Hughenden-house, Bucks.
Norris, John, Esq., Taunton, Somersetshire
*Norris, Rev. R. S., Blackburn, Lancashire
*Norris, Thomas, Esq., Bury, do.
*Norris, W. Esq., Manchester
*North, Thomas, Esq., Burton, Westmorland
North, Mr. Wm., Bishopsgate-street, London
*North and Smart, Messrs., Temple, do.
*Northcroft, Mr. A., Chancery-lane, do.
Northcroft, Mr. Wm., Egham, Surrey
NORTHAMPTON, The Most Noble the Marquis of [fordshire
Northen, F. H., Esq., M. D., Newcastle, Staf-
NORTHUMBERLAND, His Grace the Duke of
*Norton, Edward, Esq., Walbrook, London
Norton, Henry, Esq., Uxbridge
*Norton, Joseph, Esq., Wolverhampton
*Norton, L., Esq., Jewin-street, London
*Norton, W. F., Esq., Somerton, Somersetshire
*Norton, William J., Esq., New-street, London
*Norton, W. F. N., Esq., Elton Manor, Notts.
*Norton and Son, Messrs., Fenchurch-st., Lond.
*Norwich Union Fire Office, Norwich
*Norwich do. do., London
Norwood, Edward, Esq., Hertford
*Norwood, Edward, Esq., Dover
Nost, Mr. J., Lord Chamberlain's-office, Lond.
Nott, Lieut-Col., Canterbury [Leominster
Nott, Wm., Esq., Underhill, Collington, near
*Nottage, Rev. J. B., Lancaster
*Notter, Wm., Esq., Bishop-Auckland, Durham
Nottidge, Rev. J. T., St. Helens, Ipswich
*Nottingham, The Worshipful the Mayor and Corporation of
*Nottingham Law Library
Nottingham Subscription Library
*Nottingham, Mr. M., Rotherhithe, Surrey
*Nowell, A., Esq., Kirkby-Lonsdale
*Nowell, R., Esq., Essex-street, London
*Nowell, Mr. P., Pimlico, Middlesex
Noyes, Mr. James, Chippenham, Wilts.
Noyes, W. M., Esq., Calne, do.
Nugent, Rev. G., Great Berkhampstead, Herts.
*Nugent, Mr. J. R., Ross, Herefordshire
Nunn, Mr. James, Hertford
Nunn, Roger, Esq., M. D., Colchester
Nunn, William, Esq., Jesus coll., Cambridge
Nurse, Rev. J., M. A., Limington, Somersetshire
Nutt, J., Esq., Canterbury
Nutt, Mr. Joseph, Little Gate, Oxford
*Nuttall, John, Esq., Bury, Lancashire

Oakes, C. H., Esq., Merton college, Oxford
Oakes, Edward, Esq., Maidstone, Kent
Oakes, Henry James, Esq., Bury St. Edmunds
Oakes, Rev. James, Tostock, Suffolk
Oakes, James, Esq., Riddings, Derbyshire
*Oakes, R., Esq., Gravesend, Kent
*Oakley, Rev. Sir H., Bart., Ealing, Middlesex
*Oakley, Rich., jun., Esq., Harpenden, Herts.
*Oakley, Thomas, Esq., Monmouth
Obins, Rev. A., Hemingford-Abbotts, Hunts.
*O'Brien, G., Esq., Cheshunt, Herts.
*O'Brien, S., Esq., Trinity college, Cambridge
*Occleston, J., Esq., Ashton upon Mersey
*Occleston, Samuel, Esq., Manchester
*Ockleston, Mr. William, Liverpool
Odell, E., Esq., Christ-church college, Oxford
*Offley, William, Esq., University coll., do.
*Ogden, R., Esq., Portland-place, Manchester
*Ogilby, A., Esq., Trinity college, Cambridge
Ogilvey, Mr. Thomas, Colnbrook, Bucks.
*Ogilvie, Alexander, Esq., Mere, Cheshire
*Ogilvy, William F., Esq., Broxbourne, Herts.
*Oglander,—— Esq., Christ-church coll., Oxford
*Ogle, Rev. E. C., Sutton-Benger, Wilts.
*Ogle, E. L., Esq., Cornhill, London
Ogle, Mr. John, Liverpool
Ogle, Nath., Esq., Millbrook, Southampton
O'Grady, Major Standish
*Okell, Charles, Esq., Liverpool
*Okell, Rev. G., M.A., Witton, Cheshire
*Okell, John, Esq., Stretton, do.
*Okell, Joseph, Esq., do., do.
*Okell, Joseph, Esq., Northwich, do.
*Okell, Rob., Esq., Aston Grange-house, do.
Okes, John, Esq., Cambridge
*Okes, Rev. Richard, M. A., Eton college
Okey, Mr. J., Waltham-Cross, Essex
*Okill, John, Esq., Lee, near Liverpool
*Okill, Robert, Esq., Dartford, Kent
Olarenshaw, Jas., Esq., Wolverhampton
Oldaker, Day, and Co., Messrs., Evesham
Oldaker, Tomes, and Co., Messrs., Stratford on Avon, Warwickshire
Oldershaw, R., Esq., jun., Lower-st., Islington
Oldfield, Mr. T., Brampton-Moor, Derbyshire
*Oldham, C., Esq., Emanuel college, Cambridge
*Oldham, Thomas, Esq., New-Mills, Derbyshire
*Oldknow, Samuel, Esq., Mellor, do.
*Oldman, Henry, Esq., Faversham, Kent
*Oldroyd, J., Esq., Colebrook-terrace, Islington
*Oliver, Alexander, Esq., Manchester
Oliver, Mr. George, Lawrence-lane, London
*Oliver, Richard, Esq., New-Mills, Derbyshire
Oliver, Mr. R., King's Pion, Herefordshire
*Oliver, Samuel, Esq., Hatton-garden, London
*Oliver, Thomas, Esq., Spring-gardens, do.
*Ollerenshaw, Edward, Esq., Manchester
*Ollier, Henry, Esq., do.
*Ollier, James A., Esq., do.
O'Meara, B. E., Esq., Montague-sq., London
O'NEILL, The Right Honorable Earl
O'Neill, The Hon. John Bruce Richard, M.P.
Onslow, Rev. A. C., M. A., Newington, Surrey
*Onslow, Gen. Denzil, Staughton-house, Hants.
Onslow, Col. M., Woodbridge, near Guildford
*Openshaw, Charles, Esq., Bury, Lancashire
*Openshaw, James, Esq., do., do.
*Openshaw, Thomas, Esq., do., do.
*Oram, Thomas, Esq., do., do.
Oram, Mr. W., Bensington, Oxfordshire
Orange, Mr. Samuel, Cheshunt, Herts.
*Orchard, James, Esq., Cursitor-street, London
*Ord, J. T., Esq., Exeter college, Oxford
*Orde, Rev. John, Winslade, Hants.
ORDNANCE, His Majesty's Honorable Board of . . . . . . 2 Copies
O'Reiley, Mr. C., Malvern, Worcestershire
*Orme, M., Esq., Nottingham-place, London
Orme, Mr. Wm., Stourbridge, Worcestershire
Ormerod, Oliver, Esq., Brasenose coll., Oxford
Ormond, William, Esq., Wantage, Berks.
*Ormrod, Peter, Esq., Bolton, Lancashire
*Orrell, Thomas, Esq., Ashley, Cheshire
*Orrell, W., Esq., Stalybridge, Lancashire
*Orrett, Rev. W. G., A.M., Standish, do.
*Orridge, John T., Esq., Carlisle
*Orton, Thomas, Esq., Tattenhall, Cheshire
Osbaldeston, Francis S., Esq., Hatfield, Herts.
*Osborn, Latham, Esq., Margate, Kent
Osborn, R., Esq., Walton on Thames, Surrey
OSBORNE, The Right Honorable Lord
Osborne, C., Esq., Stonefield-street, Islington
*Osborne, Colonel H. S., Cecil-lodge, Herts.
Osborne, Jacob, Esq., Spondon, Derbyshire
Osborne, Jeremiah, Esq., Bristol
*Osborne, John, Esq., Trinity college, Oxford
Osborne, Mr. M. R., St. Ives, Huntingdonshire
Osborne, Mr. Philip, Birmingham
Osborne, S., Esq., Brasenose college, Oxford
Osborne, William, Esq., Spondon, Derbyshire
Oslar, Mr. T., Fulbourn St. Vigors, Cambridge
Osler, Mr. Samuel, Helston, Cornwall
Osmond, Mr. William, Reading, Berks.
*OSSORY, The Right Honorable the Earl of
*OSSULSTON, The Right Honorable Lord
Oswald, H. R., Esq., Douglas, Isle of Man
*Oswald, John, Esq., Lewisham, Kent
*O'Toole, L., Esq., Christ-church coll., Oxford
Otway, Rear-Admiral, Westwood, Southampton
Otway, Rev. C., Llanfoist, Monmouthshire
Otway, John M., Esq., Welwyn, Herts.
*Oughton, James, Esq., Manchester
Ousby, Rev. John, Chaplain, House of Correction, Cold Bath-fields
*Ouseley, The Right Honorable Sir G., Bart., F. A., R. S. K., A. N., and S. L.
*Ousey, R., Esq., Heyrod-hall, Cheshire
Overbury, Joseph, Esq., Cateaton-st., London
*Overbury, Matravers, and Overbury, Messrs., Westbury, Wilts.
Overton, George, Esq., York
Overton, Rev. J. O., M. A., do.
*Overton, W., Esq., New Broad-street, London
*Owen, Colonel, Littlebourn, Kent
*Owen, Dr., Chancery-lane, London
*Owen, Rev. E. P., M. A., Eyton, Shropshire
*Owen, E. W. S, Esq., Condover-hill, do.
*Owen, George A., Esq., Mark-lane, London
*Owen, Geo., Esq., Catharine-hall, Cambridge
*Owen, George, Esq., Manchester
*Owen, Herbert, Esq., Caius coll., Cambridge
Owen, J., Esq., Hereford
*Owen, J. C. H., Esq., Monmouth [Copies
*Owen, Mr. Jas., Little Bell-alley, London . 2
Owen, Rev. Owen, B.D., Jesus coll., Oxford
*Owen, S., Esq., Ely-place, Holborn, London
Owen, Rev. William, Gravesend, Kent
Owen, Messrs. E. and J., Manchester
*Owst, Mr. Robert, Tooley-street, London
Owthwaite, Mr. R., Henley upon Thames
Oxenden, A., Esq., University college, Oxford
*Oxenden, Rev. Chas., Bishop's Bourne, Kent
OXFORD, The Right Rev. Lord Bishop of
*Oxford, The Worshipful the Mayor and Corporation of the City of
Oxlay, T., Esq., Queen's college, Oxford
Oxley, C., Esq., do., do.
Oxley, Charles, Esq., Ripon, Yorkshire
Oxley, Joseph, and Sons, Messrs., Norwich
*OXMANTOWN, The Right Honorable Lord
Oxnayn, Rev. W., M.A., Harrow

Pacey, Rev. H. B., D.D., Boston
Pack, J. C., Esq., Christ-church coll., Oxford
Packman, Miss B., Reigate, Surrey
*Packwood, John, Esq., Cheltenham
Paddock, William, Esq., Ellesmere, Shropshire
Paddon, Joseph, Esq., Fareham, Hants.
Paddon, J. S., Esq., Clement's-inn, London
*Paddon, Rev. Thos., M. A., Mattishall, Norfolk
*Padley, Alfred, Esq., Bulwell-house, Notts.
Padley, R., Esq., Burton-Joyce, do.
Padwick, Wm., jun., Esq., Havant, Hants.
Paffard, I. H., Esq., Portsea, do
*Page, Capt., East Sheen, Surrey
Page, Rev. Edward, Bawdrip, Somersetshire
*Page, James, Esq., Erith, Kent
Page, John, Esq., Bath
*Page, G. A., Esq., Birmingham

Page, Gregory, Esq., Maidstone, Kent
Page, Robert, Esq., Charlton, Somersetshire
*Page, Samuel F., Esq., King's-road, London
*Page, T. J., Esq., Buxton, Derbyshire
*Page, Thomas, Esq., Ely, Cambridgeshire
*Page, W. E., Esq., Christ-church coll., Oxford
*Paget, Lieut. Gen. Sir Edward, Governor of Sandhurst college
Paget, Charles, Esq., Ruddington, Notts.
*Paget, E., Esq., Christ-Church college, Oxford
Paget, S., Esq., Yarmouth, Norfolk
Paget, J. M., Esq., Luckington, Somersetshire
Pain, G. H., Esq., Bridg-water, do.
Pain, Mr. John, Pittleworth, Hants.
Pain, Thomas, Esq., Dover
Paine, W. P., Esq., Farnham, Surrey
Palatine Library, Preston, Lancashire
Palairet, Charles, Esq., Queen's coll., Oxford
*Paley, John, Esq., Preston, Lancashire
*Paley, John, jun., Esq., do., do.
*Palfreman, Mr. John, Sheffield
Palgrave, F., Esq., F. R. S., F. S. A., Parliament-street, London
*Palin, Thomas, Esq., Water-street, Manchester
*Palin, William, Esq., Stapleford, Cheshire
*Palk, A. G., Esq., Christ-church coll., Oxford
Palk, Mr. John, Romsey, Hants.
*Palk, Mr. Edward, Southampton
*Palmer, A., Esq., Magdalene college, Oxford
*Palmer, C. J., Esq., Yarmouth, Norfolk
*Palmer, E. R., Esq., do., do.
Palmer, F., Esq., Christ-church coll., Oxford
Palmer, G., Esq., do., do.
Palmer, G., Esq., UpperWoburn-place, London
Palmer, George, Esq., Epping, Essex
*Palmer, Mr. George, Wallingford, Berks.
Palmer, J., Esq., Holborn-ct., Gray's-inn, Lon.
Palmer, J. H., Esq., Yarmouth, Norfolk
Palmer, Rev. J., North Pembury, Kent
*Palmer, Mr. John, Herne, do.
Palmer, N., Esq., Yarmouth, Norfolk
*Palmer, R., Esq., M. P., Holme-park, Reading
Palmer, R. S., Esq., New Boswell-ct., London
*Palmer, S. S., Esq., Timsbury-house, Somerset.
Palmer, T. C., Esq., Bromley, Kent
*Palmer, W., Esq., Magdalene college, Oxford
*Palmer, W., Esq., Bollitree, Weston under [Penyard
*Palmer & Greene, Messrs., Lichfield
Palmer and Son, Messrs., Bristol
*Pamphilon, Mr. James, Sherrard-street, London
*Panter, F.D., Trinity college, Oxford
Panting, T., Esq., Council-house, Shrewsbury
Panton, E., Esq., Elm-court, Temple, London
*Papillon, J., Esq., University college, Oxford
Papineau, Wm. M., Esq., Kennington, Surrey
*Papps, G., Esq., Six-clerks'-office, London
*Paraman, Mr. Robert, Norwich
*Pardoe, Rev. G. Dansey, Hopton-castle, Salop.
*Pardoe, George, Esq., Caius coll., Cambridge
*Parel, A. S., Esq., Surrey-street, London
*Parfett, W. B., Esq., Eversley, Hants.
*Parfitt, William, Esq., Wells, Somersetshire
Pargeter, W., Esq., Delph, Staffordshire
*Parish, Capt., R. N., Timsbury, Somersetshire
*Parish, Ambrose, Esq., Old Kent-road, London
Park, The Honorable Mr. Justice
*Park, Adam, Esq., Gravesend, Kent
*Park, James, Esq., Lancaster
Park, J. J., Esq., Southampton-buildings, Lond.
Park, Philip, Esq., Preston, Lancashire
Parken, W. P., Esq., Boswell-court, London
Parker, Sir H., Bart., Milford-hall, Suffolk
Parker, Captain, Browsholme
*Parker, Captain W., Kensington-place, Bath
Parker, Dean John, Esq., Canterbury
Parker, Rev. E., Reading, Berks.
*Parker, Mr. George, Hackney, Middlesex
*Parker, H., Esq., Preston, Lancashire
Parker, H. J., Esq., Otham, Kent
Parker, J. C., Esq., Kingston upon Hull
Parker, John, Esq., Lancaster
*Parker, John, Esq., Temple, London

Parker, John Frederick, Esq., Lewisham, Kent
Parker, Joseph, Esq., High-street, Bedford
Parker, Montague E., Esq., Oriel coll., Oxford
*Parker, R., Esq., Nantwich, Cheshire
*Parker, R. T., Esq., Preston, Lancashire
Parker, S., Esq., Great Staughton, Hunts.
Parker, T., Esq., Furnival's-inn, London
*Parker, T., Esq., Clapton, Middlesex
Parker, Thomas H., Esq., Camden Town, do.
*Parker, T., jun., Esq., Milk-street, London
*Parker, W., Esq., Henley upon Thames
*Parker, W., Esq., Skirwith Abbey, Cumberland
Parker, William, Esq., Shelton, Staffordshire
Parker, William, Esq., Grantham, Lincolnshire
*Parker, Wilmot, Esq., Lyon's-inn, London
*Parker, W. R., Esq., Oriel college, Oxford
*Parkes, Joseph, Esq., Birmingham
Parkes, Thomas, Esq., High-Onn, Staffordshire
Parkes and Ottway, Messrs., Bilston, do.
*Parkin, Benjamin, Esq., Hoylake, Cheshire
*Parkin, J., Esq., Riches-ct., Lime-st., London
Parkin, Mr. J., West-street, Finsbury-sq., do.
Parkington, M., Esq., Selby, Yorkshire
*Parkinson, Colonel, Gloucester-place, London
*Parkinson, E. C., Esq., North Brixton, Surrey
*Parkinson, Mr. J., Skinner-street, London
Parkinson, Mr. J., Radcliffe-ter., Goswell-rd., do.
*Parkinson, J. T., Esq., Bryanstone-square, do.
*Parkinson, Rev. Thomas, Bolton, Lancashire
*Parkyns, T. B., Esq., Ruddington, Notts.
*Parnell, Gervas, Esq., Gainsborough, Lincolnsh.
*Parnell & Morris, Messrs., Leicester-sq., Lond.
Parr, John, Esq., Liverpool
*Parr, Thomas, Esq., Grappenhall, Cheshire
*Parr, Thomas, Esq., Lythwood-hall, Salop.
Parr, Mr. W. B., London-lane, Norwich
*Parr, Mr. William, Throgmorton-st., London
Parr and Ward, Messrs., Liverpool
*Parrott, Thomas, Macclesfield, Cheshire
*Parry, Mr. David, Maidstone, Kent
Parry, George, Esq., Queen's college, Oxford
Parry, John, Esq., Dewlass-court, Hereford.
*Parry, T., Esq., Shipston upon Stour, Worces- [tershire
Parry, T., Esq., Wadham col., Oxford
Parsley, Samuel, Esq., Worle, Somersetshire
*Parson, Read, Esq., Furnival's-inn, London
*Parsons, Charles F., Esq., Manchester
Parsons, Mr. Edw., sen., Sawbridgeworth, Herts.
Parsons, F. C., Esq., Worcester college, Oxford
Parsons, Mr. G., Brighton
*Parsons, Geo., Esq., Birmingham
*Parsons, H., Esq., Oxford
Parsons, Rev. Henry, Godmanchester, Hunts.
Parsons, Rev. J., A. M., Redland, near Bristol
*Parsons, James, Esq., Somerton, Somersetshire
Parsons, John, Esq., Oxford
*Parsons, J. D., Esq., Croscombe, Somersetshire
*Parsons, Mr. Richard, Carpenter-street, London
Parsons, Mr. T., Fleet-street, do.
*Parsons, Mr. Thomas, Epsom, Surrey
*Parsons, Rev. W., Haslemere, do.
*Partington, James Edge, Esq., Manchester
*Partington, W., Esq., Change-alley, London
*Parton, Edward, Esq., Bow Church-yard, do.
*Parton, J., Esq., Charlotte-st., Bloomsbury, do.
Partridge, Alderman, Colchester
*Partridge, John, Esq., Canterbury
Partridge, John, Esq., Walford, Herefordshire
Partridge, Mr. John, St. Ives, Huntingdonshire
*Partridge, J. A., Esq., Breakspears, Middlesex
*Partridge, W. H., Esq., Birmingham
Partridge, R., Esq., Ambleside, Westmorland
*Partridge, W. E., Esq., Brasenose coll., Oxford
Pasmore, Mr. John, Windsor
Pasquier, Mr. E. J., Lakenham-terrace, Norwich
*Pass, William, Esq., Altrincham, Cheshire
Passman, C. B., Esq., Stafford
*Patch, M., Esq., R. N., Tintinhull, Somerset.
Patch, Robert B., Esq., Wadham coll., Oxford
*Pate, Edward, Esq., Chester
*Paterson, A., Esq., Pendleton, near Manchester
*Paterson, John, Esq., Mincing-lane, London

Paterson, W. S., Esq., Bouverie-street, London
*Pateshall, E. B., Esq., Allensmore, Herefordsh.
*Pateshall, John S. L., Esq., Hereford
Patience, Mr. John T., Norwich
*Patrick, George William, Esq., Durham
Patricke, T. C., Esq., Wakefield
*Patten, John W., Esq., Warrington
Patten, Thomas, Esq., Rochester, Kent
*Pattenson, C. Tylden, Esq., Biddenden, do.
Patterson, John, Esq., Bridge-street, London
*Patterson, J., Esq., Exeter college, Oxford
Patteson, Thomas, Esq., do., do.
Paul, Mr. Adam, Cheshunt, Herts.
Paul, Mr. Charles, St. Clement's, Norwich
*Paul, Matthew, Esq., Dillington, Somersetshire
*Paulin, John, Esq., Henley upon Thames
Paxton, Mr. Joseph, Chatsworth, Derbyshire
*PAYMASTER GENERAL'S OFFICE, His Majesty's
*Payn, Mr. John M., Stratfield-Saye, Hants.
*Payne, C., Esq., Nyton, near Lewes, Sussex
Payne, Charles, Esq., Clifton, near Bristol
*Payne, Edward, Esq., New college, Oxford
Payne, Rev. George, A. M., Exeter
Payne, J., Esq., Milverton, Somerset.
Payne, John, Esq., Maldon, Essex
*Payne, J., Esq., Wolferlow-court, Herefordshire
*Payne, R., Esq., Morning Post Newsp. Office
*Payne, Robert A., Esq., Oriel college, Oxford
*Payne, Samuel, Esq., Nottingham
*Payne, Mr. Thomas, Southampton
*Payne, William, Esq., Trinity coll., Cambridge
*Paynter, John, Esq., Blackheath, Kent
*Paynter, Samuel, Esq., Richmond, Surrey
Peace, Mr. H., Maiden-lane, Wood-st., London
*Peace, Mr. Thos. S., Manchester
Peach, Mr. B., Abergavenny, Monmouthshire
*Peach, Mr. James, Malpas, Cheshire
Peach, Samuel, Esq., Portland-place, London
*Peach, Thomas, Esq., Pudsey, Yorkshire
Peach, Rev. W., Brampton, Derbyshire
Peacock, Rev. E., St. John's coll., Cambridge
Peacock, Mr. J., Huggin-lane, Cheapside, Lond.
*Peacock, Lewis, Esq., Lincoln's-inn-fields, do.
*Peacock, M. B., Esq., Solicitor to the General Post-office, do.
*Peacock, William, Esq., Denton, Lancashire
Peake, Rev. George, Aston, near Birmingham
*Peake, Samuel, Esq., Silverdale, Staffordshire
Pearce, Mr. W. F., Camelford, Cornwall
Pearce, Rev. H., Holmer, Herefordshire
*Pearce, John, Esq., Queen's college, Oxford
Pearce, Rev. Robert, Holmer, Herefordshire
*Pearce, Rev. Thomas, Folkestone, Kent
Pearce, T., Esq., Llangarran-court, Herefordsh.
Pearce, Messrs., Swithin's-lane, London
*Peard, J. W., Esq., Exeter college, Oxford
*Pearsall, John, Esq., Bow-lane, London
*Pearse, Rev. William, Poling, Sussex
Pearson, C., Esq., Oriel college, Oxford
*Pearson, Charles, Esq., Milton, Kent
*Pearson, Edward, Esq., Ashton upon Mersey
*Pearson, F., Esq., Kirkby-Lonsdale
*Pearson, G. S., Esq., Doctors Commons, Lond.
Pearson, Henry, Esq., Carlisle
*Pearson, James, Esq., Mintridge, Herefordshire
*Pearson, J., Esq., Graisley-house, Wolverhamp- [ton
*Pearson, Joseph, Esq., Nottingham
*Pearson, Nathaniel, Esq., Macclesfield, Cheshire
*Pearson, R., Esq., Newcastle upon Tyne
*Pearson, Samuel, Esq., Macclesfield, Cheshire
*Pearson, W. W., Esq., Trinity coll., Cambridge
*Peart, John, Esq., Clifton, near Bristol
Peart, Rev. Wm., M. A., Ealing, Middlesex
Pease, Clifford, Esq., Kingston upon Hull
*Pease, J. R., Esq., Helewood-house, near do.
Peat, A., Esq., Seven-Oaks, Kent
Peaty, Mr. Charles, Southampton
Peck, Mr. David, Hertford
*Peckover, A., Esq., Wisbeach, Cambridgeshire
*Pedder, Edward, Esq., Preston, Lancashire
*Pedder, James, Esq., do., do.

*Pedder, Rev. J., A. M. Garstang, Lancashire
*Pedder, Rev. John, jun., B. A., do.
Pedder, Thomas, Esq., Preston, do.
Peed, J., Esq., Whittlesey, near Peterborough
*Peed, Samuel, Esq., Cambridge
Peel, Edmund, Esq., Church-bank, Blackburn
*Peel, George, Esq., Ardwick, near Manchester
*Peel, Rev. Giles, Haworth-Ince, Cheshire
Peel, Jonathan, Esq., Accrington-hall, Lancash.
*Peel, Jos., Esq., Broughton, near Manchester
*Peel, L., Esq., Brick-court, Temple, London
*Peel, Robert, Esq., Accrington, Lancashire
Peell, Mr. Walter, Bromyard, Herefordshire
*Peet, Samuel, Esq., Skinner-st., London
*Pegg, Mr. Henry, Tonbridge Wells, Kent
*Pegg, Mr. William, Wooburn, Bucks.
*Peipers, G., Esq., Great Coram-street, London
Peirce, Mr. James, Llanelly, Breconshire
*Peirse, James, Esq., Bucklersbury, London
*Peirson, Mr. John Hale, Altrincham, Cheshire
Pelcher, M. H., Esq., New Broad-street, Lond.
*Pelham, The Honorable John
Pelham, Jabez, Esq., Fenchurch-st., London
Pelican Life Insurance Company, do.
PEMBROKE, The Right Hon. the Earl of
*Pemberton, Christopher, Esq., Cambridge
Pemberton, J., Esq., Hertford
Pemberton, Rev. R. N., Church-Stretton, Salop.
Pemberton, Thomas, Esq., Barnes, Sunderland
*Pembrook, Mr. Richard, Littlebourn, Kent
*Pendergrass, J., Esq., Pool-cottage, Hereford
Pendleton Society, The, for Promoting Useful Knowledge
*Pendrill, John, Esq., Balliol college, Oxford
*Penfold, E., Esq., Maidstone, Kent
*Penfold, John, Esq., Haslemere, Surrey
*Penfold, Thomas, Esq., Croydon, do.
*Penfold, William, Esq., Brighton
Penhall, Rev. Samson, Whitchurch, Herefordsh.
*Penkett, J., Esq., Sea-Bank, Liscard, Cheshire
*Penleaze, J. S., Esq., Bossington, Hants.
Penleaze, John, Esq., Magdalene coll., Oxford
*Penn, J., Esq., Stoke-park, Bucks. . 2 Copies
*Pennant, G. H. D., Esq., Portland-pl., London
Pennell, Robert, Esq., Wistaston, Cheshire
Penner, Mr. Edward, Ross, Herefordshire
Penning, S., Esq., Combe-Down, Somersetshire
*Pennington, Rev. Montague, A. M., Deal
*Penny, Rev. Benj., M. A., Heswall, Cheshire
Penny, Chas., Esq., Pembroke college, Oxford
Penny, J. P., Esq., Liverpool
*Penrice, J., Esq., Yarmouth, Norfolk
Penrose, Rev. Thomas, D. C. L., Shaw-place, near Newbury, Berks.
Penton, Rev. Thomas, Wellow, Hants.
*Pepper, Benjamin, Esq., Eling, do.
Pepper, Mr. G. R., Exbury, do.
*Pepper, John, Esq., Southampton
Peppercorn, W. A., Esq., St. Neots, Hunts.
Peppercorne, W., Esq., Tokenhouse-yard, Lond.
Percival, Rev. H., Washington, Durham
*Percival, John, Esq., Northampton
Percival, S., Esq., Allerton, near Liverpool
*Peren, B., Esq., Compton-Deane, Somerset.
Perkes, Mr. J. W., Wolverhampton
*Perkins, F., Esq., Chipstead-place, Kent
Perkins, Mr. Mark, New Hall-st., Birmingham
Perkins, Samuel, Esq., Wacton, Herefordshire
Perkins, S., Esq., Blackman-street, Southwark
Perkins and Frampton, Messrs., Gray's-inn-sq., London
*Perrin, J., Esq., Wharton, Cheshire
*Perrin, W., Esq., Brickhill-lane, London
*Perry, G., Esq., Trinity college, Cambridge
*Perry, Henry, Esq., Lincoln's-inn, London
Perry, James, Esq., Sawbridgeworth, Herts.
*Perry, Rev. John, Compton-Martin, Somerset.
Perry, John, Esq., Cholstrey, Herefordshire
Perry, Mr. Joseph, Reading, Berks. [London
*Perry, R. W., Esq., Perry's-place, Oxford-st.,
Perry, Samuel, Esq., Liverpool
Perry, William, Esq., do.

*Peskett, George, Esq., Chichester, Sussex
*PETERBOROUGH, The Right Reverend Lord Bishop of
*Peters, George Frederick, Esq., Bristol
*Peters, J. W., Esq., South Petherton, Somerset.
Peters, Richard, Esq., Newcastle upon Tyne
Petersdorff, C., Esq., Temple, London
*Peterson, Andrew, Esq., Wakefield
Peterson, Henry, Esq., do.
Petley, C. R., Esq., St. John's college, Oxford
*Peto, Henry, Esq., Highbury-terrace, Islington
*PETRE, The Right Honorable Lord
Petrie, H., Esq., F. S. A., Tower, London
Pettet, Mr. Charles, Norwich
Pettet, Mr. Edward, do.
Pettipher, Mr. Samuel, Worcester
Petty, G. S., Esq., Ulverstone
*Petty, Henry, Esq., Evershot, Dorsetshire
*Petty, James, Esq., Manchester
*Petty, Jno., Esq., Froome St. Quintin, Dorset.
*Pewtress, Benjamin, Esq., Southwark, London
*Peyton, Henry, Esq., Woodstock, Oxfordshire
Peyton, Nich., Esq., Ledbury, Herefordshire
Pfeiler, John, Esq., Tokenhouse-yard, London
Phayre, Robert, Esq., Claremont, Shrewsbury
*Phelips, J., Esq., Montacute, Somersetshire
*Phelps, H. L., Esq., Puckrup, Tewkesbury
Phelps, Isaac, Esq., South Brent, Somerset.
*Phelps, Rev. J. W., Blagdon, near Bristol
*Phelps, John T., Esq., Jesus college, Oxford
*Phelps, R., Esq., Ledbury, Herefordshire
Phelps, S. F., Esq., Warminster, Wilts.
Phelps, Rev. W. A.
Phelps, W., jun., Esq., Pancras-lane, London
*Phelps, William L., Esq., Tewkesbury
*Phelps, W. L., Esq., Evesham
Phelps, Rev. W. W., M. A., Harrow, Middsx.
*Phene, Lincoln, Esq., Farnham, Surrey [Lond.
*Philip, A. P. W., Esq., M. D., Cavendish-sq.,
*Philips, J., Esq., Heath-house, Staffordshire
*Philips, John, Esq., Carlisle
*Philips, John, Esq., Royston, Herts.
*Philips, Nathaniel G., Esq., Liverpool
*Philips, Robert, Esq., Heybridge, Staffordshire
Phillimore, G., Esq., Christ-church col., Oxford
Phillimore, R. J., Esq., do., do.
*Phillimore, W. R., Esq., St. Albans
*Phillips, Sir R. B. P., Bart., M.P., Haverford West, Pembrokeshire
*Phillips, Charles, Esq., Stamford, Lincolnshire
Phillips, C. H., Esq., Wood-st., Cheapside, Lon.
Phillips, E., Esq., Upper Stamford-st., do.
*Phillips, F., Esq., Hulme, near Manchester
Phillips, George, Esq., Queen's college, Oxford
Phillips, Henry, Esq., Bermondsey-st., London
Phillips, Mr. H., Budge-row, Cannon-st., do.
Phillips, J., Esq., Bullingham-ct., Herefórdsh.
*Phillips, Rev. John, A. B., Ellesmere, Salop.
Phillips, John, Esq., Birmingham
*Phillips, John, Esq., Royston, Herts.
Phillips, John, Esq., Weslington, Herefordshire
Phillips, Mr. John, Lime-street, London
Phillips, J. E., Esq., Newcastle, Staffordshire
Phillips, J. H., Esq., Oriel college, Oxford
Phillips, Rev. John M., Louth, Lincolnshire
Phillips, Mr. Jos., jun., Stamford, do.
*Phillips, J. S., Esq., Trinity coll., Cambridge
Phillips, Rev. J. W., Fownhope, Herefordshire
Phillips, M. A., Esq., Grosmont, Monmouthsh.
Phillips, Miss M. A., do., do.
Phillips, Rev. Nathaniel, D.D., Sheffield
Phillips, Mr. Richard, Shrewsbury
*Phillips, R. Curtis, Esq., Bowlish, Somersetsh.
Phillips, Mr. Samuel, Lucton, Herefordshire
Phillips, Rev. T., King's Pion, do.
Phillips, Thomas, Esq., Newton-court, do.
Phillips, T., Esq., jun., Newport, Monmouthsh.
*Phillips, Mr. T., Carey-street, London
Phillips, Mr. Thomas, Hay, Brecon.
Phillips, Mr. Thomas, Bircher, Herefordshire
Phillips, Mr. Thomas E., Monmouth
Phillips, T. J., Esq., Newport, Monmouthshire

Phillips, Mr. W., Bromyard, Herefordshire
Phillips, W. D., Esq., Jesus college, Oxford
Phillips, W. P., Esq., Trinity college, do.
Phillips, Messrs. E. & G., Longport, Staffordsh.
*Phillott, Edward, Esq., Pembroke col., Oxford
*Phillott, Rev. J., Stanton-Priors, Somerset.
Phillott, Rev. J. R., Wookey, near Wells, do.
Phillpotts, Mr. W., St. Weonard's, Herefordsh.
Philpot, Mr. Geo., Maidstone, Kent
*Philpot, H., Esq., Catharine-hall, Cambridge
*Philpot and Stone, Messrs., Southampton-st., Bloomsbury-square, London [Man
Philpot, Rev. B., Vicar-Gen., Oak-hill, Isle of
*Philpott, ——, Esq., St. John's col., Cambdg.
*Philpott, Rev. T., Pedmore, Worcestershire
*Phipp, Thomas, Esq., London-street, London
Phippen, R., Esq., Badgworth-house, Somerset.
*Phipps, Mr. C., River, Kent
Phipps, George, Esq., Bishop-Stortford, Herts.
Phipps, John, Esq., Stratford on Avon [merset.
*Phipps, T. H. Hele, Esq., Shepton-Mallet, So-
*Pickard, Rev. J. T., L. L. D., Doctors Commons, London
*Picart, Rev. S., Hartlebury, Worcestershire
Pickering, P. A., Esq., Trinity col., Cambridge
Pickering, Mr. Robert, Ludlow, Shropshire
Pickering, T. A., Esq., Thelwall-hall, Cheshire
Pickering, T. N., Esq., St. Helen's-place, Lond.
Pickford, Mr. James, Manchester
*Pickin, J., Esq., White-moor, Notts.
*Pickin, William, Esq., Wellington, Shropshire
*Pickles, Ely, Esq., Altham, Lancashire
Pickwood, J., Esq., St. Peter's col., Cambridge
Piddocke, Rev. J., M. A., Ashby de la Zouch
Piddocke, J., Esq., do.
Pidgeon, H. C., Esq., Isleworth, Middlesex
*Pierce, Mr. J. J., Canterbury [cestersh.
Piercy, Rev. G. H., Chaddesley-Corbett, Wor-
Piercy and Oakley, Messrs., Southwark
Pierrepoint, H. B., Esq., New college, Oxford
*Pierson, Joseph M., Esq., Hitchin, Herts.
*Pieton, Mr. T., Broad-street, London
Pigeon, Henry, Esq., High-street, Borough
Piggott, Mr. J., Waltham-Abbey, Essex
Pigot, Henry, Esq., Christ-church coll., Oxford
*Pigott, John H. Smyth, Esq., Brockley-hall, Somersetshire [Essex
Pigram and Co., Messrs. C., Waltham-Abbey,
Pike, Mr. John, Oxford
*Pike, Messrs. W. and W., Derby
*Pilcher, John, Esq., Dover
*Pilgrim, John, Esq., Norwich
*Pilkington, Rev. Charles, Chichester, Sussex
*Pilkingtons, Messrs., Preston, Lancashire
*Pilling, Mr. John, Manchester
Pincke, Mrs., Sharsted-house, nr. Sittingbourne
*Pinckney, Rev. J. H., D. D., East Sheen, Surrey
*Pinder, William, Esq., Colne, Lancashire
Pineio, John D., Esq., Charlotte-st., London
Pinkardton, David, jun., Esq., Liverpool
*Pinkerton, J. S., Esq., St. John's coll., Oxford
*Pinney, John F., Esq., Somerton, Somerset.
*Pinniger, B., Esq., Chippenham, Wilts.
Pinniger, Henry, Esq., Westbury, do.
Pinscent, Mr. J., Ratcliffe-ter., Goswell-rd., Lond.
*Pirie, John, Esq., Freeman's-ct., Cornhill, do.
Pitchford, Rev. J., A. M., Colwich, Staffordsh.
*Pitman, Mr. E., Shepton-Mallet, Somersetshire
*Pitman, H., Esq., Dover
*Pitt, The Honorable George
Pitt, Mr. B., Dudley
*Pitt, Major C. H., St. Clement's, Oxford
*Pitt, H., Esq., Bodenham, Herefordshire
*Pitt, J., Esq., Lindridge, Worcestershire
*Pitt, Mr. J., Piccadilly, London
*Pittard, Rev. S. R., Martock, Somersetshire
*Pittman, Mrs. Mary Ann, Warwick-sq., Lond.
*Pix, Thomas, Esq., Peasmarsh, Sussex
*Plant, J., Esq., Manchester
Plant, Peter, Esq., Nottingham
*Platt, George E., Esq., Horsham, Sussex
Platt, J., Esq., New Boswell-court, London

*Platt, John, Esq., Altrincham, Cheshire
*Platt, Mr. Joshua, Stalybridge, Lancashire
Platt, Thomas, Esq., Lincoln's-inn, London
Platt, T. J., Esq., Farrer's-builds., Temple, do.
*Platts, H., Esq., Jewin-cresct., Aldersgate-st., do.
*Player, G., Esq., Ryde-house, Isle of Wight
Player, Mr. Thomas, Chaseley, Worcestershire
Playne, George, Esq., Gloucester
Plenty, Mr. William, Newbury, Berks.
*Plimley, Rev. Henry, Cuckfield, Sussex
*Plomer, E., Esq., George-st., Adelphi, London
Plomer, G., Esq., Canterbury
*Plowden, E., Esq., Shiffnall, Shropshire
*Plumbe, S., Esq., Peel-hall, Cheshire
Plumbe, Mr. W., Henley upon Thames
*Plumes, Dr., Library of, Maldon, Essex
Plumpton, James, Esq., Everton, near Liverpool
Plunket, —, Esq., Southampton
*PLYMOUTH, The Right Hon. the Earl of
*Pockeridge, A. S., Esq., Corsham, Wilts.
*Pocklington, Rev. H. S., M. A., Overton, near Lancaster [Cumberland
*Pocklington, J., Esq., Barrow-hall, Keswick,
*Pocock, Sir G., Bt., Twickenham-house, Surrey
*Pocock, Isaac, Esq., Maidenhead-bridge, Berks.
Podmore, C. H., Esq., Loose, Kent
Pointer, Rev. R., Southoe, Huntingdonshire
Pole, E. S. Chandos, Esq., Radbourn, Derbyshire
Pole, Rev. Reginald Chandos, do., do.
*Polehampton, Rev. E., M.A., Greenford, Midds.
*Pollard, James, Esq., Spa, near Gloucester
*Pollard, John, Esq., Chorley, Lancashire
*Pollard, Mr. John, Lewes, Sussex
Pollard, Mrs. Sarah, Hertford
*Pollen, Sir J. W., Bt., M. P., Redenham, Hants.
*Pollock, D., Esq., F. R. S., M. R. A. S., R. S. L., and V. P. S. A., Lincoln's-inn-fields, Lon.
Polmer, T. D., Esq., jun., Yarmouth, Norfolk
Pontifex, J., Esq., St. Andrew's-court, London
*Pook, John, Esq., Newington-green, Middlesex
*Poole, Charles, Esq., Altrincham, Cheshire
Poole, C. S., Esq., Staple-inn, London
Poole, D., Esq., Old Broad-street, do.
Poole, James, Esq., Oriel college, Oxford
*Poole, M., Esq., Lincoln's-inn, Old-sq., Lond.
*Poole, R., Esq., Gray's-inn, do.
Poole, R. Anthony, Esq., Carnarvon
Poole, T. Eyre, Esq., Queen's college, Oxford
*Poole & Co., Messrs., Chester
*Pooley, Henry, Esq., Manchester
*Pooley, John, sen., Esq., Hulme, near do.
*Pooley, John, jun., Esq., do., do.
Pooley, Rev. J. H., St. John's coll., Cambridge
*Poolly, Mr. George, Maidstone, Kent
Pooly, Messrs. W. & J. F., Turnwheel-lane, Lond.
Pope, Rev. B., Nether Stowey, Somersetshire
*Pope, George, Esq., Gray's-inn, London
*Pope, Joseph, Esq., Bolton, Lancashire
*Pope, Rev. Robert, Mersham, Kent
Pope, Thomas, Esq., Crawford-street, London
Pope, Rev. W. L., M. A., Tonbridge-Wells
*Popham, Lieutenant-Colonel, Littlecot, Wilts.
*Popham, F., Esq., West Bagborough-house, Somersetshire
*Popham, J. L., Esq., Wadham college, Oxford
*Porch, Mr. J., Lime-street, London
*Porter, E. R., Esq., King's-Arms-yard, do.
*Porter, Rev. G., Fellow of Queen's col., Oxford
*Porter, J. W., Esq., Birmingham
Porter, Rev. R., M. A., Draycot, Staffordshire
Porter, Thomas, Esq., Liverpool
Porter, William, Esq., Stratford on Avon
Porter, Mr. William, Yeovil, Somersetshire
*Porteus, H., Esq., Christ's college, Cambridge
*Portico Library, Manchester
*Portman, E. B., Esq., M.P., Blandford, Dorset.
*Posson, Mr. Thomas, Moccas, Herefordshire
*Postlethwaite, John, Esq., Dalton, Lancashire
Postlethwaite, William, Esq., Ulverstone
*Postlethwaite, Wooburn, Esq., do.
Potchett, Rev. William, Grantham, Lincolnshire
Pote, B. E., Esq., Lombard-street, London

*Pott, William, Esq., Bridge-street, Southwark
Potter, C. Bower, Esq., Darley-hall Derbysh.
*Potter, George, Esq., Watling-street, London
*Potter, Harold, Esq., Dinting Vale, Derbyshire
*Potter, Rev. John Cass, Tintwistle, Cheshire
Potter, Joseph, Esq., Lichfield
*Potter, Richard, Esq., Cannon-st., Manchester
*Potter, Robert, Esq., Sibbertswold, Kent
*Potter, Thomas, Esq., Manchester
*Potter, Rev. W., B.A., St. Peter's col., Cambrid.
*Potts, Henry, Esq., Chester
Potts, Rev. James, Whorlton, Durham
*Potts, John, Esq., New-Mills, Derbyshire
*Potts, Mr. John, Martin's-lane, London
*Potts, R., Esq., Serjeant's-inn, Fleet-st., do.
*Potts, Mr. T. R., Birmingham
Potts, William, Esq., do.
*Potts, W. W., Esq., New-Mills, Derbyshire
POULETT, The Right Honorable the Earl of
Poulter, J., Esq., Frome, Somersetshire
*Pound, Mr. Charles, Shrivenham, Berks.
Pountney, Rev. H., M.A., Birmingham
*Poussett, P. T., Esq., London-street, London
Pout, Mr. Alderman, Canterbury
*Powell, Charles Henry, Esq., Monmouth
Powell, G., Esq., Kingston, Somersetshire
Powell, George, Esq., Clifton, near Bristol
Powell, H. S., Esq., Trinity college, Oxford
Powell, Jas., sen., Esq., Coleford, Gloucestersh.
Powell, James, jun., Esq., do., do.
*Powell, Mr. James, Norton-Falgate, London
Powell, John, Esq., Eaton-Foy, Herefordshire
Powell, John, Esq., Little Fowley, do.
*Powell, John, Esq., Manchester
Powell, Mr. John, Monmouth
*Powell, John A., Esq., Lincoln's-inn, London
*Powell, John Folliott, Esq., Hertford
*Powell, John H., jun., Esq., Bury St. Edmunds
*Powell, J. C., Esq., St. Helen's-place, London
Powell, J. P., Esq., Quex-park, Margate
Powell, R., Esq., Trinity college, Cambridge
*Powell, Robert, Esq., Arundel-street, do.
Powell, R. J., Esq., Hinton, Herefordshire
Powell, Rev. T., Sedgley, Staffordshire
Powell, Mr. Thomas, Monmouth
Powell, Mr. William, Lyonshall, Herefordshire
*Powell, W. P., Esq., Worcester coll., Oxford
*Powell, W. W., Esq., King's Caple, Herefordsh.
Powell, Mr. Wm., Sollers-Hope, do.
Powell and Son, Messrs., Knaresborough
*Powell, Col. Thomas, Hardwick-Hay, Brecon.
*Power, Rev. Alexander, M. A., Ashford, Kent
Power, J., Esq., M. D., Lichfield
*Power, Patrick, Esq., Gifford's-hall, Suffolk
*POWIS, The Right Honorable the Earl of
Powles, Mr. Richard, Monmouth
*POWLETT, The Right Honorable Lord Wm.
*Pownall, H., Esq., Spring-grove, Middlesex
*Pownall, J., Esq., Mayfield-Wavertree, near Liverpool [Cheshire
*Pownall, J., Esq., Yarwood-heath, Rosthern,
Pownall, Mr. James E., Lambeth, Surrey
*Pownall, Messrs. J. and W., Staples-inn, Lond.
Powys, Rev. Edward, M. A., Lee-house, near Leek, Staffordshire
*Powys, H. P., Esq., Southgate, Middlesex
*Poynder, T., jun., Esq., Treasurer of Christ's Hospital, London
*Poynder, Messrs. E., and S., Clement's-lane, do.
Poynter, Rev. W., D.D., Castle-st., Holborn, do.
Pratchett, William, Esq., Ware, Herts.
*Pratt, A., Esq., Redditch, Worcestershire
Pratt, Benjamin, Esq., Pershore, do.
*Pratt, Charles, Esq., Dartford, Kent
*Pratt, Mr. H., Bilston-mill, Staffordshire
*Pratt, James, Esq., Preston, Lancashire
*Pratt, J. J., Esq., St. John's college, Oxford
Pratt, Mr. Jas., Canterbury
*Pratt, Samuel, Esq., Glastonbury, Somerset.
Preay, Charles, Esq., Liverpool
*Preece, William, Esq., Leominster
Prentice, Mr. A., Manchester

*Prentis, Henry, Esq., Rochester, Kent
*Prescott, Rev. John, Branston, Lincolnshire
Presgrave, Rev. W., M. A., Ilchester, Somerset.
Pressly, C., Esq., Somerset-house, London
Prest, John, Esq., Liverpool [Norfolk
*Preston, Sir J. H., Bart., Beeston St. Lawrence,
Preston, E., Esq., Yarmouth, do. [minster
*Preston, Rev. G., Little Dean's-yard, West-
Preston, Henry, Esq., Naburn, Yorkshire
*Preston, John H., Esq., Newcastle upon Tyne
*Preston, Overseer's Office, Lancashire
Preston, Rev. M. M., Cheshunt, Herts.
*Preston, W., Esq., Kirkby-Lonsdale
Preston and Co., Messrs. Robert, Liverpool
Prestwich, Joseph, Esq., South Lambeth, Surrey
*Pretor, Samuel, Esq., Sherborne, Dorsetshire
Pretty, J. R., Esq., Bilston, Staffordshire
*Pretyman, Rev. G. T., L. L. B., Lincoln
Pretyman, Rev. G. T., L. L. B., Wheathamp-
*Pretyman, Rev. Rich., Lincoln [stead, Herts.
*Price, Sir R., Bart., M. P., Foxley-hall, Here-
Price, David, Esq., Margate, Kent [fordsh.
Price, Rev. D. P., Llangarran-ct., Herefordsh.
Price, Fowler, Esq., Huntington, do.
*Price, F., Esq., Caroline-place, Foundling, Lon.
*Price, F. R., Esq., Bryn-y-Pys, near Wrexham
Price, G., Esq., Vern, nr. Marden, Herefordsh.
*Price, Rev. Jas., Bodnant, near Conway, Car-
Price, James, Esq., Hereford [narvonshire
Price, Mr. John, Lincoln's-inn-fields, London
*Price, Mr. John, Hay, Brecon.
*Price, Mr. Joseph, Bilston, Staffordshire
Price, L. J., Esq., Jesus college, Oxford
Price, N. G., Esq., Rolstone, Monmouth
*Price, R., Esq., Cannon-street, London
Price, Rev. S., Bodnant, nr. Conway, Carnarvon-
*Price, S. G., Esq., Gray's-inn, London [shire
Price, Rev. Thomas, Stafford
Price, Thomas, Esq., Clementhorpe, near York
Price, Thomas, Esq., Tretyre, Herefordshire
*Price, T. D., Esq., Basinghall-street, London
Price, Mr. T., Rochester, Kent
Price, Mr. Thomas, Monmouth
Price, Mr. Thos., Upton-Little, Hereford
*Price, William, Esq., Lincoln's-inn, London
*Price, Wm., Esq., Hentland, Herefordshire
Price, W., Esq., Weston super Mare, Somerset.
Price, W. B., Esq., The Wells, Herefordshire
Prichard, Thomas, Esq., Ross, do.
Prickett, Captain, R. N., Southampton
Prickett, Edward, Esq., Aylesbury, Bucks.
Prideaux, Rev. G., Sittingbourne, Kent
Pridmore, W., Esq., Coomfields, near Coventry
Priestley, Mr. Richard, Holborn, London
Prince, John, Esq., Cheltenham
*Prince, John, Esq., Manchester
Prince, Mr. Phillip, Mitcham, Surrey
Prince, R., Esq., Bullingham, Herefordshire
*Pritchard, C., Esq., Lugwardine, do.
*Pritchard, Edward, Esq., Hereford
Pritchard, J., Esq., Risca, Monmouthshire
Pritchard, R. D., Esq., Southampton
*Pritchard, Mr. Robert, Prees, Shropshire
*Pritchard, William, jun., Esq., Hereford
Pritchard, Mr. William, Bride-lane, London
Pritchett, Rev. G., Ombersley, Worcestershire
Pritchett, T. G., Esq., Norton, Herefordshire
Pritt, George, Esq., Liverpool
PRIVY COUNCIL, His Majesty's Most Hon.
Probart, F. L'Oste, Esq., Hawarden, Flintshire
Probyn, Mr. J., Lisle-st., Leicester-sq., London
*Probyn, Rev. E., A.M., Longhope, Gloucestersh.
Procter, G., Esq., King's Pion, Herefordshire
*Procter, Joseph, Esq., Lower Tooting, Surrey
*Procter and Sons, Messrs., Hay, Brecon.
*Proctor, Sir W. B., Bart., Langley-park, Norfolk
Proctor, John, Esq., Pembridge, Herefordshire
Prosser, The Rev. and Ven. Archdeacon, D. D.
Prosser, Henry, Esq., Croydon, Surrey
Prosser, Rev. Henry, Garway, Herefordshire
Prosser, Rev. Jos., Newchurch, Monmouthsh.
*Prosser, Paul, Esq., Garway, Herefordshire

* Prosser, Rev. Thomas, Dorstone, Herefordshire
Prosser, Dr. William, Monmouth [London
* Protector Fire Assurance Company, Old Jewry,
* Prothero, T., jun., Esq., Brasenose coll., Oxford
* Protheroe, Sir Henry, Knt., Llantarnan Abbey, Monmouthshire
* Proud, J. Freer, Esq., Wolverhampton
Proud, T. A., Esq., Darlaston, Staffordshire
Provand, M. Charles, Esq., Compstall, Cheshire
Pruen, E. J., Esq., Cheltenham
* Pryor, John, Esq., Baldock, Herts.
* Pryor, John Izard, Esq., Clay-hall, do.
* Pryor, Vickris, Esq., Baldock, do.
* Puddicombe, E. D., Esq., Thavies-inn, London
Pugh, Messrs. W. & C., Blackman-st., Borough
Pugh, Richard, Esq., Watford, Herts.
* Pugh, Rev. Thomas, Clifford, do.
Pugit, John Hey, Esq., Totteridge, do.
Puleston, Sir Richard, Bart., Emral, Flintshire
* Pullen, John, Esq., jun., Fore-street, London
Pullen, Samuel P., Esq., Knaresborough
* Pulley, W. M., Esq., Doctors Commons, Lond.
* Pulsford, Rev. C. H., Burnham, Somersetshire
Pumfrett, Mr. George, Betts, Huntingdon
Pumfrey, C., Esq., Droitwich, Worcestershire
Pumfrey, Mr. S., jun., Worcester
Pumfrey and Sons, Messrs., Wantage, Berks.
Purchas, John, Esq., Mordiford, Herefordshire
Purland, Mr. Theodosius, Long-Acre, London
Purlewent, W., Esq., Shepton-Mallet, Somer-
Purnell, Benjamin, Esq., Bristol [setshire
* Purves, R., Esq., Sembury-place, Middlesex
* Purvis, Captain Edward, Reading, Berks.
Pusgrave, Rev. Wm., A.M., Ilchester, Somerset
* Pybus, J. A., Esq., Newcastle upon Tyne
Pye, Wm., Esq., Christ-church college, Oxford
* Pyer, Rev. John, Canal-street, Manchester
Pyke, Mr. H., Chancery-lane, London
Pym, Rev. W. W., M. A., Willian, Herts.

* Quane, John Joseph, Esq., Nantwich, Cheshire
Quantock, J., Esq., Norton under Hambdon, So-
Quarles, Thomas James, Esq., Norwich [merset.
Queckett, Edw., Esq., Langport, and George-yard, Lombard-street, London [Wilson
* Queen's College Library, Oxford, per Rev. J.
* Quelch, William, Esq., Reading, Berks.
Quick, James C., Esq., Trinity-row, Islington
Quier, Mr. W. B., Bridg-water, Somerset. 2 Cop.
Quilter, Samuel Sacker, Esq., Walton, Suffolk
Quilton, Mr. Ambrose, Waltham-Cross, Essex
* Quin, Mr. Joseph, Coleman-street, London
* Quirk, C. T., Esq., St. John's coll., Cambridge
* Quirk, George, Esq., Castletown, Isle of Man
* Quirk, Mr. John, Union-terrace, Southampton
Quirk, Philip, Esq., Liverpool

Rackett, Rev. Thos., Upper Gower-st., London
Racster, J., Esq., Wootens, Worcestershire
* Racster, Martin, Esq., Birchin-lane, London
Racster, Mr. William, Thinghill, Herefordshire
Radcliffe, Rev. G., D.D., Salisbury
* Radcliffe, George, Esq., Witton, Lancashire
* Radcliffe, Joshua, Esq., Rochdale, do.
Radcliffe, Rev. R. B., M.A., Ashby de la Zouch
* Radcliffe, Samuel, Esq., Oldham, Lancashire
Radcliffe and Duncan, Messrs., Liverpool
Radford, A., Esq., Stoney-Middleton, Derbysh.
Radford, Edward, Esq., Matlock, do.
Radford, John, Esq., Smalley, do.
* Radley, James, Esq., Oldham, Lancashire
* Radwick, John, Esq., Rochdale, do.
Rae, Mr. James, Leominster, Herefordshire
Raffles, Rev. Thomas, L. L. D., Liverpool
Raikes, R., jun., Esq., Eastdale, Yorkshire
Raikes, Thomas, Esq., Welton, do.
* Railton, Joseph, Esq., Brook Green, Middlesex
Rain, Henry, Esq., Bread-street, London
Raincock, Fletcher, Esq., Rodney-st., Liverpool
Raine, Rev. James, M.A., Durham
* Rainshay, Rev. T., M. A., Brampton, Cumber.
* Ramadge, F. H., Esq., M. D., Ely-place, Lond.
* Ramus, Mr. H. W., Bishop's Cleeve, Glouces-
* Rampling, Mr. C., Manchester [tershire
* Ramsay, Maj.-Gen., White Friars, Canterbury
Ramsay, M., Esq., M. A., F. L. S., Fellow and Tutor of Jesus college, Cambridge
* Ramsbottom, Mr. Wm., St. Edmund's, Norwich
Ramsden, Richard, Esq., Brook-street, London
Ramsey and Andrews, Messrs., Cateaton-st., do.
* Rance, Henry, Esq., Cambridge
* Randall, A., Esq., Maidstone, Kent
* Randall, Mr. J. F., Fetter-lane, London
* Randall, Thomas, Esq., Paulton, near Bath
Randell, J. H., Esq., Liverpool
Randolph, J., jun., Esq., Milverton, Somerset
* Randolph, Rev. T., Hadham, Herts.
Ranger, Mr. E., jun., Longstock, Hants.
Ransom, W., Esq., Stow-Market, Suffolk
* Ransome, J. A., Esq., Manchester
Ransome, Mr. Richard, Norwich
Ranyard, William, Esq., Kingston, Surrey
* Raper, Matt., Esq., F. R. S., and V. P. of Antiquarian Society, Wimpole-street, London
* Rashdall, J., Esq., Corpus Christi coll., Cambridge
* Rashleigh, Rev. P., A.M., Southfleet, Kent
Rastall, Henry, Esq., Newark, Notts.
Rastrick, Mr. John, Urpeth, Stourbridge
Ratcliff, Mr. John, jun., Birmingham
* Ratcliffe, John, Esq., Templer's-street, Leeds
* Ratcliffe, Mr. Robert, Oldham, Lancashire
* Rathbone, Rev. David, Newchurch, do.
Rather, William, Esq., Grantham, Lincolnshire
Raven, Mr. H., Chapel-pl., Grosvenor-sq., Lond.
Ravenhill, William, Esq., Hereford
* Ravenhill, Rev. J., D.D., Lower Tooting, Surrey
Raver, W., Esq., Langdon, Worcestershire
Rawes, R. N., Esq., Richmond, Surrey
Rawlings, Jas., Esq., Basinghall-st., London
Rawlings, J., Esq., Catharine-hall, Cambridge
* Rawlings, Mr., Dartford, Kent
* Rawlins, Mr. G., Henley upon Thames
Rawlins, Mr. W., Paulton, near Bath
Rawlinson and Son, Messrs., Liverpool
* Rawson, B., Esq., Nidd, near Ripley, Yorksh.
* Rawson, George, Esq., Hanover-square, Leeds
* Rawson, J., Esq., Ardwick, near Manchester
* Rawson, James, jun., Esq., Leicester
* Rawson, Holdsworth, and Co., Messrs., Gracechurch-street, London
* Rawsthorne, Lawrence, Esq., Lancaster
* Rawsthorne, Thomas, Esq., do.
* Rayer, Mr. J., Forthampton, Gloucestershire
Rayment, Mr. James, Hertford
Raymond, H. A., Esq., Lincoln's-inn, London
Raymond, George, Esq., Temple, do.
Raymond, R. J., Esq., Ranelagh-walk, Chelsea
* Rayne, Rev. W. T., Leeds
* Rayner, Mr. John, Kingsland-green, Middlesex
* Rayner, William, Esq., Bury, Lancashire
Read, G. R., Esq., Magdalene col., Cambridge
* Read, John, Esq., Bayswater, Middlesex
* Read, John, Esq., Norton-house, Derbyshire
Read, John, Esq., do., Yorkshire
Read, J., Esq., Mere, near Knutsford, Cheshire
* Read, John, Esq., Holbrook, Suffolk
Read, Mr. John, Worcester
Read, Joseph, Esq., Camden Town, Middlesex
* Read, W. H. R., Esq., Trinity col., Cambridge
* Reade, F., jun., Esq., St. John's coll., do.
Reade, Thomas, Esq., Congleton, Cheshire
* Reader, William, Esq., Brunswick-sq., London
Ready, Mr. T. M., Peckham, Surrey
* Rear, F. J., Esq., Sloane-street, London
Reay, Charles, Esq., Queen's college, Oxford
* Reay, John, Esq., jun., Mark-lane, London
Reay, P., Esq., Bromyard, Herefordshire
* Redaway, George, Esq., Clement's-inn, London
Reddale, Mr. A. B., Congleton, Cheshire
* Reddish, John, Esq., Blackburn, Lancashire
* Reddish, Joseph, Esq., Northenden, Cheshire
* Reddish, T., Esq., Knurden-hall, Blackburn
Rede, Rev. Robert R., Beccles, Colchester
* Redfern, John, Esq., Ashton under Line
Redfern, William, Esq., Birmingham
Redhead, Matthew, Esq., Ulverstone
* Redhead, R., Esq., Gracechurch-street, London
* Redmayne, David M., Esq., Lancaster
* Redmayne, Leonard, Esq., do.
Redward, Mr. John, Westhide, Herefordshire
* Reece, Robert, Esq., Exeter college, Oxford
* Reed, Archibald, Esq., Newcastle upon Tyne
Reed, Rev. J., Wolverhampton
* Reed, William, Esq., Bedfont, Middlesex
* Reed, Messrs. J. and S., Newcastle upon Tyne
Reeley, Samuel, Esq., Summer-hill, Cork
Rees, Rev. William, A. M., Carlisle
Reeve, Mr. Jno., Craven-buildings, London
Reeve, Rev. Thos., Raydon, Suffolk
Reeve, W., Esq., Yarmouth, Norfolk
Reeves, Chas., Esq., Ely-place, London
Reeves, Henry, Esq., Up-Sombourn, Hants.
* Reeves, J. F., Esq., Glastonbury, Somersetshire
Reeves, John, Esq., Kingsclere, Hants
Reeves, John, Esq., F. R. S., and V. P. to the Antiquarian Society, London
Reeves, John, Esq., Parliament-place, London
* Reeves, John G., Esq., Birmingham
Reeves, Peter, Esq., Cottage, near Cork
* Reeves, Thomas W., Esq., Beckley, Sussex
Reeves, Wm., Esq., Upper Kennington-green,
* Reid, G., Esq., Regent's-park, London [Surrey
Reid, Nevile, Esq., Old Windsor
* Reid, William, Esq., Cavendish-square, London
* Reilly, James, Esq., Clement's-inn, do.
* Relph, James, Esq., Carlisle
* Remington, R., Esq., Milling, Lancashire
Rendell, E., Esq., St. John's coll., Cambridge
* Render, Henry, Esq., Dock-street, Leeds
* Renison, Mr. James P., Bradford, Wilts.
* Renshaw, John, Esq., Manchester
* Renwick, Thomas, Esq., M. D., Liverpool
Revill, Rev. S., M.A., Wingerworth, Derbysh.
Reynard, Francis, Esq., Reading, Berks.
* Reyner, J. B., Esq., Ashton under Line
* Reynolds, John, Esq., Charlton, Kent
Reynolds, Mr., Jesus college, Oxford
* Reynolds, W. F., Esq., Croydon, Surrey
Rhodes, Quintin, Esq., Ripon, Yorkshire
* Rhodes, Mr. Samuel, Halifax
Rhodes and Burch, Mess., Chancery-lane, Lond.
* Rice, Edward, Esq., Verulam-buildings, do.
* Rice, Rev. H., Norton-court, Kent
* Rice, Henry, Esq., Jermyn-street, London
* Rich, George, Esq., Gravesend, Kent
Richards, Rev. Henry, Horfield, near Bristol
Richards, Mr. C., St. Martin's-lane, London
* Richards, John, Esq., Liverpool
Richards, John, Esq., Reading, Berks.
Richards, John, Esq., Sun Fire Office, London
* Richards, J. W., Esq., Stapleton, Somerset.
Richards, Mr. J., Highgate, Warwickshire
Richards, P. M., Esq., Jesus college, Oxford
Richards, R. S., Esq., Inner Temple, London
* Richards, Silas H., Esq., Liverpool
* Richards, Thomas, Esq., Fleet-street, London
* Richards, W., Esq., Stapleton, near Martock,
* Richards, W., Esq., Reading, Berks. [Somerset.
* Richards, Clark and Nares, Messrs., Chapel-st. Bedford-row, London
Richards and Son, Messrs., Birmingham
* Richardson, Archibald, Esq., Liverpool
Richardson, Mr. C., Reading, Berks.
Richardson, Christ., and Son, Mess., Limehouse
* Richardson, Daniel, Esq., Cheapside, London
Richardson, H., Esq., Trinity col., Cambridge
* Richardson, H. K., Esq., do., do.
* Richardson, John, Esq., Lancaster
Richardson, Rev. John, Reading, Berks.
Richardson, J., Esq., jun., Spencer-st., London
* Richardson, Samuel, Esq., Hoylake, Cheshire
* Richardson, Thomas, Esq., Victualling Office, Somerset-house, London

Richardson, Thomas, Esq., Stockport, Cheshire
Richardson, Mr. Thomas, Macclesfield
* Richardson, W., Esq., Wadham coll., Oxford
* Richardson, William, Esq., Walbrook, London
* Richardson, William, Esq., Merton, Surrey
Richardson, Mr. W., Newcastle upon Tyne
Richardson, Messrs. J. and H., York
Richardson, Messrs. W., and Co., Newcastle
* Riches, Henry W., Esq., Norwich [upon Tyne
Riches, Thomas Harry, Esq., Uxbridge
Richings, Thomas, Esq., Thavies-inn, London
* RICHMOND, His Grace the Duke of
* Richmond, Christopher, Esq., Temple, London
Richmond, T., Esq., Chertsey, Surrey
* Richmond, Mr. T. P., Dorking, do.
* Rickards, G., Esq., Upper Bedford-pl., London
* Rickards and Co., Messrs., Bishopsgate-st., do.
Ricketts, Frederick, Esq., Clifton, near Bristol
* Ricketts, Henry, Esq., Brislington, do.
Ricketts, R., Esq., Bristol
Ricketts, W., Esq., Boston, Lincolnshire
Ricketts, Mrs., Shenley, Herts.
* Ricketts, W. H., Esq., Droitwich, Worcestersh.
Rickman, Thomas, Esq., Birmingham
Riddell, Rev. J., Easton, nr. Winchester, Hants.
Riddlesden, Captain, Dove Leys, Staffordshire
Rider, C., Esq., Collyhurst-hall, nr. Manchester
Ridgate, Thomas, Esq., Calverton, Notts.
* Ridge, G. Cooper, Esq., Morden-park, Surrey
* Ridge, William, Esq., Charles-st., Westminster
* Ridgen, W., Esq., Faversham, Kent
* Ridgway, I., Esq., Brom-edge, Lymm, Cheshire
Ridgway, J., Esq., Cauldon-place, Staffordshire
* Ridgway, J., Esq., Hayfield, Derbyshire
* Ridgway, John W., Esq., Manchester
* Ridgway, J., Esq., Ridgmont, Lancashire
* Ridgway, J., Esq., Liverpool
* Ridgway, Thomas, Esq., Bolton, Lancashire
Ridgway, W., Esq., Hanley, Staffordshire
Ridler, Mess. V. & C., Malvern, Worcestersh.
* Ridley, Sir Matthew White, Bart., M.P., Blagdon, Northumberland
* Ridley, Rev. T. Y., A. M., Heysham, Lancaster
Ridley, Rev. W. C., Kimbolton, Hunts.
* Ridley, Bigg, and Co., Messrs., Newcastle upon
Ridout, Rev. John, Blandford [Tyne
* Ridout, C. V., Esq., Great Russell-st., London
* Ridsdale, George, Esq., Wakefield, Yorkshire
Riebau, Mr. G., Blandford-street, London
* Rigby, Mr. John, Liverpool
* Rigby, Thomas, Esq., Marston, Cheshire
Rigby, Thomas T., Esq., Yateley-lodge, Hants.
* Rigden, W., Esq., Faversham, Kent
* Rigg, Gray, Esq., Milnthorpe, Westmorland
* Rigge, J., jun., Esq., Cook's-court, London
Riley, Richard, jun., Esq., Preston, Lancashire
Rimell, Mr. R., Aston upon Carron, Gloucester
Rindleson, D. T., Esq., Birmingham
* Ring, Thomas, Esq., Reading, Berks.
Ripley, H. A., Esq., Cateaton-street, London
Ripley, William, Esq., Liverpool
* Rippingham, M. J., Esq., Gt. Prescot-st., Lond.
* Rippon, C., Esq., Stanhope-castle, Bishop-Auckland
Rippon, John, Esq., Great Surrey-st., London
* Ritchie, Thomas M., Esq., Maidstone, Kent
* RIVERS, The Right Honorable Lord
Rivers, Miss E., Egham, Surrey
* Rivers, Mr. Joseph, Gilbert-street, London
RIVERSDALE, The Right Honorable Lord
Rix, Francis, Esq., St. Neots, Huntingdonshire
Roach, Thomas, Esq., Glastonbury, Somerset
* Roarke, James, Esq., Furnival's-Inn, London
* Robards, Thomas, Esq., Hatfield, Herefordshire
Robarts, N., Esq., Doctors Commons, London
Robarts, T. J. A., Esq., Christ-ch. col., Oxford
* Robberds, W. J., Esq., Norwich
* Robberds, C. A., Esq., Bucklersbury, London
* Roberson, Thomas, Esq., Oxford
Robert, J. M., Esq., M. D., Southampton
Roberts, Rev. ——, D. D., Bridport, Dorset.
Roberts, Lieut.-Gen., Stoke-Poges, Bucks.

* Roberts, Rev. A. W., Little Burstead, Essex
Roberts, Mr. C., Birmingham
Roberts, G., Esq., Warminster, Wilts. [dlesex
* Roberts, Rev. J., L. L. B., Harrow Weald, Mid-
Roberts, Mr. James, Canterbury
* Roberts, J. P., Esq., Holbeche-house, nr. Dudley
Roberts, J. Watson, Esq., M.D., Bishop-Stortford, Herts.
* Roberts, Richard, Esq., Manchester
* Roberts, Rev. Robert, Haverhill, Suffolk
* Roberts, Samuel, Esq., Glossop, Derbyshire
* Roberts, Thos. W., Esq., Trinity coll., Oxford
Roberts, W., Esq., New Basinghall-st., Lond.
Roberts, Wm., Esq., Coleford, Gloucestershire
Roberts, W. A., Esq., M. P., Bewdley, Worcestershire [yard, London
* Roberts, Messrs. C. and G., St. Paul's Church-
Robertson, C., Esq., Old Change, do.
* Robertson, D., Esq., Oxford
* Robertson, D. J., Esq., Tonbridge Wells
* Robertson, E., Esq., Gray's-inn, London
* Robertson, Francis, Esq., Chilcote, Derbyshire
Robertson, Mr. J., Canterbury
* Robeson, Messrs. W. and W. H., Bromsgrove
* Robin, John, Esq., West Kirby, Cheshire
* Robins, B., Esq., Wolverhampton
Robins, Charles, Esq., Fenchurch-st., London
Robins, George, Esq., Covent-garden, do.
* Robins, John, Esq., Regent-street, do.
Robins, J. R., Esq., Gower-st., Bedford-sq., do.
* Robins, Richard B., Esq., East Lavant, Sussex
* Robins, T., Esq., Magdalene coll., Cambridge
* Robinson, The Honorable Frederick
Robinson, A.W., Esq., Little St. Thomas Apostle, London [shire
Robinson, C. B., Esq., Hill Ridware, Stafford-
* Robinson, C. M., Esq., Wellington, Salop
* Robinson, D., Esq., Blackburn, Lancashire
* Robinson, E., Esq., Carey-street, London
Robinson, Frederick, Esq., Nottingham
* Robinson, F. B., Esq., Essex-street, London
* Robinson, George, Esq., Dalston, Cumberland
* Robinson, George, Esq., Wolverhampton
Robinson, George, Esq., York
Robinson, G. S., Esq., Canterbury
Robinson, J., Esq., Liverpool
Robinson, Mr. Henry, Swansea
* Robinson, J. T., Esq., Walthamstow, Essex
* Robinson, James, Esq., Pancras-lane, London
Robinson, J. E., Esq., Christ-ch. coll., Oxford
Robinson, John, Esq., Dudley
Robinson, John, Esq., Norwich [Cheshire
* Robinson, John, Esq., Dodcot cum Wilkesley,
* Robinson, John E., Esq., Cambridge
Robinson, J. J., Esq., Peckham, Surrey
Robinson, J. M., Esq., Chesterton, Cambridge
* Robinson, John R., Esq., Manchester
Robinson, Lucius H., Esq., Greek-st., London
Robinson, Rev. M., B. A., Boston, Lincolnshire
* Robinson, N., Esq., Aigburth, near Liverpool
Robinson, Rev. N. W., Bodenham, Herefordsh.
* Robinson, P. F., Esq., Lower Brook-st., Lond.
Robinson, Rev. Proctor, M. A., Head Master of the Grammar School, Dudley
Robinson, Rev. R., M. A., Whittington, Derby
Robinson, Mr. S., Dukinfield, Cheshire
Robinson, Thos. F., Esq., Maidenhead, Berks.
Robinson, Wm., Esq., Austin-friars, London
* Robinson, William, Esq., Charter-house-sq., do.
* Robinson, Rev. W. S., Dirham, Gloucester
Robinson, W., Esq., M. D., Doncaster
* Robinson, Wm., Esq., Lancaster
Robinson, W., Esq., L.L.D., Tottenham, Middsx.
Robinson, Mr. Wm., Hendon-lodge, Sunderland
Robinson and Allport, Messrs., Birmingham
Robley, Rev. J., Tedstone de la Mere, Hereford
* Robotham, J., Esq., Timperley, Cheshire
Robottom, Mr. W., Lime-street, London
* Robson, E., Esq., Dep. High Steward, Westminster
Robson, Rev. J., B. D., Tyldesley, Lancashire
* Robson, Michael, Esq., West Chirton, Durham
Roby, John, Esq., Rochdale, Lancashire

Roby, Thomas, Esq., Wigan, Lancashire
* Roby, Rev. William, Manchester
Roche, G., Esq., Charles-s., Covent-garden, Lon.
* Roche, W. N., Esq., Holborn-ct., Gray's-inn, do.
ROCHFORD, The Right Hon. the Earl of
* Rocke, Rev. John, Clungunford, Salop.
* Rockley, Mr. J., Great Surrey-street, London
* Rodbard, W., Esq., West Coker, Somerset.
* Rodenhurst, Mare, and Eyton, Messrs., Nantwich, Cheshire
* Rodenhurst, Wm., Esq., do., do.
* Rodes, Rev. C. H., Barlboro-hall, Derbyshire
Rodgers, Robert, Esq., Sheffield
* Rodgers, Thomas, Esq., Devonshire-sq., Lond.
Rodgers and Sons, Messrs., Sheffield
* Rodgerson, William, Esq., Tewkesbury
* Rodgett, Edward, Esq., Preston, Lancashire
Rodgett, Miles, Esq., do., do.
Rodham, Mr. W., Wellington, Somersetshire
* Rodmell, Thomas, Esq., Kingston upon Hull
RODNEY, The Right Honorable Lord
* RODNEY, The Right Hon. Dowager Lady
* Rodwell, William, Esq., Ipswich, Suffolk
Roe, Charles, Esq., Trinity college, Oxford
* Roe, Rev. James, Newbury, Berks.
Roe, J. C., Esq., Sidney-Sussex col., Cambrid.
* Roe, J. H., Esq., Manor-house, nr. Bromsgrove
Rofe, J., Esq., Reading, Berks.
* Rogers, E., jun., Esq., Wadham coll., Oxford
Rogers, H., Esq., Lincoln's-inn New-sq., Lond.
Rogers, H., Esq., Wolverhampton
Rogers, Henry, Esq., Cheshunt, Herts.
* Rogers, John, Esq., Babworth, Notts.
Rogers, Rev. John, Bedstone, Salop.
Rogers, Rev. John, Longtown, Monmouth
* Rogers, John, Esq., Ranby, Notts.
Rogers, Mr. John, Longtown, Monmouth
Rogers, J. B., Esq., Boston, Lincolnshire
* Rogers, John S., Esq., Green Bank, Chester
Rogers, John T., Esq., Worthing, Sussex
Rogers, R., Esq., Devonshire-square, London
* Rogers, S., Esq., Watlands, Newcastle, Staffords.
* Rogers, Thomas, Esq., St. Albans
Rogers, Mr. Thomas, Itchin-Abbas, Hants.
Rogers, Mr. Thomas, Kington, Herefordshire
Rogers, Thomas Stephens, Esq., do., do.
Rogers, W. H., Esq., Gravesend, Kent
Rogers, William, Esq., Southampton
* Rogers, William, Esq., Stanmore, Middlesex
* Rogers, Mr. William, Birmingham
Rogers and Currie, Messrs., Lincoln's-inn, Lon.
* Rogers and Son, Messrs., Manchester
* Rolfe, W. H., Esq., Sandwich, Kent
Rollason and Son, Messrs., Birmingham
* ROLLE, The Right Honorable Lord
* ROLLE, The Right Honorable Lady
* Rolles, E., Esq., Pembroke college, Oxford
Rolleston, Rev. John, Burton-Joyce, Notts.
* Rolleston, L., Esq., Watnall, do.
* Rolls, John, Esq., Bryanstone-square, London
Rolph, G., Esq., Thornbury, Gloucestershire
Rolph, William, Esq., do., do.
* Romney, F. H., Esq., Worcester coll., Oxford
* Ronalds, C., Esq., King's-Arms-yard, London
* Rondeau, James, Esq., Enfield, Middlesex
* Rooke, G., Esq., Bigswear, Gloucestershire
* Rooke, J., Esq., Cheetham, near Manchester
* Rooke, R. L., Esq., Hill-house, Bank, Leeds
* Rooke, Thos., Esq., Armourers'-hall, London
* Roope, Mr. W., Wisbeach, Cambridgeshire
* Rooth, John, Esq., Patricroft, near Manchester
Roothby, Rev. C., Sutterton, Lincolnshire
Roots, G., Esq., Brasenose college, Oxford
Roots, William, Esq., M. D., Kingston, Surrey
* Roper, C. B. T., Esq., Plas-tig-park, Flintshire
* Roper, D. R., Esq., Stamford-street, London
Roper, John, Esq., Ulverstone
* Roper, Robert, Esq., Preston, Lancashire
* Roper, T. A., Esq., Magdalene coll., Cambridge
Roper, William F., Esq., Temple, London
* Roscoe, James, Esq., Knutsford, Cheshire
* Rose, H., Esq., Great Guildford-street, London

Rose, Mr. J., Woolton-Mills, near Liverpool
Rose, Mrs. Mary, Aston, Warwickshire
* Rose, Thomas, Esq., Cowley-hall, Middlesex
Rose, W. H., Esq., Essex-street, London
* Rose, Rev. William, Glynd, Sussex
* ROSEBERY, The Right Hon. the Earl of
* Ross, A., Esq., Leadenhall-buildings, London
Ross, C., Esq., Sise-lane, Bucklersbury, do.
* Ross, John L., Esq., Oriel college, Oxford
Ross, Rev. Robert, M. D., Kidderminster
* Ross, R. L., Esq., Staffold-hall, Cumberland
* Rosser, H., Esq., Mitchell-Dean, Gloucestersh.
* Rosseter, Jas., Esq., Kennington-place, Surrey
* ROSSLYN, The Right Honorable the Earl of
Rosson, Mr. Thomas, Salford, Lancashire
* Rostron, L., Esq., Edenfield, do.
* Rostron, Laurence, Esq., Manchester
* Rothery, W., Esq., Doctors Commons, London
Rothwell, Mrs., Altrincham, Cheshire
* Rothwell, Peter, Esq., Bolton, Lancashire
Rothwell, Rev. R. R., Sefton, do.
Rotton, G., Esq., Wood-hill-side, near Bath
Rotton, Richard, Esq., Bradenham, Bucks.
* Rouch, Rev. F., M. A., St. George's, Canterbury
* Roughsedge, H., Esq., Bentham, Yorkshire
Roughsedge, Rev. R. H., M.A., Liverpool
Round, B., Esq., Wednesbury, Staffordshire
* Round, George, Esq., Colchester
Round, Mr. John, Tipton-green, Staffordshire
Roupell, G. B., Esq., Grt. Ormond-st., London
* Rous, Rev. G., Laverton, Somerset
Rouse, J., Esq., Blenheim-house, Southampton
* Routledge, R., Esq., Furnival's-inn, London
* Row, James, Esq., Tottenham, Middlesex
Rowcliffe, C., Esq., Stogumber, Somersetshire
* Rowcliffe, James, Esq., Tarporley, Cheshire
Rowden, John, Esq., Heytesbury, Wilts.
* Rowe, Dodson George, Esq., Liverpool
* Rowe, E., Esq., Lymm, Cheshire
* Rowe, Samuel, Esq., High Leigh, do.
* Rowe, Samuel, Esq., Malpas, do.
Rowell, Mr. Robert, Newbury, Berks.
* Rowland, Mr. A., Hatton-garden, London
Rowland, Michael, Esq., Bakewell, Derbyshire
Rowland, Samuel, Esq., Liverpool
Rowlands, T. W., Esq., Suffolk-place, London
* Rowley, Sir W., Bart., Tendring-hall, Suffolk
Rowley, D., Esq., St. Neots, Huntingdonshire
* Rowley, Rev. J., A. M., Lancaster
* Rowley, Mr. R., Whisken-street, London
Rowlinson, D. T., Esq., Birmingham
* Rowlinson, Frederick, Esq., Liverpool
Rowlinson, J., Esq., do.
* Rowlinson, J., Esq., Warrington
Rowlinson, William, Esq., Liverpool
Rownson, J., Esq., Doctors Commons, London
* Rowsell, T. S., Esq., Kennington, Surrey
Rowson, William, Esq., Prescot, Lancashire
Royal Exchange Assurance Office, London
Royal Union Office, Lancaster-place, do.
* Royds, Rev. E., M. A., Brereton, Cheshire
* Roylance, Peter, Esq., Manchester
Royle, J., Esq., Pendleton, near do.
* Royle, Mr. John, Chester
* Royle, Samuel, Esq., Tattenhall, Cheshire
* Royle, Thomas, Esq., Manchester
* Royle and Irwin, Messrs., do.
Roynane, R., Esq., Nicholas-street, Cork
* Royston, Mr. John, Vicar-lane, Leeds
Ruck, Lawrence, Esq., Gravesend, Kent
Rudall, George, Esq., Covent-garden, London
* Rudd, Henry, Esq., Vauxhall, Surrey
Rudd, Rev. J., Blyth, Nottinghamshire
* Rudd, Mr. Joseph, Norwich
* Rudge, E., Esq., Ewelme, Oxfordshire
Rudge, Rev. F., Eardisland, Herefordshire
Rudge, Rev. James, D.D., F.A.S., Limehouse
Rudge, James, Esq., Weston under Penyard
Ruding, Walter, Esq., Derby
* Rufford, P., Esq., Stourbridge, Worcestershire
Ruffy, W. J., Esq., Budge-row, London
* Ruge, F., Esq., Maidstone, Kent
Rugeley, H., Esq., St. Ives, Huntingdonshire
* Rumsey, John, Esq., Wycombe, Bucks.
* Runcorn, Richard, Esq., Manchester
* Rusby, Mr. James, Albion-street, Leeds
Rushbrook, Colonel, Bury St. Edmund's, Suffolk
* Rushbury, Geo., Esq., Carthusian-st., London
* Rushbury, H. D., Esq., do., do.
Rusher, Mr. James, Reading, Berks.
Rushforth, R. W., Esq., Broughton, Manchester
Rushton, Mr. William, Macclesfield, Cheshire
Russ, Harry, Esq., Castle-Cary, Somerset
* Russ, William, Esq., Rose-hill, near Oxford
* Russell, Rev. A. B., L. L. B., Richmond, Surrey
Russell, D., jun., Esq., York
Russell, Fred., Esq., St. Mary's-hall, Oxford
* Russell, Rev. J., D. D., F. A. S., Charter-house,
Russell, Mr. J., Guildford, Surrey [London
Russell, Jas., Esq., Pembroke-place, Pimlico
Russell, Mr. James, Lidbrook, Gloucestershire
* Russell, J. W., Esq., Ilam-hall, Staffordshire
* Russell, John, Esq., Leamington
* Russell, Mr. Joseph, Eccles, near Manchester
* Russell, J., Esq., Ramsbury, Wilts.
Russell, R. Greenhill, Esq., M. P., Wendover
* Russell, T. A., Esq., Cheshunt-park, Herts.
* Russell, Rev. Thomas, Hereford
* Russell, W., Esq., Brancepeth-castle, Durham
* Russell, W. C., Esq., Birmingham
Rutherford, Mr., Blithfield, Staffordshire
* RUTLAND, His Grace the Duke of
Rutter, John, Esq., M. D., Liverpool
* Rutter, R., Esq., Walsall, Staffordshire
* Rutton, Henry Loftie, Esq., Ashford, Kent
Ryall, William, Esq., Butleigh, Somersetshire
Ryde, Thos., Esq., Byfleet, Surrey
Ryder, The Right Honorable Richard
Ryder, G. D., Esq., Oriel college, Oxford
* Ryder, Rev. H. D., M. A., Tarvin, Cheshire
Rye, P. H. J. L., Esq., Lincoln coll., Oxford
* Ryland, Mr. John, Hollinghurst, near Man-
* Ryley, James, jun., Esq., Liverpool [chester
Ryley, John, Esq., High Elms, Herts.
* Ryley, Mr. R., Chancery-lane, London
* Ryton, W., Esq., Wolverhampton

Sadgrove, F., Esq., Princes-st., Bank, London
* Sadgrove, James., Esq., jun., South Moreton,
Sadler, Mr. Isaac, Oxford
* Sadler, John, Esq., Audlem, Cheshire
* Sadler, John, Esq., Broomhall, do.
Sadler, Mr. W. T., Norwich
* Sadler, Miss, Marbury, Cheshire
* Saffery, G., Esq., Market-Rasen, Lincolnshire
* Sager, Edmund, Esq., Edenfield, Lancashire
Sainsbury, Rev. H., Beckington, Somersetshire
* Sainsbury, John, Esq., Red Lion-sq., London
Sainsbury, W., jun., Esq., M. D., Corsham,
Sale, Rev. Thos., Southgate, Middlesex [Wilts.
SALISBURY, The Right Rev. Lord Bishop of
* Salisbury, T. W., Esq., Lancaster
Salisbury, E. D., Esq., Dudley
* Salmon, John, Esq., Jamaica
* Salmon, George, Esq., Cambridge
* Salmon, J. E., Esq., Holcombe-house, Somerset.
* Salmon, W. W., Esq., Devizes
* Salt, J., Esq., West Harding-street, London
* Salt, John, Esq., Bolton, Lancashire
* Salt, Mr. T. C., Easy-row, Birmingham
* Salt, Thomas, Esq., Stafford
* Salter, Richard, Esq., Arundel, Sussex
Salthouse, Elijah, Esq., Ulverstone
* Salvador, Rev. J. L., Staunton, Herefordshire
* Salvin, B. J., Esq., Burn-hall, Durham
* Salvin, T. William, Esq., Croxdale-house, do.
* Salwey, John, Esq., Richard's-Castle, Salop
* Salwey, T. Rich., Esq., the Lodge, do., do.
* Sampson, Major, East Retford, Notts.
Sampson, Edward, Esq., Henbury, near Bristol
* Sampson, George, Esq., Salisbury
Sampson, John, Esq., London-road, London
Sampson, S., Esq., Tooting, Surrey
Sampson, Rev. T., Edwinstow, Notts.
Sams, Mr., Pall-Mall, London
* Samuel, Capt. E. P., Hemel-Hempstead, Herts.
Samuel, D. M., Esq., Regent's-park, London
Samuels, Mr. John, Manchester
* Sanctuary, Thomas, Esq., Rusper, Sussex
* Sanctuary, Mrs., Catton, Norfolk
Sandars, Mr. S., jun., Gainsbro', Lincolnshire
* Sandbach, S., Esq., Woodlands, near Liverpool
* Sanders, B., jun., Esq., Bromsgrove
Sanders, Edward, Esq., Maidstone, Kent
Sanders, H., Esq., Christ-church coll., Oxford
Sanders, J. M., Esq., Stratford on Avon
Sanders, J. M., Esq., Clifton
Sanders, Samuel, Esq., Nottingham
Sanders, Mr. William, Eton
* Sanderson, Mr. C., Hampton-Court, Middlesex
Sanderson, John, Esq., Old Jewry, London
Sanderson, Isaac C., Esq., Coleman-street, do.
* Sanderson, T. B. W., Esq., Atherton, Lancash.
* Sandford, Rev. B., Farningham, Kent
* Sandford, G. B., Esq., Brasenose coll., Oxford
Sandford, Mr. Henry, Leominster
Sandford, J., Esq., Llansaintfread, Monmouth.
* Sandiford, John, Esq., Bury, Lancashire
* Sandom, John, Esq., Deptford, Kent
* Sandon, T., Esq., Shirley, near Southampton
Sands, Thomas, Esq., Liverpool
* SANDWICH, The Right Hon. the Earl of
* SANDWICH, The Right Hon. the Countess of
Sandys, Charles, Esq., Canterbury
* Sandys, Miles, Esq., Hawkeshead, Lancashire
* Sandys, M., jun., Esq., Ulverstone
* Sandys, T., Esq., Barnard's-inn, London
* Sanford, Edward Ayshford, Esq., M. P., Nine-head-court, Somersetshire
* Sanger, W. H., Esq., Salisbury
* Sankey, Richard, Esq., Holywell, Flintshire
Sankey, Richard, Esq., Ludlow, Shropshire
* Sankey, Mr. Robert, Canterbury
* Sankey, William, Esq., Wingham, Kent
* Sansome, Mr. J. T., Moseley, near Birmingham
Sant, T., Esq., Clifton on Teme, Worcestersh.
* Sarel, Andrew L., Esq., Enfield Highway
Sarel, C., Esq., Northampton-square, London
Sargant, D., Esq., Whittlesey, near Peterboro.
* Sargeant, Chas., Esq., Brasenose coll., Oxford
Sargeant, John, Esq., Isle of Dogs
Sargeaunt, Thos., Esq., Linton, Herefordshire
Sargon, Geo., Esq., Queen-st., Lincoln's-inn fields, London [dlesex
Sargon & Mann, Messrs., Kentish Town, Mid-
Satchell, John, Esq., Newbury, Berks.
* Satterthwaite, B., Esq., Castle-hill, Lancaster
Satterthwaite, Thomas, Esq., do.
* Saul, Silas, jun., Esq., Carlisle [ford
* Saunders, Rev. A. P., Christ-church coll., Ox-
Saunders, Mr. Charles, Reading, Berks.
Saunders, Rev. G. E., Tarrant Rushton, Dorset.
* Saunders, Henry, Esq., Devizes, Wilts.
Saunders, Captain James, Stratford on Avon
Saunders, J., Esq., Downes-house, Eling, Hants.
* Saunders, J. B., Esq., Wadham coll., Oxford
Saunders, J. N., Esq., Comberwell, nr. Bradford
Saunders, L., Esq., Hendon, Middlesex
Saunders, Mr. Robert, Southampton
* Saunders, T., Esq., Cheshunt, Herts.
Saunders, Thomas, Esq., Rochester, Kent
Saunders, Thomas, Esq., Park-street, Bankside
Saunders, T. B., Esq., Wadham coll., Oxford
* Saunders, T. M., Esq., Bradford, Wilts.
Saunders, Mr. William, Reading, Berks.
* Savage, Edward, Esq., Evesham
Savage, Robert, Esq., Bath, Somersetshire
* Savage, T., Esq., Midsomer-Norton, do.
Saville, The Honorable and Reverend J. L.
Savours, W., Esq., Headington, near Oxford
* Sawbridge, C., Esq., St. Peter's col., Cambridge
* Sawbridge, Samuel Elias, Esq., Wye, Kent
Sawyer, G., Esq., Dyer's-buildings, Holborn,
* Sawyer, H., Esq., Enfield, Middlesex [London
Sawyer, Rev. William, Highclere, Hants.

*Sawyer, Mr. W., Walworth, Surrey
*Saxon, George, Esq., Hartford, Cheshire
Sayce, Morris, Esq., Kington, Herefordshire
*SAYE AND SELE, The Right Honorable Lord
*Sayer, Charles, Esq., Tower-street, London
Sayer, Mr. John, Aldermanbury, do.
*Sayer, Mr. John, Gravesend, Kent
Sayer, Rev. T., Burford, Salop.
*Sayer, Wm. Myhill, Esq., Broxbourne, Herts.
*Sayor, Rev. T. M., Eythorn, Kent
*Scadding, Mr. J., Thame, Oxfordshire
*Scarisbrick, T., Esq., Ormskirk, Lancashire
*Scarlet, William, Esq., Penkridge, Staffordshire
*Scarnell, Mr. Thomas, Brighton, Sussex
*SCARSDALE, The Rt. Hon. Lord. . 2 Copies
*Scarth, J. F., Esq., Keverstone, Staindrop, Durham
*Scarth, T., Esq., do., do.
*Schofield, James, Esq., Rochdale, Lancashire
Scholefield, Rev. James, A. M., Cambridge
*Scholefield, Rev. James, Ancoats, Manchester
Scholefield, John, Esq., Horbury, Yorkshire
*Scholefield, Mess. T. and E. J., Teale, Leeds
*Scholes, Richard, Esq., Liverpool
Scholey, John, Esq., Wakefield
Schreiber, Major, Melton, Suffolk
*Schreiber, Captain George, Colchester
*Schroder, Mr. Hans, Bromyard, Herefordshire
*Schunck, Martin, Esq., Manchester
*Scobell, Captain, R. N., High Littleton-house, Somersetshire
*Scoles, Joseph J., Esq., Regent-street, London
Scotsons and Turnstall, Messrs., Kirkdale, near Liverpool
*Scott, Sir C., Bart., Lychett-Minster, Dorset.
*Scott, Captain, Draycott-house, Derby
Scott, E., Esq., Wigan, Lancashire
*Scott, Rev. E. D., M.A., Queen's college, Oxford
*Scott, E. D., Esq., Great Bar, Birmingham
Scott, E. John, Esq., St. Mildred's-ct., London
Scott, Geo. Henry, Esq., Exeter coll., Oxford
*Scott, Mr. G., Morpeth-pl., Waterloo-rd., Lond.
Scott, John, Esq., Navy-pay-office, do.
Scott, John, Esq., Great Bar, Birmingham
*Scott, John, Esq., Elm-court, Temple, London
*Scott, Page Nichol, Esq., Norwich
*Scott, Robert, Esq., Little Queen-st., London
*Scott, Rev. Russell, Portsmouth
*Scott, Thomas, Esq., Rock-house, Bath
*Scott, Thomas, Esq., Devizes
Scriven, Mr. William, Monmouth
Scroope, S. T., jun., Esq., Clifton, near Bristol
Scudamore, Edw., Esq., M. D., Lichfield
Scudamore, John L., Esq., Kent-Church Park, Herefordshire
Scurr, John, Esq., Everton, Lancashire
*Scutt, Rev. Thomas, Brighton
*Seabroke, Jonathan, Esq., Gravesend, Kent
*Seacome, Mr. John, Chester
*Seagram, C. F., Esq., M. D., Bratton-house, Wilts.
Seagram, William F., Esq., Warminster, do.
Seal, W., Esq., Holeshill-heath, near Coventry
*Seale, H. P., Esq., Christ-church coll., Oxford
Sealy, E., Esq., Bridg-water, Somersetshire
Sealy, John, Esq., Exeter college, Oxford
Sealy, Rev. W. G., Seend, Wilts.
Seaman, Francis, Esq., Norwich
*Seaman, John, Esq., Tooting, Surrey
*Searle, Mr. George, Grosvenor-street, Pimlico
*Sears, Maurice, Esq., Northop, Flintshire
*Seaton, Joseph, Esq., Sheerness, Kent
Secker, John, Esq., Windsor
Secreton, Wm. W., Esq., Usk, Monmouthshire
*Seddon, William, Esq., Manchester
Sedgwick, R., Esq., Cannon-street, London
Sedgwick, William, Esq., Maidstone, Kent
SEFTON, The Right Honorable the Earl of
*Segar, R., Esq., Preston, Lancashire
*Selby, H. C., Esq., Swansfield-house, Northum.
Sellwood, Mr. Benjamin, Aldworth, Berks.
*Sellwood, Henry, Esq., Holborn-court, London
*Selons, J. B., Esq., Winsley-street, do.

*Selwyn, Congreve, Esq., Ledbury, Herefordsh.
*Selwyn, G. A., Esq., St. John's coll., Cambdg.
*Sendale, Mr. John, Heigham-hill, Norwich
Senhouse, Mrs., Watford, Herts.
*Senhouse, H., Esq., Nether-hall, Cumberland
*Senior, Rev. Benjamin, Nantwich, Cheshire
*Sergeant, E. W., Esq., Manchester
*Serjeant and Thring, Messrs., Wilton
Sevier, J. Ford, Esq., Bristol
*Sewell, W., Esq., B. A., Fellow and Librarian of Exeter college, Oxford
*Sewell and Hearn, Messrs., Newport, Isle of Wight
*Sewers, The Honorable the Commissioners of, for Holborn and Finsbury division, Sewer's Office, London
Sexey, Mr. Chas., Fareham, Hants.
Sexty, Mr. George, Ledbury, Herefordshire
Sexty, Robert, Esq., do., do.
Seymer, H., Esq., Christ-church col., Oxford
Seymour, E. W., Esq., Crickhowel, Breconshire
*Seymour, Rev. G. T., Marksbury, Somerset.
*Seymour, Rev. J. H., Prebendary of Gloucester
Seymour, R., Esq., Christ-church coll., Oxford
Seymour, Mr. Thomas, Cheshunt, Herts.
Seymour, W. H., Esq., Coventry
*Shackel, G., Esq., Red Lands, Reading, Berks.
*Shackell, Mr. Edward, Southampton Row
*Shackell, W., Esq., 4, Great James-st., Bedford Row
Shadforth, Colonel, Witton le Wear, Durham
Shadwell, The Right Honorable Sir L., Knt.
Shadwell, John, Esq., M. D., Hill, near Southampton
Shadwell, L., Esq., New-sq., Lincoln's-inn, Lon.
*Shadwell, Thomas Caley, Esq., Gray's-inn, do.
Shafts, R. S. D., Esq., Whitworth-park, Durham
*Shakerley, C. W. T., Esq., Somerford-park, Cheshire
*Shakespear, Mr. T., Fellingley, near Coventry
Shallcross, Richard, Esq., Liverpool
Shand, Francis, Esq., Everton, Lancashire
*Shann, Thomas, Esq., Leeds
SHANNON, The Right Honorable the Earl of
*Shapland, Col. J. S., C. B., Taunton, Somerset.
*Share, Mr. Charles, Ledbury, Herefordshire
*Sharman, Mr. Richard, Windsor
*Sharman, Mr. T., jun., Islington
*Sharp, E., Esq., Stone-house, Gloucestershire
*Sharp, J., Esq., Rushulme, Lancashire
*Sharp, John, Esq., Warrington
*Sharp, J. C., Esq., Wood-st., Cheapside, Lond.
Sharp, J., Esq., Paragon, New Kent-road, do.
Sharp, Richard, Esq., Maidstone, Kent
Sharp, Mr. Richard, Stamford, Lincolnshire
*Sharp, Robert C., Esq., Manchester
*Sharp, T., Esq., Rushulme, Lancashire
*Sharp, Mr. Thomas, Swadlincote, Derbyshire
Sharp, William, Esq., Garstang, Lancashire
Sharp, W., Esq., Registrar's Office, do.
*Sharp, Mr. Wm., Canterbury
*Sharp, W. H., Esq., Burslem, Staffordshire
*Sharpe, C. V., Esq., Woodbridge, Suffolk
Sharpe, Rev. F. W., Moneyash, Derbyshire
Sharpe, Hercules, Esq., Northiam, Sussex
Sharpe, Rev. John, Doncaster
Sharpe, Mr. William, Canterbury
*Sharples, Henry, Esq., Ormskirk, Lancashire
*Sharples, Joseph, Esq., Hitchin, Herts.
*Shatwell, Mr. George, Manchester
*Shaw, Sir Robert, Bart., Bushy-park, Dublin
Shaw, Mr. B., Lombard-street, London
Shaw, Mr. C. H. C., Birmingham
*Shaw, George, Esq., M.D., Manchester
Shaw, George, Esq., Hereford
Shaw, Henry, Esq., Ulverstone
Shaw, Mr. James, Coventry
*Shaw, Rev. J., High-Ham, Somersetshire
*Shaw, John, Esq., King-st., Cheapside, Lond.
*Shaw, John, Esq., Tarporley, Cheshire
*Shaw, John, Esq., Wolverhampton
*Shaw, T., Esq., Rockpoint, Liscard, Cheshire
*Shaw, Thomas, Esq., Bollington, do.
*Shaw and Artindale, Mess., Burnley, Lancash.

*Shaw & Son, Messrs. Joseph, Leeds
*Shawe, R. N., Esq., Woodbridge, Suffolk
Shearman, C., Esq., Holborn-court, London
Shearman and Freeman, Messrs., Bartlett's-buildings, Holborn, do.
*Sheath, Rev. Martin, Wyberton, Lincolnshire
*Shee, Sir George, Bart., Mudiford, Hants.
*Sheen, Mr. John, Wallingford, Berks.
Sheen, Mr. O., Claremont-square, London
Sheen, Thomas, Esq., Kington, Herefordshire
Sheen, W. B., Esq., Wallingford, Berks.
SHEFFIELD, The Right Honorable the Earl of
*Sheild, S., Esq., St. John's coll., Cambridge
*Shelley, Sir J., Bart., M. P., Maresfield-park, Sussex
*Shelley, Sir Timothy, Bart., Field-house, do.
Shelly, Mr. John, Southampton
*Shelton, Mr. G., Henley upon Thames
Shenston, Mr. J., Somers-Town, Middlesex
Shenton, Thos., Esq., Brimfield, Herefordshire
*Shenton, William, Esq., Manchester
Shepherd, Mr. George, Abingdon, Berks.
*Shepherd, Mr. Henry, Union-street, Borough
*Shepherd, Jas., Esq., Lime-st.-square, London
*Shepherd, Mr. James, Hythe, near Southampton
Shepherd, J., Esq., Toll-end, Tipton, Staffordsh.
Shepherd, J. B., Esq., Prince's-st., Bank, Lond.
*Shepherd, J. G., Esq., Faversham, Kent
Shepherd, Samuel, Esq., do., do.
Shepherd, T., Esq., Southwell, Notts.
*Shepley, R., Esq., Glossop, Derbyshire
Sheppard, George, Esq., Frome, Somersetshire
*Sheppard, G., Esq., Chewton-Mendip, do.
*Sheppard, William, Esq., Clifton, near Bristol
*Sheppard, Thomas, and Co., Messrs., Cloak-lane, Queen-street, Cheapside, London
*Sheppards, Dr., Library, Preston, Lancashire
*Sherborn, Francis, Esq., Bedfont, Middlesex
SHERBORNE, The Right Honorable Lord
*Sherbrooke, Gen. Sir J. C., Culverton, Notts.
*Sherbrooke, W., Esq., Oxton-hall, do.
Sheriff, Mr. John, Letton, Herefordshire
Sherman, Mr. Thomas, Bensington, Oxon.
*Sherratt, Thomas, Esq., Manchester
*Sherry, J. H., Esq., West Lambrook, Somerset.
*Sherson, John Herdman, Esq., Lancaster
*Sherston, Major J. D., Wells, Somersetshire
*Sherwood, John, Esq., Reading, Berks.
Sherwood, R., Esq., do., do.
Sherwood, T., Esq., M. D., Snow-hall, Durham
*Sherwood and Son, Messrs., Southwark
Shew, Rev. H. E., Christian-Malford, Wilts.
Shield, Hugh, Esq., Poultry, London
*Shield, Joseph, Esq., Newcastle upon Tyne
Shiels, Charles, Esq., Liverpool
*Shipdern, John, Esq., Dover
Shipley, Rev. C., Twyford-house, Winchester
*Shipman, J., Esq., Charlotte-street, London
*Shipperdson, Edward, Esq., Durham
Shipton, James, Esq., Wolverhampton
*Shirley, A. G. S., Esq., Christ-ch., coll., Oxford
Shirley, Rev. W. A., A. M., Shirley, Derbysh.
Shirreff, C. T., Esq., Salisbury-st., Strand, Lond.
*Shoobridge, H., Esq., Witham, Essex
Shoolbred, Mr. A., Jermyn-street, London
*Shoolbred, Mr. J., Tottenham-court-road, do.
*Shore, Samuel, Esq., Norton-hall, Derbyshire
*Shorland, George, Esq., Manchester
*Short, John H., Esq., Trinity coll., Cambridge
Short, John James, Esq., Enfield, Middlesex
Short, Rev. William, Chippenham, Wilts.
*SHREWSBURY, The Rt. Hon. the Earl of
*SHREWSBURY, The Rt. Hon. the Countess of
Shrubsole & Lambert, Messrs., Kingston, Surrey
*Shubrick, Colonel, Leatherhead, do.
*Shugar, John S., Esq., Portsmouth
*Shuter, David, Esq., Milbank-st., Westminster
*Shuttleworth, A. A., Esq., Hathersage-hall, Derbyshire
*Shuttleworth, G., Esq., Poultry, London
Shuttleworth, Mr. J., Bread-st., Cheapside, do.
Shuttleworth, W. G., Esq., Hodsock-Park, Notts.

*Shuttleworth, Messrs, Rochdale, Lancashire
Sibley, H., Esq., Staple-inn, London
*Sibthorpe, Rev. H., Washingborough, Lincolns.
Sidaway, T., Esq., Rowley-Regis, Staffordshire
Siddons, William, Esq., Pleasley-hill, Notts.
*Sidebotham, H., Esq., Houghton, Cheshire
*Sidebotham, John, Esq., Hyde, do.
Sidebotham, Mr. J., Hovely Hyde, do.
*Sidebottom, J., Esq., Hollingworth, do.
Sidgreaves, James, Esq., Preston, Lancashire
Sigel, G. H., Esq., Brewer-st., Golden-sq., Lond.
*Sikes, Rev. J., L. L. B., Newark, Notts.
*Sikes, Rev. Thomas, M. A., Luton, Beds.
Sillitoe, Mr. William, Aldermanbury, London
*Sills, Joseph, Esq., Hoxton, Middlesex
*Silvester, J., Esq., Ashbourn-grove, Derbyshire
Sim, Rev. Henry, M. A., Bonsall, do.
*Simcox, T. G., Esq., Wadham college, Oxford
*Simes, J., Esq., Wood-st., Cheapside, London
Simmonds, G. N., Esq., Trinity college, Oxford
*Simmons, Joseph, Esq., Birmingham
Simmons, R., Esq., F. R. S.
*Simonds, Henry, Esq., Reading, Berks. [Lond.
Simonds, Mr. J., Charles-st., Commercial-road,
Simons, Rev. John, Dymock, Gloucestershire
*Simpson, A., Esq., Highbury-park, Middlesex
Simpson, Charles, Esq., Lichfield
*Simpson, Mr. Edwin, Park-place, Leeds
*Simpson, Rev. George, Sittingbourne, Kent
*Simpson, G., Esq., Camden-Town, Middlesex
Simpson, H. H., Esq., Camden-place, Bath
Simpson, Rev. John, L. L. D., Worcester
Simpson, Joseph, Esq., Liverpool
*Simpson, J. A., Esq., Austin-friars, London
*Simpson, Rich., Esq., Moreton-hall, Cheshire
Simpson, Mr. Richard, Norwood, Surrey
Simpson, Rev. Robert, M. A., F. R. S. L., and F. S. A., Derby
Simpson, Rev. J., L. L. D., Baldock, Herts.
*Simpson, S., Esq., Middle-Temple, London
*Simpson, Thomas, Esq., M. D., York
Simpson, Mr. Thomas, Stafford
*Simpson, W. W., Esq., Bucklersbury, London
*Simpson, Mr. W., Austin Friars, do.
Simpson, W. H., Esq., Peterborough
Simpson and Frear, Messrs., Derby
Sims, Mr. George, Reading, Berks.
*Sims, Thomas, Esq., Birmingham
Singer, James, Esq., Mells, Somersetshire
*Singleton, Cuthbert, Esq., New-inn, London
Singleton, James, Esq., Manchester
Sinhouse, H., Esq., Cockermouth, Cumberland
*Sirrell, Nicholas, Esq., Tarrington, Herefordshire
Sisson, Rev. Thos., M. A., Wallington, Herts.
Sivewright, John, Esq., Priory, Old Windsor
*Sivewright, Mrs., Guildford, Surrey
*Skaife, J., Esq., Blackburn, Lancashire
Skally, Mr. M., West Bromwich
Skelton, Mr. G., St. Paul's-square, Birmingham
*Skerratt, James, Esq., Sandbach, Cheshire
*Skerrett, Joseph, Esq., Nantwich, do.
*Skey, Arthur, Esq., Bewdley, Worcestershire
*Skidmore, Enmot, Esq., Rickmansworth, Herts.
*Skillicorne, W. N., Esq., Worcester coll., Oxford
Skillman, B., Esq., Tokenhouse-yard, London
Skinner, D. F. M., Esq., Downing-street, do.
Skipp, G., Esq., Ledbury, Herefordshire
Skipp, Mr. George, jun., do., do.
Skipsey, Mr. J., Carey-street, London
Skipwith, Sir G., Bart., Alveston, Warwickshire
*Skrine, Rev. J. H., M. A., Teddington, Middx.
*Skurray, Thomas, Esq., Bath
*Skynner, Rev. W., M. A., Rushden, Herts.
Skyrme, Amos Jones, Esq., Hereford
*Slack, John, Esq., Stockport, Cheshire
*Slack, J. A., Esq., Towcester, Northampton
*Slade, F., Esq., Raymond's-buildings, London
*Slade, H. R., Esq., Caius college, Cambridge
*Slade, Rev. James, M. A., Bolton, Lancashire
Slade, Wm., Esq., Doctors Commons, London
*Sladen, John B., Esq., Ripple-court, Kent
Slaney, Rev. R., M. A., Penkridge, Staffordshire

*Slaney, R. H., Esq., Garlick-hill, London
*Slark, Mr. William, Piccadilly, do.
*Slater, George, Esq., Bolton, Lancashire
*Slater, James, Esq., do., do.
*Slater, J., Esq., Newcastle upon Tyne
*Slater, Mr. J., Liverpool
Slater, J. N., Esq., Birmingham
Slatter, James, Esq., Windsor Castle
Slatter, Rev. W., Cumner, Berks.
*Sleath, Rev. J., D. D., F. R. S., F. S. A., St. Paul's school, London
*Sleath, Rev. W. B., D. D., Repton, Derbyshire
*Slee, Noah, Esq., Church-street, Bermondsey
SLIGO, The Most Noble the Marquis of
Slingsby, Chas., Esq., Knaresborough
Sloan, S., Esq., Wood-st., Cheapside, London
*Slocock, C., Esq., Donnington, near Newbury,
*Small, Rev. Henry, St. Alban's [Berks.
Smalley, C., Esq., Preston, Lancashire
Smallpiece & Son, Messrs. J., Guildford, Surrey
*Smallridge, Charles, Esq., Gloucester
Smalls, H., Esq., Durham
*Smallwood, Mr. George, Hammersmith
*Smart, George, Esq., Birmingham
*Smart, Joseph, Esq., Wolverhampton [London
Smartt, T. L., Esq., Primrose-st., Bishopsgate,
Smeeton, Rich., Esq., Congleton, Cheshire
*Smelt, Col. C., Lieut.-Governor of the I. of Man
Smethurst, Richard, Esq., Chorley, Lancashire
*Smethurst, Rev. Robt., Pilkington, do.
Smith, Miss Ann, Camden-Town, Middlesex
Smith, B., Esq., Boston, Lincolnshire
Smith, Benjamin, Esq., Chesterfield
*Smith, Rev. B. D., Timsbury, Somersetshire
*Smith, Rev. Cecil, Bishop's Lydiard, do.
Smith, C. R., Esq., Christ's coll., Cambridge
*Smith, Charles, Esq., Enfield, Middlesex
*Smith, C., Esq., Christ's college, Cambridge
Smith, Mr. Daniel, Bilston, Staffordshire
Smith, Edward, Esq., Rugeley, do.
Smith, E., Esq., Netherwood, Leominster
Smith, Rev. E. J., M. A., Whitchurch, Midsx.
*Smith, Major Gen. F., Alton, Hants.
*Smith, Frederick, Esq., Basinghall-st., London
Smith, F., Esq., Much Marcle, Herefordshire
Smith, Col. F., Hales-Owen, Salop
*Smith, G., Esq., Mercers'-hall, London
*Smith, George, Esq., Manchester
Smith, George, Esq., Liverpool
Smith, George, Esq., Frederick's-place, London
*Smith, George Henry, Esq., Bath
Smith, H., Esq., Gainsborough, Lincolnshire
*Smith, Henry, Esq., Wolverhampton
Smith, Isaac Chas., Esq., Hadlow-st., London
*Smith, James, Esq., Manchester
*Smith, James, Esq., Salford, Lancashire
Smith, James, Esq., Much-Hadham, Herts.
*Smith, J., Esq., Stone-buildings, Lincoln's-inn, London
Smith, James, Esq., Wadesmill, Herts.
Smith, James, Esq., Newport, Monmouthshire
Smith, James, Esq., Barnard's-inn, London
*Smith, Mr. James, Ashton under Line
Smith, Mr. Jas., Barton-Stacey, Hants.
Smith, Jeffery, Esq., Cotton's-wharf, London
*Smith, J., Esq., Rugeley, Staffordshire
*Smith, J., Esq., Six Clerks'-office, London
Smith, J. A., Esq., Wiveliscombe, Somerset.
Smith, J. D., Esq., Queen-st., Cheapside, Lond.
Smith, J. H., Esq., Derby
Smith, John Henry, Esq., Kingston upon Hull
*Smith, J. P., Esq., Park-place, Leeds
Smith, J. P., Esq., Burton on Trent, Staffordsh.
Smith, T. W., Esq., Fenchurch-street, London
Smith, John, Esq., Kirk-Ella, Yorkshire
Smith, John, Esq., Ledbury, Herefordshire
*Smith, John, Esq., West Gravesend, Kent
*Smith, John, Esq., Wood-street, London
Smith, John, Esq., Manchester
Smith, John, Esq., Much Marcle, Herefordsh.
*Smith, John, Esq., Preston, Lancashire
Smith, John, Esq., Walford-court, Herefordsh.

Smith, John, Esq., Chepstow, Monmouthshire
Smith, Mr. John, Kennington, Surrey
Smith, Mr. John, Cotherston, York
*Smith, J. A., Esq., M. P., Grosvenor-sq., Lond.
Smith, J. C., Esq., Stanton on Arrow, Hereford
*Smith, J. J., Esq., B. A., Caius col., Cambridge
Smith, John T., Esq., Queen's college, Oxford
*Smith, J., Esq., jun., Little Gayton-hall, Chesh.
Smith, Joseph Grace, Esq., Bristol
Smith, Joshua, Esq., Rickmansworth, Herts.
*Smith, J. B., Foaty Island, Cove of Cork
*Smith, J. T., Esq., Kidderminster
*Smith, J. W., Esq., Gray's-inn-square, London
Smith, Miss, Burnham, Bucks.
*Smith, Nicholas Hankey, Esq., Deerbolts, Suffolk
Smith, Pritchard, Esq., M. D., Reading, Berks.
*Smith, R., Esq., Temple, London
*Smith, R., Esq., Ulverstone
*Smith, R. Wordsworth, Esq., do.
*Smith, Samuel, Esq., M. P. Berkeley-square, Lon.
Smith, S., Esq., Michael-Church-Eskley, Herefordshire
*Smith, S. G., Esq., Goldings, near Hertford
*Smith, Samuel M., Esq., Nottingham
Smith, T., Esq., Hertingfordbury-park, Herts.
*Smith, Thos., Esq., Six Clerks'-Office, London
Smith, Thomas, Esq., St. Helens Place, do.
*Smith, Thomas, Esq., Hertford
Smith, T., Esq., Maidenhead, Berks.
*Smith, T., Esq., Heaton-hall, Northumberland
Smith, Thomas, Esq., Shareshill, Staffordshire
Smith, T., Esq., Whiston Eaves, do.
*Smith, T., Esq., Brentford, Middlesex
Smith, T., Esq., Huntington-hall, near York
Smith, Mr. Thomas, Waltham-Abbey, Essex
*Smith, T. A., Esq., M. P., Tidworth, Hants.
Smith, T. W., Esq., Hatton-garden, London
Smith, Timothy, Esq., Birmingham
*Smith, William, Esq., Nottingham
*Smith, William, Esq., Bucklersbury, London
Smith, Wm., Esq., Hemel-Hempstead, Herts.
*Smith, William, Esq., Wolverhampton
*Smith, William, Esq., Nantwich, Cheshire
*Smith, William, Esq., Sunderland
*Smith, William, Esq., Kingsley, Cheshire
*Smith, William, Esq., Stockport, do.
Smith, William, Esq., Uckfield, Sussex
Smith, Wm., Esq., Much Marcle, Herefordsh.
Smith, William Henry, Esq., Bristol
*Smith, W. B., Esq., Corpus-Christi coll., Oxford
Smith, W. D., Esq., Trinity college, do.
*Smith, W. H., Esq., Hawkeshead, Lancashire
Smith, Mr. W. H., Strand, London
Smith, W. F., Esq., Clement's-inn, do.
*Smith & Fletcher, Messrs., Pendleton, nr. Man-
*Smith and Hutchinson, Messrs., Leeds [chester
*Smith and Son, Alderman's-walk, London
Smither, J. S., Esq., Hale, nr. Farnham, Surrey
*Smithson, Robert, Esq., York
*Smithson, Dunn, and Hawdon, Messrs., New-inn, London
Smyth, Sir G. H., Bart., Bere-Church-hall, Essex
*Smyth, Sir John, Bart., Ashton-court, Somerset.
Smyth, Charles, Esq., Warwick
Smyth, J. F. H., Esq., Red Lion-sq., London
*Smyth, John, Esq., Shadwell, Middlesex
Smyth, J. B., Esq., Stoke-hall, Ipswich, Suffolk
*Smyth, John Vere, Esq., Hampton, Middlesex
*Smyth, Rev. Thomas, Burnley, Lancashire
*Smyth, Capt. W. H., R. N., James-st., London
*Smythe, Sir E., Bart., Acton-Burnell, Salop.
*Smythe, Lady Dowager, Wootton, Warwicksh.
*Snare, Mr. Robert, Reading, Berks.
Snead, Mr. Edwd., Peter-Church, Herefordshire
*Snell, John, Esq., Edmonton, Middlesex
Sneyd, Capt. C., Huntley-hall, Staffordshire
Sneyd, Rev. J., M. A., Bassford-hall, do.
Sneyd, W., Esq., Ashcombe, near Leek, do.
Sneyd, W., Esq., Bradwell-hall, Newcastle, do.
Sneyd, W., jun., Esq., Christ-church col., Oxford
*Snoulten, Mr. O., St. George's, Canterbury
*Snow, Mr. John, Brighton, Sussex

*Snow, Mr. John, Swanbatch, Cheshire
Snow, Wm., Esq., St. John's coll., Cambridge
Snowden, Mr. Charles, Windsor
Snowdon, William, Esq., Nottingham
Soames, W. H., Esq., Trinity col., Cambridge
*Soane, Jno., Esq., Lincoln's-inn-fields, London
*SODER AND MAN, The Right Rev. Lord Bishop of
*SOMERS, The Right Honorable Earl
*Somers, B., Esq., M. D., Langford, near Bristol
SOMERVILLE, The Right Honorable Lord
Somerville, Sir M., Bart., M. P., Somerville, Meath, Ireland
*SONDES, The Right Honorable Lord
*Sooby, Mr. M., Gainsborough, Lincolnshire
Sopp, John, Esq., Salisbury
Sorby, James, Esq., Sheffield [London
*Sotheron, Vice-Admiral, M.P., Harewood-pl.,
Soulby, George, Esq., Canterbury [tershire
*Southall, Mr. C. H., Great Malvern, Worces-
Southall, Mr. Richard, jun., Birmingham
*Southam, Messrs., and Son, Ashton under Line
*SOUTHAMPTON, The Right Honorable Lord
*Southby, Richard, Esq., Chieveley, Berks. [do.
*Southby, T. H., Esq., F. S. A., Carswell-house,
Southcomb, Rev. John, Minehead, Somerset.
Southee, Mr. Robert, Canterbury
*Southgate, F., Esq., Melton, Kent
Southouse, Capt., Millbrook, near Southampton
Southwell, Collegiate Library of the Chapter of
Southwell, Henry, Esq., St. Cross, Winchester
Southwell, Henry, Esq., Saxmundham, Suffolk
Sowerby, John P., Esq., Stokesley, Yorkshire
*Sowerby, Mr. W., Clifford-st., Bond-st., Lond.
*Sowerby, Wm., Esq., Putteridge Bury, Herts.
*Sowler, Mr. Thomas, Manchester
*Spackman, Charles, Esq., Bradford, Wilts.
*Spafford, Samuel, Esq., Salford, Lancashire
Spalding, D., Esq., Gorleston, Suffolk
Spalding, P. S., Esq., Colchester
*Spalton, Mrs. M., Dane-bank, Cranage, Chesh.
*Spargeon, Rev. T., Lowestoft, Suffolk
*Sparkes, Mess. C. & H., Friday-street, London
*Sparks, M. J. B., Esq., Christ's coll. Cambrid.
*Sparks, Mr. W., Pembroke-square, London
Sparling, William, Esq., Colchester
*Sparrow, Stephen, Esq., Clitheroe, Lancashire
Sparrow, Edwin, Esq., Wolverhampton
*Sparrow, Thomas, Esq., do.
Sparrow, W. H., Esq., do.
*Sparshall, Mr. Edward, Norwich [cashire
Speakman, T. B., Esq., Denton's-Green, Lan-
Spear, Robert, Esq., Caius college, Cambridge
Spearman, Rich., Esq., Macclesfield, Cheshire
Speed, W. J., Esq., Foster-lane, London
*Speke, Rev. Hugh, Ilminster, Somerset.
*Speke, William, Esq., Jordans, do.
*Spelman, William, Esq., Norwich
Spence, Mr. Desborough, Size-lane, London
*Spence, George, Esq., Camberwell, Surrey
*Spence, Thomas, Esq., Hertford
*SPENCER, The Right Honorable Earl
*Spencer, Charles, Esq., Ash, Kent
*Spencer, E., Esq., Highgate, Middlesex
Spencer, J., Esq., Jesus college, Cambridge
*Spencer, J., Esq., Broughton, Lancashire
*Spencer, Mr. James, Whitecross-st., London
*Spencer, John P., Esq., Oakhill, Somersetshire
Spencer, Mr. Richard, Hereford
*Spencer, Mr. Thomas, Bilston, Staffordshire
*Spencer, Timothy, Esq., Ledbury, Herefordsh.
*Spencer, Mr. William, Bunbury, Cheshire
*Spencer and James, Messrs., Hay, Brecon.
Spensley, William, Esq., Aldermanbury, London
*Spickle, Mr. Charles, Norwich
*Spiers, Joseph, Esq., Chippenham, Wilts.
*Spilling, Mr. John, Manchester
Spink, J. E., Esq., Wadham college, Oxford
Spooner, J., Esq., Caius college, Cambridge
Spooner, W., Esq., Oriel college, Oxford
Spooner, Attwood, & Co., Gracechurch-st., Lond.
Spottiswode, A., Esq., Bedford-square, do.

Spratt, William, Esq., Norwich
*Sprigge, Rev. T. D., Brockley, Suffolk
Sprott, William, Esq., Tonbridge Wells
Sproule, Anthony, Esq., Tewkesbury
*Spry, Rev. J. H., D. D., York-ter., Regent's-park, London
Spurr, William, Esq., Carlton, Notts.
*Spurway, John, Esq., Milverton, Somersetshire
*Spyring, J. S. S., Esq., Brighton, Sussex
*Squire, J. W., Esq., Walbrook, London
Squire, Richard, Esq., King's Langley, Herts.
Squire, J. W., Esq., Thavies-inn, London
*Stable, G. W., Esq., Newcastle upon Tyne
*Stable, J., Esq., Lincoln's-inn, London
Stable, J. W., Esq., Temple, do.
*Stace, Wm., Esq., Royal Arsenal, Woolwich
*Stacey, Geo., Esq., jun., Orford-mill, Norwich
*Stacey, Isaac, Esq., Jermyn-street, London
STAFFORD, The Most Noble the Marquis of
*Stafford, J., Esq., New-Mills, Derbyshire
*Stafford, J. H., Esq., Newcastle upon Tyne
*Stainbank, James, Esq., Lancaster
*ST. ALBANS, His Grace the Duke of
St. Albyn, L., Esq., Alfoxton, Somersetshire
Staley, James, Esq., Wantage, Berks.
*Stallibrass, Elisha, Esq., Hertford
*Stamford, Mr. E., Edmonton, Middlesex
*STAMFORD AND WARRINGTON, The Right Honorable the Earl of
Stamp, Rev. J. S., Oxford
Stamp, Mr. T. E., Holborn-hill, London
*STAMPS, The Hon. His Majesty's Commissioners of [rey
Stanbrough, T., Esq., Walton on Thames, Sur-
*Stanbrough, C. H., Esq., Isleworth, Middlesex
Standish, H., Esq., Doncaster
Standwell, Mr. T., Stamford, Lincolnshire
Stanfield, John, Esq., Manchester
Stanfield, Mr. S., Slough, Bucks. [ford
*Stanhope, Sir E. F., Bart., Holme-Lacy, Here-
*Stanier, John, Esq., Wellington, Shropshire
Staniforth, Samuel, Esq., Liverpool
*Stanley, Sir T. S. M., Bart, Hooton, Cheshire
*Stanley, B., Esq., New Broad-street, London
*Stanley, George, Esq., Old Broad-street, do.
Stanley, Richard, Esq., Sheffield
*Stannard, J., Esq., Gt. George's-plain, Norwich
Stannard, Mr. T., St. Peter's Mancroft, do.
*Stansbie, Mr. H., Birmingham
*Stansfield, E., Esq., Accrington, Lancashire
*Stanton, James, Esq., Thelwall, Cheshire
Stanton, John, Esq., Haydock, Lancashire
*Stanton, Thomas, Esq., Ellesmere, Salop
*Stapelton, The Honorable and Rev. M. J.
*Stapelton, Lady, per Simpkin and Marshall
Stapledon, Mr. W., Henley upon Thames
*Staples, Mr. S., jun., Staple's-inn, London
Stapleton, T. S., Esq., Littlewick, Berks.
Stapylton, Thomas, Esq., per Mr. Walther
*Star Newspaper, The Proprietors of the
*Starbuck, Mr. John James, Gravesend, Kent
*Stark, W., Esq., St. Miles's, Norwich
Starke, R. J. H., Esq., Caius coll., Cambridge
*Starkey, James, Esq., Higher Whitley, Cheshire
*Starkey, Samuel, Esq., Timperley, do.
Starkey and Co., Messrs. T., Birmingham
Starkey, Mr. J., Penkridge, Staffordshire
*Starky, S., Esq., Trinity college, Cambridge
*Starling, Mr. Thomas, Wilmington-sq., London
ST. ASAPH, The Right Rev. Lord Bishop of
*Statham, William, Esq., Liverpool
*STATIONERY OFFICE, His Majesty's
*St. Aubyn, Sir J., Bart., T.R.A., and L. S., Clowance, Cornwall
*St. Aubyn, R., Esq., Trinity coll., Cambridge
Staunton, Rev. J., L.L.D., Staunton-dale, Notts.
Stavely, Edward, Esq., Nottingham
*ST. DAVIDS, The Right Rev. Lord Bishop of . . . . 2 Copies
*Stead, Rev. A., Oldham Road, Manchester
*Steade, B., Esq., Beachiel-hall, Derbyshire
Steade, E. V., Esq., Beauchieff-abbey, Sheffield

Steavenson, R., Esq., M. D., Newcastle upon
*Stedman, Jas., Esq., Guildford, Surrey [Tyne
Stedman, Mr. Richard, Godalming, do.
*Steel, Edward, Esq., Warrington
*Steel, John, Esq., Liverpool
Steel, Mr. T., Chancery-lane, London
*Steel, J. B., Esq., Stockport, Cheshire [setshire
Steele, F. F. A., Esq., Shepton-Mallet, Somer-
*Steele, Jas., Esq., Lime-street-square, London
*Steele, Lieut. Col. Sir R., Knt., Meerhey, Dorset
*Steele, R., Esq., Christ-church college, Oxford
*Steer, Mr. James, Ripley, Surrey
*Steers, Mrs., Malvern Wells, Worcestershire
*Stelfox, Edward, Esq., Lymm, Cheshire
*Stelfox, Edward, Esq., Knutsford, do.
*Stelfox, R., Esq., Pendleton, near Manchester
*Stelfox, William, Esq., Timperley, Cheshire
*Stenning, John, Esq., East Grinstead, Sussex
Stephen, John, Esq., Chelsea, Middlesex
*Stephens, B., Esq., Serle's-place, London
*Stephens, Chas., Esq., Rickmansworth, Herts.
*Stephens, C., Esq., Stone-house, Gloucestershire
*Stephens, Gilbert, Esq., Doughty-street, London
*Stephens, J. D., Esq., Sarratt, Herts.
*Stephens, J. G., Esq., Hurst-hall, Bexley, Kent
*Stephens, John, Esq., Thames-street, London
*Stephens, J., Esq., Credenhill, Herefordshire
*Stephens, Rev. M. F. T., Thornbury, Gloucester.
*Stephens, Mr. S., St. Michael's-alley, London
*Stephens, William, Esq., Bedford-row, do.
*Stephenson, E., Esq., Somerton, Somersetshire
Stephenson, Rev. J. A., Lympsham, do.
Stephenson, M., Esq., Lawrence-lane, London
Stephenson, T., Esq., Clapham-common, Surrey
Steuart, Jas., Esq., M.P., Portland-place, Lond.
Stevens, J., Esq., Oxford-street, do.
Stevens, C. J., Esq., M. D., Carshalton, Surrey
Stevens, J., Esq., Oriel college, Oxford
Stevens, J. D., Esq., Rickmansworth, Herts.
*Stevens, Nat., Esq., Gray's-inn-square, London
Stevens, Thomas, Esq., Frant, Sussex
*Stevens, T. O., Esq., Salisbury
*Stevens, W. E., Esq., Sutton Lodge, Surrey
*Stevens and Brenchley, Messrs., Old Jewry, Lon.
Stevenson, Rev. H. I., B. A., Newark, Notts.
Stevenson, R., Esq., Gray's-inn-place, London
*Stevenson, W., Esq., Thong, Gravesend, Kent
Steward, Rev. A., Belstead, Suffolk
Steward, A. H., Esq., Stoke-park, do.
*Steward, Rev. E. T., A. B., Wem, Salop.
Steward, John, Esq., Threadneedle-st., London
Steward, John, Esq., Worcester college, Oxford
Steward, Thos., Esq., Teddington, Middlesex
Steward, T., Esq., Heigham-lodge, Norwich
Stewart, Mr. John, Islington, Liverpool
*Stewart, Rob., Esq., Great Russell-st., London
Stewart, Robert, Esq., Newbury, Berks.
*Stewart, Colonel Robert, Douglas, Isle of Man
*Stewart, T., Esq., Yarmouth, Norfolk
Stewart, W., Esq., Sackville-street, London
*Stiff, Z. C., Esq., Wellington, Somersetshire
Still, Rev. John, Inglesham, Wilts.
Still, S., Esq., Claughton-house, Lancaster, and Clapham, Surrey [shire
Stillingfleet, Rev. H. A., How Caple, Hereford-
*Stilwell, J., Esq., Thursley, Surrey
*Stilwell, J., Esq., Hillingdon, Middlesex
*Stirling, J., Esq., St. John's college, Cambridge
*ST. JOHN, The Right Honorable Lord
St. John, Rev., G., Powick, Worcestershire
St. John, Rev. G. Wm., Stanton Lacy, Salop.
*St. John, Henry, Esq., Hornsey, Middlesex
*St. John, Rev. O. D., Mottisfont, Hants.
Stock, Mr. Joseph, Birmingham
Stocken, F., Esq., Walham-green, Middlesex
Stockport New Subscription Library
*Stockport Overseers' Office, Cheshire
*Stocks, Joseph, Esq., King-street, Norwich
*Stocks, S., Esq., Hecton Mersey, nr. Stockport
*Stoddart, E., Esq., Ashford, Kent
Stoddart, W., jun., Esq., Freshford, Somerset.
*Stoddart, W. W., Esq., St. John's col., Oxford

*Stokes, Frederick, Esq., Worcester
Stokes, Rev. H. A. B., Doveridge, Derbyshire
*Stokes, John, Esq., Wolverhampton
*Stokes, J. E., Esq., Camberwell, Surrey
Stokes, J. R., Esq., Bolton, Lancashire [Lond.
Stokes and Hollingworth, Messrs., Cateaton-st.,
*Stokes and Watkins, Messrs., Bolton, Lancash.
*Stolterforth, Sigismund, Esq., M.D., Dovor
*Stonard, Rev. J., D.D., Aldingham, Lancash.
*Stonard, Nat., Esq., Tottenham, Middlesex.
Stone, D., Esq., Castle-street, London
*Stone, Rev. David, Wilton, Somersetshire
*Stone, Mr. Francis H., Norwich . . . 2 Copies
Stone, George, Esq., Taunton, Somersetshire
*Stone, Joseph, Esq., Dorchester
*Stone, Mr. O., Fish-street-hill, London
*Stone, William, Esq., Bradford, Wilts.
Stone, W. O., Esq., Mayfield, Sussex
Stone, Mr. W., Hentland, Herefordshire
*Stone and Son, Messrs., Tonbridge Wells
*STOPFORD, The Rt. Hon. Lord Viscount
Storer, Rev. John, Hawksworth, Notts.
Storey, F. W., Esq., York
Stork, Joseph, Esq., Birmingham
*Storm, A., Esq., Edgware-road, London
Story, P. L., Esq., Brighton
*Stott, Walter Barton, Esq., Manchester
STOURTON, The Right Honorable Lord
*Stow, Rich. A., Esq., Gracechurch-st., London
STOWELL, The Right Honorable Lord
*Stowell, Rev. Hugh, Salford, Lancashire
Stowkins, Mr. William, Staines, Middlesex
*St. Peter's college, Library of, Cambridge
*Stracey, John, Esq., Sprowston, Norfolk
*Strachan, J. M., Esq., Teddington, Middlesex
Stralford, John, Esq., Worcester
*Strand, James, Esq., Watling-street, London
*Strange, John, Esq., Enfield, Middlesex
*Strange, John B., Esq., Lothbury, London
*Strangways, E.S., Esq., Trinity coll., Cambridge
*Strangways, H. B., Esq., Trinity coll., Oxford
*Strangways, S. F., Esq., Christ-church coll., do.
Stratford, Mr. R., Ockbrook, Derbyshire
Stratford Library, Warwickshire
STRATHMORE, The Right Hon. the Earl of
Stratton, A., Esq., Cheapside, London
Stratton, Henry, Esq., Enfield, Middlesex
*Streachy, Capt. R., Shepton-Mallet, Somerset.
Streatfield, A. F., Esq., St. John's coll., Oxford
Streather, R., Esq., Cambridge-heath, Hackney
Street, Mr. J., Kilreage, Llangarran, Hereford.
*Street, Millington, and Co., Philpot-lane, Lond.
*Stretch, Mr. Edward, Brighton
Streeten, H. T., Esq., Queen's college, Oxford
*Stretton, C., Esq., Gloucester-place, London
*Stretton, F., Esq., Trinity college, Cambridge
*Stretton, George, Esq., Nottingham
Strickland, Eustace, Esq., York
Strickland, E. R., Esq., Trinity coll., Oxford
*Stringer, George, Esq., Dover
*Stringer, Rev. James, Emanuel col., Cambridge
*Stringer, Miles, Esq., Russell-square, London
*Stringer, W. H., Esq., Ashford, Kent
*Stringer, Cooper, and Co., Messrs., Monument-
Strong, Rev. P., Mayland, Essex [yard, Lond.
Strongitharm, Mr. J., Daw-end, Staffordshire
*Strutt, Colonel, J.H., M.P., Terling-place, Essex
Strutt, Jedediah, Esq., Belper, Derbyshire
Strutt, Joseph, Esq., Derby
Strutt, William, Esq., ditto
*Strutt, Major-Gen., W.G., Little Baddow, Essex
Strutton, Mr. George, Cannon-street, London
Stuart, Major, C., Hillingdon-grove, Middlesex
*Stubbing, Mr. William, Woolwich
*Stubbs, G. B., Esq., Walsall, Staffordshire
Stubbs, J., Esq., Longport, do.
Stubbs, J., Esq., Birmingham
Stubbs, R., Esq., Cheshunt, Herts.
Stubbs, T., jun., Esq., Boroughbridge, Yorksh.
*Stubbs, Mr. Thomas, Altrincham, Cheshire
Stubs, Peter, Esq., Warrington
Stuckey, Mr. Richard, Brighton
*Stuckey, Vincent, Esq., Langport, Somerset.
Studholme, John, Esq., Carlisle
Studholme, Rev. Joseph, M.A., Dean and Fellow of Jesus college, Cambridge
*Stulpner, J. H., Esq., Leadenhall-st., London
Sturge, Henry, Esq., Bewdley
Sturgeon, Thomas B., Esq., Rainham, Essex
Stuttard, Mr. J., Watling-street, London
Styche, Rev. G., Keele, Newcastle, Staffordshire
Sucklen, Rev. A., Wootton-hall, Norfolk
Sudlow, John, Esq., Manchester [cashire
*Sudren, Wm., Esq., Belthall, near Bury, Lan-
*Sudworth, Thomas, Esq., Blacon-point, Chester
*SUFFIELD, The Right Honorable Lord
Sulivan, George James, Esq., Langlebury, Herts.
*Sullivan, Sir C., Bart., Thames-Ditton, Surrey
Sully, H., Esq., M. D., Wiveliscombe, Somer-
*Summersby, Mr. J., Islington [setshire
*Sumner, Edward, Esq., Altrincham, Cheshire
*Sumner, Francis, Esq., Glossop, Derbyshire
Sumner, George, Esq., Lymm, Cheshire
*Sumner, Joseph, Esq., Northenden, do.
*Sun Newspaper-office, Strand, London
*Sunderland, Rev. J., M. A., Ulverstone
Surrage, T. L., Esq., Clifton, near Bristol
*Sutcliffe, John, Esq., Todmorden, Lancashire
*Sutcliffe, R., Esq., Rochdale, do.
*Sutcliffe, Mr. W., Worsley, near Manchester
*Sutcliffe, Messrs., Hebden-bridge, Lancashire
*Suter, Edward, Esq., Cheapside, London
Sutherland, A. J., Esq., Christ-ch., coll., Oxford
*Sutherland, Rev. J., A.M., Southwold, Suffolk
*Suttill, William, Esq., Bolton, Lancashire
*Sutton, Sir R., Bart., Lyndford-hall, Norfolk
*Sutton, Mr. D., Eagle-terrace, Kensington
*Sutton, E. P., Esq., Clement's-inn, London
*Sutton, James, Esq., Shardlow-hall, Derby
Sutton, John, Esq., Oriel college, Oxford
*Sutton, Joseph, Esq., Shrewsbury [bridge
Sutton, Rev. R. W., M. A., Clare-hall, Cam-
Sutton, Rev. S., Hill, near Southampton
Sutton, Rev. Thomas, Sheffield
*Swabey, H. B., Esq., Doctors Commons, Lond.
*Swaine, George, Esq., Broxbourne, Herts.
Swaine, Mr. Thomas, Waltham-Cross, do.
*Swainson, George L., Esq., Liverpool
*Swainson, J., Esq., Brasenose-coll., Oxford
Swaisland, Charles, Esq., Crayford, Kent
Swan, Henry, Esq., Doctors Commons, London
*Swan, R., Esq., Chequer-gates, Lincoln
Swann, C., Esq., Nottingham [shire
Swansborough, Mr. W., Wisbeach, Cambridge-
*Swanston, C. T., Esq., Chancery-lane, London
Swayne, John, Esq., Wilton, Wilts.
Swayne, Mr. Richard, Battersea, Surrey
Swayne, W. C., Esq., Heytesbury, Wilts.
Sweet, Rev. C. B., A.M., Kittisford, Somerset.
Sweetapple, Mr. Thomas, Godalming, Surrey
Sweeting, H., Esq., Huntingdon
Sweetlove, D. T., Esq., Maidstone, Kent
*Sweetlove, Thomas, Esq., do., do.
Swetenham, C., Esq., Somerford-Booths, Chesh.
Swettenham, J. W., Esq., Wood-end, Derby-
Swift, Mr. Edw., Walsall, Staffordshire [shire
Swift, L., Esq., Milverton, Somersetshire
Swinbourne, Mrs. Ann, Derby
*Swinburne, Thomas, Esq., Gateshead, Durham
*Swindells, Mr. John, jun., Manchester
*Swindells, Martin, Esq., do.
Swinfen, J., Esq., Swinfen-hall, near Lichfield
*Swinford, Henry K., Esq., Mark-lane, London
*Swinnerton, Mr. James, Macclesfield 2 Copies
*Swinny, Henry, Esq., Gravesend, Kent
Swinson, G. N., Esq., Birmingham
*Swire, Rev. John, Mansfield, Nottingham
*Swire, Samuel, Esq., Ashton under Line
*Swyer, Mr. Robert, Manchester
SYDNEY, The Right Hon. Lord Viscount
Sykes, Daniel, Esq., M.P., Raywell, Yorkshire
*Sykes, E., Esq., Mansfield-Woodhouse, Notts.
Sykes, John, Esq., Sheffield
*Sykes, John, Esq., Ulverstone
*Sykes, R., Esq., Edgeley, Cheshire
Sykes, Rev. Richard, West Ella, Yorkshire
*Sykes, W. A., Esq., Brasenose coll., Oxford
*Sykes, W. B., Esq., Accrington, Lancashire
Sylvester, R. J., Esq., Gloucester-st., Queen-sq., London
Symes, T., Esq., Bridg-water, Somersetshire
Symmonds, J., Esq., King's Pion, Herefordshire
Symmonds, Mr. W., Leinthall Earls, do.
Symonds, Rev. H. T., L. L. D., Hereford
Symonds, Rev. J., Great Ormsby, Norfolk
Symonds, P. H., Esq., Allensmore, Herefordsh.
*Symonds, Rev. T. P., Pengethly, do.
*Symons, H., Esq., Axbridge, Somersetshire
*Symons, T. H., Esq., Mynde-park, Herefordsh.
Sympson, E. W., Esq., Christchurch, Hants.
*Syms, Frederick G., Esq., Craven-st., London
Syms, Colonel William, East Malling, Kent

*TABLEY, DE, The Right Honorable Lord
*Tabram, R., Esq., Cambridge
*Taddy, J., Esq., Margate, Kent
Tadhunter, W., Esq., Bermondsey-st., London
*Taffnell, J. F., Esq., Langles, Great Waltham,
Tahourdin, Rev. W., Theale, Berks. [Essex
*TALBOT, The Right Honorable Earl
*Talbot, The Right Honorable Gustavus C.
Talbot, C. R. M., Esq., Penrice-castle, Swansea
*Talbot, F., Esq., Bedford-row, London
Talbot, G., Esq., Kidderminster [shire
Talbot, Rev. H. G., Mitchel-Troy, Monmouth-
Talbot, James, Esq., Evercreech, Somersetshire
*Talbot, Robert, Esq., Dartford, Kent
*Tall, John, Esq., Kingston upon Hull
Tallents and Beevor, Messrs., Newark, Notts.
*Tamlyn, Mr. George, Testwood, Southampton
*Tamplin, Richard, Esq., Brighton
*TAMWORTH, The Right Hon. Lord Visc.
*TANKERVILLE, The Rt. Hon. the Countess of
*Tanner, Jonathan, Esq., Reading, Berks.
*Tanner, R. T., Esq., Cheltenham
Tanner, Thos., Esq., Combe-house, near Bath
Tanner and Son, Messrs., Park-street, Bristol
*Taplin, Rev. J. W., B.A., Sunbury, Middlesex
*Tapster, Robert, Esq., Barnet, Herts.
Tarleton, Rev., D.D., Penley, Salop
*Tartt, Robert, Esq., Holywell
Tassell, Robert, Esq., Maidstone, Kent
Tassell, Thomas, Esq., do., do.
*Tatchill, J.T., Esq., Sedborough-house, Dorset.
*Tate, Mr. E. R., Lambeth, Surrey
Tatham, Rev. H., Summerfield-house
Tatham, Rev. R., Fellow and Librarian of St. John's college, Cambridge
*Tattershall, J., Esq., M.D., Ealing, Middlesex
Tattershall and Son, Messrs., Liverpool
*Tatton, Mrs., Withenshaw-hall, Cheshire
Taunton, T. H., Esq., Oriel college, Oxford
*Tause, George, Esq., South Lambeth, Surrey
TAXES, The Honorable the Commissioners of
*Tayler, Rev. J. J., Manchester
*Tayleure, John, Esq., Buntingsdale, Salop.
Taylor, Lieut. Gen. Sir Herbert, K.C.B. & G.H.
*Taylor, Captain Alexander, Challock, Kent
*Taylor, Rev. Charles, jun., Hereford
Taylor, C. C., Esq., Bolton-hall, Yorkshire
*Taylor, Charles S., Esq., Chippenham, Wilts.
Taylor, Mr. Edward, Culmington, Salop
Taylor, Rev. G., D. C. L., Dedham, Essex
Taylor, G., Esq., Chadnor-court, Dilwyn, Here-
Taylor, George E., Esq., Bristol [fordshire
*Taylor, George Watson, Esq., M.P., New Burlington-street, London
*Taylor, H., Esq., Uttoxeter, Staffordshire
*Taylor, H. W., Esq., Manchester
Taylor, Captain James, Hereford
*Taylor, James M., Esq., Westwood, Lancashire
Taylor, James, Esq., Moor-green, Birmingham
*Taylor, Jas., Esq., Todmorden-hall, Lancash.
Taylor, James, Esq., Wimpole-street, London
Taylor, Jeffrey, Esq., Enfield, Middlesex

*Taylor, John, Esq., Clement's-inn, London
*Taylor, John, Esq., Oldham, Lancashire
*Taylor, John, Esq., Whalley, do.
Taylor, John, Esq., Preston, do.
*Taylor, J., Esq., Strensham-ct., Worcestersh.
Taylor, John Fogg, Esq., Wigan, Lancashire
*Taylor, John H., Esq., Surrey-square
Taylor, John, Esq., Leamington, Warwickshire
*Taylor, John, Esq., Bristol
Taylor, John, Esq., Langdon-abbey, Kent
*Taylor, J. H., Esq., Crayford, do.
*Taylor, J. S., Esq., Great James'-st., London
*Taylor, Joseph, Esq., Christleton, Cheshire
Taylor, Mr. J., Washingborough, Lincolnshire
Taylor, Miss, White Friars, Chester
*Taylor, Mr. Luke, Ledbury, Herefordshire
Taylor, M., Esq., Brasenose college, Oxford
*Taylor, Mrs., Shapwick-house, Somersetshire
*Taylor, Philip, Esq., Showl-court, Herefordshire
Taylor, Richard, Esq., Weobley, do.
*Taylor, R., Esq., Featherstone-buildings, Lond.
*Taylor, R., Esq., Milnthorpe, Westmorland
*Taylor, R., Esq., Brighton
*Taylor, Robert, Esq., Lymm-hall, Cheshire
Taylor, Simon, Esq., Billiter-court, London
Taylor, Mr. S., Macclesfield
*Taylor, Mr. S. J., Fleet-street, London
*Taylor, S. W., Esq., Christ-church coll., Oxford
Taylor, Thomas, Esq., Birmingham
*Taylor, Thomas, Esq., Cricklade, Wilts.
*Taylor, Thomas, Esq., Bolton, Lancashire
*Taylor, Thomas, Esq., Overton-hall, Cheshire
Taylor, T., Esq., Wakefield
*Taylor, T., Esq., Appleton, Cheshire
*Taylor, Mr. Thomas, Manchester
Taylor, Mr. Thomas, Derby
Taylor, Rev. W., York
Taylor, W., Esq., Cloak-lane, London
Taylor, W., Esq., Birchin-lane, do.
*Taylor, William, Esq., Radcliffe on Trent
*Taylor, William, Esq., Rochdale, Lancashire
Taylor, Mr. W., Reading, Berks.
Taylor, Mr. W., Whaley, Cheshire
*Taylor, W. Garratt, Esq., Bolton, Lancashire
Taylor, W. P., Esq., Worcester college, Oxford
Taylor, Mr. W., Birchin-lane, London
*Taylor and Co., Messrs. R., Oldham
*Taylor and Garnett, Messrs., Manchester
Teale, Mr. George, Old-street, London
*Teale, Mr. Joseph, Hackney, Middlesex
*Teale, Thomas, Esq., Leeds
Tearne, T. M., Esq., Stockton, Worcestershire
Tebbertt, J., Esq., Earith, Kent
Tebbett, Mr. Robert, Windsor
*Tebbutt, T., Esq., jun., Austin-friars, London
*Tebbutt, T. R., Esq., Manchester
*Tebbutt, William, Esq., Salford, Lancashire
*Teesdale & Symes, Mess., Fenchurch-st., Lond.
Tempest, Colonel, Long-hall, York [Kent
Temple, T., Esq., sen., St. Margarett's at Cliffe,
Temple, William, Esq., Bishopstrow, Wilts.
*Temple, Rev. W. S., Durham
*Templeman, John, Esq., Bath
*Templeman, J. A., Esq., Crewkerne, Somerset.
*Templer, Rev. G. H., Shapwick, do.
*Templer, J., Esq., M.D., Tower, London
*Tennant, J., Esq., Russell-pl., Fitzroy-sq., do.
Terner, Mr. William, Stockport, Cheshire
*Terrell, Wm., Esq., Broughton, Manchester
*Terrett, Wm., Esq., L. L. B., Clare, Suffolk
*Territ, W., Esq., L. L. D., Chilcote-hall, do.
*Terry, Avison, Esq., Kingston upon Hull
Terry, Mr. H., Artillery-place, Finsbury, Lond.
Terry, J. B., Esq., Ripon, Yorkshire
*Terry, Stephen, Esq., Odiham, Hants.
*Terry, Mr. Thomas, Canterbury
*Tetlow, John, Esq., Manchester
Tetlow, Rev. John Richard, Liverpool
*Tetlow, Thomas, Esq., Oldham, Lancashire
*Thacker, W., Esq., Muchall-hall, Staffordshire
*Thackeray, Mrs. Sarah, Salford, Lancashire
*Thackeray, W. M., Esq., M. D., Chester

*Thackrah, Geo., Esq., Feltham-place, Middsx.
*Thackrey, George, Esq., Leeds
*Thackrey, John, jun., Esq., do.
Thackwell, J., Esq., Dymock, Gloucestershire
*Thackwell, S., Esq., Pembroke college, Oxford
*Thatcher, Mr. Robert, New-Mills, Derbyshire
Thatcher, Col. T., Tidenham, Gloucestershire
Thatcher, Mr. T., Paddington-green, Middlesex
*Theakstone, Francis, Esq., Fulford, near York
*Theobald, J. M., Esq., Claydon-hall, Suffolk
*Theobald, J. M., Esq., Jesus coll., Cambridge
Thew, Major, Bovingdon-grove, Herts
Thickins, Rev. William, Coventry
*Thirlwall, Rev. C., Trinity college, Cambridge
*Thiselton, H. M., Esq., Gt. Russell-st., London
*Thistlethwayte, T., jun., Esq., Christ-church college, Oxford
Thomas, Francis Henry, Esq., Hereford
Thomas, G., Esq., Cross-street, London
Thomas, Rev. G., Worcester college, Oxford
*Thomas, H., Esq., New Basinghall-st., London . . . 2 Copies
Thomas, Rev. J., Stoke-Lacy, Herefordshire
Thomas, John, Esq., Sheerness, Kent
*Thomas, John, Esq., Trinity college, Oxford
Thomas, Mr. John, Tewkesbury
*Thomas, Mr. J., King-st., Covent-garden, Lond.
Thomas, Rev. M., Abergavenny, Monmouthsh.
Thomas, M., Esq., New Boswell-court., Lond.
*Thomas, O. G., Esq., Monmouth
*Thomas, R., Esq., Kew, Surrey
Thomas, Mr. R., Purbrook, Herefordshire
*Thomas, Rees Goring, Esq., Tooting, Surrey
*Thomas, Samuel, Esq., Cornhill, London
Thomas, Thos., Esq., Canon-Pion, Herefordsh.
*Thomas, Rev. W., Wellington, Somersetshire
Thomas, W., Esq., Enfield, Middlesex
*Thomas, William, Esq., Hereford
*Thomas, W., Esq., Eye-cottage, Herefordshire
Thomas, W. B., Esq., Chesterfield, Derbyshire
Thomas, W. Lloyd, Esq., Hatfield, Hertford.
*Thomas and Co., Messrs., Cornhill, London
*Thomason, Mr. Edward, Birmingham
Thomason, Mr. S., Weobley, Herefordshire
*Thomeley, T., Esq., Hadfield-lodge, Derbysh.
*THOMOND, The Most Noble the Marquis of
Thompson, C., Esq., Rochester, Kent
*Thompson, D. V., Esq., Victualling-office, Lond.
*Thompson, Edw., Esq., Clare hall, Cambridge
*Thompson, Mr. Edward, Dover
*Thompson, Geo., Esq., Clifford's-inn, London
*Thompson, G., Esq., Lincoln's-inn-fields, do.
*Thompson, Rev. G. H., Tottenham, Middlesex
*Thompson, G. H. W., Esq., Magdalene hall, Oxford
Thompson, H. S., Esq., Trinity coll., Cambridge
*Thompson, J., Esq., Haughton-park, Notts.
Thompson, John, Esq., Gravesend, Kent
*Thompson, Jas., Esq., Tottenham, Middlesex
*Thompson, John, Esq., Manchester
Thompson, John, Esq., Liverpool
*Thompson, Mr. John, Kingston upon Hull
Thompson, John S., Esq., Hilton, Hunts.
*Thompson, Joseph, Esq., Old Change, London
*Thompson, K., Esq., Oldham, Lancashire
*Thompson, M., Esq., Southgate, Middlesex
Thompson, Mr. P., Frith-street, Soho, London
*Thompson, Richard, Esq., Oldham, Lancashire
*Thompson, R., Esq., Hemel-Hempstead, Herts.
*Thompson, Mr. R. B., Solihull, Warwickshire
Thompson, Thos., Esq., Austin-friars, London
*Thompson, Thomas, Esq., Kingston upon Hull
*Thompson, Thomas, Esq., Lancaster
*Thompson, Thomas, Esq., Sunderland
Thompson, Rev. W., Farnworth, Lancashire
*Thompson, William, Esq., Liverpool
*Thompson, William, Esq., Cothill, Berks.
*Thompson, William, jun., Esq., Lancaster
Thompson, Mr. William, Hertford
*Thompson, Messrs. J. & J., Manchester
*Thomson, Edward P., Esq., do.
*Thomson, George, Esq., Somersham, Hunts.

*Thomson, John, Esq., West-square, Lambeth
*Thomson, J., Esq., Lyndhurst, Hants.
*Thomson, J. D., Esq., King's-Arms-yard, Lon.
*Thomson, J. R., Esq., George-st., Minories, do.
Thomson, Mr. K., Paradise-row, Rotherhithe
Thomson, Robert, Esq., Jesus coll., Cambridge
Thomson, William, Esq., Uckfield, Sussex
*Thomson, Wm., Esq., Clitheroe, Lancashire
*Thoresbury, Rev. T., Cusop, Herefordshire
*Thorley, J., Esq., Tarporley, Cheshire [London
*Thorman, J., Esq., Lawrence Pountney-lane,
Thornber, W., Esq., Trinity coll., Oxford
*Thornbery, William, Esq., Worcester
*Thornbury, G., Esq., Chancery-lane, London
Thorndike, Andrew S., Esq., Staples-inn, do.
Thorneycroft, G. B., Esq., Wolverhampton
*Thornhill, B., Esq., Stanton-house, Derbyshire
*Thornhill, G., Esq., St. John's coll., Cambrid.
Thornley, Edw., Esq., Birmingham
*Thornley, R., Esq., Charlesworth, Derbyshire
Thornley, Sam., Esq., Yardley, Worcestershire
Thornton, C., Esq., Christ-church col., Oxford
*Thorold, Sir J. H., Bt., Syston-park, Lincolnsh.
*Thorold, Lady, do., do.
Thorold, M. W., Esq., Barnby-moor, Notts.
*Thoroton, Rev. Levett, B. A., Colwick, do.
Thorp, Mr., St. James's-street, London
*Thorp, Mr. John, Glossop, Derbyshire
*Thorp and Burch, Messrs., Jewry-st., London
Thorpe, Rev. John, Chester
Thorpe, Mr., St. James'-street, London
*Thorpe, G., Esq., Thavies-inn, do.
Thorpe, Rev. T., M.A., Trinity col., Cambridge
Thorpe and Grays, Messrs., York
Thould, Mr. Samuel, Ripple, Worcestershire
Threlfall, Lazarus, Esq., Preston, Lancashire
*Thring, John, Esq., Alford-house, Somerset.
Throckmorton, Sir C., Bart., Coughton-court, Alcester
Throckmorton, N., Esq., Buckland, Berks.
*Throp, William, Esq., Blackburn, Lancashire
Thursby, Rev. H., M. A., Penn, Staffordshire
*Thwaites, Daniel, Esq., Blackburn, Lancash.
Thwaites, John, Esq., do., do.
Thwaites, J., Esq., Tokenhouse-yard, London
Thwaites, W. G., Esq., Queen-st., Cheapside, do.
THYNNE, The Right Honorable Lord George
Thynne, H., Esq., Basingstoke, Hants.
Tibbatts, J., Esq., Avenbury, Herefordshire
Tibbatts, Thomas, Esq., Donnington, do.
*Tibbitts, Robert, Esq., Warwick
Tibbitts, Wm., jun., Esq., Stratford on Avon
*Tibbs, Thomas, Esq., Hill-house, Monmouth
*Tierney, Rev., M. A., Arundel, Sussex
Tilby, Mr. George, Chichester-place, London
*Tilby, James, Esq., Devizes
Tiley, William, Esq., Cross, near Bristol
*Tilleard, John, Esq., Old Jewry, London
*Tillett, Mr. A., Vine-street, Lambeth, Surrey
*Tillotson, Robert, Esq., Colne, Lancashire
*Tillsey, H., Esq., Stamp-office, Somerset-house, London
Tilson and Son, Messrs., Coleman-street, do.
Tilston, John, Esq., Ellesmere, Salop
Timbrell, The Venerable and Rev. Archdeacon, Beckford, Gloucestershire
*Timbrell, Charles, Esq., Bradford, Wilts.
*Timbrell, Thomas, Esq., Trowbridge, do.
*Times, W. G., Esq., Much-Hadham, Herts.
*Timm, Joseph, Esq., Somerset-house, London
Timmins, Charles, Esq., Birmingham
*Timperan, Jos., Esq., St. Albans
*Timperley, Mr. J., Altrincham, Cheshire
Timperley, Mr. J. P., Manchester
Tims, Thomas, Esq., Banbury, Oxfordshire
Tindal, N., Esq., Trinity college, Cambridge
Tindal, Thomas, Esq., Aylesbury, Bucks.
*Tindall, Rev. W., M. A., Wolverhampton
*Tindall, John, Esq., Manchester
*Tinley, J., Esq., North Shields, Northumberland
*Tippet, E., Esq., St. Peter's coll., Cambridge.
*Tippet, Richard E., Esq., Bread-street, London

Tippetts, J. B., Esq., Hatton-garden, London
*Tippetts, Richard, Esq., Dartford, Kent
Tipple, J. H., Esq., Wymondham, Norfolk
Tipton Furnace Company, Tipton, Staffordshire
Tittensor, T., Esq., Liverpool
*Tobin, Sir John, Knt., do.
*Tobin, John, Esq., Christ-church coll., Oxford
*Todd, Mr. H. C., Little Queen-street, London
*Todd, J. F., Esq., Trinity-college, Cambridge
Todd, John Henry, Esq., Andover
*Todd, John, Esq., Franby-park, Yorkshire
*Todd, Mr. John, Kingston upon Hull
Todd, John, Esq., Swanland-hall, near do.
Todd, Joseph, Esq., Clapham-common, Surrey
Todd, Rev. Nicholas, Corby, Lincolnshire
*Toler, The Honorable H.
Toll, William, Esq., Norwich
*Tollemache, J. J., Esq., Tarporley, Cheshire
*Toller, E., Esq., jun., Doctors Commons, Lond.
*Toller, T., Esq., Gray's-inn, do.
*Tollner, W. Michael, Esq., Sloane-st., do.
*Tolson, Major, F.S.A., Woodland-lodge, Somerset
Tombs, M., Esq., Riddox, Eardisland, Herefordshire
Tomkins, B., Esq., Upper Thames-st., London
Tomkins, G., Esq., King's Pion, Herefordshire
*Tomkins, G. J. S., Esq., Kidderminster
Tomkins, John, Esq., Weir, Herefordshire
Tomkins, William, Esq., Yeovil, Somersetshire
Tomkys, Mr. J., Bilston, Staffordshire
*Tomlin, James, Esq., Cornhill, London
*Tomlins, Sir T., Knt., Fludyer-st., Westminster
*Tomlins, J. T., Esq., Strand, London
Tomlins, T. E., Esq., Staples-inn, do.
*Tomlinson, G., Esq., Manchester
*Tomlinson, J., Esq., Cliff Ville, near Newcastle
*Tomlinson, J., Esq., Nantwich, Cheshire
*Tomlinson, Mr. R. S., St. Peter's, Norwich
*Tomlinson, Mr. W., Brookbottom, Mellor, Derby.
*Tomlinson, Mr. W., St. Peter's, Norwich
*Tompsett & Phillips, Messrs., Hastings
Tompson, Mr. Alderman, Norwich
*Tompson, C. K., Esq., Balliol college, Oxford
*Tomsom, Richard, Esq., Ramsgate, Kent
Tonge, Mr. W. S., Sittingbourne, do.
Tongue, W., Esq., Comberford-hall, Lichfield
*Tonyn, Rev. J. F., Alvechurch, Worcestershire
Tooby, Mr. Thomas, Ledbury, Herefordshire
*Toogood, J., Esq., Bridg-water, Somersetshire
*Tooke, W., Esq., F.R.S., Russell-sq., London
Tootal, J., jun., Esq., Wakefield
*Toovey, Thomas, Esq., King's Langley, Herts.
*Toovey, W., Esq., Newnham-Murren, Oxon
Topham, John, Esq., jun., Liverpool
Torin, B., Esq., Englefield-green, Surrey
*Torkington, J., Esq., Emanuel col., Cambdg.
Tottie, Richard, Esq., Kingston upon Hull
Touche, P. La, Esq., Corpus-Christi coll., Oxford
*Touchet, John, Esq., Broom-house, near Manchester
*Toulmin, Thomas, Esq., Liverpool
*Toulson, J. A. P., Esq., Skipwith, Yorkshire
Tounge, Edward, Esq., Inner Temple, London
*Tourle, T., Esq., Landport, Sussex
*Toussaint, Joseph, Esq., Feltham, Middlesex
*Towend, J., Esq., Star-ct., Broad-st., London
*Tower, C. T., Esq., Weald-hall, Brentwood
*Towers, J. G., Esq., Castle-st., Falcon-sq., Lond.
*Towgood, J., Esq., jun., Lincoln's-inn, do.
Towgood, M., Esq., St. Neots, Hunts.
*Towle, J., Esq., Borrowash-mills, Derbyshire
Towle, Samuel, Esq., Nottingham
Towle, Thomas, Esq., Draycot, Derbyshire
*Townend, H., Esq., St. John's col., Cambridge
*Townend, W., Esq., Manchester
*Townley, R. G., Esq., Fulbourn St. Vigors, Cambridgeshire
*Townley, W., Esq., Townhead, Milnthorpe, Westmorland
Townsend, B., Esq., Stratford on Avon
*Townsend, Mr. John, Manchester
*Townsend, W., Esq., Doctors Commons, Lond.
*Townshend, Rev. C. H., M.A., Baywards, Surrey, and Keswick, Cumberland
*Townshend, E. V., Esq., Wincham-hall, Chesh.
*Towry, G. E., Esq., Harewood-lodge, Berks.
*Tracy, J. C. H., Esq., Oriel college, Oxford
*Trafford, E. T., Esq., Swithamley-hall, Staffordsh.
*Trafford, T., Esq., Oughtrington-hall, Cheshire
*Trafford, T. J., Esq., Trafford-park, Manchester
Tragett, Rev. T. Heathcote, Awbridge, Hants.
*Trant, D., Esq., Malvern Wells, Worcestersh.
Travers, J. B., Esq., Furnival's-inn, London
Treacher, Mr. George, Sonning, Berks.
TREASURY, The Lords Commissioners of His Majesty's
*Trebeck, Thomas, Esq., Southwell, Notts.
*Trecothick, James, Esq., Broadstairs, Kent
Tredgold, Henry, Esq., Chilbolton, Hants.
*Trehern, C. H., Esq., New-inn, London
*Tregoning, John, Esq., Watling-street, do.
*Trench, F., Esq., Oriel college, Oxford
*Trevelyan, Rev. J. T., Milverton, Somersetshire
Trevelyan, S., Esq., Balliol college, Oxford
*Trevor, A., Esq., Gloucester-place, London
Trigg, M. T., Esq., Kingston upon Hull
*Trimmer, Rev. H. S., M. A., Heston, Middlsx.
Trinder, Charles, Esq., Devizes
*Trinity College Library, Oxford
*Trinity House, The Corporation of the
*Trinity House, The, Newcastle upon Tyne
*Tripp, R. S., Esq., Raymond-buildings, Lond.
*Trivett, Rev. W., A. M., Bradwell, Suffolk
Trodd, W. S., Esq., Romsey, Hants.
*Trollope, Admiral Sir H., Knight Banneret, Freshford, Somerset
*Trollope, Rev. W., M. A., Christ's-hospital, London
Trotman, F., Esq., Siston-court, Gloucestershire
*Trotter, Thomas, Esq., North Shields
*Troughton, John, Esq., Preston, Lancashire
*Troughton, Thomas Moore, Esq., do., do.
*Troughton and Lea, Messrs., Coventry
Trow, W., Esq., Kidderminster
Trowell, Mrs., Thorn-hill, Derby
Trower, W. J., Esq., Lincoln's-inn-fields, Lond.
*Trubshaw, J., Esq., Little Haywood, Staffordsh.
Trueman, Edw., Esq., Pontefract, Yorkshire
Trumper, Rev. John, Clifford, Herefordshire
Trumper, M., Esq., Grantsfield, do.
Trumper, —, Esq., Jesus college, Oxford
Trumper, W. W., Esq., Grosmont, Monmouth
*Trusted, Mr. Joseph, Cusop, Herefordshire
Trusted, Thos., Esq., Brampton Abbots, do.
Trye, C. B., Esq., Brasenose college, Oxford
*Trye, H. N., Esq., Leckhampton-ct., Gloucesters.
Tubb, Mr. John Benjamin, Reading, Berks.
Tubb, Prince, Esq., Oxford
Tuck, Christopher, Esq., Hoddesdon, Herts.
Tuck, William, Esq., do., do.
Tucker, Mr. John, Glastonbury, Somersetshire
Tucker, Rev. T. H., Keynsham-place, nr. Bristol
Tudor, William, Esq., Queen's-parade, Bath
*Tudway, J. P., Esq., Wells, Somersetshire
Tudway, R. C., Esq., Christ-church col., Oxford
*Tuffill, Mr. Joseph, Rochester, Kent
*Tufnel, J. J., Esq., Langley's, Essex
Tufnell, Rev. William, East Bergholt, Suffolk
*Tugwell, G. H., Esq., Bath, Somersetshire
Tugwell, Thomas, Esq., Bradford, Wilts.
*Tugwell, W. E., Esq., Devizes
*Tull, Rev. Henry, Bengeworth, Worcestershire
*Tull, Mr. John, East Lockinge, Berks.
Tull, Mr. Thomas S., Charing-cross, London
Tully, Robert, Esq., Huntington, Herefordsh.
Tunnicliff, J., Esq., Stone, Staffordshire
*Tunstall, C., Esq., Nantwich, Cheshire
Tunstall, Mr. J., Burlton-court, Herefordshire
*Tuppen, Mr. W., Brighton
Turford, J., Esq., Thornbury, Herefordshire
*Turmine, Rev. H., Minster, Kent
Turner, W., Esq., Stockport, Cheshire
*Turner, Mrs., North Ferriby, Yorkshire
*Turner, Miss Maria, Croydon, Surrey
Turner, C., Esq., Kenilworth, Warwickshire
*Turner, Cecil, Esq., Brasenose coll., Oxford
Turner, Mr. Charles, Norwich
*Turner, Daniel, Esq., St. Giles', Oxford
*Turner, Edward, Esq., Sherborne, Dorsetshire
*Turner, Mr. G., Tokenhouse-yard, London
*Turner, H. H., Esq., Percy-street, do.
Turner, James, Esq., Dudley
Turner, James, Esq., Birmingham
Turner, Rev. John, Hagley, Worcestershire
*Turner, J., Esq., Bottom's-lodge, Cheshire
*Turner, John, Esq., Nantwich, do.
*Turner, John, Esq., Middlewich, do.
Turner, John, Esq., Preston, Lancashire
Turner, J. B., Esq., Brockmanton, Herefordsh.
*Turner, Rev. Jos., M. A., Frodsham, Cheshire
*Turner, P. B., Esq., Basing-lane, London
Turner, Rev. R., Yarmouth, Norfolk
*Turner, R., Esq., Canterbury
*Turner, R., Esq., Grantham, Lincolnshire
*Turner, Richard, Esq., Lewes, Sussex
*Turner, Samuel, Esq., Chester
*Turner, Samuel, Esq., Gray's-inn-sq., London
*Turner, Samuel, Esq., Haymarket, do.
*Turner, S. A., Esq., Barnwell, Cambridge
Turner, Mr. S., Upton-Bishop, Herefordshire
*Turner, Mr. S. E., Holmer, do.
*Turner, Mr. S. G., Dudley
Turner, Rev. Thomas, B. D., Ellesmere, Salop
*Turner, Thomas, Esq., Gloucester
Turner, Mr. Thomas, Manchester
*Turner, T., Esq., Bagot's-park, Staffordshire
Turner, T. P., Esq., Millman-street, London
Turner, T. T., Esq., St. John's coll., Cambridge
Turner, Rev. W. H., Clifton, near Bristol
Turner, W., Esq., M.D., Grantham, Lincolnsh.
*Turner, Wm., Esq., Haslingdon, Lancashire
Turner, William, Esq., Reigate, Surrey
Turner, William Hammond, Esq., Birmingham
*Turner, W. H., Esq., do.
*Turnicliffe, W. Henry, Esq., Tewkesbury
*Turnley, W. S., Esq., Kennington, Surrey
*Turnor, L., Esq., Hertford
Turrell, Mr. J., Leamington, Warwickshire
Turton, George, Esq., Sheffield
*Turton, Rev. H., M. A., Betley, Staffordshire
Turton, Rev. T., D.D., Cambridge, Dean of Peterboro'
Turton, Wm., Esq., Six Clerks'-office, London
Tutton, Mr. T., Down-st., Piccadilly, do.
Tuxford, Peter, Esq., Boston, Lincolnshire
Twamley, Mr. J., jun., Dudley
*Twamley, Josiah, Esq., Warwick
*Tweddell, Rev. R., A. M., Northenden, Chesh.
*Tween, Mr. John Squire, Ware, Herts.
Tween, Mr. Thomas, do., do.
Twemlow, F., Esq., Betley-Court, Staffordshire
*Twemlow, J., Esq., Hatherton, Cheshire
*Twemlow, John, jun., Esq., do., do.
Twemlow, Mrs., Lawton, near Congleton, do.
Twigg, J., Esq., Barnfields, Baswich, Staffordsh.
Twigg, Joseph, Esq., Burslem, do.
*Twisden, Sir John, Bart., Bradbourne, Kent
*Twiss, H., Esq., M. P., Lincoln's-inn, London
Twiss, Mr. J., Congleton, Cheshire
Twitchin, Mr. John, Newbury, Berks.
Tyas, J. H., Esq., Norfolk-street, London
Tyerman, T., Esq., Kennington, Surrey
Tyers, James, Esq., St. Mary's hall, Oxford
Tyfan, Mr. Joseph Taylor, Canterbury
*Tylee, John, Esq., Devizes
*Tyler, Capt. C. H., Lynsted-lodge, Kent
*Tymbs & Deighton, Messrs., Worcester, 2 Copies
Tyndall, T., Esq., Bristol
*Tynte, C. K., Esq., M. P., Bridg-water, Somerset.
Tyrell, Charles, Esq., M.P., Hawleigh, Suffolk
Tyrer, Robert, Esq., Liverpool
*Tyrer, Messrs. William and James, do.
Tyrrell, Charles, Esq., Aldermanbury, London
*Tyrrell, Edward, Esq., Guildhall, do.
*Tyrrell, Frederick, Esq., Bridge-street, do.
*Tyrrell, R., Esq., Cross-st., Finsbury, do.
*Tyrwhitt, Rev. J., Bradshaw, Claines, Worcestershire
Tyson, Rev. E. C., M. A., Thavies-inn, Lond.

*Tyson, Mr. J. T., High-st., Canterbury
*Tyssen, J. R. D., Esq., Lincoln's-inn-fields, London

*Ullithorne, C. M., Esq., Covent-garden, Lond.
*Ullithorne and Crampton, Messrs., Lincoln's-inn-fields, do.
Ulph, Mr. John Burt, St. Ives, Hunts.
Umpleby, Rev. D., B. A., Lancaster [hampton
*Underhill, J., Esq., Parkfield, near Wolver-
Underhill, T., Esq., Tipton, Staffordshire [shire
*Underwood, Rev. J. H., Lugwardine, Hereford-
*Underwood, Rev. T., jun., Willington, do.
*Underwood and Evans, Messrs., Hereford
*Unett, C. B., Esq., Broadward-hall, nr. Ludlow
University College Library, Oxford
Unsworth, Hugh, Esq., Preston, Lancashire
Unsworth, W. G., Esq., Maghull, do.
Unwin, Rev. J. R., Langar, Nottingham
Unwin, James, Esq., Manchester
Upcott, Mr. W., Willow-walk, Bermondsey
*Upfill, Messrs. Thomas and James, Birmingham
Upsher, Mr. J., St. Ives, Hunts.
Upton and Sons, Messrs., Leeds
*Urmston, Sir James, Bart., Deal, Kent
*Urwick, Mr. E., Fetter-lane, London
Urwick, William, Esq., Ludlow, Shropshire
*Usill, Mr. A., Wisbeach, Cambridgeshire

Vale, Mr. T., Sabery-hill, Herefordshire
Vale, W., Esq., Sutton, do.
Vale, Rev. W. H., Ecclesball, near Sheffield
Valentine, J., Esq., Somerton, Somersetshire
Vallance, George, Esq., Brighton
Vallance, Mr. John, Matlock Bath, Derbyshire
Vallance, James, Esq., Chippenham, Wiltshire
*Vallance, T. T., Esq., Sittingbourne, Kent
*Vallencourt, Mr. G., Pershore, Worcestershire
*Vandeleur, C., Esq., Trinity coll., Cambridge
Vandergucht, T. G., Esq., Bedford-place, Lond.
Vanderstegen, W. H., Esq., Brasenose-coll., Oxford
*Vane, Rev. J., Wrington, Somersetshire
Vannet, Rev. P., M. A., Knutsford, Cheshire
Van Sandau and Tindale, Dowgate-hill, Lond.
*Vardon, Mr. W., Gracechurch-street, do.
*Vardy, James, Esq., Wolverhampton
*Vares, T., Esq., B. A., Wadham coll., Oxford
Varnham, Mr. Arthur, Strand, London
*Varnham, C., Esq., Bembridge, Isle of Wight
Varty, R., Esq., Bower-house, Kent
*Varty, W. N., Esq., Bishopsgate-st., London
*Vaudrey, J., Esq., Bredbury, Cheshire
*Vaudrey, John, Esq., Dukinfield, do.
Vaudrey, Thomas, Esq., Congleton, do.
Vaudrey, Messrs. W. and C., do., do.
*Vaudreys & Ryle, Messrs., Cheadle, do.
*Vaughan, Rev. V., B. D., Malpas, do.
*Vaughan, Hugh, Esq., Brasenose coll., Oxford
*Vaughan, James, Esq., Enfield, Middlesex
Vaughan, N. E., Esq., Christ-church col., Oxford
Vaughan, W., Esq., Welsh-Bicknor, Herefordsh.
Vaughan, Mr. William, Waterloo-road, Lond.
Vaughan, Mr. William, Monmouth
Vausé, Rev. J., A. M., Liverpool
*Vaux, Jas., Esq., Macclesfield
*Vaux, T., Esq., Great Russell-street, London
*Vavasour, John, Esq., Crossfield, Rochdale,
Veasey, David, Esq., Huntingdon [Lancashire
Veasey, James, Esq., Godmanchester, Hunts.
*Venables, Mr. G., Taplow, Bucks.
*Verney, Sir Harry, Bart., Winslow, do.
Vernon, The Honorable G. [fields, London
Vernon, — Esq., Stanhope-st., Lincoln's-inn-
Vernon, G. V., Esq., Grove, near East Retford
*Vernon, Rev. J., Kirkby in Ashfield, Notts.
*Vernon, John, Esq., Willington, Cheshire
*Vernon, Thomas, Esq., Tewkesbury
*Vernon, Rev. W., Wheldrake, Yorkshire
*Vernon, W. J., Esq., Ryder's-court, London

*VERULAM, The Right Hon. the Earl of
Vevers, A., Esq., Yarkhill-court, Herefordshire
Vialls, Rev. Thomas, M. A., Twickenham
Vibart, James, Esq., Pitminster, Somersetshire
*Vickers, J., Esq., Surrey-square, Old Kent-road
*Vickery, J., Esq., Ely-place, Holborn, London
*Vickery, J., Esq., Coldbath-fields, do.
*Vignoles, C., Esq., Furnival's-inn, do.
Vigor, William, Esq., Basingstoke, Hants.
*Villar, Rev. J. G., Worcester college, Oxford
*Villers, Rev. W., Kidderminster
VILLIERS, The Right Hon. Lord Viscount
Vincent, Rev. E., Rowde, near Devizes
Vincent, Rev. Frederick, Southampton
*Vincent, George, Esq., Temple, London
*Vincent, R., Esq., Basinghall-st., do.
*Vincent, Col., Hemsworth, Lane-end, Yorksh.
*Vincer, Mr. T., Dover
*Vine, Mr. John, Staining-lane, London
Viner, E., Esq., Badgeworth, near Cheltenham
Vines, C., Esq., Banner-sq., St. Lukes, Lond.
*Vines, E., Esq., Reading, Berks.
*Violett, E., Esq., Banwell, Somersetshire
*Vivian, Major Gen. Sir R. Hussey, M.P., K.C.B., and G.H.
*Vize, John, Esq., Edmonton, Middlesex
*Vizer, Robert W., Esq., Doughty-st., London
*Vizer, R. W., Esq., Basinghall-street, do.
Vogan, Rev. S. L., Newport, Monmouthshire
Vores, Thomas, Esq., Wadham college, Oxford
Voules, William James, Esq., Windsor
*Vyse, Lieut. Col., Stoke-Poges, Bucks
Vyse, Mr. Nathaniel, Birmingham
*Vyse, Mr. Richard, Gutter-lane, London

*Wackerbarth, G., Esq., Parsons-st., Radcliffe Highway, London
*Waddell, Mrs., Coleshill-house, Bucks. [Hants.
Waddington, J. H., Esq., Shawford-house,
Waddington, Messrs. S. and J., Birmingham
Wade, Mr. E., Slough, Bucks.
Wade, Mr. J., Mortimer's-Cross, Herefordshire
*Wade, Samuel, Esq., Islington, Liverpool
*Wadeson, R. S., Esq., Austin-friars, London
*Wagner, G. H. M., Esq., Hurstmonceaux, Susx.
Wagstaff, M. F., Esq., Long-lane, Southwark
Wagstaffe, C., Esq., Stockton, Worcestershire
*Waight, Mr. J. T., Southampton [Tyne
*Wailes and Brandling, Mess., Newcastle upon
*Wainewright, R., Esq., Gray's-inn, London
Wainwright, A., Esq., Dinedor-ct., Hereford-
*Wainwright, Mr. D., Park-lane, Leeds [shire
Wainwright, George J., Esq., Liverpool
*Waistell, Mr. R., Curtain-road, London
*Wait, Rev. D. G., LL. D., M. R. A. S., Blagdon, Somersetshire
Waite, Mr. D., Crawley, near Winchester [shire
*Waithman, J., Esq., Yealand-Conyers, Lanca-
*Wake, T. G., Esq., Castle-Cary, Somersetshire
Wakefield, D., Esq., Chancery-lane, London
Wakefield, J., jun., Esq., Cartmel, Lancashire
Wakefield, Rev. John, A. M., Derby
*Wakefield, Thomas, Esq., Nottingham
*Wakefield, Wm., Esq., Lancaster-castle
Wakefield, W., Esq., Earl-street, London
*Wakeham, Rev. H., Ingham, Suffolk
*Wakely, Charles, Esq., East Retford, Notts.
*Wakeman, Sir H., Bart., Perdiswell-hall, Worcestershire
*Wakeman, George, Esq., Stapeley, Cheshire
Wakeman, H., Esq., St. Paul's-sq., Birmingham
Wakeman, Mr. Stone, Staffordshire
*Walcot, H. T., Esq., Wallingford, Berks.
*WALDEGRAVE, The Right Hon. the Earl of
Waldron, E., Esq., Belbroughton, Worcestersh.
Wales, Wm., Esq., Wisbeach, Cambridgeshire
Walesby, F. P., Esq., Lincoln college, Oxford
Walford, Rev. Ellis, Woodbridge, Suffolk
*Walker, Mrs., Bury-hill, Mansfield, Notts.
Walker, E., Esq., Hampton-Wafer, Herefordsh.
Walker, Edward, Esq., M. D., Kington, do.

*Walker, F., Esq., Staunton, Worcestershire
*Walker, George, Esq., Eastwood-hall, Notts.
*Walker, Geo., Esq., Aughton, near Ormskirk,
Walker, G. C., Esq., Doncaster [Lancashire
*Walker, G. F., Esq., Chalk-lodge, Herts.
*Walker, Miss, Rusland-hall, Lancashire
*Walker, Mr. G., Old Broad-street, London
*Walker, H. B., Esq., Holt-hill, Cheshire
*Walker, Mr. Henry, Manchester
*Walker, James, Esq., Ashton under Line
Walker, John, Esq., Wolverhampton
Walker, John, Esq., Birmingham
*Walker, John, Esq., Liverpool
*Walker, John, Esq., Manchester
*Walker, J., Esq., Salford, Lancashire [tershire
Walker, J., Esq., Upton upon Severn, Worces-
Walker, Mr. John, Lyonshall, Herefordshire
*Walker, the Misses, Belle-Vue, Surrey [pool
Walker, Jos. R., Esq., Calderston, near Liver-
*Walker, Mr. J., New-sq., Lincoln's-inn, Lond.
*Walker, Oliver Ormerod, Esq., Bury, Lancash.
Walker, Proctor, Esq., Preston, do.
*Walker, Richard, Esq., Woodhill, Bury, do.
Walker, Robert, Esq., Wadham college, Oxford
Walker, R. S., Esq., Wolverhampton
Walker, Mr. Robert, Chertsey, Surrey
Walker, Robert, Canterbury
*Walker, S., Esq., Pendleton, near Manchester
Walker, Thomas, Esq., York
Walker, Rev. Thomas, Brampton, Huntingdon
*Walker, Thomas, Esq., Dartford, Kent
Walker, Thomas, Esq., Newton, Cheshire
Walker, T. A., Esq., John-street, London
Walker, W., Esq., Hatton-garden, do.
*Walker, W. F., Esq., Holborn-court, do.
*Walker, Mr. W. T., Chalk-hill, near Watford,
Walker, Mr. W., Chertsey, Surrey [Herts.
Walker, Messrs. J. and A., Bernard-st., Lond.
Walker, Messrs. D., and Sons, Gloucester
*Walkers, Parker, and Co., Messrs., Upper-Thames-street, London
*Wall, Mr. C., Highgate-hill, Middlesex
Wall, Mr. Charles, Streatham, Surrey
Wall, Rev. John, Kington, Herefordshire
Wall, J. W., Esq., Devizes
Wall, M., Esq., Yarmouth, Norfolk
Wall, S., Esq., Worthy-park, near Winchester
*Wallace, Rev. C., A. M., Hale Lowe, Cheshire
*Wallace, Hugh, Esq., Knutsford, do.
*Wallace, Rev. J. L., M.A., Edmonton, Middlesex
Wallen, Mr. W., Coleman-street, London
*Waller, Sir W., Bart., K.C.H., Pope's-villa, Twickenham, Middlesex
Waller, C. W., Esq., Annerboro, Kilkenny
Waller, G., Esq., Digswell-hill, Hertfordshire
Waller, H., Esq., Buckden, Hunts.
*Waller, Isaac Kimpton, Esq., Ware, Herts.
Waller, R., Esq., Brasenose college, Oxford
*Waller, S., Esq., Cuckfield, Sussex
*Waller, Thomas, Esq., Luton, Bedfordshire
*Waller, Wm., Esq., Chesterfield, Derbyshire
*Walley, John, Esq., Bunbury, Cheshire
*Wallington, Overbury, and Carter, Messrs., Cateaton-street, London [Middlesex
*Wallis, Mr. B., Union-place, Stepney-green,
Wallis, Edward, Esq., York
*Wallis, Preston, Esq., Bodmin, Cornwall
*Walmesley, C., Esq., Trinity college, Oxford
*Walmesley, W. G., Esq., Wigan, Lancashire
*Walmisley, John Angus, Esq., Westminster
*Walmsley, Miss Anne, Hoddesdon, Herts.
*Walmsley, B., Esq., Blackburn
Walmsley, C., Esq., Marple, Cheshire
*Walmsley, G., Esq., Bolesworth-castle, Chesh.
*Walmsley, G., Esq., Foster-hall, Burton-on-
Walmsley, J., jun., Esq., Circus, Bath [Trent
Walmsley, Richard, Esq., Preston, Lancashire
*Walmsley, Samuel, Esq., Manchester
Walmsley, Samuel, Esq., Wem, Salop
*Walmsley, Thomas, Esq., Preston, Lancashire
*Walmsley, Rev. T. T., D. D., Hanwell, Middsx.
*Walmsley, Thomas, Esq., Stockport, Cheshire

*Walmsley, Mess. J. and W., Portwood, Cheshire
*Walsh, Brigade Maj., Colonial-office, Downing-street, London
Walsh, Rev. Thomas, D.D., Wolverhampton
*Walsh, Frederick, Esq., Cheshunt, Herts.
Walsh, Rev. H., Warminster, Wilts.
Walshaw, Mr. D., Dukinfield, Cheshire
*Walter, Mr. J., Horsemonger-lane, Southwark
*Walter, Mr. R., Chertsey, Surrey
*Walter, Thomas, Esq., Luton, Bedfordshire
*Walter and Son, Mrs. E., Ashford, Kent
*Walters, D., Esq., Barnwood-house, near Gloucester [Kent
Walters, G., Esq., Park-terrace, Blackheath,
*Walters, R., Esq., Lincoln's-inn-fields, Lond.
*Walters, Ralph, Esq., Gateshead, Durham
*Walters, W. C., Esq., Gray's-inn-square, Lond.
Walthew, Mr. J., St. Paul's-sq., Birmingham
*Walton, J., Esq., Cheshunt, Herts.
Walton, John, Esq., London-dock-house
*Walton, Pearson, Esq., Walton, Yorkshire
Walton, Mr. P., Brighton
*Walton, R. T. R., Esq., Colne, Lancashire
*Walton, W., Esq., Girdler's-hall, London
Walton, Oates, and Co., Messrs., Knaresborough
Wannop, Christopher, Esq., Carlisle
Want, T., Esq., Quadrant, Regent-st., London
*Waraker, Mr. T., Chancery-lane, do.
Warbrick, Messrs. W. & J., Dukinfield, Chesh.
*Warburton, John, Esq., Altrincham, do.
*Warburton, P., Esq., Hereford
*Warburton, Peter, Esq., Audlem, Cheshire
*Warburton, T., Esq., Hale, do.
*Warburton, W., Esq., Bowdon-hall, do.
Ward, B.B., Esq., Belper, Derbyshire [2 Copies
Ward, C., Esq., jun., Maidenhead, Berkshire.
Ward, H., Esq., Lincoln's-inn-fields, London
Ward, J., Esq., Burslem, Staffordshire
*Ward, James, Esq., Sittingbourne, Kent
Ward, J., Esq., Stratford on Avon [refordsh.
Ward, J., Esq., Wamish-park, Whitbourne, He-
*Ward, John, Esq., Plumpstead, Kent
Ward, Rev. John, Stoke-Ash, Suffolk
*Ward, J. R. P., Esq., Edmonton, Middlesex
Ward, Mr. Joseph, Tixall, Staffordshire
Ward, R. B., Esq., Bristol
Ward, R. C., Esq., Trinity coll., Cambridge
Ward, Thomas, Esq., Reading, Berks.
Ward, Thos., Esq., Ledbury, Herefordshire
*Ward, Thomas A., Esq., Watford, Herts.
Ward, T., Esq., Newcastle, Staffordshire
Ward, Mr. Thos., Sandon, do.
Ward, W., Esq., Priestfields, Wolverhampton
Ward, William, Esq., Cheltenham
*Ward, William, Esq., Mark-lane, London
*Ward, W., Esq., Wood-st., Cheapside, do.
*Ward, W. H. P., Esq., Oriel college, Oxford
*Warde, J., Esq., Boughton, Kent
*Warde, Richard, Esq., Barham, do.
*Wardle, W., Esq., Clitheroe, Lancashire
Ware, H., Esq., Magdalene college, Oxford
Wareing, Wm., Esq., Ormskirk, Lancashire
Waring, Rev. W., Itchen, near Southampton
Waring, Rev. W., Creswell, Staffordshire
*Warmington, Mr. Samuel, Hoxton, Middlesex
*Warmoll, S. S., Esq., Queen's college, Oxford
*Warmsley, Mr., Belvidere-road, London
Warne, Rev. John, A.M., Exeter
*Warne, Wm., Esq., Leadenhall-st., London
*Warne and Son, Messrs., do., do.
*Warner, Charles, Esq., Everton, Lancashire
Warner, C., Esq., Somersham, Hunts.
Warner, F. Lee, Esq., Balliol college, Oxford
*Warner, Gustavus Meredith, Esq., Dublin
Warner, H. L., Esq., Oriel college, Oxford
*Warner, Joseph, Esq., Eltham, Kent
*Warner, Simion, Esq., Blackheath, do.
*Warner, William, Esq., Wolverhampton
*Warner, Rev. W., Widford, near Chelmsford
*Warner, Messrs. J. and R., Jewin-st., London
WAR OFFICE, His Majesty's [Somersetshire
Warre, Rev. F., D. C. L., Cheddon-Fitzpaine,
*Warre, H., Esq., Bishop's Lydeard, Somerset.
*Warren, F., Esq., Hemel-Hempstead, Herts.
Warren, Rev. Dawson, Edmonton, Middlesex
Warren, J. S., Esq., Langport, Somersetshire
Warren, Dr., Lower Brook-street, London
Warren, Robert, Esq., Strand, do.
Warren, S., Esq., Upper Thurlow-place, do.
Warrington, Mr. R., Farnham-Royal, Bucks.
*Warrington, Mr. R. W., Chalvey, do.
*Warry, Miss, Cossington, Somersetshire
*Warry, George, Esq., Sherborne, Dorsetshire
*Warry, Thomas, Esq., New-inn, London
Warter, J. W., Esq., Christ-church coll., Oxford
Warton, Mr. Matthew, jun., Stepney, Middlsx.
Warton, Mr. Robert, Radcliffe, do.
Warwick, J., Esq., Bencroft-place, London
*Warwick, John, Esq., Maidstone, Kent
*Wasey, J., Esq., Priors-ct., Chieveley, Berks.
*Washbourne, Mr. T. E., Cholsey, do.
Wasor, Edmund, Esq., Liverpool
*Wasor, Rigby, Esq., do. [of
*WATERFORD, The Most Noble the Marquis
*Waterhouse, Alfred, Esq., Liverpool
*Waterman, John, Esq., Rotherithe, Surrey
*Waters, R., Esq., Little Winchester-st., London
Wathen, J., Esq., sen., Hereford
Wathen, Thomas, Esq., Tretyre, Herefordshire
Watherstone, P. J., Esq., Emanuel coll., Camb.
Watier, P., Esq., Egham, Surrey
Watkin, A., Esq., Cannon-street, Manchester
Watkin, Rev. E., Cooknoe, Northamptonshire
Watkins, G., Esq., Lincoln's-inn-fields, Lond.
*Watkins, Mr., Frogmore, near Windsor
*Watkins, James, Esq., Bolton, Lancashire
Watkins, John, Esq., Foxley, Herefordshire
*Watkins, J. K., Esq., Bolton, Lancashire
Watkins, P., Esq., Cirencester
*Watkins, R., Esq., Arundel, Sussex
Watkins, Samuel, Esq., Ramsgate, Kent
*Watkins, T., Esq., Cannon-street, London
Watkins, Mr. William, Hereford
*Watling, Rev. C. H., Cheltenham
*Watmore, J. B., Esq., Windsor
*Watmore, R., Esq., Lambeth, Surrey
Watson, Sir Frederick, Knt., Windsor
Watson, The Rev. and Venerable Archdeacon, D. D., Hackney, Middlesex
Watson, Mrs., Calgarth-park, Westmorland
Watson, Mrs., Petty Cury, Cambridge
Watson, Miss, Upper George-st., Bryanstone-square, London
Watson, Colin, Esq., Everton, near Liverpool
Watson, Rev. F., Yarmouth, Norfolk [shire
Watson, G., Esq., Bronsil, Eastnor, Hereford-
*Watson, H., Esq., Great Carter-lane, London
*Watson, H., Esq., Finsbury-square, do.
*Watson, J., Esq., Gerrard-street, Soho, do.
Watson, J., Esq., Burnopfield, Durham
*Watson, Joseph, Esq., Manchester
Watson, Mr. J., Northam, near Southampton
Watson, Rev. J. S., Westbury, Wilts.
*Watson, John William, Esq., Shrewsbury
*Watson, J. W., Esq., Trinity coll., Cambridge
*Watson, T. W., Esq., Liverpool
*Watson, Thomas, Esq., Aldermanbury, London
*Watson, Mr. Thomas, St. Pancras, do.
*Watson, Major, Cheltenham
*Watson, W., Esq., Altrincham, Cheshire
Watson, W., Esq., F.L.S., Bakewell, Derbysh.
*Watson and Broughton, Messrs., Falcon-sq., London
*Watson and Son, Messrs., Bouverie-street, do.
*Watt, Fitzjames, Esq., Caius coll., Cambridge
*Watts, Mr. E., Fulham, Middlesex [London
*Watts, G., Esq., New North-st., Finsbury-sq.,
*Watts, Miss, St. Giles', Norwich
*Watts, Rev. James, Ledbury, Herefordshire
*Watts, James, Esq., Battle, Sussex
Watts, Colonel Ponsonby, Monmouth
*Watts, W. G., Esq., Dean-street, Southwark
*Waud, C., Esq., East India-house, London
Waugh, Mr. J., Reading, Berks.
Wawn, J. S., Esq., West Boldon, Durham
Wayland, Rev. C., Stratton on the Fosse, So-
*Waylen, R., Esq., Devizes [mersetshire
Wayne, Rev. W. H., M. A., F. C. P. S., Hill-cottage, near Derby
*Wayte, Samuel S., Esq., Bristol
*Wayte, Wm., Esq., Highlands, Wilts.
Weare, Major T., Hampton-Bishop, Hereford.
*Weare, William, Esq., Bristol
Weaver, H., Esq., Beckington, Somersetshire
Webb, Sir John, Knt., Woolwich, Kent
*Webb, C. H., Esq., Stafford
Webb, Charles, Esq., Beaumont-st., Oxford
Webb, C., Esq., Doctors Commons, London
Webb, H., Esq., Langley, near Norwich
Webb, James, Esq., Bedford
*Webb, John, Esq., Alcester, Warwickshire
Webb, J., Esq., Bromsberrow, Gloucestershire
*Webb, Lieut.-Col., Harbledown, nr. Canterbury
*Webb, R., Esq., Ledbury, Herefordshire
Webb, Mr. S., Fore-st., Cripplegate, London
*Webb, Miss S., Clifton downs, near Bristol
Webb, T. E., Esq., Coltishall, Norfolk
Webb, T., jun., Esq., Ledbury, Herefordshire
Webb, Rev. W., D.D., F.L.S., Master of Clare-hall, Cambridge
*Webb, W., Esq., Middle Temple-hall, London
Webb, W., Esq., Hatfield, Hertfordshire
*Webb, Mr. W., High-street, Eton
Webb, Mr. William, jun., Fleet-street, London
*Webb and Sons, Messrs. S., Reading, Berks.
Webber, The Venerable Archdeacon, M. A.
*Webber, Rev. J., D.D., Dean of Ripon
*Webber, R., Esq., Wilson-street, London
*Webber, R., Esq., Kelso, Roxburghshire
Webster, J., Esq., Moccas, Herefordshire
*Webster, T., Esq., Queen-st., Cheapside, 2 Cop.
*Webster, W., Esq., Wirrall, Cheshire
Webster and Firishaw, Messrs., Liverpool
Wedd, R., Esq., Maidstone, Kent [London
Wedge, C., Esq., Goldsmith-street, Cheapside,
*Wedge, Henry, Esq., Weobley, Herefordshire
*Wedge, T., Esq., Sealand, Flintshire
Wedlake, Mr. T., Pillgwelly, Monmouthshire
*Weedall, Rev. H., Oscott, near Birmingham
Weedon, Mr. Thomas, Rickmansworth, Herts
Weeton, Barton, Esq., Preston, Lancashire
*Weeton, Thomas R., Esq., Leigh, do.
*Wegg, R., Esq., Deptford, Kent
Weir, A., Esq., Coopers'-hall, London
Weir, C. A., Esq., Greenwich, Kent
Weir, W., Esq., Carlisle
*Welby, Miss E., Balderton-hall, Notts.
Welch, Dr., Maidstone, Kent
Welch, Mr. F. I., Birmingham
*Welch, G. A. W., Esq., Arll-lodge, Cheltenham
Welch, Miss H. E., Reading, Berks.
*Welch, J., Esq., Holborn-court, London
Welch, R. A., Esq., Pembroke college, Oxford
*Welch, R. H., Esq., Lower Gardener-street,
*Weld, S., Esq., Welbeck-st., London [Dublin
Wellbeloved, Rev. C., York . . . 2 Copies
Weller, Mr. W., Monmouth
*WELLESLEY, The Most Noble the Marquis
*WELLINGTON, His Grace the Duke of
*Wells, Edward, Esq., Wallingford, Berks.
Wells, Rev. G., Staverton, Northampton
Wells, Henry, Esq., Winchester
*Wells, Henry, Esq., Queen's college, Oxford
*Wells, J., Esq., Ramsgate, Kent
*Wells, J. B., Esq., Manchester
*Wells, J., Esq., Beckley-park, Kent
Wells, Major J. R. E., Fort, Gravesend, do.
*Wells, Major, Manor-house, Sutton, Surrey
*Wells, Samuel, Esq., Huntingdon
*Wells, Samuel, Esq., Serjeant's-inn, London
*Wells, Thomas, Esq., Wallingford, Berks.
Wells, Mr. T., New Hall-st., Birmingham
*Wells, T., Esq., Cobham, Kent
*Welman, T., Esq., Poundsford-park, Somerset.
*Welsby, W. N., Esq., Nantwich, Cheshire
Welsh, R. H., Esq., Temple, London

Welstead, B., Esq., Kimbolton, Hunts.
Welstead, F., Esq., Stonely, do.
* Weltig, L. J., Esq., Duke-street, London
* Wembridge, Mrs. C., Solihull, Warwickshire
Wemyss, Gen., M.P., Cumberland-place, Lond.
Wenn, James, Esq., Ipswich, Suffolk
* Wentworth, G., Esq., Wooley-park, Yorkshire
Wentworth, Rev. P., Oundle, Northamptonsh.
Were, W., Esq., Wellington, Somersetshire
* Werge, E., Esq., Upper Hexgrave-park, Notts.
West, E., Esq., Little Frome, Herefordshire
West, James, Esq., Beaumont-street, Oxford
West, Rev. John, Evercreech, Somersetshire
* West, Mr. John, Counter-hill, New-cross, Kent
* West, Mr. W., Marchmont-street, London
* Westall, Mr. R. P., Temple-row, Birmingham
Westall, W., Esq., King-st., Cheapside, Lond.
* Westbrook, Henry, Esq., Heston, Middlesex
Westbrook, Mr. S., Maidenhead, Berks.
Westbury, Mr. John, Worcester
* Westby, Thomas, Esq., Garstang, Lancashire
* Westcomb, J. E., Esq., Thrumpton, Notts.
* Westcote, J. B., Esq., St. Peter's coll., Camb.
* Westcote, T. P., Esq., Martock, Somersetshire
Westenra, The Honorable Henry R.
* Western, T. G., Esq., Furnival's-inn, London
* Westhead, J. P., Esq., Manchester
* Westlake, G., Esq., Great James-st., London
Westmore, Capt. Robert, Preston, Lancashire
* WESTMORLAND, The Rt. Hon. the Earl of
Weston, John, Esq., Barge-yard, London
* Weston, J. W., Esq., Manchester
* Weston, R., Esq., Brockley, Northamptonsh.
* Weston, Richard, Esq., Halewood, Lancashire
* Weston, T. E., Esq., Temple, London
Westron, T. G., Esq., Furnival's-inn, do.
* Wetherall, Rev. J., L.L.D., Streatley, Berks.
* Wetherell, T. M., Esq., Magdalene col., Oxford
* Wetmore, H., Esq., Thornbury, Gloucestershire
* WEYMOUTH, The Right Hon. Lord Viscount
Weymouth, J., Esq., Chancery-lane, London
Whaley, Dr., Bolton-street, Piccadilly, do.
Whaley, J., Esq., Camp-house, near Lancaster
* Whalley, Harry, Esq., Liverpool [Lancaster
Whalley, Lawson, Esq., M. D., F. R. S. E.,
Wharton, Rev. C., Stourport, Worcestershire
* Wharton, T., Esq., Headington, near Oxford
* Whateley, W., Esq., Temple, London
Whatley, G. L., Esq., Mitchell-Dean, Glou-
Whatley, J. C., Esq., Cheltenham [cestershire
Whatman, Jas., Esq., Bexley, Kent
* Whatton, W. R., Esq., F. A. S., Manchester
Wheable, Mr. H., Mitchelmersh, Hants.
* Wheeldon, Rev. J., M. A., St. Albans
* Wheeler, A., Esq., Lindridge, Worcestershire
* Wheeler, H., Esq., Doctors Commons, London
* Wheeler, James, Esq., Manchester
Wheeler, Rev. D., B. A., Betley, Staffordshire
Wheeler, Mr. John, Reading, Berks.
* Wheeler, R., Esq., Wycombe, Bucks.
Wheeler, Mr. S. A., Birmingham [hurst
Wheeler, W., Esq., Royal Military-col., Sand-
* Wheeler, Mr. Wm., Clifford, Herefordshire
* Wheeler and Sons, Messrs., Manchester
Wheeley, R., Esq., Blaenavon, Monmouthshire
* Wheeley, W. S., Brettell-lane, near Dudley
Wheler, Henry T., Esq., Merton coll., Oxford
* Whetham, Col. J. C., Abbot's Leigh, nr. Bristol
* Whichcord, J., Esq., Maidstone, Kent [fordsh.
* Whieldon, Rev. E., A. M., Woodhouse, Staf-
* Whieldon, G., Esq., Cotton-hall, do.
* Whiles, Henry, Esq., Clifford, Herefordshire
* Whinfield, Capt. C. R., Addiscomb, Surrey
* Whishaw, C. J., Esq., Holborn-court, London
Whiston, Mr. William, jun., Derby
* Whitaker, A., Esq., Frome, Somersetshire
* Whitaker, Charles, Esq., Kingston upon Hull
* Whitaker, Isaac, Esq., do.
Whitaker, Philip, Esq., Bratton, Wilts.
* Whitby, Rev. E., Creswell-hall, Staffordshire
* Whitby, Timothy, Esq., Tarvin, Cheshire
* Whitby, Mr. T., Thames-street, London

* Whitchurch, Samuel, Esq., Salisbury
* Whitchurch, W., Esq., Goswell-street, London
Whitcomb, S., Esq., Clirow, Hay, Brecon.
Whitcombe, H. S., Esq., Gloucester
* Whitcombe, John Aubrey, Esq., do.
* White, Sir T. W., Bart., Wallingwells, York
White, Mr. Benjamin, Eye, Suffolk
* White, Charles, Esq., Bread-street, London
White, F., Esq., Wellington, Somersetshire
* White, George, Esq., Fenchurch-st., London
White, Captain, Hartford, Hunts.
White, Mr. G. E., Reading, Berks.
White, George, Esq., Grantham, Lincolnshire
* White, H. C., Esq., Hemel-Hempstead, Herts.
White, Mr. H., Egham, Surrey
* White, J., Esq., Melton, Suffolk
White, Mr. James, Cheshunt, Herts.
* White, James, Esq., Canterbury
* White, Capt. J., Park-hall, Derbyshire
* White, J., Esq., Anfield, near Romsey, Hants.
White, Mr. John, Southampton
* White, John Sharpe, Esq., Leeds
White, Joseph, Esq., Linton, Herefordshire
* White, Mrs., Chiswell-street, London
* White, Captain Stephen, Maidstone, Kent
White, S., Esq., M.P., Suffolk-place, London
White, Rev. Thomas, Hemel-Hempstead, Herts
White, T., Esq., St. Ives, Huntingdonshire
* White, Thomas, Esq., East Bourne, Sussex
White, T., Esq., Aylton-court, Herefordshire
* White, Thomas, Esq., Foxley, do.
* White, T. W., Esq., Brasenose college, Oxford
White, Rev. T., Epperstone, Notts.
White, T., Esq., the Close, Lichfield
* White, Mr. T., Newington-causeway, Surrey
White, W., Esq., Canterbury
* White, William, Esq., Yeovil, Somersetshire
White, W. H., Esq., Serle's-place, London
White & Borrett, Messrs., Gt. St. Helen's, do.
* White, Messrs. and Sons, Coleford, Gloucester
* Whitehead, George, Esq., Bury, Lancashire
Whitehead, Henry, Esq., Rochdale, do.
Whitehead, H., Esq., Warnford-court, London
* Whitehead, H., Esq., High Crompton, Lancash.
* Whitehead, Rev. James, Bolton, do.
Whitehead, Mr. James, Tipton, Staffordshire
* Whitehead, Mr. L., Hatfield, Herts.
* Whitehead, Roger, Esq., Liverpool
* Whitehead, S., Esq., Bell Bar, Herts.
* Whitehead, Thos., Esq., Manchester
* Whitehead and Barlow, Messrs., Oldham, Lan-
Whitehouse, Mr., Gray's-inn, London [cashire
Whitehouse, Benjamin, Esq., Monmouth
Whitehouse, Mr. J., Willenhall, Staffordshire
Whitehouse, Mr. J., Goldthorn-hill, do.
Whitehouse, W. D., Esq., Hardwick Studley,
Whitehouse and Sons, Mess., Dudley [Warwick.
* Whitelegg, Miss H., Northenden, Cheshire
* Whitelegg, T., Esq., Hollins, Timperley, do.
* Whitelegg, W., Esq., Hale, do.
Whiteley, G. T., Esq., Tokenhouse-yard, Lond.
Whitelock, J., Esq., Cateaton-street, do.
Whitelock, J., Esq., Ely-place, Holborn, do.
* Whiteway, P., Esq., Runcorn, Cheshire
Whiteway, Lieut. S.N., R.N., Lyndhurst, Hants.
* Whitgreave, F., Esq., Solihull, Warwickshire
* Whitgreave, G. T., Esq., Bushbury, Staffordsh.
* Whiting, G., Esq., Southwark
* Whitle, Rev. D., Hollingworth-hall, Cheshire
Whitley, C., Esq., St. John's coll., Cambridge
* Whitley, John, Esq., Liverpool
* Whitley, Mr. J., Waltham-Abbey, Essex
* Whitley, P., Esq., Stretton, Cheshire
* Whitling, H. J., Esq., Spring-gardens, London
* Whitlow, R. M., Esq., Manchester
* Whitmarsh, F., Esq., Lincoln's-inn, London
Whitmarsh, W. B., Esq., Wilton, Wilts.
Whitmore, Mr. Felix, Lambeth, Surrey
* Whitmore, Fred., Esq., Lombard-st., London
* Whitmore, John, Esq., Auction-Mart, do.
* Whitmore, R., Esq., Montague-place, Russell-square, do.

Whitmore, T., Esq., M.P., Albemarle-st., Lond.
* Whitmore and Son, Messrs., Birmingham
Whitmore, Wells, and Whitmore, Mess., Lombard-street, London
* Whitridge, Mr. M., Cheapside, do.
* Whittaker, C. G., Esq., Barming, Kent
* Whittaker, J., Esq., Higher Hurst, Lancashire
* Whittaker, Rev. J. W., D. D., Blackburn, do.
Whittaker, P., Esq., Basinghall-st., London
* Whittaker, W., Esq., Mobberley, Cheshire
* Whittam, Joseph, Esq., Bury, Lancashire
* Whittell, Mr. Thomas, Toft, Cambridgeshire
* Whittingstall, E. J., Esq., Watford, Herts.
* Whittington, B., Esq., Dean-street, London
Whittington, G., Esq., New-inn, do.
Whittington, Richard, Esq., Stevenage, Herts.
* Whittell, J. F., Esq., Helmsley-lodge, Yorksh.
Whittle, Mr. G., Wolverhampton
* Whittle, W., Esq., Aston-Grange, Cheshire
Whittuck, S. H., Esq., Hanham-hall, Bristol
Whitwell, John, Esq., Guildford, Surrey
Whorwell, Alexander, Esq., Bolton, Lancash.
* Whorwood, Rev. T. H., Headington-house, Oxford [Hants.
* Whorwood, W. H., Esq., Portswood-cottage,
* Whyte, James, Esq., Trinity coll., Cambridge
* Wickens, Mr. G., Russell-court, London
* Wickens, J., Esq., Montague-st., do. 2 Copies
* Wickham, Rev. P., Shepton-Mallet, Somerset.
Wickham, W., Esq., Bullington, Hants.
Wickham, W. N., Esq., Winchester
Wickings, W., Esq., Barnsbury-place, Islington
* WICKLOW, The Right Honorable the Earl of
Wicks, W. H., Esq., Chippenham, Wilts.
* Wicks, Mr. W., Norwich
* Wicksteed, Mr. R., Cross-st., Finsbury-sq., Lon.
* Wienholt, Miss, Reading, Berks.
* Wigan, A., Esq., Clare-house, Kent
* Wigan, E., Esq., Lapley, Staffordshire
* Wigfield, Rev. H., B. D., Malpas, Cheshire
Wigg, Mr. F., North-place, London
Wiggins, Mr. William, Lee, Kent [fordshire
Wight, T., Esq., Rea, Bishop's Froome, Here-
* Wight, T., Esq., King's Swinford, Staffordshire
Wigley, H. R., Esq., Essex-st., Strand, London
* Wigley, J., Esq., Freeman's-court, do.
* Wigley, W., Esq., Wood-st., Cheapside, do.
Wilbraham, Captain R., R. N., Pool-Meyrick, Monmouthshire
* Wilbraham, R., Esq., Rode-hall, Cheshire
* Wilby, Thos., Esq., Christ's-hospital, London
* Wilcox, Mr. Thomas, Hereford
* Wild, Mr. G. N., Bishopsgate-street, London
* Wild, W., Esq., Martin's-lane, Cannon-st., do.
Wilday, Joseph, Esq., Birmingham
* Wilde, J., Esq., Marsden-square, Manchester
* Wilde, James, Esq., Dukinfield, Cheshire
Wilde, John, Esq., St. Albans
* Wilde and Co., Messrs. J., Oldham, Lancash.
* Wilders, W., Esq., Burton on Trent, Staffordsh.
* Wildes, E., Esq., Lincoln's-inn-fields, London
* Wilding, Samuel, Esq., All Stretton, Salop.
* Wildish, Mr. W. D., Canterbury
* Wildman, Lieut.-Col., Newstead-abbey, Notts.
Wiles, W., Esq., Pidley-lodge, Hunts.
Wiles, Mr. W., St. Neots, do.
* Wilkes, E. V., Esq., Birmingham
Wilkes, George, Esq., Blockley, Worcestersh.
Wilkins, C., Esq., Twiverton, near Bath
Wilkins, Lieut-Col. C. B., Walton on Thames
Wilkins, Rev. George, D. D., Nottingham
Wilkins, Mr. Thomas, St. Albans
Wilkins, W., Esq., Weymouth-street, London
Wilkins, W., Esq., New college, Oxford
Wilkins, Messrs. George and Son, Derby [sex
* Wilkinson, G., Esq., Tottenham-green, Middle-
Wilkinson, J., Esq., Springfield-house, Bath
Wilkinson, John, Esq., Chorley, Lancashire
Wilkinson, Mr. J., Wycombe, Bucks.
Wilkinson, Mr. J., Addle-st., Cheapside, Lond.
* Wilkinson, Rev. Thomas, A. M., Carlisle
* Wilkinson, Thomas Jones, Esq., Manchester

Wilkinson, W. W., Esq., Cottingham, York
* Wilkinson, W., Esq., Gate-street, London
Wilkinson, Rev. W. H., A.B., Gilstone, Herts.
* Wilkinson, W., Esq., Old Broad-st., London
Wilkinson and Atkinson, Messrs., Crown-ct., Broad-street, do.
* Wilks, J., Esq., Cheapside, do.
Wilks, John, Esq., M.P., Finsbury-place, do.
* Wilks, Robert, Esq., Dartford, Kent
Willan, Mr. E., jun., Bold-street, Liverpool
* Willan, Leonard, Esq., Lancaster
Willan, Rev. T., Corby, Lincolnshire
* Willans and Sons, Messrs. O., Leeds
Willats, Mr. T. Y., Reading, Berks.
* Willcox, Mr. J., Digbeth, Birmingham
* Willding, J., Esq., jun., Dartford, Kent
Wille, C., Esq., jun., Lewes, Sussex
* Willert, P. F., Esq., Ardwick-green, Manchester
* Willet, W. J., Esq., Essex-st., Strand, London
* Willett, Henry, Esq., Norwich
Willey, Rev. J., A. M., Heworth, near York
* Williams, Miss, Hereford
* Williams, Miss, Ross, Herefordshire
* Williams, B., Esq., Broughton-bridge, Lancash.
* Williams, B. P., Esq., Kennington, Surrey
* Williams, C., Esq., Maidenhead, Berks.
* Williams, Rev. D., Bleadon, Somersetshire
* Williams, E. H., Esq., Albemarle-st., London
* Williams, F., Esq., Trinity college, Oxford
Williams, Rev. F. D., Great Wishford, Wilts.
Williams, F. H., Esq., Abergavenny
Williams, G., Esq., Little Woolton, Lancashire
* Williams, G., Esq., Mill-More-house, Cheshire
* Williams, G., Esq., North-pl., Gray's-inn-road
Williams, George, Esq., Tewkesbury
Williams, G. F., Esq., Limington-house, Somersetshire
Williams, Mr. George, Hereford
Williams, Henry, Esq., Lincoln
Williams, Mr. H. H., Kinnersley, Herefordsh.
Williams, Mr. H., Waterloo-road, London
Williams, Rev. J., Mathern, Monmouthshire
Williams, J., Esq., Grange, Bermondsey, Surrey
Williams, Mr. James, Hereford
* Williams, Rev. J., Marston Magna, Somerset.
* Williams, J., Esq., Mortlake, Surrey
* Williams, John, Esq., Shrewsbury
* Williams, Mr. J., Bradford-street, Birmingham
Williams, Mr. J., Pillgwenlly, Monmouthshire
Williams, Mr. John, Dudley
Williams, Mr. John, Evesham [Gloucestershire
Williams, Mr. J. P., Beachley Old-passage,
Williams, Mr. J. C., Southampton
* Williams, John E., Esq., Sandbach, Cheshire
Williams, J. R., Esq., Clement's-lane, London
* Williams, John S., Esq., Bristol
* Williams, Mr. Matthew, Hereford
Williams, P., Esq., Christ-church coll., Oxford
Williams, Mr. R., Kingsland, Herefordshire
Williams, Mr. R. C., Ledbury, do.
Williams, R., Esq., M.P., Bridehead, Dorsetsh.
Williams, Robert, Esq., Oriel college, Oxford
* Williams, S., Esq., Altrincham, Cheshire
Williams, S. H., Esq., Woodlands, Hants.
Williams, Mr. T., St. Martin's le Grand, Lond.
Williams, Rev. Thomas, Cameley, Somerset.
Williams, Rev. T., A.M., Usk, Monmouthshire
Williams, Mr. Thomas, Norton
Williams, Mr. Thomas, Maidstone, Kent
Williams, T. W., Esq., Furnival's-inn, London
* Williams, Walter, Esq., Dudley
Williams, Rev. W., Diddington, Hunts.
* Williams, William, Esq., Durham
Williams, Wm., Esq., Wadham coll., Oxford
Williams, W., Esq., Newport, Monmouthshire
Williams, W., Esq., Tivoli-lodge, do., do.
Williams, W., Esq., Hallatrow, Somersetshire
* Williams, Wm., Esq., Jesus college, Oxford
* Williams, W.W., Esq., Broughton Priory, near Manchester
Williams, Mr. W., Back-road, Islington
Williams, Mr. W. J., East Ilsley, Berks.
* Williams, Rev. W. M. H., A.M., Somersetsh
* Williams and Bethell, Messrs., Lincoln's-inn-fields, London
* Williamson, Sir H., Bart., Whitburn, Durham
* Williamson, H. H., Esq., Greenway Bank, Staffordshire
* Williamson, J., Esq., M. D., Leeds, Yorkshire
Williamson, J., Esq., Hollings, nr. Ripley, do.
Williamson, Jos., Esq., Edge-hill, Liverpool
Williamson, Mr. S. T., Southampton
Williamson, W. M., Esq., Liverpool
* Willim, J., Esq., jun., Bilston, Staffordshire
* Willington, T., Esq., Tamworth, do.
Willis, D., Esq., Great Ryder-street, London
Willis, John, jun., Esq., Liverpool
Willis, R., Esq., Rockfield, near Monmouth
Willis, Richard, Esq., Halsnead, Lancashire
* Willock, Robert Peel, Esq., Manchester
Willoughby, Mr. John, Huntingdon
* Wills, C., Esq., Ely-place, Holborn, London
Wills, E. S., Esq., St. Peter's coll., Cambridge
* Wills, John, Esq., Doctors Commons, London
Willson, E. J., Esq., F. S. A., Newport, Lincolnshire
* Willy, Ambrose, Esq., Teddington, Middlesex
Wilmore, Mr. J., Malvern Wells, Worcestersh.
* Wilmot, E. C., Esq., Cheshunt, Herts.
* Wilmot, H. S., Esq., Chaddesden-hall, Derby
* Wilmot, John, Esq., Isleworth, Middlesex
* Wilmot, R. M., Esq., M. D., Hastings, Sussex
* Wilson, Sir T. M., Bart., Charlton, Kent
Wilson, A., Esq., Islington, Middlesex
* Wilson, C. B., Esq., Lincoln's-inn-fields, Lond.
* Wilson, Edmund, Esq., Manchester
* Wilson, Mr. F., Upperhead-row, Leeds
* Wilson, Geo., Esq., Milnthorpe, Westmorland
* Wilson, G., Esq., West Smithfield, London
Wilson, Henry, Esq., Liverpool
* Wilson, Rev. H., Kirby-Cane, Norfolk
* Wilson, Mr. Isaac, Kingston upon Hull
Wilson, J., Esq., M. P., Sneaton-castle, Whitby
* Wilson, Jas., Esq., Baxenden, Lancashire
Wilson, Rev. James, Matlock, Derbyshire
* Wilson, J., Esq., Gray's-inn-square, London
Wilson, Major John, Toxteth-park, Liverpool
* Wilson, J., Esq., Hessle, Yorkshire
* Wilson, J. B., Esq., Southborough, Kent
Wilson, Rev. J., Fellow of Queen's col., Oxford
Wilson, J., Esq., Upper Bedford-place, London
Wilson, J., Esq., jun., Islington, Middlesex
* Wilson, J., Esq., Baxenden, Lancashire
Wilson, Rev. John, Mitton
Wilson, John, Esq., Mitcham, Surrey
Wilson, Mr. John, Sheffield
Wilson, Mr. J., Wilmington-square, London
* Wilson, Jos., Esq., Carnfield-hall, Derbyshire
Wilson, Mr. J. E., Cambridge
Wilson, Rev. Richard, St. John's college, do.
Wilson, Robert F., Esq., Oriel coll., Oxford
Wilson, Rev. R. C., M. A., Preston, Lancash.
Wilson, Stephen, Esq., Goldsmith-st., London
* Wilson, T., Esq., Staples-inn, do.
* Wilson, T., Esq., Maidenhead, Berks.
Wilson, Thomas, Esq., Harraby, Carlisle
* Wilson, Thos., Esq., Cannon-st., Manchester
Wilson, Thomas, Esq., Poulton, Lancashire
* Wilson, T. D., Esq., Trinity coll., Cambridge
* Wilson, T. F., Esq., Hackney, Middlesex
Wilson, T. P., Esq., Magdalene coll., Oxford
Wilson, Mr. Thomas, Newark, Notts.
* Wilson, Rev. William, D.D., Southampton
* Wilson, Wm., Esq., St. George's-place, Hyde-park-corner, Lond.
Wilson, Mr. W., Hertford
Wilson, W., Esq., Everton, Lancashire
* Wilson, W. J., Esq., Gray's-inn-sq., London
* Wilson, W. R., Esq., Preston, Lancashire
Wilson, W. W. C., Esq., Kirkby-Lonsdale
* Wilson & Curtis, Messrs., Montague-st., Lond.
* Wilton, H., Esq., Gloucester
* Wilton, Robert, Esq., do.
Wilton, W., Esq., do.
* Wimburn and Collett, Messrs., Chancery-lane, London
* Wimpenny, A. B., Esq., Dukinfield, Cheshire
Winbolt, Mr. B. J., St. Paul's-ch-yard., Lond.
* Winder, James, Esq., Bolton, Lancashire
* Winder, Thomas, Esq., Preston, do.
Windle, H. C., Esq., Walsall, Staffordshire
Windover, Mr. William, Long-Acre, London
* Windsor, The Honorable Thomas
* Winfield, Mr. John, Birmingham
Wing, T., Esq., Holborn-ct., Gray's-inn, Lond.
Wingfield, John, Esq., Onslow, Shropshire
Winn, C., Esq., Appleby, Lincolnshire
* Winn, C., Esq., Nostall-Priory, Yorkshire
Winn, Messrs. F. and C., Broadgate, Lincoln
Winnall, J., Esq., Lady-Meadow, Herefordshire
* Winnall, T., Esq., Weston under Penyard, do.
Winnall, W., Esq., Gatley-park, do.
* Winnington, Rev. F., Upper Sapey, do.
Winnington, Sir T. E., Bart., Stanford-court, Worcestershire
Winstanley, John, Esq., Preston, Lancashire
* Winstanley, J. S., Esq., Chester-terrace, Lond.
Winstanley and Son, Messrs., Liverpool
Winter, B., Esq., Winchester
* Winter, James, Esq., Handon, Somersetshire
* Winter, Jos., Esq., Stand-house, Manchester
* Winter, T. J., Esq., Taunton, Somersetshire
Winter, W., Esq., Abbey, Romsey, Hants.
* Winter, Williams, Fossick, and Jeffries, Mess., Bedford-row, London
* Winterbottom, J. K., Esq., Stockport, Cheshire
* Winterbottom, Mr. John, Ashton under Line
Winterfold, Rev. T. H., Chaddesley-Corbett, Worcestershire
* Winthrop, S., Esq., St. John's coll., Cambridge
Wintle, Rev. Robert, Culham, Oxfordshire
Winwood, H.Q., Esq., Henbury-hill, nr. Bristol
Winwood, J., Esq., Clifton, do.
Wise, H. C., Esq., Oriel college, Oxford
Wise, H., Esq., Caldicott, Monmouthshire
Wise, S., Esq., Maidstone, Kent
Wiseman, I., Esq., Magdalen-street, Norwich
* Wishlade, Mr. B., Kington, Herefordshire
Witham, Rev. George, Durham
Witherby, C., Esq., Birchin-lane, London
* Withers, E., Esq., High-st., Whitechapel, do.
* Withington, Thomas E., Leigh, Lancashire
* Withington, T. S., Esq., Grasmere, Westmorland
Witt, Mr. T., Totton, near Southampton
Witty, Rev. J. F., Frome, Somersetshire
Wix, William, Esq., Tonbridge Wells
* Woakes, W. H., Esq., Cheltenham
* Wolfe, J. L., Esq., Change-alley, London
* Wolfenden, Mr. A., Salford, Lancashire
* Wollaston, G. H., Esq., Clapham, Surrey
* Wolley, Rev. John, Beeston, near Nottingham
Wolstenholme, Geo., Esq., Bolton, Lancashire
* Wolverhampton, The Library of, Staffordshire
Wolverhampton, The Overseers of, do.
* Wood, Abraham, Esq., Bury, Lancashire
Wood, D., Esq., Oakley-park, near Ludlow
* Wood, E., Esq., Burslem, Staffordshire
Wood, Mrs. F., Vowchurch, Herefordshire
Wood, George, Esq., Queen's college, Oxford
Wood, G.W., Esq., Somers, Billinghurst, Sussex
Wood, Rev. H., M. A., Pentrich, Derbyshire
Wood, Mr. H., Waltham-Abbey, Essex
* Wood, Rev. Isaac, M. A., Middlewich, Cheshire
Wood, The Very Rev. J., D.D., Dean of Ely, and Master of St. John's coll., Cambridge
* Wood, J., Esq., Bartholomew's-hospital, Lond.
* Wood, J., Esq., Glossop, Derbyshire
Wood, Jno., Esq., Bromsberrow, Gloucestersh.
* Wood, J. H., Esq., Emanuel coll., Cambridge
Wood, Mr. J. W., Basingstoke, Hants.
* Wood, R., Esq., Ankerden, Doddenham, Worcestershire
* Wood, Rich. M., Esq., Tottenham, Middlesex
Wood, R. S., Esq., Osmington, Dorsetshire
* Wood, R.W. K., Esq., Trinity hall, Cambridge
* Wood, Colonel S. C. B., Hoddesdon, Herts.
Wood, Mr. T., Deptford, Kent
Wood, T., Esq., Canterbury

* Wood, T., Esq., Gainsborough, Lincolnshire
* Wood, T., Esq., Lewes, Sussex
* Wood, Thomas, Esq., Mitcham, Surrey
Wood, Mr. T. K., St. Margaret at Cliffe, Kent
* Wood, W., Esq., Gt. George's-st., Westminster
* Wood, Rev. W., Staplegrove, Somersetshire
* Wood, W., Esq., Mill-hill, Leeds
* Wood, Rev. Wm., M. A., Altham, Lancashire
Wood, Wm., Esq., Vowchurch, Herefordshire
* Wood, Wm., Esq., Great Prescot-st., London
* Wood, Mr. W., Threadneedle-street, do.
* Wood, W. C., Esq., Martock, Somersetshire
Wood and Son, Messrs. J., Huntingdon
Woodall, T., Esq., Walford nr. Ross, Herefords.
Woodall, Rev. W., Abergavenny, Monmouthsh.
* Woodbridge, W., Esq., Camberwell, Surrey
* Woodburne, W. A., Esq., Manchester
Woodcock, Rev. F., Moreton, Herefordshire
Woodcock, James, Esq., Bury, Lancashire
Woodcock, James, Esq., Haslingdon, Middlsx.
Woodcock, Mr. James, Petworth, Sussex
* Woodcock, John, Esq., Watford, Herts.
Woodcock, Samuel, Esq., Bury, Lancashire
Woodcock, William, Esq., Wilton, Wilts.
* Woodcock and Co., Messrs., Coventry
* Woodd, Geo. N., Esq., Wadham coll., Oxford
* Woodford, E. W., Esq., Gravesend, Kent
Woodford, G. A., Esq., Castle-Cary, Somerset.
* Woodgate, Rev. S., Pembury, Kent
Woodhead, Mr. A., Salford, Lancashire
* Woodhouse, C., Esq., Coventry
Woodhouse, E., Esq., Leamington
Woodhouse, Mr. G. F., Norwich [colnshire
* Woodhouse, H. A., Esq., Market-Rasen, Lin-
Woodhouse, Jas., Esq., Queen-street, London
Woodhouse, Rev. J. C., D. D., Lichfield
* Woodhouse, J. T., Esq., Leominster
* Woodhouse, S., Esq., Norley-hall, Cheshire
Woodhouse, T., Esq., Longnor, Staffordshire
* Woodhouse, W., Esq., Liverpool
* Woodifield, Matthew, Esq., Durham [shire
* Woodman, Mrs., Bishop's-Cleeve, Gloucester-
Woodman, John, Esq., Marlborough, Wilts.
Woodmas, Arthur, Esq., Peter-college, Cambr.
* Woodrooffe, W., Esq., Lincoln's-inn, London
Woodrow, Mr. John, Dean-street, Soho, do.
* Woods, E., Esq., Arrow-brook, Cheshire
* Woods, H., Esq., Godalming, Surrey
Woods, W., Esq., Chatham, Kent
* Woods, W., Esq., Newcastle upon Tyne
* Woods, Mr. W., Bishopsgate-street, London
WOODS, FORESTS, AND LAND REVENUE, The Hon. the Commissioners of
* Woodthorpe, H., Esq., Guildhall, London
Woodward, C., Esq., Furnival's-inn, do.
Woodward, George, Esq., Fenchurch-st., do.
Woodward, Mr. H., Worcester
* Woodward, Jas., Esq., Chowbent, Lancashire
* Woodward, J., Esq., Appleton, Cheshire
* Woodward, J., Esq., Summer-hill, Kidderminster
* Woodyatt, J., Esq., St. John's, Worcester
Woodyer, C., Esq., Guildford, Surrey
* Woof, Mr. Richard, Worcester
Wooldridge, Mr. Thomas, Windsor
* Wooley, George, Esq., Manchester
Woollerton, Mr. J., Bethell-street, Norwich
* Woollett, Mr. George, Holborn-hill, London
* Woollett, Thomas, Esq., Monmouth
* Woolley, C., Esq., Kingsland-road, London
Woolley, G., Esq., Bread-street, do.
Woolley, S., Esq., Sutton in Ashfield, Notts.
Woolley, Mr. Wm., Ross, Herefordshire
Woolley, Rev. W., Pangbourn, Berks.
* Woolley, W., Esq., Kingston upon Hull
* Woolley and Co., Messrs. E., Bilston, Staffordshire
* Woolmore, John, Esq., Trinity House, London
* Woolner, B., Esq., Threadneedle-street, do.
* Woolrich, George, Esq., Handley, Cheshire
* Wootton, Mr. D., Rochester, Kent
* Wootton, Mr. John, Macclesfield
* WORCESTER, The Most Noble the Marquis of
Wordsworth, H., Esq., Threadneedle-st., Lon.
Workman, Rev. W., Basingstoke, Hants.
Wormald, T., Esq., Featherstone-builds., Lond.
* Wormald, Mr. S., Trafalgar-street, Leeds
* Worrall, James, jun., Esq., Manchester
* Worrall, George, Esq., Frenchay, near Bristol
Worsey, Mr. J., Stretton, Staffordshire
* Worship, Rev. M., Lowestoft, Suffolk
Worsley, Mrs. C., Winster, Derbyshire
Worsley, J., Esq., Stockport, Cheshire
Worsley, Rev. H., L. L. D., Blackheath, Kent
* Worsley, Rev. Ralph, Finchley, Middlesex
* Worsop, R. A., Esq., Howden, Yorkshire
* Wortham, T., Esq., Royston, Herts.
Worthington, Dr., Monmouth
* Worthington, Lieut. B., R. N., Dover
* Worthington, H., Esq., Altrincham, Cheshire
* Worthington, I. J., Esq., Lymm, do.
Worthington, Mr. J., Stilton, Hunts.
Worthington, J., Esq., Cheadle, Cheshire
* Worthington, T., Esq., High-st., Manchester
* Worthy, Charles, Esq., Queen's coll., Oxford
Wortle, W., Esq., Bourn, Lincolnshire
* Wotton, Wm., Esq., King's Langley, Herts.
* Wragg, G., Esq., Oakamoor, Staffordshire
* Wragg, T., Esq., Borough-road, Southwark
Wragge, Mr. F. F., Stamford, Lincolnshire
* Wray, M. O., Holborn, London
* Wreford, John, Esq., Aldermanbury, do.
* Wren, Henry, Esq., Dale-street, Manchester
Wrench, Capt. J. F., Little Orford-st, Norwich
Wright, Mr., Rochester
* Wright, C., Esq., Vivar-street, Kidderminster
Wright, C., Esq., Little Alie-street, London
* Wright, Mr. C., Dover
* Wright, Edmund, Esq., Manchester
* Wright, Mr. Edward, Hatton-garden, London
Wright, F., Esq., Queen's college, Oxford
Wright, Mr. F., Brighton, Sussex
* Wright, Geo., Esq., Hornby-castle, Lancash.
Wright, Rev. Godfrey, Doncaster
* Wright, G. H., Esq., Leeds
* Wright, Rev. H., Stockport, Cheshire
* Wright, Ichabod, Esq., Mapperley, Notts.
* Wright, James, Esq., Ashton under Line
* Wright, Mr. John, Rochester, Kent
* Wright, J., Esq., Magdalene college, Oxford
Wright, J., Esq., Ravenhill, Staffordshire
* Wright, J., Esq., Wallsend, Newcastle upon Tyne
Wright, J., Esq., Southampton-row, London
Wright, J., Esq., Ware, Herts.
Wright, J., Esq., Everton-crescent, Liverpool
* Wright, J., Esq., Hebden-bridge, Yorkshire
Wright, J. E., Esq., Hawley-sq., Margate, Kent
* Wright, John, Esq., Accrington, Lancashire
* Wright, Mr. J., West Derby, near Liverpool
Wright, Mr. J., Brampton-moor, Derbyshire
Wright, Mr. J., Clerkenwell, Middlesex
* Wright, Joseph J., Esq., Sunderland
* Wright, J. S., Esq., Rempstone-hall, Notts.
* Wright, J. W. G., Esq., Liverpool
Wright, Peter, Esq., do.
Wright, Rev. R., jun., Itchin-Abbas, Hants.
* Wright, Thomas, Esq., Bolton, Lancashire
* Wright, Thomas, jun., Esq., North Shields
Wright, Thomas, Esq., Upton-hall, Notts.
* Wright, T. S., Esq., Bucklersbury, London
Wright, Rev. W., Huntingdon
* Wright, W., Esq., Turf-Lee, Marple, Cheshire
* Wright, W., Esq., Gt. Marlborough-st., London
* Wright, Rev. W., L. L. B., Trinity hall, Cam-
* Wright, Wm., Esq., Maldon, Essex [bridge
* Wright, Bowden, & Co., Messrs., Kingston upon Hull
Wright and Son, Messrs. E., New Brampton, Derbyshire
* Wright, Taylor, and Co., Messrs., Liverpool
Wrighte, Rev. T. W., Boughton under Blean, Kent
* Wrottesley, Sir J., Bart., F. A. S., Wrottesley, Staffordshire
Wrottesley, Rev. Chas., East Knoyle, Wilts.
* Wrottesley, E. B., Esq., Trinity coll., Cambrid.
* Wrottesley and Co., Messrs., Wolverhampton
* Wulff, G., Esq., Christ's college, Cambridge
Wyatt, A., Esq., New-inn, London
Wyatt, Rev. C. F., Broughton, Oxfordshire
Wyatt, F., Esq., Ware, Herts.
* Wyatt, Mr. George, Oxford
Wyatt, Mr. James, do.
* Wyatt, J., Esq., Middle Temple, London
* Wyatt, L. W., Esq., Suffolk-st., Pall-Mall, do.
* Wyatt, R., Esq., Coleman-street, do.
* Wyatt, Mr. T., Holborn-bridge, do.
* Wyatville, Sir Jeffry, Knt., R. A., Lower Brook-street, do.
Wybault, P. R., Esq., Hythe, near Southampton
* Wych, William, Esq., Ashton under Line
* Wyer, Mr. S., Edgbaston, near Birmingham
Wykeham, A. W., Esq., Trinity coll., Oxford
* Wylde, R. H., Esq., St. John's coll., Cambrid.
* Wylde, S., Esq., Runcorn, Cheshire
Wylde, William, Esq., Southwell, Notts.
Wyldes, E., Esq., Lincoln's-inn-fields, London
* Wyley, William, jun., Esq., Admaston, Salop
* Wyllys, W., Esq., Stanton-Drew, Somersetshire
* Wyndham, W., Esq., M. P., Dinton-house, Salisbury
Wynmatt, Henry, Esq., Dymock, Gloucestersh.
Wynn, Sir W. W., Bart., M. P., Wynnstay, Denbighshire
Wynn, J., Esq., Greaseley, Staffordshire
Wynne, Rev. T., Hereford
* Wynniatt, R., Esq., Guiting-grange, Worcester.
Wyvill, R., Esq., Maidenhead, Berks.

* Yallop, T., Esq., Old-street, London
Yallop, Thomas, Esq., Furnival's-inn, do.
Yapp, Mr. R., Hope-Sollers, Herefordshire
* YARBOROUGH, The Right Hon. Lord
Yarburgh, N. E., Esq., Heslington-hall, Yorksh.
* Yard, J., Esq., Exeter college, Oxford
* Yarker, R. F., Esq., Ulverstone
Yarmouth Public Library, Norfolk
Yarrington, Mr. W., Norwich
Yate, Rev. George L., M. A., Wrackwardine, Shropshire
* Yates, E., Esq., Fairlawn, Kent
* Yates, James, Esq., Shelton, Staffordshire
Yates, John, Esq., do., do.
* Yates, Jos., Esq., Ardwick, near Manchester
Yates, Mr. S., Congleton, Cheshire
Yates, W. W., Esq., Park-fields, Staffordshire
Yea, Mrs., Pyrland-hall, Taunton, Somersetsh.
Yeates, Mr. Benjamin, Monmouth
* Yeates, J., Esq., Hyde-st., Bloomsbury, Lond.
* Yeates, J., Esq., Brighton, Sussex
Yeates, Mr. J., Acton-green, Worcestershire
Yeats, G. D., Esq., M. D., Tonbridge Wells
* Yeatman, J. C., Esq., Frome, Somersetshire
* Yeoman, Mr. J., Baker's-row, Whitechapel
Yeoman, Mr. J. T., East Lockinge, Berks.
Yerbury, F. Esq., Belcomb-house, Bradford, Wilts
* Yerbury, J., Esq., Shirehampton, near Bristol
* Yewens, W., Esq., Tokenhouse-yard, London
Yonge, D. S., Esq., Oriel college, Oxford
* YORK, His Grace the Lord Archbishop of
Yorke, Rev. H., Aspeden, Herts. [cestersh.
Yorke, J., Esq., jun., Forthampton-court, Wor-
Youle, Rev. A., West Retford, Notts.
* Young, B., Esq., Frindsbury, Kent
Young, C. A., Esq., Blackman-st., Southwark
* Young, Edward, Esq., Newcastle upon Tyne
* Young, G., Esq., Lane-End, Staffordshire
* Young, Mr. G., Arundel, Sussex
* Young, Henry, Esq., Dursley, Gloucestershire
* Young, H., Esq., Lincoln's-inn-Fields, Lond.
* Young, H. T., Esq., Balliol college, Oxford
* Young, Rev. J., Heathfield, Sussex
Young, Mr. J., Timsbury, near Romsey, Hants.
Young, J., Esq., Westridge-house, Isle of Wight
Young, J., Esq., Addle-street, London
Young, Mr. John, Leeds

Young, Mr. J. W., Reading, Berks.
*Young, J. H., Esq., Blackman-st., Southwark
Young, T., Esq., Walton on Thames, Surrey
Young, Rev. W. B., Reading, Berks.
Young, Mr. W., jun., Timsbury, near Romsey, Hants.
*Young, Son, and Elliott, Messrs., Parliament-street, London
Younge, C., Esq., Brinckcliff-edge, Yorkshire
*Younge, E., Esq., Inner Temple, London
Younge, S., Esq., jun., Sheffield
Younge, W., Esq., M. D., do.

A

TOPOGRAPHICAL DICTIONARY

OF

ENGLAND.

ABBAS-COMBE, a parish in the hundred of Horethorne, county of Somerset, 4½ miles (S. by W.) from Wincanton, containing, with Temple-Combe, 458 inhabitants. The living is a rectory, in the archdeaconry of Wells, and diocese of Bath and Wells, rated in the king's books at £9. 9. 4½., and in the patronage of the Bishop of Worcester. The church is dedicated to St. Mary. At Temple-Combe was formerly a preceptory of Knights Templars, which at the dissolution had a revenue of £128. 7. 9.

ABBERLEY, a parish in the lower division of the hundred of Doddingtree, county of Worcester, 4¾ miles (W. S. W.) from Stourport, containing 574 inhabitants. The living is a rectory, in the archdeaconry of Salop, and diocese of Hereford, rated in the king's books at £11. 10. 2½., and in the patronage of R. Bromley, Esq. The church is dedicated to St. Michael. The village of Abberley is situated in a valley to the right of the road leading from Worcester to Ludlow. The summits of the surrounding hills afford delightful prospects, and on the declivities are fine sheep-walks and thriving plantations. Coal of excellent quality, and some limestone, are found in the neighbourhood. A court leet is held annually. A charity school is supported by the daughters of Col. Bromley. William Walsh, the poet, and a correspondent of Pope and Addison, was born here, in 1663.

ABBERTON, a parish in the hundred of Winstree, county of Essex, 4¼ miles (S.) from Colchester, containing 203 inhabitants. The living is a rectory, in the archdeaconry of Colchester, and diocese of London, rated in the king's books at £14. 7. 8½., and in the patronage of the Crown. The church is dedicated to St. Andrew. There is a place of worship for Wesleyan Methodists.

ABBERTON, a parish in the upper division of the hundred of Pershore, county of Worcester, 7 miles (N. E. by N.) from Pershore, containing 82 inhabitants. The living is a discharged rectory, in the archdeaconry and diocese of Worcester, rated in the king's books at £5. 8. 1½., endowed with £200 royal bounty, and in the patronage of Mrs. Sheldon. Here is a mineral spring, the water of which is bitter and cathartic, being somewhat similar to that at Cheltenham.

ABBERWICK, a township in the parish of Edlingham, northern division of Coquetdale ward, county of Northumberland, 4 miles (W.) from Alnwick, containing 125 inhabitants. Here is a small endowed school.

ABBOT'S-ANN, a parish partly in the hundred of Wherwell, but chiefly in the hundred of Andover, Andover division of the county of Southampton, 2¼ miles (S.W. by W.) from Andover, containing, with the tything of Little-Ann, which is in the hundred of Wherwell, 526 inhabitants. The living is a rectory, in the archdeaconry and diocese of Winchester, rated in the king's books at £42. 17. 6., and in the patronage of Sir James Burrough and the Rev. Thomas Burrough. The church is dedicated to St. Mary. Here is a small endowed school.

ABBOTSBURY, a parish (formerly a market town) in the hundred of Uggscombe, Dorchester division of the county of Dorset, 8¼ miles (W. S. W.) from Dorchester, and 128 (S.W. by W.) from London, containing 907 inhabitants. The name of this place is evidently derived from its ancient possessors, the abbots of the monastery of St. Peter, supposed to have been founded, in 1044, by Orcus, or Orking, steward of the household to Canute the Great, and Tola his wife, for monks of the Benedictine order. It occupied a large extent of ground; and its revenue at the dissolution was £485. 3. 5.: there are still some remains, consisting of a gateway and portions of the walls. At the dissolution it was granted to Sir Giles Strangeways, and on its site was erected a mansion, which, having been garrisoned for the king in 1644, was attacked by Sir Anthony Ashley Cooper, and burnt to the ground. The church was also occupied by a party of royalists, who surrendered before it sustained any damage. The town, situated in a valley surrounded by lofty hills, near the sea-shore, consists of three streets, partially paved, and is well supplied with water: the western part of it was consumed by fire in 1706. Fishing is the chief occupation of the inhabitants, great quantities of mackarel being taken on the sea-coast. The weaving of cotton, which was introduced here about thirty years since, has of late much declined. The market, which was on Thursday, has fallen into disuse: a fair, for sheep and toys, is held on the 10th of July. The living is a discharged vicarage, in the archdeaconry of Dorset, and diocese of Bristol, rated in the king's books at £10, endowed with £600 private benefaction, and £600 royal bounty, and in the patronage of the Earl of Ilchester. The church, dedicated to St. Nicholas, is a large handsome structure, in the later style of English architecture, with a square embattled tower, and is supposed to have contained the remains of the founder of the abbey and his wife, which were removed hither from the conventual church at the dissolution. A school, originally founded for twenty boys, was further endowed, in 1754, by Mrs. Horner, with £21 per annum, for instructing ten additional boys. A charity school for clothing and educating twenty girls, instituted a few years since, is supported by the Countess of Ilchester, who has also established an infant school. St. Catherine's chapel, supposed to have been erected in the reign of Edward IV., stands on an eminence south-west of the town, and serves as a landmark: it is built wholly of freestone dug out of the hill on which it is situated; the roof is finely groined, and on each side is a handsome porch. Between this and the shore is a large decoy for wild fowl, and near it an extensive swannery, the property of the Earl of Ilchester. About a mile and a half to the west of Abbotsbury is an ancient intrenchment, occupying an area of nearly twenty acres; and near the town is a cromlech. The stones in the walls of the houses, which are obtained from quarries near the sea-shore, contain vast quantities of shells of marine animals.

ABBOTSHAM, a parish in the hundred of Shebbear, county of Devon, 2 miles (W.) from Bideford, containing 386 inhabitants. The living is a discharged vicarage, in the archdeaconry of Barnstaple, and diocese of Exeter, rated in the king's books at £16. 4. 7., and in the patronage of the Crown. The church is dedicated to St. Helen.

ABBOT-SIDE (HIGH), a township in the parish of Aysgarth, western division of the wapentake of Hang, North riding of the county of York, 1¼ mile (N. W. by W.) from Hawes, containing, with the chapelry of Hardrow, and the hamlets of Cotterdale, Litherskew, Lund, Sedbusk, Show, and Simonstone, 641 inhabitants. The river Ure, on which are several beautiful waterfalls, rises in this township.

ABBOT-SIDE (LOW), a township in the parish of Aysgarth, western division of the wapentake of Hang, North riding of the county of York, containing 181 inhabitants. Whitfield Gill, in which is the picturesque waterfall called Whitfield Force, separates High Abbot-Side from this township. Here is an almshouse for six widows.

ABBOTSLEY, a parish in the hundred of Toseland, county of Huntingdon, 4¼ miles (S. E.) from St. Neots, containing 392 inhabitants. The living is a discharged vicarage, in the archdeaconry of Huntingdon, and diocese of Lincoln, rated in the king's books at £8. 17., and in the patronage of the Master and Fellows of Balliol College, Oxford. The church is dedicated to St. Margaret.

ABBOTSTON, a parish in the hundred of Bountisborough, Fawley division of the county of Southampton, 2¾ miles (N. W.) from New Alresford. The population is returned with Itchin-Stoke. The living is a rectory, united to the vicarage of Itchin-Stoke, in the archdeaconry and diocese of Winchester, rated in the king's books at £13. 6. 8. The church is desecrated.

ABDASTON, a parish in the northern division of the hundred of Pirehill, county of Stafford, comprising the townships of Abdaston, Bishop's Offlow, Flashbrook, and Tunstall, and containing 596 inhabitants, of which number, 157 are in the township of Abdaston, 4¾ miles (W. by S.) from Eccleshall. The living is a perpetual curacy, in the peculiar jurisdiction and patronage of the Dean of Lichfield, endowed with £400 and £15 per annum private benefaction, and £1400 parliamentary grant. The church is dedicated to St. Margaret. In 1724, John Wright bequeathed a small portion of land for the support and education of the poor; and, in 1764, Richard Whitworth gave a house and land for similar purposes.

ABDON, a parish in the hundred of Munslow, county of Salop, 9¾ miles (N. E. by N.) from Ludlow, containing 157 inhabitants. The living is a discharged rectory, in the archdeaconry of Salop, and diocese of Hereford, rated in the king's books at £3. 6. 8., endowed with £200 private benefaction, and £200 royal bounty, and in the patronage of the Earl of Pembroke. The church is dedicated to St. Margaret.

ABERFORD, a parish (formerly a market town) in the lower division of the wapentake of Skyrack, West riding of the county of York, comprising the greater part of the township of Aberford (two portions of which are detached from the parish, one being in the liberty of St. Peter of York, and the other in the parish of Sherburn, upper division of the wapentake of Barkstone-Ash), and the townships of Parlington and Sturton-Grange, and containing 900 inhabitants, of which number, 579 are in that part of the township of Aberford which is in this parish, 16 miles (S. W.) from York, and 186¾ (N. N. W.) from London, on the road to Carlisle. The town is built on the gentle acclivity of a rock of limestone, near the small river Cock, a stream abounding with trout and eels, over which is a handsome stone bridge. It consists principally of one long street: the houses are in general built of stone, and many of them are handsome; the air is pure and salubrious, and the environs, which furnish agreeable promenades, are thickly studded with elegant villas and thriving plantations. There are extensive strata of limestone, and a productive coal mine, in the neighbourhood. The market, formerly on Wednesday, has been discontinued: fairs are held on the last Monday in April and May, the first Monday in October, the first Monday after the 18th of that month, and the first Monday after the 1st of November. Constables and other officers are appointed at the court leet of the lord of the manor. The living is a discharged vicarage, in the archdeaconry and diocese of York, rated in the king's books at £6. 1. 8., endowed with £400 private benefaction, and £400 royal bounty, and in the patronage of the Provost and Fellows of Oriel College, Oxford. The church, dedicated to St. Richard, is an ancient structure, exhibiting portions in the early, decorated, and later styles of English architecture. There is a place of worship for Wesleyan Methodists. A National school has been erected on the site of one formerly endowed by Lady Elizabeth Hastings. At the distance of a mile north of the town are vestiges of Castle-Cary, an ancient Norman fortification.

ABERGAVENNY, a market town and parish partly in the upper, but chiefly in the lower, division of the hundred of ABERGAVENNY, county of MONMOUTH, 16 miles (W. by N.) from Monmouth, and 145 (W. by N.) from London, on the road to Milford-Haven, containing, with the hamlets of Hardwicke and Lloyndû, 3592 inhabitants. This was the *Gobannium* of Antoninus, a Roman station so called from the river *Gobannius*, now the Gavenny, from which the present name of the town is formed, by prefixing the word *Aber*, denoting its situation near the mouth of that river. Soon after the Conquest, a castle was erected here by Hameline de Balun, or Baladun, one of William's followers, who also founded a priory for Benedictine monks, in honour of the Blessed Virgin, the revenue of which at the dissolution was £59. 4.: it stood in Monk-street, the site being now occupied by a modern dwelling, called the Priory House. Of the castle, the only remains are the exterior walls, which appear to have been erected in the time of Henry II., after it had been destroyed by the Welch: within these a neat modern structure has been erected for a residence. The town is beautifully situated at the extremity of a pass where the mountains abruptly terminate, and is watered by the rivers Usk, Gavenny, and Kibby, over the first of which is a beautiful ancient bridge of fifteen arches: it is lighted with gas, and well supplied with water, conveyed into the houses by pipes from springs in the vicinity. The streets are narrow, and the houses irregularly built; but considerable improvements have been made by the enlargement of the market-place, and the removal of numerous projections in front of the buildings. The salubrity of the air and the picturesque scenery attract numerous visitors during the summer months. Assemblies are occasionally held in the winter, chiefly for the promotion of charitable purposes. The trade is principally in wool, a considerable quantity being sold on the market days during the months of June and July. The mountains in the neighbourhood abound with coal and iron-stone, and in the surrounding districts numerous iron-works have been established, which are rapidly increasing. The Monmouthshire and Brecon canal, passing within half a mile of the town, affords great facility in distributing the produce of the mines to every part of the kingdom, and to the south of France. The market days are Tuesday and Saturday, the latter principally for corn: during the months of June and July a great quantity of wool is brought to the market. The fairs are held on the third Tuesday in March, May 14th (which is the principal), June 24th, the Tuesday before July 20th, September 25th, and November 19th.

The charter of incorporation, by which the government of the town was vested in a bailiff, recorder, and twenty-seven burgesses, having become forfeited in the reign of William III., the town is within the jurisdiction of the county magistrates, who hold a petty session every Tuesday. A court for the recovery of debts under 40*s*. is held under the lord of the manor, the authority of which extends over a district ten miles in circuit. The general quarter sessions of the county were formerly held here, but they have been removed to Usk. The living is a discharged vicarage, in the archdeaconry and diocese of Llandaff, rated in the king's books at £10. 0. 7½., endowed with £600 royal bounty, and in the patronage of Charles Kemeys Tynte, Esq. The church, dedicated to St. Mary, is a spacious structure in the Norman style of architecture, and contains several very ancient monuments, principally of the Herberts. There are two places of worship each for Baptists and Independents, and one each for Wesleyan Methodists and Roman Catholics. The free grammar school, founded by Henry VIII., in 1543, and formerly under the management of the corporation, was, on the forfeiture of their charter, placed under the control of the Master and Fellows of Jesus' College, Oxford, who appoint the master, whose salary is £40 per annum, giving preference to a fellow of that college. The number of scholars on the foundation is eighteen: the school-house was formerly the parochial church of St. John, which was converted to this purpose at the dissolution. About the middle of the last century it was rebuilt, but still, from its embattled tower, it presents the appearance of an ecclesiastical structure. William Prichard, in 1623, founded a scholarship in Jesus' College, Oxford, to which boys educated at this school are eligible. There are also a Lancasterian and several Sunday schools. A variety of Roman coins, among which was a gold Otho, some bricks inscribed "Leg. II. Aug.," and a sudatory, have been discovered in the town; and within half a mile of it are the remains of a Roman camp, near which was a chapel of ease, now converted into a farm-house. At Lloyndû is a mineral spring, said to have been efficacious in the cure of scrofula. Abergavenny confers the title of earl on the family of Neville; the earldom, like that of Arundel, is a local dignity, attached to the possession of the castle, and the only one, now subsisting, of those baronies with which the Norman warriors, who assisted in the subjugation of Wales, were rewarded.

ABERYSTWITH, a parish in the upper division of the hundred of ABERGAVENNY, county of MONMOUTH, 8 miles (S. W. by W.) from Abergavenny, containing 800 inhabitants. The living is a perpetual curacy, united to the rectory of Llanwenarth, in the archdeaconry and diocese of Llandaff.

Seal and Arms.

ABINGDON, a borough and market town, having separate and exclusive jurisdiction, locally in the hundred of Hormer, county of BERKS, of which it is the chief town, 6 miles (S.) from Oxford, 26 (N.W. by N.) from Reading, and 56 (W. N. W.) from London, containing, exclusively of that part of the parish of St. Helen which is in the hundred of Hormer, 5137 inhabitants, according to the census of 1821, since which period the population has considerably increased. This place, according to a manuscript in the Cottonian library, quoted by Dugdale, was, in the time of the Britons, a city of considerable importance, and distinguished as a royal residence, to which the people resorted to assist at the great councils of the nation. By the Saxons it was called *Scovechesham*, or *Sewsham*, but acquired the name of Abbendon, the town of the abbey, on the removal hither, in 680, of a monastic institution previously founded at Bagley wood, now an extra-parochial liberty in the vicinity, by Cissa, viceroy of Centwine, ninth king of Wessex, on which Ceadwalla, his son and successor, bestowed the town and its appendages. After the establishment of the monastery, Offa, King of Mercia, on a visit to Abingdon, was so much pleased with the situation, that he erected a palace here, in which he and his immediate successors, Egferth and Cenwulf, occasionally resided. The monastery continued to flourish till 871, when it was destroyed by the Danes. In 955, Edred, grandson of Alfred, laid the first stone of a new monastery, which was completed after his death by the abbot Ethelwold, and his successor Ordgar. The extent of its endowments and privileges, subsequently augmented by Edgar and Canute the Great, raised it to the dignity of a mitred abbey. William the Conqueror celebrated Easter at Abingdon, in 1084, where he was sumptuously entertained by Robert D'Oilly, one of the most powerful barons of the time, under whose inspection he left his son Henry to be educated in this convent, where the prince received that education which afterwards procured him the surname of Beauclerc. At the dissolution the revenue of the abbey was £1876. 10. 9. A nunnery was also founded here by Cilla, niece of Cissa, over which she presided till her death, when it was removed to Witham; the site of it was afterwards given, by Edward VI., to Christ's hospital in this town. The Guild of the Holy Cross, established here at a very early period, was dissolved in 1547, when its revenue amounted to £85. 15. 6. In the early part of the civil war, Charles I. garrisoned Abingdon, where he established the head-quarters of his cavalry. On the retreat of the royal forces to Oxford, in 1644, the Earl of Essex took possession of the town, and garrisoned it for the parliament; and, a few days afterwards, Waller's army, which had been stationed near Wantage, entered Abingdon, and, among other excesses, destroyed the cross in the market-place, at which, in 1641, the accommodation with the Scots was celebrated by two thousand choristers: this cross is particularly noticed by Camden for its beauty, and was the model of one afterwards erected at Coventry. Many unsuccessful attempts were subsequently made by the royalists, to regain possession of the town; the garrison, on these occasions, put every Irish prisoner to death, without trial, whence the expression "Abingdon Law."

The town, which is pleasantly situated at the influx of the small river Ock into the Thames, is handsomely built, and consists of several spacious streets diverging from the market-place; it is well paved and lighted, and amply supplied with water. Burford and Culham bridges, near the town, with the causeway between them, were constructed by the fraternity of the Holy Cross, in the reign and by license of Henry V. (the ferry being at that time dangerous for passengers and cattle); the former have been recently widened and improved by voluntary contributions, and the causeway, which is close to the town, and between the two bridges, forms a very pleasant promenade: races take place in September, when assemblies are held in the council-chamber. The manufacture of woollens, formerly carried on here to a great extent, has quite declined. Malting is now the principal business, which, with the dressing of hemp, and the making of sacking and sail-cloth, constitutes the chief employment of the labouring classes. Several wharfs and warehouses have recently been constructed, where the Wilts and Berks canal joins the Thames, near its confluence with the Ock. The market days are Monday, chiefly for corn, and Friday, for provisions only. Fairs for horses and horned cattle are held on the first Monday in Lent, May 6th, June 20th, August 5th, September 19th, the Monday before Old Michaelmas day (a statute fair), Monday after October 12th (a great market), and December 11th.

By a charter of incorporation granted by Philip and Mary, in 1557, the government of the borough is vested in a mayor, high steward, recorder, twelve principal and sixteen secondary burgesses, two bailiffs, a town clerk, and chamberlain. The mayor is chosen, on the 1st of September, from among the principal burgesses, two of whom are nominated by the inhabitants being potwallers, and returned to the chamber, which is composed of principal burgesses only, who elect one of them to the office; and two of the same body are immediately afterwards chosen justices of the peace for the ensuing year, by a common council, comprising the whole corporate body; and on the 29th of September, when the mayor is sworn into office, his immediate predecessor is sworn senior magistrate for the following year. The mayor, recorder, and justices hold a court of session quarterly, and the mayor and justices a petty session weekly on Tuesday, on which day the mayor also holds a court of record for the recovery of debts under £10. Courts leet are held by the mayor within a month after Easter and Michaelmas, the former having view of Frankpledge. This borough returns one member to parliament: the elective franchise is vested in the inhabitants paying scot and lot not receiving alms: the mayor is the returning officer. The market-house is a spacious and elegant building of freestone, erected in 1678, having a commodious hall in which the county court and the nisi prius court at the assizes are held, and public business connected with the borough or county is transacted. The county bridewell, a handsome stone edifice erected in 1811, at an expense of £26,000, comprises a neat court-house, in which the crown court at the summer assizes and the July county sessions are held; the October sessions are held here and at Reading alternately. The members for the county, who are nominated at Reading, are elected here; and the county magistrates hold a petty session on Monday in every fortnight for the Abingdon division.

Abingdon comprises the parishes of St. Helen and St. Nicholas, in the archdeaconry of Berks, and diocese of Salisbury; the former includes part of the township of Shippon and Norcott, and the whole of Sandford Barton and Pumney; and the latter, the remainder of Shippon and Norcott, also some lands in Sunningwell and Bayworth, which are all without the limits of the borough. The living of St. Helen's is a vicarage, rated in the king's books at £7, and in the patronage of the Crown: the church is a handsome structure, in the early style of English architecture, with a square embattled tower, surmounted by a lofty spire. The living of St. Nicholas' is a sinecure rectory, the vicarage being annexed to that of St. Helen's, rated in the king's books at £29. 11. 3.: the church, built about the close of the thirteenth, or commencement of the fourteenth, century, possesses some remains of Norman architecture. Mr. Wrigglesworth left lands and tenements in Abingdon, for the support of a lecture in St. Helen's church, to be delivered every Saturday evening from Michaelmas to Lady-day, and at the church at Maicham (a village two miles and a half distant) on every Sunday morning from Lady-day till Michaelmas. There are places of worship for Baptists, the Society of Friends, Independents, and Wesleyan Methodists. The free grammar school, for the education of "Threescore and thirteen" boys, was founded, in 1563, by John Royse, and endowed with two messuages in Birchin-lane, London, then known by the signs of the Bell and the Unicorn, which were afterwards destroyed by fire: the ground is now occupied by part of the premises belonging to the London Assurance Company, out of the rent of which the head master's salary is paid: according to the directions of the founder, the master is allowed to receive ten private pupils. In 1608, William Bennett of "Marleborowe" left lands in "Brodeblunsdon" for the maintenance of six poor scholars in Royse's free grammar school; these boys, who are elected by the Master and Governors of Christ's Hospital in this town, are, from the increase of the funds, clothed and instructed also in writing and arithmetic, and a handsome premium is paid with them when apprenticed. In 1609, Thomas Tesdale gave certain lands in the county of Warwick, to maintain an usher. The school is entitled to six scholarships at Pembroke College, Oxford, founded by Thomas Tesdale, two to be filled by the founder's kin, and the others from Abingdon school; and to four scholarships at the same college, founded by Richard Wightwick, two for the founder's kin. Preference is given to boys on Bennett's foundation, but, in default, the other free scholars and the master's private pupils are eligible; though, by a rule of the present head master, the latter must have been two years in the school to be qualified as candidates. In 1756, Robert Mayott bequeathed to the corporation two meadows near Oxford, for the education of poor children of Abingdon; ten boys and six girls, who are nominated by the mayor and principal burgesses, are the present number on this foundation, and they are clothed, educated, and apprenticed. John Provost, in 1703, bequeathed property for instructing ten boys in reading and writing, and for apprenticing poor children; the present number are, from the increase of the funds, clothed and taught arithmetic, in addition to the founder's directions. In 1713, Richard Belcher gave £14 per annum, and, in 1753, Joseph Tomkins £100 South Sea stock, for the instruction of children in the borough. There are also a National and a British school; to the former, Edward Beasley, Esq., in 1826, bequeathed £200.

Christ's hospital, on the west side of St. Helen's church, erected in 1446, originally belonged to the fraternity of the Holy Cross, on the dissolution of which establishment, in 1547, the inhabitants applied, through Sir John Mason, to King Edward VI., for the restoration of their lost estates, and the foundation of an hospital for the relief of the poor of the town; in compliance with which application His Majesty, by letters patent, in 1553, founded the hospital under its present name, and incorporated twelve persons, for its government by the name of "The Master and Governors of the Hospital of Christ." It consists of almshouses for six poor men and six women and a nurse, with cloisters and a handsome hall, in which the master and governors hold their meetings, and where prayers are read morning and evening to the inmates. An almshouse was built, in 1718, for eighteen poor men or women; and another, near the river Isis, for six poor men or women, to which Mr. Beasley in 1826, bequeathed £600 stock, the interest to be paid weekly. Other donations have at different times been made to the hospital, and are disposed of as directed by the donors. St. John's hospital, in the Vineyard, was endowed before the Reformation, for six poor men, and rebuilt by the corporation in 1801. B. Bedwell Esq. was a liberal contributor to it; and, in 1826, Mr. Beasley added £600 stock to the endowment. An almshouse near St. Helen's church was erected, in 1707, by Charles Twitty, for the maintenance of three men and three women, who are elected by the minister, churchwardens, and overseers of the parish of St. Helen; bequests of £200 each, by John Bedwell, in 1799, and by Samuel Cripps, in 1819, and of £600 three per cent. stock by Mr. Beasley, in 1826, have been added to the original endowment: there are also almshouses for four men and four women, endowed, in 1733, by Benjamin Tomkins. Various charitable bequests have been made to the poor of the town, the principal of which are, Mr. Frederick Klein's, by which, in pursuance of a decree of the court of Chancery, made in 1828, the interest of £1032. 12. 4. three per cent. stock is annually distributed, in the month of March, in small sums to the poor of the borough, by the mayor and principal burgesses; and £700 three per cents., bequeathed by Mr. Beasley, the dividends on which are given to the poor on Good Friday by the corporation. St. Edmund, Archbishop of Canterbury; Sir John Mason, British Ambassador at the court of France, and Chancellor of the University of Oxford; and the late Lord Colchester, were natives of this place. Abingdon confers the title of earl on the family of Bertie.

ABINGER, a parish in the first division of the hundred of WOTTON, county of SURREY, $4\frac{1}{2}$ miles (S.W. by W.) from Dorking, containing 742 inhabitants. The living is a rectory, in the archdeaconry of Surrey, and diocese of Winchester, rated in the king's books at £12. 8. $1\frac{1}{2}$., and in the patronage of Sir J. Evelyn, Bart. The church, dedicated to St. James, is in the early style of English architecture.

ABINGHALL, a parish in the hundred of ST. BRIAVELLS, county of GLOUCESTER, $4\frac{1}{2}$ miles (N. by W.) from Newnham, containing 215 inhabitants. The living is a discharged rectory, in the archdeaconry of Hereford, and diocese of Gloucester, rated in the king's books at £6. 6. 8., and in the patronage of the Rev. J. Probyn. The manufacture of paper, which is carried on to a considerable extent at Guns-mills, affords employment to from three hundred to five hundred persons of this parish and neighbourhood. A foundry for cannon balls formerly existed at this place. The church is dedicated to St. Michael. Here is a spring, the water of which is reputed to be efficacious in the cure of cutaneous eruptions.

ABINGTON, a parish in the hundred of SPELHOE, county of NORTHAMPTON, $1\frac{1}{2}$ mile (E.N.E.) from Northampton, containing 175 inhabitants. The living is a rectory, in the archdeaconry of Northampton, and diocese of Peterborough, rated in the king's books at £20, and in the patronage of J. H. Thursby, Esq. The church, dedicated to St. Peter and St. Paul, exhibits various styles of English architecture.

ABINGTON in the CLAY, or ABINGTON-PIGOTS, a parish in the hundred of ARMINGFORD, county of CAMBRIDGE, 5½ miles (W. N.W.) from Royston, containing 233 inhabitants. The living is a rectory, in the archdeaconry and diocese of Ely, rated in the king's books at £16. 2. 3½., endowed with £200 royal bounty, and in the patronage of Dr. Pigott. The church is dedicated to St. Michael.

ABINGTON (GREAT), a parish in the hundred of CHILFORD, county of CAMBRIDGE, 2¼ miles (N. W.) from Linton, containing 337 inhabitants. The living is a discharged vicarage, in the archdeaconry and diocese of Ely, rated in the king's books at £7. 16. 3., and in the patronage of the Trustees of T. Mortlock, Esq. The church is dedicated to St. Mary.

ABINGTON (LITTLE), a parish in the hundred of CHILFORD, county of CAMBRIDGE, 2¾ miles (N.W. by N.) from Linton, containing 257 inhabitants. The living is a discharged vicarage, in the archdeaconry and diocese of Ely, rated in the king's books at £7. 6. 5½., and in the patronage of the Bishop of Ely. The church is dedicated to St. Mary.

AB-KETTLEBY, a parish in the hundred of FRAMLAND, county of LEICESTER, 3½ miles (N.W. by N.) from Melton-Mowbray, containing, with the chapelry of Holwell, 319 inhabitants. The living is a vicarage, in the archdeaconry of Leicester, and diocese of Lincoln, rated in the king's books at £15. 10. 5., and in the patronage of the Rev. Thomas Bingham. The church is dedicated to St. James.

ABLINGTON, a tything in that part of the parish of BIBURY which is in the hundred of BRIGHTWELL'S-BARROW, county of GLOUCESTER, 5¼ miles (N.W. by N.) from Fairford, containing 127 inhabitants.

ABNEY, a hamlet in the parish of HOPE, hundred of HIGH PEAK, county of DERBY, 4¾ miles (N.E.) from Tideswell, containing 143 inhabitants.

ABRAM, a township in that part of the parish of WIGAN which is in the hundred of WEST DERBY, county palatine of LANCASTER, 4¼ miles (N. N. E.) from Newton in Mackerfield, containing 504 inhabitants.

ABSON, or ABSTON, a parish in the hundred of PUCKLE-CHURCH, county of GLOUCESTER, 7¼ miles (E. by N.) from Bristol, containing, with the hamlet of Wick, 715 inhabitants. The living is a perpetual curacy, united to the vicarage of Puckle-Church, in the archdeaconry and diocese of Gloucester. The church is dedicated to St. James. The village is situated at the foot of a rocky hill, rising to the height of more than two hundred feet, and consisting of alternate beds of limestone and petrosilex. Roman coins, urns, bricks, &c., have been dug up; and here is an ancient camp, supposed to be of British origin.

ABTHORPE, a parish in the hundred of TOWCESTER, county of NORTHAMPTON, 3 miles (W. S. W.) from Towcester, containing, with the hamlets of Charlock and Foscote, 417 inhabitants. The living is a vicarage, in the archdeaconry of Northampton, and diocese of Peterborough, endowed with £400 private benefaction, and £400 royal bounty, and in the patronage of Samuel Blencowe and others. The church is dedicated to St. John the Baptist. Jane Leeson, in 1646, bequeathed a rent-charge of £3 for the instruction of poor children.

ABY, a parish in the Marsh division of the hundred of CALCEWORTH, parts of LINDSEY, county of LINCOLN, 3 miles (N. W. by W.) from Alford, containing, with the hamlet of Greenfield, 192 inhabitants. The living is a discharged vicarage, united, in 1732, to the rectory of Belleau, in the archdeaconry and diocese of Lincoln, rated in the king's books at £6. 3. 6., and endowed with £200 royal bounty. The church is dedicated to All Saints.

ACASTER-MALBIS, a parish partly in the ainsty of the city of YORK, but chiefly in the wapentake of OUZE and DERWENT, East riding of the county of YORK, 4½ miles (S. by W.) from York, containing, with the township of Naburn, 657 inhabitants. The living is a discharged vicarage, in the archdeaconry and diocese of York, rated in the king's books at £5. 6. 5½., endowed with £400 royal bounty, and £200 parliamentary grant, and in the patronage of P. B. Thompson, Esq. The church is dedicated to the Holy Trinity. A school is endowed with land given by John Knowles, in 1603, which is vested in feoffees, who appoint fourteen poor children on the foundation. The navigable river Ouse passes near the village.

ACASTER-SELBY, a township in that part of the parish of STILLINGFLEET which is in the ainsty of the city, and East riding of the county, of YORK, 7¼ miles (S. by W.) from York, containing 188 inhabitants. This place formed part of the possessions of the abbot of Selby: the village is pleasantly situated on the banks of the navigable river Ouse. A college for a provost and two or three fellows, one of whom was to instruct children, was founded here by Robert Stillington; at the dissolution its revenue was £33. 10. 4. Here is a free school which is supported by a small endowment.

ACCONBURY, or ACORNBURY, a parish in the upper division of the hundred of WORMELOW, county of HEREFORD, 4½ miles (S.) from Hereford, containing 148 inhabitants. The living is a perpetual curacy with that of Callow, annexed to the vicarage of Dewsall, in the peculiar jurisdiction of the Dean of Hereford, endowed with £400 royal bounty. The church is dedicated to St. John the Baptist. A nunnery of the order of St. Augustine was founded here, in the reign of John, by Margery, wife of Walter de Lacy, to the honour of the Holy Cross, the revenue of which, at the dissolution, was £75. 7. 5¼.: the remains have been converted into a farm-house, and some stone coffins are still preserved. On the summit of Acconbury hill are traces of a large Roman encampment, of a square form, the rampart of which, on the east side, is plainly discernible.

ACCRINGTON, a considerable village, in that part of the parish of WHALLEY which is in the higher division of the hundred of BLACKBURN, county palatine of LANCASTER, 3¼ miles (N.N.W.) from Haslingden, comprising the chapelry of Old, and the township of New, Accrington, containing 5370 inhabitants, of which number, 1261 are in Old Accrington, 6¼ miles (E.), and 4109 in New Accrington, 5¼ miles (E. by S.), from Blackburn. Within the last few years this place has acquired considerable importance, from its situation in the centre of the calico-printing business. Several large establishments for spinning cotton thread, and weaving and printing calico, have been formed; in consequence of which the population has increased nearly twofold. The living of Old Accrington is a perpetual curacy, in the archdeaconry and diocese of Chester, endowed with £1000 private benefaction, £1000 royal bounty, and £1000 parliamentary grant, and in the patronage of the Vicar of Whalley. The chapel was taken down and rebuilt upon a larger scale in 1826. There are places of worship for Baptists, Wesleyan Methodists, and Swedenborgians. A National school was erected by subscription in 1806, in which about one hundred and thirty children are educated. Jonathan Peel, Esq., in 1824, gave £1000 towards its support.

ACHURCH, county of NORTHAMPTON. — See THORPE-ACHURCH.

ACKLAM, a parish in the wapentake of BUCKROSE, East riding of the county of YORK, comprising the townships of Acklam with Barthorpe, and Leavening, and containing 683 inhabitants, of which number, 389 are in the township of Acklam with Barthorpe, which is partly within the liberty of St. Peter of York, 7¼ miles (S.) from New Malton. The living is a discharged vicarage, in the peculiar jurisdiction and patronage of the Chancellor of the Cathedral Church of York, rated in the king's books at £5. The church is dedicated to St. John the Baptist. There are places of worship for Wesleyan and Primitive Methodists.

ACKLAM, a parish in the western division of the liberty of LANGBAURGH, North riding of the county of YORK, 2¾ miles (S. E. by E.) from Stockton upon Tees, containing 105 inhabitants. The living is a perpetual curacy, in the archdeaconry of Cleveland, and diocese of York, endowed with £400 royal bounty, and in the patronage of the Archbishop of York.

ACKLINGTON, a township in that part of the parish of WARKWORTH which is in the eastern division of MORPETH ward, county of NORTHUMBERLAND, 10½ miles (S. S. E.) from Alnwick, containing 269 inhabitants. Coal is obtained here.

ACKLINGTON-PARK, a township in that part of the parish of WARKWORTH which is in the eastern division of MORPETH ward, county of NORTHUMBERLAND, 9 miles (S. S. E.) from Alnwick, containing 125 inhabitants.

ACKTON, a township in that part of the parish of FEATHERSTONE which is in the lower division of the wapentake of AGBRIGG, West riding of the county of YORK, 3½ miles (W.) from Pontefract, containing 72 inhabitants.

ACKWORTH, a parish in the upper division of the wapentake of OSGOLDCROSS, West riding of the county of YORK, 3¼ miles (S.S.W.) from Pontefract, containing 1575 inhabitants. The living is a rectory, in the archdeaconry and diocese of York, rated in the king's books at £22. 1. 0½., and in the patronage of the King, as Duke of Lancaster. The church, dedicated to St. Cuthbert, is a small neat building, exhibiting various portions of ancient architecture. There is a place of worship for Wesleyan Methodists. Here was a school, originally an appendage to the Foundling Hospital. In 1777, the premises, with eighty-five acres of land, were purchased by the Society of Friends, and converted into a school for the education of youth in their own religious principles. Here is also a school, endowed with £20 a year, for the education of twenty children, besides an hospital for six women.

ACLE, a parish in the hundred of WALSHAM, county of NORFOLK, 11 miles (E.) from Norwich, containing 698 inhabitants. The living is a rectory, in the archdeaconry and diocese of Norwich, rated in the king's books at £20, and in the patronage of Lord Calthorpe. The church is dedicated to St. Edmund. The village is situated on a gentle eminence, on the banks of the navigable river Bure, near its junction with the Yare. A stone bridge of one arch, called Waybridge, forms here an important pass, there being no other bridge between this and the mouth of the Yare. At the Conquest Acle became a fief of the Crown, and was granted by the Conqueror to Roger Bigod, who obtained for it the privilege of a market and fair; and further advantages, including freedom from all tolls, and suits of shire and of hundred, were bestowed on the inhabitants by Richard II. At Waybridge a small priory of Augustine canons was founded by Roger Bigod, Earl of Norfolk, in the reign of Edward I.; at the dissolution the revenue was £7. 13. 4.

ACOMB, a parish in the ainsty of the city, and East riding of the county, of YORK, comprising the townships of Acomb and Knapton, and containing 870 inhabitants, of which number, 783 are in the township of Acomb, 2¼ miles (W.) from York. The living, a discharged vicarage, is a peculiar, rated in the king's books at £3. 9. 2., and endowed with £200 private benefaction, £200 royal bounty, and £600 parliamentary grant. The peculiar formerly belonged to the Treasurer of the Cathedral Church of York, but was surrendered, with the rectory, to the Crown in 1547; and in 1609 it was granted by James I. to Thomas Newark and his heirs. It now belongs to J. E. Baker, Esq., who has lately, by an application to the court of King's Bench, established his right to appoint a commissary to the peculiar ecclesiastical jurisdiction. The church, dedicated to St. Stephen, is a small ancient structure, occupying an elevated situation. There is a place of worship for Wesleyan Methodists. A school, built by subscription among the inhabitants, is conducted on the National plan.

ACOMB (EAST), a township in the parish of BYWELL ST. PETER, eastern division of TINDALE ward, county of NORTHUMBERLAND, 8 miles (E.) from Hexham, containing 51 inhabitants.

ACOMB (WEST), a township in the parish of ST. JOHN LEE, southern division of TINDALE ward, county of NORTHUMBERLAND, 1¾ mile (N.) from Hexham, containing 533 inhabitants. It is bounded on the south by the river Tyne: coal is obtained within its limits.

ACRISE, a parish partly in the hundred of FOLKESTONE, but chiefly in that of LONINGBOROUGH, lathe of SHEPWAY, county of KENT, 5 miles (N. N. W.) from Folkestone, containing 186 inhabitants. The living is a rectory, in the archdeaconry and diocese of Canterbury, rated in the king's books at £7, and in the patronage of the Crown. The church is dedicated to St. Martin.

ACTON, a township in the parish of WEAVERHAM, second division of the hundred of EDDISBURY, county palatine of CHESTER, 4½ miles (W. N. W.) from Northwich, containing 301 inhabitants. The Nantwich branch of the Chester canal passes through this township.

ACTON, a parish in the hundred of NANTWICH, county palatine of CHESTER, 1¼ mile (N. W. by W.) from

Nantwich, comprising the townships of Acton, Aston *juxta* Mondrum, Austerson, Baddington, Brindley, Burland, Cholmondstone, Cool-Pilate, Eddleston, Faddiley, Henhull, Hurleston, Newhall, Poole, Stoke, and Worleston, and containing 3777 inhabitants, of which number, 273 are in the township of Acton. The living is a vicarage, in the archdeaconry and diocese of Chester, rated in the king's books at £19. 9. 7., and in the patronage of the Earl of Dysart. The church, dedicated to St. Mary, exhibits some curiously ornamented windows, and the tower is partly in the early style of English architecture. In October 1643, the church and Dorfold hall were occupied by the royalists, on whose retreat both were garrisoned by the parliament. They were afterwards captured by the king's troops under Lord Byron, but on the raising of the siege of Nantwich, Sir Thomas Fairfax compelled the garrisons to surrender. Among the prisoners were sixty officers, including Col. Monk, afterwards Duke of Albemarle. Mr. Wilbraham, of Woodhay, left property for the endowment of two almshouses here, and others at Nantwich: there is also an endowed free school.

ACTON, a parish in the Kensington division of the hundred of OSSULSTONE, county of MIDDLESEX, 5 miles (W.) from London, containing 1929 inhabitants. The name is supposed to be derived from the Saxon word *Ac*, signifying oak, and *tun*, a town; the neighbourhood having, in former times, abounded with timber of that description, and some land in the parish, from time immemorial, having been called Old Oak common. Previously to the battle of Brentford, in 1642, the Earls of Essex and Warwick had their head-quarters here; and, on Cromwell's return to London, after the battle of Worcester, the lord president, the council of state, the members of the House of Commons, and the lord mayor, aldermen, and citizens of London, met him at this place, when the recorder of London delivered a congratulatory address. The village consists chiefly of one long street; it is watched by private subscription, and plentifully supplied with water. The houses in general are, from their antiquity, inferior to those in most other places within the same distance of the metropolis, but the whole place has a cleanly and cheerful appearance, and the air is considered particularly salubrious. The Paddington canal runs through the parish: a pleasure fair is held on Holy Thursday. The living is a rectory, in the archdeaconry of Middlesex, and diocese of London, rated in the king's books at £14, and in the patronage of the Bishop of London. The church, dedicated to St. Mary, which exhibits portions in the later style of English architecture, with modern insertions, was enlarged and repaired, at the expense of the inhabitants, in 1825. There is a place of worship for Independents, erected in 1815, and the detached buildings of a private mansion have been fitted up as a Roman Catholic chapel. A Lancasterian school has been erected near the church; and at that part of the village called East Acton are handsome almshouses, built and endowed by the Goldsmiths' Company, for twelve men and twelve women. In a garden, on Old Oak common, is a mineral spring, formerly held in general repute, but now disused.

ACTON, a joint township with Old Felton, in that part of the parish of FELTON which is in the eastern division of COQUETDALE ward, county of NORTHUMBERLAND, 7½ miles (S.) from Alnwick, containing, with Old Felton, 91 inhabitants.

ACTON, a parish in the hundred of BABERGH, county of SUFFOLK, 3 miles (N. E. by N.) from Sudbury, containing 555 inhabitants. The living is a vicarage, in the archdeaconry of Sudbury, and diocese of Norwich, rated in the king's books at £9. 6. 8., and in the patronage of Earl Howe. The church is dedicated to All Saints.

ACTON (IRON), a parish partly in the lower division of the hundred of GRUMBALD'S ASH, but chiefly in the lower division of the hundred of THORNBURY, county of GLOUCESTER, 3½ miles (W. N. W.) from Chipping-Sodbury, containing 1122 inhabitants. The living is a rectory, in the archdeaconry and diocese of Gloucester, rated in the king's books at £16. 10., and in the patronage of the Dean and Canons of Christ Church, Oxford. The church, dedicated to St. James, is in the latest style of English architecture: the interior contains the tomb of Robert Poyntz, who is said to have erected the tower. In the churchyard there is a beautiful cross, raised on arches, but much mutilated. The parish derives the prefix to its name from some iron-works which formerly existed here. Fairs for cattle, horses, pigs, and cheese, are held on April 25th and September 13th.

ACTON-BEAUCHAMP, a parish in the upper division of the hundred of DODDINGTREE, county of WORCESTER, 4¾ miles (S. E.) from Bromyard, containing 258 inhabitants. The living is a discharged rectory, in the archdeaconry and diocese of Worcester, rated in the king's books at £4, and in the patronage of the Rev. Henry Berry. The church is dedicated to St. Giles. Courts leet and baron are occasionally held here. There are some mineral springs in the parish.

ACTON-BURNELL, a parish in the hundred of CONDOVER, county of SALOP, 7½ miles (W. by N.) from Much-Wenlock, containing, with the chapelries of Acton-Pigot, and Ruckley with Langley, 305 inhabitants. The living is a rectory, in the archdeaconry of Salop, and diocese of Lichfield and Coventry, rated in the king's books at £6. 10., and in the patronage of Sir Edward Joseph Smythe, Bart. The church is dedicated to St. Mary. Here are some remains of an ancient castle, which belonged to the family of Burnell, from whom the place received the adjunct to its name. A great council, or parliament, was held here in the reign of Edward I., in 1283, at which a law, called the statute of Acton-Burnell, was enacted, to facilitate the recovery of debts by merchants: the king and his court were accommodated at the castle, the residence of Robert Burnell, Bishop of Bath and Wells, and Lord High Chancellor: the lords met in the hall of the castle, and the commons in a very large barn belonging to Shrewsbury abbey.

ACTON-GRANGE, a township in the parish of RUNCORN, hundred of BUCKLOW, county palatine of CHESTER, 2¾ miles (S.W. by S.) from Warrington, containing 148 inhabitants. The Mersey and Irwell canal, and the Duke of Bridgewater's canal, pass through the parish, its northern boundary being formed by the navigable river Mersey.

ACTON-PIGOT, a chapelry in the parish of ACTON-BURNELL, hundred of CONDOVER, county of SALOP, 6¾ miles (W.N.W.) from Much-Wenlock. The population is returned with the parish. The chapel is desecrated.

ACTON-REYNOLD, a township in that part of the parish of SHAWBURY which is within the liberty of SHREWSBURY, county of SALOP, 7½ miles (N.N.E.) from Shrewsbury, containing 168 inhabitants.

ACTON-ROUND, a parish in the hundred of STOTTESDEN, county of SALOP, 3¾ miles (S.S.E.) from Much-Wenlock, containing 214 inhabitants. The living is a perpetual curacy, in the archdeaconry of Salop, and diocese of Hereford, endowed with £200 private benefaction, £400 royal bounty, and £200 parliamentary grant, and in the patronage of the Vicar of Much-Wenlock.

ACTON-SCOTT, a parish in the hundred of MUNSLOW, county of SALOP, 3¼ miles (S. by E.) from Church-Stretton, containing 187 inhabitants. The living is a discharged rectory, in the archdeaconry of Salop, and diocese of Hereford, rated in the king's books at £5. 10., and in the patronage of T. P. Stackhouse, Esq. The church is dedicated to St. Margaret. The new turnpike road between Wenlock and Bishop's Castle passes through the parish.

ACTON-TRUSSELL, a chapelry in the parish of BASWICH, eastern division of the hundred of CUTTLESTONE, county of STAFFORD, 3 miles (N.N.E.) from Penkridge, containing, with Bednall, 562 inhabitants. The living is a perpetual curacy, in the peculiar jurisdiction of the Prebendary of Whittington and Baswich in the Cathedral Church of Lichfield, and in the patronage of the Rev. J. Hamilton Molineaux. The chapel is dedicated to St. James. The Staffordshire and Worcestershire canal passes through the chapelry. The poor children are instructed in the National school at Penkridge.

ACTON-TURVILLE, a chapelry in the parish of TORMARTON, lower division of the hundred of GRUMBALD'S-ASH, county of GLOUCESTER, 5¾ miles (E.) from Chipping-Sodbury, containing 215 inhabitants. The chapel is dedicated to St. Mary.

ADBASTON, county of STAFFORD.--See ABDASTON.

ADBEER, a hamlet in the parish of TRENT, hundred of HORETHORNE, county of SOMERSET, 4¾ miles (N.E. by N.) from Yeovil. The population is returned with the parish. Here was formerly a chapel, dedicated to the Virgin Mary, which was demolished during the civil war in the reign of Charles I.

ADBOLTON, formerly a parish, now a hamlet in the parish of HOLME-PIERREPOINT, southern division of the wapentake of BINGHAM, county of NOTTINGHAM, 3 miles (E.S.E.) from Nottingham. The population is returned with the parish. The living, a discharged rectory, rated in the king's books at £2. 13. 9., was, in 1707, consolidated with the rectory of Holme-Pierrepoint. The church is desecrated.

ADDERBURY (EAST), a parish in the hundred of BLOXHAM, county of OXFORD, 2¾ miles (N. by E.) from Deddington, comprising the chapelries of Earford St. John, Bodicott, and Milton, and the township of West Adderbury, and containing 2277 inhabitants. The living is a vicarage, in the archdeaconry and diocese of Oxford, rated in the king's books at £21. 4. 9½., and in the patronage of the Warden and Fellows of New College, Oxford. The church, dedicated to St. Mary, exhibits various styles of architecture, and contains some interesting specimens of early sculpture. There is a place of worship for Wesleyan Methodists. Here is a school, with an endowment of £20 per annum; and, in 1737, Lady Mary Bertie bequeathed a rent-charge of £10 for teaching ten poor children to read.

ADDERBURY (WEST), a township in the parish of EAST ADDERBURY, hundred of BLOXHAM, county of OXFORD, 2 miles (N.) from Deddington, containing 402 inhabitants.

ADDERLY, a parish in the Drayton division of the hundred of BRADFORD (North), county of SALOP, 4 miles (N. by W.) from Drayton in Hales, containing 378 inhabitants. The living is a rectory, in the archdeaconry of Salop, and diocese of Lichfield and Coventry, rated in the king's books at £11. 6. 0½., and in the patronage of H. C. Cotton, Esq. The church is dedicated to St. Peter. In 1719, the Rev. Mr. Adams bequeathed a small portion of land for the education of the poor children of this parish.

ADDERSTONE, a township in the parish of BAMBROUGH, northern division of BAMBROUGH ward, county of NORTHUMBERLAND, 3 miles (S.E. by S.) from Belford, containing 342 inhabitants.

ADDINGHAM, a parish in LEATH ward, county of CUMBERLAND, 1½ mile (S.E.) from Kirk-Oswald, comprising the townships of Gamblesby, Glassonby, Hunsonby with Winskill, and Little Salkeld, and containing 694 inhabitants. The living is a vicarage, in the archdeaconry and diocese of Carlisle, rated in the king's books at £9. 4. 7., and in the patronage of the Dean and Chapter of Carlisle. The church, dedicated to St. Michael, stands detached in the township of Glassonby. At Gamblesby are places of worship for Independents and Wesleyan Methodists, also one for the latter at Hunsonby, erected about 1823, by Mr. Thos. Hall. There are well endowed free schools at Hunsonby and Maughamby. Dr. Paley, the celebrated theological writer, held this living from 1792 to 1805, the period of his death. At Little Salkeld is a remarkable monument, supposed to be Druidical, commonly called "Long Meg and her Daughters," consisting of sixty-seven stones, varying in shape and height, which form a circle about three hundred and fifty feet in diameter. At the same place was anciently also a chapel, the site of which, according to tradition, was at a village called Addingham (which has long since disappeared), on the eastern bank of the river Eden, which forms the western boundary of the parish, where human bones, crosses, and other remains, have been dug up. The Roman road, called Maiden-way, may be traced in many parts of its course through the parish. Here are quarries of red freestone.

ADDINGHAM, a parish comprising the township of Addingham, in the eastern division of the wapentake of STAINCLIFFE and EWCROSS, and part of the township of Beamsley, in the upper division of the wapentake of CLARO, West riding of the county of YORK, and containing 1650 inhabitants, of which number, 1570 are in the township of Addingham, 6 miles (E. by S.) from Skipton. The living is a discharged rectory, in the archdeaconry and diocese of York, rated in the king's books at £9. 7. 8½., endowed with £600 private benefaction, and £1100 parliamentary grant, and in the patronage of Mrs. Mary Cunliffe. The church, dedicated to St. Peter, is an ancient structure, pleasantly situated on an eminence near the river Wharf. There is a place of worship for Wesleyan Methodists, and, in the vicinity, one for the Society of Friends. A considerable quantity of cotton goods is made here. At the distance of a mile are vestiges of a Roman encampment.

ADDINGTON, a parish in the hundred and county of BUCKINGHAM, 1¾ mile (W. N. W.) from Winslow, containing 89 inhabitants. The living is a rectory, in the archdeaconry of Buckingham, and diocese of Lincoln, rated in the king's books at £9. 9. 7., and in the patronage of John Poulett, Esq. The church is dedicated to St. Mary. A small sum of money was bequeathed by Ann Busby, in 1736, for educating and apprenticing poor children. On the border of the parish is a place called "Gallows' Gap," where, in the reign of Edward III., a gallows was erected by one of the family of Molines, who, as lord of the barony, possessed the power of trying and executing capital offenders.

ADDINGTON, a parish in the hundred of LARKFIELD, lathe of AYLESFORD, county of KENT, 7 miles (N. W. by W.) from Maidstone, containing 228 inhabitants. The living is a rectory, in the archdeaconry and diocese of Rochester, rated in the king's books at £6. 6. 8., and in the patronage of the Hon. J. W. Stratford. The church is dedicated to St. Margaret. On an eminence, at a short distance from it, are the remains of a monument, supposed to be Druidical, consisting of a circle of stones, in some degree resembling Stonehenge, with a smaller circle situated to the north-west, near which copper swords, British coins, and other relics, have been discovered. In this parish is one of those land springs which are very common in the eastern part of Kent, called the Nailbourn: the stream breaks out with great impetuosity once in seven or eight years, directing its course into a trench dug for its reception, till it arrives at the Leybourn rivulet, the trout in which, at other times white, it turns to a red colour.

ADDINGTON, a parish in the first division of the hundred of WALLINGTON, county of SURREY, 3½ miles (E. S. E.) from Croydon, containing 354 inhabitants. The living is a discharged vicarage, in the archdeaconry of Surrey, and diocese of Winchester, rated in the king's books at £4. 16. 5½., and in the patronage of the Archbishop of Canterbury. The church is dedicated to St. Mary: in the chancel lie the remains of the late Archbishop Sutton. The manor of Addington is held by the singular tenure of making and presenting to the king, at his coronation, a mess of pottage, called *maupygernon*, subject to the performance of which, a carucate of land here was granted to Tezelin, cook to William the Conqueror. On the brow of the hill adjoining Addington common are several low tumuli, in which urns have been found. Adjacent to the village is Addington Place, which, in 1807, was purchased by Dr. Sutton, Archbishop of Canterbury, with the funds arising from the sale of the archiepiscopal palace at Croydon. The mansion was originally erected by Alderman Trecothick, on the site of an ancient edifice said to have been a hunting seat of Henry VIII.; it was considerably enlarged and improved by Dr. Sutton, and is now being rebuilt by Dr. Howley, the present archbishop, for the future residence of the primates. A few years ago a water-spout burst on the adjacent eminences, and the water rushing into the village, destroyed considerable property there.

ADDINGTON (GREAT), a parish in the hundred of HUXLOE, county of NORTHAMPTON, 4½ miles (S. W.) from Thrapston, containing 256 inhabitants. The living is a rectory, in the archdeaconry of Northampton, and diocese of Peterborough, rated in the king's books at £10. 12. 8½., and in the patronage of the Rev. James Tyley. The church is dedicated to All Saints. This parish communicates with the North Sea, through the Northampton canal and the river Nen, the former of which here divides into two branches.

ADDINGTON (LITTLE), a parish in the hundred of HUXLOE, county of NORTHAMPTON, 3¼ miles (N.) from Higham-Ferrers, containing 233 inhabitants. The living is a discharged vicarage, in the archdeaconry of Northampton, and diocese of Peterborough, rated in the king's books at £7. 12., endowed with £400 private benefaction, and £400 royal bounty, and in the patronage of T. Saunderson, Esq. The church is dedicated to St. Mary. There is a free school with a small endowment. This parish, like the preceding, has a communication with the North Sea by the same means.

ADDLE, a parish in the upper division of the wapentake of SKYRACK, West riding of the county of YORK, comprising the townships of Addle *cum* Eccup and Arthington, and containing 1028 inhabitants, of which number, 699 are in the township of Addle *cum* Eccup, 5¾ miles (N. N. W.) from Leeds. The living is a rectory, in the archdeaconry and diocese of York, rated in the king's books at £16. 3. 4., and in the patronage of the Representatives of the family of Arthington. The church, one of the purest existing specimens of Norman architecture, is dedicated to St. John the Baptist. There is a free school, endowed with a portion of the income arising from £150, the gift of an unknown individual. This place was anciently called Adhill from the Ada of the Saxons, and it was the site of the *Burgodurum* of the Romans. In 1702, traces of a Roman town, with some inscribed stones, many fragments of urns, and the remains of an aqueduct, were discovered on an adjacent moor.

ADDLETHORPE, a parish in the Marsh division of the wapentake of CANDLESHOE, parts of LINDSEY, county of LINCOLN, 9½ miles (E. S. E.) from Alford, containing 176 inhabitants. The living is a discharged rectory, in the archdeaconry and diocese of Lincoln, rated in the king's books at £9. 10. 2½., and in the patronage of the Crown. The church is dedicated to St. Nicholas.

ADFORTON, a joint township with Payton and Grange, in the parish of LEINTWARDINE, hundred of WIGMORE, county of HEREFORD, 8½ miles (W. S. W.) from Ludlow, containing, with Payton and Grange, 212 inhabitants.

ADGARLEY, a township in the parish of URSWICK, hundred of LONSDALE, north of the sands, county palatine of LANCASTER, 2 miles (S. E. by E.) from Dalton. The population is returned with the parish.

ADISHAM, a parish in the hundred of DOWNHAMFORD, lathe of ST. AUGUSTINE, county of KENT, 2¾ miles (S. W. by S.) from Wingham, containing 305 inhabitants. The living is a rectory, with the perpetual curacy of Staple annexed, in the peculiar jurisdiction and patronage of the Archbishop of Canterbury, rated in the king's books at £28. 3. 1½. The church, dedicated to the Holy Innocents, is a large cruciform edifice, with a low tower, in the early style of English architecture, except the large window of the transept, which is in the decorated style.

ADLESTROP, a chapelry in the parish of BROADWELL, upper division of the hundred of SLAUGHTER, county of GLOUCESTER, 3¾ miles (E. by N.) from Stow on the Wold, containing 229 inhabitants. The chapel is dedicated to St. Mary Magdalene.

ADLINGFLEET, a parish in the lower division of the wapentake of OSGOLDCROSS, West riding of the county of YORK, comprising the townships of Adlingfleet, Fockerby, and Haldenby with Eastoft, and containing 431 inhabitants, of which number, 256 are in the township of Adlingfleet, 9½ miles (S. E.) from Howden. The living is a vicarage, in the archdeaconry and diocese of York, rated in the king's books at £9. 12. 11., and in the patronage of the Crown. The church is dedicated to All Saints. In 1743, Mary Ramsden bequeathed the sum of £200 for apprenticing boys and educating girls in Fockerby, Norton, Linton, and Adlingfleet.

ADLINGTON, a township in the parish of PRESTBURY, hundred of MACCLESFIELD, county palatine of CHESTER, 5 miles (N. by W.) from Macclesfield, containing 1057 inhabitants. There are some valuable mines of coal and quarries of flag-stone. Adlington Hall, a very ancient structure, which has long been the residence of the family of Legh, was garrisoned for Charles I. in the civil war, and taken by the parliamentarian forces, on the 14th of February, 1645, after a fortnight's siege: in the south-east angle is a small domestic chapel, handsomely fitted up, licensed by the Bishop of Lichfield and Coventry in the 25th of Henry VI. A manorial court is held twice a year, in May and December, at which debts under 40*s.* are recoverable.

ADLINGTON, a township in the parish of STANDISH, hundred of LEYLAND, county palatine of LANCASTER, 4 miles (N.) from Wigan, containing 1043 inhabitants.

ADMARSH, a chapelry in that part of the parish of LANCASTER which is in the hundred of LONSDALE, south of the sands, county palatine of LANCASTER. The population is returned with the parish. The living is a perpetual curacy, in the archdeaconry of Richmond, and diocese of Chester, endowed with £1000 royal bounty, and £200 parliamentary grant, and in the patronage of the Vicar of Lancaster.

ADMINGTON, a hamlet in the parish of QUINTON, upper division of the hundred of KIFTSGATE, county of GLOUCESTER, 6¼ miles (N. E. by N.) from Chipping-Campden, containing 162 inhabitants.

ADMISTON, or ATHELHAMPTON, a parish in the hundred of PIDDLETOWN, Dorchester division of the county of DORSET, 6¼ miles (E.N.E.) from Dorchester, containing 79 inhabitants. The living is a rectory, with that of Burleston, in the archdeaconry of Dorset, and diocese of Bristol, rated in the king's books at £2, and in the patronage of the Hon. W. T. L. P. Wellesley. This place is traditionally said to have been the principal residence of the Saxon kings of Wessex, but there is no satisfactory evidence of the truth of that opinion.

ADSTOCK, a parish in the hundred and county of BUCKINGHAM, 3 miles (N. W.) from Winslow, containing 393 inhabitants. The living is a rectory, in the archdeaconry of Buckingham, and diocese of Lincoln, rated in the king's books at £13. 16. 3., and in the patronage of the Bishop of Lincoln. The church is dedicated to St. Cecilia. In the time of the plague, in 1665, the contagion having extended to Buckingham and Winslow, a market was held at this place.

ADSTONE, a chapelry in the parish of CANONS-ASHBY, hundred of GREENS-NORTON, county of NORTHAMPTON, 6¾ miles (W. N. W.) from Towcester, containing 171 inhabitants. The chapel is dedicated to All Saints. Here is a free school for boys from the age of seven to fourteen.

ADVENT, or ST. ADVEN, a parish in the hundred of LESNEWTH, county of CORNWALL, 1¾ mile (S.) from Camelford, containing 229 inhabitants. The living is a perpetual curacy, consolidated with the rectory of Lanteglos, in the archdeaconry of Cornwall, and diocese of Exeter. The river Camel separates the two parishes. A copper mine is worked here, but it is not very productive.

ADWALTON, a hamlet in the chapelry of DRIGHLINGTON, parish of BIRSTALL, wapentake of MORLEY, West riding of the county of YORK, 5½ miles (S.E. by E.) from Bradford. The population is returned with Drighlington. On Adwalton moor a battle was fought, in 1642, between the royalists under the Earl of Newcastle, and the parliamentarians under Lord Fairfax, in which the latter were defeated. There was formerly a market in this hamlet: fairs are held February 6th, March 9th, Thursday in Easter week, the second Thursday after Easter, Whit-Thursday and every alternate Thursday till Michaelmas, November 5th, and December 23rd, all which, except the two last, are for the sale of lean cattle.

ADWELL, a parish in the hundred of LEWKNOR, county of OXFORD, 1¾ mile (S. by E.) from Tetsworth, containing 44 inhabitants. The living is a discharged rectory, in the archdeaconry and diocese of Oxford, rated in the king's books at £4. 13. 9., and in the patronage of Mrs. F. Webb. The church is dedicated to St. Mary. Here is an ancient intrenchment, called Adwell Cop, supposed by Dr. Plot to have been constructed by the Danes, about the year 1010.

ADWICK upon DEARNE, a parish in the northern division of the wapentake of STRAFFORTH and TICKHILL, West riding of the county of YORK, 6¾ miles (N. N. E.) from Rotherham, containing 168 inhabitants. The living is a perpetual curacy, in the archdeaconry and diocese of York, endowed with £400 royal bounty, and £200 parliamentary grant, and in the patronage of the Dean and Canons of Christ Church, Oxford. The river Dearne, and the Dearne and Dove canal, pass through the parish. Here is a mineral spring.

ADWICK le STREET, a parish in the northern division of the wapentake of STRAFFORTH and TICKHILL, West riding of the county of YORK, comprising the townships of Adwick le Street and Hamphall with Stubbs, and containing 486 inhabitants, of which number, 346 are in the township of Adwick le Street, 4 miles (N. W. by N.) from Doncaster. The living is a vicarage, in the archdeaconry and diocese of York, rated in the king's books at £4. 13. 4., and in the patronage of J. Fullerton, Esq. The church is dedicated to St. Lawrence. The adjunct to the name of this place is derived from its situation on a Roman road. Here is a free school, with an endowment of £10 per annum, bequeathed by the Rev. William Hedges, a late incumbent, for the education of children. A pure spring in this parish is in great repute for healing sore eyes.

AFF-PIDDLE, a parish in the hundred of HUNDRED'S BARROW, Blandford (South) division of the county of DORSET, 9 miles (E. by N.) from Dorchester, containing, with the tything of Bryant's-Piddle, 441 inhabitants. The living is a discharged vicarage, in the archdeaconry of Dorset, and diocese of Bristol, rated in the king's books at £8. 14. 9., endowed with £200 royal bounty, and in the patronage of J. Frampton, Esq. Here is a free school, endowed with £10. 10. per annum. On the summit of a hill, on the road from Piddletown to Poole, there are one hundred and twelve broad and deep pits, the largest of them sixty yards in diameter, which, in the most rainy season, never retain water: near them are some small tumuli.

AGDEN, a township in the parish of MALPAS, higher division of the hundred of BROXTON, county palatine of CHESTER, 2¾ miles (S.E.) from Malpas, containing 122 inhabitants. The Duke of Bridgewater's canal passes through the township.

AGDEN, a township partly in the parish of ROSTHERN, but chiefly in the parish of BOWDON, hundred of BUCKLOW, county palatine of CHESTER, 5½ miles (N.N.W.) from Nether Knutsford, containing 77 inhabitants.

AGELTHORPE, a township in the parish of COVERHAM, western division of the wapentake of HANG, North riding of the county of YORK, 3¼ miles (W. S. W.) from Middleham, containing 131 inhabitants.

AGLIONBY, a township in that part of the parish of WARWICK which is in CUMBERLAND ward, county of CUMBERLAND, 3¾ miles (E.) from Carlisle, containing 91 inhabitants.

AGNES (ST.), a market town and parish in the hundred of PYDER, county of CORNWALL, 8½ miles (N. W. by W.) from Truro, and 263 (W.) from London, containing 5762 inhabitants. This place, formerly named *Breanick*, or *Bryanick*, is situated in an extensive mining district on the northern coast, and consists principally of cottages, chiefly inhabited by miners: it is partially paved, and well supplied with water; the rocks on the coast are precipitous, and the scenery boldly picturesque. On a pyramidal rocky eminence, six hundred and sixty-four feet above the level of the sea, is St. Agnes' beacon, formed out of an ancient cairn, or tumulus, which, during the late war with France, was kept constantly ready in case of invasion; it has lately been much diminished by the removal of stone for repairing the fences in the vicinity. At the base of the hill are vestiges of a strong vallum, supposed to have been constructed by the Romans, which anciently extended, in a direction nearly circular, for about two miles. This district was formerly explored only for tin: the principal mine, "Sail Hole," having produced an immense quantity, was discontinued a few years since. Copper mines have been subsequently opened with very great success: in the principal mine, "Wheal Towan," eight hundred men are employed. After many fruitless attempts to form a harbour, a pier of moor-stone was constructed by a company in 1794, and a considerable trade in coal, lime, and slate, is now carried on with Ireland and Wales. The port, which is a member of that of St. Ives, has been enlarged and improved within the last few years, and is capable of affording safe anchorage to eight or ten vessels of one hundred tons' burden, but can only be entered at high water. A pilchard fishery was established in 1802, which affords employment to about forty men. The market is on Thursday, and a fair is held on April 30th. Courts for the duchy are held here annually in October, at which constables and other officers are appointed. The living is a perpetual curacy, united to the vicarage of Perranzabuloe, in the peculiar jurisdiction of the Dean and Chapter of Exeter. The church, dedicated to St. Agnes, is an ancient structure, built chiefly of granite, with a small spire of the same material. There are places of worship for Independents and Primitive and Wesleyan Methodists. The free school, founded by the Rev. St. John Eliot, in 1760, has a small endowment arising from funds bequeathed by him for charitable uses. In 1688, Mr. Nicholas Kent, of Ningoose, bequeathed a house and garden for aged widows, now used as the parish workhouse. Near the site of an ancient chapel, in a dingle called Chapelcomb, are the remains of St. Agnes' well, of which many miraculous stories are recorded. Opie, the celebrated painter, was born here, in 1761.

AIGHTON, a joint township with Bailey and Chaigley, in that part of the parish of MITTON which is in the lower division of the hundred of BLACKBURN, county palatine of LANCASTER, 5 miles (W. by S.) from Clitheroe, containing, with Bailey and Chaigley, 1487 inhabitants. Here are almshouses, towards the support of which J. Weld, Esq. contributes £92 per annum; also a free school, endowed with £20 per annum.

AIKE, a township partly in the parish of ST. JOHN, borough of BEVERLEY, but chiefly in the parish of LOCKINGTON, Bainton-Beacon division of the wapentake of HARTHILL, East riding of the county of YORK, 7 miles (N. by E.) from Beverley, containing 98 inhabitants.

AIKTON, a parish in the ward and county of CUMBERLAND, comprising the townships of Aikton, Biglands with Gamelsby, Wampool, and Wiggonby, and containing 706 inhabitants, of which number, 249 are in the township of Aikton, 4 miles (N. N. E.) from Wigton. The living is a rectory, in the archdeaconry and diocese of Carlisle, rated in the king's books at £14. 13. 1½., and in the patronage of the Earl of Lonsdale. The church is dedicated to St. Andrew.

AILESWORTH, a hamlet in the parish of CASTOR, liberty of PETERBOROUGH, county of NORTHAMPTON, 2¾ miles (E. by S.) from Wansford, containing 249 inhabitants.

AINDERBY-MYERS, a joint township with Holtby, in the parish of HORNBY, eastern division of the wapentake of HANG, North riding of the county of YORK, 3¼ miles (S. by E.) from Catterick, containing 79 inhabitants.

AINDERBY-QUERNHOW, a township in that part of the parish of PICKHILL which is in the wapentake of HALLIKELD, North riding of the county of YORK, 5¼ miles (W. S. W.) from Thirsk, containing 99 inhabitants.

AINDERBY-STEEPLE, a parish in the eastern division of the wapentake of GILLING, North riding of the county of YORK, comprising the townships of Ainderby-

Steeple, Morton, Thirntoft, and Warlaby, and containing 768 inhabitants, of which number, 266 are in the township of Ainderby-Steeple, 2¾ miles (W.S.W.) from North Allerton. The living is a discharged vicarage, in the archdeaconry of Richmond, and diocese of Chester, rated in the king's books at £13. 6. 8., and in the patronage of the Crown. The church is dedicated to St. Helen.

AINSTABLE, a parish in LEATH ward, county of CUMBERLAND, 4½ miles (N.N.W.) from Kirk-Oswald, containing, with the hamlet of Rushroft, 518 inhabitants. The living is a discharged vicarage, in the archdeaconry and diocese of Carlisle, rated in the king's books at £8. 8. 2., and in the patronage of R. L. Ross, Esq. The church is dedicated to St. Michael. The nave was rebuilt in 1816, and the chancel soon afterwards. This parish, which is bounded on the west by the river Eden, and on the east and south by the Croglin, abounds with most beautiful scenery, particularly in the vale of Croglin, and in the vicinity of Nunnery, a neat residence occupying the site of a Benedictine convent, described in the account of ARMATHWAITE. The scenery around Nunnery has been greatly improved by artificial decorations; numerous cascades, fanciful walks, &c., having been formed on both banks of the river Eden, the waters of which, near the hamlet of Armathwaite, are precipitated over a weir, four yards in height, and seventy in length, and, when the river is swollen, produce an exceedingly loud and murmuring noise. The parish contains a considerable quantity of freestone. Here is a free school, with a small endowment; and a school has been established by subscription, in which about twenty children are educated. Near the parsonage-house is a chalybeate spring. John Leake, M.D., founder of the Westminster Lying-in Hospital, and author of some esteemed medical works, was born here, in 1729.

AINSWORTH, a township in the parish of MIDDLETON, hundred of SALFORD, county palatine of LANCASTER, 3 miles (E. by N.) from Bolton le Moors, containing 1609 inhabitants.

AINTREE, a township in the parish of SEPHTON, hundred of WEST DERBY, county palatine of LANCASTER, 6 miles (N. N. E.) from Liverpool, containing 260 inhabitants.

AIRTON, a township in that part of the parish of KIRKBY in MALHAM-DALE which is in the western division of the wapentake of STAINCLIFFE and EWCROSS, West riding of the county of YORK, 6½ miles (S.E. by E.) from Settle, containing 187 inhabitants. In this township is a twist manufactory: there is also a free school, with a small endowment.

AISHOLT, or ASHOLT, a parish in the hundred of CANNINGTON, county of SOMERSET, 7¼ miles (W. by S.) from Bridg-water, containing, with the hamlet of Lower Aisholt, 176 inhabitants. The living is a rectory, in the archdeaconry of Taunton, and diocese of Bath and Wells, rated in the king's books at £7. 12. 3½., and in the patronage of the Rev. John Brice. The church is dedicated to All Saints.

AISHOLT (LOWER), a hamlet in the parish of AISHOLT, hundred of CANNINGTON, county of SOMERSET, 6¾ miles (W. by S.) from Bridg-water. The population is returned with the parish.

AISKEW, a township in that part of the parish of BEDALE which is in the eastern division of the wapentake of HANG, North riding of the county of YORK, ½ a mile (N. E.) from Bedale, containing 620 inhabitants. There are two places of worship for Anabaptists, and one for Roman Catholics. A free school has a small endowment for the instruction of children.

AISLABY, a township in the parish of EAGLESCLIFFE, south-western division of STOCKTON ward, county palatine of DURHAM, 1¼ mile (W. by N.) from Yarm, containing 166 inhabitants. This was, for several generations, the residence of the family of Pemberton, whose mansion has been converted into an inn and several other tenements.

AISLABY, or AYSLEYBY, a chapelry in that part of the parish of WHITBY which is in the eastern division of the liberty of LANGBAURGH, North riding of the county of YORK, 3 miles (S. W. by W.) from Whitby, containing 253 inhabitants. The living is a perpetual curacy, in the archdeaconry of Cleveland, and diocese of York, endowed with £200 private benefaction, and £800 royal bounty, and in the patronage of Mrs. Boulby.

AISLABY, a township in the parish of MIDDLETON, western division of PICKERING lythe, North riding of the county of YORK, 2 miles (W. N. W.) from Pickering, containing 147 inhabitants.

AISMUNDERBY, a joint township with Bondgate, in that part of the parish of RIPON which is in the liberty of RIPON, West riding of the county of YORK, containing, with Bondgate, 551 inhabitants. Here is an hospital for the support of two aged widows.

AISTHORPE, a parish in the wapentake of LAWRESS, parts of LINDSEY, county of LINCOLN, 6 miles (N. N. W.) from Lincoln, containing 70 inhabitants. The living is a discharged rectory, with the vicarage of West Thorpe annexed, in the archdeaconry of Stow, and diocese of Lincoln, rated in the king's books at £4. 10., and in the patronage of Mrs. Mangles. The church is dedicated to St. Peter.

AKEBAR, a township in the parish of FINGALL, western division of the wapentake of HANG, North riding of the county of YORK, 5 miles (N. E. by E.) from Middleham, containing 43 inhabitants.

AKELD, a township in the parish of KIRK-NEWTON, western division of GLENDALE ward, county of NORTHUMBERLAND, 2 miles (N. W. by W.) from Wooler, containing 167 inhabitants. Vestiges of a burial-place are discernible here, but there are no traces of any place of worship.

AKELY, a parish in the hundred and county of BUCKINGHAM, 2½ miles (N. by E.) from Buckingham, containing 295 inhabitants. The living is a rectory, in the archdeaconry of Buckingham, and diocese of Lincoln, rated in the king's books at £6. 2. 4., and in the patronage of the Warden and Fellows of New College, Oxford. The church is dedicated to St. James the Apostle. There was formerly a chapel of ease at Stockholt, in this parish.

AKENHAM, a parish in the hundred of BOSMERE and CLAYDON, county of SUFFOLK, 4½ miles (N. by W.) from Ipswich, containing 120 inhabitants. The living is a discharged rectory, with that of Claydon united, in the archdeaconry of Suffolk, and diocese of Norwich, rated in the king's books at £9. 11. 5½. The Rev. George Drury was patron in 1807.

Seal and Arms.

ALBANS (ST.), a borough and market town, having separate jurisdiction, locally in the hundred of Cashio, or liberty of St. Albans, county of HERTFORD, $12\frac{1}{2}$ miles (W. by S.) from Hertford, and 20 (N. W. by N.) from London, containing 4472 inhabitants. This place, separated from the site of the Roman *Verulamium* by the small river *Ver*, derived its name and origin from the magnificent monastery founded here by Offa, King of Mercia, in commemoration of St. Albanus, the proto-martyr of Britain. Verulam, according to the Roman historians, was founded by the Britons, at an earlier period than London. It was the chief station of Cassivellaunus at the time of the invasion of Cæsar, who describes it as a place of great military strength, well defended by woods and marshes. It appears to have consisted of rude dwellings constructed of wood, and to have been surrounded by a rampart and fosse. In the reign of Nero, it was accounted a *municipium*, or free city; and in that of Claudius, it was surprised by Boadicea, Queen of the Iceni, who slaughtered the chief part of the Roman and British inhabitants. After its subsequent restoration, it continued to be a primary station of the Romans until their final departure from Britain. During their occupation of it, Albanus, an eminent citizen, converted to Christianity by Amphibalus, in 293, boldly refusing to abjure his new religion, was beheaded on the hill called Holmhurst, on which spot the monastery was subsequently erected, and continued to flourish under a succession of forty abbots. About the middle of the fifth century, Verulam was occupied by the Saxons, and received the name of *Watlingceaster*, from the Roman highway, called Watling-street, on which it stood. According to Matthew Paris, the present town owes its origin to Ulsinus, or Ulsig, the sixth abbot, who, about the year 950, built a church on each of the three principal roads leading from the monastery, dedicated respectively to St. Stephen, St. Michael, and St. Peter, and encouraged the neighbouring inhabitants to erect houses, by supplying them with money and materials. Fritheric, or Frederic, the thirteenth abbot, opposed the march of the Norman conqueror, by causing the trees on the roadside, near Berkhampstead, to be cut down and laid across the way; he was also principally instrumental in exacting from him an oath to observe the ancient laws of the realm. William subsequently deprived this church of a great portion of its lands, and would have destroyed the monastery, but for the interposition of Archbishop Lanfranc. The monks and the inhabitants had frequent quarrels: and, in the reign of Richard II., the insurgents in Wat Tyler's rebellion were aided by the latter in besieging the monastery. On their dispersion, the king repaired hither, attended by Judge Tresilian and one thousand soldiers, to try the delinquents, and many of the townsmen were executed. The king remained eight days, on one of which the commons of the county assembled by his command, and, in the great court of the abbey, swore to be thenceforward faithful subjects. A sanguinary battle was fought here on the 22d of May, 1455, between Henry VI. and the Duke of York, in which the Lancastrians were defeated, their leader, the Duke of Somerset, killed, and the king himself made prisoner. On the 17th of February, 1461, another engagement took place on Bernard heath, north of the town, when Queen Margaret compelled the Earl of Warwick to retreat with considerable loss; after this action, the town was plundered and much damaged. On the introduction of printing into England, about 1471, a press was put up in the abbey, from which issued some of those early specimens which are now so eagerly sought for by collectors: the first translation of the Bible was made here. During the civil war between Charles I. and the parliament, a party of soldiers, under the Earl of Essex, garrisoned the town, and destroyed the beautiful cross, which was one of those erected by Edward I. in memory of his queen.

The town is situated chiefly on the summit and northern declivity of a considerable eminence, and consists principally of three streets, the abbey church standing on the hill near the point where they meet. That part of it which forms the old line of the great north road is narrow, and contains many ancient houses; but the other parts are spacious and well built. It is well paved and lighted under a local act, and, from the salubrity of the air, its short distance from the metropolis, and the excellence of its municipal regulations, is a desirable place of residence. By a recent diversion of the main road, extending for two miles, about three hundred yards southward from the town, the former circuitous and dangerous route through it is avoided: on this new line of road some handsome villas, and one of the most commodious inns in the county, called the Verulam Arms, have been lately erected. The manufacture of straw-plat, in which about eight hundred persons are employed, is the chief occupation of the lower class of inhabitants. A silk-mill, occupying the site of the abbey mill, affords employment to three hundred young persons of both sexes; and in a mill for spinning cotton wicks for candles, formerly applied to the cutting and polishing of diamonds, about sixty persons are engaged. The market is on Saturday, for corn, straw-plat, and provisions: there is a fair on March 25th and 26th, for cattle and horses; and a statute fair is held on Oct. 11th, and the two following days.

St. Albans is styled a borough in the record of Domesday, and is stated to have contained forty-six burgesses, who were the demesne men of the abbot, and under his jurisdiction (with the exception of a brief interval in the reigns of Edward II. and III.), until the dissolution, when the possessions of the monastery were surrendered to the crown. The inhabitants were incorporated in the 7th of Edward VI., by whose charter, modified in subsequent reigns, and confirmed in that of Charles II., the government is vested in a mayor, high steward, recorder, twelve aldermen, and twenty-four assistants, with a town clerk, who generally acts as chamberlain and coroner, two serjeants at mace, and subordinate officers. The mayor is chosen from among the aldermen, annually on the 21st of September; the high steward, recorder, and town clerk, are appointed by the mayor and aldermen, subject to approval by the crown; the aldermen are elected by a majority of their own body, as vacancies occur; and the assistants are chosen by the mayor and aldermen. The freedom of the borough is inherited by the eldest sons of freemen, acquired by servitude, and obtained by purchase, or gift. The mayor, the late mayor, the high steward, and the recorder, are justices of the peace, and hold courts of quarter session; the mayor presides at a court of aldermen, on the first Wednesday in every month, for the transaction of public business; and a court of requests, for the recovery of debts under 40*s.*, is held, under an act passed in the 25th of George II., every Saturday, the jurisdiction of which extends over the borough and liberty, including twenty-two parishes. The magistrates for the liberty hold quarter sessions here for that division, at which the recorder generally presides. The former town-hall was originally the charnel-house of the monastery; but a handsome and commodious edifice was erected in 1830, at an expense of £1200. The ancient prison of the monastery is now appropriated to the confinement of criminals committed for the borough and liberties. The borough first received the elective franchise in the 35th of Edward I., which was suspended from the 5th of Edward III. till the 1st of Edward VI., since which time it has continued to return two members to parliament. The right of election is vested in the freemen, whether resident or not, and in those householders who have been six months resident in the borough, paying scot and lot; the number of voters is about six hundred; the mayor is the returning officer, and the Earl of Verulam possesses considerable parliamentary influence.

The venerable abbey, rich in lordships and immunities, was valued at the dissolution at £2510: its abbots enjoyed both spiritual and temporal authority, having a palatine jurisdiction, similar to that possessed by the Bishops of Durham and Ely; they had also a grant of precedence from Pope Adrian IV. over all other abbots, with an exclusive exemption from the payment of Peter's pence, which, according to Camden, they possessed the power of collecting throughout the county, and applying to their own use. Henry VIII. granted the abbey to Sir Richard Lee, but retained the church, since made parochial, which Edward VI., in 1553, granted to the mayor and burgesses, for £400 and a fee-farm rent of £10, which latter, in 1684, was redeemed by the inhabitants for £200. This ancient cruciform structure is six hundred feet in length, and consists of a nave, two aisles, choir, presbytery, lady-chapel, and two transepts, with a large square tower rising from the intersection. The choir is separated from the nave by St. Cuthbert's screen, which, with the elaborately carved screen over the altar, the ceiling partly groined, and partly enriched with Mosaic paintings, and the tombs of Humphrey, Duke of Gloucester, and Abbot Ramryge, presents a rich and imposing appearance. The tower, supported on four arches, the two transepts, and a great part of the choir, were built of Roman tiles from the ancient city of Verulam, about the year 1077, and exhibit the Norman style of architecture: the remainder, erected about the reign of Henry III., is in the early English style, with sharply pointed arches. Many fine brasses, in memory of the abbots, were taken by Cromwell's soldiers, and the church was much damaged by the prisoners who were confined in it during the parliamentary war.

The town comprises the parish of St. Alban, or the abbey parish, and part of the parishes of St. Michael and St. Peter, in the archdeaconry of St. Albans, and diocese of London. The living of St. Alban's is a rectory, rated in the king's books at £10, endowed with £200 private benefaction, and £200 royal bounty, and in the patronage of the Mayor and Corporation. The living of St. Peter's is a vicarage, rated in the king's books at £9. 0. 10., and in the patronage of the Bishop of Ely: the church, erected by Abbot Ulsinus, in 948, has been rebuilt within the last thirty years. The living of St. Michael's is a vicarage, rated in the king's books at £10. 1. 8., and in the patronage of the Earl of Verulam: the church is a small edifice, erected by the same abbot. There are places of worship for Particular Baptists, the Society of Friends, Independents, Wesleyan Methodists, and Unitarians. The free grammar school was founded by Edward VI., in 1553, and further endowed, in 1570, by Queen Elizabeth, with £20 per annum, payable by the dealers in wine in the borough and within two miles of it, in consideration of certain privileges conferred on them by letters patent. The school-room, adjoining the abbey church, was formerly the beautiful chapel of the Virgin. The Blue-coat school, in which about thirty-five boys are clothed, and educated in the principles of the established church, is supported by the dividends on some funded property, and by subscription. A girls' school is supported by the Verulam family. The almshouses, called Marlborough buildings, containing apartments for thirty-six persons of both sexes, were built and endowed by Sarah, Duchess of Marlborough: they occupy three sides of a quadrangle, on the site of the old manor-house of Newland-Squillers; each inmate receives £12 per annum. There are twenty-one other almshouses, founded by different individuals.

In the town is a high square brick tower, called the Clock-house, built by one of the abbots in the reign of Henry VIII.; and, at the distance of half a mile to the south-east, are some fine remains of the nunnery of Sopwell, founded, in 1140, by Abbot Geoffrey de Gorham, of which the Lady Juliana Berners was at one time prioress; like the monastery, it was built of Roman tiles and bricks, and partly of flints. Of two hospitals, founded by the abbots, and dedicated respectively to St. Julian and St. Mary de Pratis, there is not a single vestige. On the left of the road leading to Dunstable, a few fragments of the ancient walls of Verulam are still discernible. In a field adjoining the town, called New England field, are some hills, supposed to have been the site of the camp of Ostorius, and thence vulgarly called Oyster hills. There is a mineral spring in a garden, near St. Michael's bridge. Matthew Paris, one of the most eminent of the old English historians, was a monk in the abbey. Among the most distinguished natives may be enumerated Alexander Necham, a poet and scholastic divine; Sir John Mandeville, the celebrated traveller; and Sir John King, and Sir Francis Pemberton, two eminent lawyers. Breakspear's farm-house, near the town, was the birthplace of Nicholas Breakspear, the only Englishman that ever sat in the papal chair; on his elevation he assumed the name of Adrian IV.; he was a great benefactor to the abbey. Francis, the great Lord Bacon, was buried in St. Michael's church; a finely sculptured alabaster statue has been erected to his memory, in a niche on the northern side of the chancel. St. Albans gives the title of duke to the family of Beauclerc; and the representative of the family of Grimstone enjoys the title of Earl of Verulam.

ALBERBURY, or ABBERBURY, a parish comprising the townships of Cruggion, Middleton, and Uppington, in the hundred of CAWRSE, and the township of Bauseley in the hundred of DEYTHUR, county of MONTGOMERY (Wales), and the chapelry of Wollaston, and the townships of Alberbury, Benthal with Shrawardine, Eyton, and Rowton with Amaston, in the hundred of FORD, county of SALOP, and containing 1946 inhabitants, of which number, 332 are in the township of Alberbury, 8¾ miles (W.) from Shrewsbury. The living is a discharged vicarage, in the archdeaconry of Salop, and diocese of Hereford, rated in the king's books at £5. 10., endowed with £200 private benefaction, and £200 royal bounty, and in the patronage of the Warden and Fellows of All Souls' College, Oxford. The church is dedicated to St. Michael. The Roman Watling-street passes through the parish, which is partially bounded by the river Severn. There are some remains of a castle, built in the reign of Henry II., by Fulk Fitz-Warine, who founded an abbey for Black monks of the order of Grandmont, vestiges of which may still be traced about a mile from the castle: on the suppression of Alien priories, Henry VI. gave the site to the college of All Souls', Oxford, to which it still belongs.

ALBOURNE, a parish in the hundred of TIPNOAK, rape of BRAMBER, county of SUSSEX, 2½ miles (W.N.W.) from Hurst-Pierrepoint, containing 360 inhabitants. The living is a rectory, in the archdeaconry of Lewes, and diocese of Chichester, rated in the king's books at £7. 14. 2., and in the patronage of Charles Goring, Esq. The church, dedicated to St. Bartholomew, is in the early style of English architecture, with additions of a later date.

ALBRIGHTON, a parish (formerly a market town) in the Shiffnall division of the hundred of BRIMSTREE, county of SALOP, 6 miles (S. E. by E.) from Shiffnall, containing 968 inhabitants. The living is a vicarage, in the peculiar jurisdiction of the Dean of Lichfield, rated in the king's books at £5. 10., and in the alternate patronage of the Master and Wardens of the Haberdashers' Company, and the Governors of Christ's Hospital, London. The church is dedicated to St. Mary. Here is a free school for six poor children, principally supported from the tolls of the fairs, which are held on March 5th, May 23rd, July 18th, and November 9th, for horned cattle, sheep, and hogs.

ALBRIGHTON, a parish in the hundred of PIMHILL, county of SALOP, 4 miles (N.) from Shrewsbury, containing 75 inhabitants. The living is a perpetual curacy, within the jurisdiction of the court of the royal peculiar of St. Mary's, Shrewsbury, endowed with £800 royal bounty, and in the patronage of the Dean and Chapter of Lichfield. The church is dedicated to St. John.

ALBURGH, a parish in the hundred of EARSHAM, county of NORFOLK, 3¼ miles (N.E. by N.) from Harleston, containing 601 inhabitants. The living is a rectory, in the archdeaconry of Norfolk, and diocese of Norwich, rated in the king's books at £12, and in the patronage of the Heirs of Sir R. Hill, Bart., to a fellow of St. John's College, Cambridge. The church is dedicated to All Saints.

ALBURY, a parish in the hundred of EDWINSTREE, county of HERTFORD, 4½ miles (N.W.) from Bishop-Stortford, containing 596 inhabitants. The living is a vicarage, in the peculiar jurisdiction of the Dean and Chapter of St. Paul's, London, rated in the king's books at £7. 9. 7., and in the patronage of the Treasurer in that cathedral. The church is dedicated to St. Mary.

ALBURY, a parish in the hundred of BULLINGTON, county of OXFORD, 3¼ miles (W. by S.) from Thame, containing, with the hamlet of Tiddington, 214 inhabitants. The living is a rectory, in the archdeaconry and diocese of Oxford, rated in the king's books at £9. 2. 8½., and in the patronage of the Earl of Abingdon. The church is dedicated to St. Helen. Lady Mary Bertie, in 1737, gave a rent-charge of £10 for the instruction of twelve poor boys of this parish.

ALBURY, a parish in the second division of the hundred of BLACKHEATH, county of SURREY, 4 miles (E. S. E.) from Guildford, containing 765 inhabitants. The living is a rectory, in the archdeaconry of Surrey, and diocese of Winchester, rated in the king's books at £17. 12. 8½., and in the patronage of H. Drummond, Esq. The church is dedicated to St. Peter and St. Paul; it contains two singular octangular pillars, resting upon circular bases of Sussex marble, supposed to have been removed from a Roman temple which stood on Blackheath, near the site of which is an intrenchment, with the ditch and double rampart perfect: in the neighbourhood are two chalk-pits and a quarry of stone. Courts leet and baron are held here annually. In 1754, William Resbridger bequeathed £400 for instructing children, purchasing bread for the poor, and other charitable purposes. A National school for boys is supported by subscription.

ALBY, a parish in the southern division of the hundred of ERPINGHAM, county of NORFOLK, 4¾ miles (N. by E.) from Aylsham, containing 303 inhabitants. The living is a discharged rectory, in the archdeaconry and diocese of Norwich, rated in the king's books at £7. 11. 8½., and in the patronage of the Earl of Orford. The church is dedicated to St. Ethelbert.

ALCESTER, a market town and parish in the Alcester division of the hundred of BARLICHWAY, county of WARWICK, 15 miles (W. S. W.) from Warwick, and 103 (N.W. by W.) from London, containing 2229 inhabitants. This place, from its name, from the numerous Roman relics that have been discovered, and, from being situated on the line of the Iknield-street, vestiges of which are still discernible in the immediate vicinity, is supposed to have been a Roman station. In the time of the Saxons it was a place of great importance, and of much greater extent than at present. At the Conquest it was a royal residence, and was made a free borough in the reign of Henry I. In 1141, a monastery was founded here by Ralph de Boteler, the revenue of which, at the dissolution, was £101. 14. The town is pleasantly situated in a fertile valley, surrounded with richly wooded eminences, on the eastern bank of the river Aln, near

Seal and Arms.

its junction with the Arrow, over both which rivers are neat stone bridges. It consists of one principal street, from which, near the market-place, several smaller ones diverge. Some of the houses are ancient, with projecting upper stories, though in general they are modern, and of handsome appearance: the inhabitants are well supplied with water from springs. The principal branch of manufacture is that of needles, in which about six hundred persons are employed. The market is on Tuesday: fairs are held on January 27th, March 24th, May 18th, July 28th, October 17th, and December 1st. A court leet is held annually in November, at which a bailiff and deputy bailiff are appointed; but the town is within the jurisdiction of the county magistrates. The living is a discharged rectory, in the archdeaconry and diocese of Worcester, rated in the king's books at £14. 18. 10., and in the patronage of the Marquis of Hertford. The church, formerly dedicated to St. Andrew, was, with the exception of the tower, rebuilt in 1732, and dedicated to St. Nicholas: it is partly in the early, and partly in the decorated, style of English architecture, with a fine embattled tower crowned with pinnacles; the roof is supported by pillars of the Tuscan order. There are places of worship for Particular Baptists, the Society of Friends, Wesleyan Methodists, and Unitarians. The free grammar school was founded by Mr. Walter Newport, in 1592, and endowed with £400, now producing £20 per annum. In 1780, Mr. Brook Bridges founded a school for twelve boys and twelve girls, which he endowed with £20 per annum. There is an almshouse for eight poor men. Among the Roman antiquities that have been found in the town and its environs are various urns, coins, tesselated pavements, and other relics; and in that part called the Black Fields, to which the buildings formerly extended, old foundations have been discovered. Beauchamp's Court, the ancient manorial residence, now a farm, about a mile and a half distant, gives the inferior title of baron to the Earl of Warwick.

ALCISTON, a parish in the hundred of ALCISTON, rape of PEVENSEY, county of SUSSEX, 4¾ miles (N.N.E.) from Seaford, containing 247 inhabitants. The living is a discharged rectory, at present under sequestration, in the archdeaconry of Lewes, and diocese of Chichester, rated in the king's books at £6, endowed with £200 parliamentary grant, and in the patronage of the Dean and Chapter of Chichester. The church presents some remains of Norman architecture, with an admixture of the early English style. Fragments of various kinds of coffins have been found here.

ALCONBURY, a parish in the hundred of LEIGHTONSTONE, county of HUNTINGDON, 4½ miles (N.W.) from Huntingdon, containing 783 inhabitants. The living is a discharged vicarage, in the archdeaconry of Huntingdon, and diocese of Lincoln, rated in the king's books at £8. 6. 1., endowed with £200 private benefaction, and £300 parliamentary grant, and in the patronage of the Dean and Chapter of Westminster. The church is dedicated to St. Peter and St. Paul. A fair is held on Midsummer-day. There is a place of worship for Wesleyan Methodists.

ALCONBURY-WESTON, county of HUNTINGDON. — See WESTON (ALCONBURY.)

ALCUMLOW, a joint township with Moreton, in that part of the parish of ASTBURY which is in the hundred of NORTHWICH, county palatine of CHESTER. The population is returned with Moreton.

ALDBOROUGH, a parish in the northern division of the hundred of ERPINGHAM, county of NORFOLK, 2 miles (W. by S.) from Aylsham, containing 268 inhabitants. The living is a discharged rectory, in the archdeaconry and diocese of Norwich, rated in the king's books at £8, and in the patronage of Lord Suffield. The church is dedicated to St. Mary.

Seal and Arms.

ALDBOROUGH, or ALDEBURGH, a sea-port, borough, and parish (formerly a market town), having separate jurisdiction, locally in the hundred of Plomesgate, county of SUFFOLK, 25 miles (N. E. by E.) from Ipswich, and 94 (N. E.) from London, containing 1212 inhabitants. This borough, which takes its name from its situation on the river Alde, was formerly of very considerable extent, and its importance procured for it many privileges. From the encroachment of the sea (which, within the last century, has destroyed its market-place, with an entire street and a great number of houses), it has been reduced to an inconsiderable town; but, from the salubrity of the air, and the convenience of the shore for sea-bathing, it has lately become a place of fashionable resort during the summer. The town is situated in a pleasant vale, having the river Alde on the south-west, and commanding an extensive view of the North sea on the east, and is sheltered by a steep hill, the extended summit of which forms a magnificent terrace, affording a delightful promenade, and a beautifully diversified prospect. The strand, to which the descent from the town is gradual, consists of firm sand, favourable for bathing and walking. At the southern extremity of the main street, which is nearly a mile in length, there is a battery, on which, during the late war, two eighteen-pounders were mounted, another of five guns, and a martello tower, for the protection of the coast. The old houses are in general mean and ill constructed, but those erected by families residing here during the season, or for the accommodation of visitors, are well built and respectable; among them is an elegant marine villa, in the Italian style, built by Leveson Vernon, Esq. There is a public subscription library, commanding a fine view of the bay; a neat and commodious theatre is open for a few weeks during the season; there are two billiard-tables; and assemblies are held occasionally at the principal inns. The trade of the port consists chiefly in the exportation of corn, and the importation of coal and timber, in which forty-six vessels, averaging fifty-two tons burden, are employed. The custom-house is a neat and convenient building near the quay; and the harbour, which is safe and commodious, attracts a number of seafaring people and fishermen, by whom the town is principally inhabited. Many of these are Trinity-house pilots, who form themselves into small associations, and purchase swiftly-sailing cutters, in which they traverse the North sea, frequently approaching the coast of Norway, in search of vessels that may want their assistance. The principal employment of the other inhabitants consists in the drying of herrings and sprats, which are found here in profusion, and exported to Holland; soles and lobsters of superior flavour are taken also in abundance. The market, formerly on Wednesday, has been discontinued; the fairs are held on March 1st and May 3rd. By the charter of incorporation, granted in the reign of Charles I., the government of the borough is vested in two bailiffs, and ten capital and twenty-four inferior burgesses: the freedom is inherited by birth, or obtained by gift. The bailiffs are justices of the peace, and hold a court of session annually in September; they are also empowered to hold a court of record for the recovery of debts under £30, but it has not been held for upwards of a century. The town hall is an ancient building of timber, under which is the common gaol for the borough. Aldborough first exercised the elective franchise in the 13th of Elizabeth, since which time it has returned two members to parliament. The right of election is vested in the bailiffs, and burgesses resident within the borough, and not receiving alms; the bailiffs are the returning officers. The living is a discharged vicarage, in the archdeaconry of Suffolk, and diocese of Norwich, rated in the king's books at £33. 6. 8., and in the patronage of Leveson Vernon, Esq. The church, dedicated to St. Peter and St. Paul, an ancient structure of flint and freestone, on the summit of a hill at the northern extremity of the town, has a square embattled tower surmounted with a turret, affording an excellent land-mark for mariners. There are places of worship for Particular Baptists, Independents, and Wesleyan Methodists. A National school is supported by subscription.

ALDBOROUGH, a parish, comprising the chapelry of Lower Dunsforth, and the township of Upper Dunsforth with Branton-Green, in the upper division, and the boroughs of Aldborough and Boroughbridge, the townships of Minskep and Rocliff, and part of the township of Humberton with Milby, in the lower division, of the wapentake of CLARO, West riding of the county of YORK, and containing 2129 inhabitants, of which number, 484 are in the borough of Aldborough, 16½ miles (N. W. by W.) from York, and 205½ (N. N. W.) from London. The town, which stands upon the southern bank of the river Ure, and upon the line of the northern Watling-street, was the celebrated and important Roman station called *Isurium Brigantium*, and received from the Saxons the name of *Eald-burg*, denoting its antiquity even in their time. Its destruction is attributed to the Danes, and it has now become a very inconsiderable place, being irregularly built, and the houses in general mean and detached from each other. The elective franchise was granted by Philip and Mary, in 1558. The right of election is vested in the inhabitants paying scot and lot, in number about sixty; and the bailiff, who is appointed by the lord of the manor, is the returning officer. The living is a discharged vicarage, in the peculiar jurisdiction and patronage of the Dean and Chapter of York, rated in the king's books at £9. 19. 5. The church is dedicated to St. Andrew. The foundations of the walls of the ancient city, which included a quadrilateral area of two thousand five hundred yards, may still be traced; near the centre are vestiges of a mount, called the Borough Hill, removed in 1783, and believed, from the remains then discovered, to have been the site of a Roman temple. About a hundred paces from the south wall is a semicircular outwork, called Studforth, two hundred feet long, having a slope of thirty feet, forming a lofty terrace on the south side of the town. Many Roman remains, consisting of tesselated pavements, domestic utensils, military weapons, coins, &c., have at various times been discovered.

ALDBOURN, a parish (formerly a market town) in the hundred of SELKLEY, county of WILTS, 6 miles (N. E.) from Marlborough, containing 1385 inhabitants. The name is compounded of the Saxon terms *Ald*, old, and *bourne*, a brook. Aldbourn anciently gave name to a royal chase, granted by Henry VIII. to Edward Seymour, Duke of Somerset, which, for a long period, served only as a rabbit warren, but is now enclosed and cultivated. Previously to the battle of Newbury, in the reign of Charles I., a sharp skirmish took place here between the parliamentarian forces and the royalists. In 1760, a fire consumed seventy-two houses; and, in 1817, twenty were destroyed by a similar calamity. The town is situated in a fertile valley: a considerable manufacture of fustians was formerly carried on, but it has declined. The market and fairs have been discontinued upwards of a century. The living is a vicarage, in the archdeaconry of Wilts, and diocese of Salisbury, rated in the king's books at £26. 6. 3., and in the patronage of the Bishop of Salisbury. The church, dedicated to St. Michael, is an ancient structure, exhibiting portions in the Norman style of architecture. There is a place of worship for Wesleyan Methodists. The southern part of the vicarage-house is supposed to be the remnant of a hunting seat which belonged to John of Gaunt, Duke of Lancaster. Near a farm-house, called Pierce's Lodge, are vestiges of an ancient British encampment; and in the neighbourhood artificial mounds of earth are frequently to be met with.

ALDBROUGH, a parish in the middle division of the wapentake of HOLDERNESS, East riding of the county of YORK, comprising the townships of Aldbrough, East Newton, West Newton, and a portion of the township of Cowdons, and containing 998 inhabitants, of which number, 802 are in the township of Aldbrough, 11½ miles (N. E. by E.) from Kingston upon Hull. The living is a discharged vicarage, in the archdeaconry of the East riding, and diocese of York, rated in the king's books at £13. 15., and in the patronage of the Crown. The church, dedicated to St. Bartholomew, is a large edifice in the English style of architecture: it contains a circular stone, bearing an inscription recording its erection by one Ulf, who was lord of the place, and had a castle here, every vestige of which has been destroyed. There is a place of worship for Wesleyan Methodists. Slight traces of a Roman road are discernible in the vicinity. The rental of certain land, left by Mr. Towry, is appropriated to the instruction of children and the relief of the poor.

ALDBROUGH, a township in that part of the parish of STANWICK ST. JOHN which is in the western division of the wapentake of GILLING, North riding of the county of YORK, 6½ miles (N. by E.) from Richmond, containing 544 inhabitants. There is a place of worship for Wesleyan Methodists A very good free school was built here by S. M. Barrett, Esq., which is con ducted on the Lancasterian plan, and supported by voluntary subscription.

ALDBURY, a parish in the hundred of DACORUM, county of HERTFORD, 3 miles (E. by N.) from Tring, containing 676 inhabitants. The living is a rectory, in the archdeaconry of Huntingdon, and diocese of Lincoln, rated in the king's books at £20. 8. 6½., and in the patronage of the Trustees of the late Earl of Bridgewater. The church, dedicated to St. John the Baptist, is an ancient structure in the early style of English architecture, and contains an altar-tomb of an armed knight, in a recumbent posture, and his lady, also another, with brasses, to a knight and his lady, and their nine sons and three daughters, both executed in the richest style of ancient sculpture. This village is pleasantly situated at the foot of the Chiltern hills, the summits of which are crowned with thick plantations. There are three tenements for the residence of five widowers and widows, with an annual sum for keeping them in repair, the gift of an unknown benefactor.

ALDCLIFFE, a township in that part of the parish of LANCASTER which is in the hundred of LONSDALE, south of the sands, county palatine of LANCASTER, 1½ mile (S. W.) from Lancaster, containing 85 inhabitants.

ALDEBY, a parish in the hundred of CLAVERING, county of NORFOLK, 2¾ miles (N. E.) from Beccles, containing 475 inhabitants. The living is a perpetual curacy, in the archdeaconry of Norfolk, and diocese of Norwich, endowed with £400 royal bounty, and in the patronage of the Dean and Chapter of Norwich. The church is dedicated to St. Mary. Here was a small priory, a cell to the Benedictine abbey of Norwich, which, at the dissolution, was given by Henry VIII. as part of the endowment of the dean and prebendaries of that cathedral.

ALDENHAM, a parish in the hundred of CASHIO, or liberty of ST. ALBANS, county of HERTFORD, 2¾ miles (N. E. by E.) from Watford, containing, with the hamlet of Theobald-Street, which is in the hundred of Dacorum, 1399 inhabitants. The living is a vicarage, in the archdeaconry of Huntingdon, and diocese of Lincoln, rated in the king's books at £24, and in the patronage of the Trustees of P. Thelluson, Esq. The church, dedicated to St. John the Baptist, is built in the early English style. In the 31st of Elizabeth, Richard Platt founded and endowed six almshouses, also a free grammar school for sixty children, to be chosen from among the poor of Aldenham and the families of freemen of the Brewers' Company, London; and, in default of the full number of scholars from Aldenham, the choice to be extended to the adjacent parishes, the children of the founder's name and kin to have the preference. The Master and Wardens of the Brewers' Company are the governors, and elect the master, who must have taken the degree of M.A. The annual income of the whole charity is £857. 4. 6.; of this sum the master receives £80 per annum, with a rent-free residence and a supply of coal, and the usher £40; forty-five boys are taught on the foundation.

ALDERBURY, a parish in the hundred of ALDERBURY, county of WILTS, 3 miles (S. E. by E.) from Salisbury, comprising the chapelries of Farley and Pitton, and containing 1125 inhabitants. The living is a discharged vicarage, in the peculiar jurisdiction and patronage of the Treasurer in the Cathedral Church of Salisbury. The church is dedicated to St. Mary. There is a place of worship for Wesleyan Methodists. Here is a small endowed free school. A monastery formerly existed at Ivy Church, in this parish, the site of which is now occupied by a modern residence.

ALDERFORD, a parish in the hundred of EYNSFORD, county of NORFOLK, 3¼ miles (S. E. by S.) from Reepham, containing 45 inhabitants. The living is a discharged rectory, united to the vicarage of Attlebridge, in the archdeaconry of Norfolk, and diocese of Norwich, rated in the king's books at £4. 6. 8. The church is dedicated to St. John the Baptist.

ALDERLEY, a parish in the hundred of MACCLESFIELD, county palatine of CHESTER, comprising the townships of Upper Alderley, Lower Alderley, and Great Warford, and containing 1477 inhabitants, of which number, 473 are in the township of Upper Alderley, and 668 in that of Lower Alderley, 4¾ miles (W. N. W.) from Macclesfield. The living is a rectory, in the archdeaconry and diocese of Chester, rated in the king's books at £14. 10. 10., and in the patronage of Sir J. T. Stanley, Bart. The church is dedicated to St. Mary. There is a place of worship for Baptists at Great Warford. Mines of lead, copper, and cobalt, have been worked in the neighbourhood, but the produce of ore has not been sufficient to encourage perseverance. A few of the inhabitants are engaged in weaving for the manufacturers of the neighbouring towns. A school-house, originally built in 1628 by the Rev. Hugh Shaw, curate of the parish, and since endowed with benefactions to the amount of £300, was rebuilt near the church a few years ago: there is also a small endowed free school in Lower Alderley. In Alderley park there is a large sheet of water, called Radnor mere, a wood near which contains some of the finest beech trees in England; and on the high ground of Aldersey Edge is a fine spring, called the Holy Well.

ALDERLEY, a parish in the upper division of the hundred of GRUMBALD'S ASH, county of GLOUCESTER, 2 miles (S. S. E.) from Wotton under Edge, containing 235 inhabitants. The living is a discharged rectory, in the archdeaconry and diocese of Gloucester, rated in the king's books at £11. 4. 7., and in the patronage of Mr. and Mrs. Hale. The village is situated on a hill between two streams, which unite and fall into the Lower Avon. *Cornua ammonis* and other fossils are found here. Sir Matthew Hale, Lord Chief Justice in the reign of Charles II., born here November 1st, 1609, lies interred in the church.

ALDERMASTON, a parish (formerly a market town) in the hundred of THEALE, county of BERKS, 10 miles (S. W. by W.) from Reading, containing 653 inhabitants. The living is a vicarage, in the archdeaconry of Berks, and diocese of Salisbury, rated in the king's books at £12. 12. 8½., and in the patronage of the Provost and Fellows of Queen's College, Oxford. The church is dedicated to St. Mary. Fairs are held on May 6th and July 7th. The navigable river Kennet passes through the parish.

ALDERMINSTER, a parish partly in the upper division of the hundred of OSWALDSLOW, but chiefly in the upper division of the hundred of PERSHORE, being a detached portion of the county of WORCESTER, surrounded by Warwickshire, 5 miles (S. S. E.) from Stratford upon Avon, containing 443 inhabitants. The living is a discharged vicarage, in the archdeaconry and diocese of Worcester, rated in the king's books at £7, endowed with £200 private benefaction, and £200 royal bounty, and in the patronage of the Crown. The church, dedicated to St. Mary, is a curious cruciform edifice, having a low tower; the nave is in the Norman style of architecture. A recently constructed rail-road, from Stratford upon Avon to Moreton in the Marsh, passes through the village.

ALDERSEY, a township in the parish of CODDINGTON, higher division of the hundred of BROXTON, county palatine of CHESTER, 8¾ miles (S. E. by S.) from Chester, containing 138 inhabitants. Salt-works existed here in the middle of the sixteenth century; and there is still a brine spring in the neighbourhood, which is not worked, owing to the distance whence coal must be brought for that purpose.

ALDERSHOTT, a parish in the hundred of CRONDALL, Basingstoke division of the county of SOUTHAMPTON, 3¾ miles (N. E. by N.) from Farnham, containing 525 inhabitants. The living is a donative, endowed with £1800 parliamentary grant, and in the patronage of the principal landed proprietors. The church is dedicated to St. Michael. The ancient seat of the Tichborne family has been converted into a farmhouse. This parish is within the jurisdiction of the Cheyney Court held at Winchester every Thursday, for the recovery of debts to any amount.

ALDERTON, a parish in the upper division of the hundred of TEWKESBURY, county of GLOUCESTER, 4¼ miles (N. N. W.) from Winchcomb, containing, with the hamlet of Dixon, 312 inhabitants. The living is a rectory, in the archdeaconry and diocese of Gloucester, rated in the king's books at £22. 1. 10½., and in the patronage of the Rev. Robert Townsend, D.D. The church is dedicated to St. Margaret.

ALDERTON, a parish in the hundred of CLELEY, county of NORTHAMPTON, 3¾ miles (E. S. E.) from Towcester, containing 177 inhabitants. The living is a rectory, annexed to that of Grafton Regis, in the archdeaconry of Northampton, and diocese of Peterborough, rated in the king's books at £12. The church is dedicated to St. Margaret.

ALDERTON, a parish in the hundred of WILFORD, county of SUFFOLK, 7½ miles (S. E. by S.) from Woodbridge, containing 566 inhabitants. The living is a rectory, in the archdeaconry of Suffolk, and diocese of Norwich, rated in the king's books at £14. 18. 4., and in the patronage of the lords of four neighbouring manors, who present alternately. The church is dedicated to St. Andrew.

ALDERTON, a parish forming a detached portion of the hundred of CHIPPENHAM, county of WILTS, 7½ miles (S. W. by W.) from Malmesbury, containing 176 inhabitants. The living is a perpetual curacy, annexed to the vicarage of Sherston Magna, in the archdeaconry and diocese of Salisbury. The church is dedicated to St. Giles.

ALDERWASLEY, a chapelry in that part of the parish of WIRKSWORTH which is in the hundred of APPLETREE, county of DERBY, 2¼ miles (E. by S.) from Wirksworth, containing 454 inhabitants. The chapel belongs to F. Hurst, Esq., who appoints his own chaplain. There are iron-works and furnaces for smelting leadore in the neighbourhood.

ALDFIELD, a chapelry in that part of the parish of RIPON which is in the lower division of the wapentake of CLARO, West riding of the county of YORK, 3½ miles (W. by S.) from Ripon, containing 133 inhabitants. The living is a perpetual curacy, within the jurisdiction of the peculiar court of Ripon, endowed with £200 private benefaction, and £600 royal bounty, and in the patronage of Mrs. Lawrence. This village is resorted to on account of its mineral springs, the water of which possesses a sulphureous impregnation: the neighbourhood abounds with beautiful and romantic scenery.

ALDFORD, a parish comprising the townships of Aldford and Churton, in the higher division, and the chapelry of Churton Heath, or Bruera, and the townships of Great Boughton, Buerton, and Edgerley, in the lower division, of the hundred of BROXTON, county palatine of CHESTER, and containing 1684 inhabitants, of which number, 491 are in the township of Aldford, 5½ miles (S. by E.) from Chester. The living is a rectory, in the archdeaconry and diocese of Chester, rated in the king's books at £16. 17. 8½., and in the patronage of Earl Grosvenor. The church is dedicated to St. John the Baptist. This place derives its name from an old ford on the river Dee, which bounds it on the west, and is crossed by a good bridge: it had anciently a market and a fair. A castle was erected in the reign of Henry II., the earthworks of which only remain, nearly adjoining the church: during the siege of Chester, a garrison was placed here by Sir W. Brereton. Courts leet and baron are held for the manor, and are attended by the freeholders of Thornton and Alton, who have distinct juries. Here is a free grammar school, with an endowment of £200 per annum; and a school for boys and girls is supported by contributions among the inhabitants, the school-house having been erected at the expense of Earl Grosvenor. There are also six almshouses for widows, endowed with £22 per annum. Vestiges of a Roman road, connecting the northern and southern Watling-streets, are still visible.

ALDHAM, a parish in the Witham division of the hundred of LEXDEN, county of ESSEX, 4½ miles (E. N. E.) from Great Coggeshall, containing 435 inhabitants. The living is a rectory, in the archdeaconry of Colchester, and diocese of London, rated in the king's books at £12, and in the patronage of the Bishop of London.

ALDHAM, a parish in the hundred of COSFORD, county of SUFFOLK, 2 miles (N. N. E.) from Hadleigh, containing 292 inhabitants. The living is a rectory, in the archdeaconry of Sudbury, and diocese of Norwich, rated in the king's books at £10. 13. 4., and in the patronage of Thomas Barrett Lennard, Esq. The church is dedicated to St. Mary.

ALDINGBOURN, a parish in the hundred of Box and STOCKBRIDGE, rape of CHICHESTER, county of SUSSEX, 4¼ miles (E. by N.) from Chichester, containing, with the hamlets of Lidsey and Westergate, 855 inhabitants. The living is a vicarage, in the archdeaconry and diocese of Chichester, rated in the king's books at £5. 10. 5., and in the patronage of the Dean of Chichester. The church is dedicated to St. Mary.

ALDINGHAM, a parish in the hundred of LONSDALE, north of the sands, county palatine of LANCASTER, 5¾ miles (S.) from Ulverstone, comprising the townships of Upper Aldingham, Lower Aldingham, Glaston, and Leece, and containing 760 inhabitants. The living is a rectory, in the archdeaconry of Richmond, and diocese of Chester, rated in the king's books at £39. 19. 2., and in the patronage of the Crown. The church is dedicated to St. Cuthbert. The sea has encroached upon a considerable part of the parish, in consequence of which the church, said to have been formerly in the centre of it, is now within the reach of a high tide. In the vicinity is an elevated promontory, commanding extensive views into Westmorland and Yorkshire, and surrounded by a moat, which is supposed to have been used as a "look-out," during the incursions of the Picts and Scots.

ALDINGTON, a parish partly in the liberty of ROMNEY-MARSH, but chiefly in the franchise and barony of BIRCHOLT, lathe of SHEPWAY, county of KENT, 5½ miles (W. by N.) from Hythe, containing 735 inhabitants. The living is a rectory, with the perpetual curacy of Smeeth annexed, in the peculiar jurisdiction and patronage of the Archbishop of Canterbury, rated in the king's books at £38. 6. 8. The church, dedicated to St. Martin, displays the early style of English architecture in its general structure; but, among later additions, there is a finely ornamented window of five lights.

ALDINGTON, a hamlet in the parish of BADSEY, upper division of the hundred of BLACKENHURST, county of WORCESTER, 2 miles (E.) from Evesham, containing 87 inhabitants.

ALDRIDGE, a parish in the southern division of the hundred of OFFLOW, county of STAFFORD, 3 miles (E. N. E.) from Walsall, containing, with the chapelry of Great Barr, and the liberty of Bentley, 1682 inhabitants. The living is a vicarage, in the archdeaconry of Stafford, and diocese of Lichfield and Coventry, rated in the king's books at £8. 1. 3., and in the patronage of Sir E. D. Scott, Bart. The church is dedicated to St. Mary. The neighbourhood affords a kind of clay well adapted for the manufacture of the finest sort of pottery, tiles, &c. Here is an extensive distillery; and the trade of the district is greatly facilitated by the Wyrley and Essington Extension canal, which passes through the parish. A court leet is held once in two years. There are two free schools, one with an endowment of about £110 per annum, founded in 1718, by the Rev. John Jordan, in which from thirty to forty scholars are educated; and the other, for the education of eight poor girls, endowed with £12 per annum. A National school for girls, established in 1827, is supported by subscription. The remains of a Roman encampment are visible in the parish.

ALDRINGHAM, a parish in the hundred of BLYTHING, county of SUFFOLK, 2½ miles (N. by W.) from Aldborough, containing, with the hamlet of Thorpe, 315 inhabitants. The living is a perpetual curacy, in the archdeaconry of Suffolk, and diocese of Norwich, endowed with £1000 royal bounty, and in the patronage of Lord Huntingfield. The church is dedicated to St. Andrew. There is a place of worship for Particular Baptists. A market was formerly held here, which has fallen into disuse: there is a small fair on St. Andrew's day.

ALDSTONE, county of CUMBERLAND. — See ALSTON.

ALDSWORTH, a parish in the hundred of BRIGHTWELL'S BARROW, county of GLOUCESTER, 3½ miles (S. E.) from North Leach, containing 347 inhabitants. The living is a perpetual curacy, in the peculiar jurisdiction of the Vicar of Bibury, concurrently with the Consistorial Court of the Bishop of Gloucester, endowed with £200 private benefaction, and £200 royal bounty, and in the patronage of the Dean and Canons of Christ-Church, Oxford. The church is dedicated to St. Peter.

ALDWARD, a township in the parish of ECCLESFIELD, northern division of the wapentake of STRAFFORTH and TICKHILL, West riding of the county of YORK, 2½ miles (N. E.) from Rotherham, containing 35 inhabitants.

ALDWARK, a township in that part of the parish of BRADBORNE which is in the hundred of WIRKSWORTH, county of DERBY, 5¾ miles (N. W. by W.) from Wirksworth, containing 92 inhabitants. This township is in the honour of Tutbury, duchy of Lancaster, and within the jurisdiction of a court of pleas held at Tutbury every third Tuesday, for the recovery of debts under 40*s*.

ALDWINKLE (ALL SAINTS), a parish in the hundred of HUXLOE, county of NORTHAMPTON, 4 miles (N.) from Thrapston, containing 240 inhabitants. The living is a rectory, in the archdeaconry of Northampton, and diocese of Peterborough, rated in the king's books at £12. 4. 2., and in the patronage of the Rev. R. Roberts, D.D. The church is remarkable for its beautiful tower; it has some windows in the decorated style of English architecture, and a small ornamented chapel adjoining the southern side of the chancel. Richard Thorpe, in 1671, bequeathed land, now producing £16 a year, for the support of a free school for this and the adjoining parish of St. Peter. The river Nene flows through the parish, in which there is a chalybeate spring. The poet Dryden was born at the parsonage-house, in 1631.

ALDWINKLE (ST. PETER'S), a parish in the hundred of HUXLOE, county of NORTHAMPTON, 3¾ miles (N. by E.) from Thrapston, containing 166 inhabitants. The living is a rectory, in the archdeaconry of Northampton, and diocese of Peterborough, rated in the king's books at £11. 6. 3., and in the patronage of Lord Lilford. There is a place of worship for Particular Baptists. The river Nene, which is navigable to the North sea, and communicates with the Northampton canal, flows through this parish, on the border of which are the remains of a singular cruciform building, called Liveden, erected by the Tresham family, and richly decorated with sculpture, especially round the cornice, which exhibits a Roman Catholic legend and a variety of religious symbols. Dr. Thomas Fuller, author of "The History of the Worthies of England," and other learned works, was born in this parish.

ALDWORK, a township in the parish of ALNE, partly in the liberty of ST. PETER of YORK, East riding, and partly in the wapentake of BULMER, North riding, of the county of YORK, 6½ miles (E. S. E.) from Aldborough, containing 163 inhabitants. The navigable river Ure runs through the township.

ALDWORTH, a parish in the hundred of COMPTON, county of BERKS, 4½ miles (E. by S.) from East Ilsley, containing 293 inhabitants. The living is a vicarage, in the archdeaconry of Berks, and diocese of Salisbury, rated in the king's books at £8. 16. 0½., and in the patronage of the Master and Fellows of St. John's College, Cambridge. The church, dedicated to St. Mary, is an ancient structure, containing nine monuments, elegantly sculptured, supposed to represent different members of the De la Beche family, and to have been executed in the fourteenth century: the tombs are disposed under enriched arches; six of the effigies are habited as knights in armour, the seventh is in ordinary attire, and the remaining two are those of females. Aldworth is thought by Hearne to have been a Roman settlement.

ALEMOUTH, or ALNMOUTH, a sea-port and township in that part of the parish of LESBURY which is in the southern division of BAMBROUGH ward, county of NORTHUMBERLAND, 5¼ miles (E.S.E.) from Alnwick, containing 406 inhabitants. The village is situated on a tongue of land formed by the sea and the mouth of the river Alne, whence its name. The port is subordinate to that of Berwick: about ten vessels, of from fifty to one hundred and fifty tons' burden, belong to it, which are chiefly employed in conveying goods to and from London. Corn, eggs, pork, &c., are sent to London, and wool to the manufacturing districts of Yorkshire, but the trade is not so extensive as formerly. Ship-building was carried on some years ago, but that also has declined. Alnmouth is partially resorted to, during the summer, for sea-bathing. A place of worship for Wesleyan Methodists was erected in 1826. On a small island, at the mouth of the river, was a chapel, dedicated to St. John the Baptist, the remains of which were blown down in 1806: at the time of its erection the site formed part of the main land, from which it was separated by the encroachments of the sea, and a change in the course of the river.

ALETHORPE, a hamlet in the parish of FAKENHAM, hundred of GALLOW, county of NORFOLK, 2 miles (N.E. by E.) from Fakenham, containing 9 inhabitants.

ALFOLD, a parish in the first division of the hundred of BLACKHEATH, county of SURREY, 8½ miles (S.E. by S.) from Godalming, containing 470 inhabitants. The living is a rectory, in the archdeaconry of Surrey, and diocese of Winchester, rated in the king's books at £6. 11. 2., and in the patronage of the Rev. L. W. Elliot. The Arun and Wey junction canal passes through this parish.

ALFORD, a market town and parish in the Wold division of the hundred of CALCEWORTH, parts of LINDSEY, county of LINCOLN, 34 miles (E.) from Lincoln, and 137 (N. by E.) from London, containing 1506 inhabitants. It derives its name from an ancient ford over a stream that twice crosses the town, and consists principally of one street: the houses are in general built of brick and covered with tiles, though occasionally intermixed with some having thatched roofs. A canal from this town to the sea is now in progress, which promises to be productive of great benefit. The market is on Tuesday: the fairs are on Whit-Tuesday and the 8th of November. The living is a discharged vicarage, with the perpetual curacy of Rigsby, in the archdeaconry and diocese of Lincoln, rated in the king's books at £10, and in the patronage of the Bishop of Lincoln. The church, dedicated to St. Wilfrid, is a stone edifice repaired with brick, and contains many ancient monuments. There are places of worship for Independents and Wesleyan Methodists. A court of requests, for sums not exceeding £5, is held once a month, under an act passed in the 47th of George III., the jurisdiction of which extends over several other towns in the county. The free grammar school was founded and endowed by Mr. Francis Spanning, in 1565; its revenue, which was but small, has been considerably augmented by subsequent benefactions. By a charter obtained in 1576, it was made a royal foundation, and the management vested in governors, who are a body corporate, and have a common seal. There are two quinquennial fellowships at Magdalene College, Cambridge, for its scholars, and a scholarship of £6. 8. 6. per annum at Jesus' College, Cambridge, for students from Alford, Caistor, or Louth schools. The National school, in which one hundred and thirty children of both sexes are instructed, was founded by Mr. John Spenluffe, who endowed it with an estate now producing £70 per annum. Almshouses for six people were erected and endowed by Sir Robert Christopher, Knt., in 1668; the endowment was subsequently augmented by Lord Harborough, in 1716. Alford confers the title of viscount on the family of Brownlow.

ALFORD, a parish in the hundred of CATSASH, county of SOMERSET, 1¾ mile (W. by N.) from Castle-Cary, containing 136 inhabitants. The living is a rectory, in the archdeaconry of Wells, and diocese of Bath and Wells, rated in the king's books at £9. 9. 9., and in the patronage of John Thring, Esq. The church is dedicated to All Saints. At a farm-house called Alford Well, about three quarters of a mile from the church, there is a saline chalybeate spring, now disused, but formerly in great repute for the cure of scorbutic complaints and jaundice.

ALFRETON, a market town and parish in the hundred of SCARSDALE, county of DERBY, 14 miles (N.N.E.) from Derby, and 140 (N.N.W.) from London, containing, with Alfreton-Outseats, 4689 inhabitants. This place, in King Ethelred's charter to Burton abbey, is called *Alfredingtune*, and is supposed to have derived its name from some Anglo-Saxon proprietor. It stands on the brow of a hill, and consists of two streets, intersecting each other at right angles in the market-place: the houses are irregularly built, some of them exhibiting specimens of ancient architecture. The only branches of manufacture are those of stockings and brown pottery ware. The Erewash canal passes through the parish. The market is on Friday: fairs are held on July 30th and November 22nd; the latter is also a statute fair. Constables and other officers are appointed at the court leet of the lord of the manor. The living is a discharged rectory, in the archdeaconry of Derby, and diocese of Lichfield and Coventry, rated in the king's books at £17. 8. 9., endowed with £200 private benefaction, and £200 royal bounty, and in the patronage of Mr. and Mrs. Morewood. The church, dedicated to St. Martin, appears to have been constructed at different periods, part of it prior to the reign of Henry II. There is a place of worship for Wesleyan Methodists. A free school was founded by Mrs. Eliza Turner, in 1740, and endowed with forty acres of land at Swanwick, a hamlet in this parish, for the instruction of twelve boys and eight girls of Swanwick and Greenhill-lane, in reading, writing, and arithmetic; there are now forty children in the school; the house and farm are occupied by the schoolmaster.

ALFRICK, a chapelry in the parish of SUCKLEY, upper division of the hundred of DODDINGTREE, county of WORCESTER, 7 miles (W. by S.) from Worcester, containing 445 inhabitants. The chapel is dedicated to St. Mary. Here is a free school, with an endowment of £10 per annum.

ALFRISTON, a parish in the hundred of ALCISTON, rape of PEVENSEY, county of SUSSEX, 3½ miles (N. E.) from Seaford, containing 648 inhabitants. The living is a discharged vicarage, in the archdeaconry of Lewes, and diocese of Chichester, rated in the king's books at £11. 16. 0½., and in the patronage of the Crown. The church, dedicated to St. Andrew, exhibits a mixture of the decorated and later styles of English architecture. On the neighbouring downs are several barrows, in some of which, urns, knives, spear-heads, and other articles, have been dug up. numerous wheat-ears are caught upon them in the month of August.

ALGARKIRK, a parish in the wapentake of KIRTON, parts of HOLLAND, county of LINCOLN, 7¾ miles (N. W. by N.) from Holbeach, containing 602 inhabitants. The living is a rectory, with the perpetual curacy of Fosdike, in the archdeaconry and diocese of Lincoln, rated in the king's books at £50. 18. 1½., and in the patronage of the Trustees of the Rev. B. Beridge. The church is dedicated to St. Peter and St. Paul: the burial-ground contains a stone statue, said to be that of Earl Algar, who, aided by his seneschals Wibert and Leofric, obtained a victory over the Danes near this place, in 870, but was defeated and slain the next day.

ALHAMPTON, a tything in the parish of DITCHEAT, hundred of WHITESTONE, county of SOMERSET, 2¾ miles (N. W. by N.) from Castle-Cary. The population is returned with the parish. There was formerly a chapel at this place.

ALKERTON, a tything in the parish of EASTINGTON, lower division of the hundred of WHITSTONE, county of GLOUCESTER, 3 miles (W.) from Stroud, containing 963 inhabitants.

ALKERTON, a parish in the hundred of BLOXHAM, county of OXFORD, 6 miles (W. N. W.) from Banbury, containing 158 inhabitants. The living is a rectory, in the archdeaconry and diocese of Oxford, rated in the king's books at £6. 3. 9., and in the patronage of the Rev. J. C. Townsend. The church is dedicated to St. Michael. Thomas Lydiat, the learned mathematician and chronologer, was born here, in 1572.

ALKHAM, a parish in the hundred of FOLKESTONE, lathe of SHEPWAY, county of KENT, 4 miles (W. by N.) from Dovor, containing 509 inhabitants. The living is a vicarage, with the perpetual curacy of Capel le Ferne annexed, in the archdeaconry and diocese of Canterbury, rated in the king's books at £11, and in the patronage of the Archbishop of Canterbury. The church, dedicated to St. Anthony, is partly Norman, and partly in the early style of English architecture. According to Domesday-book a church existed here in the time of Edward the Confessor.

ALKINGTON, a tything in the parish and upper division of the hundred of BERKELEY, county of GLOUCESTER, 1¼ mile (S. E.) from Berkeley, containing 1101 inhabitants.

ALKINGTON, a township in that part of the parish of WHITCHURCH which is in the Whitchurch division of the hundred of BRADFORD (North), county of SALOP, 2 miles (S. by W.) from Whitchurch, with which the population is returned.

ALKMONTON, a township in the parish of LONGFORD, hundred of APPLETREE, county of DERBY, 5¾ miles (S. by E.) from Ashbourn, containing 81 inhabitants. There was anciently an hospital, dedicated to St. Leonard, between this place and Hungry-Bentley, in the same parish, to which Walter Blount, Lord Mountjoy, was a benefactor, in 1474.

ALKRINGTON, a township in the parish of OLDHAM *cum* PRESTWICH, hundred of SALFORD, county palatine of LANCASTER, 4½ miles (N. N. E.) from Manchester, containing 365 inhabitants.

ALLARTHORP, a joint township with Swainby, in that part of the parish of PICKHILL which is in the wapentake of HALLIKELD, North riding of the county of YORK, 5 miles (E. by S.) from Bedale. The population is returned with Swainby.

ALLCANNINGS, a parish in the hundred of SWANBOROUGH, county of WILTS, 5¼ miles (E.) from Devizes, containing, with the tythings of Allington and Fullaway, 749 inhabitants The living is a rectory, with the perpetual curacy of Lea annexed, in the archdeaconry of Wilts, and diocese of Salisbury, rated in the king's books at £31. 16. 10½., and in the patronage of Paul Methuen, Esq. The church is dedicated to St. Anne. Here is a free school, endowed with £25 per annum.

ALLEN (ST.), a parish in the western division of the hundred of POWDER, county of CORNWALL, 4 miles (N. by W.) from Truro, containing 471 inhabitants. The living is a vicarage, in the archdeaconry of Cornwall, and diocese of Exeter, rated in the king's books at £8. 13. 4., and in the patronage of the Bishop of Exeter. The church is dedicated to St. Alleyn.

ALLENDALE, a parish in the southern division of TINDALE ward, county of NORTHUMBERLAND, 9¾ miles (S. W. by W.) from Hexham, and 286 (N. N. W.) from London, comprising the market town of Allendale, and the townships of West Allendale, Broadside, Cotton, Keenty, and Forest, and containing 4629 inhabitants. The town is irregularly built on an acclivity gradually rising from the eastern bank of the river Allen, from which it derives its name, and is supplied with water from springs, which abound in the neighbourhood: a bridge was erected over this river in 1825, and in the same year a subscription library was established. The inhabitants are chiefly employed in the lead mines, which are very extensive, producing upwards of two thousand five hundred tons annually: there are several walks for grinding and washing the ore, and some smelting-houses, in one of which, twenty-one tons pass through the furnace weekly, from which a considerable quantity of silver is separated. An act for making a new line of road through this parish, from Wardle, in the county of Durham, to Alston-Moor, in Cumberland, was obtained in 1826. The market is on Friday; and the fairs are held on the last Friday in April, the 22nd of August, and the first Friday after the 29th of October, for horses, cattle, and sheep: in the market-place are the ruins of a cross. The living is a perpetual curacy, in the peculiar jurisdiction of the Archbishop of York, endowed with £200 private benefaction, £200 royal bounty, and £200 parliamentary grant, and in the patronage of Col. and Mrs. Beaumont. The church is a neat edifice of stone, rebuilt in 1807.

Within the parish also are four chapels of ease, *viz.*, St. Peter's, rebuilt in 1825; the chapel at Nine-Banks, partially rebuilt about 1816; the chapel at the Carr Shield, built in 1822; and that of Allenheads, rebuilt in 1826. There are places of worship for the Society of Friends and Wesleyan Methodists. A free grammar school was founded and endowed, in 1693, by Mr. Christopher Wilkinson and others; the master's salary is about £60 per annum. There are also various other schools connected with the different places of worship in the parish. At a place called Old Town, about three miles to the north-west, are vestiges of an ancient intrenchment, of a square form, supposed to be Roman.

ALLENHEAD, or ALLONHEAD, a hamlet (formerly a distinct parish) in the parish of ALLENDALE, southern division of TINDALE ward, county of NORTHUMBERLAND, 14 miles (S. S.W.) from Hexham. The living was a vicarage, rated in the king's books at £4. 8. 1½., which has been consolidated with the perpetual curacy of St. Peter's, Allendale. Here is a domestic chapel, rebuilt by Col. Beaumont, in 1826, on the site of one erected in 1701: near it is a good house for the minister. There are several coal mines and veins of lead-ore in the neighbourhood, which are worked to a considerable extent.

ALLENSMORE, a parish in the hundred of WEBTREE, county of HEREFORD, 4 miles (S.W.) from Hereford, containing 513 inhabitants. The living is a discharged vicarage, annexed to that of Clehonger, in the peculiar jurisdiction of the Dean of Hereford, rated in the king's books at £5. 12. 6., and endowed with £400 royal bounty. The church is dedicated to St. Andrew.

ALLENTON, or ALLWINTON, a parish in the western division of COQUETDALE ward, county of NORTHUMBERLAND, comprising the townships of Allenton, Biddleston, Borrowdon, Clennell, Fairhaugh, Farnham, Linbriggs, Netherton (North side), Netherton (South side), Peals, and Sharperton, and containing 900 inhabitants, of which number, 106 are in the township of Allenton, 19 miles (W. by S.) from Alnwick. The living is a perpetual curacy, with that of Hallystone, in the archdeaconry of Northumberland, and diocese of Durham, endowed with £400 private benefaction, and £600 royal bounty, and in the patronage of the Bishop of Durham. The church is dedicated to St. Michael. The river Coquet pursues a winding course through this parish, and joins the Alwine, from which latter the name of Allwinton is derived. A free school, in which twenty-six children are instructed, is endowed with about £28 per annum, arising from a donation of £350 by Mr. John Dixon, and some minor benefactions. Here was formerly an hospital, belonging to the convent at Hallystone. On the south side of the Coquet are vestiges of an ancient structure, called Barrow Peel, to the west of which is Ridlee Cairn hill, supposed to have been burial-places of the ancient Britons.

ALLER, a parish in the hundred of SOMERTON, county of SOMERSET, 6¼ miles (W.) from Somerton, containing 454 inhabitants. The living is a rectory, in the archdeaconry of Wells, and diocese of Bath and Wells, rated in the king's books at £36. 15., and in the patronage of the Master and Fellows of Emanuel College, Cambridge. The church is dedicated to St. Andrew. At this place, Guthrum, the Danish chief, received baptism, under the sponsorship of Alfred the Great, after the famous victory obtained by that monarch over the Danes at *Ethandune*. Aller Moor was the scene of a battle between the royalists and the parliamentarians, in 1645. Dr. Ralph Cudworth, author of "The Intellectual System of the Universe," was born here, in 1617.

ALLERBY, or ALWARDBY, a joint township with Outerside, in the parish of ASPATRIA, ALLERDALE ward below Darwent, county of CUMBERLAND, 7 miles (N. N. W.) from Cockermouth. The population is returned with Outerside.

ALLERSTON, a parish in PICKERING lythe, North riding of the county of YORK, 4¾ miles (E. by S.) from Pickering, containing 401 inhabitants. The living is a perpetual curacy, united to the vicarage of Ebberston, in the peculiar jurisdiction of the Dean of York.

ALLERTHORPE, a parish partly in the liberty of ST. PETER of YORK, but chiefly in the Wilton-Beacon division of the wapentake of HARTHILL, East riding of the county of YORK, comprising the townships of Allerthorpe and Waplington, and containing 151 inhabitants, of which number, 132 are in the township of Allerthorpe, 1½ mile (S.W. by W.) from Pocklington. The living is a perpetual curacy, with the vicarage of Thornton annexed, in the peculiar jurisdiction and patronage of the Dean of York.

ALLERTON, a township in the parish of CHILDWALL, hundred of WEST DERBY, county palatine of LANCASTER, 5¼ miles (S.E.) from Liverpool, containing 328 inhabitants. Adjoining the farm on which stands the famous Allerton Oak there is a supposed Druidical monument, called Calder Stones, in digging around which, about sixty years ago, urns of the coarsest clay, containing human bones, were found.

ALLERTON, a township in the parish of BRADFORD, wapentake of MORLEY, West riding of the county of YORK, 4 miles (W. N. W.) from Bradford, containing 1488 inhabitants.

ALLERTON (CHAPEL), a parish in the hundred of BEMPSTONE, county of SOMERSET, 4¼ miles (S. W. by S.) from Axbridge, containing 335 inhabitants. The living is a discharged rectory, in the peculiar jurisdiction and patronage of the Dean of Wells, rated in the king's books at £10. 8. 4.

ALLERTON (CHAPEL), a chapelry in the parish of ST. PETER, within the liberty of the town of LEEDS, West riding of the county of YORK, 2½ miles (N. by E.) from Leeds, containing 1678 inhabitants. The living is a perpetual curacy, in the archdeaconry and diocese of York, endowed with £400 private benefaction, and £600 royal bounty, and in the patronage of the Vicar of Leeds. Robert Parker, of Browsholme, founded here an hospital for ten poor widows, and endowed it with £50 per annum.

ALLERTON-BYWATER, a township in the parish of KIPPAX, lower division of the wapentake of SKYRACK, West riding of the county of YORK, 4¾ miles (N. W.) from Pontefract, containing 329 inhabitants.

ALLERTON-MAULEVERER, a parish in the upper division of the wapentake of CLARO, West riding of the county of YORK, 5¾ miles (E. by N.) from Knaresborough, comprising the townships of Allerton-Mauleverer with Hopperton, and Clareton, and containing 290 inhabitants, of which number, 276 are in the township of Allerton-Mauleverer with Hopperton. The living is a perpetual curacy, in the archdeaconry of Richmond, and diocese of Chester, and in the patronage of Lord Stourton. The church is dedicated to St. Martin. This place obtained its distinguishing name from a family, one of whom, Richard Mauleverer, in the reign of Henry II., founded here an Alien priory of Benedictine monks, the revenue of which was given by Henry VI. to King's College, Cambridge.

ALLERTON (NORTH), a parish in the wapentake of ALLERTONSHIRE, North riding of the county of YORK, comprising the borough and market town of North Allerton, the chapelries of Brompton, Deighton, and High Worsall, and the township of Romanby, and containing 4431 inhabitants, of which number, 2626 are in the town of North Allerton, 32 miles (N. W. by N.) from York, and 224 (N. N. W.) from London. This place, supposed to have been a Roman station, and subsequently a Saxon borough, is in Domesday-book called *Alvestune* and *Alreton*, the prefix having been applied to distinguish it from Allerton-Mauleverer. It was greatly injured, if not destroyed, by Beornredus, or Earnredus, who, in 769, having invaded the kingdom of Northumberland, with a view to usurp the throne, burnt the town of Catterick, about eight miles distant. William Rufus gave the town, with the lands adjacent, to the see of Durham, and, under the patronage of the bishops, it grew into importance, and became an episcopal residence. At Cowton Moor, about three miles from the town, and within the parish, the celebrated battle of the Standard was fought, in 1138, between the English and the Scots, in which the latter were defeated, with the loss of eleven thousand men: the spot on which the standard was erected is still called Standard Hill, and the holes into which the dead were thrown, the Scots' Pits. About 1174, Henry II. ordered the demolition of the episcopal palace, supposed to have been built by Geoffrey, Bishop of Durham, and which had been strongly fortified by Bishop Pudsey; traces of the foundation are still visible on the western side of the town. In 1318, the Scots plundered and burnt the town. During the civil war, Charles I., in one of his journies to Scotland, lodged here in an old mansion, called the Porch-house; and in the rebellion of 1745, the English army, under the Duke of Cumberland, encamped on the Castle hills. The town is pleasantly situated in a valley, and consists chiefly of one spacious street, half a mile in length, partially paved, and containing some good houses. It has long given name to a district called Allertonshire, now constituting the wapentake. The principal branches of manufacture are those of linen and leather: the market is on Wednesday, and fairs are held on February 14th, September 5th and 6th, October 3rd and 4th, and the second Wednesday in the latter month. The borough first exercised the elective franchise in the 26th of Edward I., but made no subsequent return till 1640, since which time it has regularly sent two members to parliament: the right of election is vested in the proprietors of ancient burgage houses, about two hundred in number. The bailiff, who is appointed by letters patent from the Bishop of Durham, is the returning officer. The general quarter sessions for the North riding are held here, in the weeks after Christmas and Easter, and on the 11th of July and the 18th of October; and there is a weekly meeting of the county magistrates. The sessions-house is an elegant building, erected about 1790, annexed to which is a house of correction, on the plan of Mr. Howard, containing thirty cells. Westward from the sessions-house is the registrar's office for the North riding, where the Bishop of Durham holds his courts.

The living is a vicarage, in the peculiar jurisdiction and patronage of the Dean and Chapter of Durham, rated in the king's books at £17. The church, dedicated to All Saints, is supposed to have been built soon after the destruction of the town by the Scots, in 1318: it is a spacious cruciform structure, in the decorated style of English architecture, with a square tower rising from the centre, and adorned with pinnacles at the angles. There are places of worship for Independents and Wesleyan Methodists. The free grammar (now the parochial) school is of royal foundation, but the date thereof is uncertain: it has a small endowment, and an interest in five scholarships, founded by Bishop Cosins, at Peter House, Cambridge, in failure of applicants from the school at Durham; it has also a contingent interest in twelve exhibitions to Lincoln College, Oxford, founded by Lord Crewe: the school-house was rebuilt in 1777. Dr. William Palliser, Archbishop of Cashel; Dr. George Hickes, Dean of Worcester, and author of a Dictionary of the Northern Languages; Dr. Thomas Burnet, master of the Charter-house, London; Mr. Rymer, editor of the Fœdera; Dr. Radcliffe; and the Rev. John Kettlewell, were educated here. A National school for boys and girls, and a Sunday school, established in 1787, are supported by subscription. An hospital, or *Maison de Dieu*, was founded in 1476, by Richard de Moore, a draper in this town, for thirteen poor people; it has been rebuilt at the expense of the inhabitants, but the number of inmates is reduced to six. The Rev. John Kettlewell, of St. Andrew's, Holborn, London, bequeathed, in 1694, an estate in the township of Brompton, called Low Moor Farm, the proceeds of which are divided among the poor of North Allerton and Brompton. There are some remains of a monastery of Carmelites, founded by Thomas Hatfield, Bishop of Durham; and the site of St. James' hospital, about a mile from the town, is still visible. There are also vestiges of a military road leading from Aldby, the *Derventio* of the Romans, through this town to Catterick. North Allerton, in the reign of Anne, gave the title of viscount to the Elector of Hanover, afterwards George I. Edmund Guest, Bishop of Salisbury, almoner to Queen Elizabeth, was born in this town.

ALLESLEY, a parish in the Kirby division of the hundred of KNIGHTLOW, county of WARWICK, 2½ miles (N. W. by W.) from Coventry, containing 844 inhabitants. The living is a rectory, in the archdeaconry of Coventry, and diocese of Lichfield and Coventry, rated in the king's books at £17. 18. 9., and in the patronage of the Rev. William Bree. The church is dedicated to All Saints. There is a free school, towards the support of which Mrs. Flint, in 1705, gave by deed a small portion of land, and a house for the residence of the master. Vestiges of an ancient castle are discernible in the parish.

ALLESTREY, a parish in the hundred of MORLESTON and LITCHURCH, county of DERBY, 2 miles (N.)

from Derby, containing 361 inhabitants. The living is a perpetual curacy, in the archdeaconry of Derby, and diocese of Lichfield and Coventry, and in the patronage of J. Mundy, Esq. The church, dedicated to St. Andrew, is an ancient structure with a tower, containing several monuments of the Mundy family. There is a place of worship for Wesleyan Methodists. Allestrey forms part of the duchy of Lancaster, and is within the jurisdiction of a court of pleas held at Tutbury every third Tuesday, for the recovery of debts under 40*s*.

ALLEXTON, a parish in the eastern division of the hundred of GOSCOTE, county of LEICESTER, 4 miles (W. by N.) from Uppingham, containing 74 inhabitants. The living is a rectory, in the archdeaconry of Leicester, and diocese of Lincoln, rated in the king's books at £6. 18. 4., and in the patronage of Col. Wilson. The church is dedicated to St. Peter. The Union canal to Derby crosses the river Soar at this place.

ALLHALLOWS, a parish in ALLERDALE ward below Darwent, county of CUMBERLAND, 6¾ miles (S. W. by S.) from Wigton, containing 219 inhabitants. The living is a perpetual curacy, in the archdeaconry and diocese of Carlisle, endowed with £200 private benefaction, £400 royal bounty, and £200 parliamentary grant, and in the patronage of the Bishop of Carlisle. This was anciently a chapelry in the parish of Aspatria: it is bounded on the south by the river Ellen. Here are quarries of freestone and limestone, and a vein of coal of inferior quality. A little southward of Whitehall is an intrenchment, twenty-eight yards square, surrounded by a ditch.

ALLHALLOWS, a parish in the hundred of HOO, lathe of AYLESFORD, county of KENT, 9 miles (N. E.) from Rochester, containing 259 inhabitants. The living is a discharged vicarage, in the archdeaconry and diocese of Rochester, rated in the king's books at £8. 7. 11., endowed with £400 private benefaction, and £400 royal bounty, and in the patronage of the Dean and Chapter of Rochester. The church is dedicated to St. Mary. The river Thames bounds this parish on the north.

ALLINGTON, a parish in the hundred of GODDERTHORNE, Bridport division of the county of DORSET, ¾ of a mile (N. W.) from Bridport, containing 1139 inhabitants. The living is a perpetual curacy, in the archdeaconry of Dorset, and diocese of Bristol, endowed with £1200 parliamentary grant, and in the patronage of the Rev. H. Fox. The church, dedicated to St. Swithin, has been lately rebuilt, and enlarged by an addition of six hundred sittings, of which two-thirds are free, the Incorporated Society for the enlargement of churches and chapels having granted £400 towards defraying the expense. There is no burial-ground; the inhabitants inter their dead at Bridport, to which this was formerly a chapelry. Great quantities of hemp and flax are sown in the vicinity: a fair, chiefly for cheese and pedlary, is held on July 22nd. Two closes of land, containing thirty acres, are vested in trustees for the benefit of the poor in the almshouses of this parish and Charmouth. An hospital for lepers, dedicated to St. Mary Magdalene, was founded here, which at the dissolution, in 1553, was valued at £7. 8. 4.

ALLINGTON, a parish in the hundred of LARKFIELD, lathe of AYLESFORD, county of KENT, 1¾ mile (N. N. W.) from Maidstone, containing 45 inhabitants. The living is a discharged rectory, in the archdeaconry and diocese of Rochester, rated in the king's books at £6. 16. 8., endowed with £200 private benefaction, and £200 royal bounty, and in the patronage of the Earl of Romney. The church is dedicated to St. Lawrence. Allington stands on the western side of the Medway, opposite Aylesford, and was formerly a market town. Sir Thomas Wyatt, a distinguished poet in the reign of Henry VIII., was born at Allington castle, the remains of which have been converted into a farm-house.

ALLINGTON, a parish in the hundred of AMESBURY, county of WILTS, 3½ miles (E. S. E.) from Amesbury, containing 64 inhabitants. The living is a rectory, in the archdeaconry and diocese of Salisbury, rated in the king's books at £14. 13. 4., and in the patronage of the Earl of Craven. Here is a free school with a small endowment.

ALLINGTON, a tything in the parish and hundred of CHIPPENHAM, county of WILTS, 2½ miles (N. W. by W.) from Chippenham, containing 110 inhabitants.

ALLINGTON, a tything in the parish of ALLCANNINGS, hundred of SWANBOROUGH, county of WILTS, 4 miles (E. N. E.) from Devizes, containing 132 inhabitants.

ALLINGTON (EAST), a parish in the hundred of STANBOROUGH, county of DEVON, 3½ miles (N.E. by N.) from Kingsbridge, containing 615 inhabitants. The living is a rectory, in the archdeaconry of Totness, and diocese of Exeter, rated in the king's books at £32. 2. 1., and in the patronage of William Fortescue, Esq. The church, dedicated to St. Andrew, contains a wooden screen, which, with the pulpit, is much enriched with carved work.

ALLINGTON (EAST), a chapelry in the parish of SEDGEBROOK, wapentake of WINNIBRIGGS and THREO, parts of KESTEVEN, county of LINCOLN. The population is returned with the parish.

ALLINGTON (WEST), a parish in the hundred of STANBOROUGH, county of DEVON, 1 mile (W. S.W.) from Kingsbridge, containing 778 inhabitants. The living is a vicarage, with the perpetual curacies of South Huish, Malborough, and South Milton annexed, in the archdeaconry of Totness, and diocese of Exeter, rated in the king's books at £62. 16. 10½., and in the patronage of the Dean and Chapter of Salisbury. The church is dedicated to All Saints. There is a small endowed charity school. Cider of a peculiarly fine quality is made here. Bowringsleigh, an old mansion in the Elizabethan style, is still in good preservation: a more ancient seat, belonging to the family of Bastard, has been converted into a farm-house.

ALLINGTON (WEST), a parish in the wapentake of WINNIBRIGGS and THREO, parts of KESTEVEN, county of LINCOLN, 4½ miles (N.W. by W.) from Grantham, containing 357 inhabitants. The living is a rectory, in the archdeaconry and diocese of Lincoln, rated in the king's books at £3. 13. 11½., and in the patronage of the Crown. The church is dedicated to the Holy Trinity.

ALLITHWAITE (LOWER), a township in the parish of CARTMEL, hundred of LONSDALE, north of the sands, county palatine of LANCASTER, 2 miles (S.) from Cartmel, containing 839 inhabitants.

ALLITHWAITE (UPPER), a township in the parish of CARTMEL, hundred of LONSDALE, north of the sands, county palatine of LANCASTER, 3¼ miles (N. E.) from Cartmel, containing 771 inhabitants.

ALLONBY, a chapelry in that part of the parish of BROMFIELD which is in ALLERDALE ward below Darwent, county of CUMBERLAND, 9 miles (N. N. W.) from Cockermouth, containing 709 inhabitants. The living is a perpetual curacy, in the archdeaconry and diocese of Carlisle, endowed with £400 private benefaction, £600 royal bounty, and £1000 parliamentary grant, and in the patronage of the Vicar of Bromfield. The chapel, dedicated to Christ, was built at the expense of Dr. Thomlinson and some relatives, in 1744. There is a meeting-house for the Society of Friends. The village stands on the coast of Allonby bay, which opens to the Solway Firth and the Irish sea, and is much frequented as a bathing-place, the sands being extremely smooth and firm. It was noted for a herring fishery, but this has failed, owing to the herrings having deserted the neighbouring sea; a few of the inhabitants are, however, still occupied in fishing. A school, in which ten children are instructed gratuitously, was endowed, in 1755, by Mrs. Thomlinson, relict of Dr. Thomlinson, with £100, since laid out in land producing £7. 10. per annum. Six cottages, forming the wings of a dwelling-house erected by Thomas Richardson, Esq., of Stamford Hill, London, a native of this place, are appropriated as rent-free residences to as many poor families. A court baron is held annually. Captain Joseph Huddart, F. R. S., an eminent naval engineer and hydrographer, who died in 1826, was born here, in 1741.

ALLOSTOCK, a township in that part of the parish of GREAT BUDWORTH which is in the hundred of NORTHWICH, county palatine of CHESTER, 5 miles (S. by W.) from Nether Knutsford, containing 461 inhabitants. There is a place of worship for Unitarians.

ALLSTONEFIELD, a parish in the northern division of the hundred of TOTMONSLOW, county of STAFFORD, 7¼ miles (N. N. W.) from Ashbourn, comprising the chapelries of Upper Elkstone, Longnor, Quarnford, and Warslow, and the townships of Lower Elkstone, Fairfield-Head, Heathy-Lee, and Hollinsclough, and containing 5169 inhabitants. The living is a discharged vicarage, with the perpetual curacy of Warslow annexed, in the archdeaconry of Stafford, and diocese of Lichfield and Coventry, rated in the king's books at £8. 11. 4., endowed with £200 private benefaction, and £900 parliamentary grant, and in the patronage of Sir George Crewe, Bart. The church, dedicated to St. Peter, is a large structure in the early style of English architecture, with a tower ornamented with pinnacles and battlements: the pulpit, &c. were presented by Cotton, the poet, who resided here. Allstonefield forms the northern extremity of the county, being bounded by Cheshire and Derbyshire, from which it is separated by the river Dove. It belongs to the duchy of Lancaster, and is within the jurisdiction of a court of pleas held at Tutbury every third Tuesday, for the recovery of debts under 40*s*. Here is a small free school, founded by German Pole, in 1726.

ALLTON, a joint township with Idridgehay, in that part of the parish of WIRKSWORTH which is in the hundred of APPLETREE, county of DERBY, 3½ miles (S.) from Wirksworth. The population is returned with Idridgehay.

ALMELEY, a parish partly in the hundred of WOLPHY, but chiefly in the hundred of STRETFORD, county of HEREFORD, 5¼ miles (W.) from Weobley, containing, with the townships of Hopley's Green and Logaston, 699 inhabitants. The living is a vicarage, in the archdeaconry and diocese of Hereford, rated in the king's books at £6. 17. 11., and in the patronage of the Bishop of Hereford. The church is dedicated to St. Mary: at a short distance from it are two tumuli. The petty sessions for the hundred are occasionally held here.

ALMER, a parish in the hundred of LOOSEBARROW, Shaston (East) division of the county of DORSET, 5¾ miles (S. S. E.) from Blandford-Forum, containing, with the hamlet of Mapperton, 188 inhabitants. The living is a rectory, in the archdeaconry of Dorset, and diocese of Bristol, rated in the king's books at £13. 5. 8., and in the patronage of R. E. D. Grosvenor, Esq. The church, dedicated to St. Mary, is a small edifice, rebuilt by Gen. Erle.

ALMINGTON, a township in that part of the parish of DRAYTON in HALES which is in the northern division of the hundred of PIREHILL, county of STAFFORD, 1½ mile (E. by N.) from Drayton in Hales, containing 260 inhabitants.

ALMINGTON, a joint township with Stone-Delph, in that part of the parish of TAMWORTH which is in the Tamworth division of the hundred of HEMLINGFORD, county of WARWICK, 2¾ miles (E.) from Tamworth, containing, with Stone-Delph, 257 inhabitants.

ALMODINGTON, a hamlet (formerly a parish) in the parish of EARNLEY, hundred of MANHOOD, rape of CHICHESTER, county of SUSSEX, 6 miles (S. W. by S.) from Chichester. The living, a rectory, was consolidated, in 1524, with that of Earnley, with which parish the population is returned. The chapel is demolished.

ALMONDBURY, a parish in the upper division of the wapentake of AGBRIGG, West riding of the county of YORK, comprising the chapelries of South Crossland, Farnley-Tyas, Honley, Linthwaite, Lockwood, and Meltham, a portion of the chapelry of Marsden, and the townships of Almondbury, Austonley, Holme, Lingarths, Nether Thong, and Upper Thong, and containing 23,979 inhabitants, of which number, 5679 are in the township of Almondbury, 1¾ mile (S. E.) from Huddersfield. The living is a vicarage, within the jurisdiction of the peculiar court of the lord of the manor, rated in the king's books at £20. 7. 11., and in the patronage of the Governors of Clitheroe school. The church, dedicated to All Saints, is in that character of the later style of English architecture which prevails in the northern counties. New churches have been erected at Crossland, Linthwaite, and Nether Thong. There is a place of worship for Wesleyan Methodists. This is supposed to have been the *Cambodunum* of Antoninus: here was a royal palace belonging to the Anglo-Saxon monarchs, and near its site is a hill, upon which are vestiges of a rampart and the remains of a fortification. There are numerous manufactories for fancy goods and woollen cloth in the parish. A free grammar school was founded by letters patent of James I., the annual income of which amounts to about £76, arising from lands and rent-charges demised by Robert Nettleton and other benefactors. In 1724, Israel Wormall bequeathed land, the produce of which he directed to be applied towards instructing and apprenticing poor children of this place.

ALMONDSBURY, a parish comprising the tything of Almondsbury, in the lower division of the hundred of Berkeley, and the tythings of Hempton with Patchway, Over, and Lower Tockington, in the lower division of the hundred of Langley and Swinehead, county of Gloucester, and containing 1408 inhabitants, of which number, 477 are in the tything of Almondsbury, 4¼ miles (S. by W.) from Thornbury. The living is a discharged vicarage, in the peculiar jurisdiction and patronage of the Bishop of Bristol, rated in the king's books at £20. The church, situated in that part of the parish which is in the hundred of Berkeley, is dedicated to St. Mary: it is a handsome cruciform structure, in the early English style, with a tower and spire at the intersection. There is a place of worship for Wesleyan Methodists. The village is situated at the foot of a ridge of limestone rocks, near the small river Boyd, which falls into the Lower Avon: the views from the heights are remarkably grand and extensive, embracing the whole æstuary of the Severn, and the opposite coast of Wales. Here is a free school with a small endowment.

ALMSFORD, a parish in the hundred of Catsash, county of Somerset, ¾ of a mile (N.) from Castle-Cary, containing 300 inhabitants. The living is a rectory, in the archdeaconry of Wells, and diocese of Bath and Wells, rated in the king's books at £7. 12. 1., and in the patronage of J. Woodford, Esq. The church is dedicated to St. Andrew.

ALNE, a parish partly in the liberty of St. Peter of York, East riding, but chiefly in the wapentake of Bulmer, North riding, of the county of York, comprising the townships of Aldwork, Alne, Flawith, Tholthorp, Tollerton, and Youlton, and containing 1418 inhabitants, of which number, 386 are in the township of Alne, 4¾ miles (S. S. W.) from Easingwould. The living is a discharged vicarage, within the jurisdiction of the peculiar court of Alne and Tollerton, rated in the king's books at £10, and in the patronage of R. Bethell, Esq. The church is a handsome structure, dedicated to St. Mary. There is a place of worship for Wesleyan Methodists.

ALNE (GREAT), a chapelry in the parish of Kinwarton, Alcester division of the hundred of Barlichway, county of Warwick, 2¾ miles (N. E. by E.) from Alcester, containing 317 inhabitants. The chapel is dedicated to St. Mary Magdalene.

ALNHAM, a parish in the northern division of Coquetdale ward, county of Northumberland, comprising the townships of Alnham, Prendick, Screnwood, and Unthank, and containing 269 inhabitants, of which number, 143 are in the township of Alnham, 14 miles (W.) from Alnwick. The living is a discharged vicarage, in the archdeaconry of Northumberland, and diocese of Durham, rated in the king's books at £3. 17. 1., endowed with £400 royal bounty, and in the patronage of the Duke of Northumberland. The church is dedicated to St. Michael. On a hill, about a mile westward from the village, there is a semicircular encampment, defended by a high double rampart and deep trench, within which is a range of uncemented stones; and in the area, about one hundred yards in diameter, the foundations of buildings are visible.

ALNWICK, a market town and parish in the eastern division of Coquetdale ward, county of Northumberland, 34 miles (N. by W.) from Newcastle upon Tyne, and 319 (N. by W.) from London, on the great north road, containing 5927 inhabitants. This place derives its name from its situation near the river Alne. In 1093, it was besieged by Malcolm III., King of Scotland, and bravely defended by Mowbray, Earl of Northumberland. Malcolm, with his son and heir, Prince Edward, were slain during the siege, which event is commemorated by a cross, erected about a mile from the town, called Malcolm's Cross, rebuilt in 1774 by the Duchess of Northumberland, a lineal descendant of the Scottish monarch. In 1135, the town was taken by David, King of Scotland; and, in 1174, William, King of Scotland, with eighty thousand men, laid siege to it, but was defeated and captured by Ralph de Glanville, who sent him prisoner to London, whence he was afterwards ransomed by his subjects for £100,000. In 1215, Alnwick was nearly reduced to ashes by King John; but it appears to have been speedily rebuilt, for, about five years afterwards, Gualo, the pope's legate, summoned a council of the Scottish bishops to be held here. In 1328, it was again besieged by the Scots, under Robert Bruce, their king, but without success. In 1411, the castle (supposed to have been originally erected by the Saxons, on the site of a Roman fortress, and which was, at the Conquest, the baronial residence of the then Earl of Northumberland) was embattled, and the town surrounded with a strong wall, to protect it from the predatory incursions of the Scots, by whom, in 1448, it was burnt, in revenge for the burning of Dumfries by the English. After the battle of Hexham, in 1463, the castle, which was in the interest of the house of Lancaster, was summoned by the Earl of Warwick; but the garrison, though unable to sustain a protracted siege, retained possession till they were relieved by Sir George Douglas, who, at the head of a considerable force, afforded them an opportunity of retiring unmolested. Alnwick abbey was founded, in 1147, by Eustace Fitz-John, who endowed it for Premonstratensian canons: the abbots were summoned to some of the parliaments in the reigns of Edward I. and II.; its revenue, at the dissolution, was £194. 7.: only the gateway remains, which has been fitted up as a lodge to the castle. Here were also an hospital, founded by some of the Percy family, and dedicated to St. Lawrence, and a chapel, dedicated to St. Thomas.

Alnwick is situated on the irregular declivity of an eminence rising from the river Alne, over which, at the northern extremity of the town, is a neat stone bridge of three arches: the streets are spacious, well paved, and lighted with gas, under an act obtained in 1822; the houses, built of stone, are chiefly modern, and many of them elegant; and the inhabitants are amply supplied with water from cisterns and reservoirs, and by pumps erected by the corporation in various parts of the town: assemblies occasionally take place. A subscription library was established in 1783, and a scientific and mechanics' institute in 1824. The castle, now the magnificent residence of the Duke of Northumberland, is a stately structure, comprising two spacious wards, with lofty towers and exploratory turrets: it has been repaired with a due regard to its ancient style, and fitted up with the most sumptuous grandeur. The town walls were strengthened by four square and massive gateway towers, of which Bondgate is the only one remaining, and is now used as a prison. The trade and manufactures are inconsiderable: the parish contains coal, limestone, freestone, whinstone, and marble. The market is on Saturday: fairs are held on the 12th of May, the last Monday in July, the first Tuesday in October, the 28th of that month, and the last Saturday before Christmas-day; there are also statute fairs on the first Saturday in March and November. On the eve of each fair the inhabitants of the adjacent townships send deputies to attend the bailiff in the ceremony of proclamation; after which they keep watch and ward in the several quarters of the town for the remainder of the night, by which service they are exempt from toll within the borough for the next twelve months.

The corporation, which is a prescriptive body, consists of a bailiff, nominated by the Duke of Northumberland, as constable of the castle, four chamberlains, and twenty-four common council-men: the chamberlains are chosen from among the common council, and the latter from among the freemen of the several incorporated companies. The freedom is inherited by the eldest sons of freemen, or acquired by servitude. Each candidate, on taking up his freedom, is, by the provisions of King John's charter, subjected to the ludicrous ceremony of passing through a miry pool, thence called the "Freeman's Well." The officers of the corporation possess no magisterial authority, the town being within the jurisdiction of the county magistrates, who meet every alternate week: the quarter sessions for the county are held here in turn with Hexham, Newcastle, and Morpeth; the county court is held monthly, and courts leet and baron at Easter and Michaelmas, by the Duke of Northumberland, as lord of the manor: a manorial court is held also for the township of Canongate. The members of parliament and coroners for the county are elected here. The town hall is a handsome stone building surmounted by a square tower, erected in 1731, and commodiously arranged for the transaction of the public business: it is situated on the northern side of the market-place, a spacious area in the centre of the town, on the western side of which stands the market-house, a fine building in the early style of English architecture, containing seven spacious apartments, under which are the shambles, erected in 1827. The house of correction, near the Green Bat, was built in 1807. The living is a perpetual curacy, in the archdeaconry of Northumberland, and diocese of Durham, and in the patronage of the Duke of Northumberland. The church, dedicated to St. Mary, is a large building with a neat tower: the chancel was repaired and embellished, in 1781, by the Duke of Northumberland: in a niche in the south aisle are three recumbent figures in stone. There are places of worship for Antiburghers, Burghers, Independents, Primitive and Wesleyan Methodists, Presbyterians, Unitarians, and Roman Catholics. The free school, near the West-gate, for preparing the sons of freemen for the mathematical school, is principally supported by the corporation; the mathematical school, and a school for the daughters of freemen, are supported by subscription. A National school for two hundred boys was founded, in 1810, by the Duke of Northumberland, in commemoration of George III. having completed the fiftieth year of his reign; and a school for clothing and educating fifty poor girls has been instituted by the Duchess of Northumberland: there are also several Sunday schools. A dispensary was established in 1815, and a savings bank in the following year. In the vicinity are two encampments, supposed to be of Danish origin; and, about the year 1726, a considerable number of military weapons, which probably belonged to the ancient Britons, was found in Hulne park. Alnwick gives the inferior title of baron to the Earl of Beverley.

ALPHAMSTONE, a parish in the hundred of HINCKFORD, county of ESSEX, 6 miles (N. E. by E.) from Halstead, containing 244 inhabitants. The living is a rectory, in the archdeaconry of Middlesex, and diocese of London, rated in the king's books at £11, and in the patronage of the Crown.

ALPHETON, a parish in the hundred of BABERGH, county of SUFFOLK, 6¾ miles (N. by E.) from Sudbury, containing 264 inhabitants. The living is a rectory, in the archdeaconry of Sudbury, and diocese of Norwich, rated in the king's books at £10. 1. 8., and in the patronage of the Rev. T. G. Dickinson.

ALPHINGTON, a parish in the hundred of WONFORD, county of DEVON, 1½ mile (S.) from Exeter, containing 1070 inhabitants. The living is a rectory, in the archdeaconry and diocese of Exeter, rated in the king's books at £34. 6. 8., and in the patronage of the Rev. R. Ellicombe. The church, dedicated to St. Michael, has a circular Norman font, with intersecting arches and scroll ornaments. Fairs for cattle are held here on the first Wednesdays after June 20th and Michaelmas-day. The river Exe and the Exeter canal pass through the parish, in directions parallel with each other. The lord of the manor had anciently the power of inflicting capital punishment.

ALPINGTON, a parish in the hundred of LODDON, county of NORFOLK, 6 miles (S. E.) from Norwich, containing, with Yelverton, 169 inhabitants. The living is a discharged rectory, with that of Yelverton united, in the archdeaconry of Norfolk, and diocese of Norwich, and in the patronage of the Crown.

ALPRAHAM, a township in that part of the parish of BUNBURY which is in the first division of the hundred of EDDISBURY, county palatine of CHESTER, 3½ miles (S. E. by E.) from Tarporley, containing 409 inhabitants. There is a place of worship for Wesleyan Methodists.

ALRESFORD, a parish in the hundred of TENDRING, county of ESSEX, 6½ miles (S. E. by E.) from Colchester, containing 270 inhabitants. The living is a discharged rectory, in the archdeaconry of Colchester, and diocese of London, rated in the king's books at £8, and in the patronage of the Rev. T. Newman. The church is dedicated to St. Peter.

ALRESFORD (NEW), a market town and chapelry in the parish of OLD ALRESFORD, liberty of ALRESFORD, Alton (North) division of the county of SOUTHAMPTON, 6 miles (N. E. by E.) from Winchester, and 57 (S. W. by W.) from London, on the high road to Winchester, containing 1129 inhabitants. It derives its name from its situation near a ford on the river Alre. The manor was given to the church of Winchester by Cenwalh, King of the West Saxons, after his baptism by Bishop Birinus. About 1220, Godfrey de Lucy, Bishop of Winchester, restored the market, then fallen into disuse. On May-day, 1690, the town was destroyed by fire, previously to which it was so prosperous, that there was not an individual requiring parochial relief. In 1710, a similar calamity occurred. Alresford pond is a fine piece of water, through which runs the river Itchen. The northern embankment is formed by a causeway, nearly five hundred yards in length, which constituted part of the main road to London previously to 1753, when the present one was made through Bishop's Sutton. This work was accomplished by Bishop de Lucy, under a grant from King John, with a view to the improvement of his grounds, and to increase the depth of the river Itchen, which was formerly navigable to Southampton water, though of late it has ceased to be so higher than Winchester. As a recompense for this arduous undertaking, the bishop obtained, for himself and his successors, the entire royalty of the river from the reservoir to the sea. The market is on Thursday; and fairs are held on Holy Thursday, the last Thursday in July and November, and the Thursday next after Old Michaelmas-day, almost exclusively for sheep. Alresford was incorporated at a very early period, and returned one representative to parliament in the 23rd of Edward I. The corporation consists of a bailiff, appointed by the Bishop of Winchester, and eight burgesses, who, by virtue of a lease from the bishop, receive the tolls of the market, but exercise no magisterial authority. A court leet is held at Michaelmas, when the bailiff is chosen; and the county magistrates hold a petty session weekly, for the division of Alton. This place is within the jurisdiction of the Cheyney Court held at Winchester every Thursday, for the recovery of debts to any amount. There is a place of worship for Independents. H. Perin, Esq. founded a school for nineteen boys, sons of poor tradesmen in the town, and the neighbouring villages of Old Alresford, Sutton, and Tichbourne; it is endowed with a good house for the master, and fifty-two acres of land, now let for £100 per annum. At Bramdean, about three miles distant, a tesselated pavement was discovered about five years ago, one part of which represents the wrestling match between Hercules and Antæus. Among the seats in the neighbourhood are those of Lord Rodney, Sir Henry Tichbourne, Bart., and Alexander Baring, Esq., which last, called the Grange, is a beautiful copy of the Parthenon at Athens.

ALRESFORD (OLD), a parish in the hundred of Fawley, Fawley division of the county of Southampton, $\frac{3}{4}$ of a mile (N.) from New Alresford, containing 445 inhabitants. The living is a rectory, with the perpetual curacy of Medsted annexed, in the peculiar jurisdiction of the Incumbent, rated in the king's books at £49. 12. $8\frac{1}{2}$., and in the patronage of the Bishop of Winchester. The church is dedicated to St. Mary. The river Itchen runs through this parish. Old Alresford is within the jurisdiction of the Cheyney Court held at Winchester every Thursday, for the recovery of debts to any amount. Admiral Lord Rodney occupied a mansion in the neighbourhood.

ALREWAS, a parish in the northern division of the hundred of Offlow, county of Stafford, 5 miles (N. E. by N.) from Lichfield, containing, with the hamlets of Fradley and Orgreave, 1492 inhabitants. The living is a discharged vicarage, in the peculiar jurisdiction of the Prebendary of Alrewas and Weeford in the Cathedral Church of Lichfield, rated in the king's books at £5. 6. 8., and in the patronage of the Chancellor in that Cathedral. The church is dedicated to All Saints. There is a place of worship for Wesleyan Methodists. The parish is bounded by the Trent on the north, and by the Tame on the east; and the Grand Trunk and Coventry canals pass through it, the former to its junction with the Trent at this place. Courts leet and baron for the manor are held twice a year: the custom of Borough English prevails here. A National school has been established.

ALREWAS-HAYES, an extra-parochial liberty, in the northern division of the hundred of Offlow, county of Stafford, $5\frac{1}{2}$ miles (N. N. E.) from Lichfield, containing 74 inhabitants.

ALSAGER, a chapelry in that part of the parish of Barthomley which is in the hundred of Nantwich, county palatine of Chester, $5\frac{3}{4}$ miles (S. E. by S.) from Sandbach, containing 359 inhabitants. The living is a perpetual curacy, in the archdeaconry and diocese of Chester, and in the patronage of the Lord of the Manor. There is a place of worship for Wesleyan Methodists. A school, for the education of children of both sexes, was founded and endowed by Mary, Judith, and Margaret Alsager, who also built and endowed the chapel.

ALSOP le DALE, a chapelry in that part of the parish of Ashbourn which is in the hundred of Wirksworth, county of Derby, $5\frac{1}{2}$ miles (N. by W.) from Ashbourn. The population is returned with the township of Eaton. The living is a perpetual curacy, in the archdeaconry of Derby, and diocese of Lichfield and Coventry, and in the patronage of the inhabitant freeholders. The chapel, dedicated to St. Michael, is of Norman architecture, with many modern alterations. Alsop is in the honour of Tutbury, duchy of Lancaster, and within the jurisdiction of a court of pleas held at Tutbury every third Tuesday, for the recovery of debts under 40*s*.

ALSTON, or ALSTON-MOOR, a market town and parish in Leath ward, county of Cumberland, 29 miles (E. S. E.) from Carlisle, and 287 (N. N. W.) from London, containing, with the chapelry of Garrigill, 5699 inhabitants. The town is situated on the declivity of a steep hill, in a narrow valley, near the confluence of the rivers Nent and South Tyne, over each of which is a neat stone bridge. The houses, which are irregularly built, are chiefly of stone, roofed with slate, and the inhabitants are supplied with water conveyed by pipes from an excellent spring, about half a mile distant, into four punts, or cisterns, conveniently placed in different parts of the town. A subscription library was established in 1821, in commemoration of the coronation of George IV.; and races are held on Easter Monday and Tuesday. An excellent new line of road has lately been made, under the superintendence of Mr. Mc Adam, from Hexham to Penrith, through Alston, which is shorter by several miles than that by way of Carlisle. In several parts are beautiful views of the surrounding country, particularly from Hartside, which embraces the counties of Cumberland and Westmorland, including the lake of Ulswater, and the mountains of the lake district, Solway Frith, and the adjacent Scottish shore. This district, which is enclosed on the west by the mountains Cross-fell and Hartside, and on all sides by high lands, is equally remarkable for its sterility of agricultural produce, and its abundance of mineral wealth. The lead mines, in which the inhabitants are chiefly employed, are very extensive and productive; there are not less than thirty-eight in the parish, and the quantity of lead produced in the year 1830 was about five thousand tons, which is considerably less than the average quantity for several years preceding. The ore contains a proportion of silver, averaging from eight to ten ounces per ton; and one of the mines, opened at Yadmoss in 1828, has produced ore containing ninety-six ounces of silver in each ton. Copper-ore has also been found in the same vein with the lead, and in many instances the same mine has been worked for copper-ore of excellent quality, and lead-ore, which is rich in silver. The grand aqueduct level, called "Nent Force," was cut by the trustees of Greenwich Hospital, under whom the estate is held, pursuant to an act which transferred these estates from the family of James, third Earl of Derwentwater, who was beheaded for high treason in the reign of George I.: this subterraneous canal is five miles in length, from its mouth near the town to the shaft of the mine; boats and guides are kept in constant readiness to conduct those who may wish to explore it. In the mines are several extensive caverns splendidly decorated with fluor-spar, shot into chrystals of every form and hue; and where the yellow copper-ore and pyrites are intermingled, nothing can exceed the brilliancy with which the prismatic colours are reflected. Of these, Tutman's hole has been explored to the distance of a mile from the entrance; and in that at Dun fell, on the side of Alston Moor, the chambers and windings are so intricate, that visitors have been glad to avail themselves of some clue to their return. Among other minerals found here are pyrites of iron, containing small portions of gold, tesselated ore, zink, phosphate and sulphate of lead, cobalt, &c. The crow coal, found on the moor, at a small depth below the surface, contains pyrites in large proportion; it burns with little flame, but emits an intense heat, and, mixed with clay, is made into fire-balls. There are two large smelting furnaces, and several machines worked by water for crushing and washing the ore. The principal manufactures are those of shot, sewing thread, and flannel, which are extensively carried on; and there is also a public brewery on a large scale. The market is on Saturday: fairs are held on the last Thursday in May, Friday before the last day of September, and the first Thursday in November. Two of the county magistrates hold a petty session at the Swan Inn on the first Friday in every month, and courts leet and baron are held in the months next after Easter and Michaelmas.

The living is a discharged vicarage, within the jurisdiction of the Consistorial Court of Durham, rated in the king's books at £7. 13., endowed with £600 private benefaction, £800 royal bounty, and £1000 parliamentary grant, and in the patronage of the Governors of Greenwich Hospital for two turns, and of William Jackson, Esq. for one. The church, dedicated to St. Augustine, was rebuilt in 1770. A chapel of ease is situated at Garrigill, a populous village four miles south-east of the town. There are places of worship for the Society of Friends, Independents, and Primitive and Wesleyan Methodists. The grammar school was rebuilt by subscription in 1828, and is endowed with £26 per annum. No scholars are gratuitously instructed, but the master, in consideration of the endowment, is limited to a certain scale of charges for boys attending it. There is a similar school at Garrigill, endowed with £7. 4. 1. per annum; and a Lancasterian school for two hundred children was erected in 1811, and is supported by subscription. At Nent Head, a large populous village on the eastern border of the parish, where a customary market is held on Thursday, a National school was established by the London Lead Company, in 1820, and is partly supported by them, and partly by the Governors of Greenwich Hospital. On Gildersdale fell is a stagnant pool, covered with mud several inches thick, which is used by the neighbouring people as paint: it produces colours resembling yellow ochre and Spanish brown, but has not been analysed. The Roman road called Maiden-way, traces of which are distinctly visible, crosses the western part of the parish; and on Hall hill, a little below the bridge over the Tyne, are the foundations of an ancient fortress, surrounded by a moat.

ALSTON, a joint township with Hothersall, in that part of the parish of RIBCHESTER which is in the hundred of AMOUNDERNESS, county palatine of LANCASTER, 6½ miles (N.E.) from Preston, containing, with Hothersall, 948 inhabitants.

ALSTONE, a hamlet in the parish and hundred of CHELTENHAM, county of GLOUCESTER, ¾ of a mile (N. W. by W.) from Cheltenham, with which town the population is returned. Here is a chalybeate saline spa, for an account of which see CHELTENHAM.

ALSTONE, a chapelry in the parish of OVERBURY, middle division of the hundred of OSWALDSLOW, county of WORCESTER, 6½ miles (E. by S.) from Tewkesbury, containing 79 inhabitants. The chapel is dedicated to St. Margaret.

ALTCAR, a parish in the hundred of WEST DERBY, county palatine of LANCASTER, 7 miles (W. by S.) from Ormskirk, containing 499 inhabitants. The living is a perpetual curacy, in the archdeaconry and diocese of Chester, endowed with £600 royal bounty, and £1200 parliamentary grant, and in the patronage of the Earl of Sefton. The church is dedicated to St. Michael. The small river Alt runs through the parish. Here is a school, with a small endowment by the Earl of Sefton.

ALTERNON, a parish in the hundred of LESNEWTH, county of CORNWALL, 7¾ miles (W. S. W.) from Launceston, containing 885 inhabitants. The living is a vicarage, in the archdeaconry of Cornwall, and diocese of Exeter, rated in the king's books at £18. 5., and in the patronage of the Dean and Chapter of Exeter. The church is dedicated to St. Nunn. There is a place of worship for Wesleyan Methodists.

ALTHAM, a chapelry in that part of the parish of WHALLEY which is in the higher division of the hundred of BLACKBURN, county palatine of LANCASTER, 5 miles (W.) from Burnley, containing 439 inhabitants. The living is a perpetual curacy, in the archdeaconry and diocese of Chester, endowed with £10 per annum private benefaction, £400 royal bounty, and £800 parliamentary grant, and in the patronage of Earl Howe. The chapel is dedicated to St. James. Coal is obtained in the vicinity.

ALTHORNE, a parish in the hundred of DENGIE, county of ESSEX, 4 miles (N. W.) from Burnham, containing 352 inhabitants. The living is a vicarage, united to the rectory of Creeksea in 1811, in the archdeaconry of Essex, and diocese of London, rated in the king's books at £14, and endowed with £200 private benefaction, and £200 royal bounty. The church is dedicated to St. Andrew. The æstuary of the river Crouch is in this parish, in which there are very strong embankments, which are about nine feet high, intended to protect the low lands from inundation, constructed by labourers from Holland, whose descendants are still resident here.

ALTHORP, a parish in the western division of the wapentake of Manley, parts of Lindsey, county of Lincoln, 11 miles (W. by N.) from Glandford-Bridge, comprising the chapelry of Amcotts, and the township of Keadby, and containing 877 inhabitants. The living is a rectory, in the archdeaconry of Stow, and diocese of Lincoln, rated in the king's books at £25, endowed with £200 private benefaction, and £400 royal bounty, and in the patronage of the Crown. The church is dedicated to St. Oswald.

ALTOFTS, a township in the parish of Normanton, lower division of the wapentake of Agbrigg, West riding of the county of York, $3\frac{3}{4}$ miles (N.E. by E.) from Wakefield, containing 404 inhabitants.

ALTON, a market town and parish in the hundred of Alton, Alton (North) division of the county of Southampton, 30 miles (N. E.) from Southampton, and 47 (S.W. by W.) from London, containing 2499 inhabitants. The name, a contraction of Old Town, is descriptive of its great antiquity, having been a royal demesne in the reign of Alfred: it sent one member to parliament in the 23rd of Edward I. In 1643, the town was occupied by a detachment of the royal army, commanded by Sir Ralph Hopton, who was soon after defeated by Sir William Waller. It consists of three principal streets, partially paved by subscription, and lighted, and is pleasantly situated on the river Wey, which turns a silk-mill. The manufacture of bombazines, once of considerable extent, has decayed: the hop-plantations are extensive, and there are two large breweries in the town. The market, principally for corn, is on Saturday; and fairs are held on the Saturday before May 1st, and September 29th, for horses and cattle. Alton is within the jurisdiction of the county magistrates, who hold petty sessions here for the division of Alton (North). Constables and other officers are chosen at the court leet of the lord of the manor. The town hall, part of which is used as a National school-house, stands in the market-place; and a court for the recovery of debts under 40*s.* is held in it every third week. The living is a vicarage, with the perpetual curacy of Binsted annexed, in the archdeaconry and diocese of Winchester, rated in the king's books at £15, and in the patronage of the Dean and Chapter of Winchester. The church, dedicated to St. Lawrence, is a spacious structure, principally in the later style of English architecture, but with some earlier portions: it has a square embattled tower surmounted by a spire. There are places of worship for the Society of Friends, Independents, and Presbyterians. A grammar school was founded by John Egger for twenty-five boys: there are about two hundred children of both sexes in the National school. At Holybourn there is a charity school for forty boys and twenty girls. John Pitts, the biographer, and William Curtis, the botanist, were natives of this town.

ALTON-BARNES, a parish in the hundred of Swanborough, county of Wilts, 7 miles (E.) from Devizes, containing 110 inhabitants. The living is a rectory, in the archdeaconry of Wilts, and diocese of Salisbury, rated in the king's books at £6. 18. $11\frac{1}{2}$., and in the patronage of the Warden and Fellows of New College, Oxford. The church is dedicated to St. Mary.

ALTON-PANCRAS, a parish and liberty in the Cerne subdivision of the county of Dorset, $8\frac{1}{4}$ miles (N.) from Dorchester, containing 207 inhabitants. The living is a discharged vicarage, in the peculiar jurisdiction of the Dean of Salisbury, rated in the king's books at £9, and in the patronage of the Crown. The church is dedicated to St. Andrew.

ALTON-PRIORS, a chapelry in that part of the parish of Overton which is in the hundred of Elstub and Everley, county of Wilts, 7 miles (E. by N.) from Devizes, containing, with the tything of Stowell, 166 inhabitants. The chapel is dedicated to All Saints.

Arms.

ALTRINCHAM, a market town and chapelry in the parish of Bowdon, hundred of Bucklow, county palatine of Chester, 7 miles (N.by E.) from Nether Knutsford, and $179\frac{1}{2}$ (N.W. by N.) from London, containing 2302 inhabitants. The town is situated on Bowdon Downs, and, though small, contains several respectable dwelling-houses, the salubrity of the air rendering it a place of general resort for invalids from Manchester: it is watched and lighted by subscription, and is characterised throughout by cleanliness and neatness. The trade principally consists in the spinning of yarn, the making of bobbins for cotton and worsted spinners, and the weaving of cotton by hand-looms for the manufacturers at Manchester and other adjacent towns. The Duke of Bridgewater's canal from Manchester to Runcorn passes through the town, and affords a facility of conveyance for coal. Early potatoes are cultivated here to a great extent for the Manchester market. The market days are Tuesday and Saturday, the latter being only for butchers' meat: the fairs, chiefly for the sale of live stock, are held on April 29th, August 5th, and November 22nd; to the two last are attached courts of pie-powder. Altrincham was made a free borough in the reign of Edward I., by charter of Hamon de Massey, lord of the barony of Dunham-Massey, whereby the burgesses were empowered to have a guild merchant, and to choose a *præpositus*, or bailiff; but the only privilege they now possess is that of electing a mayor at a court leet held in autumn, when a jury of burgesses present three of their own body to the steward, who appoints one to the office, which is merely nominal, and the duty of which extends only to the opening of the fairs, the town being wholly within the jurisdiction of the county magistrates. Pleas were formerly held in the lord's court, but they have of late been discontinued. The living is a perpetual curacy, in the archdeaconry and diocese of Chester, endowed with £1000 parliamentary grant, and in the patronage of the Earl of Stamford and Warrington. The chapel, dedicated to St. George, is a plain brick building, erected by subscription in 1799. There are two places of worship for Methodists, and one for Unitarians. The Jubilee school, built in 1810, is supported by subscription.

ALVANLEY, a chapelry in the parish of FRODSHAM, second division of the hundred of EDDISBURY, county palatine of CHESTER, 3 miles (S. S. W.) from Frodsham, containing 284 inhabitants. The living is a perpetual curacy, in the archdeaconry and diocese of Chester, and in the patronage of J. Arden, Esq. The chapel is dedicated to St. Mary: from 1787 till within these few years the performance of divine service was discontinued in it, in consequence of the smallness of the minister's income. Alvanley gives the title of baron to the Arden family.

ALVASTON, a township in the parish and hundred of NANTWICH, county palatine of CHESTER, 2½ miles (N. E.) from Nantwich, containing 37 inhabitants. Races are held annually in this township.

ALVASTON, a chapelry in that part of the parish of ST. MICHAEL, DERBY, which is in the hundred of MORLESTON and LITCHURCH, county of DERBY, 3½ miles (S. E. by E.) from Derby, containing 399 inhabitants. The living is a perpetual curacy, annexed to that of Boulton, in the archdeaconry of Derby, and diocese of Lichfield and Coventry, endowed with £400 royal bounty. There is a place of worship for Wesleyan Methodists. A Sunday school is supported chiefly from the rental of property left by sundry persons for charitable purposes. The river Derwent and the Derby canal pass through the parish.

ALVECHURCH, a parish, forming a detached portion of the middle division of the hundred of OSWALDSLOW, locally in the upper division of the hundred of Halfshire, county of WORCESTER, 4½ miles (E. N. E.) from Bromsgrove, containing 1413 inhabitants. The living is a rectory, in the peculiar jurisdiction of the Incumbent, rated in the king's books at £24. 16. 8., and in the patronage of the Bishop of Worcester. The church, dedicated to St. Lawrence, has Norman pillars; but the chancel displays the early English style, and the tower is more modern. The Bishops of Worcester had a palace here so early as the reign of Henry II., which, after the sale of the manor by the parliament, in 1648, was suffered to fall to decay, and has now entirely disappeared. An hospital for nine persons was incorporated by Queen Elizabeth. The Birmingham and Worcester canal runs through the parish. Fairs for cattle and sheep are held on the 22nd of April and the 10th of August. In 1742, Dr. Worth bequeathed £138. 2. 2., now producing £16 per annum, for the establishment of a free school. The Roman Iknield-street passed through Alvechurch, in its course from Alcester towards Lichfield. The learned Dr. Hickes, author of the *Thesaurus Septentrionalium Linguarum*, held the rectory of this parish.

ALVELEY, a parish comprising the liberty of Romsley, within the liberty of the borough of BRIDGENORTH, and the township of King's Nordley, in the hundred of STOTTESDEN, county of SALOP, 6½ miles (S. S. E.) from Bridgenorth, containing 975 inhabitants. The living is a perpetual curacy, within the jurisdiction of the court of the royal peculiar of Bridgenorth, endowed with £200 private benefaction, £600 royal bounty, and £1000 parliamentary grant, and in the patronage of T. Whitmore, Esq. The church is dedicated to St. Mary. Alveley was one of the five prebends in the royal free chapel of the castle of Bridgenorth, having been valued, in the reign of Henry III., at sixty marks, and is still reputed and rated as such in the Office of the First Fruits. A free school was endowed, in 1616, by John Grove, who also founded almshouses for decayed labourers: the school is free to all poor children of the parish, and the master has a salary of £20 per annum, and the use of the school-house.

ALVERDISCOTT, a parish in the hundred of FREMINGTON, county of DEVON, 4¼ miles (E. by S.) from Bideford, containing 334 inhabitants. The living is a rectory, in the archdeaconry of Barnstaple, and diocese of Exeter, rated in the king's books at £13. 3. 11½., and in the patronage of J. Rowe, Esq. The church is dedicated to All Saints.

ALVERSTOKE, a parish in the liberties of ALVERSTOKE and GOSPORT, Portsdown division of the county of SOUTHAMPTON, 1½ mile (W. S. W.) from Gosport, containing, with the town of Gosport, 10,972 inhabitants. The living is a rectory, in the peculiar jurisdiction of the Incumbent, rated in the king's books at £21. 6. 0½., and in the patronage of the Bishop of Winchester. The church is dedicated to St. Mary. A new chapel is in progress of erection by the commissioners appointed under the late act for building additional churches and chapels. Alverstoke is within the jurisdiction of the Cheyney Court held at Winchester every Thursday, for the recovery of debts to any amount.

ALVERTHORPE, a chapelry in the parish of WAKEFIELD, lower division of the wapentake of AGBRIGG, West riding of the county of YORK, 1½ mile (W. N. W.) from Wakefield, containing, with the township of Thornes, 4448 inhabitants. A new chapel, in the later style of English architecture, containing one thousand five hundred and ninety sittings, of which eight hundred and thirty-two are free, was completed in 1825, at the expense of £7828, defrayed by a grant from the parliamentary commissioners. Here are three almshouses.

ALVESCOTT, a parish in the hundred of BAMPTON, county of OXFORD, 5 miles (S. S. E.) from Burford, containing 357 inhabitants. The living is a rectory, in the archdeaconry and diocese of Oxford, rated in the king's books at £8. 16. 8., and in the patronage of — Brown, Esq. Goddard Carter, Esq., in 1723, left a rent-charge of £10, directing one-half to be applied in educating poor children, and the remainder in apprenticing them.

ALVESDISTON, a parish in the hundred of CHALK, county of WILTS, 7¾ miles (E. by N.) from Shaftesbury, containing 224 inhabitants. The living is a discharged vicarage, with that of Broad-Chalk consolidated, united to the vicarage of Bower-Chalk, in the archdeaconry and diocese of Salisbury. The church is dedicated to St. Mary.

ALVESTON, a parish partly in the lower, but chiefly in the upper, division of the hundred of LANGLEY and SWINEHEAD, county of GLOUCESTER, 3 miles (S. by E.) from Thornbury, containing 657 inhabitants. The living is a vicarage with that of Olveston, in the peculiar jurisdiction of the Bishop of Bristol. The church is a small edifice, with a low tower, situated at some distance from the village. There is a place of worship for Wesleyan Methodists.

ALVESTON, a parish in the Snitterfield division of the hundred of BARLICHWAY, county of WARWICK, 2½ miles (E. N. E.) from Stratford, containing 630 inhabitants. The living is a vicarage, in the archdeaconry and diocese of Worcester, rated in the king's books at £6, and in the patronage of the Rector of Hampton-Lucy. The church is dedicated to St. James.

ALVETON, a parish in the southern division of the hundred of TOTMONSLOW, county of STAFFORD, 4½ miles (E. by S.) from Cheadle, comprising the chapelry of Cotton, and the townships of Denston and Farley, and containing 2170 inhabitants. The living is a discharged vicarage, in the archdeaconry of Stafford, and diocese of Lichfield and Coventry, rated in the king's books at £5. 16. 5½., endowed with £200 parliamentary grant, and in the patronage of the Earl of Shrewsbury. The church, dedicated to St. Peter, displays a mixture of the Norman and modern styles of architecture. There are places of worship for Calvinists and Wesleyan Methodists. The village is situated in a beautiful and romantic district, on the banks of the river Churnet, which here flows through a fertile vale. The Caldon canal passes through it, its course for some miles being parallel with that of the river, which it here crosses by means of an aqueduct. Near the side of the river is a wire-mill; and on the summit of a rock, three hundred feet above its bed, are the ruins of Alveton castle, which, in the reign of Henry II., belonged to the family of De Verdon: the property is now in the possession of the Earl of Shrewsbury, whose mansion, with its fine park and pleasure grounds, is situated on the opposite bank of the river. The remains of the castle consist of some of the outer walls, and one of the towers, overgrown with ivy; on the side opposite to the river it was defended by an intrenchment. On the summit of an adjacent eminence is a lofty tower, commanding extensive and varied prospects of the windings of the Churnet. Courts leet and baron are occasionally held here. Anthony Wall, in 1721, founded and endowed a school for the instruction of twelve boys, which is now open to all children of the parish; the school-room has been rebuilt on an enlarged plan by the Earl of Shrewsbury. At Bunbury, in this parish, are the remains of a very extensive fortress, of an irregular form, ascribed to Ceolred, King of Mercia, about 715: it is defended on three sides by a double vallum, and on the fourth by a steep declivity.

ALVINGHAM, a parish in the Marsh division of the hundred of LOUTH-ESKE, parts of LINDSEY, county of LINCOLN, 4 miles (N. E.) from Louth, containing 264 inhabitants. The living is a perpetual curacy, with that of Cockerington St. Mary annexed, in the archdeaconry and diocese of Lincoln, endowed with £1000 royal bounty, and in the patronage of the Bishop of Lincoln. The church is dedicated to St. Adelwold. A priory of Gilbertine nuns and canons, dedicated to the Virgin Mary and St. Adelwold, was founded here in the reign of Henry II., which at the dissolution was valued at £141. 15. per annum.

ALVINGTON, a parish in the hundred of BLIDESLOE, county of GLOUCESTER, 5½ miles (S. W.) from Blakeney, containing 272 inhabitants. The living is a perpetual curacy, united to the rectory of Wollastone, in the archdeaconry of Hereford, and diocese of Gloucester.

ALWALTON, a parish in the hundred of NORMANCROSS, county of HUNTINGDON, 5 miles (N. N. W.) from Stilton, containing 257 inhabitants. The living is a rectory, in the archdeaconry of Huntingdon, and diocese of Lincoln, rated in the king's books at £3. 5. 10., and in the patronage of the Dean and Chapter of Peterborough. The church, dedicated to St. Andrew, exhibits in the body of the building a singular combination of Norman and early English architecture; the chancel is chiefly in the decorated style, and there are some peculiarities in the windows, shafts, mouldings, and general details.

ALWINGTON, a parish in the hundred of SHEBBEAR, county of DEVON, 4½ miles (S.W. by W.) from Bideford, containing 386 inhabitants. The living is a rectory, in the archdeaconry of Barnstaple, and diocese of Exeter, rated in the king's books at £17. 4. 9½., and in the patronage of Richard Pine Coffin, Esq. The church is dedicated to St. Andrew. In Yeo Vale, so called from being intersected by the river Yeo, are the remains of an ancient chapel. Here are almshouses for three poor persons, endowed, in 1696, by R. Coffin, Esq.

ALWOODLEY, a township in that part of the parish of HAREWOOD which is in the upper division of the wapentake of SKYRACK, West riding of the county of YORK, 5½ miles (N.) from Leeds, containing 142 inhabitants.

AMBERLEY, a chapelry in the parish of MARDEN, hundred of BROXASH, county of HEREFORD, 5¾ miles (N. N. E.) from Hereford, containing 34 inhabitants.

AMBERLEY, a parish in the hundred of WEST EASWRITH, rape of ARUNDEL, county of SUSSEX, 5 miles (N. N. E.) from Arundel, containing, with the hamlet of Rockham, 548 inhabitants. The living is a vicarage, with that of Houghton united, in the archdeaconry and diocese of Chichester, rated in the king's books at £7. 5. 7½., and in the patronage of the Bishop of Chichester. The church has a nave of Norman, and a chancel of early English, architecture, separated by a Norman arch much enriched. The river Arun runs through this parish: on its banks are considerable remains of an ancient castle, which belonged to the Bishops of Chichester, now occupied as a farm-house.

AMBERSHAM (NORTH), a tything in the parish of STEEP, hundred of EAST MEON, Alton (South) division of the county of SOUTHAMPTON, though locally in the hundred of Easebourne, rape of Chichester, county of Sussex, 2½ miles (E. N. E.) from Midhurst, containing 134 inhabitants. This place is within the jurisdiction of the Cheyney Court held at Winchester every Thursday, for the recovery of debts to any amount.

AMBERSHAM (SOUTH), a tything in the parish of STEEP, hundred of EAST MEON, Alton (South) division of the county of SOUTHAMPTON, though locally in the hundred of Easebourne, rape of Chichester, county of Sussex, 2½ miles (E. by N.) from Midhurst, containing 175 inhabitants. This tything is within the jurisdiction of the Cheyney Court held at Winchester every Thursday, for the recovery of debts to any amount.

AMBLE, a township in that part of the parish of WARKWORTH which is in the eastern division of MORPETH ward, county of NORTHUMBERLAND, 9 miles (S.E.) from Alnwick, containing 197 inhabitants. There are valuable and extensive mines of coal in this township. The village is pleasantly situated on an eminence near the mouth of the river Coquet, and commands an extensive view of the sea: it was anciently of much greater importance, as is evident from the discovery of circular foundations of houses, of unhewn and uncemented stones, of British origin, and of Roman coins; a paved causeway was also discovered, a few years since, extending in a direction towards the old bed of the Coquet. Here was anciently a monastery, subordinate to Tynemouth priory, near the ruins of which several human bones were found a few years ago.

AMBLECOAT, a hamlet in that part of the parish of OLD SWINFORD which is in the southern division of the hundred of SEISDON, county of STAFFORD, ½ a mile (N.) from Stourbridge, containing 1157 inhabitants.

AMBLESIDE, a market town and parochial chapelry, partly in the parish of WINDERMERE, but chiefly in the parish of GRASMERE, KENDAL ward, county of WESTMORLAND, 25 miles (W. S. W.) from Appleby, and 274 (N. W. by N.) from London, containing 838 inhabitants. The name, anciently written *Hamelside,* is probably derived from the Saxon *Hamol,* signifying a sheltered habitation. The town is situated near the site of a Roman station of considerable extent, supposed by Horsley to have been the *Dictis* of the Notitia: the earthworks of the fortress remain, and various Roman relics and foundations of buildings have been discovered. It stands on the acclivity of a steep eminence near the northern extremity of the lake Windermere, in a district pre-eminently distinguished for the beauty of its scenery, and consists chiefly of one street, lighted with oil, but not paved; the houses, though detached and irregular, are well built. There are a few manufactories for linsey-woolsey. The market, granted in 1650 to the celebrated Countess of Pembroke, is on Wednesday: fairs are held on Whit-Wednesday and the 13th and 29th of October, to which a court of pie-powder is attached: the market-house was built about the year 1796, on the site of the former. The inhabitants received a charter in the reign of Charles II., under the authority of which they elect a mayor annually on Christmas-eve, but he does not possess magisterial authority, the town being entirely within the jurisdiction of the county magistrates, who hold a petty session monthly. The living is a perpetual curacy, in the archdeaconry of Richmond, and diocese of Chester, endowed with £200 private benefaction, £400 royal bounty, and £600 parliamentary grant, and in the patronage of Lady Fleming. The chapel, situated in that part of the town which is in the parish of Grassmere, was rebuilt in 1812, and exhibits some portions of ancient architecture, with many modern insertions: it was made parochial by the Bishop of Chester, in 1675. The free grammar school was founded and endowed by John Kelsick, in 1721; the annual income is about £127, which, deducting £20 for taxes, is paid to the master, who has also a house rent-free. Two Sunday schools are supported by subscription. A little below the town is the beautiful waterfall called Stockgill Force. Bernard Gilpin, surnamed "The Northern Apostle," was born at Kentmere, and Judge Wilson at Troutbeck, near this town.

AMBROSDEN, a parish in the hundred of BULLINGTON, county of OXFORD, 2½ miles (S.E. by S.) from Bicester, comprising the chapelries of Arncott and Blackthorn, and containing 843 inhabitants. The living is a discharged vicarage, in the archdeaconry and diocese of Oxford, rated in the king's books at £11. 17., endowed with £200 private benefaction, and £200 royal bounty, and in the patronage of Sir G. P. Turner, Bart. The church, dedicated to St. Mary, is stated to have been built in the latter part of the reign of Edward I., on the site of the original Saxon, or Norman, edifice, the northern entrance to which still remains. Four churchwardens are annually appointed for this parish, two by the vicar, and two by the parishioners. Bishop Kennet, who formerly held the vicarage, supposes the name to be derived from Ambrosius Aurelius, the celebrated British chief, who encamped here during the siege of Alchester by the Saxons.

AMCOTTS, a chapelry in the parish of ALTHORP, western division of the wapentake of MANLEY, parts of LINDSEY, county of LINCOLN, 11¾ miles (E. S.E.) from Glandford-Bridge, containing 346 inhabitants. The chapel is dedicated to St. Thomas à Becket. There is a place of worship for Wesleyan Methodists.

AMERSHAM, or AGMONDESHAM, a borough, market town, and parish, in the hundred of BURNHAM, county of BUCKINGHAM, 33 miles (S.E. by S.) from Buckingham, and 25¾ (W. N.W.) from London, containing 2612 inhabitants. In the reign of Henry V. several of the inhabitants were burnt at the stake for professing the tenets of the Lollards; and in that of Mary, this was again the scene of religious persecution, many individuals having suffered a similar fate for their adherence to the principles of the Reformation. The town is situated in a pleasant valley near the river Colne, surrounded by wood-crowned hills, and consists principally of one street, not lighted, but well paved: there is a plentiful supply of water. Cotton and black lace is manufactured here; many females are employed in platting straw, and wooden chairs are made for exportation. The market is on Tuesday: fairs are held on Whit-Monday and the 19th of September. A constable and other officers are appointed at the court leet of the lord of the manor. The town hall, standing in the centre of the town, is a handsome brick edifice, resting on piazzas, erected by Sir William Drake: the lower part is appropriated to the use of the market; the upper part, which is surmounted by a lantern turret, is used for transacting the public business, and holding parliamentary elections. The town, which is a borough by prescription, sent burgesses to parliament from the 28th of Edward I. until the 2nd of Edward II., but made no return until the 21st of James I., since which time it has continued to send two members to parliament. The right of election is vested in the inhabitant householders paying scot and lot: the constable is the returning officer. The poet Waller, and the celebrated Algernon Sydney, represented this borough.

The living is a rectory, in the archdeaconry of Buckingham, and diocese of Lincoln, rated in the king's books at £48. 16. 1½., and in the patronage of Thomas Tyrwhitt Drake, Esq. The church, dedicated to St. Mary, is a spacious edifice of brick, coated with stucco; the chancel and an adjoining mausoleum contain several interesting monuments. There are two places of worship for Particular Baptists, and one for the Society of Friends. The free grammar school was founded, in the reign of Elizabeth, by Dr. Robert Chaloner, canon of Windsor, who endowed it with £25 per annum; he also founded three scholarships at Christ Church College, Oxford, for boys of Amersham and Goldsborough, or Knaresborough, in Yorkshire. A Sunday school, originally supported by subscription, was endowed by William Drake, jun., Esq.; and an almshouse for six aged widows was endowed, in 1669, by Sir William Drake, Bart.

AMESBURY, a parish (formerly a market town) in the hundred of AMESBURY, county of WILTS, 7 miles (N.) from Salisbury, and 78 (W.S.W.) from London, containing 810 inhabitants. This place, anciently called *Ambresbury*, derives its name from Aurelius Ambrosius, a descendant of the Romans, who is said to have assumed the purple in Britain towards the decline of the Roman empire, and who headed the Britons in several attempts to repel their Saxon invaders. A monastery for three hundred monks is stated to have been founded here by Ambruis, a British monk, or, more probably, by Ambrosius, which was destroyed by Gurthurm, or Gurmundus, a Saxon chief. After the conversion of the Saxons to Christianity, a synod was held here, in the reign of King Edgar, to adjust the differences which existed between the regular and the secular clergy, which had been previously discussed in an assembly held at Calne. About 980, Elfrida, widow of the same king, founded here a nunnery of the Benedictine order, which she dedicated to St. Mary and St. Melorius, a Cornish saint, in expiation, it is supposed, of the murder of Edward, her step-son, at Corfe Castle. In 1177, the abbess and nuns were expelled, on the ground of incontinence; and Henry II. made it a cell to the foreign abbey of Fontevrault. Queen Eleanor, widow of Henry III., assumed the veil in this convent, where she died in 1291. It was at length made denizen; and, at the dissolution, its revenue was valued at £558. 10. 2. The mansion called the Abbey, which now occupies the site of the nunnery, was, after the French revolution, at the close of the last century, appropriated for several years to the use of a society of nuns from Louvaine in Flanders, who afterwards removed into Dorsetshire. The town is situated in a small valley, on the bank of the Upper Avon, and consists of two streets: it is neither paved nor lighted, but is well supplied with water. The market, formerly held on Friday, has been discontinued: fairs are held on the 17th of May, 21st of June, and 21st of December. Constables and other officers are appointed at the court leet of the lord of the manor.

The living is a perpetual curacy, in the archdeaconry of Wilts, and diocese of Salisbury, endowed with £400 private benefaction, and £700 parliamentary grant, and in the patronage of the Dean and Canons of Windsor. The church, which was formerly conventual, is a very ancient building, probably of Saxon architecture; it is dedicated to St. Mary and St. Melorius, and has recently been completely repaired: it is warmed by a pair of very handsome stoves, which cost £189, and were presented by Sir Edmund Antrobus, Bart. There is a place of worship for Wesleyan Methodists. An English school for twenty boys was founded and endowed, in 1677, by Mr. John Rose; and a school for teaching fifty children to read was endowed with an estate left by Mr. Spratt: a charity school for clothing and instructing fifteen boys and fifteen girls, and a National school, are supported by subscription. A fund is also appropriated to the apprenticing of children. Westward from the river there is an ancient encampment, with a vallum and deep fosse, occupying an area of forty acres, commonly attributed to Vespasian, but undoubtedly of British origin: the road from Amesbury to Warminster is cut through its rampart. Within two miles is Stonehenge, a remarkable and well-known relic of British antiquity.

AMOTHERBY, a chapelry in the parish of APPLETON le STREET, wapentake of RYEDALE, North riding of the county of YORK, 3 miles (N. W. by W.) from New Malton, containing 249 inhabitants. A school is endowed with land producing about £20 per annum, in which forty boys are educated, but only six of them are free scholars.

AMPLEFORTH, or AMPLEFORD, a parish partly in the liberty of ST. PETER of YORK, East riding, and partly in the wapentake of BIRDFORTH, but chiefly in the wapentake of RYEDALE, North riding, of the county of YORK, comprising the townships of Ampleforth and Kirk-Oswald-quarter, and containing 582 inhabitants, of which number, 214 are in the township of Ampleforth, in the last-named division of the county, 4½ miles (S.W. by S.) from Helmsley. The living is a discharged vicarage, in the peculiar jurisdiction and patronage of the Prebendary of Ampleforth in the Cathedral Church of York, rated in the king's books at £4. 6. 5½. The church is dedicated to St. Hilda. There is a place of worship for Wesleyan Methodists.

AMPNEY (ST. MARY), or ASHBROOK, a parish in the hundred of CROWTHORNE and MINETY, county of GLOUCESTER, 3½ miles (E.) from Cirencester, containing 130 inhabitants. The living is a perpetual curacy, in the archdeaconry and diocese of Gloucester, endowed with £400 private benefaction, £400 royal bounty, and £200 parliamentary grant, and in the patronage of the Crown. The church is small, exhibiting remains of early English architecture.

AMPNEY (ST. PETER), or EASINGTON, a parish in the hundred of CROWTHORNE and MINETY, county of GLOUCESTER, 4¼ miles (E. by S.) from Cirencester, containing 177 inhabitants. The living is a perpetual curacy, in the archdeaconry and diocese of Gloucester, endowed with £1600 royal bounty, and in the patronage of the Bishop of Gloucester.

AMPNEY-CRUCIS, a parish in the hundred of CROWTHORNE and MINETY, county of GLOUCESTER, 3½ miles (E.) from Cirencester, containing 590 inhabitants. The living is a discharged vicarage, in the archdeaconry and diocese of Gloucester, rated in the king's books at £6. 9. 0½., and in the patronage of the Crown. The church, dedicated to the Holy Rood, has an embattled tower, and some portions of ancient architecture. Here is a charity school.

AMPNEY-DOWN, a parish in the hundred of CROWTHORNE and MINETY, county of GLOUCESTER, 4 miles (S. W. by W.) from Fairford, containing 365 inhabitants. The living is a discharged vicarage, in the archdeaconry and diocese of Gloucester, rated in the king's books at £10. 5. 8., endowed with £200 private benefaction, and £200 royal bounty, and in the patronage of the Dean and Canons of Christ Church, Oxford. The church, dedicated to All Saints, has a tower and spire, and is chiefly in the early English style, having been built by the Knights Templars, to whom the living was given by Edward I.

AMPORT, a parish in the hundred of ANDOVER, Andover division of the county of SOUTHAMPTON, 4¼ miles (W. by S.) from Andover, containing, with the tythings of Cholderton and Sarson, 646 inhabitants. The living is a vicarage, with the perpetual curacy of Appleshaw annexed, in the archdeaconry and diocese of Winchester, rated in the king's books at £25. 7. 11., and in the patronage of the Dean and Chapter of Chichester. The church is dedicated to St. Mary. In 1812, a schoolhouse was erected here by Mrs. Sheppard, to which the Rev. Thomas Sheppard, D.D., added a bequest of £20 a year, for the education of poor children. There is an almshouse for six poor persons.

AMPTHILL, a market town and parish in the hundred of REDBORNESTOKE, county of BEDFORD, 7 miles (S. by W.) from Bedford, and 45 (N. W. by N.) from London, containing 1527 inhabitants. In the reign of Henry VI., Sir John Cornwall, created Lord Fanhope, built a castle on the manor of Ampthill, which, about the year 1530, came into the possession of the crown, and was made the head of an honour by act of parliament. Catherine of Arragon resided here while the business of the divorce was pending, where she received the summons to attend the commissioners at Dunstable, which she refused to obey. In memory of this, the Earl of Ossory, in 1770, erected on the site of the castle a handsome column, with an appropriate inscription by Horace Walpole, Earl of Orford. The modern seat is chiefly remarkable for the number of very ancient oaks which ornament the park. The town, pleasantly situated between two hills, is irregularly built, paved with pebbles, and amply supplied with water; it has been of late years considerably improved by the removal of old buildings, and the erection of a handsome market-house. The market is on Thursday: fairs are held on the 4th of May and 30th of November, for cattle. The county magistrates hold here petty sessions for the hundred; and a court for the honour of Ampthill is held in the moot-house, an ancient building, under the lord high steward, at which constables and officers are appointed.

The living is a discharged rectory, in the archdeaconry of Bedford, and diocese of Lincoln, rated in the king's books at £10. 6. 8., endowed with £300 private benefaction, and £200 royal bounty, and in the patronage of Lord Holland. The church, dedicated to St. Andrew, is a handsome cruciform structure, partaking of the decorated and later styles of English architecture, with a square embattled tower rising from the centre. There are places of worship for the Society of Friends and Wesleyan Methodists. A charity school, for twenty boys and twenty-four girls, was endowed by Mrs. Sarah Emery, in 1691, with lands producing £30 per annum; and a rent-charge of £5, given by Mr. George Watson, in 1740, is appropriated to the instruction of sixteen poor children. About a mile from the town is an hospital, founded by John Cross, in 1690, for a reader, twelve poor men, and four poor women: the reader has £15 per annum, and the others £10; they must be unmarried. The Vice-chancellor of the University of Oxford, and the Bishop of that diocese, are visitors. The interest arising from a legacy of £700, left by Mr. Arthur Whitchelner, in 1687, for apprenticing poor children, is shared by this parish conjointly with the parishes of Maulden, Millbrook, and Ridgemont.

AMPTON, a parish in the hundred of THEDWESTRY, county of SUFFOLK, 5¼ miles (N. by E.) from Bury St. Edmund's, containing 117 inhabitants. The living is a discharged rectory, in the archdeaconry of Sudbury, and diocese of Norwich, rated in the king's books at £5. 2. 1., and in the patronage of Lord Calthorpe. The church is dedicated to St. Peter. A school is endowed with £5 per annum, the gift of — Edwards, for the instruction of five children. An hospital, for clothing, maintaining, and educating six boys, for seven years, is supported by the produce of some land bequeathed by James Calthorpe, in 1705; and there is also an almshouse for four poor women.

AMWELL (GREAT), a parish in the hundred and county of HERTFORD, 1½ mile (S. E. by S.) from Ware, containing 1110 inhabitants. The living is a discharged vicarage, in the archdeaconry of Middlesex, and diocese of London, rated in the king's books at £6, endowed with £200 private benefaction, and £200 royal bounty, and in the patronage of R. C. Elwes, Esq. The church is dedicated to St. John the Baptist. In this parish is the East India College, founded in 1806, for the education of young men intended for the civil service of the Hon. East India Company in India: it will admit one hundred and five students, who are under the superintendence of a principal and several professors. On a hill above the church is an ancient mound, the remains of a fortification; and in Barrow field, on the road to Hertford, is a large barrow. Great Amwell has been the residence of some celebrated literary characters, among whom were, Izaak Walton, the noted angler; Mr. Scott, author of several poems and tracts, who built a curious grotto, containing several apartments, which still exists; and Mr. Hoole, the distinguished translator of Tasso, and biographer of Mr. Scott. The remains of Warner, the historian, were interred in the churchyard.

AMWELL (LITTLE), a liberty in that part of the parish of ALL SAINTS, HERTFORD, which is in the hundred of HERTFORD, county of HERTFORD, 1¼ mile (S. E. by S.) from Ware, containing 256 inhabitants. Here is a chapel of ease to the vicarage of All Saints. The New River, which supplies so considerable a part of the metropolis with water, has its source in a spring that rises in this liberty, called Emma's Well; of which it is supposed, the name of the place is a contraction.

ANCASTER, a parish in the wapentake of LOVEDEN, parts of KESTEVEN, county of LINCOLN, 6¾ miles (N. E.) from Grantham, containing 439 inhabitants. The living is a discharged vicarage, in the archdeaconry and diocese of Lincoln, rated in the king's books at £6. 13. 4., endowed with £200 royal bounty, and in the patronage of the Rev. J. Jowett. The church, dedicated to St. Martin, has a tower surmounted by a spire; the arches on the north side of the nave are of Norman, and those on the south of early English, architecture, while other parts exhibit a later style. Ancaster is supposed to occupy the site of the Roman station *Corisennis:* it stands on the line of the ancient Ermin-street, and various Roman coins and other relics have been found in the vicinity.

ANCROFT, a parish in ISLANDSHIRE, county palatine of DURHAM, though locally to the north of the county of Northumberland, adjoining Berwick upon Tweed, containing 1378 inhabitants. The living is a perpetual curacy, in the archdeaconry and diocese of Durham, endowed with £200 private benefaction, £400 royal bounty, and £800 parliamentary grant, and in the patronage of the Dean and Chapter of Durham. The church, which is a very ancient edifice, was formerly a chapel of ease to the perpetual curacy of Holy Island. The village appears to have been formerly of much greater extent than it is at present, from numerous foundations of houses having been discovered in a field adjoining. A school-room has lately been erected, which is conducted on the Madras system. The parish contains the villages of Ancroft, Cheswick, and Greensis. There is a large brewery at Greensis, in the vicinity of which coal is obtained: there is also a colliery at Scremerston, which village was destroyed by the Scots in 1386. The estate belonged to the Earl of Derwentwater, on whose attainder it was forfeited to the Crown, and now constitutes part of the possessions of Greenwich hospital. Haggerston House was destroyed by fire in 1618, with the exception of one of the towers, still remaining, in which Edward II. received homage from Thomas, Earl of Lancaster, for the earldom of Lincoln, in 1311: it has been rebuilt, with considerable additions and embellishments, and is situated in a spacious park.

ANDERBY, a parish in the Marsh division of the hundred of CALCEWORTH, parts of LINDSEY, county of LINCOLN, 4¼ miles (E. by S.) from Alford, containing 226 inhabitants. The living is a discharged rectory, with that of Cumberworth united, in the archdeaconry and diocese of Lincoln, rated in the king's books at £13. 10. 2½., endowed with £200 private benefaction, and £200 royal bounty, and in the patronage of the President and Fellows of Magdalene College, Cambridge. The church is dedicated to St. Andrew.

ANDERSTON, or ANDERSON, a parish in the northern division of the hundred of COOMBS-DITCH, Blandford (North) division of the county of DORSET, 6 miles (S.) from Blandford-Forum, containing 78 inhabitants. The living is a rectory, in the peculiar jurisdiction of the Dean of Salisbury, rated in the king's books at £6. 19. 1., and in the patronage of L. D. G. Tregonwell, Esq. The church is dedicated to St. Michael.

ANDERTON, a township in that part of the parish of GREAT BUDWORTH which is in the hundred of BUCKLOW, county palatine of CHESTER, 1¾ mile (N. W. by N.) from Northwich, containing 210 inhabitants. On the northern bank of the Weaver, in its course through this township, is an almost uninterrupted line of salt-works: the Grand Trunk canal passes through it.

ANDERTON, a township in the parish of STANDISH, hundred of LEYLAND, county palatine of LANCASTER, 4¾ miles (S. E. by S.) from Chorley, containing 432 inhabitants.

Seal and Arms.

ANDOVER, a borough, market town, and parish, having exclusive jurisdiction, locally in the hundred of Andover, Andover division of the county of SOUTHAMPTON, 26 miles (N. by W.) from Southampton, and 64 (W. S.W.) from London, containing, with the chapelry of Foxcote, 4219 inhabitants. Andover, or, according to the charter, seal, and official documents, *Andever*, is a corruption of the Saxon *Andeafara*, which signifies the passage of the Ande, denoting the proximity of the town to the small river Ande, or Anton. In the church at this place Anlaf, King of Norway, in 994, received the sacrament of confirmation, under the sponsorship of King Ethelred, promising that he would never more come in a hostile manner to England, which engagement he religiously performed. The town, situated on the border of the Wiltshire downs, and near the edge of an extensive tract of woodland, forming the north-west portion of the county, is neat, airy, and well built: it consists principally of three long streets, not lighted, but well paved under an act obtained in 1825, and is plentifully supplied with water. There is a small theatre; and during Weyhill fair assemblies are held in the town hall. The manufacture of silk has, of late, entirely superseded that of shalloons, which was formerly carried on to a great extent; and the construction of a canal from this town, through Stockbridge, to Southampton Water, has, by the increased facility of conveyance, materially improved its trade, particularly in corn, malt, and timber; of the last a vast quantity is forwarded from Harewood Forest, for the supply of Portsmouth dockyard. The principal market is on Saturday, and there is a smaller one on Wednesday. The fairs are on Mid-Lent Saturday and Old May-day, for horses, cattle, cheese, and leather; on the 16th of November for sheep, and on the following day for horses, hops, cheese, &c.

Three miles west of Andover, and within the out-hundred belonging to the town, is Weyhill, where an annual fair is held, which, although originating in a revel anciently kept on the Sunday before Michaelmas-day, has gradually become the largest and best attended in England; merchants and manufacturers from every part of the kingdom assembling here for the transaction of business. It is held on October 10th and six following days, by charter of Queen Elizabeth, confirmed by Charles II. The first day is noted for the sale of sheep, of which the number sold has frequently exceeded one hundred and seventy thousand; on the second, the farmers hire their servants, after which hops, cheese, horses (particularly cart colts), cloth, &c., are exposed for sale; during the first three days the bailiff of Andover holds a court of pie-powder, and receives twopence from each booth, in acknowledgment of his jurisdiction. An additional fair, principally for sheep, was instituted in 1829, and is held on the 1st of August.

The town received its first charter of incorporation from King John; but that under which it is now governed was granted by Elizabeth. The government is vested in a high steward, recorder, town clerk, twelve approved men, and twelve capital burgesses. A bailiff and two magistrates, having exclusive jurisdiction, are annually chosen, by the members of the corporation generally, from among the "approved men:" the bailiff appoints two serjeants at mace to attend him. Courts of session for the borough are held quarterly; and there is a court of record for debts and damages under £40, held every Monday, under an act passed in the 41st of Elizabeth, at which the bailiff and steward, or his deputy, preside. The town hall was erected in 1825, at an expense of £7000, towards defraying which each of the then members for the borough, Sir J. W. Pollen, Bart., and T. A. Smith, Esq., presented £1000. It is a handsome and spacious building of stone, surmounted by a cupola: on the ground-floor is the market-house, over which are a council-room for transacting the business of the corporation, and a hall for holding the quarter sessions. The borough sent representatives to all the parliaments of Edward I., but made no return after the first of Edward II. till the 27th of Elizabeth, since which period it has continued to send two members to parliament: the right of election is vested in the corporation; the bailiff is the returning officer.

The living is a vicarage, in the archdeaconry and diocese of Winchester, rated in the king's books at £17. 4. 3½., and in the patronage of the Warden and Fellows of Winchester College. The church, dedicated to St. Mary, is an ancient building with a fine Norman doorway at the west end; the chancel is separated from the nave by the belfry. There are places of worship for Baptists, the Society of Friends, Independents, and Wesleyan Methodists. The grammar school, in which ten boys are educated, each paying two guineas per annum, was founded and endowed, in 1569, by John Hanson, Esq., whose benefaction was subsequently increased by Richard Kemis: the master, who receives £20 per annum, resides in the house, and is allowed to take private pupils: the school-house was built by the corporation, on land given by Richard Blake, Esq., and is kept in repair at their expense. In 1719, John Pollen, Esq., one of the representatives of the borough, erected a school-house, and endowed it with £10 per annum, for educating twenty poor children. A National school, in which two hundred and fifty children are educated, is supported by subscription. An hospital for eight poor men was founded by John Pollen, Esq.; and six unendowed almshouses for poor women were erected with funds bequeathed by Catherine Hanson, who also gave an acre of ground, planted with trees, to be appropriated as a walk for the recreation of the inhabitants. The Roman road from Winchester to Cirencester passed near Andover, and is yet visible in Harewood coppice; and, besides two or three small encampments near the town, there is a larger one, about a mile to the south-west, on the summit of Bury hill. Some beautiful specimens of Roman pavement have recently been discovered in the neighbourhood. Andover gives the inferior title of viscount to the Earl of Suffolk.

ANGERSLEIGH, a parish in the hundred of Taunton and Taunton-Dean, county of Somerset, 4¾ miles (S.S.W.) from Taunton, containing 64 inhabitants. The living is a discharged rectory, in the archdeaconry of Taunton, and diocese of Bath and Wells, rated in the king's books at £4. 19. 4½., endowed with £200 private benefaction, and £200 royal bounty, and in the patronage of T. Southwood, Esq. The church is dedicated to St. Michael.

ANGERTON (HIGH), a township in that part of the parish of Hartburn which is in the western division of Morpeth ward, county of Northumberland, 7 miles (W.) from Morpeth, containing 87 inhabitants.

ANGERTON (LOW), a township in that part of the parish of Hartburn which is in the western division of Morpeth ward, county of Northumberland, 7½ miles (W. by S.) from Morpeth, containing 75 inhabitants.

ANGLEZARKE, a township in the parish of Bolton, hundred of Salford, county palatine of Lancaster, 4¾ miles (E.S.E.) from Chorley, containing 215 inhabitants. Lead mines are worked in this township, in which carbonate of barytes was first discovered.

ANGMERING, a parish in the hundred of Poling, rape of Arundel, county of Sussex, 3¾ miles (N.E. by E.) from Little Hampton, containing 897 inhabitants. The living comprises the rectory of West Angmering, with the vicarage of East Angmering, in the archdeaconry and diocese of Chichester, rated jointly in the king's books at £21. 9. 8., and in the patronage of Lord de la Zouche. The church is dedicated to St. Peter. A charity school was founded by William Older, in 1679, and endowed with certain houses and thirty acres of land, at East Angmering, which was formerly a distinct parish.

ANGRAM, a township in the parish of Long Marston, ainsty of the city, and East riding of the county, of York, 5 miles (N.E. by N.) from Tadcaster, containing 66 inhabitants. In 1705, Edward Randall bequeathed £200 to the poor of Marston, Hutton, and Angram, the produce of which is applied to the instruction of poor children.

ANGRAM-GRANGE, a township in the parish of Coxwold, wapentake of Birdforth, North riding of the county of York, 4¾ miles (N.) from Easingwould, containing 29 inhabitants.

ANICK, a township in the parish of St. John Lee, southern division of Tindale ward, county of Northumberland, 1¾ mile (N. E. by E.) from Hexham, containing 166 inhabitants. At Hexham Bridge End, in this township, is a large brewery.

ANICK-GRANGE, a township in the parish of St. John Lee, southern division of Tindale ward, county of Northumberland, 1½ mile (E. N. E.) from Hexham, containing 43 inhabitants.

ANLABY, a township partly in the parish of Hessle, but chiefly in the parish of Kirk-Ella, in the county of the town of Kingston upon Hull, East riding of the county of York, 3¼ miles (W.) from Kingston upon Hull, containing 307 inhabitants. There is a place of worship for Wesleyan Methodists.

ANMER, a parish in the Lynn division of the hundred of Freebridge, county of Norfolk, 5¾ miles (N.E. by E.) from Castle-Rising, containing 122 inhabitants. The living is a discharged rectory, in the archdeaconry and diocese of Norwich, rated in the king's books at £9. 0. 1. James Coldham, Esq. was patron in 1816. The church is dedicated to St. Mary.

ANNE (ST.), or BRIERS, a chapelry in the parish of Halifax, wapentake of Morley, West riding of the county of YORK, 3 miles (E. S. E.) from Halifax, with which the population is returned. The living is a perpetual curacy, in the archdeaconry and diocese of York, endowed with £400 private benefaction, £600 royal bounty, and £2100 parliamentary grant, and in the patronage of the Vicar of Halifax.

ANNESLEY, a parish in the northern division of the wapentake of BROXTOW, county of NOTTINGHAM, 6½ miles (S. S. W.) from Mansfield, containing, with the hamlet of Felly, 397 inhabitants. The living is a perpetual curacy, in the archdeaconry of Nottingham, and diocese of York, endowed with £600 royal bounty, and in the patronage of J. Musters, Esq. The church is dedicated to All Saints. There is a place of worship for Wesleyan Methodists.

ANSLEY, a parish in the Atherstone division of the hundred of HEMLINGFORD, county of WARWICK, 5½ miles (W. by N.) from Nuneaton, containing 720 inhabitants. The living is a discharged vicarage, in the archdeaconry of Coventry, and diocese of Lichfield and Coventry, rated in the king's books at £6. 6. 8., and in the patronage of the Crown. The church is dedicated to St. Lawrence. The Oxford canal passes through the village: there are some remains of an ancient castle.

ANSLOW, or ANNESLEY, a township in the parish of ROLLESTON, northern division of the hundred of OFFLOW, county of STAFFORD, 3¾ miles (N. W. by W.) from Burton upon Trent, containing 270 inhabitants. There is a place of worship for Wesleyan Methodists.

ANSTEY, a parish in the county of the city of COVENTRY, 5½ miles (N. E.) from Coventry, containing 205 inhabitants. The living is a vicarage, in the archdeaconry of Coventry, and diocese of Lichfield and Coventry, and in the patronage of the Crown. In 1719, the Rev. John Million left property for founding and endowing a free school for the education of poor children of Anstey and Skilton; of this benefaction there remains but £2 per annum, arising from the lease of a school-house, originally granted for five hundred years.

ANSTEY, a parish in the hundred of EDWINSTREE, county of HERTFORD, 3 miles (S.E.) from Barkway, containing 440 inhabitants. The living is a rectory, in the archdeaconry of Middlesex, and diocese of London, rated in the king's books at £21. 13. 4., and in the patronage of the Master and Fellows of Christ's College, Cambridge. The church is a cruciform edifice, with a central tower, and is said to have been built from the ruins of a castle erected by Eustace, Earl of Boulogne, soon after the Conquest, traces of which are still visible.

ANSTEY, a chapelry in the parish of THURCASTON, western division of the hundred of GOSCOTE, county of LEICESTER, 3¾ miles (N. W.) from Leicester, containing 784 inhabitants. The chapel is dedicated to St. Mary. There is a place of worship for Wesleyan Methodists.

ANSTEY, a parish in the hundred of DUNWORTH, county of WILTS, 5¼ miles (S. E. by S.) from Hindon, containing 327 inhabitants. The living is a perpetual curacy, in the archdeaconry and diocese of Salisbury, and in the patronage of Lord Arundel. The church, dedicated to St. James, is a very ancient structure. Here was a preceptory of the Knights Hospitallers, founded by Walter de Turberville, in the reign of John, the revenue of which at the dissolution was £81. 8. 5.; its remains have been converted into a farm-house. Dr. Richard Zouch, an eminent civilian, and judge of the court of Admiralty in the reign of Charles I., was a native of this place.

ANSTEY (EAST), a parish in the hundred of SOUTH MOLTON, county of DEVON, 3 miles (W. S. W.) from Dulverton, containing 171 inhabitants. The living is a rectory, in the archdeaconry of Barnstaple, and diocese of Exeter, rated in the king's books at £11, and in the patronage of the Mayor and Corporation of Exeter. The church is dedicated to St. Michael.

ANSTEY (WEST), a parish in the hundred of SOUTH MOLTON, county of DEVON, 3½ miles (W.) from Dulverton, containing 220 inhabitants. The living is a discharged vicarage, in the archdeaconry of Barnstaple, and diocese of Exeter, rated in the king's books at £10. 16. 8., and in the patronage of the Dean and Chapter of Exeter. The church is dedicated to St. Petrock. Here is an unendowed almshouse for the reception of the aged and infirm poor.

ANSTEY-PASTURES, an extra-parochial liberty, in the western division of the hundred of GOSCOTE, county of LEICESTER, 3¾ miles (N.W.) from Leicester, containing 11 inhabitants.

ANSTON (NORTH and SOUTH), a parish in the southern division of the wapentake of STRAFFORTH and TICKHILL, West riding of the county of YORK, 6½ miles (W. N. W.) from Worksop, containing 776 inhabitants. The living is a perpetual curacy, annexed to the prebend of Laughton en le Morthen, in the peculiar jurisdiction of the Chancellor in the Cathedral Church of York, endowed with £600 royal bounty, and £1400 parliamentary grant. The church is dedicated to St. James. Nails and starch are manufactured in this parish, and there is some business done in malt. Here is a small endowed school.

ANTHONY (ST.) in MENEAGE, a parish in the hundred of KERRIER, county of CORNWALL, 6 miles (S. by W.) from Falmouth, containing 330 inhabitants. The living is a discharged vicarage, in the peculiar jurisdiction of the Bishop of Exeter, rated in the king's books at £4. 15. 10., and in the patronage of the Crown. Here are two ancient intrenchments, Great and Little Dinas, the latter of which became the site of a small fort, which was occupied by the royalists, during the civil war, for the defence of Helford harbour, and was captured by Sir Thomas Fairfax, in March 1646. At St. Anthony was formerly a cell to the priory of Tywardreth, in the same county. In 1743, Anthony Hosken left a small endowment, to provide food, clothes, books, and instruction for poor children of this parish.

ANTHONY (ST.) in ROSELAND, a parish in the western division of the hundred of POWDER, county of CORNWALL, 9¼ miles (S. W. by S.) from Tregony, containing 179 inhabitants. The living is a perpetual curacy, in the archdeaconry of Cornwall, and diocese of Exeter, and in the patronage of the Earl of Falmouth. Here was a priory of Augustine canons, subordinate to that of Plympton.

ANTHONY (WEST), a parish in the southern division of the hundred of EAST, county of CORNWALL, 5½ miles (S. E.) from St. Germans, containing 2642 inhabitants. The living is a discharged vicarage, in the archdeaconry of Cornwall, and diocese of Exeter, rated in the king's books at £12. 17. 8½., and in the patronage of the Crown. The church is dedicated to St. James. There is a place of worship for Wesleyan Methodists. Ten poor children are instructed with the interest of £300 left for that purpose.

ANTHORN, a township in the parish of BOWNESS, ward and county of CUMBERLAND, 8 miles (N.W. by N.) from Wigton, containing 203 inhabitants.

ANTINGHAM, a parish in the northern division of the hundred of ERPINGHAM, county of NORFOLK, 2½ miles (N. W.) from North Walsham, containing 222 inhabitants. The living consists of the consolidated discharged rectories of St. Margaret and St. Mary, in the archdeaconry of Norfolk, and diocese of Norwich, and in the patronage of Lord Suffield; the former is rated in the king's books at £5. 6. 8., and the latter at £6. 3. 1½. The church is dedicated to St. Mary.

ANTROBUS, a township in that part of the parish of GREAT BUDWORTH which is in the hundred of BUCKLOW, county palatine of CHESTER, 5 miles (N.N. W.) from Northwich, containing 453 inhabitants.

ANWICK, a parish in the wapentake of FLAXWELL, parts of KESTEVEN, county of LINCOLN, 4¾ miles (N. E.) from Sleaford, containing 246 inhabitants. The living is a discharged vicarage, united to the rectories of Brauncewell and Dunsby, in the archdeaconry and diocese of Lincoln, rated in the king's books at £5. 3. 11½., and in the patronage of the Marquis of Bristol. The church is dedicated to St. Edith.

APESTHORPE, county of NOTTINGHAM.—See APPLESTHORPE.

APETHORPE, a parish in the hundred of WILLYBROOK, county of NORTHAMPTON, 4½ miles (S.W. by W.) from Wansford, containing 257 inhabitants. The living is a perpetual curacy, in the peculiar jurisdiction of the Prebendary of Nassington, and in the patronage of the Vicar of Nassington. The church, dedicated to St. Leonard, contains a sumptuous monument to the memory of Sir Anthony Mildmay, Bart., and his lady.

APETON, a township in the parish of GNOSALL, western division of the hundred of CUTTLESTONE, county of STAFFORD, containing 59 inhabitants.

APLEY, a parish in the western division of the wapentake of WRAGGOE, parts of LINDSEY, county of LINCOLN, 2 miles (S. W.) from Wragby, containing 139 inhabitants. The living is a perpetual curacy, with that of Stainfield annexed, in the archdeaconry and diocese of Lincoln, rated in the king's books at £6, endowed with £400 royal bounty, and in the patronage of Thomas Drake, Esq. The church, dedicated to St. Andrew, is desecrated. Part of the once splendid mansion of the Tyrwhitts is now occupied as a farmhouse.

APPERLEY, a joint hamlet with Whitefield, in that part of the parish of DEERHURST which is in the lower division of the hundred of WESTMINSTER, county of GLOUCESTER, 4½ miles (S. W. by S.) from Tewkesbury, containing, with Whitefield, 401 inhabitants. There is a place of worship for Wesleyan Methodists.

APPLEBY, a parish partly in the hundred of REPTON and GRESLEY, county of DERBY, but chiefly in the hundred of SPARKENHOE, county of LEICESTER, 5¼ miles (S. W. by S.) from Ashby de la Zouch, containing 1781 inhabitants. The living is a rectory, in the archdeaconry and diocese of Leicester, rated in the king's books at £20. 9. 4½., and in the patronage of Thomas Wilks, Esq. The church, which is in Leicestershire, is dedicated to St. Michael. This parish is in the honour of Tutbury, duchy of Lancaster, and within the jurisdiction of a court of pleas, held at Tutbury every third Tuesday, for the recovery of debts under 40s.

APPLEBY, a parish in the northern division of the wapentake of MANLEY, parts of LINDSEY, county of LINCOLN, 7 miles (N. W. by N.) from Glandford-Bridge, containing 534 inhabitants. The living is a discharged vicarage, in the archdeaconry of Stow, and diocese of Lincoln, rated in the king's books at £10. 4., and in the patronage of John Williamson, Esq. The church is dedicated to St. Bartholomew.

Seal and Arms.

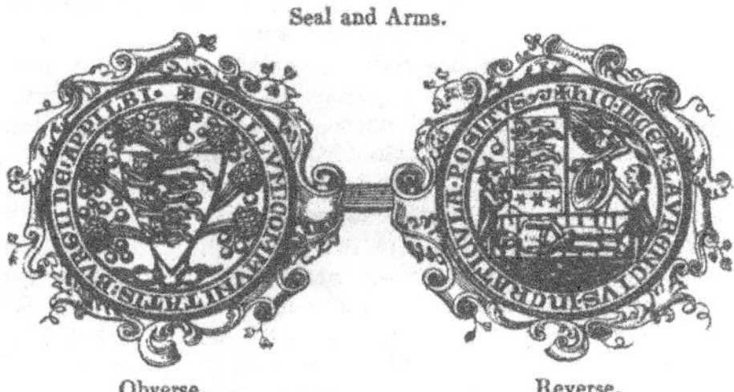

Obverse. Reverse,

APPLEBY, a borough and market town, having separate jurisdiction, locally in East ward, county of WESTMORLAND, of which it is the chief town, 274 miles (N. N. W.) from London, containing 824 inhabitants. This place is thought, but on uncertain grounds, to have been a Roman station. Camden, from a similarity of name, erroneously calls it *Aballaba*; and Horsley considers it to have been the Roman *Galacum*. A Roman road passed near it from Langton, on the east, to Redlands Bank on the north-west; and some Roman antiquities are stated to have been discovered in the vicinity. Appleby has long been the head of a barony, sometimes called the barony of Westmorland; the rest of the county, which forms the barony of Kendal, having been anciently included in Lancashire and Yorkshire. It was granted by the Conqueror to Ranulph de Meschines, whose son Ranulph, having in his mother's right succeeded to the earldom of Chester, gave it to his sister, the wife of Robert d' Estrivers; and having been in the possession of the families of Engain and Morville, it was seized by the crown, in consequence of a member of the latter family being concerned in the murder of Thomas à Becket. King John granted it, together with the "Sheriffwick and rent of the county of Westmorland," to Robert de Veteripont, lord of Curvaville in Normandy, whose grandson Robert joining the confederated barons, in the reign of Henry III., it was forfeited to the Crown, but was restored to the two younger daughters of Robert, and subsequently, by marriage, came into the possession of the illustrious family of Clifford, and was ultimately transferred, by marriage, to Lord Tufton, afterwards Earl of Thanet, whose descendants have ever since enjoyed it, with all its rights and dignities. The town was anciently of much greater magnitude than it is at present, as is evident from the situation of a township called *Burrals* (Borough Walls), a mile distant, and from the discovery of old foundations at the distance of more than two miles, to which the town and its suburbs formerly extended. An ancient record, about the period of the reign of Edward I., makes mention of a sheriff of Applebyshire; from which it appears that the town gave name to one of those districts into which Edward the Confessor divided the earldom of Northumberland. It retained its importance from the time of the Romans until the year 1176, when William, King of Scotland, surprised the castle, and destroyed the town; but from this calamity it had so far recovered in the reign of Henry III., that a court of exchequer was established in it. A Carmelite monastery was founded at Battle-Barrow, in the parish of St. Michael, in 1281, by the Lords Vesey, Clifford, and Percy; the site is now occupied by a neat modern mansion, called the Friary. In the year 1388, the town was again totally laid waste by the Scots, from the effects of which it never afterwards recovered: so that, in the reign of Philip and Mary, it was found necessary to reduce the ancient fee-farm rent, due to the Crown, from twenty marks to two. In 1598, it was nearly depopulated by the plague, and its market was consequently removed to Gilshaughlin, a village five miles distant. At the commencement of the parliamentary war, the castle was garrisoned for the king by the Countess of Pembroke, and continued in his interest until after the battle of Marston-Moor, when all the northern fortresses fell into the possession of the parliament.

The town is pleasantly situated on the river Eden, by which it is almost surrounded, and consists of one spacious street, intersected at right angles by three smaller, and terminated at one extremity by the castle, and at the other by the church of St. Lawrence: at each end also there is a handsome stone obelisk, or cross. An ancient stone bridge of two arches connects the suburb of Bongate with the borough, from which it is otherwise separated by the river. The town is well paved and amply supplied with water. The castle stands on a steep and richly wooded eminence rising from the river: it suffered much in the wars with Scotland, especially in the reigns of Richard II. and Henry IV. Of the original structure, said to be of Roman foundation, only a detached portion, called Cæsar's Tower, and a small part of the south-east end, remain; the greater part of it was rebuilt by Lord Clifford, in the reign of Henry VI. It is now occupied by the steward of the Earl of Thanet, the present proprietor, who is hereditary sheriff of the county; and has been, from time immemorial, the temporary residence of the judges travelling the northern circuit, who are entertained here at his expense. The market is on Saturday; and fairs are held on the Saturday before Whit-Sunday, for cattle; on Whit-Monday, for linen cloth and the hiring of servants; the second Wednesday in June; and the 21st of August, for woollen cloth, cheese, horses, and cattle. The market-house, or the cloisters, is a handsome structure near the church, rebuilt by the corporation in 1811, in the early style of English architecture, after a design by Mr. Smirke. Appleby, which is a borough by prescription, received a charter of incorporation from Henry I., with privileges equal to those of York, which was renewed by Henry II., King John, and Henry III., and subsequently confirmed by Edward I. Under this charter the government is vested in a mayor, recorder, twelve aldermen, and sixteen common council-men, assisted by a town clerk, two chamberlains, a sword-bearer, and a serjeant at mace. The mayor, who is elected annually by the common council-men, is a justice of the peace, though exercising only limited jurisdiction. The borough has sent members to parliament since the 23rd of Edward I.: the right of election is vested in the holders of burgage tenements, in number about two hundred; the mayor is the returning officer. The town hall is a large ancient edifice in the principal street. The assizes for the county are held in the shire hall, adjoining the gaol, erected in 1771; and the general quarter sessions are held alternately at Appleby and Kendal, the Easter and Michaelmas at the former, and the Epiphany and Midsummer at the latter. The county gaol has been recently adapted to the radiating plan, in conformity with the provisions of the late gaol act.

Appleby is situated in the parishes of St. Lawrence and St. Michael, that portion of it which is in the latter being named Bongate. The livings of both these parishes are vicarages, in the archdeaconry and diocese of Carlisle; that of St. Lawrence is rated in the king's books at £9. 5. 2½., and in the patronage of the Dean and Chapter of Carlisle; and that of St. Michael is rated at £20. 13. 9., and in the patronage of the Bishop of Carlisle. The church of St. Lawrence is an ancient structure, partly in the decorated, and partly in the later, style of English architecture; it contains the remains of Anne, the celebrated Countess of Pembroke, Dorset, and Montgomery, who died in 1675, and of her mother, the Countess of Cumberland, to the memory of each of whom there is a splendid marble monument. The church of St. Michael is situated about three quarters of a mile south-east of the town. There is a place of worship for Wesleyan Methodists. The free grammar school, founded by the burghers, existed long before the dissolution of religious houses, but was established on its present foundation in the 16th of Elizabeth, when the management was vested in ten governors, who are a corporate body. The endowment, arising from different sources, is about £200 per annum: it has five exhibitions, of £8 per annum each, to Queen's College, Oxford, founded by Thomas, Earl of Thanet, in 1720, and is entitled to send candidates for one of Lady Elizabeth Hastings' exhibitions to the same college. Dr. Bedel, Bishop of Kilmore; Dr. Barlow, Bishop of Lincoln; Drs. Smith and Waugh, Bishops of Carlisle; and Dr. Langhorne, the translator of Plutarch; were educated in this school. St. Anne's Hospital, for thirteen aged widows, was founded and endowed, in 1653, by Anne, Countess of Pembroke; the revenue arising from lands is about £490, and it has a considerable funded property; the building, which is quadrangular, comprises thirteen distinct habitations and a neat chapel: the chaplain and sisters are appointed by the Earl of Thanet, as heir of the Countess, who left also various lands at Temple-Sowerby, in this parish, for repairing the church, school-house, town hall, and bridge. In the neighbourhood were two ancient hospitals for lepers, dedicated respectively to St. Leonard and St. Nicholas; the estate of the latter was applied by the countess towards the endowment of her almshouse: there was also a chapel at the western end of the stone bridge of St. Lawrence. Thomas de Appleby, Bishop of Carlisle; and Roger de Appleby, Bishop of Ossory; were natives of this town.

APPLEDORE, a parish in the hundred of BLACKBOURNE, lathe of SCRAY, county of KENT, 6 miles (S. E. by S.) from Tenterden, containing 559 inhabitants. The living is a vicarage, with the perpetual curacy of Ebony annexed, in the archdeaconry and diocese of Canterbury, rated in the king's books at £21, and in the patronage of the Archbishop of Canterbury. The church, which is dedicated to St. Peter and St. Paul, exhibits some portions of decorated English architecture.

APPLEDRAM, a parish in the hundred of BOX and STOCKBRIDGE, rape of CHICHESTER, county of SUSSEX, 1¾ mile (S. W.) from Chichester, containing 133 inhabitants. The living is a perpetual curacy, in the archdeaconry and diocese of Chichester, rated in the king's books at £14, endowed with £600 royal bounty, and £200 parliamentary grant, and in the patronage of the Dean and Chapter of Chichester. The church, which is in the early style of English architecture, with a shingled tower, is dedicated to St. Mary: the south aisle is separated from the nave by three pointed arches springing from circular columns, and a stone on the north side bears an inscription with the date 1394. The parish is bounded on the west by the harbour of Chichester.

APPLEFORD, a chapelry in the parish of SUTTON-COURTNEY, hundred of OCK, county of BERKS, 3½ miles (S. E.) from Abingdon, containing 161 inhabitants. The chapel is dedicated to St. Peter and St. Paul. Here is a free school, founded and endowed by Edmund Bradstock, for the education of twenty poor children, seven from the chapelry of Appleford, and the remainder from the parish of Sutton.

APPLESHAW, a parish in the hundred of ANDOVER, Andover division of the county of SOUTHAMPTON, 3 miles (E. S. E.) from Ludgershall, containing 278 inhabitants. The living is a perpetual curacy, annexed to the vicarage of Amport, in the archdeaconry and diocese of Winchester, and in the patronage of the Dean and Chapter of Chichester. Fairs for the sale of sheep are held here on May 23rd and November 4th and 5th. There is a school for the education of six poor children, with an endowment of £2. 10. per annum, the bequest of Francis Offley, in 1761.

APPLESTHORPE, or APESTHORPE, a parish in the North-clay division of the wapentake of BASSETLAW, county of NOTTINGHAM, containing 103 inhabitants. The living is a perpetual curacy, in the peculiar jurisdiction and patronage of the Prebendary of Apesthorpe in the Cathedral Church of York, endowed with £200 royal bounty. The church being desecrated, the ecclesiastical rites are performed at North Leverton.

APPLETHWAITE, a township in the parish of WINDERMERE, KENDAL ward, county of WESTMORLAND, 5¼ miles (S. E.) from Ambleside, containing 417 inhabitants. There are two bobbin-mills in the township, which is interspersed with several beautiful villas, among which is Calgarth Park, commenced in 1789, by Dr. Watson, Bishop of Llandaff, who occupied it till his death, in 1816; his remains were interred at Bowness. The children of this township are entitled to the advantages of the charity school at Bowness.

APPLETON, a parish in the hundred of OCK, county of BERKS, 5½ miles (N. W.) from Abingdon, containing, with the township of Eaton, 389 inhabitants. The living is a rectory, in the archdeaconry of Berks, and diocese of Salisbury, rated in the king's books at £13. 5., and in the patronage of the President and Fellows of Magdalene College, Oxford. The church is dedicated to St. Lawrence. This parish is bounded on one side by the river Thames, which separates it from Oxfordshire, and on the other by the Ouse. Near the church is the manor-house, a moated mansion, remarkable for its great antiquity, the architecture being of the reign of Henry II. Sir R. Fettiplace, in the first of James I., endowed a free school, to which subsequent benefactions have been added; and, in 1757, George Knibb, D.D., left £3 per annum for teaching six boys. Dr. Edmund Dickinson, who published a learned work, entitled *Delphi Phœnicizantes*, tracing the origin of heathen mythology to the Bible, was born here, in 1624.

APPLETON, a joint township with Hull, in that part of the parish of GREAT BUDWORTH which is in the hundred of BUCKLOW, county palatine of CHESTER, 4¼ miles (S. S. E.) from Warrington. The population is returned with Hull.

APPLETON, a joint township with Widness, in the parish of PRESCOT, hundred of WEST DERBY, county palatine of LANCASTER, 6¾ miles (W. by S.) from Warrington. The population is returned with Widness. The navigable river Mersey runs on the south. There is a place of worship for Wesleyan Methodists.

APPLETON, a parish in the Lynn division of the hundred of FREEBRIDGE, county of NORFOLK, 3½ miles (N. E. by E.) from Castle-Rising. The living, a discharged vicarage, in the archdeaconry and diocese of Norwich, is sequestrated; it is rated in the king's books at £8, and in the patronage of E. Paston, Esq. The church is desecrated.

APPLETON, a township in that part of the parish of CATTERICK which is in the eastern division of the wapentake of HANG, North riding of the county of YORK, 2 miles (S. by W.) from Catterick, containing 87 inhabitants.

APPLETON le MOORS, a township in the parish of LASTINGHAM, wapentake of RYEDALE, North riding of the county of YORK, 3¼ miles (E. N. E.) from Kirkby-Moorside, containing 276 inhabitants. There is a place of worship for Wesleyan Methodists.

APPLETON le STREET, a parish in the wapentake of RYEDALE, North riding of the county of YORK, comprising the chapelry of Swinton, and the townships of Amotherby, Appleton le Street, Broughton, and Hildenley, and containing 873 inhabitants, of which number, 173 are in the township of Appleton le Street, 3¾ miles (W. N. W.) from New Malton. The living is a vicarage, in the archdeaconry of Cleveland, and diocese of York, rated in the king's books at £7. 8. 6½., and in the patronage of the Master and Fellows of Trinity College, Cambridge. The church is dedicated to All Saints.

APPLETON upon WISK, a parish in the western division of the liberty of LANGBRAUGH, North riding of the county of YORK, 7¼ miles (S. S. W.) from Yarm, containing 492 inhabitants. The living is a perpetual curacy, annexed to the rectory of Great Smeaton, in the archdeaconry of Cleveland, and diocese of York. There is a place of worship for Wesleyan Methodists. The manufacture of linen is here carried on to a considerable extent.

APPLETON-ROEBUCK, a township in the parish of BOLTON-PERCY, ainsty of the city, and East riding of the county, of YORK, 7½ miles (S. S. W.) from York, containing 585 inhabitants. There is a place of worship for Wesleyan Methodists.

APPLETREE, a hamlet in the parish of ASTON le WALLS, hundred of CHIPPING-WARDEN, county of NORTHAMPTON, 7 miles (N. N. E.) from Banbury, containing 88 inhabitants.

APPLETREE-WICK, a township in the parish of BURNSALL, eastern division of the wapentake of STAINCLIFFE and EWCROSS, West riding of the county of YORK, 3½ miles (N. E. by N.) from Skipton, containing 312 inhabitants.

ARBORFIELD, a parish in the hundred of SONNING, county of BERKS, 4 miles (W. by S.) from Wokingham, containing 245 inhabitants. The living is a rectory, in the peculiar jurisdiction of the Dean of Salisbury, rated in the king's books at £7. 19. 10., and in the patronage of Lord Braybrook. The church is dedicated to St. Bartholomew.

ARBURY, a joint township with Houghton and Middleton, in the parish of WINWICK, hundred of WEST DERBY, county palatine of LANCASTER, 2½ miles (N. by E.) from Warrington. The population is returned with Houghton.

ARCLEBY, a hamlet in the parish of PLUMBLAND, ALLERDALE ward below Darwent, county of CUMBERLAND, 7 miles (N. N. E.) from Cockermouth. The population is returned with the parish. There are some coal-works in the vicinity.

ARCLID, a township in that part of the parish of SANDBACH which is in the hundred of NORTHWICH, county palatine of CHESTER, 2 miles (E. N. E.) from Sandbach, containing 65 inhabitants.

ARDEN, a joint township with Ardenside, in the parish of HAWNBY, wapentake of BIRDFORTH, North riding of the county of YORK, 8 miles (N. W. by W.) from Helmsley, containing, with Ardenside, 139 inhabitants. A small Benedictine nunnery was founded here about 1150, the revenue of which, at the dissolution, was £12. In 1757, John Smales and Gregory Elsley bequeathed £120. 5., directing the produce to be applied to the instruction of six poor boys.

ARDENSIDE, a joint township with Arden, in the parish of HAWNBY, wapentake of BIRDFORTH, North riding of the county of YORK, 10½ miles (N. E.) from Thirsk. The population is returned with Arden.

ARDINGLEY, a parish in the hundred of BUTTINGHILL, rape of LEWES, county of SUSSEX, 4½ miles (N. E. by N.) from Cuckfield, containing 579 inhabitants. The living is a rectory, in the archdeaconry of Lewes, and diocese of Chichester, rated in the king's books at £19. 5. 10., and in the patronage of J. J. W. Peyton, Esq.

ARDINGTON, a parish in the hundred of WANTAGE, county of BERKS, 2¾ miles (E.) from Wantage, containing 403 inhabitants. The living is a discharged vicarage, in the archdeaconry of Berks, and diocese of Salisbury, rated in the king's books at £8. 7. 9., endowed with £200 royal bounty, and in the patronage of the Dean and Canons of Christ Church, Oxford. The church is dedicated to the Holy Trinity. The Roman Iknield-street passes through this parish, which is also intersected by the Wilts and Berks canal.

ARDLEIGH, a parish in the hundred of TENDRING, county of ESSEX, 4¾ miles (N. E.) from Colchester, containing 1387 inhabitants. The living is a discharged vicarage, in the archdeaconry of Colchester, and diocese of London, rated in the king's books at £11. 0. 10., and in the patronage of the Crown. The church is dedicated to St. Mary. There is a place of worship for Wesleyan Methodists. In 1571, William Littlebury bequeathed property, now producing £120 per annum, for instructing four poor boys.

ARDLEY, a parish in the hundred of PLOUGHLEY, county of OXFORD, 4 miles (N. W. by N.) from Bicester, containing 191 inhabitants. The living is a rectory, in the archdeaconry and diocese of Oxford, rated in the king's books at £5. 12. 8½., and in the patronage of the Duke of Marlborough. The church is dedicated to St. Mary.

ARDSLEY, a township in that part of the parish of DAREFIELD which is in the wapentake of STAINCROSS, West riding of the county of YORK, 2½ miles (E. by S.) from Barnesley, containing 992 inhabitants. There is a place of worship for Wesleyan Methodists. Richard Micklethwaite, in 1745, gave land for the instruction of five children, to which bequest an addition of £50 was made by John Micklethwaite, in 1752.

ARDSLEY (EAST), a parish in the lower division of the wapentake of AGBRIGG, West riding of the county of YORK, 3½ miles (N. W. by N.) from Wakefield, containing 832 inhabitants. The living is a perpetual curacy, in the archdeaconry and diocese of York, endowed with £10 per annum private benefaction, and £200 royal bounty, and in the patronage of the Earl of Cardigan. The neighbourhood abounds with coal, and some of the mines have been worked upwards of a century. Here is a small endowed free school.

ARDSLEY (WEST), a parish in the lower division of the wapentake of AGBRIGG, West riding of the county of YORK, 4½ miles (N. W.) from Wakefield, containing 1515 inhabitants. The living is a perpetual curacy, in the archdeaconry and diocese of York, endowed with £10 per annum private benefaction, and £200 royal bounty, and in the patronage of the Earl of Cardigan. The church is dedicated to St. Mary. This parish was anciently called Woodkirk: it contains extensive coal mines, and the manufacture of stuffs and woollen goods is carried on. In 1745, Richard Micklethwaite bequeathed land, the produce of which was to be applied to the instruction of three poor children; and, in 1752, John Micklethwaite left £50, directing the interest to be applied to a similar purpose. Here are almshouses for three widows. An old mansion, once the seat of Sir John Topcliffe, Lord Chief Justice in the reigns of Henry VII. and Henry VIII., has been converted into a farm-house.

ARDWICK, a chapelry in the parish of MANCHESTER, hundred of SALFORD, county palatine of LANCASTER, 1 mile (S. E. by E.) from Manchester, containing 3545 inhabitants. The living is a perpetual curacy, in the archdeaconry and diocese of Chester, and in the patronage of the Warden and Fellows of the Collegiate Church of Manchester. The chapel is dedicated to St. Thomas. There is a place of worship for Wesleyan

Methodists. Owing to its proximity to Manchester, Ardwick participates extensively in the trade of that place.

ARELY-KING'S, or LOWER ARELY, a parish in the upper division of the hundred of DODDINGTREE, county of WORCESTER, ¾ of a mile (S. W. by W.) from Stourport, containing 358 inhabitants. The living is a rectory, in the archdeaconry and diocese of Worcester, rated in the king's books at £9, and in the patronage of the Rector of Martley. The church, which is situated on an eminence, whence there is a remarkably fine and extensive prospect, is dedicated to St. Bartholomew. In the burial-ground is a rude sepulchral monument, composed of oblong square stones, piled on each other, and bearing a quaint rhyming distich, importing that a person named Sir Harry lies interred beneath it. Who Sir Harry was, has not been satisfactorily ascertained; but an affecting story is related of an individual who was driven into seclusion here, from the loss of an only female child, that was drowned by falling from his arms, as he held her at a window, into a moat beneath, and who is supposed to have been interred here. At Redstone Ferry, on the river Severn, which forms a boundary of this parish, is a very high rock, in the side of which was excavated a hermitage, consisting of a chapel with an altar and some apartments: over the altar was painted a figure of an archbishop saying mass; in 1736, several human bodies, supposed to have been those of the hermits, were discovered. Layamon, author of a poetical Chronicle of British History, from Brute to Cadwallader, who states himself to have been a priest residing at Erenlege on the Severn, and who lived in the latter part of the twelfth century, is said to have been born here.

ARELY (UPPER), a parish in the southern division of the hundred of SEISDON, county of STAFFORD, 5½ miles (N.W. by W.) from Kidderminster, containing 715 inhabitants. The living is a perpetual curacy, in the peculiar jurisdiction of the Dean and Chapter of Lichfield, and in the patronage of the Earl of Mountnorris. The church, dedicated to St. Peter, is situated on an eminence commanding a fine prospect. The village occupies a romantic situation near the side of the river Severn.

ARGAM, a parish in the wapentake of DICKERING, East riding of the county of YORK, 5½ miles (N. W.) from Bridlington, containing 35 inhabitants. The living is a discharged rectory, united to the perpetual curacy of Bridlington, in the archdeaconry of the East riding, and diocese of York, rated in the king's books at £4. The church, dedicated to St. John the Baptist, is desecrated.

ARKENDALE, a chapelry in that part of the parish of KNARESBOROUGH which is in the lower division of the wapentake of CLARO, West riding of the county of YORK, 4 miles (N. E.) from Knaresborough, containing 285 inhabitants. The living is a perpetual curacy, within the jurisdiction of the peculiar court of the honour of Knaresborough, endowed with £200 private benefaction, and £800 royal bounty, and in the patronage of the Vicar of Knaresborough. The chapel is dedicated to St. Bartholomew. There is a place of worship for Wesleyan Methodists.

ARKENGARTH-DALE, a parish in the western division of the wapentake of GILLING, North riding of the county of YORK, 12 miles (W. by N.) from Richmond, containing 1512 inhabitants. The living is a perpetual curacy, within the peculiar jurisdiction of the manorial court of Arkengarth-Dale, New Forest, and Hope, endowed with £200 private benefaction, £600 royal bounty, and £1000 parliamentary grant, and in the patronage of the Earl of Lonsdale. The church, dedicated to St. Mary, is a small neat stone structure, rebuilt in 1820. There is a place of worship for Wesleyan Methodists, lately erected by subscription. A free school was built by the late George Brown, Esq., lord of the manor, who endowed it with £60 per annum, payable out of the manor, for the free instruction of all children of the Dale; the master has also a house and a small piece of land rent-free. The Dale is about eight miles in length, and contains several villages and hamlets: the inhabitants are engaged in the lead mines, which are extremely productive, some of them having been worked so early as the reign of King John.

ARKESDEN, a parish in the hundred of UTTLESFORD, county of ESSEX, 5¼ miles (S. W. by W.) from Saffron-Walden, containing 415 inhabitants. The living is a discharged vicarage, in the archdeaconry of Colchester, and diocese of London, rated in the king's books at £13. 6. 8., and in the patronage of John Wolfe, Esq. The church is dedicated to St. Mary.

ARKHOLME, a chapelry in the parish of MELLING, hundred of LONSDALE, south of the sands, county palatine of LANCASTER, 5¼ miles (S. S. W.) from Kirkby-Lonsdale, containing, with the hamlet of Cawood, 357 inhabitants. The living is a perpetual curacy, in the archdeaconry of Richmond, and diocese of Chester, endowed with £600 royal bounty, and in the patronage of the Vicar of Melling.

ARKSEY, a parish in the northern division of the wapentake of STRAFFORTH and TICKHILL, West riding of the county of YORK, 3 miles (N. by E.) from Doncaster, containing, with the township of Bentley, 1171 inhabitants. The living is a vicarage, in the archdeaconry and diocese of York, rated in the king's books at £12. 17. 6., and in the patronage of Sir William Bryan Cooke, Bart. The church is dedicated to All Saints. Here is a free grammar school, erected in pursuance of the will of Sir George Cooke, with an endowment of £40 per annum, left by Sir Bryan Cooke. An hospital for twelve poor inhabitants is endowed with £120 per annum.

ARLECDON, a parish in ALLERDALE ward above Darwent, county of CUMBERLAND, 5½ miles (E. N. E.) from Whitehaven, comprising the townships of High and Low Frizington and Whillymoor, and containing 478 inhabitants. The living is a perpetual curacy, in the peculiar jurisdiction and patronage of the Bishop of Chester, endowed with £200 private benefaction, £400 royal bounty, and £200 parliamentary grant. The church, dedicated to St. Michael, has been rebuilt, and was consecrated August 25th, 1829. Fairs for cattle are held on April 24th, the first Friday in June, and September 17th. Coal, iron-ore, limestone, and freestone, are found in the parish. On an estate called Cringlegill is a chalybeate spring, the water of which is stated to possess similar properties to that of Harrogate.

ARLESCOTE, a township in the parish of WARMINGTON, Burton-Dassett division of the hundred of

KINGTON, county of WARWICK, 5½ miles (E. S. E.) from Kington. The population is returned with the parish.

ARLESTON, a joint liberty with Synfin, in that part of the parish of BARROW which is in the hundred of APPLETREE, though locally in the hundred of Repton and Gresley, county of DERBY, 4¼ miles (S. by W.) from Derby. The population is returned with Synfin. This liberty is in the honour of Tutbury, duchy of Lancaster, and within the jurisdiction of a court of pleas held at Tutbury every third Tuesday, for the recovery of debts under 40s.

ARLEY, a parish in the Kirby division of the hundred of KNIGHTLOW, county of WARWICK, 6 miles (E. by N.) from Coleshill, containing 267 inhabitants. The living is a rectory, in the peculiar jurisdiction of the Dean and Chapter of Lichfield, rated in the king's books at £9. 0. 7., and in the patronage of the Rev. R. Vaughton. The church is dedicated to St. Wilfrid. A free school is endowed with land, producing £10 per annum, left by William Avesey.

ARLINGHAM, a parish in the upper division of the hundred of BERKELEY, county of GLOUCESTER, 1½ mile (S. E. by E.) from Newnham, containing 715 inhabitants. The living is a vicarage, in the archdeaconry and diocese of Gloucester, rated in the king's books at £19. 7. 8½. Mrs. Rogers was patroness in 1814. The church is dedicated to St. Mary. There is a place of worship for Wesleyan Methodists. Arlingham is situated on a nook of land, formed by a curvature of the river Severn, by which the parish is bounded on three sides. Mrs. Mary Yate, in 1765, endowed a school for boys and girls with a rent-charge of £40, of which she directed that £20 should be paid to the master, and £10 to the mistress, the remainder to be laid out in purchasing books: she also gave an additional rent-charge of £40 for the benefit of the poor.

ARLINGTON, a parish in the hundred of SHERWILL, county of DEVON, 6¼ miles (N. E. by N.) from Barnstaple, containing 177 inhabitants. The living is a rectory, in the archdeaconry and diocese of Exeter, rated in the king's books at £13. 18. 1½., and in the patronage of J. P. B. Chichester, Esq. The church is dedicated to St. James.

ARLINGTON, a tything in that part of the parish of BIBURY which is in the hundred of BRIGHTWELL'S BARROW, county of GLOUCESTER, 4¾ miles (N. W.) from Fairford, containing 317 inhabitants.

ARLINGTON, a parish in the hundred of LONGBRIDGE, rape of PEVENSEY, county of SUSSEX, 3¾ miles (W. S. W.) from Haylsham, containing 614 inhabitants. The living is a discharged vicarage, to which that of Willingdon is annexed, in the archdeaconry of Lewes, and diocese of Chichester, rated in the king's books at £10. 6. 11., and in the patronage of the Prebendary of Woodhorne in the Cathedral Church of Chichester. The church is dedicated to St. Pancras. A priory of Black canons, in honour of the Holy Trinity, was founded here by Gilbert de Aguila, in the beginning of the reign of Henry III., the revenue of which, at the dissolution, was estimated at £191. 19. 3.

ARLSEY, a parish in the hundred of CLIFTON, county of BEDFORD, 4¾ miles (N. W. by W.) from Baldock, containing 562 inhabitants. The living is a discharged vicarage, to which the rectory of Astwick was united in 1764, in the archdeaconry of Bedford, and diocese of Lincoln, rated in the king's books at £8, and in the patronage of R. Houston, Esq. The church is dedicated to St. Peter. This place is recorded in Domesday-book as a market town, and its market, in 1270, was confirmed to Stephen Edworth, then lord of the manor, to be held on Wednesday, with a fair on the festival of St. Peter and St. Paul, both of which have been long discontinued. At Etonbury, near the road to Baldock, is an ancient intrenchment, the site of the castle of the manor.

ARMATHWAITE, a chapelry in the parish of HESKET in the FOREST, LEATH ward, county of CUMBERLAND, 5 miles (N. W.) from Kirk-Oswald. The population is returned with the parish. The living is a perpetual curacy, in the archdeaconry and diocese of Carlisle, endowed with £200 private benefaction, and £400 royal bounty, and in the patronage of the Dean and Chapter of Carlisle. The chapel was rebuilt by Richard Skelton, Esq., in 1668, having for some time previously been used as a shed for cattle. Armathwaite is a neat village, beautifully situated on the western bank of the Eden, over which is a good stone bridge of four arches. The castle, a handsome modern edifice, occupies a rocky elevation, at the foot of which flows the Eden, the site of an ancient fortress; and, in the reign of Henry VIII., was, with the estate, the property of John Skelton, the poet-laureat. A Benedictine nunnery was founded here by William II., the revenue of which, at the dissolution, was £18. 18. 8.: it stood in the parish of Ainstable, on a spot now occupied by a modern mansion, which retains the name of "Nunnery," amid scenery of a variegated and pleasing description: some trifling relics are still visible.

ARMIN, a chapelry in that part of the parish of SNAITH which is in the lower division of the wapentake of OSGOLDCROSS, West riding of the county of YORK, 3 miles (S. W. by S.) from Howden, containing 570 inhabitants. The living is a perpetual curacy, within the jurisdiction of the peculiar court of Snaith, endowed with £600 private benefaction, £600 royal bounty, and £1000 parliamentary grant, and in the patronage of N. Yarburgh, Esq. The chapel is dedicated to St. David.

ARMINGHALL, a parish in the hundred of HENSTEAD, county of NORFOLK, 3½ miles (S. E. by S.) from Norwich, containing 115 inhabitants. The living is a perpetual curacy, in the peculiar jurisdiction and patronage of the Dean and Chapter of Norwich, endowed with £400 royal bounty, and £200 parliamentary grant. The church is dedicated to St. Mary. Here is a school, with an endowment of £5 per annum. The old hall, or manor-house, has a very rich and curious porch.

ARMITAGE, a joint parish with Handsacre, in the southern division of the hundred of OFFLOW, county of STAFFORD, 2¼ miles (E. S. E.) from Rugeley, containing, with Handsacre, 793 inhabitants. The living is a perpetual curacy, in the peculiar jurisdiction and patronage of the Prebendary of Handsacre and Armitage in the Cathedral Church of Lichfield, endowed with £400 royal bounty, and £1400 parliamentary grant. The church is dedicated to St. John. There is a place of worship for Calvinists. Some earthenware is manufactured in the parish.

ARMLEY, a chapelry in the parish of ST. PETER, within the liberty of the borough of LEEDS, West riding of the county of YORK, 2½ miles (W. by N.) from Leeds, containing 4273 inhabitants. The living is a perpetual curacy, in the archdeaconry and diocese of York, endowed with £200 private benefaction, and £200 royal bounty, and in the patronage of the Vicar of Leeds. The chapel, dedicated to St. Bartholomew, was built about the year 1630. There is a place of worship for Wesleyan Methodists. The village is pleasantly situated on the south side of the river Aire, and is principally inhabited by persons occupied in the clothing business : in addition to the fulling-mills, there are cotton and corn mills on the banks of the river. The Leeds and Liverpool canal passes through the chapelry, in a parallel direction to the river, and skirts some elevations, called the Red and White War hills, where intrenchments, attributed to the Danes, were destroyed in its formation.

ARMSCOTT, a hamlet in the parish of TREDINGTON, upper division of the hundred of OSWALDSLOW, county of WORCESTER, lying in a detached portion surrounded by Warwickshire, 3 miles (N. by W.) from Shipston upon Stour, containing 131 inhabitants.

ARMSTON, a hamlet in the parish and hundred of POLEBROOK, county of NORTHAMPTON, 2¼ miles (E. S. E.) from Oundle, containing 23 inhabitants.

ARMTHORPE, a parish in the southern division of the wapentake of STRAFFORTH and TICKHILL, West riding of the county of YORK, 4 miles (E. N. E.) from Doncaster, containing 359 inhabitants. The living is a rectory, in the archdeaconry and diocese of York, rated in the king's books at £8. 18. 9., and in the patronage of the Crown. The church is dedicated to St. Mary. Here is a school, to which, in 1689, Ann Holmes bequeathed a rent-charge of £2. 10., for teaching six children and apprenticing poor boys, which endowment has been augmented with land given by Sir George Cooke, Bart.

ARNCLIFFE, a parish comprising the township of Buckden in the eastern division, and the chapelry of Haltongill, and the townships of Arncliffe, West Halton, Hawkswith, and Litton, in the western division, of the wapentake of STAINCLIFFE and EWCROSS, West riding of the county of YORK, and containing 1063 inhabitants, of which number, 189 are in the township of Arncliffe, 10½ miles (N. E.) from Settle. The living is a discharged vicarage, in the archdeaconry and diocese of York, rated in the king's books at £13. 6. 8., endowed with £200 private benefaction, and £200 royal bounty, and in the patronage of the Master and Fellows of University College, Oxford. The church is dedicated to St. Oswald. The village is pleasantly situated near the river Wharf: the scenery in the vicinity is highly picturesque.

ARNCLIFFE (INGLEBY), a parish in the western division of the liberty of LANGBAURGH, North riding of the county of YORK, 7 miles (S. W. by W.) from Stokesley, containing 331 inhabitants. The living is a perpetual curacy, in the archdeaconry of Cleveland, and diocese of York, endowed with £800 royal bounty, and £400 parliamentary grant, and in the patronage of Bryan Abbes, Esq. The church, dedicated to St. Andrew, is a small ancient edifice.

ARNCOTT, a chapelry in the parish of AMBROSDEN, hundred of BULLINGTON, though locally in the hundred of Ploughley, county of OXFORD, 2½ miles (S. E. by S.) from Bicester, containing 270 inhabitants.

ARNE, a chapelry in the parish of the HOLY TRINITY, WAREHAM, hundred of HASILOR, Blandford (South) division of the county of DORSET, 4 miles (E. by N.) from Wareham, containing 134 inhabitants. The living is a perpetual curacy, in the archdeaconry of Dorset, and diocese of Bristol, and in the patronage of the Rector of Wareham. The chapel is dedicated to St. Nicholas. The village stands on the shore of Poole harbour, between Wareham and Brownsey island. On the summit of an eminence connected with a bank of gravel or pebbles, extending north-eastward into the harbour, there is a large barrow, which has been used as a beacon.

ARNESBY, a parish in the hundred of GUTHLAXTON, county of LEICESTER, 8½ miles (S. by E.) from Leicester, containing 459 inhabitants. The living is a discharged vicarage, in the archdeaconry of Leicester, and diocese of Lincoln, rated in the king's books at £5. 16. 8., endowed with £200 royal bounty, and in the patronage of J. S. Langden, Esq. The church is dedicated to St. Peter. There is a place of worship for Particular Baptists. A small endowment has been bequeathed for the education of poor children.

ARNOLD, a parish in the northern division of the wapentake of BROXTOW, county of NOTTINGHAM, 3½ miles (N. by E.) from Nottingham, containing 3572 inhabitants. The living is a discharged vicarage, in the archdeaconry of Nottingham, and diocese of York, rated in the king's books at £7. 17. 8., and in the patronage of the Duke of Devonshire. The church, dedicated to St. Mary, and situated to the north of the village, is a large edifice in the later style of English architecture, with a tower: on a tablet in the interior are recorded various charitable bequests, amounting to about £150 per annum. There are places of worship for General and Particular Baptists and Primitive and Wesleyan Methodists. The village occupies a large plot of ground, the houses being, for the most part, detached : the inhabitants are principally employed in the manufacture of lace and hosiery for the Nottingham market. In the neighbourhood are a few mills for spinning cotton and worsted yarn. A fair for the sale of live stock is held on the first Wednesday after September 19th. A school for the instruction of poor children is endowed with £22. 18. per annum, the produce of benefactions by Daniel Chadwick and others.

ARRAM, a joint township with Atwick and Skirlington, in the parish of ATWICK, northern division of the wapentake of HOLDERNESS, East riding of the county of YORK, 11½ miles (N. E.) from Beverley. The population is returned with Atwick.

ARRETON, a parish in the liberty of EAST MEDINA, Isle of Wight division of the county of SOUTHAMPTON, 3 miles (S. E.) from Newport, containing 1757 inhabitants. The living is a discharged vicarage, in the archdeaconry and diocese of Winchester, rated in the king's books at £21, and in the patronage of J. Fleming, Esq. The church is dedicated to St. George. In 1688, John Mann, Esq. left a rent-charge of £46 for maintaining, educating, and apprenticing poor orphans and others belonging to this parish.

ARRINGTON, a parish in the hundred of WETHERLEY, county of CAMBRIDGE, 5¼ miles (S. S. E.) from

Caxton, containing 194 inhabitants. The living is a vicarage, in the archdeaconry and diocese of Ely, rated in the king's books at £7. 6. 3., endowed with £200 royal bounty, and £200 parliamentary grant, and in the patronage of the Master and Fellows of Trinity College, Cambridge. The church is dedicated to St. Nicholas.

ARROW, a township in the parish of WOODCHURCH, lower division of the hundred of WIRRALL, county palatine of CHESTER, 6¾ miles (N. by W.) from Great Neston, containing 72 inhabitants.

ARROW, a parish comprising the hamlet of Ragley in the Alcester division, and the hamlet of Oversley in the Stratford division, of the hundred of BARLICHWAY, county of WARWICK, 1 mile (S. W.) from Alcester, and containing 501 inhabitants. The living is a rectory, in the archdeaconry and diocese of Worcester, rated in the king's books at £10. 10. 7½., and in the patronage of the Marquis of Hertford. The church, dedicated to the Holy Trinity, is an ancient structure, but the tower was rebuilt about 1760.

ARROWTHORNE, a township partly in the parish of HORNBY, but chiefly in that of BROMPTON-PATRICK, eastern division of the wapentake of HANG, North riding of the county of YORK, 5 miles (S. W. by S.) from Catterick, containing 64 inhabitants.

ARTHINGTON, a township in the parish of ADDLE, upper division of the wapentake of SKYRACK, West riding of the county of YORK, 4½ miles (E.) from Otley, containing 329 inhabitants. A convent of Cluniac nuns was founded here, in the twelfth century, by Piers de Ardington, which was valued, at the dissolution, at £19: the site is occupied by a farm-house, now called the "Nunnery." There is an endowment of £3 per annum for the education of poor children.

ARTHINGWORTH, a parish in the hundred of ROTHWELL, county of NORTHAMPTON, 4½ miles (S. by E.) from Market-Harborough, containing, with the extra-parochial liberty of Barford, 219 inhabitants. The living is a rectory, in the archdeaconry of Northampton, and diocese of Peterborough, rated in the king's books at £12. 2. 8½., and in the patronage of L. Rokeby, Esq. The church is dedicated to St. Andrew. A school here is endowed with land producing £24 per annum.

ARTHURET, a parish in ESKDALE ward, county of CUMBERLAND, ¾ of a mile (S.) from Longtown, comprising the townships of Brackenhill, Lineside, Longtown, and Netherby, and containing 2953 inhabitants. The living is a rectory, in the archdeaconry and diocese of Carlisle, rated in the king's books at £3. 2. 1., and in the patronage of Sir J. Graham, Bart. The church, dedicated to St. Michael, was rebuilt in 1609, with the exception of the tower, which was not completed till 1690. In the churchyard is a rude cross, with a pierced capital, near which were interred the remains of Archibald Armstrong, court jester to James I. and Charles I., who was a native of this parish. Arthuret is situated on the border of Scotland; and at the chapel of Solom, a small oratory, which anciently stood near the spot called the Chapel Flosh, commissioners from England and Scotland met, in 1343, to settle the boundaries of the respective countries. On Solom Moss, the Scots, under Oliver Sinclair, were defeated by Sir Thomas Wharton, Lord Warden of the English Marches, in 1543. The parish was formerly much larger than it is at present, the adjoining parish of Kirk-Andrews having been separated from it in the reign of Charles I.: it includes part of the ancient parish of Easton; there are quarries of white and red freestone within its limits. A school, in which eight children are educated, was founded by Lady Widdrington, in 1754, and endowed with property producing £40 per annum.

ARTILLERY-GROUND (OLD), a liberty in the FINSBURY division of the hundred of OSSULSTONE, county of MIDDLESEX, containing 1487 inhabitants.

ARTINGTON, a tything in that part of the parish of ST. NICHOLAS, GUILDFORD, which is in the first division of the hundred of GODALMING, county of SURREY, 1 mile (S. by W.) from Guildford, containing 489 inhabitants.

Arms.

ARUNDEL, a borough, market town, and parish, having exclusive jurisdiction, locally in the hundred and rape of Arundel, county of SUSSEX, 10 miles (E. by N.) from Chichester, and 55 (S. by W.) from London, containing 2511 inhabitants. This place, which derives its name from its situation in a dale watered by the river Arun, is first noticed in the will of Alfred, who bequeathed the castle and few adjacent residences to his nephew Athelm. The castle, rebuilt by Roger de Montgomery, at the time of the Conquest, was, in the reign of Henry I., besieged and taken from his son, Robert de Belesme, who had rebelled against his sovereign. In 1397, a conspiracy to dethrone Richard II., and to murder the lords of his council, was organised here by the Earl of Arundel, the Archbishop of Canterbury, the Duke of Gloucester, and others, but was discovered before it could be carried into execution. During the parliamentary war, the possession of the castle was considered an important object by the contending parties, and it consequently sustained frequent assaults: in one of these sieges, the learned Chillingworth, who had joined the royal army, was taken prisoner, and confined in the episcopal palace at Chichester, where he died. In consequence of the dilapidation which it thus sustained, it lay for some time neglected, and some parts mouldered into ruin; but it was restored by the late Duke of Norfolk, and is now one of the most splendid baronial mansions in the kingdom. It confers on its possessor the title of earl without creation, a feudal right, which was adjudged by parliament, in the 11th of Henry VI., to an ancestor of the present Duke of Norfolk, and is the only place, with the exception of the castle of Abergavenny, in Monmouthshire, which enjoys this distinction. The town, which is pleasantly situated on rising ground, is divided into two parts by the river Arun, here navigable for vessels of three hundred tons' burden, over which is a neat stone bridge of three arches. It is much frequented as a bathing-place, being within a distance of four miles from the sea, from which ships drawing sixteen feet water can enter the port. The houses are in general well built, and many of them are modern and of handsome appearance; the streets are well paved, and the inhabitants plentifully supplied with excellent water. The theatre, which is opened occasionally, is a neat building: the environs afford pleasant promenades, and the higher grounds in the vicinity extensive prospects. The trade is principally in timber, coal, and corn; and the port also affords a facility of intercourse between London and the Mediterranean, enabling the fruit ships from the latter to perform two voyages in the season. A canal, connecting the Arun with the Thames, affords a medium of conveyance to every part of the kingdom. The market is on Tuesday, chiefly for corn, the returns of the sale of which are considerable, and on every alternate Tuesday is a large cattle market. The fairs are held May 14th, September 25th, and December 17th, chiefly for cattle and pedlary; but since the cattle markets were established they have been but little attended.

Arundel, which is a borough by prescription, was incorporated by charter of Elizabeth: the government is vested in a mayor, steward, and twelve burgesses, assisted by other officers. The mayor exercises exclusive magisterial jurisdiction within the borough, and presides at a court for the recovery of debts under 40*s.*, held every three weeks: petty sessions are also held here. A town hall, on an elegant plan, is about to be erected by the Duke of Norfolk. The borough has continued to return two members to parliament since the time of Edward I.: the right of election is vested in the inhabitants paying scot and lot, in number four hundred: the mayor is the returning officer. The living is a discharged vicarage, in the archdeaconry and diocese of Chichester, rated in the king's books at £5. 0. 10., and in the patronage of the Duke of Norfolk. The church, dedicated to the Holy Trinity, and formerly collegiate, is a very ancient and spacious cruciform structure, chiefly in the later style of English architecture, with a low tower rising from the centre. In the north aisle of the chancel, which is in a very dilapidated state, are some ancient monuments: there are also a stone pulpit and some screen-work very finely executed. Inconsiderable remains of an hospital, dedicated to the Holy Trinity, and of a convent of Black friars, founded in the reign of Edward II., are discernible. On the Causeway hill is a chalybeate spring.

ARVANS (ST.), a parish partly in the upper division of the hundred of RAGLAND, but chiefly in the upper division of the hundred of CALDICOTT, county of MONMOUTH, 2¼ miles (N.W. by N.) from Chepstow, containing, with the hamlet of Portcassegg, 307 inhabitants. The living is a perpetual curacy, in the archdeaconry and diocese of Llandaff, endowed with £600 royal bounty, and in the patronage of the Duke of Beaufort. Here are remains of two ancient chapels, dedicated respectively to St. Kingsmark and St. Lawrence. The parish is bounded on the north-east by the river Wye.

ARYHOLME, a joint township with Hawthorpe, in that part of the parish of HOVINGHAM which is in the wapentake of RYEDALE, North riding of the county of YORK, 7¼ miles (W.) from New Malton, containing 33 inhabitants.

ASBY, a parish in EAST ward, county of WESTMORLAND, 4¼ miles (S. by W.) from Appleby, comprising the townships of Asby-Coatsforth, Little Asby, and Asby-Winderwath, and containing 421 inhabitants. The living is a rectory, in the archdeaconry and diocese of Carlisle, rated in the king's books at £23. 13. 4., and in the patronage of Sir F. F. Vane, Bart. The church, dedicated to St. Peter, is a small ancient edifice. A chapel, dedicated to St. Leonard, formerly stood at Little Asby. The parish is bounded on the south by Crosby-Garret and Orton fells, and is intersected by numerous rivulets, on the margin of one of which, in a hollow called Asby Gill, is Pate Hole, a remarkable cavern, one thousand yards in depth, through which runs a small stream. Near Little Asby is a small lake, called Sunbiggin tarn. Limestone abounds in the parish, and a copper mine has been lately opened, and is successfully worked. The village of Great Asby is partly situated in the township of Asby-Coatsforth, and partly in that of Asby-Winderwath. A school-house was built in 1688, by George Smith, merchant taylor, and citizen of London, to which Dr. Thomas Smith, Bishop of Carlisle, a native of this parish, gave the sum of £100: the annual income now amounts to about £60. In 1812, an almshouse was founded for four poor widows, each of whom has an annuity of £6, and two rooms for residence. The parsonage-house occupies the site of an ancient nunnery, the chapel and prison of which remain, the latter being used as a cellar and coal-house. Near the church is St. Helen's well, supposed to have been a bath belonging to the convent; the water is reputed to be efficacious in healing sore eyes and inveterate wounds.

ASCOTE (CHAPEL), an extra-parochial liberty, in the Southam division of the hundred of KNIGHTLOW, county of WARWICK, 2 miles (N.W. by N.) from Southam, containing 12 inhabitants.

ASCOTT, a parish in the hundred of CHADLINGTON, county of OXFORD, 5¾ miles (N.E by N.) from Burford, containing 409 inhabitants. The living is a perpetual curacy, in the archdeaconry and diocese of Oxford, endowed with £200 royal bounty, and in the patronage of the Vicar of Shipton. The church is dedicated to the Holy Trinity. There are places of worship for Particular Baptists and Wesleyan Methodists.

ASCOTT, a hamlet in that part of the parish of GREAT MILTON which is in the hundred of THAME, county of OXFORD, 4½ miles (N.) from Bensington, containing 45 inhabitants.

ASENBY, a township in that part of the parish of TOPCLIFFE which is in the wapentake of HALLIKELD, North riding of the county of YORK, 5¾ miles (N.) from Boroughbridge, containing 230 inhabitants.

ASGARBY, a parish in the wapentake of ASWARDHURN, parts of KESTEVEN, county of LINCOLN, 2¾ miles (E.) from Sleaford, containing 55 inhabitants. The living is a rectory, to which that of Kirkby le Thorpe was united in 1737, in the archdeaconry and diocese of Lincoln, rated in the king's books at £10. 14. 4½., endowed with £1000 royal bounty, and £200 parliamentary grant, and in the patronage of the Marquis of Bristol. The church, dedicated to St. Andrew, exhibits the later style of English architecture, and has a lofty tower surmounted by a fine crocketed spire.

ASGARBY, a parish in the western division of the soke of BOLINGBROKE, parts of LINDSEY, county of LINCOLN, 5¼ miles (W. by N.) from Spilsby, containing 77 inhabitants. The living is a perpetual curacy, in the peculiar jurisdiction of the Dean and Chapter of Lincoln, and in the patronage of the Prebendary of Asgarby in the Cathedral Church of Lincoln. In 1667, Henry Pell bequeathed a rent-charge of £10 for the instruction of poor children of Asgarby, Howell, and Eveden, in the charity school at Ewerby.

ASH, a hamlet in the parish of SUTTON on the HILL, hundred of APPLETREE, county of DERBY, 8 miles (W. S. W.) from Derby, containing 47 inhabitants.

ASH, a hamlet in the parish of THROWLEY, hundred of WONFORD, county of DEVON, 7¼ miles (E. S. E.) from Oakhampton. The population is returned with the parish. John Churchill, Duke of Marlborough, the celebrated statesman and general, was born here, in 1650.

ASH, county of DURHAM.—See ESH.

ASH, a parish in the hundred of AXTON, DARTFORD, and WILMINGTON, lathe of SUTTON at HONE, county of KENT, 3¾ miles (N. by W.) from Wrotham, containing 505 inhabitants. The living is a rectory, in the archdeaconry and diocese of Rochester, rated in the king's books at £9. 18. 4., and in the patronage of M. Lambard, Esq. The church is dedicated to St. Peter and St. Paul. In 1735, the Rev. Samuel Attwood bequeathed a rent-charge of £22. 10., and, in 1811, James Lance gave one of £10. 10., towards the endowment of a free school, which is now united to a school on the Madras system. Girls are educated at a separate school, supported by voluntary contribution.

ASH, a parish comprising the chapelry of Frimley, in the first division of the hundred of GODLEY, and the tything of Normanby in the first division of the hundred of WOKING, county of SURREY, 5 miles (N. E. by E.) from Farnham, containing 1867 inhabitants. The living is a rectory, in the archdeaconry of Surrey, and diocese of Winchester, rated in the king's books at £15. 18. 11½., and in the patronage of the Warden and Fellows of Winchester College. The church is dedicated to St. Peter. The Basingstoke canal crosses the northern part of the parish.

ASH (GREAT), a township in that part of the parish of WHITCHURCH which is in the Whitchurch division of the hundred of BRADFORD (North), county of SALOP, 2¼ miles (S. E. by E.) from Whitchurch, with which the population is returned.

ASH (LITTLE), a township in that part of the parish of WHITCHURCH which is in the Whitchurch division of the hundred of BRADFORD (North), county of SALOP, 2¾ miles (S. E. by E.) from Whitchurch, with which the population is returned.

ASH, near SANDWICH, a parish in the hundred of WINGHAM, lathe of ST. AUGUSTINE, county of KENT, 3¼ miles (W. by N.) from Sandwich, containing 2020 inhabitants. The living is a perpetual curacy, in the archdeaconry and diocese of Canterbury, endowed with £600 private benefaction, and £1500 parliamentary grant, and in the patronage of the Archbishop of Canterbury. The church is dedicated to St. Nicholas. The hamlet of Richborough, including the ruins of the fortress called Richborough Castle, in this parish, lies near the site of one of the *Portus Rutupenses* of the Romans. The existing remains occupy the brow of a hill, about a mile north-westward from Sandwich; they were originally bounded on the eastern side by the sea, and the other three sides were defended by walls enclosing an area of nearly five acres. A portion of the walls, about two hundred feet in length, from ten to thirty feet in height, and twelve in thickness, is still standing, and forms one of the most remarkable relics of antiquity which this country affords. Fairs are held on Lady-day and Michaelmas-day. The navigable river Stour passes along the northern boundary of the parish, and is crossed by two ferries. A school is endowed with £75 per annum, left by Eleanor and Anne Cartwright, for the education of twenty-five boys and twenty-five girls: it is under the management of trustees, the master receiving £25, and the mistress £17, per annum, the remainder being expended in books and repairs: the school-room was built by Elizabeth Godfrey, on condition that ten boys and ten girls should be added to the original number.

ASH-BOCKING, a parish in the hundred of BOSMERE and CLAYDON, county of SUFFOLK, 6 miles (E. by S.) from Needham-Market, containing 248 inhabitants. The living is a discharged vicarage, in the archdeaconry of Suffolk, and diocese of Norwich, rated in the king's books at £9. 18. 6½., and in the patronage of the Crown. The church is dedicated to All Saints.

ASH-PRIORS, a parish forming, with those of Bishop's Lydeard, Fitzhead, and Wiveliscombe, one of the two unconnected portions which constitute the western division of the hundred of KINGSBURY, county of SOMERSET, 6 miles (N. W. by W.) from Taunton, containing 201 inhabitants. The living is a perpetual curacy, in the archdeaconry of Taunton, and diocese of Bath and Wells, endowed with £200 private benefaction, and £800 royal bounty, and in the patronage of Sir T. B. Lethbridge, Bart.

ASHAMSTEAD, a chapelry in the parish of BASSILDON, hundred of MORETON, county of BERKS, 6 miles (S. E. by E.) from East Ilsley, containing 337 inhabitants. The chapel is dedicated to St. Clement.

ASHAMSTEAD, a chapelry in the parish and hundred of LEWKNOR, county of OXFORD, 3¾ miles (N. W.) from Great Marlow. The population is returned with the parish. The chapel is dedicated to St. Mary de More.

ASHBOURN, a parish comprising the market town of Ashbourn, the chapelry of Alsop le Dale, the township of Eaton, and the liberties of Newton-Grange, and Offcoat with Underwood, in the hundred of WIRKSWORTH, the townships of Hulland and Hulland-Ward-Intacks, and the hamlets of Hulland-Ward, Sturston, and Yeldersley, in the hundred of APPLETREE, and the chapelry of Clifton, and the hamlet of Compton, in that of MORLESTON and LITCHURCH, county of DERBY, and containing 4708 inhabitants, of which number, 2188 are in the town of Ashbourn, 13½ miles (N. W. by W.) from Derby, and 140 (N. W. by N.) from London. This place, which at the time of the Conquest was held in royal demesne, is in Domesday-book called *Esseburn*. In 1644, a battle was fought here between the royalists and the parliamentarians, in which the former were defeated with considerable loss. Charles I. was at Ashbourn during the battle, and again, in 1645, on his march to Doncaster, at the head of thirty thousand men, when he attended divine service at the church. Charles Edward Stuart, accompanied by the Dukes of Athol and Perth, on their return from Derby in 1745, remained for one night in the town, taking forcible possession of the manor-house, from which they expelled Sir Brooke Boothby and his family. On Sir Brooke's return, he found the names of the officers written in chalk upon the doors of the apartments which they had severally occupied: of these inscriptions, which were overlaid with white paint, some are preserved, and the bed-room in which the Pretender slept is still shewn.

The town is beautifully situated in a deep vale, on the eastern bank of the river Dove, over which there is a bridge of stone: the houses are principally built of red brick, and roofed with slate; the streets are partly paved, and the inhabitants are well supplied with water. The entrance from London is highly picturesque, commanding a fine view of the beautiful vale on the left, and of Ashbourn Hall, the seat of Sir William Boothby, Bart., on the right: the vicinity abounds with pleasing and richly varied scenery. The reading and news rooms and the libraries are respectably supported. The manufacture of cotton and tambour lace is carried on to a considerable extent, and a great quantity of cheese and malt is sent to the metropolis and other towns; but the principal support of the town is derived from its markets and numerous fairs. The market is on Saturday: fairs are held on the first Tuesday in January, and February the 13th, for horses and cattle; the second Monday in March, for horses, cattle, and cheese; April 3rd, May 21st, and July 5th, for horses, cattle, and wool; August 16th and September 20th, for horses and cattle; the third Monday in September, for horses, cattle, and cheese; and November 29th, for horses. Ashbourn is in the honour of Tutbury, duchy of Lancaster, and within the jurisdiction of a court of pleas held at Tutbury every third Tuesday, for the recovery of debts under 40*s*. Courts leet and baron are held annually under the lord of the manor, at which constables and other officers for the town are appointed. The house of correction was capable of containing forty prisoners, but, as it would not admit of their classification, they are now sent to Derby, and the building has been converted into a poor-house.

The living is a discharged vicarage, with the perpetual curacy of Mappleton united, in the archdeaconry of Derby, and diocese of Lichfield and Coventry, rated in the king's books at £5. 4. 7., endowed with £600 parliamentary grant, and in the patronage of the Dean of Lincoln. The church, dedicated to St. Oswald, is a spacious cruciform edifice, having a central tower surmounted by a lofty and highly ornamented octagonal spire: it was erected in 1240, by Hugh de Patishull, Bishop of Coventry, and displays the early English style, intermixed with decorations of a later period: the northern part of the chancel, appropriated as a sepulchral chapel to the Boothby family, contains, among others, an exquisitely finished monument, from the chisel of Banks, to the memory of Penelope, only child of Sir Brooke Boothby, who died at the age of five years, which is said to have suggested to Chantrey the design of his celebrated monument in Lichfield cathedral. There are places of worship for Baptists, Wesleyan Methodists, and those in the late Countess of Huntingdon's Connexion, which last was built by Mr. John Cooper, in 1800, who endowed it with £42 per annum. The free grammar school was founded, in 1585, under a charter of Queen Elizabeth, and endowed with estates purchased by the inhabitants, now producing £210 per annum, two-thirds of which, with a house and garden, are given to the master, and the remainder, with a house, to the usher: the management is vested in three governors and twelve assistants. The English school was founded in 1710, and endowed with £10 per annum, by Mr. Spalden, for the instruction of thirty boys, till they should be fit to enter the grammar school: he also endowed a school for thirty girls under twelve years of age, the mistress of which has £10 per annum. Almshouses for four widows of Protestant clergymen, and ten almshouses in the churchyard, for poor persons of the parish, were founded and endowed by the same benevolent individual. Eight almshouses were founded by Mr. R. Owfield, in 1610, the completion and endowment of which was effected by the subsequent benefactions of various individuals; six by Mr. Pegg, in 1668, to which Mr. Jeremiah Pole bequeathed an estate; and six by Mr. John Cooper, which he endowed with £63 per annum, for poor people attending Lady Huntingdon's chapel, all which have subsequently received divers benefactions. In the neighbourhood formerly stood a chapel, dedicated to St. Mary, which, previously to its being taken down, several years ago, was used as a malt-house.

Dovedale, in the adjoining parish of Tissington, abounds with pleasingly picturesque and strikingly romantic scenery: the entrance is progressively marked with features of simple beauty, impressive grandeur, and terrific awe. Thorpe Cloud on the right, and a towering pile of massive rocks on the left, form natural ramparts of majestic elevation, between which the river Dove winds through the vale with varied course, sometimes rushing with tumultuous effort along the bases of stupendous cliffs, its stream darkened by the threatening precipices which impend above it, and at others expanding into a smooth and placid surface, reflecting, with softened beauty and milder lustre, the luxuriant verdure of its wood-crowned banks. At various intervals, rude masses of grotesque form, which have been fancifully denominated my Lady's Chair, Dovedale Castle, the Church, the Twelve Apostles, the Lion's Head, the Sugar Loaves, and the Lover's Leap, rise in succession throughout this enchanting dale, in which the simpler and the sublimer beauties of nature, in all their variety, are richly and strikingly combined.

ASHBRITTLE, a parish in the hundred of MILVERTON, county of SOMERSET, 6¾ miles (W.) from Wellington, containing 579 inhabitants. The living is a rectory, in the archdeaconry of Taunton, and diocese of Bath and Wells, rated in the king's books at £19. 3. 11½., and in the patronage of J. Quick, Esq. The church is dedicated to St. John the Baptist.

ASHBURNHAM, a parish in the hundred of FOXEARLE, rape of HASTINGS, county of SUSSEX, 4½ miles (W. by S.) from Battle, containing 768 inhabitants. The living is a vicarage, with the rectory of Penhurst annexed, in the archdeaconry of Lewes, and diocese of Chichester, rated in the king's books at £8. 13. 4., and in the patronage of the Earl of Ashburnham. The church is dedicated to St. James. A lectureship was founded in this parish, in 1631, by R. Bateman, Esq., Chamberlain of London, and others, with an endowment of £40 per annum, for two sermons; it is in the patronage of the Co-Heiresses of the late Sir Hugh Bateman, the last surviving trustee.

Seal and Arms.

ASHBURTON, a borough, market town, and parish, in the southern division of the hundred of TEIGNBRIDGE, county of DEVON, 19 miles (S. W.) from Exeter, and 192 (W. by S.) from London, on the road to Plymouth, containing 3403 inhabitants. This town, anciently called *Aisbertone*, in the time of Edward the Confessor belonged to Brietric, and at the Conquest to Jukel de Totnais: it was subsequently annexed to the see of Exeter, and, in 1310, Bishop Stapylton obtained for it a grant of a market and two fairs. In 1672, Mr. John Ford procured another market, chiefly for wool, and yarn spun in Cornwall, which has long been discontinued. It was made a stannery town by charter of Edward III., in 1328, being then noted for the mines of tin and copper which abounded in its neighbourhood. Ashburton, in the parliamentary war, having been previously occupied by the royal troops under Lord Wentworth, was taken by Sir Thomas Fairfax, on his march westward, in January 1654. The town, situated about a mile and a half from the river Dart, consists principally of one street of considerable length; the houses are built of brick and roofed with slate, which latter is obtained from quarries in the vicinity. The inhabitants are well supplied with water; the river Yeo, a rapid stream, runs through the town, and turns several mills. There is a book society; and card and dancing assemblies, and music meetings, are frequently held in a handsome suite of rooms at the Lion inn. The manufacture of serge for the East India Company is carried on to a very great extent, the annual returns being stated to exceed £100,000; there are some mills for fulling cloth and for the spinning of yarn, and, in addition to the slate-quarries, mines of tin and copper are still worked in the neighbourhood. The market is on Saturday; and fairs are held on the first Thursdays in March and June, the 10th of August, and the 11th of November, which last is a great sheep fair. Ashburton is a borough by prescription: a portreeve, bailiff, constable, and subordinate officers are appointed annually at a court leet held by the steward of the manor, but they have no magisterial authority: a stannary court is held occasionally. The borough made two returns to parliament, in the 26th of Edward I. and the 8th of Henry IV., but none subsequently until 1640, when the franchise was restored by the last parliament of Charles I., since which time it has regularly returned two members: the right of election is vested in the inhabitant freeholders; the portreeve is the returning officer.

The living is a vicarage, with the perpetual curacies of Bickington and Buckland in the Moor annexed, in the peculiar jurisdiction and patronage of the Dean and Chapter of Exeter, rated in the king's books at £38. 8. 11½. The church, dedicated to St. Andrew, was formerly collegiate: it is a venerable and spacious cruciform structure, in the later style of English architecture, with a square tower rising from the centre. There are places of worship for Particular Baptists, Independents, and Wesleyan Methodists. The free grammar school was founded, in the 36th of Elizabeth, by William Blundell, Esq., and endowed with lands, a portion of which belonged to the dissolved chantry of St. Lawrence, a fine ancient building, with a tower and a small spire, now appropriated to the use of the school, for parliamentary elections for the borough, and for other public meetings: the original endowment has been augmented by subsequent benefactions, and the management is vested in trustees chosen from among the inhabitants. The free school, in which one hundred children are educated, was endowed, in 1754, by Lord Middleton and John Harris, Esq., then representatives for the borough, in gratitude for the liberality of their constituents. There is also a school for ten poor girls, established in 1805, by Miss Mary Dunning. Inconsiderable vestiges of a chapel, which belonged to the abbot of Buckfastleigh, are still discernible in the walls of Parham House. John Dunning, Baron Ashburton, the celebrated lawyer, was born here, October 18th, 1731: he died August 18th, 1783, and was interred in the church. Dr. Ireland, Dean of Westminster, and the late Mr. Gifford, editor of the Quarterly Review, were also natives of Ashburton.

ASHBURY, a parish in the hundred of SHRIVENHAM, county of BERKS, 6¾ miles (N. W. by W.) from Lambourn, containing, with the chapelry of Chapelwick, and the tythings of Idstone and Odstone, 683 inhabitants. The living is a vicarage, in the archdeaconry of Berks, and diocese of Salisbury, rated in the king's books at £11. 8. 1½., and in the patronage of the Rector, who presents one of three candidates nominated by the President and Fellows of Magdalene College, Oxford; the rectory is a sinecure, rated at £30. 12. 6., and in the patronage of the Bishop of Bath and Wells. The church is dedicated to St. Mary. The Roman road, called the Iknield-way, passes near the village: and in the parish there is an intrenchment, called Alfred's Camp, near which are two barrows. Here are also a tumulus and cromlech, popularly called "Wayland Smith," with which a tradition, introduced by Sir Walter Scott in his romance of Kenilworth, is connected.

ASHBURY, a parish in the hundred of BLACK TORRINGTON, county of DEVON, 5¼ miles (S. W. by W.) from Hatherleigh, containing 74 inhabitants. The living is a discharged rectory, in the archdeaconry of Totness, and diocese of Exeter, rated in the king's books at £5. 13. 4., and in the patronage of the Crown. The church is dedicated to St. Mary.

ASHBY, a parish in the wapentake of BRADLEY-HAVERSTOE, parts of LINDSEY, county of LINCOLN, 6¼ miles (S. by W.) from Great Grimsby, containing, with the hamlet of Fenby, 191 inhabitants. The living is a rectory, in the archdeaconry and diocese of Lincoln, rated in the king's books at £14. 10. 10., and in the patronage of the Crown. The church is dedicated to St. Peter.

ASHBY, a parish in the Wold division of the wapentake of CANDLESHOE, parts of LINDSEY, county of LINCOLN, 2¼ miles (E. by N.) from Spilsby, containing 140 inhabitants. The living is a discharged rectory, in the archdeaconry and diocese of Lincoln, rated in the king's books at £7. 10. 2½., and in the patronage of Robert Fowler, D.D., Bishop of Ossory. The church is dedicated to St. Helen.

ASHBY, a township in that part of the parish of BOTTESFORD which is in the eastern division of the wapentake of MANLEY, parts of LINDSEY, county of LINCOLN, 6½ miles (W. by S.) from Glandford-Bridge, containing 288 inhabitants. In 1705, Stephen Caistor bequeathed a house to be used as a school-house for the children in the township.

ASHBY, a parish in the western division of the hundred of FLEGG, county of NORFOLK, 2½ miles (N.) from Acle, containing, with the parish of Oby, 72 inhabitants. The living is a rectory with Oby, united to that of Thirne, in the archdeaconry of Norfolk, and diocese of Norwich, rated in the king's books at £10. The church is dedicated to St. Mary.

ASHBY, a parish in the hundred of LODDON, county of NORFOLK, 8 miles (S. E.) from Norwich, containing 234 inhabitants. The living is a rectory, united to that of Hillington, in the archdeaconry of Norfolk, and diocese of Norwich, rated in the king's books at £6. The church is dedicated to St. Mary.

ASHBY, a parish in the hundred of MUTFORD and LOTHINGLAND, county of SUFFOLK, 6 miles (N. W.) from Lowestoft, containing 34 inhabitants. The living is a discharged rectory, in the archdeaconry of Suffolk, and diocese of Norwich, rated in the king's books at £6, and in the patronage of the Rev. George Anguish. The church, dedicated to St. Mary, is a small thatched building, having a tower circular at the base and octangular above, with battlements and embrasures.

ASHBY (CANONS), a parish in the hundred of GREENS-NORTON, county of NORTHAMPTON, 8 miles (W. by N.) from Towcester, containing, with the chapelry of Adstone, 203 inhabitants. The living is a perpetual curacy, in the archdeaconry of Northampton, and diocese of Peterborough, and in the patronage of Sir J. Dryden, Bart. The church is dedicated to St. Mary. Here was anciently a priory of Black canons, founded about the time of John, the revenue of which, at the dissolution, was £127. 19.

ASHBY (CASTLE), a parish in the hundred of WYMERSLEY, county of NORTHAMPTON, 7¾ miles (E. by S.) from Northampton, containing 128 inhabitants. The living is a rectory, in the archdeaconry of Northampton, and diocese of Peterborough, rated in the king's books at £17. 9. 7., and in the patronage of the Marquis of Northampton. The church is dedicated to St. Mary Magdalene. The castle, formerly the princely mansion of the Comptons, Earls of Northampton, is situated near the northern extremity of Yardley Chase, through which is a wide avenue, extending above three miles from the south front; it is built in the form of a quadrangle, having on the south side a screen of two stories, from a design by Inigo Jones, and, at the north-east and south-west angles, two lofty octangular towers.

ASHBY (COLD), a parish in the hundred of GUILSBOROUGH, county of NORTHAMPTON, 11½ miles (N. W. by N.) from Northampton, containing 375 inhabitants. The living is a vicarage, in the archdeaconry of Northampton, and diocese of Peterborough, rated in the king's books at £6. 0. 5., and in the patronage of the Rev. W. Mousley. The church is dedicated to St. Denis. Here is a free school for poor children, endowed with £18 per annum, being a rent-charge left by William Wickes, in 1710, and £2. 10., a moiety of the rental of a piece of land devised by Richard Ward, in 1736. Richard Knolles, the historian of the Turkish Empire, was born here, in 1540.

ASHBY de la LAUNDE, a parish in the wapentake of FLAXWELL, parts of KESTEVEN, county of LINCOLN, 6¼ miles (N. by W.) from Sleaford, containing 155 inhabitants. The living is a discharged vicarage, in the archdeaconry and diocese of Lincoln, rated in the king's books at £6. 8. 4., endowed with £200 royal bounty, and in the patronage of Neville King, Esq. The church is dedicated to St. Hybald.

ASHBY (ST. LEDGER'S), a parish in the hundred of FAWSLEY, county of NORTHAMPTON, 3½ miles (N.) from Daventry, containing 272 inhabitants. The living is a discharged vicarage, in the archdeaconry of Northampton, and diocese of Peterborough, rated in the king's books at £6. 13. 4., and in the patronage of J. Ashley, Esq. The church, dedicated to St. Mary and St. Leodgare, is in the later style of English architecture, and contains a richly ornamented screen and rood-loft, and in the windows are some portions of ancient stained glass. The parish is bounded on the east by the Watling-street.

ASHBY (MAGNA), a parish in the hundred of GUTHLAXTON, county of LEICESTER, 4 miles (N. by E.) from Lutterworth, containing 280 inhabitants. The living is a vicarage, in the archdeaconry of Leicester, and diocese of Lincoln, rated in the king's books at £7. 8. 11½., and in the patronage of the Earl of Aylesford. The church is dedicated to St. Mary.

ASHBY (PARVA), a parish in the hundred of GUTHLAXTON, county of LEICESTER, 3 miles (N. N. W.) from Lutterworth, containing 176 inhabitants. The living is a rectory, in the archdeaconry of Leicester, and diocese of Lincoln, rated in the king's books at £5. 7. 6., and in the patronage of the Crown. The church is dedicated to St. Peter. Ashby Parva is in the honour of Tutbury, duchy of Lancaster, and within the jurisdiction of a court of pleas held at Tutbury every third Tuesday, for the recovery of debts under 40*s*.

ASHBY (WEST), a parish in the soke of HORNCASTLE, parts of LINDSEY, county of LINCOLN, 1¾ mile (N.) from Horncastle, containing 378 inhabitants. The living is a perpetual curacy, in the archdeaconry and diocese of Lincoln, endowed with £400 royal bounty, and in the patronage of the Bishop of Carlisle. The church is dedicated to All Saints.

ASHBY de la ZOUCH, a market town and parish in the western division of the hundred of GOSCOTE, county of LEICESTER, 18 miles (N.W. by W.) from Leicester, and 115 (N.W. by N.) from London, containing, with the chapelry of Blackfordby, and the extra-parochial liberty of Alton-Grange, 4227 inhabitants. The name appears to be derived from the Saxon *Asc*, an ash, and *bye*, a habitation: it received the adjunct, by which it is distinguished from other towns of the same name, from the family of La Zouch, in whose possession it continued from the latter part of the twelfth to the close of the fourteenth century. Sir William Hastings, created Baron Hastings by Edward IV., who was beheaded by Richard III., built a strong castle here in the reign of the former monarch, in which Mary, Queen of Scots, while in the custody of the Earl of Huntingdon, was for some time kept in confinement: in this castle Anne, consort of James I., and her son, Prince Henry, were magnificently entertained by the Earl of Huntingdon, on their journey from York to London, in 1603. At the commencement of the parliamentary war, the Earl of Huntingdon was one of the first that appeared in arms for the king in Leicestershire. Ashby castle was garrisoned for his Majesty by the earl's second son, Col. Henry Hastings, who was made general of the king's forces in the midland counties, and, for his services to the royal cause, was, in 1643, created Baron Loughborough. The king was here, on his march to and from Leicester, in May and June 1645. After sustaining a siege of several months from the army under Sir Henry Fairfax, Lord Loughborough surrendered the castle to Col. Needham, in February 1646, on honourable terms, the garrison being allowed to march out with all the honours of war. This castle was one of the fortresses demolished by order of a committee of the House of Commons, about the end of the year 1642; portions of the walls of the hall, the chapel, and the kitchen, are still remaining, and form an extensive and interesting mass of ruins.

The town, a great part of which was destroyed by fire in 1753, is pleasantly situated on the banks of the small river Gilwisthaw, at the north-western extremity of the county, and consists principally of one very spacious street, with two smaller streets extending in a parallel direction, containing several substantial and well-built houses: there are many excellent springs in the neighbourhood, but the town is very indifferently supplied with water. The Ivanhoe baths, a splendid building erected within the last six years, in the Doric order of architecture, are supplied from the neighbouring collieries with water, strongly impregnated with muriate of soda, containing, by ten or twelve degrees, a greater proportion of salt than sea water, and efficacious in mitigating the pain of rheumatism; the baths are conveniently and elegantly fitted up for the use of invalids. There are lodging-houses, a handsome hotel, a neat theatre, and other sources of attraction requisite in a place of fashionable resort. A small mineral spring, called Griffydam, the water of which possesses highly medicinal properties, rises at a short distance from the town. The manufacture of the coarser kinds of hosiery is carried on here: bricks are made to a considerable extent; and in the neighbouring wolds, which abound with iron-stone, a furnace for smelting the ore has been recently erected. A canal passes within three miles south-westward of the town, with which it is connected by a rail-road, and, after continuing a course of more than thirty miles, unimpeded by a single lock, forms a junction with the Coventry canal. The market is on Saturday: fairs are held on Shrove-Monday, Easter-Tuesday, Whit-Tuesday, the last Monday in September, and the 10th of November, for horses and cattle: this is stated to be the best market for strong horses in England. The town is in the honour of Tutbury, duchy of Lancaster, and within the jurisdiction of a court of pleas held at Tutbury every third Tuesday, for the recovery of debts under 40*s.*: a constable and two head-boroughs are appointed at the court leet of the lord of the manor.

The living is a discharged vicarage, in the archdeaconry of Leicester, and diocese of Lincoln, rated in the king's books at £14. 10. 4., endowed with £200 private benefaction, and £200 royal bounty, and in the patronage of the Marquis of Hastings. The church, dedicated to St. Helen, is a spacious structure in the decorated style of English architecture, and contains, among many others, a handsome monument to the memory of Francis, Earl of Huntingdon, and his Countess. There are places of worship for Baptists, those in the Connexion of the late Countess of Huntingdon, Independents, and Wesleyan Methodists. The free grammar school was founded, in 1567, by Henry, Earl of Huntingdon, and others, and endowed with one hundred and twenty houses and seventy-five acres of land: it has, jointly with the school at Derby, ten exhibitions of £10 each per annum, to Emanuel College, Cambridge, founded by Francis Ash, merchant and citizen of London, a native of this town, with preference to the founder's relations. The Blue-coat school, for twenty-six boys, was founded in 1669, and endowed with £25 per annum, by Isaac Dawson; and a Green-coat school was founded and endowed by Alderman Newton, of Leicester. The Rev. Simeon Ash, a native of this town, gave £50 per annum, directing that £10 thereof should be appropriated to the apprenticing of two boys yearly in some corporate town, and that the remainder should be distributed among the poor. A great number of Roman coins has been found here within the last seven years. Bishop Hall, an eminent divine and satirist, and Dr. John Bainbridge, a celebrated astronomer and mathematician, were born at this town, the former in 1574, and the latter in 1582.

ASHBY-FOLVILLE, a parish in the eastern division of the hundred of GOSCOTE, county of LEICESTER, 6 miles (S. W. by S.) from Melton-Mowbray, containing, with the chapelry of Barsby, 405 inhabitants. The living is a discharged vicarage, in the archdeaconry of Leicester, and diocese of Lincoln, rated in the king's books at £9, and in the patronage of the Rev. J. Brown. The church is dedicated to St. Mary. Here is an hospital, founded by the Carrington family.

ASHBY-MEARS, a parish in the hundred of HAMFORDSHOE, county of NORTHAMPTON, 3¾ miles (W. by S.) from Wellingborough, containing 442 inhabitants. The living is a discharged vicarage, in the archdeaconry of Northampton, and diocese of Peterborough, rated in the king's books at £4. 13. 9., and in the patronage of Sir J. Langham, Bart. The church is dedicated to All Saints.

ASHBY-PUERORUM, a parish in the hundred of HILL, parts of LINDSEY, county of LINCOLN, 4¼ miles (E. N. E.) from Horncastle, containing, with the hamlet of Stainsby, and the extra-parochial liberty of Holbeck, 117 inhabitants. The living is a discharged vicarage, in the archdeaconry and diocese of Lincoln, rated in the king's books at £6. 3. 2., endowed with £200 royal bounty, and in the patronage of the Dean and Chapter of Lincoln. The church is dedicated to St. Andrew.

ASHCHURCH, a parish in the lower division of the hundred of TEWKESBURY, county of GLOUCESTER, 2¼ miles (E. N. E.) from Tewkesbury, comprising the tythings of Aston upon Carron, Fiddington with Natton, Northway with Newton, and Pamington, and containing 643 inhabitants. The living is a perpetual curacy, in the archdeaconry and diocese of Gloucester, endowed with £200 private benefaction, and £200 royal bounty, and in the patronage of the Rev. William Hopton. The church consists of a nave, chancel, and north aisle, with a tower at the west end, chiefly displaying the later English style, but having on the south side a Norman porch. The Carrant, a stream tributary to the Avon, flows through the parish, also a branch of the Cheltenham spring.

ASHCOMBE, a parish in the hundred of EXMINSTER, county of DEVON, 3 miles (E.) from Chudleigh, containing 283 inhabitants. The living is a rectory, in the archdeaconry and diocese of Exeter, rated in the king's books at £18, and in the patronage of the Crown. Here are two charity schools, one of which has an endowment of £3 per annum, and the other is supported by subscription.

ASHCOTT, a parish in the hundred of WHITLEY, county of SOMERSET, 5 miles (W. S. W.) from Glastonbury, containing 712 inhabitants. The living is a perpetual curacy, annexed to the vicarage of Shapwick, in the archdeaconry of Wells, and diocese of Bath and Wells. The church is dedicated to All Saints. There is a place of worship for Wesleyan Methodists. A fair for cattle is held on the 9th of January. In 1737, Richard Miles bequeathed a sum of money, since vested in land now producing £70 per annum, which is distributed among the poor of the parish.

ASHDON, a parish in the hundred of FRESHWELL, county of ESSEX, 3¾ miles (N. E. by E.) from Saffron-Walden, containing, with the hamlet of Bartlow-End, 1014 inhabitants. The living is a rectory, in the archdeaconry of Colchester, and diocese of London, rated in the king's books at £28. 3. 4., and in the patronage of the Master and Fellows of Caius College, Cambridge. The church, dedicated to All Saints, has been repaired and new pewed within the last twenty years: at the east end of the south aisle is a building termed the Old Chancel. There are four large barrows, commonly called Bartlow Hills, in this parish, one of which, on being opened, was found to contain stone coffins and a number of iron chains similar to the curb of a bridle: they are supposed to be sepulchral monuments of the Danish chiefs killed at the battle of *Assandune*, or Ashdon, in which Edmund Ironside was defeated by Canute in 1016; but the more reputable historians refer this event to Ashingdon. Here is a charity school, with an endowment of £3 per annum.

ASHE, a parish in the hundred of OVERTON, Kingsclere division of the county of SOUTHAMPTON, 5¼ miles (E. N. E.) from Whitchurch, containing 114 inhabitants. The living is a rectory, in the archdeaconry and diocese of Winchester, rated in the king's books at £9. 11. 5½., and in the patronage of Wither Bramston, Esq. The church is dedicated to the Holy Trinity. The river Test has its source in this parish.

ASHELDHAM, a parish in the hundred of DENGIE, county of ESSEX, 5 miles (S. S. W.) from Bradwell, containing 156 inhabitants. The living is a discharged vicarage, in the archdeaconry of Essex, and diocese of London, rated in the king's books at £16. 13. 4., and in the patronage of the Bishop of London. The church is dedicated to St. Lawrence.

ASHELWORTH, a parish in the upper division of the hundred of BERKELEY, though locally in the hundred of Dudstone and King's Barton, county of GLOUCESTER, 5½ miles (N. by W.) from Gloucester, containing 498 inhabitants. The living is a discharged vicarage, in the archdeaconry and diocese of Gloucester, rated in the king's books at £10. 2. 11., and in the patronage of the Bishop of Bristol. The church, dedicated to St. Andrew, consists of a nave, south aisle, and two chancels, with a tower and spire, chiefly in the later English style. Several parts of the manor-house, which stands near the church, display considerable antiquity; and the parsonage, now a farm-house, affords a peculiarly fine specimen of wood work. The navigable river Severn skirts the parish on the south-east. The Sunday school has an endowment of £3 per annum, but is chiefly supported by subscription.

ASHEN, a parish in the hundred of HINCKFORD, county of ESSEX, 2½ miles (S. W. by S.) from Clare, containing 293 inhabitants. The living is a rectory, in the archdeaconry of Middlesex, and diocese of London, rated in the king's books at £8, and in the patronage of the King, as Duke of Lancaster. According to Bishop Tanner, here was a priory of Augustine friars in the 17th of Edward II.

ASHENDON, a parish in the hundred of ASHENDON, county of BUCKINGHAM, 6½ miles (N.) from Thame, containing 339 inhabitants. The living is a perpetual curacy, in the archdeaconry of Buckingham, and diocese of Lincoln, endowed with £8 per annum private benefaction, and £600 royal bounty, and in the patronage of the Dean and Canons of Christ Church, Oxford. The church is dedicated to St. Mary.

ASHFIELD, a parish in the hundred of THREDLING, county of SUFFOLK, 6 miles (W. by S.) from Framlingham, containing, with the chapelry of Thorpe, 309 inhabitants. The living is a perpetual curacy, in the archdeaconry of Suffolk, and diocese of Norwich, endowed with £800 royal bounty, and in the patronage of Lord Henniker. The church is dedicated to St. Mary.

ASHFIELD (GREAT), a parish in the hundred of BLACKBOURN, county of SUFFOLK, 5 miles (E. S. E.) from Ixworth, containing 345 inhabitants. The living is a perpetual curacy, in the archdeaconry of Suffolk, and diocese of Norwich, endowed with £1400 royal bounty, and in the patronage of Lord Thurlow, whose ancestor, the Lord Chancellor Thurlow, was born here, in 1732. The church is dedicated to All Saints.

ASHFORD, a chapelry in the parish of BAKEWELL, hundred of HIGH PEAK, county of DERBY, 2 miles (N. W. by W.) from Bakewell, containing 728 inhabitants. The living is a perpetual curacy, in the peculiar jurisdiction of the Dean and Chapter of Lichfield, endowed with £200 private benefaction, £800 royal bounty, and £200 parliamentary grant, and in the patronage of the Vicar of Bakewell. The chapel, dedicated to the Holy Trinity, was built in 1247. There is a place of worship for General Baptists; another, originally founded by the Nonconformist divine, William Bagshaw, styled "the Apostle of the Peak," has been subsequently used by different sects. The village lies in a vale watered by the river Wye, over which are three stone bridges. Mills for sawing and polishing marble, being the first established for that purpose in England, were erected on its banks in 1786, and are supplied from the celebrated quarries of black marble in the vicinity. Ashford is in the honour of Tutbury, duchy of Lancaster, and within the jurisdiction of a court of pleas held at Tutbury every third Tuesday, for the recovery of debts under 40*s*. A school for poor children was founded by William Harris, in 1631, and endowed with £6. 13. 4. per annum, to which Thomas Roose and the Rev. Samuel Evatt added £1 per annum each. Edward Plantagenet, Earl of Kent, resided in a mansion near the church, of which there are no vestiges, except the moat that surrounded it.

ASHFORD, a parish in the hundred of Braunton, county of Devon, 2 miles (N. W.) from Barnstaple, containing 98 inhabitants. The living is a discharged vicarage, in the archdeaconry of Barnstaple, and diocese of Exeter, rated in the king's books at £8. 13. 9., endowed with £200 private benefaction, and £200 royal bounty, and in the patronage of the Crown. The church is dedicated to St. Peter. The navigable river Torr passes on the south side of the parish.

ASHFORD, a market town and parish in the hundred of Chart and Longbridge, lathe of Scray, county of Kent, 20 miles (S. E. by E.) from Maidstone, and 54 (E. S. E.) from London, containing 2773 inhabitants. This place, originally *Ass-cheford*, rose from the ruins of Great Chart, an ancient market town, which gave name to the hundred, and was destroyed during the Danish wars. The town, which is a liberty of itself, is situated on an eminence rising from the northern bank of the small river Stour, over which there is a bridge of one arch; the houses are modern and well built, and the principal street, which is nearly half a mile long, is lighted. A suite of assembly-rooms has recently been erected on the site of the ancient manor and market house, in which assemblies occasionally take place: there are two subscription libraries, and races are held annually for one day. The only branch of manufacture is that of linen, which is carried on to a small extent. The market is on Tuesday and Saturday, and there is a cattle market on the first and third Tuesday in every month: fairs are held on May 17th, September 9th, and October 24th, for general merchandise, and in the first week in August for wool. A court leet is held annually, at which a constable, borough-holder, and other officers are appointed.

The living is a vicarage, in the archdeaconry and diocese of Canterbury, rated in the king's books at £18. 4. 2., and in the patronage of the Dean and Chapter of Rochester. The church, dedicated to St. Mary, and formerly collegiate, is a spacious and handsome cruciform structure, in the later style of English architecture, with a lofty and elegant tower rising from the centre, and having at the southern entrance a fine Norman arch: it was rebuilt, in the reign of Edward IV., by Sir John Fogge, Knt., who erected the beautiful tower, and founded the college for a master, two chaplains, and two secular clerks. In a small chapel adjoining the south-western transept are three sumptuous monuments of variegated marble, to the memory of the Smyths of Westenhanger, and one to the Duchess of Athol. There are places of worship for Particular Baptists, the Society of Friends, those in the Connexion of the late Countess of Huntingdon, and Wesleyan Methodists. The free grammar school was founded, in 1636, by Sir Norton Knatchbull, who endowed it with £30 per annum, and vested the appointment of a master in his own family. A National school for ninety boys, and another for sixty girls, are supported by subscription, and by a bequest in land, producing £35 per annum, from Dr. Turner, in 1702. A mineral spring was discovered, a few years ago, in a field called Sparrows Gardens. Robert Glover, an industrious antiquary of the sixteenth century; his nephew, Thomas Miller, eminent as a herald and genealogist; and Dr. John Wallis, the celebrated mathematician, were natives of this place. Ashford confers the inferior title of baron on the family of Keppel, Earls of Albemarle.

ASHFORD, a parish in the hundred of Spelthorne, county of Middlesex, 3 miles (E.) from Staines, containing 331 inhabitants. The living is a perpetual curacy, annexed to the vicarage of Staines, in the archdeaconry of Middlesex, and diocese of London. The church is dedicated to St. Michael.

ASHFORD-BOWDLER, a parish in the hundred of Munslow, county of Salop, 2¾ miles (S. by E.) from Ludlow, containing 89 inhabitants. The living is a perpetual curacy, in the archdeaconry of Salop, and diocese of Hereford, endowed with £200 private benefaction, £200 royal bounty, and £200 parliamentary grant, and in the patronage of R. H. Green, Esq. The church is dedicated to St. Andrew.

ASHFORD-CARBONELL, a parish partly in the hundred of Munslow, but chiefly in the hundred of Stottesden, county of Salop, 3¼ miles (S.S.E.) from Ludlow, containing 316 inhabitants. The living is a perpetual curacy, annexed to the rectory of Little Hereford, in the peculiar jurisdiction of the Chancellor in the Cathedral Church of Hereford, endowed with £800 royal bounty.

ASHFORDBY, or ASFORDBY, a parish in the eastern division of the hundred of Goscote, county of Leicester, 3 miles (W.) from Melton-Mowbray, containing 424 inhabitants. The living is a rectory, in the archdeaconry of Leicester, and diocese of Lincoln, rated in the king's books at £15. 11. 8., and in the patronage of the Rev. Andrew Burnaby. The church is dedicated to All Saints. This place communicates with the Leicester and Melton-Mowbray Navigation by means of the river Wreak, over which here is a bridge. In 1769, Morris Cam bequeathed £100 towards the support of a school for poor children.

ASH-HOLM, a township in the parish of Lambley, western division of Tindale ward, county of Northumberland, 19½ miles (W. by S.) from Hexham, containing 122 inhabitants. Here is a good millstone quarry.

ASHILL, a parish in the hundred of Wayland, county of Norfolk, 3¼ miles (N. W.) from Watton, containing 579 inhabitants. The living is a rectory, in the archdeaconry and diocese of Norwich, rated in the king's books at £19. 13. 6½., and in the patronage of the Rev. B. Edwards. The church, dedicated to St. Nicholas, is chiefly in the latest style of English architecture, and has a tower built of flint. A National school was established here in 1821.

ASHILL, a parish in the hundred of Abdick and Bulstone, county of Somerset, 3½ miles (N. W.) from Ilminster, containing 378 inhabitants. The living is a discharged vicarage, in the peculiar jurisdiction and patronage of the Prebendary of Ashill in the Cathedral Church of Wells, rated in the king's books at £6. 0. 10.

and endowed with £200 private benefaction, and £200 royal bounty. The church is dedicated to St. Mary. Thomas de Multon, lord of the manor in the reign of Edward II., obtained a charter for a market on Wednesday, and fairs on the festivals of the Virgin Mary and St. Simon and St. Jude. A chalybeate spring, to which a bath has been annexed, said to be serviceable in scorbutic complaints, rises within the parish.

ASHINGDON, a parish in the hundred of ROCHFORD, county of ESSEX, 2¼ miles (N. by W.) from Rochford, containing 97 inhabitants. The living is a discharged rectory, in the archdeaconry of Essex, and diocese of London, rated in the king's books at £8. 13. 4., and in the patronage of Josiah Nottidge, Esq. The church is dedicated to St. Andrew. Here is a school, with an endowment of £2 per annum, for the education of poor children. This place is thought to have been the scene of the battle of *Assandune*, in which Canute the Dane vanquished the Saxons under Edmund Ironside.

ASHINGTON, a township in the parish of BOTHALL, eastern division of MORPETH ward, county of NORTHUMBERLAND, 4½ miles (E. by N.) from Morpeth. The population is returned with Sheepwash. The river Wansbeck is navigable for keels and small boats as far as Sheepwash, where it is crossed by a bridge.

ASHINGTON, a parish in the hundred of STONE, county of SOMERSET, 2¾ miles (E. S. E.) from Ilchester, containing 81 inhabitants. The living is a discharged rectory, in the archdeaconry of Wells, and diocese of Bath and Wells, rated in the king's books at £6. 3. 4., endowed with £200 private benefaction, and £200 royal bounty, and in the patronage of Mrs. Williams. The church is dedicated to St. Vincent. There is a provision for the education of five poor boys of this parish at the school of Marston Magna.

ASHINGTON, a parish in the hundred of WEST GRINSTEAD, rape of BRAMBER, county of SUSSEX, 5½ miles (N. W.) from Steyning, containing, with the chapelry of Buncton, 229 inhabitants. The living is a rectory, in the archdeaconry and diocese of Chichester, rated in the king's books at £8. 5., and in the patronage of the Rev. R. Clough and others. The church is dedicated to St. Peter and St. Paul.

ASHLEY, a parish in the hundred of CHEVELEY, county of CAMBRIDGE, 3¼ miles (E. by S.) from Newmarket, containing, with the parish of Silverley, 351 inhabitants. The living is a rectory, with the vicarage of Silverley annexed, in the archdeaconry of Sudbury, and diocese of Norwich, rated in the king's books at £8, and in the patronage of the Earl of Guilford. The church is dedicated to St. Mary.

ASHLEY, a township in the parish of BOWDON, hundred of BUCKLOW, county palatine of CHESTER, 5 miles (N. N. E.) from Nether Knutsford, containing 392 inhabitants. Ashley Hall, the ancient manorial mansion, is remarkable for containing eleven original portraits of the same number of gentlemen of this county, ancestors of the Grosvenors, Cholmondeleys, and other families, who formed a club during the progress of the Pretender through the north, in 1715, when the expediency of joining his standard was debated: the casting vote against the measure having been given by Thomas Asheton, the owner of the manor and mansion: this decision is considered, from the influence of the parties in Lancashire and Cheshire, to have mainly contributed to the defeat of the enterprise.

ASHLEY, a parish in the hundred of CORBY, county of NORTHAMPTON, 5 miles (W. by S.) from Rockingham, containing 367 inhabitants. The living is a rectory, in the archdeaconry of Northampton, and diocese of Peterborough, rated in the king's books at £17, and in the patronage of the Rev. Richard Farrer. The church is dedicated to St. Mary.

ASHLEY, a parish in the hundred of KING'S SOMBOURN, Andover division of the county of SOUTHAMPTON, 3 miles (S. S. E.) from Stockbridge, containing 90 inhabitants. The living is a rectory, in the archdeaconry and diocese of Winchester, rated in the king's books at £7. 16. 3., and in the patronage of the Rev. R. C. Taunton. The church is dedicated to St. Mary. In this parish are vestiges of several Roman camps, and a circular intrenchment of considerable dimensions, supposed to be British or Danish.

ASHLEY, a parish in the northern division of the hundred of PIREHILL, county of STAFFORD, 7 miles (N. W.) from Eccleshall, containing 729 inhabitants. The living is a rectory, in the archdeaconry of Stafford, and diocese of Lichfield and Coventry, rated in the king's books at £10. 2. 8½., and in the patronage of T. Kinnersley, Esq. The church is dedicated to St. John the Baptist.

ASHLEY, a parish in the hundred of MALMESBURY, county of WILTS, 5 miles (N. by W.) from Malmesbury, containing 103 inhabitants. The living is a discharged rectory, in the archdeaconry of Wilts, and diocese of Salisbury, rated in the king's books at £9. 16. 5½., and in the patronage of the King, as Duke of Lancaster. The church is dedicated to St. James.

ASHLEY-HAY, a township in that part of the parish of WIRKSWORTH which is in the hundred of APPLETREE, county of DERBY, 1¾ mile (S.) from Wirksworth, containing 223 inhabitants.

ASHMANHAUGH, a parish in the hundred of TUNSTEAD, county of NORFOLK, 2¾ miles (E. by N.) from Coltishall, containing 128 inhabitants. The living is a discharged perpetual curacy, in the archdeaconry of Norfolk, and diocese of Norwich, endowed with £200 private benefaction, and £600 royal bounty. J. Preston, Esq. was patron in 1786. The church is dedicated to St. Swithin.

ASHMANSWORTH, a parish in the hundred of EVINGAR, Kingsclere division of the county of SOUTHAMPTON, 7½ miles (N. N. W.) from Whitchurch, containing 196 inhabitants. The living is a perpetual curacy, annexed to the rectory of East Woodhay, in the peculiar jurisdiction of the Bishop of Winchester. The church is dedicated to St. James. This parish is within the jurisdiction of the Cheyney Court held at Winchester every Thursday, for the recovery of debts to any amount.

ASHMORE, a parish in that part of the hundred of CRANBORNE which is in the Shaston (West) division of the county of DORSET, 5 miles (S. E.) from Shaftesbury, containing 166 inhabitants. The living is a rectory, in the archdeaconry of Dorset, and diocese of Bristol, rated in the king's books at £7. 19. 9½., and in the patronage of the Rev. George Chisholme. The church is dedicated to St. Nicholas.

ASHOLT, county of SOUTHAMPTON. — See AISHOLT.

ASHORN, a township in the parish of Newbold-Pacey, Warwick division of the hundred of Kington, county of Warwick, 6½ miles (N. N. W.) from Kington. The population is returned with the parish.

ASHOVER, a parish partly in the hundred of Wirksworth, but chiefly in the hundred of Scarsdale, county of Derby, 7½ miles (N. W. by W.) from Alfreton, containing, with the chapelry of Dethwick-Lea, and the hamlet of Holloway, 2998 inhabitants. This place, formerly a market town, occupies a pleasant site near the rivers Amber and Milntown; and, according to Domesday-book, had a church at the time of the Conquest. Coal, iron-stone, mill-stone, grit-stone, and lead-ore are found here, and the Gregory lead mine, three hundred yards deep, is said to have once been the richest in the kingdom, though its present produce is but inconsiderable. The manufacture of stockings is carried on to a small extent, and the working of tambour lace affords employment to the greater part of the female population. Fairs for cattle and sheep are held on the 25th of April and the 15th of October. Ashover is in the honour of Tutbury, duchy of Lancaster, and within the jurisdiction of a court held at Tutbury every third Tuesday, for the recovery of debts under 40*s.*: constables and other officers are appointed at the court leet of the lord of the manor. The living is a rectory, in the archdeaconry of Derby, and diocese of Lichfield and Coventry, rated in the king's books at £24. 3. 1½., and in the patronage of the Rev. J. Browne. The church, dedicated to All Saints, is a large ancient edifice, built in 1419, with a very handsome spire, and contains a Norman font of curious design, and several monuments to the family of Babington. There are places of worship for Primitive and Wesleyan Methodists. The free school, erected in 1703, at Ashover Hill, is endowed with £23. 9. per annum, principally arising from a bequest of land by the Rev. Francis Gisborne, in 1819, for which about twenty poor children are instructed.

ASHOW, a parish in the Kenilworth division of the hundred of Knightlow, county of Warwick, 2½ miles (S. E. by E.) from Kenilworth, containing 178 inhabitants. The living is a rectory, in the archdeaconry of Coventry, and diocese of Lichfield and Coventry, rated in the king's books at £6. 2. 1., and in the patronage of Chandos Leigh, Esq. The church is dedicated to St. Mary.

ASHPERTON, a parish in the hundred of Radlow, county of Hereford, 5¼ miles (N. W. by W.) from Ledbury, containing 398 inhabitants. The living is a perpetual curacy, annexed to the vicarage of Stretton-Grandsome, in the archdeaconry and diocese of Hereford. The church is dedicated to St. Bartholomew. Courts leet and baron are held here annually.

ASHPRINGTON, a parish in the hundred of Coleridge, county of Devon, 3 miles (S. E.) from Totness, containing 619 inhabitants. The living is a rectory, in the archdeaconry of Totness, and diocese of Exeter, rated in the king's books at £29. 1. 8., and in the patronage of the Rev. G. Carwithen, and R. Newman, Esq. The church is dedicated to St. David. The navigable river Dart is joined by the Hareborn on the north-eastern border of the parish.

ASHREIGNEY, or RING'S ASH, a parish in the hundred of North Tawton with Winkley, county of Devon, 4 miles (W. by S.) from Chulmleigh, containing 858 inhabitants. The living is a rectory, in the archdeaconry of Barnstaple, and diocese of Exeter, rated in the king's books at £24, and in the patronage of the Rev. J. T. Johnson. The church is dedicated to St. James. A school for the instruction of boys and girls has been endowed with £10 per annum by Mrs. Gertrude Pyncombe.

ASHTEAD, a parish in the second division of the hundred of Copthorne, county of Surrey, 2¼ miles (S. W. by S.) from Epsom, containing 579 inhabitants. The living is a rectory, in the archdeaconry of Surrey, and diocese of Winchester, rated in the king's books at £13. 15. 5., and in the patronage of the Hon. Fulke Greville Howard. The church is dedicated to St. Giles. A mineral spring, the waters of which are similar to that of Epsom, rises in the parish. A charity school is endowed with £10 per annum; and a school for the children of the poor owes its origin and support to the Hon. Col. and Mrs. Howard. An hospital for six poor widows was founded by Lady Diana Fielding, and endowed with property producing £32. 7. 2. per annum.

ASHTON, a township in that part of the parish of Tarvin which is in the second division of the hundred of Eddisbury, county palatine of Chester, 7½ miles (E. N. E.) from Chester, containing 414 inhabitants.

ASHTON, a parish in the hundred of Exminster, county of Devon, 3¾ miles (N. by W.) from Chudleigh, containing 258 inhabitants. The living is a rectory, in the archdeaconry and diocese of Exeter, rated in the king's books at £11. 10. 2½., and in the patronage of the Rev. Thomas Hole. The church contains a very finely carved wooden screen and rood-loft. The parish is bounded by the river Teign, the sudden inundations of which frequently occasion much damage. Here are several mines of manganese, worked by contractors from Cornwall, who pay to the lord of the manor a duty on the tonnage: large quantities of this mineral are supplied to the Manchester and other manufacturers, for bleaching their goods. Jane Shepherd, in 1734, gave 12*s.* per annum for teaching two poor children of this place; and John Stooke, in 1691, gave £4. 4. per annum to the poor in the almshouse.

ASHTON, a joint township with Eye-Moreton, in the parish of Eye, hundred of Wolphy, county of Hereford, 3¾ miles (N. N. E.) from Leominster, containing, with Eye-Moreton, 278 inhabitants.

ASHTON, a joint township with Lea, Cottam, and Ingol, in the parish of Preston, hundred of Amounderness, county palatine of Lancaster, 2 miles (W. by N.) from Preston. The population is returned with Lea.

ASHTON, a joint township with Stodday, in that part of the parish of Lancaster which is in the hundred of Lonsdale, south of the sands, county palatine of Lancaster, 3¼ miles (S. S. E.) from Lancaster, containing, with Stodday, 242 inhabitants. Ashton Hall, the property of the Duke of Hamilton, is an oblong edifice, with a projecting wing to the east, and a square tower with angular turrets on the west; it was probably erected in the fourteenth century, but the numerous alterations and additions which it has undergone have left little of the ancient baronial mansion: the surrounding scenery is highly beautiful. A free school, under the management of trustees, has an income of nearly £50 per annum.

ASHTON, a parish in the hundred of CLELEY, county of NORTHAMPTON, 7 miles (S. by E.) from Northampton, containing 341 inhabitants. The living is a rectory, in the archdeaconry of Northampton, and diocese of Peterborough, rated in the king's books at £10, and in the patronage of the Crown. The church is dedicated to St. Michael. This parish has a communication with the North sea, by means of the Northampton canal and the river Nene.

ASHTON, a hamlet in the parish of UFFORD, liberty of PETERBOROUGH, county of NORTHAMPTON, 4½ miles (N. N. E.) from Ufford, containing 131 inhabitants.

ASHTON, a chapelry in the parish of OUNDLE, hundred of POLEBROOK, county of NORTHAMPTON, 1½ mile (E. by N.) from Oundle, containing 129 inhabitants.

ASHTON (COLD), a parish in the hundred of PUCKLE-CHURCH, county of GLOUCESTER, 10¼ miles (E. by S.) from Bristol, containing 284 inhabitants. The living is a rectory, in the archdeaconry and diocese of Gloucester, rated in the king's books at £17. 1. 8., and in the patronage of the Rev. J. Whittington. The church is dedicated to the Holy Trinity. Here is a school for the instruction of poor children, endowed with £8 per annum.

ASHTON under HILL, a parish partly in the upper division of the hundred of TEWKESBURY, but chiefly in the hundred of TIBALDSTONE, county of GLOUCESTER, 8 miles (E. N.E.) from Tewkesbury, containing 301 inhabitants. The living is a perpetual curacy, annexed to the vicarage of Beckford, in the archdeaconry and diocese of Gloucester. The church is dedicated to St. Barbara.

ASHTON under LINE, a parish in the hundred of SALFORD, county palatine of LANCASTER, comprising the market town of Ashton under Line, and the townships of Audenshaw, Hartshead, and Knott-Lanes, and containing 25,967 inhabitants, of which number, 9222 are in the town of Ashton under Line, 60 miles (S.E.) from Lancaster, 7 (E.) from Manchester, and 187 (N.W.) from London, on the road to Sheffield. This place, in ancient records styled *Ashtown sub Lima*, derives its name from the tree so called, and the adjunct, by which it is distinguished from other places of the same name in the county, from its situation below the Lyme of Cheshire. Its original proprietors, the Asshetons, a family distinguished in the early periods of English history, exercised the power of life and death; and a field near the old hall, called Gallows' Meadow, was the place of execution. In the reign of Henry VI., a descendant of that family, still inheriting extraordinary privileges, clad in black armour and mounted on a charger, with a numerous retinue, levied a penalty on his tenants, for neglecting to clear their lands from a pernicious weed, then called *Carr gulds*, on the discovery of which among his corn, every farmer was liable to forfeit a wether sheep. In commemoration of this, the ceremony of "riding the black lad" still takes place on Easter-Monday, when the effigy of a man in black armour is placed on horseback, and led in procession through the town; it is then dismounted and hung up at the cross in the old market-place, and, after having been shot at, is immersed in a stagnant pool by the populace, who return through the principal streets throwing it at those they meet. The town is situated on an eminence rising from the northern bank of the river Tame; the old streets are narrow and irregular, but those recently formed are spacious, and contain substantial and handsome houses. It is well paved, and is lighted with gas and supplied with water by a company incorporated by act of parliament in 1825, and is rapidly improving under the management of local commissioners, appointed under an act obtained in 1827. The principal branches of manufacture are those of calico, gingham, and muslin, and there are numerous mills for spinning the finer kinds of yarn: the various factories, which are principally worked by steam, contain four hundred and thirteen thousand one hundred and sixteen spindles, and three hundred and ninety power-looms. The manufacture of hats is also carried on extensively in this district. The neighbourhood abounds with excellent coal, which is conveyed to all parts of the kingdom by the Ashton, Huddersfield, and Peak Forest canals, which unite here. The market, which, previously to the establishment of the cotton trade, had fallen into disuse, was restored by act of parliament in 1828, under which act a convenient market-place is now being erected, but the market day has not yet been fixed. Fairs are held on March 23rd, April 29th, and on the eve, day, and morrow of St. Swithin and St. Martin, chiefly for horses and cattle. The town was formerly incorporated, but is now within the jurisdiction of the county magistrates, who sit every Monday and Wednesday, and hold a petty session, every alternate week, for the Middleton division of the hundred. The powers of the local commissioners were extended by the act obtained in 1828, whereby the internal regulation of the town is entrusted to their superintendence. The lord of the manor holds a court leet half-yearly, in April and October, for the recovery of debts under 40*s.*; and a court of requests for the recovery of debts under £5 is held on the Thursday in every third week, under an act passed in the 48th of Geo. III., having jurisdiction over the parish of Ashton under Line, and the townships of Stalybridge, Hattersley, Matley, Newton, and Duckinfield. The court-house, for the transaction of the public business, is a handsome and commodious range of building, over which are the theatre and concert-room.

The living is a rectory, in the archdeaconry and diocese of Chester, rated in the king's books at £26. 13. 4., and in the patronage of the Earl of Stamford. The parochial church, dedicated to St. Michael, is a spacious structure in the later style of English architecture, with a tower built in the reign of Henry V., but much altered by subsequent repairs: it sustained considerable injury from an accidental fire in 1821. St. Peter's, a handsome edifice in the same style, with a square embattled tower crowned with pinnacles, was erected in 1821, at the expense of £12,688. 13. 6., defrayed by the parliamentary commissioners. There are places of worship for Independents, and Primitive and Wesleyan Methodists. The National school, built partly at the expense of the Earl of Stamford and Warrington, and partly by the contributions of the inhabitants, is supported by subscription. The Roman road from Manchester to Saddleworth may still be traced in the vicinity: near the old hall are the remains of an ancient prison, and in the old market-place those of a cross.

ASHTON (LONG), a parish in the hundred of HARTCLIFFE with BEDMINSTER, county of SOMERSET, 2¾ miles (S.W. by W.) from Bristol, containing 1168 inhabitants. The living is a discharged vicarage, in the archdeaconry of Bath, and diocese of Bath and Wells, rated in the king's books at £10. 17. 11., and in the patronage of Sir J. Smyth, Bart. The church is dedicated to All Saints. There were formerly a chapel and hermitage at Rownan Ferry, in this parish. In 1661, Francis Derrick gave a piece of land producing about £8 per annum, which, exclusively of 10*s.* to the minister, and 10*s.* to the poor, is appropriated towards the support of a school. Anne Smyth, in 1760, left a rent-charge of £10, which has been applied to the support of a National school, to which, in 1822, John Stanton gave £100. On the eastern point of Ashton hill are two intrenchments, called Burwalls and Stokeleigh, now overgrown with wood, which appear to have been Roman camps; many Roman coins have been dug up in the vicinity.

ASHTON in MACKERFIELD, a chapelry in the parish of WINWICK, hundred of WEST DERBY, county palatine of LANCASTER, 2½ miles (N. W. by N.) from Newton in Mackerfield, containing 5674 inhabitants. The living is a perpetual curacy, in the archdeaconry and diocese of Chester, endowed with £200 royal bounty, and £1600 parliamentary grant, and in the patronage of the Rector of Winwick. There are places of worship for the Society of Friends, Wesleyan Methodists, and Roman Catholics. Ashton is a large village lying in the centre of a district in which are numerous potteries and cotton-manufactories.

ASHTON upon MERSEY, a parish in the hundred of BUCKLOW, county palatine of CHESTER, comprising the townships of Ashton upon Mersey and Sale, and containing 1924 inhabitants, of which number, 875 are in the township of Ashton upon Mersey, 6¾ miles (N.) from Altrincham. The living is a rectory, in the archdeaconry and diocese of Chester, rated in the king's books at £13. 4. 7., and in the patronage of W. Johnson, Esq. and another. The church is dedicated to St. Martin. There are places of worship for Calvinists, Methodists, and Unitarians. The navigable river Mersey runs through the parish. A school is endowed with land and tenements producing about £50 per annum; in addition to which, William Williamson, Esq. left an annuity of £70 for the instruction of children.

ASHTON (STEEPLE), a parish (formerly a market town) in the hundred of WHORWELSDOWN, county of WILTS, 3¼ miles (E. by S.) from Trowbridge, containing, with the chapelries of Littleton and Semington, and the tythings of West Ashton and Great Hinton, 1632 inhabitants. The living is a vicarage, in the archdeaconry and diocese of Salisbury, rated in the king's books at £17. 2. 6., and in the patronage of the Master and Fellows of Magdalene College, Cambridge. The church, dedicated to St. Mary, is a very lofty and elegant structure in the later English style, with extensive north and south porches, two small chapels, and, at the west end, a large and handsome embattled and pinnacled tower, having also a fine western window with five richly ornamented niches over it: ten clustered columns separate the aisles from the nave, and the whole interior is rich in architectural decorations: the north aisle was erected at the expense of Robert Long, a clothier, and Edith his wife, and the south chiefly at that of the parishioners. This place derives the prefix to its name from a very elevated spire, ninety-three feet high, which originally surmounted the tower of the church, but it was seriously damaged by lightning in July 1670, and again in October following, when the spire and a portion of the tower were struck down, two workmen employed in its reparation killed, and a great part of the nave and aisles damaged; the body of the church was repaired in 1675, partly from voluntary subscriptions, and partly at the expense of the parishioners. A market was granted to be held here in the reign of Edward III., and was confirmed in that of Richard II., who also added an annual fair. In the time of Henry VIII. there was a considerable clothing trade, which no longer exists; the market has been long discontinued, and the fair, now inconsiderable, is on September 18th. John Hicks gave a piece of land, producing £5 per annum, for the education of poor children.

ASHTON-GIFFORD, a township in the parish of CODFORD ST. PETER, hundred of HEYTESBURY, county of WILTS, 3 miles (S. E. by E.) from Heytesbury. The population is returned with the parish.

ASHTON-KEYNES, a parish in the hundred of HIGHWORTH, CRICKLADE, and STAPLE, county of WILTS, 4½ miles (W.) from Cricklade, containing, with the chapelry of Leigh, 1151 inhabitants. The living is a vicarage, in the archdeaconry of Wilts, and diocese of Salisbury, rated in the king's books at £16, and in the patronage of Robert Clack and others. The church is dedicated to the Holy Cross.

ASHURST, a parish in the hundred of WASHLINGSTONE, lathe of AYLESFORD, county of KENT, 4¾ miles (W.) from Tonbridge-Wells, containing 208 inhabitants. The living is a discharged rectory, in the archdeaconry and diocese of Rochester, rated in the king's books at £5. 4. 7., endowed with £200 private benefaction, and £200 royal bounty, and in the patronage of Earl De la Warr. The church, a low mean building, was, before the Reformation, famous for a rood or crucifix, the supposed miraculous powers of which attracted numerous pilgrims. The river Medway, which is here but an inconsiderable stream, bounds the parish on the north-west.

ASHURST, a parish in the hundred of WEST GRINSTEAD, rape of BRAMBER, county of SUSSEX, 3¾ miles (N.) from Steyning, containing 394 inhabitants. The living is a discharged rectory, in the archdeaconry and diocese of Chichester, and in the patronage of the President and Fellows of Magdalene College, Oxford. The navigable river Adur runs through this parish.

ASHWATER, a parish in the hundred of BLACK TORRINGTON, county of DEVON, 6½ miles (S. E. by S.) from Holsworthy, containing 774 inhabitants. The living is a rectory, in the archdeaconry of Totness, and diocese of Exeter, rated in the king's books at £26. 6. 8., and in the patronage of the Rev. T. Melhuish. The church, dedicated to St. Peter, contains some interesting monuments. Fairs for cattle are held on the first Tuesday in May, and the first Monday after the 1st of August. Freestone of excellent quality is obtained in the vicinity.

ASHWELL, a parish in the hundred of ODSEY, county of HERTFORD, 4¼ miles (N. N. E.) from Baldock, containing 915 inhabitants. The living is a vicarage, in the archdeaconry of Huntingdon, and diocese of Lincoln, rated in the king's books at £22. 3. 6½., and in the patronage of the Bishop of London. The church, dedicated to St. Mary, is a spacious edifice, with a tower and spire one hundred and seventy-five feet high. Ashwell is a place of great antiquity, and was a market town and borough at the time of the Norman survey, having also four fairs, and being held in royal demesne. Its name is derived from several springs, issuing out of a rock at the south end of the town, which were formerly surrounded by ash trees: they form the source of the small river Rhee, which soon becomes so full and rapid, as to turn several mills within a short distance. On Harborough hill, in this parish, are the remains of a quadrangular encampment of the Romans, whence the approach of an enemy, in any direction, and at a great distance, could be observed. Urns, coins, and skeletons, have been dug up, as well as near the Iknield-road, in the vicinity. The free school, in which fourteen boys are instructed, has an endowment from the estate of Sir Richard Hutchinson, paid to the master by the Merchant Taylors' Company of London. There are also six endowed almshouses for as many poor persons, and a fund for apprenticing poor children. A small manor here was held by Walter Somoner, in petit serjeantry, by the service of providing spits and roasting meat in the king's kitchen, on the day of his coronation. The only trade carried on is in malt, the barley produced in the neighbourhood being of a peculiarly excellent quality. The Rev. Ralph Cudworth, D. D., master of Christ's College, Cambridge, and author of The Intellectual System, was vicar of this parish, and died here in 1688.

ASHWELL, a parish in the hundred of ALSTOE, county of RUTLAND, 3 miles (N. by W.) from Oakham, containing 220 inhabitants. The living is a rectory, in the archdeaconry of Northampton, and diocese of Peterborough, rated in the king's books at £20. 16. 3., and in the patronage of Viscount Downe. The church is dedicated to St. Mary.

ASHWELLTHORPE, a parish in the hundred of DEPWADE, county of NORFOLK, 3½ miles (S. E. by S.) from Wymondham, containing 418 inhabitants. The living is a discharged rectory, with that of Wreningham annexed, in the archdeaconry of Norfolk, and diocese of Norwich, rated in the king's books at £6. 13. 4., and in the patronage of Robert Wilson, Esq. The church is dedicated to All Saints.

ASHWICK, a parish in the hundred of KILMERSDON, county of SOMERSET, 3¾ miles (N. by E.) from Shepton-Mallet, containing 829 inhabitants. The living is a perpetual curacy, annexed to the vicarage of Kilmersdon, in the archdeaconry of Wells, and diocese of Bath and Wells. The church is dedicated to St. James. There are places of worship for Methodists and Presbyterians. Here is a considerable brewery, and in the neighbourhood are many coal mines. On the south-western side of the parish, near the Fosse-way, there is a Roman camp, with a double intrenchment, called Masbury Castle.

ASHWICKEN, a parish in the Lynn division of the hundred of FREEBRIDGE, county of NORFOLK, 5½ miles (E. by S.) from Lynn-Regis, containing 79 inhabitants. The living is a rectory, with that of Leziate annexed, in the archdeaconry and diocese of Norwich, rated in the king's books at £6. 13. 4., and in the patronage of Earl Spencer. The church is dedicated to All Saints.

ASHWORTH, a chapelry in the parish of MIDDLETON, hundred of SALFORD, county palatine of LANCASTER, 3½ miles (W.) from Rochdale, containing 280 inhabitants. The living is a perpetual curacy, in the archdeaconry and diocese of Chester, endowed with £800 private benefaction, £1000 royal bounty, and £300 parliamentary grant, and in the patronage of W. Egerton, Esq. The chapel is dedicated to St. James.

ASKE, a township in that part of the parish of EASBY which is in the western division of the wapentake of GILLING, North riding of the county of YORK, 1¾ mile (N.) from Richmond, containing 109 inhabitants.

ASKERNE, a township in the parish of CAMPSALL, upper division of the wapentake of OSGOLDCROSS, West riding of the county of YORK, 7¼ miles (N.) from Doncaster, containing 159 inhabitants. Here is a sheet of water, called Askerne Pool, a few yards from which rises a spring with a sulphureous impregnation, the water of which is esteemed beneficial in rheumatic and scorbutic diseases, and is now extensively used; a spacious inn has lately been erected for the accommodation of visitors.

ASKERSWELL, a parish in the hundred of EGGERTON, Bridport division of the county of DORSET, 4 miles (E.) from Bridport, containing 190 inhabitants. The living is a rectory, in the archdeaconry of Dorset, and diocese of Bristol, rated in the king's books at £9. 2. 6., and in the patronage of the Rev. Edward Foyle. The church is dedicated to St. Michael.

ASKERTON, a township in the parish of LANERCOST-ABBEY, ESKDALE ward, county of CUMBERLAND, 6¼ miles (N.N.E.) from Brampton, containing 503 inhabitants. The castle, situated on the eastern bank of the Cambeck, was a small tower building with lofty turrets, but it has long been in ruins. Askerton comprises the ancient parish of Kirk-Cambeck, the church of which was destroyed by the Scots in the reign of Edward II., and the tithes are held on lease from the Dean and Chapter of Carlisle: the inhabitants repair to the church of Lanercost for the performance of ecclesiastical rites.

ASKHAM, a chapelry in the parish of EAST DRAYTON, within the liberty of SOUTHWELL and SCROOBY, which is locally in the South-clay division of the hundred of Bassetlaw, county of NOTTINGHAM, 2¾ miles (N.) from Tuxford, containing 270 inhabitants. The living is a perpetual curacy, in the peculiar jurisdiction of the Dean and Chapter of York, and in the patronage of the Vicar of East Drayton. Hops are cultivated here. There are almshouses for six widows.

ASKHAM, a parish in WEST ward, county of WESTMORLAND, comprising the townships of Askham and Helton, and containing 517 inhabitants, of which number, 355 are in the township of Askham, 4¾ miles (S.) from Penrith. The living is a discharged vicarage, in the archdeaconry and diocese of Carlisle, rated in the king's books at £6, and in the patronage of the Earl of Lonsdale. The church is a small ancient building, dedicated to St. Peter. Limestone abounds in the parish. A school was endowed, in 1813, with subscriptions amounting to £420, a great part of which has been vested in the purchase of land.

ASKHAM-BRYAN, a parish in the ainsty of the city, and East riding of the county, of YORK, 4 miles (W. S. W.) from York, containing 377 inhabitants. The living is a perpetual curacy, within the peculiar jurisdiction of the lord of the manor, endowed with £800 private benefaction, and £800 royal bounty, and in the patronage of R. J. Thompson, Esq. The church is dedicated to St. Nicholas. There is a place of worship for Wesleyan Methodists. A small endowment has been given for the education of poor children.

ASKHAM-RICHARD, a parish in the ainsty of the city, and East riding of the county, of YORK, 5¾ miles (S. W. by W.) from York, containing 249 inhabitants. The living is a discharged vicarage, in the archdeaconry and diocese of York, rated in the king's books at £4. 13. 4., endowed with £200 private benefaction, and £200 royal bounty, and in the patronage of R. J. Thompson, Esq. The church is dedicated to St. Mary. There is a place of worship for Wesleyan Methodists.

ASKRIGG, a market town and chapelry in the parish of AYSGARTH, western division of the wapentake of HANG, North riding of the county of YORK, 57 miles (W.N.W.) from York, and 247 (N.W. by N.) from London, containing 765 inhabitants. The town is situated on an eminence rising from the northern bank of the river Ure, and the surrounding country exhibits some fine waterfalls and picturesque scenery: it was formerly a place of considerable note, but has fallen into decay; there are a flax and a wool-carding mill. In the neighbourhood are lead mines, but they are not very productive. The market is on Thursday; and fairs are held on May 11th, the first Thursday in June, and October 28th. The living is a perpetual curacy, in the archdeaconry of Richmond, and diocese of Chester, endowed with £200 private benefaction, £400 royal bounty, and £1000 parliamentary grant, and in the patronage of the Vicar of Aysgarth. The chapel is an ancient structure, dedicated to St. Oswald. There is a place of worship for Wesleyan Methodists. Almshouses were founded and endowed, in 1807, by Christopher Alderson, for six poor widows of the townships of Askrigg and Low Abbotside, each of whom has a stipend of £10 per annum. In this township is the free grammar school of Yorebridge, founded by Anthony Besson, in the 43rd of Elizabeth, with an endowment of £64. 10. per annum.

ASKWITH, a township in the parish of WESTON, upper division of the wapentake of CLARO, West riding of the county of YORK, 3 miles (N.W.) from Otley, containing 367 inhabitants.

ASLACKBY, a parish in the wapentake of AVELAND, parts of KESTEVEN, county of LINCOLN, 2½ miles (S. S. E.) from Folkingham, containing, with the hamlets of Graby and Milthorpe, 425 inhabitants. The living is a vicarage, in the archdeaconry and diocese of Lincoln, rated in the king's books at £12. 10. 7½., and in the patronage of M. Barstow, Esq. The church is dedicated to St. James. Here was a preceptory of Knights Templars, which, on the abolition of their order, became a commandery of the Hospitallers: a square tower belonging to the edifice yet remains.

ASLACTON, a parish in the hundred of DEPWADE, county of NORFOLK, 3½ miles (W. by S.) from St. Mary Stratton, containing 352 inhabitants. The living is a perpetual curacy, in the archdeaconry of Norfolk, and diocese of Norwich, endowed with £800 royal bounty, and in the patronage of Mrs. Bodham. The church is dedicated to St. Michael.

ASLACTON, a township in the parish of WHATTON, northern division of the wapentake of BINGHAM, county of NOTTINGHAM, 2¾ miles (E. by N.) from Bingham, containing 273 inhabitants. It is in the honour of Tutbury, duchy of Lancaster, and within the jurisdiction of a court of pleas held at Tutbury every third Tuesday, for the recovery of debts under 40*s*. This was the birthplace of Cranmer, the first Protestant Archbishop of Canterbury, who was burnt at Oxford in 1555, a martyr to his religious tenets.

ASPALL, a parish in the hundred of HARTISMERE, county of SUFFOLK, 1¼ mile (N. by W.) from Debenham, containing 109 inhabitants. The living is a perpetual curacy, in the archdeaconry of Sudbury, and diocese of Norwich, and in the patronage of the Rev. C. Chevallier. Here is a free school, endowed with land bequeathed by the Rev. John Metcalf, in 1612, from the produce of which £50 per annum is paid to the master, and £10 to the usher.

ASPATRIA, a parish in ALLERDALE ward below Darwent, county of CUMBERLAND, comprising the townships of Aspatria with Brayton, Hayton with Melay, and Outerside with Allerby, and containing 1220 inhabitants, of which number, 632 are in the township of Aspatria with Brayton, 8 miles (N. by E.) from Cockermouth. The living is a vicarage, in the archdeaconry and diocese of Carlisle, rated in the king's books at £10. 4. 2., and in the patronage of the Bishop of Carlisle. The church, dedicated to St. Kentigern, is a finely ornamented structure, in the Norman style of architecture. A place of worship for Independents was built in 1827. Aspatria derived its name from Gospatrick, father of the first lord of Allerdale: the parish is bounded on the west by the Solway Firth, and on the south-east and south by the river Ellen, and contains a vein of red freestone at Hayton, and coal at Outerside: the village, which is long, straggling, and well built, extends along the ridge of a hill facing the south. In 1790, a barrow was opened about two hundred yards to the north of it, when the skeleton of a man, with the corroded remains of some military weapons, gold ornaments, &c., were discovered in a vault constructed of large stones, on two of which various emblematical figures were sculptured: it is supposed to have been the tomb of a warrior, interred about the close of the sixth century.

ASPEDEN, a parish in the hundred of EDWINSTREE, county of HERTFORD, ¾ of a mile (S.) from Buntingford, containing 455 inhabitants. The living is a rectory, in the archdeaconry of Huntingdon, and diocese of Lincoln, rated in the king's books at £15. 5. 2½., and in the patronage of the Earl of Hardwicke. The church is dedicated to St. Mary. The river Rib, which falls into the Lea near Hertford, flows through this parish. W. and R. Freeman, in 1668, and Mrs. Cater, in 1704, gave land for the education of children; and R. Freeman assigned an additional plot of land for clothing them. In 1684, Dr. Seth Ward, Bishop of Sarum, founded an almshouse for two men and two women, and endowed it with £41. 12. per annum.

ASPLEY, a township in the parish of **Eccleshall**, northern division of the hundred of **Pirehill**, county of **Stafford**, containing 24 inhabitants.

ASPLEY, a joint hamlet with Fordhall, in the parish of **Wootton-Wawen**, Henley division of the hundred of **Barlichway**, county of **Warwick**, containing, with Fordhall, 106 inhabitants.

ASPLEY-GUISE, a parish in the hundred of **Manshead**, county of **Bedford**, 2¼ miles (N. by W.) from Woburn, containing 848 inhabitants. The living is a rectory, consolidated, in 1796, with the vicarage of Husborn-Crawley, in the archdeaconry of Bedford, and diocese of Lincoln, rated in the king's books at £15. 16. 10½. The church, dedicated to St. Botolph, contains several ancient and interesting monuments. There is a place of worship for Wesleyan Methodists. A market on Friday, and a fair on the festival of St. Botolph, were granted to be held here in 1267; but they have been long discontinued. A small portion of this parish lies in the county of Buckingham.

ASPULL, a township in that part of the parish of **Wigan** which is in the hundred of **Salford**, county palatine of **Lancaster**, 3 miles (N.E. by E.) from Wigan, containing 1894 inhabitants. A chapel has been lately erected by the parliamentary commissioners. Cannel coal abounds in the township. Here is a small endowment for the education of poor children.

ASSELBY, a township in the parish of **Howden**, wapentake of **Howdenshire**, East riding of the county of **York**, 2 miles (W. by S.) from Howden, containing 254 inhabitants. There is a place of worship for Wesleyan Methodists.

ASSENDON, a hamlet in the parish and hundred of **Pirton**, county of **Oxford**, 4 miles (N.N.W.) from Henley upon Thames. The population is returned with the parish. Here is an almshouse, endowed with £5 per annum.

ASSINGTON, a parish in the hundred of **Babergh**, county of **Suffolk**, 2¼ miles (S.W. by W.) from Boxford, containing 533 inhabitants. The living is a discharged vicarage, in the archdeaconry of Sudbury, and diocese of Norwich, rated in the king's books at £10, endowed with £200 private benefaction, and £200 royal bounty, and in the patronage of the Rev. John Hallward. The church is dedicated to St. Edmund. In 1777, John Gurdon bequeathed £100 for the instruction of poor children.

ASTBURY, a parish comprising the township of Somerford-Booths, in the hundred of **Macclesfield**, the market town of Congleton, and the townships of Astbury-Newbold, Buglawton, Davenport, Hulme-Walfield, Moreton with Alcumlow, Oddrode, Radnor, Smallwood, and Summerford, in the hundred of **Northwich**, county palatine of **Chester**, 1½ mile (S.W.) from Congleton, and containing 10,388 inhabitants. The living is a rectory, in the archdeaconry and diocese of Chester, rated in the king's books at £68, and in the patronage of Lord Crewe. The church, dedicated to St. Mary, is a spacious and beautiful structure, in the later style of English architecture: the interior contains several stalls, a rood-loft, and some fine screen-work; the ceilings, which are of oak, are richly carved; the east window is highly finished, and there are some fine specimens of stained glass. The nave is separated from the aisles by lofty pointed arches springing from clustered columns. The tower, which stands at the north-west angle of the church, and is surmounted by an elegant spire, appears to have belonged to a former edifice. In the township of Oddrode, a church, or chapel of ease, has been erected by Mr. Dobbs, of Clapham in Surrey, which for a time was shut up, on account of some dispute respecting the patronage; but the service of the established church is now performed in it, the minister being appointed by the founder. The office of churchwarden devolves on the proprietors of six of the principal halls, and on the mayor of Congleton, who are styled *Præpositi*, here termed *Posts*, and who in rotation nominate a deputy. A railway passes through the parish from Mole-Cop to a coal wharf near Congleton; and the Macclesfield canal proceeds at a short distance east of the village. The sum of £50 per annum, the bequest of John Halford, in 1714, is partly distributed among the poor, and partly applied in apprenticing poor children.

ASTBURY (NEWBOLD), a township in that part of the parish of **Astbury** which is in the hundred of **Northwich**, county palatine of **Chester**, 3 miles (S. by E.) from Congleton, containing 569 inhabitants.

ASTERBY, a parish in the northern division of the wapentake of **Gartree**, parts of **Lindsey**, county of **Lincoln**, 7 miles (N.) from Horncastle, containing 189 inhabitants. The living is a discharged rectory, in the archdeaconry and diocese of Lincoln, rated in the king's books at £8. 0. 10., endowed with £200 private benefaction, and £200 royal bounty, and in the patronage of Lady Southwell. The church is dedicated to St. Peter. Here is a small endowment for the instruction of poor children, the bequest of Anthony Ascham, in 1638.

ASTHALL, a parish in the hundred of **Bampton**, county of **Oxford**, 3 miles (E. by S.) from Burford, containing, with the hamlet of Asthall-Leigh, 365 inhabitants. The living is a discharged vicarage, in the archdeaconry and diocese of Oxford, rated in the king's books at £7. 9. 4½., and in the patronage of the Provost and Fellows of Eton College. The church is dedicated to St. Nicholas. In this parish is a barrow of considerable height, supposed to be a sepulchral monument, near which the Roman Akeman-street passes. Sir George Fettiplace bequeathed £6 per annum for the instruction of six girls, with a house for the mistress; he also left £5 per annum for apprenticing poor boys.

ASTLEY, a chapelry in the parish of **Leigh**, hundred of **West Derby**, county palatine of **Lancaster**, 3 miles (E.) from Leigh, containing 1882 inhabitants. The living is a perpetual curacy, in the archdeaconry and diocese of Chester, endowed with £200 private benefaction, and £400 royal bounty, and in the patronage of the Vicar of Leigh. The chapel, dedicated to St. Stephen, was founded by Adam Mort, gent., in the early part of the seventeenth century, and endowed by him with property of the value of £18 per annum. In 1760, the old edifice was taken down, and a new one erected upon a more enlarged plan, by the landowners of the chapelry, the income at that time having been considerably augmented. For a long period the right of appointing the minister was a subject of dispute, and various contests took place at the time of elections; but the matter was ultimately determined by the judges of the court of King's Bench, in 1824, in favour of the present patron. There is a place of worship for Wesleyan Methodists. The manufacture of fustian is extensively carried on in the chapelry. A school is endowed with £25. 14. 8. per annum, for the education of poor children; and, in 1630, Adam Mort bequeathed land, producing about £24 per annum, for the instruction of poor children here, and in the townships of Great Bolton, Little Hulton, Bedford, and Tyldesley.

ASTLEY, a chapelry in that part of the parish of St. Mary which is within the liberties of Shrewsbury, county of Salop, 5 miles (N. N. E.) from Shrewsbury, containing 204 inhabitants. The living is a perpetual curacy, within the jurisdiction of the court of the royal peculiar of St. Mary in Shrewsbury, and in the patronage of the Perpetual Curate of that parish.

ASTLEY, a parish in the Kirby division of the hundred of Knightlow, county of Warwick, 4½ miles (W. S. W.) from Nuneaton, containing 293 inhabitants. The living is a perpetual curacy, in the archdeaconry of Coventry, and diocese of Lichfield and Coventry, endowed with £16 per annum and £400 private benefaction, and £600 royal bounty, and in the patronage of F. Newdigate, Esq. The church, dedicated to St. Mary, was made collegiate and rebuilt in the form of a cross, with a lofty spire, in the reign of Edward III., by Lord Thomas de Astley, many of whose family were interred here; the ancient choir, now forming the body of the church, is the only portion of the building remaining: the revenue of the college, at its dissolution, was £46. 8. A short distance to the north is an old mansion, erected in the sixteenth century, on the site of a more ancient baronial castle, some portion of the massive walls of which still exist.

ASTLEY, a parish in the lower division of the hundred of Doddingtree, county of Worcester, 3 miles (S. W. by S.) from Stourport, containing 784 inhabitants. The living is a rectory, in the archdeaconry and diocese of Worcester, rated in the king's books at £15. 13. 4., and in the patronage of the Rev. D. J. J. Cooks. The church, dedicated to St. Peter, is of Norman architecture. An Alien priory of Benedictine monks, founded here by Ralph de Todeni, in the reign of William I., was annexed to the college of Westbury in that of Edward IV. Here is a school, endowed with about £20 per annum. At Redstone ferry, in the vicinity, is an ancient hermitage, excavated in a lofty cliff by the side of the river.

ASTLEY (ABBOT'S), a parish in the hundred of Stottesden, county of Salop, 2 miles (N.) from Bridgenorth, containing 664 inhabitants. The living is a perpetual curacy, in the peculiar jurisdiction and patronage of T. Whitmore, Esq. The river Severn passes through the parish. Here is a school with a small endowment for poor children.

ASTON, a hamlet in the parish of Ivinghoe, hundred of Cottesloe, county of Buckingham, 1¾ mile (N.N.E.) from Ivinghoe, containing 382 inhabitants.

ASTON, a joint hamlet with Thornton, in the parish of Hope, hundred of High Peak, county of Derby, 6½ miles (N. N. E.) from Tideswell, containing, with Thornton, 102 inhabitants. This hamlet is in the honour of Tutbury, duchy of Lancaster, and within the jurisdiction of a court of pleas held at Tutbury every third Tuesday, for the recovery of debts under 40*s*.

ASTON, a parish in the hundred of Wigmore, county of Hereford, 4 miles (S.W. by W.) from Ludlow, containing 54 inhabitants. The living is a discharged rectory, in the archdeaconry of Salop, and diocese of Hereford, rated in the king's books at £2. 13. 4., and in the patronage of T. A. Knight, Esq. The church, which is very small, is dedicated to St. Giles.

ASTON, a parish in the hundred of Broadwater, county of Hertford, 3¼ miles (S.E.) from Stevenage, containing 509 inhabitants. The living is a rectory, in the archdeaconry of Huntingdon, and diocese of Lincoln, rated in the king's books at £26. 11. 8., and in the patronage of the Rev. James Ellice. The church is dedicated to St. Mary.

ASTON, a joint hamlet with Cote, in the parish and hundred of Bampton, county of Oxford, 4 miles (S. S.W.) from Witney, containing, with Cote, 659 inhabitants. A school for the education of twenty poor children is endowed with land given by Mr. Horde.

ASTON, a township in that part of the parish of Wem which is in the Whitchurch division of the hundred of Bradford (North), county of Salop, containing 262 inhabitants. There is a place of worship for Wesleyan Methodists.

ASTON, a township in that part of the parish of Muckleston which is in the northern division of the hundred of Pirehill, county of Stafford, 8 miles (W.S.W.) from Newcastle under Lyne, containing 277 inhabitants.

ASTON, a parish in the Birmingham division of the hundred of Hemlingford, county of Warwick, 2¼ miles (N.E. by E.) from Birmingham, containing, with the chapelries of Bordesley and Deritend, 19,189 inhabitants. The living is a vicarage, in the archdeaconry of Coventry, and diocese of Lichfield and Coventry, rated in the king's books at £21. 4. 9½., and in the patronage of the Rev. G. Peak. The church, dedicated to St. Peter and St. Paul, has a handsome tower and spire in the later style of English architecture, with other parts of an earlier date, but much modernized: the chancel contains some altar-tombs with effigies. The Birmingham and Fazely canal passes through this parish. In 1820, a chapel in the later style of English architecture was erected at Bordesley, at an expense of £12,722. 15. 6., by subscription of the inhabitants, aided by a grant from the parliamentary commissioners; and, in 1822, another was erected at Erdington, at the expense of £5657. 11., solely by grant of the commissioners. An almshouse for five men and five women was founded and endowed by Sir Thomas Holt, Bart., in the reign of James I.; the present building was erected by his grandson, about the year 1650.

ASTON, a parish in the southern division of the wapentake of Strafforth and Tickhill, West riding of the county of York, 5½ miles (S.S.E.) from Rotherham, containing, with the township of Aughton, 556 inhabitants. The living is a rectory, in the archdeaconry and diocese of York, rated in the king's books at £12. 15. 2½., and in the patronage of the Duke of Leeds. The church, dedicated to All Saints, contains a monument to the memory of Lord D'Arcy, who lived in the reign of Henry VIII.; also a marble tablet to that of the Rev. William Mason, the poet, rector of this parish, who died in 1797. Here is a school for the education of poor children, with a small endowment arising from a bequest of £100 by the Hon. Mrs. D'Arcy, in 1705, and from the contributions of other benefactors.

ASTON (ABBOT'S), a parish in the hundred of COTTESLOE, county of BUCKINGHAM, 5½ miles (N.N.E.) from Aylesbury, containing 321 inhabitants. The living is a vicarage, in the archdeaconry of St. Albans, and diocese of London, rated in the king's books at £6. 7. 11., and in the patronage of the Earl of Chesterfield. The church is dedicated to St. James.

ASTON by BUDWORTH, a chapelry in that part of the parish of GREAT BUDWORTH which is in the hundred of BUCKLOW, county palatine of CHESTER, 4 miles (N. N. E.) from Northwich, containing 380 inhabitants. The village is situated at the distance of about a mile from the main road between London and Liverpool, and the same distance from the Trent and Mersey canal. In the centre of the township are the remains of an ancient moated mansion, with an old bridge, and a petrifying spring rises at a place called Gore Farm. A court leet is held annually by the lord of the manor.

ASTON upon CARRON, a tything in the parish of ASHCHURCH, lower division of the hundred of TEWKESBURY, county of GLOUCESTER, 4¼ miles (E. N. E.) from Tewkesbury, containing 166 inhabitants.

ASTON (CHETWYND), a township in the parish of EDGMOND, Newport division of the hundred of BRADFORD (South), county of SALOP, 1½ mile (S. S. E.) from Newport, containing 291 inhabitants.

ASTON (CHURCH), a chapelry in the parish of EDGMOND, Newport division of the hundred of BRADFORD (South), county of SALOP, 1 mile (S.) from Newport, containing 329 inhabitants. The chapel, dedicated to St. Andrew, has recently been enlarged by the addition of two hundred sittings, one hundred and fifty of which are free, the commissioners for building and enlarging churches and chapels having contributed £100 towards defraying the expense.

ASTON sub EDGE, a parish in the upper division of the hundred of KIFTSGATE, county of GLOUCESTER, 1¼ mile (N. N. W.) from Chipping-Campden, containing 116 inhabitants. The living is a rectory, in the archdeaconry and diocese of Gloucester, rated in the king's books at £10. 2. 3½., and in the patronage of the Earl of Harrowby. The church is dedicated to St. Andrew.

ASTON (MAGNA), a hamlet in the parish of BLOCKLEY, upper division of the hundred of OSWALDSLOW, county of WORCESTER, 2¾ miles (N.) from Moreton in the Marsh, containing 254 inhabitants.

ASTON (MIDDLE), a township in the parish of STEEPLE-ASTON, hundred of WOOTTON, county of OXFORD, 3 miles (S. by E.) from Deddington, containing 120 inhabitants. Dr. Ratcliffe, in 1640, bequeathed land, now producing about £20 a year, in support of a grammar school.

ASTON juxta MONDRUM, a township in the parish of ACTON, hundred of NANTWICH, county palatine of CHESTER, 4 miles (N.) from Nantwich, containing 159 inhabitants.

ASTON (NORTH), a parish in the hundred of WOOTTON, county of OXFORD, 2½ miles (S. S. E.) from Deddington, containing 296 inhabitants. The living is a discharged vicarage, in the archdeaconry and diocese of Oxford, rated in the king's books at £6. 10., and in the patronage of John F. Willes, Esq. The church is dedicated to St. Mary. There is a place of worship for Wesleyan Methodists.

ASTON (STEEPLE), a parish in the hundred of WOOTTON, county of OXFORD, 4 miles (S. by E.) from Deddington, containing, with the township of Middle Aston, 515 inhabitants. The living is a rectory, in the archdeaconry and diocese of Oxford, rated in the king's books at £16. 2. 8½., and in the patronage of the Principal and Fellows of Brasenose College, Oxford. The church is dedicated to St. Peter. The petty sessions for the division are held here. A school for the education of poor children is endowed with about £17 per annum. A tesselated pavement was discovered in the vicinity, in the sixteenth century.

ASTON by SUTTON, a chapelry in the parish of RUNCORN, hundred of BUCKLOW, county palatine of CHESTER, 3 miles (E. by N.) from Frodsham, containing 197 inhabitants. The living is a perpetual curacy, in the archdeaconry and diocese of Chester, endowed with £200 private benefaction, £200 royal bounty, and £600 parliamentary grant, and in the patronage of H. Aston, Esq. The chapel was rebuilt on an enlarged scale in 1737.

ASTON upon TRENT, a parish (formerly a market town) in the hundred of MORLESTON and LITCHURCH, county of DERBY, 6½ miles (S. E.) from Derby, containing 552 inhabitants. The living is a rectory, in the archdeaconry of Derby, and diocese of Lichfield and Coventry, rated in the king's books at £29. 15., and in the patronage of the Rev. Charles Holden. The church is dedicated to All Saints. A grant of a market and a fair was obtained in 1256, but both have long been discontinued. The Grand Trunk Navigation joins the river Trent below Shardlow, in this parish; and here are extensive wharfs for corn and Staffordshire pottery. Aston upon Trent is in the honour of Tutbury, duchy of Lancaster, and within the jurisdiction of a court of pleas held at Tutbury every third Tuesday, for the recovery of debts under 40*s*. There is a small endowment for the education of poor children.

ASTON le WALLS, a parish in the hundred of CHIPPING-WARDEN, county of NORTHAMPTON, 8½ miles (N.N.E.) from Banbury, containing, with the hamlet of Appletree, 271 inhabitants. The living is a rectory, in the archdeaconry of Northampton, and diocese of Peterborough, rated in the king's books at £9. 9. 7., and in the patronage of the President and Fellows of St. John's College, Oxford. The church is dedicated to St. Leonard.

ASTON (WHITE LADIES), a parish in the lower division of the hundred of OSWALDSLOW, county of WORCESTER, 5 miles (E. S. E.) from Worcester, containing 342 inhabitants. The living is a vicarage, in the peculiar jurisdiction of the Bishop of Worcester, rated in the king's books at £6. 17. 3½., and in the patronage of R. Berkeley, Esq. The church is dedicated to St. John the Baptist. In the manor-house Oliver Cromwell fixed his head-quarters the night before the battle of Worcester.

ASTON-BLANK, a parish in the hundred of BRADLEY, county of GLOUCESTER, 4¼ miles (N. by E.) from

North Leach, containing 296 inhabitants. The living is a discharged vicarage, in the archdeaconry and diocese of Gloucester, rated in the king's books at £6. 12. 4., endowed with £200 private benefaction, and £200 royal bounty, and in the patronage of the Crown. The church is dedicated to St. Andrew. The parish is bounded on the north and north-east by the river Windrush, and on the south-east by the Roman Fosse-way. Here is a small endowed school.

ASTON-BOTTERELL, a parish in the hundred of Stottesden, county of Salop, 7¾ miles (N. W. by W.) from Cleobury-Mortimer, containing 230 inhabitants. The living is a rectory, in the archdeaconry of Salop, and diocese of Hereford, rated in the king's books at £7. 1. 0½., and in the patronage of the Marquis of Cleveland. The church is dedicated to St. Michael. This place formerly had a market on Tuesday, and a fair at Michaelmas, by grant from Henry III. It was then held under the Earls of Arundel by the family of Botterel, from whom it derived the adjunct to its name. The Llanymynech canal passes along the western and southern parts of the parish.

ASTON-CANTLOW, a parish in the Stratford division of the hundred of Barlichway, county of Warwick, 4 miles (N. E. by E.) from Alcester, containing 877 inhabitants. The living is a discharged vicarage, in the archdeaconry and diocese of Worcester, rated in the king's books at £9. 9. 7., endowed with £600 parliamentary grant, and in the patronage of the Rev. R. S. Carles. The church is dedicated to St. John the Baptist. The Stratford on Avon canal passes through the parish.

ASTON-CLINTON, a parish in the hundred of Aylesbury, county of Buckingham, comprising the chapelry of St. Leonard, and the township of Aston-Clinton, and containing 908 inhabitants, of which number, 723 are in the township of Aston-Clinton, 2¾ miles (W. by N.) from Tring. The living is a rectory, in the archdeaconry of Buckingham, and diocese of Lincoln, rated in the king's books at £23. 6. 10½., and in the patronage of the Principal and Fellows of Jesus' College, Oxford. The church is dedicated to St. Michael.

ASTON-EYRE, a chapelry in the parish of Morvill, hundred of Stottesden, county of Salop, 4¼ miles (W. by N.) from Bridgenorth, containing 63 inhabitants. The living is a perpetual curacy, in the archdeaconry of Salop, and diocese of Hereford, endowed with £400 private benefaction, and £1000 royal bounty, and in the patronage of the Perpetual Curate of Morvill.

ASTON-FLAMVILLE, a parish in the hundred of Sparkenhoe, county of Leicester, 2½ miles (E. S. E.) from Hinckley, containing, with the chapelry of Burbage, and the hamlet of Sketchley, 1584 inhabitants. The living is a rectory, in the archdeaconry of Leicester, and diocese of Lincoln, rated in the king's books at £33. 12. 8½., and in the patronage of the Countess de Grey. The church is dedicated to St. Peter. The Roman Watling-street passes near the border of the parish.

ASTON-GRANGE, a township in the parish of Runcorn, hundred of Bucklow, county palatine of Chester, 3¾ miles (E.) from Frodsham, containing 36 inhabitants. Here is an ancient chapel, which was rebuilt on an enlarged plan in 1737.

ASTON-INGHAM, a parish in the hundred of Greytree, county of Hereford, 5¾ miles (E.) from Ross, containing 551 inhabitants. The living is a rectory, in the archdeaconry and diocese of Hereford, rated in the king's books at £7. 7. 1., and in the patronage of the Trustees of the late Francis Lawson, Esq. Courts leet and baron are occasionally held. Here is a school, endowed with about £10 per annum. Limestone is obtained in the parish.

ASTON-MOLLINS, a hamlet in that part of the parish of Dinton which is in the hundred of Ashendon, county of Buckingham, containing 9 inhabitants.

ASTON-ROWANT, a parish in the hundred of Lewknor, county of Oxford, 3½ miles (S. E.) from Tetsworth, containing, with the liberties of Chalford and Kingston-Blount, 870 inhabitants. The living is a vicarage, with the perpetual curacy of Stokenchurch annexed, in the archdeaconry and diocese of Oxford, rated in the king's books at £16. 18. 11., and in the patronage of the Crown. The church is dedicated to St. Peter and St. Paul. Near the close of the seventeenth century, a large Roman vessel, containing five smaller ones, was discovered in Kingston field, within this parish, at the distance of about a furlong from the Iknield-street.

ASTON-SANDFORD, a parish in the hundred of Ashendon, county of Buckingham, 4 miles (E. N. E.) from Thame, containing 84 inhabitants. The living is a rectory, in the archdeaconry of Buckingham, and diocese of Lincoln, rated in the king's books at £12. 16. 0½., and in the patronage of Mrs. Susannah Barber. The church, dedicated to St. Michael, is in the later style of English architecture. The remains of the Rev. Thomas Scott, M.A., a learned and zealous commentator on the Holy Scriptures, were interred in the chancel.

ASTON-SOMERVILLE, a parish in the lower division of the hundred of Kiftsgate, county of Gloucester, 7¼ miles (N. by E.) from Winchcombe, containing 110 inhabitants. The living is a rectory, in the archdeaconry and diocese of Gloucester, rated in the king's books at £9. 3. 4., and in the patronage of Lord Somerville. This parish, with others, is within the jurisdiction of a court leet and baron held occasionally at Winchcombe. The late Lord Somerville, who first introduced the breed of Merino sheep into this country, and author of several tracts and essays on Agriculture and Rural Economy, was born here, in 1765.

ASTON-TIRROLD, a parish in the hundred of Moreton, county of Berks, 3½ miles (S. W. by W.) from Wallingford, containing 355 inhabitants. The living is a rectory, in the archdeaconry of Berks, and diocese of Salisbury, rated in the king's books at £10. 12. 11., and in the patronage of the President and Fellows of Magdalene College, Oxford. The church is dedicated to St. Michael. Bishop Gibson supposed this to be the place called in the Saxon Chronicle *Aescesdune*, where Ethelred I. and his brother Alfred defeated the Danes, in 871; but Gough, with greater probability, considers this battle to have been fought at Ashdown Park, near East Ilsley. There is a small endowment for the instruction of poor children.

ASTON-UPTHORP, a chapelry in that part of the parish of Blewberry which is in the hundred of

Moreton, county of Berks, 3¼ miles (W. S. W.) from Wallingford, containing 154 inhabitants. The chapel is said to be one of the most ancient in England.

ASTROP, a hamlet in the parish and hundred of King's Sutton, county of Northampton, 5¾ miles (W.) from Brackley. The population is returned with the parish. Here is a mineral spring, called St. Rumbald's Well, which, in the latter part of the seventeenth century, was much frequented.

ASTWELL, a hamlet partly in the parish of Syresham, but chiefly in the parish of Wappenham, hundred of King's Sutton, county of Northampton, 5½ miles (N. N. E.) from Brackley, containing 118 inhabitants.

ASTWICK, a parish in the hundred of Biggleswade, county of Bedford, 3¾ miles (N. W. by N.) from Baldock, containing 99 inhabitants. The living is a rectory, united, in 1764, to the vicarage of Arlsey, in the archdeaconry of Bedford, and diocese of Lincoln, rated in the king's books at £6. 13. 4. The church is dedicated to St. Guthlake.

ASTWOOD, a parish in the hundred of Newport, county of Buckingham, 5¾ miles (E. N. E.) from Newport-Pagnell, containing 263 inhabitants. The living is a vicarage, in the archdeaconry of Buckingham, and diocese of Lincoln, rated in the king's books at £6. 6. 8., and in the patronage of the Crown. The church is dedicated to St. Peter.

ASWARBY, a parish in the wapentake of Aswardhurn, parts of Kesteven, county of Lincoln, 4 miles (N. by W.) from Folkingham, containing 116 inhabitants. The living is a rectory, in the archdeaconry and diocese of Lincoln, rated in the king's books at £12. 4. 7., and in the patronage of Sir T. Whichcote, Bart. The church is dedicated to St. Denis.

ASWARDBY, a parish in the hundred of Hill, parts of Lindsey, county of Lincoln, 4 miles (N. W. by N.) from Spilsby, containing 80 inhabitants. The living is a discharged rectory, in the archdeaconry and diocese of Lincoln, rated in the king's books at £7. 19. 4½., and in the patronage of R. C. Breakenbury, Esq. The church is dedicated to St. Helen. There is a place of worship for Wesleyan Methodists.

ATCHAM, a parish in the Wellington division of the hundred of Bradford (South), county of Salop, 4 miles (S. E. by E.) from Shrewsbury, containing 489 inhabitants. The living is a discharged vicarage, in the archdeaconry of Salop, and diocese of Lichfield and Coventry, rated in the king's books at £11. 6. 8., and in the patronage of R. Burton, Esq. The Roman Watling-street passes through this parish, and crosses the Severn.

ATHELHAMPTON, county of Dorset.—See ADMISTON.

ATHELINGTON, a parish in the hundred of Hoxne, county of Suffolk, 5 miles (S. E. by E.) from Eye, containing 100 inhabitants. The living is a discharged rectory, in the archdeaconry of Suffolk, and diocese of Norwich, rated in the king's books at £4. 14. 2., endowed with £200 royal bounty, and in the patronage of the Crown. The church is dedicated to St. Peter.

ATHERINGTON, a parish in the hundred of North Tawton with Winkley, county of Devon, 7 miles (N. E. by E.) from Great Torrington, containing 535 inhabitants. The living is a rectory, in the archdeaconry of Barnstaple, and diocese of Exeter, rated in the king's books at £26. 2. 1., and in the patronage of Francis Basset, Esq. The church, dedicated to St. Mary, contains a richly ornamented screen and rood-loft crossing the north aisle; also the monument of a crusader, and an altar-tomb, with the figures of a knight and his two ladies on brass plates. A chapel was erected here, in the reign of Henry III., by the nuns belonging to the convent of Caen in Normandy, founded and endowed by Matilda, wife of William the Conqueror, with lands in this parish, where they had a cell.

ATHERINGTON, or ALDRINGTON, formerly a parish in the hundred of Fishergate, rape of Lewes, county of Sussex, 2½ miles (W. by N.) from Brighton. The living is a discharged rectory, in the archdeaconry of Lewes, and diocese of Chichester, rated in the king's books at £7. 10. 2½., and in the patronage of the Master and Fellows of Magdalene College, Cambridge. The church has been destroyed, and the village depopulated, by the encroachments of the sea.

ATHERSTONE, a market town and chapelry in the parish of Mancetter, Atherstone division of the hundred of Hemlingford, county of Warwick, 20 miles (N. by E.) from Warwick, and 105 (N. W. by N.) from London, on the road to Chester, containing 3434 inhabitants. The name of this place, in Domesday-book written *Aderestone*, is by Dugdale derived from *Edred*, or *Aldred*, who possessed it in the time of the Saxons, and thence called *Edredstone*, or *Aldredstone*; by others its name is deduced from its situation near Mancester, or Mancetter, the *Manduessedum* of the Romans, reckoning from which station, here was the first, or nearest, milliarium on the line of the Roman Watling-street, and thence called Hither-stone, or Atherstone. In 1485, the Earl of Richmond, previously to the battle of Bosworth Field, entered this town on the 20th of August, encamped his forces in a meadow, north of the church, still called the Royal meadow, and took up his own quarters at an ancient inn, now the Three Tuns, where he passed the night: here he had an interview with the Stanleys, and concerted those measures which secured him the victory in the celebrated battle that took place on the 22nd, and terminated the war between the houses of York and Lancaster. In 1376, Ralph, Lord Basset, of Drayton, founded a convent of Augustine friars, the church of which is now the parochial chapel; part of it is appropriated to the use of the free grammar school, and part to an endowed charity school. The town consists of one principal street, containing many ancient and several very respectable modern houses, from which another, branching off, leads to the market-place. It is paved, well lighted, and amply supplied with water: there is a subscription library and news-room; and assemblies are held occasionally in the town hall, a neat brick building on piazzas. The manufacture of hats is carried on to a considerable extent, and that of ribands upon a smaller scale. The Coventry and Fazely canal passes on the north-western extremity of the town, where extensive coal and lime wharfs have been constructed. The market is on Tuesday: fairs are held on April 7th and July 18th, for cattle; September 19th, 20th, and 21st, for cattle, cheese, and pedlary, on the Tuesday after which is a statute fair; and on December 4th is a great show fair for cattle, &c. The county magistrates hold a petty session weekly; the hundred court is held here alternately with other towns; and a court leet annually, at which constables and other officers are appointed.

The living is a perpetual curacy, in the archdeaconry of Coventry, and diocese of Lichfield and Coventry, and in the patronage of the Vicar of Mancetter. The chapel, dedicated to St. Mary, and originally belonging to the Augustine priory, is a cruciform structure, in the early and decorated styles of English architecture, with an octagonal tower rising from the centre, but its original character has been impaired by additions. There are places of worship for Wesleyan Methodists and Unitarians. The free grammar school, founded by Sir William Devereux, of Merevale, and others, and endowed with estates now producing £600 per annum, is under the management of trustees, who appoint the master; there is at present only one scholar on the foundation. Here is also an endowed charity school, in which thirty boys are instructed in reading, writing, and arithmetic. The infant school, a handsome modern building near the church, is well supported; and there is another upon a smaller scale. The self-supporting dispensary, upon the plan of Mr. Smith, of Southam, established in 1825, affords relief to a considerable number of patients. Drayton, the poet, and one of the earliest topographical writers, whose works were published by the learned Selden, was born here.

ATHERSTONE upon STOUR, a parish in the Kington division of the hundred of KINGTON, county of WARWICK, 3 miles (S.) from Stratford upon Avon, containing 94 inhabitants. The living is a rectory, in the archdeaconry and diocese of Worcester, rated in the king's books at £13. 1. 8., and in the patronage of the Rev. Dr. Cox.

ATHERTON, a chapelry in the parish of LEIGH, hundred of WEST DERBY, county palatine of LANCASTER, 1¼ mile (N. E.) from Leigh, containing 4145 inhabitants. The living is a donative, in the gift of Lord Lilford. The chapel, which is domestic, is dedicated to St. John the Baptist: it formerly belonged to the dissenters, but was consecrated for the service of the church of England by Dr. Wilson, the pious Bishop of Sodor and Man. Atherton Hall, a superb edifice built by the family of that name, in the early part of the eighteenth century, at an expense of about £63,000, was taken down in 1825, and the materials sold. This chapelry contains the populous manufacturing village of Chowbent, which see.

ATLOW, a chapelry in that part of the parish of BRADBORNE which is in the hundred of APPLETREE, county of DERBY, 5 miles (E. N. E.) from Ashbourn, containing 197 inhabitants. The living is a perpetual curacy, in the archdeaconry of Derby, and diocese of Lichfield and Coventry, endowed with £500 private benefaction, and £400 royal bounty, and in the patronage of H. F. Oakover, Esq. The church is a mean dilapidated structure, situated in the middle of a field. Near the village is a high hill, called "Magger's Bush," which affords an extensive prospect.

ATTENBOROUGH, a parish in the southern division of the wapentake of BROXTOW, county of NOTTINGHAM, 6 miles (S.W.) from Nottingham, containing, with the hamlets of Chilwell and Toton, 1031 inhabitants. The living is a discharged vicarage, with the perpetual curacy of Bramcote annexed, in the archdeaconry of Nottingham, and diocese of York, rated in the king's books at £4. 15., endowed with £200 royal bounty, and in the patronage of Sir F. Foljambe. The church is dedicated to St. Mary. The rivers Trent and Erewash run through the parish. In the hamlet of Toton is a chalybeate spring. Attenborough is the birthplace of Henry Ireton, the son-in-law of Cromwell, and Lord Deputy of Ireland in the time of the Commonwealth.

ATTERBY, a township in the parish of BISHOP'S NORTON, eastern division of the wapentake of ASLACOE, parts of LINDSEY, county of LINCOLN, 10¼ miles (W. N. W.) from Market-Rasen, containing 110 inhabitants.

ATTERCLIFFE, a chapelry in that part of the parish of SHEFFIELD which is in the southern division of the wapentake of STRAFFORTH and TICKHILL, West riding of the county of YORK, 1½ mile (N. E. by E.) from Sheffield, containing, with the hamlet of Darnall, 3172 inhabitants. The living is a perpetual curacy, in the archdeaconry and diocese of York, endowed with £400 private benefaction, £400 royal bounty, and £3000 parliamentary grant, and in the patronage of the Vicar of Sheffield. The chapel is dedicated to the Holy Jesus. A new church, in the later style of English architecture, was erected in 1822, at the expense of £11,700. 5., defrayed by a grant from the parliamentary commissioners. There are places of worship for Calvinists and Wesleyan Methodists. A Sunday school is endowed with £13. 9. 6. per annum. Almshouses have been erected for four poor people, but they are not endowed.

ATTERTON, a hamlet in the parish of WITHERLEY, hundred of SPARKENHOE, county of LEICESTER, 3¼ miles (E. by N.) from Atherstone, containing 75 inhabitants. Here was formerly a chapel, now desecrated.

ATTINGTON, an extra-parochial liberty, in the hundred of THAME, county of OXFORD, 1 mile (E. by N.) from Tetsworth, containing 8 inhabitants.

ATTLEBRIDGE, a parish in the hundred of TAVERHAM, county of NORFOLK, 4½ miles (S. S. E.) from Reepham, containing 105 inhabitants. The living is a discharged vicarage, with the rectory of Alderford united, in the archdeaconry and diocese of Norwich, rated in the king's books at £4. 6. 10½., and in the patronage of the Dean and Chapter of Norwich. The church is dedicated to St. Andrew.

ATTLEBURGH, or ATTLEBOROUGH, a market town and parish in the hundred of SHROPHAM, county of NORFOLK, 15 miles (S.W. by W.) from Norwich, and 94 (N. E. by N.) from London, containing 1659 inhabitants. This place derives its name from Atheling, or Atlinge, a Saxon prince, by whom it is supposed to have been originally founded; and from a burg, or castle, by which it was formerly defended from the incursions of the Danes: it was anciently the capital of Norfolk, and the residence of Offa and Edmund, kings of East Anglia. In the reign of Richard II., Robert de Mortimer founded a college, for a warden and four Secular priests, in the church of the Holy Cross, of which there are no remains. Though situated on the high road from Thetford to Norwich, it is now reduced to a very inconsiderable town. The market is on Thursday; and fairs are held on the Thursdays before

Easter and Whitsuntide, and on the 15th of August. Constables and other officers are appointed at the court of the lord of the manor. Attleborough formerly comprised two parishes, Attleburgh Major, a rectory, rated in the king's books at £19. 8. 9., and Attleburgh Minor, a vicarage, rated at £8. 2. 6.; they are now united, and constitute one rectory, in the archdeaconry of Norfolk, and diocese of Norwich, and in the patronage of Sir T. Smyth, Bart. The church, dedicated to St. Mary, is a spacious cruciform structure, in the decorated style of English architecture, with a square embattled tower rising from the centre, and a fine porch: the chancel, which had some portions in the Norman style, has been demolished: there are several monuments to the memory of distinguished personages, of which the most prominent are those of the Mortimers, Ratcliffs, and Blickleys. There are places of worship for Baptists and Wesleyan Methodists. A Sunday school, lately established, is supported by subscription. Two miles and a half from the town, on the road to Wymondham, said to have been the first turnpike-road constructed in England, and for which an act was granted in the 7th of William III., are the remains of an obelisk, erected by the county to the memory of Sir Edward Rich, who, in 1675, gave £200 towards repairing the highways.

ATWICK, a parish in the northern division of the wapentake of HOLDERNESS, East riding of the county of YORK, 2¼ miles (N. N. W.) from Hornsea, containing, with the township of Atwick with Arram, and Skirlington, 326 inhabitants. The living is a discharged vicarage, in the archdeaconry of the East riding, and diocese of York, rated in the king's books at £4. 7. 11., and in the patronage of the Crown. The church is dedicated to St. Lawrence. There is a place of worship for Wesleyan Methodists. The village is small, but pleasantly situated near the sea, from the encroachments of which, however, it has occasionally sustained considerable damage: in the centre stands a rude stone cross of great antiquity, with a Latin inscription upon its base, now nearly defaced. A school for the education of seventeen boys is endowed with £20 per annum, arising from a bequest of land by Edward Fenwick, in 1689; and another, for five girls, has an endowment of £18. 18., arising from land bequeathed by Ralph Burton, in 1726.

ATWORTH, a chapelry in the parish of GREAT BRADFORD, hundred of BRADFORD, county of WILTS, 4 miles (N. E. by N.) from Bradford, containing 642 inhabitants.

AUBORN, a parish in the lower division of the wapentake of BOOTHBY-GRAFFO, parts of KESTEVEN, county of LINCOLN, 6¼ miles (S. W. by S.) from Lincoln, containing, with the township of Haddington, 330 inhabitants. The living is a discharged vicarage, in the archdeaconry and diocese of Lincoln, rated in the king's books at £7. 13. 10., endowed with £200 private benefaction, £400 royal bounty, and £500 parliamentary grant, and in the patronage of C. Neville, Esq. The church is dedicated to St. Peter. There is a place of worship for Wesleyan Methodists.

AUCKLAND (ST. ANDREW), a parish comprising the townships of Byers-Green, Counden-Grange, Eldon, Middlestone, Midridge-Grange, Old-Park, Sunderland-Bridge, Westerton, and Windleston in the south-eastern division, and the market town of Bishop-Auckland, the chapelries of St. Helen Auckland and Hamsterley, and the townships of St. Andrew Auckland, West Auckland, North Bedburn, South Bedburn, Barony, Binchester, Coundon, Evenwood, Hunwick with Helmington, Lynesack with Softley, Newfield, Newton-Capp, Pollards-Lands, Shildon and East Thickley, in the north-western division, of DARLINGTON ward, county palatine of DURHAM, and containing 8253 inhabitants, of which number, 119 are in the township of St. Andrew Auckland, 1 mile (S.) from Bishop Auckland. The living is a perpetual curacy, in the archdeaconry and diocese of Durham, endowed with £800 private benefaction, and £800 royal bounty, and in the patronage of the Bishop of Durham. The church, a spacious cruciform structure, was made collegiate for Secular canons by Bishop Carileph; and in 1292 was endowed by Bishop Beck for a dean and nine prebendaries: three or four additional prebendaries were founded by Bishop Langley, in 1428. At the dissolution the deanery was valued at £100. 7. 2., and the prebends at £79. 16. 8: the dean's house and some of the prebendal houses have been converted into residences for farmers. The parish abounds with coal and limestone, and its surface is varied with highly interesting and romantic scenery. The Stockton and Darlington rail-road passes through it.

AUCKLAND (BISHOP), a market town and chapelry, in that part of the parish of ST. ANDREW, AUCKLAND which is in the north-western division of DARLINGTON ward, county palatine of DURHAM, 10½ miles (S. W.) from Durham, and 252 (N. by W.) from London, containing 2180 inhabitants. This place derives its name from the great number of oak trees which formerly grew in the neighbourhood, and its prefix from an episcopal palace, in which the bishops of the diocese, who are lords of the manor, occasionally reside. The town is pleasantly situated on a considerable eminence, near the confluence of the rivers Gaunless and Wear, in a fertile district, remarkable for the salubrity of the air, and abounding with coal and limestone; the streets are tolerably paved, the houses are well built, and the inhabitants are plentifully supplied with water. The palace, originally erected in the reign of Edward I. by Bishop Anthony Beck, and subsequently enlarged, was destroyed during the parliamentary war. After the Restoration it was rebuilt, by Bishop Cosins, in a beautiful park north-east of the town: it is a spacious structure, surrounded with plantations and pleasure grounds watered by the Gaunless. The market is on Thursday: the fairs, which are of recent origin, are in March and October, but on no fixed day; the ancient fairs, on the days of Ascension and Corpus Christi, are now obsolete. The county magistrates hold petty sessions monthly; and courts leet and baron are held annually, at the former of which a bailiff and other officers are appointed. The Bishop's chapel is a stately edifice, built about the year 1660, by Dr. John Cosins, Bishop of Durham, whose remains are therein deposited. The living is a perpetual curacy, in the archdeaconry and diocese of Durham, endowed with £600 private benefaction, and £1200 parliamentary grant, and in the patronage of the Bishop of Durham. There are places of worship for the Society of Friends, Independents, and Wesleyan Methodists. The free grammar school was founded by

James I.: the original endowment, consisting of an estate in Weardale, has been augmented by subsequent benefactions; the management is vested in twelve governors, who are a body corporate, and have a common seal; the school-room was rebuilt in 1783, and a small neat chapel, dedicated to St. Anne, erected over it by subscription. A school for twenty boys was founded by Mr. Walton, in 1772: the master has a rent-free residence, and a salary of £20 per annum; and a school on Dr. Bell's system, for two hundred children, was established in 1810, by Bishop Barrington, who also founded a school of industry for girls, in 1815. Almshouses for two men and two women were founded and endowed by Bishop Cosins, in the reign of Charles II.

AUCKLAND (ST. HELEN), a chapelry in that part of the parish of St. Andrew Auckland which is in the north-western division of Darlington ward, county palatine of Durham, 3 miles (S. S. W.) from Bishop-Auckland, containing, in the township of St. Helen Auckland (which constitutes only a small portion of the chapelry), 220 inhabitants. The living is a perpetual curacy, in the archdeaconry and diocese of Durham, rated in the king's books at £13. 9. 4., endowed with £400 private benefaction, £400 royal bounty, and £1100 parliamentary grant, and in the patronage of the Bishop of Durham. Here is a school, endowed with land producing £20 per annum.

AUCKLAND (WEST), a township in that part of the parish of St. Andrew Auckland which is in the north-western division of Darlington ward, county palatine of Durham, 3½ miles (S. W. by S.) from Bishop-Auckland, containing 1106 inhabitants. There is a place of worship for Wesleyan Methodists. A court leet, for the recovery of debts under 40*s.*, is held twice a year. A free school, founded by Mrs. Margaret Hubback in 1798, is endowed with about £20 per annum. This place gives the title of baron to the family of Eden.

AUDENSHAW, a township in the parish of Ashton under Line, hundred of Salford, county palatine of Lancaster, 5 miles (E. by S.) from Manchester, containing 3781 inhabitants. The name of this place, in ancient documents written *Aldwinshagh*, is said to be derived from the Saxon *Aldwin*, an elder or chieftain, and *Shagh*, a wood. It is supposed to have belonged, prior to the Conquest, to some Saxon thane, whose residence was on, or near, the site of the present village, which exhibits appearances of earlier cultivation than the surrounding district, which consists mostly of woods and morasses. The Ashton under Line canal passes through the township, and a large reservoir has been constructed here for supplying the town of Manchester with water. The inhabitants are chiefly employed in the various branches of the hat manufacture and in weaving. There is a place of worship for Methodists of the New Connexion. A parochial school was founded about the year 1745, and endowed by Miles Hilton with two estates in the parish of Manchester, producing £40 per annum. The school-room, with a large house for the master, has lately been erected, at an expense of nearly £1000, defrayed partly by subscription, and partly by the appropriation of the income arising from the endowment. There are also Sunday schools supported by subscription.

AUDLEM, a parish in the hundred of Nantwich, county palatine of Chester, comprising the townships of Audlem, Buerton, Dodcot with Wilkesley, Hankelow, and Tittenley, and containing 2795 inhabitants, of which number, 1307 are in the township of Audlem, 7 miles (S.) from Nantwich. The living is a vicarage, in the archdeaconry and diocese of Chester, rated in the king's books at £5. 16. 8., and in the patronage of Sir R. S. Cotton, Bart. The church is dedicated to St. James. There is a place of worship for Particular Baptists. A grant for a market, and a fair on the eve, day, and morrow of St. James the Apostle, was obtained in the 24th of Edward I., which, after long disuse, were revived a few years since. A free grammar school is endowed with £20 per annum by Ralph Bolton, a similar sum by Mr. Gamul, £7 by Tryphena Bolton, and about £40 by an unknown benefactor: here is also an endowed English school.

AUDLEY, a parish in the northern division of the hundred of Pirehill, county of Stafford, comprising the chapelry of Talk o' th' Hill, the townships of Audley, Bignall-End, Eardley-End, Knowl-End, and Park-End, and the liberty of Halmer-End, and containing 2940 inhabitants, of which number, 583 are in the township of Audley, 5 miles (N.W.) from Newcastle under Line. The living is a discharged vicarage, with the perpetual curacy of Talk o' th' Hill annexed, in the archdeaconry of Stafford, and diocese of Lichfield and Coventry, rated in the king's books at £6. 13. 4., and in the patronage of G. Tollet, Esq. The church, dedicated to St. James, is an ancient edifice having a tower crowned with pinnacles. Near the village is a place of worship for Wesleyan Methodists. This parish abounds in mines of excellent coal and iron-stone: the Grand Trunk canal crosses its eastern extremity, where it passes under the Horncastle tunnel, one thousand eight hundred and eighty-eight yards in extent. A free grammar school, in which about fifty children are educated, was founded in 1622 by Edward Vernon; it has an annual endowment amounting to £125. 18. Another school, for teaching writing and arithmetic, is endowed with £2 per annum. On the summit of a steep rock, near the western boundary of the parish, are the remains of Heyley Castle, built by the barons of Audley; and near the village are vestiges of an ancient intrenchment. Audley gives the title of baron to the family of Touchet.

AUGHTON, a chapelry in the parish of Halton, hundred of Lonsdale, south of the sands, county palatine of Lancaster, containing 199 inhabitants. The living is a perpetual curacy, in the archdeaconry of Richmond, and diocese of Chester, endowed with £200 private benefaction, and £200 royal bounty, and in the patronage of the Rector of Halton. The chapel is dedicated to St. George.

AUGHTON, a parish in the hundred of West Derby, county palatine of Lancaster, 2½ miles (S.W.) from Ormskirk, containing 1279 inhabitants. The living is a rectory, in the archdeaconry and diocese of Chester, rated in the king's books at £14. 15. 5., and in the patronage of John Plumbe Tempest, Esq. The church is dedicated to St. Michael. The Liverpool and Wigan canal passes through the parish.

AUGHTON, a parish in the Holme-Beacon division of the wapentake of Harthill, East riding of the county of York, comprising the chapelry of East Cottingwith, and the townships of Aughton and Laytham, and containing 702 inhabitants, of which number, 269 are in the township of Aughton, 8½ miles (N. N. W.) from Howden. The living is a discharged vicarage, in the archdeaconry of the East riding, and diocese of York, rated in the king's books at £4, endowed with £10 per annum private benefaction, and £200 royal bounty, and in the patronage of T. Mosley, Esq. The church is dedicated to All Souls. A castle anciently stood on the east bank of the river Derwent, of which only the moats and trenches can now be traced. This was the residence of Robert Aske, who was executed in the reign of Henry VIII., as a principal in the insurrection called the "Pilgrimage of Grace," occasioned by the suppression of the monasteries.

AUGHTON, a township in the parish of ASTON, southern division of the wapentake of STRAFFORTH and TICKHILL, West riding of the county of YORK, 4¼ miles (S. S. E.) from Rotherham. The population is returned with the parish.

AUKBOROUGH, a parish in the northern division of the wapentake of MANLEY, parts of LINDSEY, county of LINCOLN, 10½ miles (W.) from Barton upon Humber, containing 428 inhabitants. The living is a discharged vicarage, united to the rectory of Whitton, in the archdeaconry of Stow, and diocese of Lincoln, rated in the king's books at £10, endowed with £400 private benefaction, and £400 royal bounty. The church is dedicated to St. John the Baptist. There is a place of worship for Wesleyan Methodists. A free school is endowed with £16. 13. 4. per annum. Dr. Stukeley supposed Aukborough to have been the *Arquis* of the geographer of Ravennas.

AUKLEY, a township in that part of the parish of FINNINGLEY which is in the Hatfield division of the wapentake of BASSETLAW, county of NOTTINGHAM, 5¼ miles (N.) from Bawtry, containing 297 inhabitants.

AULT-HUCKNALL, a parish in the hundred of SCARSDALE, county of DERBY, 5½ miles (N. W. by W.) from Mansfield, containing, with the township of Stainsby, and a part of the township of Glapwell, 605 inhabitants. The living is a discharged vicarage, in the archdeaconry of Derby, and diocese of Lichfield and Coventry, rated in the king's books at £6. 0. 5., endowed with £200 private benefaction, £200 royal bounty, and £800 parliamentary grant, and in the patronage of the Duke of Devonshire. At Hardwicke, in this parish, there is a school for the education of poor children, towards the support of which Thomas Whitehead, in 1729, bequeathed a house and land producing £23. 15. per annum; it is also endowed with property in the parish of Edensor.

AULTON, county of DERBY.—See ALLTON.

AUNSBY, a parish in the wapentake of ASWARDHURN, parts of KESTEVEN, county of LINCOLN, 4½ miles (N. W. by W.) from Folkingham, containing 105 inhabitants. The living is a rectory, in the archdeaconry and diocese of Lincoln, rated in the king's books at £6. 0. 7½., and in the patronage of M. Newton, Esq. The church, dedicated to St. Thomas à Becket, is a small edifice, in the early style of English architecture, having in the windows some remains of beautifully stained glass: the font has some remarkable ornaments.

AUST, a chapelry in that part of the parish of HENBURY which is in the upper division of the hundred of HENBURY, county of GLOUCESTER, 4¼ miles (W. S. W.) from Thornbury, containing 192 inhabitants. This village, surrounded by salt marshes, is situated on the banks of the Severn, over which was formerly a ferry, now abandoned, in consequence of the establishment of a more convenient communication at New Passage, a mile and a half lower down the river. That rare mineral, sulphate of strontian, and carbonate of strontian, has been found in the fissures of the rocks bordering on the Severn.

AUSTELL (ST.), a market town and parish in the eastern division of the hundred of POWDER, county of CORNWALL, 34 miles (S.W.) from Launceston, and 252 (W.S.W.) from London, on the great road from Plymouth to Falmouth, containing 6175 inhabitants. The name of this place is of uncertain derivation. In the reign of Henry VIII. it was an obscure village, and first rose into importance from its vicinity to Polgooth and other considerable mines. In the parliamentary war St. Austell, in which part of the army under the Earl of Essex had been quartered, was taken by Charles I., a short time previous to the capitulation of the parliamentarians near Lostwithiel, in 1644. In 1760, the great road from Plymouth to the Land's End was brought through the town, which is now a considerable thoroughfare. St. Austell is pleasantly situated in a highly cultivated district, on the south side of a hill, which slopes gradually to a small stream; the streets are paved, and lighted with gas, and the inhabitants are well supplied with water. The trade principally consists of the produce of its numerous mines of tin and copper, and in china-stone and clay of a very superior quality, which are found here in great abundance. The Great Crinnis, East Crinnis, and Pembroke mines, which are in the parish, and the Fowey Consolidated and Lanescot mines, in the vicinity, are exceedingly productive; and, from the improved manner of working them, promise continued prosperity to the town, the population of which has been trebled within the last eighteen years. Several harbours have been formed in different parts of the parish. Of these the harbour at Charlestown, a village within a mile and a half of St. Austell, is capable of affording secure anchorage to vessels drawing about fifteen feet of water. At Par, to the east of Charlestown, a harbour with a canal is in great progress; it was projected for the especial accommodation of the Fowey Consolidated and Lanescot copper mines, but promises additional public advantages. Another harbour has been lately completed at Pentewan, about four miles to the south, with which an iron rail-road communicates from the town. Many vessels are employed in the importation of coal from Wales, for the use of the mines, and in the exportation of copper-ore for smelting; and of china-stone and clay to the different potteries, and for the use of linen-bleachers. The principal part of the grain tin produced in Cornwall is obtained here, and for melting it, blowing-houses have been erected near the town. A considerable pilchard fishery is carried on, in which many boats, fitted out from the different harbours, are employed. The market, which is considerable for corn and provisions, is on Friday; and there are fairs on November 30th and the Thursday before Trinity-Sunday. The town is within the jurisdiction of the county magistrates, by whom constables and other officers are appointed. The Blackmore, the most considerable of the Stannary courts, is held here. The living is a vicarage, with that of St. Blazey annexed, in the archdeaconry of Cornwall, and diocese of Exeter, rated in the king's books at £21, and in the patronage of the Crown. The church, dedicated to the Holy Trinity, is an ancient structure, combining various styles of English architecture, with a very handsome tower richly ornamented with sculpture. There are places of worship for Brianites, Calvinists, the Society of Friends, and Primitive and Wesleyan Methodists. At Menacuddle and Towan, in this parish, there are baptismal wells, over which are ancient buildings in the early style of English architecture, covered with arched roofs of granite. Near the new harbour of Pentewan is a large quarry, from which freestone for building many of the churches and mansions in the county has been procured; and near it, in one of the celebrated tin stream-works of Pentewan, the bones of men, of oxen of enormous size, of a whale, and of animals now unknown, have been found.

AUSTERFIELD, a chapelry in that part of the parish of Blyth which is in the northern division of the wapentake of Strafforth and Tickhill, West riding of the county of York, 1¼ mile (N. N. E.) from Bawtry, containing 242 inhabitants.

AUSTERSON, a township in the parish of Acton, hundred of Nantwich, county palatine of Chester, containing 65 inhabitants.

AUSTHORPE, a township in the parish of Whitkirk, lower division of the wapentake of Skyrack, West riding of the county of York, 3½ miles (E.) from Leeds, containing 150 inhabitants. John Smeaton, distinguished as a civil engineer, who rebuilt the Eddystone lighthouse, was born here, in 1724.

AUSTHWAITE, a joint township with Birker, in the parish of Millom, Allerdale ward above Darwent, county of Cumberland. The population is returned with Birker. This township is situated on the south side of the river Esk, and contains the lake Devockwater, and the waterfalls of Birker Force and Stanley Gill. The inhabitants have the privilege of marrying, burying, &c., at the neighbouring chapel of Eskdale.

AUSTONLEY, a township in that part of the parish of Almondbury which is in the upper division of the wapentake of Agbrigg, West riding of the county of York, 7 miles (N. by W.) from Huddersfield, containing 968 inhabitants, who are mostly engaged in the manufacture of woollen cloth, for which there are numerous mills in the township.

AUSTREY, a parish in the Tamworth division of the hundred of Hemlingford, county of Warwick, 6 miles (E. N. E.) from Tamworth, containing 542 inhabitants. The living is a vicarage, in the archdeaconry of Coventry, and diocese of Lichfield and Coventry, rated in the king's books at £8, and in the patronage of the Crown. The church is dedicated to St. Nicholas; the windows contain some curious specimens of stained glass.

AUSTWICK, a township in the parish of Clapham, western division of the wapentake of Staincliffe and Ewcross, West riding of the county of York, 5 miles (N. W.) from Settle, containing 556 inhabitants. A fair for cattle is held on the Thursday before Whitsuntide. There are two small bequests for the instruction of poor children.

AUTHORPE, a parish in the Wold division of the hundred of Louth-Eske, parts of Lindsey, county of Lincoln, 6¾ miles (N. W.) from Alford, containing 100 inhabitants. The living is a discharged rectory, in the archdeaconry and diocese of Lincoln, rated in the king's books at £5. 13. 4., and in the patronage of Robert Viner, Esq. The church is dedicated to St. Margaret.

AVEBURY, a parish in the hundred of Selkley, county of Wilts, 6¾ miles (W. by S.) from Marlborough, containing, with the tything of Beckhampton, 688 inhabitants. The living is a discharged vicarage, to which that of Winterbourne-Monkton was united in 1747, in the archdeaconry of Wilts, and diocese of Salisbury, rated in the king's books at £9, endowed with £200 private benefaction, and £200 royal bounty, and in the patronage of the Crown. The church, dedicated to St. James, is of Norman architecture. The river Kennet has its source in this parish. In 1722, Susannah Holford bequeathed £200, directing the interest to be applied to the instruction of poor children. The village occupies a portion of the area of a stupendous monument, called Abury, supposed to have been constructed by the ancient Britons, for the purposes of religious worship, or national assemblies. It consisted of an extensive ditch and rampart, including double circles of large unhewn stones, many of which have been broken, and used as materials for building the houses in the village, and for other purposes. In the vicinity are several barrows, and among them, the very large and remarkable one, close to the turnpike road, called Silbury Hill, which covers an area of five acres and thirty-four perches, and exceeds in dimensions every similar work in Great Britain, being two thousand and twenty-seven feet in circumference at the base, and one hundred and twenty at the summit; its sloping height three hundred and sixteen feet, and its perpendicular height one hundred and seventy. Within a short distance of this are the remarkable stones termed the Grey Wethers, and about a mile north of the village is a cromlech. An Alien priory, dependent on the Benedictine abbey of Bocherville in Normandy, was founded here in the reign of Henry I. Robert of Avebury, who wrote a history of Edward III., is supposed to have been a native of this place.

AVELEY, a parish (formerly a market town) in the hundred of Chafford, county of Essex, 1¾ mile (N.E.) from Purfleet, containing 733 inhabitants. The living is a discharged vicarage, in the archdeaconry of Essex, and diocese of London, rated in the king's books at £14. 10. 5., and in the patronage of the Bishop of London. The church is dedicated to St. Michael. Here is an endowed almshouse.

AVENBURY, a parish in the hundred of Broxash, county of Hereford, 1½ mile (S. E.) from Bromyard, containing 333 inhabitants. The living is a vicarage, in the archdeaconry and diocese of Hereford, rated in the king's books at £7. 8. 9., endowed with £200 royal bounty, and £200 parliamentary grant, and in the patronage of the Crown. The church is dedicated to St. Mary. A court leet is held annually. A small portion of limestone is found in the parish. Here was anciently a small priory, subordinate to the abbey of Dore.

AVENING, a parish in the hundred of Longtree, county of Gloucester, 3 miles (N.) from Tetbury, containing, exclusively of that part of the chapelry of Nailsworth which is in this parish, 1118 inhabitants.

The living is a rectory, in the archdeaconry and diocese of Gloucester, rated in the king's books at £24, and in the patronage of the Rev. T. Brooks, L.L.D. The church, dedicated to St. Mary, is supposed to have been built by the abbess of Caen in Normandy, to whom the manor belonged till the suppression of Alien priories, in the reign of Henry V. There is a place of worship for Particular Baptists. Here is an endowed school, in which six boys are clothed and educated.

AVERHAM, a parish in the northern division of the wapentake of THURGARTON, county of NOTTINGHAM, 3¼ miles (W. by N.) from Newark, containing 191 inhabitants. The living is a rectory, with that of Kelham annexed, in the archdeaconry of Nottingham, and diocese of York, rated in the king's books at £20. The church is dedicated to St. Michael. The navigable river Trent runs through the parish.

AVETON-GIFFORD, a parish in the hundred of ERMINGTON, county of DEVON, 3¼ miles (S.E.) from Modbury, containing 924 inhabitants. The living is a rectory, in the archdeaconry of Totness, and diocese of Exeter, rated in the king's books at £38. 1. 8., and in the patronage of James Pitman, Esq. The church, dedicated to St. Andrew, is an ancient structure, in the early style of English architecture, with later additions. The lords of the manor had formerly the power of inflicting capital punishment. The river Avon, which is navigable from this place to the English channel, is here crossed by a bridge, on the road leading to South Enford.

AVINGTON, a parish in the hundred of KINTBURY-EAGLE, county of BERKS, 3 miles (E. by S.) from Hungerford, containing 77 inhabitants. The living is a rectory, in the archdeaconry of Berks, and diocese of Salisbury, rated in the king's books at £8, and in the patronage of Sir Francis Burdett, Bart. The church exhibits a curious specimen of Norman architecture, having an arch separating the chancel from the nave, with an obtuse depending point in the centre: the font, which is also of Norman design, is adorned with sculptured figures under arches.

AVINGTON, a parish in the hundred of FAWLEY, Fawley division of the county of SOUTHAMPTON, 4¼ miles (N. E. by E.) from Winchester, containing 195 inhabitants. The living is a rectory, in the archdeaconry and diocese of Winchester, rated in the king's books at £11. 11. 10½., and in the patronage of the Bishop of Winchester. The church is dedicated to St. Mary. Here is an endowed school. Avington is within the jurisdiction of the Cheyney Court held at Winchester every Thursday, for the recovery of debts to any amount.

AVON, a chapelry in that part of the parish of CHRISTIAN-MALFORD which is in the hundred of CHIPPENHAM, county of WILTS, 3 miles (N. E.) from Chippenham, containing 18 inhabitants.

AVON-DASSET, county of WARWICK.— See DASSET (AVON).

AWBRIDGE, a hamlet in the parish of MITCHELMERSH, hundred of BUDDLESGATE, Fawley division of the county of SOUTHAMPTON, containing 250 inhabitants.

AWBURN, a chapelry in the parish of FRAISTHORP, wapentake of DICKERING, East riding of the county of YORK, 5 miles (S. by W.) from Bridlington. The population is returned with the parish. The living is a perpetual curacy, in the archdeaconry of the East riding, and diocese of York, endowed with £600 royal bounty, and in the patronage of Sir W. Strickland, Bart.

AWLISCOMBE, a parish in the hundred of HEMYOCK, county of DEVON, 2 miles (W. by N.) from Honiton, containing 513 inhabitants. The living is a discharged vicarage, in the archdeaconry and diocese of Exeter, rated in the king's books at £12. 10. 10., and in the patronage of the Duke of Bedford. The church, dedicated to St. Michael, has a finely ornamented window in the south transept, and a stone screen. The river Otter bounds the parish on the south.

AWNBY, a joint chapelry with Holywell, in the parish of BYTHAM-CASTLE, wapentake of BELTISLOE, parts of KESTEVEN, county of LINCOLN, 5 miles (N. by W.) from Stamford. The population is returned with Holywell.

AWRE, a parish in the hundred of BLIDESLOE, county of GLOUCESTER, 2½ miles (E. N. E.) from Blakeney, comprising the chapelry of Blakeney and the tythings of Blidesloe, Etloe, Etloe-Duchy, and Hagloe, and containing 1138 inhabitants. The living is a vicarage, in the archdeaconry of Hereford, and diocese of Gloucester, rated in the king's books at £10. 5., and in the patronage of the Master and Wardens of the Haberdashers' Company. The church is dedicated to St. Andrew. This parish forms a promontory of the Severn. The port of Gatcomb, and a town named Pomerton, which were included within it, have both been entirely destroyed: there is a large common, still called the Old Wharf.

AWSWORTH, a chapelry in the parish of NUTHALL, southern division of the wapentake of BROXTOW, county of NOTTINGHAM, 7½ miles (N. W. by W.) from Nottingham. The population is returned with the parish. The living is a perpetual curacy, in the archdeaconry of Nottingham, and diocese of York, endowed with £400 private benefaction, and £600 royal bounty, and in the patronage of the Rector of Nuthall.

AXBRIDGE, a market town and parish having separate jurisdiction, locally in the hundred of Winterstoke, county of SOMERSET, 18 miles (S. by W.) from Bristol, and 130 (W. by S.) from London, containing 988 inhabitants. This place, which derives name from its bridge over the river Axe, was formerly the residence of some of the West Saxon monarchs, by whom it was invested with many privileges. The town is of mean appearance and indifferently paved, but amply supplied with water. The chief occupation of the poorer class of inhabitants is the knitting of stockings. The navigation of the river Axe has been greatly improved by an act obtained in 1802, whereby it has also been made toll-free. The market is on Saturday: fairs are held on February 2nd, March 25th, June 11th, and October 28th; those in February and March are very large cattle fairs, and at the others great quantities of butter are brought from the adjacent country, and sold to dealers for the Bristol market.

Corporate Seal.

The government of the town, by charter of Queen Elizabeth, is vested in a mayor, bailiff, recorder, one alderman, fifteen common council-men, and twenty-two burgesses, assisted by a town clerk, two mace bearers, and subordinate officers. The corporation hold a court of session quarterly for the borough. A court of record for pleas under £10 was formerly held, but it has fallen into disuse. The council-house, an ancient building, is in a very dilapidated state. Axbridge sent members to parliament in the 23rd of Edward I., but the right was discontinued in the 17th of Edward III., on petition of the burgesses. The living is a discharged rectory, in the archdeaconry of Wells, and diocese of Bath and Wells, rated in the king's books at £11. 4. 4., endowed with £132 private benefaction, and £200 royal bounty, and in the patronage of the Bishop of Bath and Wells. The church, dedicated to St. John the Baptist, is a very ancient structure, occupying an elevated situation on the north-eastern side of the town, supposed to have been erected by one of the West Saxon monarchs, two of whose statues formerly ornamented the tower. There are places of worship for Particular Baptists and Wesleyan Methodists. Near the town is a mineral spring, which has been found efficacious in chronic diseases.

AXFORD, a tything in the parish and hundred of RAMSBURY, county of WILTS, 3¼ miles (E. N. E.) from Marlborough, containing 428 inhabitants.

AXMINSTER, a parish in the hundred of AXMINSTER, county of DEVON, comprising the market town of Axminster, and the tythings of Beerhall, Westwater, and Wyke, and containing 2742 inhabitants, of which number, 1703 are in the town of Axminster, 25 miles (E. by N.) from Exeter, and 147 (W. S. W.) from London, on the road to Exeter. The name of this place is derived from its situation near the river Axe, and from a minster founded here by King Athelstan. In the time of the Saxons it was a town of considerable importance, and the burial-place of many of their princes. In 1644, a conflict took place in the vicinity, between the royalists and the parliamentarians, in which Sir Richard Cholmondeley, who commanded the former, was slain. The town, which is irregularly built, is pleasantly situated on the summit of a hill, near the confluence of the rivers Axe and Yarty, over the former of which a bridge has been erected: the streets, which are spacious, and contain some respectable houses, are well paved and lighted, and the inhabitants are amply supplied with water from several good springs. Races are held in August at Shute-hill, three miles distant; and there are assemblies occasionally at the George hotel. The manufacture of carpets, which has been established for nearly a century, is still conducted by the family of the original proprietor, and affords employment to about a hundred men: the carpets are considered superior in beauty and durability to those of Turkey; one lately made for the Emperor of Russia measured seventy-three feet by forty-five and cost £1200: there are also manufactories for plush and tape. The market is on Tuesday, Thursday, and Saturday: the fairs are on the first Tuesday after April 25th, the first Wednesday after June 24th, and the first Wednesday after October 21st. Courts leet and baron are held annually by the lord of the manor, at the former of which constables and other officers are appointed.

The living is a vicarage, with the perpetual curacies of Kilmington and Membury annexed, in the archdeaconry and diocese of Exeter, rated in the king's books at £44. 6. 8., and in the patronage of the Chancellor in the Cathedral Church of York: there is also a sinecure rectory, rated at £40. 6. 8., belonging to the Prebendary of Warthill in the same cathedral. The church, dedicated to St. Mary, is an ancient structure, partaking of various styles of architecture: the entrance is under a fine Norman arch richly moulded; the interior is of the early English style, with later insertions; and the pulpit and reading-desk are curiously carved. There are places of worship for Independents, Wesleyan Methodists, and Roman Catholics. Twelve poor children are instructed in the parochial school, for the amount of divers benefactions made for that purpose. About a mile and a half south of the town, on the bank of the river Axe, are the remains of Newnham abbey, consisting of the chapel, kitchen, and other parts; and, at the distance of three miles, are the ruins of Musbury Castle.

AXMOUTH, a parish in the hundred of AXMINSTER, county of DEVON, 2¾ miles (S. by E.) from Colyton, containing 529 inhabitants. The living is a vicarage, in the archdeaconry and diocese of Exeter, rated in the king's books at £22. 19. 2., and in the patronage of John Hallett, Esq. The river Axe runs through the parish, and falls into the English channel, where a convenient harbour for coasting vessels of one hundred and twenty tons' burden has recently been constructed, by John Hallett, Esq. Here is a school for the education of poor children, to which William Serle, in 1726, gave a small endowment. From the numerous traces of Roman occupancy on the eastern bank of the river, it is supposed that this was the famous port *Moridunum*.

AYCLIFFE, a parish in the south-eastern division of DARLINGTON ward, county palatine of DURHAM, comprising the townships of Great Aycliffe, Brafferton, Preston le Skerne, and Woodham, and containing 1379 inhabitants, of which number, 807 are in the township of Great Aycliffe, 6 miles (N.) from Darlington. The living is a vicarage, in the archdeaconry and diocese of Durham, rated in the king's books at £20, and in the patronage of the Dean and Chapter of Durham. The church is dedicated to St. Acca. There is a place of worship for Wesleyan Methodists. Spelman supposes Aycliffe to have been the place anciently called Acled, where synods were held in 782 and 789. The Stockton and Darlington railway passes about three quarters of a mile to the west of the village. Limestone is found in abundance; and upon the river Skerne there are a spinning-mill, and a mill for the manufacture of brown paper.

AYCLIFFE (SCHOOL), a township in the parish of HEIGHINGTON, south-eastern division of DARLINGTON ward, county palatine of DURHAM, 7½ miles (N. by W.) from Darlington, containing 37 inhabitants.

AYDON, a township in the parish of CORBRIDGE, eastern division of TINDALE ward, county of NORTHUMBERLAND, 5½ miles (E. by N.) from Hexham, containing 94 inhabitants. Lead-ore and coal exist here, but in very small quantities. Several Roman relics have been found, including two urns, the effigy of a human being, &c.

AYDON-CASTLE, a township in the parish of CORBRIDGE, eastern division of TINDALE ward, county of NORTHUMBERLAND, 6½ miles (E. by N.) from Hexham, containing 31 inhabitants. The castle, now in ruins, belonged for several generations to the baronial family of Aydon, or Ayton.

AYLBURTON, a chapelry in the parish of LIDNEY, hundred of BLIDESLOE, county of GLOUCESTER, 4½ miles (S. W. by W.) from Blakeney, containing 353 inhabitants. The chapel is dedicated to St. Mary.

AYLESBEAR, a parish in the eastern division of the hundred of BUDLEIGH, county of DEVON, 4½ miles (S. W. by W.) from Ottery St. Mary, containing, with the chapelry of Newton-Poppleford, 854 inhabitants. The living is a discharged vicarage, in the archdeaconry and diocese of Exeter, rated in the king's books at £16. 2. 4., endowed with £400 private benefaction, and £600 royal bounty, and in the patronage of the Rev. W. H. Marker. The church is dedicated to St. Christopher. This parish is bounded on the east by the river Otter, on which stands a silk and riband manufactory. In 1697, Richard White bequeathed a small endowment for the instruction of poor children.

AYLESBURY, a borough, market town, and parish, in the hundred of AYLESBURY, county of BUCKINGHAM, 17 miles (S. E. by S.) from Buckingham, and 40 (N. N. W.) from London, containing, according to the last census, 4400 inhabitants, now about 5000. This town, which was one of the strongest fortresses of the ancient Britons, received the name of Æglesbury from Cuthwulf, brother of Ceawlin, King of the West Saxons, by whom it was captured in 571. About the year 600, a monastery, dedicated to St. Osyth, was erected here. At the Conquest, Aylesbury was conferred on one of the royal favourites, under the extraordinary tenure that he should provide straw for the monarch's bed, sweet herbs for his chamber, and two green geese and three eels for his table, three times in the year, if he should so often visit it. A convent of Grey friars, the only one in the county, was founded here, in 1387, by James, Earl of Ormond; its site was subsequently occupied by a mansion belonging to the Packington family, which has been long since taken down. There were also two ancient hospitals, dedicated to St. John and St. Leonard, for the benefit of lepers, which had gone to decay previously to the year 1360. In the war between Charles I. and the parliament, Aylesbury was garrisoned for the latter. The town is delightfully situated in a fertile vale, which affords pasturage to an extraordinary number of sheep: the houses are principally of stone and lath and plaister, intermixed with some handsomely built of brick; the streets are well paved, and partially lighted with oil, and the inhabitants have lately been supplied with water by means of the tread-wheel in the gaol. Much of its prosperity is due to the munificent patronage of Sir John Baldwin, Chief Justice of the Common Pleas in the reign of Henry VIII., who erected several buildings, and procured the assizes to be removed hither from Buckingham; the summer assizes, however, have been again transferred to that town. Lace-making constitutes the chief employment of the poor; and numerous ducklings are reared for the London market at Christmas. The market, which is principally for corn, and is also abundantly supplied with excellent meat, is on Saturday: fairs are held on the first Friday after January 18th, the Saturday before Palm-Sunday, May 8th, June 14th, September 25th, and October 11th.

Queen Mary, in 1550, vested the government of the borough in a corporation, who, from non-exercise of their privileges, forfeited their charter in the reign of Elizabeth; and the town is now within the jurisdiction of the county magistrates, who hold a petty session weekly: two constables and other officers are appointed at the court leet of the lord of each of the two manors, *viz.*, the manor of Aylesbury, and the manor of the rectory of Aylesbury. A court of quarter session for the county is held in the shire-hall, a handsome edifice, erected in 1723. The county gaol and house of correction admits of the classification of prisoners, and comprises one hundred and forty cells, two day-rooms, a chapel, and a tread-mill employed in raising water and grinding corn. The elective franchise was conferred in 1554, since which time the borough has continued to return two members to parliament: the right of election is vested in the inhabitant householders, and in the freeholders of the hundred, the number of both being near three thousand; the four constables are the returning officers. Concerning a disputed return for this borough in 1703, the contest between the lords and the commons was so great, that the queen deemed it expedient to prorogue the parliament. The living is a discharged vicarage, within the jurisdiction of the peculiar court of Aylesbury, belonging to the Dean and Chapter of Lincoln, rated in the king's books at £24. 18. 1., and in the patronage of the Prebendary of Aylesbury in the Cathedral Church of Lincoln. The church, dedicated to St. Mary, is a venerable and interesting structure. There are places of worship for Particular Baptists, the Society of Friends, Independents, and Wesleyan Methodists. The free grammar school, founded by Sir Henry Lee, was endowed, at the beginning of the last century, with only £8 per annum, which was augmented by John Phillips, Esq., a native of the town, with a legacy of £5000, since invested in land producing about £240 per annum: there are one hundred and twenty boys on the foundation, fifteen of whom are instructed in the classics. The school-house and residences for three masters were built in 1718. A Lancasterian school was founded by Mr. John Hull, of Uxbridge: there are also Sunday schools in connexion with the established church and the dissenting congregations. In 1694, Mr. John Bedford gave land for the repair of the highways, and for the relief of the poor, the rental of which exceeds £300 per annum. Aylesbury gives the title of marquis to the family of Brudenell Bruce.

AYLESBY, a parish in the wapentake of BRADLEY-HAVERSTOE, parts of LINDSEY, county of LINCOLN, 5½ miles (W. by S.) from Great Grimsby, containing 142 inhabitants. The living is a perpetual curacy, in the archdeaconry and diocese of Lincoln, endowed with £600 royal bounty, and in the patronage of T. D. Drake, Esq. The church is dedicated to St. Lawrence.

AYLESFORD, a parish in the hundred of LARKFIELD, lathe of AYLESFORD, county of KENT, 3½ miles (N. N. W.) from Maidstone, and 34 (S. E.) from London, containing 1136 inhabitants. This place was called *Saissenaig-hobail* by the Britons, in commemoration of their having here defeated the Saxons; and by the latter, after their settlement in the country, *Eaglesford*, of which the present name is a corruption. In the battle above mentioned, which took place in 455, Horsa, the brother of Hengist, was slain. In 893, Alfred defeated the Danes at Fenham, in this parish; and, in 1016, Edmund Ironside, in a fierce encounter with those invaders, pursued them to this place with great slaughter, and drove them hence to Sheppy. In 1240, Ralph Frisburn, on his return from the Holy Land, founded a Carmelite monastery, under the patronage of Richard, Lord Grey of Codnor, many parts of which are still entire, though the greater portion of the site is occupied by a mansion, erected by Sir William Sedley, and now the residence of the Earl of Aylesford. The town is pleasantly situated on the north-east bank of the river Medway, over which is a neat modern stone bridge of six arches: it consists of one principal street, on the east side of which the ground rises abruptly to an elevation of one hundred feet. A paper-mill, by the side of a small stream, is the only manufactory in the place: a pleasure fair is held on the 29th of June. The living is a vicarage, in the archdeaconry and diocese of Rochester, rated in the king's books at £10, and in the patronage of the Dean and Chapter of Rochester. The church, dedicated to St. Peter, is situated on rising ground to the east of the principal street. There is a place of worship for Wesleyan Methodists. A school for the education of poor children was endowed, in 1766, by Mr. William Milner, with a rent-charge of £20, which is paid to a master for instructing twenty-five boys: the school-room was built in 1773. An hospital, dedicated to the Holy Trinity, was founded for six aged persons, in 1617. Fragments of military weapons are frequently discovered here. At Horsted is a monument of upright stones, erected, as it is supposed, to the memory of Horsa; and three miles distant is another, called Kit's Cotty house, to the memory of Certigorn, brother of Vortimer, who was slain with that prince in the battle with Hengist and Horsa. Aylesford confers the title of earl on the family of Finch. Sir Charles Sedley, a celebrated wit and poet in the reign of Charles II., was a native of this parish.

AYLESTONE, a parish partly in the hundred of Guthlaxton, and partly in the hundred of Sparkenhoe, county of Leicester, 2½ miles (S. by W.) from Leicester, containing, with the chapelries of Glen Parva and Lubbesthorpe, 749 inhabitants. The living is a rectory, in the archdeaconry of Leicester, and diocese of Lincoln, rated in the king's books at £31. 8. 11½., and in the patronage of the Duke of Rutland. The church is dedicated to St. Andrew. The chapel at Lubbesthorpe has fallen to decay, and the inhabitants resort for divine service to the church at Aylestone, but pay no tithes, whence the place has been deemed extra-parochial. The Union canal passes through the parish, soon after which it joins the river Soar.

AYLMERTON, a parish in the northern division of the hundred of Erpingham, county of Norfolk, 2¾ miles (W.S.W.) from Cromer, containing 284 inhabitants. The living is a discharged rectory in medieties, with that of Runton, in the archdeaconry of Norfolk, and diocese of Norwich, rated together in the king's books at £6. 11., and in the patronage of Rear-Admiral Wyndham. The church is dedicated to St. John the Baptist.

AYLSHAM, a market town and parish in the southern division of the hundred of Erpingham, county of Norfolk, 12¼ miles (N. by W.) from Norwich, and 121 (N.E. by N.) from London, containing 1853 inhabitants. This place, situated on the southern bank of the river Bure, which is navigable for barges from Yarmouth, was formerly one of the principal manufacturing towns in the county; the linen made here was much esteemed, and distinguished by the name of Aylsham web. This branch of industry was succeeded by the woollen manufacture and the knitting of stocking pieces, which flourished until the introduction of machinery, since which it has greatly declined, a few looms only being employed for the manufacturers at Norwich: the trade at present is principally in corn and timber. The market is on Tuesday, and fairs are held on March 23rd, and the last Tuesday in September. The town is within the jurisdiction of the county magistrates: constables and other officers are appointed at the court leet of the lord of the manor. The living is a vicarage, in the archdeaconry and diocese of Norwich, rated in the king's books at £17. 19. 7., and in the patronage of the Dean and Chapter of Norwich. The church, dedicated to St. Michael, was founded by John of Gaunt, in the fourteenth century: it is a spacious structure in the decorated style of English architecture, and contains a curious and richly sculptured font. There are places of worship for Particular Baptists and Methodists. The free school, founded in 1517, by Robert Jermys, mayor of Norwich, and endowed with £10 per annum, has been incorporated with the National school. A school, founded by Robert James, has an endowment of £10 per annum, for the instruction of seven boys.

AYLTON, a parish in the hundred of Radlow, county of Hereford, 4¼ miles (W.) from Ledbury, containing 100 inhabitants. The living is a discharged rectory, in the archdeaconry and diocese of Hereford, rated in the king's books at £3. 3. 4., and in the patronage of the Earl of Oxford.

AYLWORTH, a hamlet in that part of the parish of Naunton which is in the hundred of Bradley, county of Gloucester, containing 32 inhabitants.

AYMESTREY, a parish partly in the hundred of Stretford, but chiefly in the hundred of Wigmore, county of Hereford, 8 miles (N.W.) from Leominster, comprising the chapelry of Earls Lenthall, and the townships of Conhope and Upper Ley, and containing 813 inhabitants. The living is a discharged vicarage, in the archdeaconry and diocese of Hereford, rated in the king's books at £7. 14. 2., and endowed with £200 private benefaction, and £200 royal bounty, and in the patronage of the Crown. The church is dedicated to St. John and St. Alkmund. The river Lug runs through the parish, and limestone abounds in the vicinity. A court leet for the manor is held every alternate year. A charity school is endowed with £12 per annum, and an almshouse, for one poor widow, with £2 per annum. Traces of Roman and British camps are discernible near the village.

AYNHO, a parish (formerly a market town) in the hundred of King's Sutton, county of Northampton, 2¾ miles (E. by N.) from Deddington, containing 719 inhabitants. The living is a rectory, in the archdeaconry of Northampton, and diocese of Peterborough, rated in the king's books at £25. 5. 5., and in the patronage of W. R. Cartwright, Esq. The church is dedicated to St. Michael. Robert Wild, a Presbyterian minister, and a poet and satirist, held this living during the Commonwealth; but having been ejected from it in 1662, he retired to Oundle, where he died in 1679. The village, which is of considerable size, is situated on a rocky eminence, from the foot of which issues a copious spring, called the "Town Well." A charter was obtained, in the 17th of Edward II., for a weekly market and a fair annually at Michaelmas, but both have long since been discontinued. A free school was founded by John Cartwright, and endowed with a rent-charge of £20. Here was anciently an hospital, dedicated to St. John and St. James, founded about the time of Henry II., which, in 1484, was united to Magdalene College, Oxford, by gift of the patron, William Fitz-Alan. The Roman Portway, a vicinal road, runs through this parish, and is visible at the eastern end of the village. Shakerley Marmion, a dramatic writer, was born at the manor-house, in 1602.

AYOTT (ST. LAWRENCE), a parish in the hundred of BROADWATER, county of HERTFORD, 3¼ miles (W. by N.) from Welwyn, containing 160 inhabitants. The living is a rectory, in the archdeaconry of Huntingdon, and diocese of Lincoln, rated in the king's books at £8. 13. 4., and in the patronage of Lionel Lyde, Esq. The church, dedicated to St. Lawrence, is a neat modern brick edifice, with a handsome portico of stone, of the Doric order: it was erected in 1787, at an expense of £6000, by Sir Lionel Lyde, from a design by Revett, the celebrated Italian architect. The ruins of the old church, a quarter of a mile distant, are considerable, and under the belfry of its embattled tower there is an altar-tomb, with recumbent figures of a knight and his lady. This place was anciently in the possession of King Harold. Dane-End, near Ayott, owes its name to a signal defeat of the Danes by King Ethelwulph.

AYOTT (ST. PETER), a parish in the hundred of BROADWATER, county of HERTFORD, 1¼ mile (W. by S.) from Welwyn, containing 233 inhabitants. The living is a rectory, in the archdeaconry of Huntingdon, and diocese of Lincoln, rated in the king's books at £7. 8. 6½., and in the patronage of the Earl of Hardwicke. The church, dedicated to St. Peter, a neat octagonal building, was erected about eighty years ago, by the late rector, Dr. Freeman, who built also the steeple, on the opposite side of the churchyard.

AYSGARTH, a parish in the western division of the wapentake of HANG, North riding of the county of YORK, comprising the chapelries of Askrigg and Hawes, and the townships of High Abbotside, Low Abbotside, Aysgarth, Bainbridge, Bishop-Dale, Burton with Walden, Carperby, Newbiggin, Thoralby, and Thornton-Rust, and containing 5621 inhabitants, of which number, 293 are in the township of Aysgarth, 8½ miles (W.) from Middleham. The living is a discharged vicarage, in the archdeaconry of Richmond, and diocese of Chester, rated in the king's books at £19. 6. 8., endowed with £400 private benefaction, and £200 royal bounty, and in the patronage of the Master and Fellows of Trinity College, Cambridge. The church, dedicated to St. Andrew, is a spacious structure, and has an elegant screen and rood-loft between the nave and the chancel, supposed to have been brought from the abbey of Jervaulx. There are places of worship for the Society of Friends and Wesleyan Methodists. Here is an endowed grammar school, also almshouses for six widows. The river Ure, which rises in this parish, passes over a precipitous and irregular ledge of rocks, and produces some fine waterfalls, called Aysgarth Force, Mossdale Fall, and Hardraw Fall. At some distance above there is a curious and highly ornamented bridge of one arch, having a span of seventy feet, from which a beautifully picturesque prospect may be obtained. Several veins of lead and some strata of coal exist in the neighbourhood. Mary, Queen of Scots, was imprisoned for a short time in Nappa Hall, an ancient mansion in this parish.

AYSTON, a parish in the hundred of MARTINSLEY, county of RUTLAND, 1¼ mile (N.W. by N.) from Uppingham, containing 110 inhabitants. The living is a rectory, in the archdeaconry of Northampton, and diocese of Peterborough, rated in the king's books at £8. 7. 8½., and in the patronage of G. B. Bruderell, Esq. The church is dedicated to St. Mary.

AYTON, a parish in the western division of the liberty of LANGBAURGH, North riding of the county of YORK, comprising the chapelry of Nunthorpe, and the townships of Great Ayton, and Little Ayton, and containing 1201 inhabitants, of which number, 1023 are in the township of Great Ayton, 3 miles (N.E. by E.) from Stokesley. The living is a perpetual curacy, in the archdeaconry of Cleveland, and diocese of York, endowed with £600 royal bounty, and £800 parliamentary grant, and in the patronage of the Rev. W. Marwood. The church, dedicated to All Saints, is a neat unadorned edifice of considerable antiquity, and contains a handsome monument to the memory of W. Wilson, Esq., a distinguished naval commander in the service of the Hon. East India Company. There are places of worship for the Society of Friends, Independents, and Primitive and Wesleyan Methodists. At the extremity of a ridge of hills, in this parish, is a quarry of hard blue whin-stone, or granite, which is much used in making and repairing roads. There are some linen-manufactories and oil-mills in the parish. Iron-ore has been obtained at Cliffrigg-woods, but the mine is not worked at present. There were also alum-works, but these have been abandoned. A charity school, founded in 1704, by Michael Postgate, was rebuilt in 1785; it has an endowment, of about £10 per annum, for the education of eight boys belonging to the township. At this school, the celebrated navigator, Captain Cook, received a portion of his education, at the expense of Thomas Scottowe, Esq., whom his father served as manager of a farm. Adjoining the school are three almshouses.

AYTON (EAST), a chapelry in the parish of SEAMER, PICKERING lythe, North riding of the county of YORK, 5 miles (S.W. by W.) from Scarborough, containing 333 inhabitants. The chapel is dedicated to St. John the Baptist. There is a place of worship for Wesleyan Methodists. The village is situated in a valley, remarkable for the beauty of its scenery, through which flows the river Derwent. An iron-foundry has been established here.

AYTON (LITTLE), a township in the parish of AYTON, western division of the liberty of LANGBAURGH, North riding of the county of YORK, 3½ miles (E.N.E.) from Stokesley, containing 68 inhabitants.

AYTON (WEST), a township in the parish of HUTTON-BUSHELL, PICKERING lythe, North riding of the county of YORK, 5¼ miles (S.W. by S.) from Scarborough, containing 229 inhabitants. Here are remains of an ancient castle, formerly belonging to the family of Eure, and afterwards to that of Clifford. Agreeably to the will of Lady Hewley, two-thirds of the manor are vested in seven trustees, for the support of dissenting ministers. The river Derwent separates the townships of East and West Ayton, and is here crossed by a bridge of four arches.

B.

BABCARY, a parish in the hundred of CATSASH, county of SOMERSET, 4¾ miles (E.) from Somerton, containing 422 inhabitants. The living is a rectory, in the archdeaconry of Wells, and diocese of Bath and Wells, rated in the king's books at £13. 10. 5., and in the patronage of N. and G. Messiter and John Twyford, Esqrs. The church is dedicated to the Holy Cross.

BABINGLEY, a parish in the Lynn division of the hundred of FREEBRIDGE, county of NORFOLK, 1¾ mile (N.) from Castle-Rising, containing 53 inhabitants. The living is a discharged rectory, annexed to that of Sanderingham, in the archdeaconry and diocese of Norwich, rated in the king's books at £4. 13. 4. The church, which is partly in ruins, is dedicated to St. Felix, the apostle of the East Angles, who is said to have erected the original structure.

BABINGTON, a parish in the hundred of KILMERSDON, county of SOMERSET, 5½ miles (W. N. W.) from Frome, containing 156 inhabitants. The living is a discharged rectory, in the archdeaconry of Wells, and diocese of Bath and Wells, rated in the king's books at £10, and in the patronage of J. Twyford Jolliffe, Esq. The church is dedicated to St. Margaret. There is a place of worship for Wesleyan Methodists. Coal and limestone are found in the neighbourhood. A school for poor children is endowed with £15 per annum, bequeathed in 1758, by Elizabeth Long.

BABRAHAM, a parish in the hundred of CHILFORD, county of CAMBRIDGE, 4½ miles (N. W.) from Linton, containing 238 inhabitants. The living is a discharged vicarage, in the archdeaconry and diocese of Ely, rated in the king's books at £6. 5. 10., and in the patronage of the Crown. The church is dedicated to St. Peter. Here is a school for poor children, the master of which has a salary of £20 per annum, arising from a bequest, in 1723, by Judith Bennet, who also left £25 per annum for apprenticing boys, and £30 per annum towards the support of six poor widows.

BABWORTH, a parish in the Hatfield division of the wapentake of BASSETLAW, county of NOTTINGHAM, 1¼ mile (W.) from East Retford, containing 416 inhabitants. The living is a rectory, in the archdeaconry of Nottingham, and diocese of York, rated in the king's books at £14. 19. 2., and in the patronage of the Hon. T. B. Simpson. The church is dedicated to All Saints. The Chesterfield canal passes along the northern side of the parish, the income arising from a share in which was bequeathed, in 1781, by Lindley Simpson, Esq., to support a school for the instruction of poor children.

BACH, a township in that part of the parish of ST. OSWALD, CHESTER, which is in the lower division of the hundred of BROXTON, county palatine of CHESTER, containing 21 inhabitants. Bach Hall was garrisoned for the parliament, in the early part of the civil war, and destroyed during the siege of Chester, in 1645.

BACKFORD, a parish comprising the townships of Backford, Chorlton, Lea, and Great Mollington, in the higher division of the hundred of WIRRALL, and the township of Conghall, in the lower division of the hundred of BROXTON, county palatine of CHESTER, and containing 450 inhabitants, of which number, 140 are in the township of Backford, 4 miles (N.) from Chester. The living is a discharged vicarage, in the archdeaconry and diocese of Chester, rated in the king's books at £5. 0. 5., endowed with £400 private benefaction, and £400 royal bounty, and in the patronage of the Bishop of Chester. The church is dedicated to St. Oswald. The Ellesmere canal passes along the southern side of the parish.

BACKWELL, a parish (formerly a market town) in the hundred of HARTCLIFFE with BEDMINSTER, county of SOMERSET, 7¼ miles (S. W. by W.) from Bristol, containing 863 inhabitants. The living is a discharged vicarage, in the archdeaconry of Bath, and diocese of Bath and Wells, rated in the king's books at £6. 19. 9½., endowed with £400 royal bounty, and in the patronage of the Co-heiresses of Mrs. Lox: there is also a sinecure rectory, rated at £11. 16. 3., and in the patronage of the Marquis of Bath. The church is dedicated to St. Andrew. The weekly market, granted by Edward II., has long been discontinued: there is a fair for cattle and pedlary on the 21st of September. A great number of the labouring class is employed in extensive collieries within the parish: there are also quarries which produce a reddish calcareous stone, variegated with blue and white veins, susceptible of a high polish. A National school is chiefly supported by subscription.

BACKWORTH, county of NORTHUMBERLAND.—See BLACKWORTH.

BACONSTHORPE, a parish in the southern division of the hundred of ERPINGHAM, county of NORFOLK, 3¼ miles (E. S. E.) from Holt, containing 246 inhabitants. The living is a rectory, in the archdeaconry and diocese of Norwich, rated in the king's books at £9, and in the patronage of George Chad and R. Fellowes, Esqrs. The church is dedicated to St. Mary.

BACTON, a parish in the hundred of WEBTREE, county of HEREFORD, 11½ miles (S.W. by W.) from Hereford, containing 120 inhabitants. The living is a discharged rectory, in the archdeaconry and diocese of Hereford, rated in the king's books at £3. 13. 4., and in the patronage of Sir Hungerford Hoskyns, Bart. The church is dedicated to St. Faith. A great quantity of limestone and some marble are obtained here. A court baron is held septennially. A parochial school was established in 1824, and is supported by subscription: four poor children are taught for an endowment by Mr. Oliver. Here are two chalybeate springs.

BACTON, a parish in the hundred of TUNSTEAD, county of NORFOLK, 4¼ miles (N. E. by E.) from North Walsham, containing 388 inhabitants. The living is a discharged vicarage, in the archdeaconry of Norfolk, and diocese of Norwich, rated in the king's books at £5. 3. 1½., endowed with £200 private benefaction, and £400 royal bounty, and in the patronage of the Hon. J. Wodehouse. The church is dedicated to St. Andrew.

There is a place of worship for Particular Baptists. A school is endowed with £5 per annum.

BACTON, a parish in the hundred of HARTISMERE, county of SUFFOLK, 6½ miles (N.) from Stow-Market, containing 715 inhabitants. The living is a rectory, in the archdeaconry of Sudbury, and diocese of Norwich, rated in the king's books at £19. 12. 3½., and in the patronage of the Rev. E. B. Barker. The church is dedicated to St. Mary.

BACUP, a chapelry in that part of the parish of WHALLEY which is in the higher division of the hundred of BLACKBURN, county palatine of LANCASTER, 6 miles (E. by S.) from Haslingden. The population is returned with the parish. The living is a perpetual curacy, in the archdeaconry and diocese of Chester, endowed with £200 private benefaction, £1100 royal bounty, and £1000 parliamentary grant, and in the patronage of the Vicar of Whalley. The chapel was consecrated in 1788. There are two places of worship for Particular Baptists, and one for Wesleyan Methodists. The manufacture of baize, and the spinning and manufacture of cotton, are extensively carried on in this chapelry.

BADBY, a parish in the hundred of FAWSLEY, county of NORTHAMPTON, 2¼ miles (S. S. W.) from Daventry, containing 547 inhabitants. The living is a discharged vicarage, with the perpetual curacy of Newnham annexed, in the archdeaconry of Northampton, and diocese of Peterborough, rated in the king's books at £14, endowed with £200 private benefaction, and £200 royal bounty, and in the patronage of the Dean and Canons of Christ Church, Oxford. The church is dedicated to St. Mary. There are quarries of hard blue rag-stone in the neighbourhood. On a lofty eminence, called Arbury hill, is an intrenchment enclosing an area of about ten acres, supposed to have been a Roman camp.

BADDESLEY (NORTH), a parish in the hundred of MANSBRIDGE, Fawley division of the county of SOUTHAMPTON, 3½ miles (E. by S.) from Romsey, containing 286 inhabitants. The living is a donative, in the patronage of T. Dummer, Esq.

BADDESLEY-CLINTON, a parish in the Solihull division of the hundred of HEMLINGFORD, county of WARWICK, 7 miles (N.W.) from Warwick, containing 140 inhabitants. The living is a perpetual curacy, united to the vicarage of Polesworth, in the peculiar jurisdiction of the lord of the manor, rated in the king's books as a rectory, at £4. 6. 8. The church is dedicated to St. Michael. The Warwick and Birmingham canal passes through the parish.

BADDESLEY-ENSOR, a parish in the Tamworth division of the hundred of HEMLINGFORD, county of WARWICK, 3½ miles (W. N. W.) from Atherstone, containing 535 inhabitants. The living is a perpetual curacy, in the archdeaconry of Coventry, and diocese of Lichfield and Coventry, endowed with £1200 royal bounty, and £200 parliamentary grant, and in the patronage of the Parishioners of Polesworth. The church is dedicated to St. Michael. There are some coal mines in the neighbourhood. George Abbott, in 1647, bequeathed a rent-charge of £5 in support of a free school.

BADDILEY, a parish in the hundred of NANTWICH, county palatine of CHESTER, 3 miles (W. S. W.) from Nantwich, containing 270 inhabitants. The living is a discharged rectory, in the archdeaconry and diocese of Chester, rated in the king's books at £24. 3. 6., and in the patronage of Sir H. Mainwaring, Bart. The church, dedicated to St. Michael, is constructed of English oak, and is of great antiquity; the upright timbers, being much decayed, were cased with brick in 1811, but the roof and ceiling are still in fine preservation. Baddiley Hall, once the noble residence of the Mainwarings, has been converted into a farmhouse. The Ellesmere canal passes through the parish.

BADDINGTON, a township in the parish of ACTON, hundred of NANTWICH, county palatine of CHESTER, 1½ mile (S. S. W.) from Nantwich, containing 140 inhabitants.

BADDOW (GREAT), a parish in the hundred of CHELMSFORD, county of ESSEX, 1¾ mile (S. E.) from Chelmsford, containing 1603 inhabitants. The living is a vicarage, in the archdeaconry of Essex, and diocese of London, rated in the king's books at £18. 6. 8., and in the patronage of A. Bullen, Esq. The church is dedicated to St. Mary; its tower is covered with ivy. The village is very pleasantly situated, and is inhabited by several highly respectable families. A school for the instruction of twenty children is endowed with £20 per annum, aided by a bequest of £50 from Jasper Jefferey, in 1731: there is also an endowed school for the children of dissenters, and there are nine almshouses.

BADDOW (LITTLE), a parish in the hundred of CHELMSFORD, county of ESSEX, 2½ miles (N. by W.) from Danbury, containing, with the hamlet of Little Mead, 583 inhabitants. The living is a discharged vicarage, in the archdeaconry of Essex, and diocese of London, rated in the king's books at £8. 2. 2., and in the patronage of Col. Strutt, who is also patron of the rectory, which is a sinecure, rated at £7. 13. 4. The church is dedicated to St. Mary. In 1717, Edward Butler bequeathed one hundred and ninety-six acres of land, and a wood containing thirty-six acres, directing the proceeds to be applied for clothing and educating children in this parish, and that of Boreham. A school for the instruction of twenty children is supported by the dissenters.

BADGER, a parish within the liberties of the borough of WENLOCK, locally in the hundred of Brimstree, county of SALOP, 5¾ miles (N. E.) from Bridgenorth, containing 132 inhabitants. The living is a discharged rectory, in the archdeaconry of Salop, and diocese of Hereford, rated in the king's books at £4. 13. 4., and in the patronage of the Crown. The church is dedicated to St. Giles. There is a school for poor children, with a house for the master; also six almshouses.

BADGEWORTH, a parish in the upper division of the hundred of DUDSTONE and KING'S BARTON, county of GLOUCESTER, 4 miles (S.W. by W.) from Cheltenham, containing 715 inhabitants. The living is a vicarage, with the perpetual curacy of Great Shurdington annexed, in the archdeaconry and diocese of Gloucester, rated in the king's books at £20. 11. 3., and in the patronage of W. Laurence Laurence, Esq.: there is also a sinecure rectory, in the patronage of the Principal and Fellows of Jesus' College, Oxford. The church, dedicated to St. Mary, is a handsome stone building, with a tower at the west end. There was formerly a chapel of ease at Bentham, in this parish. The village, which tradition reports to have anciently been a market town, was evidently much larger than it now is, from the foundations of houses which have been discovered in its vicinity. At Churchdown is a school for the instruction of children of that parish and Badgeworth, to which £25 per annum are paid out of an estate here, left for that purpose by William Window, Gent. The Rev. William Stanby, formerly vicar of this parish, demised an estate for apprenticing boys of the parishes of Badgeworth, Churchdown, and Cheltenham; and there are various minor charities for the benefit of the poor. On an estate called Cold Pool is a mineral spring, the water of which is similar to the Cheltenham waters.

BADGINGTON, a parish in the hundred of Crowthorne and Minety, county of Gloucester, 3¾ miles (N.) from Cirencester, containing 137 inhabitants. The living is a discharged rectory, in the archdeaconry and diocese of Gloucester, rated in the king's books at £8. 4. 4½., and in the patronage of the Principal and Fellows of Jesus' College, Oxford. The church is dedicated to St. Margaret.

BADGWORTH, a parish in the hundred of Winterstoke, county of Somerset, 2½ miles (S. W. by W.) from Axbridge, containing 319 inhabitants. The living is a rectory, in the archdeaconry of Wells, and diocese of Bath and Wells, rated in the king's books at £25. 15., and in the patronage of Sir J. Mordaunt, Bart. The church is dedicated to St. Congar.

BADINGHAM, a parish in the hundred of Hoxne, county of Suffolk, 4 miles (N. N. E.) from Framlingham, containing 816 inhabitants. The living is a rectory, in the archdeaconry of Suffolk, and diocese of Norwich, rated in the king's books at £22. 16. 8., and in the patronage of the Rev. C. Chevallier. The church is dedicated to St. John the Baptist.

BADLESMERE, a parish in the hundred of Faversham, lathe of Scray, county of Kent, 4¼ miles (S.) from Faversham, containing 113 inhabitants. The living is a discharged rectory, united to that of Leveland, in the archdeaconry and diocese of Canterbury, rated in the king's books at £5. 2., and in the patronage of Lord Sondes. The church is dedicated to St. Leonard. A fair is held here on the 6th of November.

BADLEY, a parish in the hundred of Bosmere and Claydon, county of Suffolk, 2 miles (W. N. W.) from Needham, containing 84 inhabitants. The living is a perpetual curacy, in the archdeaconry of Suffolk, and diocese of Norwich, and in the patronage of the Earl of Ashburnham and C. Boone, Esq. The church is dedicated to St. Mary. The navigable river Gep flows through the parish. The hall, once the seat of the Pooleys, is now a farm-house.

BADMINTON (GREAT), a parish in the upper division of the hundred of Grumbald's Ash, county of Gloucester, 6½ miles (E. by N.) from Chipping-Sodbury, containing 464 inhabitants. The living is a discharged vicarage, in the archdeaconry and diocese of Gloucester, rated in the king's books at £5. 5. 7½., and in the patronage of the Duke of Beaufort. The church, dedicated to St. Michael, was rebuilt by the Duke of Beaufort, in 1785. The petty sessions for the division of Sodbury and Grumbald's Ash are held here, at Cross Hands, and at Chipping-Sodbury, in rotation. In 1705, Mary, Duchess Dowager of Beaufort, gave a rent-charge of £94 for the endowment of an almshouse for three men and three women, and a school for the children of Great and Little Badminton and Littleton-Drew. The noble mansion of Badminton was erected by the first duke of Beaufort, in the reign of Charles II., on the site of an ancient seat of the Boteler family.

BADMINTON (LITTLE), a tything in the parish of Hawkesbury, upper division of the hundred of Grumbald's Ash, county of Gloucester, containing 97 inhabitants. Here was a chapel to the vicarage of Great Badminton, now desecrated.

BADSEY, a parish in the upper division of the hundred of Blackenhurst, county of Worcester, 2¼ miles (E. by S.) from Evesham, containing, with the hamlet of Aldington, 421 inhabitants. The living is a perpetual curacy, in the peculiar jurisdiction of the Bishop of Worcester, rated in the king's books at £5. 6. 8., and in the patronage of the Dean and Canons of Christ Church, Oxford. The church is dedicated to St. James. The navigable river Avon runs along the border of the parish, and receives here a small brook, which in its course turns several mills, including a silk-mill. There is a small endowed school for the instruction of poor boys. Within the limits of the parish are some mineral springs, but their properties are not thoroughly known.

BADSHOT, a tything in the parish and hundred of Farnham, county of Surrey, 2 miles (N. E. by E.) from Farnham, containing, with Runfold, 869 inhabitants.

BADSWORTH, a parish in the upper division of the wapentake of Osgoldcross, West riding of the county of York, comprising the townships of Badsworth, Thorp-Audling, and Upton, and containing 728 inhabitants, of which number, 200 are in the township of Badsworth, 5 miles (S.) from Pontefract. The living is a rectory, in the archdeaconry and diocese of York, rated in the king's books at £32. 5. 10., and in the patronage of the Earl of Derby. The church is dedicated to St. Mary. There is a place of worship for Wesleyan Methodists. A school is endowed with £5 per annum.

BADWELL-ASH, a parish in the hundred of Blackbourn, county of Suffolk, 8 miles (N. N. W.) from Stow-Market, containing 427 inhabitants. The living is a perpetual curacy, in the archdeaconry of Suffolk, and diocese of Norwich, endowed with £16 per annum private benefaction, and £800 royal bounty, and in the patronage of Miss Clough. The church is dedicated to St. Mary.

BAGBOROUGH (WEST), a parish in the hundred of Taunton and Taunton-Dean, county of Somerset, 8¼ miles (N. W. by W.) from Taunton, containing, with the hamlet of East Bagborough, 421 inhabitants. The living is a rectory, in the archdeaconry of Taunton, and diocese of Bath and Wells, rated in the king's books at £18. 10. 10., and in the patronage of the Rev. J. Guerin. The church is dedicated to the Holy Trinity.

BAGBY, a chapelry in the parish of Kirby-Knowle, wapentake of Birdforth, North riding of the county of York, 2¼ miles (E. S. E.) from Thirsk, containing 242 inhabitants. There is a place of worship for Wesleyan Methodists.

BAGGRAVE, a liberty in that part of the parish of Hungerton which is in the hundred of Gartree, county of LEICESTER, 8½ miles (E. N. E.) from Leicester, containing 15 inhabitants.

BAGINGTON, a parish in the Kenilworth division of the hundred of KNIGHTLOW, county of WARWICK, 3½ miles (S. by E.) from Coventry, containing 281 inhabitants. The living is a rectory, in the archdeaconry of Coventry, and diocese of Lichfield and Coventry, rated in the king's books at £8. 1. 8., and in the patronage of the Rev. W. D. Bromley. The church is dedicated to St. John the Baptist. Here was anciently a castle, in which the Duke of Hereford, afterwards Henry IV., lodged previously to the day appointed for the combat between him and the Duke of Norfolk, at Coventry, in the reign of Richard II.

BAGLEY-WOOD, an extra-parochial liberty, in the hundred of HORMER, county of BERKS, 3¼ miles (N. by E.) from Abingdon, containing 4 inhabitants. A monastery was founded here by Cissa, Viceroy of Centwine, ninth king of Wessex, which was removed to Abingdon, in 680, that town and its appendages having been assigned to it by Ceadwalla.

BAGNALL, a joint parish with Bucknall, in the northern division of the hundred of PIREHILL, county of STAFFORD, 3¾ miles (N. E.) from Hanley. The population is returned with Stoke upon Trent, to which parish Bagnall formerly belonged, but was separated from it, in 1807, by an act of parliament, which constituted Bucknall a distinct rectory. The living is a perpetual curacy, annexed to the rectory of Bucknall, in the archdeaconry of Stafford, and diocese of Lichfield and Coventry, endowed with £200 private benefaction, and £400 royal bounty.

BAGNOR, a joint township with Wood-Speen, in that part of the parish of SPEEN which is in the hundred of FAIRCROSS, county of BERKS, 2 miles (N. W.) from Speenhamland. The population is returned with Wood-Speen.

BAGSHOT, a chapelry in the parish of WINDLESHAM, first division of the hundred of WOKING, county of SURREY, 12 miles (N. N. W.) from Guildford, and 26 (W. S. W.) from London, on the great western road. The population is returned with the parish. The chapel, which had been destroyed by lightning, was rebuilt in 1676. This place, formerly called Holy Hall, gives name to a tract of heath land, which was anciently more extensive, a great part having been enclosed and cultivated. It was formerly the residence of some of the kings of England, who had a mansion here and a park, which was laid open after the civil war in the reign of Charles I.: it is now occupied by their Royal Highnesses the Duke and Duchess of Gloucester. On the borders of Bagshot heath are some handsome villas, but the village contains only a few respectable houses and some good inns, and is indebted to its situation as a public thoroughfare for the traffic it enjoys.

BAGTHORPE, a parish in the hundred of GALLOW, county of NORFOLK, 7 miles (S. S. W.) from Burnham-Westgate, containing 69 inhabitants. The living is a discharged rectory, in the archdeaconry of Norfolk, and diocese of Norwich, rated in the king's books at £5. 10., endowed with £400 royal bounty, and in the patronage of Sir Charles Chad, Bart. The church is dedicated to St. Mary.

BAGULEY, a township in the parish of BOWDON, hundred of BUCKLOW, county palatine of CHESTER, 6¼ miles (W. by S.) from Stockport, containing 458 inhabitants.

BAGWORTH, a chapelry in the parish of THORNTON, hundred of SPARKENHOE, county of LEICESTER, 5 miles (N. E.) from Market-Bosworth, containing, with the extra-parochial liberty of Bagworth Park, 389 inhabitants. The chapel is dedicated to the Holy Rood.

BAGWORTH-PARK, an extra-parochial liberty, in the hundred of SPARKENHOE, county of LEICESTER, 5 miles (E. N. E.) from Market-Bosworth. The population is returned with Bagworth.

BAILDON, a chapelry in that part of the parish of OTLEY which is in the upper division of the wapentake of SKYRACK, West riding of the county of YORK, 4½ miles (N. by W.) from Bradford, containing 2679 inhabitants. The living is a perpetual curacy, in the archdeaconry and diocese of York, endowed with £200 private benefaction, £200 royal bounty, and £400 parliamentary grant, and in the patronage of the Vicar of Otley. The chapel is dedicated to St. Giles. A new church, or chapel, is about to be erected here by the parliamentary commissioners. Within the limits of the chapelry are numerous manufactories for worsted, woollen, and cotton goods, and some business is done in malt and the making of nails.

BAILEY, a joint township with Aighton and Chaigley, in that part of the parish of MITTON which is in the lower division of the hundred of BLACKBURN, county palatine of LANCASTER, 8 miles (N.) from Blackburn. The population is returned with Aighton.

BAILIE, a township in the parish of BEWCASTLE, ESKDALE ward, county of CUMBERLAND, 5 miles (E. N. E.) from Longtown, containing 386 inhabitants. The scenery is of a romantic description, and there is a long range of lofty crags, which extends to the point where the kingdom of Scotland and the counties of Cumberland and Northumberland meet.

BAINBRIDGE, a township in the parish of AYSGARTH, western division of the wapentake of HANG, North riding of the county of YORK, 1½ mile (S. W.) from Askrigg, containing 872 inhabitants. The village is situated upon the river Ure, which is here crossed by a good stone bridge of three arches. A free grammar school was founded by Anthony Besson, Esq., in the 43rd of Queen Elizabeth. In this township there exists a custom of blowing a horn every night at ten o'clock, from September 27th to Shrovetide, intended as a signal to the benighted traveller, and said to have originated when the country was an open forest. On a neighbouring eminence, called Brough Hill, are vestiges of a Roman fortress, near which, among other relics, a statue of the Emperor Commodus was found.

BAINTON, a chapelry in the parish of UFFORD, liberty of PETERBOROUGH, county of NORTHAMPTON, 5 miles (N. by E.) from Wansford, containing 162 inhabitants. The chapel, dedicated to St. Mary, exhibits some interesting specimens of early English architecture.

BAINTON, a hamlet in the parish of STOKE-LYNE, hundred of PLOUGHLEY, county of OXFORD, 3 miles (N.) from Bicester, containing 58 inhabitants.

BAINTON, a parish in the Bainton-Beacon division of the wapentake of HARTHILL, East riding of the county of YORK, 5¾ miles (S. W.) from Great Driffield, containing 300 inhabitants. The living is a rectory, in the archdeaconry of the East riding, and diocese of York, rated in the king's books at £35. 14. 9½., and in the patronage of the President and Fellows of St. John's College, Oxford. The church is dedicated to St. Andrew. There are places of worship for Primitive and Wesleyan Methodists. The petty sessions for the Bainton-Beacon division are held here. A beacon was anciently erected on an eminence near the village, to give notice of approaching danger, and hence the name given to this division of the wapentake.

BAKEWELL, a parish in the hundred of HIGH PEAK, county of DERBY, comprising the market town of Bakewell, the chapelries of Ashford, Baslow, Beeley, Blackwell, Buxton, Chelmerton, Great Longstone, Monyash, Sheldon, and Taddington, the townships of Brushfield, Bubnell, Flagg, Froggatt, Over Haddon, Harthill, Holme, Priestcliffe, Rowland, Great Rowsley, and Wardlow, and the hamlets of Calver, Curbar, Hassop, and Little Longstone, and containing 9162 inhabitants, of which number, 1782 are in the town of Bakewell, 26 miles (N. W.) from Derby, and 152 (N. W. by N.) from London. The Saxon name of this place, *Baderanwylla*, or *Badde cum Well*, of which its present appellation is a contraction, is derived from a chalybeate spring, which was in great repute prior to the year 924, when Edward the Elder is said to have built a castle, or fort, in the vicinity. The town, which is in an improving state, is situated in a beautiful and picturesque vale, about four miles from the confluence of the rivers Wye and Derwent, and at nearly an equal distance from Buxton and Matlock, between which places is an excellent turnpike road, leading through a district replete with pleasingly diversified scenery. The river Wye, which flows through the town, abounds with fine trout and grayling, and is much frequented for angling during the season. The air is salubrious, and the inhabitants are amply supplied with water from numerous springs in the neighbourhood. An Agricultural Society has recently been formed, the members of which hold their meetings at Bakewell and Chesterfield alternately, generally in October. The chalybeate baths, lately re-established by the Duke of Rutland, and now in the occupation of Mr. White Watson, F.L.S., who has a good collection of minerals and fossils attached to them, constitute one of the greatest attractions: the principal bath is thirty-three feet long, sixteen wide, and of proportionate depth, and is constantly supplied with fresh water, which, on its influx, emits a considerable quantity of carbonic acid gas, and possesses a temperature of 60° of Farenheit. There are also shower baths, and a private warm bath with suitable accommodations; and a news-room has been added to the establishment. Near the entrance into the town from Ashford stands a cotton-mill, erected by the late Sir Richard Arkwright, in which about three hundred persons are employed; and in the immediate vicinity are extensive quarries of black and grey marble, and of chirt, which is used in the Staffordshire potteries, in the manufacture of earthenware. The market is on Friday, and on every alternate Monday there is a cattle market, which was established in 1825, and is now extremely well supplied with store and fat cattle and sheep. Fairs are held on Easter-Monday, Whit-Monday, August 26th, the Monday next after October 10th, and the Monday after November 11th, for horses and horned cattle. The town is within the jurisdiction of the county magistrates, and a constable and other officers are appointed at the court leet of the lord of the manor. One of the quarter sessions for the county was formerly, and a petty session for the hundred of High Peak, on the first and third Friday in every month, is still, held here. A mineral court is also held for the manor, according to the local articles and customs of the lead mines within it, which have prevailed from time immemorial. The living is a discharged vicarage, in the peculiar jurisdiction and patronage of the Dean and Chapter of Lichfield, rated in the king's books at £40. The church, dedicated to All Saints, is a spacious cruciform structure, partly in the Norman, and partly in the early style of English architecture: the tower, rising from the intersection, and surmounted by a lofty spire, having become in a dangerous state from the failure of the pillars that supported it, has been lately taken down: at the western entrance is a highly ornamented Norman arch. Within are several magnificent altar-tombs of alabaster, supporting recumbent figures, and a stone font of great antiquity; and in the churchyard is an ancient cross, decorated with rude sculpture, but greatly mutilated. There are places of worship for Independents and Wesleyan Methodists. A free school was founded here, in 1636, and endowed with £15 per annum, by Lady Grace Manners, for the instruction of poor children in reading, writing, and arithmetic; the original endowment has been augmented with £35 per annum by the Duke of Rutland, and the school is now open to the poor children of this parish and Great Rowsley: the school-room is over the town hall. Mary Hague, in 1715, gave certain houses and land, for which seven poor children are instructed, the master occupying one of the houses. St. John's hospital, for six aged men, was founded and endowed, in 1602, by Sir John Manners Sutton and his brother: the income amounts to £40 per annum. A dispensary and a lying-in institution have been established, and are supported by subscription. At the distance of two miles south of the town stands Haddon Hall, the property of the Duke of Rutland, lord of this manor, one of the largest and most perfect of the ancient baronial mansions in the kingdom; about three miles toward the north-east is Chatsworth House, the princely seat of the Duke of Devonshire, in which Mary, Queen of Scots, was confined in the year 1570; and about two miles and a half to the north is Hassop Hall, the seat of Earl Newburgh. Dr. Thomas Denman, an eminent physician and accoucheur, and father of the present Sir Thomas Denman, Attorney-general, was born here in 1733.

BALBY, a joint township with Hexthorp, in that part of the parish of DONCASTER which is in the soke of DONCASTER, West riding of the county of YORK, 1½ mile (S. S. W.) from Doncaster, containing, with Hexthorp, 392 inhabitants. The first meetings of the Society of Friends, under their founder, George Fox, were held here, and in the neighbouring village of Warmsworth.

BALCOMB, a parish partly in the hundred of STREET, but chiefly in the hundred of BUTTINGHILL, rape of LEWES, county of SUSSEX, 4½ miles (N.) from Cuckfield, containing 606 inhabitants. The living is a rectory, in the archdeaconry of Lewes, and diocese of Chichester, rated in the king's books at £15. 18. 6½., and in the patronage of the Rev. Dr. Bethune. The church is dedicated to St. Mary.

BALDERSBY, a township in that part of the parish of TOPCLIFFE which is in the wapentake of HALLIKELD, North riding of the county of YORK, 5¾ miles (N. N. E.) from Ripon, containing 241 inhabitants. Here is a school with a small endowment, bequeathed by the Rev. Mr. Day, in 1764.

BALDERSTON, a chapelry in the parish, and lower division of the hundred, of BLACKBURN, county palatine of LANCASTER, 5½ miles (E. N. E.) from Preston, containing 705 inhabitants. The living is a perpetual curacy, in the archdeaconry and diocese of Chester, endowed with £400 private benefaction, and £400 royal bounty, and in the patronage of the Vicar of Blackburn. The chapel is dedicated to St. Leonard.

BALDERTON, a parish in the southern division of the wapentake of NEWARK, county of NOTTINGHAM, 2 miles (S. E.) from Newark, containing 773 inhabitants. The living is a perpetual curacy, annexed to the vicarage of Farndon, in the archdeaconry of Nottingham, and diocese of York. The church, dedicated to St. Giles, is a very handsome edifice, principally in the later style of English architecture, with a lofty spire: it has a richly ornamented Norman porch of exceeding beauty and in good preservation. A school for the instruction of twelve boys and ten girls has been endowed by William Alvey with a rent-charge of £8.

BALDOCK, a market town and parish in the hundred of BROADWATER, county of HERTFORD, 18 miles (N. by W.) from Hertford, and 37 (N. by W.) from London, on the great north road, containing 1550 inhabitants. This place, in the reign of Stephen, belonged to the Knights Templars, to whom Gilbert, Earl of Pembroke, gave the site, which, in a charter of confirmation granted by his descendant William, is called Baudoc, of which the present name is a variation; though some antiquaries derive it from Balbec, supposing the town to have been so called by the Templars, in memory of the city of that name in Syria, from which their order had been expelled by the Saracens. The town is situated near the intersection of the great north road and the Roman Iknield-street, between two hills, which command an extensive view of a fine open country: it consists principally of one street, the houses in which are mostly ancient, interspersed with several of modern erection, and is amply supplied with water. A horticultural society, patronised by the nobility and gentry in the neighbourhood, was established in 1825. The trade is principally in malt, the land in the vicinity being highly favourable to the growth of barley: the fens and marsh land near the town form an extensive grazing district, and a great quantity of cheese of a peculiar quality is made here; there is also a very large public brewery. The general market, which was on Saturday, has been discontinued, and a market, exclusively for the sale of straw-plat, is now held on Friday. The fairs are on the festivals of St. James, St. Andrew, and St. Matthew, each continuing two days; at the last a great quantity of cheese is sold. The county magistrates hold a petty session on the first Monday in every month: constables and other officers are appointed at the court leet of the lord of the manor. The living is a discharged rectory, in the archdeaconry of Huntingdon, and diocese of Lincoln, rated in the king's books at £10. 8. 9., endowed with £800 parliamentary grant, and in the patronage of the Crown. The church, dedicated to St. Mary, was built by the Knights Templars, and nearly rebuilt in the early part of the fifteenth century: it is a spacious structure, partly in the Norman style, and partly in the later style of English architecture, with an octagonal steeple rebuilt a few years ago, and contains a finely carved oak screen, part of the ancient rood-loft, and a very curious font. There are places of worship for the Society of Friends, Independents, and Wesleyan Methodists. Almshouses for twelve aged widows were founded and endowed, in 1621, by Mr. John Winne. In cutting through Baldock hill, to form a new turnpike road, a great number of fossils, consisting of *cornua ammonis*, sharks' teeth, &c., were discovered.

BALDON-MARSH, a parish in the hundred of BULLINGTON, county of OXFORD, 6 miles (S. E. by S.) from Oxford, containing 312 inhabitants. The living is a rectory, within the jurisdiction of the peculiar court of Dorchester, rated in the king's books at £6. 13. 4., and in the patronage of Sir H. P. Willoughby, Bart. The church is dedicated to St. Peter. Elizabeth Lane, in 1770, bequeathed land, producing £6 per annum, for teaching six boys and six girls to read.

BALDON-TOOT, a parish in the hundred of BULLINGTON, county of OXFORD, 5¼ miles (S. E.) from Oxford, containing 258 inhabitants. The living is a discharged vicarage, within the jurisdiction of the peculiar court of Dorchester, and in the patronage of the Rector of Baldon-Marsh. The church is dedicated to St. Lawrence.

BALE, or BAITHLEY, a parish in the hundred of HOLT, county of NORFOLK, 4¾ miles (W. by S.) from Holt, containing 265 inhabitants. The living is a discharged rectory, united to that of Gunthorpe, in the archdeaconry and diocese of Norwich, rated in the king's books at £10. 13. 4. The church is dedicated to All Saints. Here was anciently a chapel, dedicated to St. Botolph.

BALK, a township in the parish of KIRBY-KNOWLE, wapentake of BIRDFORTH, North riding of the county of YORK, 3¾ miles (E. S. E.) from Thirsk, containing 125 inhabitants.

BALKHOLME, a township in the parish of HOWDEN, wapentake of HOWDENSHIRE, East riding of the county of YORK, 3 miles (E.) from Howden, containing 105 inhabitants.

BALLIDON, a chapelry in that part of the parish of BRADBORNE which is in the hundred of WIRKSWORTH, county of DERBY, 5¾ miles (N. N. E.) from Ashbourn, containing 102 inhabitants. This chapelry is in the honour of Tutbury, duchy of Lancaster, and within the jurisdiction of a court of pleas held at Tutbury every third Tuesday, for the recovery of debts under 40*s*.

BALLINGDON, a parochial chapelry in the hundred of HINCKFORD, county of ESSEX, ½ a mile (S. W. by W.) from Sudbury, containing, with Brundon, 662 inhabitants. The living is a perpetual curacy, consolidated with the rectory of Brundon, in the archdeaconry of Middlesex, and diocese of London. The chapel was made parochial in consequence of the decay of the church at Brundon, and all ecclesiastical rites for that parish are now performed here.

BALLINGHAM, a parish in the upper division of the hundred of WORMELOW, county of HEREFORD, 7 miles (N. by W.) from Ross, containing 127 inhabitants. The living is a perpetual curacy, in the archdeaconry and diocese of Hereford, endowed with £30 per annum private benefaction, and £200 royal bounty, and in the patronage of the Vicar of Lugwardine.

BALNE, a township in that part of the parish of SNAITH which is in the lower division of the wapentake of OSGOLDCROSS, West riding of the county of YORK, 5¼ miles (S.W. by W.) from Snaith, containing 329 inhabitants.

BALSALL, a chapelry in the parish of HAMPTON in ARDEN, Solihull division of the hundred of HEMLINGFORD, county of WARWICK, 4½ miles (S.E. by E.) from Solihull, containing 1056 inhabitants. The living is a perpetual curacy, within the peculiar jurisdiction of the manorial court of Balsall-Temple, and in the patronage of the Governors of Balsall Hospital. The chapel, dedicated to St. Mary, formerly belonged to a Society of Knights Templars, and, about 1823, was repaired at an expense of £979. Lady Katherine Leveson, of Trentham, in the county of Stafford, by will dated in 1670, devised the manor of Temple-Balsall to twelve trustees, for the erection and endowment of an hospital for twenty poor women of the chapelry, directing that £8 per annum should be paid to each of the almswomen, and £20 per annum to a minister, for reading prayers to them and for teaching twenty poor boys. By an act passed in the 1st of Queen Anne, for the better government of this hospital, it was incorporated, under the name of "The Hospital of the Lady Katherine Leveson," and eleven trustees were appointed, with power to enlarge the buildings and increase the number of inmates, which now amounts to thirty. The establishment consists of a master, under-master, an apothecary, a matron, and a nurse. The master, in addition to his salary, receives from the funds of the hospital £50 per annum, as perpetual curate of Balsall: a stipend of £50 per annum is also paid to the vicar of Long Itchington. The annual receipts of the charity now amount to about £1500.

BALSCOTT, a hamlet in the parish of WROXTON, hundred of BLOXHAM, county of OXFORD, 5 miles (W.N.W.) from Banbury, containing 214 inhabitants.

BALSHAM, a parish in the hundred of RADFIELD, county of CAMBRIDGE, 4 miles (N.E. by N.) from Linton, containing 959 inhabitants. The living is a rectory, in the peculiar jurisdiction and patronage of the Governors of the Charter-house, London, rated in the king's books at £39. 16. 8. The church is dedicated to the Holy Trinity. A little westward from the village are Gogmagog hills, on the summit of which there are remains of a circular camp with a double rampart, supposed to be British. Hugh de Balsham, founder of Peter-house College, Cambridge, was born here.

BALTONSBOROUGH, a parish in the hundred of GLASTON-TWELVE-HIDES, county of SOMERSET, 5 miles (S.E.) from Glastonbury, containing 671 inhabitants. The living is a perpetual curacy, annexed to the vicarage of Butleigh, in the archdeaconry of Wells, and diocese of Bath and Wells. The church is dedicated to St. Dunstan.

BAMBROUGH, a parish in the northern division of BAMBROUGH ward, county of NORTHUMBERLAND, comprising the chapelries of Beadnell and Lucker, and the townships of Adderstone, Bambrough, Bambrough-Castle, Bradford, Budle, Burton, Elford, Fleetham, Glororum, Hoppen, Mouson, Newham, Newstead, Outchester, Ratchwood, Shoston, Spindlestone, North Sunderland, Swinhoe, Tuggal, Warrenton, and Warnford, and containing 3342 inhabitants, of which number, 342 are in the township of Bambrough, 4¾ miles (E. by N.) from Belford. Bambrough, originally called *Bebbanburg*, was, prior to the Conquest, a royal Saxon burgh, and the residence of several of the kings of Northumbria. It sent two members to parliament in the 23rd of Edward I., and, in the reign of Edward III., furnished one ship for the expedition against Calais: it had also a market, which has long been discontinued. The surrounding district, formerly called Bambroughshire, was a separate franchise, in the possession of various privileges, now become obsolete. The village occupies an airy and pleasant situation near the sea and Budle bay. The living is a perpetual curacy, in the archdeaconry of Northumberland, and diocese of Durham, endowed with £200 private benefaction, and £500 parliamentary grant, and in the patronage of the Trustees of Lord Crewe. The church, dedicated to St. Aidan, was, with another long since desecrated, given by Henry I. to the priory of Nosthall in Yorkshire, whereupon a small convent of Augustine canons was founded here, in 1137, as a cell to that priory, the revenue of which, at the dissolution, was £124. 15. 7. There were also a college, an hospital dedicated to St. Mary Magdalene, and a house of Preaching friars.

BAMBROUGH-CASTLE, a township in the parish, and northern division of the ward, of BAMBROUGH, county of NORTHUMBERLAND, 5 miles (E. by N.) from Belford, containing 62 inhabitants. This township is principally distinguished for its castle, built about the middle of the sixth century, by Ida, the first Anglo-Saxon king of Northumbria. In 642, it was besieged by Penda, King of Mercia, who, after an unsuccessful attempt to set it on fire, was compelled to retreat. In the beginning of the eighth century, Berthfrid, guardian of Osred, the young Northumbrian king, defended it against the usurper Eadulph, who was taken prisoner and put to death. It was plundered and almost demolished by the Danes, in 993, but was soon afterwards restored. After the Norman conquest, it was held by Robert de Mowbray, on whose insurrection against William Rufus it was besieged, and, after an obstinate defence, surrendered to that monarch, who threatened, unless it were given up, to put out the eyes of Mowbray, who had been taken prisoner. During the war between Stephen and the Empress Matilda, and the protracted struggle between the houses of York and Lancaster, this castle sustained repeated sieges, and at length became dilapidated, in the reign of Henry VII. The castle and manor were granted, in the reign of James II., to John Forster, Esq., one of whose descendants having joined the Pretender, they were confiscated to the Crown, and purchased by his relative, Lord Crewe, Bishop of Durham, who, in 1720, devised this estate to trustees for charitable uses. Under the direction of Dr. Sharp, Archdeacon of Durham, the castle was repaired in 1757, and apartments were prepared, in which one of the trustees, who superintends the establishment, constantly resides. It is situated on the summit of a steep rock, which projects into the sea, and rises perpendicularly to the height of one hundred and fifty feet above low water mark, and is accessible only on the south-east side, where is the ancient gateway, flanked with a circular tower on each side, and formerly defended by a trench cut through a narrow isthmus communicating with the main land. Within a short distance of this is a more modern gateway, with a portcullis; and a little further on is a round tower. The keep, which is of Norman architecture, and the most ancient part of the building, is a lofty square structure. In 1773, the ruins of a church, or chapel, erected in the castle by King Oswald, were discovered, and the font, richly carved, is preserved, among other curiosities, in the keep. In the upper part of the building are granaries, in which corn is stored to be sold to the poor in times of scarcity: a market is opened every Tuesday and Friday, when the industrious poor are supplied with meat and grocery at the cost price. In another part of the castle is an infirmary, with a resident surgeon; the average annual number of in-patients is about thirty-five, and of out-patients upwards of one thousand. There are also two schools, in which about one hundred and sixty children of both sexes are taught on Dr. Bell's system; thirty of the girls are clothed and lodged in the castle till they are fit for service. In 1778, the trustees founded a library in the castle, to which the late Dr. Sharp bequeathed the whole of his valuable collection of books, including the greater part of the library of Dr. Sharp, Archbishop of York. But the principal object of this charitable establishment is to afford assistance to shipwrecked mariners, for whose reception, apartments comfortably furnished, and containing thirty beds, are always kept in readiness; patrols are constantly stationed along the coast in stormy nights, and when vessels are observed to be in distress, signals are made from the summit of the tower to the fishermen at Holy Island, who are rewarded for their services by the trustees.

BAMBURGH, county of LINCOLN.—See BAUMBER.

BAMFORD, a hamlet in the parish of HATHERSAGE, hundred of HIGH PEAK, county of DERBY, 6¼ miles (N. by W.) from Stoney-Middleton, containing 263 inhabitants.

BAMFORD, a joint township with Birtle, in the parish of MIDDLETON, hundred of SALFORD, county palatine of LANCASTER, 3 miles (W. S. W.) from Rochdale. The population is returned with Birtle.

BAMPTON, a market town and parish in the hundred of BAMPTON, county of DEVON, 21 miles (N. by E.) from Exeter, and 162 (W. by S.) from London, containing 1633 inhabitants. Bampton is supposed by Bishop Gibson to have been the *Beamdune* of the Saxon Chronicle, where, in 614, the Britons were defeated with great slaughter by Cynegils, King of the West Saxons. Other antiquaries, referring this event to Bindon in Dorset, derive its names *Batherm-town* and *Bathrumpton* from the river Batherm, which flows into the Exe, about three quarters of a mile below the town, whence, by contraction, its present appellation is obtained. The town is pleasantly situated in a vale watered by the river; the houses are of stone, irregularly built, and the inhabitants are amply supplied with water. The principal branch of manufacture is that of serge; and freestone and limestone are obtained in the parish. The market is on Wednesday and Saturday; and fairs are held on Whit-Tuesday, the Wednesday before Lady-day, the last Thursday in October, and the first Tuesday in November; at the two last a great number of sheep is sold, which, from the excellence of the pastures, are remarkable for size and flavour. Two portreeves, two constables, and other officers, are chosen annually by the householders. The living is a discharged vicarage, in the archdeaconry and diocese of Exeter, rated in the king's books at £21. 11., endowed with £400 private benefaction, £400 royal bounty, and £400 parliamentary grant, and in the patronage of Charles Chichester, Esq. The church, dedicated to St. Michael, is a spacious structure, in the early style of English architecture, containing several monuments to the Earls of Bath. At Pitton, four miles distant from the church, there is a chapel, in which divine service is performed once a month; and at Shillingford are the remains of another chapel. There are places of worship for Particular Baptists and Independents. A charity school has been lately built and endowed by Mrs. Penton, in which one hundred children are educated. In the vicinity is a chalybeate spring, strongly impregnated with iron. The site of an ancient castle, erected in 1336, by a member of the family of Cogan, is still discernible. John de Bampton, a Carmelite monk, and the first who read Aristotle publicly at Cambridge, was a native of this town.

BAMPTON, a market town and parish in the hundred of BAMPTON, county of OXFORD, 16 miles (W. by S.) from Oxford, and 70 (W. N. W.) from London, comprising the chapelry of Shifford, and the hamlets of Aston with Cote, Chimney, and part of that of Bright-Hampton, and containing 2304 inhabitants. This place, called by the Saxons *Bemtune*, was a town of some importance during the Octarchy, and, in the reign of Edward the Confessor, was annexed to the diocese of Exeter, by Leofric, chaplain to that monarch, and first bishop of the see. The town is situated near the river Isis, on which there are some convenient wharfs: the houses are neatly built, and the inhabitants are plentifully supplied with water, which springs through a gravelly soil; there are a subscription library and a news-room. The trade formerly consisted in supplying the counties of Bucks, Dorset, and Wilts with leather prepared by the fellmongers at Witney: the manufacture of leather was subsequently established here, but it has greatly declined. The market has recently fallen into disuse: a fair is held on the 26th and 27th of August, the former day being for the sale of horses. Constables and other officers are appointed at the court leet of the joint proprietors of the manor. The living is a vicarage, in the archdeaconry and diocese of Oxford, in three portions, each rated in the king's books at £10. 0. 10., and in the patronage of the Dean and Chapter of Exeter. The church, dedicated to St. Mary, is a spacious ancient structure, containing some interesting monuments. The free school was founded, in 1635, by Mr. Robert Vesey, of Chimney, in this parish, who endowed it with £200, which, with subsequent benefactions, was laid out in the purchase of eight acres of land, now let for £30 per ann.: in 1784, £400 stock was given to instruct ten additional scholars. The school is under the inspection of the vicars, portionists of Bampton, who appoint he master: the premises comprise a school-room, house, and garden. A National school is partly supported by an endowment, and partly by subscription; the present income is about £45 per annum. There are slight remains of an ancient castle, supposed to have been erected in the reign of John. Phillips, the author of the Splendid Shilling, a poem on Cider, &c., was born here, in 1676.

BAMPTON, a parish in West ward, county of WESTMORLAND, 9¾ miles (N. W.) from Orton, containing 614 inhabitants. The living is a discharged vicarage, in the archdeaconry and diocese of Carlisle, rated in the king's books at £7. 5., endowed with £200 private benefaction, and £400 royal bounty, and in the patronage of the Crown. The church, dedicated to St. Patrick, was rebuilt on the site of the former, in 1726: the vicarage-house was rebuilt also, about the same period, by Dr. Gibson, Bishop of London. The river Lowther runs through the parish, in which is a beautiful lake, three miles in length, called Haweswater. This lake is about three miles long, and half a mile broad, its summit being environed by an assemblage of lofty mountains, its eastern side sheltered by well-planted rocky eminences, and its western bordered by cultivated fields. A lead mine has been discovered, but it is not yet fully explored; and limestone is obtained in the parish. The free grammar school was founded, in 1627, by Thomas Sutton, D.D., who vested in trustees the sum of £500, collected in the parish of St. Saviour, Southwark, and other places, with which certain tithes were purchased, now let by the master, and producing about £60 annually: the school is free for all the children of the parish: other benefactions for the purchase of books have been added. A school at Roughill, in this parish, was founded by Edmund Noble, and endowed with £9. 15. 10. per annum. At Measand there is a school, founded in 1723, by Richard Wright, and endowed with property producing £50 per annum. Here are also three parochial libraries, established respectively in 1710, 1750, and 1757, and comprising in the aggregate upwards of eight hundred volumes; and there are some minor bequests for the benefit of the poor. Thomas Gibson, M.D., who married the daughter of Richard Cromwell, son of the Protector, physician-general to the army, and author of a "System of Anatomy," was a native of High Knipe, in this parish, where also was born, in 1669, his nephew, Edmund Gibson, D.D., Bishop of London, and author of two improved editions of Camden's Britannia, and various other learned works.

BAMPTON (KIRK), a parish in the ward and county of CUMBERLAND, comprising the townships of Kirk-Bampton, Little Bampton, and Oughterby, and containing 470 inhabitants, of which number, 193 are in the township of Kirk-Bampton, 6½ miles (W.) from Carlisle. The living is a discharged rectory, in the archdeaconry and diocese of Carlisle, rated in the king's books at £14. 17. 10., endowed with £400 parliamentary grant, and in the alternate patronage of the Earl of Lonsdale and Sir Wastel Brisco, Bart. The church, dedicated to St. Peter, is an ancient edifice. There are two chalybeate springs in the parish, one of them discovered in 1826, near Fingland Rigg.

BAMPTON (LITTLE), a township in the parish of KIRK-BAMPTON, ward and county of CUMBERLAND, 5 miles (N. by E.) from Wigton, containing 172 inhabitants.

Seal and Arms.

BANBURY, a borough, market town, and parish, having separate jurisdiction, locally in the hundred of Banbury, county of OXFORD, 22 miles (N.) from Oxford, and 73 (N. W.) from London, containing, with the hamlet of Neithrop, 5247 inhabitants. This place, by the Saxons called *Banesbyrig*, of which its present name is a contraction, is supposed to have been occupied by the Romans, and this opinion has been confirmed by the discovery of some Roman coins and an altar. A castle was built here, about 1153, by Alexander, Bishop of Lincoln, which continued an episcopal residence till the first year of the reign of Edward VI. "In this castle," says Leland, "is a terrible prison for convict men." During the war between the houses of York and Lancaster the neighbourhood was the scene of frequent conflicts: the most disastrous of these was the battle of Banbury, fought, in 1469, on a plain called Danesmore, near Edgecote, a village about three miles distant, between the forces under the celebrated Earl of Warwick, and a numerous army, which, under the command of the Earls of Pembroke and Stafford, had obtained possession of the town. The Yorkists were defeated; Pembroke and his brother, Sir Richard Herbert, were both taken and beheaded, and, in a few days, Edward IV. himself was made prisoner. At the commencement of the war between Charles I. and the parliament, the inhabitants espoused the cause of the latter, by whom the castle was garrisoned. After the battle of Edgehill, it was taken by the royalists, and defended by Sir William Compton, against Col. John Fiennes, the parliamentary officer, for thirteen weeks, till the garrison was relieved by the Earl of Northampton. It was afterwards besieged by Col. Whalley for ten weeks, when the king having joined the Scottish army, it was surrendered on honourable terms. Of this fortress, a stone vault with grated windows, supposed to have been the dungeon, and traces of the inner ditch, existed in Leland's time, and there are still some vestiges. The town is pleasantly situated in a fertile valley, on the banks of the small river Cherwell, and has been greatly improved under an act of parliament passed in the fourth year of the reign of George IV.: the houses are well built, the streets lighted with oil, and the inhabitants plentifully supplied with water. There is a public subscription library. The manufacture of plush shag and girth-webbing was formerly carried on to a considerable extent, but has greatly declined. A great quantity of cheese of a very superior quality is made, for which, and for its well-known cakes, Banbury has long been famous. The Oxford canal comes up to the town. The market, which was greatly celebrated in the time of Henry VIII., is on Thursday: fairs are held on January 22nd, March 5th, April 9th, May 28th, June 18th, July 9th, August 13th, September 10th, October 5th and 30th, and December 17th. The government, by charter of incorporation granted by Mary, confirmed by James, and enlarged by George I., is vested in a mayor, high steward, recorder, twelve aldermen, six capital burgesses, and thirty assistants, with a town clerk, chamberlain, and other officers.

The mayor, who is elected from among the aldermen, on the first Monday in September, and two of the aldermen, are justices of the peace within the borough, and hold regularly a petty session every Monday, and a general session twice a year. The corporation possess the power of holding a court of record for the recovery of debts under £40, but have discontinued the exercise of it. The elective franchise was conferred in the reign of Mary, since which time the borough has returned one member to parliament: the right of election is vested in the mayor and capital burgesses; the mayor is the returning officer, and the influence of the Marquis of Bute predominates.

The living is a discharged vicarage, within the jurisdiction of the peculiar court of Banbury, rated in the king's books at £22. 0. 2., endowed with £200 private benefaction, £400 royal bounty, and £600 parliamentary grant, and in the patronage of the Bishop of Oxford. The church, dedicated to St. Mary, is a very handsome and spacious structure, rebuilt under the authority of an act of parliament obtained in 1790, at an expense of nearly £30,000. There are places of worship for the Society of Friends, Independents, Wesleyan Methodists, and Unitarians. A free grammar school, which formerly existed here, was held in such high estimation, that the statutes of St. Paul's school, London, are said to have been drawn up on the model of those of Banbury school. One of the masters, Mr. Stanbridge, was tutor to the celebrated Sir Thomas Pope; and so great was the fame which this institution had acquired, that the statutes of the free grammar school at Manchester, dated 1524, ordain that grammar be there taught "after the manner of the school at Banbury, in Oxfordshire, which is called Stanbridge grammar." This school has been wholly abandoned for many years, and the building, formerly called the Church School, let on lease by the corporation. A Blue-coat school, established by subscription in 1705, and endowed with property to the amount of £80 per annum, was, in 1807, incorporated with a National school formed in that year, to which a Sunday school is attached, supported by the interest of £295. 1. 6. three per cent. consols., purchased by a legacy of £200 under the will of Sir John Knightley. An unendowed almshouse was rebuilt by Francis, Lord Guildford, for twelve poor persons, who are appointed by the corporation, eight of them receiving also part of a charitable fund called the widow's groats. Various other charities are periodically distributed, and certain lands are especially set apart for repairing the bridge, highways, &c. An ancient hospital, dedicated to St. John, has been converted into a farm-house. Adjoining the Ram Inn there is a sulphureous well, and, at a short distance from the town, a chalybeate spring. The *pyrites aureus*, or golden fire-stone, is frequently found in digging wells. There is also an amphitheatre, called the "Bear Garden," having two rows of seats cut in the rising ground; and on Crouch hill, a mile westward, are vestiges of a circular intrenchment, the site of which was chosen for an encampment by Sir W. Waller, in 1644.

BANHAM, a parish in the hundred of GUILT-CROSS, county of NORFOLK, 5¼ miles (E. by N.) from East Harling, containing 1195 inhabitants. The living is a rectory, in the archdeaconry of Norfolk, and diocese of Norwich, rated in the king's books at £9. 3. 6½., and in the patronage of the Crown. The church is dedicated to St. Mary. There is a place of worship for Wesleyan Methodists. The parochial school has a small endowment.

BANKFEE, or SOUTH FIELD, a hamlet in the parish of LONGBOROUGH, upper division of the hundred of KIFTSGATE, county of GLOUCESTER, 1½ mile (N. by W.) from Stow on the Wold. The population is returned with the parish.

BANKS, a township in the parish of LANERCOST-ABBEY, ESKDALE ward, county of CUMBERLAND, containing 280 inhabitants.

BANNINGHAM, a parish in the southern division of the hundred of ERPINGHAM, county of NORFOLK, 2 miles (N.E.) from Aylsham, containing 256 inhabitants. The living is a rectory, in the archdeaconry and diocese of Norwich, rated in the king's books at £10. 15. 10., and in the patronage of Sir John Lubbock, Bart.

BANSTEAD, a parish in the first division of the hundred of COPTHORNE, county of SURREY, 3½ miles (S. E. by E.) from Ewell, containing 940 inhabitants. The living is a discharged vicarage, in the archdeaconry of Surrey, and diocese of Winchester, rated in the king's books at £13. 8. 7½., and in the patronage of the Rev. W. Buckle. The church, dedicated to All Saints, contains several fine specimens of pointed arches, and has a handsome tower, surmounted by a lofty spire. Banstead downs, on which Epsom races are held, are remarkable for their verdure, and afford excellent pasturage for sheep, though a considerable portion of them has been brought under tillage of late years.

BANWELL, a parish in the hundred of WINTERSTOKE, county of SOMERSET, 5 miles (N. N. W.) from Axbridge, containing 1430 inhabitants. The living is a vicarage, within the jurisdiction of the peculiar court of Banwell at Wells, rated in the king's books at £26. 6. 0½., and in the patronage of the Dean and Chapter of Bristol. The church, dedicated to St. Andrew, is a fine specimen of the later style of English architecture: among the internal decorations are a richly carved screen and rood-loft, a finely sculptured stone pulpit, and windows of stained glass. There is a place of worship for Wesleyan Methodists. A monastery was founded at Banwell by one of the early Saxon kings, to the abbacy of which Alfred the Great appointed Asser, his subsequent biographer: it was entirely demolished in the Danish irruptions, and, although restored, never recovered its former splendour, having fallen to decay several years before the general suppression of religious houses. The manor has been in the possession of the Bishops of Bath and Wells since the time of Edward the Confessor, with the exception of the short reign of Edward VI., one of whom built an episcopal palace here, the remains of which, in the early part of the last century, were converted into a private residence, called Banwell Court, and the park has been divided into enclosures, which have been assigned on lease for lives: some of the leases have been lately bought up, and the ground disposed in a tasteful manner, by forming plantations, with drives conducting to pleasing and richly variegated prospects. The bishop also, in 1827, erected a cottage ornée for his own accommodation, and that of the numerous visitors which the recent discovery of two caverns in the rock, one denominated the Bone, and the other the

Stalactite cavern, has attracted hither. The former, when first observed, was filled, to the depth of about eight feet, with a confused mass of bones of animals, stones, and gravel; but the rubbish has been removed, and the bones, of which there are several wagon-loads, have been fancifully disposed along the sides of the cavern, about forty feet below the body of which there is a fissure, wherein the diluvia have been permitted to remain in a promiscuous state. The Stalactite cavern exhibits fine specimens of a transparent stalactite; huge fragments of the rock lie dispersed on the floor, covered with stalagmik. In this there were found two pieces of candle, incrustated with lime, which are supposed to have been left by the miners who were last employed in working for ochre, calamine, and lead-ore, minerals which, doubtless, still exist to a considerable extent, though the mines in this part of the Mendip hills have not been opened of late years. A rich vein of iron-ore, with some cobalt and manganese, has been discovered, and the working of it commenced: the ore is conveyed to the southern coast of Wales, where the smelting-works are. The village is agreeably situated under the northern declivity of the Mendip range of hills. A spring, from which the place probably derives its name, and formerly noted for possessing a medicinal property, expands into a fine sheet of water, and, after turning a large paper and grist-mill, pursues a winding course through the valley, and empties itself into the channel, near the remains of the priory at Woodspring. Fairs for the sale of cattle are held on January 18th and July 18th. An English free school was established about 1767, and a fund for its support was raised by subscription, the produce of which is £10. 10. per annum: a school-room was built in 1824, at an expense of £400. Attached to this is an endowment for the instruction of ten boys belonging to the established church. William Burgess, in 1676, gave a rent-charge of £4, to accumulate for the apprenticing of a boy every seven years. The summit of a neighbouring eminence is crowned by a British earthwork, enclosing within its irregular rampart an area of about twenty acres. About a quarter of a mile from this is an intrenchment, nearly square, in the centre of which the ground is elevated in the form of a cross.

BAPCHILD, a parish in the hundred of MILTON, lathe of SCRAY, county of KENT, 1¼ mile (E. S. E.) from Sittingbourne, containing 307 inhabitants. The living is a discharged vicarage, in the archdeaconry and diocese of Canterbury, rated in the king's books at £8, endowed with £200 private benefaction, and £200 royal bounty, and in the patronage of the Dean and Chapter of Chichester. The church, dedicated to St. Lawrence, is principally in the early style of English architecture, with modern insertions. Ecclesiastical councils were held here during the Saxon Octarchy, in commemoration of one of which, convened under Archbishop Brightwald, in 794, an oratory, or chapel, was erected, of which there are still some remains. There is a small endowment for the education of poor children.

BAPTON, a tything in the parish of FISHERTON de la MERE, hundred of WARMINSTER, though locally in the hundred of Dunworth, county of WILTS, 6 miles (N. by E.) from Hindon. The population is returned with the parish.

BARBON, a chapelry in the parish of KIRKBY-LONSDALE, LONSDALE ward, county of WESTMORLAND, 4 miles (N. N. E.) from Kirkby-Lonsdale, containing 348 inhabitants. The living is a perpetual curacy, in the archdeaconry of Richmond, and diocese of Chester, endowed with £800 royal bounty, and in the patronage of the Vicar of Kirkby-Lonsdale. The chapel, and a school-room adjoining it, were built partly by subscription, and partly by means of a rate, in 1815; the school has an endowment bequeathed by John Garnett, in 1721.

BARBY, a parish in the hundred of FAWSLEY, county of NORTHAMPTON, 5¼ miles (N. N. W.) from Daventry, containing, with the hamlet of Onely, 645 inhabitants. The living is a rectory, in the archdeaconry of Northampton, and diocese of Peterborough, rated in the king's books at £30. 2. 11., and in the patronage of the Rev. C. Williams. The church is dedicated to St. Mary. The Oxford canal crosses the parish. Property for charitable uses is vested in feoffees, and out of the produce thereof £20 per annum is paid for the daily instruction of twenty-four children, and £4 per annum to the master of a Sunday school.

BARCHESTON, a parish in the Brails division of the hundred of KINGTON, county of WARWICK, ½ a mile (E. S. E.) from Shipston upon Stour, containing, with the hamlet of Willington, 184 inhabitants. The living is a discharged rectory, in the archdeaconry and diocese of Worcester, rated in the king's books at £13. 6. 8., and in the patronage of the Rev. T. L. Snow. The church is dedicated to St. Martin.

BARCOMB, a parish in the hundred of BARCOMB, rape of LEWES, county of SUSSEX, 3 miles (N. by E.) from Lewes, containing 753 inhabitants. The living is a rectory, in the archdeaconry of Lewes, and diocese of Chichester, rated in the king's books at £18. 10. 10., and in the patronage of the Crown. The church is dedicated to St. Mary. A school established by the late Thomas Rickman, Esq., who bequeathed to it an annuity of £20 for ten years, has since been supported by the Earl of Liverpool and Mrs. Rickman.

BARDEN, a chapelry in that part of the parish of SKIPTON which is in the eastern division of the wapentake of STAINCLIFFE and EWCROSS, West riding of the county of YORK, 8 miles (N. E. by N.) from Skipton, containing 219 inhabitants. The interest of £170, being the amount of various benefactions, is appropriated to the instruction of children and the relief of the poor.

BARDFIELD (GREAT), a parish in the hundred of FRESHWELL, county of ESSEX, 4½ miles (E. by S.) from Thaxted, containing 887 inhabitants. The living is a vicarage, in the archdeaconry of Colchester, and diocese of London, rated in the king's books at £11, and in the patronage of Sir C. M. Burrell, Bart. The church is dedicated to St. Mary. The navigable river Blackwater runs through the parish. In 1584, William Benlows bequeathed property, producing about £30 per annum, for the education of children and other charitable purposes, to which sundry other endowments have since been added. Petty sessions for the hundred are held here every Thursday.

BARDFIELD (LITTLE), a parish in the hundred of FRESHWELL, county of ESSEX, 3 miles (E.) from Thaxted, containing 308 inhabitants. The living is a rectory, in the archdeaconry of Colchester, and diocese of London, rated in the king's books at £11, and in the patronage of the heir male of the Rev. T. Bernard. The church is dedicated to St. Catharine. A school was endowed by Sarah Bernard, in 1774, for eighteen poor children, to be taught by a widow; there is also an almshouse for poor widows.

BARDFIELD-SALING, a parish in the hundred of FRESHWELL, county of ESSEX, $5\frac{3}{4}$ miles (N. E.) from Great Dunmow, containing 282 inhabitants. The living is a perpetual curacy, in the archdeaconry of Essex, and diocese of London. The church is dedicated to St. Margaret.

BARDNEY, a parish in the western division of the wapentake of WRAGGOE, parts of LINDSEY, county of LINCOLN, 10 miles (W.) from Horncastle, containing 954 inhabitants. The living is a discharged vicarage, in the archdeaconry and diocese of Lincoln, rated in the king's books at £7, endowed with £220 private benefaction, £200 royal bounty, and £600 parliamentary grant, and in the patronage of the Bishop of Lincoln. The church is dedicated to St. Lawrence. There is a place of worship for Wesleyan Methodists. A free grammar school was founded, in 1711, by Thomas Kitchen, who endowed it, for the benefit of the children of Bardney, Bucknall, and Tupholme, with a salary of £35 per annum for the master, together with a house and garden. There is also an almshouse for fourteen poor widowers and widows. A monastery founded here, in which Ethelred, King of Mercia, became a monk in 704, was destroyed by the Danes in 870; and, about the period of the Conquest, it was restored for a society of Benedictine monks, by Gilbert de Gaunt, Earl of Lincoln: the revenue, at the dissolution, amounted to £429.7.

BARDON-PARK, an extra-parochial liberty, in the hundred of SPARKENHOE, county of LEICESTER, $9\frac{1}{2}$ miles (N. W. by W.) from Leicester, containing 69 inhabitants.

BARDSEA, a township in the parish of URSWICK, hundred of LONSDALE, north of the sands, county palatine of LANCASTER, 3 miles (S. by E.) from Ulverstone. The population is returned with the parish. Here are several malt-kilns, and in the neighbourhood is a copper mine. A school for the education of poor children is endowed with a rent-charge of £8, given by Wilson Braddyll, in 1781.

BARDSEY, a parish in the lower division of the wapentake of SKYRACK, West riding of the county of YORK, comprising the townships of Bardsey with Rigton, and Wothersome, and containing 372 inhabitants, of which number, 356 are in the township of Bardsey with Rigton, $4\frac{1}{2}$ miles (S. W. by S.) from Wetherby. The living is a discharged vicarage, in the archdeaconry and diocese of York, rated in the king's books at £4. 1. 8., endowed with £200 private benefaction, and £400 royal bounty, and in the patronage of George Lane Fox, Esq. The church is dedicated to All Saints: near it is a mound, called Castle Hill, the supposed site of a Roman fortress. A school was endowed with about £18 per annum by Lord Bingley, in 1726. Congreve, the poet and dramatist, supposed to have been born in Ireland, was baptized at Bardsey, in February 1670.

BARDWELL, a parish in the hundred of BLACKBOURN, county of SUFFOLK, $2\frac{1}{4}$ miles (N. by E.) from Ixworth, containing 687 inhabitants. The living is a rectory, in the archdeaconry of Sudbury, and diocese of Norwich, rated in the king's books at £7. 17. 1., and in the patronage of the President and Fellows of St. John's College, Oxford. The church is dedicated to St. Peter. There is a place of worship for Particular Baptists. The parochial school has a small endowment for the instruction of poor children: here is also an almshouse.

BARE, a township in that part of the parish of LANCASTER which is in the hundred of LONSDALE, south of the sands, county palatine of LANCASTER, $3\frac{1}{4}$ miles (N. W. by N.) from Lancaster, containing 91 inhabitants.

BARFORD, a parish in the hundred of FOREHOE, county of NORFOLK, $4\frac{3}{4}$ miles (N.) from Wymondham, containing 387 inhabitants. The living is a discharged rectory in medieties, in the archdeaconry of Norfolk, and diocese of Norwich, rated in the king's books at £4. 8. 4., endowed with £200 private benefaction, and £200 royal bounty, and respectively in the patronage of the Rev. H. Franklin and the Dean and Chapter of Norwich. The church is dedicated to St. Botolph.

BARFORD, an extra-parochial liberty, within the limits of the parish of Arthingworth, hundred of ROTHWELL, county of NORTHAMPTON, 3 miles (N. by W.) from Kettering, containing 9 inhabitants.

BARFORD, a parish in the Warwick division of the hundred of KINGTON, county of WARWICK, 3 miles (S. by W.) from Warwick, containing 671 inhabitants. The living is a rectory, in the archdeaconry and diocese of Worcester, rated in the king's books at £11. 11. $0\frac{1}{2}$., and in the patronage of Mrs. Mills. The church is dedicated to St. Peter. A free school, in which about thirty boys and thirty girls are educated, is endowed with about £48 per annum, arising chiefly from the benefaction of John Beale, in 1672, and that of the Rev. Thomas Dugard, in 1677.

BARFORD (GREAT), a parish in the hundred of BARFORD, county of BEDFORD, 6 miles (E. N. E.) from Bedford, containing 635 inhabitants. The living is a discharged vicarage, united to that of Roxton, in the archdeaconry of Bedford, and diocese of Lincoln, rated in the king's books at £9. The church is dedicated to All Saints. There is a place of worship for Wesleyan Methodists. The navigable river Ouse, here crossed by a bridge, runs along the south-eastern border of the parish.

BARFORD (GREAT), a parish in the hundred of WOOTTON, county of OXFORD, $2\frac{1}{2}$ miles (W. N. W.) from Deddington, containing 339 inhabitants. The living is a discharged vicarage, in the archdeaconry and diocese of Oxford, rated in the king's books at £6. 5., endowed with £400 private benefaction, and £600 royal bounty, and in the patronage of John Hall, Esq. The church is dedicated to St. Michael.

BARFORD (ST. JOHN), a chapelry in the parish of EAST ADDERBURY, hundred of BLOXHAM, county of OXFORD, $2\frac{3}{4}$ miles (N. W. by W.) from Deddington, containing 123 inhabitants.

BARFORD (LITTLE), a parish in the hundred of BIGGLESWADE, county of BEDFORD, $2\frac{1}{2}$ miles (S. by W.) from St. Neots, containing 123 inhabitants. The living is a rectory, in the archdeaconry of Bedford, and diocese of Lincoln, rated in the king's books at £13. 16. 3., and in the patronage of the Rev. John Alington. The church, dedicated to St. Mary, is an ancient building with a Norman arch over the south door, and a curious wooden screen between the nave and the chancel. The river Ouse forms the western boundary of the parish. Nicholas Rowe, the dramatic writer, and poet-laureat to George I., was a native of this place; he was buried with much pomp in Westminster abbey in 1718.

BARFORD (ST. MARTIN), a parish in the hundred of CAWDEN and CADWORTH, county of WILTS, 2½ miles (W.) from Wilton, containing 560 inhabitants. The living is a rectory, in the archdeaconry and diocese of Salisbury, rated in the king's books at £24. 2. 8½., and in the patronage of the Warden and Fellows of All Souls' College, Oxford. There is a place of worship for Independents. A parochial school is supported by subscription.

BARFORTH, a township in the parish of FORCETT, western division of the wapentake of GILLING, North riding of the county of YORK, 6 miles (E.) from Barnard-Castle, containing 141 inhabitants. Within this township, which is situated on the banks of the Tees, are the inconsiderable ruins of Old Richmond, a place formerly of some note, as is evident from the relics that are frequently dug up: the remains consist only of an old ruinous chapel, with some visible inequalities in the surface of the ground.

BARFRESTON, a parish in the hundred of EASTRY, lathe of ST. AUGUSTINE, county of KENT, 6 miles (S. by E.) from Wingham, containing 115 inhabitants. The living is a discharged rectory, in the archdeaconry and diocese of Canterbury, rated in the king's books at £7. 14., endowed with £400 private benefaction, and £400 royal bounty, and in the patronage of the President and Fellows of St. John's College, Oxford. The church, dedicated to St. Mary, presents a fine specimen of Norman architecture, especially in the southern porch, which is richly ornamented with varied mouldings. It is a small building, consisting of a nave and chancel, the latter much narrower than the former, and separated from it by a large circular arch, supported by two elegant wreathed pillars: the exterior is curiously ornamented with carved stone work and circular windows and arches, particularly at the east end, which has a beautiful circular upper window; the west end has also a fine circular arch, with diagonal ornaments and sculptured rows of figures: niches for statues surround the entire building. This parish, and some adjoining it, contain numerous tumuli.

BARHAM, a parish in the hundred of LEIGHTONSTONE, county of HUNTINGDON, 6 miles (N. N. E.) from Kimbolton, containing 104 inhabitants. The living is a perpetual curacy, in the peculiar jurisdiction and patronage of the Prebendary of Longstow in the Cathedral Church of Lincoln, endowed with £400 royal bounty.

BARHAM, a parish in the hundred of KINGHAMFORD, lathe of ST. AUGUSTINE, county of KENT, 6¼ miles (S. E. by S.) from Canterbury, containing 912 inhabitants. The living is a perpetual curacy, annexed to the rectory of Bishopsbourne, in the archdeaconry and diocese of Canterbury. The church is dedicated to St. John the Baptist. The Canterbury races are held annually, in the month of August, on Barham downs. Barham gives the title of baron to the family of Noel.

BARHAM, a parish in the hundred of BOSMERE and CLAYDON, county of SUFFOLK, 4 miles (N. N. W.) from Ipswich, containing, with the inmates of the house of industry for the hundred, 845 inhabitants. The living is a rectory, in the archdeaconry of Suffolk, and diocese of Norwich, rated in the king's books at £12. 10. 5., and in the patronage of the Rev. John Longe. The church, dedicated to St. Mary, is a handsome edifice with a very large chancel. The parish is bounded on the west by the navigable river Gipping. In a field, called Chapel field, the floor of an ancient chapel was lately turned up by the plough.

BARHOLME, a parish in the wapentake of NESS, parts of KESTEVEN, county of LINCOLN, 3¾ miles (W. by N.) from Market-Deeping, containing 154 inhabitants. The living is a discharged vicarage, united in 1772 to that of Stow, in the archdeaconry and diocese of Lincoln, rated in the king's books at £5. 11. 8., and in the patronage of the Governors of Oakham and Uppingham schools. The church is dedicated to St. Martin: from an inscription in verse the tower appears to have been erected in 1648.

BARKBY, a parish in the eastern division of the hundred of GOSCOTE, county of LEICESTER, 5 miles (N. E.) from Leicester, containing, with the chapelries of Barkby-Thorpe and North Thurmaston, 719 inhabitants. The living is a vicarage, in the archdeaconry of Leicester, and diocese of Lincoln, rated in the king's books at £10, and in the patronage of George Pochin, Esq.

BARKBY-THORPE, a chapelry in the parish of BARKBY, eastern division of the hundred of GOSCOTE, county of LEICESTER, 4 miles (N. E.) from Leicester, containing 70 inhabitants.

BARKHAM, a parish in the hundred of CHARLTON, county of BERKS, 2¾ miles (S. W. by W.) from Wokingham, containing 215 inhabitants. The living is a rectory, in the archdeaconry of Berks, and diocese of Salisbury, rated in the king's books at £5. 15. 7½., and in the patronage of the Rev. H. E. St. John. The church is dedicated to St. James.

BARKING, a parish in the hundred of BECONTREE, county of ESSEX, comprising the market town of Barking, and the wards of Chadwell, Ilford, and Ripple, and containing 6374 inhabitants, of which number, 2580 are in the town of Barking, 23 miles (S. W.) from Chelmsford, and 7 (N. E.) from London. The name of this place, formerly written *Berking*, is by some considered to be derived from the Saxon words *Beorce*, a birch tree, and *Ing*, a meadow; by others from *Berg-Ing*, signifying a fortification in the meadows, probably from an ancient intrenchment, at the distance of about a quarter of a mile, on the road to Ilford, of which there are still considerable vestiges. It appears to have been of an irregular quadrilateral form, enclosing an area of more than forty-eight acres, defended on the north, south, and east sides by a single, and on the west side by a double, intrenchment, and having on the north-west an outlet to a spring of fine water, protected by a high mound of earth. The town derived its ancient importance from a very extensive abbey, founded in 670, by Erkenwald, Bishop of London, for nuns of the Benedictine order, and dedicated to the Virgin Mary, which was governed by a long succession of abbesses, of whom many were of noble, and some of royal, descent. In 870, Barking was burnt by the Danes, the abbey destroyed, and the nuns (many of whom were massacred) dispersed. The abbey was afterwards rebuilt, about the year 970, by Edgar, whose queen Elfrida presided over it after his decease: at the dissolution its revenue amounted to £1084. 6. 2¾. Of the conventual buildings there remains only the gateway, over which is the chapel of the Holy Rood: the arch is finely pointed, and enriched with deeply receding mouldings; above is a canopied niche under a fine window of three lights, the whole forming a square embattled tower, with an octagonal turret at one of the angles. It is called the Fire-bell gate, from its having anciently contained the curfew. Among the ruins of the abbey were found a fibula and a gold ring, on which were engraved the Salutation of the Virgin and the letters I. M. Soon after the Conquest, William retired to this town, till the completion of the Tower of London, which he was then building, to keep the citizens in subjection; and here he was visited, during the preparation for his coronation, by Earl Edwin of Mercia, and Earl Morca of Northumberland, with many of the English nobles, who swore fealty to him on the restoration of their estates. The town is situated on the small river Roding, which, after flowing in two branches, unites with the Thames about two miles below. The inhabitants are principally occupied in the fishery, having a number of vessels which they send to the Dutch and Scotch coasts, and, on their return, the fish is sent to Billingsgate in smaller vessels. There is a convenient wharf at Barking creek, which is navigable to Ilford for ships of eighty tons' burden, by which the neighbourhood is supplied with coal and timber; and near it is a large flour-mill, formerly belonging to the abbey. Many hundred acres of land in the vicinity are appropriated to the cultivation of potatoes for the London market. The market is on Saturday: a fair is held on October 22nd. Constables and other officers for the town are appointed at a court leet, and a court under the lord of the manor is held every third Saturday, for the recovery of debts under 40*s*. The town hall is over the market-house, an ancient building, chiefly of wood, erected in the reign of Elizabeth, to which a small prison is attached. The living is a vicarage, in the archdeaconry of Essex, and diocese of London, rated in the king's books at £19. 8. 11½., and in the patronage of the Warden and Fellows of All Souls' College, Oxford. The church is dedicated to St. Margaret. There is a place of worship for Wesleyan Methodists. Sir James Campbell, in 1641, bequeathed £666. 13. 4. for founding and endowing a free school, which sum was invested in the purchase of a rent-charge of £20, on lands in the county of York. The school-house, having become ruinous, was taken down, and a workhouse erected on its site, in which the children of the poor are taught by a master and mistress, to whom the rent-charge is paid. In 1686, John Fowke, Esq. bequeathed certain estates for the maintenance of eight boys in Christ's Hospital, London, two of whom are to be chosen from this parish. National schools, for boys and girls, are supported by subscription, and a few of each sex are also clothed. An infant school, in which there are one hundred children, has been recently established. There are two unendowed almshouses, one containing four tenements, the other six.

BARKING, a parish in the hundred of BOSMERE and CLAYDON, county of SUFFOLK, 1¼ mile (S.W.) from Needham-Market, containing, with the chapelry of Needham-Market, 1687 inhabitants. The living is a rectory, in the archdeaconry of Suffolk, and diocese of Norwich, rated in the king's books at £27. 10. 7½., and in the patronage of the Earl of Ashburnham. The church is dedicated to St. Mary. There is also a chapel of ease at Darmsden, in this parish. In 1650, Francis Theobald bequeathed £30 per annum for the endowment of a free school, in which seventeen children are taught.

BARKISLAND, a township in the parish of HALIFAX, wapentake of MORLEY, West riding of the county of YORK, 5½ miles (S.W. by S.) from Halifax, containing 2224 inhabitants. The manufacture of worsted and woollen goods is carried on in the township. Sarah Gledhill, in 1657, endowed a school for twelve children, with property now producing about £40 per annum, at Ripponden in this township. Here is an almshouse for two widows.

BARKSTON, a parish in the soke of GRANTHAM, parts of KESTEVEN, county of LINCOLN, 3¾ miles (N.N.E.) from Grantham, containing 416 inhabitants. The living is a rectory, rated in the king's books at £13. 7. 6., and in the peculiar jurisdiction and patronage of the Prebendary of North Grantham in the Cathedral Church of Salisbury. The church is dedicated to St. Nicholas. There is a small endowment for instructing and apprenticing poor children, being part of the rent of some land given by Selina Towers, in 1718. An almshouse for six poor people is endowed with £43 per annum.

BARKSTON, a township in the parish of SHERBURN, upper division of the wapentake of BARKSTONE-ASH, West riding of the county of YORK, 5 miles (S. by E.) from Tadcaster, containing 251 inhabitants.

BARKSTONE, a parish in the hundred of FRAMLAND, county of LEICESTER, 6½ miles (S.E. by E.) from Bingham, containing 341 inhabitants. The living is a discharged vicarage, in the archdeaconry of Leicester, and diocese of Lincoln, rated in the king's books at £7. 5. 5., endowed with £200 royal bounty, and in the patronage of the Duke of Rutland. The church is dedicated to St. Peter and St. Paul. The Grantham and Nottingham canal passes through the parish. Daniel Smith endowed a school for the instruction of sixteen boys and sixteen girls.

BARKWAY, a parish (formerly a market town) in the hundred of EDWINSTREE, county of HERTFORD, 13¾ miles (N.N.E.) from Hertford, and 35 (N.) from London, on the road to Cambridge, containing, with the hamlet of Nuthampstead, 993 inhabitants. In the reign of Henry III. a grant of a market, now disused, and of a fair, which is still held on July 20th, was obtained for this place. Nearly the whole town was destroyed by fire in the reign of Elizabeth, and again in 1748. It is pleasantly situated on rising ground, and consists principally of one street, which is a great thoroughfare: the houses in general are modern and neatly built, and the inhabitants are well supplied with water. Constables and other officers are appointed at the court leet of the lord of the manor. The living is a vicarage, with the rectory of Reed, in the archdeaconry of Middlesex, and diocese of London, rated in the king's books at £14, and in the patronage of the Dowager Lady Selsea. The church, dedicated to St. Mary Magdalene, is a neat spacious structure with a tower. There is a place of worship for Independents. A charity school for twenty boys has an endowment of £10 per annum, and is further supported by subscription.

BARKWITH (EAST), a parish in the eastern division of the wapentake of WRAGGOE, parts of LINDSEY, county of LINCOLN, 3½ miles (N. E.) from Wragby, containing 195 inhabitants. The living is a discharged rectory, in the archdeaconry and diocese of Lincoln, rated in the king's books at £11. 10. 10., and in the patronage of G. R. Heneage, Esq. The church is dedicated to St. Mary.

BARKWITH (WEST), a parish in the eastern division of the wapentake of WRAGGOE, parts of LINDSEY, county of LINCOLN, 2½ miles (N. E.) from Wragby, containing 93 inhabitants. The living is a discharged rectory, in the archdeaconry and diocese of Lincoln, rated in the king's books at £5. 5., and in the patronage of C. D. Holland, Esq. The church is dedicated to All Saints.

BARLASTON, a parish in the southern division of the hundred of PIREHILL, county of STAFFORD, 4¼ miles (N. by W.) from Stone, containing 462 inhabitants. The living is a perpetual curacy, in the archdeaconry of Stafford, and diocese of Lichfield and Coventry, endowed with £750 private benefaction, and £600 royal bounty, and in the patronage of the Marquis of Stafford. The church, dedicated to St. John the Baptist, is a modern building of brick, with an ancient stone tower. The village is situated upon an eminence, commanding extensive, varied, and beautiful views. The Grand Trunk canal passes through the parish. There is a school for twenty-eight poor children, to which Thomas Mills, in 1800, bequeathed £12 per annum.

BARLAVINGTON, a parish in the hundred of ROTHERBRIDGE, rape of ARUNDEL, county of SUSSEX, 4½ miles (S.) from Petworth, containing 94 inhabitants. The living is a discharged rectory, in the archdeaconry and diocese of Chichester, rated in the king's books at £5. 13. 4., endowed with £200 royal bounty, and in the patronage of the Earl of Egremont.

BARLBOROUGH, a parish in the hundred of SCARSDALE, county of DERBY, 8 miles (N. E. by E.) from Chesterfield, containing 675 inhabitants. The living is a rectory, in the archdeaconry of Derby, and diocese of Lichfield and Coventry, rated in the king's books at £10. 1. 5½., and in the patronage of C. H. Rhodes, Esq. The church is dedicated to St. James. The turnpike roads from Chesterfield to Worksop, and from Sheffield to Mansfield, cross here at right angles. There are extensive collieries and mines of iron-stone in the vicinity. Margaret and Mary Pole, in 1752, founded an almshouse for six poor persons, and endowed it with an estate now producing £75 per annum. Barlborough Hall is a spacious interesting edifice of the Elizabethan era.

BARLBY, a chapelry in the parish of HEMINGBROUGH, wapentake of OUZE and DERWENT, East riding of the county of YORK, 1¾ mile (N. E. by E.) from Selby, containing 349 inhabitants. The living is a perpetual curacy, annexed to the vicarage of Hemingbrough, within the jurisdiction of the peculiar court of Howdenshire, endowed with £200 private benefaction, and £800 royal bounty. Here is a small endowed school.

BARLESTON, a chapelry in the parish of MARKET-BOSWORTH, hundred of SPARKENHOE, county of LEICESTER, 3 miles (N. E.) from Market-Bosworth, containing 617 inhabitants. The chapel is dedicated to St. Giles.

BARLEY, a parish in the hundred of EDWINSTREE, county of HERTFORD, 2¼ miles (N. E. by N.) from Barkway, containing 695 inhabitants. The living is a rectory, in the archdeaconry of Middlesex, and diocese of London, rated in the king's books at £26. 13. 4., and in the patronage of the Bishop of Ely. The church is dedicated to St. Margaret. There is a school with a small endowment.

BARLEY, a joint township with Whitley-Booths, in that part of the parish of WHALLEY which is in the higher division of the hundred of BLACKBURN, county palatine of LANCASTER, 5 miles (W. by N.) from Colne, containing, with Whitley-Booths, 765 inhabitants.

BARLEYTHORPE, a chapelry in the parish of OAKHAM-DEANSHOLD, soke of OAKHAM, county of RUTLAND, 1 mile (N. W. by W.) from Oakham. The population is returned with the parish. The chapel is dedicated to St. Peter.

BARLING, a parish in the hundred of ROCHFORD, county of ESSEX, 4¼ miles (E. N. E.) from Prittlewell, containing 293 inhabitants. The living is a vicarage, in the peculiar jurisdiction and patronage of the Dean and Chapter of St. Paul's, London, rated in the king's books at £18. The church is dedicated to All Saints.

BARLINGS, a parish in the wapentake of LAWRESS, parts of LINDSEY, county of LINCOLN, 6½ miles (E.N.E.) from Lincoln, containing 245 inhabitants. The living is a perpetual curacy, in the archdeaconry of Stow, and diocese of Lincoln, endowed with £1000 royal bounty, and in the patronage of John Dixon, Esq. The church is desecrated. A school is endowed with a rent-charge of £10. An abbey for Premonstratensian canons, dedicated to St. Mary, was founded in 1154, the revenue of which, at the dissolution, was £307. 16. 6. The last prior was Dr. Mackerel, who, having put himself at the head of an insurrection against the king's authority, was taken and executed, in 1536.

BARLOW, a chapelry in the parish of STAVELEY, hundred of SCARSDALE, county of DERBY, 3¾ miles (N. W. by W.) from Chesterfield, containing 708 inhabitants. The living is a perpetual curacy, in the archdeaconry of Derby, and diocese of Lichfield and Coventry, endowed with £400 and £10 per annum private benefaction, £400 royal bounty, and £1300 parliamentary grant, and in the patronage of the Rev. F. Gisborne. Here is a free school for ten poor children, with an endowment in land, augmented by a pecuniary donation by the Duke of Rutland.

BARLOW, a chapelry in the parish of BRAYTON, lower division of the wapentake of BARKSTONE-ASH, West riding of the county of YORK, 3¼ miles (S.E.) from Selby, containing 175 inhabitants.

BARMBY on the MARSH, a chapelry in the parish of HOWDEN, wapentake of HOWDENSHIRE, East riding of the county of YORK, 4¼ miles (W.) from Howden, containing 525 inhabitants. The living is a perpetual curacy, within the jurisdiction of the peculiar court of Howdenshire, endowed with £600 royal bounty, and in the patronage of the Vicar of Howden. The chapel is dedicated to St. Helen. There is a place of worship for

Wesleyan Methodists. Barmby is situated near the junction of the rivers Ouse and Derwent: the manufacture of sacking is carried on in the chapelry. A school is endowed for the instruction of ten boys. Here are two mineral springs, called St. Peter's and St. Helen's wells, one possessing a chalybeate, and the other a sulphureous, impregnation.

BARMBY on the MOOR, a parish (formerly a market town) within the liberty of St. Peter of York, though locally in the Wilton-Beacon division of the wapentake of Harthill, East riding of the county of York, 1¾ mile (W.) from Pocklington, containing 440 inhabitants. The living is a discharged vicarage, in the peculiar jurisdiction and patronage of the Dean of York, rated in the king's books at £5. 6. 8., and endowed with £400 royal bounty. The church is dedicated to St. Catherine. This was formerly a place of much greater importance, having received the grant of a weekly market, and various immunities, such as freedom from toll, &c., which the inhabitants still enjoy, subject to the payment of a small sum annually to the Dean and Chapter. There is a place of worship for Wesleyan Methodists. A fair is held on the Thursday preceding St. Peter's day. A school is endowed with land bequeathed by various individuals.

BARMER, in the hundred of Gallow, county of Norfolk, 5¾ miles (S. S. W.) from Burnham-Westgate, containing 25 inhabitants. The living is a perpetual curacy, in the archdeaconry of Norfolk, and diocese of Norwich, endowed with £400 royal bounty, and in the patronage of Thomas Kerslake, Esq. The church, which was dedicated to All Saints, is desecrated, and Barmer is now considered extra-parochial.

BARMING, a parish in the hundred of Maidstone, lathe of Aylesford, county of Kent, 2½ miles (W. by S.) from Maidstone, containing 406 inhabitants. The living is a rectory, in the archdeaconry and diocese of Rochester, rated in the king's books at £12. 17. 1., and in the patronage of the Crown. The church, which has a fine spire, is dedicated to St. Margaret. The river Medway, which runs through the parish, is crossed by a stone bridge leading to East Farleigh, and by another of wood, called St. Helen's bridge, on the road to West Farleigh. The soil in the neighbourhood is peculiarly adapted to the cultivation of hops, and a large quantity of fruit is sent to the London market. There was a Roman villa at this place, the foundations of which were taken up a few years ago, when coins of the Lower Empire, also of Edward I., and of later English monarchs, were found. Several urns have also been discovered in different parts of the parish. The abbess of St. Helen's, London, had a summer retreat here, but there are no remains of the house. The poet Smart resided upon his paternal estate in this parish; and the Rev. John Harris, D.D., author of a History of Kent, a Dictionary of Arts and Sciences, &c., formerly held the living.

BARMING (WEST), a hamlet (formerly a parish) in the parish of Nettlestead, hundred of Twyford, lathe of Aylesford, county of Kent. The living, which was a rectory, has been consolidated with that of Nettlestead, with which the population is returned. The church is desecrated. The river Medway, over which is a modern bridge, flows along the southern border of the hamlet.

BARMOOR, a township in the parish of Lowick, eastern division of Glendale ward, county of Northumberland, 7 miles (N. by E.) from Wooler. The population is returned with the parish. In 1417, the Lords Marchers assembled here, at the head of a force amounting to one hundred thousand men, against the Scots, who, on hearing of their approach, retreated within their own territory. The English army encamped in the vicinity prior to the battle of Flodden, on the night after which the English general slept at Barmoor wood. A fair was formerly held at Cross Hills, between this place and Lowick.

BARMPTON, a township in that part of the parish of Haughton le Skerne which is in the south-eastern division of Darlington ward, county palatine of Durham, 3¾ miles (N.E. by N.) from Darlington, containing 105 inhabitants.

BARMSTON, a township in the parish of Washington, eastern division of Chester ward, county palatine of Durham, 4¾ miles (W.) from Sunderland, containing 79 inhabitants. Here is an iron-foundry, on the banks of the river Wear.

BARMSTON, a parish in the northern division of the wapentake of Holderness, East riding of the county of York, 6½ miles (S. by W.) from Bridlington, containing 205 inhabitants. The living is a rectory, in the archdeaconry of the East riding, and diocese of York, rated in the king's books at £13. 11. 10½., and in the patronage of Sir F. Boynton, Bart. The church is dedicated to All Saints. There is a chapel in the township of Ulrome, which is partly in this parish, and partly in that of Skipsea. The village is pleasantly situated near the North sea, at the northern extremity of Holderness. A school-room, with a house for the master, has been erected by Sir Francis Boynton, Bart., lord of the manor; and an almshouse for four poor persons was founded, in 1726, by his ancestor, Sir Griffith Boynton, who endowed them with £15 per annum.

BARNACK, a parish in the liberty of Peterborough, county of Northampton, 4 miles (N.) from Wansford, containing, with the hamlets of Pilsgate and Southorpe, 649 inhabitants. The living is a rectory, in the archdeaconry of Northampton, and diocese of Peterborough, rated in the king's books at £28. 10., and in the patronage of the Bishop of Peterborough. The church, dedicated to St. John the Baptist, is an ancient structure with a square tower, the lower part of which is Norman; other parts of the edifice exhibit several varieties of English architecture. There are extensive quarries of excellent building stone near the village.

BARNACLE, a hamlet in the parish of Bulkington, Kirby division of the hundred of Knightlow, county of Warwick, 6 miles (N. E.) from Coventry, containing 219 inhabitants.

BARNACRE, a joint township with Bonds, in the parish of Garstang, hundred of Amounderness, county palatine of Lancaster, 2¼ miles (N. E.) from Garstang, containing, with Bonds, 548 inhabitants.

BARNARD-CASTLE, a market town and chapelry in that part of the parish of Gainford which is in the south-western division of Darlington ward, county palatine of Durham, 25 miles (S. W. by W.) from Durham, and 244 (N. N. W.) from London, containing 3581 inhabitants. This place is supposed to have originated, soon after the Conquest, from the decay of a more ancient town, called Marwood. About the year 1093, William II. having bestowed extensive possessions in the vicinity upon Guido Balliol, a Norman nobleman, who accompanied the Conqueror to England, and ancestor of the kings of Scotland, his eldest son Barnard, about 1178, built here a castle, and, by a grant of privileges, encouraged the erection of houses near it, thus laying the foundation of the present town, to which he imparted his own name. It was formerly a member of the ancient wapentake of Sadberge, and for a certain period was exempt from the jurisdiction of the palatinate, the illustrious family of Balliol, who held it for five successions, having exercised *jura regalia* within the franchise. Barnard Balliol, son of the founder, having espoused the cause of Galfrid, elect Bishop of Durham, the usurper Comyn despatched hither a party of soldiers, who committed great devastation, and exercised atrocious cruelty upon the inhabitants. Being forfeited to the crown, this barony, with its members, was granted to Guy Beauchamp, Earl of Warwick, and continued in the possession of his descendants until 1398, when it was given by Richard II. to Scroope, Earl of Wiltshire, but was restored, in the following year, to Thomas Beauchamp, Earl of Warwick, and subsequently passed by marriage, with Anna, daughter and coheiress of Richard Neville, Earl of Warwick, to Richard, Duke of Gloucester, afterwards Richard III., who, prior to ascending the throne, resided here, and whose crest may still be seen on the walls of the castle. In 1477, he obtained a license to found a college in the castle, for a dean and twelve secular priests, ten clerks, and six choristers, but it does not appear that this design was carried into effect. After frequent grants and reversions, the castle, honour, and privileges, with the parks, lands, and appurtenances, were purchased by an ancestor of the present Marquis of Cleveland, to whom they now belong. During the rebellion of the Earls of Northumberland and Westmorland, in the reign of Elizabeth, the castle, which then belonged to the latter nobleman, was seized and garrisoned by Sir George Bowes, of Streatham, who defended it against the insurgents, till he was relieved by the approach of the royal army. In the great civil war it was held for the king, and was besieged by Cromwell, to whom, after a severe cannonading, the garrison surrendered. After the battle of Newburn, in 1642, part of the Scottish army was quartered here. The ruins of this important baronial edifice occupy an area of nearly seven acres, on an elevated rock near the margin of the river Tees, indicating the strength and extent of the original structure: one of the towers was repaired some years ago, and fitted up as a shot-manufactory, and the inner area has been converted into a garden.

The town is situated on an eminence, rising abruptly from the southern bank of the Tees, the bridge over which was rebuilt about 1771, in which year it was swept away by a flood: it has undergone considerable improvement of late years, by the erection of new streets, and the removal of unsightly objects. The houses are built of white freestone, and have a very handsome appearance: the streets are well paved and lighted, and the inhabitants are amply supplied with water from springs in the neighbourhood. The environs are remarkably pleasant, and the vale of Tees abounds with romantic scenery. There are two book societies, one in conjunction with Staindrop. The principal articles manufactured are carpets, woollen plaids, and hats; and on the banks of the river there are several mills for spinning thread. The market is on Wednesday: fairs are held on the Wednesday in Easter and Whitsun weeks, for cattle and agricultural produce; a fair on St. Mary Magdalene's day has nearly fallen into disuse. The county magistrates hold a petty session on the first Wednesday in every month; a baronial court for the recovery of debts under 40*s.* is held quarterly; and constables and other officers are annually appointed at the court leet of the lord of the manor. The town hall, situated in the market-place, is an octagonal structure, erected in 1747, by Thos. Breaks, Esq.: the upper part is used for the transaction of business, and the lower for the market.

The living is a perpetual curacy, in the archdeaconry and diocese of Durham, endowed with £600 private benefaction, £200 royal bounty, and £1100 parliamentary grant, and in the patronage of the Vicar of Gainford. The chapel, dedicated to St. Mary, is an ancient and spacious cruciform structure, with a square embattled tower rising from the centre; it is partly Norman, and partly in the early and decorated styles of English architecture, with later insertions. There are places of worship for Independents and Primitive and Wesleyan Methodists. A National school is supported by subscription, and by the interest of £133, bequeathed by Mr. John Dent, for the instruction of ten poor boys. An hospital, for the residence and maintenance of three aged widows, was founded by John Balliol, about the 14th of Henry III., and dedicated to St. John the Baptist; the income is nearly £200 per annum. About two miles north-west of the town there is a chalybeate spring, which is approached by walks through highly varied scenery of the most pleasing description. A Roman coin of the Emperor Trajan was dug up in the churchyard, in 1824. Sir John Hullock, one of the late barons of the Exchequer; William Hutchinson, Esq., author of the History and Antiquities of the County of Durham, and various other works; and George Edwards, Esq., M.D., a political writer of considerable distinction, were natives of this place. Barnard gives the titles of viscount and baron to the Marquis of Cleveland.

BARNARDISTON, a parish in the hundred of RISBRIDGE, county of SUFFOLK, 4½ miles (N.W. by W.) from Clare, containing 164 inhabitants. The living is a discharged rectory, in the archdeaconry of Sudbury, and diocese of Norwich, rated in the king's books at £7. 10. 5., and in the patronage of the Rev. William Ellis. The church is dedicated to All Saints.

BARNBOW, a township in the parish of BARWICK in ELMETT, lower division of the wapentake of SKYRACK, West riding of the county of YORK, 7½ miles (E. N.E.) from Leeds, containing 273 inhabitants.

BARNBROUGH, a parish in the northern division of the wapentake of STRAFFORTH and TICKHILL, West riding of the county of YORK, 6¼ miles (W.) from Doncaster, containing 466 inhabitants. The living is a rectory, in the archdeaconry and diocese of York, rated in the king's books at £23, and in the patronage of the Chapter of the Collegiate Church of Southwell. The church is dedicated to St. Peter. There is a place of worship for Wesleyan Methodists. Here is a school with a small endowment for poor children.

BARNBY, a parish in the hundred of MUTFORD and LOTHINGLAND, county of SUFFOLK, 3¾ miles (E. by S.) from Beccles, containing 262 inhabitants. The living is a perpetual curacy, annexed to the rectory of Wheatacre All Saints, in the archdeaconry of Suffolk, and diocese of Norwich. The church is dedicated to St. John the Baptist.

BARNBY, a township in the parish of LYTHE, eastern division of the liberty of LANGBAURGH, North riding of the county of YORK, 5¼ miles (W. by N.) from Whitby, containing 270 inhabitants.

BARNBY upon DON, a parish in the southern division of the wapentake of STRAFFORTH and TICKHILL, West riding of the county of YORK, comprising the townships of Barnby upon Don and Thorpe in Balne, and containing 617 inhabitants, of which number, 495 are in the township of Barnby upon Don, 5¾ miles (N.E. by N.) from Doncaster. The living is a discharged vicarage, in the archdeaconry and diocese of York, rated in the king's books at £9. 12. 6., endowed with £200 private benefaction, £200 royal bounty, and £800 parliamentary grant, and in the patronage of J. Gresham, Esq. The church is dedicated to St. Peter. There is a place of worship for Wesleyan Methodists. A school for poor children is endowed with £11 per annum from the produce of land belonging to the parish, and £7. 10. bequeathed by John Martin, in 1798. Frances, Countess of Sutherland, in 1731, devised property, producing about £30 per annum, for the relief of four poor women, and for instructing poor children of Bramwith.

BARNBY in the WILLOWS, a parish in the southern division of the wapentake of NEWARK, county of NOTTINGHAM, 4¼ miles (E. by S.) from Newark, containing 247 inhabitants. The living is a discharged vicarage, in the archdeaconry of Nottingham, and diocese of York, rated in the king's books at £5. 9. 9½., and in the patronage of the Chapter of the Collegiate Church of Southwell. The church is dedicated to All Saints.

BARNBY-MOOR, a joint township with Bilby, in that part of the parish of BLYTH which is in the Hatfield division of the wapentake of BASSETLAW, county of NOTTINGHAM, 3½ miles (N.W.) from East Retford, containing, with Bilby, 182 inhabitants.

BARNES, a parish in the western division of the hundred of BRIXTON, county of SURREY, 5 miles (W. S.W.) from London, containing 1240 inhabitants. The village is pleasantly situated on the southern bank of the river Thames, and contains several well-built houses, particularly on the terrace, facing the river, which commands an extensive view of the opposite bank, and forms a peculiarly interesting promenade, from the constant traffic on the Thames, and the continued succession of pleasure boats passing between London and Richmond, and in other aquatic excursions. At Barn-Elms, in the vicinity, so called from a row of stately elm trees, there is an ancient mansion, called Queen Elizabeth's Dairy, which was afterwards the residence of Jacob Tonson, an eminent bookseller, who built a room for the meetings of the members of the "Kit-Kat-Club," portraits of some of whom adorned the walls; these have been since engraved and published, and among them are several of the most eminent English literati of the early part of the last century. Queen Elizabeth granted the manor-house to Sir Francis Walsingham, who, in 1589, entertained that sovereign and her court here: it was afterwards the residence of the Earl of Essex, who had espoused the daughter of Sir Francis, the widow of Sir Philip Sidney. A court leet is held by the lord of the manor, at which constables and other officers are appointed. The living is a rectory, in the peculiar jurisdiction of the Archbishop of Canterbury, rated in the king's books at £9. 3. 4., and in the patronage of the Dean and Chapter of St. Paul's, London. The church, dedicated to St. Mary, is an ancient edifice in the early style of English architecture, built of flint and freestone, with a square tower of brick, having an octagonal turret at one angle, which appears to have been added in 1500. There is an endowment, arising from the sum of £114, for the instruction of poor children; and a National school is supported by subscription. In 1653, Edward Rose, of London, left £20 to the poor of this parish, on condition that a tablet, erected to his memory, within a small enclosure planted with rose trees, in the churchyard, should be kept in repair. Robert Beale, who was employed by Elizabeth to communicate to Mary Queen of Scots the sentence which had been passed upon her, and afterwards sent to Fotheringay Castle, to see it carried into effect, died here in 1601. Cowley the poet resided here for some time.

BARNESLEY, a market town and chapelry in the parish of SILKSTONE, wapentake of STAINCROSS, and in the liberty of the honour of PONTEFRACT, West riding of the county of YORK, 14 miles (N.) from Sheffield, 38 (S. by W.) from York, and 177 (N.W. by N.) from London, containing 8284 inhabitants, according to the census of 1821, since which period the population has increased nearly one-third. This town, in Domesday-book called *Bernesleye*, is pleasantly situated on the acclivity of a hill, in a beautiful and richly-cultivated country, and consists of several streets, the principal of which is spacious, and contains many handsome buildings: the houses in general are built of stone obtained in the immediate neighbourhood. The town is paved, lighted with gas, watched, and regulated by commissioners appointed under the provisions of an act passed in the 3rd of George IV., and amply supplied with water from springs: considerable improvement has recently been made in the entrances and public roads. A subscription library was established in 1808, and a Philosophical Society in 1828; the members of the latter hold their meetings in the grammar school-room. The manufacture of steel wire formerly prevailed to a considerable extent, and constituted the staple trade till the close of the last century, when that of linen cloth was introduced, which is at present in a very flourishing state, and employs several thousand looms in the town and adjacent villages. The state of perfection which this branch of manufacture has attained enables the manufacturers to compete successfully with the Scotch and other markets. There are several extensive bleaching establishments, and two large calenders for finishing the cloths. The spinning of yarn is carried on to a limited extent; there are iron foundries; and the making of wire and brass is still continued on a smaller scale. Coal of excellent quality is obtained near the town; and the trade is greatly facilitated by communication with Wakefield and the West riding, by means of the Barnesley Canal Navigation and the river Calder, and with Hull and the Humber by the Dearne and Dove canal and the river Dunn. The market, on Wednesday, is free of toll for all kinds of grain; a smaller market for provisions has lately been established, which is held on Saturday. The fairs are on May 13th and October 11th, for cattle and horses; and there is a great market for live stock on the last Wednesday in February. Constables and other officers are appointed annually at the court leet of the lord of the manor; and a court for the honour of Pontefract is held on the Saturday in every third week, for the recovery of debts under £5. The living is a perpetual curacy, in the archdeaconry and diocese of York, endowed with £15 per annum and £200 private benefaction, and £800 royal bounty, and in the patronage of the Archbishop of York. The chapel, dedicated to St. Mary, has, with the exception of the tower, been rebuilt of freestone, dug in the vicinity, under an act obtained in the 59th of George III. A church, dedicated to St. George, was erected in 1823, by grant from the parliamentary commissioners, at an expense of £5918. 11. 4.; it is a neat plain edifice, in the English style of architecture, with a small tower: the living is a perpetual curacy, in the patronage of the Perpetual Curate of Barnesley. There are places of worship for the Society of Friends, Independents, Primitive and Wesleyan Methodists, and Roman Catholics. The free grammar school was founded and endowed, in 1665, by Mr. Thomas Keresforth, of Pule Hill. A National school, for children of both sexes, was erected in 1813, by the trustees of Elliss' charity. Mr. Elliss, in 1711, bequeathed land, directing the produce thereof to be applied, amongst other things, in purchasing books for twenty boys and girls of Barnesley, in compensation to a curate for catechising them, and in apprenticing a few of them. This town has the advantage of a very considerable estate, vested in trustees by Rodolph Bosville, of London, in 1558, who apply the rents for the general benefit of the inhabitants. Edmund Rogers also, by will in 1646, left an estate at Thorpe-Audlin for the benefit of the poorer inhabitants, for whom there is a yearly dole, called Cutler's charity, arising from lands devised by Thomas Cutler, in 1622, and his wife Ellen, in 1636. About a mile from the town are the remains of the Cluniac priory of Monk Bretton, founded in the 3rd of Henry II., by Adam Fitz-Swain, the revenue of which, at the dissolution, was £323. 8. 2.

BARNET (CHIPPING), a market town and parish in the hundred of Cashio, or liberty of St. Albans, county of Hertford, 14 miles (S. W. by S.) from Hertford, and 11 (N.) from London, on the great north road, containing 1755 inhabitants. This place, called also High Barnet, from its situation on the summit of a hill, derives its distinguishing name from the privilege, granted to the monks of St. Albans, of holding a market here. On the 5th of April, 1471, the decisive battle, which terminated in the defeat and death of the Earl of Warwick, and established Edward IV. on the throne, took place on Gladmore heath, a mile north-west of the town, in commemoration of which an obelisk was erected by Sir Jeremy Sambrook, at the junction of the roads from Hatfield and St. Albans, near Hadley common. The town, which is pleasantly situated, consists principally of one street, upwards of a mile in length: the houses, though interspersed occasionally with a few of more respectable appearance, are in general mean, and the inhabitants are but scantily supplied with water. A new road, entering from London, was made in 1826, by means of an embankment across the valley, at an expense of £15,000. The races, formerly held on Hadley common, and discontinued after its enclosure, have been lately revived. The market is on Monday, and is chiefly noted for the sale of pigs: a fair is held on April 8th and 9th, for cattle and horses, and on the 10th is a pleasure fair; another commences on the 4th of September, and continues the three following days, on the last of which the races are held. The magistrates for the liberty hold a meeting here on the first Thursday in every month; and the town is within the jurisdiction of a court, held at St. Albans, for the recovery of debts under 40*s.*: two constables and two headboroughs are appointed at the court leet of the lord of the manor, held at Easter.

The living is a perpetual curacy, united to the rectory of East Barnet, in the archdeaconry of St. Albans, and diocese of London. The church, dedicated to St. John the Baptist, was built by one of the abbots of St. Albans, in the fifteenth century: it is a venerable structure, in the style of that period, but has undergone several alterations. There is a place of worship for Independents. The free school was founded, in 1573, by Queen Elizabeth, for the gratuitous instruction of nine children; the rest pay 5*s.* per quarter. It was further endowed, in 1677, by Alderman Owen, and, in 1734, by the Rev. Humphrey Hall. There is also a National school, built at the expense of the parent institution, and supported partly by a bequest from Mrs. Allen, in 1725, and partly by subscription. Jesus' hospital, for six poor elderly women, was founded and endowed, in 1679, by James Ravenscroft, and further endowed with the residue of the produce of £500, left by Mrs. Barcock, in 1731, after distributing £10 to the poor. In 1729, Mr. John Garret founded and endowed six almshouses for aged widows; and six others, for aged men or women, were founded by Mr. Palmer, and endowed with part of an estate at Kentish Town, producing about £116 per annum. On Barnet common there is a mineral spring, the water of which contains a considerable portion of calcareous glauber, with a small portion of sea salt, and for the due care of it, Alderman Owen, in 1677, left £1 per annum.

BARNET (EAST), a parish in the hundred of Cashio, or liberty of St. Albans, county of Hertford, 10¼ miles (N.) from London, containing 507 inhabitants. The living is a rectory, with the perpetual curacy of Chipping-Barnet annexed, in the archdeaconry of St. Albans, and diocese of London, rated in the king's books at £22. 2. 8½., and in the patronage of the Crown. The church, dedicated to the Virgin Mary, is a very ancient structure, and formerly belonged to the monastery of St. Albans. A National school is supported by subscription. The village is pleasantly situated near the market town of Chipping-Barnet; the houses are neatly built, and the general appearance of the place pleasingly picturesque; the air is salubrious, but the supply of water is very scanty, and the quality not very good. On a hill opposite to the church, called Monk's Frith Garden, the abbots of St. Albans anciently had a villa; and in the neighbourhood are several mineral springs.

BARNET (FRYERN), a parish in the Finsbury division of the hundred of OSSULSTONE, county of MIDDLESEX, 8¾ miles (N. by W.) from London, containing, with the hamlet of Colney-Hatch, and a portion of that of Whetstone, 534 inhabitants. The living is a perpetual curacy, in the peculiar jurisdiction and patronage of the Dean and Chapter of St. Paul's, London. The church, dedicated to St. James, is a small and very ancient structure, in the Norman style of architecture: the chancel has been rebuilt within the last seven years. It is supposed that an abbey anciently existed here, and that the old manor-house, now taken down, was the summer residence of the abbots, to whom the manor belonged. The village contains several handsome houses, and the environs abound with pleasing scenery; the land is tithe-free, if cultivated by resident proprietors, but if let to tenants the exemption ceases. Courts leet and baron are held annually on the Friday in Whitsun-week. Almshouses for twelve aged persons were founded and endowed with £10 a year, in 1612, by Lawrence Kemp, Esq., of London. There is a school, supported by subscription. John Walker, an eminent philologist, and author of the English Pronouncing Dictionary, was born here, in 1732.

BARNET by the WOLD, a parish in the southern division of the wapentake of YARBOROUGH, parts of LINDSEY, county of LINCOLN, 5 miles (E. N. E.) from Glandford-Bridge, containing 316 inhabitants. The living is a discharged vicarage, in the archdeaconry and diocese of Lincoln, rated in the king's books at £6. 4. 2., and in the patronage of the Bishop of Lincoln. The church is dedicated to St. Mary.

BARNEY, a parish in the northern division of the hundred of GREENHOE, county of NORFOLK, 5 miles (E. N. E.) from Fakenham, containing 267 inhabitants. The living is a discharged vicarage, in the archdeaconry and diocese of Norwich, rated in the king's books at £6. 13. 4., and in the patronage of Sir J. D. Astley, Bart. The church is dedicated to St. Mary.

BARNHAM, a village in the hundred of BLACKBOURN, county of SUFFOLK, 3 miles (S.) from Thetford, comprising the parishes of St. Gregory and St. Martin, and containing 369 inhabitants: the living of St. Gregory's is rated in the king's books at £7. 11. 10½., and that of St. Martin's at £8. 5. 5.; they now form one consolidated rectory, with those of Euston and Little Fakenham united, in the archdeaconry of Sudbury, and diocese of Norwich, and in the patronage of the Duke of Grafton. The church of St. Gregory is the parochial church; St. Martin's is desecrated.

BARNHAM, a parish in the hundred of AVISFORD, rape of ARUNDEL, county of SUSSEX, 5½ miles (S. W. by W.) from Arundel, containing 173 inhabitants. The living is a discharged vicarage, in the archdeaconry and diocese of Chichester, rated in the king's books at £7. 15., endowed with £200 private benefaction, £600 royal bounty, and £200 parliamentary grant, and in the patronage of the Bishop of Chichester. The church is dedicated to St. Mary. The Arundel and Portsmouth canal passes through the parish.

BARNHAM-BROOM, a parish in the hundred of FOREHOE, county of NORFOLK, 4¾ miles (N. N. W.) from Wymondham, containing 388 inhabitants. The living is a rectory, united, with that of Bixton, to the vicarage of Kimberley, in the archdeaconry of Norfolk, and diocese of Norwich, rated in the king's books at £12. 8. 1½. The church is dedicated to St. Peter and St. Paul: there was formerly another, dedicated to St. Michael, but it is now desecrated. Here is a small endowment for the instruction of six poor children.

BARNHILL, a hamlet in the parish of MALPAS, higher division of the hundred of BROXTON, county palatine of CHESTER, 10 miles (S. E. by S.) from Chester. The population is returned with the parish. The petty sessions for the hundred are held here.

BARNINGHAM, a parish in the hundred of BLACKBOURN, county of SUFFOLK, 5¼ miles (N. N. E.) from Ixworth, containing 424 inhabitants. The living is a discharged rectory, with that of Coney-Weston annexed, in the archdeaconry of Sudbury, and diocese of Norwich, rated in the king's books at £13. 9. 2., and in the patronage of John Vernon, Esq. The church is dedicated to St. Andrew. There is a place of worship for Wesleyan Methodists.

BARNINGHAM, a parish in the western division of the wapentake of GILLING, North riding of the county of YORK, comprising the townships of Barningham, Hope, and Scargill, and containing 564 inhabitants, of which number, 384 are in the township of Barningham, 2 miles (S. S. W.) from Greta-Bridge. The living is a rectory, in the archdeaconry of Richmond, and diocese of Chester, rated in the king's books at £19. 17. 1., and in the patronage of the Crown. The church is dedicated to St. Michael. There is a place of worship for Wesleyan Methodists. A school, conducted on the National plan, is endowed with about £25 per annum: the school-room was rebuilt in 1820.

BARNINGHAM (LITTLE), a parish in the southern division of the hundred of ERPINGHAM, county of NORFOLK, 6 miles (N. W. by N.) from Aylsham, containing 233 inhabitants. The living is a discharged rectory, in the archdeaconry and diocese of Norwich, rated in the king's books at £5. 15. 2½., and in the patronage of J. Browne, Esq. and others. The church is dedicated to St. Andrew. A charter for a market and a fair was granted by Edward I. to Walter de Berningham, who at that time possessed the manor.

BARNINGHAM-NORWOOD, a parish in the northern division of the hundred of ERPINGHAM, county of NORFOLK, 5¼ miles (E. S. E.) from Holt, containing 82 inhabitants. The living is a discharged rectory, in the archdeaconry of Norfolk, and diocese of Norwich, rated in the king's books at £6. 13. 4. The Right Hon. W. Wyndham was patron in 1800. The church is dedicated to St. Mary.

BARNINGHAM-WINTER, a parish in the northern division of the hundred of ERPINGHAM, county of NORFOLK, 5½ miles (S. E. by E.) from Holt, containing 46 inhabitants. The living is a discharged rectory, in the archdeaconry of Norfolk, and diocese of Norwich, rated in the king's books at £6. 13. 4., and in the patronage of J. T. Mott, Esq. The church is dedicated to St. Peter. A grant of a market and a fair was obtained by Roger le Curzain, in the reign of Edward II.

BARNOLDBY le BECK, a parish in the wapentake of BRADLEY-HAVERSTOE, parts of LINDSEY, county of LINCOLN, 5¼ miles (S. W. by S.) from Grimsby, containing 220 inhabitants. The living is a rectory, in the archdeaconry and diocese of Lincoln, rated in the king's books at £14. 13. 4., and in the patronage of the Chapter of the Collegiate Church of Southwell. The church is dedicated to St. Helen. There are two almshouses, and a school for poor children, endowed with £10 per annum; and the children of this parish are also entitled to instruction at the school at Laceby, founded and endowed by Mrs. Sarah Stamford, in 1820.

BARNOLDWICK, a parish in the eastern division of the wapentake of STAINCLIFFE and EWCROSS, West riding of the county of YORK, comprising the townships of Barnoldwick, Brogden, Coates, and Salterforth, and containing 2350 inhabitants, of which number, 1334 are in the township of Barnoldwick, 9 miles (W. S. W.) from Skipton. The living is a perpetual curacy, in the peculiar jurisdiction of the Lord of the Manor, endowed with £200 private benefaction, £1100 royal bounty, and £1000 parliamentary grant, and in the patronage of Sir J. L. Kaye, Bart. The church, dedicated to St. Mary, stands on the verge of a deep glen, whence it was formerly known by the name of Gill Kirk. There are places of worship for Particular Baptists and Wesleyan Methodists. A Cistercian monastery was founded here in 1147, which was afterwards removed to Kirkstall, owing to some dissension among the monks and the inhabitants.

BARNSLEY, a parish in the hundred of BRIGHTWELL'S BARROW, county of GLOUCESTER, 4½ miles (E. N. E.) from Cirencester, containing 318 inhabitants. The living is a rectory, within the peculiar jurisdiction of the Vicar of Bibury, rated in the king's books at £13. 15. 5., and in the patronage of Sir James Musgrave, Bart. The church is dedicated to St. Mary. Here are quarries of good freestone.

Seal and Arms.

BARNSTAPLE, a port, borough, market town, and parish, having separate jurisdiction, locally in the hundred of Braunton, county of DEVON, 38 miles (N. W.) from Exeter, 8 (N. E.) from Bideford, and 193 (W. by S.) from London, containing 5079 inhabitants. This place, a Saxon burgh in the reign of Athelstan, was formerly a port of considerable trade, and a principal depôt for wool, from which circumstance it seems to have derived its name. In 1588, it fitted out three ships for the fleet of Elizabeth, to repel the Spanish Armada; and during the civil war in the reign of Charles I. it was distinguished for its adherence to the cause of the parliament, and was the scene of frequent conflicts, being alternately in the possession of each party, till its final surrender to General Fairfax, in 1646, when it was again taken possession of by Sir Thomas Fairfax. In 1606, it suffered considerably from a great flood, which inundated the town, and did much damage to the property of the inhabitants. Barnstaple is pleasantly situated in a fertile vale, sheltered by a semicircular range of hills, on the eastern bank of the river Taw, over which there is a fine stone bridge of sixteen arches. The town consists of several spacious and well-paved streets, containing many handsome houses, and is plentifully supplied with excellent water, brought by pipes from the distance of half a mile. The air is salubrious, and a walk, extending about a quarter of a mile along the winding bank of the river, which here expands into a fine bay, forms an agreeable promenade, at the end of which is a handsome piazza of the Doric order, surmounted by a statue of Queen Anne. A theatre is occasionally opened, and there are assembly and billiard rooms. The trade of the port consists principally in the importation of deals from North America and the Baltic, lime from Wales, and coal, culm, and other commodities from Bristol; and in the exportation of corn, oak timber, and bark, in which, according to the return made to parliament in 1828, forty-two vessels, averaging fifty-two tons' burden, were employed. The quay, upon which stands the custom-house, is commodious and extensive; but, from the accumulation of sand, by which the navigation of the river is obstructed, it is not accessible to vessels of more than one hundred tons' burden. Within the last few years Barnstaple has obtained the privilege of bonding wine, spirits, and other articles of colonial produce. Manufactories for serge and inferior broad cloth have recently been established; there are others for patent lace, affording employment to about eight hundred persons; and in the vicinity are six tan-yards, a paper-mill, and an iron-foundry; a great quantity of earthenware, bricks, and tiles, is also made here. Limestone abounds in the neighbourhood, and lead-ore has been discovered. The market is on Friday; and there are great markets on the Friday before the 21st of April, and the second Friday in December; a cattle market, for which this place is celebrated, is also held monthly. A fair, for horses, cattle, and sheep, commences on September 19th, and continues three days.

The government, by charter of Edward I., subsequently confirmed and extended by Edward IV., Mary, and James I., is vested in a mayor, high steward, recorder, and deputy recorder, a senior and a junior alderman, and twenty-two common council-men, assisted by a town clerk, two serjeants at mace, and subordinate officers. The mayor is elected by a majority of the corporation, annually on the Monday after the festival of St. Faith, and sworn into office in October: on retiring from office he becomes senior alderman, and the following year junior alderman. The mayor, deputy recorder (who must be a barrister of three years' standing), and the two aldermen, are justices of the peace, and hold a court of session quarterly for the borough, with power to imprison and transport; and a court of record is held, every alternate Monday, for the recovery of debts to any amount. The guildhall is a spacious handsome building, erected by the corporation in 1812; the lower part is appropriated to the use of the market. A new prison, containing twenty cells, has recently been erected upon the improved plan. The freedom of the borough is inherited by birth, or acquired by servitude. The elective franchise was granted in the reign of Edward I., since which time Barnstaple has continued to return two members to parliament: the right of election is vested in the free burgesses generally, in number about six hundred, of whom about one-third are resident: the mayor is the returning officer.

The living is a discharged vicarage, in the archdeaconry of Barnstaple, and diocese of Exeter, rated in the king's books at £15. 8. 9., and in the patronage of

Lord Wharncliffe. The church, dedicated to St. Peter and St. Paul, is a spacious ancient structure, with a spire. There are places of worship for Particular Baptists, Independents, and Wesleyan Methodists. The free grammar school was founded and endowed, in 1649, by R. Ferris, Esq., and a small annuity was added, in 1760, by the Rev. John Wright: the management is vested in the corporation, who appoint the master. The school-house is an ancient building, which formerly belonged to a Cluniac monastery, founded here by Johel de Totnes, soon after the Conquest. John Jewel, Bishop of Salisbury; Thomas Harding, the Jesuit professor at Louvain; and the poet Gay, who was born in the neighbourhood; were educated at this school. A charity school, for clothing and educating fifty boys and twenty girls, was founded in 1710, and is supported by the rent of lands purchased with several benefactions. The National school, in which one hundred and fifty children are instructed, was founded in 1813, and is supported by subscription; and there is also a school for twenty girls, who are taught reading, sewing, and knitting. Litchdon almshouse, an ancient building, consisting of a centre and two wings, in one of which is a chapel, was founded in 1624, and endowed with a considerable estate, by John Penrose, Esq., for forty aged persons of either sex: it is under the direction of two trustees, and the mayor nominates to the first vacancy that occurs during his office. Horwood's almshouses, for sixteen poor people, founded in 1658, and Paige's almshouses, founded in 1553, and enlarged in 1656, are both endowed by their respective founders. The North Devon infirmary, a lofty modern building south-east of the town, was erected under the patronage of Lord Fortescue, and is supported by subscription. On the quay there is an ancient building, now appended to the custom-house, said to have been a chantry chapel, dedicated to St. Anne.

BARNSTON, a township in the parish of WOODCHURCH, lower division of the hundred of WIRRALL, county palatine of CHESTER, 4½ miles (N. by W.) from Great Neston, containing 93 inhabitants. The Grand Trunk canal here passes through a tunnel five hundred and fifty yards long.

BARNSTON, a parish in the hundred of DUNMOW, county of ESSEX, 2¼ miles (S. E.) from Great Dunmow, containing 218 inhabitants. The living is a rectory, in the archdeaconry of Middlesex, and diocese of London, rated in the king's books at £13, and in the patronage of J. Toke, Esq. The steeple of the church was destroyed by lightning in 1665.

BARNSTONE, a chapelry in the parish of LANGAR, northern division of the wapentake of BINGHAM, county of NOTTINGHAM, 1 mile (N.E.) from Langar, with which the population is returned.

BARNTON, a township in that part of the parish of GREAT BUDWORTH which is in the hundred of BUCKLOW, county palatine of CHESTER, 1¾ mile (N.W. by W.) from Northwich, containing 612 inhabitants. There is a place of worship for Wesleyan Methodists.

BARNWELL (ALL SAINTS), a parish in the hundred of HUXLOE, county of NORTHAMPTON, 2¼ miles (S.E. by E.) from Oundle, containing 115 inhabitants. The living is a rectory, united to that of Barnwell St. Andrew by act of parliament in 1821, in the archdeaconry of Northampton, and diocese of Peterborough, rated in the king's books at £15. 6. 8., and in the patronage of Lord Montague.

BARNWELL (ST. ANDREW), a parish in the hundred of POLEBROOK, county of NORTHAMPTON, 2 miles (S. by E.) from Oundle, containing 255 inhabitants. The living is a rectory, with that of Barnwell All Saints united, in 1821, in the archdeaconry of Northampton, and diocese of Peterborough, rated in the king's books at £17. 2. 1., and in the patronage of Lord Montague. The church is an ancient structure in the early style of English architecture, with a tower and spire, and has some portions of a later date. There is an endowed free school for poor children, also an almshouse for fourteen infirm men and women. In the reign of Henry I. a castle was erected here, by Reginald le Moine, of which there are considerable remains, including the principal gateway.

BARNWOOD, a parish in the upper division of the hundred of DUDSTONE and KING'S BARTON, county of GLOUCESTER, 1½ mile (E. S. E.) from Gloucester, containing 392 inhabitants. The living is a perpetual curacy, in the archdeaconry and diocese of Gloucester, endowed with £30 per annum private benefaction, and £400 royal bounty, and in the patronage of the Dean and Chapter of Gloucester. The church is dedicated to St. Lawrence. The Gloucester and Cheltenham railway passes through the parish, which is also intersected by the Roman Foss-way. There is a small endowment for the instruction of poor children.

BARONY, a township in that part of the parish of ST. ANDREW AUCKLAND which is in the north-western division of DARLINGTON ward, county palatine of DURHAM, containing 479 inhabitants. It is situated on the north side of the river Gaunless, over which there is a bridge to Evenwood. The Bishop of Durham, as lord of the manor, holds courts leet and baron in March and October, at which debts to the amount of 40s. are recoverable.

BARR (GREAT), a chapelry in the parish of ALDRIDGE, southern division of the hundred of OFFLOW, county of STAFFORD, 3¼ miles (S. E.) from Walsall, containing 763 inhabitants. The living is a perpetual curacy, in the archdeaconry of Stafford, and diocese of Lichfield and Coventry. The chapel is dedicated to St. Margaret. John Addyes, in 1722, bequeathed property for the erection and endowment of a free school for thirteen boys, which by subsequent benefactions has been augmented for twenty, who receive an English education and are clothed. There is also a girls' school, supported by trifling bequests, in which five children are taught to read, write, and sew.

BARR (PERRY), a hamlet in the parish of HANDSWORTH, southern division of the hundred of OFFLOW, county of STAFFORD, 4 miles (N.) from Birmingham, containing 777 inhabitants.

BARRASFORD, a township in the parish of CHOLLERTON, north-eastern division of TINDALE ward, county of NORTHUMBERLAND, 7 miles (N. by W.) from Hexham, containing 193 inhabitants. Robert de Umfranville, in 1303, obtained license from Edward I. to hold a market here on Wednesdays, and a fair on November 11th, both which however have been discontinued.

BARRAWAY, a chapelry in the parish of SOHAM, hundred of STAPLOE, county of CAMBRIDGE, 2¼ miles

(S.S.E.) from Ely. The population is returned with the parish. The chapel is dedicated to St. Nicholas.

BARRINGTON, a parish in the hundred of WETHERLEY, county of CAMBRIDGE, 6¾ miles (S. W. by S.) from Cambridge, containing 483 inhabitants. The living is a discharged vicarage, in the archdeaconry and diocese of Ely, rated in the king's books at £7. 14. 4., endowed with £200 private benefaction, and £200 royal bounty, and in the patronage of the Master and Fellows of Trinity College, Cambridge. The church is dedicated to All Saints. The Master and Fellows pay £6 per annum towards the support of a school for poor children.

BARRINGTON, a parish in the southern division of the hundred of PETHERTON, county of SOMERSET, 3¾ miles (N. E.) from Ilminster, containing 453 inhabitants. The living is a perpetual curacy, in the archdeaconry of Taunton, and diocese of Bath and Wells, endowed with £800 private benefaction, and in the patronage of the Rev. Dr. W. Palmer. Hemp and flax are extensively cultivated here.

BARRINGTON (GREAT), a parish partly in the hundred of FARRINGDON, county of BERKS, but chiefly in the lower division of the hundred of SLAUGHTER, county of GLOUCESTER, 3¼ miles (N. W.) from Burford, containing 462 inhabitants. The living is a discharged vicarage, in the archdeaconry and diocese of Gloucester, rated in the king's books at £7. 6. 8., and in the patronage of Lord Dynevor. The church, which stands in the county of Gloucester, is dedicated to St. Mary: it is a handsome edifice, with a tower terminating in battlements and pinnacles, in the latest style of English architecture. The Windrush, a stream tributary to the Thames, runs through the parish. There are quarries of excellent freestone, from which the stone used in the erection and reparation of Westminster Abbey and Blenheim House was dug.

BARRINGTON (LITTLE), a parish in the lower division of the hundred of SLAUGHTER, county of GLOUCESTER, 3 miles (W.N.W.) from Burford, containing 159 inhabitants. The living is a discharged vicarage, in the archdeaconry and diocese of Gloucester, rated in the king's books at £4. 19. 2., and in the patronage of the Crown. The church is dedicated to St. Peter. Here are a parochial and a Sunday school, supported by the surplus revenue of an estate left for repairing the church.

BARRON'S-PARK, a hamlet in the parish of DESFORD, hundred of SPARKENHOE, county of LEICESTER, 5 miles (W.) from Leicester, containing 8 inhabitants.

BARROW, a parish in the second division of the hundred of EDDISBURY, county palatine of CHESTER, 5 miles (E.N.E.) from Chester, comprising the townships of Great Barrow and Little Barrow, and containing 642 inhabitants, of which number, 393 are in the township of Great Barrow. The living is a rectory, in the archdeaconry and diocese of Chester, rated in the king's books at £19. 6. 5½., and in the patronage of the Marquis of Cholmondeley. The church is dedicated to St. Bartholomew. A school for poor children is endowed with about £6 per annum. A preceptory of the Knights Hospitallers, founded here in the reign of Henry II., was valued, at the dissolution, at £107. 3. 8.

BARROW, a parish partly in the hundred of APPLETREE, and partly in the hundred of MORLESTON and LITCHURCH, county of DERBY, 5¾ miles (S.) from Derby, comprising the chapelry of Twyford, the township of Stenson, and the liberty of Synfin with Arleston, and containing 617 inhabitants. The living is a discharged vicarage, in the archdeaconry of Derby, and diocese of Lichfield and Coventry, rated in the king's books at £5. 6. 5½., endowed with £200 royal bounty, and in the patronage of Lord Scarsdale. The church is dedicated to St. Wilfrid. The parish is bounded on the south by the river Trent, and is intersected by the Trent and Mersey canal. There is a school with an endowment of £8 per annum, the gift of Elizabeth Saly, in 1702, for eight poor girls. A preceptory of Knights Commanders formerly existed here.

BARROW, a township in the parish of HALLYSTONE, western division of COQUETDALE ward, county of NORTHUMBERLAND, 22 miles (W. by S.) from Alnwick, containing 17 inhabitants.

BARROW, a chapelry in the parish of COTTESMORE, hundred of ALSTOE, county of RUTLAND, 5 miles (N. by E.) from Oakham, containing 105 inhabitants.

BARROW, a parish within the liberties of the borough of WENLOCK, county of SALOP, 3½ miles (E. by S.) from Much Wenlock, containing 462 inhabitants. The living is a perpetual curacy, in the archdeaconry of Salop, and diocese of Hereford, endowed with £200 private benefaction, £800 royal bounty, and £300 parliamentary grant, and in the patronage of the Vicar of Much Wenlock. The church is dedicated to St. Giles. Here is a free school for twenty boys, to which £10 per annum was bequeathed, in 1631, by John Slaney, who also founded and endowed an almshouse for six poor men or women.

BARROW, a tything in the parish of KINGSBURY-EPISCOPI, eastern division of the hundred of KINGSBURY, county of SOMERSET, 5 miles (N. N. E.) from Ilminster. The population is returned with the parish.

BARROW, a parish in the hundred of THINGOE, county of SUFFOLK, 6¾ miles (W.) from Bury St. Edmund's, containing 755 inhabitants. The living is a rectory, in the archdeaconry of Sudbury, and diocese of Norwich, rated in the king's books at £23. 9. 9½., and in the patronage of the Master and Fellows of St. John's College, Cambridge. The church is dedicated to All Saints. There is an endowment of about £30 per annum for the education of poor children.

BARROW upon HUMBER, a parish in the northern division of the wapentake of YARBOROUGH, parts of LINDSEY, county of LINCOLN, 2¼ miles (E.) from Barton upon Humber, containing 1307 inhabitants. The living is a discharged vicarage, in the archdeaconry and diocese of Lincoln, rated in the king's books at £9. 16., and in the patronage of the Crown. The church is dedicated to the Holy Trinity. There are places of worship for Particular Baptists and Wesleyan Methodists. Six poor children are instructed from the produce of some land devised by Richard Beck, in 1728. About a mile north-westward from the village is an intrenchment, called the Castle, supposed to have been a British camp; and near it are several barrows. A monastery was founded here, about the middle of the seventh century, by Wulphere, King of Mercia.

BARROW (LITTLE), a township in the parish of BARROW, hundred of EDDISBURY, county palatine of CHESTER, 5½ miles (N. E. by E.) from Chester, containing 249 inhabitants.

BARROW (NORTH), a parish in the hundred of Catsash, county of Somerset, 2¾ miles (S. W.) from Castle-Cary, containing 142 inhabitants. The living is a discharged rectory, in the archdeaconry of Wells, and diocese of Bath and Wells, rated in the king's books at £7. 17. 8½., and in the patronage of E. B. Portman, Esq. The church is dedicated to St. Nicholas.

BARROW upon SOAR, a parish partly in the eastern, but chiefly in the western, division of the hundred of Goscote, county of Leicester, 2 miles (W.) from Mountsorrel, comprising the chapelries of Mountsorrel, Quorndon, and Woodhouse, and containing 5560 inhabitants. The living is a vicarage, in the archdeaconry of Leicester, and diocese of Lincoln, rated in the king's books at £15. 2. 8½., and in the patronage of the Master and Fellows of St. John's College, Cambridge. The church is dedicated to the Holy Trinity. There is a place of worship for Wesleyan Methodists. Barrow is a large and pleasant village, situated near the river Soar. For many centuries it has been noted for a very fine kind of lime, which is made from a hard blue stone obtained in the vicinity; a considerable quantity is exported to Holland, and elsewhere. The Loughborough canal passes through the parish. The free grammar school is endowed with land producing £55 per annum, bequeathed by the Rev. Humphrey Perkins, in 1717. A school for six poor children has a small endowment, the produce of various benefactions. An almshouse for six poor widows, or aged bachelors, was founded in 1686, by the Rev. Humphrey Babington, who endowed it with an estate, now producing £200 per annum; he also left a fund for other charitable purposes. Dr. William Beveridge, the learned bishop of St. Asaph, was born here, in 1638; he bequeathed a rent-charge of £2 for eight poor housekeepers in this parish.

BARROW (SOUTH), a parish in the hundred of Catsash, county of Somerset, 3¾ miles (S. W. by S.) from Castle-Cary, containing 155 inhabitants. The living is a perpetual curacy, in the peculiar jurisdiction and patronage of the Dean and Chapter of Wells, endowed with £200 private benefaction, and £1100 royal bounty. The church is dedicated to St. Peter.

BARROW-GURNEY, a parish in the hundred of Hartcliffe with Bedminster, county of Somerset, 5½ miles (S.W.) from Bristol, containing 285 inhabitants. The living is a donative, in the patronage of Montague Gore, Esq. A Benedictine nunnery was founded here about 1200, the revenue of which, at the dissolution, was valued at £29. 6. 8.: the site is now occupied by a fine old mansion in the Elizabethan style.

BARROWBY, a parish in the wapentake of Winnibriggs and Threo, parts of Kesteven, county of Lincoln, 2 miles (W.) from Grantham, containing 671 inhabitants. The living is a rectory, in the archdeaconry and diocese of Lincoln, rated in the king's books at £31. 1. 5½, and in the patronage of the Duke of Devonshire. The church is dedicated to All Saints. At Neubo, in this parish, Richard de Malebisse, in 1198, founded an abbey of Premonstratensian canons, in honour of the Blessed Virgin, which at the dissolution had a revenue of £115. 11. 8.

BARROWDEN, a parish in the hundred of Wrandike, county of Rutland, 5¼ miles (E.) from Uppingham, containing 524 inhabitants. The living is a rectory, in the archdeaconry of Northampton, and diocese of Peterborough, rated in the king's books at £14. 13. 1½., and in the patronage of the Marquis of Exeter. The church is dedicated to St. Peter.

BARROWFORD, a township in that part of the parish of Whalley which is in the higher division of the hundred of Blackburn, county palatine of Lancaster, 2½ miles (W.) from Colne, containing 2168 inhabitants. There is a place of worship for Wesleyan Methodists. The spinning and manufacture of cotton prevails extensively in this township.

BARSBY, a chapelry in the parish of Ashby-Folville, eastern division of the hundred of Goscote, county of Leicester, 6 miles (S. W. by S.) from Melton-Mowbray, containing 242 inhabitants.

BARSHAM, a parish in the hundred of Wangford, county of Suffolk, 1¾ mile (W. by S.) from Beccles, containing 192 inhabitants. The living is a rectory, in the archdeaconry of Suffolk, and diocese of Norwich, rated in the king's books at £15. 6. 8., and in the alternate patronage of the Crown, and S. Lillistone, Esq. The church is dedicated to the Holy Trinity.

BARSHAM (EAST), a parish in the hundred of Gallow, county of Norfolk, 2¼ miles (N.) from Fakenham, containing 203 inhabitants. The living is a discharged vicarage, united to the rectory of Little Snoring, in the archdeaconry of Norfolk, and diocese of Norwich, rated in the king's books at £6. 13. 4., and endowed with £200 royal bounty. The church is dedicated to All Saints.

BARSHAM (NORTH), a parish in the hundred of Gallow, county of Norfolk, 2 miles (S. W. by W.) from Little Walsingham, containing 66 inhabitants. The living is a discharged rectory, in the archdeaconry of Norfolk, and diocese of Norwich, rated in the king's books at £6, and in the patronage of the Earl of Orford. The church is dedicated to All Saints.

BARSHAM (WEST), a parish in the hundred of Gallow, county of Norfolk, 2¾ miles (N. N. W.) from Fakenham, containing 66 inhabitants. The living is a discharged vicarage, in the archdeaconry of Norfolk, and diocese of Norwich, rated in the king's books at £5. 12. 1., endowed with £200 royal bounty, and in the patronage of Lady Mary Balders. A fair was formerly held here, but it has long been discontinued.

BARSTON, a parish in the Solihull division of the hundred of Hemlingford, county of Warwick, 4¼ miles (E. by S.) from Solihull, containing 344 inhabitants. The living is a perpetual curacy, annexed to the rectory of Berkeswell, in the peculiar jurisdiction of the lord of the manor. The church is dedicated to St. Swithin.

BARTESTREE, a chapelry in the parish of Dormington, hundred of Greytree, county of Hereford, 4⅓ miles (E.) from Hereford, containing 57 inhabitants. The living is a perpetual curacy, united to the vicarage of Lugwardine, in the archdeaconry and diocese of Hereford, endowed with £200 private benefaction, and £200 royal bounty. The chapel is dedicated to St. James.

BARTHERTON, a township in the parish of Wybunbury, hundred of Nantwich, county palatine of Chester, 2¼ miles (S. S. E.) from Nantwich, containing 29 inhabitants. The Grand Trunk canal passes in the vicinity.

BARTHOLOMEW-HOSPITAL (ST.), an extra-parochial liberty, in the hundred of EASTRY, lathe of ST. AUGUSTINE, county of KENT, ¾ of a mile (S.) from Sandwich, containing 61 inhabitants. The hospital, which is under the government of the corporation of Sandwich, was founded and liberally endowed, about 1190, by Sir Henry Sandwich, for the support of a master, brethren, and sisters, each of whom has a house and garden, with a considerable pecuniary allowance.

BARTHOLOMEW-HYDE-STREET (ST.), a parish partly in the city of WINCHESTER, and partly in the liberty of SOKE, county of SOUTHAMPTON, containing 730 inhabitants. The living is a discharged vicarage, in the archdeaconry and diocese of Winchester, rated in the king's books at £10, and in the patronage of the Crown. A Benedictine abbey, originally founded by Alfred the Great, on the northern side of Winchester cathedral, was re-erected here, in 1110, and richly endowed by Henry I. and other benefactors: it was one of the mitred parliamentary abbeys, and its revenue, at the dissolution, was £865. 13.: a small portion of the monastic buildings is remaining. For a more detailed account, see WINCHESTER.

BARTHOMLEY, a parish comprising the township of Batterley, in the northern division of the hundred of PIREHILL, county of STAFFORD, and the chapelries of Alsager and Haslington, and the townships of Barthomley and Crewe, in the hundred of NANTWICH, county palatine of CHESTER, and containing 2333 inhabitants, of which number, 450 are in the township of Barthomley, 6½ miles (S. by E.) from Sandbach. The living is a rectory, in the archdeaconry and diocese of Chester, rated in the king's books at £25. 7. 1., and in the patronage of Lord Crewe. The church, dedicated to St. Bertoline, exhibits various styles of architecture; it has a Norman porch on the northern side of the chancel. A school is endowed with about £10 per annum, the produce of various benefactions.

BARTHORPE, a joint township with Acklam, in the parish of ACKLAM, partly in the liberty of ST. PETER of YORK, and partly in the wapentake of BUCKROSE, East riding of the county of YORK, 9½ miles (S. by W.) from New Malton. The population is returned with Acklam.

BARTINGTON, a township in that part of the parish of GREAT BUDWORTH which is in the hundred of BUCKLOW, county palatine of CHESTER, 3¾ miles (N.W. by W.) from Northwich, containing 81 inhabitants.

BARTLOW, a parish in the hundred of CHILFORD, county of CAMBRIDGE, 1¾ mile (E. S. E.) from Linton, containing 94 inhabitants. The living is a rectory, in the archdeaconry and diocese of Ely, rated in the king's books at £19. 16. 8., and in the patronage of W. Hall, Esq. The church, dedicated to St. Mary, has a circular tower, apparently of Norman architecture.

BARTLOW-END, a hamlet in the parish of ASHDON, hundred of FRESHWELL, county of ESSEX, 2¼ miles (S. E.) from Linton, containing 212 inhabitants. It is supposed to have been formerly a distinct parish: in all temporal concerns it is included within the parish of Ashdon, and is in the jurisdiction of the magistracy for the county of Essex; but, as regards spiritual jurisdiction, it is considered to be in the parish of Bartlow, county of Cambridge, to which the inhabitants of this hamlet pay church rates, and resort to the parochial church there. Bartlow Hills are four noted hills supposed to have been thrown up by the Danes, as monumental memorials, after the sanguinary battle fought, in 1016, between Canute and Edmund Ironside, in which the latter was defeated.

BARTON, a parish in the hundred of WETHERLEY, county of CAMBRIDGE, 3¾ miles (W. S. W.) from Cambridge, containing 273 inhabitants. The living is a vicarage, in the archdeaconry and diocese of Ely, rated in the king's books at £8. 11. 3., and in the patronage of the Bishop of Ely. The church is dedicated to St. Peter.

BARTON, a township in the parish of FARNDON, higher division of the hundred of BROXTON, county palatine of CHESTER, 9½ miles (S. S. E.) from Chester, containing 168 inhabitants.

BARTON, a joint township with Bradnor and Rustrock, in the parish of KINGTON, hundred of HUNTINGTON, county of HEREFORD, ¾ of a mile (N. E.) from Kington, containing, with Bradnor and Rustrock, 357 inhabitants.

BARTON, a township in the parish of PRESTON, hundred of AMOUNDERNESS, county palatine of LANCASTER, 5¾ miles (N. N. W.) from Preston, containing 414 inhabitants.

BARTON, a parish in the northern division of the wapentake of RUSHCLIFFE, county of NOTTINGHAM, 6¾ miles (S. W. by S.) from Nottingham, containing 403 inhabitants. The living is a rectory, in the archdeaconry of Nottingham, and diocese of York, rated in the king's books at £19. 3. 9., and in the patronage of the Archbishop of York. The church is dedicated to St. George. The navigable river Trent runs along the border of the parish. There is an intrenchment on a hill near the village, which, from the coins found, is supposed to have been constructed by the Britons.

BARTON, a parish in WEST ward, county of WESTMORLAND, comprising the chapelries of Hartsop with Patterdale, and Martindale, and the townships of High Barton, Low Winder, Sockbridge, and Yanwath with Eamont-Bridge, and containing 1212 inhabitants, of which number, 322 are in the township of High Barton, 4 miles (S. W. by S.) from Penrith. The living is a vicarage, in the archdeaconry and diocese of Carlisle, rated in the king's books at £11. 1. 0½., and in the patronage of the Earl of Lonsdale. The church, dedicated to St. Michael, is a large low structure, beautifully situated in the vale of Eamont. This parish includes part of the lake of Ullswater, from which flows the river Eamont, separating Westmorland from Cumberland: at its western extremity is the lofty mountain Helvellyn, and at its eastern King Arthur's Round Table. Barton Fell contains a great variety of valuable minerals, including jasper, agate, onyx, cornelian, chalcedony, &c., besides spars, and petrifactions of fish, shells, leaves, &c. At Hartsop and Patterdale are extensive quarries of fine blue slate, and at the latter place there is a lead mine. A free grammar school was founded, in 1649, by Dr. Lancelot Dawes and Dr. Gerard Langbaine, natives of this parish, and the latter an industrious antiquary, whose endowment of it has been augmented, by subsequent benefactors, to about £90 per annum: the master has a salary of £60 per annum, and a dwelling-house. Here are several cairns, in one of which two Roman urns were found a few years ago: the vicinity also contains other relics of antiquity and various natural curiosities, and abounds with scenery of the most pleasing and picturesque character.

BARTON, a parish, comprising the chapelries of Barton St. Cuthbert and Barton St. Mary (which form one township), and the township of Newton-Morrell, in the eastern division of the wapentake of GILLING, North riding of the county of YORK, and containing 467 inhabitants, of which number, 436 are in the township of Barton, 5 miles (S. W.) from Darlington. The livings of both chapelries are perpetual curacies, in the archdeaconry of Richmond, and diocese of Chester; that of St. Cuthbert's is endowed with £800 royal bounty, and in the patronage of the Vicar of Stanwich; and that of St. Mary's is endowed with £400 royal bounty, and £200 parliamentary grant, and in the patronage of the Vicar of Gilling. The neighbourhood abounds with excellent limestone. Mark Smithson, in 1683, endowed a school with £6 per annum, which has been increased by subsequent benefactions: the school-house was purchased in 1705, with a bequest from Thomas Smithson.

BARTON, a township in the parish of HAUKSWELL, western division of the wapentake of HANG, North riding of the county of YORK, 5½ miles (S. by W.) from Richmond, containing 106 inhabitants.

BARTON in the BEANS, a township partly in the parish of SHACKERSTONE, partly in that of NAILSTONE, but chiefly in that of MARKET-BOSWORTH, hundred of SPARKENHOE, county of LEICESTER, 2¼ miles (N. by W.) from Market-Bosworth, containing 177 inhabitants. Here was formerly a chapel, now desecrated.

BARTON in the CLAY, a parish in the hundred of FLITT, county of BEDFORD, 3¼ miles (S.) from Silsoe, containing 668 inhabitants. The living is a rectory, in the archdeaconry of Bedford, and diocese of Lincoln, rated in the king's books at £26. 9. 7., and in the patronage of the Crown. The church is dedicated to St. Nicholas. There is a place of worship for Particular Baptists. A school is endowed with property producing about £50 per annum, the bequest of Edward Willes, in 1807, for the instruction of forty poor children.

BARTON (ST. DAVID), a parish in the hundred of CATSASH, county of SOMERSET, 5 miles (N. E. by N.) from Somerton, containing 368 inhabitants. The living is a discharged vicarage, in the peculiar jurisdiction and patronage of the Prebendary of Barton in the Cathedral Church of Wells, rated in the king's books at £8, endowed with £200 private benefaction, £400 royal bounty, and £300 parliamentary grant.

BARTON (EARL'S), a parish in the hundred of HAMFORDSHOE, county of NORTHAMPTON, 3¾ miles (S. W.) from Wellingborough, containing 976 inhabitants. The living is a discharged vicarage, in the archdeaconry of Northampton, and diocese of Peterborough, rated in the king's books at £10, and in the patronage of the Crown. The church, dedicated to All Saints, is a curious edifice, the tower being ornamented with ribs, or mouldings, like that at Barnack, in the Saxon, or Norman, style of architecture: the Norman style, and the early, decorated, and the later English styles, are displayed in other parts of the building. There are places of worship for Particular Baptists and Wesleyan Methodists. The navigable river Nen, by which the Northampton canal communicates with the North sea, passes through the parish.

BARTON (GREAT), a parish in the hundred of THEDWESTRY, county of SUFFOLK, 2½ miles (N. E. by E.) from Bury St. Edmund's, containing 702 inhabitants. The living is a discharged vicarage, in the archdeaconry of Sudbury, and diocese of Norwich, rated in the king's books at £10. 15. 7½., and in the patronage of Sir H. E. Bunbury, Bart. The church is dedicated to the Holy Innocents.

BARTON on the HEATH, a parish in the Brails division of the hundred of KINGTON, county of WARWICK, 5½ miles (S.) from Shipston upon Stour, containing 201 inhabitants. The living is a rectory, in the archdeaconry and diocese of Worcester, rated in the king's books at £12. 17. 11., and in the patronage of the President and Fellows of Trinity College, Oxford. The church is dedicated to St. Lawrence. The village is situated on the navigable river Avon. A Sunday school is supported by voluntary contributions, in addition to a rent-charge of £2. 8., given by the Rev. T. Haward, in 1742. In the vicinity is a large stone, called the "Four Shire Stone," where the counties of Gloucester, Worcester, Warwick, and Oxford meet.

BARTON upon HUMBER, a market town, comprising the united parishes of St. Mary and St. Peter, in the northern division of the wapentake of YARBOROUGH, parts of LINDSEY, county of LINCOLN, 34 miles (N.) from Lincoln, and 167 (N.) from London, on the road to Kingston upon Hull, containing, according to the last census, 2496 inhabitants (since increased to above 3000), of which number, 1191 are in the parish of St. Mary, and 1305 in that of St. Peter. This place is said to have been a station of considerable importance during the Saxon and Danish contests, and to have been surrounded by a rampart and a fosse, some remains of which, called the Castle Dykes, are still perceptible. At the time of the Conquest it was noted for its commerce, which continued to flourish until some time after Edward I. bestowed upon Wyke upon Hull the appellation of King's town upon Hull, and made it a free borough, when the trade of Barton began to decline. The town is pleasantly situated at the northern extremity of the Wolds, and on an acclivity rising gently from the southern bank of the river Humber, which is here from two to three miles broad: it consists of several streets, irregularly built, in which, among many old houses, are some of modern structure, and has been recently much improved, by the erection of many new buildings of various descriptions, and of several handsome and respectable dwelling-houses. The trade is chiefly in corn and flour, and there are several manufactories for rope, sacking, starch, plaister of Paris, bricks, and tiles. About six miles lower down the Humber is a ferry to Kingston upon Hull, which has existed from time immemorial, though there is little doubt that it was originally to Hessle, to which place the inhabitants on the Barton side may still demand a passage, at a proper state of the tide, on paying the ancient customary toll; it is noticed in Domesday-book, and was confirmed in the 45th of Edward III. The customary tolls and regulations, according to the records in the Tower, in the reign of Edward III., were as follows: "Every person to pay one penny; for every quarter of hard corn, twopence; for every quarter of malt, one penny; for one man and horse, sixpence; deals by the score, fourpence; nothing to be paid for under a horse-load; the boat, or boats, to return the next tide, if weather serve, and not to take in strangers from Hull, on the market day, to the prejudice of the said inhabitants; two or more of the boatmen to live in Barton; no boat to land upon the green shore but in case of necessity; also, upon request, neither boat to be denied for Hessle, paying the ancient fare; for every boat fivepence, and gift money one penny; and also to land all passengers without paying more than customary due." The ferry, which belongs to the Crown, is at present leased to the corporation of Kingston upon Hull, who have also a right of ferry from Hull to Barton, or to any of the parts of Lindsey; the occupiers have at various times attempted to raise the fares, but have been resisted by the inhabitants with success. In 1785, an attempt being made by the lessee to increase the customary tolls, a subscription was raised to try the question, and legal proceedings were instituted; but a compromise was effected, and the fares were reduced to the former amount. Since that period different lessees have attempted to raise the fares, which have been increased for passengers, and more particularly for corn and merchandise; and since the employment of a steam-packet, which the present occupiers have introduced, in addition to the regular ferry boats, and of which the fares are arbitrary, the latter have been in some degree neglected, and the inhabitants have foreborne to enforce their prescriptive rights; but, on the termination of the present lease, which will expire in 1833, they intend to enforce the observance of the ancient customary tolls, and to recover their privileges. The market is on Monday, and on every alternate Monday there is a large cattle market: the fair is on Trinity Thursday. The town is within the jurisdiction of the county magistrates: constables and other officers are appointed at the court leet of the manor, which belongs to the Crown. A court baron, formerly held every third week, for the recovery of debts under 40*s.*, has been superseded by a court of requests, for the recovery of debts under £5, which is held monthly, under an act passed in the 47th of George III.

The living is a consolidated vicarage, in the archdeaconry and diocese of Lincoln, rated in the king's books at £19. 4. 8., and in the patronage of Charles Appleby, Esq. The church of St. Peter is an ancient and spacious structure, principally in the decorated style of English architecture, with a tower, the upper stage of which is evidently in the early Norman style, and the lower of a much earlier date, being probably one of the few specimens of Saxon architecture subsisting in England. The church of St. Mary, which is supposed to have been built as a chapel of ease to St. Peters, having no endowment, is also a spacious edifice, partly in the Norman, but principally in the early style of English, architecture, of which latter the tower is an elegant specimen. There are places of worship for Independents, and Primitive and Wesleyan Methodists. The school, for the instruction of poor children in reading, writing, and arithmetic, was founded, in 1722, by Mr. William Long, who endowed it with £7. 12 per annum, to which, in 1735, Mr. Nicholas Fountain added £50. The estates are vested in nine trustees, who have lately introduced the system of mutual instruction, and have added an infant school, the accomplishment of which has been greatly facilitated by the exertions of Robert Browne, Esq., clerk to the trustees. Almshouses, for four aged women of St. Mary's parish, were founded and endowed, in 1669, by Mr. Thomas Holland. About fifteen grey coats are annually given to poor men from the rental of property left for that purpose by Magdalen George; and about thirty suits of blue cloth are annually given to poor men, and thirty dresses of the same colour to poor women, from the rental of the Blue-coat charity estate, given by John Trippe, in 1669.

BARTON upon IRWELL, a township in the parish of ECCLES, hundred of SALFORD, county palatine of LANCASTER, $5\frac{1}{2}$ miles (W. by S.) from Manchester, containing 7977 inhabitants. There is a place of worship for Wesleyan Methodists. The manufacture of calico and nankeen goods is carried on here. The Duke of Bridgewater's canal crosses the river Irwell at this place, by means of a stone aqueduct of three arches, which was the first in England constructed over a navigable river.

BARTON (ST. MARY), a hamlet in that part of the parish of ST. MARY de LODE, GLOUCESTER, which is in the middle division of the hundred of DUDSTONE and KING'S BARTON, county of GLOUCESTER, containing 670 inhabitants.

BARTON (ST. MICHAEL'S), a hamlet in that part of the parish of ST. MICHAEL, GLOUCESTER, which is in the middle division of the hundred of DUDSTONE and KING'S BARTON, county of GLOUCESTER, containing 337 inhabitants.

BARTON under NEEDWOOD, a parochial chapelry in the northern division of the hundred of OFFLOW, county of STAFFORD, 6 miles (S. W. by W.) from Burton upon Trent, containing 1287 inhabitants. The living is a perpetual curacy, in the archdeaconry of Stafford, and diocese of Lichfield and Coventry, endowed with £430 private benefaction, £200 royal bounty, and £1800 parliamentary grant, and in the patronage of the Dean of Lichfield. The chapel, dedicated to St. James, is a handsome building in the later style of English architecture, erected in the reign of Henry VIII., by Dr. John Taylor, a native of this village. Barton is the head of one of the five wards into which the ancient royal forest of Needwood has been divided: it is in the honour of Tutbury, duchy of Lancaster, and within the jurisdiction of a court of pleas held at Tutbury every third Tuesday, for the recovery of debts under 40*s.* Courts leet and baron are held annually in October. The Grand Trunk canal passes through the parish: fairs are held on May 3rd and November 28th. Thomas Russell, in 1593, gave a rent-charge of £50. 10. for the establishment of a free grammar school, under the management of a committee: about sixty-five boys are instructed on Dr. Bell's plan, and the master receives a salary of £70 per annum, arising from the endowment, and from voluntary contributions.

BARTON (STEEPLE), a parish in the hundred of WOOTTON, county of OXFORD, $4\frac{3}{4}$ miles (S. S. W.) from Deddington, containing, with the hamlets of Middle Barton and Sesswell-Barton, 404 inhabitants. The living is a discharged vicarage, in the archdeaconry and diocese of Oxford, rated in the king's books at £7. 9. 4½., and in the patronage of Mr. and Mrs. Mister. The church is dedicated to St. Mary. There is a place of worship for Wesleyan Methodists.

BARTON le STREET, a parish comprising the township of Coneysthorpe in the wapentake of BULMER, and the townships of Barton le Street and Butterwick in the wapentake of RYEDALE, North riding of the county of YORK, and containing 386 inhabitants, of which number, 176 are in the township of Barton le Street, 4¾ miles (W. N. W.) from New Malton. The living is a rectory, in the archdeaconry of Cleveland, and diocese of York, rated in the king's books at £14. 18. 6½., and in the patronage of the Marchioness of Hertford. The church, dedicated to St. Michael, is said to have been erected with materials from the ruins of St. Mary's abbey, York: it contains some curious specimens of ancient sculpture. There is a place of worship for Wesleyan Methodists. The parish is bounded on the north by the river Rye.

BARTON le WILLOWS, a township in the parish of CRAMBE, wapentake of BULMER, North riding of the county of YORK, 10½ miles (N. E.) from York, containing 188 inhabitants.

BARTON-BENDISH, a village in the hundred of CLACKCLOSE, county of NORFOLK, 4 miles (N. by E.) from Stoke-Ferry, containing 440 inhabitants. It formerly comprised three parishes, in the archdeaconry of Norfolk, and diocese of Norwich, *viz.*, St. Andrew's, St. Mary's, and All Saints'; the two latter have been united, and form a consolidated rectory, rated in the king's books at £11, and in the patronage of Sir H. Berney, Bart.; the living of St. Andrew's is a rectory, rated at £14, and in the patronage of the Crown. The church of All Saints' is desecrated. Barton derives its distinguishing name from a dyke, called Bendish, constructed here by the Saxons, as a boundary line to the hundred. Richard Jones, in 1783, bequeathed £200 for the instruction of poor children belonging to the united parishes.

BARTON-BLOUNT, a parish in the hundred of APPLETREE, county of DERBY, 11 miles (W.) from Derby, containing 73 inhabitants. The living is a discharged rectory, in the archdeaconry of Derby, and diocese of Lichfield and Coventry, rated in the king's books at £4. 19. 1., endowed with £200 private benefaction, £600 royal bounty, and £300 parliamentary grant, and in the patronage of F. Bradshaw, Esq. Barton-Blount is in the honour of Tutbury, duchy of Lancaster, and within the jurisdiction of a court of pleas held at Tutbury every third Tuesday, for the recovery of debts under 40*s*. The manor-house was garrisoned, in October 1644, by Col. Gill, on behalf of the parliamentarians.

BARTON-HARTSHORN, a parish in the hundred and county of BUCKINGHAM, 4¼ miles (W. S. W.) from Buckingham, containing 113 inhabitants. The living is a perpetual curacy, with that of Chetwood, in the archdeaconry of Bedford, and diocese of Lincoln, endowed with £200 private benefaction, and £600 royal bounty, and in the patronage of E. Lane, Esq. The church is dedicated to St. James.

BARTON-MILLS, a parish in the hundred of LACKFORD, county of SUFFOLK, 1½ mile (S. E.) from Mildenhall, containing 523 inhabitants. The living is a rectory, in the archdeaconry of Sudbury, and diocese of Norwich, rated in the king's books at £4. 15. 10., and in the patronage of the Crown. The church is dedicated to St. Mary. There is a place of worship for Particular Baptists.

BARTON-SEAGRAVE, a parish in the hundred of HUXLOE, county of NORTHAMPTON, 1¾ mile (S. E. by E.) from Kettering, containing 223 inhabitants. The living is a rectory, in the archdeaconry of Northampton, and diocese of Peterborough, rated in the king's books at £10. 17. 1., and in the patronage of the Duke of Buccleuch. The church, dedicated to St. Botolph, exhibits specimens of very ancient architecture.

BARTON-STACEY, a parish in the hundred of BARTON-STACEY, Andover division of the county of SOUTHAMPTON, 5 miles (S. S. W.) from Whitchurch, comprising the tythings of Barton-Stacey, Bransbury, Drayton, and Newton-Stacey, and containing 581 inhabitants. The living is a vicarage, in the archdeaconry and diocese of Winchester, rated in the king's books at £8. 2. 1., and in the patronage of the Dean and Chapter of Winchester. The church is dedicated to All Saints. A fair is held here on July 31st. A National school is endowed with £10. 10. per annum, being part of the rental of land, producing about £40 per annum, left for charitable uses by Dorothy and Elizabeth Wright. A Roman road passed through the parish, and there are vestiges of a strong intrenchment at Bransbury.

BARTON-TURF, a parish in the hundred of TUNSTEAD, county of NORFOLK, 5 miles (E. by N.) from Coltishall, containing 371 inhabitants. The living is a discharged vicarage, united to the rectory of Irstead, in the archdeaconry of Norfolk, and diocese of Norwich, rated in the king's books at £3. 13. 4. The church is dedicated to St. Michael.

BARTON-WESTCOTT, a parish in the hundred of WOOTTON, county of OXFORD, 4¼ miles (E.) from Neat-Enstone, containing 253 inhabitants. The living is a rectory, in the archdeaconry and diocese of Oxford, rated in the king's books at £7, and in the patronage of Thomas Coles and others. The church is dedicated to St. Edward.

BARUGH, a township in the parish of DARTON, wapentake of STAINCROSS, West riding of the county of YORK, 2½ miles (W. N. W.) from Barnesley, containing 396 inhabitants. Here is a small endowed school, also an almshouse for two poor widows.

BARUGH-AMBE, a township in the parish of KIRKBY-MISPERTON, PICKERING lythe, North riding of the county of YORK, 5¼ miles (S. W.) from Pickering, containing 241 inhabitants. There is a place of worship for Wesleyan Methodists.

BARWELL, a parish in the hundred of SPARKENHOE, county of LEICESTER, 1¾ mile (N. E. by N.) from Hinckley, containing, with the chapelries of Potters-Marston and Stapleton, 1371 inhabitants. The living is a rectory, in the archdeaconry of Leicester, and diocese of Lincoln, rated in the king's books at £20. 10. 7½., and in the patronage of the Rev. George Mettam. The church is dedicated to St. Mary. There is a place of worship for Wesleyan Methodists. A school for teaching and clothing twenty children is endowed with about £20 per annum, the bequest of Gabriel Newton, in 1760.

BARWICK, a parish in the hundred of SMITHDON, county of NORFOLK, 4¾ miles (S. S. W.) from Burnham-

Westgate, containing 29 inhabitants. The living is a discharged vicarage, in the archdeaconry of Norfolk, and diocese of Norwich, rated in the king's books at £6, endowed with £400 royal bounty, and in the patronage of Mrs. Anne Hoste. The church, now desecrated, was dedicated to St. Mary.

BARWICK, a parish in the hundred of HOUNDSBOROUGH, BERWICK, and COKER, county of SOMERSET, 1¾ mile (S. by E.) from Yeovil, containing 400 inhabitants. The living is a discharged rectory, in the archdeaconry of Wells, and diocese of Bath and Wells, rated in the king's books at £7. 14. 7., and in the patronage of John Newman, Esq. The church is dedicated to St. Mary Magdalene.

BARWICK in ELMETT, a parish in the lower division of the wapentake of SKYRACK, West riding of the county of YORK, comprising the townships of Barnbow, Barwick, Kiddal with Potterton, Morwick with Scholes, and Roundhay, and containing 1667 inhabitants, of which number, 593 are in the township of Barwick, 8 miles (N.E. by E.) from Leeds. The living is a rectory, in the archdeaconry and diocese of York, rated in the king's books at £33. 12. 6., and in the patronage of the King, as Duke of Lancaster. The church is dedicated to All Saints. A school is endowed with £14 per annum for the instruction of fourteen poor children. Here was anciently a castle of considerable extent and importance, supposed to have been a residence of some of the Northumbrian monarchs; the site was encompassed by a fortification, including an area of upwards of thirteen acres: the only remains are, a portion of the groundworks, and a mount, called Hall Tower Hill.

BARWICK-BASSETT, a parish in the hundred of CALNE, county of WILTS, 7½ miles (E. N. E.) from Calne, containing 162 inhabitants. The living is a perpetual curacy with the vicarage of Calne, annexed to the Treasurership in the Cathedral Church of Salisbury, in the archdeaconry of Wilts, and diocese of Salisbury. The church is dedicated to St. Nicholas. Henry Webb, in 1775, endowed a school with about £13 per annum, for the instruction of poor children.

BASCHURCH, a parish in the hundred of PIMHILL, county of SALOP, 8 miles (N.W. by N.) from Shrewsbury, containing 1277 inhabitants. The living is a discharged vicarage, in the archdeaconry of Salop, and diocese of Lichfield and Coventry, rated in the king's books at £10. 16., and in the patronage of the Crown. The church is dedicated to All Saints. The Ellesmere canal passes through the parish. Here is a school for teaching and clothing poor children, endowed with upwards of £140 per annum, arising from land bequeathed by Eleanor Harries, in 1716: there is also another small charity school. Vestiges of a Roman camp may be traced in the neighbourhood.

BASFORD, a township in the parish of WYBUNBURY, hundred of NANTWICH, county palatine of CHESTER, 4¾ miles (E.) from Nantwich, containing 86 inhabitants.

BASFORD, a parish in the northern division of the wapentake of BROXTOW, county of NOTTINGHAM, 2½ miles (N.W. by N.) from Nottingham, containing 3599 inhabitants. The living is a vicarage, in the archdeaconry of Nottingham, and diocese of York, rated in the king's books at £8. 17. 7., endowed with £200 royal bounty, and in the patronage of the Crown. The church, dedicated to St. Leodgarius, is situated at the southern extremity of the village, and was re-pewed in 1819, when two hundred and twelve additional free sittings were added by the Incorporated Society for the enlargement of churches and chapels, at an expense of £200. There are three places of worship for Wesleyan Methodists and those of the New Connexion, and one for Baptists, to all of which Sunday schools are attached. The house of industry, for thirty-two parishes of the county, stands in this parish, and is a neat modern stone building, capable of containing from two to three hundred persons. Basford abounds with numerous springs of soft water, which renders it peculiarly advantageous for bleaching cotton hose and lace, the manufacture of which is carried on to a great extent. The beautiful process of gassing lace was invented by Mr. Samuel Hale of this village, which is secured to him by a valuable patent obtained in 1817: there are various cotton-mills, bleaching and dye houses, corn-mills, &c.

BASFORD, a township in the parish of CHEDDLETON, northern division of the hundred of TOTMONSLOW, county of STAFFORD, 3 miles (S. by E.) from Leek, containing 282 inhabitants.

BASHALL-EAVES, a township in that part of the parish of MITTON which is in the western division of the wapentake of STAINCLIFFE and EWCROSS, West riding of the county of YORK, 3 miles (W. by N.) from Clitheroe, containing 348 inhabitants. There is a place of worship for Wesleyan Methodists.

BASILDON, a chapelry in the parish of LAINDON, hundred of BARSTABLE, county of ESSEX, 4½ miles (S.E. by S.) from Billericay, containing 142 inhabitants. The chapel is dedicated to the Holy Cross.

BASING, a parish in the hundred of BASINGSTOKE, Basingstoke division of the county of SOUTHAMPTON, 2 miles (E. N. E.) from Basingstoke, containing 1073 inhabitants. The living is a perpetual curacy, annexed to the vicarage of Basingstoke, in the archdeaconry and diocese of Winchester. The church, dedicated to St. Mary, is a large ancient structure with a central tower: it contains the family vault of the Paulets, in which all the dukes of Bolton of that family have been interred. National schools for children of both sexes have been established. This place is remarkable for having been the scene of the defeat of King Ethelred I. by the Danes, in 871. At the period of the Norman survey, Hugh de Port held fifty-five lordships in this county, of which Basing was the head. The castle was rebuilt, in a sumptuous manner, by Sir William Paulet, Knt., a lineal descendant from Hugh de Port, created Marquis of Winchester by Edward VI., and one of the most polite noblemen of the age: here, in 1560, he entertained Queen Elizabeth, who again honoured his great grandson William, the fourth marquis, with a visit, in 1601. John, the fifth marquis, was the nobleman who distinguished himself for his gallant defence of his house at Basing, in the cause of Charles I., through a series of sieges which lasted for two years, at the end of which, in October 1645, it was stormed and taken by Cromwell, who ordered it to be burnt to the ground. The fortress and its outworks occupied an area of about fourteen acres and a half, through which the Basingstoke canal now passes: the remains consist principally of the north gateway and part of the outer wall. The river Loddon also runs through the parish.

Corporate Seal.

BASINGSTOKE, a market town and parish, having separate jurisdiction, locally in the hundred of Basingstoke, and in the Basingstoke division of the county of SOUTHAMPTON, 17½ miles (N. E.) from Winchester, and 45 (W.S.W.) from London, on the great western road, containing 3165 inhabitants. In the early part of the Saxon dynasty, Basingstoke was inferior to Old Basing; but at the time of the Conquest it had obtained the superiority, since, in the record of Domesday, it is described as a royal demesne, and as being in possession of a market. In 1261, Henry III., at the request of Walter de Merton, founded an hospital here for six poor priests, giving preference to those from Merton College, Oxford. In the reign of Henry VIII., Sir William, afterwards Lord, Sandys, in conjunction with Fox, Bishop of Winchester, instituted a guild, and erected a beautiful chapel here, which he dedicated to the Holy Ghost. This fraternity was dissolved in the reign of Edward VI., and the revenue was vested in the crown; but in the reign of Mary it was re-established, and the revenue appropriated to the maintenance of a priest, for the celebration of divine service, and the instruction of young men and boys belonging to the town. During the civil war in the reign of Charles I., it was suppressed by Cromwell, and the estates were seized by the parliament; but through the intercession of Dr. Morley, Bishop of Winchester, they were restored in 1670, and appropriated to their former use. Of the chapel, and the buildings connected with it, there are some remains on an eminence on the south-western side of the town, consisting of the south and east walls, and a hexagonal tower at the north-west angle. The town is pleasantly situated in a fertile and well-cultivated district, near the source of the small river Loddon, and consists of several streets, containing neat and well-built houses: it is paved and lighted under an act of parliament granted in 1815, and is amply supplied with water. Races, which continue for two days, and are well attended, take place annually in September. The trade is principally in corn and malt, which is carried on extensively, and greatly facilitated by the situation of the town at the junction of five principal roads, and by the Basingstoke canal, which communicates with the river Wey, near its confluence with the Thames: this canal was completed in 1796, at an expense of £180,000. The market is on Wednesday, and has lately been made a pitched market for corn: fairs are held on the Wednesday next after Whitsuntide, and October 11th, which latter is also a statute fair; a fair for the sale of cheese and cattle is also held on Basingstoke down, on Easter-Tuesday. The government, by charter of incorporation granted by James I., and confirmed by Charles I., is vested in a mayor, high steward, recorder, seven aldermen, and seven burgesses, assisted by a chamberlain, who is usually the eldest member of the corporation, a town clerk, two serjeants at mace, and subordinate officers. The mayor, and two aldermen appointed by the corporation, are justices of the peace. The corporation hold courts of quarter session for the town and parish, and have power to hold a court of record for the recovery of debts under £10, but this court is falling into disuse. The county magistrates hold a petty session here for the division, on the first and third Wednesdays in every month; and a court leet is held under the lord of the manor, the jurisdiction of which extends over nineteen tythings. Basingstoke sent members to parliament from the 23rd of Edward I. to the 4th of Edward II., when, it is supposed, the privilege ceased on the solicitation of the inhabitants.

The living is a discharged vicarage, with the perpetual curacies of Basing and Upper Nately annexed, in the archdeaconry and diocese of Winchester, rated in the king's books at £30. 16. 5½., endowed with £200 private benefaction, and £200 royal bounty, and in the patronage of the President and Fellows of Magdalene College, Oxford. The church, dedicated to St. Michael, is a spacious and handsome structure, in the later style of English architecture, with a low embattled tower: it contains a small parochial library, the gift of Sir George Wheeler. There are places of worship for the Society of Friends, those in the Connexion of the late Countess of Huntingdon, Independents, and Wesleyan Methodists. The free grammar school, originally founded by Sir William Sandys, in connexion with the guild of the Holy Ghost, was re-established, after the dissolution of the fraternity in the reign of Edward VI., by Queen Mary, and has now a revenue exceeding £200: the master is appointed by the crown, and the usher by the corporation. There are twelve boys at present on the foundation, of whom those belonging to the town pay 15*s*., and those in the neighbourhood £1. 1., per quarter: the school-room is part of an ancient edifice, adjoining the remains of the chapel of the Holy Ghost, and supposed to have been originally the parish church. Dr. Joseph Warton, a poet and refined critic, and his brother Thomas, the poet-laureat, received here the early part of their education, under their father, Thomas Warton, B. D., some time Professor of Poetry in the University of Oxford, and subsequently master of this school. The Blue-coat school, in which ten boys are clothed, maintained, and educated, was founded and endowed, in 1646, by Mr. Richard Aldworth. A National school for one hundred boys was established by Dr. Sheppard, late vicar of Basingstoke; and another, for one hundred girls, by his widow, who erected a school-room, at an expense of £500; they are supported partly by endowment and partly by subscription. Almshouses for eight aged men or women, each of whom receives £6. 18. per annum, were founded and endowed by Sir James Deane, Knt., in 1607. Three almshouses, for aged widows of the Independent congregation, were founded and endowed by Mr. Joseph Page, in 1808; and several unendowed tenements, given by different individuals, are assigned rent-free to the poor of the parish, who participate in the advantages derivable from various other benefactions. On an eminence in the vicinity of the town is an ancient encampment of an elliptical form, one thousand one hundred yards in circumference, called Aubrey Camp. John de Basingstoke, a learned Greek scholar, and the intimate friend of Matthew Paris; Sir James Lancaster, an eminent navigator, who in the reign of Elizabeth explored the Arctic Sea; and Thomas Warton, above mentioned; were natives of this place.

BASINGTHORPE, a parish in the wapentake of BELTISLOE, parts of KESTEVEN, county of LINCOLN,

$3\frac{3}{4}$ miles (N. W.) from Corby, containing, with Westby, 115 inhabitants. The living is a vicarage, in the archdeaconry and diocese of Lincoln, rated in the king's books at £8. 17. 6. Sir W. Manners was patron in 1819. The church is dedicated to St. Thomas à Becket.

BASLOW, a chapelry in the parish of BAKEWELL, hundred of HIGH PEAK, county of DERBY, 3 miles (S. E.) from Stoney-Middleton, containing 872 inhabitants. The living is a perpetual curacy, in the peculiar jurisdiction of the Dean and Chapter of Lichfield, endowed with £800 royal bounty, and £1000 parliamentary grant, and in the patronage of the Duke of Devonshire. The chapel, which is chiefly in the later style of English architecture, has a tower and low spire at the western end of the north aisle. There is a place of worship for Wesleyan Methodists. Baslow is in the honour of Tutbury, duchy of Lancaster, and within the jurisdiction of a court of pleas held at Tutbury every third Tuesday, for the recovery of debts under 40*s*. About half a mile from the village is Stanton-Ford school, for the education of ten children, endowed with about £15 per annum, and a house and garden for the master.

BASSALEG, a parish partly in the lower, but chiefly in the upper, division of the hundred of WENTLLOOG, county of MONMOUTH, $2\frac{3}{4}$ miles (W.) from Newport, comprising the hamlets of Duffrin, Graig, and Rogerstone, and containing 1329 inhabitants. The living is a discharged vicarage, in the archdeaconry and diocese of Llandaff, rated in the king's books at £14. 13. $6\frac{1}{2}$., and in the patronage of the Bishop of Llandaff. The church is dedicated to St. Basil. There is a place of worship for Particular Baptists. The river Ebn, and the Monmouthshire canal, pass through the parish, which is partly bounded by the river Severn. A free school is endowed with £20 per annum. On the brow of a hill, a mile from the village, there is a circular intrenchment, called *Craeg y Saesson*, supposed to have been a Saxon camp, a mile from which is one called *Pen y Park Newydd*, probably a fortress of the Britons. A priory was founded here in 1101, which became a cell to the abbey of Glastonbury.

BASSENTHWAITE, a parish in ALLERDALE ward below Darwent, county of CUMBERLAND, 5 miles (N.W. by N.) from Keswick, containing 537 inhabitants. The living is a perpetual curacy, in the archdeaconry and diocese of Carlisle, and in the patronage of the Dean and Chapter of Carlisle. The church is dedicated to St. Bridget. The parish includes a portion of the lofty mountain Skiddaw, which is situated at its south-eastern extremity: it is intersected by the river Darwent, and contains the beautiful lake of Bassenthwaite, or Broadwater, which covers about fifteen hundred acres of ground, being enriched throughout with scenery of a sublime character. There is a mine of antimony in the neighbourhood, and lead-ore has also been found. A school-house has been erected by subscription, but it has no endowment.

BASSETT-HOUSE, an extra-parochial liberty, in the hundred of SPARKENHOE, county of LEICESTER, containing 15 inhabitants.

BASSILDON, a parish in the hundred of MORETON, county of BERKS, $7\frac{1}{2}$ miles (N. W. by W.) from Reading, containing, exclusively of the chapelry of Ashamstead, 686 inhabitants. The living is a discharged vicarage, in the archdeaconry of Berks, and diocese of Salisbury, rated in the king's books at £7. 14. $4\frac{1}{2}$., and in the alternate patronage of the Rev. R. B. Fisher and J. Hopkins, Esq. The church is dedicated to St. Bartholomew. In Domesday-book mention is made of two churches here. The river Thames separates the parish from Oxfordshire. In the reign of Edward II., a weekly market, and a fair on St. Barnabas' day, were granted. A school was endowed with a cottage and a rent-charge of £4 by William Allen, in 1720, for the instruction of ten poor children.

BASSINGBOURNE, a parish in the hundred of ARMINGFORD, county of CAMBRIDGE, $3\frac{1}{4}$ miles (N. W. by N.) from Royston, containing, with the hamlet of Kneesworth, 1213 inhabitants. The living is a vicarage, in the archdeaconry and diocese of Ely, rated in the king's books at £7. 0. 10., and in the patronage of the Dean and Chapter of Westminster. The church is dedicated to St. Peter. A room adjoining the north aisle has been appropriated to the reception of a parochial library, founded in 1717, by Edward Nightingale. A fair is held on the festival of St. Peter and St. Paul. There is an endowment of about £13 per annum for the instruction of poor children.

BASSINGHAM, a parish in the lower division of the wapentake of BOOTHBY-GRAFFO, parts of KESTEVEN, county of LINCOLN, 9 miles (S. W. by S.) from Lincoln, containing 613 inhabitants. The living is a rectory, in the archdeaconry and diocese of Lincoln, rated in the king's books at £26. 16. 3., and in the patronage of the President and Fellows of Corpus Christi College, Oxford. The church is dedicated to St. Michael. There is a place of worship for Wesleyan Methodists. The rector allows an annuity of £4 for teaching poor children. The several manor-houses in the parish are occupied as farm-houses.

BASSINGTON, a township in the parish of EGLINGHAM, northern division of COQUETDALE ward, county of NORTHUMBERLAND, $3\frac{1}{2}$ miles (N. W. by W.) from Alnwick, containing 12 inhabitants.

BASTON, a parish in the wapentake of NESS, parts of KESTEVEN, county of LINCOLN, $3\frac{1}{4}$ miles (N. N. W.) from Market-Deeping, containing, with portions of certain extra-parochial places in the fens, 682 inhabitants. The living is a discharged vicarage, in the archdeaconry and diocese of Lincoln, rated in the king's books at £6. 1. 3., and in the patronage of the Crown. The church is dedicated to St. John the Baptist.

BASTWICK, a hamlet in the parish of REPPS, western division of the hundred of FLEGG, county of NORFOLK, 5 miles (N. N. E.) from Acle. The population is returned with the parish. Here was anciently a chapel, which has long been in ruins.

BASWICH, a parish in the eastern division of the hundred of CUTTLESTONE, county of STAFFORD, $2\frac{1}{4}$ miles (E. S. E.) from Stafford, comprising the chapelries of Acton-Trussel and Bednall, and the townships of Brockton, Milford, and Walton, and containing 1376 inhabitants. The living is a perpetual curacy, in the peculiar jurisdiction of the Prebendary of Whittington and Baswich in the Cathedral Church of Lichfield, endowed with £400 private benefaction, and £2000 parliamentary grant, and in the patronage of J. Inge and J. N. Seal, Esqrs., alternately. The church is dedicated to the Holy Trinity. The Staffordshire and Worcestershire canal passes through the parish.

BATCOMBE, a parish in the hundred of **Yetminster**, Sherborne division of the county of **Dorset**, 10 miles (S. by W.) from Sherborne, containing 177 inhabitants. The living is a discharged rectory, united in 1772 to that of Frome-Vauchurch, in the archdeaconry of Dorset, and diocese of Bristol, rated in the king's books at £9. 9. 9½. The church is dedicated to St. Mary.

BATCOMBE, a parish, forming a detached portion of the hundred of **Whitestone**, county of **Somerset**, 2¾ miles (N. by E.) from Bruton, containing 792 inhabitants. The living is a rectory, with the perpetual curacy of Upton-Noble annexed, in the archdeaconry of Wells, and diocese of Bath and Wells, rated in the king's books at £26. 14. 4½., and in the patronage of the Duke of Buckingham. The church is dedicated to St. Mary. There is a place of worship for Wesleyan Methodists. A rent-charge of £2 was left by Mr. Jarvis, for the instruction of six poor children.

Arms.

BATH, a city having separate jurisdiction, locally in the hundred of Bath-Forum, county of **Somerset**, 12 miles (E. by S.) from Bristol, 19 (N. N. E.) from Wells, and 106 (W.) from London, on the direct road to Bristol, containing 36,811 inhabitants. The name of this city is obviously derived from its medicinal springs, the efficacy of which has been celebrated from remote antiquity. It is stated to have been a British town prior to the Roman invasion, and to have been named *Caer Badon*, or the place of baths, from an accidental discovery of the medicinal properties of its waters by Bladud, son of Lud Hudibras, King of Britain, who, according to the fabulous histories of those times, having been banished from court on account of leprosy, came to this place, and, being cured of that disease by using the waters, is said, after his accession to the throne, to have built a palace here, and to have encouraged the resort of persons affected with cutaneous disorders. So generally was this opinion entertained even till the eighteenth century, that his statue was erected in the king's bath, with an inscription to that effect, in 1699. The researches of modern historians, however, have induced them to reject this tradition, as entirely destitute of support, and to ascribe the foundation of the city to the Romans, in the reign of Claudius, who, having ascertained the healing quality of its waters, constructed, on a skilful and extensive plan, their *balnea*, consisting of *frigidaria, tepidaria, olothesia, sudatoria*, &c., for the better enjoyment of the luxury of the bath, and gave to the station the name *Aquæ Solis*. They erected a temple to Minerva, with many votive altars, and numerous other buildings, the remains of which, discovered at various periods, strikingly indicate their splendour and magnificence. They surrounded the city with walls twenty feet in height, and of prodigious thickness, including an area in the form of an irregular pentagon, of which the larger diameter was one thousand two hundred feet, and the smaller one thousand one hundred and forty. In the centre were the *prætorium*, the baths, and the temple; and in the walls were four gates terminating the principal streets, from which they constructed roads leading to the neighbouring stations, *Verlucio, Ischalis, Abona*, &c. After the departure of the Romans from Britain, Bath, then called *Caer Palladwr*, the city of the waters of Pallas, remained in the possession of the Britons for upwards of a century, being disturbed only by one or two unsuccessful attacks of the Saxon chieftains, Ælla and Cerdic, who were bravely repulsed by the renowned King Arthur.

In the year 577, the Saxons, having nearly overrun all the rest of the kingdom, fell with irresistible fury on the western part of England; and having gained the memorable battle of Deorham, about eight miles distant, Bath fell a prey to their ravages, and was abandoned to indiscriminate plunder. Its temple was destroyed, its altars were overthrown, and its baths and other splendid monuments of Roman grandeur reduced to a heap of ruins. How long it continued in this state of desolation is uncertain, but probably the Saxons, after having retained uninterrupted possession of it for a time, turned their attention to its restoration: they rebuilt the walls and other fortifications upon the original foundations, with the old materials, cementing them with a liquid substance which time has rendered harder than stone. It is probable that they also directed their attention to the baths, which they soon restored, for the Saxon names of the city were *Hat Bathur*, hot baths, and *Ace mannes ceaster*, city of invalids. After their conversion to Christianity, a nunnery was erected here, in 676, by King Osric, which was destroyed during the wars of the Octarchy, and on its site a college of Secular canons was founded, in 775, by Offa, King of Mercia, who had taken Bath from the king of Wessex, and annexed it to his own dominions: he also rebuilt the conventual church of St. Peter, in which Edgar was crowned king of England, by Dunstan, Archbishop of Canterbury, in 973, and the anniversary of his coronation continued to be celebrated in the time of Camden, in commemoration of the many privileges which he granted to the citizens on that occasion. Edgar converted the college into a Benedictine monastery, which, with the church, was again demolished by the Danes.

At the time of the Norman survey, Bath contained one hundred and seventy-eight burgesses, of whom sixty-four held under the king, ninety under different feudatories of the Crown, and twenty-four under the abbot of St. Peter's. In the first year of the reign of William Rufus, Geoffry, Bishop of Coutances, and Robert de Mowbray, who had risen in support of the claim of Robert, Duke of Normandy, to the throne of England, obtained possession of the city by assault, and reduced the greater part of it to ashes. From this calamity it soon recovered, under the favour of John de Villula, who, on his promotion to the see of Wells, about the year 1090, purchased the city from Henry I., for five hundred marks, and built a new and spacious church here for that see, removing the episcopal chair to this place, where, during the festival of Easter in 1107, he had the honour of entertaining Henry I. In the turbulent reign of Stephen, Bath suffered greatly from its proximity to Bristol, then the head-quarters of the Empress Matilda, and was alternately occupied by the adherents of both parties. It continued in the possession of its bishops until 1193, when Bishop Savaric transferred it to Richard I., in exchange for the abbey of Glastonbury: this monarch made it a free borough, and invested it with many privileges, in consequence of which it began to participate in the commerce of the country, and to increase in wealth and importance. The manufacture of woollen cloth, which was introduced into England in the year 1330, was established here under the auspices of the monks, in consequence of which the shuttle was introduced into the arms of the monastery. During the civil war in the reign of Charles I., Bath was fortified for the king; but the Marquis of Hertford, who commanded the royal forces, having retired into Wales, it fell into the hands of the parliamentarians, and became the head-quarters of the army raised by Waller in that part of the country, to retrieve the loss which his party had sustained in the battle of Statton. In 1643, the battle of Lansdown, in the immediate neighbourhood, took place, in which the royalists, notwithstanding many local disadvantages, drove the parliamentary forces from the field, and compelled them to retire into the city; in commemoration of which, a monument was erected on the spot by an ancestor of the present Marquis of Lansdowne, in 1720. After this battle the royalists regained possession of the city, which they held till it was finally surrendered to the parliament, in 1645. On the restoration of Charles II., the citizens presented a congratulatory address through the celebrated William Prynne, then one of their representatives; and in the autumn of 1663, the king paid a visit to Bath, on which occasion his chief physician having recommended the internal use of the waters, the adoption of this practice became general. After the suppression of Monmouth's rebellion, four persons, who had been condemned by Judge Jeffreys, were executed here.

The city continued within the limits prescribed to it by the Romans till the year 1720, and its suburbs consisted merely of a few scattered houses: celebrated only for the medicinal properties of its hot springs, it was for several years visited merely by invalids. The perseverance of Mr. John Wood, an enterprising architect, who was encouraged by the proprietors of land in the vicinity, about the year 1728, first led to its improvement, and the excellent quarries of freestone in the neighbourhood facilitated the execution of an enterprise which has embellished it with splendid edifices, and raised it to the highest rank as a place of fashionable resort. The town is pleasantly situated on the banks of the river Avon, along which its buildings extend more than two miles, decorating the acclivities, and crowning the summits, of that fine range of hills by which it is environed. Over that part of the Avon which skirts the eastern side of the town are two stone bridges, one of ancient, the other of modern, erection; and a handsome iron bridge has recently been constructed, connecting Walcot with Bathwick, and affording a direct entrance from the London road into the most improved part of the town. Among the earliest of the modern improvements is Queen's square, the houses in which are decorated with columns and pilasters of the Corinthian order; in the centre is an obelisk seventy feet high, erected in 1738, by Beau Nash, to commemorate the visit of the then Prince and Princess of Wales, who occupied a house in the square. The Circus is a noble range of uniform edifices, embellished with successive series of double pillars of the Doric, Ionic, and Corinthian orders, and enclosing an extensive area, disposed into shrubberies, with a gravel walk round a reservoir in the centre, from which the houses are supplied with water. The Royal Crescent is characterised by a simple grandeur of elevation, and adorned by a lofty colonnade of the Ionic order, rising from a rustic basement, and supporting a cornice with a rich entablature; a lawn of more than twenty acres slopes gradually to the margin of the Avon, commanding a fine view of the city, the beautiful vale below it, and the hills on the opposite side of the river. The North and South Parades are handsome ranges of building, with terraces raised on arches, and commanding extensive and varied prospects. The Orange-grove, formerly the chief place of fashionable amusement, now principally composed of lodging-houses, has been planted with trees, and in the centre is an obelisk, commemorating the restoration of the Prince of Orange to health by drinking the Bath waters. Behind the Royal Crescent are St. James' square, Lansdown Crescent, and Camden, Portland, and Somerset Places, with Mount Sion, an extensive range of houses on the summit of the Beacon-hill, Belle-Vue, Cavendish Crescent, and Lansdown Place; besides which are the Paragon, Belmont, and Belvidere, rising above each other. In the new town, on the eastern bank of the Avon, is Laura Place, a neat range of buildings in the form of a lozenge, intersected diagonally by Great Pulteney-street, a noble series of mansions, at the extremity of which are Sydney Gardens, occupying an extensive area surrounded by several ranges of building forming Sydney Place, not inferior in beauty and elegance to the most splendid part of the city. The improvements in this part of the town will speedily be extended by means of a subscription, which has been raised for that purpose.

A grand pump-room, the centre of attraction during the fashionable season, was erected in 1797; it is a handsome building, eighty-five feet in length, forty-eight in width, and thirty-four in height. The interior, which is lighted by a double range of windows, is decorated with pillars of the Corinthian order, supporting a rich entablature and a lofty coved ceiling: at the west end is a handsome orchestra, and at the eastern, a well-executed marble statue of the celebrated Beau Nash, under whose superintendence for many years, as master of the ceremonies, the elegant amusements of this place were regulated, upon a system combining the most liberal urbanity with the most refined decorum. The principal entrance is through a handsome portico of four lofty columns of the Corinthian order, supporting a triangular pediment, under the tympanum of which is inscribed "ΑΡΙΣΤΟΝ ΜΕΝ ΥΔΩΡ." The king's bath contains three hundred and sixty-four tons of water, and is conveniently fitted up with seats and recesses, having also a handsome colonnade of the Doric order, with the statue of Bladud, the traditionary patron of the waters. The queen's bath, adjoining it, has also suitable apartments. The cross bath, so called from a cross erected in the centre of it, and the hot bath, so named from its superior degree of heat, the mean temperature being 117° of Fahrenheit, have the convenience of dry and vapour baths; and a small pump-room has been recently erected. Besides these public baths, which are now principally used by the hospital patients, there are private baths belonging to the corporation, and the abbey baths, the property of Earl Manvers, which are chiefly resorted to by the wealthier visitors. The waters contain carbonic acid and nitrogen gases, sulphate and muriate of soda, sulphate and carbonate of lime, and silicious earth, with a minute portion of oxyde of iron, and are efficacious in gout, rheumatism, palsy, biliary obstruction, and cutaneous disorders. The Bath Literary and Philosophical Institution was established in 1820: the buildings, occupying the site of the lower assembly-rooms, which were burnt down in 1820, are of the Doric order, and comprise a library, lecture-room, laboratory, and two rooms for a museum, exclusively of the housekeeper's apartments: it is open to both visitors and inhabitants. The Bath and West of England Society for the encouragement of Agriculture, the Arts, Manufactures, and Commerce, by the distribution of premiums and medals, was instituted in 1777, at the suggestion of Mr. Edmund Rack. The public subscription library, established in 1800, contains an extensive and well-assorted collection of books in the various branches of science and general literature: it is conducted under judicious regulations, and is liberally supported: there are also numerous circulating libraries. The Mechanics' Institution, recently formed, occupies a commodious building at the corner of York and Abbey streets.

The chief sources of amusement are the subscription assemblies and concerts, which are held during the season, under the superintendence of a master of the ceremonies, whose office being equally honourable and lucrative, has been warmly contested by the successive candidates. The rooms are superbly elegant: the ball-room is one hundred and five feet long, forty-three wide, and twenty-two high; the card-rooms, library, and rooms for refreshment, are furnished in a style of unrivalled splendour. The subscription concerts, of which there are nine during the season, are conducted upon a scale of the most comprehensive liberality. The lower assembly-rooms, which were destroyed by fire in 1820, were nearly equal to the upper rooms in elegance of decoration and convenience of arrangement. The city assemblies, for those who are not eligible as subscribers to the upper rooms, are held, by permission of the corporation, in the banquet-room of the guildhall, every alternate Monday. The theatre, a well-adapted and handsome edifice, in the centre of the city, among the buildings of which it is distinguished by the loftiness of its elevation, is handsomely fitted up, and splendidly decorated: it contains three tiers of boxes; the ceiling is divided into compartments embellished with exquisite paintings by Cassali, which were removed from Fonthill Abbey. The building was completed in 1805, and is regularly open during the season; it has been long and deservedly eulogized for the excellence of the performances, and many actors who have attained the highest degree of eminence on the London stage have made their debût here. Sydney Gardens, the Vauxhall of Bath, are laid out with great taste and beauty; they afford an agreeable promenade at all times, and, during the summer, attract fashionable and numerous assemblages to public entertainments and exhibitions of fire-works, upon which occasions they are brilliantly illuminated. The Subscription Club-house, in York-buildings, containing a spacious suite of elegant rooms, was established in 1720, upon the plan of most of the superior club-houses in London, the members of which establishments are eligible as subscribers without ballot: the annual subscription is six guineas and a half. The Bath and West of England Subscription-rooms, in Pulteney-street, upon a similar plan, and uniting with it the accommodations of an hotel, are fitted up in a very superior style; the members of the York club, and those of the principal club-houses of London, are eligible as subscribers, the annual subscription being two guineas and a half. There are also subscription billiard-rooms in Milsom-street, to which those only are admissible who are eligible to the assembly-rooms. The Lodge of Freemasons hold their meetings in York-street, where a hall was erected in 1817, which may be ranked among the architectural ornaments of the city. There are two extensive riding-schools, well conducted on moderate terms, in one of which is a spacious covered ride for invalids in unfavourable weather. Lansdown and Claverton down afford delightful equestrian excursions, displaying much variety, and abounding in rich and interesting scenery. The races take place on Lansdown, the week after Ascot races; and there is a spring meeting in April, for half-bred mares.

The town, by means of the river, which is navigable to Bristol, and the Kennet and Avon canal, by which it maintains an inland communication with London and the intermediate places, is favourably situated for trade; but the only branch of manufacture carried on is that of coarse woollen cloth, called Bath-coating, and kerseymere, which is made in the neighbourhood. The markets are held on Wednesday and Saturday, in an area behind the guildhall, the wings of which form the principal entrances; the market-house is an extensive and commodious range of building: the corn and cattle markets are held in Walcot, and the coal market in Loo-close, where there is a weighing machine, and an officer in attendance to see all transactions equitably concluded. The fairs are on February 14th and July 10th.

Corporate Seal.

This city enjoyed, under Edgar and other Saxon monarchs, many valuable privileges, which were afterwards confirmed by Richard I., subsequently recognized and enlarged by Queen Elizabeth (who gave the citizens a charter of incorporation), and finally by George III., who made such modifications in the charter as the increasing importance of the place required. The government is vested in a mayor, recorder, two bailiffs (who act as sheriffs), a chamberlain, deputy chamberlain, ten aldermen, and twenty common council-men, assisted by a town clerk, two serjeants at mace, and subordinate officers. The mayor, who is also coroner and clerk of the market, and the two bailiffs, are chosen annually from among the aldermen, on the Monday before Michaelmas day; the mayor, aldermen, and two senior common council-men, are justices of the peace. The freedom of the city is obtained by gift from the corporation, who have power to choose citizens or free burgesses from among the inhabitants generally. The elective franchise was conferred in the reign of Edward I., since which time the city has continued to return two members to parliament: the right of election is vested solely in the corporation, and the mayor is the returning officer: the influence of the Marquis of Bath prevails in the return of one of the members. The corporation hold a court of session quarterly, and a court of record every Monday, for all personal actions arising within the city and liberty: a court of requests, for the recovery of debts under £10, is held every Monday, by commissioners appointed under an act of the 45th of George III., the jurisdiction of which extends over the city and liberty, the parish of Walcot, and the several parishes and places in the hundreds of Bath-Forum and Wellow, and the liberties of Hampton, Claverton, and Easton with Amrill, in the county of Somerset. The guildhall is an elegant structure of freestone; the front is decorated with a portico of four lofty Corinthian columns, rising from a rustic basement, and supporting a triangular pediment, with a rich entablature and cornice, in the tympanum of which are the city arms, and on the apex a finely sculptured figure of Justice; above the cornice is a handsome balustrade, with urns: this elegant building comprises, on the ground floor, a handsome vestibule, sessions hall, offices for the courts of record and requests, and for the chamberlain and town clerk; and, in the upper story, a magnificent suite of apartments for civic entertainments. In the mayor's room is a beautiful head of Minerva, or of Apollo, of gilt brass; it was discovered in 1727, at the depth of sixteen feet below the surface of the ground, in Stall-street, and is thought to be part of a mutilated statue, the remainder of which is supposed to be buried near the same spot. The prison is a spacious building, occupying an area sixty feet in front, and eighty feet in depth, with a large court-yard, and cells in which delinquents are confined previously to their committal to the county gaol.

Arms of the Bishoprick.

Jointly with Wells, Bath is the head of a diocese, which is co-extensive with the county of Somerset. The Abbey church, dedicated to St. Peter and St. Paul, is a venerable and finely proportioned cruciform structure, in the later style of English architecture, of which it forms one of the purest specimens: from the intersection, an irregularly quadrilateral tower rises to the height of one hundred and sixty-two feet. It occupies the site, and is built partly with the materials, of the conventual church of the monastery founded by Osric, which had subsisted, under different forms of government, for more than eight hundred years. This church having become dilapidated, Bishop Oliver King (as it is said, admonished in a dream, of which a memorial is sculptured on the west front,) began to rebuild it in 1495; but dying before it was completed, and the citizens refusing to purchase it from the commissioners of Henry VIII., the walls were left roofless, till Dr. James Montague, Bishop of the diocese, aided by a liberal contribution from the nobility and gentry resident in the county, completed it, in the year 1606. There are some remains of the monastery on the south side of the Abbey church, consisting chiefly of the gatehouse in which James II., Mary, consort of William III., Queen Anne and her consort, George, Prince of Denmark, successively resided: the revenue, at the dissolution, was £695. 6. 1¼. By charter of Elizabeth, the several parishes of St. Peter and St. Paul, or the Abbey parish, St. James, and St. Michael, were consolidated into one rectory, to which the vicarages of Widcomb and Lyncomb were annexed. The living is in the archdeaconry of Bath, and diocese of Bath and Wells, rated in the king's books at £20. 17. 11., and in the patronage of the Mayor and Corporation. St. James' church, rebuilt in 1768, is an elegant structure in the later style of English architecture. St. Michael's, erected in 1744, is of the Doric order, with a handsome dome. The parochial church of Walcot, a spacious edifice within the liberty of the city, was rebuilt in 1780, and has lately received an addition of two thousand one hundred sittings, of which number, one thousand eight hundred are free, and towards defraying the expense of which the Incorporated Society for building and enlarging churches and chapels granted £1000. The living is a discharged rectory, in the archdeaconry of Bath, and diocese of Bath and Wells, rated in the king's books at £6. 19. 9½., and in the patronage of the Lord of the Manor. Christ-church was erected by subscription, in 1798, for the especial accommodation of the poor; it is a fine building in the later style of English architecture. The living is a perpetual curacy, exempt from the jurisdiction of the Archdeacon, and in the patronage of the Bishop of the diocese. St. Mary Magdalene's, an ancient edifice overspread with ivy, on Beachen Cliff; and St. Michael's chapel, near the cross, are parochial chapels, the former in the gift of the Crown, and the latter in the patronage of the Rector of Bath. St. Mary's chapel, in Queen-square, built by subscription in 1735, is a handsome edifice in the Grecian style of architecture; the exterior is of the Doric, and the interior of the Ionic, order. The octagon chapel, in Milsom-street, was erected in 1767, and is much admired for the elegance of its style. Margaret chapel, in Margaret-buildings, is a spacious and handsome structure in the early style of English architecture. The chapel in Lansdown Place, erected in 1794, and dedicated to All Saints, is a good specimen of the decorated style; there are twelve fine windows, in which are painted the heads of the twelve Apostles, and the east window is ornamented with a painting of the Last Supper. Kensington chapel, a neat modern building near the London road, was erected by subscription, in 1795; and Laura chapel, an elegant and well arranged edifice in Henrietta-street, was built by tontine subscription, in 1796. There are places of worship for Baptists, the Society of Friends, Independents, Methodists, Moravians, Unitarians, and Roman Catholics.

The free grammar school was founded by Edward VI., in 1552, and endowed with lands belonging to the dissolved religious houses: the management is vested in the corporation, who appoint the master, and allow him a salary of £60 per annum, and an excellent house. The rectory of Charlcombe was annexed to the mastership of this school by the late Rev. William Robins, for the instruction of ten additional boys, sons of freemen, or inhabitants of the city, in classical and commercial learning. The Blue-coat charity school, for fifty boys and fifty girls, was founded in 1711, by Robert Nelson, Esq., and is chiefly supported by subscription; an apprentice fee of £6 is given with each boy, and one of £5 with each girl, on leaving the school. There are also two other free schools for girls, besides one for the instruction of poor children of Bath and Bath-Forum, a National school, and a Roman Catholic free school. The Bath hospital, open to the poor from every part of the kingdom, whose maladies require the use of the Bath waters, is supported by subscription, and under the direction of a president and governors, incorporated by act of parliament, who have a common seal, and are empowered to fill up vacancies in their own body. The Bath United hospital, combining the objects of the late city dispensary and casualty infirmary, recently established, and for which a spacious building has been erected near the cross bath, and the infirmary in Kingston-buildings, for curing diseases of the eye, are supported by subscription. There are three societies for the relief of women during child-birth; an asylum for the support of young females, and for instructing them in household work; a house of protection for orphans and destitute females; an establishment for aged, and an asylum for young, females; and charitable institutions of various kinds, adapted to the wants of the distressed poor, and to the mitigation of almost every species of calamity, all which are liberally supported and judiciously regulated. St. John's hospital, for the maintenance of six aged men and six women, was founded in the reign of Henry II., by Reginald Fitz-Jocelyn, who endowed it with lands then producing £22 per annum; the management is vested in the corporation: attached to this institution is a neat chapel, in which the master, who must be a clergyman of the established church, officiates daily, and receives a liberal stipend. Partis' College, a capacious range of building, occupying three sides of a quadrangle, on the upper road to Bristol, and comprising a chapel and separate dwellings for thirty decayed gentlewomen, ten of whom must be either the widows or daughters of clergymen, was founded and endowed by Mrs. Partis, in fulfilment of the intention of her husband, Fletcher Partis, Esq., who died before it was carried into effect; each of the inmates has a house containing four apartments, a garden, and a liberal pecuniary allowance.

The remains of antiquity, found at different times in this city, are of British, Roman, and Saxon origin, and clearly demonstrate the fact of its having been severally occupied by those people. Among the British antiquities are celts, or stone hatchets, hand millstones, boars' teeth, and amber beads, found in their burial-places, a small silver coin, having on the obverse a rude head in profile, and on the reverse a star, or wheel. Among the Roman was found, in 1753, a pedestal with a Latin inscription: in 1755, parts of the Roman baths, and several of the large tubulated bricks, which conveyed the heat to the *sudatoria*, were discovered; and in 1790, a votive altar, fragments of fluted Corinthian columns, basso-relievos, and other relics of the temple of Minerva, besides numerous coins of the emperors Nero, Trajan, Adrian, Antonine, Gallienus, Claudius, Gothicus, Maxentius, and Constantine, with some of Carausius, who assumed the Roman purple in Britain, were found. On digging the foundation for the new bridge over the Avon to Walcot, the remains of an old ford were observable, and a leaden vessel was found, containing some hundreds of *denarii*, and several small brass coins from the time of the Emperor Valens to that of Eugenius; for the reception of these, a room was appropriated by the corporation, in which they are deposited, with a due regard to classification. The Saxon remains, exclusively of coins, coffins, &c., consist of what is still visible in the city walls, erected by them on the Roman foundation, in which are inserted fragments of the ruined temple, pieces of sculpture, and parts of triumphal arches, intermixed with the original materials. In a stone coffin was also found a small copper box, in the form of a rouleau, divided into two parts, the upper part being covered by a slide, probably intended for perfume, and the lower part filled with small silver coins resembling the early Saxon *scattæ*. John Hales, who, in 1612, was appointed Greek Professor at Oxford, and who, in the year following, pronounced the funeral oration of Sir Thomas Bodley, founder of the Bodleian library, was a native of this city, and received the rudiments of his education in the grammar school. Benjamin Robins, a celebrated mathematician, and the writer of the account of Commodore Anson's voyage round the world, was born here in 1707. Closely connected with Bath for several years, though not a native, was Ralph Allen, Esq., of Prior Park, an elegant mansion, a few miles to the south, which was in his time the resort of several of the wits and literati of the age: this gentleman, supposed to be the original of Fielding's *Allworthy*, in his novel of Tom Jones, amassed a splendid fortune by being the first who farmed the cross-posts throughout the kingdom, and having been elected a member of the corporation of Bath, exercised great influence in the regulation of its municipal affairs: he died in 1777, and was interred at Bathampton, in the south aisle of the church, where a tablet has been erected to his memory. Bath gives the title of marquis to the family of Thynne, of Longleat House.

BATHAMPTON, a parish in the hundred or liberty of HAMPTON and CLAVERTON, though locally in the hundred of Bath-Forum, county of SOMERSET, 1¾ mile (N. E. by E.) from Bath, containing 243 inhabitants. The living is a discharged vicarage, consolidated with that of Bath-Ford, in the archdeaconry of Bath, and diocese of Bath and Wells, rated in the king's books at £7. 17. 1., and endowed with £200 private benefaction, and £200 royal bounty. The church is dedicated to St. Nicholas. The parish is within the jurisdiction of the court of requests held at Bath every Monday, for the recovery of debts under £10.

BATHEALTON, a parish in the hundred of MILVERTON, county of SOMERSET, 2½ miles (S.) from Wiveliscombe, containing 105 inhabitants. The living is a rectory, in the archdeaconry of Bath, and diocese of Bath and Wells, rated in the king's books at £7. 2. 6., and in the patronage of the Bishop of Bath and Wells. The church is dedicated to St. Bartholomew. A mile westward from it is a circular intrenchment, within the area of which some Roman coins have been discovered.

BATH-EASTON, a parish in the hundred of BATH-FORUM, county of SOMERSET, 3 miles (N. E.) from Bath, containing, with a portion of the liberty of Easton and

Amrill, 1330 inhabitants. The living is a discharged vicarage, with the perpetual curacy of St. Catherine annexed, in the archdeaconry of Bath, and diocese of Bath and Wells, rated in the king's books at £9. 6. 5., and in the patronage of the Dean and Canons of Christ Church, Oxford. The church, which has a beautiful tower, is dedicated to St. John the Baptist. There is a place of worship for Wesleyan Methodists. The village, divided into Upper and Lower Bath-Easton, is situated on the London road, between the Lower Avon and Lansdown, and at the base of a steep hill, on the summit of which there are vestiges of an intrenchment, nearly circular, supposed to have been constructed by the Saxons, when they besieged Bath, in 577: some antiquaries are of opinion that this hill was anciently crowned by a temple, erected by Bladud, in honour of Apollo. The parish is within the jurisdiction of the court of requests held at Bath every Monday, for the recovery of debts under £10. Here is a school for eight boys, with an endowment of £5. 5. per annum, the bequest of John Hellier, in 1712. The Roman Fosse-way passes through the parish: a variety of fossil shells has been found in the quarries on Lansdown. At a villa here resided Sir John Miller, whose lady established a literary festival for the recitation of prize poems, which were published, under the title of "Poetical Amusements:" she died in 1781, and was interred in the Abbey church at Bath.

BATH-FORD, a parish in the hundred of Bath-Forum, county of Somerset, 3½ miles (E. N. E.) from Bath, containing 688 inhabitants. The living is a discharged vicarage, with that of Bathampton consolidated, in the archdeaconry of Bath, and diocese of Bath and Wells, rated in the king's books at £8. 18., endowed with £200 private benefaction, and £200 royal bounty, and in the patronage of the Dean and Chapter of Bristol. The church is dedicated to St. Swithin. The village is situated in a picturesque neighbourhood, on the banks of the Avon, which was anciently crossed by a ford. The parish is within the jurisdiction of the court of requests held at Bath every Monday, for the recovery of debts under £10. Here are vestiges of a Roman camp, and a tumulus; and, in 1691, a Roman hypocaust, with a Mosaic pavement, altar, urns containing coins, and other ancient relics, were discovered.

BATHLEY, a township in the parish of North Muskham, northern division of the wapentake of Thurgarton, county of Nottingham, 4 miles (N. N. W.) from Newark, containing 172 inhabitants.

BATHWICK, a parish in the hundred of Bath-Forum, county of Somerset, ½ a mile (N. E.) from Bath, containing 4009 inhabitants. The living comprises a rectory and a vicarage, with the rectory of Wolley annexed, in the archdeaconry of Bath, and diocese of Bath and Wells: the rectory is rated in the king's books at £3. 6. 8., and the vicarage at £8. 3. 4., and in the patronage of the Marquis of Cleveland. The church, dedicated to St. Mary, was erected in 1820; it is a handsome and spacious structure in the decorated style of English architecture, with a beautiful altar-piece, painted and presented to the parish by Mr. B. Barber. This elegant suburb to the city of Bath, at the beginning of the last century, consisted only of a few scattered houses unpleasantly situated on an extensive marsh, frequently inundated by the river Avon. From the discovery here of a large portion of those interesting relics which are deposited in the museum at Bath, this place appears to have formed, at a remote period of antiquity, no inconsiderable part of that city, and to have retained its importance, during the successive occupation of Bath by the Britons, Romans, and Saxons. Since the last census, it has greatly increased in extent and population, and now contains some of the most elegant ranges of building which adorn that city: Pulteney-street, Laura Place, and Sydney Place and Gardens, are all in this parish, and several beautiful villas and handsome residences have been erected on the acclivities of the hill, extending nearly a mile, in a direction towards the pleasant and retired village of Claverton. Bathwick is connected with Bath by two handsome bridges over the river Avon, and appears to be rather an integral part of the city itself than an appendage to it. The Kennet and Avon canal, in its course through Sydney Gardens, has been made available to the introduction of a pleasing variety into the grounds; and an elegant stone bridge of one arch, with a handsome iron palisade, which has been erected over it, forms an interesting feature in the scenery of this enchanting place. In decorating these gardens, an entire pig of lead, weighing 195lb., and bearing the official stamp "IMP. HADRIANI AUG.," and several smaller pieces of that metal, were found; from which circumstance, it is very probable that this was the site of some Roman lead-works. There is a manufactory for broad cloth in the parish; and, in addition to the Kennet and Avon canal, the Somersetshire coal canal passes through it. Bathwick is in the liberty of the city of Bath, and within the jurisdiction of a court of requests held there every Monday, for the recovery of debts under £10.

BATLEY, a parish comprising the chapelry of Morley, and the township of Batley, in the lower division of the wapentake of Agbrigg, and the chapelry of Gildersome, and the township of Churwell, in the wapentake of Morley, West riding of the county of York, and containing 9154 inhabitants, of which number, 3717 are in the township of Batley, 7 miles (N. W. by W.) from Wakefield. The living is a discharged vicarage, in the archdeaconry and diocese of York, rated in the king's books at £16. 11. 8., endowed with £200 private benefaction, and £200 royal bounty, and in the patronage of the Earl of Cardigan and Lord Grey de Wilton. The church, dedicated to All Saints, and said to have been erected in the reign of Henry VI., contains several splendid monuments to the memory of the deceased lords of the manor. There is a place of worship for Wesleyan Methodists. The manufacture of blankets, carpets, coverlets, flushing, and woollen cloth, prevails to a great extent within the parish. A free school for the education of sixty children, endowed with £120 per annum and a house for the master, was founded by the Rev. William Lee, in 1612: the school-room has lately been rebuilt. A school for fifteen girls is supported by the produce of a fund raised by subscription; and one for five poor children has a small endowment, left by Joshua Scholefield, in 1806.

BATSFORD, a parish in the upper division of the hundred of Kiftsgate, county of Gloucester, 2 miles (N. W.) from Moreton in the Marsh, containing 108 inhabitants. The living is a rectory, in the archdeaconry and diocese of Gloucester, rated in the king's books at £13. 3. 9., and in the patronage of the Dean and Canons of Christ Church, Oxford. The church, dedicated to St. Mary, was rebuilt and enlarged in 1822, at the expense of Lord Redesdale. This parish enjoys the benefit of an endowed school at Moreton in the Marsh.

BATTERLEY, a township in that part of the parish of Barthomley which is in the northern division of the hundred of Pirehill, county of Stafford, 6½ miles (N. W. by W.) from Newcastle under Line, containing 242 inhabitants.

BATTERSBY, a township in the parish of Ingleby-Greenhow, western division of the liberty of Langbaurgh, North riding of the county of York, 5¼ miles (E. by S.) from Stokesley, containing 87 inhabitants.

BATTERSEA, a parish partly in the eastern, but chiefly in the western, division of the hundred of Brixton, county of Surrey, 4 miles (S.) from London, containing, with the hamlet of Penge, 4992 inhabitants. This place, in Domesday-book called *Patricesey*, or *Peters-ey*, was so named from having anciently belonged to the abbey of St. Peter, at Westminster: it was formerly of much greater extent than at present. The family of St. John had a venerable mansion here, of which there are still some remains: it was the favourite resort of Pope, who, when visiting his friend Lord Bolingbroke, usually selected as his study, in which he is said to have composed some of his celebrated works, a parlour wainscoted with cedar, overlooking the Thames. The village is pleasantly situated on the southern bank of the river, over which there is a wooden bridge, connecting it with Chelsea: the houses are irregularly built, and in detached situations; the inhabitants are supplied with water from springs. The neighbourhood has long been celebrated for the production of vegetables for the London market, especially asparagus, which was first cultivated here; but the quantity of land appropriated to that purpose has, within the last twenty years, been considerably diminished. On part of the site of Bolingbroke house a horizontal air-mill was erected, in 1790, of a conical form, one hundred and forty feet in height, and having a mean diameter of fifty feet: it was originally applied to the bruising of linseed for oil, and subsequently to the grinding of malt for distilleries, which were at that time in extensive operation here. A silk-manufactory has recently been established, but the principal business is confined to the market-gardeners, of whom there is still a considerable number in the neighbourhood. A fair was formerly held at Easter, but it has lately been suppressed. The county magistrates hold a meeting at Wandsworth, an adjoining parish, where also a court of requests, for the recovery of debts under £5, is held, under an act obtained in the 31st of George II., the powers of which were extended to the present sum by an act in the 46th of George III.; its jurisdiction includes this parish. The lord of the manor also holds a court leet at Wandsworth, at which a headborough and constables for Battersea are appointed.

The living is a vicarage, in the archdeaconry of Surrey, and diocese of Winchester, rated in the king's books at £13. 15. 2½., and in the patronage of Earl Spencer. The church, dedicated to St. Mary, was handsomely rebuilt of brick in 1777; it has a tower surmounted by a small spire, and, standing on the margin of the river, forms an interesting object from the water: the window over the altar is decorated with portraits of Henry VII., his grandmother Margaret Beauchamp, and Queen Elizabeth, in stained glass; the interior contains some interesting sepulchral monuments, among which are, one by Roubilliac, to the memory of Viscount Bolingbroke and his lady, and one to the memory of Edward Winter, an officer in the service of the East India Company, on which is recorded an account of his having, singly and unarmed, killed a tiger, and, on foot, defeated forty Moors on horseback. Collins, author of the Peerage and Baronetage of England; his grandson David Collins, Lieutenant-Governor of New South Wales, and author of a History of the English Settlement there; and William Curtis, a distinguished botanical writer, were buried here. A chapel of ease, in Battersea Fields, was erected in 1828, at the expense of £2969. 2. 10., defrayed partly by a rate, and partly by grant from the parliamentary commissioners; it is a neat building in the later style of English architecture, and contains five hundred and ninety-six sittings, of which three hundred and eighty-four are free. There are places of worship for Baptists and Wesleyan Methodists. A school, for the instruction of twenty boys, was founded and endowed by Sir Walter St. John, in 1700. A National school for ninety boys and sixty girls, and an infant school, are supported by subscription. Battersea Rise, a part of the common between Clapham and Wandsworth, is ornamented with several handsome villas, one of which was the residence of that eminent citizen, Sir John Barnard, who died in 1764.

BATTISFORD, a parish in the hundred of Bosmere and Claydon, county of Suffolk, 2½ miles (W. S. W.) from Needham-Market, containing 421 inhabitants. The living is a discharged vicarage, in the archdeaconry of Suffolk, and diocese of Norwich, rated in the king's books at £8. 0. 7½., and in the patronage of G. Paske, Esq. The church is dedicated to St. Mary. Here was anciently a preceptory of the Knights Hospitallers, the revenue of which, at the dissolution, was £53. 10.

BATTLE, or BATTEL, a market town and parish in the hundred of Battle, rape of Hastings, county of Sussex, 7 miles (N. W.) from Hastings, 63 (E. by N.) from Chichester, and 56 (S. E.) from London, containing 2852 inhabitants. This place, previously called *Epiton*, derives its present name from the memorable battle fought there, October 14th, 1066, between Harold, King of England, and William, Duke of Normandy. Though generally called the battle of Hastings, it took place at this town, where, in fulfilment of a vow, William the Conqueror founded a magnificent abbey for monks of the Benedictine order, and raised the high altar on the very spot where Harold and his valiant brothers fell, covered with wounds, by the side of the English standard. William conferred many extraordinary privileges upon this abbey, in which were preserved, until its suppression, the sword and royal robe worn by him on the day of his coronation, and the celebrated roll on which the names of the warriors who accompanied him to England were inscribed: he conferred on it the privilege of sanctuary, raised it to the dignity of a mitred abbey, and invested its abbots with the power of saving a criminal from execution, if accidentally passing at the time. At the dissolution, its revenue was £987. 0. 10½.: there are still considerable remains; the gatehouse, a beautiful specimen of the decorated style of English architecture, is in entire preservation, and many parts of the conventual buildings have been retained in the modern mansion of Battle Abbey. After the establishment of the abbey a town arose in its vicinity, which rapidly increased, and had become a place of considerable importance in the reign of Henry I., who conferred upon it many privileges, among which was the grant of a market. In 1347, the French having effected a landing at Rye, the abbot of Battel, assisted by the inhabitants, marched to that place, and drove the enemy to their ships with great slaughter. The town is situated in a beautiful valley, bounded on the west, south, and south-east by wood-crowned eminences, and consists of several streets: near the centre stands the magnificent gateway of the abbey. The houses in general are ancient and of mean appearance, but there are several modern and handsome structures; the town is lighted, and well supplied with water. The manufacture of fine gunpowder, established at a very early period, and for which this town has attained the highest celebrity, is carried on to a very great extent. The market is on Thursday: the fairs are on Whit-Monday and November 22nd; a great number of horned cattle are sent from this part of the country to the London market. The town is within the jurisdiction of the county magistrates, who hold their petty sessions here for the district; but this being a franchise, the inhabitants are exempt from serving on juries at the assizes and sessions for the county. A coroner and other officers are appointed at the court leet of the lord of the manor. The living is a vicarage, in the diocese of Chichester, and an exempt deanery, still retaining the exercise of its jurisdiction; it is rated in the king's books at £24. 13. 4., and is in the patronage of Sir Godfrey V. Webster, Bart. The church, dedicated to St. Mary, is a spacious structure, partly Norman, and partly in the early and later styles of English architecture. There are places of worship for Baptists, Wesleyan Methodists, and Unitarians. In 1791, Mrs. Elizabeth Langton bequeathed £1500 for the instruction of fifteen boys and fifteen girls, the interest of which is paid to a master; and there are three Sunday schools. Southward of the abbey grounds is a place called Tellman Hill, where William is said to have mustered his army the evening before the battle; and to the north is another, named Callback Hill, from which it is said he recalled his troops from pursuing the vanquished enemy: numerous other spots in the vicinity have names relating to circumstances connected with the battle.

BATTLEFIELD, a parish in the liberties of Shrewsbury, county of Salop, 3½ miles (N. N. E.) from Shrewsbury, containing 64 inhabitants. The living is a perpetual curacy, in the archdeaconry of Salop, and diocese of Lichfield and Coventry, endowed with £400 private benefaction, and £800 royal bounty, and in the patronage of J. Corbett, Esq. The church is dedicated to St. Mary Magdalene. A fair for horned cattle and sheep is held on the 2nd of August. This place derives its name from a sanguinary battle fought here, on the 22nd of July, 1403, between Henry IV. and the rebels under Percy, Earl of Northumberland, in which nearly two thousand three hundred gentlemen (among whom was Lord Henry Percy, the valiant Hotspur), and about six hundred private soldiers, were slain. Henry, in grateful commemoration of the victory, immediately founded on the spot a college for Secular clerks, the revenue of which, at the dissolution, was £54. 10. 4.

BATTLESDEN, a parish in the hundred of Manshead, county of Bedford, 3 miles (S. S. E.) from Woburn, containing 151 inhabitants. The living is a rectory, with that of Potsgrove annexed, in the archdeaconry of Bedford, and diocese of Lincoln, rated in the king's books at £12. 9. 7., and in the patronage of Sir G. P. Turner, Bart. The church is dedicated to St. Peter. This place affords the title of baron to Earl Bathurst.

BAUGHURST, a parish forming a detached portion of the hundred of Evingar, Kingsclere division of the county of Southampton, 7 miles (N. W. by N.) from Basingstoke, containing, with the tythings of Ham and Inhurst 434 inhabitants. The living is a rectory, in the peculiar jurisdiction of the Incumbent, rated in the king's books at £7. 12. 1., and in the patronage of the Bishop of Winchester. This parish is within the jurisdiction of the Cheyney Court held at Winchester every Thursday, for the recovery of debts to any amount.

BAULKING, a chapelry in the parish of Uffington, hundred of Shrivenham, county of Berks, 3½ miles (S. E. by S.) from Great Farringdon, containing 155 inhabitants. The chapel is dedicated to St. Nicholas.

BAUMBER, or BAMBURGH, a parish in the northern division of the wapentake of Gartree, parts of Lindsey, county of Lincoln, 4 miles (N. W.) from Horncastle, containing 319 inhabitants. The living is a perpetual curacy, in the archdeaconry and diocese of Lincoln, endowed with £400 royal bounty, and £400 parliamentary grant, and in the patronage of the Duke of Newcastle. The church is dedicated to St. Swithin.

BAUNTON, a parish in the hundred of Crowthorne and Minety, county of Gloucester, 1¾ mile (N. by E.) from Cirencester, containing 129 inhabitants. The living is a perpetual curacy, in the archdeaconry and diocese of Gloucester, endowed with £400 royal bounty, and in the patronage of John Masters, Esq. The Roman Fosse-way passes along the eastern border of the parish.

BAVERSTOCK, a parish in the hundred of Cawden and Cadworth, county of Wilts, 4 miles (W.) from Wilton, containing 135 inhabitants. The living is a rectory, in the archdeaconry and diocese of Salisbury, rated in the king's books at £11. 10. 2½., and in the patronage of the Rector and Fellows of Exeter College, Oxford. The river Nadder runs through the parish, in which there is a spring called Merrywell, the water of which is efficacious in curing diseases of the eye. The rector supports a school for poor children.

BAVINGTON (GREAT), a township in the parish of Kirk-Whelpington, north-eastern division of Tindale ward, county of Northumberland, 14 miles (N. N. E.) from Hexham, containing 74 inhabitants. There is a place of worship for Scotch Presbyterians.

BAVINGTON (LITTLE), a township in the parish of Thockrington, north-eastern division of Tindale ward, county of Northumberland, 12 miles (N.N.E.) from Hexham, containing 78 inhabitants.

BAWBURGH, a parish in the hundred of Forehoe, county of Norfolk, 4¾ miles (W.) from Norwich, containing, with Bowthorpe, 456 inhabitants. The living is a discharged vicarage, in the archdeaconry of Norfolk, and diocese of Norwich, rated in the king's books at £13. 17. 6., endowed with £400 royal bounty, and in the patronage of the Dean and Chapter of Norwich. The church is dedicated to St. Wolstan, whose birthplace this was, and who died here in 1016. His relics were enshrined in it, and became the resort of numerous pilgrims, whose presents were a source of great emolument to the vicar and officiating priests, who, in 1309, rebuilt the church, which has a round tower. An ancient hermitage, with a chapel attached to it, stood near the bridge.

BAWDESWELL, a parish in the hundred of EYNSFORD, county of NORFOLK, 4 miles (W. by S.) from Reepham, containing 590 inhabitants. The living is a discharged rectory, in the archdeaconry of Norfolk, and diocese of Norwich, rated in the king's books at £7, and in the patronage of Sir J. Lombe, Bart. The church is dedicated to All Saints. A school for the instruction of twelve boys has an endowment of about £10 per annum, arising from land bequeathed by John Leeds, in 1730.

BAWDRIP, a parish in the northern division of the hundred of PETHERTON, county of SOMERSET, 3¼ miles (N.E. by E.) from Bridg-water, containing 372 inhabitants. The living is a rectory, in the archdeaconry of Wells, and diocese of Bath and Wells, rated in the king's books at £15. 19. 7., and in the patronage of Sir Henry Nicholls, Knt., surviving trustee of Admiral Sir H. Nicholls.

BAWDSEY, a parish (formerly a market town) in the hundred of WILFORD, county of SUFFOLK, 8½ miles (S. E. by S.) from Woodbridge, containing 414 inhabitants. The living is a discharged vicarage, in the archdeaconry of Suffolk, and diocese of Norwich, rated in the king's books at £6. 13. 4., and in the patronage of the Crown. The church is dedicated to St. Mary. There is a place of worship for Wesleyan Methodists. In the 11th of Edward I. permission was obtained for a market to be held here on Friday, but it has been discontinued: there is a fair on September 8th. Bawdsey haven, at the mouth of the river Deben, affords convenient anchorage for small vessels. On the eastern side of the parish, which is bounded by the North sea, are two Martello towers, a fort, a signal-house, and a landmark.

BAWSEY, a parish in the Lynn division of the hundred of FREEBRIDGE, county of NORFOLK, 3 miles (E. by N.) from Lynn-Regis, containing 34 inhabitants. The living is a discharged rectory, in the archdeaconry and diocese of Norwich, rated in the king's books at £4, and in the patronage of Philip Hammond, Esq. The church, dedicated to St. James, is desecrated.

BAWTRY, a market town and chapelry in that part of the parish of BLYTH which is in the southern division of the wapentake of STRAFFORTH and TICKHILL, West riding of the county of YORK, 41½ miles (S. by E.) from York, and 153½ (N. by W.) from London, on the great north road, containing 1027 inhabitants. This town is situated on the river Idle, which separates the counties of York and Nottingham, and near the Roman road leading from *Agelocum*, Littleborough, to *Danum*, Doncaster. It consists of three streets, the principal of which is very spacious, and contains many handsome and well-built houses; it is partly paved, and amply supplied with water from springs and from the river, over which a neat substantial stone bridge was erected in 1811, at an expense of £4000. The trade, which has greatly declined since the construction of the Chesterfield canal, and the erection of a bridge over the Trent at Gainsborough, arises chiefly from the inland navigation, and consists in supplying London, Hull, and other places, with corn, oak timber, and stone, of which last, that called the Roche Abbey stone is much esteemed by statuaries and architects. The river is navigable for craft of from twelve to twenty-four tons' burden, by which means the town is supplied with coal, grocery, &c. The market is on Thursday: fairs for horses, horned cattle, and sheep are on the Thursday in Whitsun-week, and Old Martinmas-day. The magistrates for the West riding hold petty sessions here for the district, and constables and other officers are appointed at the court leet of the lord of the manor. The chapel, dedicated to St. Nicholas, was erected in the reign of Henry II., and rebuilt in 1686: the tower, which is strengthened by buttresses, and crowned with pinnacles, was added in 1712. There are places of worship for Independents and Wesleyan Methodists. A small school-room has been built by subscription on the waste land adjoining the town, in which eight boys are taught reading, writing, and arithmetic. At Scrooby, one mile from the town, was a palace belonging to the Archbishops of York, in which Cardinal Wolsey resided, and afterwards Archbishop Sandys, whose daughter is interred in the chancel of the chapel: the remains have been converted into a farm-house.

BAXTERLEY, a parish in the Atherstone division of the hundred of HEMLINGFORD, county of WARWICK, 4 miles (W. by S.) from Atherstone, containing 210 inhabitants. The living is a discharged rectory, in the archdeaconry of Coventry, and diocese of Lichfield and Coventry, rated in the king's books at £5, and in the alternate patronage of the Crown and John Boultbee, Esq. Coal and limestone are said to exist, but are not worked, in this parish.

BAYDON, a parish in the hundred of RAMSBURY, county of WILTS, 4¼ miles (N.) from Ramsbury, containing 313 inhabitants. The living is a perpetual curacy, in the peculiar jurisdiction of the Dean of Salisbury, endowed with £800 private benefaction, and £1000 royal bounty, and in the patronage of Sir Francis Burdett, Bart. The church is dedicated to St. Nicholas. There is a place of worship for Wesleyan Methodists.

BAYFIELD, a parish in the hundred of HOLT, county of NORFOLK, 2¾ miles (N. W.) from Holt. The population is returned with Glandford. The living is a discharged sinecure rectory, in the archdeaconry and diocese of Norwich, rated in the king's books at £4, and in the patronage of Henry Joddrell, Esq. The church, which was dedicated to St. Margaret, has long been desecrated.

BAYFORD, a parish in the hundred and county of HERTFORD, 3 miles (S. S. W.) from Hertford, containing 307 inhabitants. The living is a perpetual curacy, annexed to the rectory of Essendon, in the archdeaconry of Huntingdon, and diocese of Lincoln. The church, dedicated to St. Mary, is a neat brick edifice recently erected, containing an ancient octangular font ornamented with quatrefoils and roses.

BAYHAM, a hamlet in that part of the parish of FRANT which is in the hundred of ROTHERFIELD, rape of PEVENSEY, county of SUSSEX, 2½ miles (W.) from Lamberhurst. The population is returned with the parish. Here are some remains of a monastery of Premonstratensian canons, which is described in the article on FRANT. Bayham gives the title of viscount to the Marquis of Camden, who has a seat here.

BAYLEHAM, a parish in the hundred of BOSMERE and CLAYDON, county of SUFFOLK, 2½ miles (S. by E.) from Needham-Market, containing 237 inhabitants. The living is a rectory, in the archdeaconry of Suffolk, and diocese of Norwich, rated in the king's books at £12. 4. 9½., and in the patronage of N. Lee Acton, Esq. The church is dedicated to St. Peter. The Stow-Market and Ipswich canal bounds the parish on the north-east.

BAYNTON, a joint tything with West Coulston, in the parish of EDINGTON, hundred of WHORWELSDOWN, county of WILTS. The population is returned with West Coulston.

BAYSWATER, a hamlet in the parish of PADDINGTON, Holborn division of the hundred of OSSULSTONE, county of MIDDLESEX, 1 mile from Cumberland-gate, London, on the Uxbridge road. The population is returned with the parish. Bayswater, which may now be considered as a suburb to the metropolis, is desirable as a place of residence from its vicinity to Kensington Gardens, which are situated on the south: it is lighted with gas, and the inhabitants are supplied with water from a reservoir originally constructed for the use of Kensington Palace, and subsequently granted to the proprietors of Chelsea water-works, on the condition that the supply to the palace should be regularly continued. Sir John Hill, M.D., a voluminous writer, resided here many years, and cultivated the plants from which he prepared his medicines, on the spot now occupied by the proprietor of the Bayswater tea-gardens. An episcopal chapel was built by Mr. Edward Orme, in 1818.

BAYTON, a parish in the lower division of the hundred of DODDINGTREE, county of WORCESTER, 1¾ mile (S. E. by S.) from Cleobury-Mortimer, containing 466 inhabitants. The living is a discharged vicarage, united to that of Mamble, in the archdeaconry of Salop, and diocese of Hereford, rated in the king's books at £5. 0. 2½., endowed with £200 private benefaction, and £200 royal bounty. The church is dedicated to St. Bartholomew.

BAYWORTH, a hamlet in the parish of SUNNINGWELL, hundred of HORMER, county of BERKS. The population is returned with the parish. Here was formerly a chapel of ease to the rectory of Sunningwell, but it has gone to decay.

BEACHAMPTON, a parish in the hundred and county of BUCKINGHAM, 5½ miles (N. E. by E.) from Buckingham, containing 251 inhabitants. The living is a rectory, in the archdeaconry of Buckingham, and diocese of London, rated in the king's books at £14. 16. 5½., and in the patronage of the Master and Fellows of Caius College, Cambridge. The church is dedicated to St. Mary. The river Ouse runs through the parish. William Elmer founded a free grammar school in 1652, and endowed it with £35 per annum; he also bequeathed, in addition to other benefactions, £5 per annum for apprenticing a poor boy. Sir Simon Benet left £10 per annum for clothing six poor men.

BEACHAMWELL, county of NORFOLK. — See BEECHAMWELL.

BEACONSFIELD, a market town and parish in the hundred of BURNHAM, county of BUCKINGHAM, 36 miles (S. E. by S.) from Buckingham, and 23¼ (W. by N.) from London, containing 1736 inhabitants. This place, which is situated on a hill, is supposed to have derived its name from a beacon formerly erected there. The town consists chiefly of four streets, which meet in a convenient market-place in the centre. The principal street extends nearly three quarters of a mile along the turnpike road leading from Uxbridge to Wycombe: the houses in general are well built, and of handsome appearance, and the inhabitants are amply supplied with water. The environs, in which there are some handsome seats, abound with beautiful scenery; and the air is remarkably salubrious. The market is on Thursday; and the fairs, chiefly for horses, horned cattle, and sheep, are held on February 13th, and on Holy Thursday. Constables and other officers are appointed at the court leet of the lord of the manor. The living is a rectory, in the archdeaconry of Buckingham, and diocese of Lincoln, rated in the king's books at £26. 2. 8½., and in the patronage of the President and Fellows of Magdalene College, Oxford. The church, dedicated to All Saints, is an ancient building of stone and flint, with a tower: it formerly belonged to the Augustine monastery at Burnham, founded by Richard, Earl of Cornwall, in 1165, the revenue of which, at the dissolution, was £91. 5. 11. Within the church is a mural tablet to the memory of Edmund Burke, who died at his seat called Gregories, in this parish, and was interred here; and in the churchyard there is a monument of white marble, to the memory of Edmund Waller, the poet, who died October 21st, 1687.

BEADLAM, a township in that part of the parish of KIRKDALE which is in the wapentake of RYEDALE, North riding of the county of YORK, 2¾ miles (E.) from Helmsley, containing 143 inhabitants.

BEADNELL, a chapelry in the parish, and northern division of the ward, of BAMBROUGH, county of NORTHUMBERLAND, 10½ miles (E. S. E.) from Belford, containing 213 inhabitants. The living is a perpetual curacy, in the archdeaconry of Northumberland, and diocese of Durham, endowed with £400 private benefaction, £800 royal bounty, and £200 parliamentary grant, and in the patronage of the Perpetual Curate of Bambrough. The chapel is a small handsome structure with a spire. The village is pleasantly situated on the sea-shore, having a small harbour, and several vessels are employed in conveying lobsters, herrings, and other fish to London. Races were annually held here until 1826, when they were removed to Belford. The trustees of Lord Crewe's charity allow a schoolmaster £5 per annum, and the use of a house and garden, for educating seven boys.

BEAFORD, a parish in the hundred of SHEBBEAR, county of DEVON, 4¾ miles (S. E. by E.) from Great Torrington, containing 582 inhabitants. The living is a rectory, in the archdeaconry of Barnstaple, and diocese of Exeter, rated in the king's books at £11. 15. 7½., and in the patronage of J. Russel, Esq. The church is dedicated to All Saints.

BEAGHALL, a township in the parish of KELLINGTON, lower division of the wapentake of OSGOLDCROSS,

West riding of the county of York, 6 miles (E. N. E.) from Pontefract, containing 546 inhabitants.

BEAKSBOURNE, a parish within the cinque-port liberty of Hastings, of which it is a member, though locally in the hundred of Bridge and Petham, lathe of St. Augustine, county of Kent, 3½ miles (E. S. E.) from Canterbury, containing 311 inhabitants. The living is a vicarage, in the archdeaconry and diocese of Canterbury, rated in the king's books at £6, and in the patronage of the Archbishop of Canterbury. The church is dedicated to St. Peter.

BEALINGS (GREAT), a parish in the hundred of Carlford, county of Suffolk, 2¼ miles (W.) from Woodbridge, containing 339 inhabitants. The living is a discharged rectory, in the archdeaconry of Suffolk, and diocese of Norwich, rated in the king's books at £10. 4. 7., and in the patronage of Lord Henniker. The church is dedicated to St. Mary.

BEALINGS (LITTLE), a parish in the hundred of Carlford, county of Suffolk, 2¾ miles (W. by S.) from Woodbridge, containing 262 inhabitants. The living is a rectory, in the archdeaconry of Suffolk, and diocese of Norwich, rated in the king's books at £6. 7. 3½., endowed with £200 private benefaction, and £200 royal bounty, and in the patronage of G. Thompson, Esq. The church is dedicated to All Saints. Here is an endowment of about £10 per annum, for the instruction of poor children.

BEAMINSTER, a market town and chapelry in the parish of Netherbury, hundred of Beaminster-Forum and Redhone, Bridport division of the county of Dorset, 17½ miles (W. N. W.) from Dorchester, and 137¼ (W. S. W.) from London, containing 2806 inhabitants. During the civil war in the reign of Charles I., Prince Maurice, commanding a party of royalists engaged in besieging Lyme, took up his quarters in this town, which, in a few days after, was nearly reduced to ashes by a fire, stated by some historians to have been occasioned by accident, whilst others assert that it was the result of a quarrel between the French and the Cornish men in the service of the king, who set fire to it in five different places. It was rebuilt by means of a parliamentary grant of £2000, but was again nearly destroyed by a fire which occurred in 1684: in 1781, it experienced a similar calamity, but the greater part of the buildings having been insured, it soon recovered its former prosperity. The town is pleasantly situated on the river Birt, which is formed by the union of several small springs that rise in the immediate vicinity: the houses are in general modern and well built, and the inhabitants are amply supplied with water. The manufacture of woollen cloth, which formerly flourished here, is at present on the decline, and that of sail-cloth is now the principal source of employment: there is also a pottery for the coarser kinds of earthenware. The market, granted to William Ewel, prebendary of Sarum, in the 12th of Edward I., is on Thursday; and a fair is held on September 19th, for cattle. Constables and other officers are appointed at the court leet of the lord of the manor. The quarter sessions for the county, now held at Bridport, were formerly held here; and, in 1638, an order of session was issued for building a house of correction at the expense of the division. The town hall is a neat and commodious edifice, in which the public business is transacted.

This chapelry contains the manors of Beaminster Prima and Beaminster Secunda, forming two prebends in the Cathedral Church of Salisbury; the former is rated in the king's books at £20. 2. 6., and the latter at £22. 5. 7½. The chapel, founded in honour of the Nativity of the Blessed Virgin, is a stately edifice in the later style of English architecture, with a fine tower, one hundred feet high, and richly ornamented with sculptured designs of the Crucifixion, the Resurrection, the Ascension, and other subjects of scriptural history. There is a place of worship for Independents. The free school was founded in 1684, by Mrs. Frances Tucker, who endowed it with £20 per annum for the master, leaving also £30 per annum for apprenticing boys, one or two of whom she directed should be put to the sea service. The endowment now produces £150 per annum; the master's salary has been advanced to £40, and the present number of scholars is one hundred, who are instructed on Dr. Bell's system: it is under the direction of trustees, each of whom, on his appointment, receives £10. The Rev. Samuel Hood, father of Lords Hood and Bridport, was master of this school early in the eighteenth century, and subsequently a prebendary in the Cathedral Church of Wells. An almshouse for eight aged persons was founded, in 1630, by Sir John Strode, of Parnham, Knt., the income of which amounts to £20 per annum. Gilbert Adams, of Beaminster, Esq., in 1626, gave £200 to the poor of the parish, directing the produce to be applied to their use, at the discretion of his executors; and the Rev. William Hillary, in 1712, bequeathed the reversion, after ninety-nine years, of land in the parish of Corscombe, worth £30 per annum, for the benefit of twelve distressed families in the parish. Dr. Thomas Spratt, Bishop of Rochester, and the Rev. Thomas Russel, Fellow of New College, Oxford, who distinguished himself by his defence of Warton's History of English Poetry, were natives of this town.

BEAMISH, a township in that part of the parish of Chester le Street which is in the middle division of Chester ward, county palatine of Durham, 7½ miles (S. S. W.) from Gateshead, containing, with part of Tanfield Colliery, 1643 inhabitants. There is a great quantity of coal in this township, which also contains some iron-ore.

BEAMSLEY, a township partly in that portion of the parish of Addingham, but chiefly in that portion of the parish of Skipton, which are in the upper division of the wapentake of Claro, West riding of the county of York, 6½ miles (E. by N.) from Skipton, containing 312 inhabitants. An hospital for thirteen poor women was founded here by Margaret, Countess of Cumberland, under letters patent granted in the 35th of Elizabeth, and endowed with property which, in 1820, produced £357. 9. 4. per annum, from which sum, twelve of the alms-women receive annuities of £16 each, and the thirteenth, one of £18: they have separate apartments, and there is a chapel in which prayers are read daily.

BEANLEY, a township in the parish of Eglingham, northern division of Coquetdale ward, county of Northumberland, 9½ miles (W. N. W.) from Alnwick, containing 160 inhabitants. This was formerly the head of a barony, the lord of which had the power of inflicting capital punishment; Gallow-Haw, on the western side of the Breamish, having been the place of execution. On an elevated spot, called Beanley Plantation, are vestiges of an encampment, having a double fosse and rampart; the road which led to it is plainly discernible. Percy's Cross, erected in memory of Sir Ralph Percy, an officer attached to the Lancastrian party, who fell in battle against the Yorkists, in 1464, stands on Hedgeley moor, a short distance from the village.

BEARD, a hamlet in the parish of GLOSSOP, hundred of HIGH PEAK, county of DERBY, 4½ miles (N. W. by N.) from Chapel en le Frith, containing 332 inhabitants.

BEARL, a township in the parish of BYWELL ST. ANDREW, eastern division of TINDALE ward, county of NORTHUMBERLAND, 4 miles (E.) from Corbridge, containing 56 inhabitants.

BEARLEY, a parish in the Snitterfield division of the hundred of BARLICHWAY, county of WARWICK, 4¼ miles (N. N. W.) from Stratford upon Avon, containing 230 inhabitants. The living is a perpetual curacy, in the archdeaconry and diocese of Worcester, endowed with £200 private benefaction, and £600 royal bounty, and in the patronage of the Vicar of Wootton-Waven. The church is dedicated to St. Mary.

BEARSTEAD, a parish in the hundred of EYHORNE, lathe of AYLESFORD, county of KENT, 2½ miles (E.) from Maidstone, containing 566 inhabitants. The living is a discharged vicarage, in the archdeaconry and diocese of Canterbury, rated in the king's books at £6. 7. 4½., endowed with £200 private benefaction, and £200 royal bounty, and in the patronage of the Dean and Chapter of Rochester. The church is dedicated to the Holy Cross. A fair is held here on September 14th.

BEARSTON, a township in that part of the parish of MUCKLESTON which is in the Drayton division of the hundred of BRADFORD (North), county of SALOP, 4¾ miles (N. E. by N.) from Drayton in Hales, containing 79 inhabitants.

BEARWARD-COTE, a township in the parish of ETWALL, hundred of APPLETREE, county of DERBY. The population is returned with the parish.

BEAUCHIEF-ABBEY, an extra-parochial liberty, formerly part of the parish of Norton, in the hundred of SCARSDALE, county of DERBY, 3½ miles (N. W. by N.) from Dronfield, containing 97 inhabitants. The liberty, comprising about one thousand acres, was, by a deed executed at a court held at Richmond, March 14th, 1601, exempted from assessment for taxes. The living is a donative, in the patronage of P. Pegge Burnall, Esq. The chapel is a small edifice, erected about 1660, with the exception of the tower, which formed part of a monastery of Premonstratensian canons, founded here in 1183, by Robert Fitz-Ranulph, and dedicated to St. Thomas à Becket, the revenue of which, at the dissolution, was £157. 10. 2.

BEAUDESERT, a parish in the Henley division of the hundred of BARLICHWAY, county of WARWICK, ½ a mile (E.) from Henley in Arden, containing 209 inhabitants. The living is a rectory, in the archdeaconry and diocese of Worcester, rated in the king's books at £7. 16. 0½., and in the patronage of the Crown. The church, dedicated to St. Nicholas, is partly in the Norman, and partly in the early English, style of architecture, with a richly ornamented Norman arch between the nave and the chancel. A castle was erected here, soon after the Conquest, by Thurstan de Montfort, which was dismantled during the war between the houses of York and Lancaster; the site is still distinguishable. In the reign of Stephen, the lord of the manor obtained a grant for a market and a fair. The Rev. Richard Jago, a poet of some note, was born here in 1715, during the incumbency of his father.

BEAULIEU, a liberty in the New Forest (East) division of the county of SOUTHAMPTON, 6¼ miles (N.E.) from Lymington, containing, with an extra-parochial district within its limits, 1206 inhabitants. The living is a donative, in the patronage of Lord Montagu. The chapel, dedicated to St. Bartholomew, is a plain edifice of stone with strong buttresses, and was formerly the refectory of the ancient abbey, the church of which, situated to the south-east, has been entirely destroyed. There is a place of worship for Particular Baptists. Beaulieu is situated on a river of the same name, which rises in the New Forest, at the foot of a hill about a mile and a half to the north-east of Lyndhurst, and is navigable hence for vessels of fifty tons' burden to the Isle of Wight channel, which bounds the parish on the south. On reaching the village, it spreads into a wide surface, covering several acres, on the eastern side of which is the spot where the famous abbey formerly stood, the outer walls of which, or a large part of them, still remain. It was founded, in 1204, by King John, for thirty monks of the reformed Benedictine order, and was dedicated to the Blessed Virgin Mary: its revenue, at the dissolution in 1540, was £428. 6. 8. It possessed the privilege of sanctuary, and afforded an asylum to Margaret of Anjou, wife of Henry VI., after the battle of Barnet; and to Perkin Warbeck, in the reign of Henry VII. Various immunities, among which is exemption from arrest for debt, are still attached to the manor. The ruins stand in a beautiful valley, nearly circular in form, bounded by well-wooded hills, and surrounded by a stone wall, nearly entire in many places, and mantled with ivy. The entrance is by an ancient stone gateway, near which is an edifice of a square form, called the Palace, originally built for the abbot's lodging, but converted into a family seat after the dissolution. Over the entrance is a canopied niche, and the hall is handsomely vaulted. Eastward from the building is a long structure, supposed, from the extent and height of the apartments, to have been the dormitory, and beneath are several good cellars; the ancient kitchen is also standing. Near the abbey was a building, called an hospital, inhabited by the knights of St. John of Jerusalem, where travellers and persons in distress were relieved, the revenue of which, at the dissolution, was £100. This hospital was founded a little previously to the abbey, and, from the beauty of its situation, gave the name of *Beaulieu* to the place; it stood at the distance of about half a mile from the water's edge, at high water mark, on rising ground, having a gentle slope to the water, and commanding, toward the right, a view of Hurst Castle and the Needles; to the left, of Spithead, and the entrance to Portsmouth harbour. About two miles distant, and very near the sea-shore, is Park farm, anciently one of the granges attached to Beaulieu abbey, which, like others appertaining to that establishment, possessed the privilege of having divine service celebrated in it, under a bull of Pope Alexander I. The chapel is remaining, though much dilapidated, and adjoins the farm-house, a massive stone building of equal antiquity; its length is forty-two feet, and breadth about fourteen; the interior is divided into two compartments by a stone screen, which reaches to the roof. At a short distance from this, on the road to Beaulieu, are the ruins of the extensive barn and the chapel of St. Leonard, the former measuring in length two hundred and twenty-six feet, in breadth seventy-seven, and in height sixty, and formerly the principal grange belonging to the abbey. Buckler's Hard is a populous village in this liberty, situated on the Beaulieu river, chiefly inhabited by workmen employed in ship-building: many vessels of war have been built at this place. Beaulieu has long been noted for the manufacture of coarse sacking: near the village of Sowley, in this liberty, are two large mills belonging to some iron-works. Fairs for horses and horned cattle are held on April 15th and September 4th.

BEAU-MANOR, an extra-parochial liberty, in the western division of the hundred of Goscote, county of Leicester, 2¾ miles (W. by N.) from Mountsorrel, containing 96 inhabitants.

BEAUMONT, a parish in the ward and county of Cumberland, 4½ miles (N.W. by W.) from Carlisle, containing 323 inhabitants. The living is a discharged rectory, to which that of Kirk-Andrews upon Eden was united in 1692, in the archdeaconry and diocese of Carlisle, rated in the king's books at £8. 1. 8., endowed with £200 private benefaction, and £400 royal bounty, and in the patronage of the Earl of Lonsdale. The church, dedicated to St. Mary, stands upon a lofty hill. The river Eden and the Carlisle canal run through the parish. At the hamlet of Sandsfield, on the western bank of the Eden, vessels of sixty tons' burden, belonging to the port of Carlisle, receive and discharge their cargoes. The poor children of this parish are entitled to instruction in a school, erected by subscription, in the parish of Kirk-Andrews upon Eden, to which Thomas Pattinson, in 1785, gave a small endowment. The celebrated wall of Severus crossed this parish.

BEAUMONT, a parish in the hundred of Tendring, county of Essex, 7¾ miles (S.E. by S.) from Manningtree, containing, with the parish of Moze, 434 inhabitants. The living is a rectory, to which that of Moze was united in 1678, in the archdeaconry of Colchester, and diocese of London, rated in the king's books at £18, and in the patronage of the Governors of Guy's Hospital. The church is dedicated to St. Leonard. There is a place of worship for Wesleyan Methodists. This parish lies near the extremity of an inlet of the North sea, between the Naze and Harwich.

BEAUMONT-LEYS, an extra-parochial liberty, in the western division of the hundred of Goscote, county of Leicester, 2 miles (N.N.W.) from Leicester, containing 14 inhabitants.

BEAUSALL, a chapelry in the parish of Hatton, Snitterfield division of the hundred of Barlichway, county of Warwick, 4½ miles (N.N.W.) from Warwick, containing 269 inhabitants.

BEAWORTH, a tything in the parish of Cheriton, hundred of Fawley, Fawley division of the county of Southampton, 4¾ miles (S. by W.) from New Alresford, containing 136 inhabitants. This tything is within the jurisdiction of the Cheyney Court held at Winchester every Thursday, for the recovery of debts to any amount.

BEAWORTHY, a parish in the hundred of Black Torrington, county of Devon, 7½ miles (S.W. by W.) from Hatherleigh, containing 299 inhabitants. The living is a discharged rectory, in the archdeaconry of Totness, and diocese of Exeter, rated in the king's books at £6. 6., endowed with £200 private benefaction, and £200 royal bounty, and in the patronage of Sir William Molesworth, Bart. The church is dedicated to St. Alban.

BEBBINGTON, a parish in the lower division of the hundred of Wirrall, county palatine of Chester, comprising the townships of Higher Bebbington, Lower Bebbington, Poulton with Spittle, Storeton, and Tranmore, and containing 1678 inhabitants, of which number, 216 are in the township of Higher Bebbington, 6½ miles (N.N.E.), and 316 in that of Lower Bebbington, 5¾ (N.E. by N.), from Great Neston. The living is a rectory, in the archdeaconry and diocese of Chester, rated in the king's books at £30. 13. 4., and in the patronage of the Rev. S. Feilden and another. The church, dedicated to St. Andrew, is partly Norman, and partly in the early, decorated, and later styles of English architecture, with a tower surmounted by a spire: the nave is separated from the south aisle by a range of Norman arches, resting on massive cylindrical columns, and the chancel, with its lateral aisles, is of the later English style. Attached to the eastern end of the church is a room, used for a school, which was founded in 1655, and endowed by the parishioners with twenty acres of land, the rent of which, amounting to £25 per annum, is applied to the instruction of the poor children of Lower Bebbington. Strata of excellent freestone exist in this parish, which is of a much whiter quality than that found in any other part of the county. The navigable river Mersey runs along the northern border of the parish.

BEBSIDE, a township in the parish of Horton, eastern division of Castle ward, county of Northumberland, 5½ miles (S.E. by E.) from Morpeth, containing 123 inhabitants. It is situated on the southern bank of the river Blyth, on the opposite side of which, in the parish of Bedlington, are extensive iron-works.

BECCLES, a market town and parish in the hundred of Wangford, county of Suffolk, 44 miles (E.N.E.) from Bury St. Edmund's, and 110 (N.E. by N.) from London, containing 3493 inhabitants. This town, which suffered greatly from fire in 1586, is pleasantly situated on the river Waveney, by which it is bounded on the north and west. It consists of several spacious streets, diverging from the market-place, well paved and lighted: the houses in general are handsome and well built, and the inhabitants are amply supplied with water. The environs, which abound with pleasing scenery, afford agreeable walks; and the theatre and assembly-rooms form two handsome ornamental buildings. Races are held annually, on a fine course near the town, on which there are two commodious stands. The trade is principally in corn and malt, which is

Corporate Seal.

carried on to a considerable extent: the river Waveney is navigable from Yarmouth, and a design is now in progress for connecting it, by means of Leething lake, with the sea at Lowestoft. The market is on Saturday: the fairs are on Whit-Monday for cattle, and October 2nd for horses and pedlary; there are also statute fairs. Adjoining the town is a common, upwards of one thousand four hundred acres in extent, affording, under certain regulations, free pasturage for cattle. Under a charter of incorporation, granted by Queen Elizabeth in 1584, a portreeve, steward, twelve principal, and twenty-four inferior, burgesses are elected; the portreeve is appointed annually, by rotation, from among the principal burgesses. None of the members of the corporation exercise magisterial authority, the town being wholly within the jurisdiction of the county magistrates, who hold a quarterly court of session for the district. The town hall is a commodious building, and the gaol has recently been enlarged and improved. The living is a rectory, with the vicarage of St. Mary Endgate (the church of which is in ruins), in the archdeaconry of Suffolk, and diocese of Norwich, and in the patronage of the Earl of Gosford; the rectory is rated in the king's books at £21. 12. 3½., and the vicarage at £7. 6. 8. The church, dedicated to St. Michael, is a spacious and elegant structure, in the later style of English architecture; the porch is a fine specimen of beautiful design and elaborate execution, and the interior is appropriately ornamented. The tower, which is detached from the main building, is highly enriched with sculpture; it was built by subscription, and upon it are sculptured the arms of the donors, among which are those of Yallop, Rede (Thomas Rede having been at that time rector of the parish, and a principal contributor towards its erection), Leman, and Garneys: the churchyard commands an interesting and extensive view. There are places of worship for Baptists, Independents, and Methodists. A grammar school was founded, in 1774, and endowed by the Rev. Dr. Fauconberge, a native of the town, with an estate in the parish of Corton, producing about £200 per annum; it is under the control of the Bishop of Norwich, the Archdeacon of Suffolk, and the Rector of Beccles, who appoint the master: there are at present no scholars on the foundation, nor is there any place appropriated as a school-room for gratuitous instruction. Dr. Routh, the learned President of Magdalene College, Oxford, received the rudiments of his education at this place. A free school was founded, in 1631, and endowed with one hundred acres of land, by Sir John Leman, Knt., alderman of London, for the instruction of forty-eight boys in reading, writing, and arithmetic; and a National school, in which one hundred and twenty children of both sexes are instructed, is supported by subscription. An ancient hospital for lepers, of uncertain foundation, with a chapel dedicated to St. Mary Magdalene, was granted, in 1676, to the corporation of Beccles, for the benefit of the poor. The corporation also hold in trust for the poor a large tract of land, which was originally granted by Henry VIII., in 1540, after the dissolution of the abbey of Bury St. Edmund's (to which the manor formerly belonged), to William Rede and his heirs, in trust for the benefit of himself and other inhabitants of the town. Beccles was the birth and burial place of William de Roos, of Roos Hall, a man of considerable note; he attended Edward I. in the war with the Scots, and was present with that prince at the siege of Kaerlevrock, where he displayed great bravery.

BECCONSALL, a joint chapelry with Hesketh, in the parish of CROSTON, hundred of LEYLAND, county palatine of LANCASTER, 11 miles (N. by E.) from Ormskirk, containing, with Hesketh, 476 inhabitants. The living is a perpetual curacy, in the archdeaconry and diocese of Chester, endowed with £400 private benefaction, and £600 royal bounty, and in the patronage of the Rector of Croston.

BECHTON, a township in that part of the parish of SANDBACH which is in the hundred of NANTWICH, county palatine of CHESTER, 2¼ miles (S. E.) from Sandbach, containing 759 inhabitants. The Grand Trunk canal passes close to the salt-works here.

BECKBURY, a parish within the liberties of the borough of WENLOCK, county of SALOP, 7 miles (N.E. by N.) from Bridgenorth, containing 285 inhabitants. The living is a discharged rectory, in the archdeaconry of Salop, and diocese of Hereford, rated in the king's books at £5. 3. 4., and in the patronage of the Crown. The church is dedicated to St. Milburgh.

BECKENHAM, a parish in the hundred of BROMLEY and BECKINGHAM, lathe of SUTTON at HONE, county of KENT, 1¾ mile (W.) from Bromley, and 10 (S. S. E.) from London, containing 1180 inhabitants. The name of this place, compounded of the Saxon terms *Bec*, a brook, and *Ham*, a dwelling, is derived from a small stream which passes through the parish, and falls into the river Ravensbourne. In the reign of Henry VIII., Charles Brandon, Duke of Suffolk, entertained that monarch, when on his journey to visit Anne of Cleves, with great pomp at the manor-house in this place. The village, which is pleasantly situated, contains some neat dwelling-houses, and in the neighbourhood are many handsome villas. The Croydon canal passes along the north-western angle of the parish. A fair, chiefly for toys, is held on the Monday before St. Bartholomew's day. Beckenham is within the jurisdiction of a court of requests held every alternate Tuesday at Bromley, for the recovery of debts not exceeding 40*s*. The living is a rectory, in the archdeaconry and diocese of Rochester, rated in the king's books at £16. 18. 9., and in the patronage of John Cator, Esq. The church, dedicated to St. George, is a neat structure, erected about the beginning of the seventeenth century, with a lofty spire, which having been destroyed by lightning, in 1790, was recently rebuilt. Mrs. Mary Watson, in 1790, bequeathed property, for the instruction of poor children, after the death of two annuitants, which took place in 1807, at which period it was vested in the purchase of £1401. 12. 7. New South Sea annuities, producing an annual dividend of £42. 0. 10., the whole of which not being annually expended, the accumulation, amounting to £294. 16. 2., was, in 1818, applied in aid of a subscription for the erection of National schools for boys and girls of the parish, in which the children upon Mrs. Watson's foundation are now instructed. Capt. Leonard Bowyer, in 1717, also gave £100, the interest of which is paid out of the rental of land belonging to the parish, for the education of four additional scholars. To the east of the church are three unendowed almshouses, erected by Anthony Rawlins, Esq., in 1694. Dr. Asheton, the projector of a plan for providing for widows by survivorship, was rector of this parish towards the close of the seventeenth century.

BECKERMET (ST. BRIDGET'S), a parish in ALLERDALE ward above Darwent, county of CUMBERLAND, containing, with the township of Calder in Copeland, 545 inhabitants. The village of Great Beckermet lies partly in this parish and partly in that of Beckermet St. John, 2½ miles (S.) from Egremont. The living is a perpetual curacy, in the archdeaconry of Richmond, and diocese of Chester, endowed with £600 royal bounty, and £200 parliamentary grant, and in the patronage of the Rev. H. J. Todd. The church stands about half a mile south-west of the village. This parish is situated on the north bank of the Calder, adjoining the ocean, and contains the sequestered ruins of Calder abbey, described under Calder-Bridge. Freestone is obtained here.

BECKERMET (ST. JOHN'S), a parish in ALLERDALE ward above Darwent, county of CUMBERLAND, 2½ miles (S.) from Egremont, containing 549 inhabitants. The living is a perpetual curacy, in the archdeaconry of Richmond, and diocese of Chester, endowed with £300 private benefaction, £1200 royal bounty, and £200 parliamentary grant, and in the patronage of the Rev. H. J. Todd. The church is a small ancient edifice. A portion of the town of Egremont is included within this parish, in which also stands a private residence, called Woto-Bank, with the etymology of which is connected an interesting fabulous tale, made by Mrs. Cowley the subject of a romantic poem, entitled "Edwina," published in 1794.

BECKETT, a tything in the parish and hundred of SHRIVENHAM, county of BERKS, 4¾ miles (S. W. by S.) from Farringdon. The population is returned with the parish. The manor, soon after the Conquest, became the property of the crown, and the manor-house was occasionally made a royal residence. Dr. Shute Barrington, the late Bishop of Durham, was born here in 1734.

BECKFORD, a parish in the hundred of TIBALDSTONE, county of GLOUCESTER, 6 miles (E. N. E.) from Tewkesbury, containing, with the hamlets of Bengrave and Grafton, 442 inhabitants. The living is a vicarage, with the perpetual curacy of Ashton under Hill annexed, in the archdeaconry and diocese of Gloucester, rated in the king's books at £16. 16. 10½., and in the patronage of the Rev. John Timbrill, D.D. The church, a very ancient structure, is dedicated to St. John the Baptist. Freestone abounds in the parish. Here was an Alien priory of Augustine canons, the revenue of which, at the dissolution, was £53. 6. 8.

BECKHAM (EAST), a parish in the northern division of the hundred of ERPINGHAM, county of NORFOLK, 4½ miles (W. by S.) from Cromer, containing 48 inhabitants. The church, which was dedicated to St. Helen, has long been desecrated: it is a picturesque ruin, the southern porch and the walls of the nave and chancel, the only parts now remaining, being covered with ivy: the inhabitants resort to the church at West Beckham.

BECKHAM (WEST), a parish in the southern division of the hundred of ERPINGHAM, county of NORFOLK, 4 miles (E.) from Holt, containing 154 inhabitants. The living is a perpetual curacy, in the peculiar jurisdiction and patronage of the Dean and Chapter of Norwich, endowed with £600 royal bounty. The church is dedicated to All Saints: the tower is circular at the base and octangular above.

BECKHAMPTON, a tything in the parish of AVEBURY, hundred of SELKLEY, county of WILTS, 6½ miles (W.) from Marlborough. The population is returned with the parish. Here was formerly a chapel, now desecrated.

BECKINGHAM, a parish in the wapentake of LOVEDEN, parts of KESTEVEN, county of LINCOLN, 5 miles (E.) from Newark, containing 430 inhabitants. The living is a rectory, with the perpetual curacy of Stragglesthorpe annexed, in the archdeaconry and diocese of Lincoln, rated in the king's books at £41. 6. 8., and in the patronage of Robert Moody, Esq. The church, dedicated to All Saints, is partly Norman, and partly in the early style of English architecture: the tower, ornamented with pinnacles, is in the later English style.

BECKINGHAM, a parish within the liberty of SOUTHWELL and SCROOBY, though locally in the Northclay division of the wapentake of Bassetlaw, county of NOTTINGHAM, 3¼ miles (W. by N.) from Gainsborough, containing 515 inhabitants. The living is a vicarage, in the peculiar jurisdiction of the Chapter of the Collegiate Church of Southwell, rated in the king's books at £6. 15. 3., and in the patronage of the Prebendary of Beckingham. The church is dedicated to All Saints. There is a place of worship for Wesleyan Methodists. The navigable river Trent runs along the border of the parish. A school for ten poor children is endowed with about £15 per annum. Dr. William Howell, the historian, was born here.

BECKINGTON, a parish in the hundred of FROME, county of SOMERSET, 3 miles (N. E.) from Frome, containing 1645 inhabitants. The living is a rectory, with that of Standerwick annexed, in the archdeaconry of Wells, and diocese of Bath and Wells, rated in the king's books at £19. 11. 0½., and in the patronage of the Rev. Henry Sainsbury. The church, dedicated to St. George, contains the remains of Samuel Daniel, poet-laureat and historian, who died here in 1619; and William Huish, rector of this parish, and one of the editors of the Polyglott Bible, who died in 1688. There are places of worship for Particular Baptists and Wesleyan Methodists. The manufacture of cloth was formerly extensively carried on in this parish, and still exists to a limited degree. Thomas Beckington, Bishop of Bath and Wells, and a distinguished statesman, was born here, in 1645.

BECKLEY, a parish partly in the hundred of ASHENDON, county of BUCKINGHAM, and partly in the hundred of BULLINGTON, county of OXFORD, 4¾ miles (N. E.) from Oxford, containing, with the chapelry of Studley with Horton, 825 inhabitants. The living is a vicarage, in the archdeaconry and diocese of Oxford, rated in the king's books at £8, endowed with £400 private benefaction, £800 royal bounty, and £1300 parliamentary grant, and in the patronage of the Dean and Canons of Christ Church, Oxford. The church is dedicated to St. Mary. The manor was part of the private property of Alfred the Great: in the thirteenth century it belonged to Richard, Earl of Cornwall, who had a castellated mansion here, a portion of the site of which is now occupied by a dovecote, supposed to be a relic of the fortress. A court baron is held annually by the lord of the manor, who claims paramount authority over seven villages within the tract called Otmoor, for enclosing which an act was obtained in 1815. Here is a school with a small endowment, for the instruction of six poor children. The Roman road from Alchester to Wallingford passed through the parish, and fragments of Roman pottery have been found in the vicinity.

BECKLEY, a parish in the hundred of GOLDSPUR, rape of HASTINGS, county of SUSSEX, 6½ miles (W.N.W.) from Rye, containing 1371 inhabitants. The living is a rectory, in the archdeaconry of Lewes, and diocese of Chichester, rated in the king's books at £11. 6. 8., and in the patronage of the Master and Fellows of University College, Oxford. The church is dedicated to All Saints. There is a place of worship for Wesleyan Methodists. The river Rother bounds this parish on the north, separating the counties of Kent and Sussex.

BEDALE, a parish comprising the market town of Bedale, the townships of Aiskew, Burrel with Cowling, Crakehall, and Firby, and the hamlet of Rands-Grange, in the eastern division of the wapentake of HANG, and the township of Langthorne in the wapentake of HALLIKELD, North riding of the county of YORK, and containing 2631 inhabitants, of which number, 1137 are in the town of Bedale, 33½ miles (N. W.) from York, and 223 (N. N. W.) from London. This town, which is of prepossessing appearance, is pleasantly situated on the banks of a stream flowing into the river Swale near Scruton, and consists of one principal street. The houses are in general of brick, and irregularly built; the air is pure, and the neighbourhood, which is well cultivated, affords many pleasant walks and much picturesque scenery. The market is on Tuesday: fairs are held on Easter-Tuesday, Whit-Tuesday, and July 5th and 6th, for horses, horned cattle, and sheep; and October 10th and 11th, and the last Monday but one before Christmas-day, for cattle, sheep, hogs, and leather. Constables and other officers are appointed at the court leet of the lord of the manor. The living is a rectory, in the archdeaconry of Richmond, and diocese of Chester, rated in the king's books at £89. 4. 9½., and in the alternate patronage of Miss Pierse and Miles Stapleton, Esq. The church, dedicated to St. Gregory, is a spacious and venerable structure, in the early style of English architecture, with a square embattled tower crowned with pinnacles, of remarkable strength, having been used as a place of security from the incursions of the Scots. Within the church are several interesting monuments, one of which is to the memory of Sir Brian Fitz-Alan, Lord-Lieutenant of Scotland in the reign of Edward I., who resided here in a castle near the church, of which there are no remains. There are three places of worship for Methodists, and one each for Particular Baptists and Roman Catholics. A free grammar school, supposed to have existed here prior to the dissolution of religious houses, was endowed by Queen Elizabeth with £7. 11. 4. per annum, to which the Countess of Warwick added £13. 6. 8. per annum. The latter sum is now given to the National school, for the instruction of eighty boys, to which also is appropriated the produce of £100, bequeathed by William Heaton, in 1709, for preparing eight boys for the grammar school, which is in the churchyard. An hospital for six aged men was founded by Dr. Samwaies, in 1698, and endowed with £55. 3. 2.; it is a neat stone building, containing six apartments, to each of which a garden, comprising half an acre, is allotted: there are also almshouses for three aged women, founded by Richard and Thomas Young, in 1667, besides many bequests for the poor. Sir Christopher Wray, Lord Chief Justice of the court of King's Bench in the reign of Elizabeth, was a native of this place.

BEDBURN (NORTH), a township in that part of the parish of ST. ANDREW AUCKLAND which is in the north-western division of DARLINGTON ward, county palatine of DURHAM, 5¾ miles (N.W. by W.) from Bishop-Auckland, containing 351 inhabitants. This township is situated between the river Wear and the Bedburn rivulet, and abounds with picturesque and romantic scenery: at its north-western extremity is an ancient earthwork, called "The Castles," of an oblong form, surrounded by a lofty rampart of loose pebble stones, with an outer ditch, supposed to have been a British fortress. At Bedburn Forge is a manufactory for edge-tools, spades, &c., which, prior to the year 1820, was used for bleaching linen cloth and yarn by a chemical process.

BEDBURN (SOUTH), a township in that part of the parish of ST. ANDREW AUCKLAND which is in the north-western division of DARLINGTON ward, county palatine of DURHAM, 8½ miles (W. by N.) from Bishop-Auckland, containing 366 inhabitants.

BEDDINGHAM, a parish in the hundred of TOTNORE, rape of PEVENSEY, county of SUSSEX, 2¼ miles (S. E.) from Lewes, containing 255 inhabitants. The living is a discharged vicarage, with that of West Firle united, in the archdeaconry of Lewes, and diocese of Chichester, rated in the king's books at £9. 10. 10., and in the patronage of the Dean and Chapter of Chichester. The church is dedicated to St. Andrew. The parish is within the liberty of the duchy of Lancaster.

BEDDINGTON, a parish in the second division of the hundred of WALLINGTON, county of SURREY, 2 miles (W.) from Croydon, containing, with the hamlet of Wallington, 1327 inhabitants. The living is a rectory, in the archdeaconry of Surrey, and diocese of Winchester, rated in the king's books at £13. 16. 8., and in the patronage of Mrs. Ann Paston Gee. The church, dedicated to St. Mary, is a handsome edifice, with a fine tower, chiefly in the later style of English architecture, it was built in the reign of Richard II., and contains, together with several stalls, some handsome monuments to the memory of the Carew family, of which Sir Nicholas Carew, who was beheaded in 1539, for an alleged conspiracy against Henry VIII., was a member. The Croydon railway crosses the northern angle of the parish. The first orange-trees produced in England are said to have been planted here. A charity school is supported by subscription.

BEDFIELD, a parish in the hundred of HOXNE, county of SUFFOLK, 4¾ miles (W.N.W.) from Framlingham, containing 319 inhabitants. The living is a discharged rectory, in the archdeaconry of Suffolk, and diocese of Norwich, rated in the king's books at £14, and in the patronage of the Earl of Stradbroke. The church is dedicated to St. Nicholas.

BEDFONT (EAST), a parish in the hundred of SPELTHORNE, county of MIDDLESEX, 3¾ miles (W.S.W.)

from Hounslow, containing, with the hamlet of Hatton, 771 inhabitants. The living is a discharged vicarage, in the archdeaconry of Middlesex, and diocese of London, rated in the king's books at £6. 13. 4., and in the patronage of the Bishop of London. The church is dedicated to St. Mary. Opposite the entrance are two yew-trees, the branches of which, meeting at the top, form an arch, and have been fantastically cut so as to represent two cocks in a fighting attitude; in the thick foliage of one of them appears the date 1704 (an eccentric individual having made a bequest in that year for keeping them thus trimmed), and in that of the other are seen the initials H.I.G.R.T.

Seal and Arms.

BEDFORD, a borough and market town, having separate jurisdiction, in the county of BEDFORD, of which it is the capital, 50 miles (N. N. W.) from London, containing 5466 inhabitants. This place, called by the later Britons *Lettuydur*, and by the Saxons *Bedanford* (both which terms are expressive of its character as a place of public accommodation at the passage of a river), derives its name from its situation near an ancient ford on the river Ouse. In 571, a battle was fought here, between the Britons and the West Saxons, the latter being commanded by Ceolfulf, brother of Ceawlin, third king of Wessex, in which the Britons were defeated with considerable loss. The town having been almost destroyed by the Danes, was restored by Edward the Elder, who greatly enlarged it by erecting buildings on the opposite side of the river; but in 1010, it suffered again from an irruption of the Danes, who committed most dreadful ravages in their progress through the country. After the Conquest, Payne de Beauchamp, third baron of Bedford, built a strong castle here, which was besieged and taken by Stephen in the war with the Empress Matilda; and when the barons took up arms against King John, William de Beauchamp, who then possessed it, having taken part with the insurgents, delivered the castle into their possession, but it was subsequently besieged and ultimately taken for the king by Falco de Breant, upon whom that monarch bestowed it, as a reward for his services. In the reign of Henry III., Falco having committed excessive outrages, for which he was fined £3000 by the king's itinerant justiciaries at Dunstable, seized the principal judge and imprisoned him in the castle, which, after a vigorous siege and an obstinate defence, memorable in the history of those times, was taken, and, by the king's order, demolished, with the exception of the inner part, which was given for a residence to William de Beauchamp, to whom Henry restored the barony, which he had forfeited in the preceding reign. Of this fortress, only a part of the intrenchments, and the site of the keep, now converted into a bowling-green, remain. The ancient barons of Bedford were Lord Almoners at the coronation of the kings of England, and, as an inheritor of part of the barony, the Marquis of Exeter officiated at that of George IV., receiving the usual perquisite of a silver alms-bason, and the cloth upon which the sovereign walked from Westminster Hall to the Abbey. During the civil war in the reign of Charles I., this town, which had been garrisoned for the parliament, surrendered to Prince Rupert, in 1643: the parliamentary troops, under Col. Montague, afterwards entered it by stratagem, and carried off some money and horses, which had been brought thither for the use of the royalists.

The town is pleasantly situated in a fertile vale, watered by the river Ouse, over which a handsome stone bridge of five arches was erected in 1813, at an expense of £15,137, replacing a former bridge of great antiquity: it consists of one spacious street, nearly a mile in length, intersected at right angles by several smaller streets; the houses, many of which are ancient, are in general well built, interspersed with several of modern erection. A crescent is at present being formed on the northern side of the bridge, and the general appearance of the town is rapidly improving it is well paved and lighted, and amply supplied with water. Races are held in the spring and autumn; assemblies take place during the winter; and a small theatre is opened occasionally. The principal branches of manufacture are those of lace and straw-plat, in which many women and children are employed; and a considerable trade in corn and coal, by means of the Ouse, is carried on with Lynn-Regis and the intermediate places. The market days are Monday, for cattle; and Saturday, for corn and provisions: the former market is held in the southern, and the latter in the northern, division of the town. The fairs are on the first Tuesday in Lent, April 21st, July 5th, August 21st, October 12th, and December 19th, for cattle; and there is a wool fair on the 17th of November. The government, by charter of incorporation, granted by Charles II., by which the prescriptive privileges of the borough were confirmed, is vested in a mayor, recorder, deputy recorder, two bailiffs (who act as sheriffs), two chamberlains, an indefinite number of aldermen, and thirteen common council-men, assisted by a town clerk, three serjeants at mace, and subordinate officers. The mayor, who is a justice of the peace, and the two bailiffs, are elected annually from among the freemen: the aldermen, whose number is by custom limited to twelve, are chosen from among those who have served the office of mayor. The corporation hold a court of session quarterly, at which the deputy recorder, or, in his absence, the mayor, presides. The borough gaol has been pulled down, an arrangement having been made whereby offenders committed by the magistrates for the borough are sent to the county gaol; and a lock-up house has been built for the temporary confinement of disorderly persons. The borough first sent representatives to parliament in the 23rd of Edward I., since which time it has returned two members: the right of election is vested in the freemen and burgesses, whether resident or not, and in inhabitants, being householders and not receiving alms, in number about four hundred: the mayor and bailiffs are the returning officers. The assizes and quarter sessions for the county are held in this town. The sessions-house, rebuilt in 1753, is a neat stone edifice, in St. Paul's square: the county gaol and old house of correction, rebuilt in 1801, is a handsome structure, surrounded by a high stone wall at the north-western entrance into the town; it contains a tread-mill for grinding corn, worked by prisoners sentenced to hard labour. The county penitentiary, or new house of correction, a large brick building on the road to Kettering, was erected in 1819. The house of industry, erected by act of parliament, in 1796, at an expense of £5000, is under the control of thirteen directors resident in the town, to whom, by an act passed in the 34th of George III., the expenditure of the poor rates is entrusted. The county lunatic asylum, a handsome brick building on the road to Ampthill, was erected, by act of parliament, in 1812, at an expense of £13,000, and will accommodate sixty-five patients; private patients are admitted on paying 14*s.* each per week. The county infirmary, on the same road, is a substantial brick building, with a stone front, towards the erection and endowment of which the late Samuel Whitbread, Esq. gave £10,000, Lord Hampden £1000, and the Duke of Bedford contributes £100 per annum. The Marquis of Tavistock, at the parliamentary election for the county in 1826, presented £2000 to this institution, in lieu of entertaining the freeholders.

The town comprises the parishes of St. Cuthbert, St. John, St. Mary, St. Paul, and St. Peter Martin, within the archdeaconry of Bedford, and diocese of Lincoln. The living of St. Cuthbert's is a discharged rectory, rated in the king's books at £5. 9. 4½., endowed with £400 parliamentary grant, and in the patronage of the Crown. The living of St. John's is a rectory not in charge, in the patronage of the Corporation: the church is a neat structure in the later style of English architecture, with a handsome tower, but it has been much modernized. The living of St. Mary's is a rectory, rated in the king's books at £11. 4. 9½., endowed with £400 parliamentary grant, and in the patronage of the Bishop of Lincoln: the church is in the later style of English architecture, with a plain square tower. The living of St. Paul's is a vicarage, rated in the king's books at £10, and in the patronage of Lord Carteret. The church is a spacious and venerable structure, partly in the early, and partly in the decorated, style of English architecture, having a handsome tower surmounted by an octagonal spire, and a north and south porch in the later style: the interior, which is chiefly in the early English style, contains a stone pulpit, embellished with gilt tracery, on a blue ground, and some interesting monuments and brass plates: over the south porch there is a chamber, in which the records of the corporation are deposited, and over the northern side of the chancel, a library of valuable books. The living of St. Peter's Martin is a rectory, rated in the king's books at £11. 13. 1½., and in the patronage of the Crown: the church is an ancient edifice, with a tower, the upper part of which has been recently restored, and having, at the southern entrance, a beautiful Norman arch. There are places of worship for Baptists, Independents, Wesleyan Methodists, and Moravians.

The free grammar school was founded in 1556, and endowed with property consisting of some houses and land in Bedford, and in the united parishes of St. George the Martyr and St. Andrew above the Bars, Holborn, London, by Sir William Harpur, a native of this town, and lord mayor of London in 1561, whose statue, in white marble, is placed in a niche over the entrance. It has eight scholarships of £80 per annum each, tenable for four years, in either of the Universities of Oxford, Cambridge, or Dublin, six of which are restricted to boys whose parents are inhabitants of the town, and the remaining two are open to all scholars on the foundation. The school is under the inspection of the Warden and Fellows of New College, Oxford, who appoint the master and the usher, and under the management of eighteen trustees resident in the town, six of whom retire annually, in rotation, six others being elected in their stead. Under the same endowment there are an English school for boys, a National school for boys and girls, and an hospital for the maintenance and education of fifty children of both sexes; an apprentice fee of £30 each is given annually with ten of the boys, and one of £15 each with five of the girls, who, at the expiration of their apprenticeship, on producing a certificate of good conduct, receive a sum not less than £10, nor exceeding £20 each, to assist in setting them up in business. From the same fund were founded and endowed twenty almshouses, each containing four apartments, for ten aged men and ten aged women, decayed housekeepers, each of whom receives a weekly allowance of 10*s.*, and £3 annually for clothing; and forty-six additional almshouses have since been erected, on the northern side of Harpur-street, for aged men and women, who receive a weekly allowance of 7*s.* each, and £2 annually for clothing: small pensions are also granted to the widows who quit the almshouses on the death of their husbands. The sum of £800 is annually given, in marriage portions of £20 each, to maidens of good character, resident in the town, £500 for the relief of decayed housekeepers, and other pecuniary donations to the poor, all arising from the same endowment, which, owing to the increased rental of the estate, yields an annual income of more than £11,000. A school, for ten boys and ten girls, was founded in 1727, and endowed with lands producing £46. 10. per annum, by Mr. Alexander Leith; and a Blue-coat school, now united to the National school, was founded in 1760, and endowed with £33. 15. 6. per annum, by Alderman Newton, of Leicester, for twenty-five boys, for clothing whom the endowment is now appropriated. Eight almshouses, for unmarried persons of either sex, were founded and endowed in 1679, by Mr. Thomas Christie. An hospital, dedicated to St. John the Baptist, was founded and endowed by the inhabitants of Bedford, in the reign of Edward II., for a master and ten brethren; its revenue, at the dissolution of religious houses, was £21. 0. 8., but the charity was then confirmed, and the mastership is now annexed to the rectory of St. John's. A monastery of uncertain foundation existed here at a very early period, in the chapel of which, Offa, King of Mercia, who had been a great benefactor to it, was buried; the chapel being afterwards undermined by the Ouse, sunk with the tomb of that monarch into the river. Near St. Paul's church stands an ancient building, supposed to have been one of the prebendal houses noticed by Leland: about three quarters of a mile west of the town, on the bank of the river, are some remains of the conventual buildings of Caldwell priory, which was founded in the reign of John, by Robert, son of William de Houghton, for brethren of the order of the Holy Cross, the revenue of which, at the dissolution, was £148. 15. 10. At Newenham, a mile east of the town, are considerable remains of a priory of Black canons, which, in the reign of Henry II., was removed thither from Bedford, where it had been originally founded by Simon Beauchamp; and at Elstow church, formerly *Helenestowe*, two miles distant, on the road to Clophill, are the interesting ruins of a nunnery, founded by Judith, niece of William the Conqueror, and dedicated to the Holy Trinity, and to St. Helen, mother of Constantine the Great, the revenue of which, at the dissolution, was £325. 2. 1. John Bunyan, author of the Pilgrim's Progress, was confined for twelve years and a half in the county gaol at Bedford, from which he was ultimately released on the intercession of the Bishop of Lincoln. Bedford confers the title of duke on the noble family of Russell.

BEDFORD, a township in the parish of LEIGH, hundred of WEST DERBY, county palatine of LANCASTER, 1¼ mile (E. S. E.) from Leigh, containing 2830 inhabitants. There is a place of worship for Wesleyan Methodists. The manufacture of muslin and fustian is extensively carried on here.

BEDFORDSHIRE, an inland county, bounded on the north and north-east by Huntingdonshire, on the east by the county of Cambridge, on the south-east and south by that of Hertford, on the south-west and west by that of Buckingham, and on the north-west by that of Northampton. It lies between the parallels of 51° 50′ and 52° 21′ (N. Lat.), and between the meridians of 10′ and 42′ (W. Lon.), and includes four hundred and sixty-three square miles, or two hundred and ninety-six thousand three hundred and twenty statute acres. The population, in 1821, amounted to 83,716.

At the period of the Roman conquest of Britain, this territory, with that included in the adjoining counties of Hertford and Bucks, was inhabited by the *Cassii*; and on the consolidation of the Roman dominion, it formed part of the division of southern Britain, called by these conquerors *Flavia Cæsariensis*. During the long and sanguinary wars between the Britons and the invading Saxons, the former were defeated in a great battle fought near Bedford, in the year 580, by Cuthwulf, brother of Ceawlin, King of the West Saxons, who compelled them to abandon the districts lying immediately below the Chiltern hills, where several of their principal towns were situated, one of which, on the banks of the Ouzel in this county, was called by the Saxons *Lygeanburgh*, since corrupted into *Leighton-Buzzard*. During the Saxon Octarchy, the northern parts of this county appear to have been occupied by the South Mercians, and the southern by the East Saxons. From this period, there is no particular mention of this territory until the reign of Edward the Elder, when it was frequently the scene of contention during the furious incursions of the Danes. About the year 919, Edward came to Bedford, received the submission of the inhabitants of the surrounding country, built a fortress on the southern side of the river Ouse, and then departed after a stay of four weeks. In 921, the Danes entering from Huntingdonshire, stationed themselves at Tempsford, which place they fortified; and, in an excursion thence, attacked the town of Bedford, but the inhabitants made a vigorous sortie, and put them to flight with great slaughter. In the summer of the same year, Edward assembled a great force, and closely besieging these ravagers at Tempsford, took that city, as it is styled in the Saxon Chronicle, destroyed their fortress, and put to death their king, with a great number of his chief men. In 1009, the Danes made an incursion through the southern part of the shire to Oxford; and in the following year their army burned the towns of Bedford and Tempsford; but, in 1011, this territory was recovered by King Ethelred. In 1017, however, the power of the Danes again prevailed, and under Canute it was included in the *Dane-lege*, or Danish jurisdiction.

The first event of national importance which occurred within the limits of the county subsequently to the Conquest, was the capture of the castle of Bedford by King Stephen, in 1138, from the Beauchamps, by whom it had been held in opposition to him. The same family held this fortress against King John, who sent his favourite, Fulk de Breant, to besiege it; and after he had taken it, gave it him as a reward for his good services. All the other castles of this county appear to have been destroyed by John, in his famous march northward; and, a few years afterwards, Bedford castle itself was taken and destroyed by Henry III., one of whose justices itinerant had been arbitrarily imprisoned in it by Fulk. Thus left entirely without fortresses, this county was the scene of no important event during the wars of the Roses. In the great contest between Charles I. and the parliament, Bedfordshire was one of those counties in which, according to Lord Clarendon, the king had no visible party, nor a single fixed quarter; and was one of the first that associated to oppose him. It was included in the great district of the "Eastern Associates," for the embodying of which a special license was passed by the parliament, at the end of November, 1642, when the Earl of Manchester was appointed their commander-in-chief, under whom Cromwell commanded the horse. A strong party of royalist forces took possession of Bedford, in October, 1643: soon after, Col. Montague entered the town by a stratagem, and carried off some money and horses intended for the use of the king.

Bedfordshire is in the diocese of Lincoln, and province of Canterbury: it forms an archdeaconry, in which are included the deaneries of Bedford, Clapham, Dunstable, Eaton, Fleet, and Shefford; and contains one hundred and twenty-three parishes, of which fifty-six are rectories, sixty vicarages, and seven perpetual curacies and donatives. For purposes of civil government it is divided into nine hundreds, namely, Barford, Biggleswade, Clifton, Flitt, Manshead, Redbornestoke, Stodden, Willey, and Wixamtree. It contains the borough, market, and county town of Bedford, the corporate and market town of Dunstable, and the market towns of Ampthill, Biggleswade, Harrold, Leighton-Buzzard, Luton, Potton, and Woburn. Two knights are returned to parliament for the shire, and two burgesses for the borough of Bedford. The county is included in the Norfolk circuit, and the assizes and sessions are held in the shire-hall at Bedford, at which town are the county gaol and old house of correction, and the penitentiary, or new house of correction. There are forty-one acting magistrates. The parochial rates raised in the county for the year ending March 25th, 1827, amounted to £92,340. 11., and the expenditure to £91,359. 14., of which £81,959. 18. was applied to the relief of the poor. The form of this county is a very irregular parallelogram, the circumference of which is deeply indented by projecting, and in some instances nearly insulated, portions of the adjoining shires. The scenery is mostly of a pleasing, but rarely of an impressive kind: the loftier elevations afford cheering views of rich level tracts, watered by the slowly winding Ouse and the smaller rivers. Of these, the prospect from Ridgmont, over Buckinghamshire; that from Millbrook churchyard, over the Vale of Bedford; that from the ancient encampment called Totternhoe Castle, near Dunstable, across part of Bedfordshire and Buckinghamshire; and that afforded by a ride along the downs, from Streatley to Barton, are the most interesting. The most striking range of hills is that of chalk, which extends across the southern part of the county from Hertfordshire into Buckinghamshire, and forms the spacious downs of Luton and Dunstable. The climate, like the surface of the county, has hardly any striking peculiarities, but it is for the most part mild and genial, and favourable to the growth of corn. The crops on the colder soils of the more elevated lands to the north of Bedford, and on the chalk hills at the southern extremity of the county, are, of course, much later in arriving at maturity than those of the richer vales. The prevailing winds blow from the south-west; and the ungenial effects of those from the opposite quarter, blowing over the extensive levels of Huntingdonshire, Cambridgeshire, and Norfolk, are experienced with unmitigated severity.

Every species of soil commonly seen on the uplands of Great Britain, from the strongest clay to the lightest sand, may be found in this county. Although the various kinds are frequently found in remarkably small patches, and so intermixed that no accurate delineation of them can be given, yet the most extensively characteristic divisions may be described as follows. In the whole of the southernmost part of the county, separated from the rest of it by a line drawn from south-west to north-east, from the border of Buckinghamshire, near Eaton-Bray, to that of Hertfordshire, to the east of Barton, the prevailing soil is chalk, having a stratum of flint about six inches thick, at the depth of a foot from the surface, below which is a bed of clay, varying in thickness from six to ten feet, beneath which is found the hard chalk rock. This district is terminated on the north and north-west by the Chiltern hills, forming the abrupt extremity of the chalk strata in this direction; and contains about thirty-six thousand acres, of which four thousand acres of those elevated tracts, known by the names of Dunstable downs, Luton downs, Warden White hills, &c., are almost in a natural state. Some of the hills at Luton consist of clay towards their summits, with chalk and gravel on their declivities towards the vales; and at Sundon and Streatley, the chalky basis is covered to various depths by strata of clay, gravel, or gravelly loams. North-westward of the Chiltern hills lies a long tract of clays, extending without interruption from Billington, on the south-eastern confines of the county, north-eastward to Cockayne-Hatley, at its easternmost extremity, on the border of Cambridgeshire. These, like the other clays in the northern parts, are mostly stiff and tenacious, but interspersed with small portions of gravel, and loams on a wet basis. The clays near the Chiltern hills contain, in general, a mixture of chalk, whence they are called *white-lands*. This district again, on the north-west, is bounded by the sandy belt, which forms so distinguishing a feature in the geology of Bedfordshire, and extends, with only a small interval in the valley of the Ivel, from Leighton-Buzzard, on the confines of Buckinghamshire, by Woburn, Ampthill, and Biggleswade, to Potton, on those of Cambridgeshire. Its length is about twenty-five miles, while its ordinary breadth is about three, but in some places is as much as five, and in others not more than one. Very little sand is found out of its limits, which include about forty-two thousand acres: its surface is generally hilly, with clay and various loams in the intersecting vales, and sometimes clay on the tops of the hills, which variations, from the prevailing sandiness of the tract, added to the ferruginous peats of Tingrith, Flitwick, Westoning, Flitton, Maulden, &c., reduce the real amount of sandy surface to not more than thirty thousand acres. Many of the hills are too high and steep to be susceptible of profitable cultivation; and with regard to many others, the clay, or marl, necessary for their improvement, can be obtained only at inconvenient distances. Great efforts, however, have been made towards improvement, and only a very small portion of it remains unenclosed. The colour of this sand, though in some spots black, white, or grey, is in general a brownish yellow, which tinge it receives from the iron either combined with it, or loosely adhering to the surface of the particles of which it consists. The white and black sands are invariably barren, their natural vegetable produce being almost entirely heath, or *ling*, as it is called in this county, and the quantity of fern and natural grasses intermingled with it is very inconsiderable. Extensive tracts of gravelly loams are distributed over parts of the county, the principal of which are on the borders of the rivers Ouse and Ivel, and comprise an area of about thirty-four thousand acres. Indeed the soils of the meadows on the banks of the Ouse and Ivel consist entirely of gravels of various degrees of fineness, mixed with clay and sand. The continuous gravelly soils of these vales commence on the course of the Ouse, near Bletsoe, and on that of the Ivel, in the vicinity of Clifton; but they also frequently appear on the slopes of the hills enclosing the winding vale of the former river above Bletsoe, as far as Turvey. In some places the subsoil of gravel is covered with a thick black mould, or a reddish brown earth, both of which are of the highest fertility: in other places the upper soil is rendered sharp by the proximity of the gravel to the surface, which makes it necessary to cultivate upon it such crops as are best adapted for light land. The land immediately adjoining the rivers, by the waters of which it is annually inundated, consists every where of meadows of never-failing fertility, producing every year abundant crops of hay and aftergrass, without the aid of manure. Northward of the gravel, at the foot of the hills which bound the vale of the Ouse on the north, there is in most places a breadth of between one and two miles of peculiarly productive black and brown soils, resting on a substratum of mild clay. The rest of the county northward of the sandy tract above described consists of clays of almost every variety, but for the most part stiff and tenacious; and, with the clayey district which separates the sand from the chalk, comprises an extent of nearly one hun-

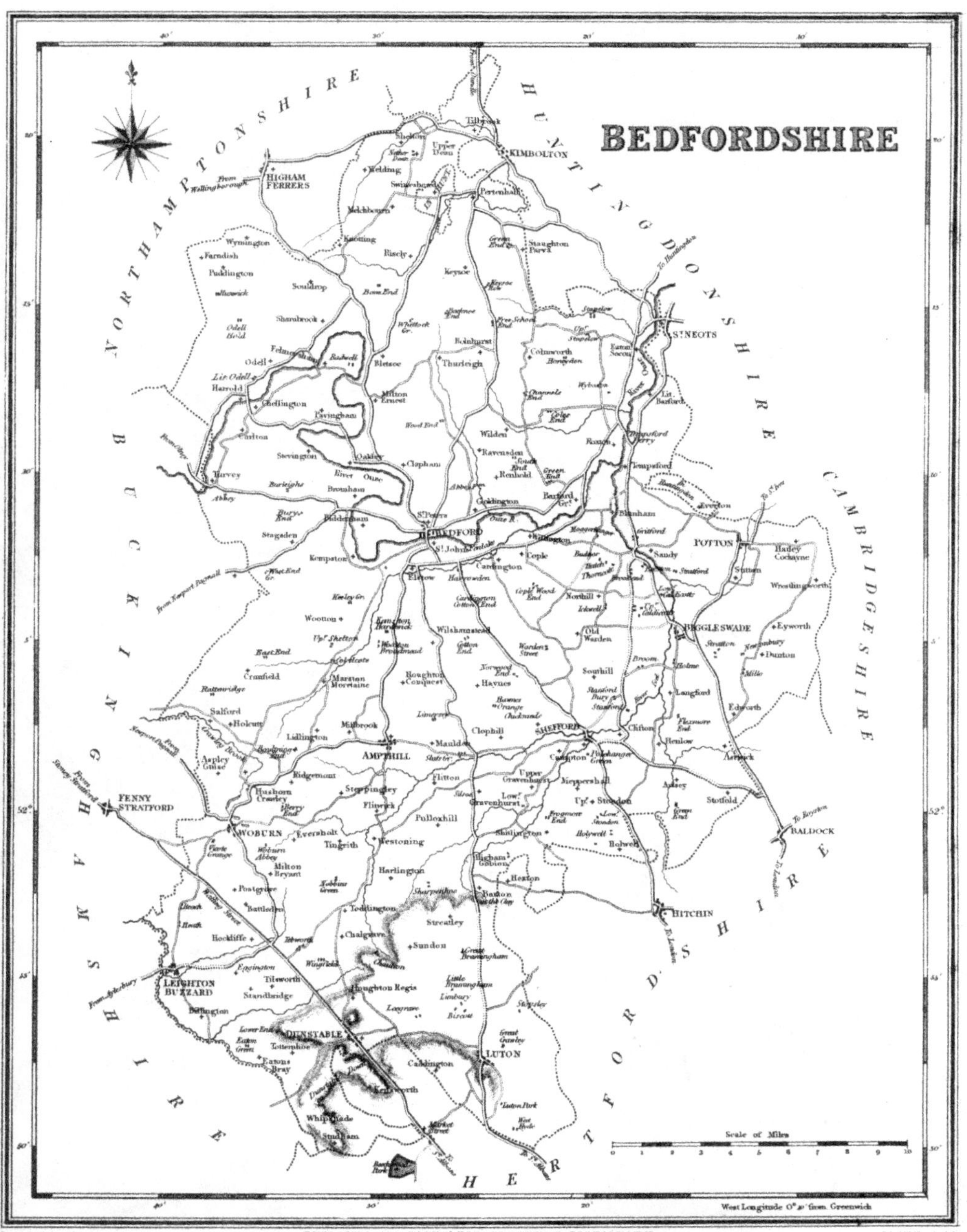

Drawn by R. Creighton. ENGRAVED FOR LEWIS'S TOPOGRAPHICAL DICTIONARY. J. & C. Walker Sculpt.

dred and ninety-eight thousand acres. Part of these clays occupies the southern portion of the Vale of Bedford, adjoining the gravelly soils above mentioned, which vale is separated by a range of hills on the east and south from the sandy tracts. Many of the summits and declivities of these hills have a peculiar shallow, light, clayey soil on a clayey, or marly, substratum, denominated *woodland*, the surface of much of which is occupied by woods. From the neighbourhood of Bedford to the northern extremity of the shire, the face of the county is tolerably uniform; and, on the upland districts, having only gentle descents, is much of this woodland, which is extremely difficult of profitable culture, and produces only the coarsest grasses. Gently rising hills of brownish clay of very various qualities bound the Vale of Bedford immediately on the north; and the smaller vallies of this part of the county have sometimes remarkably fertile soils on a substratum of gravel, more particularly that which extends from the neighbourhood of Risley through the parishes of Swineshead, Pertenhall, and Little Staughton.

The improvements that have taken place in modern times in the agriculture of this county, which have not, however, been introduced very extensively, are mainly owing to the exertions of the late Duke of Bedford. It has long been noted for its abundant produce of wheat and barley, the Vale of Bedford being one of the finest corn districts in the country. Rye and oats are very little cultivated, as beans are considered to be more profitable, and on the clay soils are less exhausting than oats. Winter and summer tares are grown in every part of the county; as also are turnips on the sandy, gravelly, and chalky soils, and sometimes on the woodlands. Much clover is sown; ray-grass, commonly called in this county *bents*, is in general use on the sandy lands; and sainfoin is cultivated by many farmers in the enclosed parts of the chalk district. The natural meadows on the banks of the rivers are distinguished for their richness, but the quantity of pasture land is not very considerable. In the southern parts of the county, and in the neighbourhoods of Ampthill and Woburn more especially, are many large dairy farms, the produce of which, being chiefly butter, is sent in considerable quantities to the London market. Very little butter is made in the northern parts of the county besides what is required for home consumption, much of the grass land being of very poor quality. The breeding and fattening of calves is carried on to a considerable extent in the neighbourhood of Biggleswade: the calves of the dairy district are sold at Leighton market, for the purpose of suckling. The irrigation of grass land was introduced by the late Duke of Bedford, and various examples of its beneficial effects may be seen in the parishes of Woburn, Crawley, Ridgmont, Flitwick, and Maulden. Marl and clay are in common use as manures on the light sandy soils; chalk and lime, in the southern parts of the county; and peat-ashes and peat dust, in different places, more particularly in the chalk district. In addition to these and the common farm-yard manures, the farmers in the southern part of the county obtain various light dressings for their land from London. The cattle are of a mixed and generally of an inferior kind, partaking of the various qualities of the Holderness, Lancashire, Leicestershire, and Alderney sorts. The sheep are also of mixed breeds: and their fleeces are of a very indifferent kind of wool, and weigh from three to four pounds. Many of the swine partake more or less of the qualities of the Berkshire kind. The farmers are chiefly supplied with horses by dealers who bring two-years-old colts from the fens of Huntingdonshire and Lincolnshire. In the southern part of the county, many road teams are kept for the purpose of conveying the produce of the soil to the metropolis, and bringing back manure. The villages of Sandy and Gritford have long been celebrated, in this and the adjacent counties, for the excellence and abundance of the culinary vegetables grown in their vicinities; for this they are chiefly indebted to the excellence of the soils in their vale lands, which consist of a fine deep sandy loam of a yellowish brown, and form the best garden grounds in the county. The soils of some parts of the parish of Potton appear to be little inferior to those of Sandy for horticultural purposes; and portions of excellent garden ground are found in other situations in the sandy district, where its surface is but little elevated, as at Biggleswade, Campton, Clophill, Maulden, &c. The produce of the extensive horticultural grounds at Sandy is sent to the surrounding markets, to the distance of sixty-miles, and in some instances even still further. The orchards are generally very small: those of cherries are most common in the southern parts of the county. The woods occupy about seven thousand acres, and are almost wholly situated on the slopes of the hills, which consist of cold wet woodland clays. A considerable portion of them clothes the hills which extend from Ampthill towards Blunham, between the sandy district and the Vale of Bedford. Others, again, are seen on the western side of the vale, at Holcutt and Marston, and nearly all the rest are dispersed over the north-western parts of the county; while, on the contrary, in many parts of the southern and eastern districts of it, wood is rarely seen. Various extensive plantations have been made by different proprietors, among which may be more particularly specified those of the Earl of Upper Ossory and Francis Moore, Esq., on the sandy district, near the western confines of the county; those of the Duke of Bedford, around Woburn Abbey; those of Lord Carteret, near his seat at Hawnes; and those of Lord St. John, in the neighbourhood of his seat at Melchbourn. Some of the sandy hills, which admit of little other improvement, have been applied in various places to the growth of furze, or whins, for the use of the bakers, lime-burners, &c. The high chalky downs, which meet the eye on every side in the southernmost part of the county, in the neighbourhoods of Luton and Dunstable, comprise about four thousand acres of bleak and barren land, which in many parts consists of nothing but a mass of hard chalk, called hurlock, or clunch, with a slight covering of loamy soil, barely sufficient to nourish a scanty crop of indifferent herbage. The northern acclivities of the Chiltern hills are, in many places, the steepest in the county, and totally inaccessible to the plough. Excepting this tract, the waste lands of Bedfordshire occupy a very small proportion of its surface.

The mineral productions are of very inferior importance. A bed of hard limestone follows the course of the river Ouse, from Turvey to Bedford, and abounds with the different kinds of shells and other marine exuviæ commonly found imbedded in the yellow limestone. This is quarried for the various purposes of building, &c. At Totternhoe, near Dunstable, is a considerable quarry of freestone; and in some of the strata which cover the principal bed of stone are found *cornua ammonis* and other shells. A small quantity of iron-stone has been observed in some pits at Bromham; and some of the strata in the sand pits of Lidlington, &c., contain a considerable proportion of the same mineral. Small quantities of imperfect coal have been found in the parish of Goldington. *Nautili* and other shells are found in a chalk pit at Caddington; sharks' teeth, ammonites, belemnites, &c., in a light-coloured clay near Leighton; and *echini* in the fields near Eaton-Bray. The manufactures are almost entirely confined to the platting of straw and the making of thread-lace, the latter being pursued in every part of the county, excepting only in the southern districts, where it has been superseded by the straw manufacture. Straw-platting was formerly confined to the chalk district, at the southernmost extremity of the county, but was so much encouraged about the commencement of the present century, as to spread rapidly over the whole southern part of it, as far as Woburn, Ampthill, and Shefford. Here many of the males, and nearly the whole female population, are employed in this manufacture; in like manner as those of the middle and northern parts of the county are in the making of thread-lace. A considerable quantity of mats is made in the vicinity of the Ouse, to the north-west of Bedford. The chief exports are the produce of the manufactures, grain, butter, and calves; the imports are horses, and the various kinds of ordinary supplies for domestic use.

The principal rivers are the Ouse and the Ivel. The former flows into this county from Buckinghamshire, in the parish of Turvey, becomes navigable at Bedford, and, passing by Tempsford, enters Huntingdonshire between Eaton-Socon and St. Neots: its course through Bedfordshire is remarkably tortuous, and about forty-five miles long. The fish in it are pike, perch, bream, chubb, bleak, cray-fish, eels, dace, roach, and gudgeon: the eels, which are particularly fine, are most abundant at Stoke mill; the bleak, at Bedford bridge. The Ivel rises near Baldock in Hertfordshire, enters the county in the vicinity of Stotfold, and, being joined by other powerful streams from the west, becomes navigable at Biggleswade, and falls into the Ouse at Tempsford. The Lea has its source near Houghton-Regis, in this county, and, flowing south-eastward through the parish of Luton, enters Hertfordshire between East and West Hide, in its progress towards the Thames. The Ouzel rises near Whipsnade, on the southern confines of the county, and, leaving Eaton-Bray on the right, takes a north-westerly course by Leighton-Buzzard, forming for a considerable distance the line of boundary between the counties of Bedford and Buckingham, in the latter of which it continues its course. The Grand Junction canal crosses a small western portion of Bedfordshire, in the valley of the Ouzel, near Leighton-Buzzard, to which town and to the neighbouring country it gives all the advantages of a cheap medium of traffic with the metropolis and with the north-western counties of England, in the articles of corn, coal, iron, &c.

The roads of the gravelly districts are in general very good; those of the sandy tract, being chiefly made and repaired with sandy gravel, are frequently loose and heavy; those of the north-western part of the county, which are mostly repaired with the limestone above-mentioned, are usually rough and uneven; while the principal roads of the clay districts afford to the traveller a sufficient idea of those of the adjacent country, which, in winter, are nearly impassable. The great northern road from London to Glasgow enters near the forty-first milestone, runs through Biggleswade and Tempsford, and passes into Huntingdonshire two miles beyond Eaton-Socon. The great road from London to Chester and Holyhead enters near the thirty-third milestone, and passing through Hockliffe, or Hockley in the Hole, quits it at the forty-second milestone for Buckinghamshire: the road to Liverpool branches off near Hockliffe, and enters the latter county two miles beyond Woburn. The road from London to Higham-Ferrers and Kettering runs into the county from Hertfordshire, near the thirty-sixth milestone, and passing through Bedford, enters Northamptonshire about eleven miles beyond it. A road from London to Bedford enters at the twenty-seventh milestone.

This county contained the Roman station called by Antonine *Durocobrivæ*, and by Richard of Cirencester *Forum Dianæ*, at Dunstable; and that called by Ptolemy Σαληναι, and by Ravennas *Salinæ*, near the village of Sandy. It was intersected by the great Roman roads, the Iknield-street and the Watling-street; by a military way, which runs for a considerable distance within its south-eastern borders; and by several vicinal ways. The Iknield, or Ikening, street, supposed to be of ancient British construction, and to have been afterwards adopted as a medium of communication by the Romans, enters Bedfordshire on its south-eastern border, from the country of the Iceni, from whom it derived its name, and crosses the turnpike-road from Luton to Bedford about the sixteenth milestone, where a branch bears off to the right through Great Bramingham and Houghton to the British camp at Maiden-Bower, near Dunstable, while the main road pursues its course along the side of the hills, and passing through the town of Dunstable, soon after enters Buckinghamshire. The Watling-street cannot, in this part of its course, be distinguished from the great road from London to Chester and Holyhead, which is carried along it from the southern to the western confines of the county: near Dunstable, through which it passes, various Roman coins have been discovered. The third great Roman road through Bedfordshire was that which enters it near Baldock in Hertfordshire, in the line of the present north road, which, however, diverges to the right at the village of Stretton, to pass through Biggleswade, while the Roman road continues its course direct to the station *Salinæ*, near the village of Sandy, the site of which is now called Chesterfield. Hence it may be traced pursuing the same direction across the road from Everton to Tempsford, through Tempsford marsh, by a tumulus on the hill beyond, called the Hen and Chickens, and to the left of Hardwick, to the Roman station at Godmanchester in Huntingdonshire. The station near Sandy appears to have communicated by different vicinal ways with others in the adjoining counties; and on its site have been found coins and every other ordinary relic of Roman occupation. On a hill overlooking this spot is a large Roman camp of an irregular oblong form; but the most remarkable military intrenchment is that called Totternhoe Castle, situated on the brow of a high hill, about two miles to the north-west of Dunstable, and consisting of a lofty circular mount, surrounded by two distinct ramparts: a little south-eastward of this is a camp in the form of a parallelogram, about five hundred feet long, and two hundred and fifty broad. About a mile from Dunstable is the large circular encampment called Maiden-Bower, about two thousand five hundred feet in circumference, and formed by a single ditch and rampart: another extensive fortification of the same kind, and nearly of a circular form, is seen near Leighton-Buzzard; and a third circular intrenchment, one hundred and twelve feet in diameter, is situated about four miles from Bedford, adjoining the road from that town to Eaton-Socon.

At the period of the Reformation, this county contained fourteen religious houses, besides a preceptory of the Knights Hospitallers, six hospitals, and one college of priests. There are considerable remains of Elstow abbey and Dunstable priory; and smaller vestiges of Warden abbey, of the Grey friars' monastery at Bedford, and of the priories of Bushmead, Harrold, Newenham, and Caldwell. The most ancient specimens of ecclesiastical architecture are seen in the church of Elstow, anciently belonging to the monastery at that place, which was founded, and the present church built, soon after the Norman Conquest. The parish church of Dunstable, also originally conventual, and built in the reign of Henry I., yet exhibits considerable remains of its original style of architecture. The other churches possessing any remarkable architectural feature are those of St. Peter at Bedford, Caddington, Little Barford, Puddington, and Thurleigh, all of which have doorways of Saxon architecture; and those of Biggleswade, Eaton-Bray, Eaton-Socon, Felmersham, Leighton-Buzzard, Luton, Marston, Northill, Odell, Studham, Willington, and Wymington. Many of the churches have richly ornamented niches, and contain fonts curiously decorated, and in some instances of great antiquity. Hardly any traces of mural fortresses now exist, excepting the strong earthworks which yet mark their ancient sites. The most remarkable of these are situated at Arlsey, Bedford, Bletsoe, Cainhoe, Meppershall, Puddington, Ridgmont, Risinghoe, Sutton, Thurleigh, Toddington, and Yielding. Among the mansions of the landed proprietors, those most worthy of particular notice are, Woburn Abbey, Ampthill Park, Luton Hoo Park, Wrest Park, Brogborough Park, Bletsoe Park, and Melchbourn Park. There are mineral springs at Barton, Bedford, Bletsoe, Blunham, Bromham, Bushmead, Clapham, Cranfield, Holcutt, Milton-Ernest, Odell, Pertenhall, Risley, Silsoe, and Turvey; they possess different properties, some being saline, others chalybeate, but none of them are much frequented.

BEDHAMPTON, a parish in the hundred of PORTSDOWN, Portsdown division of the county of SOUTHAMPTON, $\frac{3}{4}$ of a mile (W.) from Havant, containing 413 inhabitants. The living is a rectory, in the archdeaconry and diocese of Winchester, rated in the king's books at £10. 3. 9., and in the patronage of Andrew Reid, Esq. This parish is within the jurisdiction of the Cheyney Court held at Winchester every Thursday, for the recovery of debts under 40*s.*

BEDINGFIELD, a parish in the hundred of HOXNE, county of SUFFOLK, 4 miles (S. S. E.) from Eye, containing 318 inhabitants. The living is a discharged vicarage, in the archdeaconry of Suffolk, and diocese of Norwich, rated in the king's books at £8, and in the patronage of J. J. Bedingfield, Esq. The church is dedicated to St. Mary.

BEDINGHAM, a parish in the hundred of LODDON, county of NORFOLK, $4\frac{1}{4}$ miles (N. W. by W.) from Bungay, containing 343 inhabitants. The living is a discharged vicarage, in the archdeaconry of Norfolk, and diocese of Norwich, rated in the king's books at £5, endowed with £200 private benefaction, and £200 royal bounty, and in the presentation of R. Stone, Esq. on the nomination of the Bishop of Norwich. The church is dedicated to St. Andrew. Another church, dedicated to St. Mary, formerly stood in the churchyard; and the living consisted of medieties, which have long been united.

BEDLINGTON, a parish in the eastern division of CHESTER ward, county palatine of DURHAM, of which it is a detached portion, lying at the south-eastern corner of Castle ward, county of Northumberland, $5\frac{1}{2}$ miles (S. E. by E.) from Morpeth, comprising the townships of Bedlington, North Blyth with Chambois, Choppington, Netherton, East Sleckburn, and West Sleckburn, and containing 1862 inhabitants. The living is a vicarage, in the archdeaconry of Northumberland, and diocese of Durham, rated in the king's books at £13. 6. 8., and in the patronage of the Dean and Chapter of Durham. The church, dedicated to St. Cuthbert, whose remains rested here for one night in 1069, when the monks fled from Durham, at the menacing approach of the Conqueror, was enlarged and repaired in 1818. There are places of worship for Primitive and Wesleyan Methodists and Presbyterians. This parish, commonly termed Bedlingtonshire, is situated on the coast of the North sea, and is bounded on the north and south by the river Blyth: it had anciently courts within its own limits, and the officers of justice were appointed by the Bishop of Durham, to whom the manor belongs. Petty sessions for the district are held monthly at one of the inns in the village. Bedlington iron-works rank among the oldest and most extensive in the kingdom: they are romantically situated on the banks of the river Blyth, which is navigable for small craft, and affords the means of conveying their produce, consisting of chain cables, bolts, bar and sheet iron, and nearly all the heavier articles in wrought iron, to the port of Blyth, where it is shipped for London. The vicinity contains several stone quarries, producing grindstones and whetstones of a superior quality; and there are some extensive collieries. A petrifying spring rises at the western end of the village.

BEDMINSTER, a parish in the hundred of HARTCLIFFE with BEDMINSTER, county of SOMERSET, $1\frac{1}{2}$ mile (S. by W.) from Bristol, containing 7979 inhabitants. The living is a discharged vicarage, with the perpetual curacies of St. Thomas' Redcliffe and Abbot's Leigh annexed, in the archdeaconry of Bath, and diocese of Bath and Wells, rated in the king's books at £10. 3. 4., and in the patronage of the Prebendary of Bedminster in the Cathedral Church of Salisbury. The church, dedicated to St. John the Baptist, displays various portions of ancient architecture, mixed with modern insertions: a spire on the tower was thrown down in 1563. A chapel of ease is in progress of erection, under the act passed in the 58th of George III., the first stone having been laid on the 8th of September, 1829. There are places of worship for Baptists, Independents, and Methodists: that belonging to the Independents is one of the most handsome and spacious buildings of the kind in the kingdom; the principal entrance is adorned with Grecian columns, and the exterior coated with freestone. Bedminster anciently consisted only of a few cottages, but, from its proximity to Bristol (being separated from it by the new cut, whereby the natural channel of the river Avon has been converted into a floating harbour for vessels frequenting the port), and the main road to that city from the western counties passing through it, it has become a considerable suburb to Bristol, participating in its manufactures, trade, &c. Here are tan-yards and rope-walks; and in the environs are several gardens, with the produce of which the occupiers supply the city of Bristol; but many of the inhabitants, the number of whom now exceeds ten thousand, are employed in the collieries within the parish. About the close of the twelfth century, Robert de Berkeley founded an hospital, dedicated to St. Catherine, for a master and several poor brethren; it stood on the western side of a street near the extremity of Brightlow bridge, and was subsequently used as a glass-manufactory, but has since been converted into small tenements: another hospital was founded by a member of the same family, but every vestige of it has disappeared. A court baron for the prebend is held here.

BEDNALL, a joint chapelry and township with Acton-Trussell, in the parish of BASWICH, eastern division of the hundred of CUTTLESTONE, county of STAFFORD, 4 miles (N.E. by N.) from Penkridge. The population is returned with Acton-Trussell. The living is a perpetual curacy, in the peculiar jurisdiction of the Prebendary of Whittington and Baswich in the Cathedral Church of Lichfield, endowed with £600 royal bounty. The chapel is dedicated to All Saints.

BEDSTONE, a parish in the hundred of PURSLOW, county of SALOP, 4½ miles (N.E.) from Knighton, containing 165 inhabitants. The living is a discharged rectory, in the archdeaconry of Salop, and diocese of Hereford, rated in the king's books at £4. 13. 4., endowed with £200 private benefaction, and £200 royal bounty, and in the patronage of Benjamin Brown, Esq. The church is dedicated to St. Mary.

BEDWARDINE (ST. JOHN), a parish in the lower division of the hundred of OSWALDSLOW, county of WORCESTER, comprising the townships of St. John Bedwardine and Bishop's Wick, and containing 2424 inhabitants, of which number, 1161 are in the township of St. John Bedwardine, 1 mile (S.W. by W.) from Worcester. The living is a discharged vicarage, in the archdeaconry and diocese of Worcester, rated in the king's books at £13. 6. 8., and in the patronage of the Dean and Chapter of Worcester. The church, dedicated to St. John the Baptist, is an ancient edifice, partly in the Norman, but chiefly in the later style of English, architecture. The parish takes its name from its having been allotted to supply the table of the monks of Worcester with provisions. The village, pleasantly situated on an eminence rising from the western bank of the Severn, forms a suburb to the city of Worcester, from which it is separated by the river Severn. A fair is held on the Friday before Palm-Sunday, on which day (by ancient usage, originating in a grant of certain privileges to the bailiffs and corporation, by the prior of Worcester, in the reign of Edward IV.,) the mayor and corporation of Worcester walk in procession through the village.

BEDWAS, a parish comprising the hamlet of Van, in the hundred of CAERPHILLY, county of GLAMORGAN (Wales), and the hamlets of Lower and Upper Bedwas, in the lower division of the hundred of WENTLLOOG, county of MONMOUTH, and containing 650 inhabitants, of which number, 298 are in the hamlet of Upper, and 272 in that of Lower, Bedwas, 9 miles (W. by N.) from Newport. The living is a rectory, with the perpetual curacy of Ruddry annexed, in the archdeaconry and diocese of Llandaff, rated in the king's books at £10. 14. 9½., and in the patronage of the Bishop of Llandaff. The church is dedicated to St. Barrog.

BEDWELTY, a parish in the lower division of the hundred of WENTLLOOG, county of MONMOUTH, 16 miles (N.W.) from Newport, comprising the hamlets of Ishlawreoed, Mamhole, and Ushlawreoed, and containing 6382 inhabitants. The living is a perpetual curacy, in the archdeaconry and diocese of Llandaff, endowed with £600 royal bounty, and £1600 parliamentary grant, and in the patronage of the Bishop of Llandaff. The church, dedicated to St. Sannan, is of early English architecture; and the churchyard, which commands extensive and variegated prospects, is surrounded with some trifling remains of an intrenchment.

BEDWIN (GREAT), a borough, parish, and market town, in the hundred of KINWARDSTONE, county of WILTS, 5½ miles (S.W. by W.) from Hungerford, 23 (N.) from Salisbury, and 70½ (W. by S.) from London, containing, with the tythings of Crofton, East and West Grafton, Martin, Stock with Ford, Wixcombe, Wilton, and Wolfhall, 1928 inhabitants. This place, supposed by Dr. Stukeley to be the *Leucomagus* of Ravennas, derives its name from the Saxon *Beeguyn*, or *Bedgwyn*, expressive of its situation on an eminence, in a chalky soil. It was anciently a city of great extent, and the metropolis of Cissa, one of the three sons of Ælla, the Saxon chieftain, who invaded Britain in 477. Cissa, when viceroy of Wiltshire and part of Berkshire, is said to have enlarged and strengthened Chisbury Castle, now a noble relic of Saxon earthwork, about a mile to the north-east of the town, in the parish of Little Bedwin. In 674, a battle was fought here between Wulfhere, King of Mercia, and Æscuin, a nobleman in the service of Saxburga, Queen of Wessex, in which, after a desperate struggle, the latter was victorious. The soil of

Arms.

Great Bedwin is good, and the general aspect of the country luxuriant. The Kennet and Avon canal passes through the parish, and affords a medium for the conveyance of excellent coal. The market is on Tuesday; and fairs are held on April 23rd and July 26th: the market-house is an ancient building, situated in the principal street. A portreeve, who is customarily called mayor, a bailiff, and other officers, are annually chosen at the court leet of the lord of the manor. This borough sent representatives to all the parliaments of Edward I., from the close of whose reign to the 9th of Henry V. there were frequent intermissions; but since then it has constantly returned two members. The right of election is vested in the freeholders and inhabitants of the ancient burgage messuages, in number about ninety-five: the portreeve is the returning officer, and the influence of the Marquis of Ailesbury predominates. The living is a vicarage, within the jurisdiction of the peculiar court of the Lord Warden of Savernake Forest, rated in the king's books at £8. 10. 10., endowed with £400 private benefaction, £400 royal bounty, and £600 parliamentary grant, and in the patronage of the Marquis of Ailesbury. The church, dedicated to St. Mary, and the only remaining one of seven which are said to have anciently existed here, appears to have been erected at various times, and exhibits good specimens of all the styles of architecture, from the Norman to the later English; it is a cruciform structure, with a lofty embattled tower rising from the intersection, and contains several ancient memorials, among which is the figure of a Knight Templar, and the monument of Sir John Seymour, father of the Protector Somerset, and of Lady Jane Seymour, consort of Henry VIII., who were born at Wolf Hall, now a farm-house, in this parish. There is a place of worship for Wesleyan Methodists. A school is endowed for the instruction of ten boys; and Sir Andrew Hungerford, in 1694, left an annuity of £10 for apprenticing poor boys of the borough. Within the mounds of Chisbury Castle, comprising an area of fifteen acres, are the remains of an ancient chapel, now used as a barn. Half a mile to the south-west are some vestiges of a Roman building, but they are now scarcely discoverable. A fine tesselated pavement was preserved here till within the last few years. Dr. Thomas Willis, a celebrated physician, was born here in 1621, and died in London, in 1675.

Corporate Seal.

BEDWIN (LITTLE), a parish in the hundred of Kinwardstone, county of Wilts, 4½ miles (W. S. W.) from Hungerford, containing 504 inhabitants. The living is a vicarage, within the jurisdiction of the peculiar court of the Lord Warden of Savernake Forest, rated in the king's books at £9. 6. 8., and in the patronage of the Marquis of Ailesbury. The church is dedicated to St. Michael. The Kennet and Avon canal passes through the parish, which is also intersected by the ancient Wansdyke.

BEDWORTH, a parish in the Kirby division of the hundred of Knightlow, county of Warwick, 3½ miles (S.) from Nuneaton, containing 3519 inhabitants. The living is a rectory, in the archdeaconry of Coventry, and diocese of Lichfield and Coventry, rated in the king's books at £10. 3. 11½., and in the patronage of the Earl of Aylesford. The church, dedicated to All Saints, has recently received an additional number of sittings, by means of a grant of £250 from the Incorporated Society for enlarging churches and chapels. There is a place of worship for Particular Baptists. Near the village is a coal mine, from which a railroad extends to the Ashby de la Zouch and Coventry canals, which form a junction within the parish, the latter terminating here. Two charity schools, and almshouses for twenty-four persons, are endowed with land producing £700 per annum, bequeathed by the Rev. Nicholas Chamberlain, in 1715.

BEEBY, a parish in the eastern division of the hundred of Goscote, county of Leicester, 6 miles (N.E. by E.) from Leicester, containing 120 inhabitants. The living is a rectory, in the archdeaconry of Leicester, and diocese of Lincoln, rated in the king's books at £15. 2. 6., and in the patronage of the Earl of Shaftesbury. The church is dedicated to All Saints.

BEECH, a liberty in the parish of Stone, southern division of the hundred of Pirehill, county of Stafford, containing 838 inhabitants.

BEECHAMWELL, comprising the parish of All Saints, and the united parishes of St. John and St. Mary, in the hundred of Clackclose, county of Norfolk, 5½ miles (W. S. W.) from Swaffham, and containing 288 inhabitants. The living of All Saints' is a discharged rectory, with that of Shingham annexed, rated in the king's books at £6. 13. 4., and in the patronage of the Crown. St. John's and St. Mary's are discharged rectories consolidated, rated jointly at £9. 13. 4., and in the patronage of J. Motteaux, Esq.: they are in the archdeaconry of Norfolk, and diocese of Norwich.

BEECH-HILL, a tything in that part of the parish of Stratfield-Saye which is in the hundred of Reading, county of Berks, 6 miles (S. by W.) from Reading, containing 274 inhabitants. There is a place of worship for Particular Baptists.

BEECHING, or BEAUCHAMP-STOKE, a parish in the hundred of Swanborough, county of Wilts, 5¼ miles (E. by S.) from Devizes, containing 156 inhabitants. The living is a rectory, in the archdeaconry of Wilts, and diocese of Salisbury, rated in the king's books at £7. 2. 11., and in the patronage of George Wylde Heneage, Esq. The church is dedicated to St. Stephen. On opening a tumulus in this parish lately, a considerable quantity of stags' horns and human bones was discovered.

BEEDING, a parish in the hundred of Burbeach, rape of Bramber, county of Sussex, comprising Upper and Lower Beeding, and containing 904 inhabitants, of which number, 499 are in the former, 1 mile (E.), and 405 in the latter, 1½ mile (E. S. E.), from Steyning. The living is a discharged vicarage, in the archdeaconry of Lewes, and diocese of Chichester, rated in the king's books at £8, and in the patronage of the President and Fellows of Magdalene College, Oxford. The church is dedicated to St. Peter. An Alien priory of Benedictine monks was founded here about 1075, the revenue of which, amounting to £26. 9. 9., was given to the Society of Magdalene College, in the reign of Henry VI. The navigable river Adur runs in the vicinity.

BEEDON, a parish in the hundred of FAIRCROSS, county of BERKS, 2¼ miles (S. W. by W.) from East Ilsley, containing 313 inhabitants. The living is a discharged vicarage, in the archdeaconry of Berks, and diocese of Salisbury, rated in the king's books at £6. 10. 10., endowed with £250 private benefaction, and £200 royal bounty, and in the patronage of Sir J. Reade, Bart. The church is dedicated to St. Nicholas.

BEEFORD, a parish in the northern division of the wapentake of HOLDERNESS, East riding of the county of York, comprising the chapelry of Lissett, and the townships of Beeford and Dunnington, and containing 791 inhabitants, of which number, 620 are in the township of Beeford, 9 miles (E. S. E.) from Great Driffield. The living is a rectory, within the peculiar jurisdiction of the manor court of Beeford, rated in the king's books at £22, and in the patronage of the Crown. The church is dedicated to St. Leonard. There are places of worship for Independents and Wesleyan Methodists. A free school here is conducted on the National plan.

BEELEY, a chapelry in the parish of BAKEWELL, hundred of HIGH PEAK, county of DERBY, 4 miles (E. by S.) from Bakewell, containing 350 inhabitants. The living is a perpetual curacy, within the peculiar jurisdiction of the Dean and Chapter of Lichfield, endowed with £400 private benefaction, and £1200 royal bounty, and in the patronage of the Duke of Devonshire. The chapel is dedicated to St. Anne. There is a place of worship for Wesleyan Methodists. Several small benefactions have been made for the relief of the poor.

BEELSBY, a parish in the wapentake of BRADLEY-HAVERSTOE, parts of LINDSEY, county of LINCOLN, 5¾ miles (E.) from Caistor, containing 160 inhabitants. The living is a rectory, in the archdeaconry and diocese of Lincoln, rated in the king's books at £8. 17. 6., and in the patronage of the Chapter of the Collegiate Church of Southwell. The church is dedicated to St. Andrew.

BEENHAM, a parish in the hundred of READING, county of BERKS, 8¾ miles (W. S. W.) from Reading, containing 437 inhabitants. The living is a discharged vicarage, in the archdeaconry of Berks, and diocese of Salisbury, rated in the king's books at £7. 17., and in the patronage of Mrs. Stevens. The church is dedicated to St. Mary. The navigable river Kennet runs in the vicinity.

BEER, a chapelry in the parish of SEATON, hundred of COLYTON, county of DEVON, 3½ miles (S. S. W.) from Colyton, containing 1256 inhabitants. The Cove of Beer is highly favourable for fishing. In 1820, Lord Rolle obtained an act for constructing a pier and improving the harbour. Edward Colston bequeathed land, producing about £500 a year, for maintaining, clothing, and teaching one hundred poor boys of Idstock and Beer. Lady Rolle bequeathed £7000 three per cents. for charitable purposes, from which fund almshouses for twenty-five poor fishermen, and twenty infirm widows, and schools for the instruction of boys and girls, on Dr. Bell's plan, have been erected and endowed.

BEER-ALSTON, a borough in the parish of BEER-FERRIS, hundred of ROBOROUGH, county of DEVON, 14 miles (N.) from Plymouth, and 211 (W. S. W.) from London. The population is returned with the parish. This place, about the year 1295, received the grant of a weekly market and an annual fair, which have been for a considerable time discontinued. It is pleasantly situated within a mile of the navigable river Tamar, but consists only of a few mean houses. Some lead mines, opened here in the reign of Edward I., produced abundance of ore, from which a great quantity of silver was separated; after a long period of disuse they were again worked, but their produce had greatly diminished. A portreeve and other officers are annually chosen at the court leet of the lord of the manor, which is held under a large tree, where also the election of the parliamentary representatives for the borough takes place. The elective franchise was conferred in the 27th of Elizabeth, since which time the borough has returned two members to parliament: the right of election is vested by burgage tenure in those who have land in the borough, and pay an acknowledgment to the lord of the manor, upon whose will their number is entirely dependent: the portreeve is the returning officer. Here was formerly a chapel of ease to the rectory of Beer-Ferris. There is a place of worship for Wesleyan Methodists.

BEER-CROCOMBE, a parish in the hundred of ABDICK and BULSTONE, county of SOMERSET, 6 miles (N. W. by N.) from Ilminster, containing 186 inhabitants. The living is a discharged rectory, in the archdeaconry of Taunton, and diocese of Bath and Wells, rated in the king's books at £11. 12. 6., and in the patronage of the Earl of Egremont. The church is dedicated to St. James.

BEER-FERRIS, a parish in the hundred of ROBOROUGH, county of DEVON, 7½ miles (S. by W.) from Tavistock, containing, with the borough of Beer-Alston, 2198 inhabitants. The living is a rectory, in the archdeaconry of Totness, and diocese of Bath and Wells, rated in the king's books at £24. 1. 0½., and in the patronage of Viscount Valletort. The church is dedicated to St. Andrew. The parish is bounded on the west by the navigable river Tamar, and on the east by the Tavey, which unite at its southern extremity, and fall into the English channel on the western side of Devonport.

BEER-HACKET, a parish in the hundred of SHERBORNE, Sherborne division of the county of DORSET, 5 miles (S. W. by S.) from Sherborne, containing 78 inhabitants. The living is a discharged rectory, within the peculiar jurisdiction of the Dean of Salisbury, rated in the king's books at £6. 2. 8½., and in the patronage of Sir John Munden. The church is dedicated to St. Michael. There is an endowment for the instruction of children.

BEER-REGIS, a market town and parish in the hundred of BEER-REGIS, Blandford (South) division of the county of DORSET, 7 miles (N. W.) from Wareham, and 113 (S. W.) from London, containing, with the tything of Shitterton, 1080 inhabitants. This place, which is supposed by Dr. Stukeley to have been the *Ibernium* of Ravennas, derives its name from the Saxon *Byrig*, and the adjunct from its having been held in royal demesne. Elfrida, after the murder of her step-son, is said to have retired hither to avoid suspicion; and King John, who occasionally made this his residence, granted the inhabitants the privilege of a market, in the seventeenth year of his reign. Edward I. made it a free borough, but it does not appear to have ever returned any members to parliament. A great part of the town was destroyed by fire in 1634: it experienced a similar calamity in 1788, and, in 1817, another destructive fire occurred, in which the parish registers were burnt. The town is pleasantly situated on the small river Beer; the houses, in general, are modern and well built, and the inhabitants are amply supplied with water. The market is on Wednesday: a fair is held, September 18th and the four following days, on Woodbury hill, for horses, horned cattle, sheep, cloth, and cheese. The living, which, in conjunction with Charmouth, formerly constituted the golden prebend in the Cathedral Church of Salisbury, and is now in the peculiar jurisdiction of the Dean of Salisbury, is a vicarage, with the perpetual curacy of Winterbourne-Kingston annexed, rated in the king's books at £25. 5., and in the patronage of the Master and Fellows of Balliol College, Oxford. The church, dedicated to St. John the Baptist, is a spacious ancient structure, with a square embattled tower crowned with pinnacles. There are places of worship for Independents and Wesleyan Methodists; that for the Independents has an endowment of £18 per annum. A charity school was founded and endowed by Thomas Williams, Esq., and further endowed by the Rev. Thomas Williams, for two additional scholars. In 1773, the Rev. Henry Fisher bequeathed £100 to this institution: the master has a salary of £10 per annum, with a house and garden. On Woodbury hill, about half a mile from the town, there is a circular camp, comprehending an area of ten acres; and to the west of it are the site of the ancient chapel of Sancta Anchoretta, and a well called Anchoret's well. Dr. John Moreton, Archbishop of Canterbury, and a cardinal; and Dr. Tuberville, Bishop of Exeter; were natives of this place; the former also distinguished himself in the wars, and projected the union, of the houses of York and Lancaster.

BEERHALL, a tything in the parish and hundred of Axminster, county of Devon, containing 331 inhabitants.

BEES (ST.), a parish in Allerdale ward above Darwent, county of Cumberland, comprising the port and market town of Whitehaven, the chapelries of Ennerdale, Eskdale with Wasdale (including Wasdale-Head), Hensingham, and Netherwasdale, the townships of St. Bees, Kinneyside, Lowside-Quarter, Preston-Quarter, Rottington, Sandwith, and Wheddicar, and containing, according to the last census, 19,969 inhabitants (since greatly increased), of which number, 655 are in the township of St. Bees, 2¾ miles (W. by N.) from Egremont. The living is a perpetual curacy, in the archdeaconry of Richmond, and diocese of Chester, endowed with £600 private benefaction, £1000 royal bounty, and £1600 parliamentary grant, and in the patronage of the Earl of Lonsdale. The church, dedicated to St. Bega, was formerly the conventual church of a monastery, founded about 650, by Bega, or Begogh, an Irish female, who subsequently received the honour of canonization. This monastery was destroyed by the Danes, and restored, in the reign of Henry I., by William de Meschines, Lord of Copeland, as a cell to the abbey of St. Mary at York: its revenue, at the dissolution, was estimated at £149. 19. 6. The church is cruciform, having a strong tower of early Norman architecture, but the rest of the edifice is in the decorated English style: the nave is used for the celebration of divine service; and the chancel, which had long lain ruinous, was repaired in 1819, and fitted up as a school for divinity, in connexion with a clerical institution, founded by Dr. Law, a late bishop of Chester, for the benefit of young men intended for holy orders, who do not mean to complete their studies at Oxford or Cambridge, and who receive ordination after having studied for a certain period at this place; but they can only enter upon their ministry within the province of York. In addition to this, there is a celebrated free grammar school, founded by letters patent, dated April 24th, 1583, obtained by Edmund Grindall, Archbishop of Canterbury, whereby its management is entrusted to a corporation of seven governors, of whom the Provost of Queen's College, Oxford, and the Rector of Egremont, are always two, the former enjoying the privilege of nominating the master, who chooses an usher. The annual income, arising from land, is £125: of this sum, £50 are paid to the master, and £10 to the usher, but their salaries receive considerable augmentation from entrance-fees and donations at Shrovetide, and the former takes boarders: gratuitous instruction is limited to the classics. The school enjoys the advantage of a fellowship and two scholarships at Queen's College, Oxford, with the privilege of sending a candidate to be examined for one of five exhibitions, founded at the same college by Lady Elizabeth Hastings; a fellowship and three scholarships at Pembroke College, Cambridge; a scholarship of £4 a year at Magdalene College, Cambridge, and, in failure of scholars from the school at Carlisle, eligibility to two exhibitions, founded by Bishop Thomas, at Queen's College, Oxford. A good library is connected with the school. The parish extends for about ten miles along the coast, which in some parts is rocky and precipitous, and contains coal, limestone, and freestone: lead-ore is obtained at Kinneyside, where there are smelting-furnaces, and iron-ore was formerly got in Eskdale. A lighthouse was erected in 1717, on a promontory called St. Bees' Head.

BEESBY, formerly a distinct parish, now united to Hawerby, in the wapentake of Bradley-Haverstoe, parts of Lindsey, county of Lincoln, 8¼ miles (N.W. by N.) from Louth. The population is returned with Hawerby. The living is a rectory, consolidated with that of Hawerby.

BEESBY in the MARSH, a parish in the Wold division of the hundred of Calceworth, parts of Lindsey, county of Lincoln, 2½ miles (N. by E.) from Alford, containing 132 inhabitants. The living is a rectory, in the archdeaconry and diocese of Lincoln, rated in the king's books at £13. 10. 2½., and in the patronage of the Crown. The church is dedicated to St. Andrew.

BEESTON, a hamlet partly in the parish of Northill, and partly in the parish of Sandy, hundred of Wixamtree, county of Bedford, 3 miles (N.N.W.) from Biggleswade, containing 214 inhabitants.

BEESTON, a township in that part of the parish of Bunbury which is in the first division of the hundred of Eddisbury, county palatine of Chester,

$3\frac{3}{4}$ miles (S.S.W.) from Tarporley, containing 441 inhabitants. On a rocky eminence, affording a fine view over the Vale Royal, are the massive ruins of Beeston Castle, comprising part of a tower which guarded the principal entrance, flanked by semicircular ones, which formed the inner ward, occupying nearly an acre of ground, and protected by a moat excavated in the solid rock; the outer walls were guarded by eight round towers irregularly placed, and are now, for the greater part, romantically covered with ivy and other foliage: in the outer court is a considerable stone quarry. This fortress, founded by Ranulph de Blundeville, about 1220, was made a royal garrison in the war between Henry III. and the barons; and, in 1643, it was held by a detachment of the parliamentary forces. Having been subsequently taken by the royalists, it was surrendered by them for want of provisions, after a long siege, in 1645, and, early in the following year, was demolished. Courts leet and baron are held here. There is a small endowment for the instruction of poor children. A mineral spring was discovered about fifteen years ago.

BEESTON, a parish in the southern division of the wapentake of BROXTOW, county of NOTTINGHAM, $3\frac{3}{4}$ miles (S. W. by W.) from Nottingham, containing 1534 inhabitants. The living is a discharged vicarage, in the archdeaconry of Nottingham, and diocese of York, rated in the king's books at £4. 15., and in the patronage of the Duke of Devonshire. The church is dedicated to St. John the Baptist. The inhabitants are principally employed in the manufacture of hosiery and lace: a large silk-mill has also recently been erected. A branch of the Nottingham canal, called Beeston Cut, crosses the parish on the south-east, to its junction with the Trent. Considerable portions of a Roman road, uniting with the "old Coventry road" in the adjoining parish of Attenborough, and the remains of an ancient building, are discernible here. There are some wells in the village, the water of which is slightly chalybeate.

BEESTON, a chapelry in the parish of ST. PETER, within the liberty of the borough of LEEDS, though locally in the wapentake of Morley, West riding of the county of YORK, $2\frac{1}{4}$ miles (S.W. by S.) from Leeds, comprising the townships of Beeston-Shaw, Cottingley-Hall, New Hall, Parkside, Royds, and Snickells, and containing 1670 inhabitants. The living is a perpetual curacy, in the archdeaconry and diocese of York, endowed with £210 private benefaction, and £200 royal bounty, and in the patronage of the Vicar of Leeds. The chapel is a very ancient structure, dedicated to St. Mary. There is a place of worship for Wesleyan Methodists. Extensive coal mines near the village have been worked since the reign of Charles II.; and there are various establishments connected with the clothing business. An hospital is stated to have anciently existed here, but there are no remains, and even its site is not distinctly known.

BEESTON (ST. ANDREW), a parish in the hundred of TAVERHAM, county of NORFOLK, $4\frac{1}{2}$ miles (N. N. E.) from Norwich, containing 69 inhabitants. The living is a discharged rectory, in the archdeaconry and diocese of Norwich, rated in the king's books at £3. 6. 8. W. Boycott, Esq. and others were patrons in 1806. The church is desecrated.

BEESTON (ST. LAWRENCE), a parish in the hundred of TUNSTEAD, county of NORFOLK, $4\frac{1}{4}$ miles (E. by N.) from Coltishall, containing 54 inhabitants. The living is a discharged rectory, in the archdeaconry and diocese of Norwich, rated in the king's books at £6, endowed with £200 private benefaction, and £200 royal bounty, and in the patronage of J. Preston, Esq. There is a place of worship for Wesleyan Methodists.

BEESTON (ST. MARY), a parish in the hundred of LAUNDITCH, county of NORFOLK, 7 miles (N.E. by E.) from Swaffham, containing, with the parish of Little Bittering, 666 inhabitants. The living is a discharged rectory, in the archdeaconry and diocese of Norwich, rated in the king's books at £13, and in the patronage of the King, as Duke of Lancaster. A sum of money has been left for the instruction of poor children; and there is an almshouse with a small endowment.

BEESTON-REGIS, a parish in the northern division of the hundred of ERPINGHAM, county of NORFOLK, 3 miles (W. N. W.) from Cromer, containing 238 inhabitants. The living is a discharged rectory, in the archdeaconry of Norfolk, and diocese of Norwich, rated in the king's books at £16, and in the patronage of the King, as Duke of Lancaster. The church is dedicated to All Saints. The sea has made considerable encroachments on this part of the coast. Here are some remains of a priory of Augustine canons, founded in the reign of John, by Lady Isabel de Cressey, the revenue of which, at the dissolution, was £50. 6. 4.

BEETHAM, a parish in KENDAL ward, county of WESTMORLAND, comprising the chapelry of Witherslack, and the townships of Beetham, Farleton, Haverbrack, and Methop with Ulpha, and containing 1618 inhabitants, of which number, 830 are in the township of Beetham, 3 miles (N.W. by W.) from Burton in Kendal. The living is a discharged vicarage, in the archdeaconry of Richmond, and diocese of Chester, rated in the king's books at £13. 7. 4., endowed with £400 private benefaction, and £400 royal bounty, and in the patronage of the King, as Duke of Lancaster. The church is dedicated to St. Michael. This mountainous parish is situated at the south-western extremity of the county, on both sides of the æstuary of the river Kent, which is navigable for small craft as far as the hamlet of Storth, and on the shore of which are two wharfs, where slate and other articles are shipped for various ports on the western coast: there is also a ferry across the river. The Kendal and Lancaster canal, the river Belo, and some smaller streams, also intersect the parish, through which a new road was formed between Lancaster and Ulverstone, about 1820. The sands are well adapted for bathing, though the place is not much resorted to for that purpose. There is a manufactory for paper and pasteboard at the village, and limestone abounds within the parish. A grammar school, built about 1663, and rebuilt in 1827, has an endowment of about £40 per annum, arising from land, for the instruction of about fifty boys. Near the school-house stood an ancient chapel, dedicated to St. John, where human bones have frequently been dug up: the site has been converted into a garden. A court leet and baron, with view of frankpledge, are held annually by the lord of the manor. Beetham Hall, formerly a fortified mansion, situated within a spacious park, is now in ruins; and at a short distance to the south are the ruins of Helslack and Arnside towers, which were probably erected to guard the bay of Morecambe, there being remains of similar towers on the opposite shore. At Beetham Mill is a waterfall on the river Belo, near where the new road crosses that river by means of a bridge.

BEETLEY, a parish in the hundred of LAUNDITCH, county of NORFOLK, 3¾ miles (N. by W.) from East Dereham, containing 356 inhabitants. The living is a discharged rectory, in the archdeaconry and diocese of Norwich, rated in the king's books at £9. 7. 11., and in the patronage of the Rev. C. Munnings. The church is dedicated to St. Mary.

BEGBROOKE, a parish in the hundred of WOOTTON, county of OXFORD, 2¾ miles (S.E. by S.) from Woodstock, containing 102 inhabitants. The living is a rectory not in charge, in the archdeaconry and diocese of Oxford, and in the patronage of Sir G. Dashwood, Bart., for three turns, and the Principal and Fellows of Brasenose College, Oxford, for one. The church is dedicated to St. Michael. A little westward from it is an ancient military work, called Round Castle.

BEIGHTON, a parish in the hundred of SCARSDALE, county of DERBY, 7¼ miles (E. S. E.) from Sheffield, containing 856 inhabitants. The living is a discharged vicarage, in the archdeaconry of Derby, and diocese of Lichfield and Coventry, rated in the king's books at £6. 11. 10½., endowed with £10 per annum private benefaction, and £200 royal bounty, and in the patronage of Earl Manvers. The church is dedicated to St. Mary. In 1666, William Jessop bequeathed land, producing about £14 per annum, for apprenticing poor children of this parish, and other charitable purposes. A school for the instruction of ten children has an endowment of about £5 per annum.

BEIGHTON, a parish in the hundred of WALSHAM, county of NORFOLK, 2 miles (S.W. by S.) from Acle, containing 244 inhabitants. The living is a discharged rectory, in the archdeaconry and diocese of Norwich, rated in the king's books at £13, and in the patronage of R. Fellowes, Esq. The church is dedicated to All Saints.

BEIGHTON, county of SUFFOLK.—See BEYTON.

BEILBY, a chapelry in the parish of HAYTON, Holme-Beacon division of the wapentake of HARTHILL, East riding of the county of YORK, 3½ miles (S. by W.) from Pocklington, containing 239 inhabitants. The chapel is dedicated to St. Giles.

BELAUGH, a parish in the southern division of the hundred of ERPINGHAM, county of NORFOLK, 1¾ mile (S. E.) from Coltishall, containing 133 inhabitants. The living is a discharged rectory, annexed to the vicarage of Scottow, in the archdeaconry and diocese of Norwich, rated in the king's books at £6. The church is dedicated to St. Peter.

BELBANK, a township in the parish of BEWCASTLE, ESKDALE ward, county of CUMBERLAND, containing 415 inhabitants. There are collieries and limeworks at Oakshaw, a hamlet in this township.

BELBANK, a township in the parish of STAPLETON, ESKDALE ward, county of CUMBERLAND, 9 miles (N.) from Brampton, containing 137 inhabitants.

BELBROUGHTON, a parish in the lower division of the hundred of HALFSHIRE, county of WORCESTER, 5 miles (N.W. by N.) from Bromsgrove, containing 1476 inhabitants. The living is a rectory, in the archdeaconry and diocese of Worcester, rated in the king's books at £19, and in the patronage of the President and Fellows of St. John's College, Oxford. The church, dedicated to the Holy Trinity, has recently received an additional number of sittings, by means of a grant of £100 from the Incorporated Society for enlarging churches and chapels. Here is an extensive manufactory for scythes, hay-knives, &c. Fairs are held on the last Monday in April, and the Monday before St. Luke's day. A sheriff's court, for the recovery of small debts, is held on the third Wednesday in every month. There is an endowment of about £10 per annum for the instruction of poor children. The parish is divided into four yields, *viz.*, those of Belbroughton, Brian's Bell with Moor-Hall Bell, Forfield, and Broomhill.

BELBY, a township in the parish of HOWDEN, wapentake of HOWDENSHIRE, East riding of the county of YORK, 1½ mile (E. by N.) from Howden, containing 49 inhabitants.

BELCHAMP (OTTON), a parish in the hundred of HINCKFORD, county of ESSEX, 5¼ miles (N. by E.) from Castle-Hedingham, containing 352 inhabitants. The living is a rectory, in the archdeaconry of Middlesex, and diocese of London, rated in the king's books at £12, and in the patronage of the Rev. John Cox. The church is dedicated to St. Ethelbert and All Saints. Albright's chapel, formerly in this parish, has been long since demolished.

BELCHAMP (ST. PAUL'S), a parish in the hundred of HINCKFORD, county of ESSEX, 2 miles (S.E. by E.) from Clare, containing 685 inhabitants. The living is a vicarage, in the peculiar jurisdiction and patronage of the Dean and Chapter of St. Paul's, London, rated in the king's books at £14. The church is dedicated to St. Andrew.

BELCHAMP (WALTER), a parish in the hundred of HINCKFORD, county of ESSEX, 3 miles (W.) from Sudbury, containing 608 inhabitants. The living is a discharged vicarage, consolidated with that of Bulmer, in the archdeaconry of Middlesex, and diocese of London, rated in the king's books at £6, and endowed with £100 and £6 per annum private benefaction, and £200 royal bounty. The church is dedicated to St. Mary.

BELFORD, a parish partly in ISLANDSHIRE, a detached portion of the county palatine of DURHAM, but chiefly in the northern division of BAMBROUGH ward, county of NORTHUMBERLAND, comprising the market town of Belford, and the townships of Detchant, Easington, Easington-Grange, Elwick, Middleton, and Ross, and containing 1783 inhabitants, of which number, 1208 are in the town of Belford, 49 miles (N. by W.) from Newcastle upon Tyne, and 325½ (N. by W.) from London. This place, though possessing little architectural beauty, has a very pleasing appearance: it is situated on a gentle eminence within two miles of the sea, of which, and of Bambrough castle, it commands a fine view on the north-east; on all other sides it is sheltered by hills, on one of which are seen the ruins of an ancient chapel. The town consists principally of two spacious streets, intersected by a few narrow lanes, badly paved and not lighted; the houses are irregularly built, but the inhabitants are amply supplied with water: the neighbourhood abounds with pleasingly diversified scenery and agreeable walks. Belford is mainly indebted for its rise to the spirited exertions of Mr. Dixon, a former proprietor of the manor, who built several houses on a larger and more convenient scale, cleared away unsightly objects, and established a woollen manufactory, a tannery, &c. His father had previously procured the privilege of holding a market and fairs: the market is on Tuesday, and is noted for corn, much of which is sold for exportation; and the fairs are on the Tuesday before Whitsuntide, and August 23rd. The parish abounds with coal, limestone, and freestone; and considerable quantities of cockles, called Budle cockles, are got upon the coast. The town is within the jurisdiction of the county magistrates, and constables are annually appointed for the several townships. The living is a perpetual curacy, in the archdeaconry of Northumberland, and diocese of Durham, endowed with £800 private benefaction, £600 royal bounty, and £1100 parliamentary grant, and in the patronage of William Clarke, Esq., as lord of the manor. The church, dedicated to St. Mary, is a handsome structure, erected in 1700, at the north-western extremity of the town. There are places of worship for Anti-burghers, Wesleyan Methodists, and Presbyterians. A charity school is supported by subscription. About a mile to the south-west of the town is a quadrilateral intrenchment, having an entrance on the north-east, and defended by a wide ditch and a double rampart: it is by some supposed to have been a strong hold, or place of security from the incursions of the Scots, during the border wars; by others it is thought to be of Danish origin. The races, formerly held at Beadnell, have been removed hither, where a course has just been completed for holding them. There are a few mineral springs in the parish.

BELGRAVE, a parish comprising the chapelry of South Thurmaston in the eastern, and the chapelry of Birstall in the western, division of the hundred of Goscote, county of Leicester, 1¾ mile (N. N. E.) from Leicester, and containing 1904 inhabitants. The living is a vicarage, in the archdeaconry of Leicester, and diocese of Lincoln, rated in the king's books at £13. 6. 8., endowed with £8 per annum and £600 private benefaction, £400 royal bounty, and £1000 parliamentary grant, and in the patronage of the Bishop of Lichfield and Coventry. The church is dedicated to St. Peter. This parish is in the honour of Tutbury, duchy of Lancaster, and within the jurisdiction of a court of pleas held at Tutbury every third Tuesday, for the recovery of debts under 40*s*. The river Soar, or Leicester canal, which is navigable for barges, and over which there is a bridge, forms a junction with the Melton-Mowbray Navigation, by means of an artificial cut, immediately after its course through the parish. Traces of the Roman Fosse-way are visible in the vicinity. Belgrave gives the title of viscount to Earl Grosvenor.

BELLASIS, a township in the parish of Stannington, western division of Castle ward, county of Northumberland, 6 miles (S. by E.) from Morpeth. The population is returned with the parish.

BELLASIZE, a township in the parish of Eastrington, wapentake of Howdenshire, East riding of the county of York, 5¼ miles (E. by S.) from Howden, containing 197 inhabitants.

BELLCHALWELL, a parish forming, with the parishes of Shillingstone and Turnworth, a detached portion of that part of the hundred of Cranborne which is in the Shaston (West) division, being locally in the hundred of Pimperne, Blandford (North) division of the county of Dorset, 8 miles (W. N. W.) from Blandford-Forum, containing 192 inhabitants. The living is a discharged rectory, united, in 1776, to the rectory of Fifehead-Neville, in the archdeaconry of Dorset, and diocese of Bristol, rated in the king's books at £7. 15.

BELLEAU, a parish in the Marsh division of the hundred of Calceworth, parts of Lindsey, county of Lincoln, 5 miles (N.W. by W.) from Alford, containing 88 inhabitants. The living is a discharged rectory, to which the vicarage of Aby was united in 1732, in the archdeaconry and diocese of Lincoln, rated in the king's books at £13. 3. 9., and in the patronage of Lord Gwydir. The church is dedicated to St. John the Baptist. The name (*Belle eau*) is derived from a fine stream of water, which issues from a chalk hill with considerable force.

BELLERBY, a chapelry in the parish of Spennithorn, western division of the wapentake of Hang, North riding of the county of York, 1½ mile (N.) from Leyburn, containing 407 inhabitants. The living is a perpetual curacy, in the archdeaconry of Richmond, and diocese of Chester, endowed with £400 private benefaction, and £800 royal bounty, and in the patronage of W. Chaytor, Esq.

BELLESTER, a township in the parish of Haltwhistle, western division of Tindale ward, county of Northumberland, 16 miles (W. by S.) from Hexham, containing 118 inhabitants. On the bank of the South Tyne are the ruins of an ancient castle, once belonging to the Blenkinsop family.

BELLINGHAM, a parish in the north-western division of Tindale ward, county of Northumberland, comprising the market town of Bellingham, and the townships of East Charlton, West Charlton, Leemailing, the Nook, and Tarretburn, and containing 1396 inhabitants, of which number, 404 are in the town of Bellingham, 30 miles (W. N. W.) from Newcastle upon Tyne, and 298 (N. N. W.) from London. This place, from the remains of several camps apparently of Roman origin, is supposed to have been occupied by that people; but little of its early history is recorded, though the neighbourhood abounds with circular intrenchments, and the remains of British fortifications. The lords de Bellingham are said to have had a castle, or baronial seat, here, erected on an eminence still called Hall Field. In the reigns of Richard II. and Henry IV., the manor and castle were in the possession of Richard de Bellingham; the estate afterwards became the property of the Earl of Derwentwater, upon whose attainder it was given to the Governors of Greenwich Hospital. The town is pleasantly situated on the northern bank of the North Tyne, between that river and a stream called Hareshaw-burn, over which, near the eastern extremity of the town, a good stone bridge was erected in 1826. The rocks, on each side of the burn, rise precipitously to the height of one hundred feet, and the water at Hareshaw-linn has a perpendicular fall of thirty feet. In the parish there are from seven to eight thousand acres of moor-land, abounding with grouse and other game. A book club was established in the town in 1809. The market is on Saturday: a fair is held on the first Saturday after September 15th, and there are statute fairs on the Saturdays before May 12th and November 12th. This parish was formerly part of the extensive parish of Simonburn, which was divided into six distinct parishes by act of parliament obtained in 1811. The living is a rectory not in charge, in the archdeaconry of Northumberland, and diocese of Durham, and in the patronage of the Governors of Greenwich Hospital. The church, dedicated to St. Cuthbert, is a small ancient structure, with a finely groined roof of stone; the chancel contains many mural tablets and monuments: the churchyard, occupying an elevated situation, forms a beautiful terrace overlooking the river. There is a place of worship for Seceders from the Scottish church, besides a Roman Catholic chapel. A school was endowed here with £200, by Mrs. Reed of Troughead, with which sum, and a legacy of £40 left by Mr. John Charlton, in 1732, the third part of a farm was purchased, which would have now produced £50 per annum, but the Reeds of Chipchase having purchased the whole estate, sold it without any reserve, and the trustees having lost their deeds, the school has been deprived of the endowment.

BELPER, a market town and chapelry in the parish of Duffield, hundred of Appletree, county of Derby, 8 miles (N.) from Derby, and 134 (N.N.W.) from London, containing 7235 inhabitants. This place, at which was formerly a park and hunting seat belonging to John of Gaunt, Duke of Lancaster, was an inconsiderable village, inhabited principally by nailers, till the year 1777, when the cotton manufacture was introduced by Messrs. Strutt, since which time it has risen into a considerable town. It is pleasantly situated on the river Derwent, over which a handsome stone bridge of three arches has been recently erected, the former bridge, said to have been built by John of Gaunt, having been destroyed, in 1795, by a great flood. The town, consisting of several streets, is partially paved, lighted with gas, and amply supplied with water. There are five mills for the spinning of cotton, all belonging to Messrs. Strutt, who make their own machinery on the spot; two of these, and also a bleaching mill, are about a mile and a half lower down the river, over which the proprietors have built a neat stone bridge of two arches, for their own accommodation. Here is one of the largest establishments in the kingdom for silk and cotton hose, in which upwards of four thousand persons are employed, principally residing in the surrounding villages: the nails made here, especially those for the shoeing of horses, are much in demand, from the superiority of the rod iron made at Alderwasley, four miles distant, arising from the peculiar quality of the coal in that neighbourhood. The Cromford canal passes within two miles of the town, and the High Peak railway within six. The market is on Saturday: the fairs are, May 12th and October 31st, for horned cattle, sheep, and horses. The county magistrates hold a petty session for the district every Saturday: courts for the manor are held twice in the year, under the steward, at one of which constables and other officers are appointed. The living is a perpetual curacy, in the archdeaconry of Derby, and diocese of Lichfield and Coventry, endowed with £200 private benefaction, £800 royal bounty, and £2300 parliamentary grant, and in the patronage of the Vicar of Duffield. The chapel, dedicated to St. John the Baptist, was erected in 1824, at an expense of upwards of £12,000, which was partly defrayed by a parliamentary grant: it is a handsome structure in the decorated style of English architecture, with a lofty tower, and contains one thousand eight hundred and four sittings, of which one thousand two hundred and four are free. The old chapel, built by John of Gaunt, the burial-ground of which is still used, is now appropriated to the use of a Sunday school. There are places of worship for Baptists, Independents, Wesleyan Methodists, and Unitarians. A Lancasterian school is supported by the proprietors of the cotton-works, for the benefit of the children belonging to the factory. Henry Smith, Esq. endowed two almshouses for poor persons, and bequeathed an estate producing £30 per annum, directing the rental to be divided equally between the minister and the poor of Belper: two other almshouses were endowed by James Sims, with £12 per annum. In a field in the neighbourhood may still be traced the massive foundations of the mansion in which John of Gaunt resided.

BELSAY, a township in that part of the parish of Bolam which is in the north-eastern division of Tindale ward, county of Northumberland, 15 miles (N.W.) from Newcastle upon Tyne, containing 327 inhabitants. There are considerable remains of an ancient castle, occupying an elevated site, above which is a stone cross. Belsay Hall is a splendid edifice of Grecian architecture, but the entire design has not been completed.

BELSHFORD, a parish in the northern division of the wapentake of Gartree, parts of Lindsey, county of Lincoln, 4½ miles (N.E. by N.) from Horncastle, containing 490 inhabitants. The living is a rectory, in the archdeaconry and diocese of Lincoln, rated in the king's books at £18. 6. 8., and in the patronage of the Crown. The church is dedicated to St. Peter and St. Paul. The parish abounds with excellent limestone.

BELSTEAD, a parish in the hundred of Samford, county of Suffolk, 3¾ miles (S.W. by W.) from Ipswich, containing 255 inhabitants. The living is a discharged rectory, in the archdeaconry of Suffolk, and diocese of Norwich, rated in the king's books at £7. 6. 0½., and in the patronage of Ambrose Steward, Esq. The church is dedicated to St. Mary.

BELSTONE, a parish in the hundred of Black Torrington, county of Devon, 3 miles (E.S.E.) from Oakhampton, containing 157 inhabitants. The living is a discharged rectory, in the archdeaconry of Totness, and diocese of Exeter, rated in the king's books at £9. 0. 1., endowed with £200 private benefaction, and £300 parliamentary grant, and in the patronage of the Rev. John Hole. The church, dedicated to St. Mary, contains the remains of a cucking stool. The rivers Ockment and Taw, having their sources in Dartmoor, flow through the parish, in which several copper mines were formerly worked.

BELTON, a parish in the western division of the hundred of Goscote, county of Leicester, 5 miles (S.W. by S.) from Kegworth, containing, with the extra-parochial liberty of Grace-Dieu, 664 inhabitants. The living is a discharged vicarage, in the archdeaconry of

Leicester, and diocese of Lincoln, rated in the king's books at £8. 18. 4., and in the patronage of the Marquis of Hastings. The church is dedicated to St. John the Baptist. There is a place of worship for Wesleyan Methodists. A considerable fair for horses is held here annually, on the Monday next after Trinity week. A convent for nuns of the order of St. Augustine was founded at Grace-Dieu, in the reign of Henry III., the revenue of which, at the dissolution, was £101. 8. 2¼. Sir John Beaumont, author of a poem entitled "Bosworth Field," brother of Francis Beaumont, the celebrated dramatist, was born at Grace-Dieu, in 1582.

BELTON, a parish in the soke of GRANTHAM, parts of KESTEVEN, county of LINCOLN, 2¼ miles (N. N. E.) from Grantham, containing 178 inhabitants. The living is a rectory, in the archdeaconry and diocese of Lincoln, rated in the king's books at £12. 3. 6½., and in the patronage of Earl Brownlow. The church is dedicated to St. Peter and St. Paul. Here is an almshouse for six poor persons. Belton gives the title of baron to Earl Brownlow.

BELTON, a parish in the western division of the wapentake of MANLEY, parts of LINDSEY, county of LINCOLN, 1¾ mile (N.) from Epworth, containing 1437 inhabitants. The living is a perpetual curacy, in the archdeaconry of Stow, and diocese of Lincoln, and in the patronage of the Mayor and Corporation of Lincoln. The church is dedicated to All Saints. There is a place of worship for Wesleyan Methodists.

BELTON, a parish in the soke of OAKHAM, county of RUTLAND, 4 miles (W.N.W.) from Uppingham, containing, with Gunthorpe Lodge, 401 inhabitants. The living is a vicarage, annexed to the rectory of Wardley, in the archdeaconry of Northampton, and diocese of Peterborough. The church is dedicated to St. Peter. A school for the instruction of twelve poor children is endowed with about £10 per annum.

BELTON, a parish in the hundred of MUTFORD and LOTHINGLAND, county of SUFFOLK, 4½ miles (S.W.) from Great Yarmouth, containing 385 inhabitants. The living is a discharged rectory, in the archdeaconry of Suffolk, and diocese of Norwich, rated in the king's books at £17. 15., and in the patronage of the Bishop of Norwich. The church is dedicated to All Saints. The navigable river Waveney forms the western boundary of the parish.

BELVOIR, an extra-parochial liberty, partly in the soke of GRANTHAM, parts of KESTEVEN, county of LINCOLN, but chiefly in the hundred of FRAMLAND, county of LEICESTER, 7 miles (W. by S.) from Grantham, containing 88 inhabitants. Belvoir castle, the magnificent seat of the Duke of Rutland, stands on the site of an ancient fortress, said to have been built soon after the Conquest, near which a Benedictine priory was founded, in the reign of William I., the revenue of which, at the dissolution, was £135.

BEMERTON, a parish in the hundred of BRANCH and DOLE, county of WILTS, 2 miles (W. by N.) from Salisbury. The population is returned with Fugglestone. The living is a rectory, united to that of Fugglestone, in the archdeaconry and diocese of Salisbury. The church is dedicated to St. Andrew. This place is remarkable for the celebrity of three of its rectors,—George Herbert, commonly called "the Divine," who died in 1635; John Norris, a metaphysical writer, who died in 1711; and Archdeacon Coxe, the traveller and historian, who died in 1828: the first greatly repaired the church, and rebuilt the parsonage-house, at his own expense.

BEMPTON, a parish in the wapentake of DICKERING, East riding of the county of YORK, 3¼ miles (N. N. E.) from Bridlington, containing 231 inhabitants. The living is a perpetual curacy, in the archdeaconry of the East riding, and diocese of York, endowed with £800 royal bounty, and in the patronage of John Broadley, Esq. The church is dedicated to St. Michael. There is a place of worship for Wesleyan Methodists.

BENACRE, county of SUFFOLK.—See BINACRE.

BENAGER, county of SOMERSET.—See BINEGAR.

BENEFIELD, a parish in the hundred of POLEBROOK, county of NORTHAMPTON, 3½ miles (W.) from Oundle, containing 444 inhabitants. The living is a rectory, in the archdeaconry of Northampton, and diocese of Peterborough, rated in the king's books at £35. 9. 7., and in the patronage of J. Watts Russell, Esq. The church, dedicated to St. Mary, has been lately repaired at the expense of Mr. Russell: near it are the site and moat of an old castle. The parochial school is endowed with £10 per annum. About a furlong to the west of the village are nine of those cavities in the earth, commonly called "Swallows," into which the waters of the land floods flow and disappear.

BENENDEN, a parish in the hundred of ROLVENDEN, lathe of SCRAY, county of KENT, 3¼ miles (S. E.) from Cranbrooke, containing 1746 inhabitants. The living is a discharged vicarage, in the archdeaconry and diocese of Canterbury, rated in the king's books at £17. 12. 6., endowed with £200 private benefaction, and £1300 parliamentary grant, and in the patronage of T. L. Hodges, Esq. The church, dedicated to St. George, was rebuilt in 1672, the former edifice having been damaged by lightning. Fairs for horses and horned cattle are held on May 15th and August 4th. Edward Gibbon, in 1602, founded a school, which has been subsequently endowed with property producing £114 per annum. There is another school with a small endowment, the bequest of Thomas Buckland, in 1786; and there are endowments for the instruction of girls.

BENFIELD-SIDE, a township in that part of the parish of LANCHESTER which is in the western division of CHESTER ward, county palatine of DURHAM, 14 miles (N. W. by N.) from Durham, containing 341 inhabitants.

BENFLEET (NORTH), a parish in the hundred of BARSTABLE, county of ESSEX, 3¾ miles (W.) from Rayleigh, containing 303 inhabitants. The living is a rectory, in the archdeaconry of Essex, and diocese of London, rated in the king's books at £16, and in the patronage of the Rev. C. R. Rowlatt. The church, dedicated to All Saints, has a small wooden steeple. Canvey island partly belongs to this parish.

BENFLEET (SOUTH), a parish in the hundred of BARSTABLE, county of ESSEX, 4 miles (S. W. by S.) from Rayleigh, containing 515 inhabitants. The living is a discharged vicarage, in the archdeaconry of Essex, and diocese of London, rated in the king's books at £16. 5. 5., and in the patronage of the Dean and Chapter of Westminster. The church is dedicated to St. Mary. King Alfred, in the year 894, took and destroyed a castle here, built by the celebrated Danish pirate Hesting. The creek called Hadleigh Rey, or Bay, from its passing by Hadleigh, runs up between this place and Canvey island, and is navigable for small craft; and the other creeks, entering from the Thames round Benfleet, are noted for producing good oysters.

BENGEO, a parish in the hundred and county of HERTFORD, 1 mile (N. N. E.) from Hertford, containing 731 inhabitants. The living is a vicarage, in the archdeaconry of Huntingdon, and diocese of Lincoln, rated in the king's books at £7. 8. 6½., and in the patronage of T. H. Byde, Esq. The church is dedicated to St. Leonard.

BENGWORTH (ST. PETER), a parish within the jurisdiction of the borough of EVESHAM, locally in the lower division of the hundred of Blackenhurst, county of WORCESTER, ½ a mile (S.S.E.) from Evesham, containing 853 inhabitants. It is situated on the southern side of the navigable river Avon, opposite the town of Evesham, with which it was incorporated in the reign of James I. The living is a perpetual curacy, in the peculiar jurisdiction of the Bishop of Worcester, rated in the king's books at £7. 10. 10., endowed with £200 private benefaction, and £400 royal bounty, and in the patronage of the Rev. W. Alies. The church, which has a handsome tower and spire, is dedicated to St. Peter: it stands on the site of a castle which belonged to the abbey of Evesham, and which was destroyed by William D'Andeville, one of the abbots, who recovered it from William de Beauchamp, hereditary sheriff of the county, by whom it had been held, in contravention of the abbot's rights. John Deacle, alderman of London, who was born here, left £2000 for the endowment of a free school for thirty boys, who are clothed, educated, and apprenticed. See EVESHAM.

BENHALL, a parish in the hundred of PLOMESGATE, county of SUFFOLK, 2 miles (W. by S.) from Saxmundham, containing 710 inhabitants. The living is a discharged vicarage, in the archdeaconry of Suffolk, and diocese of Norwich, rated in the king's books at £7. 1. 3., and in the patronage of Edward Hollond, Esq. The church is dedicated to St. Mary. Sir Edward Duke, in 1731, bequeathed property producing about £25 per annum, for the endowment of a free school.

BENHAM, a tything in that part of the parish of SPEEN which is in the hundred of KINTBURY-EAGLE, county of BERKS, 3 miles (W.) from Speenhamland, containing 380 inhabitants.

BENNINGBROUGH, a township in the parish of NEWTON upon OUZE, wapentake of BULMER, North riding of the county of YORK, 7¾ miles (N. W.) from York, containing 99 inhabitants.

BENNINGHOLME, a joint township with Grange, in that part of the parish of SWINE which is in the middle division of the wapentake of HOLDERNESS, East riding of the county of YORK, 9¼ miles (E. by S.) from Beverley, containing, with Grange, 97 inhabitants.

BENNINGTON, a parish in the hundred of BROADWATER, county of HERTFORD, 5½ miles (E. S. E.) from Stevenage, containing 658 inhabitants. The living is a rectory, in the archdeaconry of Huntingdon, and diocese of Lincoln, rated in the king's books at £19, and in the patronage of George Procter, Esq. The church is dedicated to St. Peter. There is a place of worship for Wesleyan Methodists. On an intrenched eminence on the western side of the church anciently stood a castle. The kings of Mercia are stated to have had a palace here: several ancient coins have been found in the parish.

BENNINGTON, a parish (formerly a market town) in the wapentake of SKIRBECK, parts of HOLLAND, county of LINCOLN, 5 miles (E. N. E.) from Boston, containing 406 inhabitants. The living is a rectory, in the archdeaconry and diocese of Lincoln, rated in the king's books at £33. 8. 11½., and in the patronage of Viscount Goderich. The church is dedicated to All Saints. A free school is endowed with about £60 per annum.

BENNINGTON (LONG), a parish in the wapentake of LOVEDEN, parts of KESTEVEN, county of LINCOLN, 7 miles (N. W.) from Grantham, containing 881 inhabitants. The living is a discharged vicarage, with the perpetual curacy of Foston annexed, in the archdeaconry and diocese of Lincoln, rated in the king's books at £20. 1. 10., and in the patronage of the King, as Duke of Lancaster. The church is dedicated to All Saints. There is a place of worship for Wesleyan Methodists. The river Witham forms the north-eastern boundary of the parish, in which there is a mineral spring strongly impregnated with iron. An Alien priory of Cistercian monks was founded here about 1175, the revenue of which, in the reign of Richard II., was £50 per annum.

BENNIWORTH, a parish in the eastern division of the wapentake of WRAGGOE, parts of LINDSEY, county of LINCOLN, 6½ miles (E.N.E.) from Wragby, containing 346 inhabitants. The living is a rectory, in the archdeaconry and diocese of Lincoln, rated in the king's books at £23. 8. 6½., and in the patronage of R. Ainslie, Esq. The church is dedicated to St. Julian.

BENRIDGE, a joint township with Kirkley and Cartermoor (but formerly distinct), in the parish of PONTELAND, western division of CASTLE ward, county of NORTHUMBERLAND, 9½ miles (N. W. by N.) from Newcastle upon Tyne. The population is returned with Kirkley.

BENRIDGE, a township in that part of the parish of MITFORD which is in the western division of MORPETH ward, county of NORTHUMBERLAND, 2 miles (W. N. W.) from Morpeth, containing 57 inhabitants.

BENSINGTON, or BENSON, a parish partly in the hundred of DORCHESTER, but chiefly in that of EWELME, county of OXFORD, 11 miles (N.W. by N.) from Henley upon Thames, containing, with the hamlets of Crowmarsh-Battle and Fifield, 961 inhabitants. The living is a perpetual curacy, within the jurisdiction of the peculiar court of Dorchester, endowed with £200 private benefaction, and £200 royal bounty, and in the patronage of the Dean and Canons of Christ Church, Oxford. The church is dedicated to St. Helen. This ancient place is reported to have been taken from the Britons, about 572, by Ceawlin, third king of the West Saxons, whose successors retained it for about two hundred years, until it was surrendered to Offa, King of Mercia. The Roman way leading from Alchester to Wallingford crossed the Thames here. A royal palace anciently stood in the vicinity.

BENTFIELD, a hamlet in that part of the parish of STANSTED-MOUNTFITCHET which is in the hundred of CLAVERING, county of ESSEX, 1¾ mile (N.W. by N.) from Stansted-Mountfitchet, containing 513 inhabitants.

BENTHAL, a township in the parish of ABBERBURY, hundred of FORD, county of SALOP. The population is returned with Shrawardine.

BENTHALL, a parish within the liberties of the borough of WENLOCK, county of SALOP, 2½ miles (N.E. by N.) from Much Wenlock, containing 554 inhabitants. The living is a perpetual curacy, in the archdeaconry of Salop, and diocese of Hereford, endowed with £800 royal bounty, and £1200 parliamentary grant, and in the patronage of the Vicar of Much Wenlock. The church is dedicated to St. Bartholomew. The population are principally employed in the potteries established here. The navigable river Severn flows past this place.

BENTHAM, a parish in the western division of the wapentake of STAINCLIFFE and EWCROSS, West riding of the county of YORK, comprising the chapelry of Ingleton, and the townships of Bentham and Langcliffe, and containing 3824 inhabitants, of which number, 2102 are in the township of Bentham, 12 miles (W.N.W.) from Settle. The living is a rectory, in the archdeaconry of Richmond, and diocese of Chester, rated in the king's books at £35. 7. 8½., and in the patronage of T. L. Parker, Esq. The church, dedicated to St. John the Baptist, has lately received an addition of two hundred and eighteen sittings, one hundred and twenty-seven of which are free, the Incorporated Society for the enlargement of churches and chapels having granted £100 toward defraying the expense. Here are mills for the spinning of flax and the manufacture of linen; there are also some potteries in the parish. William Collingwood, in 1726, bequeathed property for the endowment of a free school for boys in Upper Bentham, and an hospital for six men and six women, which was vested in trustees under a decree of the Court of Chancery, in 1733, and now produces £240 per annum; some trifling donations have since been made to the school.

BENTLEY, a parish and liberty in the hundred of BASINGSTOKE, Basingstoke division of the county of SOUTHAMPTON, 4 miles (W.S.W.) from Farnham, containing 690 inhabitants. The living is a perpetual curacy, in the archdeaconry and diocese of Winchester, endowed with £600 private benefaction, £400 royal bounty, and £800 parliamentary grant. J. Andrews and others were patrons in 1820. The church is dedicated to St. Mary. Bentley is within the jurisdiction of the Cheyney Court held at Winchester every Thursday, for the recovery of debts to any amount.

BENTLEY, a liberty in the parish of ALDRIDGE, southern division of the hundred of OFFLOW, county of STAFFORD, 1¾ mile (W. by N.) from Walsall, containing 99 inhabitants.

BENTLEY, a parish in the hundred of SAMFORD, county of SUFFOLK, 6¼ miles (S.W.) from Ipswich, containing 366 inhabitants. The living is a discharged vicarage, in the archdeaconry of Suffolk, and diocese of Norwich, rated in the king's books at £6. 2. 11., and in the patronage of W. Deane, Esq. The church is dedicated to St. Mary.

BENTLEY, a chapelry in the parish of SHUSTOCK, Atherstone division of the hundred of HEMLINGFORD, county of WARWICK, 3 miles (S.W.) from Atherstone, containing 246 inhabitants.

BENTLEY, a township in the parish of ARKSEY, northern division of the wapentake of STRAFFORTH and TICKHILL, West riding of the county of YORK, 2 miles (N.W. by N.) from Doncaster. The population is returned with the parish. There is a place of worship for Wesleyan Methodists.

BENTLEY (FENNY), a parish in the hundred of WIRKSWORTH, county of DERBY, 2¼ miles (N. by W.) from Ashbourn, containing 242 inhabitants. The living is a discharged rectory, in the archdeaconry of Derby, and diocese of Lincoln, rated in the king's books at £6. 12. 10., and in the patronage of the Dean of Lincoln. The church, dedicated to St. Mary Magdalene, is a small structure with a low tower.

BENTLEY (GREAT), a parish in the hundred of TENDRING, county of ESSEX, 8 miles (E.S.E.) from Colchester, containing 794 inhabitants. The living is a discharged vicarage, in the archdeaconry of Colchester, and diocese of London, rated in the king's books at £7, endowed with £400 private benefaction, and £400 royal bounty, and in the patronage of the Bishop of London. The church is dedicated to St. Mary. There is a place of worship for Wesleyan Methodists. The parochial school is endowed with about £15 per annum.

BENTLEY (HUNGRY), a liberty in the parish of LONGFORD, hundred of APPLETREE, county of DERBY, 5¾ miles (S.) from Ashbourn, containing 88 inhabitants. Here was formerly a chapel, long since demolished.

BENTLEY (LITTLE), a parish in the hundred of TENDRING, county of ESSEX, 5½ miles (S. by E.) from Manningtree, containing 402 inhabitants. The living is a rectory, in the archdeaconry of Colchester, and diocese of London, rated in the king's books at £13, and in the patronage of Robert Foot, Esq. The church is dedicated to St. Mary. There is a place of worship for Wesleyan Methodists.

BENTON (LONG), a parish in the eastern division of CASTLE ward, county of NORTHUMBERLAND, 3¾ miles (N. E. by N.) from Newcastle upon Tyne, comprising the townships of Long Benton, Killingworth, Walker, and Weetsted, and containing 5547 inhabitants. The living is a discharged vicarage, in the archdeaconry of Northumberland, and diocese of Durham, rated in the king's books at £3. 1. 3., and in the patronage of the Master and Fellows of Balliol College, Oxford. The church, dedicated to St. Bartholomew, is a neat unadorned edifice, with a tower and spire; it was rebuilt, except the chancel, in 1791. This parish is bounded on the south by the river Tyne, on the banks of which are various extensive manufactories and coal-wharfs: it contains a very great quantity of coal, and there are some stone quarries. A parochial school-room, and a house for the master, were built some years ago, at an expense of £205, which was partly raised by subscription. The Roman wall of Severus passed through the parish, prior to its immediate termination at *Legedunum*, in the adjoining parish of Wallsend.

BENTWORTH, a parish in the hundred of ODIHAM, Basingstoke division of the county of SOUTHAMPTON, 3¾ miles (W.) from Alton, containing 548 inhabitants. The living is a rectory, in the archdeaconry and diocese of Winchester, rated in the king's books at £14. 10. 5., and in the patronage of R. Matthews, Esq. The church is dedicated to St. Mary.

BENWELL, a township in that part of the parish of St. John which is in the western division of Castle ward, county of Northumberland, 2½ miles (W.) from Newcastle upon Tyne, containing 1296 inhabitants. It is situated on the north bank of the river Tyne, and contains a great quantity of coal. In the sixteenth century, a vein of coal accidentally caught fire in the vicinity, and continued to burn upwards of thirty years, bursting out, in various places, like a volcano. It is in contemplation to erect a chapel here. Lying at a short distance southward from the wall of Severus, the site is supposed to have been occupied by the Roman station, *Condercum*. A building called the Old Tower was the summer residence of the priors of Tynemouth, who had a small chapel here, the site of the burial-ground of which is marked by a few tombstones.

BENWICK, a chapelry in the parish of Doddington, northern division of the hundred of Witchford, Isle of Ely, county of Cambridge, 8¼ miles (S. W.) from March, containing 514 inhabitants. The chapel is dedicated to St. James.

BEOLEY, a parish in the upper division of the hundred of Pershore, county of Worcester, 7½ miles (E. by S.) from Bromsgrove, containing 640 inhabitants. The living is a vicarage, in the archdeaconry and diocese of Worcester, rated in the king's books at £7. 16. 10½., and in the patronage of W. Holmes, Esq. The church is dedicated to St. Leonard. Here are some remains of an ancient castle, which belonged successively to the noble families of Mortimer, Beauchamp, and Holland. In the reign of Charles I. the manor was the property of Ralph Sheldon, a distinguished royalist, whose mansion was burnt, to prevent its falling into the possession of the parliamentarians.

BEPTON, a parish in the hundred of Easebourne, rape of Chichester, county of Sussex, 2¾ miles (S.W.) from Midhurst, containing 140 inhabitants. The living is a rectory, in the archdeaconry and diocese of Chichester, rated in the king's books at £8, and in the patronage of W. S. Poyntz, Esq.

BERDON, a parish in the hundred of Clavering, county of Essex, 5½ miles (N. W.) from Stansted-Mountfitchet, containing 338 inhabitants. The living is a perpetual curacy, in the archdeaconry of Colchester, and diocese of London, and in the patronage of the Governors of Christ's Hospital. The church is dedicated to St. Nicholas. The river Stort runs through the parish. A priory of Augustine canons was founded here in the reign of Henry III., the revenue of which, at the dissolution, was £35. 5. 1¼. The Rev. Joseph Mede, a learned commentator on the Book of Revelations, was born here, in 1586.

BERE-CHURCH, a parish within the liberties of the borough of Colchester, county of Essex, 2¼ miles (S. by W.) from Colchester, containing 122 inhabitants. The living is a perpetual curacy, in the archdeaconry of Colchester, and diocese of London, endowed with £600 private benefaction, and £800 royal bounty, and in the patronage of J. Bawtree, Esq. The church is dedicated to St. Michael.

BERGHOLT (EAST), a parish in the hundred of Samford, county of Suffolk, 3½ miles (N. W.) from Manningtree, containing 1246 inhabitants. The living is a perpetual curacy, annexed to the rectory of Brantham, in the archdeaconry of Suffolk, and diocese of Norwich. The church is dedicated to St. Mary. There is a place of worship for Independents. The navigable river Stour flows along the southern side of the parish. Lettice Dykes, in 1589, gave property, now producing about £40 per annum, to endow a free school, which was built by subscription, on land given by Edward Lamb, in 1594.

BERGHOLT (WEST), a parish in the Colchester division of the hundred of Lexden, county of Essex, 3½ miles (N. W.) from Colchester, containing 694 inhabitants. The living is a rectory, in the archdeaconry of Colchester, and diocese of London, rated in the king's books at £10, and in the patronage of William Fisher, Esq. The church is dedicated to St. Mary. There is a place of worship for Wesleyan Methodists.

BERKELEY, a market town and parish in the upper division of the hundred of Berkeley, county of Gloucester, 17 miles (S. W.) from Gloucester, and 114 (W. by N.) from London, comprising the chapelry of Stone, the tythings of Alkington, Hinton, and Ham, and the hamlets of Bradstone and Hamfollow, and containing 3835 inhabitants. This place is supposed to have been a British town in the reign of Alectus, who, as the successor of Carausius, assumed the imperial purple in Britain towards the close of the third century. It was a place of considerable importance in the time of the Saxons, and is said to have had a religious establishment, and probably a castle, prior to the Conquest, but little of their history is recorded. Henry I. visited this place in 1121, where he remained during Easter; and in the reign of Henry II., the castle, which had been erected by Roger de Berkeley, was considerably enlarged by Robert Fitz-Harding, to whom the king gave the manor (which is divided into seven considerable tythings), and who thereupon assumed the title of Baron de Berkeley. The castle, which received various additions from its successive proprietors, became one of the principal baronial seats in the country, and was connected with many transactions of intense political interest, the most important of which was the inhuman murder of the misguided king, Edward II., who was detained here in confinement under the nominal custody of the earl. During the civil war in the reign of Charles I., it was garrisoned for the king, but after a siege of nine days, in which it sustained considerable damage, it was surrendered to the parliamentarians. The principal remains of the ancient building are the keep, a fine specimen of Norman military architecture, flanked by three semicircular towers, and a square tower of later date, in a dark room in the upper part of which the inhuman murder was perpetrated. The entrance is under a massive arched portal, richly ornamented with sculpture: it occupies an area which is nearly circular, and is surrounded with a moat; part of it has been modernized, and is now the residence of Col. Berkeley, who enjoys the estate, but not the title. The town is situated on a gentle eminence in the beautiful Vale of Berkeley, at the distance of a mile from the river Severn, and consists principally of one street; the houses are indifferently built, but the inhabitants are well supplied with water. It was once of greater extent than it is at present; the diversion of the turnpike road from Gloucester to Bristol, which formerly passed through it, is supposed to have contributed to its decay. The trade is principally in timber, corn, malt, and cheese, for which last the neighbourhood is celebrated: iron-ore has been found in the vicinity, and there are appearances of some works having been formerly carried on. The Berkeley and Gloucester canal, navigable for vessels of four hundred tons' burden, passes to the north of the town, and the river Severn bounds it on the west. The market is on Thursday, but it has considerably declined of late years; the fairs are on May 14th and December 1st. The town, which was a borough in the reign of Edward I., having lost its charter of incorporation, is within the jurisdiction of the county magistrates, who hold petty sessions here for the district: a mayor is still annually elected, but the office is merely nominal; constables and other officers are appointed at the court leet of the lord of the manor, and a court for the recovery of small debts is held every third week.

The living is a vicarage, in the archdeaconry and diocese of Gloucester, rated in the king's books at £32. 15. 7½., and in the patronage of Col. Berkeley. The church, dedicated to St. Mary, is a spacious structure, consisting of a nave, aisles, and chancel, of considerable dimensions, partly of later Norman, and partly in the early style of English, architecture: the tower, which is detached, has been rebuilt within the last century. There is a place of worship for Wesleyan Methodists. The free school was founded, in 1696, by Mr. Samuel Thurner, who endowed it with lands producing £16. 5. per annum, which has received an augmentation of land producing £17 per annum, purchased with a bequest by Mr. John Smith, amounting in the whole to £33. 5. per annum, for which the master teaches thirty-nine boys. In 1626, John Attwood left by will, for the benefit of the poor inhabitants of Berkeley, lands of the value of nearly £20 per annum; and various smaller sums have been given and bequeathed at different times by other individuals, for a like purpose. Edward Jenner, M.D. and F.R.S., who introduced the practice of vaccination, was born here in 1749, and died of apoplexy in 1823.

BERKELEY, a parish in the hundred of FROME, county of SOMERSET, 2¾ miles (E. N. E.) from Frome, containing 550 inhabitants. The living is a rectory, in the archdeaconry of Wells, and diocese of Bath and Wells, rated in the king's books at £7. 9. 7., and in the patronage of the Rev. J. M. Rogers. The church, dedicated to St. Mary, was built in 1751.

BERKESWELL, a parish in the Solihull division of the hundred of HEMLINGFORD, county of WARWICK, 6¼ miles (W. by N.) from Coventry, containing 1468 inhabitants. The living is a rectory, with the perpetual curacy of Barstow annexed, in the archdeaconry of Coventry, and diocese of Lichfield and Coventry, rated in the king's books at £14. 12. 6., and in the patronage of the Disbrowe family. The church is dedicated to St. John the Baptist. There is an endowment in land, amounting to about £70 per annum, being the produce of various benefactions, for the support of a school at Berkeswell, and for various other charitable purposes.

BERKHAMPSTEAD (GREAT, or ST. PETER'S), a market town and parish in the hundred of DACORUM, county of HERTFORD, 25½ miles (W. by S.) from Hertford, and 26 (N. W. by W.) from London, on the road to Holyhead, containing 2310 inhabitants. The Saxon name of this place, *Berghamstede*, is derived from its situation, either on a hill, or near a fortress, which latter, from the site of the present town, appears to be the more probable.

Arms.

It is a town of considerable antiquity, the kings of Mercia having had a castle here, to which circumstance its early growth and subsequent importance may be attributed. According to Spelman, Wihtred, King of Kent, assisted at a council held here, in 697. At the time of the Conquest, William, on his arrival at this place, was met by Stigand, Archbishop of Canterbury, who tendered his submission; but on leaving Berkhampstead, his march was greatly obstructed by the opposition of Frederick, abbot of St. Albans, who caused the roads to be blocked up, by cutting down the trees, and, on his arrival at St. Albans, exacted from him an oath that he would observe the ancient laws of the realm, particularly those of Edward the Confessor. Robert, Earl of Moreton, to whom the Conqueror gave this town, built a castle here, which was subsequently taken from his son William, who had rebelled against Henry I., and by that monarch's order rased to the ground. Henry II. held his court here for some time, and conferred many privileges on the town. The castle was rebuilt in the reign of John, and soon after besieged by Lewis, Dauphin of France, who had come over to assist the barons that were in arms against the king. In the 11th of Edward III., Berkhampstead sent two representatives to the great council at Westminster. James I., who selected this place as a nursery for his children, granted the inhabitants a charter of incorporation; but they were so impoverished during the civil war in the reign of his son Charles I., that they were unable to maintain their privileges, whereby the charter became forfeited. The town is pleasantly situated in a deep valley, on the south-western bank of the river Bulbourne, and consists of two streets intersecting at right angles, the principal of which, nearly a mile in length, contains several handsome houses: the air is highly salubrious, and the inhabitants are amply supplied with water. Assemblies are held regularly during the season. The manufacture of wooden bowls, spoons, and other articles of a like kind, formerly prevailed, but it is on the decline; and the making of lace, which was also carried on extensively, has given place to the platting of straw, in which, at present, the female part of the population are principally employed. The Grand Junction canal, which passes by the town, affords an extensive line of inland navigation. The market is on Saturday; the market-house is an ancient building in the centre of the town. Fairs are held on Shrove-Tuesday and Whit-Monday, and there is also a statute fair at Michaelmas. The county magistrates hold a petty session on the first and third Tuesdays in every month; and courts leet for the honour of Berkhampstead, which is part of the duchy of Cornwall, are held at Whitsuntide and Michaelmas. The prison is used as a house of correction, and for the temporary confinement of malefactors previously to their committal to the county gaol.

The living is a rectory, in the archdeaconry of Huntingdon, and diocese of Lincoln, rated in the king's books at £20, and in the patronage of the King, as Duke of Cornwall. The church, dedicated to St. Peter, is a spacious cruciform structure, exhibiting some fine portions in the several styles of English architecture: the tower, rising from the intersection, and highly enriched with sculpture, was built by Richard Torrington, in the reign of Henry VIII.: within the church are two chapels at the eastern end, one dedicated to St. John, the other to St. Catherine, and some interesting monuments. There are places of worship for Baptists, the Society of Friends, and Independents. The free grammar school was founded in the reign of Henry VIII., and endowed with lands belonging to the dissolved guild of St. John the Baptist. In the succeeding reign it was made a royal foundation, the master, usher, and chaplain, were incorporated by act of parliament, and the Warden of All Souls' College, Oxford, was appointed visitor. The school was originally endowed for one hundred and forty-four scholars, but, for the last twenty years, not one boy has received any instruction; the establishment is at present under investigation in the court of Chancery. The premises are situated on one side of the churchyard, and consist of a school-room and houses for the master and usher. A charity school, for twenty boys and ten girls, was founded in 1727, by Mr. Thomas Bourne, who endowed it with £8000: the property now consists of £9300 in the New South Sea annuities, and there are at present thirty boys and twenty girls in the school. Almshouses for six aged widows were founded, in 1681, and endowed with £1000, by Mr. John Sayer; the endowment was augmented with £300 by his widow, and subsequently with £26. 5. per annum by Mrs. Martha Deere. King James I. gave £100, and Charles I. £200, for providing employment and fuel for the poor, and there are also several other bequests for charitable uses. There are slight vestiges of the ancient residence of the Mercian kings, on the north side of the town, and at the north-east end of Castle-street are the remains of the castle, consisting principally of walls of an elliptical form, defended on the north-west side by a double, and on the other sides by a triple, moat; the entrance was at the south-east angle, where there are two wide piers, between which probably was the drawbridge. At the end of the High-street is a spring of clear water, called St. James' Well, to which medicinal properties are attributed. An ancient hospital, dedicated to St. James, formerly existed here, but there are no vestiges of it. The poet Cowper was born here in 1731.

BERKHAMPSTEAD (LITTLE), a parish in the hundred and county of HERTFORD, 4¾ miles (S. W. by S.) from Hertford, containing 439 inhabitants. The living is a rectory, in the archdeaconry of Huntingdon, and diocese of Lincoln, rated in the king's books at £7. 8. 6½., and in the patronage of the Marquis of Salisbury. The church, a neat structure, is dedicated to St. Andrew. At How Green, in this parish, is a place of worship for Wesleyan Methodists. A National school for boys and girls is now in progress of erection, and there are three almshouses, the inmates of which are supported by the parish. On an elevated situation near an old manor-house, a circular tower of brick, one hundred feet in height, termed the Observatory, has been erected, which commands an extensive prospect.

BERKHAMPSTEAD (ST. MARY), or NORTHCHURCH, a parish in the hundred of DACORUM, county of HERTFORD, 1¼ mile (N. W. by W.) from Great Berkhampstead, containing 1028 inhabitants. The living is a rectory, in the archdeaconry of Huntingdon, and diocese of Lincoln, rated in the king's books at £21. 1. 3., and in the patronage of the King, as Prince of Wales.

BERKSHIRE, an inland county, bounded on the north by the county of Oxford, and a small part of the county of Buckingham, from both which it is separated by the Thames; on the east by the counties of Buckingham and Surrey; on the south by the county of Southampton; and on the west by that of Wilts: it extends from 51° 19′ to 51° 48′ (N. Lat.), and from 34½′ (E.) to 1° 43′ (W. Lon.), and, including the detached parts, contains about four hundred and sixty-four thousand acres, or seven hundred and fifty-six square miles. The population, in 1821, amounted to 134,700. This county was anciently called *Barocscire*, or *Berocscire*, softened in process of time into Barkshire and Berkshire, and probably derived its name from a thick wood, called *Barroc*, which occupied an extended tract between Lambourn and Wantage, on or near the downs; though some deduce its etymology from *Berroc*, a bare oak in some part of Windsor Forest, beneath which the Britons, as their custom was, assembled for devotional and legislatorial purposes. The *Bibroci* occupied the south-eastern extremity, and the *Segontiaci* dwelt in that part which borders on Hampshire, but the greater part was inhabited by the *Attrebatii*. The Romans included it within the district of Britannia Superior, and subsequently in that of Britannia Prima. During the Octarchy, it formed a part of the kingdom of the West Saxons, or Wessex, and, after the reduction of the Anglo-Saxon kingdom into one monarchy, it belonged to the district called West Saxon Læge. Offa, King of Mercia, after his victory over Cynewulf, King of the West Saxons, in 775, seized on all that territory lying between Iknield-street and the Thames. The Danes having made an irruption into Wessex, in 871, were repulsed near Englefield by Earl Athelwolf, who was slain in a subsequent battle between them and the army under Ethelred; a few days after which, they were again routed at Ashdown, and compelled to retreat to Reading, where they passed the winter of 872. Alfred gained a decisive victory over them at Eddington, in 878; but, in 1006, they committed great devastation in the county, and defeated the Saxons near the river Kennet. In 1011, Berkshire was under the dominion of Ethelred II., and in the year ensuing, Sweyn, King of Denmark, was at Wallingford. In the struggle between Stephen and the Empress Matilda, the castle at Wallingford was one of the strongest fortresses which were garrisoned by the empress, and was the place of her retreat when driven from Oxford: it was repeatedly besieged by Stephen, but was successfully defended until the termination of the war, when the amicable arrangement which ensued was concluded beneath its walls. During the absence of King Richard I. on a crusading expedition into Palestine, his brother John came over from Normandy, and seized the castles of Wallingford and Windsor, but the latter was retaken by the partizans of the king. Two meetings for the redress of grievances were held between John and the barons in 1213, one at Wallingford and the other at Reading: three years afterwards, the former place was fortified by the king, and the latter besieged by the barons, whose army, under Simon de Montfort, obtained possession of it in 1263: a temporary reconciliation was effected at Reading between Richard II. and the discontented nobles, in 1389. During the parliamentary war, Berkshire was frequently the scene of hostile operations. Wallingford was garrisoned for the king, and Windsor for the parliament; and each place continued in the possession of its own party until the close of the war. Reading, which had been seized on by the parliamentarians, was evacuated by them on the approach, in October 1642, of a detachment of the king's troops, the head-quarters of whose cavalry were at Abingdon. At this period, the king held the whole of the county, except the neighbourhood of Windsor, which fortress sustained but one attack during the war, and that an unsuccessful one, from Prince Rupert. In April 1643, Reading was retaken by the parliamentary army; and in the month of September following, the first battle of Newbury was fought, and the victory claimed by both parties; a few days after the action, Reading again fell into the hands of the king, who also placed a garrison in Donnington castle, near Newbury, under Col. Boys, by whom it was bravely and successfully defended against repeated attacks of the enemy. In the course of the ensuing year, Newbury, Reading (which had been dismantled of its fortifications by the king's troops), and Abingdon, fell successively into the hands of the parliament, who obtained possession of the whole county, except Wallingford. The second battle of Newbury took place in the month of October, in this year, the result of which was equally indecisive with the first. In 1645, Sir Stephen Hawkins made an unsuccessful attack on the parliamentary garrison at Abingdon; and Cromwell, with like fortune, attacked Farringdon, which was then held by the royalists, but he soon after took Sir William Vaughan and Col. Littleton prisoners, with two hundred of their troops, at Radcutt bridge. Prince Rupert attacked Abingdon in March 1646, but failed in his efforts to retake it; and this was the last event of a military nature which took place in Berkshire during the parliamentary war. Wallingford and Farringdon were surrendered to the parliament a few months afterwards, and the king passed his last Christmas in confinement at Windsor. Subsequently to the Restoration, a slight skirmish took place near Reading, in December 1688, which, with the exception of a more trifling affair at Twyford, was the only engagement that happened in this county previously to the Revolution.

Berkshire lies within the diocese of Salisbury and province of Canterbury: it forms an archdeaconry, is divided into the deaneries of Abingdon, Newbury, Reading, and Wallingford, and contains one hundred and forty-eight parishes, of which seventy-two are rectories, sixty-four vicarages, and twelve perpetual curacies. For civil purposes it is divided into twenty hundreds, namely, Beynhurst, Bray, Charlton, Compton, Cookham, Faircross, Farringdon, Ganfield, Hormer, Kintbury-Eagle, Lambourn, Moreton, Ock, Reading, Ripplesmere, Shrivenham, Sonning, Theale, Wantage, and Wargrave. It contains the boroughs and market towns of Abingdon, Reading, Wallingford, and Windsor; the incorporated market towns of Maidenhead, Newbury, and Wokingham; and the market towns of Great Farringdon, Hungerford, East Ilsley, Lambourn, and Wantage. Two knights are returned to parliament for the shire, and two representatives for each of the boroughs, except Abingdon, which sends one: the county members are nominated at Reading, and elected at Abingdon, these being the chief towns. This county is included in the Oxford circuit; the Lent assizes and the Epiphany sessions are held at Reading, the summer assizes and Hilary sessions at Abingdon, the Michaelmas sessions in either town, at the option of the magistrates, and the Easter sessions at Newbury. The county gaol and house of correction is at Reading, and the county house of correction, or bridewell, at Abingdon: there are ninety-three acting magistrates. The rates raised in the county for the year ending March 25th, 1827, amounted to £118,593, and the expenditure to £114,970, of which £99,527. 4. was applied to the relief of the poor.

Berkshire is not a manufacturing county, but there are some cotton-manufactories and a large paper-mill near Newbury, a paper-mill at Bagnor, and a large manufactory for blankets at Greenham mills, near Thatcham; the weaving of sheeting, sail-cloth, and sacking, the manufacture of floor-cloth, and that of silk ribands and galloons, are carried on at Reading; sacking and sail-cloth were formerly extensively made at Abingdon and Wantage; silk is manufactured at Wokingham to a small extent, and copper bolts for the navy, at the Temple mills in the parish of Bisham: there are also several large breweries in the county, particularly at Windsor, which is celebrated for its ale. The natural divisions of the county are four, namely, the Forest district, commencing at the eastern extremity of the county, and extending to the river Loddon westward, and from Sandhurst on the south to Maidenhead on the north; the Vale of the Kennet, stretching from near Wargrave on the east to Hungerford on the west; the Chalk hills, extending nearly across the upper part of the county; and a vale lying between Budcot and Streatley. The substratum consists of chalk, or gravel, with portions of clay at greater or less depths, according to the quality of the soil. Stones of a fine silicious grit, vulgarly called Sarsden-stones, or the Grey-weathers, are scattered over the Berkshire and Wiltshire downs, and lie on strata to which they do not naturally belong. The crops commonly produced are those of wheat, barley, oats, beans, peas, rye, buck-wheat, vetches or tares, rape of cole-seed, turnips, and potatoes; those of limited cultivation are cabbages, carrots, hops, woad, flax, dill, and lavender. The artificial grasses are red, broad, Dutch clover, ray-grass, cow or marl grass, hop-trefoil, heart-trefoil, saintfoin, lucern, burnet, and corn spurry. For pleasing and picturesque scenery, the eastern extremity of the county is pre-eminent, particularly in Windsor Forest, on the banks of the Thames between Henley and Maidenhead, and between Reading and Wallingford. The waste lands chiefly consist of Maidenhead Thicket,

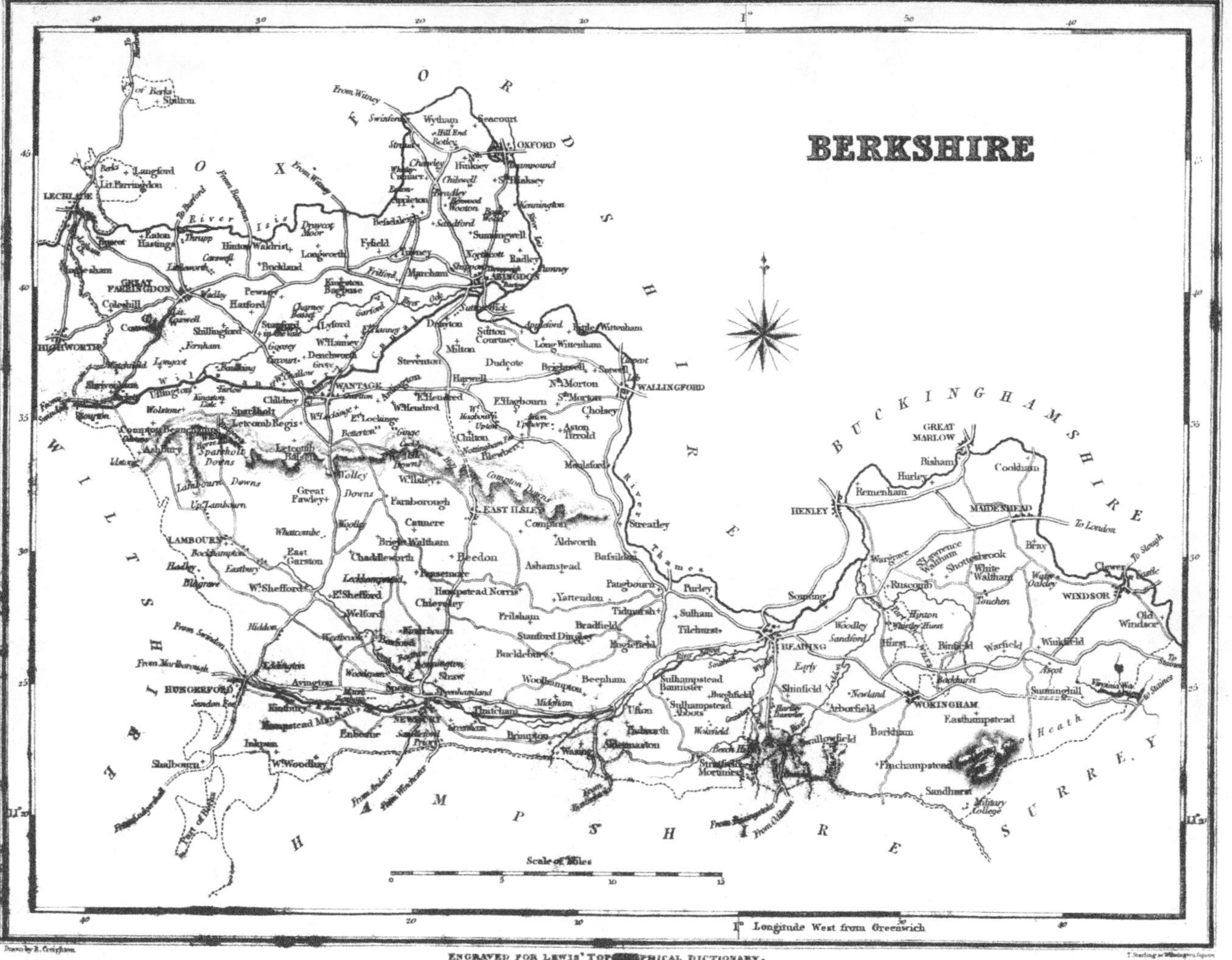

Drawn by R. Creighton.

ENGRAVED FOR LEWIS' TOPOGRAPHICAL DICTIONARY.

and some parts of Windsor Forest and its neighbourhood: this forest was formerly of much greater circuit than it is at present, having included a part of the counties of Buckingham and Surrey, and the whole of the south-eastern part of Berkshire, as far as Hungerford; its present circuit, in which is a part of Bagshot heath, is about fifty-six miles. Windsor Great park was lessened by George III., from three thousand eight hundred to one thousand eight hundred acres, two thousand acres having been brought into cultivation. From an estimate made in the year 1806, it appeared that there were in the county two hundred and fifty-five thousand acres of arable land, seventy-two thousand in meadow and dairy land, twenty-five thousand in sheep-walks, chiefly unenclosed, on the chalk hills; twenty-five thousand in other dry pastures, parks, &c., and thirty thousand waste, chiefly barren heaths. The cattle are of the long horned, or common country breed; many calves are bred for stock, but suckling for the butcher is the prevailing practice. There is a native breed of sheep, strongly marked, but the pure race is not very common. The horses are usually black, very strong and powerful, and rather of full proportions than tall. The hogs, for compactness and size, are excelled by none: in the dairy tract, the piggeries are an important appendage to the farm.

The principal rivers are the Thames and the Kennet: the former skirts the county during a course of more than one hundred miles, and is navigable as high as Lechlade; the latter flows into Berkshire at Hungerford, becomes navigable at Newbury, where it is joined by the Lambourn, and falls into the Thames near Reading: the river Loddon rises near Aldershot, in Hampshire, enters Berkshire in the parish of Swallowfield, and runs into the Thames near Wargrave; the Ock rises near Uffington and flows into the Thames at Abingdon; the Auborn rises near Inkpen, pursues an easterly course beyond Hide-End, then taking a northerly direction, falls into the Kennet a little below Wasing; the Lambourn rises amongst the hills above the town of that name, and falls into the Kennet near Shaw. The Wilts and Berks canal extends from the Thames, at Abingdon, to the eastern border of the county, in the upper part; and the Kennet and Avon canal, from the river Kennet, a little above Newbury, across the lower part of the county. The great road from London to Bath enters at Maidenhead bridge, and passing through Reading, quits near the sixty-fifth milestone; the road from London to Oxford enters at the same place, and leaves at Henley bridge; and the Cirencester road, which branches off at Dorchester, re-enters Berkshire at Abingdon, and passing through Farringdon, quits it at St. John's bridge, near Lechlade.

Within the county are many specimens of Saxon ecclesiastical architecture: the most remarkable is Avington church, which remains nearly in its original state; the churches at Abingdon, Aldermaston, Chaddleworth, Charney, Childrey, Cholsey, Hanney, Hatford, North Hinksey, Hurley, Kintbury, Shalbourn, Shaw *cum* Donnington, Stanford-Dingley, Sunninghill and Wallingford, have doors with circular arches, and Saxon mouldings and ornaments. Within the limits of the county were anciently twelve religious houses, including one Alien priory, and two preceptories of the Knights Hospitallers: there were three colleges, of which, the royal chapel of St. George at Windsor still remains; and ten hospitals, five of which are now in existence, two at Abingdon, and those at Donnington, Lambourn, and Newbury. Of the magnificent abbey built by Henry I. at Reading, little more than rude heaps of stones is now to be seen, and the church of the Grey friars has been converted into a bridewell: there are some remains of the ancient monastery at Abingdon, of that of the Benedictines at Hurley, and of the collegiate church at Wallingford. The most distinctly marked Roman road is that from Gloucester to London, which enters the county from Baydon, and falls into the modern high road from Bath to London, near the fifty-eighth milestone; the road from Silchester to London passed through the south-eastern part, bearing for Old Windsor, or Staines; the Iknield-street enters Berkshire at Streatley, and the Portway on its north-westerly border from Wiltshire; traces of the Old street are also visible between Wantage and Thatcham. Of the many ancient camps, the most remarkable are Letcomb Castle, enclosing an area of twenty-six acres, the intrenchments and ditches containing eight acres and a half; Uffington Castle, seven hundred feet in diameter from east to west, and five hundred from north to south, near which is the rude figure of a horse, of very ancient execution, formed by cutting away the turf on the side of the hill, which has hence acquired the name of White Horse hill, and the vale below, that of White Horse vale; Hardwell Castle, in form approaching to a square; Cæsar's Camp, on Bagshot heath, five hundred and sixty paces in length, and two hundred and eighty in width; Cherbury camp, near Pusey, three hundred and ten paces across; and Alfred's Castle, on the west side of Ashdown park, one hundred and forty paces in diameter. The only mineral springs of any note, are those at Cumner and Sunninghill, the first a mild cathartic, the other a very weak chalybeate; a strong chalybeate spring in the parish of Wokingham, called Gorrick Well, and some springs near Windsor, of the quality of the Epsom waters.

BERMERSLEY, a township in the parish of NORTON on the MOORS, northern division of the hundred of PIREHILL, county of STAFFORD, $6\frac{1}{4}$ miles (N. N. E.) from Newcastle under Lyne, containing 190 inhabitants.

BERMONDSEY, a parish in the eastern division of the hundred of BRIXTON, county of SURREY, $1\frac{1}{2}$ mile (S. S. E.) from London, containing 25,235 inhabitants. This place, in Domesday-book, is described as a royal demesne, and, in other ancient records, as having been occasionally the residence of William the Conqueror, and his successor, William Rufus, who had a palace here. In 1082, a priory for Cluniac monks was founded by Aldwin Child, a citizen of London, as a cell to the abbey of La Charité in France, from which establishment brethren of that order are said to have been sent hither through the influence of Lanfranc, Archbishop of Canterbury. To this monastery William Rufus and some of his successors were great benefactors. Henry I. gave the palace to the monks, for the enlargement of their cloister, reserving a part of it as a residence for himself, in which King John having subsequently resided, it obtained the appellation of King John's palace, and has been by some antiquaries considered rather the original site, than, as it was in reality, only an appendage to the monastery. This establishment increased so much in wealth and importance, that it was found necessary to enlarge the buildings; and an hospital was erected adjoining it, for the reception of their converts and the education of their children, which was dedicated to St. Thomas the Martyr. Though an Alien priory, it was exempted from sequestration in the reign of Edward III., who placed it under the superintendence of an Englishman, in whom he could confide, and whom he made prior. It was subsequently elevated into an abbey, and retained its grandeur and importance till the dissolution, when its revenue was £548. 2. 5¾. The site appears to have been very extensive, comprising the present churchyard, and an adjoining area, still called King John's Court. Vestiges of the palace and conventual buildings may still be traced in the gardens of the houses which have been erected on the site: a gateway, which was standing in 1807, has been taken down, in order to form a new street. Bermondsey owes its origin to the establishment of this monastery, in the vicinity of which, a gradual accumulation of buildings had formed an extensive village in the reign of Edward III., when a church was founded by the prior, for the use of the inhabitants. In this religious house, Catherine of France, widow of Henry V., lived in retirement, and died in 1436; and here also, in 1486, Elizabeth, queen of Edward IV., who was sentenced by the council to forfeiture of land and goods, ended her life in confinement. The village is situated on the southern bank of the Thames, and consists principally of two extensive streets, meeting obliquely near the church, and intersected by many smaller streets; the houses, in general ancient and irregularly built, are interspersed with several modern and handsome structures: the streets are paved, and well lighted with gas, and the inhabitants are supplied with water from the river and from springs. The tanning of leather is carried on to a very great extent, by a company chartered in the reign of Queen Anne; there are also numerous woolstaplers, fellmongers, curriers, and manufacturers of vellum and parchment. The situation is favourable to the carrying on of many trades: there are two small docks and several yards for boat-builders, in connexion with whom are rope-makers, anchor-smiths, and stave-merchants, and there are establishments for the printing and dyeing of calico.

The living is a rectory, in the archdeaconry of Surrey, and diocese of Winchester, rated in the king's books at £15. 8. 11½., and in the patronage of Mrs. Humbly. The church, dedicated to St. Mary Magdalene, is an ancient and very plain structure, with a low square tower. A new church was completed in 1828, partly by grant from the parliamentary commissioners, at an expense of £21,412. 19. 5.; it is a handsome edifice in the Grecian style of architecture, with a tower, and a portico of four pillars of the Ionic order, and contains two thousand sittings, of which one thousand two hundred are free. There are places of worship for Independents and Wesleyan Methodists. A free school for sixty boys, who are instructed in reading, writing, and arithmetic, was founded, in 1709, by Mr. Josiah Bacon, who left £700 for building the premises, and £150 per annum for an endowment; of this annual income, the master receives a salary of £80 per annum, and the usher one of £50, the remainder being laid out in repairs: the school-room, which was erected in 1718, in the Grange road, is a neat brick building, having a statue of the founder in a niche over the entrance. The united charity schools, established in 1712, are supported partly by subscription, and partly by an endowment of £109. 16. 4. per annum, arising from several donations: the whole income is about £550 per annum, for which two hundred and twenty boys, and one hundred and thirty girls, are instructed, of whom fifty boys and thirty girls are also clothed: there is another school with a small endowment, and numerous benefactions have been made for the relief of the poor. In 1770, a chalybeate spring was discovered here, and a spa established, which, for many years, was a celebrated place of entertainment. Israel Mauduit, an ingenious writer on politics and commerce, was born here, in 1708.

BERRICK-PRIOR, a liberty in the parish of Newington, hundred of Ewelme, county of Oxford, 4¼ miles (N. N. E.) from Wallingford, containing 152 inhabitants.

BERRICK-SALOME, a chapelry in the parish of Chalgrove, hundred of Ewelme, county of Oxford, 4 miles (N. N. E.) from Wallingford, containing 174 inhabitants. The chapel is dedicated to St. Helen. Here is a school with a small endowment.

BERRIER, a township in the parish of Greystock, Leath ward, county of Cumberland, 8 miles (W. by S.) from Penrith, containing, with the township of Murrah, 128 inhabitants. Mary Jackson, in 1799, left £230 in reversion, to found and endow a school for girls, which, having become the subject of a lawsuit, was confirmed by the court of Chancery, in 1811, and the school was built by subscription, in 1828, on ground given by the Hon. Henry Howard, of Corby Castle, and endowed with £5 per annum, the remainder of the property having been expended in the lawsuit.

BERRINGTON, a hamlet in the parish of Chipping-Campden, upper division of the hundred of Kiftsgate, county of Gloucester, containing 171 inhabitants.

BERRINGTON, a township in the parish of Eye, hundred of Wolphy, county of Hereford, 3½ miles (N. N. E.) from Leominster. The population is returned with the parish.

BERRINGTON, a parish in the hundred of Condover, county of Salop, 5½ miles (S. E. by S.) from Shrewsbury, containing 657 inhabitants. The living is a rectory, in the archdeaconry of Salop, and diocese of Lichfield and Coventry, rated in the king's books at £10. 12. 1., and in the patronage of Lord Berwick. The church is dedicated to All Saints. The navigable river Severn passes through the parish.

BERRINGTON, a hamlet in the parish of Tenbury, upper division of the hundred of Doddingtree, county of Worcester, 2 miles (W. by S.) from Tenbury, containing 195 inhabitants.

BERROW, a parish in the hundred of Brent with Wrington, county of Somerset, 9½ miles (W. by S.) from Axbridge, containing 449 inhabitants. The living is a discharged vicarage, in the archdeaconry of Wells, and diocese of Bath and Wells, rated in the king's books at £13. 11. 10½., and in the patronage of the Archdeacon of Wells. The church is dedicated to St. Mary. There is a place of worship for Wesleyan Methodists. Berrow bay, a small inlet of the Bristol channel, forms the western boundary of the parish.

BERROW, a parish in a detached part of the lower division of the hundred of OSWALDSLOW, locally in the lower division of the hundred of Pershore, county of WORCESTER, 6 miles (S. W.) from Upton upon Severn, containing 464 inhabitants. The living is a discharged vicarage, in the peculiar jurisdiction and patronage of the Dean and Chapter of Worcester, rated in the king's books at £7. 18. 4., and endowed with £1200 parliamentary grant. The church is dedicated to St. Faith.

BERRY POMEROY, a parish in the hundred of HAYTOR, county of DEVON, 1¾ mile (E.N.E.) from Totness, containing 1255 inhabitants. The living is a vicarage, in the archdeaconry of Totness, and diocese of Exeter, rated in the king's books at £18. 19. 7., and in the patronage of the Duke of Somerset. The church, dedicated to St. Mary, contains a finely carved wooden screen and rood-loft. The navigable river Dart runs along the south-western side of the parish. Here are the ruins of Berry castle, founded by Ralph de Pomeroy, soon after the Conquest.

BERRYN-ARBOR, a parish in the hundred of BRAUNTON, county of DEVON, 2¾ miles (E. by S.) from Ilfracombe, containing 648 inhabitants. The living is a rectory, in the archdeaconry of Barnstaple, and diocese of Exeter, rated in the king's books at £34. 15. 10., and in the patronage of the Bishop of Exeter and others. The church is dedicated to St. Peter. Bishop Jewell, celebrated for his controversy in support of the Protestant faith, was born here, in 1522.

BERSTED (SOUTH), a parish in the hundred of ALDWICK, rape of CHICHESTER, county of SUSSEX, 6 miles (S. E.) from Chichester, containing, with the market town of Bognor, 1851 inhabitants. The living is a vicarage, in the peculiar jurisdiction and patronage of the Archbishop of Canterbury, rated in the king's books at £7. 18. 9. The church is dedicated to St. Mary Magdalene.

BERWICK, a parish in the hundred of LONGBRIDGE, rape of PEVENSEY, county of SUSSEX, 4¾ miles (N.E. by N.) from Seaford, containing 172 inhabitants. The living is a rectory, in the archdeaconry of Lewes, and diocese of Chichester, rated in the king's books at £13. 6. 8., and in the patronage of Jeremiah Smith, Esq. This parish is separated from that of Arlington by the river Cuckmere.

BERWICK (ST. JAMES), a parish in the hundred of BRANCH and DOLE, county of WILTS, 5¼ miles (W.S.W.) from Amesbury, containing 227 inhabitants. The living is a discharged vicarage, within the peculiar jurisdiction of the Bishop of Salisbury, rated in the king's books at £8. 10., endowed with £200 private benefaction, and £500 parliamentary grant, and in the patronage of Alexander Baring, Esq.

BERWICK (ST. JOHN), a parish in the hundred of CHALK, county of WILTS, 5¼ miles (E. by S.) from Shaftesbury, containing 386 inhabitants. The living is a rectory, in the archdeaconry and diocese of Salisbury, rated in the king's books at £26. 13. 4., and in the patronage of the Warden and Fellows of New College, Oxford. About a mile southward from the village is an intrenchment, called Winkelbury Camp, supposed to have been constructed by the Romans.

BERWICK (ST. LEONARD), a parish in the hundred of DUNWORTH, county of WILTS, 1 mile (E.) from Hindon, containing 44 inhabitants. The living is a rectory, with the perpetual curacy of Sedghill annexed, in the archdeaconry and diocese of Salisbury, rated in the king's books at £8. 6. 8., and in the patronage of the Rev. Charles Henry Grove.

Arms.

BERWICK upon TWEED, a port, borough, and market town, situated between the boundary line of the northern part of the county of Durham, and that of Scotland, 64 miles (N. by W.) from Newcastle upon Tyne, and 334 (N. by W.) from London, containing 8723 inhabitants. The name, which Leland supposes to have been originally *Aberwick*, from the British terms *Aber*, the mouth of a river, and *wic*, a town, is, by Camden and other antiquaries, considered to imply only a hamlet annexed to a place of greater importance, such appendages being usually, in ancient records, styled *berewics*; and in this sense of the term Berwick is supposed to have obtained its name from having been the grange of the priory of Coldingham, ten miles distant. It is said to have been a place of considerable importance as a barrier town, in the reign of Osbert, King of Northumbria, and, according to Boëthius, was the place where the Danes, under the conduct of Hubba, landed, on their invasion of England, in the year 867. The town having come into the possession of the Saxons, they, on the defeat of their king, abandoned it, when, with that part of the kingdom of Northumberland called Bernicia, it was ceded, or sold, by Eadulf-Cudel, Earl of Northumberland, to Malcolm II., King of Scotland, in 1020. The earliest authentic notice of Berwick occurs in the reign of Henry I.; and in that of Henry II., it was, with four other towns, given up to that monarch by William the Lion, in 1176, as a pledge for the performance of the treaty of Falaise, by which, in order to obtain his release from captivity, after the battle of Alnwick, in 1174, he had engaged to do homage to the English monarch, as lord paramount, for all his Scottish dominions. Richard I., to obtain a supply of money for his expedition to the Holy Land, sold the vassalage of Scotland for ten thousand marks, and restored this and the other towns to William, content with receiving homage only for the territories which that prince held in England. King John, on retiring from an unsuccessful invasion of Scotland, burnt Berwick, which the Scots almost immediately rebuilt on an enlarged plan, and strongly fortified. In 1291, the commissioners appointed to examine and report on the validity of the title of the respective claimants to the crown of Scotland, met at Berwick, and pursued there the investigation which led to the decision in favour of John Balliol. Edward I. having compelled Balliol to resign his crown, took the town by storm, and inflicted dreadful carnage on the occasion. In 1296, he received the homage of the Scottish nobility, in the presence of a council of the whole nation, at Berwick, where, in the following year, he established a court of Exchequer for the receipt of the revenue of the kingdom of Scotland. Wallace having laid siege to the town, took possession of it, but was unsuccessful in his attempt on the castle, which was relieved by the arrival of a numerous army. Edward II., in prosecuting the war against Scotland, assembled his army here repeatedly, and made several inroads into the enemy's territory. Robert Bruce obtained possession of it in 1318, and having raised the walls, and strengthened them with towers, kept it, notwithstanding several attacks from Edward II. and Edward III., until it surrendered to the latter, after the celebrated battle of Hallidown Hill, in this neighbourhood, which took place on the 19th of July, 1333. As a frontier town it was invariably the first object of attack, on the renewal of hostilities between the two kingdoms, and, after repeated surrenders and sieges, it was ceded to Edward IV., from whom and his successors it received several charters and extensive privileges. After having been exposed, during the subsequent reigns, to the continued aggressions of the Scots and the English, it was made a free town, independent of both kingdoms, by treaty between Edward VI., King of England, and Mary, Queen of Scots, signed at Greenwich, on the part of the former, on the 10th of May, and, on the part of the latter, at Norham, in the vicinity of this town, on the 10th of June, 1551. It was strongly fortified in the reign of Elizabeth, who placed a garrison in it, which was kept up till the accession of James to the English throne, when its importance as a frontier town ceased. During the civil war in the reign of Charles I. it was garrisoned by the parliament.

The town is pleasantly situated on the northern bank, and near the mouth, of the river Tweed: the approach from the English side is over a handsome stone bridge of fifteen arches, connecting it with Tweedmouth on the south. The streets, with the exception of the High street and Hidehill, are narrow, but well paved, and lighted with gas, and the houses are in general well built: some of the inhabitants are supplied with water brought into their houses by pipes, from a spring at the distance of a mile and a half; the others are supplied from public cisterns placed in situations convenient for the purpose. The new fortifications, which are exceedingly strong, have displaced those of more ancient date, of which there remain only the ruins of the fortress at the south-west angle of the old town walls, and those near the castle. The ramparts afford an agreeable promenade, much frequented by the inhabitants. The barracks for the garrison, on the north-east side of the town, form a small quadrangle, neatly built of stone; the establishment consists of a governor, lieutenant-governor, town-major, town-adjutant, surgeon, master gunner, and a few invalid gunners: the buildings are capable of accommodating seven hundred men. Connected with the barracks are the guard-house, an hospital, and an ordnance house. A public library was established in 1812. The theatre, a small neat building, is opened annually in summer. The assembly-rooms are opened on public occasions; and subscription balls take place regularly during the winter.

The trade of the port is somewhat extensive coastwise; the exports are corn, wool, salmon, herrings, pork, and eggs; the imports are timber, deals, staves, iron, hemp, tallow, and blubber. The number of vessels belonging to the port, according to the return made to parliament in 1828, was fifty-four, averaging ninety tons' burden: the harbour is good, but, from the bar at the entrance, it is inaccessible to ships of large burden. The pier, which has been recently constructed, extends nearly half a mile in length; a lighthouse has been erected on it, to guard mariners against the rocks and shallows by which the navigation is endangered. About eight hundred men are employed in the fishery: the salmon and trout, which are caught in abundance, are packed in boxes stratified with ice, by which they are conveyed fresh to the London and other markets: a great quantity of lobsters and herrings is also found here. The annual rental of the fisheries has been estimated at £10,000, and the supply of eggs, which are sent from this place for the use of sugar refiners, has been returned as exceeding the value of £13,000 per annum, but this branch of the trade has materially diminished. The principal articles of manufacture, exclusively of such as are connected with the shipping, are damask, diaper, sacking, sail-cloth, cotton, hosiery, carpets, hats, boots, and shoes. The market, which is abundantly supplied with grain, is on Saturday; and there is a fair, for black cattle and horses, on the Friday in Trinity week; statute fairs are also held on the second Wednesday in May, the Wednesday before August 26th, and the first Wednesday in November.

The government, by charter of incorporation granted in the reign of James I., is vested in a mayor, recorder, four bailiffs, and an indefinite number of burgesses, assisted by a town clerk, coroner, four serjeants at mace, and subordinate officers. The mayor, who, with the bailiffs, is elected annually at Michaelmas, the recorder, and such of the burgesses as have filled the office of mayor, are justices of the peace by virtue of their office: the freedom of the borough is inherited by birth, acquired by servitude, or obtained by gift. The corporation hold courts of quarter session and gaol delivery for the borough, and a court of pleas every alternate Tuesday, for the recovery of debts to any amount. A court leet is held under the charter, at which a high constable and six petty constables are appointed. The town hall is a spacious, handsome building, with a portico of four massive circular columns of the Tuscan order: a portion of the lower part, called the Exchange, is appropriated to the use of the market; the first story contains two spacious halls, and other apartments in which the courts are held, and the public business of the corporation is transacted; and the upper part is used as a gaol: the whole forms a stately pile of fine hewn stone, and is surmounted with a lofty spire containing a peal of eight bells, which on the Sabbath day summon the inhabitants to the parish church, but is inconveniently situated in the centre of the High-street, by which the thoroughfare is greatly obstructed. Berwick was one of the four Scottish burghs which anciently sent representatives to the court of the four burghs in Scotland; on being annexed to the kingdom of England, its prescriptive usages were confirmed by royal charter. It first sent representatives to the English parliament in the reign of Henry VIII., since which time it has continued to return two members: the right of election is vested in the burgesses at large, in number about one thousand; the mayor and bailiffs are the returning officers.

The living is a vicarage, within the jurisdiction of the Consistorial Court of Durham, rated in the king's books at £20, endowed with £1000 private benefaction, and £1500 parliamentary grant, and in the patronage of the Dean and Chapter of Durham. The church, dedicated to the Holy Trinity, is a handsome structure in the decorated style of English architecture; it was built during the usurpation of Cromwell, and is consequently without a steeple. There are two places of worship for those connected with the Scottish Kirk, and one each for Particular Baptists, Burghers, Antiburghers, the Scottish relief, and Wesleyan Methodists. The free grammar school, founded originally by the corporation, and endowed, in the middle of the seventeenth century, by Col. Strother, with the estate of Coldmarten, is under the management of the corporation, who appoint the master; he has a salary of £80 per annum, and a house and garden, and receives ten shillings per quarter for every scholar who is not the son of a freeman. A school for the instruction of the sons of burgesses in English, Latin, and the mathematics, was founded and endowed by the corporation in 1798; to each department there is a separate master, each of whom, in addition to his salary, has a house and garden. The Blue-coat charity school, in which forty-two boys are clothed and educated, was founded by Captain James Bolton, in 1725, and endowed with £800, since augmented by various benefactions; the master has a salary of £50 per annum. The school of industry for girls, established in 1819, is supported by the ladies of Berwick, and affords instruction to one hundred and six girls. There is also a school in connexion with the workhouse, in which about one hundred children are educated; the master has a salary of £60 per annum, which is paid out of the poor's rate. A pauper lunatic asylum was erected in 1813; and there is a dispensary, established in 1814, under the patronage of the Bishop of Durham, which affords relief to the poor within twelve miles of the town, and is attended by four physicians, three surgeons, and a dispensing apothecary. There are some trifling remains of the castle, and a pentagonal tower near it, a square fort in Magdalene fields, and some intrenchments on Hallidown Hill. A Benedictine nunnery is stated to have been founded by David, King of Scotland, who died in 1153; here were also monasteries of Black, Grey, White, and Trinitarian friars, and three or four hospitals, but every vestige of them has long disappeared.

BERWICK-HILL, a township in the parish of Ponteland, western division of Castle ward, county of Northumberland, 9½ miles (N.N.W.) from Newcastle upon Tyne, containing 111 inhabitants.

BESFORD, a township in that part of the parish of Shawbury which is in the hundred of Pimhill, county of Salop, 3¾ miles (S. E. by E.) from Wem, containing 169 inhabitants.

BESFORD, a parish in the upper division of the hundred of Pershore, county of Worcester, 3 miles (W. by S.) from Pershore, containing 154 inhabitants. The living is a perpetual curacy, annexed to the vicarage of St. Andrew's, Pershore, in the archdeaconry and diocese of Worcester, rated in the king's books at £3. The church is dedicated to St. Andrew. The navigable river Avon runs along the border of the parish.

BESSELSLEIGH, a parish in the hundred of Hormer, county of Berks, 5 miles (N. W.) from Abingdon, containing 130 inhabitants. The living is a discharged rectory, in the archdeaconry of Berks, and diocese of Salisbury, rated in the king's books at £4. 17. 3½., and in the patronage of W. J. Lenthall, Esq. The church is dedicated to St. Lawrence. The parishioners are entitled to participate in the advantages of the school at Appleton, endowed by Sir R. Fettiplace. The old manor-house, formerly the seat of Lenthall, Speaker of the House of Commons in the Long Parliament, was pulled down about forty years ago. Cromwell, who was a frequent visitor here, usually concealed himself in a room to which the only access was by a chair let down and drawn up with pullies.

BESSINGBY, a parish in the wapentake of Dickering, East riding of the county of York, 2¼ miles (S. W.) from Bridlington, containing 83 inhabitants. The living is a perpetual curacy, in the archdeaconry and diocese of York, endowed with £1400 royal bounty, and in the patronage of H. Hudson, Esq. The church is dedicated to St. Magnus.

BESSINGHAM, a parish in the northern division of the hundred of Erpingham, county of Norfolk, 5¼ miles (S.W.) from Cromer, containing 149 inhabitants. The living is a discharged rectory, in the archdeaconry of Norfolk, and diocese of Norwich, rated in the king's books at £4. 6. 8., and in the patronage of Viscount Anson. The church is dedicated to St. Mary.

BESTHORPE, a parish in the hundred of Shropham, county of Norfolk, 1¼ mile (E. by S.) from Attleburgh, containing 519 inhabitants. The living is a discharged vicarage, in the archdeaconry of Norfolk, and diocese of Norwich, rated in the king's books at £5. 6. 10½., and in the patronage of the Earl of Winterton. The church is dedicated to All Saints.

BESTHORPE, a chapelry in the parish of South Scarle, northern division of the wapentake of Newark, county of Nottingham, 8 miles (N.N.E.) from Newark, containing 271 inhabitants. There is a place of worship for Wesleyan Methodists. A school is endowed with £8. 12. per annum.

BESWICK, a chapelry in the parish of Kilnwick, Bainton-Beacon division of the wapentake of Harthill, East riding of the county of York, 6½ miles (N. by W.) from Beverley, containing 192 inhabitants. The living is a perpetual curacy, in the archdeaconry of the East riding, and diocese of York, endowed with £600 royal bounty, and in the patronage of J. Denison, Esq.

BETCHWORTH, a parish in the first division of the hundred of Reigate, county of Surrey, 3¼ miles (W. by S.) from Reigate, containing 909 inhabitants. The living is a discharged vicarage, in the archdeaconry of Surrey, and diocese of Winchester, rated in the king's books at £7. 8. 11½., endowed with £200 private benefaction, and £200 royal bounty, and in the patronage of the Dean and Canons of Windsor. The church is dedicated to St. Michael. A school is endowed with £20 per annum, and is further supported by subscription.

BETHERSDEN, a parish in the hundred of Chart and Longbridge, lathe of Scray, county of Kent, 6 miles (W. S.W.) from Ashford, containing 1001 inhabitants. The living is a vicarage, in the archdeaconry and diocese of Canterbury, rated in the king's books at £12, endowed with £200 parliamentary grant, and in the patronage of the Archbishop of Canterbury. The church is dedicated to St. Beatrice. There is a place of worship for Particular Baptists. A fair is held here on the 1st of July. A considerable quantity of a species of grey marble, used for columns and the internal ornaments of various neighbouring churches, is obtained in the northern part of the parish. The inhabitants are entitled to send six children to the free school at Smarden.

BETHNAL-GREEN, a parish in the Tower division of the hundred of OSSULSTONE, county of MIDDLESEX, $2\frac{1}{2}$ miles (N.E. by E.) from St Paul's, containing 45,676 inhabitants. This very extensive parish, which was severed by act of parliament, in 1743, from the parish of Stepney, to which it was formerly a hamlet, is divided into four districts, called Church division, Green division, Hackney-road division, and Town division. It is supposed to have derived its name from Bathon Hall, the residence of a family of that name, who had considerable possessions here in the reign of Edward I., and from an extensive green, to the east of which is the site of an episcopal palace, called Bishop's Hall, which is said to have been the residence of Bonner, Bishop of London. The popular legendary ballad of the Blind Beggar of Bethnal-Green, the hero of which is said to have been Henry de Montfort, son of the Earl of Leicester, has reference to an ancient castellated mansion in this parish, built in the reign of Elizabeth, by John Kirby, a citizen of London, and now converted into a private lunatic asylum. The houses in general are meanly built of brick, and consist of large ranges of dwellings, inhabited chiefly by journeymen silk-weavers, who work at home for the master weavers in Spitalfields, in each of which two or three families live, and exercise their sedentary occupation. The parish is watched, and lighted with gas; the streets are partially paved, and the inhabitants are supplied with water by the East London Company's works. There is a very extensive cotton-factory, besides a large manufactory for water-proof hose, made of flax, without seam, and of any length and diameter, chiefly for the use of brewers and for firemen. A great quantity of land in the parish is in the occupation of market-gardeners, who raise fruit and vegetables for the London market; and there are extensive beds of clay, which is much used for the making of bricks. The fair formerly held here has been suppressed, in consequence of the riotous proceedings which usually took place during its continuance. The Regent's canal passes through the parish. This district is within the limits of the New Police act, and under the jurisdiction of a court of requests for the Tower Hamlets, for the recovery of debts under 40*s*.

The living is a rectory, in the peculiar jurisdiction of the Commissary of London, concurrently with the Consistorial Court of the Bishop, and in the patronage of the Principal and Fellows of Brasenose College, Oxford. The church, dedicated to St. Matthew, and erected in 1746, is a neat brick building, ornamented with stone. St. John's church was built in 1828, by grant from the parliamentary commissioners, at an expense of £17,638. 18.; it is a handsome edifice of stone, in the Grecian style of architecture, with a tower, and is capable of accommodating two thousand persons; one thousand two hundred of the sittings are free. There are places of worship for Baptists, Independents, and Methodists. An episcopal chapel was erected, in 1814, by the Society for Promoting Christianity among the Jews, attached to which are two schools, wherein fifty boys and nearly sixty girls are maintained and instructed. St. Matthew's school, founded in 1771, by the inhabitants, for clothing and instructing forty-five boys and forty-five girls, and a National school for one thousand children, are supported by subscription. In 1722, Mr. Thomas Parmiter left an estate in Suffolk, now producing £25 per annum, for the erection and endowment of a free school and almshouse in this parish; for the promotion of which purpose, Mrs. Elizabeth Carter gave the ground rent-free for six hundred years, and £10 per annum: Mr. William Lee also gave £10 per annum towards the maintenance of the school; and Mr. Edward Mayhew £5 towards the clothing of the children. The income, under the management of trustees, has greatly improved; there are fifty boys in the school; the master has a salary of £50, and the almspeople an allowance of £5 per annum and a supply of coal. The almshouses founded, in 1711, by Captain Fisher, and those belonging to the companies of Drapers and Dyers, are situated in this parish. Trinity Hospital, at Mile-End, was erected in 1695, on land, in this parish, given by Captain Henry Mudd, an elder brother of the Trinity House, and endowed, in 1701, by Captain Robert Sandes, for twenty-eight masters of ships, or their widows, who have each a pecuniary allowance, apartments, and other advantages. The Roman road from the western counties of England to the ferry over the river Lea at Old Ford, passes through the northern part of the parish. Sir Richard Gresham, father of Sir Thomas Gresham, who built the Royal Exchange; Sir Thomas Grey, Knt.; and Sir Balthazer Gerbier, a celebrated painter and architect, who designed the triumphal arch for the entrance of Charles II. into London, on his restoration; were residents at this place. Ainsworth, the celebrated compiler of the Latin Dictionary, kept an academy here for some years, and the noted Caslon, who established the celebrated type-foundry in Chiswell-street, lived here in retirement till his decease in 1766.

BETLEY, a parish (formerly a market town) in the northern division of the hundred of PIREHILL, county of STAFFORD, $7\frac{1}{2}$ miles (W. by N.) from Newcastle under Line, containing 932 inhabitants. The living is a perpetual curacy, in the archdeaconry of Stafford, and diocese of Lichfield and Coventry, endowed with £600 private benefaction, and £600 royal bounty, and in the patronage of George Tollet, Esq. The church, dedicated to St. Margaret, is an ancient structure, with a tower, supposed to have been erected in 1713, as that date appears on the vane: the nave is separated from the aisles by pillars and plain pointed arches of wood; several handsome monuments adorn the walls of the chancel, which is of modern construction. There is a place of worship for Wesleyan Methodists. The village is remarkably cheerful and pleasant, and contains several respectable houses; in the neighbourhood are extensive gardens, from which the town of Newcastle is supplied with vegetables, for the cultivation of which the soil is particularly adapted. Courts leet and baron are held annually; and a fair for cattle takes place on the 31st of July. Here is a charity school with a small endowment.

BETTERTON, a tything in the parish of LOCKINGE, hundred of WANTAGE, county of BERKS, 2½ miles (E. S. E.) from Wantage. The population is returned with the parish.

BETTESHANGER, a parish in the hundred of EASTRY, lathe of ST. AUGUSTINE, county of KENT, 4 miles (S. S. W.) from Sandwich, containing 21 inhabitants. The living is a discharged rectory, in the archdeaconry and diocese of Canterbury, rated in the king's books at £6. 4. 4., and in the patronage of F. E. Morrice, Esq. The church is dedicated to St. Mary.

BETTISCOMBE, a parish in the liberty of FRAMPTON, Bridport division of the county of DORSET, 6 miles (W. by S.) from Beaminster, containing 62 inhabitants. The living is a rectory, in the archdeaconry of Dorset, and diocese of Bristol, rated in the king's books at £8. 2. 3½., and in the patronage of F. J. Browne, Esq.

BETTUS, a parish in the hundred of PURSLOW, county of SALOP, 6 miles (N. W.) from Knighton, containing 341 inhabitants. The living is a perpetual curacy, in the archdeaconry of Salop, and diocese of Hereford, endowed with £600 royal bounty, and £200 parliamentary grant, and in the patronage of the Vicar of Clun. The church is dedicated to St. Mary.

BETTWS, a parish in the upper division of the hundred of WENTLLOOG, county of MONMOUTH, 2¾ miles (N. W. by W.) from Newport, containing 76 inhabitants. The living is a perpetual curacy, annexed to the vicarage of St. Woollos, in the archdeaconry and diocese of Llandaff. The church is dedicated to St. David.

BETTWS-NEWYDD, a parish in the lower division of the hundred of RAGLAND, county of MONMOUTH, 4 miles (N. by E.) from Usk, containing 84 inhabitants. The living is a perpetual curacy, annexed to the vicarage of Llanarth, in the archdeaconry and diocese of Llandaff, endowed with £200 royal bounty.

BEVERCOATES, a parish in the South-clay division of the wapentake of BASSETLAW, county of NOTTINGHAM, 2½ miles (W.N.W.) from Tuxford, containing 48 inhabitants. The living is a vicarage, united to that of West Markham, in the archdeaconry of Nottingham, and diocese of York. The church, now desecrated, was dedicated to St. Giles.

Arms.

BEVERLEY, a borough, market town, and the head of a liberty, having separate jurisdiction, in the East riding of the county of YORK, 9 miles (N.E.) from Kingston upon Hull, 29 (E.S.E.) from York, and 183 (N.) from London, containing 6728 inhabitants. This place, from the woods with which it was formerly covered, was called *Deirwalde*, implying the forest of the Deiri, the ancient inhabitants of this part of the country. By the Saxons, probably from the number of beavers with which the river Hull in this part abounded, it was called *Beverlega*, from which its present name is deduced. About the year 700, John, Archbishop of York, partly refounded the church, dedicated to St. John the Evangelist, and established an oratory, in honour of St. Martin. These he subsequently converted into a monastery, in which, after having filled the archiepiscopal see of York for thirty-three years, with a reputation for extreme sanctity, he spent the remainder of his life in retirement and devotion; and dying in 721, was canonized by the title of St. John of Beverley. In the year 867, this monastery was destroyed by the Danes, and, after remaining for three years in a state of desolation, was partly restored by the monks. In the early part of the tenth century, Athelstan, marching against the confederated Britons, Scots, and Danes, caused the standard of St. John of Beverley to be carried before his army, and having returned victorious, bestowed many privileges upon the town and monastery. He founded a college for Secular canons, which, at the dissolution, had an establishment consisting of a provost, eight prebendaries, a chancellor, precentor, seven rectors, and nine vicars choral, and a revenue of £597. 19. 6.; and he conferred on the church the privilege of sanctuary, the limits of which, extending for a mile around the town, were marked out by four crosses, erected at the four principal entrances. From this time the town began to increase rapidly in population and importance. About the year 1060, Kinsius, the twenty-third archbishop of York, built a hall, nearly rebuilt the church, to which he added a tower, and contributed greatly to its internal decoration. The memory of St. John of Beverley was held in such veneration, that William the Conqueror having advanced within seven miles of the town, gave strict orders to his army that they should not damage the church; the day of his death was appointed to be kept holy, and the festival of his translation, October 25th, was, in 1416, ordered to be annually celebrated, in commemoration of the battle of Agincourt, which was superstitiously thought to have been gained through his intercession. At the commencement of the parliamentary war, the king fixed his headquarters at Beverley, and attempted to gain possession of Kingston upon Hull, which was then defended by Sir John Hotham, who, having subsequently made overtures to the king, and entered into a negociation for surrendering the town, fled from Hull, upon the discovery of his intention, and was made prisoner at Beverley, which had fallen into the hands of the parliamentarians.

The town is situated at the foot of the Wolds, about a mile from the river Hull, and consists of several spacious streets, in which are many handsome well-built houses: the approach from the Driffield road is remarkably fine, having, particularly on the north-east side, many elegant buildings, and terminating in an ancient gateway, which leads into the town. The streets are well paved, and the inhabitants are amply supplied with water: the air is salubrious, and the environs afford agreeable walks. The races are held annually in June, on Hurn meadow, about a mile distant, on which a commodious stand has been erected. The theatre was built in 1805, assemblies are held periodically in a suite of rooms for that purpose. The trade is in coal, corn, oatmeal, malt and tanned leather, and has been greatly extended by means of a canal, called Beverley Beck, constructed under an act of parliament, in 1727, and connecting the town with the river Hull: a considerable quantity of bone lace is also made. The market is on Saturday: the market-place occupies an area of four acres, in the centre of which is a stately cross supported on eight pillars, each of one entire stone. Fairs are held on the Thursday before Old Valentine's day, Holy Thursday, July 5th, the Wednesday before September 25th, and November 6th, chiefly for horses, horned cattle, and sheep, and on every alternate Wednesday there is a great market for sheep and horned cattle.

Corporate Seal.

The government of the borough, by charter of Queen Elizabeth, is vested in a mayor, recorder, twelve aldermen, and thirteen burgesses, assisted by a town-clerk and subordinate officers: the mayor and burgesses are elected annually, and the aldermen are chosen by a majority of their own body, as vacancies occur. The freedom of the borough is inherited by the sons of freemen, if born within the liberty, acquired by servitude, or obtained by purchase: among the privileges which it conveys are, exemption from toll and custom in every town or port in England, and the right of depasturing twelve or thirteen head of cattle, at a trifling cost, on four large pastures, containing about one thousand acres. The corporation have the power of trying for capital offences, but do not exercise it; they hold courts of session for the borough and liberty which latter comprises the townships of Molscroft, Stockhill with Sandholme, Thearne, Tickton with Hull-Bridge, Weel, and Woodmansey with Beverley-Park, and part of the township of Aike, all in the parish of St. John; and a court of record is also held, called the Provost court, which takes cognizance of all pleas, except those respecting titles to landed property. A court of requests is holden under an act passed in the 21st of George III., the powers of which were extended by a subsequent act, in the 46th of the same reign, whereby debts under £5 are recoverable. The guildhall, or, as it is here called, the Hallgarth, is a neat building, containing, in addition to the apartments in which the public business of the corporation is transacted, a court-room in which the general quarter sessions for the East riding are held, and a registrar's office. The house of correction is a small neat building, about half a mile from the town. The elective franchise was conferred in the reign of Edward I., but was not exercised from the end of that reign till the 5th of Elizabeth, since which time the borough has continued to return two members to parliament: the right of election is vested in the freemen generally, whether resident or not, the number of whom is about one thousand four hundred; the mayor is the returning officer.

Beverley comprises the parishes of St. John, St. Martin, St. Mary, and St. Nicholas, all within the archdeaconry of the East riding, and diocese of York: the parish of St. John extends into the northern division of the wapentake of Holderness. It was formerly the head of a peculiar and exempt jurisdiction, under the provost of the collegiate church, which expired at the dissolution of monasteries. The living of St. John's is a perpetual curacy, with that of St. Martin's united, endowed with £200 private benefaction, and £400 royal bounty, and in the patronage of the Mayor and Corporation. The church, anciently belonging to the monastery of St. John, and still called the Minster, was almost entirely rebuilt in 1060, by Kinsius, Archbishop of York. In 1664, some workmen opening a grave in the chancel, discovered a sheet of lead, enveloping some relics, with an inscription in Latin, purporting that the ancient church having been destroyed by fire, in 1188, search was made for the relics of St. John of Beverley, which having been found, his bones were again deposited near the altar. It is not known at what precise period the present church was built, though probably it was in the early part of the reign of Henry III.; it is a venerable and spacious cruciform structure, in the early, decorated, and later styles of English architecture, with two lofty towers at the west end. Though combining these several styles, it exhibits in each of them such purity of composition, correctness of detail, and elegance of execution, as to raise it to an architectural equality with the finest of the cathedral churches, to which it is inferior only in magnitude. The west front is in the best character of the later style, and the nave and transepts are of the early English, of which the fronts of the north and south transepts are pure specimens. The choir is partly in the decorated style, with an exquisitely beautiful altar, screen, and rood-loft, which, though unequalled in elegance of design and richness of detail, has been concealed by one of very inferior composition, put up within the last century: the east window is decorated with stained glass, which has been collected from the other windows, and skilfully arranged: near the altar is the seat of refuge, formed of one entire stone, with a Latin inscription, offering an asylum to all criminals who should flee to this sanctuary; and on an ancient tablet are the portraits of St. John of Beverley and King Athelstan, with a legend recording the monarch's grant of freedom to the town. In the choir there is a superb and finely executed monument to the memory of one of the Percies, and in the north transept is a fine altar-tomb, both in the decorated style. The living of St. Mary's is a vicarage, with those of St. Nicholas' and Holme on the Wolds united, rated in the king's books at £14. 2. 8., and in the patronage of the Crown. The church is a highly interesting structure, and contains fine portions in the various styles of architecture, from the Norman to the later English: the towers at the western end are finely pierced, and the octagonal turrets flanking the nave are strikingly elegant: the roof of the chancel, which is in the decorated style, is richly groined, and the piers and arches are well proportioned; there are some interesting monuments, and a fine font in the later style. The churches of St. Martin and St. Nicholas have long since gone to decay. There are places of worship for Baptists, the Society of Friends, Independents, and Primitive and Wesleyan Methodists.

The grammar school is of uncertain origin, though it appears to have existed at a remote period: the fixed endowment is not more than £10 per annum, which was bequeathed, in 1652, by Dr. Metcalf; this is augmented with a donation of £20 per annum by the members for the borough, and one of £70 per annum by the corporation, in whom the management is vested; these sums are paid as a salary to the master, who receives also 40*s.* per annum from each of the scholars, and has the privilege of taking boarders. There are three scholarships of £6. 13. 4. per annum each, founded by Dr. Metcalf; one of £6 per annum by William Coates, Esq., in 1681; two of £8, at St. John's College, Cambridge, founded by Dr. William Lacey, in 1670; one of £20 at Corpus Christi, or St. John's, Colleges, Cambridge, founded by Dr. Green, Bishop of Lincoln, in 1778, who bequeathed £1000 for that purpose, or to the charity school; and one of £5 by Margaret Ferrer, to a student at the latter college. The Blue-coat charity school was established by subscription, in 1709, for the maintenance, clothing, and education of poor children; the annual income, arising from subsequent benefactions, is at present about £126: there are ten boys in this establishment, with each of whom, on leaving school, an apprentice fee of £3 is given. There is also a school, founded in 1804, by Mr. James Graves, who endowed it with stock in the Navy five per cents., producing £84 per annum, in which two hundred children of both sexes are instructed, the boys on the Lancasterian, and the girls on Dr. Bell's, system. Almshouses for four aged widows, each of whom receives 10*s.* per month, were founded and endowed by Mr. Thwaite Fox, in 1636. Almshouses also for thirty-two widows, who receive a weekly allowance of 5*s.* each, were founded by Mrs. Anne Routh, in 1721, and endowed with estates now producing £675 per annum; the matron receives two shillings and sixpence, and two nurses two shillings each, per week, in addition to their regular allowance. An hospital, containing fourteen apartments, was founded in 1712, by Mr. Charles Warton, who endowed it with property now producing about £400 per annum, for fourteen widows, who have a weekly allowance of 4*s.* each. There are also unendowed almshouses, erected by the corporation, comprising twenty-six tenements, the occupiers of which receive a portion of various bequests for charitable uses. Sir Michael Warton, Knt., in 1724, bequeathed £4000, as a perpetual fund for keeping the minster in repair; and Mr. Robert Stephenson, in 1711, left an estate, now producing from £70 to £100 per annum, for the maintenance of "Nonconformist preaching ministers." Alfred of Beverley, a monkish historian of the twelfth century, is supposed to have been born here; Dr. John Alcock, Bishop of Ely, and founder of Jesus' College, Cambridge; Dr. Fisher, Bishop of Rochester, a martyr to his religious tenets in the reign of Henry VIII.; and Dr. Green, Bishop of Lincoln, an elegant scholar, and one of the writers of the Athenian Letters, published by Lord Hardwicke; were natives of this town.

BEVERSTONE, a parish in the upper division of the hundred of Berkeley, county of Gloucester, 2 miles (W.N.W.) from Tetbury, containing 160 inhabitants. The living is a rectory, with the perpetual curacy of Kingscote annexed, in the archdeaconry and diocese of Gloucester, rated in the king's books at £30, and in the patronage of the Crown. The church is dedicated to St. Mary. One of the sources of the river Avon is in this parish, in which also there are quarries of stone used for roofing houses. Here are the remains of a moated castle, built by Thomas, Lord Berkeley, in the reign of Edward III., which, after repeated sieges, was taken and burnt in the early part of the parliamentary war. It is a noble ruin overgrown with ivy; and its chapel, still perfect, has a beautiful arched roof, a fine window, and an elegant shrine of tabernacle-work on the right hand side of the altar.

BEWALDETH, a joint township with Snittlegarth, in the parish of Torpenhow, Allerdale ward below Darwent, county of Cumberland, 6¼ miles (N.E. by E.) from Cockermouth, containing, with Snittlegarth, 97 inhabitants.

BEWCASTLE, a parish in Eskdale ward, county of Cumberland, comprising the townships of Bailie, Belbank, Bewcastle, and Nixons, and containing 1213 inhabitants, of which number, 188 are in the township of Bewcastle, 19 miles (N.E.) from Carlisle. The living is a rectory, in the archdeaconry and diocese of Carlisle, rated in the king's books at £2, endowed with £800 parliamentary grant, and in the patronage of the Dean and Chapter of Carlisle. The church is dedicated to St. Cuthbert. In the churchyard there is a curious antique cross, composed of a single stone, bearing inscriptions which have been variously interpreted, and some curious devices, which are supposed to be emblematical of the conversion of the Danes to Christianity, and commemorative of the death and interment of one of their kings. There is a place of worship for Presbyterians. The rivers Leven, or Line, and Irthing, have their sources in this parish. Limestone, coal, and lead-ore are obtained here. In the 7th of Edward I. license was granted to John Swinburn to hold a market and a fair. There are two schools in the parish, which are partly supported by subscription. This was a Roman station, of which there are some traces, and many coins, inscribed stones, and other relics of Roman occupation have been found: the Maiden-way passed through the parish. Bueth Castle, a fortress built by Bueth, Lord of Gilsland, soon after the Conquest, was occupied by a border garrison in the reign of Elizabeth, and, in 1641, was demolished by the parliamentarians: some vestiges are still visible, and there are various relics of antiquity in the vicinity, which abounds also with picturesque scenery. There are two mineral springs, one with a sulphureous impregnation, the other chalybeate; and at Low Grange, a quarter of a mile to the east of the church, is a petrifying spring.

Seal and Arms.

BEWDLEY, a borough, market town, and chapelry, in the parish of Ribbesford, having separate jurisdiction, locally in the lower division of the hundred of Doddingtree, county of Worcester, 14 miles (N.W.) from Worcester, and 122 (N.W.) from London, containing 3725 inhabitants. This place, from the pleasantness of its situation, and the beauty of the surrounding scenery, anciently obtained the appellation of *Beau lieu*, of which its present name is a corruption. In the 13th of Henry IV., a petition was presented to parliament from the men of "Bristowe" and Gloucester, praying that they might navigate the river Severn without being subject to new taxes levied by the men of *Beaudley*. At this time

Bewdley appears to have enjoyed many privileges, among which was that of sanctuary for persons who had shed blood: it was formerly extra-parochial, but, by letters patent granted by Henry VI., was annexed to the parish of Ribbesford. Edward IV. gave the inhabitants a charter of incorporation in the twelfth year of his reign; and Henry VII. erected a palace here for his son Arthur, in which that prince was married by proxy to Catherine of Arragon, and dying soon after at Ludlow, his corpse was removed to this town, where it lay in state previously to interment in the cathedral church of Worcester. Bewdley, formerly included in the marches of Wales, was, by an act of parliament passed in the reign of Henry VIII., added to the county of Worcester. During the civil war in the reign of Charles I., that monarch, who had been driven from Oxford by the parliamentary forces, retired with the remnant of his army to this town, where he encamped, in order to keep the river Severn between him and the enemy. Whilst staying here, he was attacked by a party of Scottish cavalry, when several of his officers, and seventy men, were made prisoners. In these attacks the palace was greatly damaged, and was subsequently taken down; the site is now occupied by a modern dwelling-house, and not a single vestige of the original edifice can, with certainty, be traced. The more ancient part of the town was built at a greater distance from the river, and the street called Load-street is supposed to have been the place where the inhabitants loaded their boats: there were formerly four gates, two of which were standing in 1811, but they have since been entirely demolished.

Bewdley is beautifully situated on the western bank of the river Severn, over which a light and elegant stone bridge was erected in 1797: the main street, leading from the bridge, diverges right and left, but extends furthest in the latter direction; it is indifferently paved and not lighted. The houses are in general well built, and of respectable appearance; and several of them, erected at different elevations on the slope of the hill rising from the bank of the river, with well cultivated gardens, and tastefully disposed pleasure grounds, present an appearance truly picturesque: the inhabitants are amply supplied with water; the air is salubrious, and the surrounding scenery richly and pleasingly diversified. Some years since, Bewdley was a place of considerable trade, having two markets and four fairs, and for a long period was the mart from which the neighbouring towns were supplied with grocery and other articles of consumption; but in consequence of the recent construction of a canal from Stourport to Stourbridge, that portion of its trade has been diverted to other towns. The manufacture of woollen caps, known by the name of Dutch caps, was introduced here in consequence of the plague prevailing at Monmouth, where it had previously been carried on, and, being encouraged by legislative enactments in the reign of Elizabeth, it continued for some time to flourish, but has now declined, and the trade is principally in malt, the tanning of leather, and the making of combs. The market is on Saturday: fairs are held on April 23rd, July 26th, and December 10th and 11th. The government of the borough, by charter of incorporation granted by James I., and confirmed by Queen Anne, is vested in a bailiff, high steward, recorder, deputy recorder (who is usually the town clerk), and twelve capital burgesses. The bailiff, who is also coroner and clerk of the market, the late bailiff, and the recorder, are justices of the peace: the freedom of the borough is obtained only by gift. The corporation hold a court of session annually, in which the bailiff, the late bailiff, and the recorder, preside; a court of record for all pleas, and for the recovery of debts under £100, in which the bailiff, or, in his absence, a deputy appointed by him from among the capital burgesses, and the recorder, preside; and a court leet, at which constables and other officers are appointed. The town hall is a neat building of stone, erected in 1818; the front is decorated with six square pilasters supporting a pediment, in which are the arms of the family of Lyttelton; under the hall is the entrance into the market-place, which has an arcade on each side for stalls, and an open area in the centre; at the extremity are two small prisons, one for malefactors, the other for debtors. The elective franchise was conferred by James I., since which time Bewdley has returned one member to parliament: the right of election is vested exclusively in the bailiff and burgesses, thirteen in number; the bailiff is the returning officer.

The living is a perpetual curacy, in the archdeaconry of Salop, and diocese of Hereford, endowed with £8 per annum, the revenue of a dissolved chantry which formerly existed here, and in the patronage of the Rector of Ribbesford. The chapel, a neat stone edifice at the upper end of the street leading from the bridge, was erected in 1748, by means of a subscription among the inhabitants, aided by a brief, and the Rev. Thomas Knight, rector of Ribbesford, principally contributed to the erection of the tower. There are places of worship for Baptists, the Society of Friends, Wesleyan Methodists, and Unitarians. The free grammar school, founded and endowed in 1591, by William Monnox, or Mormoye, and further endowed in 1599, by Humphrey Hill, was made a royal foundation by charter of James I.; the endowment, augmented by subsequent benefactions, produces a salary of £26 per annum to the master, who has also a house rent-free. A collection of books, the gift of the Rev. Thomas Wigan, is deposited in the school, under the care of the master, and the rector of Ribbesford, for the use of the clergy and laity in the neighbourhood. The Blue-coat school, for thirty boys and thirty girls, is supported by subscription. Almshouses for six aged men, founded by Mr. Sayer, of Nettlestead, in the county of Suffolk, and endowed with £30 per annum, were rebuilt in 1763, by Sir Edward Winnington, Bart., member for the borough. Burlton's almshouses, for fourteen aged women, were founded and endowed in 1645; and eight other almshouses were erected and moderately endowed in 1693, by Mr. Thomas Cook. John Tombes, a celebrated biblical critic of the seventeenth century; and Richard Willis, Bishop of Winchester, and principal founder of the Society for Promoting Christian Knowledge, were natives of this town.

BEWERLEY, a township in that part of the parish of RIPON which is in the lower division of the wapentake of CLARO, West riding of the county of YORK, 11¼ miles (W. S. W.) from Ripon, containing 1408 inhabitants. The vicinity abounds with valuable lead mines, which are worked to a considerable extent.

BEWICK (NEW), a township in the parish of EGLINGHAM, northern division of COQUETDALE ward, county of NORTHUMBERLAND, 7¼ miles (S.E.) from Wooler, containing 93 inhabitants.

BEWICK (OLD), a township in the parish of EGLINGHAM, northern division of COQUETDALE ward, county of NORTHUMBERLAND, 7 miles (S.E. by E.) from Wooler, containing 247 inhabitants. Here was anciently a chapel, dedicated to the Holy Trinity, the ruins of which are situated a little to the north-west of the village. On Bewick hill is an encampment of a semicircular form, with a double rampart; and at Hare-up-burn, half a mile eastward, is another, supposed to have been an outwork: they were probably constructed by the ancient Britons, and were afterwards occupied by the Romans.

BEXHILL, a parish in the hundred of BEXHILL, rape of HASTINGS, county of SUSSEX, 5¼ miles (W. by S.) from Hastings, containing 1907 inhabitants. The living is a vicarage, in the archdeaconry of Lewes, and diocese of Chichester, rated in the king's books at £24. 10. 2½., and in the patronage of the Bishop of Chichester. The church is dedicated to St. Peter. The hundred of Bexhill is a franchise in the enjoyment of privileges similar to those possessed by the franchise of Battle. There are several chalybeate springs in the parish.

BEXINGTON, a hamlet (formerly a parish) in the liberty of BINDON, Blandford (South) division, though locally in the parish of Abbotsbury, hundred of Uggscombe, Dorchester division of the county of DORSET, 1 mile (N. W.) from Abbotsbury, with which the population is returned. The living, which was a rectory, was, in 1451, annexed to that of Puncknoll; and the church, which was dedicated to St. Giles, and stood on the sea-shore, not far from the ruins of Abbotsbury castle, has long been desecrated.

BEXLEY, a parish partly in the hundred of LESSNESS, but chiefly in the hundred of RUXLEY, lathe of SUTTON at HONE, county of KENT, 3 miles (W.) from Dartford, containing 2311 inhabitants. The living is a vicarage, in the exempt deanery of Shoreham, the whole of which is within the peculiar jurisdiction of the Archbishop of Canterbury, rated in the king's books at £13. 4. 7., and in the patronage of Viscount Sidney. The church is dedicated to St. Mary. In the reign of Elizabeth, the manor belonged to Camden, the celebrated antiquary, who bequeathed it in trust to the Master and Fellows of University College, Oxford, for the foundation and endowment of a professorship in history. A National school for the instruction of sixty boys and sixty girls was established in 1809, and is supported by voluntary subscription and an endowment of £8 per annum: there are also almshouses for twelve persons. The Right Hon. Nicholas Vansittart, on retiring from the chancellorship of the Exchequer, was created Baron Bexley, March 1st, 1823.

BEXTON, a township in the parish of KNUTSFORD, hundred of BUCKLOW, county palatine of CHESTER, 1 mile (S. S. E.) from Nether Knutsford, containing 69 inhabitants.

BEXWELL, a parish in the hundred of CLACKCLOSE, county of NORFOLK, 1 mile (E.) from Downham-Market, containing 63 inhabitants. The living is a discharged rectory, in the archdeaconry of Norfolk, and diocese of Norwich, rated in the king's books at £7. 11. 8., and in the patronage of the Bishop of Ely. The church, dedicated to St. Mary, is built of rag-stone obtained in the vicinity. Henry III. granted to William de Bexwell permission to hold a market on Thursday, and a fair on Whit-Monday.

BEYTON, otherwise BEIGHTON, a parish in the hundred of THEDWESTRY, county of SUFFOLK, 5½ miles (E. by S.) from Bury St. Edmund's, containing 238 inhabitants. The living is a discharged rectory, in the archdeaconry of Sudbury, and diocese of Norwich, rated in the king's books at £4. 3. 9., and in the patronage of the Crown. The church is dedicated to All Saints.

BIBURY, a parish comprising the chapelry of Winson, in the hundred of BRADLEY, and the tythings of Ablington and Arlington, in the hundred of BRIGHTWELL'S BARROW, county of GLOUCESTER, 3¾ miles (N. W.) from Fairford, and containing 990 inhabitants. The living is a vicarage, within the jurisdiction of the peculiar of the vicarage of Bibury, rated in the king's books at £13. 1. 5½., and in the patronage of E. Creswell, Esq. The church is dedicated to St. Mary. Thomas Tryon, author of a curious work, entitled "The Way to Health, Long Life, and Happiness," published in 1691, was a native of this place.

BICESTER, a market town and parish in the hundred of PLOUGHLEY, county of OXFORD, 12½ miles (N.E. by N.) from Oxford, and 55 (N.W. by W.) from London, containing 2544 inhabitants. This place, by the Saxons called *Burenceaster* and *Bernaceaster*, both implying a fortified place, is supposed to derive its name either from its founder, Birinus, a canonized Saxon prelate, or from Bernwood, a forest in Buckinghamshire, on the verge of which it is situated. A priory for canons of the Benedictine order was founded in 1182, and dedicated to St. Eadburg, by Gilbert Basset, Baron of Haddington, and his wife, Oglean Courtney, the revenue of which, at the dissolution, was £167. 2. 10. In 1355, a royal license was granted to Nicholas Jurdan, warden of the chapel of St. John the Baptist, for the establishment of an hospital for poor and infirm people, but the design does not appear to have been carried into execution. During the civil war in the reign of Charles I., the inhabitants suffered by repeated exactions levied on them by both parties, and, in 1643, a skirmish took place, in which the royalists were defeated and driven through the town. Bicester, which is divided into the townships of King's-End, and Market-End, part of the latter being in the parish of Caversfield, is situated in a valley, on the banks of a tributary stream which falls into the river Cherwell at Islip; it is handsomely built, and amply supplied with water. Two book clubs have been established, one by the clergy resident in the town and neighbourhood, the other by the inhabitants. The manufacture of leather slippers is extensively carried on, and the female inhabitants are employed in making bone lace: the town is noted for excellent malt liquor. The market is on Friday; and fairs are held on the Friday in Easter week, the first Friday in June, August 5th, and the third Friday in December; there are also statute fairs on the first three Fridays after Michaelmas. The county magistrates hold their petty sessions here for the district. The living is a discharged vicarage, in the archdeaconry and diocese of Oxford, rated in the king's books at £16, and in the patronage of Sir G. P. Turner, Bart. The church, dedicated to St. Eadburg, was rebuilt in 1400, on the site of the former edifice: it is a spacious structure with a lofty square tower; the interior contains many interesting monuments and some antique sculptures. There is a place of worship for Wesleyan Methodists. A school for the instruction and clothing of thirty boys is supported partly by subscription, and partly by the dividends on £1000 stock, given in 1811 by Mr. Walker, in fulfilment of the intention of his deceased father, out of which, £14 per annum is given in moieties to a Sunday school in connexion with the established church, and to a similar institution for the children of dissenters. Lands producing £200 per annum, and a few minor charitable bequests, are appropriated to the relief of the poor. In making some excavations, in 1819, the foundations of the conventual buildings belonging to the priory, a vast mass of sculptured fragments, pieces of painted glass, and other relics, were discovered.

BICKENHALL, a parish in the hundred of Abdick and Bulstone, county of Somerset, 5½ miles (S.E. by E.) from Taunton, containing 215 inhabitants. The living is a perpetual curacy, annexed to the rectory of Staple-Fitzpaine, in the archdeaconry of Taunton, and diocese of Bath and Wells.

BICKENHILL (CHURCH), a parish in the Solihull division of the hundred of Hemlingford, county of Warwick, 4 miles (N.E.) from Solihull, containing, with Lyndon and Marston Quarters, 648 inhabitants. The living is a discharged vicarage, in the archdeaconry of Coventry, and diocese of Lichfield and Coventry, rated in the king's books at £7. 17. 3., and endowed with £1000 parliamentary grant, and in the patronage of the Earl of Aylesford. The church is dedicated to St. Peter. The Warwick and Birmingham canal passes in the vicinity. Here was anciently a castle, the site of which is now occupied by a farm-house; and a beacon formerly stood where the church now is.

BICKER, a parish in the wapentake of Kirton, parts of Holland, county of Lincoln, 1¾ mile (N.E. by N.) from Donington, containing 627 inhabitants; but, with the extra-parochial liberties of Coppin-Sike and Ferry-Corner, 644. The living is a discharged vicarage, in the archdeaconry and diocese of Lincoln, rated in the king's books at £15, and in the patronage of the Dean and Chapter of Lincoln. The church is dedicated to St. Swithin. There is a place of worship for Wesleyan Methodists. The school has a small endowment for the instruction of children.

BICKERSTAFFE, a township in the parish of Ormskirk, hundred of West Derby, county palatine of Lancaster, 3¼ miles (S.E.) from Ormskirk, containing 1212 inhabitants. Coal is obtained in this township.

BICKERTON, a township in the parish of Malpas, higher division of the hundred of Broxton, county palatine of Chester, 4¾ miles (N.N.E.) from Malpas, containing 370 inhabitants. On the summit of a hill, in this township, there is an intrenchment called Maiden Castle.

BICKERTON, a township in the parish of Rothbury, western division of Coquetdale ward, county of Northumberland, 4¾ miles (W. by S.) from Rothbury, containing 18 inhabitants. Here is a school with an endowment of about £20 per annum.

BICKERTON, a township in the parish of Bilton, ainsty of the city, and East riding of the county, of York, 3½ miles (E.N.E.) from Wetherby, containing 149 inhabitants.

BICKINGTON, a parish in the hundred of Teignbridge, county of Devon, 3¼ miles (N.E.) from Ashburton, containing 301 inhabitants. The living is a perpetual curacy, annexed to the vicarage of Ashburton, in the peculiar jurisdiction of the Dean and Chapter of Exeter. There is a place of worship for Wesleyan Methodists. A fair for cattle is held on May 14th. There are two small endowed schools.

BICKINGTON (ABBOT'S), a parish in the hundred of Black Torrington, county of Devon, 9 miles (S.W. by W.) from Great Torrington, containing 75 inhabitants. The living is a perpetual curacy, in the archdeaconry of Totness, and diocese of Exeter, endowed with £200 private benefaction, £600 royal bounty, and £300 parliamentary grant, and in the patronage of Lord Rolle. The church, dedicated to St. James, has some remains of ancient stained glass. Limestone, a kind of hard blue stone used in building, and marble, are obtained in the neighbourhood.

BICKINGTON (HIGH), a parish in the hundred of North Tawton with Winkley, county of Devon, 7¼ miles (E. by N.) from Great Torrington, containing 748 inhabitants. The living is a rectory, in the archdeaconry of Barnstaple, and diocese of Exeter, rated in the king's books at £29. 7. 6., and in the patronage of the Rev. W. Stawell. The church is dedicated to St. Mary. A school was endowed with £10 per annum by Gertrude Pyncombe, in 1740.

BICKLEIGH, a parish in the hundred of Hayridge, county of Devon, 4¼ miles (S. by W.) from Tiverton, containing 273 inhabitants. The living is a rectory, in the archdeaconry and diocese of Exeter, rated in the king's books at £18. 4. 9½., and in the patronage of Sir H. Carew, Bart. The church is dedicated to St. Mary. The navigable river Exe here receives a small stream called the Dart, and is crossed by a bridge near the point of junction. Bamfylde Moore Carew, styled King of the Beggars, was born here, in 1693, of a respectable family, his father being rector of the parish; and hither he returned, at the close of his extraordinary wanderings, where he died in 1758.

BICKLEIGH, a parish in the hundred of Roborough, county of Devon, 7 miles (N.N.E.) from Plymouth, containing 457 inhabitants. The living is a vicarage, with the perpetual curacy of Sheepstor annexed, in the archdeaconry of Totness, and diocese of Exeter, rated in the king's books at £11. 4. 7., and in the patronage of Ralph Franco, Bart. The Plymouth railway passes along this parish. Here is a charity school; also an almshouse for six widows.

BICKLEY, a township in the parish of Malpas, higher division of the hundred of Broxton, county palatine of Chester, 3½ miles (E.N.E.) from Malpas, containing 431 inhabitants. There is a place of worship for Wesleyan Methodists. On the 18th of July, 1657, about a quarter of an acre of elevated ground, covered with full-grown trees, sunk suddenly with a thundering noise to such a depth below the surface of the surrounding ground, that even the summits of the trees were not visible, from their total immersion in water: the water has long been dried up, and the chasm, called the Barrel-Fall, from being situated on the Barrel farm, is now quite dry. In a field adjoining this farm, two tablets of copper, bearing an inscription importing that certain privileges were thereby granted by Trajan to some veteran soldiers serving in this island, and now deposited in the British Museum, were discovered in 1812.

BICKMERSH, a hamlet in that part of the parish of WELFORD which is in the Stratford division of the hundred of BARLICHWAY, county of WARWICK, 5¾ miles (S. by E.) from Alcester, containing, with Little Dorsington, 61 inhabitants.

BICKNELL, county of SOMERSET.—See BICKENHALL.

BICKNOLLER, a parish in the hundred of WILLITON and FREEMANNERS, county of SOMERSET, 13½ miles (W. by N.) from Bridg-water, containing 251 inhabitants. The living is a perpetual curacy, in the archdeaconry of Taunton, and diocese of Bath and Wells, endowed with £200 private benefaction, and £400 royal bounty, and in the patronage of the Dean and Chapter of Wells. Two fortifications, named Trendle Castle and Turk's Castle, together with the ruins of a beacon, occupy the summit of an eminence near the village; and a variety of Roman coins has been found in the vicinity.

BICKNOR, a parish in the hundred of EYHORNE, lathe of AYLESFORD, county of KENT, 4½ miles (S.W.) from Milton, containing 53 inhabitants. The living is a discharged rectory, in the archdeaconry and diocese of Canterbury, rated in the king's books at £5. 10., and in the patronage of the Crown. The church is dedicated to St. James.

BICKNOR (ENGLISH), a parish in the hundred of ST. BRIAVELLS, county of GLOUCESTER, 3¾ miles (N.) from Coleford, containing 534 inhabitants. The living is a rectory, in the archdeaconry and diocese of Gloucester, rated in the king's books at £13. 6. 8., and in the patronage of the Provost and Fellows of Queen's College, Oxford. The church, dedicated to St. Mary, stands within the area of an ancient fortification, the fosse belonging to which may still be traced. This parish lies within the forest of Dean, on the eastern bank of the Wye, opposite to Welch-Bicknor, and contains mines of coal and iron: the neighbourhood produces a considerable quantity of apples, particularly of that kind from which styre cider is made.

BICKNOR (WELCH), a parish in the lower division of the hundred of SKENFRETH, county of MONMOUTH, locally in the lower division of the hundred of Wormelow, county of Hereford, 7 miles (S. by W.) from Ross, containing 113 inhabitants. The living is a discharged rectory, in the archdeaconry and diocese of Hereford, rated in the king's books at £4. 6. 8., and in the patronage of the Crown. The church, dedicated to St. Margaret, contains an antique chalice, said to have been brought into Europe with the Saracens; the lid is of beaten silver, and it bears other evidences of high antiquity. At Courtfield, a private mansion about half a mile off, there is a Roman Catholic chapel; and tradition relates that Henry V. was nursed there, under the care of the Countess of Salisbury, who, according to the same authority, is represented by a recumbent stone figure in the church. The parish is almost surrounded by the river Wye.

BICKTON, a chapelry in the parish of ST. CHAD, within the liberty of the borough of SHREWSBURY, county of SALOP, 3½ miles (N.W. by W.) from Shrewsbury. The population is returned with the parish. The living is a perpetual curacy, in the archdeaconry of Salop, and diocese of Lichfield and Coventry, endowed with £200 royal bounty, and £200 parliamentary grant, and in the patronage of the Rev. Thomas Stedman. The navigable river Severn runs through the chapelry, which is also intersected by the Roman Watling-street.

BICTON, a parish in the eastern division of the hundred of BUDLEIGH, county of DEVON, 3¾ miles (W. S. W.) from Sidmouth, containing, with a portion of the tything of Rawleigh, 204 inhabitants. The living is a rectory, in the archdeaconry and diocese of Exeter, rated in the king's books at £12. 13. 4., and in the patronage of Lord Rolle. The church is dedicated to the Holy Trinity. According to Mr. Polwhele, the possessor of the manor of Bicton is obliged to "find a county gaol."

BIDBOROUGH, a parish in the hundred of WASHLINGSTONE, lathe of AYLESFORD, county of KENT, 3 miles (S.W.) from Tonbridge, containing 192 inhabitants. The living is a discharged rectory, in the archdeaconry and diocese of Rochester, rated in the king's books at £5. 4. 4½., endowed with £200 private benefaction, and £200 royal bounty, and in the patronage of the Rev. W. Gay. The church, dedicated to St. Lawrence, has a wide Norman doorway. There are some chalybeate springs in the parish.

BIDDENDEN, a parish in the hundred of BARCLAY, lathe of SCRAY, county of KENT, 5 miles (E. by N.) from Cranbrooke, containing 1544 inhabitants. The living is a rectory, in the archdeaconry and diocese of Canterbury, rated in the king's books at £35, and in the patronage of the Archbishop of Canterbury. The church, dedicated to All Saints, is a fine structure in the later style of English architecture, with an embattled tower and turret. This place was once famous for its clothing trade, now entirely decayed. Fairs for Welch cattle are held on Old Lady-day and November 8th. John Mayne, in 1566, bequeathed a sum for the erection of a school-house, and endowed it with a rent-charge of £20. 3. 4., which is applied for teaching twelve boys. An annual distribution of bread and cheese to the poor parishioners takes place on Easter-Sunday, the expense of which is defrayed from the rental of about twenty acres of land, the reputed bequest of the Biddenden Maids, two sisters of the name of Chulkhurst, who, according to an unauthenticated tradition, were born joined together by the hips and shoulders, in the year 1100; and having lived in that state to the age of thirty-four, died within about six hours of each other. To perpetuate the remembrance of this extraordinary circumstance, cakes, bearing a corresponding impression of the figures of two females, are given, on the same day, to all who apply. Hasted, coinciding in the general opinion of the fabulousness of this tale, states that the print on the cakes is of modern origin, and considers the land to have been given by two maidens named Preston.

BIDDENHAM, a parish in the hundred of WILLEY, county of BEDFORD, 2¾ miles (W. by N.) from Bedford, containing 393 inhabitants. The living is a discharged vicarage, in the archdeaconry of Bedford, and diocese of Lincoln, rated in the king's books at £8, endowed with £400 private benefaction, and £600 royal bounty, and in the patronage of Viscount Hampden. The church is dedicated to St. James.

BIDDESCOTE, a township in that part of the parish of TAMWORTH which is in the southern division of the hundred of OFFLOW, county of STAFFORD, 1 mile (S. S. W.) from Tamworth, containing 70 inhabitants.

BIDDESHAM, a parish in the hundred of BEMPSTONE, county of SOMERSET, 3 miles (W. by S.) from Axbridge, containing 136 inhabitants. The living is a perpetual curacy, in the peculiar jurisdiction of the Dean of Wells, and in the patronage of the Dean and Chapter thereof.

BIDDESTONE (ST. NICHOLAS and ST. PETER), a parish in the hundred of CHIPPENHAM, county of WILTS, 4¼ miles (W.) from Chippenham, containing 414 inhabitants. The living is a discharged rectory, in the archdeaconry of Wilts, and diocese of Salisbury, rated in the king's books at £2. 18. 4., and in the patronage of the Warden and Fellows of Winchester College. The church contains a monument to the memory of Edmund Smith, A. M., a poet of some repute, who died in this neighbourhood in 1709.

BIDDLESDON, a parish in the hundred and county of BUCKINGHAM, 3½ miles (N. E. by E.) from Brackley, containing 175 inhabitants. The living is a perpetual curacy, in the archdeaconry of Buckingham, and diocese of Lincoln, endowed with £200 private benefaction, and £200 royal bounty, and in the patronage of Mrs. Verney. The church is dedicated to St. Margaret. An abbey of Cistercian monks was founded here in 1147, the revenue of which, at the dissolution, was £142. 1. 3. In 1315, Edward II. granted to the convent a market on Monday, and a fair on St. Margaret's day.

BIDDLESTON, a township in the parish of ALLENTON, western division of COQUETDALE ward, county of NORTHUMBERLAND, 7¾ miles (N. W. by W.) from Rothbury, containing 166 inhabitants. The manor was granted, in 1272, to Sir Walter Selby, Knt., and has ever since continued in the possession of his descendants. King James held this ancient family in such high estimation that he bestowed the honour of Knighthood upon five of its members. The manor-house, a commodious stone building of modern erection, occupies the summit of a gentle declivity, commanding, on the south, a fine prospect of the vale of Coquet.

BIDDULPH, a parish in the northern division of the hundred of PIREHILL, county of STAFFORD, 3¼ miles (S. E. by S.) from Congleton, containing 1666 inhabitants. The living is a discharged vicarage, in the archdeaconry of Stafford, and diocese of Lichfield and Coventry, rated in the king's books at £4. 9. 8., endowed with £400 private benefaction, £200 royal bounty, and £900 parliamentary grant, and in the patronage of J. Bateman, Esq. The church is dedicated to St. Lawrence. On Biddulph moor there is a place of worship for Wesleyan Methodists. The parish contains collieries, manufactories for cotton and earthenware, and iron-works. It is in the honour of Tutbury, duchy of Lancaster, and within the jurisdiction of a court of pleas held at Tutbury every third Tuesday, for the recovery of debts under 40*s*. Here is a school with an endowment of about £12 per annum.

Corporate Seal.

BIDEFORD, a sea-port, incorporated market town, and parish, having separate jurisdiction, locally in the hundred of Shebbear, county of DEVON, 39 miles (N. W. by W.) from Exeter, and 201 (W. by S.) from London, containing 4053 inhabitants. This place, called also *Bytheford*, of which its modern appellation is a variation, derives its name from being situated near an ancient ford on the river Torridge. It was a town of some importance in the time of the Saxons: in early records it is styled a borough, and in the reigns of Edward I. and II. returned members to parliament; but the burgesses having pleaded inability to supply the usual pecuniary allowance to their representatives, this distinction was withdrawn. In 1271, Richard de Grenville, to whose ancestor Bideford was granted in the reign of William Rufus, obtained for it a market and a fair; and, in 1574, Queen Elizabeth incorporated the inhabitants, and made the town a free borough. From that time it rapidly increased as a place of trade, and the expeditions of Sir Walter Raleigh to Virginia, and of Sir Richard Grenville to Carolina, established the basis of its foreign commerce. During the civil war in the reign of Charles I., two small forts were erected on the banks of the river, and a third at Appledore, which were garrisoned in the interest of the parliament, until they were taken for the king by Col. Digby, after the battle of Torrington, September 2nd, 1643, who soon after entered this town, which had been evacuated by the parliamentary troops. From this period till the beginning of the eighteenth century, Bideford was in its highest prosperity. The weaving of silk was introduced in 1650, and, after the revocation of the edict of Nantes, in 1685, many French Protestants settled in the town, and established the manufacture of silk and cotton; a great quantity of wool was imported from Spain, and, in 1699, its trade with Newfoundland was inferior only to that of London and Exeter: from 1700 to 1755, the imports of tobacco exceeded those of every port, except London. The town is situated on the river Torridge, which in spring tides rises to the height of eighteen feet above the level of high water mark: the greater part is built on the acclivity of its western bank, and is connected with that on the eastern side by a noble stone bridge of twenty-four arches, of sufficient span to allow free passage for vessels of sixty tons' burden. The bridge was erected in the early part of the fourteenth century, by a subscription raised in the counties of Devon and Cornwall, under the auspices of Grandison, Bishop of Exeter, who, being influenced by a dream of Gornard, the parish priest, granted indulgences to all who should contribute to the work: an estate, called the Bridge estate, for keeping it in repair, is vested in trustees, who are a body corporate, and have a common seal. The town consists principally of two spacious streets, well paved and lighted; the houses are in general indifferently built, many of them being of timber and brick, plaistered over, though there are some of more respectable appearance: the inhabitants are amply supplied with water. Its vicinity to Appledore renders Bideford a place of resort for company frequenting that watering-place: there are assembly-rooms on the quay. The port, including within its jurisdiction the harbours of Clovelly and Hartland, and a convenient station for wind-bound vessels, carries on a considerable colonial and coasting trade: the exports are sails, cordage, and articles of general supply to the fisheries of Newfoundland, oak-bark to Ireland, apples to Scotland, earthenware to Wales, and corn and flour to Bristol; the imports are timber from America and the Baltic, and coal from Bristol and Wales. The river, in spring tides, is navigable for vessels of three hundred tons' burden, as far as the bridge, two miles and a half above which it is connected, by means of a sea-lock, with the Torrington canal. The quay, one thousand two hundred feet in length, and of proportionate breadth, has been greatly improved by the corporation; it is very convenient for loading and unloading, and is accessible to ships of considerable burden. The number of vessels belonging to the port, according to the return of 1828, is ninety-nine, averaging a burden of ninety tons', the majority of which are employed in the coasting trade: there are also one hundred and sixty licensed boats engaged in the fishery. Ship-building is extensively carried on: during the late war, several frigates were launched at this port, and there are eight or ten dock-yards, in which smaller vessels are built. The principal articles of manufacture are ropes, sails, and common earthenware; there are also several tan-yards, and a small lace-manufactory. The market days are, Tuesday for grain, and Saturday for provisions: fairs are held on February 14th, July 18th, and November 13th. The government, by charter of incorporation granted in the 16th of Elizabeth, and confirmed and extended in the 7th of James I., is vested in a mayor, recorder, seven aldermen, and ten burgesses, assisted by a town clerk, two serjeants at mace, and subordinate officers. The mayor (who is chosen by the corporation on the 21st of September), the recorder, and one of the aldermen (who is annually elected for that purpose), are justices of the peace; a chief constable, and twelve petty constables, are appointed annually by the mayor. The corporation hold a court of general session quarterly, a court of petty session monthly, and a court of record every third week, for the recovery of debts to any amount. The town hall, erected in 1698, is a neat and commodious building; underneath are two prisons, one for malefactors, and the other for debtors: a handsome hall was erected in 1758, for the trustees of the Bridge estate, with a school-room adjoining.

The living is a rectory, in the archdeaconry of Barnstaple, and diocese of Exeter, rated in the king's books at £27. 7. 6., and in the patronage of Lewis William Buck, Esq. The church, dedicated to St. Mary, is a spacious cruciform structure, in the early style of English architecture; within are a handsome stone screen, a Norman font, and some interesting monuments. There are places of worship for Baptists, Independents, and Wesleyan Methodists. The free grammar school is of remote foundation: it was rebuilt in 1657, and, in 1689, was endowed by Mrs. Susannah Stucley, with an estate of £200 value; a good house was purchased for the master with money arising from the sale of timber on the estate: there are at present only three boys on the foundation, who are nominated by the corporation. A charity school for reading, writing, and arithmetic, is supported by the trustees of the Bridge estate; and a National school, in which one hundred and fifty boys, and one hundred and fifty girls are taught, besides other schools for the children of dissenters, are supported by subscription. Almshouses in Maiden-street, for seven poor families, were erected in 1646, by Mr. John Strange, alderman of Bideford; and an hospital in the Old town, for twelve poor families, was built pursuant to the will of Mr. Henry Amory, who died in 1663. In 1810, Mrs. Margaret Newcommen left a considerable fund for poor dissenters in this and the neighbouring parishes. Mines of culm and black mineral paint are found in the vicinity. Sir Richard Grenville, who was a native of this town, distinguished himself in 1591, in an action fought near the island of Flores, with a Spanish fleet, consisting of fifty-three sail, and ten thousand men, having only his own ship, and one hundred and eighty men; notwithstanding this inferiority of force, he gallantly repulsed the enemy fifteen times, destroyed four of their ships, and upwards of one thousand men, nor did he surrender till he had spent all his ammunition, and then only on honourable terms. Thomas Stucley, an eccentric character, the supposed original of Sterne's Captain Shandy; Dr. John Shebbeare, a noted political writer, born in 1709; the Rev. Zachary Mudge, a learned divine, and master of the grammar school; were also natives of this place. Hervey, author of the "Meditations," was curate here from 1738 till 1742.

BIDFORD, a parish (formerly a market town) in the Stratford division of the hundred of BARLICHWAY, county of WARWICK, 4 miles (S. by E.) from Alcester, comprising the hamlets of Barton, Broom, and Marlclift, and containing 1219 inhabitants. The living is a discharged vicarage, in the archdeaconry and diocese of Worcester, rated in the king's books at £7. 10. 7½., endowed with £800 parliamentary grant, and in the patronage of Lady Skipwith. The church is dedicated to St. Lawrence. This place stands on the northern bank of the navigable river Avon, and the river Arrow runs through the parish, in which there are several stone quarries. The market was held on Friday, but it has long been discontinued.

BIDICK (SOUTH), a township in the parish of HOUGHTON le SPRING, northern division of EASINGTON ward, county palatine of DURHAM, 6¾ miles (S. W. by W.) from Sunderland, containing 167 inhabitants. The unfortunate James Drummond, commonly called Duke of Perth, sought an asylum here after the rebellion of 1745, where he lived concealed until his death in 1782.

BIDSTONE, a parish in the lower division of the hundred of WIRRALL, county palatine of CHESTER, comprising the chapelry of Birkenhead, and the townships of Bidstone with Ford, Claughton with Grange, Moreton, and Saughall-Massey, and containing 1014 inhabitants, of which number, 257 are in the township of Bidstone with Ford, 9½ miles (N.) from Great Neston. The living is a perpetual curacy, in the archdeaconry and diocese of Chester, endowed with £200 and £35 per annum private benefaction, £200 royal bounty, and £1300 parliamentary grant, and in the patronage of the Bishop of Chester. A lighthouse, standing on an elevated site in this township, was purchased by the corporation of Liverpool, under an act obtained in 1762, and is supported by a duty levied on all vessels sailing to or from that port. A school is endowed with £8 per annum, and a house and garden for the master.

BIERLEY (NORTH), a chapelry in the parish of BRADFORD, wapentake of MORLEY, West riding of the county of YORK, 2 miles (S. E by S.) from Bradford, containing 6070 inhabitants. The living is a perpetual curacy, in the archdeaconry and diocese of York, endowed with £1800 parliamentary grant, and in the patronage of Miss Currer. The chapel lately received an addition of three hundred and twenty free sittings, toward defraying the expense of which the Incorporated Society for the enlargement of churches and chapels granted £200. There are extensive iron-works within this chapelry, and throughout the entire parish the woollen manufacture prevails to a very considerable extent.

BIERTON, a parish in the hundred of AYLESBURY, county of BUCKINGHAM, 1½ mile (N. E. by E.) from Aylesbury, containing, with the hamlet of Broughton, 620 inhabitants. The living is a vicarage, with the perpetual curacies of Quarrendon and Stoke-Mandeville annexed, in the peculiar jurisdiction and patronage of the Dean and Chapter of Lincoln, rated in the king's books at £20. 10. The church is dedicated to St. James. A school is endowed with £10 per annum; and Mr. Hill, in 1723, gave property, directing the proceeds to be applied in clothing poor men, and in educating and apprenticing children.

BIGBURY, a parish in the hundred of ERMINGTON, county of DEVON, 3½ miles (S.) from Modbury, containing 536 inhabitants. The living is a rectory, in the archdeaconry of Totness, and diocese of Exeter, rated in the king's books at £28. 7. 11., and in the patronage of P. Browne, Esq. The church is dedicated to St. Lawrence. The parish is bounded on the east by the river Avon, which falls into Bigbury bay, an inlet of the English channel, the navigation of which is somewhat dangerous: the coast is indented with several coves, which afford convenient retreats for smugglers.

BIGBY, a parish in the southern division of the wapentake of YARBOROUGH, parts of LINDSEY, county of LINCOLN, 4½ miles (E.) from Glandford-Bridge, containing 190 inhabitants. The living is a rectory, in the archdeaconry and diocese of Lincoln, rated in the king's books at £13. 10. 10., and in the patronage of Robert C. Elwes, Esq. The church is dedicated to All Saints.

BIGGE'S, or CARLISLE'S, QUARTER, a township in the parish of LONG HORSLEY, western division of MORPETH ward, county of NORTHUMBERLAND, containing 262 inhabitants.

BIGGIN, a township in that part of the parish of WIRKSWORTH which is in the hundred of APPLETREE, county of DERBY, 5½ miles (E. by N.) from Ashbourn, containing 160 inhabitants. This place is in the honour of Tutbury, duchy of Lancaster, and within the jurisdiction of a court of pleas held at Tutbury every third Tuesday, for the recovery of debts under 40s. Here was formerly a church, or chapel, but for many years not even the site of it has been known.

BIGGIN, a township in the parish of KIRK-FENTON, partly within the liberty of ST. PETER of YORK, East riding, and partly in the upper division of the wapentake of BARKSTONE-ASH, West riding, of the county of YORK, 6¾ miles (W. N. W.) from Selby, containing 164 inhabitants. The plant teasel (*Dipsacus Fullonum*), used in dressing woollen cloth, is said to have been first cultivated here in this county.

BIGGLESWADE, a market town and parish in the hundred of BIGGLESWADE, county of BEDFORD, 10½ miles (E. S.E.) from Bedford, and 45 (N. N. W.) from London, on the road to York, containing, with the hamlet of Holme with Stratton, 2778 inhabitants. This town is pleasantly situated on the river Ivel, which is crossed by two stone bridges, and which, by act of parliament, has been made navigable to its junction with the Ouse, whereby the neighbourhood is supplied with coal, timber, and various articles of merchandise. A considerable part of the town was destroyed by fire in 1785, to which circumstance its improved condition and handsome appearance may be attributed. The houses are uniformly built of brick, the air is pure and salubrious, and the inhabitants are amply supplied with excellent water from numerous springs. The environs, abounding with elegant villas and picturesque scenery, present a pleasing appearance. The making of white thread-lace and edging affords employment to a considerable part of the female population; but the town derives its principal support from being situated on the north road, whence the continued traffic it enjoys. The market, which is on Wednesday, is considerable for grain: fairs are held on February 13th, the Saturday in Easter week, Whit-Monday, August 2nd, and November 8th, for horses and live stock of every kind. The town is within the jurisdiction of the county magistrates, who hold a petty session for the hundreds of Biggles wade, Clifton, and Wixamtree.

The living is a discharged vicarage, in the peculiar jurisdiction and patronage of the Prebendary of Biggleswade in the Cathedral Church of Lincoln, rated in the king's books at £10. The church, dedicated to St. Andrew, and formerly collegiate, is an ancient and venerable structure, in the early style of English architecture; the chancel was rebuilt in 1467, by John Reeding, Archdeacon of Bedford, whose arms are carved on some ancient wooden stalls in the north aisle. A chantry belonging to the guild of the Holy Trinity was anciently founded in the church, the revenue of which, at the dissolution, was £7. There are places of worship for Baptists and Wesleyan Methodists. Sir John Cotton, in 1726, bequeathed £1800 for charitable uses, directing it to be laid out in the purchase of lands, two-ninths of the rental of which were to be given as a salary to a schoolmaster, who, together with the boys, is nominated by the lord of the manor, and one-ninth to the vicar of the parish: the proceeds are about £36 per annum; twelve boys are taught gratuitously. There is also an endowment of £13 a year, given by Edward Peake, in 1755, for the instruction of eight more children. In 1770, a yellow earthen pot, containing three hundred gold coins of the reign of Henry VI., was discovered by a ploughman, in a field near the manor-house; they were rather larger in diameter than a half-crown, and twenty grains less in weight than a guinea. On the obverse was a ship, with the figure of a king in armour, holding in one hand a sword, and in the other a shield, on which were quartered the arms of England and

France; on the side of the ship was a lion passant, between two fleurs de lis: on the reverse was a cross between four lions passant, crowned with the legend "*Jesus autem transiens per medium illorum ibat.*"

BIGHTON, a parish in the hundred of BISHOP'S SUTTON, Alton (North) division of the county of SOUTHAMPTON, 1¾ mile (N. E. by E.) from New Alresford, containing 231 inhabitants. The living is a rectory, in the archdeaconry and diocese of Winchester, rated in the king's books at £19. 8. 1½., and in the patronage of the Duke of Buckingham. The church is dedicated to All Saints. Bighton is within the jurisdiction of the Cheyney Court held at Winchester every Thursday, for the recovery of debts to any amount.

BIGLANDS, a joint township with Gamelsby, in the parish of AIKTON, ward and county of CUMBERLAND, 4 miles (N.) from Wigton, containing, with Gamelsby, 191 inhabitants. A sulphureous spring was discovered here about 1775, the water of which is much used for cutaneous complaints.

BIGNALL-END, a township in the parish of AUDLEY, northern division of the hundred of PIREHILL, county of STAFFORD, containing 308 inhabitants.

BIGNOR, a parish in the hundred of BURY, rape of ARUNDEL, county of SUSSEX, 5½ miles (S. by E.) from Petworth, containing 138 inhabitants. The living is a rectory, in the archdeaconry and diocese of Chichester, rated in the king's books at £8. 3. 6½., and in the patronage of the Crown. The church is chiefly in the early English style, but has some decorated portions intermixed. There are vestiges of a Roman pavement at a short distance eastward from the village.

BILBOROUGH, a parish in the southern division of the wapentake of BROXTOW, county of NOTTINGHAM, 4 miles (W. N. W.) from Nottingham, containing 291 inhabitants. The living is a discharged rectory, in the archdeaconry of Nottingham, and diocese of York, rated in the king's books at £3. 12. 6., and in the patronage of T. Webb Edge, Esq. The church is dedicated to St. Martin. Here are some coal-works. The hamlet of Broxtow, in this parish, was anciently a place of considerable importance, having given name to the wapentake.

BILBROUGH, a parish in the ainsty of the city, and East riding of the county, of YORK, 4¼ miles (N.E.) from Tadcaster, containing 260 inhabitants. The living is a perpetual curacy, in the archdeaconry and diocese of York, and in the patronage of T. L. Fairfax, Esq. Thomas, Lord Fairfax, the celebrated parliamentary general, who died in 1671, was interred in the church here. A school is endowed with about £15 per annum, for the instruction of twenty-two children.

BILBY, a joint township with Barnby-Moor, in that part of the parish of BLYTH which is in the Hatfield division of the wapentake of BASSETLAW, county of NOTTINGHAM, 4½ miles (W. N. W.) from East Retford. The population is returned with Barnby-Moor.

BILDESTON, or BILSON, a parish (formerly a market town) in the hundred of COSFORD, county of SUFFOLK, 14½ miles (W. N. W.) from Ipswich, and 66 (N. E. by N.) from London, containing 814 inhabitants. The living is a rectory, in the archdeaconry of Sudbury, and diocese of Norwich, rated in the king's books at £12. 16. 10½., and in the patronage of the Rev. Charles Johnson. The church, dedicated to St. Mary, is a handsome spacious structure. There is a place of worship for Baptists. The manufacture of blankets and woollen cloth was formerly carried on here; but at present the chief employment of the inhabitants consists in spinning yarn. The market, now disused, was held on Wednesday: there are fairs on Ash-Wednesday and Holy Thursday. In 1535, a school-house was given to the parish, but the name of the donor has not been preserved.

BILHAM, a township in that part of the parish of HOOTON-PAGNELL which is in the northern division of the wapentake of STRAFFORTH and TICKHILL, West riding of the county of YORK, 7 miles (W. N. W.) from Doncaster, containing 74 inhabitants. Strata of coal and limestone, and a kind of sand used in the foundries at Rotherham and Sheffield, exist here.

BILLERICAY, a market town and chapelry in the parish of GREAT BURSTEAD, hundred of BARSTABLE, county of ESSEX, 9½ miles (S. S. W.) from Chelmsford, and 24 (E. N. E.) from London. The population is returned with the parish. The name, anciently *Belenca*, is of uncertain derivation, and of the history of the place, few particulars of importance are recorded. From the discovery of Roman urns containing bones, glass vessels, and other relics, and from the traces of a Roman vallum and ditch at Blunt's Walls, nearly a mile distant, this place appears to have been not unknown to the Romans, who had probably a station here, though the exact site has not been ascertained. The town is pleasantly situated on an eminence overlooking an extensive and richly cultivated vale, and commanding a fine prospect of the surrounding country, which abounds with beautiful scenery, and a distant view of the shipping on the Thames: it has of late been much improved by the erection of several large and well-built houses. The only branches of manufacture are those of silk braid laces and wire riband, and they are at present declining. The market is on Tuesday: fairs are held on August 2nd and October 9th, principally for cattle. Courts leet and baron are held occasionally, at the former of which constables and other officers for the internal regulation of the town are appointed. The living is a perpetual curacy, annexed to the vicarage of Great Burstead, in the archdeaconry of Essex, and diocese of London, endowed with £1200 parliamentary grant. The chapel, dedicated to St. Mary Magdalene, is an ancient brick building in the centre of the town. There are places of worship for Baptists, the Society of Friends, and Independents. The Rev. Mr. Bayley, rector of Benfleet, in 1654, bequeathed an estate of £20 per annum for the education of ten poor children. There is a parochial almshouse for poor females.

BILLESDON, a parish in the hundred of GARTREE, county of LEICESTER, 8½ miles (E. by S.) from Leicester, containing, with the chapelries of Goadby and Rolleston, 751 inhabitants. The living is a vicarage, in the archdeaconry of Leicester, and diocese of Lincoln, rated in the king's books at £14. 10., and in the patronage of the Rev. H. Greene. The church is dedicated to St. John the Baptist. A school-house was built, in 1650, by William Sharp, which has since been endowed, by various benefactors, with property producing about £10 per annum. Here are some traces of a Roman camp, fortified with a deep ditch and a high rampart.

BILLESLEY, a parish in the Stratford division of the hundred of BARLICHWAY, county of WARWICK, 3¾ miles (W. N. W.) from Stratford upon Avon, containing 26 inhabitants. The living is a discharged rectory, in the archdeaconry and diocese of Worcester, rated in the king's books at £5. 4. 7., endowed with £400 private benefaction, and £400 royal bounty, and in the patronage of M. and J. Mills, Esqrs. The church is dedicated to All Saints.

BILLING (GREAT), a parish in the hundred of SPELHOE, county of NORTHAMPTON, 4 miles (E. N. E.) from Northampton, containing 334 inhabitants. The living is a rectory, in the archdeaconry of Northampton, and diocese of Peterborough, rated in the king's books at £19, and in the patronage of the Principal and Fellows of Brasenose College, Oxford. The church is dedicated to St. Andrew. This parish has a communication with the North sea, through the Northampton canal and the river Nen. An almshouse was founded by John Freeman, Esq., in the reign of James I., for one man and four women. Sir Isaac Wake, a distinguished scholar and diplomatist in the same reign, was born here, in 1575.

BILLING (LITTLE), a parish in the hundred of SPELHOE, county of NORTHAMPTON, 3¼ miles (E. by N.) from Northampton, containing 76 inhabitants. The living is a rectory, in the archdeaconry of Northampton, and diocese of Peterborough, rated in the king's books at £10. 2. 11., and in the patronage of Earl Brownlow. The church is dedicated to All Saints. The river Nen passes through the parish.

BILLINGBOROUGH, a parish in the wapentake of AVELAND, parts of KESTEVEN, county of LINCOLN, 3 miles (E.) from Folkingham, containing 745 inhabitants. The living is a discharged vicarage, in the archdeaconry and diocese of Lincoln, rated in the king's books at £6. 1. 8., and in the patronage of Earl Fortescue. The church, dedicated to St. Andrew, has a fine tower and spire, and displays chiefly the decorated style of English architecture. Mary Toller, in 1671, gave land producing about £25 per annum, for the endowment of a free school.

BILLINGE (CHAPEL-END), a chapelry in that part of the parish of WIGAN which is in the hundred of WEST DERBY, county palatine of LANCASTER, 5½ miles (S. W.) from Wigan, containing 1002 inhabitants. The living is a perpetual curacy, in the archdeaconry and diocese of Chester, endowed with £200 private benefaction, £200 royal bounty, and £1000 parliamentary grant, and in the patronage of the Rector of Wigan. The manufacture of cotton is here carried on to a limited extent. A charity school here has a trifling endowment.

BILLINGE (HIGHER-END), a township in that part of the parish of WIGAN which is in the hundred of WEST DERBY, county palatine of LANCASTER, 5 miles (W. S. W.) from Wigan, containing 670 inhabitants. A school here is endowed with £20 per annum.

BILLINGFORD, a parish in the hundred of EARSHAM, county of NORFOLK, 1½ mile (E.) from Scole, containing 190 inhabitants. The living is a discharged rectory, with that of Little Thorpe annexed, in the archdeaconry of Norfolk, and diocese of Norwich, rated in the king's books at £9, and in the patronage of George Wilson, Esq. The church is dedicated to St. Leonard.

BILLINGFORD, a parish in the hundred of EYNSFORD, county of NORFOLK, 3½ miles (S. S. W.) from Foulsham, containing 248 inhabitants. The living is a discharged rectory, in the archdeaconry of Norfolk, and diocese of Norwich, rated in the king's books at £7. 10., and in the patronage of T. W. Coke, Esq. A grant of a fair to be held here was obtained in the 33rd of Edward I. At Beck Hall, in this parish, now the property of Mr. Coke, an hospital, with a chapel dedicated to St. Thomas à Becket, was founded in the beginning of the reign of Henry III.

BILLINGHAM, a parish in the north-eastern division of STOCKTON ward, county palatine of DURHAM, comprising the chapelry of Wolviston, and the townships of Billingham, Cowpen-Bewley, and Newton-Bewley, and containing 1154 inhabitants, of which number, 395 are in the township of Billingham, 2½ miles (E.) from Stockton upon Tees. The living is a vicarage, in the archdeaconry and diocese of Durham, rated in the king's books at £11. 3. 1½., and in the patronage of the Dean and Chapter of Durham. The church is dedicated to St. Cuthbert. This is a place of considerable antiquity, having been the scene of a battle fought in the time of Eardulph, King of Northumberland. Here is a school with a small endowment.

BILLINGHAY, a parish in the first division of the wapentake of LANGOE, parts of KESTEVEN, county of LINCOLN, 9½ miles (N. E.) from Sleaford, containing, with the chapelry of Walcott, and the township of Dogdyke, 1554 inhabitants. The living is a discharged vicarage, in the archdeaconry and diocese of Lincoln, rated in the king's books at £13. 14., and in the patronage of Earl Fitzwilliam. The church is dedicated to St. Michael. There is a place of worship for Wesleyan Methodists.

BILLINGLEY, a township in that part of the parish of DARFIELD which is in the northern division of the wapentake of STRAFFORTH and TICKHILL, West riding of the county of YORK, 6½ miles (E. by S.) from Barnesley, containing 214 inhabitants.

BILLINGSHURST, a parish in the hundred of WEST EASWRITH, rape of ARUNDEL, county of SUSSEX, 6¾ miles (S. W. by W.) from Horsham, containing 1369 inhabitants, of which number, 794 are in East Billingshurst, and 575 in West Billingshurst. The living is a vicarage, in the archdeaconry and diocese of Chichester, rated in the king's books at £9. 6. 0½., and in the patronage of Sir Harry Goring, Bart. The church is dedicated to St. Mary. There is a place of worship for Unitarians. The river Arun rises in this parish, and the Arun and Wey Junction canal passes through it: it is also intersected by a Roman road, called Stanestreet.

BILLINGSIDE, a township in that part of the parish of LANCHESTER which is in the western division of CHESTER ward, county palatine of DURHAM, 13 miles (N. W.) from Durham, containing 45 inhabitants.

BILLINGSLEY, a parish in the hundred of STOTTESDEN, county of SALOP, 5½ miles (S. by W.) from Bridgenorth, containing 176 inhabitants. The living is a discharged rectory, in the archdeaconry of Salop, and diocese of Hereford, rated in the king's books at £4. 13. 4., endowed with £200 private benefaction, and £200 royal bounty, and in the patronage of the Marquis of Cleveland. The church is dedicated to St. Mary. Under the name *Billigesleage*, historians mention this place as the scene of a congress, in 1055, between King Harold and Griffin Prince of Wales, at which they engaged to observe mutual peace and amity. Dr. Thomas Hyde, Professor of Oriental Literature at Oxford, was born here, in 1636.

BILLINGTON, a chapelry in the parish of LEIGHTON-BUZZARD, hundred of MANSHEAD, county of BEDFORD, 2 miles (S. E.) from Leighton-Buzzard, containing 237 inhabitants. The living is a perpetual curacy, endowed with £200 parliamentary grant, and within the peculiar jurisdiction and patronage of the Prebendary of Leighton-Buzzard in the Cathedral Church of Lincoln.

BILLINGTON, a chapelry in the parish, and lower division of the hundred, of BLACKBURN, county palatine of LANCASTER, 5½ miles (N. N. E.) from Blackburn, containing 922 inhabitants. The living is a perpetual curacy, in the archdeaconry and diocese of Chester, endowed with £200 private benefaction, £600 royal bounty, and £600 parliamentary grant, and in the patronage of the Vicar of Blackburn. Here is a free school, with an endowment of about £14 per annum.

BILLISBORROW, a township in the parish of GARSTANG, hundred of AMOUNDERNESS, county palatine of LANCASTER, 4½ miles (S.S.E.) from Garstang, containing 209 inhabitants. There is a place of worship for Wesleyan Methodists. John Cross, in 1718, bequeathed property producing about £46 per annum, for the endowment of a free school for children of the townships of Billisborrow and Myerscough.

BILLOCKBY, a parish in the western division of the hundred of FLEGG, county of NORFOLK, 2½ miles (N.E.) from Acle, containing 63 inhabitants. The living is a discharged rectory, in the archdeaconry and diocese of Norwich, rated in the king's books at £2. 8. 9., endowed with £400 royal bounty, and in the patronage of Charles Lucas, Esq. The church is dedicated to All Saints.

BILL-QUAY, a village in the chapelry of NETHER HEWORTH, parish of JARROW, eastern division of CHESTER ward, county palatine of DURHAM, 3½ miles (E.) from Gateshead. The population is returned with Nether Heworth. The village lies on the southern bank of the river Tyne. The Arkendale mining company have an extensive refinery here for extracting silver from lead-ore, and an establishment for making sheet lead; and there are manufactories for glass bottles, fire-bricks, colours, and mustard; also an establishment for the distillation of oil from bones, the calx of which, after having been reduced to ashes, is used in making ivory-black, &c.; there is likewise a yard for ship-building. In a deep dene, called Catdene, now overgrown with forest trees and thorns, are extensive quarries, from which it is said the stone was obtained for building the walls of Newcastle.

BILLY-ROW, a joint township with Crook, in the parish of BRANCEPETH, north-western division of DARLINGTON ward, county palatine of DURHAM, 7 miles (N.W. by N.) from Bishop-Auckland. The population is returned with Crook.

BILNEY (EAST), a parish in the hundred of LAUNDITCH, county of NORFOLK, 5 miles (N.N.W.) from East Dereham, containing 172 inhabitants. The living is a discharged rectory, in the archdeaconry and diocese of Norwich, rated in the king's books at £5. 14. 2., endowed with £200 private benefaction, and £200 royal bounty, and in the patronage of the Rev. C. Munnings. The church is dedicated to St. Mary. Thomas Bilney, a learned divine, who was burnt at Norwich in 1531, for preaching against popery, is said to have been born here.

BILNEY (WEST), a parish in the Lynn division of the hundred of FREEBRIDGE, county of NORFOLK, 7 miles (S.E. by E.) from Lynn-Regis, containing 193 inhabitants. The living is a perpetual curacy, in the archdeaconry and diocese of Norwich, endowed with £600 royal bounty, and £200 parliamentary grant, and in the patronage of John Dalton, Esq. The church is dedicated to St. Cecilia.

BILSBY, a parish in the Wold division of the hundred of CALCEWORTH, parts of LINDSEY, county of LINCOLN, ¾ of a mile (E. by N.) from Alford, containing, with the hamlet of Thurlby, 416 inhabitants. The living is a vicarage, in the archdeaconry and diocese of Lincoln, rated in the king's books at £13. 3. 4., and in the patronage of Mrs. Wayet. The church is dedicated to the Holy Trinity. Here is a school with a small endowment.

BILSDALE (WEST SIDE), a township in the parish of HAWNBY, wapentake of BIRDFORTH, North riding of the county of YORK, 8 miles (N.W. by N.) from Helmsley, containing 127 inhabitants. In 1757, John Smales and Gregory Elsley bequeathed £120. 5., directing the proceeds to be applied to teaching six poor boys of this township.

BILSDALE-MIDCABLE, a chapelry in the parish of HELMSLEY, wapentake of RYEDALE, North riding of the county of YORK, 7 miles (N. N.W.) from Helmsley, containing, with Bilsdale-Kirkham, 780 inhabitants. The living is a perpetual curacy, in the archdeaconry of Cleveland, and diocese of York, endowed with £800 royal bounty, and £800 parliamentary grant, and in the patronage of the Vicar of Helmsley. There is a meeting-house for the Society of Friends.

BILSINGTON, a parish partly in the liberty of ROMNEY-MARSH, but chiefly in the hundred of NEWCHURCH, lathe of SHEPWAY, county of KENT, 6½ miles (S. S.E.) from Ashford, containing 299 inhabitants. The living is a perpetual curacy, in the archdeaconry and diocese of Canterbury, endowed with £200 private benefaction, and £200 royal bounty, and in the patronage of T. Rider, Esq. The church is dedicated to St. Peter and St. Paul. A fair, formerly called Woodstock fair, is held here on July 5th. The Grand Military, or Shorncliffe and Rye, canal passes through the parish. There are some remains of a priory of Augustine canons, founded in 1253, the revenue of which, at the dissolution, was £81. 1. 6.

BILSTHORPE, a parish in the South-clay division of the wapentake of BASSETLAW, county of NOTTINGHAM, 5 miles (S.) from Ollerton, containing 252 inhabitants. The living is a discharged rectory, in the archdeaconry of Nottingham, and diocese of York, rated in the king's books at £5. 1. 8., and in the patronage of the Rev. Lumley Savile. The church is dedicated to St. Margaret.

BILSTON, a market town and chapelry in that part of the parish of WOLVERHAMPTON which is in the northern division of the hundred of SEISDON, county of STAFFORD, 3 miles (S. E.) from Wolverhampton, 19 (S. by E.) from Stafford, and 120 (N. W.) from London, containing 12,003 inhabitants. This place, formerly belonging to the portionists, or prebendaries, of Wolverhampton, and in their charter called *Bilsreton*, was a royal demesne at the time of the Conquest, and in the reign of Edward III., under the name *Billestune*, was certified to be free of toll. Previously to the introduction of the iron-works, Bilston contained only a few private houses; but, from the abundance and rich quality of its mines of coal and iron-stone, it rapidly increased in extent and population, and has become one of the largest towns in the county. The town is situated on rising ground, in the centre of an extensive district abounding with numerous foundries, forges, furnaces, steam-engines, and other works necessary for the various processes of the iron trade, of which the smoke by day, and the fires by night, present a scene singularly impressive and terrific. It is irregularly built, and is nearly two miles in length; the principal streets contain several substantial and handsome houses, and throughout the neighbourhood are scattered in every direction the numerous habitations of persons employed in the different works. The manufacture of tin, japanned and enamelled wares of every kind, iron-wire, nails, screws, iron-gates, pallisades, machinery, steam-engines, and all the heavier articles in the iron trade, is carried on to a very considerable extent: there are several mills for slitting the pig-iron into bars, and many iron and brass foundries. Clay, of which the coarser kind of pottery-ware is made, and a particularly fine sand for casting, are found in great abundance: there are also quarries of a species of very hard stone, much esteemed for grindstones, troughs, and for building; it lies in horizontal strata of twelve layers, gradually increasing in thickness from the surface. The Birmingham and Staffordshire canal, which passes near the town, and several branch canals in the vicinity, afford the means of conveying the manufactures of the town, the produce of the mines, and the massive productions of the foundries, to various parts of the kingdom. The market days, established by an act of parliament obtained in 1825, are Monday and Saturday; and the fairs, which are toll-free, are on Whit-Monday and the Monday preceding the Michaelmas fair at Birmingham. Constables and other officers are appointed at the court leet of the lord of the manor. A court of requests, for the recovery of debts not exceeding £5, is held under an act passed in the 48th of George III., the jurisdiction of which extends over the townships of Bilston and Willenhall, and the parishes of Wednesbury and Darlaston, excepting the manor of Bradley, which is within the jurisdiction of a similar court previously established at Oldbury. The living is a perpetual curacy, within the jurisdiction of the court of the royal peculiar of Wolverhampton, endowed with £400 private benefaction, and £400 royal bounty, and in the patronage of the resident householders. The chapel, dedicated to St. Leonard, was rebuilt in 1826. A church, dedicated to St. Mary, and containing nine hundred and fifty-six free sittings, was erected in 1829, at an expense of £7223. 6. 1., part of which was defrayed by grant from the parliamentary commissioners; it is an elegant structure in the later style of English architecture, with a handsome tower. There are places of worship for Baptists, Independents, and Primitive and Wesleyan Methodists. A Blue-coat school was founded and endowed by Humphrey Perry, Esq., of Stafford, for clothing and instructing six boys, since which it has received a trifling bequest for the education of two more.

BILSTONE, a chapelry in the parish of NORTON juxta TWYCROSS, hundred of SPARKENHOE, county of LEICESTER, 3½ miles (N. W. by W.) from Market-Bosworth, containing 176 inhabitants. It is in the honour of Tutbury, duchy of Lancaster, and within the jurisdiction of a court of pleas held at Tutbury every third Tuesday, for the recovery of debts under 40*s*.

BILTON, a parish in the Rugby division of the hundred of KNIGHTLOW, county of WARWICK, 1½ mile (W. S. W.) from Rugby, containing 401 inhabitants. The living is a rectory, in the archdeaconry of Coventry, and diocese of Lichfield and Coventry, rated in the king's books at £16. 10. 7½., and in the patronage of the Rev. J. T. Parker. The church, dedicated to St. Mark, is principally Norman, of which style it exhibits some good specimens; the tower and spire are of later date. Bilton Hall, with the estate belonging to it, was purchased, in the early part of the last century, by Joseph Addison, Esq., the poet and moralist, who spent a considerable portion of the latter part of his life here, where he wrote his "Evidences of the Christian Religion." Miss Addison, his only child, retired hither towards the close of her life, where she died, in 1797. A school was endowed with £20 per annum, the bequest of Langton Freeman, Esq., in 1783.

BILTON, a chapelry in that part of the parish of SWINE which is in the middle division of the wapentake of HOLDERNESS, East riding of the county of YORK, 4½ miles (N. E.) from Kingston upon Hull, containing 91 inhabitants. The living is a perpetual curacy, in the archdeaconry of the East riding, and diocese of York, endowed with £400 private benefaction, and £800 royal bounty, and in the patronage of the Hon. and Rev. W. H. Dawnay. The chapel is dedicated to St. Peter.

BILTON, a parish within the ainsty of the city, and East riding of the county, of YORK, comprising the townships of Bickerton, Bilton, and Tockwith, and containing 808 inhabitants, of which number, 223 are in the township of Bilton, 5 miles (E. by N.) from Wetherby. The living is a discharged vicarage, in the peculiar jurisdiction and patronage of the Prebendary of Bilton in the Cathedral Church of York, rated in the king's books at £3. 16. 0½., endowed with £400 private benefaction, £200 royal bounty, and £300 parliamentary grant. The church is dedicated to St. Helen. At Syningthwaite, in this parish, Bertram Haget, in 1160, founded a Cistercian nunnery for a prioress and twelve nuns, in honour of the Blessed Virgin, which, at the dissolution, had a revenue of £62. 6.

BILTON, a joint township with Harrogate, in that part of the parish of KNARESBOROUGH which is in the lower division of the wapentake of CLARO, West riding of the county of YORK, 2½ miles (W.) from Knaresborough. The population is returned with Harrogate. A free school is endowed with about £30 per annum, given by Richard Taylor, in 1785. In the neighbourhood are several petrifying springs, and one with a sulphureous impregnation.

BINACRE, a parish in the hundred of BLYTHING, county of SUFFOLK, 6 miles (N. by E.) from Southwold, containing 224 inhabitants. The living is a rectory, with that of Easton-Bavents and the vicarage of North Hales consolidated, in the archdeaconry of Suffolk, and diocese of Norwich, rated in the king's books at £18, and in the patronage of Sir T. S. Gooch, Bart. The church is dedicated to St. Michael. About half a mile from the sea is Binacre Broad, a sheet of fresh water comprising an area of one hundred acres, and abounding with pike and other fish. About fifty years ago, in forming a new turnpike road from Yarmouth to London, through Binacre, the workmen discovered an urn containing coins of Vespasian, Trajan, Adrian, Antoninus Pius, and Marcus Aurelius.

BINBROOKE, a village (formerly a market town) comprising the parishes of St. Gabriel and St. Mary, in the southern division of the wapentake of WALSHCROFT, parts of LINDSEY, county of LINCOLN, 8 miles (E. N. E.) from Market-Rasen. St. Gabriel's, containing 497 inhabitants, is a discharged vicarage, within the peculiar jurisdiction of the Dean and Chapter of Lincoln, rated in the king's books at £8, endowed with £200 royal bounty, and in the patronage of the Prebendary of Milton in the Cathedral Church of Lincoln. St. Mary's, containing, with the extra-parochial liberty of Orforth, 293 inhabitants, is a discharged rectory, in the archdeaconry and diocese of Lincoln, rated in the king's books at £10. 4. 2., and in the patronage of the Crown. The Wesleyan Methodists have a place of worship here. There are extensive rabbit-warrens in the neighbourhood, and considerable business is done in the dressing of skins for furriers. A fair is held on Easter-Tuesday, on which day there are also horse-races. Here is a charity school.

BINCHESTER, a township in that part of the parish of ST. ANDREW AUCKLAND which is in the north-western division of DARLINGTON ward, county palatine of DURHAM, 2 miles (N. by E.) from Bishop-Auckland, containing 49 inhabitants. Binchester appears to have been a Roman station, called *Vinovia* by Antoninus, and *Binovium* by Ptolemy, situated on the Fosse-way. Mr. Cade considers it to have been sacred to Bacchus, and to have derived its name, *Vinovium*, from the festivals held at it, in honour of that deity. The fortress occupied an elevated site rising from the bank of the river Wear, and the station comprised a plot of about twenty-nine acres of ground, within which, and in its vicinity, the remains of a hypocaust, altars, urns, and other relics, have been found.

BINCOMBE, a parish in the liberty of FRAMPTON, Bridport division of the county of DORSET, 5 miles (S. by W.) from Dorchester, containing 178 inhabitants. The living is a rectory, annexed to that of Broadway, in the archdeaconry of Dorset, and diocese of Bristol, rated in the king's books at £9. 1. 5½. The church is dedicated to the Holy Trinity. The river Way runs through the parish, in which are quarries of fine stone, and a mineral spring. Numerous barrows are visible on the neighbouring downs.

BINDERTON, a chapelry in the parish of WEST DEAN, hundred of WESTBOURN and SINGLETON, rape of CHICHESTER, county of SUSSEX, 4 miles (N.) from Chichester, containing 67 inhabitants. The chapel is not in use, and is said to be unconsecrated.

BINEGAR, a parish in the hundred of WELLS-FORUM, county of SOMERSET, 4 miles (N.) from Shepton-Mallet, containing 363 inhabitants. The living is a rectory, within the peculiar jurisdiction of the Dean of Wells, rated in the king's books at £13. 12. 8½., and in the patronage of the Prebendary of Whitchurch in the Cathedral Church of Wells. The church is dedicated to the Holy Trinity. A large fair, noted for the sale of horses, formerly held at Wells, was removed hither in the seventeenth century, in consequence of the plague, and is held during the whole of Whitsun-week.

BINFIELD, a parish in the hundred of COOKHAM, county of BERKS, 3 miles (N. E.) from Wokingham, containing 1057 inhabitants. The living is a rectory, in the archdeaconry of Berks, and diocese of Salisbury, rated in the king's books at £18. 17. 1., and in the patronage of the Crown. The church is dedicated to All Saints. A National school is endowed with about £23 per annum. Pope, the poet, in the early part of his life, resided with his father in this village, where he wrote his poem entitled "Windsor Forest." Traces of a large intrenchment, called Cæsar's Camp, supposed to have been occupied by Julius Cæsar during his invasion of Britain, are still visible.

BINGFIELD, a chapelry in the parish of ST. JOHN LEE, southern division of TINDALE ward, county of NORTHUMBERLAND, 6½ miles (N.N.E.) from Hexham, containing 111 inhabitants. The living is a perpetual curacy, within the jurisdiction of the peculiar court of Hexham, belonging to the Archbishop of York, endowed with £200 private benefaction, and £600 royal bounty, and in the patronage of Col. and Mrs. Beaumont. The chapel is dedicated to St. Mary. A school here is endowed with £10 per annum. Near the Erring-bourn, a little northward from the village, there is a mineral spring, the water of which is so powerful, that neither fish nor any kind of insect can live in it.

BINGHAM, a market town and parish in the northern division of the wapentake of BINGHAM, county of NOTTINGHAM, 10 miles (E.) from Nottingham, and 123 (N. W. by N.) from London, containing, with part of the township of Newton, 1574 inhabitants. This place, which, previously to the Conquest, was possessed by two Saxon chieftains, appears to have been anciently more extensive than at present: it had a college, or guild, founded in honour of St. Mary. The town is pleasantly situated in the fertile vale of Belvoir, and consists principally of two parallel streets, one of which leads directly into a spacious market-place; some smaller streets have been formed within the last twenty years. The houses, though irregularly built, are neat, and several of them are of handsome appearance: the town is well paved, and amply supplied with water. The market is on Thursday: fairs are held on February 13th and 14th, for draught horses, on Whit-Monday for toys, and November 8th and 9th for young horses and hogs. The living is a rectory, in the archdeaconry of Nottingham, and diocese of York, rated in the king's books at £44. 7. 11., and in the patronage of the Earl of Chesterfield. The church, dedicated to All Saints, is an ancient and spacious cruciform structure, partaking of the early and decorated styles of English architecture, with a square embattled and highly enriched tower, crowned with the remains of statues, which have been substituted for pinnacles, and surmounted by a lofty spire, which, with the upper stage of the tower, is of later erection: within the church are some beautiful specimens of foliage and sculpture, of elegant design and elaborate execution. There are places of worship for Primitive and Wesleyan Methodists. An endowment of £8 per annum, for a free school, has been augmented with a dividend of £10 per annum, payable on the sum of £150, raised by the performance of plays, and invested in the Nottingham and Grantham canal, by a few individuals of the town. The Roman Fosse-way, in its course through the parish, passes by a large mound, called Castle Hill, the site of an ancient fortress. Mr. Robert White, the astronomer, and editor of the Ephemeris which bears his name, was a native of this parish, and is interred here; a mural tablet in the church has been inscribed to his memory. Abbot, Archbishop of Canterbury; Wren, Bishop of Ely; and Hanmer, Bishop of Bangor; were successively rectors of this parish, from which they were promoted to their respective sees, in the seventeenth century.

BINGLEY, a parish in the upper division of the wapentake of SKYRACK, West riding of the county of YORK, comprising the market town of Bingley, and the township of East and West Morton, and containing 7375 inhabitants, of which number, 6176 are in the town of Bingley (including Micklethwaite), 37 miles (W.S.W.) from York, and 202 (N.N.W.) from London. This place is pleasantly situated on an eminence near the river Aire, and consists principally of one long street, containing several respectable and well-built houses; it is plentifully supplied with water: the air is salubrious, and the environs, which are richly wooded, abound with agreeable and diversified scenery. A news-room has been recently established, which is well conducted and liberally supported. The principal branch of manufacture is that of worsted yarn, which is extensively carried on in the town and neighbourhood: there are some smaller factories for the spinning of cotton, and a manufactory for paper, together with a considerable trade in malt: the Leeds and Liverpool canal passes near the town. The market is on Tuesday: fairs are held on January 25th, and August 25th, 26th, and 27th, for linen, horses, and horned cattle. The living is a discharged vicarage, within the peculiar jurisdiction of the court of the manors of Crossley, Bingley, and Pudsey, rated in the king's books at £7. 6. 8., endowed with £400 private benefaction, £200 royal bounty, and £300 parliamentary grant, and in the patronage of the Crown. The church, dedicated to All Saints, is a neat edifice, in the later style of English architecture. There are places of worship for Baptists, Independents, and Methodists. The free grammar school was founded in the reign of Henry VIII., and endowed with land and tenements producing at present nearly £300 per annum, subject to certain payments to the poor: the premises comprise a large school-room, and a house and garden for the master. There is also a National school, capable of admitting eight hundred scholars. Mrs. Sarah Rhodes, in 1784, gave five cottages, which she endowed as almshouses for five aged widows, who receive £3 per annum each: there are also several bequests for distribution in bread and clothes among the poor, and for other charitable uses.

BING-WESTON, a quarter in that part of the parish of WORTHEN which is in the hundred of CHIRBURY, county of SALOP, containing, with Beachfield, Walton, and Rewins-Farm, 155 inhabitants.

BINHAM, a parish in the northern division of the hundred of GREENHOE, county of NORFOLK, 4 miles (N.E. by E.) from Little Walsingham, containing 438 inhabitants. The living is a discharged vicarage, in the archdeaconry and diocese of Norwich, rated in the king's books at £6. 13. 4., endowed with £200 private benefaction, and £800 royal bounty, and in the patronage of T. T. Clarke, Esq. The church, dedicated to the Holy Cross, belonged to a Benedictine priory, founded in the reign of Henry I., the revenue of which, at the dissolution, was £160. 1.: the western front affords a fine specimen of the early style of English architecture.

BINLEY, a parish in the Kirby division of the hundred of KNIGHTLOW, county of WARWICK, 2¼ miles (E. by S.) from Coventry, containing, with the liberty of Earnsford, 211 inhabitants. The living is a perpetual curacy, in the archdeaconry of Coventry, and diocese of Lichfield and Coventry, and in the patronage of Earl Craven. The church, dedicated to St. Bartholomew, was built by Lord Craven, and consecrated in 1772. The Rev. Thomas Wagstaffe, who wrote a defence of Charles I., was born here, and died at Rouen in 1770.

BINNINGTON, a township in the parish of WILLERBY, wapentake of DICKERING, East riding of the county of YORK, 8 miles (S.W. by S.) from Scarborough, containing 50 inhabitants.

BINSEY, a parish within the liberty of the city of OXFORD, locally in the hundred of Wootton, county of OXFORD, 2 miles (N.W.) from Oxford, containing 82 inhabitants. The living is a perpetual curacy, in the archdeaconry and diocese of Oxford, endowed with £600 private benefaction, and £600 royal bounty, and in the patronage of the Dean and Canons of Christ Church, Oxford. The church, dedicated to St. Margaret, is an ancient structure.

BINSTEAD, a parish in the liberty of EAST MEDINA, Isle of Wight division of the county of SOUTHAMPTON, 5½ miles (E.N.E.) from Newport, containing 225 inhabitants. The living is a discharged rectory, in the archdeaconry and diocese of Winchester, rated in the king's books at £1. 7. 1., and in the patronage of the Bishop of Winchester. The church, dedicated to the Holy Cross, exhibits marks of considerable antiquity, particularly in the arch which separates the nave from the chancel, and another in the north wall, now filled up. In the vicinity are the ancient quarries from which part of the stone used in the erection of Winchester cathedral was obtained. At Quarr, in this parish, there are remains of an abbey of Cistercian monks, which was founded, in 1132, by Baldwin de Redveriis, afterwards Earl of Devonshire; its revenue, at the dissolution, was £184. 1. 10. Their situation is very fine, having the sea on the north, and thick woods to the south and east. Most of the boundary wall, including above thirty acres, is yet standing, together with the remains of two gates, which formed the north and south entrances. The refectory, the only entire part of the buildings, is now a barn, and another part of the site is occupied by a farm-house erected out of the ruins. It was the burial-place of several distinguished persons, amongst whom were Earl Baldwin, its founder, and his countess Adeliza.

BINSTED, a parish in the hundred of ALTON, Alton (North) division of the county of SOUTHAMPTON, 3¾ miles (E. by N.) from Alton, containing 946 inhabitants. The living is a perpetual curacy, annexed to the vicarage of Alton, in the archdeaconry and diocese of Winchester. The church is dedicated to St. Nicholas. Binsted is entitled to send five children to St. Andrew's school in Holyburn. It is within the jurisdiction of the Cheyney Court held at Winchester every Thursday, for the recovery of debts to any amount.

BINSTED, a parish in the hundred of AVISFORD, rape of ARUNDEL, county of SUSSEX, 3½ miles (W. by S.) from Arundel, containing 98 inhabitants. The living is a discharged rectory, in the archdeaconry and diocese of Chichester, rated in the king's books at £5. 17. 8½., and in the patronage of the Rev. M. Smelt. The church is dedicated to St. Mary.

BINTON, a parish in the Stratford division of the hundred of BARLICHWAY, county of WARWICK, 3¾ miles (W. by S.) from Stratford upon Avon, containing 232 inhabitants. The living is a rectory, in the archdeaconry and diocese of Worcester, rated in the king's books at £8. 10., and in the patronage of the Marquis of Hertford. The church is dedicated to St. Peter. The navigable river Avon is here crossed by a bridge on the road leading to Chipping-Campden.

BINTREE, a parish in the hundred of EYNSFORD, county of NORFOLK, 1¼ mile (S. W. by W.) from Foulsham, containing 333 inhabitants. The living is a rectory, with that of Themelthorpe annexed, in the archdeaconry of Norfolk, and diocese of Norwich, rated in the king's books at £10, and in the patronage of Sir Jacob Astley, Bart. The church is dedicated to St. Swithin. The river Wensom, which separates the parish from North Elmham, is expected to be made navigable to Norwich.

BIRBECK-FELLS, a hamlet partly in the parish of ORTON, EAST ward, and partly in the parishes of CROSBY-RAVENSWORTH and SHAP, WEST ward, county of WESTMORLAND, 4 miles (W. S. W.) from Orton. The population is returned with the above parishes. A free school at Greenholme, for the education of the children of Birbeck-Fells, Bretherdale, Routhwaite, and Low Scales, is endowed with land producing about £40 per annum, purchased with a bequest of £400 by George Gibson, in 1733.

BIRCH, a chapelry in the parish of MIDDLETON, hundred of SALFORD, county palatine of LANCASTER, 2½ miles (W. N. W.) from Middleton. The population is returned with the township of Hopwood. The living is a perpetual curacy, in the archdeaconry and diocese of Chester, and in the patronage of the Rector of Middleton. The chapel, dedicated to St. Mary, was built by means of a parliamentary grant of £4000, and consecrated December 11th, 1828; it contains one thousand sittings, of which five hundred and four are free. The spinning of cotton, and the manufacture of gingham, are carried on in this chapelry to a limited extent.

BIRCH, a chapelry in the parish of WARRINGTON, hundred of WEST DERBY, county palatine of LANCASTER, 1¾ mile (E. N. E.) from Warrington, with which the population is returned. The living is a perpetual curacy, in the archdeaconry and diocese of Chester, endowed with £400 private benefaction, and £600 royal bounty, and in the patronage of J. Dickinson, Esq.

BIRCH (GREAT), a parish in the Colchester division of the hundred of LEXDEN, county of ESSEX, 5 miles (S. W.) from Colchester, containing, with the parish of Little Birch, 662 inhabitants. The living is a rectory, in the archdeaconry of Colchester, and diocese of London, rated in the king's books at £11, and in the patronage of the Bishop of London. The church is dedicated to St. Peter. Here is a small endowment for the education of poor children. The remains of Birch castle are conspicuous in the village.

BIRCH (LITTLE), a parish in the Colchester division of the hundred of LEXDEN, county of ESSEX, 4¼ miles (S. W. by W.) from Colchester. The population is returned with Great Birch. The living is a discharged rectory, in the archdeaconry of Colchester, and diocese of London, rated in the king's books at £5. 6. 8., and in the patronage of Charles Round, Esq. The church, dedicated to St. Mary, is desecrated, and religious rites are celebrated at Great Birch.

BIRCH (LITTLE), a parish in the upper division of the hundred of WORMELOW, county of HEREFORD, 6¾ miles (S.) from Hereford, containing 310 inhabitants. The living is a discharged rectory, in the archdeaconry and diocese of Hereford, rated in the king's books at £6. 12. 11., and in the patronage of the Governors of Guy's Hospital, London. The church is dedicated to St. Mary.

BIRCH (MUCH), a parish in the upper division of the hundred of WORMELOW, county of HEREFORD, 6¼ miles (S. by W.) from Hereford, containing 353 inhabitants. The living is a perpetual curacy, annexed to the vicarage of Much Dewchurch, in the archdeaconry and diocese of Hereford, endowed with £600 royal bounty. The church is dedicated to St. Mary. Wormelow, from which the hundred takes its name, is within this parish.

BIRCHAM (GREAT), a parish in the hundred of SMITHDON, county of NORFOLK, 7½ miles (S. W. by S.) from Burnham-Westgate, containing 398 inhabitants. The living is a rectory, in the archdeaconry of Norfolk, and diocese of Norwich, rated in the king's books at £22, and in the patronage of J. Spurgeon, Esq. The church is dedicated to St. Mary.

BIRCHAM-NEWTON, a parish in the hundred of SMITHDON, county of NORFOLK, 7¼ miles (S. W. by S.) from Burnham-Westgate, containing 75 inhabitants. The living is a discharged rectory, annexed to that of Bircham-Tofts, in the archdeaconry of Norfolk, and diocese of Norwich, rated in the king's books at £7. 13. 4. The church is dedicated to All Saints.

BIRCHAM-TOFTS, a parish in the hundred of SMITHDON, county of NORFOLK, 7¼ miles (S. S. W.) from Burnham-Westgate, containing 135 inhabitants. The living is a discharged rectory, with that of Bircham-Newton annexed, in the archdeaconry of Norfolk, and diocese of Norwich, rated in the king's books at £6. 13. 4., and in the patronage of the Earl of Orford. The church is dedicated to St. Andrew.

BIRCHANGER, a parish in the hundred of UTTLESFORD, county of ESSEX, 1¾ mile (S. W. by S.) from Stansted-Mountfitchet, containing 336 inhabitants. The living is a rectory, in the archdeaconry of Colchester, and diocese of London, rated in the king's books at £9. 13. 4., and in the patronage of the Warden and Fellows of New College, Oxford. The church is dedicated to St. Mary. Richard de Newport founded here, in the reign of John, an hospital dedicated to St. Mary and St. Leonard, for a master and two chaplains, the revenue of which, in the 26th of Henry VIII., was estimated at £31. 13. 11.

BIRCHER, a township in the parish of YARPOLE, hundred of WOLPHY, county of HEREFORD, 5½ miles (N. by W.) from Leominster. The population is returned with the parish.

BIRCHES, a township in that part of the parish of GREAT BUDWORTH which is in the hundred of NORTHWICH, county palatine of CHESTER, 3¼ miles (E. S. E.) from Northwich, containing 8 inhabitants. Mrs. Elizabeth Dobson, about 1695, assigned an estate here in trust for the education of two boys, one to be the son of a counsellor, and the other the son of a divine of the church of England.

BIRCHINGTON, a parish within the cinque-port liberty of DOVOR, of which it is a member, though locally in the hundred of Ringslow, or the Isle of Thanet, lathe of ST. AUGUSTINE, county of KENT, 3½ miles (W. by S.) from Margate, containing 700 inhabitants. The living is a perpetual curacy, united to the vicarage of Monkton, in the peculiar jurisdiction of the Archbishop of Canterbury. The church, dedicated to All Saints, consists of a nave, chancel, and aisles, with a lofty tower and spire rising between the east end of the north aisle and a small chapel, now the vestry-room: the nave is separated from the aisles by octangular columns supporting five pointed arches: the three east windows of the chancel are in the decorated style. On the north side of it is Quex chapel, belonging to the manor of Quex, in this parish, containing several monuments and brasses of the family of Crispe. A pleasure fair is held here on Whit-Monday and Tuesday. Hemming's bay is thought to have been so named from the landing of Hemming, a Danish chieftain, accompanied by Anlaf, in 1009. Mrs. Anna Gertrude Crispe, by will dated February 13th, 1707, bequeathed forty-seven acres of land in Birchington and Monkton for certain charitable purposes; among others for the instruction of twelve boys and girls of this parish and the vill of Acole, the remainder of the rental to be applied in apprenticing some of the boys. The master receives £36. 15. annually, for which he instructs about twenty-four children, one-half appointed by the overseers, from whom the apprentices are selected, and the rest by himself. Near the village stands the workhouse for the reception of the poor of Birchington, Monkton, Sarre, and Acole.

BIRCHOLT, a parish in the franchise and barony of BIRCHOLT, lathe of SHEPWAY, county of KENT, 4 miles (E. by S.) from Ashford, containing 33 inhabitants. The living is a rectory, in the archdeaconry and diocese of Canterbury, rated in the king's books at £2. 10. 10., and in the patronage of Lady Bankes. The church, now desecrated, was dedicated to St. Margaret.

BIRCHOVER, a chapelry in that part of the parish of YOULGRAVE which is in the hundred of HIGH PEAK, county of DERBY, 1 mile (N. by W.) from Winster, containing 121 inhabitants. It is in the honour of Tutbury, duchy of Lancaster, and within the jurisdiction of a court of pleas held at Tutbury every third Tuesday, for the recovery of debts under 40*s*.

BIRDALL, a joint township with Raisthorpe, in the parish of WHARRAM-PERCY, wapentake of BUCKROSE, East riding of the county of YORK, 8½ miles (S. E.) from New Malton. The population is returned with Raisthorpe.

BIRDBROOK, a parish in the hundred of HINCKFORD, county of ESSEX, 7 miles (N.W.) from Castle-Hedingham, containing 460 inhabitants. The living is a rectory, in the archdeaconry of Middlesex, and diocese of London, rated in the king's books at £19, and in the patronage of Sir W. Rush. The church is dedicated to St. Augustine.

BIRDFORTH, a chapelry in the parish of COXWOLD, wapentake of BIRDFORTH, North riding of the county of YORK, 4½ miles (N.W. by N.) from Easingwould, containing 42 inhabitants. The living is a perpetual curacy, in the archdeaconry of Cleveland, and diocese of York, endowed with £800 royal bounty, and in the patronage of the Archbishop of York. The antiquity of this place is evinced by its having given name to the hundred.

BIRDHAM, a parish in the hundred of MANHOOD, rape of CHICHESTER, county of SUSSEX, 4 miles (S. W. by S.) from Chichester, containing 532 inhabitants. The living is a rectory, in the archdeaconry and diocese of Chichester, rated in the king's books at £10. 0. 10., endowed with £200 private benefaction, and £200 royal bounty, and in the patronage of the Dean and Chapter of Chichester. The church is dedicated to St. Leonard. The Portsmouth and Arun canal passes through the parish, and terminates at Chichester harbour. Here is a National school, in which about one hundred boys and girls are instructed.

BIRDINBURY, a parish in the Southam division of the hundred of KNIGHTLOW, county of WARWICK, 4¾ miles (N. by E.) from Southam, containing 213 inhabitants. The living is a discharged rectory, in the archdeaconry of Coventry, and diocese of Lichfield and Coventry, rated in the king's books at £7. 10., endowed with £200 private benefaction, and £200 royal bounty, and in the patronage of Sir T. Biddulph, Bart. The church is dedicated to St. Leonard.

BIRDSALL, a parish in the wapentake of BUCKROSE, East riding of the county of YORK, 6 miles (S.S.E.) from New Malton, containing 240 inhabitants. The living is a perpetual curacy, in the archdeaconry of the East riding, and diocese of York, endowed with £400 royal bounty, and in the patronage of the Marchioness of Hertford. The church, dedicated to St. Mary, is an elegant structure, erected in 1824, at the expense of Lord Middleton. Henry Burton, a puritan divine, was born in this parish.

BIRKBY, a township in the parish of CROSS-CANNONBY, ALLERDALE ward below Darwent, county of CUMBERLAND, 1¾ mile (E.N.E.) from Maryport, containing 96 inhabitants.

BIRKBY, a township in the parish of MUNCASTER, ALLERDALE ward above Darwent, county of CUMBERLAND, 2¼ miles (E. by S.) from Ravenglass. The population is returned with the parish. Extensive ruins of a British or Danish city, called Barnscar, are visible on Birkby-Fell.

BIRKBY, a parish in the wapentake of ALLERTONSHIRE, North riding of the county of YORK, comprising the chapelry of Hutton-Bonville, and the townships of Birkby and Little Smeaton, and containing 261 inhabitants, of which number, 90 are in the township of Birkby, 6 miles (N. N. W.) from North Allerton. The living is a discharged rectory, in the peculiar jurisdiction of Allerton and Allertonshire, belonging to the Bishop of Durham, rated in the king's books at £6. 13. 4., and in the patronage of the Bishop of Durham. The church is dedicated to St. Peter.

BIRKDALE, a township in the parish of ORMSKIRK, hundred of WEST DERBY, county palatine of LANCASTER, 7½ miles (N. W.) from Ormskirk, containing 414 inhabitants.

BIRKENHEAD, a chapelry in the parish of BIDSTONE, lower division of the hundred of WIRRALL, county palatine of CHESTER, 9¼ miles (N.N.E.) from Great Neston, containing 200 inhabitants. The living is a perpetual curacy, in the archdeaconry and diocese of Chester, endowed with £1000 private benefaction £800 royal bounty, and £1200 parliamentary grant, and in the patronage of F. R. Price, Esq. A priory for sixteen Benedictine monks was founded here, about 1150, in honour of St. Mary and St. James, by Hamon de Massey, third baron of Dunham-Massey, which, according to Leland, was subordinate to the abbey of St. Werburgh, at Chester; but from the power exercised by the monks, Bishop Tanner considers it to have been an independent priory: the revenue, at the dissolution, was £102. 16. 10. The ruins, part of which has been fitted up for a chapel, stand on a peninsular rock of red freestone, formed by the æstuary of the Mersey, on the east, and a small creek on the west, opposite to Liverpool.

BIRKENSHAW, a hamlet in the parish of BIRSTALL, wapentake of MORLEY, West riding of the county of YORK, 5 miles (S.E.) from Bradford. The population is returned with the township of Gomersall. A new church is in progress of erection here. A great quantity of coal and iron-stone is found in the vicinity, and the manufacture of woollen goods is carried on to a very great extent.

BIRKER, a joint township with Austhwaite, in the parish of MILLOM, ALLERDALE ward above Darwent, county of CUMBERLAND, 7½ miles (E. by N.) from Ravenglass, containing, with Austhwaite, 101 inhabitants. This township is within the limits of the chapelry of Eskdale, in the adjoining parish of St. Bees, and the inhabitants enjoy the privilege of marrying and burying there. The lake Devock-water, and the waterfalls of Birker Force and Stanley Gill are in the neighbourhood, which abounds with picturesque scenery.

BIRKIN, a parish in the lower division of the wapentake of BARKSTONE-ASH, West riding of the county of YORK, comprising the chapelry of Chapel-Haddlesey, and the townships of Birkin, West Haddlesey, Courtney-Hurst, and Temple-Hurst, and containing 917 inhabitants, of which number, 139 are in the township of Birkin, 3½ miles (N.E. by E.) from Ferrybridge. The living is a rectory, in the archdeaconry and diocese of York, rated in the king's books at £36, and in the patronage of the devisees of the late Thomas Wright, Esq. The church is dedicated to St. Mary. The village is situated on the northern bank of the river Aire.

BIRLEY, a parish in the hundred of STRETFORD, county of HEREFORD, 4 miles (E. by N.) from Weobley, containing 119 inhabitants. The living is a discharged vicarage, consolidated with that of King's Pion, in the archdeaconry and diocese of Hereford, rated in the king's books at £5. 9. 7., and endowed with £200 royal bounty. The church is dedicated to St. Peter.

BIRLING, a parish in the hundred of LARKFIELD, lathe of AYLESFORD, county of KENT, 6¾ miles (N.W. by W.) from Maidstone, containing 459 inhabitants. The living is a vicarage, in the archdeaconry and diocese of Rochester, rated in the king's books at £6. 9. 4½., and in the patronage of the Earl of Abergavenny. The church is dedicated to All Saints. Foundations of buildings have frequently been discovered in a field near the church.

BIRLING, a township in that part of the parish of WARKWORTH which is in the eastern division of COQUETDALE ward, county of NORTHUMBERLAND, 6½ miles (S. E.) from Alnwick, containing 69 inhabitants.

BIRLINGHAM, a parish in the upper division of the hundred of PERSHORE, county of WORCESTER, 3 miles (S. S. W.) from Pershore, containing 327 inhabitants. The living is a rectory, in the archdeaconry and diocese of Worcester, rated in the king's books at £9. 17. 11., and in the patronage of A. Luders, Esq. The church is dedicated to St. James. The navigable river Avon forms a boundary to the parish.

BIRMINGHAM, a celebrated manufacturing town in the Birmingham division of the hundred of HEMLINGFORD, county of WARWICK, 18 miles (N.W. by W.) from Coventry, 20 (N. W.) from Warwick, and 109 (N. W.) from London, on the road to Holyhead, containing, with the environs, nearly 100,000 inhabitants. The earliest authentic notice of this place occurs in Domesday-book, in which it is called *Bermengeham*, whence may be easily deduced *Bromwycham*, which name, together with those of Castle and West Bromwich, two adjacent villages, is supposed to be derived from the quantity of broom growing in the neighbourhood. It is thought by some antiquaries to have been the *Bremenium* of the Romans, from its situation near the Iknield-street; and others state it to have been a British town of some importance prior to the Roman invasion, and to have been eminent for the manufacture of arms, for which the mines of iron and coal in the vicinity rendered its situation peculiarly favourable. Its history, prior to the Conquest, is involved in great obscurity, and from that period until the reign of Charles I. few incidents of moment are recorded. In the civil war during that reign, the inhabitants embraced the cause of the parliament; and in 1642, after the king had passed through the town, on his route from Shrewsbury, they seized the carriages containing the royal plate and furniture, and conveyed them to Warwick castle; they arrested all messengers and others supposed to be partizans of the king, and frequently attacked small parties of royalists, whom they sometimes defeated and sent

Arms.

prisoners to Coventry. In 1643, Prince Rupert, on his way to open a communication between Oxford and York, met with considerable resistance from a detachment of parliamentarian forces, assisted by the inhabitants, who stationed themselves at Camp-hill, and opposed his entrance into the town. A sharp conflict ensued, in which the parliamentarians were driven from their station; the Earl of Denbigh was killed, and a clergyman, who acted as governor during the action, was taken prisoner by the royalists, and, rejecting quarter, was killed after the battle, at the Red Lion inn. The prince, provoked at this resistance, set fire to the town, and, after several houses had been burnt, the inhabitants saved themselves from further suffering by the payment of a heavy fine. On the 14th of July, 1791, a party having met at an hotel, to celebrate the anniversary of the French revolution, a mob collected in front of the house, and broke the windows; they thence proceeded to the Unitarian meeting-house, which, with another, they burnt down. Doctor Priestley's dwelling-house, about a mile from the town, was the next object of attack, which, with his library, philosophical apparatus, and manuscripts, shared the same fate. For some days they continued their devastations, setting fire to several other meeting-houses and private mansions, but on the arrival of the military from Oxford and Hounslow, order was restored: at the ensuing assizes four of the ringleaders were convicted, and two of them suffered the penalty of the law. Shortly after this occurrence barracks were erected on the Vauxhall-road, near the town, consisting of a range of handsome buildings, enclosing a spacious area for the exercise of cavalry, and a smaller for parade, a riding-school, a magazine, and an hospital.

The extraordinary increase of the town, the improvement of its manufactures, the extension of its trade, and the rapid growth of its commerce, within the last century, may be attributed to the mines of iron-ore and coal with which the district abounds, to its freedom from the restrictions of incorporation, which has made it the resort of genius and of talent, and to the numerous canals by which it is connected with every part of the kingdom, and through which it not only carries on an immense inland trade, but exports its manufactures to every quarter of the world. Birmingham, in the reign of Henry VIII., was inhabited principally, as described by Leland, "by smithes that use to make knives and all manner of cutting tooles, and lorimers that make bittes, and a great many nailours." Soon after the Revolution in 1688, the manufacture of fire-arms was introduced, and continued to flourish until the close of the late war, during which, the government contracts for muskets alone generally averaged thirty thousand per month: the manufacturing of swords and army accoutrements is still carried on to a considerable extent. By an act obtained in 1813, the gun-makers were authorised to erect a proof-house, in which, under a heavy penalty, all gun and pistol barrels are subjected to a severe proof, and stamped by the master and wardens, under whose inspection the business is conducted; and since this period, the manufacture of fowling-pieces has greatly increased: the building, called the Tower, stands on the bank of the canal, and is a handsome structure, with a row of cannon in front, presenting the appearance of a military establishment. It is uncertain at what time the manufacture of buttons was begun, but it has continued to flourish in every variety from a remote period, and is still a source of wealth to many, and of employment to thousands. The buckle trade was established soon after the Revolution, and, after exercising the inventive powers of the manufacturers in every variety of size, form, and pattern, became nearly extinct in 1812. The leather trade, which formerly was extensively carried on, has very much declined; at present there is only one tan-yard in the town. The principal branches of manufacture are those of light and heavy steel goods (here called toys), gold, silver, and plated wares, trinkets, jewellery, fancy articles of every kind in the gilt-toy trade, machinery of every description, and steam-engines on every known principle: there are many iron and brass foundries, three metallic hot-house manufactories on a large scale, in one of which a hot-house has lately been made for the Duke of Northumberland, at an expense of nearly £50,000, measuring five hundred feet in length, and having in the centre a dome sixty-five feet high, and forty feet in diameter, with wings, in the purest style of modern architecture: there are also various rolling-mills of great power, worked by steam. Casting, modelling, die-sinking, and engraving, have been brought to great perfection; and several glass-houses have been erected within the last few years, besides many mills for cutting glass, of which brilliant specimens may be seen in all the show-rooms in the town. There are divers establishments for supplying the town with articles requisite for the use of the inhabitants, and for carrying on the manufactures: the Old and New Union-Mill Bread and Flour Companies, and the public and private coal-wharfs, are on an extensive scale. Of the numerous manufactories with which the neighbourhood abounds, the most ancient and extensive is the Soho Manufactory, about a mile from the town, in which, under the superintending genius of the late Mr. Boulton, the Birmingham manufactures were brought to their present high degree of perfection; and in which, under the same proprietor, assisted by his colleague, the late Mr. Watt, the most efficient application of mechanical power was produced in the construction of machinery. In this factory were coined the penny-pieces still in circulation, in a mint of great mechanical ingenuity, which, with the assistance of one or two persons, performed the whole process of coinage from the rolled metal. It was here also that the first application of gas, as a substitute for oil and tallow, was made under the auspices of Mr. Murdock, who, after a course of experiments at Redruth, in Cornwall, lighted the shops of this factory, and, in 1802, displayed the success of his researches in a splendid public illumination of the Soho, in celebration of the peace with France. Mr. Thomason's manufactory, in Church-street, has a splendid suite of show-rooms attached to it, replete with costly and elaborate specimens of workmanship, in gold, silver, plated ware, medals, bronzes, and the chrystallized bases of metals and semi-metals. Among the more massive productions is a fine statue in bronze of his late majesty, George IV., in his coronation robes: the attitude is graceful and dignified; the figure, which is more than six feet high, weighs forty-five hundred weight, and is so proportioned, as, at its proper elevation, to present a fine resemblance in countenance, form, and stature, of the monarch when at the age of fifty. In a lofty room of suitable dimensions, built for the purpose, and solely appropriated to its exhibition, is the large metallic vase, a fac-simile in size, form, and embellishment, of the celebrated Grecian vase of Lysippus, dug from the ruins of Adrian's palace, near Tivoli, which was, by the direction and at the expense of Lord Warwick, brought over to England by the late Sir William Hamilton, and placed in the gardens of Warwick castle. To this huge piece of art, which is more than twenty-one feet in circumference, six feet in height, and which weighs ninety hundred weight, the proprietor, by the peculiar process which he adopted, has imparted a soft solidity of colour, unequalled by any example of the kind, both in the porphyritic oxyde of the ground, or field, and in the ancient green bronze of the arms, visors, panthers' skins, foliage, and other ornaments with which it is embellished. Mr. Thomason's latest production is a beautiful series of sixteen scientific and philosophical medals of German silver, each containing, within a circle of three inches in diameter, a complete epitome of one of the sciences; they are enclosed in a morocco case, in the form, and of the size, of an imperial octavo volume. The manufacture of japan and papier maché has been much improved by Messrs. Jennens and Betteridge, who, by a chemical process in the preparation of pearl, by which it is reduced to the eightieth part of an inch in thickness, and made susceptible of greater transparency and brilliancy of colour, have rendered it peculiarly elegant in the decoration of cabinets, tea-trays, fans, snuff-boxes, &c., of which many beautiful specimens are exhibited in their show-rooms.

The Pantechnetheca, or General Repository, was erected in 1824, for the exhibition and sale of articles in the finer department of the arts, selected from the various manufactories in the town: the exterior of the building is fronted, on the basement story, with a Grecian Doric colonnade, supporting another of the Ionic order, surmounted by a handsome balustrade with projecting pedestals, on which are emblematical figures well sculptured; the interior consists of two handsome show-rooms, in which the manufactured articles are judiciously displayed. Mr. Phipson's pin-manufactory, by a simple but effective process, exhibits the progress of this article through all its stages, from the drawing of the wire, to sticking the pin upon paper, and occupies a thousand persons, besides affording, in many of its branches, employment to the inmates of the parish asylum, and the county bridewell. The number and variety of the manufactories, in almost all of which there is some ingenious application of machinery, either to expedite or to improve the manufacture of the article, while they preclude the possibility of enumeration, are such as to justify the assertion, that there is no species of manufacture carried on here which is not in a state of absolute or relative perfection.

The town is pleasantly situated on an eminence, at the north-western extremity of the county, bordering closely on the counties of Stafford and Worcester, from the former of which it is separated by a small brook. The streets, which are very numerous, and in general spacious, are, with the exception of a few in the more retired parts of the town, well paved, and lighted with gas, and, being on a declivity, are always clean. The houses, mostly modern and well built, are chiefly of brick, but, since the use of the Roman cement, they have assumed an improved appearance, and present, nearly throughout the town and its environs, specimens of elegance in almost every style of architecture: among those erected within the last three or four years are many splendid edifices. The inhabitants are amply supplied with water from pumps attached to their houses, and soft water is obtained from two fine wells at the lower extremity of the town. On entering Birmingham from London, the road, by a handsome stone bridge over the small river Rea, leads up an ascent into the market-place, in the centre of which is a statue in bronze of Lord Nelson, finely executed by Westmacott, at an expense of £3000, raised by subscription among the inhabitants. An act of parliament has recently been obtained for taking down the houses on one side of the present market-place, and forming an extensive area, in which it is intended to build a market-house; and under the same act, the erection of a town-hall is contemplated. The market days are Monday and Thursday, the latter being also for the sale of horses and horned cattle; and there is a market for hay on Tuesday. The cattle market and horse fair are held at Smithfield, a spacious area to the south-east of the town, conveniently divided and arranged for the purpose. A sale of horses by auction takes place also on the same day, at Beardsworth's Repository, an establishment of unequalled magnitude, near the spot. The buildings comprise a spacious quadrangular area, round which are stalls for one hundred and fifty horses, exclusively of twenty-four boxes for hunters; above these are galleries, in which there are standings for four hundred carriages, which are constantly on sale: the whole area is covered with a shed-roof supported on pillars forty feet high, and is lighted with a double range of upper windows: on one side of the quadrangle, over which the roof is continued, there is a covered ride, one hundred and eight yards in length, and forty yards in width; and on the opposite side is another of equal extent, enclosed by walls, but not roofed. In addition to the accommodations of a repository, it contains a splendid suite of apartments, elegantly furnished for the reception of gentlemen or families, who may visit Birmingham at the triennial festival, or on any other public occasion. The fairs are on the Thursday in Whitsun-week, and on the Thursday next before Michaelmas-day, each for three days; they are chiefly show fairs, though on the first day many horses and horned cattle are sold.

The town is wholly within the jurisdiction of the county magistrates, of whom, those acting for the town hold a meeting, every Monday and Thursday, at the public office: a high bailiff (who is clerk of the market, and by courtesy presides at all public meetings), a low bailiff, two constables, a headborough, two ale-conners, two flesh-conners, two affeirers, and two leather-sealers, are chosen at the court leet of the lord of the manor, which is held at Michaelmas. A court of requests for the recovery of debts under 40*s*., established by an act passed in the 25th of George II., the powers of which, by a subsequent act in the 47th of George III., were extended to the recovery of debts under £5, is held every week: it consists of seventy-two commissioners, three of whom, assisted by two clerks, who must be lawyers, form a quorum; its jurisdiction extends only to the limits of the parish. The public office is a commodious building with a handsome stone front; the court-room is well arranged, and behind it is a prison, for the confinement of malefactors previously to their committal to the county gaol. The news-room, built in 1825, is a handsome edifice with a stuccoed front, ornamented with lofty pillars of the Ionic order: the interior consists of one large room, opening through folding doors into two smaller apartments, over which are a billiard-room and a refectory; and a suite of rooms has lately been added, in which copies of the public records, and books of reference, are deposited. The old library, established in 1798, is a handsome stone building, with a circular portico; the reading-room is circular, and is lighted by a dome lanthern resting on handsome Ionic pillars of porphyry: this institution, the number of volumes in which exceeds thirty thousand, is under the direction of a committee; admission is obtained by the purchase of a share of the value of £10, and the payment of an annual subscription of £1. The new library, similarly conducted, but upon a smaller scale, is a neat building, recently erected, and internally well arranged. The Philosophical Society, which had been instituted some years previously, extended their plan in 1810, and erected a commodious theatre for the delivery of lectures by their own members, and occasionally by eminent professors, in the various branches of science: they have a museum, containing a fine collection of minerals and fossils, an extensive philosophical apparatus, a library, and a reading-room. The school of medicine and surgery was established in 1828, by Mr. W. S. Cox, and the resident physicians and surgeons lecture weekly upon subjects connected with the design of the institution; certificates of having attended these lectures qualify students to pass their examination at the Royal College of Surgeons in London: a handsome and appropriate building has been recently erected on Snow-hill for the use of this establishment.

The Society of Arts was instituted in 1821, for promoting the general study of the fine arts, by procuring from the nobility and gentry, who are its patrons, the loan of original pictures of the old and new schools, in order to stimulate the genius and industry of the members, and to enrich their annual exhibition: it comprehends also, in addition to the higher pursuits of the art, the cultivation of those particular departments of it which are connected with the manufactures of the town. The building is a chaste and elegant specimen of the Corinthian order, with a boldly projecting portico of four elegant columns, supporting a triangular pediment. An institution for promoting the fine arts, established in 1828, for the encouragement of artists resident within thirty miles of Birmingham, by appropriating its funds to the purchase of pictures from the walls at their annual exhibition, has been recently incorporated with the former. A mechanics' institution was established in 1825. The theatre is a spacious and well-arranged building, with a handsome stone front, consisting of a portico of the Ionic order, supported by a piazza, through which is the entrance to the boxes; on one side is that to a coffee-room, and on the other to a billiard-room, over which is an elegant suite of assembly-rooms: it was rebuilt in 1820, at an expense of £14,000, which was subscribed in shares; the present front is what remains of the former theatre, which was burnt down in the beginning of the same year: the season generally commences in May, and ends in October. Assemblies are held periodically, during the winter, at the Royal Hotel: the room, which is spacious and elegantly fitted up, is also appropriated to the subscription concerts, which are supported by more than three hundred subscribers, under the patronage of the nobility and gentry in the neighbourhood: the orchestra combines the first-rate talent of the metropolis with the professional skill of the town. A second concert has been recently established, which, originating, like the other, in a private meeting of amateurs, promises to equal the former in respect of numbers, though not enjoying such distinguished patronage. Triennial music meetings, the receipts of which are appropriated to the support of the general hospital, are held at the church and at the theatre; at the former, oratorios and selections of sacred music are performed, and at the latter, miscellaneous concerts in which the principal vocal and instrumental performers in the kingdom are engaged. The Vauxhall Gardens, which are brilliantly illuminated, are open during the summer, and attract much company to concerts performed there, and to grand displays of fireworks, which are frequent during the season. The Lady-well baths (so called from one of the springs by which they are supplied) form a complete establishment, consisting of hot, cold, sulphureous, vapour, and fumigating baths, attached to which are dressing-rooms and every accommodation for invalids. The swimming, or pleasure bath is one hundred and ten feet long, and fifty-two feet wide, and is supplied with a constant influx of water, at the rate of one thousand hogsheads per hour; it is surrounded with high walls, shaded with lofty trees, and furnished with alcoves and dressing-boxes. The gentlemen's cold bath is sixteen feet long, and twelve feet wide, and is supplied by a spring within itself, at the rate of twelve hogsheads per hour; the buildings are replete with every accommodation, and the gardens and pleasure grounds are extensive and retired.

Prior to the year 1715, Birmingham comprised only one parish, and for all civil purposes it is still so considered: at that time, a small portion of the original parish of St. Martin, consisting of a district in the centre of the town, was formed into the parish of St. Philip; and, in 1829, two other districts were formed into the parishes of St. George and St. Thomas: they are all within the archdeaconry of Coventry, and diocese of Lichfield and Coventry. The living of St. Martin's is a rectory, rated in the king's books at £19. 3. 6½., and in the patronage of the Executors of the late William Hawkes, Esq. The church is an ancient structure, in the decorated style of English architecture, with a square tower, and a lofty and well-proportioned spire, with the exception of which, the building, originally of stone, has been cased with brick: within are several effigies, the details of some of which are finely executed. The living of St. Philip's is a rectory not in charge, to which is annexed the prebend of Sawley, including the dignities of canon residentiary and treasurer in the Cathedral Church of Lichfield, with the patronage of the perpetual curacy of Sawley, in the county of Derby: it is in the patronage of the Bishop of Lichfield and Coventry. The church, erected in 1725, is a handsome structure, in the Grecian style of architecture, combining the

Corinthian and the Doric orders, with a tower supporting a dome and a cupola: the churchyard is a spacious area, around which are many elegant buildings of modern erection. The living of St. George's is a rectory not in charge, in the patronage of the Executors of the late William Hawkes, Esq. The church, containing one thousand three hundred and seventy-eight free sittings, was erected in 1822, by subscription among the inhabitants, aided by a grant from the parliamentary commissioners, at an expense of £12,491. 6. 6.: it is a fine specimen of the early character of the decorated style of English architecture, with a lofty square embattled tower, with pierced parapet and crocketed pinnacles. The living of St. Thomas' is a rectory not in charge, to which the Executors of the late William Hawkes, Esq. presented in 1829, in which year the church, containing one thousand four hundred and twenty-three free sittings, was completed, at an expense of £14,712. 10., which was wholly defrayed by a grant from the parliamentary commissioners: it is a chaste and elegant structure, in the Grecian style of architecture, with a handsome steeple, connected in the lower part with the sides of the church, by quadrants of the Ionic order. St. Mary's chapel, in the parish of St. Martin, erected by subscription in 1774, on a site given by Miss Weaman, is an octagonal brick building, with a small stone steeple: the living is a perpetual curacy, in the patronage of trustees appointed under the will of the late Miss Weaman. St. Paul's chapel, in the same parish, built by subscription in 1779, on a site given by Miss Colmore, is a handsome edifice in the Grecian style: the roof, which over the galleries is plainly groined, is supported on handsome pillars of the Ionic order; the altar-piece is ornamented with a painting in stained glass of the Conversion of St. Paul; the steeple, which is much admired for the lightness and elegance of its design, was added in 1820: the living is a perpetual curacy, in the patronage of Mr. Latimer. Christ Church, in the parish of St. Philip, erected in 1813, by subscription, for the especial accommodation of the poor, is a neat plain building, with a handsome portico of the Tuscan order, and a spire: the living is a perpetual curacy, to which is annexed the prebend of Tachbrook in the Cathedral Church of Lichfield; it is in the patronage of the Bishop of Lichfield and Coventry. St. Bartholomew's, a chapel of ease to the rectory of St. Martin's, is a plain brick building, with a cupola; the interior is a good specimen of the Tuscan order, and the altar-piece is richly carved. St. Peter's, a chapel of ease to the rectory of St. Philip's, containing one thousand four hundred and thirty-one free sittings, was built in 1827, at an expense of £13,365. 16. 6., part of which was defrayed by the parliamentary commissioners, and was almost destroyed by fire, in January 1831. There are places of worship for Baptists, the Society of Friends, Independents, Primitive and Wesleyan Methodists, Swedenborgians, and Unitarians; besides a Scotch church, two Roman Catholic chapels, and a synagogue. Among these, Zion chapel, Carr's Lane meeting-house, the Scotch church, and Ebenezer chapel, may be distinguished as spacious and handsome structures.

The free grammar school was founded by Edward VI., in the fifth year of his reign, and endowed with the revenue of the guild of the Holy Cross, which, prior to the dissolution, occupied the site of the present building: the endowment, arising from land, at that time amounted only to £30 per annum; at present, from the ground having been let on building leases, it produces from £8000 to £10,000 per annum, which, upon the expiration of the leases, will be greatly augmented. The management is vested in a bailiff and eighteen governors, who appoint a head-master, second master, and two ushers, with a writing-master and a drawing-master. There are seven exhibitions, of £70 per annum each, to either of the Universities; and not less than eight subordinate schools are attached to the establishment: the number of scholars on the foundation is one hundred and fifty: the premises, occupying three sides of a quadrangle, with houses for the masters, are about to be rebuilt. The Blue-coat charity school was established by subscription, in 1724, for the maintenance, clothing, and education of twenty-two boys and ten girls: its funds having been increased by additional subscriptions, donations, and legacies, the buildings were enlarged in 1794; there are at present one hundred and thirty boys and sixty girls in the school. A similar school for the children of dissenters, established in 1762, is now limited to the maintenance and instruction of forty-eight girls. The National and the Lancasterian schools are supported by subscription; and an infant school, which is under excellent regulations, is numerously attended.

The general hospital is a handsome and spacious brick building, consisting of a centre and two wings, and containing fourteen wards, in which are one hundred and sixty-five beds. This establishment has obtained extensive patronage and support: it was opened in 1779, when the committee, in order to augment its funds, had recourse to a performance of sacred music, under the direction of a London professor, the produce of which was £127. This performance, repeated every third year, formed the groundwork of the triennial musical festival, for which, under the gratuitous superintendence of Mr. Joseph Moore, a resident amateur, Birmingham has, for the last twenty years, been so justly celebrated. The receipts, which have been progressively increasing, now average a net sum of upwards of £5000, available for the benefit of the institution, which, as a school of medicine and surgery, has attained a high degree of celebrity. The dispensary was established by subscription, in 1794, and affords medical relief to about four thousand patients annually: the building, consisting of a centre and two wings, is a handsome structure of freestone, with four lofty pilasters supporting a triangular pediment, ornamented with a basso-relievo of the "Good Samaritan." The self-supporting dispensary, upon the plan of Mr. Smith, of Southam, is maintained by small annual subscriptions from the poor, aided by those of the honorary members. The infirmary for diseases of the eye and ear, established by Mr. Hodgson, surgeon, in 1823; and the infirmary for the cure of bodily deformity, established in 1817, under the patronage of the Earl of Dartmouth, are liberally supported; and a house, at the extremity of the town, has, under the superintendence of Dr. Birt Davies, been appropriated as a house of recovery from fever. The asylum for deaf and dumb children was established in 1815, and is partly supported by a weekly charge, and partly by subscription; the number at present in the institution is thirty. The school of industry is a large establishment under the management of the guardians of the poor, in which three hundred children are maintained, and employed in platting straw, heading pins, and in other kinds of work suited to their age. There are also almshouses for the aged and infirm, and numerous and extensive funds for charitable purposes. About a mile from the town is a chalybeate spring, which, though known to possess highly medicinal properties, is not much noticed; and about three miles to the west, and within a few hundred yards of the Ikniеld-street, are the remains of a large quadrangular encampment, surrounded by a triple fosse, which, from the extent of its area (being more than thirty acres), is supposed to be of Danish origin: pieces of armour, broken swords, and battle-axes, have been ploughed up in the vicinity. Inconsiderable vestiges of an ancient priory are still visible in the cellars of some houses in the square, which now occupy its site; and a great number of human bones, and sculls with teeth having the enamel perfect, have been found in the neighbourhood, parts of which still bear the names of the Upper and Lower Priory. At the western extremity of the town was an hospital, dedicated to St. Thomas the Apostle, the revenue of which, in the 26th of Henry VIII., was £8. 5. 3. Birmingham gives the title of baron to the Earl of Dudley.

BIRSTALL, a chapelry in that part of the parish of Belgrave which is in the western division of the hundred of Goscote, county of Leicester, 3¼ miles (N. by E.) from Leicester, containing 371 inhabitants. The chapel, dedicated to St. James, has lately been enlarged by the addition of one hundred and seventy-seven sittings, of which number, ninety-nine are free, and toward defraying the expense of which the Incorporated Society for the enlargement of churches granted £100. There is a communication with the Leicester and Melton-Mowbray navigation by means of the river Soar, which runs through the chapelry.

BIRSTALL, a parish in the wapentake of Morley, West riding of the county of York, 7½ miles (S. W.) from Leeds, comprising the chapelries of Clackheaton, Drighlington, Heckmondwike, Liversedge, and Tong, and the townships of Great and Little Gomersall, Hunsworth, and Wike, and containing 21,217 inhabitants. The living is a discharged vicarage, in the archdeaconry of the East riding, and diocese of York, rated in the king's books at £23. 19. 2., and in the patronage of the Archbishop of York. The church, dedicated to St. Peter, has lately been enlarged by the addition of one hundred and fifty sittings, one hundred of which are free; the Incorporated Society for the enlargement of churches and chapels having granted £150 towards defraying the expense. There is a place of worship for Wesleyan Methodists. A chapel is also being erected at Birkenshaw, in this parish. The village of Birstall is situated in the township of Gomersall: the clothing business prevails to a great extent in the parish, in which also there are some collieries. The Rev. William Armystead, in 1601, bequeathed £100 for the erection of a school; the fund now produces £8. 10. per annum, for which six children are instructed gratuitously in a National school, which was erected in 1819, at the expense of William Charlesworth, Esq. Dr. Priestley, equally distinguished for his advocacy of Unitarianism, and his discoveries in chemistry, was born at Field-head, in this parish, in 1733; he died in America, in 1804.

BIRSTWITH, a township in the parish of Hampsthwaite, lower division of the wapentake of Claro, West riding of the county of York, 8 miles (W. by N.) from Knaresborough, containing 621 inhabitants. John Richmond, in 1711, gave a rent-charge of £14 for the instruction of poor boys belonging to the townships of Birstwith and Felliscliff.

BIRTHORPE, a chapelry in the parish of Sempringham, wapentake of Aveland, parts of Kesteven, county of Lincoln, 2½ miles (E.) from Folkingham, containing 56 inhabitants.

BIRTLE, a joint township with Bamford, in the parish of Middleton, hundred of Salford, county palatine of Lancaster, 2 miles (E.N.E.) from Bury, containing, with Bamford, 1207 inhabitants. The manufacture of woollen and cotton goods, and the printing of calico, are carried on here.

BIRTLES, a township in the parish of Prestbury, hundred of Macclesfield, county palatine of Chester, 2¾ miles (W. by N.) from Macclesfield, containing 47 inhabitants. There are various tumuli in the neighbourhood, and fragments of urns, which formerly contained burnt bones, have been discovered.

BIRTLEY, a township in that part of the parish of Chester le Street which is in the middle division of Chester ward, county palatine of Durham, 5¼ miles (S. by E.) from Gateshead, containing 1386 inhabitants, many of whom are employed in the coal mines in the vicinity. There is a place of worship for Roman Catholics. A brine-spring exists in the township, from which salt is made.

BIRTLEY, a parochial chapelry in the north-eastern division of Tindale ward, county of Northumberland, 5 miles (S. E. by S.) from Bellingham, containing, with a small portion of the township of Broomhope with Buteland, 393 inhabitants. The living is a perpetual curacy, in the archdeaconry of Northumberland, and diocese of Durham, endowed with £400 private benefaction, and £800 royal bounty, and in the patronage of the Duke of Northumberland. Birtley was formed into a parochial chapelry in 1765, in which year it was separated from the parish of Chollerton. Coal and lime exist in the neighbourhood: there is a day and Sunday school in the village.

BIRTS-MORTON, a parish in the lower division of the hundred of Pershore, county of Worcester, 5¼ miles (S. W.) from Upton upon Severn, containing 236 inhabitants. The living is a rectory, in the archdeaconry and diocese of Worcester, rated in the king's books at £7. 8. 1½., and in the patronage of J. Thackwell, Esq. The church is dedicated to St. Peter and St. Paul. A charity school was endowed by Samuel Juice, in 1703, for the instruction of boys, a few of whom are clothed by means of a separate fund. The manor-house is an ancient edifice, surrounded by a moat still very perfect.

BISBROOKE, a parish in the hundred of Wrandike, county of Rutland, 1¾ mile (E.) from Uppingham, containing 223 inhabitants. The living is a discharged vicarage, in the archdeaconry of Northampton, and diocese of Peterborough, rated in the king's books at

£6. 0. 4., and in the patronage of the Duke of Rutland. The church is dedicated to St. John the Baptist. Here is a school with a trifling endowment.

BISCATHORPE, a parish in the eastern division of the wapentake of WRAGGOE, parts of LINDSEY, county of LINCOLN, 8 miles (N.E. by E.) from Wragby, containing 37 inhabitants. The living is a discharged rectory, in the archdeaconry and diocese of Lincoln, rated in the king's books at £5. 18. 4., endowed with £200 royal bounty, and in the patronage of the Crown. The church is dedicated to St. Helen.

BISCOTT, a hamlet in the parish of LUTON, hundred of FLITT, county of BEDFORD, 2 miles (N. by W.) from Luton. The population is returned with Limbury.

BISHAM, a parish in the hundred of BEYNHURST, county of BERKS, 4½ miles (N.W.) from Maidenhead, containing 707 inhabitants. The living is a discharged vicarage, in the archdeaconry of Berks, and diocese of Salisbury, rated in the king's books at £7. 13. 1., and endowed with £200 and £20 per annum private benefaction, £600 royal bounty, and £900 parliamentary grant, and in the patronage of G. Vansittart, Esq. The church, dedicated to All Saints, is pleasantly situated close to the river Thames, the banks of which are adorned with interesting scenery, and many pleasing seats. The rolling of copper into sheets, and the making of copper bolts for the navy, and of pans and other vessels in copper, are carried on here to a considerable extent. Temple mills, esteemed among the most complete and powerful of the kind in the kingdom, received this name from having been in the possession of the Knights Templars, who established a preceptory here, on receiving a grant of the manor from Robert de Ferrariis, in the reign of Stephen. This institution, on the dissolution of the society, was succeeded by an Augustine priory, founded in 1338, by William de Montacute, Earl of Salisbury, the revenue of which, in the 26th of Henry VIII., amounted to £327. 4. 6. It was surrendered in 1536, was re-founded by the king, for a mitred abbot and thirteen Benedictine monks, and was finally dissolved on the 19th of June, 1538: the abbey was frequently visited by Henry VIII., and also by Queen Elizabeth, who resided here some time, a large state apartment being still called the Queen's council-chamber; but a very small portion only of the conventual buildings can be traced in the mansion which now occupies its site.

BISHAMPTON, a parish in the middle division of the hundred of OSWALDSLOW, county of WORCESTER, 5½ miles (N. E. by N.) from Pershore, containing 374 inhabitants. The living is a discharged vicarage, in the archdeaconry and diocese of Worcester, rated in the king's books at £7. 9. 9½., endowed with £400 private benefaction, and £400 royal bounty, and in the patronage of the Bishop of Worcester. The church is dedicated to St. Peter.

BISHOP'S BOURNE, a parish in the hundred of KINGHAMFORD, lathe of ST. AUGUSTINE, county of KENT, 4 miles (S.E. by S.) from Canterbury, containing 325 inhabitants. The living is a rectory, with the perpetual curacy of Barham annexed, in the archdeaconry and diocese of Canterbury, rated in the king's books at £39. 19. 2., and in the alternate patronage of the Crown and the Archbishop of Canterbury. The church is dedicated to St. Mary.

Corporate Seal.

BISHOP'S-CASTLE, a borough, market town, and parish, having separate jurisdiction, locally in the hundred of Purslow, county of SALOP, 19 miles (N. W. by N.) from Ludlow, 20¼ (S. W. by S.) from Shrewsbury, and 157 (N. W. by W.) from London, containing 1880 inhabitants, of which number, 1616 are within the borough. This place owes its name to a castle belonging to the bishops of Hereford, that stood here, but of which the site alone, now a bowling-green belonging to the Castle Inn, and some small portions of the enclosing walls, can be traced: a subterraneous passage is said to have subsisted from this castle to another at some distance, the arched entrance to which is shown in the garden of an adjoining house; but it is scarcely distinguishable from the heaps of stones found in various parts of the hill on which the castle stood. The town is partly situated on the summit, but chiefly on the steep declivity of a hill: the houses in general are meanly built of unhewn stone, with thatched roofs; though, in detached situations, there are several handsome edifices of modern erection. Such of the inhabitants as have not pumps attached to their houses, are indifferently supplied with water, from a reservoir under the town-hall, into which it is conveyed by pipes from the neighbouring hills. The market is on Friday, and is well supplied with grain, which is sold by sample: the market-house, built within the last twenty years, by the Earl of Powis, is a handsome edifice of stone, supported on piazzas; the area is used as a corn market, and the upper part as a school-room. The fairs are on February 13th, for cattle and sheep; on the Friday preceding Good Friday, which is a very large fair for horned cattle; on the first Friday after May-day, a pleasure and statute fair; July 5th, formerly a great wool fair; September 9th, and November 13th, for horned cattle, sheep, and horses. The government, by charter granted in the 15th year of the reign of Elizabeth, and confirmed and extended by James I., is vested in a bailiff, recorder, and fifteen capital burgesses, assisted by a town-clerk, two serjeants at mace, and subordinate officers: the bailiff, late bailiff, and recorder, are justices of the peace. The bailiff is elected from among the capital burgesses, on the first Monday before Michaelmas-day, and sworn into office on the first Monday after it; the capital burgesses are chosen by a majority of the burgesses at large: the freedom is acquired only by birth. The corporation hold a court of session quarterly for the borough, on the next Wednesday after the general quarter sessions for the county, at which the bailiff, the late bailiff or justice, and the recorder, preside; and a court of record is held every alternate Saturday, for the recovery of debts under £20, under the presidency of the bailiff and two capital burgesses. The town-hall is a plain brick edifice on pillars and arches, built by the subscriptions of the burgesses, in 1750, with a prison on the basement story for criminals, and above it one for debtors. The elective franchise was conferred in the 26th of Elizabeth, since which time the borough has returned two members to parliament. The right of election is vested in the burgesses generally, about sixty in number, provided they have been resident within the borough twelve months prior to the election, in default of which they lose their title to vote: the bailiff is the returning officer.

The living is a vicarage, in the archdeaconry of Salop, and diocese of Hereford, rated in the king's books at £9. 12. 10., and in the patronage of the Earl of Powis. The church, dedicated to St. John the Baptist, is a fine old structure, principally in the Norman style, with a square embattled tower, crowned with pinnacles: it was burnt in the parliamentary war, by Cromwell, and has been rebuilt without a due regard to the original style of its architecture. The free school was founded, in 1737, by Mrs. Mary Morris, in memory of her first husband, Mr. John Wright, of Wimbledon in Surrey, merchant, a native of Bishop's Castle, and endowed with £1000 in the three per cents., for the instruction of twenty-five boys and twenty-five girls in reading, writing, and arithmetic, and the latter in sewing and knitting. Some charitable benefactions are distributed by the vicar and churchwardens, in money and bread. Jeremy Stephens, author of various doctrinal works, and the learned coadjutor of Sir Henry Spelman in the compilation of the "English Councils," was a native of the place.

BISHOP'S DALE, a township in the parish of Aysgarth, western division of the wapentake of Hang, North riding of the county of York, 12 miles (S.W. by W.) from Middleham, containing 95 inhabitants. The neighbourhood contains several waterfalls, and abounds with picturesque scenery.

BISHOP'S FEE, a liberty in the parish of St. Margaret, borough of Leicester, though locally in the hundred of Gartree, county of Leicester. The population is returned with Leicester. The magistrates for the borough, and those for the county, exercise concurrent jurisdiction throughout the liberty, the inhabitants of which pay church and poor rates to the parish of St. Margaret, but are assessed for the king's taxes with the hundred of Gartree, the petty sessions for which are occasionally held here.

BISHOP-SIDE (HIGH and LOW), a township in that part of the parish of Ripon which is within the liberty of Ripon, West riding of the county of York, 10½ miles (W. S. W.) from Ripon, containing, with the market town of Pateley-Bridge, 2072 inhabitants.

BISHOPSTON, a chapelry in the parish of Old Stratford, Stratford division of the hundred of Barlichway, county of Warwick, 2¼ miles (N.N.W.) from Stratford upon Avon, with which place the population is returned. The living is a perpetual curacy, in the archdeaconry and diocese of Worcester, endowed with £1000 royal bounty, and £200 parliamentary grant, and in the patronage of the Vicar of Stratford. The chapel, dedicated to St. Peter, is in ruins.

BISHOPSTON, a parish in the hundred of Downton, though locally in the hundred of Chalk, county of Wilts, 3½ miles (S. by W.) from Wilton, containing 663 inhabitants. The living is a vicarage, in the archdeaconry and diocese of Salisbury, rated in the king's books at £12. 1. 3.; there is also a sinecure rectory, rated at £19. 14. 2.; both are in the patronage of the Earl of Pembroke and Montgomery. The church, dedicated to St. John the Baptist, is a handsome cruciform edifice, in the decorated style of English architecture; the chancel contains three seats in canopied niches, and has a finely ornamented roof.

BISHOPSTON, a parish in the hundred of Ramsbury, county of Wilts, 5¾ miles (E.) from Swindon, containing 572 inhabitants. The living is a vicarage, in the peculiar jurisdiction and patronage of the Prebendary of Bishopston in the Cathedral Church of Salisbury, rated in the king's books at £6. 6. 8. The church is dedicated to St. Mary.

BISHOPSTONE, a parish in the hundred of Grimsworth, county of Hereford, 7 miles (W. N. W.) from Hereford, containing 270 inhabitants. The living is a discharged rectory, with the vicarage of Yazor annexed, in the archdeaconry and diocese of Hereford, rated in the king's books at £7. 7. 6., and in the patronage of Sir Uvedale Price, Bart. The church is dedicated to St. Lawrence.

BISHOPSTONE, a parish in the hundred of Bishopstone, rape of Pevensey, county of Sussex, 1¾ mile (N. W. by N.) from Seaford, containing 277 inhabitants. The living is a discharged vicarage, in the archdeaconry of Lewes, and diocese of Chichester, rated in the king's books at £8. 13. 4., endowed with £200 royal bounty, and in the patronage of the Bishop of Chichester. The church, comprising a nave, two chancels, and a tower, is chiefly in the Norman style of architecture. The Rev. James Hurdis, Professor of Poetry at Oxford, and author of the "Village Curate," and other interesting poems, was born here, in 1763.

BISHOP'S STORTFORD, county of Hertford.—See STORTFORD (BISHOP'S).

BISHOPSTROW, a parish in the hundred of Warminster, county of Wilts, 1½ mile (E. S.E.) from Warminster, containing 275 inhabitants. The living is a rectory, in the archdeaconry and diocese of Salisbury, rated in the king's books at £11. 10., and in the patronage of Sir J. D. Astley, Bart. The church is dedicated to St. Adelme. About the commencement of the present century, three urns, containing Roman brass coins, were dug up here.

BISHOP'S WOOD, a township in the parish of Brewood, eastern division of the hundred of Cuttlestone, county of Stafford. The population is returned with the parish.

BISHOP-THORPE, a parish in the ainsty of the city, and east riding of the county, of York, 3½ miles (S. by W.) from York, containing 301 inhabitants. The living is a discharged vicarage, in the archdeaconry and diocese of York, rated in the king's books at £4, endowed with £400 private benefaction, and £400 royal bounty, and in the patronage of the Archbishop of York. The church, dedicated to St. Andrew, was rebuilt by Archbishop Drummond, in 1766, and adorned with a curious window, brought from the castle of Cawood. The parish was called St. Andrew's Thorpe until the manor was purchased, in the reign of John, by Walter de Grey, Archbishop of York, who built a palace and a chapel here; on which account, the episcopal prefix was given to it, and it has been the constant residence of the archbishops since the destruction of Cawood castle, in the parliamentary war. The palace was greatly enlarged and embellished by Archbishop Drummond, when that prelate took down and rebuilt the church. A National school was erected in 1815. Attached to it is a chapel, founded by de Grey; it is in the early style of English architecture.

BISHOPTON, a parish in the south-western division of STOCKTON ward, county palatine of DURHAM, comprising the townships of Bishopton, East and West Newbiggins, and Little Stainton, and containing 453 inhabitants, of which number, 365 are in the township of Bishopton, 6 miles (W. by N.) from Stockton. The living is a discharged vicarage, in the archdeaconry and diocese of Durham, rated in the king's books at £4. 5. 10., endowed with £200 private benefaction, and £200 royal bounty, and in the patronage of the Master and Brethren of Sherburn Hospital. The church is dedicated to St. Peter. A parochial school, with a house for the master, was built a few years ago, by subscription, and is partly supported by a small annuity. In a field at the eastern extremity of the village there are vestiges of an intrenchment, which is supposed to have been part of the fortifications that guarded the mansion of the faithful Roger de Conyers, from whom William de St. Barbara, elect bishop of Durham, received powerful assistance in his struggle against Comyn, the usurper of the see, about the middle of the twelfth century, and at this secure retreat received the homage of those of his vassals who returned to their duty.

BISHOPTON, a township in that part of the parish of RIPON which is in the liberty of RIPON, West riding of the county of YORK, 2½ miles (N. by W.) from Ripon, containing 136 inhabitants.

BISHTON, a parish in the lower division of the hundred of CALDICOTT, county of MONMOUTH, 4 miles (S.E. by E.) from Caerleon, containing 153 inhabitants. The living is a perpetual curacy, in the archdeaconry and diocese of Llandaff, endowed with £1000 royal bounty, and in the patronage of the Archdeacon of Llandaff. The church is dedicated to St. Cadwallader.

BISLEY, a parish (formerly a market town) in the hundred of BISLEY, county of GLOUCESTER, 11 miles (S. E.) from Gloucester, and 97 (W.) from London, containing 5421 inhabitants. The town is situated partly on the acclivity of a hill, and partly in the vale beneath it, which is watered by a small stream. The streets are irregularly formed, and contain few houses of respectable appearance. The inhabitants are chiefly employed in the manufacture of broad cloth, which is carried on to a considerable extent. The Thames and Severn canal passes through the parish, and, near the extremity of it, enters a tunnel, through which it is conducted for nearly two miles and a half under Salperton hill. A market was formerly held here, but it has been discontinued: the fairs are on May 4th and November 12th. The town is within the jurisdiction of a court of requests held at Cirencester, for the seven hundreds of Cirencester, established by an act passed in the 32nd of George III., for the recovery of debts under 40*s.*: constables and other officers are appointed at the court leet of the lord of the manor. The living is a vicarage, in the archdeaconry and diocese of Gloucester, rated in the king's books at £19. 10. 5., and in the patronage of the Crown. The church, dedicated to All Saints, is a spacious and handsome structure, partly in the decorated, and partly in the later, style of English architecture, with a tower surmounted by a lofty spire: among other interesting monuments is a statue of one of the family of Nottingham. In the churchyard there is an octagonal cross, handsomely panelled in trefoil, and surmounted with an ancient font, erected over a well, in which a man having been drowned, the cemetery was placed under an interdict for three years, during which time the dead were carried to Bibury for interment. There is a place of worship for Wesleyan Methodists. The free school is supported by a portion of the produce of lands left for the repair of the church, the payment of the clerk, and the salary of the schoolmaster, who receives at present £13. 14. per annum. A Blue-coat school for clothing and instructing ten boys, endowed in 1820, by Mr. Taylor, has been incorporated with the free school, and the master receives a salary of £12. 12. per annum, for instructing the boys. The common, then consisting of one thousand two hundred acres, was given to the poor of this parish by Roger Mortimer, Earl of March, in the reign of Edward III.; a considerable part of it has been enclosed. At Lilly-house, a hamlet near the town, a vaulted chamber was discovered, with several adjoining apartments, having tesselated pavements, and niches in the walls; some other relics of antiquity, supposed to be Roman, have also been found at Custom-Scrubs, another adjacent hamlet.

BISLEY, a parish in the first division of the hundred of GODLEY, county of SURREY, 4 miles (S. E.) from Bagshot, containing 273 inhabitants. The living is a rectory, in the archdeaconry of Surrey, and diocese of Winchester, rated in the king's books at £7. 16. 8., and in the patronage of the Rev. John King, the Rev. Charles Simeon, and the Rev. — Ball. The church, part of which is built with timber and brick plaistered over, is dedicated to St. John the Baptist, and is said to be six centuries old: near it there is a chalybeate spring, called St. John the Baptist's well.

BISPHAM, a parish in the hundred of AMOUNDERNESS, county palatine of LANCASTER, comprising the townships of Bispham with Norbreck, and Layton with Warbrick, and containing 1072 inhabitants, of which number, 323 are in the township of Bispham with Norbreck, 3 miles (W. N. W.) from Poulton. The living is a perpetual curacy, in the archdeaconry of Richmond, and diocese of Chester, endowed with £400 private benefaction, and £400 royal bounty, and in the patronage of B. Hesketh, Esq. Richard Higginson founded a school in 1659, which he endowed with a rent-charge of £30; the income, by subsequent benefactions, has been augmented to £70 per annum.

BISPHAM, a chapelry in the parish of CROSTON, hundred of LEYLAND, county palatine of LANCASTER, 6½ miles (N. E. by E.) from Ormskirk, containing 254 inhabitants. The living is a perpetual curacy, in the archdeaconry and diocese of Chester, and in the patronage of the Trustees of the founders of the chapel, which is dedicated to St. John. A free grammar school, founded by Richard Durning, in 1692, is endowed with an estate producing about £200 per annum.

BISTERN-BARTLEY, a tything in the parish of ELING, hundred of REDBRIDGE, New Forest (East) division of the county of SOUTHAMPTON. The population is returned with the parish.

BITCHFIELD, a parish in the wapentake of BELTISLOE, parts of KESTEVEN, county of LINCOLN, 3¼ miles (N. by W.) from Corby, containing 144 inhabitants. The living is a discharged vicarage, in the archdeaconry and diocese of Lincoln, rated in the king's books at £5. 11. 5½., endowed with £200 parliamentary grant, and in the patronage of the Bishop of Lincoln. The church is dedicated to St. Mary Magdalene.

BITCHFIELD, a township in the parish of STAMFORDHAM, north-eastern division of TINDALE ward, county of NORTHUMBERLAND, 13 miles (N.W.) from Newcastle, containing 39 inhabitants.

BITTADON, a parish in the hundred of BRAUNTON, county of DEVON, 6¼ miles (N. by W.) from Barnstaple, containing 52 inhabitants. The living is a discharged rectory, in the archdeaconry of Barnstaple, and diocese of Exeter, rated in the king's books at £5. 2. 8½., and in the patronage of G. A. Barbor, Esq. The church is dedicated to St. Peter.

BITTERING (LITTLE), a parish in the hundred of LAUNDITCH, county of NORFOLK, 5 miles (N.W.) from East Dereham. The population is returned with the parish of Beeston St. Mary. The living is a discharged rectory, in the archdeaconry and diocese of Norwich, rated in the king's books at £2. 13. 6½., endowed with £800 royal bounty, and in the patronage of James Dover, Esq.

BITTERLEY, a parish partly in the hundred of MUNSLOW, but chiefly in the hundred of OVERS, county of SALOP, 4½ miles (E.N.E.) from Ludlow, containing 1064 inhabitants. The living is a rectory, in the archdeaconry of Salop, and diocese of Hereford, rated in the king's books at £18. 6. 3., and in the patronage of Sir J. D. King, Bart. The church is dedicated to St. Mary. John Newborough, in 1712, gave £400, now producing £34 per annum, toward the support of a free grammar school.

BITTERN, a tything in that part of the parish of SOUTH STONEHAM which is in the hundred of MANSBRIDGE, Fawley division of the county of SOUTHAMPTON, 2 miles (N.E.) from Southampton. The population is returned with the parish. There is a place of worship for Wesleyan Methodists. Bittern is within the jurisdiction of the Cheyney Court held at Winchester every Thursday, for the recovery of debts to any amount. This was the site of the Roman station *Clausentum*: a variety of Roman relics has been found.

BITTESBY, a liberty in the parish of CLAYBROOKE, hundred of GUTHLAXTON, county of LEICESTER, 3 miles (W. by N.) from Lutterworth, containing 11 inhabitants.

BITTESWELL, a parish in the hundred of GUTHLAXTON, county of LEICESTER, 1 mile (N. by W.) from Lutterworth, containing 427 inhabitants. The living is a vicarage, in the archdeaconry of Leicester, and diocese of Lincoln, rated in the king's books at £4. 3. 0½., and in the alternate patronage of the Master and Wardens of the Haberdashers' Company, and the Governors of Christ's Hospital, London. The church is dedicated to St. Mary. The Roman Watling-street passes along the verge of the parish, and there is a mineral spring within its limits.

BITTISCOMBE, a hamlet in the parish of UPTON, hundred of WILLITON and FREEMANNERS, county of SOMERSET. The population is returned with the parish. Here was anciently a chapel, which has been demolished.

BITTON, a parish in the upper division of the hundred of LANGLEY and SWINEHEAD, county of GLOUCESTER, comprising the chapelries of Hanham and Oldland, and the hamlet of Bitton, and containing 7171 inhabitants, of which number, 1788 are in the hamlet of Bitton, 6¼ miles (E. S. E.) from Bristol. The living is a discharged vicarage, in the archdeaconry and diocese of Gloucester, rated in the king's books at £18. 15., and in the patronage of the Prebendary of Bitton in the Cathedral Church of Salisbury. The church, dedicated to St. Mary, is a large and handsome edifice, with a finely ornamented tower, partly Norman, and partly in the later style of English architecture; it contains one thousand and nineteen sittings, of which eight hundred and eighty-eight are free, and in 1822 was constituted a district church. A chapel was built in 1820, under the provisions of a late act, toward the expense of which the parliamentary commissioners granted £2293. The river Avon flows along the southern side of the parish.

BIX-BRAND, a parish in the hundred of BINFIELD, county of OXFORD, 4 miles (N. W. by N.) from Henley upon Thames, containing, with Bix-Gibwen, 383 inhabitants. The living is a rectory, with that of Bix-Gibwen consolidated, in the archdeaconry and diocese of Oxford, rated in the king's books at £9. 15., and in the patronage of the Earl of Macclesfield. The church is dedicated to St. James.

BIX-GIBWEN, a parish in the hundred of BINFIELD, county of OXFORD, 2½ miles (N. W.) from Henley upon Thames. The population is returned with Bix-Brand. The living is a rectory, consolidated with that of Bix-Brand, in the archdeaconry and diocese of Oxford. The church, which was dedicated to St. Michael, is in ruins.

BIXLEY, a parish in the hundred of HENSTEAD, county of NORFOLK, 3 miles (S. E. by S.) from Norwich, containing 107 inhabitants. The living is a discharged rectory, with that of Earl's Framlingham united, in the archdeaconry of Norfolk, and diocese of Norwich, rated in the king's books at £5, and in the patronage of the Duke of Norfolk. The church, dedicated to St. Wandegisilus, to whose image here pilgrimages were formerly made, is an ancient edifice, built by William de Dunwich, in 1272.

BIXTON, or BICKERSTON, a parish in the hundred of FOREHOE, county of NORFOLK, 5½ miles (N. by W.) from Wymondham. The population is returned with Barnham-Broom. The living is a rectory, united, with that of Barnham-Broom, to the vicarage of Kimberley, in the archdeaconry of Norfolk, and diocese of Norwich, rated in the king's books at £2. 6. 8. The church, now desecrated, was dedicated to St. Andrew.

BLABY, a parish in the hundred of GUTHLAXTON, county of LEICESTER, 4½ miles (S. by W.) from Leicester, containing, with the chapelry of Countess-Thorpe, 1730 inhabitants. The living is a rectory, in the archdeaconry of Leicester, and diocese of Lincoln, rated in the king's books at £15. 5., and in the patronage of the Crown. The church is dedicated to All Saints. There are places of worship for Baptists and Wesleyan Methodists. The Union canal passes through the parish.

BLACKAUTON, a parish in the hundred of COLERIDGE, county of DEVON, 5 miles (W. by N.) from

Dartmouth, containing 1227 inhabitants. The living is a discharged vicarage, in the archdeaconry of Totness, and diocese of Exeter, rated in the king's books at £15. 8. 9., endowed with £200 private benefaction, and £200 royal bounty, and in the patronage of Col. Seale. The church, dedicated to St. Michael, contains a Norman font, and a wooden screen richly carved. There is a place of worship for Wesleyan Methodists.

BLACKBOROUGH, a parish in the hundred of HAYRIDGE, county of DEVON, 5 miles (E.S.E.) from Cullompton, containing 74 inhabitants. The living is a rectory, annexed to that of Bundley, in the archdeaconry and diocese of Exeter, rated in the king's books at £4. The church, which was dedicated to All Saints, is desecrated, but the cemetery is still used.

BLACKBROOK, or BLAKEBROOK, a hamlet in that part of the parish of KIDDERMINSTER which is called the Foreign, lower division of the hundred of HALFSHIRE, county of WORCESTER, ½ a mile (W.) from Kidderminster. The population is returned with the parish. Several new houses have lately been erected in this hamlet, which has become an agreeable part of the environs of Kidderminster.

BLACKBURN, a parish in the lower division of the hundred of BLACKBURN, county palatine of LANCASTER, comprising the market town of Blackburn, the chapelries of Balderston, Billington, Great Harwood, Over Darwen, Mellor, Salesbury, Samlesbury, Tockholes, and Walton le Dale, and the townships of Clayton le Dale, Cuerdale, Lower Darwen, Dinkley, Eccleshill, Little Harwood, Livesey, Osbaldeston, Pleasington, Ramsgrave, Rishton, Wilpshire, and Witton, and containing 53,350 inhabitants, of which number, 21,940 are in the town of Blackburn, 31 miles (S.E. by S.) from Lancaster, and 210 (N.N.W.) from London. This place takes its name from a small rivulet flowing near the town, which, from the turbid state of the water, was anciently called Blakeburn, or the yellow bourne. A castle is said to have been built here, probably by the Romans, which, after their departure from the island, was occupied successively by the Britons and the Saxons; but there are no vestiges of it, nor can even its site be distinctly ascertained. Blackburn was formerly the capital of a district, called Blackburnshire, which for many ages was a dreary and uncultivated waste. In the reign of Elizabeth, it was distinguished as a good market town, and, in the middle of the following century, was celebrated for its supplies of corn, cattle, and provisions. The town is pleasantly situated on the northern bank of the river Derwent, over which are three stone bridges, and in a valley sheltered by a ridge of hills, extending from the north-east to the north-west: it consists of several streets, irregularly formed, but containing several well-built, and many respectable, houses; it is well paved, lighted with gas, and amply supplied with water. In 1824, an act of parliament was obtained for constructing a new turnpike road to Preston, crossing the river Ribble at Brockholes, by which the distance is shortened nearly two miles; and under the same act the town has been greatly improved. There are assembly-rooms, a subscription library, a Linnæan Society, and a theatre, which was erected in 1818. The manufacture of Blackburn checks, and subsequently that of Blackburn greys, a mixture of linen and cotton, which formerly flourished here to a considerable extent, have been superseded by the manufacture of calico, muslin, and cotton goods: not less than forty thousand pieces of the last are, on an average, made weekly, in which about ten thousand persons are employed: the value of these goods, exclusively of dyeing and printing, is estimated at two millions sterling per annum. There are large factories for the spinning of cotton, printing and dyeing establishments, and extensive bleaching grounds.

Some of the earliest and most important improvements in the spinning and manufacture of cotton originated with James Hargreave, a carpenter in this town, who was the inventor and patentee of the spinning jenny, which has since been so generally adopted. The introduction of machinery into the factories excited a powerful sensation among the workmen of this place, and created such tumultuous proceedings on the part of the populace, who destroyed several of the factories in which it was used, that the inventor was driven from the town; and many individuals who had invested large capitals in the establishment of cotton-factories, were so intimidated, that they embraced the earliest opportunity of withdrawing their investments, and removing to places where they might employ them with greater security. There are at present about one hundred thousand spindles in operation in the town and neighbourhood, which produce about thirty-five thousand pounds of yarn weekly. The Leeds and Liverpool canal passes the town, and affords communication with the Mersey, the Dee, the Ouse, the Trent, the Humber, the Severn, and the Thames, forming a most extensive line of inland navigation. The market days are Wednesday and Saturday: the fairs are held on Easter-Monday, May 11th and 12th, and October 17th; a cattle fair is also held on the first Wednesday before February 2nd, and on every alternate Wednesday till Michaelmas. The want of a convenient market-place is strongly felt in this populous town; Fleming-square has been recently appropriated for this purpose, but the area is scarcely large enough. One side of the square is occupied by a spacious cloth-hall, erected for the exhibition and sale of Yorkshire woollen cloths, a great quantity of which is brought hither. Blackburn is within the jurisdiction of the magistrates acting for the hundred to which it gives name: two high constables are appointed, one for the upper, and one for the lower, division, for which latter, together with Whalley, a court of petty session is held here. Its local concerns are under the superintendence of commissioners appointed by a special act of parliament.

This extensive parish, which is fourteen miles in length, and ten in breadth, was formerly part of the parish of Whalley; on being separated from which, it was, on account of its sterility, endowed with a fourth part of the tithes of that parish, in addition to its own. The living is a vicarage, in the archdeaconry and diocese of Chester, rated in the king's books at £8. 1. 8., and in the patronage of the Archbishop of Canterbury. The church, dedicated to St. Mary, and formerly the conventual church of the monastery of Whalley, was rebuilt in the reign of Edward III., and again in that of Henry VIII.; but in 1819 it was taken down, with the exception of the tower, and the chapel of the Duncan family, which contains the altar, and in which baptisms and marriages are still solemnized, and the funeral service is performed. A new church was completed in 1826, on the site of the old grammar school, at an expense of £26,000, raised by a rate under an act of parliament passed in 1819: it was a spacious and elegant edifice, partly in the decorated, and partly in the later, style of English architecture, with a lofty square tower, highly enriched, and crowned with a pierced parapet and crocketed pinnacles, but was burned down in January 1831. The interior is lofty in its proportions, and elegant in its details; the nave is lighted with a fine range of double clerestory windows, and those in the aisles are enriched with flowing tracery of graceful character. The chapels of St. John and St. Peter are both neat modern edifices: St. Peter's is a chapel of ease; the living of St. John's is a perpetual curacy, in the patronage of the Vicar of Blackburn, in whom is also vested the presentation to the several perpetual curacies in the parish, with the exception of that of Salesbury. At Lower Darwen, Over Darwen, and Mellor, new churches have been erected, the expense of each having been partly defrayed by grant from the parliamentary commissioners; they are all in the later style of English architecture, with towers, and were begun in 1827, and completed in 1829. The church at Lower Darwen contains seven hundred and twenty-three free sittings, and the cost of its erection was £5491. 2. 6.: that at Over Darwen, which contains nine hundred and eighty-five free sittings, was erected at an expense of £6573. 4. 9.; and that at Mellor, which has a spire, and contains six hundred and seventy-eight free sittings, cost £5275. 6. 9. There are two places of worship each for Baptists and Independents, and one each for the Society of Friends, Primitive and Wesleyan Methodists, Swedenborgians, and Unitarians, besides two Roman Catholic chapels. The free grammar school was founded in the reign of Elizabeth, who placed it under the superintendence of fifty governors resident in the town, who are a corporate body, and appoint the master: it is endowed with land in the neighbourhood, producing £120 per annum; there are thirty boys on the foundation: the premises, consisting of a school-room and house for the master, are handsomely built of stone. The Rev. Robert Bolton, an eminent divine, and one of the compilers of the Liturgy, was a native of this town, and received the rudiments of his education in the school. In 1764, Mr. John Leyland bequeathed £250 for the instruction of poor girls in reading, writing, sewing, and knitting; this sum has been augmented by subsequent benefactions, and at present ninety girls are instructed and clothed. There is also a National school, supported by subscription, in which eight hundred children of both sexes are taught. The general dispensary was established in 1828: there are a ladies' society for the relief of poor women during child-birth at their own houses, a strangers' friend society, and several other charitable institutions.

BLACK-CHAPEL, a chapelry in the parish of Great Waltham, hundred of Chelmsford, county of Essex, 9 miles (N. by W.) from Chelmsford. The population is returned with the parish.

BLACKDEN, a township in that part of the parish of Sandbach which is in the hundred of Northwich, county palatine of Chester, 6½ miles (S. S. E.) from Knutsford, containing 191 inhabitants.

BLACKFORD, a chapelry in the parish of Wedmore, hundred of Bempstone, county of Somerset, 5¼ miles (S. by W.) from Axbridge. The population is returned with the parish. The living is a perpetual curacy, in the archdeaconry of Wells, and diocese of Bath and Wells, and in the patronage of the Dean of Wells. The chapel is of recent erection, towards defraying the expense of which the Incorporated Society for the enlargement of churches and chapels gave £200. The manor was given as part of the endowment of Bruton Hospital, by Hugh Saxey, Esq., the founder; and two boys are annually sent from this place to be educated at that institution. Here is a mineral spring.

BLACKFORD, a parish in the hundred of Whitley, though locally in the hundred of Horethorne, county of Somerset, 4¼ miles (W. S. W.) from Wincanton, containing 154 inhabitants. The living is a discharged rectory, in the archdeaconry of Wells, and diocese of Bath and Wells, rated in the king's books at £6. 11. 0½., endowed with £1200 parliamentary grant, and in the patronage of the Rev. J. Richards. The church, dedicated to St. Michael, is in the early style of English architecture, but there is a Norman arch over the entrance.

BLACKFORDBY, a chapelry in the parish of Ashby de la Zouch, western division of the hundred of Goscote, county of Leicester, 2¾ miles (W.N.W.) from Ashby de la Zouch, containing 290 inhabitants. The chapel is dedicated to St. Margaret. There is a place of worship for Wesleyan Methodists. The Ashby de la Zouch canal crosses the wolds south of this place.

BLACKHEATH, a village situated within the parishes of Greenwich, Lewisham, and Lee, in the hundred of Blackheath, lathe of Sutton at Hone, county of Kent, 5 miles (S.E.) from London, on the road to Dovor. The population is returned with the respective parishes. This place, which takes its name either from the colour of the soil, or from the bleakness of its situation, prior to the erection of the numerous villas with which it abounds, was the scene of many important political transactions. In 1011, the Danes having landed at Greenwich, encamped on the heath, and, among other barbarities, put to death Alphege, Archbishop of Canterbury, who had refused to sanction their extortions, and who was afterwards canonized. In the reign of Richard II., the insurgents under Wat Tyler, amounting to one hundred thousand men, took up their station here, whence they marched to London. In 1400, Henry IV. held an interview at this place with the Emperor of Constantinople, who came to solicit aid against Bajazet, Emperor of the Turks; and in 1415, the lord mayor and aldermen of London, in their robes of state, attended by four hundred of the principal citizens, clothed in scarlet, came hither in procession to meet Henry V., on his triumphant return after the battle of Agincourt. In 1451, Henry VI. met many of the followers of Jack Cade, who submitted to his authority, and on their knees implored and obtained his pardon; and here, the following year, that monarch assembled his forces to oppose Richard, Duke of York, who aspired to the throne. In 1497, the Cornish rebels, headed by Lord Audley, who had advanced into Kent, encamped near Eltham, and awaited the approach of Henry VII., on whose arrival a battle ensued, on the 22nd of July, in which the insurgents were defeated, and their leader, together with two of his associates who had excited the rebellion, taken and executed. In 1519, Campejo, the pope's legate, was received here in great state by the Duke of Norfolk, with a numerous retinue of bishops, knights, and gentlemen, who conducted him to a magnificent tent of cloth of gold, whence, after having arrayed himself in his cardinal's robes, he proceeded to London; and at this place, in 1540, Henry VIII. appointed an interview with Anne of Cleves, previously to their marriage, which was celebrated with great pomp in the chapel at Greenwich. Blackheath is pleasantly situated on elevated ground, commanding diversified and extensive views of the surrounding country, which is richly cultivated, and abounds with fine scenery, in which Greenwich Hospital, the park, and the river Thames, are prominent objects. There are many elegant villas, among which the Paragon, a beautiful range of building, is eminently conspicuous: on the west, and within the park, is the residence of the Princess Sophia of Gloucester, formerly occupied by the Duchess of Brunswick: the mansion in which the Princess of Wales resided has been lately taken down. Wricklemarsh House, once the noblest ornament of the heath, erected early in the last century, by Sir Gregory Page, was rased to the ground in 1787, by the different purchasers to whom it had been sold in lots by public auction; its site, now called Park-road, is occupied by handsome cottages. There are two episcopal chapels, one on that part of the heath which is in the parish of Lewisham, and the other at Kidbrook, an extra-parochial district on the north side of the heath, built by Dr. Greenlaw. The free grammar school, for thirty-one boys of Lewisham and the adjoining parishes, and for the sons of all the clergy in the hundred of Blackheath, was founded by the Rev. Abraham Colfe, vicar of Lewisham, who erected the premises in 1652, and at his death, in 1656, bequeathed the greater part of his estate in land, and £1100 in money, in trust to the Leather-sellers' Company, for its endowment, and for other charitable uses. The income is £342. 15. 6. per annum: the master, who is allowed to take twenty-six boarders, receives about £40 per annum, and resides in the house free of rent; the instruction of the free scholars is now confined to English and writing. There were seven exhibitions, of £10 each per annum, to either of the Universities; but from a failure in the funds appropriated to that use, they have been for some years discontinued. A British school for boys, and several small schools, are also supported by the liberal benevolence of the resident gentry. Morden College, a noble institution for the support of decayed merchants in the decline of life, was founded by Sir John Morden, Bart., an opulent Turkey merchant, in 1695, who endowed it with the manor of Old Court, producing £1600 per annum: the establishment consists of thirty brethren, a chaplain, and a treasurer; and the management is vested in seven trustees, who must be either Turkey merchants, or Directors of the East India Company. The premises, which occupy a spacious quadrangle, are handsomely built of brick, with quoins and cornices of stone, and are surrounded with a piazza: over the entrance are statues of the founder and his lady, whose portraits are in the hall; and in the chapel are the arms of Sir John, who was interred there in 1708.

At the distance of two or three hundred yards north of Blackheath hill, a cavern, containing several apartments, was discovered in 1780: it is supposed to have been formed as a place of security during the Saxon and Danish contests; but every attempt to explore it has been frustrated, from the falling in of the earth, and nothing has yet been found to illustrate its history. The Watling-street, or Roman road from London to Dovor, which passed over the heath, may still be traced; and in 1710, several Roman urns were dug up, two of which were of fine red clay, one of a spherical, and the other of a cylindrical, form: the former, about two feet in diameter, contained ashes, and was rudely inscribed, near the mouth, with the words "Marcus Aurelius IIII;" the latter, eighteen inches in height, contained ashes and some coins, on which, though much obliterated, the names of the emperors Claudius and Gallienus were legible. In 1803, several urns were also discovered in the gardens of the Earl of Dartmouth, about a foot below the surface of the ground, which were presented by his lordship to the British Museum.

BLACKLAND, a parish in the hundred of CALNE, county of WILTS, 1¾ mile (S. E.) from Calne, containing 44 inhabitants. The living is a discharged rectory, within the jurisdiction of the Prebendary of Calne in the Cathedral Church of Salisbury, rated in the king's books at £3. 10. 10., and in the patronage of the Rev. James Mayo. The church is dedicated to St. Peter.

BLACKLEY, a chapelry in the parish of MANCHESTER, hundred of SALFORD, county palatine of LANCASTER, 3½ miles (N. N. E.) from Manchester, containing 2911 inhabitants. The living is a perpetual curacy, in the archdeaconry and diocese of Chester, endowed with £200 royal bounty, and £600 parliamentary grant, and in the patronage of the Warden and Fellows of the Collegiate Church of Manchester. The chapel, dedicated to St. Peter, was, previously to the Reformation, a domestic chapel belonging to Blackley Hall, and, after a period of disuse, was purchased by the inhabitants, in 1610: it has lately received an addition of four hundred sittings, half of them free, toward defraying the expense of which the Incorporated Society for the enlargement of churches and chapels gave £400. There are places of worship for Wesleyan Methodists and Socinians. The inhabitants are chiefly employed in weaving, printing, bleaching, and dyeing cotton. A school, in connexion with the established church, has an endowment of £5 per annum, and is further supported by contributions: the school-room was built in 1794.

BLACKMANSTONE, a parish within the liberty of ROMNEY-MARSH, though locally in the hundred of Worth, lathe of SHEPWAY, county of KENT, 3 miles (N. by E.) from New Romney, containing 8 inhabitants. The living is a rectory, in the archdeaconry and diocese of Canterbury, rated in the king's books at £4, and in the patronage of the Archbishop of Canterbury. The church is desecrated, and the population has for several years been decreasing.

BLACKMORE, a parish in the hundred of CHELMSFORD, county of ESSEX, 3½ miles (N. W. by W.) from Ingatestone, containing 657 inhabitants. The living is a vicarage, in the archdeaconry of Essex, and diocese of London, rated in the king's books at £6. 13. 4., endowed with a rent-charge of £20 private benefaction, £400 royal bounty, and £1400 parliamentary grant. The King presented by lapse in 1808. The church, dedicated to St. Lawrence, was the conventual church of a priory of Black canons, which was built by Adam and Jordan de Samford, about the commencement of the reign of John: it was dissolved in the 17th of Henry VIII., at which time the revenue, amounting to £85. 9. 7., was applied by Cardinal Wolsey toward the endowment of his two colleges at Oxford and Ipswich, and on his attainder, in 1529, was appropriated to the crown. Henry VIII. afterwards occasionally resided in the house, which, having lately undergone a thorough repair, is now an elegant private mansion.

BLACKPOOL, a chapelry and bathing-place in the parish of BISPHAM, hundred of AMOUNDERNESS, county palatine of LANCASTER, 4 miles (S.W. by W.) from Poulton, and 25 (S.W. by W.) from Lancaster, containing 800 resident inhabitants. The living is a perpetual curacy, in the archdeaconry of Richmond, and diocese of Chester, endowed with £600 private benefaction, and £1700 parliamentary grant, and in the patronage of P. Hesketh, Esq. The chapel was built in 1821, at an expense of £1150, and the Incorporated Society for the enlargement of churches and chapels granted £200 for defraying the expense of a greater number of sittings. Blackpool, which acquired its name from a boggy pool at the southern end of the village, was, until within the last eighty years, an inconsiderable place; but, owing to its eligibility for bathing, it is now frequented every summer by a crowd of visitors, for whose accommodation commodious hotels and lodging-houses have been erected. The beach slopes gently from the site of the houses; the sands are smooth and firm; and the air is highly salubrious. The parade forms an agreeable promenade, from which there is an extensive view of the fells in Westmorland and Cumberland, and the mountains in North Wales. Excellent regulations have been introduced for the convenience of bathers; a news-room and library have been established, a theatre erected, and assemblies are occasionally held at the different hotels. Every alternate Sunday during the season the inhabitants of the surrounding district assemble at Lane End, and join in various rustic sports. The sea appears to have encroached considerably on the shore; a large stone, called Penny-stone, lying on the sands, about half a mile from the shore, is stated by tradition to mark the site on which a public-house formerly stood. A free school was established in 1817, which is conducted on Dr. Bell's plan.

BLACKROD, a chapelry in the parish of BOLTON, hundred of SALFORD, county palatine of LANCASTER, 4¾ miles (S. S. E.) from Chorley, containing 2436 inhabitants. The living is a perpetual curacy, in the archdeaconry and diocese of Chester, endowed with £200 private benefaction, and £200 royal bounty, and in the patronage of the Vicar of Great Bolton. The chapel is dedicated to St. Catherine. There is a place of worship for Wesleyan Methodists. This is the site of a Roman station, named *Coccium* by Antonine, and *Rigodunum* by Ptolemy, which was situated on the Watling-street. The spinning of cotton, and the printing of calico, are carried on within the chapelry, its trade being facilitated by a branch of the Lancaster canal, which crosses it. A fair for toys and pedlary is held on the first Thursday after July 12th. A respectable free grammar school, under the superintendence of trustees, is endowed with about £140 per annum, being the produce of various benefactions. John Holmes, in 1568, founded an exhibition at Pembroke College, Cambridge, for a scholar on this foundation; the fund having accumulated, three exhibitioners are now appointed, receiving respectively £60, £70, and £80, per annum, for four years. The house for the master was rebuilt in 1798.

BLACKTHORN, a chapelry in the parish of AMBROSDEN, hundred of BULLINGTON, county of OXFORD, 3 miles (S.E. by E.) from Bicester, containing 393 inhabitants. The chapel is in ruins. The Roman Akeman-street enters the county here, and proceeds over Blackthorn hill, in its course through the parish. The custom of running at the quintal, or quintain, the origin and practice of which are attributed to the Romans, was anciently observed on the occasion of a wedding in this chapelry.

BLACKTOFT, a parish in the wapentake of HOWDENSHIRE, East riding of the county of YORK, comprising the townships of Blacktoft and Scalby, and containing 457 inhabitants, of which number, 278 are in the township of Blacktoft, 7¾ miles (E.S.E.) from Howden. The living is a perpetual curacy, within the jurisdiction of the peculiar court of Howdenshire, endowed with £200 private benefaction, and £1000 royal bounty, and in the patronage of the Dean and Chapter of Durham. The village is situated on the northern bank of the Ouse, one mile above its confluence with the Trent, and there are usually vessels lying at anchor opposite to it.

BLACKWALL, a hamlet in the parish of STEPNEY, Tower division of the hundred of OSSULSTONE, county of MIDDLESEX, 2½ miles (E.) from London. The population is returned with Poplar. This place, which is situated near the influx of the river Lea into the Thames, consists chiefly of a few irregularly formed streets, which are paved, and lighted with gas; the houses, many of which are of wood, and of mean appearance, are inhabited chiefly by shipwrights, and persons employed in the docks: the inhabitants are supplied with water by the East London Water Company. It has long been noted for a very large private yard for ship-building, and a wet dock, formerly belonging to Mr. Perry, the former of which was purchased by Sir Robert Wigram, Bart., and is still applied to the same use; and the latter by the East India Company, for the formation of their docks, which were commenced in 1804, and completed in 1806. These docks are situated at the eastern extremity of the hamlet, and are surrounded by a lofty wall: the entrance from the shore is through a handsome gateway, surmounted by a square turret, supporting an octagonal dome, in front of which is a tablet, recording the date of their erection: they consist of an outer and an inner dock, both enclosed with walls, and communicating by locks and flood-gates. The entrance from the river is by a basin, nearly three acres in extent, from which vessels sail directly into the docks: the inner, or import dock, which is one thousand four hundred feet in length, five hundred and sixty in breadth, and of an average depth of thirty feet, occupies an area of eighteen acres, and, on the arrival of the fleets, affords accommodation for sixteen ships to unload their cargoes, though, from the custom-house regulations, only twelve landing officers being appointed, no more than twelve vessels can be unloaded at the same time. The outer, or export dock, is seven hundred and eighty feet long and five hundred and twenty feet wide, and of the same depth as the inner dock; it was enlarged in 1817 by an additional basin, prior to which its area was rather more than nine acres. Extensive ranges of warehouses have been erected within the walls: those on the north side are for saltpetre, on the south for storing the cargoes imported in shipping belonging to the private trade, and, on the east side of the import dock, for such goods as are not removed to the Company's warehouses. Sheds are also ranged round the docks, for the numerous vans employed in removing the merchandise to its several places of destination: these, of which seldom less than eighty are in constant use, are strong carriages built expressly for the purpose, and secured with bars and locks, with duplicate keys, one of which is kept at the docks, and the other at the Company's warehouses. At Blackwell Reach, adjoining this hamlet, are the West India docks, similarly constructed, but upon a more extensive scale. These consist of two spacious docks parallel with each other, and of equal dimensions, being nearly half a mile in length, excavated in a direction crossing the isthmus of the Isle of Dogs, and having an entrance basin of large extent at each extremity, by which vessels sailing in either direction may avoid the circuitous bend of the river. Between the docks are extensive ranges of warehouses, as also on the south side of the inner dock, for the convenience of forwarding goods by land carriage, and on the north side of the outer dock, in front of which is a canal three quarters of a mile in length, intersecting the Isle of Dogs, and forming a direct communication with the river at two points, between which the distance, by sailing round the isle, is nearly four miles and a half.

BLACKWATER, a large village in the parish of Yately, hundred of Crondall, Basingstoke division of the county of Southampton, 15 miles (E. N. E.) from Basingstoke. The population is returned with the parish. It occupies a low situation on the great western road, at the point of junction of the three counties of Southampton, Surrey, and Berks, on the western bank of the river Blackwater, which is here crossed by a bridge: on the northern side of the road is a range of handsome buildings, appropriated as residences for the masters of the adjoining college of Sandhurst. It is principally indebted for the traffic it enjoys to the number of coaches that pass through it daily. There is a place of worship for Particular Baptists. A fair for cattle and sheep is held on September 8th. Blackwater is within the jurisdiction of the Cheyney Court held at Winchester every Thursday, for the recovery of debts to any amount.

BLACKWELL, or BLACKHALL (HIGH), a township in that part of the parish of St. Cuthbert, Carlisle, which is in Cumberland ward, county of Cumberland, 2¼ miles (S.) from Carlisle, containing 283 inhabitants. This manor was given by Margaret de Wigton, heiress of Sir John de Wigton, to Sir Robert Parvinge, serjeant at law, and afterwards Lord High Chancellor, in the reign of Edward III., for successfully conducting her cause against Sir Robert de Bridekirk, who had impugned her title to the barony of Wigton. Thomas Lowrey, Esq., in 1779, bequeathed £200, directing that one-half of the interest should be given to a schoolmaster for teaching poor children, and the remainder to poor widows. In 1798, Grace Graham gave £100 to a school at Durdar, in this township.

BLACKWELL, or BLACKHALL (LOW), a township in that part of the parish of St. Cuthbert, Carlisle, which is in Cumberland ward, county of Cumberland, 2 miles (S.) from Carlisle, containing 124 inhabitants.

BLACKWELL, a chapelry in the parish of Bakewell, hundred of High Peak, county of Derby, 3¼ miles (S. W.) from Tideswell, containing 58 inhabitants.

BLACKWELL, a parish in the hundred of Scarsdale, county of Derby, 3¼ miles (N. E. by E.) from Alfreton, containing 457 inhabitants. The living is a discharged vicarage, in the archdeaconry of Derby, and diocese of Lichfield and Coventry, rated in the king's books at £5. 4. 2., endowed with £800 royal bounty, and in the patronage of the Duke of Devonshire. The church, dedicated to St. Werburgh, was rebuilt in 1826. Coal is obtained in the parish.

BLACKWELL, a township in the parish of Darlington, south-eastern division of Darlington ward, county palatine of Durham, 1¼ mile (S. W. by S.) from Darlington, containing 268 inhabitants. There is a place of worship for Wesleyan Methodists. The river Tees is navigable here, and a railway from Croftbridge to Darlington passes in the vicinity. At the Grange, in this township, then the property and residence of George Allan, Esq., there was formerly an extensive collection of books, manuscripts, paintings, natural and artificial curiosities, and British birds stuffed, formed at a considerable expense by that gentleman, who had also a press, with which he printed several works, some of them very scarce: this ingenious topographer, antiquary, and virtuoso, the early part of whose life was spent in the profession of the law, died of paralysis, May 18th, 1800.

BLACKWELL, a hamlet in the parish of Tredington, upper division of the hundred of Oswaldslow, county of Worcester, 2½ miles (N. N. W.) from Shipston upon Stour, containing 228 inhabitants.

BLACKWOOD, a joint township with Croborough, in the parish of Horton, northern division of the hundred of Totmonslow, county of Stafford, 4 miles (W.) from Leek, containing, with Croborough, 561 inhabitants.

BLACKWORTH, a township in the parish of Earsdon, eastern division of Castle ward, county of Northumberland, 4¾ miles (N. W.) from North Shields, containing 243 inhabitants. Here is an extensive colliery, the produce of which, known as "Northumberland Wallsend," and "Earsdon Main," is of a superior quality. A school-room has been built, chiefly at the expense of the Duke of Northumberland.

BLACON, a joint township with Crabhall, in that part of the parish of Holy Trinity, Chester, which is in the higher division of the hundred of Wirrall, county palatine of Chester, 2 miles (W. N. W.) from Chester, containing, with Crabhall, 75 inhabitants. The Ellesmere canal passes in the vicinity.

BLADON, a parish in the hundred of WOOTTON, county of OXFORD, 2 miles (S.) from Woodstock, containing, with the hamlet of Hensington, 510 inhabitants. The living is a rectory, with the chapelry of New Woodstock annexed, in the archdeaconry and diocese of Oxford, rated in the king's books at £16. 0. 5., and in the patronage of the Duke of Marlborough. The church is dedicated to St. Martin. There is a small endowment for the education of poor children.

BLAENAVON, a parochial chapelry in the hundred of ABERGAVENNY, county of MONMOUTH, 5 miles (S.W.) from Abergavenny, containing about 2500 inhabitants. The living is a perpetual curacy, in the archdeaconry and diocese of Llandaff, endowed with £400 royal bounty, and £2000 parliamentary grant, and in the patronage of Thomas Hill, Esq. There are two places of worship for Baptists. The village, which has of late assumed the appearance of a thriving town, lies in a mountainous district, near the source of the Avon Lwyd, whence it derives its name; many of the houses are excavated in the solid rock. The neighbourhood abounds with iron-ore, coal, and limestone; and iron-works, on an extensive scale, were completed here in 1789, since which they have been progressively increasing: the major portion of the pig iron is conveyed, by means of a canal and a rail-road, to Newport, whence it is exported. A customary market is held on Saturday. Near the iron-works stands a spacious English free school, endowed in 1816 by Mrs. Sarah Hopkins, for the instruction of the children of the miners: the present number, including both sexes, is about two hundred and forty.

BLAGDON, a township in the parish of STANNINGTON, western division of CASTLE ward, county of NORTHUMBERLAND, 6¾ miles (S.) from Morpeth, containing 64 inhabitants.

BLAGDON, a tything in the parish of PITMINSTER, hundred of TAUNTON and TAUNTON-DEAN, county of SOMERSET, 5 miles (S. by W.) from Taunton. The population is returned with the parish. There is a place of worship for Wesleyan Methodists.

BLAGDON, a parish in the hundred of WINTERSTOKE, county of SOMERSET, 6¼ miles (N. E. by E.) from Axbridge, containing 1068 inhabitants. The living is a rectory, in the archdeaconry of Wells, and diocese of Bath and Wells, rated in the king's books at £29. 13. 9., and in the patronage of George Thorne, Esq. The church, dedicated to St. Andrew, has lately been rebuilt, towards defraying the expense of which the Incorporated Society for the enlargement of churches and chapels granted £500. John Langhorne, D.D., a poet and miscellaneous writer, and for some time rector of this parish, lies interred in the churchyard. There is a place of worship for Methodists. *Lapis calaminaris* is found in the vicinity, and teasel, for the use of the clothiers, is cultivated to a great extent: here is also a paper-mill. Thomas Baynard, by indenture dated November 8th, 1687, gave land for the instruction of eight poor children: the endowment now produces £17. 10. per annum, for which seventeen children are gratuitously taught to read and write. There are also benefactions for the use of the poor, and a fund of £13 per annum, arising from land given by John Leman, for apprenticing children. At a place called Reg-hill-bury, where are some ruins, tradition relates that a royal palace once stood.

BLAGRAVE, a joint tything with Hadley, in the parish and hundred of LAMBOURN, county of BERKS, containing, with Hadley, 451 inhabitants.

BLAISDON, a parish in the hundred of WESTBURY, county of GLOUCESTER, 3¾ miles (E. S. E.) from Mitchel-Dean, containing 243 inhabitants. The living is a discharged rectory, in the archdeaconry of Hereford, and diocese of Gloucester, rated in the king's books at £5. 7. 3½., and in the patronage of Anna Gordon. The church is dedicated to St. Michael.

BLAKEMERE, a parish in the hundred of WEBTREE, county of HEREFORD, 10½ miles (W. by N.) from Hereford, containing 163 inhabitants. The living is a discharged vicarage, with that of Preston upon Wye united, in the peculiar jurisdiction and patronage of the Dean of Hereford, rated in the king's books at £3, endowed with £400 royal bounty, and in the patronage of the Dean and Chapter. The church is dedicated to St. Leonard.

BLAKENEY, a chapelry in the parish of AWRE, hundred of BLIDESLOE, county of GLOUCESTER, 15 miles (S. W. by W.) from Gloucester. The population is returned with the parish. The chapel, dedicated to All Saints, has lately been enlarged by the addition of five hundred sittings, three hundred and sixty-four of which are free, and towards defraying the expense the Incorporated Society for the enlargement of churches and chapels granted £110. There is a place of worship for Baptists. The navigable river Severn passes through the vicinity. Fairs for the sale of live stock are held on April 23rd and November 12th.

BLAKENEY, a small sea-port and parish in the hundred of HOLT, county of NORFOLK, 1¼ mile (N. W.) from Clay, and 125 (N. E.) from London, containing 803 inhabitants. This place is chiefly noted for its excellent harbour, which is well situated for sheltering vessels, and has a good opening to the North sea. It was called Snitterley in the reign of Henry III., who granted it a market; it first assumed its present name in the reign of Edward III., in the 31st of which a statute was passed for the regulation of the fish trade, which was then carried on to a considerable extent, and attracted a great number of German merchants, several of whom fixed their residence in the town. The harbour has been improved under an act of parliament obtained in 1817, and vessels of considerable burden can now approach the quay. The port is under the superintendence of the custom-house establishment at Clay: the trade with the northern states of Europe is rapidly increasing; a few vessels are employed in the oyster fisheries, and the coasting trade is considerable. The number of vessels belonging to the port, according to the return made in 1828, was fifty, averaging sixty-five tons' burden. There is an ancient guildhall in the town, relative to which some old deeds are yet extant. The living is a rectory, with the rectory of Cockthorpe, the vicarage of Little Langham, and the perpetual curacy of Glandford annexed, in the archdeaconry of Norfolk, and diocese of Norwich, rated in the king's books at £26. 13. 4., and in the patronage of Lord Calthorpe. The church, dedicated to St. Nicholas, is a spacious structure of stone and flint, with a square embattled tower, which serves as a land-mark to mariners: a lofty turret rises at the north-eastern corner of the chancel, and is stated to have formerly contained a light for the guidance of vessels; the roof of the chancel is curiously vaulted with stone. There is a place of worship for Methodists. The Sunday school near the church was erected by Lord Calthorpe, and is conducted upon Dr. Bell's system. There are some remains, consisting principally of several fine arches, of an ancient monastery for Carmelites, founded in 1320 to the honour of God and the Virgin Mary, in which John de Baconthorpe, a learned divine and acute metaphysician, became a friar, and ultimately Provincial of the English Carmelites; he was born here, and died in London in 1346.

BLAKENHALL, a township in the parish of WYBUNBURY, hundred of NANTWICH, county palatine of CHESTER, 5½ miles (S. E. by E.) from Nantwich, containing 225 inhabitants.

BLAKENHAM (GREAT), a parish in the hundred of BOSMERE and CLAYDON, county of SUFFOLK, 3½ miles (S. E. by S.) from Needham, containing 162 inhabitants. The living is a discharged rectory, in the archdeaconry of Suffolk, and diocese of Norwich, rated in the king's books at £6. 16. 0½., and in the patronage of the Provost and Fellows of Eton College. The church is dedicated to St. Mary. Walter Gifford, Earl of Buckingham, appropriated this manor, in the time of William II., to the abbey of Bec in Normandy, the society of which established a cell here, which was suppressed with other Alien priories, whereupon the manor was given by Henry VI. to the provost and fellows. The Stow-Market and Ipswich canal passes along the south-eastern side of the parish.

BLAKENHAM (LITTLE), a parish in the hundred of BOSMERE and CLAYDON, county of SUFFOLK, 5 miles (N. W.) from Ipswich, containing 120 inhabitants. The living is a rectory, in the archdeaconry of Suffolk, and diocese of Norwich, rated in the king's books at £10. 3. 4., and in the patronage of the Rev. Stephen Jackson. The church is dedicated to St. Mary.

BLAKESLEY, a parish in the hundred of GREENS-NORTON, county of NORTHAMPTON, 4 miles (W. N. W.) from Towcester, containing, with the hamlet of Woodend, 752 inhabitants. The living is a discharged vicarage, in the archdeaconry of Northampton, and diocese of Peterborough, rated in the king's books at £9. 17. The King, for that turn, was patron in 1828. The church is dedicated to St. Mary. A free school was founded by William Foxley, in 1669, and endowed with property now producing about £85 per annum; it is open to all boys whose parents reside in the parish. A Sunday school is endowed with a bequest of £200 by Sir John Knightley, Bart. There are also charities called Cleave's charity, the Foxley and Bidford charities, and others, some of which Blakesley enjoys in common with other parishes. Blakesley Hall is stated to have been anciently occupied by a fraternity of the order of St. John of Jerusalem.

BLANCHLAND (HIGH), a chapelry in the parish of SHOTLEY, eastern division of TINDALE ward, county of NORTHUMBERLAND, 10 miles (S. by E.) from Hexham, containing 412 inhabitants. The living is a perpetual curacy, in the archdeaconry of Northumberland, and diocese of Durham, endowed with £400 private benefaction, £600 royal bounty, and £300 parliamentary grant, and in the patronage of Lord Crewe's Trustees. The chapel was formed, in 1752, by the trustees of Bishop Crewe, out of the tower of an abbey of Premonstratensian canons, founded by Walter de Bolbec, in 1175, in honour of the Blessed Virgin, the abbot of which was elevated to the house of peers in the 23rd of Edward I.: the establishment, at the time of the dissolution, consisted of an abbot and fourteen canons, and the revenue amounted to £44. 9. 1. After having passed through various hands, the estate was purchased by Bishop Crewe, who bequeathed it for charitable purposes: besides that part converted into a chapel, the principal gateway and other portions of the conventual buildings are still visible. The trustees also endowed a free school with £50 per annum, allowing the master to charge a small quarterage in addition. This township is situated on the north side of the river Derwent, and is celebrated for its lead mines, which have been extensively worked for a very long period: the company of proprietors have a large smelting-furnace at Shildon.

BLANDFORD (ST. MARY), a parish in the hundred of COOMBS-DITCH, Blandford (North) division of the county of DORSET, ¾ of a mile (S.) from Blandford-Forum, containing 358 inhabitants. The living is a rectory, in the archdeaconry of Dorset, and diocese of Bristol, rated in the king's books at £15. 17. 8½., and in the patronage of the Rev. T. Burrough. The church, with the exception of the tower, was rebuilt in 1711. Browne Willis, L.L.D., the celebrated antiquary, was born here, September 14th, 1682; he died at Whaddon Hall, in Buckinghamshire, February 5th, 1760, and was interred in the chapel at Fenny-Stratford, which had been built chiefly through his exertions in soliciting contributions.

Corporate Seal.

BLANDFORD-FORUM, a market town and parish in the hundred of PIMPERNE, Blandford (North) division of the county of DORSET, 16 miles (N. E.) from Dorchester, and 104 (S. W.) from London, on the road to Exeter, containing 2643 inhabitants. This place derived its name from being situated near an ancient ford on the river Stour, called by the Romans *Trajectus Belaniensis*. It was nearly destroyed by an accidental fire, in the year 1579, but was soon afterwards rebuilt. During the civil war in the reign of Charles I., it suffered severely for its loyalty to that monarch. In 1644, it was plundered by the parliamentarian forces under Major Sydenham, and not being fortified, became an easy prey to the contending parties, having been frequently assailed and alternately possessed by each of them. In 1677, and in 1713, it again suffered greatly from fire, and, in 1731, was, with the exception of forty houses only, consumed by a conflagration, which destroyed also the hamlets of Blandford St. Mary and Bryanston, in which only three dwellings were left. After this calamity, which is recorded on a marble tablet over a pump near the church, it was rebuilt by act of parliament, in 1732. The town is pleasantly situated within a curve of the river Stour, over which is a bridge of six arches; there are also two other bridges, erected to facilitate the entrance into it during occasional overflowings of the river: the streets are regularly formed and well paved, the houses modern and uniformly built of brick, and the inhabitants amply supplied with water. The theatre, a neat and commodious building, is opened occasionally; and the races, which have been established for more than a century, are annually held, in August, on a fine down near the town, the course being one of the best in the kingdom. The manufacture of lace of a very fine quality, equal, if not superior, to that made in Flanders, and valued at £30 per yard, formerly flourished here: the making of shirt buttons, for which Blandford has long been noted, affords employment to a very considerable number of females in the town and the adjacent villages. The market is on Saturday: the fairs, chiefly for horses, horned cattle, and cheese, are held on March 7th, July 10th, and November 8th, to each of which a court of pie-powder is attached. The government, by charter of incorporation granted in the 3rd of James I., who made the town a free borough, and confirmed and extended the privileges which it had previously enjoyed by prescription, is vested in a bailiff, seneschal, and ten capital burgesses. The bailiff, who, with the inferior officers of the town, is chosen annually at the court leet of the lord of the manor; the seneschal, who holds his office for life, and the two senior capital burgesses, hold a court of record, for the determining of suits, and the recovery of debts under £10, but they do not exercise magisterial authority. The county magistrates hold petty sessions here for the North Blandford division of the county. The bishop's and archdeacon's courts are held monthly. The town-hall is a neat edifice of Portland stone, on pillars of the Doric order, with an entablature. The burgesses exercised the elective franchise from the 23rd of Edward I. till the 22nd of Edward III., when it was discontinued.

The living is a vicarage, in the archdeaconry of Dorset, and diocese of Bristol, rated in the king's books at £12. 8. 1½., and in the patronage of the Dean and Chapter of Winchester. The church, dedicated to St. Peter and St. Paul, is a handsome modern edifice, in the Grecian style of architecture, with a tower and spire, and ornamented with a balustrade and urns. There is a place of worship for Independents. The free school, to the north-west of the church, is of uncertain foundation; it has a small endowment. Archbishop Wake is said to have received the rudiments of his education here. The Blue-coat school, for the clothing and instruction of twelve boys, was founded in 1729, by Archbishop Wake, who endowed it with £1616, producing an annual income of £48. 9. 8. Almshouses for ten aged persons were founded and endowed by George Ryves, Esq., who, in 1685, bequeathed the residue of his estate for apprenticing poor boys: the entire annual income is about £120. In the churchyard are others for six aged persons, which were rebuilt by the corporation in 1736. William Williams, in 1621, gave £3000, since laid out in land producing £300 annually, for teaching four poor children, and other charitable purposes. On a hill to the north of the town was formerly an intrenchment, enclosing an area of three hundred paces in length, and two hundred in breadth, which has long been under cultivation, and the only relic now visible is an adjoining barrow. Sir Thomas Ryves, L.L.D., a learned antiquary and civilian; the Rev. Bruno Ryves, D.D., publisher of the *Mercurius Rusticus*, an early newspaper in the time of the parliamentary war, and one of the writers of the Polyglott Bible, born in 1596; the Rev. Thomas Creech, M.A., translator of Lucretius, born in 1659; William Wake, Archbishop of Canterbury, born in 1657; Edward Wake, uncle to that prelate, and founder of the institution for the sons of the clergy; Dr. Lindsey, Archbishop of Armagh; Dr. Samuel Lisle, Bishop of Norwich; and the Rev. Christopher Pitt, translator of Virgil's Æneid, born in 1700, and who, dying in 1748, was buried in the church; were natives of this parish. Blandford gives the inferior title of marquis to the Duke of Marlborough.

BLANKNEY, a parish in the second division of the wapentake of LANGOE, parts of KESTEVEN, county of LINCOLN, 9½ miles (N.) from Sleaford, containing 495 inhabitants. The living is a rectory, in the archdeaconry and diocese of Lincoln, rated in the king's books at £16. 10. 7½., and in the patronage of C. Chaplin, Esq. The church is dedicated to St. Oswald.

BLASTON (ST. MICHAEL), a chapelry in the parish of HALLATON, hundred of GARTREE, county of LEICESTER, 7 miles (N.E.) from Market-Harborough, containing, with Blaston St. Giles, 58 inhabitants. The chapel is a small plain building, without either tower or turret. Another chapel, called the Nether chapel, dedicated to St. Giles, was founded by Richard I., to whom the manor belonged, and rebuilt about 1710. He endowed it with all the tithes of the manor, decreeing the payment of 5*s.* annually to the rector of Medburn, for burial there: this sum is still paid, but the chapel is exempt from ecclesiastical jurisdiction, being a donative belonging to the lord of the manor.

BLATCHINGTON (EAST), a parish in the hundred of FLEXBOROUGH, rape of PEVENSEY, county of SUSSEX, 3 miles (N. E.) from Brighton, containing 187 inhabitants. The living is a discharged rectory, in the archdeaconry of Lewes, and diocese of Chichester, rated in the king's books at £14, and in the patronage of Mr. Chambers. The church is dedicated to St. Peter. This parish is bounded on the east by the river Cuckmere, and on the south-west by the English channel: here is a strong battery for the defence of the coast.

BLATCHINGTON (WEST), a parish in the hundred of WHALESBONE, rape of LEWES, county of SUSSEX, 2¼ miles (N.W. by W.) from Brighton, containing 54 inhabitants. The living is a discharged rectory, consolidated with the vicarage of Brighthelmstone, in the archdeaconry of Lewes, and diocese of Chichester, rated in the king's books at £6. 4. 4½. The church is dedicated to St. Peter.

BLATCHINWORTH, a chapelry in that part of the parish of ROCHDALE which is in the hundred of SALFORD, county palatine of LANCASTER, 3 miles (N. E.) from Rochdale, containing 3143 inhabitants. The manufacture of flannel, and the printing of calico, prevail extensively in this chapelry, which also abounds with coal-works.

BLATHERWYCKE, a parish in the hundred of CORBY, county of NORTHAMPTON, 8 miles (E. N. E.) from Rockingham, containing 240 inhabitants. The living is a rectory, in the archdeaconry of Northampton, and diocese of Peterborough, rated in the king's books at £14. 13. 3., and in the patronage of S. O'Brien, Esq. The church is dedicated to the Holy Trinity. Blatherwycke anciently comprised two parishes, which were united in 1448, since which, one of the churches, dedicated to St. Mary Magdalene, has been demolished.

BLAWITH, a chapelry in the parish of ULVERSTONE, hundred of LONSDALE, north of the sands, county palatine of LANCASTER, 7 miles (N.) from Ulverstone, containing 190 inhabitants. The living is a perpetual curacy, in the archdeaconry of Richmond, and diocese of Chester, endowed with £800 royal bounty, and in the patronage of T. R. G. Braddyll, Esq. In 1772, Margaret Lancaster bequeathed £50, and, in 1777, William Lancaster gave £110 to trustees, directing the produce to be applied toward the support of a school: a school-room has been built by the inhabitants, but only four children are taught gratuitously.

BLAXHALL, a parish in the hundred of PLOMESGATE, county of SUFFOLK, 3¾ miles (E. by N.) from Wickham-Market, containing 474 inhabitants. The living is a rectory, in the archdeaconry of Suffolk, and diocese of Norwich, rated in the king's books at £20, and in the patronage of Agnes Ingleby and others. The church is dedicated to St. Peter.

BLAXTON, a township in that part of the parish of FINNINGLEY which is in the soke of DONCASTER, West riding of the county of YORK, 4¾ miles (N. by E.) from Bawtry, containing 117 inhabitants.

BLAZEY (ST.), a parish in the eastern division of the hundred of POWDER, county of CORNWALL, 4 miles (E. N. E.) from St. Austell, containing 938 inhabitants. The living is a vicarage, annexed to that of St. Austell, in the archdeaconry of Cornwall, and diocese of Exeter. There are places of worship for Wesleyan Methodists. The parish contains tin and copper mines. Here is an almshouse of remote foundation.

BLEADON, a parish in the hundred of WINTERSTOKE, county of SOMERSET, 5¾ miles (W. N. W.) from Axbridge, containing 518 inhabitants. The living is a rectory, in the archdeaconry of Wells, and diocese of Bath and Wells, rated in the king's books at £27. 7. 8½., and in the patronage of the Bishop of Winchester. The church is dedicated to St. Peter. The Rev. Meric Casaubon, D.D., an eminent critic and divine, and son of the celebrated critic, Isaac Casaubon, was collated to this benefice about 1624. The navigable river Axe passes through the parish, and by means of it a considerable trade in coal is carried on. Here are vestiges of a British settlement, but the Roman road on which it stood can scarcely be traced. There are several barrows on an eminence in the vicinity, some of which, on being opened, were found to contain human bones, which, from their position, and the evidence of some coins lying near them, were supposed to have been those of Danes; a large quantity of ancient armour has also been dug up.

BLEANE, county of KENT.—See COSMUS (ST.) and DAMIAN.

BLEASBY, a parish in that part of the liberty of SOUTHWELL and SCROOBY which separates the northern from the southern division of the wapentake of Thurgarton, county of NOTTINGHAM, 3¾ miles (S.S.E.) from Southwell, containing 290 inhabitants. The living is a discharged vicarage, in the peculiar jurisdiction and patronage of the Chapter of the Collegiate Church of Southwell, rated in the king's books at £4, and endowed with £200 royal bounty. The church, dedicated to St. Mary, is an ancient edifice, in very good repair. The village occupies a secluded situation on the western side of the river Trent, over which there is a ferry. The free grammar school at East Retford has considerable property in this parish.

BLEASDALE, a chapelry in that part of the parish of LANCASTER which is in the hundred of AMOUNDERNESS, county palatine of LANCASTER, 4¾ miles (E. by N.) from Garstang, containing 212 inhabitants. The forest of Bleasdale, comprising eight thousand acres, was co-extensive with the township; a great part of it has been enclosed. Christopher Parkinson, by will dated July 8th, 1702, founded a school, and endowed it with an estate now yielding about £65 per annum, one-third of which is given to a schoolmaster, and the greater part of the remainder to the poor; the school is kept in a building adjoining the chapel at Admarsh. There are also some minor charities for the benefit of the poor.

BLEATARN, a hamlet in the parish of WARCOP, EAST ward, county of WESTMORLAND, 4¾ miles (W. by S.) from Brough, containing 129 inhabitants. John Tailbois, in the reign of Henry II., gave this manor to the abbot and convent of Byland, in Yorkshire, who founded a cell in the vicinity, the ruins of which indicate the conventual buildings to have been somewhat extensive. The Sawbridge estate, and others within the manor, are tithe-free, if occupied by their respective owners, but subject to the claim, if held by a tenant. Limestone abounds here.

BLECHINGDON, a parish in the hundred of PLOUGHLEY, county of OXFORD, 5 miles (E. by N.) from Woodstock, containing 570 inhabitants. The living is a rectory, in the archdeaconry and diocese of Oxford, rated in the king's books at £12. 9. 4½., and in the patronage of the Provost and Fellows of Queen's College, Oxford. The church is dedicated to St. Giles. Leonard Power, by will in 1620, endowed an almshouse for four poor persons, and a school, which he had previously built, with £200, on condition that certain parcels of land should be given by the respective owners for the same purpose, which was accordingly done: the almshouses were rebuilt about the end of the last century, and about £33 per annum is assigned for the support of the inmates: the school has been discontinued, but another, on a large scale, is supported by Arthur Annesley, Esq., in a building of his own.

BLEDINGTON, a parish in the upper division of the hundred of SLAUGHTER, county of GLOUCESTER, 3¾ miles (S.E. by E.) from Stow on the Wold, containing 340 inhabitants. The living is a discharged vicarage, in the archdeaconry and diocese of Gloucester, rated in the king's books at £6. 13. 4., endowed with £600 private benefaction, and £600 royal bounty, and in the patronage of the Dean and Canons of Christ Church, Oxford. The church is dedicated to St. Leonard.

BLEDLOW, a parish in the hundred of AYLESBURY, county of BUCKINGHAM, 5½ miles (E.S.E.) from Thame, containing, with Bledlow-Ridge, 1050 inhabitants. The living is a discharged vicarage, in the archdeaconry of Buckingham, and diocese of Lincoln, rated in the king's books at £16. 9. 7., endowed with £400 private benefaction, and £200 royal bounty, and in the patronage of Lord Carrington. The church, dedicated to the Holy Trinity, stands on the edge of a cliff, overhanging a deep glen, into which several springs fall, and uniting form a pool, called the Lyde, the water of which is stated to be continually undermining the rock, so as to have given rise to a rhyming distich, expressive of the insecure foundation of the church.

BLENCARN, a joint township with Kirkland, in the parish of KIRKLAND, LEATH ward, county of CUMBERLAND, 10½ miles (E.) from Penrith. The population is returned with Kirkland. At Blencarn-gate there is a free school, erected in 1775, and endowed with one hundred acres of land allotted to it on enclosing Culgaith common, and now let for £42 per annum, for which the master instructs gratuitously the children of Blencarn and Culgaith. Near the village is a spring, the water of which is of a powerfully astringent quality.

BLENCOGO, a township in that part of the parish of BROMFIELD which is in CUMBERLAND ward, county of CUMBERLAND, 4½ miles (W. by S.) from Wigton, containing 216 inhabitants. The Rev. Jonathan Boucher, who published a "Supplement to Dr. Johnson's Dictionary," was born here, in 1738.

BLENCOW (GREAT), a township in the parish of DACRE, LEATH ward, county of CUMBERLAND, 5 miles (W. N. W.) from Penrith. The population is returned with the parish. A grammar school, of high repute, was founded in 1576, by Thomas Burbank, who endowed it with property now producing about £200 per annum: it is free, with the exception of a small entrance-fee, to children from all parts of the world, for instruction in the classics. A new school-room, with a writing-school added to it, and a house for the master, affording extensive accommodation for boarders, were built in 1793. The late Lord Ellenborough received a small portion of his early education at this school, which has also produced several distinguished clergymen.

BLENCOW (LITTLE), a township in the parish of GREYSTOCK, LEATH ward, county of CUMBERLAND, 4¾ miles (W. N. W.) from Penrith, containing 53 inhabitants. Near an ancient house, once the residence of the family of Blencow, but now occupied by a farmer, are some dispersed ruins of buildings, particularly those of a chapel, with a burial-ground adjoining; and not far distant, near the road, there is an enclosed cemetery, in which stands a stone cross, with the arms of the family of Blencow engraved on it.

BLENDWORTH, a parish in the hundred of FINCH-DEAN, Alton (South) division of the county of SOUTHAMPTON, 8 miles (S. S. W.) from Petersfield, containing 249 inhabitants. The living is a rectory, in the archdeaconry and diocese of Winchester, rated in the king's books at £6. 7. 8½., and in the patronage of the Rev. Sir S. C. Jervoise, Bart. The church is dedicated to St. Giles. William Appleford, in 1695, gave £200 in trust, directing it to be invested in land, and the proceeds to be applied to the education of children: the income is now about £19 per annum; five boys are sent to a schoolmaster in the adjoining parish of Catherington, and twelve children are instructed by a mistress at Blendworth.

BLENHEIM-PARK, an extra-parochial district, within the liberty of OXFORD, though locally in the hundred of Wootton, county of OXFORD, containing 90 inhabitants. Blenheim castle was founded in 1704, pursuant to a parliamentary grant of £500,000, to be expended in raising the structure, and laying out the grounds, which, together with the honour of Woodstock, were bestowed on John, Duke of Marlborough, in testimony of national gratitude for his brilliant military and diplomatic services. The house was built from a design by Sir John Vanbrugh, and was called Blenheim from a village of that name on the banks of the Danube, near which this illustrious general obtained a signal victory over the French and Bavarians, on the 2nd of August, 1704, on which day annually, the inheritors of his Grace's honours and titles render at Windsor one standard, or colours, with three fleurs-de-lis painted thereon, as an acquittance for all manner of rents, suits, and services. It has all the appendages of a first-rate mansion, and the grounds and gardens are disposed with the most refined taste, and princely magnificence. The Roman road Akeman-street passes through the northern part of the park, being distinctly visible near the north lodge; and a little to the right of it, in the parish of Stonesfield, remains of Roman buildings were discovered in 1711 and 1779, and, a little further on, of a Roman villa, in 1813. For the early national events which took place at the old manor-house, see WOODSTOCK.

BLENKINSOP, a township in the parish of HALTWHISTLE, western division of TINDALE ward, county of NORTHUMBERLAND, 2¾ miles (W.) from Haltwhistle, containing 317 inhabitants. There are coal-works on a large scale in the neighbourhood. The ruins of Blenkinsop castle, once the residence of a family of that name, occupy part of an eminence in the neighbourhood, which appears to have been surrounded by a ditch.

BLENNERHASSET, a joint township with Kirkland, in the parish of TORPENHOW, ALLERDALE ward below Derwent, county of CUMBERLAND, 8¼ miles (S. W.) from Wigton, containing, with Kirkland, 224 inhabitants. A chapel for Independents was rebuilt in 1828.

BLETCHINGLEY, or BLECHINGLEY, a borough and parish (formerly a market town), in the first division of the hundred of TANDRIDGE, county of SURREY, 24 miles (E.) from Guildford, and 20 (S.) from London, containing 1187 inhabitants. The town is pleasantly situated on an eminence commanding an extensive prospect of the South Downs and other parts of Sussex: it is of considerable antiquity, and had a castle, erected soon after the Conquest, by Gilbert, Earl of Clare, which was demolished by Prince Edward after the battle of Lewes, which took place in 1264, and the foundations alone are now remaining. The market has long been discontinued: fairs are held on June 22nd and November 2nd, for horses and hogs, and for the sale of lean cattle brought from Scotland and Wales. The Croydon rail-road passes through the northern part of the parish. A bailiff and other officers for the internal regulation of the town are appointed at the court leet of the lord of the manor. The borough received the elective franchise in the 23rd of Edward I., since which time it has continued to return two members to parliament: the right of election is vested in the burgage-holders, in number one hundred and thirty. Matthew Russell, Esq. is patron of the borough; there is no returning officer, the bailiff taking no part in elections. The living is a rectory, in the archdeaconry of Surrey, and diocese of Winchester, rated in the king's books at £19. 19. 4½., and in the patronage of the Rev. J. Kenrick. The church, dedicated to St. Mary, is a spacious and venerable structure, in the early style of English architecture, with a low tower; it had a lofty spire, which was destroyed by lightning in 1606. Near the church is a charity school for twenty-five boys, founded by Mr. John Whatman, who, in the 8th of Elizabeth, endowed it with a messuage now producing £23 per annum, to which Mr. Bostock, of Tandridge, added a house and garden for the master. Almshouses for ten aged men and women were built by the inhabitants, in 1668, to which the rector, Dr. Charles Hampton, added another, and gave a rent-charge of £1. 6. 8., for supplying the alms-people with fuel. This town is near a Roman road, and at a short distance, in the parish of Caterham, is a fortification, called the Cardinal's Cap. At Pendhill, in this parish, some workmen discovered part of the foundations of a Roman bath, the different apartments in which were paved, and some of the walls lined with Roman tiles. There are inconsiderable vestiges of the residence of Earl Godwin, who retreated to this place when his estates in Kent were inundated by the sea.

BLETCHLEY, a parish in the hundred of Newport, county of Buckingham, 1½ mile (W. by S.) from Fenny-Stratford, containing, with the chapelry of Fenny-Stratford (part of which is in the parish of Simpson), and the township of Water-Eaton, 1160 inhabitants. The living is a rectory, in the archdeaconry of Buckingham, and diocese of Lincoln, rated in the king's books at £29. 13. 1½., and in the patronage of J. Fleming, Esq. The church is dedicated to St. Mary. On the enclosure of the common, an allotment of twenty-five acres was assigned for the benefit of the poor, in lieu of cutting furze.

BLETSOE, a parish in the hundred of Willey, county of Bedford, 6½ miles (N.N.W.) from Bedford, containing 383 inhabitants. The living is a rectory, in the archdeaconry of Bedford, and diocese of Lincoln, rated in the king's books at £17, and in the patronage of Lord St. John. The church is dedicated to St. Mary. The river Ouse runs through the parish, in which are the remains of an ancient castle, formerly belonging to Lord Bolingbroke, part of which has been destroyed for the materials. Here is a mineral spring, but the water is seldom used medicinally.

BLEWBERRY, a parish partly in the hundred of Moreton, but chiefly in that of Reading, county of Berks, 4½ miles (N. E. by N.) from East Ilsley, comprising the chapelries of Aston-Upthorp and Upton, and the liberty of Nottingham - Fee, and containing 941 inhabitants. The living is a discharged vicarage, in the peculiar jurisdiction of the Dean of Salisbury, rated in the king's books at £16. 6. 10½., and in the patronage of the Bishop of Salisbury. The church is dedicated to St. Michael. William Malthus, by will dated November 16th, 1700, after specifying certain bequests, directed the residue of his estate to be sold, and the purchase money to be invested in land, part of the proceeds of which was to be applied to the maintenance and education of ten boys in the Blue-coat school at Reading, and allowing the bishop of the diocese a discretionary power in the appropriation of the remainder. By deed dated May 13th, 1702, Dr. Burnett, then Bishop of Salisbury, and five other persons, were constituted governors, and agreed on a certain mode of applying the rents, which was confirmed by a decree in Chancery, on the 12th of June, but altered, pursuant to an order from Lord Chancellor King, in 1730. The clear annual income of the charity is about £916, the disbursement of which is regulated by a scheme devised in 1816, agreeably to which the trustees allow annually £161 for the support of ten boys at Reading; £50 to a master, and £20 to a mistress, for instructing thirty boys and thirty girls, who are partly clothed and provided with books and stationery; £60 for apprenticing four boys, and £25 for apprenticing four girls; £100 for clothing sixty children; and £70 in compensation to the parents of some of the children for the loss of their labour; besides paying small salaries to certain officers, and defraying incidental expenses. An almshouse for one poor man was founded, and endowed with a gift of £271. 13. 4., by Mr. Bacon, in 1732. A large edifice, called the Charter-house, supposed to have been used as a place of worship previously to the Reformation, has lately been taken down. The manor-house was formerly surrounded by an earthwork, and a deep moat crossed by a drawbridge, the remains of which have been obliterated within the memory of man. A field between Blewberry and Aston is thought to have been the scene of a severe conflict between the Saxons, under Ethelred and his brother Alfred, and the Danes, in which the latter were defeated with great slaughter: in forming a new turnpike road, in 1804, many human skeletons and military weapons were found near the spot. The parish is intersected by a Roman road and a British road, termed respectively Ickleton and Grimsditch. There is an encampment of considerable extent on a hill called Blewberton; and Loughborough hill, the loftiest eminence in this county, has been crowned by an ancient work, apparently constructed for purposes of warfare.

BLICKLING, a parish in the southern division of the hundred of Erpingham, county of Norfolk, 1¼ mile (N. W. by N.) from Aylsham, containing 359 inhabitants. The living is a rectory, in the archdeaconry and diocese of Norwich, rated in the king's books at £10. 13. 4., and in the patronage of Lord Suffield. The church is dedicated to St. Andrew. In the time of the Confessor, this ancient manor was in the possession of Harold, afterwards king of England, and, although subsequently divided, it continued exempt from the hundred, and enjoyed all the privileges of royal demesne: it was afterwards held by the bishops of Norwich, who had a palace here. Blickling Hall was built by Sir John Hobart, Knt., in 1628, at which time the domestic chapel was consecrated. The previous edifice, with the estate, was in the possession of the family of Boleyne, and in it was born Anne Boleyne, afterwards queen of Henry VIII.; this monarch is stated to have been here on a visit. Blickling was subsequently visited by Charles II. and his queen.

BLIDESLOE, a tything in the parish of Awre, hundred of Blidesloe, county of Gloucester. The population is returned with the parish.

BLIDWORTH, a parish within the liberty of Southwell and Scrooby, though locally in the wapentake of Broxtow, county of Nottingham, 5 miles

(S.E.) from Mansfield, containing 744 inhabitants. The living is a discharged vicarage, in the peculiar jurisdiction of the Chapter of the Collegiate Church of Southwell, rated in the king's books at £4, endowed with £200 private benefaction, and £200 royal bounty, and in the alternate patronage of the two prebendaries of Oxton. The church, dedicated to St. Mary, is a small edifice, built about the time of Richard III. There are places of worship for Baptists and Wesleyan Methodists, also a school with a small endowment. At the time of the Norman Survey this place formed a berewic to Oxton. The village occupies a very elevated site, nearly in the centre of the ancient forest of Sherwood, in all the perambulations of which, from the reign of Henry I. to that of Charles II., it is mentioned as a forest town: several of the inhabitants are employed in frame-work knitting. At the enclosure of waste land in the parish, pursuant to an act passed in 1806, upwards of one thousand acres were planted, and are now in a flourishing condition. In a field near the village is a rocky formation of sand and gravel, commonly called plum-pudding stone; it is fourteen feet high, and eighty-four in circumference, and is supposed to have been a Druidical idol.

BLINDBOTHEL, a township in the parish of Brigham, Allerdale ward above Darwent, county of Cumberland, 2½ miles (S.) from Cockermouth, containing 112 inhabitants.

BLINDCRAKE, a joint township with Isall and Redmain, in the parish of Isall, Allerdale ward below Darwent, county of Cumberland, 3½ miles (N. E. by N.) from Cockermouth. The population is returned with Isall.

BLISLAND, a parish in the hundred of Trigg, county of Cornwall, 4½ miles (N. N. E.) from Bodmin, containing 637 inhabitants. The living is a rectory, in the archdeaconry of Cornwall, and diocese of Exeter, rated in the king's books at £13. 10., and in the patronage of the Rev. C. Pye. The church is dedicated to St. Pratt. There is a place of worship for Wesleyan Methodists. A cattle fair is held annually on the Monday next after September 22nd.

BLISWORTH, a parish in the hundred of Wymersley, county of Northampton, 3½ miles (N.E. by N.) from Towcester, containing 696 inhabitants. The living is a rectory, in the archdeaconry of Northampton, and diocese of Peterborough, rated in the king's books at £20. 3. 9., and in the patronage of George F. Hatton, Esq. The church is dedicated to St. John the Baptist. The Grand Junction canal enters this parish by means of a tunnel from the adjoining parish of Stoke-Bruerne, and continues its course northward until it is joined by the Northampton canal.

BLITHFIELD, a parish in the southern division of the hundred of Pirehill, county of Stafford, 4¼ miles (N.) from Rugeley, containing, with the liberty of Newton, 470 inhabitants. The living is a rectory, in the archdeaconry of Stafford, and diocese of Lichfield and Coventry, rated in the king's books at £10. 19. 2., and in the patronage of Lord Bagot. The church is dedicated to St. Leonard. The river Blith runs through the parish. Elizabeth Bagot and Jane Jones, in 1729, gave land, now producing about £35 per annum, which, with voluntary contributions, is applied to the support of a school for the instruction of boys, and another for girls, in which about forty of each sex are educated on the National system.

BLOCKLEY, a parish situated in a detached portion of the upper division of the hundred of Oswaldslow, county of Worcester, surrounded by Gloucestershire and a small portion of Warwickshire, comprising the hamlets of Aston Magna, Blockley, Ditchford, Dorne, Draycott, Northwich, and Paxford, and containing 1890 inhabitants, of which number, 1158 are in the hamlet of Blockley, 3¼ miles (N. W. by W.) from Moreton in the Marsh. The living is a vicarage, in the peculiar jurisdiction and patronage of the Bishop of Worcester, rated in the king's books at £54. The church, dedicated to St. Peter and St. Paul, is partly Norman, and partly in the early style of English architecture: the tower was rebuilt in 1725, at the expense of the inhabitants. A neat chapel has recently been erected by the Baptists. The village, which is situated on elevated ground, contains several neat dwelling-houses, and presents a clean and pleasing appearance: here are several silk-mills, worked by small streams which rise in Dovedale, a short distance hence. Fairs are held on the Tuesday next after Easter-week, for cattle, and October 10th, for hiring servants. A charity school for twenty boys and six girls is partly supported by bequests, and partly by subscription. Pursuant to a statute passed in the 9th of George IV., the magistrates for the county came to a resolution, at the general quarter sessions held at Worcester, in October 1829, to alter the divisions of the county, making Blockley the head of one division, the petty sessions for which are held here. The Bishop of Worcester is lord of the manor, and, by his steward, occasionally holds a manorial court. Previously to the Reformation here was a palace in which the prelates resided, but the only memorial of it is in the name of a hill opposite to the vicarage, called the Parks. In a charter of King Buhrred, dated in 855, mention is made of a monastery, which then existed, and which was subsequently annexed to the bishoprick of Worcester. The Roman Fosse-way passed between this village and Moreton in the Marsh. Urns and other Roman remains have been found on Moor hill; and there are several chalybeate springs.

BLODWELL, county of Salop. — See LLAN-Y-BLODWELL.

BLOFIELD, a parish in the hundred of Blofield, county of Norfolk, 4½ miles (W. by S.) from Acle, containing 979 inhabitants. The living is a rectory, in the archdeaconry and diocese of Norwich, rated in the king's books at £23. 6. 8., and in the patronage of the Master and Fellows of Caius College, Cambridge. The church is dedicated to St. Andrew. The Rev. Charles Reeve, by will dated in 1729, charged some land with an annual payment toward the support of a free school, and for other charitable uses.

BLOORE in TYRLEY, a township in that part of the parish of Drayton in Hales which is in the northern division of the hundred of Pirehill, county of Stafford, 2¾ miles (E.) from Drayton, containing 214 inhabitants. Blore heath is distinguished as the scene of a sanguinary battle fought in 1459, between the Lancastrians under the command of Lord Audley, and the Yorkists under that of the Earl of Salisbury, in which the former were defeated: about two thousand four hundred persons of distinction were slain, among whom was Lord Audley; a wooden cross, resting upon a stone pedestal bearing an inscription commemorative of the event, marks the spot on which his lordship fell.

BLORE, a parish in the northern division of the hundred of TOTMONSLOW, county of STAFFORD, comprising the township of Blore with Swainscoe, and a part of the chapelry of Calton, and containing 351 inhabitants, of which number, 288 are in the township of Blore with Swainscoe, 4 miles (N.W. by W.) from Ashbourn. The living is a discharged rectory, in the archdeaconry of Stafford, and diocese of Lichfield and Coventry, rated in the king's books at £8. 8., and in the patronage of S. Shore, Esq. The church, dedicated to St. Bartholomew, is an ancient structure, with a square tower; it contains several ancient monuments to the memory of different members of the family of Basset, the site of whose mansion is now occupied by a modern farm-house. Blore is in the honour of Tutbury, duchy of Lancaster, and within the jurisdiction of a court of pleas held at Tutbury every third Tuesday, for the recovery of debts under 40*s*.

BLOWNORTON, a parish in the hundred of GUILT-CROSS, county of NORFOLK, 6 miles (S. by E.) from East Harling, containing 341 inhabitants. The living is a discharged rectory, in the archdeaconry of Norfolk, and diocese of Norwich, rated in the king's books at £5. 6. 3., and in the patronage of the Rev. Charles Brown. The church is dedicated to St. Andrew.

BLOXHAM, a parish in the wapentake of FLAXWELL, parts of KESTEVEN, county of LINCOLN, 5 miles (N. by W.) from Sleaford, containing 109 inhabitants. The living is a rectory, to which the vicarage of Digby was united in 1717, in the archdeaconry and diocese of Lincoln, rated in the king's books at £9. 9. 4½., and in the patronage of R. Manners, Esq. The church is dedicated to St. Mary.

BLOXHAM, a parish in the hundred of BLOXHAM, county of OXFORD, 4 miles (S. W. by S.) from Banbury, containing, with the chapelry of Milcombe, 1520 inhabitants. The living is a discharged vicarage, in the archdeaconry and diocese of Oxford, rated in the king's books at £17. 9. 4., endowed with £205 private benefaction, and £200 royal bounty, and in the patronage of the Provost and Fellows of Eton College. The church is dedicated to St. Mary. There is a place of worship for Baptists.

BLOXWICH, a chapelry in the parish of WALSALL, southern division of the hundred of OFFLOW, county of STAFFORD, 3 miles (N.N.W.) from Walsall, with which the population is returned. The living is a perpetual curacy, in the archdeaconry of Stafford, and diocese of Lichfield and Coventry, endowed with £600 private benefaction, and £2500 parliamentary grant. The Bishop of Lichfield and Coventry presented by lapse in 1826. The chapel, dedicated to St. Thomas, is of modern erection. There are places of worship for Wesleyan Methodists and Roman Catholics. Bloxwich, from its vicinity to Walsall, participates to a considerable extent in the manufacture and trade of that town, and derives benefit from the Essington and Wyrley canal, which passes through the chapelry.

BLOXWORTH, a parish in the hundred of COOMBS-DITCH, Blandford (North) division of the county of DORSET, 5¼ miles (N.N.W.) from Wareham, containing 210 inhabitants. The living is a rectory, in the peculiar jurisdiction of the Dean of Salisbury, rated in the king's books at £15. 7. 1., and in the patronage of J. Pickard, Esq. The church is dedicated to St. Andrew. On a hill called Woolsbarrow, situated on the heath, about a mile toward the east, are vestiges of a small fortification, supposed to be of Danish origin, the ramparts and trenches of which may be traced; near it there are several tumuli.

BLUBBER-HOUSES, a township in the parish of FEWSTON, lower division of the wapentake of CLARO, West riding of the county of YORK, 7 miles (N. by W.) from Otley, containing 126 inhabitants.

BLUNDESTON, a parish in the hundred of MUTFORD and LOTHINGLAND, county of SUFFOLK, 3½ miles (N.W.) from Lowestoft, containing 448 inhabitants. The living is a discharged rectory, with that of Flixton united, in the archdeaconry of Suffolk, and diocese of Norwich, rated in the king's books at £13. 6. 8., and in the patronage of the Rev. George Anguish. The church is dedicated to St. Mary. There is a place of worship for Wesleyan Methodists. The navigable river Waveney runs on the south-western side of the parish. The Rev. Gregory Clarke, in 1726, gave a house and some land for the instruction of poor children.

BLUNHAM, a parish (formerly a market town) in the hundred of WIXAMTREE, county of BEDFORD, 5¼ miles (N.N.W.) from Biggleswade, containing, with the hamlet of Moggerhanger, 945 inhabitants. The living is a rectory, in the archdeaconry of Bedford, and diocese of Lincoln, rated in the king's books at £46. 2. 11., and in the patronage of Countess de Grey. The church, dedicated to St. Edmund, contains several ancient monuments to the memory of different members of the families of Longueville and Bromsall. There is a place of worship for Particular Baptists. The market, which was on Wednesday, and a fair on the festival of St. James, were granted in 1315. The navigable river Ouse runs on the western, and the Ivel on the eastern, side of the parish. There is a mineral spring, called Poplarwell, but the water is not used for medicinal purposes.

BLUNSDON (ST. ANDREW), a parish in the hundred of HIGHWORTH, CRICKLADE, and STAPLE, county of WILTS, 4¼ miles (W. S. W.) from Highworth, containing 65 inhabitants. The living is a rectory, in the archdeaconry of Wilts, and diocese of Salisbury, rated in the king's books at £8. 19. 2., and in the patronage of Mrs. Barker.

BLUNSDON (BROAD), a chapelry in the parish of HIGHWORTH, hundred of HIGHWORTH, CRICKLADE, and STAPLE, county of WILTS, 3 miles (W. by S.) from Highworth, containing 552 inhabitants.

BLUNTISHAM, a parish in the hundred of HURSTINGSTONE, county of HUNTINGDON, 4½ miles (N. E. by E.) from St. Ives, containing 635 inhabitants. The living is a rectory, in the archdeaconry of Huntingdon, and diocese of Lincoln, rated in the king's books at £32. 16. 0½., and in the patronage of the Bishop of Ely. The church is dedicated to St. Mary. There is a place of worship for Particular Baptists. The Dean and Chapter of Ely are in possession of a manor here, for which they hold courts. The navigable river Ouse forms the southern boundary of the parish for the distance of about three miles. The Rev. Mr. Saywell, in 1708, gave land, now producing about £50 per annum, for the support of a charity school. Lands are held in trust, by a body of feoffees, for the use of the poor, who have also the benefit of divers small benefactions, periodically distributed. A tremendous hurricane, in September 1741, in its sweeping ravages across the country, threw down sixty barns, and about twelve dwelling-houses in this parish, besides effecting considerable damage on other kinds of property.

BLURTON, a chapelry in the parish of TRENTHAM, northern division of the hundred of PIREHILL, county of STAFFORD, 4½ miles (S.E. by E.) from Newcastle under Line, containing, with Lightwood Forest, 844 inhabitants. The living is a perpetual curacy, in the archdeaconry of Stafford, and diocese of Lichfield and Coventry, endowed with £200 private benefaction, and £200 royal bounty, and in the patronage of the Marquis of Stafford.

BLYBOROUGH, a parish in the western division of the wapentake of ASLACOE, parts of LINDSEY, county of LINCOLN, 9 miles (E. N. E.) from Gainsborough, containing 184 inhabitants. The living is a rectory, in the archdeaconry of Stow, and diocese of Lincoln, rated in the king's books at £19, and in the patronage of the Crown. The church is dedicated to St. Alkmond. There are mineral springs in the parish.

BLYMHILL, a parish in the western division of the hundred of CUTTLESTONE, county of STAFFORD, 6 miles (W.N.W.) from Brewood, containing, with Brincton, 604 inhabitants. The living is a rectory, in the archdeaconry of Stafford, and diocese of Lichfield and Coventry, rated in the king's books at £13. 10. 7½., and in the patronage of the Earl of Bradford. The church is dedicated to St. Mary. An annuity of £3. 5., the joint benefactions of the Rev. John Taylor, in 1671, and Mrs. Manning, is given to a schoolmaster, in addition to a small dwelling-house and garden, rent-free, for teaching six poor children to read.

BLYTH, a parish comprising the chapelry of Austerfield in the northern, and the chapelry of Bawtry in the southern, division of the wapentake of STRAFFORTH and TICKHILL, West riding of the county of YORK,—the township of Ranskill, within the liberty of SOUTHWELL and SCROOBY,—the market town of Blyth, the townships of Barnby-Moor with Bilby, Styrrup, and Torworth, and the lordship of Hodsock, in the Hatfield division of the wapentake of BASSETLAW, county of NOTTINGHAM, 31¼ miles (N. by E.) from Nottingham, and 151½ (N. N. W.) from London, on the old road to York, and containing 3456 inhabitants. This place, anciently called *Blia* and *Blida*, was chiefly noted in former times for its religious and charitable establishments. In 1088, a priory was founded in honour of the Blessed Virgin, by Roger de Builly and his wife Muriel, for monks of the Benedictine order, which, though considered as an Alien priory, being in some respects subordinate to the abbey of the Holy Trinity, near Rouen in Normandy, was spared at the suppression of Alien priories, and subsisted till the general dissolution, when its revenue was estimated at £126. 8. 2. An hospital for lepers, dedicated to St. John the Evangelist, was founded by Hugh de Cressy, lord of Hodsock, in the reign of John, for a warden, three chaplains, and brethren, the revenue of which, at the dissolution, was £8. 14.: of these buildings, as well as of a strong castle which is said to have been anciently erected here, there are not any remains. The town is clean, well built, pleasantly situated, and amply supplied with water. The market is on Wednesday; and the fairs are on Holy Thursday and October 20th. The living is a discharged vicarage, in the archdeaconry of Nottingham, and diocese of York, rated in the king's books at £14. 9. 4½., endowed with £220 private benefaction, and £200 royal bounty, and in the patronage of the Master and Fellows of Trinity College, Cambridge. The church, dedicated to St. Martin, is a lofty structure in the Norman style, and once formed the ante-choir of the splendid cruciform church of the priory; it has a handsome tower, in the later style of English architecture, with crocketed pinnacles. There are places of worship for the Society of Friends and Wesleyan Methodists. A school for ten poor children of the town, and for two from each of the adjoining townships, is endowed with land producing £18 per annum, to which £5 from the parish funds is annually added as a salary to the master, who is appointed by the vicar of the parish. Almshouses for six aged people, who have a small allowance of money and coal, have been lately rebuilt, and are supposed to have been originally an appendage to the hospital founded by Hugh de Cressy. There are also almshouses for two aged women, endowed with £10 per annum, under the management of seven trustees, chosen from the Society of Friends, besides other charitable bequests for the relief of the poor.

BLYTH (NORTH), a joint township with Cambois, in the parish of BEDLINGTON, eastern division of CHESTER ward, county palatine of DURHAM, 8½ miles (E.S.E.) from Morpeth. The population is returned with the parish. The village is situated on a peninsula, on the northern side of the river Blyth, opposite to the town and port of South Blyth, and is chiefly inhabited by fishermen and pilots. The manufacture of salt and earthenware was formerly carried on to a considerable extent, but has been wholly discontinued. There are a quay, several storehouses for corn, and a ship-yard, at Link-End, a hamlet situated at the extremity of the peninsula.

BLYTH (SOUTH), or BLYTH-NOOK, a small sea-port and chapelry, partly in the parish of HORTON, but chiefly in the parish of EARSDON, eastern division of CASTLE ward, county of NORTHUMBERLAND, 9½ miles (E.S.E.) from Morpeth, 13 (N.N.E.) from Newcastle, and 283 (N.N.W.) from London, containing, with the lordship of Newsham, and exclusively of that part of the town which is in the parish of Horton, 1805 inhabitants. The town is situated at the mouth of the river Blyth, where it empties itself into the North sea; and, until of late years, consisted of a few narrow and irregularly formed streets. Considerable improvement, however, has been made; but this has taken place principally in that part of it which is in the parish of Horton, owing to the tenure of property in that manor being less objectionable than that in the parish of Earsdon; so that the entire population of the town and its environs may be estimated at about three thousand. The trade of the port consists principally in the exportation of coal, and the importation of various articles of local consumption. The coal trade, during the siege of Newcastle in 1644, flourished greatly, but subsequently experienced considerable depression; it has, however, revived, and now furnishes occupation to nearly one hundred vessels, of the aggregate burden of upwards of fifteen thousand tons. The produce of the Bedlington iron-works, which are about three miles distant, is brought down the river Blyth to this port, where the articles are shipped for London. Muscles abound on the coast. The harbour, the entrance to which is at all times free from obstruction, is extremely secure, even during the most tempestuous weather. The tide formerly flowed over an extensive waste on the western side of the harbour, but, with a view to counteract this, a quay has been partly formed on the margin of the river; the undertaking, however, has been advisedly suspended, from an opinion that the free admission of the tide is essential to the preservation of the harbour. A dry dock, capable of receiving four vessels, was constructed in 1811: the custom-house is a branch of the establishment at Newcastle. A circular stone lighthouse was built by Sir M. W. Ridley, in 1788; and there is a beacon-light, called the Basket Rock-light. A detachment of troops from Tynemouth was stationed here during the late war with France, in a small fort commanding the mouth of the harbour. A chapel of ease was built by Sir M. W. Ridley, in 1751, the right of presentation to which belongs to the present baronet: attached to it is a burial-ground. A meeting-house for Presbyterians was built in 1814, one for Wesleyan Methodists in 1815, one for a congregation of the New Connexion of Methodists in 1818, and one for Scotch Seceders in 1827. George Marshall, author of a miscellaneous volume of poems, and "Letters from an Elder to a Younger Brother," was born at this place.

BLYTHBURGH, a parish (formerly a market town) in the hundred of BLYTHING, county of SUFFOLK, 4¼ miles (W. by S.) from Southwold, containing, with the hamlets of Bulcamp and Hinton, 513 inhabitants. The living is a perpetual curacy, in the archdeaconry of Suffolk, and diocese of Norwich, endowed with £400 royal bounty, and £1800 parliamentary grant, and in the patronage of Sir Charles Blois, Bart. The church, dedicated to the Holy Trinity, was profusely adorned with paintings, sculpture, and stained glass, but the former was destroyed in the time of Cromwell, and of the latter only a few fragments remain. Blythburgh, the origin of which has been ascribed to the Britons, though the only relics of antiquity that have been discovered are some Roman urns, which were dug up about 1768, was formerly a place of considerable importance, both as regards its trade and the extent of its buildings: it had a weekly market and three annual fairs. Its decay is attributed to the suppression of the priory, and also to a fire which, in 1676, destroyed a great part of the town. This priory is stated, by some, to have been founded for Black canons, by the abbot and convent of St. Osyth, in Essex, to which monastery it was subordinate; and, according to others, by Henry I. Its revenue, in 1532, two years previously to its dissolution, was estimated at £48. 8. 10.; a small portion of the ruins is visible. There are also inconsiderable remains of an ancient chapel, called Holy Rood chapel. In this parish is Westwood Lodge, a venerable edifice in the Elizabethan style of architecture. Anna, King of the East Angles, and his eldest son Ferminus, who were slain at Bulcamp, in the battle with Penda (unless we yield credence to Rapin, who states that Anna expired whilst preparing for the battle), were first interred in the church here, and subsequently removed to Bury St. Edmund's. The river Blyth is navigable hence to the North sea. Thomas Neal, in 1589, gave a small portion of land for teaching five poor children; and Burham Raymond, in 1728, assigned a rent-charge for the instruction of twelve more.

BLYTHFORD, a parish in the hundred of BLYTHING, county of SUFFOLK, 2¾ miles (E. by S.) from Halesworth, containing 163 inhabitants. The living is a perpetual curacy, in the archdeaconry of Suffolk, and diocese of Norwich, and in the patronage of the Rev. Jeremy Day. The church is dedicated to All Saints.

BLYTON, a parish in the wapentake of CORRINGHAM, parts of LINDSEY, county of LINCOLN, 4 miles (N. E.) from Gainsborough, containing, with Wharton, 504 inhabitants. The living is a vicarage, in the archdeaconry of Stow, and diocese of Lincoln, rated in the king's books at £12, and in the patronage of the Earl of Scarborough. The church is dedicated to St. Martin. There is a place of worship for Wesleyan Methodists.

BOARHUNT, a parish in the hundred of PORTSDOWN, Portsdown division of the county of SOUTHAMPTON, 1¾ mile (N. E.) from Fareham, containing 205 inhabitants. The living is a donative, in the patronage of T. Thistlethwayte, Esq. On that part of Portsdown which is within this parish a monument has been erected, in memory of Admiral Lord Nelson, which also serves as a beacon. Here was formerly a Cistercian monastery, but there are no remains of it.

BOARSTALL, a parish in the hundred of ASHENDON, county of BUCKINGHAM, 7½ miles (S. S. E.) from Bicester, containing 231 inhabitants. The living is a perpetual curacy, annexed to that of Brill, in the archdeaconry of Buckingham, and diocese of Lincoln, endowed with £15 per annum private benefaction, and £400 royal bounty. The church, dedicated to St. James, was a chapel of ease to the vicarage of Oakley until 1418, when it was made parochial. Boarstall House, in the early part of the civil war, was garrisoned for the king, but was evacuated in 1644, and immediately taken possession of by the parliamentary garrison at Aylesbury. Col. Gage recovered it again, and placed a garrison therein, but it was ultimately surrendered to Fairfax, in 1646: the only part now remaining is a large gateway, with turrets at the angles.

BOBBING, a parish in the hundred of MILTON, lathe of SCRAY, county of KENT, 1¼ mile (W. by N.) from Milton, containing 325 inhabitants. The living is a vicarage, in the archdeaconry and diocese of Canterbury, endowed with £200 private benefaction, and £200 royal bounty, and in the patronage of Miss Simpson. The church, dedicated to St. Bartholomew, is composed of two aisles, two chancels, and a western tower supporting a spire. A fair is held on the 4th of September. A benefaction of £50 from Ann Gibbon has been vested in land, now producing £6. 6. per annum, for which seven girls are instructed gratuitously. At Key-Street, a small hamlet in this parish, corruptly so called for Caius' street (*Caii stratum*), being situated on a Roman highway, there is a gravel-pit of unusual size and depth, from which Hasted conjectures the Romans obtained part of the materials for making the road.

BOBBINGTON, a parish partly in the hundred of Brimstree, county of Salop, but chiefly in the southern division of the hundred of Seisdon, county of Stafford, 9 miles (S.W.) from Wolverhampton, containing 393 inhabitants. The living is a perpetual curacy, within the jurisdiction of the court of the royal peculiar of Bridgenorth, endowed with £200 private benefaction, and £400 royal bounty, and in the patronage of T. Whitmore, Esq. The church, dedicated to St. Mary, has recently been enlarged by the addition of ninety-three free sittings, towards defraying the expense of which, the Incorporated Society for enlarging churches and chapels granted £50. A free school was built in 1792, by Hannah Cobbett, who endowed it with £1400 three per cents., for the instruction of twenty boys and twelve girls.

BOBBINGWORTH, a parish in the hundred of Ongar, county of Essex, 2½ miles (N.W.) from Chipping-Ongar, containing 277 inhabitants. The living is a rectory, in the archdeaconry of Essex, and diocese of London, rated in the king's books at £13. 6. 8., and in the patronage of Thomas Smith, Esq. The church is dedicated to St. German.

BOCKENFIELD, a township in that part of the parish of Felton which is in the eastern division of Morpeth ward, county of Northumberland, 8½ miles (N. by W.) from Morpeth, containing 107 inhabitants.

BOCKHAMPTON, a joint tything with Eastbury, in the parish and hundred of Lambourn, county of Berks, ¾ of a mile (S.E. by E.) from Lambourn. The population is returned with Eastbury.

BOCKING, a parish in the hundred of Hinckford, county of Essex, 1 mile (N.) from Braintree, containing 2786 inhabitants. The living is a rectory, and the head of a deanery, which still exercises its ancient rights, in the peculiar jurisdiction and patronage of the Archbishop of Canterbury, rated in the king's books at £35. 10. The church is dedicated to St. Mary. This village formerly enjoyed considerable trade in baize, for manufacturing one species of which it was so distinguished, that the articles were called Bockings, and a great quantity was annually sent to Portugal. The petty sessions for the division are held here. John Gauden, Bishop of Worcester, gave £21 per annum for the instruction of thirty poor children. A Lancasterian school for boys was established in 1812, and one for girls in 1825. An almshouse, consisting of nine tenements, is endowed with about £80 per annum, arising from different benefactions; and there are various minor charitable donations. Bishop Tanner states that John Doreward, Esq., in the 18th of Henry VI., founded here an hospital, called *Le maison Dieu*, or God's house, for a provost, or master, and six poor persons.

BOCKLETON, a parish partly in the hundred of Broxash, county of Hereford, but chiefly in the upper division of the hundred of Doddingtree, county of Worcester, 5 miles (S.) from Tenbury, containing, with the hamlet of Hampton-Charles, 385 inhabitants. The living is a perpetual curacy, in the archdeaconry of Salop, and diocese of Hereford, endowed with £400 private benefaction, and £400 royal bounty, and in the patronage of John Bleke Lye, Esq., M. D. The church is dedicated to St. Michael. A school, in which about one hundred and seventy boys and girls are instructed, is supported partly by subscription, but chiefly by the Rev. T. E. Miller.

BOCONNOC, a parish in the hundred of West, county of Cornwall, 3¾ miles (E.N.E.) from Lostwithiel, containing 253 inhabitants. The living is a discharged rectory, with which that of Broadoak was consolidated in 1742, in the peculiar jurisdiction of the Dean and Chapter of Exeter, rated in the king's books at £9. 17. 8., and in the patronage of Lord Grenville. In 1644, during the parliamentary war, Charles abode a short time at Boconnoc House, when he narrowly escaped death, having been fired at by a rebel whilst walking in the grounds. In the park are vestiges of lead mines, one of which was worked about that period, and again about the middle of the eighteenth century, but the produce was found too small to defray the expense.

BODDINGTON, a parish partly in the lower division of the hundred of Tewkesbury, and partly in the lower division of the hundred of Westminster, county of Gloucester, 3¾ miles (N.W. by W.) from Cheltenham, containing 413 inhabitants. The living is a perpetual curacy, annexed to the vicarage of Staverton, in the jurisdiction of the peculiar court of Deerhurst, in which, however, no spiritual authority is exercised. The church is dedicated to St. Mary Magdalene.

BODDINGTON (LOWER and UPPER), a parish in the hundred of Chipping-Warden, county of Northampton, 9¾ miles (S.W. by S.) from Daventry, containing 634 inhabitants. The living is a rectory, in the archdeaconry of Northampton, and diocese of Peterborough, rated in the king's books at £20, and in the patronage of Thomas Golightly, Esq. The church is dedicated to St. John the Baptist. Richard Lamprey, in 1758, gave a tenement for a school-house, and the interest on £300, being the amount of different benefactions, is paid to a schoolmaster for instructing sixteen poor children.

BODENHAM, a parish (anciently a market town) in the hundred of Broxash, county of Hereford, 8½ miles (N.N.E.) from Hereford, containing 964 inhabitants. The living is a vicarage, in the archdeaconry and diocese of Hereford, rated in the king's books at £12. 1. 5½., and in the patronage of R. Arkwright, Esq. The church is dedicated to St. Michael. There is a place of worship for Wesleyan Methodists. The river Lug winds through the parish. Here is a small endowed school. Walter Devereux, in 1379, obtained permission to hold a market on Tuesday, and a fair on the eve, day, and morrow of the Assumption of Our Lady, but they have been long discontinued. Thomas Mason, Esq., by will dated in 1773, gave nine acres of land, lying within the parish, directing the rental to be distributed among poor housekeepers not receiving parochial aid.

BODENHAM, a tything in the parish and hundred of Downton, county of Wilts, 3 miles (S.S.E.) from Salisbury, containing, with the chapelry of Nunton, 286 inhabitants.

BODHAM, a parish in the hundred of Holt, county of Norfolk, 3¼ miles (E.) from Holt, containing 298 inhabitants. The living is a discharged rectory, in the archdeaconry and diocese of Norwich, rated in the king's books at £9, and in the patronage of Thomas V. Mott, Esq. The church is dedicated to All Saints.

BODIAM, a parish in the hundred of Staple, rape of Hastings, county of Sussex, 9 miles (N. W.) from Winchelsea, containing 314 inhabitants. The living is a vicarage, in the archdeaconry of Lewes, and diocese of Chichester, rated in the king's books at £6. 18. 6½., and in the patronage of Sir G. V. Webster, Bart. The church, an ancient edifice, is dedicated to St. Giles. The parish is bounded on the north and south by two branches of the river Rother, which unite at its eastern extremity. The castle has become uninhabitable, and in its present mouldering state forms an extensive and interesting ruin, though still complete in some of its parts.

BODICOTT, a chapelry in the parish of East Adderbury, hundred of Bloxham, county of Oxford, 1¾ mile (S. by E.) from Banbury, containing 638 inhabitants. There is a place of worship for Particular Baptists.

Corporate Seal.

BODMIN, a parish in the hundred of Trigg, county of Cornwall, containing, with the borough of Bodmin, which possesses separate jurisdiction, 3278 inhabitants, of which number, 2902 are in the borough, 20½ miles (S. W. by W.) from Launceston, and 234½ (W. S. W.) from London, on the high western road. Bodmin, in the Cornish language called *Bosvenna*, "the houses on the hill," and in ancient charters *Bos-mana* and *Bod-minian*, "the abode of the monks," owes its origin to a monastery founded by King Athelstan, in 936, in supersedence of a cell for four brethren previously established by St. Petrock, about 518, on the site of a solitary hermitage originally occupied by St. Guron. Historians are widely at variance concerning the claims which Bodmin possesses to the distinction of having been the primary seat of the bishoprick of Cornwall. Dr. Borlase, whose opinion has been entertained by others, states that Edward the Elder, in 905, conferred this honour upon it, and it became the residence of the bishops until 981, when the town, church, and monastery having been burnt by the Danes, the episcopal chair was removed to St. German's. But this has been successfully refuted by Mr. Whitaker, in his work entitled "The ancient Cathedral of Cornwall historically surveyed," wherein he shews that the see was founded so early as 614, and that St. German's was made the original seat thereof, asserting, on the authority of a grant by King Ethelred, that the monastery of Bodmin was annexed by that monarch, in 994, to the episcopate of St. German's, and that both places combined to furnish a title to the future prelates until the annexation of the bishoprick of Cornwall to that of Crediton, in the county of Devon, in 1031, about twenty years after which Exeter was made the head of the diocese. He refers the Danish conflagration to the monastery of St. Petrock, at Padstow, and in this conclusion he is borne out by the flourishing state of the church at Bodmin, as described in Domesday-book, wherein its possessions are enumerated, including sixty-eight houses, with the privilege of a market there. This religious house, under different renewals of the establishment, the last of which was by one Algar, in 1125, appears to have been successively inhabited by Benedictine monks, nuns, secular priests, monks again, and canons regular of the order of St. Augustine. From the circumstance of his possessing a gallows and a pillory, the prior had evidently the power of inflicting capital punishment. Its revenue, at the dissolution, amounted to £289. 11. 11.; the site and demesne were granted to Thomas Sternhold, one of the first translators of the Psalms into English metre. St. Petrock was buried here; for, says Leland, "The Shrine and Tumbe of St. Petrok yet stondith in thest part of the Chirche." The town appears to have increased rapidly after the Conquest, since the same antiquary describes the market as being "lyke a fair for the confluence of people," and enumerates, in addition to the parochial church and the cantuary chapel near it, two other chapels, a house and church of Grey friars, begun by John of London, a merchant, about 1239, augmented by Edward, Earl of Cornwall, and in the time of Elizabeth converted into a house of correction for the county; and two hospitals, dedicated respectively to St. Anthony and St. George, besides the hospital of St. Lawrence, a mile off. Norden also says, "It hath bene of larger receite then now it is, as appeareth by the ruynes of sundrye buyldings decayde." William of Worcester, citing the register in the church belonging to the Grey friars, states that one thousand five hundred of the inhabitants died of the plague, about the middle of the fourteenth century. It was one of those decayed towns in the county, to repair which an act passed in the 32nd of Henry VIII.

In 1496, Perkin Warbeck, the pretended duke of York, on landing in Cornwall, assembled here a force of three thousand men, with which he marched to attack the city of Exeter; and in 1498, an insurrection of the Cornish men was organized, under the influence of Thos. Flammoc, a lawyer, and Michael Joseph, a farrier, in this town, who, being chosen leaders, conducted the insurgents to Wells, where they were joined by Lord Audley, who placed himself at their head. The rebels continued their march into Kent, and encamped at Eltham, where, in the battle of Blackheath, having been surrounded by the king's troops, they were made prisoners, and dismissed without further punishment; but Lord Audley, Flammoc, and Joseph, were executed as ringleaders. During the depression of trade and agriculture, in the reign of Edward VI., the Cornish men, superstitiously attributing their distresses to the Reformation, assembled at Bodmin to the number of ten thousand, under the command of Humphrey Arundel, governor of St. Michael's Mount, and being countenanced by the inhabitants, encamped at Castle Kynoc, near the town. The insurgents marched thence to besiege Exeter, demanding the re-establishment of the mass, and the restoration of the abbey lands; but, after having reduced the inhabitants of that city to extreme privation, they were defeated by Lord Russell, who had been sent with a reinforcement to the relief of the citizens. After their dispersion, Sir Anthony Kingston, Provost-Marshal, who had been sent to Bodmin to punish the insurgents, is said to have hanged the mayor at his own door, after having been hospitably entertained in his house. During the civil war in the reign of Charles I., the town, which had no permanent garrison, was alternately occupied by each party, till, in 1646, General Fairfax finally took possession of it for the parliament. After the Restoration, Charles II. visited Bodmin, on his journey to Scilly.

The town is situated on a gentle elevation rising out of the vale, between two hills, almost in the centre of the county: it consists of one street, nearly a mile in length, containing many ancient houses, and several neat modern edifices; it has been recently well paved, is partially lighted, and amply supplied with water. The races, which took place annually in the week after the summer assizes, have been discontinued for the last few years; the course, which is one of the best in the county, is about a mile and a half distant. Assemblies are held occasionally; and in July an annual procession of the populace, on horseback and on foot, carrying garlands of flowers, is made to a place in the vicinity, called Halgaver moor; this ceremony, the memorial of some ancient festival, now falling into disuse, is called Bodmin Riding. The manufacture of bone lace, which formerly flourished, has given place to that of shoes, a great quantity of which is exposed for sale in the markets and fairs; there is also a small manufactory for woollen cloth, and the spinning of worsted-yarn is carried on to a limited extent. The market is on Saturday: the fairs are on January 25th, the Saturday preceding Palm-Sunday, the Tuesday and Wednesday before Whitsuntide, and December 6th, for horses and horned cattle; large cattle fairs are also held in the hamlet of St. Lawrence, August 21st, and October 29th and 30th. The government, by charter of incorporation originally granted in the twelfth century, by Richard, Earl of Cornwall, confirmed by the kings Edward I. and III., and which, after having been forfeited through neglect, was renewed and extended by George III., is vested in a mayor, eleven aldermen, and twenty-four common council-men, assisted by a town-clerk, who acts as recorder, and subordinate officers. The mayor, the late mayor, and the recorder, are justices of the peace, and hold courts of session for the borough, at Easter and Michaelmas. The summer assizes, and the Epiphany, Midsummer, and Michaelmas quarter sessions for the county, are also held here. The town-hall consists of the two ends of the spacious refectory formerly belonging to an ancient convent of Grey friars, the only remains of that building, which have been fitted up as courts; the intermediate area is appropriated to the use of the corn market, and over the whole, a room for the grand jury, and a large assembly-room, have been built. The county gaol, built in 1780, on Mr. Howard's plan, has been lately enlarged for the proper classification of prisoners; it is a neat and compact building near the town, and includes also the sheriffs' ward and bridewell. The elective franchise was conferred in the 23rd of Edward I., since which time the borough has continued to return two members to parliament: the right of election is vested exclusively in the members of the corporation, in number thirty-seven, who are in the interest of the Marquis of Hertford: the mayor is the returning officer.

The living is a discharged vicarage, in the archdeaconry of Cornwall, and diocese of Exeter, rated in the king's books at £13. 6. 8., and in the patronage of Lord de Dunstanville. The church, dedicated to St. Petrock, and formerly the conventual church of the monastery, was rebuilt in 1472; it is a spacious structure, chiefly in the later style of English architecture, with a venerable tower on the north side, formerly surmounted by a lofty spire, which was destroyed by lightning in 1699. The interior, part of which is of an earlier date, contains the ashes of St. Petrock, a fine monument to Thomas Vivian, prior, and a large Norman font. There are places of worship for Bryanites and Wesleyan Methodists, and a chapel belonging to the trustees of the late Countess of Huntingdon. The grammar school was founded by Queen Elizabeth, who endowed it with £5. 6. 8. per annum, payable out of the Exchequer, to which the corporation have added £95 per annum, and, in addition to this, the master is allowed to charge annually £2. 2. for each scholar: a commodious schoolroom has been erected on the north side of the town, and the old building in the churchyard is appropriated as a National school for girls. Dr. Prideaux, Dean of Norwich, received the rudiments of his education in this school. There is also an English school, the master of which is appointed by the corporation. A commodious lunatic asylum was built at the western extremity of the town in 1820. About a mile to the east are some remains of the hospital of St. Lawrence, originally endowed for nineteen lepers, two sound men and women, and a priest, who were incorporated by Queen Elizabeth, in 1582, from whom they received the grant of a market, now discontinued, and a fair, still held on the 21st of August: the revenue, about £140 per annum, was subsequently, by a decree of the court of Chancery, transferred to the infirmary at Truro. Within a small distance is Castle Kynock, a considerable intrenchment; and on the northern side of the town there is a ruined tower, the only relic of Bury chapel, so called from a tumulus on an eminence near the spot. The curious Druidical circles, called the Hurlers, are in this neighbourhood.

BODNEY, a parish in the southern division of the hundred of Greenhoe, county of Norfolk, 5¾ miles (W. by S.) from Watton, containing 90 inhabitants. The living is a discharged rectory, united to that of Great Cressingham, in the archdeaconry of Norfolk, and diocese of Norwich, rated in the king's books at £6. 7. 3½. The church is dedicated to St. Mary.

BOGNOR, a market town and chapelry in the parish of South Bersted, hundred of Aldwick, rape of Chichester, county of Sussex, 7 miles (S.E.) from Chichester, and 68 (S.W. by S.) from London. The population is returned with the parish. This place, anciently called *Bogenor*, implying, in the Saxon language, a rocky shore, was, prior to 1790, an insignificant village, inhabited only by a few labourers and fishermen. The rocks, extending several miles along the coast, render it accessible only to ships of small burden, detracting from those commercial advantages which the situation in other respects offers: it owes its increase to the salubrity of the air, and the commodiousness of the beach, which have made it eligible as a place for bathing. In 1790, Sir Richard Hotham, Knt., member of parliament for the borough of Southwark, perceiving the natural advantages which Bognor possessed as a watering-place, erected a handsome villa for his own residence, and several lodging-houses, which he furnished at considerable expense for the accommodation of visitors. From this circumstance the town is also frequently called Hothampton, in honour of Sir Richard, whose additions to it were such as to entitle him to be considered its founder. After his decease, his estate here being sold to different purchasers, Bognor increased the more, and in a few years became a place of fashionable resort. The town is pleasantly situated near the peninsula of Selsea, and is sheltered from the north winds by a chain of hills, called the South Downs, extending from Portsdown to Dovor; but it is exposed to inundations of the sea, which frequently breaks in upon the adjacent coast: it commands an extensive view of the Isle of Wight; and, in a clear day, the Ower's light may be distinctly seen, which at night assumes the appearance of a gem in the ocean. It contains several handsome villas, respectable lodging-houses, and a commodious hotel, and is connected by good roads with the pleasant village of Aldwick, and other places in the vicinity, and by a ferry over the river Arun with Little Hampton, whence are pleasant rides to Worthing and Brighton. The warm and cold baths are conveniently arranged for the use of invalids; there are two subscription libraries, and races occasionally take place on the sands. The character of the place seems to render it peculiarly eligible to families who seek to avail themselves of the benefit of sea-bathing and a marine atmosphere in tranquillity and retirement, rather than to frequent watering-places in search of amusement. There is no other trade than what is necessary for the supply of the inhabitants, of whom several are employed in the fishery, for the supply of the London market. The Portsmouth and Arun canal passes within three miles of the town. The markets, recently established by act of parliament, and for which a spacious market-place has been formed, are on Thursday and Saturday; and a fair is held on the 5th and 6th of July. The internal regulation of the town is under the superintendence of commissioners appointed under an act, who meet once a month: they levy a duty of two shillings per chaldron upon coal, culm, and coke brought into the town, which is applied in repairing the roads. The chapel, dedicated to St. John, was built and endowed by subscription, in 1821. There are places of worship for Independents and Wesleyan Methodists. The Jubilee school, for the instruction of fifty girls, founded by the late Princess Charlotte; and a school for clothing and educating twenty girls, founded by Mrs. Smith, of Bersted Lodge, are supported by subscription. In opening the rocks various fossils have been discovered; beautiful agates and pebbles, and, after storms and high tides, pyrites, are found in profusion on the beach.

BOLAM, a township in that part of the parish of Gainford which is in the south-western division of Darlington ward, county palatine of Durham, 8½ miles (N. W.) from Darlington, containing 121 inhabitants.

BOLAM, a parish comprising the township of Trewick in the western division of Castle ward, the townships of Bolam, Bolam-Vicarage, and Gallow-Hill, in the western division of Morpeth ward, and the townships of Belsay, Bradford, Harnham, and Shortflatt, in the north-eastern division of Tindale ward, county of Northumberland, and containing 651 inhabitants, of which number, 55 are in the township of Bolam, 9½ miles (W. S. W.) from Morpeth. The living is a vicarage, in the archdeaconry of Northumberland, and diocese of Durham, rated in the king's books at £6. 13. 4., and in the patronage of the Crown. The church, an ancient edifice, is dedicated to St. Andrew. On the western side of the village are vestiges of an oblong intrenchment, consisting of a rampart with a double ditch, which was approached by a raised road. Mr. Gale ascribes it to the Britons, and is of opinion that this was the town of *Glanoventa*, which Camden fixes on the banks of the Wansbeck; some consider it to be of Roman, and others of Saxon, origin. A branch of the Watling-street, called the Devil's Causeway, may be distinctly traced about a mile westward, near which are two stone pillars, with a tumulus between them, which, on being opened, was found to contain a stone coffin. On an intrenched rock, on the north-eastern side of Bolam moor, are the ruins of some ancient buildings. The village was formerly much larger than it is at present; there are coal and limestone in the parish. The township of Bolam-Vicarage comprises only the glebe land, lying on the eastern side of the church.

BOLAS (GREAT), a parish in the Newport division of the hundred of Bradford (South), county of Salop, 7¼ miles (W. by N.) from Newport, containing, with Meeson, 274 inhabitants. The living is a rectory, in the archdeaconry of Salop, and diocese of Lichfield and Coventry, rated in the king's books at £7. 9. 4½., and in the patronage of Sir R. Hill, Bart. The church is dedicated to St. John the Baptist.

BOLD, a township in the parish of Prescot, hundred of West Derby, county palatine of Lancaster, 4½ miles (E. S. E.) from Prescot, containing 818 inhabitants. The present elegant mansion of Bold Hall was built after a design by Leoni; and the old hall, a curious edifice, is now the farm-house belonging to it. The family of Bold resided here previously to the Conquest, and preserved an uninterrupted succession of male heirs down to the death of Peter Bold, Esq., parliamentary representative for the county, who died in 1761. The Rev. Richard Barnes, promoted to the see of Carlisle in 1570, and to that of Durham in 1577; and his brother, John Barnes, the chancellor, were natives of this place.

BOLD, a chapelry in the parish of Aston-Botterell, hundred of Stottesden, county of Salop, 8¼ miles (N. N. W.) from Cleobury-Mortimer. The population is returned with the parish. The chapel is in ruins.

BOLDON, a parish in the eastern division of Chester ward, county palatine of Durham, 4½ miles (N.W.) from Sunderland, comprising the villages of East and West Boldon, and containing 733 inhabitants. The living is a rectory, in the archdeaconry and diocese of Durham, rated in the king's books at £24. 13. 4., and in the patronage of the Bishop of Durham. The church, which has a short spire, is dedicated to St. Nicholas. There is a place of worship for Wesleyan Methodists. The village of West Boldon stands on an eminence, and contains several respectable houses, some of which are occupied in summer by families from Newcastle upon Tyne and Sunderland, for the sake of enjoying the salubrity of the air. The manor has been annexed time immemorially to the see of Durham, and gave name to an early survey of the possessions of the bishoprick, called "Boldon Buke," being the first manor which occurs in that record, and on account of the numerous references in it to the services in this district. On Boldon hills, in the spring of 1644-5, some severe conflicts occurred between the army under the command of the Marquis of Newcastle, and the Scots, who then held possession of Sunderland. The parish abounds with limestone. The Rev. Henry Blackett, who died rector, in 1808, gave £10 per annum for the education of eight poor children belonging to the parish.

BOLDRE, a parish partly in the eastern division of the hundred of New Forest, New Forest (East) division, and partly in the hundred of Christchurch, New Forest (West) division, of the county of Southampton, 2 miles (N.) from Lymington, containing, with the hamlets of Sway and Walhampton, 2180 inhabitants. The living is a discharged vicarage, with the perpetual curacy of Lymington annexed, in the archdeaconry and diocese of Winchester, rated in the king's books at £12, endowed with £200 private benefaction, and £200 royal bounty, and in the patronage of J. P. Shrubb, Esq. The church is dedicated to St. John. There is a place of worship for Particular Baptists. A school for instructing and clothing twenty poor boys and twenty girls was founded at Pilley, in this parish, by the Rev. William Gilpin, vicar of Boldre, who erected the school-house, with dwellings for a master and a mistress, and, in 1803, endowed the school with the profits of his literary publications, *viz.*, "The Lives of Bernard Gilpin, Archbishop Cranmer, Bishop Latimer," "Picturesque Tours through the New Forest, and other parts of England," "Illustrations of the New Testament," "Explanation of the Church Catechism," &c. The school is under the superintendence of special visitors.

BOLDRON, a township in the parish of Bowes, western division of the wapentake of Gilling, North riding of the county of York, 2 miles (S. W. by S.) from Barnard-Castle, containing 168 inhabitants.

BOLE, a parish in the North-clay division of the wapentake of Bassetlaw, county of Nottingham, 3½ miles (S. W. by S.) from Gainsborough, containing 193 inhabitants. The living is a discharged vicarage, in the peculiar jurisdiction of the Prebendary of Bole in the Cathedral Church of York, rated in the king's books at £4. 13. 4., endowed with £200 royal bounty, and in the patronage of the Dean and Chapter of York. The church is dedicated to St. Martin. Bole ferry, across the Trent, is about a mile distant. William Nettleship, in 1780, gave a small rent-charge for the instruction of four poor children.

BOLEHALL, a joint township with Glascote, in that part of the parish of Tamworth which is in the Tamworth division of the hundred of Hemlingford, county of Warwick, 1 mile (S. S. E.) from Tamworth, containing, with Glascote, 414 inhabitants.

BOLINGBROKE, a market town and parish in the western division of the soke of Bolingbroke, parts of Lindsey, county of Lincoln, 30 miles (E. S. E.) from Lincoln, and 129 (N.) from London, containing 753 inhabitants. This town is pleasantly situated near the source of a small river, which runs into the Witham. A castle was built by William de Romara, Earl of Lincoln, of which his descendant, Allicia de Lacey, was dispossessed by Edward II. Henry IV. was born in this castle, and from it took the name of Henry of Bolingbroke: the south-west tower is still remaining, and, from the site and other vestiges, the castle appears to have been a quadrilateral building, with a tower at each angle, and to have been defended by a rampart. There is a manufactory for earthenware: the market is on Tuesday, and a fair is held on St. Peter's day. The town is within the jurisdiction of a court of requests for the recovery of debts under £5, which extends through the soke, and is held under an act passed in the 47th of George III.: constables and other officers are appointed at the court leet of the lord of the manor. The living is a discharged rectory, to which that of Hareby was united in 1739, in the archdeaconry and diocese of Lincoln, rated in the king's books at £9. 19. 2., and in the patronage of Mr. and Mrs. Warren. The church, dedicated to St. Peter and St. Paul, is a spacious and venerable structure, but a considerable part of it was destroyed in the civil war during the reign of Charles I. There is a place of worship for Wesleyan Methodists. A free school has a trifling endowment for the instruction of poor children.

BOLLEN-FEE, a township in the parish of Wilmslow, hundred of Macclesfield, county palatine of Chester, 6 miles (S. W.) from Stockport, containing 1761 inhabitants.

BOLLINGTON, a township partly in the parish of Bowdon, but chiefly in the parish of Rosthern, hundred of Bucklow, county palatine of Chester, 5½ miles (N. by W.) from Nether Knutsford, containing 264 inhabitants. There is a place of worship for Wesleyan Methodists.

BOLLINGTON, a township in the parish of Prestbury, hundred of Macclesfield, county palatine of Chester, 2½ miles (N. by E.) from Macclesfield, containing 1723 inhabitants. The village lies on the banks of a small stream, called the Bolling, from which its name is derived. Here are some silk and cotton factories, collieries, and a water-mill for grinding bark; and so prosperous has been the trade of the place, that the population has increased one-third since the census of 1821. The Macclesfield canal passes through the township. A chapel has lately been erected, by means of a grant obtained from the parliamentary commissioners. The Wesleyan Methodists have a meeting-house, attached to which is a Sunday school, wherein five hundred children are instructed. At Kerridge Hill, which is partly in this township, and partly in that of Rainow, there are quarries of freestone and slate, worked to a considerable extent, the produce being chiefly sent to the neighbouring towns; they were formerly leased by the Crown to the corporation of Macclesfield, but have been assigned, by an act passed in the 1st of Charles I., to the proprietors of land in the vicinity.

BOLNEY, a hamlet in the parish of Harpsden, hundred of Binfield, county of Oxford, 2 miles (S. S. E.) from Henley upon Thames. The population is returned with the parish. Bolney was formerly a parish, but the church having become desecrated, the living has been united to the rectory of Harpsden.

BOLNEY, a parish in the hundred of Buttinghill, rape of Lewes, county of Sussex, 3½ miles (W. S. W.) from Cuckfield, containing 560 inhabitants. The living is a discharged vicarage, in the archdeaconry of Lewes, and diocese of Chichester, rated in the king's books at £5. 5. 2½., endowed with £200 private benefaction, and £200 royal bounty, and in the patronage of the Prebendary of Hove in the Cathedral Church of Chichester. The church is dedicated to St. Mary Magdalene.

BOLNHURST, a parish in the hundred of Stodden, county of Bedford, 7 miles (N. by E.) from Bedford, containing 264 inhabitants. The living is a rectory, in the archdeaconry of Bedford, and diocese of Lincoln, rated in the king's books at £9, and in the patronage of William Guppy, Esq. The church is dedicated to St. Dunstan. A free school, founded by the Rev. Mr. Baker, in 1791, has an endowment of £12 per annum, for which about twelve children are instructed gratuitously.

BOLSOVER, a parish (formerly a market town) in the hundred of SCARSDALE, county of DERBY, 28½ miles (N. N. E.) from Derby, and 145½ (N. by W.) from London, containing, with part of the township of Glapwell, 1355 inhabitants. This place, prior to the Conquest called *Belesoure*, was, soon after the Norman survey, noted for a castle erected by William Peveril, which having been forfeited by his son, in 1153, became the occasional residence of King John; but in a few years, together with the castle of the Peak, was garrisoned by the barons against that monarch. In 1215, William, Earl Ferrars, retook both these castles from the barons, and was made governor of them, as a reward for his fidelity. That part of Bolsover castle which is now habitable was built by Sir Charles Cavendish, in 1613, in which his eldest son William, afterwards Duke of Newcastle, thrice entertained Charles I. and his court, and upon one occasion, when the queen was present, expended £15,000. In the reign of Charles II. the duke erected the splendid pile of building near it, which is now in a state of ruin. During the civil war, while the duke was abroad, the parliament having seized and sold this mansion, it was about to be pulled down, but Sir Charles, the duke's younger brother, recovered it by purchase, and restored it to the family: it occupies a lofty eminence commanding an extensive prospect. The town is large and well built, and is pleasantly situated on rising ground, environed on every side, except where the ground forms a natural rampart, with a deep intrenchment. It is within the jurisdiction of the court for the honour of Peverel, which is held at Lenton, near Nottingham: a court leet belonging to the lord of the manor is held every third week, for the recovery of debts under 40*s*. There is a fair on Midsummer-day. The living is a discharged vicarage, in the archdeaconry of Derby, and diocese of Lichfield and Coventry, rated in the king's books at £5. 19. 4., endowed with £200 and £10 per annum private benefaction, £400 royal bounty, and £200 parliamentary grant, and in the patronage of the Duke of Portland. The church, dedicated to St. Mary, is a spacious structure, having portions in the Norman style intermixed with later English architecture, and many modern insertions: within is a sepulchral chapel belonging to the Cavendish family, in which are some splendid monuments. There are places of worship for Independents and Wesleyan Methodists. A small endowed school was erected in 1756; and in 1761, Mrs. Smithson bequeathed £200 for portioning young women with £25 each, directing the overplus to be given to the poor.

BOLTBY, a chapelry in that part of the parish of FELIX-KIRK which is in the wapentake of BIRDFORTH, North riding of the county of YORK, 4¾ miles (N. E.) from Thirsk, containing 403 inhabitants. The chapel is dedicated to the Holy Trinity.

BOLTERSTONE, a chapelry in the parish of ECCLESFIELD, northern division of the wapentake of STRAFFORTH and TICKHILL, West riding of the county of YORK, 9 miles (N. W. by N.) from Sheffield. The population is returned with the parish. The living is a perpetual curacy, in the archdeaconry and diocese of York, endowed with £200 royal bounty, and £200 parliamentary grant, and in the patronage of J. Remington, Esq.

BOLTON, a parish in ALLERDALE ward below Darwent, county of CUMBERLAND, 1½ mile (N. by W.) from Ireby, containing, with the townships of Bolton High-Side, and Bolton Low-Side, 1123 inhabitants. The living is a rectory, in the archdeaconry and diocese of Carlisle, rated in the king's books at £19. 18. 4., and in the patronage of the Earl of Lonsdale. The church is dedicated to All Saints. There is a place of worship for Wesleyan Methodists. Here are collieries and lime-kilns, the neighbourhood abounding with coal and limestone to a great extent. A copper mine has been opened within the last few years, but it is not very productive. A copper battle-axe was lately found in the moss at Bolton wood, four feet below the surface. It is recorded in an old manuscript, that John Porter, of Bolton-Gate, a man of temperate habits and a sound constitution, died at the age of ninety-six, and that some time prior to that event, his hair, nails, teeth, and skin, and the whole *crasis* (temperature and constitution) was renewed, and became fresh as a child's.

BOLTON, a chapelry in the parish of EDLINGHAM, northern division of COQUETDALE ward, county of NORTHUMBERLAND, 6½ miles (W.) from Alnwick, containing 144 inhabitants. On the 5th of September, in the 5th of Henry VIII., a short time previously to the battle of Branxton, a congress was held here, at which several noblemen and other distinguished persons, with a train of about twenty-six thousand troops, were present. An hospital for a master, three chaplains, thirteen lepers, and other lay brethren, was founded and endowed prior to 1225, by Robert de Roos, Baron of Wark, in honour of St. Thomas the Martyr, or the Holy Trinity, and made subordinate to the abbey of Rivaulx, and the priory of Kirkham, in Yorkshire. Several stone chests and urns, containing ashes, charcoal, and fragments of human bones, together with a celt, have been discovered at a short distance from this place.

BOLTON, a chapelry in the parish of MORLAND, WEST ward, county of WESTMORLAND, 4 miles (N. W. by W.) from Appleby, containing 445 inhabitants. The living is a perpetual curacy, in the archdeaconry and diocese of Carlisle, endowed with £400 private benefaction, and £600 royal bounty, and in the patronage of the Landowners. The chapel is dedicated to All Saints, and a grant of £100 was lately assigned by the Incorporated Society for the enlargement of churches and chapels for its re-erection on a more extended plan. A meeting-house for the Methodists was built in 1818. A free school for the instruction of fourteen children is endowed with £14. 10. per annum, being the produce of various benefactions, and is under the control of eleven trustees: the school-room was built by subscription. In 1816, a chain bridge, thirty yards in length, was constructed across the Eden, about a mile north of the village, at the expense of the landowners. Bewley castle, which stands in the neighbourhood, and is now occupied as a farm-house, was anciently the residence of the bishops of Carlisle.

BOLTON, a township in the parish of Bishop-Wilton, partly in the liberty of St. Peter of York, and partly in the Wilton-Beacon division of the wapentake of Harthill, East riding of the county of York, $2\frac{3}{4}$ miles (N.W.) from Pocklington, containing 112 inhabitants. There is a place of worship for Wesleyan Methodists.

BOLTON, a township in the parish of Calverley, wapentake of Morley, West riding of the county of York, $2\frac{1}{2}$ miles (N.N.E.) from Bradford, containing 634 inhabitants. The woollen manufacture prevails to a great extent in the vicinity.

BOLTON, a joint township with East Halton, in that part of the parish of Skipton which is in the eastern division of the wapentake of Staincliffe and Ewcross, West riding of the county of York, 6 miles (E.) from Skipton. The population is returned with East Halton.

BOLTON-ABBEY, a chapelry in that part of the parish of Skipton which is in the eastern division of the wapentake of Staincliffe and Ewcross, West riding of the county of York, $6\frac{1}{2}$ miles (E. N.E.) from Skipton, containing 127 inhabitants. The living is a perpetual curacy, in the archdeaconry of the East riding, and diocese of York, endowed with £400 private benefaction, and £1800 parliamentary grant, and in the patronage of the Vicar of Pocklington. The chapel, dedicated to St. Mary and St. Cuthbert, was formed out of the nave of the conventual church belonging to a priory originally founded at Embsay, by William de Meschines, and his wife Cecilia, in 1121, for canons Regular of the order of St. Augustine, and removed hither, thirty-three years afterwards, by their daughter Adeliza, who was married to William Fitz-Duncan. In the 26th of Henry VIII., the revenue was valued at £302. 9. 3., and the society was dissolved in 1540. The ruins, which are extensive, are surrounded by scenery celebrated for its surpassing beauty, being composed of a variety of picturesque objects, so arranged as to constitute an almost perfect landscape. Here was also an establishment of Carmelite friars, founded by the Earl of Albemarle, or, according to some, by Lord Gray of Codnor. The Hon. Robert Boyle, in 1697, established a free grammar school, and endowed it with certain houses, lands, and a rent-charge of £20: the annual income, amounting to about £100, is, by consent of the master (the perpetual curate), paid to an usher for teaching the scholars: the premises comprise a house and garden in the occupation of the master, and a detached school-room, which is open to all children of the chapelry; the present number, about twenty, receive only an English education, though the school is free for instruction in the classics.

BOLTON by BOWLAND, a parish in the western division of the wapentake of Staincliffe and Ewcross, West riding of the county of York, $6\frac{1}{4}$ miles (N.N.E.) from Clitheroe, containing 1205 inhabitants. The living is a rectory, in the archdeaconry and diocese of York, rated in the king's books at £11. 13. 4., and in the patronage of J. P. Haywood and another. The church, dedicated to St. Peter, contains a large monumental slab of grey limestone, bearing an effigy supposed to be that of Sir Ralph Pudsay, together with effigies of his three wives and twenty-five children. Sir Ralph afforded a brief asylum to Henry VI., at his house, Bolton Hall, shortly after the battle of Hexham, so disastrous to the Lancastrian party: a pair of boots, a pair of gloves, and a spoon, are still preserved as relics of that monarch, and a well, stated to have been dug and formed into a bath by his orders, retains the name of King Henry's Well. The rivers Ribble and Skirdon run through the parish, in which there are two mineral springs, also a lead mine.

BOLTON-CASTLE, a chapelry in the parish of Wensley, western division of the wapentake of Hang, North riding of the county of York, $7\frac{1}{4}$ miles (N.W. by W.) from Middleham, containing 278 inhabitants. The living is a perpetual curacy, with that of Redmire annexed, in the archdeaconry of Richmond, and diocese of Chester, endowed with £1000 royal bounty, and in the patronage of the Rector of Wensley. The chapel is dedicated to St. Oswald. On the brow of a hill are the ruins of the castle, which was built by Richard, Lord Scrope, Chancellor of England in the reign of Richard II., in which the Queen of Scots was kept prisoner, in 1568. During the parliamentary war it sustained a pressing siege, which terminated in its surrender to the insurgents in 1645: the north-eastern tower fell down in 1761, and the eastern and northern sides are entirely in ruins; the west front, however, is in good repair. There is a small endowment in land for the instruction of poor children, bequeathed by the Rev Thomas Baynes, in 1725.

BOLTON upon DEARNE, a parish in the northern division of the wapentake of Strafforth and Tickhill, West riding of the county of York, $7\frac{1}{4}$ miles (N. by E.) from Rotherham, containing 623 inhabitants. The living is a discharged vicarage, in the archdeaconry and diocese of York, rated in the king's books at £6. 15. 5., endowed with £800 parliamentary grant, and in the patronage of W. Marsden, Esq. The church is dedicated to St. Andrew. A statute fair for hiring servants is held on the second Thursday in November. There is a charitable fund from which £11. 10. are paid annually for the instruction of twenty poor children, principally arising from a bequest by Richard Bingley, in 1756, and one by Elizabeth Pashley, in 1759.

Town Seal.

BOLTON le MOORS, a parish in the hundred of Salford, county palatine of Lancaster, comprising the market town of Bolton, the chapelries of Blackrod, Bradshaw, Darcy-Lever, Rivington, and Turton, the townships of Anglezarke, Breightmet, Edgworth, Entwisle, Harwood, Little Lever, Longworth, Quarlton, Sharples, and Tonge with Haulgh, and the hamlet of Lostock, and containing 50,197 inhabitants, of which number, 31,295 are in the town of Bolton, 43 miles (S. S. E.) from Lancaster, and 197 (N. W. by N.) from London. This place, which derives the adjunct to its name from being situated on the moors, was of little importance until about 1337, when the emigrant Flemings, who fixed their residence here, introduced the manufacture of woollen cloth, and laid the foundation of its future increase as a manufacturing town; and after the revocation of the edict of Nantz, many of the French refugees, attracted by the means of employment which its trade at that time afforded, took up their abode in the town. At the commencement of the civil war in the reign of Charles I., the inhabitants espoused the cause of the parliament, by whom the town was garrisoned, and in whose possession it remained till 1644, when Prince Rupert, advancing with ten thousand men to the relief of Latham House, which was besieged by a body of two thousand parliamentary troops, compelled them to raise the siege, and retire into this town. Having been joined by the Earl of Derby, the Prince resolved to invest Bolton, and an attempt was made to take it by storm; but the garrison, after sustaining several assaults with desperate valour, finally repulsed the assailants. The earl, placing himself at the head of his Lancashire tenantry, made a second attempt upon the town, which fell into his hands, and the parliamentary governor escaped with the remnant of the garrison into Yorkshire. After continuing for some time in possession of the royalists, Bolton was given up to the parliament; and after the disastrous battle of Worcester, the gallant earl, who had come from the Isle of Man to the assistance of Charles II., being taken prisoner, was condemned by a military tribunal at Chester, and sent under an escort to this place, where he was beheaded.

The town, comprising the townships of Great and Little Bolton, which are separated by the rivulet Croal, has been greatly enlarged, under an act of parliament obtained in 1792, for enclosing Bolton moor, of which more than two hundred and fifty acres were divided into allotments, a portion of which is occupied with buildings. The powers of the commissioners appointed under that act were extended by an act in 1817, since which time three spacious squares, several ranges of buildings, and a few public edifices, have been erected: four hundred and twenty-eight houses in Great Bolton, and one hundred and ninety-six in Little Bolton, were built during the year 1823, and considerable improvement has been made in the roads leading to the town. The houses are handsomely built; the streets, which are well paved, are lighted with gas by a company incorporated in 1820, and the inhabitants are supplied with excellent water, brought from a distance of a mile and a half, by earthenware pipes, into a reservoir which occupies a space of twenty-two acres, whence it is conveyed by an iron main of thirteen inches diameter to the various parts of the town: the water, descending from an elevation of seven hundred feet into the reservoir, rushes through the main with a pressure sufficient to raise it to the height of eighty feet, and is thus rendered available, without the assistance of an engine, to the prompt extinction of fire in the loftiest buildings. This undertaking was effected at an expense of £40,000, subscribed in shares of £50 each, by a company established by act of parliament, in 1824, for whose use a handsome stone building has been erected, in front of which is an emblematical tablet, representing a Naïad seated by a fountain, pouring water from a ewer to a thirsty child. The theatre is regularly open during the season; and a new assembly-room has been lately erected, in which also concerts take place occasionally. There are three public libraries; one of them, recently established, is conducted on principles less restrictive than either of the two former: it is held in the Exchange Buildings, a neat stone edifice, with two Ionic columns at the entrance, erected in 1825; the lower room, which is of ample dimensions, is appropriated to the transaction of general business, and fitted up as a news-room; the upper part contains the library and reading-rooms. A mechanics' institution was established in 1825.

The principal branch of manufacture, and to the introduction of which Bolton owes its present extent and importance, is that of cotton, in the improvement of which, many ingenious and valuable discoveries originated in this town. Sir Richard Arkwright, a resident here, after he had established his works at Derby and Nottingham, brought the spinning jenny and the water-frame machines to perfection; and Samuel Crompton, who was also an inhabitant of Bolton, invented a machine, called the mule, combining the properties of both, for which, after receiving two several donations of £105 and £400, subscribed as acknowledgments of his merit, he was ultimately remunerated by parliament with a grant of £5000. Previously to the introduction of the cotton trade, some weavers, who arrived in this country from the palatinate of the Rhine, had added to the manufacture of woollen cloth that of a fabric, partly composed of linen yarn, chiefly imported from Germany, and partly of cotton. The chief articles were fustian, jean, and thickset: velvet, entirely of cotton, was first made here in 1756, and muslin, quilting, and dimity, succeeded. After the introduction of the improved machinery several factories were established, but, being chiefly worked by water, they were consequently on a small scale; the subsequent employment of steam enabled the proprietors to enlarge their works, and the adoption of power-looms contributed greatly to improve and extend the trade: there are at present more than twenty factories, worked by thirty-one steam engines, of the aggregate power of seven hundred horses. The bleaching grounds are very extensive, and more than ten millions of pieces of cloth are annually bleached in the parish: among these are three large establishments, in each of which, from one hundred and thirty to one hundred and fifty thousand pieces are, on the average, bleached every month. There are ten iron-foundries, some of them on a very extensive scale, and one employing three hundred persons, chiefly in the construction of steam-engines. Machinery of all kinds, and mills of every description, are made to a great extent. The neighbourhood abounds with coal, which is brought into the town at a moderate expense, by means of a rail-road communicating with the Leeds and Liverpool canal at Leigh, eight miles distant: this work was begun under an act of parliament, in 1825, and completed at an expense of £80,000, subscribed in shares of £100 each. The canal from Manchester to Bolton was constructed in 1791; a branch to Bury diverges from it at Little Lever, in this parish. Veins of lead-ore and of calamine have been worked at Rivington, but they have not been found productive. The market days are Monday and Saturday: the fairs are on July 30th and 31st, and October 13th and 14th, for horned cattle, horses, pigs, and pedlary; a fair for lean cattle is also held every alternate Wednesday, from January 5th to May 12th. The market is held in the area of the new square, in the centre of which is a handsome cast-iron column, thirty feet high, rising from a pedestal in the form of a vase, and supporting a lantern which is lighted with gas.

The town is within the jurisdiction of the county magistrates, one of whom attends every Monday, and a petty session is held for the division every Monday and Friday. A boroughreeve, two constables, and a deputy constable, are chosen for each of the townships of Great and Little Bolton, at the court leet of the lord of the manor; under whom also a court for the recovery of debts under 40*s.* was held till the 6th of George III., when it was discontinued. A town-hall, a neat and commodious edifice, has been recently erected at Little Bolton, at an expense of £2000; and it is in contemplation to erect a similar structure in Great Bolton, more adapted to the use, and more suited to the importance, of the town than the present rooms in which the public business is transacted. The living is a discharged vicarage, in the archdeaconry and diocese of Chester, rated in the king's books at £10. 3. 1½., endowed with £200 private benefaction, and £200 royal bounty, and in the patronage of the Bishop of Chester. The church, dedicated to St. Peter, is a spacious structure, principally in the later style of English architecture, and there are some interesting monuments in the chancel. A church, dedicated to the Holy Trinity, was erected in 1825, at an expense of £13,412. 13., part of which was defrayed by grant from the parliamentary commissioners: it is a handsome structure in the later style of English architecture, with a tower, and contains nine hundred and twenty free sittings: the living is a perpetual curacy, in the patronage of the Vicar of Bolton. The church, dedicated to St. George, in Little Bolton, was erected by subscription, in 1796: the living is a perpetual curacy, in the patronage of the Trustees. The chapel, dedicated to All Saints, in Little Bolton, has been recently rebuilt: the living is a perpetual curacy, endowed with £200 private benefaction, £200 royal bounty, and £2200 parliamentary grant, and in the patronage of the lord of the manor. There are two places of worship each for Baptists, Independents, and Unitarians, one each for the Society of Friends and Swedenborgians, seven for the various denominations of Methodists, and a Roman Catholic chapel. The free grammar school was founded by Robert Lever, Esq., citizen of London, who, in 1641, bequeathed estates now producing about £400 per annum, with which the revenue of a school previously existing has been united, amounting in the whole to £485 per annum: it is under the direction of governors incorporated in 1784, who appoint a head-master, with a salary of £160 per annum; a second master, with a salary of £100; and a writing-master, with a salary of £75: there is a small exhibition to either of the Universities. Robert Ainsworth, the compiler of the Latin Dictionary, and Dr. Lempriere, the compiler of the Classical Dictionary, were masters of this school; and the former was educated here. A charity school was founded and endowed, in 1693, by Mr. Nathaniel Hulton, for the instruction of thirty boys and thirty girls; the income is £277 per annum: the school is under the management of trustees, who appoint a master and a mistress, the former with a salary of £45, and the latter with a salary of £25, per annum. A school for the clothing and education of poor children was founded, in 1714, by Thomas Marsden, Esq., who endowed it with £150, now producing £14. 10. per annum, of which the master receives £10. 10., and the remainder is expended in repairs. There are Sunday schools in connexion with the established church and the numerous dissenting congregations, in which more than seven thousand children are instructed. The school-room in connexion with the parish church is a large and handsome building of freestone, in the later style of English architecture, erected by subscription, in 1819, at an expense of £1800; it contains a good organ. A dispensary was established in 1814, and is liberally supported by subscription: the building, which is of a neat and appropriate character, was erected at an expense of £1700. A clothing society is supported chiefly by ladies, and a society for the relief of poor women during childbirth was established in 1798. John Bradshaw, president of the court which sentenced Charles I. to the scaffold, is said to have been born near this town.

BOLTON le SANDS, a parish in the hundred of LONSDALE, south of the sands, county palatine of LANCASTER, comprising the chapelry of Over Kellet, and the townships of Bolton le Sands, Nether Kellet, and Slyne with Hest, and containing 1821 inhabitants, of which number, 615 are in the township of Bolton le Sands, 4 miles (N.) from Lancaster. The living is a discharged vicarage, in the archdeaconry of Richmond, and diocese of Chester, rated in the king's books at £4. 15., endowed with £200 private benefaction, and £200 royal bounty, and in the patronage of the Bishop of Chester. The church was rebuilt in 1813. The free grammar school, for children belonging to the townships of Bolton, Nether Kellet, and Slyne with Hest, was founded in 1619, by Thomas Assheton, and has an income of £23 per annum, arising from the original endowment and subsequent benefactions. The village of Hest is considerably resorted to for sea-bathing. There are limekilns in the township of Nether Kellet.

BOLTON upon SWALE, a chapelry in the parish of CATTERICK, eastern division of the wapentake of GILLING, North riding of the county of YORK, 1¾ mile (N. E.) from Catterick, containing 100 inhabitants. The living is a perpetual curacy, in the archdeaconry of Richmond, and diocese of Chester, endowed with £600 royal bounty, and £1000 parliamentary grant, and in the patronage of the Crown. The chapel, dedicated to St. Mary, contains a neat pyramidal tablet, erected by subscription, in 1743, over the grave of Henry Jenkins, a native of this place, who died at the age of one hundred and sixty-nine, the oldest Englishman on record.

BOLTON-PERCY, a parish in the ainsty of the city, and East riding of the county, of YORK, comprising the townships of Appleton-Roebuck, Bolton-Percy, Colton, and Steeton, and containing 1054 inhabitants, of which number, 238 are in the township of Bolton-Percy, 4 miles (E. by S.) from Tadcaster. The living is a rectory, in the archdeaconry of the East riding, and diocese of York, rated in the king's books at £39. 15. 2½., and in the patronage of the Archbishop of York. The church, dedicated to All Saints, was built in 1423, by Thomas Parker, the rector: it is a neat structure, decorated with a considerable quantity of stained glass, and containing several monuments belonging to the family of Fairfax. There is a place of worship for Wesleyan Methodists.

BONBY, a parish in the northern division of the wapentake of YARBOROUGH, parts of LINDSEY, county of LINCOLN, 6½ miles (N.) from Glandford-Bridge, containing 275 inhabitants. The living is a discharged vicarage, in the archdeaconry and diocese of Lincoln, rated in the king's books at £6. 4. 4., and in the patronage of Lord Yarborough. The church, dedicated to St. Andrew, has lately received an addition of one hundred sittings, fifty of which are free, the Incorporated Society for the enlargement of churches and chapels having granted £50 towards defraying the expense. In the reign of John, an Alien priory was established by the prior and convent at Merton, to whom this church, with others, had been granted in the 4th of Henry IV., which was given to the Chartreux-house at Beauval.

BONCHURCH, a parish in the liberty of EAST MEDINA, Isle of Wight division of the county of SOUTHAMPTON, 10 miles (S. E. by S.) from Newport, containing 122 inhabitants. The living is a discharged rectory, with the perpetual curacy of Shanklin annexed, in the archdeaconry and diocese of Winchester, rated in the king's books at £6. 15. 5., and in the patronage of Lord H. Seymour and J. Popham, Esq. The church is dedicated to St. Boniface.

BONDGATE, a joint township with Aismunderby, in that part of the parish of RIPON which is within the liberty of RIPON, West riding of the county of YORK, ½ a mile (S.) from Ripon. The population is returned with Aismunderby. An hospital for two poor women was founded here, by one of the archbishops of York, about the time of King John.

BONDS, a joint township with Barnacre, in the parish of GARSTANG, hundred of AMOUNDERNESS, county palatine of LANCASTER, 1½ mile (E. N. E.) from Garstang. The population is returned with Barnacre. Here are the relics of a castle, called Greenhalgh castle.

BONEHILL, a township in that part of the parish of TAMWORTH which is in the southern division of the hundred of OFFLOW, county of STAFFORD, 1½ mile (S. W. by W.) from Tamworth, containing 279 inhabitants.

BONINGALE, or BONINGHALL, a parish in the Shiffnall division of the hundred of BRIMSTREE, county of SALOP, 5¼ miles (S. E.) from Shiffnall, containing 160 inhabitants. The living is a perpetual curacy, annexed to the rectory of Stockton, in the archdeaconry of Salop, and diocese of Lichfield and Coventry.

BONNINGTON, a parish partly in the liberty of ROMNEY-MARSH, but chiefly in the hundred of STREET, lathe of SHEPWAY, county of KENT, 6½ miles (S. E. by S.) from Ashford, containing 152 inhabitants. The living is a rectory, in the archdeaconry and diocese of Canterbury, rated in the king's books at £10. 12. 8½., and in the patronage of T. Papillon, Esq. The church is dedicated to St. Rumwald. The Grand Military, or the Shorncliff and Rye, canal crosses the parish.

BONNINGTON (SUTTON), county of NOTTINGHAM. — See SUTTON-BONNINGTON.

BONSALL, a parish (formerly a market town) in the hundred of WIRKSWORTH, county of DERBY, 3½ miles (N. by W.) from Wirksworth, containing 1396 inhabitants. The living is a rectory, in the archdeaconry of Derby, and diocese of Lichfield and Coventry, rated in the king's books at £9. 16. 0½., and in the patronage of the Dean of Lincoln. The church, dedicated to St. James, is a handsome embattled edifice, having a tower terminating in pinnacles, and supporting an octagonal spire, curiously ornamented, and encircled with coronets. There is a place of worship for General Baptists. The houses are scattered over a considerable plot of ground, and form a large village, at which a market was formerly held; the market cross, consisting of a pillar, bearing date 1687, resting on a base formed by an ascent of fifteen steps, and crowned by a ball, still remains. The vicinity is diversified with hills and dales, among which latter, the Dale of Bonsall is the most interesting; its geological formation consists of four strata of limestone, and three of toad-stone: the neighbouring hills also abound with limestone. Lead-ore and *lapis calaminaris* are obtained to a considerable extent, and prepared on the spot, the greater part of the population being engaged in the different works: here is also a comb-manufactory. A school, in which fifty boys and girls are instructed gratuitously, is endowed with about £100 per annum, arising from the gift of certain tenements by William Cragge and his wife Elizabeth, in 1704, and of some land by Elizabeth Turner, in 1763. Adjoining the school-room is a comfortable dwelling-house, with a garden attached to it, for the use of the master, whose salary is about £46 per annum: of the remainder of the income, a portion is appropriated for apprenticing boys and for purchasing religious books. Bonsall is in the honour of Tutbury, duchy of Lancaster, and within the jurisdiction of a court of pleas held at Tutbury every third Tuesday, for the recovery of debts under 40*s*. Vestiges of a Roman road may be traced within the parish.

BONWICK, a township in the parish of SKIPSEA, northern division of the wapentake of HOLDERNESS, East riding of the county of YORK, 11½ miles (E. S. E.) from Great Driffield, containing 30 inhabitants.

BOOKHAM (GREAT), a parish in the hundred of EFFINGHAM, county of SURREY, 2½ miles (W. S. W.) from Leatherhead, containing 732 inhabitants. The living is a discharged vicarage, in the archdeaconry of Surrey, and diocese of Winchester, rated in the king's books at £9. 17. 3½., and in the patronage of Dr. Heberden. The church is dedicated to St. Nicholas.

BOOKHAM (LITTLE), a parish in the hundred of EFFINGHAM, county of SURREY, 3 miles (W. S. W.) from Leatherhead, containing 153 inhabitants. The living is a discharged rectory, in the archdeaconry of Surrey, and diocese of Winchester, rated in the king's books at £6. 15. 7., and in the patronage of the Rev. G. P. Boileau Pollen. Certain tenements in London, producing about £65 per annum, were assigned by Sir Benjamin Maddox with the intent that a moiety of the rental should be given to the clergyman of this parish, and that the other moiety should be applied for the benefit of the poor and the parish clerk, and for the reparation of the church and the highways.

BOOLEY, a township in the parish of STANTON upon HINE-HEATH, Whitchurch division of the hundred of BRADFORD (North), county of SALOP, containing 134 inhabitants.

BOOTH, a hamlet in the parish of HOWDEN, wapentake of HOWDENSHIRE, East riding of the county of YORK, 2 miles (S. W.) from Howden, with which the population is returned. The village lies on the northern bank of the river Ouse, across which there is a ferry, called Booth ferry.

BOOTHBY, a parish in the higher division of the wapentake of Boothby-Graffo, parts of Kesteven, county of Lincoln, 10 miles (N.W. by N.) from Sleaford, containing 155 inhabitants. The living is a rectory, in the archdeaconry and diocese of Lincoln, rated in the king's books at £11. 12. 3½., and in the patronage of Viscount Melbourne. The church is dedicated to St. Andrew.

BOOTHBY-PAGNELL, a parish in the wapentake of Winnibriggs and Threo, parts of Kesteven, county of Lincoln, 5¼ miles (N.N.W.) from Corby, containing 110 inhabitants. The living is a rectory, in the archdeaconry and diocese of Lincoln, rated in the king's books at £11. 10. 5., and in the patronage of J. Litchford, Esq. The church is dedicated to St. Andrew.

BOOTHEN, a joint township with Penkhul, in the parish of Stoke upon Trent, northern division of the hundred of Pirehill, county of Stafford. The population is returned with Penkhul.

BOOTHS (HIGHER), a township in that part of the parish of Whalley which is in the higher division of the hundred of Blackburn, county palatine of Lancaster, 3 miles (E.) from Burnley, containing 3172 inhabitants.

BOOTHS (LOWER), a township in that part of the parish of Whalley which is in the higher division of the hundred of Blackburn, county palatine of Lancaster, containing 1513 inhabitants.

BOOTLE, a market town and parish in Allerdale ward above Darwent, county of Cumberland, 5½ miles (S.S.E.) from Ravenglass, and 282 (N.W. by N.) from London, containing 656 inhabitants. The name, formerly "Bothill," is supposed to be derived from the booths erected on a hill above the town, for the watchmen whose duty it was to light the beacon on its summit, upon the discovery of any ships in the Irish channel, which might appear to threaten a descent upon the coast. A Benedictine nunnery was founded at Seton, in this parish, by Gunild, daughter of Henry de Boyvill, fourth lord of Millorn, to which Henry IV. annexed the hospital of St. Leonard, in Lancaster: its revenue, at the dissolution, was £13. 17. 4.; there are still some remains. The town is pleasantly situated within two miles of the sea; the houses are neatly built, and the inhabitants well supplied with water: the land in the neighbourhood is in a high state of cultivation, and the environs abound with pleasing scenery. The Corney and Bootle Fells, eminences in the adjoining forest of Copeland, afford extensive views; and from Black Coombe, which is nearly two thousand feet high, may be seen the coast of Scotland, the Isle of Man, and the Welch mountains. The trade is principally in corn, pork, and bacon, which are sent to Liverpool. The market is on Saturday: the fairs are on April 5th and September 24th, for the sale of corn, and for hiring servants; and April 26th and August 3rd, for horses, horned cattle, and sheep. The living is a rectory, in the archdeaconry of Richmond, and diocese of Chester, rated in the king's books at £19. 17. 3½., and in the patronage of the Earl of Lonsdale. The church, dedicated to St. Michael, is a very ancient edifice, though much modernised by successive repairs; the interior, which has been deprived of its original character, contains some interesting monuments, among which is an effigy on a brass plate of Sir Hugh Askew, who was knighted at the battle of Musselburgh, and a large octagonal font of black marble, ornamented on each side with two ancient shields, and bearing inscriptions in old English and Saxon characters. There is a place of worship for Independents, built in 1780, by Mr. Joseph Whitridge, a native of Bootle, who endowed it with £1000, vested in trustees. The free school was founded in 1713, by Mr. Henry Singleton, who endowed it with £200, which sum, with subsequent benefactions, produces about £20 per annum, as a salary to the master, who is appointed by the rector and four trustees, and teaches six boys gratuitously: there are other bequests for the benefit of the poor. At Selker bay, a small inlet of the sea, are sometimes seen the remains of vessels, which are traditionally said to have been Roman gallies, sunk there at the time of an invasion by that people; and at Esk-Meots are vestiges of an encampment, where Roman coins and fragments of altars have been frequently discovered.

BOOTLE, a chapelry in the parish of Walton on the Hill, hundred of West Derby, county palatine of Lancaster, 3¼ miles (N.) from Liverpool, containing, with the township of Linacre, 808 inhabitants. The village comprises several good houses, and is very much resorted to during summer, for the benefit of sea-bathing.

BOOTON, a parish in the southern division of the hundred of Erpingham, county of Norfolk, 1¼ mile (E.S.E.) from Reepham, containing 204 inhabitants. The living is a discharged rectory, in the archdeaconry and diocese of Norwich, rated in the king's books at £7. 12. 6., and in the patronage of Mrs. Elwin. The church is dedicated to St. Michael.

BORDEAN, a tything in the parish and hundred of East-Meon, Alton (South) division of the county of Southampton, 3½ miles (W. by N.) from Petersfield. The population is returned with the parish.

BORDEN, a parish in the hundred of Milton, lathe of Scray, county of Kent, 2¾ miles (W. by S.) from Sittingbourne, containing 650 inhabitants. The living is a vicarage, in the archdeaconry and diocese of Canterbury, rated in the king's books at £8. 10., and in the patronage of J. Musgrave, Esq. The church, dedicated to St. Peter and St. Paul, is an ancient edifice, comprising three aisles and three chancels, with a square tower at the western end: there are some Roman bricks mixed with the flint-stones in the building, and cemented with mortar, in the composition of which pulverized cockle-shells have been used: the chief entrance is under a Saxon, or Norman, arch, and there are similar specimens of architecture in other parts of the edifice. A British coin, and several relics of Roman antiquity, together with a great quantity of round stones, like cannon-balls, have been found in the neighbourhood. Dr. Robert Plot, the natural historian of Oxfordshire and Staffordshire, was born at the manor-house of Sutton-Baron, in this parish, in 1641, where he died, April 13th, 1696.

BORDESLEY, a chapelry in the parish of Aston, Birmingham division of the hundred of Hemlingford, county of Warwick. The population is returned with the parish. The living is a perpetual curacy, in the archdeaconry of Coventry, and diocese of Lichfield and

Coventry, and in the patronage of the Vicar of Aston. The chapel, dedicated to the Holy Trinity, is in the later style of English architecture: it was built in 1820, at an expense of £12,722. 15. 6., which was raised by subscription among the inhabitants, aided by a grant from the parliamentary commissioners. This was formerly a small hamlet, consisting only of detached houses, but from its proximity to Birmingham, it has become an integral part of that town, and participates largely in its trade, manufactures, and institutions. An hospital for about twelve poor persons, an apartment in which is used for a chapel, has been built by Mr. Dowell, who appoints the inmates, but no permanent provision for their support has yet been made.

BORDESLEY, a hamlet in that part of the parish of TARDEBIGG which is in the upper division of the hundred of HALFSHIRE, county of WORCESTER, 5½ miles (E. S. E.) from Bromsgrove. The population is returned with the parish. A Cistercian abbey, in honour of the Blessed Virgin Mary, was built in 1138, by the Empress Matilda, the revenue of which, a short time previously to the dissolution, was estimated at £392. 8. 6.: the chapel, dedicated to St. Stephen, which subsisted for some time afterwards, formed part of it.

BOREHAM, a parish in the hundred of CHELMSFORD, county of ESSEX, 3½ miles (N. E. by E.) from Chelmsford, containing 918 inhabitants. The living is a vicarage, in the archdeaconry of Essex, and diocese of London, rated in the king's books at £10. 3. 9., and in the patronage of the Bishop of London. The church is dedicated to St. Andrew. The Chelmer and Blackwater canal crosses the southern part of the parish. The parochial school has an endowment of about £3 per annum, the gift of Robert Clough, in 1726; and Edmund Butler, in 1717, appropriated land for clothing and instructing poor children of Little Barlow and Boreham. New Hall, in this parish, is part of a much larger mansion supposed to have been built in the reign of Henry VII., and greatly adorned by Henry VIII., who, having obtained the manor in exchange for other property, raised it into an honour: his daughter, the Princess Mary, also resided here for several years. It afterwards came into the possession of Villiers, the first duke of Buckingham, and, on the attainder of his son, was purchased by Cromwell. After the Restoration it became the property of the Duke of Albemarle, but has since been purchased by a few opulent individuals professing the Roman Catholic faith, and is now occupied by a society of English nuns, who were driven from Liege by the fury of the French republicans, and who now superintend the education of about eighty Roman Catholic young ladies. The splendid chapel which belonged to the mansion, and which contained the painted window now in St. Margaret's church, Westminster, was taken down about eighty years ago, and the great hall of the building has since been converted into a chapel.

BORESFORD, a joint township with Pedwardine, in that part of the parish of BRAMPTON-BRYAN which is in the hundred of WIGMORE, county of HEREFORD, 3 miles (S. E.) from Knighton, containing, with Pedwardine, 112 inhabitants.

BORLEY, a parish in the hundred of HINCKFORD, county of ESSEX, 2¼ miles (N. W. by W.) from Sudbury, containing 195 inhabitants. The living is a rectory, in the peculiar jurisdiction of the Archbishop of Canterbury, rated in the king's books at £9, and in the patronage of Earl Waldegrave.

BORLEY, a township in the parish of OMBERSLEY, lower division of the hundred of OSWALDSLOW, county of WORCESTER. The population is returned with Ombersley.

BOROUGHBRIDGE, a hamlet situated within the parishes of LING, OTHERY, MIDDLEZOY, and WESTON-ZOYLAND, partly in the hundred of ANDERSFIELD, and partly in that of WHITLEY, county of SOMERSET. The population is returned with the respective parishes. Collinson, the county historian, considers the name to be derived from "a large borough or mount, very high and steep," and a stone bridge of three lofty arches, which here crosses the navigable river Parret: this mount is situated within an enclosure on the eastern side of the river, and has generally been thought to have been formed by nature; but the same author supposes it to be a work of art, raised for a tumulus. It is crowned with the ruins of an ancient cruciform chapel, which was dedicated to St. Michael, and dependent on the abbey of Athelney. Though previously in a dilapidated state, it was greatly damaged during the parliamentary war, when it was occupied as a military post by a small party of royalists, who, after having successfully resisted various assaults, were compelled to surrender to a body of parliamentarians, detached against them by General Fairfax.

BOROUGHBRIDGE, a borough, market town, and chapelry, in that part of the parish of ALDBOROUGH which is in the lower division of the wapentake of CLARO, West riding of the county of YORK, 17½ miles (N.W. by W.) from York, and 206 (N.N.W.) from London, containing 860 inhabitants. This place, which has risen into importance since the decline of Aldborough, within half a mile of which it is situated, derives its name from a bridge erected here over the river Ure, soon after the Conquest, when the road was diverted from Aldborough, and brought through this town. Near this bridge a battle took place, in 1322, between the forces of Edward II. and those of the celebrated Earl of Lancaster, in which the latter were defeated. The earl having taken refuge in the town, which was assaulted on the following day, was made prisoner and conveyed to Pontefract, where he was soon afterwards beheaded. Of this battle, a memorial has been obtained in the number of human bones, swords, fragments of armour, and other military relics, which, in raising the bank of the Ure, in 1792, were found near the spot. The town is pleasantly situated on the southern bank of the river, which is here navigable, and has been greatly improved and enlarged by the erection of several respectable houses on the opposite side of the river, over which a handsome stone bridge has been constructed, on the site of a former one, which was built of wood. The streets are partially paved, and the inhabitants are amply supplied with water from springs, and from the river. There is a small subscription library at the Crown Inn; and races are annually held in the vicinity. The trade is principally in hardware, but the town derives its chief support from being situated on the high road to Edinburgh. The market is on Saturday; and fairs are held on April 27th, June 22nd, and October 23rd, each for two days: the fair in June is chiefly for hardware and woollen cloth; the others are for cattle and sheep. In the market-place, which is conveniently situated in the centre of the town, there is a handsome fluted column of the Doric order, twelve feet high. A bailiff and other officers are chosen annually at the court leet of the lord of the manor, but they do not exercise magisterial authority. The elective franchise was conferred in the reign of Mary, since which time the borough has returned two members to parliament: the right of election is vested in the burgage tenants, in number sixty-five, who are chiefly in the interest of the Duke of Newcastle; the bailiff is the returning officer. The living is a perpetual curacy, in the archdeaconry of Richmond, and diocese of Chester, endowed with £800 royal bounty, and £1200 parliamentary grant, and in the patronage of the Vicar of Aldborough. There are places of worship for Methodists. A National school, established in 1814, is supported by subscription. To the west of the bridge are three large pyramidal stones, ranged in a straight line, in a direction from north to south, and each in a separate enclosure, the central one of which is the largest, being thirty feet and a half in height: they are vulgarly called the Devil's Arrows, and were originally four in number. The purpose of their erection is involved in obscurity; some suppose them to have been raised in memory of a reconciliation effected between Caracalla and Geta, sons of the Emperor Severus, who died at York. Camden considers them to have been Roman trophies; though they may probably have been used by that people as *metæ* in the celebration of their chariot races, yet their origin appears to be more remote. Stukeley refers them to the earliest times of the Britons, and is of opinion that here was the great Panegyre of the Druids, where the inhabitants of the neighbouring district assembled to offer the sacrifices. From its proximity to Aldborough, a celebrated Roman station, numerous relics have been found here, consisting of tesselated pavements and coins; and, in the immediate vicinity, the remains of a Roman wall are still discernible.

BOROUGH-FEN, an extra-parochial district, in the liberty of PETERBOROUGH, county of NORTHAMPTON, 5 miles (N. E. by N.) from Peterborough, containing 204 inhabitants.

BORROWBY, a township in that part of the parish of LEAK which is in the wapentake of ALLERTONSHIRE, North riding of the county of YORK, 5 miles (N.) from Thirsk, containing 267 inhabitants. There is a place of worship for Wesleyan Methodists. Some small sums have been left for the instruction of children.

BORROWBY, a township in the parish of LYTHE, eastern division of the liberty of LANGBAURGH, North riding of the county of YORK, 11¼ miles (W. N. W.) from Whitby, containing 64 inhabitants.

BORROWDALE, a chapelry in that part of the parish of CROSTHWAITE which is in ALLERDALE ward above Darwent, county of CUMBERLAND, 7 miles (S. by W.) from Keswick, containing 346 inhabitants. The living is a perpetual curacy, in the archdeaconry and diocese of Carlisle, endowed with £200 private benefaction, and £600 royal bounty, and in the patronage of the Vicar of Crosthwaite. The chapel has lately been rebuilt. There are meeting-houses for Dissenters at Grange and Rosthwaite, hamlets in this chapelry. Near Seathwaite, another hamlet, is the celebrated plumbago, wad, or black lead mine, in the side of a steep mountain, formed by a rock of grey felspar porphyry. Owing to the abundant produce, and the facility of obtaining it, the mine was formerly opened only once in five years, and that but for a short space of time; of late, however, it has been less productive, and the demand has greatly increased, so that about eight miners have been constantly engaged for several successive years in working it. The lead is found lying in lumps, or nodules, varying in weight from an ounce to fifty pounds, in the clefts of the rock. The finer sort is packed in barrels, sent to London, and deposited in the warehouse belonging to the proprietors of the mine, where it is exposed for sale to the pencil-makers on the first Monday in every month: that of an inferior description is chiefly used in the composition of crucibles, in giving a black polish to articles of cast-iron, and in various anti-attrition compositions. To protect the interests of the proprietors, an act was passed in 1752, whereby persons stealing, or receiving this article, knowing it to be stolen, are subjected to the same punishment as felons. A house has been built over the entrance, where the workmen undress and are examined, every time they leave the mine. Black lead is found in various parts of the world, but in none to so great an extent, and of the same degree of purity, as in this: an inferior kind has been discovered in the shires of Ayr and Inverness, in Scotland, but it is unfit for pencils. Here are also several quarries of blue slate: a copper mine was formerly worked; and lead-ore exists to a limited extent in the mountain. A soft, palish substance, commonly called Borrowdale soap, is found, which, having undergone a chemical process, similar to that by which the black lead is hardened, is used for slate pencils. The romantic scenery of this district has elicited deserved eulogy from the pens of numerous tourists. Bowder stone, which has often formed a subject both for the pencil and the pen, is esteemed the largest detached piece of rock entitled to the denomination of a single stone in England: it is sixty-two feet in length, and eighty-four in circumference, and contains about twenty-three thousand and ninety feet of solid stone, weighing upwards of one thousand seven hundred and seventy-one tons: the upper part projects considerably over the small base on which it rests, and it is not unusual for parties of pleasure to regale under it. On the summit of Castle Crag, a conical hill covered with wood, are vestiges of a military work. Near a lake, at the lower extremity of the dale, there is a salt-spring, the water of which is of a quality somewhat similar to that at Cheltenham. A fair for sheep is held on the first Wednesday in September.

BORROWDON, a township in the parish of ALLENTON, western division of COQUETDALE ward, county of NORTHUMBERLAND, containing 179 inhabitants.

BORWICK, a chapelry in the parish of WARTON, hundred of LONSDALE, south of the sands, county palatine of LANCASTER, 3½ miles (S.) from Burton in Kendal, containing 251 inhabitants. Charles II. lodged for one night at Borwick Hall, on his way to Worcester, and his army encamped a short distance from it.

BOSBURY, a parish in the hundred of RADLOW, county of HEREFORD, 4½ miles (N. by W.) from Ledbury, containing, with Up-Leadon, 966 inhabitants. The living is a discharged vicarage, in the archdeaconry and diocese of Hereford, rated in the king's books at

£10. 3. 8., and in the patronage of the Bishop of Hereford. The church, dedicated to the Holy Trinity, is an ancient edifice, containing some interesting monuments. A free grammar school, endowed by Sir Rodland Morton, has lately been discontinued, owing to the appropriation of the income, which is about £135 per annum, to the discharge of the costs of a suit in Chancery, which, for the next twenty years, will absorb the whole of the proceeds. Mr. Bridges, of Tiberton Court, bequeathed £5 per annum for apprenticing one poor child; and there are several other small bequests for the benefit of the poor. The bishops of Hereford had formerly a palace here, the remains of which have been converted into farm buildings.

BOSCASTLE, a small sea-port, and formerly a market town, in the parishes of Forrabury and Minster, hundred of Lesnewth, county of Cornwall, 17 miles (W. by N.) from Launceston, and 230 (W. by S.) from London. The population is returned with the parishes. This place takes its name from a castle erected by some of the family of Bottereaux, who settled here in the reign of Henry II., of which only the site remains. The town is romantically situated on the northern coast, and contains several respectable houses. A pilchard fishery, established a few years since, but soon afterwards relinquished, contributed greatly to the improvement of the quay, which is accessible to ships of three hundred tons' burden. The port is a member of the port of Padstowe, and considerable trade is carried on in corn, Delabole slate, and manganese (of which last there is a mine in the neighbourhood), which are sent coastwise, and coal and timber brought in return. The fairs are on August 5th for lambs, and November 22nd for ewes and cattle. There is a place of worship for Wesleyan Methodists; and some remains of an ancient chapel, dedicated to St. James, are visible.

BOSCOBEL, an extra-parochial district, in the Hales-Owen division of the hundred of Brimstree, county of Salop, 7½ miles (E.) from Shiffnall, containing 30 inhabitants. Boscobel House is celebrated in history as the place where Charles II. concealed himself in September, 1651, after the disastrous battle of Worcester, secure in the incorruptible integrity of five brothers, named Penderell: the house has been considerably modernised, but the place of concealment, called the *Sacred Hole*, is carefully preserved, and in front of the house is a Latin inscription, traced with white pebbles in the pavement, recording the circumstance. The Royal Oak, thought to have sprung from an acorn of the parent tree, among the branches of which the unfortunate monarch retired for greater security, when his pursuers were searching the house and out-buildings, stands near the middle of a large field adjoining the garden; it is surrounded by an iron railing, and has an inscribed brass plate affixed to it.

BOSCOMBE, a parish in the hundred of Amesbury, county of Wilts, 3¾ miles (S. E. by E.) from Amesbury, containing 128 inhabitants. The living is a rectory, in the archdeaconry and diocese of Salisbury, rated in the king's books at £13. 17. 1., and in the patronage of the Bishop of Salisbury. The church is dedicated to St. Andrew. Four almshouses, for two widows and two widowers, are endowed with a rent-charge of £24.

BOSHAM, a parish in the hundred of Bosham, rape of Chichester, county of Sussex, 4 miles (W. by S.) from Chichester, containing 1049 inhabitants. The living is a discharged vicarage, in the archdeaconry and diocese of Chichester, rated in the king's books at £6. 11. 3., endowed with £200 private benefaction, £200 royal bounty, and £400 parliamentary grant, and in the patronage of the Dean and Chapter of Chichester. The church is dedicated to the Holy Trinity. The village is situated at the upper extremity of a creek, to which it gives name, and the parish is bounded on the east and south by Chichester harbour. Two sums of £70 each, one given by George Parker the elder, in 1722, and the other by George Parker the younger, in 1733, have been laid out pursuant to a decree in Chancery, in purchasing a rent-charge of £4, which is paid to a schoolmistress for teaching poor children. So early as the year 681, here was a small monastery of five or six religious, under the government of one Dicul, a Scottish monk. Henry I. granted the place to William Warlewast, Bishop of Exeter, who founded a college of Secular canons, dedicated to the Holy Trinity, which, prior to the dissolution, was accounted a royal free chapel, exempt from the jurisdiction of the Bishop of Chichester, and that of the Archdeacon.

BOSLEY, a chapelry in the parish of Prestbury, hundred of Macclesfield, county palatine of Chester, 4¾ miles (E. N. E.) from Congleton, containing 546 inhabitants. The living is a perpetual curacy, in the archdeaconry and diocese of Chester, endowed with £800 royal bounty, and £1000 parliamentary grant, and in the patronage of the Vicar of Prestbury.

BOSSALL, a parish comprising the chapelry of Sand-Hutton, in the wapentake of Birdforth, and the townships of Bossall, Butter-Crambe, Claxton, Harton, Sand-Hutton, and a part of that of Flaxton on the Moor, in the wapentake of Bulmer, North riding of the county of York, and containing 1365 inhabitants, of which number, 31 are in the township of Bossall, 10 miles (N. E.) from York. The living is a vicarage, in the archdeaconry of Cleveland, and diocese of York, rated in the king's books at £12, and in the patronage of the Dean and Chapter of Durham. The church, dedicated to St. Botolph, is a handsome cruciform structure, with a steeple rising from the centre. The village of Bossall was formerly large, but it does not now comprise more than three or four houses: foundations of buildings have been discovered in an adjoining field, thence called "Old Bossall." Courts leet are held for the several manors within the parish, which is bounded on the south and east by the river Derwent.

BOSSINEY with TREVENA, a borough and market town in the parish of Tintagell, hundred of Lesnewth, county of Cornwall, 18 miles (W. by N.) from Launceston, and 231 (W. by S.) from London. The population is returned with the parish. This borough, comprising two villages, about a quarter of a mile distant from each other, is situated on a bleak and rugged part of the northern coast. The market is on Thursday; and the fair, which is held at Trevena, is on the first Monday after October

Seal and Arms.

19th. Bossiney was made a free borough in the reign of Henry III., by Richard, Earl of Cornwall, brother to that monarch, but it never had a royal charter. A mayor, whose office is merely nominal, is chosen annually by a jury of burgesses empannelled by his predecessor, at the court leet held in October, when constables and other inferior officers are also appointed; the burgesses are chosen in a similar manner, as vacancies occur. The freedom of the borough descends to the eldest son of a burgess possessing freehold property within it, and is obtained by presentation of the jury. The elective franchise was conferred in the 7th of Edward VI., since which time the borough has returned two members to parliament: the right of election is vested in the burgesses possessing freehold property within the borough, and residing in the parish, the present number of whom is twenty-five, who are chiefly in the interest of Lord Wharncliffe and Edward Rose Tunno, Esq. The town-hall, a small building, is appropriated also to the use of a charity school, which is chiefly supported by the mayor and burgesses, who appoint the master, and allow him a salary of £20 per annum. There are some remains of King Arthur's castle, on the top of a stupendous rock, formerly part of the main land, but now connected with it only by a narrow isthmus; the summit comprises an area of thirty acres of pasture, but the acclivities are so steep, that it is almost inaccessible to the sheep that graze on it.

BOSSINGTON, a chapelry in the parish of Broughton, hundred of Thorngate, Andover division of the county of Southampton, $3\frac{1}{2}$ miles (S. W. by S.) from Stockbridge, containing 75 inhabitants. The chapel is dedicated to St. James. The Roman road from Salisbury to Winchester passes through the parish.

BOSTOCK, a township in the parish of Davenham, hundred of Northwich, county palatine of Chester, $2\frac{3}{4}$ miles (N. W. by W.) from Middlewich, containing 174 inhabitants.

Arms.

BOSTON, a borough, port, market town, and parish, having separate jurisdiction, locally in the wapentake of Skirbeck, parts of Holland, county of Lincoln, 34 miles (S. E.) from Lincoln, and 113 (N.) from London, containing 10,330 inhabitants, and, including a small extra-parochial district, 10,373. This place derived its name from St. Botolph, a Saxon who founded a monastery here, about the year 650, from which circumstance it was called Botolph's town, of which its present name is a contraction. The monastery, which was destroyed by the Danes in 870, was erected on the northern side of the present church, and its remains have been converted into a dwelling-house, called Botolph's Priory. From the discovery of the foundations of several ancient buildings, urns and other relics of antiquity, in 1716, this place is supposed to have been of Roman origin; and according to Dr. Stukeley, the Romans built a fort at the entrance of the river Witham, over which they had a ferry, at a short distance to the south of the town. In the reign of Edward I., Robert Chamberlayne, having assembled some associates disguised as ecclesiastics, secretly set fire to the town, and, while the inhabitants were endeavouring to extinguish the flames, plundered the booths of the rich merchandise exposed for sale at the fair, and burnt such goods as they were not able to carry away: so rich is the town represented to have been at the time of this fire, that veins of melted gold and silver are said to have run, in one common current, down the streets: Chamberlayne was afterwards taken and hanged, but his confederates escaped. In 1285, Boston suffered greatly from an inundation of the river, and the mercantile ardour of the inhabitants being checked by the plunder of the fair and the conflagration of the town, its prosperity began to decline. In the early part of the reign of Edward II., it was made a staple port for wool, leather, tin, lead, and other commodities, which soon gave a new impulse to the spirit of commercial enterprise; and the settlement in England of the Hanseatic merchants, who established a guild here, tended so powerfully to revive the former prosperity of the town, that, in the reign of Edward III., Boston sent deputies to three grand councils held at Westminster, and contributed seventeen ships, and two hundred and sixty-one men, toward the armament for the invasion of Brittany. The town is situated on the banks of the river Witham, which divides it into two wards, east and west, connected by a handsome iron bridge of one arch, erected by the corporation in 1807, at an expense of £22,000, under the superintendence of Mr. Rennie. The streets are well paved, and lighted with gas, under an act passed in the 16th of George III., for the general improvement of the town, and many handsome buildings have been erected; but the inhabitants are scantily supplied with water, which the more opulent collect from rain, in cisterns attached to their houses, and the poorer bring from the river, or from pits in the neighbourhood. Frequent attempts to procure a better supply by boring have failed; and in February 1829, after expending £1800, the last undertaking was relinquished. There are two subscription libraries; a handsome suite of assembly-rooms, built by the corporation in 1820; a commodious theatre, erected in 1806; and a theatre of arts, exhibiting views of various cities, with appropriate moving figures, which is open every Wednesday evening: about half a mile from the town are Vauxhall Gardens, which, during the season, are brilliantly illuminated and very numerously attended.

Admiralty Seal.

The trade of the port, from an accumulation of silt in the river, which impeded its navigation, had begun to decline about the middle of the last century, but was revived by forming a canal, deepening the river, and enlarging the harbour. The exports consist chiefly of the agricultural produce of the county; the imports are timber, hemp, tar, and iron, from the Baltic. A considerable coasting trade is also carried on, which has rapidly increased of late years. Since the fens adjoining the town have been drained and cultivated, a tract of rich land, of nearly seventy thousand acres, has been thus obtained, which, besides producing grain, feeds a great number of sheep and oxen, remarkable for their size and fatness: oats in great quantity are shipped to various parts of the coast, and wool to the manufacturing districts in Yorkshire, whence coal and other articles are brought in return. The quay, which is conveniently adapted to the loading of vessels, is accessible to ships of one hundred tons' burden: the custom-house, a commodious building, was erected at the public expense, and the pilot-office was built in 1811; the establishment of the latter consists of a master, twelve pilots, and a few supernumeraries. The river Witham is navigable to Lincoln, from which place, by means of canals communicating with the Trent, there is an inland navigation to almost every part of the kingdom. The number of vessels belonging to the port, according to the return made in 1828, was one hundred and fifty, averaging fifty-four tons' burden. About forty boats are also employed in the fishery: shrimps of superior quality, soles, and herrings, are taken in profusion; and in 1772, the corporation erected a large fish market. The market is on Wednesday, and is abundantly supplied with poultry, a great quantity of which is sent to London every week. The fairs are on May 4th for sheep, and the day following for cattle; August 11th, which is called the Town fair; November 30th, and the three following days, for horses and horned cattle; and December 11th, for horned cattle only.

The government, according to a charter granted by Henry VIII., and enlarged by Elizabeth, who gave the corporation a court of admiralty, is vested in a mayor, recorder, deputy recorder, twelve aldermen, and eighteen common council-men, assisted by a town-clerk, judge advocate, and marshal of the admiralty court, two serjeants at mace, and other officers. The mayor is appointed from among the aldermen, who succeed to that office by rotation: the aldermen are chosen out of the common council-men, by a majority of their own body, and the common council-men are selected by the mayor and aldermen. The mayor is clerk of the market, and admiral of the port, in which latter capacity, conjointly with the common council, he holds a court of admiralty, the jurisdiction of which extends over the whole adjacent coast. The mayor, recorder, and four senior aldermen, are justices of the peace within the borough and parish. The freedom is acquired by birth, servitude, and purchase. The corporation hold a court of session quarterly for the borough, and a court of record for the recovery of debts to any amount, at which the mayor, recorder, and town-clerk preside. The petty sessions for the wapentake of Skirbeck and Kirton are held every Wednesday at the Cross chamber; and a court of requests for the recovery of debts under £5 is held once a fortnight, under an act obtained in the 47th of George III. The elective franchise was conferred in the reign of Edward VI., since which time the borough has returned two representatives to parliament: the right of election is vested in the members of the corporation, the sons of aldermen, and eldest sons of common council-men, residing as householders within the borough, and in the resident freemen generally, in number four hundred; the mayor is the returning officer. The guildhall is an ancient building, in the council-chamber of which is a fine portrait of Sir Joseph Bankes, presented by him when recorder of this borough: the borough gaol is a handsome building at the south end of the town, erected in 1811: the house of correction for the parts of Holland was built in 1809.

Corporate Seal.

The living is a vicarage, in the archdeaconry and diocese of Lincoln, rated in the king's books at £33. 6. 8., and in the patronage of the Mayor and Corporation. The church, dedicated to St. Botolph, is a spacious and magnificent structure in the decorated style of English architecture, with a lofty square tower surmounted by an octagonal lantern turret, in the later English style: it was erected in 1309, and is in an excellent state of repair: the tower, which is three hundred feet high, and was formerly illuminated during the night, forms a conspicuous land-mark for mariners traversing the North sea. Within the church, among other interesting monuments, are the effigies of Sir John Tilney and his lady, by whom the church is said to have been founded. A chapel has lately been erected by subscription. The living is a perpetual curacy, endowed with £100 per annum by the corporation, to whom the patronage, which is now vested in the subscribers, will revert after the expiration of fifteen years. There are places of worship for General and Particular Baptists, the Society of Friends, Independents, Methodists, Unitarians, and Roman Catholics; and a piece of ground has been taken, on which it is intended to build a synagogue. The free grammar school, founded and endowed in 1554, by Queen Mary, is under the control of the corporation, who appoint the master and usher, the former having a salary of £100, and the latter one of £60, per annum: the school-room was built in 1567, and a convenient house for the master in 1826. A school was founded, in 1707, by Mr. Laughton, who endowed it with lands in Skirbeck, producing about £50 per annum, which has since been augmented by other benefactors: there are at present twenty-five boys, each of whom, at the age of fourteen, is entitled to an apprentice fee of £15, provided he be put out to a free burgess. A Blue-coat school, founded in 1713, for clothing and instructing thirty-three boys and the same number of girls; and two National schools, established in 1815, in which five hundred children are instructed, are supported by subscription. A general dispensary was instituted in 1795. Of the numerous monastic establishments which formerly existed in this town and its vicinity, there remain only some slight vestiges of the Black, or Dominican friary, established in the year 1288. The ancient church of St. John, formerly the parish church, has been totally removed, but the cemetery is still used as a burying-ground. John Fox, the celebrated martyrologist, was a native of this town. Boston confers the title of viscount on the Irby family.

BOSTON, a joint township with Clifford, in the parish of Bramham, wapentake of Barkstone-Ash, West riding of the county of York, 4 miles (W.) from Tadcaster. The population is returned with Clifford. This village is of recent origin, the first house having been built in 1753. Owing to the discovery, in 1744, of a saline spring in the vicinity, it has now become a place of fashionable resort. A pump-room, with hot and cold baths, has been erected: the air is pure, and the situation being in a vale, on the southern side of the river Wharfe, is extremely picturesque. An episcopal chapel, built on land given by Mr. Samuel Tate, was consecrated in 1814. There is a place of worship for Wesleyan Methodists. A charity school was founded by Lady Elizabeth Hastings.

BOSWORTH (HUSBAND'S), a parish in the hundred of GARTREE, county of LEICESTER, 6 miles (W. S. W.) from Market-Harborough, containing 817 inhabitants. The living is a rectory, in the archdeaconry of Leicester, and diocese of Lincoln, rated in the king's books at £24. 15. 7½., and in the patronage of the Rev. J. T. Mayne. The church, dedicated to All Saints, had its spire greatly damaged during a storm of thunder and lightning, in July 1755. There are places of worship for Particular Baptists and Wesleyan Methodists. The river Welland bounds the parish on the south and south-east, and the Avon on the north-west; and the Grand Union canal crosses the western part of it, being here conducted through a tunnel, one thousand one hundred and seventy yards in length, to the northern side of the village.

BOSWORTH (MARKET), a parish in the hundred of SPARKENHOE, county of LEICESTER, comprising the town of Market-Bosworth, the chapelries of Barleston, Carlton, Shenton, and Sutton-Cheney, the township of Barton in the Beans, and part of the township of Osbaston, and containing 2677 inhabitants, of which number, 1117 are in the town of Market-Bosworth, 11½ miles (S.W.) from Leicester, and 107 (N.W.) from London. This place, in Domesday-book called *Bosworde*, takes the prefix to its name from a market granted to the inhabitants in the reign of Edward I. The neighbourhood is celebrated as the scene of a decisive battle which took place on the 22nd of August, 1485, between Richard III. and the Earl of Richmond, afterwards Henry VII.: this battle, the last of those sanguinary conflicts between the houses of York and Lancaster, which had for so many years disturbed the internal tranquillity of the kingdom, and deluged its plains with blood, was fought on a large moor, three miles from the town, formerly called Redmore, but since that event better known as Bosworth Field. It is at present enclosed, and the particular spot, called Richard's Well, is distinguished by a monument erected by subscription, through the exertions of the late Dr. Parr, who visited the site in 1813, and wrote an appropriate inscription for it in Latin: numerous swords, shields, spurs, and other military relics, have been dug up at different times in the neighbourhood. The town, which is pleasantly situated on an eminence, contains some respectable houses, and is well supplied with water. The manufacture of worsted stockings is carried on here, and in the adjacent villages, to a considerable extent; and greater facility has been given to trade by the Ashby canal, which, passing within a mile of the town, affords a medium for supplying it with coal and other articles of consumption. The market is on Wednesday: the fairs are on May 8th, for horses, horned cattle, and sheep, and July 10th, which is called the Cherry fair.

The living is a rectory, in the archdeaconry of Leicester, and diocese of Lincoln, rated in the king's books at £55. 18. 4., and in the patronage of the Dixie family. The church, dedicated to St. Peter, is a spacious ancient structure, with a beautiful spire; within are many interesting monuments, among the finest of which is one to certain members of the Dixie family. There are places of worship for Baptists and Independents. The free grammar school, open to all boys whose parents reside within the parish, was founded in 1593, and endowed with land, by Sir Wolstan Dixie, Knt., who also endowed two fellowships of £30, and four scholarships of £10, per annum each, in Emanuel College, Cambridge. In consequence of its affairs being in Chancery, the school has been discontinued for the last twenty-five years, during which period, its funds have accumulated to the amount of £15,000: of this sum it is in contemplation to appropriate a part to the foundation of additional scholarships. The premises, including commodious residences for the masters, have been handsomely rebuilt in the later style of English architecture, at an expense of £5000: the management is vested in ten governors, including the rector and churchwardens of the parish: the total income arising from the endowment is £700 per annum. The Rev. Anthony Blackwall, a distinguished critic and classical scholar, was master, and the celebrated Dr. Johnson, and Thomas Simpson, the eminent mathematician, were ushers, in this school; the latter, who was a native of the town, became Professor of Mathematics at Woolwich, and died here in 1761.

BOTCHESTON, a joint township with Newton, in the parish of RATBY, hundred of SPARKENHOE, county of LEICESTER, 6 miles (E. N. E.) from Market-Bosworth, containing, with Newton, 87 inhabitants.

BOTESDALE, a chapelry (formerly a market town) in the parish of REDGRAVE, hundred of HARTISMERE, county of SUFFOLK, 26 miles (N. N. W.) from Ipswich, and 86 (N. E. by N.) from London, on the road to Norwich, containing 584 inhabitants. The name, contracted from Botolph's Dale, is compounded of Botolph, the name of the tutelar saint of the chapel, and the dale in which the town is situated. The town consists principally of one long street, which extends into the parishes of Rickinghall Superior and Rickinghall Inferior: the houses are indifferently built, but the inhabitants are amply supplied with water. The market, formerly on Thursday, has been discontinued: a small fair for cattle and pedlary is held on Holy Thursday. Courts leet and baron are held at Whitsuntide, at the former of which constables and other officers are appointed. The chapel, which has been substantially repaired, is a neat edifice, in the later style of English architecture, of which it exhibits good specimens: within are some interesting monuments, among which may be noticed those to Sir Nicholas Bacon, and that celebrated lawyer and patriot, Lord Chief Justice Holt, whose remains are deposited here. The free grammar school was founded and endowed, in 1576, by Sir Nicholas Bacon, for a master and an usher, who are appointed by the Master and Fellows of Corpus Christi College, Cambridge, in which there are six exhibitions belonging to this school: the income is £30 per annum, of which sum, the master receives £20, and the usher £8, the remainder being expended in repairs. The school-house, which stands to the west of the chapel, was erected at the expense of Edward Britiffe, Esq.

BOTHALL, a parish in the eastern division of Morpeth ward, county of Northumberland, 3 miles (E.) from Morpeth, comprising the townships of Ashington with Sheepwash, Bothall - Deme ne, Longhurst, Old Moor, and Pegsworth, and containing 658 inhabitants. The living is a rectory, with that of Sheepwash and the perpetual curacy of Hebburn annexed, in the archdeaconry of Northumberland, and diocese of Durham, rated in the king's books at £25, and in the patronage of the Duke of Portland. The church, dedicated to St. Andrew, contains a fine alabaster tomb, representing some member of the family of Ogle, and his lady, in a recumbent position, and at the head four ecclesiastics in niches decorated with tabernacle work. The ancient parochial church stood at Sheepwash, where the parsonage-house now is. Between the village and the river Wansbeck, which bounds the parish on the south, are the ruins of an oratory, dedicated to the Virgin Mary. A school-room, with a house for the master, was built in 1817, by the Duke of Portland, who allows the master £10 per annum, in addition to the interest of £80 left by the Rev. Mr. Stafford, in 1716. There is also a school at Causey Park, built and endowed with £15 a year, by one of the Ogle family, in 1740. Coal abounds within the parish. Bothall was made a barony by Richard I., and was some time in the possession of the family of Bertram, but passed by marriage to Sir Robert Ogle, who bequeathed his paternal estate to his son Robert, and the barony of Bothall to his youngest son John; but the former, with a force of two hundred men, obtained possession of Bothall, from which, however, he was ejected by the parliament: having subsequently distinguished himself in the cause of the house of York, he was created baron of Bothall, and first Lord Ogle, of Ogle. The barony is now the property of the Duke of Portland, who holds a court leet and baron for it. The castle, which was situated near the precipice of a rock, at the foot of which flows the river Wansbeck, is in ruins, a large tower gateway, and fragments of the outer walls, being the only parts that remain.

BOTHAMSALL, a parish in the Hatfield division of the wapentake of Bassetlaw, county of Nottingham, 4½ miles (W. N. W.) from Tuxford, containing 310 inhabitants. The living is a perpetual curacy, in the archdeaconry of Nottingham, and diocese of York, and in the patronage of the Duke of Newcastle. The church is dedicated to St. Mary. The parish is bounded on the north by the river Poulter, and intersected by the Meden, which two rivers, uniting with the Maun, form the river Idle, about two miles north of the parish. Henry Walters, in 1692, founded a free school at Houghton, in this parish, which is endowed with £25 per annum. The inhabitants are entitled to the privilege of sending a certain number of children to the school at West Drayton. There is a tumulus, called Castle Hill, a little westward from the village.

BOTHEL, a township in the parish of Torpenhow, Allerdale ward below Darwent, county of Cumberland, 4 miles (W.) from Ireby, containing, with the township of Threapland, 384 inhabitants. This is a long straggling village: the vicinity abounds with limestone, and there are kilns for burning it.

BOTHENHAMPTON, a parish in the liberty of Lothers and Bothenhampton, Bridport division of the county of Dorset, 1½ mile (S. E. by S.) from Bridport, containing 385 inhabitants. The living is a perpetual curacy, in the archdeaconry of Dorset, and diocese of Bristol, and in the patronage of the Countess of Abingdon. The church is dedicated to the Holy Trinity. This parish is bounded on the west by an æstuary called Bridport harbour.

BOTH-HERGESTS, a township in the parish of Kington, hundred of Huntington, county of Hereford, containing 145 inhabitants.

BOTLEY, a tything in the parish of Cumner, hundred of Hormer, county of Berks, 1½ mile (W.) from Oxford, containing 118 inhabitants.

BOTLEY, a parish in the hundred of Mansbridge, Fawley division of the county of Southampton, 3¾ miles (S. W.) from Bishop's Waltham, containing 690 inhabitants. The living is a rectory, in the archdeaconry and diocese of Winchester, rated in the king's books at £5. 10. 2½., and in the patronage of the Duke of Rutland. The church, dedicated to All Saints, and consisting only of a nave and a chancel, stands nearly a mile to the south of the village, and contains an ancient and curious font. Considerable trade in flour is carried on: the mills are worked by the river Hamble, which is navigable up to this place for boats. Fairs, chiefly for toys and pedlary, are held on Shrove-Tuesday, Whit-Tuesday, and the Tuesday before St. Bartholomew's day; for cheese, on February 20th and May 28th; and for cattle, on July 23rd, August 20th, and November 13th. A strong chalybeate spring near the church was formerly in great repute, but is now disused.

BOTOLPH-BRIDGE, a parish in the hundred of Norman-Cross, county of Huntingdon, 2 miles (S. W. by W.) from Peterborough. The population is returned with Orton-Longville. The living is a rectory, united in 1721 to that of Orton-Longville, in the archdeaconry of Huntingdon, and diocese of Lincoln, rated in the king's books at £8. 6. 10½. The church, now desecrated, was dedicated to All Saints.

BOTTESFORD, a parish in the hundred of Framland, county of Leicester, 7 miles (W. N. W.) from Grantham, containing, with Normanton, 1070 inhabitants. The living is a rectory, in the archdeaconry of Leicester, and diocese of Lincoln, rated in the king's books at £51. 5., and in the patronage of the Duke of Rutland. The church, dedicated to St. Mary, is a spacious cruciform structure, with a tower supporting a spire at the western end: it has been the burial-place of the noble family of Manners since the dissolution of monasteries, at which period several monuments to the memory of deceased members of that family were removed hither from the conventual church at Belvoir. There is a place of worship for Particular Baptists. The Grantham canal crosses the parish. From the discovery of various relics of antiquity, this place is supposed to have been occupied by the Romans. In 1711, the Rev. Abel Ligonier and Anthony Ravell bequeathed land for the instruction of twenty-eight children.

BOTTESFORD, a parish comprising the townships of Ashby and Burringham, and the hamlets of Holm and Yaddlethorpe, in the eastern division, and the township of Crosby, in the western division, of the wapentake of Manley, parts of Lindsey, county of Lincoln, 8 miles (W.) from Glandford-Bridge, and containing 999 inhabitants. The living is a discharged vicarage, united in 1727 to the vicarage of Messingham, in the archdeaconry of Stow, and diocese of Lincoln, rated in the king's books at £10. The church is dedicated to St. Peter.

BOTTESLAW, a township in the parish of STOKE upon TRENT, northern division of the hundred of PIREHILL, county of STAFFORD. The population is returned with the parish.

BOTTISHAM, a parish in the hundred of STAINE, county of CAMBRIDGE, 6½ miles (W. S. W.) from Newmarket, containing 1123 inhabitants. The living is a discharged vicarage, in the archdeaconry and diocese of Ely, rated in the king's books at £16, and in the patronage of the Master and Fellows of Trinity College, Cambridge. The church, dedicated to the Holy Trinity, contains the tomb of Elias de Beckingham, justiciary of England in the reign of Edward I. A considerable part of the village was destroyed by fire, in 1712. Sir Roger Jenyns, Knt. founded a school in 1730, and endowed it with £20 per annum, for the gratuitous instruction and clothing of sixteen boys and four girls: the master and scholars are appointed by the proprietor of Bottisham Hall. A moiety of the income of an endowed almshouse at Eastham, founded by Giles Breame, Esq., in 1621, is paid to the poor of this place. Henry I. founded a small priory of Augustine canons at Anglesey, in this parish, and dedicated it to the Blessed Virgin and St. Nicholas, the revenue of which, in the 26th of Henry VIII., was £149. 18. 6.: the site is now occupied by a farm-house, in the walls of which a portion of the conventual buildings is visible. The petty sessions are held here. At Bottisham Lode there is a place of worship for Particular Baptists.

BOTUSFLEMING, a parish in the southern division of the hundred of EAST, county of CORNWALL, 3 miles (N. W.) from Saltash, containing 297 inhabitants. The living is a rectory, in the archdeaconry of Cornwall, and diocese of Exeter, rated in the king's books at £16. 15. 7½., and in the patronage of the Rev. William Spry. In the centre of a field, on the northern side of the village, stands a pyramidal monument, erected to the memory of Dr. William Martin of Plymouth, who died in 1762.

BOUGHTON, a parish in the hundred of CLACKCLOSE, county of NORFOLK, 1½ mile (N.) from Stoke-Ferry, containing 185 inhabitants. The living is a discharged rectory, in the archdeaconry of Norfolk, and diocese of Norwich, rated in the king's books at £10, and in the patronage of the Rev. G. Hunt. The church is dedicated to All Saints.

BOUGHTON, a hamlet in the parish of WEEKLEY, hundred of CORBY, county of NORTHAMPTON, 2½ miles (N. E. by N.) from Kettering. The population is returned with the parish. Here was formerly a chapel, but it has been demolished.

BOUGHTON, a parish in the hundred of SPELHOE, county of NORTHAMPTON, 3¾ miles (N.) from Northampton, containing 351 inhabitants. The living is a rectory, in the archdeaconry of Northampton, and diocese of Peterborough, rated in the king's books at £20. 9. 7., and in the patronage of R. W. H. H. Vyse, Esq. The church, dedicated to St. John the Baptist, is desecrated; but here is a chapel in which divine service is performed. There is a place of worship for Wesleyan Methodists. A fair, which continues for three days, is held annually on a piece of waste ground half a mile to the south of the village.

BOUGHTON, a parish in the Hatfield division of the wapentake of BASSETLAW, county of NOTTINGHAM, 1¾ mile (N. E. by E.) from Ollerton, containing 289 inhabitants. The living is a perpetual curacy, with the vicarage of Kneesall, in the archdeaconry of Nottingham, and diocese of York.

BOUGHTON under BLEAN, a parish in the hundred of BOUGHTON under BLEAN, lathe of SCRAY, county of KENT, 3 miles (S. E. by E.) from Faversham, containing 1237 inhabitants. The living is a vicarage, in the peculiar jurisdiction and patronage of the Archbishop of Canterbury, rated in the king's books at £9. 4. 9½. The church, dedicated to St. Peter and St. Paul, contains several ancient monuments: the tower formerly supported a spire, which fell down about the close of the sixteenth century. There is a place of worship for Wesleyan Methodists. Here are two charity schools for boys and girls, and an almshouse comprising two tenements. In 1716, a human skeleton, by the side of which lay a sword, and a brass coin struck in the reign of Antoninus Pius, was dug up in the vicinity. Blean Forest, from which Boughton has obtained its adjunct, was anciently the haunt of wild boars, wolves, and other beasts of chace. Boughton hill, about three quarters of a mile distant, is stated to command a more extensive prospect than any other hill in the kingdom.

BOUGHTON (GREAT), a township in that part of the parish of ALDFORD which is in the lower division of the hundred of BROXTON, county palatine of CHESTER, 1¼ mile (E.) from Chester, containing 911 inhabitants.

BOUGHTON (SPITTLE), an extra-parochial liberty, within the county of the city of CHESTER, containing 150 inhabitants.

BOUGHTON-ALUPH, a parish in the hundred of WYE, lathe of SCRAY, county of KENT, 4 miles (N.N.E.) from Ashford, containing 453 inhabitants. The living is a vicarage, in the archdeaconry and diocese of Canterbury, rated in the king's books at £6. 5., and in the patronage of Whitfield Breton, Esq. The church, dedicated to All Saints, is a spacious cruciform structure, built of flint and ashlar-stone, with a low central tower. The river Stour flows on the eastern side of this parish. A fair for toys and pedlary is held at Lees, on Midsummer-day, at which place there is an almshouse for six poor persons.

BOUGHTON-MALHERB, a parish in the hundred of EYHORNE, lathe of AYLESFORD, county of KENT, 1½ mile (S. W. by S.) from Lenham, containing 475 inhabitants. The living is a rectory, in the archdeaconry and diocese of Canterbury, rated in the king's books at £13. 15., and in the patronage of Earl Cornwallis. The church, dedicated to St. Nicholas, is a handsome edifice, with a square western tower: it stands on the summit of a ridge of hills, which divides the parish into two districts, Boughton Upland and Boughton Weald (the latter being so called from its situation within the Weald of Kent), and contains several interesting monuments to the memory of deceased members of the family of Wotton, among which is a splendid marble monument to that of Sir Thomas, and a costly one to that of Sir Edward Wotton. This family resided here for a considerable period, and this was the birthplace of its most accomplished member, Sir Henry Wotton, who was employed by James I. in several foreign embassies, and whose biography is written, in his peculiar quaintness of style, by Izaak Walton. The remains of the mansion, on a sunken pannel in which is inscribed the date 1579, have been converted into a barn.

BOUGHTON - MONCHELSEA, a parish in the hundred of EYHORNE, and extending into the hundred of Maidstone, lathe of AYLESFORD, county of KENT, 4 miles (S. by E.) from Maidstone, containing 828 inhabitants. The living is a vicarage, in the archdeaconry and diocese of Canterbury, rated in the king's books at £7. 13. 4., and in the patronage of the Dean and Chapter of Rochester. The church is dedicated to St. Peter. The parish is intersected by a ridge of hills, the summit of which forms the northern boundary of the Weald of Kent, and on the southern declivity of which there are quarries of rag-stone.

BOULBY, a hamlet in the parish of EASINGTON, eastern division of the liberty of LANGBAURGH, North riding of the county of YORK, 11 miles (N. W. by W.) from Whitby. The population is returned with the parish. This place is noted for its extensive alum-works, which were begun in 1615; they contain various petrifactions of *ammonitæ*, or snake stones, *trochitæ*, and shells of the bivalve kind.

BOULDON, a township in the parish of HOLDGATE, hundred of MUNSLOW, county of SALOP, containing 60 inhabitants.

BOULGE, a parish in the hundred of WILFORD, county of SUFFOLK, 3 miles (N. N. W.) from Woodbridge, containing 44 inhabitants. The living is a discharged rectory, with that of Debach annexed, in the archdeaconry of Suffolk, and diocese of Norwich, rated in the king's books at £3. 12. 1., endowed with £200 private benefaction, and £600 royal bounty, and in the patronage of Mrs. Reynolds. The church is dedicated to St. Michael.

BOULMER, a joint township with Seaton-House, in the parish of LONG HOUGHTON, southern division of BAMBROUGH ward, county of NORTHUMBERLAND, 6¼ miles (E. by N.) from Alnwick, containing, with Seaton-House, 104 inhabitants. This village lies on the sea-shore, and is chiefly inhabited by fishermen, whose boats are moored in Boulmer bay, a natural basin environed by rocks, eight hundred yards long, and four hundred broad, the entrance to which is twelve feet deep at low water.

BOULSTONE, a parish in the upper division of the hundred of WORMELOW, county of HEREFORD, 6 miles (S. S. E.) from Hereford, containing 75 inhabitants. The living is a perpetual curacy, annexed to the vicarage of Hom-Lacy, in the archdeaconry and diocese of Hereford.

BOULTHAM, a parish in the lower division of the wapentake of BOOTHBY-GRAFFO, parts of KESTEVEN, county of LINCOLN, 3 miles (S.W. by S.) from Lincoln, containing 74 inhabitants. The living is a discharged rectory, in the archdeaconry and diocese of Lincoln, rated in the king's books at £7. 15. 2., endowed with £400 royal bounty, and in the patronage of R. Ellison, Esq. The church is dedicated to St. Helen.

BOULTON, a chapelry in that part of the parish of ST. PETER, DERBY, which is in the hundred of MORLESTON and LITCHURCH, county of DERBY, 3½ miles (S. E. by E.) from Derby, containing 168 inhabitants. The living is a perpetual curacy, with that of Alvaston annexed, in the archdeaconry of Derby, and diocese of Lichfield and Coventry, endowed with £200 private benefaction, and £600 royal bounty, and in the patronage of the proprietors of land in the chapelry.

BOURN, a parish in the hundred of LONGSTOW, county of CAMBRIDGE, 1¾ mile (S. E. by E.) from Caxton, containing 752 inhabitants. The living is a discharged vicarage, in the archdeaconry and diocese of Ely, rated in the king's books at £9. 15. 10., endowed with £200 private benefaction, and £200 royal bounty, and in the patronage of the Master and Fellows of Christ's College, Cambridge. The church is dedicated to St. Mary. Bourn castle was destroyed in the reign of Henry III., during the war with the barons. A mineral spring here was formerly in high repute, but it is now neglected.

BOURN, a joint tything with Wrecklesham, in the parish and hundred of FARNHAM, county of SURREY. The population is returned with Wrecklesham.

BOURN - MOOR, a township in the parish of HOUGHTON le SPRING, northern division of EASINGTON ward, county palatine of DURHAM, containing 1139 inhabitants. At New Lambton, in this township, is a brine well ninety-seven fathoms deep, where salt-works were established in 1815. There is also a place of worship for Wesleyan Methodists, with a Sunday school attached, in which about one hundred and sixty children are instructed.

BOURNE, a parish in the wapentake of AVELAND, parts of KESTEVEN, county of LINCOLN, comprising the market town of Bourne, and the hamlets of Cawthorpe and Dyke, and containing 2242 inhabitants, of which number, 2029 are in the town of Bourne, 36 miles (S.) from Lincoln, and 97 (N.) from London. This place takes its name from a stream of remarkably pure water, issuing from a copious spring a short distance to the south of the town, which is so powerful as to turn a corn-mill within three hundred yards of its source, about half a mile from which it becomes navigable, and is called the Bourn Eau; it joins the river Glen, which runs on the eastern border of the parish, at a place called Tongue End, and thence the Glen shortly joins the Welland at Pinchbeck. Though little of its early history is known, it is supposed, from the discovery of Roman coins and tesselated pavements, to have been anciently a place of some importance. When the Danes invaded England in the ninth century, Marcot, the Saxon lord of Bourne, with a few of his own vassals and a detachment from Croyland abbey, after an obstinate engagement, defeated a party of them, who had made an inroad into this part of Lincolnshire. Prior to the time of Edward the Confessor, a castle was erected here, of which only the trenches and mounds are discernible, appearing to have included an area of more than eight acres. In 1138, Baldwin, a descendant of Walter Fitz-Gilbert, to whom the town was given by William Rufus, founded a priory for canons of the order of St. Augustine, the site alone of which, now called the Trenches, is visible: the revenue, at the dissolution, was £197. 17. 5. In the seventeenth century, Bourne was twice nearly destroyed by fire. The town, consisting principally of one very long street, the houses in which are in general modern and well built, is pleasantly situated, and plentifully supplied with excellent water. The trade is chiefly in leather and wool; for the former there are several extensive tan-yards. A navigable canal has been constructed from this town to Spalding and Boston, by which means it is supplied with coal, timber, and other commodities. The market is on Saturday: the fairs are on April 7th, May 7th, and October 29th. The county magistrates hold a meeting every Saturday: courts of session for the parts of Kesteven are held quarterly. The town-hall, recently erected at an expense of £2500, on the site of a former one, built by William Cecil, Lord Treasurer in the reign of Elizabeth, is a spacious handsome edifice, under which is the market-place.

The living is a discharged vicarage, under sequestration, in the archdeaconry and diocese of Lincoln, rated in the king's books at £8, and in the patronage of the Earl of Pomfret. The church, dedicated to St. Peter and St. Paul, though spacious, appears to be only part of a larger structure: it is principally in the Norman style, but contains several portions in the early and later styles of English architecture, and has two towers of mixed character, of which the southern is considerably higher than the other, and is crowned with pinnacles. Within are some interesting monuments, a finely enriched font of the later style, and a stoup under a crocketed canopy: the western entrance is a fine specimen of the later style, and over it is a large window of good composition. There are places of worship for Baptists and Wesleyan Methodists. A school for thirty children was founded in 1653, and endowed by Thomas Trollope, Esq., who also endowed an hospital for six aged men, and an almshouse for the same number of women. There is a mineral spring in the town, which was formerly in great repute. William Cecil, created Baron Burleigh by Queen Elizabeth, was born here, in 1521.

BOURNE (EAST), a parish (formerly a market town) in the hundred of Eastbourne, rape of Pevensey, county of Sussex, 7 miles (S.) from Hailsham, containing 2607 inhabitants. The living is a vicarage, in the archdeaconry of Lewes, and diocese of Chichester, rated in the king's books at £26. 1. 8., and in the patronage of the Treasurer in the Cathedral Church of Chichester. The church is dedicated to St. Mary. The town, which consists of three detached portions, is pleasantly situated beneath the brow of a lofty hill, within a short distance of the sea, and has recently been resorted to for bathing, that part called Sea Houses being chiefly appropriated to the reception of visitors, for whose recreation a library and reading-rooms, and a small theatre, have been established, and there are assembly-rooms at the Lamb Inn. The bold headland, or promontory, of Beachy head, formerly remarkable for the loss of vessels occasioned by the beating of the sea against it, the effects of which are visible in its numerous hollows and caverns, forms the south-west boundary of the parish. There are places of worship for Baptists, Independents, and Wesleyan Methodists. A strong circular fortification, called the depôt, comprising barracks, storehouses, a magazine, &c., and surrounded by a deep intrenchment, has been erected on the beach, in connexion with a line of Martello towers on the coast. The market was on Saturday, but has been discontinued: fairs are held on March 12th for pedlary, and October 11th for sheep, &c. Coins and other relics of the Romans have been discovered at various times, particularly in 1717, when a chequered pavement and a bath were exposed to the view. At Holywell, a mile west of the town, is a chalybeate spring, the water of which has properties similar to the Clifton Wells.

BOURNE (ST. MARY), a parish in the hundred of Evingar, Kingsclere division of the county of Southampton, 3 miles (N. W. by W.) from Whitchurch, containing 1053 inhabitants. The living is a perpetual curacy, annexed to the vicarage of Hurstbourne-Priors, in the archdeaconry and diocese of Winchester.

BOURNE (WEST), a parish in the hundred of Westbourne and Singleton, rape of Chichester, county of Sussex, 7¾ miles (W. N. W.) from Chichester, containing 1852 inhabitants. The living is a discharged vicarage, in the archdeaconry and diocese of Chichester, rated in the king's books at £10. 10. 5., and in the patronage of the Rector: the living is a sinecure, rated at £24. 13. 4., and in the patronage of the Rev. Lewis Way. The church, dedicated to St. John the Baptist, is a neat commodious structure, in the later style of English architecture, with a well-proportioned spire of British oak, erected by the Earl of Halifax, formerly the munificent proprietor of Stansted Park, in the adjoining parish. The parish is situated on the sea-shore, and contains several hamlets; it abounds with pleasing scenery, studded with an unusual number of genteel residences, particularly in the hamlet of Prinsted, the houses in which, each situated within a small shrubbery, or flower garden, are in the form of a crescent. On its western side is a small æstuary, which is crossed by a bridge, uniting the hamlet of Hermitage with the small brisk sea-port of Emsworth, in the county of Southampton. On the south is Thorney channel, which at low water is passable for carriages to and from Thorney island.

BOURTON, a tything in the parish and hundred of Shrivenham, county of Berks, 7 miles (S. W. by S.) from Great Farringdon, containing 275 inhabitants.

BOURTON, a hamlet in the parish, hundred, and county of Buckingham, 1½ mile (E.) from Buckingham, containing 50 inhabitants.

BOURTON, a chapelry in the parish and liberty of Gillingham, Shaston (West) division of the county of Dorset, 2½ miles (S. W. by W.) from Mere, containing 813 inhabitants. There is a place of worship for Wesleyan Methodists.

BOURTON (BLACK), a parish in the hundred of Bampton, county of Oxford, 5½ miles (S. S. E.) from Burford, containing 336 inhabitants. The living is a discharged vicarage, in the archdeaconry and diocese of Oxford, and in the patronage of the Dean and Canons of Christ Church, Oxford. The church is dedicated to St. Mary.

BOURTON upon DUNSMOOR, a parish in the Rugby division of the hundred of Knightlow, county of Warwick, 4 miles (W. by S.) from Dunchurch, containing, with the tything of Draycot, 322 inhabitants. The living is a rectory, in the archdeaconry of Coventry, and diocese of Lichfield and Coventry, rated in the king's books at £19. 17. 3½., and in the patronage of J. Shuckburgh, Esq.

BOURTON (FLAX), county of Somerset.—See FLAX-BOURTON.

BOURTON (GREAT and LITTLE), a chapelry in that part of the parish of Cropredy which is in the hundred of Banbury, county of Oxford, 3 miles (N.) from Banbury, containing 441 inhabitants. The chapel is dedicated to St. Michael. A free school, in which upwards of thirty children are instructed, is endowed with land devised by Mr. Thomas Gill, in 1666, producing a net income of £23 per annum.

BOURTON on the HILL, a parish partly in the upper division of the hundred of Tewkesbury, and partly in the upper division of the hundred of Westminster, county of Gloucester, 2 miles (W. by N.) from Moreton in the Marsh, containing 354 inhabitants. The living is a rectory, with the perpetual curacy of Moreton in the Marsh annexed, in the archdeaconry and diocese of Gloucester, rated in the king's books at £14. The Rev. Dr. Warneford was patron in 1810. The church is dedicated to St. Lawrence. Sir Thomas Overbury, an ingenious writer in the reign of James I., who was poisoned whilst a prisoner in the Tower, was born here, in 1581.

BOURTON on the WATER, a parish in the lower division of the hundred of Slaughter, county of Gloucester, 4 miles (S. S. W.) from Stow on the Wold, containing, with the chapelry of Clapton, 876 inhabitants. The living is a rectory, with the perpetual curacy of Lower Slaughter annexed, in the archdeaconry and diocese of Gloucester, rated in the king's books at £27. 2. 8½., and in the patronage of Robert Croome, Esq. The church, dedicated to St. Lawrence, is a modern edifice, having a tower at the western end, rising from a rustic basement, with Ionic pilasters at the angles, and surmounted by a balustrade, urns, and cupola; within the church is a colonnade of the Ionic order. There is a place of worship for Particular Baptists. The Roman Fosse-way passes through the parish; and about a quarter of a mile from the village there is a square intrenchment, where coins, and other relics of the Romans, have been discovered: a paved aqueduct was formerly visible on one side of it.

BOURTONHOLD, a hamlet in the parish, hundred, and county of Buckingham, containing 553 inhabitants.

BOUSTEAD-HILL, a township in the parish of Burgh upon the Sands, ward and county of Cumberland, 7½ miles (W. N. W.) from Carlisle, containing 80 inhabitants.

BOVENY (LOWER), a chapelry in the parish and hundred of Burnham, county of Buckingham, 2 miles (W.) from Eton, containing, with Upper Boveny, 202 inhabitants. The chapel is dedicated to St. Mary Magdalene.

BOVERIDGE, or BEVERIDGE, a tything in the parish of Cranborne, in that part of the hundred of Cranborne which is in the Shaston (East) division of the county of Dorset, 1¾ mile (N. N. E.) from Cranborne, with which the population is returned. An almshouse for three persons has been founded and endowed here by some member of the family of Hooper, whose descendants retain the right of appointing the inmates; there is also a small stipend for a chaplain.

BOVEY (NORTH), a parish in the hundred of Teingbridge, county of Devon, 1¾ mile (S. W. by S.) from Moreton-Hampstead, containing 603 inhabitants. The living is a rectory, in the archdeaconry of Totness, and diocese of Exeter, rated in the king's books at £22. 10. 5., and in the patronage of T. Smith and J. Pidsley, Esqrs., surviving trustees of Viscount Courtenay. The church is dedicated to St. John. This place was formerly of greater importance; its lords exercised the power of inflicting punishment for capital crimes. The vicinity is noted for mines of tin, which are worked to a considerable extent. A fair for cattle is held on the Monday next after Midsummer-day. Ten children are instructed for £11 per annum, the produce of sundry bequests for that purpose.

BOVEY-TRACEY, a parish in the hundred of Teingbridge, county of Devon, 4 miles (W. by S.) from Chudleigh, containing 1685 inhabitants. The living is a vicarage, in the archdeaconry of Totness, and diocese of Exeter, rated in the king's books at £26. 2. 1., and in the patronage of the Crown. The church, dedicated to St. Thomas à Becket, contains some interesting monuments. There are places of worship for Baptists and Wesleyan Methodists. A charity school, in which twenty-four children are instructed, is endowed with about £40 per annum, arising from land purchased with the aggregate amount of various benefactions. Bovey Tracey is under the superintendence of a portreeve and a bailiff, the latter of whom is chosen at the court leet of the lord of the manor, and, having filled the office of bailiff, is appointed, at the expiration of the period, to that of portreeve. Here are manufactories for earthenware on an extensive scale: Indiho, once a priory, and subsequently a private mansion, was, in 1772, enlarged and converted into a manufactory. Coal is obtained in this district, but it is of an inferior quality, and is divided into two species, distinguished as stone coal and wood coal, the latter, thought to be composed of a fibrous vegetable substance, presenting the appearance of charred wood. Antimony is also found to an inconsiderable extent. Bovey-Heathfield is an extensive tract lying below the level of the sea, by which it is supposed to have been formerly covered. A canal extends hence to the river Teign, at Newton-Abbots, a distance of five miles and a half, by means of which coal, sea-sand, and lime, are brought hither, and Bovey coal and pipe and potters' clay are conveyed away. The Stover railway also passes in the vicinity. A market and a fair were granted to the lord of the manor, in 1259; and fairs for cattle are still held on Easter-Monday, Holy Thursday, and the first Thursdays in July and November.

BOVINGDON, a chapelry in the parish of Hemel-Hempstead, hundred of Dacorum, county of Hertford, 4½ miles (W. by N.) from King's Langley, containing 954 inhabitants. The chapel is dedicated to St. Lawrence.

BOW, or NYMETT-TRACEY, a parish (formerly a market town) in the hundred of North Tawton with Winkley, county of Devon, 7¼ miles (W. by N.) from Crediton, containing 872 inhabitants. The living is a rectory, in the archdeaconry of Barnstaple, and diocese of Exeter, rated in the king's books at £19. 8. 9., and in the patronage of J. Marshall, Esq. The church is dedicated to St. Bartholomew. A market and a fair were granted to Henry Tracey, lord of the manor, in 1258; the former has been discontinued, but fairs for cattle are held on the third Thursday in March, Ascension-day, and November 22nd. John Gould, in 1682, endowed a school with £8. 10. per annum, and a house for the use of the master, who instructs ten children gratuitously.

BOW, or STRATFORD le BOW, a parish in the Tower division of the hundred of OSSULSTONE, county of MIDDLESEX, 4½ miles (E. N. E.) from London, containing 2349 inhabitants. This place derives its name "Stratford" from an ancient ford over the river Lea, on the line of the Roman *stratum*, or road from London to *Durolitum* (Layton in Essex). It is said that Matilda, queen of Henry I., passing this dangerous ford, narrowly escaped being drowned, and consequently ordered a bridge to be erected, from the arched form of which the village received the adjunct to its name. This bridge, which is supposed to have been the first of its kind erected in the kingdom, is by some referred to the time of Alfred the Great, whose arms are carved on the central stone: it consists of three groined arches, of which the central arch is considerably larger than the rest, and, from its inconvenient narrowness, a wooden platform has been constructed on the outside of one of the parapets, for the accommodation of foot passengers. The village is pleasantly situated: the streets are paved, and lighted with gas, and the inhabitants are supplied with water by the East London Company's works. The manufacture of porcelain, formerly carried on to a considerable extent, has been discontinued; and the fair annually held at Whitsuntide has, within the last few years, been entirely suppressed. Bow is within the jurisdiction of the court of requests held in Whitechapel, for the recovery of debts under 40*s.*: three headboroughs and a constable are annually appointed at the court leet of the lord of the manor. By an act of parliament passed in 1730, it was made a separate parish, having been severed from that of Stepney, to which it was previously a chapelry. The living is a rectory, in the archdeaconry of Middlesex, and diocese of London, and in the patronage of the Principal and Fellows of Brasenose College, Oxford, by whom an addition has recently been made to the stipend of the rector. The church, dedicated to St. Mary, was founded in the reign of Henry II.; it is an ancient structure, partly in the Norman, and partly in the early English, style of architecture, with a low square tower, having a small turret at one of the angles: the east window is ornamented with the figures of Moses and Aaron, and of the twelve Apostles, in stained glass. The churchyard being too small, a new burying-ground is nearly completed, under an act obtained in the 6th of George IV. There are places of worship for Baptists and Wesleyan Methodists; the latter, though belonging to the congregation in this place, is situated within the parish of Bromley St. Leonard. The free school was founded in 1613, by Sir John Jolles, who endowed it for thirty-four boys of this parish and that of Bromley St. Leonard: it is under the superintendence of the Drapers' Company: the school-house, which is situated in the churchyard, has been lately rebuilt. Another school for fifty boys was founded, in 1701, by Mrs. Prisca Coburne, who endowed it with houses and lands at that time producing £40 per annum; but, from the increased value of the property, the income, on the expiration of the present leases, will amount to £500 per annum: a school-room has been built for one hundred children of each sex, the school being under the inspection of the rectors of St. Mary, Stratford le Bow, and four adjoining parishes. A National school is supported by subscription. Sir John Jolles also founded and endowed almshouses for eight poor people; and there are other charitable bequests for the relief of the poor.

BOWDEN (GREAT), a parish in the hundred of GARTREE, county of LEICESTER, 1½ mile (N. E.) from Market-Harborough, containing, with the town of Market-Harborough, 2834 inhabitants. The living is a perpetual curacy, in the archdeaconry of Leicester, and diocese of Lincoln, endowed with £200 private benefaction, £200 royal bounty, and £600 parliamentary grant, and in the patronage of the Dean and Canons of Christ Church, Oxford. The church is dedicated to St. Peter. The river Welland bounds the parish on the south, and a branch of the Union Canal passes near the village. There are two trifling endowments for the instruction of poor children, one given by John Durrad, in 1723, and the other by the Rev. Robert Atkins.

BOWDEN (LITTLE), a parish in the hundred of ROTHWELL, county of NORTHAMPTON, ¾ of a mile (E.S.E.) from Market-Harborough, containing, with the hamlet of Little Oxenden, 314 inhabitants. The living is a rectory, in the archdeaconry of Northampton, and diocese of Peterborough, rated in the king's books at £15. 4. 2., and in the patronage of the Rev. John Barlow. The parochial school has a small endowment.

BOWDEN'S-EDGE, a township in the parish of CHAPEL en le FRITH, hundred of HIGH PEAK, county of DERBY, 1½ mile (N. E.) from Chapel en le Frith, containing 1093 inhabitants. This township is in the honour of Tutbury, duchy of Lancaster, and within the jurisdiction of a court of pleas held at Tutbury every third Tuesday, for the recovery of debts under 40*s.*

BOWDON, a parish in the hundred of BUCKLOW, county palatine of CHESTER, comprising the market-town of Altrincham, the chapelry of Carrington, and the townships of Agden, Ashley, Baguley, Bollington, Bowdon, Dunham-Massey, Hale, Partington, and Timperley, and containing 7442 inhabitants, of which number, 433 are in the township of Bowdon, 1 mile (S.W. by S.) from Altrincham. The living is a vicarage, in the archdeaconry and diocese of Chester, rated in the king's books at £24, and in the patronage of the Bishop of Chester. The church, dedicated to St. Nicholas, is an ancient structure on an elevated site, the churchyard commanding an extensive and pleasing panoramic view of the surrounding country; it was annexed to the See of Chester, by Henry VIII., on the dissolution of Birkenhead priory, to which it had been given by Hamon de Massey, the fifth of that name: the rectorial tithes are leased by the bishop to the Earl of Stamford and Warrington, who, as lord of the ancient barony of Dunham-Massey, appoints four churchwardens for the parish. Mr. Edward Vawdrey, about the year 1600, gave £4 per annum toward the endowment of a grammar school: the school-room was rebuilt at the expense of the parishioners, about 1670, and again in 1806, with a convenient house for the master. A charity school has also been built, and is supported by subscription. The Earl of Warrington, in 1754, gave £168. 6. for educating and apprenticing children, and for the relief of the poor. There is also a school for boys at Scamons Moss, and another for boys and girls at Littleheath, founded and endowed by the late Mr. Thomas Walton. A Roman road passed through the parish.

BOWER-CHALK, a parish in the hundred of CHALK, county of WILTS, 7½ miles (S.W. by S.) from Wilton, containing 358 inhabitants. The living is a discharged vicarage, united to the consolidated vicarage of Broadchalk and Alvediston, in the archdeaconry and diocese of Salisbury, endowed with £200 private benefaction, and £200 royal bounty. The church is dedicated to the Holy Trinity.

BOWERS-GIFFORD, a parish in the hundred of BARSTABLE, county of ESSEX, 4½ miles (S. W. by W.) from Rayleigh, containing 221 inhabitants. The living is a rectory, in the archdeaconry of Essex, and diocese of London, rated in the king's books at £25, and in the patronage of John Curtis, Esq. The church is dedicated to St. Margaret. This parish is bounded on the south by Holly and East havens, which afford a navigable communication with the Thames.

BOWES, a parish (formerly a market-town) in the western division of the wapentake of GILLING, North riding of the county of YORK, comprising the townships of Boldron, Bowes, and Gillmonby, and containing 1438 inhabitants, of which number, 1095 are in the township of Bowes, 6 miles (W. by N.) from Greta-Bridge. The living is a perpetual curacy, in the archdeaconry of Richmond, and diocese of Chester, endowed with £200 private benefaction, and £1500 parliamentary grant, and in the patronage of T. Harrison, Esq. The church, dedicated to St. Giles, contained, in the time of Camden, a hewn slab, bearing an inscription dedicatory to the Roman emperor Adrian, and at that time used for the communion table. From this and other circumstances, particularly its situation on a military way, and the discovery of an aqueduct, on a late enclosure of waste land, Bowes evidently occupies the site of a Roman station, which antiquaries identify with the *Lavatris* of Antonine. At the time of the Conquest here were the remains of a town, which had been destroyed by fire. A castle was built soon afterwards by Alan, first earl of Richmond, on the elevated site of the Roman fort, and there are still considerable remains of the building and its intrenchments. There is a place of worship for Wesleyan Methodists. Bowes, consisting principally of one street, three quarters of a mile in length, is bleakly situated on the verge of Stanemoor, and on the banks of the river Greta. The market, which was on Friday, and a fair on the 1st of October, have dwindled into insignificance. A free grammar school was founded, about 1693, by William Hutchinson, Esq., who assigned for its support an estate now producing £258 per annum, for which all children within the parish are entitled to gratuitous instruction. This place is interesting as the scene of Mallet's pathetic ballad of Edwin and Emma, a youthful pair in humble life, who, thwarted in their mutual attachment, died of grief, and, according to the parish register, were interred in the same grave, March 15th, 1714. At the distance of about two miles there is a natural bridge across the river Greta, called God's bridge, formed by a rude arch of limestone rock, sixteen feet in the span, and twenty broad at the top, along which carriages usually pass.

BOWESDEN, a hamlet in the parish of LOWICK, eastern division of GLENDALE ward, county of NORTHUMBERLAND, 9¼ miles (N.) from Wooler. The population is returned with the parish. A sepulchral urn was turned up by the plough, several years ago, at Bowesden-Hollins; and in the year 1800, some workmen, in levelling a barrow in the neighbourhood, discovered two inverted urns, containing calcined human bones.

BOWLAND, a joint township with Leagram, in that part of the parish of WHALLEY which is in the lower division of the hundred of BLACKBURN, county palatine of LANCASTER, 9 miles (W.) from Clitheroe, containing, with Leagram, 370 inhabitants.

BOWLAND-FOREST (HIGH), a township in the parish of SLAIDBURN, western division of the wapentake of STAINCLIFFE and EWCROSS, West riding of the county of YORK, containing 237 inhabitants. Here was anciently a forest, but the greater part of it has been enclosed; the office of master-forester has long been in the tenure of the family of Parker, of Browsholme Hall, an adjoining manorial residence.

BOWLAND-FOREST (LOW), a township in the parish of SLAIDBURN, western division of the wapentake of STAINCLIFFE and EWCROSS, West riding of the county of YORK, containing 360 inhabitants.

BOWLING, a township in the parish of BRADFORD, wapentake of MORLEY, West riding of the county of YORK, 1¾ mile (S. by W.) from Bradford, containing 3579 inhabitants. The spinning of worsted, and the manufacture of worsted goods, are extensively carried on in this township, in which there are also some iron-works. Bowling Hall, an ancient and stately mansion, was the head-quarters of the Earl of Newcastle, during the siege of Bradford, in 1642.

BOWNESS, a parish in the ward and county of CUMBERLAND, comprising the townships of Anthorn, Bowness, Drumburgh, and Fingland, and containing 1220 inhabitants, of which number, 471 are in the township of Bowness, 12¼ miles (W. N. W.) from Carlisle. The living is a rectory, in the archdeaconry and diocese of Carlisle, rated in the king's books at £21. 13. 11½., and in the patronage of the Earl of Lonsdale. The church is dedicated to St. Michael. The village stands on a rocky promontory, commanding a fine view of the Solway Frith, on the coast of which it is situated, and occupies the site of the Roman station *Tunnocellum*, where, according to the Notitia, a marine cohort *(cohors prima Ælia Classica)* was placed. At the distance of about a mile was the western extremity of the Picts' wall, vestiges of which are conspicuous in various parts of the parish, as well as of *Gabrosentum*, another Roman station. Coins and various other relics of the Romans, among which was an image of the god *Terminus*, have been discovered; and from the foundations of houses and streets which cultivation has exposed to the view, this place has evidently been of greater extent than it is at present. The ship canal from Carlisle terminates near the village. Thomas Pattinson, in 1785, gave £610, directing the interest to be applied for the instruction of children belonging to this and some neighbouring parishes, which has been accordingly done.

BOWNESS, a village in the parish of WINDERMERE, KENDAL ward, county of WESTMORLAND, 9 miles (W. N. W.) from Kendal. The population is returned with the township of Undermilbeck. This village is agreeably situated on the eastern shore of Windermere lake, in a district abounding with picturesque scenery, and is the principal place in the parish, the church of which stands within it. A few fishing vessels, and several pleasure boats are kept here; and there is some traffic in slate and charcoal. A small customary market, principally for butchers' meat, is held on Wednesday: a fair, formerly on the 18th of October, has been discontinued. A free school has been established by subscription among the inhabitants of Applethwaite and Undermilbeck, who, about 1637, erected a school-house, placing the institution under four trustees and ten feoffees; the endowment, arising from land, is about £50 a year.

BOWOOD, a tything in the parish of NETHERBURY, hundred of BEAMINSTER-FORUM and REDHONE, Bridport division of the county of DORSET, 2¾ miles (W. S. W.) from Beaminster. The population is returned with the parish.

BOWOOD, a liberty in the parish and hundred of CALNE, county of WILTS, 3½ miles (S. E. by E.) from Chippenham, containing 63 inhabitants.

BOWTHORP, a joint township with Menthorp, in the parish of HEMINGBROUGH, wapentake of OUZE and DERWENT, East riding of the county of YORK, 7 miles (E. by N.) from Selby. The population is returned with Menthorp.

BOWTHORPE, a parish in the hundred of FOREHOE, county of NORFOLK, 3½ miles (W. by N.) from Norwich. The population is returned with Bawburgh. The church, dedicated to St. Michael, was, at the beginning of the seventeenth century, used as a storehouse for grain; but, by a decree in Chancery, obtained in 1635, it was restored to its original purpose. The living was formerly a rectory, in the patronage of the Dean and Canons of the College of St. Mary in the Fields, at Norwich, who, in 1522, petitioned the bishop for its reduction to a curacy; since the restoration of the church, in 1635, the living has been a donative, to which the Rev. E. Frank presented in 1791.

BOX, a parish in the hundred of CHIPPENHAM, county of WILTS, 7 miles (S. W. by W.) from Chippenham, containing 1336 inhabitants. The living is a vicarage, in the archdeaconry of Wilts, and diocese of Salisbury, rated in the king's books at £15. 8. 9., and in the patronage of the Rev. J. W. W. Horlock. The church is dedicated to St. Thomas à Becket. An extensive bed of freestone of a peculiar quality exists here, called Bath stone, from the circumstance of the greater part of the city of Bath having been built with stone obtained in quarries about a mile to the east of the village. The stone, which is dug up in blocks of various sizes, is conveyed in wagons to Bath, and thence by the canal to Bristol, from which port it forms a considerable article of exportation to almost every part of the empire. At a short distance north of the village, which is beautifully situated in a rich valley, through which passes the great road from London to Bath, are two mineral springs, one strongly impregnated with neutral salts, the other clear and sparkling, and containing a very large proportion of sulphur and carbonic acid. A lodging and boarding house, pump-room, and other buildings, were erected here some time since, and the place called Middle Hill Spa; but the speculation proved unsuccessful, and the buildings are now let as private lodgings. On Cherry Court farm, north of the spa, and about four miles from Bath, a variety of Roman coins was dug up in 1813, indicating that a large Roman villa once existed on the spot where they were discovered. A charity school has an income of nearly £30 a year, the produce of various benefactions; the master has also a house and garden.

BOXFORD, a parish in the hundred of FAIRCROSS, county of BERKS, 4½ miles (N. W. by N.) from Newbury, containing, with the tything of Westbrook, 563 inhabitants. The living is a rectory, in the archdeaconry of Berks, and diocese of Salisbury, rated in the king's books at £20, and in the patronage of Mr. and Mrs. Wells. The church is dedicated to St. Andrew. There is a place of worship for Wesleyan Methodists.

BOXFORD, a parish partly in the hundred of COSFORD, but chiefly in the hundred of BABERGH, county of SUFFOLK, 16 miles (W. by S.) from Ipswich, containing, with the hamlet of Hadleigh, 944 inhabitants. The living is a rectory, in the archdeaconry of Sudbury, and diocese of Norwich, rated in the king's books at £20, and in the patronage of the Crown. The church is dedicated to St. Mary. Two fairs are held, one on Easter-Monday, and the other on the 21st of December.

BOXGROVE, a parish in the hundred of BOX and STOCKBRIDGE, rape of CHICHESTER, county of SUSSEX, 3½ miles (N. E. by E.) from Chichester, containing 868 inhabitants. The living is a vicarage, in the archdeaconry and diocese of Chichester, rated in the king's books at £9. 5. 5., and in the patronage of the Duke of Richmond. The church, dedicated to St. Mary and St. Blase, is a cruciform structure, and was the conventual church of an Alien priory, subordinate to the abbey de L'Essay in Normandy, the gross revenue of which, in the 26th of Henry VIII., was £145. 10. 2.; there are other remains of the buildings, part of which has been converted into dwelling-houses. In 1740, Mary, Countess Dowager of Derby, granted in trust some land and a rent-charge of £140 a year, for the erection and endowment of almshouses for twelve women, and a dwelling-house for a schoolmaster, who, with the aid of one of the almswomen, was to teach six boys and six girls, who are also clothed: two other children are clothed and educated under an endowment now producing £13 a year, given by Mrs. Eliz. Nash, in 1716; and two are taught under an endowment by Barnard Frederick, in 1752. In addition to the almshouses, two school-rooms have been built, in which these children, together with others from the adjacent parishes, amounting in all to about one hundred of each sex, are instructed, the additional expense being defrayed by subscription.

BOXLEY, a parish in the hundred of MAIDSTONE, lathe of AYLESFORD, county of KENT, 2¼ miles (N. E. by N.) from Maidstone, containing 1166 inhabitants. The living is a vicarage, in the archdeaconry and diocese of Canterbury, rated in the king's books at £12. 19. 2., and in the patronage of the King and the Dean and Chapter of Rochester alternately. The church is dedicated to All Saints. This parish is noted for the manufacture of paper of a superior quality; two of the mills, called the old Turkey mills, are remarkable for the extent of the buildings, the machinery, and the excellence and regularity of the arrangements: prior to the decay of the clothing trade they were used as fulling-mills, but in 1739 were purchased by Mr. James Whatman, and have ever since been appropriated to their present purpose. An abbey for Cistercian monks was founded, in 1146, by William d' Ipres, Earl of Kent, who subsequently assumed the cowl at Laon in France. Henry III.

granted to the society the privilege of holding a weekly market, and the abbot was summoned to parliament in the reign of Edward I. Edward II. resided here during the siege of Leeds castle, at which time he signed a charter for the citizens of London. At the dissolution, the revenue was estimated at £218. 19. 10.; and the site, with a portion of the estates, was granted to Sir Thomas Wyatt, the poet. The abbey contained a celebrated rood, which, together with the image of St. Rumbald, was taken away, and publicly destroyed at St. Paul's cross, in 1538: there are still some remains of the buildings. An extensive rabbit-warren, part of the possessions of the abbey, lies beneath the chalk hill; and there was another near Penenden heath (about half of which is in this parish), but it has been brought into cultivation. A small stream, which rises just below the church, runs through the village, and is stated to petrify wood with an incrustation resembling brown unpolished marble.

BOXTED, a parish in the Colchester division of the hundred of LEXDEN, county of ESSEX, 5 miles (N.) from Colchester, containing 793 inhabitants. The living is a discharged vicarage, in the archdeaconry of Colchester, and diocese of London, rated in the king's books at £7. 13. 9., endowed with £200 private benefaction, and £200 royal bounty, and in the patronage of the Bishop of London. The church is dedicated to St. Mary. The navigable river Stour runs on the northern side of this parish.

BOXTED, a parish in the hundred of BABERGH, county of SUFFOLK, 5¾ miles (N.E.) from Clare, containing 196 inhabitants. The living is a rectory not in charge, consolidated with that of Hartest, in the archdeaconry of Sudbury, and diocese of Norwich.

BOXWELL, a parish in the upper division of the hundred of GRUMBALD'S ASH, county of GLOUCESTER, 5 miles (E. by S.) from Wootton under Edge, containing, with the chapelry of Leighterton, 297 inhabitants. The living is a rectory, in the archdeaconry and diocese of Gloucester, rated in the king's books at £23. 4. 9½., and in the patronage of the Rev. R. Huntley. The church is dedicated to St. Andrew. There are quarries of freestone within the parish, which is intersected by the river Froome. A nunnery here is stated to have been destroyed by the Danes; the possessions were subsequently annexed to the abbey of Gloucester.

BOXWORTH, a parish in the hundred of PAPWORTH, county of CAMBRIDGE, 6½ miles (N.E. by N.) from Caxton, containing 317 inhabitants. The living is a rectory, in the archdeaconry and diocese of Ely, rated in the king's books at £18. 12. 3½., and in the patronage of George Thornhill, Esq. The church, dedicated to St. Peter, contains a monumental bust of Dr. Saunderson, F.R.S., the blind professor of mathematics at the University of Cambridge; he died and was buried here, in 1759.

BOYAT, a tything in the parish of OTTERBOURNE, hundred of BUDDLESGATE, Fawley division of the county of SOUTHAMPTON. The population is returned with the parish.

BOYCUTT, an extra-parochial liberty, in the hundred of PLOUGHLEY, county of OXFORD, though locally in the hundred and county of Buckingham, 3 miles (N.W. by W.) from Buckingham. The population is returned with Stowe.

BOYLSTONE, a parish in the hundred of APPLETREE, county of DERBY, 7½ miles (S.) from Ashbourn, containing 330 inhabitants. The living is a discharged rectory, in the archdeaconry of Derby, and diocese of Lichfield and Coventry, rated in the king's books at £6. 0. 2., and in the patronage of John Toples, Esq. The church is dedicated to St. John the Baptist. There is a place of worship for Wesleyan Methodists.

BOYNTON, a parish in the wapentake of DICKERING, East riding of the county of YORK, 2½ miles (W. by N.) from Bridlington, containing 123 inhabitants. The living is a discharged vicarage, in the archdeaconry of the East riding, and diocese of York, rated in the king's books at £7. 14. 2., and in the patronage of Sir W. Strickland, Bart. The church is dedicated to St. Andrew. On an eminence, south of Boynton Hall, is a lofty building, which was erected by the late Sir George Strickland, Bart., the upper story of which is encircled by a colonnade, and it commands very extensive land and sea views.

BOYTON, a parish partly in the hundred of BLACK TORRINGTON, county of DEVON, but chiefly in the hundred of STRATTON, county of CORNWALL, 5 miles (N. by W.) from Launceston, containing, with the hamlet of Northcott, 489 inhabitants. The living is a perpetual curacy, in the archdeaconry of Cornwall, and diocese of Exeter, endowed with £200 royal bounty, and £200 parliamentary grant, and in the patronage of the Rev. G. Prideaux. The Bude and Launceston, or Tamar, canal crosses the parish. A fair is held annually on the 5th of August. The old mansions of Bradridge and Beardon have been converted into farm-houses. Between this place and North Tamerton there is an ancient thatched building, called Hornacott Chapel, now occupied by a labourer.

BOYTON, a parish in the hundred of WILFORD, county of SUFFOLK, 3¼ miles (W.S.W.) from Orford, containing 284 inhabitants. The living is a rectory, in the archdeaconry of Suffolk, and diocese of Norwich, rated in the king's books at £5. 12. 1., and in the patronage of the trustees of the late Mrs. Mary Warner. The church is dedicated to St. Andrew. The river Alde runs through the parish, and communicates with Butley creek or Eye. An almshouse was built in 1743, and liberally endowed by Mrs. Warner, for six men and six women: this number has been lately increased to sixteen, each having two apartments, a garden, and an allowance of 7*s.* a week, with a suit of clothes and one chaldron of coal yearly.

BOYTON, a parish in the hundred of HEYTESBURY, county of WILTS, 3 miles (S.E.) from Heytesbury, containing, with the township of Corton, 284 inhabitants. The living is a rectory, in the archdeaconry and diocese of Salisbury, rated in the king's books at £27. 17. 3½., and in the patronage of the President and Fellows of Magdalene College, Oxford. The church is dedicated to St. Mary.

BOZEAT, a parish in the hundred of HIGHAM-FERRERS, county of NORTHAMPTON, 5¾ miles (N.) from Olney, containing 754 inhabitants. The living is a discharged vicarage, with that of Strixton consolidated, in the archdeaconry of Northampton, and diocese of Peterborough, rated in the king's books at £8, endowed with £10 per annum private benefaction, and £200 royal bounty, and in the patronage of Earl Spencer. The church is dedicated to St. Mary. There is a place of worship for Wesleyan Methodists.

BRABOURNE, a parish in the franchise and barony of BIRCHOLT, lathe of SHEPWAY, county of KENT, 6½ miles (E. by S.) from Ashford, containing 599 inhabitants. The living is a vicarage, with the rectory of Monk's Horton consolidated, in the archdeaconry and diocese of Canterbury, rated in the king's books at £11. 12. 6., and in the patronage of the Archbishop of Canterbury. The church, dedicated to St. Mary, contains numerous ancient and interesting monuments. At Brabourne-Lees there is a rabbit-warren, the rabbits in which are noted for their flavour. Extensive barracks, both for cavalry and infantry, were erected here a few years ago. A fair for toys and pedlary is held on the last day in May.

BRACEBOROUGH, a parish in the wapentake of NESS, parts of KESTEVEN, county of LINCOLN, 6 miles (W. N. W.) from Market-Deeping, containing 198 inhabitants. The living is a rectory, in the archdeaconry and diocese of Lincoln, rated in the king's books at £9. 10., and in the patronage of the Crown. The church is dedicated to St. Margaret.

BRACEBRIDGE, a parish in the liberty of the city of LINCOLN, county of LINCOLN, 2¼ miles (S. by W.) from Lincoln, containing 155 inhabitants. The living is a vicarage, in the archdeaconry and diocese of Lincoln, rated in the king's books at £3. 9. 9½., and in the patronage of the Rev. J. Penrose. The church is dedicated to All Saints. Edward Wells, in 1604, bequeathed a house and land for the instruction of poor children.

BRACEBY, a parish in the soke of GRANTHAM, parts of KESTEVEN, county of LINCOLN, 4½ miles (W. by N.) from Falkingham, containing 97 inhabitants. The living is a vicarage, united to that of South Grantham, in the archdeaconry and diocese of Lincoln. The church is dedicated to St. Margaret.

BRACE-MEOLE, a parish within the liberty of the borough of SHREWSBURY, county of SALOP, 1½ mile (S.) from Shrewsbury, containing 1348 inhabitants. The living is a discharged vicarage, in the archdeaconry of Salop, and diocese of Hereford, rated in the king's books at £5, and in the patronage of Mrs. Bather. The church is dedicated to All Saints. The Shrewsbury house of industry, a noble and spacious building, stands in this parish.

BRACEWELL, a parish in the eastern division of the wapentake of STAINCLIFFE and EWCROSS, West riding of the county of YORK, 9 miles (W. by S.) from Skipton, containing 176 inhabitants. The living is a discharged vicarage, in the archdeaconry and diocese of York, rated in the king's books at £2. 9. 9½., endowed with £600 private benefaction, and £1200 royal bounty, and in the patronage of Lord Grantham. The church is dedicated to St. Michael. There are quarries of limestone in the parish. On the summit of two eminences, Howber and Gildersber, are vestiges of military works, stated by tradition to have been constructed by Prince Rupert's forces, on their march through Craven, in 1664. A brick mansion, formerly belonging to the family of Tempest, is in ruins.

BRACKEN, a township in the chapelry of KILNWICK, Bainton-Beacon division of the wapentake of HARTHILL, East riding of the county of YORK, 6¾ miles (S.W. by S.) from Great Driffield, containing 30 inhabitants. This was formerly a populous village, and contained a chapel, the cemetery belonging to which remains undisturbed.

BRACKENBOROUGH, a chapelry in the parish of LITTLE GRIMSBY, wapentake of LUDBOROUGH, parts of LINDSEY, county of LINCOLN, 2½ miles (N.) from Louth, containing 54 inhabitants.

BRACKENFIELD, a chapelry in the parish of MORTON, hundred of SCARSDALE, county of DERBY, 4½ miles (N.W.) from Alfreton, containing 353 inhabitants. The chapel is dedicated to the Holy Trinity.

BRACKENHILL, a township in the parish of ARTHURET, ESKDALE ward, county of CUMBERLAND, 4¼ miles (E. by N.) from Longtown, containing 441 inhabitants. In this township is the small hamlet of Easton, which anciently gave name to a parish, long since included within the parishes of Arthuret and Kirk-Andrews upon Esk.

BRACKENHOLME, a joint township with Woodhall, in the parish of HEMINGBROUGH, wapentake of OUZE and DERWENT, East riding of the county of YORK, 3½ miles (N. N. W.) from Howden, containing, with Woodhall, 90 inhabitants. It occupies a pleasant site near the river Derwent.

BRACKENTHWAITE, a township in the parish of LORTON, ALLERDALE ward above Darwent, county of CUMBERLAND, 8½ miles (W. by S.) from Keswick, containing 140 inhabitants. The neighbourhood abounds with beautiful scenery, being picturesquely diversified with the lakes Loweswater, Crummock, and Buttermere, and the lofty mountain Grassmoor: lead-ore has been obtained in the township.

Seal and Arms.

BRACKLEY, a borough, market town, and parish, in the hundred of KING'S SUTTON, county of NORTHAMPTON, 20 miles (S. W. by S.) from Northampton, and 64 (N. W. by W.) from London, containing 1851 inhabitants. This place derives its name from the Anglo-Saxon *Bracken*, signifying fern, with which the neighbourhood formerly abounded: it was a Saxon burgh of considerable importance, but was greatly injured by the Danes. In the reign of John, Saher de Quincy, Earl of Winchester, joined the confederate barons at Stamford, who marched to Brackley, whence they sent a remonstrance, setting forth their grievances to the king, who was then at Oxford. In the reign of Henry III., two splendid tournaments were held, on a plain called Bayard's Green, near the town. Edward II., who conferred many privileges upon Brackley, made it a staple town for wool; and, in the reign of Edward III., having become famous for its trade, it sent three representatives, as "Merchants Staplers," to a grand council held at Westminster. In the reign of Henry VIII., the plague raging violently at Oxford, the fellows and scholars of Magdalene College removed to this town, and resided in an hospital founded by Robert le Bossu, Earl of Leicester, about the middle of the twelfth century, of which there are considerable remains, the chapel, with a broad low tower on the north-west side, being still entire. The town is on the border of Buckinghamshire, and is situated on the declivity of a hill, near a branch of the river Ouse, which has its source in the immediate vicinity: it is divided into two portions, New Brackley and Old Brackley; the latter, which is the smaller division, is without the limits of the borough. The principal street, nearly a mile in length, extends from the bridge up the acclivity of the hill, and contains many good houses, which are mostly built of stone: there is an abundant supply of water. The inhabitants are chiefly occupied in the making of bobbin lace, and boots and shoes. The market is on Wednesday: the fairs, principally for horses, horned cattle, and sheep, are on the Wednesday after February 25th, the second Wednesday in April, the Wednesday after June 22nd, the Wednesday after October 11th (a statute fair), and December 11th, which is a great fair for cattle and wearing apparel. The government, by charter of incorporation confirmed and extended in the seventh of Edward II., is vested in a mayor, six aldermen, and twenty-six burgesses: the mayor is appointed by the lord of the manor, and sworn into office at his annual court leet, which is also a court baron and port-mote, on the Monday after September 29th, when two constables, two thirdboroughs, and other officers, are also chosen. The aldermen are selected from among the burgesses, the mayor and the lord of the manor each nominating one candidate, whose election is decided by a majority of the rest: the burgesses are chosen from householders residing in New Brackley only, by the whole body, as vacancies occur. The corporation have power to hold a court of record for the recovery of debts under £20, but do not exercise it; and the mayor is not vested with magisterial authority, the town being wholly within the jurisdiction of the county magistrates. The elective franchise was conferred in the first of Edward VI., since which time the borough has returned two members to parliament: the right of election is vested in the mayor, aldermen, and burgesses, in number thirty-three, who are principally in the interest of the Marquis of Stafford: the mayor is the returning officer. The town-hall, a handsome building in the centre of the town, supported on arches, under which the market is held, was erected in 1706, by Scroop, Duke of Bridgewater, at an expense of £2000.

Brackley comprises the parishes of St. Peter and St. James, which, though ecclesiastically united, are distinct as regards civil affairs. The living is a consolidated vicarage, in the archdeaconry of Northampton, and diocese of Peterborough, rated in the king's books at £19. 1. 6., and in the patronage of the Marquis of Stafford. The church, dedicated to St. Peter, is an ancient building, with a low embattled tower; it contains a Norman font of curious design. St. James', formerly a parochial church, is now a chapel of ease to the vicarage of St. Peter. Mr. Welchman bequeathed £10 per annum to the minister, for performing evening service in the chapel every alternate Sunday. There is a place of worship for Wesleyan Methodists. The free grammar school was founded, about the year 1447, by William of Wainfleet, who endowed it with £13. 6. 8. per annum, for ten boys of the parishes of St. Peter and St. James, which sum is paid by the President and Fellows of Magdalene College, Oxford, to whom the site of the ancient hospital was granted at the time of its dissolution: there is a house for the master, who has a salary of £18 per annum, and the profits of some land attached to the school. A National school for boys was established, and is supported, by subscription. Almshouses for six aged widows were founded by Sir Thomas Crewe, in 1633, and endowed with a rent charge of £24, which was increased in 1721, by his descendant, Nathaniel, Lord Crewe, Bishop of Durham, with an additional rent-charge of £12. The site of a castle, built by one of the Norman barons, is still called the Castle hill. Samuel Clarke, an eminent orientalist, and one of the coadjutors of Walton in publishing the Polyglott Bible, was born here, in 1623.

BRACON-ASH, a parish in the hundred of HUMBLEYARD, county of NORFOLK, $5\frac{1}{4}$ miles (E. by S.) from Wymondham, containing 260 inhabitants. The living is a rectory, in the archdeaconry of Norfolk, and diocese of Norwich, rated in the king's books at £10, and in the patronage of T. T. Berney, Esq. The church is dedicated to St. Nicholas.

BRADBORNE, a parish comprising the chapelry of Atlow in the hundred of APPLETREE, and the chapelries of Ballidon and Brassington, the township of Aldwark, and the hamlet of Lea-Hall, in the hundred of WIRKSWORTH, county of DERBY, 5 miles (N. N. E.) from Ashbourn, and containing 1313 inhabitants. The living is a discharged vicarage, in the archdeaconry of Derby, and diocese of Lichfield and Coventry, rated in the king's books at £8. 3. 4., and in the patronage of the Duke of Devonshire. The church, which is in Wirksworth hundred, is dedicated to All Saints. The parish abounds with limestone. Tissington Hall was garrisoned for the king by its owner, Col. Fitz-Herbert, in 1643. Bradborne is in the honour of Tutbury, duchy of Lancaster, and within the jurisdiction of a court of pleas held at Tutbury every third Tuesday, for the recovery of debts under 40*s*.

BRADBURY, a township in the parish of SEDGEFIELD, north-eastern division of STOCKTON ward, county palatine of DURHAM, $10\frac{1}{2}$ miles (S. by E.) from Durham, containing 152 inhabitants. Mr. Cade, the antiquary, considered the name of this place to be a corruption of Brimesbury, where King Athelstan encamped in 937, when he gained a decisive victory over the Danes: but it is more probable that this battle was fought at Bramby in Lincolnshire. Here was formerly a chapel of ease, dedicated to St. Nicholas, of which there are no vestiges: the curate's house is still standing. In this township is a place called the Isle, environed by two branches of the Little Skerne; it is a distinct manor, comprising two farms.

BRADBY, a chapelry in the parish of REPTON, hundred of REPTON and GRESLEY, county of DERBY, 3 miles (E.) from Burton upon Trent, containing 302 inhabitants. The living is a donative, annexed to the perpetual curacy of Repton, at which place the inhabitants marry and bury. Near the church is the site of an ancient baronial mansion, which was fortified by royal license in the year 1300; but its materials are supposed to have been used by the first Earl of Chesterfield, in the erection of a residence, which he fortified and garrisoned for the king, in 1642. After a short defence it was captured by a strong detachment sent by Col. Gell, and was taken down in 1780. A school for teaching and clothing thirty boys, and another for thirty girls, were established and supported by the late Earl and Countess of Chesterfield, and are still continued. Bradby is in the honour of Tutbury, duchy of Lancaster, and within the jurisdiction of a court of pleas held at Tutbury every third Tuesday, for the recovery of debts under 40*s*.

BRADDEN, a parish in the hundred of GREEN'S NORTON, county of NORTHAMPTON, 3¼ miles (W.) from Towcester, containing 135 inhabitants. The living is a rectory, in the archdeaconry of Northampton, and diocese of Peterborough, rated in the king's books at £14. 6. 8., and in the patronage of C. Ives, Esq. The church is dedicated to St. Michael.

BRADENHAM, a parish in the hundred of DESBOROUGH, county of BUCKINGHAM, 4¼ miles (N. W. by N.) from High Wycombe, containing 220 inhabitants. The living is a discharged rectory, in the archdeaconry of Buckingham, and diocese of Lincoln, rated in the king's books at £5. 3. 9., endowed with £200 private benefaction, and £200 royal bounty, and in the patronage of J. Hicks, Esq. The church is dedicated to St. Botolph. Catherine Pye, by deed dated in 1713, gave land for the instruction of children in this and four other parishes.

BRADENHAM (EAST), a parish in the southern division of the hundred of GREENHOE, county of NORFOLK, 5¾ miles (S. W.) from East Dereham, containing 340 inhabitants. The living is a rectory, in the archdeaconry of Norfolk, and diocese of Norwich, rated in the king's books at £12. 2. 8½., and in the patronage of Thomas Oxley, Esq. The church, dedicated to St. Mary, is composed of flint and stones.

BRADENHAM (WEST), a parish in the southern division of the hundred of GREENHOE, county of NORFOLK, 5¾ miles (S. W. by W.) from East Dereham, containing 385 inhabitants. The living is a discharged vicarage, in the archdeaconry of Norfolk, and diocese of Norwich, rated in the king's books at £7. 1. 10½., and in the patronage of the Bishop of Ely. The church, dedicated to St. Andrew, is an ancient edifice built of flint.

BRADESTON, a parish in the hundred of BLOFIELD, county of NORFOLK, 4½ miles (W. S. W.) from Acle, containing 142 inhabitants. The living is a discharged rectory, with that of Strumpshaw united, in the archdeaconry and diocese of Norwich, rated in the king's books at £5. 6. 8., and in the patronage of the Rev. T. Woodward. The church is dedicated to St. Michael. This parish is bounded on the south by the river Yare. Three Roman urns, containing calcined bones, were found in digging a sand-pit near the site of a demolished church.

BRADFIELD, a parish in the hundred of THEALE, county of BERKS, 8 miles (W.) from Reading, containing 946 inhabitants. The living is a rectory, in the archdeaconry of Berks, and diocese of Salisbury, rated in the king's books at £19. 7. 8½., and in the patronage of the Rev. H. Stevens. The church is dedicated to St. Andrew. A monastery was founded here by King Ina, before 699, but nothing further is recorded of its history.

BRADFIELD, a parish in the hundred of TENDRING, county of ESSEX, 2¾ miles (E. S. E.) from Manningtree, containing 822 inhabitants. The living is a discharged vicarage, united to the rectory of Mistley, in the archdeaconry of Colchester, and diocese of London, rated in the king's books at £12. 13. 4., and endowed with £200 royal bounty. The church is dedicated to St. Lawrence. There is a place of worship for Wesleyan Methodists. The navigable river Stour flows along the northern part of this parish. A fair is held on the last Monday in July. Sir Harbottle Grimston, Master of the Rolls under Charles II., and an eminent writer on the law, was born here; he died in 1683.

BRADFIELD, a parish in the hundred of TUNSTEAD, county of NORFOLK, 2½ miles (N. N. W.) from North Walsham, containing 195 inhabitants. The living, consisting of one mediety, is a discharged rectory, in the archdeaconry of Norfolk, and diocese of Norwich, rated in the king's books at £3. 15. 7½., and in the patronage of Lord Suffield. The church is dedicated to St. Giles. The other mediety is a donative annexed to the vicarage of Thorpe-Market.

BRADFIELD, a chapelry in the parish of ECCLESFIELD, northern division of the wapentake of STRAFFORTH and TICKHILL, West riding of the county of YORK, 6¾ miles (N.W. by W.) from Sheffield, containing 5298 inhabitants. The living is a perpetual curacy, in the archdeaconry and diocese of York, endowed with £400 private benefaction, £400 royal bounty, and £1000 parliamentary grant, and in the patronage of the Vicar of Ecclesfield. This chapelry lies in a mountainous part of the county, and is surrounded by uncultivated and barren moors. There is a place of worship for Wesleyan Methodists. Many of the inhabitants are employed in different branches of manufacture connected with the trade at Sheffield. Fairs are held on June 17th and December 9th. An estate, called the Feoffees' estate, produces about £172 per annum, which is chiefly applied in repairing the chapel, and in defraying those local expenses for which a rate is usually imposed. A school at Lower Bradfield is endowed with a house (in which the master resides), a croft, and a garden, besides a rent-charge of £10, for which eighteen children are instructed. There is a school at Bolterstone, endowed with about £40 per annum and a house occupied by the master, chiefly from a bequest by John Hodgkinson, in 1780, for the free instruction of all children within the chapelry. The school at Onesacre has an endowment of about £14 per annum and a residence for the master, who teaches sixteen children gratuitously.

BRADFIELD (ST. CLARE), a parish in the hundred of THEDWESTRY, county of SUFFOLK, 6 miles (S.E. by S.) from Bury St. Edmund's, containing 201 inhabitants. The living is a rectory, in the archdeaconry of Sudbury, and diocese of Norwich, rated in the king's books at £7. 4. 7., and in the patronage of the Rev. R. Davers. There is a place of worship for Wesleyan Methodists.

BRADFIELD (ST. GEORGE), a parish in the hundred of THEDWESTRY, county of SUFFOLK, 5 miles (S. E.) from Bury St. Edmund's, containing 409 inhabitants. The living is a rectory, with that of Rushbrook annexed, in the archdeaconry of Sudbury, and diocese of Norwich, rated in the king's books at £11. 17. 3½., and in the patronage of the Marquis of Bristol. Thomas Sparke, in 1721, gave property for the gratuitous instruction of four children.

BRADFIELD-COMBUST, a parish in the hundred of THEDWESTRY, county of SUFFOLK, 5½ miles (S. S. E.)

from Bury St. Edmund's, containing 146 inhabitants. The living is a discharged rectory, in the archdeaconry of Sudbury, and diocese of Norwich, rated in the king's books at £4. 19. 7., endowed with £200 royal bounty, and in the patronage of the Rev. H. Hasted. The church is dedicated to All Saints. This is the birthplace of Arthur Young, the celebrated writer on agriculture, and author of various miscellaneous works.

BRADFORD, a parish in the hundred of BLACK TORRINGTON, county of DEVON, $6\frac{1}{2}$ miles (N. E. by E.) from Holsworthy, containing 384 inhabitants. The living is a rectory, in the archdeaconry of Totness, and diocese of Exeter, rated in the king's books at £13. 8. 4., and in the patronage of the Trustees of Bampfield's Charity. The church is dedicated to All Saints. The Rev. William Bickford, in 1745, gave a small endowment for the instruction of six poor children.

BRADFORD, a township in the parish of MANCHESTER, hundred of SALFORD, county palatine of LANCASTER, $1\frac{3}{4}$ mile (E. by S.) from Manchester, containing 95 inhabitants.

BRADFORD, a township in the parish of BAMBROUGH, northern division of BAMBROUGH ward, county of NORTHUMBERLAND, $4\frac{1}{2}$ miles (E. S. E.) from Belford, containing 48 inhabitants.

BRADFORD, a township in the parish of BOLAM, north-eastern division of TINDALE ward, county of NORTHUMBERLAND, 12 miles (W. S. W.) from Morpeth, containing 48 inhabitants.

BRADFORD, a parish in the hundred of TAUNTON and TAUNTON-DEAN, county of SOMERSET, $4\frac{1}{4}$ miles (W. S. W.) from Taunton, containing 525 inhabitants. The living is a discharged vicarage, in the archdeaconry of Taunton, and diocese of Bath and Wells, rated in the king's books at £10. 17. 6., endowed with £200 private benefaction, and £300 parliamentary grant, and in the patronage of the Rev. W. Burridge. The church is dedicated to St. Giles.

BRADFORD, a parish in the wapentake of MORLEY, West riding of the county of YORK, comprising the market town of Bradford, the chapelries of North Bierley, Hawarth, Heaton, Horton, Shipley, Thornton, and Wilsden, and the townships of Allerton, Bowling, Clayton, Eccleshill, and Manningham, and containing, at the census of 1821 (since which time the population has considerably increased), 52,954 inhabitants, of which number, 13,064 were in the town of Bradford, 34 miles (S. W.) from York, 10 (E. S. E.) from Leeds, and 196 (N. N. W.) from London. This place derives its name from a ford on the river Aire, at the western extremity of the town. During the civil war in the reign of Charles I., the inhabitants embraced the cause of the parliament, and on two occasions repulsed a detachment of the royal troops, sent against them from the garrison at Leeds. Sir Thomas Fairfax coming afterwards to their assistance, with eight hundred infantry and sixty cavalry, the Earl of Newcastle, with a powerful army, invested the town, and attempted to storm it in several places. After a vigorous defence, in which he had spent all his ammunition, Fairfax offered to capitulate; but the earl refusing the conditions, he, with about fifty of his horse, cut his way through the lines of the royalists, and escaped. The town is pleasantly situated at the junction of three beautiful and extensive vallies; the streets, though narrow, are well paved, and lighted with gas, under an act obtained in the 3rd of George IV., subject in its conditions to one passed in the 43rd of George III., for paving, lighting, watching, and improving the town and neighbourhood. The houses, mostly of stone, and roofed with brown slate found in the neighbourhood, are handsome and well built; and the inhabitants are plentifully supplied with water, conveyed by pipes from a fine spring at the distance of three miles. The air, though sharp, is very salubrious; and the neighbourhood abounds with pleasing and picturesque scenery. Assemblies are held in rooms in the Exchange, a handsome building of freestone, recently erected, and containing also a subscription news-room and a library. Music meetings of the Philharmonic Society are held monthly in the Exchange buildings. Bradford is in the centre of the manufacturing districts, and the inhabitants are employed principally in the manufacture of woollen cloth, worsted stuffs, and cotton goods, in the spinning of worsted yarn, and in making ivory and horn combs. The neighbourhood abounds with coal and iron-stone; and about three miles to the south-east of the town are iron-works on a very extensive scale. A branch of the Leeds and Liverpool canal has been brought to this place, and affords great facility to its commerce. The market is on Thursday: the market-house is a handsome stone building, enclosing a spacious area for the sale of provisions and various kinds of merchandise. Fairs are held on June 17th and the two following days; December 9th and the two following days, for pigs; and March 3rd and 4th, for cattle, &c. The town is within the jurisdiction of the magistrates for the West riding; two constables are appointed annually at a vestry meeting held in the parish church; a court of requests is held under an act passed in the 33rd of George III., for the recovery of debts under 40*s.*; and a court for the recovery of debts under £5, within the honour of Pontefract, on the Wednesday in every third week. The court-house is a handsome stone building in Darley-street. The Midsummer quarter sessions for the West riding are held in the Piece-hall, a spacious building in Kirkgate, divided into two apartments, one of which, besides being used for holding the courts, is for the exhibition and sale of stuffs and other articles of manufacture, which are deposited in the other.

The living is a vicarage, in the archdeaconry and diocese of York, rated in the king's books at £20, and in the patronage of Richard Fawcett, Esq. The church, dedicated to St. Peter, is an ancient structure in the decorated style of English architecture. Christ-church, a chapel of ease erected in 1814, by parliamentary grant, is a neat building in the decorated style, with a low tower crowned with pinnacles. There are places of worship for Baptists, the Society of Friends, Independents, Primitive and Wesleyan Methodists, Unitarians, and Roman Catholics. The free grammar school, founded in the reign of Edward VI., and richly endowed, was rebuilt by act of parliament, in 1818: it is a spacious and handsome edifice, with a neat house for the master, and a library for the use of the students. The management is vested in thirteen governors resident in the town and neighbourhood; and, by a charter of Charles II., bearing date October 10th, 1662, the Archbishop of York was constituted visitor. This is one of the twelve schools that have the privilege of sending candidates for Lady Elizabeth Hastings' exhibitions at Queen's College, Oxford. The dispensary, a large handsome building, was erected and is supported by voluntary contributions. The learned and eloquent Dr. John Sharp, Archbishop of York in the reign of William III., was born at Bradford, in the year 1644.

BRADFORD (GREAT), a market town and parish in the hundred of BRADFORD, county of WILTS, 8 miles (S. E.) from Bath, 31½ (N. W.) from Salisbury, and 102 (W. by S.) from London, containing with the chapelries of Atworth, Holt, Winsley with Limpley-Stoke, and South Wraxall, and the tything of Leigh-Wooley, 10,231 inhabitants. This place, from a ford over the river Avon, was called by the Saxons *Bradenford*, of which its present name is a contraction. During the Octarchy, a battle took place here, between Cenwalh, King of the West Saxons, and a formidable party of his own subjects, who had rebelled against him, under the command of his kinsman Cuthred, when the latter were defeated with great slaughter. In 706, Aldhelm, Bishop of Sherborne, founded an abbey at this place, which he dedicated to St. Lawrence, and which, after its destruction by the Danes, was rebuilt and converted into a nunnery, by Ethelred, who annexed it to a larger establishment of the same kind at Shaftesbury, in 1001. The town is beautifully situated on the acclivity of a steep hill, forming part of a line of eminences on the northern side of the river Avon, over which are an ancient bridge of four, and a modern bridge of nine, arches, both affording a most agreeable prospect. The view of the town, which consists of three regular streets ranged above each other at different elevations on the side of the hill, is strikingly picturesque: the houses, built of stone, are in general handsome, and many of them elegant; and the inhabitants are amply supplied with water from springs. Various designs have recently been carried into effect for the improvement of the town: some of the streets have been widened, and considerable alterations have been made for the furtherance of business. A book society and a news-room have been recently established, and are well supported. The principal branch of manufacture is that of woollen cloth, which is said by Leland to have flourished in the reign of Henry VIII., particularly that composed of the finer kind of Spanish and Saxony wool, for the dyeing of which the water of the river is peculiarly favourable. There are numerous factories, affording employment to many men, women, and children, in the town and neighbourhood. Ladies' cloth, kerseymere, and fancy pieces, are also manufactured to a considerable extent. Scribbling-mills and spinning-jennies were introduced about forty years since, and their adoption in the several factories excited great discontent among the workmen, several lives having been lost in the disturbances that ensued. The Kennet and Avon canal, which affords an increased facility of conveyance to various parts of the kingdom, and has contributed to the advancement of its prosperity, passes close to the town, and a commodious wharf has been constructed on its bank. The market is on Saturday: the fairs are on Trinity-Monday, and on the day after St. Bartholomew's day; the latter is held at Bradford-Leigh, a hamlet in the parish.

Bradford sent members to parliament in the 23rd of Edward I., but since that time it has made no return. The petty sessions are held here alternately with Trowbridge; and a court of requests for the recovery of debts under £5, the jurisdiction of which extends over the hundreds of Bradford, Melksham, and Whorwelsdown, is held, under an act passed in the 47th of George III., every third Tuesday, alternately with Trowbridge and Melksham. A small oratory on the south-western side of the bridge, formerly belonging to the monastery of St. Lawrence, has been converted into a place of confinement for offenders, previously to their committal to the county gaol. The living is a discharged vicarage, in the archdeaconry and diocese of Salisbury, rated in the king's books at £10. 1. 3., and in the patronage of the Dean and Chapter of Bristol. The church, dedicated to the Holy Trinity, is a spacious handsome structure; it suffered greatly from fire in 1742, and has undergone extensive repair; the windows contain some modern stained glass, and the altar is embellished with a good painting of the Last Supper; within are several stately monuments of marble. There are two places of worship each for Baptists and Independents, and one each for the Society of Friends, those in the connexion of the late Countess of Huntingdon, Wesleyan Methodists, and Unitarians. A free school for sixty boys is endowed with an estate at Holt, purchased with £250 given by Mr. Francis Smith; and with the dividends on £240 three per cents., given in 1805, by Mr. John Shawbridge, who also bequeathed £400 in the same stock, directing the interest to be distributed annually, in crowns and half-crowns, among the poor. There are two almshouses, one founded by Mr. John Hall, for aged men, the other for aged women; they are supposed to have been an appendage to the monastery, of which, and also of other religious establishments formerly existing here, there are still some slight remains. Many curious fossils have been found in the quarries adjoining the town.

BRADFORD (WEST), a township in that part of the parish of MITTON which is in the western division of the wapentake of STAINCLIFFE and EWCROSS, West riding of the county of YORK, 2 miles (N.) from Clitheroe, containing 564 inhabitants. Thomas Tarrand, in 1721, bequeathed a rent-charge of £10 for instructing poor children of the township.

BRADFORD-ABBAS, a parish in the hundred of SHERBORNE, Sherborne division of the county of DORSET, 3½ miles (W. S. W.) from Sherborne, containing 533 inhabitants. The living is a vicarage, with which the rectory of Clifton-Mabank was consolidated in 1824, in the archdeaconry of Dorset, and diocese of Bristol, rated in the king's books at £7. 17. 11., and in the patronage of the Marquis of Anglesey. The church is dedicated to St. Mary. The Rev. William Preston, in 1738, gave £14 per annum for the endowment of a charity school; and, in 1781, Mark West and William Read gave property producing an equal amount, for the same purpose.

BRADFORD-PEVERELL, a parish in the hundred of GEORGE, Dorchester division of the county of DORSET, 3¼ miles (N. W. by W.) from Dorchester, containing, with Muckleford, 277 inhabitants. The living is a rectory, in the archdeaconry of Dorset, and diocese of Bristol, rated in the king's books at £11. 2. 11., and in the patronage of the Warden and Fellows of Winchester College. The church is dedicated to St. Mary. The village is situated on the line of a Roman road; and there are several tumuli in the vicinity, some of which, on being opened, were found to contain urns, burnt bones, and various other relics of the Romans.

Corporate Seal.

BRADING, a parish (formerly a market town) in the liberty of EAST MEDINA, Isle of Wight division of the county of SOUTHAMPTON, 7 miles (E. by S.) from Newport, and 95 (S.W.) from London, containing 2023 inhabitants. This place, formerly of considerable importance, as appears from its being styled "the King's town of Brading" in the legend of its common seal, probably received name from the haven, at the upper end of which it is situated. Brading haven, a tract of marshy ground, nearly nine hundred acres in extent, is covered by the sea at every tide; so that at high water small vessels can approach the town, for unloading which a quay has been constructed. Repeated attempts have been made to exclude the sea by an embankment, and Sir Hugh Middleton, the projector of the New River, had nearly effected this, when, during a wet season, the works, which had been raised at an expense of £7000, were completely destroyed by a spring tide. The town consists principally of one long street, the houses in which are irregularly built; the inhabitants are plentifully supplied with water from public wells. Fairs are held on May 1st and September 21st. The government, by charter of incorporation granted prior to the reign of Edward VI., is vested in a senior and a junior bailiff, a recorder, and thirteen jurats, assisted by a town-clerk, who is also steward: the bailiffs are appointed at the court leet of the lord of the manor. The town-hall is a very small building; the lower part is used as a prison and for the market. The living is a discharged vicarage, in the archdeaconry and diocese of Winchester, rated in the king's books at £20, and in the patronage of the Master and Fellows of Trinity College, Cambridge. The church, dedicated to St. Mary, is one of the most ancient in the kingdom, being said to have been built in 704, by Wilfrid, Bishop of Chichester, who here baptized his first converts to Christianity: it is a spacious structure, with a tower, and some remains of Saxon architecture are preserved in the nave, though it has undergone many alterations in other parts; at the extremity of each aisle there is a small chapel. A chapel has been recently built at Bembridge, a hamlet in this parish: the living is a perpetual curacy, in the patronage of the Vicar of Brading. There is a place of worship for Wesleyan Methodists. A National school, in which about sixty children are instructed, is supported by subscription. Knight's charity supplies seven poor men annually with a suit of clothes each. In this parish is Sandown fort, a regular quadrangular fortification, flanked by four bastions, and encompassed by a ditch: it was constructed in the reign of Henry VIII., on a level with the beach, and, having been greatly neglected after the rise of the English Navy, was repaired during the late war, and is now the most considerable fortress in the island. In the American war the garrison sustained attacks from several privateers, and drove them off.

BRADLE, a tything in the parish of CHURCH-KNOWLE, hundred of HASILOR, Blandford (South) division of the county of DORSET. The population is returned with the parish.

BRADLEY, a tything in the parish of CUMNER, hundred of HORMER, county of BERKS, 5 miles (N.N.W.) from Abingdon, containing 5 inhabitants.

BRADLEY, a township in the parish of MALPAS, higher division of the hundred of BROXTON, county palatine of CHESTER, 2 miles (S.E. by E.) from Malpas, containing 78 inhabitants.

BRADLEY, a parish in the hundred of APPLETREE, county of DERBY, 3¼ miles (E. by S.) from Ashbourn, containing 320 inhabitants. The living is a rectory, in the archdeaconry of Derby, and diocese of Lichfield and Coventry, rated in the king's books at £5. 19. 9½., and in the patronage of the Dean of Lincoln. The church, dedicated to All Saints, is a small ancient structure. Within the parish is a chalybeate spring, but it is not much used.

BRADLEY, a tything in that part of the parish of CREDITON which is in the western division of the hundred of BUDLEIGH, county of DEVON, 2½ miles (N.E.) from Crediton, with which the population is returned.

BRADLEY, a tything in the parish of WOTTON under EDGE, upper division of the hundred of BERKELEY, county of GLOUCESTER, ½ a mile (W.S.W.) from Wotton under Edge, with which the population is returned.

BRADLEY, a hamlet in the chapelry of HOLT, parish of MEDBOURNE, hundred of GARTREE, county of LEICESTER, 2½ miles (N.N.W.) from Rockingham. The population is returned with Holt. A small priory of Augustine canons was founded here, in the reign of John, by Robert Bundy, or Burneby, the revenue of which, at the time of the suppression, was £20. 15. 7.

BRADLEY, a parish in the wapentake of BRADLEY-HAVERSTOE, parts of LINDSEY, county of LINCOLN, 3 miles (S.W.) from Great Grimsby, containing 78 inhabitants. The living is a discharged rectory, in the archdeaconry and diocese of Lincoln, rated in the king's books at £5. 10. 10., and in the patronage of Sir John Nelthorpe, Bart. The church is dedicated to St. George. The children of this parish are entitled to instruction at Laceby school, founded and endowed by Sarah Stamford, in 1720.

BRADLEY, a parish situated in a detached portion of the hundred of OVERTON, Kingsclere division of the county of SOUTHAMPTON, 6 miles (W.N.W.) from Alton, containing 100 inhabitants. The living is a rectory, in the archdeaconry and diocese of Winchester, rated in the king's books at £8. 13. 4., and in the patronage of J. Blackburn, Esq. The church is dedicated to All Saints. Bradley is within the jurisdiction of the Cheyney Court held at Winchester every Thursday, for the recovery of debts to any amount.

BRADLEY, a chapelry in the parish of FLADBURY, middle division of the hundred of OSWALDSLOW, county of WORCESTER, 6¾ miles (E.S.E.) from Droitwich, containing, with the hamlet of Stock, 208 inhabitants.

BRADLEY (GREAT), a parish in the hundred of RISBRIDGE, county of SUFFOLK, 6½ miles (N. by E.) from Haverhill, containing 487 inhabitants. The living is a rectory, in the archdeaconry of Sudbury, and diocese of Norwich, rated in the king's books at £17. 1. 5½., and in the patronage of the Archbishop of Dublin and others. The church is dedicated to St. Mary.

BRADLEY (LITTLE), a parish in the hundred of Risbridge, county of Suffolk, 6 miles (N. by E.) from Haverhill, containing 31 inhabitants. The living is a discharged rectory, in the archdeaconry of Sudbury, and diocese of Norwich, rated in the king's books at £5. 0. 10., and in the patronage of F. Dickens, Esq. The church is dedicated to All Saints.

BRADLEY (LOWER and UPPER), a township in the parish of Kildwick, eastern division of the wapentake of Staincliffe and Ewcross, West riding of the county of York, 2½ miles (S.S.E.) from Skipton, containing 506 inhabitants. There is a place of worship for Wesleyan Methodists.

BRADLEY (MAIDEN), a parish partly in the hundred of Norton-Ferris, county of Somerset, but chiefly in the hundred of Mere, county of Wilts, 5¾ miles (N. by W.) from Mere, containing 620 inhabitants. The living is a perpetual curacy, in the archdeaconry and diocese of Salisbury, endowed with £800 royal bounty, and £600 parliamentary grant, and in the patronage of the Dean and Canons of Christ Church, Oxford. The church is dedicated to All Saints. Fairs are held on April 25th and September 21st. An hospital for poor leprous women, under the superintendence of some Secular priests, was founded by Manasseh Biset, about the close of the reign of Stephen, or the beginning of that of Henry II. About the year 1190, Hubert, Bishop of Salisbury, changed the Seculars into a prior and canons of the Augustine order: the revenue, at the time of the dissolution, was £197. 18. 8.

BRADLEY in the MOORS, a parish in the western division of the hundred of Cuttlestone, county of Stafford, 3¾ miles (N.W.) from Penkridge, containing, with the liberties of Billington and Woollaston, part of Alstone, Brough, and Rule (the three last having been heretofore deemed extra-parochial), and part of Apeton, 723 inhabitants. The living is a perpetual curacy, in the archdeaconry of Stafford, and diocese of Lichfield and Coventry, endowed with £400 private benefaction, and £400 royal bounty, and in the patronage of Thomas Anson, Esq. The church is dedicated to All Saints. There is a place of worship for Wesleyan Methodists. The free grammar school is of early and obscure foundation: the endowment arises from land producing about £130 per annum, of which £107 are assigned as a salary to the master, and £23 to the mistress of a preparatory school on Dr. Bell's plan, each of whom has a house and a small plot of ground rent-free: these schools are free for all children within the parish, the boys being received into the grammar school so soon as they can read in the New Testament.

BRADLEY in the MOORS, a parish in the southern division of the hundred of Totmonslow, county of Stafford, 4 miles (E.S.E.) from Cheadle, containing 84 inhabitants. The living is a perpetual curacy, in the archdeaconry of Stafford, and diocese of Lichfield and Coventry, endowed with £800 royal bounty, and £200 parliamentary grant, and in the patronage of the Earl of Shrewsbury: the impropriate rectory is rated in the king's books at £17. 11. 8. The church is dedicated to All Saints.

BRADLEY (NORTH), a parish in the hundred of Whorwelsdown, county of Wilts, 2½ miles (S.) from Trowbridge, containing, with the chapelry of Southwick, 2615 inhabitants. The living is a discharged vicarage, in the archdeaconry of Wilts, and diocese of Salisbury, rated in the king's books at £11, endowed with £200 private benefaction, and £209 royal bounty, and in the patronage of the Warden and Fellows of Winchester College. The church is dedicated to St. Nicholas. An elegant chapel, called Christchurch, has been lately erected on Road hill, at one extremity of the parish, by the present vicar, Dr. Daubeny, Archdeacon of Sarum, aided by voluntary subscriptions and a grant from the commissioners for building and enlarging churches; it is endowed with £1200 private benefaction, £3400 parliamentary grant, and is in the patronage of the Vicar of North Bradley. The Incorporated Society for the enlargement of churches and chapels have also granted £1000 for the erection of seven hundred additional sittings, of which five hundred and fifty are free. There is a place of worship for Particular Baptists. The parish is bounded on the west by the river Frome, which here separates Wiltshire from Somersetshire, and is intersected by a small stream, called Bradley river.

BRADLEY (WEST), a parish in the hundred of Glaston-Twelve-Hides, county of Somerset, 4¾ miles (E.S.E.) from Glastonbury, containing 114 inhabitants. The living is a perpetual curacy, annexed to the vicarage of East Pennard, in the archdeaconry of Wells, and diocese of Bath and Wells.

BRADLEY-FIELD, a hamlet in the chapelry of Underbarrow, in that part of the parish of Kendal which is in Kendal ward, county of Westmorland, 4 miles (W.) from Kendal. The population is returned with Underbarrow.

BRADMORE, a parish in the northern division of the wapentake of Rushcliffe, county of Nottingham, 6¼ miles (S.) from Nottingham, containing 410 inhabitants. The living is a vicarage, annexed to that of Bunny, in the archdeaconry of Nottingham, and diocese of York. The church was destroyed by fire, and has not since been rebuilt: the steeple still remains.

Corporate Seal.

BRADNINCH, a parish (formerly a borough and market town), having separate jurisdiction, locally in the hundred of Hayridge, county of Devon, 8 miles (N.E.) from Exeter, and 170 (W.) from London, containing 1511 inhabitants. This place, anciently called *Braineis*, was of some importance in the time of the Saxons: in the reign of John it received many privileges, which were increased by Henry III., and in the reign of Edward III. it was annexed to the duchy of Cornwall. In this and in the preceding reign it sent representatives to parliament, from which, on account of its poverty, it was excused in the reign of Henry VII., on the payment of a fine of five marks. During the civil war in the reign of Charles I. it suffered considerably, from its proximity to Exeter, and was alternately in the possession of the royalists and the parliamentarians. In the year 1665, the town was almost destroyed by fire. It is pleasantly situated on an eminence, environed by hills on all sides except the south and south-west, and consists principally of neatly thatched and white-washed cottages. The woollen trade was formerly carried on, but little now remains; the principal branch of manufacture at present is that of paper, for which there are three mills, affording employment to sixty or seventy of the inhabitants. Iron-ore has been found in the neighbourhood, but works have not yet been established. The market has been discontinued; but small fairs are held on May 6th and October 2nd. The government, by charter of incorporation granted by Reginald, Earl of Cornwall, and renewed and enlarged by James I. and II., is vested in a mayor, recorder, twelve masters, and twenty-four inferior burgesses, assisted by a town-clerk, two serjeants at mace, a high constable, and four inferior constables. The mayor is chosen on St. Thomas' day, by the corporation at large, from among the twelve masters, who nominate two of their own body to that office; the mayor, the late mayor, and the recorder, are justices of the peace for the borough. The corporation hold a court of session quarterly: the mayor's court, for the recovery of debts under 40*s.*, is held monthly; and courts leet and baron for the duchy are also held here. The guildhall is a small building, possessing no claim to architectural notice. The living is a perpetual curacy, in the archdeaconry and diocese of Exeter, endowed with £300, and a messuage worth £400, private benefaction, £200 royal bounty, and £1300 parliamentary grant, and in the patronage of the Dean and Canons of Windsor. The church, dedicated to St. Disen, is an ancient structure, with a tower and other portions of later date; the chancel is separated from the nave by a richly carved oak screen. There is a place of worship for Particular Baptists. Bradninch gives the title of baron to the dukes of Cornwall, who are styled Barons of Braines.

BRADNOP, a township in that part of the parish of LEEK which is in the northern division of the hundred of TOTMONSLOW, county of STAFFORD, 2 miles (E. S. E.) from Leek, containing 489 inhabitants, many of whom are employed in the copper mines in the vicinity.

BRADON (NORTH and SOUTH), a parish in the hundred of ABDICK and BULSTONE, county of SOMERSET, 3¾ miles (N. by E.) from Ilminster, containing 32 inhabitants. The living is a sinecure rectory, in the archdeaconry of Taunton, and diocese of Bath and Wells, rated in the king's books at £5. 4. 4½., and in the patronage of the Earl of Egremont. The church, now desecrated, was dedicated to St. Mary Magdalene. Adjoining this parish was one called Goose, or Gouiz, Bradon, now depopulated, and the church and other buildings entirely destroyed.

BRADPOLE, a parish in the hundred of BEAMINSTER-FORUM and REDHONE, Bridport division of the county of DORSET, 1½ mile (N. N. E.) from Bridport, containing 926 inhabitants. The living is a discharged vicarage, in the archdeaconry of Dorset, and diocese of Bristol, rated in the king's books at £8. 13. 1½., and in the patronage of the Crown. The church is dedicated to the Holy Trinity. The inhabitants formerly interred their dead at Bridport, but, by a composition made in 1527, they were allowed to inter in their own churchyard, on paying annually a small acknowledgment to the rector of Bridport.

BRADSHAW, a chapelry in the parish of BOLTON, hundred of SALFORD, county palatine of LANCASTER, 3 miles (N.E.) from Bolton le Moors, containing 713 inhabitants. The living is a perpetual curacy, in the archdeaconry and diocese of Chester, endowed with £200 private benefaction, £800 royal bounty, and £400 parliamentary grant, and in the patronage of the Vicar of Bolton le Moors. A collection of books given by Mrs. Isherwood, for the use of the inhabitants, is kept in the chapel. Here are extensive bleaching-grounds. A school for the education of poor children has lately been erected. Bradshaw Hall was the property and residence of John Bradshaw, who presided at the trial of the unfortunate monarch, Charles I.

BRADSHAW-EDGE, a township in the parish of CHAPEL en le FRITH, hundred of HIGH PEAK, county of DERBY, 1½ mile (W.) from Chapel en le Frith, containing 1708 inhabitants.

BRADSTONE, a parish in the hundred of LIFTON, county of DEVON, 4¼ miles (S. E. by E.) from Launceston, containing 115 inhabitants. The living is a discharged rectory, in the archdeaconry of Totness, and diocese of Exeter, rated in the king's books at £6. 7. 2., and in the patronage of the Bishop of Exeter. The church is dedicated to St. Nun.

BRADSTONE, a hamlet in the parish, and upper division of the hundred, of BERKELEY, county of GLOUCESTER, 2¾ miles (E. N. E.) from Berkeley, containing 152 inhabitants.

BRADWELL, a parish in the hundred of NEWPORT, county of BUCKINGHAM, 3½ miles (E. by S.) from Stony-Stratford, containing 271 inhabitants. The living is a vicarage, in the archdeaconry of Buckingham, and diocese of Lincoln, rated in the king's books at £5. 11. 0½., and in the patronage of the Crown. The church is dedicated to St. Lawrence. The sum of £13. 13. is applied annually in relieving the poor, and toward instructing six or seven children.

BRADWELL, a township in the parish of SANDBACH, hundred of NORTHWICH, county palatine of CHESTER, 2 miles (N. by W.) from Sandbach, containing 282 inhabitants.

BRADWELL, a hamlet in the parish of HOPE, hundred of HIGH PEAK, county of DERBY, 4½ miles (N. N. E.) from Tideswell, containing 1130 inhabitants, who are chiefly engaged in the lead and calamine works in the vicinity, the manufacture of these articles being carried on to a considerable extent. There are places of worship for Wesleyan Methodists and Unitarians. Elias Marshall, in 1765, assigned a small portion of land, now producing £3 per annum, for which five children are educated gratuitously. About the year 1807, a huge natural excavation, called the Chrystallized Cavern, was discovered: it is approached by a narrow entrance, leading to a spacious area, the sides of which are lined with chrystallizations of singular beauty, and its separate parts are recognised by different names, such as the Grotto of Paradise, the Grotto of Calypso, Music Chamber, &c. Bradwell is in the honour of Tut bury, duchy of Lancaster, and within the jurisdiction of a court of pleas held at Tutbury every third Tuesday, for the recovery of debts under 40*s*. A place called the Castle, near the junction of the Noe and the Bradwell water, is supposed to have been the site of a Roman station, which comprised a square area, measuring three hundred and ten feet by two hundred and seventy: several Roman remains have been found.

BRADWELL, a parish in the hundred of MUTFORD and LOTHINGLAND, county of SUFFOLK, 3 miles (S.W.) from Great Yarmouth, containing 272 inhabitants. The living is a rectory, in the archdeaconry of Suffolk, and diocese of Norwich, rated in the king's books at £28. The King, by reason of lunacy, was patron in 1810. The church is dedicated to St. Nicholas. Breydon water is navigable on the northern side of this parish.

BRADWELL ABBEY, an extra-parochial liberty, in the hundred of NEWPORT, county of BUCKINGHAM, 3¾ miles (E.S.E.) from Stony-Stratford, containing 20 inhabitants. A priory of Black monks, dedicated to St. Mary, was founded, about the time of Stephen, by Meinfelin, Baron of Wolverton, originally as a cell to the monastery at Luffield, the revenue of which, in the 23rd of Henry VIII., was £53. 11. 2.: the site is now occupied by a farm-house.

BRADWELL juxta COGGESHALL, a parish in the hundred of WITHAM, county of ESSEX, 2 miles (W. by S.) from Great Coggeshall, containing 317 inhabitants. The living is a rectory, in the archdeaconry of Colchester, and diocese of London, rated in the king's books at £12, and in the patronage of the Rev. M. J. Brunwin. The church is dedicated to the Holy Trinity.

BRADWELL near the SEA, a parish in the hundred of DENGIE, county of ESSEX, 12 miles (E.) from Maldon, containing 904 inhabitants. The living is a rectory, in the archdeaconry of Essex, and diocese of London, rated in the king's books at £48, and in the patronage of the Rev. T. Schreiber. The church, dedicated to St. Thomas the Apostle, has a tower surmounted by a lofty spire. The parish lies at the mouth of the Blackwater river, which forms its northern boundary; the North sea is on the east, near which stand the remains of an ancient chapel, dedicated to St. Peter, now converted into a barn. Camden considers the Saxon city *Ithancestre* to have stood at or near this place, and identifies it also with the Roman station *Othona*, where the *Numerus Fortensium*, under a commander styled Count of the Saxon shore, was stationed, in the decline of the Roman empire. Upwards of £100, half of it arising from land given by Dr. Buckeridge, is applied annually toward the support of schools in this parish.

BRADWOOD-WIDGER, a parish in the hundred of LIFTON, county of DEVON, 6 miles (N.E.) from Launceston, containing 748 inhabitants. The living is a vicarage, in the archdeaconry of Totness, and diocese of Exeter, rated in the king's books at £8. 3. 4., and in the patronage of the Dean and Chapter of Bristol. There is a place of worship for Wesleyan Methodists.

BRADWORTHY, a parish in the hundred of BLACK TORRINGTON, county of DEVON, 7½ miles (N. by W.) from Holsworthy, containing 978 inhabitants. The living is a vicarage, with the perpetual curacy of Pancrassweek annexed, in the archdeaconry of Totness, and diocese of Exeter, rated in the king's books at £25. 5. 5., and in the patronage of the Crown. The church is dedicated to St. John the Baptist. There is a place of worship for Wesleyan Methodists.

BRAFFERTON, a township in the parish of GREAT AYCLIFFE, south-eastern division of DARLINGTON ward, county palatine of DURHAM, 4½ miles (N. by E.) from Darlington, containing 263 inhabitants. The Methodists erected a meeting-house about 1814; and a schoolroom was built by subscription, in 1823, which has been endowed with £12 per annum by the Diocesan Society.

BRAFFERTON, a parish comprising the township of Thornton-Bridge in the wapentake of HALLIKELD, the township of Brafferton in the wapentake of BULMER, and the township of Helperby, locally in the same wapentake (but included within the liberty of ST. PETER of YORK, in the East riding), North riding of the county of YORK, and containing 832 inhabitants, of which number, 178 are in the township of Brafferton, 4 miles (N.E.) from Boroughbridge. The living is a discharged vicarage, in the archdeaconry of Cleveland, and diocese of York, rated in the king's books at £9. 15. 6., endowed with £200 royal bounty, and in the patronage of the Crown. The church is dedicated to St. Peter. The village of Brafferton lies on one side of the road, and that of Helperby on the other; a school on Dr. Bell's plan is connected with both, and is supported chiefly by subscription.

BRAFIELD on the GREEN, a parish in the hundred of WYMERSLEY, county of NORTHAMPTON, 5 miles (E. by S.) from Northampton, containing 424 inhabitants. The living is a discharged vicarage, annexed to that of Little Houghton, in the archdeaconry of Northampton, and diocese of Peterborough, rated in the king's books at £6. 13. 6¼. The church is dedicated to St. Lawrence.

BRAILS, a parish in the Brails division of the hundred of KINGTON, county of WARWICK, 4 miles (E. by S.) from Shipston upon Stour, containing 1233 inhabitants. The living is a vicarage, in the archdeaconry and diocese of Worcester, rated in the king's books at £25, and in the patronage of J. Bailey, Esq. The church is dedicated to St. George. Here is a manufactory for livery shag, plush, &c. A free school was endowed, in the 23rd of Elizabeth, with an annuity of £8. 1. 8., which was augmented by Barnabas Bishopp and others, in the 18th of James I.; the annual income is £64. 8. 2., for which the school is unlimitedly free for poor children: the school-room was rebuilt in 1819.

BRAILSFORD, a parish in the hundred of APPLETREE, county of DERBY, 7¼ miles (N.W. by W.) from Derby, containing 724 inhabitants. The living is a rectory, in the archdeaconry of Derby, and diocese of Lichfield and Coventry, rated in the king's books at £9. 19. 2., and in the patronage of Earl Ferrers. The church is dedicated to All Saints. There is a place of worship for Wesleyan Methodists.

BRAINTFIELD, a parish in the hundred of CASHIO, or liberty of ST. ALBANS, though locally in the hundred of Hertford, county of HERTFORD, 3½ miles (N.W.) from Hertford, containing 232 inhabitants. The living is a rectory, in the archdeaconry of Huntingdon, and diocese of Lincoln, rated in the king's books at £11. 6. 8., and in the patronage of the Rev. E. Bouchier. The church is dedicated to St. Andrew. According to Matthew Paris, this was the first ecclesiastical preferment held by the celebrated Thomas à Becket; a small pond near the parsonage-house still bears his name.

BRAINTREE, a market town and parish in the hundred of HINCKFORD, county of Essex, 11 miles (N. by E.) from Chelmsford, and 40 (N.E.) from London, containing 2983 inhabitants. This place is described in Domesday-book under "Raines," including also the village of "Raine," to which it was at that time a hamlet, and from which it was separated in the reign of Henry II. Owing to its situation as a great thoroughfare on the road leading from London into the counties of Suffolk and Norfolk, it is supposed to have derived considerable benefit from the numerous pilgrims who passed through it, on their way to the shrines of St. Edmund, at Bury, and Our Lady of Walsingham: the population having consequently increased, it was made a market town in the reign of John. The bishops of London formerly had a palace here, but there are no remains of it. In the early part of the reign of Elizabeth, the Flemings, fleeing from the persecution of the Duke of Alva, settled at Braintree, and introduced the manufacture of woollen cloth. The town, pleasantly situated on an eminence, consists of several streets irregularly formed and inconveniently narrow; the houses are in general ancient, and many of them are built of wood. The woollen trade has given place to the manufacture of silk, which is carried on extensively. The market is on Wednesday: the fairs are on May 7th and October 2nd, each for three days. The government was formerly vested in twenty-four of the principal parishioners, who in 1584 were styled "governors of the town, and town magistrates;" but this body has been dissolved, and the county magistrates now hold a petty session here for the division every Wednesday. The living is a discharged vicarage, in the archdeaconry of Middlesex, and diocese of London, rated in the king's books at £12. 13. 4., endowed with £200 private benefaction, and £200 royal bounty, and in the patronage of Mr. and Mrs. Olmins. The church, dedicated to St. Michael, is a spacious structure, erected on the summit of a mount, apparently the site of an ancient camp; it is principally in the later style of English architecture, with a tower in the early English style, surmounted by a shingled spire of later date: it was enlarged in the reign of Henry VIII., the expense having been defrayed out of the proceeds of three plays performed in the church, of which some curious particulars are recorded in the parish register. There are places of worship for Baptists, the Society of Friends, Independents, and Methodists. A school was founded in 1702, by James Coker, Esq., a native of the town, who endowed it with a farm at Stoke, near Nayland, producing £10 per annum, for the instruction of ten boys. John Ray, a writer on natural history, was educated in this school. In the reign of Charles I., Henry Smith, Esq., alderman of London, who is said, from the habit of going about like a beggar accompanied by his dog, to have obtained the appellation of "Dog Smith," bequeathed £2800 for the relief of the poor of Braintree, and the adjoining parishes of Henham and Toxling. In conformity to his direction, that sum was invested in the purchase of an estate at Tolleshunt D'Arcy, in this county, producing a rental of £350 per annum. About half a mile from the town are the ruins of a very ancient church, formerly the parish church, consisting of the east wall of the chancel, in which are three very narrow lancet-shaped windows; and in the town and neighbourhood Roman coins and sepulchral urns have been frequently discovered.

BRAISEWORTH, a parish in the hundred of HARTISMERE, county of SUFFOLK, 1¾ mile (S. S. W.) from Eye, containing 170 inhabitants. The living is a discharged rectory, in the archdeaconry of Sudbury, and diocese of Norwich, rated in the king's books at £4. 8. 1½., and in the patronage of Earl Cornwallis.

BRAITHWAITE, a township in that part of the parish of CROSTHWAITE which is in ALLERDALE ward above Darwent, county of CUMBERLAND, 2¾ miles (W. by N.) from Keswick, containing 214 inhabitants. The village lies at the foot of Winlatter-Fell, the summit of which, gained by a steep ascent of two miles and a quarter, embraces prospects of a most sublime character. A woollen manufactory is carried on; and lead mines have been worked in the township.

BRAITHWAITE, a detached hamlet in that part of the parish of ST. MARY, CARLISLE, which is in LEATH ward, county of CUMBERLAND, 6¾ miles (E. N. E.) from Hesket-Newmarket. The population is returned with the hamlet of Middlesceugh.

BRAITHWELL, a parish in the southern division of the wapentake of STRAFFORTH and TICKHILL, West riding of the county of YORK, comprising the townships of Braithwell and Bramley, and containing 739 inhabitants, of which number, 438 are in the township of Braithwell, 7 miles (S. W. by S.) from Doncaster. The living is a discharged vicarage, in the archdeaconry and diocese of York, rated in the king's books at £7. 7. 6., and in the patronage of the Crown. The church is dedicated to St. James. There is a place of worship for Wesleyan Methodists. The school owes its foundation to Mr. John Bosvile: in 1818, the Rev. Thomas Bosvile gave £250 for the instruction of ten children: the income is £10. 10. per annum, and there are fourteen children on the foundation. Twenty-two human skeletons, supposed to be those of Roman soldiers who fell in battle with the *Brigantes*, and an urn, that probably contained the ashes of a Roman general, were discovered some years ago, in a field here, in which a variety of Roman coins has also been found at different periods.

BRAKES, a township in the parish of LEINTWARDINE, hundred of WIGMORE, county of HEREFORD, containing 125 inhabitants.

BRAMBER, a borough (formerly a market town) in the hundred of STEYNING, rape of BRAMBER, county of SUSSEX, ½ a mile (E. S. E.) from Steyning, and 50 miles (S. by W.) from London, containing 98 inhabitants. This place was formerly noted for a castle built by the descendants of William de Braiose, upon whom it was bestowed by William the Conqueror. In the reign of Edward III., this castle was garrisoned by John de Mowbray, Duke of Norfolk, for the protection of the town and shore from the expected attack of the French, who were hovering off the coast. The town is situated on the river Adar, which is navigable for small vessels; and, though formerly of considerable extent and importance, consists at present only of a few miserable hovels: there is neither trade, market, nor fair. It is a borough by prescription, and returned members to parliament in the 23rd of Edward I.; after that time it frequently omitted, and was occasionally represented in conjunction with Steyning till the 7th of Edward IV., since which it has regularly continued to return two representatives. The right of election is vested in the occupiers of burgage tenements paying scot and lot, in number about twenty: the constable is the returning officer. The living is a discharged rectory, with that of Buttolphs united, in the archdeaconry and diocese of Chichester, rated in the king's books at £10. 6. 8., and in the patronage of the President and Fellows of Magdalene College, Oxford. The church, dedicated to St. Nicholas, is a small ancient edifice, much mutilated, but containing some fine portions in the Norman style of architecture, with a low square tower. The ancient and once formidable castle occupied a quadrilateral area, six hundred feet in length, and three hundred in breadth, surrounded by a wide and deep moat: the remains consist principally of part of the entrance gateway, some detached portions of the walls to the north-west, the mount whereon stood the keep, and a noble window in the range that contained the state apartments: the prevailing style of architecture is the Norman.

BRAMCOTE, a chapelry in the parish of ATTENBOROUGH, southern division of the wapentake of BROXTOW, county of NOTTINGHAM, 4 miles (W. S. W.) from Nottingham, containing 441 inhabitants. The living is a perpetual curacy, annexed to the vicarage of Attenborough, in the archdeaconry of Nottingham, and diocese of York. The Nottingham canal passes through the chapelry. Coal is obtained on the moor.

BRAMCOTT, a hamlet in the parish of BULKINGTON, Kirby division of the hundred of KNIGHTLOW, county of WARWICK, 4 miles (S. E.) from Nuneaton, containing 35 inhabitants.

BRAMDEAN, a parish in the hundred of BISHOP'S SUTTON, Alton (North) division of the county of SOUTHAMPTON, 4 miles (S. by E.) from New Alresford, containing 232 inhabitants. The living is a rectory, in the archdeaconry and diocese of Winchester, rated in the king's books at £8. 14. 9½., and in the patronage of the Bishop of Winchester. The church is dedicated to St. Simon and St. Jude. Bramdean is within the jurisdiction of the Cheyney Court held at Winchester every Thursday, for the recovery of debts to any amount.

BRAMERTON, a parish in the hundred of HENSTEAD, county of NORFOLK, 5½ miles (S. E. by E.) from Norwich, containing 184 inhabitants. The living is a discharged rectory, in the archdeaconry of Norfolk, and diocese of Norwich, rated in the king's books at £6, and in the patronage of Robert Fellowes, Esq. The church is dedicated to St. Peter. The Rev. William Berney, in 1715, bequeathed £100 for the instruction of children, or the relief of the poor.

BRAMFIELD, a parish in the hundred of BLYTHING, county of SUFFOLK, 2¼ miles (S.S.E.) from Halesworth, containing 630 inhabitants. The living is a discharged vicarage, in the archdeaconry of Suffolk, and diocese of Norwich, rated in the king's books at £6. 7. 6., and in the patronage of the Crown. The church is dedicated to St. Andrew. Two sums, each of £3. 10. per annum, are applied for the instruction of twelve poor children; one was given by Eliz. Archer, in 1716, and the other in 1704, by Thomas Neale, whose widow, in 1725, assigned an almshouse for the reception of four poor persons.

BRAMFORD, a parish in the hundred of BOSMERE and CLAYDON, county of SUFFOLK, 3¼ miles (W. N. W.) from Ipswich, containing 855 inhabitants. The living is a vicarage, with the perpetual curacy of Burstall united, in the archdeaconry of Norfolk, and diocese of Norwich, rated in the king's books at £13. 3. 9., endowed with £800 parliamentary grant, and in the patronage of the Dean and Chapter of Canterbury. The church is dedicated to St. Mary. The Stow-Market and Ipswich canal crosses this parish.

BRAMHALL, a township in the parish of STOCKPORT, hundred of MACCLESFIELD, county palatine of CHESTER, 3 miles (S. by W.) from Stockport, containing 1359 inhabitants. The lord of this manor, in conjunction with the lords of the manors of Bredbury, Brinnington, and Norbury, has, from time immemorial, appointed the churchwardens of the parish. The manorial mansion is a curious ancient edifice of timber and brick, plaistered over, standing on elevated ground: at the south-east angle is the domestic chapel, apparently of the time of Richard III., having a flat panelled roof, and a considerable quantity of painted glass in the windows, and containing several deceased members of the family of Davenport.

BRAMHAM, a parish partly in the liberty of ST. PETER of YORK, East riding, but chiefly in the upper division of the wapentake of BARKSTONE-ASH, West riding, of the county of YORK, comprising the townships of Bramham and Clifford, and containing 1987 inhabitants, of which number, 970 are in the township of Bramham, 4¼ miles (S.S.E.) from Wetherby. The living is a discharged vicarage, in the peculiar jurisdiction of the Dean and Chapter of York, rated in the king's books at £6. 7. 6., endowed with £400 private benefaction, £400 royal bounty, and £600 parliamentary grant, and in the patronage of the Dean and Canons of Christ Church, Oxford. The church is dedicated to All Saints. There is a place of worship for Wesleyan Methodists. A battle was fought here, in 1408, between Sir Thomas Rokeby, sheriff of Yorkshire, and the earl of Northumberland, in which the earl was defeated and slain, and by which the possession of the crown was secured to Henry IV. There are visible remains of the ancient Watling-street on Bramham moor, a mile north of the village: from the middle of this moor is an extensive prospect of a well-cultivated district, which abounds also with freestone, limestone, and coal. A fund of £11 per annum, arising from land purchased by various charitable bequests, is appropriated for the instruction of six children, four from the township of Bramham, and two from that of Clifford.

BRAMHOPE, a township in that part of the parish of OTLEY which is in the upper division of the wapentake of SKYRACK, West riding of the county of YORK, 3¾ miles (E.S.E.) from Otley, containing 366 inhabitants. The school is endowed with an allotment of land producing £9 per annum, awarded to it on the enclosure of the common, for which the master instructs the children of the inhabitants on easier terms.

BRAMLEY, a parish in the hundred of BASINGSTOKE, Basingstoke division of the county of SOUTHAMPTON, 4½ miles (N. by E.) from Basingstoke, containing 455 inhabitants. The living is a discharged vicarage, in the archdeaconry and diocese of Winchester, rated in the king's books at £7. 3. 6½., and in the patronage of the Provost and Fellows of Queen's College, Oxford. The church is dedicated to All Saints.

BRAMLEY, a chapelry in the parish of SHALFORD, first division of the hundred of BLACKHEATH, county of SURREY, 3 miles (S. by E.) from Guildford, containing 707 inhabitants. The chapel, dedicated to the Holy Trinity, is partly in the early style of English architecture, with a chapel on the south side. The Arun and Wey Junction canal crosses this chapelry.

BRAMLEY, a chapelry in the parish of ST. PETER, within the liberty of the town of LEEDS, West riding of the county of YORK, 4 miles (W.N.W.) from Leeds, containing 4921 inhabitants. The living is a perpetual curacy, in the archdeaconry and diocese of York, endowed with £10 per annum private benefaction, and £200 royal bounty, and in the patronage of the Vicar of Leeds. There are places of worship for Particular Baptists and Wesleyan Methodists. Many of the inhabitants are engaged in the clothing business; and there are spacious and celebrated stone and slate quarries within the chapelry. Land producing an average rental of £21 was assigned, on the enclosure of the common, for the education of sixteen boys in the school at Leeds: having become a subject of dispute in Chancery, the income has, for the last few years, been applied in payment of the costs, but will soon be made available to the benefit of the institution. Another allotment was set apart, producing £6 per annum, for the instruction of six female children.

BRAMLEY, a township in the parish of BRAITHWELL, southern division of the wapentake of STRAFFORTH and TICKHILL, West riding of the county of YORK, 4½ miles (E.) from Rotherham, containing 301 inhabitants. There is a place of worship for Wesleyan Methodists.

BRAMPFORD-SPEKE, a parish in the hundred of WONFORD, county of DEVON, 4½ miles (N. by E.) from Exeter, containing 303 inhabitants. The living is a vicarage, in the archdeaconry and diocese of Exeter, rated in the king's books at £10, and in the patronage of the Crown. The church is dedicated to St. Peter. The river Exe forms the western boundary of this parish.

BRAMPTON, a parish in ESKDALE ward, county of CUMBERLAND, comprising the market town of Brampton, and the townships of Easby and Naworth, and containing 2921 inhabitants, of which number, 2448 are in the town of Brampton, 9½ miles (N.E. by E.) from Carlisle, and 305 (N. by W.) from London. According to Camden, this was the Roman station *Bremetenracum*, which some modern writers have fixed at Old Penrith. The town sustained extensive damage during the wars of Edward II., of which, as well as of its earlier importance, it still exhibits evident marks. It is situated between the rivers Irthing and Gelt, about one mile south of the former, and two and a half from the point where they unite, and about one mile south of the Picts' wall, in a deep narrow vale embosomed in hills. It consists of two principal streets irregularly built: the houses, excepting a few of modern erection, are generally of mean appearance; the inhabitants are well supplied with water. The only branch of manufacture is that of gingham, in which nearly seven hundred individuals are employed: there are two public breweries. The railway between Newcastle and Carlisle passes a mile and a half to the south; and the late Earl of Carlisle extended a railway from the collieries at Tindal Fell to Brampton, by which coal and lime are brought hither in abundance; in this traffic about one thousand persons are employed. The market is on Wednesday, and is well supplied with corn, admitted toll-free: fairs are held annually on the 20th of April, the second Wednesday after Whitsuntide, the second Wednesday in September, and the 23rd of October, for horned cattle, horses, and sheep. The county magistrates hold a petty session every alternate Wednesday; and courts leet and baron for the barony of Gilsland are held, at Easter and Michaelmas, in the town-hall, a neat octagonal edifice, with a cupola, erected by the Earl of Carlisle, in 1817, on the site of the former hall, in the market-place, the lower part being formed into a piazza, under which butter, eggs, poultry, &c., are sold on the market-day. The living is a vicarage, in the archdeaconry and diocese of Carlisle, rated in the king's books at £8, and in the patronage of the Earl of Carlisle. The present church was built, in 1788, out of the chapel and four tenements of an almshouse, and with the materials of the old church, dedicated to St. Martin, the chancel of which is still remaining on the southern bank of the river Irthing, about a mile west of the town, being only used for the performance of the funeral service for those who are interred in the cemetery: the new church was greatly enlarged in 1827, at an expense of £1800, on which occasion the Rev. Mr. Ramshay, vicar, presented the parish with six bells and an organ, and now pays the salaries of the organist and the ringers: he also, on every alternate Sunday, gives one shilling to each poor person attending divine service. There are places of worship for Independents, Primitive and Wesleyan Methodists, and Presbyterians. A National school, built by the Earl of Carlisle, in 1817, is supported by voluntary contributions: an infant school was established in 1825. Edward, Earl of Carlisle, built an hospital for six aged men and as many women, in 1688, to each of whom he assigned £5 per annum, besides fuel, and, by will dated in 1691, bequeathed £500 to purchase lands for its endowment; but this benevolent purpose was never carried into effect. The hospital was taken down to make room for the enlargement of the church, at the east end of which a room has been built, and is used for a grammar school; the master receives an annuity of £5 from the present earl.

Two miles east of Brampton, and about a mile south of the river Irthing, commanding a fine view of the vale of St. Mary, through which that river flows, is Naworth castle, the ancient baronial seat of the lords of Gilsland, the earliest notice of which occurs in the 18th of Richard II. The walls, including two large square towers in the front, besides others at the angles, enclose a quadrangular area, each side being forty paces in length: the entrance is through an embrasured gateway. The hall, seventy or eighty feet in length, and of proportionate width and height, displays all the magnificence of feudal grandeur, and is embellished with portraits, brought from Kirk-Oswald castle, of the kings of England prior to the union of the houses of York and Lancaster. The chapel, to which there is a descent of several steps, is very ancient, and is decorated with paintings of the patriarchs and kings of Israel and Judah; the pulpit and stalls are of carved oak. The apartments of Lord William Howard, the terror of the moss-troopers in the reign of Elizabeth, are still preserved, with their ancient furniture: they consist of a bed-room, an oratory, and a library containing several books and manuscripts, some of them bearing his autograph, and an account of the foundation of Glastonbury abbey by Joseph of Arimathea: the approach to these apartments is by a very narrow winding staircase, secured by doors of amazing strength. The dungeons of the castle, which were the prison for the barony, are still in their original state: they consist of three cells underground, and one above, and the strong iron rings to which the prisoners were chained are still remaining. To the north-east of Brampton is a high conical hill, called the Mote, from the summit of which, now planted with trees, a most extensive view of the surrounding country is obtained: at some distance from the base there are vestiges of an intrenchment, and a breastwork of considerable strength. It is supposed to have been a Danish encampment, or probably a place of security for the removal of property in case of invasion, as, from the steepness of the acclivity, a small number of men on the summit might overpower an assailing multitude. At present it forms a link in the chain of telegraphic communication between the northern parts of England and the southern parts of Scotland. To the south of the town is a fine quarry of freestone, where the Romans obtained part of the materials for building the great wall, vestiges of which are still visible; and on the rocky banks of the Gelt are some Roman inscriptions, of the time of Agricola, one of whose legions was stationed near Brampton.

BRAMPTON, a parish in the hundred of SCARSDALE, county of DERBY, 3½ miles (W. by N.) from Chesterfield, containing 2632 inhabitants. The living is a perpetual curacy, in the archdeaconry of Derby, and diocese of Lichfield and Coventry, endowed with £200 private benefaction, and £200 royal bounty, and in the patronage of the Dean of Lincoln. The church is dedicated to St. Peter. A new church, or chapel, is about to be erected in the eastern part of the parish, by subscription, and a grant from the parliamentary commissioners. There are places of worship for Primitive and Wesleyan Methodists. The parish abounds with coal and iron-stone, and the casting of iron is carried on to a limited extent: the manufactory of pottery-ware is conducted on a larger scale. There is a canal from Chesterfield to Gainsborough. A National school, used also as a Sunday school, has been established, for which the erection of a new school-room is contemplated: it is also intended to form a similar institution in connexion with the new church.

BRAMPTON, a parish in the hundred of LEIGHTONSTONE, county of HUNTINGDON, 2¼ miles (W. by S.) from Huntingdon, containing 1064 inhabitants. The living is a discharged vicarage, in the archdeaconry of Huntingdon, and diocese of Lincoln, rated in the king's qooks at £8. 1. 4., endowed with £200 private benefaction, and £200 royal bounty, and in the patronage of the Prebendary of Brampton in the Cathedral Church of Lincoln. The church, dedicated to St. Mary, is partly in the decorated, and partly in the later, style of English architecture, with a fine south porch, enriched with elegant tracery. Samuel Pepys, Esq., secretary to the Admiralty in the reigns of Charles II. and James II., and elected President of the Royal Society in 1684, was born here; his Memoirs, comprising his diary from 1659 to 1669, with a biographical sketch by Lord Braybrooke, were published, in two vols. 4to., in 1825.

BRAMPTON, a chapelry in that part of the parish of TORKSEY which is in the wapentake of WELL, parts of LINDSEY, county of LINCOLN, 7½ miles (S. S. E.) from Gainsborough, containing 98 inhabitants.

BRAMPTON, a parish in the southern division of the hundred of ERPINGHAM, county of NORFOLK, 2¾ miles (S. E.) from Aylsham, containing 145 inhabitants. The living is a discharged rectory, in the archdeaconry and diocese of Norwich, rated in the king's books at £5, and in the patronage of R. Marsham, Esq. The church, dedicated to St. Peter, has a tower circular at the base and octangular above. From several urns containing calcined bones, this is conjectured to have been the place of interment of the Roman station at Burgh, on the opposite side of the river Bure, which is here navigable.

BRAMPTON, a parish in the hundred of CORBY, county of NORTHAMPTON, 3¾ miles (E. by N.) from Market-Harborough, containing 113 inhabitants. The living is a rectory, in the archdeaconry of Northampton, and diocese of Peterborough, rated in the king's books at £21. 6. 8., and in the patronage of the President and Fellows of Corpus Christi College, Oxford. The church is dedicated to St. Mary.

BRAMPTON, a parish in the hundred of BLYTHING, county of SUFFOLK, 4½ miles (N. E.) from Halesworth, containing 255 inhabitants. The living is a discharged rectory, in the archdeaconry of Suffolk, and diocese of Norwich, rated in the king's books at £20, and in the patronage of the Rev. N. T. O. Leman. The church is dedicated to St. Peter.

BRAMPTON, a township in the parish of LONG MARTON, EAST ward, county of WESTMORLAND, 2¼ miles (N.) from Appleby. The population is returned with the parish.

BRAMPTON (CHAPEL), a parish in the hundred of NOBOTTLE-GROVE, county of NORTHAMPTON, 4½ miles (N. N. W.) from Northampton, containing 213 inhabitants. The church has long been demolished.

BRAMPTON (CHURCH), a parish in the hundred of NOBOTTLE-GROVE, county of NORTHAMPTON, 4½ miles (N. W. by N.) from Northampton, containing 179 inhabitants. The living is a rectory, in the archdeaconry of Northampton, and diocese of Peterborough, rated in the king's books at £25. 19. 7., and in the patronage of Earl Spencer. The church, dedicated to St. Botolph, is partly in the decorated, and partly in the later, style of English architecture, and contains a large circular font: the stairs of the rood-loft and some ancient benches remain.

BRAMPTON (LITTLE), a joint township with Rod and Nash, in that part of the parish of PRESTEIGNE which is in the hundred of WIGMORE, county of HEREFORD. The population is returned with Rod.

BRAMPTON en le MORTHEN, a township in the parish of TREETON, southern division of the wapentake of STRAFFORTH and TICKHILL, West riding of the county of YORK, 5¼ miles (S. E. by E.) from Rotherham, containing 136 inhabitants.

BRAMPTON-ABBOTS, a parish in the hundred of GREYTREE, county of HEREFORD, 1 mile (N.) from Ross, containing 158 inhabitants. The living is a rectory, in the archdeaconry and diocese of Hereford, rated in the king's books at £12, and in the patronage of the

Bishop of Hereford. The church is dedicated to St. Michael. Courts leet and baron are held here annually. The river Wye forms a boundary of this parish.

BRAMPTON-BIERLOW, a chapelry in the parish of WATH upon DEARNE, northern division of the wapentake of STRAFFORTH and TICKHILL, West riding of the county of YORK, 6 miles (N. by W.) from Rotherham, containing 1263 inhabitants. It stands on the line of the Dove and Dearne canal, in a district containing several iron-foundries, one of which, called Milton Furnace, is on a very extensive scale. George Ellis, in 1711, bequeathed the greater part of his estate for pious and charitable uses, and the trustees acting under the will erected, in 1818, a spacious building, at an expense of £865, for the instruction of boys and girls on Dr. Bell's plan: the master is allowed a salary of £63 per annum, and the mistress one of £15; and the sum of £12 is also paid annually to the master, from a bequest of £300 made by John Higson, in 1814. The remainder of Ellis' charity is applied in relieving the poor, and in apprentice fees.

BRAMPTON-BRYAN, a parish comprising the lordship of Stanage in the hundred of KNIGHTON, county of RADNOR (WALES), and the townships of Brampton-Bryan and Boresford with Pedwardine, in the hundred of WIGMORE, county of HEREFORD, and containing 341 inhabitants, of which number, 101 are in the township of Brampton-Bryan, 5¼ miles (E.) from Knighton. The living is a rectory, in the archdeaconry of Salop, and diocese of Hereford, rated in the king's books at £5. 11. 0½., and in the patronage of the Earl of Oxford. The church, dedicated to St. Barnabas, sustained considerable damage in the parliamentary war, during one of the sieges of the castle, which was eventually burnt by the royalists, and now lies in ruins, consisting chiefly of an arched gateway flanked by two circular towers, and fragments of the outer walls. About a mile from the church is Cornwall Knoll, on the summit of which are vestiges of a camp anciently occupied by the brave Caractacus, now overgrown with oak trees. Fairs for horned cattle, sheep, &c., are held on May 6th and August 5th. A school is endowed with property given by the Hon. Edward Harley, in 1720.

BRAMSHALL, a parish in the southern division of the hundred of TOTMONSLOW, county of STAFFORD, 2 miles (W. by S.) from Uttoxeter, containing 189 inhabitants. The living is a discharged rectory, in the archdeaconry of Stafford, and diocese of Lichfield and Coventry, rated in the king's books at £4. 3. 9., and in the patronage of Lord Willoughby de Broke. The church is dedicated to St. Lawrence. A Sunday school is supported by subscription.

BRAMSHAW, a parish partly in the hundred of CAWDEN and CADWORTH, county of WILTS, but chiefly in the northern division of the hundred of NEW FOREST, New Forest (East) division of the county of SOUTHAMPTON, 6¼ miles (N. N. W.) from Lyndhurst, containing 726 inhabitants. The living is a vicarage, in the peculiar jurisdiction and patronage of the Dean and Chapter of Salisbury, endowed with £200 private benefaction, £200 royal bounty, and £1200 parliamentary grant. The church is dedicated to St. Peter.

BRAMSHILL (GREAT), a tything in the parish of EVERSLEY, hundred of HOLDSHOTT, Basingstoke division of the county of SOUTHAMPTON, 1¾ mile (N.W. by N.) from Hartford Bridge, containing 187 inhabitants.

BRAMSHILL (LITTLE), a tything in the parish of EVERSLEY, hundred of HOLDSHOTT, Basingstoke division of the county of SOUTHAMPTON, containing 10 inhabitants.

BRAMSHOTT, a parish in the hundred of ALTON, Alton (North) division of the county of SOUTHAMPTON, 4½ miles (W. by N.) from Haslemere, containing, with the hamlet of Liphook, 1006 inhabitants. The living is a rectory, in the archdeaconry and diocese of Winchester, rated in the king's books at £18. 9. 2., and in the patronage of the Provost and Fellows of Queen's College, Oxford. The church, dedicated to St. Mary, is a small cruciform edifice, principally in the early English style, with a low tower surmounted by a spire. At Liphook fairs for the sale of live stock are held, on the first Wednesday in March and June 11th.

BRAMWITH (KIRK), a parish in the upper division of the wapentake of OSGOLDCROSS, West riding of the county of YORK, 4¾ miles (W. by S.) from Thorne, containing 252 inhabitants. The living is a rectory, in the archdeaconry and diocese of York, rated in the king's books at £12. 18. 4., and in the patronage of the King, as Duke of Lancaster. The church is dedicated to St. Mary.

BRANCASTER, a parish in the hundred of SMITHDON, county of NORFOLK, 4½ miles (W. N. W.) from Burnham-Westgate, containing 770 inhabitants. The living is a rectory, in the archdeaconry of Norfolk, and diocese of Norwich, rated in the king's books at £24, and in the patronage of the Duke of Beaufort. The church is dedicated to St. Mary. Here was the Roman station *Brannodunum*, at which an eminent commander, styled Count, or Earl, of the Saxon shore, presided over a troop of Dalmatian cavalry, for the defence of the coast against the Saxon invaders. The castle and station occupied about eight acres of ground, a little westward from the village, where numerous coins, vessels, and other relics have been found. A considerable portion of the materials was removed on the erection of a very extensive malt-house, called pre-eminently the great malt-house, three hundred and twelve feet in length, and thirty-one in breadth, adjoining a quay, or staith for ships, and all appearance of the station has been obliterated by the ploughshare. A free school and two almshouses were built by Robert Smith, about the close of the sixteenth century, and endowed with land by his sister: twenty-five boys are instructed, thirteen from this parish, and the rest, in equal numbers, from Thornham, Titchwell, and Burnham-Deepdale: the almshouses now accommodate four poor widows.

BRANCEPETH, a parish in the north-western division of DARLINGTON ward, county palatine of DURHAM, comprising the townships of Brancepeth, Brandon with Byshottles, Crook with Billy-Row, Hedley-Hope, Hemlington-Row, Stockley, and Willington, and containing 1905 inhabitants, of which number, 539 are in the township of Brancepeth, 4¼ miles (S. W.) from Durham. The living is a rectory, in the archdeaconry and diocese of Durham, rated in the king's books at £60. 10. 5., and in the patronage of R. E. D. Shaftoe, Esq. The church, dedicated to St. Brandon, is a fine cruciform edifice, highly decorated within: the chancel is stalled and wainscoted with oak carved in tabernacle work, and has an ornamented ceiling: there are several monuments to the memory of deceased members of the family of Nevill, the ancient noble owners of Brancepeth castle, which stands a little to the south-west of the village: the old castle was almost wholly pulled down by the late Matthew Russel, Esq., who erected the present magnificent edifice on its site. Brancepeth is supposed to be a corruption of *Brawn's path*, from the number of wild boars that roamed throughout the district, for the purpose of chasing which, Richard III., when Duke of Gloucester (who was maternally descended from the Nevill family), frequently repaired hither. There are some coal-works and stone-quarries in the parish, also medicinal springs of a vitriolic and sulphureous kind.

BRANDESTON, a parish in the hundred of LOES, county of SUFFOLK, 4 miles (S. W.) from Framlingham, containing 458 inhabitants. The living is a discharged rectory, in the archdeaconry of Suffolk, and diocese of Norwich, rated in the king's books at £8. 13. 4., and in the patronage of William Field, Esq. The church is dedicated to All Saints.

BRANDISTONE, a parish in the hundred of EYNSFORD, county of NORFOLK, 2¾ miles (E. S. E.) from Reepham, containing 91 inhabitants. The living is a discharged rectory, in the archdeaconry and diocese of Norwich, rated in the king's books at £7. 12. 8½., and in the patronage of the President and Fellows of Magdalene College, Oxford. The church is dedicated to St. Nicholas.

BRANDON, a joint township with Byshottles, in the parish of BRANCEPETH, north-western division of DARLINGTON ward, county palatine of DURHAM, 3¼ miles (W. S. W.) from Durham, containing, with Byshottles, 609 inhabitants. The village is occasionally called East Brandon, to distinguish it from a farm-hold within the township, bearing the name of West Brandon. Here is a paper-manufactory. On the summit of Brandon hill is an oblong mount, or tumulus, supposed to have been either the site of a beacon, or the burial-place of some departed hero.

BRANDON, a township in the parish of EGLINGHAM, northern division of COQUETDALE ward, county of NORTHUMBERLAND, 8½ miles (S. S. E.) from Wooler, containing 118 inhabitants.

BRANDON, a market town and parish in the hundred of LACKFORD, county of SUFFOLK, 40 miles (N. W.) from Ipswich, and 78 (N. N. E.) from London, containing 1770 inhabitants. The living is a rectory, with the vicarage of Wangford annexed, in the archdeaconry of Sudbury, and diocese of Norwich, rated in the king's books at £20. 18. 1½., and in the patronage of the Representatives of the late Admiral Wilson. The church is dedicated to St. Peter. There is a place of worship for Wesleyan Methodists. The town lies on the southern bank of the Little Ouse, or Brandon river, which forms the northern boundary of the county, and is here crossed by a neat stone bridge, about a mile from which goods are laden and unladen for conveyance, by means of that river, to and from the isle of Ely. Imbedded in a stratum of chalk, a mile westward from the town, lie continuous strata of the finest flint, of which gun-flints are made here in abundance, and conveyed to various parts of the kingdom: on the hills, within one hundred feet from the surface, are seven different strata of flint, separated by as many layers of pipe-clay. In addition to the trade in gun-flints there is considerable traffic in corn, malt, coal, timber, iron, bricks, tiles, &c.; and there are some extensive rabbit-warrens in the neighbourhood, that contribute to the supply of London. The market is held on Thursday; and there are fairs on February 14th, June 11th, and November 11th. A rent-charge of £30, given by Robert Wright, is applied to the instruction of children belonging to Brandon, Downham, Wangford, and Weeting; and a fund of £13 per annum was bequeathed, in 1664, by Joanna, widow of John Wright, for keeping the school-room in repair, and for the relief of the poor of Brandon, Downham, and Wangford. Brandon Camp, a square earthwork guarded by a single trench and a rampart, is supposed to have been the *Bravinium* of the Romans, and to have been occupied by Ostorius Scapula previously to the decisive victory which he obtained over the brave Caractacus. The Duke of Hamilton and Brandon takes his English title from this place.

BRANDON, a joint hamlet with Bretsford, in that part of the parish of WOLSTON which is in the Kirby division of the hundred of KNIGHTLOW, county of WARWICK, 6 miles (E. S. E.) from Coventry, containing, with Bretsford, 351 inhabitants.

BRANDON (LITTLE), a parish in the hundred of FOREHOE, county of NORFOLK, 5 miles (N. N. W.) from Wymondham, containing 236 inhabitants. The living is a discharged rectory, in the archdeaconry of Norfolk, and diocese of Norwich, rated in the king's books at £8. 3. 9., and in the patronage of F. R. Reynolds, Esq. The church is dedicated to All Saints.

BRANDSBURTON, a parish in the northern division of the wapentake of HOLDERNESS, East riding of the county of YORK, comprising the townships of Brandsburton and Moor-Town, and containing 591 inhabitants, of which number, 562 are in the township of Brandsburton, 8½ miles (N. E.) from Beverley. The living is a rectory, in the archdeaconry of the East riding, and diocese of York, rated in the king's books at £24. 13. 4., and in the patronage of the Master and Fellows of St. John's College, Cambridge. The church, dedicated to St. Mary, is principally in the later style of English architecture. There is a place of worship for Wesleyan Methodists. This is a thriving village: fairs are held on May 14th, and every alternate Wednesday throughout the year. Petty sessions take place every Thursday at the Cross Keys Inn. The sum of £24 is annually paid to a schoolmaster for teaching seventeen children. In 1601, the manor was assigned in trust to the lord mayor and aldermen of London, by Lady Dacres, for the benefit of Emanuel Hospital, Westminster, founded for old maids and bachelors.

BRANDS-FEE, a liberty partly in the parish of HITCHENDEN, hundred of DESBOROUGH, and partly in the parishes of GREAT and LITTLE MISSENDEN, hundred of AYLESBURY, county of BUCKINGHAM, 3½ miles (N. N. E.) from High Wycombe. The population is returned with the parishes.

BRANSBY, a township in the parish of STOW, wapentake of WELL, parts of LINDSEY, county of LINCOLN, 8 miles (N. W.) from Lincoln, containing 75 inhabitants.

BRANSBY, a parish in the wapentake of BULMER, North riding of the county of YORK, 6½ miles (E. N. E.)

from Easingwould, containing, with Stearsby, 277 inhabitants. The living is a rectory, in the archdeaconry of Cleveland, and diocese of York, rated in the king's books at £9. 8. 11½., and in the patronage of Thomas Smith, Esq. The church is dedicated to All Saints.

BRANSCOMBE, a parish in the hundred of COLYTON, county of DEVON, 4¾ miles (E.) from Sidmouth, containing 773 inhabitants. The living is a vicarage, in the peculiar jurisdiction and patronage of the Dean and Chapter of Exeter, rated in the king's books at £18. 15. 10. The church is dedicated to St. Winifred. Here are extensive quarries of freestone.

BRANSDALE (EAST SIDE), a township in the parish of KIRKBY-MOORSIDE, wapentake of RYEDALE, North riding of the county of YORK, 11 miles (N. W.) from Pickering, containing 455 inhabitants.

BRANSDALE (WEST SIDE), a township in that part of the parish of KIRKDALE which is in the wapentake of RYEDALE, North riding of the county of YORK, 11 miles (N. by W.) from Helmsley, containing 286 inhabitants.

BRANSFORD, a chapelry partly in the parish of POWICK, but chiefly in that of LEIGH, lower division of the hundred of PERSHORE, county of WORCESTER, 4¾ miles (W. S. W.) from Worcester, containing 264 inhabitants. The chapel is dedicated to St. John the Baptist.

BRANSGORE, a chapelry in the parish and hundred of CHRISTCHURCH, New Forest (West) division of the county of SOUTHAMPTON, 6 miles (N. E. by N.) from Christchurch, with which the population is returned. The living is a perpetual curacy, in the archdeaconry and diocese of Winchester, and in the patronage of the Vicar of Christchurch. The chapel was built in 1823, at the expense of £2800, defrayed by the parliamentary commissioners: it is a neat edifice, in the later style of English architecture, with a tower and spire, and contains four hundred and sixty-two free sittings.

BRANSON, a township in that part of the parish of BURTON upon TRENT which is in the northern division of the hundred of OFFLOW, county of STAFFORD, 2 miles (S. W. by W.) from Burton upon Trent, containing 412 inhabitants.

BRANSTON, a parish in the hundred of FRAMLAND, county of LEICESTER, 8 miles (N. E. by N.) from Melton-Mowbray, containing 282 inhabitants. The living is a rectory, in the archdeaconry of Leicester, and diocese of Lincoln, rated in the king's books at £15. 10. 5., and in the patronage of the Duke of Rutland. The church is dedicated to St. Guthlake.

BRANSTON, a parish in the liberty of the city of LINCOLN, county of LINCOLN, 4½ miles (S. E.) from Lincoln, containing 702 inhabitants. The living is a rectory, in the archdeaconry and diocese of Lincoln, rated in the king's books at £18. 17. 11., and in the patronage of the Rev. P. Curtois. The church is dedicated to All Saints. There is a place of worship for Wesleyan Methodists.

BRANTHAM, a parish in the hundred of SAMFORD, county of SUFFOLK, 2 miles (N. by E.) from Manningtree, containing 358 inhabitants. The living is a rectory, with the perpetual curacy of East Bergholt annexed, in the archdeaconry of Suffolk, and diocese of Norwich, rated in the king's books at £25. 10., and in the patronage of J. Rowley, Esq. The church is dedicated to St. Michael. The river Stour, which here branches off in two directions, is navigable on the southern side of the parish.

BRANTHWAITE, a township in the parish of DEAN, ALLERDALE ward above Derwent, county of CUMBERLAND, 6 miles (S. W.) from Cockermouth, containing 355 inhabitants. There is a meeting-house for Methodists. Several years ago, a considerable quantity of a ferruginous kind of limestone, called catscalp, was obtained here, and sent to the iron-works at Clifton and Seaton, but this branch of trade has ceased. There are quarries of white freestone, a woollen-manufactory, a paper-mill, and two corn-mills, in the township.

BRANTINGHAM, a parish comprising the township of Thorpe-Brantingham, in the Hunsley-Beacon division of the wapentake of HARTHILL, and the chapelry of Ellerker in the wapentake of HOWDENSHIRE, East riding of the county of YORK, and containing 423 inhabitants, of which number, 174 are in the township of Thorpe-Brantingham, 1¾ mile (S.E. by E.) from South Cave. The living is a discharged vicarage, within the jurisdiction of the peculiar court of Howdenshire, rated in the king's books at £12. 9. 2., and in the patronage of the Dean and Chapter of Durham. The church is dedicated to All Saints.

BRANTON, a township in the parish of EGLINGHAM, northern division of COQUETDALE ward, county of NORTHUMBERLAND, 9¼ miles (S. S. E.) from Wooler, containing 111 inhabitants. The Presbyterians have a meeting-house here.

BRANTON-GREEN, a joint township with Upper Dunsforth, in that part of the parish of ALDBOROUGH which is in the upper division of the wapentake of CLARO, West riding of the county of YORK, 3½ miles (S. E.) from Aldborough. The population is returned with Upper Dunsforth.

BRANXTON, a parish in the western division of GLENDALE ward, county of NORTHUMBERLAND, 9¼ miles (N. W.) from Wooler, containing 253 inhabitants. The living is a vicarage, in the archdeaconry of Northumberland, and diocese of Durham, rated in the king's books at £3. 6. 8., endowed with £400 private benefaction, and £400 royal bounty, and in the patronage of the Dean and Chapter of Durham. In June 1524, a skirmish took place between Lord Fowberry, at the head of one hundred cavalry, and a party of Scottish infantry, who, in number about five hundred, crossed the Tweed, for the purpose of plundering traders resorting to Berwick fair, but they were driven back with considerable loss. In Branxton West-field, about half a mile north-west of the village, stands an unhewn pillar of basalt, commemorative of the battle of Flodden, which was fought in the adjoining parish of Ford, in 1513. The Rev. Percival Stockdale, a miscellaneous writer of considerable merit, but of eccentric habits, was born here, in 1733, during the incumbency of his father.

BRASHFIELD, a hamlet in the parish of MITCHELMERSH, hundred of BUDDLESGATE, Fawley division of the county of SOUTHAMPTON, containing 284 inhabitants.

BRASSINGTON, a chapelry in that part of the parish of BRADBORNE which is in the hundred of WIRKSWORTH, county of DERBY, 3¾ miles (W. by N.)

from Wirksworth, containing 689 inhabitants. The living is a perpetual curacy, in the archdeaconry of Derby, and diocese of Lichfield and Coventry, endowed with £200 private benefaction, £800 royal bounty, and £1200 parliamentary grant, and in the patronage of the Duke of Devonshire. The chapel exhibits various styles of architecture, from the Norman to the later English. A plot of land was given by Mr. Thurston Dale, in 1742, now in the occupation of a schoolmaster, for which he instructs twelve children.

BRASTED, a parish partly in the hundred of Westerham, but chiefly in the hundred of Codsheath, lathe of Sutton at Hone, county of Kent, 5 miles (W. by N.) from Seven-Oaks, containing 970 inhabitants. The living is a rectory, in the exempt deanery of Shoreham, and in the peculiar jurisdiction and patronage of the Archbishop of Canterbury, rated in the king's books at £22. 6. 8. The church is dedicated to St. Martin. The parish is divided into Brasted-Upland and Brasted-Weald, and connected with it is a district called Brasted-Ville, not dependent on any hundred, having a high constable of its own. The rivers Eden and Darent flow through the parish. A fair is held annually on Holy Thursday.

BRATTLEBY, a parish in the wapentake of Lawress, parts of Lindsey, county of Lincoln, 6½ miles (N. N. W.) from Lincoln, containing 157 inhabitants. The living is a discharged rectory, in the archdeaconry of Stow, and diocese of Lincoln, rated in the king's books at £7. 10., and in the patronage of the Master and Fellows of Balliol College, Oxford. The church, dedicated to St. Cuthbert, has been rebuilt, but part of the ancient walls still remain.

BRATTON, a chapelry in the parish and hundred of Westbury, county of Wilts, 3 miles (E. N. E.) from Westbury, containing, with Hawkeridge and Haywood, 1295 inhabitants. There is a place of worship for Particular Baptists. Bratton Castle is a strong Danish encampment, where the Danes, after their defeat by the Saxons, held out for fourteen days. On the slope of the hill beneath it is the figure of a horse, cut out, as tradition relates, by the troops of Alfred, in memory of the victory which they obtained on Eddington down: several fragments of military weapons have been dug up in the vicinity of this earthwork.

BRATTON (ST. MAUR), a parish in the hundred of Norton-Ferris, county of Somerset, 2½ miles (W. N. W.) from Wincanton, containing 80 inhabitants. The living is a discharged rectory, in the archdeaconry of Wells, and diocese of Bath and Wells, rated in the king's books at £5. 4. 7., and in the patronage of T. and G. Messiter, Esqrs. The church is dedicated to the Holy Trinity.

BRATTON-CLOVELLY, a parish in the hundred of Lifton, county of Devon, 8 miles (W. S. W.) from Oakhampton, containing 705 inhabitants. The living is a rectory, in the archdeaconry of Totness, and diocese of Exeter, rated in the king's books at £21. 5. 2½., and in the patronage of the Bishop of Exeter. On an eminence about three miles northward is Broadbury Castle, an ancient earthwork defended by a single vallum and fosse.

BRATTON-FLEMING, a parish in the hundred of Braunton, county of Devon, 5¾ miles (N. E. by E.) from Barnstaple, containing 490 inhabitants. The living is a rectory, in the archdeaconry of Barnstaple, and diocese of Exeter, rated in the king's books at £29. 15. 5., and in the patronage of the Master and Fellows of Caius College, Cambridge. The church is dedicated to St. Peter. At Nightacott, in this neighbourhood, are six upright stones, the supposed remains of a Druidical circle.

BRAUGHIN, a parish (formerly a market town) in the hundred of Braughin, county of Hertford, 10 miles (N. E.) from Hertford, and 28 (N.) from London, containing 1228 inhabitants. This place, in the Norman survey called *Brachinges*, and by the Saxons *Brooking*, from the streams and meadows in its vicinity, was anciently a town of considerable importance, and a demesne of the Saxon kings: by some historians it is supposed to have been a Roman station, and the remains of a camp may still be distinguished. The town is pleasantly situated on the small river Quin, near its confluence with the Rib, and still exhibits traces of its former greatness. The market, which was granted in the reign of Stephen, has been discontinued, but a fair is held on Whit-Monday and the following day. The living is a vicarage, in the archdeaconry of Middlesex, and diocese of London, rated in the king's books at £19. 13. 4., and in the patronage of E. Harvey, Esq. and others. The church, dedicated to St. Mary, is a handsome and spacious edifice, with a square embattled tower, surmounted by a spire: on the north side of the chancel is a building, formerly the sepulchral chapel of the Brograve family, now divided into a school-room and a vestry-room. There is a place of worship for Independents. The school has a small endowment; and a National school for forty girls is supported by subscription. Mr. Jennings gave a rent-charge of £6. 13. 4., of which twenty shillings is applied to the repair of the bridges, and the remainder to charitable uses; he also gave a cottage, with an orchard containing one acre, for the residence of an aged couple, on condition that they should take care of the trees, in order that the fruit should be distributed annually among the poor, by the minister and churchwardens. Near the churchyard is an old house, now occupied by poor families, which was formerly fitted up for the reception of a poor couple on their marriage: it contained a furnished kitchen, a large hall for the celebration of the marriage feast, and a chamber with a bridal bed and furniture. There is also an almshouse for aged widows, who are at present nominated by Mr. Bonest, of Stonebury. On a lofty eminence to the south of the village are the remains of the ancient encampment, of which part of the vallum and fortifications may be traced; the form is quadrilateral, and the area contains nearly forty acres; the south-western angle is rounded, and on the north it is defended by a triple rampart: near it is a wood, called Camp wood.

BRAUNCEWELL, a parish in the wapentake of Flaxwell, parts of Kesteven, county of Lincoln, 4¾ miles (N. N. W.) from Sleaford, containing 77 inhabitants. The living is a discharged rectory, united with the vicarage of Anwick and the rectory of Dunsby, in the archdeaconry and diocese of Lincoln, rated in the king's books at £9. 18. 11½. The church is dedicated to All Saints.

BRAUNSTON, a parish in the hundred of Fawsley, county of Northampton, 2¾ miles (N. W.) from Daventry, containing 1236 inhabitants. The living is a rectory, in the archdeaconry of Northampton, and diocese of Peterborough, rated in the king's books at £31. 2. 11½., and in the patronage of the Principal and Fellows of Jesus College, Oxford. The church, dedicated to St. Giles, is a spacious handsome edifice, with a fine octagonal crocketed spire, one hundred and fifty feet high. There are places of worship for Baptists and Wesleyan Methodists. The Grand Junction and Oxford canals unite in this parish. Near the upper extremity of the village is an ancient cross, the shaft of which is composed of a single block of stone, eleven feet high. William Makepeace, in 1733, gave land, now producing about £30 a year, which, together with voluntary contributions, is applied towards the support of a National school. A considerable portion of this lordship is held by the following tenure :—on the death of a copyholder, his widow is obliged to appear at the succeeding manorial court, and there present a leathern purse, containing a groat, whereby she becomes tenant for life, subject to a renewal of her appearance every court day. Dr. Edward Reynolds, Bishop of Norwich, and an able polemical writer, was curate of this parish for several years.

BRAUNSTON, a parish in the soke of OAKHAM, county of RUTLAND, 2½ miles (S. W.) from Oakham, containing 423 inhabitants. The living is a perpetual curacy, annexed to the vicarage of Hambleton, in the archdeaconry of Northampton, and diocese of Peterborough. The church is dedicated to All Saints. There is a small endowment for the instruction of twenty children, given by Augustine Burton, in 1614.

BRAUNSTONE, a chapelry in the parish of GLENFIELD, hundred of SPARKENHOE, county of LEICESTER, 2¾ miles (S. W. by W.) from Leicester, containing 214 inhabitants. The chapel is dedicated to St. John the Baptist.

BRAUNSTONE-FRITH, a liberty in the parish of GLENFIELD, hundred of SPARKENHOE, county of LEICESTER, 2 miles (W. S. W.) from Leicester, containing 10 inhabitants.

BRAUNTON, a parish in the hundred of BRAUNTON, county of DEVON, 5¼ miles (W. N. W.) from Barnstaple, containing 1699 inhabitants. The living is a vicarage, in the peculiar jurisdiction and patronage of the Dean of Exeter, rated in the king's books at £16. 3. 6½. The church is dedicated to St. Brannock, from whom the parish is supposed to derive its name. There is a meeting-house for Independents. A free school was founded by the Rev. William Chaloner, in 1667, to which Arthur Acland, Esq., in 1690, gave land, now producing £75 a year: the children are instructed on the Madras system. There is also a charity school with a small endowment, the gift of Nicholas Beare, in 1751. The parish, which contains several villages, is bounded on the west by the Bristol channel, and has the navigable river Torr on the south, at the mouth of which there is a lighthouse, in addition to another structure of the same kind in the parish. A small tract of land here, formerly covered by the sea, is considered the richest in the county: some of the lands descend to younger sons, and a widow is entitled to a lifehold interest in her husband's inheritance so long as she preserves her widowhood. Within the parish are the remains of several ancient chapels.

BRAWBY, a township in the parish of SALTON, within the liberty of ST. PETER of YORK, East riding, though locally in the wapentake of Ryedale, North riding, of the county of YORK, 6½ miles (N. W.) from New Malton, containing 188 inhabitants. There is a place of worship for Wesleyan Methodists.

BRAWITH, a joint township with Knayton, in that part of the parish of LEAK which is in the wapentake of ALLERTONSHIRE, North riding of the county of YORK, 3½ miles (N. N. W.) from Thirsk. The population is returned with Knayton.

BRAXTED (GREAT), a parish in the hundred of WITHAM, county of ESSEX, 2 miles (E. by N.) from Witham, containing 508 inhabitants. The living is a rectory, in the archdeaconry of Colchester, and diocese of London, rated in the king's books at £19, and in the patronage of the Master and Fellows of Corpus Christi College, Cambridge. The church, dedicated to All Saints, has some Norman remains. There is a place of worship for Independents. A priory of Black canons, in honour of St. Nicholas, was founded at Tiptree, in this parish, in the time of Edward I., which, at the time of its dissolution, had a revenue of £22. 6. 4.

BRAXTED (LITTLE), a parish in the hundred of WITHAM, county of ESSEX, 1 mile (E.) from Witham, containing 117 inhabitants. The living is a discharged rectory, in the archdeaconry of Colchester, and diocese of London, rated in the king's books at £3. 6. 8., and in the patronage of Francis Capell, Esq. The church, dedicated to St. Nicholas, is an ancient edifice, with a circular chancel.

BRAY, a parish in the hundred of BRAY, county of BERKS, comprising the divisions of Bray, Touchen, Water-Oakley, and a part of the town of Maidenhead, and containing 3159 inhabitants, of which number, 961 are in the division of Bray, 1¾ miles (S. E.) from Maidenhead. The living is a vicarage, in the archdeaconry of Berks, and diocese of Salisbury, rated in the king's books at £25. 4. 4½., and in the patronage of the Bishop of Oxford. The church, dedicated to St. Michael, is a spacious edifice, with a tower on the south side. Bray is, by some, considered to occupy the site of the Roman station *Bibracte*. A custom prevails in the principal manor in this parish, agreeably to which, in default of male heirs, lands are not divided among females of the same degree of kindred, but descend only to the eldest. Bray now forms part of the royal demesne, being included within the liberty of Windsor Forest, and enjoys some privileges, among which is exemption from toll in the adjacent market town. A court leet is held annually. Fuller, in his "Worthies," relates a story of a vicar of this parish, who unhesitatingly conformed to every change of religion that took place during the reigns of Henry VIII. and his three immediate successors, being steady in the exercise of one principle only, which was to live and die "Vicar of Bray." A school for the instruction of twenty boys was founded by William Cherry, Esq., who endowed it with £500, to which Townley Ward, Esq. gave £100 three per cents.: the annual income is £34. 10., and the master has a rent-free residence. Jesus' Hospital was founded, in 1627, by William Goddard, Esq., for forty poor persons, six of whom must be free of the Fishmongers' Company, under whose governorship it is placed: each of the inmates is allowed eight shillings per month. Attached to the hospital is a chapel, in which divine service is regularly performed. Sir John Norris also gave eighteen tenements, which are assigned rent-free to the poor.

BRAY (HIGH), a parish in the hundred of SHERWILL, county of DEVON, 6 miles (N. by W.) from South Molton, containing 278 inhabitants. The living is a rectory, in the archdeaconry of Barnstaple, and diocese of Exeter, rated in the king's books at £14. 6. 8., and in the patronage of the Crown by reason of lunacy. The church is dedicated to All Saints.

BRAYBROOK, a parish in the hundred of ROTHWELL, county of NORTHAMPTON, 2½ miles (S.E.) from Market-Harborough, containing 379 inhabitants. The living is a rectory, in the archdeaconry of Northampton, and diocese of Peterborough, rated in the king's books at £23. 6. 10½., and in the patronage of Luke Young, Esq. The church is dedicated to All Saints. There is a place of worship for Particular Baptists. A small endowment for the instruction of poor children arises from two bequests of £50 each, one by John Mapletoft, in 1684, and the other by Samuel Hawes, in 1722. Braybrook gives the title of baron to the family of Neville-Griffin.

BRAYDON, a hamlet in the parish of PURTON, hundred of HIGHWORTH, CRICKLADE, and STAPLE, county of WILTS, 4½ miles (S.S.W.) from Cricklade, containing 70 inhabitants.

BRAYFIELD (COLD), a parish in the hundred of NEWPORT, county of BUCKINGHAM, 2¾ miles (E. by N.) from Olney, containing 80 inhabitants. The living is a perpetual curacy, annexed to the vicarage of Lavendon, in the archdeaconry of Buckingham, and diocese of Lincoln. The church is dedicated to St. Mary.

BRAYTOFT, a parish in the Wold division of the wapentake of CANDLESHOE, parts of LINDSEY, county of LINCOLN, 6 miles (E. by S.) from Spilsby, containing 179 inhabitants. The living is a discharged rectory, in the archdeaconry and diocese of Lincoln, rated in the king's books at £18. 3. 6., and in the patronage of the Crown. The church is dedicated to St. Peter and St. Paul.

BRAYTON, a joint township with Aspatria, in the parish of ASPATRIA, ALLERDALE ward below Darwent, county of CUMBERLAND, 9 miles (N.N.E.) from Cockermouth. The population is returned with Aspatria.

BRAYTON, a parish in the lower division of the wapentake of BARKSTONE-ASH, West riding of the county of YORK, comprising the chapelry of Barlow, and the townships of Brayton, Burn, Gateforth, Hambleton, and Thorpe-Willoughby, and containing 1489 inhabitants, of which number, 252 are in the township of Brayton, 1¾ miles (S.W.) from Selby. The living is a discharged vicarage, within the jurisdiction of the peculiar court of Selby, rated in the king's books at £7. 14. 4½., and in the patronage of the Hon. E. Petre. The church, dedicated to St. Wilfrid, exhibits various styles of architecture; the tower is Norman, surmounted by an octagonal lantern, from which rises a lofty spire, in the later English style; the south doorway, and the arch leading into the chancel, are Norman, highly enriched; the chancel is in the decorated, and the nave in the later, English style. Part of the parish is skirted by the river Ouse, and a canal, connecting that river with the Aire, passes through the centre of it. A rent-charge of £5 was given by the Rev. Thomas Morritt, towards the support of a school.

BREADSALL, a parish in the hundred of APPLETREE, though locally in that of Morleston and Litchurch, county of DERBY, 3 miles (N.E. by N.) from Derby, containing 544 inhabitants. The living is a rectory, in the archdeaconry of Derby, and diocese of Lichfield and Coventry, rated in the king's books at £28. 2. 8½., and in the patronage of Sir G. Crewe, Bart. The church, dedicated to All Saints, is a large handsome structure with a lofty spire: on the south side of the chancel is a monument to the memory of Erasmus Darwin, the poet, physician, and botanist, who died here in 1802. The Little Eaton canal and railway pass through the parish. John Hieron, a nonconformist divine of considerable celebrity, was incumbent of this parish from 1644 to 1662. A school-room was erected on the waste, in 1788, at the expense of Sir Henry Harpur, and some of the parishioners; it is endowed with £10. 8. per annum, arising from a bequest of £200 by the Rev. John Clayton, in 1745, for which seventeen scholars are taught reading. Here was anciently a house of friars hermits, afterwards converted into a small priory for monks of the Augustine order, the entire revenue of which, at the dissolution, was not more than £13. 0. 8.: it is supposed to have been founded by some member of the family of Dethick.

BREAGE, a parish in the hundred of KERRIER, county of CORNWALL, 3 miles (W. by N.) from Helston, containing 3668 inhabitants. The living is a rectory, with the perpetual curacies of Cury, Germoe, and Gunwalloe annexed, in the archdeaconry of Cornwall, and diocese of Exeter, rated in the king's books at £33, and in the patronage of the Crown. The parish, which is contiguous to the English channel, contains a celebrated tin mine, called Wheal-Vor. There is a small endowment, arising from various benefactions, for the support of parochial schools. On Tregonin hill are vestiges of a circular encampment.

BREAMORE, a parish and liberty in the New Forest (West) division of the county of SOUTHAMPTON, 3 miles (N.N.E.) from Fordingbridge, containing 549 inhabitants. The living is a donative, in the patronage of the Duke of Manchester. The church is dedicated to St. Mary. The river Avon is navigable on the eastern side of this parish. A priory of Black canons, dedicated to St. Michael, was founded by Baldwin de Redveriis, and his uncle Hugh, about the end of the reign of Henry I.; at the time of its suppression, the establishment consisted of a prior and nine canons, and the revenue amounted to £200. 5. 1.

BREANE, a parish in the hundred of BEMPSTONE, but locally in the hundred of Brent with Wrington, county of SOMERSET, 8½ miles (W.) from Axbridge, containing 86 inhabitants. The living is a discharged rectory, in the archdeaconry of Wells, and diocese of Bath and Wells, rated in the king's books at £7. 0. 5., and in the patronage of R. Hooper, Esq. The church is dedicated to St. Bridget. This parish has Uphill bay and the Bristol channel on the north, Berrow bay on the west (on the margin of which the village lies), and the river Axe on the east. The sea, in 1825, broke through a natural barrier of sand hills, and inundated a part of it, doing considerable damage to property. Breane Down is an elevated peninsula, extending a mile into the sea, and strikingly conspicuous from various parts of the surrounding country. A great quantity of samphire is gathered on the shore, and pickled previously to being conveyed to the inland towns.

BREARTON, a township in that part of the parish of KNARESBOROUGH which is in the lower division of the wapentake of CLARO, West riding of the county of YORK, 3½ miles (N. N. W.) from Knaresborough, containing 226 inhabitants.

BREASON, a chapelry in the parish of SAWLEY, hundred of MORLESTON and LITCHURCH, county of DERBY, 7¾ miles (E. S. E.) from Derby, containing 579 inhabitants. The living is a perpetual curacy, annexed to that of Risley, in the peculiar jurisdiction of the Prebendary of Sawley in the Cathedral Church of Lichfield, endowed with £200 private benefaction, £600 royal bounty, and £1000 parliamentary grant. The chapel is dedicated to St. Michael.

BRECCLES (LITTLE), a hamlet in the parish and hundred of SHROPHAM, county of NORFOLK. The population is returned with the parish. This was anciently a distinct parish, the living of which was a rectory, but it was finally annexed to Shropham before 1332. The church has long been demolished.

BRECKENBROUGH, a joint township with Newsham, in that part of the parish of KIRBY-WISK which is in the wapentake of BIRDFORTH, North riding of the county of YORK, 4 miles (W.) from Thirsk. The population is returned with Newsham.

BRECKLES, a parish in the hundred of WAYLAND, county of NORFOLK, 5 miles (S. E. by S.) from Watton, containing 140 inhabitants. The living is a discharged vicarage, in the archdeaconry and diocese of Norwich, rated in the king's books at £7. 17. 11., endowed with £1000 royal bounty, and in the patronage of Sir R. Gardner, Bart. The church, dedicated to St. Margaret, has a tower circular at the base and octangular above.

BREDBURY, a township in the parish of STOCKPORT, hundred of MACCLESFIELD, county palatine of CHESTER, 2¼ miles (N. E. by E.) from Stockport, containing 2010 inhabitants. The Peak Forest canal passes in the vicinity.

BREDE, a parish in the hundred of GOSTROW, rape of HASTINGS, county of SUSSEX, 6 miles (E. N. E.) from Battle, containing 902 inhabitants. The living is a rectory, in the archdeaconry of Lewes, and diocese of Chichester, rated in the king's books at £12. 10. 5., and in the patronage of Mr. and Mrs. Hele. The church, dedicated to St. George, is principally in the later style of English architecture. The parish is bounded on the south by Brede channel, over which there is a bridge. Here is a foundry for cast-iron.

BREDENBURY, a parish in the hundred of BROXASH, county of HEREFORD, 3 miles (W. N. W.) from Bromyard, containing 62 inhabitants. The living is a discharged rectory, in the archdeaconry and diocese of Hereford, rated in the king's books at £2. 1. 10½., endowed with £800 royal bounty, and in the patronage of Charles Dutton, Esq.

BREDFIELD, a parish partly in the hundred of LOES, but chiefly in the hundred of WILFORD, county of SUFFOLK, 3¼ miles (S. W. by W.) from Wickham-Market, containing 402 inhabitants. The living is a discharged vicarage, in the archdeaconry of Suffolk, and diocese of Norwich, rated in the king's books at £4. 4. 2., and in the patronage of the Crown. The church is dedicated to St. Andrew.

BREDGAR, a parish in the hundred of MILTON, lathe of SCRAY, county of KENT, 3¼ miles (S. W. by S.) from Sittingbourne, containing 508 inhabitants. The living is a discharged vicarage, in the archdeaconry and diocese of Canterbury, rated in the king's books at £9, and in the patronage of Sir E. Dering, Bart. The church, dedicated to St. John the Baptist, is partly of Norman architecture, and, prior to the dissolution, had a small college attached to it. There is a place of worship for Wesleyan Methodists. Eight children are instructed in reading by a schoolmistress, for £5 per annum, arising from an investment in land of £100 given by William Thatcher, in 1718.

BREDHURST, a parish in the hundred of EYHORNE, lathe of AYLESFORD, county of KENT, 4½ miles (S.S.E.) from Chatham, containing 134 inhabitants. The living is a perpetual curacy, in the peculiar jurisdiction of the Archbishop of Canterbury, and in the patronage of the Rector of Hollingbourn. The church, dedicated to St. Peter, consists only of one aisle and a chancel, with a tower, surmounted by a low spire: a small ruinous chapel, formerly the burial-place of the family of Kemsley, adjoins it. The ancient village is said to have stood a short distance off, near a wood, where there are several wells visible.

BREDICOT, a parish in the lower division of the hundred of OSWALDSLOW, county of WORCESTER, 3¾ miles (E.) from Worcester, containing 37 inhabitants. The living is a discharged rectory, in the archdeaconry and diocese of Worcester, rated in the king's books at £3. 18. 1½., and in the patronage of the Dean and Chapter of Worcester. The church is dedicated to St. James.

BREDON, a parish comprising the chapelry of Norton, and the hamlets of Bredon, Hardwick with Mittons, Kinsham, and Westmancote in the middle division, and the chapelry of Cutsdean in the upper division, of the hundred of OSWALDSLOW, county of WORCESTER, and containing 1239 inhabitants, 3¾ miles (N. E. by N.) from Tewkesbury. The living is a rectory, in the peculiar jurisdiction of the rector, rated in the king's books at £72. 11. 0½., and in the patronage of the Rev. John Keysall. The church, dedicated to St. Giles, has some specimens of Norman architecture, and contains, among other monuments, one to the memory of Dr. Prideaux, who was dismissed from the bishoprick of Worcester during the parliamentary war. The river Avon flows past this parish, and separates it from Gloucestershire on the west. From the summit of Bredon hill there is a pleasing view of the vales of Evesham and Cotswold, including the winding course of the Severn. About the commencement of the present century, a fissure opened in the rock in the side of this hill, nearly two hundred yards long, fifteen feet wide, and of unequal depth: the top of the hill is crowned by a Roman encampment, with a double trench. William Hancocke, in 1718, gave land, the rental of which is applied in instructing, clothing, and apprenticing twelve boys. There is an almshouse for eight poor females. Bredon was given by Ethelbald, King of Mercia, previously to the year 716, to his kinsman Eanulph, in order that he might found a monastery here, in honour of St. Peter, which, previously to the Conquest, was annexed to the bishoprick of Worcester. At Mitton, in this parish, are the ruins of a chapel.

BREDWARDINE, a parish in the hundred of Webtree, county of Hereford, 11½ miles (W. N. W.) from Hereford, containing 379 inhabitants. The living is a discharged vicarage, in the archdeaconry and diocese of Hereford, rated in the king's books at £7. 8. 1½., and in the patronage of the Rev. W. T. Spurdens. The church is dedicated to St. Andrew. On the banks of the Wye, about two miles above Moccas, are the ruins of Bredwardine castle.

BREDY (LITTLE), a chapelry in that part of the parish of Long Bredy which is in the hundred of Uggscombe, Dorchester division of the county of Dorset, 6¾ miles (W. by S.) from Dorchester, containing 126 inhabitants. The chapel is dedicated to St. Michael. Here is a large quarry, from which the stone for erecting Winterborne abbey was obtained. The river Bride, or Brede, has its source in a small lake here, called Bride Head, near which is a Druidical circle of stones. A Sunday school is supported by Robert Williams, Esq., at whose expense the children are also clothed.

BREDY (LONG), a parish in the hundred of Eggerton, Bridport division of the county of Dorset, 8 miles (W.) from Dorchester, containing 291 inhabitants. The living is a rectory, in the archdeaconry of Dorset, and diocese of Bristol, rated in the king's books at £19. 12. 1., and in the patronage of R. Williams, Esq. The church is dedicated to St. John the Baptist.

BREEDON, a parish in the western division of the hundred of Goscote, county of Leicester, 5¼ miles (N. E. by N.) from Ashby de la Zouch, comprising the chapelries of Worthington and Staunton-Harrold, the hamlets of Tongue and Willson, and the liberty of Newbold, and containing 2630 inhabitants. The living is a discharged vicarage, in the archdeaconry of Leicester, and diocese of Lincoln, rated in the king's books at £6. 2. 8., endowed with £600 royal bounty, and £1000 parliamentary grant, and in the patronage of the Earl of Stamford and Warrington. The church, dedicated to St. Mary and St. Hardulph, stands on the summit of an elevated limestone rock, at the foot of which lies the village, where are considerable lime-works. There is a place of worship for Wesleyan Methodists. Breedon is in the honour of Tutbury, duchy of Lancaster, and within the jurisdiction of a court of pleas held at Tutbury every third Tuesday, for the recovery of debts under 40*s*. By deed, in 1736, Francis Commins gave £300 towards the support of a school for boys; and Eliz. Commins £583. 1. 4½. for a school for girls. A cell for Black canons was founded, soon after 1144, by the prior and monks of St. Oswald, at Nosthall, to whom the church and some lands here had been given by Robert Ferrers, Earl of Nottingham; its revenue, at the dissolution, was £25. 8. 1.: the church which belonged to it is now the parochial church.

BREEM, a chapelry in the parish of Newland, hundred of St. Briavells, county of Gloucester, 5½ miles (W. by S.) from Blakeney, containing 417 inhabitants. The living is a perpetual curacy, in the archdeaconry of Hereford, and diocese of Gloucester, endowed with £200 private benefaction, and £400 royal bounty, and in the patronage of the Vicar of Newland. The chapel, dedicated to St. James, has lately received an addition of one hundred and twenty sittings, eighty of them free, towards defraying the expense of which the Incorporated Society for the enlargement of churches and chapels gave £100. Twelve children are taught reading for £2. 10. a year, being the interest of £50 given by Mrs. Gough.

BREIGHTMET, a township in the parish of Bolton, hundred of Salford, county palatine of Lancaster, 2¼ miles (E. by N.) from Great Bolton, containing 963 inhabitants. In 1729, William Hulton gave land for the erection of a school-house, which was built in 1750: it is endowed with £10 per annum, being the interest of £200 given by William Baguley, in 1725, and £10 per annum arising from a tenement and land given by an unknown benefactor, for which twenty-nine children are taught reading.

BREIGHTON, a township in the parish of Bubwith, Holme-Beacon division of the wapentake of Harthill, East riding of the county of York, 5¼ miles (N. W. by N.) from Howden, containing 179 inhabitants. The village lies on the eastern bank of the river Derwent, opposite to the ferry of Menthorpe.

BREINTON, a parish in the hundred of Grimsworth, county of Hereford, 2½ miles (W.) from Hereford, containing 259 inhabitants. The living is a vicarage, in the peculiar jurisdiction and patronage of the Dean of Hereford, rated in the king's books at £1. 10. The church is dedicated to St. Michael. The school has a small endowment.

BREMHILL, a parish in the hundred of Chippenham, county of Wilts, 4¼ miles (E.) from Chippenham, containing, with the chapelry of Foxham, 1443 inhabitants. The living is a vicarage, with the perpetual curacy of Highway annexed, in the archdeaconry of Wilts, and diocese of Salisbury, rated in the king's books at £15. 15., and in the patronage of the Bishop of Salisbury. The church, dedicated to St. Martin, is a venerable and interesting edifice, with a massive square tower, adorned with battlements and pinnacles: between the aisle and the chancel is a handsome and entire rood-loft, beautifully carved; the chancel contains several monuments, and in the churchyard are numerous epitaphs written by the present vicar, the Rev. Mr. Bowles, the poet, who, in 1827, published an historical description of this parish. He has also partially altered and embellished the parsonage-house, to assimilate it to the architectural style of the church, and tastefully disposed the garden and pleasure grounds. At the hamlet of Studley, in this parish, was a Roman station, supposed by Mr. Bowles to have been an outpost to the more important station of *Verlucio*, the site of which has been ascertained, by Sir Richard Colt Hoare, to be near Wanshouse, about four miles distant: numerous coins, chiefly struck in the reign of Constantine, and British earthenware, have been dug up. The Roman road Watling-street passed through the parish, and in the vicinity is the course of the ancient rampart Wansdike. Avebury, a celebrated British temple, supposed to have been raised in honour of the chief Celtic deity, Teutates, and Tan-hill and Silbury, two lofty eminences appropriated to the performance of their pagan rites, are situated within a short distance: on Tan-hill a fair is held annually on August 6th. There is a Moravian establishment at Tytherton, in this parish. Maud Heath, in 1478, gave land and houses in trust for keeping in repair an ancient paved footway between Bremhill and Chippenham, the produce of which being greater than the outlay, a considerable fund has accumulated. On the summit of Wick hill is an upright stone bearing an inscription commemorative of the bequest, and on an eminence near Chippenham is another, these being the two extremities of the road. Midway, on the banks of the Avon, is a more interesting monument, with a sun-dial, on the sides of which are monitory inscriptions in Latin, which have been translated into English verse by Mr. Bowles. Near the church are the ivy-mantled remains of a portion of the tenements belonging to the grange of the abbot of Malmesbury. The ancient mansion of the Hungerfords here has been converted into a farm-house.

BREMILHAM, a parish in the hundred of MALMESBURY, county of WILTS, 2 miles (W. by S.) from Malmesbury, containing 25 inhabitants. The living is a discharged rectory, in the archdeaconry of Wilts, and diocese of Salisbury, rated in the king's books at £4. 1. 8., endowed with £200 royal bounty, and in the patronage of Lady Northwich.

BRENCHLEY, a parish in the hundred of BRENCHLEY and HORSEMONDEN, lathe of AYLESFORD, county of KENT, 4¼ miles (N.) from Lamberhurst, containing 2264 inhabitants. The living is a vicarage, in the archdeaconry and diocese of Rochester, rated in the king's books at £12. 18. 9., and in the patronage of G. Courthope, Esq. The church, dedicated to All Saints, is an ancient cruciform structure, built chiefly of sand-stone, with a lofty tower. There is a place of worship for Particular Baptists. A rent-charge of £3 was given by John Porter, in 1763, for which five poor children are taught by a schoolmistress.

BRENDON, a parish in the hundred of SHERWILL, county of DEVON, 15½ miles (E.) from Ilfracombe, containing 275 inhabitants. The living is a discharged rectory, in the archdeaconry of Barnstaple, and diocese of Exeter, rated in the king's books at £9. 4., and in the patronage of Sir A. Chichester, Bart. The church is dedicated to St. Brendon.

BRENKLEY, a township in the parish of PONTELAND, western division of CASTLE ward, county of NORTHUMBERLAND, 7½ miles (N. by W.) from Newcastle upon Tyne, containing 37 inhabitants.

BRENT (EAST), a parish in the hundred of BRENT with WRINGTON, county of SOMERSET, 4¾ miles (W. S. W.) from Axbridge, containing 820 inhabitants. The living is a vicarage, in the archdeaconry of Wells, and diocese of Bath and Wells, rated in the king's books at £30. 11. 3., and in the patronage of the Bishop of Bath and Wells. The church is dedicated to St. Mary. There is a place of worship for Methodists. This appears to have been the scene of various military transactions at an early period: on the summit of a lofty conical hill, termed Brent Knoll, are vestiges of a large double intrenchment, of an irregular form, within which, and at the base of the hill, Roman coins, *fibulæ*, urns, heads of spears, and other Roman relics, have been found. The West Saxons are also supposed to have occupied this position, in their contests with the Mercians; and it is related that Alfred subsequently defended himself here against the Danes. A plot of ground to the south retains the name Battleborough, probably from some battle having been fought upon it. *Cornua ammonis* and other fossils have frequently been found. Here was anciently a cell to the abbey of Glastonbury.

BRENT (SOUTH), a parish (formerly a market town) in the hundred of STANBOROUGH, county of DEVON, 7¾ miles (S. W. by S.) from Ashburton, containing 1401 inhabitants. The living is a vicarage, in the archdeaconry of Totness, and diocese of Exeter, rated in the king's books at £29. 14. 4½., and in the patronage of the Rev. George Baker. The church is dedicated to St. Patrick. There is a place of worship for Wesleyan Methodists. The manor anciently belonged to the abbot of Buckfastleigh, who possessed the power of inflicting punishment for capital crimes. The river Avon pursues its course for six miles through the parish: there were formerly tin-works on Brent moor, but they have ceased operation. The market was held on Friday, but it has fallen into disuse: there are fairs for cattle on the last Tuesday in April and September. A court leet and a court baron are held for the manor. About fifty poor children are taught reading, for an annual sum of £13. 4., arising from land given by John Wilcocks, and subsequently by Thomas Acland, in 1733.

BRENT (SOUTH), a parish in the hundred of BRENT with WRINGTON, county of SOMERSET, 6 miles (S. W. by W.) from Axbridge, containing 764 inhabitants. The living is a vicarage, in the archdeaconry of Wells, and diocese of Bath and Wells, rated in the king's books at £25. 17. 8½., and in the patronage of the Archdeacon of Wells. The church is dedicated to St. Michael. There is a place of worship for Wesleyan Methodists. A fair for cattle was formerly held on Old Michaelmas-day.

BRENT-ELEIGH, or ELY, a parish (formerly a market town) in the hundred of BABERGH, county of SUFFOLK, 1¾ mile (E. by S.) from Lavenham, containing 298 inhabitants. The living is a vicarage, in the archdeaconry of Sudbury, and diocese of Norwich, rated in the king's books at £8, and in the patronage of Robert Frost, Esq. The church is dedicated to St. Mary: at the end of the chancel an apartment was built by Dr. Colman, Fellow of Trinity College, Cambridge, in which he placed a collection of useful books for a parochial library. Edward Colman, Esq., a member of the same family, assigned, in 1730, an almshouse comprising twelve apartments, with a small endowment, for six widowers and six widows. Henry III. granted permission to hold a market here, but it has long been discontinued.

BRENTFORD, a market town comprising Old Brentford, in the parish of EALING, Kensington division of the hundred of OSSULSTONE, and New Brentford, in the parish of HANWELL, hundred of ELTHORNE, county of MIDDLESEX, 7 miles (W. by S.) from Hyde-Park Corner, on the great western road. New Brentford contains 2036 inhabitants, and the population of Old Brentford is returned with Ealing. This place, anciently called *Brainforde*, takes its name from an ancient ford on the small river Brent. In 1016, Edmund Ironside having compelled the Danes to raise the siege of London, pursued them to this place, where they were routed with great slaughter. A chapter of the Order of the Garter was held at Brentford in 1445; and in the 25th of Henry VI., an hospital, for a master and several brethren, of the Nine Orders of Angels, was founded in a chapel beyond the bridge, at the western end of the town, anciently known as West Brainford: the revenue appears to have been £40, and the site was granted to Edward, Duke of Somerset, in the 1st of Edward VI. In 1558, six Protestants were here burnt at the stake, on account of their religious tenets. In the parliamentary war during the reign of Charles I., this place was the scene of a battle between the contending parties; the royalists, though victorious, were obliged to retire from the field, by the sudden arrival of a strong reinforcement to the enemy from London. For his services in this battle, which took place on the 12th of November, 1642, Patrick Ruthen, Earl of Forth, in Scotland, was created an English peer, by the title of Earl of Brentford, which title was subsequently conferred, by William III., upon Mareschal Schomberg, who accompanied him to England at the Revolution. Several skirmishes also took place, in 1647, between the royal guards stationed here and the parliamentary troops quartered at Hounslow. The town consists principally of one street, upwards of a mile in length, partly paved, and lighted with gas under an act of parliament obtained in 1825. The river Thames, on which are several wharfs, separates it from Kew Gardens on the south; and over this river, at the eastern extremity of the town, is a handsome stone bridge leading to Kew: the Brent, uniting the Grand Junction canal with the Thames, crosses it on the north, and over this is a neat stone bridge, erected by the county in 1825, replacing one of great antiquity, which was at one time supported by a toll levied upon Jewish passengers exclusively. In Old Brentford is a large malt-distillery, an extensive brewery, and a soap-manufactory, which afford employment to many of the labouring poor; but the chief trade of the town is derived from its situation on the great western road, and from the union of the Grand Junction canal with the Thames. The market is on Tuesday; and fairs are held on May 17th, 18th, and 19th, for cattle, and September 12th, 13th, and 14th, for toys and pedlary.

The town is within the jurisdiction of the county magistrates, who hold a petty session for the division every alternate week: the township of New Brentford is within the manor of Boston, but consists only of customary freeholds. A court of requests for the recovery of debts under 40*s*., the jurisdiction of which extends over the hundreds of Elthorne and Spelthorne, is held here during the summer half year, and during the winter at Uxbridge. The parliamentary elections for the county take place at New Brentford, it being the county town. The living of New Brentford is a perpetual curacy, in the archdeaconry of Middlesex, and diocese of London, endowed with £400 private benefaction, and £400 royal bounty, and in the patronage of the Rector of Hanwell. The chapel, dedicated to St. Lawrence, with the exception of the tower, was rebuilt of brick in 1762; annexed to it is a house for the residence of the minister. The chapel of Old Brentford, dedicated to St. George, was rebuilt in 1770, by subscription: it is a chapel of ease to the vicarage of Ealing. There are places of worship for Particular Baptists and Primitive and Wesleyan Methodists. A charity school for boys, established by subscription in 1703, was endowed by Lady Capel, in 1719, with the twelfth part of an estate, yielding at present £37. 10. per annum: the endowment, enlarged by subsequent benefactions, produces an annual income of £143. 7. 6. The charity school for girls is endowed with benefactions producing about £145 per annum: there is also a National school, supported by subscription. Mrs. Mary Spencer, in 1658, gave a rent-charge of £6 for apprenticing children; for which purpose also, in 1692, Lord Ossulston bequeathed £100, producing £5. 14. per annum. Several human skeletons have at various times been dug up in the neighbourhood.

BRENTINGBY, a chapelry partly in the parish of THORPE-ARNOLD, and partly in the parish of WYFORDBY, hundred of FRAMLAND, county of LEICESTER, 2½ miles (E. by S.) from Melton-Mowbray. The population is returned with Wyfordby. The chapel is dependent on the church of Thorpe-Arnold. The Melton-Mowbray and Oakham canal crosses the chapelry.

BRENTOR, a parish in the hundred of TAVISTOCK, county of DEVON, 4 miles (N.) from Tavistock, containing 151 inhabitants. The living is a perpetual curacy, in the archdeaconry of Totness, and diocese of Exeter, endowed with £1000 royal bounty, and in the patronage of the Duke of Bedford. The church, dedicated to St. Michael, occupies the summit of a lofty isolated rocky eminence, and serves as a land-mark for vessels entering Plymouth harbour. The small river Lid runs through this parish, in which there is also a fine sheet of water, called Stowford lake. Here are mines of manganese.

BRENTWOOD, a chapelry (formerly a market town) in the parish of SOUTH WEALD, hundred of CHAFFORD, county of ESSEX, 11 miles (S.W.) from Chelmsford, and 18 (E.N.E.) from London, on the road to Norwich, containing 1423 inhabitants. The name, which is of Saxon origin, signifies a burnt wood; the woods which previously occupied the site having been burnt down. The town is pleasantly situated on a commanding eminence, and consists principally of one street, the houses in which are, in general, ancient and irregularly built: the inhabitants are supplied with excellent water from wells. Races take place occasionally on a common near the town. There are cavalry barracks at Warley, about a mile and a half distant. The market has been discontinued: the fairs are on July 18th and October 15th, for cattle. Courts leet and baron are held occasionally by the lord of the manor of South Weald. Petty sessions for the division take place here every Thursday. The assizes were formerly held here: part of the old town-hall, which is still remaining, has been converted into a butcher's shop, and part into a blacksmith's shop. The living is a perpetual curacy, in the archdeaconry and diocese of London, endowed with £600 private benefaction, £800 royal bounty, and £400 parliamentary grant, and in the patronage of Christopher Thomas Tower, Esq. The chapel, dedicated to St. Thomas à Becket, is a small ancient edifice, partly in the early, and partly in the later, style of English architecture: within is a rude image of its tutelar saint, carved in wood. There is a meeting-house for Independents. The free grammar school was founded and endowed, in 1537, by Sir Anthony Browne, Knt., and is open to all boys residing within three miles of Brentwood: the income arising from the endowment is £1452. 7. per annum, which, according to the intention of the founder, is paid to the master, subject to an allowance of £10 per annum each to five alms-persons, and to the expense of keeping the school premises and almshouses in repair: the school is under the direction of a patron, the master, and two guardians. An exhibition of £6 per annum to Caius College, Cambridge, was founded by Dr. Plume, with preference to Chelmsford, Brentwood, and Maldon.

BRENZETT, a parish partly in the hundred of ALOESBRIDGE, but chiefly in the liberty of ROMNEY-MARSH, lathe of SHEPWAY, county of KENT, 4½ miles (N.W. by W.) from Romney, containing 238 inhabitants. The living is a vicarage, in the archdeaconry and diocese of Canterbury, rated in the king's books at £7. 18. 11½., and in the patronage of J. D. Brockman, Esq. The church is dedicated to St. Eanswide. There is a place of worship for Wesleyan Methodists.

BREOCK (ST.), a parish in the hundred of PYDER, county of CORNWALL, 1 mile (W.S.W.) from Wade-Bridge, containing 1225 inhabitants. The living is a rectory, in the peculiar jurisdiction of the Bishop of Exeter, rated in the king's books at £41. 10. 10., and in the patronage of Sir W. Molesworth, Bart. The river Camel flows on the northern and eastern sides of the parish, and is navigable as far as Wadebridge, where there is a fine bridge of sixteen arches over it, and a canal has been projected to extend the navigation to Bodmin. There is a cromlech on the summit of an eminence in this parish, which commands an extensive view of the coast.

BREREHURST, a hamlet in the parish of WOLSTANTON, northern division of the hundred of PIREHILL, county of STAFFORD, containing 714 inhabitants.

BRERETON with SMETHWICK, a parish in the hundred of NORTHWICH, county palatine of CHESTER, 2¾ miles (N.E. by N.) from Sandbach, containing 624 inhabitants. The living is a rectory, in the archdeaconry and diocese of Chester, rated in the king's books at £7. 0. 5., and in the patronage of James Royds, Esq. The church, dedicated to St. Oswald, is a stately structure in the later style of English architecture, with a roof of carved oak; it was formerly a chapel of ease to the church at Astbury, but was made parochial, and endowed with the tithes of Brereton and Smethwick, in the reign of Henry VIII.; it contains several monuments of the Lords Brereton and the Smethwick family. There is a place of worship for Calvinistic dissenters. Fairs for cattle are held in the second weeks in April and November. The sum of £20 per annum, arising from two farms, was given by Mr. Jupson, for the benefit of the poor.

BRESSINGHAM, a parish in the hundred of DISS, county of NORFOLK, 2¾ miles (W.) from Diss, containing 702 inhabitants. The living is a rectory, in the archdeaconry of Norfolk, and diocese of Norwich, rated in the king's books at £15, and in the patronage of the Duke of Norfolk. The church, dedicated to St. John the Baptist, was rebuilt, with the exception of the chancel, in 1527, having been commenced some time previously by Sir Roger Pilkington, Knt., lord of the manor. Conduit meadow, in this parish, is so called from a spacious conduit, now in a ruinous state, constructed by Sir Richard de Boyland, to supply some baths, and an extensive moat which encompassed his grounds.

BRETBY, county of DERBY.—See BRADBY.

BRETFORTON, a parish in the upper division of the hundred of BLACKENHURST, county of WORCESTER, 3¾ miles (E.) from Evesham, containing 451 inhabitants. The living is a discharged vicarage, in the peculiar jurisdiction of the Bishop of Worcester, rated in the king's books at £6. 5., endowed with £600 private benefaction, and £1100 parliamentary grant, and in the patronage of the Rev. Dr. Timbrill. The church is dedicated to St. Leonard.

BRETHERTON, a township in the parish of CROSTON, hundred of LEYLAND, county palatine of LANCASTER, 10 miles (N.N.E.) from Ormskirk, containing 748 inhabitants. There is a place of worship for Wesleyan Methodists. A free school was built, in 1654, at the expense of Mr. James Fletcher, who endowed it with £230, to which various donations have since been added: the annual income is now about £112, for which the boys and girls within the township are taught reading gratuitously.

BRETSFORD, a joint hamlet with Brandon, in that part of the parish of WOLSTON which is in the Kirby division of the hundred of KNIGHTLOW, county of WARWICK, 6½ miles (E. by S.) from Coventry. The population is returned with Brandon.

BRETTENHAM, a parish in the hundred of SHROPHAM, county of NORFOLK, 4 miles (E. by S.) from Thetford, containing 50 inhabitants. The living is a discharged rectory, in the archdeaconry of Norfolk, and diocese of Norwich, rated in the king's books at £5. 12. 6., and in the patronage of the Bishop of Ely. The church, dedicated to St. Mary, was, with the parsonage-house, burnt down in 1693, but the nave of the former was rebuilt soon after.

BRETTENHAM, a parish in the hundred of COSFORD, county of SUFFOLK, 3¾ miles (N.N.W.) from Bildeston, containing 280 inhabitants. The living is a rectory, in the archdeaconry of Sudbury, and diocese of Norwich, rated in the king's books at £11. 3. 11½., and in the patronage of the Crown. The church is dedicated to St. Mary. This was probably the site of the Roman station *Combretonium*; though some have endeavoured to fix it at Brettenham in Norfolk, where some Roman coins have been found.

BRETTON (MONK), a chapelry in the parish of ROYSTON, wapentake of STAINCROSS, West riding of the county of YORK, 2 miles (N. E.) from Barnesley, containing 916 inhabitants. A Cluniac monastery, dedicated to St. Mary Magdalene, was founded at the commencement of the reign of Henry II., the revenue of which, in the 26th of Henry VIII., amounted to £323. 8. 2. An almshouse, comprising six tenements, was founded, as it is thought, by Dame Mary Talbot, in 1654; the inmates are appointed by the agent of Sir George Wombwell, Bart., who allows 50*s.* annually to each, and repairs the buildings.

BRETTON (WEST), a chapelry partly in the parish of GREAT SANDALL, lower division of the wapentake of AGBRIGG, but chiefly in the parish of SILKSTONE, wapentake of STAINCROSS, West riding of the county of YORK, 6½ miles (N. W. by N.) from Barnesley, containing 518 inhabitants. The chapel is dependent on the church at Silkstone.

BREWARD (ST.), or SIMONWARD, a parish in the hundred of TRIGG, county of CORNWALL, 6¾ miles (N. by E.) from Bodmin, containing 554 inhabitants.

The living is a discharged vicarage, in the archdeaconry of Cornwall, and diocese of Exeter, rated in the king's books at £8, and in the patronage of the Dean and Chapter of Exeter. The church is dedicated to St. Bruard. Within this parish are the lofty hills Rough Tor (by contraction Rowtor) and Brown Willy, from the summits of which there is a view of the English and Bristol channels.

BREWHAM (NORTH and SOUTH), a parish in the hundred of BRUTON, county of SOMERSET, containing 989 inhabitants, of which number 389 are in North Brewham, $3\frac{1}{2}$ (E. N. E.), and 600 in South Brewham, $3\frac{1}{4}$ miles (E. by N.), from Bruton. The living is a perpetual curacy, in the archdeaconry of Wells, and diocese of Bath and Wells, endowed with £400 royal bounty, and £1200 parliamentary grant, and in the patronage of Sir R. C. Hoare, Bart. The church, dedicated to St. John the Baptist, has been enlarged by the addition of one hundred and ninety-eight sittings, one hundred and forty of which are free, and towards defraying the expense the Incorporated Society for the enlargement of churches and chapels granted £130. In the churchyard is the shaft of an old cross. The parish takes its name from the river Brew, which rises here. A chapel formerly stood at North Brewham, the remains of which have been converted into a barn.

BREWHAM-LODGE, an extra-parochial liberty, in the hundred of NORTON FERRIS, county of SOMERSET, 5 miles (E. by N.) from Bruton. It consists only of one estate, comprising nearly eight hundred acres, and acquired its extra-parochial privileges from having been one of King John's hunting seats, in memory of whom, a wood in the vicinity retains the name of King's wood: it is now the property, by purchase, of that eminent antiquary, Sir R. C. Hoare, Bart. The river Brew has its source at the distance of about half a mile. A tower, called Alfred's tower, was erected by Henry Hoare, Esq., in commemoration of a victory obtained here by that prince over the Danes: it is a triangular brick building, one hundred and fifty-five feet in height, surmounted at each angle by a turret, one of which is surrounded by a gallery: over the entrance is an inscription recording the good qualities and noble exploits of that renowned monarch. About half a mile toward the north-east there is a small oval encampment, called Jack's Castle, which is thought to be of Danish construction: human bones, spears' heads, and urns containing the ashes of burnt bones, have been dug up in the neighbourhood, which was the scene of various conflicts between the Saxons and the Danes.

BREWHOUSE-YARD, an extra-parochial liberty, in the southern division of the wapentake of BROXTOW, county of NOTTINGHAM, containing 90 inhabitants.

BREWOOD, a parish in the eastern division of the hundred of CUTTLESTONE, county of STAFFORD, comprising the townships of Brewood, Bishop's Wood, Hide with Wooley, Kiddermore-Green, and Park-Lanes, and the liberties of Chillington, Coven, and Somerford, and containing 2762 inhabitants, of which number, 2263 are in the township of Brewood, $10\frac{1}{2}$ miles (S. by W.) from Stafford. The living is a discharged vicarage, in the peculiar jurisdiction and patronage of the Dean of Lichfield, rated in the king's books at £6. 17. 8. The church, dedicated to St. Mary, is a spacious and handsome edifice, in the later style of English architecture, with a fine spire; it has recently received an addition of five hundred and sixty sittings, three hundred and seventy-two of which are free, the Incorporated Society for the enlargement of churches and chapels having granted £250 towards defraying the expense. There are places of worship for Independents and Wesleyan Methodists. Brewood, formerly a market town, is pleasantly situated on a branch of the Penk, about a mile south of the Watling-street, and consists of several ranges of houses: it is paved, and well supplied with water from springs. The market, formerly held on Friday, has been discontinued, and the ancient market-house pulled down, though butter and eggs are still exposed for sale, on that day, on its site: a fair for live stock is held on the 19th of September. A branch of the Peak Forest canal communicates with this place, and an act has been lately obtained for constructing a new canal. Here is a small manufactory for stock locks. Brewood is within the jurisdiction of the court of requests held at Wolverhampton, for the recovery of debts not exceeding £5. Courts leet and baron are held annually. The free grammar school is supposed to have been founded by Dr. Knightley, whose endowment, increased by subsequent benefactors, now produces about £412 per annum. Dr. Hurd, Bishop of Worcester, who, with other distinguished persons, was educated here, appropriated, in the year 1800, two houses for the benefit of the school, one of which was for the usher; at this period also the trust was renewed, and new regulations were adopted by the trustees and visitors. In 1827, it received a bequest of £1000 four per cents., pursuant to the will of R. Hurd, Esq., of Worcester, one-half for augmenting the master's stipend, and the remainder for repairs. It is free for the reception of children unlimitedly: the system of education is strictly classical, but there is an English free school in connexion with it; and a National school is supported by subscription. A bank for savings has been established. A small Benedictine nunnery, dedicated to the Blessed Virgin Mary, is first noticed in the time of Richard I.; at the dissolution its clear revenue was only rated at £11. 1. 6. Chillington Hall, a noble mansion in this parish, is approached by a fine avenue of trees, nearly two miles long, in a direct line: there are two Roman Catholic chapels on the estate, one at Birch, and the other at Black-Ladies. In the neighbourhood are two mineral springs, now disused.

BRIAVELL'S (ST.), a parish in the hundred of St. BRIAVELL'S, county of GLOUCESTER, 8 miles (W. by S.) from Blakeney, containing 1112 inhabitants. The living is a perpetual curacy, annexed to the vicarage of Lidney, in the archdeaconry of Hereford, and diocese of Gloucester. The church is a small cruciform edifice, principally in the Norman and early English styles of architecture. This is a place of considerable antiquity, having given name to the hundred. Milo, Earl of Hereford, built a castle here in the reign of Henry I., as a frontier fortress against the Welch: the north-western front, including two circular towers, now used as a prison for the hundred, is all that remains. It is nominally under the superintendence of a governor, whose office is a sinecure: the site of the original edifice is surrounded by a moat. Edward II. granted the inhabitants a charter for a weekly market, which has long been disused, and exempted them from the payment of toll throughout the kingdom: they still enjoy the right of cutting wood in the forest of Dean, which they form into hoops and other articles, and send to Bristol. There are several coal-works in the vicinity; and a court is held for regulating matters in dispute among the miners.

BRICETT (GREAT), a parish in the hundred of BOSMERE and CLAYDON, county of SUFFOLK, 3¾ miles (E. N. E.) from Bildeston, containing 290 inhabitants. The living is a perpetual curacy, in the archdeaconry of Suffolk, and diocese of Norwich, and in the patronage of the Provost and Fellows of King's College, Cambridge. The church is dedicated to St. Mary and St. Lawrence. A priory for Augustine canons was founded, about 1110, by Ralph Fitz-Brien, in honour of St. Leonard, the possessions of which, on the suppression of Alien priories, were given by Henry VI. to the Provost and Fellows.

BRICETT (LITTLE), a parish in the hundred of BOSMERE and CLAYDON, county of SUFFOLK, 4½ miles (S. S. W.) from Needham-Market, with which the population is returned. The living, a discharged rectory, has been united to the rectory of Offton since 1503, when the church fell into decay: it is endowed with £200 private benefaction, and £200 royal bounty, and is in the archdeaconry of Suffolk, and diocese of Norwich.

BRICKENDON, a liberty in that part of the parish of ALL SAINTS, HERTFORD, which is in the hundred of HERTFORD, county of HERTFORD, 3 miles (S. by W.) from Hertford, containing 647 inhabitants.

BRICKHILL (BOW), a parish in the hundred of NEWPORT, county of BUCKINGHAM, 2 miles (E.) from Fenny-Stratford, containing 438 inhabitants. The living is a rectory, in the archdeaconry of Buckingham, and diocese of Lincoln, rated in the king's books at £15. 0. 2½., and in the patronage of John and T. R. Ward, Esqrs. The church is dedicated to All Saints. Many of the females in this and the adjoining parish are employed in making lace. Charles Purrett, in 1633, gave a portion of land for the benefit of the poor, and for teaching and apprenticing poor children; eight boys are instructed gratuitously. The Roman Watling-street passes through the parish.

BRICKHILL (GREAT), a parish in the hundred of NEWPORT, county of BUCKINGHAM, 2¾ miles (S.E. by S.) from Fenny-Stratford, containing 558 inhabitants. The living is a rectory, in the archdeaconry of Buckingham, and diocese of Lincoln, rated in the king's books at £18. 2. 11., and in the patronage of P. D. Pauncefort, Esq. and others. The church is dedicated to St. Mary. There are places of worship for Baptists and Wesleyan Methodists.

BRICKHILL (LITTLE), a parish in the hundred of NEWPORT, county of BUCKINGHAM, 2 miles (E.S.E.) from Fenny-Stratford, containing 485 inhabitants. The living is a discharged perpetual curacy, endowed with £200 private benefaction, and £400 royal bounty, and in the peculiar jurisdiction and patronage of the Archbishop of Canterbury, as impropriator of the rectory, which is rated in the king's books at £9. The church is dedicated to St. Mary. There is a place of worship for Wesleyan Methodists. At an early period Brickhill was a place of considerable importance, and in the reign of Elizabeth it was a market and assize town, the assizes having been held here in 1638: the gallows stood on a heath, about half a mile distant. The market has been discontinued, but a fair is held on the 18th of October. Fine specimens of sulphate of lime have been found in the vicinity. There is an endowment of £5 per annum, for which twelve boys are taught to read.

BRICKLEHAMPTON, a chapelry in the parish of ST. ANDREW, PERSHORE, upper division of the hundred of PERSHORE, county of WORCESTER, 4¼ miles (S. E.) from Pershore, containing 156 inhabitants. The curacy, annexed to the vicarage of St. Andrew, Pershore, is in the archdeaconry and diocese of Worcester, and rated in the king's books at £2. 14. 2. The chapel is dedicated to St. Michael.

BRIDEKIRK, a parish in ALLERDALE ward below Derwent, county of CUMBERLAND, comprising the townships of Bridekirk, Great Broughton, Little Broughton, Dovenby, Papcastle with Goat, Ribton, and Tallentire, and containing 1694 inhabitants, of which number, 144 are in the township of Bridekirk, 2 miles (N. by W.) from Cockermouth. The living is a discharged vicarage, in the archdeaconry and diocese of Carlisle, rated in the king's books at £10. 13. 4., endowed with £600 parliamentary grant, and in the patronage of J. D. B. Dykes, Esq. The church, dedicated to St. Bridget, from whom the parish takes its name, is an ancient edifice, principally in the Norman style, containing a singular font, which, according to Camden, was brought from the Roman station at Papcastle: it exhibits in rude relief various designs symbolical of the serpent and the forbidden fruit, the expulsion of Adam and Eve from Paradise, the baptism of Christ, &c.; likewise a Runic inscription which has been variously interpreted by different antiquaries. There are quarries of limestone and white freestone within the parish. Sir Joseph Williamson, secretary of state in the reign of Charles II.; and Thomas Tickell, the poet and essayist, born in 1686, were natives of this place, each during the incumbency of his father.

BRIDE (ST.) WENTLLOOG, a parish in the upper division of the hundred of WENTLLOOG, county of MONMOUTH, 5¼ miles (S.) from Newport, containing 193 inhabitants. The living is a perpetual curacy, with that of Coedkernew united, in the archdeaconry and diocese of Llandaff, rated in the king's books at £4. 18. 1½., endowed with £600 royal bounty, and £200 parliamentary grant, and in the patronage of the Bishop of Llandaff. The parish is bounded on the east by the river Usk, and on the south by the Bristol channel. Here is a lighthouse.

BRIDE'S (ST.) NETHERWENT, a parish in the lower division of the hundred of CALDICOTT, county of MONMOUTH, 7 miles (E.S.E.) from Caerleon, containing, with the hamlet of Llandevenny, 185 inhabitants. The living is a discharged rectory, in the archdeaconry and diocese of Llandaff, rated in the king's books at £6. 16. 3., endowed with £200 royal bounty, and in the patronage of T. Matthews, Esq.

BRIDDLESFORD, a hamlet in the parish of ARRETON, liberty of EAST MEDINA, Isle of Wight division of the county of SOUTHAMPTON, 2¾ miles (E.N.E.) from Newport. The population is returned with the parish. Here was formerly a chapel.

BRIDESTOWE, a parish in the hundred of LIFTON, county of DEVON, 6 miles (S. W.) from Oakhampton, containing 787 inhabitants. The living is a rectory, with the perpetual curacy of Sourton annexed, in the archdeaconry of Totness, and diocese of Exeter, rated in the king's books at £32. 17. 11., and in the patronage of the Bishop of Exeter. The church is dedicated to St. Bridget. Fairs for cattle take place on the second Wednesday in June, and July 29th. A court baron is occasionally held here.

BRIDFORD, a parish in the hundred of WONFORD, county of DEVON, 4 miles (E. by N.) from Moreton-Hampstead, containing 491 inhabitants. The living is a rectory, in the archdeaconry and diocese of Exeter, rated in the king's books at £13. 15., and in the patronage of Sir L. V. Palk, Bart. The church, dedicated to St. Thomas à Becket, has an elegant rood-loft and screen, and a richly carved pulpit.

BRIDGE, a parish in the hundred of BRIDGE and PETHAM, lathe of ST. AUGUSTINE, county of KENT, 3 miles (S. E. by S.) from Canterbury, containing 432 inhabitants. The living is a perpetual curacy, annexed to the vicarage of Patrixbourne, in the archdeaconry and diocese of Canterbury. The church, dedicated to St. Peter, is principally in the Norman style. There is a place of worship for Wesleyan Methodists. The Little Stour runs through the parish.

BRIDGEHAM, a parish in the hundred of SHROPHAM, county of NORFOLK, 2¼ miles (W. by S.) from East Harling, containing 294 inhabitants. The living is a rectory, in the archdeaconry of Norfolk, and diocese of Norwich, rated in the king's books at £11. 1. 0½., and in the patronage of the Crown. The church is dedicated to St. Mary.

BRIDGEMERE, a township in the parish of WYBUNBURY, hundred of NANTWICH, county palatine of CHESTER, 7 miles (S. E.) from Nantwich, containing 233 inhabitants.

Arms.

BRIDGENORTH, a borough and market town, having separate jurisdiction, locally in the hundred of Stottesden, county of SALOP, 20½ miles (S.E.) from Shrewsbury, and 140 (N. W.) from London, containing 4096 inhabitants, but including the liberty of Romsley in the parish of Alveley, and part of the parish of Quatford, 4345. This place, anciently called *Brugia*, *Brug*, and (including Little Brug) *Bruges*, derives its name from a bridge over the river Severn, built by the Saxons, which, after many sanguinary conflicts with the Danes, they finally destroyed, to prevent the future incursions of these marauders. Upon the erection of a new bridge, about a mile and a half to the north of the former, it obtained the appellation of Brug North, whence its present name is deduced. Bridgenorth is supposed to have been founded by Ethelfleda, daughter of Alfred the Great; it was afterwards enlarged by Robert de Belesme, Earl of Shrewsbury, who erected, or probably rebuilt, the castle, and fortified the town with walls and six strong gates, some portions of which are still remaining. On the earl's rebellion against his sovereign, Henry I., in 1102, the town and castle were besieged, and, after an obstinate defence, were surrendered to the victorious monarch, who gave them to Hugh de Mortimer, which grant was confirmed by Stephen; but it appears to have been little more than nominal, since that king appointed "*Præpositi*," or provosts, to collect the revenue for the Crown. Mortimer having risen in rebellion against Henry II., that monarch laid siege to the castle, and nearly demolished it, and in this state it lay until the reign of John: he afterwards confirmed to the inhabitants all the privileges and franchises which they had enjoyed under Henry I. In 1216, King John passed a day in this town, on his march to Worcester, where he was soon afterwards interred. During the civil war in the reign of Charles I., Bridgenorth, being a royal garrison, was, in 1646, attacked by the parliamentarians, whose infantry forced an entrance on the south side of St. Leonard's churchyard, that part being not so well defended as the rest of the town, and a sharp skirmish ensued. Another party of them broke through a narrow defile in the rock leading to the north gate, where many of their men were killed, not only by the fire of the garrison, but by great stones rolled down upon them from the summit of the rock. The infantry having gained an entrance through the churchyard, opened the gates to the cavalry, and the royalists retiring into the castle, set fire to the town, which was nearly consumed. The parliamentarians having made the church of St. Leonard their magazine, the royalists planted cannon on the round tower of the castle, and setting fire to the church, the flames spread to an adjoining college, and entirely consumed it. The castle was now closely invested, but being strongly fortified both by nature and art, it sustained a siege of three weeks without receiving any material injury. The besiegers, despairing of success, had begun to undermine the rock on which it was built, when the garrison, having exhausted all their ammunition, capitulated on honourable terms, and retired to Worcester.

The town is most romantically situated on the banks of the river Severn, which divides it into two parts, called the Upper and the Lower Town. The Upper Town is built on the summit and steep acclivities of a rock, rising abruptly to the height of one hundred and eighty feet from the western bank of the river, and presents an appearance singularly picturesque. Crowning the summit of the rock, at the southern extremity, are the small ruins of the square tower of the castle, declining considerably from the perpendicular line, and the handsome modern church of St. Mary Magdalene; and at the northern extremity is the venerable church of St. Leonard, with its lofty square embattled tower, adorned with pinnacles. About half-way between the churches, and forming a conspicuous object, is the reservoir, a capacious flat square tank, supported on lofty pillars of brick, and assuming at a distance the appearance of a handsome portico. On the side of the rock rising from the river are several successive tiers of detached houses, many of them handsome modern buildings, the chimneys of the lower tier being below the foundation of the next upper tier, in regular gradation from the base of the rock to its summit. These are intermixed with caverns and rude dwellings excavated in the rock, with brick window and door-cases in front, and interspersed with gardens, shrubberies, and lofty trees. A road for carriages winds round the rock, and a nearer approach is afforded to foot passengers by several flights of steps, of almost perpendicular ascent, formed of pebbles, and secured by a framing of iron-work, leading through the rock into the interior of the town. A wider road for carts, from the several wharfs on the quay, has been constructed on the north side of the bridge. The walk round the castle hill is defended by a palisade, and commands a most extensive view of the surrounding country, which abounds with picturesque scenery, being richly diversified by cultivated fields, well-watered meadows, wood-crowned eminences, and barren rocks. Several streets, containing handsome well-built houses, lead from the church into the High-street, parallel with which are others of a similar character. Over the river is a handsome stone bridge of six arches, leading into the Lower Town, the streets in which contain some modern and several ancient houses. Among the latter is Canhall, an antique structure in the Elizabethan style, wherein Prince Rupert resided, in 1642, when he addressed a letter to the jury empannelled for the choice of town officers, entreating them "to select such men for their bailiffs as were well affected to his Majesty's service." The town is partially paved, and the inhabitants are supplied with soft water raised by machinery from the river into the reservoir in the Upper Town, and thence conveyed by pipes into their houses; and with spring water brought from Oldbury, at the southern extremity of the town, into several public conduits. The public library, in St. Leonard's churchyard, a handsome octagonal brick building lighted by a dome, was founded by the Rev. Mr. Stackhouse, to whose memory a marble tablet has been erected over the fire-place: it has been extended by subscription from a theological to a general library, and contains more than four thousand volumes. The theatre, a neat and commodious edifice of stone, was erected in 1824, on part of the site of the ancient moat of the castle, accidentally discovered; this being from thirty to forty feet deep, it became necessary to build strong piers, and to turn arches, to form a foundation: it is opened every alternate week for three months during the winter. The races are held in July, but they are not so well supported as formerly, the course having become damaged by being divided by moveable fences, and let out to different tenants during the interval.

The trade principally arises from the navigation of the river, which affords every facility for the transit of goods, and has made this town a thriving inland port: many vessels are built, and a great quantity of malt of very superior quality, and of grain, is sent to various parts of the country. The iron trade has greatly declined, but nails are made to a small extent: a large carpet-manufactory has been lately established, and there is a considerable manufactory for tobacco pipes. The market, held on Saturday, is abundantly supplied with wheat, barley, and beans, to the growth of which the land in the neighbourhood is particularly favourable: the fairs are on the Thursday before Shrove-Tuesday, and the nearest Thursday to March 15th, for horned cattle and sheep; May 1st, a pleasure and statute fair; June 30th, for wool and cattle; August 2nd, for lamb's wool and cattle; September 15th, for cattle, sheep, and cheese; October 29th, a great fair for salt butter, cheese, hops, and nuts; and December 15th, a large fair for cattle and general merchandise.

Corporate Seal.

The government, by a succession of charters from the reign of Henry I. to that of James II., is vested in two bailiffs, a recorder, deputy-recorder, twenty-four aldermen, forty-eight common council-men, two chamberlains, and two bridge-masters, assisted by a town-clerk, two serjeants at mace, and subordinate officers. The bailiffs, who are justices of the peace, and the senior of whom acts as coroner for the borough, are chosen, on the 21st of September, from among the aldermen not having served that office for three years preceding, by a jury, who are sworn not to eat or drink till they have made choice of proper persons; this oath has frequently compelled them to long abstinence, and, in 1739, subjected them to fast for seventy-four hours. The aldermen are chosen, as vacancies occur, either from the common council-men, or from such of the burgesses as have filled the offices of chamberlain and bridge-master two years previously, who are thus qualified to become either common council-men or aldermen. The recorder, who holds his office for life, appoints the deputy-recorder, who must be a barrister; all other officers are appointed by the bailiffs and burgesses in common council assembled. The freedom of the borough is inherited by birth; acquired by servitude for seven years and a fine of £1; by residence, paying scot and lot and a fine of £5; and by purchase, on paying a fine of £10. The corporation hold a court of petty session every alternate Monday, at which the bailiffs preside; and on the same day, a court of record, for the recovery of debts to any amount, is held by the bailiffs and deputy-recorder: as lords of the manor, they also hold courts leet in May and October, at which the town-clerk presides as their steward. The borough received the elective franchise in the 23rd of Edward I., and from that time has continued to return two members to parliament: the right of election is vested in all the burgesses, whether resident or not; the bailiffs are the returning officers. The town-hall, erected about the year 1646, is a spacious building of timber frame-work and plaister, supported on pillars and arches of brick, forming a covered area for the use of the market; above this is a large room, wherein the public business of the corporation is transacted, besides two smaller apartments, in one of which the several courts are held.

Bridgenorth comprises the parishes of St. Mary Magdalene and St. Leonard, which, with Claverley, Bobbington, Alveley, and Quatford, are within the jurisdiction of the court of the royal peculiar of Bridgenorth, belonging to Thomas Whitmore, Esq. The living of St. Mary Magdalene's is a perpetual curacy, endowed with £200 private benefaction, and £1500 parliamentary grant, and in the patronage of T. Whitmore, Esq. The church, formerly the chapel belonging to the castle, and exempted by King John from all ecclesiastical jurisdiction, was made parochial in the 4th of Edward III., and rebuilt of freestone in 1792: it is a handsome edifice in the Grecian style of architecture, with a lofty tower, surmounted by a cupola; the interior is divided by two ranges of lofty pillars of the Ionic order, supporting the roof. The living of St. Leonard's is also a perpetual curacy, endowed with £600 private benefaction, £400 royal bounty, and £700 parliamentary grant, and in the patronage of T. Whitmore, Esq. The church, formerly collegiate, was erected in 1448, on the site of a structure raised in the reign of Richard I.: it was originally a very magnificent and spacious edifice, comprising seven different chapels, the arches leading into which from the present nave, and now walled up, are still discernible. It suffered greatly while in the possession of the parliamentarians, during the civil war, and now consists only of a nave, one aisle, and a chancel; the last, parted from the nave by a screen, is used only as an entrance: its modern ceiling still exhibits vestiges of the ancient roof of pannelled oak, and some of the corbels on which its supporters rested are still remaining on the walls. There are places of worship for Baptists and Independents.

The free grammar school, founded in 1503, by the corporation, in whom the management is vested, is supported partly by an endowment of £34, and partly by contributions from the corporation and others, producing about £160 per annum, which is paid to the master: it has three exhibitions to Christ Church College, Oxford, founded by Mr. Careswell, in 1689, who endowed eighteen in that college, for the benefit of six free grammar schools of this county; *viz.*, four for that of Shrewsbury, three for that of Bridgenorth, four for that of Newport, three for that of Shiffnall, two for that of Wem, and two for that of Donnington, in the parish of Wroxeter. The management of the augmented property, which is chiefly in land situated near this town, has, since 1741, been vested in the court of Chancery; and, in 1820, the estate, including property in the funds, produced an annual income of nearly £1500, subject to certain deductions. The sums allowed to the exhibitioners, according to successive decrees of the court, are £60 to each under-graduate, £70 to each under-graduate being a commoner, £21 to each bachelor of arts, £60 to each bachelor of arts resident, and £27 to each master of arts, leaving a considerable surplus at the end of the year. The Blue-coat charity school, kept in an old castellated brick building, over an archway at the northern extremity of the town, which was one of the ancient gates, was established in 1720, and is supported partly by a small endowment arising from benefactions vested in the funds, and partly by subscription; there are thirty boys in this establishment, nominated by the subscribers in rotation, who are clothed annually, and, on leaving the school, receive £4. 2. as an apprentice fee, and £2 for clothing. There is also a National school, supported by subscription, in which two hundred boys and one hundred and fifty girls are instructed.

The hospital in St. Leonard's churchyard, for ten aged widows, who have an apartment and £10 per annum each, was founded, in 1687, by the Rev. Francis Palmer, rector of Sandby in Bedfordshire. The almshouses in Church-lane, endowed with estates producing £158 per annum, under the direction of the corporation as trustees, are for twelve widows of burgesses, who have each an apartment, two shillings and sixpence per week, with occasional additions, according to the state of the funds. At the southern extremity of the High-street, is part of an arch which formed the entrance to the castle, also some portions of the walls, which enclosed an area of fourteen acres; and at the northern extremity of the town, on the western bank of the river, are the remains of a convent of Grey friars, which have been converted into a malt-house: the great hall, or refectory, is still nearly in its pristine state: the pannelled oak ceiling, the stone fire-place, and many of the windows, though the lights are stopped with plaister, are still in entire preservation. About a quarter of a mile south of the Lower Town was an ancient hospital for lazars, converted, in the reign of Edward IV., into a priory, and now a private mansion. In making the shrubberies to the north of the house, in 1823, thirty-seven bodies were discovered lying in rows, within eighteen inches from the surface, having evidently been buried in winding sheets and without coffins; they were in good preservation, the teeth still retaining their enamel: some slight vestiges of the church may be traced in the walls of the out-buildings. There are remains of several fortifications in this neighbourhood, it having been the scene of frequent battles between the Saxons and the Danes. About a mile south of the town, on the eastern bank of the river, is a large mount, with a trench on all sides except the west, on which it is defended by a rocky precipice overhanging the Severn, where Robert de Montgomery had a strongly fortified palace. About half a mile eastward lay the ancient forest of Morfe, which, in Leland's time, was "a hilly ground, well wooded; a forest, or chase, having deer," and for which a forester and steward were appointed from the time of Edward I. to that of Elizabeth. The brother of King Athelstan is stated to have passed the life of a hermit here, and a cave in a rock, still called the Hermitage, is supposed to have been his solitary abode. On a portion of this tract are five tumuli in quincunx, under some of which the remains of human skeletons have been discovered. The sylvan features of the place have long since disappeared, and the whole, comprising between five and six thousand acres, was enclosed in 1815. Dr. Thomas Percy, Bishop of Dromore in Ireland, and compiler of "Reliques of Ancient English Poetry," was born here, in 1728.

BRIDGE-RULE, a parish comprising East Rule in the hundred of Black Torrington, county of Devon, and West Rule in the hundred of Stratton, county of Cornwall, 4½ miles (W.) from Holsworthy, containing 436 inhabitants. The living is a discharged vicarage, in the archdeaconry of Totness, and diocese of Exeter, rated in the king's books at £14, endowed with £800 private benefaction, £400 royal bounty, and £600 parliamentary grant, and in the patronage of the Rev. T. H. Kingdon. The river Tamar flows past this place, over which there is a bridge; and from this bridge, together with the manor having been held by Ruald, or Reginald, soon after the Conquest, Bridge-Rule derives its name. The church stands in that part of the parish which is in Devonshire: the part that is in Cornwall is intersected by the Bude and Launceston canal.

BRIDGE-SOLLERS, a parish in the hundred of Grimsworth, county of Hereford, 5¾ miles (W.N.W.) from Hereford, containing 58 inhabitants. The living is a discharged vicarage, in the archdeaconry and diocese of Hereford, rated in the king's books at £8. 10., endowed with £260 private benefaction, and £200 royal bounty, and in the patronage of Sir J. G. Cotterell, Bart. The church is dedicated to St. Andrew.

BRIDGFORD (EAST), a parish in the northern division of the wapentake of BINGHAM, county of NOTTINGHAM, 8 miles (E. N. E.) from Nottingham, containing 768 inhabitants. The living is a rectory, in the archdeaconry of Nottingham, and diocese of York, rated in the king's books at £19. 8. 6½., and in the alternate patronage of the President and Fellows of Magdalene College, Oxford, and J. Musters, Esq. The church is dedicated to St. Mary. There is a place of worship for Wesleyan Methodists. The village is pleasantly situated on the eastern bank of the Trent, near the spot where was anciently a ford, and where there is now a ferry. Here was the ancient *Margidunum* of the Romans, numerous relics of which people have been discovered in the vicinity, particularly gold, silver, and brass coins of various emperors. At a place called Castle Hill, on the Fosse-road, which passes through the parish, a Roman *fibula*, in good preservation, was found in 1828. There is an abundance of a fine species of gypsum in the parish. A charity school is supported by subscription.

BRIDGFORD (WEST), a parish partly in the southern division of the wapentake of BINGHAM, but chiefly in the northern division of the wapentake of RUSHCLIFFE, county of NOTTINGHAM, 1½ mile (S. S. E.) from Nottingham, containing, with the hamlet of Gampston, 310 inhabitants. The living is a rectory, in the archdeaconry of Nottingham, and diocese of York, rated in the king's books at £16. 14. 2., and in the patronage of J. C. Musters, Esq. The church is dedicated to St. Giles. At each of the hamlets of Basingfield and Gampston is a place called Chapel Yard, the supposed sites of ancient chapels. The Trent forms the northern boundary of the parish, which is intersected by the Grantham canal. The Rev. William Thompson, late rector, endowed a school with £30 per annum, of which the rector and patron are perpetual trustees.

BRIDGHAMPTON, a tything in the parish of YEOVILTON, hundred of SOMERTON, county of SOMERSET, 2½ miles (E. N. E.) from Ilchester, containing 105 inhabitants.

Arms.

BRIDG-WATER, a port, borough, market town, and parish, having separate jurisdiction, locally in the northern division of the hundred of Petherton, county of SOMERSET, 35 miles (S. W.) from Bristol, 20 (W. S. W.) from Wells, and 137 (W. by S.) from London, containing 6155 inhabitants. This place derived its name from Walter de Douay, one of William's followers, on whom it was bestowed at the time of the Conquest, and was thence called "Burgh Walter" and "Brugge Walter," by which names, both signifying Walter's burgh, or borough, it is designated in various ancient records. William de Briwere, to whom it was granted in the reign of Henry II., built a castle in the following reign, combining the strength of a fortress with the splendour of a baronial residence, and obtained from King John the grant of a market and a fair. He founded the hospital of St. John, for a master, brethren, and thirteen poor persons of the order of St. Augustine, the revenue of which, at the dissolution, was £120. 19. 1¼. He also constructed the haven, and began to erect a stone bridge of three arches over the river Parret, which was completed by Sir Thomas Trivet, in the reign of Edward I. His son William founded a monastery for Grey friars, about 1230, and dedicated it to St. Francis. The barons, during their revolt against Henry III., took possession of the town in 1260. In the parliamentary war, the inhabitants embraced the royal cause, and the castle was garrisoned by the king's forces. In this castle, on account of its being strongly fortified, and abundantly supplied with ammunition, the inhabitants of the surrounding district deposited their money, plate, and other articles of value, as in a place of security. The parliamentarians under Fairfax soon afterwards invested the town, and laid close siege to the castle, which was resolutely defended, till the town having been fired on both sides of the bridge, the garrison capitulated on terms of personal indemnity, and surrendered the fortress, with all the treasure in it, and one thousand prisoners, into the hands of the enemy. The castle, which had sustained considerable damage during this siege, was demolished in 1645; the sally-port and some detached portions of the walls are all that now remain. In the reign of James II. the inhabitants favoured the pretensions of the Duke of Monmouth, who, on his arrival from Taunton, was received with great ceremony by the corporation, and proclaimed king. He remained for some time in the town, and having from the tower of the church reconnoitred the royal army encamped on Sedgemoor, he rashly resolved to hazard the battle that terminated so fatally to his ambition. His adherents in the town suffered severely for their attachment to his cause, under the legal severity of Jeffreys, and the military executions of Kirke.

The town is pleasantly situated in a well-wooded and nearly level part of the county, the view being bounded on the north-east by the Mendip hills, and on the west by the Quantock hills: the river Parret divides it into two parts, connected with each other by a handsome iron bridge of one arch. The western part is particularly clean: the streets are spacious, well paved, and lighted; the houses, chiefly of brick, are uniform and well built; and there is an ample supply of excellent water from springs. The eastern part, termed Eastover, is inferior in appearance to the western; though very great improvement has been effected in both of late years. The foreign trade consists in the importation of wine, hemp, tallow, and timber; but the trade of the port is principally coastwise. Coal is brought free of duty from Monmouthshire and Wales, and is conveyed into the interior of the county by a canal to Taunton. The quay, which has been recently improved, is accessible to ships of two hundred tons' burden, and is furnished with every appendage requisite for the convenience of commeree: the number of vessels belonging to the port, according to the return in 1828, is forty-five, averaging sixty-two tons' burden. The principal source of employment is the making of bricks for general use; scouring-bricks, composed of a mixture of clay and sand deposited by the river within a limited distance of the bridge, beyond which it is unfit for the purpose; and a peculiar kind of brick, resembling Bath stone, of various sizes, from the ordinary dimensions to the largest size in which that stone is used: for this and the scouring-bricks patents have recently been obtained. The market days are Tuesday, for vegetables; Thursday, principally for corn and cattle; and Saturday, the general market for provisions: the market-house, lately erected, is a handsome building, surmounted with a dome and lantern, and having a semi-circular portico of the Ionic order. The fairs are on the first Monday in Lent, July 24th, October 2nd (which continues for three days, the first being noted for the sale of linen and woollen cloth, cattle, and general merchandise), and Dec. 27th.

The government, by charter of incorporation granted in the reign of John, and subsequently enlarged and confirmed by Edward IV., Elizabeth, and Charles II., is vested in a mayor, recorder, two aldermen, two bailiffs, or sheriffs, and eighteen burgesses, assisted by a town-clerk, three serjeants at mace, and subordinate officers. The mayor and bailiffs are chosen annually, but the rest usually hold their offices during life: the mayor, recorder, and aldermen, are justices of the peace within the borough and parish. The freedom is inherited by the eldest sons of freemen, and acquired by servitude and gift; among the privileges which it conveys is the freedom of all ports in England and Ireland, except those of London and Dublin. The corporation hold quarterly courts of session for the trial of all offenders, except those accused of capital crimes, and courts of record for the recovery of debts to any amount. The summer assizes, alternately with Wells, and the summer sessions for the county, are held here. The judges' mansion is a handsome modern edifice, containing apartments for the judges, the borough court-rooms, and a room for the grand jury. The borough prison contains distinct departments for debtors and criminals; the latter are only confined there previously to trial, or to their committal to the county gaol. The borough first sent representatives to parliament in the 23rd of Edward I., since which time it has continued to return two members: the right of election is vested in the inhabitants resident within the borough properly so called, paying scot and lot, the number of whom is about four hundred: the mayor is the returning officer.

Corporate Seal.

The living is a vicarage, with the rectory of Chilton-Trinity united, in the archdeaconry of Taunton, and diocese of Bath and Wells, rated in the king's books at £11. 7. 6., and in the patronage of the Crown. The church, dedicated to St. Mary, is an ancient and handsome structure, with a square embattled tower and a lofty spire: it has a rich porch in the decorated style of English architecture, and the altar is embellished with a fine painting of the Descent from the Cross, found on board a captured French privateer, and presented to the parish by the Hon. A. Poulett, member for the borough. There are places of worship for Baptists, the Society of Friends, Independents, Wesleyan Methodists, and Unitarians. The free grammar school was founded in 1561, and endowed by Queen Elizabeth with £6. 13. 4. per annum, charged on the tithes of the parish, to which two donations of £100 each were added: it is under the control of the corporation, who appoint the master, and the inspection of the bishop of the diocese; four boys are instructed gratuitously in English and the classics. A school, now conducted on Dr. Bell's system, was founded by Mr. John Morgan, in 1723, and endowed with ninety-seven acres of land: the management is vested in the corporation, the archdeacon of Taunton, the vicar of Bridg-water, and others, who, in 1816, erected a school-room, and a house for the master: there are thirty scholars, some of whom are clothed. A school was also founded, in 1781, by Mr. Edward Fackerell, who endowed it with the dividends on £3000 in the three per cent. consols., and the rents of three messuages, producing together an annual income of £174, for clothing, educating, and apprenticing the children and grandchildren of certain relatives named in his will, and so many other children as the funds might allow: the provisions of the will were afterwards restricted, by the court of Chancery, to the children of his relatives, the number of whom, at the last report, had increased to thirty: the management, by the testator's will, is vested in trustees, whose accounts are periodically audited by a master in Chancery. Almshouses, originally endowed by Major Ingram, of Westminster, with £18 per annum, are now appropriated to the poor of the parish, and the endowment is distributed among poor widows not receiving parochial relief. The infirmary, a commodious building, was established in 1813, and is supported by subscription. Admiral Blake was born here, in 1599, and received the rudiments of his education in the free grammar school. Bridg-water confers the title of earl on the family of Egerton.

BRIDLINGTON, a parish in the wapentake of Dickering, East riding of the county of York, comprising the sea-port and market town of Bridlington, the chapelries of Grindall and Specton, the townships of Buckton, Hilderthorp, and Sewerby with Marton, and the hamlet of Easton, and containing 5034 inhabitants, of which number, 4275 are in the town of Bridlington with Quay, 38 miles (E. N. E.) from York, and 201 (N.) from London. This place was chiefly remarkable for an extensive priory of Augustine canons, founded in 1106, by Walter de Gaunt, and dedicated to the Virgin Mary, which, from its vicinity to the sea, being exposed to injury from the vessels of the enemy, was, by permission of Richard II., defended by fortifications, the only remains of which are an arched gateway, with a room over it occasionally used as the town-hall, and underneath are some cells used as a temporary prison. The priors for many years enjoyed extensive privileges, granted by the popes; but in 1537, its last prior, William Wolde, being executed for treason, the priory was forfeited to the Crown: its revenue, at the dissolution, was £682. 15. 9. In 1643, the queen of Charles I., bringing a supply of arms and ammunition from Helvoetsluys, narrowly escaped the squadron under the command of Admiral Batten, who had been stationed to intercept her, and who, on her landing at this place, entered the bay with two of his ships and cannonaded the town. In 1779, a desperate naval fight took place off the coast, between the noted Paul Jones and two British ships of war, when, after a sanguinary conflict, the former was victorious.

The town is pleasantly situated on a gentle acclivity, about a mile from the sea, and consists principally of one long street intersected by some smaller ones, irregularly formed and inconveniently narrow; the houses are in general ancient and of mean appearance: the inhabitants are amply supplied with water. About a mile to the south-east is Bridlington Quay, forming in itself a small, handsome, and well-built town, consisting of one spacious street, leading directly to the harbour. This part of the town is much frequented for sea-bathing, and contains hot and cold baths conveniently fitted up for the accommodation of visitors. About a quarter of a mile from the Quay is a chalybeate spring, in much repute for its medicinal properties; and, in the harbour, an ebbing and flowing spring was discovered in 1811, that furnishes an abundant supply of fresh water.

The quay, on which is the custom-house, affords an agreeable promenade; and the two piers forming the harbour, stretching out a considerable distance into the ocean, command extensive prospects, especially the northern pier, from which are fine views of Flamborough Head and Bridlington bay. The harbour, which is defended by two batteries, one on the north, and the other on the south, side of the town, affords a secure retreat to numerous coasting vessels that shelter there during contrary winds; and the bay, protected from the north-west winds by the coast, and from the north winds by the promontory of Flamborough Head, offers safe anchorage for ships in gales of wind from those points. The port is a member of the port of Hull, and the number of vessels belonging to it, according to the return of 1829, is forty, averaging one hundred and fifty-five tons' burden; the number of vessels that entered inward and cleared outward, in 1826, was nine British and nineteen foreign, besides several engaged in the coasting trade. There is a small manufactory for hats: the trade in corn and malt, formerly flourishing, has declined since the opening of the Driffield canal to Hull; there are several windmills for corn, and a steam-mill for grinding bones. The market is on Saturday; and fairs for cattle, linen, and woollen cloth, &c., are held on the Monday before Whitsuntide and October 21st.

The living is a perpetual curacy, with the rectory of Argam united, in the archdeaconry of the East riding, and diocese of York, endowed with £200 private benefaction, £400 royal bounty, and £1600 parliamentary grant, and in the patronage of the Archbishop of York. The church is part of the ancient edifice belonging to the priory, formerly a magnificent structure, of which the two towers at the western end have been made level with the nave, and the chancel and transepts destroyed. There are places of worship for Baptists, the Society of Friends, and Primitive and Wesleyan Methodists. The free grammar school for twenty boys was founded by Mr. William Hustler, in 1637, and endowed with a rent-charge of £40, to which a considerable donation in land was added by William Bower, in 1670, for teaching twelve other children: a charity school for girls was endowed in 1671, and a National school, for two hundred children of both sexes, is supported by subscription. Numerous fossil remains have been found here; and in the vicinity the head of an enormous elk was discovered, the extremities of the horns being more than eleven feet apart. Sir George Ripley, a celebrated alchymist of the fifteenth century, author of a treatise on the philosopher's stone, and who, in the earlier part of his life, was a canon of Bridlington; William de Newburgh, an eminent historian in the reign of King John; John de Bridlington, prior of the monastery, and author of "Carmina Vaticinalia," who died in 1379; and Richard Boyle, Earl of Burlington, a great patron of the fine arts, whose title was derived from this place, and became extinct at his death in 1753; were natives of Bridlington.

Arms.

BRIDPORT, a sea-port, borough, market town, and parish, having separate jurisdiction, locally in the hundred of Whitchurch-Canonicorum, Bridport division of the county of Dorset, 14¾ miles (W.) from Dorchester, and 134 (W. S. W.) from London, on the high road to Exeter, containing 3742 inhabitants. This place takes its name from the river Bride, or Brit, which falls into the sea at the harbour, about a mile and a half to the south of it. It was a town of some importance in the time of Edward the Confessor, and is mentioned in Domesday-book as having a mint and an ecclesiastical establishment. During the civil war in the reign of Charles I., it was garrisoned by the parliament, but not being a place of much strength, was alternately in the possession of each party. In 1685, it was surprised by some troops in the interest of the Duke of Monmouth, under Lord Grey, which were defeated by the king's forces, and twelve of the principal insurgents were afterwards executed. The town is situated in a fertile vale surrounded by hills, having on the west the river Bride, or Brit, and on the east the river Asker, over which are several bridges; these rivers unite a little below the town. It is chiefly formed by three spacious streets, containing many handsome modern houses, and is well paved, and lighted with elegant lamps, adapted to the future introduction of gas; the inhabitants are amply supplied with water.

The trade of the port consists principally in the importation of hemp, flax, and timber, from Russia and the Baltic, and timber from America and Norway; there is also a considerable coasting trade, by which the adjacent towns are supplied with coal from Wales and the collieries in the north of England, and with other articles of general consumption. Many coasting vessels, particularly smacks, for the trading companies of Scotland, are built at this port, and are highly esteemed for strength, beauty, and fast sailing. The harbour is situated at the bottom of the bay, which is formed by the headlands near Portland on the east, and Torbay on the west. An act for restoring and rebuilding it was obtained in the 8th of George I., the preamble to which recites that by reason of a great sickness that had swept away the greatest part of the wealthy inhabitants, and other accidents, the haven became neglected, and was choked with sand, and the piers had fallen into ruins: the work was begun in 1742, and, by the expenditure of large sums, great improvement was made. Another act was obtained in 1823, in which, and the three succeeding years, upwards of £19,000 have been expended, in enlarging the basin, and filling the piers with masonry, so that the harbour is now perfectly safe and commodious. The number of vessels belonging to the port is from twenty to thirty, of from eighty to one hundred and thirty tons' burden each. The principal articles of manufacture are nets, lines, small twine, girth-webbing, cordage, and sail-cloth for the use of the home and colonial fisheries, particularly for those of Newfoundland and Nova Scotia, in which ten thousand persons are generally employed in the town and neighbourhood. In the reign of Henry VIII., the cordage for the whole of the English navy was ordered to be made at Bridport, or within five miles of it exclusively. The markets are on Wednesday and Saturday: fairs are held on April 6th and October 11th, for horses, horned cattle, and cheese, and there is a smaller fair on Holy Thursday.

The government, by charter of incorporation originally granted by Henry III., confirmed by Richard II., Henry VIII., and Elizabeth, and renewed and extended by James I. and Charles II., is vested in two bailiffs, a recorder, deputy-recorder, and fifteen burgesses, assisted by a town-clerk, two serjeants at mace, and subordinate officers. The bailiffs, who, with the late bailiffs, are justices of the peace within the borough (which is co-extensive with the parish), are chosen at Michaelmas, by the burgesses; the recorder, deputy-recorder, and town-clerk, are chosen by the corporation, subject to approval by the king. The corporation hold a court of session once a year, a court of record for the recovery of debts under £20 every third Monday, and a court leet annually. The elective franchise was conferred in the 23rd of Edward I., since which time the borough has regularly returned two members to parliament: the right of election is vested in the inhabitants paying scot and lot, and non-resident members of the corporation living within ten miles of the borough, of which latter the number is limited to five; the whole number of electors is about two hundred and fifty: the bailiffs are the returning officers. The town-hall is a handsome brick building faced with Portland stone, containing, in the upper story, a court for the borough sessions, a room for the grand jury, and a council-chamber; it was erected in 1786, on the site of the ancient chapel of St. Andrew, in the centre of the town, by an act of parliament, under which the town is paved and lighted: there is also a prison for the confinement of debtors.

Corporate Seal.

The living is a discharged rectory, in the archdeaconry of Dorset, and diocese of Bristol, rated in the king's books at £10. 12. 3½., and in the patronage of the Earl of Ilchester. The church, dedicated to St. Mary, is a spacious cruciform structure, chiefly in the later style of English architecture, with a square embattled tower rising from the centre, and crowned with pinnacles: within are many interesting monuments, among which is an altar-tomb of William, son of Sir Eustace Dabrigecourt, of Hainault, related to Queen Philippa. There are places of worship for the Society of Friends, Independents, Wesleyan Methodists, and Unitarians. The free school was founded and endowed, in 1708, by Daniel Taylor, one of the Society of Friends: the management is vested in trustees appointed by the members of that society, resident in Bridport and its vicinity. There is also an almshouse, founded by the same individual in 1696. Mr. Robert Bull, in 1730, left £200, directing that of the interest £4 per annum should be given for the instruction of twelve children, and £3 to twelve poor men; and a portion of the rent of eight acres and a half of land, purchased by the corporation, with money vested in them as trustees, is appropriated to the maintenance of a school. Turtle stone and *cornua ammonis* are found in the neighbouring quarries, and copperas stones on the beach, about four miles west of the harbour. Bridport confers the titles of baron and viscount on the family of Hood.

BRIDSTOW, a parish in the lower division of the hundred of Wormelow, county of Hereford, 1¼ mile (W. N. W.) from Ross, containing 541 inhabitants. The living is a vicarage, in the archdeaconry and diocese of Hereford, rated in the king's books at £9. 3. 11½., and in the patronage of the Bishop of Hereford. The church is dedicated to St. Bridget. Wilton castle, the ruins of which constitute an interesting object on the western bank of the Wye, in this neighbourhood, was anciently the baronial residence of the noble family of Grey, who assumed their title from this place: it was burnt by order of the royalist governor at Hereford, during the parliamentary war, and the walls are now overspread with ivy.

BRIERDEAN, a township in the parish of Earsdon, eastern division of Castle ward, county of Northumberland, 6¾ miles (N. N. E.) from Newcastle, containing 52 inhabitants. There are quarries of excellent freestone, and a colliery in the township: here are also the ruins of a strong fortress.

BRIERLY, a township in the parish of Felkirk, wapentake of Staincross, West riding of the county of York, 6½ miles (N. E. by E.) from Barnesley, containing 452 inhabitants. There is a place of worship for Wesleyan Methodists.

BRIERLY-HILL, a chapelry in the parish of King's Swinford, northern division of the hundred of Seisdon, county of Stafford, 2¼ miles (N. N. E.) from Stourbridge. The population is returned with the parish. The living is a perpetual curacy, in the archdeaconry of Stafford, and diocese of Lichfield and Coventry, and in the patronage of the Rector of King's Swinford. The chapel was erected in 1767. The vicinity abounds with collieries and iron-works on a large scale; and steam-boilers, and various other heavy articles in iron, are made here.

BRIERSCLIFFE, a joint township with Extwistle, in that part of the parish of Whalley which is in the higher division of the hundred of Blackburn, county palatine of Lancaster, 3 miles (N. E.) from Burnley, containing, with Extwistle, 1407 inhabitants.

BRIERTON, a township in the parish of Stranton, north eastern division of Stockton ward, county palatine of Durham, 8¼ miles (E. N. E.) from Stockton upon Tees, containing 21 inhabitants.

BRIGG, county of LINCOLN.—See GLANDFORD-BRIDGE.

BRIGHAM, a parish in ALLERDALE ward above Derwent, county of CUMBERLAND, comprising the borough and market town of Cockermouth, the chapelries of Buttermere, Embleton, Mosser, and Setmurthey, and the townships of Blindbothel, Brigham, Eaglesfield, Graysouthen, and Whinfell, and containing 6037 inhabitants, of which number, 390 are in the township of Brigham, 2 miles (W.) from Cockermouth. The living is a discharged vicarage, in the archdeaconry of Richmond, and diocese of Chester, rated in the king's books at £20. 16. 0½., and in the patronage of the Earl of Lonsdale. The church, dedicated to St. Bridget, is an ancient structure, with an elegant decorated window in the south aisle, a curious circular one in the same style, and a monumental arch, richly canopied: it stands on the southern bank of the Derwent, about half a mile from the village, which is situated on an eminence commanding a richly diversified prospect, and contains some respectable dwelling-houses. Bassenthwaite, Buttermere, Crummock, and Loweswater lakes, and the rivers Derwent and Maron, form the boundaries of the parish, which is also intersected by the river Cocker: it contains quarries of limestone, freestone, and blue slate, and a mine of coal. The surface is hilly, but the eminences are now chiefly under cultivation, the waste lands having been enclosed. Brigham is within the honour of Cockermouth, and the copyhold tenants attend at the court of dimissions held there at Christmas, and at the court leet held at Easter and Michaelmas, belonging to the Earl of Egremont, as lord paramount. On the enclosure of the common a small parcel of land was allotted toward endowing the school.

BRIGHAM, a township in the parish of FOSTON upon WOLDS, wapentake of DICKERING, East riding of the county of YORK, 5½ miles (S. E.) from Great Driffield, containing 103 inhabitants. There is a place of worship for Wesleyan Methodists.

BRIGHOUSE, a joint township with Hipperholme, in the parish of HALIFAX, wapentake of MORLEY, West riding of the county of YORK, 4 miles (N. by E.) from Huddersfield. The population is returned with Hipperholme. This village, which of late years has risen into a considerable state of prosperity, and is now rapidly thriving, is situated on the banks of the Calder. The manufacture of woollen goods, and the spinning of cotton and worsted, together with various other trades for the supply of the inhabitants, are extensively carried on; and considerable facility for the transmission of goods is afforded by the Calder and Hebble navigation, which pass through it. At a place called Cromwell Bottom, within a short distance, are some quarries of stone, the produce of which is sent to various parts of the surrounding country. There is a place of worship for Wesleyan Methodists. A fair is held at Brighouse on the day after Martinmas-day.

BRIGHTHAMPTON, a hamlet partly in the parish of BAMPTON, and partly in the parish of STANDLAKE, hundred of BAMPTON, county of OXFORD, 4¾ miles (S. E. by S.) from Witney. The former part contains 97 inhabitants, and the population of the latter is included with Standlake.

BRIGHTHELMSTONE, a sea-port, market town, and parish, in the hundred of WHALESBONE, rape of LEWES, county of SUSSEX, 30 miles (E.) from Chichester, and 54 (S.) from London, containing 24,429 inhabitants, according to the census of 1821, since which time the population has very much increased. This place, in the Saxon language termed *Brighthelmestun*, in Domesday-book *Bristlemeston*, and now, by contraction, generally Brighton, is supposed to have taken its name from the Saxon bishop, Brighthelme, who resided in the vicinity. It was anciently a fortified town of considerable importance, and by some antiquaries is supposed to have been the place where Cæsar landed on his invasion of Britain: this opinion has probably been suggested by the quantity of Roman coins found in the town, the vast number of human bones, of extraordinary size, which has been discovered for nearly a mile along the coast westward, and the traces of lines and intrenchments, in the immediate vicinity, bearing strong marks of Roman construction. From a fortified town it was, by successive encroachments of the sea, reduced to an inconsiderable village; and, soon after the Conquest, was inhabited principally by fishermen: it was frequently assaulted by the French, who, in the reign of Henry VIII., plundered and burnt it. As a protection against their future attacks, fortifications were erected, which were subsequently repaired and enlarged by Queen Elizabeth, who built a wall with four lofty gates of freestone for its better defence. After the fatal battle of Worcester, Charles II. retired in privacy to this place, whence he embarked for France. In the years 1665 and 1669, an irruption of the sea destroyed a considerable part of the town, and inundated a large tract of land adjoining; and in 1703, 1705, and 1706, the fortifications were undermined, and many houses destroyed by tremendous storms and inundations, that threatened its annihilation. In the reign of George II., Brighton began to rise into consideration as a bathing-place, from the writings of Dr. Russel, a resident physician, who recommended the sea-water here, as containing a greater proportion of salt than that of other places, and therefore more efficacious in the cure of scrofulous and glandular complaints: its progress was accelerated by the discovery of a chalybeate spring, in 1760, the water of which being successfully administered as a tonic, in cases of infirm or debilitated constitutions, made it the resort of invalids from all parts of the country; and it ultimately obtained the very high rank which it now enjoys as a fashionable watering-place, and its grandeur and importance, under the auspices of his late Majesty, George IV., who, in 1784, when Prince of Wales, erected a magnificent palace here, now the occasional residence of King William IV. and Queen Adelaide.

Town Seal.

The town is pleasantly situated on an eminence rising gently from a level called the Steyne, supposed to have been the line of the ancient *Stayne-street*, or Roman road from Arundel to Dorking, and adjoining a bay of the English channel, formed by the promontories of

Beachy Head and Worthing Point: it extends for two miles from east to west, and is sheltered by a range of hills on the north and north-east, and by the downs on the west. Its form, including the more recent additions, is quadrangular: the streets, which are spacious, and intersect each other at right angles, are well paved, and lighted with gas, and the inhabitants are plentifully supplied with water. The houses in the older part of the town are dissimilar in form and of inelegant appearance; those in the modern part are more uniform, and many of them elegant: these are chiefly situated on the cliffs, commanding extensive views of the sea, and comprise on the eastern cliff, the Royal Crescent, the buildings on the New Steyne, the Marine Parade (extending from the New to the Old Steyne,) the Pavilion Parade, and the houses on the Old Steyne (including two splendid hotels and a handsome library); and on the western cliff, Cannon-place (near which a magnificent hotel is now being erected), Bedford-square, Regency-square, and Brunswick-square and terrace, ranges of elegant houses, in front of which last is an esplanade, an extensive and fashionable promenade. On the road from Lewes are, Hanover Crescent, the area of which is tastefully laid out, Richmond Terrace, the buildings on the North Steyne; and to the east, Dorset-gardens, with a pleasure-ground in front, in which are two octagonal temples: on the London road are some neat houses in the cottage style, York-place, and St. George's-place, a handsome row of houses with circular fronts. Kemp Town, to the east, built by Thomas Read Kemp, Esq., is a splendid range of buildings, occupying three sides of a spacious quadrangle, to the extremity of each of which a row of houses of similar appearance has been added: from the area, which is elegantly disposed into pleasure-grounds, is a descent through an arch, leading down to the beach. The Pavilion, begun in 1784, and completed in 1827, by his late Majesty, is a magnificent structure in the oriental style of architecture, on the model of the Kremlin at Moscow. Toward the sea, the view of which is excluded by the buildings called Castle-square, it has a handsome stone front, of two hundred feet in length, with a circular building in the centre, surmounted by a lofty dome supported on pillars, and connected with it on the west is the royal chapel, consecrated in 1822, and capable of accommodating one thousand persons. Behind the Pavilion are the royal stables, a circular structure appropriately designed in the Arabian style, surmounted with a dome of glass, which, reflecting the rays of a meridian sun, produces an extraordinary and singularly beautiful effect; on the east side of the quadrangle, in which they are situated, is a racquet-court, and on the west a riding-house.

The hot and cold sea-water, vapour, and shower baths have been constructed with every regard to the convenience of the invalid; those at the New Steyne hotel are supplied with water raised from the sea to the height of six hundred feet, by an engine, and conveyed through a tunnel excavated in the rock. The chalybeate spring, about half a mile west of the old church, is enclosed within a neat building in the cottage style; the water, which deposits an ochrous sediment, has been found very beneficial in restoring infirm habits, and is in high repute: and the spa affords every variety of mineral water artificially prepared. The hotels, inns, and lodging-houses, are in every gradation of style, from the most sumptuous and luxurious elegance to the simpler accommodations of domestic privacy, adapted to the rank and habits of the numerous visitors; and the various shops are richly stored with every article of luxury or use. There are four public libraries, replete with choice works of every description: assemblies are held at the hotels, in which are elegant and spacious rooms, superbly fitted up. The theatre, a handsome building erected in 1807, is open for the season, during the recess of the London patent theatres, and has the assistance of the best metropolitan performers. The races, which continue for four or five days, are held on the downs, the first week in August. The royal gardens to the north of the town, including a spacious cricket-ground, are appropriated to various amusements: the park and the South Downs afford pleasant and extensive rides. The Old Steyne is adorned with a fine statue of George IV., by Chantrey; and comprises the North and South Parades and several other pleasant walks: the promenade commences after the heat of the day has subsided, and continues till night, the royal military band being occasionally in attendance.

The suspension chain pier, constructed in 1821, at an expense of £ 30,000, under the superintendence of Captain Brown, R.N., to facilitate the landing and embarkation, forms also a favourite promenade, one thousand two hundred feet in length, and fourteen feet in breadth: on the pier-head, which, in a transverse direction, is sixty feet long and twenty feet broad, are seats protected from the rain and shaded from the sun by a large awning. The foundation of this noble and ingenious structure consists of massive piers formed by clusters of piles driven ten feet into the rock, over which are carried strong chains of iron, securely fastened at one end to the shore, and at the other to the pier-head, having a dip of eighteen feet between the piers: from these chains descend perpendicular rods of iron connected by bars, and firmly bolted into the platform suspended beneath; below the pier-head are tiers of galleries, with flights of steps for the convenience of landing or embarking at any state of the tide. The Esplanade, one thousand two hundred feet long and forty feet wide, connects the chain-pier with the Steyne. Among the many recent improvements is the formation of a carriage road over the beach, thus connecting the cliff road with the Marine Parade. There are barracks for infantry in the town, and for cavalry at the distance of a mile on the road to Lewes. The artillery barracks on the western cliff, where there is a battery of heavy ordnance for the defence of the beach, are now used as dwelling-houses: a wall has been raised on the eastern side of the town, to protect it from the encroachment of the sea.

Numerous packets and steam-vessels sail from this place to Dieppe, whence the route to Paris is not only ninety miles shorter than that from Calais, but passes through Rouen and a finer part of the country; and a few vessels discharge their cargoes of coal and light goods on the beach. The principal branch of trade is that of the fishery, in which about one hundred boats are employed: the mackarel season commences in April, and the herring season in October: soles, turbot, skate, and other flat fish, are also taken in great quantities, and sent to the London market. The making of nets and tackle for the fishermen, the materials of which are brought from Bridport, affords employment to a portion of the inhabitants. In the intercourse between Brighton and London, numerous coaches are employed daily. The market was established by act of parliament, in 1773 : the principal market is on Thursday, but there are daily markets for the supply of the inhabitants : the fairs are on Holy Thursday and September 4th. A new and commodious market-house was built on the site of the old workhouse, in 1829. The town is within the jurisdiction of the county magistrates, who hold meetings every Monday and Thursday; but the direction of police and parochial affairs is entrusted, under an act of parliament, to a corporate body of one hundred and twelve commissioners, who are elected by the inhabitants paying scot and lot from among themselves, and who go out septennially by rotation; they appoint a town-clerk, surveyor, collectors of tolls and duties, police officers, criers, and watchmen : a constable, eight headboroughs, and other officers are chosen annually at the court leet for the hundred. A town-hall, more suited to the character and importance of the place than the former, which has been taken down, is now being rebuilt on the site of the old market-house.

The living is a vicarage, with the rectory of West Blatchington consolidated, in the archdeaconry of Lewes, and diocese of Chichester, rated in the king's books at £20. 2. 1½., and in the patronage of the Crown. The church, dedicated to St. Nicholas, is a spacious ancient structure, partly in the decorated, and partly in the later style of English architecture, standing on the summit of a hill, one hundred and fifty feet above the level of the sea, and having a square tower, which serves as a land-mark to mariners; within are, a fine screen of richly carved oak, and an antique font brought from Normandy in the reign of William the Conqueror, embellished with sculptured representations of the Last Supper, and of the miracles of our Saviour. St. Peter's is an elegant structure in the later style of English architecture, with a square embattled tower, erected in 1827, partly by grant from the parliamentary commissioners, and containing one thousand one hundred and nineteen free sittings; it is a chapel of ease to the church of St. Nicholas. The chapel royal in North-street, the chapels of St. James and St. Mary in St. James' street, St. Margaret's in Cannon-place, St. George's near Kemp Town, and Trinity chapel in Ship-street, are all connected with the establishment. There are two places of worship for Particular Baptists, three for Independents, and one each for the Society of Friends, those in the connexion of the late Countess of Huntingdon, Huntingtonians, Methodists, and Scotch Seceders; also Bethel chapel, in connexion with the Mariners' Friend Society, a Roman Catholic chapel, and a synagogue. There are numerous free schools for the instruction of poor children, the principal of which are the school in Gardener-street, for clothing and educating girls, founded in 1811, and endowed with £7100, by Swan Downer, Esq.; the Blue-coat school in Ship-street, for clothing and instructing boys, to which William Grimmet, Esq., in 1768, bequeathed £1932. 10. 10.; the school near Russel-street, for the children of fishermen; the orphan school, on the western road; the National, Infant, and Sunday schools, supported by subscription, to which the Countess of Gower, Mr. George Beach, Mr. Anthony Springett, and others, have been severally benefactors; and the Union charity school in Middle-street, supported by the several congregations of dissenters. The county hospital, a spacious and commodious building, on an eminence near the East Downs, is well regulated, and liberally supported by subscription: the dispensary is supported by annual subscription, and there are also six almshouses for aged widows. On White Hawke hill, near the race-course, on which a signal-house has been erected, are the remains of an encampment, having a narrow entrance on the north, where it is defended by a double intrenchment; and on Hollingsbury hill, a second station for signals, about two miles north of the town, are vestiges of a large circular encampment, in which are several tumuli. In 1750, an urn, containing one thousand silver *denarii*, of the emperors from Antoninus Pius to Philip, was found near the town; and in the immediate vicinity are numerous remains of altars and other Druidical monuments.

BRIGHTLING, a parish in the hundred of NETHERFIELD, rape of HASTINGS, county of SUSSEX, 4 miles (S. W.) from Battle, containing 641 inhabitants. The living is a rectory, in the archdeaconry of Lewes, and diocese of Chichester, rated in the king's books at £11, and in the patronage of the Rev. J. B. Hayley. The church, dedicated to St. Thomas à Becket, is principally in the later style of English architecture. Mary Herbert, in 1728, gave £200, which, aided by other benefactions, now produces £10 per annum, for which eleven girls are instructed; and there is a fund kept in reserve for the future erection of a school-room.

BRIGHTLINGSEA, a parish in the hundred of TENDRING, county of ESSEX, 9 miles (S. E.) from Colchester, containing 1528 inhabitants. The living is a discharged vicarage, in the archdeaconry of Colchester, and diocese of London, rated in the king's books at £17. 0. 5., endowed with £200 private benefaction, and £200 royal bounty, and in the patronage of the Bishop of London. The church, which is situated about a mile and a half from the village, is dedicated to All Saints. There is a place of worship for Wesleyan Methodists. The parish constitutes a peninsula, formed by the æstuary of the river Colne on the west, and that of a smaller river on the east. There is a trifling endowment for parochial schools.

BRIGHTSIDE-BIERLOW, a township in that part of the parish of SHEFFIELD which is in the northern division of the wapentake of STRAFFORTH and TICKHILL, West riding of the county of YORK, 3 miles (N. E.) from Sheffield, containing 6615 inhabitants. Here are large iron-works, and the manufacture of table knives, scythes, &c., is carried on extensively. A school at Grimesthorpe was established about 1762, and rebuilt, with a dwelling-house for the master, in 1802; it is endowed with £15. 10. per annum, for which the master teaches twelve children.

BRIGHT-WALTHAM, county of BERKS. — See WALTHAM (BRIGHT).

BRIGHTWELL, a parish in the hundred of MORETON, county of BERKS, 2½ miles (W. N. W.) from Wallingford, containing, with the hamlets of Mackney and Slade-End, 546 inhabitants. The living is a rectory, in the archdeaconry of Berks, and diocese of Salisbury, rated in the king's books at £44. 17. 11., and in the patronage of the Bishop of Winchester. The church, dedicated to St. Agatha, contains, among other monuments, one to the memory of Thomas Godwyn, D.D., author of a treatise on the Jewish and Roman antiquities, who died rector of this parish in 1642. There is a meeting-house for dissenters. The parish is bounded on the north by the river Thames, and on the south by the Tadsey. Here was anciently a castle, which, in 1153, was given up by Stephen to Henry II., then Duke of Normandy, after the treaty of peace concluded between him and Matilda at Wallingford, and probably soon afterwards demolished, for its site is not even known, though conjectured to have been within the moat where the manor farm-house now stands. Frances Riggins, in 1726, left a small annuity for the instruction of children, and for supplying the poor with bread. The Bishop of Winchester, as lord paramount, holds a court annually.

BRIGHTWELL, a parish in the hundred of CARLFORD, county of SUFFOLK, 5½ miles (E. by S.) from Ipswich, containing 73 inhabitants. The living is a rectory, with the perpetual curacy of Foxhall annexed, in the archdeaconry of Suffolk, and diocese of Norwich, endowed with £15 per annum private benefaction, £1000 royal bounty, and £200 parliamentary grant, and in the patronage of Sir John G. Shaw, Bart. The church is dedicated to St. John the Baptist.

BRIGHTWELL-BALDWIN, a parish in the hundred of EWELME, county of OXFORD, 5½ miles (S. W. by S.) from Tetsworth, containing, with the tything of Cadwell, 286 inhabitants. The living is a rectory, in the archdeaconry and diocese of Oxford, rated in the king's books at £18. 16., and in the patronage of W. White, Esq. The church is dedicated to St. Bartholomew. At a place called Bushy-Leas, between this and Chalgrave, a curious glass vessel, surrounded by twelve Roman sepulchral urns, was anciently dug up.

BRIGHTWELL-PRIOR, a chapelry in the parish of NEWINGTON, hundred of EWELME, county of OXFORD, 6¼ miles (S. S. W.) from Tetsworth, containing 44 inhabitants.

BRIGNALL, a parish in the western division of the wapentake of GILLING, North riding of the county of YORK, 1 mile (S. W. by W.) from Greta-Bridge, containing 216 inhabitants. The living is a vicarage, in the archdeaconry of Richmond, and diocese of Chester, rated in the king's books at £8. 12. 6., and in the patronage of the Crown. The church is dedicated to St. Mary. A school was established here, in 1817, by J. B. S. Morritt, Esq., who allows £15 per annum for its support.

BRIGSLEY, a parish in the wapentake of BRADLEY-HAVERSTOE, parts of LINDSEY, county of LINCOLN, 5¼ miles (S. by W.) from Great Grimsby, containing 94 inhabitants. The living is a discharged rectory, in the archdeaconry and diocese of Lincoln, rated in the king's books at £7. 4. 4., and in the patronage of the Chapter of the Collegiate Church of Southwell. The church is dedicated to St. Helen.

BRIGSTOCK, a parish in the hundred of CORBY, county of NORTHAMPTON, 22 miles (N. E.) from Northampton, containing 1037 inhabitants. The living is a vicarage, with the perpetual curacy of Stanion annexed, in the archdeaconry of Northampton, and diocese of Peterborough, rated in the king's books at £11. 7. 3½., and in the patronage of the Marquis of Cleveland. The church, dedicated to St. Andrew, has some Norman remains amidst various alterations of later date; the tower is of very rude workmanship, and plastered. There is a small endowment for parochial schools. By a custom that prevails in the manor, if any man die seized of copyhold lands or tenements which have descended to him in fee, his youngest son inherits; but if they have been purchased by him, they descend to the eldest son.

BRILL, a parish in the hundred of ASHENDON, county of BUCKINGHAM, 7 miles (N. W. by N.) from Thame, containing 1060 inhabitants. The living is a perpetual curacy, with that of Boarstall annexed, in the archdeaconry of Buckingham, and diocese of Lincoln, endowed with £15 per annum private benefaction, £400 royal bounty, and £600 parliamentary grant, and in the patronage of Sir J. Aubrey, Bart. The church is dedicated to All Saints. Here was a palace belonging to the kings of Mercia, which was a favourite residence of Edward the Confessor, who frequently came hither during the hunting season to enjoy the pleasures of the chase in Bernwood Forest. After the Conquest, Henry II., attended by his Chancellor, Thomas à Becket, kept his court here in 1160 and 1162; and Henry III. in 1224. In 1642, a garrison, which was stationed here for the king, was attacked by a detachment of the parliamentary forces, under the patriotic Hampden, but they were repulsed with considerable loss: the royalists, on the capture of Reading in the ensuing year, evacuated this place. A fair, granted to Sir John Molins in 1346, is held annually on the Wednesday next after Old Michaelmas-day. A free school has an income of about £25 per annum, arising principally from an endowment by John Pym, in 1637. Here are also almshouses with a small endowment for poor widows, given by Alice Carter, widow, in 1591. A hermitage, dedicated to St. Werburgh, anciently stood in the vicinity.

BRILLEY, a chapelry in the parish of KINGTON, hundred of HUNTINGTON, county of HEREFORD, 6¼ miles (N. E. by N.) from Hay, containing 506 inhabitants. The chapel is dedicated to St. Mary.

BRIMFIELD, a parish in the hundred of WOLPHY, county of HEREFORD, 5 miles (W.) from Tenbury, containing 532 inhabitants. The living is a perpetual curacy, in the archdeaconry and diocese of Hereford, endowed with £400 royal bounty, and in the patronage of the Bishop of Hereford.

BRIMHAM, a hamlet in the chapelry of HARTWITH, parish of KIRKBY-MALZEARD, lower division of the wapentake of CLARO, West riding of the county of YORK, 6 miles (W.) from Ripley. The population is returned with Hartwith. Brimham Craggs, an assemblage of rocks covering about forty acres of ground, are thought from their singular position, to have been thrown together by some extraordinary convulsion of the earth; the spot is also supposed to have been chosen for the performance of the sacred rites of the Druids, from the appearance of altars, rock-idols, rocking-stones, and other rude symbols.

BRIMINGTON, a chapelry in the parish of CHESTERFIELD, hundred of SCARSDALE, county of DERBY, 2¾ miles (N. E.) from Chesterfield, containing 629 inhabitants. The living is a perpetual curacy, in the archdeaconry of Derby, and diocese of Lichfield and Coventry, endowed with £200 private benefaction, £600 royal bounty, and £1200 parliamentary grant, and in the patronage of the Vicar of Chesterfield. The chapel was rebuilt in 1808. There is a place of worship for Wesleyan Methodists. The Chesterfield canal passes through the chapelry.

BRIMPSFIELD, a parish in the hundred of RAPSGATE, county of GLOUCESTER, 5¼ miles (E. N. E.) from Painswick, containing 348 inhabitants. The living is a discharged rectory, consolidated with that of Cranham, in the archdeaconry and diocese of Gloucester, rated in the king's books at £9. 12. 1. The church is dedicated to St. Michael. An Alien priory of Benedictine monks, subordinate to the abbey of St. Stephen, at Fountenay in Normandy, anciently existed here, but of its foundation and history little is known, and the only relic of it is in the name of an adjoining field. Here was also a castle, but every vestige of it has disappeared, except the moat which surrounded it. The Roman Erminstreet passed along the northern side of the parish.

BRIMPTON, a parish in the hundred of FAIRCROSS, county of BERKS, 6 miles (E. by S.) from Newbury, containing 464 inhabitants. The living is a vicarage, in the archdeaconry of Berks, and diocese of Salisbury, rated in the king's books at £7, and in the patronage of Mrs. Cove. The church is dedicated to St. Peter. At the period of the Norman survey there were two churches in the parish, and remains of an ancient ecclesiastical edifice are visible at a farm-house, about half a mile from the present church. The Knights Hospitallers appear to have had an establishment here in the time of Henry III.

BRIMPTON, a parish in the hundred of STONE, county of SOMERSET, 2¾ miles (W. S. W.) from Yeovil, containing 125 inhabitants. The living is a discharged rectory, in the archdeaconry of Wells, and diocese of Bath and Wells, rated in the king's books at £7. 7., endowed with £200 private benefaction, and £200 royal bounty, and in the patronage of Thomas S. Horner, Esq. The church is dedicated to St. Andrew.

BRIMSLADE, an extra-parochial liberty, in the hundred of KINWARDSTONE, county of WILTS, containing 110 inhabitants.

BRIMSTAGE, a township in that part of the parish of BROMBORROW which is in the lower division of the hundred of WIRRALL, county palatine of CHESTER, 3¾ miles (N. by E.) from Great Neston, containing 141 inhabitants.

BRIND, a joint township with Newsham, in the parish of WRESSEL, Holme-Beacon division of the wapentake of HARTHILL, East riding of the county of YORK, 2¾ miles (N. by W.) from Howden. The population is returned with Newsham.

BRINDLE, a parish in the hundred of LEYLAND, county palatine of LANCASTER, 4¾ miles (N. by E.) from Chorley, containing 1574 inhabitants. The living is a discharged rectory, in the archdeaconry and diocese of Chester, rated in the king's books at £12. 8. 4., and in the patronage of the Duke of Devonshire. The church, dedicated to St. James, is a small edifice. The workhouse, about a mile from the village, was formerly appropriated to the reception of pauper lunatics, and the idle and refractory poor from other townships; but since the erection of the county asylum at Lancaster, it has been open for the poor of any township, the inhabitants of which choose to contribute toward its support, and there are now about eighty townships thus incorporated. The free school, supposed to have been founded by Peter Burscough, has an endowment of £16. 16. a year, arising from various benefactions, and is open unlimitedly for poor children.

BRINDLEY, a township in the parish of ACTON, hundred of NANTWICH, county palatine of CHESTER, 4¾ miles (W.N.W.) from Nantwich, containing 167 inhabitants.

BRINDLEYS, an extra-parochial liberty, in the Holme-Beacon division of the wapentake of HARTHILL, East riding of the county of YORK, 3½ miles (N. by W.) from Howden, containing 7 inhabitants.

BRINGHURST, a parish in the hundred of GARTREE, county of LEICESTER, comprising the chapelry of Great Easton, and the townships of Bringhurst and Drayton, and containing 735 inhabitants, of which number, 102 are in the township of Bringhurst, 2¼ miles (W. by N.) from Rockingham. The living is a vicarage, in the archdeaconry of Leicester, and diocese of Lincoln, rated in the king's books at £11. 15., and in the patronage of the Dean and Chapter of Peterborough. The church is dedicated to St. Nicholas.

BRINGTON, a parish in the hundred of LEIGHTONSTONE, county of HUNTINGDON, 5¼ miles (N. by W.) from Kimbolton, containing 164 inhabitants. The living is a rectory, with the perpetual curacies of Bythorn and Old Weston united, in the archdeaconry of Huntingdon, and diocese of Lincoln, rated in the king's books at £34. 3. 6½., and in the patronage of the Master and Fellows of Clare Hall, Cambridge. The church is dedicated to All Saints.

BRINGTON, a parish in the hundred of NOBOTTLE-GROVE, county of NORTHAMPTON, 7 miles (N.W. by W.) from Northampton, containing 874 inhabitants. The living is a rectory, in the archdeaconry of Northampton, and diocese of Peterborough, rated in the king's books at £40, and in the patronage of Earl Spencer. The church, dedicated to St. Mary, contains some fine monuments to the memory of deceased members of the Spencer family, among which is that of Henry Spencer, first Earl of Sunderland, killed at the battle of Newbury, in 1644. There is a place of worship for Particular Baptists. Althorp, in this parish, which was formerly more populous, now contains only the noble mansion of Earl Spencer, to whom it gives the inferior title of viscount.

BRININGHAM, a parish in the hundred of HOLT, county of NORFOLK, 3¾ miles (S.W.) from Holt, containing 282 inhabitants. The living is a perpetual curacy, in the archdeaconry of Norfolk, and diocese of Norwich, and in the patronage of Mrs. Mary Reeve. The church is dedicated to St. Maurice.

BRINKBURN (HIGH WARD), a township in the parish of LONG FRAMLINGTON, eastern division of COQUETDALE ward, county of NORTHUMBERLAND, 9¼ miles (N.N.W.) from Morpeth, containing 197 inhabitants. Brinkburn, including also the Low Ward, was anciently extra-parochial, but has been annexed to the parish of Long Framlington. Here are extensive strata of limestone, and a rich mine of coal. A priory for Augustine canons was founded, in the time of Henry I., by Osbertus Colatarius, in honour of St. Peter: the establishment, at the time of the dissolution, consisted of ten religious, and the revenue was rated at £77. It was beautifully situated within a curvature of the river Coquet, which flows close to the walls, and now forms an interesting assemblage of ruins, consisting of the tower of its cruciform church, a small spire, a dormitory, and part of the outer walls, together with some fine pillars and arches, exhibiting various specimens of Norman architecture. On the hill above the priory are traces of a Roman town, in connexion with a military way; and the foundations of the piers of a Roman bridge across the river are plainly discernible when the water is low. Brinkburn Grove is thought to have been the spot where the Romans offered up devotions and sacrifices to their god Jupiter.

BRINKBURN (LOW WARD), a township in the parish of LONG FRAMLINGTON, eastern division of COQUETDALE ward, county of NORTHUMBERLAND, containing 55 inhabitants.

BRINKBURN (SOUTH SIDE), a township in that part of the parish of FELTON which is in the western division of MORPETH ward, county of NORTHUMBERLAND, 9 miles (N.N.W.) from Morpeth, containing 25 inhabitants.

BRINKHILL, a parish in the hundred of HILL, parts of LINDSEY, county of LINCOLN, 6½ miles (N.N.W.) from Spilsby, containing 119 inhabitants. The living is a discharged rectory, in the archdeaconry and diocese of Lincoln, rated in the king's books at £8, and in the patronage of R. Cracroft, Esq. The church is dedicated to St. Philip. There is a place of worship for Wesleyan Methodists. In a stratum of blue clay in the village are found veins of barren marcasite, a great quantity of which, after a heavy shower of rain, is usually washed down by a rill that runs near.

BRINKLEY, a parish in the hundred of RADFIELD, county of CAMBRIDGE, 3½ miles (S. by W.) from Newmarket, containing 317 inhabitants. The living is a rectory, in the archdeaconry and diocese of Ely, rated in the king's books at £13. 6. 8., and in the patronage of the Master and Fellows of St. John's College, Cambridge. The church is dedicated to St. Mary. This parish is entitled to the fifth part of an estate, producing in the whole £100 per annum, given by Mrs. Elizabeth March, in 1729, for the instruction of children.

BRINKLOW, a parish in the Kirby division of the hundred of KNIGHTLOW, county of WARWICK, 6 miles (N.W.) from Rugby, containing 757 inhabitants. The living is a rectory, in the archdeaconry of Coventry, and diocese of Lichfield and Coventry, rated in the king's books at £17. 10., and in the patronage of the Crown. The church is dedicated to St. John the Baptist. There is a place of worship for Wesleyan Methodists. Here was formerly a castle belonging to the family of Mowbray, and subsequently to that of De Stuteville: to a member of the latter King John granted permission to hold a weekly market at this place. The Oxford canal crosses the parish, and in its course through it is twice intersected by the Roman Fosse-way, on the line of which there are some traces of an encampment. The interest on £100, given by the Rev. William Fairfox, in 1761, is applied to the instruction of poor children.

BRINKWORTH, a parish in the hundred of MALMESBURY, county of WILTS, 4¼ miles (W.N.W.) from Wootton-Bassett, containing, with the tything of Grittenham, 1216 inhabitants. The living is a rectory, in the archdeaconry of Wilts, and diocese of Salisbury, rated in the king's books at £23. 9. 2., and in the patronage of Lord Holland. The church is dedicated to St. Michael. There is an endowment of about £5 per annum for teaching children.

BRINNINGTON, a township in the parish of STOCKPORT, hundred of MACCLESFIELD, county palatine of CHESTER, 2 miles (N.E. by N.) from Stockport, containing 2124 inhabitants.

BRINSOP, a parish in the hundred of GRIMSWORTH, county of HEREFORD, 5½ miles (N.W.) from Hereford, containing 107 inhabitants. The living is a discharged vicarage, in the archdeaconry and diocese of Hereford, rated in the king's books at £4, endowed with £400 private benefaction, and £400 royal bounty, and in the patronage of the Bishop of Hereford. The church is dedicated to St. George.

BRINSWORTH, a township in that part of the parish of ROTHERHAM which is in the southern division of the wapentake of STRAFFORTH and TICKHILL, West riding of the county of YORK, 2¾ miles (S.S.W.) from Rotherham, containing 225 inhabitants.

BRINTON, a parish in the hundred of HOLT, county of NORFOLK, 3½ miles (W.S.W.) from Holt, containing 221 inhabitants. The living is a discharged rectory, annexed to that of Thornage, in the archdeaconry and diocese of Norwich, rated in the king's books at £8. 11. 4. The church is dedicated to St. Andrew.

BRISCO, or BIRKSCEUGH, a township in that part of the parish of ST. CUTHBERT, CARLISLE, which is in CUMBERLAND ward, county of CUMBERLAND, 3½ miles (S.E. by S.) from Carlisle, containing 308 inhabitants. There are two establishments for printing calico on the banks of the river Petterill, in this township. The first wheat that grew in the county was produced here, about the year 1700.

BRISLEY, a parish in the hundred of LAUNDITCH, county of NORFOLK, 6 miles (N.N.W.) from East Dereham, containing 362 inhabitants. The living is a discharged rectory, with the vicarage of Gateley annexed, in the archdeaconry and diocese of Norwich, rated in the king's books at £8. 7. 8½., and in the patronage of the Master and Fellows of Christ's College, Cambridge. The church is dedicated to St. Bartholomew.

BRISLINGTON, a parish in the hundred of KEYNSHAM, county of SOMERSET, 3 miles (S.E. by E.) from Bristol, containing 1216 inhabitants. The living is a donative, in the patronage of Lieutenant-General Popham. The church, dedicated to St. Luke, has recently received an addition of two hundred and sixty-five sittings, one hundred and forty of which are free, and towards defraying the expense the Incorporated Society for the enlargement of churches and chapels granted £200. The river Avon forms the north-eastern boundary of this parish. Brislington House is an asylum for lunatics, lately erected by Edward Long Fox, M.D., who first introduced the classification of patients in such establishments: the buildings are of brick, with stone copings, and comprise a spacious central edifice, with detached wings, extending in front four hundred and ninety-five feet, and having a neatly disposed shrubbery: they are fire-proof, all the parts usually constructed of wood in other buildings being in this, with the exception of a few doors and windows in the central house, made of iron, or some other incombustible material. Attached to the establishment are warm and other baths, a bowling-green, fives-court, and similar sources of recreation; and upon the estate are other houses, remote from the principal edifice, where patients may be accommodated with servants, and keep whatever establishment their friends choose. A variety of Roman coins was found in an adjoining field in 1829. A chapel, dedicated to St. Anne, was founded by one of the lords de la Warre, in the northern part of the manor, but there are not now any vestiges of it.

Arms.

BRISTOL, a city and county of itself, and a considerable port, situated near the mouth of the Bristol channel, and between the counties of Gloucester and Somerset, 34 miles (S. W. by S.) from Gloucester, 12 (N. W.) from Bath, and 118 (W.) from London, containing 52,889 inhabitants, but including the out-parishes, which are in the hundred of Barton-Regis, and form the suburbs of Bristol, nearly 90,000. This place, called by the Britons *Caer Brito*, and supposed to have been the *Abona*, or *Trajectus*, of Antonine, notwithstanding the various conjectures of antiquaries, probably derives its name from the Saxon *Brito-stow*. In 1063, Harold set sail from this port for the subjugation of Wales; and soon after the Conquest, his sons, attempting to overthrow the government of William, made an assault upon Bristol, but were defeated by the inhabitants. At that time an extensive traffic in English slaves was carried on here, which was abolished by William, at the intercession of Archbishop Lanfranc. In 1089, Geoffrey, Bishop of Coutance, taking part in a confederacy against William Rufus, for the purpose of raising his elder brother Robert to the throne, assembled his forces here, and fortified the town with walls, portions of which still remain; and in the struggle between Stephen and Matilda, the Earl of Gloucester, having taken possession of the city for the empress, built a castle, into which she retired on her escape from Arundel, at that time besieged by her opponent. Stephen having been soon after taken prisoner, was confined in this castle, and, by Matilda's order, loaded with chains, till he was released by the capture of the earl, for whom he was exchanged. In 1142, Prince Henry, afterwards Henry II., being brought from Normandy on a visit to his mother, was placed at Bristol, under the protection of the Earl of Gloucester, where he remained for four years, and received part of his education. Edward I. kept the festival of Christmas here in 1285, where he held a council; and during the war between Edward II. and the barons, Henry de Willington and Harry de Mumford, who had been taken prisoners, were executed here, in 1322. Edward III., in 1353, removed the staple for wool from the several towns in Flanders to England, and, among other places, to this city, which, in consequence, rapidly grew into importance as a place of trade; and, in 1373, he erected it into a separate county, under the designation of the "City and County of the City of Bristol," the limits of which extend by water from Tower Haritz to Kingsroad, thence along the south side of the Bristol channel to the Holmes (the scene of the retirement of Gildas, the early historian of Britain), and eastward to Denney island, and back to Kingsroad; by land, about five miles on the side next the county of Gloucester, and nearly three on that next the county of Somerset. In 1399, the Duke of Lancaster, afterwards Henry IV., besieged the city with a powerful army, and, on its surrender, sentenced the governor, Scroop, Earl of Wiltshire, Sir Henry Green, and Sir John Bushy, to be beheaded; and in the same year, by an act of parliament, he exempted the city, by "land and water," from the jurisdiction of the Lord High Admiral. In 1471, the Duke of Somerset, the Earl of Devonshire, and other nobles in the interest of the House of Lancaster, entering into a confederacy against Edward IV., assembled their forces here, and were greatly assisted by the inhabitants, who were attached to the Lancastrian cause, in their attempts to replace Henry VI. upon the throne. Henry VII. visited Bristol in 1485, on which occasion the citizens, to evince the greater respect, appeared in their best apparel; but the king thinking their wives too richly dressed for their station, imposed a fine of twenty shillings upon every citizen who was worth £20. During the civil war in the reign of Charles I., the city was garrisoned by the parliamentarians, who appointed Nathaniel Fiennes governor. The king, sensible of the importance of the place, endeavoured to gain possession of it by means of his partisans within the town; but their proceedings having been discovered, Alderman Yeomans and Mr. Bourchier were hanged as traitors, by order of the governor. In 1643, Prince Rupert closely invested the city, which surrendered on the third day; and the king arriving soon after, remained for some days, and attended divine service in the cathedral on the following Sunday. Bristol continued in the possession of the royalists for nearly two years; but after sustaining a vigorous assault with incredible valour, the garrison capitulated to Fairfax, and Cromwell soon after ordered the castle and the fortifications to be demolished.

The city is pleasantly situated in a valley surrounded by hills, near the confluence of the rivers Avon and Frome, and, from the circumstance of many of the houses being built on the acclivities of the hills, and from its circular form, has been thought to bear a striking resemblance to ancient Rome. The old town, which forms the nucleus of the present city, consists of four principal streets, diverging at right angles from the centre, and intersected by several smaller streets. The houses in the interior of the town are mostly ancient, being built of timber and plaister, with the upper stories projecting; but in the exterior parts are spacious streets and squares, containing houses uniformly built of stone and brick, and possessing a high degree of elegance. The town is well paved, lighted with gas, and amply supplied with excellent water from springs, and from public conduits in convenient situations, of which, the conduit in Temple-street is ornamented with a fine figure of Neptune, and enclosed by an iron palisade. A handsome stone bridge of three wide arches over the Avon, which flows through the town, was completed in 1768, on the site of a former one, connecting the northern with the southern part; and over the river Frome is a drawbridge of two arches of stone, the platform being turned by machinery, to admit the passage of ships. The theatre, said to have been admired by Garrick for its just proportions and arrangement, was built by Mr. Powell, in 1766, and is opened during the winter season by the Bath company of performers. Assemblies are occasionally held in a fine suite of rooms in Princes-street, composing a handsome edifice with pillars of the Corinthian order; and equestrian performances formerly took place in the circus, a commodious building in Limekiln-lane. The city library, a handsome stone edifice, ornamented with sculptured literary emblems, contains an extensive collection of books, besides a valuable assortment of fossils given to it by the Rev. Mr. Calcott. The Philosophical Institution, a neat building with a Grecian portico, contains two reading-rooms, a theatre in which lectures on the various branches of science are periodically delivered, a laboratory, a philosophical apparatus, a museum, a room wherein casts from the Elgin marbles are deposited, and a room for the exhibition of paintings. There is also a Mechanics' Institution. The Exchange, in Cornstreet, erected about the year 1760, by the corporation, at an expense of more than £50,000, is a spacious and elegant structure, one hundred and ten feet in length, and of proportionate breadth, with a rustic basement, in the centre of which are handsome columns of the Corinthian order, forming the principal entrance, and supporting a pediment, bearing in the tympanum the king's arms, finely sculptured: this edifice is not used as an exchange, but principally for the corn market: the merchants, notwithstanding the ample accommodation it affords, having invariably transacted their business in the open street, till the year 1811, when the Commercial Rooms were erected. These buildings, to which the entrance from the street is by a portico of four pillars of the Ionic order, contain several apartments for the despatch of business, and a reading-room: the principal hall, sixty feet in length, forty feet wide, and twenty-five feet high, is lighted by a circular lantern, twenty-one feet in diameter, and crowned with a handsome dome supported by twelve caryatides. The post-office is a neat building of freestone, to the west of the Exchange.

Bristol is represented by Malmsbury as having been, so early as the reign of Henry II., a "wealthy city, full of ships from Ireland, Norway, and every part of Europe, which brought to it great commerce." It carries on an extensive trade with the West Indies, North and South America, and the countries bordering on the Baltic and Mediterranean seas. The principal articles of importation are sugar, rum, coffee, tobacco, wine, German wool, timber, and turpentine; those exported consist chiefly of the produce of the manufactories within the town and neighbourhood: it has also a very extensive coasting trade, besides considerable intercourse with Ireland. The number of ships belonging to it, according to the return in 1829, was three hundred and sixteen, the aggregate burden of which amounted to forty-nine thousand five hundred and thirty-five tons. In the year 1826, the number of vessels entered inwards from foreign ports was, three hundred and thirty-four British, and sixty foreign; and the number cleared outwards, two hundred and seventy-seven British, and thirty-five foreign: and the amount of duties paid at the custom-house, during the same year, exceeded a million sterling. In the following year, the number of coasting vessels entered inwards was five thousand one hundred and eighty-six, of which seven hundred and thirty-one were from Ireland. Within the last few years a considerable reduction has been made in the local dues of the port, the previous high rate of which, compared with those of Liverpool and other places, being considered to operate injuriously to its interests. The port was materially enlarged and improved in 1247, by diverting the course of the river Frome into another channel, but was still subject to great inconvenience, from vessels being obliged to wait for spring tides, before they could sail out of the harbour. It was further improved in 1803, by changing the course of the Avon, and damming up its former channel, to form an extensive floating-dock, communicating, by means of reservoirs, with the river and the quay, to which vessels have access at any time, and from which, at every high tide, they may sail directly into the channel. Over this new course of the Avon two handsome iron bridges have been erected: the entire work was completed in 1809, at an expense of more than £600,000. The quay, extending for more than a mile along the banks of the Avon and Frome, and secured by a strong brick wall, coped with stone, is accessible to ships of any burden, and conveniently adapted to the despatch of business. Immediately behind it, in a spacious square, in the centre of which is an equestrian statue of William III., in the Roman costume, are the mansion-house, the custom-house, and the excise-office, which are not entitled to architectural notice. On the banks of the river Avon, a little below the town, are several dock-yards, where ship-building is carried on to a considerable extent. The principal articles of manufacture are brass, copper, zinc, spelter, patent shot, lead, leather, floorcloth, china, glass, glass bottles and glass ware of every kind (for which there are fifteen furnaces), and the celebrated stone ware: the brass and copper works here are the most extensive in England, and the zinc is considered superior to that made in any other place. There is an extensive pin-manufactory, wherein, exclusively of several hundred adults, two hundred children are employed; and there are several sugar refineries, breweries, distilleries, and iron-foundries, for the supply of all which, abundance of coal is brought into the town, from the collieries in the neighbourhood. An act has lately been obtained for the construction of a rail-road from Coal Pit Heath, in the county of Gloucester, to Bristol. The market days are Monday, for fish; Tuesday, for corn, hay, and straw; Wednesday, for general provisions, fish, cheese, and hides: Thursday, for corn, cattle, and hides; Friday, for hay and straw; and Saturday, for general provisions and hides. The principal market-place forms a spacious quadrangle; one side is occupied by the back of the exchange, forming a rustic arcade, over which is a pediment ornamented with the city arms and surmounted by a handsome turret. St. James' market-house, and the Welch market-house, are neat and convenient buildings. Fairs, each continuing eight days, on the first two of which there is a considerable show of cattle, are held on March 1st and September 1st. A spacious market-place for cattle has recently been opened without the town, at an expense of £10,000: it occupies an area four hundred feet square, along the sides of which are pent-houses for fat cattle, sheep, pigs, &c. The area is formed into divisions for lean cattle, store sheep, and pigs, and showing-ground for horses: in the centre of the principal entrance is a commodious freestone residence for the clerk of the market, containing also apartments for drovers, farmers, &c.

Corporate Seal.

Obverse. Reverse.

The government, by charter of incorporation granted by Henry III., and confirmed and extended by Edward III., Queen Elizabeth, Charles II., and finally by Queen Anne, who made the election of the officers independent of royal control, is vested in a mayor, a high steward (who is usually a nobleman), a recorder (who must be a barrister of five years' standing), two sheriffs (who are also bailiffs of the ancient hundred), twelve aldermen, one for each of the twelve wards into which the city is divided, and twenty-eight common council-men, assisted by a town-clerk (who must be a barrister of three years' standing), a chamberlain, vice-chamberlain, two coroners, a sword-bearer, a water-bailiff, a clerk of the markets, eight serjeants at mace, and subordinate officers. The mayor is chosen annually on the 4th of September, from among those who have served the office of sheriff; the sheriffs are chosen annually from the common council-men, and the aldermen from those who have served the office of mayor. The freedom of the city is inherited by the sons of freemen, obtained by marriage with the daughter of a freeman, by servitude, by purchase, or by presentation. The mayor, recorder, and aldermen are justices of the peace for the city and county of the city. The corporation hold a court of session quarterly, a court of assize in April, and a court of Nisi Prius, in which one of the judges on the western circuit presides. A court, called the Tolzey court (from having been anciently held at the place where the king's tolls, or dues, were collected), is held by prescription every Monday, under the sheriffs (in their character of bailiffs of the hundred), aided by a steward, who must be a barrister of three years' standing; its jurisdiction extends over the whole of the county of the city, and on the river down to the Flat and Steep Holmes, below Kingsroad, thirty miles from the city; and it takes cognizance of all actions for debt, and other civil actions, to an unlimited amount, arising within the city: it also holds pleas of ejectment, and issues processes of attachment on the goods of foreigners sued for debt. A branch of this, and similar in all its proceedings and jurisdiction, is the court of pie-powder, which is held for fourteen days in the open air, in the Old market, commencing on the 30th of September, and during this period the proceedings in the Tolzey court are suspended. A court of conscience is held under commissioners, every Monday, pursuant to an act passed in the 1st of William and Mary, for the recovery of debts under 40*s*. A court of requests, under an act of the 56th of George III., is also held every Monday under commissioners, for the recovery of debts above 40*s*., and under any amount for which an arrest on mesne process may by law take place: its jurisdiction extends over "the city and county of the city of Bristol, and the liberties thereof, and the several parishes and out-parishes of Clifton, St. James, and St. Paul, and St. Philip and Jacob, and the tything of Stoke Bishop, in the parish of Westbury upon Trym, in the county of Gloucester, and the parish of Bedminster, in the county of Somerset." The guildhall is a very ancient building, recently fronted with stone; it is decorated with the arms of Edward VI., those of his present majesty, and a statue of Charles II. In the north wing is a small chapel, dedicated to St. George, founded in the reign of Richard II., by William Spicer, a former mayor. The new council-house, for the transaction of civic affairs, is an elegant edifice of freestone, of the Ionic order, with a handsome portico and balustrade, and ornamented with a figure of Justice over the pediment, on one side of which are the royal arms, and on the other those of the city. Merchants hall, Coopers' hall, and others, formerly belonging to the different trading companies, and many of them handsome buildings, are now appropriated to private uses. The gaol, erected in 1820, is a spacious and well-arranged quadrangular edifice of stone; at the entrance is a lodge for the turnkey, and in the centre of the court-yard is the governor's house, communicating, by means of cast-iron bridges, with the four wings of the prison, one containing rooms for forty-three male and forty-three female debtors of the first and second classes, and others for fifty of the lower class, with an infirmary for females, and two cells and a day-room for female convicts under sentence of death: the other wings are for felons, and are arranged with a due regard to classification, and to cleanliness, exercise, and health: the buildings are warmed by pneumatic stoves, and are amply supplied with water raised from a spring by a tread-wheel worked by the prisoners. The house of correction, which is also well arranged and under good regulation, is situated on the bank of the river Frome, in the parish of St. John. Lawford's Gate prison, without the city, is appropriated to that part of the suburbs lying in the county of Gloucester. The elective franchise has been exercised since the 23rd of Edward I.: the city returns two members to parliament. The right of election is vested in the freemen at large, in number about six thousand: the mayor is the returning officer.

Arms of the Bishoprick.

Bristol is the seat of a diocese, the jurisdiction of which extends over the city and county of the city, the greater part of the county of Dorset, and a few parishes in the county of Gloucester: it was separated from the diocese of Salisbury, and raised into a see in 1542. The establishment consists of a bishop, dean, six prebendaries, six minor canons, a deacon, subdeacon, and other officers. The cathedral, dedicated to the Holy Trinity, was formerly the Collegiate Church belonging to a priory of Black canons, founded by Robert Fitzharding, in 1148, and raised into an abbey in the reign of Henry II., the revenue being, at the dissolution, £767. 15. 3. It is a venerable and highly finished cruciform structure, with a lofty square embattled tower rising from the centre, strengthened with buttresses and crowned with pinnacles; it contains portions in the early, decorated, and later styles of English architecture, in all of them exhibiting specimens of the purest design and most elaborate execution. The nave was destroyed during the parliamentary war: the roofs of the choir and transepts, all of equal height and finely groined, are supported on clustered columns, richly moulded; and the remaining parts, from the striking beauty of their details, afford evidence of the grandeur of the interior when entire. At the entrance into the choir is an empannelled screen, ornamented with carvings of the minor prophets; and in several small chapels of exquisite beauty are many interesting monuments, among which may be noticed those of Robert Fitzharding, and of several of the abbots and bishops; of Mrs. Draper, the eulogized Eliza of Sterne; Lady Hesketh, celebrated by Cowper; and the wife of the Rev. William Mason, with a beautiful epitaph written by that poet. The chapter-house, a spacious edifice highly enriched, in the latest style of Norman architecture; part of the cloisters, in the later English style; and the episcopal palace, in repairing which, in 1740, a dungeon was discovered, containing human bones and several instruments of torture, are still remaining: the entrance gateway, in the lower part of the Norman style, and in the upper part of the later style of English architecture, is in a state of excellent preservation.

The city comprises the parishes of All Saints, St. Augustine, Christ Church, St. Ewin, or Owen, St. John the Baptist, St. Leonard, St. Mary le Port, St. Mary Redcliffe, St. Michael, St. Nicholas, St. Peter, St. Stephen, St. Thomas, and St. Werburgh, besides Temple parish, and part of the parishes of St. James, St. Paul, and St. Philip and St. Jacob, all within the peculiar jurisdiction of the bishop; there is also the extra-parochial ward of Castle Precincts, which has no church, and is exempted from all ecclesiastical assessments. The living of All Saints' is a discharged vicarage, rated in the king's books at £4. 3. 4., endowed with £400 private benefaction, and £400 royal bounty, and in the patronage of the Dean and Chapter of Bristol. The church, to which a tower was added in 1716, is a very ancient structure; the interior is a fine specimen of the early style of English architecture, and contains a magnificent monument, by Rysbrack, to the memory of Edward Colston, Esq., an eminent philanthropist, and a great benefactor to the city. The living of St. Augustine's is a discharged vicarage, rated in the king's books at £6, endowed with £800 royal bounty, and in the patronage of the Dean and Chapter. The church, which was built about the year 1480, combines various portions in the early, with several in the later, style of English architecture. The living of Christ Church parish is a discharged rectory, with that of St. Ewin's united, rated in the king's books at £11. 10., endowed with £200 private benefaction, and £600 royal bounty, and in the patronage of the Mayor and Corporation. The church is a handsome modern edifice in the Grecian style, with a lofty tower of two stages, decorated with light columns and pilasters, and surmounted by an octangular turret and spire. The living of St. John the Baptists' is a discharged rectory, with which that of St. Lawrence was consolidated in 1578, rated in the king's books at £7. 4. 7., endowed with £200 private benefaction, and £400 royal bounty, and in the patronage of the Mayor and Corporation. The church is a handsome edifice, chiefly in the later style of English architecture. The living of St. Leonard's is a discharged vicarage, with that of St. Nicholas united, rated in the king's books at £34. 1. 1., endowed with £400 royal bounty, and in the patronage of the Dean and Chapter. The living of the parish of St. Mary le Port is a discharged rectory, rated in the king's books at £7, endowed with £600 royal bounty, and in the patronage of the Duke of Buckingham. The church is a very ancient structure in the early style of English architecture, with a square embattled tower crowned with pinnacles. The living of St. Mary's Redcliffe is a discharged vicarage, annexed to Bedminster, rated in the king's books at £12. 6. 3. The church was founded in 1376, by Simon de Burton, mayor, and, after the damage it sustained from a violent storm, in 1445, that blew down two-thirds of the spire, it was extensively repaired by William Cannyngs, Esq. It is a spacious and magnificent cruciform structure, with a lofty and finely proportioned tower at the west end, surmounted by the remaining part of the spire, which has not been rebuilt. The interior exhibits a continued series of the richest specimens, in every variety, from the early to the later style of English architecture; the roof is elaborately groined, and supported on finely clustered columns of singular delicacy, and deeply moulded arches of graceful elevation; all the proportions are grand, and all the details rich and exquisitely finished: the beautiful east window has been blocked up with paintings, which, though from the pencil of Hogarth, cannot atone for the destruction of a feature so essential to the unity of effect that this splendid structure is calculated to produce; and the organ, which has been removed to the west end of the nave, is supported by a heavy mass of modern masonry, by no means harmonising with the character of the building. At the intersection is a fine brass eagle, formed of the refuse from the pin-manufactory, and presented by the proprietor of that establishment. The north porch, which is entirely in the decorated style, is exquisitely beautiful; and the Lady chapel, now used as a school-room, is a fine specimen of the later style. In this church are two monuments to the memory of Mr. Cannyngs, who is considered as its second founder; one bearing his effigies in magisterial robes, surmounted by a rich canopy; the other representing him as Dean of Westbury, having been promoted to that dignity on entering into holy orders towards the close of his life. The remains of Sir William Penn, father of William Penn, founder of Pennsylvania, are deposited here. The living of St. Michael's is a discharged rectory, rated in the king's books at £6, endowed with £800 royal bounty, and in the patronage of the Mayor and Corporation. The church is a neat structure in the ancient style of English architecture, with a very old tower. The living of St. Nicholas' is a discharged vicarage, with that of St. Leonard's united, endowed with £600 royal bounty, and in the patronage of the Mayor and

Corporation. The church is a neat plain modern edifice in the ancient style of English architecture; the interior forms a spacious area undivided by pillars: in the crypt is a handsome monument to the memory of Alderman John Whiston, who represented the city in four successive parliaments. The living of St. Peter's is a discharged rectory, rated in the king's books at £6. 7. 6., endowed with £200 private benefaction, and £200 royal bounty, and in the patronage of the Mayor and Corporation. The church is a very ancient and venerable structure, and though so frequently repaired as to leave little of the original building, it still retains much of its character and interest. Richard Savage, whose talents and sufferings have equally excited the admiration and the sympathy of the public, was interred in this church. The living of St. Stephen's is a discharged rectory, rated in the king's books at £16, endowed with £1200 parliamentary grant, and in the patronage of the Crown. The church, founded in 1470, by John Shipward, Esq., mayor, is a very handsome structure in the later style of English architecture, with a lofty and beautiful tower, crowned with light pierced battlements and turrets, and a porch, the details of which are exquisitely rich. The living of Temple parish is a discharged vicarage, rated in the king's books at £3. 4. 2., and in the patronage of the Mayor and Corporation. The church, founded by the Knights Templars, in 1145, is a spacious edifice, partaking of the late Norman and early English style of architecture, with a fine tower, declining considerably from the perpendicular, disunited from the body of the church by the vibration caused by ringing the bells. The living of St. Thomas' is a perpetual curacy, annexed to the vicarage of Bedminster, in the archdeaconry of Bath, and diocese of Bath and Wells. The church, founded in the twelfth century, was rebuilt in 1793; it is a handsome structure in the later style of English architecture. The living of St. Werburgh's is a discharged rectory, rated in the king's books at £10, and in the patronage of the Crown. The church, founded in 1190, and, with the exception of the tower, which was added to it in 1385, rebuilt in 1761, is in the later style of English architecture: it is highly ornamented within, and contains a handsome monument to the memory of Robert Thorne, founder of the grammar school. In this church, the litany was first celebrated in English, in 1543. The living of St. James' is a perpetual curacy, endowed with £200 private benefaction, and £600 royal bounty, and in the patronage of the Mayor and Corporation. The church, anciently collegiate, was made parochial in 1347, when the tower was added: the interior contains some fine portions in the Norman style of architecture, particularly a curious circular window. Robert, Earl of Gloucester, founder of the ancient priory of St. James, to which the church belonged, and Eleonora, niece of King John, who is said to have been forty years confined in Bristol castle, are supposed to lie interred in this church. The living of St. Paul's is a perpetual curacy, endowed with £400 private benefaction, and £400 royal bounty, and in the patronage of the Mayor and Corporation. The living of the parish of St. Philip and St. Jacob is a discharged vicarage, rated in the king's books at £15, and in the patronage of the Mayor and Corporation. The church, founded in the twelfth century, is a spacious and handsome structure, in the early style of English architecture, with a lofty square embattled tower. St. Mark's, commonly called the mayor's chapel, in College-green, formerly collegiate, is a small edifice containing elegant specimens of the early, decorated, and later styles of English architecture, with a beautiful tower; the altar-piece, which has been recently restored, contains some handsome niches in the later style, and fine tabernacle work; and to the east of the tower is a small chapel, now used for a vestry-room, with a ceiling of fan tracery of exquisite workmanship: divine service is performed every Sunday morning, by the mayor's chaplain. A new church has been erected in the parish of St. Philip, by grant from the parliamentary commissioners. There are several episcopal chapels, the principal of which are, Foster's chapel, in Steep-street; Colston's chapel, on St. Michael's Hill; Trinity chapel, a neat building in the later English style; and Great George-street chapel, a handsome structure in the Grecian style of architecture, with a portico of the Doric order; besides a chapel for French Protestants. There are places of worship for Baptists, the Society of Friends, those in the connexion of the late Countess of Huntingdon, Independents, Primitive and Wesleyan Methodists, Moravians, Scotch Seceders, Swedenborgians, Unitarians, and Roman Catholics, besides two synagogues.

The free grammar school was founded, in 1352, by Robert Thorne, who bequeathed £1000 for that purpose, which sum, together with several houses and some land belonging to the dissolved hospital of St. Bartholomew, was appropriated to its erection and endowment, and various benefactions having since been made, it now possesses five hundred and ninety acres of land and some houses: it is open to the sons of all freemen within a mile of the liberties of the city, and is under the management of the corporation, who appoint a head-master and a second master, each with a salary of £80 per annum, the head-master having also a good house, with the privilege of taking boarders: it has several exhibitions, and two small fellowships at St. John's College, Oxford. The grammar school in College-green is attached to the cathedral, for the instruction of the choristers by one of the minor canons of that establishment. The free grammar and writing school, in the parish of Redcliffe, was founded by letters patent granted in the 13th of Elizabeth, and endowed by Alderman Whiston and others, with annuities amounting to £21: it is under the management of twelve incorporated governors. Queen Elizabeth's hospital, founded in 1586, by John Carr, an opulent citizen, whose endowment of it, increased by subsequent benefactions, produces about £2400 per annum, is under the management of the corporation, and is appropriated to the clothing, maintenance, and education of forty boys. The free school in St. Augustine's parish was founded, in 1708, by Mr. Edward Colston, who endowed it for the clothing, maintenance, and education of one hundred boys; it is under the inspection of trustees, agreeably to the directions of the founder. In this school Chatterton was maintained for seven years, and within that period is thought to have composed several of his poems. The free school in Temple parish, originally supported by subscription, was endowed with £80 per annum by Mr. Edward Colston, who erected the school-house in 1711, for clothing and instructing forty boys, but the number has been reduced to thirty. The Merchants' Hall school was founded, in 1738, by Dame Susannah Holworthy, and endowed by her and other benefactors, for the instruction of forty boys in grammar, arithmetic, and geography, ten of whom are also taught navigation. The Merchants' society, in part of whose hall the school is held, provide mathematical instruments, charts, and books, and pay a master £80 per annum. The school in Pile-street, for clothing and teaching forty boys of the parishes of Redcliffe and St. Thomas, is supported partly by an endowment of £20 per annum, by Mr. Edward Colston, and partly by subscription: the income is about £170 per annum, part of it being appropriated in apprenticing a small number of the boys. The Red Maids' school was founded in 1627, and endowed by Alderman Whiston, for the clothing, maintenance, and instruction of forty girls. A school in Temple parish is endowed with a permanent fund sufficient for the clothing and instruction of forty girls. There is also a school for thirty boys, children of Protestant dissenters, who are educated and partly clothed: the buildings occupy three sides of a quadrangle in Stoke's Croft, the centre containing the school and house for the master, and the wings being used as almshouses for twelve aged persons. A school is supported by the Wesleyan Methodists, and endowed by an unknown benefactor with £700, for the clothing and instruction of thirty girls.

Trinity hospital, or almshouses, for ten aged men and thirty-six poor women, is of very ancient foundation: the original endowment, increased by successive benefactions, produces at present £790 per annum. The premises consist of two separate ranges of buildings, on opposite sides of Old Market-street, to one of which is attached a neat chapel for the use of the alms-people. Foster's almshouses, in Steep-street, were founded and endowed, in 1492, by John Foster, merchant, for fourteen aged persons; the annual revenue is at present about £330; they are firmly built of stone, and have a small chapel annexed. Temple hospital was founded and endowed, in 1613, by the Rev. Dr. White; its revenue, which has since been progressively improving, amounts at present to upwards of £600 per annum, and the number of the inmates has been increased to twenty-four: the premises consist of two parallel ranges of buildings, connected at one end by a wall, the area forming a garden for the use of the alms-people. Two almshouses, both stone structures, one in Temple-street, containing twelve tenements, and the other in the old market-place, containing sixteen apartments, were founded and endowed, in 1679, by Alderman Stevens: the endowment, consisting of three hundred and fifty-four acres of land, produces at present £750 per annum. The merchants' almshouses, in King-street, were founded by John Welch and other mariners, in the 4th of Elizabeth, and comprise thirty-one tenements, at present occupied by nineteen seamen and twelve women. Colston's almshouses, on St. Michael's Hill, were founded and endowed, in 1696, by Mr. Edward Colston, for twelve aged men and twelve aged women: the present income is about £300 per annum; the premises contain twenty-four apartments. Mrs. Sarah Ridley founded an almshouse in 1716, which she endowed with £2200, for five decayed bachelors and five decayed maids; the endowment was augmented by Mr. John Jocham, with £1000, and, with subsequent benefactions, produces at present an income of £155 per annum. The almshouses in Milk-street, were founded by Mrs. Elizabeth Blanchard, in 1722, who endowed them for five aged persons; the income is £95 per annum: there are also several others of minor importance. The revenue arising from all these various charitable endowments amounts to nearly £17,000 per annum. The infirmary, the great medical and surgical school for the western counties, is conducted on a plan of truly beneficent liberality, and embraces every possible case of calamity or disease; it was opened for the reception of patients in 1786, and is nobly supported by donations and voluntary subscription. The building, to which a new wing has been recently added, at an expense of £10,000, is spacious and well arranged, and in an open and healthy situation. The asylum for the indigent blind of both sexes, from all parts of the kingdom, who are instructed in basket-making, and in other trades suited to their situation, is a valuable institution supported by subscription. The dispensary, the hospital for diseases of the eye, the asylum for female orphans, the refuge society, the penitentiary, and numerous other charitable and benevolent institutions, are extensively patronised and liberally supported. At Clifton, about a mile from the city, are the celebrated hot wells, noticed in the account of that place.

Of the ancient fortifications, the tower gateway, a plain arch at the end of John-street, and St. John's gate, under the tower of St. John's church, decorated with statues and much ornamented, are all that remain. There are partial remains of some of the numerous religious houses anciently existing in the city and its immediate vicinity, comprised in the buildings of the schools and charitable institutions that have been established by the corporation and other individuals, into whose possession they were transferred at the dissolution. Of these the principal were, a priory of Benedictine monks, to the north-east of the city, founded by Robert, Earl of Gloucester, in the latter part of the reign of Henry I., or the beginning of that of Stephen; a nunnery to the north of the city, founded in the reign of Henry II., by Eva, widow of Robert Fitzharding, of which she was prioress, and the revenue of which, at the dissolution, was £21. 11. 3.; St. John's hospital, on the road to Bath, founded in the reign of King John, the revenue of which was £51. 10. 4.; St. Catherine's hospital, founded in the reign of Henry III., by Robert de Berkele, the revenue of which was £21. 15. 8.; St. Lawrence's hospital, for lepers, founded in the reign of Henry III.; an hospital dedicated to the Blessed Virgin and St. Mark, founded in 1229, by Maurice de Gaunt, the revenue of which was £140; a house of Black friars, by the same founder, who also erected a college of calendaries; a house of Grey friars, founded in 1234; a house of White friars, founded in 1267, by Edward I., when Prince of Wales: an establishment for Augustine friars, founded in the reign of Edward II., by Simon and William Montacute; and Trinity hospital, near Lawford-gate, founded by John Barstable, in the reign of Henry V.

This city is distinguished as the birthplace of many eminent characters, among whom may be noticed Sebastian Cabot, who first discovered the continent of North America, in 1498; Hugh Elliot, who discovered Newfoundland, in 1527; William Grocyn, Greek professor at Oxford in the beginning of the sixteenth century;

Tobias Matthew, Archbishop of York; Rev. Mr. Calcott, author of a treatise on the deluge; Sir William Draper, who distinguished himself by his epistolary replies to the strictures of Junius; Admiral Sir William Penn; the Rev. John Lewis, author of the Life of Wickliffe, History of the Translations of the Bible, &c.; the poet Chatterton; Mrs. Mary Robinson, from the sweetness of her poetry called the British Sappho; Edward Colston, merchant, who died in 1721; and Richard Reynolds, one of the Society of Friends, and a proprietor of the iron-works at Colebrook-dale, both distinguished for their munificent charities; and Thomas Edward Bowditch, the African traveller. Bristol gives the titles of earl and marquis to the family of Hervey.

BRISTON, a parish in the hundred of HOLT, county of NORFOLK, 4½ miles (S.S.W.) from Holt, containing 789 inhabitants. The living is a discharged vicarage, in the archdeaconry and diocese of Norwich, rated in the king's books at £4. 9. 9½., and in the patronage of H. Thomas Jones, Esq. The church is dedicated to All Saints. There is a place of worship for Wesleyan Methodists. Thomasine Scamler, in 1667, bequeathed £110 for teaching and apprenticing children.

BRITFORD, a parish in the hundred of CAWDEN and CADWORTH, county of WILTS, 1½ mile (S.E. by S.) from Salisbury, containing, with the hamlets of East Harnham and Longford, 713 inhabitants. The living is a vicarage, in the peculiar jurisdiction and patronage of the Dean and Chapter of Salisbury, rated in the king's books at £13. The church, dedicated to St. Peter, is a spacious cruciform structure, with a central tower: it contains a tomb which has afforded matter for controversy among writers, some considering it to be the tomb of the Duke of Buckingham, who was beheaded by Richard III., whilst others reject the opinion. A stream in this parish was cut for a canal in the reign of Charles II., to form a line of communication with Christchurch, in the county of Southampton; but, owing to the shifting of the sand, it was never completed.

BRITWELL, a liberty in the parish and hundred of BURNHAM, county of BUCKINGHAM, 4 miles (N.N.W.) from Eton. The population is returned with the parish.

BRITWELL-SALOME, a parish in the hundred of LEWKNOR, county of OXFORD, 5½ miles (S. by W.) from Tetsworth, containing 192 inhabitants. The living is a rectory, in the archdeaconry and diocese of Oxford, rated in the king's books at £6. 19. 2., and in the patronage of Mrs. Stopes. The church is dedicated to St. Nicholas.

BRIXHAM, a sea-port, market-town, and parish, in the hundred of HAYTOR, county of DEVON, 27¾ miles (S.) from Exeter, and 198 (W.S.W.) from London, containing 4503 inhabitants. This town, at which William, Prince of Orange, landed on the 5th of November, 1688, is pleasantly situated near the southern extremity of Torbay, on the west side; it is irregularly built, but contains many good houses, several of which are erected on the cliffs projecting above the harbour. The inhabitants are amply supplied with water; the air is salubrious, the environs pleasant, and its vicinity to the well-frequented bathing-place, Torquay, renders it desirable as a place of residence. The port, which is a member of the port of Dartmouth, carries on a considerable coasting trade, in which one hundred and twenty vessels, of from sixty to one hundred and fifty tons' burden, are employed. The harbour, consisting of two basins, communicating with each other, is safe and commodious; the outer basin has been recently formed, by the erection of a second pier, at the expense of £5300, raised by the inhabitants. During spring tides the water rises to the height of twenty-four feet at the pier-head. There are one hundred and five vessels, of from twenty to forty-five tons' burden, and sixty-four smaller boats, engaged in the fishing trade, which is carried on to a considerable extent: the fish caught are chiefly turbot and soles, for the supply of the London, Bath, and Exeter markets. The trade of the town has derived considerable increase from this being the rendezvous of men of war, which lay in their supply of water at this port: a considerable number of shops has been established on the shore, for the sale of slops and other articles. There are some extensive quarries of marble in the vicinity. The market days are Thursday and Saturday, established under the authority of an act of parliament passed in 1799: it is in contemplation to erect a new market-house. The fair is on Whit-Tuesday and the two following days.

The parish is divided into Higher and Lower Brixham: the living is a discharged vicarage, with the perpetual curacies of Churston-Ferrers and Kingswear annexed, in the archdeaconry of Totness, and diocese of Exeter, rated in the king's books at £52. 15., and in the patronage of the Crown. The church, dedicated to the Virgin Mary, and situated in Higher Brixham, is an ancient structure, containing some interesting monuments, among which is the cenotaph of the late Judge Buller: it has lately received an addition of eight hundred sittings, seven hundred of them free, the Incorporated Society for the enlargement of churches and chapels having granted £700 for that purpose. The chapel at Lower Brixham was erected by subscription among the inhabitants, aided by a grant of £1200 from the parliamentary commissioners; it is a neat building, in the English style of architecture, and contains three hundred free sittings. There are places of worship for Baptists and Wesleyan Methodists. A National school, founded by the society, has been incorporated with an older establishment, endowed in 1634, and also in 1692: the master has a house and garden, with a salary of about £60 per annum: two schoolrooms have been built near his dwelling, by subscription, wherein about four hundred children of both sexes are instructed. At Higher Brixham is Lay Well, the water of which ebbs and flows about nine times in an hour; the variation is about an inch and a quarter. Some ancient coins were found, in 1730, on Bury Head, which is said to have been the site of a Roman fortress.

BRIXTON, a parish in the hundred of PLYMPTON, county of DEVON, 2¼ miles (S.S.E.) from Earl's Plympton, containing 854 inhabitants. The living is a perpetual curacy, in the archdeaconry of Totness, and diocese of Exeter, endowed with £1000 parliamentary grant, and in the patronage of the Dean and Chapter of Exeter. The church first received the right of sepulture from the prior of Plympton, in 1478. The river Yealm is navigable on the south of this parish. In 1677, several elm plants were put into the ground by Edward Fortescue, Esq., in order that, when arrived at maturity, the trees might be cut down for the benefit of the poor, their places to be supplied by fresh plants.

BRIXTON, a parish in the liberty of West Medina, Isle of Wight division of the county of Southampton, 6¼ miles (S.W. by W.) from Newport, containing 686 inhabitants. The living is a rectory, in the peculiar jurisdiction of the incumbent, rated in the king's books at £32. 3. 4., and in the patronage of the Bishop of Winchester. The church is dedicated to St. Mary. In 1814, the Rev. Noel Digby conveyed an estate in trust, for the establishment of a school for the education of twenty children, to be chosen from this parish and the parish of Mottiston: the income is £20 a year.

BRIXTON, a district in the parish of Lambeth, eastern division of the hundred of Brixton, county of Surrey, 4½ miles (S.S.W.) from London. The population is returned with the parish. This is one of the most agreeable suburbs connected with the metropolis, and is divided into two parts, North Brixton and Brixton Hill: it consists principally of a line of road leading from Kennington to Streatham, upwards of two miles in length, on each side of which are ranges of neat and well-built houses, with others in detached situations surrounded by small shrubberies: it is within the limits of the new police act, and is lighted with gas. Brixton is within the jurisdiction of the court of requests for the borough of Southwark, for the recovery of debts not exceeding £5. A church, dedicated to St. Matthew, and consecrated in June 1824, has been erected, pursuant to an act of parliament, whereby the extensive and populous parish of Lambeth has been divided into five districts, Brixton being one, each of which, on the decease of the present incumbent of Lambeth, will be constituted a distinct parish and benefice: it is in the Grecian style of architecture, with a tower at the east end, and a handsome portico supported by four fluted columns of the Doric order at the west, and contains one thousand nine hundred and twenty-six sittings, of which one thousand and twenty-two are free: the expense of its erection amounted to £15,192. 9., which was defrayed by the commissioners for building new churches and chapels: attached to it is a spacious burial-ground. The living is a district incumbency, in the archdeaconry of Surrey, and diocese of Winchester, and in the patronage of the Archbishop of Canterbury. At Denmark Hill, in this district, there is also a chapel, dedicated to St. Matthew. There are three places of worship for Independents, and one for Wesleyan Methodists. Near the church is a National school, in which about two hundred boys and one hundred and twenty girls are instructed; it was erected in 1826, at an expense of £1200, and enlarged in 1829, at an expense of £366. 13. 10. An infant school was established in 1825. In Acre Lane is Trinity Asylum for aged females, founded and endowed by Thomas Bailey, Esq., in 1824: the building comprises twelve neat tenements; each inmate is entitled to £10 per annum, and twelve sacks of coal. All candidates for admission must be possessed of £20 per annum, and not less than fifty-seven years of age; and it is indispensable that they should believe in the doctrine of the Trinity. Mrs. Mary Bailey, his widow, has invested the sum of £2000 towards founding, in connexion with the above, an asylum for the education and maintenance of the orphans of gospel ministers and others. On Brixton Hill stands the house of correction for the county of Surrey, the tread-mill in which, completed in 1821, was the first established: the number of prisoners committed in 1828, according to the return made for that year, amounted to one thousand three hundred and forty.

BRIXTON-DEVERILL, a parish in the hundred of Heytesbury, county of Wilts, 4¾ miles (S.) from Warminster, containing 153 inhabitants. The living is a rectory, in the archdeaconry and diocese of Salisbury, rated in the king's books at £19. 1. 0½., and in the patronage of the Bishop of Salisbury. The church is dedicated to St. Michael. The river Willey runs through the parish.

BRIXWORTH, a parish in the hundred of Orlingbury, county of Northampton, 6½ miles (N.) from Northampton, containing 927 inhabitants. The living is a discharged vicarage, in the archdeaconry of Northampton, and diocese of Peterborough, rated in the king's books at £14. 15. 10., endowed with £200 private benefaction, and £200 royal bounty, and in the patronage of the Chancellor in the Cathedral Church of Salisbury. The church, dedicated to All Saints, is a curious and interesting edifice, exhibiting much of the original Norman structure, varied by alterations of a more recent date, in the early, decorated, and later styles of English architecture: it is built with red unhewn rag-stone, in small sizes, and the arches are turned, and most of them covered, with courses of bricks similar to the Roman bricks, or tiles, that have been discovered in Roman works in this country. There is a place of worship for Wesleyan Methodists. A fair is held annually on the Monday next after Ascension-day. Thomas Roe, in 1665, gave by deed a rent-charge of £10, for teaching ten poor children of this parish, and ten of the parish of Scaldwell.

BROADCAR, a hamlet in the parish and hundred of Shropham, county of Norfolk, 3¼ miles (N. by W.) from East Harling. The population is returned with the parish. This place, which appears to have been anciently a distinct parish, was united to Shropham previously to the reign of Edward III. The church, dedicated to St. Andrew, has long been desecrated.

BROAD-CHALK, a parish in the hundred of Chalk, county of Wilts, 5¾ miles (S.W. by S.) from Wilton, containing 706 inhabitants. The living is a discharged vicarage, consolidated with that of Alvediston, and united to the vicarage of Bower-Chalk, in the archdeaconry and diocese of Salisbury, rated in the king's books at £27. 14., and in the patronage of the Provost and Fellows of King's College, Cambridge. The church is dedicated to All Saints. Here are several vestiges of antiquity, the principal of which are, an encampment including nearly six acres, and a barrow called Gawen's Barrow.

BROAD-CLIST, county of Devon.—See CLIST (BROAD).

BROADFIELD, a parish in the hundred of Odsey, county of Hertford, 3 miles (N.W. by W.) from Buntingford, containing 23 inhabitants. The living is a rectory, annexed to that of Cottered, in the archdeaconry of Huntingdon, and diocese of Lincoln, rated in the king's books at £10. The church is desecrated.

BROADFIELD, a tything in the parish of WRINGTON, hundred of BRENT with WRINGTON, county of SOMERSET, containing 426 inhabitants.

BROADGATE, an extra-parochial liberty, in the western division of the hundred of GOSCOTE, county of LEICESTER, 5 miles (N. W.) from Leicester, containing 10 inhabitants. Here are the ruins of a fine old mansion once belonging to the noble family of Grey of Groby, of which was the accomplished and unfortunate Lady Jane Grey, who was born here, in 1537.

BROADHEMBURY, a parish (formerly a market town) in the hundred of HAYRIDGE, county of DEVON, 5 miles (N. W.) from Honiton, containing 892 inhabitants. The living is a discharged vicarage, in the archdeaconry and diocese of Exeter, rated in the king's books at £16. 17., endowed with £200 private benefaction, and £200 royal bounty, and in the patronage of the Dean and Chapter of Exeter. The church is dedicated to St. Andrew. The manor formerly belonged to the abbot of Dunkeswell, who obtained for it the grant of a market and fair; the former has long been discontinued, but the latter is still held for cattle on the 30th of November. At the village of Carswell, in this parish, was a small monastery, subordinate to the priory of Montacute. In 1725, the Rev. John Burrough gave £40 for the further support of a schoolmaster, the interest on which, together with £10 a year paid out of the great tithes of Awliscombe, is appropriated to the instruction of twenty children. The Rev. Augustus Montague Toplady, the celebrated defender of the Calvinistic principles of the church of England (whose works were collected together, after his death, in 6 vols. 8vo.), was vicar of this parish.

BROADHEMPSTON, county of DEVON.— See HEMPSTON (BROAD).

BROADHOLME, a hamlet in the parish of THORNEY, northern division of the wapentake of NEWARK, county of NOTTINGHAM, 11 miles (E. by N.) from Tuxford, containing 57 inhabitants. A small Premonstratensian nunnery was founded here in the latter part of the reign of Stephen, by Agnes de Camvile, in honour of the Blessed Virgin Mary, the revenue of which, in the 26th of Henry VIII., was estimated at £16. 15. 2.

BROADMAYNE, a parish in the hundred of GEORGE, but locally in that of Culliford-Tree, Dorchester division of the county of DORSET, 3½ miles (S. E. by S.) from Dorchester, containing 277 inhabitants. The living is a rectory, with that of West Knighton annexed, in the archdeaconry of Dorset, and diocese of Bristol, rated in the king's books at £15. 4. 2., and in the patronage of D. Urquhart, Esq. The church is dedicated to St. Martin.

BROADOAK, a parish in the hundred of WEST, county of CORNWALL, 6¾ miles (W.S.W.) from Liskeard, containing 235 inhabitants. The living is a discharged rectory, consolidated, in 1742, with the rectory of Boconnoc, in the peculiar jurisdiction of the Dean and Chapter of Exeter, rated in the king's books at £8. 13. 4. The church is dedicated to St. Mary.

BROADSTAIRS, a small sea-port and hamlet in the parish of ST. PETER, hundred of RINGSLOW, or Isle of THANET, lathe of ST. AUGUSTINE, county of KENT, 2 miles (N.E. by N.) from Ramsgate, and 75 (E.) from London. The population is returned with the parish. This place, anciently called *Bradstow*, exhibits many vestiges of its former importance; and though subsequently reduced to an inconsiderable village, inhabited only by a few fishermen, it has lately risen into celebrity as a place of fashionable resort for sea-bathing, and is visited in the season by many respectable families, for whose accommodation several new buildings have been recently erected: warm baths, arranged with every requisite appendage, have also been constructed. There are two public libraries, an assembly-room, and an excellent hotel. Leading down to the shore is a stone arch, or portal, with walls built of flint, in which were gates and a portcullis, with a drawbridge attached to it, erected to protect the inhabitants from the incursions of privateers: above the arch is the following inscription,—"York gate, built by George Culmer, A. D. 1540, repaired by Sir John Henniker, Bart., 1795." At a short distance from the gate stood a chapel, in which was placed an image of the Virgin Mary, to whom it was dedicated, in passing which all vessels lowered their topsails, as a mark of reverence. The pier, which is accessible only to vessels of small burden, was constructed in the reign of Henry VIII., for the safety of the craft employed in the fishing trade, once considerable: it is built of wood, and though an act of parliament passed, in the 32nd of George III., for the improvement of the harbour and the pier, the trade had decreased so much that its provisions were never carried into effect. The principal source of employment at present is ship-building, and that is on the decline. Fairs for toys, &c. are held on April 8th and July 10th.

A chapel was erected by subscription in 1828, the minister's stipend being derived from the rents of the seats. There is a place of worship for Wesleyan Methodists. At Kingsgate, in the vicinity, is the Bead House, built in the form of a chapel, now appropriated to the entertainment of parties of pleasure: the sea having undermined the cliff, part of the house has been taken down, the same fate, in all probability, awaiting the remainder. Near the cliff is a rude ancient building, erected on the larger of two tumuli, named Hackendon, or Hackingdown banks, where a desperate battle is said to have taken place, in 853, between the Saxons and the Danes, and to the memory of those who fell in it a tablet was inscribed by Henry, Lord Holland, who erected the building. These tumuli being opened, in 1745, were found to contain graves of an oblong form, and not more than three feet in length, excavated in the solid chalk, and covered with flat stones, and in them were many large human bones, in a perfect state; in one were found three urns of coarse earthenware. Near Broadstairs is an opening through the cliff to the shore, formerly called Bartholomew's Gate, through which Charles II., accompanied by the Duke of York, passed on landing here, in 1683, on his passage from London to Dovor; this has since been called Kingsgate, and the event is recorded by a Latin inscription, in letters of brass, on one side of the gate; on the other is an inscription in Saxon characters. In the vicinity are several curious buildings, erected by the late Lord Holland, as ornaments to his grounds at this place, where he had a villa, built on the model of that belonging to Cicero, at Baix: among them are the temple of Neptune, with an appropriate inscription, *Arx Ruochim;* a small castle, in imitation of those built by Henry VIII., for the protection of the coast; Harley tower; Whitfield tower, erected on the highest spot in the isle; Countess' fort; and an edifice originally intended for a mews, but now a handsome dwelling-house. Between Broadstairs and Kingsgate is the North Foreland, the most eastern point of England, and supposed to have been the Roman station *Cantium*, mentioned by Ptolemy, on which a lighthouse was erected in 1683. Coal was burnt here till 1794, when patent lamps, with magnifying lenses of twenty inches diameter, were introduced by the corporation of the Trinity House: the expense of maintaining this light, which may be seen at the distance of twenty or thirty miles, is defrayed by a duty of twopence per ton on English, and fourpence per ton on foreign, vessels. In 1795, a signal-house was erected near this spot, where a lieutenant and two midshipmen were stationed during the war: a telegraph was also constructed here in 1813, and one on the steeple of the church at St. Peter's, forming the commencement of a line of communication with the Nore, which was kept up till the proclamation of peace with France.

BROADWARD, a township in the parish of Leominster, hundred of Wolphy, county of Hereford, 1¼ mile (S. by E.) from Leominster, containing, with Brierley, Eaton, Hennor, Stretford and Wharton, 321 inhabitants.

BROADWAS, a parish in the lower division of the hundred of Oswaldslow, though locally in the upper division of the hundred of Doddingtree, county of Worcester, 6½ miles (W.) from Worcester, containing 272 inhabitants. The living is a rectory, in the archdeaconry and diocese of Worcester, rated in the king's books at £10. 9. 2., and in the patronage of the Dean and Chapter of Worcester. The church is dedicated to St. Mary Magdalene. The river Teme runs through the parish.

BROADWATER, a parish in the hundred of Brightford, rape of Bramber, county of Sussex, 1 mile (N.) from Worthing, containing, with the sea-port and market town of Worthing, 3725 inhabitants. The living is a rectory, in the archdeaconry and diocese of Chichester, rated in the king's books at £36, and in the patronage of William Kemp, Esq. The church, dedicated to St. Mary, is a handsome cruciform edifice, with a central tower and chapels attached, in which latter are several interesting monuments: it is partly Norman, and partly in the early style of English architecture, and has lately received an addition of three hundred and nineteen sittings, two hundred and thirty-four of which are free, the Incorporated Society for the enlargement of churches and chapels having granted £230 towards defraying the expense.

BROADWAY, a parish in the hundred of Culliford-Tree, Dorchester division of the county of Dorset, 3 miles (N. by W.) from Melcombe-Regis, containing 282 inhabitants. The living is a rectory, with that of Bincombe annexed, in the archdeaconry of Dorset, and diocese of Bristol, rated in the king's books at £7. 15. 2½., and in the patronage of the Master and Fellows of Caius College, Cambridge. The church is dedicated to St. Nicholas.

BROADWAY, a parish in the hundred of Abdick and Bulstone, county of Somerset, 2½ miles (W. by N.) from Ilminster, containing, with the tything of Capland (part only of which is in this parish), 396 inhabitants. The living is a perpetual curacy, in the archdeaconry of Taunton, and diocese of Bath and Wells, endowed with £1000 private benefaction, £800 royal bounty, and £1500 parliamentary grant, and in the patronage of the Rev. William Palmer, D.D. The church is cruciform, and in the cemetery are the remains of a cross. The name was given as being descriptive of the situation of the few scattered huts which were constructed, at an early period, along each side of a broad path leading through what was then the forest of Roche, or Neroche, so denominated from a Roman encampment, called Roche, or Rachiche, Castle, on the edge of Blackdown hill. The manufacture of serge, narrow cloth, drugget, duroy, &c., formerly prevailed to some extent, but has fallen into decay. An almshouse is endowed with about £21 per annum, for the support of seven poor men, who are appointed by the minister and parochial officers.

BROADWAY, a parish in the upper division of the hundred of Pershore, being the southern extremity of the county of Worcester, 5 miles (S. E.) from Evesham, containing 1382 inhabitants. The living is a discharged vicarage, in the peculiar jurisdiction of the Bishop of Worcester, rated in the king's books at £10. 17. 6., endowed with £200 royal bounty, and in the patronage of Miss Eliz. Mills. The church is dedicated to St. Eadburgh. There are places of worship for Independents, Wesleyan Methodists, and Roman Catholics. Thomas Hodges, in 1686, gave land for the instruction of poor boys, directing the overplus to be applied in purchasing books and clothes, or in apprenticing them. In the neighbourhood are quarries of good freestone.

BROADWELL, a parish in the upper division of the hundred of Slaughter, county of Gloucester, 1½ mile (N. N. E.) from Stow on the Wold, containing 296 inhabitants. The living is a rectory, in the archdeaconry and diocese of Gloucester, rated in the king's books at £23. 11. 10½., and in the patronage of J. H. Leigh, Esq. The church is dedicated to St. Paul. The Roman Fosse-way crosses this parish.

BROADWELL, a parish in the hundred of Bampton, county of Oxford, 5¼ miles (S.) from Burford, containing, with the chapelry of Holwell, and the hamlet of Filkins, 820 inhabitants. The living is a discharged vicarage, with the perpetual curacy of Kelmscott annexed, in the archdeaconry and diocese of Oxford, rated in the king's books at £8. 14. 4½., endowed with £200 private benefaction, and £200 royal bounty, and in the patronage of E. F. Colston, Esq. The church is dedicated to St. Peter and St. Paul.

BROADWINSOR, a parish and liberty in the Bridport division of the county of Dorset, 3 miles (W. by N.) from Beaminster, comprising the tythings of Childhay, Deberford, and Drimpton, and containing, with Little Winsor, which is in Redhone hundred, 1387 inhabitants. The living is a vicarage, in the archdeaconry of Dorset, and diocese of Bristol, rated in the king's books at £15. 8. 9. The King, for that turn, was patron in 1828. The church is dedicated to St. John the Baptist. There is an endowment of about £31, given by Robert Smith, in 1725, for the instruction of children.

BROADWOOD-KELLY, a parish in the hundred of Black Torrington, county of Devon, 5¼ miles (E. N. E.) from Hatherleigh, containing 389 inhabitants.

The living is a rectory, in the archdeaconry of Totness, and diocese of Exeter, rated in the king's books at £19. 7. 6., and in the patronage of the Rev. John Hole.

BROADWOOD-WIDGER, county of DEVON.—See BRADWOOD-WIDGER.

BROBURY, a parish in the hundred of GRIMSWORTH, county of HEREFORD, 8¾ miles (E.) from Hay, containing 79 inhabitants. The living is a discharged rectory, in the archdeaconry and diocese of Hereford, rated in the king's books at £4, endowed with £200 royal bounty, and in the patronage of the Rev. William T. Spurdens. The church is dedicated to St. Mary.

BROCKDISH, a parish in the hundred of EARSHAM, county of NORFOLK, 3¼ miles (S. W. by W.) from Harleston, containing 385 inhabitants. The living is a rectory, in the archdeaconry of Norfolk, and diocese of Norwich, rated in the king's books at £10, and in the patronage of William Wigney, Esq. The church is dedicated to St. Peter and St. Paul. There is a place of worship for Wesleyan Methodists.

BROCKENHURST, a chapelry in the parish of BOLDRE, eastern division of the hundred of NEW FOREST, New Forest (East) division of the county of SOUTHAMPTON, 4¼ miles (N. by W.) from Lymington, containing 818 inhabitants. The village is of Saxon origin, and is mentioned in Domesday-book under the name *Broceste*, wherein it is stated to contain a church: this edifice, which is a chapel of ease to Boldre, stands on an artificial mound, and, though somewhat disguised by subsequent alterations, exhibits various portions of early Norman architecture, and contains a large and curious antique font. Henry Thurston, in 1745, gave property, now producing £24 per annum, for the instruction of children; this sum, together with voluntary contributions, is applied to the support of a school on Dr. Bell's plan. The surrounding scenery is of an interesting character: Watcombe House, in Brockenhurst Park, was for three years the residence of John Howard, the philanthropist. Various tumuli are dispersed over a heath, called Sway Common, on the southwest of the village; some of them lie within the area of an intrenchment on the brow of a hill, a short distance south-east of Setley wood; and two have a regular fosse and vallum.

BROCKHALL, a parish in the hundred of NOBOTTLE-GROVE, county of NORTHAMPTON, 5 miles (E.) from Daventry, containing 69 inhabitants. The living is a rectory, in the archdeaconry of Northampton, and diocese of Peterborough, rated in the king's books at £13, and in the patronage of the Trustees of T. L. Thornton, Esq. The church, dedicated to St. Peter and St. Paul, is principally of Norman and early English architecture, with some parts in the later style. The Grand Junction canal, after being crossed by the Roman Watling-street, intersects the parish on the western side.

BROCKHAMPTON, a joint tything with Knowle, in the parish and hundred of BUCKLAND-NEWTON, Cerne subdivision of the county of DORSET, 12 miles (N. by E.) from Dorchester, containing, with Knowle, 195 inhabitants.

BROCKHAMPTON, a hamlet in the parish of BISHOP'S CLEEVE, hundred of CLEEVE, or BISHOP'S CLEEVE, county of GLOUCESTER, 3 miles (N. by W.) from Cheltenham, containing, with Southam, 248 inhabitants.

BROCKHAMPTON, a chapelry in the township of NORTON, parish of BROMYARD, hundred of BROXASH, county of HEREFORD, 3¼ miles (E. N. E.) from Bromyard. A free chapel was built here about thirty-two years ago, the right of presentation to which belongs to John Barneby, Esq.

BROCKHAMPTON, a parish in the hundred of GREYTREE, county of HEREFORD, 6¾ miles (N.) from Ross, containing 116 inhabitants. The living is a perpetual curacy, in the peculiar jurisdiction of the Dean of Hereford, endowed with £200 private benefaction, and £400 royal bounty, and in the patronage of the Dean and Chapter of Hereford. The church is dedicated to the Holy Trinity. The village lies on the eastern bank of the river Wye; and a little to the north of it are the remains of a Roman encampment, with a double trench.

BROCKHAMPTON, a tything in the parish of NEWINGTON, hundred of EWELME, county of OXFORD, 6½ miles (N.) from Wallingford, containing 92 inhabitants.

BROCKHOLES, a joint chapelry with Grimsargh, in the parish of PRESTON, hundred of AMOUNDERNESS, county palatine of LANCASTER, 3 miles (E. by N.) from Preston. The population is returned with Grimsargh.

BROCKLEBANK, a joint township with Stoneraise, in the parish of WESTWARD, ALLERDALE ward below Derwent, county of CUMBERLAND, 5½ miles (S. E.) from Wigton, containing, with Stoneraise, 621 inhabitants.

BROCKLESBY, a parish in the eastern division of the wapentake of YARBOROUGH, parts of LINDSEY, county of LINCOLN, 7 miles (N. by E.) from Caistor, containing, with the hamlet of Little Limber, 256 inhabitants. The living is a discharged rectory, in the archdeaconry and diocese of Lincoln, rated in the king's books at £7. 10. 10., endowed with £200 private benefaction, and £200 royal bounty, and in the patronage of Lord Yarborough. The church is dedicated to All Saints. A monastery of the Premonstratensian order, in honour of St. Mary and St. Martial, was founded at Newsham, in this parish, by Peter de Gousla, in 1143, which, at the dissolution, had a revenue of £114. 1. 4.

BROCKLEY, a parish forming, with the parish of Kingston-Seymour, a detached portion of the hundred of CHEWTON, county of SOMERSET, 9¾ miles (N. by E.) from Axbridge, containing 173 inhabitants. The living is a discharged rectory, in the archdeaconry of Bath, and diocese of Bath and Wells, rated in the king's books at £9. 18. 4., and in the patronage of J. H. S. Piggot, Esq. The church is dedicated to St. Nicholas. Lead-ore exists in the eastern part of the parish, and there are numerous basaltic columns, similar to those forming the Giant's Causeway, in Ireland.

BROCKLEY, a parish in the hundred of THINGOE, county of SUFFOLK, 6¾ miles (S. S. W.) from Bury St. Edmund's, containing 276 inhabitants. The living is a rectory, in the archdeaconry of Sudbury, and diocese of Norwich, rated in the king's books at £10. 4. 2., and in the patronage of the Rev. J. D. Sprigge. The church is dedicated to St. Andrew. Thomas Sparke, in 1721, bequeathed a rent-charge of £6 for the education of children.

BROCKMANTON, a township in the parish of PUDDLESTONE, hundred of WOLPHY, county of HEREFORD, 4¾ miles (E. by N.) from Leominster. The population is returned with the parish.

BROCKSFIELD, a township in the parish of EMBLETON, southern division of BAMBROUGH ward, county of NORTHUMBERLAND, 2¾ miles (N. N. E.) from Alnwick, containing 28 inhabitants.

BROCKTON, a township in the parish of BASWICH, eastern division of the hundred of CUTTLESTONE, county of STAFFORD, 4 miles (S.E. by E.) from Stafford, containing 255 inhabitants. A school here is endowed with £6. 6. per annum, arising from land, for the instruction of nine children.

BROCKWORTH, a parish in the upper division of the hundred of DUDSTONE and KING'S BARTON, county of GLOUCESTER, 4 miles (E. S. E.) from Gloucester, containing 386 inhabitants. The living is a discharged vicarage, in the archdeaconry and diocese of Gloucester, rated in the king's books at £6. 3. 4., endowed with £200 private benefaction, and £400 royal bounty, and in the patronage of Mr. Price. The church is dedicated to St. George. This parish is crossed by the ancient Ermin-street.

BRODSWORTH, a parish in the northern division of the wapentake of STRAFFORTH and TICKHILL, West riding of the county of YORK, 5½ miles (N. W. by W.) from Doncaster, comprising the townships of Brodsworth with Pickburn, and Scansby, and containing 417 inhabitants. The living is a discharged vicarage, in the peculiar jurisdiction and patronage of the Archbishop of York, rated in the king's books at £6. 6. 10½. The church is dedicated to St. Michael. Here are quarries producing a superior kind of limestone. A free school was founded, in 1696, by D'Arcy Wentworth, for ten children, for whose gratuitous instruction the sum of £10 is annually paid out of the Brodsworth estate. This estate belonged to the late Peter Thellusson, Esq., and is now vested in trustees, according to the singular will of that gentleman, who directed that the greater part of his immense property should be allowed to accumulate, and, at a future fixed period, in default of a male heir, be applied towards discharging the national debt. The late Mrs. Thellusson assigned an annual income of £4. 4., for which six girls are instructed by a schoolmistress.

BROGDEN, a township in the parish of BARNOLDWICK, eastern division of the wapentake of STAINCLIFFE and EWCROSS, West riding of the county of YORK, 9¼ miles (W. S. W.) from Skipton, containing 233 inhabitants.

BROKENBOROUGH, a parish in the hundred of MALMESBURY, county of WILTS, 1¾ mile (N. W. by N.) from Malmesbury, containing 262 inhabitants. The living is a perpetual curacy, annexed to the vicarage of Westport, in the archdeaconry of Wilts, and diocese of Salisbury. The church is dedicated to St. John the Baptist.

BROKENHAUGH, a township in the parish of WARDEN, north-western division of TINDALE ward, county of NORTHUMBERLAND, 6 miles (W. by N.) from Hexham, containing 155 inhabitants.

BROMBLOW, a quarter in that part of the parish of WORTHEN which is in the hundred of CHIRBURY, county of SALOP, containing 317 inhabitants.

BROMBORROW, a parish (formerly a market town) partly in the lower, but chiefly in the upper, division of the hundred of WIRRALL, county palatine of CHESTER, 5¼ miles (N.E.) from Great Neston, containing, with the township of Brimstage, 446 inhabitants. The living is a donative belonging to the Dean and Chapter of Chester, endowed with £200 private benefaction, and £1200 royal bounty: the lord of the manor is impropriator of the great tithes. The church, dedicated to St. Barnabas, is a small edifice, with a low wooden tower containing some specimens of early Norman architecture. The learned editor of the Saxon Chronicle has enumerated this among the places which, from the similarity of name, may claim to be the scene of the decisive action fought at *Brunanburgh*, in 937, between the Saxons under Athelstan, and the Danes under Anlaf and Constantine, in which the latter were defeated, and pursued for two days with great slaughter. A monastery was founded at this place, then called Brimesburgh, by Ethelfleda, the celebrated Countess of Mercia, about 912, which was demolished previously to the Conquest, subsequently to which period the manor was given by Ranulph de Gernons, Earl of Chester, to the monks of the abbey of St. Werburgh, to whom Prince Edward, when Earl of Chester, granted a license to hold a market here weekly on Monday, and a fair annually on the eve, festival, and morrow of St. Barnabas; but these have long been discontinued. The courts belonging to the abbey were occasionally held in the manor-house, which was one of those directed by the charter of Earl Ranulph to be kept in a state of security and convenience for that purpose. The parish is bounded on the east by the river Mersey.

BROMBY, a township in the parish of FRODINGHAM, eastern division of the wapentake of MANLEY, parts of LINDSEY, county of LINCOLN, 7½ miles (W. N. W.) from Glandford-Bridge, containing 128 inhabitants.

BROME (SOUTH), a chapelry in the parish of ALL-CANNINGS, hundred of POTTERNE and CANNINGS, county of WILTS, ¼ of a mile (S. E.) from Devizes. The chapel is dedicated to St. James.

BROMEHOLME, a hamlet (formerly a market town) in the parish of BACTON, hundred of TUNSTEAD, county of NORFOLK, 5 miles (E. by N.) from North Walsham. The population is returned with the parish. A priory for Cluniac monks, dedicated to St. Andrew, was founded in 1113, by William de Glanvill, and for some time subsisted as a cell to the monastery at Castle-Acre. Henry III., accompanied by a retinue of the nobility, was here in the eighteenth year of his reign, five years previously to which he had granted the monks license to hold a market weekly on Monday, and a fair annually on the festival of the Exaltation of the Holy Cross. The income of the monks was greatly augmented by numerous rich offerings which were presented to a cross, stated to have been made out of the wood composing the cross on which our Saviour was crucified, brought hither by an English priest, who officiated at the emperor's chapel at Constantinople: the revenue, at the dissolution, amounted to £144. 19. 1.

BROMESWELL, a parish in the hundred of WILFORD, county of SUFFOLK, 3 miles (E.N.E.) from Woodbridge, containing 185 inhabitants. The living is a discharged rectory, in the archdeaconry of Suffolk, and diocese of Norwich, rated in the king's books at £4. 15. 7½., and in the patronage of the Marquis of Bristol. The church is dedicated to St. Edmund.

BROMFIELD, a parish comprising the townships of Blencogo and Dundraw in CUMBERLAND ward, and the chapelry of Allonby, and the townships of Bromfield with Crookdake and Scales, Langrigg with Mealrigg, and West Newton, in ALLERDALE ward below Derwent, county of CUMBERLAND, and containing 2017 inhabitants, exclusively of 603 sailors employed in registered vessels, of which number, 363 are in the township of Bromfield with Crookdake and Scales, 6 miles (W. by S.) from Wigton. The living is a vicarage, in the archdeaconry and diocese of Carlisle, rated in the king's books at £22, and in the patronage of the Bishop of Carlisle. The church is dedicated to St. Kentigern. This parish lies on the shore of the Solway Frith. A free grammar school, situated in the churchyard, was founded by Richard Osmotherley, in 1612, and endowed with £10 a year, for the instruction of fifteen poor children belonging to Bromfield and Langrigg: the endowment was subsequently augmented by a donation of £100 from a member of the family of Thomlinson. In 1805, Mr. Thomlinson, another member of the same family, bequeathed £1400, to be divided among certain schools in this county, one-fourth of which was assigned to this school, which is now free for the children of all parishioners: the income is nearly £40 per annum. In a field belonging to the vicar the site of Mungo castle is visible.

BROMFIELD, a parish in the hundred of MUNSLOW, county of SALOP, comprising the chapelry of Halford, and the townships of Bromfield and Dinehope, and containing 674 inhabitants, of which number, 540 are in the township of Bromfield, 3 miles (N.W. by W.) from Ludlow. The living is a vicarage, in the archdeaconry of Salop, and diocese of Hereford, rated in the king's books at £6, and in the patronage of the Earl of Powis. The church, dedicated to St. Mary, is part of a larger conventual church, that belonged to a Benedictine priory, founded as a cell to the abbey of St. Peter at Gloucester, about 1155, on the site of a college of prebendaries, or Secular canons, of earlier foundation: its revenue, at the dissolution, was £78. 19. 4.: a small portion of the ruins is included within the grounds of Oakley Park.

BROMFLEET, a township in the parish of SOUTH CAVE, partly in the liberty of ST. PETER of YORK, and partly in the Hunsley-Beacon division of the wapentake of HARTHILL, East riding of the county of YORK, 4¼ miles (S.W.) from South Cave, containing 142 inhabitants. There is a place of worship for Wesleyan Methodists.

BROMHALL, a township in the parish of WRENBURY, hundred of NANTWICH, county palatine of CHESTER, 3¾ miles (S.S.W.) from Nantwich, containing 196 inhabitants.

BROMHAM, a parish in the hundred of WILLEY, county of BEDFORD, 3¾ miles (W.N.W.) from Bedford, containing 298 inhabitants. The living is a vicarage, in the archdeaconry of Bedford, and diocese of Lincoln, rated in the king's books at £8, and in the patronage of the Provost and Fellows of Eton College. The church, dedicated to St. Owen, contains some handsome monuments to deceased members of the families of Trevor and Dyne. The village lies on the banks of the river Ouse, over which there is a bridge: it is recorded that the channel of this river, from some unknown cause, was left so bare of water in 1399 and in 1648, that persons walked in it to the distance of three miles. Here is a mineral spring, but in disuse.

BROMHAM, a parish in the hundred of POTTERNE and CANNINGS, county of WILTS, 4 miles (N.W.) from Devizes, containing 1357 inhabitants. The living is a rectory, in the archdeaconry and diocese of Salisbury, rated in the king's books at £12. 16. 0½., and in the patronage of Dr. Starkey. The church, dedicated to St. Nicholas, contains a mural tablet to the memory of Henry Season, M.D., the projector and author of a well-known almanac, and, in an ancient chapel at the east end, several monuments of deceased members of the Baynton family. There are places of worship for Baptists and Wesleyan Methodists. The lordship belonged to Harold, Earl of the West Saxons, and afterwards king of England. Remains of a Roman bath, together with some tesselated pavement, were discovered in a field near the site of Bromham Hall, in 1767. Here is an almshouse for the support of six poor persons, to which Sir Henry Baynton, in 1614, gave land producing £20 per annum; this sum is yearly paid by the lord of the manor. Dr. George Webb, consecrated Bishop of Limerick in 1634, and esteemed one of the most effective preachers of that age, was a native of Bromham, which was also the birthplace of the Rev. John Collinson, author of the History and Antiquities of the County of Somerset, and other works on antiquarian and topographical subjects, who died in 1796. About two miles to the north, and close to the line of the Roman road from London to Bath, is Spye Park, the property and occasional residence, in the reign of Charles II., of the celebrated wit and poet, John Wilmot, Earl of Rochester.

BROMLEY, a market town and parish in the hundred of BROMLEY and BECKENHAM, lathe of SUTTON at HONE, county of KENT, 10 miles (S.E.) from London, on the road to Tonbridge, containing 3147 inhabitants. This place, supposed to have derived its name from the quantity of broom with which the neighbourhood abounds, was, in the eighth century, given by Ethelbert, King of Kent, to the bishops of Rochester, in whose possession it has remained, with very little interruption, till the present time. The episcopal palace had become so ruinous in 1184, that Gilbert de Glanville was obliged to expend a considerable sum in repairing it. In this palace was found the plot of a conspiracy, of which Spratt, Bishop of Rochester, published an account in 1692. Bishop Thomas, on being appointed to the see, finding the old building much decayed, pulled it down, and erected the present palace, which was completed in 1777: it is a plain edifice of brick, pleasantly situated on the brow of an eminence about a quarter of a mile from the town. In the gardens was anciently an oratory, much resorted to on account of certain indulgences granted by Lucas, legate of Pope Sixtus IV., to all who should offer up their devotions there during Pentecost; and near it was a well of mineral water, similar in its properties to the water at Tonbridge, but more strongly impregnated. This well, which was in honour of the saint to whom the oratory was dedicated, called St. Blaze's well, was for a considerable time in great repute; but the oratory becoming dilapidated after the

Reformation, the well was choked up and the efficacy of its water forgotten, till, being re-opened in 1756, it regained its former celebrity, and is still much esteemed for its medicinal quality. The town is pleasantly situated on the north side of the river Ravensbourne, and consists principally of one street extending for a considerable distance along the turnpike road: the houses are in general neat and well built, especially those in the market-place, in the centre of which is an ancient market-house, supported on wooden pillars: the streets are partially paved and lighted, and the inhabitants amply supplied with water. The market, granted to the bishop of Rochester in 1447, is on Thursday; and a great mart for cattle has been recently established on the third Thursday in every month. Fairs are held on February 14th and August 5th, for live stock. The county magistrates hold a meeting for the division alternately here and at Farnborough, every other week. A court of requests, for the recovery of debts under £5, is held every alternate Thursday, at the market-house, the jurisdiction of which extends over the hundreds of Blackheath, Bromley, Beckenham, Roxley, Little, and Lessness. Headboroughs and constables are appointed at the court leet of the lord of the manor.

The living is a perpetual curacy, in the archdeaconry and diocese of Rochester, and in the patronage of the Bishop of Rochester. The church, dedicated to St. Peter and St. Paul, is a spacious structure, with a square embattled tower, partly rebuilt in 1792; it contains an ancient Norman font, and various interesting monuments, among which are those of several of the bishops of Rochester; of Dr. Hawkesworth, author of the Adventurer, who was a native of this place; and of Elizabeth, wife of Dr. Johnson. There are places of worship for Independents and Methodists. A National school for children of both sexes has been erected, and is supported by subscription; fifteen of the boys and as many of the girls are clothed by means of the dividends on £1400 stock, purchased with the amount of various donations, the chief of which were by the Rev. George Wilson, in 1718, and Launcelot Tolson, in 1726. In 1631, Bishop Buckeridge gave £20 to the poor, with which a house has been purchased and is assigned rent-free to aged persons. Bromley college, at the north-eastern extremity of the town, was founded in 1666, by John Warner, Bishop of Rochester, who endowed it with £450 per annum, for the residence and support of twenty widows of loyal and orthodox clergymen, to each of whom he assigned £20 per annum, and to a chaplain £50. This endowment has been augmented by many subsequent benefactions: in 1767, the Rev. William Hetherington bequeathed £2000 Old South Sea annuities, to purchase coal and candles for the use of the establishment; in 1774, Dr. Zachary Pearce, Bishop of Rochester, gave £5000 in the same stock for the augmentation of the widows' pensions; in 1782, William Pearce, the bishop's brother, bequeathed £10,000 for the erection and endowment of ten additional houses; in 1788, Mr. Betenson left £10,000 in the three per cents., for building and endowing ten additional houses; in 1823, Walter King, Bishop of Rochester, gave £3000 three per cents., for the payment of £30 per annum each to three out-pensioners; and in 1824, Mrs. Rose bequeathed £8000, to increase the stipend of the widows. There are at present forty widows resident in the college, who receive £38 per annum each, with an allowance of coal and candles; and the chaplain's salary has been advanced to £150 per annum: the college is a handsome appropriate pile of building, surrounding two quadrangular areas, in which there is a chapel also. This institution is under the direction of fourteen trustees, among whom are the Archbishop of Canterbury, the Bishop of London, the Bishop, Archdeacon, and Chancellor of Rochester, the Dean of St. Paul's, and the Dean of the Arches, besides others who are elected.

BROMLEY, a township in the parish of ECCLESHALL, northern division of the hundred of PIREHILL, county of STAFFORD, containing 40 inhabitants.

BROMLEY (ABBOT'S), a parish (formerly a market town) in the southern division of the hundred of PIREHILL, county of STAFFORD, 12½ miles (E.) from Stafford, and 130 (N. W. by N.) from London, comprising the liberty of Bagot's Bromley, and the township of Bromley-Hurst, and containing 1533 inhabitants. This place is situated near the river Blythe, by which it is bounded on the south-west, and derives its distinguishing name from a Benedictine monastery founded at Blythebury, in this neighbourhood, in the latter part of the reign of Henry I., or in the beginning of that of Stephen, by Hugh Malveysin, and dedicated to St. Giles, which was suppressed at the instance of Cardinal Wolsey. The trade is principally in malt, which is carried on to some extent: the making of shoes, for the manufacturers at Stafford, formerly furnished a livelihood to many of the inhabitants, but it has of late declined. The market has been discontinued for many years: the market-house is an ancient building covered with shingles. The fairs are on March 11th, May 22nd, and September 4th, chiefly for cattle. Courts leet and baron for the manor are held once a year: at the former two constables and a headborough are chosen. The living is a discharged vicarage, in the archdeaconry of Stafford, and diocese of Lichfield and Coventry, rated in the king's books at £5. 1. 8., and in the patronage of the Marquis of Anglesey. The church, dedicated to St. Nicholas, is an ancient structure, partly in the decorated, and partly in the later, style of English architecture, with a Norman entrance: it has recently undergone considerable repairs, and has been much modernized. There is a place of worship for Independents. The free school was founded, in 1606, by Mr. Richard Clarke, who bequeathed £300 to purchase land for its endowment: the annual income of the school estate is £137. 11. 9., of which the master receives a salary of £20, together with a rent-free residence and about three quarters of an acre of garden-ground, for which eleven boys are taught English gratuitously, instruction in the classics having been discontinued. An hospital was founded, in 1702, by Lambard Bagot, Esq., who bequeathed £800 for its erection and endowment, for six aged men, three of this parish, and one from each of the parishes of Yoxhall, Hanbury, and Tatenhill: the endowment was augmented by Charles Bagot, Esq., and a matron has been added to the establishment, who, with each of the inmates, receives a stipend of £10 per annum.

BROMLEY (BAGOT'S), a liberty in the parish of ABBOT'S BROMLEY, southern division of the hundred of PIREHILL, county of STAFFORD, 1½ mile (N. W.) from Abbot's Bromley, with which the population is returned. This place derives its distinguishing name from the noble family of Bagot, to which it has belonged since the time of the Conquest, and was anciently their residence, which is now situated at Blithefield, about two miles distant. Sir William Bagot, Bart., was advanced to the peerage, on the 17th of October, 1780, by the title of Baron Bagot, of Bagot's Bromley. There is a chalybeate spring in the park, but it is not much resorted to.

BROMLEY (GREAT), a parish in the hundred of TENDRING, county of ESSEX, 4½ miles (S. S. W.) from Manningtree, containing 693 inhabitants. The living is a rectory, in the archdeaconry of Colchester, and diocese of London, rated in the king's books at £16. 16. 0½., and in the patronage of Valentine Warren, Esq. The church, dedicated to St. George, is a handsome and regular edifice. Petty sessions for the division are held here once in five weeks, on Monday, alternately with Mistley, Manningtree, and Thorpe. This parish participates in the benefit of two scholarships at St. John's College, Cambridge, to be filled up out of twenty candidates from the school at Dedham, of which number, Great Bromley supplies four.

BROMLEY (KING'S), a parish in the northern division of the hundred of OFFLOW, county of STAFFORD, 5½ miles (N. by E.) from Lichfield, containing 614 inhabitants. The living is a perpetual curacy, in the peculiar jurisdiction of the Prebendary of Alrewas and Weeford, and in the patronage of the Chancellor, in the Cathedral Church of Lichfield. The church is dedicated to All Saints. A free school was founded, in 1699, by Richard Crosse, who endowed it with property now producing £95 a year, for which forty-eight boys are instructed gratuitously.

BROMLEY (ST. LEONARD'S), a parish in the Tower division of the hundred of OSSULSTONE, county of MIDDLESEX, ½ a mile (S.) from Stratford le Bow, and 3½ miles (E.) from Cornhill, London, containing 4360 inhabitants. The living is a perpetual curacy, in the archdeaconry of Middlesex, and diocese of London, and in the patronage of John Walter, Esq. The church, dedicated to St. Mary, is a small plain structure, comprising only a nave and a chancel: it is surrounded by a high wall, and exhibits some remains of Norman architecture, containing also, in the southern wall of the chancel, some stone seats. It is part of a larger edifice, the conventual church of a Benedictine nunnery, founded, soon after the Conquest, by William, Bishop of London, and dedicated to St. Leonard; the society consisted of a prioress and nine nuns, whose revenue, in the 26th of Henry VIII., was rated at £121. 16. The Bow Wesleyan Methodists' chapel stands in this parish. The name appears to have been derived from *Brom*, broom, and *Ley*, a field, indicating that a great quantity of broom anciently grew in the vicinity. The village is lighted partly with gas, and partly with oil, is paved, and supplied with water by the works of the East London Water Company. There is a distillery on a large scale, near the western entrance into the village: a communication with the Regent's canal has been formed by a cut from the river Lea, made by Sir Charles Duckett. Bromley is within the jurisdiction of a court of requests held at Osborne-street, Whitechapel, for the recovery of debts under 40*s.*: two headboroughs and a constable are annually appointed at the manorial court; and the parochial affairs are under the superintendence of a select vestry. Seventeen of the children taught gratuitously in the school at Stratford le Bow, endowed by Sir John Jolles, in 1617, with £26. 13. 4. per annum, to be paid by the Drapers' Company, are chosen by the churchwardens from this parish. The same benefactor also founded eight almshouses for the equal benefit of the poor of Stratford and Bromley, which were rebuilt in 1806, by the Company of Drapers, to whom he assigned certain tenements in Mark-lane, in trust, for their support and that of the school. Opposite to these are almshouses founded for the benefit of decayed sail-makers, by John Edmonson, which are also under the superintendence of the Drapers' Company; and at the upper extremity, between the two rows of almshouses, is a neat chapel.

BROMLEY (LITTLE), a parish in the hundred of TENDRING, county of ESSEX, 3½ miles (S. S. W.) from Manningtree, containing 349 inhabitants. The living is a rectory, in the archdeaconry of Colchester, and diocese of London, rated in the king's books at £8, and in the patronage of T. Newman, Esq. The church is dedicated to St. Mary.

BROMLEY-HURST, a township in the parish of ABBOT'S BROMLEY, southern division of the hundred of PIREHILL, county of STAFFORD, 3½ miles (S.E. by S.) from Abbot's Bromley, with which the population is returned.

BROMPTON, a hamlet in the parish of GILLINGHAM, hundred of CHATHAM and GILLINGHAM, lathe of AYLESFORD, county of KENT. The population is returned with the parish. There is a place of worship for Wesleyan Methodists. This place lies at the extremity of the parish, on the brow of a hill overlooking the royal dock-yard at Chatham, and consists of a considerable collection of houses, commanding a fine prospect, and chiefly inhabited by persons connected with the dock-yard; it lies also within the fortifications called the Lines, which were constructed for the defence of the arsenal, pursuant to an act passed in 1738.

BROMPTON, a hamlet in the parish of KENSINGTON, Kensington division of the hundred of OSSULSTONE, county of MIDDLESEX, 1 mile (S. W. by W.) from Hyde-Park Corner. The population is returned with the parish. Numerous dwelling-houses have been erected here within the last few years: it is lighted with gas, and supplied with water by the Chelsea Water Works Company. A church, dedicated to the Holy Trinity, and intended as a district church for Old and New Brompton and Little Chelsea, was built in 1828, partly by a grant of £5000 from the parliamentary commissioners: it is a handsome structure in the later style of English architecture, with a square embattled tower at the west end, and contains one thousand five hundred and five sittings, of which six hundred and six are free: the living is a perpetual curacy, in the archdeaconry of Middlesex, concurrently with the Consistorial Court of the Bishop of London, and diocese of London, and in the patronage of the Vicar of Kensington. A chapel of ease was erected here in 1769. There is a meeting-house for Independents. A school for the education of one hundred boys was established in 1828, on the plan of those at Chatham, Devonport, and the Scotch public schools. Here was formerly a botanical garden, supported by subscription, but it has been converted into a nursery-ground, in common with a considerable portion of the ground in the immediate vicinity. Hale House, commonly called Cromwell House, and erroneously supposed to have been the residence of the Protector, is an ancient mansion belonging to the Earl of Harrington.

BROMPTON, a joint township with Riston, in that part of the parish of CHURCH-STOKE which is in the hundred of CHIRBURY, county of SALOP, 6 miles (N.W. by W.) from Bishop's Castle, containing, with Riston, 197 inhabitants.

BROMPTON, a chapelry in the parish of NORTH ALLERTON, wapentake of ALLERTONSHIRE, North riding of the county of YORK, 1¾ mile (N. N. E.) from North Allerton, containing 1223 inhabitants. There are places of worship for Primitive and Wesleyan Methodists. Here is an extensive linen-manufactory; and in the chapelry is Standard Hill, where the memorable battle of the Standard was fought, being thus named from a large banner having been placed on a lofty pole, with a silver crucifix on the summit, which was fixed on a wagon and carried with the troops.

BROMPTON, a parish in PICKERING lythe, North riding of the county of YORK, comprising the townships of Brompton, Sawdon, Troutsdale, and the chief part of the township of Snainton, and containing, with the whole of Snainton, 1303 inhabitants, of which number, 516 are in the township of Brompton, 8½ miles (S. W. by W.) from Scarborough. The living is a discharged vicarage, in the archdeaconry of Cleveland, and diocese of York, rated in the king's books at £12, endowed with £200 royal bounty, and £1600 parliamentary grant, and in the patronage of Sir G. Cayley, Bart. The church, dedicated to All Saints, is one of the most spacious and elegant in the county. There is a place of worship for Wesleyan Methodists. The Saxon kings of Northumberland are stated to have had a residence here; and on an eminence, called Castle Hill, are the foundations of an ancient castle, about half a mile from which is Gallows Hill, being the place of execution for criminals within the barony. John of Brompton, a monkish historian, who compiled a laborious work on the early annals of England, including the period between the years 558 and 1198, is supposed to have been born here: he lived twenty years in the Benedictine abbey of Whitby, during the abbacy of John of Skelton, which commenced in 1413.

BROMPTON upon SWALE, a township in that part of the parish of EASBY which is in the eastern division of the wapentake of GILLING, North riding of the county of YORK, 1¾ mile (N. W.) from Catterick, containing 388 inhabitants.

BROMPTON-PATRICK, a parish comprising the townships of Brompton-Patrick, Newton le Willows, and part of Arrowthorne in the eastern, and part of the chapelry of Hunton in the western, division of the wapentake of HANG, North riding of the county of YORK, and containing, with the whole of Arrowthorne and Hunton, 968 inhabitants, of which number, 158 are in the township of Brompton-Patrick, 3¾ miles (N.W. by W.) from Bedale. The living is a perpetual curacy, in the archdeaconry of Richmond, and diocese of Chester, endowed with £500 private benefaction, £200 royal bounty, and £1300 parliamentary grant, and in the patronage of the Bishop of Chester, to whom belongs the impropriate rectory, which is rated in the king's books at £34. 13. 1½. There is an endowment of about £25 per annum for the instruction of children, arising from a bequest of land by Samuel Atkinson, in 1707, and another by Mr. Clarke.

BROMPTON-RALPH, a parish in the hundred of WILLITON and FREEMANNERS, county of SOMERSET, 3½ miles (N.) from Wiveliscombe, containing 449 inhabitants. The living is a rectory, in the archdeaconry of Taunton, and diocese of Bath and Wells, rated in the king's books at £17. 10. 5., and in the patronage of the Rev. T. Sweet Escott. The church is dedicated to St. Mary: the greater part of it was rebuilt in 1738. Between Combe and Holcombe, in this parish, there are vestiges of an encampment, supposed to have been constructed by the Romans.

BROMPTON-REGIS, a parish (formerly a market town) in the hundred of WILLITON and FREEMANNERS, county of SOMERSET, 4¼ miles (N.E.) from Dulverton, containing 771 inhabitants. The living is a discharged vicarage, in the archdeaconry of Taunton, and diocese of Bath and Wells, rated in the king's books at £12. 5. 7½., and in the patronage of the Master and Fellows of Emanuel College, Cambridge. The church, dedicated to St. Mary, has a curiously carved screen, separating the nave from the chancel. This parish anciently constituted a hundred; the river Exe winds pleasingly through it, and it contains an abundance of stone used for building. A weekly market on Tuesday, and two fairs annually, each for four days, were granted to Sir Thomas de Besilles, Knt., lord of the manor; the market has long since fallen into disuse, but the fairs are held in May and October, for the sale of cattle and sheep. About two miles south of the church stands a private mansion, formed out of the remains of Barlinch priory, which was founded by William de Say, in the reign of Henry II., for Black canons, and dedicated to St. Nicholas, the revenue of which, in 1534, was valued at £98. 14. 9½.: in the burial-ground several stone coffins containing human skeletons have been found. Three Roman tumuli are visible on an adjacent eminence; and at a mount, called Hadborough, near the western extremity of Haddon hill, Roman coins have been found. Until lately a subscription hunt existed here, for the purpose of chacing the wild red deer found in the neighbouring woods; this once popular amusement, however, has been discontinued.

BROMSBERROW, a parish in the hundred of BOTLOE, county of GLOUCESTER, 3½ miles (S.E.) from Ledbury, containing 335 inhabitants. The living is a rectory, in the archdeaconry and diocese of Gloucester, rated in the king's books at £7. 15., and in the patronage of Earl Beauchamp. The church is an ancient edifice, dedicated to St. Mary; adjoining the chancel is the mausoleum of the Yate family, built about a century ago, and containing several monuments.

BROMSGROVE, a market town and parish (formerly a borough) in the upper division of the hundred of HALFSHIRE, county of WORCESTER, 13 miles (N.E. by N.) from Worcester, 13 (S.W.) from Birmingham, and 116 (N.W.) from London, on the road from Birmingham to Worcester, containing 7519 inhabitants. This place, anciently *Bremesgrave*, was a royal demesne at the time of the Conquest, and continued to be so till the reign of Henry III.: it returned members to parliament in the 23rd of Edward I. During the parliamentary war it was the head-quarters of a party of royalists employed in the siege of Hawkesley House, about three miles distant, which, in 1645, was fortified and garrisoned by the parliament. The town is pleasantly situated on the western bank of the river Salwarp, and consists principally of one street, extending for a considerable distance along the turnpike road: the houses are in general substantial and well built, and the inhabitants amply supplied with water. The principal articles of manufacture are nails, needles, and fish-hooks; and some coarse linen table-cloths and sheeting are still made: in the neighbourhood, potatoes, for the Bristol and other markets, are extensively cultivated. The Birmingham and Worcester canal passes within three miles to the east. The market is on Tuesday: the fairs are on June 24th and October 1st. The town is within the jurisdiction of the county magistrates; a bailiff and other officers are annually appointed at the court leet of the lord of the manor, held at Michaelmas; and a court is held every third week, for the recovery of debts under 40*s*. The town-hall is a neat and commodious building, under which is a market-place, in the centre of the town. The living is a vicarage, with the perpetual curacy of King's Norton annexed, in the archdeaconry and diocese of Worcester, rated in the king's books at £41. 8. 1½., and in the patronage of the Dean and Chapter of Worcester. The church, dedicated to St. John the Baptist, is a very ancient structure, combining portions in the Norman style, and others in the early, decorated, and later, styles of English architecture, of which last the tower and spire, and most of the exterior of the church, are fine specimens; the interior contains many curious and interesting monuments. There are places of worship for Baptists, Independents, Wesleyan Methodists, and Unitarians. The free grammar school was founded, with an endowment of £7 per annum, by charter of Edward VI., confirmed by Queen Mary, who vested the management in governors, whose appointment of a master is subject to the approval of the bishop of the diocese. The original endowment was augmented with £50 per annum by Sir Thomas Cookes, who in 1714 founded six scholarships, of £50 per annum each, in Worcester College, Oxford, for this school and four others in the county; and six fellowships, of £150 per annum each, in the same college, to which, as vacancies occur, those who hold the scholarships succeed. There are twelve scholars on the foundation, who are clothed, educated, and apprenticed: they are entitled to the scholarships and fellowships above mentioned, but the master's private pupils usually enjoy the benefit of them. There are some endowed almshouses in the parish. At Dodford, two miles from the town, are the remains of a small priory of Premonstratensian canons, founded by Henry I. in 1190, now part of a farm-house. At Shepley there are some traces of the Roman Iknield-street; and near Gannow is a petrifying spring. To the north of the town is Bromsgrove Lickey, a range of lofty hills, commanding an extensive and diversified prospect of the surrounding country; a considerable part, comprising a tract of two thousand acres, has been enclosed, and produces good crops of clover, turnips, and potatoes. A spring, rising among these hills, divides into two streams, one of which flowing northward, joins the river Rea, and uniting with the Trent, falls into the North sea; the other, running into the Stour, joins the Severn, and empties itself into the Irish sea.

BROMWICH (CASTLE), a chapelry in the parish of Aston, Birmingham division of the hundred of Hemlingford, county of Warwick, 4½ miles (W. by N.) from Coleshill. The population is returned with the parish. The living is a perpetual curacy, in the archdeaconry of Coventry, and diocese of Lichfield and Coventry, and in the patronage of the Earl of Bradford. The chapel is dedicated to St. Mary and St. Margaret. The Birmingham and Fazely canal passes through the chapelry.

BROMWICH (WEST), a parish in the southern division of the hundred of Offlow, county of Stafford, 3 miles (S. E. by S.) from Wednesbury, containing 9505 inhabitants, according to the census of 1821, since which time its population has increased to nearly 15,000. This place, which is in the centre of an extensive manufacturing and mining district, has, within the last few years, risen with amazing rapidity from a state of comparative insignificance to a degree of importance, for the variety and extent of its manufactures and trade, which is almost unparalleled. The rich mines of ironstone and coal beneath the soil, in almost every direction, affording the utmost facility of establishing works upon the most extensive scale, have consequently attracted the notice of the enterprising and ingenious, and, from little more than a barren heath, a populous and flourishing town has arisen. It extends for more than three miles along the high road from Birmingham to Holyhead, and, exclusively of the numerous dwellings of the people employed in the various works and manufactories, and the respectable houses of the persons who superintend them, contains many handsome private residences, and several pleasing villas inhabited by their proprietors. The parish is well lighted with gas, and the inhabitants are abundantly supplied with water from springs and pumps attached to their houses. Among the various branches of manufacture, all of which are conducted on the most extensive scale, are gun and pistol barrels and locks, swords, bayonets, fenders, fire-irons, locks, bolts, hinges, nails, sadlers' ironmongery, coach furniture, iron culinary utensils, chains, traces, spades and other implements of husbandry, steel toys, gas tubes and fittings, palisades and ornamental iron work of every kind; among the larger works are furnaces for the smelting of iron-ore, foundries, forges, slitting mills, in which, and also in the various collieries, numerous steam-engines are employed. Very extensive gas-works have been established by a company of proprietors, from which part of Birmingham, seven miles distant, is lighted: from these works, which are on a very extensive scale, Wednesbury, three miles distant; Dudley, four miles; Bilston, four miles; Darlaston, four miles; Tipton, two miles and a half; and Great Bridge, one mile and a half distant, are also supplied with gas, the conveyance of which, from the main gasometer at West Bromwich to the several places lighted by the company, employs a series of tubes of the aggregate length of nearly one hundred and fifty miles. The trade of the place, and the transport of the produce of its mines, and the heavier articles of manufacture, are greatly facilitated by the numerous branches of canals which intersect the parish. West Bromwich is within the jurisdiction of the county magistrates, who hold a petty session here every Saturday.

The living is a perpetual curacy, in the archdeaconry of Stafford, and diocese of Lichfield and Coventry, endowed with £200 royal bounty, and £2800 parliamentary grant, and in the patronage of the Earl of Dartmouth. The church, dedicated to St. Clement, is an ancient structure, of which, notwithstanding numerous alterations and additions, a portion of the original character remains. The first stone of Christ church was laid by the Earl of Dartmouth, in 1821, and the building was completed in 1828, at an expense of £12,446. 2. 6., part of which was defrayed by subscription, and the remainder by grant from the parliamentary commissioners; it is a handsome edifice of stone, in the later style of English architecture, with a lofty square embattled tower, and contains one thousand four hundred and eight sittings, of which seven hundred and thirty-seven are free. There are six places of worship for Wesleyan, and four for Primitive Methodists, three for Baptists, three for Independents, and two for Kilhamites. Two National schools, one for boys and the other for girls, are supported by subscription, and there are Sunday schools connected with the established church and the several dissenting congregations. A priory of Benedictine monks was founded at the close of the reign of Henry II., or the beginning of that of Richard I., by William, son of Guy de Opheni, at Sandwell, which was dedicated to St. Mary Magdalene; it was suppressed for the endowment of Cardinal Wolsey's intended colleges, in the 17th of Henry VIII., at which time its revenue was £38. 8. 7., the site is now occupied by the splendid mansion of the Earl of Dartmouth. The land in some parts of the parish is in a high state of cultivation, and the surface varied with pleasing undulations: the river Tame passes through it, and at a place called Wigmore is a chalybeate spring. A tesselated pavement was discovered in the village, in 1741. William Parsons, the gigantic porter of James I., whose portrait was for a long time hung up in the guard-room at Whitehall, and whose figure in bas relief, with that of Jeffrey Hudson, the celebrated dwarf, appeared in the front of a house in Newgate-street, London, was a native of this parish.

BROMYARD, a market town and parish in the hundred of BROXASH, county of HEREFORD, 14 miles (N. E.) from Hereford, and 126 (N. W. by W.) from London, on the road from Worcester to Hereford, containing, with the townships of Linton, Norton, and Winslow, 2767 inhabitants. This town is situated near the river Frome, in a district abounding with orchards, and consists of several irregular streets, indifferently paved, but well lighted: many of the houses are built of wood, and the inhabitants are tolerably supplied with water. Races were formerly held annually for two days, but they have been for some time discontinued. The market is on Monday, chiefly for grain, butter, and cheese: the fairs are on the Thursday before March 25th, May 3rd, the Thursday before St. James' day, Thursday before October 29th, and the last Monday in January. The county magistrates hold petty sessions for the hundred here weekly on Monday, and courts leet and baron are held twice in the year. The living forms a rectory and a vicarage, in the archdeaconry and diocese of Hereford: the rectory is divided into three portions, the first of which is rated in the king's books at £5, and the two others at £6 each; they are all in the patronage of the Bishop of Hereford: the vicarage is rated at £9. 10. 7½., and is in the gift of the three Portionists. The church, dedicated to St. Peter, is a spacious structure, in the Norman style of architecture. There is a meeting-house for Independents. The free grammar school was founded by Queen Elizabeth, and endowed with £16. 14. 11½. per annum, subsequently augmented with £20 per annum, by John Perrins, Esq.: though originally intended for the classics, the rudiments of an English education only are taught at present. The National school, in which ninety girls and thirty boys are instructed, is supported by subscription; the master's salary is £30 per annum. There are almshouses for seven aged women, endowed by the Rev. Phineas Jackson, formerly vicar of this parish.

BRON-Y-GARTH, a joint township with Weston-Rhyn, in the parish of ST. MARTIN, hundred of OSWESTRY, county of SALOP, 5 miles (N.) from Oswestry, containing, with Weston-Rhyn, 917 inhabitants.

BROOK, a parish partly in the hundred of WYE, but chiefly in the hundred of CHART and LONGBRIDGE, lathe of SCRAY, county of KENT, 5 miles (E. by N.) from Ashford, containing 162 inhabitants. The living is a discharged rectory, in the archdeaconry and diocese of Canterbury, rated in the king's books at £7. 7. 3., endowed with £200 private benefaction, and £200 royal bounty, and in the patronage of the Dean and Chapter of Canterbury. The church is dedicated to St. Mary.

BROOK, a parish in the liberty of WEST MEDINA, Isle of Wight division of the county of SOUTHAMPTON, 8¾ miles (S. W. by W.) from Newport, containing 123 inhabitants. The living is a discharged rectory, in the archdeaconry and diocese of Winchester, rated in the king's books at £1. 18. 9., and in the patronage of B. and J. Jolliffe, Esqrs. The church is dedicated to St. Mary. On Brook Down are several tumuli, each of which is encompassed with a fosse.

BROOKE, a parish in the hundred of CLAVERING, county of NORFOLK, 7¼ miles (S. E. by S.) from Norwich, containing 640 inhabitants. The living is a discharged vicarage, in the archdeaconry of Norfolk, and diocese of Norwich, rated in the king's books at £5, endowed with £200 royal bounty, and in the patronage of the Crown. The church is dedicated to St. Peter. This lordship was anciently part of the possessions belonging to the abbey of St. Edmund's Bury, and the abbot, in the 52nd of Henry III., pleaded exemption from the jurisdiction of the king's bailiff: in the 10th of Edward I. he received a grant of a market and a fair.

BROOKE, a parish in the soke of OAKHAM, county of RUTLAND, 3 miles (S. S. W.) from Oakham, containing 110 inhabitants. The living is a perpetual curacy, in the archdeaconry of Northampton, and diocese of Peterborough, and in the patronage of the Vicar of Oakham. The church is dedicated to St. Peter. A small priory for canons regular of the order of St. Augustine was founded by Hugh Ferrars, in the time of Richard I., as a cell to the monastery of Kenilworth in Warwickshire, and dedicated to the Blessed Virgin: the revenue, in the 26th of Henry VIII., was valued at £43. 13. 4.: only an archway remains.

BROOK-END, a hamlet in the parish of NORTHILL, hundred of WIXAMTREE, county of BEDFORD, 2¾ miles (N. W.) from Biggleswade. The population is returned with Thorncote.

BROOK-END, a hamlet in that part of the parish of SHENLEY which is in the hundred of COTTESLOE, county of BUCKINGHAM, containing 224 inhabitants.

BROOKESBY, a parish in the eastern division of the hundred of GOSCOTE, county of LEICESTER, 6 miles (W. S. W.) from Melton-Mowbray, containing 23 inhabitants. The living is a rectory, in the archdeaconry of Leicester, and diocese of Lincoln, rated in the king's books at £5. 12. 6., and in the patronage of Miss Wright. The church is dedicated to St. Michael. Here was formerly a village, but there are now only a private mansion and a farm-house. The river Wreake has been made navigable hence to Oakham. George Villiers, the first duke of Buckingham of that name, and the favourite of James I., was born here, in 1592, at the family mansion.

BROOKHAMPTON, a township in the parish of HOLDGATE, hundred of MUNSLOW, county of SALOP, containing 101 inhabitants.

BROOKHAMPTON, a township in the parish of OMBERSLEY, lower division of the hundred of OSWALDSLOW, county of WORCESTER. The population is returned with the parish.

BROOKLAND, a parish in the hundred of ALOESBRIDGE, lathe of SHEPWAY, county of KENT, 5 miles (W. by N.) from New Romney, containing 487 inhabitants. The living is a vicarage, in the archdeaconry and diocese of Canterbury, rated in the king's books at £17. 12. 8½., and in the patronage of the Dean and Chapter of Canterbury. The church, dedicated to St. Augustine, is principally in the early style of English architecture.

BROOK-STREET, a hamlet in the parish of SOUTH WEALD, hundred of CHAFFORD, county of ESSEX, 1½ mile (W. S. W.) from Brentwood. The population is returned with the parish. A free chapel, and an hospital for a master and various poor lepers, were established some time previously to the 20th of Edward I., and dedicated to St. John the Baptist.

BROOM, a hamlet in the parish of SOUTHILL, hundred of WIXAMTREE, county of BEDFORD, 2¼ miles (S. W.) from Biggleswade, containing 226 inhabitants.

BROOM, a township in that part of the parish of ST. OSWALD, city of DURHAM, which is in the middle division of CHESTER ward, county palatine of DURHAM, 2¼ miles (W.) from Durham, containing 93 inhabitants.

BROOM, a parish in the southern division of the hundred of SEISDON, county of STAFFORD, though locally in the county of Worcester, 4 miles (S.) from Stourbridge, containing 134 inhabitants. The living is a rectory, in the archdeaconry and diocese of Worcester, rated in the king's books at £5. 3. 4., and in the patronage of the Earl of Dudley. The church is dedicated to St. Peter.

BROOME, a parish in the hundred of LODDON, county of NORFOLK, 2½ miles (N. N. E.) from Bungay, containing 470 inhabitants. The living is a discharged rectory, in the archdeaconry of Norfolk, and diocese of Norwich, rated in the king's books at £6. 13. 4., and in the patronage of the Rev. N. Colville, D.D. The church is dedicated to St. Michael: here was anciently a chapel, dedicated to St. Botolph.

BROOME, a parish in the hundred of HARTISMERE, county of SUFFOLK, 2¼ miles (N.) from Eye, containing 324 inhabitants. The living is a discharged rectory, with that of Oakley annexed, in the archdeaconry of Sudbury, and diocese of Norwich, rated in the king's books at £10. 0. 2½., and in the patronage of Sir E, Kerrison, Bart: it was anciently divided into medieties. which were consolidated in 1448. The church is dedicated to St. Mary. The noble family of Cornwallis long resided here; and Charles, the fifth baron, was created Viscount Brome and Earl Cornwallis, on the 30th of June, 1753: his son and successor, Charles, having distinguished himself as a military commander in India, was advanced to a marquisate, as Marquis Cornwallis, August 15th, 1792.

BROOMFIELD, a parish in the hundred of CHELMSFORD, county of ESSEX, 2½ miles (N.) from Chelmsford, containing 624 inhabitants. The living is a discharged vicarage, in the archdeaconry of Essex, and diocese of London, rated in the king's books at £7. 13. 4., endowed with £200 private benefaction, and £200 royal bounty, and in the patronage of the Bishop of London. The church is dedicated to St. Mary.

BROOMFIELD, a parish in the hundred of EYHORNE, lathe of AYLESFORD, county of KENT, 6 miles (E. S. E.) from Maidstone, containing 115 inhabitants. The living is a perpetual curacy, united to that of Leeds, in the archdeaconry and diocese of Canterbury. The church is dedicated to St. Margaret. On the southern side of the parish extends a tract of woodland, called King's wood, and within its limits there is a rabbit-warren.

BROOMFIELD, a parish in the hundred of ANDERSFIELD, county of SOMERSET, 4¾ miles (N.) from Taunton, containing 489 inhabitants. The living is a donative, in the peculiar jurisdiction of the Dean of Wells, endowed with £400 private benefaction, and £400 royal bounty, and in the patronage of Col. Hamilton. In the churchyard is a stone cross somewhat mutilated.

BROOMHAUGH, a township in the parish of BYWELL ST. ANDREW, eastern division of TINDALE ward, county of NORTHUMBERLAND, 7¾ miles (E. S. E.) from Hexham, containing 116 inhabitants.

BROOMHILL, a member of the town and port of NEW ROMNEY, in the liberty of ROMNEY-MARSH, lathe of SHEPWAY, county of KENT, 3½ miles (E. by S.) from Rye, containing 56 inhabitants. It was anciently a parish, at which period a portion of it was within the liberty of Old Winchelsea: the church, which stood within the limits of the county of Sussex, has long since been destroyed.

BROOMHOPE, a joint township with Buteland, in the parish of BIRTLEY, north-eastern division of TINDALE ward, county of NORTHUMBERLAND, 3½ miles (E.) from Bellingham. The population is returned with Birtley and Chollerton, with the former of which this township is connected in all ecclesiastical affairs, and with the latter as regards civil matters.

BROOMLEY, a township in the parish of BYWELL ST. PETER, eastern division of TINDALE ward, county of NORTHUMBERLAND, $7\frac{3}{4}$ miles (E.S.E.) from Hexham, containing 354 inhabitants.

BROOM-PARK, a township in the parish of EDLINGHAM, northern division of COQUETDALE ward, county of NORTHUMBERLAND, $5\frac{1}{2}$ miles (W.) from Alnwick, containing 43 inhabitants.

BROOMRIDGE, a hamlet in the parish of FORD, western division of GLENDALE ward, county of NORTHUMBERLAND, $5\frac{3}{4}$ miles (N. by W.) from Wooler. The population is returned with the parish. Camden considers this to have been the place called Brunanburh, where King Athelstan, in 928, defeated Constantine, King of Scotland, Anlaf the Dane, and Eugenius, a petty prince of Cumberland. About half a mile to the south of Broomridge is Haltwell Sweire, the scene of an encounter, in 1558, between the English under Sir Henry Percy, and the Scotch under Earl Bothwell, in which the former sustained a defeat.

BROOMSTHORPE, formerly a distinct parish, now a hamlet in the parish of EAST RUDHAM, hundred of GALLOW, county of NORFOLK, $5\frac{1}{2}$ miles (W. by S.) from Fakenham, containing 11 inhabitants. The church has long been demolished.

BROSELEY, a market town and parish in the franchise of WENLOCK, county of SALOP, 4 miles (E.) from Wenlock, 14 (S.E.) from Shrewsbury, and 144 (N.W.) from London, on the road from Worcester to Shrewsbury, containing 4814 inhabitants. This place, in ancient records called *Burwardesley*, probably derived that appellation from a family of the name of *Burward*, to which it belonged; or from its vicinity to the borough of Wenlock, within the liberties of which it is comprehended. Its extent and importance are owing to the numerous mines of coal and iron-stone abounding in the neighbourhood, whereby it became the resort of miners; and in proportion as the works proceeded, it increased in population and magnitude. The town is irregularly built, but is pleasantly situated on an eminence rising abruptly from the western bank of the river Severn, to which its eastern extremity extends, and from which its western extremity is nearly two miles distant. It consists principally of one long street, from which a few smaller streets branch off irregularly, leading to the different collieries and other works: the houses, in general built of brick and of mean appearance, are occasionally intermixed with some of more respectable character; and in detached situations are several handsome and spacious edifices. It is neither paved nor lighted, and the inhabitants are but scantily supplied with water, which in winter they bring from a well about half a mile eastward from the town, and in summer from brooks at the distance of a mile and a half. The trade consists principally in mining operations; but, from the exhausted state of the mines, it is rapidly declining: there are numerous coal-pits, iron-foundries, and furnaces, and tobacco-pipes, bricks, and tiles, are made to a great extent. The fire-bricks for building furnaces are in great repute, and, by means of the river Severn, are sent to various parts of the kingdom. The market is on Wednesday: the fairs are on the last Tuesday in April and October 28th; they are chiefly pleasure fairs, though a considerable number of pigs is sold. The town is within the jurisdiction of the borough of Wenlock: courts leet for the manor are held in the town-hall in April and October, at the latter of which four constables are appointed. A court of requests, for the recovery of debts under 40*s.*, is held under an act passed in the 22nd of George III., generally every alternate Wednesday: its jurisdiction extends over "the parishes of Broseley, Benthall, Madeley, Barrow, Linley, Willey, Little Wenlock, and Dawley, and an extra-parochial place called Posnall, in the county of Salop." The town-hall is a handsome brick building, in the centre of the town, supported on pillars and arches, the basement forming a spacious market-place: on the first story is a room wherein the courts and public meetings are held (used also as an assembly-room), and two smaller apartments, appropriated to the use of the Sunday school: there is a small prison attached to it, for the confinement of debtors, and for criminals previous to their committal by the borough magistrates.

The living is a rectory, in the archdeaconry of Salop, and diocese of Hereford, rated in the king's books at £7. 18. $6\frac{1}{2}$., and in the patronage of Lord Forrester. The church, dedicated to St. Leonard, with the exception of the ancient tower, which is of stone, has been rebuilt of brick; but something of its original character is preserved in the interior, in the octangular pillars and pointed arches which support the roof. A chapel, dedicated to St. Mary, was built in 1759, by Mr. Francis Turner Blythe, in a part of the parish called Jackfield, at a considerable distance from the church: it is a neat brick building, with a square embattled tower crowned with pinnacles. The living is a perpetual curacy, in the patronage of William Yelverton Davenport, Esq., which, at his decease, becomes vested in the family of Blythe. There are two places of worship for Baptists, and one for Wesleyan Methodists. In 1750, John Barret, Esq., a native of this place, bequeathed £110 for charitable uses; this sum, augmented with a legacy of £100 by Mr. Richard Edwards, and several smaller sums, amounting in the whole to £380, was invested in the purchase of land, upon which the town-hall and other houses have been erected: after deducting the expense of keeping these in repair, the rents of the houses and of the standings in the market-place are distributed among the poor. Here is a well, the water of which, formerly containing much inflammable gas, ignited on the application of a lighted candle; but since sinking a coal-pit near the spot it has entirely lost that peculiarity.

BROTHERICK, a township in that part of the parish of WARKWORTH which is in the eastern division of COQUETDALE ward, county of NORTHUMBERLAND, containing 10 inhabitants, and only one house.

BROTHERTOFT, a chapelry in the parish and wapentake of KIRTON, parts of HOLLAND, county of LINCOLN, 4 miles (W.N.W.) from Boston, containing 111 inhabitants.

BROTHERTON, a parish comprising the township of Brotherton in the liberty of ST. PETER of YORK, East riding, and the townships of Byrome with Pool, and Sutton, partly in the same liberty, but chiefly in the lower division of the wapentake of BARKSTONE-ASH, West riding, of the county of YORK, and containing 1626 inhabitants, of which number, 1491 are in the township of Brotherton, $\frac{3}{4}$ of a mile (N.N.W.) from Ferry-Bridge. The living is a discharged vicarage, in the peculiar jurisdiction and patronage of the Dean and Chapter of York, rated in the king's books at £5. 6. 8. The church is dedicated to St. Edward the Confessor. There is a place of worship for Wesleyan Methodists. This parish is bounded on the south and west by the river Aire, and contains limestone of a fine quality, there being various kilns for burning it. In June 1300, Margaret, the second wife of Edward I., having been taken in labour whilst hunting in the neighbourhood, was delivered of a son at the village, to whom the name Thomas de Brotherton was given; he was created Earl of Norfolk and Earl Marshal of England, and from him, in the female line, descended the Mowbrays, Dukes of Norfolk: the house in which this event occurred is stated by tradition to have stood on part of a plot of land of about twenty acres, not far from the church, which the tenants are obliged, by the tenure of their land, to keep surrounded by a stone wall. There is an endowment of £5 a year for the instruction of children, arising from a bequest of £100 by Mr. Wilson, in 1731.

BROTTON, a parish in the eastern division of the liberty of LANGBAURGH, North riding of the county of YORK, comprising the townships of Brotton, Kilton, and Skinningrove, and containing 492 inhabitants, of which number, 332 are in the township of Brotton, 6 miles (N. E. by E.) from Guilsbrough. The living is a perpetual curacy, annexed to that of Skelton, in the archdeaconry of Cleveland, and diocese of York. The church was erected in 1741. There is a place of worship for Wesleyan Methodists.

BROUGH, a joint hamlet with Shatton, in the parish of HOPE, hundred of HIGH PEAK, county of DERBY, 5 miles (N. N. E.) from Tideswell, containing, with Shatton, 93 inhabitants. A place called the Castle, near the junction of two small streams, the Noe and the Bradwell Water, was evidently the site of a Roman station, probably *Crococolana*; numerous Roman relics have been discovered, coins (among which is a gold coin of Vespasian), and rude busts, one being a bust of Apollo.

BROUGH, or BURG, under STAINMOOR, a parish in EAST ward, county of WESTMORLAND, comprising the market town of Brough, the chapelry of Stainmore, the townships of Brough-Sowerby and Hilbeck, and part of the township of Kaber, and containing, exclusively of Kaber, 1837 inhabitants, of which number, 940 are in the town of Brough, 8 miles (S. E. by E.) from Appleby, and 262 (N. N. W.) from London, on the high road to Glasgow. This town occupies the site of the ancient *Verteræ, or Veteris,* where, towards the decline of the Roman empire in Britain, a prefect, with a band of *directores*, was stationed. It was partly built with the ruins of that fort, from which circumstance it probably derived its appellation, and is distinguished from other places of the same name by its vicinity to an extensive ridge of rocky mountains, that separates this county from Yorkshire. It flourished as a place of considerable importance prior to the Conquest, soon after which a conspiracy was formed here by the northern English, against the government of William. At what time the castle was erected is not precisely known; but in 1174 it was nearly demolished by William, King of Scotland, who laid waste the town: it was subsequently restored, and, in 1521, was nearly destroyed by a fire that broke out after the celebration of a Christmas festival by Lord Clifford; it remained in a ruinous state till 1660, when it was repaired by Lady Ann Clifford, Countess Dowager of Pembroke. This fortress was situated upon an eminence, abruptly steep towards the north and west; and on the south and east, where the acclivity is more gentle, it was defended by a ditch and a strong rampart: the remains consist of some massive towers, of which the keep, a large square tower with turrets at the angles, called Cæsar's tower, was almost perfect in 1792, when the lower part of one of the angles fell down, leaving the upper part adhering by the cement only to the main building. Great part of it has within the last few years been removed, and the remainder is in a state of progressive dilapidation: its present proprietor is the Earl of Thanet. The town, divided into Market-Brough and Church-Brough, is pleasantly situated, and is crossed by the Swindale Beck, which flows into the river Eden: it consists principally of one long street; the houses are rather commodious than handsome; the inhabitants are well supplied with water. Two attempts have been made to introduce the cotton manufacture into the town, but both have failed; part of the buildings has been converted into dwellings, and part into a large corn-mill: several of the female inhabitants are employed in knitting white yarn stockings. The parish contains mines of lead and coal, with strata of limestone and freestone. The market, granted in 1331, by Edward III., to Robert, Lord Clifford, is on Thursday, but is of little note; corn is admitted toll-free. Fairs are held on the Thursday before Whit-Sunday and September 30th; the latter, called Brough Hill fair, is held on a common, two miles from the town, and is celebrated for the sale of linen and woollen cloth, wearing apparel, articles of hardware, and live stock: cattle fairs are also held in the town, on the second Thursday in March and April.

This parish was formerly a chapelry within the parish of Kirkby-Stephen: the living is a vicarage, in the archdeaconry and diocese of Carlisle, rated in the king's books at £8. 8. 9., endowed with £200 private benefaction, and £200 royal bounty, and in the patronage of the Provost and Fellows of Queen's College, Oxford, to whom the rectory and advowson were given, at the request of Robert Egglesfield, founder of that college, and for several years rector of this parish. The church, dedicated to St. Michael, is a large handsome structure of great antiquity; a square embattled tower was added in 1513: the windows are ornamented with richly stained glass, which, from an inscription on one of them, appears to be of the time of Henry VIII.: the pulpit is formed of one entire stone, and within the church are several interesting monuments. There are places of worship for Independents and Primitive and Wesleyan Methodists. The free school is endowed with a portion of the revenue of a dissolved chantry and hospital, founded in 1506, by John Brunskill, the former for two chaplains, one of whom was to instruct the children of the parish in grammar: the present building was erected by Lord Thanet; and though, at the dissolution of the chantry, the pension was reserved for the continuation of the grammar school, the course of instruction is at present confined to reading, writing, and arithmetic. A National school for sixty girls was established in 1828. Many Roman coins and other antiquities have been found at various times near the castle, and, within the last thirty years, an earthen vessel full of silver *quinarii*, many of which are in good preservation, and particularly one with a perfect impression of the head of Titus Vespasian, having on the reverse the figure of a female in a weeping posture: there are several tumuli on the mountains in the neighbourhood. On Stainmoor, in that part of the parish which verges upon Yorkshire, William the Norman, and Malcolm, the Scottish king, erected a cross, called *Rey-cross*, as a boundary between the two kingdoms: the site is now marked by two stones. Cuthbert Buckle, lord mayor of London in 1593, was born here.

BROUGH, a township in that part of the parish of CATTERICK which is in the eastern division of the wapentake of HANG, North riding of the county of YORK, 1½ mile (W.) from Catterick, containing 90 inhabitants.

BROUGH-FERRY, a township in the parish of ELLOUGHTON, partly in the Hunsley-Beacon division of the wapentake of HARTHILL, and partly in the liberty of ST. PETER of YORK, East riding of the county of YORK, 3¼ miles (S. S. E.) from South Cave. The population is returned with the parish. Here is a ferry across the Humber to Wintringham, in Lincolnshire.

BROUGH-SOWERBY, a township in the parish of BROUGH, EAST ward, county of WESTMORLAND, 1¼ mile (S.) from Brough, containing 180 inhabitants.

BROUGHALL, a township in that part of the parish of WHITCHURCH which is in the Whitchurch division of the hundred of BRADFORD (North), county of SALOP, 1¾ mile (E.) from Whitchurch. The population is returned with the parish.

BROUGHAM, a parish in WEST ward, county of WESTMORLAND, 1¾ mile (S. E.) from Penrith, containing 143 inhabitants. The living is a rectory, in the archdeaconry and diocese of Carlisle, rated in the king's books at £16. 10. 7½., and in the patronage of the Earl of Thanet. The church, dedicated to St. Ninian, and hence vulgarly called the Ninekirks, stands pleasantly within a curve on the southern bank of the river Eamont. There is also a chapel of ease, supposed to be dedicated to St. Wilfrid, in the western part of the parish, which, together with the church, was rebuilt in 1659, by Anne, the celebrated Countess of Pembroke. This was the Roman station *Brovoniacum*, which appears to have comprised an area one hundred and forty paces in length, and one hundred and twenty in breadth: the vallum and some vestiges of the outworks are visible; and coins, votive altars, and other relics, have been found on the southern side of the station, where, as it is related, a city anciently stood, named by the Saxons *Burg-ham*, the Castle Town. A castle was built soon after the Conquest, principally, as appears from an inscription over the inner gateway, by the first Roger, Lord Clifford, which was demolished by the Scots, in 1412; and having been rebuilt, was honoured by the presence of James I., who was entertained by its noble owner, Francis, Earl of Cumberland, on the 6th, 7th, and 8th of August, 1617, when returning from his last progress into Scotland. Soon after this it became ruinous, and sustained much damage during the parliamentary war, but was restored by the Countess of Pembroke, in 1651. The venerable and extensive ruins are pleasingly situated on a woody eminence, at the confluence of two streams; League Tower, the only perfect part, is so called from a league having been concluded in it by commissioners from England and Scotland. Near them is a handsome pillar, embellished with heraldic bearings, and surmounted by a small obelisk, erected in 1656, by the above-named countess, as a memorial of her last parting with her mother, the Countess Dowager of Cumberland, on this spot, April 2nd, 1616: it bears an inscription, recording the gift of £4 annually to the poor of this parish, by the same distinguished female, to be distributed among them on that day, and at this stone. This parish is bounded on every side, except the south, by the rivers Eden, Eamont, and Lowther, which unite here: there are two stone bridges across the Eamont (one of them built in 1814, to afford a shorter line of communication between Penrith and Appleby), and one over the Lowther: the village of Brougham has long since disappeared. Brougham Hall, the property and residence of that distinguished orator, statesman, and scholar, Lord Brougham and Vaux, the present Lord High Chancellor of Great Britain, is a plain, lofty, and aged structure, with an embrasured parapet, erected at different periods, occupying an elevated site, which, from a similarity in the richness and diversity of the prospects it commands, has acquired for it the characteristic title of the "Windsor of the North."

BROUGHTON, a parish in the hundred of NEWPORT, county of BUCKINGHAM, 3 miles (S. S. E.) from Newport-Pagnell, containing 191 inhabitants. The living is a rectory, in the archdeaconry of Buckingham, and diocese of Lincoln, rated in the king's books at £10. 9. 7., and in the patronage of W. Praed, Esq. The church is dedicated to St. Lawrence. There is a small endowment for teaching six poor children to read.

BROUGHTON, a parish in the hundred of HURSTINGSTONE, county of HUNTINGDON, 5¾ miles (N. E. by N.) from Huntingdon, containing 351 inhabitants. The living is a rectory, in the archdeaconry of Huntingdon, and diocese of Lincoln, rated in the king's books at £21. 13. 9., and in the patronage of the Rev. Thomas Johnstone. The church is dedicated to All Saints.

BROUGHTON, a chapelry in the parish of PRESTON, hundred of AMOUNDERNESS, county palatine of LANCASTER, 4¼ miles (N. by W.) from Preston, containing 615 inhabitants. The living is a perpetual curacy, in the archdeaconry of Richmond, and diocese of Chester, endowed with £200 private benefaction, £200 royal bounty, and £800 parliamentary grant, and in the patronage of Sir H. P. Hoghton, Bart. The chapel has lately received an addition of two hundred and two sittings, one hundred and four of which are free, the Incorporated Society for the enlargement of churches and chapels having granted £150 for that purpose. A free school, for the instruction of children within the chapelry, has an endowment of £128 per annum, arising from land and tenements assigned at a remote period, by unknown donors: the master has a salary of £50 a year, with the privilege of instructing, on his own terms, children not resident within the chapelry; and an usher, one of £40. There are also some minor charities for the benefit of the poor within the township.

BROUGHTON, a township in the parish of MANCHESTER, hundred of SALFORD, county palatine of LANCASTER, 2 miles (N. N. W.) from Manchester, containing 880 inhabitants.

BROUGHTON, a parish in the eastern division of the wapentake of MANLEY, parts of LINDSEY, county of

Lincoln, 3 miles (W.N.W.) from Glandford-Bridge, containing, with Manby and Castlethorp, 827 inhabitants. The living is a rectory, in the archdeaconry of Stow, and diocese of Lincoln, rated in the king's books at £21, and in the patronage of Richard Burton, Esq. The church is dedicated to St. Mary. The interest of £200, left by Catherine Thompson, is applied to the instruction of children. Here was a Roman station, at which, about the year 400, an auxiliary troop of Dalmatian cavalry was quartered: coins, bricks, and other relics of the Romans have been found at various times. A Cistercian nunnery was founded by William de Alta Ripa, before the year 1185, the establishment of which, at the time of the dissolution, consisted of a prioress and six nuns, whose revenue was estimated at about £20; the site is now occupied by a farm-house, a doorway in which is the only relic of the conventual buildings. There is a large decoy for wild fowl on the low grounds, near the river Ancholme.

BROUGHTON, a parish in the hundred of Orlingbury, county of Northampton, 2¾ miles (S.W.) from Kettering, containing 455 inhabitants. The living is a rectory, in the archdeaconry of Northampton, and diocese of Peterborough, rated in the king's books at £21. 9. 7., and in the patronage of the Duke of Buccleuch. The church is dedicated to St. Andrew.

BROUGHTON, a parish in the hundred of Bloxham, county of Oxford, 3 miles (W.S.W.) from Banbury, containing, with the hamlet of North Newington, 517 inhabitants. The living is a rectory, in the archdeaconry and diocese of Oxford, rated in the king's books at £18. 16. 0½., and in the patronage of the Rev. Charles F. Wyatt. The church is dedicated to St. Mary.

BROUGHTON, a parish within the liberties of the borough of Shrewsbury, county of Salop, 7½ miles (N.) from Shrewsbury, containing 177 inhabitants. The living is a perpetual curacy, in the archdeaconry of Salop, and diocese of Lichfield and Coventry, endowed with £800 royal bounty, and £200 parliamentary grant, and in the patronage of R. Lister, Esq.

BROUGHTON, a parish in the hundred of Thorngate, Andover division of the county of Southampton, 3 miles (W.S.W.) from Stockbridge, containing, with the tything of French-Moor and the extra-parochial district of Pittleworth, 821 inhabitants. The living is a rectory, in the archdeaconry and diocese of Winchester, rated in the king's books at £37. 10., and in the patronage of Charles Baring Wall, Esq. The church is dedicated to St. Mary. There are places of worship for Baptists, Independents, and Wesleyan Methodists. A fair for pedlary and toys is held on the first Monday in July: the lord of the manor holds a court leet annually. Thomas Dowse, in 1601, conveyed an estate in trust for the support of a free school, the rental of which, together with minor benefactions, amounting to £68. 17. annually, is paid to the schoolmaster, who has also a house, garden, and a small plot of land, for which he instructs the children of Broughton and Bossington; the present number is about forty. Camden considers the Roman station *Brige*, noticed in Antonine's Itinerary, to have been here: Salmon fixes it on a hill near Broughton; and Mr. Gale says that, in 1719, he saw vestiges of the station in a wood near this place, on the road to Salisbury. The Roman road passed about a mile south of the village.

BROUGHTON, a chapelry in the parish of Eccleshall, northern division of the hundred of Pirehill, county of Stafford, 5¼ miles (N.W. by W.) from Eccleshall, containing 30 inhabitants. The living is a perpetual curacy, in the peculiar jurisdiction of the Prebendary of Eccleshall in the Cathedral Church of Lichfield, endowed with £1000 private benefaction, £200 royal bounty, and £1200 parliamentary grant, and in the patronage of Sir J. D. Broughton, Bart.

BROUGHTON, a township in the parish of Appleton le Street, wapentake of Ryedale, North riding of the county of York, 2 miles (N.W.) from New Malton, containing 94 inhabitants. There is a place of worship for Wesleyan Methodists. According to Bishop Tanner, an hospital, dedicated to St. Mary Magdalene, was founded here by Eustace Fitz-John, who died in the 1st of Henry II.

BROUGHTON in AREDALE, a parish in the eastern division of the wapentake of Staincliffe and Ewcross, West riding of the county of York, 3½ miles (W. by S.) from Skipton, containing, with Elslack, 427 inhabitants. The living is a discharged vicarage, in the archdeaconry and diocese of York, rated in the king's books at £5. 16. 0½., endowed with £200 private benefaction, and £200 royal bounty, and in the patronage of the Dean and Canons of Christ Church, Oxford. The church, dedicated to All Saints, contains several mural monuments belonging to the family of Tempest, who have been long resident here. The manufacture of cotton goods is carried on to a limited extent. The Saxon name of the place, implying a fortified town, is evidence of its antiquity; and there are vestiges of an early settlement, ascribed to the Romans: various instruments, supposed to have belonged to that people, or to the Britons, have also been discovered. The village suffered considerably in the civil war of the last century, when the inhabitants were plundered, and much of their property was destroyed.

BROUGHTON (CHURCH), a parish in the hundred of Appletree, county of Derby, 8½ miles (E.) from Uttoxeter, containing, with Sapperton, 536 inhabitants. The living is a discharged vicarage, in the archdeaconry of Derby, and diocese of Lichfield and Coventry, rated in the king's books at £6. 13. 4., endowed with £400 royal bounty, and in the patronage of the Crown. The church is dedicated to St. Michael; in the chancel are three stone stalls. A charity school was founded about 1745, by subscription among the freeholders, to which the Duke of Devonshire was the principal contributor; and the sum thus raised was invested in land, the rental of which is about £30 per annum. Broughton is in the honour of Tutbury, duchy of Lancaster, and within the jurisdiction of a court of pleas held at Tutbury every third Tuesday, for the recovery of debts under 40*s*.

BROUGHTON (EAST), a chapelry in the parish of Cartmel, hundred of Lonsdale, north of the sands, county palatine of Lancaster, 2 miles (N. by E.) from Cartmel, containing 381 inhabitants. The living is a perpetual curacy, in the archdeaconry of Richmond, and diocese of Chester, endowed with £200 private benefaction, £400 royal bounty, and £200 parliamentary grant, and in the patronage of Lord G. Cavendish. The chapel, which was consecrated in 1745, is dedicated to St. Peter.

BROUGHTON in FURNESS, a market town and chapelry, in the parish of KIRKBY-IRELETH, hundred of LONSDALE, north of the sands, county palatine of LANCASTER, 29 miles (N. W.) from Lancaster, and 270 (N.W. by N.) from London, containing 1253 inhabitants. The town is situated on the southern declivity of a gentle eminence, and is in the form of a square: the houses are built of stone, and roofed with blue slate. In the centre of it is a spacious square area, the ground for forming which was given by John Gilpin, Esq., whose widow erected a handsome lofty obelisk within it. Previously to the introduction of machinery, the spinning of woollen yarn prevailed to a considerable extent in private houses: the making of brush-stocks and hoops at present furnishes employment to many of the inhabitants, particularly the latter, owing to the number and extent of the coppices on Furness Fells. The surrounding country is very mountainous, abounding with mines of iron and copper ore, and with slate quarries; a great quantity of the slate is shipped at Dudden Sands, for conveyance coastwise: iron, grain, malt, oak-bark, and hoops, are also sent from the same place, in vessels averaging about sixty tons' burden; and from a place about half a mile below Dudden bridge, in vessels carrying twenty-five tons, for which the æstuary is navigable at the flow of the tide: coal and other articles of general consumption are brought to these places, whence they are distributed throughout the district. The market is on Friday: fairs are held on April 27th and August 1st, for horned cattle; and on the first Friday in October, for horned cattle and sheep; those in April and October are also statute fairs for the hiring of servants, and all are much frequented by the clothiers from Yorkshire. The living is a perpetual curacy, in the archdeaconry of Richmond, and diocese of Chester, endowed with £400 private benefaction, and £400 royal bounty, and in the patronage of J. G. Saurey, Esq. The church is dedicated to St. Mary Magdalene. There is a chapel of ease at Seathwaite. Edward Taylor, by will dated in 1784, bequeathed £100, on condition that £60 should be raised by subscription, for the benefit of a grammar school: these sums, with an additional sum of £36. 10., amounting in the whole to £196. 10., have been laid out in the purchase of premises now used as a workhouse; and the master is paid £6. 8. annually out of the poor's rate, charging also a quarterage for teaching: the school-room was built by subscription on a piece of waste ground.

BROUGHTON (GREAT), a township in the parish of BRIDEKIRK, ALLERDALE ward below Derwent, county of CUMBERLAND, 4¼ miles (W.) from Cockermouth, containing 435 inhabitants. The village lies on the southern slope of an eminence rising from the river Derwent. Mr. Joseph Ashley built an almshouse for four poor women, and a school-room for the children of Great and Little Broughton, endowing them by will dated July 18th, 1735, the former with £8, and the latter with £20. 10., per annum; between seventy and eighty children are taught gratuitously, and the master's fixed stipend is usually augmented by subscription.

BROUGHTON (GREAT and LITTLE), a township in the parish of KIRKBY in CLEVELAND, western division of the liberty of LANGBAURGH, North riding of the county of YORK, 2¼ miles (S. E.) from Stokesley, containing 517 inhabitants. On the top of a mountain near this place is a rude collection of large stones, one of them in an erect position, which some have conjectured to have been raised over the remains of a Danish warrior.

BROUGHTON (LITTLE), a township in the parish of BRIDEKIRK, ALLERDALE ward below Derwent, county of CUMBERLAND, 4¼ miles (W. by N.) from Cockermouth, containing 237 inhabitants. A meeting-house was built by the Society of Friends in 1656, and one by the Anabaptists in 1672. Here is a manufactory for tobacco-pipes and coarse earthenware. Abraham Fletcher, a self-taught mathematician of no inconsiderable eminence, author of the "Universal Measurer," was born here, in 1714; he was the son of a tobacco-pipe maker, and in early life laboured at that occupation.

BROUGHTON (NETHER), a parish in the hundred of FRAMLAND, county of LEICESTER, 5¾ miles (N. W.) from Melton-Mowbray, containing 435 inhabitants. The living is a rectory, in the archdeaconry of Leicester, and diocese of Lincoln, rated in the king's books at £11. 5. 7½., and in the patronage of the Earl of Radnor and the Hon. Francis Bowater, alternately. The church is dedicated to St. Mary. Broughton is in the honour of Tutbury, duchy of Lancaster, and within the jurisdiction of a court of pleas held at Tutbury every third Tuesday, for the recovery of debts under 40*s*.

BROUGHTON-ASTLEY, a parish in the hundred of GUTHLAXTON, county of LEICESTER, comprising the townships of Broughton-Astley, Prime-Thorp, and Sutton in the Elms, and containing 630 inhabitants, of which number, 210 are in the township of Broughton-Astley, 5½ miles (N. by W.) from Lutterworth. The living is a rectory, in the archdeaconry of Leicester, and diocese of Lincoln, rated in the king's books at £26. 10. 5, and in the patronage of the Rev. John Liptrott. The church is dedicated to St. Mary.

BROUGHTON-BRANT, a parish in the wapentake of LOVEDEN, parts of KESTEVEN, county of LINCOLN, 8 miles (E.) from Newark, containing 596 inhabitants. The living is a rectory, in the archdeaconry of Stow, and diocese of Lincoln, rated in the king's books at £35. 13. 4., and in the patronage of Sir R. Sutton, Bart The church is dedicated to St. Helen. There is a place of worship for Wesleyan Methodists. Mr. Pickering, in 1604, gave £50, the produce of which is applied to the instruction of children.

BROUGHTON-GIFFORD, a parish in the hundred of BRADFORD, county of WILTS, 2 miles (W.) from Melksham, containing 776 inhabitants. The living is a rectory, in the archdeaconry and diocese of Salisbury rated in the king's books at £19. 3. 11½., and in the patronage of the Crown. The church is dedicated to St. Mary. There is a place of worship for Particular Baptists. A fund for the instruction of children and for the relief of the poor was given by Francis Paradice and his wife, in 1782.

BROUGHTON-HACKETT, a parish in the upper division of the hundred of PERSHORE, county of WORCESTER, 5½ miles (E.) from Worcester, containing 123 inhabitants. The living is a discharged rectory, in the archdeaconry and diocese of Worcester, rated in the king's books at £8. 1. 0½., and in the patronage of the

Crown. The church is dedicated to St. Leonard. There are some stone pits in this parish, producing specimens in which marine shells are imbedded; these are susceptible of a polish that renders them in appearance not inferior to the Derbyshire marble. A valuable blueish limestone, which supplies the city of Worcester and places adjacent with lime for building and manure, abounds here.

BROUGHTON-POGGS, a parish in the hundred of BAMPTON, county of OXFORD, 5¼ miles (S. by W.) from Burford, containing 114 inhabitants. The living is a discharged rectory, in the archdeaconry and diocese of Oxford, rated in the king's books at £7. 7. 11., and in the patronage of the Rev. S. Goodenough. The church is dedicated to St. Peter.

BROUGHTON-SULNEY, a parish in the southern division of the wapentake of BINGHAM, county of NOTTINGHAM, 12¼ miles (S. E. by S.) from Nottingham, containing 348 inhabitants. The living is a rectory, in the archdeaconry of Nottingham, and diocese of York, rated in the king's books at £11. 9. 4½., and in the patronage of Sir J. Radcliffe. Broughton is in the honour of Tutbury, duchy of Lancaster, and within the jurisdiction of a court of pleas held at Tutbury every third Tuesday, for the recovery of debts under 40*s*. The water of a spring, vulgarly called Woundheal, in this parish, is noted for the cure of scorbutic eruptions.

BROWNSHALL, or BROWNSEL-LANE, a hamlet in the parish of BISHOP'S CAUNDLE, hundred of SHERBORNE, Sherborne division of the county of DORSET. The population is returned with the parish. This hamlet is of great antiquity, and was formerly of greater importance, from its having given name to the hundred of Brownshall.

BROWNSOVER, a chapelry in the parish of CLIFTON, Rugby division of the hundred of KNIGHTLOW, county of WARWICK, 2¼ miles (N. by E.) from Rugby, containing 112 inhabitants. The chapel is dedicated to St. Michael.

BROXA, a township in the parish of HACKNESS, liberty of WHITBY-STRAND, North riding of the county of YORK 7¾ miles (W. N. W.) from Scarborough, containing 61 inhabitants.

BROXBURN, a parish in the hundred and county of HERTFORD, 1¼ mile (S.) from Hoddesdon, containing, with Hoddesdon, part of which is in the parish of Great Amwell, 1888 inhabitants. The living is a discharged vicarage, in the archdeaconry of Middlesex, and diocese of London, rated in the king's books at £12. 6. 5½., and in the patronage of the Bishop of London. The church, dedicated to St. Augustine, is a large handsome edifice in the later style of English architecture, with a square tower supporting an octagonal spire, and a north and south chapel; the workmanship in the north chapel is of a superior description; there are several very fine monuments, and an ancient font. James I., on his way from Scotland, was entertained at the manor-house, where he was met by many of the nobility, and the great officers of state. Sir Richard Lacy, Knt., in 1667, bequeathed property for the erection and endowment of a school, which is free for all children within the parish. By deed in 1727, the Hon. Letitia Monson gave £1000, since laid out in Bank Annuities, for endowing an almshouse for six poor widows: there are also several minor benefactions for the poor.

BROXHOLME, a parish in the wapentake of LAWRESS, parts of LINDSEY, county of LINCOLN, 6¾ miles (N. W.) from Lincoln, containing 148 inhabitants. The living is a rectory, in the archdeaconry of Stow, and diocese of Lincoln, rated in the king's books at £9. 10., and in the patronage of George Manners, Esq. The church is dedicated to All Saints.

BROXTED, a parish in the hundred of DUNMOW, county of ESSEX, 3 miles (S. W.) from Thaxted, containing 597 inhabitants. The living is a discharged vicarage, in the archdeaconry of Middlesex, and diocese of London, rated in the king's books at £7, and in the patronage of R. De Beauvoir, Esq. The church is dedicated to St. Mary.

BROXTON, a township in the parish of MALPAS, higher division of the hundred of BROXTON, county palatine of CHESTER, 5 miles (N.) from Malpas, containing 352 inhabitants. This township has given name to a hundred, which, at the time of the Norman survey, was called *Dudestan* hundred.

BROXTOW, a chapelry in the parish of BILBOROUGH, southern division of the wapentake of BROXTOW, county of NOTTINGHAM, 3½ miles (N. W. by W.) from Nottingham. The population is returned with the parish. This place, which gave name to the hundred, in ancient records is called a parish, but appears to have been subsequently annexed to Bilborough, to which the chapel, now in ruins, was a chapel of ease.

BRUERN, an extra-parochial liberty, in the hundred of CHADLINGTON, county of OXFORD, 3¾ miles (N. by E.) from Burford, containing 64 inhabitants. An abbey for Cistercian monks, dedicated to the Blessed Virgin Mary, was founded by Nicholas Basset, in 1147, the revenue of which, at the dissolution, amounted to £124. 10. 10.

BRUISYARD, a parish in the hundred of PLOMESGATE, county of SUFFOLK, 3½ miles (N. E. by E.) from Framlingham, containing 269 inhabitants. The living is a perpetual curacy, in the archdeaconry of Suffolk, and diocese of Norwich, endowed with £1000 royal bounty, and in the patronage of the Earl of Stradbroke. The church is dedicated to St. Peter. A collegiate chapel, in honour of the Annunciation, was founded at Campsey, for a warden and four Secular priests, by Maud, Countess of Ulster, in 1347, seven years after which the establishment was removed to Bruisyard: the site and possessions, in 1366, were surrendered to an abbess and nuns of the order of St. Clare, who continued here until the general suppression, when their revenue was estimated at £56. 2. 1.

BRUMHILL, a hamlet in the parish of WEETING, hundred of GRIMSHOE, county of NORFOLK, 1 mile (N. N. E.) from Brandon. The population is returned with the parish. A priory for Augustine canons, dedicated to the Virgin Mary and St. Thomas the Martyr, was founded in or about the reign of John, by Sir Hugh de Plaiz: in the 7th of Henry III. the prior received a grant for a fair to be held here on the 7th of July, and, in the following year, permission to hold a market also. It was suppressed by a bull of Pope Clement, issued in May 1528, and the possessions were granted by the king to Cardinal Wolsey, toward endowing his intended college at Ipswich; but this design having been frustrated by the cardinal's fall, they were given, in exchange for other lands, to the Master and Fellows of Christ's College, Cambridge: the site is now occupied by a farm-house, and several stone coffins have been dug up on the spot.

BRUMSTEAD, a parish in the hundred of HAPPING, county of NORFOLK, 6¾ miles (E. S. E.) from North Walsham, containing 93 inhabitants. The living is a discharged rectory, in the archdeaconry of Norfolk, and diocese of Norwich, rated in the king's books at £6.5.7½., and in the patronage of the Earl of Abergavenny. The church is dedicated to St. Peter.

BRUNDALL, a parish in the hundred of BLOFIELD, county of NORFOLK, 6 miles (E. by S.) from Norwich, containing 54 inhabitants. The living is a discharged rectory, consolidated with those of Little Plumstead and Witton, in the archdeaconry and diocese of Norwich, rated in the king's books at £4. 10. The church is dedicated to St. Lawrence. In the 38th of Henry III., William de St. Omer received a grant of a fair to be held here.

BRUNDISH, a parish in the hundred of HOXNE, county of SUFFOLK, 4½ miles (N. by W.) from Framlingham, containing 427 inhabitants. The living is a perpetual curacy, united to the vicarage of Tannington, in the archdeaconry of Suffolk, and diocese of Norwich. The church is dedicated to St. Lawrence.

BRUNDON, a parish in the hundred of HINCKFORD, county of ESSEX, 6¾ miles (N. E.) from Castle-Hedingham. The population is returned with Ballingdon. The living is a rectory with Ballingdon, in the archdeaconry of Middlesex, and diocese of London, rated in the king's books at £6. 13. 4., and in the patronage of Admiral Wyndham. The church has been destroyed, and the inhabitants now repair to the chapel at Ballingdon, which has in consequence become parochial.

BRUNSTOCK, a township in the parish of CROSBY upon EDEN, ESKDALE ward, county of CUMBERLAND, 2¾ miles (N. E. by E.) from Carlisle, containing 53 inhabitants.

BRUNTINGTHORPE, a parish in the hundred of GUTHLAXTON, county of LEICESTER, 5¼ miles (N. E.) from Lutterworth, containing 348 inhabitants. The living is a rectory, in the archdeaconry of Leicester, and diocese of Lincoln, rated in the king's books at £10.7.6., and in the patronage of George Bridges, Esq. The church is dedicated to St. Mary.

BRUNTON (EAST), a township in that part of the parish of GOSFORTH which is in the western division of CASTLE ward, county of NORTHUMBERLAND, 4¼ miles (N. by W.) from Newcastle upon Tyne, containing 270 inhabitants.

BRUNTON (WEST), a township in that part of the parish of GOSFORTH which is in the western division of CASTLE ward, county of NORTHUMBERLAND, 4½ miles (N.W. by N.) from Newcastle upon Tyne, containing 126 inhabitants.

BRUSHFIELD, a township in the parish of BAKEWELL, hundred of HIGH PEAK, county of DERBY, 4¾ miles (W. N. W.) from Bakewell, containing 40 inhabitants.

BRUSHFORD, a parish in the hundred of NORTH TAWTON with WINKLEY, county of DEVON, 5¼ miles (S. by W.) from Chulmleigh, containing 134 inhabitants. The living is a perpetual curacy, in the archdeaconry of Barnstaple, and diocese of Exeter, endowed with £200 private benefaction, and £1000 royal bounty, and in the patronage of the Rev. J. Luxton.

BRUSHFORD, a parish in the hundred of WILLITON and FREEMANNERS, county of SOMERSET, 1¾ mile (S. by E.) from Dulverton, containing 311 inhabitants. The living is a rectory, in the archdeaconry of Taunton, and diocese of Bath and Wells, rated in the king's books at £15.1.5½., and in the patronage of the Earl of Carnarvon. The church is dedicated to St. Michael.

BRUTON, a market town and parish in the hundred of BRUTON, county of SOMERSET, 12 miles (S. E.) from Wells, and 110 (W. by S.) from London, containing, with the chapelries of Weeke-Champflower and Redlynch, and the tything of Discove, 2076 inhabitants. This place, which takes its name from the river Bri, or Bru, that rises in the adjoining forest of Selwood, was distinguished, prior to the Conquest, for an abbey founded by Algar, Earl of Cornwall, in 1005, for monks of the Benedictine order, upon the ruins of which William de Mohun, in the reign of Stephen, erected a priory for Black canons; this was raised into an abbey, in the beginning of the reign of Henry VIII., by William Gilbert, the prior, by whom it was almost rebuilt: it was dedicated to the Blessed Virgin, and its revenue, at the dissolution, was £480. 17. 2.: the remains have been recently converted into a parsonage-house, and the other vestiges consist of the altars, the tomb of the last abbot, and an ancient well. The town is pleasantly situated at the base of a steep hill, and along the side of a romantic combe, watered by the river Bru, which affords a plentiful supply of water, and over which is a stone bridge: it consists principally of one clean and well-paved street; the houses are in general neatly built. The manufactures were once considerable, but are now confined to stockings and silk. The market is on Saturday: the fairs are on September 17th and April 23rd. The town-hall is a spacious building; the lower part is used for the market, and the upper part contains a large court-room, wherein the petty sessions for the division are held.

The living is a perpetual curacy, in the archdeaconry of Wells, and diocese of Bath and Wells, endowed with £600 private benefaction, £400 royal bounty, and £1700 parliamentary grant, and in the patronage of Sir R. C. Hoare, Bart. The church, dedicated to St. Mary, is a spacious and handsome structure in the later style of English architecture; the tower at the west end is most elaborately decorated, embattled, and crowned with pinnacles: there are two porches, over the entrance into which are the arms of some of the abbots; the tomb of prior Gilbert is preserved in the church, and a neat marble monument has been erected to the memory of Captain Berkeley. There is a place of worship for Independents. The free grammar school was founded, in the reign of Edward VI., by Richard Fitzjames, Bishop of London; Sir John Fitzjames, Chief Justice of England; and Dr. John Edmonds, by deed dated September 24th, 1519, who endowed it with estates producing £350. 5. 10. per annum: it has four exhibitions, of £50 per annum each, to either of the Universities. An hospital for the maintenance and clothing of fourteen aged men, the same number of women, and sixteen boys, who are also educated and apprenticed, was founded about 1618, by Hugh Sexey, Esq., auditor of the household to Queen Elizabeth and James I., who endowed it with estates producing £1381. 11. 2½. per annum; the men and women have a weekly allowance of six shillings each, and a bushel of coal; and with the boys, on leaving school, is given an apprentice fee of £22, of which £12 is paid to the master on the signing, and £10 on the expiration, of the indenture. The chaplain has a stipend of £40 per annum; the schoolmaster, a salary of £42 per annum for teaching, and seven shillings per week each for boarding, the scholars; the treasurer and steward receives £32, and the surgeon and apothecary £20, per annum. The buildings, which were completed about 1636, form a spacious quadrangle near the west end of the town, and are in the Elizabethan style of architecture: in one of the wings is a neat chapel, with a school-room below it; and over the entrance to the hall is the bust of the founder: the eastern side of the quadrangle was rebuilt about twenty-five years since. The benevolent founder of this hospital, the two Fitzjames', and Dampier, the celebrated navigator, were born here. Many marine shells and fossils have been dug up at Creech Hill, where was an encampment, and on which also a beacon was formerly erected: human skeletons and skulls have been found at Lawyat; and at Dishcove, a small hamlet in the parish, the remains of a tesselated pavement were discovered in 1711.

BRUTON (HIGH and LOW), a township in the parish of EMBLETON, southern division of BAMBROUGH ward, county of NORTHUMBERLAND, 8¾ miles (N. by E.) from Alnwick, containing 70 inhabitants.

BRYANSTON, a parish in the hundred of PIMPERNE, Blandford (North) division of the county of DORSET, 1½ mile (N.W. by W.) from Blandford-Forum, containing 79 inhabitants. The living is a rectory, with that of Durweston consolidated, in the archdeaconry of Dorset, and diocese of Bristol, rated in the king's books at £8. 11. 5½., and in the patronage of Edward Berkeley Portman, Esq. The church is dedicated to St. Martin. The navigable river Stour forms the northern boundary of this parish.

BRYANT'S PIDDLE, a tything in the parish of AFF-PIDDLE, hundred of HUNDRED'S BARROW, Blandford (South) division of the county of DORSET, 9¼ miles (E. by N.) from Dorchester, containing 169 inhabitants.

BRYNGWYN, a parish in the lower division of the hundred of RAGLAND, county of MONMOUTH, 6½ miles (W.S.W.) from Monmouth, containing 265 inhabitants. The living is a discharged rectory, in the archdeaconry and diocese of Llandaff, rated in the king's books at £4. 8. 9., and in the patronage of the Earl of Abergavenny. The church is dedicated to St. Peter.

BRYNING, a joint township with Kellasnergh, in the parish of KIRKHAM, hundred of AMOUNDERNESS, county palatine of LANCASTER, 2¾ miles (S.W. by W.) from Kirkham, containing, with Kellasnergh, 145 inhabitants.

BUBBENHALL, a parish in the Kenilworth division of the hundred of KNIGHTLOW, county of WARWICK, 6 miles (S.S.E.) from Coventry, containing 247 inhabitants. The living is a perpetual curacy, in the peculiar jurisdiction of the Bishop of Lichfield and Coventry, endowed with £200 private benefaction, and £400 royal bounty, and in the patronage of the Prebendary of Bubbenhall in the Cathedral Church of Lichfield. The church is dedicated to St. Giles. Eight poor children are taught to read, from an endowment of £5 a year, being the interest of £100 given by Mrs. Hannah Murcott, in 1775.

BUBNELL, a township in the parish of BAKEWELL, hundred of HIGH PEAK, county of DERBY, 2¾ miles (S.E.) from Stoney-Middleton, containing 96 inhabitants. There is a small endowment for the instruction of children.

BUBWITH, a parish partly in the liberty of ST. PETER of YORK, but chiefly in the Holme-Beacon division of the wapentake of HARTHILL, East riding of the county of YORK, comprising the townships of Breighton, Bubwith, Foggathorpe, Gribthorpe with Willitoft, Harlthorpe, and Spaldington, and containing 1455 inhabitants, of which number, 540 are in the township of Bubwith, 7 miles (N.N.W.) from Howden. The living is a discharged vicarage, held in medieties; the first, which is rated in the king's books at £7. 2. 6., is in the archdeaconry of the East riding, and diocese of York, and in the patronage of the Crown; the second, rated at £8. 0. 5., is in the peculiar jurisdiction and patronage of the Dean and Chapter of York. The church is dedicated to All Saints. There is a place of worship for Wesleyan Methodists. The village is situated close to the river Derwent, which is crossed by a stone bridge of ten arches, built in 1793, and is the birthplace of Nicholas de Bubwith, Bishop of Bath and Wells, who was one of the English prelates that were present at the council of Constance, in 1415.

BUCKBY (LONG), a parish in the hundred of GUILSBOROUGH, county of NORTHAMPTON, 5 miles (N. E.) from Daventry, containing, with the hamlet of Murcott, 1843 inhabitants. The living is a discharged vicarage, in the archdeaconry of Northampton, and diocese of Peterborough, rated in the king's books at £10, endowed with £400 private benefaction, £200 royal bounty, and £1600 parliamentary grant, and in the patronage of the Bishop of Lichfield and Coventry. The church is dedicated to St. Lawrence. There is a place of worship for Particular Baptists. Langton Freeman, in 1783, gave £400 for the endowment of a school for poor children.

BUCKDEN, a parish in the hundred of TOSELAND, county of HUNTINGDON, 4½ miles (S.W. by W.) from Huntingdon, containing 973 inhabitants. The living is a discharged vicarage, rated in the king's books at £8, and in the peculiar jurisdiction and patronage of the Bishop of Lincoln. The church, dedicated to St. Mary, has a tower surmounted by an elegant spire, and contains the remains of some of the bishops of Lincoln, to one of whom the manor was granted by the abbot of Ely, in the reign of Henry I.; the episcopal palace is a venerable structure; and there are vestiges of an ancient monastic building. There is a place of worship for Wesleyan Methodists. The Grand Junction canal passes through the parish, and the river Nine has its source in the neighbourhood. Robert Raymond, in 1761, bequeathed a rent-charge of £10 for the instruction of children; and a charity school has been established by means of a bequest, in 1778, of £200 from Dr. Greenlate, Bishop of Lincoln.

BUCKDEN, a township in that part of the parish of ARNCLIFFE which is in the eastern division of the wapentake of STAINCLIFFE and EWCROSS, West riding of the county of YORK, $18\frac{1}{2}$ miles (N.E.) from Settle, containing 382 inhabitants.

BUCKENHAM, a parish in the hundred of BLOFIELD, county of NORFOLK, 5 miles (S.W.) from Acle, containing 31 inhabitants. The living is a discharged rectory, with that of Hassingham consolidated, in the archdeaconry and diocese of Norwich, rated in the king's books at £6, and in the patronage of Sir T. B. Proctor, Bart. The church is dedicated to St. Nicholas. The village lies near the river Yare, over which there is a ferry. The Romans are supposed to have had a minor station here, relics of which have been discovered in the vicinity.

BUCKENHAM (NEW), a market town and parish in the hundred of SHROPHAM, county of NORFOLK, $15\frac{1}{2}$ miles (S.W.) from Norwich, and 96 (N.E. by N.) from London, containing 720 inhabitants. This place owes its origin to William D'Albini, Earl of Chichester, who, disliking the situation of a castle which was built at Old Buckenham, about the time of the Conquest, caused that structure to be demolished, and another to be erected here, in the reign of Henry II. This castle was pleasantly situated on an eminence to the east of the former, and consisted of a keep, two round towers, a grand entrance tower, and a barbican, enclosed with embattled walls surrounded by a fosse; part of the gateway and keep is still remaining. Its lord, who had view of frank pledge, and the power of life and death, obtained from Henry II. many privileges for his new burgh, among which were those of holding a mercate court, the assize of bread and ale, and a market. The inhabitants have also the privilege of exposing goods for sale at any market or fair in the kingdom, free of toll and stallage, and are exempt from serving on juries. The lords of this manor claim the right of officiating as butler at the coronation of the kings of England. The town is pleasantly situated, the houses are neatly built, and there is an ample supply of water. A high bailiff is chosen annually at the "Portman" court; and a court baron and court leet are held by the proprietor of the manor. The market is on Saturday: the fairs are on the last Saturday in May, September 28th, and November 22nd. The living is a perpetual curacy, in the archdeaconry of Norfolk, and diocese of Norwich, endowed with £1000 parliamentary grant, and in the patronage of the parishioners. The church, dedicated to St. Martin, is an ancient structure, part of which was rebuilt in 1479; over the western entrance are sculptured the arms of several ancient families: the chancel is separated from the north aisle by a richly carved screen, and contains some interesting monuments. There is a place of worship for Methodists. A free school is endowed for a limited number of boys; and an almshouse for four aged persons was endowed by William Barber, Esq., with £28 per annum.

BUCKENHAM (OLD), a parish in the hundred of SHROPHAM, county of NORFOLK, 3 miles (S.S.E.) from Attleburgh, containing 1134 inhabitants. The living is a perpetual curacy, in the archdeaconry of Norfolk, and diocese of Norwich, endowed with £200 private benefaction, £200 royal bounty, and £800 parliamentary grant, and in the patronage of the parishioners. The church is dedicated to All Saints. There is a place of worship for Sandemanians. This was anciently a place of considerable importance, and is supposed to derive name either from *Boccen*, a beech tree, and *Ham*, a dwelling-place; or from an allusion to the bucks, or deer, that thronged the adjacent forests. A priory for Augustine canons was founded, in honour of St. James the Apostle, by William D'Albini, Earl of Chichester, about the middle of the twelfth century: at the dissolution, the establishment consisted of a prior and eight canons, whose revenue was estimated at £131. 11. It was partly built with the ruins of an old castle in the vicinity, which was entirely demolished by Sir Philip Knyvett, whose ancestors had resided in it. A little southward from the site of this castle, which is still visible, stood a chapel, dedicated to the Virgin Mary, subsequently converted into a barn, to which purpose also the present parochial church was appropriated, soon after its desecration, on being granted away as part of the possessions of the priory. Here were three guilds, dedicated respectively to St. Margaret, St. Peter, and St. Thomas the Martyr. There is a small fund for the instruction of children, besides some trifling benefactions for the poor.

BUCKENHILL, a township in the parish of WOOLHOPE, hundred of GREYTREE, county of HEREFORD, $8\frac{1}{2}$ miles (N. by E.) from Ross. The population is returned with the parish.

BUCKERELL, a parish in the hundred of HEMYOCK, county of DEVON, 3 miles (W.) from Honiton, containing 315 inhabitants. The living is a discharged vicarage, in the archdeaconry and diocese of Exeter, rated in the king's books at £10. 0. $2\frac{1}{2}$., endowed with £200 private benefaction, and £300 parliamentary grant, and in the patronage of the Dean and Chapter of Exeter. The church is dedicated to St. Mary.

BUCKFASTLEIGH, a parish (formerly a market town) in the hundred of STANBOROUGH, county of DEVON, $2\frac{1}{4}$ miles (S.W. by W.) from Ashburton, containing 2240 inhabitants. The living is a vicarage, in the archdeaconry of Totness, and diocese of Exeter, rated in the king's books at £19. 1. $0\frac{1}{2}$., and in the patronage of the Rev. Matthew Lowndes. The church, dedicated to the Holy Trinity, is situated on an eminence northward from the village, and comprises a nave, chancel, transepts, and a tower, with chapels on the north and south sides. There is a place of worship for Wesleyan Methodists. The village owed much of its past importance to a Cistercian abbey, founded in 1137, by Ethelward de Pomeroy, in honour of St. Mary, the abbot of which had power to execute capital offenders; its revenue, at the time of the dissolution, was estimated at £466. 11. 2.: the visible remains are few, many of the houses in the village having been built with its materials; and a modern mansion, in the ecclesiastical style of architecture, has been erected on part of its site. Prior to the dissolution, a weekly market was held, the market-house being still standing: fairs for live stock are held on the third Thursday in June, and the second Thursday in September. Copper-works are in active operation in the vicinity; and there are strata of indifferently good marble mixed with the limestone rock. Within the limits of the parish are vestiges of an encampment.

BUCKHOLT-FARM, an extra-parochial liberty, in the hundred of THORNGATE, Andover division of the county of SOUTHAMPTON, 5 miles (S.W.) from Stockbridge. The Roman road from Salisbury to Winchester crosses this farm.

BUCKHORN-WESTON, a parish in the hundred of Redlane, Sturminster division of the county of Dorset, 8 miles (W. by N.) from Shaftesbury, containing 327 inhabitants. The living is a rectory, in the archdeaconry of Dorset, and diocese of Bristol, rated in the king's books at £10. 1. 3., and in the patronage of Lady Stapleton. In the chancel of the church is an ancient statue, supposed to be that of the father-in-law of Gascoigne, Lord Chief Justice in the reigns of Henry IV. and V.; the gallery is said to have been painted by Sir James Thornhill, who resided in a neighbouring parish.

BUCKHOW-BANK, a township in the parish of Dalston, ward and county of Cumberland, 5½ miles (S.S.W.) from Carlisle, containing 570 inhabitants. The village lies on the eastern bank of the river Caldew, and there are several cotton-mills within the township, in connexion with the manufacturers at Carlisle: the soil is very favourable to the growth of wheat, and produces heavy crops.

Seal and Arms.

BUCKINGHAM, a parish in the hundred and county of Buckingham, comprising the borough and market town of Buckingham (which has a separate jurisdiction), the chapelry of Gawcott, the hamlets of Bourton, Bourtonhold, and Lenborough, and the precinct of Prebend-End, and containing 3465 inhabitants, of which number, 1495 are in the borough, 17 miles (N.W.) from Aylesbury, and 56 (N.W. by W.) from London. This place is supposed to have derived its name either from the Saxon *Bocce*, a beech tree, or from *Bucca*, a stag, having been equally remarkable for the extensive beech woods in its neighbourhood, and for the great number of deer with which those woods abounded: some, however, from the name having anciently been written *Boch-ing-ham*, deduce it from *Boch-ing*, a chartered or free meadow, as *boch-land*, among the Saxons, signified a charter-land, to distinguish it from *folc-land*, or copyhold. In 915, King Edward the Elder fortified both sides of the river on which the town is situated, with ramparts and turrets, to protect it from the incursions of the Danes, who, in 941, committed dreadful outrages in the neighbourhood, and, in 1010, took possession of the town. In the reign of Edward III., Buckingham sent three representatives to a great council held at Westminster, at which time it was a considerable staple town for wool; but upon the removal of that distinction to Calais, its prosperity declined, and it finally became one of those decayed towns for which relief was granted by an act of parliament in 1535. About this period, the assizes, formerly held here, were removed to Aylesbury; but in 1758 Lord Cobham obtained an act for holding the summer assizes at this town. In 1644, Charles I. fixed his head-quarters, and Sir William Waller, after the battle of Cropredy-Bridge, and Fairfax after his defeat at Borstall House, took up their stations here. In 1724, a considerable part of the town was destroyed by an accidental fire.

Buckingham is pleasantly situated on the river Ouse, by which it is environed on every side except the north, and over which are three bridges of stone: it consists principally of one long street; the houses in general are built of brick, and the town is paved, lighted with oil, and plentifully supplied with water. The trade chiefly consists in sorting wool, tanning leather, and the making of lace. Of the last, prior to the introduction of the lace manufacture into Nottingham, a great quantity was made, not only in this town, but throughout the county, affording employment to a large portion of the female inhabitants: there are several corn and paper mills on the banks of the Ouse. A branch of the Grand Junction canal, extending to the town, affords the means of supplying it with coal, and considerably facilitates its trade. There are several limestone quarries in the vicinity, besides a quarry of marble; the marble is of a darkish colour, but can neither endure the weather, nor retain a good polish, on which account it is but little worked. The market is on Saturday: fairs are held on January 12th, and on the last Monday in that month, March 7th, the second Monday in April, May 6th, Whit-Thursday, July 10th, September 4th, and October 2nd, chiefly for cattle and sheep; on the Saturday after Old Michaelmas-day, which is a statute fair; and November 8th and December 13th, for cattle. The government, by charter of incorporation granted in the reign of Edward III., confirmed by Henry VIII., and subsequently by Queen Mary, is vested in a bailiff, high steward, recorder, and twelve principal burgesses, assisted by a town-clerk and subordinate officers. There are four incorporated fraternities, *viz.*, the Mercers, Tanners, Merchant Taylors, and Butchers; but the freedom of the borough has become obsolete. The bailiff is a justice of the peace, and, with three of the burgesses, and the deputy steward, holds a court for the recovery of debts under £5. The corporation hold courts of session in April and October, for the trial of all offenders, except such as are accused of capital crimes. The town-hall is a neat and spacious brick building, nearly in the centre of the town. The borough gaol, a commodious structure, was erected by Lord Cobham, in 1748, at an expense of £7000: on a tablet over the entrance is an inscription recording the restoration of the summer assizes in 1758. The borough has constantly returned two representatives to parliament since the 36th of Henry VIII.: the right of election is vested exclusively in the officers of the corporation, thirteen in number, who are in the interest of the Duke of Buckingham: the bailiff is the returning officer.

The living is a discharged vicarage, in the peculiar jurisdiction of the Dean and Chapter of Lincoln, rated in the king's books at £22, and in the patronage of the Duke of Buckingham. The church, dedicated to St. Peter and St. Paul, was erected in 1781, on the site of an ancient castle, supposed to have been built by one of the earls of Buckingham, prior to the Conquest, the foundations of which are occasionally discovered, and constitute its only vestiges: it is a handsome structure, with a square embattled tower surmounted by a well-proportioned spire. There are places of worship for Baptists, the Society of Friends, Independents, Wesleyan Methodists, and Presbyterians. The free grammar school, now incorporated with an English school under the management of the corporation, was founded by Edward VI., who endowed it with the revenue of a dissolved chantry belonging to the guild of the Holy Trinity, and appropriated to its use the chapel founded, in 1268, by Matthew Stratton, Archdeacon of Buckingham, and dedicated to St. John the Baptist and Thomas à Becket, of which the seats, erected in the reign of Edward IV., and the original entrance, in the Norman style, are still remaining. The Green-coat school, for twenty-six boys, was founded and endowed in 1760, by Mr. Gabriel Newton, alderman of Leicester; and a National school for two hundred boys and one hundred girls, established in 1819, for which a handsome building of stone has been erected, is supported by subscription. The almshouses, called Christ's hospital, for six aged women, were founded by Queen Elizabeth, about 1597. Buckingham gives the title of duke to the family of Temple.

BUCKINGHAMSHIRE, an inland county, bounded on the south and south-west by Berkshire, from which it is separated by the river Thames; on the west by the county of Oxford; on the north-west and north by that of Northampton; on the north-east by that of Bedford; on the east by those of Bedford and Hertford; and on the south-east by Middlesex. It extends from 51° 25′ to 52° 11′ (N. Lat.), and from 0° 30′ to 1° 9′ (W. Lon.); and comprises an area of about seven hundred and forty square miles, or four hundred and seventy-three thousand statute acres. The population, in 1821, amounted to 134,068.

The ancient British inhabitants of this territory are supposed by Camden to have been the *Cassii*, or *Catti-euchlani*. Mr. Whitaker, the learned historian of Manchester, is of opinion, that only that part of Buckinghamshire which borders on the present county of Bedford, was originally inhabited by the *Cassii*; but, that they afterwards seized upon the territories of the *Dobuni*, who inhabited the other parts of it, which the latter, at a still remoter period, had conquered from the *Ancalites*. The neighbourhood of Kimble is stated to have been the scene of that action between the invading Romans and the aborigines of the island, in which the two sons of Cunobeline, or Cymbeline, were defeated by Aulus Plautius, and one of them, named Togodumnus, slain. Under the Roman dominion, the territory now constituting the county of Buckingham was included in the great division called *Flavia Cæsariensis*. The Romanized Britons, in consequence of a defeat which they had received from the Saxons under Cuthwulf, brother of Ceawlin, king of the West Saxons, at Bedford, were compelled, in the year 580, to abandon the districts lying immediately below the Chiltern Hills, in which several of their principal towns were situated, one of which, called by the victors *Eaglesbyrig*, is now the town of Aylesbury. On the complete establishment of the Saxon Octarchy, this shire became part of the powerful kingdom of Mercia. Edward the Elder, in the year 915, built a fortress on each side of the Ouse at Buckingham, where he staid four weeks: in 921, the Danes committed great depredations between Aylesbury and the forest of Bernwood. On the consolidation of the Danish power in England under Canute, this shire was included in the *Dane-lege*, or Danish jurisdiction. During the war between King John and the barons, Hanslape Castle, at Castlethorpe, was garrisoned against the former by its possessor, William Mauduit, but was taken and demolished, in 1216, by Fulk de Brent. In 1233, the lands of Richard, Earl of Cornwall, near Brill, were laid waste by Richard Sward, and others of the revolted party. At the commencement of the civil war of the seventeenth century, Buckinghamshire was one of the first that joined in an association for mutual defence on the side of the parliament: it was the address of its inhabitants, too, that first excited this body more strenuously to resist the king; and Lord Clarendon informs us that, "from the date of its presentation we may reasonably date the levying of war in England." On the breaking out of hostilities, the king had a garrison in a strong position at Brill, which, towards the close of the year 1642, was attacked by the celebrated patriot, Hampden, who, however, was repulsed with considerable loss, and the garrison continued to be a great annoyance to the parliamentarians, by its frequent excursions to Aylesbury and its vicinity. Among the terms for a cessation of hostilities, as delivered to the king, in March 1643, it was proposed that the royal forces should not advance nearer to Aylesbury than Brill, nor those of the parliament nearer to Oxford than Aylesbury. A skirmish, which took place in the following June, on Chalgrave-field, is memorable for the severe loss sustained by the parliamentarian cause in the death of Hampden, who there received a wound, which caused his death six days after. Newport-Pagnell, in the course of the same year, was for a short time garrisoned by the king's troops, but was abandoned by Sir Lewis Dyve, on the approach of the Earl of Essex, and it afterwards proved a very useful garrison to the parliament. Brill was evacuated by the royalist forces in April 1643; and about the same time Prince Rupert attacked the quarters of the parliamentarians at High Wycombe with some success. In the summer of this year, the Earl of Essex quartered his army for a considerable time about Aylesbury and Thame, near the former of which, in August, a grand rendezvous of the parliamentarian forces was held. In 1644, the king had his head-quarters for some time at Buckingham; but on the other hand a royalist garrison in Borstall House, just within the western confines of the county, which had proved troublesome to the parliamentarian garrison at Aylesbury, abandoned that strong hold in June of the same year, and it was immediately taken possession of by the parliament; but it was some time afterwards retaken for the royalists by Col. Gage. Greenland House, another garrison for the king, situated on the banks of the Thames, near Henley, after sustaining a severe siege, was surrendered in the month of July to General Browne. During the whole of the following year, neither of the contending parties here gained any advantage over the other, although Skippon and Fairfax each made successive attacks on Borstall House: from the siege of this place the parliamentarian forces marched to Marsh-Gibbon, Brickhill, and Buckingham. In 1646, Borstall House, the only remaining royal garrison in the county, was surrendered to the parliament.

Buckinghamshire is in the diocese of Lincoln, and province of Canterbury; and, with the exception of a few parishes, constitutes an archdeaconry, in which are the deaneries of Buckingham, Burnham, Mursley, Newport, Wadsden, Wendover, and Wycombe: the total number of parishes is two hundred and two, of which one hundred and one are rectories, sixty-eight vicarages, and the remainder perpetual curacies and donatives. For

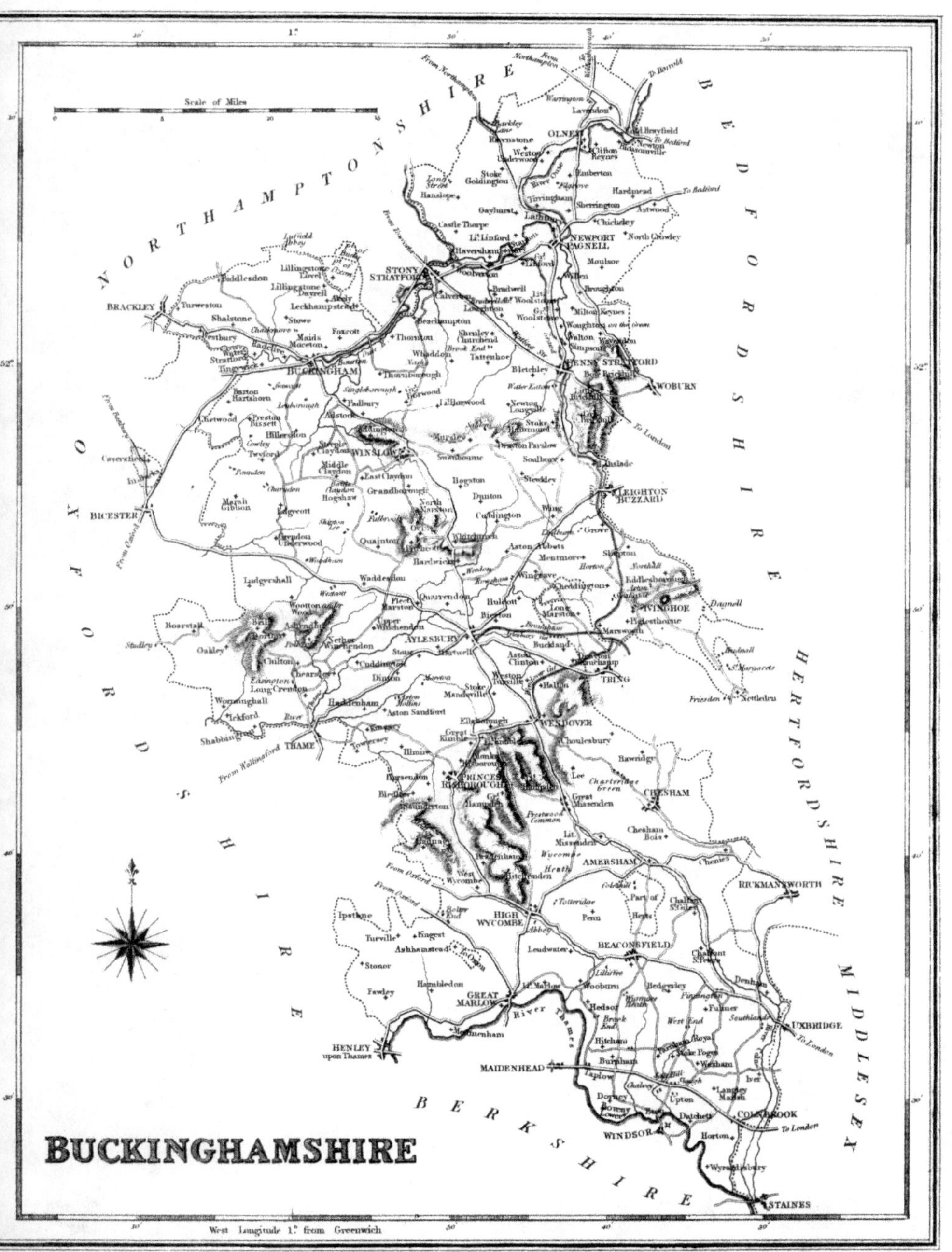

Drawn by R. Creighton.   ENGRAVED FOR LEWIS' TOPOGRAPHICAL DICTIONARY.   J. & C. Walker Sc.

purposes of civil jurisdiction, it is divided into eight hundreds, *viz.*, Ashendon, Aylesbury, Buckingham, Burnham, Cottesloe, Desborough, Newport, and Stoke. It contains the borough and market towns of Amersham, Aylesbury, Buckingham, Great Marlow, Wendover, and High or Chipping-Wycombe; and the market towns of Beaconsfield, Chesham, Ivinghoe, Newport-Pagnell, Olney, Prince's Risborough, Fenny-Stratford, Stony-Stratford, and Winslow; as also part of that of Colnbrook, the rest of which is in Middlesex. Two knights are returned to parliament for the shire, and two burgesses for each of the six boroughs: the county members are elected at Buckingham. It is included in the Oxford circuit: the summer assizes are held at Buckingham, and the Lent assizes and general quarter sessions at Aylesbury, where is situated the common gaol and house of correction for the county. There are one hundred and thirty acting magistrates. The rates raised in the county for the year ending March 25th, 1829, amounted to £146,543, and the expenditure to £143,732, of which £124,497 was applied to the relief of the poor.

There is hardly a county in England more irregular in shape and outline than this, which, although it approaches an oblong, has singular projections and indentations: its boundaries, except on the south and south-east, where they are formed by the rivers Thames and Colne, are almost entirely arbitrary. A little beyond its western confines, immediately to the north of Bicester, is a small detached portion, forming the parish of Caversfield, which is surrounded by Oxfordshire. The most striking natural feature in its surface is the range of heights called the Chiltern hills, which stretches across it from the southern extremity of Bedfordshire, by Eddlesborough, Halton, Wendover, Ellesborough, Risborough, and Bledlow, to the southern part of Oxfordshire, being part of the great chain of chalk hills which extends from Norfolk south-westward into Dorsetshire. On the western side of the county is a range of hills of calcareous stone, which runs parallel with the Chiltern hills, at the distance of only a few miles. Between these two lies the rich Vale of Aylesbury, the natural fertility of which is almost unrivalled. The country to the south of the Chilterns abounds with pleasing scenery, highly diversified with hill and dale, corn-fields, meadows, and woodlands, particularly near Amersham and the Missendens. Between Marlow and Henley the scenery is rendered still more delightful by the broad and glassy current of the Thames, and the picturesque boldness of its opposite banks. Among the more striking prospects may be particularly mentioned that from the hills above Ellesborough, over the Vale of Aylesbury; that from a field near Brill, over a great part of Oxfordshire and Northamptonshire; and that from the tower of Penn church, which is the most extensive of all, and, besides comprising a great portion of Bucks, stretches into the counties of Berks, Oxford, Bedford, Herts, Essex, Kent, Middlesex, Surrey, and even into some parts of Sussex and Northamptonshire.

The predominating soils are rich loam, strong clay, chalky mould, and loam upon gravel, all of which, however, admit of considerable variety, and are much intermingled. The subsoil of the Chiltern hills is chalk of different qualities, with occasional beds of gravel and sand, and in many places a great abundance of brick earth, especially from Chesham to Amersham, at which latter place it is very fine, and supplies a manufactory for common earthenware. The surface soil of the vallies between these hills consists of rich clays and clayey loams, which upon the declivities are, in some places, very thin, and form a clayey chalk: on some of the hills the surface is clayey; on others it is composed, in a great measure, of chalk. These kinds of soil occupy the whole southern part of the county, excepting only the district separated from the rest of it by an imaginary line drawn from Uxbridge to Maidenhead, in which a gravelly loam upon gravel prevails. In the central parts of the county, from the Chiltern hills to the Watling-street on the north-east, and to the river Ouse on the north, the prevailing soils on the uplands are various clays, upon calcareous strata. The Vale of Aylesbury consists of rich clays and loams, of almost proverbial fertility. On the border of Bedfordshire, in the neighbourhood of Wavendon, Broughton, and the Brickhills, the prevailing soil is a deep sand: in the same vicinity is also found a rich blue marl, used for manure. The northern parts of the county consist of clays and loams, with mixtures of gravel, forming good turnip land, and rich meadows along the course of the Ouse.

This county has long been famous for its produce of corn and cattle, "Buckinghamshire bread and beef" having been formerly a common expression. Agriculture is practised with greater or less diligence, according to the nature of the soils: thus, on the Chiltern hills, and in the district to the south of them, where the shallowness of the soil calls forth the industrious powers of the husbandman, a more active system of farming prevails than in the rich Vale of Aylesbury, where, indeed, the land is for the most part devoted to grazing and the dairy. One-half of the county consists of arable farms, containing not more than one-fifth of grass land, which occupy the whole of the Chiltern hills and the county southward of them to the Thames, together with the sandy lands in the neighbourhood of the Brickhills, Soulbury, and Linslade, and some parts of the Vale of Aylesbury: a sixth part of the county, situated to the north-east of the Watling-street, is composed of farms of a mixed nature, containing about two-fifths of meadows and pastures. The courses of crops are various: those most commonly cultivated are wheat, barley, beans, turnips, tares, and artificial grasses: the average produce of wheat is computed at nearly twenty-five bushels per acre; that of barley, at nearly thirty-eight bushels; and that of beans, at about twenty-four bushels. Oats and peas are very little cultivated. The turnips are chiefly eaten upon the land by sheep; the tares are applied to the feeding of sheep and horses. The artificial grasses commonly sown are red clover, white clover, trefoil, and ray-grass; sainfoin also is grown on the Chiltern hills. Besides the proportion of grass land intermixed with that under cultivation, most of the central part of the county, from the Chiltern hills to the Watling-street, consists of dairy and grazing farms, which occupy about one-third of the entire surface. The pastures are not in general so rich as those of some counties, but the meadows on the banks of the Ouse and the Thame derive such fertility from the floods to which those rivers are very liable, as seldom to require manuring. The grazing farms are very few, in comparison with those applied to the dairy, upon which latter neat stock is never grazed. The number of cows kept on these extensive pastures is computed at about twenty-seven thousand, of which upwards of twenty-one thousand are always productive to the dairy. Between four and five million pounds, or about one thousand nine hundred tons, of butter are annually made in this county, by far the greater part of which is sent by contract to London. It is made up into lumps of two pounds each, and packed in osier baskets, called flats, which are in the form of parallelopipedons of different sizes, but all of the same depth, namely, eleven inches: each of these holds from three to ten dozen of butter, or from thirty-six to one hundred and twenty pounds: the flats are the property of the carrier, who receives the butter of the dairyman at the nearest point by which he passes, its carriage being paid by the factor in London. No cheese is made, except a few cream cheeses in summer for the markets of Buckingham, Aylesbury, and Wycombe. The cattle fattened are almost wholly grazed, chiefly in the Vale of Aylesbury, and considerable numbers of them sent to Smithfield market. The manures, besides those common to other counties, are chalk, obtained by sinking pits on different parts of the Chiltern hills; marl, found at Brickhill; lime; ashes, universally applied to the clover leys; soot; and woollen rags on the Chilterns: but the most general mode of manuring land is by the folding of sheep upon it, which are sometimes hired for the purpose. The greater number of the dairy cows are of the short-horned Yorkshire kind; though some dairies are composed of the long-horned Leicester breed; others of the Suffolk, and others of the Welch: a few Alderney cows are also seen. The graziers have a great variety of cattle, among which the Hereford, Devon, and Yorkshire breeds predominate. The calves are generally sold from the dairy farms, at from four to twelve days old, to persons who suckle them: these, together with others from the northern parts of the county, are purchased at Aylesbury market by the farmers of the Chilterns, particularly such as live in the neighbourhood of Chesham and Amersham, who fatten them for the London market. The principal object of those who keep sheep is to produce fat lambs as early as possible for the London market: the prevalent breeds are, the Dorsetshire, the Gloucester, the Berkshire, and the South-Down. Hogs form an important part of the stock of the dairy farms, from which great numbers are sold as bacon between Michaelmas and Christmas, or sent as porkers to the London market from that time until the spring: they are commonly of the Berkshire sort, though the Chinese and Suffolk breeds have also been introduced. There are rabbits upon the Chiltern hills, but no warrens; considerable numbers, however, are kept by poor persons, who send the young to the London markets. At Aylesbury and its vicinity, great numbers of ducks are bred and fattened by poor people, and sent to London by the weekly carriers: in this manner are sent many thousands annually, some of them very early in the spring. The orchards, though objects of little attention, produce considerable quantities of cherries, which are sent to the Aylesbury and London markets.

It is related by ancient historians, that this shire was formerly so covered with woods as to be almost impassable, until Leofstan, abbot of St. Albans, caused several of them to be cut down, because they afforded shelter for thieves. The whole of the Chiltern district is said to have been covered with wood; and the western part of the county, bordering on Oxfordshire, was occupied by the forest of Bernwood, which was disafforested in the reign of James I. The chief of the woodlands are in the districts to the south of the Chiltern hills, of which also they occupy a considerable portion. The prevailing timber is beech, of which some of the larger woods entirely consist, and which, from its abundance, gives the country a remarkably rich appearance: this timber is generally applied to the manufacture of chairs, both in this county and in London. A tract of land on the Chiltern hills, in the parishes of Ellesborough, Little Kimble, and Great Kimble, is covered with box wood, which appears to be indigenous; and the woods on many parts of these hills, particularly at West Wycombe, contain a vast quantity of juniper: the neighbourhood of Chesham abounds with the black cherry chiefly planted in hedge-rows. The principal tract of woodland in the northern part of the county is Whaddon Chase, containing about two thousand acres of coppices, consisting of oak, ash, &c. The practice of lopping and *shrouding* trees prevails so much in some parts of the county, as to give such districts a very unsightly appearance. The most extensive tracts of waste lands are Wycombe heath, containing about fifteen hundred acres; Iver heath, about eleven hundred; Stoke heath, about one thousand; Fulmer heath, about six hundred; and Great Harwood common, about five hundred. The fuel used is chiefly coal, obtained, by means of the Grand Junction canal, from the collieries of Staffordshire: Newcastle coal is brought up the Thames, and sometimes along the Grand Junction canal from London; and fagots are burned in the places most distant from these lines of navigation, where they can be most easily procured.

The mineral productions are of scarcely any importance. Near Newport is a bed of good marble, which, however, is not worked; and in the vicinity of Olney is a quarry of freestone. At Wavendon are some very old and celebrated fullers' earth pits. At Brill is obtained ochre for painting; and umber is found in small quantities in the northern parts of the county. A yellow limestone is found near Dinton, a few miles south-westward of Aylesbury, which contains an abundance of a species of *nautilus*, with other extraneous fossils: remains of this nature have also been found in other strata at Quainton, and in its vicinity, near Aylesbury, near Amersham, on Wyrardisbury, or Raisbury, common, and in the vicinity of Ellesborough. The manufactures are those of thread-lace, straw-plat, and paper. The former is tolerably general in most parts of the county, though its prosperity has greatly declined, owing to the rise of the machine lace manufacture of Nottingham, and the populous district surrounding it, it is chiefly prevalent at Hanslope, and in its immediate vicinity: in and about Olney are made great quantities of veils and laces of the finer sorts. Both boys and girls, when about five years old, are put to the lace schools to learn the art, and by the latter it is pursued through life; some men, even, follow no other employment; and others find it a resource when out of work. The straw-plat manufacture, of which the town of Dunstable, in Bedfordshire, is the centre, extends for some distance within this county. The manufacture of paper has been carried on in the neighbourhood of Wycombe for more than a century and a quarter, and different mills on the Wyke are still actively and extensively engaged in it. The exports of the county are simply the produce of these manufactures and of its agriculture: its imports are of the ordinary kinds.

The principal rivers are, the Thames, the Ouse, the Ouzel, the Thame, and the Colne. The first of these is the boundary and chief ornament of the southern part of it, which it separates from Berkshire during a navigable course of about twenty-eight miles, first touching it about a mile north of Henley bridge, and thence flowing by Medmenham, Great Marlow, Hedsor, Taplow, Boveny, Eton, and Datchet, to the mouth of the Colne, a little above Staines, where it quits the county: the navigation of this river, as affording an immediate communication with the metropolis, is of great importance to the county. The course of the Ouse through Buckinghamshire, and as a boundary to it, is very circuitous, and in length is little less than fifty miles, in no part of which, however, is it navigable: it first becomes a boundary in the parish of Turweston, near Brackley, separating it from Northamptonshire, and, after passing Westbury, forms the boundary line of the counties of Buckingham and Oxford for a short distance: it then enters the former at Water-Stratford, and flows eastward to the borough of Buckingham, and thence north-eastward to the village of Thornton, a little beyond which it again becomes a boundary between the counties of Buckingham and Northampton: a little beyond Stony-Stratford, however, it enters the county a second time, and pursues a remarkably circuitous course eastward to Newport-Pagnell, whence it proceeds northward to Olney, and thence eastward to the border of Bedfordshire, which county it separates from that of Bucks for a short distance, and then enters the former at the north-eastern extremity of the latter. The Ouzel, which rises near Eddlesborough, on the eastern confines of the county, at the foot of the Chiltern hills, immediately becomes the boundary between it and Bedfordshire, flowing northward by Leighton-Buzzard: at Linslade, near that town, it enters Buckinghamshire, and continues to run northward by Fenny-Stratford to the Ouse, at Newport-Pagnell, which it joins, after a course of about thirty miles. Into the Ouse and Ouzel flow several brooks, which take their rise in Whaddon Chase, the highest point of land in the northern part of the county. The Thame is formed by the junction of two small streams near Quarrendon, a few miles from Aylesbury, one of which has its source near Cublington; the other on the border of Hertfordshire: being joined by various other rivulets, it becomes a considerable stream on reaching Eythorpe, in its winding course westward through the rich Vale of Aylesbury: at the town of Thame it becomes the boundary between the counties of Buckingham and Oxford, for a few miles, and entirely quits the former for the latter a little beyond the village of Ickford, after a course through Buckinghamshire, from its highest sources, of about thirty miles: this river abounds with eels, which are claimed by the king: its other fish are chiefly pike, perch, chub, roach, and gudgeons. The mouth of the Thame, where it falls into the Thames, in Oxfordshire, having, for want of cleansing, become choked up, and its channel narrowed, two commissions of sewers were issued in the early part of the last century, but, owing to disputes between the commissioners and the landowners, nothing effectual was done towards the removal of the obstruction, which, having at length so far increased that the adjacent parts of Buckinghamshire frequently presented the appearance of a lake for months together, a new commission was sued out in 1797, under which the object so long desired was accomplished, by restoring the ancient channel, which has ever since been effectually preserved. The Colne, for a course of about fourteen miles, forms the south-eastern boundary of this county, which it separates from Middlesex, flowing near Denham and Iver, through Colnbrook, and near Horton and Wyrardisbury, to the Thames, between Ankerwyke and Staines: this river, in most parts of its course, has several channels. This county derives great commercial advantage from the Grand Junction canal, which connects the Coventry canal at Braunston with the Thames navigation at Brentford and at Limehouse: it enters it from Northamptonshire, near Cosgrove in the latter, by an aqueduct about three quarters of a mile long, over the stream and valley of the Ouse; and thence proceeds eastward to within a few miles of Newport-Pagnell, where it turns southward up the valley of the Ouzel, by Fenny-Stratford and Leighton-Buzzard; passing a little to the westward of Ivinghoe, it quits for Hertfordshire a little beyond the village of Marsworth. In 1794, an act was obtained for making navigable cuts to communicate with this canal from the towns of Aylesbury, Buckingham, and Wendover: the Aylesbury branch joins the main canal near Marsworth; the Buckingham branch is carried from that town down the northern side of the valley of the Ouse, near Stony-Stratford, to the main line at Cosgrove; and the Wendover navigation joins the main canal at Bulborne, on the confines of Hertfordshire. These canals are navigated by barges of sixty tons' burden: the chief articles of traffic are iron, pottery, coal, timber, lime, and manures.

The great road from London to Chester and Holyhead enters this county in the line of the ancient Watling-street, and, passing through Fenny-Stratford and Stony-Stratford, quits it at Old Stratford, near the fifty-third milestone. That from London to Liverpool enters near the forty-third milestone, about a mile from the town of Woburn in Bedfordshire, and, proceeding through Newport-Pagnell, runs into Northamptonshire between the fifty-seventh and fifty-eighth milestones. The road from London to Oxford, Bath, &c., enters at Colnbrook, and crossing the southern extremity of the county, through Slough, quits it at Maidenhead bridge. Another road to Oxford, commonly called the Wycombe road, enters from Uxbridge, and, passing through Beaconsfield and High Wycombe, proceeds into Oxfordshire a little beyond the thirty-seventh milestone. The road from London to Banbury branches from the Wycombe road at the eighteenth milestone, and passes through Amersham, Wendover, Aylesbury, Winslow, and Buckingham, a little beyond which latter place it enters Northamptonshire, near the sixtieth milestone. That from London to Aylesbury, through Tring, enters between the thirty-second and thirty-third milestones, and joins the last-mentioned road near Aylesbury.

This county contained the Roman station *Magiovintum*, near the present town of Fenny-Stratford, and was crossed by the Roman roads Ikening, or Iknield, street, the Watling-street, and the Akeman-street, as also by several vicinal ways. The Ikening-street, supposed to have been originally of British construction, from its not being raised or paved, like other Roman roads, runs along the northern verge of the Chiltern hills through their whole extent, entering this county on its eastern border near Eddlesborough, and passing through Wendover, Aston, and Calverton, to its western confines near Chinner: although passing by many camps and earthworks of various sorts, it never diverges towards them, nor does it seem to have any connexion with them, as is the case with the roads known to be of Roman construction. Another ancient road runs nearly parallel with the above, at the northern base of the hills, and is provincially called the "Lower Acknell Way." The Watling-street, during its entire course through the northern part of the county, bears no trace of its ancient Roman construction, except its exact straightness, its line being identical with that of the great modern road to Ireland, which is carried along it from Bedfordshire, through Brickhill, Fenny-Stratford, and Stony-Stratford, across the Ouse into Northamptonshire. The ancient road called the Akeman-street, which runs parallel with the Iknield-street, on the north, is traceable only in a few places, and appears to have passed by Hide-Lane, and near Buckingham, Stony-Stratford, Stanton, and Newport-Pagnell, to Bedford. An ancient road, which by some has been falsely designated the Akeman-street, enters this county from Bicester. in Oxfordshire, and proceeds in the same line with the modern turnpike road towards the Berry-fields, near Aylesbury, and may have been part of a Roman road from Alcester to Verulam, or London. Another Roman road proceeds in a direct line north-north-eastward from Bicester, and, after forming the eastern boundary of a detached portion of Buckinghamshire, reaches the main body of the county at Water-Stratford, and appears to have crossed the northernmost part of it, by Stowe, in its way to Towcester in Northamptonshire, the Roman *Lactodorum*. Traces of another Roman road, under the usual name of the Portway, are visible in the vicinities of Stone and Hartwell, to the west of Aylesbury.

The remains of the Roman station *Magiovintum* are still visible on a small elevation in the "Auld Fields," about a quarter of a mile from Fenny-Stratford: coins and foundations of buildings have been dug up here in abundance. Camden is of opinion that there was anciently a Roman town at Burgh-hill (now contracted into Brill), in the western part of the county. Numerous traces of Roman occupation, such as coins, pavements, &c., have been found at High Wycombe and in its vicinity: coins have also been found near Prince's Risborough and Ellesborough. Above the village of Medmenham are the remains of a large camp, nearly square, formed by a single ditch and vallum, and enclosing an area of about seven acres: in a wood near Burnham is an oblong intrenchment of the same kind, about one hundred and thirty paces long and sixty broad, vulgarly called Harlequin's Moat. Near Ellesborough are some strong earthworks on the side of the Chiltern hills, at one corner of which is a high mount, eighty paces in circumference, called the Castle Hill, or Kimble Castle, and commonly supposed to have been the site of the residence of the British king Cunobeline. On the top of the hill at West Wycombe are the remains of a circular encampment; and those of another are discernible near High Wycombe, at a place called Old, or All, Hollands. At Danesfield, on the banks of the Thames, is a nearly circular intrenchment, called Danes' ditch, formed by a double vallum which environs it, except towards the river, where it is defended by a steep cliff: at Cholsbury, too, is a nearly circular camp, formed by a double ditch, two hundred and eighty-nine yards in diameter from east to west, and two hundred and seven from north to south; and the manor-house of the adjacent village of Hawridge is built within an ancient circular intrenchment. There are also some large intrenchments at Hedgerley-Dean, and a remarkable ditch runs thence to East Burnham: near the Lower Iknield Way, in the parish of Ellesborough, is a moated area of an irregular form, and in most places about fifty paces in breadth. A considerable rampart of earth, under the common name of Grimesdike, runs nearly east and west through a part of this county, upon the Chiltern hills, where it may be traced for some miles, particularly between Wigginton common in Hertfordshire and St. Leonard's common in Buckinghamshire. A great cross, called White-Leaf Cross, of unknown antiquity, is cut on the side of the chalk hills near Risborough, and has been supposed to be the memorial of some victory gained by the Anglo-Saxons over the Danes.

Before the period of the Reformation this county contained twenty-one religious houses, including four Alien priories, one preceptory of the Knights Hospitallers, and a college of the society of Bonhommes at Ashridge, near the confines of Hertfordshire, being the only house of that order in England, excepting that at Edingdon in Wiltshire: there were, besides, ten hospitals, one of which, at Newport-Pagnell, re-founded by Queen Anne, consort of James I., is still existing; and the well-known royal college of Eton, founded by Henry VI. There are very considerable remains of Nutley abbey, converted into a farm-house and offices; and vestiges of those of Burnham, Medmenham, and Great Missenden, and of the college of Bonhommes at Ashridge: part of St. Margaret's nunnery, in the parish of Ivinghoe, is yet standing, and is occupied as a dwelling-house. Among the ecclesiastical edifices, Stewkley church is entitled to primary notice, both on account of its antiquity, and as being one of the most complete specimens remaining of Saxon architecture, no part of the original structure, either internally or externally, having been altered or materially defaced; nor have any additions been made to it, excepting the porch on the southern side and the pinnacles of the tower. The doorway of Water-Stratford church is enriched with Saxon ornaments; Dinton church has another remarkable doorway of the same kind; and in that of Stanton-Bury is an arch richly ornamented with Saxon mouldings and heads of animals. Upton church retains its original form, and is on the same plan as that of Stewkley, but less ornamented and much smaller. The doorways of the churches of Caversfield, Horton, Lathbury, Twyford, Waddesdon, Westbury, and Wormenhall, and of the ancient chapel of St. Thomas à Becket, now the free school, at Buckingham, are circular, with Saxon mouldings and other ornaments: there are also remains of this style in the churches of Fingest, Hanslope, Leckhampstead, Stone,

Tingewick, and Tyrringham. Chetwood and Hillersdon churches are the only specimens of English architecture worthy of particular notice: in the chancel of the former are some of the most ancient and elegant specimens of stained glass in the kingdom; and Buckinghamshire is rich in other specimens of the same kind. There are more than seventy ancient circular fonts in the churches of this county, many of which are richly ornamented; and among these may be more particularly specified those of Aylesbury, Caversfield, Dinton, Dorney, Drayton-Beauchamp, Hambledon, Hawridge, Hedgerley, Hitchenden, Maids-Moreton, and Upton: many others are octagonal and variously ornamented; while those of Taplow and Chalfont St. Giles are square. There are no remains of the buildings of any fortress; but some earthworks point out the sites of those which formerly stood at Castlethorpe, Lavendon, and Whitchurch, the first of which was called Hanslope Castle. The most remarkable ancient mansions are, Gayhurst, which was built in the reign of Elizabeth, and Liscombe House: the gatehouse of Borstall House is yet standing. At Prince's Risborough, adjoining the churchyard, is an intrenchment nearly square, supposed to be the site of the Black Prince's palace. Among the seats of the landed proprietors, those most distinguished for their architectural beauties are, Stowe, the magnificent mansion of the Duke of Buckingham; Wycombe Abbey, the residence of Lord Carrington; Ashridge, partly in Bucks and partly in Herts, that of the late Earl of Bridgewater; and the modern mansion, at Tyrringham, of William Praed, Esq. The ordinary building materials are bricks, manufactured in various places; tiles, generally flat; freestone, dug at Olney; lime; and timber. Buckinghamshire contains no mineral waters of any note: it gives the title of earl to the family of Hampden.

BUCKINGHAM (PARVA), a parish in the hundred of Grimshoe, county of Norfolk, 6½ miles (S. W. by W.) from Watton, containing 29 inhabitants. The living is a discharged rectory, in the archdeaconry of Norfolk, and diocese of Norwich, rated in the king's books at £3, and in the patronage of the Rev. T. Newman. The church, which was dedicated to St. Andrew, has long been demolished, together with the village of Buckingham, and not even the site of the former is with certainty known.

BUCKLAND, a parish in the hundred of Ganfield, county of Berks, 4¼ miles (E. N. E.) from Great Farringdon, containing, with Carswell, 893 inhabitants. The living is a discharged vicarage, in the archdeaconry of Berks, and diocese of Salisbury, rated in the king's books at £18. 4. 7., endowed with £300 private benefaction, and £200 royal bounty, and in the patronage of Robert Throckmorton, Esq. The church is dedicated to St. Mary. Henry Southby, in 1793, gave £200 and some land; and his executrix, Sarah Hayter, gave £200 more, for the instruction of girls and for a Sunday school; and Sir J. Throckmorton, in 1793, gave a house for the charity: the income is about £40 a year, for which twenty-five children of each sex are taught and partly clothed. There is a small parochial library.

BUCKLAND, a parish in the hundred of Aylesbury, county of Buckingham, 3 miles (W. N. W.) from Tring, containing 496 inhabitants. The living is a perpetual curacy, annexed, with those of Quarrendon and Stoke-Mandeville, to the vicarage of Bierton, in the jurisdiction of the peculiar court of Bierton, which belongs to the Dean and Chapter of Lincoln. The church is dedicated to All Saints. There is a place of worship for Wesleyan Methodists.

BUCKLAND, a parish in the lower division of the hundred of Kiftsgate, county of Gloucester, 6 miles (W. S. W.) from Chipping-Campden, containing, with the hamlet of Laverton, 382 inhabitants. The living is a rectory, in the archdeaconry and diocese of Gloucester, rated in the king's books at £29. 6. 8., and in the patronage of the Marquis of Bath. The church is a fine structure, in the later style of English architecture; some of the windows exhibit specimens of ancient stained glass. Henry Fred. Thynne, Esq., by deed in 1707, gave land producing upwards of £100 per annum, for teaching poor children of the parishes of Buckland and Chipping-Campden, and for other charitable purposes.

BUCKLAND, a parish in the hundred of Edwinstree, county of Hertford, 2 miles (W. S. W.) from Barkway, containing 343 inhabitants. The living is a rectory, in the archdeaconry of Middlesex, and diocese of London, rated in the king's books at £20, and in the patronage of the Provost and Fellows of King's College, Cambridge. The church is dedicated to St. Andrew.

BUCKLAND, a parish in the hundred of Bewsborough, lathe of St. Augustine, county of Kent, 1¾ mile (N. W.) from Dover, containing 693 inhabitants. The living is a discharged perpetual curacy, in the peculiar jurisdiction and patronage of the Archbishop of Canterbury, endowed with the vicarial tithes, and with £12 per annum payable out of the great tithes; also with £200 private benefaction, £200 royal bounty, and £800 parliamentary grant. The church is dedicated to St. Andrew. There is a place of worship for Wesleyan Methodists. The river Stour is crossed by a neat brick bridge at the village: here are two large and well-constructed-paper-mills, besides a corn-mill: a fair is held on the 4th of September. In 1141, an hospital for lepers was founded within the parish, and dedicated to St. Bartholomew, but there are not now any vestiges of it; digging near its site, in 1765, a leaden vessel, filled with silver coins struck in the reigns of Edward II. and Edward III., was discovered.

BUCKLAND, a parish in the hundred of Faversham, lathe of Scray, county of Kent, 3 miles (N. W. by W.) from Faversham, containing 22 inhabitants. The living is a discharged rectory, in the archdeaconry and diocese of Canterbury, rated in the king's books at £5. 6. 8., and in the patronage of Charles Eve, Esq. The church, which was dedicated to St. Nicholas, has long been in ruins.

BUCKLAND, a parish in the first division of the hundred of Reigate, county of Surrey, 2¼ miles (W.) from Reigate, containing 292 inhabitants. The living is a rectory, in the archdeaconry of Surrey, and diocese of Winchester, rated in the king's books at £11. 12. 11., and in the patronage of the Warden and Fellows of All Souls' College, Oxford. The church is dedicated to St. Peter. The river Mole forms the southern boundary of the parish.

BUCKLAND (EAST), a parish in the hundred of BRAUNTON, though locally in the hundred of South Molton, county of DEVON, 5 miles (N. W. by N.) from South Molton, containing 165 inhabitants. The living is a rectory, consolidated with that of Buckland-Filleigh, in the archdeaconry of Barnstaple, and diocese of Exeter, rated in the king's books at £9. 1. 8. The church is dedicated to St. Michael. There is a place of worship for Wesleyan Methodists.

BUCKLAND (ST. MARY), a parish partly in the southern division of the hundred of PETHERTON, and partly in the hundred of MARTOCK, but chiefly in the hundred of ABDICK and BULSTONE, county of SOMERSET, 6 miles (W. by S.) from Ilminster, containing 565 inhabitants. The living is a rectory, in the archdeaconry of Taunton, and diocese of Bath and Wells, rated in the king's books at £12. 19. 9½., and in the patronage of Mrs. Popham. The churchyard contains a mutilated stone cross. A fair for cattle and toys is held on the Wednesday and Thursday next after September 20th. Various relics of warfare have been found in the neighbourhood, which was the scene of some sanguinary conflicts between the Saxons and the Danes: on the edge of Blackdown hill are the remains of a Roman fortification, called Neroche Castle; and on the summit of the same ridge, a little further on, by the side of the road leading to Chard, there is a huge collection of flint stones, lying in heaps upwards of sixty yards in circumference, styled Robin Hood's Butts, and supposed to be the rude sepulchral memorials of warriors who fell in battle.

BUCKLAND in the MOOR, a parish in the hundred of HAYTOR, though locally in the hundred of Lifton, county of DEVON, 3½ miles (N. W.) from Ashburton, containing 137 inhabitants. The living is a perpetual curacy, annexed to the vicarage of Ashburton, in the peculiar jurisdiction of the Dean and Chapter of Exeter. The church contains a fine wooden screen.

BUCKLAND (WEST), a parish in the hundred of BRAUNTON, though locally in the hundred of South Molton, county of DEVON, 5¾ miles (N. W.) from South Molton, containing 288 inhabitants. The living is a rectory, in the archdeaconry of Barnstaple, and diocese of Exeter, rated in the king's books at £13. 13. 4., and in the patronage of Lord de Dunstanville. The church, dedicated to St. Peter, has a carved wooden screen, highly enriched, separating the nave from the chancel.

BUCKLAND (WEST), a parish in the western division of the hundred of KINGSBURY, locally in that of Taunton and Taunton-Dean, county of SOMERSET, 2¾ miles (E.) from Wellington, containing 750 inhabitants. The living is a perpetual curacy, annexed to the vicarage of Wellington, in the archdeaconry of Taunton, and diocese of Bath and Wells. The church, dedicated to St. Mary, is partly in the Norman style of architecture, with later additions.

BUCKLAND-BREWER, a parish (formerly a market town) in the hundred of SHEBBEAR, county of DEVON, 4¾ miles (W. by N.) from Great Torrington, containing 1043 inhabitants. The living is a discharged vicarage, with the perpetual curacy of East Purtford annexed, in the archdeaconry of Barnstaple, and diocese of Exeter, rated in the king's books at £25. 17. 3½., and in the patronage of the Crown. The church, dedicated to St. Mary and St. Benedict has an enriched Norman door, and had anciently a small college, dedicated to St. Michael, attached to it, the revenue of which, at the dissolution, was £8. 7. 6. A part of the manor was anciently given by Lord Brewer to the abbot of Dunkeswell, who obtained for this place a market and a fair; the former has been discontinued, but two fairs are held, one on Whit-Monday, and the other on the 2nd of November.

BUCKLAND-DENHAM, a parish (formerly a market town) in the hundred of KILMERSDON, county of SOMERSET, 2½ miles (N. W. by N.) from Frome, containing 440 inhabitants. The living is a discharged vicarage, in the peculiar jurisdiction and patronage of the Prebendary of Buckland-Denham in the Cathedral Church of Wells, rated in the king's books at £6. 9. 7., and endowed with £200 private benefaction, and £200 royal bounty. The church is dedicated to St. Mary. There is a place of worship for Wesleyan Methodists. This was formerly a place of greater importance, having been distinguished for the manufacture of woollen cloth. The inhabitants are now chiefly engaged in the cultivation of teasel, for the use of the clothiers in the neighbouring towns. A market, to be held on Tuesday, and a fair on the eve, day, and morrow of St. Michael, were granted, in the 24th of Henry III., to Geoffrey Dinant, lord of the manor. The assizes were frequently held in a town-hall here.

BUCKLAND-EGG, a parish in the hundred of ROBOROUGH, county of DEVON, 3 miles (N. N. E.) from Plymouth, containing 954 inhabitants. The living is a vicarage, in the archdeaconry of Totness, and diocese of Exeter, rated in the king's books at £8. 4. 4½., and in the patronage of the Crown. The Methodists have a meeting-house within the parish. A fair for live stock is held on the second Wednesday in June. The Plymouth railway crosses the parish. There is a small endowment for a charity school, which is chiefly supported by subscription.

BUCKLAND-FILLEIGH, a parish in the hundred of SHEBBEAR, county of DEVON, 6½ miles (N. W. by W.) from Hatherleigh, containing 274 inhabitants. The living is a rectory, with that of East Buckland consolidated, in the archdeaconry of Barnstaple, and diocese of Exeter, rated in the king's books at £11. 16. 0½., and in the patronage of the Bishop of Exeter. The church is dedicated to St. Mary.

BUCKLAND-MONACHORUM, a parish (formerly a market town) in the hundred of ROBOROUGH, county of DEVON, 4 miles (S. by E.) from Tavistock, containing 1177 inhabitants. The living is a vicarage, in the archdeaconry of Totness, and diocese of Exeter, rated in the king's books at £19. 8. 9., and in the patronage of the Rev. A. Crymes. The church, dedicated to the Holy Trinity, stands in a cemetery planted with trees, and consists of a nave, two side aisles, two small transepts, with a fine tower supporting four octagonal turrets, embattled, and surmounted by pinnacles: within, among several others, is a noble monument, by Bacon, to the memory of Baron Heathfield, the brave defender of Gibraltar. The village, which contains some curious old houses, a mutilated stone cross, and a few ancient inscriptions, is mean in appearance, but picturesquely situated. It acquired its distinguishing name from an abbey founded, in 1278, by Amicia, Countess Dowager of Devonshire, in honour of the Virgin Mary and St. Benedict, to which she removed a society of Cistercian monks from the Isle of Wight. In 1337, the abbot obtained permission to castellate his monastery; and during the parliamentary war it was garrisoned by Sir Richard Grenville. The revenue of the society, in the 26th of Henry VIII., was estimated at £241. 17. 9.: the estate came by purchase into the possession of Sir Francis Drake, and a modern mansion, beautifully situated on the banks of the Tavy, has been erected on it; but there are still some interesting remains of the abbey. The market has been discontinued; but a fair is still held on Trinity-Monday. The Plymouth railway crosses the parish on the east. Lady Modyford, in 1702, gave two messuages, out of the rental of which, £7. 10. a year is paid for the instruction of six boys; and the interest of £100, given by Matthew Elford, in 1723, is applied in clothing four boys.

BUCKLAND-NEWTON, a parish in the hundred of Buckland-Newton, Cerne subdivision of the county of Dorset, comprising the tythings of Brockhampton with Knowle, Buckland-Newton, Duntish, Mintern Parva, and Plush, and containing 843 inhabitants, of which number, 275 are in the tything of Buckland-Newton, 10¼ miles (N.) from Dorchester. The living is a vicarage, in the archdeaconry of Dorset, and diocese of Bristol, rated in the king's books at £16. 19. 9½., and in the patronage of the Dean and Chapter of Wells. The church, dedicated to the Holy Rood, is partly in the early, and partly in the later, style of English architecture, and has lately received an addition of one hundred and twenty sittings, the Incorporated Society for the enlargement of churches and chapels having granted £50 for that purpose.

BUCKLAND-RIPERS, a parish in the hundred of Culliford-Tree, Dorchester division of the county of Dorset, 3½ miles (N. W. by N.) from Melcombe-Regis, containing 60 inhabitants. The living is a discharged rectory, in the archdeaconry of Dorset, and diocese of Bristol, rated in the king's books at £5. 9. 2., and in the patronage of J. Frampton, Esq.

BUCKLAND-TOUTSAINTS, a chapelry in that part of the parish of Loddiswell which is in the hundred of Coleridge, county of Devon, 2½ miles (N. E.) from Kingsbridge, containing 40 inhabitants.

BUCKLEBURY, a parish in the hundred of Reading, though locally in that of Faircross, county of Berks, 7½ miles (E. N. E.) from Newbury, containing 1143 inhabitants. The living is a vicarage, with the perpetual curacy of Marston, in the archdeaconry of Berks, and diocese of Salisbury, rated in the king's books at £17, and in the patronage of the Rev. W. H. H. Hartley: the vicar enjoys the great tithes of the chapelry of Marston. The church, dedicated to St. Mary, contains an organ that cost £210, presented by the present vicar, to whom the manor belongs. This parish is entitled to send scholars to the school at Thatcham, founded and endowed by Lady Frances Winchcombe, in 1707, (to whose memory there is a monument in the church of this parish), in which forty boys are clothed and educated, and six apprenticed annually, with a premium of £10 each; those who are not apprenticed receive also a small gratuity.

BUCKLESHAM, a parish in the hundred of Colneis, county of Suffolk, 5 miles (E. S. E.) from Ipswich, containing 269 inhabitants. The living is a discharged rectory, in the archdeaconry of Suffolk, and diocese of Norwich, rated in the king's books at £9. 1. 8., and in the patronage of W. Walford, Esq. The church is dedicated to St. Mary. The crag pits in this parish contain a great quantity of shells, generally considered to be antediluvian remains: bones of fishes in a state of petrefaction have also been found.

BUCKLEY, or BULKELEY, a township in the parish of Malpas, higher division of the hundred of Broxton, county palatine of Chester, 8 miles (W. by N.) from Nantwich, containing 178 inhabitants.

BUCKMINSTER, a parish in the hundred of Framland, county of Leicester, 9¼ miles (E. N. E.) from Melton-Mowbray, containing, with the chapelry of Sewstern, 625 inhabitants. The living is a vicarage, in the archdeaconry of Leicester, and diocese of Lincoln, rated in the king's books at £8. 7. 3½., and in the patronage of the Duke of Devonshire. The church, dedicated to St. John the Baptist, has a massive tower and spire, with portions in various styles of architecture. A charity school is supported by subscription; and there are several bequests for the relief of the poor. A close called the Grange was the site of a religious house subordinate to the monastery of Kirkby-Belew.

BUCKNALL, a parish in the southern division of the wapentake of Gartree, parts of Lindsey, county of Lincoln, 6¾ miles (W. by S.) from Horncastle, containing 241 inhabitants. The living is a rectory, in the archdeaconry and diocese of Lincoln, rated in the king's books at £9. 11. 10½., and in the patronage of Lord Monson. The church is dedicated to St. Margaret. There is an endowment of about £5 per annum, the gift of an unknown individual, for the instruction of poor children, paid annually by the Governors of Christ's Hospital, as trustees.

BUCKNALL, a joint parish with Bagnall, in the northern division of the hundred of Pirehill, county of Stafford, 1½ mile (E.) from Hanley. The population is returned with Stoke upon Trent. The living is a rectory not in charge, with the perpetual curacy of Bagnall annexed, in the archdeaconry of Stafford, and diocese of Lichfield and Coventry, endowed with £100 and £5 per annum, private benefaction, and £600 royal bounty, and in the patronage of the Rev. Edward Powys. The church is dedicated to St. Mary. Bucknall was formerly a chapelry in the parish of Stoke upon Trent, but, with four other chapelries, was severed from it by an act passed in 1807, by which, including the chapelry of Bagnall, this was constituted a distinct rectory. William Shallcross, in 1719, gave a rent-charge of £5 for the instruction of twelve children.

BUCKNELL, a parish in the hundred of Ploughley, county of Oxford, 2½ miles (N. W. by N.) from Bicester, containing 235 inhabitants. The living is a rectory, in the archdeaconry and diocese of Oxford, rated in the king's books at £13. 16. 0½., and in the patronage of the Warden and Fellows of New College, Oxford. The church is dedicated to St. Peter: at a short distance from it, near the verge of a coppice, are the foundations of numerous houses that constituted the village of Saxenton, the greater part of which was destroyed by the Danes, about the year 912; the site, for many generations, has been unoccupied by a single habitation.

BUCKNILL, a parish partly in the hundred of Wigmore, county of Hereford, but chiefly in the hundred of PURSLOW, county of SALOP, 3¼ miles (E. N. E.) from Knighton, containing, with the township of Buxton with Coxall, 465 inhabitants. The living is a vicarage, in the archdeaconry of Salop, and diocese of Hereford, rated in the king's books at £5. 6. 8., endowed with £400 private benefaction, and in the patronage of the Master and Wardens of the Grocers' Company. The church is dedicated to St. Mary. Bucknill is in the honour of Tutbury, duchy of Lancaster, and within the jurisdiction of a court of pleas held at Tutbury every third Tuesday, for the recovery of debts under 40*s*.

BUCKTON, a township in the parish of BRIDLINGTON, wapentake of DICKERING, East riding of the county of YORK, 4¼ miles (N. by E.) from Bridlington, containing 147 inhabitants.

BUCKWORTH, a parish in the hundred of LEIGHTONSTONE, county of HUNTINGDON, 7 miles (N. W. by W.) from Huntingdon, containing 151 inhabitants. The living is a rectory, in the archdeaconry of Huntingdon, and diocese of Lincoln, rated in the king's books at £21. 5. 2½., and in the patronage of R. E. Duncombe, Esq. The church is dedicated to All Saints.

BUDBROOK, a parish in the Snitterfield division of the hundred of BARLICHWAY, county of WARWICK, 1½ mile (W. N. W.) from Warwick, containing 438 inhabitants. The living is a discharged vicarage, in the archdeaconry and diocese of Worcester, rated in the king's books at £8, and in the patronage of the Mayor and Corporation of Warwick. The church is dedicated to St. Michael. The Warwick and Birmingham canal crosses the parish. The school is endowed with part of the rental of some land that was bequeathed by Job Marston, in 1701, the remainder of which is distributed among the poor.

BUDBY, a township in the parish of EDWINSTOW, Hatfield division of the wapentake of BASSETLAW, county of NOTTINGHAM, 3 miles (N. W. by W.) from Ollerton, containing 140 inhabitants.

BUDE, a village and small sea-port, on the coast of the Bristol channel, in the parish and hundred of STRATTON, county of CORNWALL. The population is returned with the parish. It has of late years become a place of resort for bathing. The trade of the port has recently received a stimulus from the construction of the Bude and Launceston canal: the imports are coal and limestone from Wales, and grocery, &c., from Bristol; and timber, bark, and oats, are sent coastwise. The harbour is inaccessible to ships of large burden, on account of the sands, those connected with it averaging not more than fifty tons each, though vessels of ninety tons' burden have often entered. A great quantity of sand is conveyed inland for manuring the soil. The sea is fast encroaching on the coast, having made a considerable inroad within the last fifty years.

BUDEAUX, or BUDOCK, (ST.), a parish in the hundred of ROBOROUGH, county of DEVON, 4¼ miles (N. W. by N.) from Plymouth, containing 689 inhabitants. A small portion of the parish is in the county of Cornwall. The living is a perpetual curacy, annexed to the vicarage of St. Andrew, Plymouth, in the archdeaconry of Totness, and diocese of Exeter, endowed with £1400 parliamentary grant. The church stands pleasantly on a commanding eminence, and contains some interesting monuments. The village is romantically situated on the banks of the navigable river Tamar, near the confluence of that river and the Tavy. A charity school has an endowment of about £86 per annum, arising from land purchased in 1770, for £710, of which £300 South Sea stock, and £100 Bank stock, were bequeathed by Peter Madock Docton, in 1767, in lieu of an annuity of £10, left by his father; and from some property in the funds: twelve boys and twelve girls are clothed and educated.

BUDLE, a township in the parish of BAMBROUGH, northern division of BAMBROUGH ward, county of NORTHUMBERLAND, 3¾ miles (E. by N.) from Belford, containing 99 inhabitants. The village lies on the southern shore of a fine bay; the adjacent coast abounds with large cockles of a superior flavour.

BUDLEIGH (EAST), a parish (formerly a market town) in the eastern division of the hundred of BUDLEIGH, county of DEVON, 4½ miles (W. S. W.) from Sidmouth, containing 1706 inhabitants. The living is a discharged vicarage, with the perpetual curacy of Withycombe-Rawleigh annexed, in the archdeaconry and diocese of Exeter, rated in the king's books at £30, and in the patronage of Lord Rolle. The church is dedicated to All Saints. There is a meeting-house for Independents. The river Otter flows through the parish. The antiquity of this place is evinced by its having given name to the hundred: the market was formerly held on Sunday, and afterwards on Monday, but it has been wholly discontinued: a pleasure fair is held annually on Easter-Tuesday. Budleigh-Salterton, in this parish, is rising into repute as a watering-place; hot and cold baths have been built, and there is comfortable accommodations for visitors. A chapel of ease has been erected at the expense of Lord Rolle; and there is a place of worship for Wesleyan Methodists. At Poer-Hayes is an old mansion, noted as the birthplace of Sir Walter Raleigh, in 1552, who was beheaded in 1618, besides some remains of an ancient chapel, dedicated to St. James.

BUDOCK, a parish in the hundred of KERRIER, county of CORNWALL, 2 miles (W. by S.) from Falmouth, containing, with part of the town of Falmouth, which extends into this parish, 1634 inhabitants. The living is a perpetual curacy, united to the vicarage of St. Gluvias, in the peculiar jurisdiction of the Bishop of Exeter. There is a place of worship for Wesleyan Methodists. This parish is bounded on the east by Falmouth bay and the English channel. Francis Robyns, in 1768, gave an endowment of £6. 16. per annum, for the instruction of children.

BUDWORTH (GREAT), a parish comprising the chapelry of Hartford, and the townships of Castle-Northwich and Winnington, in the second division of the hundred of EDDISBURY; the chapelries of Northwich, Nether Peover, and Witton with Twambrook, and the townships of Allostock, Birches, Hulse, Lack-Dennis, Lostock-Gralam, and a small portion of that of Rudheath, in the hundred of NORTHWICH; and the chapelries of Aston by Budworth, Little Leigh, and Stretton, and the townships of Anderton, Antrobus, Barnton, Bartington, Great Budworth, Cogshall, Comberbach, Crowley, Dutton, Hull with Appleton, Marbury, Marston, Little Peover, Pickmere, Plumley, Seven-Oaks, Tabley Inferior, Lower Whitley, Over Whitley, and Wincham, in the hundred of BUCKLOW, county palatine of CHESTER;

and containing 14,344 inhabitants, of which number, 501 are in the township of Great Budworth, 3 miles (N. by E.) from Northwich. The living is a vicarage, in the archdeaconry and diocese of Chester, rated in the king's books at £6. 10., and in the patronage of the Dean and Canons of Christ Church, Oxford. The church, dedicated to St. Mary and All Saints, consists of a nave, chancel, side aisles, and two transepts, with a fine tower; it sustained considerable damage from the parliamentarian troops in 1647, who destroyed the pipes of the organ, and perpetrated other outrages. The village is pleasantly situated on a gentle acclivity, near two sheets of water, called Budworth-mere and Pic-mere. The inhabitants are employed to a considerable extent in the manufacture of salt, which prevails throughout the entire neighbourhood. The river Weaver and the Duke of Bridgewater's canal pass through the parish. In the north-eastern angle of the churchyard is a school-room, supposed to have been built by John Dean, rector of St. Bartholomew's the Great, London, about the year 1600, and endowed with the interest of £200 given by Mr. Pickering of Thelwall, and Mrs. Glover.

BUDWORTH (LITTLE), a parish in the first division of the hundred of EDDISBURY, county palatine of CHESTER, 3¾ miles (N.E. by E.) from Tarporley, containing 524 inhabitants. The living is a perpetual curacy, in the archdeaconry and diocese of Chester, endowed with £10 per annum private benefaction, £400 royal bounty, and £800 parliamentary grant, and in the patronage of the Bishop of Chester, who is the impropriator, on the nomination of the lessee of the great tithes. The church, dedicated to St. Peter, belonged, previously to the dissolution, to St. Mary's nunnery in Chester, and was called a free chapel within the parish of Over, the church of which was also appropriated to the same convent: the nave and the chancel were rebuilt with stone, in 1798, pursuant to the will of Mr. Ralph Kirkham, a wealthy merchant in Manchester, and a native of this parish, who gave £1000 for that purpose; his remains were interred here. Horse-races were formerly held on a four-mile course, but they have long been discontinued. A school-house was erected in 1706, near the park wall at Oulton, in which about twenty children are instructed. Lady Isabella Dod, by will dated in 1720, bequeathed £2500 for the erection and endowment of almshouses for the support of twelve poor persons of Little Budworth, and eight of a town in Buckinghamshire.

BUERTON, a township in that part of the parish of ALDFORD which is in the lower division of the hundred of BROXTON, county palatine of CHESTER, 5¼ miles (S.E. by S.) from Chester, containing 60 inhabitants.

BUERTON, a township in the parish of AUDLEM, hundred of NANTWICH, county palatine of CHESTER, 2 miles (E.) from Audlem, containing 524 inhabitants.

BUGBROOKE, a parish in the hundred of NOBOTTLE-GROVE, county of NORTHAMPTON, 5¾ miles (W.S.W.) from Northampton, containing 835 inhabitants. The living is a rectory, in the archdeaconry of Northampton, and diocese of Peterborough, rated in the king's books at £34, and in the patronage of the Rev. H. B. Harrison, D.D. The church, dedicated to St. Michael, exhibits various styles of English architecture, and contains a fine wooden screen, and an octagonal font highly enriched. There is a place of worship for Particular Baptists. The Grand Junction canal passes through this parish, which is bounded on the west by the Roman Watling-street. Every inhabitant pays fourpence annually to the duchy court of Lancaster, which is held at West Haddon.

BUGLAWTON, a township in that part of the parish of ASTBURY which is in the hundred of NORTHWICH, county palatine of CHESTER, 1 mile (N.E. by E.) from Congleton, containing 948 inhabitants. There is a place of worship for Wesleyan Methodists. Extensive mills for spinning and preparing lace thread for the Nottingham and Buckingham manufacturers, are in active operation at this place. Here is a mineral spring, the water of which contains sulphur, a small quantity of Epsom salts, and calcareous earth, and has proved serviceable in scorbutic diseases.

BUGLEY, a hamlet in the parish and liberty of GILLINGHAM, Shaston (West) division of the county of DORSET, 5½ miles (W.N.W.) from Shaftesbury. The population is returned with the parish. Here was formerly a chapel.

BUGTHORPE, a parish partly in the liberty of ST. PETER OF YORK, and partly in the wapentake of BUCKROSE, East riding of the county of YORK, 7½ miles (N.N.W.) from Pocklington, containing 281 inhabitants. The living is a discharged vicarage, in the peculiar jurisdiction and patronage of the Prebendary of Bugthorpe in the Cathedral Church of York, rated in the king's books at £20, and endowed with £400 royal bounty. The church is dedicated to St. Andrew.

BUILDWAS, a parish in the Wellington division of the hundred of BRADFORD (South), county of SALOP, 4 miles (N.N.E.) from Much Wenlock, containing 240 inhabitants. The living is a perpetual curacy, in the peculiar jurisdiction and patronage of W. Moseley, Esq. The church is dedicated to the Holy Trinity. Buildwas is celebrated for the ruins of an abbey, founded in 1135, by Roger, Bishop of Chester, in honour of St. Mary and St. Chad, for monks of the order of Savigny, who were subsequently incorporated with a society of Cistercians: at the time of the dissolution, the establishment consisted of about twelve monks, whose revenue was rated at £129. 6. 10. The ruins occupy a beautiful situation on the southern bank of the Severn, and consist principally of the outer walls of the nave, transept, and tower of the cruciform church: the massive pillars of the nave, with capitals in the Norman style, support handsome pointed arches, and there are several circular arches; the western end is overspread with a thick cluster of ivy: a respectable farm-house occupies part of the site. Nearly opposite these ruins is a very handsome cast-iron bridge, constructed in 1796, on the site of an ancient stone bridge, which was swept away by a flood in the preceding year: the span of the arch is one hundred and thirty feet, and the height twenty-four: the outer ribs rise to the top of the railing, and are connected with the lower ribs by dovetailed king-posts.

BULBRIDGE, a parish in the hundred of CAWDEN and CADWORTH, county of WILTS, ¾ of a mile (S.) from Wilton, with which parish the population is returned. The living is a vicarage, united to the rectory of Wilton, in the archdeaconry and diocese of Salisbury, rated in the king's books at £11. 2. 1. The church, which was dedicated to St. Peter, has been demolished.

BULBY, a chapelry in the parish of IRNHAM, wapentake of BELTISLOE, parts of KESTEVEN, county of LINCOLN, 4¼ miles (E. by N.) from Corby, containing 105 inhabitants.

BULCOTE, a chapelry in the parish of BURTON-JOYCE, southern division of the wapentake of THURGARTON, county of NOTTINGHAM, 6 miles (N. E. by E.) from Nottingham, containing 142 inhabitants.

BULFORD, a parish in the hundred of AMESBURY, county of WILTS, 2 miles (N. E. by N.) from Amesbury, containing 269 inhabitants. The living is a perpetual curacy, in the archdeaconry and diocese of Salisbury, and in the patronage of Sir J. W. Pollen, Bart. The church is dedicated to St. John. There is a small endowment for the instruction of children, arising from a donation by Richard Duke.

BULK, a township in that part of the parish of LANCASTER which is in the hundred of LONSDALE, south of the sands, county palatine of LANCASTER, 2 miles (N. E. by N.) from Lancaster, containing 111 inhabitants.

BULKINGTON, a parish in the Kirby division of the hundred of KNIGHTLOW, county of WARWICK, 4½ miles (S. E. by S.) from Nuneaton, comprising the hamlets of Barnacle, Bramcott, Marston-Jabbett, Ryton, and Weston, and containing 1679 inhabitants. The living is a discharged vicarage, in the archdeaconry of Coventry, and diocese of Lichfield and Coventry, rated in the king's books at £6. 10. 7., and in the patronage of the Crown. The church, dedicated to St. James, has lately received an addition of three hundred and fifty sittings, three hundred of which are free, the Incorporated Society for the enlargement of churches and chapels having granted £200 for that purpose. The manufacture of ribands has recently been introduced; and the Ashby de la Zouch canal crosses the north-western angle of the parish, in which there is a quarry of excellent freestone. A National school has been established, and is supported by subscription.

BULKINGTON, a tything in that part of the parish of KEEVIL which is in the hundred of MELKSHAM, county of WILTS, 5¾ miles (S. E.) from Melksham, containing 306 inhabitants. There is a place of worship for Wesleyan Methodists.

BULKWORTHY, a chapelry in the parish of BUCKLAND-BREWER, hundred of SHEBBEAR, county of DEVON, 7½ miles (S. W. by W.) from Great Torrington, containing 155 inhabitants.

BULLER'S GREEN, a township in that part of the parish of MORPETH which is in the western division of MORPETH ward, county of NORTHUMBERLAND, containing 255 inhabitants. Part of the town of Morpeth is locally within this township.

BULLEY, a chapelry in the parish of CHURCHAM, duchy of LANCASTER, county of GLOUCESTER, 5¼ miles (S. E. by S.) from Newent, containing 237 inhabitants. The chapel is a small edifice, chiefly in the Norman style of architecture, a fine specimen of which may be seen in the arch between the nave and the chancel.

BULLINGHAM (LOWER), a hamlet in the parish of UPPER BULLINGHAM, hundred of WEBTREE, county of HEREFORD, 1¼ mile (S. by E.) from Hereford, containing 264 inhabitants.

BULLINGHAM (UPPER and LOWER), a parish in the hundred of WEBTREE, county of HEREFORD, 2 miles (S.) from Hereford, containing 376 inhabitants, of which number, 112 are in Upper Bullingham, 2 miles (S.), and 264 in Lower Bullingham, 1¼ mile (S. by E.), from Hereford. The living is a perpetual curacy, in the peculiar jurisdiction and patronage of the Prebendary of Bullinghope in the Cathedral Church of Hereford, endowed with £200 private benefaction, and £800 royal bounty.

BULLINGTON, a chapelry in the parish of GOLTHO, western division of the wapentake of WRAGGOE, parts of LINDSEY, county of LINCOLN, 2¾ miles (W.) from Wragby, containing 45 inhabitants. The chapel is dedicated to St. James. Here are inconsiderable remains of a religious house founded by Simon Fitz-William, or de Kyme, in honour of the Blessed Virgin Mary, as a priory and convent for both sexes, under the rule of St. Gilbert of Sempringham: the revenue, at the time of the dissolution, was £187. 7. 9.

BULLINGTON, a parish in the hundred of WHERWELL, Andover division of the county of SOUTHAMPTON, 5 miles (S. by W.) from Whitchurch, containing 160 inhabitants. The living is a perpetual curacy, annexed to the vicarage of Wherwell, in the archdeaconry and diocese of Winchester. The church is dedicated to St. Michael. At a place called Titbury Hill there is an intrenched area of about ten acres, in which square stones, Roman coins, and the remains of some wells, have been discovered.

BULLOCK'S HALL, a township in that part of the parish of WARKWORTH which is in the eastern division of MORPETH ward, county of NORTHUMBERLAND, 10½ miles (N. N. E.) from Morpeth, containing 14 inhabitants.

BULMER, a parish in the hundred of HINCKFORD, county of ESSEX, 2 miles (W. S. W.) from Sudbury, containing 628 inhabitants. The living is a discharged vicarage, with that of Belchamp-Walter consolidated, in the archdeaconry of Middlesex, and diocese of London, rated in the king's books at £8, and in the patronage of Samuel Milbanke Raymond, Esq. The church is dedicated to St. Andrew.

BULMER, a parish in the wapentake of BULMER, North riding of the county of YORK, comprising the chapelry of Henderskelf, and the townships of Bulmer and Welburn, and containing 850 inhabitants, of which number, 339 are in the township of Bulmer, 7 miles (W. S. W.) from New Malton. The living is a rectory, in the archdeaconry of Cleveland, and diocese of York, rated in the king's books at £11, and in the patronage of Earl Fitzwilliam. The church is dedicated to St. Martin. The river Derwent bounds this parish on the east.

BULPHAN, a parish in the hundred of BARSTABLE, county of ESSEX, 3 miles (N. W. by W.) from Horndon on the Hill, containing 242 inhabitants. The living is a rectory, in the archdeaconry of Essex, and diocese of London, rated in the king's books at £23, and in the patronage of James William Freshfield, Esq. The church is dedicated to St. Mary.

BULVERHITHE (ST. MARY), a member of the town and port of HASTINGS, locally in the parish and hundred of Bexhill, rape of HASTINGS, county of SUSSEX, 1½ mile (E.) from Bexhill, containing 34 inhabitants. William the Conqueror is supposed to have landed here, at which time it was a haven called *Bollefride:* a considerable part of the coast has been encroached upon by the sea.

BULWELL, a parish in the northern division of the wapentake of BROXTOW, county of NOTTINGHAM, 3¾ miles (N. W. by N.) from Nottingham, containing 2105 inhabitants. The living is a discharged rectory, in the archdeaconry of Nottingham, and diocese of York, rated in the king's books at £5. 5. 10., and in the patronage of the Rev. Alfred Padley. The church, dedicated to St. Mary, is a small neat edifice, situated to the east of the village, on the highest ground in the parish, and was enlarged to its present size about sixty years ago. There is a place of worship for Wesleyan Methodists. This place owes its name to a famous spring, still called the "Bull well," to which the cattle from the adjoining forest of Sherwood anciently resorted to quench their thirst, prior to its enclosure. The village contains several respectable houses; and there are three corn-mills, and one for the manufacture of cotton twist, besides some extensive bleaching-grounds, and printing establishments. To the west of the river Leen the parish abounds with excellent limestone. Courts baron and leet are held periodically, and the lord of the manor also claims the power of proving wills, and granting letters of administration, &c.: the custom of Borough English prevails throughout the manor. A free grammar school is endowed with four acres of land, producing £20 per annum, and a dwelling-house for the master: there is a good school-room.

BULWICK, a parish in the hundred of CORBY, county of NORTHAMPTON, 6½ miles (E. N. E.) from Rockingham, containing 471 inhabitants. The living is a rectory, in the archdeaconry of Northampton, and diocese of Peterborough, rated in the king's books at £18. 7. 1., and in the patronage of Thomas Tryon, Esq. The church, dedicated to St. Nicholas, is partly in the decorated, and partly in the later, style of English architecture, with a finely proportioned tower and spire; it contains three stone stalls and some screen-work, and has lately been re-pewed.

BUMPSTEAD (STEEPLE), a parish in the hundred of HINCKFORD, county of ESSEX, 8¾ miles (N. W. by N.) from Castle-Hedingham, containing 961 inhabitants. The living is a vicarage, in the archdeaconry of Middlesex, and diocese of London, rated in the king's books at £15. 2. 1., and in the patronage of the Crown. The church is dedicated to St. Mary. Ann Cole, in 1730, gave a small endowment for teaching and apprenticing children.

BUMPSTEAD-HELION, a parish in the hundred of FRESHWELL, county of ESSEX, 8¾ miles (N. N. E.) from Thaxted, containing 773 inhabitants. The living is a vicarage, in the archdeaconry of Colchester, and diocese of London, rated in the king's books at £13, and in the patronage of the Master and Fellows of Trinity College, Cambridge. The church is dedicated to St. Andrew.

BUNBURY, a parish comprising the chapelry of Burwardsley, in the higher division of the hundred of BROXTON, and the townships of Alpraham, Beeston, Bunbury, Calveley, Haughton, Peckforton, Ridley, Spurstow, Tilston-Fernall, Tiverton, and Wardle, in the first division of the hundred of EDDISBURY, county palatine of CHESTER, and containing 4021 inhabitants, of which number, 667 are in the township of Bunbury, 3½ miles (S. S. E.) from Tarporley. The living is a perpetual curacy, in the archdeaconry and diocese of Chester, endowed with £200 private benefaction, £200 royal bounty, and £1400 parliamentary grant, and in the patronage of the Master and Wardens of the Haberdashers' Company. The church, dedicated to St. Boniface, is a handsome building of red freestone, in the later style of English architecture, comprising a nave with lateral aisles, a chancel, and a square tower crowned with eight pinnacles: at the termination of each of the aisles is an ancient and elegant chapel, called Eggerton and Spurstow chapels, the former, built in 1523, containing on the north side a rich stone shrine, ornamented at the base with grotesque figures, flowers, &c., painted in *chiaro oscuro*, and on the south two arches with curious open work, and scriptural paintings. Within the church are several fine monuments, among which are a rich altar-tomb to the memory of Sir Hugh Calveley, the celebrated "Cheshire hero," who eminently distinguished himself during the invasions of France by Edward III.; and one to Sir George Beeston, one of the admirals who aided in the destruction of the Spanish Armada, in 1588. The church was fired by a detachment from the royal garrison at Cholmondeley House, on the 20th of June, 1643, and sustained considerable injury. The above Sir Hugh, about 1386, founded and endowed in the church a college for a master and six Secular chaplains: at the dissolution the establishment consisted of a dean, five vicars, and two choristers, whose clear revenue was valued at £48. 2. 8. The buildings stood in a field about two hundred yards north-west of the church; every vestige has been removed, but the site is conspicuous, from the inequality of the surface, and the remains of the moat that surrounded it. The revenue, which arose partly from the tithes of the parish, became vested in the crown, and the greater part was appropriated towards the maintenance of two ministers. In 1575, Thomas Aldersey, citizen and haberdasher of London, purchased the rectory and advowson from Queen Elizabeth, and some time afterwards leased the tithes for £130 per annum, of which he directed that £20 should be annually given to a schoolmaster, £10 to an usher, one hundred marks to a minister (each to have a house and a certain portion of land in addition), £20 to a curate, and £10 to the poor, and that the patronage should be vested in the Haberdashers' Company; all these grants were confirmed by letters patent, dated January 2nd, 1594. The ministers are nominated by the Master any Wardens, and enter upon the clerical office without and other presentation or institution, but are subject to the jurisdiction of the Ordinary. The school, which was rebuilt in 1812, at the expense of Samuel Aldersey, Esq., stands at a short distance from the church. A school, for the children of poor parishioners not resident in the township of Bunbury, was founded and endowed by Mr. Thomas Gardener, in 1750. There is a place of worship for Wesleyan Methodists. The Chester canal passes through the parish, in which courts leet and baron are held annually; and a manorial court is occasionally held, for the recovery of debts under 40*s*. Bunbury heath, by some considered to be the place described in a poem entitled the "Ancient English

Wake of Jerningham," is the scene of rustic revelry annually on the Sunday preceding the festival of St. Boniface.

BUNCTON, a chapelry in the parish of ASHINGTON, hundred of WEST GRINSTEAD, rape of BRAMBER, county of SUSSEX, $2\frac{1}{2}$ miles (N. W.) from Steyning. The population is returned with the parish.

BUNDLEY, a parish in the hundred of NORTH TAWTON with WINKLEY, county of DEVON, $6\frac{3}{4}$ miles (S. S. W.) from Chulmleigh, containing 335 inhabitants. The living is a rectory, with that of Blackborough annexed, in the archdeaconry of Barnstaple, and diocese of Exeter, rated in the king's books at £10. 17. $8\frac{1}{2}$., and in the patronage of the Hon. P. C. Wyndham, Esq. The church, dedicated to St. James, exhibits some remains of Norman architecture, and has an ancient font.

BUNGAY, a market town in the hundred of WANGFORD, county of SUFFOLK, 40 miles (N. N. E.) from Ipswich, 40 (N. E. by E.) from Bury St. Edmund's, and 109 (N. E. by N.) from London, on the road to Yarmouth, containing 3290 inhabitants. The name is supposed to have been anciently *Bon-gué*, from the goodness of a ford over the river Waveney, by which the town is nearly surrounded. In the reign of Stephen, a castle was built by one of the Bigods, earls of Norfolk, which, from its situation and the strength of its fortifications, was deemed impregnable; it was demolished in the reign of Henry III., and on its site was erected a mansion which, in the 22nd of Edward I., Roger Bigod obtained permission to embattle. In 1688, a fire broke out in an uninhabited house, and the flames spread with such rapidity that the whole town, with the exception of one small street, was reduced to ashes, destroying property of the estimated value of £30,000, together with the records of the castle: the remains of this building have been converted into cottages, and little more than some portions of the walls can now be distinguished. The town is pleasantly situated on the river Waveney, that here forms the line of boundary between the counties of Norfolk and Suffolk, and over which a handsome new bridge has been built: the streets, diverging from the market-place in the centre of the town towards the principal roads, are spacious, well paved, and lighted with oil; the houses are in general modern, having been rebuilt since the fire; and the inhabitants are amply supplied with water from springs. The theatre, a neat edifice erected in 1827, is opened occasionally; and there are assembly-rooms handsomely fitted up. On the northern side of the town is an extensive common, by the side of which is a pleasant promenade, one mile and a half in length, leading to a cold bath, where a bath-house has been built, and requisite accommodation provided. A botanical society, and a book-club, have been recently instituted. The races, after having been discontinued for more than thirty years, were re-established in 1828. The trade is principally in corn, malt, flour, and lime, there being several flour-mills, malting-houses, and limekilns, on a large scale; there are also a paper and a silk manufactory, and an extensive printing-office. The manufacture of hempen cloth for the Norwich and London markets has been wholly discontinued: several of the female inhabitants are employed in knitting stockings. The river Waveney is navigable from Yarmouth, whence the town is supplied with coal, timber, and other articles of consumption. The market is on Thursday: fairs are held on May 14th and September 25th. In the centre of the market-place is a handsome octangular building, surmounted by a dome covered with lead, and bearing on its summit a leaden statue of Justice; within is a cage for the confinement of disorderly persons. The town is within the jurisdiction of the county magistrates: a town-reeve and certain feoffees are appointed annually, who are trustees of the estates and rent-charges devised for the improvement and benefit of the town: courts leet and baron for the manor are held occasionally.

Bungay comprises the parishes of St. Mary and the Holy Trinity, both in the archdeaconry of Suffolk, and diocese of Norwich. The living of St. Mary's is a perpetual curacy, in the patronage of the Duke of Norfolk. The church is a handsome and spacious structure, with a fine tower; it was rebuilt, in 1696, with flint and freestone: the interior contains some interesting monuments, and is remarkable for the lightness and elegance of the pillars supporting the roof. The living of the parish of the Holy Trinity is a vicarage, rated in the king's books at £8. 0. 5., and in the patronage of the Bishop of Ely. The church is a small ancient edifice, with a fine round tower. There was formerly a church dedicated to St. Thomas, but it has been destroyed. There are places of worship for Wesleyan Methodists, Presbyterians, and Roman Catholics. The free grammar school is of ancient and uncertain foundation: the Rev. Thomas Popeson, in 1591, annexed the vicarage of St. Andrew Ilketshall to the mastership, and founded ten scholarships in Emanuel College, Cambridge, but these have been reduced to four: the school was endowed with forty acres of land by Mr. Scales, of Earsham: the income of the master, who is appointed by the Master and Fellows of Emanuel College, is from £180 to £200 per annum: there are ten boys upon the foundation by Mr. Scales. Henry Webster, in 1712, bequeathed land for the instruction of poor children of the parish of St. Mary. A dispensary was established in 1828, which is liberally supported; and there are almshouses in each parish for the residence of aged persons. Near St. Mary's church are some remains of a Benedictine nunnery, founded in the reign of Henry II., by Robert de Glanville and his lady, the Countess Gundreda, in honour of the Blessed Virgin and the Holy Cross, the revenue of which, at the dissolution, was estimated at £62. 2. 1. At the back of the King's Head Inn is a mineral spring, now in disuse. A few Roman coins, some seals, and ancient tokens have been found.

BUNNY, a parish in the northern division of the wapentake of RUSHCLIFFE, county of NOTTINGHAM, $7\frac{1}{4}$ miles (S.) from Nottingham, containing 395 inhabitants. The living is a discharged vicarage, with Bradmore, in the archdeaconry of Nottingham, and diocese of York, rated in the king's books at £6. 14., endowed with £200 private benefaction, and £200 royal bounty, and in the patronage of Lord Rancliffe. The church, dedicated to St. Mary, is partly in the decorated, and partly in the later, style of English architecture, with a tower surmounted by a crocketed spire. A school for the poor children of Bunny and Bradmore, the building for which was erected in 1700, has an endowment in land, producing £60 per annum, the gift of Dame Anne Parkyns, who also founded an almshouse for four poor widows, and endowed it with £16 per annum, which was augmented with £5 annually by her husband, Sir Thomas Parkyns: this benevolent lady also assigned an annuity of £30 for apprenticing poor boys.

BUNTINGFORD, a chapelry (formerly a market town) in the parishes of ASPEDEN, LAYSTON, THROCKING, and WYDDIALL, in the hundred of EDWINSTREE, county of HERTFORD, 12 miles (N. N. E.) from Hertford. The population is returned with the respective parishes. This place takes its name from a ford on the river Rib, near which a blacksmith, named Bunt, or Bunting, had a forge. The town is pleasantly situated on a gentle ascent between two hills, and consists of one street, half a mile in length: the houses are in general well built, and of respectable appearance, and the inhabitants are amply supplied with water. The trade is principally in leather and malt: the market, granted by Henry VIII., has been discontinued: the fairs, formerly on the 29th of June and the 30th of November, each for four days, are now irregularly held. The county magistrates hold petty sessions for the division at the George Inn, where also a septennial court leet is held for the hundred. The living is a perpetual curacy, in the archdeaconry of Middlesex, and diocese of London, endowed with a portion of the tithes of Layston, and in the patronage of the Vicar of that parish. The chapel, dedicated to St. Peter, is a commodious brick building, erected by subscription, and completed in 1626, through the exertions of the Rev. Alexander Strange, vicar of Layston, who is interred in it; from its convenient situation, it is appropriated to the general use of the parishioners of Layston, the parish church, half a mile distant, being resorted to only for the solemnization of marriages. There are places of worship for the Society of Friends and Independents. The free grammar school was founded also through the exertions of the Rev. Mr. Strange, and endowed, in 1630, by Mrs. Elizabeth Freeman, with lands producing £10. 10. per annum; the endowment was augmented with a moiety of the produce of lands left by Seth Ward, Bishop of Salisbury, to Christ's College, Cambridge, the other being applied to the endowment in that college of four scholarships, of £12 per annum each, for boys on this foundation, or, in default of such, for the most deserving in the university, reserving one to Hitchen. A charity school for forty girls is supported by subscription. Eight almshouses, for four aged men and four aged women, were founded in 1668, and endowed with the rent of lands in Lincolnshire, by Bishop Ward; but these are now occupied by paupers of the parish. The bishop also gave £600 to purchase lands, the rental of which is applied to the apprenticing of children: he was a native of this town, and received the rudiments of his education in the grammar school.

BUNWELL, a parish in the hundred of DEPWADE, county of NORFOLK, 3 miles (N. E. by E.) from New Buckenham, containing 774 inhabitants. The living is a rectory, in the archdeaconry of Norfolk, and diocese of Norwich, rated in the king's books at £17, and in the patronage of Sir R. J. Buxton, Bart. The church is dedicated to St. Michael.

BURASTON, a joint chapelry with Whetmore, in the parish of BURFORD, hundred of OVERS, county of SALOP, 1¾ mile (N. E.) from Tenbury, containing, with Whetmore, 226 inhabitants. The Kington canal passes on the southern side of the village.

BURBAGE, a chapelry in the parish of ASTON-FLAMVILLE, hundred of SPARKENHOE, county of LEICESTER, 1½ mile (S. E.) from Hinckley, containing, with the hamlet of Sketchley, 1504 inhabitants. There is a place of worship for Wesleyan Methodists.

BURBAGE, a parish in the hundred of KINWARDSTONE, county of WILTS, 4¾ miles (E. by N.) from Pewsey, containing 1195 inhabitants. The living is a vicarage, in the peculiar jurisdiction of the Dean of Salisbury, rated in the king's books at £7. 3. 1½., and in the patronage of the Prebendary of Hurstborne and Burbage in the Cathedral Church of Salisbury. The church, dedicated to All Saints, has recently received an addition of one hundred and twenty-eight sittings, one hundred and eight of which are free, the Incorporated Society for the enlargement of churches and chapels having granted £40 for that purpose.

BURCOMBE (SOUTH), a parish in the hundred of CAWDEN and CADWORTH, county of WILTS, 1¾ mile (W. by S.) from Wilton, containing 374 inhabitants. The living is a perpetual curacy, in the archdeaconry and diocese of Salisbury, endowed with £1000 royal bounty, and £600 parliamentary grant, and in the patronage of the Master of St. John's Hospital, Wilton.

BURCOTT, a hamlet in the parish and hundred of DORCHESTER, county of OXFORD, 5 miles (E. by S.) from Abingdon, containing 145 inhabitants.

BURDON, a township in the parish of BISHOP-WEARMOUTH, northern division of EASINGTON ward, county palatine of DURHAM, 3¾ miles (S. S. W.) from Sunderland, containing 149 inhabitants.

BURDON (GREAT), a township in that part of the parish of HAUGHTON le SKERNE which is in the south-eastern division of DARLINGTON ward, county palatine of DURHAM, 2½ miles (N. E. by E.) from Darlington, containing 76 inhabitants.

BURE, a tything in the parish and hundred of CHRISTCHURCH, New Forest (West) division of the county of SOUTHAMPTON, 2¼ miles (E.) from Christchurch, with which the population is returned.

BURES (ST. MARY), a parish partly in the hundred of HINCKFORD, county of ESSEX, but chiefly in the hundred of BABERGH, county of SUFFOLK, 5 miles (S. E. by S.) from Sudbury, containing 1292 inhabitants. The living is a vicarage, in the archdeaconry of Sudbury, and diocese of Norwich, rated in the king's books at £12. 16. 0½., and in the patronage of O. Hanbury, Esq. The church stands in the county of Suffolk. Edmund, King of the East Angles, is stated to have been crowned here. The navigable river Stour flows on the western and southern sides of the parish, and is crossed by a bridge at the village.

BURES (MOUNT), a parish in the Colchester division of the hundred of LEXDEN, county of ESSEX, 6 miles (E. by N.) from Halstead, containing 260 inhabitants. The living is a rectory, in the archdeaconry of Colchester, and diocese of London, rated in the king's books at £13. 6. 8., and in the patronage of the Rev. John Brett. The church is dedicated to St. John. The river Stour is navigable on the north-eastern side of this parish, which probably takes its distinguishing name from an artificial mount, about eighty feet in perpendicular height, covering nearly an acre and a half of ground; concerning its origin both history and tradition are silent.

Corporate Seal.

BURFORD, a market town and parish in the hundred of BAMPTON, county of OXFORD, 18½ miles (W. N. W.) from Oxford, and 73 (W. N. W.) from London, on the road from Oxford to Cheltenham, containing, with the hamlet of Upton with Signet, 1686 inhabitants. This place is of considerable antiquity, and was by the Saxons called *Beorford*, of which its present name is a variation. In 685, an ecclesiastical synod was held here by the kings Ethelred and Berthwald, at which Aldhelm, Bishop of Sherborne, was ordered to write against the error of the British church respecting Easter. In 752, a battle was fought at Battle-edge, a little westward from the town, between Ethelbald, King of Mercia, and Cuthred, King of the West Saxons, who had revolted against his authority, in which Ethelbald was defeated, and the royal standard, bearing the device of a golden dragon, captured. This event was commemorated by an annual festival on Midsummer-eve, for several ages, when the inhabitants paraded the streets, bearing the figures of a dragon and a giant. Soon after the Conquest, the town was bestowed on Robert, Earl of Gloucester, natural son of Henry I. In 1649, an encounter took place between Fairfax and the royalists, when the former was victorious. The town is pleasantly situated on the banks of the small river Windrush; the houses are indifferently built, but the inhabitants are well supplied with water. Races were formerly held here, but they have been long discontinued. The making of saddles, and a considerable trade in malt and wool, that formerly flourished, have much declined; this, added to the diversion of the line of road, which now avoids the town, instead of passing through it as before, has reduced it from a flourishing condition to a state of comparative poverty. The market is on Saturday: fairs are held on the last Saturday in April, for cattle, sheep, and cheese; July 5th, for horses; and September 25th, for horses, sheep, and cheese. A charter was granted by Henry II., conferring on the inhabitants "all customs enjoyed by the free burgesses of Oxford," of many of which they were deprived by Lord Chief Justice Tanfield, in the reign of Elizabeth. They are entitled to elect an alderman, a steward, two bailiffs, and twelve burgesses, at Easter, but of late years these officers have not been regularly appointed; they do not possess magisterial anthority, the town being wholly within the jurisdiction of the county magistrates, who hold here petty sessions for the division: a court leet and a court baron are also held.

The living is a discharged vicarage, with the perpetual curacy of Fulbrook annexed, in the archdeaconry and diocese of Oxford, rated in the king's books at £31. 13., and in the patronage of the Bishop of Oxford. The church, dedicated to St. John the Baptist, is a spacious structure, exhibiting a mixture of the Norman and the later style of English architecture, with a tower surmounted by a beautiful spire. At the west entrance is a very fine Norman arch; and the south porch, which is in the later English style, is exquisitely rich. There are places of worship for Baptists, the Society of Friends, and Wesleyan Methodists. The free school was founded by Simon Wisdom, alderman of this town, in 1571, who assigned property for its endowment, which, with subsequent benefactions, produces £84 per annum: it affords instruction in English grammar, writing, and arithmetic, to all boys resident within the parish. An apartment over the school-room is used as the town-hall, where the assizes for the county were held in 1636. Two school-wardens are annually appointed by the corporation. John Wilmot, the celebrated earl of Rochester, received the rudiments of his education in this school. The Great Almshouse was founded, in 1457, by the Earl and Countess of Warwick, for eight poor widows; and Wisdom's almshouse was founded before 1628, for four widows: the inmates of both receive, in addition, certain allowances derived from lands and tenements devised for their benefit, under the direction of feoffees. Four messuages were assigned for almshouses, in 1726, by the will of Dr. John Castle, for four aged widows, with a small endowment. There are also various charitable endowments, the principal of which are, the Church estate, which yields £56 per annum, applicable to the repairs of the church; and Pool's estate, producing £62 annually, which is distributed in various ways: some of the charities have been curtailed by the decreased value of property, and others injured by mal-administration. A small priory, or hospital, dedicated to St. John the Evangelist, was valued at the dissolution at £13. 6. 6. Lenthal, the celebrated Speaker of the Long Parliament, resided here; and his descendants occupied a mansion called the priory, near the town, erected on the site of a religious house that belonged to the abbey of Keynsham in Somersetshire. The eminent cosmographer, Dr. Peter Heylin, was born here, in 1600. Burford gives the inferior title of earl to the Duke of St. Albans.

BURFORD, a parish in the hundred of OVERS, county of SALOP, comprising the chapelries of Buraston with Whetmore, Nash with Tilsop and Weston, and Whitton, and the township of Burford, and containing 1039 inhabitants, of which number, 365 are in the township of Burford, 1½ mile (W. by S.) from Tenbury. The living is a rectory, divided into three portions, in the archdeaconry of Salop, and diocese of Hereford; the first portion is rated in the king's books at £9. 13. 4., the second at £8, and the third at £8. 13. 4., they are in the patronage of G. Bowles, Esq. The church is dedicated to St. Mary. Licence for a weekly market and an annual fair, to be held at this place, was granted by Henry III. The Kington canal crosses the parish on the northern side of the village.

BURGATE, a parish in the hundred of HARTISMERE, county of SUFFOLK, 4¼ miles (W. N. W.) from Eye, containing 344 inhabitants. The living is a rectory, in the archdeaconry of Sudbury, and diocese of Norwich, rated in the king's books at £13. 10. 10., and in the patronage of the Bishop of Ely. The church is dedicated to St. Mary.

BURGH, a parish in the southern division of the hundred of Erpingham, county of Norfolk, 2 miles (S. E. by E.) from Aylsham, containing 228 inhabitants. The living is a discharged rectory, in the archdeaconry and diocese of Norwich, rated in the king's books at £7. 17. 1., and in the patronage of G. H. Holley, Esq. The church is dedicated to St. Mary. The river Bure, which is navigable to Yarmouth, flows past this parish.

BURGH, a village (formerly a market town) comprising the consolidated parishes of St. Margaret and St. Mary, in the western division of the hundred of Flegg, county of Norfolk, 3¾ miles (N. E. by E.) from Acle, containing 396 inhabitants. The living of St. Margaret's is a discharged rectory, rated in the king's books at £8. 13. 4., and endowed with £200 royal bounty; that of St. Mary's is also a discharged rectory, rated at £4; they are in the archdeaconry and diocese of Norwich, and in the patronage of Charles Lucas, Esq. The church of St. Mary has long been in ruins. Henry III. granted permission to hold a free market here weekly on Monday, and a fair annually on the eve and festival of St. Margaret, and on the six following days.

BURGH, a parish in the hundred of Carlford, county of Suffolk, 3¾ miles (N.W.) from Woodbridge, containing 250 inhabitants. The living is a discharged rectory, in the archdeaconry of Suffolk, and diocese of Norwich, rated in the king's books at £8. 3. 4., and in the patronage of the Trustees of the late Miles Barnes, Esq. The church, dedicated to St. Botolph, is said to have been built from the ruins of an ancient castle, of which the vallum and other vestiges are still visible. A preceptory of the order of St. John of Jerusalem formerly existed here.

BURGH upon BAINE, a parish in the eastern division of the wapentake of Wraggoe, parts of Lindsey, county of Lincoln, 7 miles (W.) from Louth, containing, with the hamlet of Grisby, 128 inhabitants. The living is a vicarage, in the archdeaconry and diocese of Lincoln, rated in the king's books at £7. 10. 10., endowed with £1000 royal bounty, and in the patronage of George Lister, Esq. The church is dedicated to St. Helen.

BURGH (CASTLE), a parish in the hundred of Mutford and Lothingland, county of Suffolk, 4 miles (W. S. W.) from Great Yarmouth, containing 239 inhabitants. The living is a discharged rectory, in the archdeaconry of Suffolk, and diocese of Norwich, rated in the king's books at £6. 13. 4., and in the patronage of the Trustees of the late Miles Barnes, Esq. The church, dedicated to St. Peter, is a neat ancient edifice, with a square embattled tower on the south side, near the western end: it is stated, together with the church of Clopton adjoining, to have been built out of the ruins of a Roman fort, supposed to have been *Garianonum*, a station founded by Publius Ostorius Scapula, and garrisoned, under the command of a *Præpositus*, by a troop of cavalry called the Stablesian horse. The ramparts included an area of upwards of five acres and a half; and various coins, urns, *fibulæ*, domestic utensils, and military weapons, have been found in the fields contiguous to it. At this place, then called *Cnobheresburg*, King Sigebert gave to Fursæus, an Irish monk, some land on which he founded a monastery, the revenue of which was augmented by King Anna, and other monarchs of the East Angles. The navigable river Waveney flows on the western side of this parish, and opposite the village unites with the river Yare, forming Breydon Water, which runs on the northern side, and is navigable.

BURGH (LITTLE), a parish in the hundred of Holt, county of Norfolk, 4½ miles (S. W. by S.) from Holt. The population is returned with Melton-Constable. The living is a rectory, rated in the king's books at £4, consolidated with that of Melton-Constable, in the archdeaconry and diocese of Norwich. The church is in ruins.

BURGH in the MARSH, a parish in the Marsh division of the wapentake of Candleshoe, parts of Lindsey, county of Lincoln, 7½ miles (E. by S.) from Spilsby, containing 903 inhabitants. The living is a discharged vicarage, to which that of Winthorpe was united in 1729, in the archdeaconry and diocese of Lincoln, rated in the king's books at £13. 6. 8., endowed with £200 royal bounty, and £800 parliamentary grant, and in the patronage of the Bishop of Lincoln. The church is dedicated to St. Peter. Jane Palmer gave a rent-charge of £20 for the endowment of a free school for poor children.

BURGH upon the SANDS, a parish in the ward and county of Cumberland, comprising the townships of Boustead Hill, Burgh upon the Sands, or Burgh-Head, Longburgh, Moorhouse, and Westend, and containing 987 inhabitants, of which number, 304 are in the township of Burgh upon the Sands, 5½ miles (W. N. W.) from Carlisle. The living is a discharged vicarage, in the archdeaconry and diocese of Carlisle, rated in the king's books at £5. 1. 10½., endowed with £200 private benefaction, £400 royal bounty, and £800 parliamentary grant, and in the patronage of the Crown. The church, dedicated to St. Michael, exhibits evident marks of having been constructed, like some others on the border, as a place of occasional retreat and defence. Close to the village, on the northern side, and on a site now called the Old Castle, stood the Roman station *Axelodunum*, the sixteenth on the line of Severus' Wall, and the spot where Adrian's vallum terminated: the lines of the ramparts, which are still visible, include an area about one hundred and thirty-six yards square, in which and in the vicinity, urns, altars, and inscribed stones have been dug up. A castle, built soon after the Conquest, but of which there are no remains, is stated to have been seized in 1174, by William, King of Scotland. Several encounters between the English and the Scotch have occurred in this parish; the most sanguinary were those in 1216 and 1520. Burgh is the head of a barony including this and several other parishes, and is now the property of the Earl of Lonsdale, on whom it confers the title of baron, and who holds annually a customary court. The village, which extends into the township of Westend, is nearly three quarters of a mile in length; there were various branches of manufacture formerly carried on, but these have been chiefly removed to Carlisle. Edward I. died here, on the 7th of July, 1307, whilst on an expedition against Scotland: this event has been commemorated by the erection of an obelisk, in 1685, by Henry, Duke of Norfolk, which fell down on the 4th of March, 1795, and was rebuilt by the Earl of Lonsdale in 1803. It stands about a mile north of the village, on the marsh, a tract of ground belonging to several proprietors, each of whom pays to the baron a yearly fee rent of twopence for every stint, and which has been greatly encroached upon by the sea, so as to have rendered embankments necessary for its protection. A school-room has been erected by the parishioners, and the master receives £5 per annum from property bequeathed by Thomas Pattinson, in 1785, and Richard Hodgson previously. Such of the inhabitants as are not possessed of a real estate worth £12 per annum, are entitled to send children for instruction to the school at Wiggonby, in the parish of Aikton, founded by Mrs. Hodgson; but, owing to the distance, few avail themselves of this privilege.

BURGH (SOUTH), a parish in the hundred of Mitford, county of Norfolk, 2½ miles (N. W. by N.) from Hingham, containing 242 inhabitants. The living is a discharged rectory, in the archdeaconry of Norfolk, and diocese of Norwich, rated in the king's books at £5. 13. 6½., endowed with £200 royal bounty, and in the patronage of the Rev. P. Gurdon. The church is dedicated to St. Andrew.

BURGH-APTON, a parish in the hundred of Clavering, county of Norfolk, 8½ miles (S. E.) from Norwich, containing 388 inhabitants. The living is a rectory, to which a mediety of the rectory of Holveston is annexed, in the archdeaconry and diocese of Norwich, rated in the king's books at £13. 6. 8., and in the patronage of the Earl of Abergavenny. The church is dedicated to St. Martin.

BURGH-MATTISHALL, a parish in the hundred of Mitford, county of Norfolk, 5½ miles (E. by S.) from East Dereham, containing 219 inhabitants. The living is a discharged rectory, with that of Hockering united, in the archdeaconry of Suffolk, and diocese of Norwich, rated in the king's books at £3. 15. 10., and in the patronage of T. T. Berney, Esq. The church is dedicated to St. Peter. There is a place of worship for Wesleyan Methodists.

BURGH-WALLIS, a parish in the upper division of the wapentake of Osgoldcross, West riding of the county of York, 7¼ miles (N. N. W.) from Doncaster, containing, with Haywood and Sutton, 237 inhabitants. The living is a rectory, in the archdeaconry and diocese of York, rated in the king's books at £14. 6. 10½., and in the patronage of M. Tasburgh, Esq. The church is dedicated to St. Helen.

BURGHAM, a tything in the parish of Worplesdon, first division of the hundred of Woking, county of Surrey. The population is returned with the parish.

BURGHCLERE, a parish in the hundred of Evingar, Kingsclere division of the county of Southampton, 7½ miles (N.) from Whitchurch, containing, with Earlston, which is in Kingsclere hundred, 763 inhabitants. The living is a rectory, with the perpetual curacy of Newtown annexed, in the peculiar jurisdiction of the incumbent, rated in the king's books at £30, and in the patronage of the Earl of Carnarvon. The church is dedicated to All Saints. The wills proved in the course of the year are, at the close of it, deposited in the bishop's registry. The village lies at the base of a lofty eminence, the summit of which, now exhibiting vestiges of a military encampment, was formerly crowned by a beacon. A house and school-room are appropriated rent-free, by the Earl of Carnarvon, for the instruction of children, and his lordship allows £20 a year to the schoolmistress, who receives an additional annuity of £10, the bequest of Elizabeth Cornwallis, in 1721.

BURGHFIELD, a parish in the hundred of Theale, county of Berks, 4½ miles (S. W.) from Reading, containing 881 inhabitants. The living is a rectory, in the archdeaconry of Berks, and diocese of Salisbury, rated in the king's books at £14. 19. 2., and in the patronage of the Earl of Shrewsbury. The church is dedicated to St. Mary. The navigable river Kennet passes through the parish, and is crossed by a bridge of great antiquity. In an unsuccessful attempt to obtain coal at Hose Hill, in this parish, a few years ago, a bed of cockle-shells, firmly concreted with sand, was discovered about twelve feet beneath the surface.

BURGHILL, a parish in the hundred of Grimsworth, county of Hereford, 4 miles (N. W. by N.) from Hereford, containing, with the township of Tillington, 823 inhabitants. The living is a discharged vicarage, in the archdeaconry and diocese of Hereford, rated in the king's books at £6. 18. 2., endowed with £200 private benefaction, £600 royal bounty, and £1200 parliamentary grant, and in the patronage of B. Biddulph, Esq. The church is dedicated to St. Mary.

BURHAM, a parish in the hundred of Larkfield, lathe of Aylesford, county of Kent, 1¾ mile (N.N.W.) from Aylesford, containing 236 inhabitants. The living is a discharged vicarage, in the archdeaconry and diocese of Rochester, rated in the king's books at £8, and in the patronage of C. Milner, Esq. The church, dedicated to St. Mary, stands near the river Medway, which bounds the parish on the west; a range of chalk hills, near which are Burham Downs, forming its eastern boundary. Here is a spring, called Holy Garden, that anciently attracted numerous pilgrims, on account of the supposed miraculous efficacy of the water.

BURIAN (ST.), a parish in the hundred of Penwith, county of Cornwall, 4¾ miles (S. W. by W.) from Penzance, containing 1495 inhabitants. The living is a rectory, and a royal peculiar, rated in the king's books at £48. 12. 1., and in the patronage of the Crown. The church, which stands on an eminence, and serves as a land-mark to mariners, is a spacious edifice, containing some interesting monuments: it had a handsome carved screen and other relics of antiquity, but these were removed on its reparation in 1814: there is a small ancient cross near the south porch. St. Burian is a place of considerable antiquity, having been noted for a collegiate church founded by King Athelstan, in honour of St. Buriena, or Beriena, who had an oratory and was interred here, and on which he bestowed the privilege of sanctuary and other immunities: in the 20th of Edward I. the society consisted of a dean and three prebendaries. This establishment constituted the basis of the present independent deanery, which comprises within its jurisdiction the parishes of St. Burian, St. Levan, and Sennan: it was for a long time annexed to the bishoprick of Exeter, but was severed from it during the episcopacy of Bishop Harris, who thus became the first independent dean: every vestige of the collegiate buildings has disappeared. There is a charity school under the direction of trustees, who allow the master eight guineas a year, and a residence rent-free.

BURITON, a parish in the hundred of Finch-Dean, Alton (South) division of the county of Southampton,

$2\frac{1}{4}$ miles (S. by W.) from Petersfield, containing, with the tythings of Nursted and Weston, 767 inhabitants. The living is a rectory, with the perpetual curacy of Petersfield annexed, in the archdeaconry and diocese of Winchester, rated in the king's books at £32. 16. $10\frac{1}{2}$., and in the patronage of the Bishop of Winchester. The church is dedicated to St. Mary.

BURLAND, a township in the parish of ACTON, hundred of NANTWICH, county palatine of CHESTER, $2\frac{1}{2}$ miles (W.) from Nantwich, containing 505 inhabitants. The Whitchurch branch of the Chester canal crosses this township.

BURLATON, a chapelry in that part of the parish of SHERIFF-HALES which is in the western division of the hundred of CUTTLESTONE, county of STAFFORD, $3\frac{1}{2}$ miles (N. N. E.) from Shiffnall. The population is returned with the parish.

BURLESCOMBE, a parish partly in the hundred of HALBERTON, but chiefly in the hundred of BAMPTON, county of DEVON, 5 miles (S. W. by W.) from Wellington, containing 1073 inhabitants. The living is a discharged vicarage, in the archdeaconry and diocese of Exeter, rated in the king's books at £11. 15. 10., endowed with £200 private benefaction, and £200 royal bounty, and in the patronage of William Ayshford Sandford, Esq. The church, dedicated to St. Mary, contains several ancient monuments. A priory for Augustine canons was founded at Leigh, thence called Canonleigh, in this parish, by Walter Clavell, in the time of Henry II., in honour of the Blessed Virgin Mary, St. John the Evangelist, and St. Etheldreda: the society, in the beginning of the reign of Edward I., was changed by Matilda de Clare, Countess of Hereford and Gloucester, for an abbess and nuns of the same order, whose number, in the 26th of Henry VIII., was eighteen, and the revenue £202. 15. 3. In 1286, the abbess obtained a license for a weekly market to be held here. The gateway and the ruins of the eastern wing of the abbey are visible in the grounds belonging to Mr. Browne. There is a small chapel at Ashford, in which divine service is performed eight times during summer, a special endowment charged on the Court estate having been given for that purpose. The summit level of the Grand Western canal crosses this parish, in a direction nearly parallel with the course of the river Lynot: there are various strata of limestone, and small pieces of pure silver have been found in the limekilns. The water of a spring at Ashford possesses properties somewhat similar to those of the sulphur wells at Harrogate, and there are indications of the existence of coal in the vicinity.

BURLESTON, a parish in the hundred of PIDDLETOWN, Dorchester division of the county of DORSET, 6 miles (E. N. E.) from Dorchester, containing 63 inhabitants. The living is a rectory, united to that of Admiston, in the archdeaconry of Dorset, and diocese of Bristol, rated in the king's books at £3. 17. 1. The river Piddle passes on the southern side of the village.

BURLEY, a parish in the hundred of ALSTOE, county of RUTLAND, 2 miles (N. E. by N.) from Oakham, containing 222 inhabitants. The living is a vicarage, in the archdeaconry of Northampton, and diocese of Peterborough, rated in the king's books at £10. 13. $1\frac{1}{2}$., and in the patronage of the Earl of Winchelsea. The church is dedicated to the Holy Cross. The manor came by purchase into the possession of Villiers, the first Duke of Buckingham, who greatly enlarged and embellished the mansion, in which he successively entertained James I. and Charles I., with their respective courts. This stately edifice, on the breaking out of the civil war, was garrisoned by a small body of parliamentary troops, who, unable to sustain an attack of the royalists, set fire to the house, which, with all the costly furniture it contained, was burnt to the ground; the stables, situated at a short distance, being the only part of the buildings that escaped destruction: the site is now occupied by an elegant modern mansion.

BURLEY, a tything in that part of the parish of RINGWOOD which is in the northern division of the hundred of NEW FOREST, New Forest (East) division of the county of SOUTHAMPTON, 6 miles (W. S. W.) from Lyndhurst, containing, with the ville of Bistern-Closes, 303 inhabitants.

BURLEY, a chapelry in that part of the parish of OTLEY which is in the upper division of the wapentake of SKYRACK, West riding of the county of YORK, $2\frac{1}{2}$ miles (W. by N.) from Otley, containing 1200 inhabitants. The living is a perpetual curacy, in the archdeaconry and diocese of York, endowed with £200 royal bounty, and £1200 parliamentary grant, and in the patronage of Matthew Wilson, Esq. There is a place of worship for Wesleyan Methodists. Here are two or three cotton-mills on an extensive scale, and the manufacture of worsted goods is carried on to a limited degree.

BURLEY-DAM, a chapelry in the parish of ACTON, hundred of NANTWICH, county palatine of CHESTER, $3\frac{1}{2}$ miles (W. by S.) from Audlem. The population is returned with the parish. The living is a perpetual curacy, in the archdeaconry and diocese of Chester, endowed with £400 private benefaction, and £1000 royal bounty, and in the patronage of Viscount Combermere.

BURLEY-LODGE, an extra-parochial liberty, in the northern division of the hundred of NEW FOREST, New Forest (East) division of the county of SOUTHAMPTON, containing 30 inhabitants.

BURLINGHAM (ST. ANDREW), a parish in the hundred of BLOFIELD, county of NORFOLK, $2\frac{1}{2}$ miles (W. by S.) from Acle, containing 178 inhabitants. The living is a discharged rectory, with that of Burlingham St. Edmund annexed, in the archdeaconry of Norfolk, and diocese of Norwich, rated in the king's books at £12, and in the patronage of Mrs. Burroughes.

BURLINGHAM (ST. EDMUND), a parish in the hundred of BLOFIELD, county of NORFOLK, 3 miles (S. W.) from Acle, containing 75 inhabitants. The living is a discharged rectory, annexed to that of Burlingham St. Andrew, in the archdeaconry of Norfolk, and diocese of Norwich, rated in the king's books at £12.

BURLINGHAM (ST. PETER), a parish in the hundred of BLOFIELD, county of NORFOLK, $2\frac{1}{2}$ miles (W. by S.) from Acle, containing 97 inhabitants. The living is a discharged rectory, in the archdeaconry of Norfolk, and diocese of Norwich, rated in the king's books at £5, and in the patronage of H. N. Burroughes, Esq.

BURMARSH, a parish in the liberty of ROMNEY-MARSH, though locally in the hundred of Worth, lathe of SHEPWAY, county of KENT, $4\frac{1}{2}$ miles (W. S. W.) from Hythe, containing 94 inhabitants. The living is a rectory, in the archdeaconry and diocese of Canterbury, rated in the king's books at £20. 10. 10., and in the patronage of the Crown. The church is dedicated to All Saints.

BURMINGTON, a chapelry in the parish of Wolford, Brails division of the hundred of Kington, county of Warwick, 1½ mile (S.) from Shipston upon Stour, containing 176 inhabitants. The chapel, dedicated to St. Nicholas, was rebuilt in 1693.

BURN, a township in the parish of Brayton, lower division of the wapentake of Barkstone-Ash, West riding of the county of York, 2¾ miles (S. by W.) from Selby, containing 238 inhabitants. There is a small endowment for the instruction of children, given by George Ellis in 1711, and Edward Goodwin in 1743.

BURNAGE, a township in the parish of Manchester, hundred of Salford, county palatine of Lancaster, 5 miles (S. S. E.) from Manchester, containing 513 inhabitants.

BURNASTON, a hamlet in the parish of Etwall, hundred of Appletree, county of Derby, 5½ miles (S. W. by W.) from Derby, containing 148 inhabitants.

BURNBY, a parish in the Wilton-Beacon division of the wapentake of Harthill, East riding of the county of York, 2¾ miles (S. E. by E.) from Pocklington, containing 95 inhabitants. The living is a discharged rectory, in the archdeaconry of the East riding, and diocese of York, rated in the king's books at £7. 15., and in the patronage of the Duke of Devonshire. The church is dedicated to St. Giles.

BURNESIDE, a chapelry in the parish and ward of Kendal, county of Westmorland, 3 miles (N. by W.) from Kendal, comprising the townships of Strickland-Kettle and Strickland-Roger, and containing 731 inhabitants. The living is a perpetual curacy, in the archdeaconry of Richmond, and diocese of Chester, endowed with £400 private benefaction, and £400 royal bounty, and in the patronage of the Landowners. The chapel was rebuilt in 1823, at an expense of £1300, of which £900 was raised by subscription, and the remainder by a rate. The school was enlarged pursuant to the will of Mr. Alan Fisher, dated October 28th, 1781, whereby he endowed it with £600, bestowing also a collection of books; this endowment was augmented with a gift of £100, by the will of Mr. Joseph Harling, in 1802: these sums having been invested in the funds, produce an annual income of about £40, for which, subject to one or two small deductions, six children from Strickland-Roger are taught for Mr. Fisher's bequest, and four from Skelsmergh on account of Mr. Harling's; the rest, about forty in number, pay a small quarterage settled by the trustees. The village, situated on both sides of the river Kent, is connected by a bridge, the chapel standing in the township of Strickland-Roger. The spinning of worsted-yarn is carried on to a limited extent, and there is a manufactory for patent machines for cutting candlewicks.

BURNESTON, a parish in the wapentake of Hallikeld, North riding of the county of York, comprising the chapelry of Leeming with Exelby and Newton, and the townships of Burneston, Carthorp, Gatenby, and Theakstone, and containing 1326 inhabitants, of which number, 288 are in the township of Burneston, 4 miles (S. E. by E.) from Bedale. The living is a vicarage, in the archdeaconry of Richmond, and diocese of Chester, rated in the king's books at £37. 6. 8., and in the patronage of G. Elsley, Esq. The church is dedicated to St. Lambert. There is a place of worship for Wesleyan Methodists. Matthew Robinson, by deed dated in 1688, assigned a rent-charge of £43. 5. for the endowment of a school, and of an almshouse for five poor persons, besides an alms-master, which he had previously erected: the building contains a school-room, with apartments for the master, also rooms for the alms-master and five hospitallers: other benefactions have subsequently been added, and the present annual income is about £67, of which the schoolmaster receives £16 for teaching seventeen children, the alms-master or usher £5. 8., and the remainder is divided among the poor inmates of the hospital. An annual sum of about £20, arising from land appropriated for their benefit, is distributed among the poor of the parish. The magistrates acting for the district hold their meetings at the New Inn, in this township, and at the York Gate Inn, Melmerby, alternately.

BURNETT, a parish in the hundred of Keynsham, county of Somerset, 2 miles (S. by E.) from Keynsham, containing 75 inhabitants. The living is a discharged rectory, in the archdeaconry of Bath, and diocese of Bath and Wells, rated in the king's books at £5. 10. 7½., and in the patronage of the Mayor and Corporation of Bristol. The church is dedicated to St. Michael. The village, which is small and compact, is situated on the river Chew, and was formerly part of the manor of Keynsham, which, with the advowson, was purchased by John Whiston, Esq., alderman of Bristol, who assigned it in trust to feoffees, for the endowment of the "Red Maids' school" founded by him at Bristol.

BURNHAM, a parish in the hundred of Burnham, county of Buckingham, 3¾ miles (N. W. by N.) from Eton, comprising the chapelry of Lower Boveny, and the liberties of Upper Boveny, Britwell, East Burnham, Cippenham, Toun, and Wood, and containing 1918 inhabitants. The living is a vicarage, in the archdeaconry of Buckingham, and diocese of Lincoln, rated in the king's books at £16. 13. 4., and in the patronage of the Provost and Fellows of Eton College. The church, dedicated to St. Peter, contains a handsome monument to the memory of Lord Chief Justice Wills. There is a meeting-house for dissenters. Burnham is a place of great antiquity, having given name to the hundred. On a moated site near Cippenham stood a palace belonging to the kings of Mercia; and the kings of England of the Norman line appear to have occasionally resided in it, since the foundation charter of Burnham abbey is dated there: this abbey was founded by Richard, Earl of Cornwall, in 1165, for nuns of the order of St. Augustine, whose revenue, in the 26th of Henry VIII., amounted to £91. 5. 11.: a portion of the buildings has been converted into a farm-house and offices. The village lies at a short distance from the Thames, and had formerly a market, which has long been discontinued: fairs are held on February 23rd, May 1st, and October 2nd. A National school is supported partly by a small endowment, but chiefly by subscription among the inhabitants of Burnham, Hilcham, and Taplow; and there are various small benefactions for the poor. A court leet for the manor is held once in three years. Robert Aldrich, Bishop of Carlisle in the reign of Henry VIII., was a native of Burnham.

BURNHAM, a parish in the hundred of Dengie, county of Essex, 19½ miles (E. S. E.) from Chelmsford, containing 1371 inhabitants. The living is a vicarage, in the archdeaconry of Essex, and diocese of London, rated in the king's books at £22. 13. 4., and in the patronage of Lady Jane St. John Mildmay. The church, dedicated to St. Mary, stands about a mile south of the village, on an elevated site, the tower serving as a landmark for mariners. There is a place of worship for Wesleyan Methodists. The village is situated on the northern bank of the river Crouch, near its æstuary: there is a commodious quay; and the oyster-beds, both in the river and on the coast, are extremely productive, a considerable quantity of oysters being annually exported to Holland. There are extensive salt marshes in the vicinity. A school for the instruction of boys and girls has an endowment of about £80 per annum.

BURNHAM, a parish in the hundred of Bempstone, county of Somerset, 9¼ miles (W.S.W.) from Axbridge, containing 920 inhabitants. The living is a vicarage, in the archdeaconry of Wells, and diocese of Bath and Wells, rated in the king's books at £16. 11. 10½., and in the patronage of the Dean and Chapter of Wells. The church, dedicated to St. Andrew in 1316, is a spacious edifice, with a lofty plain tower, that serves as a landmark. It contains the fine altar-piece designed by Inigo Jones for the chapel of the intended palace of Charles II. at Whitehall, and afterwards placed in Westminster abbey, by the dean and chapter of which it was presented to Dr. King, Bishop of Rochester, for many years incumbent of this parish, who erected it in the church at his own expense. It is of white marble, and is executed in the Grecian style: the principal objects are three boys holding a bible, two children in a kneeling attitude, one pouring incense on the altar from a thuribulum, and the other bearing a paten, with two angels in the act of reverence, inclining toward the altar, as supporters. This parish lies on the coast of the Bristol channel, and the fine sandy beach has induced many respectable families to reside here during the summer. A lighthouse, formerly the property of a private individual, has lately been purchased by the Corporation of the Trinity House, for the guidance of vessels passing up the channel.

BURNHAM (EAST), a liberty in the parish and hundred of Burnham, county of Buckingham, 4 miles (N. by W.) from Eton. The population is returned with the parish.

BURNHAM-DEEPDALE, a parish in the hundred of Brothercross, county of Norfolk, 2¼ miles (N.W.) from Burnham-Westgate, containing 113 inhabitants. The living is a discharged rectory, in the archdeaconry of Norfolk, and diocese of Norwich, rated in the king's books at £11, and in the patronage of Henry Blythe, Esq. The church, dedicated to St. Mary, contained an ancient font, on which were engraved hieroglyphic characters, emblematic of the Saxon months; but, by being removed during the progress of some alteration of the edifice, about twenty years ago, it was accidentally broken. The inhabitants have the privilege of sending four children to the endowed school at Bramcaster. In this and the adjoining parishes are extensive salt marshes, for draining, embanking, and improving which, an act was obtained in 1821, whereby two hundred and fifty acres in this parish have been enclosed by a wall seventy feet broad at the base, and ten feet high, to protect it from the sea, which regularly at spring tides flowed over the whole level of the marsh. On the shore are various artificial eminences, the supposed tombs of the Saxons and Danes who fell in battle in the vicinity; and at a short distance are the vestiges of a fortification, supposed to have been raised by the Saxons, after the sanguinary battle between them and the Scots and the Picts, at Stamford in Lincolnshire.

BURNHAM-NORTON, a parish in the hundred of Brothercross, county of Norfolk, 1¼ mile (N.) from Burnham-Westgate, containing 187 inhabitants. The living, consolidated with that of Burnham-Ulph, is a rectory divided into medieties, one of which is held with Burnham-Sutton, rated jointly in the king's books at £17. 10., in the archdeaconry of Norfolk, and diocese of Norwich, and in the patronage of the Master and Fellows of Christ's College, Cambridge; the other is held with Burnham-Westgate, jointly rated at £20. 16. 8. The church is dedicated to St. Margaret. A Carmelite monastery was founded, about 1241, by Sir Ralph de Hemenhale, and Sir William de Calthorp, Knts., the revenue of which, at the time of the dissolution, was estimated at not more than £2. 5. 4. Robert Bale, the historian, was prior of this house, and, dying in the reign of Henry VII., was interred here.

BURNHAM-OVERY, a parish in the hundred of Brothercross, county of Norfolk, 1½ mile (N. E.) from Burnham-Westgate, containing 508 inhabitants. The living is a vicarage, in the archdeaconry of Norfolk, and diocese of Norwich, rated in the king's books at £8, and in the patronage of the Crown. The church is dedicated to St. Clement. This parish, together with others bearing the name of Burnham, is situated in the northern part of the county, adjoining the North sea: a considerable quantity of grain is sent from a small port here, and a few of the inhabitants are engaged in the fishery.

BURNHAM-SUTTON, a parish in the hundred of Brothercross, county of Norfolk, ¾ of a mile (S.S.E.) from Burnham-Westgate. The population is returned with Burnham-Ulph. The living is a rectory, with which a mediety of the consolidated rectories of Burnham-Norton and Burnham-Ulph is united, in the archdeaconry of Norfolk, and diocese of Norwich, rated jointly in the king's books at £17. 10. The church is dedicated to St. Albert.

BURNHAM-THORPE, a parish (formerly a market town) in the hundred of Brothercross, county of Norfolk, 1½ mile (E. by S.) from Burnham-Westgate, containing 344 inhabitants. The living is a rectory, in the archdeaconry of Norfolk, and diocese of Norwich, rated in the king's books at £19. 10., and in the patronage of the Earl of Orford. The church, dedicated to St. Peter, is principally in the later style of English architecture. In the 55th of Henry III., Sir William de Calthorp obtained a grant of a market to be held on Saturday, and a fair annually on the eve, day, and morrow of St. Peter ad Vincula. Here is a free school for a certain number of boys: the master has about £35 a year, with a house and two small plots of land. Lord Nelson, the renowned naval commander, was born here, on the 29th of September, 1758, during the incumbency of his father; he was raised to the peerage in

October, 1798, and on the 22nd of May, 1801, was created Viscount Nelson of the Nile, and of Burnham-Thorpe; his lordship was interred with the most distinguished public honours in the cathedral church of St. Paul, London, January 9th, 1806.

BURNHAM-MARKET, or BURNHAM-WESTGATE, a parish (formerly a market town) in the hundred of Brothercross, county of Norfolk, 36½ miles (N. W.) from Norwich, and 120 (N. N. E.) from London, containing 937 inhabitants. This place derives its name from the small river Burn, on which it is situated, and takes the adjunct Westgate to distinguish it from the numerous villages of the same name in this county. It is pleasantly situated in a fertile valley, environed by a range of hills on the north, west, and south, within four miles of the sea; and though its market has been discontinued, and the building appropriated to that purpose converted into dwellings, it has experienced considerable improvement of late years, and is rapidly advancing in prosperity; the houses are in general well built, and amply supplied with water from springs. The trade is chiefly in corn, which is greatly facilitated by a small harbour formed by the river, and by its proximity to the sea. A small manufactory for iron has been recently established, and hemp is prepared in the town to a limited extent. Fairs for toys are held on Easter Monday and Tuesday, and August 1st and 2nd. The county magistrates hold a meeting here once a month: courts baron are occasionally held by the lords of the respective manors. The living is a rectory, with which a mediety of the consolidated rectories of Burnham-Norton and Burnham-Ulph is united, in the archdeaconry of Norfolk, and diocese of Norwich, rated jointly in the king's books at £20. 16. 8., and in the patronage of the Master and Fellows of Caius College, Cambridge. The church, dedicated to St. Mary, is a neat structure of stone and flint, with a square embattled tower ornamented with sculptured figures; and in the chancel are some interesting monuments and a rudely sculptured statue. The site of another parochial church, dedicated to St. Margaret, is at present occupied by a carpenter's shop; and at the lower end of the town is the chapel of Burnham-Ulph, dedicated to All Saints. There is a place of worship for Independents. Mr. John Wilmot bequeathed £100 for the instruction of poor children, the produce of which is applied to the education of a certain number in a private boarding and day school. There are almshouses for the aged poor, and some bequests for charitable purposes.

BURNHAM-ULPH, a parish in the hundred of Brothercross, county of Norfolk, ¾ of a mile (N.E.) from Burnham-Westgate, containing, with Burnham-Sutton, 315 inhabitants. The living is a mediety of the consolidated rectories of Burnham-Norton and Burnham-Ulph, united to Burnham-Westgate, in the archdeaconry of Norfolk, and diocese of Norwich. The church, dedicated to All Saints, is now used as a chapel to Burnham-Westgate.

BURNISTON, a township in the parish of Scalby, Pickering lythe, North riding of the county of York, 3¼ miles (N. W.) from Scarborough, containing 347 inhabitants. There is a place of worship for Wesleyan Methodists.

BURNLEY, a market town and chapelry in that part of the parish of Whalley which is in the higher division of the hundred of Blackburn, county palatine of Lancaster, 25 miles (N.) from Manchester, 53 (E. N. E.) from Liverpool, and 210 (N. N. W.) from London, containing 6378 inhabitants. This place, anciently Brunley, derives its name from the river Burn, on which it is situated, near the confluence of that stream with the river Calder; and, from the numerous coins, fragments of pottery, and urns containing ashes and burnt bones, that have been found in the neighbourhood, is supposed to have been a Roman station. Several Saxon remains have also been discovered; and at a short distance to the east of the town is a place called *Saxifield*, said to have been the scene of a battle in the year 597. About the same period Paulinus is stated to have visited Burnley, on a mission for converting the natives to Christianity; and the remains of an ancient cross, erected to commemorate his preaching, still exist near the town, where religious rites were usually performed prior to the erection of the chapel. The town is pleasantly situated on a tongue of land formed by the rivers Burn and Calder; the greater part is of very recent erection, and the houses are neatly built of freestone found in the neighbourhood. The streets are well paved, and lighted with gas, under an act of parliament obtained in 1819, for the general improvement of the town; and the inhabitants are abundantly supplied with water from two reservoirs, one to the north, and the other to the south, of the town, under the management of a company. The barracks, standing in the adjoining township of Habergham-Eaves, were erected in 1819, at an expense of £5500, of which sum £2500 were subscribed by the inhabitants. The trade was formerly confined to the manufacture of woollen cloth and worsted goods; but that of cotton has been introduced, for the spinning, weaving, and printing of which, large establishments have been erected: on the banks of the rivers are also several mills for grinding corn, &c., and for fulling cloth. Coal, flag stone, and slate, are found in abundance within a short distance. The Leeds and Liverpool canal, which winds nearly round the town, has contributed greatly to the promotion of its trade. The market, granted in the 22nd of Edward I. to Henry de Lacy, Earl of Lincoln, is on Monday and Saturday, the former being the principal; and on every alternate Monday there is a market for cattle, established in January 1819. Fairs are held on March 6th, Easter-eve, May 9th and 13th, July 10th, and October 11th, for horses, cloth, and pedlary; there is a wool fair on the second Thursday in July, and a horse fair on the third Thursday in October. Petty sessions for the division are held here.

The living is a perpetual curacy, in the archdeaconry and diocese of Chester, endowed with various benefactions (among which is one of £400, to meet a similar donation from the commissioners of Queen Anne's bounty), and in the patronage of Robert Townley Parker, Esq. The chapel, dedicated to St. Peter, was erected soon after the Conquest; but having been partly rebuilt and enlarged at different times, it combines various styles of architecture: it is a spacious structure, and contains several monuments of the Townley family, among which is one to the memory of Charles Townley, Esq., a celebrated patron of the fine arts, whose collection of Grecian and Roman sculpture was the most select ever introduced into this country: the Townley marbles were purchased by the trustees of the British Museum for £20,000, which sum was granted by parliament for that purpose. There are places of worship for Baptists, Independents, Wesleyan Methodists, and Roman Catholics. The free grammar school was founded in the reign of Edward VI., and endowed in 1578, by Sir Robert Ingham; the endowment, originally small, has been considerably augmented by subsequent benefactions, and now produces about £140 per annum: the school has an interest in thirteen scholarships founded in Brasenose College, Oxford, by Dr. Nowell, Dean of St. Paul's, London, in 1572: the management is vested in trustees, who appoint the master, and allow him a salary of £130 per annum, with the privilege of charging each boy £3. 3. per annum for writing and arithmetic. The Rev. W. Whitaker, D.D., the learned master of St. John's College, Cambridge, and the erudite historian of the "Original parish of Whalley," received the rudiments of his education in this school. An institution for the relief of poor married women in childbirth was established in 1819; there is also a Strangers' Friend Society. The interest of £1244. 15. three per cent. consols., given by Mrs. Elizabeth Peel in 1800, and of £500 by Mrs. Molly Thompson, is distributed in clothing to the poor of Burnley and Habergham-Eaves.

BURNOP, a joint township with Hamsteels, in that part of the parish of LANCHESTER which is in the western division of CHESTER ward, county palatine of DURHAM, containing, with Hamsteels, 127 inhabitants. There is a place of worship for Wesleyan Methodists.

BURNSALL, a parish in the eastern division of the wapentake of STAINCLIFFE and EWCROSS, West riding of the county of YORK, comprising the chapelries of Coniston with Kilnsay, and Rilsdon, and the townships of Appletreewick, Burnsall with Thorp sub Montem, Craco, Harlington, and Hetton with Bordley, and containing 1423 inhabitants, of which number, 329 are in the township of Burnsall with Thorp sub Montem, 9½ miles (N. N. E.) from Skipton. The living is a rectory in medieties, in the archdeaconry and diocese of York, rated in the king's books at £36, and in the patronage of the Earl of Craven and the Archbishop of York. The church is dedicated to St. Wilfrid: at the entrance to the choir each portionist has a pulpit and a reading-desk, from which divine service is performed alternately. This parish is supposed to have been formerly a member of the parish of Linton, the rector of which still receives a modus from the greater part of it, for the tithe of corn. A grammar school was built in 1605, by Sir William Craven, Knt., who also repaired the church in 1612, erected four bridges in the vicinity, and performed various acts of charity: the income of the school is £42 per annum, arising from a rent-charge of £20 given by the founder, £200 by Dame Elizabeth Craven, in 1624, and an annuity of £10 to an usher by a subsequent benefactor: only four or five boys are taught Latin; the rest, on an average about thirty, pay for commercial instruction. Sir William was a native of Appletreewick, in this parish, and by industry and frugality amassed considerable property in London, of which city he was lord mayor in 1611.

BURNTWOOD, a chapelry in that part of the parish of ST. MICHAEL, LICHFIELD, which is in the southern division of the hundred of OFFLOW, county of STAFFORD, 3½ miles (W. by S.) from Lichfield, containing, with Edgehill and Woodhouse, 675 inhabitants. The living is a perpetual curacy, in the peculiar jurisdiction of the Dean and Chapter of Lichfield, endowed with £400 private benefaction, and £2600 parliamentary grant, and in the patronage of the Perpetual Curate of St. Michael's.

BURPHAM, a parish in the hundred of POLING, rape of ARUNDEL, county of SUSSEX, 2½ miles (N. E. by E.) from Arundel, containing 223 inhabitants. The living is a discharged vicarage, in the archdeaconry and diocese of Chichester, rated in the king's books at £7. 12. 6., endowed with £200 private benefaction, and £200 royal bounty, and in the patronage of the Dean and Chapter of Chichester. The church, dedicated to St. Mary, is principally of Norman architecture. The river Arun bounds this parish on the west.

BURRALS, a township in the parish of APPLEBY, ST. LAWRENCE, EAST ward, county of WESTMORLAND, 1¼ mile (S. by W.) from Appleby, containing 75 inhabitants. This township is supposed to have been anciently crossed by the *borough walls* of Appleby, and hence, by contraction, its name: it contains a great quantity of limestone.

BURREL, a joint township with Cowling, in that part of the parish of BEDALE which is in the eastern division of the wapentake of HANG, North riding of the county of YORK, 1¾ mile (S. W. by W.) from Bedale, containing, with Cowling, 113 inhabitants.

BURRINGHAM (EAST), a chapelry in that part of the parish of BOTTESFORD which is in the eastern division of the wapentake of MANLEY, parts of LINDSEY, county of LINCOLN, 10¾ miles (W. N. W.) from Glandford-Bridge, containing 338 inhabitants. There is a place of worship for Wesleyan Methodists. Here is a ferry over the Trent to Althorpe.

BURRINGTON, a parish in the hundred of NORTH TAWTON with WINKLEY, county of DEVON, 4 miles (N. W. by W.) from Chulmleigh, containing 939 inhabitants. The living is a vicarage, in the archdeaconry of Barnstaple, and diocese of Exeter, rated in the king's books at £13. 11. 3., and in the patronage of the Rev. J. Buckingham. The church is dedicated to the Holy Trinity.

BURRINGTON, a parish in the hundred of WIGMORE, county of HEREFORD, 4½ miles (W. S. W.) from Ludlow, containing 194 inhabitants. The living is a discharged vicarage, in the archdeaconry of Salop, and diocese of Hereford, rated in the king's books at £5, and in the patronage of the Crown. The church is dedicated to St. George.

BURRINGTON, a parish in the hundred of BRENT with WRINGTON, county of SOMERSET, 5½ miles (N.E.) from Axbridge, containing 559 inhabitants. The living is a perpetual curacy, in the archdeaconry of Bath, and diocese of Bath and Wells, and in the patronage of the inhabitants, subject to the approval of the rector of Wrington. The church, dedicated to the Holy Trinity, contains some fine screen-work. The village is romantically situated on the northern side of the Mendip range of hills. An ancient catacomb was discovered in 1795, containing about fifty skeletons lying in a great quantity of black mould, some of the bones being coated with stalagmik; and there is a cave of a similar description about a mile distant: they are supposed by Dr. Buckland to have been places of common sepulture in early times, and the circumstance of flint knives and other relics of antiquity having been found among the skeletons, corroborates the opinion of the learned professor. There is also another capacious cavern in the parish, which, owing to its intricacy, has been but little explored.

BURROUGH, a parish in the hundred of GARTREE, county of LEICESTER, 5½ miles (S.) from Melton-Mowbray, containing 183 inhabitants. The living is a rectory, in the archdeaconry of Leicester, and diocese of Lincoln, rated in the king's books at £12, and in the patronage of W. Hanbury, Esq. The church, dedicated to St. Mary, contains a circular font. Camden has fixed the Roman station *Vernometum* at this place, inferring also, from the meaning of the word, that here was a temple to one of the heathen deities: the summit of Burrough hill exhibits traces of an encampment, the lines of which enclosed an area of eighteen acres, now under cultivation.

BURROUGH-GREEN, a parish in the hundred of RADFIELD, county of CAMBRIDGE, 5 miles (S.) from Newmarket, containing 381 inhabitants. The living is a rectory, in the archdeaconry and diocese of Ely, rated in the king's books at £18. 10., and in the patronage of the Duke of Rutland. The church is dedicated to St. Augustine. A charity school is endowed with about £30 per annum, chiefly arising from a benefaction from Samuel Knight, D.D., in 1734. Editha, consort of Edward the Confessor, had a palace here.

BURROW, a township in the parish of TUNSTALL, hundred of LONSDALE, south of the sands, county palatine of LANCASTER, 2½ miles (S. by E.) from Kirkby-Lonsdale, containing 198 inhabitants.

BURROW-ASH, a hamlet in the parish of OCKBROOK, hundred of MORLESTON and LITCHURCH, county of DERBY, 4¾ miles (E. by S.) from Derby. The population is returned with the parish. Burrow-Ash is in the honour of Tutbury, duchy of Lancaster, and within the jurisdiction of a court of pleas held at Tutbury every third Tuesday, for the recovery of debts under 40*s*.

BURSCOUGH, a township in the parish of ORMSKIRK, hundred of WEST DERBY, county palatine of LANCASTER, 3¼ miles (N.E. by N.) from Ormskirk, containing 1755 inhabitants. A priory of Black canons was founded in the time of Richard I., by Robert Fitz-Henry, Lord of Latham, and dedicated to St. Nicholas: at the dissolution there were a prior, five brethren, and forty servants, and the revenue was estimated at £129. 1. 10.: previously to that period it was the burial-place of the noble family of Stanley, and the cemetery, in which stands the mutilated central arch of the church, the only relic of the conventual buildings, has subsequently been used as a place of interment by a few poor Roman Catholic families in the vicinity.

BURSLEDON, a chapelry in the parish of HOUND, in that part of the hundred of BISHOP'S WALTHAM which is in the Portsdown division of the county of SOUTHAMPTON, 4¾ miles (E.S.E.) from Southampton, containing 473 inhabitants. The chapel is dedicated to St. Leonard. This chapelry lies at the head of the æstuary of the river Hamble, about three miles from Southampton water, which is crossed by a bridge on the road from Southampton to Portsmouth. Several large vessels have been built here for the navy, the creek being very commodious for that purpose, and the water deep enough for eighty-gun ships. Bursledon is within the jurisdiction of the Cheyney Court held at Winchester every Thursday, for the recovery of debts to any amount.

BURSLEM, a market town and parish in the northern division of the hundred of PIREHILL, county of STAFFORD, 3 miles (N.E.) from Newcastle, 19 (N.) from Stafford, and 151 (N.E.) from London, containing, with the townships of Abbey-Hulton and Sneyd, 10,176 inhabitants. This place in Domesday-book is named *Barcardeslim*, the derivation of which has not been distinctly ascertained. It appears, from the most authentic records, to have been distinguished at an early period for the excellence and variety of the clay in the vicinity, and to have been noted for its manufacture of pottery and earthenware, for which, in the seventeenth century, it became the principal place in England; but it was not till after the construction of the Grand Trunk canal, begun in the year 1766, a branch of which has been formed to this town, that it rose into celebrity, under the auspices of the enterprising Mr. Wedgwood, who was a native of the place, and the principal promoter of its present importance. The town is pleasantly situated on rising ground, and contains, in addition to the dwellings of the workmen employed in the potteries, many good houses for the superintendents of the works, and some handsome edifices for the proprietors: it is lighted with gas, and supplied with water from the works of John Smith, Esq., of Hanley. Previously to the year 1766, the native clay only was used in the manufacture of earthenware; but after a facility of conveyance by water was obtained, the Devonshire and Dorsetshire clay was introduced, and the manufacture of porcelain and china established, in which the Cornwall stone, or "growan," forms an essential ingredient. A most extensive manufacture of these articles is at present carried on throughout a wide district, abounding with coal and every other requisite, and presenting the greatest facility for conveying the goods to various parts of the kingdom. The market, permanently established by act of parliament in 1825, and under the superintendence of trustees, is on Monday and Saturday; the fairs are on the Saturdays preceding Shrove-Sunday, Easter-day, and Whit-Sunday; on Midsummer-day, if Saturday, or if not, on the Saturday following; on the first Saturday after September 11th, and on the day after Christmas-day. The county magistrates hold a petty session for the whole district of the potteries once in six weeks; and a chief constable and subordinate officers are annually chosen, by resident commissioners appointed by act of parliament for managing the local affairs of the town. The town-hall is a neat building, with a cupola, in the centre of the market-place: it was erected by subscription in 1761, and has since been much improved.

Burslem, formerly a chapelry in the parish of Stoke upon Trent, was made a separate parish by act of parliament in 1807. The living is a rectory not in charge, in the archdeaconry of Stafford, and diocese of Lichfield and Coventry, and in the patronage of William Adams, Esq. The church, dedicated to St. Peter, is a small brick building, with an ancient stone steeple. The first stone of a new church, to be dedicated to St. Paul, was laid by the bishop of the diocese in 1828: the expense of its erection was estimated at £10,000, of which sum the parliamentary commissioners granted £8000, the remainder to be raised by subscription among the inhabitants. There are places of worship for Baptists, Independents, Primitive and Wesleyan Methodists, besides those in the New Connexion, and a Roman Catholic chapel. The National school, erected in 1817 by subscription, aided by a grant from the parent society, has been incorporated with a charity school, founded in 1748, by John Bourne, Esq., and endowed with twenty-seven acres of land; the school-house belonging to the latter has been converted into a private dwelling: two hundred and fifty children are instructed. There are Sunday schools in connexion with the church and the several dissenting congregations. At Abbey-Hulton are some remains of a Cistercian abbey, founded in 1223, by Henry de Audley, consisting chiefly of the out-buildings, now converted into farm-offices: the revenue, at the dissolution, was £76. 14. 11½.

BURSTALL, a parish in the hundred of SAMFORD, county of SUFFOLK, 4½ miles (W.) from Ipswich, containing 203 inhabitants. The living is a perpetual curacy, united to the vicarage of Bramford, in the archdeaconry of Suffolk, and diocese of Norwich.

BURSTEAD (GREAT), a parish in the hundred of BARSTABLE, county of ESSEX, 2 miles (S.S.E.) from Billericay, containing 1861 inhabitants. The living is a vicarage, in the archdeaconry of Essex, and diocese of London, rated in the king's books at £17. 6. 8., and in the patronage of the Rev. Edward Evans. The church is dedicated to St. Mary Magdalene. About a mile north of it are some earthworks, enclosing a space of about four acres, and called Blunt's Walls, where various Roman remains have been dug up. There is a free school at Billericay for the benefit of the children of the whole parish.

BURSTEAD (LITTLE), a parish in the hundred of BARSTABLE, county of ESSEX, 2¼ miles (S. by W.) from Billericay, containing 201 inhabitants. The living is a rectory, in the archdeaconry of Essex, and diocese of London, rated in the king's books at £12, and in the patronage of the Bishop of London. The church is dedicated to St. Mary.

BURSTOCK, a parish in the hundred of WHITCHURCH-CANONICORUM, Bridport division of the county of DORSET, 4¼ miles (W.N.W.) from Beaminster, containing 203 inhabitants. The living is a discharged vicarage, in the archdeaconry of Dorset, and diocese of Bristol, rated in the king's books at £5. 19. 4½., endowed with £200 private benefaction, and £200 royal bounty, and in the patronage of John Bragge, Esq. The church is dedicated to St. Andrew.

BURSTON, a parish in the hundred of DISS, county of NORFOLK, 2¾ miles (N.E. by N.) from Diss, containing 405 inhabitants. The living is a rectory, in the archdeaconry of Norfolk, and diocese of Norwich, rated in the king's books at £16, and in the patronage of the Crown. The church, dedicated to St. Mary, has a tower circular at the base and octangular above.

BURSTOW, a parish in the second division of the hundred of REIGATE, county of SURREY, 8 miles (S.E. by S.) from Reigate, containing 715 inhabitants. The living is a rectory, in the exempt deanery of Croydon, which is within the peculiar jurisdiction of the Archbishop of Canterbury, rated in the king's books at £15. 13. 4., and in the patronage of the Crown. The church is dedicated to St. Bartholomew.

BURSTWICK, a parish in the southern division of the wapentake of HOLDERNESS, East riding of the county of YORK, comprising the townships of Burstwick, and Ryhill with Camerton, and containing 751 inhabitants, of which number, 436 are in the township of Burstwick, 3 miles (E. by S.) from Hedon. The living is a perpetual curacy, united to the vicarage of Skeckling, in the archdeaconry of the East riding, and diocese of York. The church is principally in the later style of English architecture.

BURTHOLME, a township in the parish of LANERCOST-ABBEY, ESKDALE ward, county of CUMBERLAND, 3¼ miles (N.E. by E.) from Brampton, containing 223 inhabitants.

BURTON, a township in that part of the parish of TARVIN which is in the second division of the hundred of EDDISBURY, county palatine of CHESTER, 3¾ miles (W.N.W.) from Tarporley, containing 78 inhabitants.

BURTON, a parish (formerly a market town) in the higher division of the hundred of WIRRALL, county palatine of CHESTER, comprising the townships of Burton and Puddington, and containing 481 inhabitants, of which number, 326 are in the township of Burton, 2½ miles (S.E. by S.) from Great Neston. The living is a perpetual curacy, in the archdeaconry and diocese of Chester, endowed with £600 royal bounty, and in the patronage of R. Congreve, Esq. The church, dedicated to St. Nicholas, was rebuilt in 1721. At Denwall, in this parish, there is a colliery, opened about 1750, that extends a mile and three quarters from high water mark under the river Dee: the coal is chiefly sent to Ireland. At the same place was anciently an hospital, to which Alexander de Savensby, Bishop of Lichfield and Coventry (to which see the manor belonged) appropriated, in 1238, the tithes of Burton. Henry VII., about 1494, gave this hospital, together with all its revenue, including the rectory of this parish, to the hospital of St. John the Baptist, founded at Lichfield, by Bishop Smith, to which the estate still belongs. A free school for poor children of the township of Burton, and for four of that of Puddington, was founded in 1724, by Dr. Wilson, the pious and benevolent bishop of Sodor and Man, who was born here, on the 20th of December, 1663: he gave £400 for erecting and endowing it, and his son, Dr. Thomas Wilson, rector of St. Stephen's Walbrook, and a prebendary in the collegiate church of Westminster, added £200. The market, granted in 1298, to Bishop Langton, was held on Thursday, together with a fair for three days at the festival of St. James.

BURTON, a township in the parish of BAMBROUGH, northern division of BAMBROUGH ward, county of NORTHUMBERLAND, 5½ miles (E. by S.) from Belford, containing 85 inhabitants.

BURTON, a chapelry in the parish and liberties of MUCH WENLOCK, county of SALOP, 3 miles (S.W. by S.) from Much Wenlock, with which the population is returned. The living is a perpetual curacy, annexed to the vicarage of Much Wenlock, in the archdeaconry of Salop, and diocese of Hereford, endowed with £400 private benefaction, and £600 royal bounty.

BURTON, a tything in the parish and hundred of CHRISTCHURCH, New Forest (West) division of the county of SOUTHAMPTON, 1¼ mile (N. by E.) from Christchurch, with which the population is returned.

BURTON, or BODEKTON, a parish in the hundred of ROTHERBRIDGE, rape of ARUNDEL, county of SUSSEX, 3½ miles (S. by W.) from Petworth, containing 14 inhabitants. The living is a rectory, with that of Coates consolidated, discharged from the payment of first fruits, but paying tenths to the Bishop of Chichester, in the archdeaconry and diocese of Chichester, rated in the king's books at £7. 3. 11½., and in the patronage of the Earl of Egremont. The Rother, or Arundel navigation, forms the north-eastern boundary of this parish, where it is crossed by a bridge to Shropham.

BURTON, a hamlet in the parish of WARCOP, EAST ward, county of WESTMORLAND, 5½ miles (N. W.) from Brough, containing 52 inhabitants. There are lead-works at Kirsty Bank, in this township. This is the birthplace of Christopher Bainbridge, Archbishop of York in the reign of Henry VIII.; having been sent on a diplomatic mission to Rome by that monarch, the pontiff created him cardinal of St. Praxis: he was poisoned in 1511, by his Italian steward, with whom he had quarrelled, and was interred at Rome.

BURTON, a joint township with Walden, in the parish of AYSGARTH, western division of the wapentake of HANG, North riding of the county of YORK, 7¼ miles (W. by S.) from Middleham, containing, with Walden, 478 inhabitants. The village is situated in a district abounding with fine scenery, on a small stream which falls into the river Ure, and contains a great quantity of salmon. Wool-combing is carried on here. There is a place of worship for Wesleyan Methodists.

BURTON (BLACK), a chapelry in the parish of THORNTON in LONSDALE, western division of the wapentake of STAINCLIFFE and EWCROSS, West riding of the county of YORK, 5½ miles (S.E. by S.) from Kirkby-Lonsdale, containing 746 inhabitants. The living is a perpetual curacy, in the archdeaconry and diocese of York, endowed with £200 private benefaction, and £2100 parliamentary grant, and in the patronage of the Vicar of Thornton.

BURTON (CHERRY), a parish in the Hunsley-Beacon division of the wapentake of HARTHILL, East riding of the county of YORK, 3 miles (W.N.W.) from Beverley, containing 417 inhabitants. The living is a rectory, in the archdeaconry of the East riding, and diocese of York, rated in the king's books at £23. 6. 8., and in the patronage of the Rev. H. Ramsden. The church is dedicated to St. Michael.

BURTON in KENDAL, a parish comprising the market town of Burton in Kendal, and the township of Holme, in LONSDALE ward, and the chapelry of Preston-Patrick, in KENDAL ward, county of WESTMORLAND, and the township of Dalton in the hundred of LONSDALE, south of the sands, county palatine of LANCASTER, and containing 1642 inhabitants, of which number, 673 are in the town of Burton, 34½ miles (S. W. by S.) from Appleby, and 251 (N. W. by N.) from London, on the road to Carlisle through Manchester. The ancient name of this place, *Borton*, a contraction of *Borough town*, is still retained by the inhabitants; it takes its adjunct from being situated in the *dale*, or valley, of the river Ken, to distinguish it from Burton in Lancashire. The houses, many of which are ancient, are well built, and the general appearance of the town is prepossessing: the inhabitants are amply supplied with water. A communication with the Mersey, the Dee, the Humber, and the Trent, is afforded by the Kendal and Lancaster canal; but, notwithstanding its favourable situation, the town possesses very little trade: there are some small linen-manufactories at Holme, but the principal part of the population are employed in agriculture. The market, established in 1661, and once noted for corn, is on Tuesday: the market-place is a spacious area, adjoining which are some good houses and shops, and in the centre is a neat stone cross. A fair is held on Easter-Monday, for cattle and horses, which is also a statute fair. The county magistrates hold a petty session every alternate Tuesday; and a manorial court is held on Whit-Monday and Martinmas-day, for the renewal of fines, and for the recovery of debts under 40*s*. The living is a discharged vicarage, in the archdeaconry of Richmond, and diocese of Chester, rated in the king's books at £15. 17., endowed with £400 private benefaction, and £400 royal bounty, and in the patronage of Mrs. Johnstone. The church, dedicated to St. James, is a plain ancient structure, with a square tower: the pulpit, and the canopy over it, are richly carved; and there are two sepulchral chapels belonging to Dalton and Preston halls: in the churchyard is a monument to the memory of William Cockin, author of the "Rural Sabbath," and other literary productions. There is a place of worship for Independents. The grammar school has an income of £50 per annum, the produce of various benefactions since the year 1657: the premises, which are neat and commodious, were erected by subscription, in 1817: it has recently sustained a considerable loss from the bankruptcy of an individual who held a great part of the endowment, and is likely henceforward to be conducted on a more limited plan. Gerard Langbaine, Dr. William Lancaster, and Dr. Launcelot Dawes (prebendary of Carlisle, and forty-eight years vicar of this parish), eminent literary characters in the reign of Charles I., were natives of this town.

BURTON (KIRK), a parish in the upper division of the wapentake of AGBRIGG, West riding of the county of YORK, comprising the chapelry of Cumberworth-Half, the townships of Cartworth, Foulston, Hepworth, Kirk-Burton, Shelley, Shepley, Thurstonland, and Wooldale, and containing 13,559 inhabitants, of which number, 2153 are in the township of Kirk-Burton, 5½ miles (S. E.) from Huddersfield. The living is a vicarage, in the archdeaconry of the East riding, and diocese of York, rated in the king's books at £13. 6. 8., and in the patronage of the King, as Duke of Lancaster. The church, dedicated to St. John the Baptist, was built in the reign of Edward III. There is a place of worship for Wesleyan Methodists. A small sum is annually paid by the parishioners to the vicar of Dewsbury, in token of their ancient dependence on that parish. A school, established by the inhabitants in 1714, was endowed, in 1721, by the Rev. Henry Robinson, with a bequest of £100 for the instruction of ten poor children of this township, and three of Thurstonland; and, in the following year, with a bequest of £360, for teaching twenty more of the same places: these sums having been invested in land, produce about £66 per annum, which is paid to the master. It is thought that the Saxons had a fort here, a memorial of which probably subsists in a small dike, called the Old Saxe Dike.

BURTON by **LINCOLN**, a parish in the wapentake of Lawress, parts of Lindsey, county of Lincoln, 2¼ miles (N. N. W.) from Lincoln, containing 186 inhabitants. The living is a rectory, in the archdeaconry of Stow, and diocese of Lincoln, rated in the king's books at £11. 15. 2½., and in the patronage of Lord Monson. The church is dedicated to St. Vincent.

BURTON (LONG), a parish in the hundred of Sherborne, Sherborne division of the county of Dorset, 3 miles (S. by E.) from Sherborne, containing 327 inhabitants. The living is a discharged vicarage, within the peculiar jurisdiction of the Dean of Salisbury, rated in the king's books at £10. 15., endowed with £200 private benefaction, and £200 royal bounty, and in the patronage of the Marquis of Salisbury. The church is dedicated to St. James.

BURTON upon STATHER, a parish (formerly a market town) in the northern division of the wapentake of Manley, parts of Lindsey, county of Lincoln, 35½ miles (N. by W.) from Lincoln, and 164½ (N. by W.) from London, containing 762 inhabitants. The living is a vicarage, with which the rectory of Flixborough was consolidated in 1729, in the archdeaconry of Stow, and diocese of Lincoln, rated in the king's books at £12, and in the patronage of Sir Robert Sheffield, Bart. The church is dedicated to St. Andrew. The village is situated on the brow of a hill, at the foot of which flows the river Trent, where there is a wharf, or staith, commonly called Stather, whence the adjunct to the name. It was formerly of much greater extent than it is at present, having been greatly reduced by a tempest that entirely destroyed several of the houses, and injured the church: part of it was also damaged, in 1777, by the explosion of a brig laden with gunpowder; and the increase of Gainsborough, a neighbouring market town, has contributed still further to its decline. The market was on Tuesday: fairs are held on the first Monday in May, and the first Monday after Martinmas. On the summit of Alkborough hill is a kind of labyrinth, called the Julian tower, supposed to be the remains of a Roman fortification.

Arms.

BURTON upon TRENT, a parish comprising the market town of Burton, and the townships of Branson, Burton-Extra, Horninglow, and Stretton, in the northern division of the hundred of Offlow, county of Stafford, and the chapelry of Chilcote and the township of Winshill, in the hundred of Repton and Gresley, county of Derby, and containing 6700 inhabitants, of which number, 4114 are in the town of Burton, 24 miles (E.) from Stafford, and 124 (N. W. by N.) from London. This place derived its name from having been a Saxon burgh of considerable importance, and its adjunct from being situated on the river Trent. In the ninth century, St. Modwena, who had been expelled from her monastery in Ireland, came hither, and having obtained an asylum from King Ethelwolf, in reward for a miraculous cure that she is said to have performed on his son Alfred, erected a chapel, and dedicated it to St. Andrew: the site, still called St. Modwena's garden, is the only part visible. In 1004, Wulfric, Earl of Mercia, founded an abbey for monks of the Benedictine order, which, from the vestiges still to be traced, appears to have been one of the most considerable in the kingdom: it was a mitred abbey, richly endowed, and invested with extensive privileges; its revenue, at the dissolution, was £356. 16. 3. The remains consist principally of some fine Norman arches that formed part of the cloisters, which included an area one hundred feet square, and of part of the entrance gateway, now converted into a blacksmith's shop. In 1225, a considerable part of the town was destroyed by an accidental fire. In the reign of Edward II., Thomas, Earl of Lancaster, posted himself at Burton, and endeavoured to defend the passage of the river against the king; but being unsuccessful in his attempt, he fled with his forces into Scotland. During the parliamentary war, this town and neighbourhood were frequently the scene of action between the contending parties.

Burton is pleasantly situated in a fertile vale, on the northern bank of the river Trent, which is navigable from Gainsborough for vessels of considerable burden. Over the river is a noble bridge of freestone, five hundred and twelve yards in length, consisting of thirty-seven arches, built prior to the Conquest, and substantially repaired in the reign of Henry II.: the expense of repairing it devolves upon the Marquis of Anglesey. The town, consisting principally of one street in a direction parallel with the river, is well paved, lighted with gas, and plentifully supplied with water; the houses are in general modern and well built. There is a public subscription library and newsroom; and assemblies and concerts take place occasionally at the town-hall. The principal branch of manufacture is that of cotton, power-looms being employed in weaving it: an ancient water-mill in the vicinity of the town, noticed in the Norman survey, is now appropriated to the grinding of corn, and to making scrap-iron into bars; a few articles in iron are also made, particularly screws. This town has long been celebrated for its ale, a great quantity of which is sent to London, and other large towns in England. A company was formerly established for regulating the navigation of the river Trent; but a canal has been constructed, which joins the Grand Trunk canal, and affords a more direct medium for the transport of goods. The market is on Thursday: fairs are held on February 5th, April 5th, Holy Thursday, July 16th, and October 29th, for cattle and cheese; the last continues six days, and is a great horse fair. The government is vested in a high steward, deputy-steward, and bailiff, appointed by the Marquis of Anglesey, as lord of the manor, who holds a court leet and a court baron annually in October. The bailiff is a justice of the peace, and acts also as coroner. The power to try and execute criminals, and to hold courts of pleas to any amount, was formerly enjoyed. A court, called the Genter's court, the jurisdiction of which extends over the whole parish, is held every third Friday, before the steward, or his deputy, for the recovery of debts not exceeding 40*s*. The inhabitants, by virtue of letters patent granted in the 11th of Henry VIII., are exempt from serving the office of sheriff, and from being summoned as jurors at the assizes and sessions for the county.

The town-hall is a handsome building, erected at the expense of the Marquis of Anglesey, and containing, in addition to the offices for transacting the public business, a handsome suite of assembly-rooms.

The living is a perpetual curacy, endowed with £800 parliamentary grant, and in the peculiar jurisdiction and patronage of the lord of the manor. The ancient church, dedicated to St. Mary and St. Modwena, formerly belonged to the abbey, and was made collegiate by Henry VIII; having been greatly damaged in the parliamentary war, it was taken down, and the present edifice, a handsome structure with a tower, though less embellished than the former, was erected on its site, in 1720. A new church, dedicated to the Holy Trinity, was erected in 1823, on a piece of land given by the Marquis of Anglesey: it is a very handsome structure, in the decorated style of English architecture, and highly ornamental to the town. It was built and endowed by the executors of Isaac Hawkins, Esq.; and the living, which is a perpetual curacy, is in the patronage of the Marquis of Anglesey. There are places of worship for General and Particular Baptists, Independents, and Primitive and Wesleyan Methodists. The free grammar school was founded, in 1520, by William Beane, abbot, and endowed with lands producing at present £450 per annum, of which the master receives two-thirds, and the usher the remainder: there are sixty boys on the foundation. Richard Allsop, in 1728, bequeathed property with which land was purchased, now producing £24 per annum, to found a school for the instruction of thirty boys, for the clothing of four of whom, Francis Astle, in 1735, left a messuage producing £5 per annum. There are Sunday schools, established under the patronage of the Marquis and Marchioness of Anglesey. Almshouses were founded and endowed, in 1634, by Mrs. Ellen Parker, for six widows or maidens, who receive each an allowance of £10 annually: the management is vested in eight trustees. Other almshouses were founded in 1591, for five unmarried women, and endowed by Dame Elizabeth Pawlett, the present income of which is about £80 per annum; out of this a certain sum is paid to the master and usher of the free grammar school. There are various other charities, the principal of which, by Mrs. Almund, yields about £72 per annum. Isaac Hawkins Browne, a poet of minor celebrity, was born here, about 1705. Near Branson is a chalybeate spring.

BURTON upon URE, a township in the parish of Masham, eastern division of the wapentake of Hang, North riding of the county of York, 1 mile (N.) from Masham, containing 170 inhabitants. This township is chiefly composed of dispersed farm-houses, one of which is called High Burton, another Low Burton Hall, and a third Burton House. At a place called Aldborough was the ancient castle of William le Gros, Earl of Albemarle, who, for having gained the battle of the Standard, was created Earl of York, in 1138.

BURTON (WEST), a parish in the North-clay division of the wapentake of Bassetlaw, county of Nottingham, 3¼ miles (S. S. W.) from Gainsborough, containing 37 inhabitants. The living is a perpetual curacy, in the archdeaconry of Nottingham, and diocese of York, endowed with £20 per annum private benefaction, and £600 royal bounty, and in the patronage of David Walters, Esq. The church is dedicated to St. Helen. This parish is bounded on the east by the river Trent.

BURTON on the WOLDS, a township in the parish of Prestwould, eastern division of the hundred of Goscote, county of Leicester, 3½ miles (E. N. E.) from Loughborough, containing 416 inhabitants. The Wesleyan Methodists have a meeting-house here. There is a small endowment for teaching, clothing, and apprenticing children, chiefly arising from benefactions by Miles Newton, in 1757, and John Kirk.

BURTON-AGNES, a parish in the wapentake of Dickering, East riding of the county of York, comprising the townships of Burton-Agnes, Gransmoor, Haisthorp, and Thornholm, and containing 609 inhabitants, of which number, 321 are in the township of Burton-Agnes, 6¼ miles (N.E. by E.) from Great Driffield. The living is a vicarage, in the archdeaconry of the East riding, and diocese of York, rated in the king's books at £20. 6. 3., and in the patronage of the Rev. T. A. Mills. The church is dedicated to St. Martin. Adjoining it is an old building, used as a school-room, in which between thirty and forty children of both sexes are taught English gratuitously, from a bequest of £200 by Richard Green, in 1563, which having been invested in land, now produces £50 a year: this sum is divided into three parts, one of them being given to the schoolmaster, another to the poor, and the third expended in repairing the church. An hospital for four poor widows was founded, and endowed with an annuity of £20. 10., by the widow of the late William Boynton, Esq.

BURTON - BISHOP, a parish in the Hunsley-Beacon division of the wapentake of Harthill, East riding of the county of York, 2½ miles (W.) from Beverley, containing 534 inhabitants. The living is a discharged vicarage, in the archdeaconry of the East riding, and diocese of York, rated in the king's books at £5. 6. 8., endowed with £200 private benefaction, and £700 parliamentary grant, and in the patronage of the Prebendary of North Newbold in the Cathedral Church of York. The church is dedicated to All Saints. There is a place of worship for Particular Baptists, with a Sunday school attached, in which about one hundred children are taught. Ten poor children are instructed in English for £20 a year, being the rental of some land purchased with a legacy of £100 from Mrs. Elizabeth Gee, in 1714. Almshouses for four persons are endowed with about £70 per annum, arising from property given by Ralph Hansby, by deed dated July 24th, 1614.

BURTON-BRADSTOCK, a parish in the liberty of Frampton, though locally in the hundred of Godder-Thorne, Bridport division of the county of Dorset, 2¾ miles (S.E. by S.) from Bridport, containing 854 inhabitants. The living is a rectory, in the archdeaconry of Dorset, and diocese of Bristol, rated in the king's books at £25, and in the patronage of Lord Rivers. The church is dedicated to St. Mary. This parish has the English channel on the south, and Bridport harbour on the west; the cliffs on the beach rise perpendicularly to a considerable height, and contain a vast quantity of fossils.

BURTON-COGGLES, a parish in the wapentake of Beltisloe, parts of Kesteven, county of Lincoln, 1¾ mile (W.N.W.) from Corby, containing 245 inhabitants. The living is a rectory, in the archdeaconry and diocese of Lincoln, rated in the king's books at £16. 12. 3½., and in the patronage of the Crown. The church is dedicated to St. Thomas à Becket. A charity school has a small endowment arising from bequests by John Speight, in 1734, and Catherine Chomeley, in 1773.

BURTON-CONSTABLE, a township in the parish of FINGALL, western division of the wapentake of HANG, North riding of the county of YORK, 4¼ miles (N. E.) from Middleham, containing 204 inhabitants.

BURTON-DASSETT, a parish (formerly a market town) in the Burton-Dassett division of the hundred of KINGTON, county of WARWICK, 5¼ miles (E.) from Kington, containing 670 inhabitants. The living is a vicarage, in the archdeaconry of Coventry, and diocese of Lichfield and Coventry, rated in the king's books at £14, and in the patronage of the Duke of Buckingham. The church is dedicated to All Saints.

BURTON-EXTRA, a township in that part of the parish of BURTON upon TRENT which is in the northern division of the hundred of OFFLOW, county of STAFFORD, contiguous to the southern part of the town of Burton upon Trent, containing 910 inhabitants.

BURTON-FLEMING, or (NORTH), a parish in the wapentake of DICKERING, East riding of the county of YORK, 3¼ miles (S. by W.) from Hunmanby, containing 386 inhabitants. The living is a discharged vicarage, in the archdeaconry of the East riding, and diocese of York, rated in the king's books at £6. 4. 2., endowed with £400 royal bounty, and £200 parliamentary grant, and in the patronage of H. Osbaldeston, Esq. There is a place of worship for Wesleyan Methodists.

BURTON-GATE, a parish in the wapentake of WELL, parts of LINDSEY, county of LINCOLN, 5 miles (S.S.E.) from Gainsborough, containing 110 inhabitants. The living is a discharged rectory, in the archdeaconry of Stow, and diocese of Lincoln, rated in the king's books at £8. 10. 10., and in the patronage of W. Hutton, Esq. The church is dedicated to St. Helen.

BURTON-HASTINGS, a parish in the Kirby division of the hundred of KNIGHTLOW, county of WARWICK, 4¼ miles (E.S.E.) from Nuneaton, containing 241 inhabitants. The living is a perpetual curacy, in the archdeaconry of Coventry, and diocese of Lichfield and Coventry, endowed with £600 royal bounty, and in the patronage of G. Greenway, Esq. The church is dedicated to St. Botolph. The Ashby de la Zouch canal passes through this parish, which is also intersected by the Roman Watling-street.

BURTON-HILL, a tything in the parish and hundred of MALMESBURY, county of WILTS, ¾ of a mile (S.) from Malmesbury, containing 192 inhabitants.

BURTON-JOYCE, a parish in the southern division of the wapentake of THURGARTON, county of NOTTINGHAM, 5 miles (N.E. by E.) from Nottingham, containing, with the chapelry of Bulcote, 650 inhabitants. The living is a discharged vicarage, in the archdeaconry of Nottingham, and diocese of York, rated in the king's books at £4. 19. 2., endowed with £200 royal bounty, and in the patronage of the Earl of Chesterfield. The church, dedicated to St. Helen, is an ancient spacious structure, with a spire: in a niche of the north aisle is an upright effigy of an armed knight, standing on a lion, and bearing a shield on the left arm, said to represent Robert de Joaz, who lived in the reign of Edw. I.; and in the chancel are two altar-tombs of deceased members of the family of Stapelton, with inscriptions in Saxon characters. There is a place of worship for Wesleyan Methodists. The village is pleasantly situated on the northern bank of the river Trent. Courts leet and baron are held annually for the manor.

BURTON-LATIMER, a parish in the hundred of HUXLOE, county of NORTHAMPTON, 3½ miles (S. E.) from Kettering, containing 842 inhabitants. The living is a rectory, in the archdeaconry of Northampton, and diocese of Peterborough, rated in the king's books at £29. 10., and in the patronage of the Rev. T. Grimshaw. The church is dedicated to St. Mary. A silk-manufactory on an extensive scale has of late years been established in this parish. Here is a free school with a considerable endowment.

BURTON-LAZARS, a chapelry in the parish of MELTON-MOWBRAY, hundred of FRAMLAND, county of LEICESTER, 1¾ mile (S. E. by S.) from Melton-Mowbray, containing 249 inhabitants. The chapel is dedicated to St. James. In the reign of Stephen, an hospital, dedicated to the Blessed Virgin Mary and St. Lazarus, was founded here by a general collection throughout England, the principal contributor being Roger de Mowbray, who gave two carucates of land, a house, a mill, &c.: it was dependent on the great house at Jerusalem, and was the chief of all the lazar-houses in England: the revenue, in the 26th of Henry VIII., was estimated at £265. 10. 2. It stood near a spring, the water of which was formerly in high repute for curing the leprosy: a bath and a drinking-room were built about 1760, and are frequented by persons afflicted with scrofulous and scorbutic disorders.

BURTON-LEONARD, a parish partly in the liberty of ST. PETER of YORK, East riding, and partly in the lower division of the wapentake of CLARO, West riding, of the county of YORK, 5 miles (N. N. W.) from Knaresborough, containing 518 inhabitants. The living is a discharged vicarage, in the peculiar jurisdiction and patronage of the Dean and Chapter of York, rated in the king's books at £3. 1. 0½., and endowed with £200 royal bounty. The church, dedicated to St. Helen, is a small plain structure, built about forty years ago. There is a place of worship for Wesleyan Methodists. Many of the inhabitants are employed in the dressing of flax, and the manufacture of linen.

BURTON-OVERY, a parish in the hundred of GARTREE, county of LEICESTER, 7½ miles (S. E. by E.) from Leicester, containing 383 inhabitants. The living is a rectory, in the archdeaconry of Leicester, and diocese of Lincoln, rated in the king's books at £18. 5. 10., and in the patronage of the Rev. W. S. Lee. There is a chalybeate spring within the parish, but it is not much resorted to.

BURTON-PEDWARDINE, a parish in the wapentake of ASWARDHURN, parts of KESTEVEN, county of LINCOLN, 4½ miles (S.E. by E.) from Sleaford, containing 124 inhabitants. The living is a vicarage, in the archdeaconry and diocese of Lincoln, rated in the king's books at £7. 12. 8½., and in the patronage of T. O. Hunter, Esq. The church, dedicated to St. Andrew, has a lofty tower of considerable antiquity, but is in a very ruinous condition.

BURTON-PIDSEA, a parish partly in the liberty of ST. PETER of YORK, and partly in the middle division of the wapentake of HOLDERNESS, East riding of the county of YORK, 11½ miles (E. by N.) from Kingston upon Hull, containing 378 inhabitants. The living is a discharged vicarage, within the peculiar jurisdiction and patronage of the Dean and Chapter of York, rated in the king's books at £6, endowed with £200 royal bounty, and £200 parliamentary grant. The church is principally in the later style of English architecture. There is a place of worship for Wesleyan Methodists. The village is situated on rising ground, whence there is an extensive prospect of the surrounding country.

BURTON-SALMON, a township in the parish of MONK-FRYSTON, lower division of the wapentake of BARKSTONE-ASH, West riding of the county of YORK, 2 miles (N. by E.) from Ferry-Bridge, containing 182 inhabitants.

BURTONWOOD, a chapelry in the parish of WARRINGTON, hundred of WEST DERBY, county palatine of LANCASTER, 3¼ miles (S.W.) from Newton in Mackerfield, containing 911 inhabitants. The living is a perpetual curacy, in the archdeaconry and diocese of Chester, endowed with £600 private benefaction, £800 royal bounty, and £600 parliamentary grant, and in the patronage of the Rector of Warrington.

BURWARDSLEY, a chapelry in that part of the parish of BUNBURY which is in the higher division of the hundred of BROXTON, county palatine of CHESTER, 5¾ miles (S. S. W.) from Tarporley, containing 272 inhabitants. The living is a perpetual curacy, in the archdeaconry and diocese of Chester, endowed with £1000 royal bounty, and in the patronage of Trustees. The chapel, dedicated to St. John, was built on the waste by subscription, and consecrated in 1735.

BURWARTON, a parish in the hundred of STOTTESDEN, county of SALOP, 9¾ miles (N. E.) from Ludlow, containing 123 inhabitants. The living is a discharged rectory, in the archdeaconry of Salop, and diocese of Hereford, rated in the king's books at £4. 6. 8., and in the patronage of B. Holland, Esq. The church is dedicated to St. Lawrence.

BURWASH, a parish partly in the hundred of SHOYSWELL, partly in the hundred of HENHURST, but chiefly in the hundred of HAWKESBOROUGH, rape of HASTINGS, county of SUSSEX, 6 miles (S. E. by S.) from Wadhurst, containing 1937 inhabitants. The living is a vicarage, in the archdeaconry of Lewes, and diocese of Chichester, rated in the king's books at £18, and in the patronage of the Rev. W. Curteis. There is also a sinecure rectory, rated at £8. 10., in the gift of the same patron. The church, dedicated to St. Bartholomew, is partly in the early style of English architecture, and partly of later date. The petty sessions are held here. A National school, in which about eighty boys and the same number of girls are instructed, has an endowment of £35. 10. per annum, arising from property in land and stock, purchased with the amount of sundry contributions.

BURWELL, a parish in the Wold division of the hundred of LOUTH-ESKE, parts of LINDSEY, county of LINCOLN, 5¼ miles (S. by E.) from Louth, containing 161 inhabitants. The living is a discharged vicarage, with the perpetual curacy of Walmsgate annexed, in the archdeaconry and diocese of Lincoln, rated in the king's books at £8, endowed with £400 private benefaction, and £800 parliamentary grant, and in the patronage of M. B. Lister, Esq. The church is dedicated to St. Michael. Fairs are held annually on May 15th and Old Michaelmas-day. There are the remains of a small Alien priory of Benedictine monks, founded by John de Hay, and given by some of the lords of Kyme to the abbey of St. Mary Sylvæ Majoris, near Bordeaux. This is the birthplace of the celebrated Sarah, Duchess of Marlborough, whose ascendancy in the affections of Queen Anne had a material influence on the political events of that reign.

BURWELL, a tything in that part of the parish of HAMBLEDON which is in the hundred of MEON-STOKE, Portsdown division of the county of SOUTHAMPTON. The population is returned with the parish.

BURWELL (ST. MARY), a parish in the hundred of STAPLOE, county of CAMBRIDGE, 4 miles (N. W. by W.) from Newmarket, containing 1518 inhabitants. The living is a discharged vicarage, with which the rectory of Burwell St. Andrew is consolidated, in the archdeaconry of Sudbury, and diocese of Norwich, rated jointly in the king's books at £50. 14. 2., endowed with £200 royal bounty, and in the patronage of the Earl of Guilford, on the nomination of the University of Cambridge. The church is a beautiful edifice, in the decorated style of English architecture: the rental of one hundred acres of arable land is appropriated for preserving it in repair. The church of St. Andrew has long been demolished, and the cemetery converted into pasture ground. The village consists principally of one irregular street, about three quarters of a mile long, the houses in which are built with a peculiar kind of stone obtained in quarries in the vicinity, in which pyrites and sharks' teeth, in good preservation, have been found. A great fair for horses is held, annually on Rogation-Monday, at Reach, once a market town, now an insignificant hamlet, partly in this parish. A navigable cut extends from this place. Here are the ruins of a castle, surrounded by a moat, which was besieged in the war between Stephen and the Empress Matilda, by Geoffrey de Mandeville, Earl of Essex, who was shot by an arrow from the walls. The parish register contains the record of a melancholy event arising from a fire that broke out in a barn, in the evening of the 8th of September, 1727, whereby seventy-eight persons, who had assembled to witness a puppet-show, lost their lives; the mangled and half-consumed bodies of the sufferers were promiscuously interred in two pits, dug for them in the churchyard.

BURY, a parish in the hundred of HURSTINGSTONE, county of HUNTINGDON, 1 mile (S.) from Ramsey, containing 337 inhabitants. The living is a perpetual curacy, in the archdeaconry of Huntingdon, and diocese of Lincoln, endowed with £200 private benefaction, and £200 royal bounty, and in the patronage of George Maule, Esq. The church, dedicated to the Holy Cross, is the eastern part of a large cruciform edifice, and exhibits a mixture of Norman and early English architecture, with some interesting specimens of both; the entrance to the chancel from the nave is under a carved wooden screen. Bury formed part of the possessions of Ramsey abbey; and there is a strong stone bridge of two arches over a small brook, which is supposed to have been built by one of the abbots.

BURY, a parish comprising the market town of Bury, the chapelries of Heap, Higher Tottington, and Lower Tottington, and the townships of Elton and Walmersley, in the hundred of SALFORD, and the townships of Coupe-Lench with Newhallhey and Hall-Carr, Henheads, and Musbury, in the higher division of the hundred of BLACKBURN, county palatine of LANCASTER, and containing 34,581 inhabitants, of which number, 10,583 are in the town of Bury, 48½ miles (S.E. by S.) from Lancaster, 9 (N.N.W.) from Manchester, and 195½ (N.N.W.) from London. Some antiquaries suppose this to have been a Roman station; it was certainly a Saxon town, as its name obviously implies, the Saxon word *Byri* signifying a fortified place. Leland notices the remains of a castle near the church, the site of which, still called Castle Croft, was near the ancient bed of the river Irwell. This castle, one of the twelve baronial castles in the county, was entirely demolished about the year 1644, by the parliamentary troops, who, after having laid siege to the town, and thrown up an intrenchment at a place called Castle Steads, in the adjoining township of Walmersley, battered down the small remains that were then existing; fragments of the building are still occasionally discovered in digging the ground near its site. In 1787, nearly three hundred persons having assembled in a barn, to witness the performance of some itinerant players, the gable end gave way, and the whole building fell, and buried the audience in its ruins.

The town is situated on a gentle acclivity rising from the eastern bank of the river Irwell, over which is a stone bridge, and is skirted on the east by the river Roche, which falls into the Irwell about two miles and a half to the south. It is indifferently paved, well lighted with gas, and amply supplied with water by pumps: the houses, generally old and dilapidated, are rapidly giving place to modern structures; and among the more recent improvements may be noticed a spacious square of well-built houses at the northern extremity of the town. There are a public subscription library, a news-room, a botanical institution, and a mechanics' library; and a medical library, together with a splendid billiard-room, has been recently established by John Woodcock, Esq. The woollen trade was introduced in the reign of Edward III., and increased so as to constitute the staple trade of the town in the reign of Elizabeth, who stationed one of her aulnagers here, to stamp the cloth: it is still carried on to a considerable extent, and furnishes employment to nearly four thousand persons; the principal articles manufactured are baize, flannel, coating, blankets, &c. The cotton manufacture, improved by the various ingenious inventions of Mr. John Kay and his sons, is also carried on; and printing establishments on an extensive scale owe their introduction to the late Sir Robert Peel, Bart., whose works, together with the houses of the workmen, extend for a considerable distance along the banks of the river: there are also large bleaching-grounds in the neighbourhood. Coal abounds within the parish. A branch of the Manchester and Bolton canal, constructed under an act of parliament in 1791, affords a facility of communication with every part of the kingdom. The market is on Saturday: fairs are held on March 8th, May 3rd, and September 18th. Bury is within the jurisdiction of the county magistrates, who hold a meeting every Saturday. Petty sessions for the division are held here every alternate Saturday. Courts leet are held in April and October, and at Whitsuntide, at which last three constables are appointed for the town, subordinate to whom is a deputy constable, who holds his office for life; the jurisdiction extends over the whole parish. A court baron is also held every third week, for the recovery of debts under 40*s*. At a place called Castle Hill, not far hence, the court for the royal manor of Tottington was anciently held; it exercised jurisdiction in capital crimes, a neighbouring eminence, called Gallows Hill, having been the place of execution.

The living is a rectory, in the archdeaconry and diocese of Chester, rated in the king's books at £29. 11. 5½., and in the patronage of the Earl of Derby. The church, dedicated to St. Mary, was taken down, with the exception of the tower, which is surmounted by a low spire, and rebuilt in 1776. St. John's chapel, a neat edifice, was erected in 1770: the living is a perpetual curacy, endowed with £600 private benefaction, £400 royal bounty, and £1500 parliamentary grant, and in the patronage of the Rector, who also presents to the other chapels in the parish. There are two meeting-houses for Independents, and one each for Primitive, Wesleyan, and New Connexion of Methodists, Presbyterians, Unitarians, and Roman Catholics. The free grammar school was founded, in 1726, by the Rev. Roger Kay, prebendary in Salisbury Cathedral, who endowed it with estates now producing yearly about £440, of which the master receives £200, and the usher £100, per annum: it has two exhibitions, of £25 per annum each, to be continued for six years during residence at either of the Universities. The same foundation includes also the instruction of ten girls, for teaching whom a mistress is allowed £7 per annum: a premium is also given with such of the scholars as are apprenticed to a trade. The management is vested in thirteen trustees, seven of whom, including the rector of Bury, the warden of Manchester, and the rector of Prestwich, must be beneficed clergymen residing within ten miles of the town, and the other six, laymen of the church of England, and possessing property within the parish. The premises, comprising two school-rooms and dwellings for the masters, are handsomely built. A charity school, for the instruction of eighty boys and thirty girls, was founded and endowed, in 1748, by the Hon. and Rev. John Stanley, formerly rector: in 1815, the income having been much augmented by annual subscription, it was enlarged into a National school, and a spacious building erected, at an expense of £1000, raised by subscription; the lower apartment is for the instruction of boys, and the upper for that of girls: about sixty of the boys and forty of the girls, on an average, are clothed, in pursuance of the will of the founder. A savings bank was established in 1822, and a dispensary in 1829; there is also a lying-in charity. The Right Hon. Sir Robert Peel, Bart., late Secretary of State for the Home Department, was born at Chamber Hall, a mansion in this parish, the present residence of the family of Hardman.

BURY, a hamlet in the parish of BROMPTON-REGIS, hundred of WILLITON and FREEMANNERS, county of SOMERSET, 2¼ miles (E.) from Dulverton. The population is returned with the parish. Near this place is an intrenched mount, called Bury Castle, supposed to have been originally a military post of the Romans, on which a mansion belonging to the family of Besilles was subsequently erected.

BURY, a parish in the hundred of Bury, rape of Arundel, county of Sussex, 4 miles (N.) from Arundel, containing, with the tything of Westburton, 504 inhabitants. The living is a discharged vicarage, in the archdeaconry and diocese of Chichester, rated in the king's books at £7. 5. 5., endowed with £600 private benefaction, £800 royal bounty, and £300 parliamentary grant, and in the patronage of the Prebendary of Bury in the Cathedral Church of Chichester. The river Arun runs on the east, and the river Rother, or Arundel Navigation, on the north.

Arms.

BURY (ST. EDMUND'S), a borough and market town, having exclusive jurisdiction, locally in the hundred of Thingoe, county of Suffolk, 26½ miles (N.W. by W.) from Ipswich, and 71 (N.E. by N.) from London, containing 9999 inhabitants. This was a place of importance long before the introduction of Christianity into Britain, and is by some antiquaries supposed to have been the *Villa Faustina* of the Romans; it evidently was in the possession of that people, from the discovery of many Roman antiquities, among which are four antique heads, of colossal dimensions, cut out of single blocks of freestone, representing some of their divinities, which were found in digging up an old foundation. Soon after the settlement of the Saxons it was made a royal burgh, and called *Beodrics worthe*, signifying the dwelling of Beodric, to whom it belonged at the time of the Octarchy, and who, at his death, bequeathed it to Edmund, afterwards canonized as a martyr, from whom it was named St. Edmund's Bury. Edmund, having succeeded to the kingdom of East Anglia, on the death of Offa, was crowned here in the fifteenth year of his age; but being afterwards taken prisoner by the Danes, who in 870 made an irruption into this part of the country, he was cruelly put to death. The circumstances attending his death and burial are thus superstitiously related: on his refusal to become a vassal to the conquerors, they bound him to a tree, pierced his body with arrows, and striking off his head, threw it into a neighbouring forest. After the enemy had retired, the East Anglians assembled to perform the funeral obsequies to the remains of their sovereign; having found the body, they went into the forest to search for the head, and discovered it between the fore paws of a wolf, which immediately resigned it on their approach: the head, on being placed in contact with the trunk, is then said to have re-united so closely, that the juncture was scarcely visible. The subject of this fabulous story has been assumed for the device of the corporate seal.

Forty days after his death, the remains of Edmund were interred at Hoxne, in a small chapel built of wood, and the report of miracles wrought at his tomb being promulgated and believed, they were removed to this place in 903. A new church was built in honour of St. Edmund, by some Secular priests, who were incorporated by King Athelstan, about the year 925, and the establishment made collegiate. The town and church having been nearly destroyed by Sweyn, King of Denmark, in 1010, were restored by Canute, who being warned, as it is said, by a vision, raised the town to more than its former splendour, rebuilt the church and monastery, which he endowed with great possessions, and, expelling the Secular canons, placed in their stead monks of the Benedictine order. The monastery of St. Edmund, in process of time, became one of the most splendid establishments in the kingdom; and, in magnificent buildings, costly decorations, valuable immunities, and rich endowments, was inferior only to that of Glastonbury. It had the royalties, or franchises, of many separate hundreds, and the right of coinage; its abbot sate in parliament, and possessed the power of determining all suits within the franchise, or liberty, of Bury, and of inflicting capital punishment. These high privileges were frequently the cause of strife and bloodshed; and in the year 1327, the townsmen and neighbouring villagers, assembling to the number of twenty thousand, headed by their alderman and capital burgesses, made a violent attack upon the monastery; they demolished the gates, doors, and windows, and reduced a considerable part of the building to ashes; they wounded the monks, and pillaged the coffers, from which they took the charters, deeds, and other valuable property, including plate, £5000 sterling, and three thousand florins of gold. The king, having been informed of this outrage, sent a military force to quell the tumult; the alderman and twenty-four of the burgesses were imprisoned, and thirty carts loaded with rioters were sent to Norwich; of these, nineteen were executed, and one was pressed to death for refusing to plead: thirty-two of the parochial clergy were also convicted as abettors; and the inhabitants were adjudged to pay a fine of £140,000, which was afterwards mitigated on the restoration of the stolen property.

The monastery remained in the possession of the Benedictine monks for five hundred and nineteen years; it contained within its precincts the churches of St. Margaret, St. Mary, and St. James, and its revenue, at the dissolution, was £2336. 16. The remains consist chiefly of the abbey gate, still entire, and displaying some elegant features in the decorated style of English architecture; the abbey bridge, in good preservation; and detached portions of the walls, which still exhibit traces of its former magnificence. About the year 1256, a fraternity of the Franciscan order came to Bury, but they were compelled by the abbot to remove beyond the precincts of the town, where their establishment continued till the dissolution. Henry I., on his return from Chartres, repaired to the shrine of St. Edmund, where he presented a rich offering, in gratitude for his safe return to his own dominions; and in 1173, Henry II., having assembled a large army at this place, to oppose his rebellious sons, caused the sacred standard of St. Edmund to be borne in front of his troops, and to its influence was ascribed the victory that he obtained over them in the battle of the 27th of October. In 1214, King John was met here by the barons, who compelled him to confirm the grant of Magna Charta, to abolish the Norman laws, and to govern the kingdom by those of Edward the Confessor. Henry III. held a parliament here in 1272, which may be regarded as the outline of a British House of Commons; and in 1296, Edward I. visited this town, where he also held a parliament. In 1381, Sir John Cavendish, then Lord Chief Justice, was brought hither and beheaded by the Suffolk and Norfolk insurgents, amounting to fifty thousand men, who afterwards attacked the abbey, executed the prior, Sir John Cambridge, and continued their career of lawless outrage till they were finally dispersed by the exertions of Spencer, the martial Bishop of Norwich. In 1526, the Dukes of Suffolk and Norfolk assembled their forces here, to quell a dangerous insurrection of the inhabitants of Lavenham and the adjacent country; and on the death of Edward VI., in 1553, John Dudley, Duke of Northumberland, made this place the rendezvous of his forces, when he caused Lady Jane Grey to be proclaimed successor to the throne. In 1555-6, twelve persons were burned at the stake, in the persecutions on account of religious tenets during the reign of Mary: in 1583, her successor Elizabeth visited Bury, where she was magnificently entertained.

The town is delightfully situated on a gentle eminence, on the western bank of the river Larke, also called the Bourne, in the centre of an open and richly cultivated tract of country: the streets are spacious, well paved, and lighted with oil, under an act of parliament passed in the 51st of George III., and extended for general improvement in the 1st of George IV. The houses are in general uniform and handsomely built, and the inhabitants are amply supplied with water: the air is salubrious, the environs abound with interesting scenery, and the peculiar cleanliness of the town, and the number and variety of its public institutions, render it desirable as a place of residence. The subscription library, formed by the union of two separate institutions, one of which was established in 1790, and the other in 1795, contains a valuable collection, and is liberally supported: there are also a news-room, four circulating libraries, and a billiard-room. The botanical gardens, containing a well-arranged assortment of aquatic, alpine, and herbaceous plants, and forming an agreeable promenade, in one of the finest situations, commanding a view of the ruins of the abbey and much picturesque scenery, were established by Mr. N. S. Hodson, and are supported by an annual subscription of two guineas from each member: the theatre, a neat building, erected in 1819, is opened during the great fair, by the Norwich company of comedians. Concerts take place occasionally in the old theatre, built in 1780, which has been converted to this use; and assemblies are held during the season at the subscription rooms, erected in 1804, and handsomely fitted up. A mechanics' institution has recently been established. The spinning of yarn was formerly the principal source of employment for the poor, and the halls in which the wool was deposited are yet standing; but no particular branch of manufacture is at present carried on. About a mile from the town the river Larke becomes navigable to Lynn, whence coal and other commodities are brought hither in small barges. The market days are Wednesday and Saturday, the former for corn, &c., the latter for meat and poultry. Fairs are held on the Tuesday in Easter week, for toys, &c.; October 1st, for horses, cattle, butter, and cheese: the great fair commences on the 10th of the same month, and generally continues about three weeks; and December 1st, for cattle, butter, cheese, &c.

Corporate Seal.

The government, by charter of incorporation granted in the 4th of James I., and extended in subsequent reigns, is vested in an alderman, recorder, twelve capital burgesses, and twenty-four common councilmen, assisted by a town-clerk, four serjeants at mace, and subordinate officers. The alderman, who is chosen annually from among the capital burgesses, recorder, and coroner, are justices of the peace; there are also five assistant justices, chosen either from the burgesses, or from the inhabitants generally: these magistrates exercise exclusive jurisdiction. The freedom of the borough is acquired by servitude and gift, but is never taken up. The corporation hold courts of session for the trial of capital offenders, and a court of pleas to the amount of £200: a court for the recovery of debts under 40*s.* is held under the chief steward of the liberty of Bury. The assizes for the county and liberty are also held here: there is always a separate commission for the borough and liberty. The shire-hall, on the site of the ancient church of St. Margaret, is a neat modern building, containing two courts for civil and criminal causes. The guildhall, where the borough courts are held, has a beautiful ancient porch of flint, brick, and stone, on which are sculptured the arms of the borough; the hall contains some good portraits of members of the corporation, and representatives of the borough, among which is a portrait of Admiral Hervey, by Sir Joshua Reynolds; over the entrance is a chamber wherein the records of the corporation are deposited. The town bridewell, situated on the Hog hill, was formerly a synagogue; the circular windows bespeak its antiquity, and it appears, from other parts, to be of Norman origin. The new county gaol, erected in 1805, is a spacious building upon the radiating principle, the keeper's house being in the centre: the buildings are surrounded by a stone wall twenty feet high, enclosing an octagonal area, the diameter of which is two hundred and ninety-two feet; they consist of four wings, and have been lately enlarged; a tread-wheel has also been recently added. The house of correction, near the gaol, enclosed within a high wall, is arranged with a due regard to classification; and the internal regulations are superior to those of most others in the country. The borough first received a precept to return representatives to parliament in the 30th of Edward I., but made no subsequent return till the 4th of James I., since which it has continued to send two members: the right of election is vested exclusively in the alderman and thirty-six burgesses, who are in the interest of the Duke of Grafton and the Marquis of Bristol: the alderman is the returning officer, and has the casting vote.

Bury comprises the parishes of St. Mary and St. James; the living of each is a donative, in the patronage of the Mayor and Corporation. The church, dedicated to St. Mary, completed about the year 1433, is a spacious and elegant structure in the later style of English architecture, with a low massive tower; the north door is in the decorated style, and the porch, the roof of which is singularly beautiful, is of later date: the roof of the nave is finely carved, and supported upon slender-shafted columns; the roof of the chancel is painted and gilt, and highly embellished in compartments: on the north side of the altar is a monument of white marble to the memory of Mary Tudor, third daughter of Henry VII., wife of Louis XII. of France, and afterwards of Charles Brandon, Duke of Suffolk. The church of St. James is a large and handsome edifice, in the later style of English architecture, of which the western end is a rich and beautiful specimen: the church gate, leading to the precinct of the abbey, is surmounted by a fine Norman tower, containing the bells: the chancel has been much altered from its original character, by the insertion of modern windows. There are two places of worship for Independents, and one each for Baptists, the Society of Friends, Methodists, Unitarians, and Roman Catholics.

The grammar school, founded by Edward VI., is open to the sons of inhabitants, upon the payment of two guineas entrance, and the same sum per annum; it has four exhibitions of the value of £20 each, and two others of about the same value each, per annum, to either of the Universities: there are about one hundred scholars on the foundation: a new school-house has been erected by public contribution; over the entrance is a bust of the founder, with an appropriate inscription, and adjoining the school-room is a good house for the master: the institution, in which several distinguished individuals have received the rudiments of their education, has long occupied a high station among the schools in the country. There are four charity schools, in two of which four hundred boys, and in the others one hundred and fifty girls, are instructed and clothed, supported partly by an endowment of £70 per annum, and partly by subscription. The almshouses, about one hundred in number, were founded by Mr. Edmund King, Mrs. Margaret Drury, and others, and are under the superintendence of trustees, in whom funds, amounting to £2000 per annum, have been at various times invested for charitable uses. Clopton's asylum was founded for the support of six aged widowers, and the same number of widows, being decayed housekeepers, by Poley Clopton, M.D., who endowed it with property producing £300 per annum; it is a neat brick building with projecting wings, having the arms of the founder over the entrance in the centre. The Suffolk general hospital, established in 1825, and supported by subscription, was originally built by government for an ordnance depôt, but was afterwards purchased and converted to its present use; it contains accommodation for forty patients, and is under the superintendence of a president, vice-presidents, and governors, and gratuitously attended by the physicians and surgeons in the town and neighbourhood. Near the north gate, on the road to Thetford, are the ruins of St. Saviour's hospital, founded in the reign of King John, with an income of one hundred and fifty-three marks, where the "good" Duke of Gloucester is believed to have been murdered. A little beyond it stood St. Thomas' hospital and chapel, now a private dwelling; and about half a mile distant may be traced the site of the old priory. Various other ruins connected with the abbey and its early history are visible. Many minor institutions were dependent on it, of which there are not at present any remains: among these may be noticed a college of priests, dedicated to the Holy Name of Jesus, founded in the reign of Edward IV., and suppressed in that of Edward VI.; an hospital, dedicated to St. John, founded by one of the abbots in the reign of Edward I.; an hospital dedicated to St. Nicholas, founded also by an abbot of St. Edmund's, the revenue of which, at the dissolution, was £6. 19. 11.; and St. Peter's hospital, founded in the latter part of the reign of Henry I., or the beginning of that of Stephen, the revenue of which, at the dissolution, was £10. 18. 11. This is the native place of Sir Nicholas Bacon, Bishops Gardiner and Pretyman, and Dr. Blomfield, the present Bishop of London. Bury confers the title of viscount on the family of Keppel, earls of Albemarle.

BURYTHORP, a parish in the wapentake of Buckrose, East riding of the county of York, 4¾ miles (S.) from New Malton, containing 216 inhabitants. The living is a discharged rectory, in the archdeaconry of the East riding, and diocese of York, rated in the king's books at £6. 16. 3., and in the patronage of the Crown. The church is dedicated to All Saints. There is a place of worship for Wesleyan Methodists. In 1768, Francis Consith died here, at the age of one hundred and fifty.

BUSBY (GREAT), a township in the parish of Stokesley, western division of the liberty of Langbaurgh, North riding of the county of York, 2¼ miles (S.) from Stokesley, containing, with the hamlet of Little Busby, 117 inhabitants.

BUSCOT, or BURWASCOT, a parish in the hundred of Shrivenham, county of Berks, 4 miles (N.W. by W.) from Great Farringdon, containing 421 inhabitants. The living is a rectory, in the archdeaconry of Berks, and diocese of Salisbury, rated in the king's books at £21. 2. 8½., and in the patronage of Jeremy Baker, Esq. The church is dedicated to St. Mary.

BUSHBURY, a parish comprising the township of Essington, in the eastern division of the hundred of Cuttlestone, and the hamlet of Moseley, in the northern division of the hundred of Seisdon, county of Stafford, 2¾ miles (N. by E.) from Wolverhampton, and containing 1229 inhabitants. The living is a discharged vicarage, in the archdeaconry of Stafford, and diocese of Lichfield and Coventry, rated in the king's books at £7. 11. 5½., endowed with £200 private benefaction, and £200 royal bounty, and in the patronage of the principal land-owners. The church, dedicated to St. Mary, was built about the year 1460. There are considerable coal-works in this parish, which is intersected by the Staffordshire and Worcestershire canal. Moseley Hall was the place of temporary concealment for Charles II., when on his way to Bentley.

BUSHBY, a hamlet in the parish of Thurnby, hundred of Gartree, county of Leicester, 4¼ miles (E. by S.) from Leicester, containing 87 inhabitants.

BUSHEY, a parish in the hundred of Dacorum, though locally in the hundred of Cashio, or liberty of St. Albans, county of Hertford, 1¼ mile (S.E. by E.) from Watford, containing 1507 inhabitants. The living is a rectory, in the archdeaconry of St. Albans, and diocese of London, rated in the king's books at £18. 2. 1., and in the patronage of the Rector and Fellows of Exeter College, Oxford. The church is dedicated to St.

James. In answer to a writ of *quo warranto*, issued in the third of Edward I., David de Jarpenvil claimed the privilege of holding a market here.

BUSHLEY, a parish in the lower division of the hundred of PERSHORE, county of WORCESTER, $2\frac{1}{4}$ miles (N. W.) from Tewkesbury, containing 366 inhabitants. The living is a perpetual curacy, in the archdeaconry and diocese of Worcester, endowed with £400 royal bounty, and £200 parliamentary grant, and in the patronage of T. Dowdeswell, Esq. The church is dedicated to St. Peter. Here is a small charity school, supported by Miss Dowdeswell. The eastern boundary of this parish is formed by the river Severn, into which the Avon falls from the opposite side, below Tewkesbury, in Gloucestershire.

BUSLINGTHORPE, a parish in the wapentake of LAWRESS, parts of LINDSEY, county of LINCOLN, 4 miles (S.W. by S.) from Market-Rasen, containing 55 inhabitants. The living is a discharged rectory, in the archdeaconry of Stow, and diocese of Lincoln, rated in the king's books at £2, endowed with £200 royal bounty, and in the patronage of the Governors of the Charterhouse, London.

BUSTABECK, a township in the parish of CASTLE-SOWERBY, LEATH ward, county of CUMBERLAND, $4\frac{1}{2}$ miles (N.E.) from Hesket-Newmarket, containing 248 inhabitants.

BUSTON (HIGH), a township in that part of the parish of WARKWORTH which is in the eastern division of COQUETDALE ward, county of NORTHUMBERLAND, $4\frac{3}{4}$ miles (S.E.) from Alnwick, containing 95 inhabitants.

BUSTON (LOW), a township in that part of the parish of WARKWORTH which is in the eastern division of COQUETDALE ward, county of NORTHUMBERLAND, 5 miles (S. E. by S.) from Alnwick, containing 85 inhabitants.

BUTCOMBE, a parish in the hundred of HARTCLIFFE with BEDMINSTER, county of SOMERSET, $8\frac{1}{2}$ miles (N.E.) from Axbridge, containing 213 inhabitants. The living is a discharged rectory, in the archdeaconry of Bath, and diocese of Bath and Wells, rated in the king's books at £6. 17. 10., endowed with £200 private benefaction, and £400 royal bounty, and in the patronage of the Rev. R. P. Hassell. The church, dedicated to St. Michael, is a very old structure. A singular barrow was opened here in 1788, that exhibited an entire specimen of a well-arranged family vault: the interior consisted of an avenue formed by triplets of stones, with small cells nine feet long and two and quarter broad, in which were found skulls and other fragments of human bones.

BUTELAND, a joint township with Broomhope, in the parish of BIRTLEY, north-eastern division of TINDALE ward, county of NORTHUMBERLAND, $2\frac{1}{2}$ miles (E. by S.) from Bellingham. The population is returned with Birtley and Chollerton. This township is connected with Birtley in ecclesiastical matters only; in civil affairs it is included within the parish of Chollerton, from which Birtley was separated in 1765: an extensive farm here belongs to Greenwich hospital.

BUTLEIGH, a parish in the hundred of WHITLEY, county of SOMERSET, $4\frac{1}{2}$ miles (S. S. E.) from Glastonbury, containing, with Wootton-Butleigh, 809 inhabitants. The living is a vicarage, with the perpetual curacy of Baltonsborough annexed, in the exempt jurisdiction of Glastonbury, which belongs to the Bishop of Bath and Wells, rated in the king's books at £12. 6. 8., and in the patronage of the Hon. and Rev. G. Neville Grenville. The church is dedicated to St. Leonard. This parish abounds with blue lyas stone. Here is a chalybeate spring, but in disuse.

BUTLEY, a township in the parish of PRESTBURY, hundred of MACCLESFIELD, county palatine of CHESTER, $2\frac{3}{4}$ miles (N. by W.) from Macclesfield, containing 579 inhabitants. At the time of the Norman survey, this place, then the property of one Ulluric, a Saxon freeman, was exempted, and is consequently unnoticed in Domesday-book, a mark of clemency which the owner, who was allowed to continue in undisturbed possession, probably acquired by some signal service to the Conqueror. The manufacture of silk is carried on to some extent. There is a place of worship for Wesleyan Methodists, with a school attached, in which about one hundred children are instructed. Some tumuli were discovered in the vicinity a few years since. This is the birthplace of Thomas Newton, a distinguished writer in the sixteenth century.

BUTLEY, a parish in the hundred of LOES, county of SUFFOLK, $7\frac{1}{4}$ miles (E. by N.) from Woodbridge, containing 321 inhabitants. The living is a perpetual curacy, in the archdeaconry of Suffolk, and diocese of Norwich, endowed with £15 per annum private benefaction, and £600 royal bounty, and in the patronage of C. Thelluson, Esq. The church is dedicated to St. John the Baptist. This parish is bounded on the east by the river Butley, over which there are two ferries to Orford. A priory of Black canons, dedicated to the Blessed Virgin, was founded in 1171, by Ranulph de Glanvil, a celebrated lawyer, and afterwards Justiciary of England: the revenue, at the dissolution, was £318. 17. 2.: there are some trifling remains of the buildings.

BUTSFIELD, a township in that part of the parish of LANCHESTER which is in the western division of CHESTER ward, county palatine of DURHAM, 11 miles (W. by N.) from Durham, containing 226 inhabitants. Two Roman aqueducts, for supplying the station at Lanchester, may be traced in the neighbourhood, particularly in the grounds belonging to Thomas White, Esq., who, on the enclosure of the common lands, purchased a part which was sold to defray the expense incurred in carrying the act into effect, and out of a barren waste, in the course of a few years, has raised the thriving and well-planted estate of Woodlands.

BUTTER-CRAMBE, a township in that part of the parish of BOSSALL which is in the wapentake of BULMER, North riding of the county of YORK, $9\frac{1}{2}$ miles (N. E. by E.) from York, containing 235 inhabitants. The village is pleasantly situated on the western bank of the river Derwent, which is here navigable, and is crossed by a stone bridge. A chapel of ease has been erected here. In the vicinity is Aldby Park, on an eminence which was originally the site of a Roman station, and subsequently that of a royal Saxon ville.

BUTTERLAW, a township in that part of the parish of NEWBURN which is in the western division of CASTLE ward, county of NORTHUMBERLAND, $5\frac{1}{4}$ miles (N. W. by W.) from Newcastle, containing 28 inhabitants.

BUTTERLEIGH, a parish, forming a detached portion of the hundred of CLISTON, locally in the hundred of Hayridge, county of DEVON, 3¼ miles (S. E. by S.) from Tiverton, containing 144 inhabitants. The living is a discharged rectory, in the archdeaconry and diocese of Exeter, rated in the king's books at £10. 8. 8., and in the patronage of the Crown.

BUTTERLEY, a hamlet in the township of RIPLEY, parish of PENTRICH, hundred of MORLESTON and LITCHURCH, county of DERBY, 3 miles (S.) from Alfreston. The population is returned with Ripley. The extensive iron-works at this place belong to a company formed in 1792, who are also owners of various similar establishments, collieries, and lime-works in the vicinity. The ore and coal are conveyed to the Butterley works by railways, and by the Cromford canal, which, by means of a tunnel two thousand nine hundred and sixty-six yards in length, passes under the works; to this a shaft about thirty-six yards in depth has been sunk, up which the ore is raised by a steam-engine. There are about fifteen hundred workmen; and the number of steam-engines employed in the works and mines is twenty-six, affording an aggregate power equal to that of seven hundred and six horses. All the heavier articles in cast-iron, and machinery of various kinds, are produced at these works. Among those made for different public undertakings may be enumerated the cast-iron work for Vauxhall bridge, the great roof over the quay and other works at the West India docks, the bridges and lock-gates of the Caledonian canal, a great part of the cast-iron work for the dock-yard at Sheerness, the whole of that for the harbours and docks at Dublin and Leith, the large main pipes for supplying Edinburgh with water, and the pipes for many of the Water and Gas Companies in England: several steam-engines for vessels, and for exportation to the colonies, have been made: the entire process of constructing them, from the raising of the ore to completing the engine, is here carried on. The Cromford canal affords a medium for the conveyance of goods by water to Cromford, where the navigation terminates, and where the Cromford and High Peak railway, planned by Josias Jessop, Esq., of Butterley (the expense of constructing which is estimated at £180,000), commences, extending to Whalley bridge, near Stockport, a distance of about thirty-two miles and a half: another, called the Stockport Junction railway, has been planned connecting the former with the Manchester and Liverpool line, and thus forming a distinct medium of communication between Cromford and Liverpool.

BUTTERLEY, a township in the parish of EDWIN-RALPH, hundred of WOLPHY, though locally in the hundred of Broxash, county of HEREFORD, 3½ miles (N. W. by N.) from Bromyard. The population is returned with the parish.

BUTTERMERE, a chapelry in the parish of BRIGHAM, ALLERDALE ward above Derwent, county of CUMBERLAND, 8½ miles (S. W. by W.) from Keswick, containing 136 inhabitants. The living is a perpetual curacy, in the archdeaconry of Richmond, and diocese of Chester, endowed with £1000 royal bounty, and £200 parliamentary grant, and in the patronage of the inhabitants. The village lies in a deep winding valley, environed by high rocky mountains, between the lake of Buttermere, noted for its char, and Crummock water, and in a district celebrated for its picturesque and romantic beauty. Mines of lead and copper were formerly worked in these mountains: many of the labourers are now occupied in the extensive quarries of fine blue slate in Honister Crag.

BUTTERMERE, a parish in the hundred of KINWARDSTONE, county of WILTS, 5¼ miles (S.) from Hungerford, containing 136 inhabitants. The living is a rectory, in the archdeaconry of Wilts, and diocese of Salisbury, rated in the king's books at £10, and in the patronage of the Bishop of Winchester. The church is dedicated to St. James.

BUTTERTON, a township in the parish of TRENTHAM, northern division of the hundred of PIREHILL, county of STAFFORD, containing 22 inhabitants.

BUTTERTON, a chapelry in the parish of MAYFIELD, southern division of the hundred of TOTMONSLOW, county of STAFFORD, 6½ miles (E.) from Leek, containing 432 inhabitants. The living is a perpetual curacy, in the archdeaconry of Stafford, and diocese of Lichfield and Coventry, endowed with £400 royal bounty, and £1400 parliamentary grant, and in the patronage of the Vicar of Mayfield. William Mellor, in 1754, bequeathed property now producing £16 a year, for which twenty children are taught to read. Butterton is in the honour of Tutbury, duchy of Lancaster, and within the jurisdiction of a court of pleas held at Tutbury every third Tuesday, for the recovery of debts under 40*s*.

BUTTERWICK, a tything in the parish of FOLKE, hundred of SHERBORNE, Sherborne division of the county of DORSET, 5 miles (S. E. by S.) from Sherborne. The population is returned with the parish.

BUTTERWICK, a township in the parish of SEDGEFIELD, north-eastern division of STOCKTON ward, county palatine of DURHAM, 11 miles (S. E.) from Durham, containing 54 inhabitants.

BUTTERWICK, a parish in the wapentake of SKIRBECK, parts of HOLLAND, county of LINCOLN, 4¼ miles (E. by N.) from Boston, containing 482 inhabitants. The living is a discharged vicarage, united in 1751 to that of Frieston, in the archdeaconry and diocese of Lincoln, rated in the king's books at £8. 4. 2. The church is dedicated to St. Andrew. There is a place of worship for Wesleyan Methodists. A considerable fund is applied towards the instruction of children, besides which there are various minor sums for the relief of the poor.

BUTTERWICK, a chapelry in the parish of FOXHOLES, wapentake of DICKERING, East riding of the county of YORK, 10½ miles (N. by W.) from Great Driffield, containing 93 inhabitants. The living is a perpetual curacy, in the archdeaconry of the East riding, and diocese of York, endowed with £1000 royal bounty, and £200 parliamentary grant, and in the patronage of the Rector of Foxholes.

BUTTERWICK, a township in that part of the parish of BARTON le STREET which is in the wapentake of RYEDALE, North riding of the county of YORK, 6 miles (N. W.) from New Malton, containing 50 inhabitants.

BUTTERWICK (EAST), a township in the parish of MESSINGHAM, eastern division of the wapentake of MANLEY, parts of LINDSEY, county of LINCOLN, 10¾ miles (W.) from Glandford-Bridge, containing 248 inhabitants. There is a place of worship for Wesleyan Methodists.

BUTTERWICK (WEST), a chapelry in the parish of OWSTON, western division of the wapentake of MANLEY, parts of LINDSEY, county of LINCOLN, 4¼ miles (E. N. E.) from Epworth, containing, with the hamlet of Kelfield, 669 inhabitants. The living is a perpetual curacy, in the archdeaconry of Stow, and diocese of Lincoln, endowed with £2000 parliamentary grant, and in the patronage of the Vicar of Owston. The chapel is dedicated to St. Mary. There is a place of worship for Wesleyan Methodists.

BUTTERWORTH, a township in that part of the parish of ROCHDALE which is in the hundred of SALFORD, county palatine of LANCASTER, 4½ miles (E.) from Rochdale, containing 5554 inhabitants. A school at Milnrow, in this township, was built by Alexander Butterworth, about 1720, and endowed with a rent-charge of £20, to which £7 per annum, accumulated during a vacancy in the school from the year 1789 to 1796, has been added, and for this twenty children are taught free. There are also schools at Hollingworth and Ogden, in each of which twenty children are taught and partly clothed: that at Hollingworth is endowed with an estate producing £26 a year, and that at Ogden with one producing £54 a year, both devised by John Hill, in 1727.

BUTTOLPHS, a parish in the hundred of STEYNING, rape of BRAMBER, county of SUSSEX, 1½ mile (S. E.) from Steyning, containing 62 inhabitants. The living is a discharged rectory, annexed to that of Bramber, in the archdeaconry and diocese of Chichester. The navigable river Adur runs along the eastern boundary of this parish.

BUTTSBURY, a parish in the hundred of CHELMSFORD, county of ESSEX, 7 miles (S. W. by S.) from Chelmsford, containing 522 inhabitants. The living is a perpetual curacy, with the rectory of Ingatestone annexed, in the archdeaconry of Essex, and diocese of London, endowed with £200 royal bounty, and in the patronage of the Rev. D. Lloyd. The church is dedicated to St. Mary.

BUXHALL, a parish in the hundred of STOW, county of SUFFOLK, 3¼ miles (W. by S.) from Stow-Market, containing 457 inhabitants. The living is a rectory, in the archdeaconry of Sudbury, and diocese of Norwich, rated in the king's books at £20. 0. 5., and in the patronage of the Heirs of the late Rev. H. Hill. The church, dedicated to St. Mary, is a spacious handsome structure. The Upper and Lower Ged, and the river Bret, flow through the parish. A considerable traffic in corn and coal is carried on with Stow-Market and Ipswich. There is a school for poor children, supported by voluntary contributions.

BUXLOW, formerly a chapelry, now a hamlet in the parish of KNODISHALL, hundred of BLYTHING, county of SUFFOLK, 2½ miles (S. E.) from Saxmundham. The population is returned with the parish. The chapel, now desecrated, was dedicated to St. Peter. Buxlow was annexed to the parish of Knodishall in 1721.

BUXTED, a parish in the hundred of LOXFIELD-DORSET, rape of PEVENSEY, county of SUSSEX, 1¾ mile (N. N. E.) from Uckfield, containing 1509 inhabitants. The living is a rectory, with the perpetual curacy of Uckfield annexed, in the exempt deanery of South Malling, within the peculiar jurisdiction and patronage of the Archbishop of Canterbury, rated in the king's books at £37. 5. 2½. The church, dedicated to St. Margaret, is principally in the early style of English architecture. The Rev. Anthony Sanders left, in 1718, a considerable bequest in land, for teaching and apprenticing six poor boys, and a small donation for teaching six girls. Sir Henry Fermor bequeathed £3000, directing the interest to be applied in educating and clothing ten poor children of this parish, and thirty from Rotherfield.

BUXTON, a market town and chapelry in the parish of BAKEWELL, hundred of HIGH PEAK, county of DERBY, 33 miles (N. W.) from Derby, and 159 (N. W.) by N.) from London, on the high road from Derby to Manchester, containing 1036 inhabitants. Antiquaries agree in considering this to have been a Roman station, although they have not been able to ascertain what it was called. The name of the place subsequently was *Bawkestanes*, supposed to be a corruption of *Bathanstanes*, signifying the bath stones; and one of the Roman roads still retains the name *Bathorn-gate*. The Romans, attracted by the temperature of the waters, constructed a bath, the wall of which, covered with red cement, and other parts, are still remaining: several Roman coins have been discovered. Near this spot was the intersection of two great military roads, one connecting Little Chester with Manchester, and the other leading from Middlewich to Brough, and thence to York and Aldborough, at which places respectively were stations of considerable importance. The town is situated near the source of the small river Wye, in a valley surrounded by bleak elevated tracts of moorland; but several plantations have been formed on the adjacent eminences, which, with other improvements, will materially alter the appearance of the immediate vicinity: the older part, occupying the higher ground, consists chiefly of houses built of limestone, without order, and of mean appearance; the more modern, situated in the vale, comprises elegant lodging-houses and hotels, erected and fitted up with every regard to the comfort of its numerous visitors. The old hall, built in the sixteenth century by the Earl of Shrewsbury, for several years afforded temporary accommodation to visitors of rank; and for some time it was the abode of Mary, Queen of Scots, who, while in the custody of the earl, accompanied him and his countess in an excursion to this place. It underwent considerable alteration and enlargement in 1670, and is still the principal hotel: it contains two baths for ladies, and three for gentlemen, with distinct apartments for each; besides a bath for the gratuitous use of poor invalids: there are also warm and shower baths. The spring that supplies the baths in this establishment affords an influx of sixty gallons per minute: the mean temperature of the water is 82° of Fahrenheit. The crescent, erected in 1781, by the Duke of Devonshire, is a fine range of building in the Grecian style of architecture: it is built of grit-stone obtained near the spot, and fronted with fine freestone brought from a quarry about a mile distant, and consists of three stages; the basement story is a rustic arcade, extending round the whole of the building, and surmounted by a balustrade, above which are fluted pilasters of the Doric order, supporting a richly ornamented architrave and cornice, terminated by another balustrade: in the centre of the range are the arms of the Cavendish family. Among these buildings are several spacious lodging-houses and three hotels, called St. Anne's, the Central, and the Great hotel: the last, exclusively of other apartments, contains a splendid suite of rooms in which assemblies are held three times in the week, during the season; also a library and news-room. At the eastern extremity of the crescent, and communicating with the Great hotel, two hot baths have been recently constructed, and are supplied from Bingham's well, of which the temperature is 81° of Fahrenheit, and may be raised by means of steam to any higher degree of temperature required. In the front of the crescent is a rising ground, planted with trees, and disposed in parterres, shrubberies, and walks; and behind it is an extensive range of stabling, corresponding in character, including a spacious covered ride, affording to invalids in unfavourable weather the convenience of equestrian exercise. The new square, nearly adjoining, has an arcade communicating with that of the crescent, and forming a continued promenade of considerable extent: it contains many handsome lodging-houses, and there are also others in various parts of the town, but a preference in the use of the baths is enjoyed by those visitors who inhabit the houses belonging to the Duke of Devonshire. St. Ann's well, near the crescent, the resort of those who drink the waters, is enclosed within a handsome building in the style of a Grecian temple: the water issues from the spring into a marble basin, and opposite to it is a double pump, by which both hot and cold water are simultaneously raised from springs lying within a few inches of each other: the hot spring has a temperature of 81° of Fahrenheit. The waters are sulphureous and saline, but neither fœtid nor unpalatable, the sulphur not being united with vitriolic, and but slightly with saline, particles; they are efficacious in gout, rheumatism, and indigestion, and in nervous, scorbutic, and nephritic diseases: the season commences early in June, continuing generally till October. There is also a chalybeate spring, the water of which is strongly impregnated with iron held in solution by acidulous gas. The environs abound with picturesque and romantic scenery, and with pleasant walks and rides; of the latter, the Duke's ride, on the Bakewell road, extending over the summit of a rock called the Lover's Leap, is a favourite excursion with equestrians: a pack of harriers is kept by subscription. The principal branch of trade consists in the manufacture and sale of many beautiful ornaments in fluor spar, alabaster, and other mineral productions of the Peak. A great quantity of lime, noted for its strength, is burnt to the west of the town, the workmen and their families living in huts excavated in the limestone rocks, near which passes the Peak Forest railway. The market is on Saturday: fairs are held on February 3rd, April 1st, May 2nd, and September 8th, for cattle. The town is in the honour of Tutbury, duchy of Lancaster, and within the jurisdiction of a court held at Tutbury every third Tuesday, for the recovery of debts under 40*s*.

The living is a perpetual curacy, in the peculiar jurisdiction of the Dean and Chapter of Lichfield, endowed with £200 private benefaction, £600 royal bounty, and £800 parliamentary grant, and in the patronage of the Duke of Devonshire. A new church, an elegant structure near the town, but without the limits of the chapelry, was erected under an act passed in the 51st of George III., in 1812, at the expense of his Grace. There are places of worship for Independents, Wesleyan Methodists, and Unitarians. A school, now conducted on Dr. Bell's plan, was founded towards the close of the seventeenth century, and re-opened in 1817, after a suspension of twenty-five years, during which period its affairs were in Chancery: the income, arising from land and property in the funds, is £94 per annum: the school is held in the ancient chapel. The bath charity, for the benefit of poor invalids coming hither for the use of the waters, is liberally supported by subscription, and is under the superintendence of a president and committee: applicants, on presenting a certificate from the minister of their parish, signed by a medical practitioner, are not only permitted to bathe free of expense, but for one month receive a weekly allowance of money for their support, from a fund raised by a contribution of one shilling from every visitor who remains for more than one day in the town: according to the last annual report, one thousand one hundred persons had received relief to the amount of £450. About three quarters of a mile to the south-west of the town is Poole's Hole, a dark and dreary cavern, narrow and very low at the entrance, but spacious and lofty within, abounding with stalactites representing various natural forms; near the extremity is a rude mass, called the pillar of Mary, Queen of Scots, beyond which few persons advance: the visitors are accompanied by guides with candles, the light of which is brilliantly reflected from the various incrustations and chrystals that decorate the sides, and hang from the roof, producing a beautiful, but dazzling, effect. About one mile and a half beyond the cavern is Diamond Hill, so called from the detached chrystals found there in profusion, denominated Buxton diamonds; their form is hexagonal, and their surface and angles well defined, but of bad colour; when first found they are hard, but they soon lose that property.

BUXTON, a joint township with Coxhall, in that part of the parish of Bucknill which is in the hundred of Wigmore, county of Hereford, 4½ miles (E. by N.) from Knighton, containing, with Coxhall, 134 inhabitants.

BUXTON, a parish in the southern division of the hundred of Erpingham, county of Norfolk, 3¼ miles (N. W.) from Coltishall, containing 504 inhabitants. The living is a discharged vicarage, with the rectories of Oxnead and Skeyton annexed, in the archdeaconry and diocese of Norwich, rated in the king's books at £5. 13. 9., endowed with £200 royal bounty, and in the patronage of George Anson, Esq. The church is dedicated to St. Andrew. There is a place of worship for Particular Baptists. In this parish are two almshouses, endowed by Sir John Picto with eighteen acres of land. This was a subordinate Roman station, the name of which is not precisely known; several coins, urns, and other remains of that people have been discovered.

BWLCH, a township in that part of the parish of Cwmyoy which is in the hundred of Ewyaslacy, county of Hereford, containing 81 inhabitants.

BYAL-FEN, an extra-parochial liberty, in the hundred and Isle of Ely, county of Cambridge.

BYERS-GREEN, a township in that part of the parish of St. Andrew, Auckland, which is in the south-eastern division of Darlington ward, county palatine of Durham, 4 miles (N. N. E.) from Bishop-Auckland, containing 231 inhabitants.

BYFIELD, a parish in the hundred of Chipping-Warden, county of Northampton, 7¼ miles (S. W. by S.) from Daventry, containing 903 inhabitants. The living is a rectory, in the archdeaconry of Northampton, and diocese of Peterborough, rated in the king's books at £28, and in the patronage of the President and Fellows of Corpus Christi College, Oxford. The church is dedicated to the Holy Cross. In 1694, Samuel Greenwood bequeathed a rent-charge of £2. 14. for teaching seven poor children; and, in 1779, the Rev. John Knightly left £2. 17. 6. per annum, which is now paid to the master of a Sunday school.

BYFLEET, a parish in the first division of the hundred of Godley, county of Surrey, 2½ miles (W.N.W.) from Cobham, containing 427 inhabitants. The living is a rectory, in the archdeaconry of Surrey, and diocese of Winchester, rated in the king's books at £9. 11. 8., and in the patronage of the Crown. The church is dedicated to St. Mary. There is a place of worship for Particular Baptists. The manor was presented by Edward II. to his favourite, Piers de Gaveston; and Henry VIII. was nursed at a house in this place. The Wey and Arun Junction canal passes through the parish. An old mansion, called Byfield Park, at present a farm-house, was built by Edward the Black Prince.

BYFORD, a parish in the hundred of Grimsworth, county of Hereford, 7½ miles (W. N. W.) from Hereford, containing 211 inhabitants. The living is a rectory, in the archdeaconry and diocese of Hereford, rated in the king's books at £7. 1. 8., and in the patronage of the Crown. The church is dedicated to St. John the Baptist.

BYGRAVE, a parish in the hundred of Odsey, county of Hertford, 2 miles (N. E. by N.) from Baldock, containing 107 inhabitants. The living is a rectory, in the archdeaconry of Huntingdon, and diocese of Lincoln, rated in the king's books at £17. 9. 7., and in the patronage of the Marquis of Salisbury.

BYKER, a township in that part of the parish of All Saints, Newcastle, which is in the eastern division of Castle ward, county of Northumberland, 1¼ mile (E.) from Newcastle, containing 3852 inhabitants. The Wesleyan Methodists have a meeting-house here. There are glass-houses and other manufactories.

BYLAND cum MEMBRIS, a township in the parish of Coxwold, wapentake of Birdforth, North riding of the county of York, 7 miles (S. W. by W.) from Helmsley, containing, with Oldstead and Wass, situated in Kilburn parish, 372 inhabitants. In 1177, a convent of Cistercian monks was founded here, the revenue of which, at the dissolution, amounted to £295. 5. 4.: it was a noble building; the western front, part of a fine circular window, one end of the transept, and some parts of the lateral aisles yet remain, affording a beautiful specimen of early English architecture. On the removal of a portion of the ruins, in 1818, a stone coffin, containing, according to tradition, the remains of Roger de Mowbray, its founder, was discovered, and is still preserved at Myton. Fragments of a beautiful tesselated pavement were also found.

BYLAND (OLD), a parish in the wapentake of Birdforth, North riding of the county of York, 4¾ miles (W. N. W.) from Helmsley, containing 133 inhabitants. The living is a perpetual curacy, in the archdeaconry of Cleveland, and diocese of York, endowed with £800 royal bounty, and in the patronage of G. Wombwell, Esq.

BYLAUGH, a parish in the hundred of Eynsford, county of Norfolk, 5¼ miles (N. E.) from East Dereham, containing 93 inhabitants. The living is a perpetual curacy, in the archdeaconry and diocese of Norwich, endowed with £200 private benefaction, £600 royal bounty, and £200 parliamentary grant, and in the patronage of the Bishop of Norwich. The church, dedicated to St. Mary, is a venerable edifice, much dilapidated.

BYLEY, a joint township with Yatehouse, in that part of the parish of Middlewich which is in the hundred of Northwich, county palatine of Chester, 1¼ mile (N. E. by N.) from Middlewich, containing, with Yatehouse, 132 inhabitants.

BYRNESS, a chapelry in the parish of Elsdon, southern division of Coquetdale ward, county of Northumberland, 13¾ miles (N. N. W.) from Bellingham. The population is returned with the parish. The living is a perpetual curacy, in the archdeaconry of Northumberland, and diocese of Durham, endowed with £200 private benefaction, £400 royal bounty, and £300 parliamentary grant, and in the patronage of the Rector of Elsdon. The chapel was rebuilt, in 1793, by subscription. Here was a Druidical temple, but every vestige of it has disappeared.

BYROME, a joint township with Pool, in the parish of Brotherton, partly within the liberty of St. Peter of York, East riding, but chiefly in the lower division of the wapentake of Barkstone-Ash, West riding, of the county of York, 1¾ mile (N. N. W.) from Ferry-Bridge. The population is returned with Pool.

BYSHOTTLES, a joint township with Brandon, in the parish of Brancepeth, north-western division of Darlington ward, county palatine of Durham, 4 miles (W. S. W.) from Durham. The population is returned with Brandon.

BYTHAM (CASTLE), a parish in the wapentake of Beltisloe, parts of Kesteven, county of Lincoln, 5 miles (S. by W.) from Corby, comprising the chapelry of Holywell with Awnby, and the hamlet of Counthorpe, and containing 736 inhabitants. The living is a discharged vicarage, with which the rectory of Little Bytham is consolidated, in the archdeaconry and diocese of Lincoln, rated in the king's books at £7. 13. 6., and in the patronage of the Bishop of Lincoln and the Dean and Chapter, alternately. The church is dedicated to St. James. There is a place of worship for Wesleyan Methodists.

BYTHAM (LITTLE), a parish in the wapentake of Beltisloe, parts of Kesteven, county of Lincoln, 5 miles (S.) from Corby, containing 223 inhabitants. The living is a rectory, consolidated with the vicarage of Castle Bytham, in the archdeaconry and diocese of Lincoln, rated in the king's books at £4. 8. 4. The church is dedicated to St. Medardus.

BYTHORN, a parish in the hundred of Leightonstone, county of Huntingdon, 6½ miles (N. W. by N.) from Kimbolton, containing 293 inhabitants. The living is a perpetual curacy, united to the rectory of Brington, in the archdeaconry of Huntingdon, and diocese of Lincoln. The church is dedicated to St. Lawrence. There is a place of worship for Particular Baptists.

BYTON, a parish in the hundred of WIGMORE, county of HEREFORD, 4½ miles (E.S.E.) from Presteigne, containing 167 inhabitants. The living is a discharged rectory, in the archdeaconry and diocese of Hereford, rated in the king's books at £5, endowed with £200 royal bounty, and in the patronage of the Crown. The church is dedicated to St. Mary.

BYWELL (ST. ANDREW), a parish in the eastern division of TINDALE ward, county of NORTHUMBERLAND, comprising the townships of Bearl, Broomhaugh, Riding, Stocksfield-Hall, and Styford, and containing 399 inhabitants, exclusively of one-fourth of the population of the township of Bywell St. Andrew and St. Peter, which is in this parish, but included in the return for Bywell St. Peter. The living is a discharged vicarage, with the perpetual curacy of Shotley annexed, in the archdeaconry of Northumberland, and diocese of Durham, rated in the king's books at £3. 9. 2., endowed with £200 private benefaction, and £200 royal bounty, and in the patronage of T. W. Beaumont, Esq. The church is a small edifice with a lofty steeple. The river Tyne runs through the parish.

BYWELL (ST. PETER'S), a parish in the eastern division of TINDALE ward, county of NORTHUMBERLAND, comprising the chapelry of Whittonstall, and the townships of East Acomb, Broomley, Espershields with Millshields, High Fotherly, Heally, Newlands, Newton, Newton Hall, and Stelling, and part of the township of Bywell St. Andrew and St. Peter, and containing 1406 inhabitants, of which number, 174 are in the township of Bywell St. Andrew and St. Peter, 8 miles (E. by S.) from Hexham, on the northern bank of the Tyne. The living is a vicarage, in the archdeaconry of Northumberland, and diocese of Durham, rated in the king's books at £9. 18. 1½., endowed with £600 parliamentary grant, and in the patronage of the Dean and Chapter of Durham. There are meeting-houses in the parish for Baptists, the Society of Friends, and Wesleyan Methodists. Bywell was anciently the head of a barony, the ruins of the castle being still visible at a short distance from Bywell Hall. The village is partly situated in the parish of Bywell St. Andrew, and partly in that of Bywell St. Peter, and was formerly noted for the manufacture of saddlers ironmongery, which was in a flourishing state in the middle of the sixteenth century; it has now wholly declined, but there are still some vestiges of the works. In the river Tyne, which flows southward of this parish, two stone piers of an ancient bridge are still standing.

C.

CABOURN, a parish in the wapentake of BRADLEY-HAVERSTOE, parts of LINDSEY, county of LINCOLN, 1¾ mile (E. N. E.) from Caistor, containing 105 inhabitants. The living is a discharged vicarage, in the archdeaconry and diocese of Lincoln, rated in the king's books at £5. 18. 4., endowed with £400 royal bounty, and in the patronage of Lord Yarborough. The church is dedicated to St. Nicholas.

CABUS, a township in the parish of GARSTANG, hundred of AMOUNDERNESS, county palatine of LANCASTER, 2 miles (N.) from Garstang, containing 277 inhabitants.

CADBURY, a parish in the hundred of HAYRIDGE, county of DEVON, 6¼ miles (S.W.) from Tiverton, containing 242 inhabitants. The living is a discharged vicarage, in the archdeaconry and diocese of Exeter, rated in the king's books at £9. 4. 3., and in the patronage of the Crown. The church is dedicated to St. Michael. On the summit of a high hill, called Cadbury Castle, is an enclosure nearly circular, consisting of a single vallum and fosse, supposed to be either of British or of Roman origin.

CADBURY (NORTH), a parish in the hundred of CATSASH, county of SOMERSET, 3¼ miles (S.) from Castle-Cary, containing, with the hamlets of Galhampton, and Yarlington, with Woolston and Clapton, 1003 inhabitants. The living is a rectory, in the archdeaconry of Wells, and diocese of Bath and Wells, rated in the king's books at £28. 17. 3½., and in the patronage of the Master and Fellows of Emanuel College, Cambridge. The church, dedicated to St. Michael, is a stately and beautiful pile, pleasantly situated on the ridge of a hill. Henry V., in the fourth year of his reign, gave license to Dame Elizabeth Botreaux, relict of Sir William Botreaux the elder, to found and endow in the church (which she had then rebuilt) a college for seven secular chaplains (one of whom to be rector) and four clerks: it was to have been dedicated to St. Michael; but it does not appear ever to have been settled. On the ridge of a high hill overlooking the village is a Roman intrenchment, of an oval form, surrounded by a large double rampart composed of loose limestone, the produce of the spot on which it is situated.

CADBURY (SOUTH), a parish in the hundred of CATSASH, county of SOMERSET, 4½ miles (S.) from Castle-Cary, containing 257 inhabitants. The living is a rectory, in the archdeaconry of Wells, and diocese of Bath and Wells, rated in the king's books at £10. 3. 1½., and in the patronage of Francis Newman, Esq. The church is dedicated to St. Thomas à Becket. Near the village are the remains of one of the most famous ancient fortifications in England: it was situated on the northern extremity of a ridge of hills, and encircled by four trenches; its figure inclined to a square, but conforming to the slope of the hill: the area is upwards of thirty acres. A higher work within, surrounded by a trench, is called King Arthur's palace; the rampart is composed of large stones covered with earth, with only one entrance, from the east, guarded by six or seven trenches. Numerous Roman coins, in gold, silver, and copper, have been discovered, chiefly those of Antoninus and Faustina; and, among other antiquities, a silver horse-shoe was dug up about the middle of the sixteenth century. Antiquaries are divided as to the origin of this place: the most probable conjecture seems to be that of Stukeley, who ascribes it to the Romans.

CADDINGTON, a parish partly in the hundred of FLITT, county of BEDFORD, but chiefly in the hundred of DACORUM, county of HERTFORD, 1¾ mile (W. S. W.) from Luton, containing, with a portion of the chapelry of Market-Street, 1549 inhabitants. The living is a vicarage, in the archdeaconry of Bedford, and diocese of Lincoln, rated in the king's books at £10, and in the patronage of the Dean and Chapter of St. Paul's, London. The church, dedicated to All Saints, is in Bedfordshire. Market, originally Markgate, Cell, in this parish, was founded in 1145, chiefly by Geoffrey, Abbot of St. Albans, on land given by the Dean and Chapter of St. Paul's, for nuns of the Benedictine order, whose revenue, in the 26th of Henry VIII., was £143. 18. 3: the proprietor appropriated part of the lands to the endowment of a chapel and a school in Market-Street; but it does not appear that they were ever applied to that purpose.

CADEBY, a parish in the hundred of SPARKENHOE, county of LEICESTER, 1¼ mile (E. S. E.) from Market-Bosworth, containing, with a part of the township of Osbaston, 343 inhabitants. The living is a rectory, in the archdeaconry of Leicester, and diocese of Lincoln, rated in the king's books at £4. 10. 2½., and in the patronage of Sir Willoughby Dixie, Bart. The church is dedicated to All Saints.

CADEBY, or CATEBY, a chapelry in the parish of SPROTBROUGH, northern division of the wapentake of STRAFFORTH and TICKHILL, West riding of the county of YORK, 4½ miles (W. S. W.) from Doncaster, containing 169 inhabitants.

CADELEIGH, a parish in the hundred of HAYRIDGE, county of DEVON, 4¼ miles (S. W.) from Tiverton, containing 236 inhabitants. The living is a rectory, in the archdeaconry and diocese of Exeter, rated in the king's books at £13, and in the patronage of J. H. Moore, Esq. The church is dedicated to St. Bartholomew.

CADLEY, an extra-parochial liberty, in the hundred of KINWARDSTONE, county of WILTS, containing 45 inhabitants.

CADNAM, a hamlet partly in the parish of ELING, hundred of REDBRIDGE, and partly in the parish of MINSTEAD, northern division of the hundred of NEW FOREST, New Forest (East) division of the county of SOUTHAMPTON, 4½ miles (N.) from Lyndhurst. The population is returned with the parishes. There is a place of worship for Wesleyan Methodists.

CADNEY, a parish in the southern division of the wapentake of YARBOROUGH, parts of LINDSEY, county of LINCOLN, 2¾ miles (S. S. E.) from Glandford-Bridge, containing, with the township of Housham, 303 inhabitants. The living is a discharged vicarage, in the archdeaconry and diocese of Lincoln, rated in the king's books at £7. 18. 4., and in the patronage of Lord Yarborough. The church is dedicated to All Saints.

CADWELL, a tything in the parish of BRIGHTWELL-BALDWIN, hundred of EWELME, county of OXFORD, containing 14 inhabitants.

CAENBY, a parish in the eastern division of the wapentake of ASLACOE, parts of LINDSEY, county of LINCOLN, 7¾ miles (W.) from Market-Rasen, containing 121 inhabitants. The living is a discharged rectory, in the archdeaconry of Stow, and diocese of Lincoln, rated in the king's books at £4. 13. 4., endowed with £200 royal bounty, and in the patronage of Sir C. M. L. Monck, Bart. The church is dedicated to St Nicholas. The river Ancholme bounds the parish on the east.

CAERLEON, a market town in the parish of LLANGATTOCK, lower division of the hundred of USK, county of MONMOUTH, 20½ miles (S. W.) from Monmouth, and 151½ (W.) from London, containing 1062 inhabitants. This place, called by the Britons *Caerleon*, city of the legion, or, according to some, *Caerllian*, city of the waters, was the *Isca Silurum* of the Romans, in the time of Claudius, whose second legion, being recalled from Germany, was stationed here under the command of Vespasian. It became the metropolis of that division of the island called Britannia Secunda, and one of the chief cities of the Romans, who fortified it with strong walls three miles in circuit, enclosing a quadrilateral area, measuring five hundred and thirty yards by four hundred and sixty: they erected temples, an amphitheatre, baths, aqueducts, and splendid dwellings of various descriptions, the magnificent remains of which, in the twelfth century, are described by Giraldus Cambrensis as emulating the grandeur of Rome itself. In the reign of Domitian, St. Julian and St. Aaron, both of whom preached the doctrine of Christianity in this part of Britain, suffered martyrdom at this place; but after the final submission of the Britons to the Roman power, Caerleon became, under the auspices of Antoninus, the seat of learning and devotion. Three Christian churches were erected, two in honour of the martyrs St. Julian and St. Aaron, to which a nunnery and a priory of Cistercian canons were annexed respectively; and a third, to which was added a monastery that afterwards became the metropolitan see of Wales, and of which Dubricius, the great opponent of the Pelagian heresy, was the first archbishop. Under his successors the see continued to flourish to such an extent, that, at the time of the Saxon invasion, its college is said to have contained, among other students, not less than two hundred who were well skilled in geography and astronomy; it was afterwards translated to Menevia by St. David, and has since that time been known as the see of St. David's: there are some small remains of the monastery still existing. The castle was probably built about the time of the Conquest, but no mention of it occurs till the year 1171, when Henry II. took the town, and deposed Iorwith ap Owen, lord of Gwent, who, in 1173, retook it after a vigorous defence, and restored it to the Welch. After repeated sieges it was retained by Llewellyn ap Iorwith till the reign of Edward I., when, upon the overthrow of the independence of the Welch, the town fell into neglect, and the castle into decay: the remains of the castle are inconsiderable, consisting chiefly of heaps of stones round the base of the lofty mount on which the keep was built, and the ruins of a dilapidated portal at a distance, that probably formed the entrance. The town is pleasantly situated on a gentle acclivity on the bank of the river Usk, over which is a handsome stone bridge of modern structure, and consists of two streets indifferently paved and lighted; the houses are mostly old and irregularly built, and are fast hastening to decay: some fragments of the ancient walls are still remaining, and bear testimony to the former extent and importance of the town, which has since dwindled into comparative insignificance. The trade consists principally in the manufacture and sale of tin-plates and iron, for which there are two large establishments; the articles are conveyed to Newport by the river Usk, in vessels of small burden. The market is on Thursday: fairs are held on July 31st and October 2nd, the latter being a large fair for horses. The market-house is a dilapidated edifice, supported on four massive pillars of the Tuscan order, supposed to have belonged to some Roman structure, two bases of similar dimensions and character having been dug up near the walls.

The county magistrates hold a petty session once a fortnight. There are places of worship for Baptists, Independents, and Wesleyan Methodists. The free school, for clothing and educating twenty-five boys and twenty-five girls, was founded and endowed, in 1724, by Charles Williams, Esq.; the master's salary is £75 per annum: there is an almshouse for aged widows, who receive twenty shillings per annum each. Several remains of the Roman station are still visible, and numerous minor relics have been discovered, consisting of portions of columns, altars dedicated to Jupiter Dolichenus and the goddess Astræa, bricks inscribed "Leg. II. Aug.," tesselated pavements, coins from Cæsar to Valentinian inclusive, earthen vessels, urns, a gold ring with an intaglio representing Hercules strangling the Nemæan lion, a cornelian seal of Ceres (found about twenty years since), a mutilated statue of Jupiter in bronze, portions of the baths, &c. To the north of the town is an extensive quadrilateral encampment, with seven smaller camps near it; and on the banks of the Usk are considerable remains of the amphitheatre, called by the inhabitants King Arthur's Round Table. St. Amphibalus, the tutor of the protomartyr St. Albanus; and the martyrs St. Julian and St. Aaron; were born in this place. The renowned King Arthur is stated to have been interred here.

CAERTON, a hamlet in the parish of CHRIST-CHURCH, lower division of the hundred of CALDICOTT, county of MONMOUTH, containing 297 inhabitants.

CAER-WENT, a parish in the upper division of the hundred of CALDICOTT, county of MONMOUTH, 5½ miles (W. S. W.) from Chepstow, containing, with the hamlet of Crick, 394 inhabitants. The living is a discharged vicarage, united to that of Mathern, in the archdeaconry and diocese of Llandaff, rated in the king's books at £7. 11. 8. The church is dedicated to St. Stephen. There is a place of worship for Particular Baptists. This place, now an inconsiderable village, was anciently a Roman station, the *Venta Silurum* of Antoninus' Itinerary, and is supposed to have been the site of the capital city of the Britons in Siluria: it is still partially environed by the original Roman walls, enclosing an area of about a mile in circumference: the turnpike road to Newport, which is here upon part of the Roman road Akeman-street, passes through the centre, where formerly stood the eastern and western gates. Coins, fragments of columns, statues, sepulchral stones, and tesselated pavements belonging to that people, have been discovered: some of the latter were very curious and beautiful. At a small distance stand the magnificent ruins of Caldicott castle, formerly in the possession of the Bohuns, earls of Hereford: it is still surrounded by a moat: the side fronting the village is flanked by a large round tower, and at the northern angle is a circular tower, on a mound of earth, evidently the keep, encircled by a ditch: another circular dilapidated tower stands at the southern angle. The principal entrance consists of a fine arched gateway, flanked by massive turrets. Within are the remains of several apartments, particularly the baronial hall; and opposite to the grand gateway is another entrance, through a fine hexagonal tower, with a machicolated roof.

CAINHAM, a parish in the hundred of STOTTESDEN, county of SALOP, 3½ miles (E. S. E.) from Ludlow, containing 936 inhabitants. The living is a discharged vicarage, in the archdeaconry of Salop, and diocese of Hereford, rated in the king's books at £4. 13. 4., and in the patronage of J. Mainwaring, Esq. The church is dedicated to St. Mary.

CAIN'S CROSS, a hamlet partly in the parish of STROUD, hundred of BISLEY, and partly in the parish of STONEHOUSE, lower division, and partly in the parish of RANDWICK, upper division, of the hundred of WHITSTONE, county of GLOUCESTER, 2 miles (W.) from Stroud. The population is returned with the respective parishes. The petty sessions for Whitstone district are holden here and at Frocester alternately.

CAISTOR, or CASTOR, a market town and parish partly in the northern division of the wapentake of WALSHCROFT, but chiefly in the southern division of the wapentake of YARBOROUGH, parts of LINDSEY, county of LINCOLN, 23 miles (N. N. E.) from Lincoln, and 153 (N.) from London, containing, with the chapelry of Holton le Moor, 1388 inhabitants. This was evidently a station of the Romans; numerous coins and other Roman relics have been discovered. According to tradition, Hengist, after having repulsed the Picts and Scots, obtained from Vortigern the grant of so much land as he could encompass with the hide of an ox: having divided the hide into small thongs, he was enabled to enclose a considerable area, forming the site of the town, which, from that circumstance, was by the Saxons called *Thuang Ceastre*, or *Thong Ceastre*. But Dr. Stukeley derives the prefix from the Saxon *thegn*, a thane, or nobleman. The marriage of Rowena, daughter of Hengist, to Vortigern, was solemnized here in 453. Egbert, who finally brought the several kingdoms of the Octarchy under his dominion, obtained a signal victory at this place over Wiglof, King of Mercia, in 827, in commemoration of which a cross was erected on the castle hill, where many bodies have been dug up, and a stone with a mutilated inscription, apparently recording the dedication of the spoils by the victor to some sacred purpose. The town is well supplied with water from four springs issuing out of a grey stone rock, three of which unite their streams on the western side of the town, and fall into the river Ancholme; the other flows into the same river, near the junction of the Kelsey canal with that to Glandford-Bridge. The market is on Saturday: the fairs are on the Saturdays before Palm-Sunday, Whit-Sunday, and Old Michaelmas-day. The town is within the jurisdiction of the county magistrates, who hold a petty session here. The living is a discharged vicarage, with the perpetual curacy of Clixby annexed, rated in the king's books at £7. 6. 8., endowed with £200 royal bounty, and in the peculiar jurisdiction and patronage of the Prebendary of Caistor in the Cathedral Church of Lincoln. The church, dedicated to St. Peter and St. Paul, is a spacious structure in the early English style, with some remains of Norman architecture; it has a fine tower, with a chapel on the south side, now used as a vestry-room: it stands within the area of the ancient castle, with the materials of which it was partly built. A singular ceremony is observed here, on the performance of which depends the tenure of an estate: the holder sends an agent on Palm-Sunday, who cracks.

a whip three times in the north porch, while the minister is reading the first lesson; after which, folding the thong round the handle, and at the same time tying up some twigs of mountain-ash with it, he attaches a small purse, with some silver coin in it, to the end, enters the church, and bowing to the minister, takes his seat in front of the reading-desk; on the commencement of the second lesson, he kneels down in front of the minister, and flourishing the whip three times, keeps the purse suspended over his head till the conclusion of it, when he retires into the chancel: after the service is ended, he takes the whip and the purse to the manor-house at Hundon, where they are deposited. There are places of worship for Independents and Methodists. The free grammar school was founded, in 1630, by the Rev. Francis Rawlinson, rector of St. Nicholas', South Kelsey, who endowed it with £400, which sum was laid out in the purchase of a portion of the great tithes of Beesby, now producing £130 per annum; the endowment has been augmented with £60 per annum, arising from lands purchased with a donation by William Hansard, Esq.: the school has an exhibition of £10 per annum to Jesus' College, Cambridge, and is open to all sons of parishioners, who are instructed in the Greek, Latin, and English languages, and in writing and arithmetic, by a master and an usher.

CAISTOR (ST. EDMUND'S), a parish in the hundred of HENSTEAD, county of NORFOLK, 3¾ miles (S.) from Norwich, containing 164 inhabitants. The living is a rectory, with that of Merkshall, or Mattishall-Heath united, in the archdeaconry and diocese of Norwich, rated in the king's books at £9, and in the patronage of J. R. Dashwood, Esq. and others. Caistor, though at present an inconsiderable village, was anciently one of the most flourishing cities of the Britons, and probably the residence of the kings of the Iceni: it was the *Venta Icenorum* of the Romans, and the principal station of that people in the territory of the Iceni, the present city of Norwich having gradually arisen out of its ruins: the walls enclose a square area of about thirty acres, within which foundations of buildings may be traced. Numerous Roman coins have been discovered, principally of Constantine, and, a few years since, a bronze figure of a satyr, of very fine workmanship, about eight inches in length. But the most conspicuous Roman relic is a large fortified encampment, about a furlong south-west of Caistor: the whole space, including the rampart, exceeds thirty-two acres, and was capable of containing six thousand men: the north, east, and south sides exhibit large banks raised from a deep fosse, and the west side has one formed on the margin of the river Tees; in these are the vestiges of four gates. At each corner is an artificial mount; and on the western side the remains of a tower, thirty-three feet in circumference, are still visible. Within the area of the camp stands the church, the materials for building which were evidently taken from the ruins of the rampart.

CAISTOR near YARMOUTH, a parish in the eastern division of the hundred of FLEGG, county of NORFOLK, 19½ miles (E.) from Norwich, containing 772 inhabitants. The living is a vicarage, with the rectory of St. Edmund consolidated, in the archdeaconry and diocese of Norwich, rated in the king's books at £10, and in the patronage of John Steward, Esq. The church is dedicated to St. Edmund. The name is evidently a corrupted Saxonism of *Castrum*, it being clear, from the visible remains of fortifications and the discovery of numerous coins, that the Romans had a camp here, opposite to, and connected with, *Garianonum*. The manor was anciently in the possession of the family of Fastolf; and Sir John Fastolf, a celebrated warrior and estimable man, whose character some consider Shakspeare to have pervertedly drawn in his Sir John Falstaff, was born here. He was the founder of the castle, which at his death, in the 38th of Henry VI., he requested should be kept as a college for priests and an hospital for poor men: but it was besieged some time afterwards by the Duke of Norfolk, at the head of three thousand men, under the pretence of having purchased it, to whom the defenders were compelled to surrender it: it was supposed to be one of the oldest brick mansions in the kingdom, but is now in ruins. Caistor was formerly divided into two parishes, Castor Trinity and Castor St. Edmund's, which were consolidated September 22nd, 1608; the church belonging to the former has been suffered to fall into ruins. A line of sand-hills, called the *Meals*, or *Marum Hills*, commences here, and extends, with occasional interruptions, to Hapsbury Point, where two lighthouses have been erected, and thence to Cromer bay.

CAISTRON, a township in the parish of ROTHBURY, western division of COQUETDALE ward, county of NORTHUMBERLAND, 4½ miles (W.) from Rothbury, containing 43 inhabitants. A school was endowed by William Hall, in 1779, with £6 per annum.

CALBOURN, a parish in the liberty of WEST MEDINA, Isle of Wight division of the county of SOUTHAMPTON, 5¼ miles (W. S. W.) from Newport, containing, with the borough of Newton, 767 inhabitants. The living is a rectory, in the peculiar jurisdiction of the incumbent, rated in the king's books at £19. 12. 8½., and in the patronage of the Bishop of Winchester. The church, dedicated to All Saints, is principally in the early style of English architecture; in it is an ancient tomb, inlaid with brass, representing a knight in complete armour, with his feet resting on a dog.

CALCEBY, a parish in the Marsh division of the hundred of CALCEWORTH, parts of LINDSEY, county of LINCOLN, 4¾ miles (W.) from Alford, containing 48 inhabitants. The living is a discharged vicarage, united, in 1774, to the rectory of South Ormsby, in the archdeaconry and diocese of Lincoln, rated in the king's books at £5. 10. 2½., endowed with £200 royal bounty, and in the patronage of C. B. Massingberd, Esq. The church is dedicated to St. Andrew.

CALCETHORPE, a parish in the Wold division of the hundred of LOUTH-ESKE, parts of LINDSEY, county of LINCOLN, 6 miles (W. by N.) from Louth, containing 60 inhabitants. The living is a sinecure rectory, in the archdeaconry and diocese of Lincoln, rated in the king's books at £6. 2. 6. The Bishop of Lincoln presented by lapse in 1783. The church is dedicated to St. Faith.

CALDBECK, a parish in ALLERDALE ward below Derwent, county of CUMBERLAND, comprising the townships (locally denominated *Graves*) of High Caldbeck, Low Caldbeck, and Haltcliffe-Caldbeck, and containing 1588 inhabitants, of which number, 272 are in High Caldbeck, 720 in Low Caldbeck, and 596 in Haltcliffe-Caldbeck, 8 miles (S. E.) from Wigton. The living is a rectory, in the archdeaconry and diocese of Carlisle, rated in the king's books at £45. 13. 6½., and in the patronage of the Bishop of Carlisle. The church, dedicated to St. Kentigern, bears date 1112, and was founded soon after the establishment of an hospital for the entertainment of travellers, by the prior of Carlisle, with the permission of Ranulph D'Engain, chief forester of Inglewood: it stands in the township of Low Caldbeck, and was new roofed and greatly embellished in 1818. There are three meeting-houses in the parish for the Society of Friends, who settled here in the time of George Fox, their founder, who resided for some time at Woodhall. A manufactory for blankets, duffels, flannels, stocking-yarn, &c., has been long established; here are also a brewery, a small paper-mill, a fulling-mill, a gingham and check manufactory, and a dye-house. The parish comprises a mountainous district of eighteen thousand acres, not more than six thousand of which are enclosed, the remainder being appropriated to depasturing numerous flocks of sheep: the hills contain various mineral productions, principally lead and copper ores, limestone, and coal, and there are several establishments for working the mines: a considerable proportion of silver is occasionally extracted from the lead-ore. The summit of Carrock Fell is nearly covered with heaps of stones occupying an elliptical area of two acres, in some instances rudely piled up in huge masses; but whether they are the scattered relics of an aboriginal structure, or the production of nature, is a matter of conjecture. The river Caldew flows close to the village, about half a mile from which, in a romantic glen called the *Howk*, where it is crossed by a natural bridge of limestone, the stream dashes impetuously over the rocks, and forms two interesting cascades, by the sides of which are singular excavations, called the *Fairies' Kirk*, and *Fairies' Kettle*. At Halt Close bridge, the river enters upon a subterraneous course, which it continues for about four miles, when it emerges at a place called Spouts Dub. Robert Sewell, a natural philosopher of considerable repute, was a native of this parish.

CALDBRIDGE, a township in the parish of Coverham, western division of the wapentake of Hang, North riding of the county of York, 3¼ miles (S. W.) from Middleham, containing 103 inhabitants.

CALDECOT, a parish in the southern division of the hundred of Greenhoe, county of Norfolk, 4 miles (N. E.) from Stoke-Ferry, containing 37 inhabitants. The living is a discharged rectory, in the archdeaconry of Norfolk, and diocese of Norwich, rated in the king's books at £3. 1. 10½. The church, which was dedicated to the Virgin Mary, has been in ruins upwards of a century and a half, and the village has entirely disappeared.

CALDECOTE, a parish in the hundred of Longstow, county of Cambridge, 4 miles (E. by S.) from Caxton, containing 111 inhabitants. The living is a discharged vicarage, annexed to the rectory of Toft, in the archdeaconry and diocese of Ely, rated in the king's books at £3. 11. 0½. The church is dedicated to St. Michael.

CALDECOTE, a parish in the Atherstone division of the hundred of Hemlingford, county of Warwick, 3¼ miles (S.E. by E.) from Atherstone, containing 86 inhabitants. The living is a discharged rectory, in the archdeaconry of Coventry, and diocese of Lichfield and Coventry, rated in the king's books at £6. 15., endowed with £200 private benefaction, and £400 royal bounty, and in the patronage of S. Hemming, Esq. The church is dedicated to St. Theobald and St. Chad. In 1647, George Abbott bequeathed land, directing the annual produce to be expended in teaching poor children, and in providing them and poor families with bibles. The Coventry canal passes through this parish.

CALDECOTT, a township in the parish of Shocklach, higher division of the hundred of Broxton, county palatine of Chester, 5½ miles (N. W.) from Malpas, containing 84 inhabitants.

CALDECOTT, a parish in the hundred of Odsey, county of Hertford, 3 miles (N. by W.) from Baldock, containing 46 inhabitants. The living is a discharged rectory, in the archdeaconry of Huntingdon, and diocese of Lincoln, rated in the king's books at £8, and in the patronage of W. Hale, Esq. The church is dedicated to St. Mary Magdalene. In the year 1724, several Roman urns, containing burnt bones and ashes, were discovered in this parish.

CALDECOTT, a chapelry in the parish of Liddington, hundred of Wrandike, county of Rutland, 4¾ miles (S.) from Uppingham, containing 274 inhabitants. The chapel is dedicated to St. John. The Welland, which here separates this county from Northamptonshire, and the small river Eye, flow through the chapelry.

CALDER-BRIDGE, a hamlet in the parish of Beckermet St. Bridget's, Allerdale ward above Derwent, county of Cumberland, 5 miles (S. E.) from Egremont. The population is returned with the parish. It owes its origin and name to a bridge erected over the river Calder, and is celebrated for the remains of an abbey, founded for Cistercian monks, by Ralph de Meschines, second Earl of Chester and Cumberland, in 1134, in honour of the Blessed Virgin Mary, the revenue of which, at the suppression, was £64. 3. 9.: the ruins are situated in a sequestered and well-wooded vale, near a modern mansion of the same name, and consist principally of part of the transepts of the church, composed of five circular arches resting on clustered columns, and overspread with ivy, and a tower supported on eight clustered pillars, from the capitals of which spring beautiful pointed arches.

CALDEY (GREAT and LITTLE), a township in the parish of West Kirby, lower division of the hundred of Wirrall, county palatine of Chester, 6¾ miles (N. W. by N.) from Great Neston, containing 90 inhabitants.

CALDICOT, a parish in the upper division of the hundred of Caldicott, county of Monmouth, 6 miles (S. W.) from Chepstow, containing 498 inhabitants. The living is a discharged vicarage, in the archdeaconry and diocese of Llandaff, rated in the king's books at £6. 0. 7½., endowed with £200 royal bounty, and in the patronage of Charles Kemys Tynte, Esq. There is a place of worship for Wesleyan Methodists. In 1680, Catherine Kemys gave a small rent-charge for teaching poor children. In this parish are the remains of a castle that formerly belonged to the constable of England, and was held by the service of that office. The walls are in good preservation; they are of a square form, with round towers at the different angles: the principal entrance is under a lofty gate of smooth stone. Caldicot Level, commonly called the Moors, was formerly subject to continual inundations; but the greater part having been drained, it is now in a state of high cultivation, and forms a rich grazing district: this work was performed by the monks of a religious house in the vicinity.

CALDICOTE, a parish in the hundred of NORMAN-CROSS, county of HUNTINGDON, 1½ mile (W. S. W.) from Stilton, containing 51 inhabitants. The living is a discharged rectory, in the archdeaconry of Huntingdon, and diocese of Lincoln, rated in the king's books at £7. 3. 6., and in the patronage of James Kelwell, Esq. The church is dedicated to St. Mary Magdalene. In 1769, the Rev. James Oram bequeathed £250, directing the interest to be applied in supporting a school for girls.

CALDICOTTS (LOWER and UPPER), a hamlet in the parish of NORTHILL, hundred of WIXAMTREE, county of BEDFORD, 1½ mile (N. W. by N.) from Biggleswade, containing 369 inhabitants.

CALDWELL, a township in that part of the parish of STANWICK ST. JOHN'S which is in the western division of the wapentake of GILLING, North riding of the county of YORK, 5¼ miles (E.) from Greta-Bridge, containing 188 inhabitants. This was formerly a place of much greater extent and importance. Here is a school with a small endowment. A Roman military road passed through the township.

CALLALEY, a joint township with Yetlington, in the parish of WHITTINGHAM, northern division of COQUETDALE ward, county of NORTHUMBERLAND, 10½ miles (W. by S.) from Alnwick, containing 363 inhabitants. On Castle hill, a conical eminence embosomed in wood, is a large circular intrenchment, with vestiges of buildings denoting a Roman position.

CALLERTON (BLACK), a township in that part of the parish of NEWBURN which is in the western division of CASTLE ward, county of NORTHUMBERLAND, 6¼ miles (N. W.) from Newcastle upon Tyne, containing 173 inhabitants. T. H. Graham, Esq. allows a small yearly stipend to a schoolmaster for the instruction of poor children.

CALLERTON (HIGH), a township in the parish of PONTELAND, western division of CASTLE ward, county of NORTHUMBERLAND, 7½ miles (N. W.) from Newcastle upon Tyne, containing 104 inhabitants.

CALLERTON (LITTLE), a township in the parish of PONTELAND, western division of CASTLE ward, county of NORTHUMBERLAND, 7¾ miles (N. W. by W.) from Newcastle upon Tyne, containing 21 inhabitants.

CALLINGTON, or KELLINGTON, a borough, market town, and parish, in the middle division of the hundred of EAST, county of CORNWALL, 11 miles (S. by E.) from Launceston, 14 (N.) from Plymouth, and 213 (W. S. W.) from London, containing 1321 inhabitants. This town, formerly called *Calweton*, *Calvington*, and *Killington*, is situated on a gentle acclivity, and consists principally of one spacious street: the houses are in general of mean appearance and irregularly built; the town is badly paved, but amply supplied with water. The inhabitants formerly carried on a considerable trade in wool, which has of late declined; there is still a manufactory for fine woollen cloth. The mines in the neighbourhood, though formerly worked to a greater extent, still afford employment to a few of the labouring poor; and a mine of manganese, recently discovered, is in active operation. The market days are Wednesday and Saturday; the former is for corn and provisions, the latter for meat only: a cattle market is also held on the first Wednesday in every month. The fairs, chiefly for cattle and sheep, are on the first Thursday in May and September, and the first Wednesday and Thursday in November. The county magistrates hold a petty session here on the first Thursday in every month: a portreeve and other officers for the town are appointed annually at the court leet of the lord of the manor. The court-house, a commodious edifice, has been recently rebuilt by Lord Clinton. The borough first received the elective franchise in the 27th of Elizabeth, since which time it has continued to return two members to parliament: the right of election, by a decision of the House of Commons in 1821, is in "freeholders of houses or lands within the borough, resident or non-resident, and in persons holding lands or houses in the borough under leases granted by the owners of the freehold, for terms of years determinable on a life or lives, and in the assignees of the whole subsisting interest granted by such leases, such persons being resident householders for forty days before the day of election, and rated to the poor at forty shillings at the least:" the electors are chiefly in the interest of Alexander Baring, Esq.: the portreeve is the returning officer.

The living is a perpetual curacy, annexed to the rectory of Southill, in the archdeaconry of Cornwall, and diocese of Exeter. The church, a spacious structure dedicated to St. Mary, was built chiefly at the expense of Nicholas de Asheton, one of the judges of the court of King's Bench, who died in 1645, and to whose memory a marble tomb has been erected in the chancel: in the churchyard is the shaft of an ancient cross, on the upper part of which is sculptured a representation of the Crucifixion. There are places of worship for Independents and Wesleyan Methodists. A charity school, originally established by Lord Clinton, is at present supported by Mr. Baring, who pays the master £30 per annum for teaching poor boys of the town: there is an endowment of £12 per annum for teaching children to read, but it is usually distributed among three poor women.

CALLOW, a hamlet in that part of the parish of WIRKSWORTH which is in the hundred of WIRKSWORTH, county of DERBY, 2½ miles (S. W.) from Wirksworth, containing 100 inhabitants.

CALLOW, a parish in the hundred of WEBTREE, county of HEREFORD, 3¾ miles (S. S. W.) from Hereford, containing 139 inhabitants. The living is a perpetual curacy, united, with that of Acconbury, to the vicarage of Dewsall, which is within the peculiar jurisdiction of the Dean of Hereford, endowed with £200 royal bounty, and in the patronage of the Governors of Guy's Hospital. The church is dedicated to St. Michael: one hundred additional sittings, sixty of which are free, have been recently made, the Incorporated Society for the enlargement of churches and chapels having granted £100 for that purpose. Here are the remains of two Roman camps.

CALMSDEN, a tything in the parish of NORTH CERNEY, hundred of RAPSGATE, county of GLOUCESTER, 5¼ miles (N. N. E.) from Cirencester. The population is returned with the parish.

Seal and Arms.

CALNE, a borough, market town, and parish, in the hundred of CALNE, county of WILTS, 30 miles (N. N. W.) from Salisbury, and 87 (W. by S.) from London, on the road to Bath and Bristol, containing, with the liberty of Bowood, 4612 inhabitants. This place is of very remote antiquity, and is supposed to have risen from the ruins of a Roman station on the opposite side of the river, near the town of Studley, where numerous Roman antiquities have been discovered. Tradition states it to have been the residence of the West Saxon monarchs; but there are no vestiges of their palace, or castle, and the remembrance of it is preserved only in the name of a field thought to have been the site, and in that of a street which probably led to it. A synod, memorable from the circumstances attending it, was assembled here in 977, for adjusting the differences existing at that time between the monks and the secular clergy, at which Dunstan, Archbishop of Canterbury, presided. During the controversy the floor of the chamber gave way, and several of the secular priests were killed; but Dunstan, and the monks whose cause he advocated, having escaped unhurt, their preservation was regarded as a miraculous interposition of Heaven, and they were allowed to take immediate possession of the religious houses throughout the kingdom, to the exclusion of the secular clergy. The town consists principally of one long street, partially lighted, but not paved: the houses are in general well built of stone, and amply supplied with water from springs, and from a rivulet which, after passing through the town, falls into the Avon. Calne has been much improved under the auspices of the Marquis of Lansdowne, whose mansion is in the adjoining liberty of Bowood: it is an extensive and stately pile in the Grecian style of architecture, with a noble portico of ten columns of the Doric order, supporting an entablature and a pediment, in which are the family arms: the environs abound with pleasing scenery. The woollen manufacture, formerly carried on to a great extent, is now conducted on a very limited scale; the articles made are principally broad cloth, kerseymere, and serge. A branch of the Wilts and Berks canal passes through the town, which, uniting with the Kennet and Avon canal, and with the Thames at Abingdon, affords a facility of communication with London, Bristol, and the intermediate places. The market is on Tuesday: fairs are held on May 6th and September 29th, for cattle and sheep. The town, though a borough by prescription, is exclusively within the jurisdiction of the county magistrates: the corporation consists of two guild stewards and an indefinite number of burgesses; the former are chosen annually from among the burgesses, who add to their own number as occasion may require. A court of requests, the jurisdiction of which extends over the hundreds of Calne, Chippenham, and North Damerham, and the lordship or liberty of Corsham, is held under an act passed in the 35th of George III., for the recovery of debts under 40*s*. The town-hall is a neat and commodious building, erected by the lord of the manor, lately repaired and an upper story added by the Marquis of Lansdowne; the lower part is used as the market-place. The borough first sent members to parliament in the 23rd of Edward I., from which time it made irregular returns until the reign of Richard II., since which it has uninterruptedly returned two members: the right of election is vested in the members of the corporation, at present twenty-three in number; the guild stewards are the returning officers. The Marquis of Lansdowne possesses the preponderating influence.

The living is a vicarage, with the perpetual curacies of Cherhill and Barwick-Bassett, rated in the king's books at £8. 5., within the peculiar jurisdiction of the Prebendal Court of Calne, and in the patronage of the Treasurer in the Cathedral Church of Salisbury. The church, dedicated to St. Mary, is a venerable structure in the early style of English architecture, with a square embattled tower. There are places of worship for Baptists, the Society of Friends, Methodists, and Unitarians. The free school was founded in 1660, by John Bentley, Esq., who endowed it with property near Lincoln's Inn, London, afterwards sold by act of parliament, and the produce vested in the purchase of an annuity of £52, payable on lands in this county, for the instruction of thirty boys in English and arithmetic; but Sir Francis Bridgman, Knt., having, in 1730, founded six scholarships, of the value of £50 per annum each, in Queen's College, Oxford, of which two were for natives of this town, five of the scholars receive a classical education. The master, in addition to his salary, has a house and an acre of land rent-free. A charity school, for the instruction of children of all religious denominations, was established partly by some trifling benefactions, and is supported by subscription; a handsome school-house has lately been erected by contributions among the principal inhabitants of the town and neighbourhood. An hospital, dedicated to St. John, existed here in the reign of Henry III., the revenue of which, at the dissolution, was £2. 2. 8. At the distance of three miles to the east of the town is the figure of a horse, cut in the chalk hill, one hundred and fifty-seven feet long.

CALOW, a hamlet in the parish of CHESTERFIELD, hundred of SCARSDALE, county of DERBY, 2 miles (E. by S.) from Chesterfield, containing 395 inhabitants.

CALSTOCK, a parish in the middle division of the hundred of EAST, county of CORNWALL, 5¼ miles (E.) from Callington, containing 2388 inhabitants. The living is a rectory, in the archdeaconry of Cornwall, and diocese of Exeter, rated in the king's books at £26. 7. 8½., and in the patronage of the King, as Duke of Cornwall. The church, dedicated to St. Andrew, is a neat building, with a high tower ornamented with lofty pinnacles. There is a place of worship for Particular Baptists. The parsonage-house was built about the year 1710, by Launcelot Blackburn, then rector of this parish and Bishop of Exeter, who was afterwards Archbishop of York. Here are copper and tin mines; and a lead mine, the ore of which is intermixed with silver, has been recently opened. The Tamar canal passes through the parish, and there is a ferry over the navigable river Tamar, which forms its eastern and southern boundary, and separates it from Beer-Alston, in the county of Devon. The tide flows to about the centre of the parish, where there is a weir, and a very productive salmon fishery.

CALSTONE-WILLINGTON, a parish in the hundred of CALNE, county of WILTS, 3 miles (S. E. by E.) from Calne, containing 35 inhabitants. The living is a discharged rectory, in the archdeaconry of Wilts, and diocese of Salisbury, rated in the king's books at £4. 13. 4., endowed with £200 private benefaction, and £200 royal bounty, and in the patronage of the Marquis of Lansdowne. The church is dedicated to St. Mary. Here is a school for six children, who are taught and supplied with books at the charge of the minister.

CALTHORPE, a parish in the hundred of GUTHLAXTON, county of LEICESTER, 4¼ miles (S. by E.) from Lutterworth, containing 164 inhabitants. The living is a rectory, in the archdeaconry of Leicester, and diocese of Lincoln, rated in the king's books at £5. 5. 2½., endowed with £200 private benefaction, and £300 parliamentary grant, and in the patronage of J. Harpur, Esq. The church is dedicated to St. Mary and All Saints.

CALTHORPE, a parish in the southern division of the hundred of ERPINGHAM, county of NORFOLK, 3¼ miles (N. by W.) from Aylsham, containing 184 inhabitants. The living is a discharged vicarage, in the archdeaconry and diocese of Norwich, and in the patronage of the Mayor and Corporation of Norwich. The church is dedicated to St. Margaret.

CALTHWAITE, a township in the parish of HESKET in the FOREST, LEATH ward, county of CUMBERLAND, 7 miles (N. N. W.) from Penrith, containing 168 inhabitants. The river Petterill, over which a bridge of one arch was built by subscription in 1793, flows on the eastern side of the village.

CALTON, a chapelry partly in the parish of BLORE, northern division, and partly in the parishes of CROXDEN, MAYFIELD, and WATERFALL, southern division, of the hundred of TOTMONSLOW, county of STAFFORD, 5¾ miles (W. N. W.) from Ashbourn, containing 238 inhabitants. The living is a perpetual curacy, in the archdeaconry of Stafford, and diocese of Lichfield and Coventry, endowed with £200 royal bounty, and in the patronage of Mrs. Wilmot. The chapel, a small edifice dedicated to St. Mary, has never been consecrated. The chapelry is divided into four quarters, each maintaining its own poor.

CALTON, a township in that part of the parish of KIRKBY in MALHAM-DALE which is in the eastern division of the wapentake of STAINCLIFFE and EWCROSS, West riding of the county of YORK, 7 miles (S. E. by E.) from Settle, containing 76 inhabitants. There is a school with a small endowment. This is the birthplace of Major-General Lambert, one of the principal parliamentary leaders in the civil war.

CALVELEY, a township in that part of the parish of BUNBURY which is in the first division of the hundred of EDDISBURY, county palatine of CHESTER, 6 miles (N. W. by N.) from Nantwich, containing 221 inhabitants. The Chester canal passes in the vicinity of this township.

CALVER, a township in the parish of BAKEWELL, hundred of HIGH PEAK, county of DERBY, 1 mile (E. S. E.) from Stoney-Middleton, containing 604 inhabitants. There are extensive lime-works in this place; also cotton-mills, in which from two to three hundred persons are employed. The village is situated on the river Derwent.

CALVERHALL, a chapelry in the parish of PREES, Whitchurch division of the hundred of BRADFORD (North), county of SALOP, containing, with Williston and Millenheath, 293 inhabitants. The living is a perpetual curacy, in the peculiar jurisdiction of the Prebendary of Prees (otherwise Pipa Parva) in the Cathedral Church of Lichfield, endowed with £10 per annum and £400 private benefaction, £600 royal bounty, and £300 parliamentary grant, and in the patronage of J. W. Dodd, Esq. The chapel is dedicated to St. Bartholomew.

CALVERLEIGH, a parish in the hundred of TIVERTON, county of DEVON, 2¼ miles (N. W.) from Tiverton, containing 93 inhabitants. The living is a rectory, in the archdeaconry and diocese of Exeter, rated in the king's books at £12, and in the patronage of C. Chichester, Esq.

CALVERLEY, a parish in the wapentake of MORLEY, West riding of the county of YORK, comprising the chapelries of Idle and Pudsey, and the townships of Bolton, and Calverley with Farsley, and containing 14,134 inhabitants, of which number, 2605 are in the township of Calverley with Farsley, 4½ miles (N. E.) from Bradford. The living is a discharged vicarage, in the archdeaconry and diocese of York, rated in the king's books at £9. 11. 10., endowed with £200 private benefaction, and £200 royal bounty, and in the patronage of the Crown. The church is dedicated to St. Wilfrid. There is a small endowment for the instruction of children. At Apperley Bridge, in a most delightful part of Airedale, is a noble mansion, appropriated as a school, on the principle of that at Kingswood in Gloucestershire, for the education of the sons of Methodist ministers: it was established, in 1812, under the superintendence of the Rev. Miles Martindale, and the number is limited to seventy-two. Many of the inhabitants are employed in the woollen trade. This place is memorable as the scene of a most inhuman murder, committed in 1605, by Walter Calverley, on his two infant sons, William and Walter, aggravated by his attempt to assassinate his wife also, for which he was executed, by being pressed to death, having on his trial refused to plead: this barbarous outrage was made the subject of the "Yorkshire Tragedy," erroneously ascribed to Shakspeare.

CALVERTON, a parish in the hundred of NEWPORT, county of BUCKINGHAM, 1 mile (S.) from Stony-Stratford, containing 370 inhabitants. The living is a rectory, in the archdeaconry of Buckingham, and diocese of Lincoln, rated in the king's books at £26. 2. 11., and in the patronage of Lord Arden. The church is dedicated to All Saints. The river Ouse bounds the parish on the north. The parsonage-house occupies the site of a Roman camp, where fragments of ancient pottery have been found. The west side of Stony-Stratford, which was formerly in the parish of Calverton, has been made a separate parish by act of parliament.

CALVERTON, a parish in the southern division of the wapentake of THURGARTON, county of NOTTINGHAM, 7 miles (N. N. E.) from Nottingham, containing 1064 inhabitants. The living is a discharged vicarage, in the peculiar jurisdiction of the Chapter of the Collegiate

Church of Southwell, rated in the king's books at £4, endowed with £400 royal bounty, and in the alternate patronage of the Prebendaries of Oxton in the Collegiate Church of Southwell. The church is dedicated to St. Wilfrid. There is a place of worship for Wesleyan Methodists. This parish is in the honour of Tutbury, duchy of Lancaster, and within the jurisdiction of a court of pleas held at Tutbury every third Tuesday, for the recovery of debts under 40*s*. A school is endowed with £6 per annum, and a house and garden.

CALWICK, a township in the parish of ELLASTONE, southern division of the hundred of TOTMONSLOW, county of STAFFORD, 3½ miles (S. W. by W.) from Ashbourn, containing 120 inhabitants. A hermitage was anciently established here, which was given to the priory of Kenilworth before the year 1148, by Nicholas de Greselei Fitz-Nigell, and a small convent of Black canons placed therein. This house was given by Henry VIII. to the monastery of Merton in Surrey, in exchange for the manor of East Moulsey, as parcel of which it was again granted by that monarch to John Fleetwood.

CAM, a parish in the upper division of the hundred of BERKELEY, county of GLOUCESTER, ¾ of a mile (N. by E.) from Dursley, containing 1885 inhabitants. The living is a vicarage, in the archdeaconry and diocese of Gloucester, rated in the king's books at £6. 13. 4., endowed with £800 parliamentary grant, and in the patronage of the Bishop of Gloucester. The church is dedicated to St. George. Several of the inhabitants are employed in the manufacture of woollen cloth; and the place is also noted for the superiority of its cheese. A great part of the parish lies very low, and frequently sustains considerable injury by the inundations of the Severn. In 1730, Mrs. Frances Hopton bequeathed an estate for the erection of a school, and the education and clothing of ten boys and ten girls: the income is £163 per annum. In the reign of Edward the Elder, a battle was fought here between the Danes and the Saxons.

CAMBERWELL, a parish in the eastern division of the hundred of BRIXTON, county of SURREY, 3¼ miles (S.) from London, containing, with Dulwich and Peckham, 17,896 inhabitants. This place, in the Norman survey called *Cambrewell*, and in other ancient records *Camerwell*, appears to have been known at a very early period to the Romans, whose legions are by some antiquaries supposed to have here forded the Thames, and to have constructed a causeway leading from the river through the marshes in this parish, of which a considerable part, consisting of square chalk stones, and secured with oak piles, was discovered fifteen feet below the surface of the ground, in digging the bed of the Grand Surrey canal, in 1809. In Domesday-book mention is made of a church, and in the register of Bishop Edington, at Winchester, a commission dated 1346, for "reconciling Camberwell church, which had been polluted by bloodshed," is still in existence. The village is pleasantly situated, and the beauty of its environs, which command extensive prospects, and abound with richly diversified scenery, has made it the residence of several of the more wealthy merchants in the metropolis: it is paved, lighted with gas, and watched, under an act of parliament obtained in 1814, and the inhabitants are amply supplied with water from springs, and from the works of the South London Company. The ancient part of the village contains several spacious mansions in detached situations; the more modern is built on rising ground to the south-east, and comprises the Grove, Champion, Denmark, and Herne hills, which are occupied by elegant villas, in a pleasing and appropriate style of building. In Union-Row is a building recently purchased for the Surrey Literary Institution, which comprises a library of useful and interesting standard works, and reading and conversation-rooms, and where lectures are delivered periodically, during the winter months: the institution is under the management of a president, vice-president, honorary librarian, honorary secretary, honorary assistant secretary, and a committee of eighteen. There are several coal and coke wharfs, and a limekiln on the banks of the Surrey canal, which terminates in this parish. The magistrates for the district hold a meeting every alternate week; and the jurisdiction of the court of requests held in the borough of Southwark, for the recovery of debts under £5, was, by an act passed in the 32nd of George II., extended to this parish, in common with the other parts of the eastern division of the hundred of Brixton not previously included. A noted pleasure fair is held on the Green, annually for three days in the month of August.

The living is a vicarage, in the archdeaconry of Surrey, and diocese of Winchester, rated in the king's books at £20, and in the patronage of Sir Thomas Smyth, Bart. The church, dedicated to St. Giles, and built in the reign of Henry VIII., is in the later style of English architecture, with a low embattled tower, having a turret at one of the angles; it contains many ancient and interesting monuments. The chapel of ease, dedicated to St. Matthew, and situated on Denmark Hill, is a neat edifice of brick, ornamented with stone. St. George's, a district church, recently erected on the bank of the Surrey canal, is a handsome structure in the Grecian style of architecture: the living is a perpetual curacy, in the patronage of the Vicar of Camberwell. Camden chapel, formerly a dissenting place of worship, is now an episcopal proprietary chapel. There are places of worship for Baptists, Independents, and Methodists. The free grammar school, originally intended for twelve boys of the parish, was founded in 1618, by the Rev. Edward Wilson, vicar, who built the school-room and other premises, and gave seven acres of land for its endowment: by letters patent soon afterwards obtained, the management was vested in the patron, the vicar and churchwardens of Camberwell, the rectors of the parishes of Lambeth, Newington, and St. Olave's (Southwark), and the vicar of Carshalton. The school estate, worth £200 per annum, is let upon a beneficial lease at £60 per annum, which is given to the master, who has the privilege of taking boarders, and receiving from those who are on the foundation, not natives of the parish, a small quarterage for their instruction in the classics. The Green-coat school, on Camberwell Green, conducted on the National plan; and the Camden chapel school, instituted in 1810, besides other similar establishments, of which some have small endowments arising from successive benefactions, are supported by subscription. Sir Edmund Bowyer, in 1626, bequeathed premises and land, producing at present £98. 10. per annum, for charitable purposes; Mrs. Abigail Bowles, in 1676, bequeathed five acres of land, for the relief of the poor; and Mrs. Harriet Smith, in 1808, left £3000 three per cent. reduced annuities, the dividends on which are annually distributed amongst ten poor housekeepers in the parish. The late Dr. Lettsom, an eminent physician, lived for many years in a beautiful cottage in the Grove, where he had an extensive library, and a complete philosophical apparatus; and the uncle of the unfortunate George Barnwell, the hero of Lillo's Tragedy, resided in an ancient house, of which there are still some vestiges. On the south side of the village is Ladland's Hill, on which is a quadrilateral camp, defended on the south by a double intrenchment, and evidently of Roman origin; and in a field in the neighbourhood, called Well Hill, were discovered three large wells, thirty-five feet in circumference, and lined with cement, from which the place probably derived its name. A head of Janus, eighteen inches high, was found about a century since, at a place called St. Thomas' Watering, where pilgrims used to stop on their way to Becket's shrine, near which is a hill, called *Oak of Honour Hill,* where Queen Elizabeth is said to have dined under an oak.

CAMBLESFORTH, a township in the parish of Drax, lower division of the wapentake of Barkstone-Ash, West riding of the county of York, 2¾ miles (N.) from Snaith, containing 257 inhabitants. There is a charity school in this township, with a small endowment; besides almshouses for six poor people, endowed with £100 per annum. The poor children also participate in the advantages of the free grammar school at Drax, liberally endowed by Mr. Charles Reed, in 1669.

CAMBO, a township in that part of the parish of Hartburn which is in the north-eastern division of Tindale ward, county of Northumberland, 11½ miles (W.) from Morpeth, containing 101 inhabitants. Here is a haven for small vessels which are chiefly engaged in exporting corn and grindstones, and importing timber. There is a small subscription library in the village. The school has a small endowment left by Thomas and James Cook; and twenty-two children are taught at the expense of the Trevylian family. Here was anciently a chapel, of which there are no remains; several tombstones have been dug up near its site.

CAMBORNE, a market town and parish in the hundred of Penwith, county of Cornwall, 4 miles (W. S. W.) from Redruth, and 267 (S. W.) from London, on the road from Truro to Penzance, containing 6219 inhabitants. This town, situated in the centre of an extensive district abounding with copper, tin, and lead mines, consists of several streets, uniformly built, and contains many handsome houses, but is indifferently supplied with water obtained from wells of a great depth. There are two book clubs established in the town. In the neighbourhood are numerous cottages inhabited by the miners, dwellings for the superintendents of the works, and some handsome residences belonging to the proprietors. The Dolwath copper mine, in this parish, has been sunk to the depth of one thousand feet, and extended laterally for more than a mile, in a direction from east to west; a small vein of silver was discovered in one of the branches, about five years since, a mass of which was presented to Lord de Dunstanville, and manufactured into an elegant piece of plate: the number of persons employed in this mine exceeds one thousand, and the annual expenditure of the proprietors is more than £50,000: there are several other mines on a smaller scale, and the neighbourhood abounds with granite. The market is on Saturday: the market-house, a shed supported on pillars of granite, was erected at the expense of Lord de Dunstanville. The fairs are on March 7th, Whit-Tuesday, June 29th, and November 11th, principally for cattle. The county magistrates hold a petty session for the district on the first Tuesday in every month: a court leet is held in November, at which constables and other officers are appointed. The living is a rectory, in the archdeaconry of Cornwall, and diocese of Exeter, rated in the king's books at £39. 16. 10½., and in the patronage of Lord de Dunstanville and another. The church, dedicated to St. Martin, is an ancient structure, principally in the later style of English architecture: the altar-piece is of marble handsomely sculptured, and the pulpit of oak curiously carved: it contains a fine Norman font, and several monuments to the family of Pendarves. There are places of worship for Wesleyan Methodists and Bryanites. A free school for twelve boys and eight girls was founded, in 1763, by Mrs. Grace Percival, of Pendarves, who endowed it with a house and £21 per annum. Mrs. Basset left an endowment of £10 per annum, which is paid to a private schoolmaster for teaching ten children. Attached to the Methodist chapel is a school recently built.

CAMBRIDGE, a university, borough, and market town, having separate jurisdiction, and forming a hundred of itself, in the county of Cambridge, on the river Cam, 51 miles (N. by E.) from London. This ancient town was the *Grantan-brycge, Granta-bricge,* or *Grante-brige,* of the Saxon Chronicle, signifying the bridge over the Granta, the ancient name of the river Cam. By the substitution of cognate letters, the Saxon compound was altered after the Norman conquest into *Cantebrige,* since contracted into *Cambridge.* The earliest authenticated fact in its history is its conflagration by the Danes, in 871, who established on its desolated site one of their principal stations, which they occasionally occupied until the year 901. When the Danish army quartered here had submitted to Edward the Elder, that monarch restored the town; but, in 1010, the Danes again laid it waste. During the period that the Isle of Ely was held against William the Conqueror, by the Anglo-Saxon prelates and nobles, William built a castle at Cambridge, on the site, as it is supposed, of the Danish fortress, including also the sites of twenty-seven other houses, that, according to Domesday-book, were then destroyed. In 1088, the town and county were ravaged by Roger de Montgomery, Earl of Shrewsbury, who had espoused the cause of Robert, Duke of Normandy. Upon the agreement made in 1201, during the absence of Richard I. in Palestine, between Prince John and Chancellor Longchamp, the castle was among those which the chancellor was allowed to retain. The town was taken and despoiled by the barons in 1215. King John was at Cambridge about a month before his death: soon after his departure, the castle was taken

Seal and Arms.

by the barons, and on his decease a council was held here between them and Louis the Dauphin. In 1265, the inhabitants of the Isle of Ely being in rebellion against Henry III., the king took up his abode in this town, and began to fortify it; but being suddenly called away by the tidings of the Earl of Gloucester's success, he left Cambridge without a garrison, in consequence of which it was plundered by the rebels in the isle, the townsmen having fled at their approach. On the death of Edward VI., the Duke of Northumberland, at that time chancellor of the university, aiming to place Lady Jane Grey on the throne, came hither with an army to seize the Lady Mary, who, being at Sir John Huddleston's house at Sawston, and receiving intelligence of his design, escaped into Suffolk. The duke advanced towards Bury, but finding himself almost deserted by his forces, he returned with a small party to Cambridge, and proclaimed Queen Mary in the market-place, but was arrested for high treason the same night in King's College. In 1643, Cromwell, who, before he acquired any celebrity as a public character, was for some time an inhabitant of the Isle of Ely, and twice returned for the borough of Cambridge, took possession of it for the parliament, and placed in it a garrison of a thousand men. In August 1645, the king appeared with his army before Cambridge, but it continued in the possession of the parliamentarians until the close of the war. The town has suffered several times from accidental calamities: in 1174, the church of the Holy Trinity was destroyed by fire, and most of the other churches injured; in 1294, another conflagration destroyed St. Mary's church, and many of the adjoining houses; and, in 1630, the plague raged so violently that the summer assizes were held that year at Royston; the university commencement was postponed till October, and there was no Stourbridge fair.

Situated in a fenny agricultural district, Cambridge owes its chief picturesque attractions to the number and variety, and in several instances to the magnitude and beauty, of the buildings connected with the university, and the walks and gardens attached to them. The town, upwards of a mile in length, and in its greatest breadth more than half a mile, lies chiefly on the south-eastern side of the river: on the south it is entered by two principal streets, one forming a continuation of the road from London, the other of that from Colchester; these unite at a short distance from the iron bridge over the Cam, which connects them with the principal northern entrance, being that from Ely, Godmanchester, and Huntingdon. Notwithstanding recent alterations, the streets in general are narrow and irregularly formed; but on the whole, the town has been much improved by many elegant additions to the several colleges and university buildings; and other improvements on a very extensive scale are in contemplation, and will shortly be commenced. The town was paved under an act passed in 1787, and has lately been drained at a great expense; the streets and many of the public buildings are lighted with gas. Water is obtained from a conduit in the market-place, erected in 1614 by the eccentric and benevolent Thomas Hobson, carrier, and supplied by a small aqueduct communicating with a spring about three miles distant. Dramatic exhibitions are not permitted within nine miles of the town at any other period than that of Stourbridge fair, when, for three weeks, the Norwich company of comedians perform in a commodious theatre lately erected at Barnwell: several public concerts are held in Term-time, usually at the town-hall, when the best performers are engaged; and at the Public Commencements, which generally take place every fourth year, there are grand musical festivals. A choral society on an extensive scale has recently been formed. There are several book societies upon different plans, the most considerable of which has been established many years, and possesses a very good library, with globes, maps, &c.

Cambridge has lately become a considerable thoroughfare, particularly since the draining of the fens, and the formation of excellent roads towards the east and north-east coasts, over tracts previously impassable. There is no manufacture; but a considerable trade in corn, coal, timber, iron, &c., is carried on with the port of Lynn, by means of the Cam, which is navigable to this town. A great quantity of oil, pressed at the numerous mills in the Isle of Ely, from flax, hemp, and cole-seed, is brought up the river; and butter is also conveyed hither weekly from Norfolk and the Isle of Ely, and sent by wagons to London. The markets, which are under the sole control of the university, though the tolls belong to the corporation, are held every day in the week, Saturday's market being the largest, and are excellently supplied with provisions: the market-place consists of two spacious oblong squares. A practice peculiar to this market is that of making up the butter in rolls of such a thickness that a pound of it shall be a yard in length, in order that the butter may be more easily divisible into certain portions, called sizes, for the use of the collegians. There are two fairs; one of them, for horses, cattle, timber, and pottery, beginning on the 22nd of June, and commonly called Midsummer or Pot fair, is held on a common called Midsummer Green, between Jesus' College and Barnwell, and is proclaimed by the heads of the university and the mayor and corporation successively: the other, called Stourbridge fair, anciently one of the largest and most celebrated in the kingdom, is held in a large field a short distance to the east of Barnwell, and is proclaimed on the 18th of September by the vice-chancellor, doctors, and proctors, of the university, and by the mayor and aldermen of the town, and continues upwards of three weeks; the staple commodities exposed for sale are leather, timber, cheese, hops, wool, and cattle; the 25th is appropriated to the sale of horses: both these fairs have been for some years declining.

The town, though a borough by prescription, was first incorporated by Henry I., in the early part of his reign; and many valuable and important privileges have been granted by John, Henry III., Edward II., Richard II. and succeeding sovereigns. The officers of the corporation are a mayor, high steward, recorder, twelve aldermen, twenty-four common council-men, four bailiffs, a town-clerk, two treasurers, two coroners, with five serjeants at mace, and other inferior officers. The mayor, bailiffs, and coroners, are elected annually on the 16th of August: the mayor and his counsellors nominate one freeman, and the freemen at large another; these two then choose twelve others, and these twelve six more, by which eighteen the election is made. The aldermen and common council-men are elected in the same manner, but hold their places for life, as do also the high steward, recorder, and town-clerk, elected by the freemen at large, who also choose the treasurers annually on Hock-Tuesday. The freedom is acquired by birth, servitude, and gift: the last is vested in the freemen at large, who are entitled to take part in the transaction of all other corporation business. The justices of the peace for the town are appointed from time to time under a commission from the king, in which the names of the chancellor, vice-chancellor, and high steward of the university, with the heads of colleges and halls, and the mayor, high steward, recorder, and aldermen, of the borough, are always inserted: they have exclusive jurisdiction, and hold a court of session quarterly. By charter of Henry III. the mayor and bailiffs hold a court of pleas, taking cognizance of actions, real and personal, arising within the town, but few actions are commenced in it: they likewise hold a court leet annually, for the appointment of constables, &c. The town-hall, rebuilt in 1782, is obscurely situated behind the shire-hall. The steward of the university holds a court leet twice a year, for enquiring into matters connected with weights and measures, and for licensing victuallers in the town and the adjoining village of Chesterton. The Bishop and the Archdeacon of Ely hold their courts and have their registries here; and both the spring and the summer assizes and the quarter sessions for the county are held in the shire-hall, a handsome building standing in the market-place, containing two courts: it rests upon arches faced with stone, beneath which are shops let to butchers and fruit-sellers. Under the powers of an act of parliament recently obtained, a new and commodious town gaol, on the radiating principle, has been erected in the parish of St. Andrew the Less, on the north-east of the road to Colchester: it contains cells for forty-eight prisoners, with separate day-rooms and a tread-mill. The borough has returned members to parliament since the 23rd of Edward I.: the right of election is vested in the freemen not receiving alms, in number about one hundred and eighty, about half of whom are non-resident: the mayor is the returning officer. The privilege of sending two representatives was conferred upon the university by charter in the 1st of James I.: the right of election is vested in the members of the senate, in number about one thousand nine hundred: the vice-chancellor is the returning officer.

University Arms.

The origin of the university is enveloped in great obscurity: it is, however, probable that Cambridge first became a seat of learning in the seventh century, when, as Bede in his Ecclesiastical History informs us, Sigebert, King of the East Angles, with the assistance of Bishop Felix, instituted within his dominions a school in imitation of some that he had seen in France, and this is thought to have been established here. It is certain that at a very early period this town was the resort of numerous students, who at first resided in private apartments, and afterwards in inns, where they lived in community under a principal, at their own charge. Several of these houses were at length deserted and fell into decay; others were purchased in succession by patrons of literature, and, obtaining incorporation with right of mortmain, received permanent rich endowments. It is believed that a regular system of academical education was first introduced in 1109, when the abbot of Crowland having sent some monks, well versed in philosophy and other sciences, to his manor of Cottenham, they proceeded to the neighbouring town of Cambridge, whither a great number of scholars repaired to their lectures, which were arranged after the manner of the university of Orleans. The first charter known to have been granted to the university is that in the 15th of Henry III., conferring the privilege of appointing certain officers, called *taxors*, to regulate the rent of lodgings for students, which had been raised exorbitantly by the townsmen: this was about fifty years before the foundation of Peter-House, the first endowed college. In 1249, the discord between the scholars and the townsmen had arrived at such a pitch as to require the interference of the civil power; and, in 1261, dissensions arose in the university between the northern and the southern men, which were attended with such serious consequences that a great number of scholars, in order to pursue their studies without interruption, withdrew to Northampton, where a university was established, and continued four years. In 1270, Prince Edward came to Cambridge, and caused an agreement to be drawn up, by virtue of which certain persons were appointed by the town and the university, to preserve the peace between the students and the inhabitants. In 1333, Edward III. granted some important privileges to the university, making its authority paramount to that of the borough, and ordaining that the mayor, bailiffs, and aldermen, should swear to maintain its rights and privileges. These eminent favours caused the townsmen to be more than ever jealous of its authority: their discontents broke out into open violence in the succeeding reign, when, taking advantage of the temporary success of the rebels of Kent and Essex, in 1381, the principal townsmen, at the head of a tumultuous assemblage, seized and destroyed the university charters, plundered Benedict College, and compelled the chancellor and other members of the university to renounce their chartered privileges, and to promise submission to the usurped authority of the burgesses. These lawless proceedings were put an end to by the arrival of the Bishop of Norwich with an armed force; and the king soon after punished the burgesses, by depriving them of their charter, and bestowing all the privileges which they had enjoyed upon the university, together with a grant that no action should be brought against any scholar, or scholar's servant, by a townsman, in any other than the chancellor's court. In 1430, Pope Martin V. decided, from the testimony of ancient evidences, that the members of the university were exclusively possessed of all ecclesiastical and spiritual jurisdiction over their own scholars. Richard II. restored to the burgesses their charter, with such an abridgment of their privileges as rendered them more subordinate to the university than they had previously been. On the first symptoms of an approaching war between King Charles and the parliament, the university stood forward to demonstrate its loyalty, by tendering the college plate to be melted for his majesty's use. In 1643, the Earl of Manchester, at that time chancellor of the university, came to Cambridge, and, after a general visitation of the colleges, expelled all the members that were known to be zealously attached to the king and to the church discipline. In March 1647, Sir Thomas Fairfax visited the university, and was received with all the honours of royalty at Trinity College: on the 11th of June he kept a public fast at this place. Queen Elizabeth visited Cambridge, August 5th, 1564, and stayed five days, during which she resided at the provost's lodge, King's College, and was entertained with plays, orations, and academical exercises. On the 7th of March, 1615, James I., with his son Henry, Prince of Wales, was here, and was lodged at Trinity College, which has ever since, on the occasion of royal visits, been the residence of the sovereign. King James honoured the university with another visit, in 1625; and Charles I. and his queen were there in 1632, when they were entertained with dramatic exhibitions. It has also been visited by Charles II., October 14th, 1671, and September 27th, 1681; by William III., October 4th, 1689; by Queen Anne and the Prince of Denmark, April 16th, 1705; by George I., October 6th, 1717; and by George II., in April 1728: on all these occasions the royal guests were entertained by the university in the hall of Trinity College; and it was customary for the corporation of the town to present them with fifty broad pieces of gold.

The University of Cambridge is a society of students in all the liberal arts and sciences, incorporated in the 13th of Elizabeth, by the name of the "Chancellor, Masters, and Scholars of the University of Cambridge." It is formed by the union of seventeen colleges, or societies, devoted to the pursuit of learning and knowledge, and for the better service of the church and state. Each college is a body corporate, and bound by its own statutes, but is likewise controlled by the paramount laws of the university. The present university statutes were given by Queen Elizabeth, and, with former privileges, were sanctioned by parliament. Each of the seventeen departments, or colleges, in this literary republic, furnishes members both for the executive and the legislative branch of its government; the place of assembly is the senate-house. All persons who are masters of arts, or doctors in one of the three faculties, *viz.*, divinity, civil law, and physic, having their names upon the college boards, holding any university office, or being resident in the town, have votes in this assembly. The number of those who are entitled to the appellation of members of the senate, is at present upwards of nineteen hundred. The senate is divided into two classes, or houses; and according to this arrangement they are denominated *regents*, or *non-regents*, with a view to some particular offices allotted by the statutes to the junior division. Masters of arts of less than five years' standing, and doctors of less than two, compose the regent or upper house, or, as it is otherwise called, the white hood house, from its members wearing hoods lined with white silk. All the rest constitute the non-regent or lower house, otherwise called the black hood house, its members wearing black silk hoods. But doctors of more than two years' standing, and the public orator of the university, may vote in either house, according to their pleasure. Besides the two houses, there is a council called the *Caput*, chosen annually upon the 12th of October, by which every university grace must be approved before it can be introduced to the senate. This council consists of the vice-chancellor, a doctor in each of the three faculties, and two masters of arts, the last representing the regent and non-regent houses. A few days before the beginning of each term the vice-chancellor publishes a list of the days on which congregations will be held for transacting university business; these fixed days occur about once a fortnight, but, in case of emergency, the vice-chancellor calls a meeting of the senate, for the despatch of extraordinary affairs. Any number of members of the senate not less than twenty-five, including the proper officers, or their legal deputies, constitute a congregation. There are also statutable congregations, or days of assembling enjoined by the statutes, for the ordinary routine of affairs: a congregation may also be held without three days' previous notice, provided forty members of the senate be present. No degree is ever conferred without a grace for that purpose; after the grace has passed, the vice-chancellor is at liberty to confer the degree. The university confers no degree whatever, unless the candidate has previously subscribed a declaration that he is *bona fide* a member of the church of England, as by law established; for all other degrees, except those of B. A., M. B., and B. C. L., it is necessary that persons should subscribe to the 36th canon of the church of England, inserted in the registrar's book.

The executive branch of the university government is committed to the following officers:—A *Chancellor*, who is the head of the whole university, and presides over all cases relative to that body: his office is biennial, or tenable for such a length of time beyond two years as the tacit consent of the university chooses to allow. A *High Steward* is elected by a grace of the senate, who has special power to try scholars impeached of felony within the limits of the university (the jurisdiction of which extends a mile each way from any part of the suburbs), and to hold a court leet, according to the established charter and custom; he has power, by letters patent, to appoint a deputy. A *Vice-chancellor* is annually elected on the 4th of November by the senate: his office, in the absence of the chancellor, embraces the government of the university, according to the statutes; he acts as a magistrate both for the university and the county, and must, by an order made in 1587, be the head of some college. A *Commissary* is appointed by letters patent under the signature and seal of the chancellor; he holds a court of record for all privileged persons, and scholars under the degree of M. A. A *Public Orator* is elected by the senate, and is the oracle of that body on all public occasions; he writes, reads, and records the letters to and from the senate, and presents to all honorary degrees with an appropriate speech: this is esteemed one of the most honourable offices in the gift of the university. The *Assessor* is an officer specially appointed, by a grace of the senate, to assist the vice-chancellor in his court, *in causis forensibus et domesticis*. Two *Proctors*, who are peace-officers, are elected annually on the 10th of October by the regents only, and are chosen from the different colleges in rotation, according to a fixed cycle: it is their especial duty to attend to the discipline and behaviour of all persons *in statu pupillari*, to search houses of ill fame, and take into custody women of loose and abandoned character, and even those suspected of being so: they are also to be present at all congregations of the senate, to stand in scrutiny with the chancellor, or vice-chancellor, to take the open suffrages of the house, both by word and writing, to read them, and to pronounce the assent or dissent accordingly; to read the graces in the regent house, and to take secretly the assent or dissent, and openly to pronounce the same: they must be masters of arts of two years' standing at least, and, of whatever standing in the university, are regents by virtue of their office: they determine the seniority of all masters of arts, at the time of their taking that degree. Two *Librarians* are chosen by the senate, to whom the regulation and management of the university library are confided. A *Registrar*, elected also by the senate, is obliged, either by himself or deputy, properly authorized, to attend all congregations, to give requisite directions for the due form of such graces as are to be propounded, to receive them when passed in both houses, and to register them in the records; to register also the seniority of such as proceed yearly in any of the arts and faculties, according to the schedules delivered to him by the proctors. Two *Taxors* are elected annually on the 10th of October by the regents only, who must be masters of arts, and are regents by virtue of their office: they are appointed to regulate the markets, examine the assize of bread, the lawfulness of weights and measures, and to lay all the abuses and deficiencies thereof before the commissary. Two *Scrutators* are chosen at the same time by the non-regents only, who are non-regents, and whose duty it is to attend all congregations, to read the graces in the lower house, to gather the votes secretly, or to take them openly in scrutiny, and publicly to pronounce the assent and dissent of that house. Two *Moderators* are nominated by the proctors, and appointed by a grace of the senate: they act as the proctors' substitutes in the philosophical schools, superintending alternately the exercises and disputations in philosophy, and the examinations for the degree of bachelor of arts; they are also generally deputed to officiate in the absence of the proctors. Two *Pro-proctors* are appointed, in consequence of the increasing magnitude of the university, to assist the proctors in that part of their duty which relates to the discipline and behaviour of those who are *in statu pupillari*, and the preservation of the public morals. This office was instituted by a grace of the senate, April 29th, 1818, and bachelors in divinity, as well as masters of arts, are eligible: they are nominated by the vice-chancellor and proctors, and elected by a grace of the senate. The *Classical Examiners* are nominated by the several colleges, according to the cycle of proctors, and the election takes place at the first congregation after October 4th. There are three *Esquire Bedells*, whose duty it is to attend the vice-chancellor, and walk before him with their silver maces on all public occasions. The *University Printer*, the *Library-keeper*, and *Under Library-keeper*, and the *School-keeper*, are elected by the body at large. The *Yeoman Bedell* is appointed by letters patent under the signature and seal of the chancellor. The *University Marshal* is appointed by letters patent under the signature and seal of the vice-chancellor. The *Syndics* are members of the senate chosen to transact all special affairs relating to the university, such as the framing of laws, the regulating of fees, inspecting the library, buildings, printing, &c.

The professors have stipends allowed from various sources; some from the university chest, others from his Majesty's government, or from estates left for that purpose. *Lady Margaret's Professorship of Divinity* was founded in 1502, by Margaret, Countess of Richmond, mother of Henry VII., the election to be every two years: the electors are the chancellor, or vice-chancellor, doctors, inceptors, and bachelors in divinity, who have been regents in arts: the same person may be re-elected, but the professor usually continues in office without the observance of that ceremony. The *Regius Professorship of Divinity* was founded by Henry VIII., in 1540; the candidates must be either a bachelor or a doctor in divinity: the electors are the vice-chancellor, the master and the two senior fellows of Trinity, the provost of King's, and the masters of St. John's and Christ's Colleges. The *Regius Professorship of Civil Law* was founded also by Henry VIII., in 1540: the professor is appointed by the king, and continues in office during his Majesty's pleasure. The *Regius Professorship of Physic*, founded at the same time, may be held for life: the appointment is by the king. The *Regius Professorship of Hebrew* was founded also at the same time; the electors are the same as to the Regius Professorship of Divinity: a candidate must not be under the standing of M. A. or B. D., but doctors of all faculties are excluded. A *Professorship of Arabic* was founded by Sir Thomas Adams, Bart., in 1632; the electors are the vice-chancellor and the heads of colleges: among persons qualified, heads of houses, fellows, and masters of arts being gremials of the university, are to be preferred. The *Lord Almoner's Reader and Professorship of Arabic* is appointed to by the lord almoner, and the stipend is paid out of the almonry bounty. The *Lucasian Professorship of Mathematics* was founded in 1663, by Henry Lucas, Esq., M. P. for the university; the electors are the vice-chancellor and the masters of colleges: a candidate must be M.A. at least, and well skilled in mathematical science. The *Professorship of Casuistry* was founded in 1683, by John Knightbridge, D.D., fellow of St. Peter's: the electors are, the vice-chancellor, the Regius Professor of Divinity, the Lady Margaret's Professor, and the master of St. Peter's; in case of an equality of votes, the casting vote belongs to the last: a candidate must be a bachelor or doctor in divinity, and not less than forty years of age. The *Professorship of Music* was founded by the university, in 1684: the election is by a grace of the senate. The *Professorship of Chemistry* was founded by the university, in 1702: the election was originally by a grace of the senate, but, by a grace dated October 24th, 1793, it was determined that all subsequent elections should be *more burgensium*. The *Professorship of Astronomy and Experimental Philosophy* was founded in 1704, by Dr. Plume, Archdeacon of Rochester: the electors are, the vice-chancellor, the masters of Trinity, Christ's, and Caius Colleges, and the Lucasian professor; when any one of these masters is vice-chancellor, the master of St. John's is entitled to vote: the candidates may be single or married, Englishmen or foreigners. The *Professorship of Anatomy* was founded by the university, in 1707: the election is by a majority of the members of the senate. The *Professorship of Modern History* was founded by George I., in 1724: the professor is appointed by the king, and holds the office during his Majesty's pleasure: he must be either a master of arts, bachelor in civil law, or of a superior degree. The *Professorship of Botany* was founded by the university, in 1724, and has since been made a patent office. The *Professorship of*

Geology was founded by Dr. Woodward, in 1727: on the decease of the four executors of the founder's will, the election became vested in the members of the senate, in addition to whom the following persons were allowed to give their votes by proxy; *viz.*, the chancellor of the university, the archbishop of Canterbury, the bishop of Ely, the president of the Royal Society, the president of the College of Physicians, and the members of parliament for the university: only unmarried men are eligible. The *Professorship of Astronomy and Geometry* was founded by Thomas Lowndes, Esq., in 1749: the appointment is vested in the lord high chancellor, the lord president of the privy council, the lord privy seal, the lord high treasurer, and the lord high steward of the king's household. The *Norrisian Professorship of Divinity* was founded by John Norris, Esq., of Whitton, in the county of Norfolk, in 1768: the electors must be a majority of ten heads of houses: the professor cannot continue in office longer than five years, but may be re-elected; he may be a member of either university, may be lay or clerical, but cannot be elected under his thirtieth, nor re-elected after his sixtieth, year. The *Professorship of Natural and Experimental Philosophy* was founded in 1783, by the Rev. Richard Jackson, M.A.: the election is by those regent masters of arts who have been resident the greater part of the year previously to the day of election, excepting such as are under one year's standing, who may vote though they have not been resident for that period: a member of Trinity College is to be preferred, and next a Staffordshire, Warwickshire, Derbyshire, or Cheshire man. The *Downing Professorship of the Laws of England*, and the *Downing Professorship of Medicine*, were founded in pursuance of the will of Sir George Downing, Bart., K.B., in 1800: the electors are the archbishops of Canterbury and York, and the masters of St. John's College, Clare Hall, and Downing College. The *Professorship of Mineralogy* was founded by the university, in 1808, and afterwards endowed by his Majesty's government. The title of *Professor of Political Economy* was conferred by a grace of the senate, in May 1828, on George Pryme, Esq., M.A., late Fellow of Trinity College, and is to be a permanent professorship.

Lady Margaret's Preachership was founded in 1503: the electors are the vice-chancellor and the heads of houses: doctors, inceptors, and bachelors of divinity, are alone eligible, one of Christ's College being preferred. The *Barnaby Lectureships*, four in number, *viz.*, in mathematics, philosophy, rhetoric, and logic, are so called from the annual election taking place on St. Barnabas' day, June 11th: the mathematical lecture was founded at a very early period, by the university; and the other three were endowed in 1524, by Sir Robert Rede, Lord Chief Justice of the court of common pleas in the reign of Henry VIII. The *Sadlerian Lectureships in Algebra*, seventeen in number, were founded by Lady Sadler, and the lectures commenced in 1710: the lecturers, who are required to be bachelors of arts at least, are appointed by the heads of colleges, who are the trustees, and by the vice-chancellor for the time being, from all the colleges; the lectureships are tenable only for ten years, and no one can be elected unless previously examined and approved by the Mathematical Professor. The Rev. John Hulse, who was educated at St. John's College, and died in 1789, bequeathed his estates in Cheshire to this university, for the advancement and reward of religious learning. The purposes to which he appropriated the income are, first, the maintenance of two scholars at St. John's College; secondly, to recompense the exertions of the Hulsean prizemen; thirdly, to found and support the office of Christian Advocate; and, fourthly, that of the Hulsean Lecturer, or Christian Preacher. The *Christian Advocate* must be a learned and ingenious person, of the degree of master of arts, or of bachelor or doctor of divinity, of thirty years of age, and resident in the university; he has to compose yearly, while in office, some answer in English to objections brought against the Christian religion, or the religion of nature, by notorious infidels. The office of the *Hulsean Lecturer*, or *Christian Preacher*, is annual; but the same individual may, under certain circumstances, be re-elected for any number of successive years not exceeding six: the preacher is afterwards ineligible to the office of Christian Advocate: his duty is to preach and print twenty sermons in each year, the subject of them being to shew the evidences of revealed religion, or to explain some of the most obscure parts of the Holy Scriptures. William Worts, M.A., of Caius College, formerly one of the esquire bedells of the university, gave two pensions, of £100 per annum each, to two junior bachelors of arts, elected by the senate, who are required to visit foreign countries, to take different routes, and to write, during their travels, two Latin letters each, descriptive of customs, curiosities, &c.: the annuity is continued for three years, the period they are required to be absent.

The prizes for the encouragement of literature, the competition for which is open to the university at large, amount annually to nearly £1200 in value, three-fourths of which are given for the classics and English composition, the remainder for mathematics. The amount of the annual prizes in the different colleges is upwards of £300, two-thirds of which are given for the encouragement of classical literature. Two gold medals, value £15. 15. each, are given annually by the chancellor to two commencing bachelors of arts, who, having obtained senior optimes at least, shew the greatest proficiency in classical learning: these prizes were established in 1751, by his Grace, Thomas Holles, Duke of Newcastle, then chancellor of the university. His Royal Highness the Duke of Gloucester, the present chancellor, gives annually a third gold medal, to be conferred upon a resident undergraduate, who shall compose in English the best ode or best poem in heroic verse. The members of parliament for the university give four annual prizes, of £15. 15. each, to two bachelors of arts and two under-graduates, who compose the best dissertations in Latin prose: these prizes were established by the Hon. Edward Finch and the Hon. Thomas Townshend. Sir Edward Browne, Knt., M.D., directed three gold medals, value £5. 5. each, to be given yearly to three under-graduates on the commencement day; the first to him who writes the best Greek ode in imitation of Sappho; the second for the best Latin ode in imitation of Horace; the third for the best Greek and Latin epigrams, the former after the manner of the Anthologia, the latter on the model of Martial. The Rev. Charles Burney, D.D., and the Rev. John Cleaver Bankes, M.A., only surviving trustees of a fund raised by the friends of the late Professor Porson, and appropriated to his use during his lifetime, did, by deed bearing date November 27th, 1816, transfer to the university the sum of £400 Navy five per cents. upon trust, that the interest should be annually employed in the purchase of one or more Greek books, to be given to such resident under-graduate as shall make the best translation of a proposed passage selected from the works of Shakspeare, Ben Jonson, Massinger, or Beaumont and Fletcher, into Greek verse. The Rev. Robert Smith, D.D., late master of Trinity College, left two annual prizes, of £25 each, to two commencing bachelors of arts, the best proficients in mathematics and natural philosophy. John Morris, Esq., founder of the divinity professorship, bequeathed a premium of £12 per annum, £7. 4. of which is to be expended on a gold medal, the remainder in books, to the author of the best prose essay on a sacred subject, to be proposed by the Norrisian professor. The Rev. John Hulse directed that, out of the rents and profits of the estates which he bequeathed to the university for the advancement of religious learning, an annual premium of £40 should be given to any member, under the degree of M.A., who should compose the best dissertation on any argument proving the truth and excellence of the Christian religion. The Rev. Thomas Seaton, M.A., late fellow of Clare Hall, bequeathed to the university the rental of his estate at Kislingbury, producing a clear income of £40 per annum, to be given yearly to a master of arts who shall write the best English poem on a sacred subject.

The university scholarships are as follows:—John, Lord Craven, founded two classical scholarships, tenable for fourteen years, of £25 per annum each, arising from estates vested in trustees: by a decree of the court of Chancery in 1819, the income of the scholars has been augmented to £50, and three additional scholarships founded, which are tenable for seven years only. William Battie, M.D., fellow of King's College, left an estate, producing £18 per annum, to endow a scholarship similar to the preceding. Sir Willam Browne, Knt., M.D., left a rent-charge of £21 for endowing a scholarship tenable for seven years. The Rev. J. Davies, D.D., formerly fellow of King's College, and afterwards provost of Eton College, bequeathed, in July 1804, to the vice-chancellor for the time being, and the provost of King's College, in trust, the sum of £1000 three per cents., to found a scholarship similar to Lord Craven's, for the greatest proficient in classical learning. The Rev. William Bell, D.D., prebendary in the collegiate church of Westminster, and late fellow of Magdalene College, in 1810, transferred £15,200 three per cents. to the university in trust, to found eight new scholarships, for sons or orphans of clergymen of the church of England, whose circumstances prevent them bearing the whole expense of sending them to the university: two of these scholarships become vacant every year. By a grace of the senate, December 9th, 1813, it was directed that the sum of £1000, given by the subscribers to Mr. Pitt's statue, for the purpose of founding the Pitt scholarship, and afterwards augmented by a donation of £500 from the Pitt club in London, should be placed in the public funds until the syndics were able to vest it in land, the clear annual income to be paid to the Pitt scholar. The Rev. Robert Tyrwhitt, M.A., late fellow of Jesus' College, who died in 1817, bequeathed £4000 Navy five per cents. for the promotion and encouragement of Hebrew learning, leaving the mode of appropriating it to the discretion of the university: in 1818 the senate decreed the foundation of three Hebrew scholarships, which number, in 1826, was increased to six, two scholars to be elected annually, and called scholars of the first and second classes; a scholar of the first class receiving an annual stipend of £30, and one of the second class a stipend of £20, for three years. The annual income of the university chest is about £16,000, including about £3000 of floating capital: this arises from stock in the funds, manors, lands, houses, fees for degrees, government annuity (for the surrender of the privilege of printing almanacks), profits of the printing-office, &c. The annual expenditure is about £12,000, disbursed to the various officers, the professors, the library and schools, the university press, and in taxes, donations to charities, &c. &c. The whole is managed by the vice-chancellor for the year, and the accounts are examined by three auditors appointed annually by the senate.

The right of presentation to the rectory of Ovington, in the county of Norfolk, and of nomination to the vicarage of Burwell, in the county of Cambridge, belongs to the university at large; in addition to which the chancellor and scholars are entitled, by act of parliament passed in the 3rd of James I., and confirmed in the 1st of William and Mary, the 12th of Anne, and the 11th of George II., to the nomination, presentation, collation, and donation to every benefice, prebend, or ecclesiastical living, school, hospital, and donative, belonging to any popish recusant convict, in the following twenty-seven counties of England and Wales:—Bedfordshire, Cambridgeshire, Cheshire, Cumberland, Derbyshire, Durham, Essex, Hertfordshire, Huntingdonshire, Lancashire, Leicestershire, Lincolnshire, Norfolk, Northumberland, Nottinghamshire, Rutlandshire, Shropshire, Suffolk, Westmorland, Yorkshire, Anglesey, Caernarvonshire, Denbighshire, Flintshire, Glamorganshire, Merionethshire, and Radnorshire. The Whitehall Preacherships were established by George I., in 1721: twelve of the twenty-four are appointed from this university; the preachers must be fellows of colleges the whole time they hold the office, to which they are appointed by the Bishop of London, as dean of his Majesty's chapel.

There are two courts of law in the university:—the consistory court of the chancellor, and the consistory court of the commissary. In the former, the chancellor, or vice-chancellor, assisted by some of the heads of colleges, and one doctor or more of the civil law, administers justice in all personal pleas and actions arising within the limits of the university, wherein a member of the university is a party, which, excepting only such as concern mayhem and felony, are to be here solely heard and decided: the proceedings are according to the course of the civil law: from the judgment of this court an appeal lies to the senate, who commit the examination of it to certain delegates, in number not less than three, nor exceeding five, with power to ratify or reverse it. In the commissary's court, the commissary, by authority under the seal of the chancellor, sits both in the university, and at Midsummer and Stourbridge fairs, to proceed in all causes, excepting those of mayhem and felony, wherein one of the parties is a member of the university, excepting that within the university all causes and suits to which one of the proctors or taxors, or a master of arts, or any one of superior degree, is a party, are reserved to the sole jurisdiction of the chancellor or vice-chancellor: the manner of proceeding is the same as in the chancellor's court, to which an appeal lies, and thence to the senate. The university council are appointed by a grace of the senate, and the solicitor by the vice-chancellor. The terms, three in number, are fixed: October, or Michaelmas, term begins on the 10th of October, and ends on the 16th of December; Lent, or January, term begins on the 13th of January, and ends on the Friday before Palm-Sunday; and Easter, or Midsummer, term begins on the eleventh day after Easter-day, and ends on the Friday after Commencement day, which last is always the first Tuesday in July.

The several orders in the different colleges are as follows:—A *Head* of a college or house, who is generally a doctor in divinity; *Fellows*, who generally are doctors in divinity, civil law, or physic, bachelors in divinity, masters or bachelors of arts: the total number of the fellowships is four hundred and eight. *Noblemen Graduates, Doctors* in the several faculties, *Bachelors in Divinity* (who have been masters of arts), and *Masters of Arts*, who are not on the foundation, but whose names are kept on the boards for the purpose of being members of the senate. *Graduates*, who are neither members of the senate nor *in statu pupillari*, are bachelors in divinity denominated four-and-twenty men, or ten-year men; they are allowed by the ninth statute of Queen Elizabeth, which permits persons who are admitted at any college, twenty-four years of age and upwards, to take the degree of bachelor in divinity, when their names have remained on the boards ten years. *Bachelors in Civil Law* and in *Physic*, who sometimes keep their names upon the boards until they become doctors. *Bachelors of Arts* who are *in statu pupillari*, and pay for tuition whether resident or not, and generally keep their names on the boards, either to shew their desire to become candidates for fellowships, or members of the senate. *Fellow Commoners*, who are generally the younger sons of the nobility, or young men of fortune, and have the privilege of dining at the fellows' table; they are here equivalent to gentlemen commoners at Oxford. *Pensioners* and *Scholars*, who pay for their respective commons, rooms, &c., but the latter are on the foundation, and, from the enjoyment of scholarships, read the graces in hall, the lessons in chapel, &c. The number of scholarships and exhibitions in the university is upwards of seven hundred. *Sizars* are generally men of inferior fortune; they usually have their commons free, and receive various emoluments.

The terms required by the statutes to be kept for the several degrees are as follows:—A bachelor of arts must reside the greater part of twelve several terms, the first and last excepted. A master of arts must be a bachelor of three years' standing. A bachelor in divinity must be M.A. of seven years' standing. A bachelor in divinity (ten-year man) is allowed, by the 9th statute of Queen Elizabeth, to take the degree of B.D. at the end of ten years, without having taken any other. A doctor in divinity must be a bachelor in divinity of five years', or a master of arts of twelve years', standing. A bachelor in civil law must be of six years' standing complete, and must reside the greater part of nine several terms: a bachelor of arts of four years' standing may be admitted to this degree. A doctor in civil law must be of five years' standing from the degree of B.C.L., or a master of arts of seven years' standing. A bachelor in physic must reside the greater part of nine several terms, and may be admitted any time in his sixth year. A doctor in physic is bound by the same regulations as a doctor in civil law. A licentiate in physic is required to be M.A. or M.B. of two years' standing. A bachelor in music must enter his name at some college, and compose and perform a solemn piece of music as an exercise before the university. A doctor in music is generally a bachelor in music, and his exercise is the same.

By an interpretation made May 31st, 1786, it was determined that the following persons are entitled to honorary degrees; *viz.*—1. Privy Counsellors; 2. Bishops; 3. Noblemen—Dukes, Marquises, Earls, Viscounts, Barons; 4. Sons of Noblemen; 5. Persons related to the King by consanguinity or affinity, provided they be also Honourable; 6. The eldest sons of such persons; 7. Baronets, but only to the degree of M.A.; 8. Knights, to the same degree. By a grace of the senate, passed March 18th, 1826, all the above persons, before admission to any degree, are to be examined and approved of in the same manner as the other candidates; but they have the privilege of being examined after keeping *nine* terms, the first and last excepted: they are then entitled to the degree of master of arts. Sometimes, however, the university confers degrees without either examination or residence, on such individuals of mature age as are illustrious, not by their birth only, but also for the services they have rendered to the state, or to literature. No person taking a degree in right of nobility is entitled to a vote in the senate, unless he have previously resided three terms.

The ordinary course of study preparatory to the degree of bachelor of arts may be considered under the three heads of *Natural Philosophy, Theology and Moral Philosophy*, and the *Belles Lettres*. On these subjects, besides the public lectures delivered by the several professors, the students attend the lectures of the tutors of their respective colleges; and the instruction under each of the three general heads above named may be thus stated:—the first comprehends Euclid's Elements, the principles of algebra, plane and spherical trigonometry, conic sections, mechanics, hydrostatics, optics, astronomy, fluxions, Newton's Principia, Increments, &c.; the second, Beausobre's Introduction, Doddridge's and Paley's Evidences, the Greek Testament, Butler's Analogy, Paley's Moral Philosophy, Locke's Essay, and Duncan's Logic; the third, the most celebrated Greek and Latin classics. Besides a constant attendance on lectures, the under-graduates are examined in their respective colleges, yearly or half-yearly, on those subjects which have engaged their studies; and, according to the manner in which they acquit themselves in these examinations, their names are arranged in classes, and those who obtain the honour of a place in the first class receive prizes of books, differing in value, according to their respective merits. By this course the students are prepared for those public examinations and exercises which the university requires of all candidates for degrees. The first of these takes place in the second Lent term after the commencement of academical residence, at the general public examination held annually in the senate-house in the last week of that term, and continues for four days; two classes, each arranged alphabetically, are formed out of those examined, the first consisting of those who have passed their examination with credit, and the second of those to whom the examiners have only not refused their certificate of approval. Those who are not approved by the examiners are required to attend the examination of the following year, and so on; and no degree of B.A., M.B., or B.C.L., is granted unless a certificate be presented to the Caput that the candidate for such degree has passed, to the satisfaction of the examiners, some one of these examinations. The student having passed this preparatory step, has next to perform the exercises required by the statutes for the degree which he has in view.

By a late regulation of the court of directors of the Honourable the East India Company, with the approbation of the Board of Commissioners for the affairs of India, an examination has been appointed for those candidates for writerships in the service of the Company, who have not resided in the college at Haileybury. An examiner is appointed by each university, and the examination takes place at the India House. The candidates are examined in the Greek Testament, and in some of the works of the following Greek authors, *viz.* Homer, Herodotus, Demosthenes, or in the Greek plays; and in some of the works of the following Latin authors, *viz.* Livy, Cicero, Tacitus, and Juvenal; which part of the examination includes collateral reading in ancient history, geography, and philosophy: they are also examined in mathematics, including the four first and sixth books of Euclid, algebra, logarithms, plane trigonometry, and mechanics; in modern history, chiefly taken from Russel's "Modern Europe;" and in Paley's Evidences of Christianity. The number of members of the university, in 1828, was five thousand one hundred and four, of whom one thousand nine hundred and seventy-four were members of the senate; the number of the resident members, at the close of the year 1829, was one thousand seven hundred and seventy-one, of whom six hundred and seventy-three were in licensed lodgings.

The principal public buildings belonging to the university are, the senate-house, and the public schools and library: the former of these forms the north, and the latter the west, side of a grand quadrangle, which has Great St. Mary's church on the east, and King's College chapel on the south. The senate-house is an elegant building of Portland stone, erected from a design by Sir James Burrough, at the expense of the university, aided by an extensive subscription: the foundation was laid in 1722, but it was not entirely completed until 1766: the exterior is of the Corinthian order, and the interior of the Doric, with wainscot and galleries of Norway oak, the latter capable of accommodating one thousand persons; the room is one hundred and one feet long, forty-two broad, and thirty-two high, with a double range of windows: near the centre of one side is a marble statue of George I., by Rysbrach, executed at the expense of Lord Viscount Townshend; and opposite to it is that of George II. by Wilton, executed in 1766, at the expense of Thomas Holles, Duke of Newcastle, then chancellor of the university: at the east end, on one side of the entrance, is a statue of the Duke of Somerset, by Rysbrach; and on the other that of the Right Hon. William Pitt, by Nollekins, erected by a subscription among the members of the university, amounting to upwards of £7000. The public schools, in which disputations are held and exercises performed, were commenced on their present site in 1443, at the expense of the university, aided by liberal benefactions: they form three sides of a small court, the philosophy school being on the west, the divinity school on the north, and the schools for civil law and physic on the south; on the east is a lecture-room for the professors, fitted up in 1795: connected with the north end of the philosophy school is an apartment containing the valuable mineralogical collection presented to the university by Dr. Woodward, in 1727. The public library occupies the whole quadrangle of apartments over the schools, and consists of four large and commodious rooms, containing upwards of one hundred thousand volumes; at the commencement it occupied only the apartment on the east side, but was afterwards extended to the north side also: its most important acquisition was in the early part of the last century, when George I. having purchased of the executors of Dr. Moore, Bishop of Ely, that prelate's collection of books, amounting to upwards of thirty thousand volumes, for £6000, gave them to this university, at the same time contributing the sum of £2000 towards fitting up rooms for their reception: among the objects of the greatest curiosity in this extensive library are, a valuable and very ancient manuscript on vellum of the Gospels, and Acts of the Apostles, in Greek and Latin, presented to the university by Theodore Beza; and a large collection of the earliest printed books by Caxton, and from the foreign presses. The library has also received valuable donations of oriental books and manuscripts, chiefly from Dr. George Lewis, late archdeacon of Meath, the late Rev. Dr. Buchanan, and the Rev. C. Burckhardt. The upper part of a mutilated colossal statue, from the temple of Ceres at Eleusis, the gift of Messrs. Clarke and Cripps, of Jesus' College, by whom it was brought to England, is placed in the vestibule. The rents of the university's estate at Ovington, in the county of Norfolk, are appropriated to the purchase of books for the library, that estate having been bought with money given to the university, in 1666, by Tobias Rustat, Esq., to be so applied. William Worts, M. A., fellow of Caius College, bequeathed the annual surplus of the produce of his estate at Landbeach, in this county, to be applied to the use of the public library. A quarterly contribution of one shilling and sixpence from each member of the university, excepting sizars, is also made towards its support. This is one of the eleven libraries entitled by act of parliament to a copy of every new publication. The management is entrusted to syndics, who are the vice-chancellor, the heads of houses, all doctors in each faculty, the public orator, and all public professors, the proctors, and the scrutators. All members of the senate, bachelors in law and physic, and bachelors of arts, under certain restrictions, are entitled to the use of the library.

The superintendence of the university press is committed by the senate to syndics, who meet to transact business in the parlour of the printing-office, and cannot act unless five are present, the vice-chancellor being one. Richard, Viscount Fitz-William, formerly of Trinity Hall, who died in 1816, bequeathed to the university his splendid collection of books, paintings, drawings, engravings, &c., together with £100,000 South Sea annuities, for the erection of a museum to contain them: the old free school, in Free School-lane, has been fitted up to serve the purpose temporarily. The collection has since been augmented by many valuable donations of paintings, prints, books, &c.

The Botanical Garden occupies between three and four acres on the south-east side of the town, conveniently disposed and well watered: this piece of ground, with a large old building that formerly belonged to the Augustine friars, was purchased for £1600 by the late Dr. Richard Walker, vice-master of Trinity College. The old building having been sold, a new one has been erected for the use of the lecturers in chemistry and botany. The garden is under the government of the vice-chancellor, the provost of King's College, the masters of Trinity and St. John's Colleges, and the Professor of Physic. The Anatomical School, situated near Catharine Hall, contains a large collection of rare and valuable preparations, including the museum of the late professor, Sir B. Harwood, and a set of models beautifully wrought in wax, recently imported from Naples: it is a small building conveniently fitted up, with a theatre for the lectures on anatomy and medicine, which are delivered annually in Lent term.

Measures for the establishment of the Observatory were first adopted in 1820, when a sum of £6000 was subscribed by the members of the university, to which £5000 was added out of the public chest by a grace of the senate. The building was commenced in 1822, and is now completed: it stands on an eminence, about a mile from the college walks, on the road to Madingley, and is in the Grecian style; the centre, surmounted by a dome, is appropriated to astronomical purposes, and the wings for the residence of the observers. The superintendence is vested in the Plumian professor, under whose direction are placed two assistant observers, who must be graduates of the university, and are elected for three years, being capable of re-election at the expiration of that term. The observations are printed and published annually, and copies are presented to the principal European observatories, *viz.*, those of Greenwich, Oxford, Dublin, Paris, and Palermo. The Philosophical Society was instituted November 15th, 1819, for the purpose of promoting scientific enquiries, and of facilitating the communication of facts connected with the advancement of philosophy and natural history: it consists of fellows and honorary members, the former being elected from such persons only as are graduates of the university, and no graduate or member of the university can be admitted an honorary member: attached to the society is a reading-room, supplied with the principal literary and scientific journals, and the daily newspapers.

Arms.

St. Peter's College, commonly called Peter-house, was founded in 1257, by Hugh de Balsham, Bishop of Ely. There are fourteen fellowships on the foundation, to which no person can be elected who is M. A., or of sufficient standing to take that degree; and there cannot be more than two fellows from any one county, except those of Cambridge and Middlesex, each of which may have four: one-fourth of the foundation fellows are required to be in priest's orders. By Queen Elizabeth's license the five senior clerical fellows may hold, with their fellowships, any livings not rated higher than £20 in the king's books, and within twenty miles of the university. There are ten bye-fellows distinct from the former, and not entitled to any office or vote in the affairs of the college, but eligible to foundation fellowships. There are fifty-two scholarships, of different value, which are paid according to residence. The Bishop of Ely is visitor, and appoints to the mastership one of two candidates nominated by the society. The livings in the patronage of the master and fellows are the perpetual curacy of Little St. Mary, in the town of Cambridge; the vicarage of Cherry-Hinton, in the county of Cambridge; the vicarage of Ellington, in the county of Huntingdon; the rectory of Stathern, in the county of Leicester; the rectory of Exford, in the county of Somerset; and the rectory and vicarage of Freckenham, and the rectories of Newton, Norton, and Witnesham, in the county of Suffolk: annexed to the mastership is the rectory of Glaston, in the county of Rutland; and the master and Lord Suffield are alternate patrons of the rectory of Knapton, in the county of Norfolk. The college, which stands on the west side of Trumpington-street, consists of three courts, two of which are separated by a cloister and gallery: the largest of these is one hundred and forty-four feet long, eighty-four broad, and cased with stone; the lesser, next the street, is divided by the chapel, and has on the north side a lofty modern building faced with stone, the upper part of which commands an extensive prospect of the country toward the south: the third was completed in 1826, by means of a donation from a late fellow, the Rev. Fras. Gisborne, from whom it is called the Gisborne court. The chapel, a handsome structure erected by subscription in 1632, is chiefly remarkable for its fine east window of painted glass, representing the Crucifixion. Among the eminent persons who have been members of this society, or educated at the college, may be enumerated Cardinal Beaufort; Archbishop Whitgift; Andrew Perne, Dean of Ely; Bishops Wren, Cosin, Walton (editor of the Polyglott Bible), and Law; Moryson, the traveller; Crashawe, the poet; Dr. Sherlock, Dean of St. Paul's; Sir Samuel Garth; the learned Jeremiah Markland; the poet Gray; and Lord Chief Justice Ellenborough.

Arms.

Clare Hall was founded, in 1326, by Dr. Richard Badew, afterwards chancellor of the university, by the name of University-hall; but having been burned to the ground about the year 1342, it was rebuilt and munificently endowed, through the interest of Dr. Badew, by Elizabeth de Burgh, one of the sisters and co-heiresses of Gilbert, Earl of Clare, and from her received its present name. The society consists of a master, ten senior, or foundation fellows, nine junior, and three bye-appropriation fellows: the senior and junior fellowships are open to all counties. The master is elected by the senior and junior fellows, and must be either a bachelor or a doctor in divinity. The seniors must all be divines, except two, who, with the consent of the master and a majority of the fellows, may practise law and physic. Of the nine junior fellowships, two may be held by laymen: the other seven require priest's orders after a certain standing. The three bye-appropriation fellows hold no college office, nor have they any vote in college business, and are ever after ineligible to any other fellowship: they must take priest's orders within seven years after they are bachelors of arts. There are thirty-four scholarships, eight of which have been lately increased, four of the value of £50 per annum each, and the other four £20 each, besides a weekly allowance in the buttery of three shillings and threepence during residence. Four exhibitions of £20 per annum each were founded by Archdeacon Johnson, with preference to persons educated at Oakham and Uppingham schools. The visitors are, the chancellor, and two persons appointed by a grace of the senate. The livings in the patronage of the master and fellows are, the vicarages of Duxford St. John and Littlington, in the county of Cambridge; the rectory of Datchworth, in the county of Hertford; the rectory of Brington, with the perpetual curacies of Bythorn and Old Weston annexed, and the vicarages of Everton with Tetworth and Great Gransden, in the county of Huntingdon; the vicarage of Wrawby with the curacy of Brigg, in the county of Lincoln; the rectory of Hardingham, in the county of Norfolk; the rectories of Elmsett, Fornham All Saints with that of Westley, and Great Waldingfield, in the county of Suffolk; the rectories of Ockley and Rotherhithe, in the county of Surrey; the rectory of Orcheston St. Mary, in the county of Wilts; the rectory of Patrington, in the East riding, and the vicarage of Warmfield in the West riding, of the county of York. This hall, one of the most uniform buildings of the university, is very pleasantly situated on the eastern bank of the Cam, over which it has an elegant stone bridge, leading to a shady walk opening into a beautiful lawn surrounded by lofty elms. It was rebuilt in 1638, of Ketton stone, and consists of one grand court, one hundred and fifty feet long, and one hundred and eleven broad: the front towards the fields is very handsome, being adorned with two rows of pilasters, the lower in the Tuscan, the upper in the Ionic, order. The chapel, the rebuilding of which, from an elegant design by Sir James Burrough, was completed in 1769, at an expense of £7000, is remarkable for the neatness of its stucco-work. Among its eminent members, &c., were Thomas Philipot, the herald and antiquary; Archbishops Heath and Tillotson; Bishops Hugh Latimer, Gunning, Moore, and Henchman; George Ruggle, author of Ignoramus; Dr. Burnet, author of the Theory of the Earth; John Parkhurst, the lexicographer; Dr. Cudworth, author of the Intellectual System; William Whiston; Martin Folkes; Dr. Langhorne; Whitehead, the poet laureat; Thomas Cecil, Earl of Exeter; Thomas Holles, Duke of Newcastle; and the late Marquis Cornwallis.

Arms.

Pembroke College was founded, in 1343, by Mary, Countess of Pembroke, and its endowment greatly enlarged by Henry VI. There are fourteen foundation and two byefellowships, open to all counties, but no county to have more than three; six of the fellows must be in deacon's or priest's orders. There are twelve scholarships, varying in value from £12 to £50 per annum each, besides several of smaller amount: the lord high chancellor is visitor. The livings in the patronage of the master and fellows are, the vicarage of Soham with the curacy of Barraway, and the vicarage of Linton, in the county of Cambridge; the rectory of Rawreth, in the county of Essex; the rectory of Orton-Waterville, and the vicarage of Waresley, in the county of Huntingdon; the rectories of Cawston and Sall, and the vicarage of Saxthorpe, with the consolidated vicarages of Tilney All Saints and Tilney St. Lawrence, in the county of Norfolk; and the rectories of Framlingham and Earl-Stonham, in the county of Suffolk. The college, or hall, is situated on the east side of Trumpington-street, nearly opposite to St. Peter's College, and consists of two courts of nearly equal dimensions, being about ninety-five feet by fifty-five, with the hall between them. On the east side of the inner court is a small detached building, erected for the purpose of containing a hollow sphere, eighteen feet in diameter, turning round with ease, and having the constellations painted inside, constructed by Dr. Long, Lowndean Professor of Astronomy, and formerly master of this college: the interior is so contrived as to form an excellent astronomical lecture-room, being capable of containing conveniently about thirty persons. Among the college plate is preserved a curious gilt silver cup, of considerable antiquity, the gift of the foundress in the reign of Edward III. The chapel, built by Dr. Matthew Wren, Bishop of Ely, from a design by his nephew Sir Christopher, and consecrated by that bishop in 1665, is one of the most elegant and best proportioned in the university. Among the more eminent members, &c., may be reckoned, Archbishops Grindal and Whitgift; Bishops Lindwood, Fox, Ridley, and Andrews; the martyrs, Rogers and Bradford; the poets, Spenser, Gray, and Mason; Dr. Long, the astronomer; Stanley, editor of Æschylus; and the late illustrious statesman, the Right Hon. William Pitt.

Arms.

Gonville and Caius College, originally styled Gonville Hall, was founded in 1347, by Edmund, son of Sir Nicholas Gonville, of Terrington, in the county of Norfolk; in 1558, the hall was consolidated with the new foundation by Dr. John Caius, and under the charter then obtained the united foundations received the name they now bear. There are twenty-nine fellowships, of which twenty-one are open to all counties, and seventeen to laymen: two of the fellows must be physicians. There are twenty-six scholarships, open to all counties; three are of the value of £56 per annum each, six of £40, six of £36, six of £30, one of £24, one of £22, and three of £20: there is also a scholarship in chemistry, of the value of £20 per annum, and four studentships in physic, of upwards of £100 per annum each; in addition to these scholarships are fourteen exhibitions of different value. The visitors are, the master of Corpus Christi College, the senior doctor in physic, and the master of Trinity Hall. The livings in the patronage of the master and fellows are, the rectory of Beachampton, in the county of Buckingham; the rectory of Bratton-Fleming, in the county of Devon; the rectory of Broadway with that of Bincombe, in the county of Dorset; the rectory of Ashdon, in the county of Essex; the rectories of Blofield, Denver, Hethersett, Kirstead, the vicarage of Mattishall with the rectory of Pattesley, the rectories of Great Melton All Saints' and St. Mary's with St. Michael's Coslaney, Norwich, the rectory of St.

Clement's (Norwich) with that of Long Stratton, the rectory of Oxborough with the vicarage of Foulden, the rectories of Weeting All Saints and Weeting St. Mary, the rectory of Wheatacre All Saints with the vicarage of Mutford and the perpetual curacy of Barnaby, and the vicarage of Wilton with the rectory of Hockwold, in the county of Norfolk; and the rectory of Lavenham, in the county of Suffolk. This college stands on the west side of Trumpington-street, having Trinity College on the north, Trinity Hall on the west, and the senate-house on the south: it consists of three courts; the south court, and three remarkable gates of Grecian architecture, built by Dr. Caius, are supposed to have been designed by John of Padua, architect to Henry VIII., and to be the only works of his now remaining in the kingdom; of the principal court, part has been rebuilt, and the rest cased with stone and elegantly sashed. The chapel, though small, is admired for its beauty: on the south wall is the monument of Dr. Caius, whose body lies in a sarcophagus, under a canopy supported by Ionic columns; on the same wall is the monument of Stephen Perse, M.D., a great benefactor to the university, who died in 1615; in the ante-chapel is the gravestone of Sir James Burrough, Knt., formerly master, an ingenious architect, who designed the senate-house and other public buildings in Cambridge, and died in 1774. The library is small, but contains some exceedingly valuable books and manuscripts, particularly in heraldry and genealogy. The college has been a celebrated seminary for professors of medicine and anatomy, ever since the time of its second founder, the learned physician, Dr. Caius: of those who have most eminently conferred honour on the society in this faculty may be enumerated Dr. Francis Glisson; Sir Charles Scarborough; Dr. William Harvey, the discoverer of the circulation of the blood; and Dr. William Hyde Wollaston. Among other distinguished members, or students, were Dr. Branthwaite, one of the translators of the Bible; Sir Thomas Gresham; Sir Peter le Neve, the herald and antiquary; Richard Parker, author of the Σκελετὸς Cantabrigiensis; Dr. Brady, the historian; Henry Wharton, author of the Anglia Sacra; Sir Henry Chauncy and Francis Blomefield, the historians of Hertfordshire and Norfolk; the celebrated Bishop Taylor; Bishop Skip, one of the compilers of the Liturgy; Jeremy Collier; the learned Dr. Samuel Clarke; Shadwell, the poet; and Lord Chancellor Thurlow.

Arms.

Trinity Hall was founded, in 1350, by William Bateman, Bishop of Norwich. There are twelve fellowships, which are ordinarily held by graduates in civil law; ten of the fellows are usually laymen, and two in holy orders. The lord chancellor is visitor. The livings in the patronage of the master and fellows are, the perpetual curacy of St. Edward, in the town of Cambridge; the vicarage of Weathersfield, in the county of Essex; the vicarage of Fenstanton with the perpetual curacy of Hilton, and the vicarages of Great Stukeley and Grey-Hemingford, in the county of Huntingdon; the rectory of Swannington with the vicarage of Wood-Dalling, in the county of Norfolk; and the perpetual curacy of Cowling, and the perpetual curacy of Kentford with the vicarage of Gazeley, in the county of Suffolk. This hall stands behind the senate-house, near the river, and on the northern side of Clare Hall: the principal court is very neat, being faced with stone both within and without; the second is a convenient and handsome pile of brick and stone, recently erected for the accommodation of the under-graduates. The chapel is chiefly worthy of notice for its finely-painted altar-piece. The library contains, among other valuable books, a complete body of the canon, Roman, and common law. Among remarkable persons who have been members, or students, were Bilney, the martyr; Gardiner, Bishop of Winchester; Bishops Barlow (of Lincoln), Halifax, and Horsley (of St. Asaph); Thomas Tusser, the writer on husbandry; Sir Peter Wyche, the traveller; Dr. Haddon, master of the requests to Queen Elizabeth; Sir Robert Naunton, secretary of state to James I.; Philip, the celebrated earl of Chesterfield; Sir William de Grey, Chief Justice of the Common Pleas, and several other eminent lawyers, who have recently filled distinguished offices in that profession.

Arms.

Corpus Christi College was founded, in 1351, by the brethren of two guilds in Cambridge, bearing the names of *Gilda Corporis Christi*, and *Gilda Beatæ Mariæ Virginis*. There are twelve fellowships, four of which are appropriated, two for pupils from the school at Norwich, and two for natives of the county of Norfolk; the rest are open, with the restriction only that four of the candidates shall (if it may be) be natives of Norfolk: all the fellows are required to take orders within three years after their election. The visitors are, the vice-chancellor, and the two senior doctors in divinity; in extraordinary cases the king is visitor. The livings in the patronage of the master and fellows are the perpetual curacy of St. Benedict in the town of Cambridge; the rectory of Duxford St. Peter, the vicarage of Grantchester, and the rectories of Landbeach and Little Wilbraham, in the county of Cambridge; the rectory of Stalbridge, in the county of Dorset; the rectories of Great Braxted and Lambourne, in the county of Essex; the rectory of St. Mary Abchurch with the perpetual curacy of St. Lawrence Pounteney, in the city of London; and the rectory of Fulmodeston with the vicarage of Croxton, and the rectory of Thurning, in the county of Norfolk. This college, frequently called Bene't College, from its proximity to the church of St. Benedict, is situated in Trumpington-street, opposite to Catharine Hall; the extent and magnificence of its buildings give it a high rank among the recent improvements which have added so much to the splendour of the university. It consists of two large courts, the old and the new, the latter having been lately erected out of the funds which had accumulated for that purpose, from the munificent bequests of Archbishop Herring, and Bishops Mawson and Green, formerly masters of the college. The new buildings were commenced in July 1823; the grand west front of the new court is two hundred and twenty-two feet long, with a lofty massive tower at each extremity, and a superb entrance gateway in the centre, flanked by towers corresponding with the former; the exterior is built of Ketton stone, and richly ornamented: the court is one hundred and fifty-eight feet long, and one hundred and twenty-nine broad, having the chapel on the east side, the library on the south, and the hall on the north. The chapel, begun in 1579 by the Lord Keeper Bacon, is sixty-six feet long, and its exterior is richly adorned with sculpture. The library is a fine lofty room eighty-eight feet long, and contains the valuable manuscripts bequeathed to the college by Archbishop Parker, comprising a collection of papers relative to ecclesiastical affairs, made on the dissolution of religious houses by Henry VIII., with other interesting documents relating to the Reformation, and the original record of the Thirty-nine Articles. The old court, situated behind the hall, is a very ancient pile of building, entirely appropriated to the accommodation of the students. Among the college plate is a curious ancient drinking horn, which belonged to the guild of Corpus Christi. Of the distinguished members were, Archbishops Parker, Tenison, Herring, and Sterne; Bishops Allen, Fletcher, Jegon, Greene (Thomas), Bradford, Mawson, Green (John), Ashburnham, and Yorke; Sir Nicholas Bacon; Roger Manners, fifth earl of Rutland; Philip, second earl of Hardwicke; his brother, the Right Hon. Charles Yorke; Sir John Cust, Bart., Speaker of the House of Commons; John Fletcher, the dramatic poet; Stephen Hales, the natural philosopher; Nathaniel Salmon, the topographer; and Dr. Stukeley, Robert Masters (the historian of the college), and the late Richard Gough, three celebrated antiquaries.

Arms.

King's College was founded, in 1441, by King Henry VI. The society consists of a provost and seventy fellows and scholars; the latter are supplied by a regular succession from Eton College, and, at the expiration of three years from the day of their admission, they are elected fellows. This college possesses some remarkable privileges and exemptions: by charter it appoints its own coroner; no writ of arrest can be executed within its walls; the provost has absolute authority within the precincts; by special composition between this society and the university, the members are exempt from the power of the proctors and the university officers, within the limits of the college; neither by usage do they keep any public exercises in the schools, nor are they in any way examined for the degree of bachelor of arts. The Bishop of Lincoln is visitor. The livings in the patronage of the provost and fellows are, the rectory of Kingston, and the sinecure rectory and vicarage of Milton All Saints, in the county of Cambridge; the rectory of Sampford-Courtenay, and the curacy of Tiverton (Priors-quarter), in the county of Devon; the rectory of Stower-Provost with that of Todbere, in the county of Dorset; the rectory of Dunton, in the county of Essex; the rectory of Chalton with that of Clanfield, the rectory of Monkston, and the vicarages of Fordingbridge and Ringwood, in the county of Hants; the rectories of Buckland and Walkern, in the county of Hertford; the vicarage of Prescot, in the county of Lancaster; the rectory of Hemingby, and the vicarage of Willoughton, in the county of Lincoln, of which latter, Lord Scarborough possesses the alternate patronage; the rectory of Great Greenford, in the county of Middlesex; the rectory of Coltishall with that of Horstead, the rectory of Hempstead with that of Lessingham, and the rectory of Monks-Toft with that of Haddiscoe, in the county of Norfolk; the vicarage of Weedon-Loys, in the county of Northampton; the perpetual curacies of Great Bricett and Little Finborough, the rectory of Hepworth, and the perpetual curacies of Kersey, Lindsey, and Wattisham, in the county of Suffolk; the vicarage of Kew with that of Petersham, the vicarage of Kingston on Thames with that of Richmond, and the perpetual curacies of East Moulsey and Thames-Ditton, in the county of Surrey; the rectory of Ewhurst, in the county of Sussex; the vicarage of Wootton-Waven, in the county of Warwick; and the vicarage of Broadchalk, in the county of Wilts.

The buildings stand on the west side and near the centre of Trumpington-street, between it and the river, over which is a handsome stone bridge, communicating with the shady walks on the other side: they consist principally of the old court, now uninhabited, and purchased by the university to be taken down, in order to enlarge the public schools, and the grand court, recently completed, having Gibbs' building on the west, the magnificent chapel on the north, the library and hall on the south, and a grand entrance from Trumpington-street on the east, forming altogether the most superb groupe of buildings in Cambridge. The old court, built of stone, about one hundred and twenty feet by ninety, appears to be coeval with the foundation. A little to the south of it stands the chapel, the chief architectural ornament of the town, and one of the finest specimens of the later style of English architecture in the kingdom. This splendid structure was begun by King Henry VI., in 1441; continued by Edward IV., Richard III., and Henry VII.; and completed with money bequeathed by the latter for that purpose, in the year 1515: it forms the north side of the grand court: its extreme length is three hundred and sixteen feet, its breadth eighty-four feet, its height to the summit of the battlements ninety feet, to the top of the pinnacles one hundred and one, and to the summit of the corner towers one hundred and forty-six feet: about the middle of the interior is a wooden screen, supporting the organ gallery, and separating the ante-chapel from the choir, erected in 1534, and very curiously carved: the choir is paved with marble; the present altar-piece was erected about the year 1780. One of the most striking features of this edifice is the magnitude and beauty of its painted windows, of which there are twelve on each side, nearly fifty feet high, which, together with the east window, are enriched with various subjects from Scripture history: this beautiful glass was put up in the early part of the reign of Henry VIII., and is further interesting as presenting one of the very few instances in which this species of church decorations escaped, in such complete preservation, the destruction to which they were doomed in the time of the Commonwealth. On each side are nine small chapels, seven of which on the south side contained, until recently, the college library, to which the late learned Mr. Bryant bequeathed his valuable collection, in 1804. It was the intention of the royal founder that the chapel should form the south side of a large court, and for this purpose he granted two quarries of stone, in Yorkshire, besides £1000 per annum payable out of the duchy of Lancaster, until the college should be completed; but Edward IV. deprived the college of this money, together with nearly two-thirds of its possessions, in consequence of which nothing further was done towards completing the design, until the new building, an edifice of Portland stone, two hundred and thirty-six feet long, and intended to form the west side of the great court, was begun in 1724, and completed from a design by Mr. Gibbs. The provost's lodge, adjoining the bridge leading to the college walks, is very spacious and magnificent. The new buildings are from designs by William Wilkins, Esq. M.A. Amongst its eminent members and students may be enumerated Archbishop Rotherham; Bishops Fox, West, Aldrich, Cox, Guest, Wickham, Montagu, Pearson, Fleetwood, Hare, Weston, and Dampier; the martyrs, Fryth, Saunders, Glover, and Fuller; the statesmen, Sir John Cheke, Dr. Thomas Wilson, Sir Francis Walsingham, Walter Haddon, Sir William Temple, Sir Albert Moreton, Sir Robert Walpole, Horatio Lord Walpole, and Lord Chancellor Camden; Anthony Wooton, provost of Eton; Edward Hall, the historian; William Oughtred, the mathematician; Dr. Cowell, the civilian; Dr. Castell, author of the Heptaglott Lexicon; Waller, the poet; Dean Stanhope; Christopher Anstey; Jacob Bryant; and Horace, Earl of Orford.

Arms.

Queen's College was founded by Margaret of Anjou, consort of Henry VI., in 1446, and re-founded by Elizabeth Widville, consort of Edward IV., in 1465. There are nineteen foundation fellowships, the number of which may be increased or diminished according to certain circumstances declared by the statutes. In general there can be only *one* fellow from a county, and *two* from a diocese, the diocese of Lincoln excepted, from which there may be three; there may also be one fellow beyond the prescribed number from Middlesex, and from those counties and dioceses in which the college has property sufficient for the maintenance of a fellow: two fellows may remain laymen, and, within twelve years from M.A., one of the two must proceed to D.C.L., the other to M.D. The vice-president and the five senior fellows hold their fellowships with property; the others quit the society when possessed of a stated annual income. The five senior divines may hold livings rated in the king's books at not higher than £20 per annum, and within twenty miles of Cambridge. There is one bye-fellowship which is perfectly open, may be held by a layman, and is tenable with any property or preferment; but the holder has no vote in the society. The scholarships have recently been consolidated into twenty-six, and augmented by college grants, many of them having previously been inconsiderable: they are payable weekly according to residence. The president must be elected by a majority of the whole existing body, must have graduated B.D. at least, and must possess property to the amount of £20 per annum. The King is visitor. The livings in the patronage of the President and Fellows are, the rectory of St. Botolph's in the town of Cambridge; the rectory of Little Eversden, and the vicarage of Oakington, in the county of Cambridge; the rectory of Sandon, in the county of Essex; the rectory of Seagrave, in the county of Leicester; the rectories of Rockland and South Walsham, in the county of Norfolk; the rectory of Hickling, in the county of Nottingham; and the rectory of Newton-Toney, in the county of Wilts: the rectory of Grimstone, in the county of Norfolk, is in the patronage of the president, who must nominate one of the eight senior fellows. The buildings are situated to the west of Catharine Hall, on the banks of the river, and consist of three courts of considerable magnitude; the entrance to the outer, or principal court, which is ninety-six feet by eighty-four, is through an elegant tower gateway: the inner court is furnished with cloisters about three hundred yards in circumference, and extends to the bank of the river; Walnut-tree Court has buildings on one side only: the front of the college, next the river, has been recently rebuilt in an elegant style: the grove and gardens are particularly beautiful, and, lying on both sides of the river, are connected by a wooden bridge of one arch, built in 1746, and much admired for the ingenuity of its construction. Amongst eminent members, or students, of this college are Archbishop Grindal; Bishops Fisher, Davenant, Sparrow, and Patrick; Sir Thomas Smith, the statesman; Dr. Thomas Smith, the ecclesiastical historian; Thomas Brightman, author of the treatise on the Revelations; John Weever, author of the Funeral Monuments; Dr. Thomas Fuller, author of the Worthies of England; and Dr. John Wallis, the mathematician: the celebrated Erasmus was for some time a student of this college.

Arms.

Catharine Hall was founded, in 1475, by Robert Woodlark, D.D., chancellor of the university, and provost of King's College. There are six fellowships on the foundation, the number of which may be increased or diminished in proportion to the revenue of the college: there cannot be more than two fellows from any one county at the same time; and two of them at least must be in priest's, and one in deacon's, orders. There are also eight other fellowships; in filling up six of which, "a preference is to be given to persons born in the county of York, if duly qualified." There are forty-three scholarships, varying in value from £2 to £35 per annum each, of which thirteen are appropriated, and to several of which chambers rent-free are attached. The livings in the patronage of the master and fellows are, the rectory of Coton, in the county of Cambridge; the vicarage of Ridgwell, in the county of Essex; and the rectory of Gimingham with that of Trunch, in the county of Norfolk. The buildings form three sides of a quadrangle, one hundred and eighty feet by one hundred and twenty, the fourth side being open towards Trumpington-street, and having iron palisades, and a piece of ground planted with lofty elm-trees: the front is toward the west, and has an elegant portico in the centre. The library, a very handsome room, was fitted up at the expense of the late Dr. Thomas Sherlock, Bishop of London, who bequeathed to the college his large and valuable collection of books: he also left a stipend for the librarian. Amongst eminent members and students were Archbishops Sandys and Dawes; Bishops Overall, Brownrigg, Leng (author of the Cambridge Terence), Blackall, Hoadley, and Sherlock; John Bradford, the martyr; John Strype, the antiquary; Ray, the naturalist; and

Dr. Lightfoot, the orientalist, and author of the *Horæ Hebraicæ*.

Arms.

Jesus' College, was founded by John Alcock, Bishop of Ely, in 1496, on the site of a Benedictine nunnery, established about the year 1130, and dedicated to St. Rhadegund, the endowment of which was augmented by Malcolm, fourth king of Scotland, and the possessions of which on its dissolution, in the reign of Henry VII., were granted to the bishop: there are sixteen foundation fellowships: eight of the fellows are to be natives of the northern, and eight of the southern, counties, and six in priest's orders; but by a recent statute, granted by the Bishop of Ely, and with the king's license, the society will, from and after the 7th of Jan., 1833, be able to elect fellows from any part of England and Wales, without restriction. On each vacancy the master and fellows nominate two candidates, of whom the Bishop of Ely appoints one. There is one fellowship to which the bishop has an exclusive right both to nominate and appoint: he is also visitor, and appoints the master. There are forty-six scholarships and exhibitions, varying in value from £9 to £70 per annum each, of which twenty-seven are appropriated. The livings in the patronage of the master and fellows are, the vicarage of All Saints', and the perpetual curacy of St. Clement's, in the town of Cambridge; the vicarages of Comberton and Fordham, the rectory of Graveley, the vicarage of Guilden-Morden, the rectory of Harlton, and the vicarages of Hinxton, Swavesey, and Whittlesford, in the county of Cambridge; the vicarage of Elmstead, in the county of Essex; the rectory of Tewin, in the county of Hertford; the rectory of King's Stanley, in the county of Gloucester; and the rectory of Cavendish, the vicarage of Hundon, and the rectory of Whatfield, in the county of Suffolk. The buildings, which are situated at the extremity of the town, consist of a principal court, one hundred and forty-one feet by one hundred and twenty, which is built on three sides; and a small court surrounded by a cloister; an addition has lately been made to the eastern side of the college. The grand front looks toward the south, and is one hundred and eighty feet long, being regularly built and sashed; both the master and fellows have spacious gardens. The library contains many scarce and valuable editions of the classics. The chapel, anciently the conventual church of St. Rhadegund, exhibits, particularly in the chancel and the interior of the tower, considerable remains of the original structure; the altar-piece, representing the Presentation in the Temple, was given, in 1796, by Dr. Pearce, master of the college: in the south transept of what is now the ante-chapel are the tombs of one of the nuns, named Berta Rosata, and of Prior John de Pykenham, the latter of which is supposed to have been removed hither from the neighbouring convent of Franciscans: in the north transept is the monument of Tobias Rustat, yeoman of the robes to king Charles II., a benefactor to the college, remarkable for his great wealth and extensive charities. Amongst eminent members and students may be reckoned Archbishops Cranmer, Sterne, Herring, and Hutton; Bishop Bale, the biographer; Dr. John Nalson, the historian; Roger North the biographer; John Flamsteed, the astronomer; Fenton, the poet; Dr. Jortin; the witty Lawrence Sterne; Tyrwhitt, the founder of the Hebrew scholarships; Gilbert Wakefield, the classical editor and critic; and the celebrated traveller, Dr. Edward Daniel Clarke.

Arms.

Christ's College was originally founded, in 1456, by King Henry VI., under the name of God's House; but in 1505, the Lady Margaret, Countess of Richmond and Derby, changed the name, incorporated the former society with the present college, and endowed it liberally for the maintenance of a master and twelve fellows. This foundation is for divinity, and the fellows are required to take priest's orders within twelve months after they have attained the requisite age. The only appropriation is to the counties of England and Wales; the restrictions are, that there shall not be two of the same county, and that there shall be six, and only six, from nine specified counties in the north of England collectively. Edward VI. added another fellowship, the holder of which participates in the emolument of the original foundation: he may be from any county, and is not obliged to take holy orders. There are two other fellowships tenable by laymen, with independent revenues, and preference to the kindred of the founders. These fifteen fellows have an equal claim to the college patronage, and are allowed by the statutes to hold preferment with their fellowships, provided it does not exceed the value of ten marks, after the deductions found in the king's books. Lady Margaret founded forty-seven scholarships, now augmented to 15*s*. per week during residence; there can only be three scholars of one county: three others were added by Edward VI. Various other scholarships and exhibitions have been founded by private benefactors; and four divinity studentships, the present value of which is £113. 8. per annum each, were founded by C. Tancred, Esq. The visitors are the vice-chancellor and the two senior doctors of divinity; or, if the vice-chancellor be of this college, the provost of King's. The livings in the patronage of the master and fellows are, the vicarage of Bourn, the vicarage of Caldecote with the rectory of Toft, and the perpetual curacy of Fen-Drayton, in the county of Cambridge; the rectory of Little Canfield, in the county of Essex; the rectory of Anstey, in the county of Hertford; the rectory of Kegworth, in the county of Leicester; the rectories of Ingoldsby and Navenby, in the county of Lincoln; the rectory of Brisley with the vicarage of Gateley, the rectory of Burnham St. Mary, the vicarage of Croxton All Saints, and the perpetual curacy of Hapton, in the county of Norfolk; the rectory of Clipston (which is divided into portions), and the vicarage of Helpstone, in the county of Northampton; the vicarage of Manerbier, in the county of Pembroke; and the rectory of Moulton, in the county of Suffolk. The buildings stand north of Emanuel College, and opposite to St. Andrew's church: they consist of the principal court, a handsome quadrangle, one hundred and thirty feet by one hundred and twenty, and a second court built on two sides, that next the garden and fields being an elegant and uniform pile of stone, about one hundred and fifty feet long. The chapel is eighty-four feet long, with a floor of marble: in the east window are portraits of King Henry VII., and some others of the family of the foundress: within the rails of the altar is the gravestone of Dr. Ralph Cudworth, author of the Intellectual System, and master of the college, who died in 1688. The garden has a bowling-green and a cold bath, and contains a large mulberry-tree, planted by Milton, when a student here. Besides the great poet just mentioned, the following eminent persons have been members of this society, or students at the college: Leland, the antiquary; Archbishop John Sharp; Bishops Latimer, Law, and Porteus; Hugh Broughton, and Dr. Lightfoot, the Orientalists; the poets, John Cleland, and Francis Quarles; Dr. Joseph Mede, an eminent divine; Dr. Thomas Burnet, author of the Theory of the Earth; Dr. Lawrence Echard, the historian; Dr. Saunderson, the mathematician; and Archdeacon Paley.

Arms.

St. John's College was founded, in 1511, by the executors of Margaret, Countess of Richmond and Derby: the original endowment was for fifty fellows, but part of the foundation estates having been seized by Henry VIII., the funds were found to be sufficient only for thirty-two. These, by letters patent from King George IV., are now open to the natives of England and Wales, without any restriction of appropriation whatsoever; one of them is in the appointment of the Bishop of Ely. This being a divinity college, the fellows are obliged to be in priest's orders within six years from the degree of M.A., except four, who are allowed by the master and seniors to practise law and physic; the electors are the master and eight senior resident fellows, in whom is vested the entire management of the college concerns. Of the appropriated fellowships, twenty-one have all the privileges of the foundation fellowships, and an equal claim to the college patronage; besides these there are nine fellowships, founded by Mr. Platt, which are open to all candidates; but the fellows are not allowed to hold any college preferment. There are one hundred and fourteen scholarships, nine of which, founded by the Duchess of Somerset, have been augmented by the society to sixteen, which are appropriated to Manchester, Hertford, and Marlborough schools; and four, founded by Mr. Platt, have been increased by the college to nine. There are numerous exhibitions, varying from £70 each downwards. All livings under £30 in the king's books are tenable with the college preacherships, of which there are thirteen. The Bishop of Ely is visitor. The livings in the patronage of the master and fellows are, the rectories of Brinkley and Fulbourn, and the perpetual curacy of Horningsea, in the county of Cambridge; the rectories of Houghton-Conquest, Houghton-Gildable, Marston-Moretaine, and Meppershall, in the county of Bedford; the vicarages of Aldworth and Sunninghill, in the county of Berks; the rectory of Aberdaron, in the county of Carnarvon; the rectory of Morton, in the county of Derby, alternately with William Turbett, Esq.; the rectory of Marwood, in the county of Devon; the rectories of Lawford, Great Oakley, Great Warley, Moreton, and Thorrington with that of Frating, in the county of Essex; the vicarage of Great Hormead, and the rectories of Lilley and Little Hormead, in the county of Hertford; the rectory of Freshwater, in the Isle of Wight; the rectories of Murston and Staplehurst, and the vicarages of Higham and Ospringe, in the county of Kent; the vicarage of Barrow upon Soar, and the rectory of Medbourne with the curacy of Holt, in the county of Leicester; the vicarage of Minting, in the county of Lincoln; the vicarage of Cherry-Marham, and the rectories of Aldborough, Ditchingham, Forncett St. Mary and St. Peter, Great Snoring, Holt, and Starston, in the county of Norfolk; the rectory of Ufford with the curacy of Bainton, in the county of Northampton; the vicarage of North Stoke, and the rectory of Souldern, in the county of Oxford; the rectory of St. Florence, in the county of Pembroke; the rectories of Barrow, Cockfield, and Layham, in the county of Suffolk; the rectory of Wootton-Rivers, in the county of Wilts, alternately with the principal and fellows of Brasenose College, Oxford; the rectory of Brandsburton, and the vicarage of Holme upon Spalding-Moor with the rectory of Holme, in the East riding of the county of York; and the vicarage of Marton with Grafton, in the West riding of the county of York. Of these livings, five rectories in Norfolk are in the nomination of the Duke of Norfolk, but can be given only to the foundation fellows of the college. The buildings are situated to the north of Trinity College, and occupy the whole space between Trinity-street and the river, consisting of three courts, built for the most part of brick: the first, which is the most ancient, is about two hundred and twenty-eight feet by two hundred and sixteen, and is entered from the street by a handsome gateway, with turrets coeval with the foundation: the second court, about two hundred and seventy feet by two hundred and forty, is very handsome, and chiefly consists of the fellows' apartments; it was built by the benefaction of Mary, Countess of Shrewsbury: the third, next the river, is of smaller dimensions than the others. The north side of the first court is occupied by the chapel, that of the second by the master's lodge, and that of the third by the library; extending altogether the whole length of the college from east to west, about four hundred and eighty feet. The chapel is one hundred and twenty feet long: in the ante-chapel is the tombstone of Thomas Baker, the antiquary, sometime fellow of this college, who wrote its history; and in the chapel is a tablet, in memory of the learned Dr. Whitaker, master, who died in 1595. In the master's lodge is a spacious ancient gallery, nearly one hundred and fifty-five feet long, with a richly ornamented ceiling, now divided into a suite of rooms containing numerous portraits of benefactors and members of the college. The library, built by Archbishop Williams, is a spacious room, containing one of the most valuable and extensive collections of books in the university, among which are those presented to the college by Matthew Prior, consisting chiefly of the works of the French historians. This college suffered severely during the civil war in the reign of Charles I., having been plundered, amongst other valuable articles, of the communion plate, and of a large collection of silver coins and medals: the outer court was at the same time converted into a prison for the royalists. The spacious gardens and walks lie on the west side of the river, over which is a stone bridge of three arches, leading from the inner court: the fellows' garden has a bowling-green. A large and splendid addition to this college has been nearly completed, from a design by Rickman and Hutchinson, on the western side of the river, consisting of a spacious court, united to the three ancient courts by a covered stone bridge. The inner and the eastern and western fronts are all varied: the cloister extends from the east to the west wing, and has a lofty entrance in the centre; this building will afford additional accommodation for one hundred and seven students, including ten suites of apartments for the fellows of the college. Amongst eminent members, &c. were Roger Ascham; Sir John Cheke; Sir Thomas Wyat; Lord Treasurer Burleigh; Lord Keeper Williams; Dr. John Dee; Thomas Wentworth, Earl of Stafford; Lord Falkland; Dr. William Whitaker; Dr. William Cave; Archbishop Williams; Bishops Day, Gauden, Gunning, Stillingfleet, and Beveridge; Dr. Jenkins, who wrote on the reasonableness of Christianity; Dr. Powell; Dr. Balguy; Dr. Ogden; Thomas Stackhouse, author of the History of the Bible; Dr. William Wotton, Dr. Bentley, and Dr. Taylor, the critics; Ben Jonson; the poets, John Cleland, Ambrose Philips, Prior, Otway, Broome, Hammond, and Mason; Martin Lister, the naturalist; Francis Peck, and Thomas Baker, the antiquaries; and the late Dr. Heberden.

Arms.

Magdalene College was begun, in 1519, by Edward Stafford, Duke of Buckingham, by the name of Buckingham House, but was not completed at the time of his attainder, after which it was granted to Thomas, Baron Audley, Lord High Chancellor, who in 1542 endowed it for a master and four fellows. There are thirteen bye-fellowships; two of them are appropriated, one of the two being a travelling fellowship. All the fellows, except those of the two last-mentioned fellowships, must take orders within three years after election, if the master thinks fit. The mastership is in the appointment of the possessor of the estate at Audley End, now belonging to Lord Braybrooke. There are thirty-nine scholarships, varying in value from £3 to £70 per annum each, twelve of which are appropriated. The possessor of Audley End is visitor. The livings in the patronage of the master and fellows are, the rectory of Long Stanton St. Michael, in the county of Cambridge; the rectory of Anderby with that of Comberworth, and the perpetual curacy of Grainthorpe, in the county of Lincoln; the vicarage of St. Katherine Cree church, London; the rectory of Aldrington, in the county of Sussex; the vicarage of Steeple-Ashton (annexed to the Mastership), in the county of Wilts; and the rectory of Ellingham, in the county of Norfolk. This is the only college which stands on the north side of the river: it consists of two courts, the larger being about one hundred and ten feet by seventy-eight. On the north side of the second court is a stone building, the body of which contains the Pepysian library, and in the wings are the apartments of the fellows. This library was given to the college by Samuel Pepys, Esq., secretary to the admiralty in the reigns of Charles II. and James II.: in this repository, amongst other valuable curiosities, are preserved many very rare portraits and engravings, a large collection of ancient ballads, many of which are not elsewhere to be found, and the original narrative of the escape of Charles II., after the battle of Worcester, taken in short hand by Mr. Pepys, from the oral communication of the king himself: but the most valuable M.S. is the diary of Mr. Pepys, consisting of three thousand pages, chiefly in short hand, and relating to the maritime affairs of the kingdom from 1659 to 1669, copious extracts from which have recently been published, under the title of Memoirs of Samuel Pepys, Esq., F.R.S., &c. Among distinguished members, &c. were Archbishop Grindal; Dr. Thomas Nevile, who erected the beautiful court in Trinity College which bears his name; Pepys, the founder of the library; Dr. Duport, the celebrated Greek professor; the Lord Keeper Bridgeman; Bishop Walton, editor of the Polyglott Bible; Bishop Rainbow; Dr. Howell, the historian; Bishop Cumberland; Dr. Waterland; and the celebrated mathematician, Professor Waring.

Arms.

Trinity College stands on ground formerly occupied by seven hostels and two colleges (Michael House and King's Hall): the former college was founded, in 1324, by Hervey de Stanton, chancellor of the exchequer to Edward II.; the buildings of the latter, founded by Edward III., in 1337, for a master and thirty-two scholars, are said to have been of sufficient magnitude to accommodate Richard II. and his court, when he held a parliament at Cambridge, in 1381. Both these colleges were suppressed in 1546, and in the same year the present magnificent one was founded by Henry VIII., for a master and sixty fellows: the endowment was considerably augmented by his daughter, Queen Mary. The fellows are chosen from the scholars, ineligible if M.A., or of sufficient standing to take that degree; they are all required to go into priest's orders within seven years after they commence masters of arts, except two appointed by the master, one of whom is supposed to study law, the other physic. There are sixty-nine scholarships, which, except four or five, are open to men of any county. The government is vested in the master and eight seniors; and to so many of these as are absent the resident fellows next in seniority act as deputies: the matership is in the gift of the King, who is visitor. All livings within twenty miles of Cambridge, or such, in any part of the kingdom, as may have passed through the society; or livings from external patronage, the value of which in the king's books, after certain deductions, does not exceed £30, are tenable with college preacherships, of which there are sixteen. The livings in the patronage of the master and fellows are, the vicarages of Cardington, Eaton-Bray, Felmersham with the perpetual curacy of Pavenham, Great Barford with that of Roxton, and the vicarages of Keysoe, Shitlington, and Stotfold, in the county of Bedford; the rectory of Loughton, and the vicarage of Marsworth, in the county of Buckingham; the perpetual curacies of Great St. Mary's and St. Michael's, in the town of Cambridge; the vicarages of Arrington, Barrington, Bottisham, Chesterton, Over, Shudy-Camps, and Trumpington, and the rectories of Orwell and Papworth St. Everard, in the county of Cambridge; the vicarage of Gainford, in the county of Durham; the vicarages of Bumpstead-Helion and Hatfield-Broad-Oak, in the county of Essex; the vicarage of Great Wymondley with that of St. Ippolitts, the vicarage of Hitchin, and the vicarage of Ware with that of Thundridge, in the county of Hertford; the vicarage of Brading, in the Isle of Wight; the vicarage of Wimeswould, in the county of Leicester; the vicarage of East Ravendale (sequestrated), and those of East Randal, Little Coates, and Swineshead, in the county of Lincoln; the vicarage of Enfield, in the county of Middlesex; the rectories of Dickleburgh, Fakenham, and North Runcton, in the county of Norfolk; the vicarage of Grendon, in the county of Northampton; the vicarages of Blyth and Flintham, the perpetual curacies of Hoveringham, Thurgarton, and Langford, and the vicarages of Tuxford and Walkeringham, in the county of Nottingham; the rectory of Cheadle, in the county of Stafford; the rectory of Grundisburgh, in the county of Suffolk; the vicarages of Kirby-Monks and Withybrook, in the county of Warwick; the vicarages of Heversham, Kendal, and Kirkby-Lonsdale, in the county of Westmorland; the vicarage of Aysgarth, in the county of York; the rectory of Gilling, and the vicarage of Pickhill, in the North riding of the county of York; and the rectory and vicarage of Darfield, the rectory of Guiseley (one turn in three), the vicarage of Kellington, the vicarage of Kirkby-Malzeard with that of Masham, and the vicarages of Normanton All Saints, Sedbergh, and Whitkirk, in the West riding of the county of York.

The extensive buildings of this college are situated between those of St. John's and Caius Colleges, occupying the space between Trumpington-street and the river, and consisting of three spacious quadrangular courts. The first court, which is the largest, forms a magnificent assemblage of buildings: its form is a trapezium, approaching to a square, about six hundred and thirty yards in circuit; on the north side is the chapel; on the west the hall and the master's lodge: the other two sides comprise apartments for the fellows and students; the south end of the west side has been rebuilt in a handsome style. This court is entered from Trumpington-street by a turreted gateway, supposed to have been anciently the entrance to King's Hall. In the middle of it is a large conduit, which supplies the college and the neighbouring inhabitants with excellent water, brought by a subterraneous channel from a spring about a mile west of the town. The second court, called Nevile's Court, built in 1600, chiefly by the benefaction of Dr. Thomas Nevile, master of the college and Dean of Canterbury, is more elegant than the former, though less spacious; the length of its sides, which, like those of the first court, are unequal, vary from one hundred and thirty-two feet to two hundred and twenty-eight: the library, forming the west side, is of later date, the building having been projected by Dr. Barrow, and the north and south sides, containing fellows' and students' apartments, have been almost wholly rebuilt: the library and the cloisters, which extend along the north, west, and south sides, were designed by Sir Christopher Wren. Beyond Nevile's Court is the newly erected and magnificent quadrangle, called King's Court, in honour of King George IV., the building of which was commenced in 1823, and completed in 1825, at an expense of upwards of £40,000, a considerable part of which was defrayed by a subscription, headed by a donation of £2000 from that monarch; the buildings are from designs by William Wilkins, Esq., M.A., and the principal front, with a fine tower gateway, faces the college walks, in a line with the library. The chapel, upwards of two hundred feet long, is in the later style of English architecture, begun by Queen Mary, and finished by Queen Elizabeth; on each side of the choir are rows of very elegant stalls for the masters and scholars, with carved work by Gibbons; and the thrones for the master and the vice-master are remarkably grand and beautiful. Among the monuments in the ante-chapel, the most interesting are, a statue of Sir Isaac Newton, by Roubilliac, presented to the society by Dr. Smith, master of the college; a tablet in memory of the eminent mathematician, Roger Cotes, Plumian professor, who died in 1716; a tablet in memory of Isaac Hawkins Browne, Esq., celebrated for his poem on the Immortality of the Soul, and other works, who died in 1762; and a bust and tablet, by Chantrey, in memory of the late professor Porson. The hall, built in the later English style, is about one hundred feet long and fifty high. The master's lodge, which contains some magnificent apartments, has, ever since the reign of Elizabeth, been the residence of the sovereign, when the university has been honoured with a royal visit; and the judges always reside in it during the assizes.

The library, a magnificent room two hundred feet long, and proportionately lofty, was built by a subscription amounting to nearly £20,000, procured chiefly by the exertions of Dr. Barrow. The collection of books is large and valuable, and amongst the manuscripts are some of Milton's pieces in his own handwriting: among the busts are those of Bacon, Newton, Ray, and Willoughby, by Roubilliac; that of Roger Cotes; and one, by Scheemaker, of Edward Wortley Montagu, Esq., who presented to the society the celebrated Sigean inscription: there is also a statue of Charles Seymour, Duke of Somerset, for sixty years chancellor of the university, executed by Rysbrach in 1754; and at the upper end is a curious statue of Æsculapius, found at Samæ, about fourteen miles from Rome. Among the portraits the most interesting are, an original half-length of Shakspeare, by Mark Garrard, and an original full-length, in the hall, of Sir Isaac Newton, by Valentine Ritts. The room is paved with marble; and at the south end, opposite to the entrance, is a window of painted glass, from a design by Cipriani, representing the presentation of Sir Isaac Newton to his Majesty George II., for the execution of which £500 was bequeathed by Dr. Robert Smith, formerly master. The walks are spacious and particularly pleasant, and are connected with the college buildings by a bridge over the Cam. Amongst eminent members and students were, Archbishops Whitgift and Fowler; Bishops Powell, Wilkins, Pearson, Pearce, Hinchliffe, and Watson; Robert Devereux, Earl of Essex; Sir Francis Bacon; Sir Edward Coke; Fulke Greville; Lord Brooke; Charles, Earl of Halifax; Sir Isaac Newton; William Outram; Dr. Isaac Barrow; Dr. Bentley; Ray, the naturalist; Roger Cotes; Dr. William Whitaker; Bishop Hacket; the poets Cowley and Dryden; Dr. Donne, the satirist; Nathaniel Lee, the dramatist; George Herbert; Richard Duke; Lord Lansdowne; Sir Robert Cotton; Sir Henry Spelman; Dr. Gale; John le Neve; Francis Willoughby; Philemon Holland; Andrew Marvell; Robert Nelson; Dr. Samuel Knight; Dr. Conyers Middleton; the late professor Porson; and the late Lord Byron.

Arms.

Emanuel College was founded, in 1584, by Sir Walter Mildmay, chancellor of the exchequer and privy counsellor in the reign of Elizabeth; it occupies the site of a Dominican friary, founded about the year 1280, and subsequently enriched by Alice, widow of Robert Vere, second Earl of Oxford, which, after the dissolution, was purchased by Sir Walter, prior to the establishment of the college. The number of foundation fellowships is twelve, besides one, the holder of which receives a dividend arising from a distinct estate, but is in most respects on an equality with the foundation fellows. These thirteen fellowships are open to Englishmen of all counties, but there cannot be more than one from the same county. All the fellows must proceed to the degrees of M.A. and B.D., as soon as they are of sufficient standing; and the four seniors must take priest's orders. In addition to the above there are two fellows on the foundation by Sir Wolstan Dixie, who must proceed in their degrees equally with those on the original foundation, but have no vote in the society, nor any claim to the offices or dividends of the college. There are likewise four scholarships of the same foundation, and subject to the same restrictions. The foundation scholarships are open to Englishmen of all counties, but there can only be three from the same county: the scholars receive upwards of £12 per annum, in addition to the weekly payment of 7*s.* 6*d.* during residence. Besides these there are many scholarships and exhibitions, founded by various benefactors, to be given to the candidates most distinguished for learning and exemplary conduct. The visitors are, in some cases, the vice-chancellor and the two senior doctors in divinity, in others, the master of Christ's College and the two senior doctors. The livings in the patronage of the master and fellows are, the rectory of Wallington, in the county of Hertford; the vicarage of Standground with the curacy of Farcett, and the rectory of Thurning, in the county of Huntingdon; the rectories of Loughborough and Thurcaston, in the county of Leicester; the vicarage of Little Melton, in the county of Norfolk; the rectory of Boddington, in the county of Northampton; the rectory of North Luffenham, in the county of Rutland; the rectories of Aller, and North Cadbury, and the vicarages of King's Brompton and Winsford, in the county of Somerset; and the vicarage of Ilketshall St. Andrew, and the rectories of Preston St. Mary, and Withersdale with the vicarage of Fressingfield, in the county of Suffolk: they also nominate to the rectory of Twyford, in the county of Southampton, which is in the presentation of Lady Mildmay.

This college is very pleasantly situated in St. Andrew's street, near the south-eastern entrance into the town; the greater part of it is modern, and elegantly built of stone. It consists of one principal court, one hundred and twenty-eight feet by one hundred and seven, to which a range of buildings for the accommodation of students has recently been added, forming, with the library and the north side of the hall, a second court. The chapel, which is eighty-four feet long, and has a marble floor, was designed and commenced by Archbishop Sancroft, in 1668, and completed in 1677, the principal contribution to which was £1040, given by Sir Robert Gayer, K.B. The old chapel has been fitted up as the library, to which Archbishop Sancroft gave his own collection of books: among the works, which are principally on divinity, is a curious copy of Cicero's Offices, printed by Faust in 1465, in fine preservation. The hall is furnished with great elegance: at the upper end is a fine painting of Sir Wolstan Dixie, Knt., the founder of two bye-fellowships and two scholarships. The gardens are spacious, and have a bowling-green and a cold bath. Among eminent members were, Archbishop Sancroft; Bishops Hall, Bedell, Kidder, Hurd, Percy, and Bennet; Matthew Poole, author of the Synopsis Criticorum; Joshua Barnes; Dr. Wallis, the mathematician; Sir Robert Twiston, the antiquary; John Morton, the historian of Northamptonshire; Sir Francis Pemberton; Sir William Temple; Anthony Blackwall, author of "The Sacred Classics Defended and Illustrated;" Dr. Farmer, the sagacious commentator on Shakspeare, to whose memory there is a tablet in the cloister, near the entrance into the chapel; and the late Dr. Samuel Parr.

Arms.

Sidney Sussex College was founded, in 1598, pursuant to the will of Frances Sidney, Countess of Sussex, who died in 1589. There are nine foundation fellowships, open to natives of any part of his Majesty's dominions; besides which there are two appropriated to the scholars of this college, and one, the nomination to which is vested in the Warden and Company of Fishmongers: the two former have nearly the same privileges as those on the foundation. This being a divinity college, all the fellows must take orders within three years from the time of their election. There are twenty foundation scholarships, value seven shillings per week during residence, and two appropriated. Sir John Shelley Sidney, Bart. is visitor, as the representative of the foundress; but, by the statutes, the vice-chancellor and the two senior doctors in divinity are visitors in some cases, and the vice-chancellor, with the masters of Christ's and Emanuel Colleges, in others. The livings in the patronage of the master and fellows are, the rectory of Week St. Mary, in the county of Cornwall; the rectory of Swanscombe, in the county of Kent; the rectory of Gayton, in the county of Northampton; the vicarage of Peasmarsh, in the county of Sussex; and the rectory of South Kilvington, in the North riding of the county of York: the rectory of Rempstone, in the county of Nottingham, is in the patronage of the master. The buildings are situated on the east side of Sidney-street, and consist of two courts built of brick, and completed in 1598. The chapel and the library were rebuilt in 1780. The hall and the master's lodge have lately been cased with stone and greatly improved, and the whole college is intended to be beautified under the direction of Sir Jeffrey Wyatville. The grounds are spacious, and the fellows' garden has a large bowling-green. Amongst eminent members or students may be recorded Oliver Cromwell; Archbishop Bramall; Bishops Seth Ward, Montagu, and Garnet; Thomas Fuller, the historian; Lord Chief Baron Atkins; Sir Roger L'Estrange; Gataker, the critic; Dr. Comber, Dean of Durham; Thomas Woolston, who wrote against miracles; and William Wollaston, author of "The Religion of Nature Delineated." In the master's lodge is a portrait in crayons of Cromwell, by Cooper, and in the library, a bust by Bernini, from a cast taken after his death.

Arms.

Downing College was founded by Sir George Downing, Bart., of Gamlingay Park, in this county, who, by will dated in 1717, devised his estates in the counties of Cambridge, Bedford, and Suffolk, first to Sir Jacob Garrard Downing and afterwards to other relatives, in succession, and, in failure thereof, to found a college in this university upon a plan to be approved by the two archbishops and the masters of St. John's College and Clare Hall. Sir Jacob died in 1764, the other devisees having died previously without issue; but the estates being held by Lady Downing, and afterwards by her devisees, though without any real title, the university was obliged to sue in Chancery for the establishment of the college, a decree in favour of which was obtained in 1769. The persons named as trustees in the founder's will having died in his lifetime, the trust devolved upon the heirs-at-law, who, after combating a long series of opposition and litigation, and overcoming obstacles of various kinds, petitioned the Crown for a charter, which passed the great seal in September, 1800. By this charter the college is incorporated, with all the privileges belonging to any college in the university, and endowed with the estates devised by the founder, with power to hold landed property in addition thereto, to the value of £1500 per annum. Statutes for its government were framed in July 1805, and shortly afterwards the stipends of the members began to be paid. It is provided that no new foundation shall ever be engrafted on this college that shall be inconsistent with the charter and statutes; but the college may accept any additions to its property, in augmentation of the number or value of its present appointments, or to be applied in any other manner consistent with its constitution. A piece of land comprising nearly thirty acres, situated between Emanuel and Pembroke Colleges, having been purchased for the site, the first stone was laid May 18th, 1807, since which time the building has proceeded at intervals, at an expense of more than £60,000. The society will consist of a master, professors of law and medicine, sixteen fellows (of whom two are to be clerical), and six scholars. The object of the foundation is stated in the charter to be the study of law, physic, and other useful arts and learning. At present only the master, the professors, and three fellows are appointed, to take possession of the estates, administer the revenues, superintend the building of the college, &c.; the appointment of the remaining fellows is reserved until the completion of the buildings. The scholars will also be elected after that period, but not more than two in each year. There are two chaplains nominated by the master, who is to be elected by the archbishops of Canterbury and York, and the masters of St. John's College and Clare Hall, from among those who are, or have been, professors or fellows. The electors to the professorships are the same as to the masterships, with the addition of the master. The professor of law must be, at the time of his election, D.C.L., M.A., or B.C.L., of Cambridge or Oxford, of ten years' standing from matriculation, and a barrister at law. The professor of medicine must be an M.A., who has been licensed for two years to practise physic, or M.D. or M.B. of Cambridge or Oxford, or a member of a Scotch university, of seven years' standing, twenty-five years of age, and who shall have attended the medical lectures in one of the Scotch universities for four years. The electors to the fellowships are the master, the professors, and fellows of the degree of M.A. All graduates of Cambridge or Oxford are eligible; but after the completion of the buildings, lay fellows must be under the age of twenty-four, and clerical under thirty, at the time of election: there must not be eight fellows from one county. The clerical fellowships will be tenable for life, and subject to residence for a certain part of each term. The lay fellowships are tenable only for twelve years, and are not subject to any residence. Every lay fellow must declare either for law or physic: those who declare for law must be called to the bar within eight years after their election, and the medical fellows must take the degree of M.D. within two years after they are of sufficient standing. The visitor is the King, by the Lord Chancellor. The livings in the patronage of the master and fellows are, the rectory of East Hatley, and the vicarage of Tadlow, in the county of Cambridge. In May 1821, a portion of the buildings, sufficient for opening the college, being completed, under-graduates were admitted to reside and keep terms. The whole, when completed, will form a quadrangle, larger than the principal court of Trinity College, in the Grecian style, and faced with Ketton stone. The master's lodge is of the Ionic, and the entrance to the college will be of the Doric, order; the designs are by William Wilkins, Esq., M.A. The late Mr. John Bowtell, of this town, bequeathed to the college a collection of books, manuscripts, fossils, and antiquities, with a request that the cases containing them should be placed in the college library.

The town is divided into four distinct wards, named respectively Bridge ward, Market ward, High ward, and Preacher's ward, and contains the fourteen parishes of All Saints, St. Andrew the Great, St. Andrew the Less, St. Benedict, St. Botolph, St. Clement, St. Edward, St. Giles, St. Mary the Great, St. Mary the Less, St. Michael, St. Peter, St. Sepulchre, and the Holy Trinity, all (except the precincts of King's College, which are in the diocese of Lincoln) in the archdeaconry and diocese of Ely, excepting St. Andrew's the Less, which, being a donative, is exempt from all ecclesiastical authority. The university, by custom and composition, is exempt from episcopal and archidiaconal jurisdiction. The living of All Saints' is a discharged vicarage, rated in the king's books at £5. 6. 3., endowed with £400 parliamentary grant, and in the patronage of the Master and Fellows of Jesus College. The living of St. Andrew's the Great is a discharged vicarage, endowed with £200 private benefaction, and £400 royal bounty, and in the patronage of the Dean and Chapter of Ely. The church was repaired and a great part of it rebuilt in 1643, chiefly by the benefaction of Christopher Rose, Esq.: in the north transept is a cenotaph in memory of the celebrated navigator Captain Cook, and his three sons. The living of St. Andrew's the Less, or Barnwell, is a donative, in the patronage of the owner of the priory at Barnwell. The church stands eastward from the town, and is supposed to have been built from the ruins of the priory. The village of Barnwell has suffered from repeated fires: the last and most destructive of these was on the 30th of November 1731, when the greater part of the houses was consumed. A chapel of ease to the church of this parish has been recently erected. The living of St. Benedict's is a perpetual curacy, rated at £4. 7. 11., endowed with £200 private benefaction, £400 royal bounty, and £1200 parliamentary grant, and in the patronage of the Master and Fellows of Corpus Christi College. In the church was interred Thomas Hobson, the celebrated Cambridge carrier. The living of St. Botolph's is a discharged rectory, rated at £2. 14. 4½., endowed with £400 private benefaction, £600 royal bounty, and £200 parliamentary grant, and in the patronage of the President and Fellows of Queen's College. The living of St. Clement's is a perpetual curacy, rated at £4. 5. 7½., endowed with £400 private benefaction, £200 royal bounty, and £1100 parliamentary grant, and in the patronage of the Master and Fellows of Jesus' College. The church stands a little south of the great bridge. The living of St. Edward's is a discharged rectory, rated at 3*s.* 4*d.*, and in the patronage of the Master and Fellows of Trinity Hall. The church stands a little to the west of Trumpington-street. The living of St. Giles' is a vicarage not in charge, to which the perpetual curacy of St. Peter's is united, endowed with £200 royal bounty, for St. Giles', and £800 royal bounty for St. Peter's, and in the patronage of the Bishop of Ely. St. Giles' church stands at the north end of the town: St. Peter's, opposite to it, has been disused for many years. The living of St. Mary's the Great is a perpetual curacy, endowed with £400 private benefaction, £200 royal bounty, and £1300 parliamentary grant, and in the patronage of the Master and Fellows of Trinity College. The church, commonly called the University church, is situated nearly in the centre of the town, on the east side of Trumpington-street, and opposite to the public schools and library. It is in the later style of English architecture, and consists of a nave, the dimensions of which are about one hundred and twenty feet by sixty-eight, two aisles, and a chancel, with a lofty tower surmounted by pinnacles, and containing twelve bells, which are rung on all state holidays, &c. The rebuilding of this church, by contribution, was begun in 1478, and finished in 1519, except the tower, which was not completed until 1608. In it was interred the celebrated reformer, Martin Bucer, whose body was taken up in the reign of Mary, and burned, with that of Paul Phagius, in the market-place. Academical exercises were formerly performed, and public orations delivered, here; and, in 1564, Queen Elizabeth was present at the disputations held in it. The university sermons are still preached here: the vice-chancellor, heads of colleges, noblemen, professors, and doctors, sit in a handsome gallery raised between the nave and the chancel; the proctors, masters of arts, and fellow commoners, have seats in the area of the nave, called the pit; and the bachelors and under-graduates are provided with places in the side galleries: William Worts, Esq., who died in 1709, left the sum of £1500, to accumulate for the purpose of building the galleries, and £20 per annum for keeping them in repair. The churchwardens of this parish were made a body corporate by Henry VIII., in 1535. The living of St. Mary's the Less is a perpetual curacy, endowed with £1200 parliamentary grant, and in the patronage of the Master and Fellows of St. Peter's College. The church was built in 1327, on the site of a former church, dedicated to St. Peter, which gave name to the adjoining college of Peter-House. The living of St. Michael's is a perpetual curacy, endowed with £800 royal bounty, and in the patronage of the Master and Fellows of Trinity College. The church stands on the east side of Trumpington-street, opposite to Caius College: in the spacious chancel are held the bishop's visitations and confirmations. In 1556, this church was placed under an interdict, as being the burial-place of Paul Phagius, then esteemed an arch-heretic, and was re-consecrated by the Bishop of Chester, acting as the deputy of Cardinal Pole. The living of St. Sepulchre's is a vicarage, rated at £6. 11. 0½., endowed with £200 private benefaction, £1000 royal bounty, and £200 parliamentary grant, and in the gift of the churchwardens and parishioners. St. Sepulchre's, or the church of the Holy Sepulchre, stands on the east side of Bridge-street, and is remarkable for the antiquity and peculiarity of construction of the older part of it, which is believed to be the oldest remaining specimen of the circular churches erected by the Knights Templars, on the model of that of the Holy Sepulchre at Jerusalem, and to have been built in the reign of Henry I.: it is forty-one feet in diameter, and has a peristyle of eight rude massive pillars, supporting circular arches with chevron mouldings. This church contains a tablet in memory of Dr. Ogden, the eminent divine, who died in 1778. The living of Trinity parish is a discharged vicarage, rated at £7. 6. 8., endowed with £800 royal bounty, and £1000 parliamentary grant, and in the patronage of the Bishop of Ely. The church stands at the south end of Bridge-street. There are meeting-houses for Baptists, the Society of Friends, Independents, and Primitive and Wesleyan Methodists.

The free grammar school, situated near Corpus Christi College, was established in pursuance of the will of Stephen Perse, M.D., senior fellow of Caius College, who, in 1615, bequeathed certain property in trust for its erection and endowment; the master's salary is £40 per annum, and the usher's £20, with apartments for each; the number of free scholars is sixteen, who must be natives of Cambridge, Barnwell, Chesterton, or Trumpington, and, besides a knowledge of the Greek and Latin languages, and of Greek, Latin, and English composition, they are instructed in the ordinary branches of education, and in the elements of the mathematics: scholars educated for three years at least at this school are eligible, before all others, to the Perse fellowships and scholarships at Caius College. The new free school, situated in St. Peter's parish, founded in 1808, for the instruction of the poor of the town and the adjacent villages, was, in 1813, placed under the control of the National Society: the school-room is calculated to hold three hundred boys. The old charity schools, for both sexes, commonly called Whiston's charity schools, were instituted in 1703, chiefly by the exertions of the distinguished William Whiston, at that time Lucasian professor of the Mathematics, and to which William Worts, Esq., in 1709, bequeathed £30 per annum. On the union of the new free school with the National society, the boys from these schools also were transferred to that institution, to which, in consequence, the sum of £30 is annually allowed from the funds of the old charity schools. In 1816, a new school-room for three hundred girls was built in King-street, and the establishment put on the plan of the National society, to which it was then united. There are three infant schools.

The general hospital, or infirmary, commonly called Addenbrooke's hospital, situated at the entrance into the town from London, was founded by John Addenbrooke, M.D., fellow of Catharine Hall, who, in 1719, bequeathed about £4000 to erect and maintain a small physical hospital. The building was begun about 1753, and opened for the reception of patients in 1766, when the funds being found insufficient for its support, an act of parliament was obtained to make it a general hospital, since which it has been supported, in addition to the funds left by the founder, by donations and subscriptions. Mr. John Bowtell, late a bookbinder and stationer in this town, by will dated in September 1813, bequeathed to this institution £7000 three per cent. consolidated Bank Annuities, between £3000 and £4000 of which has been appropriated to the addition of two extensive wings: the building is faced with stone, and has a handsome colonnade in front. The number of patients annually cured or relieved is now about one thousand; and the annual expense has of late years been about £1700, of which about £600 is paid from the permanent funds. By act of parliament, the chancellor, the vice-chancellor, and the two representatives of the university, the bishop of Ely, the lord lieutenant of the county, the county members and the high sheriff, and the members for the town, the high steward, and the mayor, are perpetual governors. There are almshouses for upwards of fifty poor persons, founded and endowed by different individuals, the inmates of which receive allowances, varying from £2 to £20 per annum. John Crane, apothecary, who died in 1654, bequeathed money to purchase an estate, now producing upwards of £300 per annum, to be settled on the five following corporations, *viz.*, the university of Cambridge, and the towns of Wisbeach, Cambridge, Lynn, and Ipswich; the rents to be received in order, and to be applied by the university, in its turn, towards the relief of sick scholars. The gift to the town was to accumulate until it amounted to £200, which sum was to be disposed of in loans of £20 each, bearing no interest for twenty years, to ten young men, to set them up in trade. After the sum of £200 had been set apart, Mr. Crane directed that the rents of the estates should be applied to the relief of persons confined for debt, and of poor men and women of good character. Cambridge is also one of the twenty-five cities and towns to which Sir Thomas White gave, in rotation, the sum of £104, of which £100 was to be lent, in sums of £25 each, to five young freemen for ten years, without interest, preference being given to clothiers. William Worts, Esq., besides his other benefactions to the town and the university, left £1500 of the produce of his estates, bequeathed in trust, for making a causeway towards Gogmagog hills, which was done before the year 1767; and Thomas Hobson, by will dated in 1629, left houses to trustees, for the maintenance of a house of correction, for setting the poor to work, and other charitable objects, at the discretion of the corporation, which bequest has been increased by one of £500 by the late Mr. John Bowtell.

The religious houses at Cambridge were numerous: the most ancient was that of Augustine canons, founded near the castle, in 1092, by Picot, the sheriff, and augmented and removed to Barnwell, by Payne Peverel, standard-bearer to Robert, Duke of Normandy; its revenue, at the dissolution, was valued at £351. 15. 4.: some remains of the conventual buildings have been converted into farm offices. The Benedictine nunnery of St. Rhadegund appears to have been founded about the year 1130: it was originally dedicated to St. Mary, but was re-dedicated to St. Rhadegund by Malcolm IV., King of Scotland, who augmented its revenue, and rebuilt the conventual church about the year 1160, the remaining portion of which forms the chapel of Jesus' College; for the purpose of founding this college it was granted to Bishop Alcock by Henry VII., having escheated to the Crown in consequence of its being deserted by the nuns. The monastery of the Grey friars, or Franciscans, the site of which is occupied by Sidney-Sussex College, was founded about 1224, and was very flourishing. The Bethlemite friars settled in Cambridge, in 1257, in a house in Trumpington-street, of which they had procured a grant. The friars *De sacco*, or *De pœnitentiâ Jesu Christi*, whose order was suppressed in 1307, settled in the same street in 1258. The brethren of St. Mary settled in the parish of All Saints, near the castle, about 1274. The priory of the Black friars, the site of which is occupied by Emanuel College, was founded before 1275. The Augustine friars are supposed to have settled here about 1290: their convent, which was in the parish of St. Edward, was founded by Sir Geffrey Pitchford, Knt. The White friars, or Carmelites, the site of whose convent is occupied by the garden of the provost of King's College, settled first at Chesterton, and afterwards at the adjoining hamlet of Newenham, about 1249, from which they removed, in 1316, to a spot of ground just within the walls, given them by Edward II. A small priory of Gilbertines was founded by Bishop Fitzwalter, in 1291: the society occupied the old chapel of St. Edmund, opposite to Peter-House.

The castle, built in the reign of William the Conqueror, on the site of a Roman station, afterwards occupied by a Danish fortress, was, in early times, an occasional residence of the English sovereigns: after it had ceased to be so occupied, the buildings, which were extensive, went to decay: during the civil war it was made a garrison for the parliament. The county was in possession of it, subject to a fee-farm rent, so early as 1660; and the quarter sessions were regularly held in it from that time until after the building of the shire-hall: all that remains of the ancient building is a gate-house, which was long used as a prison, until the erection, about twenty-five years ago, of a new county gaol within the limits of the castle. Some of the earthworks that surround it are undoubtedly Roman. A somewhat curious piece of architectural antiquity exists in the ancient mansion-house of Merton Hall, in the parish of St. Giles, which has long borne the name of Pythagoras' School, though for what reason is unknown; the most remarkable part of the building is a large hall, measuring sixty-one feet by twenty-two: it had formerly an undercroft, with circular arches and plain pillars, apparently constructed in the early part of the twelfth century. There are several springs in the parish of All Saints, the water of which is strongly impregnated with iron. Amongst eminent natives of Cambridge were, Sir John Cheke, tutor, and afterwards secretary of state, to Edward VI.; Dr. Thirlebye, first and only bishop of Westminster, and afterwards, successively, bishop of Norwich and Ely; Bishop Jeremy Taylor; Dr. Goldisborowe, Bishop of Gloucester; Dr. Townson, Bishop of Salisbury; Dr. Love, Dean of Ely; Thomas Bennett, who suffered martyrdom at Exeter, in 1530; and Richard Cumberland, the dramatist. Prince Adolphus Frederick, fifth and youngest surviving son of King George III., was created Duke of Cambridge, November 27th, 1801.

CAMBRIDGE, a hamlet in the parish of SLIMBRIDGE, upper division of the hundred of BERKELEY, county of GLOUCESTER, $3\frac{1}{2}$ miles (N. by W.) from Dursley. The population is returned with the parish. In the reign of Edward the Elder a battle was fought here between the Saxons and the Danes, in which the former were victorious.

CAMBRIDGESHIRE, an inland county, bounded on the north-west by the county of Lincoln, on the north-east by the county of Norfolk, on the east by the county of Suffolk, on the south by the counties of Essex and Hertford, and on the west by the counties of Bedford, Huntingdon, and Northampton: it extends from 52° 3′ to 52° 40′ (N. Lat.), and from 25′ (E. Lon.) to 10′ (W. Lon.); and it contains eight hundred and fifty-eight square miles, or about five hundred and fifty thousand acres. The population, in 1821, amounted to 121,909.

At the time of the Roman invasion, Cambridgeshire formed part of the kingdom of the *Iceni*, being, according to Whitaker, inhabited by a tribe of that people, called the *Cenomanni*. In the first division of Britain by the Romans, it was included in *Britannia Superior;* in the second, in *Britannia Prima;* and in the last, in *Flavia Cæsariensis.* During the Saxon Octarchy, it was part of the kingdom of the East Angles. On the subsequent division of England into three great districts, this county was comprised in that called *Denelege*, or the Danish jurisdiction. The Isle of Ely, from an early period, formed a separate district, with an independent jurisdiction, being called by the Saxons *South-Girwa:* Toubert, the husband of Ethelbreda, foundress of Ely abbey, gave it her in dower, and she bestowed it on that monastery, with all its liberties and privileges. On the Danish invasion and conquest of East Anglia, in the year 870, when King Edmund was put to death, the county was entirely laid waste; and for fifty years afterwards, during which East Anglia remained under the Danish dominion, Cambridge appears to have been one of their principal military stations: there it was that, in the year 921, the Danish army surrendered to King Edward the Elder. After the destruction of Ely by the Danes, King Burrhed annexed the isle to the kingdom of Mercia. Again, in the year 1010, Cambridgeshire was ravaged by the same barbarous invaders, together with all the rest of the kingdom of East Anglia. After the battle of Hastings, and the consequent advance of the Conqueror into the interior of the kingdom, the Isle of Ely, on account of the deep fens which surrounded it, being a post of great strength, became the refuge of the Anglo-Saxon prelates and nobles who continued their resistance, in spite of repeated attempts to reduce it, under the command of the brave and vigilant Hereward: they held this post from 1067 to 1074, when it was surrendered through the treachery of the abbot and monks of Ely, to redeem from confiscation such of their lands as lay without the limits of the isle. During the civil wars in the reigns of Stephen, John, and Henry III., the county in general, and the Isle of Ely in particular, suffered severely from the devastations caused by the contending parties; and it was at Cambridge that the barons, on the death of John, were met in council by Louis the Dauphin. The only historical event of importance, from the reign of Henry III. to that of Charles I., is the proclaiming of Lady Jane Grey at Cambridge by the Duke of Northumberland, in 1553. At the beginning of the parliamentary war, Cambridgeshire and the Isle of Ely associated under Lord Grey of Werke for the parliament, and petitioned for arms for the defence of the county against the commissioners of array. Lord Clarendon enumerates this among the associated counties in which the king had no visible party, nor one fixed quarter. The university, however, voted its plate for the king's service. In 1643, Cromwell took possession of Cambridge for the parliament; and in 1645, the same commander, who had a considerable estate in that district, was sent down with three troops of horse to secure the Isle of Ely. In the month of August in the same year, the king marched towards Cambridge, but departed without attacking it. In June 1647, the parliamentarian army, under Fairfax and Cromwell, had its head-quarters at Kennet, near Newmarket. At Childerley, near Cambridge, on the 7th of the same month, Fairfax and Cromwell waited on the king, and disavowed all participation in the seizure of his person by Cornet Joyce: on the 9th, the king was removed to Newmarket. The parliamentary army, while it remained in Cambridgeshire, had a general rendezvous on Triplow heath, and another near Royston.

This county (excepting fifteen parishes in the eastern part of it, which are in the archdeaconry of Sudbury, and diocese of Norwich, and the parish of Isleham, in the peculiar jurisdiction of the Bishop of Rochester), forms an archdeaconry in the diocese of Ely, province of Canterbury, comprising the deaneries of Barton, Bourne, otherwise Knapwell, Cambridge, Camps, Chesterton, Ely, Shengay, and Wisbeach; and contains one hundred and sixty-two parishes, of which sixty-six are rectories, eighty-four vicarages, and twelve perpetual curacies. For civil purposes it is divided into seventeen hundreds, *viz.*, those of Armingford, Chesterton, Cheveley, Chilford, Ely, Flendish, Longstow, Northstow, Papworth, Radfield, Staine, Staploe, Thriplow, Wetherley, Whittlesford, Wisbeach, and Witchford. It contains the city of Ely; the university, borough, and market town of Cambridge; the market towns of Linton, March, Thorney, and Wisbeach; and part of the market towns of Newmarket and Royston. Two knights are returned to parliament for the shire, and two representatives each for the university and borough of Cambridge: the prevalent influence in county elections is possessed by the Dukes of Bedford and Rutland, and the Earl of Hardwicke. Cambridgeshire is within the Norfolk circuit: the assizes and quarter sessions for the county are held at Cambridge, where stands the county gaol: there are eighty-three acting magistrates. The Isle of Ely having been restored with all its privileges to the abbey of Ely, after the re-establishment of that monastery by King Edgar, the abbots, and afterwards the bishops, exercised the privileges of a county palatine until the reign of Henry VIII., when these privileges were, in common with those of other palatinates, considerably abridged by act of parliament. The bishop is still *custos rotulorum* of the Isle of Ely, including the three hundreds of Ely, Wisbeach, and Witchford, his jurisdiction being entitled the royal franchise, or liberty, of the Bishop of Ely. The civil officers of this franchise are, a chief justice, who holds a court of pleas above 40*s.*, under a commission from the bishop, and a court of Oyer and Terminer and gaol delivery, by virtue of a commission from the king; a chief bailiff, who exercises the same functions in the isle as the sheriff does in a county; a deputy-bailiff, two coroners, and several subordinate officers, all of whom are appointed by the bishop. The spring assizes and the April and October sessions for the isle are held at Ely; the summer assizes and the other sessions at Wisbeach; at each of these places there are a court-house and a gaol. The rates raised in the county for the year ending March 25th, 1829, amounted to £111,497, and the expenditure to £110,615, of which £94,369 was applied to the relief of the poor.

The surface of the county exhibits considerable variety: the parts adjoining the counties of Suffolk, Essex, and Hertford, have gently rising hills, with downs and open corn-fields, and a considerable portion of wood in the part contiguous to Suffolk, from Wood-Ditton to Castle-Camps; but in other parts there is a great scarcity of timber. Gogmagog hills, commencing about four miles south-east of Cambridge, though of no great height, yet being the highest in the county, command very extensive prospects. There is some pleasing scenery about Linton, Hildersham, and other villages in the valley through which the Granta runs, between Cambridge and Bartlow, which abounds with elm-trees. The views from the upper part of the Earl of Hardwicke's park, at Wimpole, are very rich. The northern part of the county, including the Isle of Ely, is for the most part fen land, and quite level, intersected by numerous canals and ditches, and containing many windmills, like those of Holland, and steam-engines for conveying the water from the land into channels formed for carrying it off to the sea: the enclosures are chiefly formed by ditches, and there are few trees except pollard willows. The great expanse of fen land in this part of the county comprises nearly half of that extensive agricultural district called the Bedford Level, the remainder being situated in the counties of Norfolk, Lincoln, Northampton, and Huntingdon. From the various remains that have been discovered in constructing the channels, it is supposed that at some remote period this county was all firm land, reduced to a marshy nature by frequent inundations of the sea, and by the obstruction of the old natural outlet, at Wisbeach, of the rivers Ouse, Nene, and Granta, and of several lodes and lakes. To prevent subsequent inundations, commissions were issued, from time to time, to enforce the repair of banks and sewers. The most important work of this kind, executed before the time of James I., was the great channel made by Bishop Morton, which carried off the overflowings of the Nene, and furnished water-carriage from Wisbeach to Peterborough. From the reign of Henry VI. down to that of James I., various commissions were granted for a general drainage, but no great progress was made under any of them: in consequence of these several failures, the king, in 1621, declared himself the principal undertaker, but was diverted from the design by other affairs towards the close of his reign. In 1630, Sir Cornelius Vermuyden, a Dutchman, at a session of sewers then held at Lynn, agreed to undertake this great work, on condition of having ninety-five thousand acres of the recovered lands insured to him, as a compensation for the expense and labour; but the landowners rejected his offer, and petitioned Francis, Earl of Bedford, who had a large property in the fens, to undertake the work on the same terms. The earl having acceded to their request, an instrument was drawn up, by which the agreement was confirmed, and various regulations for the management of the concern were determined upon: this instrument, the foundation of the laws whereby the Bedford Level Corporation is still governed, having been made and ratified at a session of sewers held at Lynn, in the year 1631, received the appellation of the Lynn Law. The Earl of Bedford associated with himself the Earl of Bolingbroke, Lord Gorges, and others, to whom he assigned shares. In 1635, the king granted the adventurers a charter of incorporation, with extensive privileges; and so rapid was the progress of the work, that in about three years afterwards, at a session of sewers held at St. Ives, in October 1638, the Great Level was adjudged to be drained according to the Lynn Law, and the ninety-five thousand acres were ordered to be allotted according to the terms of the agreement. Of this allotment, twelve thousand were made over to the king, as an acknowledgment of his gracious favour in countenancing and assisting the undertaking, and forty thousand of the remainder were made liable to taxation, for the purpose of maintaining and repairing the works: however, at a session of sewers held at Huntingdon in 1639, the whole proceedings of the last commission were annulled, the drainage was adjudged to be incomplete and defective, and it was determined that the earl and his associates had not performed their contract, and were not entitled to the land that had been allotted to them. The king (Charles I.) now proposed to undertake the whole concern, and the commissioners offered him fifty-seven thousand acres, in addition to the ninety-five thousand already mentioned, of which forty thousand were to remain to the adventurers, as a recompense for the expense incurred. In consequence of the national troubles that soon afterwards ensued, no attempt was made under the authority of the new commission to improve the drainage; meantime all the works went to decay, and remained in that condition until the year 1649, when an ordinance was passed by the Convention Parliament, declaring all the proceedings at Huntingdon null and void; and the whole management of draining the level on the general plan of the Lynn Law was committed to the care of William, Earl of Bedford, son and heir of Earl Francis, the original undertaker, who died in 1641. In 1662, an act of parliament passed for confirming the ordinance made during the interregnum, since called "the pretended act," in its most essential points. by this act taxes were laid on the ninety-five thousand acres, for maintaining the works of the level, and this taxation was further adjusted by an act of 1667. Twelve thousand acres were allotted to the crown, including

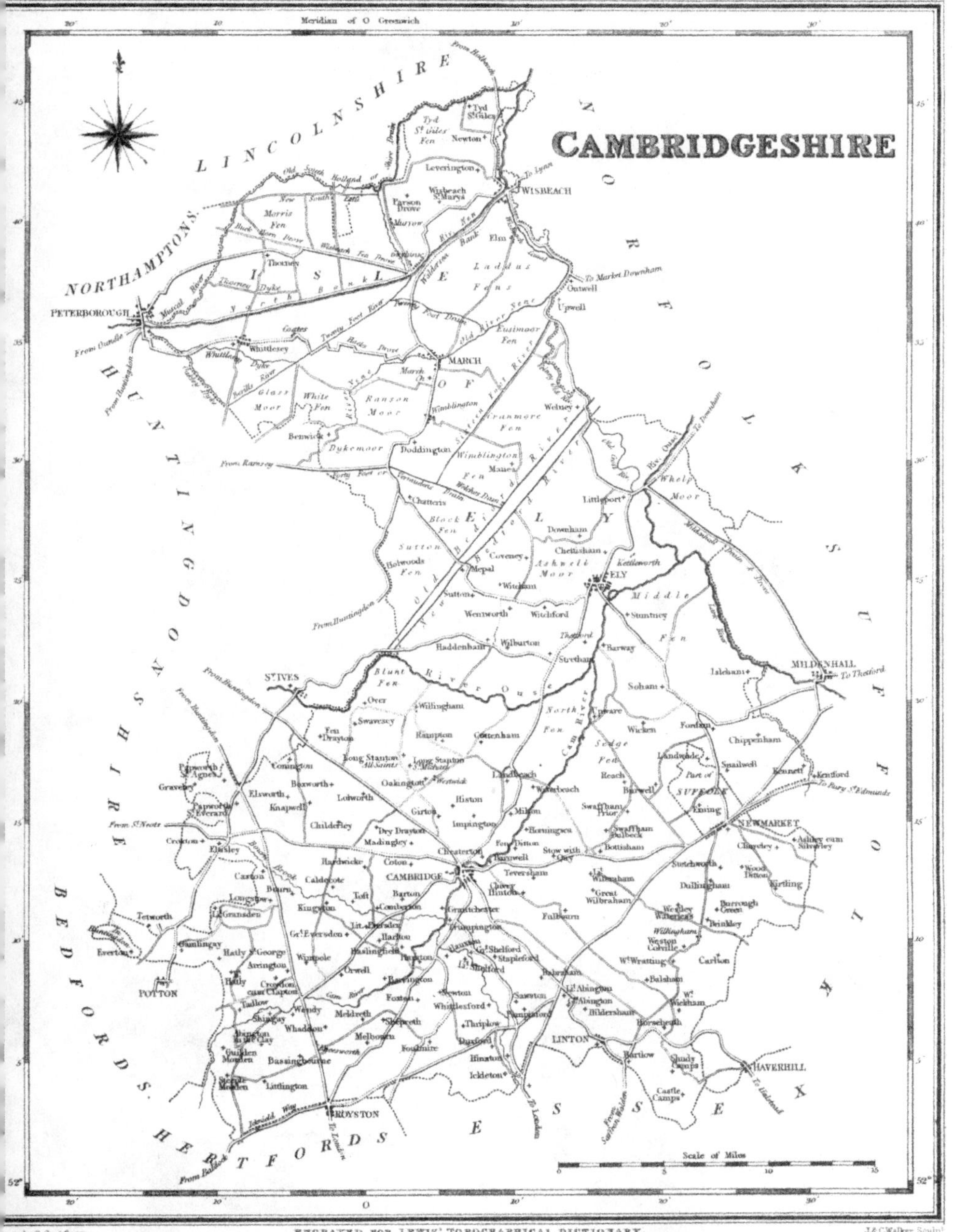

Drawn by R. Creighton. ENGRAVED FOR LEWIS' TOPOGRAPHICAL DICTIONARY. J.& C.Walker Sculpt

two thousand granted by Charles I. to Jerome, Earl of Portland; and the remaining eighty-three thousand were vested in the Corporation of the Bedford Level, which, under this act, consists of a governor, six bailiffs, twenty conservators, and commonalty. The officers are elected annually on the Wednesday in Whitsun-week: the commonalty consists of all such persons as are possessed of a hundred acres in the fens; a conservator must be possessed of two hundred; the governors and bailiffs of four hundred acres each. The Great Level, comprising a tract of about four hundred thousand acres, has been, from an early period, divided into three districts, the North Level, the Middle Level, and the South Level; the greater part of the Middle Level, and a considerable portion of the South Level, are in Cambridgeshire, including the whole of the Isle of Ely, and a few parishes to the south-east of it, and consisting nearly of two hundred thousand acres. With a view of obtaining a still more effectual drainage, an act for making a navigable cut from Lynn to Eau-Brinck passed in the year 1795, and another act to amend the former in 1805: this long-projected undertaking was commenced in 1818, and completed in 1820, the objects proposed to be accomplished by it being twofold, namely, the improvement of the drainage above, and of the harbour of Lynn below, by cutting off a considerable bend in the river Ouse immediately above that port: the old bed of the river is rapidly being filled up, and upwards of seven hundred acres of land will soon be converted to agricultural purposes.

The substrata of the county are chalk, clunch, gravel, gault, sand, silt, and peat earth: the chalk extends through the hilly part, from Royston to Newmarket; the clunch, a calcareous substance found in large masses, but neither so white nor so soft as chalk, chiefly abounds in the parish of Burwell and Isleham, and is much used for lime and fire stones; the gault is a stiff blue clay, prevailing in the eastern and western parts of the county; the stratum of sand, which crosses Bedfordshire, begins in this county in the parish of Gamlingay; the silt, a sea sand very finely pulverised by the agitation of the waters, is found in the marsh land of several parishes in the northern extremity of the county, near Wisbeach, where it is used for mending the roads; the peat earth extends through the whole of the fen district. The soil is chiefly arable, and produces an abundant supply of corn, a considerable quantity of which is sent to the London market: the average produce of wheat on the uplands is calculated at twenty-four bushels per acre; of barley, oats, &c., at thirty bushels: the fen lands are more productive, particularly of oats, yielding on an average about forty bushels per acre: it is estimated that about one-fourth of the fen lands actually in cultivation is sown with cole-seed, the plant being for the most part eaten off by sheep. Hemp and flax are cultivated to a considerable extent in the parishes of Upwell, Welney, Outwell, Elm, and Wisbeach, particularly in the two first. The parishes of Chatteris, Mepal, Sutton, Swavesey, Over, Willingham, Cottenham, Rampton, Landbeach, Waterbeach, Stretham, Ely, Littleport, Soham, and Fordham, constitute the principal dairy district, a great quantity of the butter produced in which is sent to London, and there sold under the name of Cambridge butter. In the parish of Cottenham alone, about one thousand eight hundred cows are kept; and in that of Willingham about one thousand two hundred: in these two parishes is made the cheese so much esteemed for its flavour, which goes by the name of Cottenham cheese: the parish of Soham also is celebrated for good cheese. The neighbourhood of Ely is noted for producing garden vegetables. Besides the stock common to the county, the oxen reared are usually of the Norfolk and Suffolk breed; the cows are mostly of the Cambridgeshire horned breed, although almost every parish contains various kinds: the native calves are preferred to those of Suffolk, the veal of the former being whiter. The greatest number of sheep is kept in the fens: the breed preferred is a cross between the Leicestershire and the Lincolnshire, but there are many others.

The principal rivers are the Ouse, the Cam or Granta, and the Nene. The Old Ouse crosses the county from west to east, entering it in the parish of Haddenham, near Earith bridge, and forms the southern and south-eastern boundary of the Isle of Ely, receiving the Cam at Upware, and, at a place called Prickwillow, the Lark, which is navigable to Bury St. Edmund's; it there becomes the boundary between the counties of Cambridge and Suffolk, and so continues to Brand Creek, where it receives the Little Ouse, and quits the county. The Ouse, in its modern course, enters the county about two furlongs to the north-west of Earith bridge, runs down the Hundred Feet, or New Bedford river, in a direction nearly north-east, and enters Norfolk a little to the west of Welney: it is navigable in its whole course through the county. The Cam or Granta, which is navigable to Cambridge, is formed by two small streams that unite between Grantchester and Harston, and falls into the old line of the Ouse near Thetford. The Nene, in its old course, enters at Benwick, and quits for Norfolk at Outwell: in its modern course it separates Huntingdonshire from the Isle of Ely, until it enters the isle at Moreton's Leam, whence it proceeds to the Cross Keys Wash. The rivers abound with fish: the pike and eels are especially plentiful: a considerable quantity of smelts is taken in the New Bedford river. The canals that intersect the Isle of Ely were made for the purpose of drainage, but many of them are also navigable. Vermuyden's canal commences at Ramsey: it enters the Isle of Ely near Ramsey Moor, and extends to Welche's Dam, where it joins the Old Bedford river, and, proceeding in the old course of that river, leaves the county a little to the west of Welney. The New Bedford river is the main channel for barges passing from the upper to the lower parts of the Ouse. The Old Bedford river, which runs parallel with the last from Earith to Denver sluice, is now seldom navigated, excepting the lower part of it, near Denver sluice, having been almost choked up since the making of the New Bedford river. A canal from Outwell to Wisbeach was made about thirty years ago. There is also a canal from Peterborough, by Stanground sluice and through Whittlesea dyke, to the Old Nene, a little below Benwick, and thence to March; and there are short cuts from the Ouse to Soham, Reach, and Burwell.

The great north road from London to Edinburgh enters the western part of Cambridgeshire at Royston, and quits it at Papworth St. Agnes, between the fifty-second and the fifty-third milestones. The road from London to Wisbeach, after crossing two angles of the county on its south-western border, re-enters it from Huntingdonshire at Chatteris ferry, and passes through March to Wisbeach. The road from London to Newmarket and Norfolk enters at Great Chesterford, and leaves the county about five miles beyond Newmarket. There are three turnpike-roads from Cambridge to London; one of them falls into the Newmarket road near Chesterford; the second quits the county near the eleventh milestone; and the third, branching from the latter at Hawkston, enters Huntingdonshire at Royston.

Few Roman antiquities have been discovered in Cambridgeshire, except on the site of the Roman station at Cambridge, the only one of importance within the limits of the county. The principal ancient roads that crossed it were, the Iknield-street, entering from Suffolk, near Newmarket, and quitting at Royston; the Ermin-street, which passed through it on the line of the present great north road; and the great Roman way from Colchester to Chester, which enters near Withersfield in Suffolk, and crosses the county from east to west, passing through Cambridge. The first and last, in different parts of their course, may be distinctly traced. Cambridgeshire is peculiarly rich in specimens of church architecture, Ely cathedral alone furnishing a nearly complete series of the variations in style that successively prevailed from the eleventh century to the sixteenth. The sepulchral monuments, from the thirteenth to the sixteenth century, are also numerous. Before the Reformation there were in this county thirty-two religious houses, including two houses of the Knights Templars, two preceptories of the Knights Hospitallers, and three Alien priories: there were four ancient colleges and eleven hospitals, one of which, St. John's Hospital at Cambridge, was converted into St. John's College. There are many monastic remains: those of Ely abbey are by far the most considerable. Of ancient castles there is little remaining, except the earthworks. The most considerable encampment is that called Handlebury, on the highest part of Gogmagog hills, supposed to be of British origin. The most remarkable earthworks are the trenches that extended from the woods on the east side of the county to the fens, the most entire of which is called the Devil's ditch; it runs seven miles, from Wood-Ditton to Reach, in the parish of Burwell, nearly in a straight line. Another trench, Fleam dyke, runs parallel with it, at the distance of seven miles, extending from the woodlands at Balsham to the fens at Fen-Ditton: a considerable part of it has been levelled.

CAMDEN-TOWN, a chapelry in the parish of St. Pancras, Holborn division of the hundred of Ossulstone, county of Middlesex, 3¼ miles (N.W.) from St. Paul's. The population is returned with the parish. It takes its name from Marquis Camden, lessee of the prebendal manor of Cantelows, on which it is situated. The principal part of it has been built within the last few years, and the buildings now in progress promise, when completed, to render it an elegant appendage to the western part of the metropolis. The houses are in general respectable and regularly built; the crescent, terrace, and other ranges of building in the upper part of it, are of handsome appearance, and command a partial, but pleasing, view of the Hampstead and Highgate hills. The streets, which are wide and regularly formed, are partially paved, and lighted with oil; and the inhabitants are supplied with water from a conduit into which it is conveyed from Hampstead. The Regent's canal passes through the northern part of the suburb. A veterinary college, in which lectures are delivered on the anatomy and diseases of the horse, was established in 1791, and subsequently confirmed by royal charter: it is under the management of a president, vice-president, directors, and a treasurer, who are elected annually by ballot; a subscription of two guineas per annum, or a donation of twenty guineas, qualifies persons for admission as members: the premises, which are neatly built of brick, include a spacious area, and comprise a school for the instruction of pupils, a theatre for dissections and the delivery of lectures, a museum for anatomical preparations, and an infirmary, in which is stabling for sixty horses, with paddocks adjoining. The chapel, erected in 1828, on ground given by Marquis Camden, who appoints the minister, is a neat edifice of brick, with a handsome stone portico of the Ionic order at the west end, above which rises a circular turret with a cupola. Near it are a chapel and a cemetery belonging to the parish of St. Martin's in the Fields, in connexion with which parish also there are nine almshouses in Bayham-street. Independents and Wesleyan Methodists have each a place of worship. There is a National school, in which one hundred and fifty children of Camden and Kentish Towns are instructed.

CAMEL (QUEEN), a parish in the hundred of Catsash, county of Somerset, 5½ miles (E.N.E.) from Ilchester, containing 712 inhabitants. The living is a vicarage, in the archdeaconry of Wells, and diocese of Bath and Wells, rated in the king's books at £17. 16. 8., and in the patronage of Miss Ann Mildmay. The church is dedicated to St. Barnabas. There is a place of worship for Wesleyan Methodists. This was a place of some note previously to its being burnt about the close of the sixteenth century. A charter was anciently granted, allowing a market to be held twice a week, and four fairs annually: the former has long been discontinued, and only two of the latter are now held, *viz.*, one on Trinity-Tuesday, and the other on October 25th. Opposite the hamlet of Wales, by the bank of the river Camel, there is a spring, the water of which has been successfully used in scrofulous cases.

CAMEL (WEST), a parish forming, with the parish of Yeovilton, the south-eastern portion of the hundred of Somerton, county of Somerset, 3½ miles (E. N.E.) from Ilchester, containing 304 inhabitants. The living is a rectory, in the archdeaconry of Wells, and diocese of Bath and Wells, rated in the king's books at £13. 8. 9., and in the patronage of the Crown. The church is dedicated to All Saints. In a hill, half a mile northward from this place, two catacombs, in which lay several human figures, regularly ranged in rows, were discovered near the close of the last century.

CAMELEY, a parish in the hundred of Chewton, county of Somerset, 4¾ miles (S.) from Pensford, containing 604 inhabitants. The living is a rectory, in the archdeaconry of Wells, and diocese of Bath and Wells, rated in the king's books at £6. 18. 4., and in the patronage of Lady Hippesley. The church is dedicated to St. James. Several quarries of superior Pennant stone, much of which is sent to Bath, for the purpose of flagging the pathways, are wrought within the parish.

Seal and Arms.

CAMELFORD, a borough and market town (having separate jurisdiction) in the parish of LANTEGLOS, locally in the hundred of Lesnewth, county of CORNWALL, 15 miles (W. by S.) from Launceston, and 228 (W.S.W.) from London. The population is returned with the parish. This place, supposed to have been the *Guffelford* of the Saxon Chronicle, takes its name from a ford on the river Camel, and is generally thought to be the scene of a memorable battle between King Arthur and his nephew Mordred, about the year 542, in which the former was mortally wounded, and the latter killed on the spot. About a mile to the north of the town, where the road crosses a small brook, is a place called "Slaughter Bridge," in allusion to the carnage which then ensued. In 823, a battle took place between the Britons and the Saxons under Egbert, when the former were defeated with great loss. The town, though in a dreary part of the county, has a pure air, and is considered healthy; it is indifferently built, and not lighted, but the streets are spacious and roughly paved, and the inhabitants are amply supplied with water. There is a manufactory on a small scale for the spinning of yarn. The market is on Friday: the fairs are on the Friday after March 10th, May 26th, June 17th and 18th, and September 6th, chiefly for cattle. Camelford was made a free borough by Richard, Earl of Cornwall; its privileges were confirmed by charter of Henry III., in 1259; and in the 25th of Charles II. it received a charter of incorporation, by which the government is vested in a mayor, eight aldermen, and an indefinite number of freemen, assisted by a serjeant at mace and subordinate officers. The mayor, who is elected annually on the Monday after Michaelmas, by the aldermen, from their own body, is a justice of the peace within the borough. The petty sessions for the hundred are held here. The freedom of the borough is acquired by presentation from a jury of free burgesses empanelled by the mayor at his courts held at Easter and Michaelmas. The corporation hold a court every third week, in which civil actions to the amount of £50 within the borough are cognizable; but this is mere formality, it being immediately adjourned. The elective franchise was granted in the reign of Edward VI., since which time the borough has returned two members to parliament: the right of election is vested in the free burgesses being householders residing in the borough, and paying scot and lot, whose number is about twenty: the mayor is the returning officer. The parliamentary influence is possessed by the Marquis of Cleveland, who is owner of great part of the property within the borough. The town-hall, begun in June 1806, was built at the expense of the Duke of Bedford, then proprietor of the borough: the lower part forms the market-place. Camelford does not possess a separate place of worship in connexion with the establishment, the parochial church being situated about a mile and a half to the south. An ancient chapel, dedicated to St. Thomas à Becket, has long been desecrated. There is a place of worship for Wesleyan Methodists. A charity school was founded, in 1679, by Sir James Smyth, and endowed with the tenement of Tregarth, producing £25 per annum, which is paid to the master: the school-room was rebuilt in 1823, by the corporation, who appoint the master, and nominate five children for gratuitous instruction. The renowned King Arthur is said to have been born at Tintagel castle, about five miles north-westward from the town.

CAMERTON, a parish in the hundred of WELLOW, county of SOMERSET, $6\frac{3}{4}$ miles (S. W. by S.) from Bath, containing 1004 inhabitants. The living is a rectory, in the archdeaconry of Wells, and diocese of Bath and Wells, rated in the king's books at £15. 9. 2., and in the patronage of Mrs. Jarret. The church is dedicated to St. Peter. There are meeting-houses for Baptists and Wesleyan Methodists. The Radford canal crosses this parish; and an old Roman Fosse-way traces its south-east boundary. Here is a coal mine, wherein impressions of fern, rushes, and other plants, have been discovered. Various relics of the Britons, Romans, and Saxons have been found.

CAMERTON, a joint township with Ryhill, in the parish of BURSTWICK, southern division of the wapentake of HOLDERNESS, East riding of the county of YORK, $2\frac{3}{4}$ miles (S. E. by E.) from Hedon. The population is returned with Ryhill.

CAMMERINGHAM, a parish in the western division of the wapentake of ASLACOE, parts of LINDSEY, county of LINCOLN, $7\frac{1}{4}$ miles (N. N. W.) from Lincoln, containing 142 inhabitants. The living is a discharged vicarage, in the archdeaconry of Stow, and diocese of Lincoln, rated in the king's books at £5. 4. 2., and in the patronage of Lord Monson. The church, dedicated to St. Michael, is a modern building, constructed with the materials of the former edifice. Limestone is obtained here.

CAMMERTON, a parish in ALLERDALE ward below Derwent, county of CUMBERLAND, comprising the townships of Cammerton and Seaton, and containing 706 inhabitants, of which number, 86 are in the township of Cammerton, 3 miles (E. N. E.) from Workington. The living is a perpetual curacy, in the archdeaconry and diocese of Carlisle, endowed with £600 royal bounty, and £1200 parliamentary grant, and in the patronage of the Dean and Chapter of Carlisle. The church, rebuilt in 1794, contains an effigy in full-length, the feet resting on a lamb, of a person called Black Tom of the North, whose seat here, according to tradition, was Barrow castle, now in ruins. There are some coal mines in this parish, which is bounded on the north by Solway Frith, and on the south by the river Derwent, whence passes a canal to the Seaton ironworks.

CAMPDEN (BROAD), a hamlet in the parish of CHIPPING-CAMPDEN, upper division of the hundred of KIFTSGATE, county of GLOUCESTER, 1 mile (S. E.) from Chipping-Campden, containing 250 inhabitants.

CAMPDEN (CHIPPING), a parish in the upper division of the hundred of KIFTSGATE, county of GLOUCESTER, comprising the market-town of Chipping-Campden, and the hamlets of Berrington, Broad Campden, and Wessington with Combe, and containing 1798 inhabitants, of which number, 1249 are in the town of Chipping-Campden, 29 miles (N. E. by E.) from Gloucester, and 90 (N. W. by W.) from London. This place, which is of very great antiquity, is supposed to have derived its name from an encampment formed prior to a battle between the Mercians and the West Saxons; or perhaps, with more probability, from a congress of the Saxon chiefs confederated for the conquest of Britain, that took place here in the year 687. In the fourteenth century it became noted as a staple town for wool, and was the residence of many opulent merchants, who exported a great quantity of that article to Flanders. On the emigration of the Flemings, who settled in England, and introduced the manufacture of woollen cloth, Campden lost its trade with Flanders, and its importance from that time rapidly declined. Sir Baptist Hicks erected a magnificent mansion here in the fifteenth century, which, at the commencement of the civil war in the reign of Charles I., its loyal owner demolished, to prevent its being garrisoned for the parliamentarians. The town is pleasantly situated in a fertile vale surrounded with hills richly wooded, and consists principally of one street, nearly a mile in length, neither paved nor lighted: the houses are in general ancient, and some of them fine specimens of the style of domestic architecture prevailing about the time of Elizabeth: the inhabitants are amply supplied with water from numerous springs: the environs abound with fine scenery. On Dover Hill, about a mile from the town, is still preserved, on the Thursday in Whitsuntide, some memorial of an ancient celebration of athletic exercises, instituted in the reign of James I. by Robert Dover, which was resorted to by the nobility and gentry resident in the surrounding country; prizes were awarded to such as excelled in the games, which were continued until the time of the Commonwealth, when they were suppressed. The manufacture of silk and rugs is carried on. The market is on Wednesday: fairs are held on Ash-Wednesday, April 23rd, August 5th, and December 11th. In the 3rd of James I., Campden received a charter of incorporation, by which the government was vested in two bailiffs, a steward, twelve capital and twelve inferior burgesses, who had power to hold a court of session, and a court of record for the recovery of small debts; but the charter has been forfeited from neglect, and though the bailiffs are still appointed annually on the Wednesday before New Michaelmas-day, they exercise no local authority: a court leet is held once a year: the town is wholly within the jurisdiction of the county magistrates. The court-house is situated nearly in the centre of the street, but possesses no claim to architectural description.

The living is a vicarage, in the archdeaconry and diocese of Gloucester, rated in the king's books at £20. 6. 8., and in the patronage of Lord Barham. The church, dedicated to St. James, and situated to the north of the town, in the hamlet of Berrington, is a spacious and handsome structure in the decorated style of English architecture, with a fine lofty tower, having lateral and angular buttresses, and crowned with pierced battlements and crocketed pinnacles: at the western angle of the north aisle is a circular turret, with a low dome; and at the western angle of the south aisle is an octangular turret, with a corresponding dome: some portions of the finely carved oak roof are still preserved in the north aisle, but in some instances the beauty and character of the interior have been defaced by modern alterations and repairs. It contains some beautiful sepulchral monuments to the memory of Sir Baptist Hicks, first Viscount Campden; Noel, Earl of Gainsborough; and other distinguished persons. There are places of worship for Baptists and Wesleyan Methodists. The free grammar school was founded in 1487, and endowed by Mr. John Fereby, or Verbey, with a moiety of the manor of Lynham in Oxfordshire; but, owing to mismanagement, the estate was sold, and another purchased, producing only £60 per annum, which, by a decree of Chancery in 1627, was vested in trustees for the maintenance of a master and an usher, who teach from thirty to forty boys: it has an interest in eight scholarships founded in Pembroke College, Oxford, by George Townsend, Esq., by will dated in 1682, for boys from the schools of Gloucester, Cheltenham, Chipping-Campden, and North Leach, whereby he ordained also that scholars on his foundation should be appointed to his donatives of Uxbridge and Colnbrook. A charity school, for clothing and instructing thirty girls, was endowed with £1000 by James Thynne, Esq. Almshouses for six aged men and the same number of women, were founded and endowed by Baptist, Lord Hicks, the first Viscount Campden, who rebuilt the market-house, and during his life gave £10,000 for charitable uses; he died in 1629, and was buried in the south aisle of the church. George Ballard, author of the Memoirs of learned British Ladies, was a native of Campden; he died at Oxford, in 1755. There are some petrifying springs in the neighbourhood.

CAMPSALL, a parish in the upper division of the wapentake of Osgoldcross, West riding of the county of York, comprising the townships of Askerne, Campsall, Fenwick, Moss, Norton, and Sutton, and containing 1898 inhabitants, of which number, 389 are in the township of Campsall, 8 miles (N. N. W.) from Doncaster. The living is a discharged vicarage, in the archdeaconry and diocese of York, rated in the king's books at £16. 16. 8., endowed with £600 private benefaction, and £600 royal bounty, and in the patronage of R. Yarburgh, Esq. The church is dedicated to St. Mary Magdalene.

CAMPSEA-ASH, a parish in the hundred of Loes, county of Suffolk, 2 miles (E.) from Wickham-Market, containing 342 inhabitants. The living is a rectory, in the archdeaconry of Suffolk, and diocese of Norwich, rated in the king's books at £14. 5., and in the patronage of Sir R. J. Woodford, Bart. The church is dedicated to St. John the Baptist. In the reign of Richard I., Theobald de Valoins gave his estate in this place to his two sisters, that they might build a nunnery in honour of the Virgin Mary, which they accordingly founded, and Joan, one of the sisters, was the first prioress; it was of the order of St. Clare, or the Minoresses, and at the dissolution was endowed with £182. 9. 5. per annum: a portion of the buildings still remains.

CAMPTON, a parish in the hundred of Clifton, county of Bedford, 3¾ miles (N. E. by E.) from Silsoe, containing, with the chapelry of Shefford, 1028 inhabitants. The living is a rectory, in the archdeaconry of Bedford, and diocese of Lincoln, rated in the king's books at £11. 9. 7., and in the patronage of Sir J. Osborne, Bart. The church is dedicated to All Saints. The manor, in which the small village of Campton, formerly called Camelton, is situated, was anciently possessed by the noble family of Lisle; but, upon the estates of this family devolving to the crown, it was annexed to the honour of Ampthill: the manor-house is now occupied as a school-house.

CANDLESBY, a parish in the Wold division of the wapentake of CANDLESHOE, parts of LINDSEY, county of LINCOLN, 3¼ miles (E. by N.) from Spilsby, containing 251 inhabitants. The living is a discharged rectory, in the archdeaconry and diocese of Lincoln, rated in the king's books at £9. 19. 4., and in the patronage of the President and Fellows of Magdalene College, Oxford. The church is dedicated to St. Benedict.

CANDOVER (BROWN), a parish in the hundred of MAINSBOROUGH, Fawley division of the county of SOUTHAMPTON, 4¾ miles (N. by W.) from New Alresford, containing 274 inhabitants. The living is a rectory, with the perpetual curacy of Woodmancot annexed, in the archdeaconry and diocese of Winchester, rated in the king's books at £23. 4. 2., and in the patronage of Alexander Baring, Esq. The church is dedicated to St. Peter.

CANDOVER (CHILTON), a parish in the hundred of MAINSBOROUGH, Fawley division of the county of SOUTHAMPTON, 5 miles (N.) from New Alresford, containing 87 inhabitants. The living is a rectory, in the archdeaconry and diocese of Winchester, rated in the king's books at £6. 6. 3., and in the patronage of Alexander Baring, Esq. The church is dedicated to St. Nicholas.

CANDOVER (PRESTON), a parish in the hundred of BERMONDSPIT, Basingstoke division of the county of SOUTHAMPTON, 6 miles (N. by E.) from New Alresford, containing 472 inhabitants. The living is a discharged vicarage, with the perpetual curacy of Nutley annexed, in the archdeaconry and diocese of Winchester, rated in the king's books at £18, endowed with £300 private benefaction, and £200 royal bounty, and in the patronage of the Dean and Chapter of Winchester. The church is dedicated to St. Mary. Thomas Hall, in 1772, bequeathed £4. 4. per annum for the instruction of six poor children.

CANEWDON, a parish in the hundred of ROCHFORD, county of ESSEX, 3½ miles (N. E. by N.) from Rochford, containing 732 inhabitants. The living is a vicarage, in the archdeaconry of Essex, and diocese of London, rated in the king's books at £34. 1. 8., and in the patronage of the Bishop of London. The church, dedicated to St. Nicholas, is a large structure in the later style of English architecture, with a massive western tower. Canute the Dane kept his court at Canewdon, from which circumstance its name is supposed to have been derived. The intrenchments of a strong encampment, supposed also to be Danish, including about six acres, encircle the manor-house. The river Crouch and Canewdon creek are navigable on the north of this parish.

CANFIELD (GREAT), a parish in the hundred of DUNMOW, county of ESSEX, 3½ miles (S. W.) from Great Dunmow, containing 434 inhabitants. The living is a discharged vicarage, in the archdeaconry of Middlesex, and diocese of London, rated in the king's books at £13, endowed with £600 parliamentary grant, and in the patronage of J. M. Wilson, Esq. Here are the keep-mount and intrenchments of a castle, from which this place was anciently called *Canfield ad Castrum*, or Castle-Canfield.

CANFIELD (LITTLE), a parish in the hundred of DUNMOW, county of ESSEX, 2¾ miles (W. by S.) from Great Dunmow, containing 249 inhabitants. The living is a rectory, in the archdeaconry of Middlesex, and diocese of London, rated in the king's books at £12. 0. 7½., and in the patronage of the Master and Fellows of Christ's College, Cambridge.

CANFORD (GREAT), a parish in the hundred of COGDEAN, Shaston (East) division of the county of DORSET, 2¼ miles (S. E. by E.) from Wimborne-Minster, comprising the chapelry of Kingston, and the tythings of Longfleet and Parkston, and containing 2696 inhabitants. The living is a vicarage, and a royal peculiar (including the town and county of the town of Poole, which was formerly in this parish), within the jurisdiction of the lord of the manor, rated in the king's books at £11. 9. 9½., and in the patronage of G. T. Brice, Esq. The church is a small building on a singular plan; it has a nave and a chancel, with a north aisle to each, and the tower is situated between these two aisles; there is also a south aisle to the nave and a south chapel to the chancel: one hundred and sixty-one additional sittings, one hundred and twenty-one of which are free, have been recently erected, the Incorporated Society for the enlargement of churches and chapels having granted £100 for that purpose. The navigable river Stour runs on the north of this parish, where it is crossed by a bridge on the Poole and Wimborne road.

CANN (ST. RUMBOLD), a parish in that part of the hundred of SIXPENNY-HANDLEY which is in the Shaston (West) division of the county of DORSET, 1½ mile (S. E.) from Shaftesbury, containing 365 inhabitants. The living is a rectory, in the archdeaconry of Dorset, and diocese of Bristol, rated in the king's books at £9. 2. 1., and in the patronage of the Earl of Shaftesbury.

CANNINGS (BISHOP'S), a parish in the hundred of POTTERNE and CANNINGS, county of WILTS, 3 miles (N. E.) from Devizes, containing, with the chapelry of St. James, and the tything of Chittoe, 2722 inhabitants. The living is a vicarage, in the peculiar jurisdiction and patronage of the Dean and Chapter of Salisbury, rated in the king's books at £17. 19. 2. The church, dedicated to St. Mary, is a large and handsome structure, in the early style of English architecture.

CANNINGTON, a parish in the hundred of CANNINGTON, county of SOMERSET, 3½ miles (N. W. by W.) from Bridg-water, containing, with the hamlet of Edstock, with Beer, 1228 inhabitants. The living is a vicarage, in the archdeaconry of Taunton, and diocese of Bath and Wells, rated in the king's books at £7. 10. 10., and in the patronage of W. Hodges, Esq. The church is dedicated to St. Mary. This is a place of considerable antiquity, having given name to the hundred, and it was once of much greater importance. Camden derives its name from having been occupied by a tribe of Britons, called the *Cangi*. The navigable river Parret flows on the north and east sides of this parish; and from a small harbour, called Coombwich, it is in contemplation to construct a canal to Bridg-water, to enable large vessels to sail directly up to that port. Mr. Rogers bequeathed £300 per ann., directing that £6 each should be annually given to twenty poor men, and the remainder to the poor of the parish generally. This was formerly the residence of the Cliffords, and is supposed to have been the birthplace of *Fair Rosamond.* A Benedictine nunnery was founded, in the reign of Stephen, by Robert de Courcy, and dedicated to the Blessed Virgin; it consisted of a prioress and six or seven nuns, whose revenue was estimated at £39. 15. 8. The buildings are now occupied by a society of nuns, who observe the rules of St. Benedict.

CANNOCK, a parish in the eastern division of the hundred of CUTTLESTONE, county of STAFFORD, comprising the townships of Cannock, Cannock-Wood, Cheslyn-Hay, Hednesford with Leacroft, Huntington, and Great Wyrley, and containing 2780 inhabitants, of which number, 766 are in the township of Cannock, 4½ miles (S. E. by E.) from Penkridge. The living, which is remarkable for having been the first preferment of the famous Dr. Sacheverell, is a perpetual curacy, in the peculiar jurisdiction and patronage of the Dean and Chapter of Lichfield, endowed with £15 per annum and £200 private benefaction, £200 royal bounty, and £1300 parliamentary grant. The church is dedicated to St. Luke. There are places of worship for Independents and Wesleyan Methodists. The village is supplied with water by means of a conduit and leaden pipes from Leacroft, about a mile distant, constructed by Bishop Hough. There are manufactories for edged tools at Church-bridge and Wedges Mill, which afford employment to about two hundred persons; the coal used is supplied from the immediate neighbourhood, as well as the iron-ore called Cannock-stone, or Cark, A court leet and a court baron are held annually, at which the constable and headborough, and the respective constables of the several townships, are chosen by juries; and special courts are called, when required, for the transfer of copyholds. Fairs are held on May 8th, August 24th, and October 6th, principally for cattle and sheep. A school, founded by John Wood, for the free education of children was, in 1727, enfeoffed with land by Thomas Wood, the income of which is £8 per annum; and John Biddulph, Esq. gave a meadow and garden for the use of the schoolmaster; there are thirty scholars, but none are taught free at present. In 1725, Mrs. M. Chapman bequeathed a small sum for the education of three or four children. A National school has also been recently erected at the expense of Mrs. Walhouse. This place in ancient times was a forest or chase belonging to the Mercian kings. Castle Ring, situated on the summit of Castle Hill, and supposed to have been a British encampment, is nearly a circular area of eight or ten acres, surrounded by a double trench occupying three or four acres more, exhibiting traces at its northern and southern entrances of various advanced works. Near it are the remains of a moat, enclosing an oblong square of about three acres, named the Old Nunnery, where a Cistercian abbey was founded in the reign of Stephen, which was shortly after removed to Stoneleigh in Warwickshire: a similar enclosure at a small distance is called the Moat Bank.

CANNOCK-WOOD, a township in the parish of CANNOCK, eastern division of the hundred of CUTTLESTONE, county of STAFFORD, containing 355 inhabitants.

CANNONBY (CROSS), a parish in ALLERDALE ward below Derwent, county of CUMBERLAND, comprising the market town and chapelry of Maryport, and the townships of Birkby, Cross-Cannonby, and Crosby, and containing 3870 inhabitants, of which number, 60 are in the township of Cross-Cannonby, 2¾ miles (N. E. by E.) from Maryport. The living is a perpetual curacy, in the archdeaconry and diocese of Carlisle, endowed with £1400 parliamentary grant, and in the patronage of the Dean and Chapter of Carlisle. The church, dedicated to St. John, is of early Norman architecture. This parish lies on the shore of the Solway Frith, and is bounded on the south by the river Ellen: it contains coal and freestone, and in a quarry of the latter, implements supposed to be Roman were found some years ago, from which it is thought that the stone used in erecting the Roman station at Ellenborough was obtained here.

CANON-PION, a parish in the hundred of GRIMSWORTH, county of HEREFORD, 4½ miles (S. E. by E.) from Weobley, containing 634 inhabitants. The living is a discharged vicarage, in the peculiar jurisdiction of the Dean of Hereford, rated in the king's books at £5. 13. 6½., and in the patronage of the Dean and Chapter of Hereford. The church, dedicated to St. Lawrence, is principally in the early style of English architecture, with some fine screen-work; the font is ancient, with an octagonal top enriched with quatrefoil. A court leet is held once a year.

CANON-TEIGN, a hamlet in the parish of CHRISTOW, hundred of WONFORD, county of DEVON, 4¼ miles (N. W. by N.) from Chudleigh. The population is returned with the parish. Here was formerly a chapel of ease.

CANTELOSE, or CANTELOFF, a parish in the hundred of HUMBLEYARD, county of NORFOLK, 4 miles (S. W.) from Norwich. The living is a rectory, annexed to the rectory of Hetherset in 1397, in the archdeaconry and diocese of Norwich. The church, which was dedicated to All Saints, was served as a free chapel from the time of its annexation until the Reformation, when it was demolished.

Arms.

CANTERBURY, an ancient city, and a county of itself, having separate jurisdiction, locally in the hundred of Bridge and Petham, lathe of ST. AUGUSTINE, eastern division of the county of KENT, 26 miles (S. E. by E.) from Rochester, 16 (N. W. by W.) from Dovor, and 55 (E. by S.) from London, containing 12,745 inhabitants, and, including the suburbs and portions of parishes which are without the liberties of the city, 15,373. This place, the origin of which is not distinctly known, is, from the discovery of numerous Druidical relics, supposed to have been distinguished at a very early period for the celebration of the religious rites of the Britons, prior to the Christian era. That it was a British town of considerable importance before the Roman invasion, is not only confirmed by the numerous celts, and other instruments of British warfare, that have been at various times found in the vicinity, but by the name of the station which the Romans fixed here on their establishment in the island, and which they called *Durovernum*, a name obviously derived from the British *Dwr*, a stream and *whern*, swift, being characteristic of the Stour, upon which it is situated. From this station three roads branched off to *Rhutupis, Dubræ*, and *Lemanum*, now Richborough, Dovor, and Limne. By the Saxons, who, on their arrival in Britain, were established in this part of Kent, it was called *Cantwara-byrig*, from which its present name is evidently deduced. Canterbury was the metropolis of the Saxon kingdom of Kent, and the residence of its kings, of whom Ethelbert having married Bertha of France, who had been educated in the principles of Christianity, allowed her by treaty the free exercise of her religion, and suffered her to bring over with her a limited number of ecclesiastics. The Christian religion had been partially promulgated during the occupation of the city by the Romans, and two churches had been built in the second century, one of which, on Bertha's arrival, was consecrated for her use by the Bishop of Soissons, and dedicated to St. Martin. During the reign of this monarch, Augustine, who had been sent by Pope Gregory to convert the Britons to Christianity, took up his station at Canterbury, where, through the influence of Bertha, he was courteously received: his mission was attended with success; the king, who soon became a convert, resigned to him his palace, which he converted into a priory for brethren of his own order; and, in conjunction with Ethelbert, he founded an abbey without the city walls, dedicated to St. Peter and St. Paul. Being invested by the pope with the dignity of an archbishop, he made this city the seat of the metropolitan see, which distinction it has retained for more than twelve centuries, under an uninterrupted succession of ninety archbishops, many of whom have been eminent for their talents and their virtues, and distinguished by the important offices they have held in the administration of the temporal affairs of the kingdom. Among these may be noticed Dunstan, who governed the kingdom with absolute authority during the reigns of Edred and Edwy; Stigand, who, for his opposition to William the Conqueror, was displaced from his see; Lanfranc, his successor, who rebuilt the cathedral, and founded several religious establishments; the celebrated Thomas à Becket; Stephen Langton, who was raised to the see in defiance of King John; Cranmer, who, for his zeal in promoting the Reformation, was burnt at the stake in the reign of Mary; and Laud, who, for his strenuous support of the measures of his sovereign, Charles I., was beheaded during the usurpation of Cromwell. The abbey was intended as a place of sepulture for the successors of the archbishop in the see of Canterbury, and for those of the monarch in the kingdom of Kent: the cathedral, which was not completed at the time of Augustine's decease, was dedicated to our Saviour, and is still usually called Christ Church.

The city suffered frequently from the ravages of the Danes, of whom, on their advancing against it in 1009, the inhabitants, by the advice of Archbishop Siricius, purchased a peace for the sum of £30,000, obtaining from them an oath not to renew their aggressions; but in 1011, they again landed at Sandwich, and laid siege to the city, which, after a resolute defence for three weeks on the part of the inhabitants, they took by storm and reduced to ashes. In this siege, forty-three thousand two hundred persons were slain, more than eight thousand of the inhabitants were massacred, and among the prisoners whom they carried off to their camp at Greenwich was Alphege, the archbishop, whom they afterwards put to death at Blackheath, for refusing to sanction their extortions. Canute, after his usurpation of the throne upon the death of Edmund Ironside, contributed greatly to the rebuilding of the city, and the restoration of the cathedral; and, placing his crown upon the altar, gave the revenue of the port of Sandwich for the support of the monks. From this time the city began to revive, and continued to flourish till the Norman Conquest, when, according to Stowe, it surpassed London in extent and magnificence. In Domesday-book it is described, under the title "Civitas Cantuariæ," as a populous city, having a castle, which, as there is no previous mention of it, was probably built by the Conqueror, to keep his Saxon subjects in awe; the remains now visible are evidently of Norman character. In 1080, the cathedral was destroyed by fire, but was restored with great splendour, and dedicated to the Holy Trinity, by Archbishop Lanfranc, who rebuilt the monastic edifices, erected the archbishop's palace, founded and endowed a priory, which he dedicated to St. Gregory, and built the hospitals of St. John and St. Nicholas. In 1161, the city was nearly consumed by fire, and it suffered materially from a similar calamity at several subsequent periods. In 1170, the memorable murder of Thomas à Becket was perpetrated in the cathedral, as he was ascending the steps leading from the nave into the choir: his subsequent canonization tended greatly to enrich the city and the church, by the costly offerings of numerous pilgrims of all ranks, who came not only from every part of England, but from every place in Christendom, to visit his shrine. From this source a rich fund was obtained for the enlargement and embellishment of the cathedral, which rapidly recovered from the repeated devastations to which it was exposed, and from which it invariably arose with increased magnificence. Four years after the murder of Becket, Henry II. performed a pilgrimage to Canterbury, where, prostrating himself before the shrine of the martyr, he submitted to be scourged by the monks, whom he had assembled for that purpose. In 1299, the nuptials of Edward I. and Margaret of Anjou were celebrated with great pomp in this city, which, in the reign of Edward IV., was constituted a county of itself, under the designation of the "City and County of the City of Canterbury." Little variety henceforward occurs in the civil history of this city, the interests of which were so closely interwoven with the ecclesiastical establishments, that, upon their dissolution in the reign of Henry VIII., its prosperity materially declined.

The jubilees which, by indulgence of the pope, were celebrated every fiftieth year, in honour of St. Thomas à Becket, caused a great influx of wealth into the city, which owed much of its trade to the immense number of pilgrims who came to visit his shrine: according to the civic records, more than one hundred thousand persons attended the fifth jubilee, in 1420, when the number and richness of their offerings were incredible; the last of these jubilees was celebrated in 1520. The dissolution of the priory of Christ Church was effected gradually: the festivals in honour of the martyr were successively abolished, his gorgeous shrine was stripped of its costly ornaments, and the bones of the saint were, according to Stowe, ultimately burnt to ashes, and scattered to the winds: the revenue, at the dissolution, was estimated at £2489. 4. 9., a sum greatly inferior to the actual value of its numerous and extensive possessions. At this period part of the monastery of St. Augustine was converted by Henry VIII. into a royal palace, in which Queen Elizabeth held her court for several days. During her reign, the Walloons, driven from the Netherlands by persecution on account of their religious tenets, found an asylum at Canterbury, where they introduced the weaving of silk and stuffs; their descendants are still numerous in the city and its neighbourhood, and continue to use, as their place of worship, the crypt under the cathedral, which was granted to them by Elizabeth, and where the service is performed in the French language. Charles I., in 1625, solemnized his marriage with Henrietta Maria of France at this place; and during the war in the reign of that monarch, the city was occupied by a regiment of Cromwell's horse, that committed great havoc in the ecclesiastical buildings, and wantonly mutilated and defaced the cathedral, which they used as stabling for their horses. A political tumult occurred in 1647, in which originated the celebrated Kentish Association in favour of Charles I., that terminated in the siege of Colchester, and in the execution, after its capture, of Lord Capel, Sir Charles Lucas, and Sir George Lisle. Charles II., on his return from France at the Restoration, held his court in the royal palace at Canterbury, for three days; and, in 1676, that monarch granted a charter of incorporation to the emigrant silk-weavers settled in this city, who, on the revocation of the edict of Nantes in 1685, were joined by a considerable number of other artizans from France.

The city is pleasantly situated in a fertile vale environed with gently rising hills, from which numerous streams of excellent water descend, and is intersected by the river Stour, which, dividing and re-uniting its stream, forms several islands, on one of which, anciently called Birmewith, the western part of it is built. It still occupies the original site, and is of an elliptic form; the Romans surrounded it with walls that appear to have been built of flint and chalk, and to have included an area one mile and three quarters in circumference, defended by a moat one hundred and fifty feet in width; of these nearly the whole is remaining, and on that part which forms the terrace of the promenade, called Dane John Field, are four of the ancient towers in good preservation; the arches over the river have been taken down at various times, and of the six gates that formed the principal entrances, only the west gate, through which is the entrance from the London road, is standing; it is a handsome embattled structure, erected about the year 1380, by Archbishop Sudbury, who also rebuilt a considerable portion of the city wall, and consists of a centre flanked by two round towers, having their foundations in the bed of the western branch of the Stour, over which is a stone bridge of two arches, that has been widened for the accommodation of carriages and foot passengers, an approach having been cut through the city walls for each. The principal streets, intersecting at right angles, and the smaller streets, were originally paved under an act of parliament obtained in the reign of Edward IV.; they were subsequently made more convenient by an act passed in 1787, for the improvement of the city, and are now lighted with gas by a company established under an act obtained in 1822: the inhabitants are amply supplied with water conveyed into their houses from the river, by a company established in 1824, by act of parliament; and with excellent spring water brought from St. Martin's Hill, into a spacious conduit in one of the ancient towers on the city wall, whence it is distributed to the most populous parts of the city, at the expense of the corporation. The houses in some parts retain their ancient appearance, with the upper stories projecting; the greater part of the old Checquers Inn, mentioned by Chaucer, as frequented by pilgrims visiting Becket's shrine, has been converted into a range of dwelling-houses, extending from St. Bredman's church nearly half-way down Mercery-lane; and the remains of the palace of Sir Thomas More, in the dancing-school yard in Orange-street, are now used as a warehouse for wool: in other parts of the city the houses are in general handsome, and many of them modern and well built.

The environs are pleasant, and the surrounding scenery is agreeably diversified with simple and picturesque beauty: on the road leading into the Isle of Thanet are extensive barracks for cavalry, artillery, and infantry of the line: the cavalry barracks, erected in 1794, at an expense of £40,000, are a handsome range of brick building, occupying three sides of a quadrangle, and, with the several parades and grounds for exercise, comprise sixteen acres, enclosed with lofty iron palisades: the barracks for two thousand infantry, erected near the former in 1798, have been since made a permanent station for detachments of the royal horse and foot artillery: the barracks erected on the site of St. Gregory's priory, and in other parts of the city, have been taken down, and new streets of small houses occupy their places. To the south is Dane John Field, so called from a lofty conical mount said to have been thrown up by the Danes, when they besieged the city, or, more probably from its having been the site of a keep or *donjon;* it is tastefully laid out in spiral walks and shrubberies, and planted with lime-trees: on the city wall, by which it is bounded to the south-east, is a fine broad terrace with sloping declivities covered with turf; on the promenade is a sun-dial, supported on a handsome marble pedestal, sculptured with emblematical representations of the seasons, by Mr. Henry Weeks, a native artist: on the summit of the mount, from which a fine panoramic view of the city and its environs is obtained, a stone pillar has been erected, with tablets recording, among other benefactions, a vote of £60 per annum by the corporation for keeping the promenade in order. The Philosophical and Literary Institution is a chaste and elegant edifice of the Ionic order, with a handsome portico of four columns, erected by subscription in 1825, after the model of a temple on the river Illyssus in Greece: it comprises a spacious museum, in which an extensive and valuable collection of minerals, fossils, and natural curiosities, collected by Mr. W. Masters, Mrs. Masters, and others, is scientifically arranged in an order peculiarly adapted to assist the student in natural history, also an extensive and well assorted library, and a theatre, in which lectures on literary and scientific subjects are delivered every Tuesday evening throughout the year; the museum is open to the public daily, the price of admission being one shilling each. The theatre, a neat and commodious edifice, erected by Mrs.

Sarah Baker, was opened in 1790: opposite to it is a concert-room belonging to the members of the Catch Club, in which subscription concerts take place every Wednesday evening during the winter months. Assemblies are held in a handsome suite of rooms built by subscription; and races take place, in the month of August, upon Barham Downs, within three miles of the city: the course, on which there is a commodious stand, has been greatly enlarged.

The manufacture of silk, established by the Walloons under the auspices of Queen Elizabeth, and which had flourished in such a degree as to obtain from Charles I. a charter of incorporation, gave place in 1789 to the introduction of the cotton-manufacture by Mr. John Callaway, master of the company of weavers, who discovered a method of interweaving silk with cotton in a fabric still known by the name of Canterbury, or Chamberry, muslin; what now remains of the silk manufacture, employing but few persons, is conducted by his grandson. A considerable trade in long wool is carried on, and there is an extensive manufactory for parchment; but the principal source of employment for the labouring class is the cultivation of hops, for the growth of which the soil is peculiarly favourable, and with extensive plantations of which the neighbourhood abounds: a great quantity of corn is also produced in the vicinity, and forms a material part of its trade. The city is geologically situated on the plastic clay of the London basin, with which red bricks and tiles are made; and, at a short distance to the south-east, flint imbedded in chalk is found in abundance, from which lime of an excellent quality is produced. There are numerous mills on the banks of the river, several of them extensive, particularly that called the Abbot's mill, from its having anciently belonged to the abbey of St. Augustine; it is now the property of the corporation, by whom it was purchased in 1543. Canterbury has been long celebrated for its brawn. Frequent attempts, attended with considerable expense, have been made to improve the navigation of the river Stour: an act was obtained, in 1825, to make it navigable to Sandwich, and to construct a canal from that port to a harbour to be formed near Deal, but the undertaking has not yet been commenced. In the same year an act was obtained for the formation of a railway to Whitstable, whence there is a regular conveyance by water to London: this has been carried into effect, and promises to be of great advantage to the trade of the city. The market for cattle, corn, hops, and seeds, is on Saturday, and the market for provisions daily: the cattle market is held on the site of the ancient city moat, in the parish of St. George without the walls; the corn, hop, and seed market is held in a spacious room in the Corn and Hop Exchange, a handsome building of the composite order, recently erected, and ornamented with the city arms and appropriate devices, behind which is a spacious area for the daily market for meat and vegetables; the market for eggs, poultry, and butter, is held in the ancient butter market, near Christ Church gate; and there is a convenient market-place for fish in St. Margaret's street: these markets are under the regulation of the corporation, by an act passed in 1824. The annual Michaelmas fair commences on the 10th of October, and continues during three market days.

Corporate Seal.

Obverse. Reverse.

The city, which at the time of the Conquest was governed by a *præpositus*, or prefect, appointed by the king, received from Henry II. a charter conferring enculiar privileges, in addition to those it previously pejoyed. Henry III. granted the city to the inhabitants at a fee-farm rent of £60, and empowered the citizens to elect two bailiffs, who were superseded by a mayor in the reign of Henry VI., who granted them the privilege of choosing a coroner. Edward IV. confirmed the preceding charters, remitted more than one-fourth of the fee-farm rent, and constituted the city a county of itself. Henry VII. limited the number of aldermen to twelve, and the common council-men to twenty-four; and Henry VIII., by an act in the 35th of his reign, empowered the mayor and aldermen to levy a fine of six shillings and eightpence per day upon all strangers who should keep shops, or exercise any trade in the city. James I., in the sixth year of his reign, confirmed all the former charters and privileges, and re-incorporated the citizens, under the title of the mayor and commonalty of the city of Canterbury. The government, under these several charters, is vested in a mayor, recorder, twelve aldermen (including a chamberlain and sheriff), and twenty-four common council-men, assisted by a town-clerk, who is also coroner, a sword-bearer, mace-bearer, four serjeants at mace, and subordinate officers. The mayor is chosen on Holy-rood day by the freemen, from among the twelve aldermen, who nominate two of their own body for election, and is sworn into office on the festival of St. Michael; the aldermen are selected from the common council-men by a majority of their own body, and the common council-men are chosen from the resident freemen, in the same manner; the sheriff is chosen annually by a majority of the mayor and aldermen, from among the twelve aldermen; and the recorder, chamberlain, and town-clerk, are elected by a majority of the corporation. The mayor, recorder, and such of the aldermen as have passed the chair, are justices of the peace. The freedom of the city is inherited by birth, or acquired by servitude, gift, marriage with a freeman's daughter, and by purchase. The power of purchasing their freedom was allowed to English-born Jews in 1829. The city is divided into six wards, named after the six ancient gates, over each of which two aldermen preside, who hold a court leet, with view of frankpledge, in October, when a constable, borseholder, and six commissioners of pavements are appointed for each ward. The corporation hold a court of burghmote on the first Tuesday in every month, at which the mayor or his deputy presides, assisted by the aldermen and common council-men, a majority of each of whom is necessary to constitute a court: this court, which is a court of record, and has been held from time immemorial, is convened by the blowing of a horn. They also hold courts of quarter session for the trial of capital offenders and misdemeanants, and a court of petty session on the first Thursday in every month, for determining minor offences. The mayor's court, which is also a court of record, is but rarely held; the last instance of its exercising jurisdiction in civil pleas was in February 1793. A court of requests is held every Thursday, under an act passed in the 25th of George II., for the recovery of debts under 40*s.*, within the city and liberties; but the precincts of the cathedral, the archbishop's palace, St. Augustine's abbey, and other privileged places, are exempted from its jurisdiction. The guildhall is an ancient and lofty building, containing the various court-rooms for holding the city sessions, and apartments for transacting the business of the corporation; the interior is decorated with portraits of the most distinguished benefactors to the city, and with various pieces of ancient armour. In 1453, Henry VI. granted to the corporation the custody of his gaol at Westgate, which gate from that time at least, if not previously, has been used as a city gaol; considerable additions have been recently made to it, and a house for the gaoler was erected in 1829, in a style corresponding with the character of the original building; airing-yards have lately been formed, and other improvements effected. The city has continued to return two members to parliament since the 23rd of Edward I.; the right of election is vested in the freemen at large, the number of whom is about two thousand; the sheriff is the returning officer. The quarter sessions for the eastern division of the county are regularly held here, and the petty sessions on the first Saturday in every month; and a king's commission of sewers, having jurisdiction over the several limits of East Kent, sits four times in the year at the sessions-house. The sessions-house, and common gaol and house of correction, form an extensive pile of building within the precinct of the abbey of St. Augustine; the latter comprises nine divisions, with day-rooms and airing yards for the classification of prisoners, who are employed at the tread-wheels, and in various kinds of productive labour.

The primacy, though immediately delegated by the pope to the see of Canterbury, was not maintained without considerable difficulty; its establishment was violently opposed by the native British prelates, who refused to acknowledge the supremacy either of the archbishop or the pope. Offa, King of Mercia, attempted to divide the jurisdiction, and the archbishops of York persevered in asserting their claims; but the archbishop of Canterbury was ultimately acknowledged Primate and Metropolitan of all England. In this dignity he ranks as first peer of the realm, and, with the exception of the royal family, takes precedence of all the nobility and chief officers of state; at coronations he places the crown upon the head of the sovereign; the bishops of London, Winchester, Lincoln, and Rochester, are respectively his provincial dean, subdean, chancellor, and chaplain; he is a privy councillor in right of his primacy, and has the power of conferring degrees in the several faculties of divinity, law, and physic, except within the immediate jurisdiction of the Universities of Oxford and Cambridge. The province of Canterbury comprehends the sees of twenty-one bishops, including the four Welch sees: the diocese comprises two hundred and sixty-nine parishes in the county of Kent; and nearly one hundred parishes in that and other counties are in the peculiar jurisdiction of the archbishop. The ecclesiastical establishment consists of an archbishop, dean, archdeacon, twelve prebendaries, six preachers, six minor canons, six substitutes, twelve lay clerks, ten choristers, two masters, fifty scholars, and twelve almsmen. The cathedral, dedicated to our Saviour, originally the church of the monastery founded by St. Augustine, on the site of the palace of Ethelbert, King of Kent, rebuilt by Archbishop Lanfranc soon after the Conquest, and enlarged and enriched by several of his successors, is a magnificent and splendid structure, exhibiting in their highest perfection the richest specimens in every style of architecture, from the earliest Norman to the latest English, and is equally conspicuous for the justness of its proportions, the correctness of its details, and the richness of its decoration. Its form is that of a double cross, with a lofty and elegant tower rising from the intersection of the nave and the western transepts, in the later style of English architecture, with a pierced parapet and pinnacles, and having octagonal turrets at the angles, terminating in minarets. At the west end are two massive towers, of which the north-west is in the Norman style, and the south-west, though crowned with battlements, is of similar character, and little inferior to the central tower: between the western towers is a narrow entrance, through a sharply pointed arch, with deeply receding mouldings, surmounted by canopied niches, over which is a lofty and magnificent window of six lights, decorated with richly stained glass representing figures of the saints. The south-west porch, which is the principal entrance, is a highly enriched specimen of the later style, and is profusely ornamented with niches of elegant design; the roof is elaborately groined, and at the intersections of the ribs are numerous shields. The nave, which, with the western transepts, is also in the later style, is peculiarly fine; the roof is richly groined, and supported by eight lofty piers, which on each side separate it from the aisles, and of which the clustered shafts are banded, like those of the early English: the eastern part derives a grandeur of effect from the numerous avenues leading from it to the various chapels in different parts of the interior; of these the chapel of Henry IV. is conspicuous for the elegant simplicity of its design, and the beautiful fan tracery depending from the roof; the lady chapel, separated from the eastern side of the transept by a finely carved stone screen, is small, but exquisitely beautiful; the chapel of the Holy Trinity, in which was the gorgeous shrine of St. Thomas à Becket, opens into that part of the cathedral called Becket's Crown, where is preserved the ancient stone chair in which the archbishops are enthroned: there are various other chapels equally deserving attention. A triple flight of steps leads from the nave into the choir, which are separated by a stone screen of exquisite workmanship: the roof, which is plainly

Arms of the Archbishoprick.

groined, is supported on slender-shafted columns, alternately circular and octagonal, with highly enriched capitals of various designs; this part of the structure is chiefly in the early English, intermixed with the Norman, style, which prevails also in the triforium, and other parts of the choir, and in the eastern transept: the archbishop's throne, on the south side of the choir near the centre, and the stalls of the dean and prebendaries, are strikingly elegant; a new altar-piece, in accordance with the prevailing style of architecture, has been recently erected with the Caen stone of St. Augustine's monastery: the whole length of the cathedral from east to west is five hundred and fourteen feet, the length of the choir one hundred and eighty, the length of the eastern transepts one hundred and fifty-four, and the length of the western one hundred and twenty-four. Under the whole building is a spacious and elegant crypt, the several parts of which correspond with those of the cathedral; the western part is in the Norman style, and the eastern in the early style of English architecture: the vaulted roof is about fourteen feet in height, and supported on massive pillars, of which the prevailing character is simplicity and strength, though occasionally sculptured with foliage and grotesque ornaments. Near the south end of the western transept, Edward the Black Prince, in 1363, founded a chantry, and endowed it for two chaplains with his manor of Vauxhall, near London; there are some remains of the chapel, consisting of the vaulting of the roof, supported on one central column: near the centre of the crypt are the remains of the chapel of the Virgin, in a niche, at the east end of which was her statue, supported on a pedestal sculptured in basso relievo with various subjects, among which the Annunciation may be distinctly traced. The western part is still called the French church, from its having been given by Queen Elizabeth to the Walloons and the French refugees, and from the service being still performed there in the French language. The cathedral contains many splendid and interesting monuments, and other memorials of the archbishops, deans, and other dignitaries of the church, and of illustrious persons who have been interred within its walls. In the arches surrounding the chapel of the Holy Trinity are, the tomb of Henry IV. and his queen, Joan of Navarre, whose recumbent figures, arrayed in royal robes, and crowned, are finely sculptured in alabaster; the monument of Edward the Black Prince, whose effigy in complete armour and in a recumbent posture, with the arms raised in the attitude of prayer, is finely executed in gilt brass, and surmounted by a rich canopy, in which are his gauntlets and the scabbard of his sword; and the cenotaph of Archbishop Courteney, with a recumbent figure of that prelate in his pontificals. In the north aisle of the choir are the splendid monuments of the archbishops Chicheley and Bourchier. In the chapel of the Virgin are monuments to the memory of six of the deans; and in that of St. Michael are those of the Earl of Somerset, and the Duke of Clarence, second son of Henry IV., whose effigy, with that of the duchess in her robes and coronet, is beautifully sculptured in marble; also the monuments of Archbishop Langton and Admiral Sir George Rooke. In the south aisle of the choir are those of the Archbishops Reynolds, Walter Kemp, Stratford, Sudbury, and Meopham; and within an iron palisade, on the north side of Becket's Crown, is the tomb of Cardinal Pole, the last of the archbishops who were buried in the cathedral: there are several monuments in the crypt, among which are some to the most distinguished individuals that have been connected with the county. The precincts of the cathedral comprehend an area three quarters of a mile in circumference: the principal entrance is on the south side, through Christ Church gate, erected by Prior Goldstone, in 1517, and exhibiting, though greatly mutilated, an elegant specimen of the later style of English architecture; the front is richly sculptured, and ornamented with canopied niches, and consists of two octangular embattled towers, with a larger and a smaller arched entrance between them, the wooden doors of which are carved with the arms of the see, and those of Archbishop Juxon. On the north side is the library, containing a valuable collection of books, and a series of Grecian and Roman coins; in the centre is an octagonal table of black marble, on which is sculptured the history of Orpheus, surrounded with various hunting pieces. A passage from the north transept of the cathedral to the library, leads into a circular room called "Bell Jesus," the lower part of which is of Norman character; it is lighted by a dome in the centre, under which is placed the font, removed from the nave of the cathedral. On the east side of the cloisters is the chapter-house, a spacious and elegant building, containing a hall ninety-two feet in length, thirty-seven in width, and fifty-four in height; on the sides are the ancient stone seats of the monks, surmounted by a range of trefoil-headed arches supporting a cornice and battlement; the east and west windows are large, and enriched with elegant tracery, and the roof of oak is pannelled, and decorated with shields of arms and other ornaments. The cloisters form a spacious quadrangle, on each side of which are handsome windows of four lights; the vaulted stone roof is elaborately groined, and ornamented at the points of intersection with more than seven hundred shields; against the north wall is a range of stone seats, separated from each other by pillars supporting canopied arches; on the east side are, a doorway leading into the cathedral, highly enriched, and an archway leading to the chapter-house; on the west side is an arched entrance to the archbishop's palace, the only remains of which are the porter's gallery and the surveyor's house. The treasury is a fine building in the Norman style of architecture, the staircase to which, in the same style, is of very curious design.

The city comprises the parishes of All Saints, St. Alphege, St. Andrew, St. George, the Holy Cross, St. Margaret, St. Martin, St. Mary Bredman, St. Mary Bredin, St. Mary Magdalene, St. Mary Northgate, St. Mildred, St. Peter, and St. Paul, all in the diocese, and, with the exception of St. Alphege and St. Martin, in the archdeaconry, of Canterbury. The living of All Saints' is a rectory, with which that of St. Mary in the Castle is consolidated, rated together in the king's books at £80, and united with that of St. Mildred's, rated in the king's books at £17. 17. 11., and in the patronage of the Crown. The living of the parish of St. Alphege is a rectory, exempt from archidiaconal visitation, and united with the vicarage of St. Mary Northgate, the former rated in the king's books at £8. 13. 4., and the latter at £11. 19. 4½., and in the patronage of the

Archbishop. The living of St. Andrew's is a rectory, with that of St. Mary's Bredman united, rated together in the king's books at £22. 6. 8., endowed with £400 private benefaction, and in the patronage of the Archbishop for two turns, and the Dean and Chapter for one. The living of St. George's the Martyr is a rectory, with that of St. Mary Magdalene united, the former rated in the king's books at £7. 17. 11., and the latter at £4. 10., in the patronage of the Dean and Chapter. The living of St. Margaret's is a donative, endowed with £200 parliamentary grant, and in the patronage of the Archdeacon. The living of St. Martin's is a rectory, exempt from archidiaconal visitation, and united with the vicarage of St. Paul's, the former rated in the king's books at £6. 5. 2½., and the latter at £9. 18. 9., and in the alternate patronage of the Archbishop and the Dean and Chapter. The living of St. Mary's Bredin is a vicarage, rated in the king's books at £4. 1. 5½., endowed with £1000 private benefaction, £200 royal bounty, and £2000 parliamentary grant, and in the patronage of H. Lee Warner, Esq. The living of St. Peter's is a rectory, with the vicarage of the Holy Cross united, the former rated in the king's books at £3. 10. 10., and the latter at £13. 0. 2½., in the alternate patronage of the Archbishop and the Dean and Chapter. Of the several churches, few possess any distinguishing architectural features; that of St. Martin is said to have been founded during the occupation of Canterbury by the Romans, and consecrated for the celebration of the Christian service prior to the conversion of Ethelbert. There are places of worship for Baptists, the Society of Friends, Independents, and Wesleyan Methodists, and a synagogue.

The king's free grammar school, coeval with the establishment of the cathedral, was founded by Henry VIII. for fifty scholars from all parts of the kingdom; the management is vested in the Dean and Chapter: belonging to it are two scholarships, of £3. 6. 8. per annum each, for natives of Kent, founded in Corpus Christi College, Cambridge, and endowed with a portion of the revenue of Eastbridge hospital, by Archbishop Whitgift, in 1569; one of three exhibitions, of about £15 per annum each, founded in the same college by Archbishop Parker, in 1575, in the nomination of the Dean and Chapter, for such of the sons of their Norfolk, Suffolk, and Lincolnshire tenants as are educated in this school; a medical scholarship, founded by the same archbishop in Caius College, Cambridge, for a native of Canterbury educated at any of the schools in that city; and one of three scholarships founded in the same college, by John Parker, Esq., in 1580, in the patronage of the Archbishop, for a native of Canterbury educated at the king's school: it has also four scholarships at either university, founded in 1618 by Robert Rose, Esq., who endowed them with twenty-six acres of land in Romney Marsh; two exhibitions to any college in Cambridge, founded in 1625 by William Heyman, Esq., for scholars descended from his grandfather, tenable for seven years from the time of their leaving school, and, in the event of their taking orders, to be continued for three years longer; four scholarships, of £10 per annum each, established in St. John's College, Cambridge, by a decree of the court of Chancery, in 1652, in lieu of two fellowships and two scholarships founded in that college by Henry Robinson, Esq., in 1643, for natives of the Isle of Thanet, or, in failure of such, for boys in the county, if educated at this school; five exhibitions, of £24 per annum each, to Emanuel College, Cambridge, for bachelors of arts until they proceed to their master's degree, with preference to the sons of orthodox clergymen of this diocese, founded in 1719 by Dr. George Thorpe, prebendary of Canterbury; two Greek scholarships, of £8 per annum each, founded in the same college by the Rev. John Brown, B. D.; and one exhibition, of £9 per annum, to any college in Cambridge, to cease on taking the degree of M.A., founded in 1728 by Dr. George Stanhope, Dean of Canterbury. A society of gentlemen educated at the King's school, established for more than a century, hold an anniversary meeting, when, after service at the cathedral, where a sermon suitable to the occasion is delivered by a clergyman educated in the school, a collection is made for the purpose of founding additional scholarships for students in this establishment: by the liberality and exertions of its members a fund has been raised, that has enabled them to found an exhibition of £60 per annum, to be held for four years with any of the preceding; and another of the same value is about to be added to the numerous advantages enjoyed by scholars on this foundation, which, from the zealous attention bestowed upon its management by the Dean and Chapter, promises at least to preserve, if not to increase, the high reputation it has so long maintained: in addition to the annual examinations previously established, quarterly examinations, of which the first took place in November 1829, have been instituted under two of the prebendaries, chosen for that office. Among the eminent men who have received the rudiments of their education in this school may be noticed the celebrated Dr. Harvey, who discovered the circulation of the blood; Dr. Marsh, Bishop of Peterborough; and Lord Tenterden, the present Lord Chief Justice of the court of King's Bench. The Blue-coat school was established by the mayor and commonalty, to whom Queen Elizabeth had granted an hospital founded prior to the year 1243, by Simon de Langton, Archdeacon of Canterbury, for poor priests, with all the lands belonging to it, which, by an act passed in the 1st of George II., was, for the use of the poor, transferred to guardians incorporated by the same act, upon their undertaking also to provide for sixteen poor boys of the city, to be called Blue-coat boys: the estate at present produces £795. 8. 6. per annum; and sixteen boys, nominated by the mayor and commonalty, are clothed, maintained, and instructed in reading, writing, and arithmetic, and, on leaving school, are apprenticed with premiums, which, though originally fixed at £5, are, according to circumstances, increased to £21. The Grey-coat school is supported by the Dean and Chapter, the mayor and commonalty, and other subscribers: two boys and one girl are annually apprenticed from this school by the trustees of Nixon's charity. Two schools, for children of both sexes, are conducted on Dr. Bell's plan, having been united to the National Society in 1812, in which upwards of four hundred children are instructed.

Eastbridge hospital is supposed to have been founded by Archbishop Lanfranc, for the entertainment of pilgrims, and endowed by succeeding archbishops, for a master, five brothers, and five sisters resident, and an equal number of non-resident brothers and sisters, above the age of fifty, who must have lived in the city or suburbs for seven years; the former receive £20 per annum, and the latter £2. 16. 8. per annum, each: the vacancies are filled by nomination of the mayor, who appoints two candidates, one of whom is elected by the master. A school for twenty children was annexed to it by an ordinance of Archbishop Whitgift, confirmed by act of parliament in the 27th of Elizabeth; it is endowed with a manor and an estate at Blean, and with an investment of £2624 in the three per cent. consols., arising from legacies and fines for the renewal of leases: the present income is £331. 15. 10½.: the master of the hospital has an annual income of £90. 18. 7¾., calculated upon an average balance of receipts and expenditure for several years; the schoolmaster has a salary of £30 per annum, with apartments in the hospital; there are thirty scholars at present in the school. Maynard's hospital was founded, about the year 1312, by Mayner le Rich, an opulent citizen, who endowed it with lands and tenements for the support of three unmarried brothers, one of whom is prior and reader, and four unmarried sisters: they are a corporate body by prescription, having a common seal, and, exclusively of their apartments and share of fines for the renewal of leases, receive each £18. 2. 6. per annum from the general funds. Cotton's hospital, adjoining, was founded in 1605, by Leonard Cotton, who endowed it for one aged widower and two widows, who receive £18. 11. 6. per annum each. These hospitals, which are united, are under the management of the mayor and aldermen, of whom the senior alderman is generally appointed master; the right of appointing the brothers and sisters is vested in the mayor. Jesus' hospital was founded, in 1596, by Sir John Boys, the first recorder of the city, for a warden, nine brothers, and nine sisters, above fifty-five years of age, and resident within the city for seven years, with preference to one brother and one sister of the kindred of the founder, if above the age of fifty: there are at present eight brothers and four sisters, who receive each a fixed sum of £20 per annum, and a considerable amount as surplus money: by the statutes, the warden is bound to instruct twenty children of the parishes of St. Mary Northgate, St. Paul, St. Mildred, St. Alphege, and St. Dunstan, who are called out-brothers, and clothed at the expense of the establishment; six of them are to be apprenticed annually: the mayor and aldermen, the Dean of Christ Church, and the Archdeacon of Canterbury, are visitors, and audit the accounts annually. The Rev. George Hearne, in 1805, bequeathed £37 per annum, long annuities, for the support of a Sunday school for the parishes of St. Alphege and St. Mary Northgate, which was sold in 1812 for £637. 5., and appropriated to the purchase and adaptation of a building for a National school, in which fifty-six children of those parishes are instructed. Mr. Robert Dean purchased premises for the use of a Sunday school in the parish of the Holy Cross, which he then endowed with £200 stock, and in 1818 left £800 in the four per cents., as a further endowment for teaching children on the other days of the week: there are also several smaller bequests for the instruction of poor children in the various parishes. St. John's hospital, without the North gate, was founded in 1084, by Archbishop Lanfranc, who endowed it with £70 per annum for poor infirm, lame, and blind men and women; at the time of the dissolution its revenue was £93. 15., and it is now nearly £200: the establishment consists of a prior, reader, fifteen brothers, and fifteen sisters resident, who receive each £8 per annum, with a share of some legacies left in trust to the corporation; and three brothers and three sisters non-resident, who receive something less, and do not participate in the legacies: the archbishop has the exclusive patronage, and appoints the master and prior. John Smith, Esq., in 1644, bequeathed £200 to build almshouses, and £32 per annum for their endowment. Smith's hospital, in the suburb of Langport, without the liberties of the city, for four brothers and four sisters born within the manor of Barton, was founded in 1662, by Mrs. Ann Smith, who endowed it with lands, and with a reserved rent payable by the proprietor of Barton Court, who has the sole patronage, amounting together to £171. 7. 4½. per annum, of which sum she appropriated £32 to the inmates of the hospital; £20 to the apprenticing of poor children of Hornsey, in the county of Middlesex; £20 to the minister of St. Paul's, in this city; and the residue to the apprenticing of children of that parish, with which eight children are placed out annually. Cogan's hospital was founded, in 1657, by Mr. John Cogan, who, by will, gave his mansion to the corporation in trust, for the residence of six clergymen's widows; the endowment has been augmented by numerous subsequent benefactions. The Rev. John Aucher, D.D., by deed in 1696, gave a rent-charge of £60 for six clergymen's widows, with preference to those in Cogan's hospital; and a society raises annually by subscription, £36, which is divided among three widows of clergymen. Harris' almshouses, in Wincheap, were founded in 1726, by Thomas Harris, Esq., who endowed them with houses and land producing £21 per annum, for five poor families, two of the parish of St. Mary Magdalene, two of that of Thanington, and one of St. Mildred, not receiving parochial aid. The Kent and Canterbury infirmary was opened for the reception of patients on the 26th of April, 1793, under the auspices of the late Dr. William Carter, and patronised by the principal inhabitants of the city and county: the institution is liberally supported by annual subscriptions of £2. 2., which sum (or a donation of £21) constitutes a governor; it is well regulated under the direction of a committee and a weekly board for superintending the domestic arrangements. The building, which is spacious and well adapted to the purpose, was erected on part of the ancient cemetery of St. Augustine's abbey, and contains apartments for a house surgeon and sixty patients, the latter receiving the gratuitous attendance of two physicians and four surgeons.

Of the numerous monastic establishments that anciently flourished here, the principal was the abbey which St. Augustine, in conjunction with King Ethelbert, founded for monks of the Benedictine order, and dedicated to St. Peter and St. Paul, the revenue of which, at the dissolution, was £1412. 4. 7.: the remains consist principally of the gateway entrance, a beautiful specimen of the decorated style of English architecture, with two embattled octagonal turrets highly ornamented with canopied niches, and enriched with bands, mouldings, and cornices; between these turrets is the entrance, through a finely pointed arch, in which are the original wooden doors richly carved. One of the towers, called St. Ethelbert's tower, was a fine structure in the Norman style, highly ornamented in its successive stages with a series of intersecting arches; part of it fell down in 1822, and part has been since taken down from apprehension of danger; a portion of the base of the tower, and some trifling remains of the church belonging to the abbey, are still existing. At the north-west of the cemetery are the remains of the chapel of St. Pancras, rebuilt in 1387, on the site of a previous chapel, said to have been a pagan temple, resorted to by Ethelbert before his conversion: the remains of this once splendid abbey have been converted into a public-house; the gateway is now a brewery, the room over it a cock-pit, the church a tennis-court, and the area a bowling-green. In Northgate-street was a religious house, founded in 1084, by Archbishop Lanfranc, for secular priests, and dedicated to St. Gregory, the revenue of which, at the dissolution, was £166. 4. 5.: the remains, consisting of parts of the walls, arches, and some windows in the Norman and early English styles of architecture, have been converted into a pottery, and a tobacco-pipe manufactory. To the south-east of the city was a Benedictine nunnery, founded by Archbishop Anselm, and dedicated to St. Sepulchre, the revenue of which, at the dissolution, was £38. 19. 7.: this convent obtained celebrity from the pretended inspiration of Elizabeth Barton, one of the nuns, called the holy maid of Kent, who, for denouncing the wrath of the Almighty upon Henry VIII., for his intended divorce of Catherine of Arragon, was hanged at Tyburn, with her confederate, Richard Deering, cellarer of Christ Church. To the right of the city, on the road to Dovor, was an hospital dedicated to St. Lawrence, for leprous monks, founded by Hugh, Abbot of St. Augustine's, in 1137, and endowed for a warden, chaplain, clerk, and sixteen brothers and sisters, of whom the senior sister was prioress: the revenue, at the dissolution, was £39. 8. 6. In the parish of St. Peter was an hospital, founded by William Cockyn, citizen, and dedicated to St. Nicholas and St. Catherine, which, in 1203, was united to that of St. Thomas Eastbridge. In the parish of St. Alphege was a priory of Dominicans, or Black friars, founded about the year 1221 by Henry III., the only remains of which are the hall, now a meeting-house for Baptists; and near the hospital for poor priests was a priory of Franciscans, or Grey friars, founded by the same monarch in 1224, which was the first house of that order established in the kingdom; the remains consist chiefly of some low walls and arches: there are also slight vestiges of a convent of White friars that once existed here. Numerous relics of British and Roman antiquity have been discovered; among the latter are, aqueducts, tesselated pavements, vases, and coins; and a Roman arch, called Worthgate, considered to be one of the finest and most ancient structures of the kind in England, has been carefully removed from that part of the castle yard which was crossed by the new road from Ashford, and reconstructed in a private garden. There are some chalybeate springs, and one slightly sulphureous, in the extensive nursery-grounds of Mr. W. Masters, near the west gate; and without the north gate is a fine spring of water, where a bath, called St. Rhadigund's bath, has been constructed, with requisite accommodation. Dr. Thomas Linacre, founder of the Royal College of Physicians, in London; Dr. Thomas Nevile, master of Magdalene College, and afterwards master of Trinity College, Cambridge, who was sent by Archbishop Whitgift to tender the English crown to King James; William Somner, author of the Antiquities of Canterbury, and of a Saxon Glossary; and W. Frend, M, A., author of the Ephemeris, were natives of this city. Among other literary characters that have flourished here may be noticed the Primate Langton, who first divided the Old and New Testaments into chapters; Osbern, a monk in the eleventh century, who wrote in Latin the life of St. Dunstan, and who, from his skill in music, was called the English Jubal; and John Bale, Prebendary of Canterbury and Bishop of Ossory, the Protestant historian and biographer. Isaac Casaubon, whom, on account of his learning, James I. invited over from France, and Meric, his son, were both installed prebendaries.

CANTLEY, a parish in the hundred of BLOFIELD, county of NORFOLK, 5 miles (S. by W.) from Acle, containing 251 inhabitants. The living is a rectory, in the archdeaconry and diocese of Norwich, rated in the king's books at £14, and in the patronage of R. Gilbert, Esq. The church is dedicated to St. Margaret. An allotment of thirteen acres of land was awarded on the enclosure of some waste land, which lets for £8 per annum, forming part of a salary of £30 paid to a schoolmaster, who has also a dwelling-house free, for teaching forty-five scholars.

CANTLEY, a parish in the southern division of the wapentake of STRAFFORTH and TICKHILL, West riding of the county of YORK, 4½ miles (E. by S.) from Doncaster, containing 577 inhabitants. The living is a discharged vicarage, in the archdeaconry and diocese of York, rated in the king's books at £6. 6. 5½., endowed with £200 private benefaction, and £400 royal bounty, and in the patronage of J. W. Childers, Esq. The church is dedicated to St. Wilfrid. In this parish is a cold bath, called "St. Catherine's well," that attracts numerous visitors, for whom requisite accommodation has been prepared.

CANTSFIELD, a township in the parish of TUNSTALL, hundred of LONSDALE, south of the sands, county palatine of LANCASTER, 5 miles (S. by E.) from Kirkby-Lonsdale, containing 120 inhabitants.

CANVEY - ISLAND, a chapelry partly in the parishes of NORTH and SOUTH BENFLEET, BOWERS-GIFFORD, LAINDON, PITSEA, and VANGE, in the hundred of BARSTABLE, and partly in the parishes of LEIGH, PRETTLEWELL, and SOUTHCHURCH, in the hundred of ROCHFORD, county of ESSEX, 6¾ miles (E. N. E.) from Leigh. The living is a perpetual curacy, in the archdeaconry of Essex, and diocese of London, endowed with £ 800 royal bounty, and in the patronage of the Rector of Laindon. The chapel is dedicated to St. Catherine: divine service is performed by the vicar, or curate, of South Benfleet. This island, situated near the mouth of the Thames, is about five miles in length and two in breadth, and contains three thousand six hundred acres: it is encompassed by branches of that river, but there is a passage over the strand at low water, the river being on the south side two miles wide. Numerous flocks of sheep feed here, though the low grounds are subject to inundations, one of which spread so suddenly, in 1735, that many of the sheep and other animals were drowned before they could be driven to the high grounds. Several of the inhabitants are engaged in the fishery. A fair is held on the 25th of June.

CANWELL, an extra-parochial liberty, in the southern division of the hundred of OFFLOW, county of STAFFORD, 5¼ miles (S.W. by W.) from Tamworth, containing 24 inhabitants. In 1142, a priory of Benedictine monks was founded by Geva Riddell; it subsequently went to decay, and became a poor cell for one monk, and was granted to Cardinal Wolsey by Henry VIII., towards the endowment of his two intended colleges.

CANWICK, a parish within the liberty of the city of LINCOLN, county of LINCOLN, 2¼ miles (S.E. by S.) from Lincoln, containing 223 inhabitants. The living is a discharged vicarage, in the archdeaconry and diocese of Lincoln, rated in the king's books at £5. 6. 8., endowed with £400 royal bounty, and in the patronage of the Master and Wardens of the Mercers' Company, London. The church is dedicated to All Saints. In this parish are springs strongly impregnated with iron.

CAPEL, a parish in the second division of the hundred of WOTTON, county of SURREY, 6 miles (S. by E.) from Dorking, containing 876 inhabitants. The living is a donative, in the patronage of the Duke of Norfolk. The church, dedicated to St. John the Baptist, is principally in the early style of English architecture. In Gough's additions to Camden it is mentioned that, in the reign of Elizabeth, the peaty earth of a mound on the moors within the parish glided down, and covered the lower parts, until it stopped at a farm.

CAPEL (ST. ANDREW), a hamlet in the parish of BUTLEY, hundred of WILFORD, county of SUFFOLK, 2¾ miles (W. by S.) from Orford, containing 157 inhabitants. This was formerly a distinct parish; the church, which was dedicated to St. Andrew, is in ruins.

CAPEL le FERNE, a parish in the hundred of FOLKESTONE, lathe of SHEPWAY, county of KENT, 3¼ miles (N. N.E.) from Folkestone, containing 195 inhabitants. The living is a perpetual curacy, annexed to the vicarage of Alkham, in the archdeaconry and diocese of Canterbury. The church is dedicated to St. Mary.

CAPEL (ST. MARY), a parish in the hundred of SAMFORD, county of SUFFOLK, 6 miles (S.E. by E.) from Hadleigh, containing 561 inhabitants. The living is a rectory, consolidated with that of Little Wenham, in the archdeaconry of Suffolk, and diocese of Norwich, rated in the king's books at £ 13. 18. 4., and in the patronage of the Rev. Joseph Tweed.

CAPESTHORNE, a chapelry in the parish of PRESTBURY, hundred of MACCLESFIELD, county palatine of CHESTER, 4 miles (W. by S.) from Macclesfield, containing 65 inhabitants. The living is a perpetual curacy, in the archdeaconry and diocese of Chester, endowed with £400 private benefaction, and £600 royal bounty, and in the patronage of D. Davenport, Esq. The chapel is dedicated to the Holy Trinity.

CAPHEATON, a township in the parish of KIRK-WHELPINGTON, north-eastern division of TINDALE ward, county of NORTHUMBERLAND, 13 miles (W. S. W.) from Morpeth, containing 225 inhabitants. Several Roman coins, silver vessels, &c., were discovered near Capheaton Hall by some labourers, in the early part of the last century. A school-room has been erected in the village by Sir John Swinburn, Bart., whose ancestors have resided here from a very early period.

CAPLAND, a tything partly in the parish of BEER-CROCOMBE, and partly in that of BROADWAY, hundred of ABDICK and BULSTONE, county of SOMERSET, 3 miles (W. by N.) from Ilminster. The population is returned with Broadway. Here was anciently a chapel subordinate to Beer-Crocombe.

CAPLE, a chapelry in the parish of TUDELEY, partly in the Lowey of TONBRIDGE, but chiefly in the hundred of WASHLINGSTONE, lathe of AYLESFORD, county of KENT, 3½ miles (E. S. E.) from Tonbridge, containing 330 inhabitants. The chapel is dedicated to St. Thomas à Becket.

CAPPENHURST, a township in the parish of SHOTWICK, higher division of the hundred of WIRRALL, county palatine of CHESTER, 5¾ miles (N. N. W.) from Chester, containing 161 inhabitants.

CARBROOKE, a parish in the hundred of WAYLAND, county of NORFOLK, 2¾ miles (E. N. E.) from Watton, containing 771 inhabitants. The living is a discharged vicarage, in the archdeaconry and diocese of Norwich, rated in the king's books at £7. 12. 6., endowed with £200 private benefaction, £200 royal bounty, and £1400 parliamentary grant, and in the patronage of Sir William Clayton, Bart. The church, built in the early part of the reign of Henry VI., and dedicated to St. Peter and St. Paul, has a lofty square tower, two aisles, and a chancel, and contains sixteen stalls, with several ancient monuments. A preceptory of Knights Templars was founded by Roger, Earl of Clare, who died in 1173, and subsequently given by Maud, his widowed countess, who amply endowed it, to the Knights Hospitallers of St. John of Jerusalem, as a commandery: at the dissolution it was valued at £65. 2. 9. Adjoining it was a chapel, dedicated to St. John the Baptist; they both stood on the southern side of the present churchyard, but there are not any remains of either of them.

CARBURTON, a chapelry in the parish of EDWINSTOW, Hatfield division of the wapentake of BASSETLAW, county of NOTTINGHAM, 4¼ miles (S. S. E.) from Worksop, containing 154 inhabitants.

CAR-COLSTON, a parish in the northern division of the wapentake of BINGHAM, county of NOTTINGHAM, 9 miles (S. W. by S.) from Newark, containing 213 inhabitants. The living is a discharged vicarage, in the archdeaconry of Nottingham, and diocese of York, rated in the king's books at £6. 1. 10½., and in the patronage of the Rev. R. Farmery. The church is dedicated to St. Mary. There is a place of worship for Wesleyan Methodists.

CARDEN, a township in the parish of TILSTON, higher division of the hundred of BROXTON, county palatine of CHESTER, 4½ miles (N. N. W.) from Malpas, containing 195 inhabitants. A detachment of dragoons from the parliamentary garrison at Nantwich, on the 12th of June, 1643, plundered Carden Hall, and made prisoner its owner, John Leche, Esq.

CARDESTON, a parish in the hundred of FORD, county of SALOP, 6 miles (W.) from Shrewsbury, containing, with the township of Watlesborough, 297 inhabitants. The living is a discharged rectory, in the archdeaconry of Salop, and diocese of Hereford, rated in the king's books at £3, and in the patronage of Sir B. Leighton, Bart. The church is dedicated to St. Michael. This parish is bounded on the south by the river Severn, and contains coal and limestone, but the latter only is worked.

CARDINGTON, a parish in the hundred of WIXAMTREE, county of BEDFORD, 3 miles (E. S. E.) from Bedford, containing, with the chapelry of East Cotts, 1194 inhabitants. The living is a discharged vicarage, in the archdeaconry of Bedford, and diocese of Lincoln, rated in the king's books at £7. 17., endowed with £200 private benefaction, and £200 royal bounty, and in the patronage of the Master and Fellows of Trinity College, Cambridge. The church, dedicated to St. Mary, contains several ancient monuments, also a tablet in memory of the great philanthropist, John Howard, who lived some years at this place, and served the office of sheriff for the county in 1773; and a splendid modern monument by Bacon, the last of his works, erected in 1799 to the memory of Samuel Whitbread, Esq., whose family first settled here in 1650, at a house called the Barns. There is a place of worship for Wesleyan Methodists, and at Cotton End is one for Particular Baptists. The navigable river Ouse runs along the northern side of the parish.

CARDINGTON, a parish in the hundred of MUNSLOW, county of SALOP, 4 miles (E. by N.) from Church-Stretton, containing 687 inhabitants. The living is a vicarage, in the archdeaconry of Salop, and diocese of Hereford, rated in the king's books at £6. 2. 6, and in the patronage of R. Hunt, Esq. The church is dedicated to St. James. There is an endowed school, the estate belonging to which produces £25 per annum. A species of very fine quartz, considered equal in quality to that brought from Caernarvonshire, for the use of the potteries, is found here; the parish abounds also with clay.

CARDINHAM, a parish in the hundred of WEST, county of CORNWALL, 3¾ miles (E. N. E.) from Bodmin, containing 775 inhabitants. The living is a rectory, in the archdeaconry of Cornwall, and diocese of Exeter, rated in the king's books at £24. 17. 8½., and in the alternate patronage of E. J. Glynn, Esq. and the Rev. Thomas Grylls. The church is dedicated to St. Mewbred. At a copious spring called Holy Well are vestiges of an old chapel. The manorial custom of free bench formerly prevailed here: the river Fowey passes through the parish. Here was anciently a castle, of which only the circular intrenchment is remaining; and on some high ground there is a similar intrenchment, comprehending an area of two acres, called Berry Castle. At the north-east extremity of the parish are two large tors, or rocks of granite, one called St. Bellarmine's Tor, and the other Cornet Quoit stone.

CAREBY, a parish in the wapentake of BELTISLOE, parts of KESTEVEN, county of LINCOLN, 6½ miles (N.) from Stamford, containing 51 inhabitants. The living is a rectory, in the archdeaconry and diocese of Lincoln, rated in the king's books at £8. 17. 1., and in the patronage of Lord Gwydir. The church is dedicated to St. Stephen.

CARGO, or CRAGHOW, a township in that part of the parish of STANWIX which is in CUMBERLAND ward, county of CUMBERLAND, 3¼ miles (N. W.) from Carlisle, containing 274 inhabitants.

CARHAM, a parish in the western division of GLENDALE ward, county of NORTHUMBERLAND, 3½ miles (W. S. W.) from Coldstream, comprising the townships of Carham with Shidlaw, Downham, Hagg, New Learmouth, West Learmouth, East Mindrim, West Mindrim, Moneylaws, Preston, Tythehill, Wark, and Wark Common, and containing 1370 inhabitants. The living is a perpetual curacy, in the archdeaconry of Northumberland, and diocese of Durham, and in the patronage of A. Compton, Esq. The church is dedicated to St. Cuthbert. According to Leland, a battle was fought here between the Saxons and the Danes, in which eleven bishops and two English counts were slain. In 1018, it was the scene of a sanguinary contest between the English and the Scotch, in which the latter were victorious; the loss of the English was extremely great, and the event, according to some authors, is stated to have produced such an impression on Aldun, Bishop of Durham, that he died of a broken heart. Another contest occurred in 1370, between the same people, respectively under the command of Sir John Lelburn and Sir John Gordon, in which the Scots, after a severe and arduous conflict, were again victorious, the English general, Sir John Lelburn, and his brother, having been made prisoners. An abbey of Black canons, founded at an unknown period, as a cell to the priory of Kirkham, in Yorkshire, was burnt in the 24th of Edward I., by the Scots under Wallace, whose encampment in a neighbouring field has bestowed on it the name of Campfield. The village is pleasantly situated on the south bank of the Tweed, and is surrounded by several plantations of young forest trees: there is a beautiful and extensive prospect into Scotland from a hamlet situated on a hill, called Shidlaw, on the south side.

CARHAMPTON, a parish in the hundred of CARHAMPTON, county of SOMERSET, 1½ mile (S. E.) from Dunster, containing, with the chapelry of Rode-Huish, 587 inhabitants. The living is a discharged vicarage, in the peculiar jurisdiction of the Dean of Wells, rated in the king's books at £11. 8., and in the patronage of Mrs. Langham. The church is dedicated to St. John the Baptist. There is a small endowment for the instruction of children. The petty sessions are holden here. This place, which gives name to the hundred, probably received its appellation from the British Saint Carantacus, or Carantac, who was the son of Keredic, prince of Cardigan, and who retired hither, built an oratory, and spent the remainder of his life in acts of devotion, preferring the life of a recluse to the government of his father's kingdom. In the grounds of the vicarage have been found numerous skeletons, and the foundation of an ancient building, supposed to be the remains of this chapel, which is stated to have been formerly used as the parish church. Near Dunster Park is an old encampment in excellent preservation; it is octagonal, with double ramparts and a ditch, and there are several outworks in connexion with it. In making a road through the parish, an ancient cairn was removed, when a perfect sepulchre, seven feet long, was discovered, containing a human skeleton; the place has been surrounded by a railing. Twenty poor children are educated under a schoolmistress for £5 a year, the interest of a bequest from Richard Escott, in 1785; an annuity of £3 has been left for the same purpose.

CARISBROOKE, a parish in the liberty of West Medina, Isle of Wight division of the county of Southampton, 1 mile (W. S. W.) from Newport, comprising the hamlets of Billingham, Bowcomb, and Carisbrooke, and part of the environs of the borough of Newport, and containing 4670 inhabitants. The living is a vicarage, with the perpetual curacies of Newport and Northwood annexed, in the archdeaconry and diocese of Winchester, rated in the king's books at £23. 8. 1½., and in the patronage of the Provost and Fellows of Queen's College, Oxford. The church is dedicated to St. Mary; the tower is in the later style of English architecture. This place derives its principal importance from its castle, or fortress, which stands on a commanding conical eminence rising above the village of Carisbrooke, and occupying about twenty acres. Its foundation is of very remote antiquity: the Saxon annals state that it was besieged and taken by Cerdric in 530; it received considerable additions immediately after the Conquest, and at subsequent periods: some state it to have been founded by the Romans, as a few of their coins have been discovered in the neighbourhood; but the appearance of it, especially the keep, clearly shews it has been principally a Norman erection. The whole was greatly improved in the time of Elizabeth, and surrounded by an extensive fortification, with five bastions and a deep moat, to which is attached a terrace-walk of three quarters of a mile in length: these works were raised by the inhabitants, and those who did not labour were obliged to contribute pecuniary aid. The ancient fortress, a rectangular parallelogram including the keep, an irregular polygon, occupies about an acre and a half of ground, the latter being raised on an artificial mound, to which there is an ascent of seventy-two steps, and from its summit an extensive and beautiful prospect, embracing a great portion of the island, and parts of the New Forest and Portsdown hills opposite. Here, on days of public rejoicing, and during the residence of the governor, the British flag is displayed. Within the castle are the ruins of an ancient guard-house, and the chapel of St. Nicholas, built in 1738, on the site of a more ancient one, in which the mayor and high constables of Newport are sworn into office annually. The castle was attacked and taken by Stephen, in 1136, when Baldwin, Earl of Devonshire, took refuge there, after declaring in favour of the Empress Maud; and in the reign of Richard II., it successfully resisted an attack of the French, who plundered the island. Carisbrooke Castle is, however, most remarkable for being the place in which Charles I. was confined for thirteen months, previously to his being delivered up to the parliamentary forces, and whence he made one or two unsuccessful attempts to escape: his children were also subsequently imprisoned in it. It has always been the residence of the governor of the Isle of Wight, and generally contains a strong garrison. Opposite to it, on a rising ground, stands the church, also an ancient structure, with an embattled tower, to which was formerly annexed a monastery of Cistercian monks, founded by William Fitz-Osborn, marshal to the Conqueror, who captured the island, at the same time that William conquered the kingdom; but the remains of the monastery have been converted into a farm-house, still called the Priory. On the banks of a rivulet, at the bottom of the castle hill, the village of Carisbrooke is pleasantly situated; but it was of much more consequence formerly than it is at present, having been a market town, and considered the capital of the island.

CARKIN, a township in the parish of Forcett, western division of the wapentake of Gilling, North riding of the county of York, 7½ miles (E. by N.) from Greta-Bridge, containing 24 inhabitants.

CARLATTON, an extra-parochial liberty, in Eskdale ward, county of Cumberland, 9½ miles (E. S. E.) from Carlisle, containing 54 inhabitants. This district comprises one thousand six hundred acres. Several coins, supposed to be Roman, have been discovered in ploughing a field forming part of the Low Hall estate; and at a farm called Saugh-tree-gate there is a cairn.

CARLBY, a parish in the wapentake of Ness, parts of Kesteven, county of Lincoln, 5¼ miles (N. by E.) from Stamford, containing 186 inhabitants. The living is a discharged rectory, in the archdeaconry and diocese of Lincoln, rated in the king's books at £9. 1. 10½., and in the patronage of the Marquis of Exeter. The church is dedicated to St. Stephen.

CARLEBURY, a hamlet in the parish of Conscliffe, south-eastern division of Darlington ward, county palatine of Durham, 5½ miles (W. by N.) from Darlington. The population is returned with the township of High Coniscliffe. Tradition informs us that this and several other villages in this district were burnt in one of the incursions of the Scots. At Carlebury hills, in the time of Charles I., a severe battle was fought between the royalists and a party of the parliamentary forces; and some human bones have since been dug up, presumed to have belonged to those who were slain. Extensive quarries of limestone exist here.

CARLETON, a township in the parish of Dregg, Allerdale ward above Derwent, county of Cumberland, 2 miles (N. N. W.) from Ravenglass, containing 144 inhabitants.

CARLETON, a township in that part of the parish of St. Cuthbert, Carlisle, which is in Cumberland ward, county of Cumberland, 2½ miles (S. E.) from Carlisle, containing 201 inhabitants. At Newlands, in this township, is a quarry of excellent blue freestone, in appearance like marble.

CARLETON, a chapelry in the parish of Redmarshall, south-western division of Stockton ward, county palatine of Durham, 5 miles (N. W. by W.) from Stockton upon Tees, containing 140 inhabitants. This place was restored to the see of Durham by royal charter, during the episcopacy of Bishop Flambard, the people of Northumberland having previously retained it.

CARLETON, a township in the parish of Poulton, hundred of Amounderness, county palatine of Lancaster, ¾ of a mile (W.N.W.) from Poulton, containing 356 inhabitants. In 1697, Elizabeth Wilson endowed a school with £14. 9. 4., which has been increased by subsequent benefactions, the annual income amounting to about £23; the average number of scholars is thirty.

CARLETON, a parish in the hundred of Loddon, county of Norfolk, 8½ miles (S.E. by E.) from Norwich, containing 79 inhabitants. The living is a discharged rectory, in the archdeaconry of Norfolk, and diocese of Norwich, rated in the king's books at £9, and in the patronage of Sir Charles Rich, Bart. The church is dedicated to St. Peter.

CARLETON, a parish in the western division of the liberty of LANGBAURGH, North riding of the county of YORK, 3¼ miles (S. S. W.) from Stokesley, containing 260 inhabitants. The living is a perpetual curacy, in the archdeaconry of Cleveland, and diocese of York, endowed with £800 royal bounty, and in the patronage of Joseph Reeve, Esq. The church is a small modern structure. There is a place of worship for Wesleyan Methodists. Extensive alum-works were formerly carried on here, but since the discovery of richer beds of that mineral nearer the sea they have been discontinued; various petrifactions of shells and fishes have been found.

CARLETON, a parish in the lower division of the wapentake of BARKSTONE-ASH, West riding of the county of YORK, 1½ mile (N. by E.) from Snaith, containing 775 inhabitants. The living is a perpetual curacy, within the jurisdiction of the peculiar court of Snaith, and in the patronage of William Day, Esq. The church is dedicated to St. Mary. The village is agreeably situated on the northern bank of the river Aire, across which there is a bridge on the road to Snaith. There is a small school, to which Mrs. E. Fisher, in 1726, left £4 per annum, arising from land, for teaching ten poor children to read; and there are four almshouses, to each of which Miles Stapleton, Esq. gives an annuity of £4.

CARLETON, a township in the parish of PONTEFRACT, upper division of the wapentake of OSGOLDCROSS, West riding of the county of YORK, 1¾ mile (S. by E.) from Pontefract, containing 132 inhabitants.

CARLETON, a parish in the eastern division of the wapentake of STAINCLIFFE and EWCROSS, West riding of the county of YORK, 2 miles (S. E.) from Otley, containing 1218 inhabitants. The living is a discharged vicarage, in the archdeaconry and diocese of York, rated in the king's books at £5. 2. 1., endowed with £200 private benefaction, and £200 royal bounty, and in the patronage of the Dean and Canons of Christ Church, Oxford. The church is dedicated to St. Mary. Here is an hospital or almshouse for twelve poor women, founded agreeably to the will of Ferrand Spence, who died in 1698. Six of the women are chosen from the town of Market Bosworth, in the county of Leicester. The hospital contains separate apartments for the women, also a chapel, out offices, garden, &c. The total income is about £280. A school was built by Elizabeth Wilkinson, who, in 1709, endowed it with land for clothing and educating four boys; the income is £120 per annum; twenty boys are educated, four of them being also clothed.

CARLETON-FOREHOE, a parish in the hundred of FOREHOE, county of NORFOLK, 3¼ miles (N. N. W.) from Wymondham, containing 130 inhabitants. The living is a discharged rectory, in the archdeaconry of Norfolk, and diocese of Norwich, rated in the king's books at £5. 17. 1., endowed with £200 private benefaction, and £200 royal bounty, and in the patronage of Lord Wodehouse. The church is dedicated to St. Mary. The distinguishing appellation is derived from four hills, supposed to have been artificially constructed, on one of which the court for the hundred was anciently held.

Arms.

CARLISLE, an ancient city, inland port, and market town, having separate jurisdiction, situated in the ward and county of CUMBERLAND, 302 miles (N. N. W.) from London, on the great western road to Edinburgh and Glasgow, containing 15,476 inhabitants. It was anciently called *Caer-Luil*, or *Caer-Leol*, implying the city of Luil, a British potentate, by whom it is stated to have been founded. The Romans, on selecting it for a station, changed the name to *Lugovallum*, which is probably derived from *Lugus*, or *Lucus*, a tower or fort in the Celtic tongue, and *vallum*, in allusion to Hadrian's vallum that passed near it. From its earliest foundation till the union of the English and Scottish kingdoms, it suffered those shocks of incursive warfare, to which, as a border town, it was peculiarly exposed, and by which it has been repeatedly overwhelmed. In the reign of Nero it is stated by the Scottish historians to have been burnt by the Caledonians, during the absence of the Romans from the island, who in the time of Agricola repaired it, and constructed fortifications as a barrier against the future attacks of the invaders. Soon after their final departure it was probably again destroyed, for, in the seventh century, it was rebuilt by Egfrid, King of Northumberland, in whose reign it rose into importance. About the year 875, it was demolished by the Danes, and lay in ruins till after the Norman conquest, when it was restored by William Rufus, who, in 1092, built and garrisoned the castle, and sent a colony from the south of England to inhabit the city, and cultivate the neighbouring lands. The fortifications were most probably completed by David, King of Scotland, who in 1135 took possession of Carlisle, and resided there for several years, the whole county having been subsequently ceded to him by Stephen: the Scottish historians attribute the building of the castle and the heightening of the walls to this monarch. After the disastrous battle of the Standard, in 1138, this city was the sanctuary of David, who in 1150 conferred the honour of knighthood upon Prince Henry, son of the Empress Matilda, and afterwards Henry II., with whom and the Earl of Chester he formed an alliance against Stephen. The counties of Cumberland and Northumberland having been given to Henry II., in 1157, by Malcolm IV., Carlisle was besieged in 1173, by William the Lion, brother and successor to Malcolm, by whom the garrison was reduced to the greatest distress, from which it was relieved by his capture at Alnwick: the city was afterwards taken by his successor, Alexander, but was surrendered to the English in 1217. In 1292, a great part of it was destroyed by a conflagration, originating in the vindictive malice of an incendiary, who set fire to his father's house: the priory, the convent of the Grey friars, and the church, were all consumed; the convent of the Black friars alone escaped. The public records and charters being thus destroyed, the city was taken into the king's hands, and the government was vested in justices of assize. After the battle of Falkirk, in 1298, Edward I. marched with his army to Carlisle, where he held a parliament; in 1306, he appointed here a general rendezvous of the forces destined against Scotland, under Prince Edward; and the year following, after celebrating his birthday at Carlisle, in the last stage of a decline, he reached Burgh on the Sands, where he died on the 7th of July, 1307. In 1315, Carlisle was besieged by Robert Bruce, who had been crowned King of Scotland, but was resolutely defended by its governor, Andrew de Hercla, afterwards Earl of Carlisle, who, in the year 1322, being accused of holding a treasonable correspondence with the Scots, was arrested by Lord Lucy, in the castle of which he was governor, degraded from his honours, and executed. The Scots, in 1337, laid siege to the city, and fired the suburbs; and the former, in 1345, was burnt by them, under the command of Sir William Douglas. In 1352, Edward III., in consequence of the importance of Carlisle as a frontier town, and of the many calamities it had suffered, renewed its charter, which had been destroyed in the conflagration of 1292. In 1380, a party of borderers invested the city, and fired one of the streets; and in 1385, an unsuccessful effort was made to capture it. In 1461, Carlisle was attacked by a Scottish army in the interest of Henry VI., who burnt the suburbs: this is the only event respecting it that occurred during the war between the houses of York and Lancaster. During Aske's insurrection it was besieged, in 1537, by a party of eight thousand rebels under Nicholas Musgrave and others, but without effect; the leading insurgents, except Musgrave, were apprehended, and, together with about seventy others, executed on the city wall. In 1568, Mary, Queen of Scots, in the hope of finding an asylum from the hostility of her subjects, took fatal refuge in the castle; and in 1596, Sir William Scott, afterwards Earl of Buccleuch, attacking that fortress before day-break, to rescue a noted borderer, celebrated in the ballads of those times as "Kinmont Willie," effected a breach, and triumphantly bore him away. In the following year the city was visited by a destructive pestilence, that destroyed more than one-third of the population.

On the union of the two kingdoms, and the accession of James to the English throne, the importance of Carlisle as a frontier town having ceased, the garrison was reduced. At the commencement of the civil war in the reign of Charles I., the citizens embraced the royal cause; and the city being besieged by the parliamentarian army under General Leslie, after a vigorous resistance, and incredible hardships on the part of the inhabitants, it was surrendered upon honourable terms: during this siege, a coinage of one shilling and three shilling pieces was issued from the castle, which, though very scarce, are still to be met with in the cabinets of the curious. In 1648, the city was retaken by Sir Philip Musgrave, for the royalists, who entrusted it to the custody of the Duke of Hamilton, by whom it was garrisoned with Scottish troops; at the close of the war it was surrendered by treaty to Cromwell. A dreadful famine, in 1650, caused by the consumption of the garrison, compelled the inhabitants to petition parliament for assistance; more than thirty thousand persons are said to have been destitute of bread and of money to purchase seed. The celebrated George Fox, founder of the Society of Friends, was imprisoned in the dungeons of the castle in 1653, on account of his religious tenets. During the rebellion in 1745, the young Pretender laid siege to Carlisle, which, from the weakness of its garrison, surrendered in three days, when the mayor and corporation, on their knees, presented to him the keys of the city, and proclaimed his father king, and himself regent, with all due solemnity. On the approach of the Duke of Cumberland, the Pretender retreated, leaving four hundred men in the garrison, who, unable to sustain a siege, surrendered on condition of being reserved for the king's pleasure; the officers were sent to London, where, having suffered death as traitors, their heads were sent down and exposed in the public places of the city. Cappock, whom the Pretender had created Bishop of Carlisle, was hanged, drawn, and quartered, and nine others, concerned in the rebellion, were executed in the city. The castle is situated at the north-west angle of the city, on the summit of a steep acclivity overlooking the Eden: it is of an irregular form, and consists of an outer and an inner ward; the former, two sides of which are formed by part of the city walls, is quadrangular, and contains no buildings of importance, except an armoury, in which ten thousand stand of arms were formerly deposited, and which is now converted into barracks for the infantry of the garrison, the cavalry being quartered on the innkeepers. The inner ward is triangular, and contains the keep, or dungeon tower, into which the armoury has been lately removed; it is square, and of great strength, having a circular archway leading from the outer into the inner ward, and is, no doubt, that part of the castle built by William Rufus. The other parts are evidently of later date, and correspond with the times of Richard III., Henry VIII., and Elizabeth, by all of whom it was partly rebuilt and repaired: a great part of the buildings erected by Elizabeth has been taken town. It is the head of the ancient royal manor of the soccage of Carlisle, which includes part of the city, and five hundred acres of land in its immediate vicinity.

Carlisle is pleasantly situated on a gradual eminence at the confluence of the rivers Eden and Caldew, which, with the Petterel, almost environ it. The four principal streets diverge from the market-place, and have several minor ones branching from them; they are well paved, and lighted with gas by a company formed pursuant to an act obtained in 1819, who have erected works at an expense of £10,000; the houses in general are handsome and well built, and the inhabitants have it in contemplation to conduct water into their houses by means of pipes leading from the new prison, where there is a capacious reservoir, into which it is raised from the river Caldew by a tread-wheel. In 1827, a police act, for watching, regulating, and improving the city and its suburbs, was obtained, ordaining the appointment of fifty commissioners once in three years, in addition to the higher civil and ecclesiastical authorities, whereby a police establishment has been formed: the magistrates attend at the police-office as occasion requires. A very handsome bridge of white freestone was erected over the Eden, in 1812, from a design by R. Smirke, jun., at an expense to the county of about £70,000; it consists of five elliptical arches, and is connected with the town by an arched causeway: two stone bridges, of one arch each, were built over the Caldew, on the west side of the city, in 1820; and a bridge of three arches over the Petterel, about a mile from the town, is now being erected. The environs abound with genteel residences.

the view embraces the course of the river Eden, as it winds through a fertile and well cultivated tract of country. In 1818 and 1819, a subscription was begun for the relief of the poor, who by this means were employed in completing and forming various walks near the town; the most interesting of these is the promenade on the slope and summit of the hill on which the castle stands, a terrace-walk on the opposite bank of the Eden, and a raised walk along the south margin of that river. A subscription library was established here in the year 1768, and a news-room has also lately been added to it: in January 1830, some ground was purchased opposite the Bush Inn, for the erection of a new subscription library and news-room, the foundations of which were soon afterwards laid. A commercial news-room was opened in the year 1825; and an academy of arts, for the encouragement of native and other artists in sculpture, painting, modelling, &c., was instituted in the year 1823, in which annual exhibitions are held: a mechanics' institution was formed in the year 1824. The theatre, which is a building possessing no claim to architectural notice, was erected about fourteen years since; it is constantly open during the races, and at other times. The races were first established here about the middle of the last century, and the first King's plate was given in the year 1763; they continue so be held annually in the autumn upon a fine course called the Swifts, which is situated on the south side of the Eden, and they are generally very numerously and respectably attended.

The trade principally consists in the manufacture of cotton goods and ginghams for the West India market, in which upwards of one thousand looms are employed in the town, and a greater number in the adjacent villages: there are ten gingham and check manufactories; nine cotton-spinning factories, employing eighty thousand spindles; a small mill for weaving calicoes; a carpet-manufactory; several hat-manufactories; three iron-foundries; four tan-yards; and four breweries: there are also several fisheries on the river Eden, for the regulation of which an act of parliament was passed in 1804. In 1819, a canal was begun from Carlisle to the Solway Frith at Bowness, a distance of eleven miles, and finished in 1823, at an expense of about £90,000, by means of which vessels of small burden can come up to the town. The number of vessels belonging to the port, in 1829, was forty, averaging sixty-seven tons' burden; these are chiefly employed in supplying the city and the neighbourhood with iron, slate, salt, and other merchandise, and in conveying grain, oak-bark, alabaster, freestone, lead, staves, &c., and other produce of the place, to different towns on the coast. A rail-road from Carlisle to Newcastle is about to be formed, the expense of which is estimated at £260,000. The market days are Wednesday and Saturday: fairs for cattle and horses are held on August 26th and September 19th; during their continuance all persons are free from arrest in the city. There are also fairs, or great markets, on the Saturday after Old Michaelmas-day, and on every Saturday following till Christmas; these fairs are held on the sands, near the bridge across the Eden. In April there is a great show-fair for cattle, when prizes are distributed by the Agricultural Society. The Saturdays at Whitsuntide and Martinmas are great hiring days for servants.

Corporate Seal.

Obverse. Reverse.

This city received its first charter from Richard I.; it was renewed by Edward III., and confirmed by Charles I. in 1637. The government is vested in a mayor, recorder, two bailiffs, or sheriffs, twelve aldermen, and twenty-four common council-men, assisted by a chamberlain, two coroners, a town-clerk, a sword-bearer, three serjeants at mace, and subordinate officers. The mayor is elected annually from among the aldermen, by a majority of the mayor, aldermen, bailiffs, and common council-men, on the Monday after Michaelmas-day, when the bailiffs and coroners are also chosen in like manner: the aldermen are chosen from the common council-men, by the mayor and aldermen; and vacancies in the common council are filled up from the freemen, by the court of aldermen. The mayor, recorder, and two senior aldermen are justices of the peace within the city, and hold a court of session quarterly for the trial of all but capital offenders; the mayor and bailiffs also hold a court of record every Monday, for the recovery of debts to any amount, and have the power of issuing process to hold to bail in actions for debt. A court is also held weekly on Monday, at which the mayor presides, for the recovery of debts under 40*s*. These courts are held in the town-hall, an inconsiderable structure in the centre of the town, near which are the moot-hall and council-chamber. There are eight fraternities, or companies, *viz.*, Grocers, Tanners, Skinners, Butchers, Smiths, Weavers, Tailors, and Shoemakers, who have each their public room, all in the same building, called guilds, where they hold a general meeting annually on Ascension-day. The freedom of the city is inherited by birth, and acquired by an apprenticeship of seven years to a resident freeman, and by gift from the corporation. The assizes for the county are held regularly, and the Easter and Midsummer quarter sessions (the remaining two being held at Cockermouth and Penrith) take place in the new court-houses, erected in 1810 by act of parliament, at an expense of £100,000, from a design by Robert Smirke, jun., on the site of the ancient citadel that flanked the eastern gate: they consist of two large circular towers, one on each side of the entrance into the city, in the decorated style of English architecture, and contain two court-rooms, with apartments for the grand jury, counsel, and witnesses: one is appropriated to the Crown, and the other to the Nisi Prius bar. From the former is a subterraneous passage to the county gaol and house of correction, a noble building completed under the same act, in 1827, on the site of the ancient convent of the Black friars, at an expense of £42,000, and surrounded by a stone wall twenty-five feet high. The borough first exercised the elective franchise in the

23rd of Edward I., since which time it has regularly returned two members to parliament: the right of election is vested in the free burgesses who have been previously admitted members of one of the eight fraternities, whether resident or not, the number of whom is about one thousand; the mayor is the returning officer.

Arms of the Bishoprick.

The diocese of Carlisle originally formed part of the diocese of Lindisfarn; but the see being removed from that place to Durham, and considerable inconvenience being felt from the distance of Carlisle from that city, Henry I., in 1133, constituted it a distinct bishoprick, and appointed to the episcopal chair Athelwald his confessor, who was prior of a monastery of Augustine canons, founded here in the reign of William Rufus, by Walter, a Norman priest, and completed and endowed by this monarch. It comprises the whole of Cumberland, except the ward of Allerdale above Derwent, which forms part of the diocese of Chester, and the parish of Alston, which is in the diocese of Durham; and the county of Westmorland, except the barony of Kendal, which also forms part of the diocese of Chester; and contains one hundred and two parishes, throughout the whole of which the bishop, or his chancellor, exercises sole ecclesiastical jurisdiction, the powers of the archdeacon having been anciently resigned to him for an annual pension, in consequence of the smallness of the diocese rendering their concurrent jurisdiction inconvenient. The revenue of the priory, in the 26th of Henry VIII., was estimated at £482. 8. 1. This monarch dissolved the monastic establishment in 1540, and instituted a dean and chapter, composed of a dean, four prebendaries, and eight minor canons, and endowed this body with the whole, or the greater part, of the possessions of the dissolved priory, constituting the bishop, by the same charter, visitor of the chapter; he also appointed a subdeacon, four lay clerks, a grammar master, six choristers, a master of the choristers, and inferior officers. The advowson of the prebends has, since 1557, belonged to the bishop, who also has the patronage of the archdeaconry; the deanery is in the gift of the Crown.

The cathedral, dedicated to St. Mary, is a venerable structure, exhibiting different styles of architecture: it was originally cruciform, but the western part was taken down, to furnish materials for the erection of a guard-house, in 1641; and during the interregnum, part of the nave and the conventual buildings was also pulled down for repairing the walls and the citadel; it has a square embattled central tower, and the east end is decorated with pinnacles rising above the roof. It consists of a choir, north and south transepts, and two remaining arches of the nave, walled in at the west end and used as a parish church: the choir is in the decorated style of English architecture, with large clustered columns enriched with foliage, and pointed arches with a variety of mouldings; the clerestory windows in the upper part are filled with rich tracery, and the east end has a lofty window of nine lights, of exquisite workmanship, abounding in elegance of composition, and harmony of arrangement, which render it superior to any in the kingdom; the aisles are in the early English style, with sharply-pointed windows and slender-shafted pillars; the remaining portion of the nave and the south transept are of Norman architecture, having large massive columns and circular arches, being evidently the part built in the reign of William Rufus. There are monuments to the memory of some of the bishops, and one recently erected to that of Archdeacon Paley, who wrote some of his works whilst resident in this city, and who, with his two wives, was buried in the cathedral.

Carlisle stands within the two parishes of St. Mary and St. Cuthbert, both in the diocese, and locally in the archdeaconry, of Carlisle. St. Mary's includes the townships of Abbey-street, Castle-street, Fisher-street, Scotch-street, Caldew-gate, Ricker-gate, and Cummersdale; also the chapelry of Wreay, which is without the city, and in Cumberland ward. St. Cuthbert's includes the townships of Botchard-gate, Botchardby, Brisco, and English-street, within the city; and the townships of High Blackwell, Low Blackwell, Carleton, Harraby, and Upperby, without the city, and in Cumberland ward. The parochial church of St. Mary is part of the nave of the cathedral: the living is a perpetual curacy, endowed with £200 private benefaction, £600 royal bounty, and £1000 parliamentary grant, and in the patronage of the Dean and Chapter. The church, dedicated to St. Cuthbert, Bishop of Lindisfarn, is a plain edifice, rebuilt in the year 1778, at the expense of the inhabitants, upon the site of the ancient structure: the living is a perpetual curacy, endowed with £600 private benefaction, £1200 royal bounty, and £1000 parliamentary grant, and in the patronage of the Dean and Chapter. Two new churches, or chapels of ease, were completed in September 1830, at an expense of £13,212. 0. 10., of which £4030 was subscribed by the inhabitants, and the remainder granted by the parliamentary commissioners: the first stone of each was laid on September 26th, 1828; they are in the early style of English architecture, each having a tower surmounted by a spire. There are meeting-houses for Baptists, the Society of Friends, Independents, Wesleyan Methodists, and Presbyterians, besides a Roman Catholic chapel. The grammar school was founded by Henry VIII., on instituting the dean and chapter; the endowment is £190 per annum, of which the dean and chapter and the mayor and corporation contribute each £20 per annum; the remainder arises from an estate in the parish of Addingham, purchased in 1702, with a gift of £500 by Dr. Smyth, a former bishop: the management is vested in the Dean and Chapter. Dr. Thomas, Bishop of Rochester, left £1000 stock, directing the dividends to be applied to the benefit of two sons of clergymen, instructed here, and sent to Queen's College, Oxford. Dr. Thomas, Dr. Tully, and the Rev. J. D. Carlyle, a learned orientalist, received the rudiments of their education here; the last is interred in the church of St. Cuthbert. The girls' charity school, founded in 1717, is endowed with lands purchased with a donation of £40, by Mr. Nicholas Robinson, in 1719, and one of £320 by Mr. Samuel Howe, in 1722: the dean and chapter contribute £5, and the corporation £2 annually. A Lancasterian school was instituted in 1813, and a National school in 1817: a female infant school was established in 1806. St. Patrick's day and Sunday school, for the instruction of children of all religious denominations, was erected in 1826, and is supported by subscription. Near the English gate are some almshouses for decayed freemen, or their widows. The dispensary, established in 1782; and the house of recovery from fever, erected in 1820, are supported by voluntary subscription. A savings bank was opened in 1818; and a general infirmary for the whole county is about to be erected: there are various benevolent societies and charitable donations. Near the city was an hospital, dedicated to St. Nicholas, founded prior to the 21st of Edward I., for thirteen leprous persons, which, at the dissolution, was assigned toward the endowment of the dean and chapter. In the city walls, near the castle, an ancient vaulted chamber, having a recess at each end, and accessible only by an opening through the wall, has been lately discovered; it is supposed to have been a reservoir, or fountain, in the time of the Romans. In the reign of William III., a Roman *Triclinium* with an arched roof still existed, and, from an inscription on its front which Camden read "*Marti Victori*," is supposed to have been a temple in honour of Mars. A large altar was lately found, inscribed *Deo Marti Belatucardro*; and, a few years since, a *Prefericulum*, ten inches and a quarter high, having the handles ornamented in bas relief with figures sacrificing: the latter is now in the British Museum. In the castle yard is a bas relief of two figures hooded and mantled. Carlisle confers the title of earl on the family of Howard.

CARLTON, a parish in the hundred of WILLEY, county of BEDFORD, 1½ mile (S.) from Harrold, containing 429 inhabitants. The living is a rectory, consolidated in 1769 with that of Chellington, in the archdeaconry of Bedford, and diocese of Lincoln, rated in the king's books at £15. 6. 8. The church, dedicated to St. Mary, contains a tablet on which is recorded the long incumbency of the Rev. Thomas Wills, who was minister of Carlton and Chellington three score and ten years. There is a place of worship for Particular Baptists. This parish was formerly much intermixed with that of Chellington, but, under an act of enclosure in 1801, a distinct boundary has been established.

CARLTON, a parish in the hundred of RADFIELD, county of CAMBRIDGE, 5½ miles (S.) from Newmarket, containing, with the chapelry of Willingham, 363 inhabitants. The living is a rectory, in the archdeaconry and diocese of Ely, rated in the king's books at £9, and in the patronage of Lord Dacre. The church is dedicated to St. Peter. Sir Thomas Elliot, author of a Latin dictionary, and other works, resided here, and dying in 1546, was buried in the church.

CARLTON, a chapelry in the parish of MARKET-BOSWORTH, hundred of SPARKENHOE, county of LEICESTER, 1¾ mile (N. by W.) from Market-Bosworth, containing 218 inhabitants. The chapel is dedicated to St. Mary. The Ashby de la Zouch canal crosses the south-west angle of this chapelry.

CARLTON, a hamlet in the parish of GEDLING, southern division of the wapentake of THURGARTON, county of NOTTINGHAM, 3 miles (E. N. E.) from Nottingham, containing 1345 inhabitants. There is a place of worship for Wesleyan Methodists. This is an extensive hamlet; the inhabitants are chiefly employed in the manufacture of hosiery. It is in the honour of Tutbury, duchy of Lancaster, and within the jurisdiction of a court of pleas held at Tutbury every third Tuesday, for the recovery of debts under 40*s*.

CARLTON, a parish in the hundred of HOXNE, locally in that of Plomesgate, county of SUFFOLK, ¾ of a mile (N. by W.) from Saxmundham, containing 126 inhabitants. The living is a rectory, consolidated, in 1679, with the rectory of Kelsale, in the archdeaconry of Suffolk, and diocese of Norwich, rated in the king's books at £3. 11. 0½., and in the patronage of the Rev. B. Bence. The church is dedicated to St. Peter.

CARLTON, a chapelry in the parish of HUSTHWAITE, within the liberty of ST. PETER of YORK, East riding, locally in the wapentake of Birdforth, North riding, of the county of YORK, 5¾ miles (N. N. W.) from Easingwould, containing 169 inhabitants.

CARLTON, a township in the parish of COVERHAM, western division of the wapentake of HANG, North riding of the county of YORK, 4¾ miles (S. W. by W.) from Middleham, containing 280 inhabitants.

CARLTON, a township in the parish of ROTHWELL, lower division of the wapentake of AGBRIGG, West riding of the county of YORK, 4½ miles (N.) from Wakefield, containing, with Lofthouse, 1396 inhabitants.

CARLTON, a township in the parish of GUISELEY, upper division of the wapentake of SKYRACK, West riding of the county of YORK, 2 miles (S. E.) from Otley, containing 158 inhabitants.

CARLTON, a township in the parish of ROYSTON, wapentake of STAINCROSS, West riding of the county of YORK, 3 miles (N.N.E.) from Barnesley, containing 326 inhabitants.

CARLTON (CASTLE), a parish in the Marsh division of the hundred of LOUTH-ESKE, parts of LINDSEY, county of LINCOLN, 6¾ miles (S.E. by S.) from Louth, containing 62 inhabitants. The living is a rectory not in charge, in the archdeaconry and diocese of Lincoln, endowed with £400 royal bounty, and in the patronage of John Forster, Esq. The church is dedicated to the Holy Cross. Here was once a populous market town, enjoying many privileges granted by Henry I.: there are three artificial mounts, each surrounded by a moat, on one of which was the baronial castle of Sir Hugh Bardolph.

CARLTON (EAST), comprising the united parishes of St. Mary and St. Peter the Apostle, in the hundred of HUMBLEYARD, county of NORFOLK, 4¾ miles (E.) from Wymondham, containing 262 inhabitants. The living of St. Mary's is a discharged rectory, rated in the king's books at £4, and in the patronage of the Corporation of Norwich: that of St. Peter's the Apostle is also a discharged rectory, rated in the king,s books at £6, and in the patronage of the Crown: the y are in the archdeaconry of Norfolk, and diocese of Norwich. The church of St. Peter was converted into a parsonage-house, and has subsequently fallen into ruins.

CARLTON (EAST), a parish in the hundred of CORBY, county of NORTHAMPTON, 3 miles (S.W. by W.) from Rockingham, containing 63 inhabitants. The living is a rectory, in the archdeaconry of Northampton, and diocese of Peterborough, rated in the king's books at

£12. 16. 3., and in the patronage of Sir J. H. Palmer, Bart. The church is dedicated to St. Peter. There are five almshouses in this parish, the inmates of which receive five shillings per week from the estate of Sir J. H. Palmer.

CARLTON (GREAT), a parish in the Marsh division of the hundred of LOUTH-ESKE, parts of LINDSEY, county of LINCOLN, 6½ miles (E.S.E.) from Louth, containing 242 inhabitants. The living is a vicarage not in charge, in the archdeaconry and diocese of Lincoln, and in the patronage of the Dean and Chapter of Lincoln. The church is dedicated to St. John the Baptist. There is a place of worship for Wesleyan Methodists. A school was erected by Sir Edward Smith, Bart., in 1716, which is endowed with £20 per annum, besides an annuity of £10 given by Sir John Monson, on condition that the master should teach the poor children of Great and Little Carlton, Burton, Broxholm, and those of his tenants at Saxilby; four acres of land were also added on enclosing the lordship of Carlton Castle.

CARLTON in LINDRICK, a parish in the Hatfield division of the wapentake of BASSETLAW, county of NOTTINGHAM, 3¾ miles (N. by E.) from Worksop, containing 888 inhabitants. The living is a rectory, in the archdeaconry of Nottingham, and diocese of York, rated in the king's books at £15. 13. 4., and in the patronage of the Archbishop of York. The church, dedicated to St. John, is a large structure principally in the Norman style of architecture. This appears to have been a place of some importance before the Conquest, from the many vestiges of antiquity still visible. A considerable trade is carried on in malt, which is chiefly disposed of at Manchester and Stockport.

CARLTON (LITTLE), a parish in the Marsh division of the hundred of LOUTH-ESKE, parts of LINDSEY, county of LINCOLN, 6 miles (E.S.E.) from Louth, containing 114 inhabitants. The living is a discharged rectory, in the archdeaconry and diocese of Lincoln, rated in the king's books at £5. 16. 10½., and in the patronage of John Forster, Esq. The church is dedicated to St. Edith.

CARLTON le MOOR-LANDS, a parish in the lower division of the wapentake of BOOTHBY-GRAFFO, parts of KESTEVEN, county of LINCOLN, 10 miles (S.W. by W.) from Lincoln, containing 294 inhabitants. The living is a discharged vicarage, with that of Stapleford annexed, in the archdeaconry and diocese of Lincoln, rated in the king's books at £7. 0. 10., and in the patronage of Lord Middleton. The church is dedicated to St. Mary. There is a place of worship for Particular Baptists. The parish is bounded on the east by the river Brant, and on the west by the Witham.

CARLTON (NORTH), a parish in the wapentake of LAWRESS, parts of LINDSEY, county of LINCOLN, 4½ miles (N.N.W.) from Lincoln, containing 171 inhabitants. The living is a perpetual curacy, in the peculiar jurisdiction of the Dean and Chapter of Lincoln, endowed with £400 royal bounty, and £200 parliamentary grant, and in the patronage of Lord Monson.

CARLTON (SOUTH), a parish in the wapentake of LAWRESS, parts of LINDSEY, county of LINCOLN, 3½ miles (N.N.W.) from Lincoln, containing 194 inhabitants. The living is a perpetual curacy, in the peculiar jurisdiction of the Dean and Chapter of Lincoln, endowed with £400 royal bounty, and £200 parliamentary grant, and in the patronage of Lord Monson. The family of Monson have endowed a school here, which is under their exclusive control.

CARLTON upon TRENT, a chapelry in the parish of NORWELL, northern division of the wapentake of THURGARTON, county of NOTTINGHAM, 6¾ miles (N.) from Newark, containing 287 inhabitants. At the distance of a quarter of a mile east of the village is a ferry over the Trent, which bounds the chapelry.

CARLTON-COLVILLE, a parish in the hundred of MUTFORD and LOTHINGLAND, county of SUFFOLK, 3¾ miles (S.W. by W.) from Lowestoft, containing 714 inhabitants. The living is a discharged rectory, in the archdeaconry of Suffolk, and diocese of Norwich, rated in the king's books at £12. 10. 7½., and in the patronage of the Rev. George Anguish. The church is dedicated to St. Peter. There is a place of worship for Wesleyan Methodists. This parish has the lake Lothing on the north, and the navigable river Waveney on the north-west.

CARLTON-CURLIEU, a parish in the hundred of GARTREE, county of LEICESTER, 7½ miles (N.N.W.) from Market-Harborough, containing, with the chapelry of Illston on the Hill, 174 inhabitants. The living is a rectory, in the archdeaconry of Leicester, and diocese of Lincoln, rated in the king's books at £18. 15. 10., and in the patronage of Sir J. H. Palmer, Bart. The church is dedicated to St. Mary. The ancient manor-house is curious, affording a specimen of the style of building in Queen Elizabeth's time.

CARLTON-ISLEBECK, or MINIOT, a chapelry in the parish of THIRSK, partly in the liberty of ST. PETER of YORK, East riding, and partly in the wapentake of BIRDFORTH, North riding of the county of YORK, 2½ miles (W. by S.) from Thirsk, containing 221 inhabitants. The living is a perpetual curacy, with that of Sand-Hutton, in the archdeaconry of Cleveland, and diocese of York, endowed with £800 royal bounty, and in the patronage of the Archbishop of York.

CARLTON-RODE, a parish in the hundred of DEPWADE, county of NORFOLK, 2½ miles (N.E. by E.) from New Buckenham, containing 869 inhabitants. The living is a discharged rectory, in the archdeaconry of Norfolk, and diocese of Norwich, rated in the king's books at £16, and in the patronage of Sir R. J. Buxton, Bart. The church is dedicated to All Saints: the tower was completed in 1502, and the whole was repaired and ornamented in 1717, at the expense of a few benefactors. There is a place of worship for Particular Baptists. This parish is said to take its distinguishing appellative from the existence of a remarkable rood, or cross, that stood in Rode-lane; but it is more probable that it was so called from its ancient lord, Walter de Rode, who lived in the reign of Henry III.: it is remarkable for a singular tenure, by which certain lands were held, namely, that the lord of the manor should carry to the king, in whatever part of England he might be, a hundred herrings in twenty-four pies, when they first came into season, which the town of Yarmouth was bound to supply, and send to the sheriffs of Norwich, who were to convey them to the lord of the manor: this custom was observed in the early part of the last century, by agreement between the sheriffs of Norwich and the lord of this manor, or his deputy. Here was a free chapel, dedicated to the Virgin Mary, now in ruins.

CARLTON-SCROOP, a parish in the wapentake of LOVEDEN, parts of KESTEVEN, county of LINCOLN, 6¼ miles (N. N. E.) from Grantham, containing 148 inhabitants. The living is a rectory, in the archdeaconry and diocese of Lincoln, rated in the king's books at £13. 1. 5½., and in the patronage of Earl Brownlow. The church is dedicated to St. Nicholas.

CARNABY, a parish in the wapentake of DICKERING, East riding of the county of YORK, 3 miles (S. W. by W.) from Bridlington, containing 130 inhabitants. The living is a discharged vicarage, in the archdeaconry of the East riding, and diocese of York, rated in the king's books at £7. 8. 11½., endowed with £200 royal bounty, and in the patronage of Sir W. Strickland, Bart. The church is dedicated to St. John the Baptist.

CARNFORTH, a township in the parish of WARTON, hundred of LONSDALE, south of the sands, county palatine of LANCASTER, 6 miles (N. by E.) from Lancaster, containing 294 inhabitants. A dreadful fire, in 1810, destroyed twelve houses in the village, remains of which may still be seen.

CARPERBY, a township in the parish of AYSGARTH, western division of the wapentake of HANG, North riding of the county of YORK, 9 miles (W. by N.) from Middlewich, containing 283 inhabitants.

CARRINGTON, a chapelry in the parish of BOWDON, hundred of BUCKLOW, county palatine of CHESTER, 5 miles (N. N. W.) from Altrincham, containing 531 inhabitants. The living is a perpetual curacy, in the archdeaconry and diocese of Chester, endowed with £1000 private benefaction, £1000 royal bounty, and £300 parliamentary grant, and in the patronage of the Earl of Stamford. The chapel, dedicated to St. George, was consecrated in 1759.

CARRINGTON, a parochial chapelry in the eastern division of the soke of BOLINGBROKE, parts of LINDSEY, county of LINCOLN, 1½ mile (S.) from New Bolingbroke, containing 139 inhabitants. The living is a perpetual curacy, with Frith Ville and West Ville, in the archdeaconry and diocese of Lincoln. The chapel was consecrated in 1818. Carrington was formerly in the parish of Helpringham, but was constituted a parochial chapelry in 1812, by an act of parliament, on the occasion of a very extensive drainage of fen lands.

CARROCK, or CANNOCK, PASSAGE, a chapelry in the parish of ST. VEEP, hundred of WEST, county of CORNWALL, 1 mile (N. E.) from Fowey. The population is returned with the parish. The chapel, which was dedicated to St. Cannock, is now in ruins.

CARROW, a hamlet in the parish of WARDEN, north-western division of TINDALE ward, county of NORTHUMBERLAND, 8¼ miles (N. W.) from Hexham. The population is returned with the parish. It is stated to have been the Roman station *Procolitia*, garrisoned by the *Cohors Prima Batavorum*, on the line of Severus' military way; vestiges of the works are visible on an elevated situation, where two altars, now in the Durham library, have been found. About half a mile south-westward are traces of a square fort, now called Broomdykes.

CARSHALTON, a parish (formerly a market town) in the second division of the hundred of WALLINGTON, county of SURREY, 11 miles (S. S. W.) from London, containing 1775 inhabitants. In Domesday-book this place is called *Aulton*, signifying Old Town, and this name it retained until the reign of John, when it was called Cersalton, of which the present name is a variation. The village is pleasantly situated near Banstead Downs, on a dry and chalky soil: the river Wandle runs through the parish, and, being joined in its course by other streams issuing from springs in the neighbourhood, forms in the centre of the village a broad sheet of water, through which passes the public road, constructed by subscription among the inhabitants, at an expense of £700, and renewed by the same means in 1828, when a bridge was erected, which cost £500. The environs are pleasingly diversified with rural scenery, and contain numerous elegant mansions, inhabited principally by London merchants. Near the churchyard is a fine spring, called Queen Ann Boleyne's well, that queen, as it is said, having been gratified with the flavour of the water; it is arched over with stone, and kept in good repair. The trade has lately much declined: a calico-printing establishment, on a large scale, has been discontinued; but there are extensive bleaching-grounds, and, on the banks of the river, within the limits of the parish, are several mills for the manufacture of snuff, paper, flocks, and leather, besides three large flour-mills: there are also some limekilns. A branch from the Wandsworth and Croydon railway extends to Hack bridge, in this parish. The market, granted in the reign of Henry III., has long been discontinued; but a pleasure fair is held on the 1st and 2nd of July. Carshalton is within the jurisdiction of a court of requests held at Croydon, for the recovery of debts under £5: a court for the manor is occasionally held.

The living is a vicarage, in the archdeaconry of Surrey, and diocese of Winchester, rated in the king's books at £11. 12. 6., and in the patronage of John Cator, Esq.: the vicars have received the great tithes since 1726. The church, dedicated to All Saints, is an ancient structure, containing portions in the early and decorated styles of English architecture; the chancel, which is built of flint, appears to be the oldest part, to which the other parts, built of brick, have been subsequently added; the steeple is between the chancel and the nave. The interior contains some ancient and interesting monuments belonging to the families of Fellowes and Scawen; and there are two brasses, representing Sir Nicholas Gaynesford and his lady, with a group of children. There is a Roman Catholic chapel connected with a seminary in the parish. A National school, for an unlimited number of children, is supported by subscription. Christopher Muschamp, Esq., in 1660, bequeathed £200, to be invested in the purchase of land, which now produces £25 per annum, for apprenticing poor children; and in 1726, Edward Fellowes, Esq. gave an annuity of £20, directing that half of it should be appropriated to the same purpose, and the remainder given to the poor, for whose benefit there are also some smaller bequests. A bronze figure of Cupid, about three inches and a half in height, and a brass bust of a man, both found in the river, were in 1794 exhibited to the Society of Antiquaries. Dr. Radcliffe, the munificent benefactor to the university of Oxford, resided here in the latter part of his life. Carshalton Grove has been stripped of its trees, and those beauties which once rendered it a source of considerable attraction have greatly faded.

CARSINGTON, a parish in the hundred of WIRKSWORTH, county of DERBY, 2¼ miles (W. by S.) from Wirksworth, containing 270 inhabitants. The living is a discharged rectory, in the archdeaconry of Derby, and diocese of Lichfield and Coventry, rated in the king's books at £5. 1. 10., and in the patronage of the Dean of Lincoln. The church, dedicated to St. Margaret, is a small ancient building, without a steeple, and scarcely distinguishable from the cliffs that overhang it. The village is situated in a valley surrounded by hills, in which there are quarries of limestone and lead mines. The Peak Forest railway passes through the parish. A school for twenty poor children of this parish and the adjoining township of Hopton was founded by Mrs. Temperance Gill, in 1726; it has an endowment of £60 per annum, arising from land. John Oldfield, an eminent nonconformist divine, was ejected from the benefice of this parish, in 1662; his son, Dr. Joshua Oldfield, of some literary celebrity, was born here, in 1656. Mr. Ellis Farneworth, an able translator from the Italian, was presented to the rectory in 1762. Carsington is in the honour of Tutbury, duchy of Lancaster, and within the jurisdiction of a court of pleas held at Tutbury every third Tuesday, for the recovery of debts under 40*s*.

CARSWELL (ABBOT'S), county of DEVON.—See KERSWELL (ABBOT'S).

CARTER-MOOR, a hamlet in the parish of PONTELAND, western division of CASTLE ward, county of NORTHUMBERLAND, 10½ miles (N. W. by N.) from Newcastle upon Tyne. The population is returned with the township of Kirkley, to which Carter-Moor has been annexed, having been previously a distinct township.

CARTHORP, a township in the parish of BURNESTON, wapentake of HALLIKELD, North riding of the county of YORK, 4½ miles (S. E.) from Bedale, containing 301 inhabitants. There is a place of worship for Wesleyan Methodists. Here are the remains of a Roman camp.

CARTMEL, a parish in the hundred of LONSDALE, north of the sands, county palatine of LANCASTER, comprising the market town of Cartmel, the chapelries of Broughton, Cartmel-Fell, and Staveley, and the townships of Lower Allithwaite, Upper Allithwaite, Lower Holker, and Upper Holker, and containing 4923 inhabitants: the town of Cartmel stands in the townships of Lower Allithwaite and Upper Holker, 14 miles (N. W. by N.) from Lancaster, and 254 (N. N. W.) from London. This place, supposed to have derived its name from the British words *Kert*, a camp, and *mell*, a fell, or small mountain, according to Camden, was given to St. Cuthbert in 677, by Egfrid, King of Northumberland, with all the Britons inhabiting it. In 782, Ethelred, upon his restoration to the throne of that kingdom, allured from their sanctuary at York the sons of Alfwold, who had been advanced to the crown upon his expulsion, and put them to death at this place. In 1188, William Mareschall, Earl of Pembroke, founded a priory for regular canons of the order of St. Augustine, dedicated to the Blessed Virgin, endowing it with all his lands at "Kertmell," and with other possessions, besides many privileges, among which was the exclusive right of appointing guides to conduct travellers over the extensive sands that bound this parish on the south: the establishment, at the dissolution, consisted of ten religious and forty-eight servants, and the revenue was estimated at £212. 11. 10.: the conventual church, which was also parochial, was purchased by the parishioners. The town is situated in a vale surrounded by lofty hills of varied aspect, behind which the vast fells of Coniston rise majestically to the north; the houses, with the exception of a row lately erected on the north side of the town, of modern and handsome appearance, are in general built of stone, rough-cast and white-washed: the environs abound with scenery strikingly diversified by richly wooded eminences and barren hills. The parish is bounded on the south by the bay of Morecambe, into which it extends for a considerable distance, where at low water there is a passage over the sands to Bolton: the longer course over these sands is nine miles; the shorter, over that part called the Leven sands, is four miles: guides are usually waiting to conduct over both. The scenery is romantically wild, and in some parts picturesquely beautiful. Between lake Windermere and the river is Furness point, separated from Walney island by a narrow channel, the entrance of which is defended by the Pile of Fouldrey, built by one of the abbots, on a rock in the sea. The parish abounds with rocks of limestone and marble, but very little trade is carried on; there are cotton-mills at Upper Holker. The market, formerly on Monday, is now on Tuesday: the fairs are on Whit-Monday and the Monday after October the 23rd; and cattle fairs are held on the Wednesday before Easter and November 5th.

The living is a perpetual curacy, in the archdeaconry of Richmond, and diocese of Chester, endowed with £200 parliamentary grant, and in the patronage of Lord George Cavendish. The church, dedicated to St. Mary, is a spacious cruciform structure in the early style of English architecture, with a curious tower: after having been suffered to remain in a state of neglect for nearly a century after the dissolution of the priory, during which time the conventual buildings had been removed, it was substantially repaired, in 1640, by George Preston, Esq., of Holker: the chancel contains some richly carved stalls and fine tabernacle work; on the north side of the altar is the tomb of William de Walton, one of the priors, and on the opposite side is a magnificent altar-tomb, with recumbent figures of one of the Harringtons and his lady, supposed to be Sir John Harrington, who accompanied Edward I. into Scotland, besides many other sepulchral monuments. The free grammar school, built in 1790, appears to have risen out of a parochial school supported by the churchwardens and sidesmen of the parish: various subsequent donations and legacies have produced an endowment of £117. 0. 3. per annum, of which the master receives £110: there are about fifty scholars, one-half of whom are instructed in the classics, and the rest in English only; those that learn writing and arithmetic pay a small quarterage to the master. Dr. Edmund Law, Bishop of Carlisle, whose father was curate of one of the chapels in the parish for forty-nine years, received the rudiments of his education in this school. In a wood in the vicinity, about twenty years ago, six hundred and eighty Roman coins were dug up, dated from 193 to 253, which are now in the possession of Lord George Cavendish; and at Broughton a coin of the Emperor Adrian was discovered. Three miles to the south of the town is a spring, called Holy Well, the water of which is efficacious in relieving from the pains of gout, and in nephritic and cutaneous diseases; and at Pit farm, in this parish, is an intermitting spring.

CARTMEL-FELL, a chapelry in the parish of CARTMEL, hundred of LONSDALE, north of the sands, county palatine of LANCASTER, 8 miles (W.S.W.) from Kendal, containing 371 inhabitants. The living is a perpetual curacy, in the archdeaconry of Richmond, and diocese of Chester, endowed with £800 royal bounty, and in the patronage of Lord George Cavendish, as lessee under the Bishop of Chester. The chapel is dedicated to St. Anthony. The inhabitants of a part of this chapelry contribute to the chapel of Winster, in the county of Westmorland, whither they resort for greater convenience.

CARTWORTH, a township in the parish of KIRK-BURTON, upper division of the wapentake of AGBRIGG, West riding of the county of YORK, 7¼ miles (S. by W.) from Huddersfield, containing 1211 inhabitants. There are fulling and scribbling mills, and the manufacture of woollen goods is carried on to a considerable extent.

CARWOOD, county of SALOP.—See SIBDON-CARWOOD.

CARY-COATS, a township in the parish of THOCKRINGTON, north-eastern division of TINDALE ward, county of NORTHUMBERLAND, 12 miles (N.) from Hexham, containing 50 inhabitants.

CASHIO, or CASHIOBURY, a hamlet in the parish of WATFORD, hundred of CASHIO, or liberty of ST. ALBANS, county of HERTFORD, 1½ mile (N.W.) from Watford, containing 789 inhabitants. In the time of the early Britons this was a place of importance, having been the seat of Cassibelaunus, King of the *Cassii*, from whom it derived its name; the Saxon kings of Mercia also made it their residence, and Offa included it in the possessions that he gave to the monastery of St. Albans, and called it Albaneston, which was again changed by the Normans into Caisho, since converted into Cashio. Edward IV. constituted it a liberty, and it continued annexed to the crown from the period of the dissolution until James I. granted the whole liberty of the monastery of St. Albans to Robert Whitmore, Esq., and John Eldred, Gent.

CASSINGTON, a parish in the hundred of WOOTTON, county of OXFORD, 6¾ miles (N.W.) from Oxford, containing, with the hamlet of Worton, 393 inhabitants. The living is a discharged vicarage, in the archdeaconry and diocese of Oxford, rated in the king's books at £12, and in the patronage of the Dean and Canons of Christ Church, Oxford. The church is dedicated to St. Peter. Six boys are annually clothed, educated, and apprenticed, from the produce of an estate bequeathed by Henry Alnutt.

CASSOP, a township in the parish of KELLOE, southern division of EASINGTON ward, county palatine of DURHAM, 4½ miles (S.E. by E.) from Durham, containing 78 inhabitants. The village stands on part of a range of hills that abound with limestone, commanding an extensive prospect of a variegated tract in the north-western direction.

CASTERTON, a township in the parish of KIRKBY-LONSDALE, LONSDALE ward, county of WESTMORLAND, 2 miles (N.E.) from Kirkby-Lonsdale, containing 277 inhabitants. It is supposed to have received its name from an ancient castle, every vestige of which has been removed. A chapel formerly stood at Chapel-head close, near which is a well, called St. Coume's, probably a contraction of St. Columbe, the tutelar saint of the chapel.

CASTERTON (GREAT), a parish in the hundred of EAST, county of RUTLAND, 2¼ miles (N.W. by W.) from Stamford, containing 335 inhabitants. The living is a rectory, with that of Pickworth annexed, in the archdeaconry of Northampton, and diocese of Peterborough, rated in the king's books at £11. 2. 11., and in the patronage of the Marquis of Exeter. The church is dedicated to St. Peter and St. Paul. This was anciently a Roman station, several coins having been discovered; it was subsequently demolished by the Picts and Scots, who ravaged the island as far as Stamford, whence they were driven back to their own territories by the Saxons under Hengist. Its former name was Brig-Casterton, from a bridge over the Gwash, or Wash, here; it received its present prefix to distinguish it from Little Casterton, a small village adjoining. The barony was held by various lords, until it reverted to the crown in the reign of Henry VIII., in consequence of its possessor, John, Lord Hussey, being attainted of high treason and beheaded at Lincoln, for joining a commotion raised in Lincolnshire, on account of the alterations in religion, and is now the property of the Marquis of Exeter.

CASTERTON (LITTLE), a parish in the hundred of EAST, county of RUTLAND, 2¼ miles (N.W. by N.) from Stamford, containing 84 inhabitants. The living is a rectory, in the archdeaconry of Northampton, and diocese of Peterborough, rated in the king's books at £6. 15. 5., and in the patronage of the Earl of Pomfret. The church, dedicated to All Saints, is a small neat structure; the pillars and arches are late Norman, and the windows exhibit the early and the decorated styles of English architecture.

CASTLE-ACRE, a parish in the Lynn division of the hundred of FREEBRIDGE, county of NORFOLK, 4 miles (N.) from Swaffham, containing 1100 inhabitants. The living is a discharged vicarage, in the archdeaconry and diocese of Norwich, rated in the king's books at £5. 6. 8., endowed with £200 royal bounty, and £400 parliamentary grant, and in the patronage of T. W. Coke, Esq. The church, dedicated to St. James, is a spacious and ancient structure, with a lofty square embattled tower: the east window of the chancel is ornamented with the arms, and a window in the nave with a figure in complete armour, of Earl Warren, in stained glass. There are places of worship for Baptists and Wesleyan Methodists. Castle-Acre, now an inconsiderable village, noted chiefly for the remains of its ancient castle and priory, from the former of which it takes the prefix to its name, appears, from the vestiges of a Roman road leading from Thetford to Brancaster, the discovery of a tesselated pavement, and, lately, of several coins (among which were some of Vespasian and Constantine), to have been a Roman station, on the site of which the castle was probably erected. Fairs for toys and pedlary are held on St. James' day and August 5th. The magistrates for the division hold a meeting once a fortnight; and a manorial court is held annually in October.

The castle was built by William Warren, first earl of Surrey, to whom the manor, with one hundred and thirty-nine others, was given by the Conqueror, and who made it the head of all his lordships: it was probably enlarged by his descendant, who, in 1297, entertained Edward I. as his guest: there are sufficient remains to indicate the extent of this massive pile, which, with its appendages, comprised an area of more than eighteen acres, surrounded by an embattled wall seven feet in thickness, and strengthened by three lofty buttresses built over the broad and deep moat by which the castle was surrounded. The buildings were of a circular form, and erected on the slope of a gentle eminence; below the outer wall, which reached nearly to the river, was a terrace-walk, commanding a fine view of the adjacent country: they consisted of an outer and an inner ward, in the latter of which was the keep, a lofty circular building of extraordinary strength. Through the area, in a direction from north to south, passes the principal street, at the north end of which, leading into the inner ward, is a fine arched entrance, with an outer and an inner gate, and between them a portcullis, defended by two circular bastions; at the south end of the street are traces of a similar gateway, and nearly in the centre is another gateway, leading into the outer ward, which was enclosed by an embattled wall of stone and flint, considerable portions of which are remaining; and on the eastern side of the same street, near the north gate, are the remains of the chapel that belonged to the castle, now converted into a dwelling-house. To the west of the castle are the ruins of the priory, founded by the same Earl Warren, in 1085, for monks of the Cluniac order, dedicated to the Blessed Virgin, and subordinate to a similar establishment, by the same founder, at Lewes, in the county of Sussex: its revenue, at the dissolution, was £324. 17. 5. The greater part of the west front of the priory church, a spacious cruciform structure with two towers at the west end, and a massive central tower, is still remaining, and, with the exception of a large window of later insertion over the entrance, is an elegant specimen of the most enriched style of Norman architecture. The conventual buildings, now converted into a farm-house and offices, are of later date, and, from the remains, their extent and arrangement may be distinctly ascertained: a large room, now called the prior's dining-room, has a fine oriel window, in which are the arms of the priory, of the earls Warren and Arundel, of Mowbray, Duke of Norfolk, and of France and England, all in stained glass: at the east end are vestiges of an altar, over which is a fine large window.

CASTLE-CAMPS, a parish in the hundred of CHILFORD, county of CAMBRIDGE, 5¾ miles (S. E. by E.) from Linton, containing 618 inhabitants. The living is a rectory, in the archdeaconry and diocese of Ely, rated in the king's books at £16. 4. 2., and in the patronage of the Governors of the Charter-house, London. The church is dedicated to All Saints. At this place are the ruins of a magnificent castle, formerly the seat of the Veres, earls of Oxford, one of whom received it by grant from Henry I., as lord high chamberlain of England; and it appears that they likewise held the manors of Tingrey and Weelfelmeston by sergeantry of chamberlainship to the queens of England at the coronation of their kings: the site is now occupied by a farm-house, but the moat and some slight vestiges are still visible.

CASTLE-CARROCK, a parish in ESKDALE ward, county of CUMBERLAND, 4½ miles (S. by E.) from Brampton, containing, with the outside quarters, 346 inhabitants. The living is a discharged rectory, in the archdeaconry and diocese of Carlisle, rated in the king's books at £5. 12. 11., and in the patronage of the Dean and Chapter of Carlisle. The church, dedicated to St. Peter, is a neat structure, rebuilt of freestone in 1828, by a rate on the inhabitants, with the exception of £60 given by the Incorporated Society for the enlargement of churches (for which sixty-four free sittings have been set apart), and the expense of building the chancel, which was defrayed by the rector. The former edifice is supposed to have been built out of the ruins of an ancient castle that stood within an intrenchment near the village, the lines of which are distinctly visible: there is also another intrenchment at a short distance; and on the summit of a fell are two cairns, one of which, called Hespeckraise, is of considerable magnitude. By the removal of another cairn near Geltbridge, about 1775, a human skeleton was discovered in a species of coffin made of rude stones. The parish contains both limestone and freestone: near the church is a mineral spring, the water of which is of the same quality as that of the Gilsland spa. On the enclosure of the moors, pursuant to an act passed in 1801, an allotment of twenty acres was assigned for the endowment of a school. This place is bounded on the east and north by the small river Gelt, which rises in the royal forest of Geltsdale, a hilly tract of moorland, forming the south-eastern part of the parish, and held on lease by the Earl of Carlisle.

CASTLE-CARY, a market town and parish in the hundred of CATSASH, county of SOMERSET, 11 miles (E. N. E.) from Somerton, and 113 (W. S. W.) from London, containing 1627 inhabitants. This place probably derived its name from an ancient castle originally belonging to a lord of the name of Carey, which was defended against King Stephen by its owner, Lord Lovell, one of whose descendants having embraced the cause of the deposed monarch, Richard II., was dispossessed of it by Henry VII.: the site is still called the Camp, and weapons of iron have been found in it occasionally; the only remains are some slight traces of the intrenchments. Charles II., after the battle of Worcester, took refuge in the manor-house. The town is pleasantly situated, and consists of two parts, extending together nearly a mile, partially paved, but not lighted: the houses are neatly built and amply supplied with water: the air is salubrious, the environs abound with pleasing scenery, and in many other respects this place affords an agreeable and retired residence. The market is on Tuesday, but it is very small; a great cattle market is held on each Tuesday in the seven weeks preceding Christmas: the fairs are on the Tuesday before Palm-Sunday, May 1st, and Whit-Tuesday, for cattle, broad cloth, and other merchandise. Courts leet and baron for the manor are held annually. The living is a discharged vicarage, in the archdeaconry of Wells, and diocese of Bath and Wells, rated in the king's books at £11. 16. 3., and in the patronage of the Bishop of Bath and Wells. The church, dedicated to All Saints, is a handsome structure, occupying an elevated situation; the archdeacon holds his visitations in it. There are places of worship for Independents and Wesleyan

Methodists. In 1779, two sums of £10 each, given respectively by John Francis and David Llewellin to the poor, were applied to the erection of a place of confinement for malefactors, previously to their committal to the county gaol; these sums, on the recommendation of the commissioners for inquiring concerning charities, are to be refunded from the parish rates, and made available to the benefit of the poor.

CASTLE-CHURCH, a parish in the eastern division of the hundred of CUTTLESTONE, county of STAFFORD, 1 mile (S. W.) from Stafford, containing 1118 inhabitants. The living is a perpetual curacy, in the archdeaconry of Stafford, and diocese of Lichfield and Coventry, endowed with £200 private benefaction, £700 royal bounty, and £1500 parliamentary grant, and in the patronage of the Crown. The church is dedicated to St. Lawrence. Near that part of the town of Stafford lying in this parish is a Roman Catholic chapel, built in 1822, by the late Edward Jerningham, Esq.; it is a small but elegant structure, containing seventeen of the old stalls taken from Lichfield cathedral, and has a noble organ. There is a school adjoining, founded and endowed by the same benevolent individual, which is open to children of all religious denominations.

CASTLE-COMBE, a parish (formerly a market town) in the hundred of CHIPPENHAM, county of WILTS, 6½ miles (N. W. by W.) from Chippenham, containing 635 inhabitants. The living is a rectory, in the archdeaconry of Wilts, and diocese of Salisbury, rated in the king's books at £9, and in the patronage of H. Scroop, Esq. The church, dedicated to St. Andrew, appears to be of very ancient date; it consists of a nave, north and south aisles, and a chancel, with a tower at the west end about eighty feet high, supported by angular buttresses with pinnacles. Castle-Combe is a considerable village, and was anciently celebrated for a castle built in the early part of the thirteenth century, by Walter de Dunstanville, son-in-law of Reginald, Earl of Cornwall, which was dismantled before the close of the fourteenth: it stood on a hill north of the village, where the remains of its intrenchments are still discernible. A market was obtained for this place by Bartholomew, Lord Badlesmere, one of its ancient possessors; it has been discontinued, but the market cross remains in the centre of the village.

CASTLE-EATON, a parish in the hundred of HIGHWORTH, CRICKLADE, and STAPLE, county of WILTS, 5 miles (N. W.) from Highworth, containing 334 inhabitants. The living is a rectory, in the archdeaconry of Wilts, and diocese of Salisbury, rated in the king's books at £19, and in the patronage of the Rev. T. Shepherd and another. The church is dedicated to St. Mary.

CASTLE-MORTON, a parish in the lower division of the hundred of PERSHORE, county of WORCESTER, 5 miles (W. S. W.) from Upton upon Severn, containing 788 inhabitants. The living is a discharged perpetual curacy, annexed to the vicarage of Longdon, in the archdeaconry and diocese of Worcester, rated in the king's books at £5. 8. 6½. The church, dedicated to St. Gregory, is a very ancient structure, with a fine old tower and steeple: opposite to it is an artificial mound, fifty feet high, surrounded by a moat, or ditch, supposed to have been thrown up to protect the church during the civil war in the reign of Charles I. There are charitable bequests for the poor amounting to about £30 per annum.

CASTLE-NORTHWICH, a township in that part of the parish of GREAT BUDWORTH which is in the second division of the hundred of EDDISBURY, county palatine of CHESTER, containing 575 inhabitants.

CASTLE-RISING, a borough and parish (formerly a market town) having separate jurisdiction, locally in the Lynn division of the hundred of Freebridge, county of NORFOLK, 43 miles (W. N. W.) from Norwich, and 102 (N. by E.) from London, containing 343 inhabitants. Prior to the year 1176, a castle was built by William D'Albini, the first earl of Sussex, on a hill to the south of the town, and, according to the author of the *Munimenta Antiqua*, on the site of one of King Alfred's great castles, of which some arches, included within the subsequent buildings, are supposed to be remains. In this castle, Isabel of France, queen of Edward II., after the death of Mortimer, was detained in confinement, from the year 1330 until her decease in 1358: the principal remains are the shell of the keep, a square tower, the walls of which are three yards in thickness, with some ornamented doorways and windows in the Norman style of architecture, though greatly dilapidated; the site of the great hall and some vestiges of the state apartments may be traced: the whole was surrounded by a deep moat and a bold rampart, on which was a strong wall with three turrets; the principal entrance is over a ruined bridge of one circular arch, defended by a tower gateway. This was formerly a considerable sea-port, inferior only to those of Lynn and Yarmouth, in this county; but the harbour becoming choked up with sand, its trade declined, and, from the consequent decrease of its population, the market, which was held twice a week, has been discontinued for many years: the vicinity was formerly subject to inundation from the sea, to prevent which an embankment has been constructed, and is kept in an effective state. The government was originally vested in a mayor, twelve aldermen, and an indefinite number of burgesses, aided by a recorder, high steward, &c.; there are now two aldermen only, who alternately elect each other to the office of mayor: the county magistrates, in some cases, have concurrent jurisdiction. Of the rank which this place held as an ancient borough it still retains a memorial, in the precedence given to the name of the mayor in the king's commission of the peace for the county. The elective franchise was conferred in the last year of the reign of Philip and Mary, since which time the borough has returned two members to parliament: the right of election is vested in the free burgesses, the number of whom has been reduced to two or three; the mayor is the returning officer.

Seal and Arms.

The living is a discharged rectory, with that of Roydon consolidated, in the peculiar jurisdiction of the rector, rated in the king's books at £8, and in the patronage of the Hon. Col. Howard. The church, dedicated to St. Lawrence, is an ancient structure in the Norman style of architecture, with a square tower rising from the centre; the west front, which is richly ornamented, is a fine specimen of that style; the entrance is enriched with varied mouldings, and on each side of the large window above it are series of intersecting arches: the font is very ancient and highly ornamented. A National school is supported by the family of Howard and the rector. Near the church is an hospital, containing thirteen apartments, a large hall, kitchen, and a chapel, built in 1613, by Henry Howard, Earl of Northampton, who endowed it with a rent-charge of £100 for twelve aged women and a governess. To the west of the castle is a square mount, one acre in extent, and to the east of it a circular mount surrounded by a ditch; the former is by some supposed to have been a Roman camp, though by others both are thought to have been thrown up by the people of Lynn, when they besieged the castle, and compelled the Earl of Arundel to relinquish his claim to one-third of the customs of their port. There are some chalybeate springs in the parish.

CASTLE-THORPE, a parish in the hundred of NEWPORT, county of BUCKINGHAM, 3 miles (N. N. E.) from Stony-Stratford, containing 348 inhabitants. The living is a perpetual curacy, annexed to the vicarage of Hanslope, in the archdeaconry of Buckingham, and diocese of Lincoln. The church is dedicated to St. Mary. Here was the ancient castle of the barony of Hanslope, the site of which exhibits traces of very extensive buildings; it was taken and demolished in 1217, by Fulke de Brent, when it was garrisoned by its owner, William Manduit, one of the barons who were in arms against Henry III.

CASTLEFORD, a parish in the upper division of the wapentake of OSGOLDCROSS, West riding of the county of YORK, comprising the townships of Castleford and Glass-Houghton, and containing 1434 inhabitants, of which number, 1022 are in the township of Castleford, 3½ miles (N.W.) from Pontefract. The living is a rectory, in the archdeaconry and diocese of York, rated in the king's books at £20. 13. 1½., and in the patronage of the King, as Duke of Lancaster. The church, dedicated to All Saints, is supposed to occupy the site of a Roman camp, as this place was anciently a station belonging to that people, antiquaries identifying it with *Legiolium*, or *Lagetium*, described in Antoninus' Itinerary as being situated on the river Aire, where it was crossed by a ford on the line of the ancient Herman-street, which passed between Doncaster and York; coins and other remains of the Romans have been frequently discovered. There is a place of worship for Wesleyan Methodists. Castleford is a thriving village, having an extensive pottery and a mill for grinding flint: it is situated at a short distance from the junction of the Aire and the Calder, the latter of which, in 1698, was made navigable to Wakefield. There is a peculiar regulation for the payment of tithes in this parish, sanctioned by an act of parliament; the rector receives twenty-eight quarts of wheat for every pound sterling paid by the tenant to his landlord on arable land, and twenty quarts for every two pounds on grazing land. It is related that the citizens of York being pursued by Ethelred's army, in 750, turned at this place, and committed great slaughter on their pursuers.

CASTLETON, a parish in the hundred of HIGH PEAK, county of DERBY, 4½ miles (N.) from Tideswell, containing, with the chapelry of Edale, 1428 inhabitants. The living is a discharged vicarage, in the archdeaconry of Derby, and diocese of Lichfield and Coventry, rated in the king's books at £6. 7. 6., endowed with £200 private benefaction, and £600 royal bounty, and in the patronage of the Bishop of Chester. The church, dedicated to St. Edmund, is a small ancient edifice, the arch, with its mouldings entire, separating the nave from the chancel, being a fine specimen of early English architecture; the pews are of oak curiously carved, but the exterior has been greatly modernised. There is a place of worship for Wesleyan Methodists. A school has been endowed with about £23 per annum, by Richard Bagshaw and others, for the education of poor children, in which there are about twenty-three scholars. Castleton is in the honour of Tutbury, duchy of Lancaster, and within the jurisdiction of a court of pleas held at Tutbury every third Tuesday, for the recovery of debts under 40*s*. It is said to have taken its name from a castle built by William Peverell, natural son of the Conqueror, who gave him this honour, along with thirteen other lordships in the county, which, from its situation upon a steep and high peak, was called the Castle of the Peak, or Peak Castle; but from various records it appears that a castle existed here previously, supposed to have been erected by Edward the Elder, or his heroic sister Ethelfleda, as, at the Conqueror's survey, it was described "*Castelli Wi Peverel in Pechivers*," and in the reign of Edward the Confessor it was the property of Earl Gundeburne. The extent of the ruins evinces the former magnitude of the building, the castle yard, the walls of which are in some places twenty feet high and nine feet thick, occupying almost the entire summit of the hill; the keep, consisting of two stories almost entire, and standing at the south-western point of this high and precipitous limestone rock, towering above the mouth of the great cavern of the peak, is fifty feet in height, the whole being nearly isolated, and only to be approached with difficulty from the north. Part of the arch of the principal gateway at the north-east corner is still visible, appearing to be formed of hewn gritstone. The castle remained in the possession of the Peverells until the attainder of the third William, when it was granted by Henry II. to his son John, Earl of Montaigne, afterwards King John; and, during the absence of his brother Richard I., Hugh Nonant, Bishop of Coventry, possessed it. In 1204, King John appointed Hugh Neville governor, but the disaffected barons seized it and kept possession until the reign of Henry III. From that period it had various occupiers, until settled by Edward III. upon his son, the Earl of Richmond, commonly called John of Gaunt, who having married Blanch, youngest daughter of Henry, Duke of Lancaster, in 1359, his father, in 1362, created him Duke of Lancaster, and then the castle in the peak became part of the duchy of Lancaster, and continues so to the present time. It was used in preserving the records of the miners' court down to the reign of Elizabeth, when they were removed to Tutbury castle. His Grace the Duke of Devonshire now possesses it, as lessee under the crown.

Castleton is a considerable village, situated at the

foot of the Castle hill; the inhabitants principally derive their support from the mining district by which it is surrounded: it was fortified by a rampart, the ditch being still visible, and called the Town ditch, extending from the ravines at the base of the rock, to the outworks connected with the castle, the ruins of which are boldly prominent on the verge of the hill. About half a mile east of the town is the site of an hospital, founded by King Stephen. The whole of this district abounds with greater natural curiosities than almost any other portion of the empire. Immediately under the walls of the castle is Peak Cavern, or the Devil's Cave, a succession of vast and magnificent excavations, formed in the interior of this stupendous rock. The approach to it is by the side of a clear stream, flowing from limestone rocks, that here rise to the height of two hundred and sixty feet on each side, and from the entrance to the cave, which is in a dark and gloomy recess, consisting of a tolerably well formed arch, forty-six feet high and one hundred and twenty feet wide, and exhibiting a checquered diversity of coloured stones, from which a fluid that soon petrifies is continually dropping. Immediately within the arch is a cavern of nearly the same extent, and in depth about ninety feet, where some twine-makers have established their residence and manufactory. Here the light disappears, and the rest of the cavern must be explored by torch-light. The arch leading to the next chamber is narrow and low, until arriving at a spacious opening called the Bell-house; at the end is a stream of water forty-two feet broad, over which it is necessary that visitors should be ferried. On landing, another vast vault, two hundred feet square and one hundred and forty feet high, presents itself: at the end of this is another stream generally crossed on foot; here the passage leads to what is termed Roger Rains' house, a projecting pile of rocks on which water is incessantly dropping. The next excavation is called the Chancel, which leads to what has been denominated the Devil's Cellar, and then follow numerous other immense cavities, that have received various appellations, such as Half-way House, Great Tom of Lincoln, &c., the whole extending two thousand three hundred feet from the entrance, and supposed to be six hundred and forty-five feet in depth from the summit of the mountain.

About a mile from this is the Speedwell mine, situated near the foot of what is called "the Winnets," from the gusts of wind that constantly prevail here, in consequence of the formation of this mountainous range: the mine was formerly worked for lead, but it proved unprofitable. The descent is by about one hundred steps, beneath an arched vault, leading to the sough, or level, where a boat conveys the explorer over a very broad stream, bounded by an immense gulph, the depth of which has never been accurately ascertained, though sounded by a line of three hundred and fifty feet; and above, the roof of the cavern is invisible, even with the aid of rockets and Bengal-lights. The rushing of the superfluous water through an artificial gate into this profound chasm, which has already swallowed forty thousand tons of rubbish, arising from the blasting of the rocks, without the least apparent diminution of its depth, produces an appalling effect. A little further west is the Odin lead mine, said to have been worked by the Saxons, who honoured it with the name of one of their deities, and, although in operation for so many centuries, few mines in the county are yet more productive, affording employment to about one hundred and forty persons. At some distance beyond this, raising its majestic head one thousand three hundred feet above the vale of Castleton, is the "Mam Torr," or Mother hill, having also received the name of the "Shivering Mountain," from the fragments of shale and grit-stone almost continually falling from its south side, and which have formed an elevated mount in the valley, called "Little Mam Torr." On its summit are the remains of a camp, supposed to be Saxon, with the greater part of the rampart entire; and on the south-west side are two barrows, in one of which, when opened a few years since, were found a brass celt and fragments of an unbaked urn. Near this mountain is the Water Hull mine, where the beautiful and peculiar fluor spar, locally termed "Blue John," is procured, the most esteemed of which are the violet-blue and rose-coloured, which are worked into elegant vases, urns, &c.: here is also found, between the schistus and limestone, a species of elastic bitumen, that burns with a bright flame; another variety, less elastic, is formed of filaments, and is called wood bitumen. About half a mile midway in this mountainous ravine, which exhibits in many places proofs of volcanic origin, is a place called the Cove, where large masses of basaltic rocks are conspicuous, in which are imbedded quartz, chrystals, &c. Such an assemblage of natural curiosities renders the neighbourhood of Castleton one of the most interesting districts in the kingdom.

CASTLETON, a parish in the hundred of SHERBORNE, Sherborne division of the county of DORSET, 1 mile (E. N. E.) from Sherborne, containing 174 inhabitants. The living is a perpetual curacy, in the peculiar jurisdiction of the Dean of Salisbury, endowed with £400 private benefaction, £600 royal bounty, and £300 parliamentary grant, and in the patronage of Earl Digby. The church is dedicated to St. Mary Magdalene.

CASTLETON, a township in that part of the parish of ROCHDALE which is in the hundred of SALFORD, county palatine of LANCASTER, 2 miles (S. E. by S.) from Rochdale, containing 7894 inhabitants, many of whom are employed in the woollen and cotton manufacture. The name is derived from an ancient castle, one of the twelve Saxon castles in the county, the keep of which still remains. Part of the town of Rochdale is situated within this township, where are the cisterns for supplying the town with water, and the gas-works for lighting it. The inhabitants participate in the benefactions made to the parish both for scholastic and charitable purposes.

CASTLETON, a hamlet in the parish of MARSHFIELD, upper division of the hundred of WENTLLOOG, county of MONMOUTH, 4½ miles (S. W.) from Newport. The population is returned with the parish. Here anciently stood a castle, occupied, if not built, by the Normans, to protect their conquest of Wentlloog, the only remains of which are some small ruins of the citadel, and the chapel, converted into a barn; near the site is a barrow. On the level summit of an adjoining hill there is a circular encampment, called Pen-y-Park-Newydd.

CASTLE-VIEW, an extra-parochial liberty adjoining the borough of Leicester, in the hundred of GUTH-

LAXTON, county of LEICESTER, containing 149 inhabitants.

CASTLEY, a township in the parish of LEATHLEY, upper division of the wapentake of CLARO, West riding of the county of YORK, 4½ miles (E. by N.) from Otley, containing 110 inhabitants.

CASTON, a parish in the hundred of WAYLAND, county of NORFOLK, 3½ miles (S. E.) from Watton, containing 432 inhabitants. The living is a rectory, with those of Rockland All Saints and St. Andrew annexed, in the archdeaconry and diocese of Norwich, rated in the king's books at £11. 19. 2., and in the patronage of the Rev. B. Barker. The church is dedicated to the Holy Cross. There is a place of worship for Wesleyan Methodists.

CASTOR, a parish in the liberty of PETERBOROUGH, county of NORTHAMPTON, 4½ miles (W.) from Peterborough, comprising the chapelries of Sutton and Upton, and the hamlet of Ailesworth, and containing 959 inhabitants. The living is a rectory, in the archdeaconry of Northampton, and diocese of Peterborough, rated in the king's books at £52. 12. 8½., and held in commendam with the see of Peterborough. The church, dedicated in 1124 to St. Keneburgha, who founded a nunnery here, is a spacious cruciform edifice, with a beautiful Norman tower of two stages, surmounted by a spire, rising from the intersection: the three arches on the south side of the nave are semicircular, resting on massive round pillars; the opposite three are pointed, and supported by hexagonal columns. This village, and the opposite one of Chesterton, occupy the site of the Roman station *Durobrivæ*, by the Saxons called *Dormancester*; a great quantity of coins from Trajan to Valens, fragments of urns, tiles, &c., have been discovered. The Roman highway, called Ermin-street, commenced here, and proceeding some distance, branched off into two divisions, the remains of which are still visible, one being called the *Forty foot way*, leading to Stamford, and the other *Long Ditch*, or *High-street*, running by Lolham-Bridges, through West Deeping, into Lincolnshire; together with what is termed *Lady Keneburgha's way*, which is supposed to have been an ancient paved way leading from a fortress at the other side of the Nyne, which runs through the parish, to a castle on the hill, where the Roman governor resided: the place was destroyed by the Danes. Mr. John Landen, an eminent mathematician, was born here, in 1719.

CATCHBURN, a township in that part of the parish of MORPETH which is in the eastern division of CASTLE ward, county of NORTHUMBERLAND, 1½ mile (S. by E.) from Morpeth, containing, with Morpeth Castle, Park-house, and Stobhil, 153 inhabitants.

CATCHERSIDE, a township in the parish of KIRKWHELPINGTON, north-eastern division of TINDALE ward, county of NORTHUMBERLAND, 15 miles (W.) from Morpeth, containing 15 inhabitants.

CATCLIFFE, a township in that part of the parish of ROTHERHAM which is in the southern division of the wapentake of STRAFFORTH and TICKHILL, West riding of the county of YORK, 3 miles (S.) from Rotherham, containing 202 inhabitants. Here is a manufactory for glass. In 1702, George Beardsall devised £10 per annum for a master, for which he teaches ten poor children.

CATCOTT, a chapelry in the parish of MOORLINCH, hundred of WHITLEY, county of SOMERSET, 7 miles (E. N. E.) from Bridg-water, containing 579 inhabitants. The living is a perpetual curacy, in the archdeaconry of Wells, and diocese of Bath and Wells, and in the patronage of Lord Henniker.

CATEBY, a chapelry in the parish of SPROTBROUGH, northern division of the wapentake of STRAFFORTH and TICKHILL, West riding of the county of YORK, 4½ miles (W. S. W.) from Doncaster, containing 169 inhabitants.

CATESBY-ABBEY, a parish in the hundred of FAWSLEY, county of NORTHAMPTON, 3¾ miles (S. W. by W.) from Daventry, containing, with the hamlet of Newbold-Grounds, 114 inhabitants. The living is a vicarage, in the archdeaconry of Northampton, and diocese of Peterborough, rated in the king's books at £10, and in the patronage of T. and M. Scrafton, Esqrs. The church is dedicated to St. Mary. In that part of the parish which is named Upper Catesby are some small remains of a Benedictine nunnery, founded by Robert de Esseby in the reign of Richard I.; its revenue, at the dissolution, was estimated at £145 per annum: there are also the remains of an intrenchment, named Arbury camp. Of the family of Catesby, one was beheaded after the death of his master, Richard III., and another suffered for being concerned in the Gunpowder Plot.

CATFIELD, a parish in the hundred of HAPPING, county of NORFOLK, 7½ miles (E. by N.) from Coltishall, containing 581 inhabitants. The living consists of a discharged rectory and vicarage, in the archdeaconry of Norfolk, and diocese of Norwich, rated in the king's books at £7. 10., and in the patronage of the Bishop of Norwich and the Earl of Shrewsbury, alternately. The church is dedicated to All Saints: the chancel is a fine specimen of the later style of English architecture.

CATFOSS, a township in the parish of SIGGLESTHORNE, northern division of the wapentake of HOLDERNESS, East riding of the county of YORK, 9½ miles (N. E. by E.) from Beverley, containing 49 inhabitants.

CATHERINE (ST.), a parish in the hundred of BATH-FORUM, county of SOMERSET, 4 miles (N. N. E.) from Bath, containing, with a part of the liberty of Easton and Amrill, 127 inhabitants. The living is a perpetual curacy, annexed to the vicarage of Bath-Easton, in the archdeaconry of Bath, and diocese of Bath and Wells. The valley of St. Catherine is enriched with much picturesque scenery. Catherine Court was formerly the country residence of the abbot of Bath.

CATHERINGTON, a parish in the hundred of FINCH-DEAN, Alton (South) division of the county of SOUTHAMPTON, 6¾ miles (S. W. by S.) from Petersfield, containing 798 inhabitants. The living is a discharged vicarage, in the archdeaconry and diocese of Winchester, rated in the king's books at £9. 5. 10., and in the patronage of the Rev. Joseph Hutchinson. The church is dedicated to St. Catherine. The parish is within the jurisdiction of the Cheyney Court held at Winchester every Thursday, for the recovery of debts to any amount William Appleford, porter of St. Mary's College, Winchester, founded a school in 1695, and endowed it with lands in the parish of Drayton, producing at present £15 per annum, for which forty-five children of both sexes are instructed.

CATHERSTON-LEWSTON, a parish in the hundred of WHITCHURCH-CANONICORUM, Bridport division of the county of DORSET, $2\frac{3}{4}$ miles (N. E.) from Lyme-Regis, containing 27 inhabitants. The living is a discharged rectory, in the archdeaconry of Dorset, and diocese of Bristol, rated in the king's books at £2. 16. $10\frac{1}{2}$., endowed with £400 royal bounty, and in the patronage of John Ross, Esq. The church is dedicated to St. Mary.

CATMERE, a parish in the hundred of COMPTON, county of BERKS, $3\frac{1}{2}$ miles (W. by S.) from East Ilsley, containing 89 inhabitants. The living is a rectory, in the archdeaconry of Berks, and diocese of Salisbury, rated in the king's books at £5. 5. $7\frac{1}{2}$., and in the patronage of J. A. Houblon, Esq. The church is dedicated to St. Margaret. Here was formerly a market on Monday, granted in 1306, by Edward I., together with a fair on the festival of St. Margaret.

CATON, a chapelry in that part of the parish of LANCASTER which is in the hundred of LONSDALE, south of the sands, county palatine of LANCASTER, $5\frac{1}{4}$ miles (N. E. by E.) from Lancaster, containing 1107 inhabitants. The living is a perpetual curacy, in the archdeaconry of Richmond, and diocese of Chester, endowed with £400 private benefaction, and £600 royal bounty, and in the patronage of the Vicar of Lancaster. This extensive chapelry and township lies on the southern bank of the Lune, and presents so many features of beautiful scenery as to have elicited an eulogium from the poet Gray, in a letter to Dr. Wharton. Here are several cotton-manufactories: coal and slate are found in the chapelry. Some Roman relics have been discovered, especially an ancient stone pillar with an inscription to the Emperor Adrian, found in the bed of the Fisherbeck, in 1803, besides a *milliarium* six feet in height, on the course of a Roman way that passed near the place. There are two trifling benefactions for teaching poor children.

CATSFIELD, a parish in the hundred of NINFIELD, rape of HASTINGS, county of SUSSEX, 3 miles (S. W.) from Battle, containing 575 inhabitants. The living is a rectory, in the archdeaconry of Lewes, and diocese of Chichester, rated in the king's books at £7. 9. $4\frac{1}{2}$., and in the patronage of the Earl of Ashburnham. The church, dedicated to St. Lawrence, is in the early and decorated styles of English architecture.

CATTAL, a township in the parish of HUNSINGORE, upper division of the wapentake of CLARO, West riding of the county of YORK, $5\frac{1}{4}$ miles (N. E. by N.) from Wetherby, containing 207 inhabitants.

CATTERAL, a township in the parish of GARSTANG, hundred of AMOUNDERNESS, county palatine of LANCASTER, $1\frac{3}{4}$ mile (S. S. W.) from Garstang, containing 704 inhabitants. The village contains one of the oldest and most extensive print-works in the county, situated at the confluence of the West Calder with the river Wyre.

CATTERHAM, a parish in the second division of the hundred of TANDRIDGE, county of SURREY, $3\frac{1}{4}$ miles (N. by W.) from Godstone, containing 435 inhabitants. The living is a discharged rectory, in the archdeaconry of Surrey, and diocese of Winchester, rated in the king's books at £8. 0. $1\frac{1}{2}$., and in the patronage of the Rev. James Legrew. The church is dedicated to St. Lawrence. The Croydon railway passes through this parish. A school-house has been built by Thomas Clarke, for the use of which a master teaches six poor children.

CATTERICK, a parish comprising the townships of Ellerton upon Swale, Kiplin, Scorton, Uckerby, and Whitwell, in the eastern division of the wapentake of GILLING; the chapelry of Hudswell, in the western division of the wapentake of HANG; and the chapelry of Hipswell, and the townships of Appleton, Brough, Catterick, Colbourne, St. Martin's, Killerby, Scotton, and Tunstall, in the eastern division of the wapentake of HANG, North riding of the county of YORK, and containing 2788 inhabitants, of which number, 561 are in the township of Catterick, 5 miles (S. E.) from Richmond. The living is a vicarage, in the archdeaconry of Richmond, and diocese of Chester, rated in the king's books at £25. 2. 1., and in the patronage of the Crown. The church, dedicated to St. Anne, is partly in the early style of English architecture, and partly of later date. This is a place of great antiquity, having been the site of a Roman station of some note, called *Cataractonium*, where the Ermin-street branches off in two directions; numerous Roman relics have been discovered at different periods. It also flourished during the Saxon times, but in the devastations of the Danes it was utterly destroyed, and is at present of little importance. A school, in which twelve children are instructed, and an hospital for six poor widows, were founded in 1658, by the Rev. Michael Syddall, formerly vicar of the parish, and endowed with £45 per annum, of which the schoolmaster receives £20, with a house to reside in. At the distance of a mile to the north is Catterick bridge, over the river Swale, on which was formerly a chapel; and opposite is a race-course.

CATTERLEN, a township in the parish of NEWTON-RIGNY, LEATH ward, county of CUMBERLAND, 3 miles (N. W. by N.) from Penrith, containing 124 inhabitants.

CATTERTON, a township in that part of the parish of TADCASTER which is in the ainsty of the city, and East riding of the county, of YORK, $2\frac{1}{2}$ miles (N.E. by N.) from Tadcaster, containing 63 inhabitants.

CATTISTOCK, a parish in the hundred of CERNE, TOTCOMBE, and MODBURY, Cerne subdivision of the county of DORSET, $9\frac{1}{4}$ miles (N. W.) from Dorchester, containing 382 inhabitants. The living is a rectory, in the archdeaconry of Dorset, and diocese of Bristol, rated in the king's books at £13. 13. 9., and in the patronage of P. Broadley, Esq. The church is dedicated to St. Peter and St. Paul. On a hill in the eastern part of the parish is an ancient circular fortification of about four acres, called the Castle, surrounded by a double rampart, with entrances at the north-east and west: towards the middle of the area the ground rises into a long barrow; and near the north entrance is a round tumulus, the top of which consists of flint stones.

CATTO, a joint township with Landmoth, in that part of the parish of LEAK which is in the wapentake of ALLERTONSHIRE, North riding of the county of YORK, $6\frac{1}{2}$ miles (N.) from Thirsk. The population is returned with Landmoth.

CATTON, a chapelry in that part of the parish of CROXALL which is in the hundred of REPTON and GRESLEY, county of DERBY, $7\frac{1}{2}$ miles (S. W. by S.) from Burton upon Trent, containing 89 inhabitants. This place is in the honour of Tutbury, duchy of Lancaster, and within the jurisdiction of a court of pleas held at

Tutbury every third Tuesday, for the recovery of debts under 40*s*.

CATTON, a parish in the hundred of TAVERHAM, county of NORFOLK, 2½ miles (N.) from Norwich, containing 639 inhabitants. The living is a discharged vicarage, in the peculiar jurisdiction and patronage of the Dean and Chapter of Norwich, rated in the king's books at £4. 3. 9., and endowed with £200 royal bounty. The church is dedicated to St. Margaret. In 1724, John Norman bequeathed land for teaching and apprenticing some of his relations; and, after sixty years, as his estate increased, to be applied to the erection and endowment of an hospital for boys.

CATTON, a parish comprising the townships of Kexby, and West Stamford-Bridge with Scoreby, in the wapentake of OUZE and DERWENT, and the townships of High Catton, Low Catton, and East Stamford-Bridge, in the Wilton-Beacon division of the wapentake of HARTHILL, East riding of the county of YORK, and containing 973 inhabitants, of which number, 198 are in the township of High Catton, and 177 in that of Low Catton, 9 miles (E. N. E.) from York. The living is a rectory, in the archdeaconry of the East riding, and diocese of York, rated in the king's books at £21. 12. 8½., and in the patronage of the Earl of Egremont. The church is dedicated to All Saints. There is a place of worship for Wesleyan Methodists.

CATTON, a township in that part of the parish of TOPCLIFFE which is in the wapentake of BIRDFORTH, North riding of the county of YORK, 5 miles (S.W.) from Thirsk, containing 99 inhabitants.

CATWICK, a parish in the northern division of the wapentake of HOLDERNESS, East riding of the county of YORK, 8 miles (N.E. by E.) from Beverley, containing 190 inhabitants. The living is a rectory, in the archdeaconry of the East riding, and diocese of York, rated in the king's books at £10. 5., and in the patronage of the Crown. The church, dedicated to St. Michael, is in the later style of English architecture.

CATWORTH (GREAT), a parish in the hundred of LEIGHTONSTONE, county of HUNTINGDON, 4 miles (N. by W.) from Kimbolton, containing 529 inhabitants. The living is a rectory, in the archdeaconry of Huntingdon, and diocese of Lincoln, rated in the king's books at £17. 16. 10½., and in the patronage of the Principal and Fellows of Brasenose College, Oxford. The church is dedicated to St. Leonard. Sir Wolston Dixie, who was lord mayor of London in 1585, and a considerable benefactor to Emanuel College, Cambridge, having also founded a free school at Bosworth, in Leicestershire, was born here.

CATWORTH (LITTLE), a chapelry in the parish of LONG STOW, hundred of LEIGHTONSTONE, county of HUNTINGDON, 3¾ miles (N. by E.) from Kimbolton. The population is returned with the parish.

CAUDERY, a joint township with Rudyard, in that part of the parish of LEEK which is in the southern division of the hundred of TOTMONSLOW, county of STAFFORD. The population is returned with Rudyard.

CAULDON, a parish in the northern division of the hundred of TOTMONSLOW, county of STAFFORD, 6¾ miles (W.N.W.) from Ashbourn, containing 350 inhabitants. The living is a perpetual curacy, in the archdeaconry of Stafford, and diocese of Lichfield and Coventry, endowed with £800 royal bounty, and in the patronage of Mrs. Wilmot. The church is dedicated to St. Mary. At Caldon-Low are lime-works, from which the greater part of the surrounding country is supplied with lime. The small river Hamp separates this parish from that of Waterfall, and in its course enters the ground at Waterhouses, continuing a subterraneous progress for upwards of five miles.

CAULDWELL, a chapelry in the parish of STAPENHILL, hundred of REPTON and GRESLEY, county of DERBY, 5¼ miles (S. by E.) from Burton upon Trent, containing 157 inhabitants. The chapel is dedicated to St. Giles.

CAULK, a parish in the hundred of REPTON and GRESLEY, county of DERBY, 4¼ miles (N. by E.) from Ashby de la Zouch, containing 63 inhabitants. The living is a perpetual curacy, in the archdeaconry of Derby, and diocese of Lichfield and Coventry, and in the patronage of Sir George Crewe, Bart. The church is dedicated to St. Giles. There are some lead mines in the parish. A convent of Augustine friars, in honour of St. Mary and St. Giles, was founded here before 1161, and afterwards removed to Repindon; the remains still exist, having been converted into a mansion, called the Old Abbey. The poor inhabitants are eligible to the hospital at Ticknall, founded by Charles Harpur, Esq., in 1770.

CAUNDLE (BISHOP), a parish in the hundred of SHERBORNE, Sherborne division of the county of DORSET, 5 miles (S. E. by E.) from Sherborne, containing, with Caundle-Wake, 312 inhabitants. The living is a rectory, in the archdeaconry of Dorset, and diocese of Bristol, rated in the king's books at £11. 10., and in the patronage of Earl Digby.

CAUNDLE-MARSH, a parish in the hundred of SHERBORNE, Sherborne division of the county of DORSET, 3¾ miles (S.E.) from Sherborne, containing 62 inhabitants. The living is a discharged rectory, in the peculiar jurisdiction of the Dean of Salisbury, rated in the king's books at £5. 16. 3., endowed with £200 private benefaction, and £200 royal bounty, and in the patronage of Sir R. C. Hoare, Bart. The church is dedicated to St. Peter and St. Paul.

CAUNDLE-PURSE, a parish in the hundred of SHERBORNE, Sherborne division of the county of DORSET, 1½ mile (E.S.E.) from Milborne-Port, containing 142 inhabitants. The living is a discharged rectory, in the archdeaconry of Dorset, and diocese of Bristol, rated in the king's books at £7. 8. 8., and in the patronage of Sir R. C. Hoare, Bart. The church is dedicated to St. Peter: in the chancel, under a plain marble tombstone, are interred the remains of Dr. Highmore, a distinguished writer on medical and anatomical subjects. There is a fine old mansion of stone in this parish, said to have been a hunting seat belonging to King John. Dr. Mew, Bishop of Winchester, was born here, in 1618: the year following his translation from the bishoprick of Bath and Wells to that of Winchester, he was commanded by the king to proceed against Monmouth, in the rebellion, and had the management of the artillery at the battle of Sedgmoor, where he rendered considerable service, and was rewarded with a rich medal.

CAUNDLE-STOURTON, a parish in the hundred of BROWNSHALL, Sturminster division of the county of DORSET, 3½ miles (S.E.) from Milborne-Port, containing

325 inhabitants. The living is a perpetual curacy, in the archdeaconry of Dorset, and diocese of Bristol, and in the patronage of Sir R. C. Hoare, Bart.

CAUNTON, a parish in the northern division of the wapentake of THURGARTON, county of NOTTINGHAM, 5½ miles (N. W. by N.) from Newark, containing 467 inhabitants. The living is a discharged vicarage with Beesthorpe, in the peculiar jurisdiction and patronage of the Chapter of the Collegiate Church of Southwell, rated in the king's books at £4. 2. 1. The church is dedicated to St. Andrew. Various attempts to discover coal have been made in this parish, but hitherto without success.

CAUSEY-PARK, a township in the parish of HEBBURN, western division of MORPETH ward, county of NORTHUMBERLAND, 6½ miles (N. by W.) from Morpeth, containing 88 inhabitants. Here was a chapel, dedicated to St. Cuthbert, now in ruins.

CAVE (NORTH), a parish in the Hunsley-Beacon division of the wapentake of HARTHILL, East riding of the county of YORK, comprising the townships of North Cave, South Cliff, and Drewton with Everthorp, and containing 1091 inhabitants, of which number, 783 are in the township of North Cave, 6¾ miles (S. by E.) from Market-Weighton. The living is a discharged vicarage, in the archdeaconry of the East riding, and diocese of York, rated in the king's books at £10. 7. 6., and in the patronage of Henry Barton, Esq. The church is dedicated to All Saints. There are places of worship for the Society of Friends and Primitive and Wesleyan Methodists. Four poor children are educated free, for the use of a school-room, which was erected by subscription.

CAVE (SOUTH), a parish partly within the liberty of ST. PETER of YORK, and partly in the Hunsley-Beacon division of the wapentake of HARTHILL, East riding of the county of YORK, comprising the market town of South Cave, and the townships of Bromfleet and Flaxfleet, and containing 1190 inhabitants, of which number, 885 are in the town of South Cave, 27 miles (S. E.) from York, and 183 (N. by W.) from London. The living is a discharged vicarage, within the jurisdiction of the peculiar court of South Cave, rated in the king's books at £8, and in the patronage of E. W. Barnard, Esq. The church, dedicated to All Saints, is a neat edifice, erected in 1601. There are three places of worship belonging to the Methodists. This place lies at the western extremity of the Wolds. The surrounding country is very pleasing, the eminences affording many delightful views of Lincolnshire and the Humber, which bounds the parish for three miles. At the market, which is held on Monday, considerable quantities of corn are sold for the supply of many of the manufacturing towns in the West riding; it is shipped on the Humber, and the return cargoes consist of coal, freestone, lime, flags, and a variety of other necessary commodities. A fair is held on Trinity-Monday. The petty sessions for the wapentake of Howdenshire take place here. A manorial court is held in October, at which a constable is appointed. About fifty children are taught on the National system, in a school which is supported by voluntary subscriptions and an endowment of £16 per annum. In the vicinity of the town is Cave Castle, a large and splendid structure, embattled and crowned with numerous turrets; the interior exhibits a corresponding style of magnificence, and is enriched with a noble collection of paintings, by the first artists, including a fine portrait of the celebrated American general, Washington, whose ancestors possessed a portion of the estate, and resided here prior to their emigration to Virginia, in the middle of the seventeenth century.

CAVENDISH, a parish in the hundred of BABERGH, county of SUFFOLK, 2¾ miles (E. N. E.) from Clare, containing 1215 inhabitants. The living is a rectory, in the archdeaconry of Sudbury, and diocese of Norwich, rated in the king's books at £26, and in the patronage of the Master and Fellows of Jesus' College, Cambridge. The church is dedicated to St. Mary. The village is situated upon the river Stour: it was the birthplace of John Cavendish, Esq., who, being in attendance upon Richard II., assisted Walworth, Lord Mayor of London, in slaying the rebel Wat Tyler, which the populace at this place having heard, they, under John Raw, a priest, and Robert Westbroom, seized his uncle, Sir John Cavendish, Lord Chief Justice of the court of King's Bench, and beheaded him at the market-cross in Bury, with the prior of Bury; but Dr. Spencer, the warlike bishop of Norwich, raised forces and slew many of them immediately after. By deed in 1696, Thomas Grey gave land for teaching fifteen poor boys, apprenticing two, and sending one or two to college. The noble family of Cavendish, of which the Duke of Devonshire is the representative, derives name from this place, which at an early period was in their possession.

CAVENHAM, a parish in the hundred of LACKFORD, county of SUFFOLK, 4½ miles (S. E.) from Mildenhall, containing 261 inhabitants. The living is a discharged vicarage, in the archdeaconry of Sudbury, and diocese of Norwich, rated in the king's books at £5. 5. 10., endowed with £200 private benefaction, and £200 royal bounty, and in the patronage of the Crown. The church is dedicated to St. Andrew. The river Lark is navigable on the north of this parish, where it is crossed by Temple bridge.

CAVERSFIELD, a parish partly in the hundred of PLOUGHLEY, county of OXFORD, but chiefly in the hundred and county of BUCKINGHAM, 2 miles (N.) from Bicester, containing, with a portion of the township of Bicester-Market-End, 208 inhabitants. The living is a discharged vicarage, in the archdeaconry of Buckingham, and diocese of Lincoln, rated in the king's books at £6, endowed with £8 per annum private benefaction, and £400 royal bounty, and in the patronage of the Trustees of the late Joseph Bullock, Esq. The church is dedicated to St. Lawrence. Some suppose this to have been the place where Carausius, the Roman commander, assumed the purple in 287, and where he was afterwards slain by Caius Alectus, one of the thirty tyrants: on Bayard's Green, about a mile from the church, are faint traces of Carausius' camp.

CAVERSHAM, a parish in the hundred of BINFIELD, county of OXFORD, 1 mile (N.) from Reading, containing 1317 inhabitants. The living is a perpetual curacy, in the archdeaconry and diocese of Oxford, endowed with £400 private benefaction, £200 royal bounty, and £500 parliamentary grant, and in the patronage of the Dean and Canons of Christ Church, Oxford. The church, dedicated to St. Peter, was part of the first endowment of Nutley abbey, in Buckinghamshire, the society of which here founded a cell to that monastery, in which was a chapel, where, at the time of the dissolution, was superstitiously exhibited the angel with one wing, who was stated to have brought to Caversham the spear-head by which our Saviour was pierced on the cross. The village is pleasantly situated on the banks of the Thames. Charles I. was for a short time kept a prisoner here. Caversham gives the inferior title of viscount to Earl Cadogan.

CAVERSWALL, a parish in the northern division of the hundred of TOTMONSLOW, county of STAFFORD, 3¾ miles (W.) from Cheadle, containing, with the township of Weston-Coyney with Hulme, 1082 inhabitants. The living is a discharged vicarage, in the archdeaconry of Stafford, and diocese of Lichfield and Coventry, rated in the king's books at £7. 5. 3., and in the patronage of T. H. Parker, Esq. The church, dedicated to St. Peter, contains several old monuments, and one to the lady of the late Earl St. Vincent. There is a place of worship for Wesleyan Methodists. The parish is in the honour of Tutbury, duchy of Lancaster, and within the jurisdiction of a court of pleas held at Tutbury every third Tuesday, for the recovery of debts under 40*s*. Caverswall Castle, originally founded by Sir William de Caverswall in the time of Edward II., and rebuilt in that of Elizabeth, or James I., was garrisoned for the parliament in 1645, and at the commencement of the French revolution, in 1789, was purchased, with some adjoining fields, for the English Benedictine nuns of Ghent, who had been driven from their house and possessions in Belgium, and who have since added a neat chapel of the Doric order to the building.

CAVIL, a joint township with Portingten, in the parish of EASTRINGTON, wapentake of HOWDENSHIRE, East riding of the county of YORK, 2 miles (N. N. E.) from Howden. The population is returned with Portingten.

CAWKWELL, a parish in the northern division of the wapentake of GARTREE, parts of LINDSEY, county of LINCOLN, 7½ miles (N. by E.) from Horncastle, containing 34 inhabitants. The living is a discharged vicarage, in the archdeaconry and diocese of Lincoln, rated in the king's books at £4. 8. 6½., endowed with £600 royal bounty, and in the patronage of the Crown. The church is dedicated to St. Peter.

CAWOOD, a parish (formerly a market town) partly in the liberty of St. PETER of YORK, East riding, but chiefly in the lower division of the wapentake of BARKSTONE-ASH, West riding, of the county of YORK, 9½ miles (S. by W.) from York, and 187 (N. by W.) from London, containing 1127 inhabitants. This place was the residence of the archbishops of York, having been given by King Athelstan to Wulstan, the fifteenth archbishop; and here they had a magnificent palace, or castle, in which several of the prelates lived and died, and in which Cardinal Wolsey was arrested by the Earl of Northumberland, on a charge of treason, in the reign of Henry VIII. This castle was dismantled, and in part demolished, at the conclusion of the parliamentary war, since which time, being abandoned by the archbishops, it has remained in a state of gradual dilapidation, and has nearly fallen into ruin; the remains of the great gateway, and some few fragments, are now the only vestiges. The town is pleasantly situated near the western bank of the river Ouse, over which is a good ferry: the houses are neatly built, and the inhabitants are amply supplied with water. There is a manufactory for hop-sacking. The market, which was on Wednesday, has been discontinued for many years: fairs for cattle are held on May 12th and December 19th. The quarter sessions for the liberty of Cawood, Wistow, and Otley, are held here; and the Archbishop of York, and the magistrates for the division, hold a court of session twice a year for the trial of felonies: a manorial court is held under the archbishop. The living is a perpetual curacy, in the peculiar jurisdiction of the Prebendary of Wistow in the Cathedral Church of York, endowed with £200 royal bounty, and £1400 parliamentary grant, and in the patronage of the Dean of Ripon. The church is dedicated to All Saints. There is a place of worship for Wesleyan Methodists. A charity school for boys and girls was founded, in 1731, by the Rev. Samuel Duffield, who endowed it with land now producing a considerable annual income; and £12 per annum are paid to a schoolmaster for the instruction of five poor children of this parish, out of an estate producing £213. 9. per annum, vested in trustees for the repair of the highways, and the preservation of the embankments. Dr. Harsnett, Archbishop of York, who died in 1631, gave land for teaching five poor boys, and an additional plot for apprenticing boys. An almshouse was founded about 1723, by William James, Esq., who endowed it with land producing £76 per annum, for four aged persons, who receive each a yearly stipend of £18.

CAWSTON, a parish in the southern division of the hundred of ERPINGHAM, county of NORFOLK, 3¼ miles (E. by N.) from Reepham, containing 929 inhabitants. The living is a rectory, in the archdeaconry and diocese of Norwich, rated in the king's books at £15. 13. 11½., and in the patronage of the Master and Fellows of Pembroke Hall, Cambridge. The church, dedicated to St. Agnes, is principally in the later style of English architecture. This manor is held in free socage of the King, as Duke of Lancaster, in token of which two maces are carried before the lord, or his steward, one bearing a brazen hand surmounted by a ploughshare, and the other a bearded arrow. Fairs are held on February 1st, and the last Wednesdays in April and August, that in August being a large sheep fair.

CAWTHORNE, a parish in the wapentake of STAINCROSS, West riding of the county of York, 4½ miles (W. N. W.) from Barnesley, containing 1518 inhabitants. The living is a perpetual curacy, in the archdeaconry and diocese of York, endowed with £200 private benefaction, £200 royal bounty, and £200 parliamentary grant, and in the patronage of J. S. Stanhope, Esq., and certain other landowners. The church, dedicated to All Saints, is principally in the later style of English architecture. Two hundred and fifty sittings, two hundred and eight of which are free, have recently been added, the Incorporated Society for the enlargement of churches and chapels having granted £250 towards defraying the expense. There is a place of worship for Wesleyan Methodists. A free school was founded in 1639, with a small endowment, for which six boys are taught. The Barnesley canal terminates in this parish: at its head, at Barnby bridge, is a large basin, with wharfs, warehouses, and a wet dock, besides conveniences for boat-building. A rail-road extends from this basin to the extensive collieries here, and in the adjoining parish of Silkstone. A great quantity of limestone is burnt: and there are some veins of iron-stone. There is a mineral spring, the water of which is slightly impregnated with sulphuretted hydrogen.

CAWTHORPE, a hamlet in the parish of BOURNE, wapentake of AVELAND, parts of KESTEVEN, county of LINCOLN, 1¼ mile (N. by W.) from Bourne, containing 69 inhabitants.

CAWTHORPE (LITTLE), a parish in the Marsh division of the hundred of CALCEWORTH, locally in that of Louth-Eske, parts of LINDSEY, county of LINCOLN, 3 miles (S. E. by S.) from Louth, containing 130 inhabitants. The living is a discharged vicarage, in the archdeaconry and diocese of Lincoln, rated in the king's books at £3. 4. 4½., and endowed with £600 royal bounty; it is sequestrated. The church is dedicated to St. Helen.

CAWTON, a township in that part of the parish of GILLING which is in the wapentake of RYEDALE, North riding of the county of YORK, 5½ miles (S. S. E.) from Helmsley, containing 105 inhabitants.

CAXTON, a small market town and parish in the hundred of LONGSTOW, county of CAMBRIDGE, 10½ miles (W. by S.) from Cambridge, and 49 (N.N.W.) from London, containing 406 inhabitants. This place, one of the oldest post towns in the country, is situated on the Roman Ermin-street, which passes through the town from Holm to Papworth: the houses are in general irregularly built and of mean appearance; there are some good inns, and the trade of the place arises chiefly from its situation on the old north road to York. The market, granted to Baldwin Freville in 1247, is on Tuesday: fairs, principally for pedlary, are held on May 5th and October 18th. The living is a discharged vicarage, in the archdeaconry and diocese of Ely, rated in the king's books at £7. 12. 4., and in the patronage of the Dean and Canons of Windsor. The church, dedicated to St. Andrew, contains several memorials of the Barnard family, and a handsome monument to the memory of Mary, wife of John Hanson. Robert Langwith, in 1581, bequeathed £31. 10. per annum for the benefit of eight of the poorest housekeepers, and for four sermons to be preached quarterly in the church. Matthew Paris, a Benedictine monk, who flourished in the reign of Henry III., and who wrote a history of the world from the creation to the year of his death, which happened in 1259, was a native of this place. It has been erroneously stated that Caxton, who introduced the art of printing into England, was born in this parish; his own memoirs refer his birth and education to the county of Kent.

CAYTHORPE, a parish in the wapentake of LOVEDEN, parts of KESTEVEN, county of LINCOLN, 9 miles (N. by E.) from Grantham, containing, with the hamlet of Friston, 567 inhabitants. The living is a rectory, in the archdeaconry and diocese of Lincoln, rated in the king's books at £20. 11. 10½., and in the patronage of C. J. Packe, Esq. The church, dedicated to St. Vincent, is a curious cruciform structure, principally in the decorated style of English architecture. There is a place of worship for Wesleyan Methodists.

CAYTHORPE, a township in the parish of LOWDHAM, southern division of the wapentake of THURGARTON, county of NOTTINGHAM, 8¾ miles (N. E. by E.) from Nottingham, containing 285 inhabitants.

CAYTON, a parish in PICKERING lythe, North riding of the county of YORK, comprising the townships of Cayton-Deepdale with Killerby, and Osgodby, and containing 519 inhabitants, of which number, 447 are in the township of Cayton-Deepdale, 4 miles (S. by E.) from Scarborough. The living is a perpetual curacy, annexed to the vicarage of Seamer, in the archdeaconry of the East riding, and diocese of York. The church is dedicated to St. Leonard. There are places of worship for Primitive and Wesleyan Methodists. A school is endowed with £15 a year.

CERNE, or CERNE-ABBAS, a market town and parish in the hundred of CERNE, TOTCOMBE, and MODBURY, Cerne subdivision of the county of DORSET, 8 miles (N. N. W.) from Dorchester, and 120 (S. W. by W.) from London, containing 1060 inhabitants. The name of this place is derived from its situation on the river Cerne, and its adjunct from its ancient abbey. Eadwald, brother of King Edward the Martyr, became a hermit at this place; and in the reign of Edgar, Ailmer, Earl of Cornwall, began to erect a noble abbey, and completed it in 987, for Benedictine monks, dedicating it to St. Mary, St. Peter, and St. Benedict; it was plundered, or, as some say, destroyed by King Canute, but was soon restored, and flourished till the dissolution, when its revenue was estimated at £623. 13. 2.: the remains consist principally of the gate-house, a stately square embattled tower of three stages, having two fine oriel windows above the arch, and in front various shields of armorial bearings; also a large stone barn, and a moat, with a double intrenchment that surrounded it. In 1644, the Irish troops in the service of Charles I. burnt several houses in the town; and in the following year, Cromwell, having been joined by Col. Holberne and the inhabitants, marched to oppose the king's forces that had advanced within three miles of the town, who retired on finding that he had been further reinforced with the regiments of Colonels Norton and Coke. The town is pleasantly situated in a valley surrounded by lofty hills, and consists of four or five streets, not lighted, and only partially paved; the houses are in general ancient, and possess little architectural beauty; the inhabitants are amply supplied with water from a spring, called St. Augustine's well, which, as the legend asserts, burst out to provide St. Augustine with water for baptizing his Christian converts. Considerable improvement is taking place, including the erection of some handsome modern buildings, and the formation of a new road through the town from Dorchester to Sherborne. There are manufactories for dowlas, coarse linen, gloves, and parchment; the tanning trade is carried on to a considerable extent, and many women and children are employed in winding silk. The market, granted in the 15th year of the reign of King John, is on Wednesday; the fairs are on Whit-Monday, April 28th, and October 2nd, for cattle. The petty sessions for the Cerne subdivision of the county are held here.

The living is a discharged vicarage, in the archdeaconry of Dorset, and diocese of Bristol, rated in the king's books at £8. 16., endowed with £400 royal bounty, and £600 parliamentary grant, and in the patronage of Lord Rivers. The church, dedicated to St. Mary, and supposed to have been erected on the site of the ancient hermitage, by one of the abbots of the monastery, in the fifteenth century, is a fine spacious structure in the later style of English architecture, with a square embattled tower ornamented with octagonal turrets at the angles: it has recently received an addition of three hundred free sittings, the Incorporated Society for the enlargement of churches and chapels having granted £150 for that purpose. There is a place of worship for Independents. Sir Robert Miller and Dame Margaret gave a rent-charge of £10 for apprenticing poor children. On the southern declivity of a steep chalk hill, called Trendle Hill, to the north of the town, a gigantic figure has been traced, representing a man holding a knotted club in his right hand, and extending his left arm; it is one hundred and eighty feet high, and well executed; the outlines are two feet broad, and two feet deep; between the legs is an illegible inscription, and above, the date 748. It is by some antiquaries referred to the Saxon times, and supposed to represent one of their deities; by others it is thought to be a memorial of Cenric, son of Cuthred, King of the West Saxons, who was slain in battle; and according to vulgar tradition, it was cut to commemorate the destruction of a giant who ravaged that part of the country, and was killed by the peasants: the figure is occasionally repaired by the inhabitants of the town.

CERNE (NETHER), a parish in the hundred of Cerne, Totcombe, and Modbury, Cerne subdivision of the county of Dorset, $5\frac{3}{4}$ miles (N. N. W.) from Dorchester, containing 60 inhabitants. The living is a perpetual curacy, in the archdeaconry of Dorset, and diocese of Bristol, endowed with £40 per annum private benefaction, and £600 parliamentary grant, and in the patronage of F. J. Browne, Esq. There is a small endowment for the instruction of children.

CERNE (UP), a parish in the hundred of Sherborne, being a detached portion of the Sherborne division of the county of Dorset, 9 miles (N. N. W.) from Dorchester, containing 84 inhabitants. The living is a discharged rectory, in the archdeaconry of Dorset, and diocese of Bristol, rated in the king's books at £5. 18. 4., and in the patronage of J. White, Esq.

CERNEY (NORTH), a parish in the hundred of Rapsgate, county of Gloucester, 4 miles (N.) from Cirencester, containing, with the tythings of Calmsden and Woodmancote, 562 inhabitants. The living is a rectory, in the archdeaconry and diocese of Gloucester, rated in the king's books at £21. 10. $7\frac{1}{2}$., and in the patronage of the Master and Fellows of University College, Oxford. The church is dedicated to All Saints. The Roman Fosse-way traces the eastern boundary of this parish, in which may also be seen vestiges of a Roman fortress with circumvallations. Races are annually held here.

CERNEY (SOUTH), a parish in the hundred of Crowthorne and Minety, county of Gloucester, $3\frac{3}{4}$ miles (S. E. by S.) from Cirencester, containing 922 inhabitants. The living is a discharged vicarage, in the archdeaconry and diocese of Gloucester, rated in the king's books at £6. 16. 8., and in the patronage of the Bishop of Gloucester. The church, dedicated to All Saints, consists of a nave, chancel, north aisle, and north transept, with a low central tower and spire; the south porch is of Norman architecture, with grotesque heads terminating the mouldings; between the nave and the chancel is a pointed arch rising from slender columns, the capitals of which are decorated with rich foliage; the chancel, with a fine east window of three lights, is of later date than the other parts of the edifice. The Thames and Severn canal passes through this parish.

CHACKMORE, a hamlet in the parish of Radclive, hundred and county of Buckingham, $1\frac{1}{2}$ mile (N. N. W.) from Buckingham. The population is returned with the parish. Here was formerly a chapel of ease, but it is now in ruins.

CHAD-KIRK, a chapelry in the parish of Stockport, hundred of Macclesfield, county palatine of Chester, $3\frac{1}{2}$ miles (E. by S.) from Stockport, with which the population is returned. The living is a perpetual curacy, in the archdeaconry and diocese of Chester, endowed with £400 private benefaction, £600 royal bounty, and £200 parliamentary grant, and in the patronage of the Rector of Stockport. The chapel is dedicated to St. Chadd.

CHADD (ST.), a chapelry in the higher division of the hundred of Broxton, county palatine of Chester, $2\frac{3}{4}$ miles (E. by S.) from Malpas. The living is a perpetual curacy, annexed to the first portion of the rectory of Malpas, in the archdeaconry and diocese of Chester, endowed with £600 private benefaction, and £2900 parliamentary grant, and in the patronage of the Rector of the first portion of Malpas.

CHADDENWICKE, a joint tything with Woodlands, in the parish and hundred of Mere, county of Wilts, $1\frac{3}{4}$ mile (E.) from Mere. The population is returned with Woodlands.

CHADDERTON, a chapelry in the parish of Oldham *cum* Prestwich, hundred of Salford, county palatine of Lancaster, 7 miles (N.E. by N.) from Manchester, containing 5124 inhabitants. The living is a perpetual curacy, in the archdeaconry and diocese of Chester, endowed with £400 private benefaction, £800 royal bounty, and £1900 parliamentary grant, and in the patronage of the Rector of Prestwich. The chapel is dedicated to St. Margaret. This was the birthplace of Dr. Lawrence Chadderton, an eminent divine at the period of the Reformation, of which he was a zealous promoter. There are different establishments for the spinning of cotton, the weaving of silk, and the manufacture of hats: the chapelry abounds with coal, which, by means of a branch of the Ashton canal, is conveyed to Manchester, Stockport, and other manufacturing towns in the vicinity. On the lawn in front of Chadderton Hall is a tumulus, on lowering which, at different periods, several relics of antiquity have been discovered.

CHADDESDEN, a parish in the hundred of Appletree, locally in that of Morleston and Litchurch, county of Derby, $2\frac{1}{2}$ miles (E.) from Derby, containing 486 inhabitants. The living is a perpetual curacy, in the archdeaconry of Derby, and diocese of Lichfield and Coventry, and in the patronage of Sir Robert Wilmot, Bart. The church is dedicated to St. Mary; there is a stone stall in the chancel. The Derby canal passes through the parish. In 1638, an almshouse for six poor persons was founded and endowed by Edward Wilmot, Esq.; the inmates are nominated by Sir Robert Wilmot, who repairs the almshouses, and each receives two shillings per week. There is a small donation by Robert Walker for the education of three children; and, in 1813, John Berrysford left £16. 4. per annum, to be distributed amongst the widows and orphans of the parish.

CHADDESLEY-CORBETT, a parish in the lower division of the hundred of HALFSHIRE, county of WORCESTER, 5 miles (W. N. W.) from Bromsgrove, containing 1343 inhabitants. The living is a vicarage, in the archdeaconry and diocese of Worcester, rated in the king's books at £17. 3. 4., and in the patronage of the Crown. The church, dedicated to St. Cassyon, is a fine spacious edifice of red freestone, combining different styles of English architecture, with some Norman portions, of which latter, the font is a fine specimen. Here is a free school, endowed with land and tenements, out of the annual produce of which the master is entitled to a salary of £40, and an usher to one of £10, but only a master is appointed; the remainder, amounting on an average to about £170 per annum, is applied towards the support of the poor; the present schoolroom was built in 1809. Mrs. Margaret Delabere erected and endowed an almshouse for five aged widows, who receive £10 per annum each. At the hamlet of Harvington, in this parish, is a Roman Catholic chapel, the rebuilding of which was completed in 1825, by subscription, the late Sir Charles Throckmorton, Bart. being the chief contributor. The same benevolent individual founded a school, and endowed it with a rent-charge upon the Harvington estate; it is kept in a building adjoining the moated manor-house, which is now the residence of a farmer; about thirty boys and girls, principally the children of Roman Catholics, are instructed on the Lancasterian plan, and provided with books and stationery.

CHADDLEWORTH, a parish in the hundred of KINTBURY-EAGLE, county of BERKS, 6½ miles (W.S.W.) from East Ilsley, containing, with the tything of Woolley, 448 inhabitants. The living is a discharged vicarage, in the archdeaconry of Berks, and diocese of Salisbury, rated in the king's books at £9. 4. 7., and in the patronage of the Dean and Chapter of Westminster. The church is dedicated to St. Andrew. In 1720, a school was founded and endowed in this place, by Mr. William Saunders, for the education of eight poor boys, who are also clothed and apprenticed, of which number, two belong to Chaddleworth; the income is £40 per annum. Mrs. Susannah Wynne gave also an annuity of £10 for teaching ten poor children of this parish. In 1160, a priory was founded for regular canons of the order of St. Augustine, which was dissolved by Wolsey, at which period the revenue amounted to £71. 10. 7.

CHADLINGTON (EAST), a chapelry in that part of the parish of CHARLBURY which is in the hundred of CHADLINGTON, county of OXFORD, 4 miles (S. S. E.) from Chipping-Norton, containing 125 inhabitants. The chapel is dedicated to St. Mary.

CHADLINGTON (WEST), a tything in that part of the parish of CHARLBURY which is in the hundred of CHADLINGTON, county of OXFORD, 3 miles (S. by E.) from Chipping-Norton, containing 508 inhabitants.

CHADSHUNT, a chapelry in the parish of BISHOP'S ITCHINGTON, Kington division of the hundred of KINGTON, county of WARWICK, 2¼ miles (N.E. by N.) from Kington, containing 37 inhabitants. The living is a perpetual curacy, annexed to the vicarage of Bishop's Itchington, and in the peculiar jurisdiction of the Prebendary of Colwich and Bishop's Itchington in the Cathedral Church of Lichfield. The chapel is dedicated to All Saints. The inhabitants of Gaydon marry and bury at Chadshunt, which obtained a separate register in 1813, having previously been included in Bishop's Itchington. In the burial-ground of the chapel was anciently an oratory, containing an image of St. Chad, to which numerous pilgrimages and offerings were made.

CHADWELL, a chapelry in that part of the parish of ROTHLEY which is in the eastern division of the hundred of GOSCOTE, county of LEICESTER, 5 miles (N.N.E.) from Melton-Mowbray, containing, with the hamlet of Wycomb, 101 inhabitants. The chapel is dedicated to St. Mary.

CHADWELL (ST. MARY'S), a parish in the hundred of BARSTABLE, county of ESSEX, 3 miles (S.) from Orsett, containing 202 inhabitants. The living is a rectory, in the archdeaconry of Essex, and diocese of London, rated in the king's books at £17. 13. 4., and in the patronage of the Rev. J. P. Herringham. The church is dedicated to St. Mary. This parish is bounded on the south by the Thames. In a wood near the highway leading to Stifford are several ancient excavations, termed Danes' Holes. Tilbury Fort is partly in this parish.

CHADWICK, a hamlet in the parish of BROMSGROVE, upper division of the hundred of HALFSHIRE, county of WORCESTER, 3½ miles (N. by E.) from Bromsgrove, with which the population is returned. Here was formerly a chapel, now demolished.

CHAFFCOMBE, a parish in the southern division of the hundred of PETHERTON, county of SOMERSET, 3¼ miles (S. by W.) from Ilminster, containing 225 inhabitants. The living is a discharged rectory, in the archdeaconry of Taunton, and diocese of Bath and Wells, rated in the king's books at £9. 10. 2½., and in the patronage of Earl Poulett. The church is dedicated to St. Michael.

CHAGFORD, a market town and parish in the hundred of WONFORD, county of DEVON, 15 miles (S. W. by W.) from Exeter, and 186 (S.W.) from London, containing 1503 inhabitants. This place, originally held by Dodo, a Saxon, was given by William the Conqueror to the Bishop of Constance; and in 1328 was made one of the Stannary towns by Edward III., who invested the lords of the manor with the power of inflicting capital punishment. In 1643, an action took place between the royalists and the parliamentarians, in which Sir Sidney Godolphin was killed; and in the same century a fire occurred, in which the charter for holding the market, and other records, were destroyed. The town is pleasantly situated near the river Teign, and sheltered by hills of romantic form; the houses are irregularly built, but the environs abound with pleasing and picturesque scenery. On the banks of the Teign a large woollen-manufactory has been established. The market is on Saturday: fairs are held on the last Thursday in March, the first Thursday in May, the last Thursday in September, and the last Thursday in October. The

Stannary court, in which the principal business respecting the mines is transacted, is held here. The living is a rectory, in the archdeaconry and diocese of Exeter, rated in the king's books at £39. 0. 10., and in the patronage of Mrs. Grace Hames. The church, dedicated to St. Michael, is a handsome structure, and contains a richly executed monument to the memory of Sir John Widdon, Chief Justice of the court of King's Bench in the reign of Mary. The sum of about £12 is annually paid to a schoolmaster, out of the rental of certain church lands, for teaching ten poor boys, who are appointed by the churchwardens; and a schoolmistress receives £7 per annum, arising from a benefaction of £200 by John Weekes, about 1790, for instructing six children. At the hamlets of Great Weeke and Teigncombe, in this parish, are the remains of ancient chapels: there was a chapel also at Rushford.

CHAIGLEY, a joint township with Aighton and Bailey, in that part of the parish of MITTON which is in the lower division of the hundred of BLACKBURN, county palatine of LANCASTER, 6½ miles (W. by N.) from Clitheroe. The population is returned with Aighton.

CHAILEY, a parish in the hundred of STREET, rape of LEWES, county of SUSSEX, 6½ miles (N. by W.) from Lewes, containing 946 inhabitants. The living is a rectory, in the archdeaconry of Lewes, and diocese of Chichester, rated in the king's books at £9. 4. 2., and in the patronage of T. B. Bowen, Esq., and another. The church, dedicated to St. Peter, is principally in the early style of English architecture. There is a place of worship for dissenters. In 1770, Thomas Tempest bequeathed £40, producing £3. 10. per annum, for teaching four poor children. A National school for both sexes has been established.

CHALBURY, a parish in the hundred of BADBURY, Shaston (East) division of the county of DORSET, 5 miles (N. by E.) from Wimborne-Minster, containing 135 inhabitants. The living is a rectory, in the archdeaconry of Dorset, and diocese of Bristol, rated in the king's books at £7. 10. 2½., and in the patronage of the Earl of Pembroke. The village is situated on rising ground, commanding a fine view of the Needles and the British channel. A particular sort of fine sand, used by founders, is obtained here. At Didlington, in this parish, there was anciently a chapel, now a farm-house, near which foundations of houses are often discovered in turning up the ground.

CHALCOMBE, a parish in the hundred of KING'S SUTTON, county of NORTHAMPTON, 3¾ miles (N.E. by E.) from Banbury, containing 485 inhabitants. The living is a discharged vicarage, in the archdeaconry of Northampton, and diocese of Peterborough, rated in the king's books at £7. 17., endowed with £600 private benefaction, and £400 royal bounty, and in the patronage of Charles Fox, Esq. The church is dedicated to St. Peter and St. Paul.

CHALDON, a parish in the first division of the hundred of WALLINGTON, county of SURREY, 3 miles (N.E.) from Gatton, containing 166 inhabitants. The living is a discharged rectory, in the archdeaconry of Surrey, and diocese of Winchester, rated in the king's books at £7. 10. 7½., and in the patronage of the Rev. Thomas Welton. The church is dedicated to St. Peter. The Croydon railway passes through this parish. Here are some quarries of a soft species of stone, which is not much used; and in the chalk-pits are frequently found incrustations of marine shells.

CHALDON-HERRING, a parish in the liberty of BINDON, locally in the hundred of Winfrith, Blandford (South) division of the county of DORSET, 10½ miles (W. S. W.) from Wareham, containing 240 inhabitants. The living is a vicarage, in the archdeaconry and diocese of Bristol, rated in the king's books at £8. 0. 10., endowed with £1400 royal bounty, and in the patronage of Thomas Lyte, Esq. The church is dedicated to St. Nicholas. This parish is bounded by the English channel on the south, where there is a signal station. Chaldon-Boys, or West Chaldon, now comprising only one farm, was formerly a manor and a distinct parish; the church having become desecrated, the living, a rectory, was consolidated with the vicarage of Chaldon-Herring, in 1446.

CHALE, a parish in the liberty of WEST MEDINA, Isle of Wight division of the county of SOUTHAMPTON, 7 miles (S. S. W.) from Newport, containing 473 inhabitants. The living is a rectory, in the archdeaconry and diocese of Winchester, rated in the king's books at £14. 3. 11½., and in the patronage of the Rev. C. Richards. The church, dedicated to St. Andrew, stands at the foot of St. Catherine's hill, the loftiest in the island, being seven hundred and fifty feet above the level of the sea; a chapel, dedicated to St. Catherine, was erected on its summit in 1323, the tower of which still serves as a land-mark. The land and sea views are remarkably fine from this hill; and on the south-western declivity is a rude chasm, called Black-Gang Chine, which, as seen from the shore, has a striking effect. The navigation of Chale bay is exceedingly dangerous, owing to the rocks, upon which vessels are frequently driven by the violence of the surf. A school here is endowed with £16. 14. 6., being a rent-charge purchased with the sum of £150 given by Robert Weekes, in 1784, and other benefactions.

CHALFIELD (GREAT), a parish in the hundred of BRADFORD, county of WILTS, 3½ miles (W.) from Melksham, containing, with the extra-parochial liberty of Little Chalfield and Cottles, 100 inhabitants. The living is a discharged rectory, in the archdeaconry and diocese of Salisbury, rated in the king's books at £6, endowed with £200 private benefaction, and £200 royal bounty, and in the patronage of Sir H. B. Neale, Bart. The church is dedicated to St. Catherine.

CHALFIELD (LITTLE), an extra-parochial liberty, locally in the parish of Great Chalfield, hundred of BRADFORD, county of WILTS, 3¾ miles (W.) from Melksham. The population is returned with the parish.

CHALFONT (ST. GILES), a parish in the hundred of BURNHAM, county of BUCKINGHAM, 3¾ miles (S.E.) from Amersham, containing 1104 inhabitants. The living is a rectory, in the archdeaconry of Buckingham, and diocese of Lincoln, rated in the king's books at £19. 9. 4½., and in the patronage of the Bishop of Lincoln. The church is of very great antiquity. Here are places of worship for the Society of Friends and Independents: in the cemetery attached to the former lie the remains of William Penn, founder of the colony of Pennsylvania. A charity school, now conducted on the National system, has been endowed by Sir Hugh Palliser with £30 per annum, and by Mrs. Molloy with an additional sum of £20 per annum, for twenty children of each sex: there are eight almshouses for poor men and women. During the plague that raged in London in 1665, Milton resided at this place, where he completed his celebrated poem of "Paradise Lost;" the house in which he lived is now occupied by a poor family. Here are the remains of an ancient monastery, the chapel of which is attached to the mansion of *Vach*, and in the park is a monument erected by the late Sir Hugh Palliser to the memory of Capt. Cook, the celebrated circumnavigator.

CHALFONT (ST. PETER'S), a parish in the hundred of BURNHAM, county of BUCKINGHAM, 4 miles (E. by N.) from Beaconsfield, containing 1351 inhabitants. The living is a vicarage, in the archdeaconry of Buckingham, and diocese of Lincoln, rated in the king's books at £15. 17. 1., and in the patronage of the President and Fellows of St. John's College, Oxford. The church, rebuilt in 1726, is a plain brick edifice, with quoins and window and door-cases of stone brought from the ruins of the Roman station of Verulam, now St. Albans; it contains some ancient gravestones with brasses. This parish is intersected by a tributary stream of the Colne, called Missbourne, upon which there is a silk-mill, affording employment to about fifty women. The petty sessions for the division are holden here; and a court baron is held by the lord of the manor. At Gerrard's Cross the Earl of Portland built a school, which is supported by his descendant, who appoints the master, paying him a salary for teaching poor boys of this and the adjoining parishes; and a fund is now accumulating for the purpose of endowing another school.

CHALFORD, a chapelry in the parish of LITTLE BARRINGTON, lower division of the hundred of SLAUGHTER, county of GLOUCESTER, 1¾ mile (N. E.) from Minchin-Hampton. The population is returned with the parish. There are places of worship for Baptists and Wesleyan Methodists. The village is scattered along the banks of the river Frome, in a romantic valley, through which passes the Stroudwater canal. Broad cloth is manufactured to a great extent, and among the numerous clothing-mills on the river is one said to have been erected about 1560, when the introduction of the trade into Gloucestershire took place. A petrifying spring flows from the side of the hill to the south of the river.

CHALFORD, a liberty in the parish of ASTON-ROWANT, hundred of LEWKNOR, county of OXFORD, 2 miles (E. S. E.) from Tetsworth. The population is returned with the parish.

CHALGRAVE, a parish in the hundred of MANSHEAD, county of BEDFORD, 3¾ miles (N. by W.) from Dunstable, containing 710 inhabitants. The living is a discharged vicarage, united in 1772 to the rectory of Hockcliffe, in the archdeaconry of Bedford, and diocese of Lincoln, rated in the king's books at £12. The church, dedicated to All Saints, is a venerable edifice in the ancient style of English architecture, and contains two antique tombs with statues of knights in armour. There is a place of worship for Wesleyan Methodists at Tebworth, where was formerly a chapel endowed with thirty-six acres of land. Here is a charity school for forty boys; besides which, four boys from this parish are admitted into Hockcliffe school. There are endowed almshouses for six elderly maidens, and two for six widows. At Chalgrave Field, in this parish, in June 1643, a battle took place between the royalists under Prince Rupert and a detachment of troops from the army of the Earl of Essex, in which the latter were defeated; several officers in the service of the parliament were killed, and the celebrated patriot Hampden was mortally wounded.

CHALGROVE, a parish in the hundred of EWELME, county of OXFORD, 5¾ miles (S. W.) from Tetsworth, containing, with the liberty of Rafford, 569 inhabitants. The living is a vicarage, in the archdeaconry and diocese of Oxford, rated in the king's books at £10. 5. 5., and in the patronage of the Dean and Canons of Christ Church, Oxford. The church is dedicated to St. Mary. There is a place of worship for Baptists.

CHALK, a parish in the hundred of SHAMWELL, lathe of AYLESFORD, county of KENT, 1¾ mile (E. S. E.) from Gravesend, containing, with the parish of Denton, 424 inhabitants. The living is a discharged vicarage, in the archdeaconry and diocese of Rochester, rated in the king's books at £6. 3. 8., endowed with £200 private benefaction, and £200 royal bounty, and in the patronage of the Bishop of Rochester. The church, dedicated to St. Mary, is very ancient, and has various figures carved over the entrance, the origin and meaning of which have caused much controversy among antiquaries. This parish is bounded on the north by the Thames, and is intersected by the Thames and Medway canal; it contains the villages of East and West Chalk, the former lying on the margin of an extensive marsh. There is a considerable manufactory for gun-flints, which are esteemed the best in Europe: a fair is held on Whit-Monday. In 1598, William, Lord Cobham, by will, vested £4. 6. 8. in the Warden and Commonalty of Rochester bridge, for one poor family of this parish, to inhabit Cobham College; and in 1710 a bequest, consisting of a rent-charge of £2. 18., was made by James Fry, and vested in the mayor and corporation of Gravesend, for teaching ten boys of Milton and Chalk.

CHALLACOMBE, a parish in the hundred of SHERWILL, county of DEVON, 10 miles (N. E. by E.) from Barnstaple, containing 240 inhabitants. The living is a rectory, in the archdeaconry of Barnstaple, and diocese of Exeter, rated in the king's books at £11. 9. 2., and in the patronage of Earl Fortescue. The church is dedicated to the Holy Trinity.

CHALLOCK, a parish in the hundred of FELBOROUGH, lathe of SCRAY, county of KENT, 4¼ miles (E.) from Charing, containing 381 inhabitants. The living is a perpetual curacy, annexed to the vicarage of Godmersham, in the peculiar jurisdiction of the Archbishop of Canterbury. The church, dedicated to St. Cosmus and St. Damien, is a spacious edifice in the ancient style of English architecture, with an embattled tower, steeple, and beacon turret. A fair is held on the 8th of October, for horses, cattle, and pedlary; a grant for which, and for a market now disused, was obtained in the 38th of Henry III., by Henry de Apulderfield, then lord of the manor, whose mansion is said to have stood upon a spot called Apulderfield's Garden, in the Earl of Winchelsea's park.

CHALLOW (EAST), a chapelry in the parish of LETCOMB-REGIS, hundred of KINTBURY-EAGLE, county of BERKS, 1¼ mile (W.) from Wantage, containing

256 inhabitants. The chapel is dedicated to St. Nicholas. The Wilts and Berks canal passes through this chapelry.

CHALLOW (WEST), a chapelry in the parish of LETCOMB-REGIS, hundred of KINTBURY-EAGLE, county of BERKS, 2 miles (W. N. W.) from Wantage, containing 156 inhabitants. The chapel is dedicated to St. Lawrence. The Wilts and Berks canal crosses the chapelry.

CHALTON, or CHALKTON, a parish in the hundred of FINCH-DEAN, Alton (South) division of the county of SOUTHAMPTON, 5½ miles (S. S. W.) from Petersfield, containing, with the chapelry of Idsworth, 559 inhabitants. The living is a rectory, with that of Clanfield united, in the archdeaconry and diocese of Winchester, rated in the king's books at £20. 0. 10., and in the patronage of the Provost and Fellows of King's College, Cambridge. The church is dedicated to St. Michael.

CHALVEY, a hamlet in the parish of UPTON, hundred of STOKE, county of BUCKINGHAM, 1¼ mile (N.) from Eton. The population is returned with the parish. Here is a place of worship for Independents.

CHALVINGTON, a parish in the hundred of SHIPLAKE, rape of PEVENSEY, county of SUSSEX, 5 miles (W.) from Hailsham, containing 181 inhabitants. The living is a discharged rectory, in the archdeaconry of Lewes, and diocese of Chichester, rated in the king's books at £8, and in the patronage of Augustus Elliott Fuller, Esq. The church, dedicated to St. Bartholomew, is principally in the decorated style of English architecture.

CHAMBOIS, a township in the parish of BEDLINGTON, eastern division of CHESTER ward, county palatine of DURHAM, but situated on the eastern side of the county of Northumberland, 7¼ miles (E. by S.) from Morpeth. The population is returned with the parish. The village is situated on the coast, at the mouth of the river Wansbeck; there is a small harbour, where corn, timber, and grindstones are shipped; some spacious granaries were built during the late war with France, at which period a great quantity of grain was sent from this place.

CHAPEL, or PONTISBRIGHT, county of ESSEX.—See PONTISBRIGHT.

CHAPEL en le FRITH, a market town and parish in the hundred of HIGH PEAK, county of DERBY, 41 miles (N. W. by N.) from Derby, and 167 (N.W. by N.) from London, on the road from Sheffield to Manchester, comprising the townships of Bowden's Edge, Bradshaw-Edge, and Coomb's Edge, and containing 3234 inhabitants. This town is pleasantly situated on the declivity of a hill rising from a vale embosomed in the mountains that bound this extremity of the county: it is partially paved, but not lighted, and is amply supplied with water. A small subscription library has been recently established. The principal branch of manufacture is that of cotton, in which more than three hundred persons are employed: about one hundred persons are engaged in the manufacture of paper, chiefly for the London newspapers; and there are a rope-walk and a forge for iron near the town: coal is found in the parish. There is also a large establishment for warehousing goods, this place being a medium of communication between Manchester and Sheffield. The Peak Forest canal passes within three miles to the north-west, and by means of a railway communicates with the Peak Forest limeworks, about three miles to the east of the town: there is a reservoir in this parish that occasionally supplies the canal with water. The market, which is on Thursday, has greatly declined: the fairs, most of which are very insignificant, are on the Thursday before February 13th, March 24th and 29th, the Thursday before Easter, April 30th, Holy Thursday, and the third Thursday after, for cattle; July 7th, for wool; the Thursday preceding August 24th, for sheep and cheese; the Thursday after September 29th, and the Thursday before November 11th, for cattle. The High Peak court, for the recovery of debts under £5, at which the steward of the Duke of Devonshire presides, is held every third week. The living is a perpetual curacy, in the peculiar jurisdiction of the Dean and Chapter of Lichfield, endowed with £400 private benefaction, £400 royal bounty, and £300 parliamentary grant, and in the patronage of the resident freeholders, of whom a committee of twenty-seven, chosen in equal numbers from the three "Edges" into which the parish is divided, elect the minister, by a majority. The church, dedicated to St. Thomas à Becket, is a neat edifice in the later style of English architecture, with a square embattled tower, which, with the south front, was rebuilt in the beginning of the last century, at the expense of the parishioners. There is a place of worship for Wesleyan Methodists. A school was founded in 1696, by Mrs. Mary Dixon, who endowed it with a house and land producing £18 per annum; this endowment was augmented by Robert Kirke, Esq., with a piece of land now let for £2. 10. per annum: nineteen scholars are taught reading and writing in this establishment. There is also a school at Bowden's Edge, founded by Mrs. Mary Bagshaw, who endowed it with £5 per annum, for the instruction of eight girls. A fund amounting to £13. 7. 6. per annum, arising from various benefactions, is applied to the apprenticing of poor children; and there are various bequests for distribution in bread and clothing to the poor. At Barmoor-Clough, about two miles to the east of the town, is an ebbing and flowing well; and on a hill two miles to the south are the vestiges of a Roman encampment, from which a Roman road leads to Brough, about eight miles distant.

CHAPEL-HILL, a parish in the upper division of the hundred of RAGLAND, county of MONMOUTH, 4¼ miles (N.) from Chepstow, containing 464 inhabitants. The living is a perpetual curacy, in the archdeaconry and diocese of Llandaff, endowed with £800 royal bounty, and in the patronage of the Duke of Beaufort. Within this parish stood the stately abbey of Tinterne, founded by Walter de Clare, in 1141, for Cistercian monks, and dedicated to St. Mary: its revenue, at the time of the dissolution, was estimated at £256. 11. 6. The ruins present a picturesque object on the margin of the river Wye, in a district abounding with fine scenery; they consist of nearly the entire walls of the splendid church, in a style forming a transition from the early English to the decorated, and are remarkable for harmony of design and delicacy of execution.

CHAPEL-POINT, or PORT-EAST, a sea-port and chapelry in the parish of GORRAN, eastern division of the hundred of POWDER, county of CORNWALL, 7½ miles (E. by S.) from Tregony. The population is returned with the parish. The chapel is in ruins. A great quantity of pilchards is taken and cured; some coal is also imported.

CHAPEL-SUCKEN, a township in the parish of Millom, Allerdale ward above Derwent, county of Cumberland, 12 miles (S. E. by S.) from Ravenglass, containing 251 inhabitants.

CHAPEL-THORPE, a chapelry in the parish of Great Sandall, lower division of the wapentake of Agbrigg, West riding of the county of York, 4¼ miles (S. by W.) from Wakefield. The population is returned with the parish. The living is a perpetual curacy, annexed to the vicarage of Great Sandall, in the archdeaconry and diocese of York, endowed with £200 royal bounty. The church is dedicated to St. James.

CHAPELWICK, a chapelry in the parish of Ashbury, hundred of Shrivenham, county of Berks. The population is returned with the parish.

CHARBOROUGH, a parish in the hundred of Loosebarrow, Shaston (East) division of the county of Dorset, 6¼ miles (S. S. E.) from Blandford-Forum. The population is returned with the parish of Morden. The living is a discharged rectory, annexed to the vicarage of Morden, in the archdeaconry of Dorset, and diocese of Bristol, rated in the king's books at £7. 3. 6½., and in the patronage of Richard Erle Drax, Esq. The church, dedicated to St. Mary, is now used only as the burial-place of the Drax family. Over the door of a small arched building in the grounds of Charborough House is an inscription, dated 1686, commemorating the meeting of some patriotic individuals, who here concerted the plan of the Revolution, in 1688.

CHARCOMBE, an extra-parochial liberty, in the hundred of Kilmersdon, county of Somerset.

CHARD, a parish, and one of the four unconnected portions forming the eastern division of the hundred of Kingsbury, county of Somerset, comprising the market-town of Chard, the tythings of Crim-Chard, Old Chard, South Chard, and Tatworth with Forton, and containing 3106 inhabitants, of which number, 1330 are in the town of Chard, 13 miles (S. E. by S.) from Taunton, and 139 (W. S. W.) from London. This place was of considerable importance during the Octarchy, and was by the Saxons called *Cerdre*, a name supposed to be derived from Cerdic, the founder of the kingdom of Wessex. In the 28th of Edward I. it was constituted a borough, and continued to send members to parliament until the 2nd of Edward III., since which time its privileges have been discontinued. In the parliamentary war a battle took place here, in which a party of royalists, under the command of Col. Penruddock, was defeated. The town is situated at the southern extremity of the county, and upon the highest ground between the North and the South seas, so that the course of a stream, issuing from a spring in one of the streets, may easily be diverted either into the English or the Bristol channel: it consists principally of two streets, intersecting each other; the houses are in general well built, and the inhabitants are supplied with water conveyed by leaden pipes into four conduits, from a spring at the western extremity of the town. The market is on Monday, and is noted for the sale of potatoes: the fairs are on the first Wednesdays in May, August, and November. The ancient assize-hall is now used as the market-house, to which is attached an extensive range of shambles, covered with a tiled roof, and supported on brick pillars. The town is governed by a portreeve and two bailiffs, chosen annually at the court leet of the lord of the manor. The town-hall is a very ancient edifice, and was formerly used as a chapel.

The living is a vicarage, in the archdeaconry of Taunton, and diocese of Bath and Wells, rated in the king's books at £36. 18. 9., and in the patronage of the Bishop of Bath and Wells. The church, dedicated to St. Mary, is a handsome cruciform structure, with a low tower at the west end: in the north-east corner of the south transept is a splendid monument, having the effigies of William Brewer and his wife, kneeling before an altar, with their family behind them; in the south corner of the same transept, and in various parts of the church, are other handsome and interesting monuments. There is a place of worship for Particular Baptists. An unendowed school was established by the portreeve and burgesses, to whom a house, a garden, and a field containing about one acre, were devised on certain conditions, by William Symes, in 1671: the master, who resides on the premises rent-free, receives from two to three guineas per annum from each pupil, and has the privilege of taking boarders. An hospital, or almshouse, for poor people of the parish was founded, in 1668, by Richard Harvey, Esq., of Exeter, who endowed it with two estates in the counties of Cambridge and Norfolk, formerly producing £844. 4. per annum, but, within the last few years, the income has been somewhat diminished by the reduction of the rents. In May 1831, the gardener of Henry Host Henley, Esq., of Leigh House, near this town, dug up in the garden a Roman urn, containing a great number of gold coins of the Emperor Claudius, very fresh and bright.

CHARDSTOCK, a parish in the hundred of Beaminster-Forum and Redhone, Bridport division of the county of Dorset, 4½ miles (S. S. W.) from Chard, containing 1256 inhabitants. The living is a discharged vicarage, in the peculiar jurisdiction and patronage of the Prebendary of Chardstock in the Cathedral Church of Salisbury, rated in the king's books at £14. 2. 6. The church is dedicated to St. Andrew. A great quantity of cider is made in this parish: the river Ax runs through it.

CHARFIELD, a parish in the upper division of the hundred of Grumbald's Ash, county of Gloucester, 2¼ miles (N. by W.) from Wickwar, containing 344 inhabitants. The living is a rectory, in the archdeaconry and diocese of Gloucester, rated in the king's books at £10. 1. 3., and in the patronage of the Rev. R. P. Jones. The church, dedicated to St. James, is principally in the later style of English architecture, with a low tower.

CHARFORD (NORTH), a parish in the hundred of Fordingbridge, New Forest (West) division of the county of Southampton, 3½ miles (N. by E.) from Fordingbridge, containing, with the tything of South Charford, 132 inhabitants. The living is a perpetual curacy, in the archdeaconry and diocese of Winchester, rated in the king's books at £5. 13. 4. The church, which was dedicated to St. Peter and St. Paul, is in ruins. In the Saxon annals this place is called "Cerdickford," from Cerdic, who defeated the Britons near a ford on the Avon, and subsequently became the founder of the West Saxon kingdom.

CHARFORD (SOUTH), a tything in the parish of North Charford, hundred of Fordingbridge, New Forest (West) division of the county of Southampton, containing 75 inhabitants.

CHARING, a parish in the hundred of Calehill, lathe of Scray, county of Kent, 13½ miles (E. S. E.) from Maidstone, containing 1103 inhabitants. The living is a vicarage, in the diocese of Canterbury, exempt from archidiaconal jurisdiction, rated in the king's books at £13, and in the patronage of the Dean and Chapter of St. Paul's, London. The church, dedicated to St. Peter and St. Paul, consists of an aisle, a transept, a lofty chancel, with a chapel on the south side of it, and a square tower, with a small turret at one of the angles: it is chiefly in the later style of English architecture, and contains several ancient monuments; it sustained considerable injury from a fire in 1590. There is a place of worship for Wesleyan Methodists. Fairs are held on April 29th and October 29th, for horses, cattle, and pedlary. A free school, endowed with £30 per annum, was founded in 1761, by Elizabeth Ludwell, who also established two exhibitions, of the yearly value of about £35 each, at Oriel College, Oxford, with preference to natives of this parish. The archbishops formerly had a palace here, erected before the Conquest, the remains of which have been converted into a farm-house and out-offices. Various Roman antiquities and a Roman way have been discovered in the neighbourhood.

CHARLBURY, a parish comprising the chapelries of East Chadlington and Chilson, and the tything of West Chadlington, in the hundred of Chadlington, and the hamlets of Fawler, Finstock, and Wallcott, in the hundred of Banbury, county of Oxford, 6¾ miles (W. N. W.) from Woodstock, and containing 2877 inhabitants. The living is a vicarage, with the perpetual curacy of Shorthampton annexed, in the archdeaconry and diocese of Oxford, rated in the king's books at £25. 5. 10., and in the patronage of the President and Fellows of St. John's College, Oxford. The church is dedicated to St. Mary. There is a place of worship for Wesleyan Methodists. This was formerly a market town: four fairs are still held annually, on the 1st of January, the second Friday in Lent, and the second Friday after May 12th, for live stock; and on October 10th, for cheese and cattle. A free grammar school was founded by Mrs. Ann Walker, who endowed it with land, and placed it under the special visitation of the Principal and Fellows of Brasenose College, Oxford.

CHARLCOMBE, a parish in the hundred of Hampton and Claverton, locally in that of Bath-Forum, county of Somerset, 1½ mile (N.) from Bath, containing 124 inhabitants. The living is a discharged rectory, in the archdeaconry of Bath, and diocese of Bath and Wells, rated in the king's books at £5. 15. 10., and annexed to the mastership of the free grammar school at Bath, in the patronage of the Mayor and Corporation of Bath, as trustees. The church, dedicated to St. Mary, is a small ancient edifice, which tradition relates was formerly the mother church to Bath, and received an annual acknowledgment of a pound of pepper from the abbey there. At Thelesford, in this parish, a small priory of the order of the Holy Trinity, for the redemption of captives, was founded, in the reign of John, by Sir William Lucy, Knt.

CHARLCOTE, a parish in the Warwick division of the hundred of Kington, county of Warwick, 6 miles (N. W. by W.) from Kington, containing 331 inhabitants. The living is a discharged vicarage, in the archdeaconry and diocese of Worcester, rated in the king's books at £6, endowed with £200 private benefaction, and £400 royal bounty, and in the patronage of George Lucy, Esq. The church is dedicated to St. Leonard. This parish is bounded on the west by the river Avon, which, on the south, receives the tributary stream Heile. The mansion-house, of brick faced with stone, is a fine specimen of the style of domestic architecture that prevailed in the time of Elizabeth.

CHARLCOTT, a tything in the parish of Whitchurch, hundred of Evingar, Kingsclere division of the county of Southampton, ½ a mile (S. by E.) from Whitchurch, with which the population is returned. It is within the jurisdiction of the Cheyney Court held at Winchester every Thursday, for the recovery of debts to any amount.

CHARLES, a parish in the hundred of Sherwill, county of Devon, 5 miles (N. N. W.) from South Molton, containing 322 inhabitants. The living is a rectory, in the archdeaconry of Barnstaple, and diocese of Exeter, rated in the king's books at £9. 10., and in the patronage of the Rev. John Blackmore. The church is dedicated to St. John the Baptist.

CHARLESTOWN, a sea-port in the parish of St. Austell, eastern division of the hundred of Powder, county of Cornwall, 1 mile (E. S. E.) from St. Austell, with which the population is returned. There is a place of worship for Wesleyan Methodists. This place is situated on the western side of St. Austell bay, and in 1790, when known by the name of Porthmear, contained only nine inhabitants; but since that period, owing to the spirited exertions of Charles Rashleigh, Esq., to whom it owes its modern name, it has become a thriving port, and is still increasing in extent and importance. The harbour is secured by a commodious pier, and defended by a battery of heavy ordnance on Crinnis Cliff; it contains an outer and an inner basin, the latter being capacious enough to admit vessels of five hundred tons' burden. Here are yards and dry docks for building and repairing large ships, and a rope and twine manufactory: a great quantity of lime is burnt; but the chief trade of the place consists in its extensive pilchard fishery, for which several seans have been put on, and receiving-houses erected. Most of the china clay brought from St. Stephen's is shipped at this port.

CHARLESWORTH, a chapelry in the parish of Glossop, hundred of High Peak, county of Derby, 8½ miles (N. N. W.) from Chapel en le Frith, containing 1005 inhabitants. The chapel is dedicated to St. Mary Magdalene.

CHARLETON, a parish in the hundred of Coleridge, county of Devon, 2¼ miles (S. E.) from Kingsbridge, containing 618 inhabitants. The living is a rectory, in the archdeaconry of Totness, and diocese of Exeter, rated in the king's books at £31. 8. 4., and in the patronage of the Earl of Morley. The church is dedicated to St. Mary.

CHARLETON, a hamlet partly in the parish of Newbottle, and partly in that of King's Sutton, hundred of King's Sutton, county of Northampton, 4 miles (W. by S.) from Brackley. The population is returned with Newbottle. On a neighbouring hill, called Rainsborough, is a double-trenched oval camp, about half a mile in circumference, with the inner rampart more elevated than the outer, having two entrances on the north and two on the south; urns, glass vessels, and other relics have been discovered here; and a little to the eastward, near a smaller intrenchment, a gold coin of Vespasian has been found.

CHARLETON (QUEEN), a parish in the hundred of KEYNSHAM, county of SOMERSET, 2¾ miles (N.N.E.) from Pensford, containing 147 inhabitants. The living is a perpetual curacy, in the archdeaconry of Bath, and diocese of Bath and Wells, endowed with £1000 royal bounty, and in the patronage of Miss Dickenson. The church is dedicated to St. Margaret. This place obtained its distinguishing appellation from having been settled on Catherine Parr, queen of Henry VIII. The salubrity of the air made it anciently a place of considerable resort, particularly in 1574, when the plague swept away two thousand persons at Bristol. The road to Bath formerly passed through the village. A fair, granted by Elizabeth, on her progress through this place in 1573, is held annually on the 20th of July. In 1760, Mary Freeman left £500, producing £25 per annum, for clothing and teaching twenty boys, and for supplying them with books.

CHARLEY, an extra-parochial liberty, in the western division of the hundred of GOSCOTE, county of LEICESTER, 4¾ miles (S.W. by W.) from Loughborough, containing 42 inhabitants. The ancient forest of Charley, or Charnwood, twenty miles in circuit, was disforested soon after the Conquest; its privileges were restored by Henry II., but finally abolished by Henry III. A society of eremites, of the order of St. Augustine, settled here in the reign of Henry II., by the favour of Robert Blanchmains, Earl of Leicester; but in the time of Edward II. it was united to one at Ulvescroft, where a priory of regular canons, dedicated to the Blessed Virgin Mary, continued until the dissolution, when its revenue was estimated at £101. 3. 10.

CHARLEY, a township in the parish of FAREWELL, southern division of the hundred of OFFLOW, county of STAFFORD, 4 miles (W. by N.) from Lichfield. The population is returned with the parish.

CHARLINCH, a parish in the hundred of CANNINGTON, county of SOMERSET, 4½ miles (W. by N.) from Bridg-water, containing 251 inhabitants. The living is a rectory, in the archdeaconry of Taunton, and diocese of Bath and Wells, rated in the king's books at £9. 15. 5., and in the patronage of the Rev. Dr. Starky. The church is dedicated to St. Mary. Gothelney House, an old building of the fifteenth or sixteenth century, is now occupied as a farm-house.

CHARLTON, a hamlet in the parish and hundred of WANTAGE, county of BERKS, ¾ of a mile (N.E.) from Wantage, containing 215 inhabitants.

CHARLTON, a tything in that part of the parish of HENBURY which is in the upper division of the hundred of HENBURY, county of GLOUCESTER, 5½ miles (N.) from Bristol, containing 296 inhabitants.

CHARLTON, a parish partly in the hundred of BEWSBOROUGH, but chiefly within the liberty of the cinque-port of DOVOR (of which it is a member), lathe of ST. AUGUSTINE, county of KENT, 1 mile (N.N.E.) from Dovor, containing 790 inhabitants. The living is a discharged rectory, in the archdeaconry and diocese of Canterbury, rated in the king's books at £32, and in the patronage of the Rev. John Monins. The church, dedicated to St. Peter and St. Paul, has lately received an addition of two hundred and fifty-eight free sittings, the Incorporated Society for the enlargement of churches and chapels having granted £200 towards defraying the expense. Charlton, it is conjectured, was the *Portus Dubris* of the Romans, several anchors and fragments of wreck having been discovered at various times.

CHARLTON, a parish (formerly a market town) in the hundred of BLACKHEATH, lathe of SUTTON at HONE, county of KENT, 6½ miles (E.) from London, containing 1626 inhabitants. The living is a rectory, in the archdeaconry and diocese of Rochester, rated in the king's books at £10. 7. 8½., and in the patronage of Sir T. M. Wilson, Bart. The church, dedicated to St. Luke, was rebuilt of brick about 1640; it has a square embattled tower at the west end, and in the windows are various armorial bearings in stained glass; it contains some pieces of ancient armour, banners, and several handsome monuments, among which last is one to the memory of the Right Hon. Spencer Perceval, who was interred here. A charity school was built by Sir William Langhorn, who endowed it, in 1714, with a bequest of £300; it is conducted on the National system, and affords instruction to sixty boys and forty girls. Sir William also left £1000 to increase the rector's income. An infant school is supported by subscription, and there are four ancient almshouses. Charlton, in old records called *Cerletone* and *Ceorletone*, from *Ceorle*, the Saxon term for husbandman, is a neat village, situated on rising ground, commanding a fine prospect of the Thames. A weekly market on Monday, and a fair on Trinity eve, were formerly held here, under a grant from Henry III. to the monks of Bermondsey, who possessed the manor from the close of the eleventh century until the period of the dissolution of religious houses: the market has been long discontinued; the fair, now held on St. Luke's day, is termed Horn fair, from the numerous articles made of horn brought for sale from London. The jurisdiction of the court of requests for the recovery of debts under 40*s*., which is held alternately at Bromley, Greenwich, and Woolwich, extends over this parish, the inhabitants having the right to nominate six commissioners. Sir Thomas Wilson, as lord of the manor, holds a court leet occasionally. In the vicinity are many neat villas; and nearly opposite the church stands the manor-house, a spacious building crowned with turrets, erected in 1612, in front of which there is a row of cypresses said to be the first planted in England. In 1665, the neighbourhood suffered severely from the plague, and from a violent tempest.

CHARLTON, a hamlet in the parish and hundred of KILMERSDON, county of SOMERSET, 7 miles (N.W. by W.) from Frome. The population is returned with the parish. Here was formerly a chapel.

CHARLTON, a tything in the parish of SHEPTON-MALLET, hundred of WHITESTONE, county of SOMERSET, ½ a mile (E.S.E.) from Shepton-Mallet, with which the population is returned.

CHARLTON, a tything in the parish of SINGLETON, hundred of WESTBURN and SINGLETON, rape of

Chichester, county of Sussex, containing 199 inhabitants.

CHARLTON, a tything in the parish of Donhead St. Mary, hundred of Dunworth, county of Wilts, 2¾ miles (E. by S.) from Shaftesbury. The population is returned with the parish. Here was formerly a chapel.

CHARLTON, a parish in the hundred of Malmesbury, county of Wilts, 2¼ miles (N. E. by E.) from Malmesbury, containing 563 inhabitants. The living is a perpetual curacy, annexed to the vicarage of Westport St. Mary, in the archdeaconry of Wilts, and diocese of Salisbury. The church is dedicated to St. John the Baptist.

CHARLTON, a parish in the hundred of Swanborough, county of Wilts, 4 miles (S. W.) from Pewsey, containing 193 inhabitants. The living is a discharged vicarage, in the archdeaconry and diocese of Salisbury, rated in the king's books at £6. 15. 6., and in the patronage of the Dean and Canons of Christ Church, Oxford. The church is dedicated to St. Peter. Here was an Alien priory, founded in 1187, as a cell to the abbey of L'isle Dieu, and granted at the suppression of Alien houses to St. Katherine's Hospital, London. About a mile to the westward are the remains of an intrenched camp, with a spacious prætorium, called Casterley, the area of which, comprising sixty acres, is intersected from north to south by a broad fosse.

CHARLTON, a hamlet in the parish of Cropthorn, middle division of the hundred of Oswaldslow, county of Worcester, 5¼ miles (E. by S.) from Pershore, containing 277 inhabitants.

CHARLTON (ABBOT'S), a parish in the lower division of the hundred of Kiftsgate, county of Gloucester, 2¾ miles (S. by E.) from Winchcombe, containing 87 inhabitants. The living is a perpetual curacy, in the archdeaconry and diocese of Gloucester, endowed with £200 private benefaction, and £400 royal bounty, and in the patronage of Francis Pyson, Esq.

CHARLTON (CROSS), an extra-parochial liberty, in the hundred of Kilmersdon, county of Somerset, 5 miles (N.) from Frome.

CHARLTON (EAST), a township in the parish of Bellingham, north-western division of Tindale ward, county of Northumberland, 1¾ mile (N. W. by W.) from Bellingham, containing 143 inhabitants.

CHARLTON (KING'S), a parish in the hundred of Cheltenham, county of Gloucester, 2 miles (S. S. E.) from Cheltenham, containing 1607 inhabitants. The living is a perpetual curacy, in the archdeaconry and diocese of Gloucester, endowed with £1400 parliamentary grant, and in the patronage of the Principal and Fellows of Jesus' College, Oxford. The church, dedicated to St. Mary, has lately received an addition of two hundred and twenty sittings, of which one hundred and sixty are free, the Incorporated Society for the enlargement of churches and chapels having granted £200 toward defraying the expense. There is a place of worship for Baptists. A manorial court is annually held. The sum of £6 a year is paid to a schoolmaster for the instruction of six poor children, out of the rental of land producing £30 per annum, given by Samuel Cooper, about the year 1743; the remainder is applied to the relief of the poor. A day and Sunday school, in which upwards of one hundred children are taught, is supported by subscription. The amount of divers benefactions has also been laid out in the purchase of land, now producing £39 a year, which is distributed among the deserving poor. The new road to Cirencester passes through the parish. There is a hill called Battledowns, the scene of a battle during the parliamentary war, in which many of the inhabitants who adhered to the royal cause were slain. A mineral spring, similar in its properties to the Cheltenham water, has been lately discovered in this parish.

CHARLTON (NORTH), a township in the parish of Ellingham, southern division of Bambrough ward, county of Northumberland, 6½ miles (N. by W.) from Alnwick, containing 230 inhabitants. A school erected by John Cay, Esq. has been endowed with £5 per annum by Lord Crewe's trustees, and yearly benefactions amounting to about £4 in addition.

CHARLTON upon OTMORE, a parish in the hundred of Ploughley, county of Oxford, 5¾ miles (S. S. W.) from Bicester, containing, with the hamlet of Fencot with Murcot, 581 inhabitants. The living is a rectory, in the archdeaconry and diocese of Oxford, rated in the king's books at £21. 9. 4½., and in the patronage of the Provost and Fellows of Queen's College, Oxford. The church is dedicated to St. Mary.

CHARLTON (SOUTH), a township in the parish of Ellingham, southern division of Bambrough ward, county of Northumberland, 5½ miles (N. by W.) from Alnwick, containing 170 inhabitants. Here was formerly a chapel, but at present there are no remains.

CHARLTON (WEST), a township in the parish of Bellingham, north-western division of Tindale ward, county of Northumberland, containing 187 inhabitants.

CHARLTON-ADAM, a parish in the hundred of Somerton, county of Somerset, 3 miles (E.) from Somerton, containing 377 inhabitants. The living is a discharged vicarage, in the archdeaconry of Wells, and diocese of Bath and Wells, rated in the king's books at £6. 14. 7., endowed with £200 private benefaction, £200 royal bounty, and £300 parliamentary grant, and in the patronage of H. P. Collins, Esq. The church is dedicated to St. Peter and St. Paul. A chantry, or free chapel, dedicated to St. Stephen, was anciently founded here by Lord Henry Fitz-Richard, by permission of the prior of Brewton, under whom he held the manor. The old Roman Fosse-way from Bath to Ilchester proceeds through this parish.

CHARLTON-HORETHORNE, a parish (formerly a market town) in the hundred of Horethorne, county of Somerset, 5½ miles (S. W.) from Wincanton, containing 489 inhabitants. The living is a discharged vicarage, in the archdeaconry of Wells, and diocese of Bath and Wells, rated in the king's books at £8. 10. 5., and in the patronage of Charles Gilbert, Esq. The church is dedicated to St. Peter and St. Paul. In the 22nd of Edward I., a charter was obtained by Henry de Lacy, for a weekly market, and an annual fair on the eve and day of St. Thomas the Martyr; the market has been disused. There was anciently a chantry chapel within the manor, dependent on the priory of Kenilworth.

CHARLTON-MACKREL, a parish in the hundred of Somerton, county of Somerset, 3 miles (E.) from

Somerton, containing 309 inhabitants. The living is a rectory, in the archdeaconry of Wells, and diocese of Bath and Wells, rated in the king's books at £16. 0. 2½., and in the patronage of the Rev. W. P. Brymer. The church, dedicated to St. Martin, is a handsome edifice in the ancient style of English architecture, repaired and embellished at the expense of the present incumbent. This parish is bounded on the south by the river Cary, across which there is a bridge of two arches, on the line of a modern road that passes along the course of the old Roman Fosse-way.

CHARLTON-MARSHALL, a parish in the hundred of COGDEAN, locally in that of Pimperne, Shaston (East) division of the county of DORSET, 1¾ mile (S. S. E.) from Blandford-Forum, containing 304 inhabitants. The living is a perpetual curacy, annexed to the rectory of Spetisbury, in the archdeaconry of Dorset, and diocese of Bristol. The village is situated upon the navigable river Stour: poor children are entitled to participate in the benefit of education at Spetisbury free school.

CHARLTON-MUSGRAVE, a parish in the hundred of NORTON-FERRIS, county of SOMERSET, 1 mile (N. N. E.) from Wincanton, containing 366 inhabitants. The living is a rectory, in the archdeaconry of Wells, and diocese of Bath and Wells, rated in the king's books at £13. 10., and in the patronage of the Rev. Paul Leir. The church is dedicated to St. Stephen. Dr. William Musgrave, physician and antiquary, was born here, in 1657; he died in 1721.

CHARLWOOD, a parish in the first division of the hundred of REIGATE, county of SURREY, 7 miles (S. S. W.) from Reigate, containing 1134 inhabitants. The living is a rectory, in the peculiar jurisdiction of the Archbishop of Canterbury, rated in the king's books at £19. 16. 8., and in the patronage of the Rev. H. Wise. The church, dedicated to St. Nicholas, contains several ancient monuments of the family of Sanders and others. A charity school was founded, in 1637, by the Rev. John Bristow, and endowed with a house let for £8 per annum, for teaching four children. Within this parish is Kilman bridge, so termed from a sanguinary battle fought near it, between the Danes and the inhabitants of Surrey and Sussex, in which the former were totally defeated.

CHARMINSTER, a parish in the hundred of GEORGE, Dorchester division of the county of DORSET, 2 miles (N. W. by N.) from Dorchester, containing 556 inhabitants. The living is a perpetual curacy, with that of Stratton annexed, in the peculiar jurisdiction of the Dean of Salisbury, endowed with £400 royal bounty, and £200 parliamentary grant, and in the patronage of J. Trenchard, Esq. The church is dedicated to St. Mary.

CHARMOUTH, a parish in the hundred of WHITCHURCH-CANONICORUM, Bridport division of the county of DORSET, 2 miles (N. E. by E.) from Lime-Regis, containing 607 inhabitants. The living is a discharged rectory, in the archdeaconry of Dorset, and diocese of Bristol, rated in the king's books at £8. 16. 8., endowed with £200 private benefaction, and £200 royal bounty, and in the patronage of F. P. Henville, Esq. The church is dedicated to St. Matthew. The ancient village of Charmouth derives its name from being situated at the mouth of the river Char, over which there is a bridge; it lies on the coast of the Bristol channel, at the foot of a steep hill, round the north-western side of which the road was directed in 1758, and is considerably resorted to as a watering-place. The neighbouring cliffs abound with martial pyrites, bitumen, and other inflammable matter, which, after heavy rains, have been seen to burn with a vivid flame, particularly in the year 1751. Two sanguinary battles were fought here between the Danes and the Saxons; the first, in 833, ended in the retreat of the latter, under King Egbert, and the return of the former to their ships; the second, in 840, terminated also in the defeat of the Saxons, under King Ethelwolf, who commanded in person; but the Danes so little improved their victory, as to embark precipitately without booty. After the battle of Worcester, Charles II. and his suite fled hither, with an intention to escape into France; but having been disappointed, the monarch quitted the place; soon after which, a blacksmith having discovered, from the manner of shoeing the horse of Lord Wilmot, who had tarried behind, that the party came from the north, a pursuit was immediately commenced, but without success. In the 7th of Edward I. license was granted to the abbot of Ford for a weekly market on Monday, and a fair annually on the eve, day, and morrow of St. Matthew, to be held at this place.

CHARNDON, a hamlet in the parish of TWYFORD, hundred and county of BUCKINGHAM, 7¼ miles (W. S. W.) from Winslow, containing 165 inhabitants.

CHARNES, a township (formerly a chapelry) in the parish of ECCLESHALL, northern division of the hundred of PIREHILL, county of STAFFORD, 5 miles (N. W. by W.) from Eccleshall, containing 91 inhabitants. The chapel has been destroyed.

CHARNEY, a chapelry in that part of the parish of LONGWORTH which is in the hundred of GANFIELD, county of BERKS, 4½ miles (N. by W.) from Wantage, containing 243 inhabitants. The chapel is dedicated to St. Peter. In the vicinity is a circular fortification, called Cherbury Castle, surrounded by a double trench, resembling that of Badbury in Dorsetshire, and traditionally said to have been a castle belonging to Canute the Great.

CHARNHAM-STREET, a tything in that part of the parish of HUNGERFORD which is in the hundred of KINWARDSTONE, county of WILTS, containing 348 inhabitants.

CHARNOCK-HEATH, a township in the parish of STANDISH, hundred of LEYLAND, county palatine of LANCASTER, 3 miles (S.E.) from Chorley, containing 823 inhabitants.

CHARNOCK-RICHARD, a township in the parish of STANDISH, hundred of LEYLAND, county palatine of LANCASTER, 3 miles (S.W. by W.) from Chorley, containing 794 inhabitants.

CHARSFIELD, a parish in the hundred of LOES, county of SUFFOLK, 3½ miles (W. by N.) from Wickham-Market, containing 549 inhabitants. The living is a perpetual curacy, in the archdeaconry of Suffolk, and diocese of Norwich, endowed with £600 royal bounty, and in the patronage of W. Jennens, Esq. The church is dedicated to St. Peter. There is a place of worship for Particular Baptists.

CHART, a joint tything with Pitfold, in that part of the parish of FRENSHAM which is in the hundred of FARNHAM, county of SURREY, 5¼ miles (N.W.) from Haslemere, containing, with Pitfold, 710 inhabitants.

CHART (GREAT), a parish (formerly a market town) in the hundred of CHART and LONGBRIDGE, lathe of SCRAY, county of KENT, 2 miles (W. by S.) from Ashford, containing 659 inhabitants. The living is a rectory, in the archdeaconry and diocese of Canterbury, rated in the king's books at £25. 6. 0½., and in the patronage of the Archbishop of Canterbury. The church is dedicated to St. Mary. There is a place of worship for Wesleyan Methodists. This parish, called by the Saxons *Sybertes Chert,* and in Domesday-book termed *Certh,* lies chiefly on the Quarry hills, the southern part being within the Weald, the boundary of which runs east and west, to the north of the church. Chart, now a small village, was anciently of some importance, having had a weekly market, and a great fair on the 5th of April, for sheep and oxen; the market is disused, but the remains of the market-house were formerly visible in the field where the fair is still held: the town was burnt by the Danes. From its elevated position, the village commands an extensive and picturesque view of the surrounding country. On the 1st of May, 1580, a violent earthquake was felt here.

CHART (LITTLE), a parish in the hundred of CALEHILL, lathe of SCRAY, county of KENT, 2 miles (S.W. by W.) from Charing, containing 303 inhabitants. The living is a rectory, in the archdeaconry and diocese of Canterbury, rated in the king's books at £13. 10. 10., and in the patronage of the Archbishop of Canterbury. The church is dedicated to St. Mary.

CHART (SUTTON), a parish in the hundred of EYHORNE, lathe of AYLESFORD, county of KENT, 5 miles (S.E. by S.) from Maidstone, containing 500 inhabitants. The living is a vicarage, in the archdeaconry and diocese of Canterbury, rated in the king's books at £8. 12. 8½., endowed with £200 private benefaction, and £200 royal bounty, and in the patronage of the Dean and Chapter of Rochester. The church, dedicated to St. Michael, was, with its beautiful spire, destroyed by lightning in 1779, but has since been rebuilt; it stands near Sutton-Valence, on the summit of an eminence, the slope being occupied by the village. This parish, in Domesday-book called *Certh,* is intersected from east to west by the Quarry, or northern range of hills, here forming the boundary of the Weald: the southern declivity, both from its genial aspect and the richness of the soil, is well adapted to the culture of vines.

CHARTER-HOUSE on MENDIP, a district within the liberty of WITHAM FRIARY, though locally in the hundred of Winterstoke, county of SOMERSET, 5½ miles (E.N.E.) from Axbridge, containing 115 inhabitants. Here was a cell to the priory of Witham, which, as part of the possessions of that establishment, was granted away in the 36th of Henry VIII.

CHARTHAM, a parish in the hundred of FELBOROUGH, lathe of SCRAY, county of KENT, 3½ miles (S.W. by W.) from Canterbury, containing, with the chapelry of Horton, which is situated in the hundred of Bridge and Petham, 855 inhabitants. The living is a rectory, in the archdeaconry and diocese of Canterbury, rated in the king's books at £41. 5. 10., and in the patronage of the Archbishop of Canterbury. The church, dedicated to St. Mary, is of early decorated architecture, with very fine windows and some remains of richly stained glass: the roof is of wood and the tower of flint, both being of later date than the stone work: it contains a monumental arch and some old brasses, and in the chancel lie the remains of Dr. John Reading, chaplain to Charles I., and author of some religious tracts. There is a place of worship for Wesleyan Methodists. The river Stour, which is crossed near the village by an ancient bridge of five arches, called Shalmsford bridge, passes through the parish, in which there are paper and seed mills. Numerous tumuli, raised over the slain in the decisive conflict between Cæsar and Cassivelaunus, lie thickly scattered at the distance of about three quarters of a mile from the church, on the road to Canterbury, on opening which, urns, fibulæ, &c. have been discovered.

CHARTINGTON, a township in the parish of ROTHBURY, western division of COQUETDALE ward, county of NORTHUMBERLAND, 3¼ miles (N.W. by N.) from Rothbury, containing, with Bankland, 79 inhabitants. Here are the ruins of an ancient massive castle, that originally belonged to a family of the name of Cartington, long since extinct. An almshouse for Roman Catholic widows was founded by Lady Mary Charlton, who endowed it with a rent-charge of about £6.

CHARTLEY-LODGE, an extra-parochial liberty, in the southern division of the hundred of PIREHILL, county of STAFFORD, 7½ miles (N.E. by E.) from Stafford, containing 11 inhabitants.

CHARWELTON, a parish in the hundred of FAWSLEY, county of NORTHAMPTON, 6 miles (S.W. by S.) from Daventry, containing 232 inhabitants. The living is a rectory, in the archdeaconry of Northampton, and diocese of Peterborough, rated in the king's books at £20. 2. 11., and in the patronage of Sir Charles Knightley, Bart. The church, dedicated to the Holy Trinity, has a curious octagonal font supported on a square pedestal, and richly ornamented in a peculiar style.

CHASELEY, a parish forming, with the parishes of Eldersfield and Staunton, a separate portion of the lower division of the hundred of PERSHORE, county of WORCESTER, 3 miles (S.W. by W.) from Tewkesbury, containing 337 inhabitants. The living is a discharged perpetual curacy, in the archdeaconry and diocese of Worcester, rated in the king's books at £5. 14. 7., endowed with £200 private benefaction, and £200 royal bounty, and in the patronage of the Vicar of Longdon. The church, dedicated to St. John the Baptist, is an ancient edifice, with a tower and spire. Thomas Turberville, in 1728, left a house and land, the rent-charge upon which, with other charitable gifts, produces £17 per annum, which is applied to the education of girls.

CHASEWATER, a hamlet partly in the parish of ST. KEA, and partly in the parish of KENWYN, western division of the hundred of POWDER, county of CORNWALL, 5 miles (W. by S.) from Truro. A chapel is now being erected under the late act of parliament for building additional churches, towards defraying the expense of which the commissioners granted £3000; it will contain one thousand five hundred and four sittings, of which one thousand two hundred and two will be free. There is a place of worship for Particular Baptists. In the neighbourhood are several rich copper mines: the Chasewater mine has a steam-engine, which, at the time of its erection in 1813, was the most powerful then constructed: the adit of this mine, in its course of twenty-five miles, receives the waters of many others, and discharges itself into a creek in Falmouth harbour.

CHASTLETON, a parish in the hundred of CHADLINGTON, county of OXFORD, 5 miles (W. N. W.) from Chipping-Norton, containing 250 inhabitants. The living is a rectory, in the archdeaconry and diocese of Oxford, rated in the king's books at £9. 0. 2½., and in the patronage of P. T. Adams, Esq. The church is dedicated to St. Mary. A battle was fought here in 1016, between Edmund Ironside and Canute, when the latter was defeated with great slaughter. In the vicinity are vestiges of a Danish fortification.

CHATBURN, a township in that part of the parish of WHALLEY which is in the higher division of the hundred of BLACKBURN, county palatine of LANCASTER, 2¼ miles (N. E. by E.) from Clitheroe, containing 552 inhabitants.

CHATCULL, a township in the parish of ECCLESHALL, northern division of the hundred of PIREHILL, county of STAFFORD, containing 71 inhabitants.

CHATHAM, a market town and parish, partly within the jurisdiction, and adjoining the city, of ROCHESTER, but chiefly in the hundred of CHATHAM and GILLINGHAM, lathe of AYLESFORD, county of KENT, 8 miles (N. by E.) from Maidstone, and 30 (E. by S.) from London, containing 15,268 inhabitants. This place, anciently called *Ceteham* and *Cettham*, derives its name from the Saxon *Cyte*, a cottage, and *Ham*, a village, and, till it rose into importance as the seat of one of the principal naval arsenals in the kingdom, was, as its name implies, only an inconsiderable village of cottages. Previously to the Conquest, the lord of the manor espoused the cause of Harold, and for his loyalty to that prince was, after the accession of William, deprived of his possessions, which were conferred upon Crevecœur, one of the Normans who accompanied the Conqueror to England. The town is situated on the south-east bank of the river Medway, and on the north side of Chatham hill, and, though extensive, is irregularly built, partly from the nature of the ground, and partly from the large space occupied by its vast naval establishments. The dock-yard for the royal navy was commenced in the reign of Elizabeth; it then occupied the site of the present ordnance wharf, and was protected by Upnor castle, which that queen caused to be erected for its defence. In 1622, it was removed to its present situation, and greatly enlarged by Charles I., who erected capacious storehouses, and constructed new docks, to enable ships to float in with the tide: it was still further improved by Charles II., in whose reign the Dutch Admiral de Ruyter, having cast anchor at the Nore with fifty sail of the line, sent his vice-admiral, Van Ghent, with seventeen of his lightest vessels and eight fire-ships, to destroy the shipping in the river Medway. The vice-admiral attacked and took Sheerness, though gallantly defended by Sir Edward Spragge, blew up the fortifications, burnt the storehouses, and, sailing up the Medway with six of his men of war and five fire-ships, destroyed three vessels in the river, and came in front of Upnor castle, at that time defended by Major Scot, whose warm reception of the assailant frustrated his attempt on Chatham.

The dock-yard occupies an extensive area, nearly a mile in length, enclosed on the land side by a high wall, and defended by strong fortifications, principally of modern erection; the entrance is through a spacious gateway, flanked by two embattled towers. The houses of the commissioner and the principal officers are spacious and handsome buildings, and the various offices in the several departments of the yard are neat and commodiously arranged: the numerous storehouses, one of which is six hundred and sixty feet in length, contain an immense quantity of every article necessary for the building and equipment of ships of the largest dimensions, all arranged with such order and exactness, that upon any emergency a first-rate man of war may be equipped for sea in a few days. The mast-house is two hundred and forty feet in length, and one hundred and twenty feet wide; many of the masts deposited in it are three feet in diameter and forty yards in height; the timber for making them is constantly kept floating in two capacious basins. The new rope-house is one thousand one hundred and ten feet in length, and fifty feet wide; by the aid of powerful machinery, cables of great dimensions are twisted here, some of them being one hundred fathoms in length, and twenty-five inches in circumference: the sail-loft is two hundred and ten feet long: the smith's shop, where anchors of the largest size are made, of which some weigh five tons, contains forty forges, for the manufacture also of the iron-work necessary for ship-building. At the north-eastern extremity of the dock-yard are the saw-mills, recently erected on a very extensive scale, under the superintendence of Mr. Brunel, and worked with powerful machinery propelled by steam; in the sawing-room, which is ninety feet square, are fixed eight saw-frames, each capable of carrying from one to thirty saws, and two circular saw benches, with windlases and capstans for supplying them with wood, the whole set in motion by an engine which produces eighty strokes of the saws in a minute. To the north of the mills, where the ground is appropriated to the stowage of timber, is a canal, which, on entering the rising ground, passes under a tunnel, three hundred feet long, into an elliptic basin, forty-four feet deep, of which the longer diameter is ninety feet, and the shorter seventy-two, from which the timber, having been floated into the basin from the river by means of the canal, is raised by machinery with extraordinary velocity. Connected with the steam-engine of the saw-mills are extensive water-works, for the supply of the dock-yard; and on the iron pipes laid down for that purpose in various parts of the yard are fire-plugs, from which, when opened, rises a *jet d'eau* above the summits of the highest buildings. There are four wet docks sufficiently capacious for first-rate men of war; and a new stone dock upon a still larger scale has been recently constructed. There are six slips or launches for building ships of the largest dimensions. Among the many fine vessels launched from this dock-yard may be noticed, the Royal Sovereign, of one hundred guns, built just before the Restoration of Charles II.; the new Royal George, of one hundred guns, built in 1788; the Royal Charlotte, of one hundred guns; the Ville de Paris, of one hundred and ten; the Howe, of one hundred and twenty guns; the Trafalgar, of one hundred and four guns; and the Prince Regent, of one hundred and twenty guns: the Waterloo, of one hundred and twenty guns; the London, of ninety-two, and the Monarch, of eighty-four, are now on the slips. The principal officers of the establishment are, a commissioner (who is now the commissioner belonging to Sheerness), a master attendant, master shipwright, clerk of the cheque, store-keeper, clerk of the survey, clerk of the rope-yard, master rope-maker, master sail-maker, master boat-builder, master joiner, master blacksmith, master mason and bricklayer, master house-carpenter, master painter, boatswain, warden, and surgeon. In time of war the number of artificers and labourers employed in this dock-yard exceeds three thousand. Within the walls is a neat brick chapel, erected in 1811, at an expense of £9000, for the accommodation of the families resident within the limits of the yard, and of the division of Royal Marines in garrison here. The ordnance wharf occupies a narrow site of land between the church and the river, to the west of the dock-yard, and still called the Old Dock: the guns belonging to each ship are deposited in separate tiers, with the weight of metal and the name of the ship to which they belong marked on them: the gun-carriages are laid up under cover, and immense quantities of cannon-balls and bomb-shells are piled up pyramidally in various parts of the wharf: the armoury contains hostile weapons of every kind, ranged in admirable order. The principal officers of this establishment are a storekeeper and deputy storekeeper. A large building has lately been erected for the grinding of paint, and the rolling and smelting of lead by steam.

Prior to the year 1760, the defence of the arsenal was entrusted principally to guard-ships in the river; to forts erected on its banks, especially at Sheerness, which, after the attempt made by the Dutch in 1667, had been enlarged, with new fortifications, mounted with heavy ordnance; to Upnor castle, built by Queen Elizabeth; and to a small fort below Gillingham, erected by Charles I. In 1758, an act of parliament was passed for the purchase of land, and for the construction of such works as might be requisite for the perfect security of this important arsenal, under the provisions of which act, the extensive fortifications called the Lines were constructed: these works commence above the ordnance wharf, on the bank of the Medway, and are continued round an area one mile in extent from south to north, and half a mile from west to east (including the church of Chatham, the village of Brompton, which is principally inhabited by the artificers in the yard, and the barracks, magazines, &c.), to beyond the northern extremity of the dock-yard, where they again meet the river. These fortifications were enlarged during the American war, and strengthened by the erection of a strong redoubt on the summit of an eminence commanding the river. In 1782 another act was passed, for their further improvement, under which considerable additions have been made to the lines, and they are now considered to constitute, next to Portsmouth, the most complete and regular fortress in the kingdom. Forts Pitt and Clarence, two strong redoubts flanking the southern extremity of the lines, are situated on the heights overlooking the town, and commanding the upper part of the river; since the conclusion of the war, the former has been used as an hospital for invalids. The lower, or marine barracks, adjoining the upper extremity of the dock-yard, consist of a uniform range of brick building, enclosing a spacious quadrangle: the upper barracks, in Brompton, are also neatly built of brick, and are extensive and commodious: the new artillery barracks, built in 1804, are a fine range, forming three sides of a quadrangle, and containing apartments for the officers, lodgings for one thousand two hundred men, and requisite stabling; the open side of the quadrangle commands a fine view of the Medway in the fore-gound, and of the Thames in the distance: the artillery hospital, a neat building, erected in 1809, contains wards for one hundred patients, with convenient apartments and offices for the medical establishment. Near the entrance into the town from Rochester are the premises formerly used as a victualling-office, for supplying with provisions ships lying at Chatham, Sheerness, and the Nore; they were leased by government of the Dean of Rochester, and at the expiration of the lease were converted to private purposes. The town was much improved under the provisions of an act passed in 1772, for paving it, and for lighting it, but the streets are still very narrow and inconvenient for carriages. A Philosophical and Literary Institution was established in 1827, the members of which are about to erect a building for the reception of their library, and the collection of natural curiosities, antiquities, &c.: the expense is estimated at £2000. There are two subscription libraries, one the United Service library, and the other the Marine library. Races are held annually in August, on the extensive plain without the lines. The market is on Saturday: fairs, for three days each, are held on May 15th and September 19th. Chatham is partly within the jurisdiction of the county magistrates, and partly within the limits of the city of Rochester: it is also within the jurisdiction of a court of requests held at Rochester, for the recovery of debts under £5.

The living is a perpetual curacy, in the archdeaconry and diocese of Rochester, and in the patronage of the Dean and Chapter of Rochester. The church, dedicated to St. Mary, is a neat plain structure of brick; the original edifice having been destroyed by fire, at the commencement of the fourteenth century, a new one was built under the sanction of a bull from the pope, who granted an indulgence of one year and forty days to all who should contribute to the work; in 1635 it was repaired and enlarged for the increased population arising from the dock-yard, and the steeple was rebuilt by the commissioners of the royal navy; in 1788, the body of the church was taken down, and rebuilt of brick upon a larger scale, and the churchyard being found too small, the Board of Ordnance gave three acres of ground, at a short distance from the church, for a cemetery, which was consecrated in 1828. A new church of the Grecian Doric order, with a tower, and containing one thousand six hundred and twenty-four sittings, of which one thousand and ninety are free, was completed in 1821, at an expense of nearly £15,000, which was defrayed by the parliamentary commissioners. The living is a perpetual curacy, in the gift of the Perpetual Curate of Chatham. The living of the dock-yard chapel is a perpetual curacy, in the patronage of the Lords of the Admiralty. There are places of worship for Baptists, Independents, Wesleyan Methodists, and Unitarians. An edifice for a school was built in 1828, at an expense of £1600, defrayed by one hundred shareholders of £15 each, who have each the privilege, on payment of £6 per annum, of sending one boy to be instructed in the classics and in modern languages: the head-master has a salary of £300, the second one of

£150, and the third one of £100. A National school, chiefly supported by subscription, has a small endowment of about £6. 13. 4., arising from tenements bequeathed by Mrs. Elizabeth Petty, in 1723. Melville, or Marine hospital, is a handsome range of building at a short distance from Chatham, begun in 1827, and finished in the following year, at an expense of £70,000, for the use of the whole naval department; it is built of brick and stuccoed; the front consists of three pavilions, containing apartments for the accommodation of three hundred and forty patients; a colonnade extends the whole width, which is three hundred and twenty-two feet; and at the back are neat houses for the officers of the establishment. In 1078, Gundulph, Bishop of Rochester, founded and endowed an hospital for lepers, which he dedicated to St. Bartholomew, of which the chapel only is remaining: the estate has been vested in the Dean of Rochester, who is governor and patron: there are at present four brethren, two of whom are in holy orders, and officiate as chaplains. An hospital for decayed mariners and shipwrights was founded by Sir John Hawkins, in 1592, in which twelve pensioners have each a separate house, an allowance of eight shillings per week, and an annual supply of coal: the management is vested in twenty-six governors, of which number five are elective. A fund, commonly called the chest, for the relief of sailors who have been disabled in the service, was established by Sir Francis Drake and Sir John Hawkins, Knts., in 1588, when, after the defeat of the Spanish Armada, the seamen of the royal navy agreed to contribute a portion of their pay for the relief of their distressed brethren: this chest was removed to the royal hospital at Greenwich in 1802, and the management of the funds, which was vested in the principal naval officers, has been transferred to the first lord of the admiralty, the comptroller of the navy, and the governor of Greenwich hospital. Numerous Roman remains were discovered in forming the fortifications. Chatham gives the title of earl to the family of Pitt.

CHATHILL, a township in the parish of ELLINGHAM, southern division of BAMBROUGH ward, county of NORTHUMBERLAND, 9½ miles (N. by E.) from Alnwick, containing 27 inhabitants.

CHATLEY, a hamlet in that part of the parish of GREAT LEIGHS which is in the hundred of WITHAM, county of ESSEX, 4 miles (S. by W.) from Braintree, containing 486 inhabitants.

CHATSWORTH, an extra-parochial liberty, in the hundred of HIGH PEAK, county of DERBY, 3¼ miles (E. N. E.) from Bakewell. The population is returned with the parish of Edensor. Chatsworth, as part of the duchy of Lancaster, is within the jurisdiction of a court of pleas held at Chapel en le Frith, for the recovery of debts under 40*s*. The splendid mansion of Chatsworth was begun in 1687, and completed in 1706, by William Cavendish, first duke of Devonshire, upon the site of a more ancient edifice, which was taken down about the close of the seventeenth century, and in which Mary, Queen of Scots, passed a considerable portion of her long captivity in England. Sir John Gell garrisoned it for the parliament, in 1643, but capitulated to the Earl of Newcastle, who, in December of the same year, placed Col. Eyre, with a sufficient force, therein, to hold it for the king. In 1645, it withstood the siege of four hundred parliamentarians under Col. Gell, who, at the expiration of fourteen days, raised the siege, and retired to Derby. After the battle of Blenheim, in 1704, Marshal Tallard, the French general, having been made prisoner on that occasion, was sent to reside here.

CHATTERIS, a parish in the northern division of the hundred of WITCHFORD, Isle of ELY, county of CAMBRIDGE, 8¾ miles (E. by N.) from Ramsey, containing 3283 inhabitants. The living is a vicarage, in the peculiar jurisdiction of the Bishop of Ely, rated in the king's books at £10, and in the patronage of the Rev. Dr. Chatfield. The church is dedicated to St. Peter and St. Paul. There are places of worship for Particular Baptists and Wesleyan Methodists. The river Ouse forms a boundary of the parish. A Benedictine nunnery was founded and endowed, about the year 980, by Alfwen, wife of Earl Ethelstan, by the counsel of her brother Ednod, first abbot of Ramsey, who was afterwards raised to the see of Dorchester, and murdered by the Danes in 1016: its revenue, at the dissolution, was estimated at £112. 3. 6. Chatteris is a franchise under the Bishop of Ely, who holds a court leet for appointing officers, in a house called the guildhall, given to the parish, with other premises and lands, producing together nearly £70 per annum, which is distributed amongst infirm old men and widows. There is a National school, supported by subscription, wherein from two to three hundred children of both sexes are instructed. At Hunny farm are the subterraneous remains of a chapel, supposed to have contained the bones of St. Huna. In 1757, on opening a tumulus near Somersham ferry, several human skeletons, military weapons, an urn, and a glass vase were found.

CHATTERLEY, a township in the parish of WOLSTANTON, northern division of the hundred of PIREHILL, county of STAFFORD, 3½ miles (N.) from Newcastle under Line, containing 204 inhabitants.

CHATTISHAM, a parish in the hundred of SAMFORD, county of SUFFOLK, 4½ miles (E. by S.) from Hadleigh, containing 231 inhabitants. The living is a discharged vicarage, in the archdeaconry of Suffolk, and diocese of Norwich, rated in the king's books at £4. 13. 4., endowed with £200 private benefaction, and £200 royal bounty, and in the patronage of the Provost and Fellows of Eton College. The church is dedicated to All Saints and St. Margaret. There is a place of worship for Wesleyan Methodists. Here is a school with a small endowment for teaching six boys.

CHATTON, a parish in the eastern division of GLENDALE ward, county of NORTHUMBERLAND, 4 miles (E.) from Wooler, containing 1460 inhabitants. The living is a vicarage, in the archdeaconry of Northumberland, and diocese of Durham, rated in the king's books at £12. 16. 0½., and in the patronage of the Duke of Northumberland. The church, dedicated to the Holy Cross, was rebuilt about 1763. The parish contains coal and limestone.

CHAWLEY, a tything in the parish of CUMNER, hundred of HORMER, county of BERKS, 5½ miles (N. N. W.) from Abingdon, containing 70 inhabitants.

CHAWLEY, a parish in the hundred of NORTH TAWTON with WINKLEY, county of DEVON, 2 miles (S. E. by E.) from Chulmleigh, containing 792 inhabitants. The living is a rectory, in the archdeaconry of Barnstaple, and diocese of Exeter, rated in the king's books at £25. 14. 2., and in the patronage of the Hon. N. Fellowes. The church, dedicated to St. James, has a low steeple covered with oak shingles, and contains some elegant screen work. A charity school is liberally supported by subscription. Fairs for cattle are held May 6th and December 11th.

CHAWTON, a parish in the hundred of ALTON, Alton (North) division of the county of SOUTHAMPTON, 1¼ mile (S. S. W.) from Alton, containing 417 inhabitants. The living is a rectory, in the archdeaconry and diocese of Winchester, rated in the king's books at £11. 5. 5., and in the patronage of Edward Knight, Esq. The church is dedicated to St. Nicholas. One of the sources of the river Wey is in this parish. The village is situated in a valley watered by land springs, called Lavants, which occasionally spread over the adjacent lands.

CHEADLE, a parish in the hundred of MACCLESFIELD, county palatine of CHESTER, 3 miles (W. S. W.) from Stockport, comprising the townships of Cheadle-Bulkeley, Cheadle-Moseley, and Handforth with Boxden, and containing 6508 inhabitants. The living is a rectory, in the archdeaconry and diocese of Chester, rated in the king's books at £13. 0. 7½., and in the patronage of Sir J. D. Broughton, Bart. The church, dedicated to St. Mary, is principally in the later style of English architecture, with side aisles and a tower, and contains some monuments of the Brereton and Bulkeley families. There are places of worship for Methodists and Roman Catholics in this parish. The village, situated near the Bollin, is remarkable for the beauty and salubrity of its situation, and its very neat and cleanly appearance. The chief employment of the inhabitants is in the spinning, bleaching, and printing of cotton. There are two manors in the parish, Cheadle-Bulkeley and Cheadle-Hulme, or Moseley: for the former a court is held in October; and for the latter, on the first Thursday after June 24th. A school, built by subscription among the inhabitants, was endowed by John Robinson, in 1788, with land let for about £40 per annum; and Mr. Stubbs also bequeathed land for teaching children.

CHEADLE, a market town and parish in the southern division of the hundred of TOTMONSLOW, county of STAFFORD, 14 miles (N. N. E.) from Stafford, and 147 (N. W. by N.) from London, containing 3862 inhabitants. This place is situated in a valley environed by hills, which, though formerly barren, have been recently planted with forest trees, and are gradually assuming the appearance of verdure and cultivation. The town, which is intersected by the roads from Newcastle to Ashbourn, and from Leek to Uttoxeter, consists of one principal and four smaller streets; the houses are indifferently built: the inhabitants are supplied with water from a rivulet called the Tean, and from springs: the environs, though on the confines of the moor lands, are not unpleasant, and abound with numerous seats; the summit of a hill, called Monkhouse, to the west of the town, is a favourite walk, commanding an extensive prospect of the surrounding country. The principal branch of manufacture is that of tape, which is extensively carried on in the town; and adjoining it are large brass-wire works: the neighbourhood abounds with coal, and copper-ore has been discovered, though not in sufficient quantity to repay the expense of working the mine. The Caldon branch of the Trent and Mersey canal passes within four miles of the town, by Oakmoor, where some copper works have been established. The market is on Friday; a small square has been recently appropriated for the market-place: the fairs are on Holy Thursday and August 21st, for cattle. The living is a rectory, in the archdeaconry of Stafford, and diocese of Lichfield and Coventry, rated in the king's books at £12. 9. 2., and in the patronage of the Master and Fellows of Trinity College, Cambridge. The church, dedicated to St. Giles, is an ancient structure, principally in the decorated style of English architecture; and, though much mutilated and disfigured by alterations and repairs, it still retains some features of its original character: it has a square embattled tower crowned with pinnacles. There are places of worship for Independents, Wesleyan Methodists, the New Connexion of Methodists, or Kilhamites, and Roman Catholics. A charity school was founded, in 1685, by Mr. Stubbs, who endowed it with a rent-charge of £20, for the instruction of six children of this parish and six of the parish of Kingsley; to this endowment the trustees of Mr. Andrew Newton added £30, the interest of which is paid to the master, who has also a house rent-free: there are twelve scholars on the foundation, all of the parish of Cheadle, who are instructed in reading, writing, and arithmetic. Mr. Fowler, in 1663, gave a rent-charge of £6; Mr. Charles Beech, in 1726, bequeathed land and money producing together £26 per annum; and Mrs. Francis Grosvenor, of Hale Hall, in 1727, gave a rent-charge of £10, all for distribution among the poor.

CHEAM, a parish in the second division of the hundred of WALLINGTON, county of SURREY, 1½ mile (N. E. by E.) from Ewell, containing 792 inhabitants. The living is a rectory, in the exempt deanery of Croydon, which is within the peculiar jurisdiction of the Archbishop of Canterbury, rated in the king's books at £17. 5. 5., and in the patronage of the President and Fellows of St. John's College, Oxford. The church, dedicated to St. Dunstan, is a small structure built of flint; the chancel contains some monuments to the Lumley family, who were anciently lords of the manor, and one of whom sold his collection of books to James I., which laid the foundation of the royal library now in the British Museum. It is remarkable, that of six successive rectors between 1581 and 1662, five became bishops, namely, Watson, Andrews, Mountain, Senhouse, and Hackett. About half a mile south-west from the village was situated the magnificent palace called Nonsuch, begun by Henry VIII., and finished by Henry, Earl of Arundel, which was Queen Elizabeth's favourite seat, and kept up as a royal residence till the execution of Charles I., when it came into the possession of Algernon Sidney, and at the Restoration was granted to the Duchess of Cleveland, who pulled down the house and disparked the land. There is a vein of fine clay, useful for making moulds for casting metals and for tobacco pipes.

CHEAPSIDES, an extra-parochial liberty, in the wapentake of HOWDENSHIRE, East riding of the county of YORK, 5½ miles (E.) from Howden. The population is returned with Scalby.

CHEARSLEY, a parish in the hundred of ASHENDON, county of BUCKINGHAM, 3¼ miles (N. N. E.) from

Thame, containing 263 inhabitants. The living is a perpetual curacy, in the archdeaconry of Buckingham, and diocese of Lincoln, endowed with £600 royal bounty, and £200 parliamentary grant. The church is dedicated to St. Nicholas. This parish is supposed to have been the scene of a battle which Cerdic and Cynric fought with the Britons, in 527, mentioned in the Saxon Chronicle as having occurred at *Cerdicesleagh*.

CHEBSEY, a parish in the southern division of the hundred of PIREHILL, county of STAFFORD, 2 miles (E. by S.) from Eccleshall, containing, with the township of Cold Norton, 421 inhabitants. The living is a vicarage, in the archdeaconry of Stafford, and diocese of Lichfield and Coventry, rated in the king's books at £5. 7. 6., and in the patronage of the Dean and Chapter of Lichfield. The church is dedicated to all Saints: the cemetery formerly contained a tall pyramidal stone, supposed to be the memorial of a bishop who was reputed to have been anciently slain near this place. Chebsey is in the honour of Tutbury, duchy of Lancaster, and within the jurisdiction of a court of pleas held at Tutbury every third Tuesday, for the recovery of debts under 40*s*.

CHECKENDON, a parish in the hundred of LANGTREE, county of OXFORD, 6¾ miles (S. E.) from Wallingford, containing 295 inhabitants. The living is a rectory, in the archdeaconry and diocese of Oxford, rated in the king's books at £19. 9. 4½., and in the patronage of the Master and Fellows of University College, Oxford. The church is dedicated to St. Peter and St. Paul. This parish is entitled to send two poor men to the almshouse, and four poor children to the school, established at Goring, under the will of Mr. H. Allnutt, in 1724; it has also the right of sending four children to the school at Woodcote, founded by Mrs. Newman.

CHECKLEY, a joint township with Wrinehill, in the parish of WYBUNBURY, hundred of NANTWICH, county palatine of CHESTER, 7 miles (S. E. by E.) from Nantwich, containing, with Wrinehill, 211 inhabitants.

CHECKLEY, a parish in the southern division of the hundred of TOTMONSLOW, county of STAFFORD, 5½ miles (N. W. by W.) from Uttoxeter, containing, with the hamlet of Tean, and the liberty of Madeley-Holme, 2070 inhabitants. The living is a rectory, in the archdeaconry of Stafford, and diocese of Lichfield and Coventry, rated in the king's books at £20. 2. 6., and in the patronage of Thomas Hutchinson, Esq. The church, dedicated to St. Mary and All Saints, is an ancient structure, and contains a fine marble tomb, with recumbent figures. There are places of worship for Independents and Wesleyan Methodists. A large tape-manufactory, supposed to be the most extensive of its kind in Europe, was established here in 1748, the proprietors of which, aided by a trifling annuity, support schools for children of both sexes. A fair is held on Easter-Tuesday.

CHEDBURGH, a parish in the hundred of RISBRIDGE, county of SUFFOLK, 6¼ miles (S.W.) from Bury St. Edmund's, containing 240 inhabitants. The living is a discharged rectory, with that of Ickworth united, in the archdeaconry of Sudbury, and diocese of Norwich, rated in the king's books at £4. 2. 8½., and in the patronage of the Marquis of Bristol. The church is dedicated to All Saints: one hundred and forty sittings, eighty of them free, have been recently added, the Incorporated Society for the enlargement of churches and chapels having granted £150 for that purpose.

CHEDDER, a parish (formerly a market town) in the hundred of WINTERSTOKE, county of SOMERSET, 2½ miles (E.S.E.) from Axbridge, containing 1797 inhabitants. The living is a vicarage, within the peculiar jurisdiction and patronage of the Dean and Chapter of Wells, rated in the king's books at £23. 16. 8. The church, dedicated to St. Andrew, is a large and handsome structure, with a square tower one hundred feet high, surmounted by pinnacles. There is a place of worship for Wesleyan Methodists. This place is of considerable antiquity, having been the occasional residence of the Saxon monarchs, and in the possession of Alfred the Great, who bequeathed his hunting seat at Chedder, together with his *brugge* of Ax, and the wet moor, now Nedmore, to his son. The name is generally deduced from *Ced*, a brow or height, and *Dwr*, water; a broad, clear, and rapid stream flows through the parish, on which are some paper-mills. The village consists of three or four irregular streets, in one of which stands a dilapidated hexagonal market-cross; it was once a considerable market town, the grant having been made to Joceline, Bishop of Wells, in the 19th of Henry III., but it is now principally celebrated for its excellent cheese. Several of the inhabitants are employed in the manufacture of paper, and the knitting of worsted stockings. Fairs for horned cattle and sheep are held on May 4th and October 29th. In 1751, Sarah Comer bequeathed the residue of her estate, amounting to £6052 three per cents., producing an annual dividend of £181. 11. 4., which is under the direction of trustees, who pay one-fourth to the churchwardens for the relief of decayed housekeepers, one-fourth for distribution among the general poor, a fourth to a schoolmaster for instructing thirty-five boys and thirteen girls, and the remainder for apprenticing children. Chedder cliff, a vast chasm more than a mile in length, and appearing as if the mountain had been rent by an earthquake from the summit to the base, exhibits a combination of rocky precipices and gloomy caverns, some of the rocks towering eight hundred feet above the level of the valley. The principal cavern is about one hundred feet high at the entrance, and afterwards sinks three hundred feet beneath the rocks, branching out into several collateral apartments, and producing a perfect and pleasing echo: the sides and roof are covered with stalactites that have assumed a variety of fanciful forms. A carriage road winds through this valley, opening at intervals upon the wildest and most magnificent scenery, while huge masses of rock impend on each side, with threatening aspect. The hills above the village, in common with other parts of the Mendip range, abound with metallic ores, but they are not at present worked.

CHEDDINGTON, a parish in the hundred of COTTESLOE, county of BUCKINGHAM, 2 miles (N. W.) from Ivinghoe, containing 341 inhabitants. The living is a rectory, in the archdeaconry of Buckingham, and diocese of Lincoln, rated in the king's books at £15. 9. 7., and in the patronage of the Trustees of the Earl of Bridgewater. The church is dedicated to St. Giles.

CHEDDLETON, a parish in the northern division of the hundred of TOTMONSLOW, county of STAFFORD, 3 miles (S. by W.) from Leek, containing, with the townships of Basford and Cunsall, 1525 inhabitants. The living is a perpetual curacy, in the archdeaconry of Stafford, and diocese of Lichfield and Coventry, endowed with £300 private benefaction, and £200 royal bounty, and in the patronage of the Rev. Edward Powys. The church is dedicated to St. Edward. There is a place of worship for Wesleyan Methodists. The Caldon branch of the Trent and Mersey canal, and the Uttoxeter canal, pass through the parish; the latter terminates near the village. Here are coal and lime wharfs, a silk-throwing mill, and an ale and porter brewery. At a field near Ferry hill is the shaft of a very ancient cross, eleven feet high, standing on three circular stone steps. In 1724, James Whitehall bequeathed £200 for teaching children, and £30 to build a school-room, to which charity John Bagnall gave a rent-charge of £5, the whole yielding £13 per annum, which is paid to the master.

CHEDDON-FITZPAINE, a parish in the hundred of TAUNTON and TAUNTON-DEAN, county of SOMERSET, 2¾ miles (N. by E.) from Taunton, containing 272 inhabitants. The living is a rectory, in the archdeaconry of Taunton, and diocese of Bath and Wells, rated in the king's books at £13. 10. 10., and in the patronage of the Rev. F. Warre. The navigable river Tone runs on the south of the parish, and the Taunton and Bridgwater canal passes through it. A school for children of both sexes is supported by some small bequests, and is under the direction of the minister.

CHEDGRAVE, a parish in the hundred of LODDON, county of NORFOLK, 7 miles (N. W. by N.) from Beccles, containing 302 inhabitants. The living is a discharged rectory, in the archdeaconry of Norfolk, and diocese of Norwich, rated in the king's books at £5. 6. 8., and in the patronage of Sir W. B. Proctor, Bart. The church, dedicated to All Saints, has a fine Norman door, and the steeple stands at the north-eastern end.

CHEDINGTON, a parish in the hundred of BEAMINSTER-FORUM and REDHONE, Bridport division of the county of DORSET, 4 miles (N. by E.) from Beaminster, containing 164 inhabitants. The living is a rectory, in the archdeaconry of Dorset, and diocese of Bristol, rated in the king's books at £8. 8. 4., and in the patronage of William Hody Cox, Esq. The church is dedicated to St. James. Chedington is an upland and healthful village, with scarcely a level field within the bounds of the parish; the hills, which are principally composed of a hard durable fossil rock, afford rich views over the counties of Devon, Dorset, Somerset, and Wilts, and partially of the English and Bristol channels. On one of them are the remains of a Roman encampment; and in the fields below it, the site of a Roman villa. The river Axe separates the parish on the south and south-east from that of Beaminster.

CHEDISTON, a parish in the hundred of BLYTHING, county of SUFFOLK, 2 miles (W. by N.) from Halesworth, containing 427 inhabitants. The living is a discharged vicarage, united to the rectory of Halesworth, in the archdeaconry of Suffolk, and diocese of Norwich, rated in the king's books at £6. 7. 6. The church is dedicated to St. Mary.

CHEDWORTH, a parish in the hundred of RAPSGATE, county of GLOUCESTER, 5½ miles (W. S. W.) from North Leach, containing 975 inhabitants. The living is a vicarage, in the archdeaconry and diocese of Gloucester, rated in the king's books at £7. 8. 4., and in the patronage of the Provost and Fellows of Queen's College, Oxford. The church, dedicated to St. Andrew, contains a stone pulpit. In 1760, a Roman hypocaust was discovered at Lestercomb Bottom, in this parish, with a brick floor and pillars, a spring, and a cistern, the bricks of which bore the inscription "*a'rviri.*" On a hill a little above is a large tumulus, in which, on the removal of a large stone set upright at its mouth, a great quantity of human bones was exposed. The rental of about one hundred and fifty acres of land is applied to the support of two schoolmasters and the vicar. Chedworth gave title of baron to the family of Howe, which became extinct on the death of John, Lord Chedworth.

CHEDZOY, a parish in the northern division of the hundred of PETHERTON, county of SOMERSET, 2¾ miles (E. by N.) from Bridg-water, containing 472 inhabitants. The living is a rectory, in the archdeaconry of Taunton, and diocese of Bath and Wells, rated in the king's books at £38. 7. 11., and in the patronage of the Rev. Dr. Coney. The church is dedicated to St. Mary. Roman coins have frequently been discovered within this village; and, in 1701, some earthen urns and a fibula were dug up near the church. A slight shock of an earthquake was felt on January 4th, 1682.

CHEESEBURN-GRANGE, a township in the parish of STAMFORDHAM, north-eastern division of TINDALE ward, county of NORTHUMBERLAND, 11½ miles (N. W. by W.) from Newcastle upon Tyne, containing 101 inhabitants.

CHEETHAM, a chapelry in the parish of MANCHESTER, hundred of SALFORD, county palatine of LANCASTER, 1½ mile (N. by W.) from Manchester, containing 2027 inhabitants. The living is a perpetual curacy, in the archdeaconry and diocese of Chester, and in the patronage of the Rev. C. W. Ethelston, who built the chapel, a plain brick edifice, in 1793. There is a place of worship for Wesleyan Methodists, with a burial-ground and a school attached. A charity school has been erected and is supported by subscription.

CHELBOROUGH (EAST), a parish in the hundred of TOLLERFORD, Dorchester division of the county of DORSET, 5¾ miles (N. E. by E.) from Beaminster, containing 96 inhabitants. The living is a rectory, in the archdeaconry of Dorset, and diocese of Bristol, rated in the king's books at £8, and in the patronage of the Rev. Blakeley Cooper.

CHELBOROUGH (WEST), a parish in the hundred of TOLLERFORD, Dorchester division of the county of DORSET, 5½ miles (N. E. by E.) from Beaminster, containing 56 inhabitants. The living is a discharged rectory, in the archdeaconry of Dorset, and diocese of Bristol, rated in the king's books at £4. 15. 7½., and in the patronage of Lord Rolle.

CHELDON, a parish in the hundred of WITHERIDGE, county of DEVON, 3 miles (E. by S.) from Chulmleigh, containing 96 inhabitants. The living is a discharged rectory, in the archdeaconry of Barnstable, and diocese of Exeter, rated in the king's books at £4. 18. 6½., endowed with £200 private benefaction, and £200 royal bounty, and in the patronage of the Hon. N. Fellowes. The church is dedicated to St. Mary.

CHELFORD, a chapelry in the parish of PRESTBURY, hundred of MACCLESFIELD, county palatine of CHESTER, 5¼ miles (S. E. by E.) from Knutsford, containing 203 inhabitants. The living is a perpetual curacy, in the archdeaconry and diocese of Chester, endowed with £600 private benefaction, and £600 royal bounty, and in the patronage of Mr. Parker. The chapel was rebuilt in 1776. Five roads meet in the village; and the Birtles and Henbury brooks unite immediately below the chapel, forming a fine sheet of water, which empties itself into a brook called Peover-leye. A school was built by the late Rev. John Parker, who endowed it with about £17 per annum.

CHELL, a township in the parish of WOLSTANTON, northern division of the hundred of PIREHILL, county of STAFFORD, 3¾ miles (N. by W.) from Hanley, containing 400 inhabitants.

CHELLASTON, a parish in the hundred of REPTON and GRESLEY, county of DERBY, 4½ miles (S. E. by S.) from Derby, containing 338 inhabitants. The living is a perpetual curacy, in the archdeaconry of Derby, and diocese of Lichfield and Coventry, and in the patronage of the Bishop of Carlisle. The church, dedicated to St. Peter, is in the later style of English architecture; the tower has been replaced by a bell turret of wood. There is a place of worship for Wesleyan Methodists. The Derby canal passes in the vicinity. Chellaston is in the honour of Tutbury, duchy of Lancaster, and within the jurisdiction of a court of pleas held at Tutbury every third Tuesday, for the recovery of debts under 40*s*.

CHELLESWORTH, or CHELSWORTH, a parish in the hundred of COSFORD, county of SUFFOLK, 1¼ mile (S. W.) from Bildeston, containing 311 inhabitants. The living is a rectory, in the archdeaconry of Sudbury, and diocese of Norwich, rated in the king's books at £8. 8. 9., and in the patronage of the Crown. The church is dedicated to All Saints.

CHELLINGTON, a parish in the hundred of WILLEY, county of BEDFORD, 7 miles (N. E. by E.) from Olney, containing 121 inhabitants. The living is a rectory, united in 1769 to that of Carlton, in the archdeaconry of Bedford, and diocese of Lincoln, rated in the king's books at £10. The church is dedicated to St. Nicholas.

CHELMARSH, a parish in the hundred of STOTTESDEN, county of SALOP, 4 miles (S. by E.) from Bridgenorth, containing 458 inhabitants. The living is a discharged vicarage, in the archdeaconry of Salop, and diocese of Hereford, rated in the king's books at £6. 5. 8., and in the patronage of Sir J. Sebright, Bart. The church is dedicated to St. Peter. The navigable river Severn runs at a short distance eastward from the village.

CHELMERTON, a chapelry in the parish of BAKEWELL, hundred of HIGH PEAK, county of DERBY, 4¼ miles (S. W. by S.) from Tideswell, containing 262 inhabitants. The living is a perpetual curacy, in the peculiar jurisdiction of the Dean and Chapter of Lichfield, endowed with £200 private benefaction, and £600 royal bounty, and in the patronage of the Vicar of Bakewell. The chapel has some remains of a rood-loft and screen work. There are meeting-houses for Wesleyan Methodists and Presbyterians. The village is situated at the foot of an eminence, on the summit of which are two barrows, close to each other, the circumference of the larger being about two hundred and forty feet; in this, when opened in 1782, several human skeletons were discovered, in rude stone coffins, with bones and teeth perfect. The manufacture of ribands is carried on here. There is a charity school, to which Mr. Brocklehurst, who died in 1792, gave £200, now vested in the commissioners of the Leek and Burton road, and producing £13 per annum, which is applied to the instruction of fifteen children. Chelmerton is in the honour of Tutbury, duchy of Lancaster, and within the jurisdiction of a court of pleas held at Tutbury every third Tuesday, for the recovery of debts under 40*s*.

CHELMONDISTON, a parish in the hundred of SAMFORD, county of SUFFOLK, 6¼ miles (S. S. E.) from Ipswich, containing 366 inhabitants. The living is a discharged rectory, in the archdeaconry of Suffolk, and diocese of Norwich, rated in the king's books at £8. 10., and in the patronage of the Crown. The church is dedicated to St. Andrew. The navigable river Orwell forms the northern boundary of this parish.

CHELMSFORD, a market town and parish in the hundred of CHELMSFORD, county of ESSEX, of which it is the chief town, 29 miles (N. E. by E.) from London, on the road to Yarmouth, containing, with the hamlet of Moulsham, 4994 inhabitants. This place, which is within a short distance of the *Cæsaromagus* of the Romans, derives its name from an ancient ford on the river Chelmer, near the natural confluence of that river with the Cann, into which its stream is previously diverted by an artificial channel near the bridge. In the reign of Edward the Confessor, and at the time of the Norman survey, it was in the possession of the bishops of London; and two buildings, still called Bishop's Hall and Bishop's Mill, seem to indicate its having been either permanently, or occasionally, their residence. In other respects it was an inconsiderable place till the reign of Henry I., when Maurice, Bishop of London, built a stone bridge of three arches over the river Cann; and, diverting the road, which previously passed through Writtle, made Chelmsford the great thoroughfare to the eastern parts of the county, and to Suffolk and Norfolk. From this period the town increased in importance; and its trade so much improved, that, in the reign of Edward III., it sent four representatives to a grand council at Westminster. A convent for Black, or Dominican, friars was established at an early period, the foundation of which has been erroneously attributed to Malcolm, King of Scotland: in this convent, of which only the site is visible, Thomas Langford, a friar, compiled a Universal Chronicle, from the creation to his own time: its revenue, at the dissolution, was £9. 6. 5. During the late war with France, two extensive ranges of barracks, for four thousand men, were erected near the town, both of which have been taken down; and at a short distance from it, a line of embankments, defended by star batteries, was raised to protect the approaches to the metropolis from the eastern coast, of which some traces are still remaining.

The town consists of one principal and three smaller streets, well paved, and lighted with gas; the houses, several of which, on both sides of the town, have gardens extending to the river, are in general modern and well built; and the inhabitants are amply supplied with water from a spring at the distance of half a mile, conveyed by pipes into a reservoir, over which is a handsome dome, supported on six columns of the Doric order. It has been much improved under the inspection of commissioners appointed by act of parliament, whose powers were extended by a subsequent act obtained in 1822. A handsome iron bridge has been recently constructed over the Chelmer; and an elegant stone bridge, of one fine arch, was erected in 1787, over the river Cann, connecting the town with the hamlet of Moulsham, and replacing an ancient bridge erected by Bishop Maurice, which, though calculated to endure for ages, had become too narrow in the improved state of the approaches to the town. The theatre, a neat and commodious edifice, is opened occasionally: assemblies and concerts take place periodically in the shire-hall; and races, which continue for three days, are held in the latter part of July, on Galleywood common, about two miles from the town, where there is an excellent two-mile course, of which one mile has been recently improved at a considerable expense, and on which a stand has been erected, capable of accommodating two hundred persons. The trade consists principally in corn, which is sent to London, and in the traffic arising from the situation of the town as a great public thoroughfare: there are several large corn-mills on the banks of the Chelmer. A navigable canal to the river Black-water, twelve miles distant, was constructed in 1796, and has greatly contributed to increase the trade. The market is on Friday, for corn, cattle, and provisions: fairs are held on May 12th and November 12th, the latter principally for cattle.

The town is within the jurisdiction of the county magistrates, who hold petty sessions for the division every Tuesday and Friday; and constables and other officers are appointed at the court leet of the lord of the manor, who also holds a court baron occasionally. The assizes and sessions for the county, and the election of knights for the shire, are regularly held here. The shire-hall is an elegant and commodious structure, fronted with Portland stone, and having a rustic basement, from which rise four handsome pillars of the Ionic order, supporting a triangular pediment: the upper part of the front is ornamented with appropriate figures, in basso relievo, of Wisdom, Justice, and Mercy; in the lower department are the several court-rooms, and an area for the use of the corn market; and in the upper part is a spacious assembly-room, extending the whole length of the building, over which are rooms for the grand jury and witnesses, and other apartments. The old county gaol, a spacious and handsome stone building in the hamlet of Moulsham, was completed in 1777, at an expense of upwards of £18,000: it comprises different departments for the classification of prisoners; in the front is the gaoler's house, and within the walls an infirmary and a chapel; the prisoners are employed in various kinds of work, the profits of which are applied toward the support of the establishment: it is appropriated exclusively to the reception of persons confined for debt, and of prisoners committed for trial. Adjoining the gaol, and incorporated with it, is the house of correction, now used only for convicted female prisoners: it was built in 1806, at an expense of about £7500. The new house of correction at Springfield Hill, on the road to Colchester, is a very extensive and well arranged building of brick, ornamented with stone, begun in October 1822, and completed in 1825, at an expense of £55,739. 17. 0¾., and capable of containing two hundred and fifty-four prisoners, of whom two hundred and eighteen may be confined in separate cells: it comprises seven distinct ranges of building, radiating from a spacious area comprehending, with the site of the buildings, nearly nine acres, in the centre of which is the governor's house, including a neat chapel, and commanding a view of fourteen yards, for the proper classification of the prisoners; in eight of these yards are tread-wheels, together furnishing labour for two hundred and thirteen at one time; in two others are capstans, and, in one, a windlass and machinery for raising water: there are fourteen day-rooms, two of which are used as workshops for shoemakers, eight store-rooms, one of which is used as a work-room for tailors, an infirmary, a lazaretto, a bath, and other requisite offices. Two of the tread-wheels are attached to a mill which grinds corn for the use of this prison, the county gaol, and the house of correction at Barkins: the profits of the tread-mill, from the 1st of July, 1828, to the 30th of June, 1829, were £220. 13. 5½.

The living is a rectory, in the jurisdiction of the Commissary of Essex and Herts, rated in the king's books at £31. 2. 6., and in the patronage of Lady St. John Mildmay. The church is dedicated to St. Mary; the body has been lately rebuilt, at an expense of £15,000, the former having fallen down in 1800, from the unskilfulness of some workmen, who, in digging a vault, undermined two of the principal pillars: it is a stately structure in the later style of English architecture, with a square embattled tower crowned with pinnacles and surmounted by a lofty spire. In this church the archdeacon holds his court, and the wills and records of grants of administration are deposited in an office over the south porch. A collection of books, presented by Dr. Plume, of Maldon, for the use of the clergy resident in the neighbourhood, is kept in the chancel, the east end of which is ornamented with a finely painted window, representing the Incarnation, Crucifixion, and Resurrection of our Saviour, and figures of the four Evangelists. There are two places of worship for Independents, and one each for the Society of Friends and Wesleyan Methodists. The free grammar school was founded and endowed, in 1552, by Edward VI.: in addition to the classics, a course of English instruction has been introduced. This school, in common with those at Maldon and Brentwood, has an exhibition of £6 per annum to Caius College, Cambridge: the management is vested in four hereditary trustees. The school-house was rebuilt by R. Benyon, Esq., in 1782, on the site of a more ancient one erected by Sir John Tyrrell, Bart. Philemon Holland, translator of Camden's Britannia, and a native of Chelmsford; John Dee, a celebrated mathematician; Sir William Mildmay, Bart., founder of Emanuel College, Cambridge; and Dr. Plume, Archdeacon of Rochester, received the rudiments of their education in this establishment. A charity school, for the maintenance, clothing, and instruction of fifty boys, founded in 1713; and a similar school for twenty girls, founded in 1714, are supported by subscription: there are also a Lancasterian, a National, and an infant school, for children of both sexes. Six almshouses in the hamlet of Moulsham, founded by Sir Thomas and Lady Mildmay, in 1565, were rebuilt by William Mildmay, Esq., in 1758: four almshouses in Baddow-lane, erected by the sale of a barn given by William Davis, in 1520, for the use of the poor, have also been rebuilt, and two tenements added at the expense of the parish.

CHELSEA, a parish in the Kensington division of the hundred of Ossulstone, county of Middlesex, containing, with part of the chapelry of Knightsbridge, 26,860 inhabitants. This place was anciently called *Chelcheth*, or *Chelchith*, probably from the Saxon *Ceosl*, or *Cesol*, sand, and *Hythe*, a harbour, from which its present name is derived. In 785, a synod for the reformation of the religion in England was assembled here by the legates of Pope Adrian. The beauty of its situation on the Thames, which is wider here than in any part above London bridge, made it, at an early period, the residence of illustrious persons, whose superb mansions procured for it the appellation of the village of palaces. Among these was the residence of the chancellor, Sir Thomas More, at the north end of Beaufort-row, which, after being successively in the occupation of several distinguished characters, was taken down by Sir Hans Sloane in the year 1740. The bishops of Winchester had a palace at the upper end of Cheyne-walk, which, under an act of parliament passed in 1823, enabling the bishop to alienate it from the see, was taken down in 1824. Queen Elizabeth had a palace here; and Sir Robert Walpole resided for some time in a mansion previously belonging to the crown, on the site of which a fine edifice was erected, in 1810, by General Gordon. The mansion and gardens of the Earl of Ranelagh were converted into a place of public amusement, which, after having been fashionably attended for a considerable time, was closed in 1805, and the buildings taken down; the site is now occupied by dwelling-houses. Chelsea comprehends the old town on the bank of the river, over which is a bridge of wood leading to Battersea in Surrey, and the new buildings erected since 1777, and called Hans Town, in honour of Sir Hans Sloane, a former lord of the manor. In the old town is Cheyne-walk, containing many handsome and substantial houses, commanding an interesting view of the Thames and the scenery on its opposite bank: in the new town are, Sloane-street, a regular range of respectable houses, nearly a mile in length, Sloane-square, and Upper and Lower Cadogan-places: the streets are partially paved, and well lighted with gas, under the superintendence of forty commissioners, including the rector and the churchwardens, appointed annually by act of parliament obtained about the year 1820; the inhabitants are supplied with water by the Chelsea Water Works Company, incorporated in 1724. The Botanical Gardens were established in 1673, by the Company of Apothecaries, to whom Sir Hans Sloane granted, at a quit-rent of £5 per annum, four acres of ground on the bank of the river; they contain a great variety of medicinal plants systematically arranged, a hothouse, greenhouses, and a library in which are many volumes of natural history: lectures are delivered periodically to the students, by a demonstrator appointed for that purpose: in the centre of the gardens is a fine statue of Sir Hans Sloane, by Rysbrach; and in front of the river are two remarkably fine cedars of Libanus. A second botanic garden, occupying more than six acres, well stocked with plants arranged after the Linnæan system, in seventeen compartments, was established in 1807, near Sloane-street, where lectures are delivered annually in May and June.

The Royal Hospital for veteran soldiers, a spacious and handsome structure of brick, ornamented with columns, quoins, and cornices of stone, erected after a design by Sir Christopher Wren, at an expense of £150,000, towards defraying which Sir Stephen Fox, the projector, and grandfather of the Rt. Hon. C. J. Fox, contributed £13,000, was begun in the reign of Charles II., and completed in that of William III.: the buildings occupy a spacious quadrangle, in the centre of which is a fine statue in bronze of Charles II.; the east and west sides, which are three hundred and sixty feet in length, comprise wards for the pensioners, and the governor's house; in the centre of the north side is a large vestibule, lighted by a handsome dome, with the great hall on one side, in which the pensioners dine, and on the other, the chapel, a neat and lofty edifice, containing a handsome altar-piece, in which is a good painting of the Resurrection; the south side of the quadrangle is open to the river, affording a fine view of the extensive gardens, which reach to its margin: there are smaller quadrangles, in which are the infirmaries and various offices, formed by the addition of wings to the extremities of the north side of the large quadrangle: on the north side of the college is an enclosure of thirteen acres, planted with avenues of trees. The establishment consists of a governor, lieutenant-governor, a major, adjutant, deputy-adjutant, treasurer, secretary, two chaplains, a physician, surgeon, apothecary, comptroller, steward, clerk of the works, and subordinate officers: the number of in-pensioners is about five hundred, and the number of out-pensioners indefinite; the annual expenditure is from £700,000 to £800,000. York hospital, situated in this parish, is a receptacle for wounded soldiers arriving from foreign stations, who are waiting for a vacancy in the royal college. The Royal Military Asylum was founded, in 1801, by His Royal Highness the late Duke of York, for the support and education of the orphan children of soldiers, and of those whose fathers are serving on foreign stations: there are seven hundred boys and three hundred girls, who are instructed, on Dr. Bell's plan, in reading, writing, and arithmetic, and the latter in needle-work; the boys, on leaving the asylum, enter the army with their own consent; the girls are placed out apprentices. The premises, which are handsomely built of brick, and ornamented with stone, form three sides of a quadrangle: the west front consists of a centre, with a handsome stone portico of the Doric order, connected with two wings by an arcade. There are two soap-manufactories, a brewery, and an extensive floor-cloth manufactory: a considerable trade is carried on in coal; and in the neighbourhood are large tracts of ground cultivated by market-gardeners. The county magistrates hold a petty session here for the hundred every Tuesday; and four headboroughs, nine constables, and other officers, are appointed at the court held for the manor.

The living is a rectory, in the archdeaconry and diocese of Middlesex, rated in the king's books at £13. 6. 8., and in the patronage of Earl Cadogan. The old church, dedicated to St. Luke, is a small edifice, partly in the early and partly in the decorated style of English architecture, with a low tower surmounted by a campanile turret; it is chiefly of brick, and was rebuilt in the early part of the sixteenth century: at the end of the north aisle is a chapel in the decorated style, and at the extremity of the south aisle is a chapel erected by Sir Thomas More, in 1520: the church was enlarged and the tower added about the year 1670. Among the many interesting monuments are those of Sir Thomas More; Dr. Edward Chamberlayne, author of "The present State of England;" Thomas Shadwell, poet-laureat in the reign of William and Mary; Sir Hans Sloane, and others. A new church, also dedicated to St. Luke, and containing two thousand and five sittings, of which nine hundred and twenty-seven are free, was erected in the year 1824, at an expense of £40,000, of which the parliamentary commissioners granted £8,785. 12. 4.; it is a magnificent structure in the decorated and later styles of English architecture, with a lofty square tower crowned with dome turrets at the angles; the west front is strikingly beautiful, and the aisles are surmounted by a pierced parapet, continued round the architrave of the east end, which is decorated with minarets: the interior has an impressive grandeur of effect, arising from the loftiness of the nave, which has a triforium and a fine range of clerestory windows, and is separated from the aisles by clustered columns and pointed arches of graceful elevation. The old parish church is now used as a chapel: the living is a perpetual curacy, in the patronage of the Rector of Chelsea. The chapel in Sloane-street, containing one thousand four hundred and two sittings, of which six hundred and fifty are free, was erected in 1830, at an expense of £5849. 17. 4., by grant from the parliamentary commissioners: it is a handsome edifice in the later style of English architecture, with two minaret turrets at the west end: the living is a perpetual curacy, in the patronage of the Rector of Chelsea. An episcopal chapel, called Park chapel, was built by Sir Richard Manningham, in 1718. There are two places of worship for Baptists, three for Independents, and one for Wesleyan Methodists. In 1694, John Chamberlayne, Esq. gave £10 per annum, of which £5 was to be paid to a master, for teaching five poor children, one of them to be apprenticed to a waterman, with a premium of £5; and in 1705, William Petys erected a school-room in the old churchyard, with a dwelling for the master; there are forty scholars, of whom thirty are clothed, and two apprenticed annually by the above legacy, aided by subscription. The National school in connexion with Park chapel, and the Chelsea National school, in which one hundred and fifty boys and eighty girls are instructed, are supported by subscription: for the latter, a handsome range of buildings, comprising two large school-rooms, between which are houses for the master and mistress, has been erected behind the new church, and in a style corresponding with the architecture of that splendid structure, to which they form no inelegant appendage. The western grammar school, recently established, was opened in 1829: the funds requisite for its erection and maintenance were subscribed in shares of £15, each holder, on the payment of a small sum, being entitled to present one pupil, who receives a classical and liberal education on moderate terms. Mrs. Martha Bromsall, in 1804, gave a house and premises, the proceeds from the sale of which have been vested in the purchase of £315 new four per cents.; the dividends are distributed among poor housekeepers: there are some other bequests for charitable purposes. John King, A. M., editor of some of the tragedies of Euripides; and Dr. Thomas Martyn, Regius Professor of Botany at Cambridge, and a distinguished writer on botany, were natives of this parish.

CHELSFIELD, a parish in the hundred of Ruxley, lathe of Sutton at Hone, county of Kent, 6¼ miles (S. E.) from Bromley, containing 756 inhabitants. The living is a rectory, in the archdeaconry and diocese of Rochester, rated in the king's books at £24. 14. 2., and in the patronage of the Warden and Fellows of All Souls' College, Oxford. The church, dedicated to St. Mary, is in the early style of English architecture, with a tower and spire at the north-east angle of the nave. At Farnborough, in this parish, there is a chapel of ease. There is a small endowment for the instruction of children.

CHELSHAM, a chapelry in the parish of Warlingham, second division of the hundred of Tandridge, county of Surrey, 7 miles (S. E.) from Croydon, containing 217 inhabitants. The chapel, dedicated to St. Leonard, is in the early style of English architecture. On Bottle hill, in this neighbourhood, are the remains of a Roman camp, of an oblong form, and surrounded by a single trench.

CHELTENHAM, a market town and parish in the hundred of Cheltenham, county of Gloucester, 8 miles (E. N. E.) from Gloucester, and 95 (W. N. W.) from London, containing, according to the last census, 13,396 resident inhabitants, since which the number has increased to about 22,000. This place takes its name from the small river Chilt, which rises at Dowdswell, in the vicinity, and runs through the town in its course to the Severn. Prior to the Conquest, the manor belonged to Edward the Confessor, and was afterwards held by the Conqueror; in 1199 it was granted to Henry de Bohun, Earl of Hereford, who exchanged it with King John for other lands: it was next given to the abbey of Feschamp in Normandy, and subsequently to the nunnery of Sion in Middlesex, on the dissolution of which it reverted to the Crown. Cheltenham derives its importance from the mineral springs, the oldest of which was noticed in 1716: since that time various others have been discovered, possessing different proportions of chalybeate, aperient salts, chiefly sulphate of soda, sulphate of magnesia, and oxyde of iron held in solution by carbonic acid; the last was discovered in 1803, by Dr. Thomas Jameson, according to whose analysis it contains a greater proportion of sulphureous gas than the others, and, in many instances, bears a strong affinity to the Harrogate water: they are efficacious in the cure of jaundice and other diseases of the liver, in dyspepsia, and in complaints arising from the debilitating influence of hot climates. In 1721, the old well, or spa, to the south of the town, was enclosed, and in 1738 Captain Henry Skillicorn erected over it a brick pavilion, supported on four arches, built a pump-room, and laid out walks for the accommodation of visitors. In 1780, the number of lodging-houses amounted only to thirty; but since the visit of George III., in 1788, Cheltenham has been rapidly rising into note as a fashionable place of resort, and is at present eminent for the elegance of its buildings, the extent and variety of its accommodations, and the rank and number of its visitors, of whom, in the course of the season, there are generally not less than fifteen thousand.

The town is pleasantly situated on an extensive plain, sheltered on the north and east by the Cotswold hills, and consists of numerous fine streets, the principal of which is more than a mile and a half in length, containing many handsome ranges of building, interspersed occasionally with houses of more ancient date and less pretending character: to the south are a crescent and colonnade, and the upper and the lower promenade, lately built; and on each side are dwellings, displaying much beauty and variety of architectural decoration. The masonic hall, in Portland-street, is a handsome edifice in the style of a Roman mausoleum, completed in 1823, and decorated in front and on one side with the insignia of the order of free masonry. The streets are well paved, and lighted with gas, by an act passed in the 59th of George III., and amended in the 2nd of George IV.: the Gas-light and Coke Company was formed pursuant to an act passed in 1819; and in 1824 an act was obtained for the establishment of water-works, under the direction of a company. About half a mile toward the south is the Montpelier spa: the pump-room, a spacious and handsome rotunda, has a noble colonnade in front, above the centre of which is the figure of a lion couchant; adjoining it is a long room with a viranda, and part of the building is fitted up as a conservatory. Near this spa a very handsome range of houses has been built, and a new road formed, leading more directly into the town, at the expense of P. Thompson, Esq. Nearer the town, in the same direction, is the Imperial spa, an elegant building in the Grecian style of architecture, opened in 1818; in front of the pump-room is a portico of the Ionic order, copied from a temple on the bank of the river Ilissus at Athens, and over the centre is a colossal statue of the Goddess of Health. The old well, or original spa, has been enlarged by the erection of a new pump-room in 1803. There are also the old chalybeate spa, opened in 1802; the Cambray chalybeate spa, discovered in 1807; and Alstone spa, opened in 1809. On the north side of Cheltenham is Pittville, where a new town has been planned, on a magnificent scale, by Joseph Pitt, Esq.: the pump-room, of which the first stone was laid on the 4th of May, 1825, is a splendid edifice, in the erection of which more than £20,000 has been expended; the centre of this building, which is crowned with a finely proportioned dome, embellished with richly painted glass, is decorated with a beautiful colonnade of the Ionic order, surmounted by a statue of Hygeïa; and the wings are ornamented with statues of Æsculapius and Hippocrates: in front are extensive gardens, tastefully laid out; and at the foot of the hill on which it stands is a fine sheet of water, terminated at each end by a bridge of fanciful architecture. There are warm, cold, medicated, and vapour baths, furnished with every appendage requisite for their use, and under the direction of experienced persons; hotels of the first order, affording every accommodation; and several hundred lodging-houses, many of which are splendidly fitted up for the reception of visitors of the highest rank. The various libraries, reading-rooms, and musical repositories, are richly stored and well conducted: concerts and assemblies take place regularly during the season, under the superintendence of a master of the ceremonies, in a splendid suite of rooms completed in 1816. The theatre has been rebuilt upon a more enlarged plan, and is opened regularly by the Cheltenham company: races take place annually in July, on an adjoining eminence.

The trade, exclusively of the ordinary business necessary for the supply of the inhabitants and the numerous visitors, consists principally in malt and in various kinds of medicinal salts, for the preparation of which latter there is an extensive manufactory on the road to Bath. Coal is brought from Staffordshire, Shropshire, and the Forest of Dean, by the river Severn to Gloucester, whence it is conveyed by a rail-road to the wharfs at the western extremity of the town. The market is on Thursday and Saturday: the fairs are on the second Thursday in April, August 5th, the second Thursday in September, and the third Thursday in December, for cattle and cheese; there are also statute fairs on the first and second Thursday after Michaelmas day. The market-house, a handsome and commodious building, was erected in 1823, at the expense of Lord Sherborne; it is approached by an arcade from the High-street. The town is within the jurisdiction of the county magistrates, who hold a petty session for the division at the public office, every Tuesday, Thursday, and Saturday; a high bailiff and constables are appointed at the court leet of the lord of the manor; and the local affairs are under the control of commissioners appointed by an act passed in the 2nd of George IV. By an ancient manorial custom, confirmed by act of parliament, land descends as by common law, but the eldest female inherits solely. The new gaol, near St. George's square, is a convenient edifice, erected in 1814.

The living is a perpetual curacy, in the archdeaconry and diocese of Gloucester, and in the patronage of the Society for the purchase of Livings. The church, dedicated to St. Mary, is an ancient cruciform structure, in the early, decorated, and later styles of English architecture, with a square tower rising from the intersection and surmounted by a lofty octagonal spire; on the east side of the north transept is a grand circular window, fifteen feet in diameter, divided into thirty-three compartments, and filled with tracery of the decorated and later styles intermixed; the east window of the chancel and others are also fine compositions: an antique altar-piece, presented by the Dean and Chapter of Gloucester, has been lately erected; there is also a piscina in the chancel: the churchyard, which is extensive, is planted with double rows of lime-trees; and there is an ancient stone cross of one single shaft, with an ascent of several steps. The church of the Holy Trinity, in Portland-street, a handsome structure in the later style of English architecture, was erected by subscription, having been finished by Lord Sherborne, and was consecrated in 1823: St. John's, in Berkeley-place, was built at the expense of the present incumbent: another church has lately been erected in Suffolk-square; the living of each of these is a perpetual curacy, in the patronage of trustees elected by the subscribers, for a term of forty years, at the expiration of which the right of presentation becomes vested in the Perpetual Curate of Cheltenham. A new free church is also just completed, at an expense of £6500, half of which has been defrayed by a grant from the parliamentary commissioners, the remainder having been raised by subscription among the inhabitants. A new burial-ground has also been purchased by the parishioners, but it has not yet been enclosed. There are places of worship for Baptists, the Society of Friends, those in the connexion of the late

Countess of Huntingdon, Independents, Wesleyan and other Methodists, and Roman Catholics.

The free grammar school was founded and endowed, in 1574, by Richard Pates, Esq.; the endowment, augmented by Queen Elizabeth, produces, in addition to a rent-free residence, a salary of £30 per annum to the master, who is appointed by the President and Fellows of Corpus Christi College, Oxford. There are eight scholarships in Pembroke College, Oxford, founded in 1682 by George Townsend, Esq., for boys from Gloucester, Cheltenham, Chipping-Campden, and North Leach, with preference in presentation to his donatives of Uxbridge and Colnbrook: the same benefactor also founded and endowed a school here, for the instruction of poor boys in reading, writing, and arithmetic, and similar schools in the parishes of Winchcombe, Chipping-Campden, North Leach, and Nether Guyting, or Blockley, for apprenticing whom he appropriated part of the income, which amounts to £207 per annum; the apprentice-fee, originally £5, is, according to circumstances, augmented to £15 or £20. The Rev. William Stansby, in 1704, gave land producing £25 per annum, subject to a rent-charge of £8, the residue being applied to the same purpose. A portion of an endowment by Lady Capel, amounting to £37. 10. per annum, is paid to a schoolmaster for the instruction of poor children. The National school, a school for girls under the patronage of the Bishop of Gloucester, and an infant school, the building for which was erected in 1830, are supported by subscription. Almshouses for six aged persons were founded and endowed by Richard Pates, Esq., in 1574. The dispensary and casualty ward, established in 1813, and lately enlarged, is supported by subscription; and there are many other charitable institutions, among which may be noticed the female orphan asylum, the Cobourg society for the relief of indigent married women in child-birth, and the Dorcas society: there is also a bank for savings.

CHELVESTON, a parish in the hundred of HIGHAM-FERRERS, county of NORTHAMPTON, 2 miles (E. by N.) from Higham-Ferrers, containing, with Caldecott, 317 inhabitants. The living is a perpetual curacy, united to the vicarage of Higham-Ferrers, in the archdeaconry of Northampton, and diocese of Peterborough. The church is dedicated to St. John the Baptist. There is a small endowment for the instruction of children.

CHELVEY, a parish in the hundred of HARTCLIFFE with BEDMINSTER, county of SOMERSET, 8 miles (W. S. W.) from Bristol, containing 62 inhabitants. The living is a discharged rectory, in the archdeaconry of Bath, and diocese of Bath and Wells, rated in the king's books at £4. 9. 7., and in the patronage of Lady Anne Tynte. The church is dedicated to St. Bridget.

CHELWOOD, a parish in the hundred of KEYNSHAM, county of SOMERSET, 2 miles (S. E.) from Pensford, containing 222 inhabitants. The living is a discharged rectory, in the archdeaconry of Bath, and diocese of Bath and Wells, rated in the king's books at £5. 7. 6., and in the patronage of the Bishop of Bath and Wells. The church is dedicated to St. Leonard; the tower was rebuilt in 1772. There is an endowed chapel belonging to the Independents. The parish contains extensive mines of coal.

CHELWORTH, a tything in the parish of ST. SAMPSON, borough of CRICKLADE, hundred of HIGHWORTH, CRICKLADE, and STAPLE, county of WILTS, 1¼ mile (S. W.) from Cricklade. The population is returned with the parish.

CHENIES, a parish in the hundred of BURNHAM, county of BUCKINGHAM, 5 miles (E. by N.) from Amersham, containing 595 inhabitants. The living is a rectory, in the archdeaconry of Buckingham, and diocese of Lincoln, rated in the king's books at £12. 16. 0½., and in the patronage of the Duke of Bedford. The church is dedicated to St. Michael. There is a place of worship for Particular Baptists. The old manor-house, which formerly belonged to the Cheynes, lords of the manor, and was much improved by Lord Russell, in the time of Henry VIII., yet exists at the west end of the church. Attached to it is a chapel, built in 1556, by Anne, Countess of Bedford, according to the will of her deceased lord, John, Earl of Bedford, which is used as a place of sepulture by the family; in the vault underneath are upwards of fifty coffins, with inscriptions bearing date from 1591 to 1819. Here is a large paper-mill. A National school has been established, and there is an hospital for ten poor persons, founded and endowed in 1603, by Anne, Countess of Warwick, daughter of the second earl of Bedford. John Russell, Esq., ancestor of his Grace the Duke of Bedford, was raised to the peerage in 1538-9, by the title of Baron Russell of Cheyneys, which his descendants have continued to bear.

CHEPSTOW, a port, market town, and parish, in the upper division of the hundred of CALDICOTT, county of MONMOUTH, 15 miles (S. by E.) from Monmouth, and 131 (W.) from London, containing 3008 inhabitants. This place, called by the Britons *Câs Gwent*, and by most antiquaries supposed to have risen from the ruins of the ancient city *Venta*, about four miles to the west, derives its present name from the Saxon *Chepe*, a market, and *Stowe*, a town: it obtained also the name Striguil from the earls of Pembroke, to whom it belonged at the time of the Conquest, and who, from their residing in a neighbouring castle of that name, were called lords of Striguil, by which designation the manorial courts are still held. Soon after the Conquest, a strong castle was erected, probably by William Fitz-Osborn, Earl of Hereford, on the summit of a rocky precipice overhanging the river Wye, of which there are considerable remains richly overspread with ivy, and forming a picturesque and stately object from various points of view. About the same time the town was fortified with strong walls of considerable extent, several portions of which, together with the bastions erected for their defence, are still remaining. In the reign of Stephen, a priory of Benedictine monks was founded here, and dedicated to St. Mary, the revenue of which, at the dissolution, was £32. 4. During the parliamentary war, the inhabitants adhered firmly to the royal cause, and the castle was not surrendered to the parliamentarian forces till after a vigorous siege, in which it sustained considerable damage. On the Restoration of Charles II., Henry Marten, one of those who sat in judgment on Charles I., was confined in the castle till his death.

The town is beautifully situated on the river Wye, near its confluence with the Severn, and is built on the slope of a hill, among the lofty cliffs that rise abruptly from the western bank of the river: a handsome iron bridge has been erected over the Wye, at the joint expense of the counties of Gloucester and Monmouth, of which the river forms the line of separation: it consists of several spacious and well paved streets, in which are many handsome well built houses, and is lighted with oil, towards defraying the expense of which the late J. Bowcher, Esq. bequeathed £1000; but it is very ill supplied with water, the inhabitants being obliged to procure it at the distance of a mile and a half. There is a small theatre, opened occasionally. The trade principally consists in navy timber, oak-bark, and iron; ship-building is carried on to a considerable extent, for which there are convenient docks on the banks of the Wye. The river, at spring tides, rises to the height of sixty feet at Chepstow bridge, and affords convenient access to the harbour: seventy-two ships, of an aggregate burden of five thousand eight hundred and five tons, belonged to the port in 1829: in 1826, the number of vessels entered inwards from foreign parts was thirteen British, and of those cleared outwards, three. The market days are Wednesday and Saturday; and there are also great markets on the last Monday in every month for horses, cattle, sheep, pigs, and wool: the fairs are on the Friday and Saturday in Whitsun-week, the Saturday before June 20th, August 1st, and the Friday before October 29th. The county magistrates here hold petty sessions for the division. The old passage over the Severn, within two miles of the town, has been greatly improved by the erection of stone piers, and the establishment of a regular steam-packet by some gentlemen in the neighbourhood, assisted by the Duke of Beaufort, who is lord of the manor; it may now be crossed with safety at any time of the tide: the ferry is under the direction of a superintendent, and governed by salutary regulations.

The living is a discharged vicarage, in the archdeaconry and diocese of Llandaff, rated in the king's books at £6. 16. 8., endowed with £200 private benefaction, and £200 royal bounty, and in the alternate patronage of Edward Bearan, Esq. and Mrs. Burr. The church, dedicated to St. Mary, and formerly the conventual church of the priory, exhibits a fine specimen of Norman architecture at the western entrance, and contains the tomb of Marten, who died in the castle. There are places of worship for Baptists, Independents, Wesleyan Methodists, and Roman Catholics. A charity school for thirteen poor children was endowed with land, in 1605, by Richard Clayton, Esq. A National school for an unlimited number of children of both sexes, and a philanthropic institution, are supported by subscription. Sir William Montagu's hospital, for thirteen aged persons, was founded by that gentleman, in 1614, and endowed with land. Powis' almshouse, for six men and six women, was founded, in 1716, by Thomas Powis, Esq., who bequeathed £1800 for its erection and endowment.

CHERHILL, a parish in the hundred of Calne, county of Wilts, 3 miles (E.) from Calne, containing 346 inhabitants. The living is a perpetual curacy, annexed to the vicarage of Calne, in the peculiar jurisdiction of the Treasurer in the Cathedral Church of Salisbury. The church is dedicated to St. James. On the summit of a hill near the village is Oldborough, or Oldbury, camp, to which it is supposed the Danes retreated after the battle of Ethandune; and on its slope is the figure of a white horse, one hundred and fifty-seven feet long, in the attitude of trotting, cut out of the turf on the chalk rock; it was executed about forty years ago, under the direction and at the expense of Dr. Christopher Allsop, an eminent physician of Calne, and from its lofty situation, this being the highest land between London and Bath, is visible at the distance of twenty or thirty miles, in almost every direction. There is a small endowment for the instruction of children.

CHERINGTON, a parish in the Brails division of the hundred of Kington, county of Warwick, 3¾ miles (S.E.) from Shipston upon Stour, containing 316 inhabitants. The living is a rectory, in the archdeaconry and diocese of Worcester, rated in the king's books at £11. 10. 7½., and in the patronage of the Rev. R. Nicholl. The church is dedicated to St. John the Baptist.

CHERITON, a parish in the hundred of Folkestone, lathe of Shepway, county of Kent, 2¼ miles (W. by N.) from Folkestone, containing, exclusively of the officers and men employed in the preventive service, 1121 inhabitants. The living is a rectory, with the vicarage of Newington united, in the archdeaconry and diocese of Canterbury, rated in the king's books at £16. 12. 6., and in the patronage of J. D. Brockman, Esq. The church, dedicated to St Martin, is in the early style of English architecture.

CHERITON, a parish in the hundred of Fawley, Fawley division of the county of Southampton, 2½ miles (S. by W.) from New Alresford, containing, with the tything of Beaworth, 599 inhabitants. The living is a rectory, with the perpetual curacies of Kilmeston and Titchbourn annexed, in the peculiar jurisdiction of the incumbent, rated in the king's books at £66. 2. 6., and in the patronage of the Bishop of Winchester. The church is dedicated to St. Michael. A battle was fought here in the reign of Charles I., called Alresford fight. The parish is within the jurisdiction of the Cheyney Court held at Winchester every Thursday, for the recovery of debts to any amount. Twenty poor children are instructed by a schoolmistress, for £12 per annum, the produce of a bequest by the Rev. Morgan Jones.

CHERITON (BISHOP), a parish in the hundred of Wonford, county of Devon, 6¼ miles (S. W.) from Crediton, containing 753 inhabitants. The living is a rectory, in the archdeaconry and diocese of Exeter, rated in the king's books at £22. 13. 4., and in the patronage of the Bishop of Exeter. The church is dedicated to St. Mary.

CHERITON (NORTH), a parish in the hundred of Horethorne, county of Somerset, 3 miles (S.W. by S.) from Wincanton, containing 216 inhabitants. The living is a discharged rectory, in the archdeaconry of Wells, and diocese of Bath and Wells, rated in the king's books at £8. 12. 1., and in the patronage of the Rev. Thomas Gatehouse. The church is dedicated to St. John the Baptist.

CHERITON (SOUTH), a hamlet in the parish of Horsington, hundred of Horethorne, county of Somerset, 3¼ miles (S.S.W.) from Wincanton. The population is returned with the parish. Here was formerly a chapel, but it has been demolished.

CHERITON-FITZPAINE, a parish in the western division of the hundred of Budleigh, county of Devon, 4¾ miles (N.E. by N.) from Crediton, containing 1002 inhabitants. The living is a rectory, in the archdeaconry and diocese of Exeter, rated in the king's books at £37. 6. 8., and in the patronage of — Harris, Esq. The church is dedicated to St. Mary. The tythings of Bradley and Fulford are partly in this parish, but are wholly returned with the parish of Crediton. There is an almshouse for six poor people, founded and endowed in 1594, by Andrew Scott, besides a small endowed charity school.

CHERRINGTON, a parish in the hundred of LONGTREE, county of GLOUCESTER, 4 miles (N. N. E.) from Tetbury, containing 215 inhabitants. The living is a rectory, in the archdeaconry and diocese of Gloucester, rated in the king's books at £13, and in the patronage of Mr. and Mrs. Brettingham. The church, dedicated to St. Nicholas, is a small ancient edifice, with a nave, chancel, south transept, and low tower at the west end, exhibiting, in some parts, traces of the early English style. The Rev. Joseph Trapp, Professor of Poetry at Oxford, and the translator of Virgil, was born here, in 1672; he died in 1747. There is a trifling endowment for teaching poor children.

CHERRINGTON, a township in the parish of EDGMOND, Newport division of the hundred of BRADFORD (South), county of SALOP, containing 192 inhabitants.

CHERTSEY, a market town and parish in the second division of the hundred of GODLEY, county of SURREY, 13 miles (N. N. E.) from Guildford, and 20 (W. S. W.) from London, containing 4279 inhabitants. At this place Cæsar is supposed, on landing in Britain, to have crossed the Thames to attack Cassibelaunus, King of the Trinobantes, whose army had encamped on the opposite shore: the stakes driven into the bed of the river to obstruct the passage of the Roman legions were, according to Bede, remaining in the eighth century, and vestiges of them may still be traced about a quarter of a mile below the bridge. During the Octarchy, the South Saxon kings had their residence in this town; and it became noted for a Benedictine monastery, founded in 666, by Erkenwald, afterwards Bishop of London, which, having been burnt to the ground in the war with the Danes, was refounded by King Edgar, and dedicated to St. Peter. In this abbey Henry VI. was privately interred; but his remains were subsequently removed, and deposited, with appropriate solemnities, in the royal chapel at Windsor. At the dissolution, its revenue was £774. 13. 6.: some portions of the outer walls remain, and on the site, and with part of the materials, of the abbey a private mansion, called the Abbey House, has been erected. The town is pleasantly situated upon the Thames, over which is a handsome stone bridge of seven arches, built in 1785, at an expense of £13,000, defrayed jointly by the counties of Surrey and Middlesex: the houses are in general neatly built of brick; the streets are partially paved, but not lighted; and the inhabitants are plentifully supplied with water from springs. The trade is principally in malt and flour; the manufacture of coarse thread, and the making of iron hoops and brooms, are carried on to a considerable extent; a great quantity of bricks is also made in the neighbourhood. The Guildford and Petworth canal passes within two miles of the town, and joins the river Wey at Weybridge, affording a facility of conveyance for the several articles of manufacture, and for a great quantity of vegetables, which are cultivated in the environs for the London market. The market, chartered by Queen Elizabeth in 1559, is on Wednesday: the fairs are on the first Monday and Tuesday in Lent, for cattle; May 14th, for sheep; and August 6th and September 25th, for toys and pedlary: a court of pie-powder is attached to the fair in Lent. The town is governed by a bailiff, appointed for life by letters patent from the Exchequer, and, together with the hundred, is exempt from the jurisdiction of the high sheriff for the county, but is within that of the county magistrates, who hold a meeting for the division on the first and third Wednesdays in every month. Headboroughs and other officers are appointed at the court leet of the lord of the manor, held on Tuesday in Whitsun-week, who also holds a court baron on the following day at Hardwick Court, now a farm-house, but once the manorial mansion, in which Henry VI. resided when a child.

The living is a vicarage, in the archdeaconry of Surrey, and diocese of Winchester, rated in the king's books at £13. 12. 4., and in the patronage of the Master and Wardens of the Haberdashers' Company, as trustees to certain orphans. The church, dedicated to All Saints, a handsome structure in the later style of English architecture, with a square embattled tower, was rebuilt by subscription in 1808: it contains a tablet to the memory of the celebrated statesman, Charles James Fox, and several monuments to the Mawbey family. There are places of worship for Baptists, Methodists, and Presbyterians. A charity school, originally for the instruction and clothing of twenty-five boys and twenty-five girls of this and the adjoining parishes of Thorpe, Egham, and Cobham, was founded, in 1725, by Sir William Perkins, who, during his lifetime, appropriated two houses for school-rooms, and, at his decease, endowed them with £3000 Bank Stock; this sum, augmented by an accumulating annual surplus, being vested in the same and other species of stock, produces at present nearly £400 per annum: the school, by permission of the court of Chancery, has been extended, upon the National plan, for the instruction of two hundred and thirty boys and one hundred and thirty girls, of whom thirty of each sex belonging to this parish are clothed. There are some almshouses, which are at present chiefly under the management of the overseers. The tolls and profits arising from stallage in the market and fairs were granted by Queen Elizabeth to the poor, for whose benefit there are also various other charitable benefactions. Near the town is St. Anne's hill, commanding an extensive prospect, formerly the residence of the late Rt. Hon. Charles James Fox, and now occupied by his widow, in which are some tesselated pavements collected from the ruins of the abbey: the water of St. Anne's well was formerly in repute for its efficacy in curing diseases of the eye. The poet Cowley lived for some time in an ancient house in the town, called the Porch House, in which he died: Mr. Day, author of "Sandford and Merton," also resided in the vicinity.

CHESEL, a hamlet in the parish of WEST WINTERSLOW, hundred of ALDERBURY, county of WILTS, 8 miles (E. by N.) from Salisbury. The population is returned with the parish. About a mile from this place is a curious earthwork, of an oval form, containing five acres, and supposed to have been a Roman amphitheatre; on the north side is a large rampart.

CHESELBORNE, a parish in the hundred of WHITEWAY, Cerne subdivision of the county of DORSET, $10\frac{1}{2}$ miles (S. W. by W.) from Blandford-Forum, containing 336 inhabitants. The living is a rectory, in the archdeaconry of Dorset, and diocese of Bristol, rated in the king's books at £18. 10. 5., and in the patronage of Lord Rivers. In the churchyard is an ancient stone cross.

CHESHAM, a market town and parish in the hundred of BURNHAM, county of BUCKINGHAM, 30 miles (S.E.) from Buckingham, and 29 (N. W. by W.) from London, comprising the chapelry of Lattimers, with its hamlets of Waterside and Botley, and the hamlets of Ashley-Green, Billington, Chartridge, and Hundridge with Ashridge, and containing 5032 inhabitants. The town is situated in a pleasant and fertile valley, watered by a brook flowing through it into the river Colne, which rises in the neighbourhood: it consists of three streets, and was formerly noted for its extensive manufacture of wooden ware and turnery, which has of late much declined: the prevailing branch of employment for the labouring class is the making of shoes for the London market; and many females are occupied in making lace and straw-plat: there are several mills worked by the brook for the manufacture of paper, and a small silk-mill worked by machinery. The market days are Wednesday, for corn, which is pitched in the market-place, and Saturday, for straw-plat and provisions: fairs are held on April 21st and July 22nd, for cattle; and September 28th, a statute fair. The living is a discharged vicarage, in the archdeaconry of Buckingham, and diocese of Lincoln, formerly consisting of the medieties of Chesham-Leicester and Chesham-Woburn, each rated in the king's books at £13. 1. $5\frac{1}{2}$., but consolidated in 1767, and in the patronage of the Duke of Bedford. The church, dedicated to St. Mary, is an ancient cruciform structure, with a square embattled tower surmounted by a low spire; in the chancel is a monument, from an elegant design by Bacon, to the memory of Nicholas Skottowe, Esq. There are four places of worship for dissenters, two of which are for Baptists. A National school for an unlimited number of boys has been established, and is supported by subscription. Almshouses for four aged persons were founded by Mr. Thomas Weedon, citizen and draper of London, and endowed with £35 per annum. A mineral spring has been lately discovered. At Ashridge, in this parish, a college for a rector and twenty brethren was founded, in 1283, by Edmund, Earl of Cornwall, the revenue of which, at the dissolution, was £447. 18.

CHESHAM-BOIS, a parish in the hundred of BURNHAM, county of BUCKINGHAM, $1\frac{1}{4}$ mile (S. by E.) from Chesham, containing 160 inhabitants. The living is a rectory and a donative, rated in the king's books at £5. 6. 8., and in the patronage of the Duke of Bedford. The church, dedicated to St. Leonard, contains a curious pulpit and painted window of some antiquity; it was formerly a chapel of ease to the vicarage of Chesham. The northern part of this parish is crossed by a branch of the river Coln, on which there are a paper-mill and a corn-mill.

CHESHIRE, a maritime county, and a county palatine, bounded on the north by the æstuary of the Mersey, the county palatine of Lancaster, and a small part of the county of York; on the east by the counties of Derby and Stafford; on the south by the county of Salop, and a detached portion of the county of Flint; on the west by the counties of Denbigh and Flint, and the æstuary of the Dee; and on the north-west by the Irish sea. It extends from 53° to 53° 36′ (N. Lat.), and from 1° 46′ to 3° 22′ (W. Long.); and includes, according to Holland's survey, six hundred and seventy-six thousand six hundred acres, or about one thousand and fifty-seven square miles. The population, in 1821, amounted to 270,098. The name is a contraction of Chestershire. At the time of the Roman invasion, this county formed part of the territory occupied by the Cornavii. In the first division of Britain by the Romans, it was included in Britannia Superior; and, in their subsequent subdivision, it became part of *Flavia Cæsariensis*. After the establishment of the Saxon dominion, this portion of the British territory remained free from it until the year 607, when the defeat of the Britons, by Ethelfred, King of Northumberland, rendered so memorable by the subsequent massacre of the monks of Bangor, took place here: several British princes, however, having assembled an army, marched towards Chester, defeated Ethelfred with great slaughter, and drove him away: nor was this district again subjected to the Anglo-Saxon power until the year 828, when Chester was taken by King Egbert, and made part of the kingdom of Mercia. About the close of the year 894, according to the Saxon Chronicle, an army of Danes, advancing from Northumberland by forced marches, took possession of Chester. Thither King Alfred marched with his forces, but arrived too late to prevent the Danes seizing the fortress: the Saxons, however, by destroying all the cattle and corn in the neighbourhood, and intercepting the provisions, drove the Danes to such extremities, that they quitted the city, and retreated into North Wales. Upon the division of England into three great districts by Alfred, Cheshire was included in that called *Mercenlege*, or the Mercian jurisdiction. From this period, except the rebuilding of Chester, which had been destroyed by the Danes, and the erection of several fortresses, nothing remarkable occurred until the year 981, when the coast was laid waste by pirates. In the reign of William the Conqueror, Cheshire acquired the privileges of a county palatine; that sovereign having granted to his nephew, Hugh d'Averenches, or d'Avranches, commonly called Hugh Lupus, the whole county, to hold as freely by the sword as he himself held the kingdom of England by the crown.

The next two centuries after the Norman Conquest are chiefly distinguished by the inroads of the Welch, and the preparations made by the English sovereigns to resist them, or to make irruptions into their country. During this time the city of Chester was the usual place of rendezvous for the English army; and all that part of the county bordering on Wales suffered extremely, not only from the ravages of the enemy, but from the destruction caused at intervals by the command of the English sovereigns, to prevent the Welch being benefited by plunder. From such a series of inroads and retaliations the county endured all the evils of a border warfare, until the final subjection of Wales to the English crown: the barony of Halton was held under the Earl of Chester, by the service of leading the vanguard of the earl's army, whenever he should

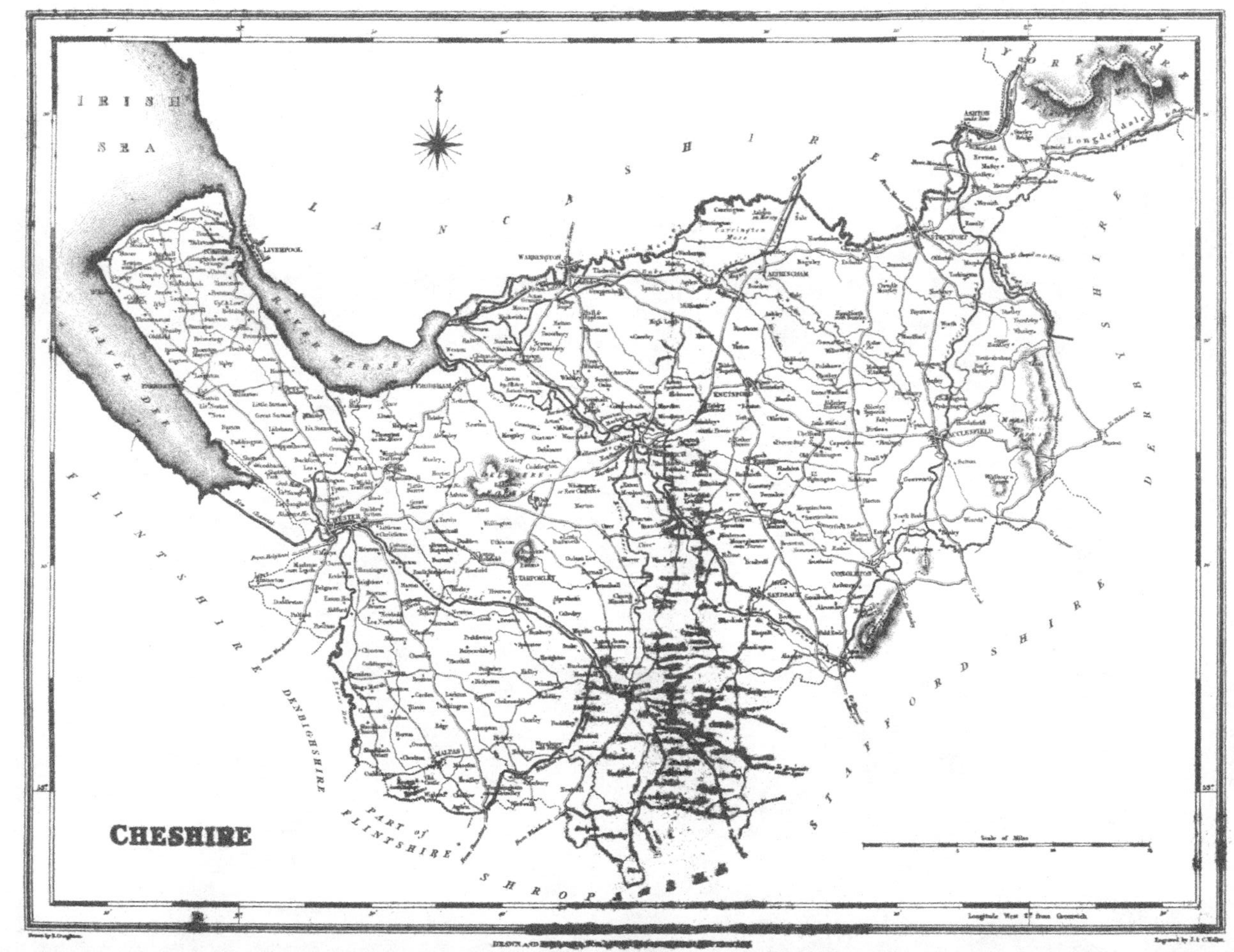
CHESHIRE
IRISH SEA
LANCASHIRE
YORKSHIRE
DERBYSHIRE
STAFFORDSHIRE
SHROPSHIRE
PART of FLINTSHIRE
DENBIGHSHIRE
FLINTSHIRE
RIVER DEE
RIVER MERSEY
LIVERPOOL
WARRINGTON
STOCKPORT
MACCLESFIELD
CONGLETON
SANDBACH
KNUTSFORD
FRODSHAM
CHESTER
TARPORLEY
MALPAS
ALTRINCHAM
Longdendale
Carrington Moss
Scale of Miles
Longitude West 2° from Greenwich
Engraved by J. & C. Walker

march into Wales. The only event worthy of notice that occurred in the baronial wars, during the reigns of John and Henry III., is the capture of Chester, in 1264, by the Earl of Derby. Soon after, Henry, Earl of Lancaster, appeared in arms against Richard II.; having received encouragement from the inhabitants of the city and the county, he came to Chester, and stayed there several days, mustering his army within sight of the city. At Chester, also, the Duke of Lancaster and the king remained one night, on their way towards London, after the conference at Flint. A few years afterwards the inhabitants of Cheshire took part in the rebellion of the Percies, the event of which was particularly disastrous to them; the greater part of the knights and esquires of the whole county, to the number of two hundred, with a great many of their retainers, being slain in the decisive battle of Shrewsbury, July 22nd, 1403. With the exception of Chester having been for a short time the head-quarters of the Duke of Lancaster's army, the county does not appear to have been the scene of any military transactions, from the reign of Henry III. to that of Charles I.; but the warlike prowess of the Cheshire heroes during that period has been highly extolled in the English annals. Soon after the commencement of the parliamentary war, an attempt was made by the principal persons of this county, who were nearly equally divided between the king and the parliament, to preserve its internal peace; and a treaty of pacification was entered into at Bunbury, on the 23rd of December, by Robert, Lord Kilmorey, and others, under the sanction of the commissioners of array; but the articles then agreed upon were rendered nugatory by an ordinance of parliament, which required the inhabitants to maintain and assist the common cause, pursuant to their former resolutions; and for their better encouragement, Sir William Brereton, a gentleman of the county, and one of its representatives in parliament, was sent down with a troop of horse and a regiment of dragoons for their protection; the king, on the other hand, sent Sir Nicholas Byron, with a commission, by which he was appointed Colonel-General of Cheshire and Shropshire, and governor of Chester, which was made the head-quarters of the royal party. Sir Nicholas, on his arrival in Cheshire, soon raised a considerable force, and had frequent skirmishes with the parliamentarian troops. Sir William Brereton, on the other hand, having taken possession of Nantwich for the parliament, fortified it, and fixed his head-quarters in that town. About the end of November 1643, a considerable body of troops arrived from Ireland, for the king's service, and were ordered to remain at Chester, under the command of Lord Byron, the governor's nephew, who employed them on various services, and with their assistance reduced several parliamentarian garrisons. In the month of December, Lord Byron, with his Irish regiments, defeated the whole of the parliament's forces, under the command of Sir William Brereton, at Middlewich. Nantwich being now the only garrison in Cheshire in possession of the parliament, was besieged during the greater part of January 1644, but was relieved by Sir Thomas Fairfax and Sir William Brereton, whose united forces defeated Lord Byron's army, the remains of which, with their commander, retreated to Chester on the 25th. Stockport was taken by Prince Rupert, without any resistance, on the 25th of May. On the 25th of August, a severe action was fought at Old Castle-heath, near Malpas, in which the royalists were defeated. The king advancing towards Chester with a large force, about the middle of May 1645, the parliament abandoned all their garrisons except Tarvin and Nantwich. On the 27th of September the battle of Rowton and Hoole-heath, near Chester, was fought, in which the king's army, commanded by Sir Marmaduke Langdale, being overpowered by the joint forces of General Poyntz and Colonel Jones, the latter of whom had hastened from the siege of Chester to the general's assistance, was defeated and put to flight, the event having been witnessed by the king himself from the walls of Chester. On the 3rd of February, 1646, the garrison of Chester, after a vigorous and obstinate defence under Lord Byron, surrendered on honourable terms; and upon this the parliament became masters of the whole county.

When the royalists in the north made an attempt to restore the king, in May 1648, the gentlemen of Cheshire in the interest of the parliament fortified the castle and city of Chester, for which they received the thanks of that body; they engaged also to raise three regiments of foot and one of horse, if they should be wanted, for the defence of the county. After the defeat of the Duke of Hamilton, at Preston, that nobleman retreating with about three thousand horse, the remains of the Scottish army, through Nantwich towards Uttoxeter, in August 1648, the gentlemen of the county took about five hundred of them. In August 1651, the Scottish army, under Charles II., was quartered for a short time at Nantwich, previously to the battle of Worcester; after which decisive action, a party of the king's cavalry, on their retreat northward, passing through Sandbach, it being the fair day, were attacked by the country people, and a hundred of them taken prisoners. During the months of June and July, 1655, many of the principal gentry were sent prisoners to the castle at Chester, on suspicion of being disaffected to Cromwell's government. In August 1659, Sir George Booth, who, as it was afterwards known, had a commission from Charles II., appointing him commander-in-chief of all his forces in Cheshire, Lancashire, and North Wales, here appeared in arms at the head of an army of upwards of three thousand men; he was accompanied by the Earl of Derby, Lord Cholmondeley, Lord Kilmorey, and several of the principal gentlemen of the county: they mustered upon Rowton heath, and there read and published a declaration, setting forth, that they took up arms for a free parliament, and to deliver the nation from the slavery of its oppressors. But General Lambert being sent by the parliament with an army against Sir George Booth, the hostile parties met at Winnington bridge, near Northwich, on the 16th of August, when an action ensued, in which Booth's forces were soon defeated. After the engagement Lambert marched to Chester, which was then held by Col. Croxton, who immediately surrendered it. To punish the revolters, the parliament passed a vote on the 17th of September, dissolving the corporation of the city of Chester, and depriving it of its independent jurisdiction. On the eve of the Revolution, Henry, Lord Delamere, having heard of the landing of the prince of Orange, raised a great force in Cheshire and Lancashire, declared in his favour, and immediately set forwards on his march to join him; meanwhile Lord Molineux and Lord Aston seized Chester for King James. In the rebellion of 1745, the young Pretender led his followers through Cheshire, on his way to Derby; and, on the approach of the Duke of Cumberland, retreated by the same route.

This county is within the diocese of Chester, and province of York: it forms an archdeaconry, and comprises the seven deaneries of Chester, Frodsham, Macclesfield, Nantwich, Malpas, Middlewich, and Wirrall, containing eighty-seven parishes, of which forty-six are rectories, twenty-three vicarages, and eighteen perpetual curacies. For civil purposes it is divided into the seven hundreds of Broxton, Bucklow, Eddisbury, Macclesfield, Nantwich, Northwich, and Wirrall. It contains the city and port of Chester (which, however, is a county within itself), and the market towns of Altrincham, Congleton, Frodsham, Knutsford, Macclesfield, Malpas, Middlewich, Nantwich, Northwich, Sandbach, Stockport, and Tarporley. The grant of this county, made by the Conqueror to his nephew Hugh Lupus, constituted the representative of the latter the first hereditary earl in England: by the terms of this grant he acquired *jura regalia* within the county, in the exercise of which he created eight parliamentary barons, one of whom was hereditary constable, and another hereditary steward; he assembled parliaments, and established courts of law. His descendants continued to enjoy this sovereignty until the death of John, Earl of Chester, in 1237, who having no male issue, Henry III. seized on the county of Chester, gave other lands in lieu of it to the sisters of the deceased earl, and bestowed the earldom on his son, Prince Edward. Richard II., having erected it into a principality, amongst his other titles, styled himself *Princeps Cestriæ:* this act was abrogated by his successor, and Cheshire again became a county palatine, and continued, under the king's eldest sons, as earls of Chester, to be governed, as in the time of its ancient earls, by a jurisdiction separate from, and independent of, the parliament of England. The city of Chester was separated from the county and erected into a county of itself by Henry VII., in the 21st year of his reign. The ancient privileges of the county palatine were much abridged in the 27th of Henry VIII., prior to which time the Lord High Chancellor of England did not appoint justices of peace, justices of quorum, or of gaol delivery, within the county. The authority of the earl in the palatinate was as absolute as that of the king throughout the realm: he had power to pardon for treason and felony, and to rescind outlawries; to make justices of eyre, assize, gaol delivery, and of the peace; and all original and judicial writs, and indictments for treason and felony, with the process thereupon, were made in his name. In consequence of this curtailment of its privileges, the county petitioned that it might send knights and burgesses to the parliament of the realm, in accordance with which an act was passed in the year 1542, enacting that thenceforward two knights should be returned to parliament for the county palatine, and two burgesses for the city of Chester. The authority of the judges and officers of the great session of the county palatine, which, says Lord Coke, is the most ancient and honourable remaining in England, extends over the counties of Chester and Flint, for both which one seal is used: the king's writ does not run in the county palatine, all writs issuing from the superior courts being directed to the chamberlain of Chester, who issues his mandate to the sheriff. The chamberlain has, within the county palatine and the county of the city of Chester, the jurisdiction of chancellor; and the court of Exchequer at Chester is the Chancery court, whereof the chamberlain, or his deputy, is the sole judge in equity; he is also judge at the common law within the said limits: the other officers of the court are, the vice-chamberlain, baron, seal-keeper, filizer, examiner, six clerks or attorneys of the court, and some inferior officers. There is also within the county palatine "the Justice of Chester," who has jurisdiction of all pleas of the crown and common pleas of all matters arising therein, as also of fines and recoveries levied and suffered, as well within the county palatine as the city of Chester; and no inhabitant of the county can be compelled by any writ or process to answer elsewhere to any matter or cause, except in cases of treason, and on writ of error. The assizes, and the Epiphany and Easter quarter sessions for the county palatine, are held at Chester; the Midsummer and Michaelmas quarter sessions take place at Knutsford. The county gaol is at Chester, and the house of correction at Knutsford. There are sixty-nine acting magistrates. The rates raised in the county for the year ending March 25th, 1829, amounted to £137,886, and the expenditure to £136,772, of which £98,105 was applied to the relief of the poor.

The cotton manufacture is carried on to a considerable extent in several parts of the county, especially in Stockport and its vicinity, Macclesfield, Marple, and Congleton. There are numerous silk-mills at Congleton, Macclesfield, Stockport, and Sandbach. The weaving of ribands is carried on at Congleton, and that of silk handkerchiefs at Macclesfield, where silk ferret also is made: at Knutsford is a considerable manufacture of thread. The manufacture of hats for exportation at Stockport, Macclesfield, and Nantwich, and of shoes at Sandbach is considerable. Some woollen cloths are made at the north-eastern extremity of the county, in the parish of Mottram: tanning is extensively carried on throughout the county, more especially in the middle and northern parts.

The surface of the county being almost uniformly level, and not abounding in wood, has little picturesque beauty. The principal hills are those on the borders of Derbyshire, which extend along the eastern side of the parishes of Astbury, Prestbury, and Mottram; a range of hills in the hundred of Broxton; Bucklow hills; Frodsham hills; and Alderley-Edge, a singular isolated hill, in the hundred of Macclesfield. According to Mr. Holland, there are six hundred and twenty thousand acres in cultivation, including parks and pleasure-grounds; twenty-eight thousand in waste lands, commons, and woods; eighteen thousand in marshes and mosses; and ten thousand in sea-sands, within the æstuaries of the Mersey and the Dee. The prevailing soil is a mixture of clay and sand, the clay for the most part predominating. There is a considerable extent of black moor, or peat-moss land, chiefly in that part of the hundred of Macclesfield which borders on Derbyshire and Yorkshire; there are some mosses of smaller extent in the neighbourhood of Coppenhall and Warmingham, but Coppenhall moss has been greatly improved. In former times Cheshire contained some very extensive forests; the forests of Delamere and Macclesfield are now large dreary tracts of waste land; the former contained ten thousand acres, but about two thousand have been enclosed. The largest tract of waste land, exclusively of the peat-mosses already described, is Rud heath, in the parishes of Great Budworth, Davenham, Middlewich, and Sandbach. Though there are now but few extensive woods, the quantity of timber growing in the county in hedge-rows and coppices greatly exceeds that in the majority of counties: the estates of the Earl of Stamford and Warrington, the Marquis of Cholmondeley, and Earl Grosvenor, in particular, abound with fine timber. Vale Royal received its distinguishing epithet from Edward I., who founded a Cistercian monastery within its limits, which was fifty-three years in building, having been begun in 1277, and completed in 1330, at an expense of £32,000. There are several small lakes, called *meres*, or *pools*. Combermere is a fine piece of water, nearly three quarters of a mile in length, close to the site of Combermere Abbey. Bar-mere, in the parish of Malpas, is nearly of the same extent: the other principal ones are, the Mere, which gives name to a township in the parish of Rosthern, Comberbach-mere, Oakhanger-mere, Pick-mere, Rosthern-mere, and Chapel-mere and Moss-mere, two beautiful sheets of water in the front of Cholmondeley castle. The richest and most extensive views are those from Alderley-Edge, Halton and Beeston castles, Mowcop and Shuttingslow hills, Carden Cliff, and Overton Sear, and from the western edge of Delamere Forest: in most of these views Beeston castle, situated on a precipitous and isolated rock of sand-stone, is a prominent object.

The staple productions of the county are cheese and salt, both having, from a very early period, been among its principal articles of exportation. The richest and best cheese is produced from land of an inferior quality; but the greatest quantity from the richest land. Among the districts most celebrated for making the prime cheese are, the neighbourhood of Nantwich for a circuit of five miles, the parish of Over, the greater part of the banks of the river Weever, and several farms near Congleton and Middlewich. It is calculated by Mr. Holland, in his survey, that the number of cows kept for the dairy in this county is about thirty-two thousand; and that the quantity of cheese annually made is about eleven thousand five hundred tons. The greater part of the cheese, particularly that made in the southern part of the county, is sold to the London cheesemongers, through the medium of factors who reside in the neighbourhood: some is sent by the Mersey to Liverpool, some inland by the Staffordshire canal, and a considerable quantity by other canals, to the markets at Stockport and Manchester. The manufacture of salt yielded a considerable revenue to the crown before the Norman Conquest. About a century ago the salt made here was not more than adequate to the consumption of this and a few adjoining counties; but partly in consequence of improvements in the art of making it, and partly from other causes, the manufacture of white salt has greatly increased. From May 1805 to May 1806, the quantity produced at the brine-pits, exclusively of that made at Nantwich and Frodsham, which was disposed of for home consumption, amounted to sixteen thousand five hundred and ninety tons and seventy-seven bushels. The annual average of white salt sent down the Weever from Winsford and Northwich, for ten years prior to 1814, was one hundred and thirty-nine thousand three hundred and seventeen tons, principally for the supply of the fisheries of Scotland, Ireland, the ports on the Baltic, the United States of America, Newfoundland, and the British Colonies. The discovery of the rock-salt in 1670 forms an important era in the history of this staple commodity. There are now ten or twelve pits of rock-salt worked in the neighbourhood of Northwich, in the townships of Witton, Marston, and Wincham, from some of which one hundred tons are raised in a day: some of the mines are worked in a circular form, and are three hundred yards in diameter. The rock-salt is sent down the Weever from Northwich: about a third of it is refined at the salt-works at Frodsham and on the Lancashire side of the Mersey; but the greater part is carried to Liverpool, whence it is exported to Ireland and the ports on the Baltic. The average quantity annually sent down the Weever from Northwich, for ten years prior to 1814, was fifty-one thousand one hundred and nine tons. In 1805 there were two thousand nine hundred and fifty persons employed in the salt manufacture. Potatoes are cultivated to a great extent in the neighbourhoods of Altrincham and Frodsham, and in the hundred of Wirrall; in the parish of Frodsham alone, it is calculated that one hundred thousand bushels have been raised annually. They are chiefly sent to the Lancashire markets by the river Mersey, and by the Duke of Bridgewater's canal: the town of Manchester is supplied with an abundance of potatoes and other vegetables from the neighbourhood of Altrincham, and that of Liverpool both from Frodsham and the hundred of Wirrall; a great quantity of early potatoes is raised in Wirrall by a peculiar mode of cultivation, and carried to market early in May.

Among the mineral products, coal is found abundant and of good quality in a district in the north-eastern part of the county, extending about ten miles from north to south, in which, especially in the townships of Poynton and Worth, are very extensive collieries that supply the populous town of Stockport. At Denwall, in the hundred of Wirrall, is a colliery, first opened about the year 1750, which extends a mile and three-quarters from high water mark under the river Dee, having two canals under the river, one of which is carried to the extremity of the works: the coal is chiefly exported to Ireland. There are lead-works at Alderley-Edge; where also a considerable quantity of cobalt has been procured, and conveyed to Ferrybridge, in Yorkshire, having been there manufactured into smalt little inferior in colour to that imported from Saxony. There are several quarries of excellent freestone, of which those of Runcorn, Manley, and Great Bebington, are the chief; the quarries at Runcorn being situated near the Duke of Bridgewater's canal, a considerable quantity of stone is sent from them to Manchester, Liverpool, and Chester. Marl exists in almost every part of the county, and is extensively used for manure. A quantity of oak and fir timber has been dug out of some of the mosses, and used for fuel, and sometimes for the interior of buildings.

The principal rivers are the Dee, the Mersey, the Weever, the Dane, the Bollin, the Peover, the Wheelock, and the Tame. The Dee rises in Merionethshire, runs through Bala Pool, and, after skirting the counties of Denbigh and Flint, becomes a boundary to Cheshire near Shocklach, passing by Farndon to Aldford, where it enters the county. It then flows past Eaton Hall and Eccleston to Chester, where it is received into an artificial channel, the first sod of which was dug on the 20th of April, 1733, and carried along the marshes, under Hawarden castle, to its æstuary, where it spreads over an extent of sands in some parts seven miles in breadth. The navigation of this river, by which, in former times, vessels were brought up to the walls of Chester, became so much obstructed by sands, from the frequent changing of the channel, as to occasion the total ruin of the haven of Chester, before the year 1449: to remedy this, a new quay, or haven, was made, nearly six miles from Chester, about the middle of the following century. In 1560, a pecuniary collection for the new haven at Chester was made in all churches throughout the kingdom; and, in 1567, there was an assessment for the same purpose in the city: it was at length completed, and for many years all goods and merchandise brought to, and conveyed from, the port of Chester, were there loaded and unloaded. In the year 1700, an act passed to enable the mayor and citizens of Chester to recover and preserve the navigation upon the river Dee. The projectors of this work were incorporated by the name of the River Dee Company; a subsequent act passed, in 1732, empowering them to enclose a large tract on the banks of the river, called the White Sands, on the condition of their making a navigable line from the sea to Chester: this new cut was begun the next year, and completed in 1754. In the year 1763, one thousand four hundred and eleven acres of land were recovered from the sea; six hundred and sixty-four acres in 1769, and three hundred and forty-eight in 1795; forming, by means of these and subsequent works, an extensive tract of reclaimed land. The new channel was at first intended only for vessels of two hundred tons' burden, but it is now navigable for ships of six hundred tons: the Dee is navigable for barges up to Bangor bridge. The Mersey is formed by the junction of the Etherow and Goyt rivers, between Compstall bridge and Marple bridge, whence it passes to Stockport from which place to Liverpool it forms the boundary between Cheshire and Lancashire: opposite Warrington, where it meets the tide, it is only forty yards wide: at Runcorn-gap, where it communicates with the Trent and Mersey, or Grand Trunk canal, and with the Duke of Bridgewater's canal, its breadth is three hundred yards; below the gap it immediately spreads into a grand æstuary three miles in width, receiving in its course the navigable river Weever, from Northwich and Frodsham. As it proceeds northward from Runcorn, it gradually diminishes for six miles, and opposite Liverpool its width is only three quarters of a mile; but it forms a fine channel, at least ten fathoms deep, at low water, very commodious for shipping: at the distance of about five miles, measuring by the Cheshire coast, it falls into the Irish sea, by two or three different channels, much obstructed by sands, but the passage is rendered secure by means of various land-marks, buoys, and lighthouses, and the good system of pilotage established by the Liverpool merchants; the whole course of this river is forty-four miles in length. The Weever rises on Bulkeley heath, and never quits the county; it passes by Nantwich to Winsford bridge, and thence to Northwich, where it joins the Dane, and soon afterwards the Peover; after this junction it passes by Frodsham to Weston, where it empties itself into the Mersey, after a course of about thirty-three miles: this river, in its natural state, having been navigable only at high tides, and for six miles above Frodsham bridge, a company of Cheshire gentlemen, in the year 1720, entered into a subscription, for the purpose of procuring an act of parliament to make it navigable from Frodsham bridge to Winsford bridge, a distance of about twenty miles. All incumbrances brought on by the undertaking were discharged in the year 1778, since which time a considerable surplus, arising from tonnage, &c., has been annually paid into the county treasury, in aid of the rate, as provided by the act, after payment of the interest to the shareholders. The expense of erecting the public buildings on the site of Chester castle has been wholly defrayed out of the revenue of the Weever navigation. In consequence of the great increase of the salt trade, an additional cut, about four miles long, has been made from the Weir, near Frodsham bridge, to Weston-point, to prevent the delays formerly occasioned by the shallowness of the river at neap-tides. The Dane rises in Macclesfield Forest, near the Three Shire Mere, and after forming for some distance a boundary between Staffordshire and Cheshire, enters the latter county within two miles of Congleton, from which town it passes near Middlewich to Northwich, where it falls into the Weever, after a course of about twenty-two miles. The Bollin rises also in Macclesfield Forest, from several sources, and passes by Macclesfield to Rixton, where it falls into the Mersey, after a course of about twenty miles. The Peover is formed by the junction of two streams that meet at Chelford, and falls into the Weever near Northwich, after a course of about fifteen miles. The Weelock is formed by the union of three streams near Sandbach, and falls into the Dane at Croxton, after a course of about twelve miles. The Tame rises in Yorkshire, and during almost the whole of its course, which is about ten miles, forms a boundary between Cheshire and Lancashire, falling into the Mersey near Stockport.

The canals that intersect various parts of the county are, the Duke of Bridgewater's, the Trent and Mersey, or Grand Trunk canal, the Ellesmere canal, the Chester and Nantwich and the Peak Forest canals. The Duke of Bridgewater's canal was begun in 1761; the communication betwen Manchester and Liverpool was opened in 1772, and the whole of the works at first projected were finished in 1776: this canal, which commences on the Duke of Bridgewater's estate, at Worsley, in Lancashire, enters Cheshire near Ashton on the Mersey, and passes near Altrincham to Runcorn, where it joins the Mersey, being conducted through a chain of ten locks: at this place is a rise of ninety-five feet, the only deviation from the level in the course of the canal, except at the vale of the Bollin, between Lymm and Altrincham, where an embankment has been made for the purpose of preserving it. The first act for making the Trent and Mersey, or Grand Trunk, canal passed in 1766: this canal communicates with the Duke of Bridgewater's at Preston-brook, and passes by Northwich and Middlewich, not far from Sandbach, to Lawton, a little beyond which it enters Staffordshire: in its course through Cheshire there are four tunnels; one at Preston on the Hill, one thousand two hundred and forty-one yards in length; another at Barnton, in the parish of Great Budworth, five hundred and seventy-two yards long; another at Saltersfield, in the same parish, three hundred and fifty yards; and another at Hermitage, one hundred and thirty yards. The Ellesmere canal communicates with the Mersey at Whitby, at a place now called Ellesmere port; it passes through the eastern extremity of the hundred of Wirrall, and the south-east part of that of Broxton, to Chester, where it joins the Dee and the Chester canal: a branch from Whitchurch, completed in 1806, enters Cheshire at Grindley brook, and forms a junction with the Chester and Nantwich canal in the township of Hurleston, after a course in this county of eleven miles. The act for making the Chester and Nantwich canal passed in 1772, and the work was completed in 1778. The Peak Forest canal, the first act for which passed in 1794, enters Cheshire from Lancashire, crossing the river Tame at Duckenfield, and quits the county near Whalley bridge: it is carried over the river Mersey, near Marple, by an aqueduct of three arches, of sixty feet in the span, and seventy-eight feet high, the whole height being one hundred feet.

One of the great roads from London to Holyhead enters Cheshire in the township of Bridgemere, and passes through Nantwich, Tarporley, and Chester, three miles and a half beyond which it enters Flintshire, ts course through this county being about thirty miles in extent. All the roads from London to Manchester pass through Cheshire; one of them enters it near Church-Lawton, passes through Knutsford and Altrincham, and quits the county a little beyond Cross-Street in the parish of Ashton: the road by way of Leek enters near Bosley mills, and passes through Macclesfield and Stockport: that through Buxton and Matlock enters at Whalley bridge, and passes through Stockport. The road from London to Liverpool enters Cheshire at Lawton, and passes through Congleton and Knutsford to Warrington: at Monk's heath, another road branches off through Alderley, Chorley, &c., towards Manchester. A road from London to Warrington enters near Lawton, and passes through Sandbach, Middlewich, and Northwich, to Latchford, opposite Warrington.

Few Roman antiquities have been discovered except within the walls of the city of Chester, which was for more than two hundred years the station of the twentieth legion, it being the only Roman station in the county the situation of which has been clearly ascertained. The Romans having placed one of their principal towns in Cheshire, and, from its convenience as a military port, fixed there the head-quarters of one of the three legions, which formed the standing army of Britain, many detached remains of their roads are discernible within the limits of the county. There is also a road, which, from its name and course, is considered of British origin; this is the northern Watling-street: it enters the county from the north at Stretford, and passes through Northwich, over Delamere Forest, to Chester, proceeding to the coast of Caernarvonshire. The principal Roman roads, of which there are various traces, are, the great Roman way from Manchester to Worcester, and a road from Kinderton to the station of Chesterton, near Newcastle under Line. Other Roman roads of considerable importance cross the county from various quarters towards Chester.

The richest specimens of church architecture are Chester cathedral and Nantwich church. Within the limits of the county, before the dissolution, were thirteen religious houses, including one preceptory of the Knights Hospitallers; there were, besides, two colleges and nine ancient hospitals: there are considerable monastic remains, especially of the abbey of St. Werburgh, at Chester. The most remarkable of the ancient mansion-houses is Little Moreton Hall; many others remain either wholly or in part, most of them having been converted into farm-houses. There are several customs peculiar to the county, but many of them are falling into non-observance; the most prevalent are the following:—On the first of May, the young men place large birchen boughs over the doors of the houses where the young women to whom they are paying their addresses reside, and an alder bough is often placed over the door of a scold. On Easter-Monday the young men deck out a chair with flowers and ribands, and carry it about, compelling every young woman they meet to get into it, and suffer herself to be lifted as high as they can reach into the air, or to be kissed, or pay a forfeit; this they call "heaving." On Easter-Tuesday, the women deck out a chair, and lift the men, or make them pay a fine: a similar custom prevails in some of the neighbouring counties. The most general custom peculiar to this county is the shouting, accompanied by particular ceremonies, of the *marlers*, or marl diggers, when any money has been given them.

CHESHUNT, a parish (formerly a market town) in the hundred and county of HERTFORD, 8 miles (S. by E.) from Hertford, comprising the three wards of Cheshunt-Street, Waltham-Cross, and Woodside, and containing 4376 inhabitants. The living is a vicarage, in the archdeaconry of Middlesex, and diocese of London, rated in the king's books at £26, and in the patronage of the Marquis of Salisbury. The church is dedicated to St. Mary. A new church, or chapel, is in progress of erection, the expense of which will be defrayed by grant from the parliamentary commissioners. Cheshunt College, for the instruction and preparation of young men for the ministry, was originally established at Talgarth, in the county of Brecon, South Wales, by the late Countess of Huntingdon, in 1768, who continued to support it until her death in 1791, when it was removed by the trustees to this place, and reopened on the 24th of August, 1792. A chapel was built in 1806, and in 1821 a new building was annexed for the accommodation of twenty additional students. The students, who, together with the masters, are appointed by the trustees, are boarded, and instructed in the knowledge of the Scriptures, in English composition on sacred subjects, in the Latin, Greek, and Hebrew languages, the elements of the mathematics, civil and ecclesiastical history, and geography; and, on leaving the college at the end of four years, or sooner if deemed able to commence the service of the ministry, are free to join any denomination of Christians they may prefer. The institution is supported by the interest on about £8000 stock, a portion of an estate called Cobham, and annual subscriptions, the whole producing about £1200 per annum.

The village is situated near the course of the river

Lea and the line of the New River, and is supposed to occupy the site of a Roman station, on the Roman road Ermin-street. The petty sessions for the division are holden here. In the parish was a bank separating the kingdoms of Mercia and East Anglia, during the Octarchy, the lands on one side of which the elder brother still inherits, and the younger those on the other side. To the north are some remains of a nunnery, founded in the reign of Stephen by Peter de Belengey, in honour of the Blessed Virgin, for nuns of the Sempringham order, in which Henry III. afterwards placed others of the Benedictine order: its revenue, in the 26th of Henry VIII., was estimated at £27. 6. 8. Cardinal Wolsey possessed the united manors of Andrews and Le Mote, in this parish, and received from the crown the appointment of bailiff of the honour, and keeper of the park of Cheshunt. Here stood also Theobalds, the favourite residence of Lord Burleigh, and afterwards of James I., who died at it in 1625; it became the occasional residence of Charles I., having been the place where he received the petition from both houses of parliament in 1642, a short time before he placed himself at the head of the army: the greater part of the palace, the park attached to which was ten miles in circuit, was taken down by the parliamentary commissioners for selling the crown lands, in 1650. Near the church is a house in which Richard Cromwell, after resigning the protectorate, lived in retirement, under the assumed name of Clark, till his death in 1712. Waltham-Cross, a considerable hamlet in this parish, is distinguished by a beautiful stone cross, erected by Edward I., in memory of his queen, Eleanor, who died at Hardeby, near Grantham, in Lincolnshire; similar crosses were erected at every town where the corpse rested, on its removal to Westminster, of which those of Geddington, Northampton, and Waltham alone remain. Roman coins of the reigns of Adrian, Claudius, Gothicus, and Constantine, were found at Cheshunt, and shewn to the Society of Antiquaries, in 1724. The free school was founded about 1642, and endowed with land by Robert Dewhurst, who built the school-house: it is under the management of twelve trustees: the master's salary is £20 per annum. The same benefactor also assigned twenty nobles each, for apprenticing six poor boys to handicraft trades, in corporate towns, appropriating five nobles to be paid as a premium, five in clothing, and the residue for expenses of indenture. There are a National school for boys, and a school of industry for girls. Almshouses for ten widows, at Turner's Hill, in this parish, are endowed with a donation of £500 from James I.: the income has been augmented by various additional benefactions. There are several minor donations for the benefit of the poor.

CHESLYN-HAY, a township in the parish of CANNOCK, eastern division of the hundred of CUTTLESTONE, county of STAFFORD, 7 miles (S. E. by S.) from Penkridge, containing 548 inhabitants.

CHESSINGTON, a parish in the second division of the hundred of COPTHORNE, county of SURREY, 2¾ miles (W. by N.) from Ewell, containing 150 inhabitants. The living is a perpetual curacy, annexed to the vicarage of Malden, in the archdeaconry of Surrey, and diocese of Winchester. The church is in the early style of English architecture. Here is a strong chalybeate spring, called Jessop's Well.

Arms.

CHESTER, a city, port, and county of itself, locally in the hundred of Broxton, county palatine of CHESTER, of which it is the capital, 17 miles (S.) from Liverpool, 36 (S.W.) from Manchester, and 181 (N.W.) from London, through Coventry and Lichfield, and 190 through Northampton and Leicester, containing 19,949 inhabitants, and, including those portions of the parishes of St. Mary on the Hill, St. Oswald, and the Holy Trinity, which are without the limits of the city, 21,176. The origin of this ancient city has been ascribed to the Cornavii, a British tribe who, at the time of the Roman invasion, inhabited that part of the island which now includes the counties of Chester, Salop, Stafford, Warwick, and Worcester; and its British name, *Caer Leon Vawr*, city of Leon the Great, has been referred to Leon, son of Brût Darian Là, eighth king of Britain. But there is no authentic account of Chester prior to the period when it was made the station of the twentieth Roman legion, after the defeat of Caractacus; and the more respectable historians deduce its names, *Caer Leon Vawr*, city or camp of the great legion, and *Caer Leon ar Dwfyr dwy*, the city of the legion on the Dee, from its connexion with that people: it was also called *Deunana* and *Deva*, from the same river. The Romans occupied it from the year 46 till their departure from the island in 446, when it reverted to the Britons, from whom it was taken by Ethelfrith, King of Northumberland, who in 607 defeated them under the King of Powysland with great slaughter. But having regained possession of it, the Britons continued to hold it till 828, when Egbert, as sole monarch of England, annexed it to his other possessions. By the Saxons it was called *Legancester* and *Legecester*. It suffered greatly from the Danes in the ninth century: on their retreat, the walls were repaired by Ethelfreda, Countess of Mercia; after her death the Britons once more became its masters, but were again driven out by Edward the Elder. In 971-3, Edgar assembled a naval force on the Dee, on which occasion that king, as mentioned by some writers, was rowed from his palace on the southern bank of the river to the conventual church of St. John, by eight tributary kings, he himself taking the helm, to denote his supremacy.

On the division of England between Canute and Edmund Ironside, in 1016, Canute retained possession of Mercia and Northumbria, and Chester, which was included in Mercia, continued to form part of it till the Norman conquest, when William bestowed it, with the earldom, on his kinsman Hugh Lupus. At this time, according to Domesday-book, the city contained four hundred and thirty-one rateable houses. For more than two centuries after the Conquest it was the head-quarters of the troops employed to defend the English border against the incursive attacks of the Welch; and, on account of its importance as a military station, was, during that period, more or less favoured by the reigning monarchs. In the war between Henry III. and the barons, Chester was held for the crown by the Earl of Derby, who captured it in 1264, till the battle of

Evesham, in which the barons were defeated with the loss of their leader, and an end put to the contest. On the subjugation of Wales in 1300 by Edward I., several of the Welch chieftains did homage to his son, Edward of Caernarvon, then an infant, in Chester castle. Richard II., by an act of parliament, which was rescinded by his successor, erected the earldom of Chester into a principality, to be held only by the king's eldest son.

The city, in common with the whole county, suffered considerably from the sanguinary conflicts between the houses of York and Lancaster, during which it was visited by Margaret of Anjou. In 1554, the inhabitants experienced the severity of the persecution by which the reign of Mary was distinguished; and the martyrdom of George Marsh, a clergyman, who was burnt for preaching the tenets of Protestantism, was rendered memorable by an attempt of one of the sheriffs to rescue him, which was defeated by the other. In 1634, the city suffered dreadfully from the plague; during its continuance, the court of Exchequer was removed to Tarvin, and the court of assize to Nantwich, and the fairs were suspended. In the memorable siege of the city by Sir William Brereton, in 1645, when the garrison was commanded by Lord Byron, the inhabitants experienced great privations for their adherence to the cause of Charles I., who had the mortification to witness, from the Phœnix tower and the great tower of the cathedral, the entire defeat of his army under Sir Marmaduke Langdale, and its pursuit by the enemy even to the very walls; the noble commander, after a gallant resistance, surrendered on honourable terms, Feb. 3rd, 1646. In 1659, Sir George Booth surprised and took possession of the city, but it was soon surrendered to the parliamentary forces under General Lambert. In 1688, the Roman Catholic Lords Molyneux and Aston raised a force, and made themselves masters of Chester, for James II.; but his abdication rendered further efforts useless. Under William III. it was chosen one of the six cities for the residence of an assay master, and allowed to issue silver coinage. In the rebellion of 1745, it was fortified against the Pretender, the last military event of importance recorded of a place celebrated as the rendezvous of troops from the earliest times.

Situated on a rocky elevation, on the northern bank of the Dee, and half encircled by a fine sweep of the river, the appearance of Chester is remarkable and picturesque. The city is entirely surrounded by a wall, and comprises four principal streets, diverging at right angles from a common centre, and extending towards the cardinal points; at the extremity of each is a gate, after which are respectively named Eastgate-street, Northgate-street, Bridgegate-street, and Watergate-street: this plan, strictly conformable to the Roman style of building, affords strong presumptive evidence of its Roman origin. Within the liberty of the city is an extensive southern suburb, called Hanbridge, which in feudal times generally fell a prey to the predatory incursions of the Welch, and thence obtained, in their language, the appellation of *Treboeth*, the burnt town. The streets, being cut out of the rock, are several feet below the general surface, which circumstance has led to a singular construction of the houses: level with the streets are low shops, or warehouses, over which is an open balustraded gallery, with steps at convenient distances into the streets. Along the galleries, or, as they are called by the inhabitants, "rows," are houses with shops; the upper stories are erected over the row, which, consequently, appears to be formed through the first floor of each house; and at the intersection of the streets are additional flights of steps. The rows in Bridge and Eastgate streets, running through the principal part of the city, are much frequented as promenades. Pennant considered them to be remnants of the ancient vestibules of the Roman houses; but other writers are of opinion that they were originally constructed for defence, especially against the sudden inroads of the Welch. The fronts of such of them as have not been modernised are bounded by a heavy wooden railing; and immense pillars of oak, supporting transverse beams, sustain the weight of the upper stories. Many of the houses in Bridge and Eastgate streets, having been rebuilt, are considerably improved and enlarged, and their appearance rendered light by iron railing. The streets, which are well lighted with gas, are indifferently paved, but the inconvenience to foot passengers, to whom the rows afford a sheltered walk, is little felt. The inhabitants are plentifully supplied with water, conducted through pipes from the Borrel on the Dee, by means of a steam-engine, into a reservoir in Northgate-street, constructed by Mr. Royle, of Chester, and capable of containing fifty thousand gallons. The city, both within and without the walls, has been much improved of late by the addition of well built houses: a new street has been made from St. Michael's church, leading to the new bridge, opposite Overleigh, which is formed on a level, and avoids the steep descent down Lower Bridge-street, and the ascent through Hanbridge; opposite to it Earl Grosvenor has erected a lodge, to form a grand entrance to the grounds of Eaton. This bridge, consisting of one arch of two hundred feet in the span, is constructed of Peckforton stone, with quoins of granite, at an expense of £40,000, from a design by Mr. Thomas Harrison. The old bridge, consisting of seven arches, has, within the last few years, been considerably widened and improved. Fine views of the city, the peninsula of Wirrall, the Welch hills, and the æstuary of the Dee, are obtained from the walls, which afford a delightful and favourite promenade. There are two public libraries: the theatre, a small neat edifice, is open during the races, and generally throughout summer; and grand musical meetings are held at distant periods. The annual races, which attract much company from Wales and the neighbouring counties, commence on the first Monday in May, and terminate on the Friday following: the grand stand has been enlarged by Royle, and is capable of holding £1000, the produce being usually applied to increase the prizes: the races take place on the Rood-eye, a fine level beneath the city walls, belonging to the corporation. All ranks are admirably accommodated, a kind of verdant amphitheatre being formed by an ascent from the course to the walls; and, from the picturesque nature of the place, the spectacle is very imposing.

The port is not of much importance, owing to the shallowness of the water; but, by the exertions of the "River Dee Company," the channel has been deepened, the navigation improved, and a tract of ground, formerly sands, but now arable land, has been gained, by altering the course of the river, and making embankments, the last of which was completed in 1824. The commerce, both domestic and foreign, was formerly somewhat extensive, but is now chiefly confined to Ireland, though a few ships trade with the Baltic, Spain, Portugal, and the Mediterranean shores. The articles imported are linen, butter, provisions, timber, hides, tallow, feathers, iron, hemp, flax, kid and lamb-skins, fruit, oil, barilla, and wine: those shipped, chiefly coastwise, are, cheese (in large quantities), coal, lead, copper, calamine, and lead, copper, and iron ores. About 1736, Chester became a great mart for Irish linen, which trade increased so much, that the fairs were principally distinguished by the quantity sold annually at them, estimated at four millions of yards. The number of vessels that entered inwards from foreign ports, in 1826, was forty-one, and outwards thirteen, all British. The manufactures are inconsiderable: the principal articles are tobacco, snuff, white lead, shot, tobacco-pipes, and leather. The skin trade was formerly extensive, and is still of consequence; but the manufacture of gloves, in which several hundred persons were employed, has much declined. The city mills, standing on the western side of the old bridge, are complete and extensive: they were erected a few years since, the previous buildings having been burnt down, and formerly were a source of considerable profit to the earls of Chester, the inhabitants not being permitted to grind their corn elsewhere. Chester is connected with Liverpool by the Ellesmere canal, which commences at Ellesmere Port, on the Mersey, and here joins the Dee and the Chester canal: these canals originally belonged to separate companies, now united; they extend to Nantwich, Whitchurch, Ellesmere, and Llanymynech, and uniting with the Montgomeryshire canal, form a line of communication by water of more than one hundred miles.

The market days are Wednesday and Saturday: the new market-place, comprising five distinct buildings, was erected at the expense of the corporation, in 1828. The fairs are on the last Thursday in February, for horses and cattle; and July 5th and October 10th, for articles in general, of which Irish linen, Manchester goods, Welch flannel, and Birmingham and Sheffield wares, are the principal. The two latter fairs were granted by Norman earls; and their antiquity is proved by the recorded jurisdiction of the Dutton family over the Cheshire minstrels, which is related to have originated in the deliverance of Earl Ranulph de Blundeville from a body of Welch invaders, by a band of minstrels and buffoons, under the command of Hugh Dutton, who had assembled at Chester fair; for which service Dutton was afterwards allowed to license minstrels and other itinerants, without their being accounted vagabonds. Fourteen days before the commencement of each general fair, a wooden hand, as the emblem of traffic and bargain, is suspended from the Pentice, adjoining St. Peter's church, where it remains during the fair (a period of twenty-nine days), when non-freemen are allowed to trade in the city; and during the continuance of the fairs, a court of pie-powder is held by the sheriffs. The Linen Hall, built about the year 1780, is a spacious pile of building, forming an oblong square; it comprises more than one hundred shops, ranged round the sides of the area, with a counting-house behind each; the upper apartment projects, and is supported by pillars, forming a covered walk all round: the entrances are in the east and west corners.

Corporate Seal.

Chester is one of the oldest corporate towns in England. At the Conquest, it ranked as a *Guilda Mercatoris*—a constitution somewhat similar to that of modern municipal corporations. It was chartered by its Norman earls, and additional privileges were conferred on the inhabitants by charters of Henry II. and John. Henry III. constituted the chief magistrate mayor. Edward II. granted to the corporation all the vacant lands within the liberty of the city; and Richard II. authorised the mayor, sheriffs, and commonalty, to hold courts of common law and other courts; which privileges were confirmed and extended by Henry IV. Henry VII., besides granting a more extensive charter, remitted four-fifths of the fee-farm rent of £100 per annum, which Henry III. and Edward I. had claimed from the citizens in consideration of continuing their privileges, and constituted the city a county of itself, under the style of the "City and County of the City of Chester." Parliament subsequently deprived the city of its privileges as a separate county; but this act was revoked at the Restoration. Charles II. disfranchised it in 1684-5: its privileges, however, were afterwards restored, with a discretionary power in the crown to displace the officers of the corporation. James II., availing himself of this prerogative, displaced the mayor, recorder, and other functionaries, but was induced, at the approach of the Revolution, to restore them to office. The charter of Henry VII. conferred on the freemen generally the important privilege of electing the officers of the corporation, which consists of a mayor, recorder, two sheriffs, twenty-four aldermen, and forty common council-men, assisted by a town-clerk, sword-bearer, mace-bearer, and subordinate officers. From the non-exercise of this privilege the election has, in effect, long been vested in the court of aldermen and common council, who now consider it their exclusive right. Several attempts have been made by the freemen to recover this lost power; but the question, after much litigation and expense, remains unsettled, and the practice continues as before. The mayor, recorder, and aldermen, who have passed the chair, are justices of the peace. The recorder and town-clerk are chosen by the corporation, who appoint, from among the common council-men, officers termed leave-lookers, whose business it is to inspect the markets and receive the dues; and, from among the senior aldermen, messengers for the superintendence of the walls of the city. The two aldermen next in rotation for the mayoralty are, respectively, by the same body, usually appointed treasurer and coroner. There are no less than twenty-four guilds, or trade companies, headed by aldermen, or wardens, and holding charters of incorporation under the city seal: by their constitution they are obliged, when required, to pay homage to the mayor, and to contribute certain sums yearly to the city plate, run for at the races on St. George's day.

By ancient usage, confirmed by the several charters,

the mayor, assisted by the recorder, holds a crown-mote and a port-mote: the earliest rolls in these courts are of the date 1277: the jurisdiction of the crown-mote extends to all crimes except that of high treason, the mayor having power to pass sentence of death, and order execution, independently of the crown; and in the port-mote pleas to any amount are cognizable. There are also two ancient courts, one called "The Pentice court," which has cognizance of personal actions to any amount; and the other "The Passage court," held before the sheriffs and a jury, with appeal to the port-mote, to which records are removable by command of the mayor without writ. The courts of session are held in the exchange, where also the magistrates and members for the city are elected; and the assizes for the county are held in the castle. The exchange is a handsome brick building, finished in 1698; it is fronted with stone, supported by columns, and surmounted by a glazed cupola. On the ground-floor are the record-room and shops; and on the first floor the council and assembly-rooms, which are decorated with a picture of George III. by Sir Joshua Reynolds, and handsome portraits of the Grosvenor, Cholmondeley, Bunbury, and Egerton families, and of several charitable individuals. The sessions have been held here before the mayor since 1377. The freedom of the city is inherited by all the sons of freemen, and acquired by servitude and purchase. On the abridgment of the privileges of the county palatine, in 1541, an act passed, empowering the county to return two knights, and the city two burgesses to parliament. The election for the city is in the mayor, aldermen, and common councilmen, whether resident or not, and freemen resident in the city a year preceding, and not having received alms: the sheriffs are the returning officers. The number of freemen who polled, during the election of 1826, was one thousand five hundred. The preponderating influence is in the Grosvenor family, members of which, or their nominees, have generally represented the city.

Of the ancient castle, built by the Conqueror, there remains only a large square tower, called "Julius Agricola's Tower," now used as a magazine for gunpowder. Though of modern appearance, having recently been newly fronted, it is undoubtedly of great antiquity, and interesting as the probable place of confinement of the Earl of Derby; and in which Richard II., and Margaret, Countess of Richmond, were imprisoned. In the second chamber James II. heard mass, on his tour through this part of the kingdom, a short time previously to the Revolution. This apartment, when opened after many years of disuse as a chapel, exhibited, from the richness of its decorations, a splendid appearance, the walls being completely covered with paintings in fresco, as vivid and beautiful as when executed. The roof, from the rich effect produced by the ribs of the groined arches, springing elegantly from slender pillars, with capitals in a chaste and curious style, was equally striking. The remainder of the original structure, which was pulled down in 1790, contained a room termed Hugh Lupus' Hall, which was regarded as a superb specimen of baronial magnificence; it was ninety-five feet long and forty-five wide, with an antique roof of wood, curiously carved and resting upon brackets. The new edifice, which has excited general admiration, was erected from a design by Mr. Harrison, and under his inspection. The principal entrance is of the Doric order, resembling the Acropolis at Athens. Opposite to the great gate is the shire-hall, a magnificent structure, internally of the semicircular form, eighty feet in diameter, in height forty-one, and in width fifty: a semicircular range of twelve Ionic pillars supports the roof, which is finely ornamented in stucco, and the effect of the whole is highly imposing. The entrance to the gaol, which is appropriated to debtors and felons of the county, is on the right of the hall. At the eastern side of the yard are barracks, fronted with white freestone, and ornamented with Ionic pillars, capable of lodging one hundred and twenty men. On the western side is a corresponding building, used as an armoury, which will contain thirty thousand stand of arms. The castle is a royal fortress: the establishment consists of a governor, lieutenant-governor, ordnance-keeper, and barrack-master. The constableship of the tower is held by patent, and is free from municipal control. The castle, although within the city walls, is extra-parochial, as is also the township of Gloverstone, now merged into the county: the sheriffs for the city attend the execution of criminals for offences committed in the county, whom they receive in form at the verge of the city, and conduct to the drop in front of the gaol; for which service, the corporation, as keepers of the north gate, were formerly entitled to a toll. Sixteen persons are named in a record of the fourteenth century as being obliged, by their tenure in the city, and the exemptions they enjoyed, to conduct the malefactors, not only of the city, but also of the county palatine, to the gallows; and the occupiers of some houses held by this tenure still continue to pay a composition, called "Execution, or Gable rent," to be relieved from this duty.

Arms of the Bishoprick.

Chester, with part of the kingdom of Mercia, at an early period gave name to a diocese, which afterwards was incorporated with that of Lichfield. In 1075, Peter, Bishop of Lichfield, restored the see to Chester, whence it was a second time removed to Lichfield, by his successor, Robert de Lindsey. It again became a diocese under Henry VIII., who named it one of the six new sees created in 1541, and endowed it with a portion of the possessions of the abbey of St. Werburgh, the revenue of which, at the dissolution, was £1073. 17. 7. The first bishop was John Bird, previously a provincial of the Carmelites, and Bishop of Bangor. In 1547 this prelate granted the manors and demesnes of the bishoprick to the king, accepting impropriations of little value in exchange, and thus rendered it one of the least valuable of the English sees. Its temporalties in Chester consist only of the palace, which was rebuilt in 1752, by Bishop Keene, and its appendages, and two houses near St. John's church. The cathedral, originally the conventual church of St. Werburgh, was first dedicated to St. Peter and St. Paul, but subsequently placed by Ethelfreda under the patronage of the Saxon saint, Walmgha, daughter of Wulphen, King of Mercia. That princess, and Leofric, Earl of Mercia, were great benefactors to the church, as well as Hugh Lupus, who substituted Benedictine monks for Secular canons. On the dissolution of the abbey, a dean, six prebendaries, and six minor canons, were appointed in lieu of the abbot and monks, the last abbot being made dean : there are also a chancellor, registrar, sacrist, and precentor. At the dissolution the cathedral was dedicated to Christ and the Blessed Virgin : it stands on the eastern side of Northgate street, and, exclusively of some interesting remains of the abbey, the present building was erected in the reigns of Henry VII. and Henry VIII. With the exception of the western end, it is, externally, a heavy irregular pile. The tower in the centre, originally intended to sustain a spire, is supported by massive piers, and is in the later style of English architecture. Within ten years, the exterior, which, from the soft nature of the stone, was greatly dilapidated, has undergone considerable repairs. The interior is elegant and impressive, and exhibits portions in the Norman and in the early and decorated styles of English architecture. The piers of the nave are in the decorated style, with flowered capitals; and the clerestory, which is in the later style, has a fine range of painted windows. To the east of the north transept are some chapels in the early English style ; the south transept, which is larger than the north, and consists of a centre and two side aisles, is in the decorated style, and, being separated from the cathedral by a wooden screen, forms the parish church of St. Oswald. The choir has a chequered floor of black and white marble, and the stalls are adorned with light tabernacle work, skilfully executed; the bishop's throne, usually deemed Werburgh's shrine, is a beautiful specimen of workmanship in the style of the early part of the fourteenth century. The chapter-house, an admirable relic of antiquity in the early English style, stands in the eastern walk of the cloister : it was built by Earl Randulph the first, and became the burial-place of the earls of the original Norman line, except Richard, who perished by shipwreck. Under part of the prebendal houses is a fine Norman crypt, in good preservation, which supported the great hall of the monastery, and had lain concealed till it was cleared out and rendered accessible by Dr. Blomfield, the present bishop of London, who then presided over this see.

The city comprises the parishes of St. Bridget, St. John the Baptist, Little St. John, St. Martin, St. Michael, St. Olave, and St. Peter ; and part of the parishes of St. Mary on the Hill, St. Oswald, and the Holy Trinity, and the precinct of the Cathedral Close ; all in the archdeaconry and diocese of Chester. The living of St. Bridget's is a rectory not in charge, endowed with £200 private benefaction, £200 royal bounty, and £200 parliamentary grant, and in the patronage of the Bishop : the church, lately built, is a chaste and elegant structure in the Grecian style of architecture, and of the Doric order ; towards its erection the Bridge Committee gave £4000, and the parishioners £500. The living of St. John the Baptist's is a vicarage not in charge, endowed with £200 royal bounty, and £2000 parliamentary grant, and in the patronage of Earl Grosvenor: the church, formerly collegiate, and, on the removal of the see of Lichfield to Chester by Bishop Peter, used as the cathedral, consists of the nave and portions of the transepts of the ancient cruciform structure, of which the eastern part has been long since destroyed ; the nave has massive Norman piers, with a triforium and clerestory of the early English character ; the north porch, in the same style, is very beautiful ; and the tower, a fine composition, though greatly mutilated, is detached from the church by the shortening of the western part of the nave. The living of Little St. John's is a perpetual curacy, endowed with £30 per annum private benefaction, £1200 royal bounty, and £600 parliamentary grant, and in the patronage of the Mayor and Corporation. The living of St. Martin's is a rectory not in charge, endowed with £200 private benefaction, £800 royal bounty, and £600 parliamentary grant, and in the patronage of the Bishop. The living of St. Michael's is a perpetual curacy, endowed with £600 royal bounty, and £1200 parliamentary grant, and in the patronage of the Bishop. The living of St. Olave's is a perpetual curacy, endowed with £200 private benefaction, £200 royal bounty, and £1400 parliamentary grant, and in the patronage of the Bishop. The living of St. Peter's is a discharged perpetual curacy, rated in the king's books at £6. 13. 4., endowed with £200 private benefaction, £400 royal bounty, and £400 parliamentary grant, and in the patronage of the Bishop. The living of the parish of St. Mary on the Hill is a rectory, rated in the king's books at £52, and in the patronage of Earl Grosvenor : the church is a venerable building in the later style of English architecture. The living of St. Oswald's is a discharged vicarage, with the perpetual curacy of Bruera annexed, rated in the king's books at £8. 18. 4., and in the patronage of the Dean and Chapter: the parochial church is formed of the south transept of the cathedral. The living of the parish of the Holy Trinity is a discharged rectory, rated in the king's books at £8. 15. 6., and in the patronage of the Earl of Derby. There are places of worship for Baptists, the Society of Friends, those in the connexion of the late Countess of Huntingdon, Independents, Welch and Wesleyan Methodists, New Connexion of Methodists, Sandemanians, Unitarians, and Roman Catholics.

The free grammar school was founded by Henry VIII., who, in the 36th year of his reign, endowed it with a rent-charge of £108. 16., for two masters and twenty-four boys, from amongst whom the choristers of the cathedral are chosen, who receive annually from the funds of the school £6. 8. each, and the other boys half that sum : the age for admission is nine years, and the term of their continuance in the school four years : it has an exhibition for a scholar at one of the Universities. The school-room, originally the refectory of the monastery, is a fine specimen of the early style of English architecture, but retaining little of the ancient edifice, except a stone pulpit, and a staircase in good preservation. The Blue-coat school was founded in 1700, on the recommendation of Bishop Stratford, and endowed for the maintenance of thirty-five boys for four years, at the end of which they are apprenticed. In 1781, the revenue being augmented, a plan was adopted for educating one hundred and twenty day-scholars in addition ; hence the origin of the Green-coat school. A similar school for girls was established in 1718, when they were only clothed and instructed, but the greater number is now boarded also, and, on leaving school, they are placed out in service. In 1811, Earl Grosvenor founded a school for instructing four hundred boys in reading, writing, and arithmetic; and the Countess established a similar school for four hundred girls: the school-rooms form a handsome building, erected by the earl, near St. John's church. The Diocesan school was instituted in 1812, under the patronage of Bishop Law, for the education of children in the principles of the church of England: the school-room, erected in 1816, will accommodate four hundred scholars. The infant school, and the working school, are of later establishment, and are supported by subscription. There are also various Sunday schools for both sexes, respectively supported by members of the church of England and dissenters.

Among the charities are divers bequests for the benefit of decayed freemen and freemen's widows; the principal is that by Mr. Owen Jones, who, in 1658, bequeathed the profits of a small estate in Denbighshire to the poor of the several city companies; which bequest, in consequence of the discovery of a lead mine, has of late enabled the trustees to distribute £400 annually. Earl Grosvenor founded ten almshouses for decayed freemen. Most of the parishes have also the distribution of benefactions; and three or four of them contain almshouses, the chief of which are for forty decayed freemen above sixty years of age. The house of industry, built in 1751, is pleasantly situated near the Rood-eye, and is under the control of the mayor, the aldermen who have passed the chair, and seventy-four guardians chosen from the several parishes. The general infirmary, a well built commodious structure, pleasantly situated on the western side of the city, is supported by a numerous body of subscribers, and possesses property to a considerable amount: it originated in 1756, from a bequest of £300 by Dr. John Stratford, and its expenditure is now nearly £3000 per annum. The establishment of fever-wards was proposed in 1774, and a few years afterwards carried into execution, chiefly through the exertions of Dr. Haygarth. There is also a lying-in institution, supported by subscriptions. A county asylum for lunatics, capable of accommodating one hundred patients, has lately been erected on the Liverpool road, from a design by Mr. William Cole, jun.: it cost upwards of £12,000, and is supported by a county rate and by payments from the more opulent patients, for whom superior accommodation is provided: the whole of the building, except the kitchens and governor's rooms, is heated by patent flues.

The walls of Chester rank amongst its principal antiquities, and are the only specimen of this species of ancient fortification in Britain remaining entire: they comprise a circuit of nearly two miles, and, in the narrowest parts, are sufficiently wide for two persons to walk abreast. Of the small towers, or turrets, erected within bow-shot of each other, only the Phœnix and Water towers exist. To keep them in repair, a small murage duty was granted by Edward I. on all merchandise brought to the town by sea. This revenue is not now very productive, in consequence of the principal articles of commerce being landed at Liverpool, and conveyed hither by canal; the corporation, however, continue the repairs. Besides the city gates before enumerated, and which, in comparison with the walls, are modern erections, there is a fifth, or postern, between East gate and Bridge gate, called New gate. The military importance of the city rendered the custody of four of the gates for centuries an honourable and lucrative office; it was held successively by the earls of Shrewsbury, Oxford, and Derby, and by Lord Crewe, and that of the fifth by one of the magistrates for the city. The custody of Water gate, connected with the office of issuing process for offences committed on the Dee, was sold, in 1778, by the Earl of Derby to the corporation. Among the ancient religious establishments may be noticed the monastery, or abbey, of St. John the Baptist, founded in 906, by Ethelred, Earl of Mercia, the revenue of which, at the dissolution, was £88. 16. 8.; the remains constitute the parish church of St. John: the monastery of St. Mary, of uncertain foundation, for Benedictine nuns, mentioned in Domesday-book, the revenue of which, at the dissolution, was £99. 16. 2.: the monastery of St. Michael, of which mention occurs in the charter of Roger, constable of Chester, and in the reign of Henry II.; a house of Grey friars in the parish of the Holy Trinity, probably founded by Henry III.; a house of Carmelites, and another of Black friars, in the parish of St. Martin; and, without the North gate, the hospital of St. John, which had a sanctuary and extensive privileges, and the revenue of which, at the dissolution, was £28. 10.

In the neighbourhood of the castle were formerly numerous Roman antiquities, particularly at Nensfield, where remains of a tesselated pavement have been discovered. The esplanade, when cleared of the ancient parts of the castle, was given by government to the county, for the erection of the splendid public buildings which now ornament the site; but the right of establishing a fortification, whenever necessary, was reserved for the crown. The eastern wall is built over part of a Roman well; but a segment of the circle is left outside the esplanade, for the purpose of clearing it. In a cellar belonging to the Feathers hotel is a Roman hypocaust, in a remarkably perfect state; and in a close at the southern end of the bridge, termed Edgar's field, the supposed site of Edgar's palace, and adjoining a cavity in a rock, is a stone figure of the goddess Pallas, a relic alluded to by ancient writers. Remains of Roman altars, with figures and inscriptions, have at different times been discovered; one in a cellar in Eastgate-street, dedicated by Telarius Longus, of the twentieth legion, to the emperors Dioclesian and Maximian; another ascribed to Jupiter the Thunderer, now preserved with the Arundelian marbles at Oxford; another, in 1693, in Eastgate-street; one in 1779, in Watergate-street, now preserved in the grounds of Oulton Park; and, in 1821, one in a field in Great Boughton: the last was purchased by Earl Grosvenor, and is placed in a temple in the garden at Eaton Hall: it is of red sandstone, with bold mouldings, and has no ornament but the scroll which supports the thuribulum. Henry Potts, Esq., of this city, has in his possession the figure of a Retiarius, armed with his trident and net, and the principal portion of the shield of the secutor, found in the market-place in 1738. Randle Higden, Roger of Chester, and Bradshaw, mention subterraneous passages under the city; one of these was discovered about the commencement of the present century, extending in a south-eastern direction from the ruins of the abbey, but it was soon closed up.

Chester has been the birthplace of several eminent men, the most distinguished of whom were, four antiquaries of the same family, all named Randle Holme; Dr. William Cowper, who made collections for a history of Chester; and the celebrated mathematicians, Edward Brerewood and Samuel Molyneux, the latter a friend and correspondent of Locke. In the church of the Holy Trinity were interred, Matthew Henry, the commentator on the Bible, and a pastor in this city from 1687 to 1713, to whose memory a brass tablet has been placed over the communion-table; and Parnell, the poet, October 24th, 1718. Chester gives the title of earl to the Prince of Wales, eldest son of the sovereign.

CHESTER (LITTLE), a township in that part of the parish of St. Alkmund, Derby, which is without the limits of the borough, in the hundred of Morleston and Litchurch, county of Derby, containing 177 inhabitants. It is situated on the eastern bank of the Derwent, about 1 mile (N. N. E.) from the town, and occupies the site of the Roman station *Derventio*, the most important in the county: it was of an oblong form, comprising nearly six acres. The wall that surrounded it was traced by Dr. Stukeley in 1721; but subsequent cultivation has removed every vestige. It stood on the line of the Iknield-street, which here crossed the river; and is noticed in Domesday-book under the name *Cestre*, being therein described as parcel of the ancient demesne of the crown. Numerous foundations, coins of gold, silver, and copper, and other remains of Roman antiquity, have been discovered.

CHESTER le STREET, a parish comprising the chapelry of Great Lumley, and the townships of Lambton and Little Lumley, in the northern division of Easington ward; and the chapelries of Lamesley and Tanfield, and the townships of Beamish, Birtley, Chester le Street, Edmondsley, Harraton, Hedley, Kibblesworth, Lintz-Green, Pelton, Plawsworth, Ravensworth, Urpeth, Ouston, and Waldridge, in the middle division of Chester ward, county palatine of Durham; and containing 13,936 inhabitants, of which number, 1892 are in the township of Chester le Street, 6¼ miles (N.) from Durham. The living is a perpetual curacy, in the archdeaconry and diocese of Durham, and in the patronage of Lord Durham and W. Joliffe, Esq., alternately. The church, anciently collegiate, is dedicated to St. Mary and St. Cuthbert, and is a well-built structure, partly in the early and partly in the later style of English architecture, with a tower square at the base, but octagonal above, supporting a beautiful spire, one hundred and fifty-six feet high, considered to be the handsomest in the north of England: the north aisle contains an interesting series, from the time of the Conqueror down to that of Elizabeth, of fourteen effigies carved in stone, and resting on the same number of altar-tombs, of the family of Lumley, of Lumley Castle. To this place Eardulph, the eighteenth prelate of the church of Lindisfarne, in 882, removed the relics of St. Cuthbert, an effigy of whom was subsequently found here, when the Danes made a devastating inroad on the coast; and having founded the church, it continued the head of the diocese, under a succession of eight bishops, until its removal to Durham, in 995. After this it was merely rectorial until 1286, when Bishop Anthony Beck founded a collegiate establishment, consisting of a dean, seven prebendaries, three deacons, and other ministers, which was included in the suppression of similar institutions in the 1st of Edward VI. There are places of worship for Independents and Primitive and Wesleyan Methodists. The village is pleasantly situated in a valley, about a quarter of a mile west of the river Wear, on the road to Berwick; it occupies the site of the Roman station *Condercum*, on the line of the Roman military way leading to Newcastle: several Roman coins, and an altar much defaced, have been found. The Saxons named it *Cunceastre*, or *Cuneagester*. The manufacture of nails, ropes, tiles, &c. is carried on, and the neighbourhood abounds with coal: a market was formerly held weekly, but it has fallen into disuse. The river Wear is navigable to this place, where it is crossed by a bridge erected in 1821. On the 17th of November, 1771, this river overflowed its banks, and greatly damaged many of the houses and other property. A mechanics' institution was established in 1825; and a Sunday school is supported by voluntary contributions. A court leet is held twice a year by the Bishop of Durham, as lord of the manor, wherein small debts are recoverable; and the petty sessions for Chester ward take place every alternate Thursday: a coroner is also specially appointed for the division. Twelve poor children are educated from a bequest by Mrs. Teward, in 1718.

CHESTERBLADE, a chapelry in the parish of Evercreech, forming, with the remainder of that parish, and the parish of West Cranmore, a detached portion of the hundred of Wells-Forum, county of Somerset, 4¼ miles (E. S. E.) from Shepton-Mallet. The population is returned with the parish. The chapel is dedicated to St. Mary. There are vestiges of a Roman encampment on a small hill in the vicinity.

Seal and Arms.

CHESTERFIELD, a parish in the hundred of Scarsdale, county of Derby, comprising the market town of Chesterfield, which has a separate jurisdiction, the chapelries of Brimington and Temple-Normanton, the townships of Hasland, Tapton, and Walton, and the hamlets of Calow, Newbold with Dunstan, and Pilsley, and containing 9190 inhabitants, of which number, 5077 are in the town of Chesterfield, 25 miles (N. by E.) from Derby, and 151 (N. N. W.) from London, on the road to Leeds. The Saxon name of this place, *Ceaster*, from which its present appellation is derived, indicates it to have been a Roman station. At the time of the Norman survey, when it was called *Cestrefeld*, it was only a bailiwick to Newbold, the latter being now a small hamlet in the parish; but within a century from that period, it appears to have risen again into such importance as to have obtained from King John, who conferred it upon William de Briwere, a charter of incorporation, with the privilege of two markets and a fair. In the reign of Henry III., a decisive battle was fought here between Henry, nephew of that monarch, and the barons, which terminated in the defeat of the latter, several of whom were slain. Robert de Ferrars,

Earl of Derby, who had espoused their cause, being taken prisoner, was sent in chains to Windsor, and afterwards, by act of parliament, degraded from his honours and deprived of his estates. During the parliamentary war, another conflict took place between the royalists, under the command of the Earl of Newcastle, and the parliamentarians, in which the former obtained a signal victory. The town is situated on an eminence between the Rother and Hipper, which at this place are inconsiderable streams; the houses are of brick, roofed with stone; the streets are indifferently paved, but well lighted with gas, by an act of parliament obtained in 1825, and are plentifully supplied with water conveyed by pipes from Holme, two miles west of the town. There are a subscription library and a theatre: assemblies are held monthly in a suite of rooms at the Castle Inn; and races take place in autumn. An agricultural society has been established within the last few years, the members of which hold their meetings alternately at Chesterfield and Bakewell, generally in October. Several of the inhabitants are employed in tambour work, and the manufacture of bobbin net-lace, gloves, and hosiery: there are also a silk-mill and a cotton-mill; and in the vicinity are some productive mines of iron-stone and coal, and some foundries, in one of which, mill-work, machinery, and steam-engines are made; about three hundred men are employed in these works: there are also several potteries, chiefly for the coarse brown stone ware, which afford employment to about two hundred men. The Chesterfield canal, communicating with the Trent and the Humber, continued for forty-six miles by sixty-five locks, and passing under two tunnels, of which that at Norwood is nearly three quarters of a mile in length, was completed in 1777, at an expense of £160,000. The market is on Saturday: fairs, principally for cattle, are held on January 27th, February 28th, the first Saturday in April, May 4th, July 4th, September 25th, and November 25th, the last being toll-free; those in May and September, at the latter of which a great quantity of cheese is sold, are attended by the clothiers from Yorkshire.

The government, by charter of incorporation granted by King John, and ratified by succeeding monarchs, enlarged by Queen Elizabeth, and confirmed by Charles II., is vested in a mayor, six aldermen, six brethren, and twelve capital burgesses, assisted by a chamberlain, town-clerk, and other officers, among whom are a master butcher and master brazier, whose duty it is to inspect the quality of the meat, and the accuracy of the weights and measures. The mayor is chosen by the corporation, on the Sunday preceding Michaelmas-day; both he and the mayor for the preceding year are justices of the peace: a constable is chosen at the court leet of the lord of the manor, held in October. The petty sessions for the division are held here; and a court of record for the recovery of debts not exceeding £20 is held under the lord of the manor, by letters patent granted by King John to William de Briwere, and confirmed by Charles I., in the seventh year of his reign, to William, Earl of Newcastle, and Sir Charles Cavendish, then lords of the manor, the jurisdiction of which extends over the hundred of Scarsdale, eight miles round Chesterfield. The town-hall, standing in the market-place, was built in 1790: on the ground-floor is a prison for debtors, and a residence for the gaoler, above which is a large room for holding the sessions and transacting public business: there is also a house of correction, under the superintendence of the county magistrates, but it is too small to admit of the classification of prisoners.

The living is a vicarage, in the archdeaconry of Derby, and diocese of Lichfield and Coventry, rated in the king's books at £15. 0. 2½., endowed with £400 parliamentary grant, and in the patronage of the Dean of Lincoln. The church, dedicated to All Saints, is a spacious cruciform structure, principally in the decorated, but partly in the early, and partly in the later style of English architecture, with a square embattled tower rising from the intersection, and surmounted by a lofty spire, which, from the peculiar mode of putting on the lead with which it is covered, though perfectly upright, appears in every direction in which it is viewed to incline considerably from the perpendicular. The clerestory windows of the nave, and the east window of the chancel, are fine compositions in the later style; and in the south transept are a beautiful screen and rood-loft: there are two very antique monuments in the nave, and three in the chancel, to members of the family of Foljambe. There are places of worship for Baptists, the Society of Friends, Independents, Primitive and Wesleyan Methodists, Sandemanians, and Unitarians. The free grammar school, for the endowment of which Godfrey Foljambe, Esq., in 1594, appropriated £13. 6. 8. annually, was founded in the reign of Elizabeth, and placed under the management of the mayor and corporation; the endowment, augmented by subsequent benefactions, produces annually £109. 10. 9., which sum, including £15 to the master and £15 to the usher, bequeathed by Cornelius Clarke, Esq. in 1690, is paid as a salary to the master, who is chosen by the mayor and corporation, subject to approval by the Archbishop of York, no usher having been appointed lately, in consequence of the small number of scholars, only five or six, attending the school. The school-house, to which are attached a garden and from four to five acres of land, was rebuilt by subscription in 1710: this school, in common with those of Ashbourn and Wirksworth, has the preference, next after the founder's relatives, to two fellowships and two scholarships, founded by the Rev. James Beresford, in St. John's College, Cambridge. A petty school, intended originally as preparatory to the grammar school, was founded in 1690, and endowed for the instruction of ten boys, by Cornelius Clarke, Esq.; the endowment was subsequently augmented by John Bright, senior, and John Bright, junior, Esqrs., for the instruction of an additional number of boys or girls, their nearest relatives, or, in default of such, of other children of the parish, nominated by the mayor and corporation; the present income arising from these endowments is £74 per annum: there is no school-room appropriated to this establishment, the children being taught in the master's house. A National school, in which one hundred and eighty boys and one hundred and twenty girls are instructed, was built in 1814, at an expense of £800, and is supported by subscription; and a Lancasterian school, in which one hundred and twelve girls are instructed, was erected in 1819. Mrs. Judith Heathcote, and other members of the same family, in 1619, appropriated estates producing £114 per annum to the apprenticing of poor children; the premium with each, originally fixed at £5, has been increased to

£10, and, within the last ten years, one hundred and three boys have been apprenticed.

Thomas Large, Esq., in 1664, gave lands and tenements, now producing about £45 per annum, for the foundation and endowment of almshouses for three aged persons: to these two more were added, in 1751, by Mrs. Sarah Rose, who also left £200 for their endowment. Almshouses for six aged persons were founded, in 1668, by George Taylor, Esq., who endowed them with property now producing £22 per annum; he also gave in trust to the mayor and corporation £120, to be lent to young tradesmen at five per cent. interest. The dispensary, erected in 1800, is liberally supported by subscription. Godfrey Foljambe, Esq., in 1594, bequeathed the rectory of Attleborough, in the county of Nottingham, and an estate at Ashover, in this county, producing together about £640 per annum, of which, after paying £40 per annum to the minister, £13. 6. 8. to the master of the free grammar school, £20 to the master and fellows of Jesus' College, and £13. 6. 8. to the master and fellows of Magdalene College, Cambridge, the remainder is appropriated to the relief of the poor. Godfrey Wolstenholme, in 1682, gave a house let for £38. 5. per annum, which is distributed in coats and gowns to the poor; and Sir Godfrey Webster, in 1720, bequeathed £1100 South Sea stock, the dividends on which, amounting to £28. 13. 4., are annually distributed in sums of £1 each to poor persons. Mrs. Hannah Hooper, in 1755, gave £2000 three per cent. consols., the dividends on which, amounting yearly to £60, are paid to six poor widows who have been resident in the parish for seven years; and Mrs. Elizabeth Bagshaw, in 1802, gave £2000 three per cent. consols., the dividends on which are distributed, in sums of £1 each, to poor housekeepers: there are also various other charitable bequests at the disposal of the corporation. An hospital for lepers, founded prior to the 10th of Richard I., and dedicated to St. Leonard, existed here till the reign of Henry VIII.; and there was a guild or fraternity, dedicated to St. Mary and the Holy Cross, founded in the reign of Richard II., the revenue of which, at the dissolution, was £19. The chantry of St. Michael, founded by Roger de Chesterfield in 1357, and the chantry of the Holy Cross, founded in the reign of Edward III., were also among the ancient religious establishments of this place. There were besides, prior to the Reformation, three free chapels, dedicated respectively to St. James, St. Thomas, and St. Helen: on the site of the last the present free grammar school was built. Chesterfield gives the title of earl to the family of Stanhope.

CHESTERFORD (GREAT), a parish (formerly a market town) in the hundred of Uttlesford, county of Essex, 4 miles (N. W. by N.) from Saffron-Walden, containing 755 inhabitants. The living is a discharged vicarage, with the rectory of Little Chesterford annexed, in the archdeaconry of Colchester, and diocese of London, rated in the king's books at £10, endowed with £200 private benefaction, and £200 royal bounty, and in the alternate patronage of the Crown and the Marquis of Bristol. The church, dedicated to All Saints, is an ancient and spacious structure, and formerly contained a chantry founded in the reign of Henry VIII., by William Howden, the revenue of which, at the dissolution, was £9. 9. 7. The market has been discontinued: a fair for horses is held on the 5th of July. There is a free school, endowed with land by John Hart, Esq., and under the management of the Master and Fellows of St. Mary Magdalene's College, Cambridge: there are also several charitable bequests for distribution among the poor. This place, which is situated on the eastern bank of the river Granta, though now only an inconsiderable village, was anciently a town of considerable importance. It is by most antiquaries identified with the *Camboricum* of Antoninus, and the foundation of walls, enclosing a quadrangular area of fifty acres, was, till very lately, plainly discernible: that it was a Roman station is evident, not only from its name, and the numerous coins and other Roman antiquities discovered at various times, but from its contiguity to several Roman roads, of which the Iknield and Ermin streets intersect each other in the immediate vicinity. Roman bricks, and coins of the earlier and later emperors, have been found in great quantities; of which, in 1769, a large number, in good preservation, was found in an earthen pot, by some workmen, who were digging up the foundation of the walls for materials to mend the road: in 1730, many coins and entire skeletons were discovered, besides a small urn of red clay, containing written scrolls of parchment, which were destroyed before they were decyphered; and in 1786 were found a bronze bust, fibulæ, gold and brass instruments, and utensils of various kinds, of which one of gold, in the form of a staple, and weighing eight pounds, lay buried under a rude mass of bronze: a stone trough, in the form of half an octagon, of which the four compartments were ornamented with human figures in relievo, was for a considerable time used as a reservoir for water in a smith's shop; it was subsequently in the possession of Dr. Gower, of Chelmsford, who referred it to that class of receptacles for ashes, called *Quietoria*. Besides the larger camp, or station, are several smaller camps; one near the church, in the grounds between which and the river are traces of an amphitheatre; at the distance of half a mile from the larger camp is another, called Hingeston barrows, and a third on the opposite side of the river. On an eminence, near the Roman road from Inckleton towards Newmarket, is Fleamsdyke, where there is a small square fort, probably the *castra exploratorum*, in the centre of which are vestiges of a building: the Roman road to Grantchester may be plainly discovered, forming a ridge of two hundred yards, in a direction towards the river, above Cambridge. The custom of Borough English, whereby the youngest son inherits prevails in this parish.

CHESTERFORD (LITTLE), a parish in the hundred of Uttlesford, county of Essex, 3 miles (N. W. by N.) from Saffron-Walden, containing 192 inhabitants. The living is a rectory, annexed to the vicarage of Great Chesterford, in the archdeaconry of Colchester, and diocese of London, rated in the king's books at £11. The church is dedicated to St. Mary.

CHESTERHOPE, a hamlet in the parish of Corsenside, north-eastern division of Tindale ward, county of Northumberland, 5 miles (E. N. E.) from Bellingham. The population is returned with the parish. Stones bearing Latin inscriptions have been found here, which are supposed to be relics of the Roman station at the adjoining village of Risingham.

CHESTERTON, a parish in the hundred of CHESTERTON, county of CAMBRIDGE, 1¼ mile (N. E.) from Cambridge, containing 1137 inhabitants. The living is a vicarage, in the archdeaconry and diocese of Ely, rated in the king's books at £10. 12. 3½., and in the patronage of the Master and Fellows of Trinity College, Cambridge. The church, dedicated to St. Andrew, is principally in the decorated and later styles of English architecture. The name signifies the town next the castle or camp, Arbury camp being at a small distance from the village, three parts of the vallum of which are still remaining, enclosing a square area of nearly six acres, in which many Roman coins have been found, particularly a silver one with the head of Romulus on the obverse, and on the reverse Castor and Pollux on horseback. It appears that every one who kept a fire here, in 1154, was bound to pay a *fly farthing*, as it was called, to St. Peter's altar in the cathedral church of Ely; and the fourth farthing arising from this town and that of Grantchester used to be paid to the castle of Norwich, by the name of *Ely ward penny*, because that place received it before. In 1729, £5 per annum, out of money left to the parish for charitable uses, was appropriated, by a decree of the court of Chancery, towards the education of ten poor children. The remains of Cambridge castle are in this parish, and the river Cam runs through it.

CHESTERTON, a parish in the hundred of NORMAN-CROSS, county of HUNTINGDON, 4½ miles (N. N. W.) from Stilton, containing 95 inhabitants. The living is a rectory, in the archdeaconry of Huntingdon, and diocese of Lincoln, rated in the king's books at £17. 3. 4., and in the patronage of the Earl of Aboyne. The church, dedicated to St. Michael, is principally in the early style of English architecture. Midway between this and Castor is the site of *Durobrivæ*, the fort of which was placed on the Huntingdonshire side of the river Nene; and at Castle field is a large tract, enclosed by a ditch and rampart, with the Roman road Ermin-street running through it obliquely. On making a turnpike road across the site of the ancient city of *Durobrivæ*, several stone coffins, urns, and coins, were dug up; and by the side of the high road near this place, in 1754, was found a coffin of yellowish stone, six feet two inches long, within which were a skeleton, three glass lachrymatories, some coins, and scraps of white wood inscribed with Greek and Roman letters.

CHESTERTON, a parish in the hundred of PLOUGHLEY, county of OXFORD, 2 miles (W. by S.) from Bicester, containing 392 inhabitants. The living is a discharged vicarage, in the archdeaconry and diocese of Oxford, rated in the king's books at £7. 8. 9., and in the patronage of the Warden and Fellows of New College, Oxford. The church is dedicated to St. Mary.

CHESTERTON, a township in the parish of WOLSTANTON, northern division of the hundred of PIREHILL, county of STAFFORD, 2½ miles (N. by W.) from Newcastle under Line, containing 974 inhabitants. There is a place of worship for Wesleyan Methodists.

CHESTERTON, a parish in the Warwick division of the hundred of KINGTON, county of WARWICK, 5½ miles (N. by E.) from Kington, containing, with the hamlet of Kington, or Little Chesterton, 231 inhabitants. The living is a perpetual curacy, in the archdeaconry of Coventry, and diocese of Lichfield and Coventry, endowed with £400 private benefaction, and £600 royal bounty, and in the patronage of Lord Willoughby de Broke. The church is dedicated to St. Giles. Here are the remains of an extensive Roman fortification, that gave name to Chesterton, which was once a populous town, situated on the line of the Roman Fosse-way.

CHESTERTON (LITTLE), county of WARWICK.—See KINGTON.

CHESWARDINE, a parish in the Drayton division of the hundred of BRADFORD (North), county of SALOP, 4½ miles (S. W.) from Drayton, containing 938 inhabitants. The living is a discharged vicarage, in the archdeaconry of Stafford, and diocese of Lichfield and Coventry, rated in the king's books at £5. 6. 8., and in the patronage of T. Smallwood, Esq. The church is dedicated to St. Swithin. There is a small bequest for teaching four poor boys of this parish.

CHETNOLE, a chapelry in the parish and hundred of YETMINSTER, Sherborne division of the county of DORSET, 7 miles (S. W. by S.) from Sherborne, containing 239 inhabitants. The chapel is dedicated to St. Peter.

CHETTISCOMBE, a chapelry in the parish and hundred of TIVERTON, county of DEVON, 2 miles (N. E. by N.) from Tiverton, with which the population is returned. The chapel is dedicated to St. Mary.

CHETTISHAM, a chapelry in the parish of ST. MARY, city and Isle of ELY, county of CAMBRIDGE, 2 miles (N. by W.) from Ely, containing 91 inhabitants. The living is a perpetual curacy, in the archdeaconry and diocese of Ely, endowed with £200 private benefaction, and £400 royal bounty, and in the patronage of the Dean and Chapter of Ely. The chapel is dedicated to St. Michael.

CHETTLE, a parish in the hundred of MONCKTON up WIMBORNE, Shaston (East) division of the county of DORSET, 7 miles (N. E.) from Blandford-Forum, containing 132 inhabitants. The living is a discharged rectory, in the archdeaconry of Dorset, and diocese of Bristol, rated in the king's books at £8. 2. 9., and in the patronage of the Lord of the Manor. The church, dedicated to St. Mary, is partly in the early and partly in the later style of English architecture. Here is a fine old mansion, built in Sir John Vanbrugh's style, but it is unoccupied.

CHETTON, a parish in the hundred of STOTTESDEN, county of SALOP, 4 miles (S. W. by W.) from Bridgenorth, containing, with the chapelry of Loughton, 573 inhabitants. The living is a rectory, consolidated in 1760 with those of Deuxhill and Glazeley, in the archdeaconry of Salop, and diocese of Hereford, rated in the king's books at £11. The church, dedicated to St. Giles, has a Norman tower; the chancel is in the early English style, and the nave is of modern erection. There is a bequest of about £8 per annum for teaching poor children, which, with additional subscriptions, is applied to the instruction of about seventy children.

CHETWOOD, a parish in the hundred and county of BUCKINGHAM, 5 miles (S. W. by W.) from Buckingham, containing 131 inhabitants. The living is a perpetual curacy, annexed to that of Barton-Hartshorn, in the archdeaconry of Buckingham, and diocese of Lincoln, endowed with £200 private benefaction, and £600 royal bounty. The church, dedicated to St. Mary and St. Nicholas, was made parochial in 1480; it is remarkable for some beautiful specimens of stained glass formerly belonging to a priory of Augustine monks, founded by Sir Ralph de Norwich, in 1244, which was dissolved on account of its poverty, in 1460, and annexed to the abbey of Nutley: there was also a hermitage, dedicated to St. Stephen and St. Lawrence, founded by a member of the Chetwode family, the representative of which claims suit and service, by prescriptive right, over this place and the neighbouring townships and hamlets of Barton, Tingewick, Preston with Cowley, Hillersdon, Gawcott, Lenborough, and Bucks Prebend-end; and accordingly requires the constables of all these villages, which were said to be included within the limits of an ancient forest of one thousand acres, called Rockwood, to be sworn at his court leet held here at Easter.

CHETWYND, a parish in the Newport division of the hundred of BRADFORD (South), county of SALOP, 1¾ mile (N. by W.) from Newport, containing 566 inhabitants. The living is a rectory, in the archdeaconry of Salop, and diocese of Lichfield and Coventry, rated in the king's books at £10. 16. 3., and in the patronage of Thomas Borough, Esq. The church, dedicated to St. Michael, is a modern brick building. A school, now conducted on the National plan, is endowed with lands producing £30 per annum.

CHEVELEY, a parish in the hundred of CHEVELEY, county of CAMBRIDGE, 3¼ miles (E. S. E.) from Newmarket, containing 521 inhabitants. The living is a rectory, in the archdeaconry of Sudbury, and diocese of Norwich, rated in the king's books at £16. 8. 1½., and in the patronage of James Thomas Hand. The church is dedicated to St. Mary. A free grammar school was founded, in 1558, by John Ray, Esq., with an endowment of forty-nine acres and a half of land in the parish, producing an annual income of about £35, to which, in augmentation of the master's salary, Lord Dover added a farm at Worlington in Suffolk. In 1748, Mr. John Warren bequeathed £300 New South Sea annuities, for teaching girls to read and sew.

CHEVENING, a parish in the hundred of CODSHEATH, lathe of SUTTON at HONE, county of KENT, 3¼ miles (N.W.) from Seven-Oaks, containing 812 inhabitants. The living is a rectory, in the exempt deanery of Shoreham, which is within the peculiar jurisdiction of the Archbishop of Canterbury, rated in the king's books at £21. 6. 8., and in the patronage of the Archbishop of Canterbury. The church, dedicated to St. Botolph, is adorned with several elegant monuments of the Lennard family, and one to Lady Frederica Stanhope. Various bequests of the Stanhope family are applied in apprenticing children. The Pilgrims' path, which led towards Becket's shrine at Canterbury, passes here, and forms a boundary of the Weald of Kent. Here is a fine seat belonging to Earl Stanhope, at which the late earl established the improved printing press bearing his name: his lordship, celebrated for his various discoveries in mechanics and natural philosophy, died here, in 1816. A fair is held on the 16th of May.

CHEVERELL (GREAT), a parish in the hundred of SWANBOROUGH, county of WILTS, 2½ miles (W.) from East Lavington, containing 442 inhabitants. The living is a rectory, in the archdeaconry and diocese of Salisbury, rated in the king's books at £16, and in the patronage of the Earl of Radnor. The church is dedicated to St. Peter. A free school is endowed with a tenement and land producing an annual income of £5. 15., for which six children are taught.

CHEVERELL (LITTLE), a parish in the hundred of SWANBOROUGH, county of WILTS, 1¾ mile (W. S. W.) from East Lavington, containing 263 inhabitants. The living is a rectory, in the archdeaconry and diocese of Salisbury, rated in the king's books at £11. 7. 3½., and in the patronage of the Earl of Radnor. The church is dedicated to St. Peter.

CHEVETT, a township in the parish of ROYSTON, wapentake of STAINCROSS, West riding of the county of YORK, 4¼ miles (S. S. E.) from Wakefield, containing 27 inhabitants.

CHEVINGTON, a parish in the hundred of THINGOE, county of SUFFOLK, 5½ miles (S. W. by W.) from Bury St. Edmunds, containing 590 inhabitants. The living is a rectory, in the archdeaconry of Sudbury, and diocese of Norwich, rated in the king's books at £16. 3. 9., and in the patronage of the Rev. J. White. The church is dedicated to All Saints.

CHEW (MAGNA), a parish in the hundred of CHEW, county of SOMERSET, 3 miles (W.) from Pensford, containing, with the tythings of Bishop-Sutton, Knowle, Knighton-Sutton, North Elm, and Stow, 1884 inhabitants. The living is a vicarage, with the perpetual curacy of Dundry annexed, in the archdeaconry of Bath, and diocese of Bath and Wells, rated in the king's books at £30. 13. 4., and in the patronage of the Rev. T. Lindsey. The church, dedicated to St. Andrew, is a massive and spacious edifice, having a tower at the west end, surmounted by a balustrade, with a turret at one angle. There is a place of worship for Wesleyan Methodists. This was anciently a borough and market town; it is sometimes called Bishop's Chew, from being the property of the bishop of the diocese. Here was a considerable manufactory for cloth, but the only trade now carried on is in stockings and edge-tools, and that to a very limited extent. The petty sessions for the division are held here. Endowments in land and money, producing about £13 per annum, are appropriated to teaching and apprenticing poor children of the parish. In an enclosure to the north-east of the church are the remains of a Druidical temple, forming a double circle of huge stones. On an eminence, which commands a fine and extensive view towards the Bristol channel, is Bow-Ditch, a circular Roman camp, with triple intrenchments. A red bole, of an astringent quality, vulgarly termed redding, is found here: it has been used by apothecaries and for marking sheep, in most parts of England, from time immemorial.

CHEW-STOKE, a parish in the hundred of CHEW, county of SOMERSET, 4¼ miles (W. S.W.) from Pensford, containing 681 inhabitants. The living is a discharged rectory, in the archdeaconry of Bath, and diocese of Bath and Wells, rated in the king's books at £7. 3. 4., endowed with £400 private benefaction, and £400 royal bounty, and in the patronage of the Rev. W. P. Wait. The church is dedicated to St. Andrew. The parsonage-house has been converted into a work-house. There is a place of worship for Wesleyan Methodists. A school for the education of twenty boys, twelve of whom are clothed, was built by subscription in 1718, to which various benefactions have since been made; the annual income is £86. A girls' school also is supported from this fund, and eight of the girls are clothed. Here are quarries of limestone, and of a reddish granulated stone suitable for building, in which are a few fossils and *cornua ammonis*. The foundations of a cell for four nuns, founded at St. Cross, by Elizabeth de Santa Cruce, are still discernible.

CHEWTON, a tything in the parish of MILTON, hundred of CHRISTCHURCH, New Forest (West) division of the county of SOUTHAMPTON, 4¼ miles (E. by N.) from Christchurch. The population is returned with the parish.

CHEWTON-MENDIP, a parish in the hundred of CHEWTON, county of SOMERSET, 5¾ miles (N.E. by N.) from Wells, containing, with the tything of Widcombe, 1327 inhabitants. The living is a discharged vicarage, with the perpetual curacies of Emborrow, Paulton, and Stone-Easton annexed, in the archdeaconry of Wells, and diocese of Bath and Wells, rated in the king's books at £29. 11. 8., and in the patronage of J. Kingsmill, Esq. The church, dedicated to St. Mary Magdalene, is in the decorated style of English architecture, with some Norman remains, having a fine tower one hundred and twenty-six feet high, surmounted by lofty pinnacles. There is a place of worship for Wesleyan Methodists. Here is an endowed school, supported by the income arising from a portion of land on Chew down, enclosed and appropriated to this purpose about ninety years since: the annual rent is about £20, which is paid to the master who is allowed to take other scholars; he is expected to teach as many boys gratuitously as he receives pounds, they are taught reading, writing, and arithmetic. The school-house was repaired a few years since, to defray the expense of which a small portion of the income arising from the land was reserved by the trustees. A school for girls was established agreeably to the will of John Dory, who bequeathed the sum of £100, which was subsequently laid out in the purchase of lands at Comb Hill, comprising about sixteen acres, now let for £7 per annum, which, with the interest of £69, an accumulation of the rent of former years, is paid to the mistress for instructing fourteen girls. The village is situated amidst the Mendip hills, where there are extensive mines of lead-ore and *lapis calaminaris*; the former are not now worked, and the trade in the latter is much reduced. There is a fair for toys, &c. on Holy Thursday: the petty sessions for the division are held here. In the reign of Henry VIII., a dispute arose between the prior of Greenoar cell upon Mendip and the tenants within this manor, relative to some infringement on his rights by the miners, to settle which, the Lord Chief Justice came expressly into the county, and laid the basis of the laws by which the miners are now governed; any miner considering himself aggrieved, complains to the ledreeve, who summons a jury of twenty-four miners, from whose decision there is no appeal: various modes of punishment are applied, the highest being expulsion from the hills. Chewton gives the title of viscount to Earl Waldegrave.

CHICH, county of ESSEX.—See OSYTH (ST.).

CHICHELEY, a parish in the hundred of NEWPORT, county of BUCKINGHAM, 2¼ miles (N.E. by E.) from Newport-Pagnell, containing 219 inhabitants. The living is a vicarage, in the archdeaconry of Buckingham, and diocese of Lincoln, rated in the king's books at £8, and in the patronage of C. Chester, Esq. The church is dedicated to St. Lawrence.

CHICHESTER, a city and market town, having exclusive jurisdiction, locally in the hundred of Box and Stockbridge, rape of CHICHESTER, county of SUSSEX, 62 miles (S.W. by S.) from London, containing 7362 inhabitants. This city, which is of very remote antiquity, derives the latter part of its name from its having been a Roman station; and the former, from its subsequent occupation by Cissa, about the close of the fifth century.

Seal and Arms.

About the year 47, Flavius Vespasian, who took possession of this portion of Britain, made this his head-quarters, and threw up an intrenchment three miles in extent, some traces of which are still apparent. In the reign of Claudius Cæsar, the Romans, as it appears from an inscription upon a stone dug up in 1723, erected a temple here, and probably surrounded their station with walls. A curious piece of tesselated pavement was found in the bishop's garden, and the priory exhibits specimens of Roman architecture. About the close of the fifth century the city was taken from the Britons by Ella, whose son Cissa rebuilt it, and called it after his own name, *Cissa's ceaster*, fortifying it also with a strong intrenchment. It afterwards became the seat of the South Saxon kings, in whose possession it remained till the middle of the seventh century, when Wulfhere, the Mercian, invaded it, and took prisoner Athelwald, its king. Upon his embracing Christianity, he was reinstated in his dominions, but was afterwards slain in battle by Ceadwalla, a prince of Wessex, who subjugated the kingdom of the South Saxons. On the union of the Saxon kingdoms by Egbert, in the year 803, Chichester was a place of considerable importance: it suffered greatly from the Danes; and, at the time of the Conquest, had declined so much, that it had scarcely a hundred houses within the walls. It, however, regained its former consequence on the transfer of the South Saxon see from Selsea, where it had remained for more than three hundred years; and in the reign of Henry I., a cathedral was built by Bishop Ralph, which being destroyed by fire, that prelate erected a second edifice, far exceeding the former in magnificence, a considerable portion of which is incorporated with the present building. In 1189, the greater part of the city was destroyed by fire, and the cathedral, having sustained great injury, was repaired and enlarged by Siffied, the seventh bishop, whose effigy in marble is placed in a niche within the interior. During the civil war in the reign of Charles I., the citizens made an ineffectual effort for the royal cause; and, using the materials of the churches without the walls to strengthen the fortifications of the town, made a resolute stand against the parliamentarian forces, who, after battering down the north-west tower of the cathedral, compelled them to surrender. In 1648, by Cromwell's orders, the cloisters of the cathedral, the bishop's palace, the deanery, and the canons' houses, were destroyed.

Chichester is pleasantly situated on a gentle eminence nearly surrounded by the Lavant, a small stream which flows at its base. It consists chiefly of four principal streets, meeting nearly at right angles in the centre of the town, where is an octagonal cross in the decorated style of English architecture, which is considered, in grandeur of design and elegance of execution, superior to every structure of its class in England: they were formerly terminated by four gates in the ancient embattled walls with which the city was surrounded; the last of these gates was taken down in 1773, and of the walls, some portions are remaining on the north and east sides, where spacious terraces were raised in 1725, covered with gravel, and shaded with rows of lofty elms, which have been lately widened and much improved, affording a pleasant promenade for the inhabitants, and highly ornamental to the city. The houses are in general handsome and well built; the streets are paved, and lighted with gas, under an act of parliament obtained in 1791, for the general improvement of the town, which is also amply supplied with water. The theatre, a neat plain edifice, was rebuilt in the year 1791: the assembly-rooms, in which assemblies are held every fortnight during the winter, and concerts also at similar intervals, were built by subscription in 1781. A public subscription library, situated in the churchyard, was established in 1794. There are several book clubs; and a mechanics' institution was formed in 1824. Races are held in August, at Goodwood, about five miles north of the city, where a new stand has been lately erected and the course greatly improved. The trade consists principally in malt, corn (of which a considerable quantity is sent coastwise), flour, timber, and coal. The Lavant empties itself into the sea at Dell-key, two miles distant from the town, where there is a small harbour, into which vessels can enter at high water; and a collector of customs is stationed to superintend the transactions of the port, which carries on a small foreign trade. Lobsters and prawns, caught at Selsea, about seven miles south of the town, and esteemed the finest on the coast, are sent in great quantities to the London market. A large quantity of salt is made at Itchenor, three miles from Chichester. A branch from the Portsmouth and Arundel canal, on the south side of the town, contributes greatly to facilitate and promote its trade. The market days are Wednesday and Saturday; and on every alternate Wednesday there is a large market for cattle, sheep, and hogs: the market-house, a convenient structure, was built in 1807: the corn market is held adjoining the Swan Inn, on Saturday, and also on the days of the cattle market. Fairs are held annually on St. George's day, Whit-Monday, St. James' day, Old Michaelmas-day, and on the 20th of October, the last being called the Sloe fair.

It is uncertain when the inhabitants were first incorporated: by charter granted in the 1st of James II. the government of the city is vested in a mayor, high steward, recorder, deputy recorder, bailiff, and an indefinite number of aldermen and common council-men, assisted by a town-clerk, four serjeants at mace, and subordinate officers. The mayor is chosen annually from among the body of aldermen, or from those who have served the office of bailiff, by a majority of the corporation, and sworn into office on the Monday before Michaelmas-day. The bailiff, who acts as sheriff, is chosen from the common council-men at the same time: the aldermen must have served the office of mayor; and the common council-men must have been nominated to the offices of portreeve and customer, by the mayor, who, from time immemorial, has appointed two burgesses annually to those nominal offices, by which appointment, or by gift, the freedom of the city alone is obtained. The mayor, the late mayor, recorder, deputy-recorder, and three of the senior aldermen chosen annually for that purpose, are justices of the peace, exercising exclusive jurisdiction for the city and its liberties, except the Close, which, though within the walls, is under the jurisdiction of the county magistrates. The corporation hold quarter sessions for the city and liberties, with power extending to capital offences, which was exercised in 1818, by executing a man for murder; but prisoners charged with capital offences have since been transferred to the judge on the circuit. A court of record is held every Monday, under the charter of King James, for the recovery of debts to any amount, at which the mayor presides. The guildhall is ancient, having been the chapel of a convent of Grey friars. The council-chamber, built by subscription in 1730, is handsome, having arcades formed by pillars of the Tuscan order. The common gaol was built in 1783; it contains only six apartments, five for males and one for females. The elective franchise was conferred in the 23rd of Edward I., since which time the city has returned two members to parliament: the right of election is vested in the corporation, in the freemen at large, and in the inhabitants paying scot and lot, about six hundred in number, with the exception only of those of the extra-parochial district of Newtown, which is within the walls: the mayor is the returning officer. The preponderating influence is possessed by the Duke of Richmond and the Earl of Egremont.

Arms of the Bishoprick.

Chichester is the seat of a diocese, the jurisdiction of which extends over the county of Sussex. The episcopal chair was first fixed at Selsea, in 681, and transferred to this place in 1070, when Stigand, chaplain to William the Conqueror, was appointed the first bishop of Chichester. The establishment consists of a bishop, dean, thirty-one prebendaries, of which four are residentiary, a procurator, chancellor, and treasurer. The cathedral, dedicated to St. Peter, was erected by Bishop Ralph, in the reign of Henry I., and subsequently repaired and enlarged by succeeding bishops: it is a spacious structure, exhibiting various Norman specimens, and of the early and decorated styles of English architecture, with a fine tower rising from the centre, surmounted by an octagonal spire, three hundred feet high, and having two fine towers on the west, of which the upper part of one was destroyed during the parliamentary war; and on the north, a fine bell tower and lantern, connected by flying buttresses, with octagonal turrets springing from the angles. The interior, which is four hundred and ten feet in length, and two hundred and twenty-seven in breadth along the transepts, is principally in the early English style; the Lady's chapel is of a later date: at the east end is a fine circular window; and the south transept, which contains a remarkably fine monument to the memory of Bishop Langton, has an elegant window of seven lights, in the decorated style. The cloisters, occupying three sides of an irregular quadrangle, are in the later style. The bishop's palace, which was repaired in 1725, contains an elegant chapel built in the thirteenth century. The deanery, built by Dean Sherlock, is a handsome edifice.

Chichester comprises the parishes of All Saints, or the Pallant, St. Andrew, St. Martin, St. Olave, St. Pancras (partly within and partly without the walls), St. Peter the Great, or the Subdeanery, St. Peter the Less, St. Bartholomew without, and the precinct of the Cathedral Close; all which were, by act of parliament in 1753, united for the better maintenance of the poor, under the inspection of perpetual guardians, consisting of the mayor, high steward, recorder, and thirty of the principal inhabitants. The livings, with the exception of that of All Saints', are all in the peculiar jurisdiction, and, with the exception of those of All Saints', St. Pancras', and St. Peter's the Less, in the patronage, of the Dean of Chichester. The living of All Saints' is a discharged rectory, rated in the king's books at £5. 17. 6., endowed with £400 royal bounty, and in the peculiar jurisdiction and patronage of the Archbishop of Canterbury. The living of St. Andrew's is a discharged rectory, rated in the king's books at £4. 13. 4., and endowed with £800 royal bounty, and £1200 parliamentary grant: the church is a neat edifice in the later style of English architecture. The living of St. Martin's is a discharged rectory, rated in the king's books at £1. 6. 8., and endowed with £800 royal bounty, and £200 parliamentary grant: the church, which was rebuilt by Mrs. Dear, of this city, is a handsome structure in the decorated style of English architecture; the interior is richly ornamented, and contains a fine monument lately erected to the memory of that lady. The living of St. Olave's is a discharged rectory, rated in the king's books at £4. 18. 9., and endowed with £200 private benefaction, and £600 royal bounty. The living of St. Pancras' is a discharged rectory, rated in the king's books at £8. 10. 8., endowed with £200 private benefaction, £200 royal bounty, and £1200 parliamentary grant, and in the patronage of the Rev. G. Bliss: the church, which was destroyed during the parliamentary war, and rebuilt by subscription in 1750, is a neat edifice in the early style of English architecture. The living of St. Peter's the Great is a discharged vicarage, rated in the king's books at £16. 8. 4., and endowed with £12 per annum private benefaction, £200 royal bounty, and £200 parliamentary grant: the church is formed of the north transept of the cathedral. The living of St. Peter's the Less is a discharged rectory, rated in the king's books at £1. 6. 8., endowed with £400 royal bounty, and in the patronage of the Crown. The living of St. Bartholomew's without is a discharged rectory, endowed with £600 royal bounty: the church, which was demolished during the parliamentary war, is now being rebuilt. There are places of worship for the Society of Friends, Huntingtonians, Independents, Wesleyan Methodists, and Unitarians.

The prebendal, or free grammar, school was founded, in 1497, by Bishop Storey, and endowed with the prebend of Highley, which is annexed to the mastership, and tithes and land in other parts of Sussex, for the benefit of all children within the diocese: the management is vested in the bishop, who confirms the appointment of a master nominated by the Dean and Chapter: it was formerly free for all boys within the diocese, but in 1828 certain regulations were formed restricting that privilege to ten boys; for several years, however, the number on the foundation has been, and is still, very inconsiderable: the master is allowed to receive boarders. Archbishop Juxon; the learned Seldon; Collins, the poet; and the late Dr. Hurdis, Professor of Poetry in the University of Oxford; received the rudiments of their education in this school. A free school, for affording nautical education to twelve boys, *viz.*, four from Chichester, and four from each of the villages of West Wettering and Harting, was founded, in 1702, by Oliver Whitby, Esq., who endowed it with lands now producing about £1230 per annum: the number of scholars has been augmented to twenty-five. Charity schools, for clothing and instructing twenty-two boys and twenty girls, are supported by subscription; the girls' school has accumulated a permanent annual income of £40. A school for the instruction of thirty boys, founded by one of the deans, was re-established by Queen Elizabeth, but the building is now occupied by two poor men and six women. There are also National and Lancasterian schools for boys and girls. St. Mary's Hospital, founded by one of the deans, in the reign of Henry II., for the maintenance of eight aged persons (two men and six women), was an ancient nunnery; the building consists of a refectory, on each side of which are rooms for the inmates, and, at the east end, a spacious chapel, in which divine service is performed twice every day: it is under the superintendence of the Dean and Chapter. The dispensary, established in 1784, and an infirmary, in 1827, about a mile north of the city, are supported by voluntary contributions. Mr. John Hardham, of London, bequeathed property producing £700 per annum, to be applied to the diminution of the poor-rates. An ancient hospital for lepers was founded in the reign of Richard I.; and to the south-east of the city was a house of Black friars, founded by Eleanor, queen of Edward I., and dedicated to St. Mary and St. Vincent. At St. Roche's hill, where was formerly a chapel dedicated to that saint, may be traced the remains of a circular Danish encampment. At Gowshill, about half a mile further, is an oblong camp; and on the same side, but nearer to the town, another of similar form, but larger, surrounded by a strong rampart and a single moat; they are both supposed to be Roman, and probably to have been occupied by Vespasian on his landing on this coast. Bradwardine and Juxon, archbishops of Canterbury; Lawrence Somercote, a great canonist and writer; and the poets Collins and Hayley, to whose memory a handsome tablet, by Flaxman, has been placed in the cathedral, by subscription among the citizens; were natives of this city. Chichester confers the title of earl on the family of Pelham.

CHICKERELL (WEST), a parish in the hundred of Culliford-Tree, Dorchester division of the county of Dorset, 3 miles (N. W. by W.) from Weymouth, containing, with the extra-parochial liberties of Winterbourne-Herringstone and Winterbourne-Farringdon, 497 inhabitants. The living is a rectory, in the archdeaconry of Dorset, and diocese of Bristol, rated in the king's books at £8. 16. 0½., and in the patronage of Lord Bolton.

CHICKLADE, a parish in the hundred of DUNWORTH, county of WILTS, 1 mile (N.) from Hindon, containing 139 inhabitants. The living is a discharged rectory, in the archdeaconry and diocese of Salisbury, rated in the king's books at £11. 5. 3., and in the patronage of H. Edgell, Esq. The church is dedicated to All Saints. Here is a charity school.

CHICKNEY, a parish in the hundred of DUNMOW, county of ESSEX, 3½ miles (S. W. by W.) from Thaxted, containing 66 inhabitants. The living is a rectory, in the archdeaconry of Middlesex, and diocese of London, rated in the king's books at £10, and in the patronage of H. Cranmer, Esq. The church is dedicated to St. Mary.

CHICKSANDS, an extra-parochial liberty, in the hundred of CLIFTON, county of BEDFORD, 1½ mile (W. N. W.) from Shefford, containing 56 inhabitants. A priory for canons and nuns of the rule of St. Gilbert of Sempringham was founded, in 1150, by Pain de Beauchamp, and the Lady Roas, his wife; the two quadrangles, with the cloisters, remain entire, and have been converted into a modern mansion.

CHICKSGROVE, a tything in the parish of TISBURY, hundred of DUNWORTH, county of WILTS, 4½ miles (E. S. E.) from Hindon. The population is returned with the parish.

CHICKSTON, a hamlet in the parish of LITTLEHAM, eastern division of the hundred of BUDLEIGH, county of DEVON. The population is returned with the parish. Here was formerly a chapel, which was dedicated to our Saviour, but it has been destroyed.

CHICKWARD, a joint township with Pembers-Oak and Lilwall, in the parish of KINGTON, hundred of HUNTINGTON, county of HEREFORD, containing, with Pembers-Oak and Lilwall, 331 inhabitants.

CHIDDEN, a tything in the parish and hundred of HAMBLEDON, Portsdown division of the county of SOUTHAMPTON, 8½ miles (S. W. by W.) from Petersfield. The population is returned with the parish. It is within the jurisdiction of the Cheyney Court held at Winchester every Thursday, for the recovery of debts to any amount.

CHIDDINGFOLD, a parish in the second division of the hundred of GODALMING, county of SURREY, 4½ miles (E. N. E.) from Haslemere, containing 999 inhabitants. The living is a rectory, with the perpetual curacy of Haslemere annexed, in the archdeaconry of Surrey, and diocese of Winchester, rated in the king's books at £26. 4. 7., and in the patronage of the Dean of Salisbury. The church, dedicated to St. Mary, is in the early style of English architecture, with some later additions.

CHIDDINGLY, a parish in the hundred of SHIPLAKE, rape of PEVENSEY, county of SUSSEX, 5½ miles (N.W.) from Hailsham, containing 870 inhabitants. The living is a discharged vicarage, in the archdeaconry of Lewes, and diocese of Chichester, rated in the king's books at £8, and in the patronage of the Duke of Dorset. The church has a handsome tower and spire, partly of early English architecture; the rest of the building is of later composition.

CHIDDINGSTONE, a parish in the hundred of SOMERDEN, lathe of SUTTON at HONE, county of KENT, 7½ miles (W. by S.) from Tonbridge, containing 1096 inhabitants. The living is a rectory, in the exempt deanery of Shoreham, and in the peculiar jurisdiction and patronage of the Archbishop of Canterbury, rated in the king's books at £28. 9. 4½. The church, dedicated to St. Mary, has considerable portions in the later style of English architecture. This parish lies in the Weald; in the Textus Roffensis, it is called *Cidingstæne;* in other records it is termed Chiding-stone, from a large stone, supposed from its name to have been the spot where judicial affairs were transacted. It is bounded on the south by a branch of the Medway, and is intersected by the river Eden, about a mile south of which, on an eminence, is the village, which is usually called High-street.

CHIDEOCK, a parish in the hundred of WHITCHURCH-CANONICORUM, Bridport division of the county of DORSET, 2¾ miles (W.) from Bridport, containing 715 inhabitants. The living is a perpetual curacy, in the archdeaconry of Dorset, and diocese of Bristol, and in the patronage of the Bishop of Bath and Wells. The church is dedicated to St. Giles. This parish is bounded on the south by the English channel.

CHIDHAM, a parish in the hundred of BOSHAM, rape of CHICHESTER, county of SUSSEX, 6 miles (W. by S.) from Chichester, containing 203 inhabitants. The living is a discharged vicarage, in the archdeaconry and diocese of Chichester, rated in the king's books at £10. 19. 2., endowed with £200 royal bounty, and in the patronage of E. M. Mundy, Esq. The church is mostly in the early style of English architecture, with later insertions and additions. This parish constitutes a peninsula formed by Bosham creek on the east, Thorney channel on the west, and Chichester harbour on the south.

CHIDLOW, a township in the parish of MALPAS, higher division of the hundred of BROXTON, county palatine of CHESTER, 2 miles (S. E.) from Malpas, containing 15 inhabitants.

CHIEVELEY, a parish in the hundred of FAIRCROSS, county of BERKS, 5¼ miles (N. by E.) from Newbury, containing, with the chapelries of Leckhampstead, Oare, and Winterbourn, and the tythings of Courage and Snelsmore, 1842 inhabitants. The living is a vicarage, in the archdeaconry of Berks, and diocese of Salisbury, rated in the king's books at £26. 11. 3., and in the patronage of W. Capel, Esq., and W. T. Wasey, Esq., alternately. The church is dedicated to St. Mary. There is a place of worship for Wesleyan Methodists. In 1759, Thomas Henshaw granted an annuity of £10, together with a school-house at North Heath, for teaching ten boys and ten girls; and in 1805, Catherine Mather bequeathed £800, producing £40. 5. per annum, for educating six children of each sex, now applied for the instruction of thirty-four boys and girls.

CHIGNAL (ST. JAMES), a parish in the hundred of CHELMSFORD, county of ESSEX, 3½ miles (N. W.) from Chelmsford, containing 217 inhabitants. The living is a rectory, with that of Mashbury united, in the archdeaconry of Essex, and diocese of London, rated in the king's books at £10. 14. 7., and in the patronage of John Strutt, Esq. Besides the present church of St. James, there was formerly one dedicated to St. Mary, long since taken down.

CHIGNAL-SMEALY, a parish in the hundred of CHELMSFORD, county of ESSEX, 4¾ miles (N. W. by N.) from Chelmsford, containing 74 inhabitants. The living is a discharged rectory, in the archdeaconry of Essex, and diocese of London, rated in the king's books at £5. 6. 8., and in the patronage of F. M. Austen, Esq. The church is dedicated to St. Nicholas.

CHIGWELL, a parish in the hundred of ONGAR, county of ESSEX, 6 miles (S.) from Epping, and 12 (N. E.) from London, containing 1696 inhabitants. The living is a vicarage, in the archdeaconry of Essex, and diocese of London, rated in the king's books at £18, and in the patronage of the Prebendary of St. Pancras' in the Cathedral Church of St. Paul, London. The church, dedicated to St. Mary, is an ancient structure, exhibiting in the south entrance and other parts some remains of early Norman architecture, with a wooden belfry and spire; on the north side of the chancel are the effigies in brass of Dr. Harsnet, Archbishop of York, many years vicar of this parish, and successively Bishop of Chichester and Norwich, and Archbishop of York, who was buried here, in 1631; on the south side is a monument in alabaster to the memory of Thomas Coleshill, Esq., an officer in the courts of Edward VI., Queen Mary, and Queen Elizabeth, inspector of the customs of the port of London, who died in 1595; there are also several other ancient monuments. There is a place of worship for Particular Baptists at Chigwell-Row. This place in ancient records is called *Cingwella*, supposed to imply the king's well, from which its present name is derived. In the forest adjoining the parish was formerly a royal mansion, called Potteles, or Langfords, the only memorial of which is preserved in the name of the site, now called King's Place Farm. The village consists principally of one long street on the public road, containing many substantial houses: at the distance of a mile to the south-east of the church is a range of good houses, called Chigwell-Row, forming one of the most populous and respectable parts of the parish. In 1629, Archbishop Harsnet, having previously built two school-houses, and a dwelling-house for a Latin master, purchased a house for another master, with a garden for each, and founded two free schools, one for the Greek and Latin languages, the other for writing and arithmetic, which he endowed with the impropriate rectory of Tottington, in Norfolk; and invested the advowson of the vicarage of that parish in trustees for presentation to such as had been educated in the grammar school of Chigwell, or, in default of such, to natives of this parish: the management of these schools he vested in governors, consisting of the Vicar of Chigwell, the Rector of Loughton, and ten of the most respectable inhabitants of the parish, by whom, with preference to such as have been educated in the school, or natives of the parish, the master is appointed; the election must take place within ten days after a vacancy occurs, otherwise the nomination lapses to the Bishop of London. William Penn, founder of the colony of Pennsylvania, was educated in this school. A charity school for twelve girls, established in 1700, is supported partly by subscription, and partly by legacies of £100 each, bequeathed by William Scott, Esq., in 1725, and Mrs. Barbara Fisher, in 1808. Almshouses were endowed by an unknown benefactor for three aged widows, who receive each an allowance of £1. 5. 8. per annum. There are several charitable benefactions for distribution among the poor; and, in 1357, Mr. John Sympson left lands, producing £15 per annum, for keeping in repair the foot-path from Abridge to Woodbridge, which passes through the parish. At Chigwell-Row is a spring, the water of which possesses a cathartic property.

CHILBOLTON, a parish in the hundred of BUDDLESGATE, Fawley division of the county of SOUTHAMPTON, 4 miles (S. E. by S.) from Andover, containing 356 inhabitants. The living is a rectory, in the peculiar jurisdiction of the incumbent, rated in the king's books at £26. 9. 4½., and in the patronage of the Bishop of Winchester. The church is dedicated to St. Mary. Here is a charity school for twenty-four children. This parish is within the jurisdiction of the Cheyney Court held at Winchester every Thursday, for the recovery of debts to any amount. The Andover canal passes through the south-western part of the parish.

CHILCOMB, a parish in the hundred of FAWLEY, Fawley division of the county of SOUTHAMPTON, 2 miles (S. E. by E.) from Winchester, containing 158 inhabitants. The living is a rectory, in the peculiar jurisdiction of the incumbent, rated in the king's books at £8. 6. 8., and in the patronage of the Bishop of Winchester. This parish is within the jurisdiction of the Cheyney Court held at Winchester every Thursday, for the recovery of debts to any amount.

CHILCOMBE, a parish in the hundred of UGGSCOMBE, Dorchester division of the county of DORSET, 4¾ miles (E. by S.) from Bridport, containing 22 inhabitants. The living is a discharged rectory, in the archdeaconry of Dorset, and diocese of Bristol, rated in the king's books at £4. 11. 8., endowed with £600 royal bounty, and £200 parliamentary grant, and in the patronage of the Rev. E. Foyle. This parish is bounded on the south by the river Bride, or Bredy. On the summit of a steep hill to the northward are vestiges of an ancient intrenchment, enclosing three barrows; from its partaking both of the Roman and Saxon modes of fortification, it is supposed to have been originally constructed by the former, and extended by the latter. The Knights Hospitallers had possessions here, with a quadrangular mansion, now a farm-house.

CHILCOMPTON, a parish in the hundred of CHEWTON, county of SOMERSET, 6¾ miles (N. N. E.) from Shepton-Mallet, containing 474 inhabitants. The living is a perpetual curacy, in the peculiar jurisdiction of the Dean of Wells, endowed with £200 private benefaction, and £200 royal bounty, and in the patronage of Miss Tooker. The church is dedicated to St. John the Baptist. There is a place of worship for Wesleyan Methodists. The name of this parish is derived from its situation in a cold, though picturesque, vale: a clear stream flows through the village, forming at intervals small cascades; several genteel villas add to the general neatness of the place. Coal is obtained here; and imbedded among the red rock in the vale are found calcareous spar, iron-ore, branches of coral, and a few *cornua ammonis*. On Blacker's hill are vestiges of a quadrangular intrenchment, enclosing about fifteen acres; and near it are several tumuli: between these and Broadway are three subterranean cavities, supposed to have been iron pits, but called by the inhabitants "The Fairy Slats."

CHILCOTE, a chapelry in that part of the parish of BURTON upon TRENT which is in the hundred of

Repton and Gresley, county of Derby, 6½ miles (S. W. by W.) from Ashby de la Zouch, containing 192 inhabitants. The chapelry is annexed to the rectory of Clifton-Campville, in the archdeaconry of Stafford, and diocese of Lichfield and Coventry. Chilcote is in the honour of Tutbury, duchy of Lancaster, and within the jurisdiction of a court of pleas held at Tutbury every third Tuesday, for the recovery of debts under 40*s*.

CHILDERDITCH, a parish in the hundred of Chafford, county of Essex, 3 miles (S. S. E.) from Brentwood, containing 289 inhabitants. The living is a discharged vicarage, in the archdeaconry of Essex, and diocese of London, rated in the king's books at £8, and in the patronage of T. B. Bramston, Esq. The church is dedicated to All Saints and St. Faith.

CHILDERLEY, a parish in the hundred of Chesterton, county of Cambridge, 7½ miles (W. N. W.) from Cambridge, containing 50 inhabitants. The living is a rectory, in the archdeaconry and diocese of Ely, rated in the king's books at £6. 9. 2., and in the patronage of N. Calvert, Esq. The church, which was dedicated to St. Mary, is in ruins. After the capture of Charles I. by Cornet Joyce, in 1647, he was conveyed hither by order of Cromwell, who visited him, in company with Fairfax, both of them disavowing all participation in the seizure of his person, and, at the king's request, caused him to be removed to Newmarket.

CHILDREY, a parish in the hundred of Wantage, county of Berks, 2½ miles (W.) from Wantage, containing 478 inhabitants. The living is a rectory, in the archdeaconry of Berks, and diocese of Salisbury, rated in the king's books at £33. 14. 7., and in the patronage of the President and Fellows of Corpus Christi College, Oxford. The church, dedicated to St. Mary, has remnants of Norman architecture, and contains several ancient monuments. There is a place of worship for Wesleyan Methodists. Here is an endowed school. Almshouses for three poor men were founded by William Fettiplace, Esq., who was a generous benefactor to Queen's College, Oxford. The Wilts and Berks canal passes through this parish, above which runs *Ickleton-way*, part of the Iknield-street. Charles I., escorted by his own troop, took up his quarters at the village, on the night of April 10th, 1664.

CHILDWALL, a parish in the hundred of West Derby, county palatine of Lancaster, comprising the chapelries of Garston, Hale, Wavertree, and Much Woolton, and the townships of Allerton, Childwall, Halewood, Speke, and Little Woolton, and containing 6648 inhabitants, of which number, 127 are in the township of Childwall, 4¼ miles (E. by S.) from Liverpool. The living is a vicarage, in the archdeaconry and diocese of Chester, rated in the king's books at £5. 11. 8., and in the patronage of the Bishop of Chester. The church, dedicated to All Saints, has some early English piers and decorated windows; but the greater portion is of modern date. In 1699, Thomas Crompton bequeathed £20 for teaching poor children. This parish is bounded on the south by the river Mersey, and at high tides is subject to inundations. Near the church was formerly a cell of monks, subordinate to the priory of St. Holme; but there are no vestiges of it. Jeremiah Markland, a learned critic and classical scholar, was born here, in 1693.

CHILFROOM, a parish in the hundred of Tollerford, Dorchester division of the county of Dorset, 9 miles (N.W. by W.) from Dorchester, containing 106 inhabitants. The living is a rectory, in the archdeaconry of Dorset, and diocese of Bristol, rated in the king's books at £5, and in the patronage of J. I. Lockhart, Esq. The church is dedicated to the Holy Trinity. A charity school was founded, in 1774, by George Brown, who endowed it with a rent-charge of £21, for teaching poor children of the parish.

CHILHAM, a parish (formerly a market town) in the hundred of Felborough, lathe of Scray, county of Kent, 6½ miles (W. S. W.) from Canterbury, containing 1025 inhabitants. The living is a vicarage, with the perpetual curacy of Moldash annexed, in the archdeaconry and diocese of Canterbury, rated in the king's books at £13. 6. 8., and in the patronage of J. S. Wildman, Esq. The church, dedicated to St. Mary, is a spacious cruciform structure, exhibiting portions in various styles of architecture, of which the early English predominates, and some painted glass: it contains several sepulchral memorials, the principal of which are, the sumptuous mausoleum of the Colebrooks, erected in 1755, on the site of an ancient chantry chapel, and that of Sir Dudley Digges, of earlier date, with his splendid monument in the centre. Here are eight almshouses, which have been converted into a poorhouse. The market has fallen into disuse; a cattle fair is held on the 8th of November: the river Stour flows through the parish. Chilham is supposed to have been a post of the ancient Britons, and afterwards a military station of the Romans, there being evident proofs of the latter in the discovery of coins, foundations of houses, and other remains. The castle is of great antiquity, and was a strong fortress and palace of the kings of Kent, till destroyed by the Danes in the middle of the ninth century; but at the Conquest it was rebuilt by one Fulbert, on whom it had been bestowed. The present stately edifice was erected by Sir Dudley Digges, in 1616, and the Norman keep converted into offices; on the north-west side there are traces of a deep fosse, enclosing an area of eight acres. It is asserted that Cæsar, on his second invasion, defeated the Britons here, who retreated and intrenched themselves in an adjoining wood, where vestiges of their rude and extensive works are still visible; and on a hill at the south-east side of the river, and eastward from the castle, is a tumulus, termed *Julaber's Grave*, supposed to be the place of sepulture of Quintus Laberius Durus, a tribune, who was slain in the conflict.

CHILHAMPTON, a chapelry in the parish of South Newton, hundred of Branch and Dole, county of Wilts, 1⅝ mile (N.) from Wilton. The population is returned with the parish.

CHILLENDEN, a parish in the hundred of Eastry, lathe of St. Augustine, county of Kent, 3¾ miles (S. E. by S.) from Wingham, containing 147 inhabitants. The living is a discharged rectory, in the archdeaconry and diocese of Canterbury, rated in the king's books at £5, endowed with £200 private benefaction, and £200 royal bounty, and in the patronage of the Crown. The church is dedicated to All Saints. A fair for pedlary, &c. is held on Whit-Monday.

CHILLESFORD, a parish in the hundred of Plomesgate, county of Suffolk, 3¼ miles (W. N. W.)

from Orford, containing 140 inhabitants. The living is a discharged rectory, in the archdeaconry of Suffolk, and diocese of Norwich, rated in the king's books at £5. 3. 4., endowed with £200 private benefaction, £200 royal bounty, and in the patronage of the Rev. Christopher Smear. The church is dedicated to St. Peter. The navigable river Butley runs on the west and south sides of this parish.

CHILLINGHAM, a parish in the eastern division of GLENDALE ward, county of NORTHUMBERLAND, comprising the townships of Chillingham, Hebburn, and Newton, and containing 356 inhabitants, of which number, 146 are in the township of Chillingham, 5 miles (E. by S.) from Wooler. The living is a vicarage, in the archdeaconry of Northumberland, and diocese of Durham, rated in the king's books at £4, and in the patronage of the Bishop of Durham. The church is dedicated to St. Peter. Courts leet and baron are occasionally held here. A school with a small endowment is chiefly supported by the Earl of Tankerville, who provides a schoolhouse and £10 per annum for teaching ten poor children. This parish is intersected by the river Till, and by the Roman way from Newcastle to Berwick upon Tweed: coal and limestone are found in it, and there are kilns for burning the latter. On an eminence eastward from Chillingham park is a double intrenchment, called Ros Castle, supposed to have been a British fort; and there are tumuli, formed of irregular heaps of stones, out of which urns containing human ashes have been dug: at Newton is an ancient cross, termed the Hurle Stone, twelve feet high. Chillingham castle is a very ancient structure: in the park is a breed of wild cattle, the only one in the island; these animals are white, with a reddish tinge on the ear. At Hebburn are the remains of an ancient keep, a strong vaulted building, similar to many others in the northern counties.

CHILLINGTON, a parish in the southern division of the hundred of PETHERTON, county of SOMERSET, 4 miles (W. by N.) from Crewkerne, containing 270 inhabitants. The living is a perpetual curacy, in the archdeaconry of Taunton, and diocese of Bath and Wells, endowed with £600 royal bounty, and £400 parliamentary grant, and in the patronage of Earl Poulett. The church is dedicated to St. James.

CHILLINGTON, a liberty in the parish of BREWOOD, eastern division of the hundred of CUTTLESTONE, county of STAFFORD. The population is returned with the parish.

CHILMARK, a parish in the hundred of DUNWORTH, county of WILTS, 4 miles (E.) from Hindon, containing, with the tything of Ridge, 524 inhabitants. The living is a rectory, in the archdeaconry and diocese of Salisbury, rated in the king's books at £19. 13. 4., and in the patronage of the Earl of Pembroke. The church, dedicated to St. Margaret, is cruciform, having a tower with a handsome spire rising from the intersection; some parts of the building are in the early style of English architecture, others of later date. The ancient Iknield way proceeds through this parish, which is also intersected by the river Nadder and several streams tributary to it, and by the Wilts and Berks canal. Its celebrated quarries of freestone, whence the materials were drawn for the erection of Salisbury cathedral, have almost fallen into disuse, the stone having been superseded by Bath-stone, which is wrought at less expense. A great fair for live stock is held on the 30th of July. This is the birthplace of John de Chilmarke, a celebrated mathematician and philosophical writer in the thirteenth century.

CHILSON, a tything in that part of the parish of CHARLBURY which is in the hundred of CHADLINGTON, county of OXFORD, 5¼ miles (S. by W.) from Chipping-Norton, containing, with the chapelry of Shorthampton, and the tything of Pudlicott, 252 inhabitants.

CHILSWELL, a liberty in the parish of CUMNER, hundred of HORMER, county of BERKS, 5 miles (N. by W.) from Abingdon, containing 16 inhabitants. Here was formerly a chapel.

CHILTERN (ALL SAINTS), a parish in the hundred of HEYTESBURY, county of WILTS, 4 miles (E.N.E.) from Heytesbury, containing 381 inhabitants. The living is a discharged vicarage, to which is united the vicarage of Chiltern St. Mary, in the archdeaconry and diocese of Salisbury, rated in the king's books at £7. 0. 10., and in the patronage of the Bishop and the Dean and Chapter of Salisbury alternately. Chiltern lies adjacent to the Chiltern downs, a chain of chalk hills which, from the nature of the soil, was called by the Saxons Cilt, or Chilt. They were anciently covered with impenetrable woods, infested by robbers, until Leofstan, abbot of St. Albans, thinned them, and the Danes burnt them down in 1009. By accepting the nominal stewardship of this district under the crown, a member of parliament is enabled to vacate his seat. Westward from this place is a small Roman camp, named Knooke Castle; and near it an irregular ditch running in various directions, as if intended to form some ancient boundary-line.

CHILTERN (ST. MARY), a parish in the hundred of HEYTESBURY, county of WILTS, 3¾ miles (E. by N.) from Heytesbury, containing 169 inhabitants. The living is a discharged vicarage, united to that of Chiltern All Saints, in the archdeaconry and diocese of Salisbury, rated in the king's books at £6.

CHILTHORNE-DOMER, a parish in the hundred of STONE, county of SOMERSET, 2 miles (S.) from Ilchester, containing 234 inhabitants. The living is a discharged vicarage, in the archdeaconry of Wells, and diocese of Bath and Wells, rated in the king's books at £5. 7. 1., and in the patronage of the Rev. John Bayly. The church is dedicated to St. Mary. In 1755, Christopher Brown gave a rent-charge of £2. 16., for teaching six children of the parish.

CHILTINGTON (EAST), a chapelry in the parish of WESTMESTON, hundred of STREET, rape of LEWES, county of SUSSEX, 6 miles (N. W. by N.) from Lewes, containing 243 inhabitants. Here is a charity school for the instruction of eight children, supported by a rent-charge of £4. 6. 8., bequeathed by John Marten, in 1797.

CHILTINGTON (WEST), a parish partly in the eastern division of the hundred of EASWRITH, rape of BRAMBER, but chiefly in the western division of the same hundred, rape of ARUNDEL, county of SUSSEX, 8½ miles (N. W. by N.) from Steyning, containing 638 inhabitants. The living is a rectory, in the archdeaconry and diocese of Chichester, rated in the king's books at £12. 16. 10½., and in the patronage of the Earl of Abergavenny. The church is a neat structure in the early style of English architecture, with a spire. A charity school was founded, in 1634, by William Smyth, with an endowment, since vested in land producing £47 per annum, for which fifty children are taught. In the higher parts of the parish some curious circular nodules of blue limestone are found, imbedded in the steep banks of clay overhanging the road.

CHILTON, a parish in the hundred of COMPTON, county of BERKS, 3¼ miles (N.) from East Ilsley, containing 229 inhabitants. The living is a rectory, in the archdeaconry of Berks, and diocese of Salisbury, rated in the king's books at £13. 8. 4., and in the patronage of Mrs. Heneage. The church is dedicated to All Saints.

CHILTON, a parish in the hundred of ASHENDON, county of BUCKINGHAM, 3½ miles (N. by W.) from Thame, containing, with the hamlet of Easington, 379 inhabitants. The living is a perpetual curacy, in the archdeaconry of Buckingham, and diocese of Lincoln, endowed with £8 per annum and £200 private benefaction, and £800 royal bounty, and in the patronage of Sir J. Aubrey, Bart. The church, dedicated to St. Mary, contains some fine monuments belonging to the Croke family. In 1639, Sir George Croke, Knt. founded eight almshouses at Studley, in the county of Oxford, with an endowment producing annually £41. 12., for four men and four women belonging to the parishes of Chilton, Hadleigh, and Waterstoke, alternately. Sir George Croke, the celebrated lawyer, famous for his determined opposition to the tax of ship-money, in the reign of Charles I., was born, and lies buried, here.

CHILTON, a township in the parish of MERRINGTON, south-eastern division of DARLINGTON ward, county palatine of DURHAM, 9 miles (S. by E.) from Durham, containing 182 inhabitants.

CHILTON, a parish in the hundred of BABERGH, county of SUFFOLK, 1¾ mile (N. E. by E.) from Sudbury, containing 97 inhabitants. The living is a discharged rectory, in the archdeaconry of Sudbury, and diocese of Norwich, rated in the king's books at £5. 6. 5½., and in the patronage of Mrs. Windham.

CHILTON, a hamlet in the parish of CLARE, hundred of RISBRIDGE, county of SUFFOLK, 1 mile (W. by N.) from Clare. The population is returned with the parish. Here was formerly a chapel, now demolished. A small priory of Augustine canons, dedicated to the Blessed Virgin Mary, was founded here; but the income not exceeding £10 per annum, and the buildings becoming dilapidated, it was given, in 1468, to the Dean and Chapter of the college of Stoke: the remains have been converted into a dwelling-house.

CHILTON upon POLDON, a chapelry in the parish of MOORLINCH, hundred of WHITLEY, county of SOMERSET, 5¼ miles (E. N. E.) from Bridg-water, containing 352 inhabitants.

CHILTON-CANTILO, a parish forming a detached portion of the hundred of HOUNDSBOROUGH, BERWICK, and COKER, locally in that of Horethorne, county of SOMERSET, 3¾ miles (E.) from Ilchester, containing 140 inhabitants. The living is a discharged rectory, in the archdeaconry of Wells, and diocese of Bath and Wells, rated in the king's books at £9. 11. 5½., and in the patronage of Richard Messiter, Esq. The church is dedicated to St. James.

CHILTON-FOLIATT, a parish partly in the hundred of KINTBURY-EAGLE, county of BERKS, but chiefly in the hundred of KINWARDSTONE, county of WILTS, 2¼ miles (N. W. by W.) from Hungerford, containing, with the tything of Leverton, 777 inhabitants. The living is a rectory, in the archdeaconry of Wilts, and diocese of Salisbury, rated in the king's books at £14. 8. 9., and in the patronage of E. W. L. Popham, Esq. The church is dedicated to St. Mary. There is a place of worship for Wesleyan Methodists. In 1770, Roger and Elizabeth Ipanswick founded a charity school, with an endowment now producing £20 per ann., to which Walter Bigg, in 1772, bequeathed £100, for teaching poor boys and girls. This parish is crossed by a small stream, called the Chilt, whence it derives its name.

CHILTON-TRINITY, a parish in the northern division of the hundred of PETHERTON, county of SOMERSET, 1½ mile (N. by W.) from Bridg-water, containing 49 inhabitants. The living is a discharged rectory, united to the vicarage of Bridg-water, in the archdeaconry of Taunton, and diocese of Bath and Wells, rated in the king's books at £7. 0. 2½., and in the patronage of the Crown. The church, dedicated to the Holy Trinity, is a neat structure covered with lead, with a tower rebuilt in 1728. This is a place of great antiquity, having formerly given name to a hundred, called Chilton-Trinitatis. There is an endowment in land, given by Edward Colston, for a charity school. The navigable river Parret runs on the eastern side of the parish; and the neighbourhood contains a great quantity of coal lying beneath a stony stratum, here called *wark*, on which, when split, impressions of fern and other plants are visible; much of the coal is tinged with sulphur, and in one mine a considerable quantity of lead-ore was found adhering to it.

CHILVERS-COTON, a parish in the Atherstone division of the hundred of HEMLINGFORD, county of WARWICK, ¾ of a mile (S. W.) from Nuneaton, containing 2169 inhabitants. The living is a discharged vicarage, in the archdeaconry of Coventry, and diocese of Lichfield and Coventry, rated in the king's books at £7. 4., endowed with £1400 parliamentary grant, and in the patronage of the Chancellor of the diocese. The church is dedicated to All Saints. There is a place of worship for Wesleyan Methodists. The manufacture of ribands is carried on extensively here, and there are some coal-works in the parish: the Coventry canal passes through it. In the reign of Henry II. Ralph de Sudley founded an Augustine priory at Erdbury, in this parish, in honour of the Blessed Virgin Mary, the revenue of which, at the dissolution, was £122. 8. 6.

CHILWELL, a hamlet in the parish of ATTENBOROUGH, southern division of the wapentake of BROXTOW, county of NOTTINGHAM, 4¾ miles (S. W. by W.) from Nottingham, containing 823 inhabitants. Here are two endowed almshouses.

CHILWORTH, a hamlet in that part of the parish of GREAT MILTON which is in the hundred of BULLINGTON, county of OXFORD, 3½ miles (W. N. W.) from Tetsworth, containing 63 inhabitants.

CHILWORTH, a parish in the hundred of MANSBRIDGE, Fawley division of the county of SOUTHAMPTON, 4 miles (S. E. by E.) from Romsey, containing 147 inhabitants. The living is a perpetual curacy, in the archdeaconry and diocese of Winchester, endowed with £600 royal bounty, and £200 parliamentary grant, and in the patronage of John Fleming, Esq. The church is a small, but neat, edifice, rebuilt a few years since by the late patron, P. Serle, Esq. The soil is peculiarly favourable to the growth of oak, which is here produced in great luxuriance.

CHILWORTH, or ST. MARTHA, a parish in the first division of the hundred of BLACKHEATH, county of SURREY, 2¾ miles (S. E.) from Guildford, containing 197 inhabitants. The living is a donative, in the gift of the Proprietor of the Chilworth estate.

CHIMNELL, a township in that part of the parish of WHITCHURCH which is in the Whitchurch division of the hundred of BRADFORD (North), county of SALOP, 1¾ mile (N. N. E.) from Whitchurch, with which the population is returned.

CHIMNEY, a hamlet in the parish and hundred of BAMPTON, county of OXFORD, 6¼ miles (S. by W.) from Witney, containing 46 inhabitants. The river Isis flows past the village.

CHINEHAM, a tything in that part of the parish of MONK'S SHERBORNE which is in the hundred of BASINGSTOKE, Basingstoke division of the county of SOUTHAMPTON, 1¼ mile (N. N. E.) from Basingstoke, containing 41 inhabitants.

CHINGFORD, a parish in the hundred of WALTHAM, county of ESSEX, 9½ miles (N. N. E.) from London, containing 837 inhabitants. The living is a rectory, in the archdeaconry of Essex, and diocese of London, rated in the king's books at £14. 5. 5., and in the patronage of J. Heathcote, Esq. The church, dedicated to All Saints, is a small building of flint and stone, with a low tower; it is in the later style of English architecture, and much overgrown with ivy. This parish lies on the border of Epping Forest, in which there is a house termed Queen Elizabeth's Lodge, where the courts under the forest laws are held. A day and a Sunday school are supported by subscription.

CHINLEY, a chapelry in the parish of GLOSSOP, hundred of HIGH PEAK, county of DERBY, 2½ miles (N. by W.) from Chapel en le Frith, containing, with Brownside and Bugsworth, 1038 inhabitants. There is a place of worship for Wesleyan Methodists. Here is a trifling endowment for teaching poor children, besides which five are educated by means of Trickett's charity at Bowden, and others partake of Jenkinson's, jointly with Brownside.

CHINNOCK (EAST), a parish in the hundred of HOUNDSBOROUGH, BERWICK, and COKER, county of SOMERSET, 5 miles (S. W. by W.) from Yeovil, containing 581 inhabitants. The living is a rectory, in the archdeaconry of Wells, and diocese of Bath and Wells, rated in the king's books at £6. 7. 8½., and in the patronage of the Crown. About a mile west from the church there is a spring of brackish water, whence salt may be extracted. A school is endowed with a small annuity paid by the trustees of property bequeathed for divers charitable purposes.

CHINNOCK (MIDDLE), a parish in the hundred of HOUNDSBOROUGH, BERWICK, and COKER, county of SOMERSET, 3½ miles (N. E. by N.) from Crewkerne, containing 173 inhabitants. The living is a rectory, in the archdeaconry of Wells, and diocese of Bath and Wells, rated in the king's books at £7. 9. 7., and in the patronage of the Earl of Ilchester. The church, dedicated to St. Margaret, has a Norman arch over the southern entrance. Hemp and flax are produced in this parish, and the poor are employed in spinning and weaving them into sail-cloth, &c.

CHINNOCK (WEST), a parish in the hundred of HOUNDSBOROUGH, BERWICK, and COKER, county of SOMERSET, 3 miles (N.E. by N.) from Crewkerne, containing 477 inhabitants. The living is a perpetual curacy, annexed to the rectory of Chisleborough, in the archdeaconry of Wells, and diocese of Bath and Wells. The church has lately received an addition of one hundred and fifty-two sittings, of which eighty-four are free, the Incorporated Society for the enlargement of churches and chapels having granted £50 towards defraying the expense. There is a place of worship for Wesleyan Methodists.

CHINNOR, a parish in the hundred of LEWKNOR, county of OXFORD, 3½ miles (N. E. by E.) from Watlington, containing, with the liberty of Henton, 1097 inhabitants. The living is a rectory, in the archdeaconry and diocese of Oxford, rated in the king's books at £26. 0. 5., and in the patronage of Sir James Musgrave, Bart. The church is dedicated to St. Andrew. The Roman Iknield-street enters the county at this place.

CHIPCHASE, a chapelry in the parish of CHOLLERTON, north-eastern division of TINDALE ward, county of NORTHUMBERLAND, 9 miles (N. N.W.) from Hexham, containing, with the township of Gunnerton, 409 inhabitants. The chapel was rebuilt in 1732, by John Reed, Esq., on the lawn of Chipchase Castle, a large and beautiful structure standing upon a lofty eminence, at the foot of which flows the North Tyne: of the ancient building only a tower remains; its roof rests on corbels, and has openings for missiles, or scalding water, to be thrown upon an enemy; some tattered fragments of paintings on the walls are exceedingly curious.

CHIPPENHAM, a parish in the hundred of STAPLOE, county of CAMBRIDGE, 4½ miles (N. N. E.) from Newmarket, containing 607 inhabitants. The living is a discharged vicarage, in the archdeaconry of Sudbury, and diocese of Norwich, rated in the king's books at £11. 12. 6., and in the patronage of the Trustees of J. Tharp, Esq. The church, dedicated to St. Margaret, was rebuilt by means of a grant of indulgences, shortly after the destruction of the ancient edifice by fire, in the fifteenth century. A charity school was founded in 1714, by the Earl of Orford, with an endowment of £20 per annum, for teaching all the poor children of the parish. William de Mandeville, Earl of Essex, gave this manor to the society of Knights Hospitallers, whereupon a subordinate establishment was fixed here. Charles I., during the civil war, enjoyed the diversion of bowling at Chippenham Park, the seat of Sir William Russel; and George I. was entertained here by Admiral Russel, October 4th, 1717. About the middle of the seventeenth century the mansion and estate were possessed by Sir Francis Russel, Bart., whose daughter married the fourth son of the Protector Cromwell. Sir Edward Russel, created Earl of Orford, expended a considerable sum in improving the park and embellishing the mansion, which latter was taken down and the materials sold.

Seal and Arms.

CHIPPENHAM, a parish in the hundred of CHIPPENHAM, county of WILTS, comprising the borough and market town of Chippenham, and the tythings of Allington, and Tytherton-Stanley with Nethermore, and containing 3506 inhabitants, of which number, 3201 are in the borough, 33 miles (N.W. by N.) from Salisbury, and 93 (W.) from London. This place, which derives its name from the Saxon *Cyppanham*, a market town, was of considerable importance during the Octarchy, and is supposed to have been the residence of the West Saxon kings. Ethelwolf, on his return from an excursion against the Welch, in 853, remained for some time at this place, where he celebrated the marriage of his daughter Ethelswitha with Burhred, King of Mercia. In the reign of Alfred, the Danes, who, after their defeat, had engaged by treaty to quit the kingdom, retreated to this town, of which they obtained possession by treachery; and that monarch, after the dispersion of his army, was compelled to take refuge in the cottage of a neat-herd: on their subsequent defeat by Alfred, the Danes again took refuge here, where the treaty between that monarch and the Danish prince Guthrum was negociated. The town is pleasantly situated on the side of a hill, on the south bank of the river Avon, which here expands into a noble sheet of water, over which, terminating the western extremity of the principal street, is a handsome stone bridge of twenty-two arches, widened about thirty years since, and ornamented with balustrades, for the repair of which, and of a stone causeway of nearly three miles in length, a considerable estate is vested in the corporation. It consists of one spacious street, half a mile in length and well paved, containing many respectable houses, and of several smaller streets; it is lighted, and tolerably well supplied with water from the river, by which it is bounded on three sides. The woollen manufacture, consisting chiefly of the finer broad cloths and kerseymeres, formerly flourished to a considerable extent; but it has altogether declined: there are a few grist-mills and tanneries; and the town is greatly benefited by the trade arising from its situation as a great thoroughfare on the road to Bath and Bristol. The Wilts and Berks canal passes close to it. The market is on Saturday: fairs are held on May 17th, June 22nd, October 29th, and December 11th, for horses, cattle, and sheep. The government, by charter of Queen Mary, granted in the first year of her reign, and, after its surrender to Charles II., renewed in the reign of James II., is vested in a bailiff and twelve capital burgesses, assisted by a town-clerk and subordinate officers: the bailiff is elected by the burgesses, but he does not exercise magisterial authority. The petty sessions for the division are held here; and a court of requests, for the recovery of debts under 40*s.*, is held on the Tuesday in every sixth week by commissioners, under an act passed in the 35th of George III., the jurisdiction of which extends over the hundreds of Chippenham, Calne, and North Damerham, and the liberty of Corsham. The town-hall market-house, and shambles are very inconveniently situated: it has long been in contemplation to remove them, but this desirable object has not yet been carried into effect. Chippenham is a borough by prescription, and first sent members to parliament in the reign of Edward I.; it made two returns in the reign of Edward II., and four in that of Edward III., from which period it discontinued till the 2nd of Richard II.; after the 12th of that reign it again ceased to make any return till the first of Henry VI., since which time it has regularly sent two members: the right of election is vested in the resident burgage-holders, of whom the number is one hundred and twenty-eight, the addition of one more having been for many years a subject of litigation; one-half of them are in the interest of Joseph Nield, Esq.: the bailiff is the returning officer.

The living is a discharged vicarage, in the archdeaconry of Wilts, and diocese of Salisbury, rated in the king's books at £13. 19. 4., endowed with £200 private benefaction, and £200 royal bounty, and in the patronage of the Dean and Canons of Christ Church, Oxford. The church, dedicated to St. Andrew, is a spacious ancient building, containing portions in different styles of English architecture, of which the tower and spire are in the early style; it contains several interesting monuments. There is a chapel of ease at Tytherton-Lucas, in this parish. There are places of worship for Baptists, Independents, and Wesleyan Methodists. William Woodroffe, in 1664, gave land producing £5 per annum, for teaching ten poor children, to which Mrs. Mary Bridges added £15, for two additional boys. The Rev. Robert Cock, in 1719, gave £50 towards the establishment of a charity school for girls; and a Lancasterian school, recently established, is supported by subscription. Thomas Ray, Esq., in 1615, bequeathed nine houses in New Sarum, directing the rents to be distributed among poor clothiers in Chippenham, Marlborough, Trowbridge, and Westbury. Mr. Gabriel Goldney, in 1620, gave a rent-charge of £6, to furnish great coats for six aged men. Sir Francis Popham gave lands, producing £12 per annum, to be divided among six poor burgesses; and, in 1769, Sir Edward Baynton and Sir Thomas Fludyer, who in that year were returned as members for the borough, invested £1000 in the three per cent. Bank Annuities, for the support of such freemen, or their widows, living in burgage-houses, as the trustees should consider deserving objects. There are various other bequests, both for the benefit of the poor and for the repair of the causeway. At the distance of about two miles is the site of Stanley abbey, founded by the Empress Matilda and Henry II., in 1154, who removed hither a society of Cistercian monks, established at Lockswell three years previously; its revenue, in the 26th of Henry VIII., was estimated at £222. 19. 4.: there are no visible remains, but fragments are occasionally found upon the site. Monkton, the name of an estate on the north bank of the river, seems to indicate the remote existence of some religious establishment, of which no vestige or historical account remains. There are two chalybeate springs in the parish, which were formerly in great repute; one of them is now occasionally used, but the other is entirely closed up.

CHIPPING, a parish in the lower division of the hundred of BLACKBURN, county palatine of LANCASTER, comprising the townships of Chipping, and Thornley with Wheatley, and containing 1735 inhabitants, of which number, 1229 are in the township of Chipping, 9¼ miles (W. by N.) from Clitheroe. The living is a discharged vicarage, in the archdeaconry of Richmond, and diocese of Chester, rated in the king's books at £36. 13. 4., endowed with £400 private benefaction, £400 royal bounty, and £200 parliamentary grant, and in the patronage of the Bishop of Chester, as impropriator of the rectory, which is rated at £24. 16. 5½. The church is dedicated to St. Bartholomew. This parish contains limestone, a considerable quantity of which is burned in the neighbourhood. Fairs for cattle are held on Easter-Tuesday and August 24th. A free school was founded, in 1684, by the trustees of John Brabin, Esq., with an endowment in land producing £60 per annum; there is another endowment, of £4 per annum, by C. Parkinson, in 1702, in support of an usher: sixteen boys are clothed, educated, and supplied with books. Three almshouses were also founded by the same trust, for six poor women, who receive twelve shillings each monthly. Three apprentices are bound annually from a bequest by the Rev. Mr. Carlisle.

CHIPPINGHURST, a hamlet in the parish of Cuddesden, hundred of Bullington, county of Oxford, 7¼ miles (N. by W.) from Bensington, containing 28 inhabitants.

CHIPSTABLE, a parish in the hundred of Williton and Freemanners, county of Somerset, 2¾ miles (W. by S.) from Wiveliscombe, containing 337 inhabitants. The living is a rectory, in the archdeaconry of Taunton, and diocese of Bath and Wells, rated in the king's books at £11. 1. 8., and in the patronage of the Rev. S. S. Richards. The church is dedicated to All Saints.

CHIPSTEAD, a parish in the second division of the hundred of Reigate, county of Surrey, 2¾ miles (N. by E.) from Gatton, containing 440 inhabitants. The living is a rectory, in the archdeaconry of Surrey, and diocese of Winchester, rated in the king's books at £17. 13. 11½., and in the patronage of Col. Hylton Jolliffe. The church, dedicated to St. Margaret, was thoroughly repaired in 1829: on the north side is a fine Norman arch. Here is a charity school, endowed with a house and land given by Mary Stephens, in 1746, producing £70 per annum, for teaching and apprenticing six children, who are bound with premiums of from £10 to £20 each. The Croydon railway passes through this parish.

CHIRBURY, a parish in the hundred of Chirbury, county of Salop, 3¼ miles (E. N. E.) from Montgomery, containing 1442 inhabitants. The living is a vicarage, in the archdeaconry of Salop, and diocese of Hereford, rated in the king's books at £9. 6. 8., and in the patronage of the Mayor and Corporation of Shrewsbury. The church, dedicated to St. Michael, is in the early style of English architecture, with a fine square tower at the west end, surmounted by open-worked battlements and eight pinnacles: it consists of the nave of the conventual church of an abbey of Augustine friars, founded in the reign of Henry III., by Robert de Boulers, and removed to this place, the revenue of which, at the dissolution, was £87. 7. 4. A considerable endowment in land was given, in 1675, by Edward Lewis, for the maintenance of a schoolmaster. The castle, a stately structure, which formerly stood on the bank of the Severn, was erected by Ethelfreda, Countess of Mercia, to repel the incursions of the Welch. Edward, the celebrated Lord Herbert, was created baron of Chirbury, but the title became extinct at his death.

CHIRDON, a township in the parish of Gaystead, north-western division of Tindale ward, county of Northumberland, 6 miles (W. by S.) from Bellingham, containing 83 inhabitants.

CHIRTON, a township in the parish of Tynemouth, eastern division of Castle ward, county of Northumberland, 1 mile (W. S. W.) from North Shields, containing 4351 inhabitants. The village is situated on the western side of the town of North Shields, and has increased upwards of three-fourths in size and population since 1811, owing chiefly to the extension of the coal-works, from which railways have been formed to the Tyne: at the north end of it is a burying-ground belonging to the Jews.

CHISELHAMPTON, a parish in the hundred of Dorchester, county of Oxford, 7 miles (S. E.) from Oxford, containing 118 inhabitants. The living is a perpetual curacy, consolidated with that of Stadhampton, claimed to be in the jurisdiction of the peculiar court of Dorchester, endowed with £16 per annum private benefaction, £800 royal bounty, and £400 parliamentary grant. The church is dedicated to St. Mary. The river Thame runs through this parish.

CHISELHURST, a parish in the hundred of Ruxley, lathe of Sutton at Hone, county of Kent, 11 miles (S. E.) from London, containing, with a portion of the hamlet of Mottingham, which extends into this parish, 1586 inhabitants. The living is a rectory, in the archdeaconry and diocese of Rochester, rated in the king's books at £16. 3. 6½., and in the patronage of the Bishop of Rochester. The church, dedicated to St. Nicholas, is built of flint, with a shingled spire. There is a place of worship for Wesleyan Methodists. A school is endowed with £15 per annum and a house for the master, for teaching six boys; but fifty are educated on this foundation on the National system. There are two schools for girls, one affording clothing and instruction to six, and the other to twelve, supported by various bequests and donations producing £24 per annum, besides subscriptions. Children of this parish are also admitted into the National school established at Foot's Cray. In 1680, Thomas Philpott made a bequest for building six almshouses at Eltham, two of them to be inhabited by poor persons of this parish. Sir Nicholas Bacon was a native of Chiselhurst: here also was born, in 1500, Sir Francis Walsingham, secretary of state to Queen Elizabeth; and at this place, in 1623, died Camden, the celebrated antiquary, from whom Camden Place, in this parish (whence Lord Chancellor Pratt took the title of baron, and which now confers the title of marquis on his descendants), derives its name. Viscount Sydney enjoys the title of Baron Sydney of Chiselhurst, which was conferred in 1783.

CHISENBURY, a tything in the parish of Nether Avon, hundred of Elstub and Everley, county of Wilts, 9 miles (W. by N.) from Ludgershall, containing 41 inhabitants. This tything forms part of the endowment of the prebend of Chute and Chisenbury in the Cathedral Church of Salisbury, and is within the peculiar jurisdiction of the prebendary.

CHISHALL (GREAT), a parish in the hundred of Uttlesford, county of Essex, 8¼ miles (W. by N.) from Saffron-Walden, containing 353 inhabitants. The living is a discharged vicarage, in the archdeaconry of Colchester, and diocese of London, rated in the king's books at £10, endowed with £200 royal bounty, and in the patronage of J. Wilkes, Esq. The church is dedicated to St. Swithin.

CHISHALL (LITTLE), a parish in the hundred of Uttlesford, county of Essex, 8¼ miles (W. by S.) from Saffron-Walden, containing 71 inhabitants. The living is a rectory, with that of Haydon annexed, in the archdeaconry of Colchester, and diocese of London, rated in the king's books at £14. 10., and in the patronage of Sir P. Soame, Bart. The church is dedicated to St. Nicholas.

CHISLEBOROUGH, a parish in the hundred of Houndsborough, Berwick, and Coker, county of Somerset, 4 miles (N. N. E.) from Crewkerne, containing 434 inhabitants. The living is a rectory, with the perpetual curacy of West Chinnock annexed, in the archdeaconry of Wells, and diocese of Bath and Wells, rated in the king's books at £14. 5. 7½., and in the patronage of the Earl of Ilchester. The church is dedicated to St. Peter and St. Paul. A fair for horses, cattle, and toys, is held on the last Tuesday in October. The river Parret runs through this parish.

CHISLEDON, a parish in the hundred of Kingsbridge, county of Wilts, 3½ miles (S. E.) from Swindon, containing 1077 inhabitants. The living is a discharged vicarage, in the archdeaconry of Wilts, and diocese of Salisbury, rated in the king's books at £8. 8. 9., endowed with £400 private benefaction, £200 royal bounty, and £300 parliamentary grant, and in the patronage of T. Cally, Esq. The church is dedicated to the Holy Cross. There is an endowment of £10. 10. per annum for teaching poor children.

CHISLETT, a parish in the hundred of Bleangate, lathe of St. Augustine, county of Kent, 7 miles (N. E.) from Canterbury, containing 1135 inhabitants. The living is a vicarage, in the archdeaconry and diocese of Canterbury, rated in the king's books at £29. 19. 9½., and in the patronage of the Archbishop of Canterbury. The church, dedicated to St. Mary, is in the early style of English architecture. In 1811, the archbishop demised certain lands, which let for £40 per annum, for the education of children of the parish: the income is applied to teaching twenty-seven boys and girls, and in support of a Sunday school for sixty children.

CHISWICK, a parish in the Kensington division of the hundred of Ossulstone, county of Middlesex, 4½ miles (W. by S.) from London, containing 4236 inhabitants. The living is a vicarage, in the peculiar jurisdiction and patronage of the Dean and Chapter of St. Paul's, London, rated in the king's books at £9. 18. 4. The church is dedicated to St. Nicholas: in the churchyard are some ancient tombs, and a monument to the memory of Hogarth, the painter. Here are charity schools, founded in the year 1719, by Lady Capel, and endowed with £39 per annum, for teaching and clothing twenty boys and ten girls. Chiswick is pleasantly situated on the margin of the Thames, to the left of the great western road from London, and contains many elegant seats belonging to the nobility and gentry, the principal of which, Devonshire House, is adorned on each side with fine rows of cedars: in this mansion died the Right Hon. Charles James Fox, in 1806, and the Right Hon. George Canning, in 1827. Here are the extensive gardens belonging to the Horticultural Society of London, incorporated by charter in 1808, for the improvement of horticulture in all its branches, the concerns of which are under the superintendence of a council, president, treasurer, and secretary: the general meetings of the Fellows take place on the first and third Tuesdays in every month, at the house belonging to the Society, in Regent-street, London: a selection from the papers read to the Society is occasionally published. The Society has formed a collection of drawings of the most approved fruits and ornamental plants, together with models of fruit in wax; and the members have free access to a library of horticultural works; the terms are six guineas on admission, and four guineas per annum.

CHISWORTH, a joint township with Ludworth, in the parish of Glossop, hundred of High Peak, county of Derby, 9 miles (N. N. W.) from Chapel en le Frith. The population is returned with Ludworth.

CHITHURST, a chapelry in the parish of Iping, hundred of Dumpford, rape of Chichester, county of Sussex, 3¾ miles (W. N. W.) from Midhurst, containing 146 inhabitants. The chapel is in the early style of English architecture.

CHITTLEHAMPTON, a parish in the hundred of South Molton, county of Devon, 5¼ miles (W.) from South Molton, containing 1748 inhabitants. The living is a vicarage, in the archdeaconry of Barnstaple, and diocese of Exeter, rated in the king's books at £34. 18. 11½., and in the patronage of Lord Rolle. The church, dedicated to St. Urith, is a handsome structure, with a fine tower in the later style of English architecture, containing a pulpit richly carved with figures of saints and vine leaves, besides some interesting monuments. Culm is obtained in the parish; and limestone is found enclosed in a bed of thick slate, or flag-stone. At Brightley are some remains of an ancient mansion and a chapel.

CHITTOE, a tything in the parish of Bishop's Cannings, hundred of Potterne and Cannings, county of Wilts, 5 miles (N. W.) from Devizes, containing 233 inhabitants.

CHIVELSTONE, a parish in the hundred of Coleridge, county of Devon, 6 miles (S. E. by S.) from Kingsbridge, containing 637 inhabitants. The living is a perpetual curacy, annexed to the vicarage of Stokingham, in the archdeaconry of Totness, and diocese of Exeter. The church is dedicated to St. Sylvester. At Ford there is a meeting-house for dissenters.

CHIVESFIELD, county of Hertford. — See GRAVELEY.

CHIVINGTON (EAST), a township in that part of the parish of Warkworth which is in the eastern division of Morpeth ward, county of Northumberland, 10½ miles (N. N. E.) from Morpeth, containing 207 inhabitants.

CHIVINGTON (WEST), a township in that part of the parish of Warkworth which is in the eastern division of Morpeth ward, county of Northumberland, 8 miles (N. by E.) from Morpeth, containing 108 inhabitants. Here was formerly a chapel, which has long been in ruins. From the foundations of houses, still to be seen, extending one mile and a half in a direct line from this place to East Chivington, it seems to have been formerly a place of much greater importance.

CHOBHAM, a parish in the first division of the hundred of GODLEY, county of SURREY, $4\frac{1}{2}$ miles (E. S. E.) from Bagshot, containing 1719 inhabitants. The living is a vicarage, in the archdeaconry of Surrey, and diocese of Winchester, rated in the king's books at £10. 2. 1., and in the patronage of Samuel Thornton, Esq. The church is dedicated to St. Lawrence. There is a place of worship for Wesleyan Methodists. Bagshot heath forms a large portion of this parish, but little more than a third of it is in cultivation, the soil being for the most part sandy, with beds of gravel underneath. At Chobham park are the remains of a large mansion, in which Archbishop Heath died. There is a school for about one hundred and fifty children, supported by subscription.

CHOCKNELL, a hamlet in the parish of LEIGH, lower division of the hundred of PERSHORE, county of WORCESTER, $5\frac{3}{4}$ miles (W. S. W.) from Worcester. The population is returned with the parish. This was formerly a distinct parish: the living, which was a vicarage, rated in the king's books at £16. 1. $5\frac{1}{2}$., has been consolidated with the rectory of Leigh; it is in the archdeaconry and diocese of Worcester. The church has been demolished.

CHOLDERTON, a chapelry in the parish of AMPORT, hundred of ANDOVER, Andover division of the county of SOUTHAMPTON, 5 miles (W.) from Andover. The population is returned with the parish.

CHOLDERTON, a parish in the hundred of AMESBURY, county of WILTS, 5 miles (E. by N.) from Amesbury, containing 149 inhabitants. The living is a rectory, in the archdeaconry and diocese of Salisbury, rated in the king's books at £11. 0. $7\frac{1}{2}$., and in the patronage of the Provost and Fellows of Oriel College, Oxford. The church is dedicated to St. Nicholas. By deed in 1753, Anthony Cratcherode gave land for teaching children, and for the poor of this parish.

CHOLLERTON, a parish in the north-eastern division of TINDALE ward, county of NORTHUMBERLAND, comprising the chapelry of Chipchase with Gunnerton, and the townships of Barrasford, Chollerton, and Colwell with Swinburn, and the greater part of the township of Broomhope with Buteland, and containing 1241 inhabitants, of which number, 403 are in the township of Chollerton, 6 miles (N.) from Hexham. The living is a vicarage, in the archdeaconry of Northumberland, and diocese of Durham, rated in the king's books at £6. 14. $4\frac{1}{2}$., and in the patronage of Colonel and Mrs. Beaumont. The church is dedicated to St. Giles. A cross, still called St. Oswald's cross, was set up here by Oswald, King of Northumberland, to commemorate his victory at Haledon, in this parish, over Ceadwall, King of Cumberland, after which he became a Christian. About a mile from the village of Chollerton was the line of the Picts' wall, erected by the Romans and South Britons, in 430, to protect themselves from the incursions of the Picts, the remains of which still exist, extending above eighty miles through this county and that of Cumberland, from the North sea to the Solway Frith: it was eight feet broad and twelve high, with towers situated about a mile from each other; and at short distances were erected several small fortified places, called *Chesters* by the Saxons, many vestiges of which are still conspicuous. Within this parish also are the remains of two ancient and extensive castles, called *Chipchase* and *Swinburn*, which have partly been converted into elegant modern structures.

CHOLMONDELEY, a township in the parish of MALPAS, higher division of the hundred of BROXTON, county palatine of CHESTER, $7\frac{1}{2}$ miles (W.) from Nantwich, containing 297 inhabitants. Cholmondeley House was garrisoned, in 1643, by four hundred royalists, who, in April, were attacked and defeated by the parliamentary troops from Nantwich, having lost fifty men and six hundred horses. It afterwards fell into the hands of the parliamentarians, and was re-captured by the royalists, who were driven from it again on the 30th of June, 1644. The present splendid mansion of Cholmondeley castle, about half a mile from the former, the seat of the Marquis of Cholmondeley, was begun in 1801, and completed in 1804. A domestic chapel, to which the tenants enjoy the privilege of resorting, has long been attached to it.

CHOLMONDSTONE, a township in the parish of ACTON, hundred of NANTWICH, county palatine of CHESTER, $4\frac{1}{2}$ miles (N. by W.) from Nantwich, containing 208 inhabitants. Thomas Fillcock left a small bequest for teaching poor children.

CHOLSEY, a parish in the hundred of READING, though locally in the hundred of Moreton, county of BERKS, $2\frac{1}{2}$ miles (S. W.) from Wallingford, containing 975 inhabitants. The living is a vicarage, with the perpetual curacy of Moulsford united, in the archdeaconry of Berks, and diocese of Salisbury, rated in the king's books at £18. 9. $9\frac{1}{2}$., and in the patronage of the Crown. The church, dedicated to St. Mary, contains some remains of Norman architecture. The Baptists have a place of worship here. A monastery was founded, in 986, by Ethelred, as an atonement for the murder of his brother, Edward the Martyr, which was destroyed by the Danes in 1006, together with the village wherein it was situated. The abbot of Reading had a seat here, which was granted, in 1555, to Sir Francis Englefield, and conveyed afterwards by the crown to William Knollys, Viscount Wallingford, subsequently created Earl of Banbury.

CHOPPINGTON, a township in the parish of BEDLINGTON, eastern division of CHESTER ward, county palatine of DURHAM, though locally on the east side of the county of Northumberland, 4 miles (E. by S.) from Morpeth. The population is returned with the parish. There is a bridge of four arches over the Wansbeck at Sheepwash, in this township.

CHOPWELL, a township in the parish of RYTON, western division of CHESTER ward, county palatine of DURHAM, $11\frac{1}{2}$ miles (W. S. W.) from Gateshead, containing 237 inhabitants. This township contains some coal; and at Black-hall, on the river Derwent, is a manufactory for German steel, which is stated to have been first carried on here by some emigrants from Germany. Lady Liddell supports a school for boys and another for girls.

CHORLEY, a township in the parish of WILMSLOW, hundred of MACCLESFIELD, county palatine of CHESTER, $5\frac{3}{4}$ miles (N. W. by W.) from Macclesfield, containing 478 inhabitants.

CHORLEY, a township in the parish of Wrenbury, hundred of Nantwich, county palatine of Chester, 5¼ miles (W. by S.) from Nantwich, containing 183 inhabitants.

CHORLEY, a market town and parish in the hundred of Leyland, county palatine of Lancaster, 32 miles (S. by E.) from Lancaster, and 208 (N. W. by N.) from London, on the road to Scotland, containing 7315 inhabitants. The name of this place is derived from its situation on the river Chor, about a mile from its confluence with the Yarrow, and either from the Saxon word *Ley*, a field, or from the family of Ley, who were its ancient proprietors. The town is pleasantly situated on the summit of a considerable elevation, and, though in Leland's time described as "a wonderful poore or rather no market," has, from the excellent quarries in the neighbourhood, and from the enterprising spirit of its inhabitants, been rapidly rising into consideration and importance, and increasing in population and extent: since the census of 1821, more than three hundred houses have been erected. The town is well lighted with gas by a company established in 1819, who enlarged and appropriated to that purpose some works previously erected for lighting a private manufactory: it is amply supplied with water, which, under the direction of a company formed in 1823, is conveyed by pipes from a large reservoir, into which it is raised by a steam-engine of twelve-horse power, from a spring that affords an abundant supply: from the elevated situation of the reservoir, the water descends with a velocity sufficient to raise it to the roofs of the highest buildings. The environs, in which are many elegant mansions, abound with pleasing and diversified scenery: the hills are rich in coal, slate, ashler, and millstone. Mines of lead-ore and alum-shale exist in the neighbourhood: the lead mine is worked at Anglezark, and contains an abundance of carbonate of barytes. The principal branch of manufacture is that of cotton, which is carried on to a considerable extent; the chief articles are muslins and calicoes: there are large printing and bleaching establishments on the banks of the streams in the vicinity; many of the factories are worked by water, and several by steam-engines of considerable power. The Lancaster canal, and the Leeds and Liverpool canal, which unite to the south-west of Whittle le Woods, pass within half a mile of the town. The market is on Tuesday: fairs are held on March 26th, May 5th, and August 20th, principally for cattle; and September 4th, 5th, and 6th, for woollen cloth, hardware, and pedlary. The county magistrates hold a petty session for the division, once in five weeks, alternately with Cuerdon, Leyland, Penwortham, and Rufford; and the lord of the manor holds a court leet once a year. The town-hall, a neat stone building, in the area under which the market is held, was erected in 1802, at the sole expense of the late John Hollingshead, Esq.; the upper part contains a large room in which the petty sessions are held, and a smaller for the transaction of parochial business: adjoining it is a small prison for the temporary confinement of offenders prior to their committal to the county gaol.

Chorley was originally a chapelry in the parish of Croston, from which it was separated in 1793, when that extensive parish was divided into three distinct parishes. The living is a rectory not in charge, in the archdeaconry and diocese of Chester, and in the patronage of the Rev. John Whalley Master, B.D. The church, dedicated to St. Lawrence, is an ancient structure, retaining several features of Norman character, of which the south entrance is a fine specimen: it formerly contained a relic, said to be the head of its tutelar saint, which, according to a manuscript in the British Museum, was brought from Normandy by Sir Rowland Stanley, Knt., and presented to the parish by his brother. St. George's church, completed in 1825, at an expense of £11,845. 12. 5., defrayed by the parliamentary commissioners, is a handsome and spacious structure in the later style of English architecture, with a square embattled tower, and contains two thousand and twelve sittings, of which one thousand five hundred and ninety are free. The living is a perpetual curacy, in the patronage of the Rector of Chorley. There are places of worship for Independents, Wesleyan Methodists, Unitarians, and Roman Catholics. The grammar school was originally established by the churchwardens of the parish, who, in 1634, built a schoolroom, partly in the churchyard, and partly in the yard of an adjoining tythe-barn; it has a small endowment, not exceeding £10 per annum, arising from several subsequent benefactions, and a new schoolroom was erected in 1824: the course of instruction is rather commercial than classical, and every scholar pays a quarterage to the master, none being gratuitously instructed. A charity school, for which a new building was erected at an expense of £600, raised by subscription in 1824, is conducted on the National plan: there are also similar schools in which about one thousand children are educated. An almshouse was erected and endowed, in 1682, by Hugh Cooper, Esq., for six aged persons, who have each an apartment, a garden, and an allowance of £2 per annum in money.

CHORLTON, a township in the parish of Malpas, higher division of the hundred of Broxton, county palatine of Chester, 2¼ miles (W. by N.) from Malpas, containing 124 inhabitants. A quantity of Roman coins, of the reigns of the emperors Valerian and Posthumus, was dug up, in March 1818, by some workmen, in a field in this township.

CHORLTON, a township in the parish of Wybunbury, hundred of Nantwich, county palatine of Chester, 5¾ miles (E. by S.) from Nantwich, containing 91 inhabitants.

CHORLTON, a township in that part of the parish of Backford which is in the higher division of the hundred of Wirrall, county palatine of Chester, 4½ miles (N.) from Chester, containing 78 inhabitants.

CHORLTON, a chapelry in the parish of Manchester, hundred of Salford, county palatine of Lancaster, 3½ miles (S. S. W.) from Manchester, containing, with Hardy, 624 inhabitants. The living is a perpetual curacy, in the archdeaconry and diocese of Chester, endowed with £400 private benefaction, and £600 royal bounty, and in the patronage of the Warden and Fellows of the Collegiate Church of Manchester. In 1741, Margaret Usherwood bequeathed £160, for clothing and teaching six poor children.

CHORLTON, a chapelry in the parish of Eccleshall, northern division of the hundred of Pirehill, county of Stafford, 6¼ miles (N. by W.) from Eccleshall, containing 237 inhabitants. The living is a perpetual curacy, within the peculiar jurisdiction of the Prebendary of Eccleshall in the Cathedral Church of Lichfield and Coventry, endowed with £200 private benefaction, and £1000 royal bounty, and in the patronage of certain Trustees. The chapel, dedicated to St. Lawrence, had sixty free sittings recently erected in it, towards defraying the expense of which the Incorporated Society for the enlargement of churches and chapels granted £50.

CHORLTON-HILL, a township in the parish of Eccleshall, northern division of the hundred of Pirehill, county of Stafford, containing 94 inhabitants.

CHORLTON-ROW, a chapelry in the parish of Manchester, hundred of Salford, county palatine of Lancaster, containing 8209 inhabitants. It is situated adjacent to the town of Manchester, and consists of several good streets, being well lighted with gas, paved, and amply supplied with water, and is inhabited by many of the merchants and manufacturers of that town, in the trade of which it greatly participates, there being several large spinning mills in the chapelry. The chapel, dedicated to St. Luke, was built by the late Rev. Edward Smith, and opened in 1804; it is a small neat structure of brick, with a turret. There are places of worship for Independents and Wesleyan Methodists. An infant school was established in 1825, in which there are about two hundred children; and there are Sunday schools attached to the different places of worship. This chapelry is within the jurisdiction of the court of requests for the recovery of debts under £5, held at Manchester. The building lately erected for a town-hall, dispensary, and constables' dwelling-house, is described in the account of Manchester.

CHOULESBURY, a parish in the hundred of Cottesloe, county of Buckingham, 4 miles (N. W. by N.) from Chesham, containing 132 inhabitants. The living is a perpetual curacy, in the archdeaconry of Buckingham, and diocese of Lincoln, endowed with £8 per annum private benefaction, and £600 royal bounty, and in the patronage of the Trustees of Mr. Neale. The church is dedicated to St. Lawrence.

CHOWBENT, a hamlet in the parish of Leigh, hundred of West Derby, county palatine of Lancaster, 2¼ miles (N. E.) from Leigh, containing 4145 inhabitants. A chapel, which formerly belonged to a congregation of dissenters, was consecrated by Dr. Wilson, the pious and benevolent bishop of Sodor and Man: the living is a donative, in the gift of Lord Lilford. There is a place of worship for Unitarians. This is a large village, in which the manufacture of nails is carried on to some extent; several carding-engines, spinning-frames, &c., were formerly made here. There are two fairs for toys, pedlary, &c., on June 29th and August 24th; but a market, formerly held by custom, has fallen into disuse.

CHOWLEY, a township in the parish of Coddington, higher division of the hundred of Broxton, county palatine of Chester, 9¼ miles (S. E. by S.) from Chester, containing 78 inhabitants.

CHRISHALL, a parish in the hundred of Uttlesford, county of Essex, 6½ miles (W. by N.) from Saffron-Walden, containing 411 inhabitants. The living is a discharged vicarage, in the archdeaconry of Essex, and diocese of London, rated in the king's books at £13, endowed with £200 private benefaction, and £200 royal bounty, and in the patronage of the Bishop of London. The church is dedicated to the Holy Trinity.

CHRIST-CHURCH, county of Middlesex.—See SPITALFIELDS.

CHRISTCHURCH, a parish in the lower division of the hundred of Caldicott, county of Monmouth, 2¼ miles (E. N. E.) from Newport, containing, with the hamlet of Caerton-ultra-Pontem, 854 inhabitants. The living is a discharged vicarage, in the archdeaconry and diocese of Llandaff, rated in the king's books at £13. 4. 2., and in the patronage of the Provost and Fellows of Eton College. The church is a large and elegant edifice, occupying an elevated situation. The petty sessions for the lower division of the hundred are held here, and also at Magor. The river Usk partly bounds this parish, in which there is an abundance of limestone.

Seal and Arms.

CHRISTCHURCH, a borough, sea port, market town, and parish, having separate jurisdiction, locally in the hundred of Christchurch, New Forest (West) division of the county of Southampton, 21½ miles (S. W. by W.) from Southampton, and 100 (S. W. by W.) from London, containing, with the chapelries of Bransgore, Hinton, and the tythings of Street, Bure with Hinton, Hurn with Parly, Iford with Tuckton (in Westover liberty), and Winkton with Burton, 4644 inhabitants. This place is of great antiquity, and, from some relics discovered in the church, is supposed to have been of Roman origin; by the Saxons it was called *Twyneham-Bourne* and *Tweon-ea*, from its situation between two rivers. The earliest historical notice of it occurs in the Saxon Chronicles, which records its occupation by Ethelwold, during his revolt against his kinsman, Edward the Elder. In Domesday-book it is mentioned, under the name *Thuinam*, as a burgh and royal manor, containing thirty-one messuages. Its present name is derived from its church and priory, founded prior to the Conquest for a dean and twenty-four Secular canons, and dedicated to the Holy Trinity, which was rebuilt in the reign of William Rufus, and dedicated to our Saviour Christ, by Ralph Flambard, Bishop of Durham, and formerly dean of the priory; it was largely endowed by Richard de Rivers, Earl of Devon, to whom Henry I. gave the manor. Earl Baldwin, son and successor to Earl Richard, placed canons regular of the order of St. Augustine in this priory, which flourished till the dissolution, at which time its revenue was £544. 6. Some portions of the walls that enclosed the conventual buildings are still remaining: the ancient lodge is now occupied as a dwelling-house, and the site of the refectory may be traced by the remnants of its walls. The town was fortified by Richard de Rivers, who either erected or rebuilt the castle, of which there are some remains to the north of the priory; these consist chiefly of the ruins of the keep, on the summit of an artificial mount, the walls of which are more than ten feet in thickness, and part of the range that comprised the state apartments: the Norman style of architecture prevails and the arches of some remaining windows are divided by Norman pillars.

Christchurch is situated on the borders of the New Forest, and between the rivers Avon and Stour, which uniting their streams at a short distance below, expand into a broad sheet of water and fall into Christchurch bay, in connexion with which they form a harbour. The current of the Avon, to the east of the town, is intercepted and divided into two parts by an island, from each side of which a bridge to the opposite bank of the river forms the continuation of the road to Lymington: on the site of several houses, destroyed by a fire within the last few years, a new street of respectable houses has been erected: the town is not lighted, nor regularly paved, but is amply supplied with water. The harbour is accessible only at high tides to small vessels drawing not more than from five to six feet of water, the entrance being obstructed by a bar, or lodge of sand, extending from Hengistbury Head, on the Hampshire side, where Hengist, King of the Saxons, landed, to St. Catherine's Cliff, in the Isle of Wight, and occasionally shifting its position, according to the prevalence of successive rains, or sea-storms, attended with southerly winds. In this harbour, as in the neighbouring port of Pool, there is high water twice at every tide: this peculiarity arises from the situation of the coast with respect to the Isle of Wight, and from the projection of the point of land on which Hurst Castle is situated, which, by obstructing the free passage of the water at the influx of the tide, occasions its rise in the bay and harbour to take place earlier than at Portsmouth and Chichester, by three hours and a half at the full and change of the moon; and, by confining the water which has spread over the channel and Southampton water, its reflux is sufficiently violent to cause a second rise in Christchurch bay of nearly three feet. The river Avon was made navigable to Salisbury in 1680, but the accumulation of sand has rendered the navigation useless. The sâlmon fishery, which formerly afforded employment to a considerable number of the labouring class, has very much declined: there are two breweries; and many females are employed in the knitting of stockings, and in the manufacture of watch-spring, or fusee, chains, the latter of which has been lately established. The market is on Monday: fairs are held on Trinity-Thursday, and October 17th, for cattle and horses. The government is vested in a mayor, recorder, two bailiffs, aldermen, and common council-men, in all twenty-four; but the officers of the corporation do not exercise magisterial authority, the town being wholly within the jurisdiction of the county magistrates. The borough was summoned in the 35th of Edward I. and the 2nd of Edward II., but made no subsequent return till the 13th of Elizabeth, since which time it has regularly sent two members to parliament: the right of election is claimed by the resident householders paying scot and lot, but is at present exercised exclusively by the members of the corporation, who are in the interest of Sir George H. Rose: the mayor is the returning officer. Courts leet and baron are held here.

The living is a vicarage, with the perpetual curacy of Holdenhurst annexed, in the archdeaconry and diocese of Winchester, rated in the king's books at £16, and in the patronage of the Dean and Chapter of Winchester. The church, dedicated to the Holy Trinity, and anciently the collegiate church of the priory, is a magnificent cruciform structure, partly in the Norman style, and partly in the early and later styles of English architecture, with a finely proportioned and embattled tower at the west end, which was erected by the Montacutes, earls of Salisbury, in the fifteenth century. The piers and arches of the nave, which is of Norman character, are bold and simple; the clerestory is of later date; the northern entrance is a fine specimen of the early, and the chancel of the later, English style. The altar is decorated with a rude, but interesting, representation of the genealogy of Christ, carved in the style of the age in which the church was founded: to the north of it is a beautiful sepulchral chapel, built in the reign of Henry VII., by the celebrated countess of Salisbury, who, in the 70th year of her age, was beheaded by Henry VIII.; and at the east is a spacious chapel, dedicated to the Virgin Mary, erected in the fourteenth century by the ancestor of Lord Delaware, over which is a large room, called St. Michael's loft, which, since 1662, has been appropriated to the use of the grammar school; there are some other chapels of fine execution, chiefly in the later English style. The west front, principally in the early style, in which a large and handsome window has been recently inserted, is ornamented with a figure of Christ in a canopied niche: the length of this church is three hundred and eleven feet, its breadth at the western extremity sixty feet, and along the transepts one hundred and four feet. There is a place of worship for Independents in the town; and at Burton, a mile and a half to the north, is a Roman Catholic chapel. The free grammar school is of uncertain foundation: in 1707, it had an annuity of £25 for ninety-nine years, payable from the Exchequer; since the expiration of which, in 1805, the amount of various benefactions, vested in the South Sea funds, produces an income of £15 per annum, for which ten boys are instructed in reading, writing, and arithmetic, by a master, who occupies the room over the chapel at the east end of the church. A National and a Lancasterian school, recently established, are supported by subscription; and there are several charitable bequests for distribution among the poor. An intrenchment, six hundred and thirty yards in length, extends across the isthmus which connects Hengistbury Head, with the main land; and near its northern extremity is a large barrow, in which human bones and an urn have been found. On a ridge of hills, about a mile and a half to the north of Christchurch, and a mile to the west of the Avon, called St. Catherine's hill, are traces of an exploratory camp, fifty-five yards square, round which are six small tumuli; and near the base of the hill are ten large barrows, one of which has been discovered to contain human bones. To the north of the camp is an elliptical earthwork, of which the greater diameter is thirty-five, and the less twenty-five, yards: the remains of other intrenchments may be traced in the vicinity.

CHRIST-CHURCH, a parish partly in the eastern division of the hundred of Brixton, but chiefly within the borough of Southwark, county of Surrey, containing 13,339 inhabitants. The living is a rectory, in the archdeaconry of Surrey, and diocese of Winchester.

The Trustees of Mr. Marshall's charities were patrons in 1809. This parish, situated on the south side of Blackfriars' bridge, was anciently termed the liberty of Paris Garden, and formed a part of the parish of St. Saviour until 1706, when it was made a distinct parish by act of parliament. It constituted a portion of the borough of Southwark under a charter of Edward VI., though the inhabitants cannot vote for its parliamentary members, in consequence of having allowed the privilege to fall into disuse. The parish is within the jurisdiction of the court of requests for the town and borough of Southwark, established by an act passed in the 22nd of George II., for the recovery of debts under 40*s*. In 1713, a school for boys was established in Blackfriars' road; and in 1720, a school for girls was added to it, both by subscription: the school-room belonging to the former was enlarged, and that belonging to the latter rebuilt, in 1819, when the Lancasterian system was introduced: they have a permanent endowment of about £180 per annum, and the annual amount of subscriptions, &c., is upwards of £300 more: a few children of each sex are clothed. Almshouses for forty-four poor persons are endowed with nearly £300 per annum, arising from property given by Edward Edwardes, in 1717. Hopton's almshouses, founded by Charles Hopton, in 1730, are endowed with about £500 per annum, affording an asylum to twenty-six poor men. There are various charities for general purposes, all of minor amount except Marshall's charity, founded by John Marshall in 1627, and producing nearly £900 per annum; Hammerton's, producing £230 per annum; and Boyse's, producing £160 per annum.

CHRISTIAN-MALFORD, a parish partly in the hundred of CHIPPENHAM, comprising the chapelry of Avon, but chiefly in the northern division of the hundred of DAMERHAM (of which it is a detached portion), county of WILTS, 5½ miles (N.E. by N.) from Chippenham, and containing 896 inhabitants. The living is a rectory, in the archdeaconry of Wilts, and diocese of Salisbury, rated in the king's books at £27, and in the patronage of the Bishop of Bath and Wells. The church is dedicated to All Saints. There is a place of worship for Independents. The origin and name of this large parish are involved in obscurity, though it was evidently of greater importance in former times than it is at present; but tradition says that the Saxons having been defeated by the Danes in this neighbourhood, the place being before called Melford, from the badness of the passage across the river, it assumed the prefix of Christian for having proved disastrous to the former. The village is built near an old ford on the Avon, which here turns a fulling-mill. There is a National school for children of both sexes.

CHRISTLETON, a parish in the lower division of the hundred of BROXTON, county palatine of CHESTER, comprising the townships of Christleton, Cotton-Abbots, Cotton-Edmund's, Littleton, and Rowton, and containing 954 inhabitants, of which number, 701 are in the township of Christleton, 2¼ miles (E. by S.) from Chester. The living is a rectory, in the archdeaconry and diocese of Chester, rated in the king's books at £39. 5., and in the patronage of Sir Thomas Mostyn, Bart. The church, dedicated to St. James, existed prior to the Conquest: the body has been wholly rebuilt of brick, but the stone tower bears the date 1530. There is a place of worship for Wesleyan Methodists. This place formed, at the time of the Norman survey, a part of the barony of Malpas, at which period it is said to have been very populous; it continued of some importance, and was fortified for the parliament, having been made the head-quarters of Sir William Brereton; but on the siege of Chester being raised, in February 1645, it was, in a sally of the citizens, very nearly destroyed by fire. The Chester and Ellesmere canal passes close to the village. In 1779, John Sellers, of Littleton, left a small bequest for teaching poor children; and a school-house was built in 1800, principally by a bequest from John Hignett, Esq.

CHRISTON, a parish in the hundred of WINTERSTOKE, county of SOMERSET, 5 miles (N.W. by W.) from Axbridge, containing 55 inhabitants. The living is a discharged rectory, in the archdeaconry of Wells, and diocese of Bath and Wells, rated in the king's books at £6. 1. 8., and in the patronage of Montague Gore, Esq. The church is principally in the early style of English architecture.

CHRISTOW, a parish in the hundred of WONFORD, county of DEVON, 5½ miles (N.N.W.) from Chudleigh, containing 531 inhabitants. The living is a discharged vicarage, in the archdeaconry and diocese of Exeter, rated in the king's books at £8. 6. 8., endowed with £200 private benefaction, and £200 royal bounty, and in the patronage of Viscount Exmouth. The church, dedicated to St. James, has a Norman font, and some fine screen-work across the nave and aisles. In this neighbourhood are many excellent cherry orchards. Pope House is said to have been a cell to the priory of Cowick, near Exeter.

CHUDLEIGH, a market town and parish in the hundred of EXMINSTER, county of DEVON, 9 miles (S.S.W.) from Exeter, and 182 (W.S.W.) from London, containing 2053 inhabitants. This place, anciently called *Chidleighe*, was formerly the residence of the bishops of Exeter, who had a sumptuous palace, of which there are some small remains. In the year 1309, Bishop Stapleton procured for it the grant of a weekly market and an annual fair. During the parliamentary war, the army under General Fairfax was quartered in this town: in 1807, nearly half of it was destroyed by fire, the loss of property having been estimated at £60,000 value. The town is pleasantly situated on an eminence near the eastern bank of the river Teign, and consists principally of one long street; the houses are in general modern and neatly built, and are well supplied with water: the environs are pleasant, and abound with woodland scenery. The trade, which consisted principally in the manufacture of woollen cloth, has lately declined: extensive quarries of good marble and excellent limestone, which abound in the vicinity, afford employment to many of the inhabitants; and the neighbourhood is famed for cider of superior quality. The market is on Saturday: the fairs, chiefly for cattle and sheep, are on Easter-Tuesday, the third Tuesday and Wednesday in June, and October 2nd, unless it falls on Saturday, Sunday, or Monday, in which case it is postponed till the Tuesday following. The living is a vicarage, in the peculiar jurisdiction of the Bishop of Exeter, rated in the king's books at £21, and in the patronage of the parishioners possessing freehold property to the amount of £5 per annum. The church, which is small and not entitled to architectural notice, is dedicated to St. Martin. There is a place of worship for Independents. The free grammar school was founded, in 1668, by Mr. John Pynsent, of Combe, in the county of Surrey, who built the schoolroom, with suitable accommodations for the master, and endowed it with a rent-charge of £30 per annum, founding also three exhibitions for its benefit at Cambridge, of £5 each, tenable for four years. There is also an endowment of £5 per annum for teaching poor children; and a National school, recently established, is supported by subscription. Half a mile from the town is Chudleigh Rock, a stupendous mass of limestone, in which is a cavern of considerable extent; and near it are very perfect remains of an elliptical encampment, supposed from its form to be of Danish origin, but, from its proximity to a Roman road, to have been previously occupied by that people. The quarries yield argillaceous slate; antimony and cobalt may be found in the neighbourhood, and many organic remains have been discovered. Chudleigh confers the title of baron on the family of Clifford.

CHULMLEIGH, a market town and parish in the hundred of WITHERIDGE, county of DEVON, 21½ miles (N.W.) from Exeter, and 194 (W. by S.) from London, containing 1506 inhabitants. This place, anciently called *Chimleighe*, is not connected with many events of historical importance: in the reign of Henry III., John de Courtenay, Earl of Devonshire, obtained for it the grant of a weekly market. During the parliamentary war, a skirmish took place here between the royalists and the parliamentarians, in 1645. The town, a considerable portion of which was destroyed by fire in 1803, is situated on an eminence rising gently from the eastern bank of the river Taw: the houses, with the exception of a few which are modern and well built, are low and covered with thatch; but there is an ample supply of water. Though formerly a place of considerable trade for wool-combing, it does not now possess any particular branch of manufacture. The market is on Friday: fairs are held on the third Friday in March, the Wednesday in Easter week, and the last Wednesday in July. A portreeve, whose office is merely nominal, and other officers, are appointed annually at the court leet and baron of the lord of the manor. The living is a rectory, in the archdeaconry of Barnstable, and diocese of Exeter, rated in the king's books at £20. 18. 1½., and in the patronage and incumbency of the Rev. George Hole: in the church are five prebends, endowed with glebe and a portion of the tithes of the parish, *viz.*, Brookland, rated at £4. 8. 4.; Denes, at £4. 6. 8.; Higher Heyne, at £5. 13. 4.; Lower Heyne, at £5; and Penels, at £5; they are distinct from the rectory, but are now held with it, the advowson both to the rectory and the prebends having been in the family of the present rector since 1773, when they were purchased from the Duke of Beaufort, then lord of the manor. The church, dedicated to St. Mary Magdalene, was damaged by lightning in 1797; it is an ancient and spacious structure in the decorated style of English architecture, with a square embattled tower; the interior is fine, and contains an ancient screen of oak richly carved. There are places of worship for Independents and Wesleyan Methodists. A small charity school was endowed by Mrs. Pyncombe with £10 per annum, for the instruction of twelve boys and twelve girls.

CHUNAT, a township in the parish of GLOSSOP, hundred of HIGH PEAK, county of DERBY, 7½ miles (N. by W.) from Chapel en le Frith, containing 145 inhabitants.

CHURCHAM, a parish partly in the lower division of the hundred of DUDSTONE and KING'S BARTON, but chiefly in the hundred of WESTBURY, county of GLOUCESTER, 4½ miles (W. by N.) from Gloucester, containing, with the hamlets of Highnam, Over, and Linton, 733 inhabitants. The living is a vicarage, in the archdeaconry of Hereford, and diocese of Gloucester, rated in the king's books at £20. 5., and in the patronage of the Dean and Chapter of Gloucester. The church, dedicated to St. Andrew, is a small edifice, with some remains of Norman architecture. There is a chapel of ease at Bulley, in this parish.

CHURCHDOWN, a parish in the upper division of the hundred of DUDSTONE and KING'S BARTON, county of GLOUCESTER, 3¾ miles (E. by N.) from Gloucester, containing, with the hamlet of Hucklecot, 954 inhabitants. The living is a perpetual curacy, in the archdeaconry and diocese of Gloucester, endowed with £400 private benefaction, £400 royal bounty, and £400 parliamentary grant, and in the patronage of the Dean and Chapter of Bristol. The church is dedicated to St. Bartholomew. The village is singularly situated on the top of an oval eminence, nearly four miles in circuit at the base, and rising from the vale to the height of about two thousand five hundred feet. The Gloucester and Cheltenham railway passes through the parish. There are two charity schools, for boys and girls, supported by an endowment of about £25 per annum, devised in 1734, by H. Window, Esq.; and four almshouses, for four poor widows, are endowed with about £4 per annum each. John Harmer, Professor of Greek in the University of Oxford, author of a Life of Cicero, a Greek Etymological Dictionary, and other learned works, was born here; he died in 1670. His father, who died in 1613, master of Winchester school, and one of the translators of the Bible, appears to have been minister of this parish.

CHURCH-END, a township in that part of the parish of SHENLEY which is in the hundred of NEWPORT, county of BUCKINGHAM, containing 225 inhabitants.

CHURCHENFORD, a hamlet in the parish of CHURCH-STANTON, hundred of HEMYOCK, county of DEVON, 9¼ miles (N. N. E.) from Honiton. The population is returned with the parish. The village is noted for its excellent cider: there are cattle fairs on the 25th of January and the 6th of March.

CHURCHFIELD, a hamlet (formerly a chapelry) in the parish of OUNDLE, hundred of POLEBROOKE, county of NORTHAMPTON, 2½ miles (W.) from Oundle, with which the population is returned. The chapel has been demolished.

CHURCHILL, a parish in the hundred of CHADLINGTON, county of OXFORD, 3 miles (S. W. by W.) from Chipping-Norton, containing 665 inhabitants. The living is a discharged vicarage, in the archdeaconry and diocese of Oxford, rated in the king's books at £7. 16. 0½., endowed with £200 private benefaction, and £200 royal bounty, and in the patronage of the Crown. The church is dedicated to All Saints. There is a school for educating and clothing girls.

CHURCHILL, a parish in the hundred of WINTERSTOKE, county of SOMERSET, 4¾ miles (N. by E.) from Axbridge, containing 824 inhabitants. The living is a perpetual curacy, within the jurisdiction of the peculiar court of Banwell at Wells, endowed with £200 private benefaction, £200 royal bounty, and £1400 parliamentary grant, and in the patronage of the Dean and Chapter of Bristol. The church, dedicated to St. John the Baptist, is a handsome structure, with an embattled tower, and contains a fine altar-piece representing the Lord's Supper, and several interesting monuments. This is a very ancient place, occurring in old deeds under the names of *Curichill, Cheuchill,* and *Cherchill:* immediately after the Conquest it was held by Roger de Leon, who came over with the Conqueror, and who appears to have assumed the name of Courcill, or Curcelle, from this property; he is said have been the remote ancestor of John Churchill, the great Duke of Marlborough. On a very high point of the Mendip range of hills, above the village, is an old encampment, called Dolberry Castle, forming a parallelogram of five hundred and forty yards by two hundred and twenty, and enclosed by a ditch, varying from sixteen to thirty feet in depth, on all sides but the south-east, where the steepness of the hill rendered it unnecessary; within it many Roman and Saxon coins and some fragments of weapons have been found. In 1820, James Symons, Esq. left three acres of land, directing the income to be applied to the education of eight poor children; there are several benefactions for the relief of the poor.

CHURCHILL, a parish in the lower division of the hundred of HALFSHIRE, county of WORCESTER, 3½ miles (N. E. by E.) from Kidderminster, containing 141 inhabitants. The living is a discharged rectory, in the archdeaconry and diocese of Worcester, rated in the king's books at £5. 6. 8., and in the patronage of Lord Lyttelton. The church is dedicated to St. James. Here is a chalybeate spring, which was formerly much frequented.

CHURCHILL, a parish in the lower division of the hundred of OSWALDSLOW, county of WORCESTER, 5½ miles (E. by S.) from Worcester, containing 102 inhabitants. The living is a discharged rectory, in the archdeaconry and diocese of Worcester, rated in the king's books at £13. 6. 8., and in the patronage of Lord Lyttelton. The church is dedicated to St. Michael.

CHURCHOVER, a parish in the Rugby division of the hundred of KNIGHTLOW, county of WARWICK, 4¼ miles (N. by E.) from Rugby, containing 322 inhabitants. The living is a rectory, in the archdeaconry of Coventry, and diocese of Lichfield and Coventry, rated in the king's books at £15, and in the patronage of Abraham Grimes, Esq. The church, dedicated to the Holy Trinity, is a small edifice with a spire and a side aisle. The river Swift runs through the parish.

CHURCH-STANTON, a parish in the hundred of HEMYOCK, county of DEVON, 11 miles (N. by E.) from Honiton, containing 862 inhabitants. The living is a rectory, in the archdeaconry and diocese of Exeter, rated in the king's books at £26. 5. 5., and in the patronage of the Rev. J. Clarke. The church is dedicated to St. Paul: one hundred and fourteen free sittings have recently been added, towards defraying the expense of which the Incorporated Society for the enlargement of churches and chapels granted £80. There is a small endowed school.

CHURCHSTOW, a parish in the hundred of STANBOROUGH, county of DEVON, 1¾ mile (N. W. by W.) from Kingsbridge, containing 316 inhabitants. The living is a discharged vicarage, annexed to that of Kingsbridge, in the archdeaconry of Totness, and diocese of Exeter, rated in the king's books at £16. 16. 11., endowed with £200 private benefaction, and £200 royal bounty. The church is dedicated to St. Mary. The great tithes, which formerly belonged to the abbot of Buckfastleigh, are now vested in the Dean and Chapter of Exeter. The river Avon bounds the parish on the north-west.

CHURCH-TOWN, a chapelry in that part of the parish of WHALLEY which is in the lower division of the hundred of BLACKBURN, county palatine of LANCASTER, 4¾ miles (E.) from Blackburn, containing 752 inhabitants. The living is a perpetual curacy, in the archdeaconry and diocese of Chester, endowed with £10 per annum and £200 private benefaction, £200 royal bounty, and £700 parliamentary grant, and in the patronage of Earl Howe. The chapel is dedicated to St. James. There is a place of worship for Wesleyan Methodists.

CHURSTON-FERRERS, a parish in the hundred of HAYTOR, county of DEVON, 1½ mile (N. W.) from Brixham, containing 726 inhabitants. The living is a perpetual curacy, annexed to the vicarage of Brixham, in the archdeaconry of Totness, and diocese of Exeter, and in the patronage of the Crown. The church contains an ancient wooden screen. This parish lies on the coast of the English channel, having the navigable river Dart running along its western side, and Torbay bounding it on the north. There is an almshouse for seven poor people.

CHURTON, a township in that part of the parish of ALDFORD which is in the higher division of the hundred of BROXTON, county palatine of CHESTER, 4½ miles (S. E. by S.) from Chester, containing 210 inhabitants.

CHURTON, a township in the parish of FARNDON, higher division of the hundred of BROXTON, county palatine of CHESTER, 7 miles (S. by E.) from Chester, containing 117 inhabitants. The river Dee bounds this township on the west.

CHURTON, or CHIRKTON, a parish in the hundred of SWANBOROUGH, county of WILTS, 4¼ miles (N. E. by E.) from East Lavington, containing, with the tything of Conock, 401 inhabitants. The living is a discharged vicarage, in the archdeaconry and diocese of Salisbury, rated in the king's books at £11. 0. 5., and in the patronage of the Crown.

CHURTON-HEATH, or BRUERA, a chapelry in that part of the parish of ALDFORD which is in the lower division of the hundred of BROXTON, county palatine of CHESTER, 5½ miles (S. E. by S.) from Chester, containing 8 inhabitants. The living is a perpetual curacy, annexed to the vicarage of St. Oswald, city of Chester, in the archdeaconry and diocese of Chester. The chapel, dedicated to St. Mary, is a very ancient structure, with a Norman arch between the nave and the chancel, and a rich Norman door at the south end; various carved stones are conspicuous in the walls.

CHURWELL, a township in that part of the parish of BATLEY which is in the wapentake of MORLEY, West riding of the county of YORK, 3 miles (S.W. by S.) from Leeds, containing 814 inhabitants, who are chiefly employed in the manufacture of woollen cloth. There is a place of worship for Wesleyan Methodists.

CHUTE, a parish in the hundred of KINWARDSTONE, county of WILTS, 3¾ miles (N.E.) from Ludgershall, containing 489 inhabitants. The living is a vicarage, in the peculiar jurisdiction and patronage of the Prebendary of Chute and Chisenbury in the Cathedral Church of Salisbury, rated in the king's books at £11. The church is dedicated to St. Nicholas. Jeremy Corderoy, a divine of some celebrity in the seventeenth century, was born here: there is a small endowment for the instruction of children.

CHUTE-FOREST, an extra-parochial district, in the hundred of KINWARDSTONE, county of WILTS, 4¾ miles (N.E. by N.) from Ludgershall, containing 144 inhabitants.

CIPPENHAM, a liberty in the parish and hundred of BURNHAM, county of BUCKINGHAM, 2¼ miles (N.W. by N.) from Eton. The population is returned with the parish. This is said to have been a place of residence for the Saxon kings; but it is more certain that here was a palace for the monarchs of the Norman line.

CIRCOURT, a joint chapelry with Goosey, in that part of the parish of STANFORD in the VALE which is in the hundred of OCK, county of BERKS. The population is returned with Goosey.

Arms.

CIRENCESTER, an unincorporated borough, market town, and parish, in the hundred of CROWTHORNE and MINETY, county of GLOUCESTER, 17 miles (S.E.) from Gloucester, and 88 (W. by N.) from London, containing 4987 inhabitants. Prior to the arrival of the Romans, this was a British city, called *Caer Cori*, the town on the river Corin, now Churn, which the Romans converted into a military station, denominated *Corinium:* this station, from its situation near the intersection of the Fosse-way with the Ermin and Iknield streets, was one of considerable extent and importance; vestiges of the vallum and rampart are yet visible on the south-eastern side of the town, where Roman inscriptions, tesselated pavements, coins, urns, vases, the remains of an hypocaust, and various fragments of masonry, have been found. The Saxons added the name *Ceaster*, of which, and its Roman name, the present is a corruption. It was the metropolis of the *Dobuni*, an ancient British tribe, from whom, in 577, it was taken by Ceawlin, King of Wessex; in 656 it was annexed to the kingdom of Mercia; and, in 879, the Danes under Guthrum, after their memorable defeat by Alfred, in the battle of *Ethandune*, retired hither, where they remained for a year, during the progress of the negociations which led to their conversion to Christianity, and their settlement in the island. Canute the Great held a general council here in 1020, when, according to the Saxon Chronicle, "Alderman Ethelward was outlawed, and Edwy, King of the Churls." In the war between Stephen and Matilda, Cirencester castle, of which the earliest notice then occurs, being garrisoned by Robert, Earl of Gloucester, on the part of Matilda, was taken and burnt by the king's troops, in 1142; having been rebuilt, it was afterwards garrisoned by the disaffected barons against Henry III., but was taken by the king, who issued his warrant for its immediate demolition. The wall and gates that defended the town continued entire for some time afterwards. In 1322, Edward II. spent the festival of Christmas here, and soon afterwards convened an assembly of his nobles, to devise means for crushing the conspiracy formed by Thomas, Earl of Lancaster, and other barons, against his favourite, Hugh le Despencer; and the whole of the royal army was subsequently assembled here. Early in the reign of Henry IV., the Dukes of Albemarle, Surrey, and Exeter, and the Earls of Gloucester and Salisbury, with other persons of distinction, entered into a conspiracy to assassinate the king, and restore the deposed monarch, Richard II. Henry being informed of this, led an army against them, when some of the principal conspirators, with the forces under them, retired to Cirencester, where they encamped: here they were attacked by surprise by the townsmen; and the Duke of Surrey and the Earl of Salisbury were taken and immediately beheaded, on which the troops dispersed. Henry subsequently granted the town a charter for the encouragement of trade, which, after a contested dispute in Chancery, was cancelled in the 37th of Elizabeth. The explosion of hostilities against Charles I. is stated to have occurred in this town, by a personal attack upon Lord Chandos, who had been appointed to execute the commission of array on behalf of the king; and it was soon afterwards garrisoned for the parliament. Having been assaulted by Prince Rupert, it was captured, after a sharp conflict of two hours, on the 2nd of February, 1642; but was recovered for the parliament by the Earl of Essex, on the 16th of September in the following year: it again fell into the hands of the royalists, but was ultimately surrendered to the parliament. On the landing of the Prince of Orange, in 1688, the inhabitants, influenced by the Duke of Beaufort, declared for James II.; and Lord Lovelace, on his march through the town, with a party to join the prince, was attacked by Captain Lorange, of the county militia, made prisoner, and sent to Gloucester gaol; in this encounter flowed the first blood that was shed in the revolution.

The town is pleasantly situated, and consists of four principal, and several smaller, streets. It was formerly of much greater extent, the walls having enclosed an area of two miles in circuit. The houses, which are chiefly of stone, are well built, and many of the more respectable are detached: the town is lighted, and the foot-paths paved with small stones; it is well supplied with water. There is a society, called the Cirencester and Gloucestershire Agricultural Association: races are held annually near the town. But little trade is carried on, the cloth manufacture, formerly extensive, having declined: some knives of a peculiar and superior quality are made for the use of curriers; and there are a small carpet-manufactory and two breweries. The Thames and Severn canal passes in the vicinity, and a branch of it comes up to the town. The market is on Monday for corn and provisions, and on Friday for provisions only; the latter was formerly considerable for wool, but, since the decline of the woollen manufacture, is much neglected. Fairs are held on Easter-Thursday, July 18th, and November 8th; and statute fairs on the Monday before, and the Monday after, October the 10th. The borough is within the jurisdiction of the county magistrates, who hold petty sessions here for the seven hundreds of Cirencester, which comprise nearly a fourth part of the county. A court of requests, for the recovery of debts under 40*s*., established by act of parliament in 1792, is also held for the same division. A court leet is held annually, at which the steward for the manor appoints two high, and fourteen petty, constables, two of the latter being for each of the seven wards into which the borough is divided. By charter of incorporation granted by Henry IV., Cirencester was constituted a separate hundred, which was co-extensive with the borough, but this charter having been set aside in the reign of Elizabeth, it has merged into the adjoining hundred. The borough sent representatives to a great council in the 11th of Edward III., but did not acquire the permanent privilege of returning two burgesses until the year 1571, by grant from Elizabeth: the right of election is vested in the resident householders not receiving alms, except "inhabitants of the abbey, and Emery and Spiringate-lane," about five hundred in number, and in the interest of Earl Bathurst: the steward and bailiff of the manor are the returning officers.

The living is a perpetual curacy, in the archdeaconry and diocese of Gloucester, and in the patronage of the Bishop of Gloucester. The church, dedicated to St. John the Evangelist, is a magnificent structure in the decorated style of English architecture, erected in the fifteenth century, with a lofty embattled tower crowned with pinnacles; its interior and exterior are richly adorned in the most elaborate style, and it contains several chapels of exquisite beauty, and many sepulchral monuments. A fund, producing £267. 9. 4. per annum, was bequeathed for keeping it in repair. Two other churches, one dedicated to St. Cecilia, and the other to St. Lawrence, have long since been desecrated. There are places of worship for Baptists, the Society of Friends, Wesleyan Methodists, and Unitarians. The free grammar school was founded by Bishop Ruthal; the original endowment was augmented by Queen Mary, with £20 per annum, payable out of the Exchequer; the master is appointed by the Lord Chancellor. The Blue-coat school, established by subscription in 1714, was afterwards endowed by Thomas Powell, Esq. with £15 per annum, part of an annuity issuing from the Exchequer for ninety-nine years, and a moiety of the revenue of Maskelyne's estate, to which the Lord Chancellor, in 1737, added £20 per annum, out of property left for charitable uses by Mrs. Rebecca Powell, and, in 1744, with the interest of £562. 7. 6., as a provisional supply after the expiration of the annuity: the income is about £60 per annum. The Yellow-coat school was founded, in 1737, by Mrs. Rebecca Powell, who endowed it for the instruction of twenty boys of Cirencester, in reading, writing, arithmetic, and frame-work knitting, and for clothing and teaching twenty girls: it is under the superintendence of trustees, and the annual income is about £320: the entire amount appropriated for schools in this parish is about £870 per annum. St. John's hospital, for three men and three women, was founded by Henry I., and endowed with land and reserved rents amounting to between £30 and £40 per annum. St. Lawrence's hospital, for a master and two poor women, was founded in the time of Edward III., by Edith, proprietress of the manor of Wiggold; it has a small endowment, and is under the control of Earl Bathurst. St. Thomas' hospital was erected by Sir William Nottingham, attorney-general to Henry IV., and endowed with £6. 18. 8. per annum, which is divided between four persons. In 1620, Mrs. Elizabeth Bridges founded an almshouse, with a small endowment, which has been subsequently augmented; and there are various minor bequests for the benefit of the poor, and for apprenticing children.

Henry I., in 1117, built an abbey for Black canons, in honour of the Blessed Virgin Mary, which he and his successors richly endowed, insomuch that, in the 26th of Henry VIII., its revenue was estimated at £1051. 7. 1.: it was a mitred abbey: the remains consist of two gateways and a large barn. In a field called the Querns, to the west of the town, near the Roman wall, are the remains of an amphitheatre. Grismond's Tower, a circular hill about a quarter of a mile westward, was discovered, on examination, to be a Roman tumulus, containing several large urns full of ashes and burnt bones. Richard of Cirencester, author of a History and Itinerary of Britain in the time of the Romans; Thomas Ruthall, Bishop of Durham, and counsellor to Henry VII.; and Caleb Hillier Parry, M. D., eminent in his profession, and father of the celebrated navigator, were natives of this place.

CLACK, a hamlet in the parish of Lineham, hundred of Kingsbridge, county of Wilts, 5¼ miles (S.W.) from Wootton-Bassett. The population is returned with the parish. Fairs are held on April 5th and October 10th, for horned cattle, pigs, sheep, horses, and cheese.

CLACKHEATON, a chapelry in the parish of Birstall, wapentake of Morley, West riding of the county of York, 5½ miles (S.S.E.) from Bradford, containing, with the hamlets of Scholes and Oakenshaw, 2436 inhabitants. The living is a perpetual curacy, in the archdeaconry and diocese of York, endowed with £540 private benefaction, £600 royal bounty, and £400 parliamentary grant. Miss Currer was patroness in 1805. The chapel is called White chapel: another is now being erected, under the late act for building additional churches, the patronage of which will be in the Vicar of Birstall. The village is situated in a fine fertile valley, stretching from north to south, the acclivities on both sides being well wooded: it has recently undergone great improvement, and several elegant villas have been erected in the vicinity. There are meeting-houses for Independents and Moravians. Worsted, coarse woollen goods, and machinery for carding and spinning, are manufactured here. Coal abounds in the neighbourhood, and is wrought to some extent. Here stood a small Roman town, the name of which is unknown, and every vestige of it has been obliterated by the plough.

CLACTON (GREAT), a parish in the hundred of Tendring, county of Essex, 14½ miles (S.E. by E.) from Colchester, containing 1075 inhabitants. The living is a discharged vicarage, with Little Holland, in the archdeaconry of Colchester, and diocese of London, rated in the king's books at £10, and in the patronage of F. Nassau, Esq. The church is dedicated to St. John the Baptist. There is a place of worship for Wesleyan Methodists. The bishops of London had formerly a palace here. This parish is bounded on the south by the North sea, and contains three Martello towers and a battery for the defence of the coast. A fair for toys is held on the 29th of June.

CLACTON (LITTLE), a parish in the hundred of Tendring, county of Essex, 12½ miles (E. S. E.) from Colchester, containing 494 inhabitants. The living is a discharged vicarage, in the archdeaconry of Colchester, and diocese of London, rated in the king's books at £6. 13. 4., and in the patronage of F. Nassau, Esq. A fair for toys is held on the 25th of July.

CLAIFE, a township in the parish of Hawkeshead, hundred of Lonsdale, north of the sands, county palatine of Lancaster, 2 miles (S. E.) from Hawkeshead, containing 452 inhabitants. This place is bounded on the east by Easthwaite water, and on the west by the beautiful lake of Windermere, which at this point is only a quarter of a mile in breadth, and across which there is a constant ferry for horses and foot passengers. Here is a charity school, founded in 1766, by a bequest of £309 from William Braithwaite, now producing £16. 16. per annum.

CLAINES, a parish in the lower division of the hundred of Oswaldslow, county of Worcester, 2½ miles (N.) from Worcester, containing, with the tything of Whistons, 3853 inhabitants. The living is a perpetual curacy, in the peculiar jurisdiction of the Bishop of Worcester, endowed with £200 private benefaction, and £900 parliamentary grant, and in the patronage of Sir H. Wakeman, Bart. The church is dedicated to St. John the Baptist. A chapel is now being erected, by a grant of £3345. 10. 8. from the commissioners under the act passed in the 58th of George III., for building additional churches and chapels, to contain seven hundred and twelve sittings, of which three hundred and fifty-eight will be free. Here is a school with an endowment of £7. 7. per annum. The Birmingham canal passes on the south of this parish; and the Droitwich canal, on the north, passes along the western boundary, where it forms a junction with the Severn. The ancient hospital of St. Oswald was founded here prior to 1268. On the site of the mansion of White Ladies was the Benedictine nunnery of Whitestone, or Whistons, founded by Walter de Cantelupe, Bishop of Worcester, in 1255: to this house Charles II. retired after the decisive battle of Worcester. In this parish is the island of Bevere, formed by the rivulet Beverhern, remarkable as having twice afforded refuge to the inhabitants of Worcester; first, in 1041, from the fury of King Hardicanute, on account of their refusing to pay the Danegelt, and next, in 1637, from a dreadful pestilence then raging in the city.

CLANABOROUGH, a parish in the hundred of North Tawton with Winkley, county of Devon, 2 miles (E. by N.) from Bow, containing 56 inhabitants. The living is a rectory, in the archdeaconry of Barnstaple, and diocese of Exeter, rated in the king's books at £5. 17. 3½., and in the patronage of the Crown. The church is dedicated to St. Petrock.

CLANDON (EAST), a parish in the second division of the hundred of Woking, county of Surrey, 4 miles (E. N. E.) from Guildford, containing 230 inhabitants. The living is a rectory, in the archdeaconry of Surrey, and diocese of Winchester, rated in the king's books at £10. 6. 10½., and in the patronage of Lord King.

CLANDON (WEST), a parish in the second division of the hundred of Woking, county of Surrey, 3 miles (N. E. by E.) from Guildford, containing 361 inhabitants. The living is a rectory, in the archdeaconry of Surrey, and diocese of Winchester, rated in the king's books at £13. 10., and in the patronage of the Earl of Onslow.

CLANFIELD, a parish in the hundred of Bampton, county of Oxford, 5 miles (E. N. E.) from Lechlade, containing 490 inhabitants. The living is a discharged vicarage, in the archdeaconry and diocese of Oxford, rated in the king's books at £7. 6. 5½., endowed with £200 private benefaction, £200 royal bounty, and £300 parliamentary grant, and in the patronage of the Crown. The church is dedicated to St. Stephen.

CLANFIELD, a parish in the hundred of Finchdean, Alton (South) division of the county of Southampton, 5¾ miles (S. W.) from Petersfield, containing 196 inhabitants. The living is a rectory, annexed to that of Chalton, in the archdeaconry and diocese of Winchester, rated in the king's books at £11. The church is dedicated to St. James.

CLAPCOT, a liberty in that part of the parish of Allhallows, Wallingford, which is in the hundred of Moreton, county of Berks, containing 38 inhabitants.

CLAPHAM, a parish forming, with the parishes of Milton-Ernest and Oakley, a detached portion of the hundred of Stodden, county of Bedford, 2½ miles (N. W. by N.) from Bedford, containing 204 inhabitants. The living is a discharged vicarage, in the archdeaconry of Bedford, and diocese of Lincoln, rated in the king's books at £5. 13. 4., endowed with £600 private benefaction, and £600 royal bounty, and in the patronage of the Earl of Ashburnham. The church, dedicated to St. Thomas à Becket, is a very ancient structure, with a Norman, or Saxon, tower remarkable for the simplicity and rudeness of its architecture. Clapham was formerly a chapelry in the parish of Oakley; the inhabitants still bury there. Here are charitable donations, producing £20 per annum, for the purpose of apprenticing boys.

CLAPHAM, a parish in the eastern division of the hundred of Brixton, county of Surrey, 4 miles (S.) from London, containing 7151 inhabitants. This village has, for many years, been considered as one of the most respectable in the environs of the metropolis. The road from London, particularly that part of it which is called Clapham Rise, has on each side large and handsome houses, with gardens and lawns in front, forming a continuous line leading to the common, which occupies a space of two hundred acres, surrounded by noble mansions and elegant villas; and, from the improvements that have been made by the formation of carriage drives, and the plantation of exotic and native trees and shrubs, assumes the appearance of a park. On the east side a handsome crescent has been recently formed, opposite to which is a range of houses, called the Grove: the area is tastefully laid out in shrubberies, and planted with evergreens, and the approach from the common is formed by a handsome iron palisade, on each side of which is a stately mansion. In that part of the parish situated towards Brixton, which was formerly called Bleakhall Farm, considerable alterations and improvements are taking place: new roads have been made; a new church and several villas have been erected, and the spot is now designated Clapham New Park. The parish, previously watched and lighted under an act of parliament obtained in 1785, is now within the limits of the new police establishment; the road from London is lighted with gas, main pipes having been laid down by the Phœnix gas company, from which a plentiful supply is distributed to every part of the village and its vicinity. The inhabitants are supplied with water from the South Lambeth water-works, and from an excellent spring on the side of the common leading to Wandsworth, opened in 1825, near another which had supplied the village for more than a century: this spring, the water of which is peculiarly soft, supplies upwards of six hundred hogsheads per day, and nearly twenty families derive employment and support by conveying it to the houses of the inhabitants at a moderate expense. The subscription library, to which a commodious reading-room has been added, contains a well-assorted and extensive collection of volumes, in various branches of literature; it has been established for nearly half a century, and is liberally supported. There is no trade except what is necessary for the accommodation of the numerous opulent families residing in the neighbourhood. Clapham is within the jurisdiction of the county magistrates, who hold a petty session at the office of their clerk, every Saturday; and within that of the court of requests for the borough of Southwark, for the recovery of debts under £5, which, by an act passed in the 32nd of George III., was extended to this parish, in common with other places in the eastern division of the hundred of Brixton, not previously included. The acting coroner for the district is appointed at the court of the duchy of Lancaster, within the jurisdiction of which a part of the parish is comprehended: the parochial affairs are under the direction of a select vestry.

The living is a rectory, in the archdeaconry of Surrey, and diocese of Winchester, rated in the king's books at £8. 0. 10., and in the patronage of William Atkins, Esq. The church, dedicated to the Holy Trinity, and which anciently belonged to the priory at Merton, was, with the exception of the north aisle, which was left standing for the performance of the burial service, taken down under an act of parliament in 1774, and a new church erected in the following year, at an expense of £11,000, on the north side of the common: it is a neat structure of brick ornamented with stone, with a dome turret, and having a handsome portico of stone, extending the whole width of the western front, which was added to it in 1812. The interior is characterized by a chaste simplicity of style: the east window is ornamented with a modern and well executed painting on glass, and there are some monumental tablets; but no person is buried either in the church or churchyard, the cemetery of the old church being exclusively reserved for interments. The remaining aisle of the old church, which was situated in that part of the village leading to Wandsworth, and near the old manor-house, of which an octagonal tower is still remaining, was taken down in 1815, and a neat proprietary chapel, in some respects dependent on the mother church, was erected, under an act of parliament, at an expense of £5000, and dedicated to St. Paul. The burial-ground, which is spacious, contains many ancient tombs and monuments; and such of the latter as were in the old church have been put up against the exterior walls of the chapel. A proprietary episcopal chapel, dedicated to St. James, has recently been erected at Clapham New Park, under an act of parliament; it is a small handsome structure, in the later style of English architecture, with a square embattled tower crowned with pinnacles. There are two places of worship for Independents, and one for Baptists. The parochial school is supported by subscription: the premises were originally built at the expense of the inhabitants, on ground given for that purpose by Richard Atkins, Esq., lord of the manor; the school-house was taken down and rebuilt in 1781, and in 1809 it was considerably enlarged: upwards of two hundred children now receive instruction.

CLAPHAM, a parish in the hundred of BRIGHTFORD, rape of BRAMBER, county of SUSSEX, 5 miles (E. by S.) from Arundel, containing 245 inhabitants. The living is a discharged rectory, in the archdeaconry and diocese of Chichester, rated in the king's books at £14, and in the patronage of R. W. Walker, Esq.

CLAPHAM, a parish in the western division of the wapentake of STAINCLIFFE and EWCROSS, West riding of the county of YORK, comprising the townships of Austwick, Clapham with Newby, and Lawkland, and containing 1889 inhabitants, of which number, 982 are in the township of Clapham with Newby, 6 miles (N.W. by W.) from Settle. The living is a discharged vicarage, in the archdeaconry of Richmond, and diocese of Chester, rated in the king's books at £5. 17. 1., endowed with £200 private benefaction, and £200 royal bounty, and in the patronage of the Bishop of Chester. In 1711, George Ellis bequeathed property now let for £89 per annum, out of which he directed £6. 13. 4. to be paid to a schoolmaster, for teaching twenty children of Clapham and Newby; the residue, after deducting trifling sums for books, and annual expenses to the trustees, is paid to the minister for preaching two sermons every Sunday: there is a school-room at Newby, and another, built by subscription in 1824, at Clapham, for the purposes of this charity, which has been augmented to upwards of £15 per annum by the subsequent bequests of Henry and Grace Winterburn. A fair for sheep is held on the 21st of September.

CLAPTON, a parish in the hundred of ARMINGFORD, county of CAMBRIDGE, 6 miles (S. E. by S.) from Caxton. The population is returned with the parish of Croydon. The living is a discharged rectory, consolidated with the vicarage of Croydon, in the archdeaconry and diocese of Ely, rated in the king's books at £4. 9. 7.

CLAPTON, a chapelry in the parish of BOURTON on the WATER, lower division of the hundred of SLAUGHTER, county of GLOUCESTER, 4¾ miles (N. E.)

from North Leach, containing 118 inhabitants. The chapel is dedicated to St. James.

CLAPTON, a hamlet in the parish of St. John, Hackney, Tower division of the hundred of Ossulstone, county of Middlesex, 3 miles (N. by E.) from London. The population is returned with the parish. It is divided into Upper and Lower Clapton, and extends from Hackney church to Stamford Hill: the houses, in general well built and respectable, are supplied with water by means of pipes leading from a reservoir at Lower Clapton, belonging to the East London Water Works Company, into which it is conveyed from the river Lea by a steam-engine. A proprietary chapel was built at Upper Clapton in 1777, which has lately been enlarged. There are places of worship for Independents and Wesleyan Methodists. The London Orphan Asylum, founded in 1813, for the maintenance and education of destitute orphans, is a handsome building of light-coloured brick, consisting of a centre and two projecting wings, with a lawn in front and gardens behind, situated on a gentle elevation at Lower Clapton, at the distance of one hundred yards from the road: the number of children in this institution at the general annual meeting held on the 25th of January, 1830, including boys and girls, was three hundred and thirty-four.

CLAPTON, a parish in the hundred of Navisford, county of Northampton, 5¼ miles (E. N. E.) from Thrapston, containing 94 inhabitants. The living is a rectory, in the archdeaconry of Northampton, and diocese of Peterborough, rated in the king's books at £17. 3. 9., and in the patronage of W. P. Williams, Esq. The church is dedicated to St. Peter.

CLAPTON, a tything in the parish of Midsummer-Norton, hundred of Chewton, county of Somerset, 6¾ miles (N. by E.) from Shepton-Mallet, containing 106 inhabitants.

CLAPTON, a parish in the hundred of Portbury, county of Somerset, 9¼ miles (W.) from Bristol, containing 157 inhabitants. The living is a discharged rectory, in the archdeaconry of Bath, and diocese of Bath and Wells, rated in the king's books at £10. 9. 2., and in the patronage of Mrs. Colston and others. The church is dedicated to St. Michael.

CLARE, a market town and parish in the hundred of Risbridge, county of Suffolk, 18 miles (S. S. W.) from Bury St. Edmund's, and 55½ (N. E. by N.) from London, containing 1487 inhabitants. This place, which is of great antiquity, derived considerable importance during the Saxon Octarchy from being on the frontier of the kingdom of East Anglia; and after the Conquest it was distinguished for having given the title of earl to the family of De Clare, and that of duke to Lionel, third son of Edward III., who was created Duke of Clarence. To the south of the town are the ruins of a castle, formerly the baronial residence of the earls of Clare, and equal to any of those structures in feudal grandeur and magnificence: the site of the fortifications, which may be distinctly traced, comprehended an area of thirty acres, divided into an outer and an inner ward, of which the latter only was enclosed by walls; the whole was surrounded with a deep fosse: on the summit of a high mount, evidently of artificial construction, are the remains of the ancient keep, a circular building of flints, strongly cemented with mortar, and strengthened with buttresses, which, from its situation near the frontier, is supposed to have been erected either prior to or during the Octarchy. The town is situated on the river Stour, which separates this county from Essex, on the south: the houses are in general of mean appearance, and the streets, though spacious, are neither paved nor lighted; the inhabitants are amply supplied with water, and the approaches to the town are gradually improving. The market is on Monday: the fairs are on Easter-Tuesday and July 26th, chiefly for toys and pedlary. The county magistrates hold petty sessions for the division here: the courts baron of Erbury, and Stoke with Chilton, and a court for the duchy of Lancaster, are also held.

The living is a discharged vicarage, in the archdeaconry of Sudbury, and diocese of Norwich, rated in the king's books at £4. 18. 9., and in the patronage of the King, as Duke of Lancaster. The church, dedicated to St. Peter and St. Paul, is a large, handsome, and ancient structure, chiefly in the decorated style of English architecture, with a square tower, strengthened with buttresses, and of an earlier date than the body: the interior, which has been improved by the heightening of the nave, and the addition of side aisles, is richly ornamented, and contains an octagonal and elegantly designed font in the later English style, and a brass eagle, on a pedestal, with wings displayed, forming the reading-desk: in the chancel are said to have been interred the remains of Lionel, Duke of Clarence, who died in 1368, at Piedmont, and is supposed to have been born here, but there is no monument to his memory. There are places of worship for Baptists and Independents. Mr. William Cadge, in 1669, bequeathed a farm, now let for £60 per annum, appropriating £10 per annum to a master, for teaching ten poor boys, and £15 per annum to the clothing of eight or ten poor widows. A Sunday school, for children of both sexes, is supported by subscription; and there are several charitable bequests for distribution among the poor, who have also the privilege of depasturing forty milch cows on a piece of land granted by Queen Mary for that purpose. To the south-west of the town are the remains of Clare priory, founded by Eluric, or Alfric, Earl of Clare, for Secular canons, which Gilbert de Clare, in 1090, gave to the Benedictine abbey of Bec in Normandy, to which it was a cell till 1124, when his son Richard removed the monks to the village of Stoke. Joan d'Acre, daughter of Edward I., and wife of Gilbert de Clare, who was a great benefactress to this establishment, is traditionally said to have been interred in the chapel, which has been converted into a barn: the priory, now a private residence, though it has undergone considerable repairs and alterations, still retains much of its original character. A monastery for Augustine monks is said to have been founded here in 1248, but by whom is not known. To the north-west of the town are evident marks of a Roman camp.

CLAREBOROUGH, a parish in the North-clay division of the wapentake of Bassetlaw, county of Nottingham, 2½ miles (N. E. by E.) from East Retford, containing 1929 inhabitants. The living is a discharged vicarage, in the archdeaconry of Nottingham, and diocese of York, rated in the king's books at £9. 15. 4., and in the patronage of the Duke of Devonshire. The church, dedicated to St. John the Baptist, is a small edifice, built by Sewell, Archbishop of York, in 1258. The

Chesterfield canal passes through the parish. At Bolam are the remains of an ancient chapel, and some caves hewn in the rock, in which many of the inhabitants reside.

CLARENDON-PARK, an extra-parochial liberty, in the hundred of ALDERBURY, county of WILTS, 3½ miles (E. by S.) from Salisbury, containing 183 inhabitants. Here were anciently two palaces, termed the King's and the Queen's. At a very remote period this was a royal chase and residence: here Edward the Martyr spent the day preceding his assassination in hunting; Henry II. frequently kept his court here, and in 1164 held the council which enacted the celebrated edicts, called "The Constitutions of Clarendon," defining the limits of ecclesiastical authority in England: Richard, John, and Henry III., often resided at this place; and in 1357, when the plague was raging in London, and in many of the principal towns in the kingdom, Edward III., with his royal prisoners, the kings of France and Scotland, passed the summer at his palace of Clarendon, of which no part is now standing, save a lofty wall. The park was enclosed by act of parliament in the sixteenth of Charles II., and granted to General Monk, who had been created Duke of Albemarle; and in the same reign Clarendon gave the title of earl to Edward Hyde, a native of Dinton, in this county, Lord High Chancellor of England, ancestor of the queens Mary II. and Anne, and author of the History of the Rebellion. The Roman way from Winchester to Old Sarum passes through this liberty.

CLARETON, a township in the parish of ALLERTON-MAULEVERER, upper division of the wapentake of CLARO, West riding of the county of YORK, 5¼ miles (E.N.E.) from Knaresborough, containing 14 inhabitants. Claro hill, which gives name to the wapentake, is in this township; it is supposed to have been the place on which the Wittenagemote, or public meetings of the district, were anciently held.

CLAREWOOD, a township in the parish of CORBRIDGE, eastern division of TINDALE ward, county of NORTHUMBERLAND, 8½ miles (N. E. by E.) from Hexham, containing 62 inhabitants.

CLATFORD, a chapelry in the parish of PRESHUTE, hundred of SELKLEY, county of WILTS, 1½ mile (W.S.W.) from Marlborough. The population is returned with the parish. The living is a perpetual curacy, in the archdeaconry of Wilts, and diocese of Salisbury, and in the patronage of the Provost and Fellows of Eton College. An Alien priory to the abbey of St. Victor in Caleto, in Normandy, was founded here by Sir Roger Mortimer, in the time of William the Conqueror, and granted by Henry VI. to Eton College. In the valley termed Clatford Bottom is a large cromlech.

CLATFORD (GOODWORTH), a parish in the hundred of WHERWELL, Andover division of the county of SOUTHAMPTON, 2 miles (S.) from Andover, containing 382 inhabitants. The living is a discharged vicarage, in the archdeaconry and diocese of Winchester, rated in the king's books at £10, and in the patronage of Colonel Iremonger. The church is dedicated to St. Peter.

CLATFORD (UPPER), a parish in the hundred of ANDOVER, Andover division of the county of SOUTHAMPTON, 1 mile (S.) from Andover, containing 370 inhabitants. The living is a rectory, in the archdeaconry and diocese of Winchester, rated in the king's books at £22, and in the patronage of R. Willis, Esq. The church is dedicated to All Saints. A school is supported by charitable donations producing £9 per annum. The Andover canal crosses this parish.

CLATTERCOTT, an extra-parochial liberty, in the hundred of BANBURY, county of OXFORD, 6 miles (N.) from Banbury, containing 8 inhabitants. Here was, in the reign of John, a small religious house of the Sempringham order, dedicated to St. Leonard, and once an hospital for lepers, which, at the dissolution, consisted of a prior and four canons, whose revenue was estimated at £34. 19. 11. per annum.

CLATWORTHY, a parish in the hundred of WILLITON and FREEMANNERS, county of SOMERSET, 4 miles (N. W.) from Wiveliscombe, containing 280 inhabitants. The living is a rectory, in the archdeaconry of Taunton, and diocese of Bath and Wells, rated in the king's books at £13. 10. 5., and in the patronage of J. Bernard, Esq. The church is dedicated to St. Mary.

CLAUGHTON, a joint township with Grange, in the parish of BIDSTONE, lower division of the hundred of WIRRALL, county palatine of CHESTER, 9½ miles (N. by E.) from Great Neston, containing, with Grange, 119 inhabitants.

CLAUGHTON, a township in the parish of GARSTANG, hundred of AMOUNDERNESS, county palatine of LANCASTER, 2 miles (S. S. E.) from Garstang, containing 943 inhabitants. The linen manufacture has been established here of late years.

CLAUGHTON, a parish in the hundred of LONSDALE, south of the sands, county palatine of LANCASTER, 7½ miles (N. E. by E.) from Lancaster, containing 123 inhabitants. The living is a discharged rectory, in the archdeaconry of Richmond, and diocese of Chester, rated in the king's books at £9. 13. 10., and in the patronage of Thomas Fenwick, Esq. The church is dedicated to St. Chad. The river Lune passes through this parish. Here are several quarries of flag-stone. Near Claughton Hall, an ancient building in a dilapidated state, are the remains of a Roman Catholic chapel.

CLAVERDON, a parish in the Henley division of the hundred of BARLICHWAY, county of WARWICK, 3½ miles (E. by S.) from Henley in Arden, containing, with the hamlets of Langley and Pindley, 683 inhabitants. The living is a discharged vicarage, with the perpetual curacy of Norton-Lindsey annexed, in the archdeaconry and diocese of Worcester, rated in the king's books at £5. 12. 1., endowed with £200 private benefaction, and £200 royal bounty, and in the patronage of the Archdeacon of Worcester. The church is dedicated to St. Michael. John Matthews, about the year 1526, gave £12. 12. per annum for the instruction of children.

CLAVERING, a parish in the hundred of CLAVERING, county of ESSEX, 7½ miles (N. W. by N.) from Stansted-Mountfitchet, containing 1081 inhabitants. The living is a vicarage, with the perpetual curacy of Langley annexed, in the archdeaconry of Colchester, and diocese of London, rated in the king's books at £22. 13. 11½., and in the patronage of the Archbishop of Canterbury. The church is dedicated to St. Mary and St. Clement. The river Stort has its source in this parish, which is crossed also by the river Darenth. Here are remains of the keep and moat of the ancient castle of the Claverings, a family which became extinct in the reign of Edward III.

CLAVERLEY, a parish in the Hales-Owen division of the hundred of Brimstree, county of Salop, 5½ miles (E.) from Bridgenorth, containing 1305 inhabitants. The living is a perpetual curacy, within the jurisdiction of the court of the royal peculiar of Bridgenorth, endowed with £200 private benefaction, £200 royal bounty, and £1200 parliamentary grant, and in the patronage of Thomas Whitmore, Esq. The church is dedicated to All Saints. A free school was founded, in 1659, by Richard Dovey, who endowed it with an estate for the education of fourteen boys; and, in 1702, John Sanders devised £5 a year for clothing them. Richard Bennett, in 1794, left £100 in aid of this charity, the total annual income being £36. 5. There are three small tenements appropriated for poor families.

CLAVERTON, a parish in the hundred of Hampton and Claverton, though locally in the hundred of Bath-Forum, county of Somerset, 2½ miles (E. S. E.) from Bath, containing 137 inhabitants. The living is a discharged rectory, in the archdeaconry of Bath, and diocese of Bath and Wells, rated in the king's books at £10. 6. 10½., and in the patronage of John Vivian, Esq. This is a pretty retired village, separated from Bath by a hill round which the Avon winds its course; it is situated in a romantic valley, environed by bold and beautifully wooded hills, through which passes the Kennet and Avon canal. Here is a small endowment, bequeathed by Ann Tucker, with which, and some trifling subscriptions, sixteen poor children are educated. In the reign of Henry III. a grant was obtained, whereby Claverton and the village of Hampton were exempted from the jurisdiction of the hundred, and constituted a liberty, which is now within the jurisdiction of the court of requests held in the city of Bath, for the recovery of debts under £10. Graves, the author of the Spiritual Quixote, was rector of this parish.

CLAWRPLWYF, a hamlet in the parish of Mynyddyslwyn, lower division of the hundred of Wentlloog, county of Monmouth, containing 1250 inhabitants.

CLAWTON, a parish in the hundred of Black Torrington, county of Devon, 3½ miles (S.) from Holsworthy, containing 534 inhabitants. The living is a discharged perpetual curacy, in the archdeaconry of Totness, and diocese of Exeter, endowed with £1600 parliamentary grant, and in the patronage of the Rev. T. Melhuish, jun. There is good stone for building in this neighbourhood.

CLAXBY, a parish in the Wold division of the hundred of Calceworth, parts of Lindsey, county of Lincoln, 3 miles (S.) from Alford, containing 97 inhabitants. The living is a discharged vicarage, united to the rectory of Well, in the archdeaconry and diocese of Lincoln, rated in the king's books at £5. 3. 1½. The church, dedicated to St. Andrew, is a small thatched building without a cemetery. A fine spring has its source from a chalk hill in the centre of the parish, and flows eastward. Here are vestiges of a Roman camp, and several tumuli covered with trees.

CLAXBY, a parish in the northern division of the wapentake of Walshcroft, parts of Lindsey, county of Lincoln, 4 miles (N.) from Market-Rasen, containing 184 inhabitants. The living is a discharged rectory, to which the rectory of Normanby on the Wolds was united in 1740, in the archdeaconry and diocese of Lincoln, rated in the king's books at £8. 10. 10., and in the patronage of R. Atkinson, Esq. The church is dedicated to St. Mary.

CLAXBY-PLUCKACRE, a parish in the hundred of Hill, parts of Lindsey, county of Lincoln, 5¼ miles (S. E. by E.) from Horncastle, containing 36 inhabitants. The living is a discharged rectory, in the archdeaconry and diocese of Lincoln, rated in the king's books at £6. 10. 10., and in the patronage of Henry Dymoke, Esq. The church is dedicated to St. Andrew.

CLAXTON, a township in the parish of Greatham, north-eastern division of Stockton ward, county palatine of Durham, 7 miles (N. N. E.) from Stockton upon Tees, containing 38 inhabitants. This place gives name to an ancient family, from which Thomas Claxton, a celebrated antiquary, was descended.

CLAXTON, a parish in the hundred of Loddon, county of Norfolk, 7½ miles (S. E. by E.) from Norwich, containing 160 inhabitants. The living is a vicarage, in the archdeaconry of Norfolk, and diocese of Norwich, endowed with £200 parliamentary grant, and in the patronage of Sir Charles Rich, Bart. The church is dedicated to St. Andrew. There is a place of worship for Baptists.

CLAXTON, a township in that part of the parish of Bossall which is in the wapentake of Bulmer, North riding of the county of York, 8½ miles (N.) from York, containing 135 inhabitants. The petty sessions for the division are held here.

CLAXTON, or LONG CLAWSON, a parish in the hundred of Framland, county of Leicester, 6 miles (N. N. W.) from Melton-Mowbray, containing 678 inhabitants. The living is a discharged vicarage, in the archdeaconry of Leicester, and diocese of Lincoln, rated in the king's books at £9. 10. 2., and in the patronage of Lord F. Osborne. The church is dedicated to St. Remigius. There is a place of worship for Wesleyan Methodists. Here are two free schools, toward the endowment of which Anthony Wadd gave certain lands, in 1758, now producing a considerable income: for the same purpose, in 1772, Mrs. Briggs bequeathed £100, and the Duke of Rutland gave £21 towards the erection of a schoolroom.

CLAYBROOKE, a parish comprising the chapelry of Little Wigston, the townships of Great Claybrooke and Little Claybrooke, the liberty of Bittesby, and the hamlet of Ullesthorpe, in the hundred of Guthlaxton, county of Leicester; and the hamlet of Wibtoft, in the Kirby division of the hundred of Knightlow, county of Warwick, and containing 1312 inhabitants, of which number, 458 are in the township of Great Claybrooke, 4¾ miles (N. W. by W.) from Lutterworth. The living is a vicarage, in the archdeaconry of Leicester, and diocese of Lincoln, rated in the king's books at £30. 10. 5., and in the patronage of the Crown. The church, dedicated to St. Peter, is partly in the decorated, and partly in the later, style of English architecture. There is a small endowment for a boys' school, which, with another for girls, is principally supported by the Dicey family. At a place termed High Cross, two miles westward, is the intersection of two great Roman roads, which traverse the kingdom obliquely. This was the Roman station *Benonæ*, or *Vennones*.

CLAYBROOKE (LITTLE), a township in that part of the parish of Claybrooke which is in the hundred of Guthlaxton, county of Leicester, 4 miles (N.W. by N.) from Lutterworth, containing 54 inhabitants.

CLAYDON, a chapelry in that part of the parish of Cropredy which is in the hundred of Banbury, county of Oxford, 6½ miles (N.) from Banbury, containing 252 inhabitants. The village is the most northern in the county; a small spring which rises in it has the peculiarity of emitting the largest quantity of water in the driest weather. The inhabitants enjoy the privilege of sending fifteen children to the free school at Farnborough, in Warwickshire. Here are found the *pyrites aureus*, or golden fire-stone; also the *asteria*, or star-stone, called by Gesner "*sigillum stellæ*," from its use in sealing: in splitting some of these, the figure of a rose is plainly discernible in the centre.

CLAYDON, a parish in the hundred of Bosmere and Claydon, county of Suffolk, 3½ miles (N.N.W.) from Ipswich, containing 328 inhabitants. The living is a rectory, united to that of Akenham, in the archdeaconry of Suffolk, and diocese of Norwich, rated in the king's books at £10. The church is dedicated to St. Peter: the churchyard is tastefully laid out as a garden. The Stow-Market and Ipswich navigation crosses this parish.

CLAYDON (EAST), a parish in the hundred of Ashendon, county of Buckingham, 2¾ miles (S.W. by W.) from Winslow, containing, with Bottle-Claydon, 339 inhabitants. The living is a discharged vicarage, in the archdeaconry of Buckingham, and diocese of Lincoln, rated in the king's books at £7. 17., and in the patronage of Mrs. Verney. The church, which was dedicated to St. Mary, was demolished during the parliamentary war, by Cornelius Holland, one of the judges who sat upon the trial of Charles I. In 1673, Maurice Griffith left a trifling endowment for the education of two boys, and for apprenticing one of them every six years.

CLAYDON (MIDDLE), a parish in the hundred of Ashendon, county of Buckingham, 4 miles (W.S.W.) from Winslow, containing 160 inhabitants. The living is a rectory, in the archdeaconry of Buckingham, and diocese of Lincoln, rated in the king's books at £15, and in the patronage of Mrs. Verney. The church, dedicated to All Saints, contains a monument to the memory of Sir Edward Verney, standard-bearer to Charles I., who was killed at the battle of Edge-Hill, in 1642. Almshouses for six poor widows were built, in 1696, by Sir Ralph Verney, but they have no endowment.

CLAYDON (STEEPLE), a parish in the hundred and county of Buckingham, 5½ miles (W.) from Winslow, containing 804 inhabitants. The living is a vicarage, in the archdeaconry of Buckingham, and diocese of Lincoln, rated in the king's books at £13. 3. 9., and in the patronage of Mrs. Verney. The church is dedicated to St. Michael. Thomas Chaloner, Esq., in 1656, built a school-house, and endowed it with £12 per annum, but the endowment having been lost, the proprietor of the estate pays to the schoolmistress two shillings per week. At the period of the Conquest, this was the most populous place in the hundred: in an adjoining wood, an earthen vessel, filled with coins of Carausius and Alectus, has been discovered.

CLAYHANGER, a parish in the hundred of Bampton, county of Devon, 4¾ miles (E. by N.) from Bampton, containing 342 inhabitants. The living is a rectory in the archdeaconry and diocese of Exeter, rated in the king's books at £15. 7. 3½., and in the patronage of R. Harrison, Esq. The church contains a rood-loft and an ancient wooden screen; it formerly belonged to the Knights Templars, who had a preceptory here. A charity school was founded, in 1747, by Hannah Nutcombe Bluett, with an endowment of £3 per annum, which, by the subsequent gifts of John Norman and Buckland Nutcombe Bluett, in 1785, has been increased to £7. 10., that sum being paid to a schoolmistress for teaching as many children as choose to apply.

CLAYHEDON, a parish in the hundred of Hemyock, county of Devon, 4 miles (S.S.E.) from Wellington, containing 822 inhabitants. The living is a rectory, in the archdeaconry and diocese of Exeter, rated in the king's books at £38. 5., and in the patronage of the Rev. W. Clarke. The church is dedicated to St. Andrew. A charity school was endowed with £110, by Mary Waldron, in 1749, producing £7. 10. per annum, for teaching children of this parish and the parish of Hemyock.

CLAY-LANE, a township in the parish of North Wingfield, hundred of Scarsdale, county of Derby, 5½ miles (S.) from Chesterfield, containing 465 inhabitants.

CLAYPOLE, a parish in the wapentake of Loveden, parts of Kesteven, county of Lincoln, 5 miles (S.E.) from Newark, containing 605 inhabitants. The living is a rectory in medieties, in the archdeaconry and diocese of Lincoln; the north mediety is rated in the king's books at £16. 8. 4., and the south at £15. 15.; they are in the patronage of J. Plumtre, Esq. The church, dedicated to St. Peter, is an ancient structure, with a tower surmounted by a spire. There is a place of worship for Wesleyan Methodists. Charles Gretton, in 1727, endowed a school for the instruction of ten boys, with a rent-charge of £9 per annum, subject to a deduction of £2. 10.

CLAYTHORPE, a chapelry in the parish of Belleau, Marsh division of the hundred of Calceworth, parts of Lindsey, county of Lincoln, 4 miles (N.W. by W.) from Alford, containing 57 inhabitants.

CLAYTHORPE, a hamlet in that part of the parish of Burton in Kendal which is in Lonsdale ward, county of Westmorland, 1 mile (N.E. by N.) from Burton in Kendal, with which the population is returned. About a mile from the village is Farlton Knot, a huge limestone mountain, resembling in form the rock of Gibraltar: on the edge of another mountain is a natural curiosity, called Claythorpe Clints, consisting of a limestone rock, forming an inclined plain to the horizon, deeply rent in many places by the supposed ebbing of a great body of water, or the retiring of the ocean, by which it is conjectured that this, with some other plains in the neighbourhood, was once covered.

CLAYTON, a liberty in the parish of Stoke upon Trent, northern division of the hundred of Pirehill, county of Stafford, 2 miles (S. by E.) from Newcastle under Line, containing 152 inhabitants.

CLAYTON, a parish in the hundred of Buttinghill, rape of Lewes, county of Sussex, 2¼ miles (S.S.E.) from Hurst-Pierrepoint, containing 453 inhabitants. The living is a rectory, with the perpetual curacy of Keymer annexed, in the archdeaconry of Lewes, and diocese of Chichester, rated in the king's books at £21. 0. 10., and in the patronage of the Principal and Fellows of Brasenose College, Oxford. The church is dedicated to St. John the Baptist.

CLAYTON, a township in the parish of SOUTH STAINLEY, lower division of the wapentake of CLARO, West riding of the county of YORK, 2½ miles (N. E. by N.) from Ripley. The population is returned with the parish.

CLAYTON, a township in the parish of BRADFORD, wapentake of MORLEY, West riding of the county of YORK, 3½ miles (W. by S.) from Bradford, containing 3609 inhabitants, who are chiefly employed in the manufacture of cotton and worsted goods. There are places of worship for Wesleyan Methodists here and at Clayton Heights.

CLAYTON, a joint parish with Frickley, in the northern division of the wapentake of STRAFFORTH and TICKHILL, West riding of the county of YORK, 9 miles (E. by N.) from Barnesley. The population is returned with Frickley. The living is a perpetual curacy, with that of Frickley, in the archdeaconry and diocese of York. The church is dedicated to All Saints.

CLAYTON le DALE, a township in the parish of BLACKBURN, lower division of the hundred of BLACKBURN, county palatine of LANCASTER, 4¼ miles (N. by W.) from Blackburn, containing 598 inhabitants. In 1744, Edward Bootle gave a school-house and land, the annual rental of which is £9. 10., for the free education of five boys in Latin and English.

CLAYTON le MOORS, a township in that part of the parish of WHALLEY which is in the lower division of the hundred of BLACKBURN, county palatine of LANCASTER, 5½ miles (N. E. by E.) from Blackburn, containing 1963 inhabitants.

CLAYTON (WEST), a township in the parish of HIGH HOYLAND, wapentake of STAINCROSS, West riding of the county of YORK, 7 miles (N. W. by W.) from Barnesley, containing 854 inhabitants, of whom several are occupied in the manufacture of stuffs, fancy goods, &c.

CLAYTON le WOODS, a township in the parish and hundred of LEYLAND, county palatine of LANCASTER, 3¾ miles (N. by W.) from Chorley, containing 801 inhabitants.

CLAYTON-GRIFFITH, a township in the parish of TRENTHAM, northern division of the hundred of PIREHILL, county of STAFFORD, containing 34 inhabitants.

CLAYWORTH, a parish in the North-clay division of the wapentake of BASSETLAW, county of NOTTINGHAM, 6 miles (N. N. E.) from East Retford, containing, with the township of Wiseton, 557 inhabitants. The living is a rectory, in the archdeaconry of Nottingham, and diocese of York, rated in the king's books at £26. 10. 10., and in the patronage of the Dean of Lincoln. The church is dedicated to St. Peter. There is a place of worship for Wesleyan Methodists. The Rev. William Sampson, in 1700, bequeathed land now producing £58 per annum, to endow a school for the instruction of six boys: there is an orchard, the gift of Christopher Johnson, in 1707, in the possession of the master, who enjoys a salary of £48 per annum, with a house for his residence, the last having been devised by Francis Otter, in 1813, for instructing one boy; thirteen boys are educated upon this foundation. The Chesterfield canal passes through this parish.

CLEADON, a township in the parish of WHITBURN, eastern division of CHESTER ward, county palatine of DURHAM, 3½ miles (N. by W.) from Sunderland. The population is returned with the parish. Limestone is obtained in this township; and near Marston rock is found a species of indurated marl, in thin laminæ, very pliant, and hence termed flexible limestone.

CLEARWELL, a chapelry in the parish of NEWLAND, hundred of ST. BRIAVELLS, county of GLOUCESTER, 7 miles (W. by N.) from Blakeney, containing 583 inhabitants. The chapel has lately received four hundred and fifty additional sittings, three hundred and eighty of them free, towards defraying the expense of which the Incorporated Society for the enlargement of churches and chapels granted £400. There is a curious stone cross at this place.

CLEASBY, a parish in the eastern division of the wapentake of GILLING, North riding of the county of YORK, 3 miles (W. by S.) from Darlington, containing 147 inhabitants. The living is a perpetual curacy, in the archdeaconry of Richmond, and diocese of Chester, endowed with £35 per annum private benefaction, and £200 royal bounty, and in the patronage of the Dean and Chapter of Ripon. The church is a mean, low, and narrow structure, rebuilt, together with the parsonage-house, by Dr. John Robinson, a native of this parish, Bishop of London, and one of the plenipotentiaries at the treaty of Utrecht. He also founded a school for six poor boys, in 1723, and endowed it with sixteen acres of land, of which the Dean and Chapter of Ripon are visitors. The river Tees flows past the village.

CLEATHAM, a township in that part of the parish of MANTON which is in the wapentake of CORRINGHAM, parts of LINDSEY, county of LINCOLN, 6 miles (S. W.) from Glandford-Bridge, containing 117 inhabitants.

CLEATLAM, a township partly in the parish of STAINDROP, but chiefly in that part of the parish of GAINFORD which is in the south-western division of DARLINGTON ward, county palatine of DURHAM, 4½ miles (E. by N.) from Barnard-Castle, containing 126 inhabitants.

CLEATOR, a parish in ALLERDALE ward above Derwent, county of CUMBERLAND, 2¼ miles (N.) from Egremont, containing 818 inhabitants. The living is a perpetual curacy, in the archdeaconry of Richmond, and diocese of Chester, endowed with £200 private benefaction, £600 royal bounty, and £800 parliamentary grant, and in the patronage of T. R. G. Braddyll, Esq. The church is dedicated to St. Leonard. The manor-house is stated to have been burnt, about 1315, by a party of Scots under the command of James Douglas. The parish contains coal, limestone, and iron-ore, a great quantity of lime being burnt and sent into Scotland: here are also two forges for the manufacture of spades and other edged tools, besides an extensive establishment for spinning hemp and tow, making sewing-thread, &c. The mine of iron-ore at Crowgarth is of a superior description; it is twelve fathoms below the surface, and the vein of solid ore is from twenty-four to twenty-five feet in thickness: it was not much worked until 1784, but, about 1790 and a few years afterwards, twenty thousand tons of ore were annually shipped from Whitehaven to Hull and the Carron works, though the produce of late has greatly declined. The village is large, containing a few good houses, besides a number of cottages occupied by the workmen employed in the different manufactories: the inhabitants claim a right of common on the adjacent mountain of Dent. A Roman causeway formerly passed through the parish, from Egremont to Papcastle, near Cockermouth, but few traces of it are at present apparent.

CLEE, a parish in the wapentake of BRADLEY-HAVERSTOE, parts of LINDSEY, county of LINCOLN, $2\frac{1}{2}$ miles (S. E. by E.) from Great Grimsby, containing, with the township of Cleethorpe, 560 inhabitants. The living is a discharged vicarage, in the archdeaconry and diocese of Lincoln, rated in the king's books at £8, endowed with £800 royal bounty, and £600 parliamentary grant, and in the patronage of the Bishop of Lincoln. The church, dedicated to the Holy Trinity, has some fine Norman piers and arches, and contains an ancient circular font. In this parish are many of those fountains called Blow Wells, which are deep circular pits, supplying a continual flow of water. The custom of strewing the floor of the church, on Trinity-Sunday, with grass mown for that purpose, is perpetuated by a small legacy in land, left by a widow lady.

CLEE (ST. MARGARET'S), a parish in the hundred of MUNSLOW, county of SALOP, $8\frac{1}{4}$ miles (N. E. by N.) from Ludlow, containing 229 inhabitants. The living is a rectory, in the archdeaconry of Salop, and diocese of Hereford, rated in the king's books at £2. 8. 4., endowed with £600 private benefaction, £400 royal bounty, and £2100 parliamentary grant, and in the patronage of John C. Pelham, Esq.

CLEER (ST.), a parish in the hundred of WEST, county of CORNWALL, $2\frac{3}{4}$ miles (N. by W.) from Liskeard, containing 985 inhabitants. The living is a vicarage, in the archdeaconry of Cornwall, and diocese of Exeter, rated in the king's books at £19. 6. 8., and in the patronage of the Crown. The church is a handsome and spacious structure. The parish contains a great quantity of granite, locally termed moor-stone, and porphyry; and a copper mine has recently been opened. The river Fowey runs through it, and several rivulets empty themselves near Looe: there are also a few chalybeate springs, and an ancient Druidical monument, called the Hurlers, consisting of rude upright stones arranged in three circles, their centres in a right line, and the middle circle the largest.

CLEETHORPE, a township in the parish of CLEE, wapentake of BRADLEY-HAVERSTOE, parts of LINDSEY, county of LINCOLN, 3 miles (E. S. E.) from Great Grimsby, containing 154 inhabitants. There is a place of worship for Wesleyan Methodists. Here is a fishing hamlet, situated at the mouth of the Humber, which in summer is much resorted to for sea-bathing.

CLEEVE (BISHOP'S), a parish forming the hundred of CLEEVE, or BISHOP'S CLEEVE, in the county of GLOUCESTER, comprising the chapelry of Stoke-Orchard, the township of Bishop's Cleeve, and the hamlets of Gotherington, Southam with Brockampton, and Woodmancott, and containing 1548 inhabitants, of which number, 458 are in the township of Bishop's Cleeve, $3\frac{1}{4}$ miles (N. by E.) from Cheltenham. The living is a rectory, in the peculiar jurisdiction of the rector, in concurrence with the consistory court of the Bishop of Gloucester, wills and administrations being deposited in the bishop's registry: it is rated in the king's books at £84. 6. 8., and is in the patronage of the Rev. W. L. Townsend. The church, dedicated to St. Michael, is a curious and spacious structure, principally of Norman architecture, with a noble arch of exquisite workmanship in that style over the western entrance: the spire fell down in 1696, and caused considerable dilapidation, and, in 1700, it was replaced by the tower that now rises from the centre of the building, which underwent a thorough repair at the same time. The village occupies an eminence on the high road from Cheltenham to Evesham: its name, Clive, or Cleeve, is probably derived from the Saxon term *Cliv*, a steep ascent; and its adjunct given to distinguish it from Prior's Cleeve, it having been the property of the bishops of Worcester, whose ancient residence is now the rectory-house. On the ridge of Cleeve-Cloud hill, upon which races are annually held, is a large double intrenchment, called the Camps, in form of a crescent, three hundred and fifty yards in length, but accessible only in front.

CLEEVE (CHAPEL), a hamlet in the parish of OLD CLEEVE, hundred of WILLITON and FREEMANNERS, county of SOMERSET, $3\frac{1}{4}$ miles (E.) from Dunster. The chapel, which gave to this place its distinguishing appellation, was dedicated to the Blessed Virgin, but has long since fallen to ruin; it stood on a rock, and was the resort of numerous pilgrims.

CLEEVE (OLD), a parish in the hundred of WILLITON and FREEMANNERS, county of SOMERSET, $3\frac{3}{4}$ miles (E. S. E.) from Dunster, containing 1251 inhabitants. The living is a discharged vicarage, with the perpetual curacy of Leighland annexed, in the archdeaconry of Taunton, and diocese of Bath and Wells, rated in the king's books at £7, endowed with £200 private benefaction, and £200 royal bounty, and in the patronage of the Rev. John Newton. The church is dedicated to St. Andrew. There is a place of worship for Wesleyan Methodists. The parish adjoins the Bristol channel, and is remarkable for its craggy rocks, which abound with alabaster. On the beach a great quantity of kelp is gathered and burnt, previously to being sold in the market at Bristol; lodging-houses have been recently erected for the accommodation of persons resorting hither for the benefit of sea-bathing. A Cistercian abbey, in honour of the Virgin Mary, was founded here, in 1188, by William de Romara, the revenue of which, in 1534, was valued at £155. 9. $4\frac{1}{2}$.: there are still some remains, part having been converted into a private mansion, called Cleeve Abbey.

CLEEVE (PRIOR'S), a parish in the upper division of the hundred of OSWALDSLOW, locally in the upper division of that of Blackenhurst, county of WORCESTER, $5\frac{1}{2}$ miles (N. E.) from Evesham, containing 343 inhabitants. The living is a vicarage, in the archdeaconry and diocese of Worcester, rated in the king's books at £8, and in the patronage of the Dean and Chapter of Worcester. The church is dedicated to St. Andrew. The village is situated on an eminence, but the grounds immediately round it are flat, and the meadows on the banks of the Avon, which receives the Arrow, and enters Worcestershire from this parish, are sometimes subject to floods. The parish contains blue limestone; and there are quarries of valuable paving stone, and a species of marble which bears a polish like the Derbyshire marble; in working one of which, in 1812, two earthen jars of Roman coins, one containing gold and the other silver, principally of the reigns of Gratian, Valentinian, and Theodosius, and in good preservation, were found at the depth of three feet from the surface.

CLEHONGER, a parish in the hundred of WEBTREE, county of HEREFORD, 3½ miles (W. S. W.) from Hereford, containing 339 inhabitants. The living is a discharged vicarage, with that of Allensmore, in the peculiar jurisdiction and patronage of the Dean of Hereford, rated in the king's books at £4. 4. 2., and endowed with £200 royal bounty. The church is dedicated to All Saints.

CLEMENT'S (ST.), a parish in the western division of the hundred of POWDER, county of CORNWALL, containing 2306 inhabitants. Part of the town of Truro is situated in this parish. The living is a vicarage, in the archdeaconry of Cornwall, and diocese of Exeter, rated in the king's books at £9, and in the patronage of the King, as Duke of Cornwall. The river Fal runs through the parish, in which are some mineral springs. Charles I., after his defeat at this place, in 1646, took refuge at Polwhele, anciently a castle, and the family seat of the ancestors of the historian of the county of Cornwall.

CLEMENT'S (ST.), a parish in the hundred of BULLINGTON, county of OXFORD, containing 770 inhabitants. The parish is bounded on the west by the Cherwell, over which is a handsome bridge leading into the city of Oxford. The living is a rectory not in charge, in the archdeaconry and diocese of Oxford, endowed with £600 parliamentary grant, and in the patronage of the Crown. Owing to the inadequate accommodation which the old church afforded, a new church, in the Norman style, has been erected by subscription, on ground given by Sir Joseph Locke; it is situated near the margin of the Cherwell, and, as seen from Magdalene bridge, forms an interesting feature in the vale. Between it and the bridge, but nearer the latter, baths on an extensive scale have been constructed, consisting principally of a spacious swimming-bath, with dressing-rooms, a reading-room, and other conveniences. Stone's hospital, for the residence and support of poor persons, was founded pursuant to the will of the Rev. William Stone, Principal of New Inn Hall, dated May 12th, 1685, for eight poor women, each of whom has about £12 per annum; and Boulter's almshouses, agreeably to the will of Cutler Boulter, dated March 21st, 1736, for eight single men, one from each of the parishes of Wimple in Cambridgeshire, Wherwell in Hampshire, Haseley in Oxfordshire, Barlings in Lincolnshire, Deptford with Brockley in Kent, and Harewood in Yorkshire, who have each eight shillings weekly: they are both under the superintendence of special visitors. Various lands and tenements, producing about £400 per annum, have been left for the benefit of the poor, and for repairing the church. Henry I., in 1126, founded an hospital for infirm lepers, which, having suffered considerable impoverishment, was granted by Edward III. to Oriel College, on condition that the society should maintain a chaplain and eight almsmen in perpetuity. Respecting this charity there have been various suits at law between the society and the mayor and corporation of Oxford, and notwithstanding several legal decisions, the funds afford a very inadequate means of support to the hospitallers, who are eight in number, besides a chaplain, and who generally reside in the city, labouring at some kind of employment. About the time of the siege of Oxford, the house was demolished, and rebuilt by the society in 1649: it was afterwards used as a laboratory for making magnesia, by a private individual, and the remains are now appropriated to stabling and cow-houses. Anciently the funds of the establishment were augmented by the contributions of the fellows of New College, at their annual procession to the chapel of St. Bartholomew, on Holy Thursday: the students of Oriel and Magdalene Colleges, and the citizens of Oxford, were also accustomed to assemble here on May-day, bringing with them the earliest productions of the season, as oblations to the saint, and further celebrating the festive day with music and dancing. This custom is supposed to have originated in the pious intention of Burgwast, bishop of the diocese, who granted forty days' indulgence to all who came to the chapel on the festival of the saint, and contributed to the relief of the leprous almsmen. Here too were preserved relics of various saints, the supposed efficacy of which, in performing miraculous cures, attracted numerous pilgrims.

CLENCHWHARTON, a parish in the Marshland division of the hundred of FREEBRIDGE, county of NORFOLK, 2¾ miles (W.) from Lynn-Regis, containing 456 inhabitants. The living is a rectory, in the archdeaconry and diocese of Norwich, rated in the king's books at £14. 6. 8., and in the patronage of Miss Docker. At the time of the Norman survey this place was called *Ecleuuartuana*, signifying a watery situation by a river, and was divided into north and south.

CLENNELL, a township in the parish of ALLENTON, western division of COQUETDALE ward, county of NORTHUMBERLAND, 10¼ miles (W.N.W.) from Rothbury, containing 27 inhabitants.

CLENT, a parish in the southern division of the hundred of SEISDON, county of STAFFORD, though locally in the lower division of the hundred of Halfshire, county of Worcester, 3¼ miles (S. S. E.) from Stourbridge, containing 885 inhabitants. The living is a vicarage, with the perpetual curacy of Rowley-Regis annexed, in the archdeaconry and diocese of Worcester, rated in the king's books at £8. 16. 5½., and in the patronage of the Crown. The church is dedicated to St. Leonard. There are places of worship for Baptists and Wesleyan Methodists. The infant king of Mercia, St. Kenelm, is supposed to have been murdered here in 819, by order of his sister Quendrida, but the body, having been subsequently discovered, was buried in Winchcombe abbey, which had been founded by his father. Here is a free school for the children of poor parishioners, founded by John Amphlett, Esq., in 1704; the master, who instructs thirty children, has a house to reside in, with a garden attached, and the interest of £200. A Sunday school was also commenced, in 1788, by Thomas Waldron, Esq., who supported it during his lifetime, and at his death, in 1800, bequeathed £500 for that purpose; eighty children receive instruction.

CLEOBURY-MORTIMER, a market town and parish in the hundred of STOTTESDEN, county of SALOP, 32 miles (S. S. E.) from Shrewsbury, and 137 (N. W.) from London, on the road to Ludlow, containing 1602 inhabitants. The name of this place is derived from its situation in a district abounding with clay, and from the Saxon word *byrig*, a town; the adjunct, by which it is distinguished from North Cleobury, in the same county, is taken from its ancient possessor, Ralph de Mortimer, who held it at the time of the general survey. Hugh de Mortimer, his son, built a castle here, but having revolted in favour of the heir of Stephen, he fortified it against Henry II., who, with a powerful army, besieged and entirely demolished it. During the war between Henry III. and the barons, Cleobury suffered greatly from the incursions of the Welch, who at that time made frequent irruptions into this part of the country. The town is situated on an eminence rising gradually from the western bank of the river Rea, over which is a neat stone bridge: it consists principally of one long street, in which are many good houses, and the mutilated remains of an old cross; but it is neither paved nor lighted: the inhabitants are plentifully supplied with excellent water from a spring rising in the Brown Clee hills, and falling into a capacious basin in the lower part of the town. The trade is rapidly declining; formerly there were very extensive iron-works, but there are now only two forges: a few of the inhabitants are employed in the manufactory of paper, for which there are two mills. On the Clee hills, about three miles west of the town, are extensive collieries producing excellent coal; and on the higher part of them is a remarkably fine, though not extensive, vein of cannel coal, of which many beautiful specimens have been worked into snuff-boxes and ornaments of various kinds. The market, granted to Sir Francis Lacon, in 1614, is held on Wednesday: the fairs are on April 21st, Trinity-Monday, and October 27th. A constable is annually appointed at the court leet of the lord of the manor, held in April.

The living is a vicarage, in the archdeaconry of Salop, and diocese of Hereford, rated in the king's books at £13, and in the patronage of William Lacon Childe, Esq. The church, dedicated to St. Mary, is an ancient structure, with a plain square tower, surmounted by an octagonal spire of wood, considerably curved from the perpendicular. There are two places of worship for Wesleyan Methodists; and a Roman Catholic chapel is attached to Mawley Hall, the mansion of Sir Edward Blount, Bart., within a mile of the town. The free school was founded pursuant to the will of Sir Lacon William Childe, Knt., dated in 1714, whereby he bequeathed the residue of his personal estate, after the death of his wife, for its endowment: by a decree of the court of Exchequer, in 1735, a plot of ground was purchased, in 1739, on which the buildings were erected; the surplus of the endowment was vested in land, which, with property in the funds (of which £1000 in the three per cents. was given, in 1810, by Mr. John Winwood, of Bristol, formerly a scholar on the foundation), produces about £450 per annum: the management is vested in ten trustees. The master, who is appointed by W. L. Childe, Esq., as representative of the founder, has £60 per annum, and an usher £40: the boys are taught reading, writing, and arithmetic: a mistress is also appointed by the trustees, with a salary of £20 per annum, for teaching girls. The income is about £450 per annum: the present number of scholars is two hundred: thirty boys and forty girls are annually clothed, and a fee is occasionally given for apprenticing the boys on their leaving the school. Adjoining the town are a large schoolroom and dwelling-house, with a garden and a piece of waste ground attached, unoccupied and falling to decay: the premises were built by subscription, about 1727, for a free grammar school, but the institution has long since been dissolved, owing to the want of a permanent fund for its support. To the east of the free school are the remains of a Danish encampment; and within the distance of a mile and a half were the three castles of Cleobury, Toot, and Wall-town, of all which there is not a single vestige. Robert Langford, author of the Visions of Pierce Plowman, a satirical poem on the clergy of the fourteenth century, was a native of this town.

CLEOBURY (NORTH), a parish in the hundred of STOTTESDEN, county of SALOP, 8 miles (S. W. by W.) from Bridgenorth, containing 173 inhabitants. The living is a rectory, in the archdeaconry of Salop, and diocese of Hereford, rated in the king's books at £5. 12. 3½., and in the patronage of Mrs. Brazier. The church is dedicated to St. Peter.

CLERKENWELL, an extensive parish, in the Finsbury division of the hundred of OSSULSTONE, county of MIDDLESEX, adjoining the city of London, containing 39,105 inhabitants. Its name originated from an ancient well, round which the parish clerks of London were in the habit of assembling, at certain periods, for the performance of sacred dramas, noticed in the reign of Henry II. by Fitz-Stephen, under the appellation of *Fons Clericorum*. The parish is not mentioned in Domesday-book, being probably at the time of the survey an undistinguished portion of the great forest of Middlesex, or included in the parish of Islington, which, under the name Isendone, is noticed in that record. The site appears to have been well adapted to the celebration of those sacred festivals for which it was selected, from being in the centre of gently rising grounds, which formed an extensive and natural amphitheatre, for the accommodation of the numerous spectators who attended on such occasions. The most celebrated of these festivals took place in 1391, in the reign of Richard II., and continued for three days, during which several sacred dramas were performed by the clerks, in presence of the king and queen, attended by the whole court. About the year 1100, Lord Jordan Briset and his wife founded a priory here for nuns of the Benedictine order, dedicated to St. Mary, the site being now occupied by the parish church of St. James: the revenue, at the dissolution, was £282. 16. 5. The same Jordan founded also an hospital for Knights Hospitallers of the order of St. John of Jerusalem, which was liberally endowed with lands, and invested with many privileges by several successive monarchs; the lord prior had precedence of all lay barons in parliament, and power over all preceptories and smaller establishments of that order in the kingdom; the revenue, at the dissolution, was £2385. 12. 8.: this institution was partly restored in the reign of Philip and Mary, but was suppressed in that of Elizabeth: the remains are, the gate, in the later style of English architecture, now a private residence, and the vaults of the old church, in the Norman character, upon the site of which St. John's church was subsequently restored. The establishment of these monasteries naturally drew around them a number of dependent dwellings, but the parish made little progress in the number of its inhabitants prior to the time of Elizabeth, in whose reign, with the exception of some "banquetting houses and summer houses," it contained only a few straggling cottages, and some good houses in the immediate neighbourhood of the religious houses; its increase was afterwards more rapid, and in 1619 several noblemen and gentlemen were numbered among its inhabitants. Since then, the formation of numerous streets, and the more recent laying out of Spa-fields and the New River Company's estate, in a variety of new streets and squares, have rendered this one of the most populous parishes in the vicinity of the metropolis.

Among the more recent improvements may be noticed Claremont-square, in the centre of which is the reservoir of the New River water-works, surrounded by a high embankment, planted with shrubs; Myddelton and Wilmington squares, and numerous spacious streets and ranges of modern and respectable buildings. St. John's street and Goswell roads, the former leading from Smithfield, and the latter from Aldersgate, and the New Road, leading to Paddington, are the principal thoroughfares. The parish is lighted with gas, and the pathways are well flagged; it is within the limits of the new police establishment: the inhabitants are supplied with water by the New River Company, whose works are situated in this parish, where the river terminates. This stupendous undertaking was projected in the reign of Elizabeth, and, in the following reign, James I. granted an act of parliament, enabling the mayor and commonalty of London to carry it into effect; but the commissioners, dreading the difficulty and expense, made no advances for some years. In 1609, Mr. Hugh Myddelton, citizen and goldsmith of London, made proposals to the common council of the city to undertake the work at his own risk, and to complete it in four years, for which purpose the commissioners transferred to him the powers with which they had been invested by the act. After having persevered in the enterprise till the water was brought to Enfield, the city refusing to grant him any pecuniary assistance, Mr. Myddelton applied to the king, who agreed to pay him one-half of the expense, on condition of having a moiety of the concern transferred to him, and at various times, from Easter 1612, to Michaelmas 1614, advanced sums of money, amounting in the whole to £6347. 4. 11½., with which assistance the work was completed on the 29th of September, 1613, on the afternoon of which day, the lord mayor and corporation went in state to the "great cistern," called the New River Head, in this parish, when, after an oration delivered by a person especially selected, the flood-gates were thrown open, and the water rushed from the river into the cistern, amidst the joyous acclamations of an assembled multitude. The river, from its source at Amwell in Hertfordshire to Spa-fields, is thirty-eight miles, three quarters, and sixteen poles in length: there are nearly three hundred bridges erected over it, and its course is continued through the varying levels of the districts through which it passes, by means of forty sluices. The property of the company was divided into seventy-two shares, of which one-half was vested in Mr. Myddelton and twenty-eight other persons incorporated by charter of James I., in 1619, proprietors of the thirty-six shares constituting what is called the adventurers' moiety; the other moiety, vested in the crown, was re-granted by Charles I. to Sir Hugh Myddelton, who had been created a baronet on the 22nd of October, 1622: an adventurer's share in this company has been sold for £14,000. The Regent's canal passes on the north side of the parish, and enters a tunnel near White Conduit House; after proceeding in a direct line for nearly one thousand yards, in the course of which it passes under the New River, it terminates about twenty yards eastward from that part of it which flows between Colebrook-row and the City-road, in the parish of Islington.

Of the numerous wells with which this parish abounded, several were in great repute for their medicinal properties, and houses of public entertainment were erected near their site: of these, which were generally tea-gardens, and rendered more attractive by musical performances, the chief were Bagnigge Wells, White Conduit House, and New Tunbridge Wells, or Islington Spa, all still remaining: of those which have for many years been discontinued were, the Pantheon in Spa-fields, now a chapel belonging to a congregation in the late Countess of Huntingdon's connexion; the Cold Bath, in Cold Bath fields, of which the bath alone is still frequented; the Mulberry and Vineyard gardens; the celebrated Bear garden at Hockley in the Hole; and Sadler's Wells, near the New River Head, which has for many years been converted into a theatre for dramatic representations. *Fons Clericorum*, or the *Clerks' well*, is still in existence, being situated in Ray-street, where the spot is marked by a pump, with an inscription. The manufacture of clocks and watches, of which the several parts form distinct and separate departments of the trade, has for more than a century been carried on here to a considerable extent: when the duty on clocks and watches was imposed, in 1791, not less than seven thousand of the inhabitants were deprived of employment, and obliged to have recourse to parochial aid. There is a large manufactory for tin goods, which during the late war supplied the chief of the government contracts, also some extensive distilleries and soap-manufactories. The sessions for the county, and the meetings of the county magistrates, for the assessment of the county rates, and for other affairs, are held at the sessions-house, Clerkenwell Green, which was erected at an expense of £13,000, and has lately been repaired and beautified: it is a spacious and handsome edifice fronted with stone, having in the centre four pillars of the Ionic order, rising from a rustic basement and supporting a pediment: in the tympanum and on each side are emblematical figures in basso relievo. The entrance, by a flight of steps, opens into a hall thirty-four feet square, lighted by a dome which surmounts the building; from this hall, contiguous to which are the offices of the county treasurer and clerk of the peace, a double flight of steps leads into the court-room, which is of a semicircular form, commodiously arranged for the business of the sessions, and furnished with galleries for the accommodation of auditors: there are, on this story, rooms for the grand jury, for the commissioners of the land and assessed taxes, for the meetings of the magistrates, and for other purposes. The new prison, for the confinement of prisoners awaiting their trial at the sessions, was erected on the site of the old bridewell, in 1780, at an expense of £2500: it was partly rebuilt and greatly enlarged in 1818, and again enlarged in 1830, and comprises a house for the governor, a chapel, twenty wards, ten day-rooms, and twelve airing-yards, for the classification of prisoners, and two infirmaries, one for males and the other for females. The house of correction for the county, in Cold Bath Fields, was erected in 1794, at an expense of £70,000: it is a spacious brick building, enclosed with high walls, including an area divided into eighteen airing-yards, in one of which is a tread-mill upon an improved principle: this prison has also been considerably enlarged recently. Clerkenwell manor, formerly denominated the manor of St. John of Jerusalem, includes several out-portions of the parishes of St. Sepulchre, St. Luke (Old-street), and Hornsey, with those parts of the parish of Clerkenwell called the liberties of Cold Bath Fields, St. John of Jerusalem, Clerkenwell Close, Wood's Close, and Pentonville: constables and headboroughs for these liberties are chosen by the inhabitants of each, and presented at the manorial court for the approbation of the proprietor. The custom of Borough English, whereby the youngest son inherits, prevails in this manor.

The church of St. James was formerly the only church within the parish, which is now divided into three districts, namely St. James', St. John's, and St. Mark's, all in the archdeaconry and diocese of London. The living of St. James' is a perpetual curacy, in the patronage of the inhabitants generally, paying church and poor rates: the church is a modern structure of brick, with a handsome stone steeple, erected on the site of the ancient church of the priory of St. Mary, which had been previously modernised, but which, prior to its being taken down, for the erection of the present edifice, retained many vestiges of its Norman character, and contained the ashes of the last prioress of the nunnery; the last prior of St. John's; Weever, the antiquary; Bishop Burnet, and many other distinguished characters. The living of St. John's is a rectory not in charge, endowed with £600 royal bounty, and £1800 parliamentary grant, and in the patronage of the Crown: the church, with large curtailments and alterations, is that anciently belonging to the priory of the Knights Hospitallers, of which the choir only remained, being restored by the commissioners appointed under the act for building fifty new churches, passed in the tenth of Queen Anne's reign, by virtue of which a district was annexed to it, and the benefice constituted a rectory, in 1723. Notwithstanding it enjoys the privilege of religious rites, the incumbent of St. James' is entitled to the surplice fees: there are separate churchwardens for St. John's church, but the inhabitants of both districts contribute to the repairs of the two churches, and the same overseers of the poor act for the whole. St. Mark's, a district church, in Myddelton-square, containing one thousand six hundred and twenty-two sittings, of which eight hundred and forty-seven are free, was erected in 1826, by a grant from the parliamentary commissioners, at an expense of £16,000: it is a neat edifice in the later style of English architecture, with a handsome western front and a square tower with pierced parapet and pinnacles: the expense of furnishing it, which amounted to £2000, was defrayed by the parishioners. The living is a district incumbency, in the patronage of the Rev. Thomas Sheppard, the present incumbent of St. James', after whose decease the right of presentation becomes vested in the Bishop of London. A chapel of ease to St. Mark's is now in progress of erection, under the auspices of the Commissioners. The chapel at Pentonville, a neat modern edifice of brick, ornamented with stone, and having a small cupola, was erected in 1791, for a chapel of ease to St. James'. Spa-Fields chapel, formerly the Pantheon, as before noticed, was appropriated for a place of worship by the late Countess of Huntingdon, who for many years resided at the chapel house adjoining; and at her decease it was vested in trustees, with other chapels in various parts of the kingdom, agreeably to her will: there are likewise places of worship for Baptists, the Society of Friends, Independents, and Wesleyan and other Methodists, besides a Scotch church and a Welch chapel. The parish has the right of sending six scholars to the free grammar school, founded by Lady Alice Owen, for natives of this parish and of that of Islington, and of having three boys in Christ's hospital, the latter under the will of Giles Russell, Esq., who, in 1664, devised property to that establishment, for nine boys of the town of Sherborne, in the county of Dorset, and of the parishes of St. Anne, Blackfriars, and St. James, Clerkenwell. The parochial school, founded about the year 1700, has recently been removed from the school-house in Aylesbury-street, to a more convenient premises in Amwell-street, erected in 1829, forming a spacious and handsome range of building in the Elizabethan style of architecture, and capable of accommodating upwards of one thousand children: there are at present three hundred and forty-five boys and two hundred and twenty-six girls, of whom ninety boys and sixty girls are clothed. A charity school at Pentonville was instituted in 1788: the number of children amounts to one hundred and sixty, of whom sixty are clothed. The London Female Penitentiary at Pentonville, established in 1807, is a large range of building, comprising an infirmary, and apartments for one hundred females, who are chiefly employed in needlework and domestic occupations, to qualify them for service: since the establishment of this institution, one thousand four hundred and sixty-nine females have been received into it, of whom the greater number has been placed out in respectable situations, or restored to their friends. The Finsbury Dispensary was established in 1780, since which time it has extended relief to more than one hundred and fifty thousand of the labouring and necessitous poor; the number of patients annually relieved is, on an average, four thousand. A portion of the Roman Watling-street, and the river of Wells (the *Fleta* of the Romans), form part of the boundaries of the parish. Among the distinguished natives and residents of Clerkenwell the following may be enumerated:—Sir Thomas Chaloner, Bishop Burnet, Sir John Oldcastle, Baron Cobham, and Cave, who established the Gentleman's Magazine, and whose printing-office was in St. John's gate.

CLETHER (ST.), a parish in the hundred of LESNEWTH, county of CORNWALL, 7 miles (E.) from Camelford, containing 175 inhabitants. The living is a discharged vicarage, in the archdeaconry of Cornwall, and diocese of Exeter, rated in the king's books at

£6. 11. 10½., and in the patronage of J. Carpenter and T. J. Phillips, Esqrs.

CLEVEDON, a parish in the hundred of PORTBURY, county of SOMERSET, 14 miles (W. by S.) from Bristol, containing 581 inhabitants. The living is a discharged vicarage, in the archdeaconry of Bath, and diocese of Bath and Wells, rated in the king's books at £15. 14. 4., endowed with £400 private benefaction, and £200 royal bounty, and in the patronage of the Bishop of Bristol. The church, dedicated to St. Andrew, stands at the western extremity of the parish, and occupies a high and prominent situation on the shore of the Bristol channel: it is a cruciform structure, with a central tower. On the top of some of the hills are the remains of lead mines; and *lapis calaminaris* has also been found here. The old manor-house, a spacious building principally in the Elizabethan style, occupies a pleasant situation on the southern slope of the mountainous range that bounds the greater portion of the hundred. The Yeo flows through the village, and thence into the Bristol channel, a little southward from the church: several houses have been recently erected near the shore, for the reception of bathers; and a pier is also about to be constructed. As a watering-place, Clevedon is inferior to its rival neighbour, Weston, on account of the fine sandy beach of the latter, but greatly superior in the beauty of its scenery: myrtles and other delicate shrubs flourish in the gardens at all seasons. In 1650, Thomas Gwilliam, or Phillips, gave six acres of land, producing £11 per annum, for apprenticing poor children; and in 1727, Sir A. Elton bequeathed £5 per annum, for the instruction of children.

CLEVEDON (MILTON), a parish in the hundred of BRUTON, county of SOMERSET, 2¼ miles (N.W. by N.) from Bruton, containing 189 inhabitants. The living is a discharged vicarage, in the archdeaconry of Wells, and diocese of Bath and Wells, rated in the king's books at £6. 13. 4., endowed with 200 private benefaction, and £200 royal bounty, and in the patronage of the Earl of Ilchester. The church is dedicated to St. James. This parish lies under the western declivity of the Burton hills, and contains limestone, with various fossils imbedded in it. There are vestiges of an ancient fortification on Small-down, which, from the circumstance of several gigantic skeletons having been found near the spot, is supposed to have been the scene of a battle.

CLEVELAND-PORT, a hamlet in the parish of ORMESBY, western division of the liberty of LANGBAURGH, North riding of the county of YORK, 9 miles (N. by E.) from Stokesley. The population is returned with the parish. It is situated near the mouth of the Tees, affording a convenient point for shipping the greater part of the produce of Cleveland Vale and the surrounding neighbourhood for the London and other markets, and was formerly called Cargo Fleet.

CLEVELEY, a hamlet in the parish of CHURCH-ENSTONE, hundred of CHADLINGTON, county of OXFORD, 1½ mile (E.S.E.) from Neat Enstone, containing 214 inhabitants.

CLEVELY, a township partly in the parish of COCKERHAM, hundred of LONSDALE, south of the sands but chiefly in the parish of GARSTANG, hundred of AMOUNDERNESS, county palatine of LANCASTER, 4¼ miles (N. by E.) from Garstang, containing 148 inhabitants.

CLEVERTON, a township in the parish of LEA, hundred of MALMESBURY, county of WILTS, 3¼ miles (E. S. E.) from Malmesbury. The population is returned with the parish.

CLEWER, a parish in the hundred of RIPPLESMERE, county of BERKS, 1 mile (W.) from New Windsor, containing 2115 inhabitants. The living is a rectory, in the archdeaconry of Berks, and diocese of Salisbury, rated in the king's books at £14. 1. 0½., and in the patronage of the Provost and Fellows of Eton College. The church is dedicated to St. Andrew. There are places of worship for Wesleyan Methodists and Roman Catholics. The parish, situated on the south bank of the Thames, comprises part of the town of Windsor. On a patent roll of the 13th of Edward II. is a grant to John the Hermit, of the chapel of St. Leonard, of Loffield, in Windsor Forest, to enclose some land, parcel of the forest, which probably gave name to St. Leonard's Hill, an elegant mansion built by the Duchess of Gloucester, when Countess Waldegrave, on the site of a cottage. In 1809, Sir James Poultney, Bart. left by will £666. 13. 4. in the three per cent. consols., for the benefit of the master of a school; and, in 1815, Earl Harcourt conveyed two cottages, a schoolroom, and £500 Navy five per cents., for the instruction of poor boys and girls; about eighty of the former and seventy of the latter are taught on the National system. There are, besides, some trifling bequests for the poor, and for apprenticing children. A court leet is held annually; and a fair for toys and pedlary takes place on the 29th of May. A mineral spring has recently been discovered, but the quality of the water has not yet been accurately ascertained.

CLEY, a small sea-port, market town, and parish, in the hundred of HOLT, county of NORFOLK, 26 miles (N.N.W.) from Norwich, and 124 (N.N.E.) from London, containing 742 inhabitants. In 1406, Prince James of Scotland, on his voyage to France, to receive his education, was driven by stress of weather upon this coast; and being detained here, he was sent to London by order of Henry IV., who committed him and his attendant, the Earl of Orkney, to the Tower, where they remained for seventeen years in confinement; they were released in the 3rd of Henry VI., and the prince ascended the Scottish throne. The town is situated on the banks of a small river which falls into the harbour, at the north-eastern extremity of the county, and consists principally of one street, in the centre of which is the custom-house, a neat and commodious edifice, containing apartments for a resident collector, comptroller, &c.: it is plentifully supplied with water from springs. The trade of the port (of which the jurisdiction extends for thirty miles along the coast, from Morston on the west, to Barton Coal Gap on the east), consists principally in corn, coal, timber and deals, hemp, iron, tar, tallow, oil-cakes, &c., of which the importation is considerable; a small trade is also carried on in malt: the exports are comparatively trifling, consisting principally of salt, for the manufacture of which there are considerable works in the neighbourhood. The haven is good, but the channel leading from it to the town abounds with shoals, to the exclusion of ships of large burden. Under an act of enclosure obtained in 1822, a considerable quantity of land has been rescued from the sea by an embankment. The market is on Saturday; and a fair for horses is held annually on the last Friday in July.

The living is a rectory, in the archdeaconry and diocese of Norwich, rated in the king's books at £22. 13. 4., and in the patronage of John Winn Thomlinson, Esq. The church, dedicated to St. John, is a fine spacious structure in the early style of English architecture, and contains an ancient stone font, adorned with sculptured representations of the seven Sacraments of the church of Rome. Here is a place of worship for Wesleyan Methodists.

CLEYGATE, a manor in that part of the parish of Thames-Ditton which is in the second division of the hundred of Kingston, county of Surrey, 1¾ mile (E. S. E.) from Esher, containing 559 inhabitants.

CLIBURN, a parish in West ward, county of Westmorland, 7¼ miles (N. W. by W.) from Appleby, containing 205 inhabitants. The living is a discharged rectory, in the archdeaconry and diocese of Carlisle, rated in the king's books at £9. 1. 5½., and in the patronage of the Bishop of Carlisle. The church is dedicated to St. Cuthbert. This parish is bounded on two sides by the Eden and the Lyvennet, and the Lethe rivulet flows through it. A small school has been established for the education of the children of parishioners, endowed with an allotment of land by the commissioners under an act of parliament, which produces an income of £21 per annum; the average number of scholars is twenty. A market was held at Gilshauglin, in this parish, in 1598, when the plague raged at Appleby.

CLIDDESDEN, a parish in the hundred of Basingstoke, Basingstoke division of the county of Southampton, 1¾ mile (S. by W.) from Basingstoke, containing 264 inhabitants. The living is a rectory, united to that of Farleigh-Wallop, in the archdeaconry and diocese of Winchester, rated in the king's books at £10. 16. 3. There is a school for the instruction of poor children, endowed by Mrs. Ann Dorrington with £10 per annum, to which the Earl of Portsmouth gave an additional sum of £10 per annum, with a house for a schoolmistress.

CLIEVELOAD, a chapelry in the parish of Powick, lower division of the hundred of Pershore, county of Worcester, 5½ miles (S. S. W.) from Worcester, containing 36 inhabitants. The chapel has been demolished. The river Severn flows past the village.

CLIFF, a joint township with Lund, in the parish of Hemingbrough, wapentake of Ouze and Derwent, East riding of the county of York, 3½ miles (E.) from Selby, containing, with Lund, 501 inhabitants. There is a place of worship for Wesleyan Methodists. In 1708, Mary Ward bequeathed £220 for the building and endowment of a school, towards the further support of which Mr. Whittall gave £100; the income is £40. 16. 6., for which thirty scholars are educated.

CLIFFE, a parish in the hundred of Shamwell, lathe of Aylesford, county of Kent, 5 miles (N. by W.) from Rochester, containing 673 inhabitants. The living is a rectory, in the peculiar jurisdiction of the incumbent, rated in the king's books at £50, and in the patronage of the Archbishop of Canterbury. The church, dedicated to St. Helen, is considered to be the finest in the county, being a large handsome cruciform structure in the early style of English architecture, with an embattled central tower, and containing several curious monuments and remains of antiquity, together with six stalls that belonged to a dean and five prebendaries, it having been formerly collegiate. The parish is bounded on the north by the Thames: the village, which is supposed to take name from the cliff or rock on which it stands, at present consists of West-street and Church-street, but was formerly of much greater extent, a great part of it having been destroyed by fire in 1520. It was anciently the scene of several provincial councils: a fair is held on the 28th of September. The school-house, which has been recently put into a state of complete repair, was founded in 1679, by John Browne, who bequeathed two tenements and other appurtenances, for educating twelve poor children, directing his executors and the churchwardens to appoint a poor man and woman teachers, and to choose the scholars. One of the cottages is occupied by the school-mistress, who receives £10 per annum for teaching eight poor children.

CLIFFE, a township in that part of the parish of Manfield which is in the western division of the wapentake of Gilling, North riding of the county of York, 5¾ miles (W. by N.) from Darlington, containing 53 inhabitants. There is a Roman Catholic chapel at Cliffe Hall.

CLIFFE (KING'S), a parish in the hundred of Willybrook, county of Northampton, 31 miles (N. E. by N.) from Northampton, and 88 (N. N. W.) from London, containing 1080 inhabitants. The living is a rectory, in the archdeaconry of Northampton, and diocese of Peterborough, rated in the king's books at £13. 16. 3., and in the patronage of the Earl of Westmorland. The church is dedicated to All Saints. This was formerly a market town; the market, which was held on Tuesday, has fallen into disuse, but there is still a fair on the 29th of October. The Rev. William Law, a nonjuring divine and polemical writer, was born at this place, in 1686, where, after residing in it during the last twenty years of his life, he died in 1761. A school for twenty boys and fourteen girls, and three alms-houses, were endowed, principally with a bequest of lands and houses, by Elizabeth Hutchinson, in 1745, which yield an annual income of £260.

CLIFFE (NORTH), a township in the parish of Sancton, Hunsley-Beacon division of the wapentake of Harthill, East riding of the county of York, 3 miles (S.) from Market-Weighton, containing 89 inhabitants.

CLIFFE (SOUTH), a township in the parish of North Cave, Hunsley-Beacon division of the wapentake of Harthill, East riding of the county of York, 3½ miles (S.) from Market-Weighton, containing 131 inhabitants.

CLIFFE (ST. THOMAS), county of Sussex.— See LEWES.

CLIFFE (WEST), a parish in the hundred of Bewsborough, lathe of St. Augustine, county of Kent, 2¾ miles (N.E.) from Dovor, containing 52 inhabitants. The living is a discharged vicarage, in the archdeaconry and diocese of Canterbury, endowed with £200 royal bounty, and in the patronage of the Archbishop of Canterbury. The church is dedicated to St. Peter.

CLIFFE-PYPARD, a parish in the hundred of Kingsbridge, county of Wilts, 4¼ miles (S. by E.) from Wootton-Bassett, containing 815 inhabitants. The living is a vicarage, in the archdeaconry of Wilts, and diocese of Salisbury, rated in the king's books at £9, and in the patronage of the Rev. E. Goddard. The church, dedicated to St. Peter, and in which are some remains of painted glass, was founded by one Cobham, a knight templar, whose effigy lies near the wall of the north aisle. This place takes its name from a cliff, and its adjunct from a court anciently kept, called Pypard; it is situated at the foot of a chain of hills (a very steep one separating the north part of the parish from the south) that runs along the north side of the vale of White Horse: there is a hill composed of a kind of freestone, as white as chalk, but considerably harder, and much used for paving and building. A free school is supported by an annuity of about £30.

CLIFFORD, a parish in the hundred of HUNTINGTON, county of HEREFORD, 9½ miles (S.W. by S.) from Kington, containing, with a part of the township of Vowmine, 816 inhabitants. The living is a discharged vicarage, in the archdeaconry and diocese of Hereford, rated in the king's books at £4. 10., endowed with £200 private benefaction, and £200 royal bounty, and in the patronage of the Rev. W. Trumper. The church is dedicated to St. Mary. There are some portions of Clifford castle remaining, in a ruinous condition: it stood on a bold eminence, projecting over the river Wye, and was the baronial residence of the lords de Clifford for two centuries, being, as it is supposed, the birthplace of Fair Rosamond. Here was anciently a convent of Cluniac monks, founded by one of the lords de Clifford, as a cell to the priory of Lewes, in Sussex; at the dissolution, its revenue was estimated at £75. 7. 5.

CLIFFORD, a township in the parish of BRAMHAM, upper division of the wapentake of BARKSTONE-ASH, West riding of the county of YORK, 3¼ miles (S.E. by S.) from Wetherby, containing 1017 inhabitants. There is a place of worship for Wesleyan Methodists.

CLIFFORD-CHAMBERS, a parish in the upper division of the hundred of TEWKESBURY, though locally in that of the hundred of Kiftsgate, county of GLOUCESTER, 2¾ miles (S. by W.) from Stratford upon Avon, containing 305 inhabitants. The living is a rectory, in the archdeaconry and diocese of Gloucester, rated in the king's books at £18. 15. 7½., and in the patronage of L. Dighton, Esq. The church, dedicated to St. Helen, is a small structure, with a south door of Norman architecture.

CLIFTON, a parish in the hundred of CLIFTON, county of BEDFORD, 1½ mile (E. by N.) from Shefford, containing 483 inhabitants. The living is a rectory, in the archdeaconry of Bedford, and diocese of Lincoln, rated in the king's books at £20. 2. 11., and in the patronage of the Rev. D. J. Olivier. The church, dedicated to All Saints, contains some ancient monumental brasses, and a fine altar-tomb in memory of Sir Michael Fisher, who died lord of the manor in 1549. The river Ivel, lately made navigable, runs through the parish. There is a day and Sunday school, founded and endowed in 1827, by the late rector, the Rev. D. S. Olivier, for eighteen children.

CLIFTON, or ROCK-SAVAGE, a township in the parish of RUNCORN, hundred of BUCKLOW, county palatine of CHESTER, 2¼ miles (N.N.E.) from Frodsham, containing 26 inhabitants. This place has been called Rock-Savage since the erection of a splendid mansion by Sir John Savage, in 1565. The township comprises only the manorial mansion and its demesne land, now in the possession of the Marquis of Cholmondeley, who enjoys also the title of Earl of Rock-Savage.

CLIFTON, a chapelry in that part of the parish of ASHBOURN which is in the hundred of MORLESTON and LITCHURCH, though locally in the hundred of Wirksworth county of DERBY, 1¾ mile (S. W.) from Ashbourn, containing, with the hamlet of Compton, 768 inhabitants.

CLIFTON, a parish and favourable watering-place, in the hundred of BARTON-REGIS, county of GLOUCESTER, 1¼ mile (W.) from Bristol, 14 miles (N. W.) from Bath, and 121 (W. by S.) from London, containing 8811 inhabitants. This place, by some antiquaries supposed to have been a British town prior to the Roman invasion, and to have been called *Caer-oder*, or city of the chasm, derives its present name from its romantic situation on the acclivities and summit of a precipitous cliff, apparently separated by some convulsion of nature, from a chain of rocks in the Bristol channel. The river Avon, which is navigable for ships of the greatest burden, flows with a rapid current through this natural chasm, forming the south-western boundary of the parish, and separating the counties of Gloucester and Somerset. On the summit of the cliff, which rises to the height of three hundred feet above the bed of the river, was anciently a small chapel, dedicated to St. Vincent, from which the rock on the north-east bank takes its name. The town is indebted for its present grandeur and importance to the efficacy of its hot wells, originally noticed, in 1480, by William of Worcester, but not brought into general use till 1632, when the water was first applied externally in cases of scrofula and cancer, and internally, in 1672, in cases of inflammation, dysentery, and hœmorrhage. These waters issue from an aperture in the cliff, about ten feet above low water-mark, and about twenty-six below high water-mark, and are pumped into reservoirs for use, besides being conveyed by pipes into many of the houses; the aperture is secured from the water of the river, which in spring tides rises to the height of thirty-six feet. Their mean temperature is 68° of Fahrenheit, and they contain a portion of sulphuric acid, but are soft and pleasant to the taste, and free from any fœtid smell; they are generally drunk in the morning before breakfast, and in the afternoon. At the time of the earthquake at Lisbon, the water became so red and turbid as to be unfit for use.

That part of the town called the Hot Wells, and formerly the more populous, is situated at the base of the cliff, and has a mild and genial atmosphere, peculiarly suited to delicate constitutions; from which circumstance it has been not unaptly denominated the Montpelier of England. A new pump-room, a handsome edifice of the Tuscan order, containing also apartments for the residence of invalids, has been erected near the site of the old house, which was built by subscription about the year 1770. Immediately above this is an observatory, in which are a camera obscura, embracing a comprehensive view of the surrounding scenery; and powerful telescopes, constructed by an untaught genius, to whom the lord of the manor granted the materials and an advantageous lease of an ancient mill occupying the site: near this a suspension bridge, long in contemplation, was commenced in the summer of 1831, which will form an interesting addition to the beautiful scenery of this picturesque spot. Gloucester House, formerly the only hotel of any consideration in the place, and now the Gloucester and Steam-packet hotel, whence the packets to Ireland regularly sail, is still much frequented, from its proximity to the waters and the excellence of its accommodations: Dowry-square and parade, Hope-square, Albemarle-row, St. Vincent's parade, and Granby-hill, all contain respectable lodging-houses, fitted up with due regard to the comfort and convenience of visitors. Ascending the cliff, on which is situated that part of the town properly called Clifton, are baths and a pump-room for drinking the water, which issues from a spring of similar quality to that at the Hot Wells, or more probably from the same spring, recently opened at a greater elevation, for the accommodation of invalids residing in this part of the town: to the pump-room are attached a reading-room and lodging-rooms; and a little below Mardyke, on the road to the Hot Wells, is a spa, where saline mineral water is obtained, which is said to be efficacious in visceral and other disorders. The acclivities are occupied by ranges of stately edifices, under the respective names of crescent, circus, paragon, and terrace, among which York-crescent is distinguished for its superior extent and magnificence: the summit, on which formerly there were only a few scattered dwellings, is now crowned with superb mansions and elegant villas, commanding extensive prospects of romantic beauty. Here is an elegant mansion built by Sir William Draper, Knt., the celebrated opponent of Junius, in the front court of which are, an obelisk, erected to the memory of William Pitt, Earl of Chatham, and a cenotaph to the memory of those of the seventy-ninth regiment who fell at Arott, Manilla, Pondicherry, and the Philippine Islands. The Clifton Hotel is a splendid edifice, occupying the whole eastern extremity of the mall: the front, which is of freestone, exhibits a pleasing combination of tasteful elegance; the centre comprises a suite of three spacious rooms, handsomely fitted up, and appropriated to the public subscription concerts and assemblies, one of them during the morning being open as a reading-room: the north side is occupied as private lodging-houses, and the rooms over the centre and the south side are appropriated to the uses of the hotel. Concerts and assemblies frequently take place during the season: the terraces afford delightful promenades; and the nursery ground, comprising several acres, beautifully laid out and interspersed with parterres of flowers, adorned with grottos, and embellished with numerous fossils and natural curiosities, is also a favourite place of resort: the town is brilliantly lighted with oil-gas, and plentifully supplied with water. Many of the labouring class are employed in blasting the rocks, the fragments of which being broken are shipped to the counties of Devon and Cornwall, and used for mending the roads. St. Vincent's rock is composed of hard variegated marble, susceptible of a high polish; it is burnt into a fine white lime, much esteemed by plasterers, and a considerable quantity is packed in barrels and exported to the East and West Indies. In the fissures of the rocks are found beautiful spars, and those quartz chrystals called Bristol diamonds, which are equal in transparency, and inferior only in hardness, to those of India; they are remarkable for their naturally formed and highly polished hexagonal surfaces, and are found imbedded in nodulæ of stone of the same colour as the soil; in these rocks have been also discovered veins of lead and iron ore. That part of the parish which is situated between Rownham Ferry and Lime-kiln Dock, on the south side of the Hot Well road, is within the jurisdiction of the city of Bristol; the remainder is within that of the magistrates for the Bristol division of the county of Gloucester: the town is within the jurisdiction of the court of requests for the city and county of the city of Bristol, established under an act passed in the 56th of George III., for the recovery of debts from 40*s.* to any amount under that for which an arrest on mesne process may issue. The living is a perpetual curacy, in the archdeaconry of Gloucester, and diocese of Bristol, endowed with £200 private benefaction, and £400 royal bounty, and in the patronage of the Rev. C. Simeon. The church, dedicated to St. Andrew, is a spacious structure in the later style of English architecture, erected in 1822. There is a private episcopal chapel; and it is in contemplation to build another church at the Hot Wells, for the especial accommodation of the poor. There are a chapel for those in the late Countess of Huntingdon's connexion, a floating chapel for seamen, called Clifton Ark, and a place of worship for Wesleyan Methodists. A National and an infant school, and a dispensary, for which a neat building was erected at the sole expense of Mr. Whippie, are supported by subscription. On the summit of St. Vincent's rock are the remains of an encampment, three or four acres in extent, defended by three ramparts and two ditches; the inner rampart, which is in no part more than five feet in height, is supposed to have been surmounted by a wall: its extent, from one side of the rock to the other, is two hundred and ninety-three yards; and on the side next the river there is a deep trench, said to have been cut during the civil war in the reign of Charles I. Its origin is by some antiquaries ascribed to the Britons, and by others to the Romans, who placed there the first of that chain of forts erected to defend the passage of the Severn: in the immediate neighbourhood, and in various parts of the parish, numerous Roman and Saxon coins have been discovered. Anne Yearsley, who, in the humble station of a milk-woman, displayed much poetical talent, and produced several literary works, was a native of this place; she died in 1806 at Melksham, in the county of Wilts.

CLIFTON, a joint township with Salwick, in the parish of KIRKHAM, hundred of AMOUNDERNESS, county palatine of LANCASTER, 3 miles (E. S. E.) from Kirkham, containing, with Salwick, 608 inhabitants. In 1682, John Dickson left a small bequest for teaching poor children.

CLIFTON, a township in the parish of ECCLES, hundred of SALFORD, county palatine of LANCASTER, 5 miles (N. W. by W.) from Manchester, containing 1168 inhabitants. New collieries have been opened at this place, whereby its population has greatly increased.

CLIFTON, a joint township with Coldwell, in the northern division of the parish of STANNINGTON, western division of CASTLE ward, county of NORTHUMBERLAND, 2½ miles (S.) from Morpeth. The population is returned with the parish.

CLIFTON, a parish in the northern division of the wapentake of RUSHCLIFFE, county of NOTTINGHAM, 4¼ miles (S. W. by S.) from Nottingham, containing, with Glapton, 470 inhabitants. The living is a rectory, in the archdeaconry of Nottingham, and diocese of

York, rated in the king's books at £21. 6. 10½., and in the patronage of Sir Robert Clifton, Bart. The church, dedicated to St. Mary, is a fine structure, though much dilapidated; it has a massive tower, and contains several monuments to the Clifton family. Here was anciently a small college for a warden and two priests, dedicated to the Holy Trinity, and founded in the time of Edward IV., by Sir Gervase Clifton, which, at the dissolution, was valued at £20 per annum. There is a small bequest for the instruction of children and the support of an hospital. Clifton is in the honour of Tutbury, duchy of Lancaster, and within the jurisdiction of a court of pleas held at Tutbury every third Tuesday, for the recovery of debts under 40*s*.

CLIFTON, a township in the parish of DEDDINGTON, hundred of WOOTTON, county of OXFORD, 1¼ mile (E.) from Deddington, containing 271 inhabitants. There is a place of worship for Wesleyan Methodists.

CLIFTON, a parish in WEST ward, county of WESTMORLAND, 2¾ miles (S. E. by S.) from Penrith, containing 283 inhabitants. The living is a rectory, in the archdeaconry and diocese of Carlisle, rated in the king's books at £8. 3. 4., and in the patronage of the Bishop of Carlisle. The church, dedicated to St. Cuthbert, is a small and indifferently built structure. The parish is bounded on the north and west by the river Lowther, in the vale of which the village is situated, deriving its name from the rock or cliff on which it stands. At Clifton moor, which was enclosed in 1812, a slight skirmish took place in 1745, between the Duke of Cumberland and a party of the Pretender's army, on its retreat to Scotland. There is a medicinal spring, the water of which is efficacious in the cure of scorbutic complaints. Mary Scott, in 1764, made a small bequest towards the support of a schoolmaster.

CLIFTON, a township partly in the parish of ST. MICHAEL le BELFREY, within the liberty of ST. PETER of YORK, and partly in the parish of ST. OLAVE, MARY-GATE, wapentake of BULMER, North riding of the county of YORK, 1¼ mile (N. W.) from York, containing 469 inhabitants.

CLIFTON, a joint township with Norwood, in the parish of FEWSTON, lower division of the wapentake of CLARO, West riding of the county of YORK, 6 miles (N. by E.) from Otley, containing, with Norwood, 420 inhabitants. Clifton is within the jurisdiction of the court of the honour of Knaresborough. A school is endowed with a small annuity for the instruction of eight poor children.

CLIFTON, a joint township with Newhall, in that part of the parish of OTLEY which is in the upper division of the wapentake of CLARO, West riding of the county of YORK, 2 miles (N. N. W.) from Otley. The population is returned with Newhall.

CLIFTON, a joint chapelry with Hartshead, in that part of the parish of DEWSBURY which is in the wapentake of MORLEY, West riding of the county of YORK, 5 miles (N. N. E.) from Huddersfield, containing, with Hartshead, 2007 inhabitants. The living is a perpetual curacy, in the archdeaconry and diocese of York, endowed with £460 private benefaction, £400 royal bounty, and £800 parliamentary grant.

CLIFTON upon DUNSMOOR, a parish in the Rugby division of the hundred of KNIGHTLOW, county of WARWICK, 2¼ miles (E. N. E.) from Rugby, containing, with the hamlet of Newton with Biggin, 612 inhabitants. The living is a discharged vicarage, in the archdeaconry of Coventry, and diocese of Lichfield and Coventry, rated in the king's books at £8. 1. 8., and in the patronage of the Earl of Bradford. The church is dedicated to St. Mary. The Oxford canal passes through this parish. Thomas Carte, author of an elaborate History of England, was born here, in 1686; he died in 1754.

CLIFTON (GREAT), a chapelry in the parish of WORKINGTON, ALLERDALE ward above Derwent, county of CUMBERLAND, 2½ miles (E.) from Workington, containing 251 inhabitants. The living is a perpetual curacy, in the archdeaconry of Richmond, and diocese of Chester, endowed with £800 royal bounty, and £1000 parliamentary grant, and in the patronage of the Rector of Workington. The chapel is situated in the township of Little Clifton: an additional piece of ground was consecrated for a cemetery in 1821, the former burial-ground having been disused from the year 1736. Here are the remains of an ancient cross, where, according to tradition, a market was formerly held. The Rev. Jeremiah Seed, a theological writer, was a native of this place; he died in 1747.

CLIFTON (LITTLE), a township in the parish of WORKINGTON, ALLERDALE ward above Derwent, county of CUMBERLAND, 3¼ miles (E.) from Workington, containing 203 inhabitants.

CLIFTON (NORTH), a parish in the northern division of the wapentake of NEWARK, county of NOTTINGHAM, 6 miles (E. by N.) from Tuxford, comprising the township of South Clifton, and the hamlets of Harby and Spalford, and containing 864 inhabitants. The living is a discharged vicarage, in the archdeaconry of Nottingham, and diocese of York, rated in the king's books at £7. 6., and in the patronage of the Prebendary of Clifton in the Cathedral Church of Lincoln. The church is dedicated to St. George. The parish is bounded on the west by the river Trent, over which there is a ferry, which is free to the inhabitants. The small village of Harby contained a palace belonging to Queen Eleanor, consort of Edward I., who expired here on the 29th of November, 1290; and here her august husband erected the first cross to her memory. A schoolmaster receives £10. 10. per annum, a schoolroom and residence having been built for him by subscription in 1799, arising from land bequeathed by Simon Nicholson, in 1669, for instructing fifteen poor children of North and South Clifton.

CLIFTON (SOUTH), a township in the parish of NORTH CLIFTON, northern division of the wapentake of NEWARK, county of NOTTINGHAM, 6 miles (E. by S.) from Tuxford, containing 292 inhabitants.

CLIFTON upon TEME, a parish in the upper division of the hundred of DODDINGTREE, county of WORCESTER, 10¼ miles (N. W. by W.) from Worcester, containing 520 inhabitants. The living is a discharged vicarage, in the archdeaconry of Salop, and diocese of Hereford, rated in the king's books at £6. 19. 2., and in the patronage of Sir T. E. Winnington, Bart. The church, dedicated to St. Killom, contains some ancient monuments. There is a place of worship for Wesleyan Methodists. The village is beautifully situated on a steep cliff, overlooking the serpentine course of the river

Teme, by means of which the meadows and hop plantations in the neighbourhood are irrigated. Edward III. made it a free borough, granting also a weekly market, now disused. Near it are the remains of Ham castle, formerly the residence of the family of Jefferies, which was nearly destroyed in 1646, by the parliamentary troops; it is now occupied as a farmhouse. There was anciently a chapel at Overton, in this parish, but, in 1532, Charles, Bishop of Hereford, with the consent of the vicar of Clifton and the inhabitants, united it to the parish of Slandford, reserving to the vicar an annual pension of 13*s*. 4*d*., in lieu of tithes and offerings due from the inhabitants of the chapelry.

CLIFTON upon URE, a township in the parish of Thornton-Watlass, eastern division of the wapentake of Hang, North riding of the county of York, 4 miles (S. W.) from Bedale, containing 50 inhabitants.

CLIFTON-CAMPVILLE, a parish in the northern division of the hundred of Offlow, county of Stafford, 5¾ miles (N. E. by N.) from Tamworth, comprising the chapelry of Harleston and the township of Haunton, and containing 838 inhabitants. The living is a rectory, in the archdeaconry of Stafford, and diocese of Lichfield and Coventry, rated in the king's books at £30, and in the patronage of the Rev. John Watkins. The church is dedicated to St. Andrew.

CLIFTON-HAMPDEN, a parish in the hundred of Dorchester, county of Oxford, 3¼ miles (E. S. E.) from Abingdon, containing 277 inhabitants. The living is a perpetual curacy, in the jurisdiction of the peculiar court of Dorchester, endowed with £666 private benefaction, £200 royal bounty, and £2100 parliamentary grant, and in the patronage of Miss Noyes. The church is dedicated to St. Michael.

CLIFTON-MABANK, a parish in the hundred of Yetminster, Sherborne division of the county of Dorset, 5½ miles (W. S. W.) from Sherborne, containing 66 inhabitants. The living is a rectory, formerly within the peculiar jurisdiction of the Dean of Salisbury, but united in 1824 to the vicarage of Bradford-Abbas, and now within the archdeaconry of Dorset, and diocese of Bristol, rated in the king's books at £4. 16. 0½. The church, which was dedicated to All Saints, has been in ruins for a century. The river Ivel runs through this parish.

CLIFTON-REYNES, a parish in the hundred of Newport, county of Buckingham, 2½ miles (E.) from Olney, containing 230 inhabitants. The living is a rectory, in the archdeaconry of Buckingham, and diocese of Lincoln, rated in the king's books at £13. 6. 10½., and in the patronage of Trustees for William Harry Alexander Small, Esq. The church is dedicated to St. Mary. The principal manor here was given by William the Conqueror to Robert de Todeni, one of the companions of his expedition, and it afterwards passed into the family of Reynes, from which the parish takes its adjunct.

CLIMPING, a parish in the hundred of Avisford, rape of Arundel, county of Sussex, 7 miles (S. S. W.) from Arundel, containing 258 inhabitants. The living is a vicarage, in the archdeaconry and diocese of Chichester, rated in the king's books at £9. 11. 0½., and in the patronage of the Provost and Fellows of Eton College. The church is cruciform, and principally in the early style of English architecture, with a Norman tower at the end of the south transept. The parish is bounded on the east by the river Arun, over which there is a ferry, and on the south by the English channel. There is a small fund for the instruction of children.

CLINCH, a joint township with Fawdon and Hartside, in the parish of Ingram, northern division of Coquetdale ward, county of Northumberland, 12½ miles (W.) from Alnwick. The population is returned with Fawdon.

CLINT, a township in that part of the parish of Ripley which is in the lower division of the wapentake of Claro, West riding of the county of York, 1¼ mile (W. by S.) from Ripley, containing 412 inhabitants. Here are the remains of an ancient mansion, called Clint Hall. The Roman road from Ilkley over the forest of Knaresborough branched off in two directions at this place, one leading to Catterick, the other to Aldborough.

CLIPPESBY, a parish in the western division of the hundred of Flegg, county of Norfolk, 3 miles (N. E.) from Acle, containing 50 inhabitants. The living is a discharged rectory, in the archdeaconry and diocese of Norwich, rated in the king's books at £6. 13. 4., and in the patronage of D. Colby, Esq. and another. The church is dedicated to St. Peter.

CLIPSHAM, a parish in the soke of Oakham, locally in the hundred of Alstoe, county of Rutland, 9¾ miles (N. E. by E.) from Oakham, containing 221 inhabitants. The living is a rectory, in the archdeaconry of Northampton, and diocese of Peterborough, rated in the king's books at £10. 0. 5., and in the patronage of Mrs. Snow. The church is dedicated to St Mary.

CLIPSTON, a parish in the hundred of Rothwell, county of Northampton, 4 miles (S. S. W.) from Market-Harborough, containing 813 inhabitants. The living is a rectory in three portions, two of which are valued in the king's books at £11. 12. 8½., and the third at £6; it is in the archdeaconry of Northampton, and diocese of Peterborough, and in the patronage of the Master and Fellows of Christ's College, Cambridge. The church is dedicated to All Saints. In 1667, Sir George Boswell bequeathed land and tenements to endow a school and an hospital; and Francis Horton also bequeathed £200 to increase the endowment: they are for the benefit of the inhabitants of Clipston, Merston, Nussell, East Farndon, Oxendon, Kilmarsh, and Haselbeck. The river Ise rises in this parish.

CLIPSTON, a township in that part of the parish of Plumtree which is in the southern division of the wapentake of Bingham, county of Nottingham, 6¾ miles (S. E.) from Nottingham, containing 72 inhabitants. Richard I., after returning from the captivity brought on by his crusade to the Holy Land, had an interview with the king of Scotland at this place, in 1194, where they spent several days.

CLIPSTONE, a township in the parish of Edwinstow, Hatfield division of the wapentake of Bassetlaw, county of Nottingham, 3¾ miles (W. S. W.) from Ollerton, containing 142 inhabitants. On an eminence above the village are some remains of a very ancient palace that belonged to the Anglo-Saxon kings; it is of Norman architecture, and is said to have been erected by one of the kings of Northumberland; after the Conquest it was frequently the residence of King John, both before and after his accession to the throne, and the charter which he granted to Nottingham, in the first year of his reign, is dated at this place; as were also the orders issued by Edward II., on September 25th, 1307, to the seneschal of Gascony, and constable of Bourdeaux, to provide a thousand pipes of good wine to be sent to London before the following Christmas, for his approaching coronation. To this palace also all the kings of England down to Henry V. appear to have repaired for the diversion of hunting in the royal forest of Sherwood, as we find that Henry de Fauconberge, in the reign of Henry III., held the neighbouring manor of Cuckney in serjeantry by the shoeing of the king's palfrey on coming to Mansfield. A parliament was held here by Edward I. in 1290, and an old oak at the edge of the park is still called the Parliament oak. Clipston is in the honour of Tutbury, duchy of Lancaster, and within the jurisdiction of a court of pleas held at Tutbury every third Tuesday, for the recovery of debts under 40*s*.

CLIST (BROAD), a parish in the hundred of CLISTON, county of DEVON, 5¾ miles (N. E.) from Exeter, containing 1885 inhabitants. The living is a vicarage, in the archdeaconry and diocese of Exeter, rated in the king's books at £26, and in the patronage of Sir T. D. Acland, Bart. The church, dedicated to St. John the Baptist, is a handsome edifice in the later style of English architecture, containing three stone stalls with buttresses and pinnacles, having rich canopies, and embellished with varied foliage, with an effigy in plate armour within them. The river Clist runs through the parish, in which there is a paper-mill. This place was burnt down by the Danes in 1001. The old mansion of Columbjohn, in this parish, was garrisoned for Charles I. by his loyal adherent, Sir John Acland: it has a chapel, in which divine service is still regularly performed. On the manor of Clist-Gerald is a barn, once the chapel of St. Leonard; there were also chapels dedicated to St. David and St. Catherine. A charity school, founded in 1691, is supported partly by an endowment of about £15 per annum, and partly by subscription: a good school-house for boys and girls, who are instructed on the National plan, has been erected by Sir T. D. Acland, and another for girls only by Lady Acland. An almshouse for twelve poor persons was built by Mr. Burrough, who endowed it, in 1605, with £23. 11. per annum, and placed it under the direction of the 'Eight Men' of the parish. Adjoining it is a dwelling called the New House, and, at a little distance, one called the Parish House, both inhabited by paupers.

CLIST (ST. GEORGE), a parish in the eastern division of the hundred of BUDLEIGH, county of DEVON, 1½ mile (N. E. by E.) from Topsham, containing 345 inhabitants. The living is a rectory, in the archdeaconry and diocese of Exeter, rated in the king's books at £17. 16. 8., and in the patronage of the Rev. W. R. Ellicombe. In the windows of the church are some remains of ancient stained glass. A school for boys and girls was founded, in 1703, by Sir Edward and Dame Seward; the income is about £42 per annum, and it has an exhibition of £4 per annum at either of the Universities: £3 per annum is received by this parish from the Holbrook estate in the parish of Clist-Honiton, the gift of Thomas Weare for instructing four poor children.

CLIST (ST. LAWRENCE), a parish in the hundred of CLISTON, county of DEVON, 5 miles (S. by E.) from Cullompton, containing 149 inhabitants. The living is a rectory, in the archdeaconry and diocese of Exeter, rated in the king's books at £9. 4. 4½., and in the patronage of the Mayor and Corporation of Exeter. The church contains an elegant wooden screen.

CLIST (ST. MARY), a parish in the eastern division of the hundred of BUDLEIGH, county of DEVON, 2¼ miles (N. E. by N.) from Topsham, containing 145 inhabitants. The living is a rectory, in the archdeaconry and diocese of Exeter, rated in the king's books at £5. 1. 3., and in the patronage of the Rev. Thomas Strong. This parish is memorable for having been the scene of one of the principal contests between the adherents of the old religion and the Reformers, in 1549, when the former were defeated, and pursued with great slaughter through the village to the heath adjoining. This parish is entitled to an annuity of £3 per annum from an estate called Holbrook, in the parish of Clist-Honiton, bequeathed by Thomas Weare for the education of six poor children.

CLIST-HONITON, a parish in the eastern division of the hundred of BUDLEIGH, county of DEVON, 4½ miles (E. by N.) from Exeter, containing 383 inhabitants. The living is a perpetual curacy, within the peculiar jurisdiction and patronage of the Dean and Chapter of Exeter, endowed with £200 private benefaction, and £300 parliamentary grant. The Clyst, though an insignificant stream, imparts its name to this and the other parishes through which it passes. Thomas Weare by his will bearing date 28th April, 1691, charged his estate, called Holbrook, with the annual payment of £4. 10. for educating six children. This sum is regularly paid by the owner of the property, and with subscriptions, affords instruction to all the poor children of the parish who apply.

CLIST-HYDON, a parish in the hundred of CLISTON, county of DEVON, 3¾ miles (S. S. E.) from Cullompton, containing 297 inhabitants. The living is a rectory, in the archdeaconry and diocese of Exeter, rated in the king's books at £20. 0. 7½., and in the patronage of the Rev. John Huyshe. The church is dedicated to St. Andrew. A charity school is endowed with about £20 per annum, principally from a bequest by the Rev. Robert Hall, D.D., in 1667, part of which is also applied in apprenticing poor children, with a fee of £5.

CLIST-SACKVILLE, a chapelry in the parishes of CLIST ST. MARY, FARRINGDON, and SOWTON, eastern division of the hundred of BUDLEIGH, county of DEVON, 2¼ miles (N. by E.) from Topsham. The population is returned with the parishes of Farringdon and Sowton. The chapel, which was dedicated to St. Gabriel, has been demolished. This place was mortgaged by Sir Ralph Sackville to Walter Brownscomb, Bishop of Exeter, to enable him to proceed with Edward I. on a crusade to the Holy Land, promising to refund the money at a fixed period, and to defray all charges on the estate during his absence; on which the bishop erected a palace, still standing, and fenced the ground at great charge, so that the expense exceeded the value of the land, in consequence of which it remained with him and his successors, until Bishop Vesey alienated it to the Earl of Bedford.

Arms.

CLITHEROE, an unincorporated borough, market town, and parochial chapelry, in that part of the parish of WHALLEY which is in the higher division of the hundred of BLACKBURN, county palatine of LANCASTER, on the eastern bank of the Ribble, 30 miles (N.) from Manchester, 49 (N.E.) from Liverpool, 26 (S.E.) from Lancaster, and 216 (N.N.W.) from London, containing 3213 inhabitants. Its ancient name, *Cliderhow*, is of a mixed derivation, from the British *Cled-dwr*, which signifies *the hill, or rock, by the waters*, and the final syllable *how*, a Saxon word for *hill*, being descriptive of its situation, which is on an isolated eminence, terminating in one direction in a lofty rock of limestone, on which stands the decayed keep of a castle, erected either in the reign of William the Conqueror, or in that of his son: some ascribe the foundation to Robert de Lacy the first, but, on the authority of a manuscript in the Bodleian Library, it is assigned to Robert de Lacy the second, in 1179, which account is confirmed by Dugdale, who states that the castle, and the chapel of St. Michael annexed thereto, were built by the latter. The castle originally consisted of a keep, with a tower and arched gateway, and was surrounded by a strong lofty wall built on the margin of the rock: it was used as a species of fortress for dispensing justice and receiving tribute by the Lacies, who were lords paramount of the honour. This honour, which extends over the parishes of Whalley, Blackburn, Chipping, and Ribchester, the forest of Bowland, and the manors of Tottington and Rochdale, and includes twenty-eight manors, formed part of the possessions of the house of Lancaster, from the time of the marriage of Thomas Plantagenet, Earl of Lancaster, with Alice, sister and heiress of Henry de Lacy, until that of the Restoration, when Charles II. bestowed it upon General Monk and his heirs: it is now divided between his Grace the Duke of Buccleuch and Lord Montague; all manors and estates, of whatsoever tenure, within its limits, being held of the castle: it has also a court for the recovery of small debts, extending over the hundred of Blackburn. During the wars of the roses, Henry VI., on his deposition, sought a temporary refuge here among the hereditary dependents of the house of Lancaster, but was betrayed to his rival by the Talbots of Bashall and Colebry, and sent bound to London. In the civil war this fortress was among the last surrendered to the parliament, by whose directions, in 1649, it was dismantled, the keep, a square tower rapidly mouldering away, being all that remains: the site, and a certain portion of ground occupied by the demesne and forests of the baronial edifice, are extra-parochial, and commonly designated the Castle parish. A modern castellated edifice has been erected within the precincts of the castle. Clitheroe was the scene of an engagement, in 1138, between a small party of the English army and the Scotch, in which the former was totally defeated by superior numbers; some traces of this sanguinary conflict have been discovered near Edisforth bridge and along the banks of the Ribble. An hospital for lepers, called the Hospital of Edisforth, was founded here by some of the earliest burgesses, and dedicated to St. Nicholas, which shared the fate of the smaller monasteries at the dissolution.

The town, from its elevated position, is clean and pleasantly situated; the houses, which are generally of an inferior order, are built of stone; the streets are well paved, but not lighted, and the inhabitants are amply supplied with water from several springs. The neighbourhood abounds with an almost inexhaustible bed of limestone; and at Pimlico, a short distance northward from the town, ten kilns are kept burning forty weeks in the year, and produce in the aggregate four thousand windles, or twenty-eight thousand strikes weekly. Horse-races of an inferior description were re-established in 1821, and are held annually on the 21st and 22nd of June, on Salt-hill moor. There are extensive cotton-manufactories and print-works in the town and its vicinity, which have flourished to such a degree that the population has nearly doubled during the last ten years. A communication by water has been opened with the principal navigable rivers and canals, thus affording a facility of conveyance to all parts of the kingdom. The market is on Tuesday: fairs are held annually on the 24th and 25th of March, 1st and 2nd of August, on the fourth Friday and Saturday after the 29th of September, and on the 6th and 7th of December; there is also a fair for cattle and sheep every alternate Tuesday.

Corporate Seal.

Clitheroe is a borough by prescription: its first charter, dated in the time of Henry de Lacy, who died in 1147, was confirmed by Edward I., who granted the burgesses the same privileges as those enjoyed by the citizens of Chester, and subsequently by Edward III., Henry VIII., and James II. The civil power is vested in two bailiffs, chosen annually by the burgesses at large, from their own body, at a court held for that purpose on the first Friday after the 9th of October: their joint authority is equal to that of one magistrate; they are coroners and lords of the manor, for which they hold a court leet twice a year: in addition to this, there are a court baron and a court of enquiry, held under one or both of the bailiffs: these courts are held in the moot-hall, a neat modern edifice, ornamented in front with the borough arms cut in stone, and surmounted by a spire sixty-two feet high. There is also a court of pleas, having jurisdiction to an unlimited amount in actions of debt arising within the borough: it is holden every three weeks before the two bailiffs, and has existed from time immemorial. In addition to the bailiffs are the recorder, who is elected by the burgesses, and officiates as assessor to the bailiffs in the trial of causes in the borough court; the town-clerk, who is also steward of the court leet; and the town-serjeant, who is the executive officer and keeper of the gaol: the two last officers are appointed by the bailiffs. The borough did not return members to parliament until the first year of the reign of Elizabeth, since which period it has regularly sent two: in consequence of a petition to the House of

Commons, that assembly determined, in 1694, "that the right of election was in the burgesses and freemen; the burgesses were such as had, in any land or houses in the borough, an estate of freehold inheritance, and they were of two sorts; out-burgesses, who lived out of the borough, and in-burgesses, who lived in the borough, and had such an estate in houses or land there, and both these had a right of electing: the freemen were such as lived in the houses within the borough as tenants, and they had the right of electing when the landlords did not vote for these houses, but when they did, the tenants had no right of electing:" there are about one hundred voters: the bailiffs are the returning officers. The parliamentary influence is principally possessed by Earl Brownlow and Earl Howe, who concur in the nomination of one member each.

The living is a perpetual curacy, endowed with £10 per annum and £200 private benefaction, £200 royal bounty, and £1900 parliamentary grant, and in the patronage of Earl Howe. The church, dedicated to St. Michael, is of great antiquity, being designated the church of St. Mary Magdalene, in a deed of the 13th of Edward IV.: between the nave and the choir is a fine Norman arch; and a brass plate against the southern wall of the nave bears a curious enigmatical diagram, and an inscription in Latin to the memory of Dr. John Webster, the celebrated judicial astrologer, and formerly curate of Clitheroe, who was interred here, June 21st, 1682. There are places of worship for Independents, Methodists, and Roman Catholics. The free grammar school was founded, in 1554, by Philip and Mary, and endowed with the rectorial tithes of the parish of Almondbury, and with certain messuages, burgages, and lands in the district of Craven, in Yorkshire: its concerns are under the superintendence of six governors, who appoint the master and usher, subject to the approval of the Bishop Chester, as visitor. The head-master receives a salary of £200, and has a handsome residence, recently erected, which he occupies rent-free: the second master is allowed £100 per annum, and both receive gratuities at Shrovetide. The surplus revenue of the institution is appropriable to the repairs of the school, and to the support of poor scholars at the university, but the latter purpose is seldom carried into effect. The Rev. James King, afterwards chaplain to the House of Commons, and father of Captain James King, who accompanied Captain Cook in his voyage of discovery round the globe, also of the Right Rev. Walker King, late Bishop of Rochester, was, during the early part of his ministry, incumbent of Clitheroe.

CLIVE, a township in that part of the parish of MIDDLEWICH which is in the hundred of NORTHWICH, county palatine of CHESTER, 2 miles (W. by S.) from Middlewich, containing 29 inhabitants.

CLIVE, a chapelry in that part of the parish of ST. MARY which is within the liberties of the town of SHREWSBURY, county of SALOP, 3½ miles (S.) from Wem, containing 306 inhabitants. The living is a perpetual curacy, within the jurisdiction of the court of the royal peculiar of St. Mary, in Shrewsbury, endowed with £400 royal bounty, and in the patronage of the Mayor and Head-master of the free grammar school of Shrewsbury. The chapel is dedicated to All Saints. William Wycherley, the poet and comic writer, was born here, in 1640.

CLIVIGER, a chapelry in that part of the parish of WHALLEY which is in the higher division of the hundred of BLACKBURN, county palatine of LANCASTER, 3½ miles (S. E. by S.) from Burnley, containing 1314 inhabitants. There is a small bequest for the instruction of children.

CLIXBY, a chapelry in the parish of CAISTOR, southern division of the hundred of YARBOROUGH, parts of LINDSEY, county of LINCOLN, 2½ miles (N. by W.) from Caistor, containing 67 inhabitants. The living is a perpetual curacy, annexed to the vicarage of Caistor, in the peculiar jurisdiction of the Prebendary of Caistor in the Cathedral Church of Lincoln.

CLOATLY, a tything in the parish of HANKERTON, hundred of MALMESBURY, county of WILTS, 3½ miles (N. E.) from Malmesbury, containing 87 inhabitants.

CLODOCK, a parish in the hundred of EWYAS-LACY, county of HEREFORD, 16 miles (S. W. by W.) from Hereford, comprising the chapelries of Crasswall, Llanveynoe, and Longtown, and the township of Newton, and containing 1796 inhabitants. The living is a vicarage not in charge, in the archdeaconry of Brecon, and diocese of St. David's, and in the patronage of Walter Wilkins, Esq. The church is dedicated to St. Cleodocus. Fairs are held on April 29th, June 22nd, and September 21st. Here is a school with an endowment of £4 per annum. The rivers Olchon and Munnow have their source in this parish, and the river Eskley runs through it. At Longtown are the remains of an ancient castle, formerly of great strength, and a Roman camp in a very perfect state.

CLOFFOCK, an extra-parochial liberty adjoining the parish of Workington, in ALLERDALE ward above Derwent, county of CUMBERLAND, containing 15 inhabitants. This is a large common, lying on the north side of the town of Workington, and is completely surrounded by the river Derwent and a small stream. Races are held annually upon it; and at the west end are a quay and a patent slip. A portion of the ground is called Chapel Flat, whence it is thought to have been the site or property of a religious house.

CLOFORD, a parish in the hundred of FROME, county of SOMERSET, 4½ miles (S.W.) from Frome, containing 312 inhabitants. The living is a discharged vicarage, in the archdeaconry of Wells, and diocese of Bath and Wells, rated in the king's books at £7. 17. 6., and in the patronage of S. T. Horner, Esq. The church is dedicated to St. Mary. There is a place of worship for Wesleyan Methodists. The ancient liberty of Hillhouse includes this parish and the parish of Elm.

CLOPHILL, a parish in the hundred of FLITT, county of BEDFORD, 1¾ mile (N. by E.) from Silsoe, containing 838 inhabitants. The living is a vicarage, in the archdeaconry of Bedford, and diocese of Lincoln, rated in the king's books at £12, and in the patronage of the Countess De Grey. The church, dedicated to St. Mary, stands upon an eminence at some distance from the village. There is a place of worship for Wesleyan Methodists. The river Ivel passes through the parish. At Cainhoe are vestiges of the ancient moated castle of the Barons d'Albini; the hill on which it stood is high and steep, and overgrown with coppice wood. Here was a religious house, probably a cell to St. Alban's abbey.

CLOPTON, a parish in the hundred of CARLFORD, county of SUFFOLK, 4 miles (N. W.) from Woodbridge, containing 413 inhabitants. The living is a rectory, in the archdeaconry of Suffolk, and diocese of Norwich, rated in the king's books at £16. 13. 4., and in the patronage of the Rev. J. G. Spurgeon. The church is dedicated to St. Mary.

CLOSWORTH, a parish in the hundred of HOUNDSBOROUGH, BERWICK, and COKER, county of SOMERSET, 4½ miles (S. by E.) from Yeovil, containing 187 inhabitants. The living is a discharged rectory, in the archdeaconry of Wells, and diocese of Bath and Wells, rated in the king's books at £6. 8. 11½., and in the patronage of E. B. Portman, Esq. The church is dedicated to All Saints.

CLOTHALL, a parish in the hundred of ODSEY, county of HERTFORD, 2¼ miles (S. E.) from Baldock, containing 358 inhabitants. The living is a rectory, in the archdeaconry of Huntingdon, and diocese of Lincoln, rated in the king's books at £16. 0 7½., and in the patronage of the Marquis of Salisbury. The church, dedicated to St. Mary, is built of flint and stone, and has a square tower surmounted by a spire; it contains several ancient effigies and inscriptions in brass. Here was a free chapel, or college, of ancient foundation, dedicated to St. Mary Magdalene, for a master, brethren, and sisters, which was valued at £4. 2. 8., and continued till the dissolution. Thomas Stanley, son of Sir Thomas Stanley, Knt., and author of The History of the Philosophers, was born here, in 1625; he died in 1678, and was buried in the parish church.

CLOTHERHOLME, a township in that part of the parish of RIPON which is within the liberty of RIPON, West riding of the county of YORK, 2 miles (N. W. by W.) from Ripon, containing 16 inhabitants.

CLOTTON-HOOFIELD, a township in that part of the parish of TARVIN which is in the second division of the hundred of EDDISBURY, county palatine of CHESTER, 2 miles (W. N. W.) from Tarporley, containing 388 inhabitants.

CLOUGHTON, a chapelry in the parish of SCALBY, PICKERING lythe, North riding of the county of YORK, 4¼ miles (N. W. by N.) from Scarborough, containing 366 inhabitants. Here is a large quarry of excellent freestone.

CLOVELLY, a parish in the hundred of HARTLAND, county of DEVON, 12 miles (W. by S.) from Bideford, containing 941 inhabitants. The living is a rectory, in the archdeaconry of Barnstaple, and diocese of Exeter, rated in the king's books at £19. 11. 5½., and in the patronage of Sir J. H. Williams, Bart. The church, dedicated to All Saints, and made collegiate for a warden and six chaplains by one of the family of Carew, in the 11th of Richard II., stands at the distance of half a mile from the village, and at a considerable height above it. There is a place of worship for Wesleyan Methodists. At this place was a Roman *trajectus* from Caermarthen, and till within the last few years the remains of a fort, erected by the Romans for the defence of the pass, were plainly to be distinguished. The village is romantically situated on the declivities of a shelving and precipitous rock, rising abruptly from the Bristol channel to the height of several hundred feet above the harbour, and crowned with luxuriant verdure; beneath this the houses are irregularly scattered in narrow ranges, descending in direct and spiral lines from the summit to the base. The prospect from the heights is extensive, and embraces numerous interesting objects, among which the views of the isle of Lundy in the channel, of Barnstaple bay, of the opposite coast as far as the Severn, and of the vessels in the small harbour beneath, are eminently fine: the appearance of the village from the harbour is strikingly picturesque, presenting a singular combination of romantic cottages, rugged precipices, and masses of rock of remarkable configuration, fringed with woods and occasionally interspersed with spots of ground in a high state of cultivation. The harbour, which, together with that of Hartland, is an appendage to the port of Bideford, though small, is remarkable for its security, and is formed partly by the projecting rocks of the coast, and partly by a substantial pier erected by a member of the family of Carew, by one of whom the manor was purchased in the reign of Richard II. A considerable trade is still carried on in the herring fishery, for which Clovelly was formerly the most noted place on the coast: the herrings are esteemed the finest taken in the channel, and the fishery furnishes employment to the principal part of the labouring class. The neighbourhood abounds with geological attractions, but possesses no organic remains; the rocks, of which the strata incline in every direction, consist of alternate beds of dun-stone and shillat. There is a small charity school, partly supported by the rental of the seats in the gallery of the church, and partly by subscription. On the summit of the heights above the village is a large encampment, called Dichen, or the Clovelly ditches, consisting of three trenches, or dykes, enclosing a quadrilateral area three hundred and sixty feet in length, and three hundred in breadth.

CLOWHOUSE, a joint township with Houghton, in that part of the parish of HEDDON on the WALL which is in the eastern division of TINDALE ward, county of NORTHUMBERLAND, 7¼ miles (W. by N.) from Newcastle. The population is returned with Houghton.

CLOWN, a parish in the hundred of SCARSDALE, county of DERBY, 8 miles (E. N. E.) from Chesterfield, containing 616 inhabitants. The living is a rectory, in the archdeaconry of Derby, and diocese of Lichfield and Coventry, rated in the king's books at £7. 0. 10., and in the patronage of the Crown. The church, dedicated to St. John the Baptist, has Norman portions, amidst various later styles of architecture. Charles Basseldine, in 1730, founded a charity school, with an endowment of thirteen acres of land, now producing £26 per annum, with a house for the master and a schoolroom; twenty children are educated upon this foundation, and four others for £2 per annum, the gift of John Slater, in 1727. In 1770 an information and bill were filed in the court of Chancery, to recover some part of the school property left by Mr. Basseldine, when a decree was given in favour of the charity, and the rectors of Clown, Staveley, and Barlbrough, for the time being, were appointed the trustees of the estate: but other trustees were subsequently chosen upon the report of the Master. Limestone is obtained here. There is a chalybeate spring, called Shuttlewood Spa, in this parish; and several rivulets, tributary to the stream running down to Welbeck, flow through it: there is also a piece of water called Harlesthorpe Dam, covering about four acres.

Corporate Seal.

CLUN, a parish in the hundred of Purslow, county of Salop, comprising the borough and market town of Clun, and the townships of Edeclift, Hobendrid, and Newcastle, and containing 1781 inhabitants, of which number, 792 are in the town of Clun, 26 miles (S. W.) from Shrewsbury, and 157 (N. W. by W.) from London. This place takes its name from the river Colun, or Clun, which, rising in the forest of that name, six miles to the west, divides the town into two parts, and pursues an easterly course towards Ludlow. In the reign of Stephen, or, according to Camden, in that of Henry III., a castle was erected here by Fitz-Alan, afterwards Earl of Arundel, on a lofty eminence overlooking the river, the proprietor of which anciently possessed the power of life and death over his tenants; it was demolished by Owen Glyndwr in his rebellion against Henry IV. The remains still present an interesting and picturesque object in the surrounding landscape; they consist of the lofty and massive walls of the keep and the banquet-hall; and considerable masses of the ruins in various parts of the area indistinctly mark out both the ancient form and extent of this once stately pile. In the reign of Henry VIII. this parish was by statute annexed to, and made part of, the newly formed county of Montgomery, from which it was afterwards severed, and included in that of Salop. The town is pleasantly and romantically situated on a gentle eminence surrounded by hills of bolder elevation, and consists principally of one long irregular street on the north bank of the river, over which is an ancient stone bridge of five sharply-pointed arches, leading to that part of the town in which the church stands: the houses are in general built of rag-stone, and roofed with thatch, though occasionally interspersed with some of more modern structure; and the inhabitants are well supplied with water. The market is on Wednesday: the fairs are on Whit-Tuesday and September 23rd, for cattle, sheep, and pigs; and November 22nd, which is a statute and a large cattle fair. Clun, formerly a lordship in the marches, was first incorporated by the Lords Marchers, whose charter was confirmed to Thomas, Earl of Arundel, in the reign of Edward II., at which time its prescriptive right was admitted; the charter not having been enrolled in Chancery, and all the records of the Lords Marchers having been destroyed, its being an incorporated borough was proved by parole evidence: it was formerly the head of a hundred of the same name, which has been incorporated with that of Purslow. The government is vested in two bailiffs and thirty burgesses, assisted by a town-clerk, two serjeants at mace, and subordinate officers. The bailiffs are chosen annually by the burgesses, from among their own body, on the first Sunday after the 19th of September, and sworn into office at the ensuing court leet, held in October; they are justices of the peace, and hold a court of record for the recovery of debts to any amount. The hundred court, for the recovery of debts under 40*s.*, is held every third Wednesday, and courts leet in May and October: at that held in October constables for the town and the several townships in the parish are appointed. The town-hall, a neat modern stone building supported on arches, consists of one large upper room, in which the several courts are held; under it is an area for the use of the market, in which is a small prison for the temporary confinement of malefactors.

The living is a vicarage, in the archdeaconry of Salop, and diocese of Hereford, rated in the king's books at £13. 10. 5., and in the patronage of the Earl of Powis. The church, dedicated to St. George, is a very ancient structure in the earliest period of the Norman style of architecture, and has evidently been of much greater extent than it is at present, having had several chapels attached to it: it has a low tower of very large dimensions and of great strength, with a pyramidal roof, from the centre of which rises another of similar form, but smaller; the arch under the tower, which forms the western entrance, bears a strong resemblance to the Saxon arch, and it is not improbable that this part of the building existed before the Conquest: the northern entrance is under a highly ornamented Norman arch, on the east side of which is an arched recess, richly cinquefoiled, and probably intended for the tomb of its founder: the interior contains a fine old font and many interesting monuments; the roof is supported on massive circular columns and obtusely pointed arches, with flat mouldings; and in the north aisle the original oak ceiling, carved in quatrefoil, is still preserved. There is a place of worship for Wesleyan Methodists. A charity school for twenty poor girls was built by the Rev. Mr. Swainson, the present vicar, who pays a mistress for teaching them reading, sewing, and knitting, and also the master of a similar school for boys, for teaching them to write. The charity school for boys, held in the town-hall, is supported partly by the vicar, and partly by subscription; in both these schools articles of clothing are given in reward for good conduct.

Clun Hospital, dedicated to the Holy Trinity, was founded in 1614, and endowed, by Henry Howard, Earl of Northampton, with tithes in the several parishes of Church-Stoke in Montgomeryshire, Knighton in Radnorshire, and Weston in the county of Salop, producing a revenue of £1000 per annum; the establishment consists of fourteen poor brethren, and a warden, who reads morning and evening prayers daily; the brethren have each a house and garden, and receive £2 per month; in addition to this, the warden receives a gratuity at the discretion of the Earl of Powis, as lord of the honour, by whom he is appointed; they occasionally wear a silver badge, on which is the crest of the founder: the management is vested in the vicar of Clun, the bailiff of Bishop's Castle, and the rector of Hopesay; the Bishop of Hereford is visitor. The buildings comprise a quadrangle of forty yards in length, and the same in breadth, in one angle of which is a very neat chapel, and behind the buildings is a large extent of additional garden-ground, apportioned to the several houses. Within a quarter of a mile to the north-west of the town is a single intrenchment, said to have been raised by Owen Glyndwr, as a shelter for his troops during their attack on the castle; and within half a mile to the south is Walls Castle, the station from which it was battered. About two miles and a half to the north-east is the camp of Ostorius, the station occupied by that general in his last battle with Caractacus; and about five miles to the south-east, near the confluence of the rivers Clun and Teind, and within a mile of Walcott, the seat of the Earl of Powis, are the Caer, or Bury Ditches, the station of the British hero, and the scene of his last effort against the Roman power: the camp, which is of an elliptic form, comprehends an area of from three to four acres, on the summit of a very lofty eminence, commanding an extensive view of the surrounding country; the steep acclivities are defended by a triple intrenchment of amazing strength, which, though overgrown with turf, is still in a state of entire preservation; the ramparts, varying from fifty to sixty feet in height, are constructed of stones and earth firmly compacted, and the intermediate spaces are from twenty to thirty yards in breadth: this fortification, evidently a work of prodigious labour, is one of the most interesting in the country, and, under the care of the Earl of Powis, is preserved with a due regard to its historical importance. In making a turnpike road from Clun to Bishop's Castle, in 1780, several cannon balls were found.

CLUNBURY, a parish in the hundred of PURSLOW, county of SALOP, comprising the townships of Clunbury with Obley, and Clunton with Rempton, and containing 800 inhabitants, of which number, 359 are in the township of Clunbury with Obley, 6½ miles (S. S. E.) from Bishop's Castle. The living is a perpetual curacy, in the archdeaconry of Salop, and diocese of Hereford, endowed with £800 private benefaction, and £1800 parliamentary grant, and in the patronage of the Earl of Powis. The church is dedicated to St. Swithin. Here is a small endowed school.

CLUNGUNFORD, a parish in the hundred of PURSLOW, county of SALOP, 9 miles (S. E. by S.) from Bishop's Castle, containing, with the extra-parochial liberty of Dinmore, 486 inhabitants. The living is a rectory, in the archdeaconry of Salop, and diocese of Hereford, rated in the king's books at £16, and in the patronage of John Rocke, Esq. The church is dedicated to St. Cuthbert. The trustees of Francis Walker, in 1682, founded and endowed a charity school, the income of which, increased by sundry other bequests in 1725 and 1776, amounts to £46 per annum, for teaching the children of Clungunford, and the adjoining township of Broome, in the parish of Hopesay; about eighty are educated upon this foundation. The river Clun and the Roman Watling-street intersect this parish from north to south. In the neighbourhood are two tumuli, and limestone in abundance.

CLUNTON, a joint township with Rempton, in the parish of CLUNBURY, hundred of PURSLOW, county of SALOP, 5½ miles (S. by E.) from Bishop's Castle, containing, with Rempton, 441 inhabitants.

CLUTTON, a township in the parish of FARNDON, higher division of the hundred of BROXTON, county palatine of CHESTER, 10 miles (S. S. E.) from Chester, containing 96 inhabitants.

CLUTTON, a parish in the hundred of CHEW, county of SOMERSET, 3¼ miles (S. by E.) from Pensford, containing 1206 inhabitants. The living is a rectory, in the archdeaconry of Bath, and diocese of Bath and Wells, rated in the king's books at £9. 4. 2., and in the patronage of the Earl of Upper Ossory. The church is dedicated to St. Augustine. There are places of worship for Methodists and Independents. In 1728, the trustees of a legacy of £200, bequeathed by Mr. Perry, and of another of £98 by Mr. Adams, vested the money in land, and founded a free school, the income of which is £20 per annum, for teaching and apprenticing ten children of the parish. A school is carried on in a large room built upon the church lands, from a charge upon which, and the interest arising from some charities at Chewstoke and Clutton, all the poor boys of the parish are taught upon the National system. There are extensive coal-mines worked in the parish. In the vicinity are vestiges of an ancient fortification, called Highbury, where British weapons have been found; which, from the discovery of some foundations, seems to have been surrounded with walls.

CLYTHA, a chapelry in that part of the parish of LLANARTH which is in the lower division of the hundred of RAGLAND, county of MONMOUTH, 5¾ miles (N. by W.) from Usk, containing 376 inhabitants. On the summit of an eminence at the extremity of the Clytha hills is a small encampment, which retains marks of having been strongly fortified.

COAL-ASTON, a township in the parish of DRONFIELD, hundred of SCARSDALE, county of DERBY, ¾ of a mile (N. by E.) from Dronfield, containing 304 inhabitants. Here is a school with a trifling endowment.

COALEY, a parish in the upper division of the hundred of BERKELEY, county of GLOUCESTER, 3¾ miles (N. N. E.) from Dursley, containing 1117 inhabitants. The living is a discharged vicarage, in the archdeaconry and diocese of Gloucester, rated in the king's books at £8. 2. 2., and in the patronage of the Crown. The church is dedicated to St. Bartholomew. There is a place of worship for Wesleyan Methodists.

COANWOOD (EAST), a township in the parish of HALTWHISTLE, western division of TINDALE ward, county of NORTHUMBERLAND, 5 miles (S.) from Haltwhistle, containing 165 inhabitants.

COASTAMOOR, a township in the parish of HEIGHINGTON, south-eastern division of DARLINGTON ward, county palatine of DURHAM, 5½ miles (N. N. W.) from Darlington, containing 12 inhabitants. This township consists of only two farms.

COATES, a parish in the hundred of CROWTHORNE and MINETY, county of GLOUCESTER, 3¾ miles (W. by S.) from Cirencester, containing 309 inhabitants. The living is a rectory, in the archdeaconry and diocese of Gloucester, rated in the king's books at £9. 6. 8., and in the patronage of William Tombs, Esq. The church is dedicated to St. Matthew. The Thames and Severn canal is crossed by a bridge on the line of the old Ackmanway, as it passes through this parish. In the neighbourhood is Trewsbury castle, also vestiges of a Roman encampment.

COATES, a township in the parish of PRESTWOULD, eastern division of the hundred of GOSCOTE, county of LEICESTER, 1½ mile (N. E. by E.) from Loughborough, containing 74 inhabitants.

COATES, a parish in the western division of the wapentake of ASLACOE, parts of LINDSEY, county of LINCOLN, 9½ miles (N. W. by N.) from Lincoln, containing 45 inhabitants. The living is a discharged vicarage, in the archdeaconry of Stow, and diocese of Lincoln, rated in the king's books at £3. 16. 8., endowed with £600 royal bounty, and £200 parliamentary grant; it is held by sequestration. The church is dedicated to St. Edith.

COATES, a parish in the hundred of BURY, rape of ARUNDEL, county of SUSSEX, 4 miles (S. E. by S.) from Petworth, containing 41 inhabitants. The living is consolidated with the rectory of Burton, in the archdeaconry and diocese of Chichester. The church is in the early style of English architecture. The Rother, or Arundel, navigation traces the northern boundary of this parish.

COATES, a township in the parish of BARNOLDWICK, eastern division of the wapentake of STAINCLIFFE and EWCROSS, West riding of the county of YORK, 8 miles (W. S. W.) from Skipton, containing 97 inhabitants.

COATES (GREAT), a parish in the wapentake of BRADLEY-HAVERSTOE, parts of LINDSEY, county of LINCOLN, 4 miles (W.) from Great Grimsby, containing 237 inhabitants. The living is a rectory, in the archdeaconry and diocese of Lincoln, rated in the king's books at £11. 10. 10., and in the patronage of Sir R. Sutton, Bart. The church is dedicated to St. Nicholas.

COATES (LITTLE), a parish in the wapentake of BRADLEY-HAVERSTOE, parts of LINDSEY, county of LINCOLN, 3¼ miles (W. by S.) from Great Grimsby, containing 47 inhabitants. The living is a discharged vicarage, in the archdeaconry and diocese of Lincoln, rated in the king's books at £4. 18. 4., endowed with £200 private benefaction, and £200 royal bounty, and in the patronage of the Master and Fellows of Trinity College, Cambridge. The church is dedicated to St. Nicholas.

COATES (NORTH), a parish in the wapentake of BRADLEY-HAVERSTOE, parts of LINDSEY, county of LINCOLN, 10 miles (N. N. E.) from Louth, containing 154 inhabitants. The living is a rectory, in the archdeaconry and diocese of Lincoln, rated in the king's books at £12. 10. 10., and in the patronage of the King, as Duke of Lancaster. The church is dedicated to St. Nicholas.

COATHAM (EAST), a hamlet in the parish of KIRKLEATHAM, eastern division of the liberty of LANGBAURGH, North riding of the county of YORK, 6¾ miles (N. by W.) from Guilsborough. The population is returned with the parish. East Coatham is a small fishing village near the mouth of the Tees, much resorted to for sea-bathing: the sands in the neighbourhood are well adapted for the promenade or the carriage; and the prospect is often rendered pleasing from the number of trading vessels sailing in the offing. There are several machines for sea-bathing, and accommodation can also be afforded for taking warm baths. The village consists of about seventy houses. A school for forty boys is supported by an income of £47, arising principally from the revenues of Kirkleatham school; and £12. 12. is also paid from the same fund to a schoolmistress, for teaching younger children.

COTHAM-MUNDEVILLE, a township in that part of the parish of HAUGHTON le SKERNE which is in the south-western division of STOCKTON ward, county palatine of DURHAM, 4½ miles (N.) from Darlington, containing 184 inhabitants.

COATHILL, a joint township with Cumwhinton, in that part of the parish of WETHERAL which is in CUMBERLAND ward, county of CUMBERLAND, 5½ miles (S. E.) from Carlisle. The population is returned with Cumwhinton. Here is a quarry of gypsum.

COATON, a hamlet in that part of the parish of RAVENSTHORPE which is in the hundred of GUILSBOROUGH, county of NORTHAMPTON, 9½ miles (N. W. by N.) from Northampton, containing 120 inhabitants.

COATON-CLAY, a parish in the hundred of GUILSBOROUGH, county of NORTHAMPTON, 6¼ miles (E. by N.) from Rugby, containing 90 inhabitants. The living is a rectory, in the archdeaconry of Northampton, and diocese of Peterborough, rated in the king's books at £10, and in the patronage of the Rev. Thomas Smith. The church is dedicated to St. Andrew.

COAT-YARDS, or COAL-YARDS, a township in the parish of NETHER WITTON, western division of MORPETH ward, county of NORTHUMBERLAND, 6 miles (S. by E.) from Rothbury, containing 14 inhabitants.

COBHAM, a parish (formerly a market town) in the hundred of SHAMWELL, lathe of AYLESFORD, county of KENT, 5 miles (W.) from Rochester, containing 646 inhabitants. The living is a vicarage not in charge, in the archdeaconry and diocese of Rochester, endowed with £600 parliamentary grant, and in the patronage of the Earl of Darnley. The church, dedicated to St. Mary Magdalene, has parapets and an embattled tower, which, with the north porch, and a fine basin, or water drain, under a richly canopied niche, are in the later style of English architecture; but the chancel and some other portions of the fabric are of early date: it contains some very ancient monuments and brasses to the noble families of Cobham and Brooke. In 1362, John, Lord Cobham, made it collegiate, erecting the college contiguous to the churchyard, and amply endowing it for five chaplains, which number he afterwards increased to eleven: at the suppression it was valued at £128. 1. 2., and was confirmed by the crown to George, Lord Cobham, whose executors, in 1598, built upon its site the present college, and endowed it with the former possessions, for the maintenance of twenty poor persons. It is a neat quadrangular building of stone, comprising part of the ancient structure, and containing a spacious hall, and an apartment with a garden for each inmate: in the 39th of Elizabeth the incorporated wardens of Rochester bridge were declared to be perpetual presidents of "the New College," in whose successors the government is solely vested. The village stands upon an eminence, and is supplied with water from works constructed for the purpose by the family of Cobham: it had formerly a weekly market on Monday, and a fair on St. Mary Magdalene's day, granted to John, Lord Cobham, in the 41st of Edward III.; the fair is held annually on the 2nd of August, but the market has been long disused. The course of the Roman Watling-street is visible in the parish; and on a hill in Cobham Park is a splendid mausoleum, in the Doric style, erected by the Earl of Darnley, at an expense of £15,000.

COBHAM, a parish in the second division of the hundred of ELMBRIDGE, county of SURREY, 10 miles (N. E.) from Guildford, and 20 (S. W.) from London, containing 1340 inhabitants. The living is a discharged vicarage, in the archdeaconry of Surrey, and diocese of Winchester, rated in the king's books at £9. 17. 11., endowed with £200 private benefaction, and £400 royal bounty, and in the patronage of H. P. Weston Esq. The church, dedicated to St. Andrew, is partly in the early, and partly in the decorated, style of English architecture, and has lately received an addition of two hundred and ten sittings, of which one hundred and ten are free, the Incorporated Society for the enlargement of churches and chapels having granted £100 towards defraying the expense. In pursuance of the will of Henry Smith, a charity school was founded in 1642, with an endowment in land, which was augmented, in 1680, by a bequest from Henry Smith, together producing £15 per annum, for teaching and apprenticing children; in 1722, two trifling donations were left to this charity, by Gainsford Thomas and Mary Hope, increasing the annual income to £17. 5. The river Mole flows through this parish: it abounds with pike, trout, perch, &c., and its banks are adorned with many elegant villas. Fairs for horses and sheep are held on March 17th and December 11th. In the vicinity are some copper and iron works. A little westward is a barrow, near which a considerable number of Roman coins of the Lower Empire was ploughed up, in 1772.

COBRIDGE, a hamlet partly in the parish of BURSLEM, and partly in that of STOKE upon TRENT, northern division of the hundred of PIREHILL, county of STAFFORD, 2¼ miles (N. N. E.) from Newcastle under Line. The population is returned partly with the township of Shelton, and partly with the parish of Stoke upon Trent. The village contains several manufactories for china and earthenware, and there is an abundant supply of coal in the neighbourhood. Here are a chapel and a school belonging to Roman Catholics, and a meeting-house for the New Connexion of Methodists. School-rooms were erected by subscription in 1766, for children of both sexes, which are let at trifling rents to a master and a mistress, but there are no free pupils. The ancient vill of Rushton, which has been superseded by Cobridge, is described in Domesday-book under the name Risetone. It was given by Henry de Audley to Hulton abbey, to which it became the grange, and after the dissolution was a demesne; for which reason, and as having belonged to Cistercian monks, it is exempt from the payment of tithes, and has never been assessed to the church rate; for all other purposes (the repairing of highways excepted) it is considered a member of Burslem.

COCKEN, a township in the parish of HOUGHTON le SPRING, northern division of EASINGTON ward, county palatine of DURHAM, 4 miles (N. N. E.) from Durham, containing 59 inhabitants. Cocken was separated from the constablery of West Rainton, and made a distinct constablery, in 1726. It is situated on the river Wear: coal is obtained in the neighbourhood. The manor-house, which is surrounded by beautiful scenery, became, at the commencement of the present century, the residence of a convent of nuns of the order of St. Theresa, who were driven by the revolutionists from their former settlement at Lier in Flanders, by which they were deprived of all their property in that country.

COCKERHAM, a parish in the hundred of LONSDALE, south of the sands, county palatine of LANCASTER, comprising the chapelry of Ellel, and the township of Cockerham, and containing 2624 inhabitants, of which number, 773 are in the township of Cockerham, 5½ miles (N. N. W.) from Garstang. The living is a discharged vicarage, in the archdeaconry of Richmond, and diocese of Chester, rated in the king's books at £10. 16. 8., and in the patronage of the Lords of Cockerham manor. There is a school-house at the north-east corner of the churchyard, erected by subscription in 1681, with an endowment in land, producing £15 per annum: about eighteen children are taught upon this foundation. A fair for pedlary is held on Easter-Monday. Courts leet and baron are attached to the manor.

COCKERINGTON (ST. LEONARD), a parish in the Wold division of the hundred of LOUTH-ESKE, parts of LINDSEY, county of LINCOLN, 4¼ miles (E. N. E.) from Louth, containing 186 inhabitants. The living is a discharged vicarage, in the archdeaconry and diocese of Lincoln, rated in the king's books at £5. 1. 5½., endowed with £400 royal bounty, and in the patronage of the Bishop of Lincoln. The church is dedicated to St. Leonard.

COCKERINGTON (ST. MARY), a parish in the Wold division of the hundred of LOUTH-ESKE, parts of LINDSEY, county of LINCOLN, 4¾ miles (N. E.) from Louth, containing 206 inhabitants. The living is a perpetual curacy, annexed to that of Alvingham, in the archdeaconry and diocese of Lincoln. The church is dedicated to St. Mary.

COCKERMOUTH, an unincorporated borough, market town, and parochial chapelry, in the parish of BRIGHAM, ALLERDALE ward above Derwent, county of CUMBERLAND, 25 miles (S. W.) from Carlisle, and 305 (N. W. by N.) from London, containing 3790 inhabitants. The name is derived from the situation of the town at the *mouth* of the river *Cocker*, which here unites with the Derwent. The barony, now called the Honour of Cockermouth, was assigned, soon after the Conquest, by William de Meschines to Waldeof, Lord of Allerdale, son of Gospatrick, Earl of Northumberland, from whom it descended to Fitz-Duncan, nephew to Malcolm, King of Scotland; and his co-heiresses, one of whom married into the family of Albemarle, and the other into that of Lucy, shared it in moieties. On the death of William de Fortibus, Earl of Albemarle, and his countess Isabel, without issue, their moiety of the castle and honour lapsed to the crown, and was bestowed upon Piers Gavestone, in whose possession it continued for some time; but, in 1323, it was granted by Edward II. to Anthony, Lord Lucy, proprietor of the other moiety by inheritance. After his death, which took place in 1369, Maud, his sister and heiress, settled the castle and honour on her second husband, Percy, Earl of Northumberland. They next passed to Charles Seymour, Duke of Somerset, by marriage with the only daughter of Joceline, the last earl of Northumberland, and ultimately, in like manner, came into the possession of the earls of Egremont, the present earl being lord paramount of the honour.

The castle, formerly the baronial seat of the lords of Allerdale, stands on the edge of a precipitous eminence, on the northern side of the town, opposite the confluence of the two rivers; it is supposed to have been erected by Waldeof, soon after the Conquest (although the remains are not, apparently, of earlier date than the fourteenth century), and to have been constructed with the materials of an older castle, called Papcastle, the former residence of Waldeof, a Roman fortress, about a mile and a half distant, on the other side of the Derwent; it was originally an extensive and very strong building, and was garrisoned for the royal cause, but reduced and dismantled in 1648, after a month's siege, by the parliamentarians, who are stated to have destroyed part of the town also. The only perfect and habitable parts are the gate-house, with two rooms adjoining, and the court-house at the eastern angle of the area: underneath the ruins of the great tower is a spacious vault, thirty feet square, the roof of which is formed of groined and intersecting arches, and supported by an octagonal central pillar, with pilasters at the corners and sides; this vault, from being called Mary Kirk, is supposed to have been the chapel, dedicated to St. Mary. On each side of the entrance gateway is a dungeon, capable of containing fifty prisoners, who probably entered through a small aperture visible in the corner of the arch. Mary, Queen of Scots, after her escape from the castle of Dunbar, rested some time at Cockermouth, on her way from Workington to Carlisle, and was also hospitably entertained at Hutton Hall, then belonging to the Fletchers. In 1647, the plague swept off nearly two hundred of the inhabitants.

The town is situated in a narrow valley, amid scenery richly diversified with hill and dale, wood and water: the Derwent flows on the northern side of it, and is crossed by a handsome stone bridge of two arches, connecting the town with the hamlet of Goat, two hundred and seventy feet in length, and completed in 1822, at an expense to the county of £3000: on the margin of this river is an agreeable promenade, about one mile in length, terminated at one extremity by lofty well-wooded cliffs, and at the other by the ruins of the castle, and the elevated bowling green. The river Cocker divides the town into two parts, and is crossed by a bridge of one arch, rebuilt on a wider and improved plan in 1828, at an expense of £2600. The streets, with the exception of the High-street, a fine broad street, are but indifferently paved, and not lighted: there is an ample supply of water from the rivers Derwent and Cocker, from some streams which flow through the town, and from pumps connected with most of the dwellings: the houses are in general built of stone, roofed with blue slate, and of respectable appearance. Considerable improvement has lately been effected, particularly in the erection and widening of the bridges, and in the market-place, above the bridge over the Cocker. There is a small subscription library; also a parochial library over the grammar school, containing upwards of five hundred volumes, founded by Dr. Bray and his associates, to which Dr. Keene, Bishop of Chester, was a great benefactor.

Cockermouth is a town of considerable trading importance, enjoying, within a very limited distance, the advantage of three sea-ports. A great trade is carried on in cotton, linen, and woollen articles, for which there are some extensive manufactories; also in the tanning and dressing of leather, and the manufacture of hats, stockings, paper, &c.: in the vicinity are considerable coal mines. The moor, containing about twelve hundred acres, was enclosed and divided under an act obtained in 1813. The market is held on Monday, at which a considerable quantity of grain is pitched in the market-place; and there is an inferior market on Saturday, for provisions, &c. Fairs for cattle are held on every alternate Wednesday from the beginning of May till the end of September; and there is a great fair for horses and horned cattle on the 10th of October: there are also two great annual fairs, or statutes, for hiring servants, on the Mondays at Whitsuntide and Martinmas. This town has no separate jurisdiction: the chief officer is a bailiff, who is chosen annually at Michaelmas, at the court leet for the manor, from among the burghers, by a jury of burghers, which is a special jury appointed for regulating the internal affairs of the town; he acts as clerk of the market, but exercises no magisterial functions, and has no local authority, the county magistrates having jurisdiction in the borough, and holding a petty session every Monday, to transact the business of the borough and regulate the police. The steward of the manor holds a court every three weeks, for the recovery of debts under 40*s*., and a court leet at Michaelmas and Easter: he also, aided by commissioners appointed for the government of the several manors comprised within the honour, holds a court of dimissions at Christmas, in the castle. The Epiphany quarter session for the county is held here in January. The moot-hall, formerly an old dilapidated structure inconveniently situated in the market-place, has been recently rebuilt in a more commodious manner, and on a more eligible site. There is a small house of correction in St. Helen's street. In the 23rd of Edward I. this borough returned members to parliament, but from that date till the 16th of Charles I. the elective franchise was suspended; it was then restored by a resolution of the House of Commons, determining, "That the borough of Cockermouth be restored to the ancient privilege of sending burgesses to parliament;" and has from that period regularly returned two members, who are elected by the burgage tenants, about three hundred in number, chiefly in the interest of the Earl of Lonsdale: the bailiff is the returning officer. The election of knights for the shire takes place here.

The living is a perpetual curacy, in the archdeaconry of Richmond, and diocese of Chester, endowed with £800 private benefaction, £200 royal bounty, and £1900 parliamentary grant, and in the patronage of the Earl of Lonsdale. The old church, or chapel, erected in the reign of Edward III., was taken down, with the exception of the tower, and the present edifice of freestone built by means of a brief in 1711, and dedicated to All Saints: it was enlarged and beautified in 1825, towards defraying the expense of which the Incorporated Society for building new churches contributed £175; it contains one thousand free sittings. There are places of worship for the Society of Friends, Independents, and Wesleyan Methodists. The free grammar school was founded in 1676, by Lord Wharton, Sir Richard Graham, and others; it was further endowed with £10 annually, charged upon the great tithes, and paid by the Earl of Lonsdale, who also contributes £10 annually as a gratuity, the whole income being not more than £24 per annum; the children pay a quarterage. A charity school, founded in 1784, is supported by voluntary contributions, and contains at present sixty-three scholars. There is a free school, supported in a similar manner, for thirty girls, who are admitted from the age of eight to fourteen, and taught reading, writing, and needlework. In 1785, a Sunday school was founded by subscription, for the instruction of one hundred children. In 1760, the Rev. Thomas Leathes gave a house in Kirk-gate, and the interest of £100, to which his daughter added £50, for the maintenance of six poor widows, or unmarried women, above sixty years of age. The interest of about £800, the amount of several benefactions, is distributed by the church-wardens among the poor inhabitants weekly, in bread and money. A dispensary, established in 1785, is liberally supported; and there are four friendly societies, comprising in the whole about five hundred members. In addition to these, there are different benevolent societies, established at various periods. A savings bank was opened in May 1818, which, in November 1827, contained deposits to the amount of £17,167.15.5. The hills on each side of the Derwent are interesting to the naturalist, consisting of calcareous stone, almost entirely composed of shells of the genus *ammoniæ*. On the north side of the town is a tumulus, called Toot-hill; and one mile westward are the rampart and ditch of a fort, or encampment, triangular in form, and nearly seven hundred and fifty feet in circumference. The Honour of Cockermouth confers the title of baron on the family of Wyndham, Earls of Egremont.

COCKERSAND-ABBEY, an extra-parochial liberty, in the hundred of LONSDALE, south of the sands, county palatine of LANCASTER, 7 miles (S. W. by S.) from Lancaster. This was originally a hermitage, then an hospital dedicated to St. Mary, for a prior and several infirm brethren: it was endowed by William of Lancaster, in the time of Henry III., and was subordinate to the abbey of Leicester; but about the year 1196 it was changed into an abbey of Premonstratensian canons: by favour of the crown it survived, for a short time, the general dissolution, when it consisted of twenty-one religious and fifty-seven servants, and was valued at £282. 7. 7. per annum: the principal relic is an octagonal chapter-house.

COCKERTON, a township in the parish of DARLINGTON, south-eastern division of DARLINGTON ward, county palatine of DURHAM, 1¼ mile (N.W. by N.) from Darlington, containing 469 inhabitants. Cockerton is a considerable village, the inhabitants of which are chiefly employed in the manufacture of linen. A schoolroom was erected by subscription in 1825, with an endowment of £5 per annum, by the trustees of the late Lord Crewe: divine service is performed in it every Wednesday evening, by the curate of the parish. A meeting-house for Wesleyan Methodists was built in 1823.

COCKEY, a chapelry in the parish of MIDDLETON, hundred of SALFORD, county palatine of LANCASTER, 3¼ miles (W. by S.) from Bury. The population is returned with the parish. The living is a perpetual curacy, in the archdeaconry and diocese of Chester, endowed with £200 private benefaction, £600 royal bounty, and £600 parliamentary grant, and in the patronage of the Rector of Middleton. In the village of Cockey-Moor there is a place of worship for Unitarians.

COCKFIELD, a parish in the south-western division of DARLINGTON ward, county palatine of DURHAM, 8½ miles (N. E.) from Barnard-Castle, containing 533 inhabitants. The living is a discharged rectory, with the perpetual curacy of Staindrop annexed, in the archdeaconry and diocese of Durham, rated in the king's books at £9. 18., and in the patronage of the Marquis of Cleveland. A colliery was wrought so early as 1375, since which period coal has been constantly obtained here. On Cockfield Fell are traces of ancient intrenchments.

COCKFIELD, a parish in the hundred of BABERGH, county of SUFFOLK, 4¼ miles (N. by W.) from Lavenham, containing 897 inhabitants. The living is a rectory, in the archdeaconry of Sudbury, and diocese of Norwich, rated in the king's books at £30, and in the patronage of the Master and Fellows of St. John's College, Cambridge. The church, dedicated to St. Peter, has a large and handsome tower.

COCKING, a parish in the hundred of EASEBOURNE, rape of CHICHESTER, county of SUSSEX, 2½ miles (S.) from Midhurst, containing 340 inhabitants. The living is a vicarage, in the archdeaconry and diocese of Chichester, rated in the king's books at £13. 6. 8., and in the patronage of the Bishop of Chichester. The church is in the early style of English architecture, with some later additions. In 1730, Stephen Challen bequeathed certain messuages in trust, for the education of twenty children of this parish and the parish of Oving; but the rental is now only £4 a year, a moiety of which is paid to a schoolmistress for teaching four children of this parish to read.

COCKINGTON, a parish (formerly a market town) in the hundred of HAYTOR, county of DEVON, 2½ miles (W.) from Torbay, containing 280 inhabitants. The living is a perpetual curacy, with that of Tor-Moham annexed, in the archdeaconry of Totness, and diocese of Exeter, endowed with £200 private benefaction, £400 royal bounty, and £1900 parliamentary grant, and in the patronage of the Rev. Roger Mallock. The church contains an octagonal font and a wooden screen. Queen Elizabeth leased the rectory of Tor-Moham, and the church of Cockington, to Sir George Cary, who, in 1609, erected almshouses here for seven poor persons, with an endowment of £30 per annum, paid out of the rental of Cockington and Chilston manors: the old buildings were taken down in 1810, and new ones erected on a more convenient site. Cockington is said to have received the privilege of a market and a fair about the year 1297.

COCKLAW, a township in the parish of ST. JOHN LEE, southern division of TINDALE ward, county of NORTHUMBERLAND, 4½ miles (N. by E.) from Hexham, containing 199 inhabitants. It extends from the North Tyne along the eastern side of the Erring-bourn. Here are remains of an ancient castle of the Erringtons, called Cocklaw Tower.

COCKLE-PARK, a township in the parish of HEBBURN, western division of MORPETH ward, county of NORTHUMBERLAND, 4 miles (N.) from Morpeth, containing 57 inhabitants. Cockle Park tower stands on an eminence, and was formerly a strong hold of the family of Bertram, and their tenants, who fled to it, with their cattle, &c., in time of danger: the south part was destroyed by lightning several centuries ago.

COCKLEY-CLEY, a parish in the southern division of the hundred of GREENHOE, county of NORFOLK, 4 miles (S. W. by S.) from Swaffham, containing 238 inhabitants. The living is a discharged rectory, with the vicarage of St. Peter consolidated, in the archdeaconry of Norfolk, and diocese of Norwich, rated in the king's books at £8. 17. 1., and in the patronage of R. Dashwood, Esq. The church is dedicated to All Saints. There was formerly a church, dedicated to St. Peter, which has been demolished; and a chapel, which was dedicated to St. Mary, has been converted into the parsonage-house.

COCKSHUT, a chapelry in the parish of ELLESMERE, hundred of PIMHILL, county of SALOP, 4¼ miles (S. E. by S.) from Ellesmere, with which the population is returned. The living is a perpetual curacy, annexed to the vicarage of Ellesmere, in the archdeaconry of Salop, and diocese of Lichfield and Coventry, endowed with £200 private benefaction, and £1000 royal bounty. The chapel is dedicated to St. Helen.

COCKTHORPE, a parish in the northern division of the hundred of GREENHOE, county of NORFOLK, 5½ miles (W. by S.) from Clay, containing 32 inhabitants. The living is a rectory, annexed, with the vicarage of Little Langham, and the perpetual curacy of Glandford, to the rectory of Blakeney, in the archdeaconry and diocese of Norwich, rated in the king's books at £5. The church is dedicated to All Saints. At this inconsiderable place, now comprising only three or four houses, Admirals Sir Cloudesley Shovel, Sir John Narborough, and Sir Christopher Mynnes, were born.

COCKTHORPE, a chapelry in the parish of DUCKLINGTON, hundred of BAMPTON, county of OXFORD, 2¾ miles (S. by E.) from Witney. The population is returned with the parish. The chapel is dedicated to St. Mary.

CODDENHAM, a parish in the hundred of BOSMERE and CLAYDON, county of SUFFOLK, 3¾ miles (E. S. E.) from Needham-Market, containing 847 inhabitants. The living is a vicarage, with the perpetual curacy of Crowfield annexed, in the archdeaconry of Suffolk, and diocese of Norwich, rated in the king's books at £12. 0. 5., and in the patronage of the Rev. J. Longe. The church, dedicated to St. Mary, was granted in the reign of Henry II. for the founding of a Cistercian nunnery, but whether the design was carried into effect or not is unknown. There is a place of worship for Wesleyan Methodists. In 1758, Lady Catherine Gardenau erected a commodious school-house, with an endowment in land now producing a rental of £120 per annum, for teaching fifteen boys and fifteen girls of the parish: at present, twenty-five of each sex are partly clothed, and taught upon the National system. A fair is held on the 2nd of October.

CODDINGTON, a parish in the higher division of the hundred of BROXTON, county palatine of CHESTER, comprising the townships of Aldersey, Chowley, and Coddington, and containing 346 inhabitants, of which number, 130 are in the township of Coddington, 6 miles (N. N. W.) from Malpas. The living is a discharged rectory, in the archdeaconry and diocese of Chester, rated in the king's books at £5. 4. 2., endowed with £200 private benefaction, and £200 royal bounty, and in the patronage of the Dean and Chapter of Chester. The church, dedicated to St. Mary, is an ancient structure, with a wooden belfry, supposed to have been founded in the eleventh century; it was granted with the living to Chester abbey, by Fitz-Hugh, and was one of the few possessions remaining to the abbey that were confirmed to the Dean and Chapter by Queen Elizabeth. Coddington is thought to have been a habitation of the Britons, which seems probable from the artificial embankments and tumuli discernible in the vicinity.

CODDINGTON, a parish in the hundred of RADLOW, county of HEREFORD, 7 miles (N.) from Ledbury, containing 184 inhabitants. The living is a discharged rectory, in the archdeaconry and diocese of Hereford, rated in the king's books at £4. 18. 4., and in the patronage of the Bishop of Hereford. The church is dedicated to All Saints.

CODDINGTON, a parish in the southern division of the wapentake of NEWARK, county of NOTTINGHAM, 2¼ miles (E. by N.) from Newark, containing 374 inhabitants. The living is a perpetual curacy, annexed to the vicarage of East Stoke, in the archdeaconry of Nottingham, and diocese of York. The church, dedicated to All Saints, is a small structure, principally in the early English and decorated styles of architecture.

CODFORD (ST. MARY), a parish in the hundred of HEYTESBURY, county of WILTS, 4 miles (E. S. E.) from Heytesbury, containing 258 inhabitants. The living is a rectory, in the archdeaconry and diocese of Salisbury, rated in the king's books at £18, and in the patronage of the President and Fellows of St. John's College, Oxford.

CODFORD (ST. PETER), a parish in the hundred of HEYTESBURY, county of WILTS, 3½ miles (E. S. E.) from Heytesbury, containing, with the township of Ashton-Gifford, 347 inhabitants. The living is a rectory, in the archdeaconry and diocese of Salisbury, rated in the king's books at £17. 15., and in the patronage of the Master and Fellows of Pembroke College, Oxford.

CODICOTE, a parish in the hundred of CASHIO, or liberty of ST. ALBANS, though locally in the hundred of Broadwater, county of HERTFORD, 2 miles (N. N. W.) from Welwyn, containing 795 inhabitants. The living is a discharged vicarage, in the archdeaconry of St. Albans, and diocese of London, rated in the king's books at £7. 5. 10., and in the patronage of the Bishop of Ely. At the general dissolution, the advowson was granted to the Bishop of Ely, one of whose successors gave an augmentation of £30 per annum out of the great tithes. The church, dedicated to St Giles, is a small building, with a chapel attached, and has an embattled tower surmounted by a spire. There is a place of worship for Baptists. A market on Friday, and a fair on St. James' day, were granted by Henry III.; they are both disused, but a small market, for the sale of straw-plat, is held on Thursday, and a pleasure fair on Whit-Monday. Thirty girls are clothed and educated at the joint expense of the Hon. Mrs. Leesom and Mrs. Staple, and there is a charitable fund, out of which one boy is apprenticed every seven years. On Codicote heath are the remains of a Roman fortification.

CODNOR, a joint township with Loscow, in the parish of HEANOR, hundred of MORLESTON and LITCHURCH, county of DERBY, 4¾ miles (S. by E.) from Alfreton, containing, with Loscow, 1329 inhabitants.

CODNOR-CASTLE, an extra-parochial district, in the hundred of MORLESTON and LITCHURCH, county of DERBY, 5 miles (S. S.E.) from Alfreton, containing, with the Park liberty, 693 inhabitants. Here was an ancient castle belonging to the noble family of Grey, styled lords Grey of Codnor, the last of whom, Henry, a philosopher and alchymist in the reign of Edward IV., obtained a license to practise the transmutation of metals. The

Cromford canal passes on the east side of this district, where there are extensive iron-works, and a railway on the south communicates with the collieries in the neighbourhood.

CODRINGTON, a tything in the parish of WAPLEY, lower division of the hundred of GRUMBALD'S ASH, county of GLOUCESTER, 3 miles (S. by W.) from Chipping-Sodbury. The population is returned with the parish.

CODSALL, a parish in the southern division of the hundred of SEISDON, county of STAFFORD, 5 miles (N.W.) from Wolverhampton, containing 659 inhabitants. The living is a perpetual curacy, in the jurisdiction of the royal peculiar court of Tettenhall, endowed with £600 private benefaction, £400 royal bounty, and £1500 parliamentary grant, and in the patronage of Sir J. Wrottesley, Bart. The church is dedicated to St. Nicholas. A school was founded in 1716, by Dorothy Derby, with an endowment increased, by a subsequent bequest from Margaret Somerford, in 1730, to £3. 3. per annum, for teaching children of this parish.

COEDKERNEW, a parish in the upper division of the hundred of WENTLLOOG, county of MONMOUTH, 4¼ miles (S.S.W.) from Newport, containing 128 inhabitants. The living is a perpetual curacy, united to that of St. Bride's Wentlloog, in the archdeaconry and diocese of Llandaff, endowed with £800 royal bounty. The church is dedicated to All Saints.

COFFINSWELL, a parish in the hundred of HAYTOR, county of DEVON, 3 miles (S.E. by E.) from Newton-Bushell, containing 255 inhabitants. The living is a perpetual curacy, annexed to the vicarage of St. Mary Church, in the peculiar jurisdiction and patronage of the Dean and Chapter of Exeter. The church is dedicated to St. Bartholomew.

COGDEAN, a hamlet in the parish of STURMINSTER-MARSHALL, hundred of COGDEAN, Shaston (East) division of the county of DORSET, 2 miles (S.W. by S.) from Wimborne-Minster. The population is returned with the parish. This place gave name to the hundred.

COGENHOE, a parish in the hundred of WYMERSLEY, county of NORTHAMPTON, 5¼ miles (E.) from Northampton, containing 255 inhabitants. The living is a rectory, in the archdeaconry of Northampton, and diocese of Peterborough, rated in the king's books at £17, and in the patronage of the Rev. E. Watkins. The church, dedicated to St. Peter, is small, and partly in the early style of English architecture, but a considerable portion of it is of later date. The village is situated upon an eminence, at the foot of which runs the river Nen, separating this parish from that of Ecton. Limestone is obtained here.

COGGES, a parish in the hundred of WOOTTON, county of OXFORD, 1¼ mile (S.E. by E.) from Witney, containing 452 inhabitants. The living is a vicarage not in charge, in the archdeaconry and diocese of Oxford, endowed with £15 per annum private benefaction, and £600 royal bounty, and in the patronage of the Provost and Fellows of Eton College. The church is dedicated to St. Mary. In 1695, William Blake, Esq. bequeathed land producing about £50 per annum, out of which £6 is paid for teaching twenty-four children at High Cogges, £6 for a like purpose at Newland in Cogges, and £20 for clothes, books, and other charitable uses. Some of the family of Arsic, who were lords of the barony, founded here an Alien priory of Black monks, subordinate to the abbey of Fescamp in Normandy; after the dissolution of foreign cells its possessions were granted by Henry VI. toward the endowment of Eton College.

COGGESHALL (GREAT), a market town and parish in the Witham division of the hundred of LEXDEN, county of ESSEX, 16 miles (N.E.) from Chelmsford, and 45 (N.E.) from London, containing 2896 inhabitants. This place is supposed by some antiquaries to have been the Roman station *Ad Ansam*, and by others the *Canonium* of Antoninus, with the distance of which latter from *Cæsaromagus* its situation precisely corresponds. Numerous vestiges of Roman antiquity have been discovered here, among which were a silver coin of Domitian, a glass lamp, an urn containing ashes and bones, and some Roman pottery of red earth, which were found in an arched vault constructed of Roman brick; and at Westfield, about three quarters of a mile from the town, was discovered, by the plough, a large brazen pot, enclosing a smaller one of earth, within which was an urn wrapped in stuff like velvet, containing bones and fragments of bones enveloped in silk. The present town appears to have risen from the establishment of an abbey, in 1242, by King Stephen and his queen Matilda, for monks of the Cistercian order, and dedicated to the Blessed Virgin, to the abbot and monks of which King John granted several privileges, among which, probably, was the power of life and death, as inferred from the ancient name of one of the streets, which is still by some called Gallows-street. Henry III. gave them a grant of free warren, a weekly market, and an annual fair for eight days. The revenue of the abbey, at the dissolution, was £298. 8.: the remains, which exhibit specimens of early English architecture, are now occupied as a farm-house; the exterior has some lancet-shaped windows in good preservation, and in the interior are some good windows and vaulted roofs plainly groined. Near the abbey is an ancient bridge of three arches, built by King Stephen, over a canal cut for conveying water from the river to the monastery, which has been recently repaired. The town is situated near the river Blackwater, and consists of several narrow streets, indifferently paved, lighted by subscription, and amply supplied with water from springs in the neighbourhood, the principal of which is called Peter's well. The manufacture of baize and serge, which was formerly extensive, is still continued on a more confined scale; but the principal branch of trade at present is silk-weaving, which has been established within the last ten years. The market is on Thursday: a fair is held on Whit-Tuesday, for cattle and pedlary.

Coggeshall anciently comprised the parishes of Great and Little Coggeshall, now consolidated: in the latter, which is now only a hamlet to the former, were two churches, built by the monks; one for their own use, which has been entirely demolished, and the other for a parochial church, of which the remains have been converted into a barn. The living is a vicarage, in the archdeaconry of Colchester, and diocese of London, rated in the king's books at £11. 3. 4., and in the patronage of Peter Du Cane, Esq. The church, dedicated to St. Peter, is a spacious handsome structure in the later style of English architecture, with a large square tower; the aisles are embattled, and strengthened with empannelled buttresses. There are places of worship for Baptists, the Society of Friends, Independents, and Wesleyan Methodists. A school, under the direction of the Master and Fellows of Pembroke Hall, Cambridge, who appoint the master, was founded in 1636, by Sir Robert Hitcham, Knt., who bequeathed to them, in trust, lands at Framlingham and Saxted, in the county of Suffolk, producing £300 per annum, for educating from thirty to forty boys, with whom a premium of £10 each is given for apprenticing them: about £50 per annum is paid to Levington, and £9 to Nacton; the remainder is distributed among the poor. A Lancasterian school for boys was established here in 1811, and another for girls in 1826. There are six unendowed almshouses; and among the charitable bequests for the benefit of the poor is one of £70 per annum, called wood money, given by Thomas Pycocke, Esq., in 1580.

COGGESHALL (LITTLE), a hamlet in the parish of GREAT COGGESHALL, hundred of WITHAM, county of ESSEX, ½ a mile (S.) from Great Coggeshall, containing 362 inhabitants. This was anciently a distinct parish, within the limits of which stood the abbey described in the account of Great Coggeshall, together with a church erected by the abbot for himself and the monks, who agreed to build a chapel also for their servants and tenants.

COGSHALL, a township in that part of the parish of GREAT BUDWORTH which is in the hundred of BUCKLOW, county palatine of CHESTER, 3½ miles (N.N.W.) from Northwich, containing 110 inhabitants. This place consists of only two farms. Tradition says that on a steep sandy eminence, called Butter hill, the market people from the hundred of Wirrall deposited their butter and other produce when the plague excluded them from the market-place at Chester.

COKER (EAST), a parish in the hundred of HOUNDSBOROUGH, BERWICK, and COKER, county of SOMERSET, 2½ miles (S.S.W.) from Yeovil, containing, with the hamlet of North Coker, 1103 inhabitants. The living is a vicarage, in the archdeaconry of Wells, and diocese of Bath and Wells, rated in the king's books at £12. 6. 3., and in the patronage of the Dean and Chapter of Exeter. The church, dedicated to St. Michael, is a neat cruciform edifice, with a tower rising from the intersection: near it are almshouses endowed with an estate at Whitchurch in Dorsetshire, for the maintenance of twelve poor widows. In a field in this parish the foundations of a Roman building were discovered in 1753; one of the rooms had a beautiful tesselated pavement, representing persons lying on a couch, beneath which were found a hypocaust, several coffins, burnt bones, &c. Dampier, the celebrated circumnavigator, was born here, in 1652.

COKER (NORTH), a hamlet (formerly a chapelry) in the parish of EAST COKER, hundred of HOUNDSBOROUGH, BERWICK, and COKER, county of SOMERSET, 2 miles (S.S.W.) from Yeovil. The population is returned with the parish. The chapel has been demolished, and a workhouse occupies its site

COKER (WEST), a parish in the hundred of HOUNDSBOROUGH, BERWICK, and COKER, county of SOMERSET, 3½ miles (S.W. by W.) from Yeovil, containing 928 inhabitants. The living is a rectory, in the archdeaconry of Wells, and diocese of Bath and Wells, rated in the king's books at £12. 19. 7., and in the patronage of Joseph Jekyll, Esq. The church is dedicated to St. Martin. Almshouses for five poor persons were founded about 1719, pursuant to the will of William Ruddock, who endowed them with a rent-charge on his estates of 10*s*. per week.

COLAN, a parish in the hundred of PYDER, county of CORNWALL, 3½ miles (S.W. by W.) from St. Columb-Major, containing 259 inhabitants. The living is a discharged vicarage, in the archdeaconry of Cornwall, and diocese of Exeter, rated in the king's books at £6. 13. 4., and in the patronage of the Bishop of Exeter. The church is dedicated to St. Colan. There is a place of worship for Wesleyan Methodists. Here is a charity school. In this parish is a celebrated spring, called Our Lady of Nantz' well.

COLBOURNE, a township in that part of the parish of CATTERICK which is in the eastern division of the wapentake of HANG, North riding of the county of YORK, 2½ miles (S.E. by E.) from Richmond, containing 133 inhabitants.

COLBY, a parish in the southern division of the hundred of ERPINGHAM, county of NORFOLK, 3¼ miles (N.E. by N.) from Aylsham, containing 267 inhabitants. The living is a discharged rectory, in the archdeaconry and diocese of Norwich, rated in the king's books at £8. 15. 10., and in the patronage of Lord Suffield. The church is dedicated to St. Giles.

COLBY, a township in the parish of ST. LAWRENCE, APPLEBY, EAST ward, county of WESTMORLAND, 1½ mile (W. by N.) from Appleby, containing 141 inhabitants. The village is situated on an eminence, at the base of which flows the river Eden.

Arms.

COLCHESTER, a borough and market town having separate jurisdiction, locally in the Colchester division of the hundred of Lexden, county of ESSEX, 22 miles (N.E. by E.) from Chelmsford, and 51 (N.E. by E.) from London, containing 12,005 inhabitants, and, including the parishes of Bere-Church, Greenstead, Lexden, and Mile-End, which are within the liberties, 14,016. The name of this place, which by some antiquaries is supposed to have been the *Camalodunum* of the Romans, is derived from its situation on the river Colne, and its history may be traced to a period of very remote antiquity. It was by the Britons called *Caer Colun*, and appears to have been a town of considerable importance prior to the invasion of the Romans, who, according to Tacitus and other historians, having, under the conduct of Claudius, subdued the Trinobantes and taken possession of this town, garrisoned it with the second, ninth, and fourteenth legions, styled by him the conquerors of Britain, and named the place *Colonia*. Claudius having reduced the adjacent country to a Roman province, appointed Plautius his proprætor, and returned in triumph to Rome. After his departure, Boadicea, queen of the Iceni, taking advantage of the absence of part of the Roman legions, attacked *Camalodunum*, which, after a feeble resistance, she entirely demolished. According to Pliny, and the evidence of Roman coins and other ancient inscriptions, it appears to have been soon rebuilt with increased splendour, and to have been adorned with public edifices, a temple to Claudius, a triumphal arch, and a statue to the Goddess of Victory. Constantine the Great is traditionally said to have been born in this city, which continued to flourish as a primary station of the Romans till their final departure from Britain. The Saxons, by whom it was afterwards occupied, gave it the name of *Colne-ceaster,* and it retained its consequence as a place of strength for a considerable time, but began to decline in proportion as London rose into importance. On the irruption of the Danes it became the residence of that people, who, by treaty with Alfred, were established in the city and country adjacent; but commencing their barbarous system of plunder and devastation, Edward the Elder took the town by assault, and, putting them all to the sword, re-peopled it with West Saxons: according to the Saxon Chronicles he repaired the walls in 922, at which time he is stated to have erected the castle, now falling to decay, but the remains of that edifice are evidently of Norman character. Colchester was a considerable town at the time of the Norman survey, but suffered greatly in the wars of the succeeding reigns. During the turbulent reign of John, Saher de Quincy, Earl of Winchester, having assembled an army of foreigners, laid siege to the city in 1215, but, on the approach of the barons, who were advancing from London to its relief, he drew off his forces and retired to Bury St. Edmund's; he afterwards got possession of the town, and, having plundered it, left a garrison in the castle, which, having been invested by the king, was compelled to surrender: it was subsequently besieged and taken by the troops of Prince Louis, whom the barons had invited into England to their assistance, and who, thinking the opportunity favourable for conquest, kept possession of it for himself, and hoisted the banner of France upon its walls; but the barons having submitted to their new sovereign, Henry III., retook the castle from the prince, and expelled him from the kingdom. In the reign of Edward III., the town contributed five ships and one hundred and seventy mariners towards the naval armament for the blockade of Calais. The inhabitants, during the attempt to raise Lady Jane Grey to the throne, steadfastly adhered to the interests of Mary, whose cause they supported with so much zeal, that very soon after her accession, that queen visited the town, for the express purpose of testifying her gratitude: her majesty was received with every public demonstration of joy, and, on her departure, was presented with a silver cup, and £20 in gold. During her reign many of the Protestant inhabitants were put to death on account of their religious tenets. In 1648, the town was besieged by the parliamentary forces under Fairfax: after a close blockade for eleven weeks, during which period it was gallantly defended by the Earl of Norwich, Lord Capel, Sir Charles Lucas, and Sir George Lisle, the garrison, reduced to the extremity of want and suffering, surrendered to Fairfax, when Sir Charles Lucas and Sir George Lisle were shot under the castle walls.

The town is built on the summit and northern acclivity of an eminence rising gently from the river Colne, over which are three bridges, and occupies a quadrilateral area enclosed by the ancient walls, within which the houses to the south and south-east are irregularly disposed: the streets are spacious, and the High-street contains many excellent houses: the town is well paved, lighted with gas, and supplied with water by an engine worked by steam. The theatre, a neat and commodious edifice erected in 1812, is opened annually by the Norwich company of comedians. A literary and philosophical society was established in 1820, the members of which in rotation deliver a lecture at their monthly meetings; attached to it is a museum of shells, fossils, and natural curiosities. A botanical society was instituted in 1823: there is a medical society, established in 1774; and there are a private subscription library, and a musical society of amateurs. The barracks, with a park of artillery, were capable of accommodating ten thousand troops, but since the conclusion of the war they have been taken down. The woollen manufacture appears to have been carried on so early as the reign of Edward III., but the weaving of baizes was probably introduced by the Flemings in the reign of Elizabeth, and at that time employed a considerable number of the inhabitants: the baize was subject to certain regulations prescribed by the Baize-hall; but the trade has been transferred to other towns, and is here succeeded by a large silk-manufactory. The oyster fishery on the river Colne, granted to the free burgesses by Richard I., confirmed by subsequent charters, and for the preservation of which courts of admiralty were usually held on the borough walls, affords employment to a great number of men, and some hundreds of smacks are engaged in conveying to London the oysters dredged from the river, for which there is a very great demand, especially for those of Pyfleet, which are found in a small creek, and are remarkable for their goodness and flavour: the river is navigable for vessels of two hundred tons' burden to the Hythe, where there are a spacious quay and a custom-house. The market days are Saturday and Wednesday, the former being the principal, on which corn and cattle are sold: a market for meat, fish, and vegetables, is held daily on the north side of the High-street, where a convenient and spacious market-place has been constructed. The corn-exchange, a handsome building supported on columns, was erected a few years since, of which the lower part is appropriated to the corn market, and the upper part occupied as offices by the Essex and Suffolk Insurance Society. The fairs are on July 5th and the following day, and July 23rd and the two following days, for cattle; and October 20th for cattle, and the three following days for general merchandise.

Corporate Seal.

Obverse. Reverse.

The borough was first incorporated in 1089, by charter of Richard I., who conferred on the inhabitants many valuable privileges, which were confirmed by succeeding sovereigns, and extended by Henry V. By its charter, which, having been forfeited on several occasions, was renewed by George III. in 1818, the government is vested in a mayor, high steward, recorder, chamberlain, twelve aldermen, eighteen assistants, and eighteen common council-men, aided by a town-clerk, two coroners, a water-bailiff, four serjeants at mace, and other officers. The mayor, recorder, the late mayor, and four of the aldermen, are justices of the peace for the borough, the freedom of which is inherited by birth, and acquired by servitude within the borough, and by presentation. The corporation hold quarterly courts of session for the borough and liberties, together extending over sixteen parishes, and two courts of pleas for the recovery of debts to any amount, the jurisdiction of which, by Edward IV., was extended to the adjoining parishes of Bere-Church, Greenstead, Lexden, and Mile-End: these courts are held at stated periods; one, called the Law Hundred, for actions against free burgesses, is held on Monday; and the other, called the Foreign Court, for actions against foreigners, or non-freemen, is held on Thursday: the petty sessions for the division are also held in this town, every Saturday. The moot-hall is an ancient edifice, originally erected by Eudo, dapifer, or steward, to Henry I., and containing the hall and the exchequer-chamber, in part of which the records are deposited; over these is the council-chamber, a spacious room in which the public business of the corporation is transacted; underneath is the town gaol. The borough first exercised the elective franchise in the 23rd of Edward I., since which time it has, with occasional intermissions, returned two members to parliament: the right of election is vested in the free burgesses generally not receiving alms, whose number is about one thousand four hundred, but may be augmented at the will of the corporation in common council assembled: the mayor is the returning officer.

Colchester is, but upon very disputed authority, supposed to have been the seat of a diocese in the early period of Christianity in Britain; Henry VIII. made it the seat of a suffragan bishop, and two bishops were successively consecrated. The town comprises the parishes of All Saints, St. James, St. Martin, St. Mary at the Walls, St. Nicholas, St. Peter, St. Runwald, and the Holy Trinity, within the walls, and the parishes of St. Botolph, St. Giles, St. Leonard, or the Hythe, and St. Mary Magdalene, without the walls, all in the archdeaconry of Colchester, and diocese of London. The living of All Saints' is a rectory not in charge, endowed with £400 private benefaction, and £400 royal bounty, and in the patronage of the Master and Fellows of Balliol College, Oxford: the church was erected in the year 1309, near the east gate of the monastery of Grey friars, which had been founded by Robert Fitz-Walter in that year. The living of St. James' is a discharged rectory, rated in the king's books at £11. 10., endowed with £400 private benefaction, £200 royal bounty, and £500 parliamentary grant, and in the patronage of the Crown: the church is a spacious structure built prior to the reign of Edward II.; it has a fine altar-piece representing the Adoration of the Shepherds. The living of St. Martin's is a discharged rectory, rated in the king's books at £6. 13. 4., endowed with £800 royal bounty, and £800 parliamentary grant. The Bishop of London, for that turn, was patron in 1825: the church was much damaged during the siege of the town in 1648; the steeple, which was built with Roman bricks, is now in a ruinous state. The living of St. Mary's at the Walls is a rectory, rated in the king's books at £10, and in the patronage of the Bishop of London: the church was rebuilt in 1713, with the exception of the ancient steeple, which, becoming ruinous, was repaired in 1729. The living of St. Nicholas' is a discharged rectory, rated in the king's books at £10, endowed with £800 royal bounty, and £600 parliamentary grant, and in the patronage of the Master and Fellows of Balliol College, Oxford: the church is ancient; the tower some years since fell down upon the nave and the chancel, the latter of which is still in a ruinous state. The chapel of St. Helen, in this parish, rebuilt by Eudo in 1076, was lately used as a place of worship by the Society of Friends, and is now used for a Sunday school. The living of St. Peter's is a discharged vicarage, rated in the king's books at £10, endowed with £600 private benefaction, and £600 royal bounty, and in the patronage of John Thornton, Esq.: the church, an ancient structure, was erected before the Conquest, and in Domesday-book is noticed as the only church in Colchester; it was extensively repaired and modernised in 1758, when the tower at the west end was erected, and was some time since greatly beautified at an expense of £3000; the altar-piece is embellished with a fine painting by Halls, the subject of which is the raising of Jairus' daughter. The living of St. Runwald's is a discharged rectory, rated in the king's books at £7. 13. 4., endowed with £600 private benefaction, and £1000 royal bounty, and in the patronage of C. Round, Esq.: the church, which is small, was erected about the close of the thirteenth century. The living of the parish of the Holy Trinity is a discharged rectory, rated in the king's books at £6. 13. 4., endowed with £200 private benefaction, and £200 royal bounty, and in the patronage of the Master and Fellows of Balliol College, Oxford: the church was erected in the year 1349. The living of St. Botolph's is a perpetual curacy, united to the rectory of All Saints': the church has been in ruins since the siege in 1648, exhibiting indications of its original magnificence, and of the antiquity of its style, which appears to have been the early Norman, and of the same date as the neighbouring priory; it was built with bricks of extraordinary hardness, supposed to have been taken from the Roman station: in the interior are several plain massive piers and circular arches, and part of the arches of the triforium is remaining: the west front has a central doorway, on the south side of which is a deeply receding Norman arch; over these are two series of intersecting arches. The living of St. Giles' is a discharged rectory, rated in the king's books at £30, endowed with £200 private benefaction, and £200 royal bounty, and in the patronage of the Devisees of the Rev. J. W. Morgan: the church, a very ancient structure, and formerly greatly dilapidated, has lately undergone a thorough repair. The living of St. Leonard's is a discharged rectory, rated in the king's books at £10, endowed with £200 private benefaction, £400 royal bounty, and £200 parliamentary grant, and in the patronage of the Master and Fellows of Balliol College, Oxford: the church is a spacious structure in good preservation. The living of St. Mary Magdalene's is a rectory, rated in the king's books at £11, and in the patronage of the Crown: the church, which is small, is pleasantly situated on Magdalene Green. On the site of the chapel of St. Anne, which stood in the parish of St. James, and was formerly a hermitage, a barn has been erected, part of the chapel having been incorporated with the building. There are two places of worship for Baptists, two for Independents, and one each for the Society of Friends, Wesleyan Methodists, and Unitarians.

The free grammar school was founded and endowed by the corporation, to whom Queen Elizabeth, in the twenty-sixth year of her reign, granted certain ecclesiastical revenues for that purpose: the present income is £117 per annum; the number of scholars on the foundation is generally from thirty to forty. A scholarship for boys educated at this school was founded in St. John's College, Cambridge, by the Rev. Robert Lewes, in 1620: two scholarships, founded in the same college by the Rev. Ambrose Gilbert, in 1642, revert to this school on failure of applicants of the surnames of Gilbert, or Torbington; and four founded in Pembroke College, Cambridge, by Mr. Ralph Scrivener, in 1601, on failure of boys from the grammar school at Ipswich. Dr. Harsnet, Archbishop of York, received the rudiments of his education in this institution. Two charity schools, for the education of fifty-five boys and thirty girls, who are also clothed, were established in 1708; towards the purchase of the school-house Mr. Samuel Rush, in 1711, gave £100, and £50 was given for the same purpose by his widow. Mr. William Naggs, in 1747, gave a freehold messuage and twenty-five acres of land, in the county of Essex, to certain trustees, for the better maintenance of these schools, to which seven other benefactions have been added. The National school constitutes an extension of the original plan of the charity school: the number of children educated is about four hundred, of whom one hundred and forty-eight are clothed. A Lancasterian school for children of both sexes is supported by subscription; there are schools also supported by the several dissenting congregations. A school for the children of members of the Society of Friends was established in 1816, and endowed with a sum of money and an extensive library by John Kendall, to which has been added a legacy by the late Francis Freshfield, Esq.: the election of the master is vested in eight trustees, subject to the sanction of the society at their quarterly meeting; in consideration of the dividend arising from the legacies, he instructs gratuitously six day-scholars, sons of members of the society, or, in failure of such, sons of necessitous parents of sober conduct, in addition to the boarding and education of the pupils for whom he is regularly paid. Mr. Arthur Winsley, in 1726, founded and endowed almshouses for twelve poor men, to which six others have since been added; each of the almsmen receives seven shillings and sixpence per week, and a chaldron of coal annually. Mr. John Wenock, in 1679, erected and endowed almshouses for six aged widows, which number, by a bequest from Mrs. Bardfield, has since been increased to fourteen. Ralph Finch also, in 1552, founded and endowed almshouses for four poor persons. Those erected by Lady Mary D'Arcy, and others situated in Eld-lane, having no endowment, are occupied by persons requiring parochial relief: there are also several charitable bequests for distribution among the poor. The Essex and Colchester general hospital, completed in 1820, and supported by subscription, is a neat building of white brick, situated on the south side of the London road, comprising a front receding curvilinearly from the rear at both angles, so as to present the appearance of wings.

Of the monastic establishments anciently existing here, the hospital, originally founded at the command of Henry I., for a master and leprous brethren, and dedicated to St. Mary Magdalene, by Eudo, who had been a principal officer of the household to William the Conqueror and his two sons, of which, at the dissolution, the revenue was £11, was refounded in 1610 by James I., for three poor brethren and a master, who is always the clergyman of the parish. Of the other ancient establishments, the principal was St. John's abbey, founded in the reign of Henry I. by the same Eudo, for monks of the Benedictine order, the revenue of which, at the dissolution, was £523. 17.; of this only the gateway is remaining, a handsome structure in the later style of English architecture, and, consequently, either rebuilt since the foundation of the abbey, or a subsequent addition to it. To the south of the town was a monastery of Augustine canons, founded in the reign of Henry I., and dedicated to St. Julian and St. Botolph, by Ernulphus, who afterwards became prior: at the dissolution its revenue was £113. 12. 8.: the only remains are its stately church, now in ruins, which was previously the parish church of St. Botolph. Without the walls was an hospital, or priory, of Crutched friars, an order introduced into England about the year 1244, the revenue of which, at the dissolution, was £7. 7. 8. The priory of Franciscan, or Grey, friars was founded, in 1309, by Robert Fitz-Walter, the only probable remains of which are the parish church of All Saints. Of the walls by which the city was surrounded, and in consideration of repairing which, Richard II. is recorded to have exempted the burgesses from sending members to three of his parliaments, only some detached portions are remaining: they were strengthened by bastions, and defended on the west by an ancient fort of Roman construction, the remaining arches of which are built with Roman bricks; and the north and west sides, where the town was most exposed, were protected by deep intrenchments: the entrance to the town was by four principal gates and three posterns, which have been mostly demolished. The ruins of the castle occupy an elevated site to the north-east of the town; the form is quadrilateral, and the walls of the keep, twelve feet in thickness, are almost entire: the building is of flint, stone, and Roman brick intermixed, and is supposed to have been originally erected by the Romans, though subsequently repaired by Edward the Elder; the solidity of the structure has frustrated repeated attempts to demolish it for the sake of the materials. The town and environs abound with ancient relics, among which are, a quantity of Roman bricks in several of the churches and other buildings, tesselated pavements, sepulchral urns, statues, lamps, rings, coins, medals, and almost every species of Roman antiquities. William Gilbert, physician to Elizabeth and James I., and author of a work on the qualities of the loadstone, entitled "*De Magnete*;" and Dr. Samuel Harsnett, Archbishop of York, were natives of this place. The late Right Hon. Charles Abbot, Speaker of the House of Commons, who was born in the neighbourhood, was elevated to the peerage, June 3rd, 1817, by the title of Baron Colchester, which is now enjoyed by his son.

COLDCOATS, a township in the parish of PONTELAND, western division of CASTLE ward, county of NORTHUMBERLAND, 9¼ miles (N. W.) from Newcastle, containing 45 inhabitants.

COLD-DUNGHILLS, an extra-parochial district, adjoining the parish of ST. CLEMENT, borough of IPSWICH, county of SUFFOLK. The population is returned partly with the parish of St. Clement, and partly with that of St. Margaret.

COLD-MARTIN, a township in the parish of CHATTON, eastern division of GLENDALE ward, county of NORTHUMBERLAND, 1 mile (E. by S.) from Wooler. The population is returned with the parish.

COLDMEECE, a township in the parish of ECCLESHALL, northern division of the hundred of PIREHILL, county of STAFFORD, containing 61 inhabitants.

COLDRED, a parish in the hundred of BEWSBOROUGH, lathe of ST. AUGUSTINE, county of KENT, 5 miles (N.W. by N.) from Dover, containing 125 inhabitants. The living is a vicarage, annexed to that of Sibbertswold, in the archdeaconry and diocese of Canterbury, rated in the king's books at £6. 2. 6. The church, dedicated to St. Pancras, is surrounded by a trench, enclosing about two acres, with an artificial mount on the northern side, which tradition ascribes to Ceoldred, King of Mercia, from whom the parish is named, who fought a battle near this spot, in 694, with Ina, King of the West Saxons; it is, however, probably of Roman origin, various relics of that people having been discovered on the site.

COLDSBORNE, a parish in the hundred of RAPSGATE, county of GLOUCESTER, 7½ miles (N. by W.) from Cirencester, containing 245 inhabitants. The living is a discharged rectory, in the archdeaconry and diocese of Gloucester, rated in the king's books at £5. 6. 10½., endowed with £400 private benefaction, £200 royal bounty, and £300 parliamentary grant, and in the patronage of F. Eyre and J. Elwes, Esqrs. The church is dedicated to St. James.

COLDWALTHAM, county of SUSSEX.—See WALTHAM (COLD).

COLDWELL, a township in the parish of KIRKWHELPINGTON, north-eastern division of TINDALE ward, county of NORTHUMBERLAND, 14 miles (W.) from Morpeth, containing 7 inhabitants. It consists of a large sheep farm and one house.

COLE, a tything in the parish of PITCOMB, hundred of BRUTON, county of SOMERSET, 2 miles (S. W.) from Bruton. The population is returned with the parish.

COLE, a joint tything with West Park, in the parish and hundred of MALMESBURY, county of WILTS, 1¾ mile (S.S.E.) from Malmesbury, containing, with West Park, 37 inhabitants.

COLEBROKE, a parish in the hundred of CREDITON, county of DEVON, 4½ miles (W.) from Crediton, containing 875 inhabitants. The living is a vicarage, in the peculiar jurisdiction and patronage of the Dean and Chapter of Exeter, rated in the king's books at £20. The church is dedicated to St. Mary. There are ruins of chapels at Coplestone, Hooke, Horwell, Land's End, and Wolmstone, in this parish; and near the latter is a well, dedicated to the Virgin Mary.

COLEBY, a parish in the higher division of the wapentake of BOOTHBY-GRAFFO, parts of KESTEVEN, county of LINCOLN, 6¾ miles (S.) from Lincoln, containing 322 inhabitants. The living is a discharged vicarage, in the archdeaconry and diocese of Lincoln, rated in the king's books at £6. 12. 1., endowed with £200 private benefaction, and £200 royal bounty, and in the patronage of the Provost and Fellows of Oriel College, Oxford. The church, dedicated to All Saints, has a tower, the lower part of which, with the south door and nave, exhibits fine specimens of Norman architecture; the rest of the building is in the early English style, with later additions, particularly the upper portion of the tower and spire.

COLEDALE, a joint township with Portingscale, in that part of the parish of CROSTHWAITE which is in ALLERDALE ward above Derwent, county of CUMBERLAND, 3 miles (W.) from Keswick, containing 294 inhabitants.

COLEFORD, a market town and chapelry in the parish of NEWLAND, hundred of ST. BRIAVELLS, county of GLOUCESTER, 19 miles (W. S. W.) from Gloucester, and 124 (W. by N.) from London, containing 1804 inhabitants. This place, which is pleasantly situated on the verge of the county, next Monmouthshire, obtained the grant of a market from James I. During the parliamentary war, a skirmish took place previously to the siege of Gloucester, between a party of the royalists commanded by Lord Herbert and the parliamentary forces under Col. Barrow, in which the market-house was destroyed, and Sir Richard Lawdy, major-general of South Wales, and several officers, were killed: at a subsequent period, during the same war, the ancient chapel was demolished. The town consists principally of one spacious street, in which is the market-place; the houses are in general neat and well built; the environs are pleasant, and in some points beautifully picturesque; and in the vicinity are several elegant mansions and handsome villas. The inhabitants are principally employed in agriculture, and many of the labouring class are occupied in the extensive iron-works in the neighbourhood; a great quantity of apples is cultivated for cider. The market is on Friday: fairs are held on June 20th for wool, and November 24th for cattle and cheese. The market-house was rebuilt in 1679, towards defraying the expense of which Charles II. contributed £50. The living is a perpetual curacy, in the archdeaconry of Hereford, and diocese of Gloucester, endowed with £200 private benefaction, £600 royal bounty, and £1200 parliamentary grant, and in the patronage of the Bishop of Gloucester. The chapel, rebuilt in the reign of Queen Anne, who contributed £300 towards its erection, is dedicated to All Saints. There is a place of worship for Particular Baptists. Vestiges of King Offa's dyke may be distinctly traced in some parts of the town.

COLEFORD, a hamlet in the parish and hundred of KILMERSDON, county of SOMERSET, 6¼ miles (W. by N.) from Frome. The population is returned with the parish. A chapel of ease is in progress of erection here.

COLEMORE, a parish in the hundred of BARTON-STACEY, Andover division, though locally in the hundred of Selborne, Alton (North) division, of the county of SOUTHAMPTON, 5¾ miles (S. by W.) from

Alton, containing 123 inhabitants. The living is a rectory, in the archdeaconry and diocese of Winchester, rated in the king's books at £22. 9. 4½., and in the patronage of the Rev. James Cookson. There is a chapel of ease at Prior's Dean. The greater part of this parish lay formerly in the forest of Wolmer, where a considerable quantity of charcoal was made; and from the mere, or boundary, to the westward, it had its former name, Colemere, by which it is noticed in Domesday-book and other ancient records. John Graves, the astronomer and mathematician, was born here, in 1602.

COLE-ORTON, a parish in the western division of the hundred of Goscote, county of Leicester, 2 miles (E.) from Ashby de la Zouch, containing 883 inhabitants. The living is a rectory, in the archdeaconry of Leicester, and diocese of Lincoln, rated in the king's books at £10. 6. 0½., and in the patronage of Sir G. H. Beaumont, Bart. The church, dedicated to St. Mary, has a tower and spire, with some of its portions in the decorated style of architecture. Extensive collieries have been wrought here for a great length of time. Thomas, Viscount Beaumont, in 1701, bequeathed a rent-charge of £90 for the erection of a school-house, and an hospital for six poor widows, who have each a separate house and garden.

COLERIDGE, a parish in the hundred of North Tawton with Winkley, county of Devon, 5 miles (S. by E.) from Chulmleigh, containing 632 inhabitants. The living is a discharged vicarage, in the archdeaconry of Barnstaple, and diocese of Exeter, rated in the king's books at £7. 8. 9., and in the patronage of the Bishop of Exeter. The church, dedicated to St. Mary, contains an ancient wooden screen. A charity school is chiefly supported by the Hon. Newton Fellowes.

COLERNE, a parish in the hundred of Chippenham, county of Wilts, 7 miles (W. by S.) from Chippenham, containing 888 inhabitants. The living is a discharged vicarage, in the archdeaconry of Wilts, and diocese of Salisbury, rated in the king's books at £9. 16.: there is also a sinecure rectory, rated at £16. 11. 10½., and annexed to the Wardenship of New College, Oxford, the Warden being patron of the vicarage. The church is dedicated to St. John the Baptist. There is a meeting-house for Independents. Colerne, or, as it was formerly called, Coldhorn, derives its name from its bleak situation upon the summit of one of the highest hills in the vicinity of Bath: the tower of the church and a large brewery are conspicuous objects for miles round the country, which is singularly intersected by deep combes in all directions. About sixty years ago the village was destroyed by fire, and rebuilt with stone, without much regard to uniformity. The neighbourhood was the scene of many sanguinary conflicts between the Saxons and the Danes: the Wansdyke touches the parish in two places, constituting the boundary of the county. On Colerne down is an ancient double intrenchment, called Northwood Camp; and in the park is another ancient fortification. There is a spring holding a quantity of lime in solution, the water of which incrusts, and gives the appearance of a petrifaction to any thing upon which it falls.

COLESHILL, a chapelry partly in the parish of Amersham, hundred of Dacorum, county of Hertford, and partly in the parish of Beaconsfield, hundred of Burnham, county of Buckingham, 1¾ mile (S. by W.) from Amersham, containing 492 inhabitants. Since the demolition of the chapel the inhabitants have attended divine service at the parish church of Amersham; they still pay their own poor and highway rates. Here are manufactories for lace and common red earthenware. Edmund Waller, the lyric poet, was born here; he represented the borough of Amersham in three parliaments, and died in 1687.

COLESHILL, a parish partly in the hundred of Highworth, Cricklade, and Staple, county of Wilts, but chiefly in the hundred of Shrivenham, county of Berks, 3¾ miles (W. S. W.) from Great Farringdon, containing, with the tything of Lynt, 324 inhabitants. The living is a vicarage, in the archdeaconry of Berks, and diocese of Salisbury, rated in the king's books at £17. 11. 8., and in the patronage of the Earl of Radnor. The church, dedicated to All Saints, has, at the west end, an embattled tower with pinnacles, and contains some handsome monuments; the eastern window of the chancel exhibits some fine stained glass, representing the Nativity, presented by the Earl of Radnor, in 1787. Lord Simon Digby, in 1694, gave £500 for teaching and apprenticing poor children of the parish, and for other charitable purposes: in the same year, Offalia Rawlins made a donation of £100, with similar directions for its use; and, in 1706, the Rev. John Pinsent gave an estate, producing about £15 per annum, for apprenticing the children of such of the inhabitants of Coleshill and Great Coxwell as had never received parochial relief, with £5 to each. This parish derives its name from the elevated situation of the village above the river Cole, which forms the western boundary, and gives the title of baron to the Earl of Radnor.

COLESHILL, a market town and parish in the Birmingham division of the hundred of Hemlingford, county of Warwick, 18 miles (N. by W.) from Warwick, and 103½ (N. W.) from London, containing 1760 inhabitants. This place derives its name from being situated on the acclivity and summit of an eminence rising gradually from the south bank of the river Cole, over which is a neat brick bridge of six arches leading into the town: it consists principally of one long street, from the centre of which a shorter street of considerable width diverges towards the church, and affords a convenient area for the market-place, in which is a portico of brick. The houses are in general well built, and several of them are handsome and of modern date; the inhabitants are amply supplied with water from springs, and from the rivers Thame and Blyth, which run through the parish. The market is on Wednesday: the fairs are on the first Monday in January for cattle and sheep, on Shrove-Monday for horses, which is the principal fair, May 6th, the first Monday in July, and the first Monday after September 25th, all for cattle. The county magistrates occasionally hold here a petty session for the division; two constables, two headboroughs, two clerks of the market, and two pinners, are chosen at the court of the lord of the manor, held in October: the bishop holds his annual visitation in August, and a court of probate quarterly. Part of the workhouse is appropriated to the confinement of malefactors previously to their committal.

The living is a vicarage, in the archdeaconry of Coventry, and diocese of Lichfield and Coventry, rated in the king's books at £10. 18. 6½., and in the patronage of Earl Digby. The church, dedicated to

St. Peter and St. Paul, is an ancient and spacious structure, in the decorated style of English architecture, with a lofty tower surmounted by an octagonal spire, crocketed at the angles, part of which was taken down and rebuilt in the same style in 1812: it contains an ancient Norman font, with an effigy of St. Peter, and a representation of the Crucifixion, rudely sculptured on it. There is a place of worship for Wesleyan Methodists. The free grammar school was founded in the reign of James I., by Lord Digby, who, in conjunction with some of the parishioners, endowed it with seventy acres of land and several houses in the parish; the management is vested in thirteen trustees, of whom Earl Digby nominates three: it comprises two schoolrooms, one exclusively for classical literature, the other for English, writing, and arithmetic: the head-master's salary is £80 per annum, with a house and seven or eight acres of land; the second master has a salary of £70 per annum; both are nominated by the trustees, and their appointment is confirmed by Earl Digby. A charity school was endowed, in 1694, by Simon, Lord Digby, with £500, which has been vested in the purchase of a house and land, for clothing and instructing poor girls, and apprenticing poor children; and under the same trust is a small endowment for the distribution of bibles and prayer-books. There are two almshouses for widows; and a house, which has lately been rebuilt, is endowed with land for the accommodation of poor travellers for one night, with a small hospital attached to it for those that are sick. About a mile to the east of the town is Maxstoke castle, in a high state of preservation, and inhabited by a descendant of the founder: the buildings occupy an irregular quadrilateral area, enclosed by an embattled wall, and defended at the angles by octagonal towers: the entrance on the east side is under a finely groined arch in the gateway tower, which is square and strengthened with angular turrets, and was formerly defended by a portcullis. About a mile and a half to the south-east of the castle are the remains of Maxstoke priory, consisting of part of the walls and the entrance gateway; the conventual buildings have been converted into farm-offices: the castle and the remains of the priory are in the decorated style of English architecture, and appear to be of the same date with the church, to which it is said there was a subterraneous passage leading from the priory. Coleshill gives the title of viscount to Earl Digby.

COLEY, a chapelry in the parish of HALIFAX, wapentake of MORLEY, West riding of the county of YORK, 3 miles (N. E. by E.) from Halifax, with which the population is returned. The living is a perpetual curacy, in the archdeaconry and diocese of York, endowed with £200 private benefaction, £200 royal bounty, and £1400 parliamentary grant, and in the patronage of the Vicar of Halifax.

COLKERK, a parish in the hundred of LAUNDITCH, county of NORFOLK, 2 miles (S.) from Fakenham, containing 358 inhabitants. The living is a discharged rectory, with that of Stibbard annexed, in the archdeaconry and diocese of Norwich, rated in the king's books at £10, and in the patronage of Lord J. Townsend. The church is dedicated to St. Mary.

COLLIERLY, a township in that part of the parish of LANCHESTER which is in the western division of CHESTER ward, county palatine of DURHAM, 12½ miles (N. W.) from Durham, containing, with the villages of Dipton and Pontop, 556 inhabitants. Here was formerly a chapel. At Collierly Dykes there is a place of worship for Wesleyan Methodists. This township contains several coal-works, from which it derives its name.

COLLINGBOURN-DUCIS, a parish in the hundred of ELSTUB and EVERLEY, county of WILTS, 2¾ miles (N. W.) from Ludgershall, containing 476 inhabitants. The living is a rectory, within the jurisdiction of the peculiar court of the Lord Warden of Savernake Forest, rated in the king's books at £16. 6. 8., and in the patronage of the Marquis of Ailesbury. The church is dedicated to St. Andrew. This was formerly part of the duchy of Lancaster, from which it acquired the adjunct to its name; but Henry VIII. alienated it to the Earl of Hertford, afterwards Duke of Somerset, and Protector of England, upon whose attainder it reverted to the crown, and was granted by Queen Elizabeth to Edward, Earl of Hertford, whose descendants inherited all the former possessions of the Duke of Somerset.

COLLINGBOURN-KINGSTONE, a parish in the hundred of KINWARDSTONE, county of WILTS, 4 miles (N. N. W.) from Ludgershall, containing 817 inhabitants, of which number, 251 are in Collingbourn-Southon, 233 in Collingbourn-Kingston, and 333 in Collingbourn-Vallance. The living is a vicarage, in the archdeaconry of Wilts, and diocese of Salisbury, rated in the king's books at £15. 7. 3½., and in the patronage of the Dean and Chapter of Winchester. The church is dedicated to St. Mary. There is a place of worship for Wesleyan Methodists. John Norris, eminent as a divine and philosopher, was born at the vicarage-house, in 1567.

COLLINGHAM, a parish in the lower division of the wapentake of SKYRACK, West riding of the county of YORK, 2 miles (S. S. W.) from Wetherby, containing 286 inhabitants. The living is a discharged vicarage, in the archdeaconry and diocese of York, rated in the king's books at £3. 11. 5½., endowed with £400 private benefaction, and £200 royal bounty, and in the patronage of Mrs. Wheeler. The church is dedicated to St. Oswald. A charity school was founded, in 1738, by Lady Elizabeth Hastings, with an endowment, producing £24 per annum, for teaching twenty children, and providing them with books.

COLLINGHAM (NORTH), a parish in the northern division of the wapentake of NEWARK, county of NOTTINGHAM, 5¾ miles (N. N. E.) from Newark, containing 805 inhabitants. The living is a discharged vicarage, in the archdeaconry of Nottingham, and diocese of York, rated in the king's books at £8. 14. 2., endowed with £200 private benefaction, £200 royal bounty, and £1400 parliamentary grant, and in the patronage of the Dean and Chapter of Peterborough. The church, dedicated to All Saints, is a very ancient structure, in the Norman style of architecture. There is a place of worship for Particular Baptists. A school is supported by charitable donations amounting to £41 per annum.

COLLINGHAM (SOUTH), a parish in the northern division of the wapentake of NEWARK, county of NOTTINGHAM, 5½ miles (N. N. E.) from Newark, containing

686 inhabitants. The living is a rectory, in the archdeaconry of Nottingham, and diocese of York, rated in the king's books at £14. 1. 10½., and in the patronage of the Bishop of Peterborough. The church is dedicated to St. John the Baptist. There is a place of worship for Wesleyan Methodists. Here is a school with a very trifling endowment. This parish is bounded on the west by the navigable river Trent. There is a lofty tumulus, called Potter's hill, where many Roman relics have been found. South of this, on the Fosse-road, on the Lincolnshire boundary, is the site of the *Crococolana* of Antoninus, now occupied by the village of Brough, where coins, termed *Brugh pennies,* have been ploughed up, and ancient foundations often discovered: human bones, with remains of coffins, have also been turned up in a place called the Chapel Close, which was the burying-ground attached to a chapel that formerly stood there, and belonged to the rectory of Hawton.

COLLINGTON, a parish in the hundred of BROXASH, county of HEREFORD, 4½ miles (N.) from Bromyard, containing 145 inhabitants. The living is a discharged rectory, in the archdeaconry and diocese of Hereford, rated in the king's books at £2. 18. 10., and in the patronage of Mrs. Pytts. The church is dedicated to All Saints. Limestone is obtained here.

COLLINGTREE, a parish in the hundred of WYMERSLEY, county of NORTHAMPTON, 3½ miles (S.) from Northampton, containing 194 inhabitants. The living is a rectory, in the archdeaconry of Northampton, and diocese of Peterborough, rated in the king's books at £16. 10. 5., and in the patronage of the Rev. Benjamin Hill. The church is dedicated to St. Columbus. There is a place of worship for Wesleyan Methodists.

COLLITON-ROW, a tything in the parish of the HOLY TRINITY, DORCHESTER, hundred of GEORGE, Dorchester division of the county of DORSET. The population is returned with the parish. It forms a small street on the south of Gildepath hill, and, though within the walls of the town, is properly without the borough, and lost its right of voting at elections for members of parliament in 1720, before which period it had constantly exercised it.

COLLUMPTON, county of DEVON.—See CULLOMPTON.

COLLY-WESTON, a parish in the hundred of WILLYBROOK, county of NORTHAMPTON, 3¾ miles (S. W. by S.) from Stamford, containing 353 inhabitants. The living is a rectory, in the archdeaconry of Northampton, and diocese of Peterborough, rated in the king's books at £12. 9. 7., and in the patronage of the Crown. The church is dedicated to St. Andrew. Extensive quarries of slate are wrought in the neighbourhood.

COLMWORTH, a parish in the hundred of BARFORD, county of BEDFORD, 5½ miles (W. by S.) from St. Neots, containing 450 inhabitants. The living is a rectory, in the archdeaconry of Bedford, and diocese of Lincoln, rated in the king's books at £18, and in the patronage of William Guppy, Esq. The church, dedicated to St. Denis, is a handsome structure with a lofty spire; it is in the early style of English architecture, and contains several ancient monuments.

COLN (ST. ALDWIN'S), a parish in the hundred of BRIGHTWELLS-BARROW, county of GLOUCESTER, 3 miles (N.) from Fairford, containing 393 inhabitants. The living is a discharged vicarage, in the archdeaconry and diocese of Gloucester, rated in the king's books at £8. 19. 4½., endowed with £200 private benefaction, and £200 royal bounty, and in the patronage of T. Ingram, Esq. and another. The church is dedicated to St. John the Baptist.

COLN (ST. DENIS), a parish in the upper division of the hundred of DEERHURST, though locally in the hundred of Bradley, county of GLOUCESTER, 3 miles (S. W. by S.) from North Leach, containing 179 inhabitants. The living is a rectory, in the archdeaconry and diocese of Gloucester, rated in the king's books at £9. 19. 4½., and in the patronage of the Master and Fellows of Pembroke College, Oxford. This parish is bounded on the south-west by the river Coln, and on the north-west by the old Roman Fosse-way.

COLN-ROGERS, a parish in the hundred of BRADLEY, county of GLOUCESTER, 4 miles (S. W. by S.) from North Leach, containing 139 inhabitants. The living is a rectory, in the archdeaconry and diocese of Gloucester, rated in the king's books at £7. 0. 5., and in the patronage of the Dean and Chapter of Gloucester. The church is dedicated to St. Andrew. This parish is bounded on the north by the river Coln, which is crossed by Fosse-bridge, on the Roman way of the same name.

COLNBROOK, a chapelry (formerly a market town) partly in the parish of STANWELL, hundred of SPELTHORNE, county of MIDDLESEX, but chiefly in the parishes of HORTON, IVER, and LANGLEY-MARSH, in the hundred of STOKE, county of BUCKINGHAM, 46 miles (S. E. by S.) from Buckingham, and 17 (W. by S.) from London, on the road to Bath. The population is returned with the several parishes. This place, which is of great antiquity, is supposed to have been the station *Ad Pontes* of Antoninus: it derives its name from the river Colne, by which it is separated from Middlesex, and is intersected by different branches of that river, over each of which is a small bridge. The town consists principally of one long street; the houses are in general neatly built and of respectable appearance. The trade principally arises from its situation as a great thoroughfare, which has made it a considerable posting town. The market has been long discontinued, and the market-house and the chapel, which were inconveniently situated in the narrower part of the town, have been removed by the commissioners of the turnpike roads, who have rebuilt the chapel, a neat modern edifice, dedicated to St. Mary, on the opposite side of the road, in the parish of Horton. Fairs are held on April 5th and May 3rd, for cattle and horses. The government, by charter of Henry VIII., which was renewed in the reign of Charles I., is vested in a bailiff and burgesses. The living is a perpetual curacy, in the archdeaconry of Buckingham, and diocese of Lincoln, and in the patronage of the Trustees of the late George Townsend, Esq., for Fellows of Pembroke College, Oxford. There is a place of worship for Baptists; and there are several charitable bequests for distribution among the poor.

COLNE, a parish in the hundred of HURSTINGSTONE, county of HUNTINGDON, 2¼ miles (S. E. by S.) from Somersham, containing 480 inhabitants. The living is a perpetual curacy, annexed to the rectory of Somersham, in the archdeaconry of Huntingdon, and diocese of Lincoln. The church, dedicated to St. Helen, is in the early style of English architecture, with a western tower; it contains some remains of figures and armorial bearings in stained glass, and is situated about half a mile from the village.

COLNE, a market town and chapelry in that part of the parish of WHALLEY which is in the higher division of the hundred of BLACKBURN, county palatine of LANCASTER, 35 miles (S. E.) from Lancaster, and 217 (N. N. W.) from London, containing 7274 inhabitants. This place is supposed by the geographer of Ravenna to have been a Roman station, the site of which is by Whitaker, the historian of Manchester, referred to Castor Cliff, a lofty eminence about a mile south of the town, where are still the vestiges of a quadrilateral camp, one hundred and twenty yards in length, and one hundred and ten in breadth, surrounded by a double vallum and fosse. This camp is by Whitaker, the historian of the "Ancient parish of Whalley," considered only as the *castra æstiva* of the primary station, which, perhaps on better authority, he places in the low grounds beneath the town, and near the bank of the Colne-water, but of which every vestige has been obliterated by cultivation. Numerous Roman coins have been found at various times, and among them several of Gordianus and other emperors, enclosed in a large silver cup turned up by the plough in 1696. The town, which is of great antiquity, appears to have arisen with Lancaster, Manchester, and other towns in the county, soon after its conquest by Agricola, in the year seventy-nine, and derives its name either from *Colunio*, the supposed name of the Roman station, or from the Saxon *Culme*, coal, with which the neighbourhood abounds: it is situated on an elevated point of land between the river Calder and the Leeds and Liverpool canal; the streets are paved, and the inhabitants are amply supplied with water conveyed by pipes from Flass spring, about two miles distant, under the management of a company formed for that purpose. A subscription library has been established under good regulations, and is well conducted. The woollen manufacture was carried on here previously to the arrival of the Flemings in England in the time of Edward III., as appears from the rent-roll of the last Henry de Lacy, lord of the manor, in 1311, in which a fulling-mill is returned as being valued at 6*s*. 8*d*. per annum: the manufacture of shalloons, calimancoes, and tammies, was also extensively carried on, for the sale of which a Piece Hall was erected in 1775, by a company of proprietors, on a plot of ground on the south side of the town, presented by Banastre Watson, Esq., of Marsden Hall; it is a substantial stone building, containing two spacious rooms, and was for many years the principal mart in the district for woollen and worsted goods, but is now appropriated to the sale of general merchandise at the annual fairs only. The cotton manufacture is at present the principal branch of business; the chief articles are calico and dimity for the Manchester market, both of them being made to a considerable extent: the machinery for spinning the cotton is chiefly put in motion by water, but partly by steam. The Leeds and Liverpool canal passes through a tunnel a mile in length, at a small distance from the town, affording a facility of conveyance for the coal, freestone, slate, and lime, with which the neighbouring hills abound, and for the produce of the manufactories. The market days are Wednesday and Saturday; and on the last Wednesday in every month is a large cattle market: the fairs are on March 7th, May 13th for cattle, and 15th for pedlary, October 11th, and December 21st. The town is within the jurisdiction of the county magistrates: a constable is annually chosen by such of the inhabitants as are assessed to the county rate; and a court baron is held by the lord of the manor.

The living is a perpetual curacy, in the archdeaconry and diocese of Chester, endowed with £600 parliamentary grant, and in the patronage of the Vicar of Whalley. The chapel, dedicated to St. Bartholomew, is a very ancient structure, erected probably soon after the Conquest: in the reign of Henry I. it was given to the priory of Pontefract by Hugh de Val; it was substantially repaired, or partly rebuilt, in the reign of Henry VIII., when the only remains preserved of the original building were the finely carved screen at the entrance and on the sides of the choir, and three massive circular columns in the north aisle, one of which, being undermined by some recent interments, suddenly gave way in 1815, and endangered the whole building, which has since been rendered firm and secure. There are places of worship for Baptists, Independents, Wesleyan Methodists, and Methodists of the New Connexion. The grammar school is of very uncertain foundation: it is endowed with about £15 per annum, for which six boys are taught free, four of them by means of a bequest of £40 from Thomas Blakey, Esq., in 1687. The old school-room was taken down, and on its site a new one erected by subscription, in 1812. Dr. Tillotson, Archbishop of Canterbury, received the rudiments of his education at this school. A school was founded in 1746, at Laneshaw Bridge, by John Emmot, Esq., in which twenty children of the tenants on the Emmot estate are gratuitously instructed. There are also Sunday schools for one thousand four hundred and fifty children, in connexion with the established church and the several dissenting congregations.

COLNE (EARL'S), a parish in the Witham division of the hundred of LEXDEN, county of ESSEX, 3½ miles (E. S. E.) from Halstead, containing 1229 inhabitants. The living is a vicarage, in the archdeaconry of Colchester, and diocese of London, rated in the king's books at £8. 10. 10., and in the patronage of W. Reeve, and Arthur Clarence, Esqrs. The church, dedicated to St. Andrew, contains several monuments of the de Veres, Earls of Oxford, which were removed from the church of a Benedictine priory, founded here in the eleventh century by Aubrey de Vere, who himself became one of the monks: it was dedicated to St. Mary and St. John the Evangelist, and was made a cell to the abbey of Abingdon in Berkshire; at the dissolution it had a prior and ten monks, with a revenue of £175. 14. 8. There is a place of worship for Particular Baptists. Here is an ancient free school, endowed by the Earls of Oxford, the annual income of which is £12. 17. A fair for cattle and toys is held on the 25th of March. The river Colne, which is here crossed by a bridge on the line of the Roman road from Colchester, runs through this parish.

COLNE (ENGAIN), a parish in the Witham division of the hundred of LEXDEN, county of ESSEX, 2¼ miles (E.) from Halstead, containing 547 inhabitants. The living is a rectory, in the archdeaconry of Colchester, and diocese of London, rated in the king's books at £13. 17. 6., and in the patronage of the Governors of Christ's Hospital. The church is dedicated to St. Andrew. This parish is bounded on the south by the river Colne, near which passes the Roman road from Colchester. There is a small endowment for the instruction of children.

COLNE (WAKES), a parish in the Witham division of the hundred of LEXDEN, county of ESSEX, 5½ miles (E. by S.) from Halstead, containing 417 inhabitants. The living is a rectory, in the archdeaconry of Colchester, and diocese of London, rated in the king's books at £12. 0. 5., and in the patronage of the Earl of Verulam. The church is dedicated to All Saints. The Roman road from Colchester passes through this parish, to the southward of which flows the river Colne.

COLNE (WHITE), a parish in the Witham division of the hundred of LEXDEN, county of ESSEX, 4½ miles (E.) from Halstead, containing 298 inhabitants. The living is a perpetual curacy, in the archdeaconry of Colchester, and diocese of London, endowed with £200 royal bounty, and in the patronage of W. E. Hume, Esq. This parish has the river Colne on the south, where also passes the Roman road from Colchester.

COLNEY, a parish in the hundred of HUMBLEYARD, county of NORFOLK, 2¾ miles (W. by S.) from Norwich, containing 78 inhabitants. The living is a discharged rectory, in the archdeaconry of Norfolk, and diocese of Norwich, rated in the king's books at £6. 13. 4., and in the patronage of J. Postle, Esq. The church, dedicated to St. Andrew, has a round tower.

COLSTERWORTH, a parish partly in the wapentake of BELTISLOE, comprising the township of Twyford, but chiefly in the soke of GRANTHAM, parts of KESTEVEN, county of LINCOLN, 32½ miles (S. by W.) from Lincoln, containing 776 inhabitants. The living is a rectory, in the archdeaconry and diocese of Lincoln, rated in the king's books at £14. 10., and in the patronage of the Prebendary of South Grantham in the Cathedral Church of Lincoln. The church, dedicated to St. John the Baptist, is a small structure of early English architecture, with a good tower in the later style. There is a place of worship for Wesleyan Methodists. The village is situated in a beautiful valley, through which winds the river Witham. Sir Isaac Newton was born here, on Christmas-day, 1642, about three months after the death of his father, who was lord of the manor; he received the rudiments of his education at the free grammar school at Grantham, and was admitted at Trinity College, Cambridge, in 1660.

COLSTON-BASSET, a parish in the southern division of the wapentake of BINGHAM, county of NOTTINGHAM, 10 miles (S. E. by E.) from Nottingham, containing 310 inhabitants. The living is a vicarage, in the archdeaconry of Nottingham, and diocese of York, rated in the king's books at £8. 7. 6., and in the patronage of the Crown. The church, dedicated to St. Mary, is an ancient cruciform structure, standing on a hill at a short distance from the village.

COLTISHALL, a parish in the southern division of the hundred of ERPINGHAM, county of NORFOLK, 8½ miles (N. N. E.) from Norwich, containing 685 inhabitants. The living is a rectory, in the archdeaconry and diocese of Norwich, rated in the king's books at £7. 2. 6., and in the patronage of the Provost and Fellows of King's College, Cambridge. The church, dedicated to St. John the Baptist, was rebuilt in 1824. There is a place of worship for Wesleyan Methodists. John Chapman, in 1718, bequeathed land for the endowment of a school, the annual income of which, amounting to £14, is paid for teaching English to ten boys, the sons of poor parishioners: a schoolroom has since been built by subscription. A fair for pedlary is held on Whit-Monday.

COLTON, a parish in the hundred of FOREHOE, county of NORFOLK, 5¾ miles (N.) from Wymondham, containing 267 inhabitants. The living is a discharged rectory, in the archdeaconry of Norfolk, and diocese of Norwich, rated in the king's books at £6. 9. 9½., endowed with £200 private benefaction, and £200 royal bounty, and in the patronage of the Crown. The church is dedicated to St. Andrew. The Rev. Henry Rix, in 1726, bequeathed certain land in trust for the endowment of a school and other charitable purposes, the annual income of which, with a subsequent gift by an unknown benefactor for teaching six children, amounts to £12. 7.

COLTON, a parish in the southern division of the hundred of PIREHILL, county of STAFFORD, 2 miles (N. by E.) from Rugeley, containing 569 inhabitants. The living is a rectory, in the archdeaconry of Stafford, and diocese of Lichfield and Coventry, rated in the king's books at £5, and in the patronage of the Rev. C. S. Landor. The church, dedicated to St. Mary, is very ancient, and has a square tower. Here is a school, with a house for the master, founded by contribution in 1763, for teaching twenty children, and since endowed with £500 by the late John Spencer, Esq.: there is also a school for younger children, endowed by the late Mr. Webb with land and a house called the Bell Inn, producing £5 per annum. The Grand Trunk canal passes through the south-west part of this parish.

COLTON, a township in the parish of BOLTON-PERCY, in the ainsty of the city, and East riding of the county, of YORK, 6¼ miles (S. W.) from York, containing 148 inhabitants. A school is endowed with an annuity of £6.

COLUMB (ST.) MAJOR, a market town and parish in the hundred of PYDER, county of CORNWALL, 32 miles (S. W. by W.) from Launceston, and 245 (W. by S.) from London, containing 2493 inhabitants. This place takes its name from an ancient church erected by the founder of Bodmin priory, and dedicated to St. Columba, and its adjunct, to distinguish it from a smaller town of that name in the same hundred. The town is situated on the summit of an eminence which is supposed to have been occupied as a Danish fortification, and is surrounded by extensive tracts of fine meadow land: the houses are in general well built, the streets are roughly paved, but not lighted, and the inhabitants are well supplied with water. The market, granted to Sir John Arundel in 1333, by Edward III., is on Thursday, for corn and provisions; there is also a market for butchers' meat only, on Saturday: the market-house is an ancient building in the principal street. The fairs are on the Thursday after Mid-Lent Sunday, for cattle and sheep, and on the Thursday after November 13th, for sheep only. It is in contemplation to construct a canal from Mawgan Porth to this place, the expense of which is estimated at £7000. The county magistrates hold a petty session for the hundred once a month. The living is a rectory, in the archdeaconry of Cornwall, and diocese of Exeter, rated in the king's books at £53. 6. 8., and in the patronage of —— Walker, Esq. The church, dedicated to St. Columba, is an ancient and venerable structure, with a lofty square embattled tower crowned with pinnacles; within are several interesting monuments. There are places of worship for Independents and Wesleyan Methodists. In 1628, James Jenkins, Esq. gave by will £200, which has been invested in the purchase of land, producing £25. 5. per annum, for distribution among the poor. About two miles to the south-east of the town is a large elliptical encampment, called Castle an Dinas, defended by a double vallum, and having only one entrance; the longer diameter of the inner area is one thousand seven hundred feet, and the shorter one thousand five hundred; within it are two tumuli, one of which is surrounded by a small ditch: it is supposed to have been erected by the Danes, and to have been the residence of one of their chiefs.

COLUMB (ST.) MINOR, a parish in the hundred of Pyder, county of Cornwall, 5¼ miles (W. by S.) from St. Columb Major, containing 1297 inhabitants. The living is a perpetual curacy, in the archdeaconry of Cornwall, and diocese of Exeter, endowed with £200 private benefaction, £600 royal bounty, and £1000 parliamentary grant, and in the patronage of James Buller, Esq. and others. The church is dedicated to St. Columb. John Francis Buller gave £5 per annum for teaching four children of this parish and two of Crantock; and in 1782, John Martyn gave £5 per annum for the like purpose. This parish is bounded on the west by Towan and Watergate bays and the small harbour of Porth on the Bristol channel. A fair is held annually on the 9th of June: there are considerable remains of a religious house, formerly a cell to the priory of Bodmin.

COLUMB-DAVID, a tything in the parish and hundred of Hemyock, county of Devon, 4¾ miles (S. S. W.) from Wellington. The population is returned with the parish.

COLVESTON, a parish in the hundred of Grimshoe, county of Norfolk, 6½ miles (N. by E.) from Brandon, containing 42 inhabitants. The living is a discharged rectory, consolidated with the vicarage of Didlington, in the archdeaconry of Norfolk, and diocese of Norwich. The church, which was dedicated to St. Mary, and dependent on the church of St. Bartholomew at Ickburgh, has been, with the village, long since demolished.

COLWALL, a parish in the hundred of Radlow, county of Hereford, 3¾ miles (N. E. by N.) from Ledbury, containing 782 inhabitants. The living is a rectory, in the archdeaconry and diocese of Hereford, rated in the king's books at £20. 6. 8., and in the patronage of the Bishop of Hereford. The church, dedicated to St. James, is an ancient structure with a square tower. Colwall is thought to have derived its name from a corruption of *Collis Vallum*, a fortified hill, which is descriptive of the situation of the place. The Herefordshire Beacon, an ancient encampment on one of the highest of the Malvern hills, is supposed to have been formed by the Britons to repel the Romans; near it a coronet of gold, set with diamonds, was discovered by a cottager in 1650, who, ignorant of its value, sold it for £31, though it afterwards fetched £1500. Here is a free grammar school, founded in 1612, by Humphrey Walwine, Esq., and under the patronage of the Grocers' Company: there are two schoolrooms, one for the free boys, the other for private pupils. The water of Colwall is equal in purity to the most celebrated of the Malvern springs.

COLWELL, a joint township with Swinburn, in the parish of Chollerton, north-eastern division of Tindale ward, county of Northumberland, 8¾ miles (N. by E.) from Hexham, containing, with Swinburn, 403 inhabitants. Colwell is situated at the intersection of Watling-street and the Cambo road, and is the property of Ralph Riddell, Esq., who has erected a schoolroom and a house for the master, who teaches eighteen free children.

COLWICH, a parish in the southern division of the hundred of Pirehill, county of Stafford, comprising the chapelry of Fradswell, and the township of Colwich, and containing 1865 inhabitants, of which number, 1646 are in the township of Colwich, 3 miles (N. W. by N.) from Rugeley. The living is a discharged vicarage, in the peculiar jurisdiction of the Prebendary of Colwich and Bishop's Itchington in the Cathedral Church of Lichfield, and in the patronage of the Bishop of Lichfield and Coventry, rated in the king's books at £6. 0. 5., endowed with £235 private benefaction, and £200 royal bounty. The church, dedicated to St. Michael, is of some antiquity, and contains a monument to the memory of the celebrated navigator, George, Lord Anson, who was interred in the family cemetery at this place, June 14th, 1762. The Staffordshire and Worcestershire canal forms a junction with the Grand Trunk canal near Great Heywood, in this parish. A fair for cattle, called Wolseley Meeting, is held at Wolseley annually on the Wednesday before Mid-Lent Sunday.

COLWICK, a parish in the southern division of the wapentake of Thurgarton, county of Nottingham, 2½ miles (E.) from Nottingham, containing 120 inhabitants. The living is a rectory, in the archdeaconry of Nottingham, and diocese of York, rated in the king's books at £6. 1. 0½., and in the patronage of J. Musters, Esq. The church is dedicated to St. John the Baptist. A school was founded by the Rev. William Thompson, late rector, with an endowment of £20 per annum. The navigable river Trent flows through this parish.

COLYFORD, a hamlet in the parish and hundred of Colyton, county of Devon, 1 mile (S. S. E.) from Colyton, with which the population is returned. Colyton was made a borough before the reign of Edward I.: it is governed by a mayor, who is chosen annually at the court of the lord of the manor. The tolls of a large cattle fair, held on the first Wednesday after March 11th, belong to the mayor, and the great tithes within the limits of the borough to the vicar of Colyton. Sir T. Gates, who discovered the Bermuda Isles, was born here.

COLYTON, a market town and parish in the hundred of Colyton, county of Devon, 22 miles (E.) from Exeter, and 151 (W. S. W.) from London, containing 1945 inhabitants. This place derives its name from the river Cole, on which it is situated, near its confluence with the river Axe. In the reign of Edward III. it obtained the grant of a weekly market and an annual fair. During the parliamentary war, the royal forces in possession of the town were attacked and defeated by a detachment of the parliamentarian army stationed at Lyme. The town is pleasantly situated in a fertile vale, surrounded by fine pasture land and orchards, and abounding with excellent timber: the houses, many of which are very ancient, are in general irregularly built of flint, with thatched roofs; the inhabitants are supplied with water from two conduits connected with springs a little south of the town. The principal branch of manufacture is that of blue, brown, and common white paper; there are also two tanneries. The market days are Tuesday, Thursday, and Saturday, which last is the principal market: the fairs are on May 1st and November 30th, for cattle. The petty sessions for the division are held here; and two constables and a tythingman are annually appointed at the court leet of the lord of the manor. The living is a vicarage, with which the perpetual curacies of Monkton and Shute are annexed, rated in the king's books at £40. 10. 10., and in the peculiar jurisdiction and patronage of the Dean and Chapter of Exeter. The church, dedicated to St. Andrew, is a spacious and handsome cruciform structure, in the later style of English architecture, with a low square embattled tower rising from the centre, and surmounted by a handsome octagonal lantern turret with pierced parapets: the south transept is separated from the nave by an elaborately carved stone screen; and in the chancel is a beautiful altar-tomb, with the effigy of the daughter of one of the Courtenays, earls of Devonshire, richly enshrined in tabernacle work. There are places of worship for Independents and Unitarians. A school, in which twenty boys are taught reading, writing, and arithmetic, is supported by part of a fund given to the parish by Henry VIII. for divers charitable purposes, amounting to about £220 per annum, out of which the schoolmaster is paid a salary of £30; and a Sunday school for one hundred and forty children is supported partly by an endowment of £200 in the five per cents., given in 1816, by its founder, the Rev. James How, and partly by subscription.

COLYTON-RAWLEIGH, a parish in the eastern division of the hundred of Budleigh, county of Devon, 3¼ miles (W.) from Sidmouth, containing 770 inhabitants. The living is a vicarage, in the archdeaconry and diocese of Exeter, rated in the king's books at £16. 4. 9½., and in the patronage of the Dean of Exeter. The church is dedicated to St. John the Baptist: near it are the remains of an ancient vicarage-house, which had a chapel attached to it: there was also a chapel in the parish, dedicated to St. Theobald.

COMBE, a tything in the parish of Wotton under Edge, upper division of the hundred of Berkeley, county of Gloucester, 1 mile (N.E. by E.) from Wotton under Edge, with which the population is returned.

COMBE, a tything in the parish and hundred of Crewkerne, county of Somerset. The population is returned with the parish.

COMBE, a parish in the hundred of Pastrow, Kingsclere division of the county of Southampton, 6¾ miles (E. S. E.) from Great Bedwin, containing 188 inhabitants. The living is a discharged vicarage, in the archdeaconry and diocese of Winchester, rated in the king's books at £6. 13. 4., endowed with £200 private benefaction, and £200 royal bounty, and in the patronage of the Dean and Canons of Windsor. The church is dedicated to St. Swithin.

COMBE, a tything in the parish of Endford, hundred of Elstub and Everley, county of Wilts, 8¼ miles (W.) from Ludgershall. The population is returned with the parish.

COMBE (ABBAS), county of Somerset. — See ABBAS-COMBE.

COMBE (ENGLISH), a parish in the hundred of Wellow, county of Somerset, 2¾ miles (S.W.) from Bath, containing 311 inhabitants. The living is a discharged vicarage, in the archdeaconry of Bath, and diocese of Bath and Wells, rated in the king's books at £9. 3. 11½., endowed with £400 private benefaction, and £400 royal bounty, and in the patronage of the Rev. D. Hughes. The church is a very handsome structure. Here was formerly a castle belonging to the family of Gurnay, but little more than the fosse which encompassed it is distinguishable. The ancient road Wansdyke crosses this parish, passing by an eminence called Roundbarrow, or Barrow Hill, which has been erroneously considered of artificial construction; at its base a coin of Antoninus Pius was found in 1786.

COMBE (LONG), a parish in the hundred of Wootton, county of Oxford, 5 miles (W. by S.) from Woodstock, containing 564 inhabitants. The living is a perpetual curacy, in the peculiar jurisdiction and patronage of the Rector and Fellows of Lincoln College, Oxford. The church is dedicated to St. Lawrence.

COMBE (MONCTON), a parish in the hundred of Bath-Forum, county of Somerset, 3½ miles (S.E. by S.) from Bath, containing 855 inhabitants. The living is a perpetual curacy, annexed to the vicarage of South Stoke, in the archdeaconry of Wells, and diocese of Bath and Wells. The church is dedicated to St. Michael. Here is a large paper-manufactory. On Combe down are extensive quarries, at which stone was obtained for erecting many of the best houses in Bath; in the cavities of it clusters of hexagonal brown chrystals are found, and in the fissures of the rocks are some fine and curiously frosted stalactites.

COMBE (ST. NICHOLAS), a parish in the eastern division of the hundred of Kingsbury, county of Somerset, 2½ miles (N. W.) from Chard, containing 1046 inhabitants. The living is a vicarage, in the peculiar jurisdiction of the Dean and Chapter of Wells, rated in the king's books at £15. 4. 4½., and in the patronage of the Dean of Wells. Fairs are held on the 18th of June, and on the Wednesday before December 11th.

COMBE-FIELDS, or COMBE-ABBEY, an extra-parochial liberty, in the Kirby division of the hundred of Knightlow, county of Warwick, 5¼ miles (E.) from Coventry, containing 173 inhabitants. Richard de Camvilla, in 1150, founded here a Cistercian abbey, which was dedicated to St. Mary, and richly endowed: at the dissolution it contained about fourteen monks, and was valued at £343. 0. 5. per annum: the site, which was granted by Edward VI. to the Earl of Warwick, is occupied by the manor-house; there are still some vestiges of the cloisters.

COMBE-FLOREY, a parish in the hundred of Taunton and Taunton-Dean, county of Somerset, 6 miles (N. E. by E.) from Wiveliscombe, containing 306 inhabitants. The living is a rectory, in the archdeaconry of Bath, and diocese of Bath and Wells, rated in the king's books at £11. 13. 9., and in the patronage of the Crown. The church is dedicated to St. Peter.

COMBE-HAY, a parish in the hundred of WELLOW, county of SOMERSET, 3½ miles (S. by W.) from Bath, containing 237 inhabitants. The living is a rectory, in the archdeaconry of Wells, and diocese of Bath and Wells, rated in the king's books at £9. 12. 3½., and in the patronage of H. Hanbury Tracey, Esq. The Roman Fosse-way passes near this place: the ditch on each side, which gives name to it, is here very perfect. The Radford canal has its course through the parish, and joins the Kennet and Avon canal.

COMBE-HILL, a joint township with Healy, in the parish of NETHERWITTON, western division of MORPETH ward, county of NORTHUMBERLAND, 6½ miles (S. by E.) from Rothbury. The population is returned with Healy.

COMBE-MARTIN, a market town and parish in the hundred of BRAUNTON, county of DEVON, 4½ miles (E.) from Ilfracombe, and 176 (W. by S.) from London, containing 1032 inhabitants. This place derives its name from its situation in a deep valley, and its adjunct from its proprietor at the time of the Conquest. In the reign of Edward I. some mines of lead, containing a considerable portion of silver, were discovered, which in the reign of Edward III. produced such a quantity of that metal as to assist him materially in defraying the expense of carrying on the war with France. These mines, after remaining in a neglected state for many years, were re-opened in the reign of Elizabeth, and worked with considerable advantage under the direction of Sir Beavis Bulmer; a cup made of silver found here was presented to William Bourchier, Earl of Bath, and another, weighing one hundred and thirty-seven ounces, to Sir Richard Martyn, Lord Mayor of London. They were unsuccessfully explored in 1790: in 1813 a more profitable attempt was made; but after four years, during which time two hundred and eighty tons of silver were extracted, the works were discontinued. The town is situated in a deep romantic glen, extending in a north-west direction, and opening into a small cove on the Bristol channel, which formed a convenient port for shipping the mineral produce, and still affords the inhabitants the means of conveying coal and lime to other towns, from which they receive corn and bark in return. The houses, many of which are in ruins and overgrown with ivy, extend for nearly a mile in an irregular line along the side of the vale: the surrounding scenery is strikingly magnificent, and in many points of view highly picturesque. The market has been discontinued; but the charter, granted to Nicholas Fitz-Martin by Henry III., in 1264, is still retained by the exposure of some trifling article for sale on the market days; the market-house is rapidly falling to decay: a fair is held on Whit-Monday. The county magistrates hold a petty session for the division, on the first Monday in every month, at a small inn. The living is a rectory, in the archdeaconry of Barnstaple, and diocese of Exeter, rated in the king's books at £39. 8. 9., and in the patronage of the Rev. William Toms. The church, which is a handsome structure, is dedicated to St. Peter. There is a place of worship for Wesleyan Methodists. A school for teaching forty children reading, writing, and arithmetic, was endowed, in 1733, by George Ley, Esq., with a house and land producing £25 per annum: the premises have been lately rebuilt. Thomas Harding, a learned Roman Catholic divine and controversialist, was born here, in 1512.

COMBERBACH, a township in that part of the parish of GREAT BUDWORTH which is in the hundred of BUCKLOW, county palatine of CHESTER, 3 miles (N. by W.) from Northwich, containing 226 inhabitants. There is a place of worship for Wesleyan Methodists.

COMBERTON, a parish in the hundred of WETHERLEY, county of CAMBRIDGE, 5¾ miles (W.S.W.) from Cambridge, containing 383 inhabitants. The living is a discharged vicarage, in the archdeaconry and diocese of Ely, rated in the king's books at £6. 18. 11½., and in the patronage of the Master and Fellows of Jesus' College, Cambridge. The church is dedicated to St. Mary.

COMBERTON (GREAT), a parish in the upper division of the hundred of PERSHORE, county of WORCESTER, 2¾ miles (S. by E.) from Pershore, containing 206 inhabitants. The living is a discharged rectory, in the archdeaconry and diocese of Worcester, rated in the king's books at £10, endowed with £400 private benefaction, and £400 royal bounty, and in the patronage of Miss Myddleton. The church is dedicated to St. Michael. The river Avon flows through this parish.

COMBERTON (LITTLE), a parish in the upper division of the hundred of PERSHORE, county of WORCESTER, 2½ miles (S.E. by S.) from Pershore, containing 172 inhabitants. The living is a discharged rectory, in the archdeaconry and diocese of Worcester, rated in the king's books at £9. 0. 2½., and in the patronage of Col. Davies. The church is dedicated to St. Peter.

COMBINTINHEAD, a parish forming, with Stoke-intinhead, Shaldon Green, and Haccombe, a detached portion of the hundred of WONFORD, locally in that of Haytor, county of DEVON, 3 miles (E.) from Newton-Bushell, containing 403 inhabitants. The living is a rectory, in the archdeaconry and diocese of Exeter, rated in the king's books at £32. 2. 8½., and in the patronage of Sir B. Wrey, Bart. The church contains an ancient wooden screen. The church-house, now occupied by the poor, is of ancient foundation. Here is a school, founded by Margaret Burgoyne, in 1783, with an endowment of £100 stock, for teaching ten children. The navigable river Teign bounds this parish on the north.

COMB-PYNE, a parish in the hundred of AXMINSTER, county of DEVON, 3¾ miles (E.S.E.) from Colyton, containing 132 inhabitants. The living is a discharged rectory, in the archdeaconry and diocese of Exeter, rated in the king's books at £8. 11. 8., and in the patronage of Charles Edwards, Esq. This place was anciently called Comb-Coffin, from the Coffin family; its present adjunct is derived from the Pynes, its later possessors. Here is a school, endowed with £7 per annum, also nine dwellings occupied by poor persons.

COMB-RAWLEIGH, a parish in the hundred of AXMINSTER, county of DEVON, 1½ mile (N.N.W.) from Honiton, containing 285 inhabitants. The living is a rectory, in the archdeaconry and diocese of Exeter, rated in the king's books at £20. 0. 10., and in the patronage of J. R. Drewe, Esq. The church, dedicated to St. Nicholas, contains a monument to the memory of John

Sheldon, Esq., F.R.S., and anatomical professor, who died in 1808. This parish was formerly denominated Comb-Baunton and Comb-Matthew.

COMBROOK, a chapelry in the parish of KINGTON, Kington division of the hundred of KINGTON, county of WARWICK, 2¼ miles (W. by N.) from Kington, containing 289 inhabitants. The chapel is dedicated to St. Margaret. There is a place of worship for Wesleyan Methodists. In 1641, Sir Grevill Verney gave an annuity of £8 towards supporting the free school founded by his mother, with an endowment of £25 per annum for instructing all the poor children of Combrook and Compton-Verney; and in 1763, Lady Tryphena Verney, agreeably to a bequest of £300 by her husband, George Verney, Esq., conveyed to trustees an estate at South Littleton, in the county of Worcester, for the maintenance of two scholars at Trinity College, Cambridge, to be chosen from this school, or, in default, out of the grammar school at Warwick.

COMBS, a parish in the hundred of STOW, county of SUFFOLK, 2 miles (S. by E.) from Stow-Market, containing 736 inhabitants. The living is a rectory, in the archdeaconry of Sudbury, and diocese of Norwich, rated in the king's books at £25. 17. 8½., and in the patronage of the Earl of Ashburnham. The church, dedicated to St. Mary, is in the early style of English architecture. The river Orwell flows along the north-eastern boundary of the parish, and is navigable from Ipswich to Stow-Market. Here is a considerable tannery.

COMMON-DALE, a township in the parish of GUILSBROUGH, eastern division of the liberty of LANGBAURGH, North riding of the county of YORK, 6½ miles (S.E.) from Guilsbrough, containing 86 inhabitants. Common-dale is corrupted from Colman-dale, so called from Colman, Bishop of Lindisfarne, who had a hermitage here.

COMP (GREAT), a hamlet in the parish and hundred of WROTHAM, lathe of AYLESFORD, county of KENT, 3¼ miles (S. E.) from Wrotham, with which the population is returned. Here was formerly a chapel, now demolished.

COMPSTALL, a village in the parish of STOCKPORT, hundred of MACCLESFIELD, county palatine of CHESTER, 5 miles from Stockport, containing about 1600 inhabitants, of which, 1200 are employed in spinning, power-loom-weaving, bleaching, and printing, and the remainder at the extensive coal-works in the neighbourhood. There is a place of worship for Wesleyan Methodists. Twenty-five years ago, Compstall consisted of only a few straggling cottages, but, since the establishment of the cotton manufacture, it has been gradually rising to its present thriving condition.

COMPTON, a parish in the hundred of COMPTON, county of BERKS, 2¼ miles (E. S. E.) from East Ilsley, containing 482 inhabitants. The living is a discharged vicarage, in the archdeaconry of Berks, and diocese of Salisbury, rated in the king's books at £11. 14. 4½., and in the patronage of Sir W. J. James, Bart.

COMPTON, a hamlet in that part of the parish of ASHBOURN which is in the hundred of MORLESTON and LITCHURCH, though locally in the hundred of Appletree, county of DERBY, ½ a mile (S. E.) from Ashbourn. The population is returned with the chapelry of Clifton. A chapel, called Sion chapel, with a house for the minister, and six almshouses attached to it, and under the direction of the trustees of the Countess of Huntingdon's college, were built here by John Cooper, who, by deed in 1801, endowed them with £4500 three per cent. reduced annuities, yielding now a dividend of about £130 per annum, of which sum, £68 is paid to the minister, and £10. 10. to each of the six inmates of the hospital, who, together with the minister, are appointed by the trustees: the premises were substantially repaired in 1824.

COMPTON, a tything in the parish of NEWENT, hundred of BOTLOE, county of GLOUCESTER, containing 403 inhabitants.

COMPTON, a tything in that part of the parish of HENBURY which is in the upper division of the hundred of HENBURY, county of GLOUCESTER, containing 151 inhabitants.

COMPTON, a parish in the hundred of BUDDLESGATE, Fawley division of the county of SOUTHAMPTON, 2½ miles (S. S. W.) from Winchester, containing 267 inhabitants. The living is a rectory, in the peculiar jurisdiction of the incumbent, rated in the king's books at £23. 6. 8., and in the patronage of the Bishop of Winchester. The church, dedicated to All Saints, is small, and has portions in various styles of architecture, the Norman predominating. Compton is within the jurisdiction of the Cheyney Court held at Winchester every Thursday, for the recovery of debts to any amount. The Itchen line of navigation passes through this parish.

COMPTON, a parish in the first division of the hundred of GODALMING, county of SURREY, 3¼ miles (S. W. by W.) from Guildford, containing 423 inhabitants. The living is a rectory, in the archdeaconry of Surrey, and diocese of Winchester, rated in the king's books at £15. 4. 9½., and in the patronage of J. M. Molyneux, Esq. The church, dedicated to St. Nicholas, has a low tower and spire, and a curious chancel with a groined roof and a chapel over it; these portions are in the early style of English architecture, but there are others of decorated character.

COMPTON, a parish in the hundred of WESTBOURN and SINGLETON, rape of CHICHESTER, county of SUSSEX, 9 miles (S.W. by. W.) from Midhurst, containing 233 inhabitants. The living is a vicarage, with the perpetual curacy of Up-Marden annexed, in the archdeaconry and diocese of Chichester, rated in the king's books at £13. 6. 8., and in the patronage of the Bishop of Chichester. The church, dedicated to St. Mary, has a mixture of the early English and decorated styles of architecture. Edward Flower, in 1521, founded a free grammar school, with an endowment of £100, to be laid out in land. Thomas Pelham gave £80, with a rent-charge of £20, and, in 1528, William Spicer conveyed other lands in furtherance of this charity, the total income of which, amounting to £28 per annum, is paid to the master of a boarding-school, to whom no application has ever been made to teach children gratuitously. The Rev. Dr. Cox, in 1741, bequeathed £100 for teaching poor children of Compton and Up-Marden. A donation of £30 by the Rev. Robert Middleton, and one of £20 by Timothy Burrell, Esq., in 1716, for the education of poor children, have been, with a further sum of £100 given by the latter, appropriated for a workhouse, in which a school is kept.

COMPTON (EAST), a tything in the parish of PILTON, hundred of WHITESTONE, county of SOMER-

SET, 2½ miles (S. S. W.) from Shepton-Mallet. The population is returned with the parish.

COMPTON (FENNY), a parish in the Burton-Dassett division of the hundred of KINGTON, county of WARWICK, 5¾ miles (E. by N.) from Kington, containing 572 inhabitants. The living is a rectory, in the archdeaconry of Coventry, and diocese of Lichfield and Coventry, rated in the king's books at £15. 8. 4., and in the patronage of the President and Fellows of Corpus Christi College, Oxford. The church is dedicated to St. Peter. Sir Henry Bate Dudley, a comic writer of some note, was born here, in 1745; he died in 1824.

COMPTON (LITTLE), a parish in the upper division of the hundred of DEERHURST, county of GLOUCESTER, though locally in the hundred of Chadlington, county of Oxford, 4½ miles (N. W. by W.) from Chipping-Norton, containing 314 inhabitants. The living is a perpetual curacy, in the archdeaconry and diocese of Gloucester, endowed with £400 private benefaction, and £400 royal bounty, and in the patronage of the Dean and Canons of Christ Church, Oxford. The church is dedicated to St. Denis. Here is an old mansion, formerly the residence of Bishop Juxon, chaplain to Charles I.

COMPTON (LONG), a parish in the Brails division of the hundred of KINGTON, county of WARWICK, 4¼ miles (N. N. W.) from Chipping-Norton, containing 860 inhabitants. The living is a discharged vicarage, in the archdeaconry and diocese of Worcester, rated in the king's books at £12. 15. 7½., endowed with £200 private benefaction, and £200 royal bounty, and in the patronage of the Provost and Fellows of Eton College. The church is dedicated to St. Peter and St. Paul. There is a place of worship for Wesleyan Methodists. A weekly market and an annual fair, now disused, were granted in the 15th of Henry III. About a mile southward, and near the Oxfordshire boundary, is that remarkable monument of antiquity, called Rolle-rich, or Rowlright, stones, of which there is an absurd vulgar tradition that they were once men, and that the highest of them would have been king of England, if he could have seen this village before they were turned into stone.

COMPTON (NETHER), a parish in the hundred of SHERBORNE, Sherborne division of the county of DORSET, 2¾ miles (W. N. W.) from Sherborne, containing 458 inhabitants. The living is a discharged rectory, annexed to that of Over Compton, in the peculiar jurisdiction of the Dean of Salisbury, rated in the king's books at £7. 18. The church is dedicated to St. Nicholas.

COMPTON (OVER), a parish in the hundred of SHERBORNE, Sherborne division of the county of DORSET, 3½ miles (W. by N.) from Sherborne, containing 149 inhabitants. The living is a rectory, with that of Nether Compton annexed, in the peculiar jurisdiction of the Dean of Salisbury, rated in the king's books at £11. 9. 4½., and in the patronage of R. Gooden, Esq. The church is dedicated to St. Michael.

COMPTON (WEST), a tything in the parish of PILTON, hundred of WHITESTONE, county of SOMERSET, 2 miles (W. S. W.) from Shepton-Mallet. The population is returned with the parish.

COMPTON-ABBAS, or WEST COMPTON, a parish in the hundred of CERNE, TOTCOMBE, and MODBURY, Cerne subdivision of the county of DORSET, 9 miles (W. N. W.) from Dorchester, containing 80 inhabitants. The living is a discharged rectory, in the archdeaconry of Dorset, and diocese of Bristol, rated in the king's books at £8. 0. 5., and in the patronage of D. R. Mitchell, Esq. The church is dedicated to St. Michael. Compton-Abbas derives its adjunct from having once formed part of the possessions of Milton abbey, and is termed West Compton from its relative position to East Compton.

COMPTON-ABBAS, a parish in that part of the hundred of SIXPENNY-HANDLEY which is in the Shaston (West) division of the county of DORSET, 3½ miles (S. by E.) from Shaftesbury, containing 368 inhabitants. The living is a rectory, in the archdeaconry of Dorset, and diocese of Bristol, rated in the king's books at £9. 10. 2½., and in the patronage of D. R. Mitchell, Esq. The church, dedicated to St. Mary, is a small ancient edifice. The village is situated in a *combe*, or vale, whence its name; it derives its adjunct from having formed part of the endowment of Shaston abbey.

COMPTON-ABDALE, a parish in the hundred of BRADLEY, county of GLOUCESTER, 4¼ miles (W. N. W.) from North Leach, containing 184 inhabitants. The living is a perpetual curacy, in the archdeaconry and diocese of Gloucester, endowed with £200 private benefaction, and 600 royal bounty, and in the patronage of the Dean and Chapter of Bristol. The church, dedicated to St. Oswald, is a small ancient building. Here is a school with a trifling endowment. The river Coln runs through this parish, which is well wooded.

COMPTON-BASSETT, a parish in the hundred of CALNE, county of WILTS, 2¼ miles (E. N. E.) from Calne, containing 480 inhabitants. The living is a rectory, in the peculiar jurisdiction of the Prebendary of Combe and Harnham in the Cathedral Church of Salisbury, rated in the king's books at £13. 6. 10½., endowed with £600 royal bounty, and in the patronage of the Bishop of Salisbury. The church is dedicated to St. Swithin. Robert Rawlings, in 1786, bequeathed land producing £11 per annum, for teaching ten children, prior to which, in 1706, Elizabeth Giddes gave £8 for educating one.

COMPTON-BEAUCHAMP, a parish in the hundred of SHRIVENHAM, county of BERKS, 6½ miles (S. by W.) from Great Farringdon, containing 103 inhabitants. The living is a rectory, in the archdeaconry of Berks, and diocese of Salisbury, rated in the king's books at £9. 18. 9., and in the patronage of J. A. Wright, Esq. The church is dedicated to St. Swithin. Here is an extensive double-trenched encampment, thought to be Roman, from the coins discovered upon the spot, near which, and to the south of the church, passes the Iknield road. The Wilts and Berks canal has its course along the northern parts of this parish.

COMPTON-BISHOP, a parish in the hundred of WINTERSTOKE, county of SOMERSET, 2¼ miles (W. N. W.) from Axbridge, containing 513 inhabitants. The living is a discharged vicarage, in the peculiar jurisdiction and patronage of the Prebendary of Compton-Bishop in the Cathedral Church of Wells, rated in the king's books at £11, endowed with £400 private benefaction, and 400 royal bounty. The church is dedicated to St. Andrew: in the churchyard is an ancient cross, with six rows of steps. The village lies in a hollow, under the southern declivity of the Mendip range of hills, presenting a very picturesque appearance. A little to the south-west is a spacious natural cave, entered by a perpendicular shaft: proceeding by a difficult winding passage, a still more extensive cavern opens to the sight: from the roof, which expands into a kind of arch, hung formerly some beautiful specimens of stalactites; and various incrustations, assuming the most fantastic shapes, lay scattered about, but all have been defaced or removed by visitors. William Cray, in 1728, bequeathed land, now producing £17 per annum, for teaching poor children in two schoolrooms. At the village of Cross, in this parish, are some good posting-houses: and by a recent regulation it has been made the station of a general post-office, whence bags of letters are sent to the neighbouring parishes.

COMPTON-CHAMBERLAIN, a parish forming a detached portion of the southern division of the hundred of Damerham, locally in the hundred of Cawden and Cadworth, county of Wilts, 4½ miles (W. by S.) from Wilton, containing 267 inhabitants. The living is a discharged vicarage, in the archdeaconry and diocese of Salisbury, rated in the king's books at £13, endowed with £200 private benefaction, and £400 royal bounty, and in the patronage of J. H. Penruddock, Esq. The church is dedicated to St. Michael. There is a charity school. Col. Penruddock, who was executed at Exeter, in 1655, for an attempt to restore Charles II. to the throne, resided in this parish.

COMPTON-DANDO, a parish in the hundred of Keynsham, county of Somerset, 2 miles (E. by N.) from Pensford, containing 344 inhabitants. The living is a discharged vicarage, in the archdeaconry of Bath, and diocese of Bath and Wells, rated in the king's books at £5. 10. 5., and in the patronage of the Bishop of Bath and Wells. The church is dedicated to St. Mary. There is a place of worship for Wesleyan Methodists. The river Chew runs through this parish, which is also crossed by the ancient Belgic boundary line, called Wansdyke.

COMPTON-DUNDON, a parish in the hundred of Whitley, county of Somerset, 2¾ miles (N.) from Somerton, containing, with the hamlet of Littleton, 544 inhabitants. The living is a discharged vicarage, in the peculiar jurisdiction and patronage of the Prebendary of Compton-Dundon in the Cathedral Church of Wells, rated in the king's books at £9. 6. 10., endowed with £200 private benefaction, and £200 royal bounty. The church is dedicated to St. Andrew. The ruins of a mansion that formerly belonged to the family of Beauchamp adjoin the churchyard. An adjacent hill is called Dundon Beacon, from a beacon having anciently been erected on it.

COMPTON-DURVILLE, a tything in the parish of South Petherton, southern division of the hundred of Petherton, county of Somerset, 1½ mile (W.N.W.) from South Petherton, with which the population is returned.

COMPTON-GIFFORD, a tything in that part of the parish of Charles the Martyr, Plymouth, which is in the hundred of Roborough, county of Devon, 1½ mile (N. N. E.) from Plymouth, containing 175 inhabitants.

COMPTON-GREENFIELD, a parish in the upper division of the hundred of Henbury, county of Gloucester, 6¼ miles (N. by W.) from Bristol, containing 42 inhabitants. The living is a discharged rectory, in the peculiar jurisdiction of the Bishop of Bristol, rated in the king's books at £7, and in the patronage of John Ward, Esq. The navigable river Severn flows on the western side of this parish.

COMPTON-MARTIN, a parish in the hundred of Chewton, county of Somerset, 8 miles (N.) from Wells, containing 534 inhabitants. The living is a rectory, with the perpetual curacy of Nempnett-Thrubwell annexed, in the archdeaconry of Bath, and diocese of Bath and Wells, rated in the king's books at £10. 6. 8., and in the patronage of the Duke of Buckingham. The church, dedicated to St. Michael, is a fine specimen of the Norman style of architecture, and the interior is particularly neat. John King, in 1773, bequeathed an annuity of £1 for a charity school, which was established in 1776, and is endowed with about £13 per annum. The village lies at the edge of an extensive valley under the north ridge of Mendip, and derives its adjunct from its ancient proprietors.

COMPTON-PAUNCEFOOT, a parish in the hundred of Catsash, county of Somerset, 5 miles (W.S.W.) from Wincanton, containing 228 inhabitants. The living is a rectory, in the archdeaconry of Welis, and diocese of Bath and Wells, rated in the king's books at £8. 10. 10., and in the patronage of John H. Hunt, Esq. The church is dedicated to St. Mary.

COMPTON-VALLENCE, a parish in the liberty of Frampton, Bridport division of the county of Dorset, 7¼ miles (W.N.W.) from Dorchester, containing 86 inhabitants. The living is a rectory, in the archdeaconry of Dorset, and diocese of Bristol, rated in the king's books at £12. 5. 2½., and in the patronage of R. Williams, Esq. The church, dedicated to St. Thomas à Becket, is a small building with a plain tower. The village, which is situated on the banks of a small stream, was formerly more considerable than it is at present.

COMPTON-VERNEY, an extra-parochial liberty, in the Kington division of the hundred of Kington, county of Warwick, 2 miles (N.W.) from Kington, containing 37 inhabitants. Here is a free school, which is entitled to two exhibitions in Trinity College, Cambridge, jointly with that at Combrook.

COMPTON-WYNIATES, a parish in the Brails division of the hundred of Kington, county of Warwick, 5¼ miles (E. by N.) from Shipston upon Stour, containing 28 inhabitants. The living is a rectory, with the vicarage of Tysoe united, in the archdeaconry and diocese of Worcester, rated in the king's books at £10, and in the patronage of the Marquis of Northampton. The manor-house, erected in the reign of Henry VIII., was garrisoned by some troops belonging to the parliament, in 1646.

CONDERTON, a hamlet in the parish of Overbury, middle division of the hundred of Oswaldslow, county of Worcester, containing 89 inhabitants.

CONDICOTE, a parish partly in the upper division of the hundred of Kiftsgate, and partly in the upper division of the hundred of Slaughter, county of Gloucester, 3½ miles (N.W. by W.) from Stow on the Wold, containing 165 inhabitants. The living is a discharged rectory, in the archdeaconry and diocese of Gloucester, rated in the king's books at £7. 1. 0½., and in the patronage of Thomas Davies, Esq. The church is dedicated to St. Nicholas. Here is a school with a trifling endowment.

CONDOVER, a parish in the hundred of CONDOVER, county of SALOP, 4½ miles (S.) from Shrewsbury, containing 1378 inhabitants. The living is a discharged vicarage, in the archdeaconry of Salop, and diocese of Lichfield and Coventry, rated in the king's books at £4. 14., and in the patronage of E. W. S. Owen, Esq. The church is dedicated to St. Andrew. A school is supported by divers donations, amounting in the whole to £25 per annum. Here is a small lake, termed Bomere, in and near which have been found several rare botanical plants. There is a mine of coal in the parish.

CONEYSTHORPE, a township in that part of the parish of BARTON in the STREET which is in the wapentake of BULMER, North riding of the county of YORK, 5 miles (W.) from New Malton, containing 160 inhabitants.

CONEYTHORPE, a township in the parish of GOLDSBOROUGH, upper division of the wapentake of CLARO, West riding of the county of York, 4¼ miles (E. N. E.) from Knaresborough, containing 112 inhabitants.

CONGERSTON, a parish in the hundred of SPARKENHOE, county of LEICESTER, 3¾ miles (N. W. by W.) from Market-Bosworth, containing 149 inhabitants. The living is a rectory, in the archdeaconry of Leicester, and diocese of Lincoln, rated in the king's books at £5. 3. 6½., and in the patronage of Earl Howe. The church is dedicated to St. Mary. Charles Jennins, in 1773, left £333. 6. 8. in trust for teaching poor children of the parish, the annual produce of which is £16. 13. There is also a school on the National system, supported by Earl and Countess Howe, in which one hundred and fifty children are clothed and educated. The Ashby de la Zouch canal passes through this parish. Congerston is in the honour of Tutbury, duchy of Lancaster, and within the jurisdiction of a court of pleas held at Tutbury every third Tuesday, for the recovery of debts under 40*s*.

CONGHALL, or COUGHALL, a township in that part of the parish of BACKFORD which is in the lower division of the hundred of BROXTON, county palatine of CHESTER, 3½ miles (N. by E.) from Chester, containing 23 inhabitants. The Ellesmere canal passes near this place.

CONGHAM, a parish in the Lynn division of the hundred of FREEBRIDGE, county of NORFOLK, 3½ miles (E. by S.) from Castle-Rising, containing 279 inhabitants. The living is a rectory, with which that of Congham St. Mary was consolidated in 1684, in the archdeaconry and diocese of Norwich, rated together in the king's books at £12. 10., and in the patronage of Mrs. Nelson. The church is dedicated to St. Andrew: that of St. Mary has been demolished. The rector also receives the tithes of Congham All Saints, subject to an annual payment to the impropriator. Here are almshouses for twelve women, with an endowment of £100 per annum. The learned antiquary and historian, Sir Henry Spelman, was born at this place, in 1562, and died in 1641: he first prosecuted his studies at Trinity College, Cambridge, whence he was called to the bar, and was sheriff for the county in the year 1605. His chief works were, the Glossary, History of Sacrilege, a treatise *De non temerandis Ecclesiis*, Icenia, &c., which were collected and published, with a biographical sketch prefixed, by Bishop Gibson.

Corporate Seal.

CONGLETON, an incorporated market town and chapelry, in the parish of ASTBURY, having separate jurisdiction, locally in the hundred of Northwich, county palatine of CHESTER, 31 miles (E. by S.) from Chester, and 161 (N. W. by W.) from London, containing 6405 inhabitants. Some writers have considered this the site of *Condate*, an aboriginal settlement of the Cornavii; but Whitaker, in his history of Manchester, has convincingly refuted this opinion, and fixed that station at Kinderton. In Domesday-book it is called *Cogletone*, but its origin has not been satisfactorily ascertained: it is not distinguished by any events of historical importance. In the beginning of the fourteenth century a free charter was granted to it by Henry de Lacey, Earl of Lincoln, who, in 1282, obtained for it the grant of a weekly market. In the reign of Henry VI., an inundation having done considerable damage to the town, the inhabitants obtained permission to divert the course of the river, and subsequently a grant of the king's mills, which stood on its banks. The town is situated in a valley embosomed in richly wooded hills, on the south bank of the river Daven, or Dane, over which a handsome bridge was built in 1782, and, notwithstanding some recent improvements, consists of narrow and irregularly formed streets: the houses in the eastern part are old, and chiefly of timber and brickwork; those in the western part are in general modern and of handsome appearance: the inhabitants are supplied with water from springs, and from the rivulet Howtey, which intersects the town. The environs abound with scenery beautifully diversified by the windings of the river, on the banks of which are numerous stately mansions and elegant villas. Assemblies are held periodically in the market-house, and races take place annually in August. The manufacture of gloves, and leather laces called *Congleton points*, for which the town was celebrated, has given place to the throwing of silk and the spinning of cotton, for the former of which not less than fifty mills have been erected since 1752, when that branch of manufacture was introduced by Mr. Pattison, of London, who built the first mill, an edifice comprising five stories of rooms, each two hundred and forty feet in length, and of proportionate width; this establishment, which is considered in point of extent the second in the kingdom, is still conducted by the descendants of the founder: ribands and handkerchiefs also are woven to a limited extent. A canal from Marple, to join the Grand Trunk canal at Lawton, is now being constructed, which, passing within a quarter of a mile of the town, will materially facilitate its trade. The market is on Saturday: the fairs, chiefly for cattle, are on the Thursday before Shrovetide, May 12th, July 12th, and November 22nd. The market-house, a neat and commodious edifice, containing a handsome assembly-room, was built in 1822, at the sole expense of Sir Edmund Antrobus, Bart. The government, by charter of incorporation granted by James I., in 1625, is vested in a mayor, high steward, eight aldermen, and sixteen capital burgesses, assisted by a town-clerk and subordinate officers: the mayor, who is elected annually by a majority of the corporation, on the Monday before Michaelmas-day, and two of the aldermen, who at the same time are chosen for that purpose, are justices of the peace within the borough; the high steward and town-clerk hold their respective offices for life. The freedom of the borough is inherited by the eldest sons of freemen, and acquired by servitude, purchase, and gift. The corporation hold quarterly courts of session, for trying prisoners charged with misdemeanors and felonies not capital; and courts of record for the recovery of debts to any amount, in which, though they do not exercise it, they have the privilege of proceeding according to the statute of Acton-Burnell, otherwise the law of statute-merchant: a court leet is also held in August, at which the high steward, or his deputy, presides. The guildhall is a neat brick building, with a piazza in front, supported on four pillars of stone; it was rebuilt in 1805, and, in addition to the court-rooms and apartments for transacting the public business of the corporation, comprises a room for debtors, and cells for the confinement of criminals.

The living is a perpetual curacy, in the archdeaconry and diocese of Chester, endowed with £200 private benefaction, £200 royal bounty, and £400 parliamentary grant, and in the patronage of the Mayor and Corporation. The chapel, dedicated to St. Peter, was rebuilt of brick in 1740, and a square tower of stone was added to it in 1786; it stands on elevated ground, and commands a fine and extensive prospect. There was formerly another chapel at the end of the bridge, on the opposite side of the river Dane, which, having long since become desecrated, was appropriated to the reception of the poor; it was pulled down in 1810, when a spacious one was erected at Coughton-moss. There are places of worship for Independents, Primitive and Wesleyan Methodists, Unitarians, and Roman Catholics. The grammar school, free for the sons of burgesses exclusively, and under the management of the corporation, who appoint the master, is of uncertain foundation, but existed prior to 1590, and was endowed with a house and garden and one acre of land, to which £16 per annum is added by the corporation, as a salary to the master, who receives a quarterly payment of fifteen shillings each for instructing the sons of non-freemen in English and the mathematics, and has the privilege of taking boarders. A spacious schoolroom, detached from the house, was erected in 1814 by the corporation, on condition that the present master, during his lifetime, should give up his claim to the £16 per annum. Adjoining the chapel a handsome brick building, capable of accommodating eight hundred children, was erected in 1828, for the use of the Sunday school, which is supported by subscription. At Buglawton, a township in this parish, is a mineral spring, the water of which is said to be efficacious in scrofula and other diseases: by the breaking in of the banks, and the consequent admixture of other water, its power has been considerably weakened, but it is in contemplation to repair the well, and to erect baths for the accommodation of invalids. John Bradshaw, Chief Justice of Chester, and president of the tribunal which passed sentence of death on Charles I., was articled to an attorney in this town, of which he became mayor in 1637, and was subsequently appointed high steward. John Whitehurst, a celebrated mechanic, and author of a treatise on the Theory of the Earth, was born here, in 1713.

CONGRESBURY, a parish (formerly a market town) in the hundred of Winterstoke, county of Somerset, 7½ miles (N. by W.) from Axbridge, containing 1202 inhabitants. The living is a vicarage, with the perpetual curacy of Wick St. Lawrence annexed, in the archdeaconry of Wells, and diocese of Bath and Wells, rated in the king's books at £42. 1. 8., and in the patronage of the Mayor and Corporation of Bristol. The church, dedicated to St. Andrew, is a handsome structure with a tower and lofty spire. This is a very large parish, bounded on the west by extensive marshes stretching to the Bristol channel: the legendary account of it states that the name is derived from St. Congar, son of an eastern monarch, who in 711 fled from his father's court, to avoid a marriage to which he was disinclined, and ultimately settled here, where he built an oratory, received a grant of land from Ina, King of the West Saxons, and founded an establishment for twelve canons; he then proceeded on a pilgrimage to Jerusalem, where he died, and was brought hither for interment. Jocelyn, Bishop of Bath, obtained from Henry III. a grant of a weekly market and an annual fair; the market is disused, but the fair is held on the 14th of September: a large and lofty cross stands in the centre of the village.

CONHOPE, a township in that part of the parish of Aymestrey which is in the hundred of Stretford, county of Hereford, 4½ miles (N. by E.) from Pembridge, containing 96 inhabitants.

CONINGSBY, a parish in the soke of Horncastle, parts of Lindsey, county of Lincoln, 1 mile (E. N. E.) from Tattershall, containing 1651 inhabitants. The living is a rectory, in the archdeaconry and diocese of Lincoln, rated in the king's books at £39. 10. 2½., and in the patronage of Sir Gilbert Heathcote, Bart. The church is dedicated to St. Michael. There are places of worship for General Baptists and Primitive and Wesleyan Methodists. The rivers Bane and Witham, and the Horncastle canal, pass through this parish: the Witham is navigable from Lincoln to Boston. An annual feast is held on the Sunday nearest St. Michael's day.

CONINGTON, a parish in the hundred of Papworth, county of Cambridge, 3¼ miles (S. by E.) from St. Ives, containing 202 inhabitants. The living is a rectory, in the archdeaconry and diocese of Ely, rated in the king's books at £9. 15. 10., and in the patronage of the Bishop of Ely. The church is dedicated to St. Mary. There is an endowed school. Traces of the moat surrounding the site of an ancient fortress, called Bruce Castle, may be discerned.

CONINGTON, a parish in the hundred of Norman-Cross, county of Huntingdon, 3 miles (S. E. by S.) from Stilton, containing 215 inhabitants. The living is a rectory, in the archdeaconry of Huntingdon, and diocese of Lincoln, rated in the king's books at £19. 6. 8., and in the patronage of Dr. Procter. The church, dedicated to All Saints, is a large handsome structure, having an embattled tower with octagonal pinnacles, and the windows adorned with stained glass; it contains many monuments to the Cottons, and an inscribed tablet to the memory of Prince Henry of Scotland, Lord of

Conington, &c.: the font is characteristic of the Norman and early English styles. The Rev. James Oram, in 1769, left £500 for teaching poor children. At the village, within a square intrenchment, are vestiges of an ancient castle, which, with the lordship, was given by Canute to Turkill, a Danish lord, who, taking advantage of his residence among the East Angles, invited over Sueno to plunder the country. After Turkill's departure it fell to Waldeof, Earl of Huntingdon, who married Judith, niece to the Conqueror, from whom it descended to the royal line of Scotland, and thence to the Cottons, ancestors of Sir Robert Cotton, celebrated for his valuable collection of books and MSS., known by the name of the Cottonian Library. Sir Robert Cotton, Bart., on making an excavation for a pond, found the skeleton of a sea-fish, twenty feet long, lying in perfect silt, about six feet below the surface of the ground, and as much above the present level of the fens.

CONISBROUGH, a parish in the southern division of the wapentake of STRAFFORTH and TICKHILL, West riding of the county of YORK, 6½ miles (N. E. by E.) from Rotherham, containing 1142 inhabitants. The living is a discharged vicarage, in the archdeaconry and diocese of York, rated in the king's books at £8. 12. 8½., and in the patronage of the Archbishop of York. The church, dedicated to St. Peter, is of Norman character, combined with the early, the decorated, and later style, of English architecture: it had a chantry, founded in the 14th of Edward II.: there are several monuments, together with a curious stone, adorned with many hieroglyphics. There is a place of worship for Wesleyan Methodists. A schoolroom was erected upon waste land by subscription in 1812; the income, amounting to £7. 10. per annum, arises from the rent of the old school premises, and an endowment of £2 a year. This is a place of high antiquity, having been connected with all the different dynasties by which Britain has been governed. The Britons called it *Caer Conan*; the Saxons *Cyning*, or *Conan Burgh*, both signifying a royal town. A Roman road is discoverable not far hence. Conisbrough is stated to have been the seat of a civil jurisdiction, which comprised twenty-eight towns. The castle, standing upon an eminence above the river Don, is of uncertain foundation; some consider it to have been built by Queen Cartismandua, others by the Romans, and others again by the Saxons. It is first mentioned as a fortress belonging to Hengist, the Saxon leader, who was defeated here, in 487, by Aurelius Ambrosius, and again in 489, at which period, according to Geoffry of Monmouth, he was made prisoner, and subsequently beheaded at the northern gate of the citadel; a tumulus near the place is stated to cover his relics. This account, however, has not been universally credited: there can be little doubt that a fortress existed here previously to the Conquest; but the structure, the ruins of which now constitute so interesting an object, was probably erected by Earl Warrenne, to whom the Conqueror gave the manor. In this castle Richard, Earl of Cambridge, second son of the Duke of York, and grandson of Edward III., was born; he was beheaded for conspiring against Henry V. The round tower, or keep, is almost perfect; the rest forms a picturesque ruin. Several human skeletons have been discovered.

CONISCLIFFE, a parish in the south-eastern division of DARLINGTON ward, county palatine of DURHAM, comprising the townships of High Coniscliffe and Low Coniscliffe, and containing 391 inhabitants, of which number, 245 are in the township of High Coniscliffe, 4 miles (W. by N.) from Darlington. The living is a vicarage, in the archdeaconry and diocese of Durham, rated in the king's books at £7. 18. 1½., and in the patronage of the Bishop of Durham. The church, dedicated to St. Edwin, has a tower and spire, and is in the early and later styles of English architecture: it stands at the village of High Coniscliffe, on the north bank of the Tees, occupying an eminence nearly surrounded by quarries of limestone, deeply wrought but now disused, though a large quantity is still obtained and burnt in other parts of the parish. The village of Low Coniscliffe is situated about a mile east from the church, and on the same side of the river. Coniscliffe was a considerable Roman station, the outworks of which, with the foundations of an aqueduct, and the military road called Broadway, from Binchester to the remains of an ancient stone bridge a little below the present one, are still discernible. Horsley places the *Magæ* of the Notitia here, the station being occupied by a field called the Tofts. Numerous Roman coins have been found; and there are two tumuli in the neighbourhood.

CONISCLIFFE (LOW), a township in the parish of CONISCLIFFE, south-eastern division of DARLINGTON ward, county palatine of DURHAM, 3 miles (W.) from Darlington, containing 146 inhabitants.

CONISHOLM, a parish in the Marsh division of the hundred of LOUTH-ESKE, parts of LINDSEY, county of LINCOLN, 8¼ miles (N. E. by E.) from Louth, containing 127 inhabitants. The living is a discharged rectory, in the archdeaconry and diocese of Lincoln, rated in the king's books at £9. 13. 6½., and in the patronage of Viscount and Viscountess Goderich. The church is dedicated to St. Peter. There is a place of worship for Wesleyan Methodists.

CONISTON, a township in that part of the parish of SWINE which is in the middle division of the wapentake of HOLDERNESS, East riding of the county of YORK, 5½ miles (N. E. by N.) from Kingston upon Hull, containing 137 inhabitants.

CONISTON, a chapelry in the parish of BURNSALL, eastern division of the wapentake of STAINCLIFFE and EWCROSS, West riding of the county of YORK, 11¾ miles (E. N. E.) from Settle, containing, with the hamlet of Kilnsay, 137 inhabitants.

CONISTON (COLD), a township in the parish of GARGRAVE, eastern division of the wapentake of STAINCLIFFE and EWCROSS, West riding of the county of YORK, 5¾ miles (N. W. by W.) from Skipton, containing 345 inhabitants. On a lofty mount near the village is an oval encampment, supposed to be Danish. Tradition relates that at a place called Sweet-Gap, on the north-western side of Coniston moor, the inhabitants endeavoured to arrest the progress of a party of Scottish invaders, and nearly the whole of them were killed.

CONISTON (MONK), a joint township with Skelwith, in the parish of HAWKESHEAD, hundred of LONSDALE, north of the sands, county palatine of LANCASTER, 4 miles (W. by N.) from Hawkeshead, containing, with Skelwith, 426 inhabitants. The village, consisting of groups of houses and neat cottages covered with slate, the produce of the adjacent mountains, is beautifully situated at the head of Coniston lake; this lake extends from north to south about six miles, is half a mile across its widest part, and in depth, at some places, not less than forty fathoms, abounding with char.

CONISTONE (CHURCH), a chapelry in the parish of ULVERSTONE, hundred of LONSDALE, north of the sands, county palatine of LANCASTER, 4 miles (W.) from Hawkeshead, containing 566 inhabitants. The living is a perpetual curacy, in the archdeaconry of Richmond, and diocese of Chester, endowed with £200 private benefaction, £400 royal bounty, and £800 parliamentary grant, and in the patronage of W. Bradyll, Esq.

CONOCK, a tything in the parish of CHURTON, hundred of SWANBOROUGH, county of WILTS, 4½ miles (N. E. by E.) from East Lavington, containing 144 inhabitants.

CONONLEY, a joint township with Farnhill, in the parish of KILDWICK, eastern division of the wapentake of STAINCLIFFE and EWCROSS, West riding of the county of YORK, 3 miles (S.) from Skipton. The population is returned with Farnhill.

CONSIDE, a joint township with Knitsley, in that part of the parish of LANCHESTER which is in the western division of CHESTER ward, county palatine of DURHAM, 14½ miles (N.W. by W.) from Durham, containing 141 inhabitants.

CONSTANTINE, a parish in the hundred of KERRIER, county of CORNWALL, 6¾ miles (S. W. by W.) from Falmouth, containing 1671 inhabitants. The living is a discharged vicarage, in the archdeaconry of Cornwall, and diocese of Exeter, rated in the king's books at £19. 3. 10½., and in the patronage of the Dean and Chapter of Exeter. The church is dedicated to St. Constantine. There is a place of worship for Wesleyan Methodists. The navigable river Hel runs on the southern side of this parish, and the village is situated upon an eminence nearly surrounded by tin works. The petty sessions for the division are held here. On the right of the road from Penryn to Helston is a vast rock of granite, computed to weigh seven hundred and fifty tons, called the *Tolmen*, from the Cornish words, *Toll*, a hole, and *Maen*, a stone: it is in the shape of an egg, with several excavations on the top, and is curiously poised on two others: at a short distance there is another mass of a circular form, resembling a cap. At Boscawen, in this parish, is a subterraneous passage, termed Piskey Hall, thirty feet long, five feet wide, and six feet high, formed of rude stones. The sites of decayed chapels are still discernible at Benallock and Budockwean. Near the church, where formerly stood a cross, a bag full of silver coins of kings Arthur and Canute was discovered about the close of the seventeenth century.

COOKBURY, a parish in the hundred of BLACK TORRINGTON, county of DEVON, 4¾ miles (E. N. E.) from Holsworthy, containing 282 inhabitants. The living is a perpetual curacy, annexed to the rectory of Milton-Damerell, in the archdeaconry of Totness, and diocese of Exeter.

COOKHAM, a parish (formerly a market town) in the hundred of COOKHAM, county of BERKS, 2½ miles (N. by E.) from Maidenhead, containing 2734 inhabitants. The living is a vicarage, in the archdeaconry of Berks, and diocese of Salisbury, rated in the king's books at £14. 14. 2., and in the patronage of — Rogers, Esq. The church is dedicated to the Holy Trinity. There is a place of worship for Independents. This parish includes the northern portion of the town of Maidenhead: the market has been discontinued, but fairs are held on May 16th and October 11th: it is bounded on the east and north by the river Thames. There is a manufactory for coarse paper. Courts leet and baron are held annually. There are eight almshouses, the inmates of which receive some trifling gratuities, and a small endowed school. Several descendants of Gen. Washington, and Mr. Hooke, the historian of the Roman empire, are interred in the church.

COOKLEY, a parish in the hundred of BLYTHING, county of SUFFOLK, 2½ miles (W. S. W.) from Halesworth, containing 274 inhabitants. The living is a discharged rectory, united to that of Huntingfield, in the archdeaconry of Suffolk, and diocese of Norwich, rated in the king's books at £6. 13. 4. The church is dedicated to St. Michael. There is a small endowed school.

COOLING, a parish in the hundred of SHAMWELL, lathe of AYLESFORD, county of KENT, 2 miles (N. by E.) from Rochester, containing 124 inhabitants. The living is a rectory, in the archdeaconry and diocese of Rochester, rated in the king's books at £14, and in the patronage of T. Best, Esq. and H. Fox. The church is dedicated to St. James. This parish, originally called *Colniges*, or *Colneges*, from its bleak situation, comprehends the two villages of Cooling-street and Church-Cooling, and contains the remains of a castle formerly of great strength, but long since dismantled.

COOL-PILATE, a township in the parish of ACTON, hundred of NANTWICH, county palatine of CHESTER, 4 miles (S.) from Nantwich, containing 48 inhabitants.

COOMBE, a township in that part of the parish of PRESTEIGNE which is in the hundred of WIGMORE, county of HEREFORD, 2½ miles (E. S. E.) from Presteigne, containing 67 inhabitants.

COOMBE-BISSETT, a parish in the hundred of CAWDEN and CADWORTH, county of WILTS, 3½ miles (S. W.) from Salisbury, containing 331 inhabitants. The living is a discharged vicarage, with the perpetual curacy of West Harnham annexed, in the archdeaconry and diocese of Salisbury, rated in the king's books at £7, endowed with £600 royal bounty, and in the patronage of the Prebendary of Coombe and Harnham in the Cathedral Church of Salisbury. The church is dedicated to St. Michael. This place received its distinguishing name from the family that formerly possessed it; the other arose from its situation in one of the narrow bourns, or combes, with which Salisbury plain is so frequently intersected.

COOMBE-KEYNES, a parish in the hundred of WINFRITH, Blandford (South) division of the county of DORSET, 6 miles (W. S. W.) from Wareham, containing 128 inhabitants. The living is a discharged vicarage, with the perpetual curacy of Wool annexed, in the archdeaconry of Dorset, and diocese of Bristol, rated in the king's books at £13. 18. 11½., and in the patronage of John Bond, Esq. The church, dedicated to the Holy Rood, is partly in the early style of English architecture, and partly of later date. The court leet is held by the tenure that the tythingman shall proceed to do suit at Winfrith court, repeating a few doggerel lines, and paying a fine of threepence. There is a small endowed school.

COOMBS, a parish in the hundred of STEYNING, rape of BRAMBER, county of SUSSEX, 2 miles (S.E. by S.) from Steyning, containing 70 inhabitants. The living is a rectory, in the archdeaconry and diocese of Chichester, rated in the king's books at £10. 0. 2½., and in the patronage of the Earl of Egremont. The church is in the early style of English architecture. The navigable river Adur runs on the eastern side of this parish.

COOMBS-EDGE, a township in the parish of CHAPEL en le FRITH, hundred of HIGH PEAK, county of DERBY, 2¼ miles (N. W. by W.) from Buxton, containing 433 inhabitants.

COPDOCK, a parish in the hundred of SAMFORD, county of SUFFOLK, 3¾ miles (W. S. W.) from Ipswich, containing 278 inhabitants. The living is a discharged rectory, with the vicarage of Washbrook annexed, in the archdeaconry of Suffolk, and diocese of Norwich, rated in the king's books at £9. 12. 8½., and in the patronage of Lord Walsingham. The church is dedicated to St. Peter. Clopdock hall was once the residence of Lord Chief Justice de Grey, and of Dr. Foster, a zealot of the church of Rome.

COPFORD, a parish in the Witham division of the hundred of LEXDEN, county of ESSEX, 4 miles (W. S. W.) from Colchester, containing 592 inhabitants. The living is a rectory, in the archdeaconry of Colchester, and diocese of London, rated in the king's books at £15. 3. 4., and in the patronage of the Crown. The church is principally of Norman architecture.

COPGROVE, a parish in the lower division of the wapentake of CLARO, West riding of the county of YORK, 4¾ miles (S. W. by W.) from Boroughbridge, containing 87 inhabitants. The living is a discharged rectory, in the archdeaconry of Richmond, and diocese of Chester, rated in the king's books at £5. 9. 7., and in the patronage of T. Duncombe, Esq. The church is dedicated to St. Michael. St. Mongah's well, in this village, was formerly celebrated for its medicinal properties. There is a trifling bequest, by means of which three poor children are educated.

COPLE, a parish in the hundred of WIXAMTREE, county of BEDFORD, 4 miles (E. by S.) from Bedford, containing 524 inhabitants. The living is a discharged vicarage, in the archdeaconry of Bedford, and diocese of Lincoln, rated in the king's books at £7. 17., endowed with £200 private benefaction, and £400 royal bounty, and in the patronage of the Dean and Canons of Christ Church, Oxford. The church, dedicated to All Saints, contains some ancient brasses. The navigable river Ouse passes along the northern boundary of this parish.

COPLESTONE, a hamlet in the parish of COLEBROKE, hundred of CREDITON, county of DEVON, 4¼ miles (W. N. W.) from Crediton. The village formerly contained a chapel, and, according to some authorities, a mint and a prison, long since destroyed: there are still some remains of an ancient cross.

COPMANTHORPE, a chapelry in that part of the parish of ST. MARY BISHOPSHILL JUNIOR which is in the ainsty of the city, and East riding of the county, of YORK, 4½ miles (S. W. by S.) from York, containing 281 inhabitants. There is a place of worship for Wesleyan Methodists, also a small endowment for the instruction of children.

COPP, a chapelry in the parish of ST. MICHAEL upon WYRE, hundred of AMOUNDERNESS, county palatine of LANCASTER. The population is returned with the parish.

COPPENHALL, a parish in the hundred of NANTWICH, county palatine of CHESTER, comprising the townships of Church-Coppenhall and Monks-Coppenhall, and containing 512 inhabitants, of which number, 366 are in the township of Church-Coppenhall, 5 miles (N.E.) from Nantwich, and 146 in the adjoining township of Monks-Coppenhall. The living is a rectory, in the archdeaconry and diocese of Chester, rated in the king's books at £6. 10., and in the patronage of the Bishop of Lichfield and Coventry. The church, dedicated to St. Michael, is built of wood and plaister, in the style which prevailed in the reign of Queen Elizabeth.

COPPENHALL, a chapelry in that part of the parish of PENKRIDGE which is in the eastern division of the hundred of CUTTLESTONE, county of STAFFORD, 4 miles (N. N. W.) from Penkridge, containing 108 inhabitants. The living is a perpetual curacy, in the jurisdiction of the court of the royal peculiar of Penkridge, endowed with £800 royal bounty, and in the patronage of E. J. Littleton, Esq. The chapel, dedicated to St. Lawrence, is built of timber and brick-work, apparently of the reign of Elizabeth.

COPPINGFORD, a parish in the hundred of LEIGHTONSTONE, county of HUNTINGDON, 6½ miles (S.) from Stilton, containing 70 inhabitants. The living is a rectory, consolidated with that of Upton, in the archdeaconry of Huntingdon, and diocese of Lincoln, rated in the king's books at £18. 13. 1½., and in the patronage of Lord Montague. The church, which was dedicated to All Saints, is in ruins.

COPPIN-SIKE, an extra-parochial liberty with Ferry-Corner, in the wapentake of KIRTON, parts of HOLLAND, county of LINCOLN, containing 17 inhabitants.

COPPULL, a chapelry in the parish of STANDISH, hundred of LEYLAND, county palatine of LANCASTER, 4 miles (S. S. W.) from Chorley, containing 1017 inhabitants. The living is a perpetual curacy, in the archdeaconry and diocese of Chester, endowed with £400 private benefaction, £400 royal bounty, and £400 parliamentary grant, and in the patronage of the Rector of Standish.

COPSTON (MAGNA), a chapelry in the parish of MONKS-KIRBY, Kirby division of the hundred of KNIGHTLOW, county of WARWICK, 6¾ miles (E. S. E.) from Nuneaton, containing 98 inhabitants. The chapel is in ruins.

COPSTON (PARVA), a hamlet in the parish of WOLVEY, Kirby division of the hundred of KNIGHTLOW, county of WARWICK, 6½ miles (S. E. by E.) from Nuneaton. There was formerly a village at this place, but it is now depopulated.

CORBRIDGE, a parish (formerly a borough and market town) in the eastern division of TINDALE ward, county of NORTHUMBERLAND, comprising the chapelry of Halton, and the townships of Aydon, Aydon-

Castle, Clarewood, Corbridge, Dilston, Halton-Shields, Thornborough, Great Whittington, and Little Whittington, and containing 2037 inhabitants, of which number, 1254 are in the township of Corbridge, 4½ miles (E.) from Hexham. The living is a vicarage, in the archdeaconry of Northumberland, and diocese of Durham, rated in the king's books at £11. 11. 8., and in the patronage of the Dean and Chapter of Carlisle. The church, dedicated to St. Andrew, is supposed to have been built out of the ruins of a neighbouring Roman station; it is a neat edifice, having undergone frequent repairs. There are places of worship for Independents, Wesleyan Methodists, and Roman Catholics. The village, formerly a borough and market town of considerable extent, stands north of the river Tyne, over which there is a bridge of seven arches; but, though well built, and in repute for its healthy situation, it has lost its former importance; the privilege of returning members having been found too expensive, and the market falling into disuse. Near the centre of the market-place is a cross, erected in 1814, by the Duke of Newcastle, who, in 1815, constructed a fountain near it, which, together with another fountain erected by the inhabitants, is supplied with water from a reservoir in the vicinity. A fair, held on the eve, day, and morrow of St. John the Baptist, has fallen into disuse; but fairs are held at Stagshaw Bank, in this parish, for the sale of live stock, annually on Whitsun-eve and July 4th, and a tryst fair on the 24th of November, the last established in 1820: at the fair in July a great quantity of linen and woollen cloth, brought from Scotland, is exposed for sale. At this place David, King of Scots, encamped in 1138. Corbridge was burnt by the Scots in 1296 and 1311. Two battles are said to have been fought here, one between the royalists and the Scottish troops, during the parliamentary war; the scene of the other is termed the Bloody Acre. To the west are vestiges of a Roman station, on the line of the ancient Watling-street, supposed by Camden to be the *Curia Ottadinarum* of Ptolemy, and by Horsley the *Corstopitum* of Antoninus, now called Corchester, where coins and numerous other antiquities have been found; and, in 1735, a large piece of Roman plate, twenty inches long and fifteen broad, and weighing one hundred and forty-eight ounces, was discovered in an enclosure south of the place, near the Tyne, which was claimed by the Duke of Somerset, as lord of the manor. In the churchyard, two altars, with Greek inscriptions, were dug up, one of them in honour of the Tyrian Hercules, which is esteemed the greatest curiosity of the kind in Britain. King John, expecting, from the past importance of the place, to discover buried treasure, ordered a diligent search to be made, but without effect: about a century and a half since, some bones and teeth, of an extraordinary size, were accidentally exposed by the flooding of the stream Cor, and were supposed to be the remains of oxen sacrificed at the above-mentioned altar of Hercules. In addition to the present parochial church, there were three others, *viz.*, St. Mary's, St. Helen's, and Trinity church, of which there are not any remains, though the site of each is well known. South of the church stands a venerable tower, once used as the town gaol; and a little to the east is an eminence called Gallow Hill, where criminals were executed. The parish contains lead-ore, coal, and lime-stone: several tanners' and skinners' pits, built of brick, were discovered in a field in the neighbourhood, in 1760. A court leet and court baron is held on Easter-Tuesday, under the authority of the Duke of Northumberland, as lord of the manor. A school, supported by subscription, was established in 1824.

CORBY, a market town and parish in the wapentake of Beltisloe, parts of Kesteven, county of Lincoln, 33 miles (S. by E.) from Lincoln, and 103 (N. by W.) from London, containing 581 inhabitants. This place, though situated on a Roman road leading to Ancaster, traces of which are still perceptible, is not distinguished by any event of historical importance, nor by any features of architectural interest. The market, which has nearly fallen into disuse, is on Wednesday: the fairs are on the 6th of August and the Monday before October 10th, for cattle and horses. The living is a discharged vicarage, united to the rectory of Irnham, in the archdeaconry and diocese of Lincoln, rated in the king's books at £5. 12. 1½. The church is dedicated to St. John the Evangelist. The grammar school was founded, in 1669, by Charles Reed, Esq., who endowed it with a rent-charge of £48. 15., for an unlimited number of boys of this parish.

CORBY, a parish in the hundred of Corby, county of Northampton, 2½ miles (S. E.) from Rockingham, containing 707 inhabitants. The living is a rectory, in the archdeaconry of Northampton, and diocese of Peterborough, rated in the king's books at £13. 16. 3., and in the patronage of the Earl of Cardigan. The church is dedicated to St. John the Baptist.

CORBY (GREAT), a township in that part of the parish of Wetheral which is in Eskdale ward, county of Cumberland, 6¼ miles (E. S. E.) from Carlisle, containing 303 inhabitants. The village is pleasantly situated on the east bank of the Eden; and contiguous to it, on the summit of a precipitous cliff, stands Corby castle, anciently the seat of the Salkelds, who inherited it from Hubert de Vallibus, Baron of Gilsland, from whom it passed by purchase to its present possessors, the Howards, a branch of the Norfolk family. The mansion was much modernised and improved in 1813, and the scenes and walks surrounding it abound in natural beauties. A court leet, a court baron, and a customary court, are held. A school, with a house and garden attached, was endowed, in 1720, with twenty-five acres of land, yielding about £20 per annum; the master receives a small quarterage from the scholars.

CORBY (LITTLE), a township in that part of the parish of Warwick which is in Eskdale ward, county of Cumberland, 5½ miles (E. by N.) from Carlisle, containing 170 inhabitants. The village is situated at the junction of the Eden and Irthing rivers.

CORELY, a parish in the hundred of Stottesden, county of Salop, 4 miles (W. by S.) from Cleobury-Mortimer, containing 566 inhabitants. The living is a discharged rectory, in the archdeaconry of Salop, and diocese of Hereford, rated in the king's books at £5. 5. 10., and in the patronage of the Rev. J. Corbet. The church is dedicated to St. Peter.

CORFE, a parish in the hundred of Taunton and Taunton-Dean, county of Somerset, 3½ miles (S.) from Taunton, containing 232 inhabitants. The living is a perpetual curacy, in the archdeaconry of Taunton, and diocese of Bath and Wells, and in the patronage of F. G. Cooper, Esq. and Mrs. Cooper.

Seal and Arms.

CORFE-CASTLE, a borough and parish (formerly a market town) possessing separate jurisdiction, locally in the hundred of Corfe-Castle, Blandford (South) division of the county of DORSET, 23 miles (E. S. E.) from Dorchester, and 120 (S. W.) from London, containing, with the tythings of North division and South division, 1465 inhabitants. This place, which in the Saxon Chronicle is termed *Corve* and *Corves-geate*, appears to have derived its importance from a formidable castle erected by Edgar, prior to the year 980, at the gate of which Edward the Martyr, when calling to visit his step-mother Elfrida, was, by her order, treacherously murdered. In the reign of Stephen the castle was taken by Baldwin de Rivers, Earl of Devonshire, who held it against the king: it was frequently the residence of King John, who kept the regalia at it, and by whose orders twenty-two prisoners, some of whom were among the principal nobility of Poictiers, were starved to death in its dungeons. Richard II., after his deposition in 1327, was removed from Kenilworth to this fortress, where he was detained for a short time prior to his tragical death at Berkeley castle. During the parliamentary war, Lord Chief Justice Bankes, who then resided in the castle, being with the king at York, Sir Walter Earl and Sir Thomas Trenchard assaulted the place, thinking to obtain easy possession of it for the parliament, but it was heroically defended by Lady Bankes and her daughters, with the assistance only of their domestics; until, on the approach of the king to Blandford, Captain Lawrence was sent to her assistance, when, having raised a small guard of her tenantry, she sustained a siege for six weeks, and, with the loss of two men only, preserved the castle for the king. In 1645, Corfe Castle was again besieged by the parliamentarian forces under Fairfax, when, by the treachery of Lieut.-Colonel Pitman, an officer of the garrison, who deserted from the king's service, it was taken and demolished. The remains of this stupendous edifice are extensive and interesting, and plainly indicate its former prodigious strength; they occupy the summit of a lofty and steep eminence to the north of the town, with which they are connected by a bridge of four narrow circular arches, crossing a deep ravine, and leading to the principal entrance between two massive circular towers: the walls, which enclose a spacious area divided into four wards, were defended by numerous circular towers at convenient distances, of which several have declined from the perpendicular line, by the attempts made to undermine them at the siege, and of which, together with the walls, vast fragments have fallen into the vale: at the western angle are the remains of the keep, a massive octagonal tower, and in the inner ward those of the king's and queen's towers, between which is part of the chapel, with two pointed windows; the east end of the king's tower, which is separated from the main building, is overgrown with ivy, and forms a picturesque feature in these extensive ruins, which, from their elevated situation, are conspicuously grand and majestic.

The town is situated on an eminence, nearly in the centre of the Isle of Purbeck, and consists principally of two streets diverging from the market-place, in the centre of which is an ancient stone cross. The houses are in general built of stone obtained from the neighbouring quarries, and approached by a flight of steps; the inhabitants are well supplied with water. The bridge connecting the castle with the town is called St. Edward's bridge, and is said to be the spot where Edward, fainting from the loss of blood, fell from his horse and expired. At the entrance from the London road is an ancient stone bridge over the small river Corfe, by which the town is bounded on the east. The inhabitants are principally employed in the quarries and clay-pits, for which the isle is celebrated: from the principal of these, called Norden, about a mile from the town, a railway has been constructed, to facilitate the communication with Poole harbour, where the clay is shipped for the Staffordshire and other potteries: a few of the female inhabitants are employed in the knitting of stockings. The market, which was held on Thursday, has been for some time discontinued: the fairs are on May 12th and October 29th. The lord of the manor of Corfe was anciently hereditary lord-lieutenant of the Isle of Purbeck, and had the power of appointing all officers, and determining all actions or suits by his bailiff or deputy; he was also admiral of the isle, and exercised the authority of Lord High Admiral, in which capacity he was entitled to all wrecks, except in cases where there was a special grant to the contrary, and had power to array the militia: these privileges ceased on the passing of the militia act, in 1757, Mr. Bankes, then lord of the manor, having omitted to enforce his claims. Though a borough by prescription, the town was not incorporated till the 18th of Queen Elizabeth, who invested it with the same privileges as were enjoyed by the cinque-ports. Under the existing charter of Charles II. the corporation consists of a mayor, who is annually elected at the court leet of the lord of the manor, held at Michaelmas, and eight barons, who have previously served the office of mayor: the mayor and the late mayor are justices of the peace. The elective franchise was granted in the 14th of Elizabeth, since which time the borough has returned two members to parliament: the right of election is vested in the freeholders, and in holders of leases determinable on life or lives, paying scot and lot, who are chiefly in the interest of Henry Bankes, Esq.: the mayor is the returning officer.

The living is a rectory, within the jurisdiction of the royal peculiar court of Corfe-Castle, rated in the king's books at £40. 14. 7., and in the patronage of Henry Bankes, Esq. The church, dedicated to St. Edward the Martyr, is a spacious and ancient structure, partly Norman, and partly in the early style of English architecture, with a lofty square embattled tower, crowned with pinnacles and ornamented with niches, in which are some sculptured decorations of singular design: it contains a few old monuments and several altar-tombs of Purbeck marble. This parish is the centre of a district of considerable extent, in which the earliest of the Sunday schools were established, under the auspices of William Morton Pitt, Esq., of Kingston House; there are thirteen of these schools, supported by subscription, in which more than four hundred children are instructed. A National school has been recently established, which is also supported by subscription. The almshouses in East-street, for six aged persons, have an endowment in land. In making a turnpike road near the town, in 1768, two stone coffins, formed of flat stones placed edgeways, and containing a skeleton, were found; and in 1753, an urn containing burnt bones was discovered, with the mouth downwards, near St. Edward's bridge. About two miles to the east of the town is an eminence called Nine Barrow Down, on which are sixteen barrows of various dimensions, chiefly circular, nine of which are in a straight line, and from this circumstance the hill has derived its name; eight or ten of them are surrounded by a narrow trench: the eminence commands a beautiful view of the port and bay of Sandwich, the British channel, and the Isle of Wight.

CORFE-MULLEN, a chapelry in the parish of Sturminster-Marshall, hundred of Cogdean, Shaston (East) division of the county of Dorset, 3 miles (S.W. by W.) from Wimborne-Minster, containing 544 inhabitants. The chapel is dedicated to St. Nicholas. The navigable river Stour runs on the north of this chapelry. There is an annuity of £27 for the support of a parish school, to which Richard Lockyer, in 1706, bequeathed £17 for teaching poor children.

CORHAMPTON, a parish in the hundred of Meon-Stoke, Portsdown division of the county of Southampton, 4 miles (N. E. by E.) from Bishop's Waltham, containing 168 inhabitants. The living is a perpetual curacy, in the archdeaconry and diocese of Winchester, endowed with £400 private benefaction, and £400 royal bounty, and in the patronage of H. P. Wyndham, Esq. The church is a curious edifice, apparently of early Norman construction. In 1669, William Collins gave a school-house and £450, producing an income of £22, for which about eight poor boys are instructed.

CORLEY, a parish in the Atherstone division of the hundred of Hemlingford, county of Warwick, 4¾ miles (N. N. W.) from Coventry, containing 316 inhabitants. The living is a vicarage, in the archdeaconry of Coventry, and diocese of Lichfield and Coventry, and in the patronage of F. Gregory, Esq.

CORNARD (GREAT), a parish in the hundred of Babergh, county of Suffolk, 1¼ mile (S. E.) from Sudbury, containing 656 inhabitants. The living is a discharged vicarage, in the archdeaconry of Sudbury, and diocese of Norwich, rated in the king's books at £9, and in the patronage of J. G. Sparrow, Esq. The church is dedicated to St. Andrew. The navigable river Stour passes on the west of this parish.

CORNARD (LITTLE), a parish in the hundred of Babergh, county of Suffolk, 2½ miles (S.E.) from Sudbury, containing 297 inhabitants. The living is a rectory, in the archdeaconry of Sudbury, and diocese of Norwich, rated in the king's books at £8. 2. 8½., and in the patronage of Mrs. Green. The church is dedicated to All Saints. The navigable river Stour flows on the south-west of the parish.

CORNBROUGH, a township in the parish of Sheriff-Hutton, wapentake of Bulmer, North riding of the county of York, 11 miles (N. by E.) from York, containing 63 inhabitants.

CORNELLY, a parish in the western division of the hundred of Powder, county of Cornwall, ¾ of a mile (W. by S.) from Tregoney, containing 168 inhabitants. The living is a perpetual curacy, annexed to the vicarage of Probus, in the archdeaconry of Cornwall, and diocese of Exeter, endowed with £200 parliamentary grant. The church is dedicated to St. Cornelius. The river from Tregoney is navigable on the south of this parish.

CORNEY, a parish in Allerdale ward above Derwent, county of Cumberland, 4 miles (S. E. by S.) from Ravenglass, containing 289 inhabitants. The living is a discharged rectory, in the archdeaconry of Richmond, and diocese of Chester, rated in the king's books at £9. 17. 1., endowed with £200 royal bounty, and in the patronage of the Earl of Lonsdale. The church is dedicated to St. John the Baptist. A little northward from the village are ruins of considerable magnitude, the history of which has never been developed: Druidical remains are also abundant in the neighbourhood. Mr. Troughton, an ingenious and eminent philosophical instrument-maker, who invented and constructed the mural circle for the Royal Observatory at Greenwich, was born here. A manor court is held at Middleton-Place, a small hamlet in this parish.

CORNFORTH, a township in the parish of Bishop's Middleham, north-eastern division of Stockton ward, county palatine of Durham, 6¼ miles (S. S. E.) from Durham, containing 330 inhabitants. The hill at the bottom of which the village lies contains a vast quantity of limestone; and the houses are disposed in the form of a square, with a green of several acres in the centre. Dr. Hutchinson, a learned writer, was born here.

CORNHILL, a chapelry in the parish of Norham, otherwise Norhamshire, county palatine of Durham, 1½ mile (E. by S.) from Coldstream, containing 863 inhabitants. The living is a perpetual curacy, in the archdeaconry of Northumberland, and diocese of Durham, endowed with £400 private benefaction, and £400 royal bounty, and in the patronage of the Vicar of Norham. The chapel, dedicated to St. Helen, was rebuilt in 1751, when a stone coffin, containing fragments of a human skeleton, and two urns of coarse earthenware, were found: in an adjoining wood is a well called St. Helen's Well, the water of which is serviceable in scorbutic and gravel complaints, but is not much used; a neat cold bath has been erected near it. A fair is held annually on the 6th of December. The castle was demolished by the Scots in 1385, and again in 1549, when a considerable booty fell into their possession: the remains consist of a tower surrounded by a ditch. Here are some medicinal springs. To the south-east is an encampment of unusual construction, the outworks having been mistaken for tumuli, the history of which has baffled the enquiries of different writers; and a quarter of a mile west is another large camp, the most remarkable north of the wall for variety and extent.

CORNSAY, a township in the parish of Lanchester, north-western division of Darlington ward, county palatine of Durham, 6¼ miles (N. E.) from Wolsingham, containing 249 inhabitants. In 1811, William Russell, Esq., of Brancepeth castle, gave an endowment for a schoolmaster and a schoolmistress, who are gratuitously to instruct twenty poor boys and girls, and also built and endowed almshouses for six poor men and six poor widows, each receiving £6 per annum, with other gratuities.

CORNWALL, a maritime county, bounded on the north by the Bristol channel, on the west by the Atlantic ocean, on the south by the English channel, and on the east by Devonshire; extending from 49° 57′ 30″ to about 51° (N.Lat.), and from about 4° to 5° 40′ (W.Lon.): it contains eight hundred and forty-nine thousand two hundred and eighty acres, or one thousand three hundred and twenty-seven square miles. The population, exclusively of the Scilly islands, amounted in 1821 to 257,447. The name is thus derived:—the part of Britain including this county and a portion of Devonshire, from its shape, was called by its ancient British inhabitants *Kernou*, or, as it is written by the Welch, *Kerniw*, signifying the horn, which word was latinized to *Carnubia*, or *Cornubia*: when the Saxons gave the name of *Weales* to the Britons, they distinguished those who had retired into Kernou, or Cornubia, by that of *Cornweales*; and their country was thus called Cornuwall, or Cornwall, that is, Cornish Wales. At the time of the arrival of the Romans, the northern part was inhabited by the Cimbri, the eastern by the Danmonii, and the remaining portion by the Carnabii. The Danmonii had subdued the two other tribes, and taken possession of their territories; but the Romans having effected the conquest of the whole island, and divided it into districts, Cornwall was included in that of Britannia Prima. Of the less authenticated portion of Cornish history are the traditions relative to the birth of King Arthur, at Tintagell castle, and his death at a battle fought near Camelford with his rebellious nephew Mordred. At a later period occurred various acts of hostility between the Saxons and the Cornish Britons, which obliged the latter to call in the Danes to their assistance. The Danish fleet arrived on the coast of Cornwall in 806; notwithstanding which, King Egbert, in 813, overran the territory from east to west. In 823, a great battle was fought at Camelford, between the Cornish Britons and the Saxons of Devonshire. Twelve years afterwards, another severe battle was fought at Hengston Hill, in the parish of Stoke-Chinsland, in which the Britons and their allies, the Danes, were defeated by Egbert. They were at length finally brought under the Saxon yoke by Athelstan, prior to which time they had occupied a great part of Devonshire, and inhabited Exeter in common with the Saxons. Athelstan having defeated Howell, King of Cornwall, near Exeter, drove the Britons out of that city, and obliged them to retire to the west of the river Tamar. Nine years after, the Cornish men having shewn symptoms of revolt, Athelstan entered their territory, and traversed without opposition to the Land's End, where he embarked his army, and, having reduced the Scilly islands, is considered to have thus completed the conquest of Cornwall. In 997, the Danes ravaged the territory, which, in 1068, was again plundered by Godwin and Edmund, sons of Harold, on their return to Ireland.

Owing probably to its remote situation, this county participated only in a very trifling degree in the military transactions of the three following centuries. In the reign of Stephen, the Cornish people declared openly for the Empress Matilda, and, although the war did not extend into their own county, they fought for her under the Earl of Cornwall, her brother. During the foreign captivity of Richard I. some slight skirmishing took place, in consequence of the seizure of St. Michael's Mount, by Henry de la Pomeroy, in behalf of Prince John. In 1471, when Queen Margaret had landed at Weymouth, the whole force of Cornwall and Devonshire joined her at Exeter, and accompanied her to the field of Tewkesbury. In September of the same year, John de Were, Earl of Oxford, having by stratagem got possession of St. Michael's Mount, established himself in that fortress, with a garrison of nearly four hundred men, and held it till the 3rd of February, 1472, when he surrendered it on condition that his life should be spared. The year 1497 is memorable for the rebellion of the commons of Cornwall, under Lord Audley, occasioned by the levy of a tax for the Scottish war; as also for the subsequent landing of Perkin Warbeck, who raised in this county a force of three thousand men, with which he marched to besiege Exeter. In 1548 occurred here the rebellion (one of those occasioned by the recent change in religion) of which Hugh Arundel, governor of St. Michael's, was one of the principal leaders. In July 1595, a small party of Spaniards, having landed near Mousehole, burned that town, Newlyn, and Penzance.

During the parliamentary war, the partisans of the king, being very numerous in Cornwall, had, about the close of the year 1642, secured entire possession of it, and volunteer regiments were raised, which made occasional incursions into Devonshire. The parliamentarian forces having entered the county from Dorsetshire and Somersetshire, were defeated on the 9th of January, 1643, on Broadoak, or Bradock down, and soon after driven out of the county. Not long after this a treaty was concluded between the contending parties, for adjusting the strife in the counties of Cornwall and Devon, and for removing the war into other parts, but it was annulled by the parliament. The subsequent hostilities, owing to the strength of the royal party, were various and important: on the 16th of May, 1643, the battle of Stratton was fought, in which the royalists obtained a brilliant victory over their opponents, and drove them entirely out of the county, proceeding immediately afterwards to join their party in Somersetshire, under Prince Maurice and the Marquis of Hertford: they particularly distinguished themselves at the battle of Lansdown, and at the siege of Bristol, for which services the king addressed a letter of thanks to the county, dated Sudeley Castle, Sep. 10th, 1643, commanding it to be printed and published, and a copy to be read in every church and chapel therein, which copies are still preserved in many of the churches. In the middle of July 1644, the queen, having retreated to Pendennis castle, embarked there for France. On the 20th of the same month, the Earl of Essex entered the county at Newbridge on the Tamar, and was pursued by the king, who entered it at Polston bridge, on the 1st of August; on the 1st of September, the army under Essex capitulated at Fowey, the earl himself having the same morning made his escape thence by water. The parliamentary army, under Sir Thomas Fairfax, again entered Cornwall, in the beginning of March 1646, and the whole county was subjected to the parliament by the 23rd of April, excepting only Pendennis castle, which held out until the middle of August. In May 1648, a small force which had been raised here,

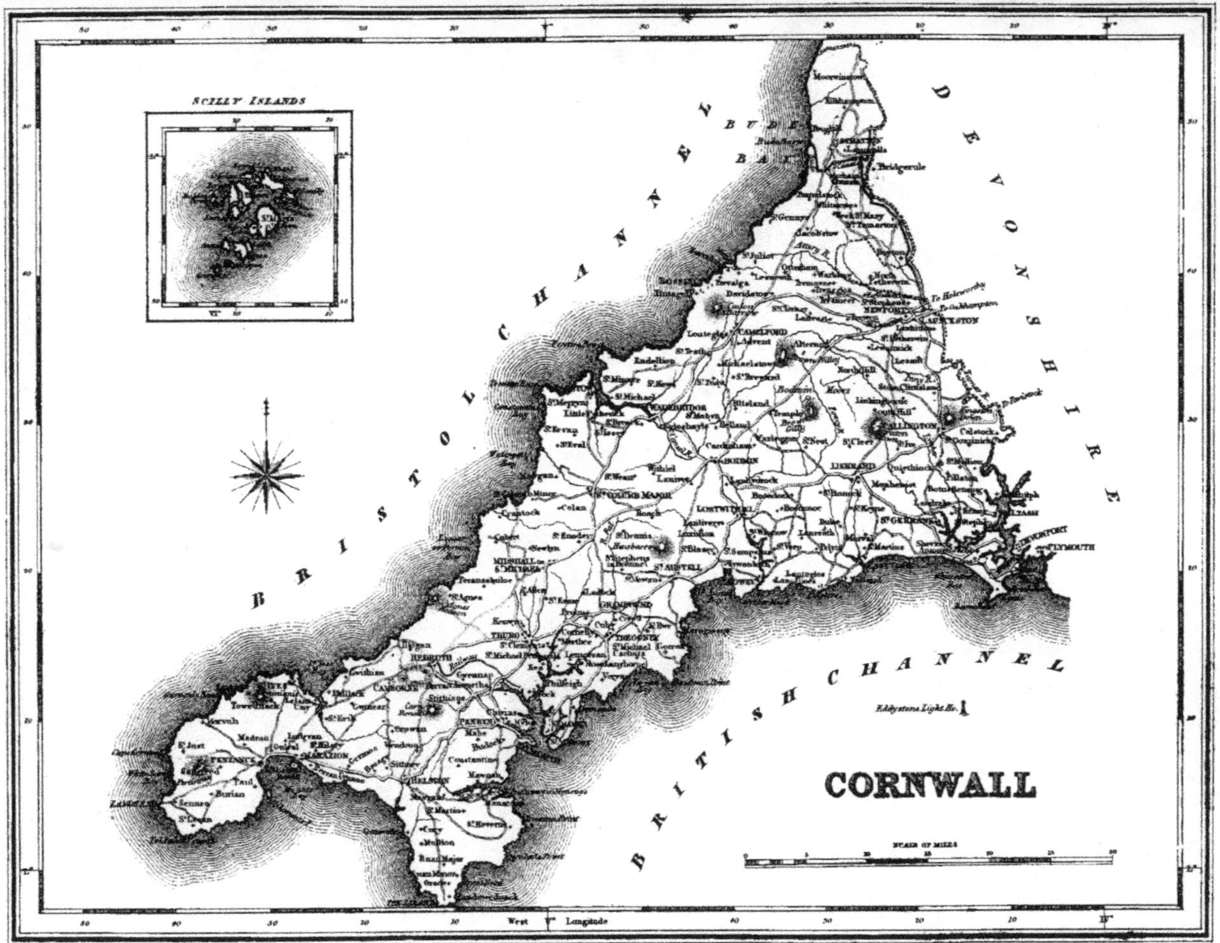
SCILLY ISLANDS
DEVONSHIRE
BUDE BAY
BRISTOL CHANNEL
BRITISH CHANNEL
CORNWALL
Eddystone Light Ho.
SCALE OF MILES
LAUNCESTON
To Holsworthy
To Okehampton
CAMELFORD
WADEBRIDGE
CALLINGTON
BODMIN
LISKEARD
LOSTWITHIEL
ST. AUSTELL
TRURO
REDRUTH
CAMBORNE
HELSTON
PENZANCE
PLYMOUTH
West Longitude

Drawn by R. Creighton.

ENGRAVED FOR LEWIS' TOPOGRAPHICAL DICTIONARY.

T. Starling sculpt Wilmington Square London.

in the hope of restoring Charles I., was defeated by Sir Hardress Waller. Sir John Berkeley and Col. Slingsby having been sent into Cornwall, in the autumn of 1649, to encourage their friends to take up arms for Charles II., were seized at Col. Trevanion's house, and sent prisoners to Truro. In 1650, the Scilly islands were held against the parliament by a considerable body of English and Irish forces. In May 1651, Admiral Sir George Ayscough, acting for the parliament, took all these islands, excepting St. Mary's, which was not surrendered until June. In 1667, the Dutch made an attempt to land near Cawland, in this county, but were driven back by the infantry on shore; they also made an attempt on Fowey harbour, but were repulsed.

Cornwall is within the diocese of Exeter, and province of Canterbury, and forms, together with three parishes in Devonshire, an archdeaconry, comprising the deaneries of East, Kerrier, Penwith, Powder, Pyder, Trigg-Major, Trigg-Minor, and West, and containing two hundred and three parishes, of which eighty-five are rectories, ninety-six vicarages, and twenty-two perpetual curacies; there are also three donatives, and several chapels: the spiritual court is held at Bodmin every second Friday, except during the Easter and Christmas holidays; and the archdeacon's visitations are held annually, about a month after Easter, at Launceston, Liskeard, Bodmin, Truro, Helston, and Penzance. The office of rural dean, which in many parts of the kingdom has become nearly nominal, is in Cornwall an efficient office: the rural deans are appointed annually, make regular visitations to every church within their deanery, and report the state of each at the archdeacon's visitations. For civil purposes the county is divided into the nine hundreds of East, Kerrier, Lesnewth, Penwith, Powder, Pyder, Stratton, Trigg, and West, in which are sixteen borough and market towns, *viz.*, Bodmin, Bossiney, Callington, Camelford, East Looe, Fowey, Helston, Launceston, Liskeard, Lostwithiel, Penryn, St. Ives, St. Mawes, Saltash, Tregoney, and Truro; four boroughs which have no market, *viz.*, Newport, St. Germans, St. Michaels, and West Looe; and fifteen market towns which are not boroughs, *viz.*, Boscastle, Camborne, Falmouth, Grampound, Marazion, Mevagissey, Padstow, Penzance, Polperro, Redruth, St. Agnes, St. Austell, St. Columb, St. Day, and Stratton. Of the above towns, ten are sea-ports, *viz.*, Falmouth, Fowey, Looe, Marazion, Mevagissey, Padstow, Penryn, Penzance, Polperro, and St. Ives; besides which there are the smaller ports of Bude, Charlestown, Hayle, Helford, Porth, Port-Isaac, Portreath, or Basset's Cove, and Trevaunance. Two knights are returned to parliament for the shire, and two representatives for each of the twenty boroughs. It is included in the western circuit: the spring assizes are held at Launceston; the summer assizes, and the Michaelmas quarter sessions, at Bodmin; the Easter quarter sessions at Truro; and the Epiphany and Midsummer quarter sessions at Lostwithiel. The county gaol and house of correction is at Bodmin, and there is also a county gaol at Launceston. There are ninety-nine acting magistrates. The rates raised in the county for the year ending March 25th, 1829, amounted to £118,628, and the expenditure to £115,641, of which, £98,520 was applied to the relief of the poor.

Cornwall is a royal duchy, settled by act of parliament upon the eldest son of the king. The immediate government of the county is vested in the duke, who has his chancellor, attorney-general, solicitor-general, and other officers, and his court of exchequer, with the appointment of sheriffs, &c. The important concerns of the mining trade are under a separate jurisdiction, the miners being, by ancient privilege confirmed to them by Edward III., exempt from all other civil jurisdiction than that of the stannary courts, except in cases affecting land, life, or limb. At the head of this jurisdiction is the lord-warden of the stannaries, under whom is the vice-warden; the final appeal being to the duke and his council. The vice-warden's court, held generally once a month, is a court of equity for all matters relating to the tin mines and trade, from which no writ of error lies to the courts at Westminster, but there is an appeal to the lord-warden, and from him to the duke and his council. Issues are frequently directed by the vice-warden to be tried in the stannary courts, which are held at the end of every three weeks (except in the stannary of Foymore, in which there is scarcely any business for the court), before the steward of each stannary and a jury, for determining on all civil actions arising within the stannaries, in which either the plaintiff or defendant is a privileged tinner; but the decision of each of these courts is subject to an appeal to the vice-warden, and from him to the superior authorities. Henry VII., on confirming their ancient privileges, granted that no new laws affecting the miners should be enacted by the duke and his council, without the consent of twenty-four persons, called stannators, six being chosen out of each of the four stannaries, or mining districts, of Foymore, Blackmore, Tywarnhaile, and Penwith and Kerrier. The stannators for Foymore are chosen by the mayor and corporation of Lostwithiel, those for Blackmore by the mayor and corporation of Launceston, those for Tywarnhaile by the mayor and corporation of Truro, and those for Penwith and Kerrier by the mayor and corporation of Helston; they are some of the principal gentlemen of property in the mining districts: on assembling, they elect a speaker, and their meeting is called a stannary parliament. These parliaments have been convened occasionally by the lord-warden, as the circumstances of the times have required new laws, or the revision of the old; the last met at Truro, in 1752, and continued by adjournments until September 11th, 1753. The stannary prison is at Lostwithiel, where the ancient records of the stannaries were kept previously to their being burned during the parliamentary war. The amount of the annual revenue of the duchy, in 1814, was £22,000, of which, £8,500 arose from the tin duty in this county, and £3,500 from rents of manors, fines, &c. The tin duty, before the late continental war, amounted to nearly £ 14,000 per annum.

The climate is remarkably salubrious, the southern coast, especially towards the Land's End, being, on account of the superior mildness of the air, much resorted to by invalids in the winter season. The surface of the county is hilly, and a large portion of it is occupied by uncultivated heaths and moors. The moors extend from near Blisland on the west, to near Northill on the east, about ten miles, and from near Davidstow on the north, to near St. Neots on the south, about twelve miles, lying in the four hundreds of Lesnewth, East, West, and Trigg; they abound with picturesque hills, and tors composed of immense masses of granite. The height of the principal elevations in the county, according to Col. Mudge's observations, is as follows: Brown Willey, by far the highest, is one thousand three hundred and sixty-eight feet above the level of the sea at low water; Carraton hill, one thousand two hundred and eight feet; Kil hill, one thousand and sixty-seven feet; Henborough, one thousand and thirty-four feet; and Cadonborough, one thousand and eleven feet. The rivers and smaller streams, owing to the inequalities of the surface, and to the many springs, are very numerous. The most considerable lakes, or pools, are, the Lo pool, about two miles long and a furlong wide, between the town of Helston and the sea, noted for excellent trout; and Dosmery pool, in the parish of Alternon, about a mile in circumference, formed by the union of the waters from the surrounding hills. The high grounds, through which the great roads chiefly pass, present a dreary aspect; but there is much beautiful scenery near the southern coast, particularly at East and West Looe, Fowey, and Polperro, and on the banks of the Lynher, near Trematon castle, and Nottarbridge. Falmouth bay and Mount's bay are considered equal in beauty to any spot in Great Britain. The banks of the Tamar, in the neighbourhood of Calstock, Cothele, Pentillie, &c., abound with fine scenery. The surface of the ground in many parts of the mining district has been greatly disfigured, particularly by the stream-works of successive ages. Some of the most remarkable and interesting scenes occur along a bold line of broken coast, bounded by the Atlantic ocean and the British channel, where, amidst a great variety of striking objects, may be enumerated the magnificent groups of granite rocks at the Land's End, Cape Cornwall, and Castle Treryn, the rocks of schistus at Tintagel, and the stupendous rocks near Portreath, with a lofty perforation called Tabbin's Hole. The rocks of serpentine at Kynan's Cove, near the Lizard Point, exhibit a variety of picturesque forms. The interior of the county also presents some remarkable objects in the rude masses of granite, in various fantastic shapes, which appear above the surface. The soil is various, the prevailing kinds being the black growan, or gravelly: the shelfy, or slaty; and loam, differing in colour, texture, and degree of fertility. The first abounds in all the higher grounds, and occupies a considerable part of the area of the county, the substratum being granite, frequently in a decomposed state. This soil is not generally so fertile as the others, but is particularly well suited to the culture of potatoes; and in some parts, where the growan is mixed with a large portion of loam, the land is remarkably productive. The shelfy, or slaty, soil takes its name from the rock schistus, or soft slate, on which it lies, and of which, with a mixture of light loam, it is composed. There are three extensive and very fertile districts in which it prevails, *viz.*, on the banks of the Alan, the Fowey, and the Fal. The loamy or alluvial soils of various descriptions, more or less mixed with clay, which is their substratum, are very fertile, and occur in many parts of the county, chiefly in the valleys and on the banks of the rivers. The serpentine soil, or that which covers the serpentine rock on Goonhilly downs, is noted for the production of that remarkable plant, the *erica vagans*, which is peculiar to Cornwall. Some of the high grounds on the north coast are covered to the depth of many feet with sea sand, which is composed of very minute fragments of sea shells, or coral, and appears to have been deposited by the spray of the sea at a remote period. The sea has considerably encroached upon the coast, within the last sixty years, in the hundreds of Stratton and Lesnewth, especially near Bude harbour, where the waves are rapidly wasting the sand hills. The substratum which prevails in the greater part of the county is that species of stratified rock usually called slate, or schistus, but known in the mining district by the name of killas; this, varying in substance and in colour, is found in every part of Cornwall, with the exception of those spaces which are occupied by the granite, or moorstone, the serpentine, and a few others of small extent. Of the granite there are four considerable districts: the first is nearly bounded by the church-towns of Northill, St. Neots, Blisland, St. Breward, and St. Clether; the second by those of Llanlivery, Roach, St. Denis, St. Stephens, St. Austell, and St. Blazey; the third by those of Constantine, Crowan, Redruth, and Stithians; the fourth occupying the western extremity of the county, from St. Paul and Zennor to the Land's End; and four small spots, one of them between Calstock and Callington, another east of Redruth, a third west of Breage, and St. Michael's Mount. In the southern part of the district of Meneage the substratum is serpentine, except a small portion of green-stone, being a species of trap, in the parish of St. Keverne. There are also three narrow veins of what is called irestone, or iron-stone, two of them bounding the granite of the Land's End toward the east and west, the third bounding the granite in the neighbourhood of Redruth, to the north-west. Some thin beds of limestone occur alternately with the slate near Padstow, and in the parishes of Carantoc and Lower St. Columb; and there are some isolated strata of limestone between Liskeard and the Tamar. Beds of clay of various colours are also found in several parts.

Some districts produce an abundance of corn, particularly that part extending from Endellion to St. Columb on the north coast, that called Meneage, the neighbourhoods of Burian and St. Germans, the lands near the Fawy, and a great part of the hundred of Stratton; but the fertility of these districts scarcely compensates for the barrenness of other parts of the county. The crops commonly cultivated are wheat, barley, and oats, including the naked oat, called in Cornwall *pillis*, or pill-corn, from the Cornish word *pilez*, bald, which brings the same price as wheat; its chief use is in making gruel for calves, and as food for poultry. The manures are sea-sand, sea-weed, and damaged pilchards; the sand being well adapted for manure, from the abundant mixture of pulverized shells and coral, is conveyed into the interior in great quantities, sometimes to the distance of twenty miles. Potatoes have been cultivated to a great extent in Cornwall longer than in other parts of the kingdom: in the vicinity of Penzance the land produces two crops of them in the year; and an acre has been known to yield three hundred bushels (Winchester measure) of the early kidney potatoes, at the first crop, and at the second six hundred bushels of apple potatoes: a large quantity is sent to London, Plymouth, and Portsmouth. There are numerous orchards in all the southern parts of the county, in some parts of the hundred of Stratton, and in that part of the hundred of East which borders on the Tamar. The parishes of Calstock and Stoke-Climsland abound also in cherry orchards. Owing to the cooling effect which the sea breezes produce upon the atmosphere, the harvest is later here than in the midland counties. Nearly a fourth part of the surface of the county, from one hundred and fifty thousand to two hundred thousand acres, consists of unenclosed waste lands, which are appropriated to no other purpose than as a scanty pasture for an inferior breed of sheep, and for goats, throughout the year; and about ten thousand acres to the summer pasture of cattle and sheep. Many of the valleys are well wooded, particularly in the south-eastern part of the county, and in the vicinity of Lostwithiel and Bodmin; and there are extensive plantations at Tregothnan, Clowance, Tehidy, Port-Eliot, Carclew, &c.: the principal landowners having of late directed their attention to planting, the face of the county, in the course of twenty or thirty years, will present extensive woodland scenery, both useful and ornamental. Much of the waste land in the mining district has been rendered more valuable by assigning on lease, for ninety-nine years, determinable on three lives, to the operative miners, portions of about three acres each, at an annual rental of ten shillings, on condition that they build a cottage and cultivate the land. It is worthy of observation, that the common sea-rush, which is very abundant on the northern coast, is planted there, as the only means of arresting, by the spread of its fibrous roots, the progress of the moving heaps of sand. Several plants indigenous to the south-eastern parts of Europe grow wild in this county. The Devonshire breed of cattle, more or less mixed, prevails throughout Cornwall; those of the larger sort, which are very numerous, are sold annually to graziers and contractors: the native cattle are very small and hardy, black, short-horned, and thick-boned; draught oxen are much used. Several mules, too, are bred and employed in the mining district, where also are many goats, these animals being much more numerous in Cornwall than in any part of South Wales. The Cornish choughs, once so abundant, and so well known as having afforded an armorial device to many of the Cornish gentry, have become rather scarce.

Cornwall has been celebrated for the produce of its tin mines from very remote antiquity. Strabo, Herodotus, and other ancient writers, relate that the Phœnicians, and after them the Greeks and the Romans, traded for tin to Cornwall and the Scilly islands, under the name of the islands Cassiterides, from a very early period; and Diodorus Siculus, who wrote in the reign of Augustus, gives a particular account of the manner in which the tin-ore was dug and prepared by the Britons. At what period the coinage of the tin obtained within the earldom of Cornwall was first established, is not certain, but it was practised so early as the reign of King John. In the reign of Edward I. it was first ordered, for better securing the payment of the duty to the earl, that all tin should be brought to certain places appointed for that purpose, to be weighed and stamped, or, as it is usually termed, *coined;* and that no tin should be sold until this stamp had been affixed. The quantity raised annually from the Cornish mines has varied with circumstances: the average annual quantity raised in the years 1799, 1800, and 1801, was sixteen thousand eight hundred and twenty blocks; each block weighing about three hundred and a quarter, and about six blocks and a sixth making a ton: in 1811, the quantity produced was fourteen thousand six hundred and ninety-eight blocks; in 1824, twenty-eight thousand three hundred and ten; in 1825, twenty-four thousand four hundred and seventy-nine; and in 1826, twenty-five thousand seven hundred and eighty-seven. At the commencement of the present century, according to Dr. Berger, there were twenty-eight tin mines then in operation in Cornwall, of which seven were in the parish of St. Agnes, four in that of Wendron, three in Gulval, and two each in Lelant, Redruth, and Perran-Zabuloe; besides which there were thirteen mines producing tin and copper, of which four were in the parish of Redruth, four in Gwennap, three in St. Agnes', and two in St. Neot's; and one mine worked for tin and cobalt in Madron. Drakewall's tin mine, on Hingeston down, in the parish of Calstock, is said to be the oldest mine now wrought, having been in operation about one hundred and sixty years. The principal tin mines are, Huel-Vor, in the parish of Breagne; Poldice, in the parish of Gwennap; Huel-Reeth, in the parish of Lelant; and Beam, in the parish of Roche: tin-ore is also found in beds usually thought diluvial; the most extensive deposits of this description occurring at Carnon, in the parish of Feock; Pentewan, in the parish of St. Ewe; and the Gorse and Fore moors, in the parishes of Roche and St. Columb. The mineral rights of tin in the duchy manors were, about fifteen years ago, sold for a term of years. The tin-ore has always been smelted in the county: in the year 1705 a patent was obtained for smelting it in iron furnaces. Soon afterwards reverberatory furnaces were introduced; and the blowing-houses, in which the metal had before been smelted, fell into disuse. For some purposes, however, particularly for fixing the grain of the scarlet dye, the tin smelted in blowing-houses is esteemed more valuable than the other, and it bears a higher price: the smelting establishments are principally at St. Austell's, Hayle, Huel-Vor, Penzance, Porheath, and Truro.

The working of copper mines was not carried on in this county to any great extent until the close of the seventeenth century, since which the quantity of ore raised has been gradually increasing, so that, in the year 1824, were obtained one hundred and ten thousand tons of ore, producing eight thousand four hundred and seventeen tons of copper, of the value of £743,253; in 1825, one hundred and eighteen thousand seven hundred and sixty-eight of ore, producing nine thousand one hundred and forty of copper, of the value of £798,790; in 1826, one hundred and twenty-eight thousand four hundred and fifty-nine of ore, producing ten thousand four hundred and fifty of copper, of the value of £755,358. The average depth of the mines is about one hundred fathoms, but Dolcoath mine, in the parish of Camborne, which is the deepest, is about two hundred and thirty fathoms, being one hundred and eighty fathoms below the level of the sea. At Botallock and Huel-Cock, in the parish of St. Just, the workings extend beneath the ocean, the noise of which is distinctly heard by the workmen. About the year 1800 there were forty-five copper mines in operation, of which eleven were in the parish of Gwennap, six in that of St. Agnes, five in that of Camborne, four in that of Gwinear, four in that of St. Hillary, three in each of the parishes of Germoe, Crowan, and Illogan, and two in St. Neots, the remainder being scattered singly in other parishes. Besides these were the mines already described as being worked both for copper and tin; a mine in Gwinear, for copper and silver; and one in Camborne, for copper and cobalt. The most productive copper mines in 1813 were, one near Hayle, one near St. Austell, one in the parish of Camborne, four in Gwennap, one in Crowan, one in St. Agnes', and one in Calstock; the two first were the most profitable, it being calculated that the one near St. Austell yielded about £2000 a month, and that near Hayle about half as much: the Huel-Damul mine, in the parish of Gwennap, in the course of about seven years, yielded a profit to the proprietors of about £230,000: the monthly expense of working Dolcoath mine is about £4000; and that of the Consolidated mines £6000. There are about one hundred and twenty steam-engines employed in drawing the water, rubbish, and ore out of the mines, and in working the apparatus for crushing the ore: the steam power in operation at the Consolidated mines, in the parish of Gwennap, is equal to that of two thousand five hundred horses; there are several engines of four hundred and sixty horse power each. Copper-ore is said to have been first smelted in Cornwall at Polruddan, in the parish of St. Austell: about the year 1754, some gentlemen of Camborne erected furnaces for smelting the ore at Entrall, in that parish; but, for the convenience of importing coal, the works were removed to Hayle, where are now the only copper smelting-houses in the county: in these about six thousand tons of ore are smelted annually; but the greater part is still shipped to be smelted in Wales.

The produce of the lead mines is inconsiderable; the ore is chiefly found at Huel Rose, in the parish of Newlyn, and Huel Penrose, in the parish of Sithney. Gold-ore has never been found in sufficient quantities to have been regarded as an object of profit. Some portion of silver was obtained so early as the reign of Edward I.: of late years the principal silver mines have been, one in each of the parishes of Cubert, Gwinear, and Calstock; of these, the only one now worked is the Calstock mine, which about the year 1814 yielded a profit of £5000. Other minerals of less importance, which are occasionally objects of commerce, are, cobalt-ore, found at Huel-Sparnon, near Redruth; antimony-ore at North Downs, in the parish of St. Agnes; and manganese-ore in the neighbourhood of Calstock. There are iron-foundries at Perran wharf and Hayle; manufactories for gunpowder at Kennall Vale, in the parish of Stythians, and at Coscawes, in the parish of St. Gluvias; for paint and colours at Penryn; and for the preparation of oxyde of arsenic at Perran-Arworthal. The ores are found in veins, of which the prevailing direction is from east to west, being crossed by other veins extending from north to south: most of the productive mines are situated near the union of the slate and granite strata. The ores are not found indiscriminately throughout the county, but lie chiefly in fields, or districts: these are, first the "Eastern," near Calstock; secondly, the "St. Austell," in the parish of St. Blazey; thirdly, the "Gwennap and Redruth," in the parishes of Gwennap, Redruth, St. Agnes, Stythian, Kenwyn, and Kea; fourthly, the "Camborne," in the parishes of Camborne and Illogan; fifthly, the "Huel-Vor," in the parishes of Crowan, Breagne, Germoe, and Gwinear; and sixthly, the "Western," extending along the north coast from Lelant to the Land's End: in each of these there are several mines, but there are also some in the intervening tracts. The mineral rights of copper, lead, &c., in the duchy manors were sold, about the year 1812, for a term of thirty-one years. The mines are private property, and are let during a term of years for a pecuniary consideration, varying in amount from one-twelfth to one-thirtieth of the produce. A debenture is allowed by government on Norway timber and coal consumed in the mines. The Cornish slate is a considerable article of commerce: the principal quarries are those on the southern coast, those between Liskeard and the Tamar, those in the parishes of Padstow and Tintagel, and the celebrated quarry of Delabole, or Dennybal, in the parish of St. Teath, the produce of which is held in the highest esteem, and is shipped in large quantities from Port-Isaac, about five miles distant, both coastwise and to the continent: this remarkable quarry was described by Dr. Borlase, about sixty years ago, as being three hundred yards long, one hundred yards wide, and forty fathoms deep; the quartz chrystals found in it are of great brilliancy. There is a great quantity of stone in various parts of the county suitable for building; it is principally taken from the porphyry dykes, or courses, which traverse both the granite and slate strata, in a direction from east to west; the granite, or moorstone, which abounds on the surface of the moors, has of late years been exported for the erection of bridges and other public buildings. An abundance of felspar clay, resulting from the decomposition of granite, is found in the parishes of Roche, St. Stephen, and St. Denis, and is shipped, chiefly at the neighbouring port of Charlestown, for the manufacture of china and fine earthenware. A yellow sandy clay, which from its resisting intense heat is called fire-clay, found near Lelant, is sent to Wales for laying the bottoms of copper furnaces.

The abundance of fish on the coast, besides supplying a great portion of food to the inhabitants, once furnished an important article of commerce, but of late years has greatly declined: the most esteemed fish, such as the turbot, sole, piper, dory, red mullet, whiting, mackarel, &c., are still caught. The London market is said to be chiefly supplied with mackarel, in the early part of the season, from the fisheries at Newlyn. But the most important branch of the Cornish fishery is that of herrings and pilchards, particularly the latter, which are peculiar to these coasts, the opposite coasts of Britanny, and those of the south of Ireland. The pilchard trade had become so extensive before the late continental war, that sixty thousand hogsheads, caught in St. Austell's bay, were exported from Fowey in one year. During the war this fishery almost wholly declined, so that in 1808 and 1810 there was no trade coastwise. In 1811 it revived a little, in consequence of the exportation of pilchards to the West Indies. Of late years a great quantity has been sold for manure, the oil being first extracted. The chief pilchard fisheries at present are in St. Austell bay and Mount's bay, on the south coast, and at St. Ives and New Quay on the north coast. Good oysters are found in great abundance in the creeks of the Hele.

Cornwall has few branches of manufacture, except such as relate to the smelting and preparation of its metallic ores: there is a carpet-manufactory at Truro; and coarse woollen cloths are made at Truro and Perran-Arworthal. The principal articles of export are tin, copper, and fish; to which may be added slate, granite, china-stone, china-clay, and potatoes. The principal imports are coal, timber, iron, hemp, and other articles of consumption in mining and fishing, besides a considerable quantity of grain and flour, grocery, and various manufactured goods. With respect to the state of the harbours, the mouths of nearly all the tide rivers on the northern coast have been nearly choked with sand cast up by the surge, or drifted in by the north-westerly winds.

The principal rivers are the Tamar, the Lynher or Lyner, the Tide or Tidi, the Leaton, the East Looe, the Duloe, the Fawy, the Fal, the Hele or Heyl, and the Alan or Camel. The Tamar rises in the parish of Moorwinstow, about three miles from the Bristol channel, and, after receiving the Tavy on the east, and the Lynher creek on the west, constitutes the fine harbour of Hamoaze; then, after forming two large creeks on the west, and one on the east, it falls into the English channel, between Mount-Edgecumbe and the lands of Stonehouse and St. Michael's island, in Plymouth Sound: its course is about forty miles, nearly south, in which it receives numerous small rivers, and forms from the sea up to its source (excepting only for the space of about three miles) the boundary between this county and Devonshire. The Lynher rises about eight miles west of Launceston, and flows south-south-east, near Callington, to Noddetor, or Notter, bridge, where it becomes navigable, and spreads into the Lynher creek; four miles further it falls into the Tamar, after a course of about twenty-four miles. The Tide, or Tidi, rises on the south side of Carraton hill, near Liskeard, and becomes navigable two miles above St. Germans, below which town it is called St. German's creek, which forms a junction with the Lynher creek. The Leaton rises about four miles north-east of Liskeard, and, passing near that town, falls into the sea, after a course of twelve miles. The East Looe river rises in the parish of St. Cleer, and, becoming navigable at Sand-place, falls into the sea between East and West Looe, after a course of ten miles; the West Looe river rises in the parish of St. Pinnock, and becoming navigable at Trelawn-wear, falls into the East Looe river near its mouth. The Fawy rises in the parish of Alternon, near the hill called Brown Willey, and becomes navigable (at high water) at Lostwithiel, three miles below which it joins the Leryn creek, and forms a wide and deep haven; two miles further it passes the town of Fowey, and falls into the sea after a course of twenty-six miles. The Fal rises about two miles west of Roach hills, and a mile below Tregoney its waters begin to spread, and form Lamorran creek, which is joined by Maples, or Mopas road, formed by the junction of Truro and St. Clement's creeks: two miles below this junction it reaches Falmouth harbour, which is four miles long, and upwards of a mile broad, and on the eastern side has fourteen fathoms of water; on the western side it has three creeks. At the bottom of this harbour the Fal opens into the sea, between Pendennis castle and St. Mawe's and Anthony point, its channel being there nearly a mile broad. The river Hele rises on the hills in the parish of Wendron, becomes navigable (at high tide) at Gweek, and, being joined in the latter part of its course by several small creeks, forms Helford haven, within a mile below which it falls into the sea, after a course of twelve miles, with an æstuary of about a mile broad. The Alan, or Camel, rises about two miles north of Camelford, and becomes navigable at Polbrock: flowing by Padstow, where it is about a mile broad, it falls into the sea about two miles below. An act of parliament was passed, in 1774, for making a navigable canal from Bude harbour to join the river Tamar, in the parish of Calstock; and another in 1769, for making a navigable canal, to be called the Polbrock canal, from Guinea port, near Wade bridge, to Dunmeer bridge, in the parish of Bodmin, with a collateral cut to, or near, Ruthern bridge, in the same parish.

The great mail-coach road from London to Falmouth, Penzance, &c., enters Cornwall at Poulston bridge, one mile and three quarters from Launceston, and passes through that town, Bodmin, Truro, the borough of Michell, and Penryn. The road to Penzance branches off between Truro and Penryn, at the village of Perranwell, and joins the turnpike road from Penryn to Helston, six miles from the latter town, through which and Marazion it passes to Penzance. The great road from London to the Land's End, by way of Devonport, enters Cornwall at Tor-point, and passes near St. Germans, through Liskeard, Lostwithiel, St. Austell, and Grampound, to Truro, where it joins the other great road. The mail-coach roads are very good; there is little travelling on the cross roads.

Cornwall abounds with rude monuments of its aboriginal inhabitants, much resembling those found in Ireland, Wales, and North Britain, consisting of large unwrought stones placed erect, either singly or in circles, or with others laid across; and barrows and tumuli; the numerous circles of erect stones are generally termed *Dawns-mên*, the stone dance. There are also several circular enclosures of stone, or earth, within which are rows of seats, having formed amphitheatres, originally designed for the exhibition of various sports, and where, in later times, the Cornish plays were acted: these are called *rounds*, or *Plan an guare*, the place of sport. Tumuli and barrows, the latter commonly called by the British name of cairns, are found in all parts of the county. Another kind of rude stone monument, most probably sepulchral, is found in many places, *viz.*, the cromlech, which consists of a large flat stone, laid horizontally upon several others fixed upright in the ground, and is provincially called the quoit, or the giant's quoit. Those ancient instruments of mixed metal, commonly called celts, have been found here more abundantly than in any other part of the kingdom. Several artificial caves, or subterranean passages, have been discovered, consisting of long galleries running in various directions, formed of upright stones with others laid across. In the year 1749, a great number of gold coins, believed to be British, were found in the middle of the ridge of Carnbrê hill. In several parts of the county may be seen rude upright stones of granite, with inscriptions of a date anterior to the Norman Conquest, and some of them coeval with the time of the Romans. The other Roman antiquities consist for the most part of coins, which of late years have been discovered in abundance in the western part of the county; and of spear-heads, swords, and other weapons of mixed metal, which have frequently been found in the ancient mines and stream-works. The situation of any of the Roman stations has not been ascertained. Ancient roads, or fragments of them, are visible in various parts of the county: one of these, believed to be British, traverses the hills, with barrows at intervals along its line, from the Land's End towards Stratton and the north of Cornwall, passing near the great British station of Carnbrê. Two Roman roads enter the county from Devonshire, one of which was a continuation of the great road from Dorchester and Exeter; the other appears to lead from Torrington and the northern part of Devonshire towards Stratton. Several of the Cornish churches retain traces of Saxon, or early Norman, architecture, some of them exhibiting curious specimens; the most considerable of which appears in the church of St. Germans, anciently the cathedral of the bishoprick of Cornwall, which was founded in 614, and annexed to the see of Crediton, in the county of Devon, in 1031: most of these churches appear to have been rebuilt in the fifteenth and sixteenth centuries: the towers are extremely well constructed, and those of St. Austell and Probus are highly ornamented. In the churches of St. Kew, St. Neot, and St. Winnow, are considerable remains of ancient painted glass. Several others contain richly ornamented screens, rood-lofts, pulpits, &c. Of the ancient fonts, many are in the grotesque Saxon style. There is a great number of sepulchral monuments of the sixteenth century, consisting of large slabs of slate, with effigies carved in bas-relief. Before the Reformation there were about twenty religious houses in Cornwall, including two Alien houses, and one preceptory of the Knights Hospitallers; there were also eleven colleges, and seven ancient hospitals: the monastic remains are few, and, excepting those of St. German's priory, not remarkable. Small chapels, or oratories, erected over wells or springs to which extraordinary properties have been attributed, abound in most parts of the county, the greater part of them in ruins; and in every part of it, are ancient stone crosses, not only in the churchyards, but also on the moors, and in other solitary situations. There are also, particularly in the narrowest parts of the county, from St. Michael's Mount to the Land's End, remains of several rude circular buildings on the summits of hills, of very remote antiquity, and still denominated castles; besides several cliff castles, formed by stone walls running across necks of land from cliff to cliff on the sea coast. Of more regular fortresses the principal remains are those of the castles of Launceston, Carnbrê, Tintagel, Trematon, and Restormel, all of high antiquity, and the first believed to be of British origin. St. Catharine's castle at Fowey, and those of Pendennis and St. Mawes, were built in the reign of Henry VIII., and resemble other castles, or blockhouses, erected by that sovereign for the defence of the southern coast. The most perfect specimen of ancient domestic architecture is Cothele House, erected in the reign of Henry VII. Ancient camps and earthworks are here particularly abundant, the greater part of them being nearly round or oval. In many places along the coast, a single vallum runs across from the edge of one cliff to that of another, with a ditch on the land side. There are considerable remains of a vallum called the Giant's Hedge, which appears to have been originally about seven miles and a half in length, extending in an irregular line from the river Looe, a little above the town of West Looe, to Leryn.

Of peculiar customs still observed, the following are the most remarkable. The lighting of bonfires on the eve of St. John the Baptist's day, and on that of St. Peter's day; the custom among the reapers of dressing up the last handful of corn, and parading about with it; and that of saluting the apple-trees at Christmas, which prevails also in Devonshire; to which may be added, the Furry at Helston, and the Bodmin riding, described in the account of those places. The Cornish were formerly much addicted to sports and pastimes, especially to the miracle-play, wrestling, and hurling; the practice of wrestling, after that particular mode, still prevails here more generally than in any other part of England. The miracle-plays having been composed in the Cornish language, a dialect of the ancient British, have not survived its extinction: that language was generally spoken until the time of Henry VIII., when, by the introduction of the English Liturgy, it gradually fell into disuse, and towards the close of the last century it had entirely ceased to be spoken.

CORNWELL, a parish in the hundred of Chadlington, county of Oxford, 4 miles (W.) from Chipping-Norton, containing 97 inhabitants. The living is a discharged rectory, in the archdeaconry and diocese of Oxford, rated in the king's books at £7. 4. 2., and in the patronage of the Crown.

CORNWOOD, a parish in the hundred of Ermington, county of Devon, 5 miles (N. E. by E.) from Earl's Plympton, containing 1057 inhabitants. The living is a vicarage, in the archdeaconry of Totness, and diocese of Exeter, rated in the king's books at £33. 4. 7., and in the patronage of the Bishop of Exeter. The church, dedicated to St. Michael, contains three stone stalls. The ground is hilly, with several small mountain streams encompassing the parish, the river Yealm running through it, and the Erme separating it from the adjoining parish of Harford. A charity school is supported by subscription, aided by an endowment of £10 per annum, left by the late vicar, the Rev. Duke Young, who also bequeathed £20 per annum for medical assistance to poor people not receiving parochial relief. Cattle fairs are held on the first Monday in May, and the fourth Monday in September.

CORNWORTHY, a parish in the hundred of Coleridge, county of Devon, 4¼ miles (S. E. by S.) from Totness, containing 607 inhabitants. The living is a discharged vicarage, in the archdeaconry of Totness, and diocese of Exeter, rated in the king's books at £10, endowed with £200 royal bounty, and in the patronage of the Rev. Charles Barter. The church is dedicated to St. Peter. An ancient priory for seven nuns of the order of St. Augustine, said to have been founded by the ancestors of the family of Edgecombe, and valued at the time of the dissolution at £63 per annum, formerly stood here: two arched gateways that belonged to it still remain. The parish, mentioned as a borough in old records, contains several acres of good productive orchard ground. The river Harborne, separating it from Ashprington, on the north, falls into the Dart, which then forms the line of separation from Stoke-Gabriel, for a short distance, making it a kind of peninsula. At Tuckerhay, a hamlet in this parish, is a flax-manufactory. There is a school for poor children, male and female, founded in 1609, by Dame Elizabeth Harris, and endowed by her with land producing about £25 per annum. Sir John Peters bequeathed a small sum from the great tithes of the parish, to be distributed to poor people not receiving parochial relief.

CORPUSTY, a parish in the southern division of the hundred of ERPINGHAM, county of NORFOLK, 6 miles (W.N.W.) from Aylsham, containing 451 inhabitants. The living is a discharged vicarage, in the archdeaconry and diocese of Norwich, rated in the king's books at £4. 12. 8½., endowed with £800 royal bounty, and £200 parliamentary grant, and is sequestrated. The church is dedicated to St. Peter.

CORRIDGE, a township in that part of the parish of HARTBURN which is in the western division of MORPETH ward, county of NORTHUMBERLAND, 11 miles (W. by S.) from Morpeth, containing 27 inhabitants.

CORRINGHAM, a parish in the hundred of BARSTABLE, county of ESSEX, 3 miles (E.) from Horndon on the Hill, containing 235 inhabitants. The living is a rectory, in the archdeaconry of Essex, and diocese of London, rated in the king's books at £22. 13. 4., and in the patronage of the Rev. W. R. Stephenson. The church, dedicated to St. Mary, has a tower apparently Norman, with two tiers of plain round arches; at the upper end are some pierced windows, and a low wooden spire. This parish is situated between Tilbury Fort and Canvey Island, and is bounded on the south by the Thames.

CORRINGHAM, a parish comprising the villages of Great and Little Corringham, in the wapentake of CORRINGHAM, parts of LINDSEY, county of LINCOLN, 4 miles (E. by N.) from Gainsborough, containing 479 inhabitants. The living is a vicarage, in the peculiar jurisdiction and patronage of the Prebendary of Corringham in the Cathedral Church of Lincoln, rated in the king's books at £12. The church is dedicated to St. Lawrence. There is a place of worship for Wesleyan Methodists.

CORSCOMBE, a parish in the hundred of BEAMINSTER-FORUM and REDHONE, Bridport division of the county of DORSET, 3½ miles (N.E.) from Beaminster, containing 632 inhabitants. The living is a rectory, in the archdeaconry of Dorset, and diocese of Bristol, rated in the king's books at £21. 3. 4., and in the patronage of the Rev. J. Munden. The church, dedicated to St. Michael, is a neat modern structure, erected about one hundred and fifty years since. The village is situated on the north side of a hill, and commands extensive views over the county of Somerset to the Bristol channel, and the mountains of Wales. The court-house, belonging to John Disney, Esq., lord of the manor, and now occupied as a farm-house, is nearly encompassed by a moat, over which there was formerly a drawbridge.

CORSE, a parish in the lower division of the hundred of WESTMINSTER, county of GLOUCESTER, 5½ miles (E. by N.) from Newent, containing 446 inhabitants. The living is a discharged vicarage, in the archdeaconry and diocese of Gloucester, rated in the king's books at £6. 2. 9., and in the patronage of the Crown. The church is dedicated to St. Margaret. This parish is beautifully situated, and has recently been improved by the enclosure of upwards of one thousand three hundred acres of land, which anciently abounded with wood, and was called "Corse Lawn."

CORSENSIDE, a parish in the north-eastern division of TINDALE ward, county of NORTHUMBERLAND, 5¾ miles (N.E. by N.) from Bellingham, containing 487 inhabitants. The living is a discharged vicarage, in the archdeaconry of Northumberland, and diocese of Durham, endowed with £250 private benefaction, and £600 royal bounty, and in the patronage of Francis Tweddell, Esq. The church, which formerly belonged to Halystone priory, is a small ancient edifice, inconveniently situated at the north-west end of the parish. The river Reed passes through the centre of the parish, the soil on its banks being of a light gravelly nature, and the best in the vicinity. Limestone and coal are found here, and in the western part of the parish a lead mine was formerly worked.

CORSHAM, a parish in the hundred of CHIPPENHAM, county of WILTS, 4 miles (S.W. by W.) from Chippenham, containing 2727 inhabitants. The living is a discharged vicarage, in the peculiar jurisdiction of the incumbent, rated in the king's books at £10. 16., and in the patronage of P. Methuen, Esq. The church, dedicated to St. Bartholomew, is a large structure, consisting of a nave, three aisles, and a chancel, with a tower and spire in the centre, and a chapel separated from the north aisle by a richly carved screen. There are two places of worship for Independents, one for Baptists, and a disused meeting-house, formerly belonging to the Society of Friends. Corsham, or, as it is sometimes named, Corsham Regis, from King Ethelred's having had a villa here, is a considerable village, having a separate jurisdiction, the bailiff of the manor, who is chosen by the tenants from among themselves, being vested with the power of sheriff and coroner within the same. Before the Conquest, it was a lordship belonging to Tostig, Earl of Northumberland, and at the time of the Norman survey it was held by the Crown; but in the reign of Henry III. it was possessed by that sovereign's brother, Richard, Earl of Cornwall, who, as well as his successors, granted and procured for it many important and peculiar privileges, which were confirmed in later times, some of them being still enjoyed by the inhabitants. Here was anciently an Alien priory, a cell to the monastery of Marmonstier, in Touraine. During the last century, Corsham was noted for its manufacture of woollen cloths, which has been entirely discontinued; though, with a view to the revival of its disused market, Mr. Methuen built, in 1784, a market or court-house, in the centre of the village, which consists principally of one long street of well-built houses, the situation being flat, dry, and salubrious. At the south end is an hospital for six poor aged women, erected in 1688, to which a free school was formerly attached: it is under the government of a master, who occupies an adjoining lodge, and who is appointed by the Earl of Radnor, as descendant of the foundress, Lady Margaret Hungerford, relict of Sir E. Hungerford, Knt., who also bequeathed land producing £20 per annum for a school. Edward Hasted, Esq., the historian of the county of Kent, was master of this hospital, and died there in 1812. Sir Richard Blackmore, a physician and minor poet, was a native of this place. A neat free school-house, for poor children of both sexes, has recently been erected, at the expense of Paul Methuen, Esq., the present lord of the manor. Fairs for cattle are held on March 7th and September 4th.

CORSLEY, a parish comprising Great and Little Corsley, in the hundred of WARMINSTER, county of WILTS, 3¼ miles (W.N.W.) from Warminster, containing 1609 inhabitants. The living is a discharged rectory, in the archdeaconry and diocese of Salisbury, rated in the king's books at £11. 0. 10., and in the patronage of the Marquis of Bath. The church is dedicated to St. Margaret. There is a bequest yielding £9 per annum, for the instruction of children.

CORSTON, a parish in the hundred of WELLOW, county of SOMERSET, 3¾ miles (W.) from Bath, containing 368 inhabitants. The living is a discharged vicarage, in the archdeaconry of Bath, and diocese of Bath and Wells, rated in the king's books at £6. 3. 9., endowed with £200 private benefaction, and £200 royal bounty, and in the patronage of the Bishop of Bath and Wells. The church is dedicated to All Saints. The river Avon bounds the parish on the north-east: *cornua ammonis*, and various petrified shells, abound in the quarries here.

CORSTON, a chapelry in that part of the parish of MALMESBURY which is in the hundred of MALMESBURY, county of WILTS, 2½ miles (S. by W.) from Malmesbury, containing 171 inhabitants. The chapel, dedicated to All Saints, exhibits some portions of early English architecture.

CORTON, a hamlet in the parish of PORTISHAM, hundred of UGGSCOMBE, Dorchester division of the county of DORSET, 6 miles (S. W.) from Dorchester. The population is returned with the parish. Here was formerly a chapel, which has long been desecrated, and converted into a barn.

CORTON, a parish in the hundred of MUTFORD and LOTHINGLAND, county of SUFFOLK, 3 miles (N.) from Lowestoft, containing 375 inhabitants. The living is a discharged vicarage, in the archdeaconry of Suffolk, and diocese of Norwich, endowed with £600 royal bounty, and in the patronage of the Crown. The church, dedicated to St. Bartholomew, is partly in ruins, the porch and the lateral walls of the nave being nearly overspread with ivy, but divine service is still performed in the chancel; though, from its beautiful tower, still perfect, and which, from its elevated position, serves as a land-mark for mariners, and its extensive ruins, there is reason to presume that it was a structure of much magnificence: the remains of another church, or chapel, still visible at a place called the Gate, together with old ruins and foundations discovered in many parts, lead to the inference that the village of Corton was in former times much larger than it is at present, and probably the resort of fishermen at the period when the mouth of Yarmouth harbour extended nearly to this place. Coins, fossils, &c., have been found within the base of the cliff, which borders on the North sea, on its being undermined by the tide; and a stratum of oak, several feet thick, and extending in length more than two hundred yards, was exposed to the view, after a severe storm in 1812. About the same time, a part of the *pelvis*, or haunch bones, of the mammoth, now in Mr. Sowerby's museum, London, together with other antediluvian remains, were found half a mile northward of the place.

CORTON, a township in the parish of BOYTON, hundred of HEYTESBURY, county of WILTS, 2½ miles (S. E. by S.) from Heytesbury. The population is returned with the parish.

CORTON, a hamlet in the parish of CLIFFE-PYPARD, hundred of KINGSBRIDGE, county of WILTS, 5 miles (N. E.) from Calne. The population is returned with the parish. Here was formerly a chapel, now demolished.

CORTON-DENHAM, a parish in the hundred of HORETHORNE, county of SOMERSET, 4 miles (N.) from Sherborne, containing 469 inhabitants. The living is a rectory, in the archdeaconry of Wells, and diocese of Bath and Wells, rated in the king's books at £13. 9. 4½., and in the patronage of E. B. Portman, Esq. The church is dedicated to St. Andrew. Some workmen, in 1723, discovered a Roman urn in the vicinity, containing about two quarts of coins, in good preservation, of the emperors, from Valerian and Galienus to Probus.

CORTON-HACKET, a parish in the upper division of the hundred of HALFSHIRE, county of WORCESTER, 5 miles (N. E.) from Bromsgrove, containing 187 inhabitants. The living is a perpetual curacy, annexed to the rectory of Northfield, in the archdeaconry and diocese of Worcester. The church, dedicated to St. Michael, is a small curious edifice, with a bell gable, having some decorated and ornamented portions in the later style of English architecture.

CORYTON, a parish in the hundred of LIFTON, county of DEVON, 6¼ miles (N. by W.) from Tavistock, containing 258 inhabitants. The living is a rectory, in the archdeaconry of Totness, and diocese of Exeter, rated in the king's books at £8. 13. 9., and in the patronage of T. W. N. Newman, Esq. The church is dedicated to St. Andrew.

COSBY, a parish in the hundred of GUTHLAXTON, county of LEICESTER, 6¾ miles (S. S. W.) from Leicester, containing, with Little Thorpe, 883 inhabitants. The living is a discharged vicarage, in the archdeaconry of Leicester, and diocese of Lincoln, rated in the king's books at £4. 15., endowed with £400 royal bounty, and £200 parliamentary grant, and in the patronage of Thomas Pares, Esq. The church is dedicated to St. Michael.

COSFORD, a hamlet in the parish of NEWBOLD upon AVON, Rugby division of the hundred of KNIGHTLOW, county of WARWICK, 3 miles (N. by W.) from Rugby, containing 55 inhabitants.

COSGROVE, a parish in the hundred of CLELEY, county of NORTHAMPTON, 1½ mile (N. N. E.) from Stony-Stratford, containing, with a portion of the hamlet of Old Stratford, 559 inhabitants. The living is a rectory, in the archdeaconry of Northampton, and diocese of Peterborough, rated in the king's books at £14. 11. 3., and in the patronage of J. C. Mansell, Esq. The church is dedicated to St. Peter. This parish is situated on the borders of Buckinghamshire, the Buckingham canal passing on its southern side, and there joining the Grand Junction canal, which enters the county here, by crossing the Ouse near its conflux with the Tow. A mineral spring, named St. Vincent's or Finche's well, exists in this parish.

COSMUS (ST.) and DAMIAN in the BLEAN, a parish in the hundred of WHITSTABLE, lathe of ST. AUGUSTINE, county of KENT, 2¼ miles (N. W. by N.) from Canterbury, containing 438 inhabitants. The living is a vicarage, in the archdeaconry and diocese of Canterbury, rated in the king's books at £10, and in the patronage of the Master of Eastbridge Hospital. The church is dedicated to St. Cosmus and St. Damian. There are four parcels of land within this parish which are reputed to be within the ville of Christ Church, the inheritance belonging to the Dean and Chapter of Canterbury.

COSSAL, a parish in the southern division of the wapentake of BROXTOW, county of NOTTINGHAM, 6½ miles (W.N.W.) from Nottingham, containing 317 inhabitants. The living is a perpetual curacy, annexed to the rectory of Wollaton, in the archdeaconry of Nottingham, and diocese of York, endowed with £200 private benefaction, and £200 royal bounty. The Nottingham canal proceeds through this parish to the northward, in a serpentine direction; and the river Erewash runs on the west side, separating it from Derbyshire. In the village is an hospital, founded by the ancient family of Willoughby, for four old men and four old women, who have coal, clothing, and two shillings per week each: there is a small bequest for a free school.

COSSINGTON, a parish in the eastern division of the hundred of GOSCOTE, county of LEICESTER, 2¾ miles (S. E. by E.) from Mountsorrel, containing 237 inhabitants. The living is a rectory, in the archdeaconry of Leicester, and diocese of Lincoln, rated in the king's books at £17. 7. 6., and in the patronage of T. Babington, Esq. The church is dedicated to All Saints. The parish is bounded on the west and on the south by the rivers Soar and Wreake, near which latter is a large oblong tumulus, three hundred and fifty feet long, one hundred and twenty broad, and forty high, and very steep, extending due north and south, called "Shipley hill," supposed to be the monument of some Danish king.

COSSINGTON, a parish in the hundred of WHITLEY, county of SOMERSET, 4¼ miles (N. E. by E.) from Bridg-water, containing 268 inhabitants. The living is a rectory, in the archdeaconry of Wells, and diocese of Bath and Wells, rated in the king's books at £13. 10., and in the patronage of the Rev. T. Hobbs. The church is dedicated to St. Mary. The village is one of the neatest in the county, the cottages being fitted up in a tasteful style, and the gardens ornamentally laid out.

COSTESSY, a parish in the hundred of FOREHOE, county of NORFOLK, 4½ miles (N.W. by W.) from Norwich, containing 824 inhabitants. The living is a perpetual curacy, in the archdeaconry of Norfolk, and diocese of Norwich, and in the patronage of the Mayor and Corporation of Norwich. The church is dedicated to St. Edmund. Here is a handsome Roman Catholic chapel, with pointed arched windows and painted glass, erected by Edward Jerningham, Esq.

COSTOCK, or CORTLINGSTOCK, a parish in the southern division of the wapentake of RUSHCLIFFE, county of NOTTINGHAM, 9½ miles (S.) from Nottingham, containing 341 inhabitants. The living is a rectory, in the archdeaconry of Nottingham, and diocese of York, rated in the king's books at £7. 18. 4., and in the patronage of the Rev. William Beetham. The church is dedicated to St. Giles. Costock is situated in a vale running east and west, and extending to the summit of a hill on each side, lying north and south, with a small brook at the bottom, dividing it into two nearly equal parts.

COSTON, a parish in the hundred of FRAMLAND, county of LEICESTER, 7 miles (N. E. by E.) from Melton-Mowbray, containing 162 inhabitants. The living is a rectory, in the archdeaconry of Leicester, and diocese of Lincoln, rated in the king's books at £16. 6. 3., and in the patronage of the Crown. The church is dedicated to St. Andrew.

COSTON, a parish in the hundred of FOREHOE, county of NORFOLK, 4½ miles (N. W.) from Wymondham, containing 65 inhabitants. The living is a perpetual curacy, in the archdeaconry of Norfolk, and diocese of Norwich, and in the patronage of the Archdeacon of Norfolk. The church is dedicated to St. Michael.

COTE, a joint hamlet with Aston, in the parish and hundred of BAMPTON, county of OXFORD, 2¼ miles (W. by S.) from Bampton. The population is returned with Aston.

COTES, a township in the parish of ECCLESHALL, northern division of the hundred of PIREHILL, county of STAFFORD, containing 241 inhabitants.

COTES de VAL, a hamlet in the parish of KIMCOTE, hundred of GUTHLAXTON, county of LEICESTER, 3½ miles (E. N. E.) from Lutterworth, containing 7 inhabitants. Here was formerly a chapel, but it has long since been destroyed.

COTGRAVE, a parish in the southern division of the wapentake of BINGHAM, county of NOTTINGHAM, 6 miles (S. E. by E.) from Nottingham, containing 779 inhabitants. The living is a rectory, consisting of two consolidated medieties, the first being rated in the king's books at £10. 7. 3½., and the second at £9. 14. 9½., in the archdeaconry of Nottingham, and diocese of York, and in the patronage of Earl Manvers. The church, dedicated to All Saints, is in the later style of English architecture, with a lofty octagonal spire. Here is a place of worship for Wesleyan Methodists. The Nottingham and Grantham canal passes through the parish, and the Fosse-road proceeds along its eastern boundary. Limestone is plentiful, and gypsum is occasionally found here. There is a small bequest for teaching poor children, and for bread for the poor, the school-house having been erected by a gift from a person unknown. A court, called the "Court of St. John of Hierusalem," which was anciently held at Shelford, under the prior of St. John of Jerusalem, and then styled the "Master and Lieutenant's Court of Shelford," is held here, and has a common seal: its jurisdiction extends over the extra-parochial liberty of Brewhouse-Yard, Kneighton, Owthorpe Tollerton, Hoveringham, Gedling, Barnby in the Willows, Stanford, Ruddington, Rempstone, Normanton upon Soar, Flintham, Hickling, Willoughby, Normanton on the Wolds, Cotgrave, Whatton, Aslackton, Scarrington, Carcolston, Carlton, and Ratcliff: all wills within the above places are proved in this court, and charters of exemption from toll throughout the king's dominions are granted to the tenants in each of these manors.

COTHAM, a hamlet in the parish of KEELBY, eastern division of the wapentake of YARBOROUGH, parts of LINDSEY, county of LINCOLN, 9 miles (N. W. by W.) from Great Grimsby. In the reign of Stephen, Alan Muncels, or Munceaux, built here a Cistercian nunnery, in honour of the Virgin Mary, in which, at the suppression, were a prioress and twelve nuns, whose revenue was estimated at £46 per annum.

COTHAM, a parish in the southern division of the wapentake of NEWARK, county of NOTTINGHAM, $4\frac{1}{2}$ miles (S.) from Newark, containing 74 inhabitants. The living is a discharged vicarage, in the archdeaconry of Nottingham, and diocese of York, rated in the king's books at £7. 18., endowed with £400 royal bounty, and in the patronage of the Duke of Portland. The church, dedicated to St. Michael, is a small dilapidated building.

COTHELSTON, a parish in the hundred of TAUNTON and TAUNTON-DEAN, county of SOMERSET, 7 miles (N.W. by N.) from Taunton, containing 108 inhabitants. The living is a perpetual curacy, annexed to the vicarage of Kingston, in the archdeaconry of Taunton, and diocese of Bath and Wells, endowed with £200 private benefaction, and £800 royal bounty. Cothelston hill is one thousand two hundred and fifty feet above the level of the sea, commanding an extensive view over eleven counties: on the summit is a round tower of great antiquity. The old manor-house, formerly the residence of the Stawells, who held the manor from the period of the Conquest until it was alienated to the family of its present possessor, still exists, but is inhabited by a farmer. A curious and very ancient custom prevails in this manor, certain tenements being held by the payment annually of so many bushels of rye, on Martinmas-day, at the manor-house; from which practice the tenants are called "Rye Renters." Limestone strata of blue lyas run north and south through the parish; and some indications of copper having been observed, an attempt at mining was made, but it was soon discontinued.

COTHERIDGE, a parish in the upper division of the hundred of DODDINGTREE, county of WORCESTER, $3\frac{3}{4}$ miles (W.) from Worcester, containing 277 inhabitants. The living is a perpetual curacy, in the archdeaconry and diocese of Worcester, rated in the king's books at £5. 16. 8., and in the patronage of the Rev. H. R. Berkeley. The church is dedicated to St. Leonard.

COTHERSTON, a township in the parish of ROMALD-KIRK, western division of the wapentake of GILLING, North riding of the county of YORK, $3\frac{3}{4}$ miles (N. W. by W.) from Barnard-Castle, containing 706 inhabitants. There are places of worship for the Society of Friends, Independents, and Wesleyan Methodists. A free school on the National system has been established for fifty children, of whom twelve are annually clothed. The village is pleasantly situated on the banks of the Tees, contiguous to which are the remains of a castle that formerly belonged to the Fitz-Hughs, lords of the manor, but was destroyed in one of the devastating inroads of the Scots.

COTLEIGH, a parish in the hundred of COLYTON, county of DEVON, 3 miles (E. N. E.) from Honiton, containing 239 inhabitants. The living is a rectory, in the archdeaconry and diocese of Exeter, rated in the king's books at £9, and in the patronage of the Rev. William Michell.

COTNESS, a township in the parish of HOWDEN, wapentake of HOWDENSHIRE, East riding of the county of YORK, 5 miles (S. E.) from Howden, containing 29 inhabitants.

COTON, a parish in the hundred of WETHERLEY, county of CAMBRIDGE, 3 miles (W. by N.) from Cambridge, containing 228 inhabitants. The living is a discharged rectory, in the archdeaconry and diocese of Ely, rated in the king's books at £6. 12. 11., and in the patronage of the Master and Fellows of Catharine Hall, Cambridge. The church is dedicated to St. Peter. Dr. Andrew Downes, Greek Professor at Cambridge, and translator of the Apocrypha, died here in 1627.

COTON, a township in the parish of HANBURY, northern division of the hundred of OFFLOW, county of STAFFORD, $6\frac{3}{4}$ miles (S. E. by E.) from Uttoxeter, containing 42 inhabitants. William Wollaston, author of a learned work entitled "The Religion of Nature Delineated," was born here, in 1650; he died in 1724.

COTON, a joint liberty with Hopton, in that part of the parish of ST. MARY, STAFFORD, which is in the southern division of the hundred of PIREHILL, county of STAFFORD, $5\frac{3}{4}$ miles (E. by S.) from Stone. The population is returned with Hopton.

COTON in the ELMS, a township in the parish of LULLINGTON, hundred of REPTON and GRESLEY, county of DERBY, $6\frac{1}{4}$ miles (S. by W.) from Burton upon Trent, containing 285 inhabitants. There is a trifling bequest, made in 1773, by Thomas Wagstaff, for which five poor boys are educated.

COTTAM, a joint township with Lea, Ashton, and Ingol, in the parish of PRESTON, hundred of AMOUNDERNESS, county palatine of LANCASTER, 4 miles (W. N. W.) from Preston. The population is returned with Lea.

COTTAM, a chapelry in the parish of SOUTH LEVERTON, North-clay division of the wapentake of BASSETLAW, county of NOTTINGHAM, 8 miles (E. by S.) from East Retford, containing 74 inhabitants. The chapel is dedicated to the Holy Trinity.

COTTENHAM, a parish in the hundred of CHESTERTON, locally in that of Northstow, county of CAMBRIDGE, $6\frac{3}{4}$ miles (N.) from Cambridge, containing 1488 inhabitants. The living is a rectory, in the archdeaconry and diocese of Ely, rated in the king's books at £36. 15., and in the patronage of the Bishop of Ely. The church is dedicated to All Saints. There is a place of worship for Particular Baptists. The dairies, which are numerous in this parish and neighbourhood, are famed for producing excellent cheese. The adventurers' land, chiefly enclosed from the old river Ouse and the common adjoining, was sometimes subject to inundation, but, in consequence of late improvements, this has been in a great measure prevented. A branch of the old Ouse passes near the village, and meets the river Cam below Streatham. It was to this village that Geoffrey, abbot of Crowland, sent the monks who first established a regular course of academical education at Cambridge: in 1676 two-thirds of it were destroyed by fire. A charity school was founded by Mrs. Catherine Pepys, in 1703, who gave a house for a schoolmaster, and £100 to purchase land, directing the rent to be paid as a salary for teaching sixteen poor children; and, in 1728, Mrs. Alice Rogers augmented this endowment with £10 per annum, for five more, and the same sum annually for apprenticing poor children, a bequest for the same purpose having been previously made, in 1671, by Mr. Moreton, who gave a moiety of an estate in the parish of St. Andrew, Holborn: in 1715, Mrs. Jane Bingham gave £15 per annum for the like use. This is the birthplace of Archbishop Tenison, author of several theological works, who died in 1715.

COTTERED, a parish in the hundred of ODSEY, county of HERTFORD, 3¾ miles (W.) from Buntingford, containing 410 inhabitants. The living is a rectory, with that of Broadfield annexed, in the archdeaconry of Huntingdon, and diocese of Lincoln, rated in the king's books at £20. 8. 6½., and in the patronage of the Misses Jones. The church is dedicated to St. Mary.

COTTERSTOCK, a parish in the hundred of WILLYBROOK, county of NORTHAMPTON, 2 miles (N. N. E.) from Oundle, containing 159 inhabitants. The living is a discharged vicarage, with that of Glapthorn united, in the archdeaconry of Northampton, and diocese of Peterborough, endowed with £200 private benefaction, and £200 royal bounty, and in the patronage of the Earl of Westmorland. The church, dedicated to St. Andrew, with its tower, is an interesting edifice, exhibiting portions in every style of English architecture, and some remains of stained glass in the fine tracery of the windows: it anciently had a college for a provost, twelve chaplains, and two clerks, founded in 1336, by John Gifford, clerk, a canon in the cathedral church of York; three stone stalls still remain in the chancel. In 1658, Clement Bellamy bequeathed land, producing about £5 per annum, for two exhibitions to two poor scholars at Cambridge, and for apprenticing poor children.

COTTESBACH, a parish in the hundred of GUTHLAXTON, county of LEICESTER, 1½ mile (S. by W.) from Lutterworth, containing 118 inhabitants. The living is a rectory, in the archdeaconry of Leicester, and diocese of Lincoln, rated in the king's books at £10. 6. 8., and in the patronage of the Rev. R. Marriott. The church is dedicated to St. Mary.

COTTESBROOK, a parish in the hundred of GUILSBOROUGH, county of NORTHAMPTON, 8¾ miles (N. N. W.) from Northampton, containing 297 inhabitants. The living is a rectory, in the archdeaconry of Northampton, and diocese of Peterborough, rated in the king's books at £26. 0. 10., and in the patronage of Sir J. Langham, Bart. The church is dedicated to All Saints. An hospital for two widowers and six widows was founded by Sir James Langham, in 1651, and endowed with fifty-three acres of land in Sibbertoft, as specified in a deed enrolled in Chancery at that period. A cell of Premonstratensian canons existed here, foundations of which have been dug up, the site appearing to have been surrounded by a moat.

COTTESFORD, a parish in the hundred of PLOUGHLEY, county of OXFORD, 6 miles (N.) from Bicester, containing 140 inhabitants. The living is a discharged rectory, in the archdeaconry and diocese of Oxford, rated in the king's books at £6. 13. 4., endowed with £200 private benefaction, and £200 royal bounty, and in the patronage of the Provost and Fellows of Eton College. The church is dedicated to St. Mary.

COTTESMORE, a parish in the hundred of ALSTOE, county of RUTLAND, 4¼ miles (N. N. E.) from Oakham, containing, with the chapelry of Barrow, 602 inhabitants. The living is a rectory, in the archdeaconry of Northampton, and diocese of Peterborough, rated in the king's books at £25. 16. 3., and in the patronage of Sir Gerard Noel, Bart. The church is dedicated to St. Nicholas. The Oakham canal passes through this parish, in which limestone is obtained.

COTTINGHAM, a parish in the hundred of CORBY, county of NORTHAMPTON, 2 miles (S. W. by W.) from Rockingham, containing, with the township of Middleton, 839 inhabitants. The living is a rectory, in the archdeaconry of Northampton, and diocese of Peterborough, rated in the king's books at £23. 7. 3½., and in the patronage of the Principal and Fellows of Brasenose College, Oxford. The church is dedicated to St. Mary Magdalene. There is a place of worship for Wesleyan Methodists. In an ancient record it is stated that a house for leprous persons existed here in the time of Henry III.

COTTINGHAM, a parish (formerly a market town) in the Hunsley-Beacon division of the wapentake of HARTHILL, East riding of the county of YORK, 4½ miles (N. W.) from Kingston upon Hull, containing, with a part of the township of Willerby, 2479 inhabitants. The living is a vicarage, with the perpetual curacy of Skidley annexed, in the archdeaconry of the East riding, and diocese of York, endowed with £200 private benefaction, £300 royal bounty, and £800 parliamentary grant, and in the patronage of the Bishop of Chester, as impropriator of the rectory, which is rated in the king's books at £106. 13. 4. The church, dedicated to St. Mary the Virgin, is a spacious handsome edifice, built in 1272, with a light and beautiful tower rising from the centre: within are several elegant monuments, particularly those of the family of Burton, and in the chancel is an ancient tombstone, without date, to the memory of the founder, Nicholas de Stuteville. There are places of worship for Independents and Primitive and Wesleyan Methodists. Leland, in his Collectanea, states that William d'Estoteville, or Stuteville, being then sheriff of Yorkshire, entertained King John here, and obtained from that monarch, in the year 1200, permission to hold a market and fair, and to embattle and fortify his residence. This noble mansion, called Baynard castle, continued for ages a distinguished monument of feudal grandeur, but it was destroyed by fire in 1541, and only the ramparts and ditches are visible. In the 15th of Edward II., Thomas, Lord Wake, began to establish here a monastery for Augustine canons, which, about the year 1324, was removed to the extra-parochial liberty of Newton, or Howdenprice: its revenue, at the dissolution, was estimated at £178. 0. 10.: there are no remains. The village, which is very agreeably situated, is large, and contains several highly respectable dwelling-houses; there are two breweries and a carpet-manufactory. A considerable portion of the land in the parish is appropriated to the cultivation of vegetables and other horticultural produce, for the market at Hull, which place is also, in a great measure, supplied with milk and butter from this neighbourhood. The market and one of the fairs have been discontinued, but a fair is held annually on the festival of St. Martin. A free school is principally supported from a bequest of land, producing about £40 per annum, by Mr. Mark Kirby, in 1712, for which twenty children are instructed. There are various minor benefactions for the poor, including a dole of £10 per annum, left by Mr. Robert Mills, for distribution at Christmas. The parish officers, in 1819, assigned about twelve acres of land, the proceeds of which were previously applied toward the repairs of the church, to twenty poor men, each of whom has erected a cottage, for which he pays annually an acknowledgment of two shillings. Adjoining the ancient road called Keldgate are some intermitting springs, which will sometimes flow copiously after remaining quiescent for several years.

COTTINGWITH (EAST), a chapelry in the parish of AUGHTON, Holme-Beacon division of the wapentake of HARTHILL, East riding of the county of YORK, 8½ miles (S. W. by W.) from Pocklington, containing 308 inhabitants. There is a place of worship for Wesleyan Methodists. A trifling bequest has been made for the instruction of children.

COTTINGWITH (WEST), a township in the parish of THORGANBY, wapentake of OUZE and DERWENT, East riding of the county of YORK, 9¾ miles (S. E.) from York. The population is returned with the parish. Four poor children are educated for £3. 10., being a portion of the produce of town lands.

COTTLES, an extra-parochial liberty with Little Chalfield, in the hundred of BRADFORD, county of WILTS, 3½ miles (W.) from Melksham. The population is returned with Great Chalfield.

COTTON, a township in that part of the parish of SANDBACH which is in the hundred of NORTHWICH, county palatine of CHESTER, 2¾ miles (E. by N.) from Middlewich, containing 81 inhabitants.

COTTON, a township in that part of the parish of WEM which is in the Whitchurch division of the hundred of BRADFORD (North), county of SALOP, containing 458 inhabitants.

COTTON, a chapelry in the parish of ALVETON, southern division of the hundred of TOTMONSLOW, county of STAFFORD, 5¼ miles (N. E.) from Cheadle, containing 439 inhabitants. The living is a perpetual curacy, in the archdeaconry of Stafford, and diocese of Lichfield and Coventry, endowed with £400 private benefaction, and £1000 royal bounty, and in the patronage of George Whieldon, Esq. The chapel was built in 1795, at the sole expense of the late Thomas Gilbert, Esq., who also endowed it, and left the payment of the repairs a perpetual charge upon his property. There are extensive quarries of limestone, worked by the Trent and Mersey Canal Company. Cotton is in the honour of Tutbury, duchy of Lancaster, and within the jurisdiction of a court of pleas held at Tutbury every third Tuesday, for the recovery of debts under 40*s*.

COTTON, a parish in the hundred of HARTISMERE, county of SUFFOLK, 2 miles (W.N.W.) from Mendlesham, containing 527 inhabitants. The living is a rectory, in the archdeaconry of Sudbury, and diocese of Norwich, rated in the king's books at £15. 10. 2½., and in the patronage of the Rev. P. Eade. The church is dedicated to St. Andrew. There is a place of worship for Wesleyan Methodists. A bequest from an unknown donor produces about £9 per annum, for the instruction of children.

COTTON, or COTTAM, a chapelry in the parish of LANGTOFT, partly within the liberty of ST. PETER of YORK, and partly in the wapentake of DICKERING, East riding of the county of YORK, 5¾ miles (N.N.W.) from Great Driffield, containing 16 inhabitants. The living is a perpetual curacy, in the peculiar jurisdiction of the Prebendary of Langtoft in the Cathedral Church of York, and in the patronage of the Vicar of Langtoft.

COTTON, a township in that part of the parish of HOVINGHAM which is in the wapentake of RYEDALE, North riding of the county of YORK, 8 miles (S. by E.) from Helmsley, containing 112 inhabitants.

COTTON (ABBOT'S), a township in the parish of CHRISTLETON, lower division of the hundred of BROXTON, county palatine of CHESTER, 4 miles (E. by N.) from Chester, containing 17 inhabitants.

COTTON (EDMUND'S), a township in the parish of CHRISTLETON, lower division of the hundred of BROXTON, county palatine of CHESTER, 4¼ miles (E. by S.) from Chester, containing 85 inhabitants. It derives its name from Edmund de Cotton, who formerly possessed it.

COTTON-FAR, a hamlet in the parish of HARDINGSTONE, hundred of WYMERSLEY, county of NORTHAMPTON, ½ a mile (S.) from Northampton, containing, with Paper Mills and Delapree Abbey, 356 inhabitants. An hospital, dedicated to St. Leonard, for a master and leprous brethren and sisters, is stated to have been founded here by William the Conqueror, which was under the superintendence of the mayor and burgesses of Northampton: its revenue, in the 26th of Henry VIII., was estimated at £12. 6. 8.

COUGHTON, a hamlet in the parish of WALFORD, hundred of GREYTREE, county of HEREFORD, 2¾ miles (S. by E.) from Ross. The population is returned with the parish. Here was formerly a chapel, now in ruins.

COUGHTON, a parish in the Alcester division of the hundred of BARLICHWAY, county of WARWICK, 2 miles (N. by W.) from Alcester, containing, with the hamlet of Sambourn, 926 inhabitants. The living is a discharged vicarage, in the archdeaconry and diocese of Worcester, rated in the king's books at £9. 10. 7½., endowed with £400 royal bounty, and in the patronage of Sir Charles Throckmorton, Bart. The church is dedicated to St. Peter.

COULDSNOUTH, a joint township with Thompson's Walls, in the parish of KIRKNEWTON, western division of GLENDALE ward, county of NORTHUMBERLAND, 7½ miles (W. by N.) from Wooler, containing, with Thompson's Walls, 44 inhabitants.

COULSDON, a parish in the first division of the hundred of WALLINGTON, county of SURREY, 5 miles (S. by W.) from Croydon, containing 516 inhabitants. The living is a rectory, in the archdeaconry of Surrey, and diocese of Winchester, rated in the king's books at £21. 16. 5½., and in the patronage of the Archbishop of Canterbury. The church is dedicated to St. John the Evangelist.

COULSTON (EAST), a parish in the hundred of WHORWELSDOWN, county of WILTS, 5 miles (E. N. E.) from Westbury, containing 99 inhabitants. The living is a rectory, in the archdeaconry of Wilts, and diocese of Salisbury, rated in the king's books at £7. 14. 2., and in the patronage of the Crown. The church is dedicated to St. Thomas à Becket.

COULSTON (WEST), a joint tything with Baynton, in the parish of Edington, hundred of Whorwelsdown, county of Wilts, containing, with Baynton, 168 inhabitants.

COULTON, a parish in the hundred of Lonsdale, north of the sands, county palatine of Lancaster, comprising the chapelries of Finthwaite, Haverthwaite, and Rusland, and the townships of East Coulton, West Coulton, and Nibthwaite, and containing 1627 inhabitants. East Coulton is 5½ miles (N. N. E.), and West Coulton 5 miles (N. by E.), from Ulverstone. The living is a perpetual curacy, in the archdeaconry of Richmond, and diocese of Chester, endowed with £400 private benefaction, £400 royal bounty, and £600 parliamentary grant, and in the patronage of the Landowners, who pay their quotas to the minister's stipend. The church is dedicated to the Holy Trinity. This parish is bounded on the east and south by the lake Windermere, and the river Leven, which issues from it, and on the west by the lake Coniston and the river Crake. There is a meeting-house for the Society of Friends. The parochial school is endowed with fifty acres of land given by Adam Sandys, Esq., besides a small bequest from Bartholomew Pennington.

COUND, a parish in the hundred of Condover, county of Salop, 6½ miles (N.W.) from Much Wenlock, containing, with the chapelry of Cressage, 799 inhabitants. The living is a rectory, in the archdeaconry of Salop, and diocese of Lichfield and Coventry, rated in the king's books at £33, and in the patronage of John C. Pelham, Esq. The church is dedicated to St. Peter. The river Severn runs through the parish.

COUNDEN-GRANGE, a township in that part of the parish of St. Andrew Auckland which is in the south-eastern division of Darlington ward, county palatine of Durham, 1¾ mile (E. S. E.) from Bishop-Auckland, containing 28 inhabitants.

COUNDON, a township in that part of the parish of St. Andrew Auckland which is in the north-western division of Darlington ward, county palatine of Durham, 2 miles (E. by S.) from Bishop-Auckland, containing 222 inhabitants.

COUNDON, a hamlet in that part of the parish of the Holy Trinity, Coventry, which is in the Kirby division of the hundred of Knightlow, county of Warwick, containing 213 inhabitants.

COUNTESS-THORPE, a chapelry in the parish of Blaby, hundred of Guthlaxton, county of Leicester, 6 miles (S.) from Leicester, containing 741 inhabitants.

COUNTHORPE, a hamlet in the parish of Bytham-Castle, wapentake of Beltisloe, parts of Kesteven, county of Lincoln, 3½ miles (S.) from Corby, containing 43 inhabitants.

COUNTISBURY, a parish in the hundred of Sherwill, county of Devon, 15½ miles (E. by N.) from Ilfracombe, containing 118 inhabitants. The living is a perpetual curacy, annexed to that of Linton, in the archdeaconry of Barnstaple, and diocese of Exeter, endowed with £600 royal bounty, and £200 parliamentary grant. The church is dedicated to St. John the Baptist. The parish borders on the Bristol channel, and is bounded for some miles on the south and west by the small but rapid stream Lyn.

COUPE-LENCH, a joint township with Newhall-hey and Hall-Carr, in that part of the parish of Bury which is in the higher division of the hundred of Blackburn, county palatine of Lancaster, 4¼ miles (S. S. E.) from Haslingden, containing, with Newhall-hey and Hall-Carr, 1224 inhabitants.

COUPLAND, a township in the parish of Kirk-newton, western division of Glendale ward, county of Northumberland, 4½ miles (N.W.) from Wooler, containing 98 inhabitants.

COURAGE, a tything in the parish of Chieveley, hundred of Faircross, county of Berks, 4¼ miles (N.N.E.) from Newbury. The population is returned with the parish.

COURTEENHALL, a parish in the hundred of Wymersley, county of Northampton, 5¼ miles (S.) from Northampton, containing 144 inhabitants. The living is a rectory, in the archdeaconry of Northampton, and diocese of Peterborough, rated in the king's books at £12. 10. 10., and in the patronage of the Crown. The church is dedicated to St. Peter and St. Paul. A free school was founded and endowed, in the year 1670, by Sir Samuel Jones, for boys who must reside within four miles of the village of Courteenhall; the founder bequeathed £500 for the purpose of building the school-house, and a rent-charge of £80 for a master, and £20 for an usher, besides a bequest of £500 for repairing the church.

COVE, a tything in the parish of Yately, hundred of Crondall, Basingstoke division of the county of Southampton, 9 miles (E. N. E.) from Odiham, containing 403 inhabitants. It is within the jurisdiction of the Cheyney Court held at Winchester every Thursday, for the recovery of debts to any amount.

COVE (CHAPEL), a chapelry in Pitt quarter of the parish of Tiverton, hundred of Tiverton, county of Devon, 5 miles (N.) from Tiverton. The population is returned with Pitt quarter. The chapel is dedicated to St. John the Baptist.

COVE (NORTH), a parish in the hundred of Wangford, county of Suffolk, 2¾ miles (E. by S.) from Beccles, containing 219 inhabitants. The living is a discharged rectory, with that of Willingham annexed, in the archdeaconry of Suffolk, and diocese of Norwich, rated in the king's books at £10, and in the patronage of the Crown. The church is dedicated to St. Botolph. There is a place of worship for Wesleyan Methodists. The navigable river Waveney passes on the north side of this parish.

COVE (SOUTH), a parish in the hundred of Blything, county of Suffolk, 3 miles (N.) from Southwold, containing 186 inhabitants. The living is a discharged rectory, in the archdeaconry of Suffolk, and diocese of Norwich, rated in the king's books at £6. 2. 11., endowed with £200 royal bounty, and in the patronage of Sir T. S. Gooch, Bart. The church is dedicated to St. Lawrence.

COVEHITHE, county of Suffolk.—See NORTH-HALES.

COVEN, a liberty in the parish of Brewood, eastern division of the hundred of Cuttlestone, county of Stafford, 2 miles (E. S. E.) from Brewood, containing 499 inhabitants. The Staffordshire and Worcestershire canal passes through this liberty. There is a place of worship for Wesleyan Methodists.

COVENEY, a parish in the southern division of the hundred of WITCHFORD, Isle of ELY, county of CAMBRIDGE, 6 miles (W. N. W.) from Ely, containing, with the chapelry of Manea, 982 inhabitants. The living is a rectory, in the archdeaconry and diocese of Ely, rated in the king's books at £5, and in the patronage of Lord Rokeby. The church is dedicated to St. Peter.

COVENHAM (ST. BARTHOLOMEW), a parish in the wapentake of LUDBOROUGH, parts of LINDSEY, county of LINCOLN, 5½ miles (N. N. E.) from Louth, containing 219 inhabitants. The living is a discharged rectory, in the archdeaconry and diocese of Lincoln, rated in the king's books at £17. 12. 8., and in the patronage of the Rev. John Fretwell. There is a place of worship for Wesleyan Methodists. Here was formerly a cell belonging to the monastery of St. Carilephus, in the diocese of Mains.

COVENHAM (ST. MARY), a parish in the wapentake of LUDBOROUGH, parts of LINDSEY, county of LINCOLN, 5 miles (N. N. E.) from Louth, containing 142 inhabitants. The living is a discharged rectory, in the archdeaconry and diocese of Lincoln, rated in the king's books at £10, endowed with £200 royal bounty, and in the patronage of the Crown.

Arms.

COVENTRY, an ancient city, and a county of itself, locally in the county of Warwick, 10 miles (N. E.) from Warwick, 18 (S. E.) from Birmingham, and 91 (N. N. W.) from London, on the road to Holyhead, containing, exclusively of those portions of the parishes of the Holy Trinity, St. John the Baptist, and St. Michael, which are without the city, 21,242 inhabitants. In ancient records this place is called *Coventre* and also *Conventrey*, from the foundation of a convent by Canute, of which St. Osburg was abbess, in 1016, when it was burnt by Edric, the traitor, who having invaded Mercia, destroyed many towns in Warwickshire. On the site of this convent, Leofric, Earl of Mercia, and his countess Godiva, in the reign of Edward the Confessor, erected a monastery, which they munificently endowed, and decorated with such a profusion of costly ornaments, that, according to William of Malmesbury, the walls were covered with gold and silver. About this time Leofric, at the intercession of his countess, granted the citizens a charter conferring various privileges and immunities, the same being commemorated, in the south window of Trinity church, by portraits of the Earl and Countess, with a poetical legend. Leofric died in 1057, and was interred in the monastery which he had founded. Shortly after the Norman Conquest, the lordship of Coventry became vested in the earls of Chester, by marriage with the grand-daughter of Leofric. In the contest between Stephen and the Empress Matilda, the Earl of Chester taking part with the latter, his castle of Coventry was occupied by the king's forces: the earl besieged it, but the king came in person to its relief, and repulsed the earl after an obstinate conflict. In 1141, Robert Marmion, the inveterate enemy of the Earl of Chester, took possession of this monastery, from which he expelled the monks, fortified the church, and cut deep trenches in the adjoining fields, concealing them only with a slight covering: on the earl's approach to dislodge him, Marmion drew out his forces, but, forgetting the exact situation of the trenches, his horse fell with him to the ground, and in this situation his head was severed from his body by a private soldier. In 1355, the city was surrounded with walls three miles in circuit, three yards in thickness, and six yards in height, strengthened with thirty-two towers, and containing twelve principal gates, each defended by a portcullis. In 1397, Richard II. appointed this town for the decision, by single combat, of the quarrel between the Dukes of Hereford and Norfolk; and magnificent preparations were made on Gosford Green for this encounter, which, however, was prevented by the banishment of the combatants, a measure which ultimately caused the deposition of the king. In 1404, the Duke of Hereford, who had become Duke of Lancaster, by the death of his father, John of Gaunt, on his return from exile, having succeeded to the crown by the title of Henry IV., held a parliament here in the great chamber of the priory, which, from the exclusion of all lawyers, was called *Parliamentum Indoctorum.* In 1411, the Prince of Wales, afterwards Henry V., was arrested at the priory by John Horneby, mayor of the city, probably for some tumultuous excess, the particulars of which are not recorded. The city, with a district of four miles around it, was severed from Warwickshire, and erected into a county of itself, under the designation of the "City and County of the City of Coventry," by charter of Henry VI., in 1451; and in 1459 the same monarch held a parliament in the chapter-house of the priory, which, from the number of attainders passed against the Duke of York and others, was, by the Yorkists, called *Parliamentum Diabolicum.* In 1465, Edward IV. and his queen kept the festival of Christmas at Coventry; and three years after, the Earl of Rivers and his son, who had been seized by a party of the northern rebels at Grafton, were beheaded on Gosford Green. In the war between the houses of York and Lancaster, Richard, Earl of Warwick, marched with all his ordnance and warlike stores into this city, where he remained for a short time, during which Edward IV., on his route from Leicester, attempted to force an entrance; but being repulsed, he passed on to Warwick, and thence to London, where having gained a battle in which the Earl of Warwick was slain, he returned to Coventry, and deprived the citizens of their charter, for the restoration of which they were compelled to pay a fine of five hundred marks. In 1472, severe enactments were passed by the magistrates against women of immoral character, who were publicly exhibited in carts on the market days. Henry VII., on his route from Bosworth Field in 1475, was received here with every demonstration of congratulation and respect.

In the early part of the sixteenth century, Coventry became the theatre of religious persecution: the Bishop of Chester, coming to examine persons accused of heresy, condemned seven to the stake, which sentence was executed in the little park: in 1554, Mr. Hopkins, sheriff for the city, was confined in the Fleet prison, on a charge of heresy, but was liberated after great intercession, and fled the kingdom; and in the following year Mr. Lawrence Saunders, Robert Glover, A.M., and Cornelius Bongey, were burnt for their religious tenets. In 1565, Queen Elizabeth visited the city; and in 1566, Mary, Queen of Scots, was conducted to this place, where she was detained a prisoner; and in 1569, on her removal from Tutbury castle, she was for some time at the Bull Inn, in the custody of the Earls of Shrewsbury and Huntingdon. In 1607, the city suffered considerable damage from an inundation, which entered two hundred and fifty-seven houses, washing away furniture and utensils of various kinds: the flood rose to the height of three yards, and, after remaining for three or four hours, suddenly subsided; clusters of white snails were afterwards found in the houses and in the trees, supposed to have collected prior to the influx of the water, which, though observed at the distance of nearly a mile from the town, was so instantaneous in its approach, as to preclude all means of precaution. King James, attended by a large retinue of the nobility, visited the city in 1617, on which occasion a cup of pure gold, weighing forty-five ounces, and containing £100, was presented to him by the corporation, which his Majesty ordered to be preserved with the royal plate for the heirs of the crown. During the parliamentary war, Charles I., having erected his standard at Nottingham in 1641, sent orders to the mayor and sheriffs of Coventry to attend him at that place; but the majority of the citizens embraced the cause of the parliament, and a party having obtained possession of the magazine in Spon tower, which the Earl of Northampton had directed the aldermen to secure for the royalists, kept it for Lord Brooke, who removed it to Warwick castle. The parliamentarian party in the city, having been reinforced with four hundred men from Birmingham, held it against the king, who sent a herald to demand entrance, which being refused, some cannon were planted in the great park and on Stivichall hill, which played upon the town, but without effect. Finding the citizens resolved to defend their gates, and learning that Lord Brooke was approaching with his army from London, the king drew off his forces, and the city was now regularly garrisoned by the parliament, and further preparations made for its defence. The women were employed to fill up the quarries in the park, that they might not afford any shelter to the royal troops; and for this purpose they assembled in companies, by beat of drum, and marched in military array, with mattocks and spades, headed by an amazon who carried an Herculean club on her shoulder, and conducted from their work by another, who discharged a pistol as a signal of dismissal. On the Restoration of Charles II., that monarch was proclaimed by the mayor and aldermen, attended by a vast concourse of the inhabitants, with the most triumphant acclamation: the greatest rejoicings took place, and the public conduits of the city were made to flow with wine; a deputation was sent to present to him a basin and ewer, and fifty pieces of gold, and to surrender all the king's lands. In 1662, the Earl of Northampton, with a large retinue of the neighbouring gentry, and a detachment of the county troops, was sent with a commission from the king to make a breach in the walls, as a punishment to the inhabitants for shutting their gates against his father; but the earl so far exceeded the limits of his commission as to leave only a few fragments of them remaining: of the gates, which were only dismantled, there are some yet standing; the Bastille, Swanswell, and Cook-street gates, are the most entire.

The city is pleasantly situated on a gentle eminence, bounded on the north-east by the river Shirburn and the Radford brook, which, running from north to south, unite within the town. In the more ancient part, the streets, with the exception of that part of the High-street called the Cross-cheaping, or the market-place, are generally narrow, partially paved, and lighted partly with oil and partly with gas: many of the houses are in the style of the sixteenth century, built of timber frame-work and brick, with the upper stories projecting, and present a dark and sombre appearance, occasionally enlivened by an intermixture of others of more modern structure, of which several are spacious and handsome: the suburbs have within the last few years been greatly extended, several new streets have been formed, and ranges of handsome houses erected: the inhabitants are amply supplied with water from conduits made by the corporation, and by water-works under the superintendence of two public companies. The public library, established in 1791, has a proprietary of about two hundred members, and is well regulated by a committee: the theatre, a neat and conveniently arranged building, is opened occasionally; and assemblies and concerts take place periodically at St. Mary's and Drapers' Halls: the environs are pleasant, abounding with interesting scenery, and with some agreeable promenades. The barracks, erected in 1792, on the site of the old Bull Inn, are a handsome range of building, fronted with stone, and ornamented with the king's arms over a window above the principal gate-way: the establishment is for a field officer and fifteen subalterns, and comprises a riding-house, an hospital, and stabling for one hundred and eighty-eight horses. The making of caps was the principal trade of the town prior to the year 1436, when the manufacture of woollen and broad cloth was introduced, and continued to flourish till the end of the sixteenth century: at this time Coventry was celebrated for a peculiar kind of blue thread, which, from the permanence of its colour, obtained the appellation of "Coventry true blue." About the beginning of the eighteenth century, striped and mixed tammies, camlets, shalloons, and calimancoes, were manufactured to a considerable extent, to which succeeded the throwing of silk, the weaving of gauzes, broad silks, and ribands, and the manufacture of watches. The weaving of ribands forms at present the staple trade: a great quantity is exported; an immense number of pieces are sent off weekly for the supply of the wholesale dealers in London, and a considerable quantity is, by means of travelling agents, distributed to every town in the kingdom. In 1808 there were two thousand eight hundred and nineteen silk and riband looms in the city alone, exclusively of those in the adjacent villages; but since that time the number has considerably increased. The trade, though at present greatly depressed, affords employment to nearly sixteen thousand persons in the city and suburbs; and, from the introduction of the French looms and machinery, an infinite variety in the pattern, and an elegance in the texture, have been attained, which give a distinguished superiority to the ribands manufactured here. The manufacture of watches, for which Coventry was for many years so celebrated, has of late been rapidly declining. The situation of the town is peculiarly advantageous for trade, being central to the ports of London, Liverpool, Bristol, and Hull, and having, by means of the Oxford and Coventry canals, which form a junction at a short distance to the north, a direct communication with the manufacturing districts of Lancashire and Yorkshire: the canal office is a small but handsome building, with a portico of the Grecian Ionic order. The market, which is on Friday, is held in various parts of the town; for corn, in the Cross-cheaping, now a spacious area enlarged by the removal of a middle range of old houses, by which it was divided, and in which was the ancient cross, one of the most beautiful in the kingdom, taken down in 1771; for cattle, in Bishop-street; for pigs, in Cook-street; and for butter, eggs, and poultry, in an area behind the mayor's parlour, where a market-house has been erected. Fairs for three days each are held on April 21st, August 16th, and October 21st, for cattle and merchandise; to these fairs are attached courts of pie-powder, and the corporation are entitled to the same tolls as are taken at Smithfield market, in London. The great shew-fair takes place on the Friday after Corpus Christi day, and continues for eight days, on the first of which the commemoration of Lady Godiva's procession is occasionally revived, by a representative obtained for that purpose: this ceremony has its origin in a tradition that the citizens being greatly oppressed by the severe exactions imposed on them by Leofric, his countess undertook to intercede for their relief, but was apparently frustrated in her suit by a promise of exemption only upon the condition of her riding naked through the city on horseback; it is further recorded in the traditionary legends of the city, that, having obtained her husband's permission, and trusting for concealment to the length of her hair, and to the discretion of the inhabitants, who were ordered, upon pain of death, to shut themselves up in their houses, she performed the task, and obtained for the city a charter of "freedom from servitude, evil customs, and exactions." The tradition also records that a tailor, who disobeyed the injunction, was instantly struck blind; and a figure, called Peeping Tom, carved in wood, and placed in a niche at the corner of a house in High-street, is still preserved in memory of this event, which, whether real or fictitious, is closely interwoven with the history of the place.

The city received its first charter of incorporation from Edward III., in 1344: in 1384, Richard II. ordered the sword of state to be borne behind the mayor in civic processions, as a mark of disgrace, for his not having duly administered justice in the execution of his office, which order that monarch revoked in 1392. Under the charter of Edward III., confirmed in succeeding reigns, and extended in that of James I., the government is vested in a mayor, recorder, two sheriffs, a steward (who must be a barrister), a coroner, two chamberlains, two wardens, ten aldermen, a superior council of thirty-one, and a second council, or grand inquest, of twenty-five members, assisted by a town-clerk, sword-bearer, mace-bearer, and subordinate officers. The mayor, sheriffs, steward, and coroner, are chosen annually by the council of thirty-one, in the council-chamber in St. Mary's Hall, and sworn into office on All Saints' day: the aldermen are elected by the same body, from the grand inquest, as vacancies occur: the mayor, recorder, and aldermen, are justices of the peace, and have exclusive jurisdiction within the city and county of the city. The city is divided into ten wards, each under its respective aldermen, and comprises thirteen fraternities, or trading companies, the numbers of which, with the exception of the Drapers' company, who still retain their hall, have been greatly reduced. The freedom is obtained only by a servitude of seven years to one trade within the city and liberties. Among the privileges enjoyed by the freemen is that of depasturing cattle upon the "Lammas Grounds," a tract of three thousand acres, appropriated to that use from Lammas to Candlemas by especial grant. The corporation hold quarterly courts of session, at which the mayor, assisted by the steward, presides: these courts are held by adjournment in the mayor's parlour, on the last Friday in every month; they have power to try capital offenders, but this they generally delegate to the judge travelling the midland circuit. A court of record has been held by prescription from a very remote period, the date of which is certainly anterior to the reign of Henry VI., for the recovery of debts to any amount, at which the mayor and sheriffs preside; and a county court is held monthly by adjournment, in the mayor's parlour, where also either the mayor, or some of the city magistrates attend daily, to decide on affairs of police.

Corporate Seal.

The city first exercised the elective franchise in the 26th of Edward I., but there were partial intermissions until the 31st of Henry VI., since which time it has regularly returned two members to parliament: the right of election is vested in the freemen not receiving alms, of whom the number is about three thousand: the sheriffs are the returning officers. The county-hall, in which the sessions and other courts are held, is a neat modern building faced with stone, and ornamented with pillars of the Tuscan order, rising from a rustic basement, and supporting a handsome cornice in the centre of the front: adjoining is the gaoler's house, a neat brick edifice; and behind it the prison, which has been recently rebuilt. St. Mary's Hall, appropriated to the larger meetings and civic entertainments of the corporation, is a beautiful and magnificent structure in the later style of English architecture: it was originally built by the master and wardens of St. Mary's Guild, in the fourteenth century, and subsequently enlarged and beautified for the use of the corporation: the exterior, with its richly decorated windows, and elaborately groined archway, has an imposing grandeur of effect; the interior, which is replete with the richest ornaments of the decorated style, comprises a splendid banquet-hall, adorned with well painted portraits of several of the sovereigns, who have been entertained within its walls; the windows, of which the tracery is gracefully elegant, are ornamented with painted glass: at the upper end is a fine piece of tapestry, elegantly worked in compartments; and on the north side is a small recess, with a beautiful oriel window, above which the original carved roof is still entire: the council-chamber is fitted up in the ancient style, and retains, among its ornaments, many relics of feudal grandeur. The Drapers' Hall, nearly adjoining, is a neat building, with a stone front of the Tuscan order, of chaste and pleasing design.

Coventry forms a diocese jointly with Lichfield, of which the seat was fixed in this city from 1102 till 1188, when it was removed to Lichfield: the diocese comprehends the whole counties of Derby and Stafford (excepting the parishes of Broom and Clent in the latter), the greater part of Warwickshire, and nearly half of the county of Salop, and comprises five hundred and fifty-seven parishes. Of the cathedral, once a sumptuous and magnificent structure, formerly the Benedictine monastery founded by Leofric, of which at the dissolution the revenue was £731. 19. 5., only the slightest vestiges are discernible, in the mouldings of arches and outlines of windows and doors worked in with the materials of a modern building, which has been erected on the site of one of its ancient towers, and some indistinct remains of what are supposed to have been the conventual buildings. The city comprises the parishes of St. Michael, the Holy Trinity, and St. John the Baptist, the last having been constituted a parish by act of parliament in 1734, all in the archdeaconry of Coventry, and diocese of Lichfield and Coventry. The living of St. Michael's is a vicarage, rated in the king's books at £26. 15. 5., and in the patronage of the Crown. The church is a splendid structure, principally in the later style of English architecture, with a lofty tower of four stages, panelled and ornamented with niches in which were finely sculptured figures, and surmounted by a lofty and finely proportioned octagonal spire, the whole height being, from the base of the tower, three hundred feet, exactly equal to the length of the church: the interior is finely arranged, and derives great beauty from the loftiness of its elevation, and the delicacy of the piers which support the roof; the clerestory windows of the nave form a noble range of large dimensions, and are ornamented with ancient stained glass: the chancel, which is of earlier date, was formerly a chapel erected in 1133, to which the nave and aisles were subsequently added; it deviates from a straight line, and forms an angle with the line of the nave, which sensibly offends the eye. The living of the parish of the Holy Trinity is a vicarage, rated in the king's books at £10, and in the patronage of the Crown: the church, which is of earlier date than the more recent part of St. Michael's, is a venerable cruciform structure in the later style of English architecture, with a well proportioned tower rising from the intersection, and surmounted by a handsome octagonal spire: the proportions of the interior are more massive than those of St. Michael's; and, though less elaborate in its details, this church preserves throughout a consistent unity of design: the oak roof is divided into panels, decorated with gilded mouldings; the pulpit is of stone similarly ornamented. The living of St. John's is a rectory not in charge, endowed with £600 parliamentary grant, and in the patronage of the Mayor and Corporation: it is always annexed to the head-mastership of the free school, and includes also a lectureship for the second master, the former taking two-thirds and the latter one-third of the income. The church, formerly a chapel erected in honour of our Saviour, upon ground given by Isabel, queen-mother of Edward III., is an interesting structure, quadrangular in the lower part, and cruciform in the upper; from the centre rises a square embattled tower, with circular turrets at the angles, and supported on four finely clustered piers and arches of singular beauty: the interior is characterised by a simple grandeur of style, which more than compensates for the want of elaborate embellishment. To the south of the city was the monastery of the Grey friars, the brethren of which were famous for their skill in the representation of religious dramas: it was originally founded in 1234, and the church was built in 1358, for which Edward the Black Prince granted the friars permission to take stone from the quarries in his park at Cheylesmere: the monastery was destroyed at the dissolution; all that remains is the very beautiful steeple of the church, consisting of an octagonal tower, with a pierced parapet, from which rises a lofty and finely proportioned octagonal spire; to this a body is now being annexed by subscription among the inhabitants, aided by a grant from the parliamentary commissioners. There are places of worship for Baptists, the Society of Friends, Independents, Wesleyan Methodists, Unitarians, and Roman Catholics.

The free grammar school was founded, in the reign of Henry VIII., by John Hales, Esq., who endowed it with lands at that time of the value of two hundred marks, but which now produce an annual income of £900, of which the head-master receives two-thirds and the second master the remainder; it is under the management of the corporation, by whom the masters are appointed: there are three exhibitions of £10 each, and two of £5 each per annum, to either of the Universities; two fellowships in St. John's College, Oxford; and one fellowship and one scholarship in Catharine Hall, Cambridge, belonging to this establishment. The schoolroom is the remaining part of a church which anciently belonged to the hospital of St. John, built in the reign of Henry II., the revenue of which, at the dissolution, was £83. 3. 8.; it is a spacious room, lighted with windows in the decorated style, with rich tracery, and fitted up with the ancient carved seats, removed from the choir of the church belonging to the monastery of the White friars: the western end, taken down to widen the street, has been rebuilt in an appropriate style, and ornamented with two handsome turrets. Sir William Dugdale, the celebrated antiquary, and Archbishop Secker, received the rudiments of their education at this school. The Bablake Blue-coat school, occupying one side of the quadrangle of the Bablake hospital, was founded, in 1566, by Mr. Thomas Wheatley, ironmonger, and mayor of the city, in consequence of an accidental acquisition of wealth, by the delivery of barrels of cochineal and ingots of silver in mistake for steel gads, which he sent his agent to purchase in Spain. The original endowment, increased by subsequent benefactions, produces £340 per annum, which is applied to the clothing, maintenance, and instruction of twenty-six boys, who receive a small sum as an apprentice-fee on their leaving school; they are nominated by the corporation, who are trustees. A charity school, for clothing and instructing forty girls, of which number six are maintained in the house for the last year, and qualified for service, is supported by subscription. The National school, also supported by subscription, for an unlimited number of children of both sexes, is a large handsome building of brick, in the antique style, having the master's house in the centre, and on each side of it a large schoolroom, supported on brick columns and groined arches, affording a sheltered area for a playground. Another school, situated in Cow-lane, for clothing and instructing forty children, has an endowment in land, with a house for the master, given by Mr. W. Baker, and augmented by subsequent benefactions: there is also a Lancasterian school, supported by subscription; and there are Sunday schools connected with the church and the dissenting congregations. Bond's hospital was founded, in 1506, by Mr. Thomas Bond, draper, who endowed it with lands for the maintenance of ten poor men and one woman: the number of pensioners, in consequence of the improvement of the income, has been increased to forty-eight, who receive each a weekly allowance of six shillings; thirteen of them are resident in the hospital, and have each an apartment, firing, and washing, free of expense. The building, occupying one side of the Bablake quadrangle, is an ancient edifice of timber frame-work and brick, in the Elizabethan style, but much of its original character has been destroyed by repairs and alterations. The Grey friars' hospital, so called from its proximity to a monastery of that order formerly existing here, was founded in 1529, by Mr. William Ford, who endowed it for five aged men and one woman; from the increased amount of the income, there are at present eighteen women in this establishment, who receive a weekly allowance of 2*s.* 6*d.*, with additional advantages: the buildings, which form a long and narrow quadrangular area, almost darkened by the projection of the upper stories, are in the style of domestic architecture prevailing in the reign of Elizabeth; the timber frame-work, richly carved, and decorated with cornices and canopies over the central windows and doorways is, as perfect as when first erected, and these beautiful almshouses are deservedly admired as the most entire and elegant specimen of the kind in the kingdom. The house of industry occupies the site, and includes the remains, of an ancient monastery of Carmelites, founded in 1342, by Sir John Pulteney, lord mayor of London, the revenue of which, at the dissolution, was £7. 13. 8.: part of the arched cloisters, beautifully groined, the refectory, and dormitory, are still remaining, with the beautiful entrance gateway, richly groined and ornamented with three canopied niches in front; to these remains has been added a large and handsome brick building, well adapted to the purpose: the management of this establishment, which is also a comfortable asylum for the aged poor, is vested in a body of guardians. The corporation have at their disposal funds to the amount of £3000 per annum, for distribution among the poor, arising chiefly from Sir Thomas White's donation of £1400 in the reign of Henry VIII., exclusively of considerable sums to be lent for nine years to apprentices of good character, on the expiration of their indentures; in this loan natives of Leicester, Northampton, Nottingham, and Warwick, participate. At Allesley, about a mile distant, is a petrifying spring, not much used. William Macclesfield, created Cardinal by Pope Benedict XI.; John Bird, Bishop of Chester, who was deprived of his see in the reign of Mary; Humphrey Wanley, the antiquary; and Nehemiah Grew, the botanist, were natives of this city; and Dr. Philemon Holland, the translator of Camden's Britannia, resided here for the greater part of his life. Coventry gives the title of earl to the family of that name.

COVERHAM, a parish in the western division of the wapentake of HANG, North riding of the county of YORK, 1¾ mile (S. W. by W.) from Middleham, comprising the townships of Agelthorpe, Caldbridge, Carlton, Carlton-Highdale, Melmerby, and West Scrafton, and containing 1170 inhabitants. The living is a perpetual curacy, in the archdeaconry of Richmond, and diocese of Chester, endowed with £800 private benefaction, £400 royal bounty, and £1200 parliamentary grant, and in the patronage of the Rev. S. Hardcastle. The church is dedicated to the Holy Trinity. The river Cover runs near this village, over which there is a bridge of one arch, and near it are the remains of a priory of White canons, founded in the thirteenth century, at Swainby, in the parish of Pickhall, and removed hither soon afterwards: its revenue, in the 26th of Henry VIII., was valued at £207. 14. 8. A school, in which between twenty and thirty children are educated, is endowed with a bequest of a messuage and lands by John Constantine, in 1724, producing £23 per annum.

COVINGTON, a parish in the hundred of LEIGHTONSTONE, county of HUNTINGDON, 3¼ miles (W.N.W.) from Kimbolton, containing 139 inhabitants. The living is a rectory, in the archdeaconry of Huntingdon, and diocese of Lincoln, rated in the king's books at £10. 1. 8., and in the patronage of Earl Fitzwilliam. The church is dedicated to All Saints.

COWARNE (LITTLE), a parish in the hundred of BROXASH, county of HEREFORD, 4¼ miles (S. W. by W.) from Bromyard, containing 134 inhabitants. The living is a perpetual curacy, annexed to the rectory of Ullingswick, in the archdeaconry and diocese of Hereford.

COWARNE (MUCH), a parish in the hundred of BROXASH, county of HEREFORD, 5¾ miles (S. S. W.) from Bromyard, containing 585 inhabitants. The living is a discharged vicarage, in the archdeaconry and diocese of Hereford, rated in the king's books at £14. 19. 7., and in the patronage of the Bishop of Gloucester. The church is dedicated to St. Mary.

COWBIT, a parish in the wapentake of ELLOE, parts of HOLLAND, county of LINCOLN, 5½ miles (N. by E.) from Crowland, containing 511 inhabitants. The living is a perpetual curacy, in the archdeaconry and diocese of Lincoln, and in the patronage of the Devisees of Mrs. Miller. The church, dedicated to St. Mary, was, with the cemetery, consecrated in 1486, by Bishop Russell. There is a place of worship for Wesleyan Methodists. In 1712, Joseph Andrew endowed a school with £12. 10. per annum, arising from a bequest of land.

COWDEN, a parish in the hundred of SOMERDEN, lathe of SUTTON at HONE, county of KENT, 9 miles (W.) from Tonbridge-Wells, containing 683 inhabitants. The living is a rectory, in the archdeaconry and diocese of Rochester, rated in the king's books at £9. 18. 11½., and in the patronage of the Rev. T. Harvey. The church, dedicated to St. Mary Magdalene, is a small building, with a handsome spire. One of the four principal heads of the Medway, which rises at Gravelley hill, in Sussex, directs its course eastward along the southern side of this parish, and separates it from the county of Sussex. Iron-ore is found in the parish. A fair is held on the 2nd of August, for oxen and pedlary. There is a trifling endowment for the support of five almshouses.

COWDON (GREAT and LITTLE), a parish partly in the middle, but chiefly in the northern, division of the wapentake of HOLDERNESS, East riding of the county of YORK, containing 146 inhabitants. Great Cowdon is 14¼ miles, and Little Cowdon 12¾, (N. E.) from Kingston upon Hull. The living is a discharged rectory, in the archdeaconry of the East riding, and diocese, of York, rated in the king's books at £2. 13. 4., and in the patronage of the Crown. The church has long been swallowed up by the sea, and the parish is commonly considered a township partly in the parish of Aldborough, but chiefly in the parish of Mappleton.

COWES (EAST), a hamlet in the parish of WHIPPINGHAM, liberty of EAST MEDINA, Isle of Wight division of the county of SOUTHAMPTON, ¾ of a mile (S. E. by E.) from West Cowes. The population is returned with the parish. This village is situated on the eastern side of the mouth of the river Medina, and owes its origin to a fort, or blockhouse, erected by Henry VIII., for the defence of the harbour, of which no traces are discernible. Here is a custom-house, where vessels arriving in the harbour pay the government duties.

COWES (WEST), a sea-port and chapelry in the northern division of the parish of NORTHWOOD, liberty of WEST MEDINA, Isle of Wight division of the county of SOUTHAMPTON, 4½ miles (N.) from Newport, and 86 (S. W.) from London. The population is returned with the parish. This place owes its origin to the erection of a small castle on the western bank of the river Medina, which commands the entrance of the harbour: this fortress, which was built in the reign of Henry VIII., is a small edifice with a semicircular battery mounting eleven pieces of heavy ordnance, and contains accommodation for a captain and a company of artillery. From the excellence of the harbour, in which ships may find shelter in stormy weather, and from which they may sail out either to the east or west, as the wind may serve, Cowes has become a populous and flourishing town; and, from its advantageous situation for ship-building, a private dock-yard has been established, in which several men of war have been built for the royal navy. The town is pleasantly and romantically situated on the declivity of an eminence rising from the mouth of the river Medina, by which it is separated from East Cowes. The streets are narrow, and the houses in general inelegant, but, rising above each other from the margin of the river to the summit of the acclivity on which they are built, they have a pleasing and picturesque appearance from the opposite bank, and are seen with peculiar advantage from the sea, of which they command interesting and extensive views. The excellence of its beach, the pleasantness of its situation, and the salubrity of the air, have rendered it a fashionable place for sea-bathing, for which purpose several respectable lodging-houses have been erected for the accommodation of visitors, and numerous bathing-machines are ranged on the beach, to the west of the castle: the environs abound with elegant mansions and marine villas, the grounds being laid out with exquisite taste. In addition to the amusements which the town affords, there are frequent opportunities for aquatic excursions. The Yacht club, consisting of His Majesty and about sixty noblemen and gentlemen, established here for many years, celebrate their annual regatta generally in August or September, on which occasion more than two hundred yachts and other vessels are assembled, forming a spectacle truly splendid and magnificent. An extensive trade is carried on in provisions and other articles for the supply of the shipping: the principal exports of the island are wheat, flour, malt, barley, wool, and salt, large quantities of which are shipped for France, Spain, Portugal, and the Mediterranean shores. The number of vessels belonging to this port in 1829 was one hundred and fifty-one, averaging thirty-nine tons' burden; in 1826, nine British and four foreign vessels entered inwards from foreign ports, and nine British and two foreign vessels cleared outwards. Packets sail daily to Southampton and Portsmouth, and passage boats to Newport and Ryde. The living is a perpetual curacy, in the archdeaconry and diocese of Winchester, endowed with £400 private benefaction, £400 royal bounty, and £1400 parliamentary grant, and in the patronage of the Vicar of Carisbrooke. The chapel, erected in 1657, and consecrated in 1662, is on the summit of the hill on which the town is situated. There is a place of worship for Wesleyan Methodists.

COWFOLD, a parish in the hundred of WINDHAM and EWHURST, rape of BRAMBER, county of SUSSEX, 7 miles (S. S. E.) from Horsham, containing 822 inhabitants. The living is a vicarage, in the archdeaconry of Lewes, and diocese of Chichester, rated in the king's books at £10. 6. 8., and in the patronage of the Bishop of Chichester.

COWGROVE, a tything in the parish of WIMBORNE-MINSTER, hundred of BADBURY, Shaston (East) division of the county of DORSET, 2 miles (W.) from Wimborne-Minster, containing 638 inhabitants.

COWICK, a chapelry in the parish of ST. THOMAS the APOSTLE, EXETER, hundred of WONFORD, county of DEVON, 1 mile (S. W. by S.) from Exeter. The population is returned with the parish. The chapel is dedicated to St. Thomas à Becket. A Benedictine monastery, a cell to the abbey of Bec in Normandy, was established here by William, son of Balwine, in the time of Henry II., but there are not any remains of it.

COWICK, a township in that part of the parish of SNAITH which is in the lower division of the wapentake of OSGOLDCROSS, West riding of the county of YORK, ½ a mile (S. E. by E.) from Snaith, containing 905 inhabitants. There is a small endowed school.

COWLAM, a parish in the wapentake of BUCKROSE, East riding of the county of YORK, 6¼ miles (N. W. by N.) from Great Driffield, containing 33 inhabitants. The living is a discharged rectory, in the archdeaconry of the East riding, and diocese of York, rated in the king's books at £11. 11. 3., and in the patronage of the Rev. T. F. F. Bowes. The church contains a curious ancient font. From numerous foundations discovered here, it is probable that Cowlam was once a large town.

COWLEY, a hamlet in the parish of DRONFIELD, hundred of SCARSDALE, county of DERBY, 1¼ mile (W. S. W.) from Dronfield, with which the population is returned. Here is a sulphureous spring.

COWLEY, a parish in the hundred of RAPSGATE, county of GLOUCESTER, 6½ miles (S. by E.) from Cheltenham, containing 273 inhabitants. The living is a rectory, in the archdeaconry and diocese of Gloucester, rated in the king's books at £9. 1. 10½., and in the patronage of the Crown. The church is dedicated to St. Mary. The Ermin-street traces the southern boundary of this parish.

COWLEY, a parish in the hundred of ELTHORNE, county of MIDDLESEX, 1½ mile (S. by E.) from Uxbridge, containing 349 inhabitants. The living is a rectory, in the archdeaconry of Middlesex, and diocese of London, rated in the king's books at £11, and in the patronage of E. Hilliard, Esq. The church is dedicated to St. Lawrence. Barnard Dognall, in 1761, bequeathed four acres of land, producing £10 per annum, for the parish clerk, on condition of his keeping the church free from dust, and the churchyard from weeds and other annoyances.

COWLEY, a parish in the hundred of BULLINGTON, county of OXFORD, 2½ miles (S. E. by E.) from Oxford, containing 472 inhabitants. The living is a perpetual curacy, in the archdeaconry and diocese of Oxford, endowed with £600 private benefaction, and £600 royal bounty, and in the patronage of the Dean and Canons of Christ Church, Oxford. The church is dedicated to St. James. There was anciently a preceptory of the Knights Templars in this parish.

COWLEY, a township in the parish of GNOSALL, western division of the hundred of CUTTLESTONE, county of STAFFORD, 5 miles (E.) from Newport, containing 498 inhabitants.

COWLING, a parish in the hundred of RISBRIDGE, county of SUFFOLK, 8¾ miles (N.N.W.) from Clare, containing 790 inhabitants. The living is a perpetual curacy, in the archdeaconry of Sudbury, and diocese of Norwich, endowed with £200 royal bounty, and £1000 parliamentary grant, and in the patronage of the Master and Fellows of Trinity Hall, Cambridge. The church is dedicated to St. Margaret. There are fairs on the 31st of July and the 17th of October.

COWLING, a joint township with Burrel, in that part of the parish of BEDALE which is in the eastern division of the wapentake of HANG, North riding of the county of YORK, 2¼ miles (W. by S.) from Bedale. The population is returned with Burrel.

COWLING, a township in the parish of KILDWICK, eastern division of the wapentake of STAINCLIFFE and EWCROSS, West riding of the county of YORK, 5¼ miles (S. S.W.) from Skipton, containing 1870 inhabitants, who are chiefly employed in the cotton manufacture. A school is endowed with about £16 per annum, arising from land bequeathed by Hugh Smith, in 1665.

COWPEN, a township in the parish of HORTON, eastern division of CASTLE ward, county of NORTHUMBERLAND, 8 miles (E.S.E.) from Morpeth, containing 1765 inhabitants. Here are extensive coal mines.

COWPEN-BEWLEY, a township in the parish of BILLINGHAM, north-eastern division of STOCKTON ward, county palatine of DURHAM, 4½ miles (N.E. by N.) from Stockton upon Tees, containing 132 inhabitants.

COWSBY, a parish in the wapentake of BIRDFORTH, North riding of the county of YORK, 6¼ miles (N.N.E.) from Thirsk, containing 91 inhabitants. The living is a discharged rectory, within the jurisdiction of the peculiar court of Allerton and Allertonshire, belonging to the Bishop of Durham, rated in the king's books at £5. 11. 0½., and in the patronage of Thomas Alston, Esq. Here is an hospital for decayed tenants, supposed to have been founded by Lord Crewe.

COWSHUISH, a tything comprising the hamlet of Toulton in the parish of KINGSTON, hundred of TAUNTON and TAUNTON-DEAN, county of SOMERSET, 5½ miles (N.W. by N.) from Taunton. The population is returned with the parish.

COWTHORN, a township in the parish of MIDDLETON, PICKERING lythe, North riding of the county of YORK, 4 miles (N.N.W.) from Pickering, containing 22 inhabitants.

COWTHORP, a parish in the upper division of the wapentake of CLARO, West riding of the county of YORK, 3¾ miles (N.E. by N.) from Wetherby, containing 120 inhabitants. The living is a discharged rectory, in the archdeaconry and diocese of York, rated in the king's books at £4. 15. 10., and in the patronage of T. Starkie, Esq. The church is dedicated to St. Michael.

COWTON (EAST), a parish in the eastern division of the wapentake of GILLING, North riding of the county of YORK, 7 miles (N. E. by E.) from Catterick, containing 338 inhabitants. The living is a discharged vicarage, in the archdeaconry of Richmond, and diocese of Chester, rated in the king's books at £4. 6. 10½. The patronage is attached conditionally to the Mastership of Kirkby-Ravensworth Hospital, or otherwise in the patronage of the Wardens and Hospitallers. The church is dedicated to St. Mary. A free school established here has an annuity of £27 from Kirkby-Ravensworth school fund.

COWTON (NORTH), a township in that part of the parish of GILLING which is in the eastern division of the wapentake of GILLING, North riding of the county of YORK, 6¼ miles (N. E.) from Catterick, containing 270 inhabitants.

COWTON (SOUTH), a chapelry in that part of the parish of GILLING which is in the eastern division of the wapentake of GILLING, North riding of the county of YORK, 5¼ miles (N. E. by E.) from Catterick, containing 148 inhabitants. The living is a perpetual curacy, in the archdeaconry of Richmond, and diocese of Chester, endowed with £600 royal bounty, and £200 parliamentary grant, and in the patronage of the Vicar of Gilling. The chapel is dedicated to St. Mary. On the moor between this and North Cowton was fought the famous battle of the Standard, in 1138, between the English and the Scotch, when the latter were defeated with the loss of eleven thousand men: the spot is still called Standard Hill, and the holes into which the slain were thrown, the Scots' Pits.

COXFORD, a hamlet in the parish of EAST RUDHAM, hundred of GALLOW, county of NORFOLK, 5¼ miles (W.) from Fakenham. The population is returned with the parish. William Chene founded a priory at Rudham, in the reign of Stephen, which was subsequently removed to this place. Among other grants, the prior obtained license, in the 11th of Henry III., to hold a fair annually on the festival of the Translation of St. Thomas the Martyr; and in the 3rd and 15th of Edward I. a free market on Monday, and a fair on the eve and day of St. Matthew the Apostle, were granted. The annual revenue, in 1428, amounted to £222. 12. 8.; but at the dissolution it was only estimated at £153. 7. 1. A small vessel, containing some Roman coins, is stated to have been found among the ruins in 1719.

COXHALL, a joint township with Buxton, in that part of the parish of BUCKNILL which is in the hundred of WIGMORE, county of HEREFORD, 3¾ miles (E. by N.) from Knighton. The population is returned with Buxton. Here are traces of an ancient circular camp.

COXHOE, a township in the parish of KELLOE, southern division of EASINGTON ward, county palatine of DURHAM, 5½ miles (S.E. by S.) from Durham, containing 132 inhabitants. Coal is obtained in this neighbourhood to a considerable extent; there are also limestone quarries, and a good seam of clay for making earthenware.

COXLODGE, a township in that part of the parish of GOSFORTH which is in the western division of CASTLE ward, county of NORTHUMBERLAND, 2¼ miles (N.) from Newcastle, containing 633 inhabitants. A place of worship for Wesleyan Methodists and a Sunday school were built in 1819. There are several collieries in the township. In 1800, the grand stand for the Newcastle racecourse was erected here, near which is a reservoir for the supply of that town with water, which is raised by a windmill pump.

COXWELL (GREAT), a parish in the hundred of FARRINGDON, county of BERKS, 1¾ mile (S. W.) from Great Farringdon, containing 306 inhabitants. The living is a discharged vicarage, in the archdeaconry of Berks, and diocese of Salisbury, rated in the king's books at £7. 7. 11., endowed with £400 private benefaction, and £400 royal bounty, and in the patronage of the Bishop of Salisbury. The church is dedicated to St. Giles. Limestone and fossil remains are met with here. There are the remains of a religious establishment in this parish, formerly built by the abbots of Beaulieu, to whom the manor was granted by King John in 1204, now used as a barn: the adjoining farmhouse was occupied by the monks. On Badbury hill is an ancient circular encampment, supposed to be Danish. The Rev. David Collier, in 1724, imposed a charge of eight bushels of barley on lands in Little Coxwell, for teaching two poor children; and the sum of £3. 10. is paid to a schoolmaster for instructing three children; besides which, the Rev. John Pynsent, in 1705, bequeathed land, producing about £20 per annum, for apprenticing the children of labourers of this parish and Coleshill: there is likewise a curious bequest from the Earl of Radnor, in 1771, charging his lands with an annuity of £45, to be applied to the apprenticing of the children of poor persons of Coleshill and this parish, so often as the vicar of Coleshill shall be absent from the parish more than sixty days in any one year, and shall accept any other preferment with cure of souls.

COXWELL (LITTLE), a chapelry in that part of the parish of FARRINGDON which is in the hundred of FARRINGDON, county of BERKS, 1½ mile (S.) from Great Farringdon, containing 271 inhabitants. The chapel is dedicated to St. Mary. The remains of a camp, apparently in the form of a square, are visible here, the double ditch on the western side being nearly entire; and there are also, in an enclosed field of about fourteen acres, two hundred and seventy-three pits, called Cole's Pits, excavated in the sand and varying in depth, supposed to have been the habitations, or hiding-places, of the ancient Britons.

COXWOLD, a parish in the wapentake of BIRDFORTH, North riding of the county of YORK, comprising the chapelry of Birdforth, and the townships of Angram-Grange, Byland *cum* Membris, Coxwold, Newborough, Oulston, Thornton with Baxly, Wildon-Grange, and Yearsley, and containing 1447 inhabitants, of which number, 348 are in the township of Coxwold, 5 miles (N.) from Easingwould. The living is a perpetual curacy, in the archdeaconry of Cleveland, and diocese of York, and in the patronage of G. Wombwell, Esq. The church, dedicated to St. Michael, is a small ancient structure, said to have been erected so early as 700, with an octagonal tower: the chancel was rebuilt in 1777, by the Earl of Fauconberg: there is some stained glass in the windows, and within are many handsome monuments of the Belasyse family. A free grammar school was founded, in 1603, by Sir John Harte, alderman of London, who endowed it with £36. 13. 4. per annum, charged on certain lands in this county: only a few boys are instructed in writing and arithmetic, paying a small quarterage also. An hospital for ten poor men was founded, in 1696, by Thomas, Earl of Fauconberg, the endowment of which consists of a rent-charge of £59, and is divided among ten poor persons, only two of whom reside in the hospital, which comprises a chapel, with a small chamber above, and two apartments on each side: an hospital for eight poor women was also established here, which has long since gone to decay. There is a fair on the 25th of August. Sterne wrote his Tristram Shandy and some other works at Shandy Hall, near this place, where he resided about seven years.

COZENLEY, a township in the parish of KIRKBY-MALZEARD, lower division of the wapentake of CLARO, West riding of the county of YORK, 4½ miles (N.W. by W.) from Ripon, containing 579 inhabitants.

CRABHALL, a joint township with Blacon, in that part of the parish of the HOLY TRINITY, CHESTER, which is in the higher division of the hundred of WIRRALL, county palatine of CHESTER, 2½ miles (N.W. by N.) from Chester. The population is returned with Blacon.

CRACKENTHORPE, a township in the parish of BONGATE, or ST. MICHAEL, APPLEBY, EAST ward, county of WESTMORLAND, 2½ miles (N.W.) from Appleby, containing 134 inhabitants. At a place called Chapel-hill are the ruins of a chapel, dedicated to St. Giles. On the road from this place to Kirkby-Thore, and to the southward of the ancient Roman road, are traces of a quadrilateral camp; and further on is a small outwork, called Maiden-hold. In digging for clay at Machel's Bank, three urns containing calcined bones and ashes were found covered with similar relics; and in another pit, fifty yards from the former, a large quantity of ashes and bones, without any urn, was also discovered.

CRACO, a township in the parish of BURNSALL, eastern division of the wapentake of STAINCLIFFE and EWCROSS, West riding of the county of YORK,

6½ miles (N.) from Skipton, containing 179 inhabitants. There is a place of worship for Wesleyan Methodists.

CRADLEY, a parish in the hundred of RADLOW, county of HEREFORD, comprising the townships of East and West Cradley, and containing 1459 inhabitants, of which number, 739 are in the township of East Cradley, 7 miles (N. by E.) from Ledbury. The living is a rectory, in the archdeaconry and diocese of Hereford, rated in the king's books at £18, and in the patronage of the Bishop of Hereford. The church is dedicated to St. James.

CRADLEY, a chapelry in that part of the parish of HALES-OWEN which is in the lower division of the hundred of HALFSHIRE, county of WORCESTER, 2 miles (N.W. by N.) from Hales-Owen, containing 1696 inhabitants. The living is a perpetual curacy, in the archdeaconry and diocese of Worcester, endowed with £400 private benefaction, and £1400 parliamentary grant, and in the patronage of Lord Calthorpe, the Rev. Mr. Gisborne, and W. Wilberforce, Esq. The chapel, a modern structure, pleasantly situated on the brow of a hill, commanding an agreeable prospect, has lately received an addition of two hundred free sittings, the Incorporated Society for the enlargement of churches and chapels having granted £75 towards defraying the expense. There are places of worship for Baptists, Wesleyan Methodists, and Unitarians. A National school for boys and girls is supported by charitable contributions. The river Stour runs on the north and north-western sides of the chapelry, and separates it from Staffordshire. A mine of coal has been worked upon its banks, but is now discontinued. Beautifully situated in a woody spot, amid pleasing walks, and on the banks of a large pool, or artificial lake, is Cradley Spa, where warm and cold baths have been erected: the water is impregnated with sulphate of soda, magnesia, &c., and is greatly used by invalids during the summer: an attempt was formerly made to manufacture salt here. In a large wood, called Cradley Park, are vestiges of the moat of an ancient building. The chapelry is hilly, and the vicinity abounds with pleasing and picturesque scenery.

CRADLEY (WEST), a township in the parish of CRADLEY, hundred of RADLOW, county of HEREFORD, 7 miles (N. by E.) from Ledbury, containing 720 inhabitants. A charity school is supported by subscriptions amounting to about £20 per annum.

CRAIKE, a parish in the south-western division of STOCKTON ward, county palatine of DURHAM, though locally in the wapentake of Bulmer, North riding of the county of York, 3¼ miles (E. by N.) from Easingwould, containing 538 inhabitants. The living is a rectory, in the peculiar jurisdiction of the Dean and Chapter of Durham, rated in the king's books at £10, and in the patronage of the Bishop of Durham. The church is dedicated to St. Cuthbert. There is a place of worship for Wesleyan Methodists. A school is supported by charitable donations amounting to about £4. 10. per annum. Egfrid, King of Northumberland, in 685, gave this place, with land extending three miles round it, to St. Cuthbert, the founder of a monastery here, every vestige of which has for ages been removed. There are remains of a castle of remote and uncertain date, converted into a farm-house.

CRAKEHALL, a joint township with Elmer, in that part of the parish of TOPCLIFFE which is in the wapentake of BIRDFORTH, North riding of the county of YORK, 6½ miles (N.N.E.) from Boroughbridge. The population is returned with Elmer.

CRAKEHALL, a township in that part of the parish of BEDALE which is in the eastern division of the wapentake of HANG, North riding of the county of YORK, 1¾ mile (N.W. by W.) from Bedale, containing, with Rands-Grange, 550 inhabitants. There are places of worship for Baptists and Wesleyan Methodists. The village forms a spacious quadrangle, enclosing an extensive and pleasant green, ornamented with stately trees.

CRAKEMARSH, a township in the parish of UTTOXETER, southern division of the hundred of TOTMONSLOW, county of STAFFORD, 2¼ miles (N. by E.) from Uttoxeter, with which the population is returned. Crakemarsh is in the honour of Tutbury, duchy of Lancaster, and within the jurisdiction of a court of pleas held at Tutbury every third Tuesday, for the recovery of debts under 40*s*.

CRAMBE, a parish in the wapentake of BULMER, North riding of the county of YORK, comprising the townships of Barton le Willows, Crambe, and Whitwell on the Hill, and containing 522 inhabitants, of which number, 152 are in the township of Crambe, 6¼ miles (S.W. by S.) from New Malton. The living is a discharged vicarage, in the archdeaconry of Cleveland, and diocese of York, rated in the king's books at £9. 1. 8., and in the patronage of the Archbishop of York. The church is dedicated to St. Michael.

CRAMLINGTON, a chapelry in that part of the parish of ST. ANDREW, NEWCASTLE, which is in the eastern division of CASTLE ward, county of NORTHUMBERLAND, 8¾ miles (N. by E.) from Newcastle, containing 330 inhabitants. The living is a perpetual curacy, in the archdeaconry of Northumberland, and diocese of Durham, endowed with £200 private benefaction, £600 royal bounty, and £200 parliamentary grant, and in the patronage of Sir M. W. Ridley, Bart., and C. Lawson, Esq. The chapel is dedicated to St. Nicholas. The village, which is situated on a pleasant slope, commanding a fine sea-view, has gradually risen to its present improved state from the period of opening the adjacent collieries, the coal from which is conveyed by a rail-road to the river Tyne, near Howden Pans. Sir M. W. Ridley, Bart. has provided a schoolroom here, with a house and garden for the master.

CRANAGE, a township in that part of the parish of SANDBACH which is in the hundred of NORTHWICH, county palatine of CHESTER, 3¾ miles (E.N.E.) from Middlewich, containing 433 inhabitants. Thomas Hall, Esq. erected two schoolrooms here, one of which he endowed with £10 per annum, for ten boys, and the other with £4 per annum, for ten girls, all of them being partly clothed. In the reign of Henry VI. a bridge of stone was erected across the river Dane, at the expense of Sir John Nedham, but a few years ago it gave place to the present structure, which is built of wood, from a design by Mr. Harrison, of Chester.

CRANBORNE, a market town and parish, comprising the tythings of Alderholt, Beveridge, and Farewood, and the hamlet of Crendall, in the hundred of CRANBORNE, and the tythings of Blagdon and Monckton up Wimborne, in the hundred of MONCKTON up WIMBORNE, Shaston (East) division of the county of DORSET, 30 miles (N.E. by E.) from Dorchester, and 92 (W.S.W.) from London, and containing 1823 inhabitants. This place, which is of great antiquity, derives its name from the Saxon *Gren*, a crane, and *Burn*, a river, either from the tortuous windings of a stream, which, rising in the parish, falls into the Stour, or from the number of cranes that frequented its banks. In 980, Ailward de Meaw founded here a Benedictine monastery, dedicated to St. Bartholomew; but in 1102 the abbot retired with his brethren to Tewkesbury, where Robert Fitz-Hamon had founded a magnificent abbey, to which the original establishment became a cell. The old manor-house, from having been embattled, was called the castle, and was the occasional residence of the king, when he came to hunt in Cranborne Chase, an extensive tract reaching almost to Salisbury: the chase courts were regularly held in it, in which was a room, called the dungeon, for the confinement of offenders against the chase laws.

The town is pleasantly situated at the north-eastern extremity of the county, in the centre of a fine open expanse of champaign land: the houses are in general neat and well built, and the inhabitants are amply supplied with water. Riband-weaving formerly flourished here, but has declined, and the majority of the labouring class are employed in agriculture. The market is on Thursday: fairs are held on August 24th and December 6th, for cheese and sheep. The town is within the jurisdiction of the county magistrates, and is divided into the liberties of the tything, the priory, and the borough, for which a constable, tythingman, and bailiff, are appointed respectively. The living is a discharged vicarage, in the archdeaconry of Dorset, and diocese of Bristol, rated in the king's books at £6. 13. 4., endowed with £1000 private benefaction, and £2700 parliamentary grant, and in the patronage of the Marquis of Salisbury. The church, dedicated to St. Bartholomew, and formerly the conventual church of the priory, is an ancient structure, partly Norman, and partly in the early style of English architecture, with a large and handsome tower in the later style; the pulpit is of oak, richly carved, and supported on a pedestal of stone: there are some remains of stained glass in the large window of the south aisle, representing the Virgin Mary and the heads of some of the Saints. An almshouse for three single persons was founded and endowed by Thomas Hooper, Esq., who also gave a rent-charge of £6 for the steward. On Castle hill, to the south of the town, is a circular fortification, consisting of two deep trenches and ramparts, and including an area of six acres, in which is a well; and in the environs are numerous barrows, of which some have been opened and found to contain urns with bones. The learned Bishop Stillingfleet was born here, in 1635, and died in 1699. Cranborne gives the title of viscount to the Marquis of Salisbury.

CRANBROOKE, a market town and parish in the hundred of CRANBROOKE, lathe of SCRAY, county of KENT, 14 miles (S. by E.) from Maidstone, and 48 (S.E. by E.) from London, containing 3683 inhabitants. This place, anciently called *Crane-broke*, derives its name from its situation upon a brook called the Crane. When the manufacture of woollen cloth was introduced into England by Edward III., it was principally carried on in the Weald of Kent, and Cranbrooke, situated in the centre of that district, became, and continued to be for centuries, a very flourishing town, and the principal seat of the clothing trade, by the removal of which into the counties of Gloucester and Somerset, within the last fifty years, its trading importance has been almost annihilated. The town consists chiefly of one wide street, extending three quarters of a mile in length, from which a smaller street branches off at right angles: it is indifferently paved, and partially lighted, contains some well-built, houses, and is well supplied with water. The trade is now principally in hops, which is carried on to a considerable extent. The market, formerly on Saturday, and considerable for corn, hops, &c., has, within the last few years, been altered to Wednesday; there is also a cattle market on every alternate Wednesday: the market-house, a neat octagonal building supported on double columns at the angles, and surmounted by a cupola, was erected by William Coleman, Esq., a great benefactor to the town. The fairs are on May 30th and September 29th, for horses and cattle; the latter is also a great hop fair.

The living is a vicarage, in the archdeaconry and diocese of Canterbury, rated in the king's books at £19. 19. 4½., endowed with £200 private benefaction, and £1100 parliamentary grant, and in the patronage of the Archbishop of Canterbury. The church, dedicated to St. Dunstan, is a spacious handsome structure in the later style of English architecture, with a square embattled tower: in the year 1725, one of the columns giving way, a part of the church fell down; it was repaired at an expense of £2000. There are places of worship for Particular Baptists, Huntingtonians, Independents, Wesleyan Methodists, and Unitarians. The free grammar school was founded, in 1574, by Simon Lynch, Esq., and endowed by Queen Elizabeth with land producing at present about £140 per annum, which has been augmented by subsequent benefactors to £300 per annum: the management is vested in thirteen trustees, including the vicar. A writing school was founded, in 1573, by Mr. Alexander Dence, who endowed it with a house for the master, a schoolroom, and the interest of £160; of this sum, £60 was expended in the enlargement of the premises, the interest of the remainder only being available to the payment of the master. A National school for the instruction of an unlimited number of boys and girls is supported by subscription. In the hamlet of Milkhouse-street, are the remains of an ancient chapel, dedicated to the Holy Trinity. There are several mineral springs in the vicinity, the properties of which are similar to those of Tonbridge-Wells. Sir Richard Baker, author of the English Chronicles, was born in this parish, about the year 1568. The celebrated William Huntington, late minister of Providence chapel, Gray's Inn Lane, London, and founder of a sect called "Huntingtonians," holding high Calvinistic principles, was born at a place called "The Four Wents," in this parish: he died July 1st, 1813, aged 69, and was interred in the burial-ground of Jireh chapel, Lewes, Sussex. He wrote and published eighty-one separate works, most of which went through several editions during his lifetime; and, added to six volumes of Letters, &c., published since his death, his works extend to thirty-four volumes 8vo.

CRANFIELD, a parish in the hundred of REDBORNE-STOKE, county of BEDFORD, 7 miles (W. N. W.) from Ampthill, containing 1153 inhabitants. The living is a rectory, in the archdeaconry of Bedford, and diocese of Lincoln, rated in the king's books at £33. 2. 1., and in the patronage of the Rev. James Beard. The church is dedicated to St. Peter and St. Paul. There is a place of worship for Particular Baptists. A school is supported by charitable donations amounting to about £15 per annum. A mineral spring rises in the parish, but it is very little resorted to. Cranfield gives the inferior title of baron to the Duke of Dorset.

CRANFORD, a parish in the hundred of ELTHORNE, county of MIDDLESEX, 2½ miles (N. W. by W.) from Hounslow, containing 288 inhabitants. The living is a rectory, in the archdeaconry of Middlesex, and diocese of London, rated in the king's books at £16, and in the patronage of the Dowager Countess of Berkeley. The church is dedicated to St. Dunstan. The river Colne runs through the parish, and is crossed by a bridge at the village, called Cranford-bridge.

CRANFORD (ST. ANDREW), a parish in the hundred of HUXLOE, county of NORTHAMPTON, 4¼ miles (E. by S.) from Kettering, containing, with the parish of Cranford St. John, 515 inhabitants. The living is a rectory, in the archdeaconry of Northampton, and diocese of Peterborough, rated in the king's books at £9. 9. 7., and in the patronage of Sir G. Robinson, Bart.

CRANFORD (ST. JOHN), a parish in the hundred of HUXLOE, county of NORTHAMPTON, 4 miles (E. S. E.) from Kettering. The population is returned with Cranford St. Andrew. The living is a rectory, in the archdeaconry of Northampton, and diocese of Peterborough, rated in the king's books at £12, and in the patronage of the Bishop of Lincoln.

CRANHAM, a parish in the hundred of CHAFFORD, county of ESSEX, 2¾ miles (E. S. E.) from Hornchurch, containing 289 inhabitants. The living is a rectory, in the archdeaconry of Essex, and diocese of London, rated in the king's books at £13. 13. 4., and in the patronage of the President and Fellows of St. John's College, Oxford. The church is dedicated to All Saints. This parish was formerly known by the names of Bishop's Ockingdon and Cravenham.

CRANHAM, a parish in the hundred of RAPSGATE, county of GLOUCESTER, 2½ miles (N. E. by E.) from Painswick, containing 321 inhabitants. The living is a discharged rectory, consolidated with that of Brimpsfield, in the archdeaconry and diocese of Gloucester, rated in the king's books at £6. 6. 8., endowed with £200 royal bounty, and in the patronage of the Earl of Mount-Edgecumbe. The church is dedicated to St. James. There are manufactories for earthenware in the parish.

CRANLEY, a parish in the second division of the hundred of BLACKHEATH, county of SURREY, 7¾ miles (S. E. by E.) from Godalming, containing 1182 inhabitants. The living is a rectory, in the archdeaconry of Surrey, and diocese of Winchester, rated in the king's books at £20. 18. 1½., and in the patronage of the Rev. John Wolfe. The church, dedicated to St. Nicholas, is a large and handsome edifice in the ancient style of English architecture, having a richly ornamented chapel, enclosed with curious and elegant lattice-work at the termination of each aisle. At Vacharie are foundations, encompassed by a moat, of the ancient baronial residence of the lords of Shire. Cranley gives the title of viscount to the Earls of Onslow.

CRANMORE (EAST), a parish in the hundred of FROME, county of SOMERSET, 4¼ miles (E.) from Shepton-Mallet, containing 68 inhabitants. The living is a perpetual curacy, annexed to the vicarage of Doulting, in the archdeaconry of Wells, and diocese of Bath and Wells. The church is dedicated to St. James. The district which now comprises East and West Cranmore was exempted from all suit and service to the hundred courts, and raised into a liberty by Henry I. The inhabitants bury at West Cranmore.

CRANMORE (WEST), a parish forming, with the parish of Evercreech and the chapelry of Chesterblade, a detached portion of the hundred of WELLS-FORUM, county of SOMERSET, 3½ miles (E.) from Shepton-Mallet, containing 270 inhabitants. The living is a perpetual curacy, annexed to the vicarage of Doulting, in the archdeaconry of Wells, and diocese of Bath and Wells. The church is dedicated to St. Bartholomew.

CRANOE, a parish in the hundred of GARTREE, county of LEICESTER, 6 miles (N. N. E.) from Market-Harborough, containing 101 inhabitants. The living is a rectory, in the archdeaconry of Leicester, and diocese of Lincoln, rated in the king's books at £8. 16. 8., and in the patronage of the Earl of Cardigan. The church is dedicated to St, Michael.

CRANSFORD, a parish in the hundred of PLOMESGATE, county of SUFFOLK, 2¼ miles (E. N. E.) from Framlingham, containing 294 inhabitants. The living is a discharged vicarage, in the archdeaconry of Suffolk, and diocese of Norwich, rated in the king's books at £6. 13. 4., endowed with £200 private benefaction, and £200 royal bounty, and in the patronage of the Rev. C. Chevallier. The church is dedicated to St. Peter.

CRANSLEY, a parish in the hundred of ORLINGBURY, county of NORTHAMPTON, 3 miles (W. S. W.) from Kettering, containing 250 inhabitants. The living is a discharged vicarage, in the archdeaconry of Northampton, and diocese of Peterborough, rated in the king's books at £8. 5., endowed with £400 private benefaction, and £400 royal bounty, and in the patronage of J. C. Rose, Esq. The church is dedicated to St. Andrew.

CRANTOCK, a parish in the hundred of PYDER, county of CORNWALL, 7 miles (N. W. by W.) from St. Michael, containing 389 inhabitants. The living is a perpetual curacy, in the archdeaconry of Cornwall, and diocese of Exeter, endowed with £800 royal bounty, and in the patronage of Mr. Buller and others. The church is dedicated to St. Cadock, a corruption of St. Carantocus: in the time of Edward the Confessor it was made collegiate for Secular canons, who continued till the dissolution, when its annual revenue of £89. 15. 8. was divided amongst the dean, nine prebendaries, and four vicars choral. This parish is bounded on the north by the Bristol channel, and has a small harbour at the mouth of the river Gannel.

CRANWELL, a parish in the hundred of FLAXWELL, parts of KESTEVEN, county of LINCOLN, 4 miles (N. W.) from Sleaford, containing 155 inhabitants. The living is a discharged vicarage, in the archdeaconry and diocese of Lincoln, endowed with £200 private benefaction, and £600 royal bounty, and in the patronage of Sir John H. Thorold. The church is dedicated to St. Andrew. A school is supported by charitable donations amounting to about £3 per annum.

CRANWICK, a parish in the hundred of GRIMSHOE, county of NORFOLK, 6 miles (S. E. by E.) from Stoke-Ferry, containing 70 inhabitants. The living is a discharged rectory, with the vicarage of Methwold annexed, in the archdeaconry of Norfolk, and diocese of Norwich, rated in the king's books at £8. 9. 7., and in the patronage of H. S. Partridge, Esq. The church, dedicated to St. Mary, is a small ancient building of flint, having at the west end a tower of similar materials, supposed to have been erected by King Harold, one of whose freemen possessed a moiety of this place in the time of Edward the Confessor. The river Wissy bounds the parish on the north.

CRANWORTH, a parish in the hundred of MITFORD, county of NORFOLK, 6 miles (N. E. by E.) from Watton, containing 331 inhabitants. The living is a rectory, with that of Letton consolidated, in the archdeaconry of Norfolk, and diocese of Norwich, rated in the king's books at £5. 18. 6½., and in the patronage of T. T. Gurdon, Esq. The church is dedicated to St. Mary.

CRASSWALL, a chapelry in the parish of CLODOCK, hundred of EWYASLACY, county of HEREFORD, 5 miles (S. E.) from Hay, containing 374 inhabitants. The living is a perpetual curacy, in the archdeaconry of Brecon, and diocese of St. David, endowed with £200 royal bounty, and in the patronage of the Earl of Oxford. The chapel is dedicated to St. Mary. About the close of the reign of King John a monastery was founded here, probably by Walton de Lacy, for a prior and ten religious of the order of Grandmont in Normandy: at the seizure of Alien priories it was valued at 40*s*. per annum, and granted, in the 2nd of Edward IV., to God's House, now Christ's College, Cambridge. There is a fine stone quarry in the neighbourhood.

CRASTER, a township in the parish of EMBLETON, southern division of BAMBROUGH ward, county of NORTHUMBERLAND, 6¼ miles (N. E.) from Alnwick, containing 146 inhabitants. The village, which is called Craster Sea Houses, is situated on the coast of the North sea.

CRATFIELD, a parish in the hundred of BLYTHING, county of SUFFOLK, 5½ miles (W. S. W.) from Halesworth, containing 717 inhabitants. The living is a discharged vicarage, annexed to that of Laxfield, in the archdeaconry of Suffolk, and diocese of Norwich, rated in the king's books at £5. 7. 11., and in the patronage of Lord Huntingfield. The church is dedicated to St. Mary. There is an endowed Sunday school in this parish, also a school supported by charitable donations amounting to £8. 8. per annum.

CRATHORNE, a parish in the western division of the liberty of LANGBAURGH, North riding of the county of YORK, 3¼ miles (S. S. E.) from Yarm, containing 330 inhabitants. The living is a rectory, in the archdeaconry of Cleveland, and diocese of York, rated in the king's books at £10. 11. 10½., and in the patronage of Godfrey Wentworth and Robert Chaloner, Esqrs. The church, dedicated to All Saints, is an ancient structure; in the chancel is the figure of an armed knight lying cross-legged, with the arms of Crathorne on the shield, and near it is a mural monument of a member of the same family. There are places of worship for Primitive Methodists and Roman Catholics. Thomas Baxter, in 1769, gave £100, now producing, with other subscriptions, £13. 6. per annum, which is applied to the education of twenty poor children. Here are a linen-manufactory and an extensive bleaching-ground. At a short distance from the village is a mineral spring.

CRAWCROOK, a township in the parish of RYTON, western division of CHESTER ward, county palatine of DURHAM, 9¾ miles (W.) from Gateshead, containing 308 inhabitants. Coal is obtained in this township. Miss Simpson, of Bradley Hall, endowed a school with £25 per annum, for teaching twenty-six children; and another has been established by Lady Ravensworth, who annually contributes £20 for the education of girls.

CRAWFORD-TARRANT, a parish in the hundred of BADBURY, Shaston (East) division of the county of DORSET, 3½ miles (S. E. by E.) from Blandford-Forum, containing, with Preston, 76 inhabitants. The living is a perpetual curacy, in the archdeaconry of Dorset, and diocese of Bristol, and in the patronage of E. B. Portman, Esq. The church is dedicated to St Mary. Richard Poor, successively Bishop of Chichester, Salisbury, and Durham, founded, about 1230, an abbey of Cistercian nuns, in honour of the Blessed Virgin and All Saints; at the dissolution, its revenue was estimated at £239. 11. 10.

CRAWLEY, a township in the parish of EGLINGHAM, northern division of COQUETDALE ward, county of NORTHUMBERLAND, 9¼ miles (W. N. W.) from Alnwick, containing 23 inhabitants. It was anciently called Crawlawe, from *Caer-law*, a fortified hill. Crawley tower, a Roman structure, stands on an eminence near an old and strong intrenchment, which is thought to be the *Alauna Amnis* of Richard of Cirencester, though some place this station at Alnwick, and others at Glanton: it commands a fine view of the vale of Whittingham, with the river Breamish, from its source to Horton castle; and no less than seven British and Saxon fortifications may be discerned within four miles round this spot.

CRAWLEY, a hamlet in the parish of WITNEY, hundred of BAMPTON, county of OXFORD, 1¾ mile (N. W. by N.) from Witney, containing 221 inhabitants.

CRAWLEY, a parish in the hundred of BUDDLESGATE, Fawley division of the county of SOUTHAMPTON, 5 miles (N. W.) from Winchester, containing, with the chapelry of Hunton, 476 inhabitants. The living is a rectory, in the peculiar jurisdiction of the incumbent, rated in the king's books at £35. 13. 4., and in the patronage of the Bishop of Winchester. The church is dedicated to St. Mary. Crawley is within the jurisdiction of the Cheyney Court held at Winchester every Thursday, for the recovery of debts to any amount.

CRAWLEY, a parish in the hundred of BUTTINGHILL, rape of LEWES, county of SUSSEX, 9½ miles (N. by W.) from Cuckfield, containing 334 inhabitants. The living is a discharged rectory, in the archdeaconry of Lewes, and diocese of Chichester, rated in the king's books at £6. 15., endowed with £200 private benefaction, and £200 royal bounty, and in the patronage of

James Clitherow, Esq. The church, dedicated to St. John the Baptist, is partly in the decorated and partly in the later style of English architecture, and has lately received an addition of ninety free sittings, the Incorporated Society for the enlargement of churches and chapels having granted £17 toward defraying the expense. Fairs for horned cattle are held on May 8th and September 29th.

CRAWLEY (HUSBORN), county of BEDFORD.—See HUSBORN-CRAWLEY.

CRAY (FOOT'S), a parish in the hundred of RUXLEY, lathe of SUTTON at HONE, county of KENT, 12½ miles (S. E.) from London, containing 221 inhabitants. The living is a discharged rectory, in the archdeaconry and diocese of Rochester, rated in the king's books at £8. 3. 4., endowed with £200 private benefaction, and £200 royal bounty, and in the patronage of the Crown. The church, dedicated to All Saints, is a small plain building, supposed to be of high antiquity. This parish probably derived its name from Fot, or Vot, its proprietor in the time of Edward the Confessor, and from the river Cray, which runs by the eastern end of the village, there turning a mill, and then directing its course towards North Cray. A National school was established in 1815, for which the Rev. Francis Wollaston left £200 five per cents.; and Benjamin Harence, Esq., in 1817, gave land whereon a school-house had been previously erected by subscription; from seventy to eighty children of both sexes are taught at this school, which is supported by contributions in aid of the original bequest.

CRAY (ST. MARY'S), a parish in the hundred of RUXLEY, lathe of SUTTON at HONE, county of KENT, 2 miles (S. by W.) from Foot's Cray, containing 874 inhabitants. The living is a perpetual curacy, annexed to the vicarage of Orpington, in the peculiar jurisdiction of the Archbishop of Canterbury. The church contains several ancient brasses and some memorials of the Mannings. A charity school was established here in 1710, for the education of six children; and Sir Thomas Dyke, in 1816, erected another, with a residence for the master and mistress, extending its benefits to the children of Orpington; it is supported by a rent-charge upon estates at Hunton, bequeathed in 1715 by Catherine Withens, which, with a weekly contribution of twopence paid by each pupil sent from Orpington, produces an annual income of £80 to the master and mistress, who also receive an allowance of £5 a year, coal, &c.: about one hundred children are instructed upon the National system. "The Crays," so called from the river Cray, which runs through it, is reckoned one of the most beautiful tracts in Kent, and produces a vast quantity of birch; it comprehends four parishes, with as many villages, distinguished by their prefixes, of which St. Mary's Cray was the most considerable, and had the privilege of a market so early as the reign of Edward I.; but the market-house having been destroyed by a tempest in 1703, the market has never since been held.

CRAY (NORTH), a parish in the hundred of RUXLEY, lathe of SUTTON at HONE, county of KENT, 1 mile (N. by E.) from Foot's Cray, containing 245 inhabitants. The living is a rectory with Ruxley, in the archdeaconry and diocese of Rochester, rated in the king's books at £13. 9. 9½., and in the patronage of T. W. Coventry, Esq. The church is dedicated to St. James. In 1771, the Rev. William Hetherington, and Elizabeth Hetherington, gave a tenement for a school, in support of which the latter bequeathed £100 in 1776, which, with other donations for the same purpose, produce about £11. 11. per annum; in 1777, the former left £200 for repairs and other uses, which, with additions since made, yields an annual dividend of £12. 8. From these funds £10 a year is paid to a mistress for teaching an unlimited number of young children, who, on attaining the age of seven years, are admitted into the National school at Bexley, the master and mistress of which receive from this charity £5 per annum each, with an allowance of 20*s.* a year for books and rewards. This parish is pleasingly diversified with villas and well cultivated domains, of which Mount Mascall and Vale Mascall claim distinction; in the grounds of the latter the river Cray forms a cascade much admired for its picturesque beauty. In 1723 a subterraneous fire broke out, and the inhabitants for several days afterwards employed themselves with wagons in conveying water from Bexley, for the purpose of quenching the flames.

CRAY (ST. PAUL'S), a parish in the hundred of RUXLEY, lathe of SUTTON at HONE, county of KENT, 1½ mile (S.) from Foot's Cray, containing 364 inhabitants. The living is a rectory, in the archdeaconry and diocese of Rochester, rated in the king's books at £12. 13. 4., and in the patronage of Viscount Sidney. The church is dedicated to St. Paulinus. In 1729, Richard Chapman bequeathed a rent-charge of £2 towards endowing a school, in furtherance of which the Rev. Thomas Kingsman, in 1752, left £50 three per cents., producing annually about £1. 10., which sums are paid to a schoolmistress for teaching six girls. The river Cray runs through this parish.

CRAYFORD, a parish (formerly a market town) in the hundred of LESSNESS, lathe of SUTTON at HONE, county of KENT, 13 miles (E. by S.) from London, containing 1866 inhabitants. The living is a rectory, in the peculiar jurisdiction of the Archbishop of Canterbury, rated in the king's books at £35. 13. 4., and in the patronage of Thomas Austen, Esq. The church, dedicated to St. Paulinus, is a spacious modern structure, adorned with an elegant altar-piece; it stands on an eminence at the upper end of the village, which consists of an irregular street, branching off to the left of the road from London to Dartford. There is a place of worship for Particular Baptists. Crayford is so called from *Creccanford*, an ancient ford on the river Creccan, now Cray, which here flows in two streams, having upon its banks several extensive establishments for printing calico, and a large mill for making iron hoops. One of the archbishops of Canterbury, who formerly had possessions here, procured a weekly market on Tuesday, and a fair on our Lady's Nativity; the market has long been disused, but an annual fair is still held on the 8th of September. In the immediate vicinity of Crayford some antiquaries have placed the Roman station *Noviomagus*, near which a great battle was fought, in 457, between Hengist the Saxon and the British king Vortimer, which ended in the secure establishment of the kingdom of Kent under the rule of the former. In this parish are many ancient caves, of which some are from fifteen to twenty fathoms deep, increasing in circumference from the mouth downwards, and containing several large apartments, supported by pillars of chalk: it is conjectured that they were used as places of security for the wives, children, and moveable goods of the Saxons, during their wars with the Britons. The manor-house, which was built and occupied by Sir Cloudesley Shovel, is moated, and is now occupied by a farmer.

CREACOMBE, a parish in the hundred of WITHERIDGE, county of DEVON, $8\frac{1}{4}$ miles (S. E. by E.) from South Molton, containing 40 inhabitants. The living is a discharged rectory, in the archdeaconry of Barnstaple, and diocese of Exeter, rated in the king's books at £4. 18. 9., endowed with £700 private benefaction, and £900 royal bounty, and in the patronage of the Rev. W. Karslake. The church is dedicated to St. Michael.

CREAKE (NORTH), a parish in the hundred of BROTHERCROSS, county of NORFOLK, 3 miles (S.E. by S.) from Burnham-Westgate, containing 618 inhabitants. The living is a rectory, in the archdeaconry of Norfolk, and diocese of Norwich, rated in the king's books at £33. 6. 8., and in the patronage of Earl Spencer and the Bishop of Norwich alternately. The church is dedicated to St. Mary, besides which there was formerly one dedicated to St. Michael, also parochial. At Lingerscroft, between Creake and Burnham, Sir Robert de Hereford, in 1206, founded a church, and subsequently a chapel and hospital, dedicated in 1221 to St. Bartholomew, in which he placed a master, four chaplains, and thirteen poor lay brethren: this foundation soon afterwards acquired the distinction of a priory, and in the 15th of Henry III. was elevated into an abbey: that monarch also confirmed the grant of a fair previously made, changing the period to the eve and festival of St. Thomas the Martyr; in the 14th of Edward I. the abbot claimed the right of holding four fairs annually at Creake. In consequence of the death of the abbot, and there being no convent to elect another, the abbey was deemed dissolved, and its possessions were granted, in the 22nd of Henry VII., to the Countess of Richmond, by whom they were given to Christ's College, Cambridge. In 1815 a school-house was erected here, upon land given for the purpose by a charitable individual. There are four cottages appropriated for the benefit of the poor.

CREAKE (SOUTH), a parish in the hundred of BROTHERCROSS, county of NORFOLK, 4 miles (S. S. E.) from Burnham-Westgate, containing 728 inhabitants. The living is a discharged vicarage, in the archdeaconry of Norfolk, and diocese of Norwich, rated in the king's books at £22, and in the patronage of H. Goggs, Esq. The church is dedicated to St. Mary. There is a place of worship for Particular Baptists. In the neighbourhood is a Saxon fortification, the way leading from which is called Blood-gate, from the dreadful slaughter made there in a battle between the Saxons and the Danes.

CREATON (GREAT), a parish in the hundred of GUILSBOROUGH, county of NORTHAMPTON, $7\frac{1}{4}$ miles (N.N.W.) from Northampton, containing 492 inhabitants. The living is a rectory, in the archdeaconry of Northampton, and diocese of Peterborough, rated in the king's books at £ 11. 1. 8., and in the patronage of the Rev. Mr. Beynon. The church is dedicated to St. Michael. In 1825, six cottages, for the accommodation of aged widows, were built on a piece of waste land in the village, by the Rev. Thomas Jones, late curate of the parish. In this parish are the remains of Holmby House, where Charles I. suffered imprisonment.

CREATON (LITTLE), a hamlet in the parish of SPRATTON, hundred of SPELHOE, county of NORTHAMPTON, $7\frac{3}{4}$ miles (N.N.W.) from Northampton, containing 106 inhabitants.

CREDENHILL, a parish in the hundred of GRIMSWORTH, county of HEREFORD, $4\frac{1}{2}$ miles (N. W. by W.) from Hereford, containing 199 inhabitants. The living is a discharged rectory, in the archdeaconry and diocese of Hereford, rated in the king's books at £17. 19. 4., and in the patronage of the Rev. Edmund Eckley. The church is dedicated to St. Mary. On the summit of a steep and lofty hill, the declivity of which is well wooded, are the remains of an ancient and almost inaccessible camp, having an outer and an inner trench, enclosing an area of nearly forty acres: from its irregular form some have attributed this work to the Britons, while others, with greater probability, suppose it to have been constructed by the Romans, for the defence of their adjacent station at Kenchester, the *Magna Castra* of Antoninus: the view from it is one of the most extensive and beautiful in the county.

CREDITON, a borough, market town, and parish, in the hundred of CREDITON, and extending also into that of West Budleigh, county of DEVON, 8 miles (N. W.) from Exeter, and 180 (W. by S.) from London, containing, with the tythings of Bradley, Canon-Fee, Fulford, Knowle, Rudge, Town, Uford, Uton, and Woodland, 5515 inhabitants. This place, which takes its name from its situation on the river Creedy, was for many years the seat of a diocese, of which a collegiate church, founded here in 905, and dedicated to the Holy Cross, became the cathedral. In the reign of Canute, Levinus, Bishop of Crediton, prevailed upon that monarch, with whom he had great influence, to annex the see of St. Germans to that of Crediton, the united see having been removed to Exeter, by Edward the Confessor, in 1050. A chapter, consisting of a dean and twelve prebendaries, was still maintained in the old collegiate church, under the jurisdiction of the Bishop of Exeter, the revenue of which, at the dissolution, was £332. 17. 5.: the church, with some lands belonging to it, was granted to the governors of the free school in the reign of Edward VI. In the reign of Edward I. this borough sent members to a parliament held at Carlisle; and, in 1310, Bishop Stapleton obtained for it the grant of a weekly market and two annual fairs. Towards the middle of the sixteenth century, the opponents of the Reformation assembled their forces at Crediton, but were compelled to withdraw by Sir Peter Carew, who was sent against them with a superior force. In 1644, Charles I. reviewed his troops in this town, which was subsequently possessed by the army under Sir Thomas Fairfax: in 1743 a fire destroyed a considerable part of it, and a similar calamity occurred in 1769.

Crediton is pleasantly situated in a vale on the banks of the river Creedy, and within three quarters of a mile of the river Exe, with which the Creedy unites between this place and Exeter: it is divided into two parts, east and west, of which the former, containing the church, is the more ancient, and the latter the more extensive; and consists principally of one main street, nearly a mile in length, roughly paved, and containing low cottages at each extremity, with a few well-built houses in the centre, in which is also a range of shambles: it is amply supplied with water. Assemblies and concerts take place periodically, during the winter, in a good assembly-room, conveniently fitted up for the purpose. The principal branch of manufacture is that of serge, which is sent to Exeter to be finished for exportation; dowlas, long ells, and flannel, are also manufactured here, but not to a great extent: it is in contemplation to bring the road to Barnstaple through the town, within a short distance of which it now passes. The market, which is very well attended, is on Saturday; and on the Saturday preceding the last Wednesday in April is a large market for cattle, in which more than one thousand head are frequently sold. Fairs for cattle are held, in the eastern division of the town, on May 11th and September 21st, and in the western division on the 21st of August, unless it happen on Friday, Saturday, or Sunday, in which case it is postponed till the following Tuesday; this fair continues for three days, on the first of which a great number of cattle is sold. The town is within the jurisdiction of the county magistrates, who hold a petty session every month; and its local affairs are under the superintendence of a portreeve, bailiff, and constables, chosen annually by a jury at the court leet of the lord of the manor, the bailiff for the year preceding being invariably appointed to the office of portreeve.

The living is a vicarage, in the peculiar jurisdiction of the Bishop of Exeter, rated in the king's books at £30, and in the patronage of twelve lay governors, incorporated by charters of Edward VI. and Elizabeth, by whom the church is kept in repair. The church, dedicated to the Holy Cross, is a spacious and magnificent cruciform structure, with a square embattled tower rising from the centre; it was erected, or rather rebuilt, in the reign of Henry VII., and is a fine specimen of the later English style of architecture, which at that time was in its highest perfection. There are places of worship for Baptists, Independents, Wesleyan Methodists, and Unitarians. The grammar school was founded by Edward VI., and further endowed by Queen Elizabeth, who by her charter provided for the gratuitous instruction of four boys, to each of whom forty shillings are annually given; the school, which is open to all boys of the parishes of Crediton and Sandford, on the payment of £5 per annum, is under the management of the twelve governors, who appoint the master, to whom they pay a salary of £30 per annum, and nominate the four free boys: there are three exhibitions, of £6. 13. 4. each, to either of the Universities, tenable for five years, belonging to this school; and annexed to the mastership is the perpetual curacy of Kennerley. The Blue-coat school, founded about the year 1730, by subscription, and since endowed with various benefactions, was incorporated with an English school in 1814, and placed under one master, in a house erected, in 1806, by the trustees of Sir John Hayward's charity; the annual income of these united schools is £116. 12.: about one hundred and fifty children are instructed on Dr. Bell's system, eighty of them being also clothed. A mathematical school was founded, in 1794, by Mr. Samuel Dunn, who endowed it with £600 stock, now in the four per cents.; in this school twelve boys are instructed in reading, writing, and arithmetic, and in navigation and land-surveying, if required. Almshouses with small endowments were founded by Mr. Humphrey Sparway, in 1557, and by Mr. John Davie, in 1620. Near the church are some slight remains of the episcopal palace, and of the chapel of St. Lawrence, anciently connected with one of the prebends of the collegiate church: in North-street is an ancient building, said to have formed part of the dean's house, in a portion of which, supposed to have been the refectory, the ancient ceiling is still preserved. Winifred, Archbishop of Mentz, and legate under several of the popes, who was eminently successful in promulgating the doctrines of Christianity among the Mercians, and suffered martyrdom in the year 354, was a native of this place.

CREECH (EAST), a tything in the parish of Church-Knowle, hundred of Hasilor, Blandford (South) division of the county of Dorset, 3¼ miles (S.) from Wareham. The population is returned with the parish.

CREECH (ST. MICHAEL), a parish forming, with the parish of Lyng, which includes the Isle of Athelney, a distinct portion of the hundred of Andersfield, locally in the hundred of Taunton and Taunton-Dean, county of Somerset, 3½ miles (E. N. E.) from Taunton, containing 812 inhabitants. The living is a vicarage, in the archdeaconry of Taunton, and diocese of Bath and Wells, rated in the king's books at £16. 18. 9., and in the patronage of E. Cresswell, Esq. The church is dedicated to St. Michael. Henry Stodgel, in 1701, and Ann Seager, in 1741, bequeathed a rent-charge of £2 each for teaching poor children. The navigable river Tone runs through this parish, and is crossed by a bridge at the village.

CREED, a parish in the western division of the hundred of Powder, county of Cornwall, ¾ of a mile (S.) from Grampound, containing, with the whole of the chapelry of Grampound, part of which is in the parish of Probus, 947 inhabitants. The living is a rectory, in the archdeaconry of Cornwall, and diocese of Exeter, rated in the king's books at £13. 6. 8., and in the patronage of Sir Christopher Hawkins. The church is dedicated to St. Creed. There is a small chapel of ease at Grampound, in a ruinous condition. The parish is bounded on the west by the river Fal; and in the neighbourhood are vestiges of two ancient intrenchments, each enclosing about one acre.

CREEKSEA, a parish in the hundred of Dengie, county of Essex, 2 miles (N. W. by W.) from Burnham, containing 152 inhabitants. The living is a discharged rectory, to which the vicarage of Althorne was united in 1811, in the archdeaconry of Essex, and diocese of London, rated in the king's books at £9. 8. 10., and in the patronage of J. Robinson, Esq. The church is dedicated to All Saints. There is a ferry over Crouch river to Wallisea island, from the south side of the parish, where the marshes are protected from inundation by strong embankments, about nine feet in height.

CREETING (ALL SAINTS), a parish in the hundred of Bosmere and Claydon, county of Suffolk, 1¾ mile (N.) from Needham-Market, containing 271 inhabitants. The living is a discharged rectory, with which the rectories of Creeting St. Mary and Creeting St. Olave are consolidated, in the archdeaconry of Sudbury, and diocese of Norwich, rated in the king's books at £10. 0. 5., and in the patronage of the Provost and

Fellows of Eton College. The church is demolished. The StowMarket and Ipswich navigation passes along the south-western boundary.

CREETING (ST. MARY), a parish in the hundred of BOSMERE and CLAYDON, county of SUFFOLK, 1½ mile (N. N. E.) from Needham-Market, containing 167 inhabitants. The living is a discharged rectory, consolidated with the rectories of Creeting All Saints and Creeting St. Olave, in the archdeaconry of Suffolk, and diocese of Norwich, rated in the king's books at £7. 14. 2., endowed with £200 private benefaction, and £200 royal bounty. Here was formerly a cell to the abbey of Bernay, in Normandy, the revenue of which, at the suppression of Alien establishments, was applied towards the endowment of Eton College.

CREETING (ST. OLAVE), a parish in the hundred of BOSMERE and CLAYDON, county of SUFFOLK, 2½ miles (N. N. E.) from Needham-Market, containing 35 inhabitants. The living is a discharged rectory, consolidated with the rectories of Creeting All Saints and Creeting St. Mary, in the archdeaconry of Suffolk, and diocese of Norwich, rated in the king's books at £4. 17. 8½. The church has been demolished.

CREETING (ST. PETER, or WEST), a parish in the hundred of STOW, county of SUFFOLK, 2½ miles (N. by W.) from Needham-Market, containing 169 inhabitants. The living is a discharged rectory, in the archdeaconry of Sudbury, and diocese of Norwich, rated in the king's books at £10. 2. 6., and in the patronage of George Paske, Esq.

CREETON, a parish in the wapentake of BELTISLOE, parts of KESTEVEN, county of LINCOLN, 3¾ miles (S. by E.) from Corby, containing 51 inhabitants. The living is a discharged rectory, in the archdeaconry and diocese of Lincoln, rated in the king's books at £4. 15. 10., and in the patronage of the Crown. The church is dedicated to St. Peter.

CREIGHTON, a township in the parish of UTTOXETER, southern division of the hundred of TOTMONSLOW, county of STAFFORD, 2 miles (N. by W.) from Uttoxeter, with which the population is returned.

CRENDAL, a hamlet in the parish of CRANBORNE, in that part of the hundred of CRANBORNE which is in the Shaston (East) division of the county of DORSET, 2 miles (E.) from Cranborne, with which the population is returned. Potter's clay is dug here, and a considerable quantity of earthenware is made from it.

CRENDON (LONG), a parish in the hundred of ASHENDON, county of BUCKINGHAM, 2¼ miles (N. by W.) from Thame, containing 1212 inhabitants. The living is a perpetual curacy, in the archdeaconry of Buckingham, and diocese of Lincoln, endowed with £800 private benefaction, £800 royal bounty, and £200 parliamentary grant, and in the patronage of the Duke of Marlborough. The church, dedicated to St. Mary, is a spacious edifice with a tower rising from the centre. There is a place of worship for Particular Baptists. A school is supported by donations producing from £5 to £6 per annum. Many of the inhabitants are employed in the manufacture of needles. Walter Giffard, Earl of Buckingham, and his countess, in 1162, built and endowed the abbey of Nuttley for regular canons of the order of St. Augustine; it was dedicated to the Virgin Mary and St. John the Baptist, and, at the dissolution, possessed a revenue valued at £495. 18. 5.: the remains have been converted into a farm-house; part of the cloisters is still discernible, and round the cornice of an ancient room is the Stafford knot, repeatedly labelled in black letter, with the motto *En lui Plaisance.*

CRESLOW, a parish in the hundred of COTTESLOE, county of BUCKINGHAM, 5¾ miles (N.) from Aylesbury, containing 5 inhabitants. The living is a rectory, in the archdeaconry of Buckingham, and diocese of Lincoln, rated in the king's books at £3. The church, which was dedicated to the Holy Trinity, is desecrated, and the inhabitants attend divine service at Whitchurch.

CRESSAGE, a chapelry in the parish of COUND, hundred of CONDOVER, county of SALOP, 4 miles (N.W. by N.) from Much Wenlock, containing 295 inhabitants.

CRESSING, a parish in the hundred of WITHAM, county of ESSEX, 3¼ miles (S. E.) from Braintree, containing 489 inhabitants. The living is a discharged vicarage, in the archdeaconry of Colchester, and diocese of London, rated in the king's books at £7. 15. 5., and in the patronage of Andrew Downs, Esq. The church is dedicated to All Saints. Cressing Temple, anciently a commandery of the Knights Templars, was given by King Stephen, with the advowson of the church, in perpetual alms to that order; on its dissolution these possessions passed to the Knights Hospitallers of St. John of Jerusalem, and reverted to the crown at the general suppression.

CRESSINGHAM (GREAT), a parish in the southern division of the hundred of GREENHOE, county of NORFOLK, 4½ miles (W. by N.) from Watton, containing 400 inhabitants. The living is a discharged rectory, with the curacy of St. George, and the rectory of Bodney united, and a royal peculiar, in which the rector exercises jurisdiction, rated in the king's books at £17. 18. 1½., and in the patronage of the Crown. The church, dedicated to St. Michael, is composed of flint and freestone, with a tower at the west end, and is ornamented in many places with the letter M, surmounted by a crown, also an erect sword, with a crown on the point, supposed to be memorials of the victory of the patron saint; the nave and chancel are separated by a screen curiously painted and carved, behind which are six stalls, similar to those in collegiate churches. About a mile from the village, in a field called Stone-close, stood the parochial chapel of St. George, previously the chapel of a hermit, in right of which the rector holds a fair annually on the 12th of August, for horses and toys.

CRESSINGHAM (LITTLE), a parish in the southern division of the hundred of GREENHOE, county of NORFOLK, 3 miles (W.) from Watton, containing 160 inhabitants. The living is a discharged rectory, in the archdeaconry of Norfolk, and diocese of Norwich, rated in the king's books at £13. 12. 6., and in the patronage of the Rev. Thomas Baker. The church is dedicated to St. Andrew.

CRESSWELL, a township in the parish of WOODHORN, eastern division of MORPETH ward, county of NORTHUMBERLAND, 8½ miles (N. E.) from Morpeth, containing 303 inhabitants. The village is situated on the coast of the North sea, and is inhabited chiefly by fishermen.

CRESSY HALL, a chapelry in the parish of SURFLEET, wapentake of KIRTON, parts of HOLLAND, county of LINCOLN, 6¼ miles (N. N. W.) from Spalding. The population is returned with the parish.

CRESWELL, an extra-parochial liberty, in the southern division of the hundred of PIREHILL, county of STAFFORD, 3 miles (S. W. by S.) from Cheadle, containing 12 inhabitants.

CRETINGHAM, a parish in the hundred of LOES, county of SUFFOLK, 4½ miles (W. S. W.) from Framlingham, containing 375 inhabitants. The living is a discharged vicarage, in the archdeaconry of Suffolk, and diocese of Norwich, rated in the king's books at £9. 10. 10., and in the patronage of the Crown. The church is dedicated to St. Andrew.

CREWE, a township in the parish of FARNDON, higher division of the hundred of BROXTON, county palatine of CHESTER, 6¼ miles (N. W.) from Malpas, containing 47 inhabitants. It is bounded on the west by the river Dee.

CREWE, a township in that part of the parish of BARTHOMLEY which is in the hundred of NANTWICH, county palatine of CHESTER, 4½ miles (S. W. by S.) from Sandbach, containing 297 inhabitants. A charity school was founded in 1729, pursuant to the will of Thomas Leadbeater, Esq., who bequeathed £30 for the erection of a school-house, and £120 for the maintenance of a master.

CREWKERNE, a market town and parish in the hundred of CREWKERNE, county of SOMERSET, 10 miles (S. W. by S.) from Ilchester, and 132 (W. S. W.) from London, containing 3434 inhabitants. This place, being a royal manor, anciently enjoyed many privileges, and in the reign of Henry II. was exempt from taxation. The town is pleasantly situated in a fertile valley, watered by branches of the rivers Parret and Axe, and sheltered by hills richly planted; it consists of five principal streets, diverging from a spacious market-place, in the centre of which a large and commodious market-house has been erected: the houses are in general well built and of handsome appearance, and the inhabitants are amply supplied with water. Sail-cloth, stockings, and dowlas, are manufactured here. The market, which is well supplied with corn, is on Saturday: the fair is on the 4th of September, for horses, bullocks, linen-drapery, cheese, and toys. The living is a perpetual curacy, in the archdeaconry of Taunton, and diocese of Bath and Wells, endowed with £800 parliamentary grant, and in the patronage of the Dean and Chapter of Winchester. The church, dedicated to St. Bartholomew, is a spacious cruciform structure, in the decorated style of English architecture, with a lofty and highly enriched tower rising from the intersection, crowned with battlements and ornamented with angular turrets: the interior is finely arranged, the windows are large and filled with rich tracery, and the piers and arches which support the tower are lofty and of graceful elevation; behind the altar is a small room, formerly the confessional, having a door at each end. There are places of worship for Particular Baptists and Unitarians. The free grammar school was founded, in 1449, by John de Combe, Precentor of the cathedral of Exeter, who endowed it with lands now producing £300 per annum: there are four exhibitions, of £5 per annum each, to any college at Oxford, founded by the Rev. William Owsley, who gave a rent-charge of £20, which, from want of applications, has been for some time accumulating for the augmentation of the exhibitions. A charity school is supported by subscription; and there are two almshouses, one of which, for six aged men and six aged women, was, in 1707, endowed with a rent-charge of £29, by Mrs. Mary Davis.

CRICH, a parish comprising the township of Crich, in the hundred of MORLESTON and LITCHURCH, the township of Wessington, in the hundred of SCARSDALE, and the hamlet of Tansley, in the hundred of WIRKSWORTH, county of DERBY, and containing 2961 inhabitants, of which number, 2024 are in the township of Crich, 4¾ miles (W. by S.) from Alfreton. The living is a discharged vicarage, in the archdeaconry of Derby, and diocese of Lichfield and Coventry, rated in the king's books at £6. 10. 10., endowed with £200 private benefaction, £200 royal bounty, and £600 parliamentary grant. The Lord Chancellor, by reason of lunacy, presented in 1801. The church, dedicated to St. Mary, has a tower surmounted by a spire, and contains several ancient monuments of the Dixie family. There are two places of worship for Wesleyan Methodists, one at Crich, the other at Tansley. This place, which is situated on an eminence commanding extensive prospects, was, not long since, an inconsiderable village, and rose into importance from the establishment of a cotton-manufactory at Frichly, in 1793: in 1810 it received the grant of a market, which was discontinued on the decline of the manufactory; fairs for cattle are held on April 6th and October 11th. Several of the inhabitants are employed in the adjacent quarries, which produce limestone of a superior quality, a considerable quantity being sent to London and Manchester; here are also kilns for burning it: the manufacture of stockings is carried on to a limited degree. The Cromford canal passes along the western side of the parish, and through a tunnel at its north-western and southern extremities: from the latter point a railway runs northward to within a short distance of the village. In 1825, an infant school was established in the parish. Crich is evidently a place of some antiquity, coins of Adrian and Dioclesian having been found in an adjacent lead mine, whence it is conjectured that lead was first obtained here by the Romans: at the period of the Norman survey, "Leuric had a lead mine at Cric," which is still wrought to a small extent. The manor of Wakebridge, in this parish, which formerly belonged to Darley abbey, still enjoys the privilege of exemption from king's duty on lead-ore, the mine of which is considered the richest in the county. About one mile north of the village is Crich cliff, a lofty hill, upon the summit of which an observatory was erected in 1789; it is principally composed of limestone, and contains mines of lead-ore, which were formerly more productive than at present.

CRICK, a hamlet in the parish of CAERWENT, upper division of the hundred of CALDICOTT, county of MONMOUTH, 4½ miles (S. W. by. W.) from Chepstow. The population is returned with the parish. The road leading from this village to Caerwent was evidently a Roman way, the foundations being plainly discernible; on each side lie large stones covered with moss, which appear to have formed part of the old causeway.

CRICK, a parish in the hundred of GUILSBOROUGH, county of NORTHAMPTON, 6½ miles (N. by E.) from

Daventry, containing 968 inhabitants. The living is a rectory, in the archdeaconry of Northampton, and diocese of Peterborough, rated in the king's books at £32. 13. 1½., and in the patronage of the President and Fellows of St. John's College, Oxford. The church is dedicated to St. Margaret. A school was endowed upwards of fifty years ago, by William Henfray, with a bequest of about £10 per annum, for the education of twelve poor children. Richard Rayson, in 1806, bequeathed £15 a year for teaching twenty children free; and Elizabeth Heygate, in 1822, left £10 in trust, that the interest should be applied for a Sunday school: the schoolmaster to whom these several sums are paid has the use of a schoolroom, house, and garden. The Grand Union canal, in its course through this parish, passes under an arch, or tunnel, one thousand five hundred and twenty-four yards in length; and the Roman Watling-street traces the entire western boundary.

CRICKET (ST. THOMAS), a parish in the southern division of the hundred of PETHERTON, county of SOMERSET, 4¼ miles (W. by S.) from Crewkerne, containing 75 inhabitants. The living is a discharged rectory, in the archdeaconry of Taunton, and diocese of Bath and Wells, rated in the king's books at £9. 17. 6., and in the patronage of Lord Bridport. The church is dedicated to St. Thomas.

CRICKET-MALHERBIE, a parish in the hundred of ABDICK and BULSTONE, county of SOMERSET, 2¼ miles (S.) from Ilminster, containing 73 inhabitants. The living is a discharged rectory, in the archdeaconry of Taunton, and diocese of Bath and Wells, rated in the king's books at £6. 6. 3., and in the patronage of Mrs. Pitt. The church is dedicated to St. Mary Magdalene.

CRICKLADE, a borough and market town, in the hundred of HIGHWORTH, CRICKLADE, and STAPLE, county of WILTS, 44½ miles (N. by W.) from Salisbury, and 83 (W. by N.) from London, containing, with the township of Whidhill, 1506 inhabitants. This place, which is of great antiquity, is by some antiquaries supposed to have derived its name from the British *Cerigwlâd*, signifying a country abounding with stones; and by others from the Saxon *Cræcca*, a brook, and *Lædian*, to empty; the small rivers Churn and Rey here discharging themselves into the river Isis. It is thought by Dr. Stukeley to have been a Roman station, from its situation on the Roman road which connected *Corinium*, now Cirencester, with *Spinæ*, now Spene. About the year 905, Ethelwald, opposing the election of Edward the Elder to the throne, collected a large body of troops, consisting principally of East Anglians, and advanced to this place on a predatory excursion, from which he retreated with his plunder before Edward, who was marching to attack him, had reached the town. In 1016, the town was plundered by Canute the Dane. Since the Conquest, Cricklade has not been distinguished by any event of historical importance. The town is situated in a level tract of country, on the south bank of the Isis, which has its source in the vicinity, and consists principally of one long street: a fund of £160 per annum, arising from an early bequest, which has been for a long time misapplied, is about to be appropriated to the paving of it; it is but indifferently supplied with spring water. An attempt to introduce the manufacture of pins has recently been made, but without success. The Thames and Severn canal passes to the north of the town. The market is on Saturday, but has greatly declined, owing to the proximity of Cirencester: the fairs have been discontinued, except a small pleasure fair, which is still held on the 29th of September. The county magistrates hold a meeting here on the first Saturday in every month: a bailiff and other officers are appointed by a jury at the court leet of the lord of the manor, who holds a court every third week, for the recovery of debts under 40*s*. Cricklade is a borough by prescription, and exercised the elective franchise from the reign of Edward I., but with various intermissions till that of Henry VI., since which time it has uninterruptedly continued to return two members to parliament: in consequence of notorious bribery, the elective franchise was, in 1782, extended to the five adjoining divisions, *viz*. Highworth, Cricklade, Staple, Kingsbridge, and Malmesbury. The right of election is vested in the freeholders, copyholders, and leaseholders for not less than three years, within the borough, and in the freeholders of the five divisions: the number of voters is about one thousand two hundred; the bailiff is the returning officer.

Cricklade comprises the parishes of St. Sampson and St. Mary, both in the archdeaconry of Wilts, and diocese of Salisbury. The living of St. Sampson's is a vicarage, rated in the king's books at £18. 11. 10½., and in the patronage of the Dean and Chapter of Winchester: the church is a spacious and ancient cruciform structure, with a handsome square tower rising from the intersection, crowned with a pierced parapet and pinnacles, and highly ornamented with niches and pedestals: the south porch was formerly a chapel built by one of the Hungerford family; and towards the east is another porch, with large battlements, having in the centre the figure of a lion couchant: the interior is of corresponding character. The piers and arches which support the tower are lofty and of graceful elevation; and the interior of the tower, which is open to a considerable height, is decorated with numerous escutcheons, among which are the cognizances of the earls of Warwick, one of whom contributed largely to the building of the church: a stone cross, which formerly stood in the principal street, was removed into the churchyard, when the old town-hall was taken down. The living of St. Mary's is a discharged rectory, rated in the king's books at £4. 14. 0½., endowed with £200 private benefaction, and £1900 royal bounty, and in the alternate patronage of the King and the Bishop of Salisbury: the church is a very ancient structure; the chancel is separated from the nave by a circular Norman arch, and the interior contains many vestiges of its original character: in the churchyard is a handsome stone cross of one shaft on a flight of steps; the head is richly ornamented with small sculptured figures in canopied niches. There are places of worship for Independents and Wesleyan Methodists. There was formerly a free school, founded and endowed by Robert Jenner, Esq., citizen and goldsmith of London; but the endowment has been lost, and the building converted into tenements for paupers: in each of the parishes is a National school for girls; and there are Sunday schools for both sexes, supported by subscription. Among the several bequests for charitable uses is one of a hundred acres of land in the neighbourhood, now producing £125 per annum, of which £15 is appropriated to the apprenticing of poor children, and the remainder distributed among the poor. In the parish of St. Mary are the remains of the priory of St. John the Baptist, founded in the reign of Henry III., now converted into a residence for the poor: there was also an hospital, dedicated to the same patron, the revenue of which, at the dissolution, was £4. 10. 7.; some land belonging to it, in the parish of St. Sampson, is still called the Spital.

CRIDLING-STUBBS, a township in the parish of WOMERSLEY, lower division of the wapentake of OSGOLDCROSS, West riding of the county of YORK, 4¾ miles (E.) from Pontefract, containing 96 inhabitants.

CRIGGLESTONE, a township in that part of the parish of GREAT SANDALL which is in the lower division of the wapentake of AGBRIGG, West riding of the county of YORK, 3¾ miles (S. by W.) from Wakefield, containing 1265 inhabitants. There is a place of worship for Particular Baptists. Here are two tanneries and several malt-kilns.

CRIMPLESHAM, a parish in the hundred of CLACKCLOSE, county of NORFOLK, 2½ miles (E.) from Downham-Market, containing 279 inhabitants. The living is a discharged vicarage, in the archdeaconry of Norfolk, and diocese of Norwich, rated in the king's books at £8, and in the patronage of the Bishop of Ely. The church is dedicated to St. Mary.

CRINGLEFORD, a parish in the hundred of HUMBLEYARD, county of NORFOLK, 2½ miles (S. W. by W.) from Norwich, containing 150 inhabitants. The living is a perpetual curacy, in the archdeaconry of Norfolk, and diocese of Norwich, and in the patronage of the Mayor and Corporation of Norwich. The church is dedicated to St. Albert. Within the parish was anciently a free chapel, dedicated to St. Ethelred, to which pilgrims used to resort in great numbers. Cringleford derives its name from the gravelly ford, which has been superseded by a stone bridge, separating the liberties of Norwich from the rest of the county.

CRIPTON, a tything in that part of the parish of WINTERBOURN-CAME which is in the hundred of CULLIFORD-TREE, Dorchester division of the county of DORSET, 3½ miles (S. by E.) from Dorchester, containing 20 inhabitants.

CRITCHELL (LONG), a parish in the hundred of KNOWLTON, Shaston (East) division of the county of DORSET, 6½ miles (W. S. W.) from Cranborne, containing 108 inhabitants. The living is a rectory, with which the rectory of Moor-Critchell was united in 1774, in the archdeaconry of Dorset, and diocese of Bristol, rated in the king's books at £12. 13. 8½., and in the patronage of Charles Sturt, Esq. The church, dedicated to St. Mary, has a tower at the west end, with a massive buttress on its north side, in which there is a niche, and beneath it three shields much defaced. Long Critchell, which received its distinguishing appellation from its greater length in comparison with the adjoining parish of Moore-Critchell, is divided into two tythings, called Critchell-Gouis and Critchell-Lucy, so called from their ancient lords.

CRITCHELL (MOORE), a parish in the hundred of BADBURY, Shaston (East) division of the county of DORSET, 6 miles (S. W. by W.) from Cranborne, containing 267 inhabitants. The living is a rectory, united in 1774 to that of Long Critchell, in the archdeaconry of Dorset, and diocese of Bristol, rated in the king's books at £10. 9. 7. The church, dedicated to All Saints, is a small ancient fabric, having at the west end an embattled tower, with a porch of modern erection: it had a chantry well endowed with certain messuages and land, one hundred sheep, and twelve hogs, by John de Bridport, in the 2nd of Edward III., for a chaplain to pray daily for his soul.

CROBOROUGH, a joint township with Blackwood, in the parish of HORTON, northern division of the hundred of TOTMONSLOW, county of STAFFORD, 5½ miles (W.) from Leek. The population is returned with Blackwood.

CROCK-STREET, a hamlet partly in the parish of COMBE ST. NICHOLAS, eastern division of the hundred of KINGSBURY, and partly in the parish of DONYATT, hundred of ABDICK and BULSTONE, county of SOMERSET, 3 miles (W. S. W.) from Ilminster. A considerable quantity of coarse earthenware is made at the potteries in this hamlet.

CROCKERN-WELL, a hamlet partly in the parish of BISHOP-CHERITON, and partly in that of DREWSTEINGTON, hundred of WONFORD, county of DEVON, 7 miles (S. W.) from Crediton. The hamlet is divided into three parts, and abounds with beautiful scenery. Here was formerly a chapel, but there are no remains of it.

CROCKERNE-PILL, a hamlet in the parish of EASTON in GORDANO, hundred of PORTBURY, county of SOMERSET, 5½ miles (N. W.) from Bristol. The population is returned with the parish. This hamlet, which had its rise in the seventeenth century, is chiefly inhabited by mariners, who are principally engaged in piloting vessels to and from Bristol, and down the channel, under the regulations of the company of merchant adventurers of Bristol: it is situated on the banks of the Avon, near the junction of that river with the Severn.

CROFT, a parish in the hundred of WOLPHY, county of HEREFORD, 5½ miles (N. N. W.) from Leominster, containing, with the township of Newton, 119 inhabitants. The living is a discharged rectory, with the perpetual curacies of Elton and Yarpole united, in the archdeaconry and diocese of Hereford, rated in the king's books at £7. 11. 3., endowed with £200 private benefaction, and £200 royal bounty, and in the patronage of the Rev. James Keville. The church is dedicated to St. Michael. At Castle Parke, on an eminence to the north-west of the village, is Croft Ambrey, an ancient British camp, with a double ditch and rampart.

CROFT, a joint township with Southworth, in the parish of WINWICK, hundred of WEST DERBY, county palatine of LANCASTER, 4 miles (E. S. E.) from Newton in Mackerfield. The population is returned with Southworth.

CROFT, a parish in the hundred of SPARKENHOE, county of LEICESTER, 6¼ miles (E. by N.) from Hinckley, containing 297 inhabitants. The living is a rectory, in the archdeaconry of Leicester, and diocese of Lincoln, rated in the king's books at £12. 3. 4., and in the patronage of the Rev. Robert Thomas Adnutt. The village is situated on a granite rock rising from the edge of a brook which falls into the Soar, and continuing in a ridge northward, until it terminates in a remarkable conical hill that is conspicuous for many miles round.

CROFT, a parish in the Marsh division of the wapentake of CANDLESHOE, parts of LINDSEY, county of LINCOLN, 1¾ mile (N.N.E.) from Wainfleet, containing 483 inhabitants. The living is a vicarage, in the archdeaconry and diocese of Lincoln, rated in the king's books at £23. 7. 3½., and in the patronage of Lord Monson. The church is dedicated to All Saints. There is a trifling bequest for the benefit of the poor.

CROFT, a parish partly within the liberty of ST. PETER of YORK, East riding, but chiefly in the eastern division of the wapentake of GILLING, North riding, of the county of YORK, comprising the townships of Croft, Dalton upon Tees, and part of Stapleton, the remaining portion of the last being in the parish of St. John Stanwick, and containing 647 inhabitants, of which number, 367 are in the township of Croft, 3½ miles (S.) from Darlington. The living is a rectory, in the archdeaconry of Richmond, and diocese of Chester, rated in the king's books at £12. 8. 4., and in the patronage of the Crown. The church, dedicated to St. Peter, exhibits specimens of the various styles of English architecture. The village is situated on the banks of the Tees, half a mile to the west of which is a sulphureous mineral spring, the water of which is used both for drinking and bathing: commodious baths were fitted up about fifteen years ago. Certain lands are held in this place by the owner presenting on the bridge, at the coming of every new bishop of Durham, an old sword, pronouncing a legendary address, and delivering the sword to the bishop, who returns it immediately. A charity school, in which twenty-five children are instructed, is supported by a small bequest from Lady Crew, and by voluntary contributions, the whole amounting to about £25 per annum.

CROFTON, a township in the parish of THURSBY, ward and county of CUMBERLAND, 3¼ miles (E. N. E.) from Wigton, containing 65 inhabitants.

CROFTON, in the parish of ORPINGTON, hundred of RUXLEY, lathe of SUTTON at HONE, county of KENT, 3½ miles (S. by W.) from Foot's Cray. This is said to have been once a parish, and the village to have been destroyed by fire.

CROFTON, a township in the parish of DIDDLEBURY, hundred of MUNSLOW, county of SALOP, 7½ miles (N. by W.) from Ludlow. The population is returned with the parish.

CROFTON, a chapelry in the parish and hundred of TITCHFIELD, Portsdown division of the county of SOUTHAMPTON, 2½ miles (S. W. by W.) from Fareham. The population is returned with the parish. The chapel is dedicated to the Holy Rood.

CROFTON, a parish in the lower division of the wapentake of AGBRIGG, West riding of the county of YORK, 3¾ miles (E. S. E.) from Wakefield, containing 459 inhabitants. The living is a rectory, in the archdeaconry and diocese of York, rated in the king's books at £10. 0. 2½., and in the patronage of the King, as Duke of Lancaster. The church, dedicated to All Saints, is a small cruciform structure in the later English style, with a low central tower.

CROGDEAN, a township in the parish of KIRKWHELPINGTON, north-eastern division of TINDALE ward, county of NORTHUMBERLAND, containing 6 inhabitants.

CROGLIN, a parish in LEATH ward, county of CUMBERLAND, 5 miles (N. N. E.) from Kirk-Oswald, containing 348 inhabitants. The living is a discharged rectory, in the archdeaconry and diocese of Carlisle, rated in the king's books at £8, and in the patronage of H. Chaytor, Esq. and others. The church is dedicated to St. John the Baptist. The river Croglin bounding it on the south, gives its name to this parish: veins of coal extend through it, and there are quarries of limestone and red freestone, besides a species of porphyry, or bastard marble. The land is chiefly mountainous, with a remarkable lofty eminence, named Croglin fell. In a deep vale on the north side of the river is the village, near which are the remains of an old border fortification, termed *Scarromanwick*. The school, built by subscription in 1724, is endowed with the interest of £50, given in 1723 by the Rev. J. Hunter, then rector, and an allotment of twenty-four acres, appropriated on the enclosure of waste lands pursuant to an act passed in 1808, yielding about £24 per annum; thirty-five children are taught.

CROKEHAM, a hamlet in that part of the parish of THATCHAM which is in the hundred of FAIRCROSS, county of BERKS, 4¼ miles (S. E.) from Newbury. The population is returned with the parish. Here was formerly a chapel, which has been demolished.

CROMER, a parish (formerly a market town) in the northern division of the hundred of ERPINGHAM, county of NORFOLK, 21 miles (N.) from Norwich, and 130 (N.N.E.) from London, containing 1023 inhabitants. This place, originally of much greater extent, included the town of Shipden, which, with its church and a considerable number of houses forming another parish, was destroyed by an inundation of the sea. It is situated on a high cliff, on the north-eastern coast of the North sea, commanding a fine view of Cromer bay, which, from its dangerous navigation, is by seamen called the "Devil's Throat." The town was formerly inhabited only by a few fishermen, but, from the excellence of its beach, the salubrity of its air, and the beauty of its scenery, it has become a bathing-place of some celebrity: there are still some remains of the walls with which it was anciently surrounded; and a fort and two half-moon batteries were, during the last war, erected upon a commanding eminence for its defence: the houses are in general badly built and of mean appearance, but those near the sea are commodious and pleasantly situated, and there are several respectable inns for the accommodation of visitors; the inhabitants are amply supplied with water from springs. There are a circulating library and a subscription news-room; and a regatta is annually celebrated. The coast between this place and Yarmouth being extremely dangerous, it has been found necessary to erect within that short distance not less than four lighthouses, of which that at Cromer, three quarters of a mile to the east of the town, is built of brick coated with Roman cement; it is three stories high, and has a revolving lantern, twenty-four feet in circumference, lighted by twenty-one patent lamps with highly polished metallic reflectors, presenting every other minute a brilliant light, which may be distinctly seen from all points: a life-boat, constructed on Greathead's principle, and Captain Manby's apparatus for preserving the lives of shipwrecked mariners, are in constant readiness, and have often been used with success. Several vessels discharge their cargoes of coal and timber on the beach: lobsters and crabs of superior flavour are taken in great numbers, and sent to the different markets. Many attempts have been made to construct a pier, but the works have invariably been washed away by the sea. The market, formerly held on Saturday, has been discontinued; but a fair, chiefly for toys, is held on Whit-Monday. The county magistrates hold a meeting here every fortnight.

The living is a vicarage, in the archdeaconry of Norfolk, and diocese of Norwich, rated in the king's books at £9. 4., endowed with £400 royal bounty, and £800 parliamentary grant, and in the patronage of the Bishop of Ely. The church, dedicated to St. Peter and St. Paul, was built in the reign of Henry IV.; it is a handsome structure of freestone and flint, in the later style of English architecture, with a lofty square embattled tower crowned with pinnacles: the western entrance, the north porch, and the chancel, though much dilapidated, are fine specimens of the later style. There is a place of worship for Wesleyan Methodists. A National school for an unlimited number of children of both sexes is supported by subscription.

CROMFORD, a chapelry in the parish and hundred of WIRKSWORTH, county of DERBY, 15 miles (N.) from Derby, containing 1242 inhabitants. This place, which is pleasantly situated on the river Derwent, was an inconsiderable village prior to the year 1776, when Sir Richard Arkwright, having purchased the manor, erected mills, and established a cotton-manufactory of very considerable extent. Since this period it has greatly increased, and is now a flourishing place: it consists chiefly of dwellings for the persons employed in the factories, which are neat and commodious; of these many are built round an open space in which a small customary market is held on Saturday; the others are chiefly in detached situations. The cotton-manufactory affords employment to more than one thousand persons, including a proportionate number of children, who are not admitted into the factory till they have been for a certain time at a school supported by the proprietor for their instruction: there is also a manufactory for hats, and one for ginghams, on a small scale, and a paper-manufactory, in which about forty persons are occupied: a great quantity of *lapis calaminaris* is made here, of which from one hundred to four hundred tons are exported annually. In the neighbourhood are extensive mines of lead and calamine, also quarries of marble and limestone. The Cromford canal, communicating with the Erewash canal near Langley bridge, and the Cromford and Peak Forest railway afford every facility for the conveyance of minerals, coal, and limestone to various parts of the kingdom. The chapel, a small neat building, begun by Sir Richard Arkwright, and completed by his son, Richard Arkwright, Esq., who endowed it with £50 per annum in perpetuity, was consecrated in 1797. The living is a perpetual curacy, in the archdeaconry of Derby, and diocese of Lichfield and Coventry, endowed with £200 private benefaction, £200 royal bounty, and £800 parliamentary grant, and in the patronage of Richard Arkwright, Esq. The Wesleyan Methodists have a place of worship here. There are day and Sunday schools, founded and supported by the Arkwright family, for the instruction of the children employed in the factory. Almshouses for six poor widows were founded, in 1651, by Dame Mary Talbot. Cromford is in the honour of Tutbury, duchy of Lancaster, and within the jurisdiction of a court of pleas held at Tutbury every third Tuesday, for the recovery of debts under 40*s*.

CROMHALL (ABBOT'S), a parish in the upper division of the hundred of BERKELEY, locally in the lower division of the hundred of Thornbury, county of GLOUCESTER, 2½ miles (N. W. by W.) from Wickwar, containing, with the tything of Lygon-Cromhall, 703 inhabitants. The living is a rectory, in the archdeaconry and diocese of Gloucester, rated in the king's books at £16. 9. 2., and in the patronage of the Provost and Fellows of Oriel College, Oxford. The church, dedicated to St. Andrew, is partly in the early and partly in the later style of English architecture. The prefix to the name of this parish arises from its having belonged to the abbot and convent of St. Augustine, in Bristol, to which society it was given by Lord Berkeley, in 1148. A coal mine has been lately opened in the neighbourhood.

CROMHALL (LYGON), a tything in the parish of ABBOT'S CROMHALL, upper division of the hundred of BERKELEY, county of GLOUCESTER, 4¼ miles (N.W) from Wickwar. The population is returned with the parish. This place derives its distinguishing name from having anciently belonged to the family of Lygon.

CROMPTON, a township in the parish of OLDHAM *cum* PRESTWICH, hundred of SALFORD, county palatine of LANCASTER, 4¼ miles (S. E.) from Rochdale, containing 6482 inhabitants.

CROMWELL, a parish in the northern division of the wapentake of THURGARTON, county of NOTTINGHAM, 5¼ miles (N.) from Newark, containing 184 inhabitants. The living is a rectory, in the archdeaconry of Nottingham, and diocese of York, rated in the king's books at £13. 2. 3½., and in the patronage of the Duke of Newcastle. The church is dedicated to St. Giles.

CRONDALL, a parish in the hundred of CRONDALL, Basingstoke division of the county of SOUTHAMPTON, comprising the tythings of Ewshott, Dippenhall, Crondall with Swanthorpe, and Crookham, and containing 1894 inhabitants, of which number, 470 are in the township of Crondall with Swanthorpe, 3 miles (W. N. W.) from Farnham. The living is a vicarage, in the archdeaconry and diocese of Winchester, rated in the king's books at £22. 5. 7½., and in the patronage of the Master and Brethren of the Hospital of St. Cross, Winchester. The church, dedicated to All Saints, is a large ancient structure, partly in the Norman style. The Basingstoke canal passes through this parish. At Badley Pound farm, a mile south of the village, a beautiful Roman Mosaic pavement, twelve feet square, was discovered a few years since, and is still preserved: foundations of buildings, with some coins and other remains of the Romans, have since been found there, as well as in a contiguous field; and at Turksbury hill are the remains of a Roman encampment. The Dean and Chapter of Winchester are lords of the manor, and hold a court leet annually at the manor-house. A National school, erected by voluntary contributions, is partly supported by a bequest from Elizabeth Oliver, in 1802, of £37. 3. per annum. There is another school, founded in 1818, by Henry Maxwell, Esq., with an endowment of £1238. 15. 2. three per cents., for teaching the poor children of the parish.

CRONTON, a township in the parish of PRESCOT, hundred of WEST DERBY, county palatine of LANCASTER, 3¾ miles (S. S. E.) from Prescot, containing 358 inhabitants. A trifling endowment for teaching children was bequeathed by Margaret Wright.

CROOK, a joint township with Billyrow, in the parish of BRANCEPETH, north-western division of DARLINGTON ward, county palatine of DURHAM, 5½ miles (N. W. by N.) from Bishop-Auckland, containing 228 inhabitants. Crook is a scattered village, partly extending into the adjoining township of Helmington Row.

CROOK, a chapelry in the parish and ward of KENDAL, county of WESTMORLAND, 4¾ miles (W.N.W.) from Kendal, containing 227 inhabitants. The living is a perpetual curacy, in the archdeaconry of Richmond, and diocese of Chester, endowed with £200 private benefaction, and £600 royal bounty, and in the patronage of the landowners in the parish. The chapel, an ancient building with a tower, stands in the centre of the chapelry, which is very extensive. The Society of Friends have a meeting-house and burial-ground near How. There is a woollen mill at the hamlet of Crook-Mill, where also the turning of bobbins is carried on. In the mountainous part of this district is a vein of lead, containing *barytes*, similar to that used in the manufacture of Wedgwood's jasper vases.

CROOKDAKE, a joint township with Bromfield and Scales, in that part of the parish of BROMFIELD which is in ALLERDALE ward below Derwent, county of CUMBERLAND, 6½ miles (S. W.) from Wigton. The population is returned with Bromfield.

CROOKHAM, a tything in the parish and hundred of CRONDALL, Basingstoke division of the county of SOUTHAMPTON, 4 miles (N. E. by E.) from Odiham, containing 623 inhabitants.

CROOKHOUSE, a township in the parish of KIRK-NEWTON, western division of GLENDALE ward, county of NORTHUMBERLAND, 7 miles (W. N. W.) from Wooler, containing 18 inhabitants.

CROOM (EARL'S), a parish in the lower division of the hundred of OSWALDSLOW, county of WORCESTER, 2 miles (N.E. by E.) from Upton upon Severn, containing 186 inhabitants. The living is a discharged rectory, in the archdeaconry and diocese of Worcester, rated in the king's books at £7. 8. 1½., and in the patronage of the Rev. Charles Dunne. The church, dedicated to St. Nicholas, is an old building in the Norman style.

CROOM-D'ABITOT, a parish in the lower division of the hundred of OSWALDSLOW, county of WORCESTER, 4 miles (W. by S.) from Pershore, containing 129 inhabitants. The living is a rectory, with that of Pirton, in the archdeaconry and diocese of Worcester, rated in the king's books at £7, and in the patronage of the Earl of Coventry. The church, dedicated to St. Mary Magdalene, was rebuilt in 1763: it is a neat edifice in the later style of English architecture.

CROOM-HILL, a parish in the lower division of the hundred of OSWALDSLOW, county of WORCESTER, 3¼ miles (E.) from Upton upon Severn, containing 18 inhabitants. The living is a rectory, in the archdeaconry and diocese of Worcester, rated in the king's books at £7. 10. 5., and in the patronage of the Crown. The church is dedicated to St. Mary. Courts leet and baron are held annually.

CROPREDY, a parish comprising the chapelry of Mollington, which is partly in the Burton-Dassett division of the hundred of KINGTON, county of WARWICK, but chiefly in the hundred of BLOXHAM, county of OXFORD, and the chapelries of Bourton, Claydon, and Wardington, and the hamlet of Prescott, in the hundred of BANBURY, county of OXFORD, 4 miles (N. by E.) from Banbury, and containing 2395 inhabitants. The living is a vicarage, within the peculiar jurisdiction of the Dean and Chapter of Lincoln, rated in the king's books at £26. 10. 10., and in the patronage of the Bishop of Oxford. The church is dedicated to St. Mary. There is a place of worship for Wesleyan Methodists. Walter Calcott founded a free school, and endowed it with an annuity of £13, for teaching forty children; two others are educated for a rent-charge of £2, given by John Ditchfield in 1708. The river Cherwell and the Oxford canal pass through this parish.

CROPSTON, a township in the parish of THURCASTON, western division of the hundred of GOSCOTE, county of LEICESTER, 3¼ miles (S. W. by S.) from Mountsorrel, containing 98 inhabitants.

CROPTHORN, a parish in the middle division of the hundred of OSWALDSLOW, county of WORCESTER, 4¼ miles (E. by S.) from Pershore, containing, with the chapelry of Netherton, and the hamlet of Charlton, 687 inhabitants. The living is a vicarage, in the archdeaconry and diocese of Worcester, rated in the king's books at £14. 17. 3½., and in the patronage of the Dean and Chapter of Worcester. The church is dedicated to St. Michael. A school is endowed with about £10 per annum, bequeathed by Mary Holland, in 1740.

CROPTON, a township in the parish of MIDDLETON, PICKERING lythe, North riding of the county of YORK, 4¼ miles (N. W. by N.) from Pickering, containing 321 inhabitants. There is a place of worship for Wesleyan Methodists. An estate forming part of the parish charity lands, producing about £23 per annum, has been appropriated to the support of a school in which twelve children are educated. There are various tumuli within the township, thought to be British, and a high mount called Cropton Castle, at the base of which are distinct traces of a Roman road, and near it vestiges of a Roman camp.

CROPWELL (BISHOP), a parish in the southern division of the wapentake of BINGHAM, county of NOTTINGHAM, 8 miles (E. S. E.) from Nottingham, containing 392 inhabitants. The living is a discharged vicarage, in the peculiar jurisdiction of the Collegiate Church of Southwell, rated in the king's books at £5. 3. 4., endowed with £200 private benefaction, and £200 royal bounty, and in the patronage of the Prebendaries of Oxton in the Collegiate Church of Southwell. The church is dedicated to St. Giles. There is a place of worship for Wesleyan Methodists. The old Fosse-road and the Grantham canal pass through this parish.

CROPWELL-BUTLER, a chapelry in the parish of TYTHBY, southern division of the wapentake of BINGHAM, county of NOTTINGHAM, 8¼ miles (E. S. E.) from Nottingham, containing 489 inhabitants. There is a place of worship for Wesleyan Methodists.

CROSBY, a township in the parish of CROSS-CANNONBY, ALLERDALE ward below Derwent, county of CUMBERLAND, 3 miles (N. W. by W.) from Maryport, containing 200 inhabitants. There is a school in the village, endowed by John Nicholson with £10 per ann. for teaching twenty children of Birkby, Crosby, and Cross-Cannonby.

CROSBY, a township in that part of the parish of BOTTESFORD which is in the northern division of the wapentake of MANLEY, parts of LINDSEY, county of LINCOLN, 8¼ miles (N. W. by W.) from Glandford-Bridge, containing 146 inhabitants. A school is partly supported by charitable donations amounting to about £2. 10. per annum, for the education of children belonging to this and the adjoining township of Brumby and Scunthorpe.

CROSBY, a township in that part of the parish of LEAK which is in the wapentake of ALLERTONSHIRE, North riding of the county of YORK, 5¾ miles (N. by W.) from Thirsk, containing 39 inhabitants.

CROSBY upon EDEN, a parish in ESKDALE ward, county of CUMBERLAND, comprising the townships of Brunstock, High Crosby, Low Crosby, and Walby, and containing 419 inhabitants, of which number, 184 are in the township of Low Crosby, 3¾ miles (N. E. by E.) from Carlisle. The living is a discharged vicarage, in the archdeaconry and diocese of Carlisle, rated in the king's books at £3. 11. 5½., endowed with £200 royal bounty, and in the patronage of the Bishop of Carlisle. The church, dedicated to St. John, is a small ancient building, situated in the village of Low Crosby. Joseph Jackson, in 1773, bequeathed £40 for the education of four children, and in 1803 a schoolroom was built by subscription. The southern part of the parish forms a gentle slope to the river Eden. A fine red freestone is obtained in the neighbouring quarries. In the time of Henry I. a cross was erected on the spot now occupied by the church, to which the inhabitants resorted for prayer. The military road from Newcastle to Carlisle passes through this parish, and a portion of the site of the Picts' wall is also discernible in it.

CROSBY (GREAT), a chapelry in the parish of SEPHTON, hundred of WEST DERBY, county palatine of LANCASTER, 7 miles (N. by W.) from Liverpool, containing 674 inhabitants. The living is a perpetual curacy, in the archdeaconry and diocese of Chester, endowed with £200 private benefaction, and £1000 royal bounty, and in the patronage of the Rector of Sephton. The chapel was rebuilt in 1774. The village is in a very thriving state, from being much resorted to for sea-bathing. A grammar school was founded, in 1618, by John Harrison, a native of this place, citizen and merchant of London, with an endowment of £50 a year for a master and an usher, besides £8 for repairs: the school-house is a good building of freestone, and the school is under the direction of the Merchant Taylors' Company in London: there is also a charity school for boys and girls, founded under the will of Catherine Halsall, with an endowment of £18 per annum.

CROSBY (HIGH), a township in the parish of CROSBY upon EDEN, ESKDALE ward, county of CUMBERLAND, 4¼ miles (N.E. by E.) from Carlisle, containing 136 inhabitants.

CROSBY (LITTLE), a township in the parish of SEPHTON, hundred of WEST DERBY, county palatine of LANCASTER, 7¾ miles (N. by W.) from Liverpool, containing 359 inhabitants. At Harkirk, in this township, a number of Saxon and other ancient coins was discovered in 1611.

CROSBY (LOW), a township in the parish of CROSBY upon EDEN, ESKDALE ward, county of CUMBERLAND, 3¾ miles (N.E. by E.) from Carlisle, containing 184 inhabitants. The village is pleasantly situated on the line of the military road from Newcastle to Carlisle.

CROSBY-GARRETT, a parish in EAST ward, county of WESTMORLAND, comprising the townships of Crosby-Garrett and Little Musgrave, and containing 273 inhabitants, of which number, 193 are in the township of Crosby-Garrett, 3 miles (W. by N.) from Kirkby-Stephen. The living is a discharged rectory, in the archdeaconry and diocese of Carlisle, rated in the king's books at £19. 4. 4½., endowed with £200 private benefaction, and £200 royal bounty, and in the patronage of Richard Bunn, L.L.D., and Mrs. Coulston. The church, dedicated to St. Andrew, is a spacious edifice in the ancient style of English architecture. A charity school was founded in 1629, and a schoolroom has been since erected by subscription: it is endowed with about £12 per annum, arising from a sum of £40 bequeathed by Thomas Wilson in 1767, and from various other benefactions. This parish consists of two detached portions, the chapelry of Soulby lying between them: it has the river Eden on the north-east, and on the south-west a lofty verdant hill, termed Crosby Fell, at the foot of which the village is situated, in a deep and romantic valley.

CROSBY-RAVENSWORTH, a parish in WEST ward, county of WESTMORLAND, 4 miles (N. by E.) from Orton, containing, with a portion of Birkbeck Fells, 863 inhabitants. The living is a discharged vicarage, in the archdeaconry and diocese of Carlisle, rated in the king's books at £7. 13. 4., endowed with £200 private benefaction, and £200 royal bounty, and in the patronage of the Hon. F. G. Howard. The church, dedicated to St. Lawrence, a handsome structure with a square tower, was rebuilt in 1814: near it stands the ancient manorial mansion, a tower building embosomed in trees, and formerly moated. A school was founded and endowed by the Rev. William Willan, in 1630; the schoolroom was rebuilt, in 1784, by William Dent, Esq., who, in conjunction with others, raised the income to about £30 per annum, for which twenty-five children are educated and supplied with books. A great quantity of limestone is obtained in the parish, and several hogs are fattened in it, the hams being noted for a peculiarly fine flavour. The village is situated in a valley through which runs the small rivers Birkbeck and Lyvennet; at Black Dub, where the latter has its source, Charles II., with his Scottish army, halted in 1651. A little higher up, on the eastern side, is a heap of stones, called Penhurrock, probably a tumulus raised by the Britons. Tradition records the ancient existence of a friary here, but there are no remains except the names Monk-garth, Monks' barn, and Monks' bridge.

CROSCOMBE, a parish (formerly a market town) in the hundred of WHITESTONE, county of SOMERSET, 1¾ mile (W. N. W.) from Shepton-Mallet, containing 742 inhabitants. The living is a discharged rectory, in the archdeaconry of Wells, and diocese of Bath and Wells, rated in the king's books at £12. 6. 10½., and in the patronage of Miss Elizabeth Wylie. The church is dedicated to St. Mary. There is a place of worship for Particular Baptists. Near it stands an ancient cross, fourteen feet high. There are manufactories for woollen goods and stockings in the village, at which a market, granted by Edward I., was formerly held, but it has fallen into disuse: a fair is held annually on Lady-day. A small river runs through the parish, and turns several mills in its course. In the vicinity are vestiges of a Roman encampment, called Masbury Castle.

CROSS (ST.), county of SOUTHAMPTON. — See WINCHESTER.

CROSS-HANDS, a hamlet in the parish of OLD SODBURY, lower division of the hundred of GRUMBALD'S ASH, county of GLOUCESTER, 3¾ miles (E.) from Chipping-Sodbury, with which the population is returned. The petty sessions for the division are held here alternately with Badminton and Chipping-Sodbury.

CROSSLAND (NORTH and SOUTH), a chapelry in the parish of ALMONDBURY, upper division of the wapentake of AGBRIGG, West riding of the county of YORK, 3¾ miles (S. W.) from Huddersfield, containing 1583 inhabitants. The chapel was lately erected at the expense of £2321. 4. 1., granted by the commissioners under the act passed in the 58th of George III., for building additional churches, and contains three hundred and twenty-two free sittings. The manufacture of woollen cloth is extensively carried on here; and there is a scribbling-mill in the neighbourhood. A rent-charge of £3 was given by Godfrey Beamont towards the support of a school; and in 1749, Sir John Lester Kaye, Bart., gave land for the erection of a schoolroom, which has since been rebuilt.

CROSSTONE, a chapelry in the parish of HALIFAX, wapentake of MORLEY, West riding of the county of YORK, 11½ miles (W.) from Halifax, with which the population is returned. The living is a perpetual curacy, in the archdeaconry and diocese of York, endowed with £600 private benefaction, and £3300 parliamentary grant, and in the patronage of the Vicar of Halifax. This place derives its name from an ancient cross, which has fallen to decay.

CROSTHWAITE, a parish comprising the chapelries of Borrowdale, Newlands, and Thornthwaite, and the townships of Braithwaite and Coledale, or Portingscale, in ALLERDALE ward above Derwent, and the chapelry of St. John Castlerigg with Wythburn, the town of Keswick, and the township of Under Skiddaw, in ALLERDALE ward below Derwent, county of CUMBERLAND, ½ a mile (N. by W.) from Keswick, and containing 4087 inhabitants. The living is a vicarage, in the archdeaconry and diocese of Carlisle, rated in the king's books at £50. 8. 11½., endowed with £300 private benefaction, and £800 royal bounty, and in the patronage of the Bishop of Carlisle. The church, dedicated to St. Kentigern, an ancient fabric, was roofed with slate in 1812, having been previously covered with lead. Adjoining the churchyard is a free grammar school, founded and endowed prior to 1571: the income is about £100 per annum, of which £65 is paid to the master, and £30 to the usher, for teaching one hundred and twenty children; the remainder is applied for repairing the school-house, which was built at the expense of the inhabitants. Near the source of the Derwent are two saline springs, in great repute among the inhabitants. This parish produces copper and lead ores, with plumbago, or black lead, and abounds with numerous interesting objects, for a description of which see KESWICK.

CROSTHWAITE, a parochial chapelry in the parish of HEVERSHAM, KENDAL ward, county of WESTMORLAND, 5 miles (W. S. W.) from Kendal, containing, with the hamlet of Lyth, 781 inhabitants. The living is a perpetual curacy, in the archdeaconry of Richmond, and diocese of Chester, endowed with £630 private benefaction, £200 royal bounty, and £800 parliamentary grant, and in the patronage of the Inhabitants and the Vicar of Heversham. Crosthwaite contains several hamlets, and the small but pleasant village of Church-town, near which, and in the centre of a picturesque and fertile vale, stands the chapel, dedicated to the Virgin Mary, which was rebuilt about 1813, at the expense of the inhabitants: the ancient structure had parochial privileges granted, in 1556, by the diocesan, on account of its great distance from the mother church. George Cocke, in 1665, gave £60 for the building and maintenance of a school: the schoolroom was erected by subscription, and the endowment is about £37 per annum, arising from the foregoing gift, the interest of £300 left by Tobias Atkinson in 1817, and the sum of £13 appropriated out of the general charities; there are about thirty free scholars. Here are a paper-manufactory, a corn-mill, and a malthouse. Lyth is a distinct constablewick on the south side of this extensive chapelry, and is bounded on the south-west by the mountainous ridge called Lyth Fell, or Whitbarrow Scar. At the hamlet of Raw, in Lyth, there are several limekilns, and at Pool-bank a manufactory of wood-hoops. In Lyth-moss several large trees have been discovered beneath the surface.

CROSTON, a parish (formerly a market town) in the hundred of LEYLAND, county palatine of LANCASTER, comprising the chapelries of Becconsall with Hesketh, and Tarleton, and the townships of Bispham, Bretherton, Croston, Mawdesley, and Ulnes-Walton, and containing 5831 inhabitants, of which number, 1367 are in the township of Croston, 6½ miles (W.) from Chorley. The living comprises a rectory and a vicarage, in the archdeaconry and diocese of Chester, rated in the king's books at £31. 11. 10½., and in the patronage of Mrs. Master. The church, dedicated to St. Michael, stands in a valley upon the margin of the river Yarrow, and was rebuilt in 1743, at an expense of £1834, which was defrayed by a brief. In the churchyard the Rev. James Hiet, in 1660, built a school-house, and endowed it with £400, producing about £15 a year, appropriated to the free education of thirty-six poor children. A school of industry was established by subscription in 1802, in aid of which Elizabeth Master, in 1809, bequeathed £200; the annual income, amounting to £14, is applied to the instruction of thirty girls. Croston was anciently one of the most extensive and valuable benefices in the county: for many ages the limits of the parish remained unaltered, but, at various periods since, it has been divided by authority of parliament into six entire and independent parishes, *viz.*, Croston, Hoole separated in 1642, Chorley and Rufford in 1793, and Tarleton and Hesketh with Becconsall in 1821. The market has fallen into disuse; but there is a cattle fair on the Monday before Shrove-Tuesday.

CROSTWICK, a parish in the hundred of TAVERHAM, county of NORFOLK, 3 miles (S. S. W.) from Coltishall, containing 136 inhabitants. The living is a discharged rectory, in the archdeaconry of Norfolk, and diocese of Norwich, rated in the king's books at £2. 17. 6., and in the patronage of the Bishop of Norwich. The church is dedicated to St. Peter.

CROSTWIGHT, a parish in the hundred of TUNSTEAD, county of NORFOLK, 3½ miles (E. by S.) from North Walsham, containing 84 inhabitants. The living is a discharged rectory, in the archdeaconry and diocese of Norwich, rated in the king's books at £5. 6. 8., and in the patronage of Sir R. Kerrison, Knt. The church is dedicated to All Saints.

CROUCH-END, a hamlet in the parish of HORNSEY, Finsbury division of the hundred of OSSULSTONE, county of MIDDLESEX, 5 miles (N. by W.) from London. The population is returned with the parish (which see).

CROUGHTON, a township in that part of the parish of ST. OSWALD, CHESTER, which is in the higher division of the hundred of WIRRALL, county palatine of CHESTER, 4½ miles (N. by E.) from Chester, containing 27 inhabitants. The Ellesmere canal passes through this township.

CROUGHTON, a parish in the hundred of KING'S SUTTON, county of NORTHAMPTON, 3½ miles (S. W.) from Brackley, containing 376 inhabitants. The living is a rectory, in the archdeaconry of Northampton, and diocese of Peterborough, rated in the king's books at £15. 3. 6½., and in the patronage of Viscount Ashbrook. The church is dedicated to All Saints. Dr. John Friend, the learned author of a "History of Physick," was born here, in 1675.

CROWAN, a parish in the hundred of PENWITH, county of CORNWALL, 6 miles (N. by W.) from Helston, containing 3973 inhabitants. The living is a vicarage, in the archdeaconry of Cornwall, and diocese of Exeter, rated in the king's books at £11. 9. 2., and in the patronage of Sir J. St. Aubyn, Bart. The church is dedicated to St. Crewenne. A charity school was founded, in 1730, by the family of St. Aubyn, and endowed with the interest of £100.

CROWBOROUGH, county of STAFFORD. — See CROBOROUGH.

CROWCOMBE, a parish (formerly a borough and market town) in the hundred of WILLITON and FREEMANNERS, county of SOMERSET, 7 miles (N. E. by N.) from Wiveliscombe, containing 600 inhabitants. The living is a rectory, in the archdeaconry of Taunton, and diocese of Bath and Wells, rated in the king's books at £32. 14. 4½., and in the patronage of Robert Harvey, Esq. The church, dedicated to the Holy Trinity, is an ancient edifice, built of hewn stone, having a tower formerly surmounted by an octagonal spire, which was struck down by lightning in 1725: the interior was neatly fitted up in 1534, with well-carved oak; and the north aisle, a handsome addition to the original structure, was built by the Carews, who have their place of sepulture underneath, there being several fine monuments to different members of that family. Elizabeth Carew, in 1668, bequeathed £400, directing a moiety thereof to be appropriated to the instruction of fifteen boys; and, in 1766, a rent-charge of £12 was devised by Thomas Carew, in aid of this charity, the annual income of which is about £40. Another school was endowed, in 1716, by Dr. Henry James, who left £100, producing now about £10 a year, for teaching eighteen girls: there is also a Sunday school, supported by voluntary contributions. Crowcombe was formerly of greater importance than it is at present: it was a borough, and the inhabitants being incorporated, enjoyed various privileges: a portreeve is still annually chosen at the court leet of the lord of the manor. A market, now disused, existed so early as the reign of Henry III.; fairs are held on the first Friday in May, Monday after August 1st, and October 31st, for cattle and drapery. A cross, in good preservation, stands at the entrance to the village, and fragments of another are visible in the churchyard. Near the court-house there is a spring which ebbs and flows with the tide. Some veins of copper have been found in the sides of the Quantock hills.

CROWELL, a parish in the hundred of LEWKNOR, county of OXFORD, 5 miles (E. S. E.) from Tetsworth, containing 159 inhabitants. The living is a rectory, in the archdeaconry and diocese of Oxford, rated in the king's books at £7. 9. 9½., and in the patronage of Miss Wykeham. The church is dedicated to St. Mary. Crowell is situated at the foot of the Chiltern hills: the Roman Iknield-street passes through the parish.

CROWFIELD, a chapelry in the parish of CODDENHAM, hundred of BOSMERE and CLAYDON, county of SUFFOLK, 5 miles (E. N. E.) from Needham-Market, containing 345 inhabitants. The living is a perpetual curacy, annexed to the vicarage of Coddenham, in the archdeaconry of Suffolk, and diocese of Norwich. The church is dedicated to All Saints.

CROWHURST, a parish in the first division of the hundred of TANDRIDGE, county of SURREY, 4½ miles (S. E.) from Godstone, containing 214 inhabitants. The living is a vicarage, in the archdeaconry of Surrey, and diocese of Winchester, and in the patronage of George Ruck, Esq. The church is dedicated to St. George.

CROWHURST, a parish in the hundred of BALDSLOW, rape of HASTINGS, county of SUSSEX, 2¾ miles (S.) from Battle, containing 340 inhabitants. The living is a rectory, in the archdeaconry of Lewes, and diocese of Chichester, rated in the king's books at £10, and in the patronage of J. C. Pelham, Esq. The church, dedicated to St. George, is principally in the later style of English architecture.

CROWLAND, or CROYLAND, a parish (formerly a market town) in the wapentake of ELLOE, parts of HOLLAND, county of LINCOLN, 51 miles (S. S. E.) from Lincoln, and 89 (N.) from London, containing 2113 inhabitants. During the Octarchy this place was the retreat of St. Guthlac, who in the reign of Cenred, eighth king of Mercia, retired from the persecution of the pagan Britons into a hermitage, near which Ethelbald, in 716, founded a Benedictine monastery to the honour of St. Mary, St. Bartholomew, and St. Guthlac, endowing it with a considerable sum of money, and with "the whole island of Croyland, formed by the four waters of *Shepishea* on the east, *Nena* on the west, *Southea* on the south, and *Asendyk* on the north, with a portion of the adjoining marshes, and with the fishery of the Nene and Welland." This monastery, which, from the marshy nature of the soil, was built upon an artificial foundation of piles, having been destroyed by the Danes in 870, was rebuilt by King Edred, in the year 948; in 1091 it was by an accidental fire reduced to a heap of ruins, from which, under the influence of its abbot, who granted a plenary indulgence to such as should contribute to its restoration, it was again rebuilt in 1112, but was destroyed, by a like cause, about forty years afterwards; it was a third time restored, with increased splendour, and continued to flourish till the dissolution, at which time its revenue was £1217. 5. 11.: the conventual buildings, which from neglect were gradually falling to decay, were almost entirely demolished during the parliamentary war, when the monastery was occupied as a garrison: the remains are highly interesting, consisting chiefly of the western piers of the eastern portion, in the Norman style, and of some portion of the nave and aisles of the abbey church, in which the south piers and arches, and part of the clerestory, are remaining, the western part of which is partly Norman, and partly in the early and later styles of English architecture: the north aisle of the nave has been restored, and is now used as the parish church. The town, which is accessible only by artificial roads, consists of four principal streets, separated by water-courses, and communicating with each other by means of an ancient triangular stone bridge of singular construction, erected in the reign of Edward II., and consisting of one principal and finely groined arch, from which diverge three pointed arches over the streams Welland, Nene, and Catwater: it is in the decorated style of English architecture, and on one side is a mutilated figure of Ethelbald, in a sitting posture, holding a globe in the right hand. The principal employment of the inhabitants is agriculture, the feeding of cattle, and the management of the dairy: a great number of geese and wild fowl are sold for the neighbouring markets, and an extensive fishery is carried on, for the privilege of which £300 per annum, formerly paid to the abbot, is now paid to the crown: the soil, under the influence of an efficient system of irrigation, has been greatly improved, and much of the land, formerly unprofitable from the morasses with which it was overspread, has been converted into rich pastures and fruitful cornfields: the engines employed in draining the water from the fens are of considerable power, and are set in motion by wind; one of them, which has twelve sails, throws up forty tons of water every minute. The market formerly held here has been removed to Thorney, in the county of Cambridge; but a fair is held annually, commencing on the festival of St. Bartholomew, and continuing for twelve days.

The living is a rectory not in charge, in the archdeaconry and diocese of Lincoln, and in the alternate patronage of T. O. Hunter and James Whitsed, Esqrs. The church, dedicated to St. Bartholomew and St. Guthlac, though consisting only of the north aisle of the nave of the abbey church, is a commodious and very handsome edifice, chiefly in the later style of English architecture, with a low massive tower; the west front, which is highly enriched, is ornamented with several statues of kings and abbots, among which are those of St. Guthlac and St. Bartholomew, and of King Ethelbald, the first of whom was interred in a small stone building near the abbey, probably his abode while leading the life of an anchorite, from which circumstance, perhaps, originated its modern names, "Anchorage House" and "Anchor Church House;" the interior contains an ancient font, divided into compartments, a cylindrical stoup, and some well-executed screen-work; the roof is finely groined, and the windows are large, and decorated with elegant tracery. There is a place of worship for Wesleyan Methodists. Between the river Welland and the marshes is a causeway, on which, at the distance of two miles from the town, is St. Guthlac's pyramid; and in the neighbourhood are many stone crosses.

CROWLE, a parish (formerly a market town) in the western division of the wapentake of Manley, parts of Lindsey, county of Lincoln, 35 miles (N. N.W.) from Lincoln, and 164 (N. by W.) from London, containing 1729 inhabitants, and, including the chapelry of East Toft, 1961. The town is situated in the northwest extremity of the Isle of Axholme, near the river Don, and within a mile of the Stainforth and Keadby canal, which passes it on the north. The market, formerly on Saturday, has been discontinued; but from March till the end of May a market for sheep and cattle is held every alternate Monday, and there are fairs on the last Monday in May and November 22nd, for cattle, flax, and hemp. The county magistrates hold here a petty session for the division; and constables are appointed at the court leet of the lord of the manor. The living is a vicarage, in the archdeaconry of Stowe, and diocese of Lincoln, rated in the king's books at £14. 10., and in the patronage of Mrs. Egremont. The church, dedicated to St. Oswald, is a very ancient structure, of which the original character is concealed by repeated alterations and repairs. There are places of worship for Independents and Wesleyan Methodists. A charity school, for teaching poor children reading, writing, and arithmetic, is partly supported by subscription, and by an endowment of £60 per annum arising from various bequests; there are thirty children in the school. In 1747, the body of a woman was found in an erect position in the peat moor, near the town, at the depth of six feet beneath the surface; from the sandals on the feet it appeared to have been there for several centuries; the hair and nails were entire, and the skin, though discoloured, was soft and apparently sound.

CROWLE, a parish partly in the upper division of the hundred of Halfshire, but chiefly in the middle division of the hundred of Oswaldslow, county of Worcester, $5\frac{1}{2}$ miles (S. by E.) from Droitwich, containing 461 inhabitants. The living is a vicarage, in the archdeaconry and diocese of Worcester, rated in the king's books at £16, and in the patronage of the Rev. R. Harrison, M.A. The church is dedicated to St. Peter. On entering the parish from Worcester, there is a beautiful range of hills, forming an amphitheatre, and commanding extensive prospects. Crowle Court, the interior of which clearly shews it to have been a religious house, is a very ancient edifice, surrounded by a deep moat. In the neighbourhood are considerable quarries of a blue stone, which burns into excellent lime.

CROWLEY, a township in that part of the parish of Great Budworth which is in the hundred of Bucklow, county palatine of Chester, $6\frac{3}{4}$ miles (N.) from Northwich, containing 149 inhabitants.

CROWLEY (NORTH), a parish in the hundred of Newport, county of Buckingham, $3\frac{1}{2}$ miles (E. by N.) from Newport-Pagnell, containing 775 inhabitants. The living is a rectory, in the archdeaconry of Buckingham, and diocese of Lincoln, rated in the king's books at £27. 10., and in the patronage of Miss Duncombe. The church is dedicated to St. Firmin, to whom a monastery is mentioned in Domesday-book as having been founded here before the time of Edward the Confessor; which was in existence after the Conquest.

CROWMARSH-GIFFORD, a parish in the hundred of LANGTREE, county of OXFORD, ½ a mile (E.) from Wallingford, containing 230 inhabitants. The living is a rectory, in the archdeaconry and diocese of Oxford, rated in the king's books at £12. 6. 0½., and in the patronage of C. Turner, Esq. The church is dedicated to St. Mary Magdalene.

CROWNTHORPE, a parish in the hundred of FOREHOE, county of NORFOLK, 2¼ miles (N. W. by W.) from Wymondham, containing 103 inhabitants. The living is a discharged rectory, in the archdeaconry of Norfolk, and diocese of Norwich, rated in the king's books at £4. 12. 6., and in the patronage of Lord Wodehouse. The church is dedicated to St. James.

CROWTON, a township in the parish of WEAVERHAM, second division of the hundred of EDDISBURY, county palatine of CHESTER, 5¼ miles (W. by N.) from Northwich, containing 455 inhabitants.

CROXALL, a parish comprising the township of Oakley, in the hundred of OFFLOW, county of STAFFORD, and the chapelry of Catton, in the hundred of REPTON and GRESLEY, county of DERBY, 7½ miles (N.) from Tamworth, and containing, with a part of the parish of Edinghall, 305 inhabitants. The living is a vicarage, in the archdeaconry of Derby, and diocese of Lichfield and Coventry, rated in the king's books at £5, and in the patronage of the Crown. The church is dedicated to St. John the Baptist. There is a school on the Madras system, supported by subscription. The river Meuse flows through this parish, and the Tame touches upon its boundary. Croxall is in the honour of Tutbury, duchy of Lancaster, and within the jurisdiction of a court of pleas held at Tutbury every third Tuesday, for the recovery of debts under 40*s*.

CROXBY, a parish in the southern division of the wapentake of WALSHCROFT, parts of LINDSEY, county of LINCOLN, 5¼ miles (E. S. E.) from Caistor, containing 67 inhabitants. The living is a discharged rectory, in the archdeaconry and diocese of Lincoln, rated in the king's books at £6. 4. 2., and in the patronage of the Crown. The church is dedicated to All Saints.

CROXDALE, a chapelry in that part of the parish of ST. OSWALD, DURHAM, which is in the southern division of EASINGTON ward, county palatine of DURHAM, 3½ miles (S. by W.) from Durham. The population is returned with the parish. The living is a perpetual curacy, in the archdeaconry and diocese of Durham, endowed with £200 private benefaction, and £200 royal bounty. The chapel is dedicated to the Holy Cross. There is a private Roman Catholic chapel at the hall.

CROXDEN, a parish in the southern division of the hundred of TOTMONSLOW, county of STAFFORD, 5½ miles (N. N. W.) from Uttoxeter, containing, with the township of Great Yate, and a portion of the chapelry of Calton, 273 inhabitants. The living is a perpetual curacy, in the archdeaconry of Stafford, and diocese of Lichfield and Coventry, endowed with £2. 11. 10. per annum and £137. 16. private benefaction, £400 royal bounty, and £1000 parliamentary grant, and in the patronage of the Earl of Macclesfield. The church is dedicated to St. Giles. Gervase, Lord Pierrepoint, in 1715, bequeathed a rent-charge of £5 for the education of twelve poor children. Bertram de Verdun, in 1176, gave the monks of Aulney, in Normandy, a piece of land at Chotes, or Chotene (probably Cotton), to build a Cistercian abbey, which three years afterwards was removed to Croxden, where he and all his family were buried, and also King John's heart; it was dedicated to the Blessed Virgin, and at the general dissolution had an abbot and twelve religious, whose revenue was valued at £103. 6. 7.: the remains of this once stately and sumptuous edifice, situated near the Derbyshire border, exhibit good specimens of the early style of English architecture.

CROXTETH-PARK, an extra-parochial liberty, in the hundred of WEST DERBY, county palatine of LANCASTER, 4 miles (W. N. W.) from Prescot, containing 30 inhabitants.

CROXTON, a parish in the hundred of LONGSTOW, county of CAMBRIDGE, 4½ miles (W. N. W.) from Caxton, containing 225 inhabitants. The living is a rectory, in the archdeaconry and diocese of Ely, rated in the king's books at £14. 8. 6½., endowed with £200 royal bounty, and in the patronage of Sir G. W. Leeds, Bart. The church is dedicated to St. James. A school has been recently built by Sir G. W. Leeds, Bart., for children of Croxton, Eltisley, and the adjoining parishes, which is endowed with £6 per annum bequeathed by John Leeds, Esq., in 1705.

CROXTON, a township in that part of the parish of MIDDLEWICH which is in the hundred of NORTHWICH, county palatine of CHESTER, 1 mile (N. N. W.) from Middlewich, containing 52 inhabitants. The Grand Trunk canal passes through this parish.

CROXTON, a parish in the eastern division of the wapentake of YARBOROUGH, parts of LINDSEY, county of LINCOLN, 7½ miles (N. E. by E.) from Glandford-Bridge, containing, with the hamlet of Yarborough, 87 inhabitants. The living is a discharged rectory, in the archdeaconry and diocese of Lincoln, rated in the king's books at £8. 14. 2., and in the patronage of the Crown. The church is dedicated to St. John the Evangelist. Upon a lofty eminence about half a mile westward of the village are remains of a large intrenchment, called Yarborough Camp, supposed to be a Roman work, from the coins found in the area and near its site.

CROXTON, a chapelry in the parish of FULMONDESTON, hundred of GALLOW, county of NORFOLK, 4 miles (E. by N.) from Fakenham. The population is returned with the parish. The chapel is dedicated to St. John the Baptist.

CROXTON, a parish in the hundred of GRIMSHOE, county of NORFOLK, 2 miles (N.) from Thetford, containing 246 inhabitants. The living is a discharged vicarage, in the archdeaconry of Norfolk, and diocese of Norwich, rated in the king's books at £6. 13. 4., endowed with £400 royal bounty, and in the patronage of the Master and Fellows of Corpus Christi College, Cambridge. The church is dedicated to All Saints.

CROXTON, a township in the parish of ECCLESHALL, northern division of the hundred of PIREHILL, county of STAFFORD, 3¾ miles (N.W. by W.) from Eccleshall, containing 683 inhabitants.

CROXTON (SOUTH), a parish in the eastern division of the hundred of GOSCOTE, county of LEICESTER;

8¾ miles (N.E. by E.) from Leicester, containing 316 inhabitants. The living is a discharged rectory, in the archdeaconry of Leicester, and diocese of Lincoln, rated in the king's books at £8. 3. 4., and in the patronage of the Duke of Rutland. The church is dedicated St. John the Baptist.

CROXTON-KEYRIAL, a parish in the hundred of FRAMLAND, county of LEICESTER, 7 miles (S.E.) from Grantham, containing, with Beskaby, 527 inhabitants. The living is a discharged vicarage, in the archdeaconry of Leicester, and diocese of Lincoln, rated in the king's books at £7. 14. 7., and in the patronage of the Duke of Rutland. The church, dedicated to St. John, is in the later style of English architecture, with a tower rising from the centre. William Smith, in 1711, bequeathed land producing about £5 per annum for the endowment of a free school. Croxton abbey, dedicated to St. John the Evangelist, was founded in 1162, by William Porcarius de Linus, for Premonstratensian canons, whose revenue, at the dissolution, was valued at £458. 19. 11.: one of the abbots was physician to King John, whose bowels were interred in the church.

CROYDON, a parish in the hundred of ARMINGFORD, county of CAMBRIDGE, 6 miles (S. by E.) from Caxton, containing, with Clapton, 368 inhabitants. The living is a discharged vicarage, with the rectory of Clapton consolidated, in the archdeaconry and diocese of Ely, rated in the king's books at £7. 9. 7., and in the patronage of the Rev. T. Gape. The church is dedicated to All Saints.

CROYDON, a market town and parish in the first division of the hundred of WALLINGTON, county of SURREY, 9½ miles (S.) from London, containing 9254 inhabitants. This place, called by Camden *Cradeden*, and in ancient records *Croindene* and *Croiden*, derives its present name from *Croie*, chalk, and *Dune*, a hill, denoting its situation on the summit of an extensive basin of chalk. By some antiquaries it has been identified with the *Noviomagus* of Antonine; and the Roman road from Arundel to London, which passed through that station, may still be traced on Broad Green, near the present town. At the time of the Conquest it was given to Lanfranc, Archbishop of Canterbury, whose successors had for several centuries a residence here, which is said to have been originally a royal palace. During the war between Henry III. and the barons, in 1264, the citizens of London, who had taken up arms against their sovereign, after having been driven from the field at Lewes, retreated to this town, where they endeavoured to make a stand; but part of the royal army, then stationed at Tonbridge, marching hither, attacked and defeated them with great slaughter. The archiepiscopal palace, which in 1278 was in its original state, built chiefly of timber, was enlarged by Archbishop Stafford, and subsequently improved by his successors in the see, of whom Archbishop Parker, in 1573, had the honour of entertaining Queen Elizabeth and her court for several days in this palace; which, having afterwards fallen into a state of dilapidation, was alienated from the see by act of parliament, and sold in 1780: the remains are now occupied by the proprietor of a calico-manufactory, who has converted the gardens into bleaching-grounds. With the produce of the sale, and other funds vested in the see of Canterbury, was purchased, in 1807, for about £25,000, Addington park, three miles and a half from Croydon, with a noble mansion built by the late Alderman Trecothick, on the site of an ancient edifice said to have been a hunting-seat belonging to Henry VIII.: this mansion, which has been considerably enlarged and improved, is now the residence of the archbishops.

Croydon is pleasantly situated on the borders of Bansted downs, and near the source of the river Wandle, a small stream abounding with excellent trout, which, in its course through Beddington, Carshalton, and Mitcham, is considerably increased, and falls into the Thames at Wandsworth. The town consists principally of one long street, and is tolerably well paved, lighted with gas, and watched, under the direction of commissioners appointed by an act passed in the 10th of George IV. for its general improvement: the houses are mostly substantial and well built, and many of them are handsome and of modern structure; the inhabitants are plentifully supplied with water. There is a theatre, but it is seldom opened. The barracks, at the entrance into the town from Mitcham, were erected in 1794, as a temporary station for cavalry during the preparation of troops for foreign service: they form a neat range of building, originally consisting of six wings, three of which were taken down in 1827, and contain complete accommodation for three troops of cavalry, with an hospital for thirty-four patients, infirmary, stabling for twelve horses, a storeroom for one thousand sets of harness, with field equipments, riding-house, and other requisite offices: they are at present the depôt of the royal wagon train, established here in 1803; and, in addition to their previous accommodation for cavalry, contain sheds for three hundred carriages, and sadlers', smiths', and wheelwrights' shops, in which is made a variety of implements and carriages for the service of the troops in and out of the field. Within the distance of a mile east by north of the town is Addiscombe House, formerly the residence of the first Lord Liverpool, which in 1809 was purchased by the Honourable the East India Company, for the establishment of their military college, previously formed at Woolwich common, for the education of cadets for the engineers and artillery, but since 1825 open to the reception of cadets for the whole military service of the company, with the exception of the cavalry: there are generally from one hundred and twenty to one hundred and fifty students, under the inspection of an officer of high rank in the company's service, assisted by an officer of distinction in his Majesty's corps of engineers or artillery, to whom is entrusted the examination of the cadets previously to their obtaining commissions: there are fourteen professors and masters employed in the several departments of instruction; and two public examinations take place annually, at which the chairman and deputy-chairman of the Court of Directors preside, assisted by some of the superior officers of the state. Under the auspices and patronage of the Hon. the Court of Directors, this establishment has obtained a rank equal to that of any military institution in the kingdom; and the services performed in India, by which many of the officers educated at Addiscombe have distinguished themselves, bear honourable testimony to its claims to that high reputation which it has already acquired. The buildings which have been at various times added to the original mansion, for the completion of the college, and for its adaptation in every respect to the intended purposes, have cost the proprietors more than £40,000.

The trade is principally in corn: the calico-printing and bleaching, which were formerly carried on extensively, have materially declined; there is a large brewery, which has been established more than a century. An iron rail-road from Wandsworth passes through the town to Merstham, near Reigate; and a branch communicating with the Grand Surrey canal, near the Thames, affords a facility of water carriage. The market is on Saturday: fairs are held on July 6th for cattle, and October 2nd for horses, cattle, sheep, and pigs; at the latter, which is also a large pleasure fair, a great quantity of walnuts is sold. The town is within the jurisdiction of the county magistrates, of whom those acting for the division hold a petty session weekly: a head constable, two petty constables, and two headboroughs, are appointed at the court leet of the Archbishop of Canterbury, who is lord of the manor. A court of requests, for the recovery of debts under £5, is held every alternate week, under an act passed in the 47th of George III., the jurisdiction of which extends over the hundred of Wallington. The summer assizes for the county are held here and at Guildford alternately. The town-hall was erected in 1807, at an expense of £10,000, defrayed by the proceeds of the sale of waste lands belonging to the parish: it is a neat stone edifice surmounted by a cupola, comprising in the upper part a convenient court for the trial of civil causes at the assizes, with rooms for the judges, sheriffs, and grand jury, and for holding the court of requests; and in the lower part, a court for criminal causes, and an area which, except when the assizes are held, is appropriated to the use of the corn market. The prison was erected by subscription among the inhabitants, on the site of the old town-hall: it is a large and substantial building, of which the lower part, containing several rooms, is used as the town gaol, and for the confinement of prisoners during the assizes, and the upper part let for warehouses: behind it is a house occupied by one of the beadles, who has the care of the prisoners: near the town-hall is a convenient edifice for the butter and poultry market.

The living is a discharged vicarage, rated in the king's books at £21. 18. 9., and in the peculiar jurisdiction and patronage of the Archbishop of Canterbury. The church, dedicated to St. John the Baptist, was begun by Archbishop Courteney, and completed by Archbishop Chicheley: it is a spacious and elegant structure of freestone and flint, in the later style of English architecture, having a lofty square embattled tower with crocketed pinnacles: within are some interesting monuments to the memory of Gundall, Whitgift, Sheldon, and other archbishops whose remains were interred here; of these, the monument to Archbishop Sheldon, from the excellence of the sculpture for the period of its execution, has been erroneously attributed to a foreign artist: the finely painted windows of the church were wantonly destroyed during the Commonwealth. Two new chapels have been erected, partly by grant and partly by a loan of £7000, to be repaid by instalments, from the parliamentary commissioners; one near Croydon common, in the later style of English architecture, with a small campanile tower, containing one thousand two hundred sittings, four hundred of them free, for the erection of which the commissioners granted £3500; and one at Beaulieu Hill, Norwood, also in the later style of English architecture, with four turrets, containing one thousand and five sittings, of which six hundred and thirty-two are free, and toward the erection of which the commissioners granted £3000. The livings are perpetual curacies, in the patronage of the Vicar of Croydon. There are places of worship for Baptists, the Society of Friends, Independents, and Wesleyan Methodists. The free school, for ten boys and ten girls, was founded and endowed in 1714, by Archbishop Tenison; the income arising at present from the endowment, part of which is in houses and land, and part vested in the three per cent. consols., is £130 per annum: the children are taught by the master and his wife, who have a joint salary of £50 per annum, and a house which, with two schoolrooms, was erected in 1792, at an expense of nearly £1000, on a piece of land adjoining the old school-house, which, having become unfit for the purpose, was let by the trustees: a National and a British school are supported by subscription. The Society of Friends have a large establishment, removed to this place, in 1825, from Islington, where it had existed for more than a century, supported by subscription, for the maintenance and education of one hundred and fifty boys and girls. A free school originally founded and endowed by Archbishop Whitgift, in conjunction with the hospital of the Holy Trinity, is now the parish charity school.

The hospital of the Holy Trinity was founded and endowed by that primate, in 1596, for a warden, schoolmaster, chaplain, and any number above thirty and not exceeding forty, of poor brothers and sisters, not less than sixty years of age, of the parishes of Croydon and Lambeth, who were to be a body corporate and have a common seal; it is under the inspection of the Archbishop of Canterbury, as visitor: the income arising from the endowment, in land and houses, originally not more than £200 per annum, has increased to £2000 per annum: there are thirty-four brothers and sisters now in the hospital. The building, occupying three sides of a quadrangle, in which is a small chapel, is a handsome specimen of the style of domestic architecture prevailing at the time of its foundation: the schoolroom is at present occupied by the children of the National school. Davy's almshouses, for the reception and maintenance of seven aged men and women, were founded in 1447, by Elys Davy, citizen and mercer of London, who endowed them with lands and tenements in the parish, now producing about £130 per annum: the premises were rebuilt about sixty years since. The Little almshouses, containing originally nine rooms, were erected principally with money given by the Earl of Bristol, in consideration of lands enclosed on Norwood common; they have been enlarged by the addition of fifteen apartments, erected at the expense of the parish, for the residence of the poor. A school of industry for female children is supported by subscription: the chapel belonging to the archiepiscopal palace has been appropriated to its use. In 1656, Archbishop Laud gave £300, which sum having been invested in the purchase of a farm and in the funds, produces £62 per annum, which, according to the intention of the donor, is applied to the apprenticing of poor children. Henry Smith, Esq., of London, in 1627, left lands and houses producing £213 per annum, of which about £150 is distributed among the inmates of the Little almshouses: there are various other charitable bequests for the relief of the poor. On a hill towards Addington is a cluster of twenty-five tumuli, one of which is forty feet in diameter; they appear to have been opened, and, according to Salmon, to have contained urns: and on Thunderfield common is a circular encampment, including an area of two acres, surrounded by a double moat. In 1719, a gold coin of the Emperor Domitian was found at Whitehorse farm, in this parish, where also, within the last four or five years, a gold coin of Lælius Cæsar, in good preservation, and several others, were discovered; and in digging for a foundation in the town, in 1791, two gold coins of Valentinian, and a brass coin of Trajan, were found.

CRUCKTON, a township in the parish of PONTESBURY, hundred of FORD, county of SALOP, 4 miles (S.W. by W.) from Shrewsbury, containing 377 inhabitants.

CRUDWELL, a parish in the hundred of MALMESBURY, county of WILTS, 4 miles (N.N.E.) from Malmesbury, containing, with the tything of Eastcourt, 570 inhabitants. The living is a rectory, in the archdeaconry of Wilts, and diocese of Salisbury, rated in the king's books at £17. 5. 2½., and in the patronage of the Earl of Hardwicke. The church, dedicated to All Saints, is a large and handsome edifice in the Norman style of architecture; on one side of the nave the columns are short and massive, while on the other side they are lofty and light. A free school, founded by John, Lord Lucas, is supported by donations of about £6 per annum. Near this place runs the old Fosseway to Cirencester.

CRUMPSALL, a township in the parish of MANCHESTER, hundred of SALFORD, county palatine of LANCASTER, 2½ miles (N. by W.) from Manchester, containing 910 inhabitants. In 1785, two cottages were erected by John Bowker and John Taylor, for the purpose of a school, which are now let for £22 per annum, £13 of which is paid in support of St. Mark's charity school, Cheetham. Humphrey Chetham, founder of Manchester college, or Blue-coat hospital, was born here, in 1580.

CRUNDALE, a parish in the hundred of WYE, lathe of SCRAY, county of KENT, 8 miles (S.W. by S.) from Canterbury, containing 250 inhabitants. The living is a rectory, in the archdeaconry and diocese of Canterbury, rated in the king's books at £11. 10. 10., and in the patronage of Sir J. Filmer, Bart. The church is dedicated to St. Mary. The Rev. Richard Forster, in 1728, bequeathed a house and land, now producing £5. 16. per annum, which is applied to teaching eight children. At Crundale Green considerable remains of a Roman sepulchre were discovered in 1703, in which were several skeletons, urns, and other vessels, both of earthenware and glass, with some coins, trinkets for females, &c., supposed to have existed so early as the second century.

CRUTCH, an extra-parochial district, in the upper division of the hundred of HALFSHIRE, county of WORCESTER, 2 miles (N.) from Droitwich.

CRUWYS-MORCHARD, a parish in the hundred of WITHERIDGE, county of DEVON, 5¼ miles (W.) from Tiverton, containing 652 inhabitants. The living is a rectory, in the archdeaconry of Barnstaple, and diocese of Exeter, rated in the king's books at £21. 11. 8., and in the patronage of Beauvis Wood, Esq. and another. The church, dedicated to the Holy Cross, was struck by lightning in 1689, which rent the steeple and melted the bells.

CRUX-EASTON, a parish in the hundred of PASTROW, Kingsclere division of the county of SOUTHAMPTON, 6¼ miles (N.N.W.) from Whitchurch, containing 74 inhabitants. The living is a rectory, in the archdeaconry and diocese of Winchester, rated in the king's books at £12. 12. 6., and in the patronage of R. G. Temple, Esq. The church is dedicated to St. Michael. There is also a chapel of ease, called New chapel. Here was the celebrated grotto constructed by nine sisters, daughters of Edward Lisle, Esq., and commemorated by Pope; it has been suffered to go to ruin, the shell only remaining.

CUBBERLY, a parish in the hundred of RAPSGATE, county of GLOUCESTER, 5½ miles (S. by E.) from Cheltenham, containing 237 inhabitants. The living is a rectory, in the archdeaconry and diocese of Gloucester, rated in the king's books at £10, and in the patronage of Henry Elwes, Esq. The church, dedicated to St. Giles, contains some curious monuments. There is a place of worship for Baptists. One of the principal sources of the river Thames, called the Seven Springs, is in this parish.

CUBBINGTON, a parish in the Kenilworth division of the hundred of KNIGHTLOW, county of WARWICK, 5 miles (N.E. by E.) from Warwick, containing 614 inhabitants. The living is a discharged vicarage, in the archdeaconry of Coventry, and diocese of Lichfield and Coventry, rated in the king's books at £6. 6. 8., endowed with £200 private benefaction, and £200 royal bounty, and in the patronage of Chandos Leigh, Esq. The church is dedicated to St. Mary. A National school was established in 1821, and a bequest by John Glover, in 1762, of £250, for educating poor children, and one by Hannah Murcott, in 1775, of £100, for the establishment of a charity school, are applied towards its support; all the poor children of the parish may receive free instruction.

CUBERT, a parish in the hundred of PYDER, county of CORNWALL, 5¼ miles (W.N.W.) from St. Michaels, containing 322 inhabitants. The living is a discharged vicarage, in the archdeaconry of Cornwall, and diocese of Exeter, rated in the king's books at £8. 6. 8., and in the patronage of the Rev. T. Stabback. The church is dedicated to St. Cuthbert. This place is situated on the coast of the Bristol channel: it was visited in 1564 with the pestilence, which carried off a very large portion of the inhabitants.

CUBLEY, a parish in the hundred of APPLETREE, county of DERBY, 6 miles (S. by W.) from Ashbourn, containing 439 inhabitants. The living is a rectory, with the perpetual curacy of Marston-Montgomery annexed, in the archdeaconry of Derby, and diocese of Lichfield and Coventry, rated in the king's books at £13. 16. 3., and in the patronage of the Earl of Chesterfield. The church is dedicated to St. Andrew. A fair is held here on the 30th of November.

CUBLINGTON, a parish in the hundred of COTTESLOE, county of BUCKINGHAM, 6¾ miles (N. by E.) from Aylesbury, containing 259 inhabitants. The living is a rectory, in the archdeaconry of Buckingham, and diocese of Lincoln, rated in the king's books at £9. 16. 3., and in the patronage of the Rector and Fellows of Lincoln College, Oxford. The church is dedicated to St. Nicholas.

CUBY, a parish in the western division of the hundred of POWDER, county of CORNWALL, ¼ of a mile (N. by E.) from Tregoney, containing, with the borough of Tregoney, 1175 inhabitants. The living is a vicarage, with Tregoney, in the archdeaconry of Cornwall, and diocese of Exeter, and in the patronage of the Marquis of Cleveland. The church is dedicated to St. Keby. An hospital for decayed housekeepers was founded here, in 1646, by Hugh Boscaw, who endowed it with lands now producing £30 per annum, and which are expected to yield a much larger income on the expiration of the present leases.

CUCKFIELD, a market town and parish in the hundred of BUTTINGHILL, rape of LEWES, county of SUSSEX, 25 miles (N. E. by E.) from Chichester, and 40 (S.) from London, on the road to Brighton, containing 2385 inhabitants. This place is situated on a pleasant eminence, nearly in the centre of the county, and is handsomely built of freestone, of which there are excellent quarries in the neighbourhood: the pathways in the town are laid with bricks of a very firm and durable quality, formed of red clay, which is found within the distance of four miles, where also are strata of pipe-clay of peculiar whiteness: the inhabitants are supplied with water from springs. The market is on Friday: fairs are held on May 28th, Whit-Thursday, September 16th, and November 29th, for horses and cattle. The county magistrates hold petty sessions for the division at the court-house. The living is a vicarage, in the archdeaconry of Lewes, and diocese of Chichester, rated in the king's books at £20. 14. 2., and in the patronage of the Bishop of Chichester. The church, dedicated to the Holy Trinity, is a large and handsome structure, in the decorated style of English architecture, with a square tower surmounted by a spire covered with shingles, which, from its elevated situation, has been frequently injured by lightning. There is a place of worship for Unitarians. The free grammar school was founded in 1528, and endowed by Edward Flower, Esq., of London, and the Rev. William Spicer, of Balcomb, in this county, with the manor of Redstone, in the parish of Reigate, and other estates, for the instruction of the sons of parishioners of Cuckfield and Balcomb; the master's salary is £28 per annum: there are at present not more than five or six scholars on the foundation, though more than fifty pupils receive a classical education on payment of a quarterage to the master.

CUCKLINGTON, a parish (formerly a market town) in the hundred of NORTON-FERRIS, county of SOMERSET, 2¾ miles (E. by S.) from Wincanton, containing, with Clap on-Forms, 320 inhabitants. The living is a rectory, with that of Stoke-Trister united, in the archdeaconry of Wells, and diocese of Bath and Wells, rated in the king's books at £12. 19. 4½., and in the patronage of John Phelips, Esq. The church is dedicated to St. Lawrence. There is a small school, in which four poor children are educated, endowed with land producing £1. 5. a year, the bequest of Thomas Knight, in 1722. A license for a market on Tuesday, and a fair annually on the eve, day, and morrow of the festival of All Saints, and the seven succeeding days, was granted in the 32nd of Edward I., to Henry de Ortiaco, or L'Orti, lord of the manor, but both have been discontinued.

CUCKNEY, or NORTON-CUCKNEY, a parish in the Hatfield division of the wapentake of BASSETLAW, county of NOTTINGHAM, 5½ miles (S. S. W.) from Worksop, comprising the townships of Holbeck, Langwith, and Norton, and containing 1435 inhabitants. The living is a discharged vicarage, in the archdeaconry of Nottingham, and diocese of York, rated in the king's books at £9. 8. 6½., endowed with £200 royal bounty, and in the patronage of Earl Manvers. The church is dedicated to St. Mary. A market and a fair were formerly held, but both have been long discontinued. There are some large worsted and cotton mills, which give employment to a number of children from the Foundling Hospital, in London. There is also a mill for polishing marble.

CUDDESDEN, a parish in the hundred of BULLINGTON, county of OXFORD, 6½ miles (E. S. E.) from Oxford, comprising the chapelries of Denton and Wheatley, and the hamlet of Chippinghurst, and containing 1328 inhabitants. The living is a vicarage, annexed to the bishoprick of Oxford, in the archdeaconry and diocese of Oxford, rated in the king's books at £17. 0. 5. The church is dedicated to All Saints. A school is endowed, by a bequest from Dr. Moss, a late bishop of Oxford, with £1500 three per cent. stock, for the education of one hundred and fifty poor children of Cuddesden, Wheatley, Denton, and Chippinghurst, the produce of which, with contributions, amounts to about £100 a year: twelve poor girls are also educated at the expense of the Bishop of Oxford, who has a palace here, which was rebuilt by Bishops Paul and Fell, the old palace, erected by Bishop Bancroft, having been burnt down, in 1644, to prevent its falling into the possession of the parliament.

CUDDINGTON, a parish in the hundred of AYLESBURY, county of BUCKINGHAM, 5¼ miles (W. S. W.) from Aylesbury, containing 547 inhabitants. The living is a perpetual curacy, annexed to the vicarage of Haddenham, in the archdeaconry of Buckingham, and diocese of Lincoln, and in the patronage of the Dean and Chapter of Rochester. The church is dedicated to St. Nicholas. There is a place of worship for Particular Baptists. The river Teme runs on the north-west of the parish, in which there are quarries of stone.

CUDDINGTON, a township in the parish of MALPAS, higher division of the hundred of BROXTON, county palatine of CHESTER, 2¼ miles (W. by S.) from Malpas, containing 247 inhabitants.

CUDDINGTON, a township in the parish of WEAVERHAM, second division of the hundred of EDDISBURY, county palatine of CHESTER, 4¾ miles (W. by S.) from Northwich, containing 282 inhabitants.

CUDDINGTON, a parish in the second division of the hundred of COPTHORNE, county of SURREY, ¾ of a mile (N. N. E.) from Ewell, containing 117 inhabitants. The living is a vicarage, in the archdeaconry of Surrey, and diocese of Winchester, rated in the king's books at £7. 12. 3½. The church, which was dedicated to St. Mary, has been demolished. The celebrated palace called Nonsuch, built by Henry VIII., was situated here.

CUDHAM, a parish in the hundred of RUXLEY, lathe of SUTTON at HONE, county of KENT, 7¼ miles (S. E. by S.) from Bromley, containing 683 inhabitants. The living is a discharged vicarage, in the archdeaconry and diocese of Rochester, rated in the king's books at £13. 2. 2., endowed with £200 private benefaction, and £200 royal bounty, and in the patronage of the Crown. The church is dedicated to St. Peter and St. Paul. A grant for a weekly market here was made by Henry III.

CUDWORTH, a parish in the southern division of the hundred of PETHERTON, county of SOMERSET, 3 miles (S. S. E.) from Ilminster, containing 144 inhabitants. The living is a perpetual curacy, in the peculiar jurisdiction and patronage of the Prebendary of Cudworth in the Cathedral Church of Wells, endowed with £200 private benefaction, and £400 royal bounty. The church is dedicated to St. Michael.

CUDWORTH, a township in the parish of ROYSTON, wapentake of STAINCROSS, West riding of the county of YORK, 4 miles (N. E. by E.) from Barnesley, containing 487 inhabitants. There is a place of worship for Wesleyan Methodists. A school has been endowed by a bequest from William Poppleton, in 1747, of £50 for the erection of a schoolroom, and £300 to support the master; the income is £12. 12. per annum, for which seventeen children are educated.

CUERDALE, a township in the parish and lower division of the hundred of BLACKBURN, county palatine of LANCASTER, 3¾ miles (E.) from Preston, containing 166 inhabitants.

CUERDEN, a township in the parish and hundred of LEYLAND, county palatine of LANCASTER, 5 miles (N. N. W.) from Chorley, containing 569 inhabitants. Petty sessions for the division are held on Mondays, once in five weeks, alternately with Chorley, Leyland, Penwortham, and Rufford. A school was erected by Andrew Dandy, in 1673, who bequeathed a rent-charge of £5 towards the support of a master: arrears on this annuity have increased it to £6 per annum, for which twenty poor children are educated at a trifling charge; five are instructed gratuitously in the same school from a bequest of £5 a year by Samuel Crooke.

CUERDLEY, a township in the parish of PRESCOT, hundred of WEST DERBY, county palatine of LANCASTER, 4½ miles (W. by S.) from Warrington, containing 321 inhabitants.

CULBONE, otherwise KILNER, a parish in the hundred of CARHAMPTON, county of SOMERSET, 9 miles (W. by N.) from Minehead, containing 45 inhabitants. The living is a discharged rectory, in the archdeaconry of Taunton, and diocese of Bath and Wells, rated in the king's books at £3. 18. 11½., endowed with £200 royal bounty, and in the patronage of Lord King. The church is dedicated to St. Culbone. This parish is bounded on the north by the Bristol channel, and exhibits the most romantic scenery; the village, from the steepness of the surrounding hills, was, until within the last few years, scarcely approachable, except on foot.

CULCHETH, a township in the parish of WINWICK, hundred of WEST DERBY, county palatine of LANCASTER, 5½ miles (E.) from Newton in Mackerfield, containing 2163 inhabitants. In 1727, Henry Johnson bequeathed £612. 6. for educating and clothing children; there are also two small bequests of £10 each, made in 1691 and 1702, for six children.

CULFORD, a parish in the hundred of BLACKBOURN, county of SUFFOLK, 4¾ miles (N. N. W.) from Bury St. Edmund's, containing 291 inhabitants. The living is a discharged rectory, with those of Ingham and Timworth consolidated, in the archdeaconry of Sudbury, and diocese of Norwich, rated in the king's books at £8, and in the patronage of R. B. De Bevoir, Esq. The church is dedicated to St. Mary. The navigable river Larke runs through the parish.

CULGAITH, a chapelry in the parish of KIRKLAND, LEATH ward, county of CUMBERLAND, 8¼ miles (E.) from Penrith, containing 257 inhabitants. The living is a perpetual curacy, in the archdeaconry and diocese of Carlisle, endowed with £200 private benefaction, and £600 royal bounty, and in the patronage of the Vicar of Kirkland. The chapel is dedicated to All Saints.

CULHAM, a parish in the hundred of DORCHESTER, county of OXFORD, 1 mile (S. S. E.) from Abingdon, containing 359 inhabitants. The living is a vicarage not in charge, in the archdeaconry and diocese of Oxford, and in the patronage of the Bishop of Oxford. The church is dedicated to St. Paul. Here is a small endowed school.

CULLERCOATS, a township in the parish of TYNEMOUTH, eastern division of CASTLE ward, county of NORTHUMBERLAND, 1½ mile (N. by W.) from Tynemouth, containing 536 inhabitants.

CULLINGWORTH, a hamlet in the parish of BINGLEY, upper division of the wapentake of SKYRACK, West riding of the county of YORK, 3¼ miles (S. by E.) from Keighley. The population is returned with the parish. There is a place of worship for Wesleyan Methodists. The manufacture of worsted is carried on here. A school having a small endowment was built by subscription in 1780, in which from thirty to forty scholars are educated at a moderate charge.

CULLOMPTON, a market town and parish in the hundred of HAYRIDGE, county of DEVON, 12 miles (N.E. by N.) from Exeter, and 166 (W. by S.) from London, containing 3410 inhabitants. This place, which derives its name from being situated on the river Culme, or Columb, was held in royal demesne during the Octarchy. A collegiate church was founded here, at a very early period, by one of the Saxon monarchs, which was annexed by William the Conqueror to the abbey of Battle, in Sussex. In 1278, the inhabitants obtained the grant of a market from Edward I., which was confirmed by his successor in 1317, with the addition of an annual fair. The town is pleasantly situated in an extensive vale, surrounded by a large tract of level country, and consists of one principal street, roughly paved, from which some smaller streets diverge: the houses are in general neat and well built, and several of them retain evident vestiges of ancient magnificence: the inhabitants are amply supplied with water, and the environs abound with pleasant walks. The principal articles of manufacture are broad and narrow woollen cloth, kerseymere, and serge, which afford employment to several hundred persons, and are still increasing: on a stream between the river and the town are two flour-mills, a paper-mill, and a mill for spinning yarn; there are other manufacturing establishments in the parish, also four tanneries. The market is on Saturday: the fairs are on the first Wednesdays in May and November, which are large marts for bullocks and sheep. The county magistrates hold here monthly a petty session for the division: a high constable is chosen alternately in this parish and that of Kentisbear adjoining, who presides over both parishes; and six petty constables are annually appointed by the parishioners, three for the town, and three for the rest of the parish.

The living is a vicarage, in the archdeaconry and diocese of Exeter, rated in the king's books at £47. 4. 2., and in the patronage of Henry Skinner, Esq. The church, dedicated to St. Andrew, is an elegant and spacious structure in the later style of English architecture, with a lofty square tower, strengthened with highly enriched buttresses, and crowned with pierced battlements and crocketed pinnacles: opening into the south aisle is a beautiful chapel, erected in 1528, in the richest style of that period, by Mr. John Lane, whose remains are deposited in it: the roof of the nave and aisle of the church is of oak, richly carved and decorated with gilding. There are places of worship for Baptists, Brianites, the Society of Friends, Independents, Wesleyan Methodists, and Unitarians. A National school for two hundred children of both sexes is supported by subscription. A fund of nearly £100 per annum, arising from land purchased with a donation from George Spicer, Esq., in 1624, is appropriated to the apprenticing of poor children; and £54. 10. per annum, arising from land purchased with a donation from John and Henry Hill, Esqrs., is distributed in clothing to poor aged men: there are also several other charitable benefactions, by means of which £100 is annually distributed among the poor. At Langford-Barton, in this parish, are the remains of an ancient chapel.

CULMINGTON, a parish in the hundred of Munslow, county of Salop, 5½ miles (N. by W.) from Ludlow, containing 569 inhabitants. The living is a rectory, in the archdeaconry of Salop, and diocese of Hereford, rated in the king's books at £18. 9. 2., and in the patronage of the Rev. Mr. Johnstone. The church is dedicated to All Saints. Courts leet and baron are held occasionally.

CULMSTOCK, a parish in the hundred of Hemyock, county of Devon, 7 miles (N. E.) from Cullompton, containing 1357 inhabitants. The living is a discharged vicarage, in the peculiar jurisdiction and patronage of the Dean and Chapter of Exeter, rated in the king's books at £16. The church, dedicated to All Saints, contains a handsome stone screen with a doorway enriched and canopied with foliage. There are meeting-houses for Baptists, the Society of Friends, and Wesleyan Methodists. Fairs for cattle are held on the 21st of May, and the Wednesday before September 29th. Here is a small endowed school.

CULPHO, a parish in the hundred of Carlford, county of Suffolk, 3½ miles (W. by N.) from Woodbridge, containing 55 inhabitants. The living is a discharged rectory, in the archdeaconry of Suffolk, and diocese of Norwich, rated in the king's books at £5. 8. 1½., endowed with £200 private benefaction, £600 royal bounty, and £700 parliamentary grant, and in the patronage of B. G. Dillingham, Esq. The church is dedicated to St. Botolph.

CULVERLANDS, a tything in the parish and hundred of Farnham, county of Surrey, 1½ mile (S. S. E.) from Farnham, containing, with Tilford, 457 inhabitants.

CULVERTHORPE, a chapelry in that part of the parish of Haydor which is in the wapentake of Aswardhurn, parts of Kesteven, county of Lincoln, 5½ miles (S. W. by W.) from Sleaford, containing 61 inhabitants. The chapel is dedicated to St. Bartholomew.

CULWORTH, a parish in the hundred of King's Sutton, county of Northampton, 7¾ miles (N. E.) from Banbury, containing 581 inhabitants. The living is a vicarage, in the archdeaconry of Northampton, and diocese of Peterborough, rated in the king's books at £10, and in the patronage of Mrs. Grace Greenwood. The church is dedicated to St. Mary. A school-house was built by Mrs. Danvers, and in 1795 was endowed with an annuity of £65 by Martha and Frances Rich; from seventy to eighty children are instructed gratuitously.

CUMBERLAND, the extreme north-western county, is bounded on the east by the counties of Northumberland and Durham; on the south-east by Westmorland and Lancashire, being partly separated from the former by Ullswater lake and the river Eamont, and from the latter by the river Dudden; on the west by the Irish sea; and on the north by Scotland, from which it is separated by the Solway Firth, and the rivers Liddel and Sark: it is situated between 54° 6′ and 55° 7′ (N. Lat.), and between 2° 13′ and 3° 30′ (W. Lon.), and contains one thousand four hundred and seventy-eight square miles, or nine hundred and forty-five thousand nine hundred and twenty acres: the population, in 1821, amounted to 156,124. Cumberland, or, according to the Saxon orthography, *Cumbra-land*, signifying the land of the Cumbrians, derived its name from having been inhabited, at the time of the Saxon conquests in Britain, by a remnant of the ancient Britons, called *Cambri*, or *Cumbri*. At the time of the Roman invasion it was, according to Whitaker, occupied by the *Volantii*, or *Voluntii* (people of the forests), a tribe of the *Brigantes*, whose territory was not subjugated by the Romans until the reign of the Emperor Vespasian. It was also called *Caerleyl-schire*, or *Caerlielleshire*, from its chief town *Caerleyl*, now Carlisle. On the first division of the island by the victorious Romans, this county was included in the province of Britannia Inferior; and on the second, in the northern district, which they named Valentia. During the Saxon Octarchy it formed part of the kingdom of Northumberland. About the middle of the tenth century Cumberland was ceded to the Scots, from which period it was sometimes under the dominion of their monarchs, and sometimes under that of the English kings, till the year 1237, when it was finally annexed to the crown of England by Henry III. The earliest event of importance which historians concur in authenticating, with respect to this province, is the conquest of the whole kingdom of Northumberland by the Danes under Halfden, in the year 875, who, however, were soon expelled. The accounts given by the English and Scottish writers

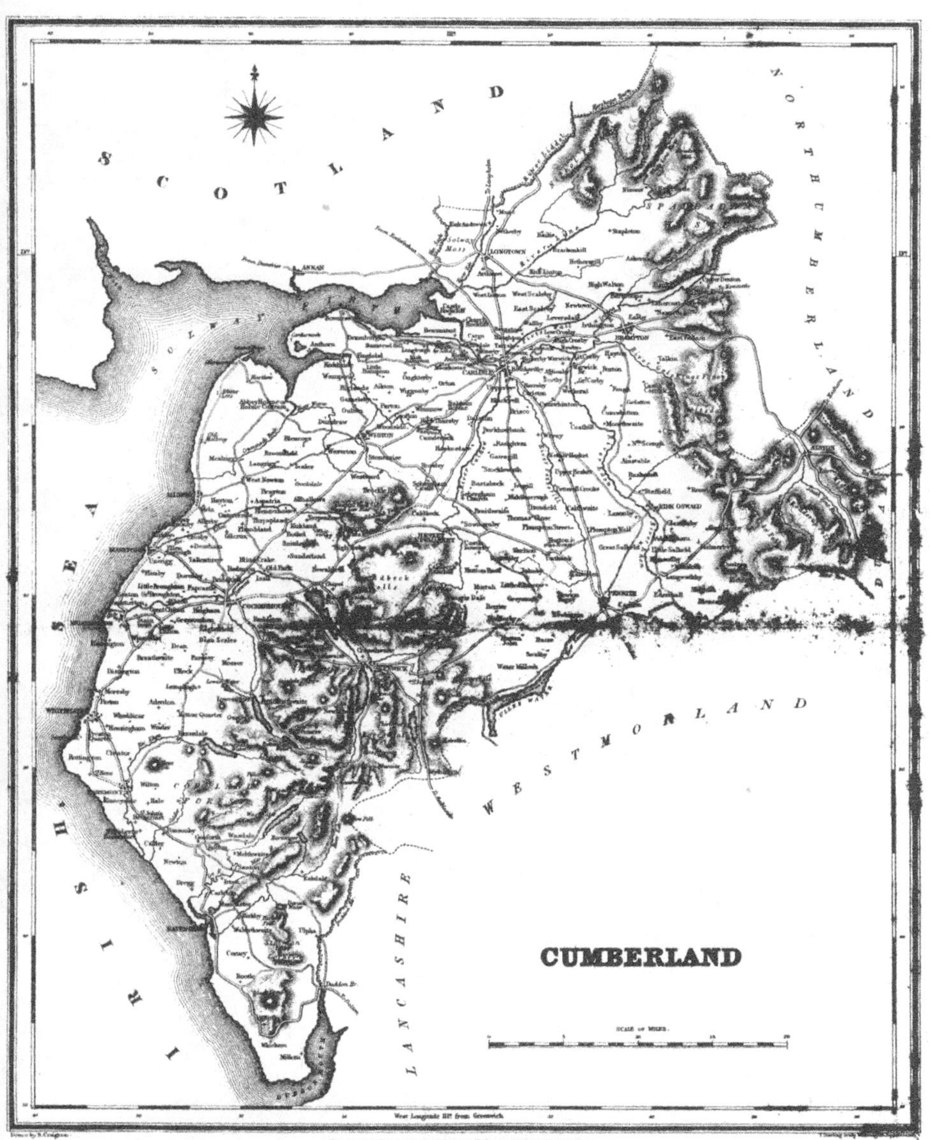
SCOTLAND
NORTHUMBERLAND
WESTMORLAND
LANCASHIRE
IRISH SEA
CUMBERLAND
CARLISLE
LONGTOWN
BRAMPTON
PENRITH
ANNAN
Solway Moss
SCALE OF MILES
DRAWN AND ENGRAVED FOR LEWIS' TOPOGRAPHICAL DICTIONARY.

respecting other historical transactions are contradictory and uncertain, up to the period when King Athelstan obtained at Bruningfield, or Brunford (a corruption of the Saxon *Brunan-burh*), a victory over the king of Scotland, and his ally, the king of Northumberland, whereby he acquired possession of Cumberland and Westmorland; but these counties were ceded to the Scottish king by his successor Edmund, by treaty; and it was agreed that the heir apparent of Scotland should possess Cumberland, as before, rendering homage for it to the king of England: accordingly Indulph, son of King Malcolm, was proclaimed Prince of Cumberland. The insurrectionary inhabitants having shortly afterwards set up an independent sovereign, named Dunmaile, apparently of British origin, King Edmund marched against them in 945, laid waste their territory, and restored it to Malcolm on the condition of his firm alliance. About the year 1000, King Ethelred invaded Cumberland, because the Scottish prince had refused to pay his quota of the contributions levied for prosecuting the war against the Danes. In the early part of the eleventh century, Othred, Earl of Northumberland, in alliance with the Danes, began to commit depredations in this county, but was defeated by Malcolm, after a desperate engagement, near Burgh upon the Sands: the Danes and Northumbrians afterwards made an irruption, and were defeated by Duncan, grandson of Malcolm, who had been invested with the princedom of Cumberland. Canute, having ascended the English throne, summoned the Scottish prince to do homage, which the latter refused, on the plea that he was not the lawful sovereign of England: Canute, in consequence, marched northward with his army in 1033, but it is very uncertain whether an engagement or an accommodation ensued, so little are the contradictory statements of the ancient historians to be relied on. Duncan succeeded to the crown of Scotland in the next year; and after his murder, Malcolm, his son and heir, finding himself unable to resist the usurper Macbeth, retired with his brother Donald Bain to his principality of Cumberland, and, having remained there some time, repaired subsequently to the English court. In the year 1053, Edward the Confessor gave Cumberland and the other northern counties to Siward, Earl of Northumberland, who thereupon invaded Scotland, defeated Macbeth, and placed Prince Malcolm on the throne.

Shortly after the Norman Conquest, a war broke out between King William and Malcolm of Scotland, who had granted an asylum to the English refugees. In 1069, or the following year, the Scottish monarch passed through this county, which then belonged to him, and ravaged Tees-dale; Gospatrick, Earl of Northumberland, retaliated in Cumberland, where his soldiers committed the most wanton cruelties. About this period the Conqueror bestowed the county on Ranulph de Meschines, who allotted it among his followers, dividing it into eleven baronies, the lords of which granted numerous manors to their dependents, most of which, having passed through various hands, continue to be held under such baronies as still exist; but on William's return from Scotland, in 1072, he revoked the grant, and gave the earldom of Chester in its stead. William had just then concluded a peace with the king of Scots, to whom a tract of land between Cumberland, Stainmore and the Tweed, was ceded in lieu of this county. When William Rufus was at Carlisle, in 1092, as he came back from Scotland, he gave orders for rebuilding the city (which had lain in ruins since its destruction by the Danes two centuries before), and for erecting a castle: these works advanced but slowly, for when Henry I. was there, thirty years afterwards, he ordered more money to be disbursed for their completion. David, King of Scotland, took possession of Carlisle and all the fortresses in Cumberland and Northumberland, except Bambrough castle, in the year 1135, for the Empress Matilda; tidings of this having reached Stephen, he marched with his army towards the north, but a treaty being shortly after concluded, Carlisle was given to David, and some time after the county of Cumberland. In 1138, the king of Scots occupied that city with a strong garrison; and in the same year, on the 25th of September, Alberic, the pope's legate, arrived, and found him attended by the barons, bishops, and priors of Scotland. David being defeated the following year in the battle of the Standard, near York, fled to Carlisle, where he was joined by his son three days afterwards. In 1142, a dispute arose between the Scottish prince, Henry, and Ralph, Earl of Chester, respecting the county of Cumberland, the latter claiming it as his inheritance under King William's grant to Ranulph de Meschines, but it was agreed that the earl should have the honour of Lancaster in lieu, and espouse one of Henry's daughters. The English and Scottish monarchs again took up arms, in 1149, Stephen lying at York, and David at Carlisle, but they both retired without coming to an engagement. In the following year a league was entered into against Stephen, at the latter city, between King David, Henry Plantagenet (afterwards Henry II. of England), and the Earl of Chester, on which occasion Henry was knighted by the king of Scotland, and swore that when he came to the throne he would confirm to him and his heirs the territories which the Scots possessed in England. In 1152, David, and his son Henry (who died in that year), met John, the pope's legate, at Carlisle: in the next, or the following year, the king expired in that city, and was succeeded by his grandson, Malcolm IV. When Henry II. ascended the English throne, disregarding the oath made to David, he demanded the counties of Cumberland and Northumberland of Malcolm, who, being unable to withstand against so powerful an adversary, yielded them in the year 1157, receiving in lieu a confirmation of the county of Huntingdon. During the contest between Henry II. and his son, William (surnamed the Lion), King of Scotland, availing himself of so favourable an apportunity to recover possession of Cumberland, invaded it in 1173, and laid siege to Carlisle; but on hearing that Richard de Lucy, the justiciary and regent during the king's absence in France, was advancing with a large army, he raised the siege. William again invaded Cumberland in the following year, and regularly invested Carlisle: during the siege, which lasted some months, Liddell castle and other fortresses were captured by the Scots; the garrison, being at length reduced to great extremities, agreed to surrender the castle at Michaelmas, if not previously relieved, but before that period arrived, William was made prisoner at Alnwick. King Henry, in order to assist the Scottish king in subduing Roland, a rebellious subject in Galloway, stationed himself at

Carlisle with a strong force, in the year 1186. Eight years afterwards, William demanded Cumberland and the other English possessions, which had been held by the ancestors of Richard I., but the statements of the historians of that period are greatly at variance regarding his having been put in possession of them. Prince Alexander succeeded to the throne of Scotland in 1214, and two years after, during the war with the barons, he invaded Cumberland, pillaged the abbey of Holme-Cultram, and besieged Carlisle, which was surrendered to him on the 8th of August, by order of the barons. He then repaired to Louis, the Dauphin of France, who was in possession of the greater part of England, and received from him and the barons of his party a recognition of his claim to the counties of Cumberland, Northumberland, and Westmorland, for which he did homage.

Soon after the accession of Henry III. a general pacification ensued, and Carlisle was given up to the English in 1217: it was then agreed that the sovereignty of Cumberland should remain with Alexander, but Henry appears to have retained firm hold of it, for in 1235 and 1237 the Scottish monarch demanded that county and those of Northumberland and Westmorland, as his lawful inheritance; however, at a conference held at York in the last mentioned year, he was induced to relinquish his claim, and to accept in lieu lands then of the yearly value of £200. The Scottish dominion over the northern counties of England thus finally ceased, but the feuds between the two kingdoms raged with unabated violence for more than three centuries, during which Cumberland was seldom long exempt from the horrors of invasion, or the cruelties and depredations of border warfare. Life and property could only be preserved by a most vigilant system of watch and ward, and the construction of numerous fortresses; almost every gentleman's residence, particularly on the sea-side, or near the border, had its fortified tower, sufficiently capacious to afford refuge to the inhabitants of the domain, and in some parishes the church towers were so constructed as to serve this purpose. The border service and laws were instituted in the reign of Edward I.; the former, for the purpose of keeping a strict watch, establishing beacons, and regulating the musters in time of war; the latter, for the punishment of private rapine and murders committed by individuals of either nation on the other, in time of peace. A Lord Warden of the Marches, whose authority was partly civil, and partly military, was appointed on each side of the borders; the first English Lord Warden having been appointed in 1296. The English borders were divided into three districts, called Marches, the Eastern, Middle, and Western, Cumberland being included in the last. The wardens held courts, but offenders were frequently executed without trial. On the attempt of Baliol, who had been acknowledged King of Scotland, to emancipate himself from the English yoke, Edward I. immediately seized on Penrith, Salkeld, and the other manors belonging to the crown of Scotland, which became the object of contention in subsequent wars, but were never afterwards restored. The Scottish troops, commanded by the Earl of Buchan, made an inroad into Cumberland, in 1296, and invested Carlisle, before which they remained four days, and burned the suburbs; but meeting with the most vigorous resistance from the inhabitants, they raised the siege and retreated. The same army, in its career of devastation, arrived at Lanercost on the 8th of April, and burnt the priory, but retired on receiving intelligence that the English forces were advancing. In October of the following year, William Wallace entered Cumberland with his victorious army, and summoned Carlisle, but finding that the garrison resolutely held out, he marched forward, and laid waste the Forest of Inglewood, and the whole of Allerdale, as far as Cockermouth. Shortly after the battle of Falkirk, in 1298, in which the Scots under Wallace were defeated, King Edward proceeded with his army to Carlisle, and there held a parliament on the 15th of September. Two years afterwards, about Midsummer, he set out on a new expedition against Scotland, and, passing through that city, marched with his army to the western border. In the year 1306, Robert le Brus, Earl of Carrick, having been crowned King of Scotland, Edward ordered his army to assemble at Carlisle on Midsummer-day, to accompany his son to that kingdom; he had been for some time in Northumberland, and arrived at Carlisle with the queen about the end of August, where they stayed till the 10th of September. On the 12th of March following, the court removed to Carlisle, where the parliament was then sitting. The king, though daily declining in health, did not relax in his efforts against Scotland, and ordered all his vassals to assemble at Carlisle on the 8th of July; he quitted that city on the 28th of June, being then in so weak a state as to be unable to travel more than two miles a day, and reached Burgh on the Sands on the 5th of July, where he expired two days afterwards. An express having been sent to Prince Edward, he reached Carlisle on the 11th, and two days afterwards received the homage of almost all the principal men in the kingdom. He then returned into Scotland, but having abandoned the vigorous prosecution of the war against that nation, he arrived at the above-mentioned city in the month of September.

In the year 1311, two inroads were made into Cumberland by Robert le Brus, King of Scotland, who ravaged Gilsland; during his second incursion he stayed three days at Lanercost with his army, and imprisoned several of the monks, but set them at liberty before his departure. In the autumn of the year 1314, Edward le Brus, brother of the Scottish monarch, attended by Sir James Douglas, advanced into England as far as Richmond in Yorkshire, after the battle of Bannockburn, and on his return burnt Kirk-Oswald. About Christmas the Scots made another inroad into Gilsland, and exacted large tributes from the inhabitants. The following year, King Robert le Brus again devastated the county and invested Carlisle, which was so obstinately defended by its governor, Andrew de Hercla, that the siege was raised on the eleventh day, when the garrison sallied out on the besiegers, and made some of them prisoners. The whole country from Carlisle to York was at this time overrun, and there was no safety for the inhabitants but in the principal fortified towns; the western part of Cumberland was also ravaged during this invasion, the monastery of St. Bees pillaged, and the manor-houses of Cleator and Stainburn destroyed. The Scots under James Douglas and Thomas Randolf laid waste Gilsland and other parts of

Cumberland in 1319: three years afterwards, England was again invaded by Robert le Brus, who burnt Rose castle (the bishop's palace), plundered the abbey of Holme-Cultram, in which the remains of his father had been deposited, laid waste all the western side of Cumberland, as far as Dudden sands, and entered Lancashire; on his return he encamped near Carlisle, and there remained five days. Edward II. retaliated upon Scotland, but was compelled to retire in consequence of the scarcity of provisions, and a dysentery which raged in his army; whereupon Le Brus again entered Cumberland, and lay with his army for five days at Beaumont, whence he sent forth detachments to ravage the surrounding country.

Shortly after the accession of Edward III., in 1327, the lords Ufford and Mowbray were sent with a reinforcement to Lord Lucy, the governor of Carlisle; in July, the Earl of Murray and Lord Douglas entered England with a large army, and marched through Cumberland, devastating the country. Edward Baliol having, in 1332, made an attempt to recover his father's crown, after narrowly escaping assassination at Annan, fled to Carlisle, where he was hospitably received by Lord Dacre, the governor. The following year that nobleman's estates in Gilsland were ravaged by Lord Archibald Douglas, who stayed four days with his army in Cumberland. When Edward III. was in Scotland, at the close of the year 1334, he sent Edward Baliol and the Earls of Oxford and Warwick to defend Carlisle against the Scots; large reinforcements having joined them from the northern counties, they made a successful incursion into Scotland, and returned to that city: the next year, on the 11th of July, the king quitted it with his army, on his way to Scotland. The Scots entered England at Arthuret in 1337, and, marching eastward, destroyed and sacked about twenty villages: during a subsequent invasion in the same year, they surrounded Carlisle, and fired the suburbs, with the hospital of St. Nicholas; they also burnt Rose castle, and pillaged the surrounding country. Five years after this they invaded Gilsland, and, having penetrated as far as Penrith, burnt that town, with several of the villages in its neighbourhood. Carlisle and Penrith were again burnt by them in 1345. In the next year, David le Brus invaded Cumberland in person, and took Liddell castle by assault; the Scots then plundered the monks of Lanercost of their money and jewels, and, after committing great destruction, marched by way of Naworth to Ridpath.

Although a truce had been established between the two nations, the borderers continued their hostilities. In the summer of 1380, the Scots laid waste the forest of Inglewood, and having surprised the town of Penrith during the time of the fair, they slew a great number of the people, and carried off several prisoners, besides a large booty; for which, however, they paid very dearly, as they became infected with a pestilence then raging, of which vast numbers of the inhabitants of Scotland died. On their return, they made an attempt on Carlisle, and set fire to one of the streets by discharging burning arrows, but were deterred from prosecuting the siege by a report that a numerous army was coming to the relief of the city. Three years after this, the abbot of Holme-Cultram paid a large sum of money to the Earl of Douglas, to prevent the monastery from being burned. The Scots, assisted by the French, invaded Cumberland in 1385, ravaged the estates of the Lord of Greystock and the Musgraves, and made an unsuccessful attack on Carlisle. Two years after this, the Earls of Douglas and Fife, with other Scottish noblemen, invaded Cumberland, devastated the country, surprised Cockermouth, where they remained three days, and carried off Peter Tilliol, sheriff for the county; during this inroad another attack was made on Carlisle, and the suburbs burnt. In 1388, the Scots entered Gilsland, and, on Lord Dacre's demesne, barbarously set fire to some houses, in which they had shut up more than two hundred decrepid persons, women, and children. No further mention is made of this county till the year 1461, when an army of Scots, in the interest of Henry VI., besieged Carlisle, and burnt the suburbs. In 1522, the Duke of Albany marched to the borders with a large army, and approached within four miles of Carlisle, with an intention to besiege it; but having received intelligence that it was well defended, and in every respect prepared for a siege, he retired, and made proposals to Lord Dacre for a truce. The next year, Lord Maxwell, having made an inroad into Cumberland, a skirmish took place, in which, after a sharp conflict, he overcame his opponents, and returned with three hundred prisoners to Scotland. Nicholas Musgrave and others, having excited an insurrection in 1537, besieged Carlisle, but were repulsed by the inhabitants, and afterwards defeated by the Duke of Norfolk, who ordered seventy-four of their officers to be hanged on the walls of that city; Musgrave, however, escaped. Lord Maxwell, Lord Warden of the Marches, passed the Eske in 1542, and burnt some houses on the borders. The battle of Solway-moss was fought soon afterwards, in the parish of Kirk-Andrews, when the Scots, notwithstanding their superior numbers, were defeated by the English army, commanded by Sir Thomas Dacre, who took above a thousand prisoners, among whom were two hundred noblemen, esquires, and gentlemen. In the year 1569, Lord Scrope, the Lord Warden, held Carlisle against the Earls of Northumberland and Westmorland, who were then in open rebellion; these noblemen advanced from Northumberland as far as Naworth, but, after a conference with Leonard Dacre, finding that their cause was hopeless, disbanded their forces in the month of December. Early in the following year, Dacre, who laid claim to the baronies of Gilsland and Greystock, having raised from among the tenants of those baronies a force of two thousand infantry and six hundred cavalry, garrisoned Naworth and Rockcliffe castles. Lord Hunsdon was sent against him, and on the 20th of February approached Naworth, but instead of investing the castle, passed on towards Carlisle; Dacre thereupon made a sally with one thousand five hundred foot and six hundred horse, and attempted to intercept Hunsdon's progress, but was repulsed, and fled with his cavalry to Scotland; Lord Hunsdon proceeded to Carlisle, and immediately took possession of Naworth, Rockcliffe, and Greystock castles for the queen.

The last hostile inroad, prior to the union of the two kingdoms, was immediately after the accession of James I., when a party of Scots, amounting to between two and three hundred, entered Cumberland,

and penetrated as far as Penrith, committing various depredations. James, who was then at Berwick, on his way to London, immediately despatched the governor, Sir William Selby, against them, with a detachment of the garrison, who soon defeated these freebooters, and sent all the prisoners he took to the castle of Carlisle. As the two countries were now united under James VI. of Scotland and I. of England, and frontier garrisons were no longer necessary, the king reduced those at Carlisle and Berwick; he also took active measures for ensuring the peace of the borders, and appointed George Clifford, Earl of Cumberland, Lord Warden of the Marches. In order to abolish as much as possible the distinction between the two kingdoms, he ordered that the counties of England and Scotland, which had been called the Borders, should be styled the Middle Shires, and thus described them in his proclamation. He soon after banished the Græmes, or Grahams, a numerous clan, occupying what was called *the debateable ground*, near the river Eske, who had long been an annoyance both to their own countrymen and the inhabitants of Cumberland; they embarked at Workington, some being sent to the Netherlands, but the greater number to Ireland, and, in 1606, there was an assessment on the county to defray the expense of their removal: some of them having returned from exile, the king issued a proclamation for apprehending them in 1614. For some time after the accession of James, outrages and robberies continued to be perpetrated on the borders; as a further check to them, the king issued several special commissions, under which various regulations were adopted. All persons, "saving noblemen and gentlemen unsuspected of felony or theft, and not being of broken clans," in the counties lately called the Borders, were forbidden to wear any armour, or weapons offensive or defensive, or to keep any horse above the value of fifty shillings, on pain of imprisonment. Slough-dogs, or blood-hounds, for pursuing the offenders through the mosses, sloughs, or bogs (who thus acquired the name of moss-troopers), were ordered to be kept at the charge of the inhabitants of certain districts; and Lord William Howard maintained a small garrison at Naworth, in order to check their marauding, enforcing the laws against them with the utmost severity; his great grandson, the Earl of Carlisle, was not more lenient, but they were not finally extirpated until the reign of Queen Anne.

Carlisle and Bewcastle were garrisoned in 1639, in consequence of the commotions in Scotland: in the month of June of the following year, the Scottish army being daily expected to enter Cumberland, necessary precautions were taken; orders were issued for keeping strict watch, and for preparing the beacons. The garrison at the former place was kept up till the month of October, 1641, when, in pursuance of a treaty with the Scots, it was disbanded. Soon after the commencement of the war between Charles I. and the parliament, at the end of 1642, the northern counties associated and raised forces for the king, but Cumberland was not often the scene of action: during the following year, the troops levied in this county distinguished themselves in Lancashire, under the command of Col. Hudleston. The royalists had an army in Cumberland and Westmorland in 1644, which was joined by Prince Rupert, after the battle of Marston Moor; and in that year a force was first raised in this county for the parliament, which menaced Carlisle, but, being pursued by the *posse comitatûs* towards Abbey-Holme, quickly dispersed and fled. At this period the Marquis of Montrose, being hard pressed by the Earl of Calendar, retreated from Scotland to that city; a skirmish took place in the town on the 17th of May, when Montrose retired to the castle, where he was besieged; but it does not appear to have been surrendered, as the earl, five days afterwards, was employed in the siege of Morpeth. After the capture of York, in July, Sir Thomas Glenham, with the garrison, retired to Carlisle, where he assumed the command; and about the end of September, Sir Philip Musgrave and Sir Henry Fletcher, being defeated near Great Salkeld by the Scottish army under General Lesley, escaped with difficulty to the same place: as Lesley did not then stay to invest it, the townsmen were enabled to lay in a stock of provisions; but after the storming of Newcastle, in October, he returned with part of his forces and laid siege to the city. About the end of February, it being found necessary to put the garrison and inhabitants on short allowance, they experienced the most severe distress; but nevertheless held out till all hopes of relief had vanished by the fatal issue of the battle of Naseby, and did not surrender till the 25th of June, 1645, when the most honourable terms were granted them. In the month of October, Lord Digby and Sir Marmaduke Langdale were defeated by Sir John Brown, governor of Carlisle, at Carlisle sands, and, their forces being dispersed, were obliged to take refuge in the Isle of Man. Carlisle had been garrisoned by the Scots from the time of its capture by General Lesley, but on the general evacuation of fortified towns by the Scottish garrisons, it was relinquished in February 1647. An army was raised in Scotland for the service of the king, in 1648, under the Duke of Hamilton, and, about the end of April in the same year, Sir Thomas Glenham and Sir Philip Musgrave surprised Carlisle: shortly after that event, a force of about three thousand infantry and seven hundred cavalry, raised in Cumberland and Westmorland, assembled, under the command of Sir Marmaduke Langdale, upon a heath five miles from that city, where they were joined by five hundred cavalry from the bishoprick of Durham. General Lambert, who commanded the parliamentary army in the north, took Penrith on the 15th of June, and established his head-quarters there for a month; detachments from his army captured Greystock, Rose, and Scaleby castles. Langdale retreated towards Carlisle, on which the citizens, dreading the recurrence of a famine, petitioned Sir Philip Musgrave not to admit his army within the walls. The Duke of Hamilton arrived there early in July, and superseded Musgrave, conferring the command of the garrison on Sir William Levingston: his forces, which were quartered in the neighbourhood of the city and at Wigton, having joined those under the command of Langdale, at Rose castle, making together a body of about twelve thousand men, he marched to the south; on his approach, General Lambert quitted Penrith, on the 15th of July, and retreated into Westmorland.

Cumberland was much harassed and plundered by General Munroe, who followed the Duke of Hamilton out of Scotland with six thousand men, both on his march to the south, and in his way home after the battle of

Preston. Sir Philip Musgrave, returning about this time with his forces to Carlisle, was refused admittance by the governor. Cockermouth castle was besieged by a body of five hundred Cumberland royalists, in August 1648, and relieved on the 29th of September by Lieutenant-Colonel Ashton, who had been despatched from Lancashire by Cromwell for that purpose. On the 1st of October, Carlisle was surrendered to Cromwell, and garrisoned by eight hundred infantry and a regiment of cavalry: a garrison, consisting of six hundred infantry and one thousand two hundred cavalry, was afterwards established there for the purpose of suppressing the insurrections of the moss-troopers. The county was at this time in a deplorable state; people of the highest rank had scarce ly bread enough for their consumption, and no better beverage than water; many died on the highways for want of sustenance, and there were thousands of families in a state of utter destitution: parliament ordered a collection to be made for their relief, but it proved very inefficient.

In the month of November, 1715, a large force under the command of Mr. Forster, who had received a general's commission from James Steuart, entered England, marched to Brampton, where they proclaimed him, and, advancing to Penrith, took possession of the town, the *posse comitatûs*, amounting to twelve thousand men, fleeing at their approach. This county was once more the scene of military operations in 1745, when the young chevalier, as he was styled, made an attempt to regain the crown, which had been forfeited by his grandfather: the van-guard of his army entered Cumberland on the 8th of November, near Longtown, and encamped the next day within four miles of Carlisle, which was garrisoned by the militia of Cumberland and Westmorland; the main body having joined them on the 10th, they summoned the town, but the siege was not commenced till the 13th, two days after which it surrendered. A garrison having been left there, the advanced guard marched on the 21st to Penrith, on their route to the south, and the next day, Charles arrived there with the remainder of his army. He proceeded as far as Derby, but, after holding a council of war, made a hasty retreat towards the north, followed by the Duke of Cumberland. The main body of the Highland army reached Penrith on its retreat, on the 17th of December, and a skirmish took place on the following day between the rear and a part of the duke's forces at Clifton. On the 20th the Highlanders quitted Carlisle, after leaving a garrison in the castle, and fled towards Scotland; the Duke of Cumberland arrived before the place the next morning, but, being obliged to wait for cannon from Whitehaven, did not erect his batteries till the 28th, two days after which the city was surrendered at discretion. In 1778, during the American war, a daring attempt was made on the port of Whitehaven by the famous Paul Jones; but one of his men having deserted, gave timely notice to the inhabitants of his intentions, who were thus fully prepared to repel the attack.

Cumberland is chiefly in the archdeaconry and diocese of Carlisle, which include also part of Westmorland, but that part of Allerdale ward which is above the river Derwent is in the deanery of Copeland, archdeaconry of Richmond, and diocese of Chester, and in the province of Canterbury: it comprises the deaneries of Allendale and Carlisle, and part of that of Cumberland, the remainder being in Westmorland. It contains one hundred and four parishes, of which thirty-eight are rectories, twenty-nine vicarages, and thirty-seven perpetual curacies. For civil purposes it is divided into four districts, called wards (a term peculiar to the border counties), which have always borne the same appellation; Allerdale (above and below Derwent), Cumberland, Eskdale, and Leath wards. It comprises the city of Carlisle, the borough and market town of Cockermouth, and the market towns of Alston Moor, Bootle, Brampton, Egremont, Hesket-Newmarket, Keswick, Kirk-Oswald, Longtown, Maryport, Penrith, Ravenglass, Whitehaven, Wigton, and Workington. This county returns six members to parliament; two knights of the shire, two burgesses for Carlisle, and two for Cockermouth, at which latter place the election of the county members takes place. It is in the northern circuit: the assizes and the spring and summer quarter sessions are held at Carlisle, where stands the county gaol and house of correction; the autumnal session at Penrith, and the Epiphany session at Cockermouth. There are fifty-five acting magistrates. The rates raised in the county for the year ending March 25th, 1829, amounted to £57,888, and the expenditure to £55,920, of which £43,783 was applied to the relief of the poor.

The manufacture of calico and gingham was first established at Dalston, and soon extended to Carlisle and Penrith, where there are large cotton works. The cotton-printing is chiefly carried on at Carlisle, and the population has, in consequence, greatly increased. At Cleator, Egremont, and Whitehaven, sail-cloth is manufactured on an extensive scale, and coarse woollen cloths and blankets at Keswick. Coarse earthenware is made at Dearham and Whitehaven, and bottles are manufactured at the Ginns. There are iron-foundries at Carlisle, Dalston, and Seaton near Workington: paper-mills at Cockermouth, Egremont, and Kirk-Oswald; and several yards for ship-building at Maryport, Whitehaven, and Workington, as well as every kind of manufacture for the supply of the shipping.

The climate is extremely salubrious, the county being throughout remarkable for the longevity of its inhabitants. The surface is much diversified; the northern and western parts are generally level, and do not afford any interesting scenery, except in the courses of the several rivers. The eastern and south-western parts are chiefly occupied by mountains, many of which are of considerable height: between these and the level district are lower ranges of smooth hills, most of which are denominated *fells*. The mountainous tract which forms the eastern boundary is a long continued range of mountains and hills, none of them picturesque, the summits being for the most part very little broken. The numerous mountains in the south-west part of the county present a great variety of grand and picturesque forms, and are interspersed with lakes of considerable extent, and highly cultivated vallies, in many parts well wooded; forming altogether some of the most remarkable and beautiful scenery in the kingdom. The principal mountains are Black-Comb, Skiddaw, Saddleback, Bow-fell, Grasmere-fell, Helvellyn, Hardknot, Wry-nose, High-pike, Pillar, Sca-fell, and the Screes, of which several are very rugged and precipitous. The principal elevations, as computed from the observations made in the course of the trigonometrical survey of the kingdom, are as follows :—Sca-fell (high point), three thousand one hundred and sixty-six feet; Sca-fell (low point), three thousand and ninety-two; Helvellyn, three thousand and fifty-five; Skiddaw, three thousand and twenty-two; Bow-fell, two thousand nine hundred and eleven; Cross-fell, two thousand nine hundred and one; Pillar, two thousand eight hundred and ninety-three; Saddleback, two thousand seven hundred and eighty-seven; Grasmere-fell, two thousand seven hundred and fifty-six; High-pike, two thousand one hundred and one; Black-Comb, one thousand nine hundred and nineteen; Dent-hill, one thousand one hundred and fifteen. The largest of the lakes is Ulswater, which for about six miles forms the boundary between Cumberland and Westmorland: its whole length somewhat exceeds eight miles, and, its breadth being in no part quite a mile, it has much the appearance of a wide river: its scenery is remarkably beautiful and picturesque; the most prominent feature of it is the mountain Helvellyn, which, with some lower ones, being seen over Patterdale, with sharp peaks, are said to resemble the Alpine forms more than any others in this country. The same mountain is also the most conspicuous amongst the rugged and barren masses seen from the lake of Thirlemeer, or Leatheswater, which is long and narrow, like Ulswater, but of smaller dimensions, and is situated at the entrance of the small but beautiful vale of St. John's. Amongst the finest scenery is the Vale of Keswick, containing the lakes of Derwentwater and Bassenthwaite, or Broad-water, connected by a small stream. The borders of Derwentwater, consisting of fine oak woods and rich enclosures, over which are seen the mountain Skiddaw at the northern extremity, and Borrowdale at the southern, present a great variety of magnificent and beautiful scenes, a considerable addition to which is made in rainy seasons by the Lowdore waterfall, the height of which is two hundred feet. Borrowdale itself, a narrow valley, bounded on each side by steep rocky mountains, presents a great diversity of picturesque scenery, among the most remarkable objects of which are the conical hill called Castle-Cragg, and the immense and singularly detached rock, called the Bowder-stone. The lake of Buttermere lies a short distance north-west of Borrowdale, surrounded by rugged mountains; and a little further northward lie Crummock-water and Lowes-water, connected with each other and with Buttermere by a small stream. At the western extremity of this group of mountains are those called Hard-knot, Wry-nose, Sca-fell, and the Screes; the three first form the eastern boundary of Eskdale, and, as seen from its opposite extremity, present one of the finest of the Cumberland views; the precipitous side of the Screes forms the southern boundary of Wast-water, and, by descending quite into the lake, gives its scenery a peculiar character. Besides the lakes already mentioned, the principal are Ennerdale-water and Devock lake. There is also a number of smaller lakes, or *tarns*, as they are provincially termed. The lakes abound with trout, and with the giviniad, or schelly, as well as pike and other fish: there are char in Ulswater, Crummock-water, Buttermere, and Ennerdale-water, and abundance of carp in Tarn-Wadlin. Among the mountains are several interesting waterfalls, the principal of which are, Stock-Gill Force; Rydal Waterfalls; the Force, on the river Brathay, above Skelwith bridge; Lowdore cascade, near the south-east corner of Derwentwater, one of the most magnificent scenes in England; Barrow cascade; Scale Force; and Airey Force.

The soil may be classed under four different heads: first, rich strong loam, which covers but a small portion of the county, and produces excellent crops of grain. Second, dry loams, which occupy a larger portion of it than any other, and prevail, not only in the lower districts, but on the steep sides of the mountains, and even their summits are sometimes covered with a dry sound earth, producing green sward and a little heath. It is estimated that one-half of the lower district is covered with this valuable soil, which is well adapted to the culture of turnips, artificial grasses, and the various species of grain, and for breeding and feeding the best kinds of stock, particularly sheep. Third, wet loam, generally on a clay bottom, the fertility of which varies greatly, as it depends on the depth of the soil, and the nature of the clay beneath; although unsafe for sheep, cows for the dairy may be kept upon it with advantage, and young cattle and horses bred; it is also well suited to the culture of wheat, oats, clover, and ray-grass. Fourth, black peat earth, which prevails on the mountainous districts bordering on Northumberland and Durham, and occasionally on commons in the lowlands, in some places only a few inches thick, reposing on a bed of white sand. The crops commonly cultivated are barley, oats, peas, turnips, and potatoes; those less commonly cultivated are beans, cabbages, carrots, and flax: the artificial grasses are red and white clover, common hay seeds, with a little rib-grass, and ray-grass. The land is ploughed by horses yoked abreast, and guided by the ploughman with cords; oxen are never employed for this purpose: the swing plough, in which no improvement has been made, is used in this and all the northern counties. The carts are drawn by a single horse, three of them, and sometimes more, being driven without difficulty by a man or a boy: the women are frequently employed in the labours of the field. This county, until lately, did not produce much more corn than was sufficient for the consumption of its inhabitants, but since the large enclosures which have been made within the last five and thirty years, considerable quantities of flour and oatmeal have been sent coastwise to other parts of the kingdom: the chief exports are from Whitehaven, but smaller shipments of flour and oatmeal are also made from Maryport and Ravenglass. Wheat is chiefly grown in the north-west part of the county; Gilsland also, in the north-east, is a corn district, where the turnip and barley system is very prevalent. The north-east, south-east, and southern parts of the county are chiefly appropriated to grazing, and a great deal of butter is sent in firkins to distant markets. Cranberries grow in great profusion on the moors, and form an article of trade: besides those which are sent in barrels to the metropolis, the sale is very extensive at Longtown and other markets. The fisheries are of some importance, a great quantity of cod being taken on the coast; there are herring-fisheries at Allonby, Maryport, and Whitehaven, the last on a very extensive scale. There are valuable salmon-fisheries in the Eske, Eden, and Derwent; the produce is sent from Carlisle and Bowness to London, to which place the char taken in the lakes is also forwarded, having been first potted at Keswick.

The pearls, still occasionally found in the muscles of the Irt, were once highly esteemed.

Copper was formerly exported to a large amount, and a considerable quantity of silver extracted from the mines; lead and coal are now the most valuable subterranean productions. The principal lead mines are those at Alston Moor, discovered and worked by Francis Radcliffe, the first earl of Derwentwater; upon the attainder of the third earl, they were vested in Greenwich Hospital, with the manor and his other estates: the number of mines held under that establishment, in the year 1814, amounted to one hundred and two. Lead mines have been worked with tolerable success for some years on Cross-fell, in the parish of Kirkland, and there are three in operation at Newlands, but they are not profitable. The principal collieries on the coast are at Whitehaven and Workington, the former being by far the most extensive in the kingdom, and there is one at Scalegill, worked only for inland sale. Howgill on the west, and Whingill to the east, of Whitehaven, are the largest collieries; there are three entrances to the former, and four to the latter, called Bear-mouths, or Day-holes, by which both men and horses descend to the bottom. Thwaite pit, which in the year 1816 was one hundred and fifty fathoms in depth, and King pit, which was one hundred and twenty, both in Howgill, are the deepest pits that have yet been sunk; the former was at that period one hundred and twelve fathoms below the sea; the greatest distance to which workings had then been carried in a direct line from the shore was one thousand yards. The first steam-engine for raising water at Whitehaven was erected early in the last century, at the Ginns; the first for raising coal was used at George pit, in Whingill colliery, in 1787; others were soon afterwards erected for the same purpose. Howgill and Whingill have each two steam-engines for pumping water, and three for raising coal: these collieries produce, on an average, about two hundred and twenty-five thousand tons annually. The coal was formerly conveyed from the works to the sea-side in packs on horseback, but, about the year 1720, small wagons were introduced; in 1813, the wagon-ways, which were before of wood, were laid with cast-iron, and on the Howgill side, a self-acting inclined plane was constructed, two hundred and ninety yards long, with a perpendicular altitude of one hundred and fifteen feet. About nine hundred persons are employed in the works at Whitehaven. The next colliery in point of extent on the coast is at Workington, which affords employment to four hundred persons; there are four pits now in operation from sixty-five to ninety-five fathoms in depth, and six steam-engines are at work in this colliery.

At Crowgarth, in the parish of Cleator, and Bigrigg, in the parish of Egremont, there are iron mines. Some years ago a considerable quantity of a ferruginous sort of limestone was sent from the parish of Arlochden to the iron-works at Carron; and a black stone, called Catscalp, raised at Braithwaite, in the parish of Dean, was used in the iron works at Seaton, for the purpose of making pig-iron: upon the sea-shore near Harrington iron-stone is collected, and a few hundred tons annually sent to Ulverstone. The celebrated mine of wad, or black lead, is at the head of Borrowdale (under which place an account of it is given). Limestone is very abundant in various parts of the county, and near the sea-coast is burnt in great quantities for exportation, particularly at Overend, near Hensingham, and at Distington, from each of which places about three hundred and fifty thousand Winchester bushels are annually sent to Scotland. At All-hallows, Brigham, Cleator, Hodbarrow in Millom, Ireby, Plumbland, Sebergham, Uldale, &c., there are limeworks for inland consumption, and the barony of Gilsland is supplied from the parishes of Castle-Carrock, Denton, and Farlam. Gypsum, or alabaster, abounds in the parishes of Wetherall, St. Cuthbert, and in St. Bees, on the sea-coast, about a mile from Whitehaven, whence five or six hundred tons are annually exported to Dublin, Glasgow, and Liverpool, where it is principally used in the composition of stucco. There are several quarries of excellent freestone, both red and white, in the neighbourhood of Whitehaven, where a great deal is shipped for Ireland, Scotland, and the Isle of Man. At Ivegill and Barngill, near that port, there are quarries for grindstones, which are also exported in considerable quantities; and in the townships of Bassenthwaite, Borrowdale, Buttermere, Cockermouth, and Ulpha, are quarries of excellent blue slate.

The cattle are small, with long horns, but the Galloway breed is sometimes intermixed, particularly along the coast from Whitehaven to Carlisle: the native breed is not distinguished by any particularly good qualities, little attention being paid to its improvement, but it appears better adapted to this county than any other kind: the Galloway polled cattle also thrive well. The dairies are generally small; the butter which they produce is of excellent quality; the cheese, however, is very indifferent, being mostly made of skimmed milk. The sheep (except the Herdwicks, a breed peculiar to the mountainous district, known as Hardknot, Sca-fell, Wry-nose, &c.) are descended from a race with black faces and coarse wool, but, by crossing with some other kind, many of them have acquired a large portion of white on their faces and legs; they have thick, rough, hairy legs, and coarse long wool. The management of sheep is very similar all over the county; during the summer the flock is turned on the commons and allowed to range at large; in Autumn they are driven in and salved, when the old sheep are turned loose again, but on the first appearance of snow are brought to the enclosures and daily foddered with hay. Swine are bred in considerable numbers, as every farmer fattens one or more of them, and most labourers rear and feed a pig; their weight is from fifteen to twenty stone.

The Eden and the Derwent are the principal rivers: the former rises in Westmorland, and enters this county about a mile south of Edenhall, flowing by Kirk-Oswald, Warwick-bridge, Carlisle, and Rowcliffe; at a short distance from the latter place it falls into the sea, its course through Cumberland being about thirty-five miles. The Derwent rises in Borrowdale, five miles south-west from Derwentwater, and, after feeding that lake, flows on to Bassenthwaite water, which it also feeds, then passes by Cockermouth (where it is joined by the Cocker), and Workington, near which it runs into the sea; its course from Derwentwater being about twenty miles. The other rivers are the Bleng, the Calder, Caldew, Cocker, Croglin, Dudden, Eamont, Ellen or Elne,

Enn, Esk, Gelt, Greeta, Irt, Irthing, Kershope, King-water, Levon, or Line, Liddell, Lowther, Mite, Nent, Petterell, Sark, Tees, Tyne, Wampool, and Waver. A ship canal connects Carlisle with the Solway Frith at Bowness, and a rail-road is about to be commenced from Carlisle to Newcastle upon Tyne.

The main roads are remarkably good, limestone having been employed in their construction; but the cross roads are usually narrow and bad. The great road from London to Glasgow enters the county at the bridge over the Eamont, near Penrith, passing through Carlisle and Longtown, and four miles beyond the latter place runs into Scotland, crossing the Sark to Springfield and Gretna-Green. The road from Carlisle to Edinburgh branches off at Longtown, and crosses the borders a little beyond Kirk-Andrews. That from Carlisle to Newcastle passes through Crosby to Brampton, and about six miles further on enters Northumberland. The road from Carlisle to Cockermouth, Workington, and Whitehaven, runs through Wigton, thence by Cockbridge to Cockermouth, and, in the direction of Great and Little Clifton, proceeds to Workington; at Little Clifton it turns off through Distington and Moresby to Whitehaven.

Athough remains of early Norman architecture are to be seen in many of the churches of Cumberland, few of them are entitled to particular notice, except the nave and south transept of Carlisle cathedral (the style of which is plain and massy), and the churches of Aspatria and Torpenhow: the great arch and south doorway of the former are profusely adorned with braids and chevron mouldings, and some of the original small round-headed windows are still remaining in the north wall of the nave and of the belfry. The great arch in Torpenhow church is enriched with chevron mouldings: the ornaments of the capitals of the half pillars on each side are very singular, consisting of an assemblage of grotesque heads and human figures with interlaced arms. The great arches and the doorways of Bridekirk, Irthington, Isell, and Kirk-Bampton churches are in the same style, but less decorated; there is a bas-relief of indifferent execution within the arch of the north doorway of the latter, representing three grotesque figures, one of which is an abbot. Kirklinton is a complete Norman church, not having undergone any alteration. Warwick church is in the same style, and very plain. The great west door of the church of St. Bees is ornamented with grotesque heads and chevron mouldings; and the churches of Bromfield, Burgh on the Sands, Dearham, Edenhall, Grinsdale, and Great Salkeld, have doorways with circular arches and Saxon ornaments. The remains of the churches of Holme-Cultram abbey and of Lanercost priory exhibit specimens of the earliest English architecture of the middle and latter part of the twelfth century, having the pointed arch united to the massy pillars of the Norman style. The east end of the church of St. Bees, now dilapidated, and the aisles of the choir of Carlisle cathedral, are early English with lancet-shaped windows and slender shafts between them; the east end of Egremont church, and the remains of Seton priory, are in the same style. The large clustered pillars in the choir of Carlisle cathedral, the capitals of which are much enriched with sculptured foliage, are the work of the latter part of the thirteenth century: the roof of the choir, and the east end of it, which was rebuilt in the reign of Edward III., after the church had been partially destroyed by fire, and a fine window at the east end of the south aisle of Brigham church, are the only remains of ecclesiastical architecture of the fourteenth century in this county. The only example of later English architecture occurs at the west end of Abbey-Holme church, where there are two niches, the arches and pinnacles of which are ornamented with crockets. There are some remarkable churches on the borders of Scotland, which have hitherto been little noticed; the towers of two of these, Newton-Arlosh, near the western coast, and Burgh on the Sands, near the Solway Firth, appear to have been very strong, and capable of affording protection to the inhabitants of the villages upon any sudden invasion. The tower of the church of Burgh on the Sands is strongly fortified, the walls on three sides being from six to seven feet thick. The tower of Great Salkeld church was also strongly fortified: at the entrance from the nave is a massy grated iron door, lined with oak; the chamber on the ground-floor is vaulted, like those of Newton-Arlosh and Burgh on the Sands. The Augustine monks had a priory at Carlisle, and another at Lanercost; the Benedictines had priories at St. Bees and Wetherall, both cells to the abbey of St. Mary at York, and nunneries at Armathwaite and Seton; the Cistercians had abbeys at Calder and Holme-Cultram; the Black friars had a convent in Carlisle; and the Grey friars had one in the same city, and another at Penrith. The churches of Greystock and Kirk-Oswald were collegiate. At Carlisle there was an hospital for thirteen lepers, dedicated to St. Nicholas, and at Wigton an hospital and free chapel, dedicated to St. Leonard.

A great trackway, probably of British construction, extended from the banks of the Eamont to Carlisle, nearly in the line of the present turnpike road; and the Maiden-way, from Kirby-Thore to Bewcastle, seems to have been another British road. The principal Roman way, called the larger road of Severus, may be traced very distinctly in the neighbouring county of Northumberland, but disappears at Foultown, near the borders: it soon after becomes visible at Willowford, in Cumberland, to the south of the works of Severus and Adrian. On approaching the Irthing, the road descends the steep bank to the river, and ascends on the other side; between High House and Walbours it is very conspicuous, but a little way beyond the latter, where the ground has been ploughed, it is completely lost for some miles; on approaching Watchcross, it is again discerned in the direction from Cambeck fort towards High Crosby, as if bearing for Stanwix, and soon afterwards finally disappears. A second Roman road, and one of the most considerable in the north, crosses the county from Westmorland to the Roman wall, in the line of a great British trackway, passing the Eamont on the spot traversed by the present turnpike road, and proceeding, in the same direction due north, to the stations at Plumpton-wall and Carlisle: it approaches the former within two hundred yards, being in that part at least twenty-two feet broad, passes the wall at Stanwix, and runs by the village of Blackford to Longtown on the Eske, where another large road branches off to the north-east, bearing evidently for the station at Netherby, and thence to a Roman post at the junction of the Eske and Liddell; after passing these rivers it may be traced to Castle-Over, which was originally a British, and afterwards a Roman, city. The principal road, having crossed the Eske at Longtown, runs through the centre of Solway moss, passes the Sark at Barrowslacks, and through the *Procestrium* of the Roman camp at Burrens, in its course to the northern vallum. A third road, called the Maiden-way, may be traced among the moors on the eastern border of the county: it leaves the Roman road at Kirby-Thore, passes between Crossfell and Kirkland, crosses Blackburn, and, running within two miles west of Alston-Moor, enters Northumberland, bearing for Whitley castle, a well known station in that county, and thence to Carvorran: it passes the Roman wall at Dead-water, and, re-entering Cumberland, proceeds towards the station at Bewcastle, which it leaves a little to the left; then, under the name of the Wheel causeway, crossing the Kirksop, enters Scotland. No less than three Roman roads diverge in different directions from Ellenborough, the station above Maryport; one of these is very distinct two or three miles beyond Allonby, and again near Old Mawburgh, and, where last seen, evidently points for Bowness. A second military way from the same station has been traced with more certainty to the Roman town at Papcastle, near Cockermouth. The third crosses the road from Crosby to Cross-Cannonby, traverses Allerby, passes over Outerside common, through Baggray, Bolton pasture, and Shaking bridge, and by Red Dial to the station at Old Carlisle, which it leaves to the left, and, from the village beyond Thursby, proceeds in a direct line towards Carlisle cathedral. A Roman road, which connected the stations of Ambleside and Plumpton-wall, is visible at Kirkstone hill, and again at Gowbarrow-park-head, near Ulswater; it runs thence between two hills, called Mill-fells, to the camp at Whitbarrow, near the eighth milestone on the turnpike road from Keswick to Penrith, which was a station between the two Roman towns: it crosses this road in a direction from south-west to north-east, and was entire a few years ago upon Greystock low moor, till it was converted into a modern road leading to Greystock; then, after having made an inclination to the left, it continues in a straight line towards Blencow, and is still visible in a field two hundred yards north of Little Blencow, pointing at Couch-gate: leaving Kulbarrow to the south, it runs through Cow-close and over Whitrigg, becomes again visible at the edge of the road on Fair-bank, in Low-street, and through the enclosures, to the south gate of the station at Plumpton-wall. A Roman road came from the station at Brougham, through Stainton to Whitbarrow, which was a post of some consequence. Another of these roads passed in a direct line through the Town-head and Wood-end estates, in the parish of Egremont, the Cleator hall property, and close by the village of Cleator; the estate of Todholes, and part of that of Warth, in the parish of Cleator; across the parish of Arlochden, and the township of Frisington; the parish of Lamplugh, close by Lamplugh-Cross, and Street-gate, whence it approached Cockermouth in a straight line: this road is eighteen feet wide, and formed of cobbles and freestone.

The celebrated wall, constructed by the Roman legions, which crosses the northern part of this county, commences on the west side of a small stream, called Poltross-Burn, at the distance of about two miles from the station at Carvorran, in Northumberland, but is only seen occasionally as a green bank until it reaches the station at Burdoswald, a little to the west of which the face of the wall appears in some places to the height of about three feet and a half, consisting of five courses of hewn stone, one of which is nine inches thick, and the others eight. A great deal of the wall was laid open in 1807 and the following year, when Banks-Fell was enclosed, and the lower parts of several of the watch towers were discovered at Banks-head, but it was destroyed for the sake of the materials, except in a few places, where some of the lower courses of stone, serving as the foundations of some modern fences, have been preserved. At Hare Hill, half a mile north of Lanercost priory, a part of it remains, ten feet in height, and fifteen in length, but no further traces are to be seen above ground, till within about a mile of its termination on the Solway Firth, where a piece, several hundred yards in length, and about three feet high, is standing at Kirkland, with a hedge on it; the facing stones, however, have been removed. In following the course of the wall from Northumberland through this county, the station of Burdoswald, one of the most remarkable on the whole line, first occurs, its northern side being formed by the wall, so that the garrison could enter the country beyond by sallying out at its northern gate: the ditch, gates, and rampart, enclose a square of five or six acres, within which are the remains of several buildings: the turrets on each side of the south gate are still visible. Six miles and a quarter further on is Castlesteads, or Cambeck fort, about four hundred yards south of the wall; the situation is convenient, owing to its proximity to the river, an advantage of which the Romans always availed themselves. Three miles west of this is Watchcross: the next station is at Stanwix, just opposite to Carlisle. Burgh on the Sands, about four miles and a half from Stanwix, was the *Axelodunum* of the Romans; urns, altars, and inscriptions of that people have been frequently found there. These stations were placed much closer together on the west than on the east side of the wall; most probably with the view of preventing the incursions of the Irish.

The castle of Carlisle, which stands at the north-west angle of the city, is of an irregular form; it was originally erected by William Rufus, but parts of it are of much more recent date, considerable additions and repairs having been made in the reigns of Richard III., Henry VIII., and Elizabeth. Egremont castle, which was built by William de Meschines, soon after the Conquest, is in a very dilapidated state, the gateway being the only part remaining. Cockermouth castle, the greater part of which is in ruins, does not appear to be older than the fourteenth century, though it has been referred to a much earlier period. The castle which stands within the site of the Roman station at Bewcastle is a plain square tower, apparently of great antiquity, but nothing certain is known of its founder, or the period of its foundation. Naworth castle, which is in a very perfect state, was erected in the reign of Edward III., when Ralph, Lord Dacre, obtained the king's license to castellate the mansion: it is chiefly in the style of the early part of the sixteenth century, and built round a court of irregular form. At the south-east angle stands a tower, evidently part of the original edifice; the upper story contains the private apartment of Lord William Howard, who resided here in the reign of Elizabeth and her successor, consisting of a library, chapel, and bedchamber, all of very small dimensions; the entrance is by a very strong door, well secured with iron-grating and bolts. Nothing now remains of Kirk-Oswald castle, except a ruined tower and some fragments of walls on a hill above the church. A great part of Millom castle, which was fortified and embattled by Sir John Huddlestone, in the year 1335, in pursuance of the king's license, is still standing, but is not worthy of particular notice. Of Rose castle, the residence of the bishops of Carlisle, which was first castellated in 1336, little of the ancient edifice now exists, except a gateway and a large square tower. Scaleby castle was erected about the year 1307, by Robert de Tilliol. The ruins of Penrith castle excite but little interest. High-head castle stands on the rocky precipitous bank of the Ivebeck; the embattled gate-house, which serves as an entrance to the more modern mansion, is all that remains of the original structure. Dacre castle is a plain square building, with four square turrets at the corners. Askerton castle, of small dimensions, erected as a protection against the inroads of the borderers, contains nothing remarkable; the stables are vaulted. Greystock castle was constructed soon after the year 1353, when William de Greystoke had the king's license to castellate his manor-house.

The sulphuretted spring at Gilsland, so celebrated for the cure of cutaneous disorders, has long been resorted to on account of its valuable properties; it contains a considerable proportion of sulphur, a small quantity of sea-salt, and a very little earth. There is a strong sulphureous spring in the township of Biglands, in the parish of Aikton, which is much weakened in the winter by its mixture with fresh water. At Stanger, two miles north of Lorton, is a saline spring, nearly resembling the Cheltenham water, which turns white on the infusion of spirit of hartshorn, and precipitates considerably on the application of oil of tartar: a gallon of it will yield one thousand one hundred and seventy grains of sediment, of which one thousand and eighty are sea-salt. Many other springs exist, but the nature of some of them has not been accurately ascertained. On Newyear's-day, in many parts of this county and that of Westmorland adjoining, the common people assemble, carrying *stangs* (poles) and baskets, and hoist up every man, who refuses to join them, on the pole, or woman on the basket, and carry them to the next public-house, where they must pay a fine. In the parish of Cumwhitton they hold the wake on St. John's eve, with lighting fires (called the *bel-tien*), dancing, &c.: in that of Whitbeck, newly-married peasants beg corn to sow for their first crop, and are called *cornlaiters*; and here, as well as in several other places in the county, the people keep *wake* with the dead. The bride-ale (here called a bridewain), and usually observed towards an industrious couple in the decline of life in reduced circumstances, prevails in several parts of the county.

CUMBERWORTH, a parish in the Marsh division of the hundred of CALCEWORTH, parts of LINDSEY, county of LINCOLN, 4¼ miles (S. E. by E.) from Alford, containing 170 inhabitants. The living is a discharged rectory, united in 1733 to the rectory of Anderby, in the archdeaconry and diocese of Lincoln, rated in the king's books at £10. 10. 2½., endowed with £200 private benefaction, and £200 royal bounty, and in the patronage of the Master and Fellows of Magdalene College, Cambridge. The church is dedicated to St. Helen.

CUMBERWORTH, a chapelry partly in the parish of KIRK-BURTON, upper division of the wapentake of AGBRIGG, but chiefly in the parish of SILKSTONE, wapentake of STAINCROSS, West riding of the county of YORK, 9 miles (S. E.) from Huddersfield, containing, with the township of Skelmanthorpe, 2451 inhabitants. The chapel is dedicated to St. Nicholas. Here are several manufacturers of fancy goods. There is a small endowment for a school.

CUMDEVOCK, a township in the parish of DALSTON, ward and county of CUMBERLAND, 6 miles (S. S. W.) from Carlisle, containing 333 inhabitants.

CUMMERSDALE, a township in that part of the parish of ST. MARY which is within the liberty of the city of CARLISLE, county of CUMBERLAND, 2¼ miles (S. by W.) from Carlisle, containing 512 inhabitants.

CUMNER, a parish in the hundred of HORMER, county of BERKS, comprising the chapelry of Wootton, the township of Cumner, the tythings of Botley, Bradley, Chawley, Henwood, Hill-end, Stroud, Swinford, and Whitley, and the liberty of Chilswell, and containing 1303 inhabitants, of which number, 508 are in the township of Cumner, 5¼ miles (N. N. W.) from Abingdon. The living is a discharged vicarage, in the archdeaconry of Berks, and diocese of Salisbury, rated in the king's books at £24. 17., and in the patronage of the Earl of Abingdon. The church is dedicated to St. Michael: in the south transept are two ancient tombs of abbots of Abingdon: they had formerly a residence here, called Cumner hall, but few vestiges of it are now to be seen. It is noted as the scene of the murder of the Countess of Leicester, by the direction of her husband, the favourite of Queen Elizabeth. There is a small endowment for a school. A mineral spring here was formerly in great repute, but is now disused.

CUMREW, a parish in ESKDALE ward, county of CUMBERLAND, 6 miles (N.) from Kirk-Oswald, comprising the townships of Cumrew-Inside and Cumrew-Outside, the former containing 148, and the latter 83, inhabitants. The living is a perpetual curacy, in the archdeaconry and diocese of Carlisle, endowed with £600 royal bounty, and in the patronage of the Dean and Chapter of Carlisle. It is bounded on the east by the river Gelt, and near it are the ruins of a large castle, formerly belonging to the Dacres; there are also several cairns, one of which, Carduneth, on the summit of a hill, is of immense size.

CUMWHINTON, a joint township with Coathill, in that part of the parish of WETHERAL which is in CUMBERLAND ward, county of CUMBERLAND, 4 miles (S. E. by E.) from Carlisle, containing 472 inhabitants. There is a place of worship for Wesleyan Methodists.

CUMWHITTON, a parish in ESKDALE ward, county of CUMBERLAND, comprising the townships of Cumwhitton, and Moorthwaite with Northsceugh, and containing 544 inhabitants, of which number, 285 are in the township of Cumwhitton, 9¼ miles (E. S. E.) from Carlisle. The living is a perpetual curacy, in the archdeaconry and diocese of Carlisle, endowed with £400 private benefaction, £600 royal bounty, and £300 parliamentary grant, and in the patronage of the Dean and Chapter of Carlisle. The church is dedicated to St. Mary. On an eminence called "King Harry' is a Druidical temple, the stones of which, ninety in number, are placed in a circular position, and the lines of ancient intrenchments may be traced on the common.

CUNDALL, a parish in the wapentake of HALLIKELD, North riding of the county of YORK, comprising the townships of Cundall with Leckby, and Norton le Clay, and containing 312 inhabitants, of which number, 170 are in the township of Cundall with Leckby, 5 miles (N. N. E.) from Boroughbridge. The living is a vicarage, in the archdeaconry of Richmond, and diocese of Chester, rated in the king's books at £3. 6. 8., endowed with £400 royal bounty, and £200 parliamentary grant, and in the patronage of N. Cholmley, Esq. The church is dedicated to All Saints. A school, in which thirty poor children are educated, is supported by the proceeds of the parish poor lands and subscriptions, in addition to a small endowment.

CUNSALL, a township in the parish of CHEDDLETON, northern division of the hundred of TOTMONSLOW, county of STAFFORD, 3¾ miles (N. N. W.) from Cheadle, containing 182 inhabitants.

CUNSCOUGH, a district in the parish of HALSALL, hundred of WEST DERBY, county palatine of LANCASTER, 4 miles (S. by E.) from Ormskirk. The population is returned with the parish.

CUPERNHAM, a tything in that part of the parish of ROMSEY styled ROMSEY EXTRA, hundred of KING'S SOMBOURN, Andover division of the county of SOUTHAMPTON, 1 mile (N. E.) from Romsey. The population is returned with the parish.

CURBAR, a hamlet in the parish of BAKEWELL, hundred of HIGH PEAK, county of DERBY, 1½ mile (E. by S.) from Stoney-Middleton, containing 392 inhabitants.

CURBOROUGH, a joint township with Elmhurst, in that part of the parish of ST. CHAD, LICHFIELD, which is in the northern division of the hundred of OFFLOW, county of STAFFORD, 2 miles (N. N. E.) from Lichfield, containing 250 inhabitants.

CURBRIDGE, a hamlet in the parish of WITNEY, hundred of BAMPTON, county of OXFORD, 2¼ miles (W. S. W.) from Witney, containing 372 inhabitants. There are six almshouses endowed with £110 per annum.

CURDWORTH, a parish in the Birmingham division of the hundred of HEMLINGFORD, county of WARWICK, 3 miles (N. W. by N.) from Coleshill, containing, with the township of Minworth, 555 inhabitants. The living is a vicarage, in the archdeaconry of Coventry, and diocese of Lichfield and Coventry, rated in the king's books at £5, and in the patronage of the Rev. W. Wakefield and C. B. Adderley, Esq. The church is dedicated to St. Nicholas. The Birmingham and Fazely canal passes through this parish, and is conducted under a short tunnel near the village.

CURLAND, a parish in the hundred of ABDICK and BULSTONE, county of SOMERSET, 5¾ miles (S. E. by E.) from Taunton, containing 168 inhabitants. The living is a perpetual curacy, annexed to the rectory of Curry-Mallet, in the archdeaconry of Taunton, and diocese of Bath and Wells. The church is dedicated to All Saints. There is a place of worship for Wesleyan Methodists.

CURRY-MALLET, a parish (formerly a market town) in the hundred of ABDICK and BULSTONE, county of SOMERSET, 5¾ miles (N. N. W.) from Ilminster, containing 461 inhabitants. The living is a rectory, with the perpetual curacy of Curland annexed, in the archdeaconry of Taunton, and diocese of Bath and Wells, rated in the king's books at £24. 1. 3., and in the patronage of the Crown. The church is dedicated to All Saints. The act of parliament passed in the 2nd of Edward III., which vested the duchy of Cornwall in the king's eldest son, annexed Curry-Mallet to it, and it still continues a part thereof. A weekly market, and a fair annually on the eve, day, and morrow of All Saints, were granted by Edward II. to Hugh Poyntz, then owner of the manor, who, in the 18th of the same reign, was summoned to parliament by the title of Lord Poyntz, Baron of Curry-Mallet.

CURRY (NORTH), a parish (formerly a market town) in the hundred of NORTH CURRY, county of SOMERSET, 6½ miles (E. by N.) from Taunton, containing, with the tythings of Knapp, Lillistone, and Wrantage, 1645 inhabitants. The living is a discharged vicarage, with the perpetual curacies of Stoke St. Gregory and West Hatch annexed, in the peculiar jurisdiction and patronage of the Dean and Chapter of Wells, rated in the king's books at £21. The church is dedicated to St. Peter and St. Paul. There are places of worship for Particular Baptists and Wesleyan Methodists. This place appears to have been not unknown to the Romans, an urn containing a quantity of the silver coins of that people having been discovered in 1748: it was subsequently held by the Saxon kings, and retained in demesne by the Conqueror. King John granted it a market, which was formerly held on Wednesday, but has been long discontinued. The navigable river Tone passes in the vicinity. Newport, in this parish, anciently possessed the privileges and officers of a corporate town, and is still called a borough: it had also a chapel.

CURRY-REVELL, a parish in the hundred of ABDICK and BULSTONE, county of SOMERSET, 2½ miles (W. S. W.) from Langport, containing 1192 inhabitants. The living is a vicarage, with Weston, in the archdeaconry of Taunton, and diocese of Bath and Wells, rated in the king's books at £13. 16. 0½., and in the patronage of the Earl of Chatham. The church is dedicated to St. Andrew. This parish contains several quarries of blue limestone and white lyas, in which bivalve shells of different sorts are frequently found. Fairs for cattle and sheep are held on the Monday next after Lammas and the 5th of August. The house and beautiful grounds of Burton-Pynsent, once the property and residence of the celebrated Earl of Chatham, who enjoyed the title of Viscount Pitt of Burton-Pynsent, add greatly to the interesting scenery of this neighbourhood.

CURY, a parish in the hundred of KERRIER, county of CORNWALL, 4¾ miles (S. S. E.) from Helston, containing 505 inhabitants. The living is a perpetual curacy, annexed to the vicarage of St. Breage, in the archdeaconry of Gornwall, and diocese of Exeter, and in the patronage of the Crown. The church is dedicated to St. Ninian. There is a place of worship for Wesleyan Methodists. The English channel bounds this parish on the west.

CUSOP, a parish in the hundred of EWYASLACY, county of HEREFORD, 2 miles (E. S. E.) from Hay, containing 266 inhabitants. The living is a discharged rectory, in the archdeaconry and diocese of Hereford, rated in the king's books at £5. 19. 7., endowed with £200 private benefaction, and £200 royal bounty, and in the patronage of the Earl of Oxford. The church is dedicated to St. Mary.

CUSTHORPE, a hamlet in that part of the parish of WEST-ACRE which is in the southern division of the hundred of GREENHOE, county of NORFOLK, 4¼ miles (N. W.) from Swaffham. The population is returned with the parish. Here are the ruins of a chapel, dedicated to St. Thomas à Becket, supposed to have been founded by the monks of Westacre priory, who received permission to hold a fair annually on the 7th of July: connected with it was a house, the residence of a custos and one or two monks, who were engaged in serving the chapel.

CUTCOMBE, a parish in the hundred of CARHAMPTON, county of SOMERSET, 5¼ miles (S. W. by S.) from Dunster, containing 664 inhabitants. The living is a vicarage, with the perpetual curacy of Luxborough annexed, in the archdeaconry of Taunton, and diocese of Bath and Wells, rated in the king's books at £14. 0. 7½., and in the patronage of the Crown. The church is dedicated to St. John. A school was founded and endowed, in 1720, by Richard Elsworth, in which from fifty to sixty children are instructed. Dunkery, the highest mountain in the western counties of England, is in this parish, on the summit of which are the ruins of several large hearths belonging to the beacons formerly erected on this elevated spot, to alarm the country in times of civil discord or foreign invasion.

CUTSDEAN, a chapelry in that part of the parish of BREDON which is in the upper division of the hundred of OSWALDSLOW, county of WORCESTER, though locally in the upper division of the hundred of Kiftsgate, county of Gloucester, 7 miles (W. by S.) from Moreton in the Marsh, containing 112 inhabitants. There is a trifling endowment for educating children.

CUTTHORPE, a hamlet in the parish of BRAMPTON, hundred of SCARSDALE, county of DERBY, containing 315 inhabitants.

CUXHAM, a parish in the hundred of EWELME, county of OXFORD, 5 miles (S. S. W.) from Tetsworth, containing 182 inhabitants. The living is a rectory, in the archdeaconry and diocese of Oxford, rated in the king's books at £9. 10. 5., and in the patronage of the Warden and Fellows of Merton College, Oxford. The church is dedicated to the Holy Rood.

CUXTON, a parish in the hundred of SHAMWELL, lathe of AYLESFORD, county of KENT, 2¾ miles (W. S. W.) from Rochester, containing 384 inhabitants. The living is a rectory, in the archdeaconry and diocese of Rochester, rated in the king's books at £14. 15. 5., and in the patronage of the Bishop of Rochester. The church is dedicated to St. Michael.

CUXWOLD, a parish in the wapentake of BRADLEY-HAVERSTOE, parts of LINDSEY, county of LINCOLN, 4 miles (E.) from Caistor, containing 60 inhabitants. The living is a discharged rectory, in the archdeaconry and diocese of Lincoln, rated in the king's books at £5. 7. 6., endowed with £200 royal bounty, and in the patronage of H. Thorold Esq. The church is dedicated to St. Nicholas.

CWMCARVAN, a parish in the upper division of the hundred of RAGLAND, county of MONMOUTH, 3½ miles (S. S. W.) from Monmouth, containing 293 inhabitants. The living is a perpetual curacy, annexed to the rectory of Mitchel-Troy, in the archdeaconry and diocese of Llandaff.

CWMYOY, a parish partly in the hundred of EWYASLACY, county of HEREFORD, and partly in the lower division of the hundred of ABERGAVENNY, county of MONMOUTH, 8½ miles (N. by W.) from Abergavenny, containing, with the townships of Bwlch and Toothog, 679 inhabitants. The living is a perpetual curacy, in the archdeaconry of Brecon, and diocese of St. David, endowed with £200 private benefaction, and £400 royal bounty, and in the patronage of — Lander, Esq. The church is dedicated to St. Michael. Soon after the year 1108, a priory, dedicated to St. John the Baptist, and afterwards known by the name of Llantony abbey, was founded here by Hugh Lacy, for canons regular of the order of St. Augustine, many of whom, by reason of the privations and hardships which they sustained in this place, removed first to the episcopal palace at Hereford, and afterwards, in 1136, to a place near Gloucester, leaving a few of their brethren at the original settlement at Llantony, whose revenue, in the 26th of Henry VIII., was estimated at about £100: the remains, which are nearly in the centre of the parish, are in a tolerable state of preservation.

THE END OF VOLUME I.

www.ingramcontent.com/pod-product-compliance
Lightning Source LLC
Chambersburg PA
CBHW072058040426
42334CB00040B/1301

* 9 7 8 0 8 0 6 3 5 8 6 7 3 *